The Bill James Handbook 2008

Baseball Info Solutions

www.baseballinfosolutions.com

Published by ACTA Sports

A Division of ACTA Publications

Cover by Tom A. Wright

Cover Photos by Scott Jordan Levy

First Edition: November 2007

Published by:
ACTA Sports, a division of ACTA Publications
5559 W. Howard Street, Skokie, IL 60077
(800) 397-2282
www.actasports.com www.actapublications.com

ISBN-13: 978-0-87946-340-3

Printed in the United States of America

Table of Contents

Introduction...1

2007 Team Statistics 3

Team Efficiency Summary (by Bill James)..............................9

The Fielding Bible Awards (by John Dewan) 11

Plus/Minus Leaders (by John Dewan) 19

Career Register 23

2007 Fielding Statistics..289

Player Baserunning (by Bill James)...................................301

Team Baserunning (by Bill James)....................................311

Pitchers Hitting, Fielding & Holding Runners / Hitters Pitching 313

Manufactured Runs (by Bill James) 325

Manager's Record (by Bill James) 331

2007 Park Indices...341

2007 Lefty/Righty Statistics 357

2007 Leader Boards 377

Win Shares...411

Young Talent Inventory (by Bill James) 421

Hitter Projections (by Bill James).....................................431

Projected Career Totals for Active Players..........................449

Pitcher Projections (by Bill James)....................................451

Career Targets (by Bill James) 463

300-Win Candidates (by Bill James)..................................465

Baseball Glossary 467

Baseball Info Solutions...481

Dedication

I dedicate this book to my family, both immediate and extended. I am so blessed to be part of a large family of loving, supportive people—especially my wife of more than 18 years, Cindy— and our 15-year-old daughter, Chelsea.

Pat Quinn

Acknowledgements

A friend of mine once told me that the only people who read the Acknowledgements are the folks mentioned. That's probably true. In any case, I'll try and give this year's Acknowledgements a baseball feel for a baseball book.

Bill James and John Dewan are the David Ortiz and Alex Rodriguez of Baseball Info Solutions. The public faces of the company, their search for baseball truth guarantees BIS' position as the most innovative firm in the business.

Damon Lichtenwalner is Ichiro Suzuki. Despite the fact that he's often in the background, Damon is a superstar nonetheless, hitting well over .300 every baseball season.

Jon Vrecsics and Jim Swavely are Jay Bruce, our Minor League Players of the Year. Jon and Jim run our Double-A and Triple-A operation, an enormous task, to say the least.

Matt Lorenzo and Todd Radcliffe are Tim Wakefield. Veterans of Baseball Info Solutions, they take the ball whenever asked and are vital to the overall quantity and quality of data that BIS produces.

Joel Kammeyer is Troy Tulowitzki, our 2007 Rookie of the Year. With Joel moving on into the baseball world, we're planning on the same kind of star performance from his successor, Dan Casey.

If there was a particular Advanced Scout who was famous enough to be a household name, that would be Pat Quinn. Pat doesn't work in the Pennsylvania office, but the support he provides remotely for John Dewan is top-notch.

New programmer Tony Pellegrino is Ryan Braun. Tony has only been at BIS since August, but he has superstar potential written all over him.

Our Video Scout crew from 2007 are Placido Polanco. If you can hit .341 and still go relatively unnoticed, that's these guys. Thanks to Ben Baroody, Mike Berman, Dedan Brozino, Chris Calo, James Conrad, Austin Diamond, Brett Gilliland, Sven Jenkins, Wes Koser, Gary Read, Colin Runt, Eric Schulhaus and Mark Shive.

Our colleagues at ACTA Sports are our MLB-caliber Public Relations Department, helping spread the good word about Baseball Info Solutions. Thanks to Greg Pierce, Andrew Yankech, Charles Fiore and the rest of the ACTA staff.

Thanks to our remote video crew, who is like—what else?—a remote video crew. Thanks to James Davis, Jr., Brian Dewberry-Jones, David Dick, Joe Dimino, Mariusz Robert Dudek, Don Masi, Al Melchior, John Menna, Gus Papadopoulos, Theo Papadopoulos, Daryl Ravani, Harold Richter, Bob Routier, Kyle Schmidt, Wayne Sit and John Wagner.

Thanks to our friends and helpers with a connection to the baseball industry: Greg Ambrosius, Andy Andres, Jeff Barton, Matthew Berry, Jim Callis, Mike Canter, Gary

Cohen, David Creamer, Doug Dennis, Jeff Erickson, Jason Grey, Durward Hamil, Gene McCaffrey, Peter Kreutzer, Sig Mejdal, Bob Meyerhoff, Rob Neyer, Mat Olkin, Scott Pianowski, Mike Phillips, David Pinto, Nate Ravitz, Hal Richman, Steve Ruskowski, Mike Salfino, Peter Schoenke, Ron Shandler, John Sickels, Sam Walker, Mark Watson, Rick Wilton, Rick Wolf, Trace Wood and Todd Zola.

And who am I? I am the Walrus. Goo goo g'joob.

Steve Moyer
President
Baseball Info Solutions

Introduction

Baseball fans have it the worst. You know this, deep down. No matter what anyone says, no matter how many times your spouse rolls his or her eyes when you complain about the winter, you know we have the absolute longest and dreariest off-season of any fan base in sports.

The weather plays no small part in this, of course, and those of us here at ACTA Sports—just outside Chicago—take baseball's hot-stove season pretty literally. But now that we're publishing *The Bill James Handbook* in-house, along with the brilliant folks at Baseball Info Solutions, maybe we won't mind the winter quite so much when we settle into our armchairs and look back over the year that was.

In 2007, Barry Bonds wrapped up his impressive but somehow not-all-that-exciting assault on Hank Aaron's home run record—and eclipsed 755 in early August. There were incredible pennant races; the ascension of the Arizona "Baby-backs;" and perhaps the last game in pinstripes by Jorge Posada, Mariano Rivera and Alex Rodriguez. We watched Bobby Jenks tie the record for consecutive batters retired; we saw David Wright assert himself as, if not the top third basemen in New York, then no worse than 1a.

But if 2007 was a disappointment (as it was for *half* of our office here at ACTA Sports, the half who aren't Cubs fans—oh wait, they were disappointed too), the *Handbook* allows us to look toward next year and dream for just a little while about what moves our favorite teams might make at the winter meetings, or what a pennant might feel like in our hometown. Pure fantasy? Maybe. But then that's why we offer projections as well, so you can go into your respective fantasy game drafts prepared.

We offer new features this year such as: Bill James' "Young Talent Inventory," in which he analyzes the best new players in baseball. Don't miss the 2007 Fielding Bible Awards (inspired by John Dewan's book *The Fielding Bible*, the cutting edge of fielding statistical analysis). And as always, errata (hopefully none!) will be available at www.BaseballInfoSolutions.com beginning Feb. 1.

My advice? Keep a copy of the *Handbook* near you at all times, or at least wherever you wind up watching football on weekends, or basketball during the week. As soon as you lose interest in the dreary march between hash-marks, or in the eternal last two minutes of a basketball game, pick up this book. Guaranteed: You'll feel just a note of spring in the air, no matter what the weather is like outside.

Enjoy the cold. Recharge. After all, pitchers and catchers report in just a few short months.

L.C. Fiore
ACTA Sports

2007 Team Statistics

As Bill Taylor said, "Players win games, teams win championships."

For all the attention paid to individual achievement in the game of baseball, it is only in the context of "team" that these achievements have relevance. So it feels right that in the first section of this book we examine the teams—a comprehensive look at the statistics behind the successes and failures of the past season.

In the next few pages, teams are evaluated in aggregate against every other team in baseball. If you want to know which team had the highest fielding percentage in the AL Central, the best record in June in the NL East, or the lowest number of home runs in the American League, it's all here.

Enjoy.

2007 American League Standings

Overall

EAST

Team	W-L	Pct	GB	D1	LD1	LLd
Boston Red Sox	96-66	.593	0.0	172	10/1	11.5
New York Yankees*	94-68	.580	2.0	5	4/10	0.5
Toronto Blue Jays	83-79	.512	13.0	10	4/17	1.0
Baltimore Orioles	69-93	.426	27.0	0	-	0.0
Tampa Bay Devil Rays	66-96	.407	30.0	2	4/7	0.5

CENTRAL

Team	W-L	Pct	GB	D1	LD1	LLd
Cleveland Indians	96-66	.593	0.0	121	10/1	8.0
Detroit Tigers	88-74	.543	8.0	59	8/16	2.0
Minnesota Twins	79-83	.488	17.0	18	4/23	1.5
Chicago White Sox	72-90	.444	24.0	0	-	0.0
Kansas City Royals	69-93	.426	27.0	1	4/2	0.0

WEST

Team	W-L	Pct	GB	D1	LD1	LLd
Los Angeles Angels	94-68	.580	0.0	172	10/1	9.5
Seattle Mariners	88-74	.543	6.0	7	4/17	1.5
Oakland Athletics	76-86	.469	18.0	9	5/8	2.0
Texas Rangers	75-87	.463	19.0	0	-	0.0

* Clinched Wild Card Birth on 9/26. Division Clinch Dates: Cleveland 9/23, Los Angeles 9/23, Boston 9/28.
D1 = Number of days a team had at least a share of first place of their division; LD1 = Last date the team had at least a share of first place; LLd = The largest number of games that a team led their division

East Division

Tm	AT Home	AT Road	VERSUS East	Cent	West	NL	LHS	RHS	COND Day	Night	Grass	Turf	GAME 1-Rn	5+Rn	XInn	April	May	June	July	Aug	S/O	ALL-STAR Pre	Post
Bos	51-30	45-36	42-30	22-13	20-17	12-6	25-23	71-43	32-15	64-51	83-58	13-8	22-28	36-17	2-5	16-8	20-8	13-14	15-12	16-13	16-11	53-34	43-32
NYY	52-29	42-39	39-33	30-11	15-16	10-8	20-19	74-49	29-27	65-41	82-59	12-9	18-21	46-19	4-9	9-14	13-15	16-11	19-9	18-11	19-8	43-43	51-25
Tor	49-32	34-47	36-36	19-18	18-17	10-8	26-17	57-62	28-25	55-54	27-38	56-41	29-25	23-14	8-9	13-12	12-16	14-13	14-12	15-13	15-13	43-44	40-35
Bal	35-46	34-47	34-38	16-19	13-24	6-12	19-27	50-66	15-25	54-68	61-80	8-13	13-31	14-24	10-7	12-14	15-13	8-18	15-10	9-19	10-19	38-50	31-43
TB	37-44	29-52	29-43	14-24	16-18	7-11	21-25	45-71	22-24	44-72	26-45	40-51	22-21	19-33	8-3	11-14	11-15	11-17	7-20	15-14	11-16	34-53	32-43

Central Division

Tm	AT Home	AT Road	VERSUS East	Cent	West	NL	LHS	RHS	COND Day	Night	Grass	Turf	GAME 1-Rn	5+Rn	XInn	April	May	June	July	Aug	S/O	ALL-STAR Pre	Post
Cle	51-29	45-37	18-18	48-24	21-15	9-9	32-19	64-47	28-19	68-47	84-60	12-6	29-24	26-15	11-8	14-8	19-11	15-13	12-14	17-11	19-9	52-36	44-30
Det	45-36	43-38	20-15	36-36	18-19	14-4	28-15	60-59	30-25	58-49	77-69	11-5	27-19	26-21	8-10	14-11	16-12	16-10	15-12	11-18	16-11	52-34	36-40
Min	41-40	38-43	19-19	28-44	21-13	11-7	22-24	57-59	29-26	50-57	37-38	42-45	22-22	23-25	5-7	14-11	13-14	15-12	13-14	13-16	11-16	45-43	34-40
CWS	38-43	34-47	17-23	39-33	12-20	4-14	16-28	56-62	25-40	47-50	63-82	9-8	16-26	10-27	6-7	12-11	12-14	10-18	14-15	9-20	15-12	39-47	33-43
KC	35-46	34-47	11-26	29-43	19-16	10-8	19-26	50-67	21-23	48-70	62-84	7-9	21-22	22-30	5-8	8-18	11-17	15-12	13-12	13-15	9-19	38-50	31-43

West Division

Tm	AT Home	AT Road	VERSUS East	Cent	West	NL	LHS	RHS	COND Day	Night	Grass	Turf	GAME 1-Rn	5+Rn	XInn	April	May	June	July	Aug	S/O	ALL-STAR Pre	Post
LAA	54-27	40-41	26-18	22-21	32-25	14-4	19-21	75-47	30-23	64-45	91-62	3-6	25-19	25-19	7-3	15-11	18-11	17-9	12-12	18-11	14-14	53-35	41-33
Sea	49-33	39-41	25-19	23-20	31-26	9-9	28-13	60-61	24-22	64-52	83-67	5-7	27-20	24-29	5-2	10-10	16-14	18-9	14-14	15-13	15-14	49-36	39-38
Oak	40-41	36-45	21-20	21-25	24-33	10-8	24-22	52-64	27-30	49-56	70-78	6-8	25-24	22-17	11-5	12-13	14-13	15-13	9-18	17-12	9-17	44-44	32-42
Tex	47-34	28-53	20-25	17-25	27-30	11-7	22-25	53-62	19-21	56-66	72-77	3-10	26-18	19-24	5-9	10-15	9-20	14-12	14-12	14-14	14-14	38-50	37-37

Team vs. Team Breakdown

	EAST Bos	NYY	Tor	Bal	TB	CENTRAL Cle	Det	Min	CWS	KC	WEST LAA	Sea	Oak	Tex
Boston Red Sox	-	8	9	12	13	5	3	4	7	3	6	4	4	6
New York Yankees	10	-	10	9	10	6	4	5	6	9	3	5	2	5
Toronto Blue Jays	9	8	-	10	9	2	3	6	4	4	4	5	4	5
Baltimore Orioles	6	9	8	-	11	3	1	0	5	7	3	2	4	4
Tampa Bay Devil Rays	5	8	9	7	-	2	4	4	1	3	2	3	6	5
Cleveland Indians	2	0	4	4	8	-	12	14	11	11	5	4	6	6
Detroit Tigers	4	4	4	5	3	6	-	12	7	11	3	6	4	5
Minnesota Twins	3	2	4	7	3	4	6	-	9	9	3	6	5	7
Chicago White Sox	1	4	3	3	6	7	11	9	-	12	5	1	4	2
Kansas City Royals	3	1	3	0	4	7	7	9	6	-	5	3	6	5
Los Angeles Angels	4	6	3	7	6	5	5	6	4	2	-	13	9	10
Seattle Mariners	5	5	4	7	4	3	4	3	7	6	6	-	14	11
Oakland Athletics	4	4	5	4	4	4	6	2	5	4	10	5	-	9
Texas Rangers	4	1	5	6	4	3	4	2	4	4	9	8	10	-

4

2007 National League Standings

Overall

EAST Team	W-L	Pct	GB	D1	LD1	LLd
Philadelphia Phillies	89-73	.549	0.0	5	10/1	1.0
New York Mets	88-74	.543	1.0	159	9/29	7.0
Atlanta Braves	84-78	.519	5.0	32	5/15	2.0
Washington Nationals	73-89	.451	16.0	0	-	0.0
Florida Marlins	71-91	.438	18.0	2	4/3	0.0

CENTRAL Team	W-L	Pct	GB	D1	LD1	LLd
Chicago Cubs	85-77	.525	0.0	45	10/1	3.5
Milwaukee Brewers	83-79	.512	2.0	133	9/18	8.5
St Louis Cardinals	78-84	.481	7.0	4	4/12	0.0
Houston Astros	73-89	.451	12.0	1	4/20	0.5
Cincinnati Reds	72-90	.444	13.0	11	4/17	1.0
Pittsburgh Pirates	68-94	.420	17.0	8	4/10	1.0

WEST Team	W-L	Pct	GB	D1	LD1	LLd
Arizona Diamondbacks	90-72	.556	0.0	69	10/1	5.0
Colorado Rockies*	90-73	.552	0.5	2	4/6	0.5
San Diego Padres	89-74	.546	1.5	51	9/4	2.0
Los Angeles Dodgers	82-80	.506	8.0	67	7/30	3.0
San Francisco Giants	71-91	.438	19.0	1	4/26	0.0

* Clinched Wild Card Birth on 10/1. Division Clinch Dates: Chicago 9/28, Arizona 9/29, Philadelphia 9/30.
D1 = Number of days a team had at least a share of first place of their division; LD1 = Last date the team had at least a share of first place; LLd = The largest number of games that a team led their division

East Division

Tm	AT Home	Road	VERSUS East	Cent	West	AL	LHS	RHS	CONDITIONS Day	Night	Grass	Turf	GAME 1-Rn	5+Rn	XInn	MONTHLY April	May	June	July	Aug	S/O	ALL-STAR Pre	Post
Phi	47-34	42-39	42-30	25-16	14-20	8-7	26-26	63-47	27-23	62-50	89-73	0-0	14-23	27-20	11-8	11-14	15-13	15-13	15-10	16-12	17-11	44-44	45-29
NYM	41-40	47-34	35-37	28-12	17-18	8-7	29-24	59-50	30-22	58-52	88-74	0-0	22-15	29-18	7-8	15-9	19-9	12-15	13-14	15-13	14-14	48-39	40-35
Atl	44-37	40-41	39-33	22-20	19-14	4-11	31-32	53-46	24-22	60-56	84-75	0-3	18-25	24-20	6-9	16-9	14-14	13-15	13-13	13-15	15-12	47-42	37-36
Was	40-41	33-48	32-40	21-18	11-22	9-9	25-24	48-65	24-22	49-67	70-86	3-3	27-24	12-27	5-9	9-17	13-15	10-16	14-12	12-17	15-12	36-52	37-37
Fla	36-45	35-46	32-40	18-20	12-22	9-9	21-28	50-63	19-24	52-67	68-91	3-0	22-24	21-30	7-6	12-13	14-15	11-16	12-14	9-19	13-14	42-47	29-44

Central Division

Tm	AT Home	Road	VERSUS East	Cent	West	AL	LHS	RHS	CONDITIONS Day	Night	Grass	Turf	GAME 1-Rn	5+Rn	XInn	MONTHLY April	May	June	July	Aug	S/O	ALL-STAR Pre	Post
ChC	44-37	41-40	15-21	46-21	17-18	8-4	19-24	66-53	43-38	42-39	85-77	0-0	23-22	27-17	2-8	10-14	12-15	17-11	17-9	12-16	17-12	44-43	41-34
Mil	51-30	32-49	16-17	43-36	16-19	8-7	28-23	55-50	24-31	59-48	81-70	2-1	22-21	26-21	8-6	16-9	14-15	17-9	11-16	9-18	16-12	49-39	34-40
StL	43-38	35-46	14-21	43-37	15-17	6-9	29-27	49-57	26-24	52-60	78-84	0-0	16-20	26-38	7-4	10-14	12-15	13-13	15-11	15-13	13-18	40-45	38-39
Hou	42-39	31-50	13-18	35-44	16-18	6-9	22-23	51-66	18-27	55-62	73-89	0-0	25-26	19-30	9-10	10-14	12-17	12-10	12-13	15-14	12-15	39-50	34-39
Cin	39-42	33-48	15-19	36-43	14-17	7-11	23-36	49-54	19-26	53-64	72-90	0-0	26-24	18-27	10-8	12-13	9-21	10-16	14-12	17-11	10-17	36-52	36-38
Pit	37-44	31-50	13-18	36-44	14-22	5-10	23-25	45-69	22-30	46-64	68-94	0-0	16-22	20-32	8-7	12-12	11-18	12-15	7-17	17-13	9-19	40-48	28-46

West Division

Tm	AT Home	Road	VERSUS East	Cent	West	AL	LHS	RHS	CONDITIONS Day	Night	Grass	Turf	GAME 1-Rn	5+Rn	XInn	MONTHLY April	May	June	July	Aug	S/O	ALL-STAR Pre	Post
Ari	50-31	40-41	24-9	22-20	36-36	8-7	28-17	62-55	21-24	69-48	90-72	0-0	32-20	20-26	8-6	16-11	16-12	14-13	13-13	16-12	15-11	47-43	43-29
Col	51-31	39-42	17-15	20-20	43-30	10-8	20-24	70-49	26-21	64-52	90-70	0-3	19-19	29-18	11-10	13-13	18-9	15-11	15-9	15-14	21-8	44-44	46-29
SD	47-34	42-40	17-16	26-16	40-33	6-9	22-22	60-52	23-19	66-55	87-73	2-1	23-26	27-23	11-10	13-13	18-9	15-11	18-11	15-14	13-18	49-38	40-36
LAD	43-38	39-42	20-16	23-16	34-38	5-10	26-22	56-58	25-22	57-58	79-77	3-3	28-20	24-22	9-4	15-11	16-11	14-14	12-13	13-15	12-16	49-40	33-40
SF	39-42	32-49	18-17	20-20	28-44	5-10	22-26	49-65	20-30	51-61	71-91	0-0	24-28	17-17	6-15	13-11	12-16	9-18	12-13	16-15	9-18	38-48	33-43

Team vs. Team Breakdown

	EAST Phi	NYM	Atl	Was	Fla	CENTRAL ChC	Mil	StL	Hou	Cin	Pit	WEST Ari	Col	SD	LAD	SF
Philadelphia Phillies	-	12	9	12	9	4	4	6	3	4	4	1	3	4	2	4
New York Mets	6	-	9	9	11	5	4	5	5	5	4	4	2	2	5	4
Atlanta Braves	9	9	-	11	10	5	5	3	3	1	5	2	4	5	4	4
Washington Nationals	6	9	7	-	10	1	2	5	5	6	2	1	3	2	1	4
Florida Marlins	9	7	8	8	-	6	2	2	2	3	3	1	3	3	4	1
Chicago Cubs	3	2	4	6	0	-	9	11	8	9	8	2	5	3	2	5
Milwaukee Brewers	3	2	2	4	5	6	-	7	13	7	10	5	2	2	3	4
St Louis Cardinals	3	2	4	1	4	5	8	-	9	9	12	3	4	4	3	1
Houston Astros	3	2	3	2	3	7	5	7	-	11	5	2	4	4	4	2
Cincinnati Reds	2	2	6	1	4	9	8	6	4	-	9	4	2	2	2	4
Pittsburgh Pirates	2	2	1	4	4	7	6	6	10	7	-	4	3	1	2	4
Arizona Diamondbacks	5	3	4	6	6	4	2	4	5	2	5	-	8	10	8	10
Colorado Rockies	4	4	2	4	3	2	4	3	3	4	4	10	-	11	12	10
San Diego Padres	3	4	2	4	4	5	5	3	4	4	6	8	8	-	10	14
Los Angeles Dodgers	4	5	3	5	3	5	3	3	3	4	5	10	6	8	-	10
San Francisco Giants	4	2	3	3	6	2	5	4	2	3	2	8	8	4	8	-

American League Batting

Tm	G	AB	H	2B	3B	HR	(Hm	Rd)	TB	R	RBI	TBB	IBB	SO	HBP	SH	SF	ShO	SB	CS	SB%	GDP	LOB	Avg	OBP	Slg
NYY	162	5717	1656	326	32	201	(107	94)	2649	968	929	637	32	991	78	41	54	8	123	40	.75	138	1249	.290	.366	.463
Det	162	5757	1652	352	50	177	(99	78)	2635	887	857	474	45	1054	56	31	45	3	103	30	.77	128	1148	.287	.345	.458
Bos	162	5589	1561	352	35	166	(79	87)	2481	867	829	689	54	1042	64	30	54	7	96	24	.80	146	1291	.279	.362	.444
LAA	162	5554	1578	324	23	123	(61	62)	2317	822	776	507	15	883	40	32	65	8	139	55	.72	146	1100	.284	.345	.417
Tex	162	5555	1460	298	36	179	(95	84)	2367	816	768	503	27	1224	56	57	42	8	88	25	.78	129	1092	.263	.328	.426
Cle	162	5604	1504	305	27	178	(100	78)	2397	811	784	590	56	1202	80	32	59	7	72	41	.64	114	1215	.268	.343	.428
Sea	162	5684	1629	284	22	153	(77	76)	2416	794	754	389	32	861	62	33	40	7	81	30	.73	154	1128	.287	.337	.425
TB	162	5593	1500	291	36	187	(96	91)	2424	782	750	545	31	1324	53	34	52	7	131	48	.73	119	1166	.268	.336	.433
Bal	162	5631	1529	306	30	142	(83	59)	2321	756	718	500	31	939	47	38	47	4	144	42	.77	139	1152	.272	.333	.412
Tor	162	5536	1434	344	24	165	(90	75)	2321	753	719	533	32	1044	47	33	48	4	57	22	.72	127	1112	.259	.327	.419
Oak	162	5577	1430	295	16	171	(77	94)	2270	741	711	466	29	1119	49	18	56	10	52	20	.72	142	1258	.256	.338	.407
Min	162	5522	1460	273	36	118	(48	70)	2159	718	671	512	41	839	48	34	45	14	112	30	.79	149	1121	.264	.330	.391
KC	162	5534	1447	300	46	102	(49	53)	2145	706	660	428	34	1069	89	41	47	11	78	44	.64	151	1089	.261	.322	.388
CWS	162	5441	1341	249	20	190	(110	80)	2200	693	667	532	33	1149	52	41	35	11	78	45	.63	138	1074	.246	.318	.404
AL	1134	78294	21181	4299	433	2252	(1171	1081)	33102	11114	10593	7503	532	14740	821	495	689	109	1354	496	.73	1920	16195	.271	.338	.423

American League Pitching

Tm	G	CG	Rel	IP	BFP	H	R	ER	HR	SH	SF	HB	TBB	IBB	SO	WP	Bk	W	L	Pct.	ShO	Sv-Op	Hld	OAvg	OOBP	OSlg	ERA
Bos	162	5	451	1438.2	6071	1350	657	618	151	32	34	62	482	20	1149	33	0	96	66	.593	13	45-56	78	.247	.314	.392	3.87
Tor	162	11	420	1448.2	6108	1383	699	644	157	17	44	55	479	34	1067	42	3	83	79	.512	9	44-69	64	.251	.315	.391	4.00
Cle	162	9	395	1462.2	6206	1519	704	658	146	32	45	56	410	42	1047	42	2	96	66	.593	8	49-63	71	.268	.322	.407	4.05
Min	162	5	438	1436.2	6133	1505	725	663	185	34	40	51	420	33	1094	46	5	79	83	.488	8	38-52	65	.269	.324	.431	4.15
LAA	162	5	396	1435.0	6161	1480	731	674	151	28	40	51	477	22	1156	69	5	94	68	.580	9	43-57	74	.266	.328	.412	4.23
Oak	162	4	446	1448.0	6247	1468	758	689	138	40	60	43	530	60	1036	52	4	76	86	.469	9	36-61	66	.263	.329	.404	4.28
NYY	162	1	522	1450.2	6308	1498	777	724	150	31	51	60	578	33	1009	59	6	94	68	.580	5	34-55	71	.268	.340	.417	4.49
KC	162	2	448	1437.1	6253	1547	778	716	168	38	59	41	520	54	993	56	4	69	93	.426	6	36-54	74	.277	.339	.445	4.48
Det	162	1	443	1447.1	6345	1498	797	735	174	35	49	68	566	41	1047	75	8	88	74	.543	9	44-65	73	.266	.338	.427	4.57
Sea	162	6	456	1434.1	6313	1578	813	754	147	37	50	62	546	39	1020	59	10	88	74	.543	12	43-58	74	.281	.349	.431	4.73
CWS	162	9	463	1440.2	6293	1556	839	763	174	46	58	59	499	50	1015	45	0	72	90	.444	9	42-65	73	.276	.338	.435	4.77
Tex	162	0	467	1430.0	6389	1525	844	755	155	38	51	70	668	38	976	66	4	75	87	.463	6	42-56	80	.274	.356	.423	4.75
Bal	162	4	490	1438.2	6418	1491	868	827	161	41	50	72	696	37	1087	55	8	69	93	.426	9	30-55	78	.268	.354	.412	5.17
TB	162	2	483	1429.2	6403	1649	944	879	199	41	47	63	568	31	1194	55	2	66	96	.407	2	28-49	58	.290	.358	.467	5.53
AL	1134	64	6318	20178.1	87648	21047	10934	10099	2256	500	678	813	7439	534	14890	754	61	1145	1123	.505	115	554-815	999	.269	.336	.421	4.50

American League Fielding

Team	G	Inn	PO	Ast	OFAst	E	(Throw	Field)	TC	DP	GDP	SB	CS	SB%	CPkof	PPkof	PB	UER	UERA	FPct
Baltimore	162	1438.2	4316	1690	28	79	37	42	6085	155	133	109	32	.77	2	4	19	41	0.26	.987
Boston	162	1438.2	4316	1538	24	81	39	42	5935	145	115	107	32	.77	1	4	10	39	0.24	.986
New York	162	1450.2	4352	1588	33	88	31	57	6028	174	151	136	44	.76	1	1	16	53	0.33	.985
Oakland	162	1448.0	4344	1687	20	90	46	44	6121	153	135	101	26	.80	0	2	16	69	0.43	.985
Seattle	162	1434.1	4303	1656	29	90	43	47	6049	167	140	69	45	.61	3	8	8	59	0.37	.985
Cleveland	162	1462.2	4388	1697	24	92	38	54	6177	167	136	93	46	.67	1	7	8	46	0.28	.985
Minnesota	162	1436.2	4310	1611	32	95	48	47	6016	151	128	65	41	.61	0	2	6	62	0.39	.984
Toronto	162	1448.2	4346	1853	27	102	52	50	6301	160	146	134	24	.85	2	3	6	55	0.34	.984
Detroit	162	1447.1	4342	1635	25	99	47	52	6076	148	125	73	31	.70	2	7	10	62	0.39	.984
Los Angeles	162	1435.0	4305	1550	30	101	44	57	5956	154	133	107	31	.78	8	3	8	57	0.36	.983
Kansas City	162	1437.1	4312	1553	36	106	49	57	5971	160	138	70	26	.73	0	6	5	62	0.39	.982
Chicago	162	1440.2	4322	1604	27	108	53	55	6034	168	138	98	23	.81	0	5	20	76	0.47	.982
Tampa Bay	162	1429.2	4289	1548	42	117	56	61	5954	155	128	96	44	.69	0	2	14	65	0.41	.980
Texas	162	1430.0	4290	1744	35	124	59	65	6158	179	143	98	47	.68	1	3	14	89	0.56	.980
American League	1134	20178.1	60535	22954	412	1372	642	730	84861	2236	1889	1356	492	.73	21	57	160	835	0.37	.984

National League Batting

Tm	G	AB	H	2B	3B	HR	(Hm)	(Rd)	TB	R	RBI	TBB	IBB	SO	HBP	SH	SF	ShO	SB	CS	SB%	GDP	LOB	Avg	OBP	Slg
Phi	162	5688	1558	326	41	213	(116)	(97)	2605	892	850	641	74	1205	90	65	52	3	138	19	.88	125	1295	.274	.354	.458
Col	163	5691	1591	313	36	171	(103)	(68)	2489	860	823	622	51	1152	58	83	44	8	100	31	.76	140	1251	.280	.354	.437
Atl	162	5689	1562	328	27	176	(82)	(94)	2472	810	781	534	43	1149	49	55	47	10	64	30	.68	137	1205	.275	.339	.435
NYM	162	5605	1543	294	27	177	(83)	(94)	2422	804	761	549	64	981	54	77	58	5	200	46	.81	114	1196	.275	.342	.432
Mil	162	5554	1455	310	37	231	(121)	(110)	2532	801	774	501	60	1137	76	60	47	5	96	32	.75	112	1117	.262	.329	.456
Fla	162	5627	1504	340	38	201	(110)	(91)	2523	790	749	521	46	1332	82	72	42	9	105	34	.76	107	1192	.267	.336	.448
Cin	162	5607	1496	293	23	204	(117)	(87)	2447	783	747	536	51	1113	66	73	46	6	97	31	.76	140	1170	.267	.335	.436
ChC	162	5643	1530	340	28	151	(84)	(67)	2379	752	711	500	48	1054	40	48	37	5	86	33	.72	127	1190	.271	.333	.422
SD	163	5612	1408	322	31	171	(72)	(99)	2305	741	704	557	45	1229	49	64	44	8	55	24	.70	113	1152	.251	.322	.411
LAD	162	5613	1544	276	35	129	(69)	(60)	2277	735	706	511	41	864	41	58	55	12	137	50	.73	116	1200	.275	.337	.406
StL	162	5529	1513	279	13	141	(62)	(79)	2241	725	690	506	47	909	54	68	54	12	56	33	.63	154	1167	.274	.337	.405
Pit	162	5569	1463	322	31	148	(65)	(83)	2291	724	694	463	31	1135	71	60	51	13	68	30	.69	130	1119	.263	.325	.411
Hou	162	5605	1457	293	30	167	(83)	(84)	2311	723	700	547	40	1043	55	77	40	7	65	33	.66	142	1181	.260	.330	.412
Ari	162	5398	1350	286	40	171	(91)	(80)	2229	712	687	532	38	1111	57	55	58	7	109	24	.82	121	1090	.250	.321	.413
SF	162	5538	1407	267	37	131	(54)	(77)	2141	683	641	532	74	907	39	67	36	12	119	33	.78	142	1141	.254	.322	.387
Was	162	5520	1415	309	31	123	(48)	(75)	2155	673	646	524	38	1128	53	63	41	12	69	23	.75	143	1163	.256	.325	.390
NL	1297	89488	23796	4898	505	2705	(1360)	(1345)	37819	12208	11664	8576	791	17449	934	1045	752	134	1564	506	.76	2063	18829	.266	.334	.423

National League Pitching

Tm	G	CG	Rel	IP	BFP	H	R	ER	HR	SH	SF	HB	TBB	IBB	SO	WP	Bk	W	L	Pct.	ShO	Sv-Op	Hld	OAvg	OOBP	OSlg	ERA
SD	163	1	485	1484.2	6254	1406	666	611	119	58	39	48	474	48	1136	42	6	89	74	.546	20	45-67	76	.250	.311	.374	3.70
ChC	162	2	478	1446.2	6186	1340	690	650	165	68	33	59	573	46	1211	42	3	85	77	.525	10	39-53	67	.246	.322	.399	4.04
SF	162	5	496	1453.2	6299	1442	720	677	133	73	50	47	593	41	1057	49	4	71	91	.438	10	37-60	86	.261	.335	.405	4.19
LAD	162	4	483	1450.0	6196	1443	727	677	146	70	42	38	518	34	1184	44	5	82	80	.506	6	43-60	73	.261	.326	.399	4.20
Ari	162	7	469	1441.0	6216	1446	732	662	169	94	35	61	546	38	1088	48	9	90	72	.556	12	51-66	85	.262	.334	.420	4.13
Atl	162	1	528	1456.1	6263	1442	733	665	172	76	49	42	537	89	1106	48	5	84	78	.519	6	36-51	64	.259	.327	.415	4.11
NYM	162	2	499	1452.1	6293	1415	750	687	165	66	38	61	570	40	1134	36	3	88	74	.543	10	39-56	78	.255	.329	.409	4.26
Col	162	9	472	1472.0	6293	1497	758	706	164	60	50	69	504	61	967	35	8	90	73	.552	7	39-68	80	.266	.330	.423	4.32
Mil	162	3	492	1444.1	6285	1513	776	708	161	58	48	52	507	37	1174	57	2	83	79	.512	6	49-69	95	.269	.333	.422	4.41
Was	162	0	588	1446.2	6333	1502	783	736	187	66	61	42	580	44	931	52	4	73	89	.451	6	46-73	95	.269	.000	.433	4.58
Hou	162	2	476	1464.2	6417	1566	813	763	206	63	52	63	510	62	1109	40	3	73	89	.451	6	38-63	65	.273	.337	.454	4.68
Phi	162	5	498	1458.1	6385	1555	821	767	198	66	47	72	558	62	1050	46	3	89	73	.549	5	42-63	90	.276	.346	.451	4.73
StL	162	2	516	1435.2	6283	1514	829	741	168	53	53	73	509	25	945	39	6	78	84	.481	8	34-45	63	.271	.336	.431	4.65
Pit	162	4	495	1447.2	6374	1627	846	793	174	66	60	76	518	55	997	45	3	68	94	.420	5	32-51	45	.288	.352	.447	4.93
Cin	162	6	522	1449.2	6354	1605	853	796	198	61	49	73	482	47	1068	54	5	72	90	.444	7	34-62	59	.282	.343	.456	4.94
Fla	162	0	560	1443.2	6544	1617	891	793	176	77	57	76	661	60	1142	67	9	71	91	.438	4	40-64	106	.285	.364	.442	4.94
NL	1297	48	8114	23247.1	100975	23930	12388	11430	2701	1040	763	942	8640	789	17299	744	78	1286	1308	.496	128	644-971	1250	.267	.335	.424	4.43

National League Fielding

Team	G	Inn	PO	Ast	OFAst	E	(Throw)	(Field)	TC	DP	GDP	SB	CS	SB%	CPkof	PPkof	PB	UER	UERA	FPct
Colorado	163	1472.0	4416	1842	25	68	38	30	6326	180	154	96	25	.79	2	4	9	52	0.32	.989
Pittsburgh	162	1447.2	4343	1721	31	83	26	57	6147	190	163	110	35	.76	1	2	13	53	0.33	.986
Philadelphia	162	1458.1	4375	1723	39	89	34	55	6187	162	135	84	39	.68	5	1	8	54	0.33	.986
San Francisco	162	1453.2	4361	1666	19	88	32	56	6115	148	130	77	33	.70	3	0	21	43	0.27	.986
San Diego	163	1484.2	4454	1766	23	92	39	53	6312	147	126	189	20	.90	0	4	9	55	0.33	.985
Chicago	162	1446.2	4340	1535	35	94	40	54	5969	134	117	116	24	.83	0	2	16	40	0.25	.984
Cincinnati	162	1449.2	4349	1517	28	95	35	60	5961	155	130	88	31	.74	2	7	14	57	0.35	.984
Houston	162	1464.2	4394	1689	30	103	39	64	6186	148	112	84	28	.75	3	2	6	52	0.32	.983
New York	162	1452.1	4357	1518	23	101	50	51	5976	124	110	105	29	.78	3	3	5	63	0.39	.983
Atlanta	162	1456.1	4369	1657	30	107	50	57	6133	141	119	98	30	.77	0	5	10	68	0.42	.983
Arizona	162	1441.0	4323	1635	28	106	44	62	6064	157	138	88	42	.68	1	6	15	70	0.44	.983
Washington	162	1446.2	4340	1567	17	109	58	51	6016	153	134	80	37	.68	0	7	9	47	0.29	.982
Milwaukee	162	1444.1	4333	1529	27	109	50	59	5971	144	125	99	24	.80	0	4	6	68	0.42	.982
Los Angeles	162	1450.0	4350	1651	20	114	58	56	6115	160	142	96	46	.68	4	2	5	50	0.31	.981
St Louis	162	1435.2	4307	1672	23	121	47	74	6100	155	131	58	34	.63	2	5	10	88	0.55	.980
Florida	162	1443.2	4331	1510	36	137	68	69	5978	159	128	94	33	.74	9	3	19	98	0.61	.977
National League	1297	23247.1	69742	26198	434	1616	708	908	97556	2437	2094	1562	510	.75	35	57	175	958	0.37	.983

Team Efficiency Summary

Bill James

The concept of "Team Efficiency" is essentially a comparison of a team's wins to the statistics of their individual players. We ask three questions:

1) How many runs did the team score, compared to the number we would expect them to score based on their hitting stats?

2) How many runs did the team allow, compared to the number we would have expected to allow?

3) How many games did the team win, based on the number of runs they scored and allowed?

2007 American League Team Efficiency Summary

	RC	Runs	Hit Eff	Exp RA	RA	Pit Eff	Exp Wins	Wins	Runs Eff	Eff Wins	Wins	Overall Eff
Seattle Mariners	793	794	100	796	813	98	79	88	111	81	88	109
Los Angeles Angels	790	822	104	724	731	99	90	94	104	88	94	107
Chicago White Sox	677	693	102	790	839	94	66	72	110	69	72	105
Texas Rangers	763	816	107	837	844	99	78	75	96	74	75	102
Cleveland Indians	821	811	99	694	704	99	92	96	104	95	96	102
Minnesota Twins	712	718	101	740	725	102	80	79	98	78	79	101
Kansas City Royals	671	706	105	786	778	101	73	69	94	68	69	101
Detroit Tigers	891	887	100	789	797	99	90	88	98	91	88	97
Tampa Bay Devil Rays	808	782	97	922	944	98	66	66	100	70	66	94
New York Yankees	973	968	99	754	777	97	99	94	95	101	94	93
Toronto Blue Jays	743	753	101	662	699	95	87	83	95	90	83	92
Baltimore Orioles	770	756	98	810	868	93	70	69	99	77	69	90
Boston Red Sox	902	867	96	636	657	97	103	96	93	108	96	89
Oakland Athletics	768	741	97	703	758	93	79	76	96	88	76	86

2007 National League Team Efficiency Summary

	RC	Runs	Hit Eff	Exp RA	RA	Pit Eff	Exp Wins	Wins	Runs Eff	Eff Wins	Wins	Overall Eff
Arizona Diamondbacks	714	712	100	746	732	102	79	90	114	77	90	116
Washington Nationals	690	673	98	797	783	102	69	73	106	69	73	105
St Louis Cardinals	744	725	97	780	829	94	70	78	111	77	78	101
Houston Astros	747	723	97	828	813	102	72	73	102	73	73	100
Philadelphia Phillies	931	892	96	825	821	100	88	89	101	91	89	98
Florida Marlins	835	790	95	922	891	104	71	71	100	73	71	97
Pittsburgh Pirates	727	724	100	825	846	98	68	68	99	71	68	96
Milwaukee Brewers	814	801	98	760	776	98	84	83	99	87	83	96
New York Mets	844	804	95	725	750	97	87	88	102	93	88	94
San Diego Padres	731	741	101	622	666	93	90	89	99	95	89	94
Chicago Cubs	775	752	97	682	690	99	88	85	97	91	85	93
Cincinnati Reds	805	783	97	840	853	98	74	72	97	78	72	93
Atlanta Braves	821	810	99	726	733	99	89	84	94	91	84	92
Los Angeles Dodgers	778	735	94	701	727	96	82	82	100	90	82	92
Colorado Rockies	882	860	98	710	758	94	92	90	98	99	90	91
San Francisco Giants	686	683	100	708	720	98	77	71	93	78	71	91

It was very widely noted in 2007 that the Arizona Diamondbacks had over-achieved relative to their expectations, which is a way of saying that they were almost phenomenally efficient. Based on that, perhaps we can assume that the concept of Team Efficiency is by now pretty generally understood.

Albert Pujols   Eric Byrnes
Aaron Hill   Andruw Jones
Pedro Feliz   Alex Rios
Troy Tulowitzki   Yadier Molina
Johan Santana

THE FIELDING BIBLE
AWARDS 2007

The Fielding Bible Awards

John Dewan

This is our second year of The Fielding Bible Awards. There are quite a few new award winners and we think that's great. Through our extensive fielding research over the past few years, we're finding that, just like hitters and pitchers, fielders have good seasons and bad seasons. We were somewhat worried the awards might turn into a mirror of the Gold Glove Awards, in which it seems once a player wins, he keeps winning until retirement, injury, trade or a position switch. With a second year now in the books, that is definitely not the case with the Fielding Bible Awards.

Plus, this year we have a true rookie, Troy Tulowitzki of the Rockies, winning a Fielding Bible Award. That rarely happens in the Gold Glove voting.

Here are the Fielding Bible Awards for the 2007 season:

The Fielding Bible Awards 2007

First Base – Albert Pujols, St. Louis

Albert Pujols is the only repeat winner from last year, and it was a landslide. He received the highest vote total of any position (91 out of a possible 100 points) and received 7 of 10 first place votes, plus three additional first place votes from our three tie-breakers. His excellent defense is beginning to become as well known as his incredible offense.

Second Base – Aaron Hill, Toronto

Aaron Hill edged out last year's winner, Orlando Hudson, by a margin of 82 to 80 points. Hudson's injury late in the year (he missed most of September) may have come into play, but it's Hill who has led the majors in plus/minus at second base in each of the last two years (+22 each year).

Third Base – Pedro Feliz, San Francisco

After last year's incredible battle between Adrian Beltre, Scott Rolen and Joe Crede for the third base award (won by Beltre), a new combatant, Pedro Feliz, emerged and won. Rolen once again locked horns but then lost to the winner (Feliz 89 points, Rolen 83). Feliz is especially good at handling bunts and rates an A+ in this area over the last three years.

Shortstop – Troy Tulowitzki, Colorado

A rookie wins the award! You can't say that too often about the Gold Gloves. But the Fielding Bible Award voters are not afraid to stand up and say, "This is our man," even in his first year. On my own personal ballot, I placed annual Gold Glove winner Omar Vizquel on top, with Tulowitzki second. But the final decision of the award panel was that Tulowitzki was the best defensive shortstop in the game in 2007. He did get some help; last year's winner, Adam Everett, was injured about a third of the way into the season but still managed to place second on the strength of his incredible defense in that short time.

Left Field – Eric Byrnes, Arizona

Another close vote as Eric Byrnes gets the nod over the incumbent, Carl Crawford, by three points. Byrnes, heralded in an article in *Sports Illustrated* as the second coming of Pete Rose based on his constant aggressiveness and hustle, was the Major League leader in left field in plus/minus (+28) as well as one of the leaders in Good Fielding Plays (23), a new defensive category being tracked by Baseball Info Solutions.

Center Field – Andruw Jones, Atlanta

Last year Carlos Beltran won the award with Andruw Jones coming in second. This year Jones returned the favor, tipping the scales at 86 points to 80 for Beltran. Jones and Beltran both have great range, but it was probably Jones' intimidating throwing arm that swayed the voters. It's interesting that just a year ago Jones seemed to be slipping slightly from the consensus best center fielder he was a few years before. Perhaps we should also crown him "Comeback Fielder of the Year."

Right Field – Alex Rios, Toronto

Where's Ichiro? In center field this year, that's where. He came in third behind Jones and Beltran. Last year's runner-up in right field, Alex Rios, takes over Suzuki's vacated spot. It was a strong battle between three great right fielders, as Rios scored 73 points to 66 each for Austin Kearns and Jeff Francouer.

Catcher – Yadier Molina, St. Louis

Move over, Pudge. Last year, Ivan Rodriguez and Yadier Molina were neck-and-neck in the battle for the Fielding Bible Award at catcher as they were named first or second on nearly every ballot. Molina maintained his incredible performance controlling the running game in 2007 throwing out 49% of would-be base stealers. Rodriguez' drop from 46% last year to 26% this year convinced our voters to bestow the award on Molina.

Pitcher – Johan Santana, Minnesota

Oh my! The winner of last year's first Fielding Bible Award (and 16 of the last 17 National League Gold Gloves) has been dethroned. Greg Maddux finished a close second but it was Johan Santana who won his first award for defensive excellence. The voting was exceptionally interesting. Five voters, plus all three tie-breakers, had Maddux in first place on their ballots. But then, one voter placed him tenth while two others (including Bill James) didn't rank him in their top ten at all. Why is that? The answer lies in how much emphasis each voter puts on a pitcher's control over the running game. Base stealers have always had their way with Maddux, and 2007 was no exception as 32 of 34 attempts were successful against him. Johan Santana, on the other hand, has always been one of the best in baseball in this area. Base stealers were not only caught more often (45% vs. 6% for Maddux), but Santana held runners on so much better that they attempted to steal far less often (only 11 attempts against Santana versus 34 against Maddux).

Background of the Fielding Bible Awards

While *The Fielding Bible* puts a lot of emphasis on the numbers, especially my Plus-Minus System, I feel that visual observation and subjective judgment are still very important parts of determining the best defensive players. Also, I think people have a right to know who is voting and all the players they are voting for. Therefore, in setting up the Fielding Bible Awards, I took the following steps:

1. *I appointed a panel of experts to vote.* We have a panel of ten experts plus three "tie-breaker" ballots. (See below.)

2. *We rate everybody in one group.* The Gold Glove vote is divided into National League and American League. We make ours different by putting everybody together. Besides, is playing shortstop in the American League one thing and playing shortstop in the National League a different thing, or are they really very much the same thing? We want to say who the best fielder was at each position last year in the Major Leagues, period. So we have a single ballot.

3. *We use a ten-man ballot.* We use a ten-man ballot (I'm referring to the players listed, not the panel of experts). Ten points for first place, nine points for second place, etc., down to one point for tenth place. We feel strongly that a ten-man ballot with weighted positions leads to more accurate outcomes.

4. *We defined the list of candidates.* Only players who actually were regulars at the position are candidates. This eliminates the possibility of a vote going to somebody who wasn't really playing the position.

5. *We are publishing the balloting.* We summarize the voting at each position, clearly identifying whom everybody voted for. Publishing the actual vote totals encourages the voters to take their votes more seriously because they understand those ballots are going to be published. Also, we feel the public will have more respect for the voting if they have more insight into the process.

There is something cool about having 10 experts and a 10-man ballot, because that gives each position 100 possible points. If all 10 voters place one player first on their ballot, he scores 100. It hasn't happened yet.

Here are the tie-breaker rules we are using:
    1. Most first-place votes wins.
    2. Count the tie-breaker ballots.
    3. Award goes to player with the higher plus/minus rating.

Ballots were due on the Tuesday after the end of the regular season. Here is this year's panel:

Since you have this book, you probably know **Bill James**, a baseball writer and analyst published for more than thirty years. Bill is the Senior Baseball Operations Advisor for the Boston Red Sox.

The **BIS Video Scouts** at Baseball Info Solutions (BIS) study every game of the season, sometimes multiple times, with the task of examining a huge list of valuable game details.

The man who created Strat-O-Matic Baseball, **Hal Richman**, continues to lead his company's annual in-depth analysis of each player's season. Hal cautions SOM players that his voting on this ballot may or may not reflect the eventual 2007 fielding ratings for players in his game. Ballots were due prior to the completion of his annual research effort to evaluate player defense.

Named the best sports columnist in America by the Associated Press Sports Editors in 2003 and 2005, **Joe Posnanski** writes for the *Kansas City Star*.

For over twenty years, BIS owner **John Dewan** has collected, analyzed, and published in-depth baseball statistics. He wrote *The Fielding Bible* in February 2006. An update to this book is planned for 2009.

Now Seattle Mariners Player Acquisition Consultant to GM Bill Bavasi, **Mat Olkin** studied, analyzed, and wrote about baseball players for almost fifteen years.

On Chicago sports radio for more than fifteen years, **Mike Murphy's** many strengths include keen baseball observations. He currently hosts a daily show on WSCR 670 The Score.

Joel Kammeyer oversees the BIS data collection operation and manages the team of BIS Video Scouts. Prior to working at BIS, he was employed by the Louisville Bats of the International League.

Rob Neyer writes baseball for ESPN.com and appears regularly on ESPN radio and ESPN News.

The **Tom Tango Fan Poll** represents the results of a poll taken at the website, Tango on Baseball (www.tangotiger.net). Besides hosting the website, Tom writes research articles devoted to sabermetrics.

Our three tie-breakers are **Steve Moyer**, president of BIS, **Todd Radcliffe**, lead Video Scout at BIS and **Dave Studenmund**, one of the founders of www.hardballtimes.com and the editor of *The Hardball Times Baseball Annual*.

The Fielding Bible Awards

Below we show the final point tally for The Fielding Bible Awards in the 2007 season. We asked a panel of experts to complete a ten-man ballot ranking the defensive ability of players from 1 to 10. We show the ranks in the tables below. We then awarded points in the same way as Major League Baseball's MVP voting: ten points for a first place vote, nine for second, etc., down to one point for tenth place. We cover all nine positions, looking at only their fielding work for the 2007 season. Non-pitchers are only eligible if they played at least 500 innings. Pitchers require a minimum of 100 innings pitched

.

First Basemen

First Basemen	Bill James	BIS Video Scouts	Hal Richman	Joe Posnanski	Joel Kammeyer	John Dewan	Mat Olkin	Mike Murphy	Rob Neyer	Tango Fan Poll	Total Points
Albert Pujols	1	1	3	1	1	1	1	7	1	2	91
Casey Kotchman	7	2	5	2	2	2	5	3	2	5	75
Kevin Youkilis	2	5	6	3	8	4	4	1	3	9	65
Todd Helton	4	3	7	6	3	6	3	2	7	7	62
Lyle Overbay	5	4	10	4	5	3	2	6	4		56
Derrek Lee	8	6	2		4	7	6	4		1	50
Mark Teixeira	6	8	1	7	7	5	8		6	6	45
Carlos Pena	3	7	9	10		8		8		10	22
Adrian Gonzalez			4							4	14
James Loney									5	3	14
Justin Morneau					6	9	10	5			14

Others receiving points: Ross Gload 12, Adam LaRoche 10, Sean Casey 9, Ryan Klesko 7, Scott Thorman 2, Brad Wilkerson 1, Lance Berkman 1

Second Basemen

Second Basemen	Bill James	BIS Video Scouts	Hal Richman	Joe Posnanski	Joel Kammeyer	John Dewan	Mat Olkin	Mike Murphy	Rob Neyer	Tango Fan Poll	Total Points
Aaron Hill	1	1		2	1	1	1	2	2	6	82
Orlando Hudson	2	4	1	3	4	2	3	6	3	2	80
Brandon Phillips	6	2	2	4	3	6	5	7	7	3	65
Mark Ellis	4	6	6	5	7	4	4	5	4	1	64
Chase Utley	7	3		1	2	3	7	9	1	7	59
Robinson Cano	3	5	10	7		10	2	1	6		44
Placido Polanco	8	8	4			5	6		9	5	32
Dustin Pedroia	5	7	7		5	9	9	10			25
Mark Grudzielanek			8	6	6	7		8	8		23
Brian Roberts		10	5	9			10			4	17

Others receiving points: Kaz Matsui 16, Luis Castillo 13, Jose Lopez 12, Howie Kendrick 6, Aaron Miles 3, Ian Kinsler 3, Jamey Carroll 3, Freddy Sanchez 2, Josh Barfield 1

Third Basemen

Third Basemen	Bill James	BIS Video Scouts	Hal Richman	Joe Posnanski	Joel Kammeyer	John Dewan	Mat Olkin	Mike Murphy	Rob Neyer	Tango Fan Poll	Total Points
Pedro Feliz	1	1	8	1	1	1	2	1	1	4	89
Scott Rolen	2	3	2	2	3	3	1	2	8	1	83
Ryan Zimmerman	6	2	3	4	4	2	4	3	3	7	72
Brandon Inge	4	6	7	3	7	4	3	8	2	6	60
Nick Punto		4	6	9	2	5		4	4	8	46
Adrian Beltre	7		1	5	10	7	6		6	2	44
David Wright	3	5		6	8	6	5	9	5		41
Eric Chavez	8		5	8		8	8	5	7	3	36
Aramis Ramirez	5		7		9	9	7	10			23
Mike Lowell	10		4	10		10	7		9		16

Others receiving points: Akinori Iwamura 12, Abraham Nunez 6, Jose Bautista 5, Troy Glaus 5, Alex Gordon 4, Alex Rodriguez 3, Craig Counsell 2, Melvin Mora 2, Chipper Jones 1

Shortstops

Shortstops	Bill James	BIS Video Scouts	Hal Richman	Joe Posnanski	Joel Kammeyer	John Dewan	Mat Olkin	Mike Murphy	Rob Neyer	Tango Fan Poll	Total Points
Troy Tulowitzki	1	1	5	1	3	2	1	1	2	6	87
Adam Everett	8	8	1	5	4	5	2	4	3	1	69
John McDonald	2	2		6	2	3	3		1	2	67
Omar Vizquel	6	6	2	2	5	1	4	6	8	3	67
Jose Reyes	4	4	3	3	8	10	6	3	7	4	58
Jack Wilson	3	3	9	8	1	4	7	7	6	9	53
Jimmy Rollins	5	6	4	6	9		5			5	37
Tony F. Pena	9			7		7	5	8	5		25
Jason Bartlett	10	5		9	10	6	9		4		24
Rafael Furcal	7	7		9		8	8		9	8	21

Others receiving points: Orlando Cabrera 15, Ryan Theriot 9, Khalil Greene 8, Derek Jeter 4, J.J. Hardy 3, Yuniesky Betancourt 3

Left Fielders

Left Fielders	Bill James	BIS Video Scouts	Hal Richman	Joe Posnanski	Joel Kammeyer	John Dewan	Mat Olkin	Mike Murphy	Rob Neyer	Tango Fan Poll	Total Points
Eric Byrnes	3	1	2	2	1	1	5	1	1	8	85
Carl Crawford	1	2	1	1	3	4	1		3	1	82
Alfonso Soriano	2	10	9	6	10	3	3	2	5	4	56
Geoff Jenkins	7	5	8	3	8	5	7	5		3	48
Willie Harris	4	4			2	2		4	10	7	44
Reggie Willits	8	9	4	10	5		4	8		2	38
Shannon Stewart	6			5		8	2	3	4		38
Ryan Church	9	6	5		7	6			2		31
Matt Holliday	10	7	10	4	9		6	6			25
Matt Diaz		3			6	7					17

Others receiving points: Hidoki Matsui 13, Jason Michaels 11, Emil Brown 9, Jason Bay 9, Jason Tyner 9, Josh Willingham 7, Jay Payton 6, Jose Cruz 6, Barry Bonds 5, Garret Anderson 4, Moises Alou 4, Carlos Lee 3

Center Fielders

Center Fielders	Bill James	BIS Video Scouts	Hal Richman	Joe Posnanski	Joel Kammeyer	John Dewan	Mat Olkin	Mike Murphy	Rob Neyer	Tango Fan Poll	Total Points
Andruw Jones	2	1	2	2	2	1	4	5	2	3	86
Carlos Beltran	4	3	9	1	1	3	2	4	1	2	80
Ichiro Suzuki	9	4	4	7	6	6	1	2	6	1	64
Coco Crisp	1	2	10	3	3	4	6	6	3		61
Curtis Granderson	3	6		4	5	2	3	3	5	7	61
Torii Hunter	5	5	1	8	8		8	7	8	4	45
Mike Cameron	8	8	7	9	7	10	9	10	7	8	27
Vernon Wells	6		3	5		9				5	27
Aaron Rowand			5	10		8		1			20
Nook Logan		10		6	10	5			4		20

Others receiving points: Gary Matthews Jr. 16, Grady Sizemore 12, Alfredo Armezaga 11, Jim Edmonds 7, Chris Duffy 5, Melky Cabrera 4, Jerry Owens 3, Chris Young 1

Right Fielders

Right Fielders	Bill James	BIS Video Scouts	Hal Richman	Joe Posnanski	Joel Kammeyer	John Dewan	Mat Olkin	Mike Murphy	Rob Neyer	Tango Fan Poll	Total Points
Alex Rios	2	5	1	3	6	3	1		1	4	73
Austin Kearns	4	8	4	1	10	2	4	2	3	6	66
Jeff Francoeur	1	1	5		2	1	3	4		5	66
Andre Ethier	8	3		4	3	7	5	6	4	9	50
Nick Markakis	3	2	2		1	8		10		2	49
Shane Victorino	7	7	8	10		6	2	3	7	1	48
Franklin Gutierrez		6	7		4	5			2	3	39
Corey Hart		4		2	5	9	10	5	8	10	35
Randy Winn			6	8	7	4	8	8	5		31
Magglio Ordonez	5			5			6		10		18

Others receiving points: Mark Teahen 16, J.D. Drew 15, Delmon Young 14, Carlos Quentin 8, Michael Cuddyer 8, Brian Giles 4, Jeremy Hermida 4, Jose Guillen 3, Ken Griffey Jr. 2, Travis Buck 1

Catchers

Catchers	Bill James	BIS Video Scouts	Hal Richman	Joe Posnanski	Joel Kammeyer	John Dewan	Mat Olkin	Mike Murphy	Rob Neyer	Tango Fan Poll	Total Points
Yadier Molina	2	3	2		1	1	1	2	1	3	83
Russell Martin	7	1	4	4	4	4	10	1	2	2	71
Joe Mauer	1	10	3	10	3	2	5	3	5	1	67
Kenji Johjima		4	7	1	2	3	2	5	3		61
Jason Varitek	5	2	6	7	5		4		6	10	43
Brad Ausmus		7	1	5	8	8	9		9	7	34
Gerald Laird		5		6		7	8	7	4	6	34
Ivan Rodriguez	3		9	2		6		8		4	34
Carlos Ruiz		9		3	9	10	3	9	7	9	29
Chris Snyder			8		7		6	4		5	25

Others receiving points: Dave Ross 24, Brian Schneider 19, Bengie Molina 6, Gregg Zaun 5, John Buck 4, Jason Kendall 3, Dioner Navarro 2, Victor Martinez 2, A.J. Pierzynski 1, Brian McCann 1, Ronny Paulino 1, Yorvlt Torrealba 1

Pitchers

Pitchers	Bill James	BIS Video Scouts	Hal Richman	Joe Posnanski	Joel Kammeyer	John Dewan	Mat Olkin	Mike Murphy	Rob Neyer	Tango Fan Poll	Total Points
Johan Santana	5	5	2	3	6	2	2		1		62
Greg Maddux		1	1	1	1	1			10	3	59
Chien-Ming Wang	7		3	2	3	4		2	4		52
Mark Buehrle	2	7				3	3	7	2		42
Tim Hudson	4	4	10	6	5	10		4			34
Dontrelle Willis	6	2	9		9	6			3		31
Jon Garland	1					5	4				23
Shaun Marcum							1	9		1	22
Jake Westbrook					4	9		10		4	17
John Smoltz		3			2						17

Others receiving points: Aaron Cook 16, Woody Williams 16, Brandon Webb 13, Jeff Suppan 13, Jake Peavy 12, Tom Glavine 12, Jarrod Washburn 10, Jeff Francis 10, Jose Contreras 10, Steve Trachsel 9, Erik Bedard 8, Roy Oswalt 8, Adam Eaton 7, Livan Hernandez 7, Andy Pettitte 6, Brian Bannister 6, Chris Capuano 6, Orlando Hernandez 6, Chris Sampson 4, James Shields 4, Fausto Carmona 3, Daisuke Matsuzaka 2, Mike Mussina 2, Javier Vazquez 1

Plus/Minus Leaders

John Dewan

The next two pages summarize the leaders in plus/minus by position for the last three years, and for 2007 by itself. We're expanding the section to include trailers this year. ("Trailers" is our polite word for those bringing up the rear.)

The Plus/Minus System is a way to evaluate defensive ability in baseball. A number greater than zero (plus "+") is above average. Below zero (minus "-") is below average. Please see the Glossary (or my book, *The Fielding Bible*) for a more complete description.

Some observations:

- Manny Ramirez has the worst plus/minus in all of Major League Baseball over the last three years (-109). Does that make him baseball's worst defender? Maybe, but there is a question because of the wall in Fenway Park. Are his numbers hurt by the wall? The answer is clearly yes. Balls that hit the wall might be catchable in other parks. It's an adjustment we need to make but haven't gotten around to as of yet, mostly because unique park configurations like Fenway are not as common elsewhere. Ramirez was below average in road games as well, though nowhere near as poor as his overall numbers would suggest.
- OK, if it's not Manny, is Derek Jeter the worst defender? Jeter has the second worst three-year plus/minus figure at -90. Well, Jeter's poor numbers do not have a caveat like Manny's do. There are no significant park effects clouding his stats. The numbers suggest that Jeter has hurt his team defensively as much or more than any other player in baseball. Having said that, you can still make a good case for Jeter being the best shortstop in the game. Given all that he brings to the team—hitting, baserunning, leadership, overall baseball savvy (including as a defender)—nearly every baseball general manager would prefer Jeter over almost any other shortstop. But defensively, he's not the best. Do I personally think he's the worst defensive shortstop in baseball? No, but he's far from deserving to be a guy who will probably win his fourth Gold Glove in as many years. He's a below-average defender who should never have received a Gold Glove in the first place.
- Scott Podsednik of the White Sox leads all left fielders in plus/minus over the last three years (tied with Fielding Bible Award winner, Eric Byrnes). Scotty Pods didn't qualify for this year's Fielding Bible Award ballot because of his injuries, but there's no question he covers a ton of ground in left field. It's pretty amazing that, on a few occasions over the last two years, the White Sox have removed him for a defensive replacement. Rob Mackoviak has been the main guy. The reason, I surmise, is Podsednik's throwing arm. It's not strong, and Sox manager Ozzie Guillen clearly likes a better thrower out there. But here's something for Ozzie to consider. Podsednik's arm may not be as strong as that of some other outfielders, but his tremendous speed in getting to the ball negates a lot of the problem. In fact, Podsednik ranks eighth (out of 25 qualified left fielders) in the last three years in preventing baserunners from taking an extra base.

Plus/Minus Leaders
2005-2007

First Basemen Leaders		Second Basemen Leaders		Third Basemen Leaders		Shortstops Leaders	
Albert Pujols	+72	Chase Utley	+64	Pedro Feliz	+64	Adam Everett	+92
Doug Mientkiewicz	+31	Orlando Hudson	+53	Brandon Inge	+61	Jason Bartlett	+45
Lyle Overbay	+24	Aaron Hill	+48	Scott Rolen	+50	Clint Barmes	+43
Kevin Youkilis	+19	Mark Ellis	+43	Joe Crede	+44	Jimmy Rollins	+42
Mark Teixeira	+15	Mark Grudzielanek	+36	Adrian Beltre	+42	Jack Wilson	+41
Justin Morneau	+14	Placido Polanco	+28	David Bell	+30	Rafael Furcal	+36
Nick Johnson	+6	Brian Roberts	+25	Nick Punto	+28	John McDonald	+33
Dan Johnson	+6	Jamey Carroll	+17	Eric Chavez	+27	Omar Vizquel	+31
Chris Shelton	+5	Adam Kennedy	+16	Ryan Zimmerman	+24	Troy Tulowitzki	+30
Ryan Howard	+2	Ronnie Belliard	+13	Morgan Ensberg	+16	J.J. Hardy	+24
Travis Lee	+2	Josh Barfield	+13			Bill Hall	+24

First Basemen Trailers		Second Basemen Trailers		Third Basemen Trailers		Shortstops Trailers	
Prince Fielder	-33	Rickie Weeks	-41	Miguel Cabrera	-37	Derek Jeter	-90
Adam LaRoche	-28	Jeff Kent	-36	Mark Teahen	-30	Michael Young	-64
Carlos Delgado	-26	Craig Biggio	-33	Hank Blalock	-28	Hanley Ramirez	-43
Mike Jacobs	-25	Jose Vidro	-31	Edwin Encarnacion	-25	Felipe Lopez	-34
Richie Sexson	-25	Jorge Cantu	-29	Garrett Atkins	-21	Marco Scutaro	-33
						Angel Berroa	-33

Left Fielders Leaders		Center Fielders Leaders		Right Fielders Leaders		Pitchers Leaders	
Scott Podsednik	+34	Andruw Jones	+63	Austin Kearns	+36	Greg Maddux	+25
Eric Byrnes	+34	Nook Logan	+46	Alex Rios	+29	Johan Santana	+18
Carl Crawford	+32	Curtis Granderson	+45	Randy Winn	+27	Kenny Rogers	+17
Reed Johnson	+27	Carlos Beltran	+40	Jeff Francoeur	+24	Brandon Webb	+14
Matt Murton	+21	Joey Gathright	+33	Ichiro Suzuki	+24	Dontrelle Willis	+14
Alfonso Soriano	+16	Corey Patterson	+31	Geoff Jenkins	+19	Kirk Saarloos	+14
Shannon Stewart	+12	Jeremy Reed	+28	Brian Giles	+18	Chien-Ming Wang	+13
Matt Holliday	+9	Willy Taveras	+26	Casey Blake	+18	Horacio Ramirez	+11
Jason Michaels	+8	Aaron Rowand	+21	J.D. Drew	+17	Mark Mulder	+11
Kevin Mench	+3	Vernon Wells	+21	Trot Nixon	+11	Jake Westbrook	+10

Left Fielders Trailers		Center Fielders Trailers		Right Fielders Trailers		Pitchers Trailers	
Manny Ramirez	-109	Ken Griffey Jr.	-53	Jermaine Dye	-57	Daniel Cabrera	-14
Adam Dunn	-63	Kenny Lofton	-25	Michael Cuddyer	-51	Jeremy Bonderman	-11
Pat Burrell	-50	Dave Roberts	-24	Brad Hawpe	-40	Scott Kazmir	-10
Josh Willingham	-34	Mark Kotsay	-17	Bobby Abreu	-40	Jorge Sosa	-9
Carlos Lee	-19	Johnny Damon	-15	Shawn Green	-21	Cliff Lee	-9

Plus/Minus Leaders
2007

First Basemen
Leaders

Albert Pujols	+37
Casey Kotchman	+24
Lyle Overbay	+13
Kevin Youkilis	+10
Todd Helton	+9
Ryan Klesko	+8
Ross Gload	+5
Carlos Pena	+4
Adam LaRoche	+3
James Loney	+2
Scott Thorman	+2

Second Basemen
Leaders

Aaron Hill	+22
Chase Utley	+22
Orlando Hudson	+20
Mark Ellis	+19
Robinson Cano	+17
Kaz Matsui	+12
Brandon Phillips	+11
Placido Polanco	+10
Ian Kinsler	+7
Mark Grudzielanek	+7
Howie Kendrick	+7

Third Basemen
Leaders

Pedro Feliz	+27
Brandon Inge	+22
Ryan Zimmerman	+21
Aramis Ramirez	+15
Scott Rolen	+15
David Wright	+13
Nick Punto	+10
Eric Chavez	+10
Troy Glaus	+9
Adrian Beltre	+7
Mike Lowell	+7

Shortstops
Leaders

Troy Tulowitzki	+35
John McDonald	+26
Omar Vizquel	+20
Tony F. Pena	+18
Jason Bartlett	+18
Adam Everett	+18
Jose Reyes	+13
Jack Wilson	+10
Jimmy Rollins	+7
Khalil Greene	+7
J.J. Hardy	+7

First Basemen
Trailers

Dmitri Young	-22
Nomar Garciaparra	-18
Richie Sexson	-15
Prince Fielder	-15
Scott Hatteberg	-10
Mike Jacobs	-10

Second Basemen
Trailers

Dan Uggla	-19
Rickie Weeks	-17
Craig Biggio	-17
Jeff Kent	-13
Ray Durham	-10

Third Basemen
Trailers

Ryan Braun	-41
Garrett Atkins	-29
Miguel Cabrera	-24
Jose Bautista	-23
Josh Fields	-19

Shortstops
Trailers

Hanley Ramirez	-37
Derek Jeter	-34
Brendan Harris	-19
Michael Young	-15
David Eckstein	-14

Left Fielders
Leaders

Eric Byrnes	+28
Willie Harris	+21
Geoff Jenkins	+19
Ryan Church	+12
Matt Diaz	+12
Adam Lind	+11
Scott Hairston	+11
Matt Holliday	+9
Emil Brown	+9
Shannon Stewart	+8

Center Fielders
Leaders

Carlos Beltran	+25
Andruw Jones	+24
Coco Crisp	+22
Curtis Granderson	+21
Nook Logan	+21
Alfredo Amezaga	+15
Jacque Jones	+13
Jerry Owens	+11
Juan Pierre	+5
Ichiro Suzuki	+4

Right Fielders
Leaders

Franklin Gutierrez	+22
Austin Kearns	+18
Andre Ethier	+16
Corey Hart	+13
Randy Winn	+13
Alex Rios	+12
Jeff Francoeur	+10
Jeremy Hermida	+7
Shane Victorino	+6
Nelson Cruz	+6
Carlos Quentin	+6

Pitchers
Leaders

Greg Maddux	+10
Chien-Ming Wang	+7
Aaron Cook	+6
Tim Hudson	+5
Dustin McGowan	+5
Jake Peavy	+5
Woody Williams	+5
Jeff Francis	+5
Johan Santana	+5
5 tied with	+4

Left Fielders
Trailers

Manny Ramirez	-38
Adam Dunn	-29
Josh Willingham	-28
Pat Burrell	-24
Raul Ibanez	-23

Center Fielders
Trailers

Gary Matthews Jr.	-26
Melky Cabrera	-22
Dave Roberts	-19
Kenny Lofton	-12
Jim Edmonds	-10

Right Fielders
Trailers

Jermaine Dye	-37
Michael Cuddyer	-29
Brad Hawpe	-25
Bobby Abreu	-12
Delmon Young	-10

Pitchers
Trailers

Daniel Cabrera	-9
Edwin Jackson	-6
Scott Kazmir	-6
Scott Olsen	-6
3 tied with	-5

Career Register

The Career Register includes complete career statistics through the 2007 season for every major league player who played in 2007. We've included a few bonus players as well, guys who missed the entire 2007 season, for example Francisco Liriano or Mark Prior, and potential foreign imports for 2008 such as Kosuke Fukudome (pronounced KOH-soo-kay foo-koo-DOH-may).

For players who have appeared in fewer than three major league seasons, we included their full minor league statistics. For those players with three or more years in the big leagues who also spent time in the minor leagues in 2007 (for example, if they had a rehab assignment) we included only their 2007 minor league statistics—indicated by an asterisk. Those players who split time between the majors and the minors last season but have fewer than three years of major league experience still have their full minor league stats included.

If a player led the league in a particular category, that register total will appear in **boldface**.

The Register also features Runs Created (RC) for hitters and Component ERA (ERC) for pitchers, in addition to the more traditional statistics. Developed by Bill James, Runs Created is a method of measuring every facet of a hitter's strengths and weaknesses and combining those factors into one number, indicative of a player's production. Component ERC estimates what a pitcher's ERA *should* have been based upon his raw pitching statistics and gives us a good indication of whether or not a pitcher actually deserved his ERA. An explanation of Bill's most-current formulas for both RC and ERC can be found in the Baseball Glossary at the end of the *Handbook*.

It's been an entire year since our last edition, so here's a little refresher:

Age is seasonal as of June 30, 2008.

For pitchers, **BFP** is Batters Facing Pitcher; **TBB** is Total Bases on Balls (or, Total Walks, intentional and unintentional); **Sv-Op** is Save Opportunities; **Hld** is Holds.

For varying levels of Class-A ball, we have used "A+" to indicate High A and "A-" to indicate Low A.

Finally, Bill James decided two years ago that we should start referring to all incarnations of the Los Angeles Angels of Anaheim as LAA. He cited the Philadelphia Blue Jays of 1943 and 1944 as a historical example of a very temporary team name being forgotten and eventually assimilated into the name they were called going forward: the Phillies.

David Aardsma

Pitches: R Bats: R Pos: RP-25   Ht: 6'4" Wt: 205 Born: 12/27/1981 Age: 26

			HOW MUCH HE PITCHED						WHAT HE GAVE UP										THE RESULTS							
Year Team	Lg	G	GS	CG	GF	IP	BFP	H	R	ER	HR	SH	SF	HB	TBB	IBB	SO	WP	Bk	W	L	Pct	ShO	Sv-Op	Hld	ERC	ERA
2007 Charltt*	AAA	28	0	0	24	35.1	143	26	18	17	7	1	0	0	11	1	45	1	0	3	2	.600	0	15--	-	2.85	4.33
2004 SF	NL	11	0	0	5	10.2	61	20	8	8	1	0	1	2	10	0	5	0	0	1	0	1.000	0	0-1	1	13.38	6.75
2006 ChC	NL	45	0	0	9	53.0	225	41	25	24	9	1	3	1	28	0	49	1	0	3	0	1.000	0	0-0	5	3.88	4.08
2007 CWS	AL	25	0	0	7	32.1	151	39	24	23	4	2	1	1	17	3	36	2	0	2	1	.667	0	0-3	3	5.93	6.40
3 ML YEARS		81	0	0	21	96.0	437	100	57	55	14	3	5	4	55	3	90	3	0	6	1	.857	0	0-4	9	5.49	5.16

Reggie Abercrombie

Bats: R Throws: R Pos: CF-17; PH-9; PR-9; LF-3; RF-2   Ht: 6'3" Wt: 215 Born: 7/15/1980 Age: 27

					BATTING															BASERUNNING				AVERAGES		
Year Team	Lg	G	AB	H	2B	3B	HR	(Hm	Rd)	TB	R	RBI	RC	TBB	IBB	SO	HBP	SH	SF	SB	CS	SB%	GDP	Avg	OBP	Slg
2000 Gr Falls	R+	54	220	60	7	1	2	(-	-)	75	40	29	32	22	0	66	8	3	0	32	8	.80	1	.273	.360	.341
2001 Wilmg	A	125	486	110	17	3	10	(-	-)	163	63	41	49	19	1	154	12	12	2	44	11	.80	3	.226	.272	.335
2002 VeroB	A+	132	526	145	23	13	10	(-	-)	224	80	56	74	27	0	158	9	6	1	41	17	.71	3	.276	.321	.426
2002 Jaxnvl	AA	1	4	1	0	0	0	(-	-)	1	1	0	0	0	0	1	0	0	0	1	0	1.00	0	.250	.250	.250
2003 Jaxnvl	AA	116	448	117	25	7	15	(-	-)	201	59	54	62	16	2	164	9	3	3	28	9	.76	3	.261	.298	.449
2004 VeroB	A+	34	133	36	4	5	5	(-	-)	65	18	12	21	6	0	33	1	2	1	16	5	.76	1	.271	.305	.489
2004 Lancst	A+	29	120	41	10	2	3	(-	-)	64	24	19	23	2	0	24	1	0	0	8	1	.89	1	.342	.358	.533
2004 Jaxnvl	AA	41	168	29	6	4	4	(-	-)	55	17	20	9	4	0	66	1	1	3	3	3	.50	2	.173	.193	.327
2005 Jupiter	A+	76	299	82	12	3	15	(-	-)	145	51	45	47	14	2	87	5	2	1	19	6	.76	5	.274	.317	.485
2005 Carlina	AA	49	178	45	7	2	10	(-	-)	86	28	23	27	11	0	40	6	0	2	7	5	.58	1	.253	.315	.483
2007 Albq	AAA	93	353	114	23	9	17	(-	-)	206	71	55	77	11	0	95	11	2	2	41	6	.87	3	.323	.361	.584
2006 Fla	NL	111	255	54	12	2	5	(1	4)	85	39	24	24	18	2	78	3	4	1	6	5	.55	2	.212	.271	.333
2007 Fla	NL	35	76	15	3	0	2	(0	2)	24	16	5	3	2	0	22	2	0	0	7	1	.88	1	.197	.238	.316
2 ML YEARS		146	331	69	15	2	7	(1	6)	109	55	29	27	20	2	100	5	4	1	13	6	.68	3	.208	.263	.329

Bobby Abreu

Bats: L Throws: R Pos: RF-157; PH-4; DH-1; PR-1   Ht: 6'0" Wt: 210 Born: 3/11/1974 Age: 34

					BATTING															BASERUNNING				AVERAGES		
Year Team	Lg	G	AB	H	2B	3B	HR	(Hm	Rd)	TB	R	RBI	RC	TBB	IBB	SO	HBP	SH	SF	SB	CS	SB%	GDP	Avg	OBP	Slg
1996 Hou	NL	15	22	5	1	0	0	(0	0)	6	1	1	1	2	0	3	0	0	0	0	0	-	1	.227	.292	.273
1997 Hou	NL	59	188	47	10	3	3	(3	0)	72	22	26	25	21	0	48	1	0	0	7	2	.78	0	.250	.329	.372
1998 Phi	NL	151	497	155	29	6	17	(10	7)	247	68	74	101	84	14	133	0	4	4	19	10	.66	6	.312	.409	.497
1999 Phi	NL	152	546	183	35	11	20	(13	7)	300	118	93	131	109	8	113	3	0	4	27	9	.75	13	.335	.446	.549
2000 Phi	NL	154	576	182	42	10	25	(14	11)	319	103	79	130	100	9	116	1	0	3	28	8	.78	12	.316	.416	.554
2001 Phi	NL	162	588	170	48	4	31	(13	18)	319	118	110	125	106	11	137	1	0	9	36	14	.72	13	.289	.393	.543
2002 Phi	NL	157	572	176	50	6	20	(8	12)	298	102	85	112	104	9	117	3	0	6	31	12	.72	11	.308	.413	.521
2003 Phi	NL	158	577	173	35	1	20	(11	9)	270	99	101	120	109	13	126	2	0	7	22	9	.71	13	.300	.409	.468
2004 Phi	NL	159	574	173	47	1	30	(13	17)	312	118	105	139	127	10	116	5	0	5	40	5	.89	5	.301	.428	.544
2005 Phi	NL	162	588	168	37	1	24	(15	9)	279	104	102	116	117	15	134	6	0	8	31	9	.78	7	.286	.405	.474
2006 2 Tms		156	548	163	41	2	15	(8	7)	253	98	107	123	124	6	138	3	2	9	30	6	.83	13	.297	.424	.462
2007 NYY	AL	158	605	171	40	5	16	(10	6)	269	123	101	101	84	0	115	3	0	7	25	8	.76	11	.283	.369	.445
06 Phi	NL	98	339	94	25	2	8	(5	3)	147	61	65	76	91	5	86	2	0	6	20	4	.83	8	.277	.427	.434
06 NYY	AL	58	209	69	16	0	7	(3	4)	106	37	42	47	33	1	52	1	2	3	10	2	.83	5	.330	.419	.507
12 ML YEARS		1643	5881	1766	415	49	221	(118	103)	2942	1074	984	1224	1087	95	1296	28	6	64	296	92	.76	105	.300	.408	.500

Tony Abreu

Bats: B Throws: R Pos: 3B-28; 2B-25; PH-10; SS-7; PR-2   Ht: 5'9" Wt: 200 Born: 11/13/1984 Age: 23

					BATTING															BASERUNNING				AVERAGES		
Year Team	Lg	G	AB	H	2B	3B	HR	(Hm	Rd)	TB	R	RBI	RC	TBB	IBB	SO	HBP	SH	SF	SB	CS	SB%	GDP	Avg	OBP	Slg
2003 Ddgrs	R	45	163	48	7	5	0	(-	-)	65	30	20	24	11	1	24	5	0	0	9	3	.75	3	.294	.358	.399
2003 VeroB	A+	3	10	0	0	0	0	(-	-)	0	0	0	0	1	0	2	0	0	0	0	0	-	0	.000	.091	.000
2004 Clmbs	A	104	359	108	21	8	8	(-	-)	169	50	54	54	8	0	59	7	6	3	16	12	.57	5	.301	.326	.471
2004 VeroB	A+	11	43	18	3	1	0	(-	-)	23	8	3	9	1	0	8	1	1	1	4	1	.80	1	.419	.435	.535
2005 VeroB	A+	96	394	129	23	7	4	(-	-)	178	54	43	62	15	1	56	5	3	4	14	10	.58	9	.327	.356	.452
2005 Jaxnvl	AA	24	96	24	3	2	0	(-	-)	31	10	9	8	4	0	21	1	0	1	2	.00	2		.250	.284	.323
2006 Jaxnvl	AA	118	457	131	24	3	6	(-	-)	179	66	55	65	33	2	69	9	4	6	9	4	.69	15	.287	.343	.392
2007 LsVgs	AAA	54	234	83	22	5	2	(-	-)	121	48	18	48	14	1	34	4	0	1	5	0	1.00	3	.355	.399	.517
2007 LAD	NL	59	166	45	14	1	2	(0	2)	67	19	17	18	7	1	21	3	0	2	0	0		5	.271	.309	.404

Winston Abreu

Pitches: R Bats: R Pos: RP-26   Ht: 6'2" Wt: 150 Born: 4/5/1977 Age: 31

			HOW MUCH HE PITCHED						WHAT HE GAVE UP										THE RESULTS							
Year Team	Lg	G	GS	CG	GF	IP	BFP	H	R	ER	SH	SF	HB	TBB	IBB	SO	WP	Bk	W	L	Pct	ShO	Sv-Op	Hld	ERC	ERA
1994 Braves	R	13	11	0	1	57.1	257	57	35	26	2	0	4	24	0	53	3	4	0	8	.000	0	0--	-	3.81	4.08
1995 Danvle	R	13	13	1	0	74.0	277	54	29	19	5	0	4	13	0	90	2	0	6	3	.667	0	0--	-	1.84	2.31
1996 Macon	A	12	12	0	0	60.0	247	51	29	20	4	1	0	25	1	60	3	1	4	3	.571	0	0--	-	3.22	3.00
1998 Eugene	A-	17	10	0	3	45.1	206	39	36	32	6	0	2	31	0	52	6	0	0	4	.000	0	0--	-	5.11	6.35
1999 Macon	A	14	14	0	0	69.1	272	41	17	13	3	0	2	26	0	95	7	1	7	2	.778	0	0--	-	1.81	1.69
1999 MrtlBh	A+	13	12	0	0	68.2	290	53	26	25	7	2	4	41	0	76	3	1	3	2	.600	0	0--	-	3.66	3.28
2000 Braves	R	2	2	0	0	3.0	14	2	1	1	1	0	0	2	0	2	0	0	0	0	-	0	0--	-	6.25	3.00
2000 Macon	A	11	0	0	8	28.2	103	11	6	6	2	0	0	6	0	48	1	0	2	1	.667	0	3--	-	0.80	1.88
2000 Grnville	AA	1	1	0	0	4.0	17	4	1	1	0	0	0	3	0	5	0	0	0	1	.000	0	0--	-	5.14	2.25
2000 Rchmd	AAA	3	0	0	0	9.0	42	7	8	7	2	1	1	10	0	5	0	0	1	0	1.000	0	0--	-	7.52	7.00
2001 Grnville	AA	34	7	0	4	73.2	319	56	40	38	5	2	5	45	2	93	2	1	3	5	.375	0	0--	-	3.96	4.64

24

Year	Team	Lg	G	GS	CG	GF	IP	BFP	H	R	ER	HR	SH	SF	HB	TBB	IBB	SO	WP	Bk	W	L	Pct	ShO	Sv-Op	Hld	ERC	ERA
2002	WTenn	AA	11	0	0	3	15.0	75	9	12	12	2	2	0	0	20	0	20	2	1	1	0	1.000	0	0--	-	5.50	7.20
2002	Wichta	AA	23	1	0	9	40.2	169	29	16	15	1	1	1	0	21	3	52	3	0	3	0	1.000	0	2--	-	2.38	3.32
2004	Jaxnvl	AA	3	2	0	0	9.2	46	10	7	6	4	0	0	1	7	0	12	0	0	1	1	.500	0	0--	-	8.70	5.59
2004	LsVgs	AAA	14	1	0	2	23.0	109	20	20	20	5	0	0	2	20	0	23	0	1	1	2	.333	0	0--	-	6.51	7.83
2004	Tucsn	AAA	28	0	0	9	44.1	205	44	28	28	10	0	1	2	25	1	41	6	0	1	0	1.000	0	3--	-	5.64	5.68
2005	Tucsn	AAA	27	0	0	10	33.1	150	37	24	24	6	0	0	1	15	0	42	2	0	2	3	.400	0	2--	-	5.47	6.48
2006	Ottawa	AAA	46	0	0	11	65.1	274	54	22	18	4	4	2	3	20	6	78	8	0	9	4	.692	0	1--	-	2.52	2.48
2007	Clmbs	AAA	37	0	0	14	52.1	202	24	7	7	2	0	0	1	20	5	82	3	2	3	0	1.000	0	5--	-	1.17	1.20
2006	Bal	AL	7	0	0	2	8.0	42	10	10	9	1	0	1	1	6	1	6	0	0	0	0	-	0	0-0	0	7.17	10.13
2007	Was	NL	26	0	0	3	30.1	133	37	21	20	7	1	0	0	9	1	26	2	1	0	1	.000	0	0-1	3	5.90	5.93
2 ML YEARS			33	0	0	5	38.1	175	47	31	29	8	1	2	1	15	2	32	2	1	0	1	.000	0	0-1	3	6.19	6.81

Jeremy Accardo

Pitches: R Bats: R Pos: RP-64   Ht: 6'2" Wt: 189 Born: 12/8/1981 Age: 26

Year	Team	Lg	G	GS	CG	GF	IP	BFP	H	R	ER	HR	SH	SF	HB	TBB	IBB	SO	WP	Bk	W	L	Pct	ShO	Sv-Op	Hld	ERC	ERA
2005	SF	NL	28	0	0	7	29.2	124	26	13	13	2	1	1	1	9	1	16	1	0	1	5	.167	0	0-1	4	2.87	3.94
2006	2 Tms		65	0	0	27	69.0	297	76	42	41	7	1	4	1	20	5	54	4	1	2	4	.333	0	3-8	10	4.17	5.35
2007	Tor	AL	64	0	0	48	67.1	275	51	19	16	4	0	1	2	24	2	57	0	1	4	4	.500	0	30-35	2	2.44	2.14
06	SF	NL	38	0	0	16	40.1	170	38	23	22	2	0	4	1	11	3	40	2	0	1	3	.250	0	3-6	8	2.88	4.91
06	Tor	AL	27	0	0	11	28.2	127	38	19	19	5	1	0	0	9	2	14	2	1	1	1	.500	0	0-2	2	6.25	5.97
3 ML YEARS			157	0	0	82	166.0	696	153	74	70	13	2	6	4	53	8	127	5	2	7	13	.350	0	33-44	16	3.20	3.80

Manny Acosta

Pitches: R Bats: R Pos: RP-21   Ht: 6'4" Wt: 170 Born: 5/1/1981 Age: 27

Year	Team	Lg	G	GS	CG	GF	IP	BFP	H	R	ER	HR	SH	SF	HB	TBB	IBB	SO	WP	Bk	W	L	Pct	ShO	Sv-Op	Hld	ERC	ERA
2000	Yanks	R	12	10	0	1	62.1	270	64	28	24	3	4	0	0	21	0	46	1	0	4	2	.667	0	0--	-	3.56	3.47
2001	Tampa	A+	2	2	0	0	7.0	31	7	7	6	1	0	0	0	6	0	8	4	0	0	1	.000	0	0--	-	6.78	7.71
2001	Grnsbr	A	10	10	1	0	65.2	267	37	14	11	2	4	1	2	37	0	67	7	2	5	2	.714	1	0--	-	2.09	1.51
2002	Grnsbr	A	13	10	0	0	52.0	257	65	47	37	4	3	3	1	44	0	35	5	0	2	5	.286	0	0--	-	7.41	6.40
2002	StlsInd	A-	3	3	0	0	15.1	70	20	9	7	0	0	1	0	8	0	12	4	0	2	1	.667	0	0--	-	5.74	4.11
2003	Btl Crk	A	15	11	0	3	61.0	290	80	58	45	3	3	7	3	29	0	45	4	0	0	8	.000	0	0--	-	5.97	6.64
2003	MrtlBh	A+	8	0	0	3	12.2	70	19	14	9	1	1	0	0	11	1	10	1	0	2	0	1.000	0	1--	-	8.35	6.39
2004	MrtlBh	A+	11	0	0	4	23.1	102	20	12	11	1	0	0	1	11	0	21	3	0	4	0	1.000	0	0--	-	3.25	4.24
2004	Braves	R	2	0	0	1	2.2	13	5	2	1	0	0	0	0	2	0	2	1	0	0	0	-	0	0--	-	11.62	3.38
2005	Danvle	R+	3	2	0	0	6.0	20	3	2	2	0	1	0	0	1	0	8	2	0	0	0	-	0	0--	-	0.88	3.00
2005	MrtlBh	A+	18	0	0	16	22.1	100	22	12	11	1	2	0	2	9	0	18	3	0	2	2	.500	0	7--	-	3.85	4.43
2006	Miool	AA	13	0	0	9	15.1	68	7	4	4	1	0	0	0	15	3	13	0	0	0	0	-	0	4--	-	2.92	2.35
2006	Rchmd	AAA	38	0	0	33	44.2	204	38	19	18	4	6	2	5	32	3	44	0	0	1	6	.143	0	17--	-	4.72	3.63
2007	Rchmd	AAA	40	0	0	30	59.2	247	46	18	14	0	0	1	0	35	3	56	1	3	9	3	.750	0	12--	-	2.87	2.11
2007	Atl	NL	21	0	0	5	23.2	93	13	6	6	2	0	0	1	14	1	22	1	0	1	1	.500	0	0-0	4	2.39	2.28

Russ Adams

Bats: L Throws: R Pos: 3B 16; DH 7; PR-7; PH-4; 2B-2   Ht: 6'1" Wt: 180 Born: 8/30/1980 Age: 27

Year	Team	Lg	G	AB	H	2B	3B	HR	(Hm	Rd)	TB	R	RBI	RC	TBB	IBB	SO	HBP	SH	SF	SB	CS	SB%	GDP	Avg	OBP	Slg
2007	Syrcse*	AAA	113	431	113	23	2	11	(-	-)	173	62	54	60	41	0	57	5	6	1	3	3	.50	9	.262	.333	.401
2004	Tor	AL	22	72	22	2	1	4	(1	3)	38	10	10	11	5	0	5	1	0	0	1	0	1.00	3	.306	.359	.528
2005	Tor	AL	139	481	123	27	5	8	(5	3)	184	68	63	66	50	1	57	3	3	3	11	2	.85	5	.256	.325	.383
2006	Tor	AL	90	251	55	14	1	3	(2	1)	80	31	28	23	22	0	41	1	3	3	1	2	.33	5	.219	.282	.319
2007	Tor	AL	27	60	14	3	0	2	(2	0)	23	14	12	9	7	1	14	0	2	0	2	1	.67	1	.233	.313	.383
4 ML YEARS			278	864	214	46	7	17	(10	7)	325	123	113	109	84	2	117	5	8	11	15	5	.75	14	.248	.314	.376

Jon Adkins

Pitches: R Bats: L Pos: RP-1   Ht: 6'1" Wt: 218 Born: 8/30/1977 Age: 30

Year	Team	Lg	G	GS	CG	GF	IP	BFP	H	R	ER	HR	SH	SF	HB	TBB	IBB	SO	WP	Bk	W	L	Pct	ShO	Sv-Op	Hld	ERC	ERA
2007	NewOr*	AAA	48	0	0	22	65.1	281	70	33	28	8	4	6	2	17	0	44	3	0	2	4	.333	0	5--	-	4.17	3.86
2003	CWS	AL	4	0	0	2	9.1	42	8	5	5	1	1	1	1	7	0	3	0	0	0	0	-	0	0-0	0	5.27	4.82
2004	CWS	AL	50	0	0	19	62.0	271	75	35	32	13	3	1	1	20	3	44	1	0	2	3	.400	0	0-0	5	5.90	4.65
2005	CWS	AL	5	0	0	4	8.1	42	13	8	8	0	0	0	1	4	2	1	0	0	0	1	1.000	0	0-0	0	6.94	8.64
2006	SD	NL	55	0	0	15	54.1	232	55	26	24	3	5	2	2	20	4	30	0	0	2	1	.667	0	0-0	8	3.77	3.98
2007	NYM	NL	1	0	0	0	1.0	3	0	0	0	0	0	0	0	0	0	0	0	0	0	0	-	0	0-0	0	0.00	0.00
5 ML YEARS			115	0	0	40	135.0	590	151	74	69	17	9	4	5	51	9	78	1	0	4	5	.444	0	0-0	13	4.97	4.60

Jeremy Affeldt

Pitches: L Bats: L Pos: RP-75   Ht: 6'4" Wt: 225 Born: 6/6/1979 Age: 29

Year	Team	Lg	G	GS	CG	GF	IP	BFP	H	R	ER	HR	SH	SF	HB	TBB	IBB	SO	WP	Bk	W	L	Pct	ShO	Sv-Op	Hld	ERC	ERA
2002	KC	AL	34	7	0	4	77.2	353	85	41	40	8	2	1	3	37	4	67	5	2	3	4	.429	0	0-1	1	4.97	4.64
2003	KC	AL	36	18	0	5	126.0	533	126	58	55	12	2	5	5	38	1	98	2	2	7	6	.538	0	4-4	3	3.82	3.93
2004	KC	AL	38	8	0	26	76.1	344	91	49	42	6	4	4	3	32	2	49	4	3	3	4	.429	0	13-17	5	5.26	4.95
2005	KC	AL	49	0	0	13	49.2	232	56	35	29	3	0	1	0	29	2	39	5	0	2	2	.000	0	0-0	12	5.08	5.26
2006	2 Tms		54	9	0	12	97.1	448	102	74	67	13	4	4	2	55	3	48	2	0	8	8	.500	0	1-3	5	5.21	6.20

Year	Team	Lg	G	GS	CG	GF	IP	BFP	H	R	ER	HR	SH	SF	HB	TBB	IBB	SO	WP	Bk	W	L	Pct	ShO	Sv-Op	Hld	ERC	ERA
2007	Col	NL	75	0	0	11	59.0	253	47	26	23	3	3	6	3	33	9	46	6	1	4	3	.571	0	0-4	9	3.19	3.51
06	KC	AL	27	9	0	3	70.0	320	71	51	46	9	3	3	1	42	0	28	2	0	4	6	.400	0	0-0	2	5.18	5.91
06	Col	NL	27	0	0	9	27.1	128	31	23	21	4	1	1	1	13	3	20	0	0	4	2	.667	0	1-3	3	5.29	6.91
6 ML YEARS			286	42	0	71	486.0	2163	507	283	256	45	15	21	16	224	21	347	24	8	25	27	.481	0	18-29	30	4.55	4.74

Jonathan Albaladejo

Pitches: R **Bats:** R **Pos:** RP-14 **Ht:** 6'5" **Wt:** 260 **Born:** 10/30/1982 **Age:** 25

			HOW MUCH HE PITCHED						WHAT HE GAVE UP												THE RESULTS							
Year	Team	Lg	G	GS	CG	GF	IP	BFP	H	R	ER	HR	SH	SF	HB	TBB	IBB	SO	WP	Bk	W	L	Pct	ShO	Sv-Op	Hld	ERC	ERA
2001	Pirates	R	10	2	0	5	19.0	85	22	13	10	1	2	3	1	2	0	24	2	0	0	3	.000	0	1--	-	3.44	4.74
2002	Pirates	R	12	10	0	1	60.0	247	71	20	16	2	3	0	3	6	0	37	1	0	3	2	.600	0	0--	-	3.78	2.40
2003	Hickory	A	29	20	5	2	139.0	536	114	53	48	14	2	4	4	19	1	110	5	1	12	5	.706	0	1--	-	2.32	3.11
2004	Lynbrg	A+	24	24	1	0	131.0	561	150	72	63	10	8	7	5	25	0	92	6	0	8	8	.500	1	0--	-	4.04	4.33
2005	Lynbrg	A+	28	6	0	6	78.1	333	74	40	34	9	2	7	2	21	0	76	2	1	4	3	.571	0	2--	-	3.37	3.91
2006	Altna	AA	18	1	0	4	36.0	153	41	18	16	4	3	2	3	5	1	27	1	0	1	2	.333	0	1--	-	4.20	4.00
2006	Pirates	R	3	2	0	0	12.1	48	21	4	4	1	0	0	0	3	0	16	0	0	1	0	1.000	0	0--	-	9.50	2.92
2007	Hrsbrg	AA	21	0	0	13	36.2	156	30	20	17	3	4	0	1	15	3	35	4	0	4	3	.571	0	2--	-	2.92	4.17
2007	Clmbs	AAA	15	0	0	4	24.0	95	14	3	3	2	0	0	3	7	1	21	2	1	3	0	1.000	0	0--	-	1.86	1.13
2007	Was	NL	14	0	0	1	14.1	51	7	3	3	1	0	1	1	2	0	12	0	0	1	1	.500	0	0-1	2	1.10	1.88

Matt Albers

Pitches: R **Bats:** L **Pos:** SP-18; RP-13 **Ht:** 6'0" **Wt:** 205 **Born:** 1/20/1983 **Age:** 25

			HOW MUCH HE PITCHED						WHAT HE GAVE UP												THE RESULTS							
Year	Team	Lg	G	GS	CG	GF	IP	BFP	H	R	ER	HR	SH	SF	HB	TBB	IBB	SO	WP	Bk	W	L	Pct	ShO	Sv-Op	Hld	ERC	ERA
2002	Mrtnsvl	R+	13	13	0	0	59.2	273	61	38	34	2	2	3	7	38	0	72	5	1	2	3	.400	0	0--	-	5.19	5.13
2003	TriCity	A-	15	14	0	0	86.1	355	69	37	28	1	3	0	5	25	0	94	4	1	5	4	.556	0	0--	-	2.24	2.92
2004	Lxngtn	A	22	21	0	0	111.1	474	95	51	41	3	4	6	6	57	0	140	11	0	8	3	.727	0	0--	-	3.45	3.31
2005	Salem	A+	28	27	0	0	148.2	669	161	86	77	15	2	4	8	62	0	146	7	0	8	12	.400	0	0--	-	4.78	4.66
2006	CpChr	AA	19	19	0	0	116.0	496	96	40	28	4	4	2	12	47	2	95	9	0	10	2	.833	0	0--	-	3.05	2.17
2006	RdRck	AAA	4	4	0	0	25.0	107	24	11	11	2	0	0	2	10	0	26	0	0	2	1	.667	0	0--	-	4.09	3.96
2007	RdRck	AAA	9	9	1	0	53.0	223	50	28	22	6	1	3	2	22	0	43	3	0	2	3	.400	0	0--	-	4.17	3.74
2006	Hou	NL	4	2	0	0	15.0	66	17	10	10	1	2	0	0	7	0	11	0	0	0	2	.000	0	0-0	0	4.97	6.00
2007	Hou	NL	31	18	0	2	110.2	508	127	77	72	18	6	8	7	50	6	71	7	0	4	11	.267	0	0-0	0	5.76	5.86
2 ML YEARS			35	20	0	2	125.2	574	144	87	82	19	8	8	7	57	6	82	7	0	4	13	.235	0	0-0	0	5.66	5.87

Antonio Alfonseca

Pitches: R **Bats:** R **Pos:** RP-61 **Ht:** 6'5" **Wt:** 250 **Born:** 4/16/1972 **Age:** 36

			HOW MUCH HE PITCHED						WHAT HE GAVE UP												THE RESULTS							
Year	Team	Lg	G	GS	CG	GF	IP	BFP	H	R	ER	HR	SH	SF	HB	TBB	IBB	SO	WP	Bk	W	L	Pct	ShO	Sv-Op	Hld	ERC	ERA
1997	Fla	NL	17	0	0	2	25.2	123	36	16	14	3	1	0	1	10	3	19	1	0	1	3	.250	0	0-2	0	6.41	4.91
1998	Fla	NL	58	0	0	27	70.2	316	75	36	32	10	7	6	3	33	9	46	1	0	4	6	.400	0	4-18	9	4.96	4.08
1999	Fla	NL	73	0	0	49	77.2	325	79	28	28	4	3	1	4	29	6	46	1	0	4	5	.444	0	21-25	5	3.96	3.24
2000	Fla	NL	68	0	0	62	70.0	311	82	35	33	7	3	1	1	24	3	47	0	2	5	6	.455	0	**45**-49	0	4.79	4.24
2001	Fla	NL	58	0	0	52	61.2	268	68	24	21	6	5	1	5	15	3	40	2	0	4	4	.500	0	28-34	0	4.24	3.06
2002	ChC	NL	66	0	0	55	74.1	330	73	34	33	5	4	3	3	36	3	61	1	0	2	5	.286	0	19-28	5	4.12	4.00
2003	ChC	NL	60	0	0	17	66.1	296	76	43	43	7	4	1	2	27	3	51	0	0	3	1	.750	0	0-4	9	5.05	5.83
2004	Atl	NL	79	0	0	11	73.2	313	71	24	21	5	6	1	0	28	5	45	5	0	6	4	.600	0	0-1	13	3.47	2.57
2005	Fla	NL	33	0	0	1	27.1	118	29	15	15	2	3	2	2	14	4	16	1	0	1	1	.500	0	0-2	8	4.96	4.94
2006	Tex	AL	19	0	0	3	16.0	74	23	10	10	3	0	1	0	7	0	5	0	0	0	0	-	0	0-0	8	7.86	5.63
2007	Phi	NL	61	0	0	22	49.2	236	65	31	30	3	0	1	1	27	6	24	1	0	5	2	.714	0	8-13	15	6.03	5.44
11 ML YEARS			592	0	0	301	613.0	2710	677	296	280	55	36	18	22	250	45	400	13	2	35	37	.486	0	129-172	67	4.67	4.11

Eliezer Alfonzo

Bats: R **Throws:** R **Pos:** C-17; PH-10 **Ht:** 5'11" **Wt:** 210 **Born:** 2/7/1979 **Age:** 29

			BATTING																				BASERUNNING				AVERAGES		
Year	Team	Lg	G	AB	H	2B	3B	HR	(Hm	Rd)	TB	R	RBI	RC	TBB	IBB	SO	HBP	SH	SF	SB	CS	SB%	GDP	Avg	OBP	Slg
1997	JhsCty	R+	38	120	33	11	1	2	(-	-)	52	15	15	18	7	0	34	6	0	0	0	1	.00	1	.275	.346	.433
1998	NewJrs	A-	48	175	43	4	1	2	(-	-)	55	16	19	15	6	0	49	2	1	3	1	0	1.00	5	.246	.274	.314
1999	NewJrs	A-	46	178	58	12	2	3	(-	-)	83	14	28	27	3	0	39	4	1	1	3	4	.43	5	.326	.349	.466
2000	Peoria	A	49	175	54	16	0	5	(-	-)	85	28	21	30	6	0	35	6	1	2	2	0	1.00	6	.309	.349	.486
2000	Beloit	A	60	221	59	10	0	5	(-	-)	84	22	27	25	8	0	58	3	0	2	2	2	.50	6	.267	.299	.380
2001	Beloit	A	106	397	110	28	2	14	(-	-)	184	52	48	58	13	3	65	8	3	3	0	1	.00	10	.277	.311	.463
2002	Hi Dsrt	A+	12	43	15	2	0	2	(-	-)	23	7	9	9	3	0	14	2	1	0	0	0	-	1	.349	.417	.535
2002	Hntsvl	AA	69	244	63	15	1	7	(-	-)	101	23	38	29	9	0	55	3	1	1	2	3	.40	8	.258	.292	.414
2004	Jupiter	A+	105	399	112	12	2	18	(-	-)	182	51	70	61	22	2	105	12	0	3	6	4	.60	16	.281	.335	.456
2004	Carlina	AA	4	4	0	0	0	0	(-	-)	0	0	0	0	0	0	4	0	0	0	0	0	-	0	.000	.000	.000
2005	SnJos	A+	53	196	70	16	0	13	(-	-)	125	35	45	47	11	0	49	8	0	2	1	3	.25	2	.357	.410	.638
2005	Nrwich	AA	49	176	55	9	0	9	(-	-)	91	30	31	32	8	2	39	4	0	1	1	0	1.00	5	.313	.354	.517
2005	Fresno	AAA	4	14	4	1	0	1	(-	-)	8	3	3	2	1	0	2	1	0	0	0	0	-	0	.286	.375	.571
2006	Conn	AA	20	65	18	3	0	0	(-	-)	21	8	7	8	7	0	16	1	0	1	1	0	1.00	0	.277	.351	.323
2006	Fresno	AAA	24	74	14	0	1	2	(-	-)	22	5	6	6	4	0	18	6	2	1	0	0	-	0	.189	.282	.297
2007	Giants	R	5	13	6	0	0	0	(-	-)	6	2	5	5	0	0	1	1	0	1	0	0	-	0	.462	.467	.462
2007	Fresno	AAA	18	64	19	6	0	3	(-	-)	34	9	10	10	1	0	8	1	0	0	0	0	-	0	.297	.308	.531
2006	SF	NL	87	286	76	17	2	12	(3	9)	133	27	39	36	9	7	74	7	4	3	1	0	1.00	10	.266	.302	.465
2007	SF	NL	26	64	16	2	1	1	(1	0)	23	5	6	5	2	2	23	1	0	0	0	2	.00	2	.250	.284	.359
2 ML YEARS			113	350	92	19	3	13	(4	9)	156	32	45	41	11	9	97	8	4	3	1	2	.33	12	.263	.298	.446

Sandy Alomar Jr.

Bats: R Throws: R Pos: C-6; PH-2   Ht: 6'3" Wt: 235 Born: 6/18/1966 Age: 42

Year	Team	Lg	G	AB	H	2B	3B	HR	(Hm	Rd)	TB	R	RBI	RC	TBB	IBB	SO	HBP	SH	SF	SB	CS	SB%	GDP	Avg	OBP	Slg
2007	NewOr*	AAA	45	144	42	8	1	4	(-	-)	64	15	29	21	8	0	24	0	1	3	1	0	1.00	4	.292	.323	.444
2007	Bnghtn*	AA	5	16	3	0	0	0	(-	-)	3	1	1	0	0	0	2	0	0	0	0	0	-	0	.188	.188	.188
1988	SD	NL	1	1	0	0	0	0	(0	0)	0	0	0	0	0	0	1	0	0	0	0	0	-	0	.000	.000	.000
1989	SD	NL	7	19	4	1	0	1	(1	0)	8	1	6	2	3	1	3	0	0	0	0	0	-	1	.211	.318	.421
1990	Cle	AL	132	445	129	26	2	9	(5	4)	186	60	66	60	25	2	46	2	5	6	4	1	.80	10	.290	.326	.418
1991	Cle	AL	51	184	40	9	0	0	(0	0)	49	10	7	10	8	1	24	4	2	1	0	4	.00	4	.217	.264	.266
1992	Cle	AL	89	299	75	16	0	2	(1	1)	97	22	26	26	13	3	32	5	3	0	3	3	.50	7	.251	.293	.324
1993	Cle	AL	64	215	58	7	1	6	(3	3)	85	24	32	28	6	1	4	3	1	.75	3	.270	.318	.395
1994	Cle	AL	80	292	84	15	1	14	(4	10)	143	44	43	48	25	2	31	2	0	1	8	4	.67	7	.288	.347	.490
1995	Cle	AL	66	203	61	6	0	10	(4	6)	97	32	35	30	7	0	26	3	4	1	3	1	.75	8	.300	.332	.478
1996	Cle	AL	127	418	110	23	0	11	(3	8)	166	53	50	44	19	0	42	3	2	2	1	0	1.00	20	.263	.299	.397
1997	Cle	AL	125	451	146	37	0	21	(9	12)	246	63	83	78	19	2	48	3	6	1	0	2	.00	16	.324	.354	.545
1998	Cle	AL	117	409	96	26	2	6	(3	3)	144	45	44	33	18	0	45	3	5	3	0	1	.00	15	.235	.270	.352
1999	Cle	AL	37	137	42	13	0	6	(4	2)	73	19	25	23	4	0	23	0	1	2	0	1	.00	1	.307	.322	.533
2000	Cle	AL	97	356	103	16	2	7	(5	2)	144	44	42	45	16	1	41	4	4	4	2	2	.50	9	.289	.324	.404
2001	CWS	AL	70	220	54	8	1	4	(1	3)	76	17	21	20	12	1	17	2	3	2	1	2	.33	6	.245	.288	.345
2002	2 Tms		89	283	79	14	1	7	(5	2)	116	29	37	30	9	0	33	1	1	2	0	0	-	11	.279	.302	.410
2003	CWS	AL	75	194	52	12	0	5	(3	2)	79	22	26	21	4	0	17	0	5	1	0	0	-	4	.268	.281	.407
2004	CWS	AL	50	146	35	4	0	2	(1	1)	45	15	14	14	11	2	13	2	3	2	0	0	-	4	.240	.298	.308
2005	Tex	AL	46	128	35	7	0	0	(0	0)	42	11	14	14	5	0	12	1	3	0	0	0	-	3	.273	.306	.328
2006	2 Tms		46	108	30	8	0	1	(1	0)	41	8	17	13	3	0	14	0	0	0	0	0	-	3	.278	.292	.380
2007	NYM	NL	8	22	3	1	0	0	(0	0)	4	1	0	0	0	0	3	0	0	0	0	0	-	0	.136	.136	.182
02	CWS	AL	51	167	48	10	1	7	(5	2)	81	21	25	22	5	0	14	1	1	2	0	0	-	5	.287	.309	.485
02	Col	NL	38	116	31	4	0	0	(0	0)	35	8	12	8	4	0	19	0	0	0	0	0	-	6	.267	.292	.302
06	LAD	NL	27	62	20	5	0	0	(0	0)	25	3	9	10	0	0	7	0	0	0	0	0	-	3	.323	.323	.403
06	CWS	AL	19	46	10	3	0	1	(1	0)	16	5	8	3	3	0	7	0	0	0	0	0	-	0	.217	.255	.348
	20 ML YEARS		1377	4530	1236	249	10	112	(53	59)	1841	520	588	537	212	15	499	41	48	34	25	24	.51	132	.273	.309	.406

Moises Alou

Bats: R Throws: R Pos: LF-84; PH-3   Ht: 6'3" Wt: 229 Born: 7/3/1966 Age: 41

Year	Team	Lg	G	AB	H	2B	3B	HR	(Hm	Rd)	TB	R	RBI	RC	TBB	IBB	SO	HBP	SH	SF	SB	CS	SB%	GDP	Avg	OBP	Slg
2007	Mets*	R	5	15	5	1	0	1	(-	-)	9	2	3	3	1	0	2	1	0	0	0	0	-	0	.333	.412	.600
2007	Bklyn*	A-	1	4	1	0	0	0	(-	-)	1	0	1	0	0	0	0	0	0	0	0	0	-	1	.250	.250	.250
1990	2 Tms		16	20	4	0	1	0	(0	0)	6	4	0	1	0	0	3	0	1	0	0	0	-	1	.200	.200	.300
1992	Mon	NL	115	341	96	28	2	9	(6	3)	155	53	56	53	25	0	46	1	5	5	16	2	.89	5	.282	.328	.455
1993	Mon	NL	136	482	138	29	6	18	(10	8)	233	70	85	79	38	9	53	5	3	7	17	6	.74	9	.286	.340	.483
1994	Mon	NL	107	422	143	31	5	22	(9	13)	250	81	78	92	42	10	63	2	0	5	7	6	.54	7	.339	.397	.592
1995	Mon	NL	93	344	94	22	0	14	(4	10)	158	48	58	52	29	6	56	9	0	4	4	3	.57	9	.273	.342	.459
1996	Mon	NL	143	540	152	28	2	21	(14	7)	247	87	96	81	49	7	83	2	0	7	9	4	.69	15	.281	.339	.457
1997	Fla	NL	150	538	157	29	5	23	(12	11)	265	88	115	97	70	9	85	4	0	7	9	5	.64	13	.292	.373	.493
1998	Hou	NL	159	584	182	34	5	38	(19	19)	340	104	124	130	84	11	87	5	0	6	11	3	.79	14	.312	.399	.582
2000	Hou	NL	126	454	161	28	2	30	(17	13)	283	82	114	104	52	4	45	2	0	9	3	3	.50	21	.355	.416	.623
2001	Hou	NL	136	513	170	31	2	27	(15	12)	284	79	108	104	57	14	57	3	0	8	5	1	.83	18	.331	.396	.554
2002	ChC	NL	132	484	133	23	1	15	(7	8)	203	50	61	59	47	4	61	0	0	3	8	0	1.00	15	.275	.337	.419
2003	ChC	NL	151	565	158	35	1	22	(14	8)	261	83	91	94	63	7	67	7	0	3	3	1	.75	16	.280	.357	.462
2004	ChC	NL	155	601	176	36	3	39	(29	10)	335	106	106	114	68	2	80	0	0	6	3	0	1.00	12	.293	.361	.557
2005	SF	NL	123	427	137	21	3	19	(12	7)	221	67	63	74	56	1	43	3	0	4	5	1	.83	11	.321	.400	.518
2006	SF	NL	98	345	104	25	1	22	(13	9)	197	52	74	65	28	2	31	1	0	4	2	1	.67	15	.301	.352	.571
2007	NYM	NL	87	328	112	19	1	13	(6	7)	172	51	49	52	27	5	30	2	0	3	3	0	1.00	13	.341	.392	.524
90	Pit	NL	2	5	1	0	0	0	(0	0)	1	0	0	0	0	0	0	0	0	0	0	0	-	1	.200	.200	.200
90	Mon	NL	14	15	3	0	1	0	(0	0)	5	4	0	1	0	0	3	0	1	0	0	0	-	0	.200	.200	.333
	16 ML YEARS		1927	6988	2117	419	39	332	(187	145)	3610	1105	1278	1251	735	91	890	46	9	81	105	36	.74	194	.303	.369	.517

Chip Ambres

Bats: R Throws: R Pos: PH-2; RF-1   Ht: 6'1" Wt: 232 Born: 12/19/1979 Age: 28

Year	Team	Lg	G	AB	H	2B	3B	HR	(Hm	Rd)	TB	R	RBI	RC	TBB	IBB	SO	HBP	SH	SF	SB	CS	SB%	GDP	Avg	OBP	Slg
1999	Mrlns	R	37	139	49	13	3	1	(-	-)	71	29	15	36	25	0	19	2	0	2	22	3	.88	0	.353	.452	.511
1999	Utica	A-	28	105	28	3	6	5	(-	-)	58	24	15	23	21	0	25	1	0	2	11	4	.73	1	.267	.388	.552
2000	Kane	A	84	320	74	16	3	7	(-	-)	117	46	28	46	52	0	72	3	3	2	26	8	.76	3	.231	.342	.366
2001	Kane	A	96	377	100	26	8	5	(-	-)	157	79	41	61	53	0	81	11	5	3	19	15	.56	7	.265	.369	.416
2002	Jupiter	A+	123	509	120	25	7	9	(-	-)	186	88	37	66	57	0	98	9	2	1	23	8	.74	6	.236	.323	.365
2003	Carlina	AA	127	380	98	23	8	10	(-	-)	167	75	55	67	72	1	81	2	0	2	9	6	.60	3	.258	.376	.439
2004	Carlina	AA	137	452	109	28	3	20	(-	-)	203	81	62	79	76	2	117	6	4	8	26	9	.74	7	.241	.352	.449
2005	Pwtckt	AAA	84	279	82	20	3	10	(-	-)	138	47	50	59	47	2	64	4	0	2	19	5	.79	7	.294	.401	.495
2006	Omha	AAA	56	187	38	8	1	3	(-	-)	57	19	15	16	22	0	41	0	2	2	4	4	.33	5	.203	.284	.305
2007	NewOr	AAA	120	427	117	23	0	21	(-	-)	203	80	71	82	71	2	107	3	0	3	7	0	1.00	11	.274	.379	.475
2005	KC	AL	53	145	35	8	0	4	(2	2)	55	25	9	13	16	1	32	2	3	1	3	2	.60	5	.241	.323	.379
2007	NYM	NL	3	3	1	0	0	0	(0	0)	1	0	1	1	0	0	1	0	0	0	0	0	-	0	.333	.333	.333
	2 ML YEARS		56	148	36	8	0	4	(2	2)	56	25	10	14	16	1	33	2	3	1	3	2	.60	5	.243	.323	.378

Alfredo Amezaga

Bats: B **Throws:** R **Pos:** CF-87; PH-26; SS-18; 3B-12; 2B-11; PR-6; 1B-4; RF-3; LF-2   **Ht:** 5'10" **Wt:** 180 **Born:** 1/16/1978 **Age:** 30

Year Team	Lg	G	AB	H	2B	3B	HR	(Hm	Rd)	TB	R	RBI	RC	TBB	IBB	SO	HBP	SH	SF	SB	CS	SB%	GDP	Avg	OBP	Slg
2002 LAA	AL	12	13	7	2	0	0	(0	0)	9	3	2	6	0	0	1	0	0	0	1	0	1.00	1	.538	.538	.692
2003 LAA	AL	37	105	22	3	2	2	(0	2)	35	15	7	7	9	0	23	1	5	0	2	2	.50	2	.210	.278	.333
2004 LAA	AL	73	93	15	2	0	2	(0	2)	23	12	11	5	3	0	24	3	6	0	3	2	.60	2	.161	.212	.247
2005 2 Tms	NL	5	6	1	0	0	0	(0	0)	1	2	0	0	1	0	0	0	0	0	1	0	1.00	0	.167	.286	.167
2006 Fla	NL	132	334	87	9	3	3	(0	3)	111	42	19	32	33	4	46	3	7	1	20	12	.63	5	.260	.332	.332
2007 Fla	NL	133	400	105	14	9	2	(1	1)	143	46	30	38	35	0	52	4	4	5	13	7	.65	4	.263	.324	.358
05 Col	NL	2	3	1	0	0	0	(0	0)	1	1	0	0	0	0	0	0	0	0	0	0	-	0	.333	.333	.333
05 Pit	NL	3	3	0	0	0	0	(0	0)	0	1	0	0	1	0	0	0	0	0	0	1	1.00	0	.000	.250	.000
6 ML YEARS		392	951	237	30	14	9	(1	8)	322	120	69	88	81	4	146	11	22	6	40	23	.63	14	.249	.314	.339

Brian Anderson

Bats: R **Throws:** R **Pos:** LF-5; CF-3; PH-3; DH-2; PR-2   **Ht:** 6'2" **Wt:** 220 **Born:** 3/11/1982 **Age:** 26

Year Team	Lg	G	AB	H	2B	3B	HR	(Hm	Rd)	TB	R	RBI	RC	TBB	IBB	SO	HBP	SH	SF	SB	CS	SB%	GDP	Avg	OBP	Slg
2007 Charltt*	AAA	57	200	51	8	2	8	(-	-)	87	29	31	28	19	0	47	1	0	3	3	2	.60	4	.255	.318	.435
2005 CWS	AL	13	34	6	1	0	2	(0	2)	13	3	3	2	0	0	12	0	1	0	1	0	1.00	2	.176	.176	.382
2006 CWS	AL	134	365	82	23	1	8	(7	1)	131	46	33	32	30	2	90	5	2	3	4	7	.36	3	.225	.290	.359
2007 CWS	AL	13	17	2	1	0	0	(0	0)	3	3	0	0	2	0	7	0	0	0	0	0	-	2	.118	.211	.176
3 ML YEARS		160	416	90	25	1	10	(7	3)	147	52	36	34	32	2	109	5	3	3	5	7	.42	7	.216	.279	.353

Garret Anderson

Bats: L **Throws:** L **Pos:** LF-85; DH-20; PH-3   **Ht:** 6'3" **Wt:** 225 **Born:** 6/30/1972 **Age:** 36

Year Team	Lg	G	AB	H	2B	3B	HR	(Hm	Rd)	TB	R	RBI	RC	TBB	IBB	SO	HBP	SH	SF	SB	CS	SB%	GDP	Avg	OBP	Slg
2007 RCuca*	A+	6	18	4	1	0	0	(-	-)	5	3	2	1	1	0	3	0	0	0	0	0	-	1	.222	.263	.278
1994 LAA	AL	5	13	5	0	0	0	(0	0)	5	0	1	2	0	0	0	0	0	0	0	0	-	0	.385	.385	.385
1995 LAA	AL	106	374	120	19	1	16	(7	9)	189	50	69	63	19	4	65	1	2	4	6	2	.75	8	.321	.352	.505
1996 LAA	AL	150	607	173	33	2	12	(7	5)	246	79	72	68	27	5	84	0	5	3	7	9	.44	22	.285	.314	.405
1997 LAA	AL	154	624	189	36	3	8	(5	3)	255	76	92	80	30	6	70	2	1	5	10	4	.71	20	.303	.334	.409
1998 LAA	AL	156	622	183	41	7	15	(4	11)	283	62	79	88	29	8	80	1	3	3	8	3	.73	13	.294	.325	.455
1999 LAA	AL	157	620	188	36	2	21	(10	11)	291	69	80	81	34	8	81	0	0	6	3	4	.43	15	.303	.336	.469
2000 LAA	AL	159	647	185	40	3	35	(20	15)	336	92	117	95	24	5	87	0	1	9	7	6	.54	21	.286	.307	.519
2001 LAA	AL	161	672	194	39	2	28	(13	15)	321	83	123	97	27	4	100	0	0	5	13	6	.68	12	.289	.314	.478
2002 LAA	AL	158	638	195	56	3	29	(13	16)	344	93	123	108	30	11	80	0	0	10	6	4	.60	11	.306	.332	.539
2003 LAA	AL	159	638	201	49	4	29	(12	17)	345	80	116	114	31	10	83	0	0	4	3	3	.67	15	.315	.345	.541
2004 LAA	AL	112	442	133	20	1	14	(4	10)	197	57	75	70	29	6	75	1	0	3	2	1	.67	3	.301	.343	.446
2005 LAA	AL	142	575	163	34	1	17	(5	12)	250	68	96	82	23	8	84	0	0	5	1	1	.50	13	.283	.308	.435
2006 LAA	AL	141	543	152	28	2	17	(8	9)	235	63	85	75	38	11	95	0	0	7	1	0	1.00	8	.280	.323	.433
2007 LAA	AL	108	417	124	31	1	16	(11	5)	205	67	80	65	27	9	54	0	0	6	1	0	1.00	8	.297	.336	.492
14 ML YEARS		1868	7432	2205	462	32	257	(119	138)	3502	958	1208	1099	368	95	1040	5	12	70	71	43	.62	169	.297	.327	.471

Josh Anderson

Bats: L **Throws:** R **Pos:** CF-15; LF-3; PH-3; RF-1; PR-1   **Ht:** 6'2" **Wt:** 195 **Born:** 8/10/1982 **Age:** 25

Year Team	Lg	G	AB	H	2B	3B	HR	(Hm	Rd)	TB	R	RBI	RC	TBB	IBB	SO	HBP	SH	SF	SB	CS	SB%	GDP	Avg	OBP	Slg
2003 TriCity	A-	74	297	85	11	4	3	(-	-)	113	44	30	42	16	2	53	10	2	4	26	9	.74	2	.286	.339	.380
2004 Lxngtn	A	73	299	97	12	3	4	(-	-)	127	69	31	59	33	1	47	7	2	2	47	9	.84	0	.324	.402	.425
2004 Salem	A+	66	280	75	13	6	2	(-	-)	106	45	21	38	13	1	53	6	7	0	31	4	.89	3	.268	.314	.379
2005 CpChr	AA	127	524	148	17	9	1	(-	-)	186	67	25	66	29	2	80	8	10	2	50	18	.74	4	.282	.329	.355
2006 CpChr	AA	131	561	173	26	4	3	(-	-)	216	83	50	81	27	2	73	10	8	4	43	13	.77	9	.308	.349	.385
2007 RdRck	AAA	132	513	140	17	6	2	(-	-)	175	64	43	64	32	2	75	8	10	1	40	8	.83	11	.273	.325	.341
2007 Hou	NL	21	67	24	3	0	0	(0	0)	27	10	11	13	5	0	6	2	0	1	1	1	.50	0	.358	.413	.403

Marlon Anderson

Bats: L **Throws:** R **Pos:** PH-50; LF-12; 1B-3; CF-3; DH-3; 2B-1; RF-1; PR-1   **Ht:** 5'11" **Wt:** 200 **Born:** 1/6/1974 **Age:** 34

Year Team	Lg	G	AB	H	2B	3B	HR	(Hm	Rd)	TB	R	RBI	RC	TBB	IBB	SO	HBP	SH	SF	SB	CS	SB%	GDP	Avg	OBP	Slg
2007 LsVgs*	AAA	11	29	7	2	1	1	(-	-)	14	6	11	6	7	0	5	1	0	1	2	0	1.00	2	.241	.395	.483
2007 NewOr*	AAA	6	23	4	1	0	0	(-	-)	5	1	1	1	3	0	6	0	0	0	0	0	-	2	.174	.269	.217
1998 Phi	NL	17	43	14	3	0	1	(1	0)	20	4	4	7	1	0	6	0	0	1	2	0	1.00	0	.326	.333	.465
1999 Phi	NL	129	452	114	26	4	5	(4	1)	163	48	54	49	24	1	61	2	4	2	13	2	.87	6	.252	.292	.361
2000 Phi	NL	41	162	37	8	1	1	(1	0)	50	10	15	12	12	0	22	0	0	2	2	2	.50	5	.228	.282	.309
2001 Phi	NL	147	522	153	30	2	11	(7	4)	220	69	61	72	35	5	74	2	10	5	8	5	.62	12	.293	.337	.421
2002 Phi	NL	145	539	139	30	6	8	(4	4)	205	64	48	53	42	14	71	5	2	4	5	1	.83	16	.258	.315	.380
2003 TB	AL	145	482	130	27	3	6	(2	4)	181	59	67	70	41	5	60	3	4	5	19	3	.86	5	.270	.328	.376
2004 StL	NL	113	253	60	12	0	8	(2	6)	96	31	28	23	12	1	38	1	0	5	6	2	.75	5	.237	.269	.379
2005 NYM	NL	123	235	62	9	0	7	(3	4)	92	31	19	23	18	0	45	1	4	2	6	1	.86	2	.264	.316	.391
2006 2 Tms	NL	134	279	83	16	4	12	(4	8)	143	43	38	42	25	1	49	1	4	3	4	6	.40	4	.297	.354	.513
2007 2 Tms	NL	66	95	28	7	0	3	(2	1)	44	17	27	17	8	1	17	0	1	2	4	1	.80	2	.295	.343	.463
06 Was	NL	109	215	59	13	2	5	(0	5)	91	31	23	28	18	1	41	1	3	2	2	4	.33	1	.274	.331	.423
06 LAD	NL	25	64	24	3	2	7	(4	3)	52	12	15	14	7	0	8	0	1	1	2	2	.50	3	.375	.431	.813
07 StL	NL	23	26	6	0	0	0	(0	0)	6	3	2	2	3	0	5	0	0	0	1	0	1.00	0	.231	.310	.231
07 NYM	NL	43	69	22	7	0	3	(2	1)	38	14	25	15	5	1	12	0	1	2	3	1	.75	2	.319	.355	.551
10 ML YEARS		1060	3062	820	168	20	62	(30	32)	1214	376	361	368	218	28	443	15	29	29	69	23	.75	58	.268	.317	.396

Robert Andino

Bats: R Throws: R Pos: PH-4; SS-3   Ht: 6'0" Wt: 170 Born: 4/25/1984 Age: 24

							BATTING													BASERUNNING				AVERAGES		
Year	Team	Lg	G	AB	H	2B	3B	HR	(Hm | Rd)	TB	R	RBI	RC	TBB	IBB	SO	HBP	SH	SF	SB	CS	SB%	GDP	Avg	OBP	Slg
2007	Albq*	AAA	142	598	166	25	13	13	(- | -)	256	85	50	83	40	1	129	1	2	3	21	13	.62	11	.278	.322	.428
2005	Fla	NL	17	44	7	4	0	0	(0 | 0)	11	4	1	1	5	1	8	0	1	0	1	0	1.00	2	.159	.245	.250
2006	Fla	NL	11	24	4	1	0	0	(0 | 0)	5	0	2	0	1	0	6	0	1	2	1	0	1.00	0	.167	.185	.208
2007	Fla	NL	7	13	5	1	0	0	(0 | 0)	6	0	0	1	0	0	2	0	0	0	0	0	-	0	.385	.385	.462
	3 ML YEARS		35	81	16	6	0	0	(0 | 0)	22	4	3	2	6	1	16	0	2	2	2	0	1.00	2	.198	.247	.272

Rick Ankiel

Bats: L Throws: L Pos: RF-27; CF-22; PH-6; LF-2   Ht: 6'1" Wt: 210 Born: 7/19/1979 Age: 28

							BATTING													BASERUNNING				AVERAGES		
Year	Team	Lg	G	AB	H	2B	3B	HR	(Hm | Rd)	TB	R	RBI	RC	TBB	IBB	SO	HBP	SH	SF	SB	CS	SB%	GDP	Avg	OBP	Slg
2005	QuadC	A	51	185	50	10	1	11	(- | -)	95	33	45	37	27	1	37	5	0	6	0	0	-	4	.270	.368	.514
2005	Sprgfld	AA	34	136	33	7	0	10	(- | -)	70	18	30	21	10	0	29	0	0	0	0	0	-	4	.243	.295	.515
2007	Memp	AAA	102	387	104	15	3	32	(- | -)	221	62	89	70	25	5	89	4	0	5	4	3	.57	11	.269	.316	.571
1999	StL	NL	9	10	1	0	0	0	(0 | 0)	1	0	0	0	0	0	3	0	1	0	0	0	-	0	.100	.100	.100
2000	StL	NL	33	68	17	1	1	2	(2 | 0)	26	8	9	0	4	0	20	0	1	0	0	0	-	1	.250	.292	.382
2001	StL	NL	6	8	0	0	0	0	(0 | 0)	0	1	0	0	1	0	5	0	1	0	0	0	-	0	.000	.111	.000
2004	StL	NL	5	1	0	0	0	0	(0 | 0)	0	0	0	0	1	0	1	0	0	0	0	0	-	0	.000	.500	.000
2007	StL	NL	47	172	49	8	1	11	(9 | 2)	92	31	39	32	13	0	41	0	1	4	1	0	1.00	3	.285	.328	.535
	5 ML YEARS		100	259	67	9	2	13	(11 | 2)	119	40	48	32	19	0	70	0	4	4	1	0	1.00	4	.259	.305	.459

Greg Aquino

Pitches: R Bats: R Pos: RP-15   Ht: 6'1" Wt: 192 Born: 1/11/1978 Age: 30

			HOW MUCH HE PITCHED					WHAT HE GAVE UP											THE RESULTS						
Year	Team	Lg	G	GS	CG	GF	IP	BFP	H	R	ER	HR	SH	SF	HB	TBB	IBB	SO	WP	Bk	W	L	Pct	ShO	Sv-Op	Hld	ERC	ERA
2007	Nashv*	AAA	35	0	0	17	38.2	162	26	12	10	2	2	3	3	19	2	45	4	0	3	2	.600	0	7--	-	2.55	2.33
2004	Ari	NL	34	0	0	26	35.1	147	24	15	12	4	2	2	2	17	2	26	4	0	0	2	.000	0	16-19	1	2.87	3.06
2005	Ari	NL	35	0	0	11	31.1	155	42	29	27	7	1	1	4	17	1	34	2	1	0	1	.000	0	1-3	3	8.22	7.76
2006	Ari	NL	42	0	0	12	48.1	220	54	27	24	8	1	0	4	24	2	51	2	0	2	0	1.000	0	0-0	2	5.99	4.47
2007	Mil	NL	15	0	0	8	14.0	59	13	9	7	2	1	0	0	5	1	12	2	0	0	1	.000	0	0-2	2	3.69	4.50
	4 ML YEARS		126	0	0	57	129.0	581	133	80	70	21	5	3	10	63	6	123	10	1	2	4	.333	0	17-24	8	5.31	4.88

Alberto Arias

Pitches: R Bats: R Pos: RP-6   Ht: 5'11" Wt: 155 Born: 10/14/1983 Age: 24

			HOW MUCH HE PITCHED					WHAT HE GAVE UP											THE RESULTS						
Year	Team	Lg	G	GS	CG	GF	IP	BFP	H	R	ER	HR	SH	SF	HB	TBB	IBB	SO	WP	Bk	W	L	Pct	ShO	Sv-Op	Hld	ERC	ERA
2003	Casper	R+	13	13	1	0	73.0	313	69	45	29	4	2	2	3	23	0	64	5	1	4	4	.500	0	0--	-	3.23	3.58
2004	Ashvll	A	26	24	4	2	135.0	572	153	86	75	23	5	8	3	36	0	83	6	2	8	9	.471	1	1--	-	5.01	5.00
2005	Mdest	A+	37	7	0	4	90.2	394	99	48	44	4	2	3	6	25	0	53	6	0	4	4	.500	0	2--	-	3.95	4.37
2006	Tulsa	AA	49	9	0	10	111.2	479	102	59	54	15	4	4	10	45	1	83	11	2	8	6	.571	0	0--	-	4.22	4.35
2007	ColSpr	AAA	10	3	0	1	26.1	111	32	12	11	1	1	1	0	8	0	15	1	0	2	2	.500	0	0--	-	4.69	3.76
2007	Col	NL	6	0	0	0	7.1	32	8	4	4	1	1	0	0	5	0	3	0	0	1	0	1.000	0	0-1	0	6.51	4.91

Tony Armas Jr.

Pitches: R Bats: R Pos: RP-16; SP-15   Ht: 6'3" Wt: 225 Born: 4/29/1978 Age: 30

			HOW MUCH HE PITCHED					WHAT HE GAVE UP											THE RESULTS						
Year	Team	Lg	G	GS	CG	GF	IP	BFP	H	R	ER	HR	SH	SF	HB	TBB	IBB	SO	WP	Bk	W	L	Pct	ShO	Sv-Op	Hld	ERC	ERA
1999	Mon	NL	1	1	0	0	6.0	28	8	4	1	0	0	1	0	2	1	2	2	0	0	1	.000	0	0-0	0	4.53	1.50
2000	Mon	NL	17	17	0	0	95.0	403	74	49	46	10	7	3	3	50	2	59	3	0	7	9	.438	0	0-0	0	3.49	4.36
2001	Mon	NL	34	34	0	0	196.2	851	180	101	88	18	15	6	10	91	6	176	9	1	9	14	.391	0	0-0	0	3.95	4.03
2002	Mon	NL	29	29	0	0	164.1	705	149	87	81	22	6	2	7	78	12	131	14	2	12	12	.500	0	0-0	0	4.19	4.44
2003	Mon	NL	5	5	0	0	31.0	124	25	9	9	4	2	2	1	8	0	23	0	0	1	2	.667	0	0-0	0	2.84	2.61
2004	Mon	NL	16	16	0	0	72.0	320	66	41	39	2	3	2	4	45	6	54	0	0	2	4	.333	0	0-0	0	5.26	4.88
2005	Was	NL	19	19	0	0	101.1	452	100	57	56	16	4	1	5	54	4	59	6	2	7	7	.500	0	0-0	0	5.11	4.97
2006	Was	NL	30	30	0	0	154.0	693	167	96	86	19	12	6	13	64	7	97	6	1	9	12	.429	0	0-0	0	5.04	5.03
2007	Pit	NL	31	15	0	6	97.0	442	111	68	65	18	2	7	8	38	3	73	2	0	4	5	.444	0	0-0	0	5.77	6.03
	9 ML YEARS		182	166	0	6	917.1	4018	880	512	471	120	50	30	51	430	41	674	42	6	52	65	.444	0	0-0	0	4.50	4.62

Bronson Arroyo

Pitches: R Bats: R Pos: SP-34   Ht: 6'5" Wt: 194 Born: 2/24/1977 Age: 31

			HOW MUCH HE PITCHED					WHAT HE GAVE UP											THE RESULTS						
Year	Team	Lg	G	GS	CG	GF	IP	BFP	H	R	ER	HR	SH	SF	HB	TBB	IBB	SO	WP	Bk	W	L	Pct	ShO	Sv-Op	Hld	ERC	ERA
2000	Pit	NL	20	12	0	1	71.2	338	88	61	51	10	5	2	4	36	6	50	3	1	2	6	.250	0	0-0	0	6.18	6.40
2001	Pit	NL	24	13	1	1	88.1	390	99	54	50	12	4	6	4	34	6	39	4	1	5	7	.417	0	0-0	2	5.09	5.09
2002	Pit	NL	9	4	0	1	27.0	123	30	14	12	1	1	1	0	15	3	22	0	0	2	1	.667	0	0-0	1	4.64	4.00
2003	Bos	AL	6	0	0	2	17.1	66	10	5	4	0	0	0	1	4	2	14	0	0	0	0	-	0	1-1	0	1.14	2.08
2004	Bos	AL	32	29	0	0	178.2	764	171	99	80	17	5	4	20	47	3	142	5	0	10	9	.526	0	0-0	0	3.65	4.03
2005	Bos	AL	35	32	0	1	205.1	878	213	116	103	22	4	4	14	54	3	100	5	1	14	10	.583	0	0-0	0	4.04	4.51
2006	Cin	NL	35	35	3	0	240.2	992	222	98	88	31	9	2	5	64	7	184	6	0	14	11	.560	1	0-0	0	3.37	3.29
2007	Cin	NL	34	34	1	0	210.2	921	232	109	99	28	10	7	13	63	6	156	4	0	9	15	.375	0	0-0	0	4.68	4.23
	8 ML YEARS		195	159	5	6	1039.2	4472	1065	556	487	121	38	26	61	317	36	707	27	3	56	59	.487	1	1-1	3	4.12	4.22

Jose Ascanio

Pitches: R **Bats:** R **Pos:** RP-13 **Ht:** 6'0" **Wt:** 170 **Born:** 5/2/1985 **Age:** 23

			HOW MUCH HE PITCHED						WHAT HE GAVE UP									THE RESULTS						
Year	Team	Lg	G	GS	CG	GF	IP	BFP	H	R	ER	HR	SH	SF	HB	TBB	IBB	SO	WP	Bk	W	L	Pct	ShO	Sv-Op Hld	ERC	ERA
2003	Braves	R	8	0	0	0	26.1	104	26	4	4	0	0	1	2	5	0	17	4	0	4	0	1.000	0	0-- -	3.01	1.37
2004	Rome	A	34	0	0	18	65.2	274	58	39	28	6	0	0	4	15	1	64	5	3	3	3	.500	0	9-- -	2.89	3.84
2005	MrtlBh	A+	5	3	0	2	20.2	94	26	17	14	5	1	0	0	9	0	12	2	0	3	1	.750	0	0-- -	6.95	6.10
2006	MrtlBh	A+	8	6	0	1	31.0	148	38	18	17	0	1	2	4	20	0	23	0	0	1	1	.500	0	0-- -	6.24	4.94
2006	Missi	AA	24	0	0	6	38.0	171	37	20	18	2	1	1	6	17	3	37	1	1	4	2	.667	0	0-- -	4.21	4.26
2007	Missi	AA	44	1	0	20	78.0	314	66	26	22	1	4	5	5	18	0	71	8	1	2	2	.500	0	10-- -	2.35	2.54
2007	Atl	NL	13	0	0	6	16.0	74	17	11	9	3	1	0	0	6	2	13	0	0	1	1	.500	0	0-0 0	4.43	5.06

Scott Atchison

Pitches: R **Bats:** R **Pos:** RP-22 **Ht:** 6'2" **Wt:** 200 **Born:** 3/29/1976 **Age:** 32

			HOW MUCH HE PITCHED						WHAT HE GAVE UP									THE RESULTS						
Year	Team	Lg	G	GS	CG	GF	IP	BFP	H	R	ER	HR	SH	SF	HB	TBB	IBB	SO	WP	Bk	W	L	Pct	ShO	Sv-Op Hld	ERC	ERA
2007	Fresno*	AAA	38	1	0	15	53.2	214	44	17	12	1	2	1	1	8	0	51	3	0	3	2	.600	0	4-- -	1.79	2.01
2004	Sea	AL	25	0	0	8	30.2	133	29	12	12	4	2	1	0	14	2	36	2	0	2	3	.400	0	0-0 2	4.08	3.52
2005	Sea	AL	6	0	0	2	6.2	27	7	5	5	1	0	0	0	1	0	9	0	0	0	0	-	0	0-0 0	3.77	6.75
2007	SF	NL	22	0	0	4	30.2	131	32	14	14	5	1	2	1	10	0	25	2	0	0	0	-	0	0-1 5	4.65	4.11
	3 ML YEARS		53	0	0	14	68.0	291	68	31	31	10	3	3	1	25	2	70	4	0	2	3	.400	0	0-1 7	4.31	4.10

Garrett Atkins

Bats: R **Throws:** R **Pos:** 3B-154; 1B-10; PH-2 **Ht:** 6'3" **Wt:** 215 **Born:** 12/12/1979 **Age:** 28

			BATTING																BASERUNNING				AVERAGES		
Year	Team	Lg	G	AB	H	2B	3B	HR	(Hm | Rd)	TB	R	RBI	RC	TBB	IBB	SO	HBP	SH	SF	SB	CS	SB%	GDP	Avg	OBP	Slg
2003	Col	NL	25	69	11	2	0	0	(0 | 0)	13	6	4	2	3	0	14	1	0	0	0	0	-	1	.159	.205	.188
2004	Col	NL	15	28	10	2	0	1	(1 | 0)	15	3	8	8	4	0	3	0	0	1	0	0	-	0	.357	.424	.536
2005	Col	NL	138	519	149	31	1	13	(9 | 4)	221	62	89	74	45	1	72	5	0	4	0	2	.00	18	.287	.347	.426
2006	Col	NL	157	602	198	48	1	29	(15 | 14)	335	117	120	129	79	6	76	7	0	7	4	0	1.00	24	.329	.409	.556
2007	Col	NL	157	605	182	35	1	25	(10 | 15)	294	83	111	106	67	3	96	2	0	10	3	1	.75	16	.301	.367	.486
	5 ML YEARS		492	1823	550	118	3	68	(35 | 33)	878	271	332	319	198	10	261	15	0	22	7	3	.70	59	.302	.371	.482

Rich Aurilia

Bats: R **Throws:** R **Pos:** 1B-55; 3B-22; SS-12; PH-12; 2B-9 **Ht:** 6'1" **Wt:** 190 **Born:** 9/2/1971 **Age:** 36

			BATTING																BASERUNNING				AVERAGES		
Year	Team	Lg	G	AB	H	2B	3B	HR	(Hm | Rd)	TB	R	RBI	RC	TBB	IBB	SO	HBP	SH	SF	SB	CS	SB%	GDP	Avg	OBP	Slg
2007	Fresno*	AAA	2	6	2	0	0	0	(- | -)	2	1	2	0	1	0	1	0	0	0	0	0	-	0	.333	.429	.333
1995	SF	NL	9	19	9	3	0	2	(0 | 2)	18	4	4	7	1	0	2	0	1	1	1	0	1.00	1	.474	.476	.947
1996	SF	NL	105	318	76	7	1	3	(1 | 2)	94	27	26	29	25	2	52	1	6	2	4	1	.80	1	.239	.295	.296
1997	SF	NL	46	102	28	8	0	5	(1 | 4)	51	16	19	16	8	0	15	0	1	2	1	1	.50	3	.275	.321	.500
1998	SF	NL	122	413	110	27	2	9	(5 | 4)	168	54	49	54	31	3	62	2	5	3	3	3	.50	3	.266	.319	.407
1999	SF	NL	152	558	157	23	1	22	(9 | 13)	248	68	80	79	43	3	71	5	3	5	2	3	.40	16	.281	.336	.444
2000	SF	NL	141	509	138	24	2	20	(12 | 8)	226	67	79	74	54	2	90	0	4	4	1	2	.33	15	.271	.339	.444
2001	SF	NL	156	636	206	37	5	37	(15 | 22)	364	114	97	124	47	2	83	0	3	3	1	3	.25	14	.324	.369	.572
2002	SF	NL	133	538	138	35	2	15	(4 | 11)	222	76	61	61	37	0	90	4	3	7	1	2	.33	15	.257	.305	.413
2003	SF	NL	129	505	140	26	1	13	(6 | 7)	207	65	58	56	36	0	82	1	0	3	2	2	.50	18	.277	.325	.410
2004	2 Tms		124	399	98	21	2	6	(3 | 3)	141	49	44	39	37	1	71	4	7	3	1	0	1.00	12	.246	.314	.353
2005	Cin	NL	114	426	120	23	2	14	(11 | 3)	189	61	68	70	37	2	67	1	1	3	2	0	1.00	8	.282	.338	.444
2006	Cin	NL	122	440	132	25	1	23	(13 | 10)	228	61	70	72	34	1	51	1	2	4	3	0	1.00	8	.300	.349	.518
2007	SF	NL	99	329	83	19	2	5	(2 | 3)	121	40	33	33	22	1	45	4	0	3	0	0	-	8	.252	.304	.368
	04	Sea	AL	73	261	63	13	0	4	(2 | 2)	88	27	28	25	22	1	43	2	6	1	1	0	1.00	10	.241	.304	.337
	04	SD	NL	51	138	35	8	2	2	(1 | 1)	53	22	16	14	15	0	28	2	1	2	0	0	-	2	.254	.331	.384
	13 ML YEARS		1452	5192	1435	278	21	174	(82 | 92)	2277	702	688	714	412	17	781	23	36	42	22	17	.56	124	.276	.330	.439

Brad Ausmus

Bats: R **Throws:** R **Pos:** C-114; 1B-5; 3B-2; PH-2; 2B-1; PR-1 **Ht:** 5'11" **Wt:** 190 **Born:** 4/14/1969 **Age:** 39

			BATTING																BASERUNNING				AVERAGES		
Year	Team	Lg	G	AB	H	2B	3B	HR	(Hm | Rd)	TB	R	RBI	RC	TBB	IBB	SO	HBP	SH	SF	SB	CS	SB%	GDP	Avg	OBP	Slg
1993	SD	NL	49	160	41	8	1	5	(4 | 1)	66	18	12	19	6	0	28	0	0	0	2	0	1.00	2	.256	.283	.413
1994	SD	NL	101	327	82	12	1	7	(6 | 1)	117	45	24	36	30	12	63	1	6	2	5	1	.83	8	.251	.314	.358
1995	SD	NL	103	328	96	16	4	5	(2 | 3)	135	44	34	49	31	3	56	2	4	4	16	5	.76	6	.293	.353	.412
1996	2 Tms		125	375	83	16	0	5	(2 | 3)	114	46	35	32	39	1	72	5	6	2	4	8	.33	8	.221	.302	.304
1997	Hou	NL	130	425	113	25	1	4	(1 | 3)	152	45	44	51	38	4	78	3	6	6	14	6	.70	7	.266	.326	.358
1998	Hou	NL	128	412	111	10	4	6	(2 | 4)	147	62	45	51	56	11	60	3	3	1	10	3	.77	18	.269	.356	.357
1999	Det	AL	127	458	126	25	6	9	(5 | 4)	190	62	54	69	51	0	71	14	3	1	12	9	.57	11	.275	.365	.415
2000	Det	AL	150	523	139	25	3	7	(3 | 4)	191	75	51	64	69	0	79	6	4	2	11	5	.69	19	.266	.357	.365
2001	Hou	NL	128	422	98	23	4	5	(4 | 1)	144	45	34	38	30	6	64	1	6	2	4	1	.80	13	.232	.284	.341
2002	Hou	NL	130	447	115	19	3	6	(4 | 2)	158	57	50	44	38	3	71	6	2	3	2	3	.40	30	.257	.322	.353
2003	Hou	NL	143	450	103	12	2	4	(1 | 3)	131	43	47	44	46	1	66	4	4	5	5	3	.63	8	.229	.303	.291
2004	Hou	NL	129	403	100	14	1	5	(2 | 3)	131	43	34	34	33	11	56	2	7	3	2	2	.50	13	.248	.306	.325
2005	Hou	NL	134	387	100	19	0	3	(1 | 2)	128	35	47	42	51	8	48	5	7	1	5	3	.63	17	.258	.351	.331
2006	Hou	NL	139	439	101	16	1	2	(1 | 1)	125	37	39	36	45	2	71	6	9	3	3	1	.75	21	.230	.308	.285
2007	Hou	NL	117	349	82	16	3	3	(2 | 1)	113	38	25	28	37	3	74	6	4	1	6	1	.86	11	.235	.318	.324
	96	SD	NL	50	149	27	4	0	1	(0 | 1)	34	16	13	6	13	0	27	3	1	0	1	4	.20	4	.181	.261	.228
	96	Det	AL	75	226	56	12	0	4	(2 | 2)	80	30	22	26	26	1	45	2	5	2	3	4	.43	4	.248	.328	.354
	15 ML YEARS		1833	5905	1490	256	34	76	(41 | 35)	2042	690	572	641	597	65	957	64	71	36	101	51	.66	193	.252	.326	.346

Luis Ayala

Pitches: R Bats: R Pos: RP-44   Ht: 6'2" Wt: 175 Born: 1/12/1978 Age: 30

			HOW MUCH HE PITCHED						WHAT HE GAVE UP											THE RESULTS							
Year	Team	Lg	G	GS	CG	GF	IP	BFP	H	R	ER	HR	SH	SF	HB	TBB	IBB	SO	WP	Bk	W	L	Pct	ShO	Sv-Op	Hld	ERC	ERA
2007	Ptomc*	A+	3	1	0	0	2.2	10	1	0	0	0	0	0	0	1	0	1	0	0	0	0	-	0	0- -	-	0.85	0.00
2007	Clmbs*	AAA	5	0	0	1	7.0	26	4	1	1	1	0	0	1	2	0	5	0	1	0	0	-	0	0- -	-	2.41	1.29
2003	Mon	NL	65	0	0	24	71.0	288	65	27	23	8	3	1	5	13	3	46	1	0	10	3	.769	0	5 8	19	3.11	2.92
2004	Mon	NL	81	0	0	28	90.1	367	92	30	27	6	2	2	5	15	2	63	3	1	6	12	.333	0	2-7	21	3.32	2.69
2005	Was	NL	68	0	0	18	71.0	293	75	23	21	7	8	3	6	14	4	40	0	0	8	7	.533	0	1-3	22	3.95	2.66
2007	Was	NL	44	0	0	11	42.1	181	43	16	15	5	3	4	1	12	0	28	1	0	2	2	.500	0	1-2	6	3.88	3.19
	4 ML YEARS		258	0	0	81	274.2	1129	275	96	86	26	16	10	17	54	9	177	5	1	26	24	.520	0	9-20	68	3.51	2.82

Erick Aybar

Bats: B Throws: R Pos: 2B-43; SS-20; PH-20; LF-6; RF-2; DH-2; PR-2; 3B-1   Ht: 5'10" Wt: 170 Born: 1/14/1984 Age: 24

						BATTING															BASERUNNING				AVERAGES		
Year	Team	Lg	G	AB	H	2B	3B	HR	(Hm	Rd)	TB	R	RBI	RC	TBB	IBB	SO	HBP	SH	SF	SB	CS	SB%	GDP	Avg	OBP	Slg
2002	Provo	R+	67	273	89	15	6	4	(-	-)	128	64	29	50	21	1	43	11	2	1	15	10	.60	4	.326	.395	.469
2003	CRpds	A	125	496	153	30	10	6	(-	-)	221	83	57	80	17	0	54	13	6	3	32	9	.78	6	.308	.346	.446
2004	RCuca	A+	136	573	189	25	11	14	(-	-)	278	102	65	98	26	1	66	13	10	5	51	36	.59	3	.330	.370	.485
2005	Ark	AA	134	535	162	29	10	9	(-	-)	238	101	54	86	29	0	51	14	4	8	49	23	.68	13	.303	.350	.445
2006	Salt Lk	AAA	81	339	96	20	3	6	(-	-)	140	63	45	46	21	2	36	3	1	4	32	18	.64	5	.283	.327	.413
2007	RCuca	A+	2	5	2	0	0	0	(-	-)	2	3	0	1	1	0	1	0	0	0	3	1	.75	1	.400	.500	.400
2007	Salt Lk	AAA	3	12	4	0	0	0	(-	-)	4	2	2	1	0	0	2	0	0	0	2	1	.67	0	.333	.333	.333
2006	LAA	AL	34	40	10	1	1	0	(0	0)	13	5	2	4	0	0	8	0	0	0	1	0	1.00	1	.250	.250	.325
2007	LAA	AL	79	194	46	5	1	1	(0	1)	56	18	19	16	10	0	32	2	3	2	4	4	.50	8	.237	.279	.289
	2 ML YEARS		113	234	56	6	2	1	(0	1)	69	23	21	20	10	0	40	2	3	2	5	4	.56	9	.239	.274	.295

Willy Aybar

Bats: B Throws: R Pos: SS   Ht: 5'11" Wt: 200 Born: 3/9/1983 Age: 25

						BATTING															BASERUNNING				AVERAGES		
Year	Team	Lg	G	AB	H	2B	3B	HR	(Hm	Rd)	TB	R	RBI	RC	TBB	IBB	SO	HBP	SH	SF	SB	CS	SB%	GDP	Avg	OBP	Slg
2000	Gr Falls	R+	70	266	70	15	1	4	(-	-)	99	39	49	37	36	2	45	0	6	2	5	5	.50	3	.263	.349	.372
2001	Wilmg	A	120	431	102	25	2	4	(-	-)	143	45	48	45	43	3	64	3	3	5	7	9	.44	4	.237	.307	.332
2001	VeroB	A+	2	7	2	0	0	0	(-	-)	2	0	0	0	1	0	2	0	0	0	0	0	-	0	.286	.375	.286
2002	VeroB	A+	108	372	80	18	2	11	(-	-)	135	56	65	52	69	4	54	3	2	4	15	8	.65	7	.215	.339	.363
2003	VeroB	A+	119	445	122	29	3	11	(-	-)	190	47	74	65	41	1	70	3	1	5	9	9	.50	3	.274	.336	.427
2004	Jaxnvl	AA	126	482	133	27	0	15	(-	-)	205	56	77	72	50	4	77	3	0	2	8	10	.44	11	.276	.346	.425
2005	LsVgs	AAA	108	401	119	26	4	5	(-	-)	168	47	60	61	40	0	56	1	1	7	1	6	.14	8	.297	.356	.419
2006	LsVgs	AAA	50	197	62	12	1	10	(-	-)	106	30	41	39	22	1	24	1	0	2	1	3	.25	6	.315	.383	.538
2006	Rchmd	AAA	3	10	3	1	0	0	(-	-)	4	2	1	1	2	0	3	0	0	0	0	0	-	1	.300	.417	.400
2005	LAD	NL	26	86	28	8	0	1	(0	1)	39	12	10	21	18	0	11	1	0	0	3	1	.75	0	.326	.448	.453
2006	2 Tms	NL	79	243	68	18	0	4	(3	1)	98	32	30	33	28	0	36	4	3	0	1	2	.33	7	.280	.364	.403
06	LAD	NL	43	128	32	12	0	3	(2	1)	53	15	22	19	18	0	17	3	2	0	1	0	1.00	5	.250	.356	.414
06	Atl	NL	36	115	36	6	0	1	(1	0)	45	17	8	14	10	0	19	1	1	0	0	2	.00	2	.313	.373	.391
	2 ML YEARS		105	329	96	26	0	5	(3	2)	137	44	40	54	46	0	47	5	3	0	4	3	.57	7	.292	.387	.416

Brandon Backe

Pitches: R Bats: R Pos: SP-5   Ht: 6'0" Wt: 195 Born: 4/5/1978 Age: 30

				HOW MUCH HE PITCHED					WHAT HE GAVE UP											THE RESULTS							
Year	Team	Lg	G	GS	CG	GF	IP	BFP	H	R	ER	HR	SH	SF	HB	TBB	IBB	SO	WP	Bk	W	L	Pct	ShO	Sv-Op	Hld	ERC	ERA
2007	CpChr*	AA	1	1	0	0	5.0	21	5	3	3	1	0	0	0	2	0	4	0	0	1	0	1.000	0	0- -	-	4.93	5.40
2007	RdRck*	AAA	5	5	0	0	25.0	106	27	12	12	4	0	0	0	11	1	25	0	0	3	2	.600	0	0- -	-	5.32	4.32
2002	TB	AL	9	0	0	4	13.0	61	15	10	10	3	0	0	2	7	0	6	0	0	0	0	-	0	0-0	0	7.37	6.92
2003	TB	AL	28	0	0	8	44.2	192	40	28	27	6	2	1	2	25	1	36	3	0	1	1	.500	0	0-0	5	4.64	5.44
2004	Hou	NL	33	9	0	0	67.0	293	75	33	32	10	5	1	1	27	4	54	1	0	5	3	.625	0	0-0	0	5.18	4.30
2005	Hou	NL	26	25	1	0	149.1	653	151	82	79	19	7	1	4	67	1	97	5	2	10	8	.556	1	0-0	0	4.65	4.76
2006	Hou	NL	8	8	0	0	43.0	189	43	18	18	4	1	2	3	18	0	19	2	0	3	2	.600	0	0-0	0	4.37	3.77
2007	Hou	NL	5	5	0	0	28.2	123	27	13	12	4	0	1	2	11	0	11	0	0	3	1	.750	0	0-0	0	4.26	3.77
	6 ML YEARS		109	47	1	20	345.2	1511	351	184	178	46	15	6	14	155	6	223	11	2	22	15	.595	1	0-0	8	4.78	4.63

Mike Bacsik

Pitches: L Bats: L Pos: SP-20; RP-9   Ht: 6'3" Wt: 190 Born: 11/11/1977 Age: 30

				HOW MUCH HE PITCHED					WHAT HE GAVE UP											THE RESULTS							
Year	Team	Lg	G	GS	CG	GF	IP	BFP	H	R	ER	HR	SH	SF	HB	TBB	IBB	SO	WP	Bk	W	L	Pct	ShO	Sv-Op	Hld	ERC	ERA
2007	Clmbs*	AAA	9	5	0	2	36.0	152	40	18	16	6	2	2	4	6	0	28	0	0	1	3	.250	0	0- -	-	4.78	4.00
2001	Cle	AL	3	0	0	0	9.0	45	13	10	9	0	0	1	1	3	1	4	0	0	0	0	-	0	0-0	0	5.56	9.00
2002	NYM	NL	11	9	1	1	55.2	247	63	29	27	8	5	1	4	19	3	30	0	0	3	2	.600	0	0-0	0	5.13	4.37
2003	NYM	NL	5	3	0	1	17.2	85	28	21	20	5	0	1	0	8	0	12	0	0	1	2	.333	0	0-0	0	9.79	10.19
2004	Tex	AL	3	3	0	0	15.2	63	16	8	8	2	0	0	2	1	0	6	0	0	1	1	.500	0	0-0	0	3.67	4.60
2007	Was	NL	29	20	0	0	118.0	520	141	73	67	26	3	4	6	29	3	45	4	0	5	8	.385	0	0-0	0	5.61	5.11
	5 ML YEARS		51	35	1	2	216.0	960	261	141	131	41	8	7	13	60	7	97	4	0	10	13	.435	0	0-0	0	5.65	5.46

Cha Seung Baek

Pitches: R Bats: R Pos: SP-12; RP-2   Ht: 6'4" Wt: 220 Born: 5/29/1980 Age: 28

Year	Team	Lg	G	GS	CG	GF	IP	BFP	H	R	ER	HR	SH	SF	HB	TBB	IBB	SO	WP	Bk	W	L	Pct	ShO	Sv-Op	Hld	ERC	ERA
2007	Ms*	R	1	0	0	0	3.0	11	1	0	0	0	0	0	0	0	0	6	0	0	0	0	-	0	0--	-	0.23	0.00
2007	Wisc*	A-	1	1	0	0	3.2	16	5	2	2	1	0	0	0	0	0	6	0	1	0	0	-	0	0--	-	5.60	4.91
2007	Tacom*	AAA	6	6	0	0	31.0	135	33	13	11	1	1	2	1	10	0	18	1	0	1	1	.500	0	0--	-	3.74	3.19
2004	Sea	AL	7	5	0	2	31.0	139	35	23	19	5	0	0	2	11	1	20	2	0	2	4	.333	0	0-0	0	5.26	5.52
2006	Sea	AL	6	6	0	0	34.1	140	26	15	14	6	0	0	2	13	0	23	1	0	4	1	.800	0	0-0	0	3.44	3.67
2007	Sea	AL	14	12	1	1	73.1	321	87	45	42	6	1	1	3	14	1	49	1	0	4	3	.571	0	0-0	0	4.24	5.15
	3 ML YEARS		27	23	1	3	138.2	600	148	83	75	17	1	1	7	38	2	92	4	0	10	8	.556	0	0-0	0	4.26	4.87

Danys Baez

Pitches: R Bats: R Pos: RP-53   Ht: 6'1" Wt: 230 Born: 9/10/1977 Age: 30

Year	Team	Lg	G	GS	CG	GF	IP	BFP	H	R	ER	HR	SH	SF	HB	TBB	IBB	SO	WP	Bk	W	L	Pct	ShO	Sv-Op	Hld	ERC	ERA
2007	Bowie*	AA	3	0	0	0	4.0	16	3	1	1	1	1	0	0	2	1	4	1	0	0	0	-	0	0--	-	3.91	2.25
2001	Cle	AL	43	0	0	8	50.1	202	34	22	14	5	1	0	3	20	4	52	3	0	5	3	.625	0	0-1	14	2.51	2.50
2002	Cle	AL	39	26	1	9	165.1	726	160	84	81	14	2	8	9	82	5	130	6	1	10	11	.476	0	6-8	0	4.35	4.41
2003	Cle	AL	73	0	0	46	75.2	318	65	36	32	9	6	1	4	23	0	66	5	0	2	9	.182	0	25-35	5	3.22	3.81
2004	TB	AL	62	0	0	59	68.0	295	60	31	27	6	5	1	7	29	4	52	3	1	4	4	.500	0	30-33	1	3.73	3.57
2005	TB	AL	67	0	0	64	72.1	308	66	27	23	7	4	2	2	30	0	51	0	0	5	4	.556	0	41-49	0	3.74	2.86
2006	2 Tms	NL	57	0	0	28	59.2	257	60	35	30	3	4	5	7	17	3	39	3	0	5	6	.455	0	9-17	12	3.69	4.53
2007	Bal	AL	53	0	0	25	50.1	233	50	36	36	8	3	1	7	29	5	29	0	0	0	6	.000	0	3-5	14	5.56	6.44
06	LAD	NL	46	0	0	27	49.2	213	53	29	24	3	4	5	6	11	2	29	3	0	5	5	.500	0	9-16	6	3.90	4.35
06	Atl	NL	11	0	0	1	10.0	44	7	6	6	0	0	0	1	6	1	10	0	0	0	1	.000	0	0-1	6	2.64	5.40
	7 ML YEARS		394	26	1	239	541.2	2339	495	271	243	52	24	19	39	230	21	419	20	2	31	43	.419	0	114-148	46	3.88	4.04

Homer Bailey

Pitches: R Bats: R Pos: SP-9   Ht: 6'4" Wt: 205 Born: 5/3/1986 Age: 22

Year	Team	Lg	G	GS	CG	GF	IP	BFP	H	R	ER	HR	SH	SF	HB	TBB	IBB	SO	WP	Bk	W	L	Pct	ShO	Sv-Op	Hld	ERC	ERA
2004	Reds	R	6	3	0	0	12.1	54	14	7	6	0	0	0	0	3	0	9	1	1	0	1	.000	0	0--	-	3.42	4.38
2005	Dayton	A	28	21	0	1	103.2	458	89	64	51	5	4	6	3	62	0	125	11	5	8	4	.667	0	0--	-	3.76	4.43
2006	Srsota	A+	13	13	0	0	70.2	290	49	35	26	6	2	1	5	22	0	79	2	0	3	5	.375	0	0--	-	2.26	3.31
2006	Chatt	AA	13	13	0	0	68.0	276	50	13	12	1	7	0	2	28	0	77	6	0	7	1	.875	0	0--	-	2.32	1.59
2007	Srsota	A+	2	2	0	0	8.0	44	15	9	9	2	0	0	0	5	0	7	0	0	1	0	1.000	0	0--	-	11.94	10.13
2007	Lsvlle	AAA	12	12	0	0	67.1	278	49	29	23	4	5	1	0	32	0	59	4	1	6	3	.667	0	0--	-	2.65	3.07
2007	Cin	NL	9	9	0	0	45.1	205	43	32	29	3	1	6	3	28	1	28	1	1	4	2	.667	0	0-0	0	4.61	5.76

Jeff Bailey

Bats: R Throws: R Pos: 1B-3; PH-1   Ht: 6'2" Wt: 200 Born: 11/26/1978 Age: 29

Year	Team	Lg	G	AB	H	2B	3B	HR	(Hm	Rd)	TB	R	RBI	RC	TBB	IBB	SO	HBP	SH	SF	SB	CS	SB%	GDP	Avg	OBP	Slg
1997	Mrlns	R	5	7	1	0	0	0	(-	-)	1	0	0	0	1	0	2	0	0	0	0	0	-	1	.143	.250	.143
1998	Mrlns	R	37	127	42	10	0	2	(-	-)	58	21	28	27	19	0	31	7	0	1	3	2	.60	3	.331	.442	.457
1999	Kane	A	76	277	77	19	1	10	(-	-)	128	49	53	48	34	2	77	6	0	5	1	1	.50	8	.278	.363	.462
2000	BrvdCt	A+	125	458	113	19	3	14	(-	-)	180	56	66	62	50	2	116	7	1	4	3	3	.50	9	.247	.328	.393
2001	Portlnd	AA	129	432	104	28	2	13	(-	-)	175	56	66	66	64	1	136	8	0	3	7	2	.78	4	.241	.347	.405
2002	Hrsbrg	AA	99	309	87	17	1	13	(-	-)	145	45	52	46	63	4	78	10	1	3	3	3	.50	3	.282	.416	.469
2003	Hrsbrg	AA	103	362	89	18	3	13	(-	-)	152	54	57	52	35	2	74	8	2	6	2	1	.67	14	.246	.321	.420
2003	Edmtn	AAA	5	17	7	3	0	1	(-	-)	13	5	6	6	3	0	5	1	0	0	0	0	-	1	.412	.524	.765
2004	Portlnd	AA	91	299	88	23	3	13	(-	-)	156	57	58	4	46	0	80	11	0	3	80	0	1.00	7	.294	.404	.522
2004	Pwtckt	AAA	3	10	3	1	0	0	(-	-)	4	2	0	2	3	0	3	0	0	0	1	0	-	0	.300	.462	.400
2005	Pwtckt	AAA	31	95	25	5	0	6	(-	-)	48	15	12	16	8	0	26	1	0	0	1	0	1.00	3	.263	.327	.505
2005	Pwtckt	AAA	43	132	33	7	0	7	(-	-)	61	21	26	25	20	0	36	8	1	0	3	1	.75	2	.250	.381	.462
2006	Pwtckt	AAA	134	458	126	22	5	22	(-	-)	224	64	82	89	74	3	116	10	0	6	1	2	.33	11	.275	.383	.489
2007	Pwtckt	AAA	115	404	99	22	1	15	(-	-)	168	64	60	64	59	1	99	13	0	2	9	6	.60	8	.245	.358	.416
2007	Bos	AL	3	9	1	0	0	1	(0	1)	4	1	1	0	0	0	1	0	0	0	0	0	-	0	.111	.111	.444

Jeff Baker

Bats: R Throws: R Pos: PH-51; 1B-20; RF-13; LF-6; 3B-2; DH-2   Ht: 6'2" Wt: 210 Born: 6/21/1981 Age: 27

Year	Team	Lg	G	AB	H	2B	3B	HR	(Hm	Rd)	TB	R	RBI	RC	TBB	IBB	SO	HBP	SH	SF	SB	CS	SB%	GDP	Avg	OBP	Slg
2007	ColSpr*	AAA	7	26	6	1	0	1	(-	-)	10	3	2	2	1	0	8	0	0	0	0	0	-	1	.231	.259	.385
2005	Col	NL	12	38	8	4	0	1	(1	0)	15	6	4	4	5	0	12	0	0	0	0	0	-	1	.211	.302	.395
2006	Col	NL	18	57	21	7	2	5	(4	1)	47	13	21	17	1	0	14	0	0	0	2	0	1.00	0	.368	.379	.825
2007	Col	NL	85	144	32	2	2	4	(4	0)	50	17	12	8	13	1	40	2	0	0	0	0	-	7	.222	.296	.347
	3 ML YEARS		115	239	61	13	4	10	(9	1)	112	36	37	29	19	1	66	2	0	0	2	0	1.00	8	.255	.315	.469

Scott Baker

Pitches: R **Bats:** R **Pos:** SP-23; RP-1   **Ht:** 6'4" **Wt:** 220 **Born:** 9/19/1981 **Age:** 26

			HOW MUCH HE PITCHED						WHAT HE GAVE UP											THE RESULTS						
Year	Team	Lg	G	GS	CG	GF	IP	BFP	H	R	ER	HR	SH	SF	HB	TBB	IBB	SO	WP	Bk	W	L	Pct	ShO	Sv-Op Hld	ERC	ERA
2007	Roch*	AAA	7	6	0	1	42.2	162	34	16	15	3	0	2	1	4	0	41	1	0	3	2	.600	0	1-- -	1.88	3.16
2005	Min	AL	10	9	0	0	53.2	217	48	21	20	5	2	2	0	14	0	32	0	0	3	3	.500	0	0-0 1	2.97	3.35
2006	Min	AL	16	16	0	0	83.1	377	114	63	59	17	2	4	3	16	1	62	0	0	5	8	.385	0	0-0 0	6.26	6.37
2007	Min	AL	24	23	2	0	143.2	606	162	70	68	15	6	2	5	29	4	102	0	0	9	9	.500	1	0-0 1	4.19	4.26
	3 ML YEARS		50	48	2	0	280.2	1200	324	154	147	37	10	8	8	59	5	196	0	0	17	20	.459	1	0-0 2	4.53	4.71

Paul Bako

Bats: L **Throws:** R **Pos:** C-57; PH-4   **Ht:** 6'2" **Wt:** 207 **Born:** 6/20/1972 **Age:** 36

						BATTING																BASERUNNING				AVERAGES		
Year	Team	Lg	G	AB	H	2B	3B	HR	(Hm	Rd)	TB	R	RBI	RC	TBB	IBB	SO	HBP	SH	SF	SB	CS	SB%	GDP	Avg	OBP	Slg
1998	Det	AL	96	305	83	12	1	3	(2	1)	106	23	30	34	23	4	82	0	1	4	1	1	.50	3	.272	.319	.348
1999	Hou	NL	73	215	55	14	1	2	(2	0)	77	16	17	26	26	3	57	0	3	3	1	1	.50	4	.256	.332	.358
2000	3 Tms	NL	81	221	50	10	1	2	(2	0)	68	18	20	20	27	10	64	1	1	1	0	0	-	6	.226	.312	.308
2001	Atl	NL	61	137	29	10	1	2	(0	2)	47	19	15	15	20	2	34	0	0	0	1	0	1.00	3	.212	.312	.343
2002	Mil	NL	87	234	55	8	1	4	(2	2)	77	24	20	20	20	3	46	0	3	0	0	2	.00	4	.235	.295	.329
2003	ChC	NL	70	188	43	13	3	0	(0	0)	62	19	17	21	22	3	47	1	1	1	0	1	.00	2	.229	.311	.330
2004	ChC	NL	49	138	28	8	0	1	(1	0)	39	13	10	11	15	3	29	2	1	1	1	0	1.00	4	.203	.288	.283
2005	LAD	NL	13	40	10	2	0	0	(0	0)	12	1	4	6	7	1	12	0	0	0	0	0	-	0	.250	.362	.300
2006	KC	AL	56	153	32	3	0	0	(0	0)	35	7	10	9	11	0	46	0	2	1	0	0	-	3	.209	.261	.229
2007	Bal	AL	60	156	32	3	1	1	(0	1)	40	13	8	6	15	0	50	1	1	1	0	1	.00	5	.205	.254	.256
00	Hou	NL	1	2	0	0	0	0	(0	0)	0	0	0	0	0	0	1	0	0	0	0	0	-	0	.000	.000	.000
00	Fla	NL	56	161	39	6	1	0	(0	0)	47	10	14	16	22	7	48	1	1	1	0	0	-	4	.242	.335	.292
00	Atl	NL	24	58	11	4	0	2	(2	0)	21	8	6	4	5	3	15	0	0	0	0	0	-	2	.190	.254	.362
	10 ML YEARS		646	1787	417	83	9	15	(9	6)	563	153	151	168	186	29	467	5	13	12	4	6	.40	33	.233	.306	.315

Rocco Baldelli

Bats: R **Throws:** R **Pos:** CF-20; DH-15   **Ht:** 6'4" **Wt:** 200 **Born:** 9/25/1981 **Age:** 26

						BATTING																BASERUNNING				AVERAGES		
Year	Team	Lg	G	AB	H	2B	3B	HR	(Hm	Rd)	TB	R	RBI	RC	TBB	IBB	SO	HBP	SH	SF	SB	CS	SB%	GDP	Avg	OBP	Slg
2007	VeroB*	A+	2	5	0	0	0	0	(-	-)	0	1	0	0	1	0	1	0	0	0	0	0	-	0	.000	.167	.000
2007	Drham*	AAA	2	8	1	0	0	1	(-	-)	4	2	1	0	1	1	2	0	0	0	0	0	-	0	.125	.222	.500
2003	TB	AL	156	637	184	32	8	11	(2	9)	265	89	78	77	30	4	128	8	3	6	27	10	.73	10	.289	.326	.416
2004	TB	AL	136	518	145	27	3	16	(6	10)	226	79	74	70	30	2	88	8	3	6	17	4	.81	12	.280	.326	.436
2006	TB	AL	92	364	110	24	6	16	(6	10)	194	59	57	65	14	1	70	7	0	2	10	1	.91	2	.302	.339	.533
2007	TB	AL	35	137	28	6	0	5	(4	1)	49	16	12	14	9	1	35	3	1	0	4	1	.80	1	.204	.268	.358
	4 ML YEARS		419	1656	467	89	17	48	(18	30)	734	243	221	226	83	8	321	26	7	14	58	16	.78	25	.282	.324	.443

John Bale

Pitches: L **Bats:** L **Pos:** RP-26   **Ht:** 6'4" **Wt:** 220 **Born:** 5/22/1974 **Age:** 34

			HOW MUCH HE PITCHED						WHAT HE GAVE UP											THE RESULTS						
Year	Team	Lg	G	GS	CG	GF	IP	BFP	H	R	ER	HR	SH	SF	HB	TBB	IBB	SO	WP	Bk	W	L	Pct	ShO	Sv-Op Hld	ERC	ERA
2007	Wichta*	AA	3	3	0	0	4.0	18	5	2	2	1	0	0	0	2	0	0	0	0	0	0	-	0	0-- -	7.44	4.50
2007	Omha*	AAA	8	4	0	0	12.2	51	13	5	4	0	0	1	0	1	0	12	0	0	0	1	.000	0	0-- -	2.38	2.84
1999	Tor	AL	1	0	0	0	2.0	10	2	3	3	1	0	0	0	2	0	4	0	0	0	0	-	0	0-0 0	9.87	13.50
2000	Tor	AL	2	0	0	0	3.2	22	5	7	6	1	0	0	0	3	0	6	0	0	0	0	-	0	0-0 0	8.10	14.73
2001	Bal	AL	14	0	0	0	26.2	113	18	14	9	2	0	0	0	17	0	21	0	0	1	0	1.000	0	0-0 0	3.05	3.04
2003	Cin	NL	10	9	0	0	46.1	195	50	24	23	7	1	2	2	12	2	37	1	0	1	2	.333	0	0-0 0	4.52	4.47
2007	KC	AL	26	0	0	5	40.0	179	45	18	18	1	3	3	1	17	2	42	2	0	1	1	.500	0	0-1 5	4.32	4.05
	5 ML YEARS		53	9	0	5	118.2	519	120	66	59	12	4	5	3	51	4	110	3	0	3	3	.500	0	0-1 5	4.31	4.47

Wladimir Balentien

Bats: R **Throws:** R **Pos:** RF-2; PH-2; LF-1   **Ht:** 6'2" **Wt:** 190 **Born:** 7/2/1984 **Age:** 23

						BATTING																BASERUNNING				AVERAGES		
Year	Team	Lg	G	AB	H	2B	3B	HR	(Hm	Rd)	TB	R	RBI	RC	TBB	IBB	SO	HBP	SH	SF	SB	CS	SB%	GDP	Avg	OBP	Slg
2003	Ms	R	50	187	53	12	5	16	(-	-)	123	42	52	44	22	0	55	3	1	3	4	2	.67	4	.283	.363	.658
2004	Wisc	A-	76	260	72	12	3	15	(-	-)	135	39	46	43	12	2	77	3	3	1	10	2	.83	8	.277	.315	.519
2004	InldEm	A+	10	38	11	1	0	2	(-	-)	18	5	5	6	4	0	10	0	0	0	1	0	1.00	0	.289	.357	.474
2005	InldEm	A+	123	492	143	38	8	25	(-	-)	272	76	93	93	33	0	160	6	1	7	9	2	.82	7	.291	.338	.553
2006	SnAnt	AA	121	444	102	23	1	22	(-	-)	193	76	82	69	70	5	140	4	4	7	14	7	.67	10	.230	.337	.435
2007	Tacom	AAA	124	477	139	24	4	24	(-	-)	243	77	84	91	54	3	105	3	2	8	15	4	.79	14	.291	.362	.509
2007	Sea	AL	3	3	2	1	0	1	(1	0)	6	1	4	4	0	0	0	0	0	1	0	0	-	0	.667	.500	2.000

Grant Balfour

Pitches: R **Bats:** R **Pos:** RP-25   **Ht:** 6'2" **Wt:** 192 **Born:** 12/30/1977 **Age:** 30

			HOW MUCH HE PITCHED						WHAT HE GAVE UP											THE RESULTS						
Year	Team	Lg	G	GS	CG	GF	IP	BFP	H	R	ER	HR	SH	SF	HB	TBB	IBB	SO	WP	Bk	W	L	Pct	ShO	Sv-Op Hld	ERC	ERA
2007	Hntsvl*	AA	8	0	0	5	11.1	47	8	3	3	0	1	0	0	4	0	21	0	1	0	0	-	0	2-- -	1.71	2.38
2007	Nashv*	AAA	24	0	0	11	32.0	121	17	6	6	2	2	0	0	11	0	47	0	0	1	1	.500	0	5-- -	1.47	1.69
2001	Min	AL	2	0	0	0	2.2	14	3	4	4	2	0	0	0	3	0	2	0	0	0	0	-	0	0-0 0	13.78	13.50
2003	Min	AL	17	1	0	6	26.0	115	23	12	12	4	2	1	0	14	2	30	0	0	1	0	1.000	0	0-1 1	4.14	4.15
2004	Min	AL	36	0	0	14	39.1	172	35	19	19	4	2	0	2	21	1	42	3	0	4	1	.800	0	0-1 4	4.16	4.35

Year	Team	Lg	G	GS	CG	GF	IP	BFP	H	R	ER	HR	SH	SF	HB	TBB	IBB	SO	WP	Bk	W	L	Pct	ShO	Sv-Op	Hld	ERC	ERA
2007	2 Tms		25	0	0	8	24.2	121	30	21	21	2	2	3	1	20	0	30	0	0	1	2	.333	0	0-0	1	7.15	7.66
07	Mil	NL	3	0	0	2	2.2	18	4	6	6	1	1	0	1	4	0	3	0	0	0	2	.000	0	0-0	0	15.83	20.25
07	TB	AL	22	0	0	6	22.0	103	26	15	15	1	1	3	0	16	0	27	0	0	1	0	1.000	0	0-0	1	6.19	6.14
4 ML YEARS			80	1	0	28	92.2	422	91	56	56	12	6	4	3	58	3	104	3	0	6	3	.667	0	0-2	6	5.16	5.44

Josh Banks

Pitches: R **Bats:** R **Pos:** RP-2; SP-1 **Ht:** 6'3" **Wt:** 215 **Born:** 7/18/1982 **Age:** 25

			HOW MUCH HE PITCHED						WHAT HE GAVE UP												THE RESULTS							
Year	Team	Lg	G	GS	CG	GF	IP	BFP	H	R	ER	HR	SH	SF	HB	TBB	IBB	SO	WP	Bk	W	L	Pct	ShO	Sv-Op	Hld	ERC	ERA
2003	Auburn	A-	15	15	0	0	66.2	264	58	21	18	1	0	4	1	10	0	81	5	0	7	2	.778	0	0--	-	2.03	2.43
2004	Dnedin	A+	11	11	0	0	60.0	230	49	17	12	4	2	1	1	8	0	60	6	0	7	1	.875	0	0--	-	2.07	1.80
2004	NHam	AA	18	17	1	0	91.1	381	89	54	51	15	2	3	0	28	0	76	1	1	6	6	.500	0	0--	-	4.03	5.03
2005	NHam	AA	27	27	2	0	162.1	645	159	76	69	18	4	7	0	11	0	145	3	0	8	11	.421	0	0--	-	2.77	3.83
2006	Syrcse	AAA	29	29	0	0	170.2	727	184	108	98	35	3	3	3	28	0	126	2	0	10	11	.476	0	0--	-	4.25	5.17
2007	Syrcse	AAA	27	27	3	0	169.0	714	192	89	87	22	3	6	4	24	0	101	8	0	12	10	.545	0	0--	-	4.10	4.63
2007	Tor	AL	3	1	0	1	7.1	35	11	6	6	1	0	1	0	2	0	2	0	0	0	0	-	0	0-0	0	6.66	7.36

Brian Bannister

Pitches: R **Bats:** R **Pos:** SP-27 **Ht:** 6'2" **Wt:** 210 **Born:** 2/28/1981 **Age:** 27

			HOW MUCH HE PITCHED						WHAT HE GAVE UP												THE RESULTS							
Year	Team	Lg	G	GS	CG	GF	IP	BFP	H	R	ER	HR	SH	SF	HB	TBB	IBB	SO	WP	Bk	W	L	Pct	ShO	Sv-Op	Hld	ERC	ERA
2003	Bklyn	A-	12	9	0	1	46.0	179	27	12	11	0	3	1	1	18	0	42	4	2	4	1	.800	0	1--	-	1.54	2.15
2004	StLuci	A+	20	20	0	0	110.1	462	111	63	52	6	10	4	10	27	1	106	10	1	5	7	.417	0	0--	-	3.59	4.24
2004	Bnghtn	AA	8	8	0	0	44.1	180	45	23	20	2	2	0	2	17	0	28	4	0	3	3	.500	0	0--	-	4.19	4.06
2005	Bnghtn	AA	18	18	1	0	109.0	428	91	36	31	11	1	1	6	27	0	94	2	1	9	4	.692	1	0--	-	2.96	2.56
2005	Norfolk	AAA	8	8	0	0	45.1	197	48	19	16	0	1	4	1	13	0	48	4	0	4	1	.800	0	0--	-	3.28	3.18
2006	StLuci	A+	2	2	0	0	12.0	49	10	4	2	0	0	1	1	4	0	9	0	0	1	0	1.000	0	0--	-	2.65	1.50
2006	Norfolk	AAA	6	6	1	0	30.1	128	34	15	13	4	1	0	0	5	0	24	1	0	3	3	.500	0	0--	-	4.01	3.86
2007	Omha	AAA	4	4	0	0	20.2	80	16	11	6	4	1	0	0	4	1	14	0	0	1	1	.500	0	0--	-	2.63	2.61
2006	NYM	NL	8	6	0	1	38.0	171	34	18	18	4	1	4	2	22	2	19	2	0	2	1	.667	0	0-0	0	4.27	4.26
2007	KC	AL	27	27	1	0	165.0	683	156	76	71	15	2	4	6	44	1	77	4	0	12	9	.571	0	0-0	0	3.36	3.87
2 ML YEARS			35	33	1	1	203.0	854	190	94	89	19	3	8	8	66	3	96	6	0	14	10	.583	0	0-0	0	3.53	3.95

Rod Barajas

Bats: R **Throws:** R **Pos:** C-38; PH-9; 1B-1 **Ht:** 6'2" **Wt:** 230 **Born:** 9/5/1975 **Age:** 32

			BATTING																				BASERUNNING				AVERAGES		
Year	Team	Lg	G	AB	H	2B	3B	HR	(Hm	Rd)	TB	R	RBI	RC	TBB	IBB	SO	HBP	SH	SF	SB	CS	SB%	GDP	Avg	OBP	Slg
2007	Lakwd*	A-	6	16	6	2	0	0	(-	-)	8	0	2	3	3	0	6	0	0	0	0	0	-	1	.375	.474	.500
2007	Rdng*	AA	2	5	1	0	0	0	(-	-)	1	0	0	0	0	0	0	0	0	0	0	0	-	0	.200	.200	.200
1999	Ari	NL	5	16	4	1	0	1	(1	0)	8	3	3	2	1	0	1	0	1	0	0	0	-	0	.250	.294	.500
2000	Ari	NL	5	13	3	0	0	1	(1	0)	6	1	3	1	0	0	4	0	0	0	0	0	-	0	.231	.231	.462
2001	Ari	NL	51	106	17	3	0	3	(2	1)	29	9	9	4	4	0	26	0	0	0	0	0	-	0	.160	.191	.274
2002	Ari	NL	70	154	36	10	0	3	(1	2)	55	12	23	15	10	4	25	3	2	3	1	0	1.00	4	.234	.288	.357
2003	Ari	NL	80	220	48	15	0	3	(3	0)	72	19	28	19	14	7	43	1	1	3	0	0	-	6	.218	.265	.327
2004	Tex	AL	108	358	89	26	1	15	(8	7)	162	50	58	43	13	0	63	3	8	7	0	1	.00	3	.249	.276	.453
2005	Tex	AL	120	410	104	24	0	21	(7	14)	191	53	60	56	26	0	70	6	4	3	0	0	-	6	.254	.306	.466
2006	Tex	AL	97	344	88	20	0	11	(6	5)	141	49	41	36	17	0	51	4	5	1	0	0	-	6	.256	.298	.410
2007	Phi	NL	48	122	28	8	0	4	(1	3)	48	16	10	12	21	3	24	2	1	0	0	1	.00	5	.230	.352	.393
9 ML YEARS			584	1743	417	107	1	62	(30	32)	712	212	235	188	106	14	307	19	22	17	1	2	.33	33	.239	.288	.408

Josh Bard

Bats: B **Throws:** R **Pos:** C-108; PH-12; DH-1 **Ht:** 6'3" **Wt:** 210 **Born:** 3/30/1978 **Age:** 30

			BATTING																				BASERUNNING				AVERAGES		
Year	Team	Lg	G	AB	H	2B	3B	HR	(Hm	Rd)	TB	R	RBI	RC	TBB	IBB	SO	HBP	SH	SF	SB	CS	SB%	GDP	Avg	OBP	Slg
2002	Cle	AL	24	90	20	5	0	3	(2	1)	34	9	12	7	4	0	13	0	1	0	0	0	-	6	.222	.255	.378
2003	Cle	AL	91	303	74	13	1	8	(5	3)	113	25	36	34	22	1	53	0	1	3	0	2	.00	9	.244	.293	.373
2004	Cle	AL	7	19	8	2	0	1	(1	0)	13	5	4	6	3	0	0	0	0	1	0	0	-	0	.421	.478	.684
2005	Cle	AL	34	83	16	4	0	1	(0	1)	23	6	9	8	9	0	11	0	1	2	0	0	-	2	.193	.266	.277
2006	2 Tms		100	249	83	20	0	9	(5	4)	130	30	40	44	30	1	42	1	2	2	1	0	1.00	9	.333	.404	.522
2007	SD	NL	118	389	111	27	2	5	(4	1)	157	42	51	65	50	7	58	0	1	3	0	1	.00	16	.285	.364	.404
06	Bos	AL	7	18	5	1	0	0	(0	0)	6	2	0	2	3	0	3	0	0	0	0	0	-	0	.278	.381	.333
06	SD	NL	93	231	78	19	0	9	(5	4)	124	28	40	42	27	1	39	1	2	2	1	0	1.00	9	.338	.406	.537
6 ML YEARS			374	1133	312	71	3	27	(17	10)	470	117	152	164	118	9	177	1	6	11	1	3	.25	42	.275	.341	.415

Brian Barden

Bats: R **Throws:** R **Pos:** PH-13; SS-6; 3B-4; 2B-2; PR-1 **Ht:** 5'11" **Wt:** 185 **Born:** 4/2/1981 **Age:** 27

			BATTING																				BASERUNNING				AVERAGES		
Year	Team	Lg	G	AB	H	2B	3B	HR	(Hm	Rd)	TB	R	RBI	RC	TBB	IBB	SO	HBP	SH	SF	SB	CS	SB%	GDP	Avg	OBP	Slg
2002	Yakima	A-	4	15	5	1	0	0	(-	-)	6	5	2	2	1	0	1	1	0	0	0	0	-	1	.333	.412	.400
2002	Lancst	A+	64	269	90	19	1	8	(-	-)	135	58	46	49	16	0	63	1	2	3	3	1	.75	3	.335	.370	.502
2003	ElPaso	AA	109	383	110	24	5	3	(-	-)	153	50	57	56	29	0	78	3	4	5	10	4	.71	8	.287	.348	.399
2004	ElPaso	AA	48	195	59	10	6	3	(-	-)	90	33	28	30	10	1	48	2	1	5	1	2	.33	3	.303	.335	.462
2004	Tucsn	AAA	89	332	94	30	5	8	(-	-)	158	50	50	52	17	0	83	5	2	4	3	1	.75	6	.283	.324	.476
2005	Tucsn	AAA	135	518	159	36	5	15	(-	-)	250	78	85	93	38	3	111	11	3	6	14	5	.74	15	.307	.363	.483
2006	Tucsn	AAA	128	494	147	35	3	16	(-	-)	236	80	96	86	44	2	92	7	2	3	1	3	.25	11	.298	.361	.478

Year	Team	Lg	G	AB	H	2B	3B	HR	(Hm	Rd)	TB	R	RBI	RC	TBB	IBB	SO	HBP	SH	SF	SB	CS	SB%	GDP	Avg	OBP	Slg
																					BATTING			BASERUNNING		AVERAGES	
2007	Tucsn	AAA	83	284	77	9	2	2	(-	-)	96	36	25	37	31	1	55	7	5	0	2	3	.40	11	.271	.357	.338
2007	Memp	AAA	20	68	16	3	0	2	(-	-)	25	7	12	7	5	0	13	1	0	3	0	0	-	3	.235	.286	.368
2007	2 Tms	NL	23	35	6	1	0	0	(0	0)	7	6	0	1	2	0	7	0	0	0	0	0	-	2	.171	.216	.200
07	Ari	NL	8	12	1	0	0	0	(0	0)	1	0	0	0	0	0	3	0	0	0	0	0	-		.083	.083	.083
07	StL	NL	15	23	5	1	0	0	(0	0)	6	6	0	1	2	0	4	0	0	0	0	0	-	2	.217	.280	.261

Josh Barfield

Bats: R **Throws:** R **Pos:** 2B-120; PR-13; DH-2; PH-1   **Ht:** 6'0" **Wt:** 190 **Born:** 12/17/1982 **Age:** 25

Year	Team	Lg	G	AB	H	2B	3B	HR	(Hm	Rd)	TB	R	RBI	RC	TBB	IBB	SO	HBP	SH	SF	SB	CS	SB%	GDP	Avg	OBP	Slg
2001	Idaho	R+	66	277	86	15	4	4	(-	-)	121	51	53	44	16	1	54	3	0	4	12	4	.75	7	.310	.350	.437
2002	FtWyn	A	129	536	164	22	3	8	(-	-)	216	73	57	77	26	0	105	4	3	5	26	8	.76	13	.306	.340	.403
2002	Lk Els	A+	6	23	2	0	0	0	(-	-)	2	2	4	0	1	0	4	0	1	1	0	0	-	1	.087	.120	.087
2003	Lk Els	A+	135	549	185	46	6	16	(-	-)	291	99	128	114	50	3	122	4	1	11	16	4	.80	11	.337	.389	.530
2004	Mobile	AA	138	521	129	28	3	18	(-	-)	217	79	90	71	48	4	119	5	0	7	4	2	.67	6	.248	.313	.417
2005	Portlnd	AAA	137	516	160	25	1	15	(-	-)	232	74	72	90	52	1	108	1	2	7	20	5	.80	10	.310	.370	.450
2006	SD	NL	150	539	151	32	3	13	(6	7)	228	72	58	69	30	7	81	2	2	5	21	5	.81	8	.280	.318	.423
2007	Cle	AL	130	420	102	19	3	3	(2	1)	136	53	50	42	14	0	90	3	3	4	14	5	.74	3	.243	.270	.324
	2 ML YEARS		280	959	253	51	6	16	(8	8)	364	125	108	111	44	7	171	5	5	9	35	10	.78	11	.264	.297	.380

Sean Barker

Bats: R **Throws:** R **Pos:** PH-2; LF-1; CF-1   **Ht:** 6'3" **Wt:** 220 **Born:** 5/26/1980 **Age:** 28

Year	Team	Lg	G	AB	H	2B	3B	HR	(Hm	Rd)	TB	R	RBI	RC	TBB	IBB	SO	HBP	SH	SF	SB	CS	SB%	GDP	Avg	OBP	Slg
2002	TriCity	A-	45	166	37	9	1	1	(-	-)	51	21	15	14	12	0	38	2	2	0	4	2	.67	6	.223	.283	.307
2003	Visalia	A+	104	378	106	24	4	10	(-	-)	168	61	41	57	25	0	71	7	1	3	6	3	.67	3	.280	.334	.444
2004	Visalia	A+	105	412	127	29	5	20	(-	-)	226	75	96	85	40	1	89	7	2	7	11	3	.79	9	.308	.373	.549
2004	Tulsa	AA	22	83	19	3	0	2	(-	-)	28	9	12	8	7	0	24	0	1	0	2	0	1.00	2	.229	.289	.337
2005	Tulsa	AA	125	468	122	24	8	14	(-	-)	204	72	76	67	37	2	133	4	2	2	15	7	.68	10	.261	.319	.436
2006	ColSpr	AAA	106	330	98	14	9	13	(-	-)	169	53	55	61	29	0	104	5	0	1	17	7	.71	4	.297	.362	.512
2007	ColSpr	AAA	72	261	86	23	2	6	(-	-)	131	52	46	49	14	1	65	6	1	3	13	5	.72	4	.330	.373	.502
2007	Col	NL	3	2	0	0	0	0	(0	0)	0	0	0	0	0	0	1	1	0	0	0	0	-	0	.000	.333	.000

Clint Barmes

Bats: R **Throws:** R **Pos:** PH-11; SS-8; 2B-5; CF-5; PR-4; 3B-1   **Ht:** 6'0" **Wt:** 210 **Born:** 3/6/1979 **Age:** 29

Year	Team	Lg	G	AB	H	2B	3B	HR	(Hm	Rd)	TB	R	RBI	RC	TBB	IBB	SO	HBP	SH	SF	SB	CS	SB%	GDP	Avg	OBP	Slg
2007	ColSpr*	AAA	108	428	128	20	6	11	(-	-)	193	68	44	71	22	4	52	22	4	1	8	6	.57	5	.299	.364	.451
2003	Col	NL	12	25	8	2	0	0	(0	0)	10	2	2	3	0	0	10	2	0	1	0	0	-	0	.320	.357	.400
2004	Col	NL	20	71	20	3	1	2	(0	2)	31	14	10	12	3	0	10	1	2	0	0	1	.00	2	.282	.320	.437
2005	Col	NL	81	350	101	19	1	10	(7	3)	152	55	46	49	16	1	36	6	4	1	6	4	.60	4	.289	.330	.434
2006	Col	NL	131	478	105	26	4	7	(3	4)	160	57	56	47	22	6	72	9	19	7	5	4	.56	2	.220	.264	.335
2007	Col	NL	27	37	8	3	0	0	(0	0)	11	5	1	1	1	1	13	0	1	0	0	0	-	1	.216	.237	.297
	5 ML YEARS		271	961	242	53	6	19	(10	9)	364	133	115	112	42	8	141	18	26	9	11	9	.55	9	.252	.293	.379

Daniel Barone

Pitches: R **Bats:** R **Pos:** RP-10; SP-6   **Ht:** 6'2" **Wt:** 185 **Born:** 4/24/1983 **Age:** 25

Year	Team	Lg	G	GS	CG	GF	IP	BFP	H	R	ER	HR	SH	SF	HB	TBB	IBB	SO	WP	Bk	W	L	Pct	ShO	Sv-Op Hld	ERC	ERA
2004	Jmstwn	A-	19	2	0	5	51.1	225	60	31	29	7	1	0	2	11	0	45	3	0	3	6	.333	0	0-- -	4.92	5.08
2005	Jmstwn	A-	9	0	0	3	19.2	77	14	2	1	1	1	1	0	4	0	17	1	0	2	0	1.000	0	2-- -	1.80	0.46
2005	JhsCty	R+	1	0	0	0	1.0	4	1	1	1	1	0	0	0	0	0	1	0	0	0	0	-	0	0-- -	7.45	9.00
2005	Grnsbr	A	12	6	0	2	39.1	164	35	19	18	4	3	0	4	10	0	29	3	0	2	2	.500	0	1-- -	3.32	4.12
2006	Grnsbr	A	9	6	0	1	49.0	193	36	15	13	1	0	0	3	9	0	60	0	0	4	0	1.000	0	0-- -	1.70	2.39
2006	Jupiter	A+	17	8	0	2	73.1	321	84	44	35	9	5	3	4	18	0	57	1	0	3	5	.375	0	0-- -	4.63	4.30
2006	Carlina	AA	3	2	0	0	20.0	77	13	4	4	1	0	0	0	6	0	13	0	0	1	0	1.000	0	0-- -	1.70	1.80
2007	Carlina	AA	13	13	0	0	74.2	306	68	35	32	7	3	6	2	18	0	60	2	0	1	3	.250	0	0-- -	3.05	3.86
2007	Albq	AAA	10	10	0	0	61.2	253	60	30	28	6	2	2	1	14	0	31	3	0	7	0	1.000	0	0-- -	3.34	4.09
2007	Fla	NL	16	6	0	4	41.0	183	50	29	26	11	0	2	1	19	2	18	1	0	1	3	.250	0	0-0 0	7.23	5.71

Michael Barrett

Bats: R **Throws:** R **Pos:** C-95; PH-8   **Ht:** 6'3" **Wt:** 210 **Born:** 10/22/1976 **Age:** 31

Year	Team	Lg	G	AB	H	2B	3B	HR	(Hm	Rd)	TB	R	RBI	RC	TBB	IBB	SO	HBP	SH	SF	SB	CS	SB%	GDP	Avg	OBP	Slg
2007	Portlnd*	AAA	3	11	2	1	0	0	(-	-)	3	2	1	0	0	0	2	0	0	0	0	0	-	1	.182	.182	.273
1998	Mon	NL	8	23	7	2	0	1	(0	1)	12	3	2	5	3	0	6	1	0	0	0	0	-	0	.304	.407	.522
1999	Mon	NL	126	433	127	32	3	8	(5	3)	189	53	52	59	32	4	39	3	0	1	0	2	.00	18	.293	.345	.436
2000	Mon	NL	89	271	58	15	1	1	(0	1)	78	28	22	19	23	5	35	1	1	1	0	1	.00	7	.214	.277	.288
2001	Mon	NL	132	472	118	33	2	6	(3	3)	173	42	38	46	25	2	54	2	4	3	2	1	.67	14	.250	.289	.367
2002	Mon	NL	117	376	99	20	1	12	(4	8)	157	41	49	49	40	7	65	1	6	5	6	3	.67	14	.263	.332	.418
2003	Mon	NL	70	226	47	9	2	10	(5	5)	90	33	30	25	21	7	37	2	2	1	0	0	-	6	.208	.280	.398
2004	ChC	NL	134	456	131	32	6	16	(9	7)	223	55	65	67	33	4	64	5	4	8	1	4	.20	13	.287	.337	.489
2005	ChC	NL	133	424	117	32	3	16	(9	7)	203	48	61	67	40	3	61	7	2	4	0	3	.00	7	.276	.345	.479
2006	ChC	NL	107	375	115	25	3	16	(9	7)	194	48	53	58	54	5	41	5	2	3	0	1	.00	12	.307	.368	.517

Year	Team	Lg	G	AB	H	2B	3B	HR	(Hm	Rd)	TB	R	RBI	RC	TBB	IBB	SO	HBP	SH	SF	SB	CS	SB%	GDP	Avg	OBP	Slg
2007	2 Tms	NL	101	344	84	17	0	9	(6	3)	128	29	41	29	19	3	57	0	0	4	2	2	.50	10	.244	.281	.372
07	ChC	NL	57	211	54	9	0	9	(6	3)	90	23	29	22	17	3	36	0	0	3	2	2	.50	5	.256	.307	.427
07	SD	NL	44	133	30	8	0	0	(0	0)	38	6	12	7	2	0	21	0	0	1	0	0	-	5	.226	.235	.286
10 ML YEARS			1017	3400	903	217	21	95	(50	45)	1447	386	413	424	269	37	459	27	21	30	11	17	.39	101	.266	.322	.426

Kevin Barry

Pitches: R **Bats:** R **Pos:** RP-1   **Ht:** 6'2" **Wt:** 235 **Born:** 8/18/1978 **Age:** 29

			HOW MUCH HE PITCHED						WHAT HE GAVE UP											THE RESULTS						
Year	Team	Lg	G	GS	CG	GF	IP	BFP	H	R	ER	HR	SH	SF	HB	TBB	IBB	SO	WP	Bk	W	L	Pct	ShO	Sv-Op	Hld	ERC	ERA
2001	Jmstwn	A-	29	0	0	23	31.1	126	14	5	3	0	0	1	0	18	0	54	0	0	1	0	1.000	0	12--	-	1.41	0.86
2002	MrtlBh	A+	47	0	0	43	50.0	197	37	14	14	2	3	4	1	17	1	67	0	0	4	2	.667	0	26--	-	2.24	2.52
2003	Grnville	AA	51	0	0	19	56.1	257	54	36	31	1	2	3	3	32	0	68	3	0	4	4	.500	0	5--	-	4.00	4.95
2004	Grnville	A	20	0	0	19	24.2	100	15	2	2	1	0	1	2	20	2	31	2	0	2	1	.667	0	4--	-	3.21	0.73
2004	Rchmd	AAA	30	0	0	13	35.2	157	25	15	10	1	0	0	0	25	2	40	0	0	3	3	.500	0	2--	-	2.92	2.52
2005	Missi	AA	3	0	0	0	7.1	31	3	1	1	0	0	0	0	6	0	7	0	0	0	0	-	0	0--	-	1.83	1.23
2005	Rchmd	AAA	32	8	0	12	79.0	336	60	28	25	8	2	2	2	44	4	73	0	0	5	3	.625	0	1--	-	3.40	2.85
2006	Rchmd	AAA	18	15	0	2	95.1	409	87	40	35	5	5	5	2	36	2	73	1	0	4	5	.444	0	0--	-	3.18	3.30
2007	Rchmd	AAA	24	22	0	0	112.2	491	118	59	53	13	9	7	1	41	0	83	3	0	5	7	.417	0	0--	-	4.58	4.23
2006	Atl	NL	19	1	0	7	25.2	115	24	16	16	2	3	2	1	14	0	19	0	0	1	1	.500	0	0-1	1	4.21	5.61
2007	Atl	NL	1	0	0	1	2.0	14	6	5	5	0	0	0	0	2	0	4	1	0	0	0	-	0	0-0	0	19.55	22.50
2 ML YEARS			20	1	0	8	27.2	129	30	21	21	2	3	2	1	16	0	23	1	0	1	1	.500	0	0-1	1	5.12	6.83

Jason Bartlett

Bats: R **Throws:** R **Pos:** SS-138; PH-2; PR-2   **Ht:** 6'0" **Wt:** 185 **Born:** 10/30/1979 **Age:** 28

			BATTING																	BASERUNNING				AVERAGES		
Year	Team	Lg	G	AB	H	2B	3B	HR	(Hm	Rd)	TB	R	RBI	RC	TBB	IBB	SO	HBP	SH	SF	SB	CS	SB%	GDP	Avg	OBP	Slg
2004	Min	AL	8	12	1	0	0	0	(0	0)	1	2	1	1	1	0	1	0	1	0	1	0	1.00	0	.083	.154	.083
2005	Min	AL	74	224	54	10	1	3	(2	1)	75	33	16	22	21	0	37	4	2	1	4	0	1.00	6	.241	.316	.335
2006	Min	AL	99	333	103	18	2	2	(0	2)	131	44	32	50	22	1	46	11	1	5	10	5	.67	8	.309	.367	.393
2007	Min	AL	140	510	135	20	7	5	(2	3)	184	75	43	65	50	3	73	8	0	2	23	3	.88	8	.265	.339	.361
4 ML YEARS			321	1079	293	48	10	10	(4	6)	391	154	92	138	94	4	157	23	4	8	39	8	.83	22	.272	.341	.362

Daric Barton

Bats: L **Throws:** R **Pos:** 1B-18   **Ht:** 6'0" **Wt:** 225 **Born:** 8/16/1985 **Age:** 22

			BATTING																	BASERUNNING				AVERAGES		
Year	Team	Lg	G	AB	H	2B	3B	HR	(Hm	Rd)	TB	R	RBI	RC	TBB	IBB	SO	HBP	SH	SF	SB	CS	SB%	GDP	Avg	OBP	Slg
2003	JhsCty	R+	54	170	50	10	0	4	(-	-)	72	29	29	32	37	0	48	2	0	3	0	3	.00	2	.294	.420	.424
2004	Peoria	A	90	313	98	23	0	13	(-	-)	160	63	77	74	69	9	44	8	0	3	4	4	.50	7	.313	.445	.511
2005	Stcktn	A+	79	292	93	16	2	8	(-	-)	137	60	52	64	62	0	49	3	0	4	0	1	.00	6	.318	.438	.469
2005	Mdland	AA	56	212	67	20	1	5	(-	-)	104	38	37	43	35	1	30	0	0	2	1	2	.33	4	.316	.410	.491
2006	Scrmto	AAA	43	147	38	6	4	2	(-	-)	58	25	22	25	32	0	26	0	0	1	1	0	1.00	6	.259	.389	.395
2006	As	R	2	5	1	1	0	0	(-	-)	2	1	2	0	0	0	0	0	0	0	0	0	-	0	.200	.200	.400
2007	Scrmto	AAA	136	516	151	38	5	9	(-	-)	226	84	70	93	78	0	69	6	0	4	3	4	.43	14	.293	.389	.438
2007	Oak	AL	18	72	25	9	0	4	(2	2)	46	16	8	14	10	0	11	1	0	1	1	0	1.00	2	.347	.429	.639

Chris Basak

Bats: R **Throws:** R **Pos:** 3B-3; SS-1; PH-1; PR-1   **Ht:** 6'2" **Wt:** 190 **Born:** 12/6/1978 **Age:** 29

			BATTING																	BASERUNNING				AVERAGES		
Year	Team	Lg	G	AB	H	2B	3B	HR	(Hm	Rd)	TB	R	RBI	RC	TBB	IBB	SO	HBP	SH	SF	SB	CS	SB%	GDP	Avg	OBP	Slg
2000	Pittsfld	A-	63	249	87	18	4	0	(-	-)	113	46	15	49	26	2	36	3	3	0	32	12	.73	1	.349	.417	.454
2000	StLuci	A+	4	17	7	1	0	0	(-	-)	8	2	3	4	4	0	2	0	0	0	3	1	.75	1	.412	.524	.471
2001	StLuci	A+	126	472	110	19	4	4	(-	-)	149	71	46	51	47	0	125	5	4	8	30	9	.77	8	.233	.305	.316
2001	Bnghtn	AA	13	43	16	6	1	1	(-	-)	27	11	7	11	3	0	10	2	0	1	2	0	1.00	1	.372	.429	.628
2002	Bnghtn	AA	109	377	96	18	3	4	(-	-)	132	54	34	44	38	3	94	2	6	4	19	14	.58	0	.255	.323	.350
2002	Norfolk	AAA	17	60	13	1	0	0	(-	-)	16	6	6	4	3	0	14	0	0	0	5	0	1.00	0	.217	.254	.267
2003	Bnghtn	AA	113	404	110	25	2	7	(-	-)	160	59	42	56	35	0	101	5	8	8	18	10	.64	9	.272	.332	.396
2003	Norfolk	AAA	19	71	17	6	0	0	(-	-)	23	10	8	7	7	0	24	1	2	0	3	3	.50	0	.239	.316	.324
2004	Bnghtn	AA	80	276	71	21	5	8	(-	-)	126	42	41	47	39	1	67	3	2	2	10	5	.67	4	.257	.353	.457
2004	Norfolk	AAA	58	193	43	11	4	6	(-	-)	80	25	19	21	10	0	58	0	9	1	5	3	.63	0	.223	.260	.415
2005	Norfolk	AAA	93	279	76	17	4	8	(-	-)	125	52	41	48	30	1	54	3	9	5	17	3	.85	0	.272	.344	.448
2006	Norfolk	AAA	119	371	99	22	3	8	(-	-)	151	36	36	56	39	0	76	5	2	0	17	3	.85	3	.267	.345	.407
2007	S-WB	AAA	84	308	78	19	1	7	(-	-)	120	47	38	40	21	0	55	4	3	4	13	3	.81	4	.253	.306	.390
2007	Roch	AAA	12	33	8	1	0	0	(-	-)	9	3	4	2	1	0	9	0	1	0	1	0	1.00	0	.242	.265	.273
2007	NYY	AL	5	1	0	0	0	0	(0	0)	0	0	0	0	0	0	0	0	0	0	0	0	-	0	.000	.000	.000

Miguel Batista

Pitches: R **Bats:** R **Pos:** SP-32; RP-1   **Ht:** 6'1" **Wt:** 197 **Born:** 2/19/1971 **Age:** 37

			HOW MUCH HE PITCHED						WHAT HE GAVE UP											THE RESULTS						
Year	Team	Lg	G	GS	CG	GF	IP	BFP	H	R	ER	HR	SH	SF	HB	TBB	IBB	SO	WP	Bk	W	L	Pct	ShO	Sv-Op	Hld	ERC	ERA
1992	Pit	NL	1	0	0	1	2.0	13	4	2	2	1	0	0	0	3	0	1	0	0	0	0	-	0	0-0	0	20.26	9.00
1996	Fla	NL	9	0	0	4	11.1	49	9	8	7	0	3	0	0	7	2	6	1	0	0	0	-	0	0-0	0	2.77	5.56
1997	ChC	NL	11	6	0	2	36.1	168	36	24	23	4	4	1	0	24	2	27	2	0	0	5	.000	0	0-0	0	5.09	5.70
1998	Mon	NL	56	13	0	12	135.0	598	141	66	57	12	7	5	6	65	7	92	6	1	3	5	.375	0	0-3	4	4.70	3.80
1999	Mon	NL	39	17	2	3	134.2	606	146	88	73	10	8	11	7	58	0	95	6	0	8	7	.533	1	1-1	0	4.62	4.88
2000	2 Tms	NL	18	9	0	2	65.1	310	85	68	62	19	1	2	2	37	2	37	4	0	2	7	.222	0	0-2	0	8.37	8.54

Year	Team	Lg	HOW MUCH HE PITCHED						WHAT HE GAVE UP												THE RESULTS							
			G	GS	CG	GF	IP	BFP	H	R	ER	HR	SH	SF	HB	TBB	IBB	SO	WP	Bk	W	L	Pct	ShO	Sv-Op	Hld	ERC	ERA
2001	Ari	NL	48	18	0	6	139.1	581	113	57	52	13	9	3	10	60	2	90	6	0	11	8	.579	0	0-0	4	3.43	3.36
2002	Ari	NL	36	29	1	2	184.2	790	172	99	88	12	5	8	6	70	3	112	9	2	8	9	.471	0	0-0	2	3.45	4.29
2003	Ari	NL	36	29	2	5	193.1	822	197	85	76	13	10	6	8	60	3	142	7	0	10	9	.526	1	0-0	0	3.77	3.54
2004	Tor	AL	38	31	2	7	198.2	867	206	115	106	22	7	6	3	96	1	104	12	0	10	13	.435	1	5-5	0	4.84	4.80
2005	Tor	AL	71	0	0	62	74.2	331	80	39	34	9	2	2	2	27	5	54	3	0	5	8	.385	0	31-39	4	4.39	4.10
2006	Ari	NL	34	33	3	0	206.1	910	231	116	105	18	12	5	6	84	5	110	14	1	11	8	.579	1	0-0	0	4.82	4.58
2007	Sea	AL	33	32	0	0	193.0	860	209	101	92	18	5	5	8	85	3	133	15	2	16	11	.593	0	0-0	0	4.81	4.29
00	Mon	NL	4	0	0	0	8.1	49	19	14	13	2	1	1	2	3	0	7	0	0	0	1	.000	0	0-2	0	14.73	14.04
00	KC	AL	14	9	0	2	57.0	261	66	54	49	17	0	1	0	34	2	30	4	0	2	6	.250	0	0-0	0	7.50	7.74
13 ML YEARS			430	217	10	106	1574.2	6905	1629	868	777	151	73	57	59	676	37	1003	85	6	84	90	.483	4	37-47	9	4.49	4.44

Tony Batista

Bats: R **Throws:** R **Pos:** PH-63; 1B-27; 3B-2   **Ht:** 6'0" **Wt:** 208 **Born:** 12/9/1973 **Age:** 34

Year	Team	Lg	BATTING																	BASERUNNING				AVERAGES		
			G	AB	H	2B	3B	HR	(Hm	Rd)	TB	R	RBI	RC	TBB	IBB	SO	HBP	SH	SF	SB	CS	SB%	GDP	Avg	OBP	Slg
2007	Clmbs*	AAA	30	107	31	7	1	6	(-	-)	58	14	22	20	8	0	16	3	0	2	1	0	1.00	3	.290	.350	.542
1996	Oak	AL	74	238	71	10	2	6	(1	5)	103	38	25	37	19	0	49	1	0	2	7	3	.70	2	.298	.350	.433
1997	Oak	AL	68	188	38	10	1	4	(0	4)	62	22	18	14	14	0	31	2	3	0	2	2	.50	8	.202	.265	.330
1998	Ari	NL	106	293	80	16	1	18	(9	9)	152	46	41	46	18	0	52	3	0	4	1	1	.50	7	.273	.318	.519
1999	2 Tms		142	519	144	30	1	31	(10	21)	269	77	100	87	38	4	96	6	3	7	4	0	1.00	3	.277	.330	.518
2000	Tor	AL	154	620	163	32	2	41	(25	16)	322	96	114	94	35	1	121	6	0	3	5	4	.56	15	.263	.307	.519
2001	2 Tms		156	579	138	27	6	25	(14	11)	252	70	87	70	32	1	113	4	0	7	5	2	.71	9	.238	.280	.435
2002	Bal	AL	161	615	150	36	1	31	(14	17)	281	90	87	79	50	9	107	11	0	6	5	4	.56	13	.244	.309	.457
2003	Bal	AL	161	631	148	20	1	26	(10	16)	248	76	99	66	28	4	102	5	0	6	4	3	.57	20	.235	.270	.393
2004	Mon	NL	157	606	146	30	2	32	(13	19)	276	76	110	69	26	4	78	4	4	10	14	6	.70	14	.241	.272	.455
2006	Min	AL	50	178	42	12	0	5	(2	3)	69	24	21	23	15	1	27	2	0	0	0	1	.00	5	.236	.303	.388
2007	Was	NL	80	101	26	3	0	2	(0	2)	35	10	16	14	12	3	14	3	0	2	0	0	-	4	.257	.347	.347
99	Ari	NL	44	144	37	5	0	5	(1	4)	57	16	21	21	16	3	17	2	0	2	2	0	1.00	1	.257	.335	.396
99	Tor	AL	98	375	107	25	1	26	(9	17)	212	61	79	66	22	1	79	4	3	5	2	0	1.00	1	.285	.328	.565
01	Tor	AL	72	271	56	11	1	13	(9	4)	108	29	45	27	13	1	66	4	0	3	0	1	.00	2	.207	.251	.399
01	Bal	AL	84	308	82	16	5	12	(5	7)	144	41	42	43	19	0	47	0	0	4	5	1	.83	7	.266	.305	.468
11 ML YEARS			1309	4568	1146	226	17	221	(98	123)	2069	625	718	599	287	27	790	47	10	47	47	26	.64	109	.251	.299	.453

Denny Bautista

Pitches: R **Bats:** R **Pos:** RP-8; SP-1   **Ht:** 6'5" **Wt:** 190 **Born:** 8/23/1980 **Age:** 27

Year	Team	Lg	HOW MUCH HE PITCHED						WHAT HE GAVE UP													THE RESULTS							
			G	GS	CG	GF	IP	BFP	H	R	ER	HR	SH	SF	HB	TBB	IBB	SO	WP	Bk	W	L	Pct	ShO	Sv-Op	Hld	ERC	ERA
2007	ColSpr*	AAA	51	0	0	21	64.2	276	54	22	21	1	3	4	31	0	63	10	0	3	2	.600	0	0-0	0	3.14	2.92
2004	2 Tms	AL	7	5	0	0	29.2	142	44	28	28	3	0	1	3	13	1	19	3	2	0	4	.000	0	0-0	0	7.76	8.10
2005	KC	AL	7	7	0	0	35.2	160	36	23	23	2	1	1	2	17	0	23	3	0	2	2	.500	0	0-0	0	4.27	5.80
2006	2 Tms		12	8	0	3	41.2	194	47	34	26	5	1	2	4	21	0	27	5	0	0	3	.000	0	0-0	0	5.75	5.62
2007	Col	NL	9	1	0	0	8.2	48	18	12	12	0	1	0	1	4	0	8	0	0	2	1	.667	0	0-0	2	10.84	12.46
04	Bal	AL	2	0	0	0	2.0	15	6	8	8	1	0	1	1	2	0	1	1	0	0	0	-	0	0-0	0	28.67	36.00
04	KC	AL	5	5	0	0	27.2	127	38	20	20	2	0	0	2	11	1	18	2	2	0	4	.000	0	0-0	0	6.50	6.51
06	KC	AL	8	7	0	0	35.0	161	38	24	22	5	1	2	4	17	0	22	5	0	0	2	.000	0	0-0	0	5.70	5.66
06	Col	NL	4	1	0	3	6.2	33	9	10	4	0	0	0	0	4	0	5	0	0	0	1	.000	0	0-0	0	5.98	5.40
4 ML YEARS			35	21	0	5	115.2	544	145	97	89	10	3	4	10	55	1	77	11	2	4	10	.286	0	0-0	2	6.12	6.93

Jose Bautista

Bats: R **Throws:** R **Pos:** 3B-126; RF-16; CF-5; LF-2; PH-1   **Ht:** 6'0" **Wt:** 195 **Born:** 10/19/1980 **Age:** 27

Year	Team	Lg	BATTING																	BASERUNNING				AVERAGES		
			G	AB	H	2B	3B	HR	(Hm	Rd)	TB	R	RBI	RC	TBB	IBB	SO	HBP	SH	SF	SB	CS	SB%	GDP	Avg	OBP	Slg
2007	Pirates*	R	2	8	3	2	0	0	(-	-)	5	1	1	1	0	0	1	0	0	0	0	0	-	0	.375	.375	.625
2004	4 Tms		64	88	18	3	0	0	(0	0)	21	6	2	2	7	0	40	0	1	0	0	1	.00	1	.205	.263	.239
2005	Pit	NL	11	28	4	1	0	0	(0	0)	5	3	1	0	3	0	7	0	0	0	1	0	1.00	0	.143	.226	.179
2006	Pit	NL	117	400	94	20	3	16	(11	5)	168	58	51	55	46	2	110	16	3	4	2	4	.33	12	.235	.335	.420
2007	Pit	NL	142	532	135	36	2	15	(8	7)	220	75	63	71	68	1	101	4	4	6	6	3	.67	16	.254	.339	.414
04	Bal	AL	16	11	3	0	0	0	(0	0)	3	3	0	1	1	0	3	0	0	0	0	0	-	0	.273	.333	.273
04	TB	AL	12	12	2	0	0	0	(0	0)	2	1	1	0	3	0	7	0	1	0	0	1	.00	0	.167	.333	.167
04	KC	AL	13	25	5	1	0	0	(0	0)	6	1	1	0	1	0	12	0	0	0	0	0	-	0	.200	.231	.240
04	Pit	NL	23	40	8	2	0	0	(0	0)	10	1	0	1	2	0	18	0	1	0	0	0	-	1	.200	.238	.250
4 ML YEARS			334	1048	251	60	5	31	(19	12)	414	142	117	128	124	3	258	20	8	10	9	8	.53	31	.240	.329	.395

Jason Bay

Bats: R **Throws:** R **Pos:** LF-142; PH-2; DH-1   **Ht:** 6'2" **Wt:** 205 **Born:** 9/20/1978 **Age:** 29

Year	Team	Lg	BATTING																	BASERUNNING				AVERAGES		
			G	AB	H	2B	3B	HR	(Hm	Rd)	TB	R	RBI	RC	TBB	IBB	SO	HBP	SH	SF	SB	CS	SB%	GDP	Avg	OBP	Slg
2003	2 Tms	NL	30	87	25	7	1	4	(2	2)	46	15	14	19	19	0	29	1	0	1	3	1	.75	0	.287	.421	.529
2004	Pit	NL	120	411	116	24	4	26	(15	11)	226	61	82	75	41	2	129	10	5	5	4	6	.40	9	.282	.358	.550
2005	Pit	NL	162	599	183	44	6	32	(9	23)	335	110	101	128	95	9	142	6	0	7	21	1	.95	12	.306	.402	.559
2006	Pit	NL	159	570	163	29	3	35	(13	22)	303	101	109	103	102	9	156	8	0	9	11	2	.85	15	.286	.396	.532
2007	Pit	NL	145	538	133	25	2	21	(7	14)	225	78	84	74	59	3	141	9	0	8	4	1	.80	8	.247	.327	.418
03	SD	NL	3	8	2	1	0	1	(0	1)	6	2	2	2	1	0	1	0	0	0	0	0	-	0	.250	.400	.750
03	Pit	NL	27	79	23	6	1	3	(2	1)	40	13	12	17	18	0	28	1	0	1	3	1	.75	0	.291	.423	.506
5 ML YEARS			616	2205	620	129	16	118	(46	72)	1135	365	390	399	316	23	597	34	5	29	43	11	.80	44	.281	.375	.515

37

Jonah Bayliss

Pitches: R Bats: R Pos: RP-39
Ht: 6'2" Wt: 200 Born: 8/13/1980 Age: 27

Year	Team	Lg	G	GS	CG	GF	IP	BFP	H	R	ER	HR	SH	SF	HB	TBB	IBB	SO	WP	Bk	W	L	Pct	ShO	Sv-Op	Hld	ERC	ERA
2007	Indy*	AAA	16	0	0	9	21.2	97	23	19	17	5	1	3	0	10	1	17	0	0	3	2	.600	0	0- -	-	5.51	7.06
2005	KC	AL	11	0	0	7	11.2	48	7	6	6	2	0	0	2	4	0	10	0	0	0	0	-	0	0-0	1	2.80	4.63
2006	Pit	NL	11	0	0	5	14.2	69	13	7	7	1	2	1	1	11	2	15	2	0	1	1	.500	0	0-0	1	4.46	4.30
2007	Pit	NL	39	0	0	11	37.2	179	51	36	35	8	0	1	2	18	2	29	1	0	4	3	.571	0	0-1	4	7.65	8.36
3 ML YEARS			61	0	0	23	64.0	296	71	49	48	11	2	2	5	33	4	54	3	0	5	4	.556	0	0-1	5	5.92	6.75

Yorman Bazardo

Pitches: R Bats: R Pos: RP-9; SP-2
Ht: 6'2" Wt: 220 Born: 7/11/1984 Age: 23

Year	Team	Lg	G	GS	CG	GF	IP	BFP	H	R	ER	HR	SH	SF	HB	TBB	IBB	SO	WP	Bk	W	L	Pct	ShO	Sv-Op	Hld	ERC	ERA
2002	Jmstwn	A-	25	0	0	21	36.1	154	39	11	11	0	0	2	1	6	0	26	7	0	5	0	1.000	0	6- -	-	2.95	2.72
2003	Grnsbr	A	21	21	4	0	130.0	548	132	56	45	8	3	4	9	26	0	70	4	2	9	8	.529	2	0- -	-	3.38	3.12
2004	Jupiter	A+	25	25	2	0	154.1	654	161	78	56	3	9	13	10	30	0	95	9	1	5	9	.357	2	0- -	-	3.20	3.27
2005	Carlina	AA	19	19	0	0	108.1	469	108	60	48	12	9	5	8	36	3	73	8	1	8	7	.533	0	0- -	-	4.10	3.99
2005	SnAnt	AA	6	6	0	0	33.2	150	38	16	16	4	0	1	0	11	0	26	0	2	3	1	.750	0	0- -	-	4.54	4.28
2006	SnAnt	AA	25	25	0	0	138.1	589	144	65	56	10	6	6	9	45	0	80	9	1	6	5	.545	0	0- -	-	4.15	3.64
2007	Toledo	AAA	23	21	2	0	136.2	568	134	66	57	8	4	6	6	43	3	69	1	1	10	6	.625	0	0- -	-	3.58	3.75
2005	Fla	NL	1	0	0	0	1.2	12	5	5	4	0	0	0	0	2	0	2	1	0	0	0	-	0	0-0	0	20.56	21.60
2007	Det	AL	11	2	0	6	23.2	96	19	7	6	2	0	1	3	5	0	15	1	0	2	1	.667	0	0-0	1	2.71	2.28
2 ML YEARS			12	2	0	6	25.1	108	24	12	10	2	0	1	3	7	0	17	2	0	2	1	.667	0	0-0	1	3.61	3.55

Colter Bean

Pitches: R Bats: R Pos: RP-3
Ht: 6'6" Wt: 255 Born: 1/16/1977 Age: 31

Year	Team	Lg	G	GS	CG	GF	IP	BFP	H	R	ER	HR	SH	SF	HB	TBB	IBB	SO	WP	Bk	W	L	Pct	ShO	Sv-Op	Hld	ERC	ERA
2007	S-WB*	AAA	28	5	0	7	59.0	274	66	40	39	3	1	1	14	31	0	56	5	0	2	0	1.000	0	0- -	-	6.01	5.95
2005	NYY	AL	1	0	0	1	2.0	9	1	1	1	0	0	0	0	2	0	2	0	0	0	0	-	0	0-0	0	2.80	4.50
2006	NYY	AL	2	0	0	1	2.0	10	2	2	2	0	0	1	1	2	0	1	0	0	0	0	-	0	0-0	0	8.25	9.00
2007	NYY	AL	3	0	0	0	3.0	19	5	4	4	0	0	0	0	5	0	2	0	0	0	1	.000	0	0-0	0	12.68	12.00
3 ML YEARS			6	0	0	2	7.0	38	8	7	7	0	0	1	1	9	0	5	0	0	0	1	.000	0	0-0	0	8.29	9.00

Josh Beckett

Pitches: R Bats: R Pos: SP-30
Ht: 6'5" Wt: 220 Born: 5/15/1980 Age: 28

Year	Team	Lg	G	GS	CG	GF	IP	BFP	H	R	ER	HR	SH	SF	HB	TBB	IBB	SO	WP	Bk	W	L	Pct	ShO	Sv-Op	Hld	ERC	ERA
2001	Fla	NL	4	4	0	0	24.0	99	14	9	4	3	0	0	1	11	0	24	1	0	2	2	.500	0	0-0	0	2.36	1.50
2002	Fla	NL	23	21	0	0	107.2	454	93	56	49	13	5	3	1	44	2	113	5	0	6	7	.462	0	0-0	0	3.50	4.10
2003	Fla	NL	24	23	0	1	142.0	601	132	54	48	9	5	1	2	56	4	152	6	1	9	8	.529	0	0-0	0	3.44	3.04
2004	Fla	NL	26	26	1	0	156.2	654	137	72	66	16	9	3	6	54	3	152	5	0	9	9	.500	1	0-0	0	3.32	3.79
2005	Fla	NL	29	29	2	0	178.2	729	153	75	67	14	8	2	7	58	2	166	5	0	15	8	.652	1	0-0	0	3.06	3.38
2006	Bos	AL	33	33	0	0	204.2	869	191	120	114	36	2	3	10	74	1	158	11	1	16	11	.593	0	0-0	0	4.28	5.01
2007	Bos	AL	30	30	1	0	200.2	822	189	76	73	17	3	2	5	40	0	194	3	0	20	7	.741	0	0-0	0	2.99	3.27
7 ML YEARS			169	166	4	1	1014.1	4228	909	462	421	108	32	14	32	337	12	959	36	2	77	52	.597	2	0-0	0	3.41	3.74

Erik Bedard

Pitches: L Bats: L Pos: SP-28
Ht: 6'1" Wt: 196 Born: 3/6/1979 Age: 29

Year	Team	Lg	G	GS	CG	GF	IP	BFP	H	R	ER	HR	SH	SF	HB	TBB	IBB	SO	WP	Bk	W	L	Pct	ShO	Sv-Op	Hld	ERC	ERA
2002	Bal	AL	2	0	0	0	0.2	4	2	1	1	0	0	0	0	0	0	1	0	0	0	0	-	0	0-0	0	14.52	13.50
2004	Bal	AL	27	26	0	0	137.1	633	149	83	70	13	0	4	7	71	1	121	7	2	6	10	.375	0	0-0	0	5.11	4.59
2005	Bal	AL	24	24	0	0	141.2	606	139	66	63	10	3	6	5	57	1	125	4	1	6	8	.429	0	0-0	0	3.95	4.00
2006	Bal	AL	33	33	0	0	196.1	844	196	92	82	16	4	4	5	69	0	171	6	0	15	11	.577	0	0-0	0	3.83	3.76
2007	Bal	AL	28	28	1	0	182.0	733	141	66	64	19	2	4	5	57	0	221	3	0	13	5	.722	1	0-0	0	2.71	3.16
5 ML YEARS			114	111	1	0	658.0	2820	627	308	280	58	11	18	22	254	2	639	20	3	40	34	.541	1	0-0	0	3.80	3.83

Joe Beimel

Pitches: L Bats: L Pos: RP-83
Ht: 6'3" Wt: 215 Born: 4/19/1977 Age: 31

Year	Team	Lg	G	GS	CG	GF	IP	BFP	H	R	ER	HR	SH	SF	HB	TBB	IBB	SO	WP	Bk	W	L	Pct	ShO	Sv-Op	Hld	ERC	ERA
2001	Pit	NL	42	15	0	9	115.1	511	131	72	67	12	3	1	6	49	4	58	3	0	7	11	.389	0	0-0	0	5.24	5.23
2002	Pit	NL	53	8	0	8	85.1	389	88	49	44	9	7	3	4	45	12	53	2	0	2	5	.286	0	0-1	5	4.68	4.64
2003	Pit	NL	69	0	0	11	62.1	276	69	35	35	7	3	5	4	33	6	42	0	1	1	3	.250	0	0-5	12	5.62	5.05
2004	Min	AL	3	0	0	0	1.2	15	8	8	8	1	0	0	0	2	0	2	0	0	0	0	-	0	0-0	0	44.44	43.20
2005	TB	AL	7	0	0	3	11.0	51	15	4	4	1	0	0	0	4	1	3	1	0	0	0	-	0	0-0	1	5.80	3.27
2006	LAD	NL	62	0	0	10	70.0	295	70	26	23	7	4	3	0	21	3	30	6	1	2	1	.667	0	2-2	10	3.62	2.96
2007	LAD	NL	83	0	0	10	67.1	281	63	30	29	1	5	2	1	24	6	39	3	2	4	2	.667	0	1-1	16	2.93	3.88
7 ML YEARS			319	23	0	51	413.0	1818	444	224	210	38	22	14	15	178	32	227	15	4	16	22	.421	0	3-9	43	4.62	4.58

Matt Belisle

Pitches: R Bats: R Pos: SP-30   Ht: 6'3" Wt: 230 Born: 6/6/1980 Age: 28

			HOW MUCH HE PITCHED						WHAT HE GAVE UP										THE RESULTS						
Year	Team	Lg	G	GS	CG	GF	IP	BFP	H	R	ER	HR	SH	SF	HB	TBB	IBB	SO	WP	Bk	W	L	Pct	ShO	Sv-Op Hld	ERC	ERA
2007	Lsvlle*	AAA	1	1	0	0	6.0	28	7	4	2	0	0	0	0	2	0	7	0	0	0	1	.000	0	0- - -	3.75	3.00
2003	Cin	NL	6	0	0	2	8.2	39	10	5	5	1	2	1	1	2	0	6	0	0	1	1	.500	0	0-1 1	4.73	5.19
2005	Cin	NL	60	5	0	17	85.2	382	101	49	42	11	4	2	6	26	6	59	3	0	4	8	.333	0	1-4 8	5.08	4.41
2006	Cin	NL	30	2	0	5	40.0	180	43	18	16	5	1	2	3	19	1	26	3	0	2	0	1.000	0	0-1 0	5.29	3.60
2007	Cin	NL	30	30	1	0	177.2	771	212	111	105	26	7	9	7	43	4	125	6	1	8	9	.471	0	0-0 0	5.05	5.32
4 ML YEARS			126	37	1	24	312.0	1372	366	183	168	43	14	14	17	90	11	216	12	1	15	18	.455	0	1-6 8	5.08	4.85

Heath Bell

Pitches: R Bats: R Pos: RP-81   Ht: 6'3" Wt: 226 Born: 9/29/1977 Age: 30

			HOW MUCH HE PITCHED						WHAT HE GAVE UP										THE RESULTS						
Year	Team	Lg	G	GS	CG	GF	IP	BFP	H	R	ER	HR	SH	SF	HB	TBB	IBB	SO	WP	Bk	W	L	Pct	ShO	Sv-Op Hld	ERC	ERA
2004	NYM	NL	17	0	0	2	24.1	94	22	9	9	5	1	0	0	6	0	27	0	0	0	2	.000	0	0-1 1	3.86	3.33
2005	NYM	NL	42	0	0	12	46.2	206	56	30	29	3	4	0	1	13	3	43	0	1	1	3	.250	0	0-0 4	4.42	5.59
2006	NYM	NL	22	0	0	6	37.0	166	51	25	21	6	1	0	0	11	2	35	1	0	0	0	-	0	0-0 0	6.40	5.11
2007	SD	NL	81	0	0	16	93.2	363	60	21	21	3	4	1	2	30	1	102	4	0	6	4	.600	0	2-6 34	1.67	2.02
4 ML YEARS			162	0	0	36	201.2	829	189	85	80	17	10	1	3	60	6	207	5	1	7	9	.438	0	2-7 39	3.30	3.57

Rob Bell

Pitches: R Bats: R Pos: RP-30   Ht: 6'5" Wt: 215 Born: 1/17/1977 Age: 31

			HOW MUCH HE PITCHED						WHAT HE GAVE UP										THE RESULTS						
Year	Team	Lg	G	GS	CG	GF	IP	BFP	H	R	ER	HR	SH	SF	HB	TBB	IBB	SO	WP	Bk	W	L	Pct	ShO	Sv-Op Hld	ERC	ERA
2007	Norfolk*	AAA	10	10	0	0	66.2	277	61	25	22	5	2	3	2	17	0	59	6	0	4	3	.571	0	0- - -	2.99	2.97
2000	Cin	NL	26	26	1	0	140.1	618	130	84	78	32	8	2	1	73	6	112	11	0	7	8	.467	0	0-0 0	4.98	5.00
2001	2 Tms		27	27	0	0	149.2	670	176	115	111	32	3	9	7	64	1	97	9	0	5	10	.333	0	0-0 0	6.40	6.67
2002	Tex	AL	17	15	0	0	94.0	425	113	69	65	16	1	6	1	35	0	70	7	0	4	3	.571	0	0-0 0	5.67	6.22
2003	TB	AL	19	18	0	0	101.0	440	103	64	62	15	2	2	5	39	1	44	0	0	5	4	.556	0	0-0 0	4.67	5.52
2004	TB	AL	24	19	1	3	123.0	529	121	71	61	16	2	2	5	41	0	57	10	0	8	8	.500	0	0-0 0	4.06	4.46
2005	TB	AL	8	3	0	4	25.0	129	41	25	23	7	0	1	2	12	0	13	3	0	1	1	.500	0	0-0 0	10.30	8.28
2007	Bal	AL	30	0	0	8	53.0	251	73	37	35	7	1	3	0	24	5	28	2	0	4	3	.571	0	0-0 0	6.61	5.94
01	Cin	NL	9	9	0	0	44.1	188	46	28	27	9	0	1	3	17	1	33	1	0	0	5	.000	0	0-0 0	5.43	5.48
01	Tex		18	18	0	0	105.1	482	130	87	84	23	3	8	4	47	0	64	8	0	5	5	.500	0	0-0 0	6.82	7.18
7 ML YEARS			151	108	2	15	686.0	3062	757	465	435	125	17	25	21	288	13	421	42	0	34	37	.479	1	0-0 0	5.45	5.71

Mark Bellhorn

Bats: B Throws: R Pos: PH-10; 3B-2; 2B-1   Ht: 6'1" Wt: 205 Born: 8/23/1974 Age: 33

			BATTING																	BASERUNNING				AVERAGES		
Year	Team	Lg	G	AB	H	2B	3B	HR	(Hm	Rd)	TB	R	RBI	RC	TBB	IBB	SO	HBP	SH	SF	SB	CS	SB%	GDP	Avg	OBP	Slg
2007	Lsvlle*	AAA	98	326	83	23	0	12	(-	-)	142	38	57	59	63	3	93	6	1	3	0	0	-	7	.255	.382	.436
1997	Oak	AL	68	224	51	9	1	6	(3	3)	80	33	19	29	32	0	70	0	5	0	7	1	.88	1	.228	.324	.357
1998	Oak	AL	11	12	1	1	0	0	(0	0)	2	1	1	1	3	0	4	1	0	0	2	0	1.00	0	.083	.313	.167
2000	Oak	AL	9	13	2	0	0	0	(0	0)	2	2	0	1	2	0	6	0	0	0	0	0	-	0	.154	.267	.154
2001	Oak	AL	38	74	10	1	2	1	(1	0)	18	11	4	3	7	0	37	0	1	0	0	0	-	1	.135	.210	.243
2002	ChC	NL	146	445	115	24	4	27	(15	12)	228	80	56	79	76	3	144	6	2	0	7	5	.58	6	.258	.374	.512
2003	2 Tms	NL	99	249	55	10	1	2	(1	1)	73	27	26	26	50	1	78	3	1	4	5	6	.45	3	.221	.353	.293
2004	Bos	AL	138	523	138	37	3	17	(11	6)	232	93	82	95	88	1	177	5	1	3	6	1	.86	8	.264	.373	.444
2005	2 Tms	NL	94	300	63	20	0	8	(3	5)	107	43	30	28	52	1	112	0	0	3	3	0	1.00	4	.210	.324	.357
2006	SD	NL	115	253	48	11	2	8	(6	2)	87	26	27	24	32	0	90	2	0	1	0	0	-	3	.190	.285	.344
2007	Cin	NL	13	14	1	0	0	0	(0	0)	1	2	1	0	4	0	5	0	0	0	0	0	-	0	.071	.278	.071
03	ChC	NL	51	139	29	7	1	2	(1	1)	44	15	22	17	29	1	46	1	0	4	3	5	.50	2	.209	.341	.317
03	Col	NL	48	110	26	3	0	0	(0	0)	29	12	4	9	21	0	32	2	1	0	2	3	.40	1	.236	.368	.264
05	Bos	AL	85	283	61	20	0	7	(3	4)	102	41	28	28	49	1	109	0	0	3	3	0	1.00	4	.216	.328	.360
05	NYY	AL	9	17	2	0	0	1	(0	1)	5	2	2	0	3	0	3	0	0	0	0	0	-	0	.118	.250	.294
10 ML YEARS			731	2107	484	113	13	69	(40	29)	830	324	246	286	346	6	723	17	10	11	30	13	.70	26	.230	.341	.394

Ronnie Belliard

Bats: R Throws: R Pos: 2B-115; PH-19; 1B-9; SS-4; 3B-2; DH-2; PR-2   Ht: 5'8" Wt: 195 Born: 4/7/1975 Age: 33

			BATTING																	BASERUNNING				AVERAGES		
Year	Team	Lg	G	AB	H	2B	3B	HR	(Hm	Rd)	TB	R	RBI	RC	TBB	IBB	SO	HBP	SH	SF	SB	CS	SB%	GDP	Avg	OBP	Slg
1998	Mil	NL	8	5	1	0	0	0	(0	0)	1	1	0	0	0	0	0	0	0	0	0	0	-	0	.200	.200	.200
1999	Mil	NL	124	457	135	29	4	8	(5	3)	196	60	58	72	64	0	59	0	6	4	4	5	.44	16	.295	.379	.429
2000	Mil	NL	152	571	150	30	9	8	(4	4)	222	83	54	81	82	4	84	3	4	7	5	5	.58	12	.263	.354	.389
2001	Mil	NL	101	364	96	30	3	11	(7	4)	165	69	36	56	35	2	65	5	4	2	5	2	.71	5	.264	.335	.453
2002	Mil	NL	104	289	61	13	0	3	(0	3)	83	30	26	15	18	0	46	1	6	3	2	3	.40	9	.211	.257	.287
2003	Col	NL	116	447	124	31	2	8	(6	2)	183	73	50	71	49	2	71	2	6	1	7	2	.78	7	.277	.351	.409
2004	Cle	AL	152	599	169	48	1	12	(4	8)	255	78	70	87	60	5	98	2	0	2	3	2	.60	18	.282	.348	.426
2005	Cle	AL	145	536	152	36	1	17	(7	10)	241	71	78	71	35	2	72	1	8	7	2	2	.50	17	.284	.325	.450
2006	2 Tms	NL	147	544	148	30	4	13	(5	8)	219	63	67	62	36	2	81	5	3	2	2	3	.40	17	.272	.322	.403
2007	Was	NL	147	511	148	35	1	11	(5	6)	218	57	58	64	34	1	72	1	6	5	3	0	1.00	12	.290	.332	.427
06	Cle	AL	93	350	102	21	0	8	(3	5)	147	43	44	47	21	0	45	4	2	2	2	0	1.00	8	.291	.337	.420
06	StL	NL	54	194	46	9	4	5	(2	3)	72	20	23	15	15	2	36	1	1	0	0	3	.00	9	.237	.295	.371
10 ML YEARS			1196	4323	1184	282	22	91	(43	48)	1783	585	497	579	413	14	648	20	43	33	35	24	.59	113	.274	.338	.412

Edwin Bellorin

Bats: R **Throws:** R **Pos:** C-2; PH-1   **Ht:** 5'9" **Wt:** 225 **Born:** 2/21/1982 **Age:** 26

Year	Team	Lg	G	AB	H	2B	3B	HR	(Hm	Rd)	TB	R	RBI	RC	TBB	IBB	SO	HBP	SH	SF	SB	CS	SB%	GDP	Avg	OBP	Slg
2001	Ddgrs	R	28	80	14	1	0	0	(-	-)	15	11	6	5	8	0	6	4	2	0	1	0	1.00	0	.175	.283	.188
2002	SoGA	A	92	318	89	13	1	0	(-	-)	104	28	38	37	19	2	39	6	7	1	4	2	.67	8	.280	.331	.327
2003	VeroB	A+	67	233	57	9	0	3	(-	-)	75	19	28	21	10	0	32	5	2	3	0	2	.00	8	.245	.287	.322
2003	Jaxnvl	AA	17	57	11	2	1	0	(-	-)	15	2	3	2	2	0	13	0	1	0	0	0	-	0	.193	.220	.263
2004	Jaxnvl	AA	86	285	80	15	1	1	(-	-)	100	27	30	35	18	0	51	4	2	1	1	0	1.00	5	.281	.331	.351
2005	VeroB	A+	87	308	84	18	2	3	(-	-)	115	36	33	36	14	2	44	4	1	2	1	1	.50	9	.273	.311	.373
2006	LsVgs	AAA	96	321	75	13	1	7	(-	-)	111	32	49	30	14	1	59	2	8	5	1	2	.33	12	.234	.266	.346
2007	ColSpr	AAA	59	221	72	18	0	9	(-	-)	117	38	45	43	16	1	27	2	0	5	1	0	1.00	6	.326	.369	.529
2007	Col	NL	3	2	0	0	0	0	(0	0)	0	0	0	0	0	0	0	0	0	0	0	0	-	1	.000	.000	.000

Carlos Beltran

Bats: B **Throws:** R **Pos:** CF-141; PH-3   **Ht:** 6'1" **Wt:** 205 **Born:** 4/24/1977 **Age:** 31

Year	Team	Lg	G	AB	H	2B	3B	HR	(Hm	Rd)	TB	R	RBI	RC	TBB	IBB	SO	HBP	SH	SF	SB	CS	SB%	GDP	Avg	OBP	Slg
1998	KC	AL	14	58	16	5	3	0	(0	0)	27	12	7	9	3	0	12	1	0	1	3	0	1.00	2	.276	.317	.466
1999	KC	AL	156	663	194	27	7	22	(12	10)	301	112	108	100	46	2	123	4	0	10	27	8	.77	17	.293	.337	.454
2000	KC	AL	98	372	92	15	4	7	(4	3)	136	49	44	43	35	2	69	0	2	4	13	0	1.00	12	.247	.309	.366
2001	KC	AL	155	617	189	32	12	24	(7	17)	317	106	101	118	52	2	120	5	1	5	31	1	.97	7	.306	.362	.514
2002	KC	AL	162	637	174	44	7	29	(19	10)	319	114	105	117	71	1	135	4	3	7	35	7	.83	12	.273	.346	.501
2003	KC	AL	141	521	160	14	10	26	(10	16)	272	102	100	117	72	4	81	2	0	7	41	4	.91	8	.307	.389	.522
2004	2 Tms		159	599	160	36	9	38	(15	23)	328	121	104	124	92	10	101	7	3	7	42	3	.93	8	.267	.367	.548
2005	NYM	NL	151	582	155	34	2	16	(6	10)	241	83	78	88	56	5	96	2	4	6	17	6	.74	9	.266	.330	.414
2006	NYM	NL	140	510	140	38	1	41	(15	26)	303	127	116	121	95	6	99	4	1	7	18	3	.86	6	.275	.388	.594
2007	NYM	NL	144	554	153	33	3	33	(11	22)	291	93	112	97	69	10	111	2	1	10	23	2	.92	8	.276	.353	.525
04	KC	AL	69	266	74	19	2	15	(8	7)	142	51	51	57	37	7	44	2	1	3	14	3	.82	4	.278	.367	.534
04	Hou	NL	90	333	86	17	7	23	(7	16)	186	70	53	67	55	3	57	5	2	4	28	0	1.00	4	.258	.368	.559
10 ML YEARS			1320	5113	1433	278	58	236	(99	137)	2535	919	875	934	591	42	947	31	15	64	250	34	.88	89	.280	.354	.496

Adrian Beltre

Bats: R **Throws:** R **Pos:** 3B-147; DH-2; PR-1   **Ht:** 5'11" **Wt:** 220 **Born:** 4/7/1979 **Age:** 29

Year	Team	Lg	G	AB	H	2B	3B	HR	(Hm	Rd)	TB	R	RBI	RC	TBB	IBB	SO	HBP	SH	SF	SB	CS	SB%	GDP	Avg	OBP	Slg
1998	LAD	NL	77	195	42	9	0	7	(5	2)	72	18	22	20	14	0	37	3	2	0	3	1	.75	4	.215	.278	.369
1999	LAD	NL	152	538	148	27	5	15	(6	9)	230	84	67	84	61	12	105	6	4	5	18	7	.72	4	.275	.352	.428
2000	LAD	NL	138	510	148	30	2	20	(7	13)	242	71	85	85	56	2	80	2	3	4	12	5	.71	13	.290	.360	.475
2001	LAD	NL	126	475	126	22	4	13	(4	9)	195	59	60	60	28	1	82	5	1	5	13	4	.76	9	.265	.310	.411
2002	LAD	NL	159	587	151	26	5	21	(7	14)	250	70	75	74	37	4	96	4	1	6	7	5	.58	17	.257	.303	.426
2003	LAD	NL	158	559	134	30	2	23	(13	10)	237	50	80	66	37	4	103	5	1	6	2	2	.50	13	.240	.290	.424
2004	LAD	NL	156	598	200	32	0	48	(23	25)	376	104	121	120	53	9	87	2	0	4	7	2	.78	15	.334	.388	.629
2005	Sea	AL	156	603	154	36	1	19	(7	12)	249	69	87	75	38	6	108	5	0	4	3	1	.75	15	.255	.303	.413
2006	Sea	AL	156	620	166	39	4	25	(16	9)	288	88	89	85	47	4	118	10	1	3	11	5	.69	15	.268	.328	.465
2007	Sea	AL	149	595	164	41	2	26	(11	15)	287	87	99	79	38	2	104	2	0	4	14	2	.88	18	.276	.319	.482
10 ML YEARS			1427	5280	1433	292	25	217	(99	118)	2426	700	785	748	409	44	920	44	14	41	90	34	.73	123	.271	.327	.459

Armando Benitez

Pitches: R **Bats:** R **Pos:** RP-55   **Ht:** 6'4" **Wt:** 260 **Born:** 11/3/1972 **Age:** 35

			HOW MUCH HE PITCHED						WHAT HE GAVE UP												THE RESULTS						
Year	Team	Lg	G	GS	CG	GF	IP	BFP	H	R	ER	HR	SH	SF	HB	TBB	IBB	SO	WP	Bk	W	L	Pct	ShO	Sv-Op	Hld	ERC	ERA
1994	Bal	AL	3	0	0	1	10.0	42	8	1	1	0	0	0	1	4	0	14	0	0	0	0	-	0	0-0	0	2.71	0.90
1995	Bal	AL	44	0	0	18	47.2	221	37	33	30	8	2	3	5	37	2	56	3	1	1	5	.167	0	2-5	6	5.06	5.66
1996	Bal	AL	18	0	0	8	14.1	56	7	6	6	2	0	1	0	6	0	20	1	0	1	0	1.000	0	4-5	1	1.78	3.77
1997	Bal	AL	71	0	0	26	73.1	307	49	22	20	7	2	4	1	43	5	106	1	0	4	5	.444	0	9-10	20	2.92	2.45
1998	Bal	AL	71	0	0	54	68.1	289	48	29	29	10	3	2	4	39	2	87	0	0	5	6	.455	0	22-26	3	3.63	3.82
1999	NYM	NL	77	0	0	42	78.0	312	40	17	16	4	0	0	0	41	4	128	2	0	4	3	.571	0	22-28	17	1.69	1.85
2000	NYM	NL	76	0	0	68	76.0	304	39	24	22	10	2	1	0	38	2	106	0	0	4	4	.500	0	41-46	0	2.08	2.61
2001	NYM	NL	73	0	0	64	76.1	320	59	32	32	12	2	1	1	40	6	93	5	0	6	4	.600	0	43-46	5	3.67	3.77
2002	NYM	NL	62	0	0	52	67.1	275	46	20	17	8	3	2	3	25	0	79	1	0	1	0	1.000	0	33-37	0	2.55	2.27
2003	3 Tms		69	0	0	49	73.0	313	59	27	24	6	0	1	0	41	3	75	3	1	4	4	.500	0	21-29	5	3.45	2.96
2004	Fla	NL	64	0	0	59	69.2	262	36	11	10	6	3	1	0	21	4	62	0	0	2	2	.500	0	47-51	0	1.36	1.29
2005	SF	NL	30	0	0	27	30.0	127	25	17	15	5	0	2	0	16	0	23	0	0	2	3	.400	0	19-23	0	4.20	4.50
2006	SF	NL	41	0	0	33	38.1	171	39	15	15	6	1	3	0	21	2	31	1	0	4	2	.667	0	17-25	1	5.11	3.52
2007	2 Tms		55	0	0	24	50.1	228	49	37	30	8	6	1	1	29	2	57	1	3	2	8	.200	0	9-16	11	5.01	5.36
03	NYM	NL	45	0	0	40	49.1	209	41	18	17	5	0	1	0	24	1	50	3	1	3	3	.500	0	21-28	0	3.46	3.10
03	NYY	AL	9	0	0	2	9.1	40	8	4	2	0	0	0	0	6	1	10	0	0	1	1	.500	0	0-0	4	3.40	1.93
03	Sea	AL	15	0	0	7	14.1	64	10	5	5	1	0	0	0	11	1	15	0	0	0	0	-	0	0-1	1	3.40	3.14
07	SF	NL	19	0	0	17	17.1	78	17	9	9	3	2	0	0	9	1	18	0	2	0	3	.000	0	9-11	0	4.77	4.67
07	Fla	NL	36	0	0	7	33.0	150	32	28	21	5	4	1	1	20	1	39	1	1	2	5	.286	0	0-5	11	5.14	5.73
14 ML YEARS			754	0	0	525	772.2	3227	541	291	267	92	24	22	16	401	32	937	18	5	40	46	.465	0	289-347	64	3.05	3.11

40

Gary Bennett

Bats: R **Throws:** R **Pos:** C-52; PH-9; 1B-1   **Ht:** 6'0" **Wt:** 210 **Born:** 4/17/1972 **Age:** 36

							BATTING														BASERUNNING				AVERAGES		
Year	Team	Lg	G	AB	H	2B	3B	HR	(Hm	Rd)	TB	R	RBI	RC	TBB	IBB	SO	HBP	SH	SF	SB	CS	SB%	GDP	Avg	OBP	Slg
1995	Phi	NL	1	1	0	0	0	0	(0	0)	0	0	0	0	0	0	1	0	0	0	0	0	-	0	.000	.000	.000
1996	Phi	NL	6	16	4	0	0	0	(0	0)	4	0	1	1	2	1	6	0	0	0	0	0	-	0	.250	.333	.250
1998	Phi	NL	9	31	9	0	0	0	(0	0)	9	4	3	4	5	0	5	0	0	1	0	0	-	1	.290	.378	.290
1999	Phi	NL	36	88	24	4	0	1	(0	1)	31	7	21	7	4	0	11	0	0	2	0	0	-	7	.273	.298	.352
2000	Phi	NL	31	74	18	5	0	2	(0	2)	29	8	5	12	13	0	15	2	0	0	0	0	-	0	.243	.371	.392
2001	3 Tms		46	131	32	6	1	2	(2	0)	46	15	10	15	12	4	24	1	2	2	0	0	-	1	.244	.308	.351
2002	Col	NL	90	291	77	10	2	4	(2	2)	103	26	26	29	15	2	45	6	2	0	1	3	.25	10	.265	.314	.354
2003	SD	NL	96	307	73	15	0	2	(1	1)	94	26	42	33	24	3	48	2	3	2	3	0	1.00	8	.238	.296	.306
2004	Mil	NL	75	219	49	14	0	3	(3	0)	72	18	20	15	22	3	32	2	0	3	1	0	1.00	9	.224	.297	.329
2005	Was	NL	68	199	44	7	0	1	(1	0)	54	11	21	17	21	3	37	2	3	3	0	1	.00	7	.221	.298	.271
2006	StL	NL	60	157	35	5	0	4	(2	2)	52	13	22	13	11	2	30	0	2	0	0	0	-	3	.223	.274	.331
2007	StL	NL	59	155	39	7	0	2	(0	2)	52	12	17	14	8	1	16	1	2	4	1	1	.50	6	.252	.286	.335
01	Phi	NL	26	75	16	3	1	1	(1	0)	24	8	6	7	9	1	19	0	1	1	0	0	-	1	.213	.294	.320
01	NYM	NL	1	1	1	0	0	0	(0	0)	1	0	0	1	0	0	0	0	0	0	0	0	-	0	1.000	1.000	1.000
01	Col	NL	19	55	15	3	0	1	(1	0)	21	7	4	7	3	3	5	1	1	1	0	0	-	0	.273	.317	.382
12 ML YEARS			577	1669	404	73	3	21	(11	10)	546	140	188	160	137	19	270	16	14	17	6	5	.55	52	.242	.303	.327

Jeff Bennett

Pitches: R **Bats:** R **Pos:** SP-2; RP-1   **Ht:** 6'3" **Wt:** 200 **Born:** 6/10/1980 **Age:** 28

			HOW MUCH HE PITCHED						WHAT HE GAVE UP											THE RESULTS						
Year	Team	Lg	G	GS	CG	GF	IP	BFP	H	R	ER	HR	SH	SF	HB	TBB	IBB	SO	WP	Bk	W	L	Pct	ShO	Sv-Op	Hld	ERC	ERA
1998	Pirates	R	13	11	0	0	46.2	212	50	29	24	4	0	2	7	13	0	18	2	0	2	4	.333	0	0--	-	4.33	4.63
1999	Pirates	R	8	8	0	0	44.2	191	53	27	21	1	2	1	0	9	0	28	2	3	3	4	.429	0	0--	-	3.80	4.23
1999	Hickory	A	8	6	0	2	35.0	161	48	25	23	5	2	0	1	9	0	16	2	0	2	2	.500	0	0--	-	6.06	5.91
2000	Hickory	A	27	27	1	0	171.2	761	189	116	84	14	5	7	16	47	1	126	11	2	10	13	.435	0	0--	-	4.30	4.40
2001	Lynbrg	A+	25	25	2	0	166.0	691	171	78	63	14	6	2	13	30	1	98	2	0	11	10	.524	1	0--	-	3.62	3.42
2001	Altna	AA	1	1	0	0	7.0	34	9	3	3	0	0	0	2	2	0	6	0	0	0	1	.000	0	0--	-	5.48	3.86
2002	Lynbrg	A+	24	20	0	1	124.1	535	137	64	50	7	2	5	8	30	0	90	2	0	10	6	.625	0	0--	-	3.97	3.62
2003	Altna	AA	33	2	0	9	59.2	249	45	22	18	2	0	1	1	23	3	62	0	0	4	4	.500	0	1--	-	2.24	2.72
2003	Nashv	AAA	9	5	0	1	23.1	111	26	21	17	4	2	2	1	12	0	16	1	0	1	3	.250	0	0--	-	5.69	6.56
2005	Nashv	AAA	49	0	0	30	62.1	256	44	24	21	6	3	3	5	25	0	56	7	0	2	3	.400	0	13--	-	2.80	3.03
2007	Missi	AA	6	0	0	0	8.2	40	7	4	4	0	0	0	1	6	0	7	1	0	0	0	-	0	0--	-	3.71	4.15
2007	Rchmd	AAA	36	6	0	8	86.1	365	84	32	32	5	2	4	9	34	1	45	2	1	3	5	.375	0	1--	-	4.14	3.34
2004	Mil	NL	60	0	0	20	71.1	316	78	43	38	12	2	5	2	26	2	45	6	0	1	5	.167	0	0-1	8	4.98	4.79
2007	Atl	NL	3	2	0	0	13.0	57	14	5	5	3	1	1	0	3	1	14	1	0	2	1	.667	0	0--	-	4.41	3.46
2 ML YEARS			63	2	0	20	84.1	373	92	48	43	15	3	6	2	29	3	59	7	0	3	6	.333	0	0-1	8	4.90	4.59

Joaquin Benoit

Pitches: R **Bats:** R **Pos:** RP-70   **Ht:** 6'3" **Wt:** 220 **Born:** 7/26/1977 **Age:** 30

			HOW MUCH HE PITCHED						WHAT HE GAVE UP											THE RESULTS						
Year	Team	Lg	G	GS	CG	GF	IP	BFP	H	R	ER	HR	SH	SF	HB	TBB	IBB	SO	WP	Bk	W	L	Pct	ShO	Sv-Op	Hld	ERC	ERA
2001	Tex	AL	1	1	0	0	5.0	26	8	6	6	3	0	1	0	3	0	4	0	0	0	0	-	0	0-0	0	13.11	10.80
2002	Tex	AL	17	13	0	2	84.2	405	91	51	50	6	4	3	5	58	2	59	7	0	4	5	.444	0	1-1	0	5.52	5.31
2003	Tex	AL	25	17	0	0	105.0	462	99	67	64	23	1	4	3	61	0	87	3	1	8	5	.615	0	1-0	0	5.03	5.49
2004	Tex	AL	28	15	0	2	103.0	456	113	67	65	19	2	10	8	31	0	95	3	0	3	5	.375	0	0-0	0	5.10	5.68
2005	Tex	AL	32	9	0	6	87.0	369	69	39	36	9	2	1	2	38	0	78	1	0	4	4	.500	0	0-0	5	3.15	3.72
2006	Tex	AL	56	0	0	7	79.2	347	68	49	43	5	0	3	3	38	4	85	3	0	1	1	.500	0	0-2	7	3.30	4.86
2007	Tex	AL	70	0	0	22	82.0	337	68	28	26	6	3	2	2	28	2	87	3	0	7	4	.636	0	6-13	19	2.83	2.85
7 ML YEARS			229	55	0	40	546.1	2402	516	307	290	71	12	24	23	247	8	495	20	1	27	24	.529	0	7-16	31	4.27	4.78

Kris Benson

Pitches: R **Bats:** R **Pos:** P   **Ht:** 6'4" **Wt:** 205 **Born:** 11/7/1974 **Age:** 33

			HOW MUCH HE PITCHED						WHAT HE GAVE UP											THE RESULTS						
Year	Team	Lg	G	GS	CG	GF	IP	BFP	H	R	ER	HR	SH	SF	HB	TBB	IBB	SO	WP	Bk	W	L	Pct	ShO	Sv-Op	Hld	ERC	ERA
1999	Pit	NL	31	31	2	0	196.2	840	184	105	89	16	6	7	6	83	5	139	2	1	11	14	.440	0	0-0	0	3.78	4.07
2000	Pit	NL	32	32	2	0	217.2	936	206	104	93	24	7	6	10	86	5	184	5	0	10	12	.455	1	0-0	0	3.97	3.85
2002	Pit	NL	25	25	0	0	130.1	576	152	76	68	18	5	3	3	50	8	79	3	1	9	6	.600	0	0-0	0	5.31	4.70
2003	Pit	NL	18	18	0	0	105.0	475	127	67	58	14	3	4	1	36	4	68	7	0	5	9	.357	0	0-0	0	5.20	4.97
2004	2 Tms	NL	31	31	1	0	200.1	854	202	106	96	15	8	6	10	61	8	134	5	0	12	12	.500	1	0-0	0	3.71	4.31
2005	NYM	NL	28	28	0	0	174.1	737	171	86	80	24	5	3	4	49	5	95	4	0	10	8	.556	0	0-0	0	3.78	4.13
2006	Bal	AL	30	30	3	0	183.0	781	199	105	98	33	9	13	5	58	2	88	6	0	11	12	.478	0	0-0	0	5.06	4.82
04	Pit	NL	20	20	0	0	132.1	564	137	69	62	7	7	4	6	44	5	83	2	0	8	8	.500	0	0-0	0	3.84	4.22
04	NYM	NL	11	11	1	0	68.0	290	65	37	34	8	1	2	4	17	3	51	3	0	4	4	.500	1	0-0	0	3.45	4.50
7 ML YEARS			195	195	8	0	1207.1	5199	1241	649	582	144	43	42	41	423	37	787	32	2	68	73	.482	2	0-0	0	4.27	4.34

Jason Bergmann

Pitches: R **Bats:** R **Pos:** SP-21   **Ht:** 6'4" **Wt:** 203 **Born:** 9/25/1981 **Age:** 26

			HOW MUCH HE PITCHED						WHAT HE GAVE UP											THE RESULTS						
Year	Team	Lg	G	GS	CG	GF	IP	BFP	H	R	ER	HR	SH	SF	HB	TBB	IBB	SO	WP	Bk	W	L	Pct	ShO	Sv-Op	Hld	ERC	ERA
2007	Nats*	R	1	1	0	0	3.0	14	2	0	0	0	0	0	0	2	0	4	1	0	0	0	-	0	0--	-	2.31	0.00
2007	Clmbs*	AAA	5	5	0	0	24.0	94	20	4	4	0	2	0	0	6	1	22	1	1	2	1	.667	0	0--	-	2.05	1.50

			HOW MUCH HE PITCHED						WHAT HE GAVE UP											THE RESULTS							
Year	Team	Lg	G	GS	CG	GF	IP	BFP	H	R	ER	HR	SH	SF	HB	TBB	IBB	SO	WP	Bk	W	L	Pct	ShO	Sv-Op	Hld	ERC	ERA
2005	Was	NL	15	1	0	4	19.2	85	14	6	6	1	1	1	2	11	1	21	1	0	2	0	1.000	0	0-0	1	3.05	2.75
2006	Was	NL	29	6	0	7	64.2	303	81	49	48	12	6	4	6	27	6	54	3	0	0	2	.000	0	0-0	1	6.50	6.68
2007	Was	NL	21	21	0	0	115.1	480	99	59	57	18	6	1	2	42	1	86	4	0	6	6	.500	0	0-0	0	3.59	4.45
3 ML YEARS			65	28	0	11	199.2	868	194	114	111	31	13	6	10	80	8	161	7	0	8	8	.500	0	0-0	2	4.43	5.00

Lance Berkman

Bats: B **Throws:** L **Pos:** 1B-126; RF-31; PH-3; CF-1; DH-1

Ht: 6'1" **Wt:** 220 **Born:** 2/10/1976 **Age:** 32

					BATTING														BASERUNNING				AVERAGES		
Year	Team	Lg	G	AB	H	2B	3B	HR	(Hm Rd)	TB	R	RBI	RC	TBB	IBB	SO	HBP	SH	SF	SB	CS	SB%	GDP	Avg	OBP	Slg
1999	Hou	NL	34	93	22	2	0	4	(2 2)	36	10	15	12	12	0	21	0	0	1	5	1	.83	2	.237	.321	.387
2000	Hou	NL	114	353	105	28	1	21	(10 11)	198	76	67	76	56	1	73	1	0	7	6	2	.75	6	.297	.388	.561
2001	Hou	NL	156	577	191	55	5	34	(13 21)	358	110	126	144	92	5	121	13	0	6	7	9	.44	8	.331	.430	.620
2002	Hou	NL	158	578	169	35	2	42	(20 22)	334	106	128	130	107	20	118	4	0	3	8	4	.67	10	.292	.405	.578
2003	Hou	NL	153	538	155	35	6	25	(11 14)	277	110	93	115	107	13	108	9	1	3	5	3	.63	10	.288	.412	.515
2004	Hou	NL	160	544	172	40	4	30	(8 22)	308	104	106	126	127	14	101	10	0	6	9	7	.56	10	.316	.450	.566
2005	Hou	NL	132	468	137	34	1	24	(13 11)	245	76	82	88	91	12	72	4	0	2	4	1	.80	18	.293	.411	.524
2006	Hou	NL	152	536	169	29	0	45	(24 21)	333	95	136	138	98	22	106	4	0	5	3	2	.60	11	.315	.420	.621
2007	Hou	NL	153	561	156	24	2	34	(13 21)	286	95	102	105	94	11	125	8	0	5	7	3	.70	11	.278	.386	.510
9 ML YEARS			1212	4248	1276	282	20	259	(114 145)	2375	782	855	934	784	98	845	53	1	41	54	32	.63	86	.300	.412	.559

Angel Berroa

Bats: R **Throws:** R **Pos:** SS-4; PR-4; DH-2; PH-2; 2B-1; 3B-1

Ht: 6'0" **Wt:** 195 **Born:** 1/27/1978 **Age:** 30

					BATTING														BASERUNNING				AVERAGES		
Year	Team	Lg	G	AB	H	2B	3B	HR	(Hm Rd)	TB	R	RBI	RC	TBB	IBB	SO	HBP	SH	SF	SB	CS	SB%	GDP	Avg	OBP	Slg
2007	Omha*	AAA	81	307	92	17	0	8	(- -)	133	47	40	50	25	0	44	9	6	5	2	2	.50	13	.300	.364	.433
2001	KC	AL	15	53	16	2	0	0	(0 0)	18	8	4	6	3	0	10	0	0	0	2	0	1.00	2	.302	.339	.340
2002	KC	AL	20	75	17	7	1	0	(0 0)	26	8	5	8	7	1	10	1	0	0	3	0	1.00	1	.227	.301	.347
2003	KC	AL	158	567	163	28	7	17	(6 11)	256	92	73	90	29	3	100	18	13	8	21	5	.81	13	.287	.338	.451
2004	KC	AL	134	512	134	27	6	8	(3 5)	197	72	43	62	23	0	87	12	5	2	14	8	.64	10	.262	.308	.385
2005	KC	AL	159	608	164	21	5	11	(6 5)	228	69	55	68	18	3	108	14	10	2	7	5	.58	13	.270	.305	.375
2006	KC	AL	132	474	111	18	1	9	(6 3)	158	45	54	32	14	1	88	3	9	3	3	1	.75	21	.234	.259	.333
2007	KC	AL	9	11	1	0	0	0	(0 0)	1	0	1	0	0	0	4	1	1	0	0	1	.00	1	.091	.167	.091
7 ML YEARS			627	2300	606	103	20	45	(21 24)	884	293	235	258	94	8	407	49	38	15	50	20	.71	61	.263	.305	.384

Rafael Betancourt

Pitches: R **Bats:** R **Pos:** RP-68

Ht: 6'2" **Wt:** 200 **Born:** 4/29/1975 **Age:** 33

				HOW MUCH HE PITCHED						WHAT HE GAVE UP											THE RESULTS							
Year	Team	Lg	G	GS	CG	GF	IP	BFP	H	R	ER	HR	SH	SF	HB	TBB	IBB	SO	WP	Bk	W	L	Pct	ShO	Sv-Op	Hld	ERC	ERA
2003	Clo	AL	33	0	0	13	38.0	154	27	11	9	5	1	1	1	13	2	36	1	0	2	2	.500	0	1-3	4	2.54	2.13
2004	Cle	AL	68	0	0	21	66.2	286	71	32	29	7	1	2	0	18	6	76	5	1	5	6	.455	0	4-11	12	3.77	3.92
2005	Cle	AL	54	0	0	12	67.2	272	57	23	21	7	1	0	0	17	2	73	0	0	4	3	.571	0	1-3	10	2.49	2.79
2006	Cle	AL	50	0	0	17	56.2	231	52	25	24	7	2	2	0	11	5	48	0	0	3	4	.429	0	3-6	7	2.84	3.81
2007	Cle	AL	68	0	0	15	79.1	289	51	13	13	4	0	2	0	9	3	80	0	0	5	1	.833	0	3-6	31	1.24	1.47
5 ML YEARS			273	0	0	78	308.1	1232	258	104	96	28	5	7	1	68	18	313	6	1	19	16	.543	0	12-29	64	2.42	2.80

Yuniesky Betancourt

Bats: R **Throws:** R **Pos:** SS-152; PH-3; PR-2

Ht: 5'10" **Wt:** 190 **Born:** 1/31/1982 **Age:** 26

					BATTING														BASERUNNING				AVERAGES		
Year	Team	Lg	G	AB	H	2B	3B	HR	(Hm Rd)	TB	R	RBI	RC	TBB	IBB	SO	HBP	SH	SF	SB	CS	SB%	GDP	Avg	OBP	Slg
2005	Sea	AL	60	211	54	11	5	1	(1 0)	78	24	15	21	11	0	24	2	2	2	1	3	.25	2	.256	.296	.370
2006	Sea	AL	157	558	161	28	6	8	(2 6)	225	68	47	60	17	0	54	1	7	1	11	8	.58	10	.289	.310	.403
2007	Sea	AL	155	536	155	38	2	9	(6 3)	224	72	67	73	15	3	48	1	3	4	5	4	.56	10	.289	.308	.418
3 ML YEARS			372	1305	370	77	13	18	(9 9)	527	164	129	154	43	3	126	4	12	7	17	15	.53	22	.284	.307	.404

Wilson Betemit

Bats: B **Throws:** R **Pos:** 3B-67; PH-38; 1B-14; SS-10; 2B-3; PR-2; LF-1; RF-1

Ht: 6'3" **Wt:** 230 **Born:** 11/2/1981 **Age:** 26

					BATTING														BASERUNNING				AVERAGES		
Year	Team	Lg	G	AB	H	2B	3B	HR	(Hm Rd)	TB	R	RBI	RC	TBB	IBB	SO	HBP	SH	SF	SB	CS	SB%	GDP	Avg	OBP	Slg
2001	Atl	NL	8	3	0	0	0	0	(0 0)	0	1	0	0	2	0	3	0	0	0	1	0	1.00	0	.000	.400	.000
2004	Atl	NL	22	47	8	0	0	0	(0 0)	8	2	3	0	4	0	16	0	0	1	0	1	.00	0	.170	.231	.170
2005	Atl	NL	115	246	75	12	4	4	(0 4)	107	36	20	36	22	4	55	0	4	2	1	3	.25	5	.305	.359	.435
2006	2 Tms	NL	143	373	98	23	0	18	(7 11)	175	49	53	52	36	6	102	0	1	2	3	1	.75	11	.263	.326	.469
2007	2 Tms	NL	121	240	55	12	0	14	(8 6)	109	33	50	42	38	0	82	1	2	3	0	0	-	2	.229	.333	.454
06	Atl	NL	88	199	56	16	0	9	(3 6)	99	30	29	35	19	3	57	0	1	0	2	1	.67	4	.281	.344	.497
06	LAD	NL	55	174	42	7	0	9	(4 5)	76	19	24	17	17	3	45	0	0	2	1	0	1.00	7	.241	.306	.437
07	LAD	NL	84	156	36	8	0	10	(6 4)	74	22	26	26	32	0	49	1	0	3	0	0	-	1	.231	.359	.474
07	NYY	AL	37	84	19	4	0	4	(2 2)	35	11	24	16	6	0	33	0	2	0	0	0	-	1	.226	.278	.417
5 ML YEARS			409	909	236	47	4	36	(15 21)	399	121	126	130	102	10	258	1	7	8	5	5	.50	18	.260	.332	.439

42

Craig Biggio

Bats: R **Throws:** R **Pos:** 2B-114; PH-23; DH-4; C-1; PR-1   **Ht:** 5'11" **Wt:** 185 **Born:** 12/14/1965 **Age:** 42

								BATTING													BASERUNNING				AVERAGES		
Year	Team	Lg	G	AB	H	2B	3B	HR	(Hm	Rd)	TB	R	RBI	RC	TBB	IBB	SO	HBP	SH	SF	SB	CS	SB%	GDP	Avg	OBP	Slg
1988	Hou	NL	50	123	26	6	1	3	(1	2)	43	14	5	11	7	2	29	0	1	0	6	1	.86	1	.211	.254	.350
1989	Hou	NL	134	443	114	21	2	13	(6	7)	178	64	60	64	49	8	64	6	6	5	21	3	.88	7	.257	.336	.402
1990	Hou	NL	150	555	153	24	2	4	(2	2)	193	53	42	68	53	1	79	3	9	1	25	11	.69	11	.276	.342	.348
1991	Hou	NL	149	546	161	23	4	4	(0	4)	204	79	46	79	53	3	71	2	5	3	19	6	.76	2	.295	.358	.374
1992	Hou	NL	162	613	170	32	3	6	(3	3)	226	96	39	95	94	9	95	7	5	2	38	15	.72	5	.277	.378	.369
1993	Hou	NL	155	610	175	41	5	21	(8	13)	289	98	64	105	77	7	93	10	4	5	15	17	.47	10	.287	.373	.474
1994	Hou	NL	114	437	139	44	5	6	(4	2)	211	88	56	94	62	1	58	8	2	2	39	4	.91	5	.318	.411	.483
1995	Hou	NL	141	553	167	30	2	22	(6	16)	267	123	77	116	80	1	85	22	11	7	33	8	.80	6	.302	.406	.483
1996	Hou	NL	162	605	174	24	4	15	(8	7)	251	113	75	105	75	0	72	27	8	8	25	7	.78	10	.288	.386	.415
1997	Hou	NL	162	619	191	37	8	22	(7	15)	310	146	81	139	84	6	107	34	0	7	47	10	.82	0	.309	.415	.501
1998	Hou	NL	160	646	210	51	2	20	(10	10)	325	123	88	135	64	6	113	23	1	4	50	8	.86	10	.325	.403	.503
1999	Hou	NL	160	639	188	56	0	16	(10	6)	292	123	73	117	88	9	107	11	5	6	28	14	.67	5	.294	.386	.457
2000	Hou	NL	101	377	101	13	5	8	(2	6)	148	67	35	63	61	3	73	16	7	5	12	2	.86	10	.268	.388	.393
2001	Hou	NL	155	617	180	35	3	20	(10	10)	281	118	70	109	66	4	100	28	0	6	7	4	.64	11	.292	.382	.455
2002	Hou	NL	145	577	146	36	3	15	(7	8)	233	96	58	77	50	2	111	17	9	2	16	2	.89	15	.253	.330	.404
2003	Hou	NL	153	628	166	44	2	15	(6	9)	259	102	62	97	57	3	116	27	3	2	8	4	.67	4	.264	.350	.412
2004	Hou	NL	156	633	178	47	0	24	(13	11)	297	100	63	88	40	0	94	15	9	3	7	2	.78	8	.281	.337	.469
2005	Hou	NL	155	590	156	40	1	26	(19	7)	276	94	69	80	37	2	90	17	4	3	11	1	.92	10	.264	.325	.468
2006	Hou	NL	145	548	135	33	0	21	(15	6)	231	79	62	62	40	1	84	9	5	5	3	2	.60	15	.246	.306	.422
2007	Hou	NL	141	517	130	31	3	10	(7	3)	197	68	50	49	23	0	112	3	7	5	4	3	.57	5	.251	.285	.381
20 ML YEARS			2850	10876	3060	668	55	291	(143	148)	4711	1844	1175	1747	1160	68	1753	285	101	81	414	124	.77	150	.281	.363	.433

Chad Billingsley

Pitches: R **Bats:** R **Pos:** RP-23; SP-20   **Ht:** 6'1" **Wt:** 245 **Born:** 7/29/1984 **Age:** 23

			HOW MUCH HE PITCHED						WHAT HE GAVE UP										THE RESULTS						
Year	Team	Lg	G	GS	CG	GF	IP	BFP	H	R	ER	HR	SH	SF	HB	TBB	IBB	SO	WP	Bk	W	L	Pct	ShO	Sv-Op	Hld	ERC	ERA
2003	Ogden	R+	11	11	0	0	54.0	225	49	24	17	0	3	2	3	15	0	62	8	0	5	4	.556	0	0--	-	2.66	2.83
2004	VeroB	A+	18	18	0	0	92.0	386	68	32	24	6	6	2	2	49	0	111	3	0	7	4	.636	0	0--	-	3.03	2.35
2004	Jaxnvl	AA	8	8	0	0	42.1	169	32	16	14	1	1	0	1	22	0	47	2	0	4	0	1.000	0	0--	-	2.97	2.98
2005	Jaxnvl	AA	28	26	2	0	146.0	604	116	60	57	12	5	3	4	50	0	162	10	0	13	6	.684	1	0--	-	2.72	3.51
2006	LsVgs	AAA	13	13	0	0	70.2	297	57	32	31	7	2	2	3	32	0	78	4	0	6	3	.667	0	0--	-	3.40	3.95
2006	LAD	NL	18	16	0	0	90.0	403	92	43	38	7	4	0	3	58	3	59	5	0	7	4	.636	0	0-0	0	5.22	3.80
2007	LAD	NL	43	20	1	6	147.0	623	131	56	64	15	9	3	3	64	3	141	5	0	12	5	.706	0	0-1	3	3.70	3.31
2 ML YEARS			61	36	1	6	237.0	1026	223	99	92	22	13	3	6	122	6	200	10	0	19	9	.679	0	0-1	3	4.26	3.49

Kurt Birkins

Pitches: L **Bats:** L **Pos:** RP-17; SP-2   **Ht:** 6'2" **Wt:** 190 **Born:** 8/11/1080 **Age:** 27

			HOW MUCH HE PITCHED						WHAT HE GAVE UP										THE RESULTS						
Year	Team	Lg	G	GS	CG	GF	IP	BFP	H	R	ER	HR	SH	SF	HB	TBB	IBB	SO	WP	Bk	W	L	Pct	ShO	Sv-Op	Hld	ERC	ERA
2001	Orioles	R	5	4	0	1	22.0	85	13	5	5	2	0	0	4	3	0	24	1	0	2	1	.667	0	0--	-	1.69	2.05
2001	Bluefld	R+	6	6	0	0	37.0	144	28	14	12	2	1	0	2	5	0	42	3	0	4	1	.800	0	0--	-	1.81	2.92
2002	Dlmrva	A	27	25	3	0	143.2	607	140	66	56	10	6	1	10	46	1	102	7	0	9	7	.563	0	0--	-	3.72	3.51
2003	Frdrck	A+	25	25	0	0	126.1	576	152	82	66	10	5	6	13	40	0	79	12	0	8	11	.421	0	0--	-	5.12	4.70
2004	Frdrck	A+	27	6	0	8	68.0	291	70	36	34	9	5	6	13	22	1	55	3	0	5	2	.714	0	2--	-	4.27	4.50
2005	Bowle	AA	26	24	0	0	129.0	552	134	69	56	8	5	2	11	42	0	114	10	0	7	11	.389	0	0--	-	4.14	3.91
2006	Ottawa	AAA	5	5	0	0	25.1	101	20	10	9	2	0	0	1	11	0	19	0	0	1	3	.250	0	0--	-	3.26	3.20
2006	Frdrck	A+	1	0	0	0	1.0	3	0	0	0	0	0	0	0	1	0	1	0	0	0	0	-	0	0--	-	1.26	0.00
2006	Abrdn	A-	2	0	0	0	2.2	10	3	1	1	0	0	1	1	0	0	2	0	0	1	1	.500	0	0--	-	4.72	3.38
2006	Bowie	AA	2	0	0	0	4.0	17	5	4	4	2	0	0	0	1	0	5	0	0	1	0	1.000	0	0--	-	8.20	9.00
2007	Norfolk	AAA	20	19	0	0	105.2	449	102	39	36	6	2	4	5	38	2	98	7	1	8	4	.667	0	0--	-	3.61	3.07
2006	Bal	AL	35	0	0	4	31.0	136	25	19	17	4	2	2	3	16	0	27	3	0	5	2	.714	0	0-1	4	3.98	4.94
2007	Bal	AL	19	2	0	7	34.1	170	52	31	31	3	0	0	3	14	0	30	1	0	1	2	.333	0	0-0	0	7.41	8.13
2 ML YEARS			54	2	0	11	65.1	306	77	50	48	7	2	2	6	30	0	57	4	0	6	4	.600	0	0-1	4	5.71	6.61

Joe Bisenius

Pitches: R **Bats:** R **Pos:** RP-2   **Ht:** 6'4" **Wt:** 205 **Born:** 9/18/1982 **Age:** 25

			HOW MUCH HE PITCHED						WHAT HE GAVE UP										THE RESULTS						
Year	Team	Lg	G	GS	CG	GF	IP	BFP	H	R	ER	HR	SH	SF	HB	TBB	IBB	SO	WP	Bk	W	L	Pct	ShO	Sv-Op	Hld	ERC	ERA
2004	Batvia	A-	11	11	0	0	50.1	199	39	12	8	5	3	3	1	14	0	38	4	1	0	1	.000	0	0--	-	2.55	1.43
2005	Lakwd	A	40	4	1	14	64.1	300	66	45	42	5	3	4	6	37	0	56	10	3	6	4	.600	0	4--	-	5.03	5.88
2006	Clrwtr	A+	35	0	0	9	60.2	250	48	17	13	4	4	1	1	22	0	62	2	0	4	1	.800	0	2--	-	2.65	1.93
2006	Rdng	AA	16	0	0	9	23.1	87	14	9	8	2	1	1	0	8	0	33	0	0	4	2	.667	0	5--	-	1.88	3.09
2007	Ottawa	AAA	35	0	0	11	46.0	212	52	29	28	5	3	5	0	31	2	41	7	1	3	4	.429	0	0--	-	6.07	5.48
2007	Phi	NL	2	0	0	0	2.0	9	2	0	0	0	0	0	0	2	0	3	0	0	0	0	-	0	0-0	0	6.15	0.00

Nick Blackburn

Pitches: R **Bats:** R **Pos:** RP-6   **Ht:** 6'4" **Wt:** 230 **Born:** 2/24/1982 **Age:** 26

			HOW MUCH HE PITCHED						WHAT HE GAVE UP										THE RESULTS						
Year	Team	Lg	G	GS	CG	GF	IP	BFP	H	R	ER	HR	SH	SF	HB	TBB	IBB	SO	WP	Bk	W	L	Pct	ShO	Sv-Op	Hld	ERC	ERA
2002	Elizab	R+	13	13	0	0	66.2	293	70	41	37	6	2	0	2	21	0	62	1	0	3	3	.500	0	0--	-	3.97	5.00
2003	QuadC	A	16	10	2	4	76.0	320	78	44	41	13	4	3	4	18	0	40	5	0	2	9	.182	1	1--	-	4.30	4.86
2004	QuadC	A	20	13	1	5	84.1	342	69	37	26	3	3	5	2	23	1	66	2	1	6	4	.600	1	1--	-	2.31	2.77
2004	FtMyrs	A+	9	7	0	0	37.1	171	51	30	26	7	4	2	2	7	1	21	1	0	3	3	.500	0	0--	-	6.08	6.27
2005	FtMyrs	A+	15	15	1	0	93.2	381	95	43	35	5	0	2	5	16	0	55	1	0	7	5	.583	0	0--	-	3.25	3.36

(continued)

Year Team	Lg	G	GS	CG	GF	IP	BFP	H	R	ER	HR	SH	SF	HB	TBB	IBB	SO	WP	Bk	W	L	Pct	ShO	Sv-Op	Hld	ERC	ERA
2005 NwBrit	AA	7	7	2	0	49.0	186	35	16	10	1	3	1	2	10	1	27	1	0	2	4	.333	1	0--	-	1.66	1.84
2005 Roch	AAA	3	3	0	0	14.0	65	20	11	8	2	1	0	0	3	0	7	0	0	0	0	-	0	0--	-	6.02	5.14
2006 NwBrit	AA	30	19	2	3	132.1	565	141	72	65	11	3	5	8	37	2	81	7	0	7	8	.467	1	0--	-	4.11	4.42
2007 NwBrit	AA	8	7	0	0	38.0	160	36	21	13	1	1	1	1	7	0	18	1	0	3	1	.750	0	0--	-	2.51	3.08
2007 Roch	AAA	17	17	3	0	110.2	433	96	32	26	7	5	1	2	12	0	57	3	0	7	3	.700	2	0--	-	2.17	2.11
2007 Min	AL	6	0	0	3	11.2	54	19	12	10	2	0	0	0	2	0	8	0	0	0	2	.000	0	0-1	1	7.61	7.71

Travis Blackley

Pitches: L **Bats:** L **Pos:** SP-2

Ht: 6'3" **Wt:** 200 **Born:** 11/4/1982 **Age:** 25

Year Team	Lg	G	GS	CG	GF	IP	BFP	H	R	ER	HR	SH	SF	HB	TBB	IBB	SO	WP	Bk	W	L	Pct	ShO	Sv-Op	Hld	ERC	ERA
2001 Everett	A-	14	14	0	0	78.2	319	60	34	29	7	2	2	1	29	0	90	3	0	6	1	.857	0	0--	-	2.70	3.32
2002 SnBrn	A+	21	20	1	1	121.1	505	102	52	47	11	4	0	7	44	0	152	11	2	5	9	.357	0	0--	-	3.25	3.49
2003 SnAnt	AA	27	27	0	0	162.1	658	125	55	47	11	5	4	6	62	0	144	9	2	17	3	.850	0	0--	-	2.77	2.61
2004 Tacom	AAA	19	18	2	0	110.1	455	100	49	47	14	6	1	3	47	0	80	9	3	8	6	.571	2	0--	-	4.12	3.83
2006 SnAnt	AA	25	25	0	0	144.0	615	139	77	65	18	5	4	15	45	2	100	11	1	8	11	.421	0	0--	-	4.13	4.06
2006 Tacom	AAA	2	2	0	0	11.0	48	10	5	5	2	0	0	0	5	0	5	0	0	1	1	.500	0	0--	-	4.26	4.09
2007 Fresno	AAA	28	28	0	0	162.1	687	156	87	84	21	5	4	7	68	0	121	14	1	10	8	.556	0	0--	-	4.43	4.66
2004 Sea	AL	6	6	0	0	26.0	134	35	31	29	9	1	1	1	22	0	16	3	1	1	3	.250	0	0-0	0	10.52	10.04
2007 SF	NL	2	2	0	0	8.2	40	10	7	7	2	1	0	0	5	0	5	0	1	0	0	-	0	0-0	0	6.78	7.27
2 ML YEARS		8	8	0	0	34.2	174	45	38	36	11	2	1	1	27	0	21	3	2	1	3	.250	0	0-0	0	9.55	9.35

Casey Blake

Bats: R **Throws:** R **Pos:** 3B-145; 1B-12; RF-7; PH-7; DH-1

Ht: 6'2" **Wt:** 210 **Born:** 8/23/1973 **Age:** 34

Year Team	Lg	G	AB	H	2B	3B	HR	(Hm	Rd)	TB	R	RBI	RC	TBB	IBB	SO	HBP	SH	SF	SB	CS	SB%	GDP	Avg	OBP	Slg
1999 Tor	AL	14	39	10	2	0	1	(0	1)	15	6	1	4	2	0	7	0	0	0	0	0	-	1	.256	.293	.385
2000 Min	AL	7	16	3	2	0	0	(0	0)	5	1	1	2	3	0	7	1	0	1	0	0	-	1	.188	.333	.313
2001 2 Tms	AL	19	37	9	1	0	1	(0	1)	13	3	4	5	4	1	12	0	0	0	3	0	1.00	0	.243	.317	.351
2002 Min	AL	9	20	4	1	0	0	(0	0)	5	2	1	1	2	0	7	0	0	0	0	0	-	0	.200	.273	.250
2003 Cle	AL	152	557	143	35	0	17	(2	15)	229	80	67	68	38	1	109	10	8	3	7	9	.44	11	.257	.312	.411
2004 Cle	AL	152	587	159	36	3	28	(13	15)	285	93	88	88	68	2	139	9	1	3	5	8	.38	19	.271	.354	.486
2005 Cle	AL	147	523	126	32	1	23	(7	16)	229	72	58	53	43	3	116	10	2	5	4	5	.44	9	.241	.308	.438
2006 Cle	AL	109	401	113	20	1	19	(9	10)	192	63	68	62	45	5	93	4	1	5	6	0	1.00	11	.282	.356	.479
2007 Cle	AL	156	588	159	36	4	18	(11	7)	257	81	78	69	54	2	123	10	5	5	4	5	.44	14	.270	.339	.437
01 Min	AL	13	22	7	1	0	0	(0	0)	8	1	2	4	1	0	8	0	0	0	1	0	1.00	0	.318	.400	.364
01 Bal	AL	6	15	2	0	0	1	(0	1)	5	2	2	1	1	0	4	0	0	0	2	0	1.00	0	.133	.188	.333
9 ML YEARS		765	2768	726	165	9	107	(42	65)	1230	401	366	352	259	14	613	44	17	27	29	27	.52	66	.262	.332	.444

Hank Blalock

Bats: L **Throws:** R **Pos:** 3B-39; DH-18; PH-2

Ht: 6'1" **Wt:** 200 **Born:** 11/21/1980 **Age:** 27

Year Team	Lg	G	AB	H	2B	3B	HR	(Hm	Rd)	TB	R	RBI	RC	TBB	IBB	SO	HBP	SH	SF	SB	CS	SB%	GDP	Avg	OBP	Slg
2002 Tex	AL	49	147	31	8	0	3	(2	1)	48	16	17	15	20	1	43	1	2	2	0	0	-	2	.211	.306	.327
2003 Tex	AL	143	567	170	33	3	29	(18	11)	296	89	90	90	44	1	97	1	0	3	2	3	.40	16	.300	.350	.522
2004 Tex	AL	159	624	172	38	3	32	(16	16)	312	107	110	119	75	7	149	6	0	8	2	2	.50	13	.276	.355	.500
2005 Tex	AL	161	647	170	34	0	25	(20	5)	279	80	92	86	51	1	132	3	0	4	1	0	1.00	16	.263	.318	.431
2006 Tex	AL	152	591	157	26	3	16	(8	8)	237	76	89	87	51	6	98	2	0	2	1	0	1.00	15	.266	.325	.401
2007 Tex	AL	58	208	61	16	3	10	(7	3)	113	32	33	38	21	1	38	1	0	2	4	1	.80	8	.293	.358	.543
6 ML YEARS		722	2784	761	155	12	115	(71	44)	1285	400	431	435	262	17	557	14	2	21	10	6	.63	70	.273	.337	.462

Henry Blanco

Bats: R **Throws:** R **Pos:** C-14; PH-6; 1B-2

Ht: 5'11" **Wt:** 220 **Born:** 8/29/1971 **Age:** 36

Year Team	Lg	G	AB	H	2B	3B	HR	(Hm	Rd)	TB	R	RBI	RC	TBB	IBB	SO	HBP	SH	SF	SB	CS	SB%	GDP	Avg	OBP	Slg
2007 Peoria*	A	8	19	6	1	0	1	(-	-)	10	3	5	4	3	1	3	1	0	1	0	0	-	0	.316	.417	.526
2007 Iowa*	AAA	3	10	2	0	0	0	(-	-)	2	2	1	0	0	0	3	0	0	0	0	0	-	0	.200	.200	.200
1997 LAD	NL	3	5	2	0	0	0	(0	1)	5	1	1	2	0	0	1	0	0	0	0	0	-	0	.400	.400	1.000
1999 Col	NL	88	263	61	12	3	6	(3	3)	97	30	28	32	34	1	38	1	3	2	1	1	.50	4	.232	.320	.369
2000 Mil	NL	93	284	67	24	0	7	(3	4)	112	29	31	33	36	6	60	0	0	4	0	3	.00	9	.236	.318	.394
2001 Mil	NL	104	314	66	18	3	6	(4	2)	108	33	31	30	34	6	72	2	5	2	3	1	.75	10	.210	.290	.344
2002 Atl	NL	81	221	45	9	1	6	(4	2)	74	17	22	15	20	5	51	1	2	5	0	2	.00	5	.204	.267	.335
2003 Atl	NL	55	151	30	8	0	1	(0	1)	41	11	13	13	10	2	21	1	3	1	0	0	-	3	.199	.252	.272
2004 Min	NL	114	315	65	19	1	10	(4	6)	116	36	37	25	21	0	56	3	11	3	0	3	.00	8	.206	.260	.368
2005 ChC	NL	54	161	39	6	0	6	(2	4)	63	16	25	17	11	1	24	0	4	2	0	0	-	6	.242	.287	.391
2006 ChC	NL	74	241	64	15	2	6	(2	4)	101	23	37	26	14	1	38	0	4	2	0	0	-	8	.266	.304	.419
2007 ChC	NL	22	54	9	3	0	0	(0	0)	12	3	4	2	2	0	12	0	1	1	0	0	-	0	.167	.193	.222
10 ML YEARS		688	2009	448	114	10	49	(22	27)	729	199	229	195	182	22	373	8	33	22	4	10	.29	53	.223	.287	.363

Joe Blanton

Pitches: R Bats: R Pos: SP-34 Ht: 6'3" Wt: 250 Born: 12/11/1980 Age: 27

Year	Team	Lg	G	GS	CG	GF	IP	BFP	H	R	ER	HR	SH	SF	HB	TBB	IBB	SO	WP	Bk	W	L	Pct	ShO	Sv-Op	Hld	ERC	ERA
2004	Oak	AL	3	0	0	1	8.0	30	6	5	5	1	0	0	0	2	0	6	0	0	0	0	-	0	0-0	0	2.52	5.63
2005	Oak	AL	33	33	2	0	201.1	835	178	86	79	23	2	7	5	67	3	116	4	2	12	12	.500	0	0-0	0	3.37	3.53
2006	Oak	AL	32	31	1	0	194.1	856	241	111	104	17	3	9	5	58	4	107	3	0	16	12	.571	0	0-0	0	5.09	4.82
2007	Oak	AL	34	34	3	0	230.0	950	240	106	101	16	5	8	4	40	4	140	3	1	14	10	.583	1	0-0	0	3.30	3.95
4 ML YEARS			102	98	6	1	633.2	2671	665	308	289	57	10	24	14	167	11	369	10	3	42	34	.553	2	0-0	0	3.84	4.10

Jerry Blevins

Pitches: L Bats: L Pos: RP-6 Ht: 6'6" Wt: 185 Born: 9/6/1983 Age: 24

Year	Team	Lg	G	GS	CG	GF	IP	BFP	H	R	ER	HR	SH	SF	HB	TBB	IBB	SO	WP	Bk	W	L	Pct	ShO	Sv-Op	Hld	ERC	ERA
2004	Boise	A-	23	0	0	11	33.1	141	17	7	6	1	0	0	3	21	1	42	2	0	6	1	.857	0	5--	-	2.13	1.62
2005	Peoria	A	48	2	0	29	76.1	344	75	51	47	6	9	3	5	38	0	96	5	0	3	7	.300	0	14--	-	4.39	5.54
2006	Dytona	A+	8	0	0	3	11.0	56	18	12	11	0	1	1	1	4	0	9	0	1	1	1	.000	0	1--	-	7.14	9.00
2006	Boise	A-	16	0	0	6	22.1	109	27	22	15	3	1	3	3	8	0	19	1	0	1	2	.333	0	1--	-	5.57	6.04
2006	WTenn	AA	5	0	0	2	6.1	25	5	1	1	0	0	0	1	1	0	8	0	0	0	0	-	0	1--	-	2.11	1.42
2007	Dytona	A+	15	0	0	10	23.2	89	13	1	1	0	1	1	1	5	2	32	0	0	1	0	1.000	0	6--	-	1.02	0.38
2007	Tenn	AA	23	0	0	11	29.1	120	23	5	5	1	2	2	1	8	1	37	1	0	2	2	.500	0	3--	-	2.11	1.53
2007	Mdland	AA	17	0	0	11	22.0	86	18	10	8	2	2	2	0	5	1	29	2	0	1	3	.250	0	1--	-	2.42	3.27
2007	Scrmto	AAA	1	0	0	0	2.2	9	1	0	0	0	0	0	0	0	0	4	0	0	1	0	1.000	0	0--	-	0.31	0.00
2007	Oak	AL	6	0	0	1	4.2	25	8	6	5	1	0	0	2	0	0	3	0	0	0	1	.000	0	0--	-	9.08	9.64

Willie Bloomquist

Bats: R Throw: R Pos: 2B-20; 3B-20; SS-20; PR-19; LF-13; CF-7; 1B-4; RF-4; DH-2; PH-2 Ht: 5'11" Wt: 195 Born: 11/27/1977 Age: 30

Year	Team	Lg	G	AB	H	2B	3B	HR	(Hm	Rd)	TB	R	RBI	RC	TBB	IBB	SO	HBP	SH	SF	SB	CS	SB%	GDP	Avg	OBP	Slg
2002	Sea	AL	12	33	15	4	0	0	(0	0)	19	11	7	10	5	0	2	0	0	0	3	1	.75	0	.455	.526	.576
2003	Sea	AL	89	196	49	7	2	1	(1	0)	63	30	14	18	19	1	39	1	2	2	4	1	.80	6	.250	.317	.321
2004	Sea	AL	93	188	46	10	0	2	(0	2)	62	27	18	18	10	0	48	0	3	0	13	2	.87	2	.245	.283	.330
2005	Sea	AL	82	249	64	15	2	0	(0	0)	83	27	22	26	11	0	38	1	4	4	14	1	.93	5	.257	.289	.333
2006	Sea	AL	102	251	02	6	2	1	(0	1)	75	36	15	27	24	0	40	4	2	2	16	3	.84	3	.247	.320	.299
2007	Sea	AL	91	173	48	3	0	2	(1	1)	57	28	13	16	10	0	35	1	4	0	7	5	.58	7	.277	.321	.329
6 ML YEARS			469	1090	284	45	6	6	(2	4)	359	159	89	115	79	1	202	7	15	6	57	13	.81	23	.261	.313	.329

Geoff Blum

Bats: B Throws: R Pos: 2B-61; PH-40; 3B-13; SS-12; LF-9; DH-3; 1B-1 Ht: 6'3" Wt: 205 Born: 4/26/1973 Age: 35

Year	Team	Lg	G	AB	H	2B	3B	HR	(Hm	Rd)	TB	R	RBI	RC	TBB	IBB	SO	HBP	SH	SF	SB	CS	SB%	GDP	Avg	OBP	Slg
1999	Mon	NL	45	133	32	7	2	8	(0	8)	67	21	18	22	17	3	25	0	3	0	1	0	1.00	4	.241	.327	.504
2000	Mon	NL	124	343	97	20	2	11	(5	6)	154	40	45	50	26	2	60	3	3	4	1	4	.20	4	.283	.335	.449
2001	Mon	NL	148	453	107	25	0	9	(6	3)	159	57	50	49	43	8	94	10	3	5	9	5	.64	12	.236	.313	.351
2002	Hou	NL	130	368	104	20	4	10	(6	4)	162	45	52	62	49	5	70	1	1	2	2	0	1.00	8	.283	.367	.440
2003	Hou	NL	123	420	110	19	0	10	(6	4)	159	51	52	40	20	1	50	2	2	5	0	0	-	15	.262	.295	.379
2004	TB	AL	112	339	73	21	0	8	(2	6)	118	38	35	29	24	1	58	0	4	2	2	3	.40	4	.215	.266	.348
2005	2 Tms		109	319	73	15	2	6	(1	5)	110	32	25	27	28	0	43	3	0	1	3	3	.50	6	.229	.296	.345
2006	SD	NL	109	276	70	17	1	4	(0	4)	101	27	34	26	17	1	51	0	2	4	0	1	.00	5	.254	.293	.366
2007	SD	NL	122	330	83	21	1	5	(1	4)	121	34	33	38	32	4	52	2	3	3	0	1	.00	10	.252	.319	.367
05	SD	NL	78	224	54	13	1	5	(1	4)	84	26	22	23	24	0	28	3	0	1	3	2	.60	5	.241	.321	.375
05	CWS	AL	31	95	19	2	1	1	(0	1)	26	6	3	4	4	0	15	0	0	0	0	1	.00	1	.200	.232	.274
9 ML YEARS			1022	2981	749	165	12	71	(27	44)	1151	345	344	343	256	25	503	21	21	26	18	16	.53	67	.251	.312	.386

Hiram Bocachica

Bats: R Throws: R Pos: RF-15; CF-12; PH-6; PR-4; LF-2 Ht: 5'11" Wt: 195 Born: 3/4/1976 Age: 32

Year	Team	Lg	G	AB	H	2B	3B	HR	(Hm	Rd)	TB	R	RBI	RC	TBB	IBB	SO	HBP	SH	SF	SB	CS	SB%	GDP	Avg	OBP	Slg
2007	Scrmto*	AAA	35	131	41	11	1	9	(-	-)	81	27	32	35	25	1	21	6	0	0	8	3	.73	3	.313	.444	.618
2007	Portlnd*	AAA	13	38	7	1	0	0	(-	-)	8	3	3	5	12	0	5	1	0	1	2	0	1.00	1	.184	.385	.211
2000	LAD	NL	8	10	3	0	0	0	(0	0)	3	2	0	1	0	0	2	0	0	0	0	0	-	0	.300	.300	.300
2001	LAD	NL	75	133	31	11	1	2	(2	0)	50	19	5	15	9	0	33	1	0	0	4	1	.80	1	.233	.287	.376
2002	2 Tms		83	168	37	7	0	8	(2	6)	68	26	17	13	10	0	41	0	1	0	3	3	.50	3	.220	.264	.405
2003	Det	AL	6	22	1	1	0	0	(0	0)	2	1	0	0	0	0	7	0	0	0	0	0	-	0	.045	.045	.091
2004	Sea	AL	50	90	22	5	0	3	(3	0)	36	9	6	9	12	0	27	1	3	1	5	4	.56	1	.244	.337	.400
2005	Oak	AL	9	19	2	0	0	0	(0	0)	2	2	0	0	0	0	7	0	0	0	0	0	-	0	.105	.105	.105
2006	Oak	AL	8	13	3	0	0	0	(0	0)	3	3	0	1	3	0	4	0	0	0	1	0	1.00	0	.231	.375	.231
2007	2 Tms		33	80	16	4	0	2	(0	2)	26	11	5	5	7	0	18	0	1	0	3	2	.60	1	.200	.261	.325
02	LAD	NL	49	65	14	3	0	4	(1	3)	29	12	9	6	5	0	19	0	0	0	1	1	.50	1	.215	.271	.446
02	Det	AL	34	103	23	4	0	4	(1	3)	39	14	8	7	5	0	22	0	1	0	2	2	.50	2	.223	.259	.379
07	Oak	AL	6	17	1	0	0	0	(0	1)	4	2	0	0	2	0	5	0	0	0	0	0	-	1	.059	.150	.235
07	SD	NL	27	63	15	4	0	1	(0	1)	22	9	5	5	5	0	13	0	0	0	3	2	.60	0	.238	.294	.349
8 ML YEARS			272	535	115	28	1	15	(7	8)	190	69	37	44	41	0	139	2	4	2	16	10	.62	6	.215	.272	.355

Jeremy Bonderman

Pitches: R Bats: R Pos: SP-28 Ht: 6'2" Wt: 220 Born: 10/28/1982 Age: 25

			HOW MUCH HE PITCHED					WHAT HE GAVE UP											THE RESULTS					
Year	Team	Lg	G	GS	CG	GF	IP	BFP	H	R	ER	HR	SH	SF	HB	TBB	IBB	SO	WP	Bk	W	L	Pct	ShO	Sv-Op Hld	ERC	ERA
2003	Det	AL	33	28	0	0	162.0	727	193	118	100	23	3	6	4	58	2	108	12	2	6	19	.240	0	0-0 0	5.39	5.56
2004	Det	AL	33	32	2	0	184.0	793	168	101	100	24	10	5	10	73	5	168	7	0	11	13	.458	2	0-0 0	3.93	4.89
2005	Det	AL	29	29	4	0	189.0	801	199	101	96	21	3	3	4	57	0	145	5	1	14	13	.519	0	0-0 0	4.20	4.57
2006	Det	AL	34	34	0	0	214.0	903	214	104	97	18	3	6	3	64	7	202	3	1	14	8	.636	0	0-0 0	3.58	4.08
2007	Det	AL	28	28	0	0	174.1	753	193	105	97	23	2	4	4	48	6	145	12	1	11	9	.550	0	0-0 0	4.44	5.01
5 ML YEARS			157	151	6	0	923.1	3977	967	529	490	109	21	24	25	300	20	768	39	5	56	62	.475	2	0-0 0	4.24	4.78

Barry Bonds

Bats: L Throws: L Pos: LF-110; PH-10; DH-6 Ht: 6'2" Wt: 240 Born: 7/24/1964 Age: 43

						BATTING												BASERUNNING				AVERAGES		
Year	Team	Lg	G	AB	H	2B	3B	HR	(Hm | Rd)	TB	R	RBI	RC	TBB	IBB	SO	HBP	SH	SF	SB	CS	SB%	GDP	Avg	OBP	Slg
1986	Pit	NL	113	413	92	26	3	16	(9 | 7)	172	72	48	64	65	2	102	2	2	2	36	7	.84	4	.223	.330	.416
1987	Pit	NL	150	551	144	34	9	25	(12 | 13)	271	99	59	92	54	3	88	3	0	3	32	10	.76	4	.261	.329	.492
1988	Pit	NL	144	538	152	30	5	24	(14 | 10)	264	97	58	97	72	14	82	2	0	2	17	11	.61	3	.283	.368	.491
1989	Pit	NL	159	580	144	34	6	19	(7 | 12)	247	96	58	91	93	22	93	1	1	4	32	10	.76	9	.248	.351	.426
1990	Pit	NL	151	519	156	32	3	33	(14 | 19)	293	104	114	121	93	15	83	3	0	6	52	13	.80	8	.301	.406	.565
1991	Pit	NL	153	510	149	28	5	25	(12 | 13)	262	95	116	113	107	25	73	4	0	13	43	13	.77	8	.292	.410	.514
1992	Pit	NL	140	473	147	36	5	34	(15 | 19)	295	109	103	134	127	32	69	5	0	7	39	8	.83	9	.311	.456	.624
1993	SF	NL	159	539	181	38	4	46	(21 | 25)	365	129	123	155	126	43	79	2	0	7	29	12	.71	11	.336	.458	.677
1994	SF	NL	112	391	122	18	1	37	(15 | 22)	253	89	81	105	74	18	43	6	0	3	29	9	.76	4	.312	.426	.647
1995	SF	NL	144	506	149	30	7	33	(16 | 17)	292	109	104	125	120	22	83	5	0	4	31	10	.76	12	.294	.431	.577
1996	SF	NL	158	517	159	27	3	42	(23 | 19)	318	122	129	148	151	30	76	1	0	6	40	7	.85	11	.308	.461	.615
1997	SF	NL	159	532	155	26	5	40	(24 | 16)	311	123	101	140	145	34	87	8	0	5	37	8	.82	13	.291	.446	.585
1998	SF	NL	156	552	167	44	7	37	(21 | 16)	336	120	122	141	130	29	92	8	1	6	28	12	.70	15	.303	.438	.609
1999	SF	NL	102	355	93	20	2	34	(16 | 18)	219	91	83	85	73	9	62	3	0	3	15	2	.88	6	.262	.389	.617
2000	SF	NL	143	480	147	28	4	49	(25 | 24)	330	129	106	139	117	22	77	3	0	7	11	3	.79	6	.306	.440	.688
2001	SF	NL	153	476	156	32	2	73	(37 | 36)	411	129	137	191	177	35	93	9	0	2	13	3	.81	5	.328	.515	.863
2002	SF	NL	143	403	149	31	2	46	(19 | 27)	322	117	110	160	198	68	47	9	0	2	9	2	.82	4	.370	.582	.799
2003	SF	NL	130	390	133	22	1	45	(23 | 22)	292	111	90	129	148	61	58	10	0	2	7	0	1.00	7	.341	.529	.749
2004	SF	NL	147	373	135	27	3	45	(26 | 19)	303	129	101	171	232	120	41	9	0	3	6	1	.86	5	.362	.609	.812
2005	SF	NL	14	42	12	1	0	5	(2 | 3)	28	8	10	9	9	3	6	0	0	-	0	0	-	0	.286	.404	.667
2006	SF	NL	130	367	99	23	0	26	(12 | 14)	200	74	77	103	115	38	51	10	0	1	3	0	1.00	9	.270	.454	.545
2007	SF	NL	126	340	94	14	0	28	(16 | 12)	192	75	66	88	132	43	54	3	0	2	5	0	1.00	13	.276	.480	.565
22 ML YEARS			2986	9847	2935	601	77	762	(379 | 383)	5976	2227	1996	2601	2558	688	1539	106	4	91	514	141	.78	165	.298	.444	.607

Emilio Bonifacio

Bats: B Throws: R Pos: 2B-6; PH-3; PR-2 Ht: 5'11" Wt: 180 Born: 4/23/1985 Age: 23

						BATTING												BASERUNNING				AVERAGES		
Year	Team	Lg	G	AB	H	2B	3B	HR	(Hm | Rd)	TB	R	RBI	RC	TBB	IBB	SO	HBP	SH	SF	SB	CS	SB%	GDP	Avg	OBP	Slg
2003	Msoula	R+	54	146	29	1	1	0	(- | -)	32	20	16	12	18	0	43	3	4	1	15	3	.83	1	.199	.298	.219
2004	Sbend	A	120	411	107	9	6	1	(- | -)	131	59	37	45	25	3	122	3	9	2	40	10	.80	9	.260	.306	.319
2005	Sbend	A	127	522	141	14	7	1	(- | -)	172	81	44	68	56	0	90	2	7	4	55	17	.76	9	.270	.341	.330
2006	Lancst	A+	130	546	175	35	7	7	(- | -)	245	117	50	100	44	0	104	6	8	4	61	14	.81	5	.321	.375	.449
2007	Mobile	AA	132	551	157	21	5	2	(- | -)	194	84	40	70	38	1	105	2	4	1	41	13	.76	6	.285	.333	.352
2007	Ari	NL	11	23	5	1	0	0	(0 | 0)	6	2	2	4	4	0	3	0	0	0	0	1	.00	0	.217	.333	.261

Boof Bonser

Pitches: R Bats: R Pos: SP-30; RP-1 Ht: 6'4" Wt: 260 Born: 10/14/1981 Age: 26

						HOW MUCH HE PITCHED					WHAT HE GAVE UP											THE RESULTS					
Year	Team	Lg	G	GS	CG	GF	IP	BFP	H	R	ER	HR	SH	SF	HB	TBB	IBB	SO	WP	Bk	W	L	Pct	ShO	Sv-Op Hld	ERC	ERA
2000	SlmKzr	A-	10	9	0	0	33.0	145	21	23	22	2	1	2	1	29	0	41	4	0	1	4	.200	0	0-- -	3.77	6.00
2001	Hgrstn	A	27	27	0	0	134.0	548	91	40	37	7	2	3	9	61	2	178	10	1	16	4	.800	0	0-- -	2.53	2.49
2002	Shreve	AA	5	5	0	0	24.1	112	30	15	15	3	0	2	1	14	0	23	0	0	1	2	.333	0	0-- -	6.76	5.55
2002	SnJos	A+	23	23	0	0	128.1	537	89	44	41	9	1	2	7	70	0	139	7	1	8	6	.571	0	0-- -	3.01	2.88
2003	Nrwich	AA	24	24	1	0	135.0	579	122	80	60	11	7	7	0	67	0	103	10	0	7	10	.412	1	0-- -	3.81	4.00
2003	Fresno	A	4	4	0	0	23.0	97	17	13	8	4	1	1	0	8	0	28	2	0	1	2	.333	0	0-- -	2.79	3.13
2004	NwBrit	AA	27	27	0	0	154.1	658	160	89	75	22	2	8	3	56	1	146	4	0	12	9	.571	0	0-- -	4.58	4.37
2004	Roch	AAA	1	1	0	0	7.0	26	5	1	1	1	0	0	0	1	0	7	0	0	1	0	1.000	0	0-- -	1.99	1.29
2005	Roch	AAA	28	28	0	0	160.1	684	153	80	71	22	7	8	2	57	0	168	3	0	11	9	.550	0	0-- -	3.92	3.99
2006	Roch	AAA	14	14	0	0	86.1	361	68	31	27	4	0	1	3	35	0	83	0	0	6	4	.600	0	0-- -	2.72	2.81
2006	Min	AL	18	18	0	0	100.1	419	104	50	47	18	2	2	1	24	0	84	2	0	7	6	.538	0	0-0 0	4.25	4.22
2007	Min	AL	31	30	0	0	173.0	772	199	108	98	27	4	3	5	65	4	136	3	1	8	12	.400	0	0-0 0	5.33	5.10
2 ML YEARS			49	48	0	0	273.1	1191	303	158	145	45	6	5	6	89	4	220	5	1	15	18	.455	0	0-0 0	4.93	4.77

Chris Booker

Pitches: R Bats: R Pos: RP-3 Ht: 6'3" Wt: 235 Born: 12/9/1976 Age: 31

						HOW MUCH HE PITCHED					WHAT HE GAVE UP											THE RESULTS					
Year	Team	Lg	G	GS	CG	GF	IP	BFP	H	R	ER	HR	SH	SF	HB	TBB	IBB	SO	WP	Bk	W	L	Pct	ShO	Sv-Op Hld	ERC	ERA
2007	Clmbs*	AAA	55	0	0	51	58.0	246	37	19	19	4	5	1	0	39	0	83	2	0	2	5	.286	0	30-- -	2.94	2.95
2005	Cin	NL	3	0	0	1	2.0	15	6	8	7	2	0	0	0	2	0	0	0	0	0	0	-	0	0-0 0	40.92	31.50
2006	2 Tms		11	0	0	2	8.1	38	10	9	9	4	0	0	0	4	0	7	1	0	0	0	-	0	0-0 2	8.66	9.72

46

Year	Team	Lg	G	GS	CG	GF	IP	BFP	H	R	ER	HR	SH	SF	HB	TBB	IBB	SO	WP	Bk	W	L	Pct	ShO	Sv-Op	Hld	ERC	ERA
2007	Was	NL	3	0	0	1	1.0	5	1	2	2	1	0	1	0	1	0	1	1	0	0	1	.000	0	0-1	0	14.27	18.00
06 KC		AL	1	0	0	0	1.0	11	5	6	6	3	0	1	0	3	0	0	0	0	0	0	-	0	0-0	0	94.96	54.00
06 Was		NL	10	0	0	2	7.1	27	5	3	3	1	0	0	0	1	0	7	1	0	0	0	-	0	0-0	2	1.78	3.68
3 ML YEARS			17	0	0	4	11.1	58	17	19	18	7	0	1	0	9	0	10	2	0	0	1	.000	0	0-1	2	14.08	14.29

Aaron Boone

Bats: R Throws: R Pos: 1B-48; PH-14; 3B-12; PR-1   **Ht: 6'2" Wt: 200 Born: 3/9/1973 Age: 35**

							BATTING														BASERUNNING				AVERAGES		
Year	Team	Lg	G	AB	H	2B	3B	HR	(Hm	Rd)	TB	R	RBI	RC	TBB	IBB	SO	HBP	SH	SF	SB	CS	SB%	GDP	Avg	OBP	Slg
2007	Jupiter*	A+	1	3	0	0	0	0	(-	-)	0	1	1	0	0	0	0	0	0	0	0	0	-	0	.000	.000	.000
1997	Cin	NL	16	49	12	1	0	0	(0	0)	13	5	5	3	2	0	5	0	1	0	1	0	1.00	1	.245	.275	.265
1998	Cin	NL	58	181	51	13	2	2	(2	0)	74	24	28	27	15	1	30	5	3	2	6	1	.86	3	.282	.350	.409
1999	Cin	NL	139	472	132	26	5	14	(7	7)	210	56	72	70	30	2	79	8	5	5	17	6	.74	6	.280	.330	.445
2000	Cin	NL	84	291	83	18	0	12	(5	7)	137	44	43	50	24	1	52	10	2	4	6	1	.86	5	.285	.356	.471
2001	Cin	NL	103	381	112	26	2	14	(10	4)	184	54	62	63	29	1	71	8	3	6	6	3	.67	9	.294	.351	.483
2002	Cin	NL	162	606	146	38	2	26	(14	12)	266	83	87	83	56	4	111	10	9	4	32	8	.80	9	.241	.314	.439
2003	2 Tms		160	592	158	32	3	24	(13	11)	268	92	96	89	46	2	104	8	6	2	23	3	.88	13	.267	.327	.453
2005	Cle	AL	143	511	124	19	1	16	(5	11)	193	61	60	52	35	3	92	9	4	6	9	3	.75	16	.243	.299	.378
2006	Cle	AL	104	354	89	19	1	7	(1	6)	131	50	46	46	27	1	62	6	4	1	5	4	.56	4	.251	.314	.370
2007	Fla	NL	69	189	54	11	0	5	(1	4)	80	27	28	32	21	4	41	13	1	4	2	0	1.00	9	.286	.388	.423
03 Cin		NL	106	403	110	19	3	18	(10	8)	189	61	65	65	35	2	74	5	3	0	15	3	.83	6	.273	.349	.469
03 NYY		AL	54	189	48	13	0	6	(3	3)	79	31	31	24	11	0	30	3	3	2	8	0	1.00	7	.254	.302	.418
10 ML YEARS			1038	3626	961	203	16	120	(58	62)	1556	496	527	515	285	19	653	77	38	34	107	29	.79	66	.265	.329	.429

Chris Bootcheck

Pitches: R Bats: R Pos: RP-51   **Ht: 6'5" Wt: 200 Born: 10/24/1978 Age: 29**

					HOW MUCH HE PITCHED				WHAT HE GAVE UP										THE RESULTS						
Year	Team	Lg	G	GS	CG	GF	IP	BFP	H	R	ER	HR	SH	SF	HB	TBB	IBB	SO	WP	Bk	W	L	Pct	ShO	Sv-Op	Hld	ERC	ERA
2003	LAA	AL	4	1	0	2	10.1	53	16	13	11	5	0	0	0	6	0	7	0	0	0	1	.000	0	0-0	0	11.53	9.58
2005	LAA	AL	5	2	0	1	18.2	79	19	7	7	1	0	1	0	4	1	8	1	0	0	1	.000	0	1-1	0	3.00	3.38
2006	LAA	AL	7	0	0	5	10.1	54	16	12	12	3	1	0	0	9	0	7	1	0	0	1	.000	0	0-0	0	11.63	10.45
2007	LAA	AL	51	0	0	17	77.1	331	81	43	41	7	2	4	5	24	3	56	6	1	3	3	.500	0	0-1	4	4.16	4.77
4 ML YEARS			67	3	0	25	116.2	517	132	75	71	16	3	5	5	43	4	78	8	1	3	6	.333	0	1-2	4	5.11	5.48

Joe Borchard

Bats: B Throws: R Pos: PH-41; RF-34; LF-14; PR-1   **Ht: 6'4" Wt: 230 Born: 11/25/1978 Age: 29**

							BATTING														BASERUNNING				AVERAGES		
Year	Team	Lg	G	AB	H	2B	3B	HR	(Hm	Rd)	TB	R	RBI	RC	TBB	IBB	SO	HBP	SH	SF	SB	CS	SB%	GDP	Avg	OBP	Slg
2007	Albq*	AAA	22	76	27	3	0	8	(-	-)	54	19	28	22	15	3	12	0	0	2	1	2	.33	2	.355	.452	.711
2002	CWS	AL	16	36	8	0	0	2	(0	2)	14	5	5	5	1	0	14	0	0	0	0	0	-	0	.222	.243	.389
2003	CWS	AL	16	49	9	1	0	1	(0	1)	13	5	5	2	5	0	18	0	0	3	0	1	.00	0	.184	.246	.265
2004	CWS	AL	63	201	35	4	1	9	(6	3)	68	26	20	13	19	1	57	1	1	0	1	0	1.00	4	.174	.249	.338
2005	CWS	AL	7	12	5	2	0	0	(0	0)	7	0	0	2	0	0	4	0	0	0	0	0	-	0	.417	.417	.583
2006	2 Tms		114	239	55	7	1	10	(5	5)	94	33	28	26	28	3	69	3	0	0	0	3	.00	4	.230	.319	.393
2007	Fla	NL	85	179	35	9	0	4	(4	0)	56	20	19	15	21	3	60	2	0	0	4	0	1.00	10	.196	.287	.313
06 Sea		AL	6	9	2	0	0	0	(0	0)	2	3	0	0	0	0	3	0	0	0	0	1	.00	0	.222	.222	.222
06 Fla		NL	108	230	53	7	1	10	(5	5)	92	30	28	26	28	3	66	3	0	0	0	2	.00	4	.230	.322	.400
6 ML YEARS			301	716	147	23	2	26	(15	11)	252	89	77	63	74	7	222	6	1	3	5	5	.50	13	.205	.284	.352

Dave Borkowski

Pitches: R Bats: R Pos: RP-64   **Ht: 6'1" Wt: 230 Born: 2/7/1977 Age: 31**

					HOW MUCH HE PITCHED				WHAT HE GAVE UP										THE RESULTS						
Year	Team	Lg	G	GS	CG	GF	IP	BFP	H	R	ER	HR	SH	SF	HB	TBB	IBB	SO	WP	Bk	W	L	Pct	ShO	Sv-Op	Hld	ERC	ERA
1999	Det	AL	17	12	0	0	76.2	351	86	58	52	10	4	6	4	40	0	50	3	0	0	4	.250	0	0-	0	5.75	6.10
2000	Det	AL	2	1	0	0	5.1	34	11	13	13	2	0	1	0	7	1	1	0	0	0	1	.000	0	0-	0	17.78	21.94
2001	Det	AL	15	0	0	7	29.2	135	30	21	21	5	0	2	3	15	3	30	0	0	0	2	.000	0	0-	0	5.28	6.37
2004	Bal	AL	17	8	0	3	56.0	247	65	37	32	6	2	2	3	15	1	45	2	1	3	4	.429	0	0-1	3	4.67	5.14
2006	Hou	NL	40	0	0	12	71.0	299	70	38	37	8	2	2	0	23	7	52	2	0	3	2	.600	0	0-0	1	3.65	4.69
2007	Hou	NL	64	0	0	18	71.2	325	76	46	41	8	3	6	4	34	9	63	3	0	5	3	.625	0	1-4	8	4.76	5.15
6 ML YEARS			155	21	0	41	310.1	1391	338	213	196	39	8	15	14	134	21	241	10	1	13	18	.419	0	1-5	10	4.95	5.68

Joe Borowski

Pitches: R Bats: R Pos: RP-69   **Ht: 6'2" Wt: 225 Born: 5/4/1971 Age: 37**

					HOW MUCH HE PITCHED				WHAT HE GAVE UP										THE RESULTS						
Year	Team	Lg	G	GS	CG	GF	IP	BFP	H	R	ER	HR	SH	SF	HB	TBB	IBB	SO	WP	Bk	W	L	Pct	ShO	Sv-Op	Hld	ERC	ERA
1995	Bal	AL	6	0	0	3	7.1	30	5	1	1	0	0	0	0	4	0	3	0	0	0	0	-	0	0-0	0	2.32	1.23
1996	Atl	NL	22	0	0	8	26.0	121	33	15	14	4	5	0	1	13	4	15	1	0	2	4	.333	0	0-0	1	6.46	4.85
1997	2 Tms		21	0	0	9	26.0	123	29	13	12	2	1	0	0	20	5	18	0	0	2	3	.400	0	0-2	0	5.74	4.15
1998	NYY	AL	8	0	0	3	9.2	42	11	7	7	0	0	0	0	4	0	7	0	0	1	0	1.000	0	0-0	0	4.27	6.52
2001	ChC	NL	1	1	0	0	1.2	13	6	6	6	1	1	0	0	3	0	1	0	0	0	1	.000	0	0-0	0	39.91	32.40
2002	ChC	NL	73	0	0	25	95.2	391	84	31	29	10	5	3	1	29	6	97	1	0	4	4	.500	0	2-6	12	3.05	2.73
2003	ChC	NL	68	0	0	59	68.1	280	53	23	20	5	4	0	1	19	1	66	0	0	2	2	.500	0	33-37	1	2.26	2.63
2004	ChC	NL	22	0	0	19	21.1	106	27	19	19	3	1	1	0	15	2	17	0	0	2	4	.333	0	9-11	0	6.92	8.02
2005	2 Tms		43	0	0	17	46.1	184	38	23	23	9	4	1	0	12	1	27	1	0	1	5	.167	0	0-4	20	3.04	4.47
2006	Fla	NL	72	0	0	60	69.2	304	63	31	29	7	1	0	2	33	7	64	1	0	3	5	.500	0	36-43	0	3.74	3.75

Year Team	Lg	G	GS	CG	GF	IP	BFP	H	R	ER	HR	SH	SF	HB	TBB	IBB	SO	WP	Bk	W	L	Pct	ShO	Sv-Op	Hld	ERC	ERA
2007 Cle	AL	69	0	0	58	65.2	292	77	39	37	9	3	4	2	17	4	58	2	0	4	5	.444	0	45-53		4.68	5.07
97 Atl	NL	20	0	0	8	24.0	111	27	11	10	2	1	0	0	16	4	6	0	0	2	2	.500	0	0-0	2	5.51	3.75
97 NYY	AL	1	0	0	1	2.0	12	2	2	2	0	0	0	0	4	1	2	0	0	0	1	.000	0	0-0	0	8.25	9.00
05 ChC	NL	11	0	0	3	11.0	47	12	8	8	5	0	0	0	1	0	11	0	0	0	0	-	0	0-0	1	5.36	6.55
05 TB	AL	32	0	0	4	35.1	137	26	15	15	3	1	0	0	11	1	16	1	0	1	5	.167	0	0-4	19	2.33	3.82
11 ML YEARS		405	1	0	254	437.2	1886	426	208	197	49	22	8	7	169	30	363	6	0	21	31	.404	0	125-154	36	3.89	4.05

Jason Botts

Bats: B **Throws:** R **Pos:** LF-28; DH-18; PH-2   **Ht:** 6'5" **Wt:** 250 **Born:** 7/26/1980 **Age:** 27

Year Team	Lg	G	AB	H	2B	3B	HR	(Hm	Rd)	TB	R	RBI	RC	TBB	IBB	SO	HBP	SH	SF	SB	CS	SB%	GDP	Avg	OBP	Slg
2007 Okla*	AAA	102	369	118	36	4	13	(-	-)	201	69	78	90	81	6	102	1	0	8	0	1	.00	10	.320	.436	.545
2005 Tex	AL	10	27	8	0	0	0	(0	0)	8	4	3	3	3	0	13	0	0	0	0	0	-	1	.296	.367	.296
2006 Tex	AL	20	50	11	4	0	1	(1	0)	18	8	6	6	8	1	18	0	0	2	0	0	-	0	.220	.317	.360
2007 Tex	AL	48	167	40	8	1	2	(1	1)	56	19	14	17	19	0	59	3	0	1	1	0	1.00	8	.240	.326	.335
3 ML YEARS		78	244	59	12	1	3	(2	1)	82	31	23	26	30	1	90	3	0	3	1	0	1.00	9	.242	.329	.336

Michael Bourn

Bats: L **Throws:** R **Pos:** LF-79; PR-34; CF-12; PH-12; RF-6   **Ht:** 5'11" **Wt:** 180 **Born:** 12/27/1982 **Age:** 25

Year Team	Lg	G	AB	H	2B	3B	HR	(Hm	Rd)	TB	R	RBI	RC	TBB	IBB	SO	HBP	SH	SF	SB	CS	SB%	GDP	Avg	OBP	Slg
2003 Batvia	A-	35	125	35	0	1	0	(-	-)	37	12	4	21	23	0	28	3	2	0	23	5	.82	2	.280	.404	.296
2004 Lakwd	A	109	413	131	20	14	5	(-	-)	194	92	53	98	85	2	88	2	6	4	57	6	.90	1	.317	.433	.470
2005 Rdng	AA	135	544	146	18	8	6	(-	-)	198	80	44	76	63	5	123	3	4	0	38	12	.76	2	.268	.348	.364
2006 Rdng	AA	80	318	87	5	6	4	(-	-)	116	62	26	48	36	2	67	2	4	1	30	4	.88	3	.274	.350	.365
2006 S-WB	AAA	38	152	43	5	7	1	(-	-)	65	34	15	27	20	0	33	1	0	1	15	1	.94	2	.283	.368	.428
2006 Phi	NL	17	8	1	0	0	0	(0	0)	1	2	0	0	1	0	3	0	2	0	1	2	.33	1	.125	.222	.125
2007 Phi	NL	105	119	33	3	3	1	(1	0)	45	29	6	19	13	2	21	0	1	0	18	1	.95	1	.277	.348	.378
2 ML YEARS		122	127	34	3	3	1	(1	0)	46	31	6	19	14	2	24	0	3	0	19	3	.86	1	.268	.340	.362

Rob Bowen

Bats: B **Throws:** R **Pos:** C-56; PH-4; PR-4   **Ht:** 6'3" **Wt:** 225 **Born:** 2/24/1981 **Age:** 27

Year Team	Lg	G	AB	H	2B	3B	HR	(Hm	Rd)	TB	R	RBI	RC	TBB	IBB	SO	HBP	SH	SF	SB	CS	SB%	GDP	Avg	OBP	Slg
2003 Min	AL	7	10	1	0	0	0	(0	0)	1	0	1	0	0	0	4	0	0	1	0	0	-	1	.100	.091	.100
2004 Min	AL	17	27	3	0	0	1	(0	1)	6	1	2	2	4	0	10	0	1	0	0	0	-	1	.111	.226	.222
2006 SD	NL	94	94	23	5	0	3	(2	1)	37	22	13	12	13	0	26	1	1	1	0	1	.00	1	.245	.339	.394
2007 3 Tms		61	156	36	10	0	4	(1	3)	58	21	18	20	27	3	61	1	2	2	1	2	.33	2	.231	.344	.372
07 SD	NL	30	82	22	8	0	2	(1	1)	36	12	11	12	13	3	28	1	1	1	1	2	.33	0	.268	.371	.439
07 ChC	NL	10	31	2	1	0	0	(0	0)	3	3	2	0	4	0	13	0	0	1	0	0	-	2	.065	.167	.097
07 Oak	AL	21	43	12	1	0	2	(0	2)	19	6	5	8	10	0	20	0	1	0	0	0	-	0	.279	.415	.442
4 ML YEARS		179	287	63	15	0	8	(3	5)	102	44	34	34	44	3	101	2	4	4	1	3	.25	5	.220	.323	.355

Micah Bowie

Pitches: L **Bats:** L **Pos:** RP-22; SP-8   **Ht:** 6'4" **Wt:** 221 **Born:** 11/10/1974 **Age:** 33

Year Team	Lg	G	GS	CG	GF	IP	BFP	H	R	ER	HR	SH	SF	HB	TBB	IBB	SO	WP	Bk	W	L	Pct	ShO	Sv-Op	Hld	ERC	ERA
2007 Nats*	R	2	1	0	0	5.0	22	6	3	2	0	0	0	1	1	0	7	0	0	0	0	-	0	0- -	-	4.56	3.60
2007 Clmbs*	AAA	3	3	0	0	13.2	60	12	6	6	1	4	3	1	5	0	8	0	0	0	2	.000	0	0- -	-	3.23	3.95
1999 2 Tms	NL	14	11	0	2	51.0	265	81	60	58	9	3	3	2	34	2	41	4	2	2	7	.222	0	0-0	0	9.69	10.24
2002 Oak	AL	13	0	0	4	12.0	55	12	2	2	1	0	0	0	8	1	8	0	0	2	0	1.000	0	0-0	5	5.26	1.50
2003 Oak	AL	6	0	0	3	8.1	38	13	7	7	1	0	0	0	2	0	4	0	0	0	1	.000	0	0-0	1	7.15	7.56
2006 Was	NL	15	0	0	3	19.2	75	11	3	3	1	1	0	0	7	0	11	0	0	0	1	.000	0	0-5	1	1.54	1.37
2007 Was	NL	30	8	0	2	57.1	248	55	30	29	7	4	4	2	27	0	42	0	0	4	3	.571	0	0-1	1	4.48	4.55
99 Atl	NL	3	0	0	2	4.0	23	8	6	6	1	0	0	0	4	0	2	0	0	1	1	1.000	0	0-0	0	15.43	13.50
99 ChC	NL	11	11	0	0	47.0	242	73	54	52	8	3	3	2	30	2	39	4	2	2	6	.250	0	0-0	0	9.23	9.96
5 ML YEARS		78	19	0	14	148.1	681	172	102	99	19	8	7	5	78	3	106	4	2	8	12	.400	0	0-1	9	5.88	6.01

Blaine Boyer

Pitches: R **Bats:** R **Pos:** RP-5   **Ht:** 6'3" **Wt:** 215 **Born:** 7/11/1981 **Age:** 26

Year Team	Lg	G	GS	CG	GF	IP	BFP	H	R	ER	HR	SH	SF	HB	TBB	IBB	SO	WP	Bk	W	L	Pct	ShO	Sv-Op	Hld	ERC	ERA
2007 Rchmd*	AAA	21	12	0	2	73.1	333	76	40	35	1	6	6	7	50	3	62	5	0	4	3	.571	0	2- -	-	5.20	4.30
2005 Atl	NL	43	0	0	5	37.2	158	32	13	13	1	1	1	2	17	0	33	2	0	4	2	.667	0	0-2	9	3.21	3.11
2006 Atl	NL	2	0	0	0	0.2	7	4	3	3	0	0	0	0	1	0	0	0	0	0	0	-	0	0-0	1	47.92	40.50
2007 Atl	NL	5	0	0	2	5.1	26	10	3	2	0	1	0	0	1	1	3	2	0	0	0	-	0	0-0	1	7.41	3.38
3 ML YEARS		50	0	0	7	43.2	191	46	19	18	1	2	1	2	19	1	36	4	0	4	2	.667	0	0-2	11	4.14	3.71

Dallas Braden

Pitches: L Bats: L Pos: SP-14; RP-6   Ht: 6'1" Wt: 185 Born: 8/13/1983 Age: 24

			HOW MUCH HE PITCHED						WHAT HE GAVE UP												THE RESULTS							
Year	Team	Lg	G	GS	CG	GF	IP	BFP	H	R	ER	HR	SH	SF	HB	TBB	IBB	SO	WP	Bk	W	L	Pct	ShO	Sv-Op	Hld	ERC	ERA
2004	Vancvr	A-	7	0	0	4	16.1	63	15	7	5	1	0	0	0	3	0	26	0	0	2	0	1.000	0	2--	-	2.73	2.76
2004	Kane	A	5	5	0	0	23.0	101	22	13	12	2	3	1	0	6	1	33	1	1	2	1	.667	0	0--	-	2.94	4.70
2005	Stcktn	A+	7	7	1	0	43.2	170	31	14	13	4	2	0	3	11	0	64	4	2	6	0	1.000	0	0--	-	2.29	2.68
2005	Mdland	AA	16	16	0	0	97.0	413	104	43	39	5	5	5	1	32	1	71	8	3	9	5	.643	0	0--	-	3.94	3.62
2006	As	R	6	6	0	0	21.0	74	12	2	2	0	2	0	0	3	0	36	1	0	2	0	1.000	0	0--	-	0.98	0.86
2006	Stcktn	A+	3	3	0	0	13.0	57	12	9	9	3	0	0	2	5	0	17	0	0	2	0	1.000	0	0--	-	5.13	6.23
2006	Mdland	AA	1	1	0	0	3.1	19	9	6	6	1	1	0	0	0	0	2	0	0	0	0	-	0	0--	-	15.42	16.20
2007	Mdland	AA	2	2	0	0	12.0	42	5	3	3	2	0	0	0	3	0	13	0	0	1	0	1.000	0	0--	-	1.30	2.25
2007	Scrmto	AAA	11	11	2	0	64.0	263	51	22	21	4	3	0	2	18	1	74	2	2	2	3	.400	1	0--	-	2.38	2.95
2007	Oak	AL	20	14	0	1	72.1	332	91	59	54	9	4	0	2	26	1	55	6	1	1	8	.111	0	0-0	1	5.63	6.72

Chad Bradford

Pitches: R Bats: R Pos: RP-78   Ht: 6'5" Wt: 212 Born: 9/14/1974 Age: 33

			HOW MUCH HE PITCHED						WHAT HE GAVE UP												THE RESULTS							
Year	Team	Lg	G	GS	CG	GF	IP	BFP	H	R	ER	HR	SH	SF	HB	TBB	IBB	SO	WP	Bk	W	L	Pct	ShO	Sv-Op	Hld	ERC	ERA
1998	CWS	AL	29	0	0	8	30.2	125	27	16	11	0	0	0	0	7	0	11	1	1	2	1	.667	0	1-3	9	2.16	3.23
1999	CWS	AL	3	0	0	0	3.2	24	9	8	8	1	0	0	0	5	0	0	1	0	0	0	-	0	0-0	0	21.34	19.64
2000	CWS	AL	12	0	0	5	13.2	52	13	4	3	0	0	0	0	1	1	9	0	0	1	0	1.000	0	0-0	2	2.01	1.98
2001	Oak	AL	35	0	0	19	36.2	154	41	12	11	6	1	0	1	6	0	34	0	0	2	1	.667	0	1-4	4	4.36	2.70
2002	Oak	AL	75	0	0	14	75.1	311	73	29	26	2	2	2	5	14	5	56	0	1	4	2	.667	0	2-5	24	2.77	3.11
2003	Oak	AL	72	0	0	12	77.0	322	67	28	26	7	1	0	7	30	9	62	0	1	7	4	.636	0	2-5	23	3.50	3.04
2004	Oak	AL	68	0	0	16	59.0	251	51	32	29	5	3	1	5	24	9	34	0	0	5	7	.417	0	1-4	14	3.35	4.42
2005	Bos	AL	31	0	0	2	23.1	104	29	10	10	1	3	1	3	4	1	10	2	0	2	1	.667	0	0-1	8	4.54	3.86
2006	NYM	AL	70	0	0	15	62.0	252	59	22	20	1	4	3	0	13	4	45	0	0	4	2	.667	0	2-3	10	2.48	2.90
2007	Bal	AL	78	0	0	14	64.2	289	77	28	24	1	4	1	6	16	3	29	0	0	4	7	.364	0	2-7	19	4.16	3.34
10 ML YEARS			473	0	0	105	446.0	1884	446	189	168	24	18	8	27	120	32	290	4	3	31	25	.554	0	11-32	113	3.39	3.39

Milton Bradley

Bats: B Throws: R Pos: LF-40; CF-15; RF-4; PH-3   Ht: 6'0" Wt: 225 Born: 4/15/1978 Age: 30

			BATTING																			BASERUNNING				AVERAGES		
Year	Team	Lg	G	AB	H	2B	3B	HR	(Hm	Rd)	TB	R	RBI	RC	TBB	IBB	SO	HBP	SH	SF		SB	CS	SB%	GDP	Avg	OBP	Slg
2007	Scrmto*	AAA	2	5	0	0	0	0	(-	-)	0	1	0	0	2	0	4	0	0	0		0	0	-	0	.000	.286	.000
2000	Mon	NL	42	154	34	8	1	2	(1	1)	50	20	15	14	14	0	32	1	1	1		2	1	.67	3	.221	.288	.325
2001	2 Tms		77	238	53	17	3	1	(0	1)	79	22	19	21	21	0	65	1	2	0		8	5	.62	7	.223	.288	.332
2002	Cle	AL	98	325	81	18	3	9	(4	5)	132	48	38	40	32	2	58	0	1	0		6	3	.67	12	.249	.317	.406
2003	Cle	AL	101	377	121	34	2	10	(4	6)	189	61	56	77	64	8	73	5	0	5		17	7	.71	10	.321	.421	.501
2004	LAD	NL	141	510	138	24	0	19	(8	11)	219	72	67	70	71	3	123	6	3	1		15	11	.58	12	.267	.362	.424
2005	LAD	NL	75	283	82	14	1	13	(6	7)	137	49	38	40	25	1	47	2	4	1		6	1	.86	6	.290	.350	.484
2006	Oak	AL	96	351	97	14	2	14	(7	7)	157	53	52	60	51	1	65	2	0	1		10	2	.83	13	.276	.370	.447
2007	2 Tms		61	209	64	9	1	13	(7	6)	114	37	37	42	31	3	41	3	0	1		5	2	.71	5	.306	.402	.545
01	Mon	NL	67	220	49	16	3	1	(0	1)	74	19	19	20	19	0	62	1	2	0		7	4	.64	6	.223	.288	.336
01	Cle	AL	10	18	4	1	0	0	(0	0)	5	3	0	1	2	0	3	0	0	0		1	1	.50	1	.222	.300	.278
07	Oak	AL	19	65	19	4	0	2	(1	1)	29	6	7	10	8	1	14	1	0	1		2	1	.67	2	.292	.373	.446
07	SD	NL	42	144	45	5	1	11	(6	5)	85	31	30	32	23	2	27	2	0	0		3	1	.75	3	.313	.414	.590
8 ML YEARS			691	2453	670	138	13	81	(37	44)	1077	362	322	364	309	18	504	20	11	10		69	32	.68	68	.273	.358	.439

Russell Branyan

Bats: L Throws: R Pos: PH-44; 3B-34; LF-13; 1B-4; DH-3   Ht: 6'3" Wt: 195 Born: 12/19/1975 Age: 32

			BATTING																			BASERUNNING				AVERAGES		
Year	Team	Lg	G	AB	H	2B	3B	HR	(Hm	Rd)	TB	R	RBI	RC	TBB	IBB	SO	HBP	SH	SF		SB	CS	SB%	GDP	Avg	OBP	Slg
2007	Buffalo*	AAA	1	4	0	0	0	0	(-	-)	0	0	0	0	0	0	3	0	0	0		0	0	-	0	.000	.000	.000
1998	Cle	AL	1	4	0	0	0	0	(0	0)	0	0	0	0	0	0	2	0	0	0		0	0	-	0	.000	.000	.000
1999	Cle	AL	11	38	8	2	0	1	(0	1)	13	4	6	4	3	0	19	1	0	0		0	0	-	0	.211	.286	.342
2000	Cle	AL	67	193	46	7	2	16	(13	3)	105	32	38	34	22	1	76	4	0	1		0	0	-	2	.238	.327	.544
2001	Cle	AL	113	315	73	16	2	20	(11	9)	153	48	54	50	38	1	132	3	0	5		1	1	.50	2	.232	.316	.486
2002	2 Tms		134	378	86	13	1	24	(5	19)	173	50	56	49	51	3	151	2	0	4		4	3	.57	5	.228	.320	.458
2003	Cin	NL	74	176	38	12	0	9	(7	2)	77	22	26	23	27	0	69	1	0	1		0	0	-	1	.216	.322	.438
2004	Mil	NL	51	158	37	11	1	11	(8	3)	83	21	27	23	20	0	68	2	0	1		1	0	1.00	1	.234	.324	.525
2005	Mil	NL	85	202	52	11	0	12	(3	9)	99	23	31	38	39	10	80	0	1	0		1	0	1.00	3	.257	.378	.490
2006	2 Tms		91	241	55	11	0	18	(9	9)	120	37	36	34	34	1	89	3	1	3		2	0	1.00	1	.228	.327	.498
2007	3 Tms		89	163	32	5	1	10	(6	4)	69	22	26	23	28	1	69	2	0	1		1	0	1.00	2	.196	.320	.423
02	Cle	AL	50	161	33	4	0	8	(1	7)	61	16	17	14	17	0	65	0	0	2		1	2	.33	3	.205	.278	.379
02	Cin	NL	84	217	53	9	1	16	(4	12)	112	34	39	35	34	3	86	2	0	2		3	1	.75	2	.244	.349	.516
06	TB	AL	64	169	34	10	0	12	(7	5)	80	23	27	22	19	0	62	2	1	2		2	0	1.00	1	.201	.286	.473
06	SD	NL	27	72	21	1	0	6	(2	4)	40	14	9	12	15	1	27	1	0	1		0	0	-	0	.292	.416	.556
07	SD	NL	61	122	24	5	1	7	(5	2)	52	16	19	18	21	1	48	2	0	1		1	0	1.00	2	.197	.322	.426
07	Phl	NL	7	9	2	0	0	2	(0	2)	8	2	5	2	0	0	6	0	0	0		0	0	-	0	.222	.222	.889
07	StL	NL	21	32	6	0	0	1	(1	0)	9	4	2	3	7	0	15	0	0	0		0	0	-	0	.188	.333	.281
10 ML YEARS			716	1868	427	88	7	121	(62	59)	892	259	300	278	262	17	755	18	2	17		10	4	.71	17	.229	.327	.478

Ryan Braun

Bats: R **Throws:** R **Pos:** 3B-112; PH-1   **Ht:** 6'2" **Wt:** 200 **Born:** 11/17/1983 **Age:** 24

								BATTING												BASERUNNING				AVERAGES		
Year	Team	Lg	G	AB	H	2B	3B	HR	(Hm Rd)	TB	R	RBI	RC	TBB	IBB	SO	HBP	SH	SF	SB	CS	SB%	GDP	Avg	OBP	Slg
2005	Helena	R+	10	41	14	2	1	2	(- -)	24	6	10	9	2	0	6	2	0	2	2	1	.67	0	.341	.383	.585
2005	WV	A	37	152	54	16	2	8	(- -)	98	21	35	35	9	1	34	2	2	1	2	4	.33	7	.355	.396	.645
2006	BrvdCt	A+	59	226	62	12	2	7	(- -)	99	34	37	37	23	1	54	4	3	4	14	4	.78	3	.274	.346	.438
2006	Hntsvl	AA	59	231	70	19	1	15	(- -)	136	42	40	51	21	1	46	3	1	1	12	0	1.00	6	.303	.367	.589
2007	Nashv	AAA	34	117	40	12	0	10	(- -)	82	28	22	31	15	0	11	1	0	1	4	3	.57	1	.342	.418	.701
2007	Mil	NL	113	451	146	26	6	34	(17 17)	286	91	97	94	29	1	112	7	0	5	15	5	.75	13	.324	.370	.634

Ryan Braun

Pitches: R **Bats:** R **Pos:** RP-26   **Ht:** 6'1" **Wt:** 220 **Born:** 7/29/1980 **Age:** 27

			HOW MUCH HE PITCHED						WHAT HE GAVE UP												THE RESULTS							
Year	Team	Lg	G	GS	CG	GF	IP	BFP	H	R	ER	HR	SH	SF	HB	TBB	IBB	SO	WP	Bk	W	L	Pct	ShO	Sv-Op	Hld	ERC	ERA
2003	Royals	R	18	0	0	13	21.1	90	15	9	7	0	0	0	0	10	0	25	0	0	0	0	-	0	3- -	-	2.06	2.95
2004	Wilmg	A+	51	0	0	42	57.0	248	48	25	14	2	1	0	3	25	4	58	4	0	2	3	.400	0	23- -	-	2.92	2.21
2005	Wichta	AA	6	0	0	3	4.2	35	15	10	9	0	0	0	0	7	1	1	1	0	1	0	.000	0	0- -	-	23.82	17.36
2005	Hi Dsrt	A+	2	0	0	0	4.0	16	3	2	2	0	0	0	0	2	0	6	0	0	1	0	1.000	0	0- -	-	2.58	4.50
2006	Wichta	AA	26	0	0	22	40.2	170	30	11	10	2	3	0	4	16	3	58	2	0	1	6	.143	0	10- -	-	2.56	2.21
2006	Omha	AAA	17	0	0	11	25.0	109	23	9	6	0	2	1	0	13	2	22	0	0	2	0	.000	0	3- -	-	3.23	2.16
2007	Omha	AAA	23	0	0	20	33.0	123	19	7	4	1	1	0	0	12	1	36	1	0	2	2	.500	0	9- -	-	1.54	1.09
2006	KC	AL	9	0	0	2	10.2	46	13	8	8	2	1	1	0	3	0	6	0	0	0	1	.000	0	0-2	0	5.63	6.75
2007	KC	AL	26	0	0	10	39.1	183	46	32	29	4	2	5	0	22	1	24	3	0	2	0	1.000	0	0-0	1	5.64	6.64
	2 ML YEARS		35	0	0	12	50.0	229	59	40	37	6	3	6	0	25	1	30	3	0	2	1	.667	0	0-2	1	5.65	6.66

Bill Bray

Pitches: L **Bats:** L **Pos:** RP-19   **Ht:** 6'3" **Wt:** 222 **Born:** 6/5/1983 **Age:** 25

			HOW MUCH HE PITCHED						WHAT HE GAVE UP												THE RESULTS							
Year	Team	Lg	G	GS	CG	GF	IP	BFP	H	R	ER	HR	SH	SF	HB	TBB	IBB	SO	WP	Bk	W	L	Pct	ShO	Sv-Op	Hld	ERC	ERA
2004	BrvdCt	A+	6	0	0	4	7.1	32	9	5	4	0	0	0	0	1	0	6	0	0	0	2	.000	0	1- -	-	3.51	4.91
2005	Ptomc	A+	8	0	0	5	12.2	50	8	3	3	1	0	0	0	3	0	18	0	0	1	0	1.000	0	3- -	-	1.53	2.13
2005	Hrsbrg	AA	3	0	0	1	5.2	27	10	4	4	1	0	0	0	1	0	6	0	0	1	0	1.000	0	1- -	-	8.61	6.35
2005	NewOr	AAA	23	0	0	12	21.1	99	23	16	12	3	2	2	2	9	3	25	1	0	1	4	.200	0	2- -	-	4.87	5.06
2006	NewOr	AAA	21	0	0	7	31.2	131	26	14	14	3	1	0	0	2	0	45	0	0	4	1	.800	0	5- -	-	3.25	3.98
2007	Srsota	A+	2	0	0	0	2.0	6	0	0	0	0	0	0	0	1	0	2	0	0	0	0	-	0	0- -	-	0.32	0.00
2007	Lsvlle	AAA	18	0	0	1	19.0	84	19	10	9	1	1	0	0	6	1	29	1	0	1	2	.333	0	0- -	-	3.17	4.26
2006	2 Tms	NL	48	0	0	10	50.2	223	57	27	23	5	2	1	1	18	3	39	0	0	3	2	.600	0	2-3	3	4.58	4.09
2007	Cin	NL	19	0	0	5	14.1	63	16	10	10	1	0	1	0	5	1	14	0	0	3	3	.500	0	1-1	3	4.16	6.28
06	Was	NL	19	0	0	4	23.0	100	24	11	10	2	1	1	1	9	2	16	0	0	1	1	.500	0	0-0	1	4.25	3.91
06	Cin	NL	29	0	0	6	27.2	123	33	16	13	3	1	0	0	9	1	23	0	0	2	1	.667	0	2-3	2	4.85	4.23
	2 ML YEARS		67	0	0	15	65.0	286	73	37	33	6	2	2	1	23	4	53	0	0	6	5	.545	0	3-4	6	4.48	4.57

Craig Brazell

Bats: L **Throws:** R **Pos:** PH-4; 1B-1   **Ht:** 6'3" **Wt:** 210 **Born:** 5/10/1980 **Age:** 28

								BATTING												BASERUNNING				AVERAGES		
Year	Team	Lg	G	AB	H	2B	3B	HR	(Hm Rd)	TB	R	RBI	RC	TBB	IBB	SO	HBP	SH	SF	SB	CS	SB%	GDP	Avg	OBP	Slg
1998	Mets	R	13	47	14	3	1	1	(- -)	22	6	6	7	2	0	13	1	0	0	0	0	-	0	.298	.340	.468
1999	Kngspt	R+	59	221	85	16	1	6	(- -)	121	27	39	45	7	4	34	8	2	1	6	5	.55	5	.385	.422	.548
2000	Clmbia	A	112	406	98	28	0	8	(- -)	150	35	57	39	15	1	82	9	1	8	3	3	.50	6	.241	.279	.369
2001	Clmbia	A	83	331	102	25	5	19	(- -)	194	51	72	61	15	3	74	5	0	5	3		.00	3	.308	.343	.586
2002	StLuci	A+	100	402	107	25	3	16	(- -)	186	38	82	52	13	3	78	6	0	10	2	1	.67	7	.266	.292	.463
2002	Bnghtn	AA	35	130	40	8	0	6	(- -)	66	14	19	20	1	0	28	6	0	0	2	0		2	.308	.343	.508
2003	Bnghtn	AA	111	432	126	23	2	17	(- -)	204	58	76	66	23	4	97	6	0	7	2	1	.67	4	.292	.331	.472
2003	Norfolk	AAA	12	46	12	3	0	0	(- -)	15	4	1	4	1	1	8	1	0		1	0	1.00		.261	.292	.326
2004	Norfolk	AAA	121	475	126	22	2	23	(- -)	221	66	67	63	21	5	99	3	5	1	2	2	.33	5	.265	.300	.465
2005	Norfolk	AAA	52	173	43	11	2	6	(- -)	76	22	28	23	13	3	32	0	1	0	2	0	1.00	4	.249	.301	.439
2006	Jaxnvl	AA	117	421	104	26	1	21	(- -)	195	56	61	57	19	1	93	4	0	4	1	0	1.00	19	.247	.283	.463
2007	Wichta	AA	30	109	38	5	0	7	(- -)	64	15	15	24	11	1	19	0	0	0	0	0	-	0	.349	.408	.587
2007	Omha	AAA	105	433	133	33	0	32	(- -)	262	68	76	85	20	2	83	0	1				.00	12	.307	.337	.605
2004	NYM	NL	24	34	9	2	0	1	(1 0)	14	3	3	2	1	0	7	0	0	0	0	0		1	.265	.286	.412
2007	KC	AL	5	4	1	0	0	0	(0 0)	1	1	0	0	1	0	1	0	0	0	0	0	-	0	.250	.400	.250
	2 ML YEARS		29	38	10	2	0	1	(1 0)	15	4	3	2	2	0	8	0	0	0	0	0	-	1	.263	.300	.395

Yhency Brazoban

Pitches: R **Bats:** R **Pos:** RP-4   **Ht:** 6'1" **Wt:** 250 **Born:** 6/11/1980 **Age:** 28

			HOW MUCH HE PITCHED						WHAT HE GAVE UP												THE RESULTS							
Year	Team	Lg	G	GS	CG	GF	IP	BFP	H	R	ER	HR	SH	SF	HB	TBB	IBB	SO	WP	Bk	W	L	Pct	ShO	Sv-Op	Hld	ERC	ERA
2007	InldEm*	A+	3	3	0	0	4.1	20	4	5	1	0	0	0	0	2	0	5	0	0	0	1	.000	0	0- -	-	2.92	2.08
2007	LsVgs*	AAA	11	0	0	5	13.2	48	6	3	3	2	0	0	0	3	0	14	0	0	0	0	-	0	3- -	-	1.23	1.98
2004	LAD	NL	31	0	0	10	32.2	133	25	9	9	2	4	0	0	15	2	27	1	0	6	2	.750	0	2-6		2.76	2.48
2005	LAD	NL	74	0	0	44	72.2	317	70	46	43	11	7	2	5	32	4	61	1	0	4	10	.286	0	21-27	8	4.60	5.33
2006	LAD	NL	5	0	0	2	5.0	23	7	3	3	0	0	1	0	2	0	4	1	0	0	0	-	0	0-1	0	5.74	5.40
2007	LAD	NL	4	0	0	1	1.2	12	3	4	3	0	0	0	0	3	1	5	0	0	0	0	-	0	0-0	0	11.51	16.20
	4 ML YEARS		114	0	0	57	112.0	485	105	62	58	13	11	3	5	52	7	97	3	0	10	12	.455	0	21-28	13	4.19	4.66

Chris Britton

Pitches: R **Bats:** R **Pos:** RP-11   **Ht:** 6'3" **Wt:** 275 **Born:** 12/16/1982 **Age:** 25

			HOW MUCH HE PITCHED						WHAT HE GAVE UP											THE RESULTS					
Year	Team	Lg	G	GS	CG	GF	IP	BFP	H	R	ER	HR	SH	SF	HB	TBB	IBB	SO	WP	Bk	W	L	Pct	ShO	Sv-Op Hld	ERC	ERA
2001	Orioles	R	12	3	0	2	32.2	153	35	20	10	3	2	2	5	12	1	20	1	0	2	3	.400	0	0-- -	4.63	2.76
2002	Bluefld	R+	9	8	0	1	35.2	145	30	21	18	5	1	2	0	10	0	27	0	0	3	0	1.000	0	0-- -	3.01	4.54
2004	Dlmrva	A	27	8	1	3	84.0	356	76	38	35	11	2	3	2	31	2	80	2	0	9	4	.692	0	0-- -	3.68	3.75
2005	Frdrck	A+	46	0	0	15	78.2	298	47	15	14	5	0	0	1	23	0	110	1	0	6	1	.000	0	6-- -	1.60	1.60
2006	Bowie	AA	13	0	0	4	16.0	67	14	5	5	0	1	0	0	6	1	24	0	0	1	0	1.000	0	2-- -	2.54	2.81
2007	S-WB	AAA	37	0	0	17	57.1	233	51	19	16	3	1	2	0	14	0	58	0	0	4	2	.667	0	8-- -	2.60	2.51
2006	Bal	AL	52	0	0	12	53.2	221	46	22	20	4	1	1	0	17	3	41	0	0	0	2	.000	0	1-3 6	2.74	3.35
2007	NYY	AL	11	0	0	4	12.2	51	9	5	5	2	1	0	0	4	0	5	0	0	0	1	.000	0	0-0 0	2.55	3.55
	2 ML YEARS		63	0	0	16	66.1	272	55	27	25	6	2	1	0	21	3	46	0	0	0	3	.000	0	1-3 6	2.71	3.39

Lance Broadway

Pitches: R **Bats:** R **Pos:** RP-3; SP-1   **Ht:** 6'2" **Wt:** 210 **Born:** 8/20/1983 **Age:** 24

			HOW MUCH HE PITCHED						WHAT HE GAVE UP											THE RESULTS					
Year	Team	Lg	G	GS	CG	GF	IP	BFP	H	R	ER	HR	SH	SF	HB	TBB	IBB	SO	WP	Bk	W	L	Pct	ShO	Sv-Op Hld	ERC	ERA
2005	WinSa	A+	11	11	0	0	55.0	253	68	31	28	4	4	0	7	20	0	58	2	0	1	3	.250	0	0-- -	5.64	4.58
2006	Brham	AA	25	25	2	0	154.1	659	160	59	47	10	9	5	10	40	0	111	11	0	8	8	.500	1	0-- -	3.74	2.74
2006	Charltt	AAA	2	2	1	0	9.2	40	8	4	4	1	0	0	0	3	0	13	1	0	0	0	-	0	0-- -	2.78	3.72
2007	Charltt	AAA	27	27	2	0	155.0	684	155	86	80	17	7	4	8	78	2	108	12	0	8	9	.471	0	0-- -	4.79	4.65
2007	CWS	AL	4	1	0	1	10.1	41	5	2	1	0	0	1	0	5	0	14	0	0	1	1	.500	0	0-0 0	1.34	0.87

Doug Brocail

Pitches: R **Bats:** L **Pos:** RP-67   **Ht:** 6'5" **Wt:** 250 **Born:** 5/16/1967 **Age:** 41

			HOW MUCH HE PITCHED						WHAT HE GAVE UP											THE RESULTS					
Year	Team	Lg	G	GS	CG	GF	IP	BFP	H	R	ER	HR	SH	SF	HB	TBB	IBB	SO	WP	Bk	W	L	Pct	ShO	Sv-Op Hld	ERC	ERA
2007	Lk Els*	A+	1	1	0	0	2.0	8	2	0	0	0	0	0	0	0	0	3	0	0	0	0	-	0	0-- -	1.95	0.00
1992	SD	NL	3	3	0	0	14.0	64	17	10	10	2	2	0	0	5	0	15	0	0	0	0	-	0	0-0 0	5.33	6.43
1993	SD	NL	24	24	0	0	128.1	571	143	75	65	16	10	8	4	42	4	70	4	1	4	13	.235	0	0-0 0	4.60	4.56
1994	SD	NL	12	0	0	4	17.0	78	21	13	11	1	1	1	2	5	3	11	1	1	0	0	-	0	0-1 0	4.79	5.82
1995	Hou	NL	36	7	0	12	77.1	339	87	40	36	10	1	1	4	22	2	39	1	1	6	4	.600	0	1-1 0	4.68	4.19
1996	Hou	NL	23	4	0	4	53.0	231	58	31	27	7	3	2	2	23	1	34	0	0	1	5	.167	0	0-0 1	5.26	4.58
1997	Det	AL	61	4	0	20	78.0	332	74	31	28	10	1	3	4	36	4	60	6	0	3	4	.429	0	2-9 16	4.42	3.23
1998	Det	AL	60	0	0	24	62.2	247	47	23	19	2	2	3	1	18	3	55	6	0	5	2	.714	0	0-1 11	1.99	2.73
1999	Det	AL	70	0	0	22	82.0	326	60	23	23	7	4	2	4	25	1	78	4	1	4	4	.500	0	2-4 23	2.43	2.52
2000	Det	AL	49	0	0	10	50.2	221	57	25	23	5	3	3	1	14	2	41	1	1	5	4	.556	0	0-5 19	4.35	4.09
2004	Tex	AL	43	0	0	14	52.1	232	54	29	24	2	4	2	5	20	1	43	2	1	4	1	.800	0	1-1 4	4.05	4.13
2005	Tex	AL	61	0	0	13	73.1	344	90	45	45	2	3	4	4	34	3	61	4	0	5	3	.626	0	1-4 5	5.15	5.52
2006	SD	NL	25	0	0	6	28.1	119	27	16	15	1	3	1	0	8	2	19	1	0	2	2	.500	0	0-0 0	2.80	4.76
2007	SD	NL	67	0	0	16	76.2	319	66	33	26	8	2	1	2	24	3	43	2	0	5	1	.833	0	0-0 10	3.03	3.05
	13 ML YEARS		534	42	0	145	793.2	3423	801	397	352	73	39	31	32	276	29	569	32	6	44	43	.506	0	7-26 89	3.96	3.99

Ben Broussard

Bats: L **Throws:** L **Pos:** 1B-52; PH-29; RF-12; LF-10; DH-2   **Ht:** 6'2" **Wt:** 220 **Born:** 9/24/1976 **Age:** 31

			BATTING																BASERUNNING				AVERAGES		
Year	Team	Lg	G	AB	H	2B	3B	HR	(Hm | Rd)	TB	R	RBI	RC	TBB	IBB	SO	HBP	SH	SF	SB	CS	SB%	GDP	Avg	OBP	Slg
2002	Cle	AL	39	112	27	4	0	4	(2 | 2)	43	10	9	9	7	1	25	1	0	0	0	0	-	3	.241	.292	.384
2003	Cle	AL	116	386	96	21	3	16	(7 | 9)	171	53	55	53	32	2	75	5	3	3	5	2	.71	6	.249	.312	.443
2004	Cle	AL	139	418	115	28	5	17	(9 | 8)	204	57	82	79	52	3	95	12	1	2	4	2	.67	7	.275	.370	.488
2005	Cle	AL	142	466	119	30	5	19	(11 | 8)	216	59	68	60	32	5	98	4	0	3	2	2	.50	4	.255	.307	.464
2006	2 Tms	AL	144	432	125	21	0	21	(12 | 9)	209	61	63	64	26	3	103	3	0	4	2	1	.67	8	.289	.331	.484
2007	Sea	AL	99	240	66	10	0	7	(4 | 3)	97	27	29	30	17	2	50	4	0	3	2	0	1.00	7	.275	.330	.404
06	Cle	AL	88	268	86	14	0	13	(11 | 2)	139	44	46	48	17	1	58	1	0	2	0	1	.00	5	.321	.361	.519
06	Sea	AL	56	164	39	7	0	8	(1 | 7)	70	17	17	16	9	2	45	2	0	2	2	0	1.00	3	.238	.282	.427
	6 ML YEARS		679	2054	548	114	13	84	(45 | 39)	940	267	306	295	166	16	446	29	4	15	15	7	.68	35	.267	.328	.458

Jim Brower

Pitches: R **Bats:** R **Pos:** RP-3   **Ht:** 6'3" **Wt:** 215 **Born:** 12/29/1972 **Age:** 35

			HOW MUCH HE PITCHED						WHAT HE GAVE UP											THE RESULTS					
Year	Team	Lg	G	GS	CG	GF	IP	BFP	H	R	ER	HR	SH	SF	HB	TBB	IBB	SO	WP	Bk	W	L	Pct	ShO	Sv-Op Hld	ERC	ERA
2007	Indy*	AAA	6	0	0	5	7.1	32	9	3	3	0	0	0	2	0	0	4	0	0	1	0	1.000	0	1-- -	4.15	3.68
2007	S-WB*	AAA	38	0	0	34	47.2	194	44	12	12	2	2	0	6	13	0	45	2	0	4	2	.667	0	21-- -	3.41	2.27
1999	Cle	AL	9	2	0	1	25.2	113	27	13	13	8	1	1	1	10	1	18	0	0	3	1	.750	0	0-0 0	5.96	4.56
2000	Cle	AL	17	11	0	1	62.0	293	80	45	43	11	1	0	2	31	1	32	3	0	2	3	.400	0	0-0 0	6.95	6.24
2001	Cin	NL	46	10	0	13	129.1	559	119	65	57	17	9	3	5	60	5	94	5	1	7	10	.412	0	1-2 0	4.21	3.97
2002	2 Tms	NL	52	0	0	23	80.1	344	77	40	39	7	2	1	4	32	2	57	1	0	3	2	.600	0	0-1 6	3.94	4.37
2003	SF	NL	51	5	0	13	100.0	411	90	48	44	8	5	4	1	39	2	65	4	0	8	5	.615	0	2-3 2	3.46	3.96
2004	SF	NL	89	0	0	21	93.0	401	90	42	34	6	11	2	4	36	2	63	10	0	7	7	.500	0	1-5 24	3.72	3.29
2005	2 Tms	NL	69	0	0	12	60.1	282	73	36	36	11	2	1	5	32	3	53	4	0	3	3	.500	0	1-3 12	6.86	5.37
2006	2 Tms	NL	18	0	0	4	20.0	106	32	27	27	2	0	1	5	14	1	14	2	0	0	1	.000	0	0-1 1	10.42	12.15
2007	NYY	AL	3	0	0	0	3.1	21	8	7	5	0	0	2	1	2	0	1	0	0	0	0	-	0	0-0 1	14.45	13.50
02	Cin	NL	22	0	0	11	39.1	158	38	18	17	2	1	1	0	10	1	24	0	0	2	0	1.000	0	0-0 0	3.08	3.89
02	Mon	NL	30	0	0	12	41.0	186	39	22	22	5	1	0	4	22	1	33	1	0	1	2	.333	0	0-1 6	4.79	4.83
05	SF	NL	32	0	0	8	30.1	144	40	22	22	5	1	1	2	15	0	25	2	0	2	1	.667	0	1-3 5	7.24	6.53

Year	Team	Lg	G	GS	CG	GF	IP	BFP	H	R	ER	HR	SH	SF	HB	TBB	IBB	SO	WP	Bk	W	L	Pct	ShO	Sv-Op	Hld	ERC	ERA
			HOW MUCH HE PITCHED						**WHAT HE GAVE UP**												**THE RESULTS**							
05	Atl	NL	37	0	0	4	30.0	138	33	14	14	6	1	0	3	17	3	28	2	0	1	2	.333	0	0-0	7	6.47	4.20
06	Bal	AL	12	0	0	1	12.1	71	21	19	19	1	0	1	3	13	1	9	2	0	0	1	.000	0	0-1	1	12.48	13.86
06	SD	NL	6	0	0	3	7.2	35	11	8	8	1	0	0	2	1	0	5	0	0	0	0	-	0	0-0	0	7.15	9.39
9 ML YEARS			354	28	0	88	574.0	2530	596	323	298	70	31	15	28	256	17	397	29	1	33	32	.508	0	5-15	48	4.82	4.67

Andrew Brown

Pitches: R **Bats:** R **Pos:** RP-33 **Ht:** 6'6" **Wt:** 230 **Born:** 2/17/1981 **Age:** 27

Year	Team	Lg	G	GS	CG	GF	IP	BFP	H	R	ER	HR	SH	SF	HB	TBB	IBB	SO	WP	Bk	W	L	Pct	ShO	Sv-Op	Hld	ERC	ERA
			HOW MUCH HE PITCHED						**WHAT HE GAVE UP**												**THE RESULTS**							
1999	Braves	R	11	11	0	0	42.1	183	40	15	11	4	1	0	3	16	0	57	1	4	1	1	.500	0	0- -		3.90	2.34
2001	Jmstwn	A-	14	12	0	0	64.1	267	50	29	28	5	0	0	3	31	0	59	5	0	3	4	.429	0	0- -		3.27	3.92
2002	VeroB	A+	25	24	1	0	127.0	530	97	63	58	13	3	6	8	62	0	129	9	3	10	10	.500	1	0- -		3.44	4.11
2003	Jaxnvl	AA	1	1	0	0	1.0	3	0	0	0	0	0	0	0	0	0	1	0	0	0	0	-	0	0- -		0.00	0.00
2004	Jaxnvl	AA	8	8	0	0	40.1	173	36	23	18	5	3	1	2	14	0	58	3	0	1	3	.250	0	0- -		3.56	4.02
2004	Akron	AA	17	17	0	0	77.1	335	66	44	40	7	7	7	3	36	1	67	4	0	3	6	.333	0	0- -		3.53	4.66
2004	Buffalo	AAA	1	1	0	0	5.0	21	4	0	0	0	0	0	0	3	0	4	1	0	1	0	1.000	0	0- -		3.13	0.00
2005	Buffalo	AAA	49	0	0	21	69.2	279	52	28	26	7	0	2	3	19	0	81	4	0	4	2	.667	0	4- -		2.44	3.36
2006	Buffalo	AAA	39	0	0	17	62.1	276	52	21	18	5	5	3	4	36	1	53	9	0	5	4	.556	0	5- -		3.87	2.60
2007	Portlnd	AAA	32	0	0	7	35.2	148	26	14	11	3	1	0	2	15	0	43	5	0	2	3	.400	0	0- -		2.80	2.78
2007	Scrmto	AAA	5	0	0	4	5.0	21	6	2	2	1	0	0	1	0	0	6	0	0	0	0	-	0	4- -		5.26	3.60
2006	Cle	AL	9	0	0	4	10.0	44	6	4	4	0	0	0	1	8	1	7	1	0	0	0	-	0	0-0	0	2.87	3.60
2007	Oak	AL	33	0	0	5	41.2	178	38	21	21	1	2	1	3	17	3	43	6	0	3	3	.500	0	0-2	3	3.27	4.54
2 ML YEARS			42	0	0	9	51.2	222	44	25	25	1	2	1	4	25	4	50	7	0	3	3	.500	0	0-2	3	3.20	4.35

Dee Brown

Bats: L **Throws:** R **Pos:** LF-4; RF-4 **Ht:** 6'0" **Wt:** 220 **Born:** 3/27/1978 **Age:** 30

Year	Team	Lg	G	AB	H	2B	3B	HR	(Hm	Rd)	TB	R	RBI	RC	TBB	IBB	SO	HBP	SH	SF	SB	CS	SB%	GDP	Avg	OBP	Slg
			BATTING																		**BASERUNNING**				**AVERAGES**		
2007	Tucsn*	AAA	41	131	37	7	0	2	(-	-)	50	25	24	18	13	0	24	1	0	0	1	1	.50	4	.282	.352	.382
2007	Scrmto*	AAA	62	245	73	14	0	14	(-	-)	129	47	54	47	24	0	52	2	0	6	2	0	1.00	4	.298	.357	.527
1998	KC	AL	5	3	0	0	0	0	(0	0)	0	2	0	0	0	0	1	0	0	0	0	0	-	0	.000	.000	.000
1999	KC	AL	12	25	2	0	0	0	(0	0)	2	1	0	0	2	0	7	0	0	0	0	0	-	0	.080	.148	.080
2000	KC	AL	15	25	4	1	0	0	(0	0)	5	4	4	1	3	0	9	0	0	0	0	0	-	0	.160	.250	.200
2001	KC	AL	106	380	93	19	0	7	(4	3)	133	39	40	34	22	4	81	1	1	2	5	3	.63	12	.245	.286	.350
2002	KC	AL	16	51	12	3	1	1	(0	1)	20	5	7	4	4	0	20	0	0	0	0	0	-	0	.235	.291	.392
2003	KC	AL	50	132	30	7	0	2	(1	1)	43	16	14	15	8	1	37	2	0	1	1	1	.50	0	.227	.280	.326
2004	KC	AL	59	195	49	7	0	4	(2	2)	68	19	24	21	11	0	50	1	1	1	2	2	.50	1	.251	.293	.349
2007	Oak	AL	8	3	0	0	0	0	(0	0)	0	0	0	0	0	0	2	0	0	0	0	0	-	0	.000	.000	.000
8 ML YEARS			271	814	190	37	1	14	(7	7)	271	86	89	75	50	5	207	4	2	4	8	6	.57	13	.233	.280	.333

Emil Brown

Bats: R **Throws:** R **Pos:** LF-78; RF-21; DH-11; PH-8; PR-7 **Ht:** 6'2" **Wt:** 210 **Born:** 12/29/1974 **Age:** 33

Year	Team	Lg	G	AB	H	2B	3B	HR	(Hm	Rd)	TB	R	RBI	RC	TBB	IBB	SO	HBP	SH	SF	SB	CS	SB%	GDP	Avg	OBP	Slg
			BATTING																		**BASERUNNING**				**AVERAGES**		
1997	Pit	NL	66	95	17	2	1	2	(1	1)	27	16	6	9	10	1	32	7	0	0	5	1	.83	1	.179	.304	.284
1998	Pit	NL	13	39	10	1	0	0	(0	0)	11	2	3	3	1	0	11	1	0	0	0	0	-	0	.256	.293	.282
1999	Pit	NL	6	14	2	1	0	0	(0	0)	3	0	0	0	0	0	3	0	0	0	0	0	-	0	.143	.143	.214
2000	Pit	NL	50	119	26	5	0	3	(2	1)	40	13	16	11	11	0	34	3	1	1	3	1	.75	3	.218	.299	.336
2001	2 Tms	NL	74	137	26	4	1	3	(2	1)	41	21	13	12	16	1	49	2	0	0	12	4	.75	2	.190	.284	.299
2005	KC	AL	150	545	156	31	5	17	(8	9)	248	75	86	91	48	1	108	8	1	7	10	1	.91	14	.286	.349	.455
2006	KC	AL	147	527	151	41	2	15	(6	9)	241	77	81	79	59	3	95	5	0	10	6	3	.67	15	.287	.358	.457
2007	KC	AL	113	366	94	13	1	6	(1	5)	127	44	62	49	24	2	71	1	0	6	12	2	.86	7	.257	.300	.347
01	Pit	NL	61	123	25	4	1	3	(2	1)	40	18	13	12	15	1	42	2	0	0	10	4	.71	2	.203	.300	.325
01	SD	NL	13	14	1	0	0	0	(0	0)	1	3	0	0	1	0	7	0	0	0	2	0	1.00	0	.071	.133	.071
8 ML YEARS			619	1842	482	98	10	46	(20	26)	738	248	267	254	169	8	403	27	2	24	48	12	.80	42	.262	.329	.401

Matt Brown

Bats: R **Throws:** R **Pos:** 3B-4; PH-1 **Ht:** 6'0" **Wt:** 200 **Born:** 8/8/1982 **Age:** 25

Year	Team	Lg	G	AB	H	2B	3B	HR	(Hm	Rd)	TB	R	RBI	RC	TBB	IBB	SO	HBP	SH	SF	SB	CS	SB%	GDP	Avg	OBP	Slg
			BATTING																		**BASERUNNING**				**AVERAGES**		
2001	Angels	R	46	141	23	7	1	1	(-	-)	35	14	21	9	18	1	30	5	1	3	1	3	.25	1	.163	.275	.248
2002	Angels	R	28	97	35	7	0	2	(-	-)	48	16	22	22	15	0	14	1	0	2	3	1	.75	2	.361	.443	.495
2002	Provo	R+	32	108	32	5	1	0	(-	-)	39	14	11	17	15	0	21	5	0	0	3	3	.50	3	.296	.406	.361
2003	CRpds	A	49	164	34	6	1	3	(-	-)	51	22	15	17	19	0	36	5	0	1	1	0	1.00	4	.207	.307	.311
2003	Provo	R+	65	233	68	19	0	11	(-	-)	120	58	52	51	42	2	56	9	0	5	2	3	.40	1	.292	.412	.515
2004	CRpds	A	122	437	102	20	4	23	(-	-)	199	67	82	62	33	1	126	13	2	5	6	6	.50	4	.233	.303	.455
2005	RCuca	A+	125	488	128	39	4	12	(-	-)	211	68	65	71	40	0	125	11	3	5	4	5	.44	10	.262	.329	.432
2006	Ark	AA	134	515	151	41	3	19	(-	-)	255	77	79	92	47	0	108	10	2	2	7	6	.54	8	.293	.362	.495
2007	Salt Lk	AAA	110	391	108	30	2	19	(-	-)	199	69	60	69	45	0	106	5	1	0	5	9	.36	12	.276	.358	.509
2007	LAA	AL	4	5	0	0	0	0	(0	0)	0	0	0	0	2	0	1	0	0	0	1	0	1.00	0	.000	.286	.000

Jonathan Broxton

Pitches: R **Bats:** R **Pos:** RP-83 **Ht:** 6'2" **Wt:** 290 **Born:** 6/16/1984 **Age:** 24

Year Team	Lg	G	GS	CG	GF	IP	BFP	H	R	ER	HR	SH	SF	HB	TBB	IBB	SO	WP	Bk	W	L	Pct	ShO	Sv-Op	Hld	ERC	ERA
2005 LAD	NL	14	0	0	5	13.2	68	13	11	9	0	0	2	1	12	2	22	2	0	1	0	1.000	0	0-1	1	4.65	5.93
2006 LAD	NL	68	0	0	20	76.1	320	61	25	22	7	3	1	1	33	6	97	7	0	4	1	.800	0	3-7	12	2.97	2.59
2007 LAD	NL	83	0	0	18	82.0	334	69	30	26	6	0	1	1	25	3	99	4	0	4	4	.500	0	2-8	32	2.71	2.85
3 ML YEARS		165	0	0	43	172.0	722	143	66	57	13	3	4	3	70	11	218	13	0	9	5	.643	0	5-16	45	2.98	2.98

Brian Bruney

Pitches: R **Bats:** R **Pos:** RP-58 **Ht:** 6'2" **Wt:** 245 **Born:** 2/17/1982 **Age:** 26

Year Team	Lg	G	GS	CG	GF	IP	BFP	H	R	ER	HR	SH	SF	HB	TBB	IBB	SO	WP	Bk	W	L	Pct	ShO	Sv-Op	Hld	ERC	ERA
2007 S-WB*	AAA	4	0	0	2	6.0	26	5	4	4	1	0	0	1	2	0	5	1	0	2	0	1.000	0	1--	-	3.92	6.00
2004 Ari	NL	30	0	0	14	31.1	135	20	16	15	2	1	0	1	27	5	34	2	0	3	4	.429	0	0-1	3	3.54	4.31
2005 Ari	NL	47	0	0	21	46.0	230	56	39	38	6	2	1	5	35	2	51	2	0	1	3	.250	0	12-16	4	7.48	7.43
2006 NYY	AL	19	0	0	2	20.2	90	14	2	2	1	0	0	1	15	0	25	2	0	1	1	.500	0	0-0	4	3.37	0.87
2007 NYY	AL	58	0	0	16	50.0	228	44	28	26	5	1	6	3	37	2	39	4	0	3	2	.600	0	0-2	6	4.92	4.68
4 ML YEARS		154	0	0	53	148.0	683	134	85	81	14	4	7	10	114	9	149	10	0	8	10	.444	0	12-19	17	5.14	4.93

Eric Bruntlett

Bats: R **Throws:** R **Pos:** SS-63; PR-10; PH-7; LF-4; 3B-3; CF-2; RF-1 **Ht:** 6'0" **Wt:** 190 **Born:** 3/29/1978 **Age:** 30

Year Team	Lg	G	AB	H	2B	3B	HR	(Hm	Rd)	TB	R	RBI	RC	TBB	IBB	SO	HBP	SH	SF	SB	CS	SB%	GDP	Avg	OBP	Slg
2007 RdRck*	AAA	61	227	63	9	5	1	(-	-)	85	31	21	35	31	3	36	1	2	1	13	4	.76	4	.278	.365	.374
2003 Hou	NL	31	54	14	3	0	1	(1	0)	20	3	4	5	0	0	10	0	1	1	0	0	-	1	.259	.255	.370
2004 Hou	NL	45	52	13	2	0	4	(3	1)	27	14	8	9	7	0	13	0	0	2	4	0	1.00	0	.250	.328	.519
2005 Hou	NL	91	109	24	5	2	4	(2	2)	45	19	14	12	10	0	25	1	1	0	7	2	.78	4	.220	.292	.413
2006 Hou	NL	73	119	33	8	0	0	(0	0)	41	11	10	15	13	1	21	1	2	1	3	1	.75	2	.277	.351	.345
2007 Hou	NL	80	138	34	5	0	0	(0	0)	39	16	14	19	20	1	27	1	6	0	6	3	.67	1	.246	.346	.283
5 ML YEARS		320	472	118	23	2	9	(6	3)	172	63	50	60	50	2	96	3	10	4	20	6	.77	8	.250	.323	.364

Clay Buchholz

Pitches: R **Bats:** L **Pos:** SP-3; RP-1 **Ht:** 6'3" **Wt:** 190 **Born:** 8/14/1984 **Age:** 23

Year Team	Lg	G	GS	CG	GF	IP	BFP	H	R	ER	HR	SH	SF	HB	TBB	IBB	SO	WP	Bk	W	L	Pct	ShO	Sv-Op	Hld	ERC	ERA
2005 Lowell	A-	15	15	0	0	41.1	166	34	15	12	2	0	1	4	9	0	45	0	1	0	1	.000	0	0--	-	2.24	2.61
2006 Grnville	A	21	21	0	0	103.0	411	78	34	30	10	5	3	5	29	0	117	8	1	9	4	.692	0	0--	-	2.55	2.62
2006 Wilmg	A+	3	3	0	0	16.0	61	10	4	2	0	1	0	1	4	0	20	1	0	2	0	1.000	0	0--	-	1.30	1.13
2007 Portlnd	AA	16	15	1	0	86.2	332	55	18	17	4	2	1	2	22	0	116	1	1	7	2	.778	0	0--	-	1.57	1.77
2007 Pwtckt	AAA	8	8	0	0	38.2	164	32	21	17	5	2	3	1	13	0	55	1	3	1	3	.250	0	0--	-	3.08	3.96
2007 Bos	AL	4	3	1	0	22.2	88	14	6	4	0	0	1	1	10	0	22	0	0	3	1	.750	1	0-0	0	1.90	1.59

Taylor Buchholz

Pitches: R **Bats:** R **Pos:** RP-33; SP-8 **Ht:** 6'4" **Wt:** 220 **Born:** 10/13/1981 **Age:** 26

Year Team	Lg	G	GS	CG	GF	IP	BFP	H	R	ER	HR	SH	SF	HB	TBB	IBB	SO	WP	Bk	W	L	Pct	ShO	Sv-Op	Hld	ERC	ERA
2000 Phillies	R	12	7	0	2	44.0	188	46	22	11	2	0	1	2	14	0	41	3	1	2	3	.400	0	0--	-	3.84	2.25
2001 Lakwd	A	28	26	5	0	176.2	741	165	83	66	8	5	7	11	57	0	136	1	0	9	14	.391	3	0--	-	3.32	3.36
2002 Clrwtr	A+	23	23	4	0	158.2	666	140	66	58	11	3	3	7	51	1	129	7	0	10	6	.625	2	0--	-	3.07	3.29
2002 Rdng	AA	4	4	0	0	23.0	102	29	19	19	5	2	1	1	6	0	17	0	0	2	0	.000	0	0--	-	6.14	7.43
2003 Rdng	AA	25	24	1	0	144.2	600	136	62	57	14	3	7	9	33	0	114	3	0	9	11	.450	0	0--	-	3.31	3.55
2004 NewOr	AAA	20	17	1	0	98.0	425	107	60	57	16	2	8	2	29	0	74	8	0	6	7	.462	0	0--	-	4.69	5.23
2005 RdRck	AAA	20	14	0	4	76.2	323	79	41	41	14	3	2	4	27	0	45	2	0	6	0	1.000	0	0--	-	5.03	4.81
2006 RdRck	AAA	7	7	0	0	44.0	192	47	27	24	2	3	2	1	17	0	37	0	0	1	3	.250	0	0--	-	4.11	4.91
2006 Hou	NL	22	19	1	1	113.0	479	107	80	74	21	5	6	3	34	4	77	5	0	6	10	.375	1	0-0	0	3.97	5.89
2007 Col	NL	41	8	0	6	93.2	396	105	47	44	8	5	5	2	20	4	61	3	1	6	5	.545	0	0-0	1	3.97	4.23
2 ML YEARS		63	27	1	7	206.2	875	212	127	118	29	10	11	5	54	8	138	8	1	12	15	.444	1	0-0	1	3.97	5.14

John Buck

Bats: R **Throws:** R **Pos:** C-112; PH-3 **Ht:** 6'3" **Wt:** 220 **Born:** 7/7/1980 **Age:** 27

Year Team	Lg	G	AB	H	2B	3B	HR	(Hm	Rd)	TB	R	RBI	RC	TBB	IBB	SO	HBP	SH	SF	SB	CS	SB%	GDP	Avg	OBP	Slg
2004 KC	AL	71	238	56	9	0	12	(6	6)	101	36	30	26	15	0	79	0	4	1	1	1	.50	6	.235	.280	.424
2005 KC	AL	118	401	97	21	1	12	(3	9)	156	40	47	43	23	2	94	3	1	2	2	2	.50	9	.242	.287	.389
2006 KC	AL	114	371	91	21	1	11	(6	5)	147	37	50	43	26	2	84	7	4	1	0	2	.00	7	.245	.306	.396
2007 KC	AL	113	347	77	18	0	18	(6	12)	149	41	48	37	36	0	92	10	0	6	0	1	.00	11	.222	.308	.429
4 ML YEARS		416	1357	321	69	2	53	(21	32)	553	154	175	149	100	4	349	20	9	10	3	6	.33	33	.237	.297	.408

Travis Buck

Bats: L **Throws:** R **Pos:** RF-65; LF-18; CF-5; PH-2; PR-1   **Ht:** 6'2" **Wt:** 225 **Born:** 11/18/1983 **Age:** 24

Year	Team	Lg	G	AB	H	2B	3B	HR	(Hm	-)	TB	R	RBI	RC	TBB	IBB	SO	HBP	SH	SF	SB	CS	SB%	GDP	Avg	OBP	Slg
																										BATTING												**BASERUNNING**				**AVERAGES**		
2005	Vancvr	A-	9	36	13	1	0	2	(-	-)	20	7	9	8	5	0	8	0	0	0	1	1	.50	3	.361	.439	.556
2005	Kane	A	32	123	42	13	0	1	(-	-)	58	17	22	25	19	1	19	0	1	1	3	1	.75	4	.341	.427	.472
2006	Stcktn	A+	34	126	44	17	3	3	(-	-)	76	24	26	30	14	0	18	0	0	5	2	1	.67	3	.349	.400	.603
2006	Mdland	AA	50	212	64	22	1	4	(-	-)	100	32	22	39	22	1	39	3	1	0	9	1	.90	5	.302	.376	.472
2007	Scrmto	AAA	2	7	1	0	1	0	(-	-)	3	0	1	1	2	0	2	0	0	0	0	0	-	0	.143	.333	.429
2007	Oak	AL	82	285	82	22	5	7	(3	4)	135	41	34	48	39	2	66	4	2	4	4	1	.80	9	.288	.377	.474

Billy Buckner

Pitches: R **Bats:** R **Pos:** SP-5; RP-2   **Ht:** 6'2" **Wt:** 215 **Born:** 8/27/1983 **Age:** 24

Year	Team	Lg	G	GS	CG	GF	IP	BFP	H	R	ER	HR	SH	SF	HB	TBB	IBB	SO	WP	Bk	W	L	Pct	ShO	Sv-Op	Hld	ERC	ERA
			HOW MUCH HE PITCHED						**WHAT HE GAVE UP**												**THE RESULTS**							
2004	Idaho	R+	7	5	0	0	30.0	128	36	14	11	4	2	1	4	0	0	37	3	0	2	1	.667	0	0--	-	4.51	3.30
2005	Burlgtn	A	11	11	0	0	60.1	269	66	36	26	9	1	3	2	17	0	60	3	0	3	7	.300	0	0--	-	4.45	3.88
2005	Hi Dsrt	A+	17	17	0	0	94.0	421	105	65	56	10	1	2	4	46	0	92	14	2	5	6	.455	0	0--	-	5.42	5.36
2006	Hi Dsrt	A+	16	16	0	0	90.0	397	92	44	39	6	2	4	4	47	0	85	7	0	7	1	.875	0	0--	-	4.70	3.90
2006	Wichta	AA	13	13	0	0	75.2	344	78	40	39	7	5	1	5	39	0	63	9	0	5	3	.625	0	0--	-	4.88	4.64
2007	Wichta	AA	4	3	0	1	19.1	85	20	10	10	4	0	0	0	6	0	13	1	1	1	3	.250	0	0--	-	4.49	4.66
2007	Omha	AAA	27	15	0	3	104.2	439	108	49	44	11	6	4	5	26	1	83	3	0	9	7	.563	0	0--	-	3.91	3.78
2007	KC	AL	7	5	0	1	34.0	143	37	20	20	5	0	1	0	16	0	17	0	0	1	2	.333	0	0-0	0	5.57	5.29

Ryan Budde

Bats: R **Throws:** R **Pos:** C-10; DH-2; PH-2   **Ht:** 5'11" **Wt:** 205 **Born:** 8/15/1979 **Age:** 28

Year	Team	Lg	G	AB	H	2B	3B	HR	(Hm	Rd)	TB	R	RBI	RC	TBB	IBB	SO	HBP	SH	SF	SB	CS	SB%	GDP	Avg	OBP	Slg
																										BATTING												**BASERUNNING**				**AVERAGES**		
2002	RCuca	A+	87	307	74	17	1	5	(-	-)	108	40	39	34	27	1	60	2	1	2	2	1	.67	4	.241	.305	.352
2002	Ark	AA	3	9	1	0	0	1	(-	-)	4	1	1	0	1	0	2	0	0	0	0	0	-	0	.111	.200	.444
2003	Ark	AA	96	342	73	9	1	10	(-	-)	114	45	41	34	35	1	76	2	1	2	1	1	.50	5	.213	.289	.333
2003	RCuca	A+	14	50	12	3	1	1	(-	-)	20	6	6	5	2	1	10	0	0	2	0	0	-	1	.240	.259	.400
2004	RCuca	A+	99	359	90	17	0	13	(-	-)	146	54	51	47	27	2	76	8	2	5	3	5	.38	3	.251	.313	.407
2004	Salt Lk	AAA	5	17	4	0	0	0	(-	-)	4	0	1	1	1	0	7	0	0	0	0	0	-	0	.235	.263	.235
2005	Salt Lk	AAA	58	196	45	10	3	6	(-	-)	79	26	25	21	9	0	41	1	2	0	3	1	.75	3	.230	.267	.403
2006	Salt Lk	AAA	72	215	50	15	0	8	(-	-)	89	32	33	30	22	1	55	7	0	0	1	1	.50	8	.233	.324	.414
2007	Clrwtr	A+	3	10	2	1	0	0	(-	-)	3	1	0	0	0	0	3	0	0	0	0	0	-	0	.200	.200	.300
2007	Salt Lk	AAA	47	156	46	12	0	4	(-	-)	70	21	28	26	18	0	27	1	0	2	2	2	.50	10	.295	.367	.449
2007	LAA	AL	12	18	3	1	0	0	(0	0)	4	0	1	0	0	0	6	0	0	0	0	0	-	1	.167	.167	.222

Mark Buehrle

Pitches: L **Bats:** L **Pos:** SP-30   **Ht:** 6'2" **Wt:** 220 **Born:** 3/23/1979 **Age:** 29

Year	Team	Lg	G	GS	CG	GF	IP	BFP	H	R	ER	HR	SH	SF	HB	TBB	IBB	SO	WP	Bk	W	L	Pct	ShO	Sv-Op	Hld	ERC	ERA
			HOW MUCH HE PITCHED						**WHAT HE GAVE UP**												**THE RESULTS**							
2000	CWS	AL	28	3	0	6	51.1	225	55	27	24	5	1	0	3	19	1	37	0	0	4	1	.800	0	0-2	3	4.56	4.21
2001	CWS	AL	32	32	4	0	221.1	885	188	89	81	24	9	4	8	48	2	126	1	5	16	8	.667	2	0-0	0	2.79	3.29
2002	CWS	AL	34	34	5	0	239.0	984	236	102	95	25	9	3	3	61	7	134	6	1	19	12	.613	2	0-0	0	3.53	3.58
2003	CWS	AL	35	35	2	0	230.1	978	250	124	106	22	7	7	5	61	2	119	1	0	14	14	.500	0	0-0	0	4.10	4.14
2004	CWS	AL	35	35	4	0	245.1	1016	257	119	106	33	4	6	8	51	0	165	0	0	16	10	.615	1	0-0	0	4.00	3.89
2005	CWS	AL	33	33	3	0	236.2	971	240	99	82	20	7	4	4	40	4	149	2	2	16	8	.667	1	0-0	0	3.21	3.12
2006	CWS	AL	32	32	1	0	204.0	876	247	124	113	36	6	7	6	48	5	98	0	1	12	13	.480	0	0-0	0	5.37	4.99
2007	CWS	AL	30	30	3	0	201.0	835	208	86	81	22	7	5	5	45	5	115	1	0	10	9	.526	1	0-0	0	3.75	3.63
	8 ML YEARS		259	234	22	6	1629.0	6770	1681	770	688	187	50	36	42	373	28	943	11	9	107	75	.588	7	0-2	3	3.80	3.80

Ryan Bukvich

Pitches: R **Bats:** R **Pos:** RP-45   **Ht:** 6'2" **Wt:** 250 **Born:** 5/13/1978 **Age:** 30

Year	Team	Lg	G	GS	CG	GF	IP	BFP	H	R	ER	HR	SH	SF	HB	TBB	IBB	SO	WP	Bk	W	L	Pct	ShO	Sv-Op	Hld	ERC	ERA
			HOW MUCH HE PITCHED						**WHAT HE GAVE UP**												**THE RESULTS**							
2007	Charltt*	AAA	23	0	0	19	28.0	118	24	9	9	2	2	1	0	9	1	32	1	0	1	3	.250	0	9--	-	2.69	2.89
2002	KC	AL	26	0	0	2	25.0	121	26	19	17	2	4	3	1	19	3	20	1	0	1	0	1.000	0	0-1	5	5.39	6.12
2003	KC	AL	9	0	0	6	10.1	52	12	11	11	2	1	1	0	9	0	8	1	0	1	0	1.000	0	0-0	0	7.65	9.58
2004	KC	AL	9	0	0	6	7.1	30	4	3	3	0	1	0	0	7	0	7	0	0	0	0	-	0	1-1	1	3.21	3.68
2005	Tex	AL	4	0	0	0	4.0	19	2	5	5	0	1	0	0	6	0	4	0	0	0	0	-	0	0-0	1	4.74	11.25
2007	CWS	AL	45	0	0	7	35.2	170	36	23	20	5	1	2	3	24	1	18	3	0	1	0	1.000	0	0-1	4	5.70	5.05
	5 ML YEARS		93	0	0	21	82.1	392	80	61	56	9	8	6	4	65	4	57	5	0	3	0	1.000	0	1-3	11	5.58	6.12

Jason Bulger

Pitches: R **Bats:** R **Pos:** RP-6   **Ht:** 6'4" **Wt:** 215 **Born:** 12/6/1978 **Age:** 29

Year	Team	Lg	G	GS	CG	GF	IP	BFP	H	R	ER	HR	SH	SF	HB	TBB	IBB	SO	WP	Bk	W	L	Pct	ShO	Sv-Op	Hld	ERC	ERA
			HOW MUCH HE PITCHED						**WHAT HE GAVE UP**												**THE RESULTS**							
2007	Salt Lk*	AAA	49	0	0	23	52.2	233	51	24	22	4	2	1	2	24	1	81	3	1	5	2	.714	0	10--	-	3.91	3.76
2005	Ari	NL	9	0	0	4	10.0	48	14	6	6	1	1	0	0	5	1	9	0	0	1	0	1.000	0	0-0	0	6.68	5.40
2006	LAA	AL	2	0	0	1	1.2	9	1	3	3	0	0	0	0	3	0	1	1	0	0	0	-	0	0-0	0	6.15	16.20
2007	LAA	AL	6	0	0	4	6.1	25	5	2	2	0	0	0	0	3	0	8	1	0	0	0	-	0	0-0	0	2.74	2.84
	3 ML YEARS		17	0	0	10	18.0	82	20	11	11	1	1	0	0	11	1	18	2	0	1	0	1.000	0	0-0	0	5.18	5.50

Bryan Bullington

Pitches: R **Bats:** R **Pos:** SP-3; RP-2 **Ht:** 6'4" **Wt:** 220 **Born:** 9/30/1980 **Age:** 27

Year	Team	Lg	G	GS	CG	GF	IP	BFP	H	R	ER	HR	SH	SF	HB	TBB	IBB	SO	WP	Bk	W	L	Pct	ShO	Sv-Op	Hld	ERC	ERA
2003	Hickory	A	8	7	0	0	45.1	172	25	10	7	3	3	2	0	11	0	46	1	0	5	1	.833	0	0--	-	1.29	1.39
2003	Lynbrg	A+	17	17	2	0	97.1	428	101	39	33	5	4	2	8	27	0	67	3	0	8	4	.667	1	0--	-	3.69	3.05
2004	Altna	AA	26	26	0	0	145.0	642	160	77	66	18	10	9	9	47	1	100	5	0	12	7	.632	0	0--	-	4.73	4.10
2005	Indy	AAA	18	18	1	0	109.1	458	104	48	41	11	10	2	4	26	1	82	0	0	9	5	.643	0	0--	-	3.28	3.38
2007	Indy	AAA	26	26	0	0	150.2	635	146	70	67	10	9	4	6	59	3	89	3	0	11	9	.550	0	0--	-	3.85	4.00
2005	Pit	NL	1	0	0	0	1.1	7	1	2	2	0	0	1	1	1	0	1	0	0	0	0	-	0	0-0	0	5.91	13.50
2007	Pit	NL	5	3	0	0	17.0	76	24	11	10	3	1	0	0	5	0	7	1	0	0	3	.000	0	0-0	0	6.90	5.29
	2 ML YEARS		6	3	0	0	18.1	83	25	13	12	3	1	1	1	6	0	8	1	0	0	3	.000	0	0-0	0	6.85	5.89

Ambiorix Burgos

Pitches: R **Bats:** R **Pos:** RP-17 **Ht:** 6'3" **Wt:** 244 **Born:** 4/19/1984 **Age:** 24

Year	Team	Lg	G	GS	CG	GF	IP	BFP	H	R	ER	HR	SH	SF	HB	TBB	IBB	SO	WP	Bk	W	L	Pct	ShO	Sv-Op	Hld	ERC	ERA
2007	Mets*	R	3	1	0	1	4.0	15	0	1	0	0	0	0	1	0	0	1	0	0	0	0	-	0	1--	-	0.06	0.00
2007	NewOr*	AAA	8	0	0	1	9.1	42	10	7	7	2	0	1	0	4	0	13	1	0	0	0	-	0	0--	-	5.32	6.75
2005	KC	AL	59	0	0	17	63.1	278	60	29	28	6	2	1	5	31	1	65	8	2	3	5	.375	0	2-6	11	4.41	3.98
2006	KC	AL	68	1	0	41	73.1	336	83	49	45	16	1	4	6	37	4	72	11	3	4	5	.444	0	18-30	5	6.51	5.52
2007	NYM	NL	17	0	0	5	23.2	98	17	10	9	3	1	1	2	9	0	19	2	0	1	0	1.000	0	0-0	1	2.97	3.42
	3 ML YEARS		144	1	0	63	160.1	712	160	88	82	25	4	6	13	77	5	156	21	5	8	10	.444	0	20-36	17	5.10	4.60

Chris Burke

Bats: R **Throws:** R **Pos:** 2B-58; CF-26; RF-20; PH-19; SS-7; PR-4; LF-3 **Ht:** 5'11" **Wt:** 180 **Born:** 3/11/1980 **Age:** 28

Year	Team	Lg	G	AB	H	2B	3B	HR	(Hm	Rd)	TB	R	RBI	RC	TBB	IBB	SO	HBP	SH	SF	SB	CS	SB%	GDP	Avg	OBP	Slg
2007	RdRck*	AAA	18	66	16	1	0	2	(-	-)	23	14	7	8	5	0	7	2	0	3	5	2	.71	2	.242	.303	.348
2004	Hou	NL	17	17	1	0	0	0	(0	0)	1	2	0	0	3	0	3	0	0	0	0	0	-	0	.059	.200	.059
2005	Hou	NL	108	318	79	19	2	5	(2	3)	117	49	26	35	23	0	62	6	9	3	11	6	.65	7	.248	.309	.368
2006	Hou	NL	123	366	101	23	1	9	(3	6)	153	58	40	49	27	0	77	14	4	2	11	1	.92	6	.276	.347	.418
2007	Hou	NL	111	319	73	19	2	6	(3	3)	114	39	28	33	27	1	52	8	8	1	9	3	.75	10	.229	.304	.357
	4 ML YEARS		359	1020	254	61	5	20	(8	12)	385	148	94	117	80	1	194	28	21	6	31	10	.76	23	.249	.319	.377

Jamie Burke

Bats: R **Throws:** R **Pos:** C-48; PH-2 **Ht:** 6'0" **Wt:** 225 **Born:** 9/24/1971 **Age:** 36

Year	Team	Lg	G	AB	H	2B	3B	HR	(Hm	Rd)	TB	R	RBI	RC	TBB	IBB	SO	HBP	SH	SF	SB	CS	SB%	GDP	Avg	OBP	Slg
2001	LAA	AL	9	5	1	0	0	0	(0	0)	1	1	0	0	0	0	2	0	0	0	0	0	-	0	.200	.200	.200
2003	CWS	AL	6	8	3	0	0	0	(0	0)	3	0	2	2	0	0	0	0	0	0	0	0	-	0	.375	.375	.375
2004	CWS	AL	57	120	40	9	0	0	(0	0)	49	22	15	21	10	0	13	1	1	1	0	0	-	3	.333	.386	.408
2005	CWS	AL	1	1	0	0	0	0	(0	0)	0	0	0	0	0	0	0	0	0	0	0	0	-	0	.000	.000	.000
2007	Sea	AL	50	113	34	8	0	1	(1	0)	45	19	12	16	7	0	17	4	5	0	0	1	.00	2	.301	.363	.398
	5 ML YEARS		123	247	78	17	0	1	(1	0)	98	42	29	39	17	0	32	5	6	1	0	1	.00	5	.316	.370	.397

A.J. Burnett

Pitches: R **Bats:** R **Pos:** SP-25 **Ht:** 6'4" **Wt:** 230 **Born:** 1/3/1977 **Age:** 31

Year	Team	Lg	G	GS	CG	GF	IP	BFP	H	R	ER	HR	SH	SF	HB	TBB	IBB	SO	WP	Bk	W	L	Pct	ShO	Sv-Op	Hld	ERC	ERA
2007	Syrcse*	AAA	1	1	0	0	5.0	19	3	1	1	0	0	0	0	1	0	7	0	0	0	0	-	0	0--	-	1.11	1.80
1999	Fla	NL	7	7	0	0	41.1	182	37	23	16	3	1	3	0	25	2	33	0	0	4	2	.667	0	0-0	0	4.00	3.48
2000	Fla	NL	13	13	0	0	82.2	364	80	46	44	8	6	3	2	44	3	57	2	0	3	7	.300	0	0-0	0	4.45	4.79
2001	Fla	NL	27	27	2	0	173.1	733	145	82	78	20	6	8	7	83	3	128	7	1	11	12	.478	1	0-0	0	3.76	4.05
2002	Fla	NL	31	29	7	0	204.1	844	153	84	75	12	9	4	9	90	5	203	14	0	12	9	.571	5	0-1	0	2.77	3.30
2003	Fla	NL	4	4	0	0	23.0	106	18	13	12	2	2	1	2	18	2	21	2	0	0	2	.000	0	0-0	0	4.36	4.70
2004	Fla	NL	20	19	1	0	120.0	490	102	50	49	9	3	3	4	38	0	113	7	0	7	6	.538	0	0-0	0	2.95	3.68
2005	Fla	NL	32	32	4	0	209.0	873	184	97	80	12	7	5	7	79	1	198	12	0	12	12	.500	2	0-0	0	3.20	3.44
2006	Tor	AL	21	21	2	0	135.2	577	138	67	60	14	4	3	8	39	3	118	6	1	10	8	.556	1	0-0	0	3.97	3.98
2007	Tor	AL	25	25	2	0	165.2	691	131	74	69	23	0	2	12	66	2	176	5	0	10	8	.556	0	0-0	0	3.47	3.75
	9 ML YEARS		180	177	18	0	1155.0	4860	988	536	483	103	38	32	51	482	21	1047	55	2	69	66	.511	9	0-1	0	3.44	3.76

Pat Burrell

Bats: R **Throws:** R **Pos:** LF-138; PH-12; DH-5 **Ht:** 6'4" **Wt:** 234 **Born:** 10/10/1976 **Age:** 31

Year	Team	Lg	G	AB	H	2B	3B	HR	(Hm	Rd)	TB	R	RBI	RC	TBB	IBB	SO	HBP	SH	SF	SB	CS	SB%	GDP	Avg	OBP	Slg
2000	Phi	NL	111	408	106	27	1	18	(7	11)	189	57	79	69	63	2	139	1	0	2	0	0	-	5	.260	.359	.463
2001	Phi	NL	155	539	139	29	2	27	(10	17)	253	70	89	86	70	7	162	5	0	4	2	1	.67	12	.258	.346	.469
2002	Phi	NL	157	586	165	39	2	37	(18	19)	319	96	116	104	89	9	153	3	0	6	1	0	1.00	16	.282	.376	.544
2003	Phi	NL	146	522	109	31	4	21	(9	12)	211	57	64	57	72	2	142	4	0	1	0	0	-	18	.209	.309	.404
2004	Phi	NL	127	448	115	17	0	24	(14	10)	204	66	84	72	78	7	130	2	0	6	2	0	1.00	10	.257	.365	.455
2005	Phi	NL	154	562	158	27	1	32	(20	12)	283	78	117	109	99	6	160	3	0	5	0	0	-	11	.281	.389	.504
2006	Phi	NL	144	462	119	24	1	29	(12	17)	232	80	95	81	98	5	131	3	0	4	0	0	-	11	.258	.388	.502
2007	Phi	NL	155	472	121	26	0	30	(16	14)	237	97	97	98	114	1	120	4	0	8	0	0	-	10	.256	.400	.502
	8 ML YEARS		1149	3999	1032	220	11	218	(106	112)	1928	581	741	676	683	39	1137	25	0	36	5	1	.83	94	.258	.367	.482

Brian Burres

Pitches: L Bats: L Pos: RP-20; SP-17   Ht: 6'1" Wt: 180 Born: 4/8/1981 Age: 27

Year	Team	Lg	G	GS	CG	GF	IP	BFP	H	R	ER	HR	SH	SF	HB	TBB	IBB	SO	WP	Bk	W	L	Pct	ShO	Sv-Op	Hld	ERC	ERA
2001	SlmKzr	A-	14	6	0	2	40.2	174	43	20	14	2	3	2	1	11	0	38	5	0	3	1	.750	0	1--	-	3.61	3.10
2002	Hgrstn	A	32	16	0	4	119.1	522	114	78	63	15	4	4	9	53	0	119	8	1	5	10	.333	0	1--	-	4.49	4.75
2003	SnJos	A+	39	0	0	16	60.2	276	55	33	26	4	2	4	3	36	3	64	7	0	3	3	.500	0	1--	-	4.06	3.86
2004	SnJos	A+	36	15	0	6	123.2	506	115	49	39	10	4	4	7	30	0	114	6	0	12	1	.923	0	0--	-	3.24	2.84
2005	Nrwich	AA	26	24	0	1	128.2	563	130	66	60	13	6	3	10	57	0	105	8	1	9	6	.600	0	0--	-	4.69	4.20
2006	Ottawa	AAA	26	26	1	0	139.0	596	133	63	58	14	6	3	8	57	1	110	8	0	10	6	.625	1	0--	-	4.14	3.76
2007	Norfolk	AAA	2	0	0	0	4.0	15	2	1	1	1	0	0	0	1	0	5	0	0	1	0	1.000	0	0--	-	1.80	2.25
2006	Bal	AL	11	0	0	2	8.0	31	6	2	2	1	0	0	0	1	0	6	0	0	0	0	-	0	0-0	4	1.91	2.25
2007	Bal	AL	37	17	0	9	121.0	559	140	81	80	14	2	0	5	66	1	96	8	0	6	8	.429	0	0-0	-	5.89	5.95
	2 ML YEARS		48	17	0	11	129.0	590	146	83	82	15	2	0	5	67	1	102	8	0	6	8	.429	0	0-0	4	5.61	5.72

Jared Burton

Pitches: R Bats: R Pos: RP-47   Ht: 6'5" Wt: 225 Born: 6/2/1981 Age: 27

Year	Team	Lg	G	GS	CG	GF	IP	BFP	H	R	ER	HR	SH	SF	HB	TBB	IBB	SO	WP	Bk	W	L	Pct	ShO	Sv-Op	Hld	ERC	ERA
2002	Vancvr	A-	13	5	0	2	37.2	164	32	22	15	0	2	1	2	14	0	38	2	1	0	4	.000	0	1--	-	2.57	3.58
2003	Kane	A	15	2	0	3	31.2	120	19	9	8	2	2	0	2	7	0	33	4	0	2	1	.667	0	1--	-	1.55	2.27
2004	As	R	5	5	0	0	21.2	91	21	12	10	2	0	0	2	4	0	15	2	0	1	0	1.000	0	0--	-	3.35	4.15
2004	Mdest	A+	10	3	0	1	32.0	147	34	19	17	6	0	0	1	20	1	25	4	0	3	2	.600	0	0--	-	6.16	4.78
2005	Stcktn	A+	52	0	0	35	55.1	234	44	21	16	2	2	0	4	20	0	67	8	1	4	4	.500	0	24--	-	2.63	2.60
2006	Mdland	AA	53	0	0	19	74.0	314	71	36	34	7	4	2	3	27	3	66	9	0	6	5	.545	0	1--	-	3.80	4.14
2007	Chatt	AA	4	0	0	1	5.1	31	10	7	7	0	0	0	1	5	0	3	1	0	1	0	1.000	0	0--	-	12.09	11.81
2007	Lsvlle	AAA	10	0	0	3	14.0	53	11	1	1	0	0	0	0	4	0	13	1	0	1	0	1.000	0	1--	-	2.08	0.64
2007	Cin	NL	47	0	0	12	43.0	176	28	15	12	2	1	1	2	22	4	36	3	1	4	2	.667	0	0-3	11	2.37	2.51

Brian Buscher

Bats: L Throws: R Pos: 3B-27; PH-7; PR-1   Ht: 6'0" Wt: 200 Born: 4/18/1981 Age: 27

Year	Team	Lg	G	AB	H	2B	3B	HR	(Hm	Rd)	TB	R	RBI	RC	TBB	IBB	SO	HBP	SH	SF	SB	CS	SB%	GDP	Avg	OBP	Slg
2003	Hgrstn	A	54	200	55	7	1	0	(-	-)	64	19	26	21	10	0	25	4	0	3	0	0	-	4	.275	.318	.320
2004	SnJos	A+	88	343	100	14	7	4	(-	-)	140	50	56	53	33	0	61	6	0	5	5	4	.56	8	.292	.359	.408
2005	Nrwich	AA	64	215	49	8	1	1	(-	-)	62	19	23	21	20	0	36	6	0	6	6	3	.67	10	.228	.304	.288
2005	SnJos	A+	55	206	58	12	1	5	(-	-)	87	37	29	33	27	0	47	2	0	2	0	2	.00	7	.282	.367	.422
2006	Conn	AA	130	467	121	23	3	7	(-	-)	171	43	49	58	39	3	75	6	7	5	5	4	.56	12	.259	.321	.366
2007	NwBrit	AA	63	247	76	19	1	7	(-	-)	118	37	37	47	31	4	30	4	0	2	2	2	.50	3	.308	.391	.478
2007	Roch	AAA	40	132	41	7	0	7	(-	-)	69	21	22	26	13	1	11	1	0	1	1	0	1.00	2	.311	.374	.523
2007	Min	AL	33	82	20	1	0	2	(0	2)	27	8	10	8	10	0	16	0	1	1	1	0	1.00	2	.244	.323	.329

David Bush

Pitches: R Bats: R Pos: SP-31; RP-2   Ht: 6'2" Wt: 209 Born: 11/9/1979 Age: 28

Year	Team	Lg	G	GS	CG	GF	IP	BFP	H	R	ER	HR	SH	SF	HB	TBB	IBB	SO	WP	Bk	W	L	Pct	ShO	Sv-Op	Hld	ERC	ERA
2004	Tor	AL	16	16	1	0	97.2	412	95	47	40	11	4	4	6	25	2	64	3	0	5	4	.556	1	0-0	0	3.65	3.69
2005	Tor	AL	25	24	2	1	136.1	575	142	73	68	20	3	2	13	29	3	75	2	0	5	11	.313	0	0-0	0	4.28	4.49
2006	Mil	NL	34	32	3	0	210.0	869	201	111	103	26	9	6	18	38	2	166	6	0	12	11	.522	2	0-0	1	3.47	4.41
2007	Mil	NL	33	31	0	2	186.1	810	217	110	106	27	6	2	11	44	1	134	3	0	12	10	.545	0	0-0	0	4.93	5.12
	4 ML YEARS		108	103	6	3	630.1	2666	655	341	317	84	22	14	48	136	8	439	14	0	34	36	.486	3	0-0	1	4.09	4.53

Billy Butler

Bats: R Throws: R Pos: DH-70; 1B-13; PH-7; LF-6   Ht: 6'1" Wt: 240 Born: 4/18/1986 Age: 22

Year	Team	Lg	G	AB	H	2B	3B	HR	(Hm	Rd)	TB	R	RBI	RC	TBB	IBB	SO	HBP	SH	SF	SB	CS	SB%	GDP	Avg	OBP	Slg
2004	Idaho	R+	74	260	97	22	3	10	(-	-)	155	74	68	75	57	0	63	4	0	3	5	0	1.00	6	.373	.488	.596
2005	Hi Dsrt	A+	92	379	132	30	2	25	(-	-)	241	70	91	95	42	3	80	6	0	3	0	0	-	12	.348	.419	.636
2005	Wichta	AA	29	112	35	9	0	5	(-	-)	59	14	19	20	7	3	18	0	0	0	0	0	-	3	.313	.353	.527
2006	Wichta	AA	119	477	158	33	1	15	(-	-)	238	82	96	93	41	3	67	8	1	8	1	0	1.00	25	.331	.388	.499
2007	Omha	AAA	57	203	59	10	1	13	(-	-)	110	40	46	48	43	2	32	3	1	6	1	0	1.00	8	.291	.412	.542
2007	KC	AL	92	329	96	23	2	8	(5	3)	147	38	52	50	27	5	55	2	0	2	0	0	-	8	.292	.347	.447

Freddie Bynum

Bats: L Throws: R Pos: PR-27; LF-23; SS-15; PH-9; DH-7; CF-6; 2B-4   Ht: 6'1" Wt: 190 Born: 3/15/1980 Age: 28

Year	Team	Lg	G	AB	H	2B	3B	HR	(Hm	Rd)	TB	R	RBI	RC	TBB	IBB	SO	HBP	SH	SF	SB	CS	SB%	GDP	Avg	OBP	Slg
2007	Dlmrva*	A-	1	1	0	0	0	0	(-	-)	0	0	0	0	1	0	0	0	0	0	1	0	1.00	0	.000	.500	.000
2007	Frdrck*	A+	5	17	4	1	0	0	(-	-)	6	3	2	2	1	0	4	1	0	0	0	0	-	0	.235	.316	.353
2007	Bowie*	AA	1	3	0	0	0	0	(-	-)	0	0	0	0	0	0	2	0	0	0	0	0	-	0	.000	.000	.000
2005	Oak	AL	7	7	2	1	0	0	(0	0)	3	0	1	1	0	0	3	0	0	0	0	0	-	0	.286	.286	.429
2006	ChC	NL	71	136	35	5	5	4	(3	1)	62	20	12	18	9	0	44	1	2	0	8	4	.67	2	.257	.308	.456
2007	Bal	AL	70	96	25	8	2	2	(0	2)	43	21	11	12	2	0	30	2	1	0	8	1	.89	2	.260	.290	.448
	3 ML YEARS		148	239	62	14	7	6	(3	3)	108	41	24	31	11	0	77	3	3	0	16	5	.76	4	.259	.300	.452

Marlon Byrd

Bats: R **Throws:** R **Pos:** CF-63; RF-40; LF-18; PH-5   **Ht:** 6'0" **Wt:** 235 **Born:** 8/30/1977 **Age:** 30

Year	Team	Lg	G	AB	H	2B	3B	HR	(Hm	Rd)	TB	R	RBI	RC	TBB	IBB	SO	HBP	SH	SF	SB	CS	SB%	GDP	Avg	OBP	Slg
2007	Okla*	AAA	45	176	63	15	2	6	(-	-)	100	29	32	39	13	0	30	5	0	1	3	2	.60	4	.358	.415	.568
2002	Phi	NL	10	35	8	2	0	1	(1	0)	13	2	1	0	1	0	8	0	0	0	0	2	.00	0	.229	.250	.371
2003	Phi	NL	135	495	150	28	4	7	(3	4)	207	86	45	72	44	3	94	7	4	3	11	1	.92	8	.303	.366	.418
2004	Phi	NL	106	346	79	13	2	5	(3	2)	111	48	33	35	22	1	68	7	2	1	2	2	.50	10	.228	.287	.321
2005	2 Tms		79	229	61	15	2	2	(0	2)	86	20	26	30	19	1	50	2	5	4	5	1	.83	5	.266	.323	.376
2006	Was	NL	78	197	44	8	1	5	(1	4)	69	28	18	18	22	1	47	6	1	2	3	3	.50	6	.223	.317	.350
2007	Tex	AL	109	414	127	17	8	10	(4	6)	190	60	70	68	29	3	88	5	0	6	5	3	.63	9	.307	.355	.459
05	Phi	NL	5	13	4	0	0	0	(0	0)	4	0	0	2	1	0	3	1	0	0	0	0	-	0	.308	.400	.308
05	Was	NL	74	216	57	15	2	2	(0	2)	82	20	26	28	18	1	47	1	5	4	5	1	.83	5	.264	.318	.380
	6 ML YEARS		517	1716	469	83	17	30	(12	18)	676	244	193	223	137	9	355	27	12	16	26	12	.68	38	.273	.334	.394

Paul Byrd

Pitches: R **Bats:** R **Pos:** SP-31   **Ht:** 6'1" **Wt:** 190 **Born:** 12/3/1970 **Age:** 37

Year	Team	Lg	G	GS	CG	GF	IP	BFP	H	R	ER	HR	SH	SF	HB	TBB	IBB	SO	WP	Bk	W	L	Pct	ShO	Sv-Op	Hld	ERC	ERA
1995	NYM	NL	17	0	0	6	22.0	91	18	6	5	1	0	2	1	7	1	26	1	2	2	0	1.000	0	0-0	3	2.53	2.05
1996	NYM	NL	38	0	0	14	46.2	204	48	22	22	7	1	1	0	21	4	31	3	0	1	2	.333	0	0-2	3	4.67	4.24
1997	Atl	NL	31	4	0	9	53.0	236	47	34	31	6	2	2	4	28	4	37	3	1	4	4	.500	0	0-0	1	4.15	5.26
1998	2 Tms	NL	9	8	2	0	57.0	233	45	19	17	6	2	1	0	18	1	39	2	0	5	2	.714	1	0-0	0	2.62	2.68
1999	Phi	NL	32	32	1	0	199.2	872	205	119	102	34	5	6	17	70	2	106	11	3	15	11	.577	0	0-0	0	4.87	4.60
2000	Phi	NL	17	15	0	0	83.0	371	89	67	60	17	3	1	3	35	2	53	1	0	2	9	.182	0	0-0	0	5.42	6.51
2001	2 Tms		19	16	1	1	103.1	444	120	54	51	12	4	6	2	26	1	52	2	0	6	7	.462	0	0-0	0	4.62	4.44
2002	KC	AL	33	33	7	0	228.1	935	224	111	99	36	2	13	7	38	1	129	3	1	17	11	.607	2	0-0	0	3.55	3.90
2004	Atl	NL	19	19	0	0	114.1	482	123	57	50	18	3	3	2	19	0	79	1	0	8	7	.533	0	0-0	0	3.98	3.94
2005	LAA	AL	31	31	2	0	204.1	842	216	95	85	22	7	7	7	28	1	102	1	0	12	11	.522	1	0-0	0	3.56	3.74
2006	Cle	AL	31	31	1	0	179.0	805	232	120	97	26	1	6	6	38	3	88	2	0	10	9	.526	0	0-0	0	5.40	4.88
2007	Cle	AL	31	31	2	0	192.1	835	239	107	98	27	4	4	6	28	3	88	5	0	15	8	.652	2	0-0	0	4.80	4.59
98	Atl	NL	1	0	0	0	2.0	11	4	3	3	0	0	0	0	1	0	1	0	0	0	0	-	0	0-0	0	9.72	13.50
98	Phi	NL	8	8	2	0	55.0	222	41	16	14	6	2	1	0	17	1	38	2	0	5	2	.714	1	0-0	0	2.41	2.29
01	Phi	NL	3	1	0	1	10.0	45	10	9	9	1	2	2	1	4	0	3	1	0	0	1	.000	0	0-0	0	4.36	8.10
01	KC		16	15	1	0	93.1	399	110	45	42	11	2	4	1	22	1	49	1	0	6	6	.500	0	0-0	0	4.65	4.05
	12 ML YEARS		308	220	16	30	1483.0	6350	1606	811	717	212	34	52	55	366	23	030	35	7	97	81	.545	6	0-2	7	4.32	4.35

Tim Byrdak

Pitches: L **Bats:** L **Pos:** RP-39   **Ht:** 5'11" **Wt:** 195 **Born:** 10/31/1973 **Age:** 34

Year	Team	Lg	G	GS	CG	GF	IP	BFP	H	R	ER	HR	SH	SF	HB	TBB	IBB	SO	WP	Bk	W	L	Pct	ShO	Sv-Op	Hld	ERC	ERA
2007	Toledo*	AAA	17	0	0	5	24.1	100	22	7	7	3	2	1	0	8	1	30	2	1	0	1	1.000	0	0- -	3	3.41	2.59
1998	KC	AL	3	0	0	0	1.2	9	5	1	1	1	0	0	0	0	0	1	0	0	0	0	-	0	0-0	0	23.52	5.40
1999	KC	AL	33	0	0	5	24.2	128	32	24	21	5	3	0	1	20	2	17	3	1	0	3	.000	0	1-4	10	8.29	7.66
2000	KC	AL	12	0	0	1	6.1	34	11	8	8	3	0	0	0	4	0	8	1	0	0	1	.000	0	0-2	3	13.14	11.37
2005	Bal	AL	41	0	0	3	26.2	131	27	14	12	1	2	1	1	21	1	31	5	0	0	1	.000	0	1-1	11	5.04	4.05
2006	Bal	AL	16	0	0	2	7.0	42	14	10	10	2	2	0	0	8	1	2	1	0	0	0	-	0	0-0	3	15.90	12.86
2007	Det	AL	39	0	0	3	45.0	199	38	23	16	3	2	5	1	26	4	49	3	0	3	0	1.000	0	1 2	8	3.53	3.20
	6 ML YEARS		144	0	0	14	111.1	543	127	80	68	15	9	6	3	79	8	108	13	1	4	5	.444	0	3-9	35	6.28	5.50

Eric Byrnes

Bats: R **Throws:** R **Pos:** LF-123; RF-35; CF-23   **Ht:** 6'2" **Wt:** 210 **Born:** 2/16/1976 **Age:** 32

Year	Team	Lg	G	AB	H	2B	3B	HR	(Hm	Rd)	TB	R	RBI	RC	TBB	IBB	SO	HBP	SH	SF	SB	CS	SB%	GDP	Avg	OBP	Slg
2000	Oak	AL	10	10	3	0	0	0	(0	0)	3	5	0	1	0	0	1	1	0	0	2	1	.67	0	.300	.364	.300
2001	Oak	AL	19	38	9	1	0	3	(2	1)	19	9	5	7	4	0	6	1	0	0	1	0	1.00	0	.237	.326	.500
2002	Oak	AL	90	94	23	4	2	3	(2	1)	40	24	11	10	4	0	17	3	1	2	3	0	1.00	3	.245	.291	.426
2003	Oak	AL	121	414	109	27	9	12	(7	5)	190	64	51	68	42	4	71	2	0	2	10	2	.83	3	.263	.333	.459
2004	Oak	AL	143	569	161	39	3	20	(10	10)	266	91	73	87	46	0	111	12	0	5	17	1	.94	11	.283	.347	.467
2005	3 Tms		126	412	93	24	3	10	(5	5)	153	49	40	41	32	0	71	8	3	1	7	2	.78	7	.226	.294	.371
2006	Ari	NL	143	562	150	37	3	26	(12	14)	271	82	79	78	34	2	88	5	2	3	25	3	.89	12	.267	.313	.482
2007	Ari	NL	160	626	179	30	8	21	(11	10)	288	103	83	103	57	5	98	10	1	4	50	7	.88	12	.286	.353	.460
05	Oak	AL	59	192	51	15	2	7	(3	4)	91	30	24	29	14	0	27	7	1	1	2	2	.50	1	.266	.336	.474
05	Col	NL	15	53	10	2	0	0	(0	0)	12	2	5	4	7	0	11	0	0	0	2	0	1.00	1	.189	.283	.226
05	Bal	AL	52	167	32	7	1	3	(2	1)	50	17	11	8	11	0	33	1	2	0	3	0	1.00	5	.192	.246	.299
	8 ML YEARS		812	2725	727	162	28	95	(49	46)	1230	427	342	395	219	11	463	42	7	17	115	16	.88	48	.267	.329	.451

Asdrubal Cabrera

Bats: B **Throws:** R **Pos:** 2B-40; SS-7; PH-4; 3B-1; PR-1   **Ht:** 6'0" **Wt:** 170 **Born:** 11/13/1985 **Age:** 22

Year	Team	Lg	G	AB	H	2B	3B	HR	(Hm	Rd)	TB	R	RBI	RC	TBB	IBB	SO	HBP	SH	SF	SB	CS	SB%	GDP	Avg	OBP	Slg
2004	Everett	A-	63	239	65	16	3	5	(-	-)	102	44	41	35	21	1	43	2	7	5	7	5	.58	3	.272	.330	.427
2005	Wisc	A	51	192	61	12	3	4	(-	-)	91	26	30	37	30	1	32	1	2	3	2	6	.25	6	.318	.407	.474
2005	InldEm	A+	55	225	64	15	6	1	(-	-)	94	31	26	31	15	0	47	0	1	3	3	1	.75	8	.284	.325	.418
2005	Tacom	AAA	6	23	5	0	1	0	(-	-)	7	4	3	1	1	0	4	0	1	0	0	0	-	1	.217	.250	.304
2006	Tacom	AAA	60	203	48	12	2	3	(-	-)	73	27	22	25	24	1	51	3	1	2	7	5	.58	4	.236	.323	.360

57

Year	Team	Lg	G	AB	H	2B	3B	HR	(Hm	Rd)	TB	R	RBI	RC	TBB	IBB	SO	HBP	SH	SF	SB	CS	SB%	GDP	Avg	OBP	Slg
2006	Buffalo	AAA	52	190	50	11	0	1	(-	-)	64	26	14	19	8	0	39	3	4	6	5	4	.56	4	.263	.295	.337
2007	Akron	AA	96	368	114	23	3	8	(-	-)	167	78	54	69	45	0	42	3	2	7	23	7	.77	8	.310	.383	.454
2007	Buffalo	AAA	9	38	12	3	0	0	(-	-)	15	6	3	5	2	0	8	0	0	0	2	0	1.00	1	.316	.350	.395
2007	Cle	AL	45	159	45	9	2	3	(1	2)	67	30	22	27	17	0	29	2	5	3	0	0	-	7	.283	.354	.421

Daniel Cabrera

Pitches: R **Bats:** R **Pos:** SP-34   **Ht:** 6'9" **Wt:** 270 **Born:** 5/28/1981 **Age:** 27

			HOW MUCH HE PITCHED						WHAT HE GAVE UP												THE RESULTS							
Year	Team	Lg	G	GS	CG	GF	IP	BFP	H	R	ER	HR	SH	SF	HB	TBB	IBB	SO	WP	Bk	W	L	Pct	ShO	Sv-Op	Hld	ERC	ERA
2004	Bal	AL	28	27	1	1	147.2	662	145	85	82	14	4	7	2	89	2	76	12	0	12	8	.600	0	1-1	0	4.79	5.00
2005	Bal	AL	29	29	0	0	161.1	716	144	92	81	14	2	3	11	87	2	157	9	1	10	13	.435	0	0-0	0	4.13	4.52
2006	Bal	AL	26	26	2	0	148.0	662	130	82	78	11	5	8	5	104	1	157	17	1	9	10	.474	0	0-0	0	4.55	4.74
2007	Bal	AL	34	34	1	0	204.1	922	207	133	126	25	13	5	15	108	6	166	7	2	9	18	.333	0	0-0	0	5.08	5.55
	4 ML YEARS		117	116	4	1	661.1	2962	626	392	367	64	24	23	33	388	11	556	45	4	40	49	.449	2	1-1	0	4.66	4.99

Fernando Cabrera

Pitches: R **Bats:** R **Pos:** RP-33   **Ht:** 6'4" **Wt:** 220 **Born:** 11/16/1981 **Age:** 26

			HOW MUCH HE PITCHED						WHAT HE GAVE UP												THE RESULTS							
Year	Team	Lg	G	GS	CG	GF	IP	BFP	H	R	ER	HR	SH	SF	HB	TBB	IBB	SO	WP	Bk	W	L	Pct	ShO	Sv-Op	Hld	ERC	ERA
2007	Norfolk*	AAA	3	0	0	0	3.0	11	1	1	1	0	1	0	0	2	0	2	0	0	0	0	-	0	0- --	-	1.37	3.00
2004	Cle	AL	4	0	0	2	5.1	20	3	3	2	0	0	1	0	1	0	6	0	0	0	0	-	0	0-0	0	0.99	3.38
2005	Cle	AL	15	0	0	6	30.2	124	24	7	5	1	0	0	0	11	1	29	1	1	2	1	.667	0	0-0	1	2.33	1.47
2006	Cle	AL	51	0	0	20	60.2	256	53	36	35	12	1	4	1	32	2	71	5	0	3	3	.500	0	0-4	6	4.72	5.19
2007	2 Tms		33	0	0	13	43.2	207	50	36	35	9	0	2	0	31	3	48	2	0	1	2	.333	0	1-1	1	6.98	7.21
07	Cle	AL	24	0	0	9	33.2	157	38	22	21	7	0	2	0	22	3	39	1	0	1	2	.333	0	0-0	1	6.61	5.61
07	Bal	AL	9	0	0	4	10.0	50	12	14	14	2	0	0	0	9	0	9	1	0	0	0	-	0	1-1	0	8.26	12.60
	4 ML YEARS		103	0	0	41	140.1	607	130	82	77	22	1	7	1	75	6	154	8	1	6	6	.500	0	1-5	8	4.62	4.94

Melky Cabrera

Bats: B **Throws:** L **Pos:** CF-131; LF-18; PH-6; RF-5; PR-1   **Ht:** 5'11" **Wt:** 200 **Born:** 8/11/1984 **Age:** 23

Year	Team	Lg	G	AB	H	2B	3B	HR	(Hm	Rd)	TB	R	RBI	RC	TBB	IBB	SO	HBP	SH	SF	SB	CS	SB%	GDP	Avg	OBP	Slg
2005	NYY	AL	6	19	4	0	0	0	(0	0)	4	1	0	0	0	0	2	0	0	0	0	0	-	0	.211	.211	.211
2006	NYY	AL	130	460	129	26	2	7	(3	4)	180	75	50	68	56	3	59	2	5	1	12	5	.71	9	.280	.360	.391
2007	NYY	AL	150	545	149	24	8	8	(4	4)	213	66	73	70	43	0	68	5	10	9	13	5	.72	14	.273	.327	.391
	3 ML YEARS		286	1024	282	50	10	15	(7	8)	397	142	123	138	99	3	129	7	15	10	25	10	.71	23	.275	.340	.388

Miguel Cabrera

Bats: R **Throws:** R **Pos:** 3B-154; DH-3; PH-1   **Ht:** 6'4" **Wt:** 240 **Born:** 4/18/1983 **Age:** 25

Year	Team	Lg	G	AB	H	2B	3B	HR	(Hm	Rd)	TB	R	RBI	RC	TBB	IBB	SO	HBP	SH	SF	SB	CS	SB%	GDP	Avg	OBP	Slg
2003	Fla	NL	87	314	84	21	3	12	(7	5)	147	39	62	51	25	3	84	2	4	1	0	2	.00	12	.268	.325	.468
2004	Fla	NL	160	603	177	31	1	33	(14	19)	309	101	112	92	68	5	148	6	0	8	5	2	.71	20	.294	.366	.512
2005	Fla	NL	158	613	198	43	2	33	(11	22)	344	106	116	108	64	12	125	2	0	6	1	0	1.00	20	.323	.385	.561
2006	Fla	NL	158	576	195	50	2	26	(15	11)	327	112	114	132	86	27	108	10	0	4	9	6	.60	18	.339	.430	.568
2007	Fla	NL	157	588	188	38	2	34	(19	15)	332	91	119	122	79	23	127	5	1	7	2	1	.67	17	.320	.401	.565
	5 ML YEARS		720	2694	842	183	10	138	(66	72)	1459	449	523	505	322	70	592	25	5	26	17	11	.61	87	.313	.388	.542

Orlando Cabrera

Bats: R **Throws:** R **Pos:** SS-153; DH-2   **Ht:** 5'9" **Wt:** 185 **Born:** 11/2/1974 **Age:** 33

Year	Team	Lg	G	AB	H	2B	3B	HR	(Hm	Rd)	TB	R	RBI	RC	TBB	IBB	SO	HBP	SH	SF	SB	CS	SB%	GDP	Avg	OBP	Slg
1997	Mon	NL	16	18	4	0	0	0	(0	0)	4	2	0	1	0	0	3	0	1	1	1	2	.33	1	.222	.263	.222
1998	Mon	NL	79	261	73	16	5	3	(2	1)	108	44	22	34	18	1	27	0	5	1	2	2	.75	6	.280	.325	.414
1999	Mon	NL	104	382	97	23	5	8	(6	2)	154	48	39	42	18	4	38	3	4	0	2	2	.50	9	.254	.293	.403
2000	Mon	NL	125	422	100	25	1	13	(7	6)	166	47	55	43	25	3	28	1	3	3	4	4	.50	12	.237	.279	.393
2001	Mon	NL	162	626	173	41	6	14	(7	7)	268	64	96	85	43	5	54	4	4	7	19	7	.73	15	.276	.324	.428
2002	Mon	NL	153	563	148	43	1	7	(3	4)	214	64	56	61	48	4	53	2	9	4	25	7	.78	16	.263	.321	.380
2003	Mon	NL	162	626	186	47	2	17	(8	9)	288	95	80	92	52	3	64	1	3	9	24	2	.92	18	.297	.347	.460
2004	2 Tms		161	618	163	38	3	10	(2	8)	237	74	62	67	39	0	54	3	3	10	16	4	.80	16	.264	.306	.383
2005	LAA	AL	141	540	139	28	3	8	(2	6)	197	70	57	61	38	4	50	3	4	2	21	2	.91	10	.257	.309	.365
2006	LAA	AL	153	607	171	45	1	9	(3	6)	245	95	72	77	51	0	58	3	3	11	27	3	.90	12	.282	.335	.404
2007	LAA	AL	155	638	192	35	1	8	(3	5)	253	101	86	95	44	0	64	5	3	11	20	4	.83	12	.301	.345	.397
04	Mon	NL	103	390	96	19	2	4	(1	3)	131	41	31	37	28	0	31	2	2	3	12	3	.80	12	.246	.298	.336
04	Bos	AL	58	228	67	19	1	6	(1	5)	106	33	31	30	11	0	23	1	1	7	4	1	.80	4	.294	.320	.465
	11 ML YEARS		1411	5301	1446	341	28	97	(43	54)	2134	706	627	657	377	24	493	25	42	58	165	39	.81	127	.273	.321	.403

Matt Cain

Pitches: R **Bats:** R **Pos:** SP-32   **Ht:** 6'3" **Wt:** 235 **Born:** 10/1/1984 **Age:** 23

		HOW MUCH HE PITCHED						WHAT HE GAVE UP										THE RESULTS						
Year	Team	Lg	G	GS	CG	GF	IP	BFP	H	R	ER	HR	SH	SF	HB	TBB	IBB	SO	WP	Bk	W	L	Pct	ShO	Sv-Op Hld	ERC	ERA
2005	SF	NL	7	7	1	0	46.1	181	24	12	12	4	2	1	0	19	1	30	1	0	2	1	.667	0	0-0 0	1.61	2.33
2006	SF	NL	32	31	1	1	190.2	818	157	93	88	18	11	6	6	87	1	179	9	2	13	12	.520	1	0-0 0	3.35	4.15
2007	SF	NL	32	32	1	0	200.0	832	173	84	81	14	8	5	5	79	3	163	12	0	7	16	.304	0	0-0 0	3.23	3.65
	3 ML YEARS		71	70	3	1	437.0	1831	354	189	181	36	21	12	11	185	5	372	22	2	22	29	.431	1	0-0 0	3.09	3.73

Miguel Cairo

Bats: R **Throws:** R **Pos:** 1B-24; 3B-22; SS-16; PH-13; 2B-12; PR-11; LF-4; DH-3   **Ht:** 6'1" **Wt:** 208 **Born:** 5/4/1974 **Age:** 34

			BATTING																	BASERUNNING				AVERAGES		
Year	Team	Lg	G	AB	H	2B	3B	HR	(Hm	Rd)	TB	R	RBI	RC	TBB	IBB	SO	HBP	SH	SF	SB	CS	SB%	GDP	Avg	OBP	Slg
2007	Memp*	AAA	9	31	9	2	0	0	(-	)	11	0	3	5	5	0	6	2	0	0	2	0	1.00	0	.290	.421	.355
1996	Tor	AL	9	27	6	2	0	0	(0	0)	8	5	1	2	2	0	9	1	0	0	0	0	-	1	.222	.300	.296
1997	ChC	NL	16	29	7	1	0	0	(0	0)	8	7	1	3	2	0	3	1	0	0	0	0	-	0	.241	.313	.276
1998	TB	AL	150	515	138	26	5	5	(3	2)	189	49	46	58	24	0	44	6	11	2	19	8	.70	9	.268	.307	.367
1999	TB	AL	120	465	137	15	5	3	(1	2)	171	61	36	57	24	0	46	7	7	5	22	7	.76	13	.295	.335	.368
2000	TB	AL	119	375	98	18	2	1	(0	1)	123	49	34	42	29	0	34	2	6	5	28	7	.80	7	.261	.314	.328
2001	2 Tms	NL	93	156	46	8	1	3	(2	1)	65	25	16	23	18	1	23	0	7	1	2	1	.67	4	.295	.366	.417
2002	StL	NL	108	184	46	9	2	2	(1	1)	65	28	23	19	13	2	36	3	6	2	1	1	.50	5	.250	.307	.353
2003	StL	NL	92	261	64	15	2	5	(2	3)	98	41	32	25	13	1	30	6	3	7	4	1	.80	6	.245	.289	.375
2004	NYY	AL	122	360	105	17	5	6	(4	2)	150	48	42	50	18	1	49	14	12	4	11	3	.79	7	.292	.346	.417
2005	NYM	NL	100	327	82	18	0	2	(1	1)	106	31	19	29	19	2	31	4	12	5	13	3	.81	5	.251	.296	.324
2006	NYY	AL	81	222	53	12	3	0	(0	0)	71	28	30	26	13	0	31	1	5	3	13	1	.93	4	.239	.280	.320
2007	2 Tms		82	174	44	9	2	0	(0	0)	57	20	15	21	11	1	24	2	5	1	10	2	.83	3	.253	.303	.328
01	ChC	NL	66	123	35	3	1	2	(1	1)	46	20	9	17	16	1	21	0	7	1	2	1	.67	3	.285	.364	.374
01	StL	NL	27	33	11	5	0	1	(1	0)	19	5	7	6	2	0	2	0	0	0	0	0	-	1	.333	.371	.576
07	NYY	AL	54	107	27	7	0	0	(0	0)	34	12	10	12	8	1	19	1	4	1	8	1	.89	3	.252	.308	.318
07	StL	NL	28	67	17	2	2	0	(0	0)	23	8	5	9	3	0	5	1	1	0	2	1	.67	0	.254	.296	.343
	12 ML YEARS		1092	3095	826	150	27	27	(14	13)	1111	392	295	355	186	8	360	47	74	35	123	34	.78	64	.267	.315	.359

Kiko Calero

Pitches: R **Bats:** R **Pos:** RP-46   **Ht:** 6'1" **Wt:** 203 **Born:** 1/9/1975 **Age:** 33

			HOW MUCH HE PITCHED						WHAT HE GAVE UP											THE RESULTS						
Year	Team	Lg	G	GS	CG	GF	IP	BFP	H	R	ER	HR	SH	SF	HB	TBB	IBB	SO	WP	Bk	W	L	Pct	ShO	Sv-Op Hld	ERC	ERA
2003	StL	NL	26	1	0	7	38.1	162	29	12	12	5	1	3	1	20	2	51	3	1	1	1	.500	0	1-4 5	3.44	2.82
2004	StL	NL	41	0	0	4	45.1	168	27	14	14	5	4	0	1	10	1	47	1	0	3	1	.750	0	2-3 12	1.62	2.78
2005	Oak	AL	58	0	0	15	55.2	229	45	20	20	6	1	1	1	18	2	52	2	0	4	1	.800	0	1-2 12	2.80	3.23
2006	Oak	AL	70	0	0	17	58.0	241	50	22	22	4	0	1	0	24	3	67	1	0	3	2	.600	0	2-5 23	3.13	3.41
2007	Oak	AL	46	0	0	6	40.2	185	46	26	26	3	0	5	2	21	2	31	1	0	1	6	.107	0	1-4 9	5.26	5.75
	5 ML YEARS		211	1	0	49	238.0	985	197	94	94	23	6	10	5	93	10	248	8	1	12	10	.545	0	7 18 57	3.13	3.55

Carmen Cali

Pitches: L **Bats:** L **Pos:** RP-24   **Ht:** 5'10" **Wt:** 185 **Born:** 11/4/1978 **Age:** 29

			HOW MUCH HE PITCHED						WHAT HE GAVE UP											THE RESULTS						
Year	Team	Lg	G	GS	CG	GF	IP	BFP	H	R	ER	HR	SH	SF	HB	TBB	IBB	SO	WP	Bk	W	L	Pct	ShO	Sv-Op Hld	ERC	ERA
2007	Roch*	AAA	31	0	0	11	47.2	187	42	17	13	1	2	3	0	14	1	28	2	1	5	1	.833	0	1- --	2.64	2.45
2004	StL	NL	10	0	0	2	7.1	40	13	7	7	1	0	1	0	6	1	8	1	0	0	0	-	0	0-0 0	10.96	8.59
2005	StL	NL	6	0	0	3	6.0	33	10	8	7	3	0	1	0	6	1	5	1	0	0	0	-	0	0-0 0	14.93	10.50
2007	Min	AL	24	0	0	7	21.0	101	22	11	11	2	0	0	2	16	3	14	2	0	0	1	.000	0	0-1 2	5.87	4.71
	3 ML YEARS		40	0	0	12	34.1	174	45	26	25	6	0	2	2	28	5	27	4	0	0	1	.000	0	0-1 2	8.36	6.55

Alberto Callaspo

Bats: B **Throws:** R **Pos:** 3B-18; PH-18; 2B-10; SS-9; RF-7; LF-3; PR-1   **Ht:** 5'10" **Wt:** 175 **Born:** 4/19/1983 **Age:** 25

			BATTING																	BASERUNNING				AVERAGES		
Year	Team	Lg	G	AB	H	2B	3B	HR	(Hm	Rd)	TB	R	RBI	RC	TBB	IBB	SO	HBP	SH	SF	SB	CS	SB%	GDP	Avg	OBP	Slg
2002	Provo	R+	70	299	101	16	10	3	(-	-)	146	70	60	55	17	0	14	2	3	3	13	4	.76	6	.338	.374	.488
2003	CRpds	A	133	514	168	38	4	2	(-	-)	220	86	67	87	42	4	28	3	0	6	20	6	.77	8	.327	.377	.428
2004	Ark	AA	136	550	156	29	2	6	(-	-)	207	76	48	72	47	1	25	0	11	4	15	14	.52	16	.284	.338	.376
2005	Ark	AA	89	350	104	9	0	10	(-	-)	143	53	49	51	28	1	17	1	1	5	9	8	.53	4	.297	.346	.409
2005	Salt Lk	AAA	50	212	67	21	2	1	(-	-)	95	28	31	32	10	1	13	1	2	3	2	5	.29	7	.316	.345	.448
2006	Tucsn	AAA	114	490	165	24	12	7	(-	-)	234	93	68	96	56	3	27	2	2	4	8	5	.62	5	.337	.404	.478
2007	Tucsn	AAA	59	226	77	15	2	5	(-	-)	111	48	30	46	28	2	17	1	0	6	1	2	.33	8	.341	.406	.491
2006	Ari	NL	23	42	10	1	1	0	(0	0)	13	2	6	5	4	0	6	0	0	0	0	1	.00	0	.238	.298	.310
2007	Ari	NL	56	144	31	8	0	0	(0	0)	39	10	7	7	9	0	14	1	1	1	1	1	.50	8	.215	.265	.271
	2 ML YEARS		79	186	41	9	1	0	(0	0)	52	12	13	12	13	0	20	1	1	2	1	2	.33	8	.220	.272	.280

Kevin Cameron

Pitches: R **Bats:** R **Pos:** RP-48   **Ht:** 6'1" **Wt:** 180 **Born:** 12/15/1979 **Age:** 28

			HOW MUCH HE PITCHED						WHAT HE GAVE UP											THE RESULTS						
Year	Team	Lg	G	GS	CG	GF	IP	BFP	H	R	ER	HR	SH	SF	HB	TBB	IBB	SO	WP	Bk	W	L	Pct	ShO	Sv-Op Hld	ERC	ERA
2001	Elizab	R+	22	0	0	22	23.0	94	16	4	4	0	0	0	3	5	0	30	3	0	1	1	.500	0	13- --	1.67	1.57
2003	QuadC	A	39	0	0	16	62.0	281	57	30	27	2	5	1	2	33	5	58	13	0	1	5	.167	0	2- --	3.50	3.92
2004	FtMyrs	A+	22	0	0	10	31.2	131	23	13	11	1	0	0	0	13	1	22	2	0	2	3	.400	0	1- --	2.16	3.13

59

			HOW MUCH HE PITCHED						WHAT HE GAVE UP												THE RESULTS							
Year	Team	Lg	G	GS	CG	GF	IP	BFP	H	R	ER	HR	SH	SF	HB	TBB	IBB	SO	WP	Bk	W	L	Pct	ShO	Sv-Op	Hld	ERC	ERA
2004	NwBrit	AA	26	0	0	10	46.1	209	47	20	12	1	0	0	2	21	2	47	2	0	1	3	.250	0	3- -	-	3.78	2.33
2005	NwBrit	AA	42	0	0	16	75.2	331	75	38	24	8	2	2	1	26	1	57	1	1	6	2	.750	0	6- -	-	3.76	2.85
2006	Roch	AAA	40	0	0	23	66.1	280	53	25	22	2	3	2	3	26	1	65	3	0	6	4	.600	0	9- -	-	2.61	2.98
2007	SD	NL	48	0	0	20	58.0	263	55	24	18	0	4	2	0	36	5	50	2	0	2	0	1.000	0	0-0	1	3.67	2.79

Mike Cameron

Bats: R **Throws:** R **Pos:** CF-150; PH-2; PR-1   **Ht:** 6'2" **Wt:** 200 **Born:** 1/8/1973 **Age:** 35

			BATTING																	BASERUNNING				AVERAGES		
Year	Team	Lg	G	AB	H	2B	3B	HR	(Hm	Rd)	TB	R	RBI	RC	TBB	IBB	SO	HBP	SH	SF	SB	CS	SB%	GDP	Avg	OBP	Slg
1995	CWS	AL	28	38	7	2	0	1	(0	1)	12	4	2	3	3	0	15	0	3	0	0	0	-	0	.184	.244	.316
1996	CWS	AL	11	11	1	0	0	0	(0	0)	1	1	0	1	1	0	3	0	0	0	0	1	.00	0	.091	.167	.091
1997	CWS	AL	116	379	98	18	3	14	(10	4)	164	63	55	63	55	1	105	5	2	5	23	2	.92	6	.259	.356	.433
1998	CWS	AL	141	396	83	16	5	8	(5	3)	133	53	43	39	37	0	101	6	1	3	27	11	.71	6	.210	.285	.336
1999	Cin	NL	146	542	139	34	9	21	(12	9)	254	93	66	96	80	2	145	6	5	3	38	12	.76	4	.256	.357	.469
2000	Sea	AL	155	543	145	28	4	19	(15	4)	238	96	78	91	78	0	133	9	7	6	24	7	.77	10	.267	.365	.438
2001	Sea	AL	150	540	144	30	5	25	(7	18)	259	99	110	96	69	3	155	10	1	13	34	5	.87	13	.267	.353	.480
2002	Sea	AL	158	545	130	26	5	25	(7	18)	241	84	80	78	79	3	176	7	4	5	31	8	.79	5	.239	.340	.442
2003	Sea	AL	147	534	135	31	5	18	(11	7)	230	74	76	80	70	1	137	5	1	2	17	7	.71	13	.253	.344	.431
2004	NYM	NL	140	493	114	30	1	30	(11	19)	236	76	76	70	57	2	143	8	1	3	22	6	.79	5	.231	.319	.479
2005	NYM	NL	76	308	84	23	2	12	(7	5)	147	47	39	52	29	0	85	4	1	1	13	1	.93	5	.273	.342	.477
2006	SD	NL	141	552	148	34	9	22	(11	11)	266	88	83	98	71	2	142	6	0	5	25	9	.74	8	.268	.355	.482
2007	SD	NL	151	571	138	33	6	21	(10	11)	246	88	78	83	67	1	160	8	2	3	18	5	.78	5	.242	.328	.431
13 ML YEARS			1560	5452	1366	305	54	216	(96	120)	2427	866	786	849	696	15	1500	74	28	49	272	74	.79	89	.251	.341	.445

Shawn Camp

Pitches: R **Bats:** R **Pos:** RP-50   **Ht:** 6'1" **Wt:** 200 **Born:** 11/18/1975 **Age:** 32

			HOW MUCH HE PITCHED						WHAT HE GAVE UP												THE RESULTS							
Year	Team	Lg	G	GS	CG	GF	IP	BFP	H	R	ER	HR	SH	SF	HB	TBB	IBB	SO	WP	Bk	W	L	Pct	ShO	Sv-Op	Hld	ERC	ERA
2007	Drham*	AAA	12	0	0	8	15.1	61	13	2	2	0	1	0	2	2	0	16	0	0	0	1	.000	0	4- -	-	2.18	1.17
2004	KC	AL	42	0	0	12	66.2	286	74	37	29	10	2	3	5	16	1	51	2	1	2	2	.500	0	2-3	5	4.74	3.92
2005	KC	AL	29	0	0	7	49.0	228	69	40	35	4	0	3	4	13	3	28	3	0	1	4	.200	0	0-2	0	6.00	6.43
2006	TB	AL	75	0	0	15	75.0	328	93	43	39	9	2	3	7	19	3	53	4	0	7	4	.636	0	4-6	12	5.48	4.68
2007	TB	AL	50	0	0	8	40.0	198	63	33	32	7	5	1	3	18	6	36	2	0	0	3	.000	0	0-2	11	8.59	7.20
4 ML YEARS			196	0	0	42	230.2	1040	299	153	135	30	9	10	19	66	13	168	11	1	10	13	.435	0	6-13	28	5.89	5.27

Jorge Campillo

Pitches: R **Bats:** R **Pos:** RP-5   **Ht:** 6'1" **Wt:** 190 **Born:** 8/10/1978 **Age:** 29

			HOW MUCH HE PITCHED						WHAT HE GAVE UP												THE RESULTS							
Year	Team	Lg	G	GS	CG	GF	IP	BFP	H	R	ER	HR	SH	SF	HB	TBB	IBB	SO	WP	Bk	W	L	Pct	ShO	Sv-Op	Hld	ERC	ERA
2007	Tacom*	AAA	24	22	0	0	149.1	623	151	55	51	11	2	4	5	39	0	99	2	0	9	6	.600	0	0- -	-	3.59	3.07
2005	Sea	AL	2	1	0	1	2.0	9	1	0	0	0	0	0	0	1	0	1	0	0	0	0	-	0	0-0	0	1.26	0.00
2006	Sea	AL	1	0	0	0	2.1	11	4	4	4	0	0	0	0	0	0	1	0	0	0	0	-	0	0-0	0	5.71	15.43
2007	Sea	AL	5	0	0	2	13.1	63	18	12	10	2	1	1	1	6	0	9	0	0	0	0	-	0	0-0	0	7.18	6.75
3 ML YEARS			8	1	0	3	17.2	83	23	16	14	2	1	1	1	7	0	11	0	0	0	0	-	0	0-0	0	6.11	7.13

Robinson Cano

Bats: L **Throws:** R **Pos:** 2B-159; PH-3   **Ht:** 6'0" **Wt:** 205 **Born:** 10/22/1982 **Age:** 25

			BATTING																	BASERUNNING				AVERAGES		
Year	Team	Lg	G	AB	H	2B	3B	HR	(Hm	Rd)	TB	R	RBI	RC	TBB	IBB	SO	HBP	SH	SF	SB	CS	SB%	GDP	Avg	OBP	Slg
2005	NYY	AL	132	522	155	34	4	14	(5	9)	239	78	62	59	16	1	68	3	7	3	1	3	.25	16	.297	.320	.458
2006	NYY	AL	122	482	165	41	1	15	(9	6)	253	62	78	74	18	3	54	2	1	5	5	2	.71	9	.342	.365	.525
2007	NYY	AL	160	617	189	41	7	19	(10	9)	301	93	97	94	39	5	85	8	1	4	4	5	.44	19	.306	.353	.488
3 ML YEARS			414	1621	509	116	12	48	(24	24)	793	233	237	227	73	9	207	13	9	12	10	10	.50	54	.314	.346	.489

Jorge Cantu

Bats: R **Throws:** R **Pos:** PH-23; 1B-21; DH-7; 2B-2; 3B-1   **Ht:** 6'3" **Wt:** 200 **Born:** 1/30/1982 **Age:** 26

			BATTING																	BASERUNNING				AVERAGES		
Year	Team	Lg	G	AB	H	2B	3B	HR	(Hm	Rd)	TB	R	RBI	RC	TBB	IBB	SO	HBP	SH	SF	SB	CS	SB%	GDP	Avg	OBP	Slg
2007	Drham*	AAA	24	91	22	5	1	1	(-	-)	32	12	10	10	8	0	21	0	0	1	0	0	-	1	.242	.300	.352
2007	Lsvlle*	AAA	24	94	29	9	0	2	(-	-)	44	12	13	16	5	1	15	3	0	0	0	0	-	0	.309	.363	.468
2004	TB	AL	50	173	52	20	1	2	(0	2)	80	25	17	22	9	0	44	2	0	1	0	0	-	5	.301	.341	.462
2005	TB	AL	150	598	171	40	1	28	(16	12)	297	73	117	88	19	1	83	6	0	7	1	0	1.00	24	.286	.311	.497
2006	TB	AL	107	413	103	18	2	14	(7	7)	167	40	62	42	26	2	91	3	0	6	1	1	.50	16	.249	.295	.404
2007	2 Tms		52	115	29	9	0	1	(0	1)	41	12	13	12	12	0	26	3	0	3	0	0	-	6	.252	.331	.357
07	TB	AL	25	58	12	1	0	0	(0	0)	13	4	4	3	5	0	16	1	0	1	0	0	-	3	.207	.277	.224
07	Cin	NL	27	57	17	8	0	1	(0	1)	28	8	9	9	7	0	10	2	0	2	0	0	-	3	.298	.382	.491
4 ML YEARS			359	1299	355	87	4	45	(23	22)	585	150	209	164	66	3	244	14	0	17	2	1	.67	51	.273	.312	.450

Jose Capellan

Pitches: R **Bats:** R **Pos:** RP-17   **Ht:** 6'4" **Wt:** 235 **Born:** 1/13/1981 **Age:** 27

Year	Team	Lg	G	GS	CG	GF	IP	BFP	H	R	ER	HR	SH	SF	HB	TBB	IBB	SO	WP	Bk	W	L	Pct	ShO	Sv-Op	Hld	ERC	ERA
2007	Nashv*	AAA	17	3	0	8	28.0	121	23	15	12	1	1	2	1	14	0	22	1	2	3	2	.600	0	1--	-	3.13	3.86
2007	Toledo*	AAA	9	0	0	9	9.1	41	12	7	6	3	1	0	0	1	1	5	0	0	0	1	.000	0	3--	-	5.78	5.79
2004	Atl	NL	3	2	0	0	8.0	42	14	10	10	2	1	1	0	5	0	4	0	0	0	1	.000	0	0 0	0	11.31	11.25
2005	Mil	NL	17	0	0	7	15.2	67	17	6	5	1	2	2	0	5	0	14	0	0	1	1	.500	0	0-3	3	4.01	2.87
2006	Mil	NL	61	0	0	12	71.2	310	65	37	35	11	8	2	3	31	7	58	3	0	4	2	.667	0	0-2	16	4.04	4.40
2007	2 Tms		17	0	0	9	26.0	115	28	19	16	7	0	1	1	9	2	20	3	0	0	3	.000	0	0-0	1	5.49	5.54
07	Mil	NL	7	0	0	3	12.0	52	10	6	6	2	0	1	0	6	1	8	2	0	0	2	.000	0	0-0	0	3.79	4.50
07	Det	AL	10	0	0	6	14.0	63	18	13	10	5	0	0	1	3	1	12	1	0	0	1	.000	0	0-0	1	7.07	6.43
4 ML YEARS			98	2	0	28	121.1	534	124	72	66	21	11	6	4	50	9	96	6	0	5	7	.417	0	0-2	20	4.76	4.90

Matt Capps

Pitches: R **Bats:** R **Pos:** RP-76   **Ht:** 6'2" **Wt:** 245 **Born:** 9/3/1983 **Age:** 24

Year	Team	Lg	G	GS	CG	GF	IP	BFP	H	R	ER	HR	SH	SF	HB	TBB	IBB	SO	WP	Bk	W	L	Pct	ShO	Sv-Op	Hld	ERC	ERA
2005	Pit	NL	4	0	0	0	4.0	16	5	2	2	0	0	1	0	3	0	3	0	0	0	0	-	0	0-0	0	4.62	4.50
2006	Pit	NL	85	0	0	15	80.2	329	81	37	34	12	8	2	3	12	5	56	4	0	9	1	.900	0	1-10	13	3.52	3.79
2007	Pit	NL	76	0	0	47	79.0	315	64	22	20	5	3	2	3	16	10	64	1	0	4	7	.364	0	18-21	15	2.10	2.28
3 ML YEARS			165	0	0	62	163.2	660	150	61	56	17	11	4	7	28	15	123	5	0	13	8	.619	0	19-31	28	2.84	3.08

Chris Capuano

Pitches: L **Bats:** L **Pos:** SP-25; RP-4   **Ht:** 6'2" **Wt:** 220 **Born:** 8/19/1978 **Age:** 29

Year	Team	Lg	G	GS	CG	GF	IP	BFP	H	R	ER	HR	SH	SF	HB	TBB	IBB	SO	WP	Bk	W	L	Pct	ShO	Sv-Op	Hld	ERC	ERA
2003	Ari	NL	9	5	0	2	33.0	139	27	19	17	3	4	1	6	11	1	23	3	0	2	4	.333	0	0-0	1	3.45	4.64
2004	Mil	NL	17	17	0	0	88.1	385	91	55	49	18	4	1	5	37	1	80	3	1	6	8	.429	0	0-0	0	5.37	4.99
2005	Mil	NL	35	35	0	0	219.0	949	212	105	97	31	14	5	12	91	6	176	3	4	18	12	.600	0	0-0	0	4.44	3.99
2006	Mil	NL	34	34	3	0	221.1	936	229	108	99	29	9	8	4	47	4	174	7	0	11	12	.478	2	0-0	0	3.84	4.03
2007	Mil	NL	29	25	0	0	150.0	669	170	93	85	20	10	3	8	54	2	132	10	0	5	12	.294	0	0-0	0	5.11	5.10
5 ML YEARS			124	116	3	2	711.2	3078	729	380	347	101	41	18	40	240	14	585	26	5	42	48	.467	2	0-0	1	4.46	4.39

Buddy Carlyle

Pitches: R **Bats:** L **Pos:** SP-20; RP-2   **Ht:** 6'3" **Wt:** 185 **Born:** 12/21/1977 **Age:** 30

Year	Team	Lg	G	GS	CG	GF	IP	BFP	H	R	ER	HR	SH	SF	HB	TBB	IBB	SO	WP	Bk	W	L	Pct	ShO	Sv-Op	Hld	ERC	ERA
2007	Rchmd*	AAA	9	9	1	0	48.2	189	40	15	14	5	0	0	2	9	1	66	1	0	5	2	.714	1	0--	-	2.50	2.59
1999	SD	NL	7	7	0	0	37.2	162	36	28	25	7	1	2	2	17	0	29	1	0	1	3	.250	0	0-0	0	4.95	5.97
2000	SD	NL	4	0	0	2	3.0	18	6	7	7	0	0	0	0	3	0	2	0	0	0	0	-	0	0-0	0	12.01	21.00
2005	LAD	NL	10	0	0	2	14.0	62	16	13	13	4	2	0	1	4	0	13	0	0	0	0	-	0	0-1	0	6.07	8.36
2007	Atl	NL	22	20	0	1	107.0	462	117	67	62	19	11	5	2	32	8	74	3	0	8	7	.533	0	0-1	0	4.71	5.21
4 ML YEARS			43	27	0	5	161.2	704	175	115	107	30	14	7	5	56	8	118	4	0	9	10	.474	0	0-1	0	5.01	5.96

Fausto Carmona

Pitches: R **Bats:** R **Pos:** SP-32   **Ht:** 6'4" **Wt:** 220 **Born:** 12/7/1983 **Age:** 24

Year	Team	Lg	G	GS	CG	GF	IP	BFP	H	R	ER	HR	SH	SF	HB	TBB	IBB	SO	WP	Bk	W	L	Pct	ShO	Sv-Op	Hld	ERC	ERA
2002	Burlgtn	A	13	11	0	2	76.1	326	89	36	28	4	4	4	6	10	0	42	1	3	2	4	.333	0	1--	-	3.93	3.30
2002	MhVlly	A-	3	0	0	2	4.0	13	2	0	0	0	0	0	0	1	0	0	0	0	0	0	-	0	0--	-	1.09	0.00
2003	Lk Cty	A	24	24	1	0	148.1	573	117	48	34	10	7	2	3	14	0	83	3	0	17	4	.810	0	0--	-	1.78	2.06
2003	Akron	AA	1	1	0	0	6.0	27	8	3	3	1	0	0	1	0	0	3	0	0	0	0	-	0	0--	-	5.41	4.50
2004	Knstn	A+	12	12	0	0	70.0	297	68	28	22	6	3	2	2	20	0	57	4	0	5	2	.714	0	0--	-	3.52	2.83
2004	Akron	AA	15	15	0	0	87.0	381	114	52	48	3	7	5	2	21	0	63	4	1	4	8	.333	0	0--	-	4.93	4.97
2004	Buffalo	AAA	1	1	0	0	6.0	26	6	4	4	0	0	0	0	3	0	2	0	0	1	0	1.000	0	0--	-	3.79	6.00
2005	Akron	AA	14	14	0	0	90.2	398	100	46	41	7	5	2	8	20	1	57	2	0	6	5	.545	0	0--	-	4.03	4.07
2005	Buffalo	AAA	13	12	1	0	83.0	336	76	32	30	10	4	2	3	15	0	49	2	0	7	4	.636	0	0--	-	3.06	3.25
2006	Buffalo	AAA	6	5	0	0	27.2	118	28	21	17	2	0	3	1	8	0	28	3	0	1	3	.250	0	0--	-	3.64	5.53
2006	Cle	AL	38	7	0	12	74.2	340	88	46	45	9	2	4	7	31	3	58	3	1	1	10	.091	0	0-3	10	5.69	5.42
2007	Cle	AL	32	32	2	0	215.0	879	199	78	73	16	2	4	11	61	2	137	5	1	19	8	.704	1	0-0	0	3.32	3.06
2 ML YEARS			70	39	2	12	289.2	1219	287	124	118	25	4	8	18	92	5	195	8	2	20	18	.526	1	0-3	10	3.90	3.67

Chris Carpenter

Pitches: R **Bats:** R **Pos:** SP-1   **Ht:** 6'6" **Wt:** 230 **Born:** 4/27/1975 **Age:** 33

Year	Team	Lg	G	GS	CG	GF	IP	BFP	H	R	ER	HR	SH	SF	HB	TBB	IBB	SO	WP	Bk	W	L	Pct	ShO	Sv-Op	Hld	ERC	ERA
2007	PlmBh*	A+	2	2	0	0	4.1	22	7	5	3	0	0	0	0	1	0	4	0	0	0	1	.000	0	0--	-	5.77	6.23
1997	Tor	AL	14	13	1	0	81.1	374	108	55	46	7	1	2	2	37	0	55	7	1	3	7	.300	0	0-0	0	6.38	5.09
1998	Tor	AL	33	24	1	4	175.0	742	177	97	85	18	4	5	5	61	1	136	5	0	12	7	.632	1	0-0	0	4.12	4.37
1999	Tor	AL	24	24	4	0	150.0	663	177	81	73	16	4	6	3	48	1	106	9	1	9	8	.529	1	0-0	0	4.90	4.38
2000	Tor	AL	34	27	2	1	175.1	795	204	130	122	30	3	1	5	83	1	113	3	0	10	12	.455	0	0-0	0	6.04	6.26
2001	Tor	AL	34	34	3	0	215.2	930	229	112	98	29	3	1	16	75	5	157	5	0	11	11	.500	2	0-0	0	4.82	4.09
2002	Tor	AL	13	13	1	0	73.1	327	89	45	43	11	1	4	4	27	0	45	3	0	4	5	.444	0	0-0	0	5.91	5.28
2004	StL	NL	28	28	1	0	182.0	746	169	75	70	24	6	3	8	38	2	152	4	0	15	5	.750	0	0-0	0	3.32	3.46

Year	Team	Lg	G	GS	CG	GF	IP	BFP	H	R	ER	HR	SH	SF	HB	TBB	IBB	SO	WP	Bk	W	L	Pct	ShO	Sv-Op	Hld	ERC	ERA
							HOW MUCH HE PITCHED				WHAT HE GAVE UP													THE RESULTS				
2005	StL	NL	33	33	7	0	241.2	953	204	82	76	18	7	7	3	51	0	213	5	0	21	5	.808	4	0-0	0	2.49	2.83
2006	StL	NL	32	32	5	0	221.2	896	194	81	76	21	12	4	10	43	3	184	3	0	15	8	.652	3	0-0	0	2.75	3.09
2007	StL	NL	1	1	0	0	6.0	29	9	5	5	0	1	0	1	1	0	3	0	0	0	1	.000	0	0-0	0	5.80	7.50
	10 ML YEARS		246	229	25	6	1522.0	6455	1560	763	694	174	42	33	57	464	13	1164	44	2	100	69	.592	12	0-0	0	4.11	4.10

Hector Carrasco

Pitches: R **Bats:** R **Pos:** RP-28; SP-1   **Ht:** 6'2" **Wt:** 235 **Born:** 10/22/1969 **Age:** 38

Year	Team	Lg	G	GS	CG	GF	IP	BFP	H	R	ER	HR	SH	SF	HB	TBB	IBB	SO	WP	Bk	W	L	Pct	ShO	Sv-Op	Hld	ERC	ERA
2007	Clmbs*	AAA	15	0	0	1	18.1	89	23	22	18	4	0	1	0	15	0	10	6	0	1	2	.333	0	0- -	-	8.63	8.84
1994	Cin	NL	45	0	0	29	56.1	237	42	17	14	3	5	0	2	30	1	41	3	1	5	6	.455	0	6-8	3	3.01	2.24
1995	Cin	NL	64	0	0	28	87.1	391	86	45	40	1	2	6	2	46	5	64	15	0	2	7	.222	0	5-9	11	3.77	4.12
1996	Cin	NL	56	0	0	10	74.1	325	58	37	31	6	4	4	1	45	5	59	8	1	4	3	.571	0	0-2	15	3.41	3.75
1997	2 Tms		66	0	0	22	86.0	388	80	46	42	7	4	3	8	41	5	76	11	2	2	8	.200	0	0-2	8	4.00	4.40
1998	Min	AL	63	0	0	20	61.2	287	75	30	30	4	0	8	1	31	1	46	8	0	4	2	.667	0	1-2	10	5.47	4.38
1999	Min	AL	39	0	0	11	49.0	204	48	29	27	3	0	1	1	18	0	35	4	0	2	3	.400	0	1-2	7	3.76	4.96
2000	2 Tms	AL	69	1	0	20	78.2	364	90	46	41	8	8	4	4	38	1	64	14	1	5	4	.556	0	1-6	8	5.37	4.69
2001	Min	AL	56	0	0	12	73.2	317	77	40	38	8	6	3	0	30	3	70	7	1	4	3	.571	0	1-2	1	4.42	4.64
2003	Bal	AL	40	0	0	10	38.1	174	40	22	21	5	4	0	2	20	3	27	0	0	2	6	.250	0	1-3	8	5.09	4.93
2005	Was	NL	64	5	0	13	88.1	358	59	23	20	6	4	4	6	38	7	75	6	1	5	4	.556	0	2-4	8	2.41	2.04
2006	LAA	AL	56	3	0	24	100.1	417	93	42	38	10	2	2	5	27	1	72	6	0	7	3	.700	0	1-2	1	3.36	3.41
2007	LAA	AL	29	1	0	9	38.1	187	44	34	28	8	0	1	1	23	1	33	3	0	2	1	.667	0	0-0	2	6.40	6.57
97	Cin	NL	38	0	0	11	51.1	237	51	25	21	3	3	1	4	25	2	46	3	2	1	2	.333	0	0-0	5	4.14	3.68
97	KC	AL	28	0	0	11	34.2	151	29	21	21	4	1	2	4	16	3	30	8	0	1	6	.143	0	0-2	3	3.79	5.45
00	Min	AL	61	0	0	18	72.0	324	75	38	34	6	6	4	3	33	0	57	14	0	4	3	.571	0	1-5	7	4.52	4.25
00	Bos	AL	8	1	0	2	6.2	40	15	8	7	2	2	0	1	5	1	7	0	1	1	1	.500	0	0-1	1	16.76	9.45
	12 ML YEARS		647	10	0	208	832.1	3649	792	411	370	69	39	36	33	387	33	662	85	7	44	50	.468	0	19-42	82	4.00	4.00

Brett Carroll

Bats: R **Throws:** R **Pos:** CF-12; LF-7; RF-5; PR-4; PH-3   **Ht:** 6'0" **Wt:** 190 **Born:** 10/3/1982 **Age:** 25

Year	Team	Lg	G	AB	H	2B	3B	HR	(Hm	Rd)	TB	R	RBI	RC	TBB	IBB	SO	HBP	SH	SF	SB	CS	SB%	GDP	Avg	OBP	Slg
2004	Jmstwn	A-	60	211	53	16	1	6	(-	-)	89	27	28	29	15	1	57	7	2	1	1	0	1.00	2	.251	.321	.422
2005	Grnsbr	A	118	412	100	28	1	18	(-	-)	184	57	54	54	17	2	108	15	3	2	10	10	.50	4	.243	.296	.447
2006	Jupiter	A+	59	216	52	12	1	8	(-	-)	90	31	30	31	18	1	48	9	0	1	9	3	.75	3	.241	.324	.417
2006	Carlina	AA	74	251	58	15	3	9	(-	-)	106	29	30	33	18	1	62	8	3	0	4	1	.80	8	.231	.303	.422
2007	Carlina	AA	30	100	27	13	0	3	(-	-)	49	9	12	17	12	0	20	3	0	2	0	2	.00	3	.270	.359	.490
2007	Albq	AAA	88	317	100	21	6	19	(-	-)	190	60	70	65	18	0	68	7	0	3	0	4	.00	7	.315	.362	.599
2007	Fla	NL	23	49	9	1	0	0	(0	0)	10	10	2	0	3	0	15	0	1	0	0	0	-	1	.184	.231	.204

Jamey Carroll

Bats: R **Throws:** R **Pos:** 2B-60; 3B-35; PR-20; PH-14; SS-11; RF-2; CF-1   **Ht:** 5'9" **Wt:** 170 **Born:** 2/18/1974 **Age:** 34

Year	Team	Lg	G	AB	H	2B	3B	HR	(Hm	Rd)	TB	R	RBI	RC	TBB	IBB	SO	HBP	SH	SF	SB	CS	SB%	GDP	Avg	OBP	Slg
2002	Mon	NL	16	71	22	5	3	1	(1	0)	36	16	6	12	4	0	12	0	4	0	1	0	1.00	1	.310	.347	.507
2003	Mon	NL	105	227	59	10	1	1	(1	0)	74	31	10	18	19	0	39	3	9	2	2	.71	10	.260	.323	.326
2004	Mon	NL	102	218	63	14	2	0	(0	0)	81	36	16	28	32	1	21	1	2	3	5	1	.83	3	.289	.378	.372
2005	Was	NL	113	303	76	8	1	0	(0	0)	86	44	22	38	34	1	55	5	13	3	3	4	.43	2	.251	.333	.284
2006	Col	NL	136	463	139	23	5	5	(2	3)	187	84	36	65	56	1	66	3	9	3	10	12	.45	10	.300	.377	.404
2007	Col	NL	108	227	51	9	1	2	(1	1)	68	45	22	24	28	1	34	4	6	3	6	2	.75	2	.225	.317	.300
	6 ML YEARS		580	1509	410	69	13	9	(5	4)	532	256	112	185	173	4	227	16	43	14	30	21	.59	28	.272	.350	.353

Marcos Carvajal

Pitches: R **Bats:** R **Pos:** RP-3   **Ht:** 6'4" **Wt:** 175 **Born:** 8/19/1984 **Age:** 23

Year	Team	Lg	G	GS	CG	GF	IP	BFP	H	R	ER	HR	SH	SF	HB	TBB	IBB	SO	WP	Bk	W	L	Pct	ShO	Sv-Op	Hld	ERC	ERA
2002	Ddgrs	R	13	5	0	3	42.0	169	30	12	8	0	0	1	4	15	0	35	1	0	3	2	.600	0	0- -	-	2.18	1.71
2003	Ogden	R+	23	0	0	21	38.0	173	32	16	13	1	2	2	4	22	0	50	6	1	2	1	.667	0	2- -	-	3.63	3.08
2004	Clmbs	A	36	0	0	21	72.0	299	50	19	15	2	3	4	5	35	0	72	7	0	4	2	.667	0	1- -	-	2.57	1.88
2004	Jaxnvl	AA	1	0	0	0	3.0	13	2	0	0	0	0	0	0	2	0	2	1	0	0	0	-	0	0- -	-	2.54	0.00
2006	Mont	AA	39	0	0	14	72.1	321	66	34	31	7	3	1	2	39	0	69	6	0	2	2	.500	0	0- -	-	4.16	3.86
2007	Bnghtn	AA	28	22	0	2	119.0	545	120	82	69	13	5	8	5	63	1	92	10	1	5	10	.333	0	0- -	-	4.74	5.22
2005	Col	NL	39	0	0	11	53.0	229	52	30	30	8	2	2	3	21	0	47	4	0	0	0	.000	0	0-1	0	4.57	5.09
2007	Fla	NL	3	0	0	3	4.0	24	8	4	3	0	0	1	0	2	0	2	0	0	0	0	-	0	0-0	0	8.87	6.75
	2 ML YEARS		42	0	0	14	57.0	253	60	34	33	8	2	3	3	23	0	49	4	0	0	2	.000	0	0-1	0	4.87	5.21

Raul Casanova

Bats: B **Throws:** R **Pos:** C-23; PH-6; DH-1; PR-1   **Ht:** 6'0" **Wt:** 235 **Born:** 8/23/1972 **Age:** 35

Year	Team	Lg	G	AB	H	2B	3B	HR	(Hm	Rd)	TB	R	RBI	RC	TBB	IBB	SO	HBP	SH	SF	SB	CS	SB%	GDP	Avg	OBP	Slg
2007	Drham*	AAA	44	141	41	9	0	5			65	14	21	22	12	0	32	0	0	0	0	0	-	3	.291	.346	.461
1996	Det	AL	25	85	16	1	0	4	(1	3)	29	6	9	5	6	0	18	0	0	0	0	0	-	6	.188	.242	.341
1997	Det	AL	101	304	74	10	1	5	(5	0)	101	27	24	29	26	1	48	3	0	1	1	1	.50	10	.243	.308	.332
1998	Det	AL	16	42	6	2	0	1	(1	0)	11	4	3	3	5	0	10	1	0	0	0	0	-	0	.143	.250	.262
2000	Mil	NL	86	231	57	13	3	6	(4	2)	94	24	36	31	26	1	48	4	2	2	1	2	.33	5	.247	.331	.407

Year	Team	Lg	G	AB	H	2B	3B	HR	(Hm	Rd)	TB	R	RBI	RC	TBB	IBB	SO	HBP	SH	SF	SB	CS	SB%	GDP	Avg	OBP	Slg
										BATTING											BASERUNNING				AVERAGES		
2001	Mil	NL	71	192	50	10	0	11	(7	4)	93	21	33	28	12	2	29	1	0	3	0	0	-	3	.260	.303	.484
2002	2 Tms		33	88	16	1	0	1	(0	1)	20	3	8	4	10	4	19	1	0	1	0	0	-	3	.182	.270	.227
2005	CWS	AL	6	5	1	0	0	0	(0	0)	1	0	0	1	0	0	1	0	0	0	0	0	-	3	.200	.200	.200
2007	TB	AL	29	79	20	1	1	6	(0	6)	41	12	11	9	7	1	17	1	0	2	0	0	-	3	.253	.315	.519
02	Mil	AL	31	87	16	1	0	1	(0	1)	20	3	8	4	10	4	18	1	0	1	0	0	-	3	.184	.273	.230
02	Bal	AL	2	1	0	0	0	0	(0	0)	0	0	0	0	0	0	0	0	0	0	0	0	*	0	.000	.000	.000
8 ML YEARS			367	1026	210	00	5	54	(18	16)	390	93	124	110	92	9	190	11	2	9	2	3	.40	30	.234	.301	.380

Sean Casey

Bats: L Throws: R Pos: 1B-131; PH-13; DH-7   **Ht: 6'4" Wt: 235 Born: 7/2/1974 Age: 33**

Year	Team	Lg	G	AB	H	2B	3B	HR	(Hm	Rd)	TB	R	RBI	RC	TBB	IBB	SO	HBP	SH	SF	SB	CS	SB%	GDP	Avg	OBP	Slg
										BATTING											BASERUNNING				AVERAGES		
1997	Cle	AL	6	10	2	0	0	0	(0	0)	2	1	1	1	1	0	2	1	0	0	0	0	-	0	.200	.333	.200
1998	Cin	NL	96	302	82	21	1	7	(3	4)	126	44	52	45	43	3	45	3	0	3	1	1	.50	11	.272	.365	.417
1999	Cin	NL	151	594	197	42	3	25	(11	14)	320	103	99	119	61	13	88	9	0	5	0	2	.00	15	.332	.399	.539
2000	Cin	NL	133	480	151	33	2	20	(9	11)	248	69	85	91	52	4	80	7	0	6	1	0	1.00	16	.315	.385	.517
2001	Cin	NL	145	533	165	40	0	13	(5	8)	244	69	89	86	43	8	63	9	0	3	3	1	.75	16	.310	.369	.458
2002	Cin	NL	120	425	111	25	0	6	(3	3)	154	56	42	45	43	6	47	5	0	3	2	1	.67	11	.261	.334	.362
2003	Cin	NL	147	573	167	19	3	14	(8	6)	234	71	80	84	51	4	58	2	0	3	4	0	1.00	19	.291	.350	.408
2004	Cin	NL	146	571	185	44	2	24	(9	15)	305	101	99	104	46	5	36	10	0	6	1	0	1.00	16	.324	.381	.534
2005	Cin	NL	137	529	165	32	0	9	(4	5)	224	75	58	72	48	3	48	5	0	5	1	0	1.00	27	.312	.371	.423
2006	2 Tms		112	397	108	22	0	8	(3	5)	154	47	59	57	33	9	43	7	0	3	0	1	.00	10	.272	.336	.388
2007	Det	AL	143	453	134	30	1	4	(2	2)	178	40	54	57	39	11	42	2	0	2	2	2	.50	9	.296	.353	.393
06	Pit	NL	59	213	63	15	0	3	(1	2)	87	30	29	33	23	5	22	6	0	2	0	0	-	7	.296	.377	.408
06	Det	AL	53	184	45	7	0	5	(2	3)	67	17	30	24	10	4	21	1	0	1	0	1	.00	3	.245	.286	.364
11 ML YEARS			1336	4867	1467	308	12	130	(57	73)	2189	676	718	761	460	66	552	60	0	39	17	8	.68	150	.301	.366	.450

Kevin Cash

Bats: R Throws: R Pos: C-12   **Ht: 6'0" Wt: 190 Born: 12/6/1977 Age: 30**

Year	Team	Lg	G	AB	H	2B	3B	HR	(Hm	Rd)	TB	R	RBI	RC	TBB	IBB	SO	HBP	SH	SF	SB	CS	SB%	GDP	Avg	OBP	Slg
										BATTING											BASERUNNING				AVERAGES		
2007	Pwtckt*	AAA	59	176	31	7	0	7	(-	-)	59	22	25	17	23	0	56	2	5	2	0	0	-	4	.176	.276	.335
2002	Tor	AL	7	14	2	0	0	0	(0	0)	2	1	0	0	1	0	4	0	0	0	0	0	-	1	.143	.200	.143
2003	Tor	AL	34	106	15	3	0	1	(1	0)	21	10	8	0	4	0	22	1	5	1	0	0	-	6	.142	.179	.198
2004	Tor	AL	60	181	35	9	0	4	(2	2)	56	18	21	11	10	0	59	4	0	2	0	0	-	3	.193	.249	.309
2005	TB	AL	13	31	5	1	0	2	(1	1)	12	4	2	0	1	0	13	1	0	0	0	0	-	3	.161	.212	.387
2007	Bos	AL	12	27	3	1	0	0	(0	0)	4	2	4	1	4	0	13	1	0	1	0	0	-	2	.111	.242	.148
5 ML YEARS			126	359	60	14	0	7	(4	3)	95	35	35	12	20	0	111	7	5	4	0	0	-	15	.167	.223	.265

Alexi Casilla

Bats: B Throws: R Pos: 2B-52; SS-5; PR-4; PH-1   **Ht: 5'9" Wt: 178 Born: 7/20/1984 Age: 23**

Year	Team	Lg	G	AB	H	2B	3B	HR	(Hm	Rd)	TB	R	RBI	RC	TBB	IBB	SO	HBP	SH	SF	SB	CS	SB%	GDP	Avg	OBP	Slg
										BATTING											BASERUNNING				AVERAGES		
2004	Angels	R	45	163	42	1	4	0	(-	-)	51	29	10	20	15	0	10	4	2	2	24	8	.75	3	.258	.332	.313
2004	CRpds	A	9	29	9	2	1	0	(-	-)	13	6	1	6	5	0	4	0	0	0	1	1	.50	0	.310	.412	.448
2004	Provo	R+	4	12	4	1	1	0	(-	-)	7	4	1	4	4	0	0	1	0	0	1	0	1.00	0	.333	.529	.583
2005	CRpds	A	78	308	100	11	3	3	(-	-)	126	62	17	56	29	0	31	6	3	1	47	12	.80	6	.325	.392	.409
2005	Ark	AA	7	19	4	0	0	0	(-	-)	4	4	4	1	2	0	3	0	0	0	1	1	.50	0	.211	.286	.211
2005	Salt Lk	AAA	13	39	10	0	0	0	(-	-)	10	3	1	3	3	0	6	0	4	0	1	1	.50	1	.256	.310	.256
2006	FtMyrs	A+	78	323	107	12	6	0	(-	-)	131	56	33	57	30	0	36	2	3	1	31	6	.84	8	.331	.390	.406
2006	NwBrit	AA	45	170	50	10	1	1	(-	-)	65	28	13	28	18	0	20	4	7	0	19	4	.83	1	.294	.375	.382
2007	Roch	AAA	84	320	86	13	1	3	(-	-)	110	53	20	41	34	1	50	4	6	1	24	12	.67	6	.269	.345	.344
2006	Min	AL	9	4	1	0	0	0	(0	0)	1	1	0	1	2	0	1	0	0	0	0	0	-	0	.250	.500	.250
2007	Min	AL	56	189	42	5	1	0	(0	0)	49	15	9	11	9	0	29	0	5	1	11	1	.92	5	.222	.256	.259
2 ML YEARS			65	193	43	5	1	0	(0	0)	50	16	9	12	11	0	30	0	5	1	11	1	.92	5	.223	.263	.259

Santiago Casilla

Pitches: R Bats: R Pos: RP-46   **Ht: 6'0" Wt: 202 Born: 7/25/1980 Age: 27**

Year	Team	Lg	G	GS	CG	GF	IP	BFP	H	R	ER	HR	SH	SF	HB	TBB	IBB	SO	WP	Bk	W	L	Pct	ShO	Sv-Op	Hld	ERC	ERA
			HOW MUCH HE PITCHED						WHAT HE GAVE UP												THE RESULTS							
2007	Scrmto*	AAA	22	0	0	10	24.0	100	16	10	10	1	0	2	0	14	2	29	4	0	2	1	.667	0	3--	-	2.48	3.75
2004	Oak	AL	4	0	0	2	5.2	32	5	8	8	3	0	0	1	9	0	5	0	0	0	0	-	0	0-0	0	13.22	12.71
2005	Oak	AL	3	0	0	3	3.0	12	2	1	1	0	0	0	0	1	0	1	1	0	0	0	-	0	0-0	0	1.57	3.00
2006	Oak	AL	2	0	0	1	2.1	10	2	3	3	0	0	0	0	2	0	2	0	0	0	0	-	0	0-0	0	4.61	11.57
2007	Oak	AL	46	0	0	10	50.2	219	43	25	25	6	0	3	1	23	6	52	5	0	3	1	.750	0	2-5	12	3.39	4.44
4 ML YEARS			55	0	0	16	61.2	273	52	37	37	9	0	3	2	35	6	60	6	0	3	1	.750	0	2-5	12	4.08	5.40

Jack Cassel

Pitches: R Bats: R Pos: SP-4; RP-2   **Ht: 6'2" Wt: 190 Born: 8/8/1980 Age: 27**

Year	Team	Lg	G	GS	CG	GF	IP	BFP	H	R	ER	HR	SH	SF	HB	TBB	IBB	SO	WP	Bk	W	L	Pct	ShO	Sv-Op	Hld	ERC	ERA
			HOW MUCH HE PITCHED						WHAT HE GAVE UP												THE RESULTS							
2000	Idaho	R+	7	0	0	2	12.2	52	10	8	2	1	0	1	0	3	1	13	0	1	0	0	-	0	0--	-	2.06	1.42
2000	FtWyn	A	22	0	0	6	36.1	160	42	24	19	2	0	2	2	12	0	25	4	0	2	2	.500	0	0--	-	4.61	4.71
2001	FtWyn	A	25	23	0	1	128.1	591	163	104	79	7	5	4	12	35	0	89	6	5	4	14	.222	0	0--	-	5.06	5.54
2002	FtWyn	A	27	0	0	9	50.2	222	58	22	17	0	0	2	1	11	3	34	4	1	4	1	.800	0	0--	-	3.44	3.02

			HOW MUCH HE PITCHED						WHAT HE GAVE UP													THE RESULTS							
Year	Team	Lg	G	GS	CG	GF	IP	BFP	H	R	ER	HR	SH	SF	HB	TBB	IBB	SO	WP	Bk	W	L	Pct	ShO	Sv-Op	Hld	ERC	ERA
2002	Lk Els	A+	23	0	0	4	37.0	154	33	15	10	0	1	0	3	11	0	25	0	1	1	1	.500	0	1--	-	2.76	2.43
2003	Lk Els	A+	64	0	0	22	72.2	300	69	34	29	0	4	0	4	18	1	52	7	0	5	4	.556	0	3--	-	2.78	3.59
2004	Mobile	AA	57	0	0	19	74.2	333	76	35	31	4	1	2	8	27	2	52	6	1	4	2	.667	0	1--	-	3.99	3.74
2005	Mobile	AA	24	3	0	9	43.0	184	45	18	16	1	1	0	2	16	4	29	5	0	3	3	.500	0	1--	-	3.78	3.35
2005	Portlnd	AAA	23	3	0	8	39.0	183	54	25	20	2	2	1	2	17	2	21	2	1	3	2	.600	0	0--	-	6.32	4.62
2006	Portlnd	AAA	18	11	0	0	76.1	346	96	60	55	12	1	1	2	28	2	44	4	0	3	5	.375	0	0--	-	5.98	6.48
2006	Mobile	AA	12	12	1	0	78.2	321	66	30	20	3	0	2	7	18	0	75	4	0	6	3	.667	0	0--	-	2.52	2.29
2007	Portlnd	AAA	27	24	3	0	156.2	705	203	94	68	13	9	3	6	42	6	117	10	1	7	14	.333	0	0--	-	5.21	3.91
2007	SD	NL	6	4	0	0	22.2	98	30	10	10	1	0	0	1	5	0	11	1	0	1	1	.500	0	0-0	0	5.17	3.97

Alberto Castillo

Bats: R **Throws:** R **Pos:** C-11   **Ht:** 6'0" **Wt:** 215 **Born:** 2/10/1970 **Age:** 38

					BATTING															BASERUNNING				AVERAGES		
Year	Team	Lg	G	AB	H	2B	3B	HR	(Hm	Rd)	TB	R	RBI	RC	TBB	IBB	SO	HBP	SH	SF	SB	CS	SB%	GDP	Avg	OBP	Slg
2007	Norfolk*	AAA	64	203	55	6	0	3	(-	-)	70	24	24	29	32	0	34	0	3	2	0	0	-	5	.271	.367	.345
1995	NYM	NL	13	29	3	0	0	0	(0	0)	3	2	0	0	3	0	9	1	0	0	1	0	1.00	0	.103	.212	.103
1996	NYM	NL	6	11	4	0	0	0	(0	0)	4	1	0	1	0	0	4	0	0	0	0	0	-	0	.364	.364	.364
1997	NYM	NL	35	59	12	1	0	0	(0	0)	13	3	7	3	9	0	16	0	2	1	0	1	.00	3	.203	.304	.220
1998	NYM	NL	38	83	17	4	0	2	(0	2)	27	13	7	7	9	0	17	1	6	0	0	2	.00	1	.205	.290	.325
1999	StL	NL	93	255	67	8	0	4	(2	2)	87	21	31	29	24	1	48	2	5	4	0	0	-	6	.263	.326	.341
2000	Tor	AL	66	185	39	7	0	1	(1	0)	49	14	16	14	21	0	36	0	2	3	0	0	-	3	.211	.287	.265
2001	Tor	AL	66	131	26	4	0	1	(0	1)	33	9	4	7	7	0	30	3	5	0	1	1	.50	2	.198	.255	.252
2002	NYY	AL	15	37	5	1	1	0	(0	0)	8	3	4	1	1	0	12	0	3	0	0	0	-	2	.135	.158	.216
2003	SF	NL	11	15	3	1	0	1	(1	0)	7	2	4	2	0	0	5	0	0	0	0	0	-	0	.200	.200	.467
2004	KC	AL	29	89	24	6	0	1	(0	1)	33	12	11	10	14	0	10	0	1	1	0	2	.00	1	.270	.365	.371
2005	2 Tms	AL	35	101	21	5	1	1	(1	0)	31	13	14	12	12	0	22	0	1	1	1	0	1.00	2	.208	.289	.307
2007	Bal	AL	11	31	5	2	0	1	(0	1)	10	5	3	1	3	0	10	0	1	1	0	0	-	1	.161	.229	.323
05	KC	AL	34	100	21	5	1	1	(1	0)	31	13	14	12	12	0	21	0	1	1	1	0	1.00	2	.210	.292	.310
05	Oak	AL	1	1	0	0	0	0	(0	0)	0	0	0	0	0	0	1	0	0	0	0	0	-	0	.000	.000	.000
12 ML YEARS			418	1026	226	39	2	12	(5	7)	305	98	101	87	103	1	219	7	26	11	3	6	.33	21	.220	.293	.297

Jose Castillo

Bats: R **Throws:** R **Pos:** 3B-34; PH-32; 2B-20; SS-8; RF-1; PR-1   **Ht:** 6'1" **Wt:** 219 **Born:** 3/19/1981 **Age:** 27

					BATTING															BASERUNNING				AVERAGES		
Year	Team	Lg	G	AB	H	2B	3B	HR	(Hm	Rd)	TB	R	RBI	RC	TBB	IBB	SO	HBP	SH	SF	SB	CS	SB%	GDP	Avg	OBP	Slg
2004	Pit	NL	129	383	98	15	2	8	(3	5)	141	44	39	40	23	5	92	1	5	2	3	2	.60	12	.256	.298	.368
2005	Pit	NL	101	370	99	16	3	11	(2	9)	154	49	53	43	23	3	59	0	1	4	2	3	.40	11	.268	.307	.416
2006	Pit	NL	148	518	131	25	0	14	(10	4)	198	54	65	53	32	8	98	5	1	6	6	4	.60	22	.253	.299	.382
2007	Pit	NL	87	221	54	18	1	0	(0	0)	74	18	24	16	6	2	48	2	0	1	0	0	-	11	.244	.270	.335
4 ML YEARS			465	1492	382	74	6	33	(15	18)	567	165	181	152	84	18	297	8	7	13	11	9	.55	56	.256	.297	.380

Luis Castillo

Bats: B **Throws:** R **Pos:** 2B-135   **Ht:** 5'11" **Wt:** 190 **Born:** 9/12/1975 **Age:** 32

					BATTING															BASERUNNING				AVERAGES		
Year	Team	Lg	G	AB	H	2B	3B	HR	(Hm	Rd)	TB	R	RBI	RC	TBB	IBB	SO	HBP	SH	SF	SB	CS	SB%	GDP	Avg	OBP	Slg
1996	Fla	NL	41	164	43	2	1	1	(0	1)	50	26	8	19	14	0	46	0	2	0	17	4	.81	0	.262	.320	.305
1997	Fla	NL	75	263	63	8	0	0	(0	0)	71	27	8	21	27	0	53	0	1	0	16	10	.62	6	.240	.310	.270
1998	Fla	NL	44	153	31	3	2	1	(0	1)	41	21	10	14	22	0	33	1	1	0	3	0	1.00	1	.203	.307	.268
1999	Fla	NL	128	487	147	23	4	0	(0	0)	178	76	28	78	67	0	85	0	6	3	50	17	.75	3	.302	.384	.366
2000	Fla	NL	136	539	180	17	3	2	(1	1)	209	101	17	95	78	0	86	0	9	0	62	22	.74	11	.334	.418	.388
2001	Fla	NL	134	537	141	16	10	2	(1	1)	183	76	45	67	67	0	90	1	4	3	33	16	.67	6	.263	.344	.341
2002	Fla	NL	146	606	185	18	5	2	(0	2)	219	86	39	84	55	4	76	2	4	1	48	15	.76	7	.305	.364	.361
2003	Fla	NL	152	595	187	19	6	6	(2	4)	236	99	39	87	63	0	60	2	15	1	21	19	.53	7	.314	.381	.397
2004	Fla	NL	150	564	164	12	7	2	(1	1)	196	91	47	84	75	2	68	1	4	3	21	4	.84	15	.291	.373	.348
2005	Fla	NL	122	439	132	12	4	4	(0	4)	164	72	30	61	65	1	32	1	18	1	10	7	.59	11	.301	.391	.374
2006	Min	AL	142	584	173	22	6	3	(3	0)	216	84	49	80	56	0	58	1	9	2	25	11	.69	14	.296	.358	.370
2007	2 Tms	NL	135	548	165	19	5	1	(0	1)	197	91	38	76	53	0	45	0	12	2	19	6	.76	5	.301	.362	.359
07	Min	AL	85	349	106	11	3	0	(0	0)	123	54	18	45	29	0	28	0	5	1	9	4	.69	3	.304	.356	.352
07	NYM	NL	50	199	59	8	2	1	(0	1)	74	37	20	31	24	0	17	0	7	1	10	2	.83	2	.296	.371	.372
12 ML YEARS			1405	5479	1611	171	53	24	(8	16)	1960	850	358	766	642	7	732	9	86	17	325	131	.71	86	.294	.368	.358

Kory Casto

Bats: L **Throws:** R **Pos:** LF-12; PH-4; 1B-2   **Ht:** 6'1" **Wt:** 195 **Born:** 12/8/1981 **Age:** 26

					BATTING															BASERUNNING				AVERAGES		
Year	Team	Lg	G	AB	H	2B	3B	HR	(Hm	Rd)	TB	R	RBI	RC	TBB	IBB	SO	HBP	SH	SF	SB	CS	SB%	GDP	Avg	OBP	Slg
2003	Vrmnt	A-	71	259	62	14	2	4	(-	-)	92	26	28	31	30	1	47	2	0	1	1	1	.50	3	.239	.322	.355
2004	Savann	A	124	483	138	35	4	16	(-	-)	229	67	88	78	31	1	70	8	1	3	1	2	.33	5	.286	.337	.474
2005	Ptomc	A+	135	500	145	36	4	22	(-	-)	255	86	90	104	84	1	98	5	0	5	6	3	.67	5	.290	.394	.510
2006	Hrsbrg	AA	140	489	133	24	6	20	(-	-)	229	84	80	92	81	4	104	8	4	8	6	5	.55	13	.272	.379	.468
2007	Clmbs	AAA	113	408	101	20	2	11	(-	-)	158	56	55	56	54	0	105	2	1	3	4	4	.50	7	.248	.336	.387
2007	Was	NL	16	54	7	2	0	0	(0	0)	9	1	3	0	2	0	17	0	0	0	0	0	-	3	.130	.158	.167

Fabio Castro

Pitches: L Bats: L Pos: RP-9; SP-1
Ht: 5'7" Wt: 183 Born: 1/20/1985 Age: 23

		HOW MUCH HE PITCHED				WHAT HE GAVE UP											THE RESULTS					
Year Team	Lg	G GS CG GF	IP	BFP	H	R	ER	HR	SH	SF	HB	TBB	IBB	SO	WP	Bk	W	L	Pct	ShO	Sv-Op Hld	ERC	ERA
2003 Bristol	R+	19 0 0 10	47.0	190	29	14	9	1	1	1	1	19	1	59	6	2	6	2	.750	0	2-- -	1.69	1.72
2003 Knapol	A-	2 2 0 0	11.0	45	8	5	4	0	0	0	0	5	0	16	0	0	0	2	.000	0	0-- -	2.21	3.27
2004 Knapol	A-	37 0 0 15	51.0	222	44	20	17	2	0	0	3	23	0	44	2	0	4	0	1.000	0	3-- -	3.26	3.00
2004 WinSa	A+	6 0 0 0	7.2	27	2	2	2	0	0	0	1	2	0	9	1	0	1	1	.500	0	0-- -	0.64	2.35
2005 WinSa	A+	53 0 0 20	79.0	321	58	23	20	7	4	4	3	37	0	75	4	0	5	5	.500	0	6-- -	3.07	2.28
2006 Frisco	AA	5 4 0 0	13.2	62	14	7	3	1	0	0	0	8	0	10	1	0	0	1	.000	0	0-- -	4.71	1.98
2006 Okla	AAA	1 1 0 0	3.2	17	5	2	2	0	0	0	0	1	0	5	0	0	0	0	-	0	0-- -	4.76	4.91
2007 Ottawa	AAA	21 7 0 3	58.1	257	53	32	26	7	4	6	1	33	1	47	0	0	5	5	.500	0	1-- -	4.39	4.01
2007 Rdng	AA	11 0 0 3	16.2	68	12	5	5	0	0	0	0	6	0	24	3	0	2	0	1.000	0	1-- -	1.84	2.70
2006 2 Tms		20 0 0 11	31.2	125	18	9	8	1	2	2	2	13	0	18	0	1	0	1	.000	0	1-2 0	1.76	2.27
2007 Phi	NL	10 1 0 4	12.0	56	9	8	8	2	0	0	0	13	0	14	0	0	0	0	-	0	0-0 1	5.99	6.00
06 Tex	AL	4 0 0 2	8.1	37	6	5	4	0	0	0	0	7	0	5	0	0	0	0	-	0	0-0 0	3.47	4.32
06 Phi	NL	16 0 0 9	23.1	88	12	4	4	1	2	2	2	6	0	13	0	1	0	1	.000	0	1-2 0	1.34	1.54
2 ML YEARS		30 1 0 15	43.2	181	27	17	16	3	2	2	2	26	0	32	0	1	0	1	.000	0	1-2 1	2.77	3.30

Juan Castro

Bats: R Throws: R Pos: PH-18; 3B-17; SS-16; 2B-8; PR-3
Ht: 5'11" Wt: 195 Born: 6/20/1972 Age: 36

		BATTING																		BASERUNNING				AVERAGES		
Year Team	Lg	G	AB	H	2B	3B	HR	(Hm Rd)	TB	R	RBI	RC	TBB	IBB	SO	HBP	SH	SF		SB	CS	SB%	GDP	Avg	OBP	Slg
1995 LAD	NL	11	4	1	0	0	0	(0 0)	1	0	0	1	1	0	1	0	0	0		0	0	-	0	.250	.400	.250
1996 LAD	NL	70	132	26	5	3	0	(0 0)	37	16	5	8	10	0	27	0	4	0		1	0	1.00	3	.197	.254	.280
1997 LAD	NL	40	75	11	3	1	0	(0 0)	16	3	4	2	7	1	20	0	2	0		0	0	-	2	.147	.220	.213
1998 LAD	NL	89	220	43	7	0	2	(0 2)	56	25	14	12	15	0	37	0	9	2		0	0	-	5	.195	.245	.255
1999 LAD	NL	2	1	0	0	0	0	(0 0)	0	0	0	0	0	0	1	0	0	0		0	0	-	0	.000	.000	.000
2000 Cin	NL	82	224	54	12	2	4	(1 3)	82	20	23	20	14	1	33	0	4	2		0	2	.00	9	.241	.283	.366
2001 Cin	NL	96	242	54	10	0	3	(0 3)	73	27	13	16	13	2	50	0	4	2		0	0	-	9	.223	.261	.302
2002 Cin	NL	54	82	18	3	0	2	(0 2)	27	5	11	11	7	0	18	0	1	1		0	0	-	0	.220	.278	.329
2003 Cin	NL	113	320	81	14	1	9	(4 5)	124	28	33	36	18	1	58	0	7	3		2	3	.40	7	.253	.290	.388
2004 Cin	NL	111	299	73	21	2	5	(3 2)	113	36	26	26	14	1	51	0	2	1		1	0	1.00	11	.244	.277	.378
2005 Min	AL	97	272	70	18	1	5	(2 3)	105	27	33	28	9	1	39	0	9	2		0	1	.00	8	.257	.279	.386
2006 2 Tms		104	251	63	10	3	3	(3 0)	88	18	28	26	11	0	36	0	1	1		1	2	.33	6	.251	.281	.351
2007 Cin	NL	54	89	16	5	0	0	(0 0)	21	5	5	2	4	0	21	0	3	2		0	0	-	2	.180	.211	.236
06 Min	AL	50	156	36	5	2	1	(1 0)	48	10	14	11	6	0	23	0	1	1		1	1	.50	6	.231	.258	.308
06 Cin	NL	54	95	27	5	1	2	(2 0)	40	8	14	15	5	0	13	0	0	0		0	1	.00	0	.284	.320	.421
13 ML YEARS		923	2211	510	108	13	33	(13 20)	743	210	195	188	123	7	392	0	46	16		5	8	.38	62	.231	.269	.336

Ramon Castro

Bats: R Throws: R Pos: C-50; PH-6
Ht: 6'0" Wt: 256 Born: 3/1/1976 Age: 32

		BATTING																		BASERUNNING				AVERAGES		
Year Team	Lg	G	AB	H	2B	3B	HR	(Hm Rd)	TB	R	RBI	RC	TBB	IBB	SO	HBP	SH	SF		SB	CS	SB%	GDP	Avg	OBP	Slg
1999 Fla	NL	24	67	12	4	0	2	(0 2)	22	4	4	6	10	3	14	0	0	1		0	0	-	1	.179	.282	.328
2000 Fla	NL	50	138	33	4	0	2	(0 2)	43	10	14	14	16	7	36	1	0	2		0	0	-	1	.239	.318	.312
2001 Fla	NL	7	11	2	0	0	0	(0 0)	2	0	1	0	1	0	1	0	0	0		0	0	-	0	.182	.250	.182
2002 Fla	NL	54	101	24	4	0	6	(4 2)	46	11	18	14	14	3	24	0	1	3		0	0	-	4	.238	.322	.455
2003 Fla	NL	40	53	15	2	0	5	(4 1)	32	6	8	8	4	0	11	0	0	0		0	0	-	4	.283	.333	.604
2004 Fla	NL	32	96	13	3	0	3	(0 3)	25	9	8	4	11	2	30	1	0	0		0	0	-	1	.135	.231	.260
2005 NYM	NL	99	209	51	16	0	8	(5 3)	91	26	41	30	25	2	58	0	3	3		1	0	1.00	7	.244	.321	.435
2006 NYM	NL	40	126	30	7	0	4	(1 3)	49	13	12	11	15	2	40	1	1	1		0	0	-	2	.238	.322	.389
2007 NYM	NL	52	144	41	6	0	11	(3 8)	80	24	31	23	10	0	39	1	0	2		0	0	-	1	.285	.331	.556
9 ML YEARS		398	945	221	46	0	41	(17 24)	390	103	137	110	106	19	253	4	5	12		1	0	1.00	17	.234	.310	.413

Frank Catalanotto

Bats: L Throws: R Pos: LF-64; DH-17; 1B-14; PH-11; PR-1
Ht: 6'0" Wt: 195 Born: 4/27/1974 Age: 34

		BATTING																		BASERUNNING				AVERAGES		
Year Team	Lg	G	AB	H	2B	3B	HR	(Hm Rd)	TB	R	RBI	RC	TBB	IBB	SO	HBP	SH	SF		SB	CS	SB%	GDP	Avg	OBP	Slg
2007 Frisco*	AA	1	4	0	0	0	0	(- -)	0	1	0	0	1	0	2	0	0	0		0	0	-	0	.000	.200	.000
2007 Okla*	AAA	4	13	5	2	0	0	(- -)	7	5	0	3	2	0	1	1	0	0		0	0	-	0	.385	.500	.538
1997 Det	AL	13	26	8	2	0	0	(0 0)	10	2	3	4	3	0	7	0	0	0		0	0	-	0	.308	.379	.385
1998 Det	AL	89	213	60	13	2	6	(3 3)	95	23	25	30	12	1	39	4	0	5		3	2	.60	4	.282	.325	.446
1999 Det	AL	100	286	79	19	0	11	(6 5)	131	41	35	42	15	1	49	9	0	5		3	4	.43	4	.276	.327	.458
2000 Tex	AL	103	282	82	13	2	10	(6 4)	129	55	42	49	33	0	36	6	3	2		6	2	.75	5	.291	.375	.457
2001 Tex	AL	133	463	153	31	5	11	(4 7)	227	77	54	88	39	3	55	8	1	1		15	5	.75	5	.330	.391	.490
2002 Tex	AL	68	212	57	16	6	3	(2 1)	94	42	23	39	25	0	27	8	3	2		9	5	.64	3	.269	.364	.443
2003 Tor	AL	133	489	146	34	6	13	(7 6)	231	83	59	84	35	1	62	6	2	2		5	5	.50	9	.299	.351	.472
2004 Tor	AL	75	249	73	19	1	1	(1 0)	97	27	26	34	17	1	33	4	1	3		1	0	1.00	7	.293	.344	.390
2005 Tor	AL	130	419	126	29	5	8	(3 5)	189	56	59	80	37	0	53	10	4	5		2	0	.00	9	.301	.367	.451
2006 Tor	AL	128	437	131	36	2	7	(2 5)	192	56	56	72	52	0	37	4	2	4		1	3	.25	11	.300	.376	.439
2007 Tex	AL	103	331	86	20	4	11	(9 2)	147	52	44	51	28	0	37	11	6	1		2	1	.67	6	.260	.337	.444
11 ML YEARS		1075	3407	1001	232	33	81	(43 38)	1542	514	426	573	296	7	435	70	22	31		42	26	.62	63	.294	.359	.453

Troy Cate

Pitches: L **Bats:** L **Pos:** RP-14   **Ht:** 6'1" **Wt:** 220 **Born:** 10/21/1980 **Age:** 27

Year	Team	Lg	G	GS	CG	GF	IP	BFP	H	R	ER	HR	SH	SF	HB	TBB	IBB	SO	WP	Bk	W	L	Pct	ShO	Sv-Op	Hld	ERC	ERA
2002	Everett	A-	16	12	1	1	85.1	323	62	21	19	6	5	0	2	11	0	95	4	0	6	1	.857	1	0--	-	1.67	2.00
2003	InldEm	A+	27	25	0	0	160.0	680	165	79	73	10	6	3	10	37	1	153	7	2	9	11	.450	0	0--	-	3.55	4.11
2003	Tacom	AAA	1	1	0	0	5.1	24	4	3	1	2	0	0	1	2	0	6	0	0	1	0	1.000	0	0--	-	4.87	1.69
2004	SnAnt	AA	12	12	0	0	56.2	256	74	44	40	7	2	3	2	20	0	35	1	1	2	5	.286	0	0--	-	6.12	6.35
2004	InldEm	A+	7	3	0	0	20.2	85	21	8	6	2	1	0	0	6	0	24	0	0	3	0	1.000	0	0--	-	3.83	2.61
2005	InldEm	A+	23	0	0	10	42.2	198	36	21	12	1	3	0	7	25	0	54	5	1	4	4	.500	0	1--	-	3.83	2.53
2006	PlmBh	A+	34	0	0	13	41.0	154	19	8	7	3	3	0	1	13	0	58	1	0	2	2	.500	0	1--	-	1.28	1.54
2006	Sprgfld	AA	10	0	0	3	15.2	59	5	2	1	1	0	0	1	6	0	20	1	0	1	1	.500	0	1--	-	1.05	0.57
2007	Memp	AAA	33	9	0	5	71.1	328	88	61	54	14	6	3	0	30	3	60	2	0	2	5	.286	0	0--	-	6.14	6.81
2007	StL	NL	14	0	0	4	16.0	74	18	7	6	1	1	2	0	9	0	12	0	0	0	0	-	0	0-0	2	5.10	3.38

Andy Cavazos

Pitches: R **Bats:** R **Pos:** RP-17   **Ht:** 6'3" **Wt:** 225 **Born:** 1/5/1981 **Age:** 27

Year	Team	Lg	G	GS	CG	GF	IP	BFP	H	R	ER	HR	SH	SF	HB	TBB	IBB	SO	WP	Bk	W	L	Pct	ShO	Sv-Op	Hld	ERC	ERA
1999	Rngrs	R	10	7	0	1	36.1	151	35	16	15	3	3	1	0	12	0	15	1	1	2	0	1.000	0	0--	-	3.54	3.72
2000	Savann	A	20	15	0	1	82.1	364	67	49	43	13	2	1	3	55	0	71	10	0	2	5	.286	0	1--	-	4.66	4.70
2001	Savann	A	29	19	1	3	122.0	569	149	87	75	13	1	3	10	63	0	96	10	3	6	10	.375	0	0--	-	6.32	5.53
2002	Charltt	A+	33	10	0	13	82.2	345	66	40	36	7	2	1	2	33	4	63	6	1	6	5	.545	0	1--	-	2.89	3.92
2003	Peoria	A	36	13	0	16	103.2	445	106	51	46	9	3	6	1	40	2	56	7	2	5	4	.556	0	10--	-	4.09	3.99
2004	Tenn	AA	46	0	0	14	51.1	253	67	40	35	6	0	0	1	32	3	41	2	0	2	5	.286	0	1--	-	6.81	6.14
2005	Sprgfld	AA	23	0	0	4	29.0	121	27	15	13	4	2	1	2	7	4	24	0	0	1	2	.333	0	1--	-	3.39	4.03
2005	PlmBh	A+	28	0	0	12	31.2	137	36	20	12	1	1	0	0	7	0	43	0	1	1	5	.167	0	1--	-	3.59	3.41
2006	Sprgfld	AA	16	0	0	5	20.0	77	6	2	1	0	1	0	0	12	1	19	3	0	2	2	.500	0	0--	-	1.01	0.45
2006	Memp	AAA	44	0	0	13	56.1	231	47	23	22	2	5	3	1	16	1	55	0	0	1	5	.167	0	4--	-	2.38	3.51
2007	Memp	AAA	44	0	0	12	47.2	203	40	18	17	5	3	1	0	26	1	48	2	0	2	5	.286	0	0--	-	3.79	3.21
2007	StL	NL	17	0	0	5	20.0	104	27	27	23	5	2	3	2	16	0	15	2	0	0	0	-	0	0-0	0	9.65	10.35

Ronny Cedeno

Bats: R **Throws:** R **Pos:** SS-15; PH-11; 2B-8; PR-7; 3B-4   **Ht:** 6'0" **Wt:** 180 **Born:** 2/2/1983 **Age:** 25

Year	Team	Lg	G	AB	H	2B	3B	HR	(Hm	Rd)	TB	R	RBI	RC	TBB	IBB	SO	HBP	SH	SF	SB	CS	SB%	GDP	Avg	OBP	Slg
2007	Iowa*	AAA	75	287	103	15	3	10	(-	-)	154	52	37	63	30	3	46	2	7	1	6	4	.60	9	.359	.422	.537
2005	ChC	NL	41	80	24	3	0	1	(0	1)	30	13	6	11	5	1	11	2	2	0	1	0	1.00	4	.300	.356	.375
2006	ChC	NL	151	534	131	18	7	6	(4	2)	181	51	41	41	17	4	109	3	15	3	8	8	.50	10	.245	.271	.339
2007	ChC	NL	38	74	15	2	0	4	(2	2)	29	6	13	8	3	0	18	0	2	1	2	1	.67	0	.203	.231	.392
	3 ML YEARS		230	688	170	23	7	11	(6	5)	240	70	60	60	25	5	138	5	19	4	11	9	.55	14	.247	.277	.349

Gustavo Chacin

Pitches: L **Bats:** L **Pos:** SP-5   **Ht:** 5'11" **Wt:** 193 **Born:** 11/4/1980 **Age:** 27

Year	Team	Lg	G	GS	CG	GF	IP	BFP	H	R	ER	HR	SH	SF	HB	TBB	IBB	SO	WP	Bk	W	L	Pct	ShO	Sv-Op	Hld	ERC	ERA
2007	Syrcse*	AAA	3	3	0	0	9.2	44	13	8	8	1	0	1	1	3	0	5	2	0	0	2	.000	0	0--	-	6.35	7.45
2004	Tor	AL	2	2	0	0	14.0	52	8	4	4	0	0	0	1	3	0	6	0	0	1	1	.500	0	0-0	0	1.24	2.57
2005	Tor	AL	34	34	0	0	203.0	872	213	93	84	20	8	10	8	70	3	121	3	0	13	9	.591	0	0-0	0	4.30	3.72
2006	Tor	AL	17	17	0	0	87.1	384	90	51	49	19	2	0	6	38	2	47	0	0	9	4	.692	0	0-0	0	5.57	5.05
2007	Tor	AL	5	5	0	0	27.1	118	29	17	17	6	0	0	2	7	1	11	0	0	2	1	.667	0	0-0	0	4.90	5.60
	4 ML YEARS		58	58	0	0	331.2	1426	340	165	154	45	10	10	17	118	6	185	3	0	25	15	.625	0	0-0	0	4.52	4.18

Shawn Chacon

Pitches: R **Bats:** R **Pos:** RP-60; SP-4   **Ht:** 6'3" **Wt:** 220 **Born:** 12/23/1977 **Age:** 30

Year	Team	Lg	G	GS	CG	GF	IP	BFP	H	R	ER	HR	SH	SF	HB	TBB	IBB	SO	WP	Bk	W	L	Pct	ShO	Sv-Op	Hld	ERC	ERA
2001	Col	NL	27	27	0	0	160.0	711	157	96	90	26	6	3	10	87	10	134	6	0	6	10	.375	0	0-0	0	5.22	5.06
2002	Col	NL	21	21	0	0	119.1	537	122	84	76	25	5	2	7	60	3	67	0	1	5	11	.313	0	0-0	0	5.63	5.73
2003	Col	NL	23	23	0	0	137.0	596	124	73	70	12	10	5	12	58	4	93	8	0	11	8	.579	0	0-0	0	3.82	4.60
2004	Col	NL	66	0	0	60	63.1	316	71	52	50	12	7	0	5	52	7	52	9	0	1	9	.100	0	35-44	0	7.30	7.11
2005	2 Tms		27	24	0	0	151.2	652	135	59	58	14	9	5	14	66	4	79	6	1	8	10	.444	0	0-0	1	3.89	3.44
2006	2 Tms		26	20	0	0	109.0	516	124	86	77	23	7	7	9	63	3	62	4	1	7	6	.538	0	0-0	0	6.76	6.36
2007	Pit	NL	64	4	0	11	96.0	428	95	42	42	9	10	4	7	48	11	79	1	0	5	4	.556	0	1-8	12	4.46	3.94
05	Col	NL	13	12	0	0	72.2	322	69	33	33	7	9	4	8	36	4	39	3	0	1	7	.125	0	0-0	0	4.51	4.09
05	NYY	AL	14	12	0	0	79.0	330	66	26	25	7	0	1	6	30	0	40	3	1	7	3	.700	0	0-0	1	3.35	2.85
06	NYY	AL	17	11	0	0	63.0	306	77	54	49	11	3	5	5	36	2	35	3	0	5	3	.625	0	0-0	0	6.86	7.00
06	Pit	NL	9	9	0	0	46.0	210	47	32	28	12	4	2	4	27	1	27	1	1	2	3	.400	0	0-0	0	6.61	5.48
	7 ML YEARS		254	119	0	71	836.1	3756	828	492	463	121	54	26	64	434	42	566	34	3	43	58	.426	0	36-52	13	5.05	4.98

Joba Chamberlain

Pitches: R Bats: R Pos: RP-19   Ht: 6'2" Wt: 230 Born: 9/23/1985 Age: 22

			HOW MUCH HE PITCHED						WHAT HE GAVE UP										THE RESULTS					
Year	Team	Lg	G	GS	CG	GF	IP	BFP	H	R	ER	HR	SH	SF	HB	TBB	IBB	SO	WP	Bk	W	L	Pct	ShO	Sv-Op Hld	ERC	ERA
2007	Tampa	A+	7	7	0	0	40.0	156	25	10	9	0	0	1	1	11	0	51	2	0	4	0	1.000	0	0- - -	1.39	2.03
2007	Trntn	AA	8	7	0	1	40.1	166	32	15	15	4	1	1	2	15	1	66	3	0	4	2	.667	0	0- - -	3.03	3.35
2007	S-WB	AAA	3	1	0	0	8.0	29	5	0	0	0	0	0	0	1	0	18	1	0	1	0	1.000	0	0- - -	1.07	0.00
2007	NYY	AL	19	0	0	3	24.0	91	12	2	1	1	1	0	1	6	0	34	1	0	2	0	1.000	0	1-1 8	1.16	0.38

Endy Chavez

Bats: L Throws: L Pos: LF-37; RF-24; CF-10; PR-9; PH-6   Ht: 6'0" Wt: 165 Born: 2/7/1978 Age: 30

			BATTING																			BASERUNNING				AVERAGES		
Year	Team	Lg	G	AB	H	2B	3B	HR	(Hm	Rd)	TB	R	RBI	RC	TBB	IBB	SO	HBP	SH	SF	SB	CS	SB%	GDP	Avg	OBP	Slg
2007	Mets*	R	2	8	5	0	0	0	(-	-)	5	2	4	2	1	0	2	0	0	1	0	0	-	0	.625	.600	.625
2007	StLuci*	A+	4	16	8	1	0	0	(-	-)	9	3	2	3	0	0	0	0	0	0	0	1	.00	0	.500	.500	.563
2007	Bnghtn*	AA	1	3	0	0	0	0	(-	-)	0	0	0	0	2	0	0	0	0	0	0	0	-	0	.000	.400	.000
2001	KC	AL	29	77	16	2	0	0	(0	0)	18	4	5	2	3	0	8	0	0	0	0	2	.00	3	.208	.234	.234
2002	Mon	NL	36	125	37	8	5	1	(0	1)	58	20	9	14	5	0	16	0	7	1	3	5	.38	0	.296	.321	.464
2003	Mon	NL	141	483	121	25	5	5	(4	1)	171	66	47	56	31	3	59	0	9	3	18	7	.72	7	.251	.294	.354
2004	Mon	NL	132	502	139	20	6	5	(4	1)	186	65	34	56	30	0	40	1	12	2	32	7	.82	6	.277	.318	.371
2005	2 Tms	NL	98	116	25	4	3	0	(0	0)	35	19	11	8	7	0	14	0	7	0	2	2	.50	3	.216	.260	.302
2006	NYM	NL	133	353	108	22	5	4	(2	2)	152	48	42	54	24	3	44	0	11	2	12	3	.80	7	.306	.348	.431
2007	NYM	NL	71	150	43	7	2	1	(1	0)	57	20	17	20	9	0	16	0	5	1	5	2	.71	5	.287	.325	.380
05	Was	NL	7	9	2	1	0	0	(0	0)	3	2	1	1	3	0	1	0	0	0	0	1	.00	1	.222	.417	.333
05	Phi	NL	91	107	23	3	3	0	(0	0)	32	17	10	7	4	0	13	0	7	0	2	1	.67	2	.215	.243	.299
7 ML YEARS			640	1806	489	88	26	16	(11	5)	677	242	165	210	109	6	197	1	51	9	72	28	.72	31	.271	.311	.375

Eric Chavez

Bats: L Throws: R Pos: 3B-88; PR-2; DH-1; PH-1   Ht: 6'1" Wt: 230 Born: 12/7/1977 Age: 30

			BATTING																			BASERUNNING				AVERAGES		
Year	Team	Lg	G	AB	H	2B	3B	HR	(Hm	Rd)	TB	R	RBI	RC	TBB	IBB	SO	HBP	SH	SF	SB	CS	SB%	GDP	Avg	OBP	Slg
1998	Oak	AL	16	45	14	4	1	0	(0	0)	20	6	6	7	3	1	5	0	0	0	1	1	.50	1	.311	.354	.444
1999	Oak	AL	115	356	88	21	2	13	(8	5)	152	47	50	50	46	4	56	0	0	0	1	1	.50	7	.247	.333	.427
2000	Oak	AL	153	501	139	23	4	26	(15	11)	248	89	86	86	62	8	94	1	0	5	2	2	.50	9	.277	.355	.495
2001	Oak	AL	151	552	159	43	0	32	(14	18)	298	91	114	99	41	9	99	4	0	7	8	2	.80	7	.288	.338	.540
2002	Oak	AL	153	585	161	31	3	34	(17	17)	300	87	109	103	65	13	119	1	0	3	8	3	.73	8	.275	.348	.513
2003	Oak	AL	156	588	166	39	5	29	(12	17)	302	94	101	97	62	10	89	1	0	3	8	3	.73	14	.282	.350	.514
2004	Oak	AL	125	475	131	20	0	29	(15	14)	238	87	77	84	95	10	99	3	0	4	6	3	.67	21	.276	.397	.501
2005	Oak	AL	160	625	168	40	1	27	(15	12)	291	92	101	95	58	4	129	2	0	9	6	0	1.00	19	.269	.329	.466
2006	Oak	AL	137	485	117	24	2	22	(8	14)	211	74	72	70	84	6	100	1	0	6	3	0	1.00	19	.241	.351	.435
2007	Oak	AL	90	341	82	21	2	15	(10	5)	152	43	46	30	34	2	78	0	0	4	4	2	.67	9	.240	.306	.446
10 ML YEARS			1256	4553	1225	266	20	227	(114	113)	2212	710	762	729	550	67	866	13	0	40	47	17	.73	104	.269	.347	.486

Bruce Chen

Pitches: L Bats: L Pos: RP-5   Ht: 6'1" Wt: 215 Born: 6/19/1977 Age: 31

			HOW MUCH HE PITCHED						WHAT HE GAVE UP										THE RESULTS					
Year	Team	Lg	G	GS	CG	GF	IP	BFP	H	R	ER	HR	SH	SF	HB	TBB	IBB	SO	WP	Bk	W	L	Pct	ShO	Sv-Op Hld	ERC	ERA
2007	Okla*	AAA	4	4	0	0	16.0	68	17	11	10	3	0	1	1	3	0	12	0	0	1	1	.500	0	0- - -	4.40	5.63
1998	Atl	NL	4	4	0	0	20.1	91	23	9	9	3	1	0	1	9	1	17	0	0	2	0	1.000	0	0-0 0	5.55	3.98
1999	Atl	NL	16	7	0	3	51.0	214	38	32	31	11	1	1	2	27	3	45	0	0	2	2	.500	0	0-0 0	4.07	5.47
2000	2 Tms	NL	37	15	0	4	134.0	559	116	54	49	18	8	3	2	46	4	112	4	1	7	4	.636	0	0-0 0	3.35	3.29
2001	2 Tms	NL	27	27	0	0	146.0	634	146	90	79	29	4	7	1	59	4	126	5	0	7	7	.500	0	0-0 0	4.75	4.87
2002	3 Tms	NL	55	6	0	9	77.2	360	85	53	48	16	2	3	2	43	5	80	4	0	2	5	.286	0	0-0 4	5.99	5.56
2003	2 Tms	NL	16	2	0	4	24.1	110	26	16	15	6	3	3	2	10	1	20	0	0	0	1	.000	0	0-0 0	5.81	5.55
2004	Bal	AL	8	7	1	0	47.2	196	39	19	16	7	2	1	0	16	0	32	0	0	2	1	.667	0	0-0 0	3.13	3.02
2005	Bal	AL	34	32	1	0	197.1	832	187	94	84	33	3	9	9	63	0	133	2	1	13	10	.565	0	0-0 0	4.12	3.83
2006	Bal	AL	40	12	0	16	98.2	453	137	81	76	28	3	5	0	35	3	70	1	0	0	7	.000	0	0-0 0	7.73	6.93
2007	Tex	AL	5	0	0	3	10.0	46	11	11	8	3	0	0	0	6	1	7	0	0	0	0	-	0	0-0 0	6.90	7.20
00	Atl	NL	22	0	0	4	39.2	176	35	15	11	4	3	2	1	19	2	32	0	1	4	0	1.000	0	0-0 0	3.62	2.50
00	Phi	NL	15	15	0	0	94.1	383	81	39	38	14	5	1	1	27	2	80	4	0	3	4	.429	0	0-0 0	3.22	3.63
01	Phi	NL	16	16	0	0	86.1	381	90	53	48	19	2	4	1	31	4	79	2	0	4	5	.444	0	0-0 0	4.87	5.00
01	NYM	NL	11	11	0	0	59.2	253	56	37	31	10	2	3	0	28	0	47	3	0	3	2	.600	0	0-0 0	4.58	4.68
02	NYM	NL	1	0	0	0	0.2	3	1	0	0	0	0	0	0	0	0	0	0	0	0	0	-	0	0-0 0	4.47	0.00
02	Mon	NL	15	5	0	4	37.1	179	47	29	29	9	0	1	0	23	3	43	3	0	2	3	.400	0	0-0 4	7.69	6.99
02	Cin	NL	39	1	0	5	39.2	178	37	24	19	7	2	3	1	20	2	37	1	0	0	2	.000	0	0-0 0	4.55	4.31
03	Hou	NL	11	0	0	2	12.0	60	14	8	8	2	3	2	2	8	1	8	0	0	0	0	-	0	0-0 0	7.11	6.00
03	Bos	AL	5	2	0	2	12.1	50	12	8	7	4	0	1	0	2	0	12	0	0	0	1	.000	0	0-0 0	4.40	5.11
10 ML YEARS			242	112	2	39	807.0	3495	808	459	415	154	27	26	19	314	22	642	16	2	35	37	.486	0	0-0 6	4.73	4.63

Rocky Cherry

Pitches: R Bats: R Pos: RP-22   Ht: 6'5" Wt: 225 Born: 8/19/1979 Age: 28

			HOW MUCH HE PITCHED						WHAT HE GAVE UP										THE RESULTS					
Year	Team	Lg	G	GS	CG	GF	IP	BFP	H	R	ER	HR	SH	SF	HB	TBB	IBB	SO	WP	Bk	W	L	Pct	ShO	Sv-Op Hld	ERC	ERA
2003	Lansng	A	8	4	0	0	29.1	119	23	10	9	1	2	0	4	7	0	18	3	0	2	0	1.000	0	0- - -	2.45	2.76
2003	Boise	A-	10	10	0	0	54.0	222	36	21	13	1	1	1	2	18	0	55	2	0	5	2	.714	0	0- - -	1.70	2.17
2004	Dytona	A+	27	22	1	0	124.2	557	138	79	72	16	11	8	9	46	1	104	4	0	5	10	.333	1	0- - -	5.03	5.20
2005	WTenn	AA	3	3	0	0	9.1	41	8	5	2	0	1	0	1	4	0	9	0	0	0	0	-	0	0- - -	3.03	1.93
2006	WTenn	AA	31	0	0	16	48.2	200	43	14	12	3	5	3	3	14	3	50	6	0	4	1	.800	0	2- - -	2.95	2.22

Year	Team	Lg	G	GS	CG	GF	IP	BFP	H	R	ER	HR	SH	SF	HB	TBB	IBB	SO	WP	Bk	W	L	Pct	ShO	Sv-Op	Hld	ERC	ERA
2006	Iowa	AAA	2	0	0	0	2.2	12	3	3	3	0	0	0	0	1	0	2	1	0	1	0	1.000	0	0--	-	3.84	10.13
2007	Cubs	R	2	2	0	0	2.0	7	0	0	0	0	0	0	1	1	0	2	0	0	0	0	-	0	0--	-	1.08	0.00
2007	Iowa	AAA	43	1	0	16	51.0	220	50	27	26	5	0	0	1	18	0	56	5	0	2	0	1.000	0	7--	-	3.80	4.59
2007	2 Tms		22	0	0	2	31.1	145	30	20	19	4	2	2	3	19	2	23	0	0	1	1	.500	0	0-1	0	5.05	5.46
07	ChC	NL	12	0	0	2	15.0	66	13	6	5	1	0	1	1	6	1	13	0	0	1	1	.500	0	0-1	0	3.14	3.00
07	Bal	AL	10	0	0	0	16.1	79	17	14	14	3	2	1	2	13	1	10	0	0	0	0	-	0	0-0	0	7.06	7.71

Matt Chico

Pitches: L Bats: L Pos: SP-31 Ht: 6'0" Wt: 205 Born: 6/10/1983 Age: 25

Year	Team	Lg	G	GS	CG	GF	IP	BFP	H	R	ER	HR	SH	SF	HB	TBB	IBB	SO	WP	Bk	W	L	Pct	ShO	Sv-Op	Hld	ERC	ERA
2003	Yakima	A-	17	13	0	0	71.1	309	75	28	28	4	3	2	5	25	1	71	9	1	7	4	.636	0	0--	-	4.15	3.53
2004	Sbend	A	14	14	2	0	87.2	344	59	26	25	4	1	2	3	27	0	89	5	0	8	5	.615	1	0--	-	2.22	2.57
2004	ElPaso	AA	14	12	0	0	62.1	300	82	53	40	7	3	5	2	36	1	59	7	1	3	7	.300	0	0--	-	6.91	5.78
2005	Tenn	AA	10	10	0	0	52.2	246	75	44	36	8	5	4	2	15	1	35	2	2	1	7	.125	0	0--	-	6.62	6.15
2005	Lancst	A+	18	18	0	0	110.0	462	101	50	46	13	0	5	3	39	0	102	4	1	7	2	.778	0	0--	-	3.70	3.76
2006	Lancst	A+	10	10	0	0	50.1	215	48	25	21	5	1	1	1	11	0	49	4	0	3	4	.429	0	0--	-	3.06	3.75
2006	Tenn	AA	13	13	0	0	81.0	319	62	22	20	6	1	2	0	21	0	63	8	1	7	2	.778	0	0--	-	2.21	2.22
2006	Hrsbrg	AA	4	4	0	0	22.0	98	28	9	8	3	0	0	2	8	0	13	3	1	2	0	1.000	0	0--	-	6.45	3.27
2007	Clmbs	AAA	2	2	0	0	11.0	44	9	4	4	1	0	0	0	5	0	7	0	0	1	1	.500	0	0--	-	3.42	3.27
2007	Was	NL	31	31	0	0	167.0	747	183	96	86	26	6	10	5	74	3	94	7	0	7	9	.438	0	0-0	0	5.31	4.63

Randy Choate

Pitches: L Bats: L Pos: RP-2 Ht: 6'1" Wt: 195 Born: 9/5/1975 Age: 32

Year	Team	Lg	G	GS	CG	GF	IP	BFP	H	R	ER	HR	SH	SF	HB	TBB	IBB	SO	WP	Bk	W	L	Pct	ShO	Sv-Op	Hld	ERC	ERA
2007	Tucsn*	AAA	54	0	0	16	62.2	274	67	27	21	3	2	2	5	16	2	60	5	0	3	1	.750	0	3--	-	3.72	3.02
2000	NYY	AL	22	0	0	6	17.0	75	14	10	9	3	0	1	1	8	0	12	1	0	0	1	.000	0	0-0	2	3.99	4.76
2001	NYY	AL	37	0	0	13	48.1	207	34	21	18	0	2	1	9	27	2	35	3	0	3	1	.750	0	0-0	3	3.03	3.35
2002	NYY	AL	18	0	0	11	22.1	101	18	18	15	1	0	0	3	15	0	17	3	0	0	0	-	0	0-0	6	4.13	6.04
2003	NYY	AL	5	0	0	2	3.2	16	7	3	3	0	0	0	0	1	0	0	0	0	0	0	-	0	0-0	0	9.72	7.36
2004	Ari	NL	74	0	0	17	50.2	232	52	26	26	1	0	4	5	28	11	49	1	1	2	4	.333	0	0-2	11	4.18	4.62
2005	Ari	NL	8	0	0	0	7.0	35	8	7	7	0	0	0	1	5	1	4	1	0	0	0	-	0	0-0	0	5.48	9.00
2006	Ari	NL	30	0	0	3	16.0	75	21	9	7	0	0	0	3	5	0	12	0	0	0	1	.000	0	0-0	5	4.87	3.94
2007	Ari	NL	2	0	0	0	0.0	3	3	0	0	0	0	0	0	0	0	0	0	0	0	0	-	0	0-0	0	-	-
8 ML YEARS			196	0	0	52	165.0	744	157	94	85	5	2	6	22	87	14	129	9	1	5	7	.417	0	0-2	23	4.14	4.64

Shin-Soo Choo

Bats: L Throws: L Pos: LF-3; RF-2; PH-1; PR-1 Ht: 5'11" Wt: 210 Born: 7/13/1982 Age: 25

Year	Team	Lg	G	AB	H	2B	3B	HR	(Hm	Rd)	TB	R	RBI	RC	TBB	IBB	SO	HBP	SH	SF	SB	CS	SB%	GDP	Avg	OBP	Slg
2007	Indns*	R	2	5	1	1	0	0	(-	-)	2	0	2	0	0	0	1	1	0	0	0	0	-	0	.200	.333	.400
2007	Buffalo*	AAA	59	208	54	11	2	3	(-	-)	78	34	26	28	21	0	40	3	0	6	10	3	.77	6	.260	.328	.375
2005	Sea	AL	10	18	1	0	0	0	(0	0)	1	1	1	0	3	0	4	0	0	0	0	0	-	0	.056	.190	.056
2006	2 Tms	AL	49	157	44	12	3	3	(2	1)	71	23	22	24	18	2	50	2	1	1	5	3	.63	3	.280	.360	.452
2007	Cle	AL	6	17	5	0	0	0	(0	0)	5	5	5	3	2	1	5	0	0	1	0	1	.00	0	.294	.350	.294
06	Sea	AL	4	11	1	1	0	0	(0	0)	2	0	0	0	0	0	4	1	0	0	0	0	-	1	.091	.167	.182
06	Cle	AL	45	146	43	11	3	3	(2	1)	69	23	22	24	18	2	46	1	1	1	5	3	.63	2	.295	.373	.473
3 ML YEARS			65	192	50	12	3	3	(2	1)	77	29	28	27	23	3	59	2	1	2	5	4	.56	3	.260	.342	.401

Vinnie Chulk

Pitches: R Bats: R Pos: RP-57 Ht: 6'1" Wt: 195 Born: 12/19/1978 Age: 29

Year	Team	Lg	G	GS	CG	GF	IP	BFP	H	R	ER	HR	SH	SF	HB	TBB	IBB	SO	WP	Bk	W	L	Pct	ShO	Sv-Op	Hld	ERC	ERA
2003	Tor	AL	3	0	0	2	5.1	25	6	3	3	0	0	0	0	3	0	2	0	0	0	0	-	0	0-1	0	4.53	5.06
2004	Tor	AL	47	0	0	10	56.0	248	59	30	29	6	1	1	1	27	1	44	2	0	1	3	.250	0	2-5	13	4.83	4.66
2005	Tor	AL	62	0	0	10	72.0	301	68	33	31	9	3	4	1	26	3	39	5	0	0	1	.000	0	0-1	13	3.83	3.88
2006	2 Tms		48	0	0	13	46.1	205	46	29	27	6	0	2	3	20	2	43	4	0	1	3	.250	0	0-2	6	4.53	5.24
2007	SF	NL	57	0	0	15	53.0	222	53	22	21	3	1	4	2	14	2	41	2	0	5	4	.556	0	0-2	9	3.37	3.57
06	Tor	AL	20	0	0	8	24.0	107	29	16	14	4	0	1	2	5	0	18	1	0	1	0	1.000	0	0-1	1	5.25	5.25
06	SF	NL	28	0	0	5	22.1	98	17	13	13	2	0	1	1	15	2	25	3	0	0	3	.000	0	0-1	5	3.74	5.24
5 ML YEARS			217	0	0	50	232.2	1001	232	117	111	24	5	11	7	90	8	169	13	0	7	11	.389	0	2-11	41	4.11	4.29

Ryan Church

Bats: L Throws: L Pos: LF-91; CF-41; PH-15; DH-1; PR-1 Ht: 6'1" Wt: 190 Born: 10/14/1978 Age: 29

Year	Team	Lg	G	AB	H	2B	3B	HR	(Hm	Rd)	TB	R	RBI	RC	TBB	IBB	SO	HBP	SH	SF	SB	CS	SB%	GDP	Avg	OBP	Slg
2004	Mon	NL	30	63	11	1	0	1	(0	1)	15	6	6	2	7	1	16	0	1	0	0	0	-	3	.175	.257	.238
2005	Was	NL	102	268	77	15	3	9	(5	4)	125	41	42	34	24	0	70	5	1	3	3	2	.60	6	.287	.353	.466
2006	Was	NL	71	196	54	17	1	10	(6	4)	103	22	35	36	26	0	60	3	3	2	6	1	.86	4	.276	.366	.526
2007	Was	NL	144	470	128	43	1	15	(5	10)	218	57	70	70	49	4	107	8	0	3	3	2	.60	12	.272	.349	.464
4 ML YEARS			347	997	270	76	5	35	(16	19)	461	126	153	142	106	5	253	16	5	8	12	5	.71	25	.271	.348	.462

Alex Cintron

Bats: B **Throws:** R **Pos:** 3B-19; SS-17; PH-16; 2B-14; DH-6; PR-5   **Ht:** 6'1" **Wt:** 205 **Born:** 12/17/1978 **Age:** 29

Year	Team	Lg	G	AB	H	2B	3B	HR	(Hm	Rd)	TB	R	RBI	RC	TBB	IBB	SO	HBP	SH	SF	SB	CS	SB%	GDP	Avg	OBP	Slg
2001	Ari	NL	8	7	2	0	1	0	(0	0)	4	0	0	1	0	0	0	0	0	0	0	0	-	0	.286	.286	.571
2002	Ari	NL	38	75	16	6	0	0	(0	0)	22	11	4	5	12	2	13	0	3	0	0	0	-	2	.213	.322	.293
2003	Ari	NL	117	448	142	26	6	13	(6	7)	219	70	51	70	29	0	33	2	5	3	2	3	.40	7	.317	.359	.489
2004	Ari	NL	154	564	148	31	7	4	(1	3)	205	56	49	59	31	2	59	2	12	4	3	3	.50	11	.262	.301	.363
2005	Ari	NL	122	330	90	19	2	8	(5	3)	137	36	48	35	12	3	33	1	2	3	1	2	.33	8	.273	.298	.415
2006	CWS	AL	91	288	82	10	3	5	(3	2)	113	35	41	33	10	0	35	2	1	3	10	3	.77	10	.285	.310	.392
2007	CWS	AL	68	185	45	7	1	2	(1	1)	60	23	19	21	9	1	35	1	0	1	2	1	.67	5	.243	.281	.324
7 ML YEARS			598	1897	525	99	20	32	(16	16)	760	231	212	224	103	8	208	8	23	14	18	12	.60	43	.277	.315	.401

Jeff Cirillo

Bats: R **Throws:** R **Pos:** PH-27; 3B-26; DH-24; 1B-10; 2B-2; PR-1   **Ht:** 6'1" **Wt:** 205 **Born:** 9/23/1969 **Age:** 38

Year	Team	Lg	G	AB	H	2B	3B	HR	(Hm	Rd)	TB	R	RBI	RC	TBB	IBB	SO	HBP	SH	SF	SB	CS	SB%	GDP	Avg	OBP	Slg
2007	FtMyrs*	A+	1	3	0	0	0	0	(0	0)	0	0	0	0	0	0	0	0	0	0	0	0	-	0	.000	.000	.000
1994	Mil	AL	39	126	30	9	0	3	(1	2)	48	17	12	14	11	0	16	2	0	0	0	1	.00	4	.238	.309	.381
1995	Mil	AL	125	328	91	19	4	9	(6	3)	145	57	39	55	47	0	42	4	1	4	7	2	.78	8	.277	.371	.442
1996	Mil	AL	158	566	184	46	5	15	(6	9)	285	101	83	105	58	0	69	7	6	6	4	9	.31	14	.325	.391	.504
1997	Mil	AL	154	580	167	46	2	10	(4	6)	247	74	82	91	60	0	74	14	4	3	4	3	.57	13	.288	.367	.426
1998	Mil	NL	156	604	194	31	1	14	(6	8)	269	97	68	103	79	3	88	4	5	2	10	4	.71	26	.321	.402	.445
1999	Mil	NL	157	607	198	35	1	15	(6	9)	280	98	88	111	75	4	83	5	3	7	7	4	.64	15	.326	.401	.461
2000	Col	NL	157	598	195	53	2	11	(9	2)	285	111	115	108	67	4	72	6	1	12	3	4	.43	19	.326	.392	.477
2001	Col	NL	138	528	165	26	4	17	(9	8)	250	72	83	89	43	6	63	5	1	9	12	2	.86	15	.313	.364	.473
2002	Sea	AL	146	485	121	20	0	6	(2	4)	159	51	54	52	31	0	67	9	13	9	8	4	.67	12	.249	.301	.328
2003	Sea	AL	87	258	53	11	0	2	(1	1)	70	24	23	23	24	1	32	5	4	2	1	1	.50	6	.205	.284	.271
2004	SD	NL	33	75	16	3	0	1	(0	1)	22	12	7	6	5	0	14	0	0	1	0	0	-	0	.213	.259	.293
2005	Mil	NL	77	185	52	15	0	4	(1	3)	79	29	23	30	23	0	22	4	7	0	4	2	.67	3	.281	.373	.427
2006	Mil	NL	112	263	84	16	0	3	(1	2)	109	33	23	38	21	0	33	1	3	2	1	1	.50	8	.319	.369	.414
2007	2 Tms	NL	78	193	48	13	2	2	(0	2)	71	24	27	26	19	0	19	1	3	2	2	0	1.00	10	.249	.316	.368
07	Min	AL	50	153	40	9	2	2	(0	2)	59	18	21	22	15	0	13	1	3	2	2	0	1.00	9	.261	.327	.386
07	Ari	NL	28	40	8	4	0	0	(0	0)	12	6	6	4	4	0	6	0	0	0	0	0	-	1	.200	.273	.300
14 ML YEARS			1617	5396	1598	343	21	112	(54	58)	2319	800	727	851	563	18	694	67	51	59	63	37	.63	153	.296	.366	.430

Brady Clark

Bats: R **Throws:** R **Pos:** LF-38; RF-15; CF-14; PR-7; PH-6   **Ht:** 6'2" **Wt:** 205 **Born:** 4/18/1973 **Age:** 35

Year	Team	Lg	G	AB	H	2B	3B	HR	(Hm	Rd)	TB	R	RBI	RC	TBB	IBB	SO	HBP	SH	SF	SB	CS	SB%	GDP	Avg	OBP	Slg
2007	Pwtckt*	AAA	5	19	5	2	0	1	(-	-)	10	2	3	3	3	0	1	1	0	1	0	1	.00	0	.263	.375	.526
2007	Portlnd*	AAA	14	59	20	6	0	0	(-	-)	26	12	8	11	5	0	11	3	0	0	1	0	1.00	0	.339	.418	.441
2000	Cin	NL	11	11	3	1	0	0	(0	0)	4	1	2	1	0	0	2	0	0	0	0	0	-	0	.273	.273	.364
2001	Cin	NL	89	129	34	3	0	6	(4	2)	55	22	18	21	22	1	16	1	4	1	4	1	.80	6	.264	.373	.426
2002	2 Tms	NL	61	78	15	4	0	0	(0	0)	19	9	10	7	7	2	11	1	1	0	1	2	.33	7	.192	.267	.244
2003	Mil	NL	128	315	86	21	1	6	(5	1)	127	33	40	40	21	0	40	9	2	7	13	2	.87	12	.273	.330	.403
2004	Mil	NL	138	353	99	18	1	7	(1	6)	140	41	46	56	53	2	48	9	1	3	15	8	.65	9	.280	.385	.397
2005	Mil	NL	145	599	183	31	1	13	(8	5)	255	94	53	92	47	1	55	18	8	2	10	13	.43	13	.306	.372	.426
2006	Mil	NL	138	415	109	14	2	4	(3	1)	139	51	29	47	43	4	60	14	5	5	3	4	.43	9	.263	.348	.335
2007	2 Tms	NL	68	107	28	5	2	0	(0	0)	37	13	11	11	14	2	18	1	1	0	1	3	.25	3	.262	.352	.346
02	Cin	NL	51	66	10	3	0	0	(0	0)	13	6	9	5	6	2	9	1	1	0	1	2	.33	2	.152	.233	.197
02	NYM	NL	10	12	5	1	0	0	(0	0)	6	3	1	2	1	0	2	0	0	0	0	0	-	0	.417	.462	.500
07	LAD	NL	47	58	13	4	0	0	(0	0)	17	7	5	4	6	0	11	1	1	0	1	2	.33	1	.224	.308	.293
07	SD	NL	21	49	15	1	2	0	(0	0)	20	6	6	7	8	2	7	0	0	0	0	1	.00	2	.306	.404	.408
8 ML YEARS			778	2007	557	97	7	36	(21	15)	776	264	209	275	207	12	250	53	22	18	47	33	.59	54	.278	.358	.387

Howie Clark

Bats: L **Throws:** R **Pos:** PH-12; 3B-10; DH-4; PR-4; 1B-3; 2B-3; SS-2   **Ht:** 5'10" **Wt:** 195 **Born:** 2/13/1974 **Age:** 34

Year	Team	Lg	G	AB	H	2B	3B	HR	(Hm	Rd)	TB	R	RBI	RC	TBB	IBB	SO	HBP	SH	SF	SB	CS	SB%	GDP	Avg	OBP	Slg
2007	NHam*	AA	1	3	1	0	0	0	(-	-)	1	0	0	0	1	0	0	0	0	0	0	0	-	0	.333	.500	.333
2007	Syrcse*	AAA	22	81	22	3	0	3	(- | -)	34	8	15	11	6	0	6	1	0	1.00	2					.272	.322	.420
2002	Bal	AL	14	53	16	5	0	0	(0	0)	21	3	4	3	3	0	6	2	0	0	-	5			.302	.362	.396
2003	Tor	AL	38	70	25	3	1	0	(0	0)	30	9	7	13	3	0	6	2	2	0	1	.00	3		.357	.400	.429
2004	Tor	AL	40	115	25	6	0	3	(3	0)	40	17	12	11	13	0	15	0	3	2	0	0	-	0	.217	.292	.348
2006	Bal	AL	7	7	1	0	0	0	(0	0)	1	1	0	1	2	0	2	0	1	0	0	0	-	0	.143	.333	.143
2007	Tor	AL	31	49	10	2	0	0	(0	0)	12	6	2	3	7	1	5	0	0	1	1	0	1.00	1	.204	.298	.245
5 ML YEARS			130	294	77	16	1	3	(3	0)	104	36	25	31	28	1	34	4	6	3	1	1	.50	11	.262	.331	.354

Tony Clark

Bats: B **Throws:** R **Pos:** 1B-83; PH-36   **Ht:** 6'7" **Wt:** 245 **Born:** 6/15/1972 **Age:** 36

Year	Team	Lg	G	AB	H	2B	3B	HR	(Hm	Rd)	TB	R	RBI	RC	TBB	IBB	SO	HBP	SH	SF	SB	CS	SB%	GDP	Avg	OBP	Slg
1995	Det	AL	27	101	24	5	1	3	(0	3)	40	10	11	11	8	0	30	0	0	0	0	0	-	2	.238	.294	.396
1996	Det	AL	100	376	94	14	0	27	(17	10)	189	56	72	55	29	1	127	0	0	6	0	1	.00	7	.250	.299	.503
1997	Det	AL	159	580	160	28	3	32	(18	14)	290	105	117	107	49	3	144	3	0	5	1	3	.25	11	.276	.376	.500
1998	Det	AL	157	602	175	37	0	34	(18	16)	314	84	103	107	63	5	128	3	0	5	3	3	.50	16	.291	.358	.522
1999	Det	AL	143	536	150	29	0	31	(12	19)	272	74	99	94	64	7	133	6	0	3	2	1	.67	14	.280	.361	.507

Year	Team	Lg	G	AB	H	2B	3B	HR	(Hm	Rd)	TB	R	RBI	RC	TBB	IBB	SO	HBP	SH	SF	SB	CS	SB%	GDP	Avg	OBP	Slg
2000	Det	AL	60	208	57	14	0	13	(6	7)	110	32	37	35	24	2	51	0	0	0	0	0	-	10	.274	.349	.529
2001	Det	AL	126	428	123	29	3	16	(7	9)	206	67	75	74	62	10	108	1	0	6	0	1	.00	14	.287	.374	.481
2002	Bos	AL	90	275	57	12	1	3	(1	2)	80	25	29	19	21	0	57	1	0	1	0	0	-	11	.207	.265	.291
2003	NYM	NL	125	254	59	13	0	16	(9	7)	120	29	43	29	24	2	73	1	0	1	0	0	-	8	.232	.300	.472
2004	NYY	AL	106	253	56	12	0	16	(5	11)	116	37	49	37	26	3	92	2	0	2	0	0	-	6	.221	.297	.458
2005	Ari	NL	130	349	106	22	2	30	(19	11)	222	47	87	71	37	6	88	1	0	6	0	0	-	10	.304	.366	.636
2006	Ari	NL	79	132	26	4	0	6	(3	3)	48	13	16	10	13	2	40	2	0	0	0	0	-	5	.197	.279	.364
2007	Ari	NL	113	221	55	5	1	17	(14	3)	113	31	51	28	21	3	59	0	0	3	0	0	-	8	.249	.310	.511
13 ML YEARS			1415	4315	1142	224	11	244	(129	115)	2120	610	789	677	485	54	1130	20	0	38	6	9	.40	122	.265	.339	.491

Darren Clarke

Pitches: R **Bats:** R **Pos:** RP-2 **Ht:** 6'8" **Wt:** 235 **Born:** 3/18/1981 **Age:** 27

Year	Team	Lg	G	GS	CG	GF	IP	BFP	H	R	ER	HR	SH	SF	HB	TBB	IBB	SO	WP	Bk	W	L	Pct	ShO	Sv-Op	Hld	ERC	ERA
2001	Casper	R+	14	14	0	0	55.1	271	76	47	37	3	1	3	8	33	0	42	5	0	3	6	.333	0	0--	-	7.53	6.02
2002	TriCity	A-	12	9	0	1	40.0	194	51	34	31	3	2	3	3	19	0	38	3	1	4	3	.571	0	0--	-	5.93	6.98
2003	Ashvll	A	27	25	1	0	157.1	676	155	80	67	22	5	8	6	59	0	107	5	2	8	6	.571	0	0--	-	4.34	3.83
2004	Visalia	A+	8	7	0	0	35.1	181	54	35	29	6	2	3	2	16	0	27	5	1	1	3	.250	0	0--	-	8.06	7.39
2005	TriCity	A-	12	0	0	5	14.0	52	9	1	1	0	0	0	1	2	0	18	2	0	0	0	-	0	3--	-	1.31	0.64
2005	Mdest	A+	5	0	0	0	6.0	33	13	8	6	2	0	0	0	3	0	4	1	0	0	0	-	0	0--	-	14.78	9.00
2006	Mdest	A+	25	0	0	16	26.2	101	13	5	4	1	0	0	1	7	0	37	2	0	1	1	.500	0	5--	-	1.13	1.35
2007	Tulsa	AA	10	1	0	4	11.0	37	5	2	2	2	0	0	0	1	0	16	0	0	1	1	.500	0	0--	-	1.10	1.64
2007	Col	NL	2	0	0	0	1.1	7	2	0	0	0	0	0	0	1	0	1	0	0	0	0	-	0	0-0	0	7.52	0.00

Brandon Claussen

Pitches: L **Bats:** R **Pos:** P **Ht:** 6'1" **Wt:** 200 **Born:** 5/1/1979 **Age:** 29

Year	Team	Lg	G	GS	CG	GF	IP	BFP	H	R	ER	HR	SH	SF	HB	TBB	IBB	SO	WP	Bk	W	L	Pct	ShO	Sv-Op	Hld	ERC	ERA
2007	Nats*	R	3	3	0	0	15.0	59	14	6	5	2	0	1	1	9	0	18	2	0	0	0	-	0	0--	-	2.96	3.00
2007	Clmbs*	AAA	4	4	0	0	19.1	95	29	19	15	2	1	0	1	7	0	13	1	0	1	1	.500	0	0--	-	7.01	6.98
2003	NYY	AL	1	1	0	0	6.1	28	8	2	1	1	0	0	0	1	0	5	0	0	1	0	1.000	0	0-0	0	4.89	1.42
2004	Cin	NL	14	14	0	0	66.0	313	80	50	45	9	5	3	2	35	2	45	3	0	2	8	.200	0	0-0	0	6.11	6.14
2005	Cin	NL	29	29	0	0	166.2	731	178	89	78	24	8	6	7	57	5	121	2	1	10	11	.476	0	0-0	0	4.63	4.21
2006	Cin	NL	14	14	0	0	77.0	351	93	56	53	14	6	2	6	28	1	57	2	0	3	8	.273	0	0-0	0	6.06	6.19
4 ML YEARS			58	58	0	0	316.0	1423	359	197	177	48	19	11	15	121	8	228	7	1	16	27	.372	0	0-0	0	5.28	5.04

Royce Clayton

Bats: R **Throws:** R **Pos:** SS-69; PR-8; 3B-3; DH-2; PH-1 **Ht:** 6'0" **Wt:** 200 **Born:** 1/2/1970 **Age:** 38

Year	Team	Lg	G	AB	H	2B	3B	HR	(Hm	Rd)	TB	R	RBI	RC	TBB	IBB	SO	HBP	SH	SF	SB	CS	SB%	GDP	Avg	OBP	Slg
2007	Pwtckt*	AAA	7	28	4	3	0	0	(-	-)	7	2	3	1	2	0	10	0	0	0	0	0	-	0	.143	.200	.250
1991	SF	NL	9	26	3	1	0	0	(0	0)	4	0	2	0	1	0	6	0	0	0	0	0	-	1	.115	.148	.154
1992	SF	NL	98	321	72	7	4	4	(3	1)	99	31	24	25	26	3	63	0	3	2	8	4	.67	11	.224	.281	.308
1993	SF	NL	153	549	155	21	5	6	(5	1)	204	54	70	64	38	2	91	5	8	7	11	10	.52	16	.282	.331	.372
1994	SF	NL	108	385	91	14	6	3	(1	2)	126	38	30	40	30	2	74	3	3	2	23	3	.88	7	.236	.295	.327
1995	SF	NL	138	509	124	29	3	5	(2	3)	174	56	58	53	38	1	109	3	4	3	24	9	.73	7	.244	.298	.342
1996	StL	NL	129	491	136	20	4	6	(6	0)	182	64	35	56	33	4	89	1	2	4	33	15	.69	13	.277	.321	.371
1997	StL	NL	154	576	153	39	5	9	(5	4)	229	75	61	67	33	3	109	3	2	5	30	10	.75	19	.266	.306	.398
1998	2 Tms		142	541	136	31	2	9	(2	7)	198	89	53	62	53	1	83	3	6	5	24	11	.69	16	.251	.319	.366
1999	Tex	AL	133	465	134	21	5	14	(6	8)	207	69	52	71	39	1	100	4	9	3	11	8	.57	6	.288	.346	.445
2000	Tex	AL	148	513	124	21	5	14	(9	5)	197	70	54	54	42	1	92	3	12	3	11	7	.61	21	.242	.301	.384
2001	CWS	AL	135	433	114	21	4	9	(6	3)	170	62	60	50	33	2	72	3	9	7	10	7	.59	16	.263	.315	.393
2002	CWS	AL	112	342	86	14	2	7	(4	3)	125	51	35	37	20	0	67	3	7	4	5	1	.83	7	.251	.295	.365
2003	Mil	NL	146	483	110	16	1	11	(5	6)	161	49	39	37	49	10	92	3	4	4	5	2	.71	25	.228	.301	.333
2004	Col	NL	146	574	160	36	4	8	(6	2)	228	95	54	75	48	0	125	4	24	2	10	5	.67	13	.279	.338	.397
2005	Ari	NL	143	522	141	28	4	2	(1	1)	183	59	44	55	38	0	105	1	10	2	13	3	.81	19	.270	.320	.351
2006	2 Tms	NL	137	454	117	30	1	2	(2	0)	155	49	40	43	30	3	85	5	7	6	14	6	.70	11	.258	.307	.341
2007	2 Tms	NL	77	195	48	14	0	1	(0	1)	65	24	12	18	14	0	53	1	3	3	2	1	.67	10	.246	.296	.333
98	StL	NL	90	355	83	19	1	4	(1	3)	116	59	29	37	40	1	51	2	3	2	19	6	.76	10	.234	.313	.327
98	Tex	AL	52	186	53	12	1	5	(1	4)	82	30	24	25	13	0	32	1	3	3	5	5	.50	6	.285	.330	.441
06	Was	NL	87	305	82	22	1	0	(0	0)	106	36	27	32	19	3	53	4	5	5	8	3	.73	8	.269	.315	.348
06	Cin	NL	50	149	35	8	0	2	(2	0)	49	13	13	11	11	0	32	1	2	1	6	3	.67	3	.235	.290	.329
07	Tor	AL	69	189	48	14	0	1	(0	1)	65	23	12	18	14	0	50	1	3	3	2	1	.67	8	.254	.304	.344
07	Bos	AL	8	6	0	0	0	0	(0	0)	0	1	0	0	0	0	3	0	0	0	0	0	-	2	.000	.000	.000
17 ML YEARS			2108	7379	1904	363	55	110	(63	47)	2707	935	723	807	565	34	1415	45	113	62	231	100	.70	218	.258	.312	.367

Roger Clemens

Pitches: R **Bats:** R **Pos:** SP-17; RP-1 **Ht:** 6'4" **Wt:** 235 **Born:** 8/4/1962 **Age:** 45

Year	Team	Lg	G	GS	CG	GF	IP	BFP	H	R	ER	HR	SH	SF	HB	TBB	IBB	SO	WP	Bk	W	L	Pct	ShO	Sv-Op	Hld	ERC	ERA
2007	Tmpa*	A+	1	1	0	0	4.0	15	3	1	1	1	0	0	0	0	0	2	0	0	0	0	-	0	0--	-	2.05	2.25
2007	Trntn*	AA	1	1	0	0	5.1	27	6	3	3	0	1	0	1	4	0	5	1	0	0	0	-	0	0--	-	5.97	5.06
2007	SWB*	AAA	1	1	0	0	6.0	22	2	0	0	0	0	0	0	2	0	6	0	0	1	0	1.000	0	0--	-	0.69	0.00
1984	Bos	AL	21	20	5	0	133.1	575	146	67	64	13	2	3	2	29	3	126	4	0	9	4	.692	1	0-0	0	3.81	4.32
1985	Bos	AL	15	15	3	0	98.1	407	83	38	36	5	1	2	3	37	0	74	1	3	7	5	.583	1	0-0	0	2.96	3.29
1986	Bos	AL	33	33	10	0	254.0	997	179	77	70	21	4	6	3	67	0	238	11	3	24	4	.857	1	0-0	0	2.03	2.48
1987	Bos	AL	36	36	18	0	281.2	1157	248	100	93	19	6	4	9	83	4	256	3	3	20	9	.690	7	0-0	0	2.94	2.97

Year	Team	Lg	G	GS	CG	GF	IP	BFP	H	R	ER	HR	SH	SF	HB	TBB	IBB	SO	WP	Bk	W	L	Pct	ShO	Sv-Op	Hld	ERC	ERA
1988	Bos	AL	35	35	14	0	264.0	1063	217	93	86	17	6	3	6	62	4	291	4	7	18	12	.600	8	0-0	0	2.36	2.93
1989	Bos	AL	35	35	8	0	253.1	1044	215	101	88	20	9	5	8	93	5	230	7	0	17	11	.607	3	0-0	0	3.13	3.13
1990	Bos	AL	31	31	7	0	228.1	920	193	59	49	7	7	5	7	54	3	209	8	0	21	6	.778	4	0-0	0	2.33	1.93
1991	Bos	AL	35	35	13	0	271.1	1077	219	93	79	15	6	8	5	65	12	241	6	0	18	10	.643	4	0-0	0	2.23	2.62
1992	Bos	AL	32	32	11	0	246.2	989	203	80	66	11	5	5	9	62	5	208	3	0	18	11	.621	5	0-0	0	2.38	2.41
1993	Bos	AL	29	29	2	0	191.2	808	175	99	95	17	5	7	11	67	4	160	3	1	11	14	.440	1	0-0	0	3.53	4.46
1994	Bos	AL	24	24	3	0	170.2	692	124	62	54	15	2	5	4	71	1	168	4	0	9	7	.563	1	0-0	0	2.72	2.85
1995	Bos	AL	23	23	0	0	140.0	623	141	70	65	15	2	3	14	60	0	132	9	0	10	5	.667	0	0-0	0	4.67	4.18
1996	Bos	AL	34	34	6	0	242.2	1032	216	106	98	19	4	7	4	106	2	257	8	1	10	13	.435	2	0-0	0	3.52	3.63
1997	Tor	AL	34	34	9	0	264.0	1044	204	65	60	9	5	2	12	68	0	292	4	0	21	7	.750	3	0-0	0	2.17	2.05
1998	Tor	AL	33	33	5	0	234.2	961	169	78	69	11	8	2	7	88	0	271	6	0	20	6	.769	3	0-0	0	2.27	2.65
1999	NYY	AL	30	30	1	0	187.2	822	185	101	96	20	10	5	9	90	0	163	8	0	14	10	.583	1	0-0	0	4.59	4.60
2000	NYY	AL	32	32	1	0	204.1	878	184	96	84	26	1	2	10	84	0	188	2	1	13	8	.619	0	0-0	0	3.93	3.70
2001	NYY	AL	33	33	0	0	220.1	918	205	94	86	19	4	4	6	72	1	213	14	0	20	3	.870	0	0-0	0	3.43	3.51
2002	NYY	AL	29	29	0	0	180.0	768	172	94	87	18	5	5	7	63	6	192	14	0	13	6	.684	0	0-0	0	3.72	4.35
2003	NYY	AL	33	33	1	0	211.2	878	199	99	92	24	3	6	5	58	1	190	5	0	17	9	.654	1	0-0	0	3.44	3.91
2004	Hou	NL	33	33	0	0	214.1	878	169	76	71	15	8	7	6	79	5	218	5	0	18	4	.818	0	0-0	0	2.72	2.98
2005	Hou	NL	32	32	1	0	211.1	838	151	51	44	11	9	3	3	62	5	185	3	1	13	8	.619	0	0-0	0	1.96	1.87
2006	Hou	NL	19	19	0	0	113.1	451	89	34	29	7	5	1	4	29	1	102	3	0	7	6	.538	0	0-0	0	2.33	2.30
2007	NYY	AL	18	17	0	0	99.0	420	99	52	46	9	2	3	5	31	0	68	7	0	6	6	.500	0	0-0	0	3.90	4.18
24 ML YEARS			709	707	118	0	4916.2	20240	4185	1885	1707	363	119	103	159	1580	63	4672	143	20	354	184	.658	46	0-0	0	2.92	3.12

Jeff Clement

Bats: L **Throws:** R **Pos:** PH-6; DH-4   **Ht:** 6'1" **Wt:** 210 **Born:** 8/21/1983 **Age:** 24

							BATTING												BASERUNNING				AVERAGES		
Year	Team	Lg	G	AB	H	2B	3B	HR	(Hm | Rd)	TB	R	RBI	RC	TBB	IBB	SO	HBP	SH	SF	SB	CS	SB%	GDP	Avg	OBP	Slg
2005	Wisc	A	30	113	36	5	0	6	(- | -)	59	17	20	22	12	0	25	1	0	1	1	2	.33	0	.319	.386	.522
2006	SnAnt	AA	15	59	17	6	1	2	(- | -)	31	7	10	12	7	0	8	3	0	1	0	0	-	1	.288	.386	.525
2006	Tacom	AAA	67	245	63	10	0	4	(- | -)	85	23	32	28	16	1	53	8	1	2	0	2	.00	8	.257	.321	.347
2007	Tacom	AAA	125	455	125	35	3	20	(- | -)	226	76	80	86	61	4	88	10	0	4	0	0	-	8	.275	.370	.497
2007	Sea	AL	9	16	6	1	0	2	(2 | 0)	13	4	3	6	3	0	3	0	0	0	0	0	-	0	.375	.474	.813

Matt Clement

Pitches: R **Bats:** R **Pos:** P   **Ht:** 6'3" **Wt:** 210 **Born:** 8/12/1974 **Age:** 33

Year	Team	Lg	G	GS	CG	GF	IP	BFP	H	R	ER	HR	SH	SF	HB	TBB	IBB	SO	WP	Bk	W	L	Pct	ShO	Sv-Op	Hld	ERC	ERA
1998	SD	NL	4	2	0	0	13.2	62	15	8	7	0	2	0	0	7	1	13	2	0	2	0	1.000	0	0-0	0	4.14	4.61
1999	SD	NL	31	31	0	0	180.2	803	190	110	90	18	7	6	9	86	2	135	11	0	10	12	.455	0	0-0	0	4.89	4.48
2000	SD	NL	34	34	0	0	205.0	940	194	131	117	22	12	5	16	125	4	170	23	0	13	17	.433	0	0-0	0	4.87	5.14
2001	Fla	NL	31	31	0	0	169.1	760	172	102	95	15	14	3	15	85	2	134	15	0	9	10	.474	0	0-0	0	4.81	5.05
2002	ChC	NL	32	32	3	0	205.0	858	162	84	82	10	11	4	6	85	7	215	7	0	12	11	.522	2	0-0	0	2.96	3.60
2003	ChC	NL	32	32	2	0	201.2	851	169	100	92	22	10	2	14	79	2	171	13	0	14	12	.538	1	0-0	0	3.47	4.11
2004	ChC	NL	30	30	0	0	181.0	775	155	79	74	23	5	4	12	77	4	190	14	1	9	13	.409	0	0-0	0	3.78	3.68
2005	Bos	AL	32	32	1	0	191.0	830	192	102	97	18	2	6	16	68	1	146	13	0	13	6	.684	0	0-0	0	4.22	4.57
2006	Bos	AL	12	12	0	0	65.1	310	77	50	48	8	1	0	6	38	0	43	3	0	5	5	.500	0	0-0	0	6.44	6.61
9 ML YEARS			238	236	6	0	1412.2	6189	1326	762	702	144	64	30	94	650	23	1217	101	1	87	86	.503	3	0-0	0	4.21	4.47

Brent Clevlen

Bats: R **Throws:** R **Pos:** LF-8; RF-4; PR-3; CF-1; DH-1; PH-1   **Ht:** 6'2" **Wt:** 190 **Born:** 10/27/1983 **Age:** 24

							BATTING												BASERUNNING				AVERAGES		
Year	Team	Lg	G	AB	H	2B	3B	HR	(Hm | Rd)	TB	R	RBI	RC	TBB	IBB	SO	HBP	SH	SF	SB	CS	SB%	GDP	Avg	OBP	Slg
2002	Tigers	R	28	103	34	2	3	3	(- | -)	51	14	21	19	8	0	24	0	0	2	2	1	.67	0	.330	.372	.495
2003	WMich	A	138	481	125	22	7	12	(- | -)	197	67	63	76	72	0	111	4	0	3	6	3	.67	16	.260	.359	.410
2004	Lkland	A+	117	420	94	23	6	6	(- | -)	147	49	50	47	44	1	127	4	0	5	2	1	.67	12	.224	.300	.350
2005	Lkland	A+	130	494	149	28	4	18	(- | -)	239	77	102	95	65	8	118	5	2	2	14	5	.74	16	.302	.384	.484
2006	Erie	AA	109	395	91	17	0	11	(- | -)	141	47	45	48	47	3	138	3	1	5	6	2	.75	9	.230	.313	.357
2007	Tigers	R	14	48	15	1	0	2	(- | -)	22	10	8	8	3	0	8	0	0	1	1	0	1.00	2	.313	.346	.458
2007	Toledo	AAA	90	322	71	14	5	7	(- | -)	116	33	36	36	39	1	113	1	1	3	4	4	.50	5	.220	.304	.360
2006	Det	AL	31	39	11	1	2	3	(0 | 3)	25	9	6	6	2	0	15	0	1	0	0	0	-	0	.282	.317	.641
2007	Det	AL	13	10	1	0	0	0	(0 | 0)	1	2	0	0	0	0	7	0	0	1	0	0	-	1	.100	.100	.100
2 ML YEARS			44	49	12	1	2	3	(0 | 3)	26	11	6	6	2	0	22	0	1	0	0	0	-	1	.245	.275	.531

Tyler Clippard

Pitches: R **Bats:** R **Pos:** SP-6   **Ht:** 6'4" **Wt:** 170 **Born:** 2/14/1985 **Age:** 23

Year	Team	Lg	G	GS	CG	GF	IP	BFP	H	R	ER	HR	SH	SF	HB	TBB	IBB	SO	WP	Bk	W	L	Pct	ShO	Sv-Op	Hld	ERC	ERA
2003	Yanks	R	11	5	0	0	43.2	168	33	16	14	3	1	1	5	5	0	56	4	0	3	3	.500	0	0--	0	2.07	2.89
2004	Btl Crk	A	26	25	1	0	149.0	636	153	71	57	12	7	2	15	32	0	145	4	0	10	10	.500	0	0--	0	3.74	3.44
2005	Tampa	A+	26	25	0	1	147.1	589	118	56	52	12	2	5	9	34	0	169	5	1	10	9	.526	0	0--	0	2.53	3.18
2005	CtnSC	A	1	1	0	0	6.0	29	9	5	5	1	0	0	2	0	0	10	1	0	0	1	.000	0	0--	0	7.19	7.50
2005	Clmbs	AAA	1	0	0	0	1.0	3	0	0	0	0	0	0	0	0	0	2	0	0	0	0	-	0	0.00	0.00
2006	Trntn	AA	28	28	1	0	166.1	672	118	72	62	14	6	3	17	55	1	175	3	0	12	10	.545	1	0--	0	2.59	3.35
2007	S-WB	AAA	14	14	0	0	69.1	317	82	40	32	7	2	3	3	35	0	55	3	0	4	4	.500	0	0--	0	5.83	4.15
2007	Trntn	AA	6	6	0	0	26.2	113	22	18	16	5	1	1	2	12	0	28	2	0	2	1	.667	0	0--	0	4.24	5.40
2007	NYY	AL	6	6	0	0	27.0	124	29	19	19	6	0	0	0	17	1	18	2	1	3	1	.750	0	0-0	0	6.37	6.33

Buck Coats

Bats: L Throws: R Pos: PH-10; LF-5; RF-5; CF-2   Ht: 6'3" Wt: 195 Born: 6/9/1982 Age: 26

Year	Team	Lg	G	AB	H	2B	3B	HR	(Hm	Rd)	TB	R	RBI	RC	TBB	IBB	SO	HBP	SH	SF	SB	CS	SB%	GDP	Avg	OBP	Slg
2000	Cubs	R	30	98	29	6	3	0	(-	-)	41	20	14	18	12	2	24	4	0	0	7	1	.88	1	.296	.395	.418
2001	Cubs	R	33	123	32	3	3	1	(-	-)	44	11	18	12	4	0	19	2	1	1	3	4	.43	1	.260	.292	.358
2002	Lansng	A	133	501	129	21	4	4	(-	-)	170	65	47	55	31	4	67	4	2	6	14	3	.82	5	.257	.303	.339
2003	Lansng	A	132	488	135	25	7	1	(-	-)	177	64	59	71	64	5	93	4	6	2	32	15	.68	13	.277	.364	.363
2004	Dytona	A+	112	414	120	22	4	8	(-	-)	174	64	55	62	32	2	90	1	3	3	28	9	.76	6	.290	.340	.420
2005	WTenn	AA	127	439	124	32	6	1	(-	-)	171	47	49	62	38	1	80	2	1	4	17	5	.77	10	.282	.340	.390
2006	Iowa	AAA	124	450	127	21	0	7	(-	-)	169	60	51	62	38	1	87	4	4	2	17	4	.81	9	.282	.342	.376
2007	Iowa	AAA	123	455	138	21	3	11	(-	-)	198	81	59	77	44	3	74	2	1	6	18	2	.90	10	.303	.363	.435
2007	Lsvlle	AAA	4	16	7	2	0	0	(-	-)	9	1	4	4	1	1	5	0	0	0	2	0	1.00	1	.438	.471	.563
2006	ChC	NL	18	18	3	1	0	1	(0	1)	7	2	1	0	0	0	6	0	0	0	0	0	-	1	.167	.167	.389
2007	Cin	NL	20	34	7	4	0	0	(0	0)	11	2	2	2	3	0	15	0	0	1	0	0	-	1	.206	.263	.324
	2 ML YEARS		38	52	10	5	0	1	(0	1)	18	4	3	2	3	0	21	0	0	1	0	0	-	2	.192	.232	.346

Todd Coffey

Pitches: R Bats: R Pos: RP-58   Ht: 6'5" Wt: 255 Born: 9/9/1980 Age: 27

Year	Team	Lg	G	GS	CG	GF	IP	BFP	H	R	ER	HR	SH	SF	HB	TBB	IBB	SO	WP	Bk	W	L	Pct	ShO	Sv-Op	Hld	ERC	ERA
2007	Lsvlle*	AAA	19	0	0	3	27.0	103	17	4	4	0	2	2	2	5	0	25	3	0	2	0	1.000	0	1--	-	1.33	1.33
2005	Cin	NL	57	0	0	14	58.0	265	84	33	29	5	3	2	5	11	2	26	1	0	4	1	.800	0	1-2	3	6.11	4.50
2006	Cin	NL	81	0	0	28	78.0	340	85	34	31	7	0	1	2	27	5	60	4	0	6	7	.462	0	8-12	15	4.29	3.58
2007	Cin	NL	58	0	0	8	51.0	242	70	36	33	12	1	0	5	19	4	43	4	0	2	1	.667	0	0-3	7	7.58	5.82
	3 ML YEARS		196	0	0	50	187.0	847	239	103	93	24	4	3	12	57	11	129	9	0	12	9	.571	0	9-17	25	5.71	4.48

Willie Collazo

Pitches: L Bats: L Pos: RP-6   Ht: 5'9" Wt: 175 Born: 11/7/1979 Age: 28

Year	Team	Lg	G	GS	CG	GF	IP	BFP	H	R	ER	HR	SH	SF	HB	TBB	IBB	SO	WP	Bk	W	L	Pct	ShO	Sv-Op	Hld	ERC	ERA
2001	Jmstwn	A-	9	0	0	7	15.0	55	9	2	1	0	1	0	1	0	0	13	2	0	3	1	.750	0	1--	-	0.87	0.60
2001	Macon	A	12	0	0	6	23.1	88	13	9	7	3	3	3	2	4	0	23	2	0	3	2	.600	0	1--	-	1.57	2.70
2002	Grnville	AA	51	0	0	26	72.2	309	70	34	28	7	2	1	2	27	2	74	4	1	4	2	.667	0	4--	-	3.82	3.47
2003	Grnville	AA	39	0	0	11	46.2	202	41	22	19	3	7	3	1	21	1	34	3	2	6	2	.750	0	0--	-	3.34	3.66
2003	MrtlBh	A+	11	0	0	2	14.2	59	12	5	5	1	0	0	1	4	0	15	0	0	0	1	.000	0	0--	-	2.74	3.07
2004	Ark	AA	32	20	3	2	148.0	642	156	88	75	11	3	6	12	38	0	100	8	0	6	10	.375	2	1--	-	3.91	4.56
2005	Salt Lk	AAA	11	1	0	2	23.1	103	29	20	20	7	2	2	4	9	0	12	1	0	0	1	.000	0	0--	-	8.37	7.71
2005	Ark	AA	26	10	0	1	71.2	329	85	60	54	16	3	3	4	29	1	58	1	0	1	5	.167	0	0--	-	6.28	6.78
2006	Bnghtn	AA	18	18	1	0	118.2	467	104	44	41	7	5	3	4	16	0	79	2	1	7	6	.538	1	0--	-	2.49	3.11
2006	Norfolk	AAA	7	5	0	0	41.1	178	45	24	22	4	1	2	1	13	0	26	1	2	3	3	.500	0	0--	-	4.34	4.79
2007	NewOr	AAA	53	4	0	24	98.2	396	91	33	27	5	6	3	7	19	1	69	2	0	6	5	.545	0	4--	-	2.89	2.46
2007	NYM	NL	6	0	0	1	5.2	27	7	4	4	0	0	0	0	5	1	0	0	0	0	0	-	0	0-0	0	6.54	6.35

Jesus Colome

Pitches: R Bats: R Pos: RP-61   Ht: 6'2" Wt: 200 Born: 12/23/1977 Age: 30

Year	Team	Lg	G	GS	CG	GF	IP	BFP	H	R	ER	HR	SH	SF	HB	TBB	IBB	SO	WP	Bk	W	L	Pct	ShO	Sv-Op	Hld	ERC	ERA
2007	Nats*	R	2	1	0	0	3.0	11	2	0	0	0	0	0	0	0	0	2	0	0	1	0	1.000	0	0--	-	0.91	0.00
2007	Clmbs*	AAA	1	0	0	0	1.0	3	0	0	0	0	0	0	0	0	0	2	0	0	0	0	-	0	0--	-	0.00	0.00
2001	TB	AL	30	0	0	9	48.2	209	37	22	18	8	2	2	2	25	4	31	2	0	2	3	.400	0	0-0	6	3.62	3.33
2002	TB	AL	32	0	0	15	41.1	204	56	41	38	6	4	1	2	33	5	33	5	0	2	7	.222	0	0-5	3	8.57	8.27
2003	TB	AL	54	0	0	24	74.0	334	69	37	37	9	2	4	3	46	5	69	7	0	3	7	.300	0	2-8	11	4.76	4.50
2004	TB	AL	33	0	0	9	41.1	169	28	16	15	4	5	0	1	18	1	40	1	1	2	2	.500	0	3-4	8	2.54	3.27
2005	TB	AL	36	0	0	18	45.1	212	54	29	23	7	1	0	2	18	3	28	5	0	2	3	.400	0	0-1	2	5.46	4.57
2006	TB	AL	1	0	0	0	0.1	2	0	1	1	0	0	0	0	1	0	0	0	0	0	0	-	0	0-0	0	7.00	27.00
2007	Was	NL	61	0	0	16	66.0	286	64	30	28	6	4	6	1	27	3	43	4	0	5	1	.833	0	1-4	12	3.83	3.82
	7 ML YEARS		247	0	0	91	317.0	1416	308	176	160	40	18	13	11	168	21	244	24	1	16	23	.410	0	6-22	42	4.62	4.54

Bartolo Colon

Pitches: R Bats: R Pos: SP-18; RP-1   Ht: 5'11" Wt: 245 Born: 5/24/1973 Age: 35

Year	Team	Lg	G	GS	CG	GF	IP	BFP	H	R	ER	HR	SH	SF	HB	TBB	IBB	SO	WP	Bk	W	L	Pct	ShO	Sv-Op	Hld	ERC	ERA
2007	RCuca*	A+	2	2	0	0	9.2	38	6	2	2	0	0	0	0	1	0	10	0	0	1	0	1.000	0	0--	-	0.93	1.86
2007	Salt Lk*	AAA	3	3	0	0	15.0	60	12	4	4	0	0	1	0	3	0	8	0	0	2	0	1.000	0	0--	-	1.70	2.40
1997	Cle	AL	19	17	1	0	94.0	427	107	66	59	12	4	1	3	45	1	66	5	0	4	7	.364	0	0-0	0	5.53	5.65
1998	Cle	AL	31	31	6	0	204.0	883	205	91	84	15	10	2	3	79	5	158	4	0	14	9	.609	2	0-0	0	3.87	3.71
1999	Cle	AL	32	32	1	0	205.0	858	185	97	90	24	5	4	7	76	5	161	4	0	18	5	.783	1	0-0	0	3.68	3.95
2000	Cle	AL	30	30	2	0	188.0	807	163	86	81	21	2	3	4	98	4	212	4	0	15	8	.652	1	0-0	0	3.97	3.88
2001	Cle	AL	34	34	1	0	222.1	947	220	106	101	26	8	4	2	90	2	201	4	1	14	12	.538	0	0-0	0	4.24	4.09
2002	2 Tms		33	33	8	0	233.1	966	219	85	76	20	19	6	2	70	5	149	4	0	20	8	.714	3	0-0	0	3.29	2.93
2003	CWS	AL	34	34	9	0	242.0	984	223	107	104	30	5	8	5	67	3	173	8	3	15	13	.536	3	0-0	0	3.47	3.87
2004	LAA	AL	34	34	1	0	208.1	897	215	122	116	38	5	8	3	71	1	158	1	0	18	12	.600	0	0-0	0	4.64	5.01
2005	LAA	AL	33	33	2	0	222.2	906	215	93	86	26	9	4	3	43	0	157	2	1	21	8	.724	0	0-0	0	3.28	3.48
2006	LAA	AL	10	10	1	0	56.1	251	71	39	32	11	4	1	0	11	0	31	1	0	1	5	.167	1	0-0	0	5.61	5.11

Year	Team	Lg	G	GS	CG	GF	IP	BFP	H	R	ER	HR	SH	SF	HB	TBB	IBB	SO	WP	Bk	W	L	Pct	ShO	Sv-Op	Hld	ERC	ERA
							HOW MUCH HE PITCHED					WHAT HE GAVE UP												THE RESULTS				
2007	LAA	AL	19	18	0	0	99.1	453	132	74	70	15	4	3	5	29	1	76	1	0	6	8	.429	0	0-0	1	6.17	6.34
02	Cle	AL	16	16	4	0	116.1	467	104	37	33	11	6	3	2	31	1	75	3	0	10	4	.714	2	0-0	0	3.09	2.55
02	Mon	NL	17	17	4	0	117.0	499	115	48	43	9	13	3	0	39	4	74	1	0	10	4	.714	1	0-0	0	3.48	3.31
11 ML YEARS			309	306	31	0	1975.1	8379	1955	966	899	238	75	44	40	679	27	1542	38	5	146	95	.606	8	0-0	1	4.02	4.10

Steve Colyer

Pitches: L Bats: L Pos: RP-7　　　　**Ht: 6'4" Wt: 235 Born: 2/22/1979 Age: 29**

Year	Team	Lg	G	GS	CG	GF	IP	BFP	H	R	ER	HR	SH	SF	HB	TBB	IBB	SO	WP	Bk	W	L	Pct	ShO	Sv-Op	Hld	ERC	ERA
							HOW MUCH HE PITCHED					WHAT HE GAVE UP												THE RESULTS				
2007	Rchmd*	AAA	2	0	0	1	2.0	8	2	0	0	0	0	0	0	0	0	1	0	0	0	0	-	0	0--	-	1.95	0.00
2003	LAD	NL	13	0	0	3	19.2	84	22	6	6	0	1	0	0	9	0	16	1	0	0	0	-	0	0-0	0	4.44	2.75
2004	Det	AL	41	0	0	9	32.0	147	33	24	23	8	0	0	1	24	1	31	3	0	1	0	1.000	0	0-0	4	7.19	6.47
2007	Atl	NL	7	0	0	1	3.2	22	9	2	2	1	0	0	0	4	0	4	1	0	0	1	.000	0	0-0	1	20.81	4.91
3 ML YEARS			61	0	0	13	55.1	253	64	32	31	9	1	0	1	37	1	51	5	0	1	1	.500	0	0-0	5	6.93	5.04

Clay Condrey

Pitches: R Bats: R Pos: RP-39　　　　**Ht: 6'3" Wt: 215 Born: 11/19/1975 Age: 32**

Year	Team	Lg	G	GS	CG	GF	IP	BFP	H	R	ER	HR	SH	SF	HB	TBB	IBB	SO	WP	Bk	W	L	Pct	ShO	Sv-Op	Hld	ERC	ERA
							HOW MUCH HE PITCHED					WHAT HE GAVE UP												THE RESULTS				
2007	Ottawa*	AAA	10	0	0	5	22.0	85	20	7	6	0	2	0	1	5	0	10	0	0	1	0	1.000	0	1--	-	2.66	2.45
2002	SD	NL	9	3	0	2	26.2	106	20	7	5	1	2	2	2	8	1	16	1	1	1	2	.333	0	0-0	3	2.29	1.69
2003	SD	NL	9	6	0	0	34.0	168	43	32	32	7	3	0	3	21	4	25	0	0	1	2	.333	0	0-0	0	7.50	8.47
2006	Phi	NL	21	0	0	10	28.2	122	35	11	10	3	2	1	0	9	2	16	0	0	2	2	.500	0	0-1	1	5.14	3.14
2007	Phi	NL	39	0	0	14	50.0	228	61	30	28	4	1	3	5	16	3	27	1	0	5	0	1.000	0	2-2	2	5.14	5.04
4 ML YEARS			78	9	0	26	139.1	624	159	80	75	15	8	6	10	54	10	84	2	1	9	6	.600	0	2-3	6	5.08	4.84

Jeff Conine

Bats: R Throws: R Pos: 1B-67; PH-37; LF-2; RF-2; 3B-1; DH-1; PR-1　　　　**Ht: 6'1" Wt: 227 Born: 6/27/1966 Age: 42**

Year	Team	Lg	G	AB	H	2B	3B	HR	(Hm	Rd)	TB	R	RBI	RC	TBB	IBB	SO	HBP	SH	SF	SB	CS	SB%	GDP	Avg	OBP	Slg
									BATTING											BASERUNNING				AVERAGES		
1990	KC	AL	9	20	5	2	0	0	(0	0)	7	3	2	2	2	0	5	0	0	0	0	0	-	1	.250	.318	.350
1992	KC	AL	28	91	23	5	2	0	(0	0)	32	10	9	10	8	1	23	0	0	0	0	0	-	1	.253	.313	.352
1993	Fla	NL	162	595	174	24	3	12	(5	7)	240	75	79	83	52	2	135	5	0	6	2	2	.50	14	.292	.351	.403
1994	Fla	NL	115	451	144	27	6	18	(8	10)	237	60	82	84	40	4	92	1	0	4	1	2	.33	8	.319	.373	.525
1995	Fla	NL	133	483	146	26	2	25	(13	12)	251	72	105	93	66	5	94	1	0	12	2	0	1.00	13	.302	.379	.520
1996	Fla	NL	157	597	175	32	2	26	(15	11)	289	84	95	99	62	4	121	4	0	7	1	4	.20	17	.293	.360	.484
1997	Fla	NL	151	405	98	13	1	17	(7	10)	164	46	61	55	57	3	89	2	0	2	2	0	1.00	11	.242	.337	.405
1998	KC	AL	93	309	79	26	0	8	(4	4)	129	30	43	40	26	1	68	2	0	6	3	0	1.00	8	.256	.312	.417
1999	Bal	AL	139	444	129	31	1	13	(7	6)	201	54	75	64	30	4	40	3	1	7	0	3	.00	12	.291	.335	.453
2000	Bal	AL	119	409	116	20	2	13	(6	7)	179	53	46	58	36	1	53	2	0	4	4	3	.57	14	.284	.341	.438
2001	Bal	AL	139	524	163	23	2	14	(5	9)	232	75	97	89	64	6	75	5	0	8	12	8	.60	12	.311	.386	.443
2002	Bal	AL	116	451	123	26	4	15	(12	3)	202	44	63	61	25	6	66	2	0	10	8	0	1.00	10	.273	.307	.448
2003	2 Tms		149	577	163	36	3	20	(11	9)	265	88	95	84	50	5	70	5	1	13	5	0	1.00	16	.282	.338	.459
2004	Fla	NL	140	521	146	35	1	14	(9	5)	225	55	83	78	48	3	78	2	2	6	5	5	.50	15	.280	.340	.432
2005	Fla	NL	131	335	102	20	2	3	(1	2)	135	42	33	46	38	2	58	3	2	6	2	0	1.00	12	.304	.374	.403
2006	2 Tms	NL	142	489	131	26	4	10	(6	4)	195	54	66	59	40	4	65	4	1	5	3	2	.60	13	.268	.325	.399
2007	2 Tms	NL	101	256	65	13	1	6	(4	2)	98	25	37	35	27	2	36	0	2	7	4	0	1.00	5	.254	.317	.383
03	Bal	AL	124	493	143	33	3	15	(8	7)	227	75	80	73	37	5	60	5	0	12	5	0	1.00	14	.290	.338	.460
03	Fla	NL	25	84	20	3	0	5	(3	2)	38	13	15	11	13	0	10	0	1	1	0	0	-	2	.238	.337	.452
06	Bal	AL	114	389	103	20	3	9	(6	3)	156	43	49	45	35	2	53	2	1	5	3	2	.60	12	.265	.325	.401
06	Phi	NL	28	100	28	6	1	1	(0	1)	39	11	17	14	5	2	12	2	0	0	0	0	-	1	.280	.327	.390
07	Cin	NL	80	215	57	11	1	6	(4	2)	88	23	32	31	20	0	28	0	1	6	4	0	1.00	4	.265	.328	.409
07	NYM	NL	21	41	8	2	0	0	(0	0)	10	2	5	4	7	2	8	0	1	1	0	0	-	1	.195	.306	.244
17 ML YEARS			2024	6957	1982	385	36	214	(113	101)	3081	870	1071	1040	671	46	1168	41	9	103	54	29	.65	182	.285	.347	.443

Jose Contreras

Pitches: R Bats: R Pos: SP-30; RP-2　　　　**Ht: 6'4" Wt: 245 Born: 12/6/1971 Age: 36**

Year	Team	Lg	G	GS	CG	GF	IP	BFP	H	R	ER	HR	SH	SF	HB	TBB	IBB	SO	WP	Bk	W	L	Pct	ShO	Sv-Op	Hld	ERC	ERA
							HOW MUCH HE PITCHED					WHAT HE GAVE UP												THE RESULTS				
2003	NYY	AL	18	9	0	2	71.0	293	52	27	26	4	0	1	5	30	1	72	2	0	7	2	.778	0	0-1	1	2.71	3.30
2004	2 Tms	AL	31	31	0	0	170.1	758	166	114	104	31	3	6	8	84	1	150	17	0	13	9	.591	0	0-0	0	5.05	5.50
2005	CWS	AL	32	32	1	0	204.2	857	177	91	82	23	7	2	9	75	2	154	20	2	15	7	.682	0	0-0	0	3.46	3.61
2006	CWS	AL	30	30	1	0	196.0	833	194	101	93	20	2	8	10	55	4	134	16	0	13	9	.591	1	0-0	0	3.72	4.27
2007	CWS	AL	32	30	2	2	189.0	858	232	134	117	21	8	10	15	62	1	113	3	0	10	17	.370	2	0-0	0	5.49	5.57
04	NYY	AL	18	18	0	0	95.2	425	93	66	60	22	1	4	6	42	1	82	10	0	8	5	.615	0	0-0	0	5.18	5.64
04	CWS	AL	13	13	0	0	74.2	333	73	48	44	9	2	2	2	42	0	68	7	0	5	4	.556	0	0-0	0	4.87	5.30
5 ML YEARS			143	132	4	4	831.0	3599	821	467	422	99	20	27	47	306	9	623	58	2	58	44	.569	3	0-1	1	4.21	4.57

Aaron Cook

Pitches: R Bats: R Pos: SP-25   Ht: 6'3" Wt: 215 Born: 2/8/1979 Age: 29

Year	Team	Lg	G	GS	CG	GF	IP	BFP	H	R	ER	HR	SH	SF	HB	TBB	IBB	SO	WP	Bk	W	L	Pct	ShO	Sv-Op	Hld	ERC	ERA
2007	ColSpr*	AAA	1	1	0	0	1.0	8	4	3	3	0	0	1	0	1	0	0	0	0	0	1	.000	0	0--	-	27.72	27.00
2002	Col	NL	9	5	0	1	35.2	154	41	18	18	4	0	0	2	13	0	14	0	0	2	1	.667	0	0-0	1	5.31	4.54
2003	Col	NL	43	16	1	4	124.0	579	160	89	83	8	4	6	8	57	7	43	10	0	4	6	.400	0	0-0	1	5.95	6.02
2004	Col	NL	16	16	1	0	96.2	433	112	47	46	7	5	1	7	39	5	40	6	1	6	4	.600	0	0-0	0	5.05	4.28
2005	Col	NL	13	13	2	0	83.1	357	101	38	34	8	1	3	2	16	2	24	3	0	7	2	.778	0	0-0	0	4.53	3.67
2006	Col	NL	32	32	0	0	212.2	915	242	107	100	17	8	5	7	55	11	92	2	0	9	15	.375	0	0-0	0	4.23	4.23
2007	Col	NL	25	25	2	0	166.0	698	178	87	76	15	6	3	6	44	6	61	0	0	8	7	.533	0	0-0	0	4.05	4.12
6 ML YEARS			138	107	6	5	718.1	3136	834	386	357	59	24	18	32	224	31	274	21	1	36	35	.507	0	0-0	2	4.67	4.47

Alex Cora

Bats: L Throws: R Pos: 2B-47; SS-33; PH-12; PR-5; DH-3; 1B-1   Ht: 6'0" Wt: 200 Born: 10/18/1975 Age: 32

Year	Team	Lg	G	AB	H	2B	3B	HR	(Hm	Rd)	TB	R	RBI	RC	TBB	IBB	SO	HBP	SH	SF	SB	CS	SB%	GDP	Avg	OBP	Slg
1998	LAD	NL	29	33	4	0	1	0	(0	0)	6	1	0	1	2	0	8	1	2	0	0	0	-	0	.121	.194	.182
1999	LAD	NL	11	30	5	1	0	0	(0	0)	6	2	3	0	0	0	4	1	0	0	0	0	-	1	.167	.194	.200
2000	LAD	NL	109	353	84	18	6	0	(2	2)	126	39	32	38	26	4	53	7	6	2	4	1	.80	6	.238	.302	.357
2001	LAD	NL	134	405	88	18	3	4	(2	2)	124	38	29	30	31	6	58	8	3	2	0	2	.00	16	.217	.285	.306
2002	LAD	NL	115	258	75	14	4	5	(4	1)	112	37	28	46	26	4	38	7	2	0	7	2	.78	3	.291	.371	.434
2003	LAD	NL	148	477	119	24	3	4	(3	1)	161	39	34	46	16	3	59	10	9	2	4	2	.67	5	.249	.287	.338
2004	LAD	NL	138	405	107	9	4	10	(4	6)	154	47	47	63	47	10	41	18	12	2	3	4	.43	5	.264	.364	.380
2005	2 Tms	AL	96	250	58	8	4	3	(1	2)	83	25	24	21	11	0	30	5	4	3	7	2	.78	6	.232	.275	.332
2006	Bos	AL	96	235	56	7	2	1	(1	0)	70	31	18	24	19	1	29	6	4	0	6	2	.75	4	.238	.312	.298
2007	Bos	AL	83	207	51	10	5	3	(0	3)	80	30	18	19	7	2	23	9	7	2	1	1	.50	5	.246	.298	.386
05	Cle	AL	49	146	30	5	2	1	(1	0)	42	11	8	9	5	0	18	4	1	1	6	0	1.00	3	.205	.250	.288
05	Bos	AL	47	104	28	3	2	2	(0	2)	41	14	16	12	6	0	12	1	3	2	1	2	.33	3	.269	.310	.394
10 ML YEARS			959	2653	647	109	32	34	(17	17)	922	289	233	288	185	30	343	72	49	13	32	16	.67	55	.244	.309	.348

Tim Corcoran

Pitches: R Bats: R Pos: RP-9   Ht: 6'2" Wt: 210 Born: 4/15/1978 Age: 30

Year	Team	Lg	G	GS	CG	GF	IP	BFP	H	R	ER	HR	SH	SF	HB	TBB	IBB	SO	WP	Bk	W	L	Pct	ShO	Sv-Op	Hld	ERC	ERA
2007	Drham*	AAA	10	0	0	4	14.1	60	13	4	4	1	1	0	0	6	0	13	0	0	1	1	.500	0	0--	-	3.48	2.51
2007	Mont*	AA	14	0	0	5	18.1	77	12	7	7	1	2	1	1	9	0	20	0	0	2	1	.667	0	3--	-	2.45	3.44
2005	TB	AL	10	1	0	4	22.2	97	19	15	15	1	0	0	1	12	0	13	2	0	0	0	-	0	0-0	0	3.49	5.96
2006	TB	AL	21	16	0	2	90.1	396	92	48	44	10	1	4	4	48	3	59	0	1	5	9	.357	0	0-0	0	5.04	4.38
2007	TB	AL	9	0	0	3	17.1	79	17	14	13	2	0	0	1	12	3	6	1	0	0	0	-	0	0-0	0	5.25	6.75
3 ML YEARS			40	17	0	9	130.1	572	128	77	72	13	1	4	6	72	6	78	3	1	5	9	.357	0	0-0	0	4.79	4.97

Chad Cordero

Pitches: R Bats: R Pos: RP-76   Ht: 6'0" Wt: 195 Born: 3/18/1982 Age: 26

Year	Team	Lg	G	GS	CG	GF	IP	BFP	H	R	ER	HR	SH	SF	HB	TBB	IBB	SO	WP	Bk	W	L	Pct	ShO	Sv-Op	Hld	ERC	ERA
2003	Mon	NL	12	0	0	4	11.0	40	4	2	2	1	1	0	0	3	1	12	1	0	1	0	1.000	0	1-1	1	0.86	1.64
2004	Mon	NL	69	0	0	40	82.2	357	68	28	27	8	2	4	1	43	4	83	5	0	7	3	.700	0	14-18	8	3.47	2.94
2005	Was	NL	74	0	0	62	74.1	300	55	24	15	9	2	1	2	17	2	61	0	0	2	4	.333	0	47-54	0	2.22	1.82
2006	Was	NL	68	0	0	59	73.1	307	59	27	26	13	6	2	3	22	5	69	0	0	7	4	.636	0	29-33	0	3.10	3.19
2007	Was	NL	76	0	0	59	75.0	321	75	31	28	8	2	1	0	29	3	62	5	1	3	3	.500	0	37-46	1	4.02	3.36
5 ML YEARS			299	0	0	224	316.1	1325	261	112	98	39	13	8	6	114	15	287	11	1	20	14	.588	0	128-152	10	3.09	2.79

Francisco Cordero

Pitches: R Bats: R Pos: RP-66   Ht: 6'2" Wt: 235 Born: 5/11/1975 Age: 33

Year	Team	Lg	G	GS	CG	GF	IP	BFP	H	R	ER	HR	SH	SF	HB	TBB	IBB	SO	WP	Bk	W	L	Pct	ShO	Sv-Op	Hld	ERC	ERA
1999	Det	AL	20	0	0	4	19.0	91	19	7	7	2	2	4	0	18	2	19	1	0	2	2	.500	0	0-0	6	6.19	3.32
2000	Tex	AL	56	0	0	13	77.1	365	87	51	46	11	2	6	4	48	3	49	7	0	1	2	.333	0	0-3	4	6.15	5.35
2001	Tex	AL	3	0	0	2	2.1	12	3	1	1	0	0	0	0	2	1	1	1	0	0	1	.000	0	0-0	1	5.73	3.86
2002	Tex	AL	39	0	0	25	45.1	177	33	12	9	2	0	0	2	13	1	41	1	0	2	0	1.000	0	10-12	1	2.11	1.79
2003	Tex	AL	73	0	0	36	82.2	352	70	33	27	4	3	4	2	38	6	90	1	0	5	8	.385	0	15-25	18	3.08	2.94
2004	Tex	AL	67	0	0	63	71.2	304	60	19	17	1	5	1	1	32	2	79	3	2	3	4	.429	0	49-54	0	2.78	2.13
2005	Tex	AL	69	0	0	60	69.0	302	61	28	26	5	4	3	4	30	2	79	0	0	3	1	.750	0	37-45	0	3.47	3.39
2006	2 Tms	NL	77	0	0	47	75.1	322	69	32	31	7	3	5	3	32	2	84	4	0	10	5	.667	0	22-33	16	3.79	3.70
2007	Mil	NL	66	0	0	58	63.1	261	52	23	21	4	2	1	1	18	1	86	2	0	0	4	.000	0	44-51	0	2.45	2.98
06	Tex	AL	49	0	0	21	48.2	210	49	27	26	5	1	5	3	16	1	54	3	0	7	4	.636	0	6-15	15	4.05	4.81
06	Mil	NL	28	0	0	26	26.2	112	20	5	5	2	2	0	0	16	1	30	1	0	3	1	.750	0	16-18	1	3.30	1.69
9 ML YEARS			470	0	0	308	506.0	2186	454	206	185	36	21	24	17	231	20	528	20	2	26	27	.491	0	177-223	46	3.57	3.29

74

Bryan Corey

Pitches: R **Bats:** R **Pos:** RP-9   Ht: 6'0" Wt: 180 Born: 10/21/1973 Age: 34

			HOW MUCH HE PITCHED						WHAT HE GAVE UP									THE RESULTS							
Year	Team	Lg	G	GS	CG	GF	IP	BFP	H	R	ER	HR	SH	SF	HB	TBB	IBB	SO	WP	Bk	W	L	Pct	ShO	Sv-Op Hld	ERC	ERA
2007	Pwtckt*	AAA	58	0	0	20	68.2	282	57	31	28	6	7	2	3	20	1	67	1	0	6	8	.429	0	3-- -	2.81	3.67
1998	Ari	NL	3	0	0	2	4.0	20	6	4	4	1	1	0	1	2	0	1	0	0	0	0	-	0	0-0 0	10.40	9.00
2002	LAD	NL	1	0	0	1	1.0	3	0	0	0	0	0	0	0	0	0	0	0	0	0	0	-	0	0-0 0	0.00	0.00
2006	2 Tms	AL	32	0	0	3	39.0	166	35	16	16	1	1	3	2	15	0	28	0	0	2	1	.667	0	0-0 3	3.13	3.69
2007	Bos	AL	9	0	0	2	9.1	32	6	2	2	0	1	1	0	4	0	6	0	0	1	0	1.000	0	0-0 1	2.13	1.93
06	Tex	AL	16	0	0	3	17.1	75	15	5	5	0	1	1	0	8	0	13	0	0	1	0	.500	0	0-0 0	2.82	2.60
06	Bos	AL	16	0	0	0	21.2	91	20	11	11	1	0	2	2	7	0	15	0	0	1	0	1.000	0	0-0 3	3.39	4.57
	4 ML YEARS		45	0	0	8	53.1	221	47	22	22	2	3	4	3	21	0	35	0	0	3	1	.750	0	0-0 4	3.28	3.71

Lance Cormier

Pitches: R **Bats:** R **Pos:** SP-9; RP-1   Ht: 6'1" Wt: 200 Born: 8/19/1980 Age: 27

			HOW MUCH HE PITCHED						WHAT HE GAVE UP									THE RESULTS							
Year	Team	Lg	G	GS	CG	GF	IP	BFP	H	R	ER	HR	SH	SF	HB	TBB	IBB	SO	WP	Bk	W	L	Pct	ShO	Sv-Op Hld	ERC	ERA
2007	Rome*	A-	1	1	0	0	2.0	11	5	1	1	0	0	0	0	0	0	4	1	0	0	0	-	0	0-- -	10.86	4.50
2007	Missi*	AA	2	2	0	0	8.0	30	8	4	4	1	0	0	0	0	0	6	0	0	1	1	.500	0	0-- -	2.85	4.50
2007	Rchmd*	AAA	10	10	1	0	52.0	212	56	22	20	4	1	0	1	15	0	31	2	1	4	2	.667	1	0-- -	4.22	3.46
2004	Ari	NL	17	5	0	3	45.1	218	62	42	41	13	2	3	2	25	2	24	2	1	1	4	.200	0	0-0 2	8.76	8.14
2005	Ari	NL	67	0	0	13	79.1	356	86	50	45	7	4	1	5	43	5	63	6	0	7	3	.700	0	0-1 13	5.30	5.11
2006	Atl	NL	29	9	0	5	73.2	333	90	44	40	8	1	4	2	39	7	43	2	0	4	5	.444	0	0-0 2	6.13	4.89
2007	Atl	NL	10	9	0	1	45.2	210	56	38	36	16	3	0	0	22	3	27	4	0	2	6	.250	0	0-0 0	7.66	7.09
	4 ML YEARS		123	23	0	22	244.0	1117	294	174	162	44	10	8	9	129	17	157	14	1	14	18	.438	0	0-1 17	6.62	5.98

Rheal Cormier

Pitches: L **Bats:** L **Pos:** RP-6   Ht: 5'10" Wt: 195 Born: 4/23/1967 Age: 41

			HOW MUCH HE PITCHED						WHAT HE GAVE UP									THE RESULTS							
Year	Team	Lg	G	GS	CG	GF	IP	BFP	H	R	ER	HR	SH	SF	HB	TBB	IBB	SO	WP	Bk	W	L	Pct	ShO	Sv-Op Hld	ERC	ERA
2007	Rchmd*	AAA	5	0	0	2	7.2	30	4	1	1	0	1	0	0	3	1	7	0	0	1	0	1.000	0	0-- -	1.15	1.17
1991	StL	NL	11	10	2	1	67.2	281	74	35	31	5	1	3	2	8	1	38	2	1	4	5	.444	0	0-0 0	3.41	4.12
1992	StL	NL	31	30	3	1	186.0	772	194	83	76	15	11	3	5	33	2	117	4	2	10	10	.500	0	0-0 0	3.42	3.68
1993	StL	NL	38	21	1	4	145.1	619	163	80	70	18	10	4	4	27	3	75	6	0	7	6	.538	0	0-0 0	4.13	4.33
1994	StL	NL	7	7	0	0	39.2	169	40	24	24	6	1	2	3	7	0	26	2	0	3	2	.600	0	0-0 0	3.80	5.45
1995	Bos	AL	48	12	0	3	115.0	488	131	60	52	12	6	2	3	31	2	69	4	0	7	5	.583	0	0-2 9	4.56	4.07
1996	Mon	NL	33	27	1	1	159.2	674	165	80	74	16	4	8	9	41	3	100	0	1	7	10	.412	1	0-0 0	3.93	4.17
1997	Mon	NL	1	1	0	0	1.1	9	4	5	5	1	0	0	0	1	0	0	0	0	0	1	.000	0	0-0 0	27.46	33.75
1999	Bos	AL	60	0	0	7	63.1	275	61	34	26	4	1	3	5	18	2	39	1	0	2	0	1.000	0	0-3 15	3.33	3.69
2000	Bos	Al	64	0	0	12	68.1	293	74	40	35	7	5	2	0	17	2	43	1	0	3	3	.500	0	0-2 9	3.86	4.61
2001	Phi	NL	60	0	0	16	51.1	222	49	28	24	5	3	0	4	17	4	37	1	0	5	6	.455	0	1-6 12	3.67	4.21
2002	Phi	NL	54	0	0	7	60.0	268	61	38	35	6	2	0	4	32	6	49	4	0	5	6	.455	0	0-3 9	4.85	5.25
2003	Phi	NL	65	0	0	21	84.2	327	54	18	16	4	4	0	1	25	2	67	0	1	8	0	1.000	0	1-4 14	1.63	1.70
2004	Phi	NL	84	0	0	8	81.0	330	70	32	32	7	3	1	5	26	6	46	1	0	4	5	.444	0	0-7 28	3.16	3.56
2005	Phi	NL	57	0	0	10	47.1	211	56	33	31	9	2	2	2	16	1	34	3	0	4	2	.667	0	0-2 17	5.71	5.89
2006	2 Tms	NL	64	0	0	13	48.0	205	48	13	13	5	5	0	3	17	3	19	2	0	2	3	.400	0	0-4 14	4.13	2.44
2007	Cin	NL	6	0	0	1	3.0	14	4	3	3	1	1	0	1	1	0	1	0	0	0	0	-	0	0-0 3	9.77	9.00
06	Phi	NL	43	0	0	6	34.0	139	27	6	6	2	3	0	3	13	3	13	2	0	2	2	.500	0	0-4 12	2.91	1.59
06	Cin	NL	21	0	0	7	14.0	66	21	7	7	3	2	0	0	4	0	6	0	0	0	1	.000	0	0-0 2	7.48	4.50
	16 ML YEARS		683	108	7	105	1221.2	5157	1248	604	547	121	57	32	51	317	37	760	39	4	71	64	.526	1	2-33 130	3.77	4.03

Manny Corpas

Pitches: R **Bats:** R **Pos:** RP-78   Ht: 6'3" Wt: 170 Born: 12/3/1982 Age: 25

			HOW MUCH HE PITCHED						WHAT HE GAVE UP									THE RESULTS							
Year	Team	Lg	G	GS	CG	GF	IP	BFP	H	R	ER	HR	SH	SF	HB	TBB	IBB	SO	WP	Bk	W	L	Pct	ShO	Sv-Op Hld	ERC	ERA
2002	Casper	R+	29	0	0	20	33.0	159	37	24	21	4	4	0	2	18	3	42	3	1	2	4	.333	0	2-- -	5.37	5.73
2003	TriCity	A-	15	15	0	0	84.0	375	98	61	54	7	4	6	7	22	1	47	3	0	5	6	.455	0	0-- -	4.60	5.79
2004	Ashvll	A	43	0	0	20	44.1	199	48	20	15	3	0	0	6	13	1	52	2	1	2	2	.500	0	3-- -	4.29	3.05
2005	Mdest	A+	47	0	0	19	69.0	305	83	33	29	2	2	2	3	14	1	52	3	0	3	2	.600	0	2-- -	4.00	3.78
2006	Tulsa	AA	34	0	0	30	36.2	134	22	7	4	0	3	0	3	4	1	35	1	0	2	1	.667	0	19-- -	1.11	0.98
2006	ColSpr	AAA	8	0	0	5	8.2	32	5	1	1	0	0	0	0	2	0	7	0	0	0	0	-	0	0-- -	1.56	1.04
2006	Col	NL	35	0	0	3	32.1	136	36	13	13	9	0	0	2	8	1	27	2	0	1	2	.333	0	0-2 7	4.39	3.62
2007	Col	NL	78	0	0	46	78.0	306	63	20	18	6	2	1	2	20	3	58	0	0	4	2	.667	0	19-22 16	2.51	2.08
	2 ML YEARS		113	0	0	49	110.1	442	99	33	31	9	2	1	4	28	4	85	2	0	5	4	.556	0	19-24 23	3.02	2.53

Kevin Correia

Pitches: R **Bats:** R **Pos:** RP-51; SP-8   Ht: 6'3" Wt: 200 Born: 8/24/1980 Age: 27

			HOW MUCH HE PITCHED						WHAT HE GAVE UP									THE RESULTS							
Year	Team	Lg	G	GS	CG	GF	IP	BFP	H	R	ER	HR	SH	SF	HB	TBB	IBB	SO	WP	Bk	W	L	Pct	ShO	Sv-Op Hld	ERC	ERA
2003	SF	NL	10	7	0	1	39.1	173	41	16	16	6	1	1	4	18	1	28	2	0	3	1	.750	0	0-0 0	5.46	3.66
2004	SF	NL	12	1	0	5	19.0	92	25	20	17	3	3	3	1	10	0	14	0	0	0	1	.000	0	0-0 0	7.12	8.05
2005	SF	NL	16	11	0	1	58.1	264	61	31	30	12	5	1	4	31	2	44	2	0	2	5	.286	0	0-0 0	5.94	4.63
2006	SF	NL	48	0	0	9	69.2	295	64	27	27	5	4	3	1	22	0	57	0	0	2	0	1.000	0	0-1 10	3.25	3.49
2007	SF	NL	59	8	0	9	101.2	437	94	39	39	9	4	3	2	40	7	80	1	1	4	7	.364	0	0-3 12	3.48	3.45
	5 ML YEARS		145	27	0	25	288.0	1261	285	133	129	35	14	12	14	121	10	223	5	1	11	14	.440	0	0-4 22	4.37	4.03

Fernando Cortez

Bats: L **Throws:** R **Pos:** 2B-6; PH-2; PR-1   **Ht:** 6'1" **Wt:** 175 **Born:** 8/10/1981 **Age:** 26

Year	Team	Lg	G	AB	H	2B	3B	HR	(Hm	Rd)	TB	R	RBI	RC	TBB	IBB	SO	HBP	SH	SF	SB	CS	SB%	GDP	Avg	OBP	Slg
2001	HudVal	A-	55	234	65	14	3	1	(-	-)	88	36	25	30	15	1	26	3	3	2	6	3	.67	5	.278	.327	.376
2002	CtnSC	A	127	475	127	14	5	2	(-	-)	157	60	49	56	41	0	59	4	2	6	37	16	.70	9	.267	.327	.331
2003	Bkrsfld	A+	102	384	108	19	0	1	(-	-)	130	53	53	53	41	2	61	2	2	9	32	9	.78	7	.281	.346	.339
2003	Orlndo	AA	30	114	36	3	1	1	(-	-)	44	15	6	14	3	0	22	0	1	0	1	2	.33	2	.316	.333	.386
2004	Mont	AA	94	359	103	20	5	3	(-	-)	142	51	30	50	32	1	60	1	6	2	7	7	.50	3	.287	.345	.396
2005	Mont	AA	55	219	73	11	4	0	(-	-)	92	39	23	37	15	0	42	2	1	3	12	3	.80	5	.333	.377	.420
2005	Drham	AAA	58	238	54	8	2	2	(-	-)	72	26	26	21	10	0	38	3	3	1	13	1	.93	6	.227	.266	.303
2006	Drham	AAA	60	203	45	6	2	0	(-	-)	55	21	7	14	11	0	37	1	2	0	8	3	.73	7	.222	.265	.271
2006	Omha	AAA	67	258	63	6	2	0	(-	-)	73	29	13	19	12	0	30	1	3	0	5	6	.45	8	.244	.280	.283
2007	Omha	AAA	82	304	88	15	1	4	(-	-)	117	40	24	44	25	1	42	1	8	2	12	1	.92	6	.289	.343	.385
2005	TB	AL	8	13	1	0	0	0	(0	0)	1	0	1	0	1	0	3	0	0	0	0	0	-	0	.077	.143	.077
2007	KC	AL	8	14	4	1	0	0	(0	0)	5	3	1	2	1	0	0	0	1	0	0	0	-	0	.286	.333	.357
2 ML YEARS			16	27	5	1	0	0	(0	0)	6	3	2	2	2	0	3	0	1	0	0	0	-	0	.185	.241	.222

Shane Costa

Bats: L **Throws:** R **Pos:** PH-25; LF-15; RF-13; DH-7; PR-3   **Ht:** 6'0" **Wt:** 190 **Born:** 12/12/1981 **Age:** 26

Year	Team	Lg	G	AB	H	2B	3B	HR	(Hm	Rd)	TB	R	RBI	RC	TBB	IBB	SO	HBP	SH	SF	SB	CS	SB%	GDP	Avg	OBP	Slg
2007	Omha*	AAA	59	233	76	20	3	5	(-	-)	117	46	14	48	26	1	20	5	1	2	8	2	.80	3	.326	.402	.502
2005	KC	AL	27	81	19	2	0	2	(1	1)	27	13	7	7	5	0	11	1	1	0	0	0	-	3	.235	.287	.333
2006	KC	AL	72	237	65	20	1	3	(1	2)	96	23	23	26	6	2	29	5	2	2	2	0	1.00	5	.274	.304	.405
2007	KC	AL	55	103	23	6	1	0	(0	0)	31	13	12	8	5	0	23	0	0	1	0	1	.00	2	.223	.257	.301
3 ML YEARS			154	421	107	28	2	5	(2	3)	154	49	42	41	16	2	63	6	3	3	2	1	.67	10	.254	.289	.366

Chris Coste

Bats: R **Throws:** R **Pos:** C-31; PH-16; 1B-1   **Ht:** 6'1" **Wt:** 215 **Born:** 2/4/1973 **Age:** 35

Year	Team	Lg	G	AB	H	2B	3B	HR	(Hm	Rd)	TB	R	RBI	RC	TBB	IBB	SO	HBP	SH	SF	SB	CS	SB%	GDP	Avg	OBP	Slg
2000	Akron	AA	65	240	80	20	4	2	(-	-)	114	32	31	43	15	2	12	4	0	1	1	2	.33	7	.333	.381	.475
2000	Buffalo	AAA	31	96	29	2	0	4	(-	-)	43	15	8	13	3	0	3	1	1	0	0	1	.00	4	.302	.330	.448
2001	Akron	AA	6	24	3	0	0	0	(-	-)	3	1	0	0	1	0	50	0	0	0	0	1	.00	0	.125	.160	.125
2001	Buffalo	AAA	75	271	78	16	2	7	(-	-)	119	31	50	40	15	1	54	4	1	4	0	1	.00	11	.288	.330	.439
2002	Buffalo	AAA	124	478	152	32	1	8	(-	-)	210	59	67	82	34	2	18	13	0	3	0	0	-	14	.318	.377	.439
2003	Pwtckt	AAA	29	96	18	5	0	1	(-	-)	26	5	8	5	4	0	5	0	1	1	0	0	-	3	.188	.218	.271
2003	RedSx	R	11	30	7	2	1	1	(-	-)	14	3	6	5	7	1	37	0	0	0	0	0	-	2	.233	.378	.467
2004	Indy	AAA	78	262	77	21	1	2	(-	-)	106	34	26	38	20	0	85	5	2	2	2	3	.40	6	.294	.353	.405
2005	S-WB	AAA	134	506	148	26	1	20	(-	-)	236	73	89	84	40	0	85	9	0	7	3	4	.43	25	.292	.351	.466
2006	S-WB	AAA	39	147	26	8	0	2	(-	-)	40	12	14	8	9	1	28	3	0	2	1	1	.50	2	.177	.236	.272
2007	Clrwtr	A+	3	10	4	1	0	0	(-	-)	5	3	1	1	0	0	1	0	0	0	0	0	-	0	.400	.400	.500
2007	Ottawa	AAA	26	90	21	5	0	0	(-	-)	26	8	10	9	10	0	14	1	1	0	0	0	-	0	.233	.317	.289
2007	Rdng	AA	27	108	31	5	0	5	(-	-)	51	14	31	16	5	1	13	1	0	2	0	0	-	5	.287	.319	.472
2006	Phi	NL	65	198	65	14	0	7	(4	3)	100	25	32	36	10	1	31	5	0	0	0	0	-	6	.328	.376	.505
2007	Phi	NL	48	129	36	3	0	5	(5	0)	54	15	22	17	4	1	20	2	2	0	0	0	-	1	.279	.311	.419
2 ML YEARS			113	327	101	17	0	12	(9	3)	154	40	54	53	14	2	51	7	2	0	0	0	-	7	.309	.351	.471

Humberto Cota

Bats: R **Throws:** R **Pos:** C-5   **Ht:** 6'0" **Wt:** 210 **Born:** 2/7/1979 **Age:** 29

Year	Team	Lg	G	AB	H	2B	3B	HR	(Hm	Rd)	TB	R	RBI	RC	TBB	IBB	SO	HBP	SH	SF	SB	CS	SB%	GDP	Avg	OBP	Slg
2007	Indy*	AAA	30	95	27	6	0	0	(-	-)	33	9	9	12	7	0	8	0	1	1	2	0	1.00	4	.284	.330	.347
2001	Pit	NL	7	9	2	0	0	0	(0	0)	2	0	1	0	0	0	5	0	0	0	0	0	-	0	.222	.222	.222
2002	Pit	NL	7	17	5	1	0	0	(0	0)	6	2	0	1	1	1	4	0	0	0	0	0	-	0	.294	.333	.353
2003	Pit	NL	10	16	4	1	0	0	(0	0)	5	1	1	0	1	0	5	0	0	0	0	0	-	0	.250	.294	.313
2004	Pit	NL	36	66	15	1	1	5	(3	2)	33	10	8	7	3	1	20	1	0	0	0	0	-	1	.227	.271	.500
2005	Pit	NL	93	297	72	20	1	7	(5	2)	115	29	43	30	17	2	80	2	1	3	0	0	-	8	.242	.285	.387
2006	Pit	NL	38	100	19	1	0	0	(0	0)	20	5	5	3	8	0	26	0	1	1	0	0	-	3	.190	.248	.200
2007	Pit	NL	5	14	4	1	0	0	(0	0)	5	1	3	3	2	0	2	1	0	1	0	0	-	0	.286	.389	.357
7 ML YEARS			196	519	121	25	2	12	(8	4)	186	48	61	44	32	4	142	4	2	5	0	0	-	12	.233	.280	.358

Neal Cotts

Pitches: L **Bats:** L **Pos:** RP-16   **Ht:** 6'1" **Wt:** 200 **Born:** 3/25/1980 **Age:** 28

Year	Team	Lg	G	GS	CG	GF	IP	BFP	H	R	ER	HR	SH	SF	HB	TBB	IBB	SO	WP	Bk	W	L	Pct	ShO	Sv-Op	Hld	ERC	ERA
2007	Iowa*	AAA	24	6	0	1	50.1	217	43	28	27	4	2	2	1	30	0	48	3	2	2	2	.500	0	0--	0	4.02	4.83
2003	CWS	AL	4	4	0	0	13.1	69	15	12	12	1	1	0	0	17	0	10	0	0	1	1	.500	0	0-0	0	8.43	8.10
2004	CWS	AL	56	1	0	12	65.1	281	61	45	41	13	0	1	3	30	2	58	8	0	4	4	.500	0	0-2	4	4.84	5.65
2005	CWS	AL	69	0	0	10	60.1	248	38	15	13	1	0	3	4	29	5	58	3	0	4	0	1.000	0	0-2	13	2.03	1.94
2006	CWS	AL	70	0	0	14	54.0	251	64	33	31	12	3	1	3	24	6	43	3	0	1	2	.333	0	1-4	14	6.24	5.17
2007	ChC	NL	16	0	0	4	16.2	76	15	9	9	1	1	2	3	9	0	14	0	0	1	0	1.000	0	0-0	2	4.41	4.86
5 ML YEARS			215	5	0	40	209.2	925	193	114	106	28	5	7	13	109	13	183	14	0	10	8	.556	0	1-8	33	4.48	4.55

Craig Counsell

Bats: L **Throws:** R **Pos:** 3B-50; PH-35; SS-27; 2B-24   **Ht:** 6'0" **Wt:** 175 **Born:** 8/21/1970 **Age:** 37

									BATTING											BASERUNNING				AVERAGES		
Year	Team	Lg	G	AB	H	2B	3B	HR	(Hm	Rd)	TB	R	RBI	RC	TBB	IBB	SO	HBP	SH	SF	SB	CS	SB%	GDP	Avg	OBP	Slg
1995	Col	NL	3	1	0	0	0	0	(0	0)	0	0	0	0	1	0	0	0	0	0	0	0	-	0	.000	.500	.000
1997	2 Tms	NL	52	164	49	9	2	1	(1	0)	65	20	16	24	18	2	17	3	3	1	1	1	.50	5	.299	.376	.396
1998	Fla	NL	107	335	84	19	5	4	(2	2)	125	43	40	48	51	7	47	4	8	1	3	0	1.00	5	.251	.355	.373
1999	2 Tms	NL	87	174	38	7	0	0	(0	0)	45	24	11	12	14	0	24	0	5	2	1	0	1.00	2	.218	.274	.259
2000	Ari	NL	67	152	48	8	1	2	(0	2)	64	23	11	25	20	0	18	2	1	1	3	3	.50	4	.316	.400	.421
2001	Ari	NL	141	458	126	22	3	4	(4	0)	166	76	38	61	61	3	76	2	6	6	6	8	.43	9	.275	.359	.362
2002	Ari	NL	112	436	123	22	1	2	(0	2)	153	63	51	65	45	3	52	1	4	3	7	5	.58	10	.282	.348	.351
2003	Ari	NL	89	303	71	6	3	3	(3	0)	92	40	21	29	41	0	32	2	3	2	11	4	.73	4	.234	.328	.304
2004	Mil	NL	140	473	114	19	5	2	(1	1)	149	59	23	48	59	9	88	5	5	3	17	4	.81	5	.241	.330	.315
2005	Ari	NL	150	578	148	34	4	9	(5	4)	217	85	42	80	78	4	69	8	2	4	26	7	.79	8	.256	.350	.375
2006	Ari	NL	105	372	95	14	4	4	(3	1)	129	56	30	45	31	0	47	9	2	1	15	8	.65	1	.255	.327	.347
2007	Mil	NL	122	282	62	12	2	3	(0	3)	87	31	24	29	41	4	47	3	6	2	4	2	.67	7	.220	.323	.309
97	Col	NL	1	0	0	0	0	0	(0	0)	0	0	0	0	0	0	0	0	0	0	0	0	-	0			
97	Fla	NL	51	164	49	9	2	1	(1	0)	65	20	16	24	18	2	17	3	3	1	1	1	.50	5	.299	.376	.396
99	Fla	NL	37	66	10	1	0	0	(0	0)	11	4	2	1	5	0	10	0	2	0	0	0	-	1	.152	.211	.167
99	LAD	NL	50	108	28	6	0	0	(0	0)	34	20	9	11	9	0	14	0	3	2	1	0	1.00	1	.259	.311	.315
12 ML YEARS			1175	3728	958	172	30	34	(19	15)	1292	520	307	466	460	32	517	39	45	26	94	42	.69	60	.257	.343	.347

Jon Coutlangus

Pitches: L **Bats:** L **Pos:** RP-64   **Ht:** 6'1" **Wt:** 185 **Born:** 10/21/1980 **Age:** 27

			HOW MUCH HE PITCHED						WHAT HE GAVE UP										THE RESULTS							
Year	Team	Lg	G	GS	CG	GF	IP	BFP	H	R	ER	HR	SH	SF	HB	TBB	IBB	SO	WP	Bk	W	L	Pct	ShO	Sv-Op	Hld	ERC	ERA
2004	Giants	R	1	0	0	0	1.0	4	1	0	0	0	0	0	0	0	0	0	0	0	0	0	-	0	0--	-	1.95	0.00
2005	SnJos	A+	50	0	0	14	77.0	315	64	27	26	3	2	5	4	29	0	79	9	0	4	0	1.000	0	3--	-	2.94	3.04
2006	Chatt	AA	48	0	0	27	63.0	264	40	24	20	0	6	1	9	32	3	56	5	0	1	3	.250	0	9--	-	2.33	2.86
2006	Lsvlle	AAA	2	0	0	0	2.2	10	2	0	0	0	0	0	0	1	0	2	0	0	0	0	-	0	0--	-	2.27	0.00
2007	Lsvlle	AAA	9	0	0	0	11.1	54	14	9	8	3	1	1	0	7	0	14	0	0	2	0	1.000	0	0--	-	7.74	6.35
2007	Cin	NL	64	0	0	9	41.0	187	38	22	20	3	2	2	4	27	0	38	6	0	4	2	.667	0	0-3	9	4.88	4.39

Jesse Crain

Pitches: R **Bats:** R **Pos:** RP-18   **Ht:** 6'1" **Wt:** 204 **Born:** 7/5/1981 **Age:** 26

			HOW MUCH HE PITCHED						WHAT HE GAVE UP										THE RESULTS							
Year	Team	Lg	G	GS	CG	GF	IP	BFP	H	R	ER	HR	SH	SF	HB	TBB	IBB	SO	WP	Bk	W	L	Pct	ShO	Sv-Op	Hld	ERC	ERA
2004	Min	AL	22	0	0	3	27.0	109	17	6	6	2	1	0	1	12	1	14	1	0	3	0	1.000	0	0-1	2	2.25	2.00
2005	Min	AL	75	0	0	17	79.2	326	61	28	24	6	9	3	5	29	7	25	2	0	12	5	.706	0	1-4	11	2.66	2.71
2006	Min	AL	68	0	0	24	76.2	325	79	31	30	6	1	2	2	18	2	60	1	0	4	5	.444	0	1-4	10	3.48	3.52
2007	Min	AL	18	0	0	5	16.1	71	19	16	10	4	0	1	1	4	0	10	0	1	1	2	.333	0	0-0	6	5.73	5.51
4 ML YEARS			183	0	0	49	199.2	831	176	81	70	18	11	6	9	63	10	109	4	1	20	12	.625	0	2-9	29	3.14	3.16

Carl Crawford

Bats: L **Throws:** L **Pos:** LF-139; DH-3; PH-2; PR-1   **Ht:** 6'2" **Wt:** 215 **Born:** 8/5/1981 **Age:** 26

									BATTING											BASERUNNING				AVERAGES		
Year	Team	Lg	G	AB	H	2B	3B	HR	(Hm	Rd)	TB	R	RBI	RC	TBB	IBB	SO	HBP	SH	SF	SB	CS	SB%	GDP	Avg	OBP	Slg
2002	TB	AL	63	259	67	11	6	2	(1	1)	96	23	30	34	9	0	41	3	6	1	9	5	.64	0	.259	.290	.371
2003	TB	AL	151	630	177	18	9	5	(5	0)	228	80	54	80	26	4	102	1	1	3	55	10	.85	5	.281	.309	.362
2004	TB	AL	152	626	185	26	19	11	(6	5)	282	104	55	96	35	2	81	1	4	6	59	15	.80	2	.296	.331	.450
2005	TB	AL	156	644	194	33	15	15	(5	10)	302	101	81	102	27	1	84	5	5	6	46	8	.85	11	.301	.331	.469
2006	TB	AL	151	600	183	20	16	18	(7	11)	289	89	77	113	37	3	85	4	9	2	58	9	.87	8	.305	.348	.482
2007	TB	AL	143	584	184	37	9	11	(6	5)	272	93	80	97	32	5	112	5	1	2	50	10	.83	11	.315	.355	.466
6 ML YEARS			816	3343	990	145	74	62	(30	32)	1469	490	377	522	166	15	505	19	26	20	277	57	.83	37	.296	.331	.439

Joe Crede

Bats: R **Throws:** R **Pos:** 3B-46; DH-1   **Ht:** 6'2" **Wt:** 230 **Born:** 4/26/1978 **Age:** 30

									BATTING											BASERUNNING				AVERAGES		
Year	Team	Lg	G	AB	H	2B	3B	HR	(Hm	Rd)	TB	R	RBI	RC	TBB	IBB	SO	HBP	SH	SF	SB	CS	SB%	GDP	Avg	OBP	Slg
2000	CWS	AL	7	14	5	1	0	0	(0	0)	6	2	3	2	0	0	3	0	0	0	0	0	-	0	.357	.333	.429
2001	CWS	AL	17	50	11	1	1	0	(0	0)	14	1	7	4	3	0	11	1	0	1	1	0	1.00	1	.220	.273	.280
2002	CWS	AL	53	200	57	10	0	12	(7	5)	103	28	35	31	8	0	40	0	0	1	0	2	.00	1	.285	.311	.515
2003	CWS	AL	151	536	140	31	2	19	(11	8)	232	68	75	69	32	1	75	6	2	4	1	1	.50	11	.261	.308	.433
2004	CWS	AL	144	490	117	25	0	21	(12	9)	205	67	69	58	34	0	81	10	4	5	1	2	.33	14	.239	.299	.418
2005	CWS	AL	132	432	109	21	0	22	(12	10)	196	54	62	62	33	3	66	8	2	4	1	1	.50	7	.252	.303	.454
2006	CWS	AL	150	544	154	31	0	30	(16	14)	275	76	94	84	28	1	58	7	0	7	0	2	.00	18	.283	.323	.506
2007	CWS	AL	47	167	36	5	0	4	(0	4)	53	13	22	18	10	0	24	0	0	1	0	1	.00	1	.216	.258	.317
8 ML YEARS			701	2433	629	125	3	108	(58	50)	1084	309	367	328	140	5	358	32	8	24	4	9	.31	53	.259	.305	.446

Coco Crisp

Bats: B **Throws:** R **Pos:** CF-144; PR-4   **Ht:** 6'0" **Wt:** 180 **Born:** 11/1/1979 **Age:** 28

								BATTING												BASERUNNING				AVERAGES		
Year	Team	Lg	G	AB	H	2B	3B	HR	(Hm | Rd)	TB	R	RBI	RC	TBB	IBB	SO	HBP	SH	SF	SB	CS	SB%	GDP	Avg	OBP	Slg
2002	Cle	AL	32	127	33	9	2	1	(1 | 0)	49	16	9	19	11	0	19	0	3	2	4	1	.80	0	.260	.314	.386
2003	Cle	AL	99	414	110	15	6	3	(3 | 0)	146	55	27	48	23	1	51	0	7	3	15	9	.63	4	.266	.302	.353
2004	Cle	AL	139	491	146	24	2	15	(8 | 7)	219	78	71	72	36	4	69	0	9	2	20	13	.61	8	.297	.344	.446
2005	Cle	AL	145	594	178	42	4	16	(4 | 12)	276	86	69	92	44	1	81	0	13	5	15	6	.71	7	.300	.345	.465
2006	Bos	AL	105	413	109	22	2	8	(4 | 4)	159	58	36	51	31	1	67	1	7	0	22	4	.85	5	.264	.317	.385
2007	Bos	AL	145	526	141	28	7	6	(1 | 5)	201	85	60	68	50	1	84	1	9	5	28	6	.82	12	.268	.330	.382
6 ML YEARS			665	2565	717	140	23	49	(21 | 28)	1050	378	272	350	195	8	371	2	48	17	104	39	.73	36	.280	.329	.409

Bobby Crosby

Bats: R **Throws:** R **Pos:** SS-92; PR-1   **Ht:** 6'3" **Wt:** 217 **Born:** 1/12/1980 **Age:** 28

								BATTING												BASERUNNING				AVERAGES		
Year	Team	Lg	G	AB	H	2B	3B	HR	(Hm | Rd)	TB	R	RBI	RC	TBB	IBB	SO	HBP	SH	SF	SB	CS	SB%	GDP	Avg	OBP	Slg
2003	Oak	AL	11	12	0	0	0	0	(0 | 0)	0	1	0	0	1	0	5	1	0	0	0	0	-	0	.000	.143	.000
2004	Oak	AL	151	545	130	34	1	22	(11 | 11)	232	70	64	60	58	0	141	9	5	6	7	3	.70	20	.239	.319	.426
2005	Oak	AL	84	333	92	25	4	9	(3 | 6)	152	66	38	47	35	0	54	1	1	1	0	0	-	10	.276	.346	.456
2006	Oak	AL	96	358	82	12	0	9	(3 | 6)	121	42	40	38	36	1	76	0	2	2	8	1	.89	11	.229	.298	.338
2007	Oak	AL	93	349	79	16	0	8	(7 | 1)	119	40	31	26	23	1	62	2	0	0	10	2	.83	11	.226	.278	.341
5 ML YEARS			435	1597	383	87	5	48	(24 | 24)	624	219	173	171	153	2	338	13	8	9	25	6	.81	52	.240	.310	.391

Enrique Cruz

Bats: R **Throws:** R **Pos:** SS-1   **Ht:** 6'1" **Wt:** 205 **Born:** 11/21/1981 **Age:** 26

								BATTING												BASERUNNING				AVERAGES		
Year	Team	Lg	G	AB	H	2B	3B	HR	(Hm | Rd)	TB	R	RBI	RC	TBB	IBB	SO	HBP	SH	SF	SB	CS	SB%	GDP	Avg	OBP	Slg
1999	Mets	R	54	183	56	14	2	4	(- | -)	86	34	24	34	28	0	41	1	0	1	0	0	-	3	.306	.399	.470
2000	Clmbia	A	49	157	29	12	0	1	(- | -)	44	19	12	13	25	1	44	1	1	1	1	3	.25	1	.185	.299	.280
2000	Kngspt	R+	63	223	56	14	0	9	(- | -)	97	35	39	32	26	1	56	3	4	2	19	7	.73	3	.251	.335	.435
2001	Clmbia	A	124	438	110	20	2	9	(- | -)	161	60	59	61	59	0	106	6	3	3	33	7	.83	7	.251	.346	.368
2002	StLuci	A+	124	467	136	21	2	6	(- | -)	179	69	45	58	32	2	76	2	3	5	33	16	.67	15	.291	.336	.383
2004	Hntsvl	AA	35	101	19	3	1	2	(- | -)	30	14	5	8	14	1	37	0	1	1	2	1	.67	1	.188	.284	.297
2004	Hi Dsrt	A+	97	361	102	19	0	17	(- | -)	172	53	65	57	36	1	82	2	0	5	12	7	.63	6	.283	.347	.476
2005	Hntsvl	AA	137	496	149	34	3	14	(- | -)	231	67	59	82	37	7	107	5	2	1	4	4	.50	14	.300	.354	.466
2006	Nashv	AAA	25	69	18	5	0	1	(- | -)	26	6	10	8	6	0	23	0	1	0	2	2	.50	3	.261	.320	.377
2006	Frisco	AA	76	281	76	17	1	3	(- | -)	104	32	32	34	19	0	82	3	4	0	8	6	.57	7	.270	.323	.370
2007	Chatt	AA	128	484	129	29	1	7	(- | -)	181	60	62	62	41	0	116	1	7	6	12	4	.75	8	.267	.321	.374
2003	Mil	NL	60	71	6	1	0	0	(0 | 0)	7	6	2	0	4	0	30	1	0	0	0	0	-	2	.085	.145	.099
2007	Cin	NL	1	1	0	0	0	0	(0 | 0)	0	0	0	0	0	0	0	0	0	0	0	0	-	0	.000	.000	.000
2 ML YEARS			61	72	6	1	0	0	(0 | 0)	7	6	2	0	4	0	30	1	0	0	0	0	-	2	.083	.143	.097

Jose Cruz

Bats: B **Throws:** R **Pos:** LF-49; PH-28; RF-23; CF-3   **Ht:** 6'0" **Wt:** 210 **Born:** 4/19/1974 **Age:** 34

								BATTING												BASERUNNING				AVERAGES		
Year	Team	Lg	G	AB	H	2B	3B	HR	(Hm | Rd)	TB	R	RBI	RC	TBB	IBB	SO	HBP	SH	SF	SB	CS	SB%	GDP	Avg	OBP	Slg
2007	S-WB*	AAA	16	62	17	4	0	1	(- | -)	24	12	7	10	9	2	12	0	0	0	3	0	1.00	0	.274	.366	.387
1997	2 Tms	AL	104	395	98	19	1	26	(11 | 15)	197	59	68	63	41	2	117	0	1	5	7	2	.78	5	.248	.315	.499
1998	Tor	AL	105	352	89	14	3	11	(4 | 7)	142	55	42	57	57	3	99	0	0	4	11	4	.73	0	.253	.354	.403
1999	Tor	AL	106	349	84	19	3	14	(8 | 6)	151	63	45	57	64	5	91	0	1	0	14	4	.78	5	.241	.358	.433
2000	Tor	AL	162	603	146	32	5	31	(15 | 16)	281	91	76	91	71	3	129	2	2	3	15	5	.75	11	.242	.323	.466
2001	Tor	AL	146	577	158	38	4	34	(15 | 19)	306	92	88	101	45	4	138	1	2	2	32	5	.86	8	.274	.326	.530
2002	Tor	AL	124	466	114	26	5	18	(11 | 7)	204	64	70	71	51	1	106	0	1	4	7	1	.88	8	.245	.317	.438
2003	SF	NL	158	539	135	26	1	20	(9 | 11)	223	90	69	71	102	6	121	0	0	2	5	8	.38	14	.250	.366	.414
2004	TB	AL	153	545	132	25	8	21	(13 | 8)	236	76	78	79	76	8	117	2	5	8	11	6	.65	6	.242	.333	.433
2005	3 Tms	NL	115	370	93	24	2	18	(11 | 7)	175	46	50	55	66	3	101	0	0	1	0	2	.00	10	.251	.364	.473
2006	LAD	NL	86	223	52	16	1	5	(2 | 3)	85	34	17	27	43	2	54	0	4	3	5	1	.83	3	.233	.353	.381
2007	LAD	NL	91	256	60	12	3	6	(3 | 3)	96	37	21	26	31	1	65	0	5	1	6	1	.86	3	.234	.316	.375
97	Sea	AL	49	183	49	12	1	12	(7 | 5)	99	28	34	31	13	0	45	0	1	1	1	0	1.00	3	.268	.315	.541
97	Tor	AL	55	212	49	7	0	14	(4 | 10)	98	31	34	32	28	2	72	0	0	4	6	2	.75	2	.231	.316	.462
05	Ari	NL	64	202	43	9	0	12	(6 | 6)	88	23	28	25	42	2	54	0	0	1	0	1	.00	6	.213	.347	.436
05	Bos	AL	4	12	3	1	0	0	(0 | 0)	4	0	0	1	1	0	4	0	0	0	0	0	-	0	.250	.308	.333
05	LAD	NL	47	156	47	14	2	6	(5 | 1)	83	23	22	29	23	1	43	0	0	0	0	1	.00	4	.301	.391	.532
11 ML YEARS			1350	4675	1161	251	36	204	(102 | 102)	2096	707	623	696	647	38	1138	5	23	38	113	39	.74	73	.248	.338	.448

Juan Cruz

Pitches: R **Bats:** R **Pos:** RP-53   **Ht:** 6'2" **Wt:** 155 **Born:** 10/15/1978 **Age:** 29

				HOW MUCH HE PITCHED						WHAT HE GAVE UP											THE RESULTS						
Year	Team	Lg	G	GS	CG	GF	IP	BFP	H	R	ER	HR	SH	SF	HB	TBB	IBB	SO	WP	Bk	W	L	Pct	ShO	Sv-Op	Hld	ERC	ERA
2007	Tucsn*	AAA	1	0	0	0	2.0	6	0	0	0	0	0	0	0	0	0	0	0	0	0	0	0--	-	0--	-	0.00	0.00
2001	ChC	NL	8	8	0	0	44.2	185	40	16	16	4	2	0	2	17	1	39	5	0	3	1	.750	0	0-0	-	3.59	3.22
2002	ChC	NL	45	9	0	14	97.1	431	84	56	43	11	7	8	8	59	4	81	1	0	3	11	.214	0	1-4	3	4.49	3.98
2003	ChC	NL	25	6	0	3	61.0	284	66	44	41	7	7	2	7	28	0	65	4	0	2	7	.222	0	0-1	1	5.23	6.05
2004	Atl	NL	50	0	0	22	72.0	300	59	24	22	7	4	1	2	30	1	70	1	0	6	2	.750	0	0-0	5	3.25	2.75
2005	Oak	AL	28	0	0	14	32.2	159	38	33	27	5	0	2	4	22	4	34	3	0	0	3	.000	0	0-0	0	6.87	7.44
2006	Ari	NL	31	15	0	5	94.2	413	80	45	44	7	5	2	11	47	2	88	2	0	5	6	.455	0	0-0	0	3.82	4.18
2007	Ari	NL	53	0	0	15	61.0	262	45	28	21	7	2	2	5	32	3	87	1	2	6	1	.857	0	0-0	4	3.43	3.10
7 ML YEARS			240	38	0	73	463.1	2034	412	246	214	48	27	17	39	235	15	464	12	2	25	31	.446	0	1-5	10	4.17	4.16

Nelson Cruz

Bats: R **Throws:** R **Pos:** RF-82; LF-16; PH-5; PR-2; DH-1   **Ht:** 6'3" **Wt:** 230 **Born:** 7/1/1980 **Age:** 27

Year	Team	Lg	G	AB	H	2B	3B	HR	(Hm	Rd)	TB	R	RBI	RC	TBB	IBB	SO	HBP	SH	SF	SB	CS	SB%	GDP	Avg	OBP	Slg
2007	Okla*	AAA	44	162	57	9	1	15	(-	-)	113	32	45	44	21	1	34	2	0	2	1	2	.33	3	.352	.428	.698
2005	Mil	NL	8	5	1	1	0	0	(0	0)	2	1	0	1	2	0	0	0	0	0	0	0	-	0	.200	.429	.400
2006	Tex	AL	41	130	29	3	0	6	(3	3)	50	15	22	18	7	0	32	0	0	1	1	0	1.00	1	.223	.261	.385
2007	Tex	AL	96	307	72	15	2	9	(4	5)	118	35	34	32	21	1	87	2	1	1	2	4	.33	5	.235	.287	.384
	3 ML YEARS		145	442	102	19	2	15	(7	8)	170	51	56	51	30	1	119	2	1	2	3	4	.43	6	.231	.282	.385

Michael Cuddyer

Bats: R **Throws:** R **Pos:** RF-140; 1B-4   **Ht:** 6'2" **Wt:** 220 **Born:** 3/27/1979 **Age:** 29

Year	Team	Lg	G	AB	H	2B	3B	HR	(Hm	Rd)	TB	R	RBI	RC	TBB	IBB	SO	HBP	SH	SF	SB	CS	SB%	GDP	Avg	OBP	Slg
2001	Min	AL	8	18	4	2	0	0	(0	0)	6	1	1	2	2	0	6	0	0	0	1	0	1.00	1	.222	.300	.333
2002	Min	AL	41	112	29	7	0	4	(2	2)	48	12	13	14	8	0	30	1	1	1	2	0	1.00	3	.259	.311	.429
2003	Min	AL	35	102	25	1	3	4	(1	3)	44	14	8	10	12	0	19	0	0	0	1	1	.50	6	.245	.325	.431
2004	Min	AL	115	339	89	22	1	12	(8	4)	149	49	45	51	37	2	74	3	2	1	5	5	.50	8	.263	.339	.440
2005	Min	AL	126	422	111	25	3	12	(8	4)	178	55	42	43	41	5	93	3	1	3	3	4	.43	19	.263	.330	.422
2006	Min	AL	150	557	158	41	5	24	(15	9)	281	102	109	101	62	5	130	10	0	6	6	0	1.00	11	.284	.362	.504
2007	Min	AL	144	547	151	28	5	16	(8	8)	237	87	81	82	64	1	107	7	0	5	5	0	1.00	19	.276	.356	.433
	7 ML YEARS		619	2097	567	126	17	72	(42	30)	943	320	299	303	226	13	459	24	4	16	23	10	.70	67	.270	.346	.450

Jack Cust

Bats: L **Throws:** R **Pos:** DH-56; RF-48; LF-14; PH-9   **Ht:** 6'1" **Wt:** 231 **Born:** 1/16/1979 **Age:** 29

Year	Team	Lg	G	AB	H	2B	3B	HR	(Hm	Rd)	TB	R	RBI	RC	TBB	IBB	SO	HBP	SH	SF	SB	CS	SB%	GDP	Avg	OBP	Slg
2007	Portlnd*	AAA	25	80	24	7	0	9	(-	-)	58	17	20	23	19	0	29	0	0	1	0	0	-	0	.300	.430	.725
2001	Ari	NL	3	2	1	0	0	0	(0	0)	1	0	0	1	1	0	0	0	0	0	0	0	-	0	.500	.667	.500
2002	Col	NL	35	65	11	2	0	1	(0	1)	16	8	8	6	12	0	32	0	0	1	0	1	.00	3	.169	.295	.246
2003	Bal	AL	27	73	19	7	0	4	(2	2)	38	7	11	17	10	0	25	1	0	0	0	0	-	0	.260	.357	.521
2004	Bal	AL	1	1	0	0	0	0	(0	0)	0	0	0	0	0	0	1	0	0	0	0	0	-	0	.000	.000	.000
2006	SD	NL	4	3	1	0	0	0	(0	0)	1	1	0	0	0	0	1	0	0	0	0	0	-	0	.333	.333	.333
2007	Oak	AL	124	395	101	18	1	26	(14	12)	199	61	82	87	105	2	**164**	1	0	6	0	2	.00	6	.256	.408	.504
	6 ML YEARS		194	539	133	27	1	31	(16	15)	255	77	101	111	128	2	223	2	0	7	0	3	.00	9	.247	.389	.473

Johnny Damon

Bats: L **Throws:** L **Pos:** CF-48; DH-48; LF-32; PH-12; 1B-5; PR-2; RF-1   **Ht:** 6'2" **Wt:** 205 **Born:** 11/5/1973 **Age:** 34

Year	Team	Lg	G	AB	H	2B	3B	HR	(Hm	Rd)	TB	R	RBI	RC	TBB	IBB	SO	HBP	SH	SF	3D	OC	CB%	GDP	Avg	OBP	Slg
1995	KC	AL	47	188	53	11	5	3	(1	2)	83	32	23	29	12	0	22	1	2	3	7	0	1.00	2	.282	.324	.441
1996	KC	AL	145	517	140	22	5	6	(3	3)	190	61	50	64	31	3	64	3	10	5	25	5	.83	4	.271	.313	.368
1997	KC	AL	146	472	130	12	8	8	(3	5)	182	70	48	63	42	2	70	3	6	1	16	10	.62	3	.275	.338	.386
1998	KC	AL	161	642	178	30	10	18	(11	7)	282	104	66	98	58	4	84	4	3	3	26	12	.68	4	.277	.339	.439
1999	KC	AL	145	583	179	39	9	14	(5	9)	278	101	77	108	67	5	50	3	3	4	36	6	.86	13	.307	.379	.477
2000	KC	AL	159	655	214	42	10	16	(10	6)	324	**136**	88	124	65	4	60	1	8	12	**46**	9	.84	7	.327	.382	.495
2001	Oak	AL	155	644	165	34	4	9	(2	7)	234	108	49	79	61	1	70	5	5	4	27	12	.69	7	.256	.324	.363
2002	Bos	AL	154	623	178	34	11	14	(5	9)	276	118	63	101	65	5	70	6	3	5	31	6	.84	4	.286	.356	.443
2003	Bos	AL	145	608	166	32	6	12	(5	7)	246	103	67	92	68	4	74	2	6	6	30	6	.83	5	.273	.345	.405
2004	Bos	AL	150	621	189	35	6	20	(9	11)	296	123	94	115	76	1	71	2	0	3	19	8	.70	8	.304	.380	.477
2005	Bos	AL	148	624	197	35	6	10	(3	7)	274	117	75	105	53	3	69	2	0	9	18	1	.95	5	.316	.366	.439
2006	NYY	AL	149	593	169	35	5	24	(13	11)	286	115	80	99	67	1	85	4	2	5	25	10	.71	4	.285	.359	.482
2007	NYY	AL	141	533	144	27	2	12	(5	7)	211	93	63	84	66	1	79	2	1	3	27	3	.90	4	.270	.351	.396
	13 ML YEARS		1845	7303	2102	388	87	166	(75	91)	3162	1281	843	1166	731	34	868	38	49	63	333	88	.79	70	.288	.353	.433

John Danks

Pitches: L **Bats:** L **Pos:** SP-26   **Ht:** 6'1" **Wt:** 200 **Born:** 4/15/1985 **Age:** 23

Year	Team	Lg	G	GS	CG	GF	IP	BFP	H	R	ER	HR	SH	SF	HB	TBB	IBB	SO	WP	Bk	W	L	Pct	ShO	Sv-Op	Hld	ERC	ERA
2003	Rngrs	R	5	3	0	0	13.0	48	6	3	1	0	0	0	0	4	0	22	1	0	1	0	1.000	0	0--	-	0.97	0.69
2003	Spkane	A-	5	5	0	0	12.2	55	12	12	12	0	1	2	0	7	0	13	0	0	0	2	.000	0	0--	-	3.69	8.53
2004	Clinton	A	14	8	0	2	49.2	200	38	17	12	4	2	2	1	14	0	64	1	0	3	2	.600	0	0--	-	2.35	2.17
2004	Stcktn	A+	13	13	0	0	55.0	247	62	38	32	5	3	6	1	26	0	48	3	1	1	4	.200	0	0--	-	5.13	5.24
2005	Bkrsfld	A+	10	10	0	0	57.2	237	50	18	16	5	0	0	2	16	0	53	1	0	3	3	.500	0	0--	-	2.94	2.50
2005	Frisco	AA	18	17	0	0	98.1	436	117	66	60	12	2	2	5	34	1	85	4	0	4	10	.286	0	0--	-	5.38	5.49
2006	Frisco	AA	13	13	0	0	69.1	300	74	38	32	11	4	1	2	22	0	82	3	0	5	4	.556	0	0--	-	4.65	4.15
2006	Okla	AAA	14	13	0	0	70.2	311	67	43	34	11	4	2	1	34	0	72	2	0	4	5	.444	0	0--	-	4.51	4.33
2007	CWS	AL	26	26	0	0	139.0	622	160	92	85	28	7	4	4	54	4	109	3	0	6	13	.316	0	0-0	0	5.73	5.50

Jeff DaVanon

Bats: B **Throws:** R **Pos:** CF-23; RF-8; PH-6; LF-3; PR-3   **Ht:** 6'0" **Wt:** 200 **Born:** 12/8/1973 **Age:** 34

Year	Team	Lg	G	AB	H	2B	3B	HR	(Hm	Rd)	TB	R	RBI	RC	TBB	IBB	SO	HBP	SH	SF	SB	CS	SB%	GDP	Avg	OBP	Slg
2007	Visalia*	A+	12	42	14	5	1	1	(-	-)	24	5	5	10	10	0	3	0	0	0	1	3	.25	1	.333	.462	.571
2007	Tucsn*	AAA	5	15	5	0	0	0	(-	-)	5	3	0	2	1	0	2	1	0	0	0	0	-	0	.333	.412	.333
2007	Scrmto*	AAA	7	28	9	1	0	1	(-	-)	13	7	2	5	7	0	5	0	0	0	1	3	.25	0	.321	.457	.464
1999	LAA	AL	7	20	4	0	1	1	(1	0)	9	4	4	2	2	0	7	0	0	0	0	1	.00	0	.200	.273	.450
2001	LAA	AL	40	88	17	2	1	5	(3	2)	36	7	9	9	11	0	29	0	0	1	1	3	.25	1	.193	.280	.409
2002	LAA	AL	16	30	5	3	0	1	(0	1)	11	3	4	4	2	0	6	0	1	0	1	0	1.00	0	.167	.219	.367
2003	LAA	AL	123	330	93	16	1	12	(3	9)	147	56	43	56	42	0	59	1	4	5	17	5	.77	6	.282	.360	.445
2004	LAA	AL	108	285	79	11	4	7	(4	3)	119	41	34	47	46	2	54	0	1	5	18	3	.86	2	.277	.372	.418
2005	LAA	AL	108	225	52	10	1	2	(1	1)	70	42	15	26	39	1	44	2	3	2	11	6	.65	6	.231	.347	.311
2006	Ari	NL	87	221	64	12	4	5	(3	2)	99	38	35	42	31	0	42	0	0	4	10	4	.71	6	.290	.371	.448
2007	2 Tms		39	89	19	3	1	0	(0	0)	24	14	6	7	12	0	27	1	0	2	1	1	.50	3	.213	.308	.270
07	Ari	NL	13	26	4	2	0	0	(0	0)	6	5	1	1	5	0	8	1	0	1	1	1	.50	1	.154	.303	.231
07	Oak	AL	26	63	15	1	1	0	(0	0)	18	9	5	6	7	0	19	0	0	1	0	0	-	2	.238	.310	.286
	8 ML YEARS		528	1288	333	57	13	33	(15	18)	515	205	150	193	185	3	268	4	9	19	59	23	.72	24	.259	.349	.400

Dave Davidson

Pitches: L **Bats:** L **Pos:** RP-2   **Ht:** 6'1" **Wt:** 190 **Born:** 4/23/1984 **Age:** 24

			G	GS	CG	GF	IP	BFP	H	R	ER	HR	SH	SF	HB	TBB	IBB	SO	WP	Bk	W	L	Pct	ShO	Sv-Op	Hld	ERC	ERA
Year	Team	Lg																										
2003	Pirates	R	7	0	0	2	7.2	41	10	12	11	0	0	2	4	7	0	8	1	0	0	2	.000	0	0- -	-	9.86	12.91
2004	Pirates	R	7	1	0	2	18.1	89	16	11	7	0	1	1	5	14	0	24	2	0	1	0	1.000	0	0- -	-	4.94	3.44
2005	Wmspt	A-	5	4	0	0	17.0	72	14	7	6	0	0	0	2	8	0	23	2	0	1	1	.500	0	0- -	-	3.19	3.18
2005	Hickory	A	10	2	0	3	19.1	96	16	22	21	4	1	3	3	21	0	23	5	0	1	2	.333	0	0- -	-	7.41	9.78
2006	Hickory	A	27	0	0	2	56.0	229	39	18	12	2	1	3	4	21	0	72	5	0	2	1	.667	0	0- -	-	2.24	1.93
2006	Altna	AA	10	1	0	3	11.2	53	8	4	3	0	0	0	0	10	1	13	0	1	1	1	.500	0	0- -	-	3.10	2.31
2006	Lynbrg	A+	5	0	0	1	8.1	24	6	2	2	0	0	0	1	2	0	11	1	0	0	0	-	0	0- -	-	2.83	2.16
2007	Altna	AA	39	0	0	10	59.2	254	45	30	29	3	2	3	4	30	2	55	5	1	3	1	.750	0	2- -	-	2.98	4.37
2007	Indy	AAA	6	0	0	0	7.2	33	6	2	1	0	1	0	1	3	0	9	1	0	1	0	1.000	0	0- -	-	2.62	1.17
2007	Pit	NL	2	0	0	1	2.0	17	6	6	5	1	0	0	2	2	0	0	0	0	0	0	-	0	0-0	0	29.58	22.50

Kyle Davies

Pitches: R **Bats:** R **Pos:** SP-28   **Ht:** 6'2" **Wt:** 205 **Born:** 9/9/1983 **Age:** 24

Year	Team	Lg	G	GS	CG	GF	IP	BFP	H	R	ER	HR	SH	SF	HB	TBB	IBB	SO	WP	Bk	W	L	Pct	ShO	Sv-Op	Hld	ERC	ERA
2007	Rchmd*	AAA	2	2	0	0	10.0	46	11	5	5	1	1	1	0	6	0	12	1	0	0	1	.000	0	0- -	-	5.46	4.50
2005	Atl	NL	21	14	0	2	87.2	403	98	51	48	8	3	0	1	49	5	62	4	0	7	6	.538	0	0-1	2	5.25	4.93
2006	Atl	NL	14	14	1	0	63.1	312	90	60	59	14	3	2	3	33	0	51	3	0	3	7	.300	0	0-0	0	8.33	8.38
2007	2 Tms		28	28	0	0	136.0	628	155	102	92	22	5	3	5	70	4	99	8	1	7	15	.318	0	0-0	0	5.90	6.09
07	Atl	NL	17	17	0	0	86.0	389	92	61	55	12	3	2	2	44	3	59	1	1	4	8	.333	0	0-0	0	5.24	5.76
07	KC	AL	11	11	0	0	50.0	239	63	41	37	10	2	1	3	26	1	40	7	0	3	7	.300	0	0-0	0	7.09	6.66
	3 ML YEARS		63	56	1	2	287.0	1343	343	213	199	44	11	5	9	152	9	212	15	1	17	28	.378	0	0-1	2	6.22	6.24

Doug Davis

Pitches: L **Bats:** R **Pos:** SP-33   **Ht:** 6'4" **Wt:** 213 **Born:** 9/21/1975 **Age:** 32

Year	Team	Lg	G	GS	CG	GF	IP	BFP	H	R	ER	HR	SH	SF	HB	TBB	IBB	SO	WP	Bk	W	L	Pct	ShO	Sv-Op	Hld	ERC	ERA
1999	Tex	AL	2	0	0	0	2.2	20	12	10	10	3	0	0	0	0	0	3	0	0	0	0	-	0	0-0	0	41.42	33.75
2000	Tex	AL	30	13	1	4	98.2	450	109	61	59	14	6	4	3	58	3	66	5	1	7	6	.538	0	0-3	2	5.93	5.38
2001	Tex	AL	30	30	1	0	186.0	828	220	103	92	14	4	6	3	69	1	115	7	2	11	10	.524	0	0-0	0	4.90	4.45
2002	Tex	AL	10	10	1	0	59.2	262	67	36	33	7	3	3	2	22	0	28	2	2	3	5	.375	1	0-0	0	5.05	4.98
2003	3 Tms		21	20	1	0	109.1	491	123	55	49	16	6	2	1	51	1	62	7	0	7	8	.467	0	0-0	0	5.46	4.03
2004	Mil	NL	34	34	0	0	207.1	880	192	84	78	14	11	5	7	79	3	166	4	1	12	12	.500	0	0-0	0	3.49	3.39
2005	Mil	NL	35	35	2	0	222.2	946	196	103	95	26	12	2	4	93	5	208	3	2	11	11	.500	1	0-0	0	3.62	3.84
2006	Mil	NL	34	34	1	0	203.1	904	206	118	111	19	16	8	5	102	1	159	3	0	11	11	.500	1	0-0	0	4.59	4.91
2007	Ari	NL	33	33	0	0	192.2	862	211	100	91	21	10	2	5	95	7	144	10	1	13	12	.520	0	0-0	0	5.15	4.25
03	Tex	AL	1	1	0	0	3.0	17	4	4	4	2	0	0	0	4	0	2	0	0	0	0	-	0	0-0	0	15.81	12.00
03	Tor	AL	12	11	0	0	54.0	250	70	33	30	6	3	0	1	26	1	25	6	0	4	6	.400	0	0-0	0	6.39	5.00
03	Mil	NL	8	8	1	0	52.1	224	49	18	15	8	3	2	0	21	0	35	1	0	3	2	.600	0	0-0	0	4.06	2.58
	9 ML YEARS		229	209	7	4	1282.1	5643	1336	670	618	134	68	32	31	569	21	951	41	9	75	75	.500	3	0-3	2	4.60	4.34

Jason Davis

Pitches: R **Bats:** R **Pos:** RP-24   **Ht:** 6'6" **Wt:** 210 **Born:** 5/8/1980 **Age:** 28

Year	Team	Lg	G	GS	CG	GF	IP	BFP	H	R	ER	HR	SH	SF	HB	TBB	IBB	SO	WP	Bk	W	L	Pct	ShO	Sv-Op	Hld	ERC	ERA
2007	Tacom*	AAA	5	5	0	0	25.1	123	37	21	20	2	0	2	0	14	0	16	1	0	0	2	.000	0	0- -	-	7.40	7.11
2002	Cle	AL	3	2	0	0	14.2	60	12	3	3	1	1	0	0	4	0	11	0	1	1	0	1.000	0	0-0	0	2.40	1.84
2003	Cle	AL	27	27	1	0	165.1	696	172	101	86	25	7	3	8	47	4	85	9	2	8	11	.421	0	0-0	0	4.44	4.68
2004	Cle	AL	26	19	0	2	114.1	540	148	81	70	13	7	2	4	51	1	72	7	1	2	7	.222	0	0-0	1	6.17	5.51
2005	Cle	AL	11	4	0	2	40.1	182	44	22	21	4	0	3	3	20	0	32	2	0	4	2	.667	0	0-0	0	5.34	4.69
2006	Cle	AL	39	0	0	10	55.1	246	67	28	23	1	3	4	3	14	2	37	3	0	3	2	.600	0	1-3	6	4.20	3.74
2007	2 Tms	AL	24	0	0	9	37.0	177	42	27	24	4	1	3	2	25	2	19	2	2	2	0	1.000	0	0-0	1	6.14	5.84
07	Cle	AL	8	0	0	4	11.1	56	13	6	6	0	0	1	0	9	1	5	0	0	0	0	-	0	0-0	0	5.37	4.76
07	Sea	AL	16	0	0	5	25.2	121	29	21	18	4	1	2	2	16	1	14	2	2	2	0	1.000	0	0-0	1	6.48	6.31
	6 ML YEARS		130	52	1	23	427.0	1901	485	262	227	48	19	15	20	161	9	256	23	6	20	22	.476	0	1-3	8	5.02	4.78

Kane Davis

Pitches: R **Bats:** R **Pos:** RP-11 — **Ht:** 6'3" **Wt:** 190 **Born:** 6/25/1975 **Age:** 33

Year	Team	Lg	G	GS	CG	GF	IP	BFP	H	R	ER	HR	SH	SF	HB	TBB	IBB	SO	WP	Bk	W	L	Pct	ShO	Sv-Op	Hld	ERC	ERA
2007	Ottawa*	AAA	41	0	0	21	53.0	229	46	21	18	2	5	2	2	26	2	60	5	0	3	3	.500	0	4- -	-	3.33	3.06
2000	2 Tms		8	2	0	1	15.0	85	27	24	21	4	0	0	2	13	0	4	0	1	0	3	.000	0	0-0	0	13.77	12.60
2001	Col	NL	57	0	0	6	68.1	301	66	36	33	11	2	4	1	32	4	47	4	0	2	4	.333	0	0-5	9	4.50	4.35
2002	NYM	NL	16	0	0	5	14.0	70	15	11	11	2	2	1	1	11	2	24	1	0	1	1	.500	0	0-0	1	6.19	7.07
2005	Mil	NL	15	0	0	3	16.2	70	10	6	5	2	0	0	0	10	0	11	1	0	1	1	.500	0	0-2	2	2.78	2.70
2007	Phi	NL	11	0	0	1	11.1	59	17	7	7	2	0	1	0	8	2	10	0	0	0	1	.000	0	0-0	3	8.60	5.56
00	Cle	AL	5	2	0	0	11.0	61	20	21	18	3	0	0	1	8	0	2	0	1	0	3	.000	0	0-0	0	12.94	14.73
00	Mil	NL	3	0	0	1	4.0	24	7	3	3	1	0	0	1	5	0	2	0	0	0	0	-	0	0-0	0	16.04	6.75
	5 ML YEARS		107	2	0	16	125.1	585	135	84	77	21	4	6	4	74	8	96	6	1	4	10	.286	0	0-7	15	5.75	5.53

Rajai Davis

Bats: R **Throws:** R **Pos:** CF-58; PH-13; LF-7; PR-7; RF-1 — **Ht:** 5'11" **Wt:** 195 **Born:** 10/19/1980 **Age:** 27

Year	Team	Lg	G	AB	H	2B	3B	HR	(Hm	Rd)	TB	R	RBI	RC	TBB	IBB	SO	HBP	SH	SF	SB	CS	SB%	GDP	Avg	OBP	Slg
2001	Pirates	R	26	84	22	1	0	0	(-	-)	23	19	4	11	13	0	26	1	3	1	11	3	.79	5	.262	.364	.274
2001	Wmspt	A-	6	12	1	0	0	0	(-	-)	1	1	0	0	2	0	4	0	0	0	0	1	.00	0	.083	.214	.083
2002	Pirates	R	58	224	86	16	5	4	(-	-)	124	38	35	54	20	0	25	3	0	3	24	6	.80	3	.384	.436	.554
2002	Wmspt	A-	1	4	0	0	0	0	(-	-)	0	0	0	0	0	0	1	0	0	0	0	0	-	0	.000	.000	.000
2002	Hickory	A	6	14	6	0	0	0	(-	-)	6	4	3	4	6	0	2	1	1	0	2	2	.50	1	.429	.619	.429
2003	Hickory	A	125	478	146	21	7	6	(-	-)	199	84	54	83	55	0	65	6	8	2	40	13	.75	7	.305	.383	.416
2004	Lynbrg	A+	127	509	160	27	7	5	(-	-)	216	91	38	92	59	2	60	0	4	0	57	15	.79	8	.314	.386	.424
2005	Altna	AA	123	499	140	22	5	4	(-	-)	184	82	34	74	43	2	76	12	6	1	45	9	.83	6	.281	.351	.369
2006	Indy	AAA	100	385	109	17	1	2	(-	-)	134	53	21	50	27	0	59	3	2	0	45	13	.78	3	.283	.335	.348
2007	Indy	AAA	53	211	67	12	4	4	(-	-)	99	31	30	41	21	0	25	3	2	2	28	9	.76	5	.318	.384	.469
2006	Pit	NL	20	14	2	1	0	0	(0	0)	3	1	0	0	2	0	3	0	1	0	1	3	.25	0	.143	.250	.214
2007	2 Tms	NL	75	190	53	11	2	1	(0	1)	71	32	9	26	21	1	28	4	3	1	22	6	.79	1	.279	.361	.374
07	Pit	NL	24	48	13	2	1	0	(0	0)	17	6	2	6	7	0	3	0	1	1	5	2	.71	1	.271	.357	.354
07	SF	NL	51	142	40	9	1	1	(0	1)	54	26	7	20	14	1	25	4	2	0	17	4	.81	0	.282	.363	.380
	2 ML YEARS		95	204	55	12	2	1	(0	1)	74	33	9	26	23	1	31	4	4	1	23	9	.72	1	.270	.353	.363

Dewon Day

Pitches: R **Bats:** R **Pos:** RP-13 — **Ht:** 6'4" **Wt:** 210 **Born:** 9/29/1980 **Age:** 27

Year	Team	Lg	G	GS	CG	GF	IP	BFP	H	R	ER	HR	SH	SF	HB	TBB	IBB	SO	WP	Bk	W	L	Pct	ShO	Sv-Op	Hld	ERC	ERA
2003	Pulaski	R+	26	0	0	24	30.0	127	21	8	6	0	1	0	3	9	0	26	1	0	2	0	1.000	0	12- -	-	1.79	1.80
2003	Auburn	A-	2	0	0	1	1.1	5	1	0	0	0	0	0	0	0	0	1	0	0	0	0	-	0	0- -	-	1.13	0.00
2004	Auburn	A-	27	0	0	22	24.0	108	24	8	4	0	0	0	2	10	2	28	2	0	0	3	.000	0	8- -	-	3.49	1.50
2005	Auburn	A-	3	0	0	1	3.0	17	4	2	1	0	0	0	0	3	0	4	1	0	0	0	-	0	0- -	-	7.03	3.00
2005	Lansng	A	9	0	0	3	13.1	62	15	6	6	2	0	1	2	9	0	14	4	0	0	0	-	0	0- -	-	7.31	4.05
2006	WinSa	A+	40	0	0	24	47.2	210	40	23	18	3	4	0	5	21	0	63	2	0	1	4	.200	0	8- -	-	3.39	3.40
2007	Brham	AA	20	0	0	12	25.0	113	26	13	10	1	1	0	0	12	3	48	2	0	2	3	.400	0	2- -	-	3.86	3.60
2007	Charltt	AAA	14	0	0	5	14.1	75	10	10	10	0	0	0	3	20	1	15	3	1	0	2	.000	0	0- -	-	5.93	6.28
2007	CWS	AL	13	0	0	6	12.0	65	19	15	15	1	0	0	2	9	0	7	1	0	0	1	.000	0	0-0	1	9.76	11.25

Alejandro De Aza

Bats: L **Throws:** L **Pos:** CF-35; PH-11 — **Ht:** 6'0" **Wt:** 175 **Born:** 4/11/1984 **Age:** 24

Year	Team	Lg	G	AB	H	2B	3B	HR	(Hm	Rd)	TB	R	RBI	RC	TBB	IBB	SO	HBP	SH	SF	SB	CS	SB%	GDP	Avg	OBP	Slg
2002	Ddgrs	R	38	128	29	6	1	1	(-	-)	40	27	14	18	22	0	17	2	2	1	16	2	.89	3	.227	.346	.313
2003	Ogden	R+	55	208	48	11	1	2	(-	-)	67	36	24	26	23	0	34	10	5	0	15	6	.71	2	.231	.336	.322
2004	Clmbs	A	102	341	87	17	2	4	(-	-)	120	63	45	46	38	1	54	10	3	1	24	10	.71	3	.255	.346	.352
2005	Jupiter	A+	123	472	135	24	9	3	(-	-)	186	75	37	75	58	3	87	8	11	5	34	17	.67	8	.286	.370	.394
2006	Carlina	AA	69	230	64	12	2	2	(-	-)	86	40	16	33	21	0	46	4	9	2	28	10	.74	5	.278	.346	.374
2006	Mrlns	R	7	24	11	1	0	0	(-	-)	12	7	4	6	4	0	2	0	0	0	3	2	.60	0	.458	.536	.500
2006	Jupiter	A+	2	7	1	0	1	0	(-	-)	3	1	0	0	0	0	2	0	1	0	0	1	.00	0	.143	.143	.429
2007	Mrlns	R	4	9	6	2	0	0	(-	-)	8	2	1	4	2	0	1	1	0	0	2	2	.50	0	.667	.750	.889
2007	Carlina	AA	5	20	7	2	0	2	(-	-)	15	7	3	5	3	0	2	0	0	0	0	0	-	0	.350	.435	.750
2007	Jupiter	A+	2	8	4	1	1	0	(-	-)	7	1	0	2	1	0	1	0	0	0	0	1	.00	0	.500	.556	.875
2007	Fla	NL	45	144	33	8	2	0	(0	0)	45	14	8	11	6	1	37	1	5	2	2	0	1.00	2	.229	.261	.313

Jordan De Jong

Pitches: R **Bats:** R **Pos:** RP-6 — **Ht:** 6'2" **Wt:** 180 **Born:** 4/12/1979 **Age:** 29

Year	Team	Lg	G	GS	CG	GF	IP	BFP	H	R	ER	HR	SH	SF	HB	TBB	IBB	SO	WP	Bk	W	L	Pct	ShO	Sv-Op	Hld	ERC	ERA
2002	MdHat	R+	33	0	0	27	44.0	170	23	10	7	1	1	0	5	10	2	62	11	1	6	1	.857	0	16- -	-	1.21	1.43
2002	Auburn	A-	2	0	0	1	4.1	13	0	0	0	0	0	0	0	1	0	3	0	0	1	0	1.000	0	0- -	-	0.07	0.00
2003	Dnedin	A+	28	0	0	25	29.0	129	23	10	9	2	2	0	1	18	2	30	2	0	2	3	.400	0	17- -	-	3.49	2.79
2003	NwHav	AA	27	0	0	11	27.2	124	27	16	11	0	1	2	2	17	0	29	3	0	4	5	.444	0	1- -	-	4.36	3.58
2004	NHam	AA	57	0	0	29	69.1	317	69	24	22	2	1	1	7	30	2	57	9	0	6	2	.750	0	14- -	-	3.85	2.86
2005	NHam	AA	45	0	0	18	67.1	300	82	49	44	5	3	3	3	21	1	63	8	0	1	4	.200	0	2- -	-	4.95	5.88
2006	NHam	AA	23	0	0	10	37.1	156	26	8	6	2	0	0	5	13	0	38	2	0	4	0	1.000	0	0- -	-	2.43	1.45

Year	Team	Lg	G	GS	CG	GF	IP	BFP	H	R	ER	HR	SH	SF	HB	TBB	IBB	SO	WP	Bk	W	L	Pct	ShO	Sv-Op	Hld	ERC	ERA
							HOW MUCH HE PITCHED					WHAT HE GAVE UP											THE RESULTS					
2006	Syrcse	AAA	22	0	0	7	39.1	162	38	19	18	3	0	0	2	13	0	33	1	0	2	0	1.000	0	0--	-	3.79	4.12
2007	NHam	AA	8	0	0	1	14.0	53	6	1	1	0	0	0	0	6	0	18	0	0	0	0	-	0	0--	-	1.10	0.64
2007	Syrcse	AAA	30	0	0	9	52.2	233	49	28	23	4	1	1	4	20	1	61	7	1	6	5	.545	0	2--	-	3.58	3.93
2007	Tor	AL	6	0	0	4	9.0	42	11	9	8	0	0	0	0	5	0	7	0	0	0	0	-	0	0-0	0	5.19	8.00

Eulogio de la Cruz

Pitches: R **Bats:** R **Pos:** RP-6   **Ht:** 5'11" **Wt:** 175 **Born:** 3/12/1984 **Age:** 24

			HOW MUCH HE PITCHED						WHAT HE GAVE UP											THE RESULTS							
Year	Team	Lg	G	GS	CG	GF	IP	BFP	H	R	ER	HR	SH	SF	HB	TBB	IBB	SO	WP	Bk	W	L	Pct	ShO	Sv-Op	Hld	ERC	ERA
2002	Tigers	R	20	0	0	7	37.2	179	40	24	11	0	1	1	2	21	0	46	1	4	1	1	.500	0	1--	-	4.28	2.63
2002	Oneont	A-	2	0	0	1	2.1	20	7	8	6	0	1	1	2	4	0	4	0	0	0	0	-	0	0--	-	24.01	23.14
2003	Tigers	R	22	0	0	18	24.1	105	18	10	7	0	1	0	1	15	0	30	4	0	2	2	.500	0	7--	-	2.92	2.59
2003	Oneont	A-	2	0	0	0	3.1	17	6	4	4	0	0	0	1	1	0	4	1	0	0	0	-	0	0--	-	9.38	10.80
2004	WMich	A	54	0	0	38	54.0	249	51	30	23	2	0	0	3	33	0	44	13	1	2	4	.333	0	17--	-	4.22	3.83
2005	Lkland	A+	40	10	0	11	95.2	395	66	46	36	5	5	3	5	36	0	97	13	0	4	3	.571	0	5--	-	2.22	3.39
2005	Erie	AA	1	0	0	0	1.2	11	2	3	3	0	0	0	0	4	0	0	0	0	1	0	1.000	0	0--	-	12.62	16.20
2006	Erie	AA	38	12	0	9	105.0	454	103	46	40	3	6	1	3	45	4	87	7	2	5	6	.455	0	2--	-	3.63	3.43
2006	Toledo	AAA	1	1	0	0	2.1	14	4	3	3	1	0	0	0	2	0	3	1	0	0	0	-	0	0--	-	12.72	11.57
2007	Erie	AA	11	11	2	0	66.0	262	54	31	25	5	0	2	0	19	0	57	8	1	4	5	.444	1	0--	-	2.60	3.41
2007	Toledo	AAA	22	1	0	2	38.1	167	41	17	15	0	0	4	3	18	1	25	3	0	3	0	1.000	0	0--	-	4.41	3.52
2007	Det	AL	6	0	0	4	6.2	32	10	8	5	1	0	0	0	4	1	5	3	0	0	0	-	0	0-0	0	8.47	6.75

Jorge de la Rosa

Pitches: L **Bats:** L **Pos:** SP-23; RP-3   **Ht:** 6'1" **Wt:** 210 **Born:** 4/5/1981 **Age:** 27

			HOW MUCH HE PITCHED						WHAT HE GAVE UP											THE RESULTS							
Year	Team	Lg	G	GS	CG	GF	IP	BFP	H	R	ER	HR	SH	SF	HB	TBB	IBB	SO	WP	Bk	W	L	Pct	ShO	Sv-Op	Hld	ERC	ERA
2007	Wichta*	AA	3	2	0	1	5.2	32	10	8	7	3	1	0	0	4	0	7	2	0	0	1	.000	0	0--	-	13.85	11.12
2004	Mil	NL	5	5	0	0	22.2	113	29	20	16	1	1	3	1	14	0	5	3	0	0	3	.000	0	0-0	0	6.12	6.35
2005	Mil	NL	38	0	0	13	42.1	208	48	23	21	1	2	2	0	38	4	42	6	0	2	2	.500	0	0-2	5	6.04	4.46
2006	2 Tms		28	13	0	4	79.0	367	81	59	57	14	2	4	2	54	1	67	6	1	5	6	.455	0	0-0	1	6.05	6.49
2007	KC	AL	26	23	0	1	130.0	589	160	88	84	20	2	4	3	53	6	82	4	1	8	12	.400	0	0-0	0	5.93	5.82
06	Mil	NL	18	3	0	4	30.1	146	32	30	29	4	1	3	1	22	1	31	4	0	2	2	.500	0	0-0	1	5.90	8.60
06	KC	AL	10	10	0	0	48.2	221	49	29	28	10	1	1	1	32	0	36	2	1	3	4	.429	0	0-0	0	6.14	5.18
	4 ML YEARS		97	41	0	18	274.0	1277	318	190	178	36	7	13	6	159	11	196	19	2	15	23	.395	0	0-2	6	6.02	5.85

David DeJesus

Bats: L **Throws:** L **Pos:** CF-156; PH-1   **Ht:** 6'0" **Wt:** 190 **Born:** 12/20/1979 **Age:** 28

			BATTING																		BASERUNNING				AVERAGES		
Year	Team	Lg	G	AB	H	2B	3B	HR	(Hm	Rd)	TB	R	RBI	RC	TBB	IBB	SO	HBP	SH	SF	SB	CS	SB%	GDP	Avg	OBP	Slg
2003	KC	AL	12	7	2	0	1	0	(0	0)	4	0	0	2	1	0	2	1	1	0	0	0	-	0	.286	.444	.571
2004	KC	AL	96	363	104	15	3	7	(2	5)	146	58	39	53	33	0	53	9	8	0	8	11	.42	6	.287	.360	.402
2005	KC	AL	122	461	135	31	6	9	(6	3)	205	69	56	77	42	1	76	9	5	6	5	5	.50	6	.293	.359	.445
2006	KC	AL	119	491	145	36	7	8	(4	4)	219	83	56	76	43	4	70	12	2	4	6	3	.67	10	.295	.364	.446
2007	KC	AL	157	605	157	29	9	7	(3	4)	225	101	58	87	64	7	83	23	7	4	10	4	.71	10	.260	.351	.372
	5 ML YEARS		506	1927	543	111	26	31	(15	16)	799	311	209	295	183	12	284	54	23	14	29	23	.56	32	.282	.358	.415

Manny Delcarmen

Pitches: R **Bats:** R **Pos:** RP-44   **Ht:** 6'2" **Wt:** 190 **Born:** 2/16/1982 **Age:** 26

			HOW MUCH HE PITCHED						WHAT HE GAVE UP											THE RESULTS							
Year	Team	Lg	G	GS	CG	GF	IP	BFP	H	R	ER	HR	SH	SF	HB	TBB	IBB	SO	WP	Bk	W	L	Pct	ShO	Sv-Op	Hld	ERC	ERA
2007	Pwtckt*	AAA	20	0	0	10	29.1	130	28	13	11	1	1	0	0	14	1	37	3	0	3	2	.600	0	0--	-	3.50	3.38
2005	Bos	AL	10	0	0	2	9.0	41	8	3	3	0	0	0	1	7	0	9	0	0	0	0	-	0	0-0	0	4.68	3.00
2006	Bos	AL	50	0	0	11	53.1	243	68	32	30	2	3	1	2	17	2	45	0	0	2	0	1.000	0	0-4	14	4.90	5.06
2007	Bos	AL	44	0	0	5	44.0	176	28	11	10	4	2	2	2	17	1	41	0	0	0	0	-	0	1-2	11	2.23	2.05
	3 ML YEARS		104	0	0	18	106.1	460	104	46	43	6	5	3	5	41	3	95	0	0	2	0	1.000	0	1-6	25	3.72	3.64

Carlos Delgado

Bats: L **Throws:** R **Pos:** 1B-138; DH-1   **Ht:** 6'3" **Wt:** 264 **Born:** 6/25/1972 **Age:** 36

			BATTING																		BASERUNNING				AVERAGES		
Year	Team	Lg	G	AB	H	2B	3B	HR	(Hm	Rd)	TB	R	RBI	RC	TBB	IBB	SO	HBP	SH	SF	SB	CS	SB%	GDP	Avg	OBP	Slg
1993	Tor	AL	2	1	0	0	0	0	(0	0)	0	0	0	0	1	0	0	0	0	0	0	0	-	0	.000	.500	.000
1994	Tor	AL	43	130	28	2	0	9	(5	4)	57	17	24	20	25	4	46	3	0	1	1	1	.50	5	.215	.352	.438
1995	Tor	AL	37	91	15	3	0	3	(2	1)	27	7	11	5	6	0	26	0	0	2	0	0	-	1	.165	.212	.297
1996	Tor	AL	138	488	132	28	2	25	(12	13)	239	68	92	83	58	2	139	9	0	8	0	0	-	13	.270	.353	.490
1997	Tor	AL	153	519	136	42	3	30	(17	13)	274	79	91	94	64	9	133	8	0	4	0	3	.00	6	.262	.350	.528
1998	Tor	AL	142	530	155	43	1	38	(20	18)	314	94	115	117	73	13	139	11	0	6	3	0	1.00	8	.292	.385	.592
1999	Tor	AL	152	573	156	39	0	44	(17	27)	327	113	134	121	86	7	141	15	0	7	1	1	.50	11	.272	.377	.571
2000	Tor	AL	162	569	196	57	1	41	(30	11)	378	115	137	164	123	18	104	15	0	4	0	1	.00	12	.344	.470	.664
2001	Tor	AL	162	574	160	31	1	39	(13	26)	310	102	102	126	111	22	136	16	0	3	3	0	1.00	8	.279	.408	.540
2002	Tor	AL	143	505	140	34	2	33	(17	16)	277	103	108	117	102	18	126	13	0	8	1	0	1.00	8	.277	.406	.549
2003	Tor	AL	161	570	172	38	1	42	(24	18)	338	117	145	146	109	23	137	19	0	7	0	0	-	9	.302	.426	.593
2004	Tor	AL	128	458	123	26	0	32	(18	14)	245	74	99	88	69	12	115	13	0	11	0	1	.00	11	.269	.372	.535

Year	Team	Lg	G	AB	H	2B	3B	HR	(Hm	Rd)	TB	R	RBI	RC	TBB	IBB	SO	HBP	SH	SF	SB	CS	SB%	GDP	Avg	OBP	Slg
2005	Fla	NL	144	521	157	41	3	33	(16	17)	303	81	115	110	72	20	121	17	0	6	0	0	-	16	.301	.399	.582
2006	NYM	NL	144	524	139	30	2	38	(18	20)	287	89	114	101	74	11	120	10	0	10	0	0	-	12	.265	.361	.548
2007	NYM	NL	139	538	139	30	0	24	(9	15)	241	71	87	70	52	8	118	11	0	6	4	0	1.00	12	.258	.333	.448
15 ML YEARS			1850	6591	1848	444	16	431	(218	213)	3617	1130	1374	1362	1025	167	1601	160	0	83	13	7	.65	133	.280	.386	.549

David Dellucci

Bats: L Throws: L Pos: LF-51; PH-11; DH-3; PR-1   Ht: 5'11" Wt: 195 Born: 10/31/1973 Age: 34

Year	Team	Lg	G	AB	H	2B	3B	HR	(Hm	Rd)	TB	R	RBI	RC	TBB	IBB	SO	HBP	SH	SF	SB	CS	SB%	GDP	Avg	OBP	Slg
1997	Bal	AL	17	27	6	1	0	1	(0	1)	10	3	3	3	4	1	7	1	0	0	0	0	-	2	.222	.344	.370
1998	Ari	NL	124	416	108	19	12	5	(1	4)	166	43	51	51	33	2	103	3	0	1	3	5	.38	6	.260	.318	.399
1999	Ari	NL	63	109	43	7	1	1	(0	1)	55	27	15	24	11	0	24	3	0	0	2	0	1.00	3	.394	.463	.505
2000	Ari	NL	34	50	15	3	0	0	(0	0)	18	2	2	6	4	0	9	0	0	0	2	0	1.00	1	.300	.352	.360
2001	Ari	NL	115	217	60	10	2	10	(5	5)	104	28	40	36	22	4	52	2	0	0	2	1	.67	2	.276	.349	.479
2002	Ari	NL	97	229	56	11	2	7	(2	5)	92	34	29	26	28	5	55	1	0	3	2	4	.33	7	.245	.326	.402
2003	2 Tms		91	216	49	12	3	3	(1	2)	76	26	23	23	23	1	58	5	2	2	12	0	1.00	6	.227	.313	.352
2004	Tex	AL	107	331	80	13	1	17	(9	8)	146	59	61	56	47	3	88	5	1	3	9	4	.69	4	.242	.342	.441
2005	Tex	AL	128	435	109	17	5	29	(14	15)	223	97	65	81	76	0	121	6	0	2	5	3	.63	7	.251	.367	.513
2006	Phi	NL	132	264	77	14	5	13	(6	7)	140	41	39	43	28	0	62	6	0	3	1	3	.25	1	.292	.369	.530
2007	Cle	AL	56	178	41	11	2	4	(0	4)	68	25	20	18	17	2	40	1	0	3	2	1	.67	4	.230	.296	.382
03	Ari	NL	70	165	40	11	3	2	(2	0)	63	18	19	21	19	1	45	3	1	2	9	0	1.00	4	.242	.328	.382
03	NYY	AL	21	51	9	1	0	1	(1	0)	13	8	4	2	4	0	13	2	1	0	3	0	1.00	2	.176	.263	.255
11 ML YEARS			964	2472	644	118	33	90	(40	50)	1098	385	348	367	293	18	619	32	3	17	38	23	.62	43	.261	.344	.444

Ryan Dempster

Pitches: R Bats: R Pos: RP-66   Ht: 6'2" Wt: 215 Born: 5/3/1977 Age: 31

Year	Team	Lg	G	GS	CG	GF	IP	BFP	H	R	ER	HR	SH	SF	HB	TBB	IBB	SO	WP	Bk	W	L	Pct	ShO	Sv-Op	Hld	ERC	ERA
2007	Iowa*	AAA	2	1	0	1	2.0	8	1	0	0	0	0	0	0	1	0	4	0	0	0	0	-	0	0--	-	1.41	0.00
1998	Fla	NL	14	11	0	1	54.2	272	72	47	43	6	5	6	9	38	1	35	5	0	1	5	.167	0	0-1	0	8.14	7.08
1999	Fla	NL	25	25	0	0	147.0	666	146	77	77	21	3	6	6	93	2	126	8	0	7	8	.467	0	0-0	0	5.49	4.71
2000	Fla	NL	33	33	2	0	226.1	974	210	102	92	30	4	5	5	97	7	209	4	0	14	10	.583	1	0-0	0	4.04	3.66
2001	Fla	NL	34	34	2	0	211.1	954	218	123	116	21	15	7	10	112	5	171	5	0	15	12	.556	1	0-0	0	4.91	4.94
2002	2 Tms	NL	33	33	4	0	209.0	915	228	127	125	28	9	6	10	93	2	153	2	0	10	13	.435	0	0-0	0	5.35	5.38
2003	Cin	NL	22	20	0	1	115.2	545	134	89	84	14	9	4	5	70	4	84	3	0	3	7	.300	0	0-0	0	6.11	6.54
2004	ChC	NL	23	0	0	8	20.2	93	16	9	9	1	1	0	2	13	0	18	1	0	1	1	.500	0	2-2	3	3.61	3.92
2005	ChC	NL	63	6	0	53	92.0	401	83	35	32	4	5	0	4	49	7	89	4	0	5	3	.625	0	33-35	0	3.69	3.13
2006	ChC	NL	74	0	0	64	75.0	342	77	47	40	5	5	4	3	36	3	67	6	0	1	9	.100	0	24-33	2	4.26	4.80
2007	ChC	NL	66	0	0	58	66.2	282	59	36	35	8	3	2	1	30	4	55	2	1	2	7	.222	0	28-31	0	3.77	4.73
02	Fla	NL	18	18	3	0	120.1	521	126	66	64	12	7	3	7	55	1	87	0	0	5	8	.305	0	0-0	0	4.06	4.70
02	Cin	NL	15	15	1	0	88.2	394	102	61	61	16	2	3	3	38	1	66	2	0	5	5	.500	0	0-0	0	5.90	6.19
10 ML YEARS			387	162	8	185	1218.1	5444	1243	692	653	138	59	40	55	631	35	1007	40	1	59	75	.440	2	87-102	5	4.91	4.82

Chris Denorfia

Bats: R Throws: R Pos: OF   Ht: 6'0" Wt: 195 Born: 7/15/1980 Age: 27

Year	Team	Lg	G	AB	H	2B	3B	HR	(Hm	Rd)	TB	R	RBI	RC	TBB	IBB	SO	HBP	SH	SF	SB	CS	SB%	GDP	Avg	OBP	Slg
2002	Reds	R	57	200	68	9	2	0	(-	-)	81	38	19	38	31	0	23	0	0	2	18	8	.69	8	.340	.425	.405
2002	Dayton	A	3	10	0	0	0	0	(-	-)	0	2	0	0	0	0	3	0	0	0	0	0	-	0	.000	.000	.000
2002	Chatt	AA	3	7	3	2	1	0	(-	-)	7	0	0	3	2	0	1	0	0	0	0	0	-	0	.429	.556	1.000
2003	Ptomc	A+	128	470	111	10	5	4	(-	-)	143	60	39	51	54	0	106	3	11	3	20	7	.74	10	.236	.317	.304
2004	Ptomc	A+	75	269	84	18	4	11	(-	-)	143	52	51	60	48	0	66	1	1	2	10	6	.63	3	.312	.416	.532
2004	Chatt	AA	61	221	55	10	2	6	(-	-)	87	30	27	32	30	1	42	1	3	1	5	2	.71	1	.249	.340	.394
2005	Chatt	AA	46	188	62	17	3	7	(-	-)	106	40	26	39	17	1	38	2	2	0	4	3	.57	1	.330	.391	.564
2005	Lsvlle	AAA	91	323	100	12	6	13	(-	-)	163	50	61	65	41	1	54	4	3	3	8	3	.73	7	.310	.391	.505
2006	Lsvlle	AAA	83	312	109	19	1	7	(-	-)	151	46	45	65	34	4	41	1	1	5	15	1	.94	12	.349	.409	.484
2005	Cin	NL	18	38	10	3	0	1	(1	0)	16	8	2	3	6	0	9	0	0	0	1	0	1.00	1	.263	.364	.421
2006	Cin	NL	49	106	30	6	0	1	(0	1)	39	14	7	13	11	1	21	1	2	0	1	1	.50	1	.283	.356	.368
2 ML YEARS			67	144	40	9	0	2	(1	1)	55	22	9	16	17	1	30	1	2	0	2	1	.67	2	.278	.358	.382

Julio DePaula

Pitches: R Bats: R Pos: RP-16   Ht: 6'0" Wt: 180 Born: 12/31/1982 Age: 25

Year	Team	Lg	G	GS	CG	GF	IP	BFP	H	R	ER	HR	SH	SF	HB	TBB	IBB	SO	WP	Bk	W	L	Pct	ShO	Sv-Op	Hld	ERC	ERA
2002	Twins	R	7	6	1	1	39.2	164	39	16	8	0	2	0	4	5	0	21	2	0	3	2	.600	0	0--	-	2.67	1.82
2002	Elizab	R+	5	5	0	0	23.2	118	40	25	24	1	1	2	1	9	1	15	9	0	0	2	.000	0	0--	-	7.85	9.13
2003	Elizab	R+	22	0	0	17	26.1	106	19	7	5	1	0	2	1	8	2	24	2	0	2	3	.400	0	5--	-	1.93	1.71
2004	QuadC	A	49	0	0	19	91.1	398	81	37	31	4	0	0	5	39	2	88	6	3	12	7	.632	0	9--	-	3.27	3.05
2005	FtMyrs	A+	36	0	0	15	64.1	263	52	18	16	0	1	0	7	25	0	51	2	4	4	3	.571	0	4--	-	2.84	2.24
2006	FtMyrs	A+	8	0	0	7	15.1	62	8	4	0	1	0	1	0	6	0	10	1	0	1	1	.500	0	3--	-	1.47	0.00
2006	NwBrit	AA	43	0	0	27	66.2	288	58	25	19	1	3	0	6	27	0	43	3	0	2	2	.500	0	7--	-	3.10	2.57
2007	Roch	AAA	49	0	0	11	83.2	332	66	33	27	8	11	1	6	27	4	63	3	2	12	5	.706	0	2--	-	2.69	2.90
2007	Min	AL	16	0	0	7	20.0	99	30	20	19	5	1	1	3	10	1	8	0	0	0	1	.000	0	0-0	1	9.69	8.55

Mark DeRosa

Bats: R **Throws:** R **Pos:** 2B-93; 3B-37; RF-22; 1B-9; PH-5; SS-1; LF-1; PR-1   **Ht:** 6'1" **Wt:** 205 **Born:** 2/26/1975 **Age:** 33

					BATTING																	BASERUNNING				AVERAGES		
Year	Team	Lg	G	AB	H	2B	3B	HR	(Hm	Rd)	TB	R	RBI	RC	TBB	IBB	SO	HBP	SH	SF	SB	CS	SB%	GDP	Avg	OBP	Slg
1998	Atl	NL	5	3	1	0	0	0	(0	0)	1	2	0	0	0	0	1	0	0	0	0	0	-	0	.333	.333	.333
1999	Atl	NL	7	8	0	0	0	0	(0	0)	0	0	0	0	0	0	2	0	0	0	0	0	-	0	.000	.000	.000
2000	Atl	NL	22	13	4	1	0	0	(0	0)	5	9	3	2	2	0	1	0	0	0	0	0	-	0	.308	.400	.385
2001	Atl	NL	66	164	47	8	0	3	(3	0)	64	27	20	22	12	6	19	5	1	2	2	1	.67	3	.287	.350	.390
2002	Atl	NL	72	212	63	9	2	5	(3	2)	91	24	23	27	12	3	24	3	2	3	2	3	.40	5	.297	.339	.429
2003	Atl	NL	103	266	70	14	0	6	(3	3)	102	40	22	28	16	0	49	5	0	1	1	0	1.00	6	.263	.316	.383
2004	Atl	NL	118	309	74	16	0	3	(0	3)	99	33	31	24	23	3	53	3	4	6	1	3	.25	6	.239	.293	.320
2005	Tex	AL	66	148	36	5	0	8	(7	1)	65	26	20	20	16	0	35	2	0	0	1	0	1.00	5	.243	.325	.439
2006	Tex	AL	136	520	154	40	2	13	(5	8)	237	78	74	78	44	1	102	6	0	2	4	4	.50	13	.296	.357	.456
2007	ChC	NL	149	502	147	28	3	10	(5	5)	211	64	72	76	58	2	93	7	3	4	1	2	.33	17	.293	.371	.420
10 ML YEARS			744	2145	596	121	7	48	(26	22)	875	303	265	277	183	15	379	31	10	18	12	13	.48	55	.278	.341	.408

Matt DeSalvo

Pitches: R **Bats:** R **Pos:** SP-6; RP-1   **Ht:** 6'0" **Wt:** 180 **Born:** 9/11/1980 **Age:** 27

Year	Team	Lg	G	GS	CG	GF	IP	BFP	H	R	ER	HR	SH	SF	HB	TBB	IBB	SO	WP	Bk	W	L	Pct	ShO	Sv-Op	Hld	ERC	ERA
			HOW MUCH HE PITCHED						WHAT HE GAVE UP												THE RESULTS						
2003	StIsInd	A-	10	10	1	0	49.0	205	42	18	10	2	1	0	4	19	1	52	2	2	3	3	.500	0	0--	-	3.17	1.84
2003	Btl Crk	A	3	3	0	0	22.0	82	15	5	2	0	0	0	0	5	1	21	0	0	2	0	1.000	0	0--	-	1.42	0.82
2004	Tampa	A+	13	13	0	0	75.1	310	48	20	12	1	1	5	3	30	1	80	6	0	6	3	.667	0	0--	-	1.75	1.43
2004	Trntn	AA	5	5	0	0	27.1	116	27	20	20	3	1	1	1	10	0	24	5	0	2	2	.500	0	0--	-	4.15	6.59
2005	Trntn	AA	25	24	0	1	149.0	609	108	55	49	8	5	4	9	67	1	151	11	0	9	5	.643	0	0--	-	2.76	2.96
2006	Clmbs	AAA	11	8	0	1	38.2	193	47	39	33	4	1	0	4	34	0	30	3	1	1	6	.143	0	0--	-	8.00	7.68
2006	Trntn	AA	16	16	0	0	78.0	367	80	60	50	7	1	6	3	59	3	52	5	0	5	4	.556	0	0--	-	5.67	5.77
2007	S-WB	AAA	20	20	0	0	113.1	483	92	39	34	4	4	2	6	56	2	102	4	0	9	5	.643	0	0--	-	3.14	2.70
2007	NYY	AL	7	6	0	0	27.2	135	34	20	19	2	1	0	3	18	0	10	2	0	1	3	.250	0	0-0	0	6.68	6.18

Elmer Dessens

Pitches: R **Bats:** R **Pos:** RP-12; SP-5   **Ht:** 5'11" **Wt:** 200 **Born:** 1/13/1971 **Age:** 37

Year	Team	Lg	G	GS	CG	GF	IP	BFP	H	R	ER	HR	SH	SF	HB	TBB	IBB	SO	WP	Bk	W	L	Pct	ShO	Sv-Op	Hld	ERC	ERA
			HOW MUCH HE PITCHED						WHAT HE GAVE UP												THE RESULTS						
2007	Nashv*	AAA	3	3	0	0	11.2	42	7	2	2	0	0	0	0	0	0	10	0	0	1	0	1.000	0	0--	-	0.75	1.54
2007	ColSpr*	AAA	1	0	0	0	3.0	10	1	0	0	0	0	0	0	1	0	1	0	0	1	0	1.000	0	0--	-	0.75	0.00
1996	Pit	NL	15	3	0	1	25.0	112	40	23	23	2	3	1	0	4	0	13	0	0	0	2	.000	0	0-0	3	6.77	8.28
1997	Pit	NL	3	0	0	1	3.1	13	2	0	0	0	0	0	1	0	0	2	0	0	0	0	-	0	0-0	0	1.31	0.00
1998	Pit	NL	43	5	0	8	74.2	332	90	50	47	10	4	3	0	25	2	43	1	0	2	6	.250	0	0-1	6	5.19	5.67
2000	Cin	NL	40	16	1	6	147.1	640	170	73	70	10	12	7	3	43	7	85	4	0	11	5	.688	0	1-1	1	4.31	4.28
2001	Cin	NL	34	34	1	0	205.0	862	221	103	102	32	7	7	1	56	1	128	4	1	10	14	.417	1	0-0	0	4.49	4.48
2002	Cin	NL	30	30	0	0	178.0	737	173	70	60	24	7	1	7	49	8	93	3	1	7	8	.467	0	0-0	0	3.82	3.03
2003	Ari	NL	34	30	0	1	175.2	781	212	107	99	22	9	3	4	57	6	113	3	2	8	8	.500	0	0-0	0	5.19	5.07
2004	2 Tms	NL	50	10	0	9	105.0	468	123	61	52	15	4	3	1	31	4	73	2	0	2	6	.250	0	2-5	4	4.83	4.46
2005	LAD	NL	28	7	0	4	65.2	277	63	30	26	6	1	3	1	19	2	37	1	0	1	2	.333	0	0-0	1	3.35	3.56
2006	2 Tms	NL	62	0	0	12	77.0	334	86	43	39	8	5	1	1	22	8	52	3	0	5	8	.385	0	2-7	18	4.17	4.56
2007	2 Tms	NL	17	5	0	7	34.0	156	45	32	27	6	2	1	0	12	0	22	0	0	2	2	.500	0	0-0	0	6.37	7.15
04	Ari		38	9	0	7	85.1	386	107	54	45	11	4	3	1	23	4	55	2	0	1	6	.143	0	2-4	4	5.08	4.74
04	LAD		12	1	0	2	19.2	82	16	7	7	4	0	0	0	8	0	18	0	0	1	0	1.000	0	0-1	0	3.74	3.20
06	KC	AL	43	0	0	10	54.0	234	63	31	27	4	3	1	1	13	6	36	2	0	5	7	.417	0	2-7	12	4.08	4.50
06	LAD	NL	19	0	0	2	23.0	100	23	12	12	4	2	0	0	9	2	16	1	0	0	1	.000	0	0-0	6	4.37	4.70
07	Mil	NL	12	0	0	7	15.0	69	24	16	11	3	0	1	0	3	0	12	0	0	1	1	.500	0	0-0	0	7.85	6.60
07	Col	NL	5	5	0	0	19.0	87	21	16	16	3	2	0	0	9	0	10	0	0	1	1	.500	0	0-0	0	5.29	7.58
11 ML YEARS			356	140	2	49	1090.2	4712	1225	592	545	135	54	30	19	318	38	661	21	4	48	61	.440	1	5-14	33	4.54	4.50

Ross Detwiler

Pitches: L **Bats:** R **Pos:** RP-1   **Ht:** 6'5" **Wt:** 185 **Born:** 3/6/1986 **Age:** 22

Year	Team	Lg	G	GS	CG	GF	IP	BFP	H	R	ER	HR	SH	SF	HB	TBB	IBB	SO	WP	Bk	W	L	Pct	ShO	Sv-Op	Hld	ERC	ERA
			HOW MUCH HE PITCHED						WHAT HE GAVE UP												THE RESULTS						
2007	Nats	R	4	4	0	0	12.0	50	11	3	3	1	0	0	2	3	0	15	0	0	0	0	-	0	0--	-	3.65	2.25
2007	Ptomc	A+	5	4	0	1	21.1	100	27	11	10	1	0	1	3	9	0	13	1	0	2	2	.500	0	0--	-	5.91	4.22
2007	Was	NL	1	0	0	1	1.0	4	0	0	0	0	0	0	0	0	0	1	0	0	0	0	-	0	0-0	0	0.00	0.00

Joey Devine

Pitches: R **Bats:** R **Pos:** RP-10   **Ht:** 5'11" **Wt:** 205 **Born:** 9/19/1983 **Age:** 24

Year	Team	Lg	G	GS	CG	GF	IP	BFP	H	R	ER	HR	SH	SF	HB	TBB	IBB	SO	WP	Bk	W	L	Pct	ShO	Sv-Op	Hld	ERC	ERA
			HOW MUCH HE PITCHED						WHAT HE GAVE UP												THE RESULTS						
2007	Missi*	AA	33	0	0	31	35.0	143	26	9	8	1	1	2	4	13	0	51	4	0	2	4	.333	0	16--	-	2.61	2.06
2007	Rchmd*	AAA	17	0	0	12	22.0	88	15	5	4	1	2	0	0	6	0	27	0	0	3	0	1.000	0	4--	-	1.65	1.64
2005	Atl	NL	5	0	0	1	5.0	26	6	7	7	2	0	0	0	5	1	3	0	0	0	1	.000	0	0-0	1	9.97	12.60
2006	Atl	NL	10	0	0	1	6.1	36	8	7	7	1	0	0	1	9	1	10	4	1	0	0	-	0	0-1	0	11.11	9.95
2007	Atl	NL	10	0	0	5	8.1	39	7	1	1	0	1	1	0	8	2	7	1	0	1	0	1.000	0	0-0	0	4.08	1.08
3 ML YEARS			25	0	0	7	19.2	101	21	15	15	3	1	1	1	22	4	20	5	1	1	1	.500	0	0-1	1	7.70	6.86

Matt Diaz

Bats: R **Throws:** R **Pos:** LF-95; PH-51; RF-5; 1B-2; DH-1; PR-1 **Ht:** 6'1" **Wt:** 205 **Born:** 3/3/1978 **Age:** 30

Year	Team	Lg	G	AB	H	2B	3B	HR	(Hm	Rd)	TB	R	RBI	RC	TBB	IBB	SO	HBP	SH	SF	SB	CS	SB%	GDP	Avg	OBP	Slg
2003	TB	AL	4	9	1	0	0	0	(0	0)	1	2	0	0	1	0	3	0	0	0	0	0	-	0	.111	.200	.111
2004	TB	AL	10	21	4	1	1	1	(1	0)	10	3	3	2	1	0	6	2	0	0	0	0	-	0	.190	.292	.476
2005	KC	AL	34	89	25	4	2	1	(0	1)	36	7	9	11	4	0	15	2	1	1	0	1	.00	1	.281	.323	.404
2006	Atl	NL	124	297	97	15	4	7	(3	4)	141	37	32	40	11	3	49	9	1	4	5	5	.50	9	.327	.364	.475
2007	Atl	NL	135	358	121	21	0	12	(5	7)	178	44	45	53	16	3	63	4	1	5	4	0	1.00	8	.338	.368	.497
	5 ML YEARS		307	774	248	41	7	21	(9	12)	366	93	89	106	33	6	136	17	3	10	9	6	.60	20	.320	.357	.473

Victor Diaz

Bats: R **Throws:** R **Pos:** RF-24; PH-11; DH-5; LF-3; PR-1 **Ht:** 6'0" **Wt:** 200 **Born:** 12/10/1981 **Age:** 26

Year	Team	Lg	G	AB	H	2B	3B	HR	(Hm	Rd)	TB	R	RBI	RC	TBB	IBB	SO	HBP	SH	SF	SB	CS	SB%	GDP	Avg	OBP	Slg
2007	Okla*	AAA	69	271	87	15	2	14	(-	-)	148	39	65	54	21	1	81	3	0	4	3	0	1.00	7	.321	.371	.546
2004	NYM	NL	15	51	15	3	0	3	(1	2)	27	8	8	6	1	0	15	1	0	0	0	0	-	3	.294	.321	.529
2005	NYM	NL	89	280	72	17	3	12	(4	8)	131	41	38	35	30	7	82	1	0	2	6	2	.75	13	.257	.329	.468
2006	NYM	NL	6	11	2	1	0	0	(0	0)	3	0	2	1	0	0	5	0	0	0	0	0	-	0	.182	.182	.273
2007	Tex	AL	37	104	25	4	0	9	(2	7)	56	13	25	13	1	0	33	2	0	1	0	0	-	4	.240	.259	.538
	4 ML YEARS		147	446	114	25	3	24	(7	17)	217	62	73	55	32	7	135	4	0	3	6	2	.75	20	.256	.309	.487

Mike DiFelice

Bats: R **Throws:** R **Pos:** C-16 **Ht:** 6'2" **Wt:** 223 **Born:** 5/28/1969 **Age:** 39

Year	Team	Lg	G	AB	H	2B	3B	HR	(Hm	Rd)	TB	R	RBI	RC	TBB	IBB	SO	HBP	SH	SF	SB	CS	SB%	GDP	Avg	OBP	Slg
2007	NewOr*	AAA	72	248	70	9	0	7	(-	-)	100	37	38	34	20	0	61	2	1	1	0	1	.00	5	.282	.339	.403
1996	StL	NL	4	7	2	1	0	0	(0	0)	3	0	2	1	0	0	1	0	0	0	0	0	-	0	.286	.286	.429
1997	StL	NL	93	260	62	10	1	4	(1	3)	86	16	30	23	19	0	61	3	6	1	1	1	.50	11	.238	.297	.331
1998	TB	AL	84	248	57	12	3	3	(1	2)	84	17	23	19	15	0	56	1	3	2	0	0	-	12	.230	.274	.339
1999	TB	AL	51	179	55	11	0	6	(5	1)	84	21	27	29	8	0	23	3	0	1	0	0	-	1	.307	.346	.469
2000	TB	AL	60	204	49	13	1	6	(4	2)	82	23	19	21	12	0	40	0	5	2	0	0	-	8	.240	.280	.402
2001	2 Tms		60	170	32	5	1	2	(0	2)	45	14	10	10	8	0	49	4	3	2	1	1	.50	3	.188	.239	.265
2002	StL	NL	70	174	40	11	0	4	(3	1)	63	17	19	17	17	3	42	1	2	3	0	0	-	4	.230	.297	.362
2003	KC	AL	62	189	48	16	1	3	(1	2)	75	29	25	26	9	0	30	4	1	2	1	0	1.00	6	.254	.299	.397
2004	2 Tms		17	25	3	0	1	0	(0	0)	5	3	2	1	3	0	4	0	0	0	0	0	-	3	.120	.214	.200
2005	NYM	NL	11	17	2	0	0	0	(0	0)	2	0	0	0	2	0	5	0	0	0	0	0	-	1	.118	.211	.118
2006	NYM	NL	15	25	2	1	0	0	(0	0)	3	3	1	1	5	0	10	0	0	0	0	0	-	0	.080	.233	.120
2007	NYM	NL	16	40	10	2	1	0	(0	0)	14	1	5	6	2	0	12	2	2	1	0	0	-	2	.250	.311	.350
01	TB	AL	48	149	31	5	1	2	(0	2)	44	13	9	10	8	0	39	3	2	1	1	1	.50	3	.208	.259	.295
01	AiI	NL	12	21	1	0	0	0	(0	0)	1	1	1	0	0	0	10	1	1	0	0	0	-	0	.048	.091	.048
04	Det	AL	13	22	3	0	1	0	(0	0)	5	3	2	1	3	0	3	0	0	0	0	0	-	3	.136	.240	.227
04	ChC	NL	4	3	0	0	0	0	(0	0)	0	0	0	0	0	0	1	0	0	0	0	0	-	0	.000	.000	.000
	12 ML YEARS		543	1538	362	82	9	28	(15	13)	546	144	163	154	100	3	333	18	22	14	3	2	.60	51	.235	.287	.355

Joe Dillon

Bats: R **Throws:** R **Pos:** PH-22; LF-0; 1D-5; 2B-3; 3B-3; RF-1; PR-1 **Ht:** 6'2" **Wt:** 215 **Born:** 8/2/1975 **Age:** 32

Year	Team	Lg	G	AB	H	2B	3B	HR	(Hm	Rd)	TB	R	RBI	RC	TBB	IBB	SO	HBP	SH	SF	SB	CS	SB%	GDP	Avg	OBP	Slg
1997	Spkane	A-	19	70	15	3	0	2	(-	-)	24	6	6	7	5	0	13	1	0	0	1	0	1.00	2	.214	.276	.343
1998	Lansng	A	73	268	70	17	2	15	(-	-)	136	37	43	49	36	1	57	0	4	0	9	2	.82	5	.261	.349	.507
1999	Wilmg	A	134	503	133	31	2	16	(-	-)	216	73	90	78	59	4	124	7	2	5	9	6	.60	12	.264	.347	.429
2000	Wichta	AA	62	220	70	16	2	10	(-	-)	120	35	43	53	39	1	38	7	2	5	0	0	-	6	.318	.428	.545
2000	Omha	AAA	45	149	42	11	2	1	(-	-)	60	19	11	23	17	0	26	2	0	0	1	0	1.00	6	.282	.363	.403
2001	Wichta	AA	101	369	106	19	3	15	(-	-)	176	62	59	65	36	1	60	8	1	3	4	3	.57	10	.287	.361	.477
2002	NwBrit	AA	103	344	90	20	2	9	(-	-)	141	47	50	57	54	3	62	6	0	4	3	1	.75	10	.262	.368	.410
2002	Edmtn	AAA	6	18	3	1	0	0	(-	-)	4	5	0	1	2	0	2	0	0	0	1	0	1.00	1	.167	.250	.222
2004	Carlina	AA	33	117	40	13	0	9	(-	-)	80	26	31	31	14	0	29	4	0	1	3	2	.60	1	.342	.426	.684
2004	Albq	AAA	108	403	131	33	7	30	(-	-)	268	96	86	104	46	0	85	10	0	9	12	3	.80	7	.325	.400	.665
2005	Albq	AAA	98	350	126	21	1	24	(-	-)	221	80	72	100	57	4	59	12	0	6	11	1	.92	7	.360	.459	.631
2007	Nashv	AAA	94	319	101	28	2	20	(-	-)	193	69	73	78	50	3	34	2	0	7	6	1	.86	12	.317	.405	.605
2005	Fla	NL	27	36	6	1	0	1	(1	0)	10	6	1	0	1	0	8	1	1	0	0	0	-	3	.167	.211	.278
2007	Mil	NL	39	76	26	8	2	0	(1	0)	38	12	10	13	5	0	14	1	0	0	0	0	-	2	.342	.390	.500
	2 ML YEARS		66	112	32	9	2	1	(1	0)	48	18	11	13	6	0	22	2	1	0	0	0	-	5	.286	.333	.429

Lenny DiNardo

Pitches: L **Bats:** L **Pos:** SP-20; RP-15 **Ht:** 6'4" **Wt:** 190 **Born:** 9/19/1979 **Age:** 28

Year	Team	Lg	G	GS	CG	GF	IP	BFP	H	R	ER	HR	SH	SF	HB	TBB	IBB	SO	WP	Bk	W	L	Pct	ShO	Sv-Op	Hld	ERC	ERA
2004	Bos	AL	22	0	0	6	27.2	130	34	17	13	1	1	1	2	12	1	21	1	0	0	0	-	0	0-0	0	5.17	4.23
2005	Bos	AL	8	1	0	3	14.2	62	13	6	3	1	1	1	0	5	1	15	1	0	1	0	1.000	0	0-0	0	2.86	1.84
2006	Bos	AL	13	6	0	3	39.0	190	61	35	34	6	0	1	1	20	1	17	1	0	1	2	.333	0	0-0	1	8.80	7.85
2007	Oak	AL	35	20	0	9	131.1	555	136	74	60	13	7	6	3	50	2	59	2	0	8	10	.444	0	0-0	0	4.39	4.11
	4 ML YEARS		78	27	0	18	212.2	937	244	132	110	21	9	9	6	87	5	112	5	0	9	13	.409	0	0-0	1	5.12	4.66

Greg Dobbs

Bats: L **Throws:** R **Pos:** 3B-68; PH-57; 1B-14; LF-14; 2B-4; RF-3; DH-1   **Ht:** 6'1" **Wt:** 205 **Born:** 7/2/1978 **Age:** 29

Year	Team	Lg	G	AB	H	2B	3B	HR	(Hm	Rd)	TB	R	RBI	RC	TBB	IBB	SO	HBP	SH	SF	SB	CS	SB%	GDP	Avg	OBP	Slg
2004	Sea	AL	18	53	12	1	0	1	(1	0)	16	4	9	5	1	0	14	1	0	1	0	0	-	0	.226	.250	.302
2005	Sea	AL	59	142	35	7	1	1	(0	1)	47	8	20	16	9	3	25	0	1	2	1	0	1.00	4	.246	.288	.331
2006	Sea	AL	23	27	10	3	1	0	(0	0)	15	4	3	5	0	0	4	1	0	0	0	1	.00	0	.370	.393	.556
2007	Phi	NL	142	324	88	20	4	10	(5	5)	146	45	55	42	29	4	67	1	0	4	3	0	1.00	7	.272	.330	.451
	4 ML YEARS		242	546	145	31	6	12	(6	6)	224	61	87	68	39	7	110	3	1	7	4	1	.80	11	.266	.314	.410

Scott Dohmann

Pitches: R **Bats:** R **Pos:** RP-31   **Ht:** 6'1" **Wt:** 200 **Born:** 2/13/1978 **Age:** 30

Year	Team	Lg	G	GS	CG	GF	IP	BFP	H	R	ER	HR	SH	SF	HB	TBB	IBB	SO	WP	Bk	W	L	Pct	ShO	Sv-Op	Hld	ERC	ERA
2007	Drham*	AAA	37	0	0	21	48.2	191	37	12	11	2	2	0	2	13	1	48	2	0	4	1	.800	0	5--	-	2.16	2.03
2004	Col	NL	41	0	0	13	46.0	198	41	22	21	8	2	3	0	19	0	49	3	0	3	0	.000	0	0-4	4	3.94	4.11
2005	Col	NL	32	0	0	10	31.0	143	33	21	21	6	0	0	0	19	1	35	0	0	2	1	.667	0	0-3	7	5.94	6.10
2006	2 Tms		48	0	0	18	48.1	231	59	39	38	9	4	0	4	33	7	44	5	0	2	4	.333	0	1-3	6	7.54	7.08
2007	TB	AL	31	0	0	8	32.2	136	29	13	12	3	2	3	0	18	1	26	0	0	3	0	1.000	0	0-0	4	4.13	3.31
06	Col	NL	27	0	0	9	24.2	114	26	18	17	4	2	0	2	15	2	22	2	0	1	1	.500	0	1-2	3	5.94	6.20
06	KC	AL	21	0	0	9	23.2	117	33	21	21	5	2	0	2	18	5	22	3	0	1	3	.250	0	0-1	3	9.34	7.99
	4 ML YEARS		152	0	0	49	158.0	708	162	95	92	26	8	6	4	89	9	154	8	0	7	8	.467	0	1-10	21	5.42	5.24

Brendan Donnelly

Pitches: R **Bats:** R **Pos:** RP-27   **Ht:** 6'3" **Wt:** 245 **Born:** 7/4/1971 **Age:** 36

Year	Team	Lg	G	GS	CG	GF	IP	BFP	H	R	ER	HR	SH	SF	HB	TBB	IBB	SO	WP	Bk	W	L	Pct	ShO	Sv-Op	Hld	ERC	ERA
2002	LAA	AL	46	0	0	11	49.2	199	32	13	12	2	1	1	3	19	3	54	1	0	1	1	.500	0	1-3	13	1.89	2.17
2003	LAA	AL	63	0	0	15	74.0	307	55	14	13	2	3	1	4	24	1	79	1	0	2	2	.500	0	3-5	29	2.12	1.58
2004	LAA	AL	40	0	0	10	42.0	172	34	14	14	5	2	2	1	15	0	56	0	0	5	2	.714	0	0-0	5	3.12	3.00
2005	LAA	AL	66	0	0	14	65.1	271	60	30	27	9	3	1	2	19	3	53	3	0	9	3	.750	0	0-5	16	3.52	3.72
2006	LAA	AL	62	0	0	17	64.0	278	58	32	28	8	2	2	4	28	3	53	0	0	6	0	1.000	0	0-1	11	4.02	3.94
2007	Bos	AL	27	0	0	14	20.2	90	19	8	7	0	0	0	4	5	0	15	2	0	2	1	.667	0	0-0	8	3.00	3.05
	6 ML YEARS		304	0	0	71	315.2	1317	258	111	101	26	13	7	17	110	10	310	13	0	25	9	.735	0	4-14	82	2.92	2.88

Octavio Dotel

Pitches: R **Bats:** R **Pos:** RP-33   **Ht:** 6'0" **Wt:** 210 **Born:** 11/25/1973 **Age:** 34

Year	Team	Lg	G	GS	CG	GF	IP	BFP	H	R	ER	HR	SH	SF	HB	TBB	IBB	SO	WP	Bk	W	L	Pct	ShO	Sv-Op	Hld	ERC	ERA
2007	Wichta*	AA	3	1	0	2	3.0	11	2	1	1	0	1	0	0	0	0	4	1	0	0	1	.000	0	1--	-	0.91	3.00
1999	NYM	NL	19	14	0	1	85.1	368	69	52	51	12	3	5	6	49	1	85	3	2	8	3	.727	0	0-0	0	4.30	5.38
2000	Hou	NL	50	16	0	25	125.0	563	127	80	75	26	7	8	7	61	3	142	6	0	3	7	.300	0	16-23	0	5.47	5.40
2001	Hou	NL	61	4	0	20	105.0	438	79	35	31	5	2	2	2	47	2	145	4	0	7	5	.583	0	2-4	14	2.62	2.66
2002	Hou	NL	83	0	0	22	97.1	376	58	21	20	7	3	7	4	27	2	118	2	0	6	4	.600	0	6-10	31	1.61	1.85
2003	Hou	NL	76	0	0	13	87.0	346	53	25	24	9	2	1	3	31	2	97	2	0	6	4	.600	0	4-6	33	2.02	2.48
2004	2 Tms		77	0	0	70	85.1	356	68	38	35	13	4	2	4	33	7	122	4	1	6	6	.500	0	36-45	0	3.31	3.69
2005	Oak	AL	15	0	0	13	15.1	65	10	6	6	2	0	0	0	11	2	16	1	0	1	2	.333	0	7-11	0	3.44	3.52
2006	NYY	AL	14	0	0	7	10.0	59	18	13	12	2	0	1	0	11	1	7	3	0	0	0	-	0	0-0	1	12.97	10.80
2007	2 Tms		33	0	0	25	30.2	138	29	16	14	4	1	0	4	12	4	41	2	0	2	1	.667	0	11-15	1	4.12	4.11
04	Oak	AL	32	0	0	29	34.2	146	27	15	12	4	2	1	1	15	4	50	3	1	0	4	.000	0	14-17	0	3.01	3.12
04	Oak	AL	45	0	0	41	50.2	210	41	23	23	9	2	1	3	18	3	72	1	0	6	2	.750	0	22-28	0	3.52	4.09
07	KC	AL	24	0	0	22	23.0	108	24	11	10	3	1	0	4	11	4	29	2	0	2	1	.667	0	11-14	0	5.13	3.91
07	Atl	NL	9	0	0	3	7.2	30	5	5	4	1	0	0	0	1	0	12	0	0	0	0	-	0	0-1	1	1.51	4.70
	9 ML YEARS		428	34	0	196	641.0	2709	511	286	268	80	22	26	30	282	24	773	27	3	39	32	.549	0	82-114	80	3.40	3.76

Ryan Doumit

Bats: B **Throws:** R **Pos:** RF-38; C-28; PH-18; 1B-3; DH-1   **Ht:** 6'1" **Wt:** 218 **Born:** 4/3/1981 **Age:** 27

Year	Team	Lg	G	AB	H	2B	3B	HR	(Hm	Rd)	TB	R	RBI	RC	TBB	IBB	SO	HBP	SH	SF	SB	CS	SB%	GDP	Avg	OBP	Slg
2007	Indy*	AAA	16	53	22	4	0	4	(-	-)	38	15	20	17	8	2	12	3	0	3	3	2	.60	2	.415	.493	.717
2005	Pit	NL	75	231	59	13	1	6	(4	2)	92	25	35	32	11	1	48	13	1	1	2	1	.67	5	.255	.324	.398
2006	Pit	NL	61	149	31	9	0	6	(3	3)	58	15	17	17	15	1	42	11	1	2	0	0	-	3	.208	.322	.389
2007	Pit	NL	83	252	69	19	2	9	(7	2)	119	33	32	34	22	2	59	4	0	1	1	2	.33	5	.274	.341	.472
	3 ML YEARS		219	632	159	41	3	21	(14	7)	269	73	84	83	48	4	149	28	2	4	3	3	.50	13	.252	.330	.426

Dennis Dove

Pitches: R **Bats:** R **Pos:** RP-3   **Ht:** 6'4" **Wt:** 205 **Born:** 8/31/1981 **Age:** 26

Year	Team	Lg	G	GS	CG	GF	IP	BFP	H	R	ER	HR	SH	SF	HB	TBB	IBB	SO	WP	Bk	W	L	Pct	ShO	Sv-Op	Hld	ERC	ERA
2003	NewJrs	A-	7	7	0	0	25.2	120	29	15	10	1	0	2	1	15	0	15	4	0	1	3	.250	0	0--	-	5.20	3.51
2004	Peoria	A	3	3	0	0	12.2	58	11	8	7	1	0	0	1	10	0	4	0	0	1	0	1.000	0	0--	-	5.07	4.97
2004	NewJrs	A-	6	6	0	0	22.1	106	31	20	20	3	0	1	2	13	0	24	7	0	0	5	.000	0	0--	-	8.25	8.06
2005	QuadC	A	18	18	2	0	102.0	422	93	47	44	6	2	3	2	30	0	72	5	1	7	5	.583	1	0--	-	3.01	3.88
2005	PlmBh	A+	8	8	0	0	42.2	189	48	24	23	1	1	2	3	15	0	23	6	0	2	4	.333	0	0--	-	4.31	4.85

Year	Team	Lg	G	GS	CG	GF	IP	BFP	H	R	ER	HR	SH	SF	HB	TBB	IBB	SO	WP	Bk	W	L	Pct	ShO	Sv-Op	Hld	ERC	ERA
2006	PlmBh	A+	41	0	0	15	51.1	203	38	20	16	3	6	2	3	13	0	56	5	1	3	3	.500	0	4--	-	2.18	2.81
2006	Sprgfld	AA	13	0	0	5	14.1	72	18	16	14	6	0	1	2	8	1	15	9	0	3	0	.000	0	0--	-	9.16	8.79
2007	Memp	AAA	12	0	0	5	14.0	60	15	7	7	2	0	1	0	7	1	10	3	0	1	0	1.000	0	0--	-	5.33	4.50
2007	StL	NL	3	0	0	1	3.0	15	5	5	5	2	0	0	0	1	0	1	0	0	0	0	-	0	0-0	0	12.68	15.00

Scott Downs

Pitches: L **Bats:** L **Pos:** RP-81   **Ht:** 6'2" **Wt:** 190 **Born:** 3/17/1976 **Age:** 32

Year	Team	Lg	G	GS	CG	GF	IP	BFP	H	R	ER	HR	SH	SF	HB	TBB	IBB	SO	WP	Bk	W	L	Pct	ShO	Sv-Op	Hld	ERC	ERA
2000	2 Tms	NL	19	19	0	0	97.0	442	122	62	57	13	2	4	5	40	1	63	1	0	4	3	.571	0	0-0	0	6.19	5.29
2003	Mon	NL	1	1	0	0	3.0	17	5	5	5	2	0	0	0	3	2	4	0	1	0	1	.000	0	0-0	0	15.01	15.00
2004	Mon	NL	12	12	1	0	63.0	284	79	47	36	9	2	1	3	23	2	38	2	0	3	6	.333	0	0-0	0	5.97	5.14
2005	Tor	AL	26	13	0	0	94.0	407	93	49	45	12	0	1	5	34	0	75	3	0	4	3	.571	0	0-0	0	4.25	4.31
2006	Tor	AL	59	5	0	13	77.0	327	73	38	35	9	1	1	2	30	6	61	7	0	6	2	.750	0	1-4	6	3.87	4.09
2007	Tor	AL	81	0	0	13	58.0	239	47	15	14	3	1	2	1	24	3	57	2	1	4	2	.667	0	1-4	24	2.81	2.17
00	ChC	NL	18	18	0	0	94.0	426	117	59	54	13	2	4	5	37	1	63	1	0	4	3	.571	0	0-0	0	6.07	5.17
00	Mon	NL	1	1	0	0	3.0	16	5	3	3	0	0	0	0	3	0	0	0	0	0	0	-	0	0-0	0	10.34	9.00
	6 ML YEARS		198	50	1	26	392.0	1716	419	216	192	48	6	9	16	154	14	298	15	2	21	17	.553	1	2-8	30	4.74	4.41

Cory Doyne

Pitches: R **Bats:** R **Pos:** RP-5   **Ht:** 6'0" **Wt:** 240 **Born:** 8/13/1981 **Age:** 26

Year	Team	Lg	G	GS	CG	GF	IP	BFP	H	R	ER	HR	SH	SF	HB	TBB	IBB	SO	WP	Bk	W	L	Pct	ShO	Sv-Op	Hld	ERC	ERA
2000	Mrtnsvl	R+	12	8	0	0	39.2	177	25	25	24	1	0	1	1	35	0	54	8	0	3	6	.333	0	0--	-	3.39	5.45
2001	Mrtnsvl	R+	13	13	0	0	61.0	264	57	31	24	2	2	2	3	30	0	56	5	1	4	3	.571	0	0--	-	3.82	3.54
2002	Mich	A	27	26	0	1	141.2	610	131	76	67	8	2	3	3	63	0	101	11	2	9	8	.529	0	0--	-	3.60	4.26
2003	Lxngtn	A	9	9	0	0	54.2	220	34	18	13	4	2	1	6	19	0	48	2	0	3	1	.750	0	0--	-	2.17	2.14
2003	FtWyn	A	12	12	0	0	47.0	214	44	31	22	2	1	1	4	29	0	37	4	1	4	6	.400	0	0--	-	4.44	4.21
2004	NewJrs	A-	30	0	0	22	38.2	148	19	10	10	2	0	0	1	12	1	48	3	0	2	0	1.000	0	12--	-	1.24	2.33
2005	QuadC	A	2	0	0	1	2.1	7	0	0	0	0	0	0	0	0	0	5	0	0	0	0	-	0	0--	-	0.00	0.00
2005	Sprgfld	AA	48	0	0	31	55.1	241	38	14	11	5	1	2	5	36	4	53	5	0	2	1	.667	0	19--	-	3.46	1.79
2005	PlmBh	A+	6	0	0	3	9.0	32	3	0	0	0	0	0	0	2	0	11	0	0	1	0	1.000	0	0--	-	0.52	0.00
2006	Sprgfld	AA	54	0	0	27	66.1	280	48	29	25	1	2	1	0	42	1	78	6	1	1	7	.125	0	6--	-	2.89	3.39
2006	Memp	AAA	2	0	0	2	5.0	20	3	0	0	0	1	0	0	3	0	3	1	0	0	0	-	0	0--	-	2.16	0.00
2007	Norfolk	AAA	42	0	0	36	44.1	171	23	11	11	0	2	0	2	16	0	49	3	0	0	1	.000	0	29--	-	1.31	2.23
2007	Bal	AL	5	0	0	3	3.2	22	7	6	6	1	0	1	1	3	0	2	0	0	0	0	-	0	0-0	0	14.78	14.73

J.D. Drew

Bats: L **Throws:** R **Pos:** RF-133; PH-11; CF-4; PR-2; DH-1   **Ht:** 6'1" **Wt:** 200 **Born:** 11/20/1975 **Age:** 32

Year	Team	Lg	G	AB	H	2B	3B	HR	(Hm	Rd)	TB	R	RBI	RC	TBB	IBB	SO	HBP	SH	SF	SB	CS	SB%	GDP	Avg	OBP	Slg
1998	StL	NL	14	36	15	3	1	5	(4	1)	35	9	13	12	4	0	10	0	0	1	0	0	-	4	.417	.463	.972
1999	StL	NL	104	368	89	16	6	13	(5	8)	156	72	39	58	50	0	77	6	3	3	19	3	.86	4	.242	.340	.424
2000	StL	NL	135	407	120	17	2	18	(11	7)	195	73	57	80	67	4	99	6	5	1	17	9	.65	3	.295	.401	.479
2001	StL	NL	109	375	121	18	5	27	(15	12)	230	80	73	92	57	4	75	4	3	4	13	3	.81	6	.323	.414	.613
2002	StL	NL	135	424	107	19	1	18	(9	9)	182	61	56	65	57	4	104	8	3	4	8	2	.80	6	.252	.349	.429
2003	StL	NL	100	287	83	13	3	15	(7	8)	147	60	42	58	36	0	48	3	2	0	2	2	.50	6	.289	.374	.512
2004	Atl	NL	145	518	158	28	8	31	(14	17)	295	118	93	121	118	2	116	5	1	3	12	3	.80	7	.305	.436	.569
2005	LAD	NL	72	252	72	12	1	15	(10	5)	131	48	36	49	51	3	50	5	0	3	1	1	.50	3	.286	.412	.520
2006	LAD	NL	146	494	140	34	6	20	(12	8)	246	84	100	92	89	8	106	4	1	6	2	3	.40	4	.283	.393	.498
2007	Bos	AL	140	466	126	30	4	11	(4	7)	197	84	64	68	79	10	100	1	0	6	4	2	.67	12	.270	.373	.423
	10 ML YEARS		1100	3627	1031	190	37	173	(91	82)	1814	689	573	695	608	35	785	42	18	31	78	28	.74	53	.284	.390	.500

Stephen Drew

Bats: L **Throws:** R **Pos:** SS-147; PH-3   **Ht:** 6'1" **Wt:** 185 **Born:** 3/16/1983 **Age:** 25

Year	Team	Lg	G	AB	H	2B	3B	HR	(Hm	Rd)	TB	R	RBI	RC	TBB	IBB	SO	HBP	SH	SF	SB	CS	SB%	GDP	Avg	OBP	Slg
2005	Lancst	A+	38	149	58	16	3	10	(-	-)	110	33	39	47	26	2	25	2	0	0	1	1	.50	1	.389	.486	.738
2005	Tenn	AA	27	101	22	5	0	4	(-	-)	39	11	13	11	12	0	24	0	0	0	2	3	.40	1	.218	.301	.386
2006	Tucsn	AAA	83	342	97	16	3	13	(-	-)	158	55	51	55	33	2	50	0	1	7	3	3	.50	7	.284	.340	.462
2006	Ari	NL	59	209	66	13	7	5	(3	2)	108	27	23	31	14	4	50	0	2	1	2	0	1.00	1	.316	.357	.517
2007	Ari	NL	150	543	129	28	4	12	(6	6)	201	60	60	71	60	5	100	3	5	8	9	0	1.00	4	.238	.313	.370
	2 ML YEARS		209	752	195	41	11	17	(9	8)	309	87	83	102	74	9	150	3	7	9	11	0	1.00	5	.259	.325	.411

Travis Driskill

Pitches: R **Bats:** R **Pos:** RP-2   **Ht:** 6'0" **Wt:** 215 **Born:** 8/1/1971 **Age:** 36

Year	Team	Lg	G	GS	CG	GF	IP	BFP	H	R	ER	HR	SH	SF	HB	TBB	IBB	SO	WP	Bk	W	L	Pct	ShO	Sv-Op	Hld	ERC	ERA
2007	RdRck*	AAA	44	0	0	25	65.1	264	60	28	27	7	5	4	1	16	3	63	1	0	4	3	.571	0	9--	-	3.13	3.72
2002	Bal	AL	29	19	0	6	132.2	589	150	78	73	21	2	2	8	48	1	78	6	0	8	8	.500	0	0-0	0	5.36	4.95
2003	Bal	AL	20	0	0	6	48.0	215	62	35	32	8	3	2	1	9	2	33	3	0	3	5	.375	0	1-1	0	5.30	6.00
2004	Col	NL	5	0	0	1	8.1	39	13	6	6	0	0	0	0	3	0	6	0	0	0	0	-	0	0-1	0	6.62	6.48
2005	Hou	NL	1	0	0	1	1.0	4	1	0	0	0	0	0	0	0	0	2	0	0	0	0	-	0	0-0	0	1.95	0.00
2007	Hou	NL	2	0	0	1	6.0	29	10	6	3	1	0	1	0	1	0	4	0	0	1	0	1.000	0	0-0	0	7.50	4.50
	5 ML YEARS		57	19	0	15	196.0	876	236	125	114	30	5	5	9	61	3	123	9	0	11	14	.440	0	1-2	0	5.45	5.23

Justin Duchscherer

Pitches: R **Bats:** R **Pos:** RP-17 **Ht:** 6'3" **Wt:** 203 **Born:** 11/19/1977 **Age:** 30

| | | | | | | HOW MUCH HE PITCHED | | | | | | | | WHAT HE GAVE UP | | | | | | | | | THE RESULTS | | | | | |
Year	Team	Lg	G	GS	CG	GF	IP	BFP	H	R	ER	HR	SH	SF	HB	TBB	IBB	SO	WP	Bk	W	L	Pct	ShO	Sv-Op	Hld	ERC	ERA
2007	Stcktn*	A+	1	1	0	0	1.0	3	0	0	0	0	0	0	0	0	0	1	0	0	0	0	-	0	0-0	0	0.00	0.00
2001	Tex	AL	5	2	0	1	14.2	76	24	20	20	5	0	0	4	4	0	11	1	0	1	1	.500	0	0-0	0	10.68	12.27
2003	Oak	AL	4	3	0	0	16.1	71	17	7	6	1	1	0	2	3	0	15	0	0	1	1	.500	0	0-0	0	3.58	3.31
2004	Oak	AL	53	0	0	18	96.1	398	85	37	35	13	7	1	5	32	6	59	1	1	7	6	.538	0	0-2	6	3.57	3.27
2005	Oak	AL	65	0	0	24	85.2	338	67	25	21	7	4	2	2	19	3	85	2	0	7	4	.636	0	5-7	10	2.23	2.21
2006	Oak	AL	53	0	0	17	55.2	224	52	18	18	4	1	0	1	9	0	51	3	0	2	1	.667	0	9-11	17	2.73	2.91
2007	Oak	AL	17	0	0	2	16.1	75	18	9	9	3	1	2	0	8	3	13	0	0	3	3	.500	0	0-2	5	5.22	4.96
	6 ML YEARS		197	5	0	62	285.0	1182	263	116	109	33	14	5	14	75	12	234	7	1	21	16	.568	0	14-22	38	3.37	3.44

Brandon Duckworth

Pitches: R **Bats:** R **Pos:** RP-23; SP-3 **Ht:** 6'1" **Wt:** 215 **Born:** 1/23/1976 **Age:** 32

| | | | | | | HOW MUCH HE PITCHED | | | | | | | | WHAT HE GAVE UP | | | | | | | | | THE RESULTS | | | | | |
Year	Team	Lg	G	GS	CG	GF	IP	BFP	H	R	ER	HR	SH	SF	HB	TBB	IBB	SO	WP	Bk	W	L	Pct	ShO	Sv-Op	Hld	ERC	ERA
2007	Wilmg*	A+	2	2	0	0	4.0	20	6	4	4	0	0	0	0	2	0	5	0	0	0	1	.000	0	0--	-	6.48	9.00
2007	Omha*	AAA	3	3	0	0	15.0	57	12	6	6	2	0	0	0	1	0	15	2	0	0	1	.000	0	0--	-	2.02	3.60
2001	Phi	NL	11	11	0	0	69.0	289	57	29	27	2	7	3	6	29	5	40	2	0	3	2	.600	0	0-0	0	2.98	3.52
2002	Phi	NL	30	29	0	0	163.0	725	167	103	98	26	7	3	7	69	5	167	10	0	8	9	.471	0	0-0	0	4.80	5.41
2003	Phi	NL	24	18	0	2	93.0	424	98	58	51	12	9	1	10	44	3	68	5	0	4	7	.364	0	0-0	0	5.25	4.94
2004	Hou	NL	19	6	0	6	39.1	180	55	30	30	11	3	1	0	13	3	23	3	0	1	2	.333	0	0-0	0	7.56	6.86
2005	Hou	NL	7	2	0	1	16.1	82	24	20	20	4	0	1	5	7	1	10	0	0	0	1	.000	0	0-0	0	9.78	11.02
2006	KC	AL	10	8	0	0	45.2	216	62	36	31	3	1	2	2	24	4	27	4	0	1	5	.167	0	0-0	0	6.58	6.11
2007	KC	AL	26	3	0	6	46.2	211	51	30	24	3	1	1	1	23	2	21	7	0	3	5	.375	0	1-1	5	4.69	4.63
	7 ML YEARS		127	77	0	15	473.0	2127	514	306	281	61	28	12	31	209	23	356	31	0	20	31	.392	0	1-1	5	5.14	5.35

Chris Duffy

Bats: L **Throws:** L **Pos:** CF-68; PH-4; PR-1 **Ht:** 5'9" **Wt:** 180 **Born:** 4/20/1980 **Age:** 28

| | | | | | | | BATTING | | | | | | | | | | | | BASERUNNING | | | | AVERAGES | | |
Year	Team	Lg	G	AB	H	2B	3B	HR	(Hm	Rd)	TB	R	RBI	RC	TBB	IBB	SO	HBP	SH	SF	SB	CS	SB%	GDP	Avg	OBP	Slg
2007	Pirates*	R	4	13	4	1	0	0	(-	-)	5	1	1	2	1	0	1	0	0	0	0	0	-	0	.308	.400	.385
2005	Pit	NL	39	126	43	4	2	1	(0	1)	54	22	9	22	7	0	22	2	1	0	2	2	.50	1	.341	.385	.429
2006	Pit	NL	84	314	80	14	3	2	(0	2)	106	46	18	36	19	1	71	10	4	1	26	1	.96	1	.255	.317	.338
2007	Pit	NL	70	241	60	11	3	3	(1	2)	86	31	22	29	21	0	43	3	2	3	13	4	.76	2	.249	.313	.357
	3 ML YEARS		193	681	183	29	8	6	(1	5)	246	99	49	87	47	1	136	15	7	4	41	7	.85	4	.269	.328	.361

Zach Duke

Pitches: L **Bats:** L **Pos:** SP-19; RP-1 **Ht:** 6'2" **Wt:** 220 **Born:** 4/19/1983 **Age:** 25

| | | | | | | HOW MUCH HE PITCHED | | | | | | | | WHAT HE GAVE UP | | | | | | | | | THE RESULTS | | | | | |
Year	Team	Lg	G	GS	CG	GF	IP	BFP	H	R	ER	HR	SH	SF	HB	TBB	IBB	SO	WP	Bk	W	L	Pct	ShO	Sv-Op	Hld	ERC	ERA
2007	Pirates*	R	2	2	0	0	6.2	25	5	1	1	0	0	0	0	2	0	3	0	0	0	0	-	0	0--	-	1.97	1.35
2007	StCol*	A-	1	1	0	0	5.2	23	3	1	1	0	0	0	1	2	0	3	0	0	1	0	1.000	0	0--	-	1.56	1.59
2007	Indy*	AAA	1	1	0	0	3.2	18	7	2	2	0	0	0	0	2	0	1	0	0	1	0	.000	0	0--	-	10.41	4.91
2005	Pit	NL	14	14	0	0	84.2	341	79	20	17	3	3	1	2	23	2	58	1	0	8	2	.800	0	0-0	0	2.96	1.81
2006	Pit	NL	34	34	2	0	215.1	935	255	116	107	17	13	4	7	68	6	117	8	1	10	15	.400	1	0-0	0	4.82	4.47
2007	Pit	NL	20	19	0	0	107.1	482	161	74	66	14	2	4	3	25	2	41	0	1	3	8	.273	0	0-0	0	6.96	5.53
	3 ML YEARS		68	67	2	0	407.1	1758	495	210	190	34	18	9	12	116	10	216	9	2	21	25	.457	1	0-0	0	4.94	4.20

Elijah Dukes

Bats: R **Throws:** R **Pos:** CF-38; DH-9; LF-3; PH-3; RF-1 **Ht:** 6'2" **Wt:** 250 **Born:** 6/26/1984 **Age:** 24

| | | | | | | | BATTING | | | | | | | | | | | | BASERUNNING | | | | AVERAGES | | |
Year	Team	Lg	G	AB	H	2B	3B	HR	(Hm	Rd)	TB	R	RBI	RC	TBB	IBB	SO	HBP	SH	SF	SB	CS	SB%	GDP	Avg	OBP	Slg
2003	CtnSC	A	117	383	94	17	4	7	(-	-)	140	51	53	53	45	1	130	10	4	3	33	11	.75	5	.245	.338	.366
2004	CtnSC	A	43	163	47	12	2	2	(-	-)	69	26	15	28	18	3	47	3	0	1	14	1	.93	1	.288	.368	.423
2004	Bkrsfld	A+	58	211	70	16	2	8	(-	-)	114	44	34	47	26	1	50	5	1	1	16	7	.70	1	.332	.416	.540
2005	Mont	AA	120	446	128	21	5	18	(-	-)	213	73	75	78	45	2	83	4	0	3	21	8	.72	11	.287	.355	.478
2006	Drham	AAA	80	283	83	15	5	10	(-	-)	138	58	50	57	44	3	47	7	0	0	9	4	.69	6	.293	.401	.488
2007	TB	AL	52	184	35	3	2	10	(4	6)	72	27	21	20	33	0	44	2	0	1	2	4	.33	6	.190	.318	.391

Phil Dumatrait

Pitches: L **Bats:** R **Pos:** SP-6 **Ht:** 6'2" **Wt:** 200 **Born:** 7/12/1981 **Age:** 26

| | | | | | | HOW MUCH HE PITCHED | | | | | | | | WHAT HE GAVE UP | | | | | | | | | THE RESULTS | | | | | |
Year	Team	Lg	G	GS	CG	GF	IP	BFP	H	R	ER	HR	SH	SF	HB	TBB	IBB	SO	WP	Bk	W	L	Pct	ShO	Sv-Op	Hld	ERC	ERA
2000	RedSx	R	6	6	0	0	16.1	73	10	6	3	0	1	0	2	12	0	12	0	0	0	1	.000	0	0--	-	2.88	1.65
2001	RedSx	R	8	8	0	0	32.2	128	27	10	10	0	1	0	0	9	0	33	1	0	3	0	1.000	0	0--	-	2.17	2.76
2001	Lowell	A-	2	2	0	0	10.1	44	9	4	4	0	0	0	0	4	0	15	1	0	1	1	.500	0	0--	-	2.60	3.48
2002	Augsta	A	22	22	1	0	120.1	492	109	44	37	5	1	1	5	47	0	108	7	0	8	5	.615	1	0--	-	3.43	2.77
2002	Srsota	A+	4	4	0	0	14.0	68	10	9	6	0	0	1	0	15	0	16	2	0	0	2	.000	0	0--	-	4.07	3.86
2003	Srsota	A+	21	20	0	1	104.1	429	74	41	35	4	2	2	4	59	0	74	4	0	7	5	.583	0	1--	-	2.96	3.02
2003	Ptomc	A+	7	7	1	0	37.2	162	36	17	14	2	2	0	1	14	0	32	3	0	4	1	.800	0	0--	-	3.46	3.35
2005	Srsota	A+	3	2	0	0	10.0	41	8	4	3	0	0	0	0	3	0	13	0	0	0	0	-	0	0--	-	2.00	2.70
2005	Chatt	AA	24	24	0	0	127.2	551	115	58	45	6	4	4	2	70	4	101	13	0	4	12	.250	0	0--	-	3.66	3.17

Year	Team	Lg	G	GS	CG	GF	IP	BFP	H	R	ER	HR	SH	SF	HB	TBB	IBB	SO	WP	Bk	W	L	Pct	ShO	Sv-Op	Hld	ERC	ERA
2006	Chatt	AA	10	10	0	0	49.2	206	39	24	20	4	1	3	1	22	2	45	3	1	3	4	.429	0	0--	-	2.99	3.62
2006	Lsvlle	AAA	16	15	1	0	87.2	392	104	49	46	10	7	2	1	36	1	58	1	0	5	7	.417	0	0--	-	5.38	4.72
2007	Lsvlle	AAA	22	22	0	0	125.0	537	114	57	49	10	9	1	6	49	0	76	1	0	10	6	.625	0	0--	-	3.58	3.53
2007	Cin	NL	6	6	0	0	18.0	104	39	30	30	6	2	2	1	12	0	9	0	0	0	4	.000	0	0-0	0	15.81	15.00

Chris Duncan

Bats: L **Throws:** R **Pos:** LF-99; PH-31; 1B-11; DH-3   **Ht:** 6'5" **Wt:** 230 **Born:** 5/5/1981 **Age:** 27

| | | | | | BATTING | | | | | | | | | | | | | | | | BASERUNNING | | | | AVERAGES | | |
Year	Team	Lg	G	AB	H	2B	3B	HR	(Hm	Rd)	TB	R	RBI	RC	TBB	IBB	SO	HBP	SH	SF	SB	CS	SB%	GDP	Avg	OBP	Slg
2005	StL	NL	9	10	2	1	0	0	(1	0)	6	2	3	1	0	0	5	0	0	0	0	0	-	1	.200	.200	.600
2006	StL	NL	90	280	82	11	3	22	(9	13)	165	60	43	47	30	0	69	2	0	2	0	0	-	4	.293	.363	.589
2007	StL	NL	127	375	97	20	0	21	(8	13)	180	51	70	69	55	3	123	1	0	1	2	1	.67	4	.259	.354	.480
3 ML YEARS			226	665	181	32	3	44	(18	26)	351	113	116	117	85	3	197	3	0	3	2	1	.67	9	.272	.350	.528

Shelley Duncan

Bats: R **Throws:** R **Pos:** DH-14; 1B-9; RF-8; PH-6; PR-5; LF-4   **Ht:** 6'5" **Wt:** 215 **Born:** 9/29/1979 **Age:** 28

| | | | | | BATTING | | | | | | | | | | | | | | | | BASERUNNING | | | | AVERAGES | | |
Year	Team	Lg	G	AB	H	2B	3B	HR	(Hm	Rd)	TB	R	RBI	RC	TBB	IBB	SO	HBP	SH	SF	SB	CS	SB%	GDP	Avg	OBP	Slg
2001	StIslnd	A-	70	273	67	17	2	8	(-	-)	112	43	39	36	21	1	62	6	0	2	5	3	.63	5	.245	.311	.410
2002	Grnsbr	A	101	356	95	23	2	14	(-	-)	164	58	56	66	59	1	88	3	0	1	15	3	.83	4	.267	.375	.461
2003	Tampa	A+	91	330	87	19	2	8	(-	-)	134	42	47	48	35	0	83	4	0	6	5	1	.83	8	.264	.336	.406
2004	Tampa	A+	123	424	105	27	1	19	(-	-)	191	65	78	68	54	5	119	7	0	9	6	3	.67	7	.248	.336	.450
2005	Trntn	AA	142	537	130	28	2	34	(-	-)	264	86	92	88	56	3	140	11	0	2	3	2	.60	14	.242	.325	.492
2006	Trntn	AA	92	351	90	24	0	19	(-	-)	171	47	61	58	34	3	77	5	0	4	3	1	.75	9	.256	.327	.487
2006	Clmbs	AAA	12	43	8	1	0	1	(-	-)	12	1	4	3	5	1	10	0	0	0	0	0	-	1	.186	.271	.279
2007	S-WB	AAA	91	336	99	18	1	25	(-	-)	194	58	79	73	45	3	82	3	0	3	2	2	.50	4	.295	.380	.577
2007	NYY	AL	34	74	19	1	0	7	(6	1)	41	16	17	14	8	0	20	0	1	0	0	0	-	2	.257	.329	.554

Adam Dunn

Bats: L **Throws:** R **Pos:** LF-144; PH-7; DH-3   **Ht:** 6'6" **Wt:** 275 **Born:** 11/9/1979 **Age:** 28

| | | | | | BATTING | | | | | | | | | | | | | | | | BASERUNNING | | | | AVERAGES | | |
Year	Team	Lg	G	AB	H	2B	3B	HR	(Hm	Rd)	TB	R	RBI	RC	TBB	IBB	SO	HBP	SH	SF	SB	CS	SB%	GDP	Avg	OBP	Slg
2001	Cin	NL	66	244	64	18	1	19	(8	11)	141	54	43	51	38	2	74	4	0	0	4	2	.67	4	.262	.371	.578
2002	Cin	NL	158	535	133	28	2	26	(13	13)	243	84	71	96	128	13	170	9	1	3	19	9	.68	4	.249	.400	.454
2003	Cin	NL	116	381	82	12	1	27	(16	11)	177	70	57	61	74	8	126	10	0	4	8	2	.80	4	.215	.354	.465
2004	Cin	NL	161	568	151	34	0	46	(25	21)	323	105	102	108	108	11	195	5	0	0	6	1	.86	8	.266	.388	.569
2005	Cin	NL	160	543	134	35	2	40	(26	14)	293	107	101	112	114	14	168	12	0	2	4	2	.67	8	.247	.387	.540
2006	Cin	NL	160	561	131	24	0	40	(22	18)	275	99	92	96	112	12	194	6	1	3	7	0	1.00	8	.234	.365	.490
2007	Cin	NL	152	522	138	27	2	40	(19	21)	289	101	106	103	101	8	165	5	0	4	9	2	.82	12	.264	.386	.554
7 ML YEARS			973	3354	833	178	8	238	(129	109)	1741	620	572	627	675	68	1092	51	2	16	57	18	.76	50	.248	.381	.519

Chad Durbin

Pitches: R **Bats:** R **Pos:** SP-19; RP-17   **Ht:** 6'2" **Wt:** 200 **Born:** 12/3/1977 **Age:** 30

| | | | HOW MUCH HE PITCHED | | | | | | WHAT HE GAVE UP | | | | | | | | | | | THE RESULTS | | | | | | | |
Year	Team	Lg	G	GS	CG	GF	IP	BFP	H	R	ER	HR	SH	SF	HB	TBB	IBB	SO	WP	Bk	W	L	Pct	ShO	Sv-Op	Hld	ERC	ERA
1999	KC	AL	1	0	0	0	2.1	9	1	0	0	0	0	0	0	1	0	3	1	0	0	0	-	0	0-0	0	1.08	0.00
2000	KC	AL	16	16	0	0	72.1	349	91	71	66	14	1	3	0	43	1	37	7	0	2	5	.286	0	0-0	0	7.05	8.21
2001	KC	AL	29	29	2	0	179.0	777	201	109	98	26	2	7	11	58	0	95	6	0	9	16	.360	0	0-0	0	5.15	4.93
2002	KC	AL	2	2	0	0	8.1	43	13	11	11	3	0	0	1	4	0	5	0	0	0	1	.000	0	0-0	0	10.58	11.88
2003	Cle	AL	3	1	0	0	8.2	45	18	12	7	2	0	0	0	3	0	8	2	0	0	1	.000	0	0-0	0	12.37	7.27
2004	2 Tms		24	8	1	5	60.2	291	72	50	47	11	2	2	5	35	3	48	5	0	6	7	.462	0	0-0	1	6.75	6.97
2006	Det	AL	3	0	0	1	6.0	24	6	1	1	1	0	0	0	0	0	3	0	0	0	0	-	0	0-0	0	2.87	1.50
2007	Det	AL	36	19	0	7	127.2	561	131	71	67	21	1	7	8	49	4	66	2	0	8	7	.533	0	1-2	3	4.92	4.72
04	Cle	AL	17	8	1	5	51.1	239	63	40	38	10	0	2	4	24	3	38	3	0	5	6	.455	0	0-0	0	6.70	6.66
04	Ari	NL	7	0	0	0	9.1	52	9	10	9	1	2	0	1	11	0	10	2	0	1	1	.500	0	0-0	1	6.92	8.68
8 ML YEARS			114	75	3	13	465.0	2099	535	325	297	78	6	19	25	193	8	265	23	0	25	37	.403	0	1-2	4	5.73	5.75

J.D. Durbin

Pitches: R **Bats:** R **Pos:** SP-10; RP-9   **Ht:** 6'0" **Wt:** 210 **Born:** 2/24/1982 **Age:** 26

| | | | HOW MUCH HE PITCHED | | | | | | WHAT HE GAVE UP | | | | | | | | | | | THE RESULTS | | | | | | | |
Year	Team	Lg	G	GS	CG	GF	IP	BFP	H	R	ER	HR	SH	SF	HB	TBB	IBB	SO	WP	Bk	W	L	Pct	ShO	Sv-Op	Hld	ERC	ERA
2000	Twins	R	2	0	0	0	2.0	9	2	2	0	0	0	0	0	0	0	4	0	0	0	0	-	0	0--	-	1.68	0.00
2001	Elizab	R+	8	7	0	0	33.2	145	23	13	7	2	1	1	4	17	0	39	5	1	3	2	.600	0	0--	-	2.87	1.87
2002	QuadC	A	27	27	0	0	161.0	666	144	66	57	14	3	4	5	51	1	163	6	1	13	4	.765	0	0--	-	3.23	3.19
2003	FtMyrs	A+	14	14	0	0	87.1	355	73	35	30	3	1	3	3	22	0	69	3	1	9	2	.818	0	0--	-	2.37	3.14
2003	NwBrit	AA	14	14	2	0	94.2	401	102	39	33	10	0	0	4	29	0	70	1	0	6	3	.667	0	0--	-	4.46	3.14
2004	NwBrit	AA	13	13	0	0	64.1	274	62	21	18	4	3	0	4	22	0	53	1	0	4	1	.800	0	0--	-	3.64	2.52
2004	Roch	AAA	7	7	0	0	35.2	168	49	27	18	4	0	0	1	16	0	38	1	0	3	2	.600	0	0--	-	6.78	4.54
2005	Roch	AAA	22	19	0	0	104.0	460	97	52	50	8	3	3	6	51	1	90	10	0	5	5	.500	0	0--	-	4.05	4.33
2006	Roch	AAA	16	16	0	0	89.0	381	67	27	23	3	5	0	5	50	1	81	3	0	4	3	.571	0	0--	-	3.08	2.33
2007	Ottawa	AAA	10	10	0	0	59.1	256	67	33	30	9	1	1	0	21	0	44	4	0	2	4	.333	0	0--	-	5.10	4.55
2004	Min	AL	4	1	0	2	7.1	38	12	6	6	0	0	1	0	6	0	6	1	0	0	1	.000	0	0-0	0	9.19	7.36

Year	Team	Lg	G	GS	CG	GF	IP	BFP	H	R	ER	HR	SH	SF	HB	TBB	IBB	SO	WP	Bk	W	L	Pct	ShO	Sv-Op	Hld	ERC	ERA
							HOW MUCH HE PITCHED						**WHAT HE GAVE UP**											**THE RESULTS**				
2007	2 Tms	NL	19	10	1	4	65.1	305	78	49	44	6	4	1	2	37	4	40	2	0	6	5	.545	1	1-1	0	5.85	6.06
07	Ari	NL	1	0	0	0	0.2	10	7	7	7	0	0	0	0	1	0	1	0	0	0	0	-	0	0-0	0	89.93	94.50
07	Phi	NL	18	10	1	4	64.2	295	71	42	37	6	4	1	2	36	4	39	2	0	6	5	.545	1	1-1	0	5.25	5.15
	2 ML YEARS		23	11	1	6	72.2	343	90	55	50	6	4	2	2	43	4	46	3	0	6	6	.500	1	1-1	0	6.17	6.19

Ray Durham

Bats: B **Throws:** R **Pos:** 2B-124; PH-20   **Ht:** 5'8" **Wt:** 190 **Born:** 11/30/1971 **Age:** 36

Year	Team	Lg	G	AB	H	2B	3B	HR	(Hm	Rd)	TB	R	RBI	RC	TBB	IBB	SO	HBP	SH	SF	SB	CS	SB%	GDP	Avg	OBP	Slg
					BATTING																**BASERUNNING**				**AVERAGES**		
1995	CWS	AL	125	471	121	27	6	7	(1	6)	181	68	51	57	31	2	83	6	5	4	18	5	.78	8	.257	.309	.384
1996	CWS	AL	156	557	153	33	5	10	(3	7)	226	79	65	87	58	4	95	10	7	7	30	4	**.88**	6	.275	.350	.406
1997	CWS	AL	155	634	172	27	5	11	(3	8)	242	106	53	83	61	0	96	6	2	8	33	16	.67	14	.271	.337	.382
1998	CWS	AL	158	635	181	35	8	19	(10	9)	289	126	67	110	73	3	105	6	6	3	36	9	.80	5	.285	.363	.455
1999	CWS	AL	153	612	181	30	8	13	(7	6)	266	109	60	103	73	1	105	4	3	2	34	11	.76	9	.296	.373	.435
2000	CWS	AL	151	614	172	35	9	17	(5	12)	276	121	75	100	75	0	105	7	5	8	25	13	.66	13	.280	.361	.450
2001	CWS	AL	152	611	163	42	10	20	(9	11)	285	104	65	97	64	3	110	4	6	6	23	10	.70	10	.267	.337	.466
2002	2 Tms	AL	150	564	163	34	6	15	(11	4)	254	114	70	96	73	1	93	7	10	5	26	7	.79	15	.289	.374	.450
2003	SF	NL	110	410	117	30	5	8	(3	5)	181	61	33	56	50	2	82	3	4	2	7	7	.50	4	.285	.366	.441
2004	SF	NL	120	471	133	28	8	17	(8	9)	228	95	65	83	57	3	60	6	4	4	10	4	.71	6	.282	.364	.484
2005	SF	NL	142	497	144	33	0	12	(6	6)	213	67	62	67	48	2	59	7	1	7	6	3	.67	19	.290	.356	.429
2006	SF	NL	137	498	146	30	7	26	(10	16)	268	79	93	93	51	6	61	2	2	2	7	2	.78	17	.293	.360	.538
2007	SF	NL	138	464	101	21	2	11	(2	9)	159	56	71	47	53	6	75	2	0	9	10	2	.83	18	.218	.295	.343
02	CWS	AL	96	345	103	20	2	9	(6	3)	154	71	48	61	49	0	59	5	8	4	20	5	.80	13	.299	.390	.446
02	Oak	AL	54	219	60	14	4	6	(5	1)	100	43	22	35	24	1	34	2	2	1	6	2	.75	2	.274	.350	.457
	13 ML YEARS		1847	7038	1947	405	79	186	(78	108)	3068	1185	830	1079	767	33	1129	70	55	67	265	93	.74	144	.277	.351	.436

Jermaine Dye

Bats: R **Throws:** R **Pos:** RF-135; DH-3   **Ht:** 6'5" **Wt:** 240 **Born:** 1/28/1974 **Age:** 34

Year	Team	Lg	G	AB	H	2B	3B	HR	(Hm	Rd)	TB	R	RBI	RC	TBB	IBB	SO	HBP	SH	SF	SB	CS	SB%	GDP	Avg	OBP	Slg
					BATTING																**BASERUNNING**				**AVERAGES**		
1996	Atl	NL	98	292	82	16	0	12	(4	8)	134	32	37	36	8	0	67	3	0	3	1	4	.20	11	.281	.304	.459
1997	KC	AL	75	263	62	14	0	7	(3	4)	97	26	22	26	17	0	51	1	1	1	2	1	.67	6	.236	.284	.369
1998	KC	AL	60	214	50	5	1	5	(3	2)	72	24	23	17	11	2	46	1	0	4	2	2	.50	8	.234	.270	.336
1999	KC	AL	158	608	179	44	8	27	(15	12)	320	96	119	106	58	4	119	1	0	6	2	3	.40	17	.294	.354	.526
2000	KC	AL	157	601	193	41	2	33	(15	18)	337	107	118	125	69	6	99	3	0	6	0	1	.00	12	.321	.390	.561
2001	2 Tms	AL	158	599	169	31	1	26	(16	10)	280	91	106	99	57	6	112	7	1	11	9	1	.90	8	.282	.346	.467
2002	Oak	AL	131	488	123	27	1	24	(13	11)	224	74	86	70	52	2	108	10	0	5	2	0	1.00	15	.252	.333	.459
2003	Oak	AL	65	221	38	6	0	4	(3	1)	56	28	20	10	25	2	42	3	0	4	1	0	1.00	11	.172	.261	.253
2004	Oak	AL	137	532	141	29	4	23	(12	11)	247	87	80	69	49	4	128	4	0	5	4	2	.67	16	.265	.329	.464
2005	CWS	AL	145	529	145	29	2	31	(15	16)	271	74	86	80	39	3	99	9	0	2	11	4	.73	15	.274	.333	.512
2006	CWS	AL	146	539	170	27	3	44	(21	23)	335	103	120	116	59	4	118	6	0	7	7	3	.70	15	.315	.385	.622
2007	CWS	AL	138	508	129	34	0	28	(14	14)	247	68	78	67	45	2	107	4	0	4	2	1	.67	17	.254	.317	.486
01	KC	AL	97	367	100	14	0	13	(8	5)	153	50	47	54	30	3	68	6	1	6	7	1	.88	2	.272	.333	.417
01	Oak	AL	61	232	69	17	1	13	(8	5)	127	41	59	45	27	3	44	1	0	5	2	0	1.00	6	.297	.366	.547
	12 ML YEARS		1468	5394	1481	303	22	264	(134	130)	2620	810	895	821	489	35	1096	52	2	58	43	22	.66	151	.275	.337	.486

Damion Easley

Bats: R **Throws:** R **Pos:** 2B-39; PH-25; RF-6; LF-3; 1B-2; 3B-2   **Ht:** 5'11" **Wt:** 195 **Born:** 11/11/1969 **Age:** 38

Year	Team	Lg	G	AB	H	2B	3B	HR	(Hm	Rd)	TB	R	RBI	RC	TBB	IBB	SO	HBP	SH	SF	SB	CS	SB%	GDP	Avg	OBP	Slg
					BATTING																**BASERUNNING**				**AVERAGES**		
1992	LAA	AL	47	151	39	5	0	1	(1	0)	47	14	12	14	8	0	26	3	2	1	9	5	.64	2	.258	.307	.311
1993	LAA	AL	73	230	72	13	2	2	(0	2)	95	33	22	37	28	2	35	3	1	2	6	6	.50	5	.313	.392	.413
1994	LAA	AL	88	316	68	16	1	6	(4	2)	104	41	30	28	29	0	48	4	4	2	4	5	.44	8	.215	.288	.329
1995	LAA	AL	114	357	77	14	2	4	(1	3)	107	35	35	30	32	1	47	6	6	4	5	2	.71	11	.216	.288	.300
1996	2 Tms	AL	49	112	30	2	0	4	(1	3)	44	14	17	16	10	0	25	1	5	1	3	1	.75	0	.268	.331	.393
1997	Det	AL	151	527	139	37	3	22	(12	10)	248	97	72	88	68	3	102	16	4	5	28	13	.68	18	.264	.362	.471
1998	Det	AL	153	594	161	38	2	27	(19	8)	284	84	100	94	39	2	112	16	0	2	15	5	.75	8	.271	.332	.478
1999	Det	AL	151	549	146	30	1	20	(12	8)	238	83	65	82	51	2	124	19	2	6	11	3	.79	15	.266	.346	.434
2000	Det	AL	126	464	120	27	2	14	(5	9)	193	76	58	69	55	1	79	11	4	1	13	4	.76	11	.259	.350	.416
2001	Det	AL	154	585	146	27	7	11	(4	7)	220	77	65	72	52	3	90	13	4	4	10	5	.67	10	.250	.323	.376
2002	Det	AL	85	304	68	14	1	8	(4	4)	108	29	30	29	27	3	43	11	1	3	1	3	.25	4	.224	.307	.355
2003	TB	AL	36	107	20	3	1	1	(0	1)	28	8	7	3	2	0	18	0	1	0	0	0	-	3	.187	.202	.262
2004	Fla	NL	98	223	53	20	1	9	(5	4)	102	26	43	34	24	1	36	8	0	2	4	1	.80	6	.238	.331	.457
2005	Fla	NL	102	267	64	19	1	9	(5	4)	112	37	30	33	26	3	47	4	3	4	4	1	.80	6	.240	.312	.419
2006	Ari	NL	90	189	44	6	1	9	(3	6)	79	24	28	29	21	0	30	5	3	2	1	1	.50	4	.233	.323	.418
2007	NYM	NL	76	193	54	6	0	10	(6	4)	90	24	26	34	19	1	35	5	0	1	0	1	.00	2	.280	.358	.466
96	LAA	AL	28	45	7	1	0	2	(1	1)	14	4	7	4	6	0	12	0	3	0	0	0	-	0	.156	.255	.311
96	Det	AL	21	67	23	1	0	2	(0	2)	30	10	10	12	4	0	13	1	2	1	3	1	.75	0	.343	.384	.448
	16 ML YEARS		1593	5168	1301	277	25	157	(82	75)	2099	702	640	692	491	22	897	125	40	40	114	56	.67	113	.252	.329	.406

Adam Eaton

Pitches: R **Bats:** R **Pos:** SP-30   **Ht:** 6'2" **Wt:** 200 **Born:** 11/23/1977 **Age:** 30

Year	Team	Lg	G	GS	CG	GF	IP	BFP	H	R	ER	HR	SH	SF	HB	TBB	IBB	SO	WP	Bk	W	L	Pct	ShO	Sv-Op	Hld	ERC	ERA
2007	Rdng*	AA	1	1	0	0	2.0	9	3	2	2	0	0	1	1	0	0	1	0	0	0	0	-	0	0--	-	7.26	9.00
2000	SD	NL	22	22	0	0	135.0	583	134	63	62	14	1	3	2	61	3	90	3	0	7	4	.636	0	0-0	0	4.34	4.13
2001	SD	NL	17	17	2	0	116.2	499	108	61	56	20	3	2	5	40	3	109	3	0	8	5	.615	0	0-0	0	4.01	4.32
2002	SD	NL	6	6	0	0	33.1	142	28	20	20	5	2	2	2	17	0	25	2	0	1	1	.500	0	0-0	0	4.28	5.40
2003	SD	NL	31	31	1	0	183.0	789	173	91	83	20	5	5	7	68	6	146	7	1	9	12	.429	0	0-0	0	3.78	4.08
2004	SD	NL	33	33	0	0	199.1	848	204	113	102	28	12	7	10	52	3	153	5	0	11	14	.440	0	0-0	0	4.10	4.61
2005	SD	NL	24	22	0	2	128.2	568	140	70	61	14	4	6	5	44	6	100	5	0	11	5	.688	0	0-0	0	4.44	4.27
2006	Tex	AL	13	13	0	0	65.0	291	78	38	37	11	1	1	4	24	0	43	0	0	7	4	.636	0	0-0	0	5.98	5.12
2007	Phi	NL	30	30	0	0	161.2	734	192	117	113	30	10	5	11	71	4	97	6	0	10	10	.500	0	0-0	0	6.33	6.29
	8 ML YEARS		176	174	3	2	1022.2	4454	1057	573	534	142	38	31	46	377	25	763	31	1	64	55	.538	0	0-0	0	4.56	4.70

David Eckstein

Bats: R **Throws:** R **Pos:** SS-114; PH-4   **Ht:** 5'7" **Wt:** 175 **Born:** 1/20/1975 **Age:** 33

Year	Team	Lg	G	AB	H	2B	3B	HR	(Hm	Rd)	TB	R	RBI	RC	TBB	IBB	SO	HBP	SH	SF	SB	CS	SB%	GDP	Avg	OBP	Slg
2001	LAA	AL	153	582	166	26	2	4	(3	1)	208	82	41	80	43	0	60	21	16	2	29	4	.88	11	.285	.355	.357
2002	LAA	AL	152	608	178	22	6	8	(3	5)	236	107	63	93	45	0	44	27	14	8	21	13	.62	7	.293	.363	.388
2003	LAA	AL	120	452	114	22	1	3	(1	2)	147	59	31	53	36	0	45	15	10	4	16	5	.76	9	.252	.325	.325
2004	LAA	AL	142	566	156	24	1	2	(2	0)	188	92	35	60	42	1	49	13	14	2	16	5	.76	11	.276	.339	.332
2005	StL	NL	158	630	185	26	7	8	(3	5)	249	90	61	103	58	0	44	13	8	4	11	8	.58	13	.294	.363	.395
2006	StL	NL	123	500	146	18	1	2	(0	2)	172	68	23	60	31	0	41	15	3	7	7	6	.54	7	.292	.350	.344
2007	StL	NL	117	434	134	23	0	3	(1	2)	166	58	31	55	24	0	22	12	7	7	10	1	.91	9	.309	.356	.382
	7 ML YEARS		965	3772	1079	161	18	30	(13	17)	1366	556	285	504	279	1	305	116	72	30	110	42	.72	67	.286	.351	.362

Jim Edmonds

Bats: L **Throws:** L **Pos:** CF-103; PH-15; 1B-1   **Ht:** 6'1" **Wt:** 210 **Born:** 6/27/1970 **Age:** 38

Year	Team	Lg	G	AB	H	2B	3B	HR	(Hm	Rd)	TB	R	RBI	RC	TBB	IBB	SO	HBP	SH	SF	SB	CS	SB%	GDP	Avg	OBP	Slg
1993	LAA	AL	18	61	15	4	1	0	(0	0)	21	5	4	4	2	1	16	0	0	0	0	2	.00	1	.246	.270	.344
1994	LAA	AL	94	289	79	13	1	5	(3	2)	109	35	37	38	30	3	72	1	1	1	4	2	.67	3	.273	.343	.377
1995	LAA	AL	141	558	162	30	4	33	(16	17)	299	120	107	100	51	4	130	5	1	5	1	4	.20	10	.290	.352	.536
1996	LAA	AL	114	431	131	28	3	27	(17	10)	246	73	66	88	46	2	101	4	0	2	4	0	1.00	8	.304	.375	.571
1997	LAA	AL	133	502	146	27	0	26	(14	12)	251	82	80	90	60	5	80	4	0	5	5	7	.42	8	.291	.368	.500
1998	LAA	AL	154	599	184	42	1	25	(9	16)	303	115	91	104	57	7	114	1	1	1	7	5	.58	16	.307	.368	.506
1999	LAA	AL	55	204	51	17	2	5	(3	2)	87	34	23	30	28	0	45	0	0	1	5	4	.56	3	.250	.339	.426
2000	StL	NL	152	525	155	25	0	42	(22	20)	306	129	108	126	103	3	167	6	1	8	10	3	.77	5	.295	.411	.583
2001	StL	NL	150	500	152	38	1	30	(16	14)	282	95	110	113	93	12	136	4	1	10	5	5	.50	8	.304	.410	.564
2002	StL	NL	144	476	148	31	2	28	(17	11)	267	96	83	101	86	14	134	8	0	6	4	3	.57	9	.311	.420	.561
2003	StL	NL	137	447	123	32	2	39	(17	22)	276	89	89	87	77	6	127	4	1	2	1	3	.25	11	.275	.385	.617
2004	StL	NL	153	498	150	38	3	42	(24	18)	320	102	111	115	101	12	150	5	0	8	8	3	.73	4	.301	.418	.643
2005	StL	NL	142	467	123	37	1	29	(15	14)	249	88	89	95	91	10	139	4	1	4	5	5	.50	6	.263	.385	.533
2006	StL	NL	110	350	90	18	0	19	(11	8)	165	52	70	51	53	7	101	4	0	5	4	0	1.00	9	.257	.350	.471
2007	StL	NL	117	365	92	15	2	12	(5	7)	147	39	53	43	41	2	75	0	2	3	0	2	.00	9	.252	.325	.403
	15 ML YEARS		1814	6272	1801	395	23	362	(189	173)	3320	1154	1121	1185	919	88	1587	46	9	61	63	48	.57	112	.287	.379	.531

Scott Elarton

Pitches: R **Bats:** R **Pos:** SP-9   **Ht:** 6'7" **Wt:** 255 **Born:** 2/23/1976 **Age:** 32

Year	Team	Lg	G	GS	CG	GF	IP	BFP	H	R	ER	HR	SH	SF	HB	TBB	IBB	SO	WP	Bk	W	L	Pct	ShO	Sv-Op	Hld	ERC	ERA
2007	Wichta*	AA	2	2	0	0	8.2	44	9	5	3	0	1	0	1	5	0	4	1	0	1	1	.500	0	0--	-	4.19	3.12
2007	Omha*	AAA	8	8	0	0	44.1	192	51	34	33	13	0	1	0	14	0	19	4	0	2	3	.400	0	0--	-	6.08	6.70
2007	Buffalo*	AAA	9	0	0	2	18.0	75	17	7	5	2	0	1	0	5	1	14	1	0	1	0	1.000	0	0--	-	3.27	2.50
1998	Hou	NL	28	2	0	7	57.0	227	40	21	21	5	1	1	1	20	0	56	1	0	2	1	.667	0	2-3	2	2.35	3.32
1999	Hou	NL	42	15	0	8	124.0	524	111	55	48	8	7	4	4	43	0	121	3	0	9	5	.643	0	1-4	5	3.16	3.48
2000	Hou	NL	30	30	2	0	192.2	855	198	117	103	29	5	7	6	84	1	131	8	0	17	7	.708	0	0-0	0	4.82	4.81
2001	2 Tms	NL	24	24	0	0	132.2	595	146	105	104	34	7	2	6	59	2	87	5	0	4	10	.286	0	0-0	0	6.21	7.06
2003	Col	NL	11	10	0	0	51.2	253	73	46	36	13	3	4	4	20	3	20	3	0	4	4	.500	0	0-0	0	7.79	6.27
2004	2 Tms		29	29	1	0	158.2	697	164	107	104	33	5	7	4	62	3	103	8	0	3	11	.214	1	0-0	0	5.04	5.90
2005	Cle	AL	31	31	1	0	181.2	774	189	100	93	32	3	10	6	48	1	103	4	1	11	9	.550	0	0-0	0	4.40	4.61
2006	KC	AL	20	20	0	0	114.2	501	117	73	68	26	2	2	6	52	1	49	3	0	4	9	.308	0	0-0	0	5.64	5.34
2007	KC	AL	9	9	0	0	37.0	185	53	44	43	12	0	3	3	21	0	13	2	0	2	4	.333	0	0-0	0	9.76	10.46
01	Hou	NL	20	20	0	0	109.2	499	126	88	87	26	7	2	6	49	1	76	5	0	4	8	.333	0	0-0	0	6.42	7.14
01	Col	NL	4	4	0	0	23.0	96	20	17	17	8	0	0	0	10	1	11	0	0	0	2	.000	0	0-0	0	5.18	6.65
04	Col	NL	8	8	0	0	41.1	199	57	45	45	8	2	3	0	20	1	23	5	0	0	6	.000	0	0-0	0	7.35	9.80
04	Cle	AL	21	21	1	0	117.1	498	107	62	59	25	3	4	4	42	2	80	3	0	3	5	.375	1	0-0	0	4.28	4.53
	9 ML YEARS		224	170	4	15	1050.0	4611	1091	668	620	192	33	40	40	409	11	683	37	1	56	60	.483	1	3-7	7	4.97	5.31

Brad Eldred

Bats: R **Throws:** R **Pos:** RF-8; PH-7; 1B-4; DH-1　　　　**Ht:** 6'5" **Wt:** 275 **Born:** 7/12/1980 **Age:** 27

Year	Team	Lg	G	AB	H	2B	3B	HR	(Hm	Rd)	TB	R	RBI	RC	TBB	IBB	SO	HBP	SH	SF	SB	CS	SB%	GDP	Avg	OBP	Slg
2002	Wmspt	A-	72	276	78	22	3	10	(-	-)	136	43	48	48	18	4	74	6	0	2	10	1	.91	4	.283	.338	.493
2003	Hickory	A	115	420	105	22	0	28	(-	-)	211	62	80	71	38	2	142	11	0	3	7	1	.88	5	.250	.326	.502
2004	Lynbrg	A+	91	335	104	22	1	21	(-	-)	191	54	77	75	35	3	97	15	0	3	5	2	.71	4	.310	.397	.570
2004	Altna	AA	39	147	41	9	0	17	(-	-)	101	24	60	32	6	0	51	5	0	0	0	0	-	3	.279	.329	.687
2005	Altna	AA	21	84	28	6	0	13	(-	-)	73	22	27	25	8	1	25	0	0	1	1	1	.50	0	.333	.387	.869
2005	Indy	AAA	54	195	55	13	1	15	(-	-)	115	31	48	39	14	1	57	3	0	2	4	0	1.00	3	.282	.336	.590
2006	Indy	AAA	18	62	14	7	0	3	(-	-)	30	10	10	9	8	0	18	0	0	1	1	1	.50	1	.226	.310	.484
2007	Indy	AAA	86	311	65	10	2	15	(-	-)	124	37	45	36	20	1	90	9	0	2	9	3	.75	5	.209	.275	.399
2005	Pit	NL	55	190	42	9	0	12	(4	8)	87	23	27	14	13	0	77	3	0	2	1	1	.50	5	.221	.279	.458
2007	Pit	NL	19	46	5	1	0	2	(1	1)	12	3	3	0	1	1	16	0	0	0	0	0	-	1	.109	.128	.261
2 ML YEARS			74	236	47	10	0	14	(5	9)	99	26	30	14	14	1	93	3	0	2	1	1	.50	6	.199	.251	.419

Mark Ellis

Bats: R **Throws:** R **Pos:** 2B-150; PH-1　　　　**Ht:** 5'11" **Wt:** 190 **Born:** 6/6/1977 **Age:** 31

Year	Team	Lg	G	AB	H	2B	3B	HR	(Hm	Rd)	TB	R	RBI	RC	TBB	IBB	SO	HBP	SH	SF	SB	CS	SB%	GDP	Avg	OBP	Slg
2002	Oak	AL	98	345	94	16	4	6	(6	0)	136	58	35	55	44	1	54	4	8	3	4	2	.67	3	.272	.359	.394
2003	Oak	AL	154	553	137	31	5	9	(7	2)	205	78	52	69	48	4	94	7	9	5	6	2	.75	7	.248	.313	.371
2005	Oak	AL	122	434	137	21	5	13	(8	5)	207	76	52	78	44	1	51	4	4	0	1	3	.25	10	.316	.384	.477
2006	Oak	AL	124	441	110	25	1	11	(7	4)	170	64	52	53	40	1	76	8	4	7	4	0	1.00	13	.249	.319	.385
2007	Oak	AL	150	583	161	33	3	19	(10	9)	257	84	76	76	44	1	94	10	2	3	9	4	.69	10	.276	.336	.441
5 ML YEARS			648	2356	639	126	18	58	(35	23)	975	360	267	331	220	8	369	33	27	18	24	11	.69	43	.271	.340	.414

Jason Ellison

Bats: R **Throws:** R **Pos:** RF-41; LF-32; PR-20; PH-16; CF-8　　　　**Ht:** 5'10" **Wt:** 180 **Born:** 4/4/1978 **Age:** 30

Year	Team	Lg	G	AB	H	2B	3B	HR	(Hm	Rd)	TB	R	RBI	RC	TBB	IBB	SO	HBP	SH	SF	SB	CS	SB%	GDP	Avg	OBP	Slg
2003	SF	NL	7	10	1	0	0	0	(0	0)	1	1	0	0	0	0	1	0	0	0	0	0	-	0	.100	.100	.100
2004	SF	NL	13	4	2	0	0	0	(0	1)	5	4	3	3	0	0	1	0	0	0	2	0	1.00	0	.500	.500	1.250
2005	SF	NL	131	352	93	18	2	4	(2	2)	127	49	24	34	24	1	44	3	6	1	14	6	.70	7	.264	.316	.361
2006	SF	NL	84	81	18	5	1	2	(0	2)	31	14	4	4	5	0	14	1	3	1	2	2	.50	3	.222	.273	.383
2007	2 Tms	NL	100	94	22	1	0	1	(0	2)	26	16	2	5	6	0	27	1	3	0	4	3	.57	1	.234	.287	.277
07	Sea	AL	63	46	13	0	0	0	(0	0)	13	9	0	2	1	0	12	0	1	0	3	3	.50	1	.283	.298	.283
07	Cin	NL	37	48	9	1	0	1	(0	2)	13	7	2	3	5	0	15	1	2	0	1	0	1.00	0	.188	.278	.271
5 ML YEARS			335	541	136	24	3	8	(2	6)	190	84	33	46	35	1	87	5	12	2	22	11	.67	11	.251	.302	.351

Jacoby Ellsbury

Bats: L **Throws:** L **Pos:** LF-22; CF-16; RF-1; PH-1; PR-1　　　　**Ht:** 6'1" **Wt:** 185 **Born:** 9/11/1983 **Age:** 24

Year	Team	Lg	G	AB	H	2B	3B	HR	(Hm	Rd)	TB	R	RBI	RC	TBB	IBB	SO	HBP	SH	SF	SB	CS	SB%	GDP	Avg	OBP	Slg
2005	Lowell	A-	35	139	44	3	5	1	(-	-)	60	28	19	30	24	0	20	1	0	1	23	3	.88	4	.317	.418	.432
2006	Wilmg	A+	61	244	73	7	5	4	(-	-)	102	35	32	42	25	3	28	7	4	1	25	9	.74	5	.299	.379	.418
2006	Portlnd	AA	50	198	61	10	3	3	(-	-)	86	29	19	34	24	2	25	2	0	1	16	8	.67	1	.308	.387	.434
2007	Portlnd	AA	17	73	33	10	2	0	(-	-)	47	16	13	23	6	0	7	4	0	0	8	1	.89	0	.452	.518	.644
2007	Pwtckt	AAA	87	363	108	14	5	2	(-	-)	138	66	28	56	32	2	47	4	1	1	33	6	.85	5	.298	.360	.380
2007	Bos	AL	33	116	41	7	1	3	(3	0)	59	20	18	26	8	0	15	1	0	2	9	0	1.00	2	.353	.394	.509

Alan Embree

Pitches: L **Bats:** L **Pos:** RP-68　　　　**Ht:** 6'2" **Wt:** 190 **Born:** 1/23/1970 **Age:** 38

Year	Team	Lg	G	GS	CG	GF	IP	BFP	H	R	ER	HR	SH	SF	HB	TBB	IBB	SO	WP	Bk	W	L	Pct	ShO	Sv-Op	Hld	ERC	ERA
1992	Cle	AL	4	4	0	0	18.0	81	19	14	14	3	0	2	1	8	0	12	1	1	0	2	.000	0	0-0	0	5.25	7.00
1995	Cle	AL	23	0	0	8	24.2	111	23	16	14	2	2	2	0	16	0	23	1	0	3	2	.600	0	1-1	6	4.51	5.11
1996	Cle	AL	24	0	0	2	31.0	141	30	26	22	10	1	3	0	21	3	33	3	0	1	1	.500	0	0-0	1	6.58	6.39
1997	Atl	NL	66	0	0	15	46.0	190	36	13	13	1	4	1	2	20	2	45	3	1	3	1	.750	0	0-0	16	2.66	2.54
1998	2 Tms	NL	55	0	0	16	53.2	237	56	32	25	7	4	1	1	23	0	43	3	0	4	2	.667	0	1-3	12	4.71	4.19
1999	SF	NL	68	0	0	13	58.2	244	42	22	22	6	3	2	3	26	2	53	3	0	3	2	.600	0	0-3	22	2.86	3.38
2000	SF	NL	63	0	0	21	60.0	263	62	34	33	4	4	5	3	25	2	49	1	0	3	5	.375	0	2-5	9	4.24	4.95
2001	2 Tms	NL	61	0	0	17	54.0	245	65	47	44	14	0	6	3	17	2	59	3	0	1	4	.200	0	0-3	9	6.20	7.33
2002	2 Tms	NL	68	0	0	20	62.0	251	47	19	15	6	1	2	1	20	3	81	1	0	4	6	.400	0	2-7	18	2.48	2.18
2003	Bos	AL	65	0	0	15	55.0	221	49	26	26	5	2	2	0	16	3	45	0	0	4	1	.800	0	1-2	14	3.01	4.25
2004	Bos	AL	71	0	0	11	52.1	217	48	29	24	7	2	2	1	11	1	37	0	0	2	2	.500	0	0-1	20	3.21	4.13
2005	2 Tms	AL	67	0	0	15	52.0	231	62	47	44	10	3	3	2	14	3	38	1	1	2	5	.286	0	1-3	10	5.34	7.62
2006	SD	NL	73	0	0	11	52.1	221	50	21	19	4	2	3	0	15	2	53	0	0	4	3	.571	0	0-1	15	3.13	3.27
2007	Oak	AL	68	0	0	36	68.0	284	67	30	30	5	1	4	0	19	5	51	0	0	1	2	.333	0	17-21	16	3.24	3.97
98	Atl	NL	20	0	0	5	18.2	87	23	14	9	2	1	1	0	10	0	19	0	0	1	0	1.000	0	0-1	6	6.06	4.34
98	Ari	NL	35	0	0	10	35.0	150	33	18	16	5	3	0	1	13	0	24	3	0	3	2	.600	0	1-2	6	4.03	4.11
01	SF	NL	22	0	0	7	20.0	106	34	26	25	7	0	3	2	10	2	25	1	0	0	2	.000	0	0-1	9	11.29	11.25
01	CWS	AL	39	0	0	10	34.0	139	31	21	19	7	0	3	1	7	0	34	2	0	1	2	.333	0	0-2	9	3.61	5.03
02	SD	NL	36	0	0	13	28.2	118	23	7	4	2	0	0	0	9	2	38	1	0	3	4	.429	0	0-2	10	2.38	1.26
02	Bos	AL	32	0	0	7	33.1	133	24	12	11	4	1	2	1	11	1	43	0	0	1	2	.333	0	2-5	8	2.56	2.97
05	Bos	AL	43	0	0	11	37.2	163	42	33	32	8	1	2	1	11	2	30	1	0	1	4	.200	0	1-3	4	5.14	7.65
05	NYY	AL	24	0	0	4	14.1	68	20	14	12	2	2	1	1	3	1	8	0	1	1	1	.500	0	0-0	6	5.85	7.53
14 ML YEARS			776	4	0	200	687.2	2937	657	375	345	84	27	38	17	251	28	622	20	3	35	38	.479	0	25-49	169	3.86	4.52

Edwin Encarnacion

Bats: R **Throws:** R **Pos:** 3B-137; PH-3   **Ht:** 6'1" **Wt:** 216 **Born:** 1/7/1983 **Age:** 25

								BATTING															BASERUNNING				AVERAGES		
Year	Team	Lg	G	AB	H	2B	3B	HR	(Hm	Rd)	TB	R	RBI	RC	TBB	IBB	SO	HBP	SH	SF		SB	CS	SB%	GDP	Avg	OBP	Slg
2007	Lsvlle*	AAA	11	46	19	3	0	3	(-	-)	31	12	7	11	1	0	4	0	0	0		1	0	1.00	0	.413	.426	.674
2005	Cin	NL	69	211	49	16	0	9	(3	6)	92	25	31	24	20	2	60	3	0	0		3	0	1.00	8	.232	.308	.436
2006	Cin	NL	117	406	112	33	1	15	(7	8)	192	60	72	66	41	3	78	13	0	3		6	3	.67	9	.276	.359	.473
2007	Cin	NL	139	502	145	25	1	16	(10	6)	220	66	76	86	39	4	86	14	0	1		8	1	.89	5	.289	.356	.438
	3 ML YEARS		325	1119	306	74	2	40	(20	20)	504	151	179	176	100	9	224	30	0	4		17	4	.81	22	.273	.348	.450

Juan Encarnacion

Bats: R **Throws:** R **Pos:** RF-74; PH-4; CF-2   **Ht:** 6'3" **Wt:** 215 **Born:** 3/8/1976 **Age:** 32

								BATTING															BASERUNNING				AVERAGES		
Year	Team	Lg	G	AB	H	2B	3B	HR	(Hm	Rd)	TB	R	RBI	RC	TBB	IBB	SO	HBP	SH	SF		SB	CS	SB%	GDP	Avg	OBP	Slg
2007	Sprgfld*	AA	15	58	9	4	0	0	(-	-)	13	5	4	3	6	0	11	1	0	0		1	0	1.00	1	.155	.246	.224
1997	Det	AL	11	33	7	1	1	1	(1	0)	13	3	5	4	3	0	12	2	0	0		3	1	.75	1	.212	.316	.394
1998	Det	AL	40	164	54	9	4	7	(4	3)	92	30	21	31	7	0	31	1	0	3		7	4	.64	2	.329	.354	.561
1999	Det	AL	132	509	130	30	6	19	(6	13)	229	62	74	64	14	1	113	9	4	2		33	12	.73	12	.255	.287	.450
2000	Det	AL	141	547	158	25	6	14	(4	10)	237	75	72	76	29	1	90	7	3	4		16	4	.80	15	.289	.330	.433
2001	Det	AL	120	417	101	19	7	12	(4	8)	170	52	52	48	25	1	93	6	5	4		9	5	.64	9	.242	.292	.408
2002	2 Tms	NL	152	584	158	22	5	24	(8	16)	262	77	85	74	46	0	113	4	3	7		21	9	.70	18	.271	.324	.449
2003	Fla	NL	156	601	162	37	6	19	(9	10)	268	80	94	76	37	0	82	4	5	6		19	8	.70	17	.270	.313	.446
2004	2 Tms	NL	135	484	114	30	2	16	(8	8)	196	63	62	60	38	2	86	7	1	2		5	4	.56	11	.236	.299	.405
2005	Fla	NL	141	506	145	27	3	16	(8	8)	226	59	76	79	41	2	104	9	4	3		6	5	.55	9	.287	.349	.447
2006	StL	NL	153	557	155	25	5	19	(10	9)	247	74	79	79	30	6	86	4	1	6		6	5	.55	11	.278	.317	.443
2007	StL	NL	78	283	80	17	1	9	(5	4)	126	43	47	32	18	0	43	1	1	4		2	2	.50	11	.283	.324	.445
02	Cin	NL	83	321	89	11	2	16	(6	10)	152	43	51	42	26	0	63	1	3	3		9	4	.69	7	.277	.330	.474
02	Fla	NL	69	263	69	11	3	8	(2	6)	110	34	34	32	20	0	50	3	0	4		12	5	.71	11	.262	.317	.418
04	LAD	NL	86	324	76	18	1	13	(6	7)	135	42	43	38	21	0	53	4	0	1		3	3	.50	9	.235	.289	.417
04	Fla	NL	49	160	38	12	1	3	(2	1)	61	21	19	22	17	2	33	3	1	1		2	1	.67	2	.238	.320	.381
	11 ML YEARS		1259	4685	1264	242	46	156	(67	89)	2066	618	667	623	288	13	853	54	27	41		127	59	.68	116	.270	.317	.441

John Ennis

Pitches: R **Bats:** R **Pos:** RP-2; SP-1   **Ht:** 6'5" **Wt:** 220 **Born:** 10/17/1979 **Age:** 28

			HOW MUCH HE PITCHED						WHAT HE GAVE UP												THE RESULTS						
Year	Team	Lg	G	GS	CG	GF	IP	BFP	H	R	ER	HR	SH	SF	HB	TBB	IBB	SO	WP	Bk	W	L	Pct	ShO	Sv-Op	Hld	ERC	ERA
2007	Ottawa*	AAA	37	7	0	6	88.0	377	90	40	33	7	4	3	3	32	1	83	2	0	4	4	.500	0	1- -	-	4.07	3.38
2002	Atl	NL	1	1	0	0	4.0	18	5	2	2	0	1	1	0	3	0	1	0	0	0	0	-	0	0-0	0	6.70	4.50
2004	Det	AL	12	0	0	5	16.0	75	20	16	15	3	0	1	0	5	0	13	1	1	0	0	-	0	1-2	0	5.53	8.44
2007	Phi	NL	3	1	0	1	7.2	38	12	7	7	1	0	0	0	3	0	8	0	0	0	0	-	0	1-1	0	7.56	8.22
	3 ML YEARS		16	2	0	6	27.2	131	37	25	24	4	1	2	0	11	0	22	1	1	0	0	-	0	2-3	0	6.26	7.81

Morgan Ensberg

Bats: R **Throws:** R **Pos:** 3B-80; PH-42; 1B-1; PR-1   **Ht:** 6'2" **Wt:** 220 **Born:** 8/26/1975 **Age:** 32

								BATTING															BASERUNNING				AVERAGES		
Year	Team	Lg	G	AB	H	2B	3B	HR	(Hm	Rd)	TB	R	RBI	RC	TBB	IBB	SO	HBP	SH	SF		SB	CS	SB%	GDP	Avg	OBP	Slg
2000	Hou	NL	4	7	2	0	0	0	(0	0)	2	0	0	1	0	0	1	0	0	0		0	0	-	0	.286	.286	.206
2002	Hou	NL	49	132	32	7	2	3	(2	1)	52	14	19	13	18	0	25	3	0	0		2	0	1.00	8	.242	.346	.394
2003	Hou	NL	127	385	112	15	1	25	(16	9)	204	69	60	71	48	1	60	6	1	1		7	2	.78	10	.291	.377	.530
2004	Hou	NL	131	411	113	20	3	10	(9	1)	169	51	66	57	36	1	46	0	5	4		6	4	.60	17	.275	.330	.411
2005	Hou	NL	150	526	149	30	3	36	(20	16)	293	86	101	107	85	9	119	8	0	5		6	7	.46	12	.283	.388	.557
2006	Hou	NL	127	387	91	17	1	23	(16	7)	179	67	58	73	101	7	96	4	0	3		1	4	.20	3	.235	.396	.463
2007	2 Tms	NL	115	282	65	13	0	12	(5	7)	114	47	39	34	38	0	67	0	2	2		0	1	.00	7	.230	.320	.404
07	Hou	NL	85	224	52	10	0	8	(2	6)	86	36	31	27	31	0	48	0	2	2		0	1	.00	6	.232	.323	.384
07	SD	NL	30	58	13	3	0	4	(3	1)	28	11	8	7	7	0	19	0	0	0		0	0	-	1	.224	.308	.483
	7 ML YEARS		703	2130	564	102	10	109	(68	41)	1013	334	343	356	326	18	414	21	8	15		22	18	.55	57	.265	.366	.476

Darin Erstad

Bats: L **Throws:** L **Pos:** CF-45; 1B-22; LF-12; RF-9; PH-4; DH-3   **Ht:** 6'2" **Wt:** 220 **Born:** 6/4/1974 **Age:** 34

								BATTING															BASERUNNING				AVERAGES		
Year	Team	Lg	G	AB	H	2B	3B	HR	(Hm	Rd)	TB	R	RBI	RC	TBB	IBB	SO	HBP	SH	SF		SB	CS	SB%	GDP	Avg	OBP	Slg
2007	Charltt*	AAA	12	47	6	0	0	0	(-	-)	6	3	2	0	5	0	15	0	0	0		0	0	-	0	.128	.212	.128
1996	LAA	AL	57	208	59	5	1	4	(1	3)	78	34	20	26	17	1	29	0	1	3		3	3	.50	3	.284	.333	.375
1997	LAA	AL	139	539	161	34	4	16	(8	8)	251	99	77	92	51	4	86	4	5	6		23	8	.74	5	.299	.360	.466
1998	LAA	AL	133	537	159	39	3	19	(9	10)	261	84	82	94	43	7	77	6	1	3		20	6	.77	2	.296	.353	.486
1999	LAA	AL	142	585	148	22	5	13	(6	7)	219	84	53	64	47	3	101	1	2	3		13	7	.65	16	.253	.308	.374
2000	LAA	AL	157	676	240	39	6	25	(11	14)	366	121	100	145	64	9	82	1	2	4		28	8	.78	8	.355	.409	.541
2001	LAA	AL	157	631	163	35	1	9	(3	6)	227	89	63	79	62	7	113	10	1	7		24	10	.71	8	.258	.331	.360
2002	LAA	AL	150	625	177	28	4	10	(2	8)	243	99	73	74	27	4	67	2	5	4		23	3	.88	9	.283	.313	.389
2003	LAA	AL	67	258	65	7	1	4	(1	3)	86	35	17	22	18	1	40	4	2	2		9	1	.90	8	.252	.309	.333
2004	LAA	AL	125	495	146	29	1	7	(3	4)	198	79	69	76	37	1	74	4	3	4		16	1	.94	9	.295	.346	.400
2005	LAA	AL	153	609	166	33	3	7	(4	3)	226	86	66	79	47	3	109	1	4	2		10	3	.77	8	.273	.325	.371
2006	LAA	AL	40	95	21	8	1	0	(0	0)	31	8	5	6	6	0	18	2	1	1		1	1	.50	2	.221	.279	.326
2007	CWS	AL	87	310	77	13	1	4	(2	2)	104	33	32	36	28	0	44	0	6	1		7	2	.78	4	.248	.310	.335
	12 ML YEARS		1407	5568	1582	292	31	118	(51	67)	2290	851	657	793	447	40	840	35	33	40		177	53	.77	82	.284	.339	.411

Alex Escobar

Bats: R Throws: R Pos: OF   Ht: 6'1" Wt: 190 Born: 9/6/1978 Age: 29

									BATTING												BASERUNNING				AVERAGES		
Year	Team	Lg	G	AB	H	2B	3B	HR	(Hm	Rd)	TB	R	RBI	RC	TBB	IBB	SO	HBP	SH	SF	SB	CS	SB%	GDP	Avg	OBP	Slg
2007	Ptomc*	A+	2	8	1	0	0	0	(-	-)	1	1	1	0	1	0	1	0	0	0	0	0	-	0	.125	.222	.125
2007	Hrsbrg*	AA	5	16	3	2	0	0	(-	-)	5	0	1	1	0	0	2	0	0	1	1	0	1.00	0	.188	.176	.313
2007	Clmbs*	AAA	7	27	4	1	0	0	(-	-)	5	3	1	1	4	0	9	0	0	0	0	0	-	2	.148	.258	.185
2001	NYM	NL	18	50	10	1	0	3	(3	0)	20	3	8	5	3	0	19	0	0	0	1	0	1.00	1	.200	.245	.400
2003	Cle	AL	28	99	27	2	0	5	(4	1)	44	16	14	9	7	1	33	1	0	1	1	0	1.00	0	.273	.324	.444
2004	Cle	AL	46	152	32	8	2	1	(0	1)	47	20	12	17	23	0	42	1	3	0	1	1	.50	1	.211	.318	.309
2006	Was	NL	33	87	31	3	2	4	(2	2)	50	14	18	16	8	0	18	0	0	4	2	0	1.00	3	.356	.394	.575
4 ML YEARS			125	388	100	14	4	13	(9	4)	161	53	52	47	41	1	112	2	3	5	5	1	.83	5	.258	.328	.415

Kelvim Escobar

Pitches: R Bats: R Pos: SP-30   Ht: 6'1" Wt: 230 Born: 4/11/1976 Age: 32

				HOW MUCH HE PITCHED						WHAT HE GAVE UP										THE RESULTS						
Year	Team	Lg	G	GS	CG	GF	IP	BFP	H	R	ER	HR	SH	SF	HB	TBB	IBB	SO	WP	Bk	W	L	Pct	ShO	Sv-Op	Hld	ERC	ERA
1997	Tor	AL	27	0	0	23	31.0	139	28	12	10	1	2	0	0	19	2	36	0	0	3	2	.600	0	14-17	1	3.68	2.90
1998	Tor	AL	22	10	0	2	79.2	342	72	37	33	5	0	3	0	35	0	72	0	0	7	3	.700	0	0-1	5	3.41	3.73
1999	Tor	AL	33	30	1	2	174.0	795	203	118	110	19	2	8	10	81	2	129	6	1	14	11	.560	0	0-0	0	5.62	5.69
2000	Tor	AL	43	24	3	8	180.0	794	186	118	107	26	5	4	3	85	3	142	4	0	10	15	.400	1	2-3	3	4.94	5.35
2001	Tor	AL	59	11	1	15	126.0	517	93	51	49	8	2	5	3	52	5	121	2	0	6	8	.429	1	0-0	13	2.54	3.50
2002	Tor	AL	76	0	0	68	78.0	355	75	39	37	10	1	0	5	44	6	85	4	0	5	7	.417	0	38-46	0	4.77	4.27
2003	Tor	AL	41	26	1	12	180.1	797	189	94	86	15	5	5	9	78	3	159	9	0	13	9	.591	1	4-5	0	4.53	4.29
2004	LAA	AL	33	33	0	0	208.1	878	192	91	91	21	3	6	7	76	2	191	9	0	11	12	.478	0	0-0	0	3.65	3.93
2005	LAA	AL	16	7	0	2	59.2	242	45	21	20	4	2	0	2	21	1	63	4	0	3	2	.600	0	1-1	2	2.51	3.02
2006	LAA	AL	30	30	1	0	189.1	789	192	93	76	17	6	3	4	50	2	147	7	0	11	14	.440	0	0-0	0	3.67	3.61
2007	LAA	AL	30	30	3	0	195.2	812	182	79	74	11	5	4	3	66	2	160	9	0	18	7	.720	1	0-0	0	3.25	3.40
11 ML YEARS			410	201	10	132	1502.0	6460	1457	753	693	137	33	38	46	607	28	1305	54	1	101	90	.529	4	59-73	24	3.97	4.15

Yunel Escobar

Bats: R Throws: R Pos: SS-53; 3B-22; 2B-21; PH-12; PR-2   Ht: 6'2" Wt: 200 Born: 11/2/1982 Age: 25

									BATTING												BASERUNNING				AVERAGES		
Year	Team	Lg	G	AB	H	2B	3B	HR	(Hm	Rd)	TB	R	RBI	RC	TBB	IBB	SO	HBP	SH	SF	SB	CS	SB%	GDP	Avg	OBP	Slg
2005	Danvle	R	8	30	12	2	1	2	(-	-)	22	9	8	9	5	0	4	0	0	1	0	0	-	1	.400	.472	.733
2005	Rome	A	48	198	62	13	3	4	(-	-)	93	30	19	32	14	0	30	0	2	0	2	2	.00	6	.313	.358	.470
2006	Missi	AA	121	428	112	21	4	2	(-	-)	147	55	45	57	58	1	76	9	2	4	7	9	.44	20	.262	.359	.343
2007	Rchmd	AAA	46	180	60	10	3	2	(-	-)	82	20	29	31	14	1	27	0	0	1	7	3	.70	10	.333	.379	.456
2007	Atl	NL	94	319	104	25	0	5	(3	2)	144	54	28	52	27	1	44	5	2	2	5	3	.63	6	.326	.385	.451

Brian Esposito

Bats: R Throws: R Pos: C-1   Ht: 6'1" Wt: 205 Born: 2/24/1979 Age: 29

									BATTING												BASERUNNING				AVERAGES		
Year	Team	Lg	G	AB	H	2B	3B	HR	(Hm	Rd)	TB	R	RBI	RC	TBB	IBB	SO	HBP	SH	SF	SB	CS	SB%	GDP	Avg	OBP	Slg
2000	Lowell	A-	42	154	37	9	1	3	(-	-)	57	15	20	17	11	0	31	1	1	2	0	1	.00	2	.240	.292	.370
2001	Augsta	A	90	311	59	13	0	3	(-	-)	81	21	30	16	13	0	81	2	2	5	0	0	-	5	.190	.224	.260
2002	Augsta	A	40	154	39	5	0	5	(-	-)	59	20	15	18	7	0	32	5	2	0	0	0	-	4	.253	.307	.383
2002	Srsota	A+	31	99	16	5	0	2	(-	-)	27	8	7	4	5	0	20	1	1	1	0	0	-	1	.162	.208	.273
2003	Srsota	A+	2	7	0	0	0	0	(-	-)	0	0	0	0	0	0	0	0	0	0	0	0	-	0	.000	.000	.000
2003	Provo	R+	3	11	1	0	0	0	(-	-)	1	0	0	0	0	0	4	0	0	0	0	0	-	1	.091	.091	.091
2003	RCuca	A	9	32	11	2	0	0	(-	-)	13	2	2	4	0	0	5	0	1	0	0	0	-	1	.344	.344	.406
2004	Stcktn	A+	22	78	20	2	1	5	(-	-)	39	10	13	12	6	1	17	0	0	1	0	1	1.00	1	.256	.310	.500
2004	Frisco	AA	31	92	19	4	0	1	(-	-)	26	11	11	5	4	0	27	0	2	3	0	1	.00	3	.207	.232	.283
2004	OKC	AAA	1	4	0	0	0	0	(-	-)	0	1	0	0	0	0	1	0	0	0	0	0	-	0	.000	.000	.000
2005	Frisco	AA	38	136	31	7	0	0	(-	-)	38	12	5	10	7	0	33	2	2	0	1	0	1.00	2	.228	.276	.279
2005	Okla	AAA	8	27	11	1	0	0	(-	-)	12	6	4	5	1	0	6	1	0	0	0	0	-	1	.407	.448	.444
2006	Memp	AAA	55	175	41	9	0	2	(-	-)	56	13	12	14	3	0	32	4	4	0	0	1	.00	8	.234	.264	.320
2007	Memp	AAA	77	242	43	6	0	4	(-	-)	61	11	16	10	11	0	52	1	0	0	0	2	.00	10	.178	.217	.252
2007	StL	NL	1	0	0	0	0	0	(0	0)	0	0	0	0	0	0	0	0	0	0	0	0	-	0	-	-	-

Shawn Estes

Pitches: L Bats: R Pos: P   Ht: 6'2" Wt: 220 Born: 2/18/1973 Age: 35

				HOW MUCH HE PITCHED						WHAT HE GAVE UP										THE RESULTS						
Year	Team	Lg	G	GS	CG	GF	IP	BFP	H	R	ER	HR	SH	SF	HB	TBB	IBB	SO	WP	Bk	W	L	Pct	ShO	Sv-Op	Hld	ERC	ERA
2007	Padres*	R	4	3	0	0	7.0	29	6	3	3	1	0	0	0	1	0	10	1	0	0	0	-	0	0--	-	2.45	3.86
2007	Lk Els*	A+	3	3	0	0	14.0	54	12	5	3	0	0	1	0	3	0	14	1	0	0	1	.000	0	0--	-	2.13	1.93
2007	Portlnd*	AAA	4	2	0	0	7.1	38	13	8	8	3	0	0	1	3	0	3	1	0	0	1	.000	0	0--	-	12.67	9.82
1995	SF	NL	3	3	0	0	17.1	76	16	14	13	2	0	1	1	5	0	14	4	0	0	3	.000	0	0-0	0	3.37	6.75
1996	SF	NL	11	11	0	0	70.0	305	63	30	28	3	5	0	2	39	3	60	4	0	3	5	.375	0	0-0	0	3.78	3.60
1997	SF	NL	32	32	3	0	201.0	849	162	80	71	12	13	2	8	100	2	181	10	2	19	5	.792	2	0-0	0	3.28	3.18
1998	SF	NL	25	25	1	0	149.1	661	150	89	84	14	15	4	5	80	6	136	6	1	7	12	.368	1	0-0	0	4.71	5.06
1999	SF	NL	32	32	1	0	203.0	914	209	121	111	21	14	5	7	112	2	159	15	1	11	11	.500	1	0-0	0	4.96	4.92
2000	SF	NL	30	30	4	0	190.1	829	194	99	90	11	7	6	3	108	1	136	11	0	15	6	.714	2	0-0	0	4.75	4.26
2001	SF	NL	27	27	0	0	159.0	693	151	78	71	11	5	9	5	77	7	109	10	2	9	8	.529	0	0-0	0	3.96	4.02
2002	2 Tms	NL	29	29	1	0	160.2	713	171	94	91	13	7	6	9	83	9	109	3	1	5	12	.294	1	0-0	0	5.00	5.10
2003	ChC	NL	29	28	1	0	152.1	699	182	113	97	20	11	7	1	83	1	103	6	0	8	11	.421	1	0-0	0	6.15	5.73
2004	Col	NL	34	34	1	0	202.0	904	223	133	131	30	13	8	11	105	5	117	4	2	15	8	.652	0	0-0	0	5.86	5.84
2005	Ari	NL	21	21	2	0	123.2	535	132	70	66	15	10	4	4	45	0	63	4	0	7	8	.467	0	0-0	0	4.65	4.80

			HOW MUCH HE PITCHED					WHAT HE GAVE UP												THE RESULTS							
Year	Team	Lg	G	GS	CG	GF	IP	BFP	H	R	ER	HR	SH	SF	HB	TBB	IBB	SO	WP	Bk	W	L	Pct	ShO	Sv-Op	Hld	ERC	ERA
2006	SD	NL	1	1	0	0	6.0	27	5	3	3	0	0	0	1	3	0	4	0	0	0	1	.000	0	0-0	0	3.35	4.50
02	NYM	NL	23	23	1	0	132.2	580	133	70	67	12	7	4	5	66	9	92	2	1	4	9	.308	1	0-0	0	4.51	4.55
02	Cin	NL	6	6	0	0	28.0	133	38	24	24	1	0	2	4	17	0	17	1	0	1	3	.250	0	0-0	0	7.52	7.71
	12 ML YEARS		274	273	14	0	1634.2	7205	1658	924	856	152	100	49	55	840	36	1191	77	9	99	90	.524	8	0-0	0	4.72	4.71

Johnny Estrada

Bats: B **Throws:** R **Pos:** C-113; PH-5; DH-2   **Ht:** 5'11" **Wt:** 209 **Born:** 6/27/1976 **Age:** 32

			BATTING																		BASERUNNING				AVERAGES		
Year	Team	Lg	G	AB	H	2B	3B	HR	(Hm	Rd)	TB	R	RBI	RC	TBB	IBB	SO	HBP	SH	SF	SB	CS	SB%	GDP	Avg	OBP	Slg
2001	Phi	NL	89	298	68	15	0	8	(7	1)	107	26	37	25	16	6	32	4	2	4	0	0	-	15	.228	.273	.359
2002	Phi	NL	10	17	2	1	0	0	(0	0)	3	0	2	0	2	1	2	0	0	0	0	0	-	0	.118	.211	.176
2003	Atl	NL	16	36	11	0	0	0	(0	0)	11	2	2	2	0	0	3	0	0	0	0	0	-	1	.306	.359	.306
2004	Atl	NL	134	462	145	36	0	9	(4	5)	208	56	76	78	39	7	66	11	1	4	0	0	-	18	.314	.378	.450
2005	Atl	NL	105	357	93	26	0	4	(2	2)	131	31	39	36	20	6	38	3	0	3	0	0	-	13	.261	.303	.367
2006	Ari	NL	115	414	125	26	0	11	(7	4)	184	43	71	59	13	7	40	7	1	8	0	0	-	17	.302	.328	.444
2007	Mil	NL	120	442	123	25	0	10	(3	7)	178	40	54	41	12	3	43	2	1	7	0	0	-	16	.278	.296	.403
	7 ML YEARS		589	2026	567	129	0	42	(23	19)	822	198	281	241	102	30	224	30	5	26	0	0	-	80	.280	.320	.406

Andre Ethier

Bats: L **Throws:** L **Pos:** RF-102; LF-60; PH-12; PR-2   **Ht:** 6'2" **Wt:** 210 **Born:** 4/10/1982 **Age:** 26

			BATTING																		BASERUNNING				AVERAGES		
Year	Team	Lg	G	AB	H	2B	3B	HR	(Hm	Rd)	TB	R	RBI	RC	TBB	IBB	SO	HBP	SH	SF	SB	CS	SB%	GDP	Avg	OBP	Slg
2003	Vancvr	A-	10	41	16	4	1	1	(-	-)	25	7	7	10	3	1	3	1	0	0	2	1	.67	3	.390	.444	.610
2003	Kane	A	40	162	44	10	0	0	(-	-)	54	23	11	20	19	2	25	2	0	0	2	2	.50	4	.272	.355	.333
2004	Mdest	A+	99	419	131	23	5	7	(-	-)	185	72	53	72	45	0	64	4	1	2	2	5	.29	12	.313	.383	.442
2005	Mdland	AA	131	505	161	30	3	18	(-	-)	251	104	80	97	48	4	93	11	0	8	1	4	.20	18	.319	.385	.497
2005	Scrmto	AAA	4	15	4	1	0	0	(-	-)	5	0	2	1	2	0	3	0	0	0	0	0	-	0	.267	.353	.333
2006	LsVgs	AAA	25	86	30	4	3	1	(-	-)	43	15	12	19	14	0	16	2	0	1	2	1	.67	1	.349	.447	.500
2006	LAD	NL	126	396	122	20	7	11	(9	2)	189	50	55	62	34	2	77	5	0	6	5	5	.50	11	.308	.365	.477
2007	LAD	NL	153	447	127	32	2	13	(8	5)	202	50	64	65	46	12	68	4	0	8	0	4	.00	10	.284	.350	.452
	2 ML YEARS		279	843	249	52	9	24	(17	7)	391	100	119	127	80	14	145	9	0	14	5	9	.36	21	.295	.357	.464

Terry Evans

Bats: R **Throws:** R **Pos:** RF-6; LF-1; DH-1; PH-1; PR-1   **Ht:** 6'3" **Wt:** 205 **Born:** 1/19/1982 **Age:** 26

			BATTING																		BASERUNNING				AVERAGES		
Year	Team	Lg	G	AB	H	2B	3B	HR	(Hm	Rd)	TB	R	RBI	RC	TBB	IBB	SO	HBP	SH	SF	SB	CS	SB%	GDP	Avg	OBP	Slg
2002	JhsCty	R+	60	230	66	22	2	7	(-	-)	113	42	41	43	29	1	67	0	0	2	17	4	.81	5	.287	.364	.491
2003	Peoria	A	104	382	94	28	1	10	(-	-)	154	35	41	45	19	0	86	3	4	2	13	6	.00	8	.246	.286	.403
2004	Peoria	A	101	365	81	21	1	13	(-	-)	143	48	59	45	35	1	105	7	1	1	8	3	.73	7	.222	.301	.392
2004	PlmBh	A+	19	58	13	4	0	2	(-	-)	23	7	7	7	4	0	16	1	0	1	1	0	1.00	0	.224	.281	.397
2005	PlmBh	A+	114	385	85	16	1	8	(-	-)	127	34	47	37	29	1	110	7	1	3	12	6	.67	5	.221	.285	.330
2006	PlmBh	A+	60	238	74	10	1	15	(-	-)	131	43	45	51	20	0	50	4	0	1	21	1	.95	6	.311	.373	.550
2006	Sprgfld	AA	21	75	23	4	0	7	(-	-)	48	13	20	17	3	0	21	5	0	1	5	1	.83	0	.307	.369	.640
2006	Ark	AA	52	188	58	9	2	11	(-	-)	104	48	22	39	18	1	56	6	0	1	11	6	.65	4	.309	.385	.553
2007	Salt Lk	AAA	120	475	150	40	4	15	(-	-)	243	70	75	85	26	1	119	2	2	2	24	9	.73	6	.316	.352	.512
2007	LAA	AL	8	11	1	0	0	1	(1	0)	4	3	2	2	2	0	4	0	0	0	0	0	-	1	.091	.231	.364

Dana Eveland

Pitches: L **Bats:** L **Pos:** RP-4; SP-1   **Ht:** 6'1" **Wt:** 240 **Born:** 10/29/1983 **Age:** 24

			HOW MUCH HE PITCHED						WHAT HE GAVE UP												THE RESULTS							
Year	Team	Lg	G	GS	CG	GF	IP	BFP	H	R	ER	HR	SH	SF	HB	TBB	IBB	SO	WP	Bk	W	L	Pct	ShO	Sv-Op	Hld	ERC	ERA
2007	Visalia*	A+	2	2	0	0	5.0	19	1	1	0	0	0	0	0	2	0	9	0	0	0	0	-	0	0- -	-	0.48	0.00
2007	Tucsn*	AAA	7	5	0	0	27.2	119	29	7	6	0	1	1	0	10	1	15	1	0	1	0	1.000	0	0- -	-	3.43	1.95
2005	Mil	NL	27	0	0	3	31.2	146	40	21	21	2	0	1	1	18	3	23	1	0	1	1	.500	0	1-2	7	6.16	5.97
2006	Mil	NL	9	5	0	1	27.2	141	39	25	25	4	1	1	5	16	2	32	2	0	0	3	.000	0	0-1	8	8.30	8.13
2007	Ari	NL	5	1	0	0	5.0	28	8	8	8	0	0	1	0	5	0	3	1	0	1	0	1.000	0	0-0	0	9.25	14.40
	3 ML YEARS		41	6	0	4	64.1	315	87	54	54	6	1	3	6	39	5	58	4	0	2	4	.333	0	1-3	7	7.31	7.55

Adam Everett

Bats: R **Throws:** R **Pos:** SS-66; PH-1   **Ht:** 6'0" **Wt:** 170 **Born:** 2/5/1977 **Age:** 31

			BATTING																		BASERUNNING				AVERAGES		
Year	Team	Lg	G	AB	H	2B	3B	HR	(Hm	Rd)	TB	R	RBI	RC	TBB	IBB	SO	HBP	SH	SF	SB	CS	SB%	GDP	Avg	OBP	Slg
2001	Hou	NL	9	3	0	0	0	0	(0	0)	0	1	0	0	0	0	1	0	0	0	1	0	1.00	0	.000	.000	.000
2002	Hou	NL	40	88	17	3	0	0	(0	0)	20	11	4	6	12	1	19	1	2	0	3	0	1.00	1	.193	.297	.227
2003	Hou	NL	128	387	99	18	3	8	(5	3)	147	51	51	50	28	6	66	9	11	1	8	1	.89	7	.256	.320	.380
2004	Hou	NL	104	384	105	15	2	8	(5	3)	148	66	31	51	17	0	56	9	22	3	13	2	.87	4	.273	.317	.385
2005	Hou	NL	152	549	136	27	2	11	(7	4)	200	58	54	61	26	1	103	8	8	4	21	7	.75	5	.248	.290	.364
2006	Hou	NL	150	514	123	28	6	6	(2	4)	181	52	59	50	34	5	71	4	10	4	9	6	.60	5	.239	.290	.352
2007	Hou	NL	66	220	51	11	1	2	(1	1)	70	18	15	21	14	0	31	1	1	0	4	2	.67	3	.232	.281	.318
	7 ML YEARS		649	2145	531	102	14	35	(20	15)	766	257	214	239	131	13	347	32	54	12	59	18	.77	25	.248	.299	.357

Scott Eyre

Pitches: L **Bats:** L **Pos:** RP-55   **Ht:** 6'1" **Wt:** 217 **Born:** 5/30/1972 **Age:** 36

			HOW MUCH HE PITCHED						WHAT HE GAVE UP										THE RESULTS							
Year	Team	Lg	G	GS	CG	GF	IP	BFP	H	R	ER	HR	SH	SF	HB	TBB	IBB	SO	WP	Bk	W	L	Pct	ShO	Sv-Op	Hld	ERC	ERA
1997	CWS	AL	11	11	0	0	60.2	267	62	36	34	11	1	2	1	31	1	36	2	0	4	4	.500	0	0-0	0	5.37	5.04
1998	CWS	AL	33	17	0	10	107.0	491	114	78	64	24	2	3	2	64	0	73	7	0	3	8	.273	0	0-0	0	6.31	5.38
1999	CWS	AL	21	0	0	8	25.0	129	38	22	21	6	0	1	1	15	2	17	1	0	1	1	.500	0	0-0	1	9.23	7.56
2000	CWS	AL	13	1	0	3	19.0	93	29	15	14	3	0	2	1	12	0	16	0	0	1	1	.500	0	0-0	0	9.49	6.63
2001	Tor	AL	17	0	0	5	15.2	66	15	6	6	1	0	1	1	7	2	16	2	0	1	2	.333	0	2-3	3	3.96	3.45
2002	2 Tms		70	3	0	6	74.2	333	80	41	37	4	2	4	0	36	8	58	5	0	2	4	.333	0	0-1	18	4.26	4.46
2003	SF	NL	74	0	0	10	57.0	256	60	23	21	4	2	3	1	26	0	35	6	0	2	1	.667	0	1-3	20	4.37	3.32
2004	SF	NL	83	0	0	12	52.2	229	43	26	24	8	3	3	0	27	3	49	3	0	2	2	.500	0	1-5	23	3.67	4.10
2005	SF	NL	86	0	0	15	68.1	277	48	21	20	3	4	3	4	26	0	65	3	0	2	2	.500	0	0-2	32	2.32	2.63
2006	ChC	NL	74	0	0	15	61.1	266	61	25	23	11	2	4	0	30	4	73	6	0	1	3	.250	0	0-3	18	4.94	3.38
2007	ChC	NL	55	0	0	17	52.1	240	59	26	24	3	2	1	1	35	5	45	3	0	2	1	.667	0	0-4	5	5.61	4.13
02	Tor	AL	49	3	0	3	63.1	283	69	37	35	4	2	4	0	29	7	51	4	0	2	4	.333	0	0-1	12	4.32	4.97
02	SF	NL	21	0	0	3	11.1	50	11	4	2	0	0	0	0	7	1	7	1	0	0	0	-	0	0-0	6	3.91	1.59
11 ML YEARS			537	32	0	101	593.2	2647	609	319	288	78	18	27	12	309	25	483	38	0	21	29	.420	0	4-21	120	4.96	4.37

Willie Eyre

Pitches: R **Bats:** R **Pos:** RP-31; SP-2   **Ht:** 6'2" **Wt:** 205 **Born:** 7/21/1978 **Age:** 29

			HOW MUCH HE PITCHED						WHAT HE GAVE UP										THE RESULTS							
Year	Team	Lg	G	GS	CG	GF	IP	BFP	H	R	ER	HR	SH	SF	HB	TBB	IBB	SO	WP	Bk	W	L	Pct	ShO	Sv-Op	Hld	ERC	ERA
1999	Elizab	R+	16	10	1	1	57.2	270	60	38	29	4	2	0	4	34	0	59	7	1	6	3	.667	0	0- -	-	5.00	4.53
1999	QuadC	A	2	2	0	0	12.2	51	8	6	6	0	0	1	1	6	0	10	1	0	1	0	1.000	0	0- -	-	2.13	4.26
2000	QuadC	A	26	18	1	3	99.2	457	104	64	51	9	2	3	5	56	0	81	9	0	5	7	.417	1	0- -	-	5.06	4.61
2001	FtMyrs	A+	17	0	0	6	22.1	87	19	6	6	1	0	0	1	2	0	21	1	0	3	0	1.000	0	4- -	-	2.02	2.42
2001	FtMyrs	A+	32	0	0	10	64.1	280	54	27	18	2	2	7	4	33	2	51	5	0	2	5	.286	0	1- -	-	3.30	2.52
2002	FtMyrs	A+	19	0	0	6	33.2	136	28	9	9	0	1	1	1	13	1	25	1	0	4	1	.800	0	2- -	-	2.62	2.41
2002	NwBrit	AA	28	0	0	9	50.0	209	40	21	18	1	1	2	3	21	0	43	5	0	6	4	.600	0	1- -	-	2.78	3.24
2003	NwBrit	AA	29	10	1	8	96.1	416	93	42	37	6	2	2	6	38	4	66	5	0	6	5	.545	1	0- -	-	3.78	3.46
2003	Roch	AAA	6	5	0	1	24.0	116	30	18	16	2	0	1	2	16	0	23	2	1	0	2	.000	0	0- -	-	6.96	6.00
2004	Roch	AAA	36	21	1	5	136.0	569	131	60	55	13	8	7	4	53	1	91	6	0	6	7	.462	1	4- -	-	4.02	3.64
2005	Roch	AAA	56	0	0	23	82.2	349	79	30	25	3	3	0	4	28	1	74	4	0	10	3	.769	0	7- -	-	3.35	2.72
2007	Okla	AAA	5	0	0	1	7.1	25	2	0	0	0	0	0	0	1	0	8	0	0	1	0	1.000	0	1- -	-	0.31	0.00
2006	Min	AL	42	0	0	20	59.1	275	75	36	35	8	3	1	6	22	4	26	4	0	1	0	1.000	0	0-0	6	6.07	5.31
2007	Tex	AL	33	2	0	10	68.0	307	78	42	39	8	5	1	1	32	4	42	5	0	4	6	.400	0	1-1	1	5.32	5.16
2 ML YEARS			75	2	0	30	127.1	582	153	78	74	16	6	4	7	54	8	68	9	0	5	6	.455	0	1-1	1	5.67	5.23

Brandon Fahey

Bats: L **Throws:** R **Pos:** SS-18; PR-10; 2B-9; LF-7; DH-3; 3B-2; PH-2   **Ht:** 6'2" **Wt:** 170 **Born:** 1/18/1981 **Age:** 27

			BATTING																			BASERUNNING				AVERAGES		
Year	Team	Lg	G	AB	H	2B	3B	HR	(Hm	Rd)	TB	R	RBI	RC	TBB	IBB	SO	HBP	SH	SF	SB	CS	SB%	GDP	Avg	OBP	Slg
2002	Abrdn	A-	63	253	71	10	6	0	(-	-)	93	31	15	30	20	1	34	1	4	2	5	8	.38	1	.281	.333	.368
2003	Frdrck	A+	107	365	85	11	3	1	(-	-)	105	41	22	30	22	0	56	2	13	2	4	2	.67	7	.233	.279	.288
2004	Frdrck	A+	62	181	49	7	0	3	(-	-)	65	20	19	25	22	1	20	2	6	1	3	3	.50	3	.271	.354	.359
2004	Bowie	AA	63	208	49	7	1	1	(-	-)	61	20	15	19	17	0	27	0	7	0	3	1	.75	5	.236	.293	.293
2005	Bowie	AA	139	502	146	21	4	3	(-	-)	184	63	47	70	44	0	71	4	22	6	17	8	.68	12	.291	.349	.367
2006	Ottawa	AAA	20	68	19	1	1	0	(-	-)	22	8	3	10	10	0	5	4	2	0	4	3	.57	1	.279	.402	.324
2007	Norfolk	AAA	91	343	81	8	8	2	(-	-)	111	37	28	36	30	0	46	3	4	3	12	5	.71	7	.236	.301	.324
2006	Bal	AL	91	251	59	8	2	2	(2	0)	77	36	23	27	23	0	48	3	9	0	3	3	.50	2	.235	.307	.307
2007	Bal	AL	40	54	9	1	1	0	(0	0)	12	10	1	2	2	0	9	0	0	0	2	1	.67	1	.167	.196	.222
2 ML YEARS			131	305	68	9	3	2	(2	0)	89	46	24	29	25	0	57	3	9	0	5	4	.56	3	.223	.288	.292

Brian Falkenborg

Pitches: R **Bats:** R **Pos:** RP-16   **Ht:** 6'6" **Wt:** 230 **Born:** 1/18/1978 **Age:** 30

			HOW MUCH HE PITCHED						WHAT HE GAVE UP										THE RESULTS							
Year	Team	Lg	G	GS	CG	GF	IP	BFP	H	R	ER	HR	SH	SF	HB	TBB	IBB	SO	WP	Bk	W	L	Pct	ShO	Sv-Op	Hld	ERC	ERA
2007	Memp*	AAA	51	0	0	42	52.2	230	54	22	19	2	2	3	0	17	2	58	6	0	3	4	.429	0	23- -	-	3.32	3.25
1999	Bal	AL	2	0	0	0	3.0	12	2	0	0	0	0	0	0	2	0	1	0	0	0	0	-	0	0-0	0	2.79	0.00
2004	LAD	NL	6	0	0	1	14.1	73	19	14	12	2	2	0	3	9	0	11	1	0	1	0	1.000	0	0-0	0	8.19	7.53
2005	SD	NL	10	0	0	3	11.0	54	17	11	10	2	0	0	0	5	1	10	2	0	0	0	-	0	0-0	0	8.14	8.18
2006	StL	NL	5	0	0	3	6.1	25	5	2	2	0	1	0	1	0	0	5	0	0	0	1	.000	0	0-0	0	1.57	2.84
2007	StL	NL	16	0	0	2	18.2	84	22	10	10	2	0	0	1	8	0	16	1	0	0	1	.000	0	0-0	1	5.58	4.82
5 ML YEARS			39	0	0	9	53.1	248	65	37	34	6	3	0	5	24	1	43	4	0	1	2	.333	0	0-0	1	6.02	5.74

Kyle Farnsworth

Pitches: R **Bats:** R **Pos:** RP-64   **Ht:** 6'4" **Wt:** 235 **Born:** 4/14/1976 **Age:** 32

			HOW MUCH HE PITCHED						WHAT HE GAVE UP										THE RESULTS							
Year	Team	Lg	G	GS	CG	GF	IP	BFP	H	R	ER	HR	SH	SF	HB	TBB	IBB	SO	WP	Bk	W	L	Pct	ShO	Sv-Op	Hld	ERC	ERA
1999	ChC	NL	27	21	1	1	130.0	579	140	80	73	28	6	2	3	52	1	70	7	1	5	9	.357	1	0-0	0	5.39	5.05
2000	ChC	NL	46	5	0	8	77.0	371	90	58	55	14	4	4	4	50	8	74	3	0	2	9	.182	0	1-6	6	6.72	6.43
2001	ChC	NL	76	0	0	24	82.0	339	65	26	25	8	2	2	1	29	2	107	2	2	4	6	.400	0	2-3	24	2.76	2.74
2002	ChC	NL	45	0	0	17	66.0	301	53	47	38	9	2	5	1	24	7	46	1	0	4	6	.400	0	1-7	6	5.89	7.33
2003	ChC	NL	77	0	0	13	76.1	312	53	31	28	6	4	1	0	36	1	92	6	0	3	2	.600	0	0-3	19	2.58	3.30
2004	ChC	NL	72	0	0	25	66.2	298	67	39	35	10	5	0	2	33	1	78	1	0	4	5	.444	0	0-4	18	4.91	4.73
2005	2 Tms		72	0	0	34	70.0	277	44	18	17	5	2	1	3	27	0	87	3	1	1	1	.500	0	16-18	19	2.12	2.19
2006	NYY	AL	72	0	0	24	66.0	289	62	34	32	8	3	2	1	28	3	75	5	1	3	6	.333	0	6-10	19	3.88	4.36

Year Team	Lg	HOW MUCH HE PITCHED						WHAT HE GAVE UP												THE RESULTS						
		G	GS	CG	GF	IP	BFP	H	R	ER	HR	SH	SF	HB	TBB	IBB	SO	WP	Bk	W	L	Pct	ShO	Sv-Op	Hld	ERC	ERA
2007 NYY	AL	64	0	0	11	60.0	266	60	35	32	9	1	2	2	27	2	48	4	2	2	1	.667	0	0-3	15	4.67	4.80
05 Det	AL	46	0	0	16	42.2	174	29	12	11	1	1	1	1	20	0	55	2	0	1	1	.500	0	6-8	15	2.26	2.32
05 Atl	NL	26	0	0	11	27.1	103	15	6	6	4	1	0	2	7	0	32	1	1	0	0	-	0	10-10	4	1.86	1.98
9 ML YEARS		551	26	1	157	674.2	2944	634	368	335	97	29	19	17	306	25	677	32	7	28	45	.384	1	26-54	126	4.26	4.47

Sal Fasano

Bats: R **Throws:** R **Pos:** C-16   **Ht:** 6'2" **Wt:** 225 **Born:** 8/10/1971 **Age:** 36

Year Team	Lg	BATTING																BASERUNNING				AVERAGES		
		G	AB	H	2B	3B	HR	(Hm | Rd)	TB	R	RBI	RC	TBB	IBB	SO	HBP	SH	SF	SB	CS	SB%	GDP	Avg	OBP	Slg
2007 Syrcse*	AAA	47	145	38	4	0	8	(- | -)	66	18	14	23	6	0	33	11	0	1	1	0	1.00	2	.262	.337	.455
1996 KC	AL	51	143	29	2	0	6	(1 | 5)	49	20	19	13	14	0	25	2	1	0	1	1	.50	3	.203	.283	.343
1997 KC	AL	13	38	8	2	0	1	(0 | 1)	13	4	1	2	1	0	12	0	0	0	0	0	-	1	.211	.231	.342
1998 KC	AL	74	216	49	10	0	8	(4 | 4)	83	21	31	26	10	1	56	16	3	2	1	0	1.00	4	.227	.307	.384
1999 KC	AL	23	60	14	2	0	5	(2 | 3)	31	11	16	12	7	0	17	7	0	1	0	1	.00	1	.233	.373	.517
2000 Oak	AL	52	126	27	6	0	7	(4 | 3)	54	21	19	16	14	0	47	3	0	1	0	0	-	3	.214	.306	.429
2001 3 Tms		39	85	17	5	0	3	(3 | 0)	31	12	9	10	5	0	31	4	2	0	0	0	-	3	.200	.277	.365
2002 LAA	AL	2	1	0	0	0	0	(0 | 0)	0	0	0	0	0	0	1	0	0	0	0	0	-	0	.000	.000	.000
2005 Bal	AL	64	160	40	3	0	11	(1 | 10)	76	25	20	17	9	0	41	5	0	0	0	0	-	5	.250	.310	.475
2006 2 Tms		78	189	41	12	0	5	(2 | 3)	68	12	15	12	7	0	61	6	4	0	0	1	.00	5	.217	.267	.360
2007 Tor	AL	16	45	8	3	0	1	(0 | 1)	14	5	4	2	2	0	19	1	1	0	0	0	-	0	.178	.229	.311
01 Oak	AL	11	21	1	0	0	0	(0 | 0)	1	2	0	0	1	0	12	1	0	0	0	0	-	0	.048	.130	.048
01 KC	AL	3	1	0	0	0	0	(0 | 0)	0	0	0	0	0	0	0	0	0	0	0	0	-	1	.000	.000	.000
01 Col	NL	25	63	16	5	0	3	(3 | 0)	30	10	9	10	4	0	19	3	2	0	0	0	-	2	.254	.329	.476
06 Phi	NL	50	140	34	8	0	4	(2 | 2)	54	9	10	9	5	0	47	3	1	0	0	1	.00	4	.243	.284	.386
06 NYY	AL	28	49	7	4	0	1	(0 | 1)	14	3	5	3	2	0	14	3	3	0	0	0	-	1	.143	.222	.286
10 ML YEARS		412	1063	233	45	0	47	(17 | 30)	419	131	134	110	69	1	310	44	11	4	2	3	.40	25	.219	.293	.394

Ryan Feierabend

Pitches: L **Bats:** L **Pos:** SP-9; RP-4   **Ht:** 6'3" **Wt:** 190 **Born:** 8/22/1985 **Age:** 22

Year Team	Lg	HOW MUCH HE PITCHED						WHAT HE GAVE UP												THE RESULTS						
		G	GS	CG	GF	IP	BFP	H	R	ER	HR	SH	SF	HB	TBB	IBB	SO	WP	Bk	W	L	Pct	ShO	Sv-Op	Hld	ERC	ERA
2003 Ms	R	6	5	0	1	20.2	89	23	11	6	0	1	1	1	6	0	12	1	1	2	3	.400	0	1--	-	3.79	2.61
2004 Wisc	A	26	26	1	0	161.0	666	158	78	65	17	4	10	7	44	0	100	14	0	9	7	.563	1	0--	-	3.77	3.63
2005 InldEm	A+	29	29	0	0	150.2	689	186	80	65	16	5	1	8	51	0	122	3	0	8	7	.533	0	0--	-	5.38	3.88
2006 SnAnt	AA	28	28	0	0	153.2	654	156	87	73	16	1	6	7	55	1	127	6	1	9	12	.429	0	0--	-	4.27	4.28
2007 Tacom	AAA	19	19	1	0	108.1	475	131	57	48	9	6	2	5	30	0	70	6	0	6	4	.600	0	0--	-	5.04	3.99
2006 Sea	AL	4	2	0	2	17.0	73	15	7	7	3	1	0	0	7	0	11	1	2	0	1	.000	0	0-0	0	3.91	3.71
2007 Sea	AL	13	9	0	0	49.1	236	73	44	44	10	0	2	4	23	2	27	3	0	1	6	.143	0	0-0	0	8.71	8.03
2 ML YEARS		17	11	0	2	66.1	000	88	51	51	13	1	2	4	30	2	38	4	2	1	7	.125	0	0-0	0	7.37	6.92

Scott Feldman

Pitches: R **Bats:** L **Pos:** RP-29   **Ht:** 6'5" **Wt:** 210 **Born:** 2/7/1983 **Age:** 25

Year Team	Lg	HOW MUCH HE PITCHED						WHAT HE GAVE UP												THE RESULTS						
		G	GS	CG	GF	IP	BFP	H	R	ER	HR	SH	SF	HB	TBB	IBB	SO	WP	Bk	W	L	Pct	ShO	Sv-Op	Hld	ERC	ERA
2007 Okla	AAA	21	0	0	13	30.0	129	28	18	15	1	0	2	1	12	2	24	5	0	1	1	.500	0	2--	3	3.24	4.50
2005 Tex	AL	8	0	0	3	9.1	37	9	1	1	0	0	0	0	2	1	4	0	0	0	1	.000	0	0-0	1	2.48	0.96
2006 Tex	AL	36	0	0	5	41.1	175	42	19	18	4	2	1	4	10	0	30	0	0	0	2	.000	0	0-1	7	3.94	3.92
2007 Tex	AL	29	0	0	10	39.0	192	44	26	25	3	0	2	3	32	5	19	2	2	1	2	.333	0	0-0	0	6.40	5.77
3 ML YEARS		73	0	0	18	89.2	404	95	46	44	7	2	3	7	44	6	53	2	2	1	5	.167	0	0-1	8	4.82	4.42

Pedro Feliciano

Pitches: L **Bats:** L **Pos:** RP-78   **Ht:** 5'10" **Wt:** 192 **Born:** 8/25/1976 **Age:** 31

Year Team	Lg	HOW MUCH HE PITCHED						WHAT HE GAVE UP												THE RESULTS						
		G	GS	CG	GF	IP	BFP	H	R	ER	HR	SH	SF	HB	TBB	IBB	SO	WP	Bk	W	L	Pct	ShO	Sv-Op	Hld	ERC	ERA
2002 NYM	NL	6	0	0	3	6.0	26	9	5	5	0	0	0	0	1	0	4	0	0	0	0	-	0	0-0	0	5.56	7.50
2003 NYM	NL	23	0	0	8	48.1	218	52	21	18	5	0	1	3	21	3	43	3	1	0	0	-	0	0-0	0	4.77	3.35
2004 NYM	NL	22	0	0	8	18.1	82	14	12	11	2	1	1	1	12	0	14	1	0	1	1	.500	0	0-0	2	3.93	5.40
2006 NYM	NL	64	0	0	10	60.1	256	56	15	14	4	4	3	3	20	1	54	1	0	7	2	.778	0	0-3	10	3.34	2.09
2007 NYM	NL	78	0	0	12	64.0	275	47	26	22	3	2	2	5	31	4	61	1	1	2	2	.500	0	2-3	18	2.74	3.09
5 ML YEARS		193	0	0	36	197.0	857	178	79	70	14	7	7	12	85	8	176	6	2	10	5	.667	0	2-6	30	3.59	3.20

Pedro Feliz

Bats: R **Throws:** R **Pos:** 3B-143; PH-6; 1B-4; LF-2; C-1; RF-1   **Ht:** 6'1" **Wt:** 210 **Born:** 4/27/1975 **Age:** 33

Year Team	Lg	BATTING																BASERUNNING				AVERAGES		
		G	AB	H	2B	3B	HR	(Hm | Rd)	TB	R	RBI	RC	TBB	IBB	SO	HBP	SH	SF	SB	CS	SB%	GDP	Avg	OBP	Slg
2000 SF	NL	8	7	2	0	0	0	(0 | 0)	2	1	0	1	0	0	1	0	0	0	0	0	-	0	.286	.286	.286
2001 SF	NL	94	220	50	9	1	7	(3 | 4)	82	23	22	20	10	2	50	2	3	3	2	1	.67	5	.227	.264	.373
2002 SF	NL	67	146	37	4	1	2	(1 | 1)	49	14	13	12	6	1	27	0	0	0	0	0	-	2	.253	.281	.336
2003 SF	NL	95	235	58	9	3	16	(6 | 10)	121	31	48	34	10	0	53	1	1	2	2	2	.50	7	.247	.278	.515
2004 SF	NL	144	503	139	33	3	22	(11 | 11)	244	72	84	56	23	8	85	0	0	5	5	2	.71	18	.276	.305	.485
2005 SF	NL	156	569	142	30	4	20	(10 | 10)	240	69	81	58	38	1	102	1	1	6	0	2	.00	20	.250	.295	.422
2006 SF	NL	160	603	147	35	5	22	(6 | 16)	258	75	98	71	33	4	112	1	1	6	1	1	.50	18	.244	.281	.428
2007 SF	NL	150	557	141	28	2	20	(8 | 12)	233	61	72	67	29	2	70	1	0	3	2	2	.50	15	.253	.290	.418
8 ML YEARS		874	2840	716	148	19	109	(45 | 64)	1229	346	418	319	149	11	500	6	6	26	12	10	.55	85	.252	.288	.433

Robert Fick

Bats: L **Throws:** R **Pos:** 1B-84; PH-26; LF-14; PR-8; RF-7   **Ht:** 6'1" **Wt:** 200 **Born:** 3/15/1974 **Age:** 34

Year Team	Lg	G	AB	H	2B	3B	HR	(Hm	Rd)	TB	R	RBI	RC	TBB	IBB	SO	HBP	SH	SF	SB	CS	SB%	GDP	Avg	OBP	Slg
1998 Det	AL	7	22	8	1	0	3	(0	3)	18	6	7	6	2	0	7	0	0	0	1	0	1.00	1	.364	.417	.818
1999 Det	AL	15	41	9	0	0	3	(1	2)	18	6	10	6	7	0	6	0	0	1	1	0	1.00	1	.220	.327	.439
2000 Det	AL	66	163	41	7	2	3	(0	3)	61	18	22	21	22	2	39	1	0	2	2	1	.67	4	.252	.340	.374
2001 Det	AL	124	401	109	21	2	19	(8	11)	191	62	61	62	39	3	62	4	0	4	0	3	.00	10	.272	.339	.476
2002 Det	AL	148	556	150	36	2	17	(12	5)	241	66	63	70	46	4	90	7	0	5	0	1	.00	17	.270	.331	.433
2003 Atl	NL	126	409	110	26	1	11	(4	7)	171	52	80	68	42	4	47	2	0	7	1	0	1.00	9	.269	.335	.418
2004 2 Tms		89	226	45	5	2	6	(3	3)	72	14	26	22	22	2	36	3	0	2	0	0	-	2	.199	.277	.319
2005 SD	NL	93	230	61	10	2	3	(0	3)	84	25	30	29	26	2	33	1	1	2	0	2	.00	4	.265	.340	.365
2006 Was	NL	60	128	34	4	0	2	(1	1)	44	14	9	11	10	1	24	1	2	0	1	1	.50	4	.266	.324	.344
2007 Was	NL	118	197	46	6	1	2	(1	1)	60	24	16	17	19	1	42	3	1	1	0	1	.00	9	.234	.309	.305
04 TB	AL	76	214	43	5	2	6	(3	3)	70	12	26	21	20	2	32	2	0	2	0	0	-	2	.201	.273	.327
04 SD	NL	13	12	2	0	0	0	(0	0)	2	2	0	1	2	0	4	1	0	0	0	0	-	0	.167	.333	.167
10 ML YEARS		846	2373	613	116	12	69	(30	39)	960	287	324	312	235	19	386	22	4	24	6	9	.40	61	.258	.328	.405

Nate Field

Pitches: R **Bats:** R **Pos:** RP-1   **Ht:** 6'2" **Wt:** 200 **Born:** 12/11/1975 **Age:** 32

Year Team	Lg	G	GS	CG	GF	IP	BFP	H	R	ER	HR	SH	SF	HB	TBB	IBB	SO	WP	Bk	W	L	Pct	ShO	Sv-Op	Hld	ERC	ERA
2007 Albq*	AAA	44	0	0	26	46.1	197	37	20	18	6	2	1	2	17	1	45	8	0	6	6	.500	0	11--	-	3.09	3.50
2002 KC	AL	5	0	0	0	5.0	26	8	5	5	2	1	0	0	3	1	3	2	0	0	-	0	0-0	-	10.82	9.00
2003 KC	AL	19	0	0	7	21.2	97	19	10	10	3	0	1	1	14	1	19	0	0	1	1	.500	0	0-0	2	4.74	4.15
2004 KC	AL	43	0	0	23	44.1	191	40	25	21	5	1	2	2	19	2	30	2	0	2	3	.400	0	3-5	2	3.82	4.26
2005 KC	AL	7	0	0	3	6.2	35	13	7	7	1	0	0	0	5	2	4	1	0	0	-	0	0-0	1	12.38	9.45
2006 Col	NL	14	0	0	1	9.0	40	9	4	4	2	0	0	0	5	1	14	1	0	1	1	.500	0	0-1	0	5.45	4.00
2007 Fla	NL	1	0	0	1	1.0	7	3	3	3	0	0	0	0	1	0	2	0	0	0	-	0	0-0	0	19.55	27.00
6 ML YEARS		89	0	0	35	87.2	396	92	54	50	13	2	3	3	47	7	72	6	0	4	5	.444	0	3-6	9	5.28	5.13

Prince Fielder

Bats: L **Throws:** R **Pos:** 1B-153; DH-4; PH-2   **Ht:** 6'0" **Wt:** 260 **Born:** 5/9/1984 **Age:** 24

Year Team	Lg	G	AB	H	2B	3B	HR	(Hm	Rd)	TB	R	RBI	RC	TBB	IBB	SO	HBP	SH	SF	SB	CS	SB%	GDP	Avg	OBP	Slg
2005 Mil	NL	39	59	17	4	0	2	(2	0)	27	2	10	10	2	0	17	0	0	1	0	0	-	0	.288	.306	.458
2006 Mil	NL	157	569	154	35	1	28	(11	17)	275	82	81	84	59	5	125	12	0	8	7	2	.78	17	.271	.347	.483
2007 Mil	NL	158	573	165	35	2	50	(27	23)	354	109	119	125	90	21	121	14	0	4	2	2	.50	9	.288	.395	.618
3 ML YEARS		354	1201	336	74	3	80	(40	40)	656	193	210	219	151	26	263	26	0	13	9	4	.69	26	.280	.369	.546

Josh Fields

Bats: R **Throws:** R **Pos:** 3B-79; LF-21   **Ht:** 6'1" **Wt:** 215 **Born:** 12/14/1982 **Age:** 25

Year Team	Lg	G	AB	H	2B	3B	HR	(Hm	Rd)	TB	R	RBI	RC	TBB	IBB	SO	HBP	SH	SF	SB	CS	SB%	GDP	Avg	OBP	Slg
2004 WinSa	A+	66	256	73	12	4	7	(-	-)	114	36	39	38	18	1	74	2	0	3	0	0	-	2	.285	.333	.445
2005 Brham	AA	134	477	120	27	0	16	(-	-)	195	76	79	70	55	2	142	13	9	6	7	6	.54	4	.252	.341	.409
2006 Charltt	AAA	124	462	141	32	4	19	(-	-)	238	85	70	94	54	2	136	3	4	3	28	5	.85	6	.305	.379	.515
2007 Charltt	AAA	56	205	58	14	0	10	(-	-)	102	28	37	42	39	1	60	1	0	4	8	5	.62	3	.283	.394	.498
2006 CWS	AL	11	20	3	2	0	1	(1	0)	8	4	2	1	5	0	8	0	0	0	0	0	-	0	.150	.320	.400
2007 CWS	AL	100	373	91	17	1	23	(15	8)	179	54	67	56	35	0	125	1	6	3	1	1	.50	11	.244	.308	.480
2 ML YEARS		111	393	94	19	1	24	(16	8)	187	58	69	57	40	0	133	1	6	3	1	1	.50	11	.239	.309	.476

Chone Figgins

Bats: B **Throws:** R **Pos:** 3B-99; RF-11; 2B-9; DH-1; PH-1; PR-1   **Ht:** 5'8" **Wt:** 180 **Born:** 1/22/1978 **Age:** 30

Year Team	Lg	G	AB	H	2B	3B	HR	(Hm	Rd)	TB	R	RBI	RC	TBB	IBB	SO	HBP	SH	SF	SB	CS	SB%	GDP	Avg	OBP	Slg
2007 Salt Lk*	AAA	4	14	5	1	0	0	(-	-)	6	3	1	2	1	0	0	0	0	0	0	1	.00	0	.357	.400	.429
2002 LAA	AL	15	12	2	1	0	0	(0	0)	3	6	1	0	0	0	5	0	0	0	2	1	.67	1	.167	.167	.250
2003 LAA	AL	71	240	71	9	4	0	(0	0)	88	34	27	39	20	0	38	0	6	4	13	7	.65	1	.296	.345	.367
2004 LAA	AL	148	577	171	22	17	5	(3	2)	242	83	60	93	49	0	94	0	10	2	34	13	.72	6	.296	.350	.419
2005 LAA	AL	158	642	186	25	10	8	(2	6)	255	113	57	94	64	1	101	0	9	5	62	17	.78	9	.290	.352	.397
2006 LAA	AL	155	604	161	23	8	9	(2	7)	227	93	62	84	65	1	100	2	5	7	52	16	.76	7	.267	.336	.376
2007 LAA	AL	115	442	146	24	6	3	(1	2)	191	81	58	88	51	0	81	0	2	8	41	12	.77	7	.330	.393	.432
6 ML YEARS		662	2517	737	104	45	25	(8	17)	1006	410	265	398	249	2	419	2	32	26	204	66	.76	30	.293	.354	.400

Luis Figueroa

Bats: B **Throws:** R **Pos:** PH-5; SS-1; LF-1   **Ht:** 5'9" **Wt:** 185 **Born:** 2/16/1974 **Age:** 34

Year Team	Lg	G	AB	H	2B	3B	HR	(Hm	Rd)	TB	R	RBI	RC	TBB	IBB	SO	HBP	SH	SF	SB	CS	SB%	GDP	Avg	OBP	Slg
2007 Fresno*	AAA	117	443	134	22	4	4	(-	-)	176	68	53	62	28	0	34	5	13	3	7	9	.44	11	.302	.349	.397
2001 Pit	NL	4	2	0	0	0	0	(0	0)	0	0	0	0	0	0	0	0	0	0	0	0	-	0	.000	.000	.000
2006 Tor	AL	8	9	1	1	0	0	(0	0)	2	1	0	0	0	0	2	0	0	0	0	0	-	0	.111	.111	.222
2007 SF	NL	6	5	1	0	0	0	(0	0)	1	1	0	0	0	0	0	0	0	0	0	0	-	0	.200	.200	.200
3 ML YEARS		18	16	2	1	0	0	(0	0)	3	2	0	0	0	0	2	0	0	0	0	0	-	0	.125	.125	.188

Steve Finley

Bats: L **Throws:** L **Pos:** CF-26; PH-22; RF-3   **Ht:** 6'2" **Wt:** 195 **Born:** 3/12/1965 **Age:** 43

												BATTING									BASERUNNING				AVERAGES		
Year	Team	Lg	G	AB	H	2B	3B	HR	(Hm	Rd)	TB	R	RBI	RC	TBB	IBB	SO	HBP	SH	SF	SB	CS	SB%	GDP	Avg	OBP	Slg
1989	Bal	AL	81	217	54	5	2	2	(0	2)	69	35	25	23	15	1	30	1	6	2	17	3	.85	3	.249	.298	.318
1990	Bal	AL	142	464	119	16	4	3	(1	2)	152	46	37	47	32	3	53	2	10	5	22	9	.71	8	.256	.304	.328
1991	Hou	NL	159	596	170	28	10	8	(0	8)	242	84	54	80	42	5	65	2	10	6	34	18	.65	8	.285	.331	.406
1992	Hou	NL	**162**	607	177	29	13	5	(5	0)	247	84	55	93	58	6	63	3	16	2	44	9	.83	10	.292	.355	.407
1993	Hou	NL	142	545	145	15	13	8	(1	7)	210	69	44	64	28	1	65	3	6	3	19	6	.76	8	.266	.304	.385
1994	Hou	NL	94	373	103	16	5	11	(4	7)	162	64	33	54	28	0	52	2	13	1	13	7	.65	3	.276	.329	.434
1995	SD	NL	139	562	167	23	8	10	(4	6)	236	104	44	90	59	5	62	3	4	2	36	12	.75	8	.297	.366	.420
1996	SD	NL	161	655	195	45	9	30	(15	15)	348	126	95	117	56	5	87	4	1	5	22	8	.73	20	.298	.354	.531
1997	SD	NL	143	560	146	26	5	28	(5	23)	266	101	92	84	43	2	92	3	2	7	15	3	.83	10	.261	.313	.475
1998	SD	NL	159	619	154	40	6	14	(8	6)	248	92	67	76	45	0	103	3	3	4	12	3	.80	9	.249	.301	.401
1999	Ari	NL	156	590	156	32	10	34	(17	17)	310	100	103	105	63	7	94	3	2	5	8	4	.67	4	.264	.336	.525
2000	Ari	NL	152	539	151	27	5	35	(17	18)	293	100	96	104	65	7	87	8	2	0	12	6	.67	9	.280	.361	.544
2001	Ari	NL	140	495	136	27	4	14	(8	6)	213	66	73	71	47	9	67	1	2	3	11	7	.61	8	.275	.337	.430
2002	Ari	NL	150	505	145	24	4	25	(14	11)	252	82	89	94	65	7	73	3	1	3	16	4	.80	10	.287	.370	.499
2003	Ari	NL	147	516	148	24	10	22	(10	12)	258	82	70	85	57	4	94	6	0	3	15	8	.65	10	.287	.363	.500
2004	2 Tms		**162**	628	170	28	1	36	(23	13)	308	92	94	86	61	1	82	1	9	7	9	7	.56	14	.271	.333	.490
2005	LAA	AL	112	406	90	20	3	12	(3	9)	152	41	54	39	26	3	71	3	1	4	8	4	.67	6	.222	.271	.374
2006	SF	NL	139	426	105	21	12	6	(2	4)	168	66	40	52	46	2	55	2	3	4	7	0	1.00	6	.246	.320	.394
2007	Col	NL	43	94	17	3	0	1	(0	1)	23	9	2	3	8	1	4	0	0	0	0	0	-	2	.181	.245	.245
04	Ari	NL	104	404	111	16	1	23	(14	9)	198	61	48	52	40	1	52	1	6	5	8	4	.67	9	.275	.338	.490
04	LAD	NL	58	224	59	12	0	13	(9	4)	110	31	46	34	21	0	30	0	3	2	1	3	.25	5	.263	.324	.491
19 ML YEARS			2583	9397	2548	449	124	304	(138	166)	4157	1443	1167	1367	844	69	1299	53	91	75	320	118	.73	152	.271	.332	.442

Jesus Flores

Bats: R **Throws:** R **Pos:** C-55; PH-27   **Ht:** 6'1" **Wt:** 185 **Born:** 10/26/1984 **Age:** 23

												BATTING									BASERUNNING				AVERAGES		
Year	Team	Lg	G	AB	H	2B	3B	HR	(Hm	Rd)	TB	R	RBI	RC	TBB	IBB	SO	HBP	SH	SF	SB	CS	SB%	GDP	Avg	OBP	Slg
2004	Mets	R	45	141	45	12	3	4	(-	-)	75	16	25	27	8	0	26	4	1	2	1	1	.50	2	.319	.368	.532
2004	Bklyn	A-	3	6	2	0	0	1	(-	-)	5	1	3	1	0	0	1	0	0	0	0	0	-	1	.333	.333	.833
2005	Hgrstn	A	82	319	69	18	0	7	(-	-)	108	34	42	26	12	0	90	3	1	2	2	2	.50	6	.216	.250	.339
2006	StLuci	A+	120	429	114	32	0	21	(-	-)	209	66	70	72	28	1	127	18	2	3	2	0	1.00	6	.266	.335	.487
2007	Was	NL	79	180	44	9	0	4	(1	3)	65	21	25	19	14	0	48	3	0	0	0	1	.00	5	.244	.310	.361

Randy Flores

Pitches: L **Bats:** L **Pos:** RP-70   **Ht:** 6'0" **Wt:** 190 **Born:** 7/31/1975 **Age:** 32

			HOW MUCH HE PITCHED						WHAT HE GAVE UP												THE RESULTS							
Year	Team	Lg	G	GS	CG	GF	IP	BFP	H	R	ER	HR	SH	SF	HB	TBB	IBB	SO	WP	Bk	W	L	Pct	ShO	Sv-Op	Hld	ERC	ERA
2002	2 Tms		28	2	0	9	29.0	140	40	26	24	7	2	2	3	16	3	14	4	0	0	2	.000	0	1-2	2	8.69	7.45
2004	StL	NL	9	1	0	3	14.0	57	13	3	3	0	1	1	3	3	1	7	0	0	1	0	1.000	0	0-0	0	3.15	1.93
2005	StL	NL	50	0	0	6	41.2	174	37	22	16	5	1	3	3	13	0	43	2	0	3	1	.750	0	1-3	11	3.55	3.46
2006	StL	NL	65	0	0	10	41.2	196	49	29	26	5	3	1	1	22	3	40	1	0	1	1	.500	0	0-1	18	5.64	5.62
2007	StL	NL	70	0	0	11	55.0	253	71	31	26	2	4	2	3	15	0	47	3	0	3	0	1.000	0	1-2	14	4.87	4.25
02	Tex	AL	20	0	0	5	12.0	52	11	7	6	2	1	2	0	8	2	7	3	0	0	0	-	0	1-2	2	5.07	4.50
02	Col	NL	8	2	0	4	17.0	88	29	19	18	5	1	0	3	8	1	7	1	0	0	2	.000	0	0-0	0	11.52	9.53
5 ML YEARS			222	3	0	39	181.1	820	210	111	95	19	11	9	13	69	7	151	10	0	8	4	.667	0	3-8	45	5.15	4.72

Ron Flores

Pitches: L **Bats:** L **Pos:** RP-17   **Ht:** 5'10" **Wt:** 193 **Born:** 8/9/1979 **Age:** 28

			HOW MUCH HE PITCHED						WHAT HE GAVE UP												THE RESULTS							
Year	Team	Lg	G	GS	CG	GF	IP	BFP	H	R	ER	HR	SH	SF	HB	TBB	IBB	SO	WP	Bk	W	L	Pct	ShO	Sv-Op	Hld	ERC	ERA
2007	Scrmto*	AAA	40	0	0	4	36.1	166	38	22	11	4	4	1	1	17	5	26	2	1	1	2	.333	0	1-	-	4.41	2.72
2005	Oak	AL	11	0	0	4	8.2	34	8	1	1	1	0	0	0	0	0	6	1	0	0	0	-	0	0-0	1	2.22	1.04
2006	Oak	AL	25	0	0	11	29.2	122	28	11	11	3	0	2	0	10	2	20	1	0	1	2	.333	0	1-1	3	3.51	3.34
2007	Oak	AL	17	0	0	4	17.2	81	16	8	7	2	0	1	0	12	5	15	0	0	0	2	.000	0	0-1	1	4.14	3.57
3 ML YEARS			53	0	0	19	56.0	237	52	20	19	6	0	3	0	22	7	41	2	0	1	4	.200	0	1-2	3	3.51	3.05

Cliff Floyd

Bats: L **Throws:** R **Pos:** RF-63; PH-30; LF-17; DH-2   **Ht:** 6'4" **Wt:** 230 **Born:** 12/5/1972 **Age:** 35

												BATTING									BASERUNNING				AVERAGES		
Year	Team	Lg	G	AB	H	2B	3B	HR	(Hm	Rd)	TB	R	RBI	RC	TBB	IBB	SO	HBP	SH	SF	SB	CS	SB%	GDP	Avg	OBP	Slg
1993	Mon	NL	10	31	7	0	0	1	(0	1)	10	3	2	2	0	0	9	0	0	0	0	0	-	0	.226	.226	.323
1994	Mon	NL	100	334	94	19	4	4	(2	2)	133	43	41	46	24	0	63	3	2	3	10	3	.77	3	.281	.332	.398
1995	Mon	NL	29	69	9	1	0	1	(1	0)	13	6	8	2	7	0	22	1	0	0	3	0	1.00	1	.130	.221	.188
1996	Mon	NL	117	227	55	15	4	6	(3	3)	96	29	26	35	30	1	52	5	1	3	7	1	.88	3	.242	.340	.423
1997	Fla	NL	61	137	32	9	1	6	(2	4)	61	23	19	23	24	0	33	2	1	1	6	2	.75	3	.234	.354	.445
1998	Fla	NL	153	588	166	45	3	22	(10	12)	283	85	90	92	47	7	112	3	0	3	27	14	.66	10	.282	.337	.481
1999	Fla	NL	69	251	76	19	1	11	(4	7)	130	37	49	45	30	5	47	2	0	2	5	6	.45	4	.303	.379	.518
2000	Fla	NL	121	420	126	30	0	22	(13	9)	222	91	79	92	50	5	82	8	0	9	24	3	.89	4	.300	.378	.529
2001	Fla	NL	149	555	176	44	4	31	(16	15)	321	123	103	121	59	12	101	10	0	5	18	3	.86	9	.317	.390	.578
2002	3 Tms	NL	146	520	150	43	4	28	(13	15)	277	86	79	92	76	19	106	10	0	5	15	5	.75	6	.288	.388	.533
2003	NYM	NL	108	365	106	25	2	18	(10	8)	189	57	68	68	51	2	66	3	0	6	3	0	1.00	10	.290	.376	.518
2004	NYM	NL	113	396	103	26	0	18	(7	11)	183	55	63	64	47	6	103	11	0	3	11	4	.73	8	.260	.352	.462
2005	NYM	NL	150	550	150	22	2	34	(21	13)	278	85	98	99	63	13	98	11	0	5	12	2	.86	5	.273	.358	.505
2006	NYM	NL	97	332	81	19	1	11	(5	6)	135	45	44	45	29	3	58	12	0	3	6	0	1.00	5	.244	.324	.407

Year	Team	Lg	G	AB	H	2B	3B	HR	(Hm	Rd)	TB	R	RBI	RC	TBB	IBB	SO	HBP	SH	SF	SB	CS	SB%	GDP	Avg	OBP	Slg
2007	ChC	NL	108	282	80	10	1	9	(3	6)	119	40	45	43	35	5	47	5	0	0	0	0	-	6	.284	.373	.422
02	Fla	NL	84	296	85	20	0	18	(7	11)	159	49	57	64	58	18	68	7	0	1	10	5	.67	0	.287	.414	.537
02	Mon	NL	15	53	11	2	0	3	(3	0)	22	7	4	2	3	1	10	1	0	0	1	0	1.00	0	.208	.263	.415
02	Bos	AL	47	171	54	21	0	7	(3	4)	96	30	18	26	15	0	28	2	0	2	2	0	1.00	6	.316	.374	.561
15 ML YEARS			1531	5057	1411	327	23	222	(110	112)	2450	792	826	866	572	85	999	86	4	43	147	43	.77	81	.279	.359	.484

Gavin Floyd

Pitches: R Bats: R Pos: SP-10; RP-6   Ht: 6'4" Wt: 225 Born: 1/27/1983 Age: 25

			HOW MUCH HE PITCHED					WHAT HE GAVE UP										THE RESULTS						
Year	Team	Lg	G	GS	CG	GF	IP	BFP	H	R	ER	HR	SH	SF	HB	TBB	IBB	SO	WP	Bk	W	L	Pct	ShO	Sv-Op	Hld	ERC	ERA
2007	Charltt*	AAA	17	17	0	0	106.2	442	93	39	37	9	4	0	7	34	0	96	3	1	7	3	.700	0	0- -	-	3.25	3.12
2004	Phi	NL	6	4	0	0	28.1	126	25	11	11	1	1	0	5	16	0	24	1	1	2	0	1.000	0	0-0	0	4.33	3.49
2005	Phi	NL	7	4	0	0	26.0	127	30	31	29	5	1	1	3	16	2	17	2	0	1	2	.333	0	0-0	0	6.82	10.04
2006	Phi	NL	11	11	1	0	54.1	264	70	48	44	14	2	5	3	32	3	34	2	0	4	3	.571	1	0-0	0	8.02	7.29
2007	CWS	AL	16	10	0	4	70.0	314	85	45	41	17	3	2	6	19	0	49	1	0	1	5	.167	0	0-0	0	6.22	5.27
4 ML YEARS			40	29	1	4	178.2	831	210	135	125	37	7	8	17	83	5	124	6	1	8	10	.444	1	0-0	0	6.55	6.30

Josh Fogg

Pitches: R Bats: R Pos: SP-29; RP-1   Ht: 6'0" Wt: 205 Born: 12/13/1976 Age: 31

			HOW MUCH HE PITCHED					WHAT HE GAVE UP										THE RESULTS						
Year	Team	Lg	G	GS	CG	GF	IP	BFP	H	R	ER	HR	SH	SF	HB	TBB	IBB	SO	WP	Bk	W	L	Pct	ShO	Sv-Op	Hld	ERC	ERA
2007	ColSpr*	AAA	1	1	0	0	5.0	22	6	3	2	0	0	0	0	0	0	3	0	0	0	1	.000	0	0- -	-	2.73	3.60
2001	CWS	AL	11	0	0	4	13.1	53	10	3	3	0	0	1	3	1	1	17	0	0	0	0	-	0	0-0	2	1.73	2.03
2002	Pit	NL	33	33	0	0	194.1	832	199	102	94	28	6	3	8	69	12	113	2	0	12	12	.500	1	0-0	0	4.46	4.35
2003	Pit	NL	26	26	1	0	142.0	625	166	90	83	22	6	4	9	40	0	71	0	0	10	9	.526	0	0-0	0	5.25	5.26
2004	Pit	NL	32	32	0	0	178.1	770	193	98	92	17	9	6	8	66	8	82	4	1	11	10	.524	0	0-0	0	4.59	4.64
2005	Pit	NL	34	28	0	1	169.1	742	196	106	95	27	4	6	6	53	11	85	2	1	6	11	.353	0	0-0	0	5.13	5.05
2006	Col	NL	31	31	1	0	172.0	765	206	115	105	24	6	5	6	60	13	93	3	0	11	9	.550	0	0-0	0	5.36	5.49
2007	Col	NL	30	29	0	0	165.2	745	194	99	91	23	5	5	13	59	7	94	3	0	10	9	.526	0	0-0	0	5.44	4.94
7 ML YEARS			197	179	2	5	1035.0	4532	1164	613	563	141	36	30	51	350	52	555	16	2	60	60	.500	1	0-0	2	4.97	4.90

Mike Fontenot

Bats: L Throws: R Pos: 2B-62; PH-25; SS-3   Ht: 5'8" Wt: 170 Born: 6/9/1980 Age: 28

			BATTING																	BASERUNNING				AVERAGES		
Year	Team	Lg	G	AB	H	2B	3B	HR	(Hm	Rd)	TB	R	RBI	RC	TBB	IBB	SO	HBP	SH	SF	SB	CS	SB%	GDP	Avg	OBP	Slg
2002	Frdrck	A+	122	481	127	16	4	8	(-	-)	175	61	53	61	42	1	117	10	9	5	13	9	.59	3	.264	.333	.364
2003	Bowie	AA	126	449	146	24	5	12	(-	-)	216	63	66	89	50	3	89	8	4	4	16	5	.76	6	.325	.399	.481
2004	Ottawa	AAA	136	524	146	30	10	8	(-	-)	220	73	49	80	48	0	111	9	4	5	14	7	.67	9	.279	.346	.420
2005	Iowa	AAA	111	379	103	22	10	6	(-	-)	163	60	39	66	59	3	77	6	3	2	3	2	.60	4	.272	.377	.430
2006	Iowa	AAA	111	362	107	28	2	8	(-	-)	163	54	36	63	47	2	64	2	2	5	5	4	.56	4	.296	.375	.450
2007	Iowa	AAA	55	211	71	17	4	6	(-	-)	114	46	34	43	16	2	32	1	2	1	3	1	.75	10	.336	.384	.540
2005	ChC	NL	7	2	0	0	0	0	(0	0)	0	4	0	1	2	0	1	0	0	0	0	0	-	0	.000	.600	.000
2007	ChC	NL	86	234	65	12	4	3	(2	1)	94	32	29	26	22	0	43	0	1	3	5	4	.56	5	.278	.336	.402
2 ML YEARS			93	236	65	12	4	3	(2	1)	94	36	29	27	24	0	43	1	1	3	5	4	.56	5	.275	.341	.398

Lew Ford

Bats: R Throws: R Pos: LF-35; CF-14; PR-8; PH-7; RF-3; DH-3   Ht: 6'0" Wt: 200 Born: 8/12/1976 Age: 31

			BATTING																	BASERUNNING				AVERAGES		
Year	Team	Lg	G	AB	H	2B	3B	HR	(Hm	Rd)	TB	R	RBI	RC	TBB	IBB	SO	HBP	SH	SF	SB	CS	SB%	GDP	Avg	OBP	Slg
2007	Roch*	AAA	35	122	32	12	0	2	(-	-)	50	14	17	18	17	0	30	0	0	0	2	1	.67	2	.262	.353	.410
2003	Min	AL	34	73	24	7	1	3	(2	1)	42	16	15	16	8	0	9	1	1	0	2	0	1.00	1	.329	.402	.575
2004	Min	AL	154	569	170	31	4	15	(6	9)	254	89	72	101	67	3	75	13	2	7	20	2	.91	15	.299	.381	.446
2005	Min	AL	147	522	138	30	4	7	(6	1)	197	70	53	70	45	2	85	16	2	5	13	6	.68	9	.264	.338	.377
2006	Min	AL	104	234	53	6	1	4	(2	2)	73	40	18	22	16	0	43	4	1	0	9	1	.90	5	.226	.287	.312
2007	Min	AL	55	116	27	6	0	3	(1	2)	42	13	14	13	11	0	24	3	0	0	3	1	.75	4	.233	.315	.362
5 ML YEARS			494	1514	412	80	10	32	(17	15)	608	228	172	222	147	5	236	37	6	12	47	10	.82	34	.272	.349	.402

Casey Fossum

Pitches: L Bats: L Pos: RP-30; SP-10   Ht: 6'1" Wt: 170 Born: 1/9/1978 Age: 30

			HOW MUCH HE PITCHED					WHAT HE GAVE UP										THE RESULTS						
Year	Team	Lg	G	GS	CG	GF	IP	BFP	H	R	ER	HR	SH	SF	HB	TBB	IBB	SO	WP	Bk	W	L	Pct	ShO	Sv-Op	Hld	ERC	ERA
2007	Portlnd*	AAA	3	3	0	0	13.1	67	26	12	12	0	0	1	5	7	1	7	0	0	0	2	.000	0	0- -	-	10.73	8.10
2001	Bos	AL	13	7	0	3	44.1	197	44	26	24	4	0	1	6	20	1	26	1	1	3	2	.600	0	0-0	0	4.70	4.87
2002	Bos	AL	43	12	0	13	106.2	461	113	56	41	12	2	4	4	30	0	101	3	0	5	4	.556	0	1-1	3	4.14	3.46
2003	Bos	AL	19	14	0	2	79.0	346	82	55	48	9	1	3	4	34	4	63	4	0	6	5	.545	0	1-1	0	4.77	5.47
2004	Ari	NL	27	27	0	0	142.0	652	171	111	105	31	8	4	10	63	5	117	4	2	4	15	.211	0	0-0	0	6.67	6.65
2005	TB	AL	36	25	0	1	162.2	725	170	100	89	21	3	5	18	60	3	128	8	1	8	12	.400	0	0-1	0	4.80	4.92
2006	TB	AL	25	25	0	0	130.0	594	136	89	77	18	2	3	12	63	3	88	4	1	6	6	.500	0	0-0	0	5.25	5.33
2007	TB	AL	40	10	0	7	76.0	364	109	71	65	15	2	7	6	27	1	53	3	0	5	8	.385	0	0-4	2	7.59	7.70
7 ML YEARS			203	120	0	26	740.2	3339	825	508	449	110	18	27	60	297	13	576	27	5	37	52	.416	0	2-7	5	5.39	5.46

Jake Fox

Bats: R **Throws:** R **Pos:** RF-3; PH-3; 1B-1 **Ht:** 6'0" **Wt:** 210 **Born:** 7/20/1982 **Age:** 25

									BATTING											BASERUNNING				AVERAGES		
Year	Team	Lg	G	AB	H	2B	3B	HR	(Hm | Rd)	TB	R	RBI	RC	TBB	IBB	SO	HBP	SH	SF	SB	CS	SB%	GDP	Avg	OBP	Slg
2003	Cubs	R	15	50	12	5	0	1	(- | -)	20	4	6	6	5	0	14	1	0	0	0	1	.00	0	.240	.321	.400
2003	Lansng	A	29	100	26	8	0	5	(- | -)	49	13	12	16	8	0	19	3	0	1	0	0	-	3	.260	.330	.490
2004	Lansng	A	97	366	105	19	3	14	(- | -)	172	49	55	57	17	0	75	8	2	2	2	1	.67	7	.287	.331	.470
2005	Dytona	A+	83	270	76	20	0	9	(- | -)	123	37	40	46	26	3	48	8	1	4	5	2	.71	8	.281	.357	.456
2006	Dytona	A+	66	249	78	15	1	16	(- | -)	143	45	61	55	27	3	49	6	1	8	4	1	.80	4	.313	.383	.574
2006	WTenn	AA	55	193	52	17	0	5	(- | -)	84	20	25	25	9	0	44	1	0	1	0	0	-	10	.269	.304	.435
2007	Tenn	AA	91	359	102	23	1	18	(- | -)	181	60	60	60	17	3	72	8	0	4	6	2	.75	8	.284	.327	.504
2007	Iowa	AAA	25	99	28	7	0	6	(- | -)	53	18	19	18	5	0	23	4	0	0	2	0	1.00	0	.283	.343	.535
2007	ChC	NL	7	14	2	2	0	0	(0 | 0)	4	3	1	1	1	0	2	0	0	0	0	0	-	1	.143	.200	.286

Jeff Francis

Pitches: L **Bats:** L **Pos:** SP-34 **Ht:** 6'5" **Wt:** 205 **Born:** 1/8/1981 **Age:** 27

			HOW MUCH HE PITCHED						WHAT HE GAVE UP											THE RESULTS						
Year	Team	Lg	G	GS	CG	GF	IP	BFP	H	R	ER	HR	SH	SF	HB	TBB	IBB	SO	WP	Bk	W	L	Pct	ShO	Sv-Op	Hld	ERC	ERA
2004	Col	NL	7	7	0	0	36.2	164	42	22	21	8	2	1	1	13	1	32	2	0	3	2	.600	0	0-0	0	5.62	5.15
2005	Col	NL	33	33	0	0	183.2	828	228	119	116	26	6	10	8	70	5	128	2	0	14	12	.538	0	0-0	0	5.94	5.68
2006	Col	NL	32	32	1	0	199.0	843	187	101	92	18	7	7	13	69	15	117	0	1	13	11	.542	1	0-0	0	3.63	4.16
2007	Col	NL	34	34	1	0	215.1	922	234	103	101	25	7	4	7	63	7	165	1	1	17	9	.654	1	0-0	0	4.37	4.22
	4 ML YEARS		106	106	2	0	634.2	2757	691	345	330	77	22	22	29	215	28	442	5	1	47	34	.580	2	0-0	0	4.64	4.68

Ben Francisco

Bats: R **Throws:** R **Pos:** LF-14; RF-5; PH-5; PR-3; DH-2 **Ht:** 6'1" **Wt:** 190 **Born:** 10/23/1981 **Age:** 26

									BATTING											BASERUNNING				AVERAGES		
Year	Team	Lg	G	AB	H	2B	3B	HR	(Hm	Rd)	TB	R	RBI	RC	TBB	IBB	SO	HBP	SH	SF	SB	CS	SB%	GDP	Avg	OBP	Slg
2002	MhVlly	A-	58	235	82	23	2	3	(-	-)	118	55	23	51	22	1	28	7	2	3	22	6	.79	5	.349	.416	.502
2003	Lk Cty	A	80	289	83	21	1	11	(-	-)	139	57	48	52	31	1	50	4	1	5	15	6	.71	7	.287	.359	.481
2004	Akron	AA	133	497	126	29	3	15	(-	-)	206	72	71	73	50	2	86	6	4	6	21	5	.81	10	.254	.326	.414
2005	Akron	AA	83	323	99	19	7	7	(-	-)	153	45	46	56	24	1	60	2	2	1	15	4	.79	4	.307	.357	.474
2005	Buffalo	AAA	4	16	8	1	0	0	(-	-)	9	4	3	4	1	0	3	0	0	1	1	0	1.00	1	.500	.500	.563
2006	Buffalo	AAA	134	515	143	32	4	17	(-	-)	234	80	59	86	45	0	72	10	5	4	25	5	.83	9	.278	.345	.454
2007	Buffalo	AAA	95	377	120	27	2	12	(-	-)	187	60	51	73	36	3	66	4	6	2	22	8	.73	11	.318	.382	.496
2007	Cle	AL	25	62	17	5	0	3	(2	1)	31	10	12	6	3	0	19	0	0	1	2	2	.00	2	.274	.303	.500

Frank Francisco

Pitches: R **Bats:** R **Pos:** RP-50 **Ht:** 6'2" **Wt:** 235 **Born:** 9/11/1979 **Age:** 28

				HOW MUCH HE PITCHED					WHAT HE GAVE UP											THE RESULTS						
Year	Team	Lg	G	GS	CG	GF	IP	BFP	H	R	ER	HR	SH	SF	HB	TBB	IBB	SO	WP	Bk	W	L	Pct	ShO	Sv-Op	Hld	ERC	ERA
2007	Okla*	AAA	5	0	0	5	6.0	23	0	0	0	0	0	1	0	3	0	14	0	0	1	0	1.000	0	2- -	-	0.44	0.00
2004	Tex	AL	45	0	0	7	51.1	216	36	19	19	4	2	1	3	28	2	60	4	1	5	1	.833	0	0-3	10	3.04	3.33
2006	Tex	AL	8	0	0	2	7.1	32	8	4	4	2	0	0	0	2	0	6	1	0	0	1	.000	0	0-0	2	5.17	4.91
2007	Tex	AL	59	0	0	16	59.1	268	57	33	30	3	6	1	2	38	4	49	8	0	1	1	.500	0	0-0	21	4.44	4.55
	3 ML YEARS		112	0	0	25	118.0	510	101	56	53	9	8	2	5	68	6	115	13	1	6	3	.667	0	0-3	33	3.87	4.04

Julio Franco

Bats: R **Throws:** R **Pos:** PH-37; 1B-16; 3B-2; DH-1 **Ht:** 6'1" **Wt:** 210 **Born:** 8/23/1958 **Age:** 49

									BATTING											BASERUNNING				AVERAGES		
Year	Team	Lg	G	AB	H	2B	3B	HR	(Hm	Rd)	TB	R	RBI	RC	TBB	IBB	SO	HBP	SH	SF	SB	CS	SB%	GDP	Avg	OBP	Slg
2007	Rome*	A-	4	13	4	0	0	0	(-	-)	4	3	2	2	1	0	2	2	0	0	1	0	1.00	1	.308	.438	.308
2007	Rchmd*	AAA	4	14	4	0	0	0	(-	-)	4	2	1	2	3	0	0	0	0	0	0	0	-	1	.286	.412	.286
1982	Phi	NL	16	29	8	1	0	0	(0	0)	9	3	3	2	2	1	4	0	1	0	0	2	.00	1	.276	.323	.310
1983	Cle	AL	149	560	153	24	8	8	(6	2)	217	68	80	62	27	1	50	2	3	6	32	12	.73	21	.273	.306	.388
1984	Cle	AL	160	658	188	22	5	3	(1	2)	229	82	79	72	43	1	68	6	1	10	19	10	.66	23	.286	.331	.348
1985	Cle	AL	160	636	183	33	4	6	(3	3)	242	97	90	90	54	2	74	4	0	9	13	9	.59	26	.288	.343	.381
1986	Cle	AL	149	599	183	30	5	10	(4	6)	253	80	74	76	32	1	66	0	0	5	10	7	.59	28	.306	.338	.422
1987	Cle	AL	128	495	158	24	3	8	(5	3)	212	86	52	81	57	2	56	3	0	5	32	9	.78	23	.319	.389	.428
1988	Cle	AL	152	613	186	23	6	10	(3	7)	251	88	54	89	56	4	72	2	1	4	25	11	.69	17	.303	.361	.409
1989	Tex	AL	150	548	173	31	5	13	(9	4)	253	80	92	93	66	11	69	1	0	6	21	3	.88	27	.316	.386	.462
1990	Tex	AL	157	582	172	27	1	11	(4	7)	234	96	69	94	82	3	83	2	2	2	31	10	.76	12	.296	.383	.402
1991	Tex	AL	146	589	201	27	3	15	(7	8)	279	108	78	113	65	8	78	3	0	2	36	9	.80	13	.341	.408	.474
1992	Tex	AL	35	107	25	7	0	2	(2	0)	38	19	8	12	15	2	17	0	1	0	1	1	.50	3	.234	.328	.355
1993	Tex	AL	144	532	154	31	3	14	(6	8)	233	85	84	83	62	4	95	1	5	7	9	3	.75	16	.289	.360	.438
1994	CWS	AL	112	433	138	19	2	20	(10	10)	221	72	98	87	62	4	75	5	0	5	8	1	.89	14	.319	.406	.510
1996	Cle	AL	112	432	139	20	1	14	(7	7)	203	72	76	79	61	2	82	0	3	3	8	8	.50	14	.322	.407	.470
1997	2 Tms	AL	120	430	116	16	1	7	(5	2)	155	68	44	58	69	4	116	1	1	4	15	6	.71	17	.270	.369	.360
1999	TB	AL	1	1	0	0	0	0	(0	0)	0	0	0	0	0	0	1	0	0	0	0	0	-	0	.000	.000	.000
2001	Atl	NL	25	90	27	4	0	3	(2	1)	40	13	11	14	10	1	20	1	0	0	0	0	-	3	.300	.376	.444
2002	Atl	NL	125	338	96	13	1	6	(3	3)	129	51	30	39	39	3	75	1	2	3	5	1	.83	13	.284	.357	.382
2003	Atl	NL	103	197	58	12	2	5	(1	4)	89	28	31	31	25	5	43	0	0	1	1	0	1.00	8	.294	.372	.452
2004	Atl	NL	125	320	99	18	3	6	(5	1)	141	37	57	57	36	4	68	1	1	3	4	2	.67	10	.309	.378	.441
2005	Atl	NL	108	233	64	12	0	9	(3	6)	105	30	42	36	27	1	57	1	1	3	4	0	1.00	10	.275	.348	.451
2006	NYM	NL	95	165	45	10	0	2	(0	2)	61	14	26	21	13	2	49	1	0	0	6	1	.86	11	.273	.330	.370
2007	2 Tms	NL	55	90	20	3	0	1	(0	1)	26	6	11	16	12	1	14	0	0	2	1	0	.67	2	.222	.321	.289
	97	Cle	78	289	82	13	1	3	(2	1)	106	46	25	37	38	2	75	0	1	0	8	5	.62	13	.284	.367	.367

Year	Team	Lg	G	AB	H	2B	3B	HR	(Hm	Rd)	TB	R	RBI	RC	TBB	IBB	SO	HBP	SH	SF	SB	CS	SB%	GDP	Avg	OBP	Slg
97	Mil	AL	42	141	34	3	0	4	(3	1)	49	22	19	21	31	2	41	1	0	4	7	1	.88	4	.241	.373	.348
07	NYM	NL	40	50	10	0	0	1	(0	1)	13	7	8	6	10	0	13	0	0	1	2	1	.67	1	.200	.328	.260
07	Atl	NL	15	40	10	3	0	0	(0	0)	13	1	8	6	4	1	10	0	0	1	0	0	-	1	.250	.311	.325
23 ML YEARS			2527	8677	2586	407	54	173	(86	87)	3620	1285	1194	1289	917	67	1341	38	19	80	281	107	.72	312	.298	.365	.417

Jeff Francoeur

Bats: R Throws: R Pos: RF-162 **Ht: 6'4" Wt: 220 Born: 1/8/1984 Age: 24**

Year	Team	Lg	G	AB	H	2B	3B	HR	(Hm	Rd)	TB	R	RBI	RC	TBB	IBB	SO	HBP	SH	SF	SB	CS	SB%	GDP	Avg	OBP	Slg
2005	Atl	NL	70	257	77	20	1	14	(11	3)	141	41	45	50	11	3	58	4	0	2	3	2	.60	4	.300	.336	.549
2006	Atl	NL	162	651	169	24	6	29	(19	10)	292	83	103	91	23	6	132	9	0	3	1	6	.14	15	.260	.293	.449
2007	Atl	NL	162	642	188	40	0	19	(7	12)	285	84	105	97	42	5	129	5	0	7	5	2	.71	14	.293	.338	.444
3 ML YEARS			394	1550	434	84	7	62	(37	25)	718	208	253	238	76	14	319	18	0	12	9	10	.47	33	.280	.319	.463

Kevin Frandsen

Bats: R Throws: R Pos: 2B-49; PH-27; SS-22; LF-10; 3B-9; PR-4; RF-3 **Ht: 6'0" Wt: 180 Born: 5/24/1982 Age: 26**

Year	Team	Lg	G	AB	H	2B	3B	HR	(Hm	Rd)	TB	R	RBI	RC	TBB	IBB	SO	HBP	SH	SF	SB	CS	SB%	GDP	Avg	OBP	Slg
2004	SlmKzr	A-	25	98	29	5	0	3	(-	-)	43	22	14	3	9	0	9	3	1	1	0	1	.00	1	.296	.369	.439
2005	SnJos	A+	75	291	102	22	3	2	(-	-)	136	57	40	58	26	0	22	15	2	1	13	11	.54	12	.351	.429	.467
2005	Nrwich	AA	33	129	37	8	0	2	(-	-)	51	22	20	18	4	0	14	6	2	1	7	3	.70	3	.287	.336	.395
2005	Fresno	AAA	20	94	33	10	1	2	(-	-)	51	18	16	18	2	0	5	2	0	0	1	1	.50	6	.351	.378	.543
2006	SnJos	A+	2	7	3	0	0	0	(-	-)	3	1	1	1	0	0	0	2	0	0	0	0	-	0	.429	.556	.429
2006	Fresno	AAA	71	293	89	25	3	3	(-	-)	129	46	30	47	12	0	30	14	7	2	7	4	.64	9	.304	.358	.440
2007	Fresno	AAA	19	67	27	5	0	1	(-	-)	35	13	7	17	9	0	6	5	2	0	4	2	.67	1	.403	.506	.522
2006	SF	NL	41	93	20	4	0	2	(0	2)	30	12	7	7	3	0	14	6	0	0	0	1	.00	3	.215	.284	.323
2007	SF	NL	109	264	71	12	1	5	(1	4)	100	26	31	29	21	3	24	5	3	3	4	3	.57	17	.269	.331	.379
2 ML YEARS			150	357	91	16	1	7	(1	6)	130	38	38	36	24	3	38	11	3	3	4	4	.50	20	.255	.319	.364

Ryan Franklin

Pitches: R Bats: R Pos: RP-69 **Ht: 6'3" Wt: 190 Born: 3/5/1973 Age: 35**

Year	Team	Lg	G	GS	CG	GF	IP	BFP	H	R	ER	HR	SH	SF	HB	TBB	IBB	SO	WP	Bk	W	L	Pct	ShO	Sv-Op	Hld	ERC	ERA
1999	Sea	AL	6	0	0	2	11.1	51	10	6	6	2	0	0	1	8	1	6	0	0	0	0	-	0	0-0	1	5.52	4.76
2001	Sea	AL	38	0	0	14	78.1	335	76	32	31	13	1	2	4	24	4	60	2	0	5	1	.833	0	0-1	5	4.08	3.56
2002	Sea	AL	41	12	0	10	118.2	495	117	62	53	14	5	5	5	22	1	65	0	0	7	5	.583	0	0-1	3	3.40	4.02
2003	Sea	AL	32	32	2	0	212.0	877	199	93	84	34	8	5	9	61	3	99	1	2	11	13	.458	1	0-0	0	3.90	3.57
2004	Sea	AL	32	32	2	0	200.1	870	224	116	109	33	2	11	10	61	1	104	0	3	4	16	.200	1	0-0	0	5.08	4.90
2005	Sea	AL	32	30	2	0	190.2	832	212	110	108	28	3	3	7	62	4	93	3	1	8	15	.348	1	0-0	0	4.89	5.10
2006	2 Tms		66	0	0	19	77.1	343	86	42	39	13	2	2	4	33	10	43	2	0	6	7	.462	0	0-3	8	5.41	4.54
2007	StL	NL	69	0	0	8	80.0	317	70	28	27	8	2	2	3	11	0	44	2	0	4	4	.500	0	1-6	25	2.59	3.04
06	Phi	NL	46	0	0	13	53.0	233	59	28	27	10	0	1	4	17	4	25	1	0	1	5	.167	0	0-1	8	5.26	4.58
06	Cin	NL	20	0	0	6	24.1	110	27	14	12	3	2	1	0	16	6	18	1	0	5	2	.714	0	0-2	0	5.67	4.44
8 ML YEARS			316	106	6	53	968.2	4120	994	489	457	145	23	30	43	282	24	514	10	6	45	61	.425	3	1-11	42	4.30	4.25

Jason Frasor

Pitches: R Bats: R Pos: RP-51 **Ht: 5'10" Wt: 170 Born: 8/9/1977 Age: 30**

Year	Team	Lg	G	GS	CG	GF	IP	BFP	H	R	ER	HR	SH	SF	HB	TBB	IBB	SO	WP	Bk	W	L	Pct	ShO	Sv-Op	Hld	ERC	ERA
2004	Tor	AL	63	0	0	37	68.1	299	64	31	31	4	3	4	2	36	3	54	4	2	4	6	.400	0	17-19	8	3.97	4.08
2005	Tor	AL	67	0	0	12	74.2	305	67	31	27	8	2	1	3	28	2	62	1	0	3	5	.375	0	1-3	15	3.72	3.25
2006	Tor	AL	51	0	0	12	50.0	215	47	24	24	8	0	3	2	17	1	51	3	0	3	2	.600	0	0-1	12	3.98	4.32
2007	Tor	AL	51	0	0	18	57.0	242	47	29	29	3	1	2	2	23	1	59	2	1	1	5	.167	0	3-6	4	2.88	4.58
4 ML YEARS			232	0	0	79	250.0	1061	225	115	111	23	6	9	9	104	7	226	10	3	11	18	.379	0	21-29	39	3.65	4.00

Ryan Freel

Bats: R Throws: R Pos: CF-59; 3B-19; PH-7; 2B-2; LF-1 **Ht: 5'10" Wt: 180 Born: 3/8/1976 Age: 32**

Year	Team	Lg	G	AB	H	2B	3B	HR	(Hm	Rd)	TB	R	RBI	RC	TBB	IBB	SO	HBP	SH	SF	SB	CS	SB%	GDP	Avg	OBP	Slg
2007	Lsvlle*	AAA	8	33	11	2	0	0	(-	-)	13	6	3	5	3	0	2	0	0	0	2	0	1.00	0	.333	.389	.394
2001	Tor	AL	9	22	6	1	0	0	(0	0)	7	1	3	3	1	0	4	1	0	0	2	1	.67	0	.273	.333	.318
2003	Cin	NL	43	137	39	6	1	4	(0	4)	59	23	12	17	9	1	13	4	2	1	9	4	.69	2	.285	.344	.431
2004	Cin	NL	143	505	140	21	8	3	(1	2)	186	74	28	73	67	0	88	12	8	0	37	10	.79	7	.277	.375	.368
2005	Cin	NL	103	369	100	19	3	4	(2	2)	137	69	21	55	51	0	59	8	3	0	36	10	.78	9	.271	.371	.371
2006	Cin	NL	132	454	123	30	2	8	(6	2)	181	67	27	59	57	0	98	9	3	0	37	11	.77	5	.271	.363	.399
2007	Cin	NL	75	277	68	13	3	3	(2	1)	96	44	16	31	18	0	47	7	2	0	15	8	.65	4	.245	.308	.347
6 ML YEARS			505	1764	476	90	17	22	(11	11)	666	278	107	238	203	1	309	41	18	1	136	44	.76	27	.270	.358	.378

Brian Fuentes

Pitches: L Bats: L Pos: RP-64   Ht: 6'4" Wt: 230 Born: 8/9/1975 Age: 32

			HOW MUCH HE PITCHED						WHAT HE GAVE UP												THE RESULTS							
Year	Team	Lg	G	GS	CG	GF	IP	BFP	H	R	ER	HR	SH	SF	HB	TBB	IBB	SO	WP	Bk	W	L	Pct	ShO	Sv-Op	Hld	ERC	ERA
2007	Ashvll*	A-	1	0	0	0	1.0	3	0	0	0	0	0	0	0	0	0	2	0	0	0	0	-	0	0--	-	0.00	0.00
2007	ColSpr*	AAA	2	1	0	0	2.0	7	2	0	0	0	0	0	0	0	0	2	0	0	0	0	-	0	0--	-	2.31	0.00
2001	Sea	AL	10	0	0	3	11.2	47	6	6	6	2	0	1	3	8	0	10	1	0	1	1	.500	0	0-1	1	4.39	4.63
2002	Col	NL	31	0	0	9	26.2	118	25	14	14	4	0	2	3	13	0	38	1	0	2	0	1.000	0	0-0	0	4.91	4.73
2003	Col	NL	75	0	0	23	75.1	320	64	24	23	7	0	3	6	34	2	82	2	1	3	3	.500	0	4-6	19	3.71	2.75
2004	Col	NL	47	0	0	12	44.2	201	46	30	28	5	7	0	4	19	6	48	3	0	2	4	.333	0	0-1	13	4.50	5.64
2005	Col	NL	78	0	0	55	74.1	321	59	25	24	6	5	1	10	34	4	91	8	0	2	5	.286	0	31-34	6	3.44	2.91
2006	Col	NL	66	0	0	58	65.1	274	50	25	25	8	2	1	6	26	4	73	6	0	3	4	.429	0	30-36	5	3.19	3.44
2007	Col	NL	64	0	0	38	61.1	255	46	26	21	6	1	1	7	23	0	56	2	0	3	5	.375	0	20-27	8	3.06	3.08
	7 ML YEARS		371	0	0	108	359.1	1536	296	150	141	38	15	9	39	157	16	398	23	1	16	22	.421	0	85-105	47	3.65	3.53

Kosuke Fukudome

Bats: L Throws: R Pos: OF   Ht: 6'0" Wt: 187 Born: 4/26/1977 Age: 31

						BATTING													BASERUNNING				AVERAGES		
Year	Team	Lg	G	AB	H	2B	3B	HR	(Hm | Rd)	TB	R	RBI	RC	TBB	IBB	SO	HBP	SH	SF	SB	CS	SB%	GDP	Avg	OBP	Slg
1999	Chnchi	Jap	132	461	131	25	2	16	(- | -)	208	76	52	68	50	-	121	5	8	2	4	7	.36	3	.284	.359	.451
2000	Chnchi	Jap	97	316	80	18	2	13	(- | -)	141	50	42	51	45	-	79	3	2	2	8	5	.62	5	.253	.350	.446
2001	Chnchi	Jap	120	375	94	22	2	15	(- | -)	165	51	56	62	56	-	90	4	4	3	8	4	.67	4	.251	.352	.440
2002	Chnchi	Jap	140	542	186	42	3	19	(- | -)	291	85	65	116	56	2	96	5	0	5	4	2	.67	4	.343	.406	.537
2003	Chnchi	Jap	140	528	165	30	11	34	(- | -)	319	107	96	125	78	1	118	4	1	6	10	5	.67	5	.313	.401	.604
2004	Chnchi	Jap	92	350	97	19	7	23	(- | -)	199	61	81	73	48	0	93	3	1	2	8	3	.73	3	.277	.367	.569
2005	Chnchi	Jap	142	515	169	39	6	28	(- | -)	304	102	103	128	93	3	128	1	0	3	13	5	.72	8	.328	.430	.590
2006	Chnchi	Jap	130	496	174	47	5	31	(- | -)	324	117	104	135	76	4	94	3	0	3	11	2	.85	4	.351	.438	.653
2007	Chnchi	Jap	81	269	79	22	0	13	(- | -)	140	64	48	67	69	-	66	6	0	4	5	-		5	.294	.443	.520

Sam Fuld

Bats: L Throws: L Pos: PR-7; RF-6; PH-2; LF-1; CF-1   Ht: 5'10" Wt: 180 Born: 11/20/1981 Age: 26

						BATTING													BASERUNNING				AVERAGES		
Year	Team	Lg	G	AB	H	2B	3B	HR	(Hm | Rd)	TB	R	RBI	RC	TBB	IBB	SO	HBP	SH	SF	SB	CS	SB%	GDP	Avg	OBP	Slg
2005	Peoria	A	125	443	133	32	6	5	(- | -)	192	82	37	75	50	0	44	7	4	4	18	11	.62	16	.300	.377	.433
2006	Dytona	A+	89	353	106	19	6	4	(- | -)	149	63	40	62	40	5	54	5	6	1	22	3	.88	6	.300	.378	.422
2007	Tenn	AA	90	335	97	23	2	2	(- | -)	130	56	27	54	41	1	38	5	8	3	11	3	.79	2	.290	.372	.388
2007	Iowa	AAA	14	52	14	4	1	1	(- | -)	23	13	2	10	9	0	5	2	0	0	2	0	1.00	1	.269	.397	.442
2007	ChC	NL	14	6	0	0	0	0	(0 | 0)	0	3	0	0	3	0	3	0	0	0	0	0	-	0	.000	.333	.000

Aaron Fultz

Pitches: L Bats: L Pos: RP-49   Ht: 6'0" Wt: 210 Born: 9/4/1973 Age: 34

			HOW MUCH HE PITCHED						WHAT HE GAVE UP												THE RESULTS							
Year	Team	Lg	G	GS	CG	GF	IP	BFP	H	R	ER	HR	SH	SF	HB	TBB	IBB	SO	WP	Bk	W	L	Pct	ShO	Sv-Op	Hld	ERC	ERA
2007	Lk Cty*	A-	1	0	0	0	1.0	3	0	0	0	0	0	0	0	0	0	1	0	0	0	0	-	0	0--	-	0.00	0.00
2007	Akron°	AA	1	1	0	0	1.0	3	0	0	0	0	0	0	0	0	0	1	0	0	0	0	-	0	0--	-	0.00	0.00
2000	SF	NL	58	0	0	18	69.1	299	67	38	36	8	7	6	3	28	0	62	0	2	5	2	.714	0	1-3	7	4.19	4.67
2001	SF	NL	66	0	0	17	71.0	300	70	40	36	9	3	4	1	21	3	67	1	0	3	1	.750	0	1-2	12	3.75	4.56
2002	SF	NL	43	0	0	12	41.1	185	47	22	22	4	2	1	3	19	3	31	1	0	2	2	.500	0	0-1	4	5.36	4.79
2003	Tex	AL	64	0	0	10	67.1	296	75	43	39	9	4	2	2	27	7	53	1	1	1	3	.250	0	0-0	19	4.99	5.21
2004	Min	AL	55	0	0	16	50.0	216	50	28	28	5	1	4	1	23	2	37	3	0	3	3	.500	0	1-4	5	4.40	5.04
2005	Phi	NL	62	0	0	12	72.1	286	47	21	18	6	4	1	5	23	2	54	0	0	4	0	1.000	0	0-1	2	2.11	2.24
2006	Phi	NL	66	1	0	12	71.1	317	80	39	36	7	3	6	2	28	8	62	5	0	3	1	.750	0	0-2	9	4.64	4.54
2007	Cle	AL	49	0	0	10	37.0	158	31	12	12	2	0	3	1	18	2	28	1	0	4	3	.571	0	0-1	11	3.21	2.92
	8 ML YEARS		463	1	0	111	479.2	2057	467	243	227	50	24	27	18	187	27	394	12	3	25	15	.625	0	3-14	69	4.00	4.26

Rafael Furcal

Bats: B Throws: R Pos: SS-138   Ht: 5'9" Wt: 195 Born: 10/24/1977 Age: 30

						BATTING													BASERUNNING				AVERAGES		
Year	Team	Lg	G	AB	H	2B	3B	HR	(Hm | Rd)	TB	R	RBI	RC	TBB	IBB	SO	HBP	SH	SF	SB	CS	SB%	GDP	Avg	OBP	Slg
2007	InldEm*	A+	2	6	1	0	0	0	(- | -)	1	0	0	0	2	0	1	0	0	0	1	0	1.00	0	.167	.375	.167
2000	Atl	NL	131	455	134	20	4	4	(1 | 3)	174	87	37	78	73	0	80	3	9	2	40	14	.74	2	.295	.394	.382
2001	Atl	NL	79	324	89	19	0	4	(3 | 1)	120	39	30	41	24	1	56	1	4	6	22	6	.79	5	.275	.321	.370
2002	Atl	NL	154	636	175	31	8	8	(4 | 4)	246	95	47	80	43	0	114	3	9	2	27	15	.64	8	.275	.323	.387
2003	Atl	NL	156	664	194	35	10	15	(4 | 11)	294	130	61	107	60	2	76	3	3	4	25	2	.93	9	.292	.352	.443
2004	Atl	NL	143	563	157	24	5	14	(5 | 9)	233	103	59	82	58	4	71	1	5	5	29	6	.83	9	.279	.344	.414
2005	Atl	NL	154	616	175	31	11	12	(9 | 3)	264	100	58	98	62	3	78	1	5	5	46	10	.82	11	.284	.348	.429
2006	LAD	NL	159	654	196	32	9	15	(12 | 3)	291	113	63	110	73	3	98	1	5	3	37	13	.74	7	.300	.369	.445
2007	LAD	NL	138	581	157	23	4	6	(4 | 2)	206	87	47	65	55	3	68	1	2	3	25	6	.81	11	.270	.333	.355
	8 ML YEARS		1114	4493	1277	215	51	78	(42 | 36)	1828	754	402	661	448	16	641	14	42	30	251	72	.78	54	.284	.349	.407

J.J. Furmaniak

Bats: R **Throws:** R **Pos:** PR-7; 2B-4; DH-4; SS-3; 3B-2; RF-2; LF-1   **Ht:** 5'11" **Wt:** 185 **Born:** 7/31/1979 **Age:** 28

Year	Team	Lg	G	AB	H	2B	3B	HR	(Hm	Rd)	TB	R	RBI	RC	TBB	IBB	SO	HBP	SH	SF	SB	CS	SB%	GDP	Avg	OBP	Slg
2000	Idaho	R+	62	245	84	18	2	5	(-	-)	121	72	38	57	44	1	48	5	0	4	10	3	.77	8	.343	.446	.494
2001	FtWyn	A	123	436	96	24	3	5	(-	-)	141	57	35	48	55	0	117	4	3	7	11	6	.65	10	.220	.309	.323
2002	Lk Els	A+	106	381	98	16	6	7	(-	-)	147	50	43	46	26	1	100	6	5	5	11	9	.55	8	.257	.311	.386
2003	Lk Els	A+	78	309	97	22	8	9	(-	-)	162	65	54	65	36	1	55	8	3	2	10	4	.71	5	.314	.397	.524
2003	Mobile	AA	31	103	27	4	1	3	(-	-)	42	10	11	14	8	0	27	4	1	1	0	0	-	0	.262	.336	.408
2004	Mobile	AA	14	51	10	4	0	1	(-	-)	17	10	8	5	7	0	15	1	0	0	1	0	1.00	0	.196	.305	.333
2004	Portlnd	AAA	120	425	125	24	4	17	(-	-)	208	71	73	73	33	2	86	6	2	7	8	5	.62	10	.294	.348	.489
2005	Portlnd	AAA	99	387	103	16	4	14	(-	-)	169	54	47	56	28	0	86	6	5	2	9	5	.64	8	.266	.324	.437
2005	Indy	AAA	36	139	40	5	3	2	(-	-)	57	12	21	18	4	0	32	2	1	1	5	3	.63	1	.288	.315	.410
2006	Indy	AAA	114	371	79	12	3	6	(-	-)	115	43	27	31	25	2	85	2	4	1	15	5	.75	11	.213	.266	.310
2007	Scrmto	AAA	106	424	124	18	2	15	(-	-)	191	70	51	75	49	1	105	8	5	4	21	8	.72	10	.292	.373	.450
2005	Pit	NL	13	26	5	1	1	0	(0	0)	8	3	1	2	4	0	4	0	0	0	0	0	-	0	.192	.300	.308
2007	Oak	AL	16	17	3	1	0	0	(0	0)	4	5	1	2	3	0	8	2	0	0	0	0	-	0	.176	.364	.235
	2 ML YEARS		29	43	8	2	1	0	(0	0)	12	8	2	4	7	0	12	2	0	0	0	0	-	0	.186	.327	.279

Kason Gabbard

Pitches: L **Bats:** L **Pos:** SP-15   **Ht:** 6'3" **Wt:** 205 **Born:** 4/8/1982 **Age:** 26

			HOW MUCH HE PITCHED						WHAT HE GAVE UP										THE RESULTS						
Year	Team	Lg	G	GS	CG	GF	IP	BFP	H	R	ER	HR	SH	SF	HB	TBB	IBB	SO	WP	Bk	W	L	Pct	ShO	Sv-Op	Hld	ERC	ERA
2001	RedSx	R	6	6	0	0	14.1	65	11	11	9	1	0	2	1	9	0	17	3	0	0	1	.000	0	0- -	-	3.56	5.65
2002	Augsta	A	7	7	0	0	38.0	150	31	14	8	0	1	0	2	7	0	31	9	0	0	4	.000	0	0- -	-	1.95	1.89
2003	Srsota	A+	2	2	0	0	7.0	34	13	8	8	0	2	1	0	3	0	4	0	0	0	1	.000	0	0- -	-	9.24	10.29
2004	Srsota	A+	10	7	0	1	43.1	191	43	17	13	2	3	0	4	16	1	30	5	1	3	2	.600	0	1- -	-	3.79	2.70
2004	Portlnd	AA	14	14	0	0	53.0	242	61	42	37	5	1	3	2	26	0	35	4	0	3	6	.333	0	0- -	-	5.44	6.28
2005	Portlnd	AA	27	25	0	0	132.2	580	128	80	68	10	5	4	4	65	1	96	9	1	9	11	.450	0	0- -	-	4.17	4.61
2006	Portlnd	AA	13	13	1	0	73.2	298	51	26	21	4	1	0	6	25	0	68	5	0	9	2	.818	0	0- -	-	2.27	2.57
2006	Pwtckt	AAA	9	8	0	0	51.2	220	51	31	30	8	4	0	0	26	0	48	3	0	1	7	.125	0	0- -	-	4.99	5.23
2007	Pwtckt	AAA	14	14	0	0	75.0	313	66	29	27	10	4	0	3	25	1	64	2	0	7	2	.778	0	0- -	-	3.52	3.24
2006	Bos	AL	7	4	0	1	25.2	111	24	11	10	0	1	0	0	16	0	15	1	1	1	3	.250	0	0-0	-	3.96	3.51
2007	2 Tms	AL	15	15	1	0	81.1	344	68	42	42	8	1	1	7	41	1	55	5	0	6	1	.857	1	0-0	-	3.99	4.65
07	Bos	AL	7	7	1	0	41.0	165	28	17	17	3	0	0	4	18	0	29	0	0	4	0	1.000	1	0-0	-	2.83	3.73
07	Tex	AL	8	8	0	0	40.1	179	40	25	25	5	1	1	3	23	1	26	5	0	2	1	.667	0	0-0	-	5.27	5.58
	2 ML YEARS		22	19	1	1	107.0	455	92	53	52	8	2	1	7	57	1	70	6	1	7	4	.636	1	0-0	-	3.98	4.37

Eric Gagne

Pitches: R **Bats:** R **Pos:** RP-54   **Ht:** 6'0" **Wt:** 240 **Born:** 1/7/1976 **Age:** 32

			HOW MUCH HE PITCHED						WHAT HE GAVE UP										THE RESULTS						
Year	Team	Lg	G	GS	CG	GF	IP	BFP	H	R	ER	HR	SH	SF	HB	TBB	IBB	SO	WP	Bk	W	L	Pct	ShO	Sv-Op	Hld	ERC	ERA
2007	Frisco*	AA	3	2	0	1	2.2	11	2	1	1	0	0	0	0	1	0	3	0	0	0	1	.000	0	0- -	-	4.26	3.38
1999	LAD	NL	5	5	0	0	30.0	119	18	8	7	3	1	0	0	15	0	30	1	0	1	1	.500	0	0-0	-	2.42	2.10
2000	LAD	NL	20	19	0	0	101.1	464	106	62	58	20	5	3	3	60	1	79	4	0	4	6	.400	0	0-0	-	5.97	5.15
2001	LAD	NL	33	24	0	3	151.2	649	144	90	80	24	6	8	16	46	1	130	3	1	6	7	.462	0	0-0	-	4.22	4.75
2002	LAD	NL	77	0	0	68	82.1	314	55	18	18	6	3	2	2	16	4	114	1	0	4	1	.800	0	52-56	1	1.60	1.97
2003	LAD	NL	77	0	0	67	82.1	306	37	12	11	2	4	0	3	20	2	137	2	0	2	3	.400	0	55-55	0	0.93	1.20
2004	LAD	NL	70	0	0	59	82.1	326	53	24	20	5	4	2	5	22	3	114	2	0	7	3	.700	0	45-47	0	1.72	2.19
2005	LAD	NL	14	0	0	13	13.1	53	10	4	4	2	0	0	0	3	0	22	3	0	1	0	1.000	0	8-8	0	2.38	2.70
2006	LAD	NL	2	0	0	2	2.0	8	0	0	0	0	0	0	1	1	0	3	0	0	0	0	-	0	1-1	0	0.95	0.00
2007	2 Tms	AL	54	0	0	41	52.0	222	49	22	22	3	0	0	1	21	0	51	1	0	4	2	.667	0	16-20	4	3.56	3.81
07	Tex	AL	34	0	0	30	33.1	133	23	8	8	2	0	0	1	12	0	29	1	0	2	0	1.000	0	16-17	1	2.21	2.16
07	Bos	AL	20	0	0	11	18.2	89	26	14	14	1	0	0	0	9	0	22	0	0	2	2	.500	0	0-3	3	6.37	6.75
	9 ML YEARS		352	48	0	253	597.1	2461	472	240	220	65	23	15	31	204	11	680	17	1	29	23	.558	0	177-187	5	2.95	3.31

Armando Galarraga

Pitches: R **Bats:** R **Pos:** RP-2; SP-1   **Ht:** 6'4" **Wt:** 180 **Born:** 2/15/1982 **Age:** 26

			HOW MUCH HE PITCHED						WHAT HE GAVE UP										THE RESULTS						
Year	Team	Lg	G	GS	CG	GF	IP	BFP	H	R	ER	HR	SH	SF	HB	TBB	IBB	SO	WP	Bk	W	L	Pct	ShO	Sv-Op	Hld	ERC	ERA
2001	Expos	R	14	1	0	5	34.2	157	37	21	12	2	2	2	3	15	1	24	3	1	1	3	.250	0	2- -	-	4.51	3.12
2002	Expos	R	2	2	0	0	3.2	12	1	1	1	1	0	0	0	0	0	1	0	0	0	0	-	0	0- -	-	0.55	2.45
2003	Expos	R	5	5	0	0	15.0	60	13	5	3	0	0	0	1	5	0	7	1	0	1	1	.500	0	0- -	-	2.84	1.80
2004	Savann	A	23	19	2	1	110.1	470	104	64	57	14	6	6	8	31	0	94	3	1	5	5	.500	0	0- -	-	3.71	4.65
2005	Ptomc	A+	14	14	0	0	80.0	337	69	30	22	7	1	1	10	23	0	79	4	2	3	4	.429	0	0- -	-	3.28	2.48
2005	Hrsbrg	AA	13	13	1	0	77.1	328	80	46	43	10	5	3	4	22	0	59	2	1	3	4	.429	1	0- -	-	4.27	5.00
2006	Frisco	AA	9	9	0	0	41.0	192	56	34	25	5	1	1	6	13	0	38	1	1	1	6	.143	0	0- -	-	6.76	5.49
2006	Rngrs	R	6	6	0	0	16.1	69	18	8	6	0	0	0	1	6	0	16	4	0	0	2	.000	0	0- -	-	4.24	3.31
2006	Spkane	A-	1	1	0	0	4.0	16	4	2	2	1	0	0	0	3	0	3	0	0	1	0	1.000	0	0- -	-	3.33	4.50
2006	Bkrsfld	A+	2	2	0	0	8.2	41	6	9	6	2	0	0	0	7	0	7	1	0	0	1	.000	0	0- -	-	4.55	6.23
2007	Frisco	AA	23	22	2	0	127.2	542	122	58	57	14	4	0	12	47	0	114	4	0	9	6	.600	2	0- -	-	4.23	4.02
2007	Okla	AAA	4	4	1	0	24.2	109	23	13	13	1	0	0	1	11	0	21	2	1	2	2	.500	1	0- -	-	3.52	4.74
2007	Tex	AL	3	1	0	2	8.2	40	8	6	6	2	0	1	0	7	0	6	0	0	0	0	-	0	0-0	0	6.35	6.23

John Gall

Bats: R **Throws:** R **Pos:** PH-2; RF-1 **Ht:** 6'0" **Wt:** 195 **Born:** 4/2/1978 **Age:** 30

											BATTING									BASERUNNING					AVERAGES		
Year	Team	Lg	G	AB	H	2B	3B	HR	(Hm	Rd)	TB	R	RBI	RC	TBB	IBB	SO	HBP	SH	SF	SB	CS	SB%	GDP	Avg	OBP	Slg
2007	Albq*	AAA	113	413	124	28	3	13	(-	-)	197	75	58	73	38	1	49	3	0	2	10	4	.71	17	.300	.362	.477
2005	StL	NL	22	37	10	3	0	2	(1	1)	19	5	10	6	1	0	8	0	0	1	0	0	-	0	.270	.282	.514
2006	StL	NL	8	12	3	0	0	0	(0	0)	3	1	1	2	0	0	5	0	0	0	0	0	-	0	.250	.250	.250
2007	Fla	NL	3	4	0	0	0	0	(0	0)	0	0	0	0	0	0	1	1	0	0	0	0	-	1	.000	.200	.000
3 ML YEARS			33	53	13	3	0	2	(1	1)	22	6	11	8	1	0	14	1	0	1	0	0	-	1	.245	.268	.415

Sean Gallagher

Pitches: R **Bats:** R **Pos:** RP-8 **Ht:** 6'2" **Wt:** 225 **Born:** 12/30/1985 **Age:** 22

			HOW MUCH HE PITCHED						WHAT HE GAVE UP										THE RESULTS						
Year	Team	Lg	G	GS	CG	GF	IP	BFP	H	R	ER	HR	SH	SF	HB	TBB	IBB	SO	WP	Bk	W	L	Pct	ShO	Sv-Op Hld	ERC	ERA
2004	Cubs	R	10	9	0	0	34.2	152	38	19	12	0	0	3	11	0	44	1	0	1	2	.333	0	0- -	3.91	3.12
2005	Peoria	A	26	26	0	0	146.0	600	107	53	44	10	6	5	15	55	0	139	5	0	14	5	.737	0	0- -	2.77	2.71
2005	Dytona	A+	1	1	0	0	5.0	21	6	1	1	1	0	0	0	0	0	7	0	0	0	0	-	0	0- -	4.14	1.80
2006	Dytona	A+	13	13	0	0	78.1	322	75	24	20	5	6	2	5	21	0	80	3	0	4	0	1.000	0	0- -	3.42	2.30
2006	WTenn	AA	15	15	0	0	86.1	374	74	30	26	4	5	3	1	55	2	91	9	0	7	5	.583	0	0- -	3.88	2.71
2007	Tenn	AA	11	11	0	0	61.0	260	54	25	23	3	0	1	3	24	0	54	3	0	7	2	.778	0	0- -	3.24	3.39
2007	Iowa	AAA	8	8	0	0	40.2	163	33	12	12	1	3	2	3	13	0	37	3	0	3	1	.750	0	0- -	2.65	2.66
2007	ChC	NL	8	0	0	3	14.2	74	19	15	14	3	0	1	1	12	0	5	0	0	0	0	-	0	1-1 0	8.95	8.59

Yovani Gallardo

Pitches: R **Bats:** R **Pos:** SP-17; RP-3 **Ht:** 6'1" **Wt:** 209 **Born:** 2/27/1986 **Age:** 22

			HOW MUCH HE PITCHED						WHAT HE GAVE UP										THE RESULTS						
Year	Team	Lg	G	GS	CG	GF	IP	BFP	H	R	ER	HR	SH	SF	HB	TBB	IBB	SO	WP	Bk	W	L	Pct	ShO	Sv-Op Hld	ERC	ERA
2004	Brewrs	R	6	6	0	0	19.1	74	14	3	1	0	0	0	1	4	0	23	2	0	0	0	-	0	0- -	1.65	0.47
2004	Beloit	A	2	2	0	0	7.1	34	12	10	10	2	0	0	0	4	0	8	3	0	0	1	.000	0	0- -	11.30	12.27
2005	WV	A	26	18	0	5	121.1	503	100	46	37	5	7	1	8	51	0	110	8	0	8	3	.727	0	1- -	3.12	2.74
2006	BrvdCt	A+	13	13	0	0	77.2	307	54	24	19	4	4	1	4	23	0	103	5	0	6	3	.667	0	0- -	2.05	2.20
2006	Hntsvl	AA	13	13	0	0	77.1	303	50	18	14	2	6	1	1	28	0	85	3	0	5	2	.714	0	0- -	1.78	1.63
2007	Nashv	AAA	13	13	0	0	77.2	315	53	26	25	4	3	1	2	28	0	110	4	0	8	3	.727	0	0- -	2.06	2.90
2007	Mil	NL	20	17	0	1	110.1	466	103	48	45	8	4	3	2	37	2	101	3	0	9	5	.643	0	0-0	3.30	3.67

Anderson Garcia

Pitches: R **Bats:** R **Pos:** RP-1 **Ht:** 6'2" **Wt:** 170 **Born:** 3/23/1981 **Age:** 27

			HOW MUCH HE PITCHED						WHAT HE GAVE UP										THE RESULTS						
Year	Team	Lg	G	GS	CG	GF	IP	BFP	H	R	ER	HR	SH	SF	HB	TBB	IBB	SO	WP	Bk	W	L	Pct	ShO	Sv-Op Hld	ERC	ERA
2001	StIsInd	A-	1	1	0	0	4.2	20	7	3	3	0	0	0	0	1	0	1	1	0	0	1	.000	0	0- -	5.90	5.79
2002	Yanks	R	11	9	1	0	58.2	237	43	22	15	1	3	0	1	22	0	41	8	0	4	1	.800	1	0- -	2.15	2.30
2003	Btl Crk	A	16	11	1	2	76.0	317	57	35	28	2	1	2	4	36	0	62	5	3	3	6	.333	0	0- -	2.74	3.32
2003	CptCty	A	6	2	0	0	12.2	50	10	6	6	1	1	0	1	2	0	12	1	0	0	1	.000	0	0- -	2.27	4.26
2004	CptCty	A	35	5	0	15	84.0	396	92	57	44	7	1	1	9	47	2	75	8	1	9	2	.818	0	2- -	5.45	4.71
2005	StLuci	A+	16	0	0	9	26.2	112	21	9	8	2	2	1	1	9	0	20	2	1	2	2	.500	0	3- -	2.61	2.70
2005	Bnghtn	AA	30	1	0	18	50.2	214	55	31	28	7	1	2	0	18	1	41	1	1	4	1	.800	0	5- -	4.78	4.97
2006	Bnghtn	AA	11	0	0	2	21.0	89	21	5	3	0	2	1	1	6	1	17	2	0	1	1	.500	0	1- -	3.06	1.29
2006	Norfolk	AAA	20	0	0	2	31.1	138	35	25	22	4	1	2	0	14	1	18	0	0	1	4	.200	0	0- -	5.17	6.32
2006	Mets	R	2	0	0	0	3.0	11	0	1	1	0	0	0	0	2	0	3	1	2	0	0	-	0	0- -	0.46	3.00
2006	Bowie	AA	4	0	0	2	8.1	31	6	2	2	0	0	0	1	0	0	8	0	0	2	1	.667	0	0- -	1.33	2.16
2006	Ottawa	AAA	5	1	0	2	6.2	27	4	2	2	0	0	0	1	3	0	3	1	0	0	0	-	0	0- -	2.12	2.70
2007	Rdng	AA	14	0	0	13	17.1	69	16	6	6	1	1	0	0	1	1	19	1	0	0	2	.000	0	7- -	2.04	3.12
2007	Ottawa	AAA	37	1	0	21	59.2	263	63	35	34	7	2	6	2	20	3	42	0	0	1	5	.167	0	4- -	4.22	5.13
2007	Phi	NL	1	0	0	0	0.2	4	2	1	1	0	0	0	0	0	0	0	0	0	0	0	-	0	0-0 0	14.52	13.50

Freddy Garcia

Pitches: R **Bats:** R **Pos:** SP-11 **Ht:** 6'4" **Wt:** 260 **Born:** 6/10/1976 **Age:** 32

			HOW MUCH HE PITCHED						WHAT HE GAVE UP										THE RESULTS						
Year	Team	Lg	G	GS	CG	GF	IP	BFP	H	R	ER	HR	SH	SF	HB	TBB	IBB	SO	WP	Bk	W	L	Pct	ShO	Sv-Op Hld	ERC	ERA
2007	Phillies*	R	1	1	0	0	2.0	9	2	1	1	0	0	0	1	0	0	2	0	0	0	0	-	0	0- -	3.63	4.50
2007	Clrwtr*	A+	2	2	0	0	6.1	24	5	0	0	0	0	0	0	1	0	8	0	0	0	0	-	0	0- -	1.64	0.00
1999	Sea	AL	33	33	2	0	201.1	888	205	96	91	18	3	6	10	90	4	170	12	3	17	8	.680	1	0-0	4.46	4.07
2000	Sea	AL	21	20	0	0	124.1	538	112	62	54	16	6	1	2	64	4	79	4	2	9	5	.643	0	0-0	4.20	3.91
2001	Sea	AL	34	34	4	0	238.2	971	199	88	81	16	8	5	5	69	6	163	3	1	18	6	.750	3	0-0	2.61	3.05
2002	Sea	AL	34	34	1	0	223.2	955	227	110	109	30	4	8	6	63	3	181	7	1	16	10	.615	0	0-0	3.98	4.39
2003	Sea	AL	33	33	1	0	201.1	862	196	109	101	31	2	8	11	71	2	144	11	0	12	14	.462	0	0-0	4.33	4.51
2004	2 Tms	AL	31	31	1	0	210.0	878	192	92	89	22	8	3	7	64	3	184	8	0	13	11	.542	0	0-0	3.37	3.81
2005	CWS	AL	33	33	2	0	228.0	943	225	102	98	26	5	5	3	60	2	146	20	1	14	8	.636	0	0-0	3.65	3.87
2006	CWS	AL	33	33	1	0	216.1	917	228	116	109	32	1	6	7	48	3	135	4	0	17	9	.654	0	0-0	4.09	4.53
2007	Phi	NL	11	11	0	0	58.0	264	74	39	38	12	4	3	5	19	3	50	5	0	1	5	.167	0	0-0	6.57	5.90
04	Sea	AL	15	15	1	0	107.0	446	96	39	38	8	4	1	2	32	1	82	5	0	4	7	.364	0	0-0	3.00	3.20
04	CWS	AL	16	16	0	0	103.0	432	96	53	51	14	4	2	5	32	2	102	3	0	9	4	.692	0	0-0	3.77	4.46
9 ML YEARS			263	262	12	0	1701.2	7216	1658	814	770	203	41	45	56	548	30	1252	74	8	117	76	.606	4	0-0	3.87	4.07

Harvey Garcia

Pitches: R Bats: R Pos: RP-8   Ht: 6'2" Wt: 170 Born: 3/16/1984 Age: 24

		HOW MUCH HE PITCHED					WHAT HE GAVE UP											THE RESULTS						
Year Team	Lg	G	GS	CG	GF	IP	BFP	H	R	ER	HR	SH	SF	HB	TBB	IBB	SO	WP	Bk	W	L	Pct	ShO	Sv-Op	Hld	ERC	ERA
2003 RedSx	R	9	8	0	0	33.1	132	21	11	7	2	0	2	1	12	0	32	4	0	3	0	1.000	0	0--	-	1.92	1.89
2004 Lowell	A-	14	14	0	0	61.0	272	61	40	35	8	3	7	4	30	0	54	7	0	4	6	.400	0	0--	-	4.94	5.16
2005 Grnville	AA	32	0	0	22	44.2	206	49	18	10	3	2	3	5	18	0	54	2	0	3	5	.375	0	6--	-	4.72	2.01
2006 Jupiter	A+	54	0	0	42	63.2	281	54	27	21	5	4	1	0	32	0	81	0	0	0	7	.000	0	20--	-	3.35	2.97
2007 Carlina	AA	18	0	0	5	24.1	108	21	14	11	3	0	0	0	17	0	25	5	1	2	2	.500	0	0--	-	4.69	4.07
2007 Albq	AAA	42	0	0	13	48.0	223	59	35	33	9	2	3	1	22	2	45	5	0	4	1	.800	0	1--	-	6.31	6.19
2007 Fla	NL	8	0	0	0	12.1	55	14	6	6	3	1	0	0	7	1	15	2	0	0	1	.000	0	0-0	0	6.78	4.38

Nomar Garciaparra

Bats: R Throws: R Pos: 1B-68; 3B-43; PH-11   Ht: 6'0" Wt: 190 Born: 7/23/1973 Age: 34

		BATTING																		BASERUNNING				AVERAGES		
Year Team	Lg	G	AB	H	2B	3B	HR	(Hm	Rd)	TB	R	RBI	RC	TBB	IBB	SO	HBP	SH	SF	SB	CS	SB%	GDP	Avg	OBP	Slg
1996 Bos	AL	24	87	21	2	3	4	(3	1)	41	11	16	13	4	0	14	0	1	1	5	0	1.00	0	.241	.272	.471
1997 Bos	AL	153	684	209	44	11	30	(11	19)	365	122	98	122	35	2	92	6	2	7	22	9	.71	9	.306	.342	.534
1998 Bos	AL	143	604	195	37	8	35	(17	18)	353	111	122	117	33	1	62	8	0	7	12	6	.67	20	.323	.362	.584
1999 Bos	AL	135	532	190	42	4	27	(14	13)	321	103	104	125	51	7	39	8	0	4	14	3	.82	11	.357	.418	.603
2000 Bos	AL	140	529	197	51	3	21	(7	14)	317	104	96	127	61	20	50	2	0	7	5	2	.71	8	.372	.434	.599
2001 Bos	AL	21	83	24	3	0	4	(3	1)	39	13	8	13	7	0	9	1	0	0	0	1	.00	1	.289	.352	.470
2002 Bos	AL	156	635	197	56	5	24	(10	14)	335	101	120	113	41	4	63	6	0	11	5	2	.71	17	.310	.352	.528
2003 Bos	AL	156	658	198	37	13	28	(18	10)	345	120	105	114	39	1	61	11	1	10	19	5	.79	10	.301	.345	.524
2004 2 Tms		81	321	99	21	3	9	(6	3)	153	52	41	53	24	2	30	6	1	2	4	1	.80	10	.308	.365	.477
2005 ChC	NL	62	230	65	12	0	9	(5	4)	104	28	30	28	12	0	24	2	0	3	0	0	-	6	.283	.320	.452
2006 LAD	NL	122	469	142	31	2	20	(9	11)	237	82	93	87	42	9	30	8	0	4	3	0	1.00	15	.303	.367	.505
2007 LAD	NL	121	431	122	17	0	7	(6	1)	160	59	59	60	31	5	41	0	0	4	3	1	.75	6	.283	.328	.371
04 Bos	AL	38	156	50	7	3	5	(3	2)	78	24	21	26	8	2	16	4	0	1	2	0	1.00	4	.321	.367	.500
04 ChC	NL	43	165	49	14	0	4	(3	1)	75	28	20	27	16	0	14	2	1	1	2	1	.67	6	.297	.364	.455
12 ML YEARS		1314	5263	1659	353	52	218	(109	109)	2770	886	892	972	380	51	515	58	5	60	92	30	.75	113	.315	.364	.526

Lee Gardner

Pitches: R Bats: R Pos: RP-62   Ht: 6'0" Wt: 210 Born: 1/16/1975 Age: 33

		HOW MUCH HE PITCHED					WHAT HE GAVE UP											THE RESULTS						
Year Team	Lg	G	GS	CG	GF	IP	BFP	H	R	ER	HR	SH	SF	HB	TBB	IBB	SO	WP	Bk	W	L	Pct	ShO	Sv-Op	Hld	ERC	ERA
2007 Albq*	AAA	9	0	0	4	13.1	49	10	8	7	0	2	0	0	2	1	9	0	0	0	2	.000	0	1--	-	1.45	4.73
2002 TB	AL	12	0	0	3	13.1	65	12	11	6	3	1	2	3	8	0	8	0	0	1	1	.500	0	0-2	1	5.86	4.05
2005 TB	AL	5	0	0	2	7.1	37	12	9	4	2	0	1	0	2	0	4	0	0	0	0	-	0	0-0	0	8.45	4.91
2007 Fla	NL	62	0	0	20	74.1	311	72	19	16	2	3	3	3	18	4	52	1	0	3	4	.429	0	2-2	9	2.87	1.94
3 ML YEARS		79	0	0	25	95.0	413	96	39	26	7	4	6	6	28	4	64	1	0	4	5	.444	0	2-4	10	3.65	2.46

Ryan Garko

Bats: R Throws: R Pos: 1B-125; PH-11; DH-6   Ht: 6'2" Wt: 225 Born: 1/2/1981 Age: 27

		BATTING																		BASERUNNING				AVERAGES		
Year Team	Lg	G	AB	H	2B	3B	HR	(Hm	Rd)	TB	R	RBI	RC	TBB	IBB	SO	HBP	SH	SF	SB	CS	SB%	GDP	Avg	OBP	Slg
2005 Cle	AL	1	1	0	0	0	0	(0	0)	0	0	0	0	0	0	1	0	0	0	0	0	-	0	.000	.000	.000
2006 Cle	AL	50	185	54	12	0	7	(4	3)	87	28	45	32	14	0	37	7	0	3	0	0	-	5	.292	.359	.470
2007 Cle	AL	138	484	140	29	1	21	(12	9)	234	62	61	71	34	1	94	20	0	3	0	1	.00	12	.289	.359	.483
3 ML YEARS		189	670	194	41	1	28	(16	12)	321	90	106	103	48	1	132	27	0	6	0	1	.00	17	.290	.358	.479

Jon Garland

Pitches: R Bats: R Pos: SP-32   Ht: 6'6" Wt: 215 Born: 9/27/1979 Age: 28

		HOW MUCH HE PITCHED					WHAT HE GAVE UP											THE RESULTS						
Year Team	Lg	G	GS	CG	GF	IP	BFP	H	R	ER	HR	SH	SF	HB	TBB	IBB	SO	WP	Bk	W	L	Pct	ShO	Sv-Op	Hld	ERC	ERA
2000 CWS	AL	15	13	0	1	69.2	324	82	55	50	10	0	2	1	40	0	42	4	0	4	8	.333	0	0-0	1	6.26	6.46
2001 CWS	AL	35	16	0	8	117.0	510	123	59	48	16	2	5	4	55	2	61	3	0	6	7	.462	0	1-1	2	5.16	3.69
2002 CWS	AL	33	33	1	0	192.2	827	188	109	98	23	3	4	9	83	1	112	5	0	12	12	.500	1	0-0	0	4.46	4.58
2003 CWS	AL	32	32	0	0	191.2	813	188	103	96	28	4	8	4	74	1	108	8	0	12	13	.480	0	0-0	0	4.38	4.51
2004 CWS	AL	34	33	1	0	217.0	923	223	135	118	34	9	5	4	76	2	113	3	0	12	11	.522	0	0-0	0	4.56	4.89
2005 CWS	AL	32	32	3	0	221.0	901	212	93	86	26	9	8	7	47	3	115	2	0	18	10	.643	3	0-0	0	3.39	3.50
2006 CWS	AL	33	32	1	0	211.1	900	247	112	106	26	5	8	6	41	4	112	4	0	18	7	.720	0	0-0	0	4.50	4.51
2007 CWS	AL	32	32	2	0	208.1	883	219	114	98	19	3	7	4	57	3	98	1	0	10	13	.435	1	0-0	0	3.87	4.23
8 ML YEARS		246	223	8	9	1428.2	6081	1482	770	700	182	35	47	39	473	16	761	30	0	92	81	.532	6	1-1	3	4.35	4.41

Matt Garza

Pitches: R Bats: R Pos: SP-15; RP-1   Ht: 6'4" Wt: 205 Born: 11/26/1983 Age: 24

		HOW MUCH HE PITCHED					WHAT HE GAVE UP											THE RESULTS						
Year Team	Lg	G	GS	CG	GF	IP	BFP	H	R	ER	HR	SH	SF	HB	TBB	IBB	SO	WP	Bk	W	L	Pct	ShO	Sv-Op	Hld	ERC	ERA
2005 Elizab	R+	4	4	0	0	19.2	79	14	10	8	3	1	0	1	6	0	25	2	0	1	1	.500	0	0--	-	2.71	3.66
2005 Beloit	A	10	10	0	0	56.0	236	53	24	22	5	1	4	1	15	0	64	1	0	3	3	.500	0	0--	-	3.46	3.54
2006 FtMyrs	A+	8	8	0	0	44.1	77	27	13	7	3	2	2	2	11	0	53	0	0	5	1	.833	0	0--	-	4.16	1.42
2006 NwBrit	AA	10	10	0	0	57.1	228	40	22	16	2	1	3	1	14	0	68	3	0	6	2	.750	0	0--	-	1.76	2.51
2006 Roch	AAA	5	5	2	0	34.0	126	20	7	7	1	1	0	3	7	0	33	0	0	3	1	.750	1	0--	-	1.44	1.85

Year Team Lg	HOW MUCH HE PITCHED			WHAT HE GAVE UP			THE RESULTS		
	G GS CG GF	IP BFP	H R ER	HR SH SF HB	TBB IBB	SO WP Bk	W L Pct ShO	Sv-Op Hld	ERC ERA
2007 Roch AAA	16 16 1 0	92.0 401	93 43 37	5 5 2 5	31 0	95 6 0	4 6 .400 0	0-- -	3.73 3.62
2006 Min AL	10 9 0 0	50.0 232	62 33 32	6 0 3 0	23 0	38 1 0	3 6 .333 0	0-0 0	5.82 5.76
2007 Min AL	16 15 0 1	83.0 367	96 44 34	8 1 4 4	32 4	67 4 0	5 7 .417 0	0-0 0	5.08 3.69
2 ML YEARS	26 24 0 1	133.0 599	158 77 66	14 1 7 4	55 4	105 5 0	8 13 .381 0	0-0 0	5.36 4.47

Joey Gathright

Bats: L Throws: R Pos: LF-64; CF-10; PH-5; DH-1; PR-1   Ht: 5'10" Wt: 185 Born: 4/27/1981 Age: 27

Year Team Lg	BATTING					BASERUNNING	AVERAGES
	G AB H 2B 3B HR	(Hm Rd) TB	R RBI RC	TBB IBB SO	HBP SH SF	SB CS SB% GDP	Avg OBP Slg
2007 Omha* AAA	60 223 76 10 4 0	(- -) 94	44 25 50	43 0 24	7 1 3	25 8 .76 3	.341 .457 .422
2004 TB AL	19 52 13 0 0 0	(0 0) 13	11 1 4	2 0 14	3 0 0	6 1 .86 2	.250 .316 .250
2005 TB AL	76 203 56 7 3 0	(0 0) 69	29 13 22	10 0 39	7 3 0	20 5 .80 5	.276 .316 .340
2006 2 Tms AL	134 383 91 12 3 1	(1 0) 112	59 41 46	42 0 75	7 9 4	22 9 .71 3	.238 .321 .292
2007 KC AL	74 228 70 8 0 0	(0 0) 78	28 19 31	20 0 36	3 10 0	9 8 .53 2	.307 .371 .342
06 TB AL	55 154 31 6 0 0	(0 0) 37	25 13 15	20 0 30	3 5 0	12 3 .80 1	.201 .305 .240
06 KC AL	79 229 60 6 3 1	(1 0) 75	34 28 31	22 0 45	4 4 4	10 6 .63 2	.262 .332 .328
4 ML YEARS	303 866 230 27 6 1	(1 0) 272	127 74 103	74 0 164	15 22 4	57 23 .71 12	.266 .333 .314

Chad Gaudin

Pitches: R Bats: R Pos: SP-34   Ht: 5'10" Wt: 180 Born: 3/24/1983 Age: 25

Year Team Lg	HOW MUCH HE PITCHED			WHAT HE GAVE UP			THE RESULTS		
	G GS CG GF	IP BFP	H R ER	HR SH SF HB	TBB IBB	SO WP Bk	W L Pct ShO	Sv-Op Hld	ERC ERA
2003 TB AL	15 3 0 5	40.0 173	37 18 16	4 0 2 1	16 0	23 1 0	2 0 1.000 0	0-0 0	3.70 3.60
2004 TB AL	26 4 0 5	42.2 201	59 27 23	4 2 4 4	16 4	30 0 0	1 2 .333 0	0-1 5	6.46 4.85
2005 Tor AL	5 3 0 0	13.0 74	31 19 19	6 0 1 1	6 0	12 0 0	1 3 .250 0	0-0 0	18.35 13.15
2006 Oak AL	55 0 0 13	64.0 276	51 24 22	3 0 3 1	42 2	36 2 2	4 2 .667 0	2-3 11	3.62 3.09
2007 Oak AL	34 34 1 0	199.1 886	205 100 98	21 3 6 8	100 8	154 3 1	11 13 .458 0	0-0 0	4.80 4.42
5 ML YEARS	135 44 1 23	359.0 1610	383 196 178	38 5 16 15	180 14	255 6 3	19 20 .487 0	2-4 16	5.04 4.46

Geoff Geary

Pitches: R Bats: R Pos: RP-57   Ht: 6'0" Wt: 180 Born: 8/26/1976 Age: 31

Year Team Lg	HOW MUCH HE PITCHED			WHAT HE GAVE UP			THE RESULTS		
	G GS CG GF	IP BFP	H R ER	HR SH SF HB	TBB IBB	SO WP Bk	W L Pct ShO	Sv-Op Hld	ERC ERA
2007 Ottawa* AAA	14 0 0 1	25.0 101	28 9 7	0 0 0 0	1 0	21 0 0	2 1 .667 0	0-- -	2.73 2.52
2003 Phi NL	5 0 0 2	6.0 28	8 3 3	1 0 0 0	3 0	3 0 0	- - - 0	0-0 0	5.70 4.50
2004 Phi NL	33 0 0 0	44.2 200	52 29 27	8 1 2 3	16 3	30 2 1	1 0 1.000 0	0-0 0	5.63 5.44
2005 Phi NL	40 0 0 12	58.0 247	54 29 24	5 2 4 1	21 4	42 3 0	2 1 .667 0	0-1 3	3.38 3.72
2006 Phi NL	81 0 0 17	91.1 390	103 34 30	6 3 1 6	20 4	60 2 0	7 1 .875 0	1-4 15	4.07 2.96
2007 Phi NL	57 0 0 10	67.1 296	72 44 33	8 5 3 9	25 6	38 3 0	3 2 .600 0	0-3 9	4.98 4.41
5 ML YEARS	216 0 0 57	267.1 1161	289 139 117	27 12 10 19	85 17	173 10 1	13 4 .765 0	1-8 27	4.43 3.94

Esteban German

Bats: R Throws: R Pos: 2B-56; 3B-46; PH-26; LF-8; SS-4, DH-3; PR-3   Ht: 5'9" Wt: 195 Born: 1/26/1978 Age: 30

Year Team Lg	BATTING					BASERUNNING	AVERAGES
	G AB H 2B 3B HR	(Hm Rd) TB	R RBI RC	TBB IBB SO	HBP SH SF	SB CS SB% GDP	Avg OBP Slg
2002 Oak AL	9 35 7 0 0 0	(0 0) 7	4 0 2	4 0 11	1 0 0	1 0 1.00 0	.200 .300 .200
2003 Oak AL	5 4 1 0 0 0	(0 0) 1	0 1 1	0 0 1	0 0 0	0 0 - 1	.250 .250 .250
2004 Oak AL	31 60 15 1 1 0	(0 0) 18	9 7 8	4 0 13	0 1 0	0 1 .00 1	.250 .297 .300
2005 Tex AL	5 4 3 1 0 0	(0 0) 4	3 1 2	0 0 1	0 0 0	2 0 1.00 0	.750 .750 1.000
2006 KC AL	106 279 91 18 5 3	(2 1) 128	44 34 55	40 0 49	6 6 0	7 3 .70 8	.326 .422 .459
2007 KC AL	121 348 92 15 6 4	(3 1) 131	49 37 48	43 0 60	5 6 3	11 7 .61 11	.264 .351 .376
6 ML YEARS	277 730 209 35 12 7	(5 2) 289	109 80 116	91 0 135	12 13 3	21 11 .66 21	.286 .373 .396

Justin Germano

Pitches: R Bats: R Pos: SP-23; RP-3   Ht: 6'3" Wt: 205 Born: 8/6/1982 Age: 25

Year Team Lg	HOW MUCH HE PITCHED			WHAT HE GAVE UP			THE RESULTS		
	G GS CG GF	IP BFP	H R ER	HR SH SF HB	TBB IBB	SO WP Bk	W L Pct ShO	Sv-Op Hld	ERC ERA
2007 Portlnd* AAA	5 5 0 0	32.0 122	23 7 6	0 1 0 1	3 1	20 1 0	4 0 1.000 0	0-- -	1.28 1.69
2004 SD NL	7 5 0 0	21.1 109	31 24 21	2 3 1 0	14 0	16 0 0	1 2 .333 0	0-0 0	7.69 8.86
2006 Cin NL	2 1 0 0	6.2 31	8 4 4	1 0 0 1	3 1	4 0 0	1 0 1.000 0	0-0 0	6.26 5.40
2007 SD NL	26 23 0 3	133.1 566	133 72 66	14 4 0 8	40 3	78 1 0	7 10 .412 0	0-0 0	3.93 4.46
3 ML YEARS	35 29 0 3	161.1 706	172 100 91	17 7 1 9	57 4	102 1 0	8 13 .381 0	0-0 0	4.49 5.08

Jason Giambi

Bats: L Throws: R Pos: DH-56; 1B-18; PH-14   Ht: 6'3" Wt: 235 Born: 1/8/1971 Age: 37

Year Team Lg	BATTING					BASERUNNING	AVERAGES
	G AB H 2B 3B HR	(Hm Rd) TB	R RBI RC	TBB IBB SO	HBP SH SF	SB CS SB% GDP	Avg OBP Slg
2007 Tampa* A+	5 13 4 1 0 0	(- -) 5	0 1 2	3 0 5	0 0 0	0 0 - 0	.308 .438 .385
2007 S-WB* AAA	4 9 1 0 0 1	(- -) 4	1 1 2	6 1 2	0 0 0	0 1 .00 0	.111 .467 .444
1995 Oak AL	54 176 45 7 0 6	(3 3) 70	27 25 27	28 0 31	3 1 2	2 1 .67 4	.256 .364 .398
1996 Oak AL	140 536 156 40 1 20	(6 14) 258	84 79 88	51 3 95	1 1 5	0 1 .00 15	.291 .355 .481
1997 Oak AL	142 519 152 41 2 20	(14 6) 257	66 81 91	55 3 89	6 0 8	0 1 .00 11	.293 .362 .495
1998 Oak AL	153 562 166 28 0 27	(12 15) 275	92 110 103	81 7 102	5 0 9	2 2 .50 16	.295 .384 .489

BATTING / BASERUNNING / AVERAGES

Year	Team	Lg	G	AB	H	2B	3B	HR	(Hm	Rd)	TB	R	RBI	RC	TBB	IBB	SO	HBP	SH	SF	SB	CS	SB%	GDP	Avg	OBP	Slg
1999	Oak	AL	158	575	181	36	1	33	(17	16)	318	115	123	132	105	6	106	7	0	8	1	1	.50	11	.315	.422	.553
2000	Oak	AL	152	510	170	29	1	43	(23	20)	330	108	137	152	137	6	96	9	0	8	2	0	1.00	9	.333	.476	.647
2001	Oak	AL	154	520	178	47	2	38	(27	11)	343	109	120	153	129	24	83	13	0	9	2	0	1.00	17	.342	.477	.660
2002	NYY	AL	155	560	176	34	1	41	(19	22)	335	120	122	139	109	4	112	15	0	5	2	2	.50	18	.314	.435	.598
2003	NYY	AL	156	535	134	25	0	41	(12	29)	282	97	107	120	129	9	140	21	0	5	2	1	.67	9	.250	.412	.527
2004	NYY	AL	80	264	55	9	0	12	(5	7)	100	33	40	42	47	1	62	8	0	3	0	1	.00	5	.208	.342	.379
2005	NYY	AL	139	417	113	14	0	32	(16	16)	223	74	87	102	108	5	109	19	0	1	0	0	-	7	.271	.440	.535
2006	NYY	AL	139	446	113	25	0	37	(20	17)	249	92	113	106	110	12	106	16	0	7	2	0	1.00	6	.253	.413	.558
2007	NYY	AL	83	254	60	8	0	14	(6	8)	110	31	39	41	40	2	66	8	0	1	1	0	1.00	1	.236	.356	.433
13 ML YEARS			1705	5874	1699	343	8	364	(180	184)	3150	1048	1183	1296	1129	82	1197	135	2	71	16	10	.62	133	.289	.411	.536

Jay Gibbons

Bats: L **Throws:** L **Pos:** LF-43; DH-29; PH-12; RF-2   **Ht:** 6'0" **Wt:** 197 **Born:** 3/2/1977 **Age:** 31

Year	Team	Lg	G	AB	H	2B	3B	HR	(Hm	Rd)	TB	R	RBI	RC	TBB	IBB	SO	HBP	SH	SF	SB	CS	SB%	GDP	Avg	OBP	Slg
2001	Bal	AL	73	225	53	10	0	15	(9	6)	108	27	36	31	17	0	39	4	0	0	0	1	.00	7	.236	.301	.480
2002	Bal	AL	136	490	121	29	1	28	(17	11)	236	71	69	71	45	3	66	2	0	4	1	3	.25	9	.247	.311	.482
2003	Bal	AL	160	625	173	39	2	23	(12	11)	285	80	100	94	49	11	89	3	0	5	0	1	.00	12	.277	.330	.456
2004	Bal	AL	97	346	85	14	1	10	(4	6)	131	36	47	38	29	0	64	1	1	3	1	1	.50	11	.246	.303	.379
2005	Bal	AL	139	488	135	33	3	26	(13	13)	252	72	79	73	28	3	56	1	0	1	0	0	-	15	.277	.317	.516
2006	Bal	AL	90	343	95	23	0	13	(8	5)	157	34	46	50	32	2	48	2	0	1	0	0	-	12	.277	.341	.458
2007	Bal	AL	84	270	62	14	0	6	(1	5)	94	28	28	23	15	1	52	2	0	3	0	0	-	5	.230	.272	.348
7 ML YEARS			779	2787	724	162	7	121	(64	57)	1263	348	405	380	215	20	414	15	1	17	2	6	.25	71	.260	.314	.453

Dan Giese

Pitches: R **Bats:** R **Pos:** RP-8   **Ht:** 6'3" **Wt:** 200 **Born:** 5/19/1977 **Age:** 31

			HOW MUCH HE PITCHED						WHAT HE GAVE UP											THE RESULTS						
Year	Team	Lg	G	GS	CG	GF	IP	BFP	H	R	ER	HR	SH	SF	HB	TBB	IBB	SO	WP	Bk	W	L	Pct	ShO	Sv-Op	Hld	ERC	ERA
1999	Lowell	A-	18	0	0	8	34.1	131	17	8	7	2	1	1	2	10	1	27	2	0	3	0	1.000	0	2--	-	1.31	1.83
1999	Augsta	A	9	0	0	1	17.1	71	15	4	4	1	1	0	3	5	0	11	1	0	1	0	1.000	0	0--	-	3.42	2.08
2000	Lowell	A-	15	0	0	13	19.2	75	12	3	2	1	1	0	0	1	0	20	1	0	0	0	-	0	9--	-	0.98	0.92
2000	Srsota	A+	8	0	0	2	14.1	64	19	8	8	2	0	1	0	2	0	13	0	0	1	0	1.000	0	0--	-	5.05	5.14
2001	Augsta	A	46	0	0	39	74.0	297	65	27	18	2	0	0	1	8	3	95	2	0	6	4	.600	0	9--	-	1.89	2.19
2002	Trntn	AA	23	0	0	9	49.1	204	53	24	21	6	3	3	1	9	3	39	1	0	1	2	.333	0	3--	-	3.82	3.83
2002	Mobile	AA	32	0	0	8	52.2	222	56	24	17	3	2	3	0	13	6	51	1	0	4	5	.444	0	0--	-	3.36	2.91
2003	Mobile	AA	2	0	0	0	4.0	15	1	1	1	1	0	0	2	0	0	4	0	0	1	0	1.000	0	0--	-	1.58	2.25
2003	Portlnd	AAA	3	0	0	1	6.0	32	12	9	9	2	0	0	0	3	0	6	0	0	1	0	1.000	0	0--	-	13.48	13.50
2003	Rdng	AA	9	0	0	4	12.1	46	8	2	2	1	1	0	1	1	0	16	0	0	2	1	.667	0	0--	-	1.49	1.46
2003	S-WB	AAA	34	0	0	11	48.1	189	37	19	17	8	0	2	1	10	0	49	0	0	2	0	1.000	0	0--	-	2.61	3.17
2004	S-WB	AAA	54	0	0	23	83.1	332	63	27	26	8	0	0	1	18	3	54	1	0	12	5	.706	0	3--	-	2.08	2.81
2005	S-WB	AAA	26	0	0	5	38.0	166	51	28	24	9	2	1	1	1	0	28	1	1	3	4	.429	0	2--	-	5.49	5.68
2006	Rdng	AA	23	0	0	10	36.1	144	27	11	11	5	1	2	0	14	1	27	0	0	1	2	.333	0	1--	-	2.94	2.48
2006	S-WB	AAA	25	0	0	8	35.2	154	46	17	12	3	3	2	0	4	1	33	0	1	2	2	.500	0	0--	-	4.39	3.03
2007	Fresno	AAA	47	0	0	14	73.1	291	65	26	23	2	2	2	1	10	1	76	3	1	3	1	.750	0	2--	-	2.10	2.82
2007	SF	NL	8	0	0	3	9.1	37	8	5	5	4	1	0	0	2	0	7	0	0	0	2	.000	0	0-0	0	4.61	4.82

Geronimo Gil

Bats: R **Throws:** R **Pos:** C-4; PH-1   **Ht:** 6'2" **Wt:** 225 **Born:** 8/7/1975 **Age:** 32

Year	Team	Lg	G	AB	H	2B	3B	HR	(Hm	Rd)	TB	R	RBI	RC	TBB	IBB	SO	HBP	SH	SF	SB	CS	SB%	GDP	Avg	OBP	Slg
2001	Bal	AL	17	58	17	2	0	0	(0	0)	19	3	6	7	5	0	7	2	1	0	0	0	-	1	.293	.369	.328
2002	Bal	AL	125	422	98	19	0	12	(5	7)	153	33	45	33	21	1	88	1	5	1	2	2	.50	12	.232	.270	.363
2003	Bal	AL	54	169	40	4	0	3	(2	1)	53	22	16	18	12	0	34	3	2	0	0	0	-	2	.237	.299	.314
2004	Bal	AL	12	32	9	2	0	0	(0	0)	11	1	4	5	3	1	5	0	0	0	0	0	-	0	.281	.343	.344
2005	Bal	AL	64	125	24	3	0	4	(1	3)	39	7	17	6	5	0	23	0	2	2	0	0	-	10	.192	.220	.312
2007	Col	NL	5	14	1	0	0	0	(0	0)	1	1	0	0	1	0	5	0	1	0	0	0	-	1	.071	.133	.071
6 ML YEARS			277	820	189	30	0	19	(8	11)	276	67	88	69	47	2	162	6	11	3	2	2	.50	31	.230	.276	.337

Jerry Gil

Bats: R **Throws:** R **Pos:** PR-1   **Ht:** 6'3" **Wt:** 195 **Born:** 10/14/1982 **Age:** 25

Year	Team	Lg	G	AB	H	2B	3B	HR	(Hm	Rd)	TB	R	RBI	RC	TBB	IBB	SO	HBP	SH	SF	SB	CS	SB%	GDP	Avg	OBP	Slg
2000	Msoula	R+	58	227	51	10	2	0	(-	-)	65	24	20	15	11	1	63	2	0	1	7	3	.70	5	.225	.266	.286
2001	Sbend	A	105	363	78	14	5	2	(-	-)	108	40	31	20	8	0	103	4	8	0	19	7	.73	12	.215	.240	.298
2002	Lancst	A+	10	37	8	0	0	1	(-	-)	11	4	4	2	1	0	11	0	0	0	1	1	.50	0	.216	.237	.297
2002	Yakima	A-	65	224	56	11	2	2	(-	-)	77	21	28	21	6	0	47	2	2	2	14	1	.93	6	.250	.274	.344
2003	Sbend	A	116	429	111	16	6	4	(-	-)	151	52	58	40	10	0	90	2	10	6	19	10	.66	7	.259	.275	.352
2004	Tucsn	AAA	114	421	117	31	8	11	(-	-)	197	58	59	58	12	1	94	2	5	3	12	1	.92	4	.278	.299	.468
2005	Tenn	AA	55	199	51	7	3	10	(-	-)	94	28	29	26	8	1	52	1	4	0	10	7	.59	3	.256	.288	.472
2006	Tenn	AA	112	446	120	27	6	26	(-	-)	237	71	86	71	18	3	111	5	8	4	6	6	.50	7	.269	.302	.531
2006	Tucsn	AAA	16	47	6	1	0	1	(-	-)	10	6	3	0	0	0	15	1	1	0	1	0	1.00	0	.128	.146	.213
2004	Ari	NL	29	86	15	2	1	0	(0	0)	19	3	8	4	0	0	33	1	0	1	2	0	1.00	2	.174	.182	.221
2007	Cin	NL	1	0	0	0	0	0	(0	0)	0	0	0	0	0	0	0	0	0	0	0	0	-	0	-	-	-
2 ML YEARS			30	86	15	2	1	0	(0	0)	19	3	8	4	0	0	33	1	0	1	2	0	1.00	2	.174	.182	.221

Brian Giles

Bats: L Throws: L Pos: RF-120; CF-1; PH-1   Ht: 5'10" Wt: 205 Born: 1/20/1971 Age: 37

Year	Team	Lg	G	AB	H	2B	3B	HR	(Hm	Rd)	TB	R	RBI	RC	TBB	IBB	SO	HBP	SH	SF	SB	CS	SB%	GDP	Avg	OBP	Slg
2007	Lk Els*	A+	3	10	4	0	0	1	(-	-)	7	2	3	3	4	0	2	0	0	0	0	0	-	1	.400	.571	.700
1995	Cle	AL	6	9	5	0	0	1	(0	1)	8	6	3	3	0	0	1	0	0	0	0	0	-	0	.556	.556	.889
1996	Cle	AL	51	121	43	14	1	5	(2	3)	74	26	27	29	19	4	13	0	0	3	3	0	1.00	6	.355	.434	.612
1997	Cle	AL	130	377	101	15	3	17	(7	10)	173	62	61	66	63	2	50	1	3	7	13	3	.81	10	.268	.368	.459
1998	Cle	AL	112	350	94	19	0	16	(10	6)	161	56	66	66	73	8	75	3	1	3	10	5	.67	7	.269	.396	.460
1999	Pit	NL	141	521	164	33	3	39	(24	15)	320	109	115	127	95	7	80	3	0	8	6	2	.75	14	.315	.418	.614
2000	Pit	NL	156	559	176	37	7	35	(16	19)	332	111	123	139	114	13	69	7	0	8	6	0	1.00	15	.315	.432	.594
2001	Pit	NL	160	576	178	37	7	37	(18	19)	340	116	95	131	90	14	67	4	0	4	13	6	.68	10	.309	.404	.590
2002	Pit	NL	153	497	148	37	5	38	(15	23)	309	95	103	128	135	24	74	7	0	5	15	6	.71	10	.298	.450	.622
2003	2 Tms	NL	134	492	147	34	6	20	(12	8)	253	93	88	102	105	12	58	8	0	4	4	3	.57	12	.299	.427	.514
2004	SD	NL	159	609	173	33	7	23	(10	13)	289	97	94	102	89	6	80	4	0	9	10	3	.77	12	.284	.374	.475
2005	SD	NL	158	545	164	38	8	15	(6	9)	263	92	83	112	119	9	64	2	0	8	13	5	.72	14	.301	.423	.483
2006	SD	NL	158	604	159	37	1	14	(6	8)	240	87	83	95	104	6	60	5	0	4	9	4	.69	18	.263	.374	.397
2007	SD	NL	121	483	131	27	2	13	(1	12)	201	72	51	74	64	5	61	4	0	1	4	6	.40	8	.271	.361	.416
03	Pit	NL	105	388	116	30	4	16	(10	6)	202	70	70	79	85	11	48	6	0	2	0	3	.00	8	.299	.430	.521
03	SD	NL	29	104	31	4	2	4	(2	2)	51	23	18	23	20	1	10	2	0	2	4	0	1.00	4	.298	.414	.490
	13 ML YEARS		1639	5743	1683	361	50	273	(127	146)	2963	1022	992	1174	1070	110	752	48	4	64	106	43	.71	136	.293	.404	.516

Marcus Giles

Bats: R Throws: R Pos: 2B-112; PH-4   Ht: 5'8" Wt: 175 Born: 5/18/1978 Age: 30

Year	Team	Lg	G	AB	H	2B	3B	HR	(Hm	Rd)	TB	R	RBI	RC	TBB	IBB	SO	HBP	SH	SF	SB	CS	SB%	GDP	Avg	OBP	Slg
2001	Atl	NL	68	244	64	10	2	9	(5	4)	105	36	31	33	28	0	37	0	1	0	2	5	.29	8	.262	.338	.430
2002	Atl	NL	68	213	49	10	1	8	(4	4)	85	27	23	22	25	3	41	2	1	1	1	1	.50	5	.230	.315	.399
2003	Atl	NL	145	551	174	49	2	21	(9	12)	290	101	69	101	59	2	80	11	10	4	14	4	.78	7	.316	.390	.526
2004	Atl	NL	102	379	118	22	2	8	(6	2)	168	61	48	67	36	0	79	9	3	7	17	4	.81	6	.311	.378	.443
2005	Atl	NL	152	577	168	45	4	15	(11	4)	266	104	63	96	64	1	108	5	4	4	16	3	.84	13	.291	.365	.461
2006	Atl	NL	141	550	144	32	2	11	(7	4)	213	87	60	82	62	0	105	6	5	3	10	5	.67	12	.262	.341	.387
2007	SD	NL	116	420	96	19	3	4	(2	2)	133	52	39	46	44	0	82	3	6	3	10	3	.77	10	.229	.304	.317
	7 ML YEARS		792	2934	813	187	16	76	(44	32)	1260	468	333	447	318	6	523	36	30	22	70	25	.74	61	.277	.353	.429

Troy Glaus

Bats: R Throws: R Pos: 3B-114; PH-3   Ht: 6'5" Wt: 240 Born: 8/3/1976 Age: 31

Year	Team	Lg	G	AB	H	2B	3B	HR	(Hm	Rd)	TB	R	RBI	RC	TBB	IBB	SO	HBP	SH	SF	SB	CS	SB%	GDP	Avg	OBP	Slg
1998	LAA	AL	48	165	36	9	0	1	(0	1)	48	19	23	13	15	0	51	0	0	2	1	0	1.00	3	.218	.280	.291
1999	LAA	AL	154	551	132	29	0	29	(12	17)	248	85	79	84	71	1	143	6	0	3	5	1	.83	9	.240	.331	.450
2000	LAA	AL	159	563	160	37	1	47	(24	23)	340	120	102	129	112	6	163	2	0	1	14	11	.56	14	.284	.404	.604
2001	LAA	AL	161	588	147	38	2	41	(22	19)	312	100	108	114	107	7	158	6	0	7	10	3	.77	16	.250	.367	.501
2002	LAA	AL	156	569	142	24	1	30	(13	17)	258	99	111	100	88	4	144	6	0	8	10	3	.77	12	.250	.352	.453
2003	LAA	AL	91	319	79	17	2	16	(9	7)	148	53	50	48	46	4	73	1	0	1	7	2	.78	8	.248	.343	.464
2004	LAA	AL	58	207	52	11	1	18	(9	9)	119	47	42	41	31	3	52	3	0	1	2	3	.40	6	.251	.355	.575
2005	Ari	NL	149	538	139	29	1	37	(20	17)	281	78	97	87	84	2	145	7	0	5	4	2	.67	7	.258	.363	.522
2006	Tor	AL	153	540	136	27	0	38	(25	13)	277	105	104	84	80	6	134	3	0	5	3	2	.60	25	.252	.355	.513
2007	Tor	AL	115	385	101	19	1	20	(7	13)	182	60	62	65	61	2	102	5	0	5	0	1	.00	7	.262	.366	.473
	10 ML YEARS		1244	4425	1124	240	9	277	(141	136)	2213	766	778	765	701	35	1165	39	0	38	56	28	.67	107	.254	.358	.500

Tom Glavine

Pitches: L Bats: L Pos: SP-34   Ht: 6'0" Wt: 204 Born: 3/25/1966 Age: 42

Year	Team	Lg	G	GS	CG	GF	IP	BFP	H	R	ER	HR	SH	SF	HB	TBB	IBB	SO	WP	Bk	W	L	Pct	ShO	Sv-Op	Hld	ERC	ERA
1987	Atl	NL	9	9	0	0	50.1	238	55	34	31	5	2	3	3	33	4	20	1	1	2	4	.333	0	0-0	0	5.70	5.54
1988	Atl	NL	34	34	1	0	195.1	844	201	111	99	12	17	11	8	63	7	84	2	2	7	17	.292	0	0-0	0	3.74	4.56
1989	Atl	NL	29	29	6	0	186.0	766	172	88	76	20	11	4	2	40	3	90	2	0	14	8	.636	4	0-0	0	2.99	3.68
1990	Atl	NL	33	33	1	0	214.1	929	232	111	102	18	21	2	1	78	10	129	8	1	10	12	.455	0	0-0	0	4.24	4.28
1991	Atl	NL	34	34	9	0	246.2	989	201	83	70	17	7	6	2	69	6	192	10	2	20	11	.645	1	0-0	0	2.47	2.55
1992	Atl	NL	33	33	7	0	225.0	919	197	81	69	6	2	6	2	70	7	129	5	0	20	8	.714	5	0-0	0	2.61	2.76
1993	Atl	NL	36	36	4	0	239.1	1014	236	91	85	16	10	2	2	90	7	120	4	0	22	6	.786	2	0-0	0	3.70	3.20
1994	Atl	NL	25	25	2	0	165.1	731	173	76	73	10	9	6	1	70	10	140	8	1	13	9	.591	0	0-0	0	4.02	3.97
1995	Atl	NL	29	29	3	0	198.2	822	182	76	68	9	7	5	5	66	0	127	3	0	16	7	.696	1	0-0	0	3.14	3.08
1996	Atl	NL	36	36	1	0	235.1	994	222	91	78	14	15	2	0	85	7	181	4	0	15	10	.600	0	0-0	0	3.29	2.98
1997	Atl	NL	33	33	5	0	240.0	970	197	86	79	20	11	4	2	79	9	152	3	0	14	7	.667	2	0-0	0	2.80	2.96
1998	Atl	NL	33	33	4	0	229.1	934	202	67	63	13	6	2	2	74	2	157	3	0	20	6	.769	3	0-0	0	2.93	2.47
1999	Atl	NL	35	35	2	0	234.0	1023	259	115	107	18	22	10	4	83	14	138	2	0	14	11	.560	0	0-0	0	4.31	4.12
2000	Atl	NL	35	35	4	0	241.0	992	222	101	91	24	9	5	4	65	6	152	0	0	21	9	.700	0	0-0	0	3.19	3.40
2001	Atl	NL	35	35	1	0	219.1	929	213	92	87	24	5	8	2	97	10	116	2	0	16	7	.696	1	0-0	0	4.21	3.57
2002	Atl	NL	36	36	2	0	224.2	936	210	85	74	21	12	6	8	78	8	127	2	0	18	11	.621	1	0-0	0	3.61	2.96
2003	NYM	NL	32	32	0	0	183.1	791	205	94	92	21	7	4	2	66	7	82	2	0	9	14	.391	0	0-0	0	4.77	4.52
2004	NYM	NL	33	33	1	0	212.1	904	204	94	85	20	13	10	0	70	10	109	0	0	11	14	.440	1	0-0	0	3.43	3.60
2005	NYM	NL	33	33	2	0	211.1	901	227	88	83	12	19	3	3	61	5	105	1	0	13	13	.500	1	0-0	0	3.79	3.53
2006	NYM	NL	32	32	0	0	198.0	842	202	94	84	22	11	7	6	62	7	131	1	0	15	7	.682	0	0-0	0	4.01	3.82
2007	NYM	NL	34	34	1	0	200.1	855	219	102	99	23	5	2	4	64	2	89	2	0	13	8	.619	1	0-0	0	4.53	4.45
	21 ML YEARS		669	669	56	0	4350.0	18323	4231	1860	1695	345	221	110	65	1463	141	2570	65	7	303	199	.604	25	0-0	0	3.57	3.51

Ross Gload

Bats: L Throws: L Pos: 1B-89; PH-9; LF-8; DH-2; PR-1 **Ht: 6'1" Wt: 190 Born: 4/5/1976 Age: 32**

Year	Team	Lg	G	AB	H	2B	3B	HR	(Hm	Rd)	TB	R	RBI	RC	TBB	IBB	SO	HBP	SH	SF	SB	CS	SB%	GDP	Avg	OBP	Slg
2007	Omha*	AAA	1	4	2	0	0	1	(-	-)	5	1	1	1	0	0	0	0	0	0	0	0	-	0	.500	.500	1.250
2000	ChC	NL	18	31	6	0	1	1	(0	1)	11	4	3	3	3	0	10	0	0	1	0	0	-	1	.194	.257	.355
2002	Col	NL	26	31	8	1	0	1	(1	0)	12	4	4	3	3	0	7	0	0	0	0	0	-	0	.258	.324	.387
2004	CWS	AL	110	234	75	16	0	7	(3	4)	112	28	44	41	20	1	37	2	1	3	0	3	.00	11	.321	.375	.479
2005	CWS	AL	28	42	7	2	0	0	(0	0)	9	2	5	2	2	0	9	0	0	0	0	0	-	1	.167	.205	.214
2006	CWS	AL	77	156	51	8	2	3	(1	2)	72	22	18	24	6	0	15	1	3	1	6	0	1.00	6	.327	.354	.462
2007	KC	AL	102	320	92	22	3	7	(2	5)	141	37	51	45	16	2	39	2	0	8	2	2	.50	13	.288	.318	.441
	6 ML YEARS		361	814	239	49	6	19	(7	12)	357	97	125	118	50	3	117	5	4	13	8	5	.62	29	.294	.333	.439

Gary Glover

Pitches: R Bats: R Pos: RP-67 **Ht: 6'5" Wt: 225 Born: 12/3/1976 Age: 31**

			HOW MUCH HE PITCHED					WHAT HE GAVE UP										THE RESULTS						
Year	Team	Lg	G	GS	CG	GF	IP	BFP	H	R	ER	HR	SH	SF	HB	TBB	IBB	SO	WP	Bk	W	L	Pct	ShO	Sv-Op	Hld	ERC	ERA
1999	Tor	AL	1	0	0	1	1.0	3	0	0	0	0	0	0	0	1	0	0	0	0	0	0	-	0	0-0	0	1.26	0.00
2001	CWS	AL	46	11	0	10	100.1	429	98	61	55	16	2	2	4	32	3	63	4	0	5	5	.500	0	0-1	7	4.12	4.93
2002	CWS	AL	41	22	0	10	138.1	604	136	86	80	21	6	2	7	52	1	70	6	0	7	8	.467	0	1-1	2	4.39	5.20
2003	2 Tms		42	0	0	15	62.2	279	77	33	33	6	0	5	3	22	3	37	2	0	2	0	1.000	0	0-0	1	5.37	4.74
2004	Mil	NL	4	3	0	0	18.0	82	18	9	7	2	2	2	2	8	1	8	1	0	2	1	.667	0	0-0	1	4.57	3.50
2005	Mil	NL	15	11	0	1	64.2	284	74	41	40	10	3	2	2	20	0	58	3	0	5	4	.556	0	0-0	0	5.06	5.57
2007	TB	AL	67	0	0	18	77.1	334	87	44	42	12	1	3	1	27	3	51	2	0	6	5	.545	0	2-4	11	5.07	4.89
	03 CWS	AL	24	0	0	8	35.2	160	43	18	18	3	0	3	2	14	2	23	1	0	1	0	1.000	0	0-0	1	5.32	4.54
	03 LAA	AL	18	0	0	7	27.0	119	34	15	15	3	0	2	1	8	1	14	1	0	1	0	1.000	0	0-0	0	5.44	5.00
	7 ML YEARS		216	47	0	55	462.1	2015	490	274	257	67	14	16	19	162	11	287	18	0	27	23	.540	0	3-6	21	4.67	5.00

Jimmy Gobble

Pitches: L Bats: L Pos: RP-74 **Ht: 6'3" Wt: 200 Born: 7/19/1981 Age: 26**

			HOW MUCH HE PITCHED					WHAT HE GAVE UP										THE RESULTS						
Year	Team	Lg	G	GS	CG	GF	IP	BFP	H	R	ER	HR	SH	SF	HB	TBB	IBB	SO	WP	Bk	W	L	Pct	ShO	Sv-Op	Hld	ERC	ERA
2003	KC	AL	9	9	0	0	52.2	230	56	32	27	8	1	3	4	15	0	31	1	0	4	5	.444	0	0-0	0	4.61	4.61
2004	KC	AL	25	24	1	0	148.0	638	157	94	88	24	4	7	3	43	0	49	4	0	9	8	.529	0	0-0	0	4.47	5.35
2005	KC	AL	28	4	0	11	53.2	249	64	34	34	9	3	1	1	30	4	38	2	0	1	1	.500	0	0-0	4	6.39	5.70
2006	KC	AL	60	6	0	17	84.0	370	95	51	48	12	3	0	1	29	1	80	4	0	4	6	.400	0	2-4	11	4.93	5.14
2007	KC	AL	74	0	0	12	53.2	233	56	23	18	6	1	5	2	23	6	50	6	1	4	1	.800	0	1-3	16	4.56	3.02
	5 ML YEARS		196	43	1	40	392.0	1720	428	234	215	59	12	16	11	140	11	248	17	1	22	21	.512	0	3-7	31	4.85	4.94

Jonny Gomes

Bats: R Throws: R Pos: DH-45; RF-32; LF-26; PH-8 **Ht: 6'1" Wt: 225 Born: 11/22/1980 Age: 27**

Year	Team	Lg	G	AB	H	2B	3B	HR	(Hm	Rd)	TB	R	RBI	RC	TBB	IBB	SO	HBP	SH	SF	SB	CS	SB%	GDP	Avg	OBP	Slg
2007	Drham*	AAA	13	43	13	2	0	1	(-	-)	18	6	7	10	11	0	15	2	0	0	4	1	.80	1	.302	.464	.419
2003	TB	AL	8	15	2	1	0	0	(0	0)	3	1	0	0	0	0	6	1	0	0	0	0	-	0	.133	.188	.200
2004	TB	AL	5	14	1	0	0	0	(0	0)	1	0	1	0	1	0	6	0	0	0	0	0	-	0	.071	.133	.071
2005	TB	AL	101	348	98	13	6	21	(11	10)	186	61	54	62	39	1	113	14	1	5	9	5	.64	6	.282	.372	.534
2006	TB	AL	117	385	83	21	1	20	(7	13)	166	53	59	53	61	2	116	6	0	9	1	5	.17	10	.216	.325	.431
2007	TB	AL	107	348	85	20	2	17	(10	7)	160	48	49	47	35	1	126	7	0	4	12	4	.75	1	.244	.322	.460
	5 ML YEARS		338	1110	269	55	9	58	(28	30)	516	163	163	162	136	4	367	28	1	18	22	14	.61	17	.242	.335	.465

Carlos Gomez

Bats: R Throws: R Pos: LF-27; RF-22; PH-6; PR-5; CF-4 **Ht: 6'4" Wt: 195 Born: 12/4/1985 Age: 22**

Year	Team	Lg	G	AB	H	2B	3B	HR	(Hm	Rd)	TB	R	RBI	RC	TBB	IBB	SO	HBP	SH	SF	SB	CS	SB%	GDP	Avg	OBP	Slg
2004	Kngspt	R+	38	150	43	10	4	1	(-	-)	64	24	20	23	5	1	29	6	1	1	8	1	.89	2	.287	.333	.427
2004	Mets	R	19	71	19	7	0	0	(-	-)	26	10	11	9	2	0	9	2	0	1	9	1	.90	1	.268	.303	.366
2005	Hgrstn	A	120	487	134	13	6	8	(-	-)	183	75	48	66	32	0	88	9	10	1	64	24	.73	6	.275	.331	.376
2006	Bnghtn	AA	120	430	121	24	8	7	(-	-)	182	53	48	71	27	0	97	20	6	3	41	9	.82	6	.281	.350	.423
2007	StLuci	A+	5	13	2	0	0	0	(-	-)	2	1	0	0	1	0	4	1	0	0	2	0	1.00	0	.154	.267	.154
2007	NewOr	AAA	36	140	40	8	2	2	(-	-)	58	24	13	23	15	0	23	2	0	0	17	4	.81	2	.286	.363	.414
2007	NYM	NL	58	125	29	3	0	2	(1	1)	38	14	12	11	8	2	27	3	0	3	12	3	.80	0	.232	.288	.304

Chris Gomez

Bats: R Throws: R Pos: 1B-44; 3B-31; 2B-10; SS-10; PH-9; PR-8; DH-1 **Ht: 6'1" Wt: 190 Born: 6/16/1971 Age: 37**

Year	Team	Lg	G	AB	H	2B	3B	HR	(Hm	Rd)	TB	R	RBI	RC	TBB	IBB	SO	HBP	SH	SF	SB	CS	SB%	GDP	Avg	OBP	Slg
1993	Det	AL	46	128	32	7	1	0	(0	0)	41	11	11	12	9	0	17	1	3	0	2	2	.50	2	.250	.304	.320
1994	Det	AL	84	296	76	19	0	8	(5	3)	119	32	53	39	33	0	64	3	3	1	5	3	.63	8	.257	.336	.402
1995	Det	AL	123	431	96	20	2	11	(5	6)	153	49	50	43	41	0	96	3	3	4	4	1	.80	13	.223	.292	.355
1996	2 Tms		137	456	117	21	1	4	(2	2)	152	53	45	52	57	1	84	7	6	2	3	3	.50	16	.257	.347	.333
1997	SD	NL	150	522	132	19	2	5	(2	3)	170	62	54	64	53	1	114	5	3	3	5	8	.38	16	.253	.326	.326
1998	SD	NL	145	449	120	32	3	4	(3	1)	170	55	39	58	51	7	87	5	7	3	1	3	.25	11	.267	.346	.379
1999	SD	NL	76	234	59	8	1	1	(1	0)	72	20	15	23	27	3	49	1	2	1	1	2	.33	6	.252	.331	.308
2000	SD	NL	33	54	12	0	0	0	(0	0)	12	4	3	4	7	0	5	0	1	1	0	0	-	1	.222	.306	.222
2001	2 Tms		98	301	78	19	0	8	(5	3)	121	37	43	36	17	0	38	2	6	5	4	0	1.00	9	.259	.298	.402

Year Team	Lg	G	AB	H	2B	3B	HR	(Hm	Rd)	TB	R	RBI	RC	TBB	IBB	SO	HBP	SH	SF	SB	CS	SB%	GDP	Avg	OBP	Slg
2002 TB	AL	130	461	122	31	3	10	(2	8)	189	51	46	51	21	0	58	7	6	3	1	3	.25	8	.265	.305	.410
2003 Min	AL	58	175	44	9	3	1	(0	1)	62	14	15	15	7	1	13	0	2	1	2	1	.67	10	.251	.279	.354
2004 Tor	AL	109	341	96	11	1	3	(1	2)	118	41	37	48	28	0	41	2	3	3	3	2	.60	4	.282	.337	.346
2005 Bal	AL	89	219	61	11	0	1	(1	0)	75	27	18	24	27	1	17	1	6	1	2	1	.67	14	.279	.359	.342
2006 Bal	AL	55	132	45	7	0	2	(0	2)	58	14	17	22	7	1	11	3	0	0	1	2	.33	7	.341	.387	.439
2007 2 Tms	AL	92	222	66	12	1	1	(1	0)	83	21	21	23	10	1	26	0	6	2	1	2	.33	6	.297	.325	.374
96 Det	AL	48	128	31	5	0	1	(1	0)	39	21	16	13	18	0	20	1	3	0	1	1	.50	5	.242	.340	.305
96 SD	NL	89	328	86	16	1	3	(1	2)	113	32	29	39	39	1	64	6	3	2	2	2	.50	11	.262	.349	.345
01 SD	NL	40	112	21	3	0	0	(0	0)	24	6	7	4	9	0	14	0	2	2	1	0	1.00	5	.188	.244	.214
01 TB	AL	58	189	57	16	0	8	(5	3)	97	31	36	32	8	0	24	2	4	3	3	0	1.00	4	.302	.332	.513
07 Bal	AL	73	169	51	10	1	1	(1	0)	66	17	16	20	10	1	20	0	5	1	1	2	.33	5	.302	.339	.391
07 Cle	AL	19	53	15	2	0	0	(0	0)	17	4	5	3	0	0	6	0	1	1	0	0	-	1	.283	.278	.321
15 ML YEARS		1425	4421	1156	226	18	59	(27	32)	1595	491	467	502	395	16	720	40	57	30	35	33	.51	131	.261	.326	.361

Adrian Gonzalez

Bats: L **Throws:** L **Pos:** 1B-161 **Ht:** 6'2" **Wt:** 220 **Born:** 5/8/1982 **Age:** 26

Year Team	Lg	G	AB	H	2B	3B	HR	(Hm	Rd)	TB	R	RBI	RC	TBB	IBB	SO	HBP	SH	SF	SB	CS	SB%	GDP	Avg	OBP	Slg
2004 Tex	AL	16	42	10	3	0	1	(1	0)	16	7	7	7	2	0	6	0	0	0	0	0	-	0	.238	.273	.381
2005 Tex	AL	43	150	34	7	1	6	(3	3)	61	17	17	13	10	2	37	0	0	0	0	0	-	3	.227	.272	.407
2006 SD	NL	156	570	173	38	1	24	(10	14)	285	83	82	82	52	9	113	3	1	5	0	1	.00	24	.304	.362	.500
2007 SD	NL	161	646	182	46	3	30	(10	20)	324	101	100	108	65	9	140	3	0	6	0	0	-	6	.282	.347	.502
4 ML YEARS		376	1408	399	94	5	61	(24	37)	686	208	206	210	129	20	296	6	1	13	0	1	.00	33	.283	.343	.487

Alberto Gonzalez

Bats: R **Throws:** R **Pos:** SS-11; 3B-1; PH-1; PR-1 **Ht:** 5'11" **Wt:** 167 **Born:** 4/18/1983 **Age:** 25

Year Team	Lg	G	AB	H	2B	3B	HR	(Hm	Rd)	TB	R	RBI	RC	TBB	IBB	SO	HBP	SH	SF	SB	CS	SB%	GDP	Avg	OBP	Slg
2004 Sbend	A	100	319	76	15	6	2	(-	-)	109	39	25	33	16	0	44	11	5	2	9	7	.56	10	.238	.296	.342
2005 Sbend	A	95	352	112	21	7	1	(-	-)	150	60	42	56	20	1	42	5	5	5	12	5	.71	7	.318	.359	.426
2006 Tenn	AA	129	434	126	20	3	6	(-	-)	170	67	50	65	37	6	42	8	13	2	5	1	.83	11	.290	.356	.392
2006 Tucsn	AAA	4	15	3	0	0	0	(-	-)	3	2	1	0	1	0	1	1	0	0	0	0	-	0	.200	.294	.200
2007 S-WB	AAA	106	384	95	21	10	1	(-	-)	139	44	35	44	24	2	49	6	9	3	12	5	.71	12	.247	.300	.362
2007 Trntn	AA	28	109	36	10	1	0	(-	-)	48	18	16	19	10	0	14	1	3	2	1	1	.50	3	.330	.385	.440
2007 NYY	AL	12	14	1	0	0	0	(0	0)	1	3	1	0	1	0	1	0	0	0	0	1	.00	1	.071	.133	.071

Alex Gonzalez

Bats: R **Throws:** R **Pos:** SS-103, PH-0 **Ht:** 6'0" **Wt:** 200 **Born:** 2/15/1977 **Age:** 31

Year Team	Lg	G	AB	H	2B	3B	HR	(Hm	Rd)	TB	R	RBI	RC	TBB	IBB	SO	HBP	SH	SF	SB	CS	SB%	GDP	Avg	OBP	Slg
1998 Fla	NL	25	86	13	2	0	3	(1	2)	24	11	7	5	9	0	30	1	2	0	0	0	-	2	.151	.240	.279
1999 Fla	NL	136	560	155	28	8	14	(7	7)	241	81	59	69	15	0	113	12	1	3	3	5	.38	13	.277	.308	.430
2000 Fla	NL	109	385	77	17	4	7	(5	2)	123	35	42	26	13	0	77	2	5	2	7	1	.88	7	.200	.229	.319
2001 Fla	NL	145	515	129	36	1	9	(5	4)	194	57	48	56	30	6	107	10	3	3	2	2	.50	13	.250	.303	.377
2002 Fla	NL	42	151	34	7	1	2	(1	1)	49	15	18	14	12	1	32	4	3	2	3	1	.75	2	.225	.296	.325
2003 Fla	NL	150	528	135	33	6	18	(7	11)	234	52	77	67	33	13	106	13	3	5	0	4	.00	8	.256	.313	.443
2004 Fla	NL	159	561	130	30	3	23	(13	10)	235	67	79	58	27	9	126	4	3	4	3	1	.75	17	.232	.270	.419
2005 Fla	NL	130	435	115	30	0	5	(2	3)	160	45	45	47	31	10	81	5	4	3	5	3	.63	11	.264	.319	.368
2006 Bos	AL	111	388	99	24	2	9	(4	5)	154	48	50	40	22	1	67	5	7	7	1	0	1.00	6	.255	.299	.397
2007 Cin	NL	110	393	107	27	1	16	(8	8)	184	55	55	51	24	1	75	8	2	3	0	1	.00	13	.272	.325	.468
10 ML YEARS		1117	4002	994	234	26	106	(53	53)	1598	466	480	433	216	41	814	64	33	32	24	18	.57	92	.248	.295	.399

Andy Gonzalez

Bats: R **Throws:** R **Pos:** 3B-25; LF-18; CF-10; RF-10; PH-7; 1B-5; 2B-4; PR-3; SS-1 **Ht:** 6'2" **Wt:** 190 **Born:** 12/15/1981 **Age:** 26

Year Team	Lg	G	AB	H	2B	3B	HR	(Hm	Rd)	TB	R	RBI	RC	TBB	IBB	SO	HBP	SH	SF	SB	CS	SB%	GDP	Avg	OBP	Slg
2001 WhSox	R	48	189	61	18	1	5	(-	-)	96	33	30	38	15	0	36	3	0	0	13	2	.87	5	.323	.382	.508
2002 Bristol	R+	66	254	71	17	0	1	(-	-)	91	48	45	36	32	1	43	3	0	7	5	4	.56	3	.280	.358	.358
2003 Knapol	A-	123	429	99	17	1	1	(-	-)	121	58	39	50	69	1	82	7	4	0	22	10	.69	8	.231	.347	.282
2004 Knapol	A-	14	48	13	1	0	1	(-	-)	17	6	3	5	4	0	6	1	0	1	1	2	.33	0	.271	.333	.354
2004 WinSa	A+	80	309	78	18	0	8	(-	-)	120	59	28	48	49	0	53	7	1	2	2	3	.40	4	.252	.365	.388
2004 Brham	AA	36	112	19	3	0	3	(-	-)	31	19	8	8	10	0	17	4	1	0	1	0	1.00	3	.170	.262	.277
2005 Brham	AA	122	433	120	19	2	4	(-	-)	155	51	63	63	60	1	91	5	5	8	5	5	.50	9	.277	.366	.358
2006 Charltt	AAA	117	403	110	27	0	6	(-	-)	155	48	51	59	46	2	77	7	5	2	16	8	.67	9	.273	.356	.385
2007 Charltt	AAA	35	124	30	7	1	3	(-	-)	48	15	17	19	22	1	39	1	0	1	6	1	.86	2	.242	.358	.387
2007 CWS	AL	67	189	35	6	0	2	(1	1)	47	17	11	12	25	1	61	0	1	0	1	5	.17	4	.185	.280	.249

Edgar Gonzalez

Pitches: R **Bats:** R **Pos:** RP-20; SP-12 **Ht:** 6'0" **Wt:** 225 **Born:** 2/23/1983 **Age:** 25

Year Team	Lg	G	GS	CG	GF	IP	BFP	H	R	ER	HR	SH	SF	HB	TBB	IBB	SO	WP	Bk	W	L	Pct	ShO	Sv-Op	Hld	ERC	ERA
2003 Ari	NL	9	2	0	1	18.1	85	28	10	10	3	1	1	0	7	2	14	2	0	2	1	.667	0	0-1	0	7.81	4.91
2004 Ari	NL	10	10	0	0	46.1	228	72	49	48	15	5	1	5	18	4	31	3	1	0	9	.000	0	0-0	0	9.78	9.32

Year	Team	Lg	HOW MUCH HE PITCHED						WHAT HE GAVE UP												THE RESULTS							
			G	GS	CG	GF	IP	BFP	H	R	ER	HR	SH	SF	HB	TBB	IBB	SO	WP	Bk	W	L	Pct	ShO	Sv-Op	Hld	ERC	ERA
2005	Ari	NL	1	0	0	0	0.1	5	2	4	4	1	0	0	0	2	0	1	1	0	0	0	-	0	0-0	0	124.7	108.0
2006	Ari	NL	11	5	0	1	42.2	182	45	20	20	7	4	1	3	9	0	28	2	0	3	4	.429	0	0-0	1	4.33	4.22
2007	Ari	NL	32	12	0	5	102.0	437	110	61	57	18	2	3	4	28	4	62	5	1	8	4	.667	0	0-0	0	4.67	5.03
	5 ML YEARS		63	29	0	7	209.2	937	257	144	139	44	12	6	12	64	10	136	13	2	13	18	.419	0	0-1	1	6.02	5.97

Enrique Gonzalez

Pitches: R **Bats:** R **Pos:** RP-1   **Ht:** 5'10" **Wt:** 210 **Born:** 7/14/1982 **Age:** 25

Year	Team	Lg	HOW MUCH HE PITCHED						WHAT HE GAVE UP												THE RESULTS							
			G	GS	CG	GF	IP	BFP	H	R	ER	HR	SH	SF	HB	TBB	IBB	SO	WP	Bk	W	L	Pct	ShO	Sv-Op	Hld	ERC	ERA
1999	DBcks	R	12	11	1	0	71.0	267	41	21	13	0	0	0	0	24	0	82	0	0	7	3	.700	0	0- -	-	1.37	1.65
2000	DBcks	R	11	0	0	8	17.2	80	16	13	3	0	0	0	1	12	0	17	3	0	1	0	1.000	0	1- -	-	4.08	1.53
2000	Tucsn	AAA	1	0	0	0	4.0	12	1	0	0	0	0	0	0	1	0	1	0	0	1	0	1.000	0	0- -	-	0.47	0.00
2001	Sbend	A	26	26	1	0	146.0	630	142	81	65	9	3	11	10	53	0	92	10	0	4	12	.250	0	0- -	-	3.77	4.01
2002	Lancst	A+	5	5	0	0	18.1	100	34	27	25	3	1	1	1	14	0	11	4	0	1	4	.200	0	0- -	-	12.36	12.27
2002	Yakima	A-	11	11	0	0	66.0	278	53	27	18	2	1	5	7	23	0	57	7	0	5	2	.714	0	0- -	-	2.73	2.45
2002	Sbend	A	4	4	0	0	21.2	95	23	16	9	1	0	1	0	9	0	20	0	0	1	2	.333	0	0- -	-	4.08	3.74
2003	Sbend	A	55	0	0	18	72.0	300	58	22	17	5	3	0	2	29	3	63	3	0	4	3	.571	0	3- -	-	2.88	2.13
2004	Lancst	A+	42	17	0	5	142.1	586	128	64	51	13	5	3	6	44	0	110	3	0	13	6	.684	0	0- -	-	3.33	3.22
2005	Tenn	AA	27	27	2	0	161.1	676	160	76	62	8	6	7	6	52	0	146	9	0	11	8	.579	2	0- -	-	3.59	3.46
2006	Tucsn	AAA	10	10	0	0	60.1	251	62	25	15	2	2	1	2	14	0	35	3	0	4	3	.571	0	0- -	-	3.19	2.24
2007	Tucsn	AAA	27	27	0	0	153.2	701	186	105	88	11	7	7	5	61	1	118	5	1	8	10	.444	0	0- -	-	5.15	5.15
2006	Ari	NL	22	18	0	1	106.1	462	114	71	67	14	7	3	4	34	0	66	1	0	3	7	.300	0	0-0	0	4.53	5.67
2007	Ari	NL	1	0	0	0	2.0	11	4	4	3	0	0	0	0	1	0	0	0	0	0	0	-	0	0-0	0	9.72	13.50
	2 ML YEARS		23	18	0	2	108.1	473	118	75	70	14	7	3	4	35	0	66	1	0	3	7	.300	0	0-0	0	4.62	5.82

Luis Gonzalez

Bats: L **Throws:** R **Pos:** LF-127; PH-12; DH-1   **Ht:** 6'2" **Wt:** 210 **Born:** 9/3/1967 **Age:** 40

Year	Team	Lg	BATTING																	BASERUNNING				AVERAGES		
			G	AB	H	2B	3B	HR	(Hm	Rd)	TB	R	RBI	RC	TBB	IBB	SO	HBP	SH	SF	SB	CS	SB%	GDP	Avg	OBP	Slg
1990	Hou	NL	12	21	4	2	0	0	(0	0)	6	1	0	2	2	1	5	0	0	0	0	0	.00	-	.190	.261	.286
1991	Hou	NL	137	473	120	28	9	13	(4	9)	205	51	69	64	40	4	101	8	1	4	10	7	.59	9	.254	.320	.433
1992	Hou	NL	122	387	94	19	3	10	(4	6)	149	40	55	41	24	3	52	2	1	2	7	7	.50	6	.243	.289	.385
1993	Hou	NL	154	540	162	34	3	15	(8	7)	247	82	72	90	47	7	83	10	3	10	20	9	.69	9	.300	.361	.457
1994	Hou	NL	112	392	107	29	4	8	(3	5)	168	57	67	57	49	6	57	3	0	6	15	13	.54	10	.273	.353	.429
1995	2 Tms	NL	133	471	130	29	8	13	(6	7)	214	69	69	72	57	8	63	6	1	6	6	8	.43	16	.276	.357	.454
1996	ChC	NL	146	483	131	30	4	15	(6	9)	214	70	79	75	61	8	49	4	1	6	9	6	.60	13	.271	.354	.443
1997	Hou	NL	152	550	142	31	2	10	(4	6)	207	78	68	73	71	7	67	5	0	5	10	7	.59	12	.258	.345	.376
1998	Det	AL	154	547	146	35	4	23	(15	8)	260	84	71	89	57	7	62	8	0	8	12	7	.63	9	.267	.340	.475
1999	Ari	NL	153	614	206	45	4	26	(10	16)	337	112	111	129	66	6	63	7	1	5	9	5	.64	13	.336	.403	.549
2000	Ari	NL	162	618	192	47	2	31	(14	17)	336	106	114	128	78	6	85	15	2	12	2	4	.33	13	.311	.392	.544
2001	Ari	NL	162	609	198	36	7	57	(26	31)	419	128	142	164	100	24	83	14	0	5	1	1	.50	14	.325	.429	.688
2002	Ari	NL	148	524	151	19	3	28	(11	17)	260	90	103	114	97	8	76	5	0	7	9	2	.82	12	.288	.400	.496
2003	Ari	NL	156	579	176	46	4	26	(6	20)	308	92	104	113	94	17	67	3	0	3	5	3	.63	19	.304	.402	.532
2004	Ari	NL	105	379	98	28	5	17	(10	7)	187	69	48	62	68	11	58	2	0	2	2	2	.50	9	.259	.373	.493
2005	Ari	NL	155	579	157	37	0	24	(10	14)	266	90	79	87	78	12	90	11	0	4	4	1	.80	14	.271	.366	.459
2006	Ari	NL	153	586	159	52	2	15	(8	7)	260	93	73	81	69	10	58	7	0	6	0	1	.00	14	.271	.352	.444
2007	LAD	NL	139	464	129	23	2	15	(5	10)	201	70	68	65	56	4	56	4	0	2	6	2	.75	11	.278	.359	.433
95	Hou	NL	56	209	54	10	4	6	(1	5)	90	35	35	26	18	3	30	3	1	3	1	3	.25	8	.258	.322	.431
95	ChC	NL	77	262	76	19	4	7	(5	2)	124	34	34	46	39	5	33	3	0	3	5	5	.50	8	.290	.384	.473
	18 ML YEARS		2455	8816	2502	570	67	346	(150	196)	4244	1382	1392	1506	1114	149	1175	111	10	93	127	85	.60	203	.284	.368	.481

Mike Gonzalez

Pitches: L **Bats:** R **Pos:** RP-18   **Ht:** 6'2" **Wt:** 213 **Born:** 5/23/1978 **Age:** 30

Year	Team	Lg	HOW MUCH HE PITCHED						WHAT HE GAVE UP												THE RESULTS							
			G	GS	CG	GF	IP	BFP	H	R	ER	HR	SH	SF	HB	TBB	IBB	SO	WP	Bk	W	L	Pct	ShO	Sv-Op	Hld	ERC	ERA
2003	Pit	NL	16	0	0	2	8.1	38	7	7	7	4	1	0	0	6	0	6	1	0	0	1	.000	0	0-0	3	7.18	7.56
2004	Pit	NL	47	0	0	12	43.1	169	32	7	6	2	3	0	1	6	0	55	4	0	3	1	.750	0	1-4	13	1.60	1.25
2005	Pit	NL	51	0	0	15	50.0	212	35	15	15	2	0	2	1	31	2	58	3	0	1	3	.250	0	3-3	15	2.90	2.70
2006	Pit	NL	54	0	0	47	54.0	234	42	13	13	1	3	1	2	31	2	64	0	0	3	4	.429	0	24-24	3	3.00	2.17
2007	Atl	NL	18	0	0	5	17.0	70	15	3	3	0	0	1	0	8	0	13	0	0	2	0	1.000	0	2-2	5	3.13	1.59
	5 ML YEARS		186	0	0	81	172.2	723	131	45	44	9	7	5	4	82	4	196	8	0	9	9	.500	0	30-33	39	2.79	2.29

Alex Gordon

Bats: L **Throws:** R **Pos:** 3B-137; 1B-32; PH-3; SS-1   **Ht:** 6'1" **Wt:** 220 **Born:** 2/10/1984 **Age:** 24

Year	Team	Lg	BATTING																	BASERUNNING				AVERAGES		
			G	AB	H	2B	3B	HR	(Hm	Rd)	TB	R	RBI	RC	TBB	IBB	SO	HBP	SH	SF	SB	CS	SB%	GDP	Avg	OBP	Slg
2006	Wichta	AA	130	485	158	39	1	29	(-	-)	286	111	100	123	73	0	112	16	0	2	23	3	.88	4	.326	.429	.590
2007	KC	AL	151	543	134	36	4	15	(8	7)	223	60	60	69	41	4	137	13	1	2	14	4	.78	12	.247	.314	.411

Tom Gordon

Pitches: R **Bats:** R **Pos:** RP-44 **Ht:** 5'10" **Wt:** 200 **Born:** 11/18/1967 **Age:** 40

Year	Team	Lg	G	GS	CG	GF	IP	BFP	H	R	ER	HR	SH	SF	HB	TBB	IBB	SO	WP	Bk	W	L	Pct	ShO	Sv-Op	Hld	ERC	ERA
2007	Phillies*	R	2	2	0	0	2.1	13	5	5	5	0	0	0	0	1	0	3	0	0	0	1	.000	0	0- -	-	10.38	19.29
2007	Clrwtr*	A+	2	2	0	0	2.2	10	1	0	0	0	0	0	0	1	0	1	0	0	0	0	-	0	0- -	-	0.85	0.00
1988	KC	AL	5	2	0	0	15.2	67	16	9	9	1	0	0	0	7	0	18	0	0	0	2	.000	0	0-0	2	4.22	5.17
1989	KC	AL	49	16	1	16	163.0	677	122	67	66	10	4	4	1	86	4	153	12	0	17	9	.654	1	1-7	3	2.97	3.64
1990	KC	AL	32	32	6	0	195.1	858	192	99	81	17	8	2	3	99	1	175	11	0	12	11	.522	1	0-0	0	4.37	3.73
1991	KC	AL	45	14	1	11	158.0	684	129	76	68	16	5	3	4	87	6	167	5	0	9	14	.391	0	1-4	4	3.67	3.87
1992	KC	AL	40	11	0	13	117.2	516	116	67	60	9	2	6	4	55	4	98	5	2	6	10	.375	0	0-2	0	4.17	4.59
1993	KC	AL	48	14	2	18	155.2	651	125	65	62	11	6	6	1	77	5	143	17	0	12	6	.667	0	1-6	2	3.18	3.58
1994	KC	AL	24	24	0	0	155.1	675	136	79	75	15	3	8	3	87	3	126	12	1	11	7	.611	0	0-0	0	4.04	4.35
1995	KC	AL	31	31	2	0	189.0	843	204	110	93	12	7	11	4	89	4	119	9	0	12	12	.500	0	0-0	0	4.59	4.43
1996	Bos	AL	34	34	4	0	215.2	998	249	143	134	28	2	11	4	105	5	171	6	1	12	9	.571	1	0-0	0	5.50	5.59
1997	Bos	AL	42	25	2	16	182.2	774	155	85	76	10	3	4	3	78	1	159	5	0	6	10	.375	0	11-13	0	3.08	3.74
1998	Bos	AL	73	0	0	69	79.1	317	55	24	24	2	2	2	0	25	1	78	9	0	7	4	.636	0	46-47	0	1.72	2.72
1999	Bos	AL	21	0	0	15	17.2	82	17	11	11	2	0	0	1	12	2	24	0	0	0	2	.000	0	11-13	1	5.04	5.60
2001	ChC	NL	47	0	0	40	45.1	187	32	18	17	4	0	0	1	16	1	67	2	0	1	2	.333	0	27-31	0	2.27	3.38
2002	2 Tms	NL	34	0	0	10	42.2	181	42	19	16	3	3	0	1	16	3	48	0	0	1	3	.250	0	0-0	6	3.71	3.38
2003	CWS	AL	66	0	0	35	74.0	310	57	29	26	4	4	3	4	31	3	91	5	0	7	6	.538	0	12-17	7	2.74	3.16
2004	NYY	AL	80	0	0	15	89.2	342	56	23	22	5	5	2	1	23	5	96	3	0	9	4	.692	0	4-10	36	1.50	2.21
2005	NYY	AL	79	0	0	17	80.2	324	59	25	23	8	1	3	0	29	4	69	1	1	5	4	.556	0	2-9	33	2.45	2.57
2006	Phi	NL	59	0	0	53	59.1	253	53	23	22	9	2	1	1	22	4	68	3	0	3	4	.429	0	34-39	0	3.62	3.34
2007	Phi	NL	44	0	0	11	40.0	170	40	21	21	7	1	2	2	13	0	32	1	0	3	2	.600	0	6-11	14	4.55	4.73
02	ChC	NL	19	0	0	7	23.2	104	27	12	9	1	1	0	1	10	1	31	0	0	1	1	.500	0	0-0	4	4.75	3.42
02	Hou	NL	15	0	0	3	19.0	77	15	7	7	2	2	0	0	6	2	17	0	0	0	2	.000	0	0-0	2	2.53	3.32
19 ML YEARS			853	203	18	339	2076.2	8909	1855	993	906	173	58	68	38	957	56	1902	106	5	133	121	.524	4	156-209	108	3.63	3.93

Nick Gorneault

Bats: R **Throws:** R **Pos:** LF-2 **Ht:** 6'3" **Wt:** 200 **Born:** 4/19/1979 **Age:** 29

Year	Team	Lg	G	AB	H	2B	3B	HR	(Hm	Rd)	TB	R	RBI	RC	TBB	IBB	SO	HBP	SH	SF	SB	CS	SB%	GDP	Avg	OBP	Slg
2001	Provo	R+	54	168	53	12	4	6	(-	-)	91	38	30	33	11	1	65	5	2	1	5	2	.71	0	.315	.373	.542
2002	CRpds	A	103	346	100	17	7	10	(-	-)	161	60	53	57	30	0	106	2	2	3	12	5	.71	3	.289	.346	.465
2003	RCuca	A+	97	374	120	36	2	14	(-	-)	202	67	72	71	20	3	82	5	0	1	11	6	.65	3	.321	.363	.540
2003	Ark	AA	29	110	38	6	4	2	(-	-)	58	19	19	22	8	0	25	1	2	0	2	0	1.00	3	.345	.395	.527
2004	Ark	AA	130	496	139	28	4	21	(-	-)	238	91	81	82	45	2	128	3	5	5	7	5	.58	8	.280	.341	.480
2004	Salt Lk	AAA	6	19	6	1	0	1	(-	-)	10	4	5	3	1	0	7	1	0	0	0	0	-	0	.316	.381	.526
2005	Salt Lk	AAA	130	488	143	25	11	26	(-	-)	268	106	107	97	58	1	118	2	1	6	7	6	.54	11	.293	.366	.549
2006	Salt Lk	AAA	107	407	115	25	9	15	(-	-)	203	66	78	70	38	0	106	2	0	5	6	4	.60	8	.283	.343	.499
2007	Salt Lk	AAA	128	471	123	24	1	19	(-	-)	206	82	59	74	68	1	108	3	1	0	17	8	.68	11	.261	.346	.437
2007	LAA	AL	2	4	0	0	0	0	(0	0)	0	0	0	0	1	0	1	0	0	0	0	0	-	0	.000	.200	.000

Tom Gorzelanny

Pitches: L **Bats:** L **Pos:** SP-32 **Ht:** 6'2" **Wt:** 219 **Born:** 7/12/1982 **Age:** 25

Year	Team	Lg	G	GS	CG	GF	IP	BFP	H	R	ER	HR	SH	SF	HB	TBB	IBB	SO	WP	Bk	W	L	Pct	ShO	Sv-Op	Hld	ERC	ERA
2005	Pit	NL	3	1	0	0	6.0	32	10	8	8	1	1	0	0	3	0	3	0	0	0	1	.000	0	0-0	0	8.76	12.00
2006	Pit	NL	11	11	0	0	61.2	267	50	29	26	3	7	4	4	31	2	40	3	0	2	5	.286	0	0-0	0	3.23	3.79
2007	Pit	NL	32	32	1	0	201.2	874	214	90	87	18	3	9	11	68	3	135	5	1	14	10	.583	1	0-0	0	4.31	3.88
3 ML YEARS			46	44	1	0	269.1	1173	274	127	121	22	11	13	15	102	5	178	8	1	16	16	.500	1	0-0	0	4.15	4.04

Mike Gosling

Pitches: L **Bats:** L **Pos:** RP-23 **Ht:** 6'2" **Wt:** 210 **Born:** 9/23/1980 **Age:** 27

Year	Team	Lg	G	GS	CG	GF	IP	BFP	H	R	ER	HR	SH	SF	HB	TBB	IBB	SO	WP	Bk	W	L	Pct	ShO	Sv-Op	Hld	ERC	ERA
2007	Lsvlle*	AAA	13	13	0	0	78.0	328	71	31	26	7	6	3	3	22	0	65	2	0	5	3	.625	0	0- -	-	3.23	3.00
2004	Ari	NL	6	4	0	0	25.1	112	26	13	13	5	2	0	2	13	1	14	2	0	1	1	.500	0	0-0	0	5.83	4.62
2005	Ari	NL	13	5	0	5	32.1	154	40	20	16	2	2	0	0	19	2	14	0	0	0	3	.000	0	0-0	0	5.74	4.45
2006	Cin	NL	1	0	0	0	1.1	7	1	2	2	1	0	0	1	1	0	1	0	0	0	0	-	0	0-0	0	12.98	13.50
2007	Cin	NL	23	0	0	7	33.0	164	42	22	18	5	2	1	1	28	8	32	1	0	2	0	1.000	0	0-1	0	7.81	4.91
4 ML YEARS			43	9	0	12	92.0	437	109	57	49	13	6	1	4	61	11	61	3	0	3	4	.429	0	0-1	0	6.60	4.79

Ruben Gotay

Bats: B **Throws:** R **Pos:** PH-57; 2B-37; SS-5; 3B-2; PR-1 **Ht:** 5'11" **Wt:** 190 **Born:** 12/25/1982 **Age:** 25

Year	Team	Lg	G	AB	H	2B	3B	HR	(Hm	Rd)	TB	R	RBI	RC	TBB	IBB	SO	HBP	SH	SF	SB	CS	SB%	GDP	Avg	OBP	Slg
2007	NewOr*	AAA	23	82	21	7	1	2	(-	-)	36	12	13	14	14	0	14	1	0	1	1	1	.50	2	.256	.367	.439
2004	KC	AL	44	152	41	7	3	1	(1	0)	57	17	16	17	9	0	36	2	1	2	0	1	.00	4	.270	.315	.375
2005	KC	AL	86	282	64	14	2	5	(2	3)	97	32	29	31	22	0	51	4	4	5	2	2	.50	3	.227	.288	.344
2007	NYM	NL	98	190	56	12	0	4	(2	2)	80	25	24	28	16	1	42	1	3	1	3	3	.50	2	.295	.351	.421
3 ML YEARS			228	624	161	33	5	10	(5	5)	234	74	69	76	47	1	129	7	8	8	5	6	.45	9	.258	.313	.375

John Grabow

Pitches: L Bats: L Pos: RP-63   Ht: 6'2" Wt: 205 Born: 11/4/1978 Age: 29

Year Team	Lg	G	GS	CG	GF	IP	BFP	H	R	ER	HR	SH	SF	HB	TBB	IBB	SO	WP	Bk	W	L	Pct	ShO	Sv-Op	Hld	ERC	ERA
2007 Indy*	AAA	4	0	0	1	4.0	16	4	1	1	1	0	0	0	2	0	4	0	0	0	0	-	0	0--	-	6.22	2.25
2003 Pit	NL	5	0	0	1	5.0	22	6	3	2	0	0	0	0	0	0	9	0	0	0	0	-	0	0-0	0	2.73	3.60
2004 Pit	NL	68	0	0	10	61.2	286	81	39	35	8	6	1	0	28	7	64	5	0	2	5	.286	0	1-7	11	6.21	5.11
2005 Pit	NL	63	0	0	8	52.0	222	46	31	28	6	2	0	2	25	2	42	1	0	2	3	.400	0	0-1	14	4.00	4.85
2006 Pit	NL	72	0	0	17	69.2	303	68	34	32	7	5	3	3	30	3	66	0	0	4	2	.667	0	0-2	11	4.17	4.13
2007 Pit	NL	63	0	0	14	51.2	228	56	27	26	6	4	2	1	19	2	42	3	0	3	2	.600	0	1-2	8	4.51	4.53
5 ML YEARS		271	0	0	50	240.0	1061	257	134	123	27	17	6	6	102	14	223	9	0	11	12	.478	0	2-12	44	4.67	4.61

Tony Graffanino

Bats: R Throws: R Pos: 2B-30; 3B-23; PH-23; 1B-9; LF-3; SS-1; PR-1   Ht: 6'1" Wt: 190 Born: 6/6/1972 Age: 36

Year Team	Lg	G	AB	H	2B	3B	HR	(Hm	Rd)	TB	R	RBI	RC	TBB	IBB	SO	HBP	SH	SF	SB	CS	SB%	GDP	Avg	OBP	Slg
1996 Atl	NL	22	46	8	1	1	0	(0	0)	11	7	2	3	4	0	13	1	0	1	0	0	-		.174	.250	.239
1997 Atl	NL	104	186	48	9	1	8	(5	3)	83	33	20	29	26	1	46	1	3	5	6	4	.60	3	.258	.344	.446
1998 Atl	NL	105	289	61	14	1	5	(3	2)	92	32	22	22	24	0	68	2	1	1	1	4	.20	7	.211	.275	.318
1999 TB	AL	39	130	41	9	4	2	(1	1)	64	20	19	23	9	0	22	1	2	0	3	2	.60	1	.315	.364	.492
2000 2 Tms	AL	70	168	46	6	1	2	(1	1)	60	33	17	23	22	0	27	2	1	1	7	4	.64	2	.274	.363	.357
2001 CWS	AL	74	145	44	9	0	2	(1	1)	59	23	15	22	16	0	29	1	4	3	4	1	.80	4	.303	.370	.407
2002 CWS	AL	70	229	60	12	4	6	(4	3)	98	35	31	35	22	1	38	2	4	2	2	1	.67	2	.262	.329	.428
2003 CWS	AL	90	250	65	15	3	7	(4	3)	107	51	23	36	24	1	37	3	3	1	8	0	1.00	1	.260	.331	.428
2004 KC	AL	75	278	73	11	0	3	(0	3)	93	37	26	35	27	0	38	3	4	2	10	2	.83	5	.263	.332	.335
2005 2 Tms	AL	110	379	117	17	3	7	(4	3)	161	68	38	58	31	2	51	4	2	1	7	2	.78	14	.309	.366	.425
2006 2 Tms		129	456	125	33	3	7	(3	4)	185	68	59	67	45	1	68	5	4	1	5	4	.56	10	.274	.345	.406
2007 Mil		86	231	55	8	0	9	(7	2)	90	34	30	24	24	6	44	3	0	2	0	1	.00	7	.238	.315	.390
00 TB	AL	13	20	6	1	0	0	(0	0)	7	8	1	2	1	0	2	1	0	0	0	0	-		.300	.364	.350
00 CWS	AL	57	148	40	5	1	2	(1	1)	53	25	16	21	21	0	25	1	1	1	7	4	.64	2	.270	.363	.358
05 KC	AL	59	191	57	5	2	3	(1	2)	75	29	18	32	22	1	28	2	2	0	3	1	.75	6	.298	.377	.393
05 Bos	AL	51	188	60	12	1	4	(3	1)	86	39	20	26	9	1	23	2	0	1	4	1	.80	8	.319	.355	.457
06 KC	AL	69	220	59	16	0	5	(2	3)	90	34	32	31	25	1	31	1	4	0	3	4	.43	4	.268	.346	.409
06 Mil	NL	60	236	66	17	3	2	(1	1)	95	34	27	36	20	0	37	4	0	1	2	0	1.00	6	.280	.345	.406
12 ML YEARS		974	2787	743	144	21	58	(32	26)	1103	441	302	377	274	12	481	28	28	20	53	25	.68	56	.267	.336	.396

Curtis Granderson

Bats: L Throws: R Pos: CF-157; PH-6; LF-2; PR-1   Ht: 6'1" Wt: 185 Born: 3/16/1981 Age: 27

Year Team	Lg	G	AB	H	2B	3B	HR	(Hm	Rd)	TB	R	RBI	RC	TBB	IBB	SO	HBP	SH	SF	SB	CS	SB%	GDP	Avg	OBP	Slg
2004 Det	AL	9	25	6	1	1	0	(0	0)	9	2	0	2	3	0	8	0	0	0	0	0	-	1	.240	.321	.360
2005 Det	AL	47	162	44	8	3	8	(5	3)	80	18	20	26	10	0	43	0	2	2	1	1	.50	2	.272	.314	.494
2006 Det	AL	159	596	155	31	9	19	(7	12)	261	90	68	89	66	0	174	4	7	6	8	5	.62	4	.260	.335	.438
2007 Det	AL	158	612	185	38	23	23	(10	13)	338	122	74	106	52	3	141	5	5	2	26	1	.96	3	.302	.361	.552
4 ML YEARS		373	1395	390	76	36	50	(22	28)	688	232	162	223	131	3	366	9	14	8	35	7	.83	10	.280	.343	.493

Nick Green

Bats: R Throws: R Pos: SS-3; PH-3; 2B-2   Ht: 6'0" Wt: 180 Born: 9/10/1978 Age: 29

Year Team	Lg	G	AB	H	2B	3B	HR	(Hm	Rd)	TB	R	RBI	RC	TBB	IBB	SO	HBP	SH	SF	SB	CS	SB%	GDP	Avg	OBP	Slg
2007 Indy*	AAA	26	102	25	6	0	5	(-	-)	46	9	20	11	2	0	28	1	0	1	1	2	.33	2	.245	.264	.451
2007 Tacom*	AAA	66	285	96	15	6	16	(-	-)	171	52	46	62	21	0	67	2	4	1	4	3	.57	7	.337	.385	.600
2004 Atl	NL	95	264	72	15	3	3	(3	0)	102	40	26	36	12	1	63	4	8	2	1	2	.33	0	.273	.312	.386
2005 TB	AL	111	318	76	15	2	5	(2	3)	110	53	29	38	33	0	86	11	10	3	3	1	.75	5	.239	.329	.346
2006 2 Tms	AL	63	114	21	5	0	2	(1	1)	32	12	4	10	11	0	40	1	1	0	1	4	.20	1	.184	.262	.281
2007 Sea	AL	6	7	0	0	0	0	(0	0)	0	0	0	0	0	0	3	0	0	0	0	0	-	0	.000	.000	.000
06 TB	AL	17	39	3	0	0	0	(0	0)	3	4	0	0	6	0	11	0	0	0	0	3	.00	2	.077	.200	.077
06 NYY	AL	46	75	18	5	0	2	(1	1)	29	8	4	10	5	0	29	1	1	0	1	1	.50	-	.240	.296	.387
4 ML YEARS		275	703	169	35	5	10	(6	4)	244	105	59	84	56	1	192	16	19	5	5	7	.42	7	.240	.309	.347

Sean Green

Pitches: R Bats: R Pos: RP-64   Ht: 6'6" Wt: 230 Born: 4/20/1979 Age: 29

Year Team	Lg	G	GS	CG	GF	IP	BFP	H	R	ER	HR	SH	SF	HB	TBB	IBB	SO	WP	Bk	W	L	Pct	ShO	Sv-Op	Hld	ERC	ERA
2000 Portlnd	A-	22	0	0	4	28.2	155	45	32	27	2	1	2	5	19	2	17	5	0	1	4	.200	0	0--	-	8.87	8.48
2001 Ashvll	A	43	0	0	9	58.0	271	66	43	38	4	4	1	4	28	1	37	8	2	3	4	.429	0	0--	-	5.10	5.90
2002 Salem	A+	52	0	0	17	67.0	319	92	41	29	5	6	4	1	31	8	26	8	0	2	5	.286	0	2--	-	6.15	3.90
2003 Visalia	A+	46	2	0	17	80.0	370	90	54	43	2	3	1	8	38	2	56	4	0	3	4	.429	0	0--	-	4.82	4.84
2004 Tulsa	AA	52	0	0	19	77.1	330	83	32	26	5	0	1	7	29	1	50	6	0	3	4	.571	0	2--	-	3.01	3.03
2005 SnAnt	AA	21	0	0	19	24.1	100	17	11	8	1	1	0	1	8	1	18	6	0	0	1	.000	0	14--	-	1.93	2.96
2005 Tacom	AAA	33	0	0	14	49.1	217	40	23	20	1	1	2	4	29	0	44	8	0	4	2	.667	0	1--	-	3.47	3.65
2006 Tacom	AAA	15	0	0	12	24.0	96	18	6	6	0	3	0	2	11	1	12	0	0	4	1	.800	0	5--	-	2.69	2.25
2007 Tacom	AAA	10	0	0	3	17.1	72	13	5	4	0	1	1	0	8	1	10	2	0	2	1	.667	0	1--	-	2.23	2.08
2006 Sea	AL	24	0	0	11	32.0	139	34	16	16	2	1	2	2	13	1	15	2	0	0	0	-	0	0-1	3	4.47	4.50
2007 Sea	AL	64	0	0	10	68.0	304	77	31	29	2	4	5	3	34	6	53	2	0	5	2	.714	0	0-3	13	4.81	3.84
2 ML YEARS		88	0	0	21	100.0	443	111	47	45	4	5	6	5	47	7	68	4	0	5	2	.714	0	0-4	16	4.70	4.05

Shawn Green

Bats: L **Throws:** L **Pos:** RF-110; 1B-17; PH-9; PR-1   **Ht:** 6'4" **Wt:** 205 **Born:** 11/10/1972 **Age:** 35

							BATTING														BASERUNNING				AVERAGES		
Year	Team	Lg	G	AB	H	2B	3B	HR	(Hm	Rd)	TB	R	RBI	RC	TBB	IBB	SO	HBP	SH	SF	SB	CS	SB%	GDP	Avg	OBP	Slg
1993	Tor	AL	3	6	0	0	0	0	(0	0)	0	0	0	0	0	0	1	0	0	0	0	0	-	0	.000	.000	.000
1994	Tor	AL	14	33	3	1	0	0	(0	0)	4	1	1	1	1	0	8	0	0	0	1	0	1.00	1	.091	.118	.121
1995	Tor	AL	121	379	109	31	4	15	(5	10)	193	52	54	61	20	3	68	3	0	3	1	2	.33	4	.288	.326	.509
1996	Tor	AL	132	422	118	32	3	11	(7	4)	189	52	45	64	33	3	75	8	0	2	5	1	.83	9	.280	.342	.448
1997	Tor	AL	135	429	123	22	4	16	(10	6)	201	57	53	70	36	4	99	1	1	4	14	3	.82	6	.287	.340	.469
1998	Tor	AL	158	630	175	33	4	35	(21	14)	321	106	100	108	50	2	142	1	1	3	35	12	.74	6	.278	.334	.510
1999	Tor	AL	153	614	190	45	0	42	(20	22)	361	134	123	132	66	4	117	11	0	5	20	7	.74	13	.309	.384	.588
2000	LAD	NL	162	610	164	44	4	24	(15	9)	288	98	99	107	90	9	121	8	0	6	24	5	.83	18	.269	.367	.472
2001	LAD	NL	161	619	184	31	4	49	(19	30)	370	121	125	134	72	10	107	5	0	5	20	4	.83	10	.297	.372	.598
2002	LAD	NI	158	582	166	31	1	42	(18	24)	325	110	114	106	93	22	112	5	0	5	8	5	.62	26	.285	.385	.558
2003	LAD	NL	160	611	171	49	2	19	(10	9)	281	84	85	92	68	2	112	6	0	6	6	2	.75	18	.280	.355	.460
2004	LAD	NL	157	590	157	28	1	28	(16	12)	271	92	86	76	71	6	114	8	0	2	5	2	.71	17	.266	.352	.459
2005	Ari	NL	158	581	166	37	4	22	(12	10)	277	87	73	78	62	6	95	5	0	8	8	4	.67	18	.286	.355	.477
2006	2 Tms	NL	149	530	147	31	3	15	(9	6)	229	73	66	69	45	5	82	10	0	3	4	4	.50	17	.277	.344	.432
2007	NYM	NL	130	446	130	30	1	10	(5	5)	192	62	46	59	37	4	62	5	1	1	11	1	.92	14	.291	.352	.430
06	Ari	NL	115	417	118	22	3	11	(6	5)	179	59	51	57	37	4	64	6	0	2	4	4	.50	9	.283	.348	.429
06	NYM	NL	34	113	29	9	0	4	(3	1)	50	14	15	12	8	1	18	4	0	1	0	0	-	8	.257	.325	.442
15 ML YEARS			1951	7082	2003	445	35	328	(167	161)	3502	1129	1070	1156	744	80	1315	80	3	53	162	52	.76	175	.283	.355	.494

Khalil Greene

Bats: R **Throws:** R **Pos:** SS-153   **Ht:** 5'11" **Wt:** 195 **Born:** 10/21/1979 **Age:** 28

							BATTING														BASERUNNING				AVERAGES		
Year	Team	Lg	G	AB	H	2B	3B	HR	(Hm	Rd)	TB	R	RBI	RC	TBB	IBB	SO	HBP	SH	SF	SB	CS	SB%	GDP	Avg	OBP	Slg
2003	SD	NL	20	65	14	4	1	2	(0	2)	26	8	6	4	4	0	19	1	0	0	1	0	1.00	3	.215	.271	.400
2004	SD	NL	139	484	132	31	4	15	(3	12)	216	67	65	73	53	10	94	8	1	8	4	2	.67	9	.273	.349	.446
2005	SD	NL	121	436	109	30	2	15	(6	9)	188	51	70	58	25	3	93	6	3	6	5	0	1.00	8	.250	.296	.431
2006	SD	NL	122	412	101	26	2	15	(6	9)	176	56	55	48	39	0	87	7	0	2	5	1	.83	15	.245	.320	.427
2007	SD	NL	153	611	155	44	3	27	(12	15)	286	89	97	77	32	3	128	5	0	11	4	0	1.00	12	.254	.291	.468
5 ML YEARS			555	2008	511	135	12	74	(27	47)	892	271	293	260	153	16	421	27	4	27	18	4	.82	47	.254	.312	.444

Kevin Gregg

Pitches: R **Bats:** R **Pos:** RP-74   **Ht:** 6'6" **Wt:** 235 **Born:** 6/20/1978 **Age:** 30

			HOW MUCH HE PITCHED						WHAT HE GAVE UP										THE RESULTS							
Year	Team	Lg	G	GS	CG	GF	IP	BFP	H	R	ER	HR	SH	SF	HB	TBB	IBB	SO	WP	Bk	W	L	Pct	ShO	Sv-Op	Hld	ERC	ERA
2003	LAA	AL	5	3	0	0	24.2	97	18	9	9	3	0	0	1	8	0	14	0	0	2	0	1.000	0	0-0	0	2.74	3.28
2004	LAA	AL	55	0	0	23	87.2	377	86	43	41	6	4	5	3	28	3	84	13	1	5	2	.714	0	1-2	3	3.47	4.21
2005	LAA	AL	33	2	0	9	64.1	290	70	37	36	8	1	1	3	29	2	52	5	0	1	2	.333	0	0-1	1	5.08	5.04
2006	LAA	AL	32	3	0	12	78.1	341	88	41	36	10	0	3	2	21	0	71	6	0	3	4	.429	0	0-0	0	4.51	4.14
2007	Fla	NL	74	0	0	55	84.0	355	63	34	33	7	3	0	6	40	1	87	6	0	0	5	.000	0	32-36	6	3.15	3.54
5 ML YEARS			199	8	0	99	339.0	1460	325	164	155	34	8	9	15	126	6	308	30	1	11	13	.458	0	33-39	10	3.86	4.12

Zack Greinke

Pitches: R **Bats:** R **Pos:** RP-38; SP-14   **Ht:** 6'2" **Wt:** 185 **Born:** 10/21/1983 **Age:** 24

			HOW MUCH HE PITCHED						WHAT HE GAVE UP										THE RESULTS							
Year	Team	Lg	G	GS	CG	GF	IP	BFP	H	R	ER	HR	SH	SF	HB	TBB	IBB	SO	WP	Bk	W	L	Pct	ShO	Sv-Op	Hld	ERC	ERA
2004	KC	AL	24	24	0	0	145.0	599	143	64	64	26	3	2	8	26	3	100	1	1	8	11	.421	0	0-0	0	3.85	3.97
2005	KC	AL	33	33	2	0	183.0	829	233	125	118	23	4	4	13	53	0	114	4	2	5	17	.227	0	0-0	0	5.71	5.80
2006	KC	AL	3	0	0	1	6.1	28	7	3	3	1	0	0	0	3	2	5	0	0	1	0	1.000	0	0-0	0	4.93	4.26
2007	KC	AL	52	14	0	7	122.0	507	122	52	50	12	3	4	3	36	5	106	3	1	7	7	.500	0	1-1	12	3.77	3.69
4 ML YEARS			112	71	2	8	456.1	1963	505	244	235	62	10	10	24	118	10	325	8	4	21	35	.375	0	1-1	12	4.57	4.63

Ken Griffey Jr.

Bats: L **Throws:** L **Pos:** RF-133; PH-9; DH-3   **Ht:** 6'3" **Wt:** 228 **Born:** 11/21/1969 **Age:** 38

							BATTING														BASERUNNING				AVERAGES		
Year	Team	Lg	G	AB	H	2B	3B	HR	(Hm	Rd)	TB	R	RBI	RC	TBB	IBB	SO	HBP	SH	SF	SB	CS	SB%	GDP	Avg	OBP	Slg
1989	Sea	AL	127	455	120	23	0	16	(10	6)	191	61	61	64	44	8	83	2	1	4	16	7	.70	4	.264	.329	.420
1990	Sea	AL	155	597	179	28	7	22	(8	14)	287	91	80	101	63	12	81	2	0	4	16	11	.59	12	.300	.366	.481
1991	Sea	AL	154	548	179	42	1	22	(16	6)	289	76	100	112	71	21	82	1	4	9	18	6	.75	10	.327	.399	.527
1992	Sea	AL	142	565	174	39	4	27	(16	11)	302	83	103	102	44	15	67	5	0	3	10	5	.67	15	.308	.361	.535
1993	Sea	AL	156	582	180	38	3	45	(21	24)	359	113	109	137	96	25	91	6	0	7	17	9	.65	14	.309	.408	.617
1994	Sea	AL	111	433	140	24	4	40	(18	22)	292	94	90	107	56	19	73	2	0	2	11	3	.79	9	.323	.402	.674
1995	Sea	AL	72	260	67	7	0	17	(13	4)	125	52	42	49	52	6	53	0	0	2	4	2	.67	4	.258	.379	.481
1996	Sea	AL	140	545	165	26	2	49	(26	23)	342	125	140	131	78	13	104	7	1	7	16	1	.94	7	.303	.392	.628
1997	Sea	AL	157	608	185	34	3	56	(27	29)	393	125	147	142	76	23	121	8	0	12	15	4	.79	12	.304	.382	.646
1998	Sea	AL	161	633	180	33	3	56	(30	26)	387	120	146	136	76	11	121	7	0	4	20	5	.80	14	.284	.365	.611
1999	Sea	AL	160	606	173	26	3	48	(27	21)	349	123	134	132	91	17	108	7	0	2	24	7	.77	8	.285	.384	.576
2000	Cin	NL	145	520	141	22	3	40	(22	18)	289	100	118	111	94	17	117	9	0	8	6	4	.60	7	.271	.387	.556
2001	Cin	NL	111	364	104	20	2	22	(12	10)	194	57	65	69	44	6	72	4	1	4	2	0	1.00	6	.286	.365	.533
2002	Cin	NL	70	197	52	8	0	8	(4	4)	84	17	23	27	28	6	39	3	0	4	1	2	.33	6	.264	.358	.426
2003	Cin	NL	53	166	41	12	1	13	(5	8)	94	34	26	26	27	5	44	6	1	1	1	0	1.00	3	.247	.370	.566
2004	Cin	NL	83	300	76	18	0	20	(11	9)	154	49	60	56	44	3	67	2	0	2	1	0	1.00	8	.253	.351	.513

					BATTING															BASERUNNING				AVERAGES		
Year	Team	Lg	G	AB	H	2B	3B	HR	(Hm	Rd)	TB	R	RBI	RC	TBB	IBB	SO	HBP	SH	SF	SB	CS	SB%	GDP	Avg	OBP	Slg
2005	Cin	NL	128	491	148	30	0	35	(15	20)	283	85	92	89	54	3	93	3	0	7	0	1	.00	9	.301	.369	.576
2006	Cin	NL	109	428	108	19	0	27	(13	14)	208	62	72	55	39	6	78	2	0	3	0	0	-	13	.252	.316	.486
2007	Cin	NL	144	528	146	24	1	30	(17	13)	262	78	93	87	85	14	99	1	0	9	6	1	.86	14	.277	.372	.496
19 ML YEARS			2378	8826	2558	473	37	593	(311	282)	4884	1545	1701	1733	1162	230	1593	77	8	94	184	68	.73	177	.290	.374	.553

John-Ford Griffin

Bats: L **Throws:** L **Pos:** RF-3; DH-3; PH-2; PR-1   **Ht:** 6'2" **Wt:** 215 **Born:** 11/19/1979 **Age:** 28

					BATTING															BASERUNNING				AVERAGES		
Year	Team	Lg	G	AB	H	2B	3B	HR	(Hm	Rd)	TB	R	RBI	RC	TBB	IBB	SO	HBP	SH	SF	SB	CS	SB%	GDP	Avg	OBP	Slg
2001	StIsInd	A-	66	238	74	17	1	5	(-	-)	108	46	43	48	40	0	41	3	1	2	10	4	.71	5	.311	.413	.454
2002	Tampa	A+	65	255	68	16	1	3	(-	-)	95	32	31	35	29	0	45	3	0	4	1	0	1.00	9	.267	.344	.373
2002	Nrwich	AA	18	67	22	3	0	5	(-	-)	40	17	10	15	8	1	13	0	0	0	0	1	.00	5	.328	.400	.597
2002	Mdland	AA	2	7	1	0	0	0	(-	-)	1	0	0	0	0	0	3	1	0	0	0	0	-	0	.143	.250	.143
2003	NwHav	AA	104	373	104	23	3	13	(-	-)	172	48	75	65	49	4	85	2	0	5	2	0	1.00	8	.279	.361	.461
2004	NHam	AA	129	467	116	28	1	22	(-	-)	212	66	81	73	56	2	128	4	0	6	1	1	.50	15	.248	.330	.454
2005	Syrcse	AAA	135	512	130	21	1	30	(-	-)	243	80	103	84	62	4	140	3	0	5	1	2	.33	10	.254	.335	.475
2006	Syrcse	AAA	60	227	51	19	0	6	(-	-)	88	30	22	26	19	1	59	2	0	1	2	0	1.00	4	.225	.289	.388
2007	Syrcse	AAA	133	484	122	28	4	26	(-	-)	236	69	83	82	59	1	144	1	0	7	4	0	1.00	11	.252	.330	.488
2005	Tor	AL	7	13	4	2	0	1	(1	0)	9	3	6	2	0	0	4	0	0	0	0	0	-	0	.308	.308	.692
2007	Tor	AL	6	10	3	1	0	1	(1	0)	7	4	3	3	3	0	5	0	0	1	0	0	-	0	.300	.429	.700
2 ML YEARS			13	23	7	3	0	2	(2	0)	16	7	9	5	3	0	9	0	0	1	0	0	-	0	.304	.370	.696

Jason Grilli

Pitches: R **Bats:** R **Pos:** RP-57   **Ht:** 6'5" **Wt:** 225 **Born:** 11/11/1976 **Age:** 31

			HOW MUCH HE PITCHED						WHAT HE GAVE UP													THE RESULTS							
Year	Team	Lg	G	GS	CG	GF	IP	BFP	H	R	ER	HR	SH	SF	HB	TBB	IBB	SO	WP	Bk	W	L	Pct	ShO	Sv-Op	Hld	ERC	ERA
2000	Fla	NL	1	1	0	0	6.2	35	11	4	4	0	2	0	2	2	0	3	0	0	1	0	1.000	0	0-0	0	7.84	5.40
2001	Fla	NL	6	5	0	1	26.2	115	30	18	18	6	1	0	2	11	0	17	0	0	2	2	.500	0	0-0	0	6.44	6.08
2004	CWS	AL	8	8	1	0	45.0	203	52	38	37	11	2	1	3	20	0	26	2	0	2	3	.400	0	0-0	0	6.67	7.40
2005	Det	AL	3	2	0	0	16.0	63	14	6	6	1	1	1	0	6	0	5	0	0	1	1	.500	0	0-0	0	3.27	3.38
2006	Det	AL	51	0	0	18	62.0	270	61	31	29	6	2	4	5	25	3	31	5	0	2	3	.400	0	0-9	9	4.23	4.21
2007	Det	AL	57	0	0	13	79.2	352	81	46	42	5	1	5	5	32	1	62	5	0	5	3	.625	0	0-2	11	4.09	4.74
6 ML YEARS			126	16	1	32	236.0	1038	249	143	136	29	9	11	17	96	4	144	12	0	13	12	.520	0	0-2	20	4.89	5.19

Lee Gronkiewicz

Pitches: R **Bats:** R **Pos:** RP-1   **Ht:** 5'11" **Wt:** 180 **Born:** 8/21/1978 **Age:** 29

			HOW MUCH HE PITCHED						WHAT HE GAVE UP													THE RESULTS							
Year	Team	Lg	G	GS	CG	GF	IP	BFP	H	R	ER	HR	SH	SF	HB	TBB	IBB	SO	WP	Bk	W	L	Pct	ShO	Sv-Op	Hld	ERC	ERA
2001	Burlgtn	R	25	0	0	23	31.2	124	18	11	9	1	1	1	2	8	0	47	2	0	3	3	.500	0	11--	-	1.35	2.56
2001	Akron	AA	2	0	0	2	2.0	10	4	0	0	0	0	0	0	1	0	1	0	0	0	0	-	0	0--	-	7.48	0.00
2002	Clmbs	A	50	0	0	48	61.1	271	58	19	16	4	8	1	5	27	6	72	5	0	4	2	.667	0	27--	-	3.78	2.35
2003	Knstn	A+	51	0	0	47	56.0	226	50	19	15	4	2	1	0	14	0	46	3	0	2	3	.400	0	37--	-	2.78	2.41
2004	Akron	AA	52	0	0	45	65.1	288	65	24	22	5	0	0	4	21	3	68	1	0	1	4	.200	0	20--	-	3.62	3.03
2004	Buffalo	AAA	1	0	0	1	1.0	0	0	0	0	0	0	0	0	0	0	0	0	0	0	0	-	0	0--	-		0.00
2005	NHam	AA	38	0	0	34	38.1	147	24	7	6	2	2	1	0	10	1	45	0	0	2	0	1.000	0	24--	-	1.50	1.41
2005	Syrcse	AAA	28	0	0	12	28.1	118	21	9	7	3	1	1	0	13	2	26	1	0	1	0	1.000	0	6--	-	2.82	2.22
2006	Syrcse	AAA	41	0	0	29	44.0	184	47	18	16	4	2	1	0	8	2	33	1	0	2	3	.400	0	17--	-	3.45	3.27
2007	NHam	AA	24	0	0	22	30.0	121	31	7	6	3	1	1	4	0	1	37	0	0	2	3	.600	0	11--	-	3.38	1.80
2007	Syrcse	AAA	23	1	0	8	44.2	184	38	19	14	4	0	0	3	6	0	46	1	0	3	1	.750	0	2--	-	2.39	2.82
2007	Tor	AL	1	0	0	0	4.0	15	2	1	1	1	0	0	0	2	0	2	0	0	0	0	-	0	0-0	0	2.92	2.25

Gabe Gross

Bats: L **Throws:** R **Pos:** RF-45; PH-42; CF-5; LF-3; DH-3; PR-1   **Ht:** 6'3" **Wt:** 210 **Born:** 10/21/1979 **Age:** 28

					BATTING															BASERUNNING				AVERAGES		
Year	Team	Lg	G	AB	H	2B	3B	HR	(Hm	Rd)	TB	R	RBI	RC	TBB	IBB	SO	HBP	SH	SF	SB	CS	SB%	GDP	Avg	OBP	Slg
2007	Nashv*	AAA	20	76	27	3	2	4	(-	-)	46	13	10	20	14	0	14	0	0	0	2	0	1.00	1	.355	.456	.605
2004	Tor	AL	44	129	27	4	0	3	(2	1)	40	18	16	15	19	0	31	0	0	0	2	2	.50	1	.209	.311	.310
2005	Tor	AL	40	92	23	4	1	1	(1	0)	32	11	7	11	10	0	21	0	0	0	1	1	.50	0	.250	.324	.348
2006	Mil	NL	117	208	57	15	0	9	(5	4)	99	42	38	42	36	3	60	2	3	3	1	0	1.00	3	.274	.382	.476
2007	Mil	NL	93	183	43	12	2	7	(4	3)	80	28	24	23	25	2	37	1	0	1	3	1	.75	1	.235	.329	.437
4 ML YEARS			294	612	150	35	3	20	(12	8)	251	99	85	91	90	5	149	3	3	4	7	4	.64	5	.245	.343	.410

Mark Grudzielanek

Bats: R **Throws:** R **Pos:** 2B-116; SS-3; PH-1   **Ht:** 6'1" **Wt:** 200 **Born:** 6/30/1970 **Age:** 38

					BATTING															BASERUNNING				AVERAGES		
Year	Team	Lg	G	AB	H	2B	3B	HR	(Hm	Rd)	TB	R	RBI	RC	TBB	IBB	SO	HBP	SH	SF	SB	CS	SB%	GDP	Avg	OBP	Slg
1995	Mon	NL	78	269	66	12	2	1	(1	0)	85	27	20	24	14	4	47	7	3	0	8	3	.73	7	.245	.300	.316
1996	Mon	NL	153	657	201	34	4	6	(5	1)	261	99	49	90	26	3	83	9	1	3	33	7	.83	10	.306	.340	.397
1997	Mon	NL	156	649	177	54	3	4	(1	3)	249	76	51	75	23	0	76	10	3	3	25	9	.74	13	.273	.307	.384
1998	2 Tms	NL	156	589	160	21	1	10	(5	5)	213	62	62	64	26	2	73	11	8	7	18	5	.78	18	.272	.311	.362
1999	LAD	NL	123	488	159	23	5	7	(4	3)	213	72	46	76	31	1	65	10	2	3	6	6	.50	13	.326	.376	.436
2000	LAD	NL	148	617	172	35	6	7	(4	3)	240	101	49	80	45	0	81	9	2	3	12	3	.80	16	.279	.335	.389
2001	LAD	NL	133	539	146	21	3	13	(8	5)	212	83	55	66	28	0	83	11	3	5	4	4	.50	9	.271	.317	.393
2002	LAD	NL	150	536	145	23	0	9	(5	4)	195	56	50	53	22	4	89	3	1	4	1	1	.80	17	.271	.301	.364
2003	ChC	NL	121	481	151	38	1	3	(2	1)	200	73	38	71	30	0	64	11	7	2	6	2	.75	12	.314	.366	.416

Year	Team	Lg	G	AB	H	2B	3B	HR	(Hm	Rd)	TB	R	RBI	RC	TBB	IBB	SO	HBP	SH	SF	SB	CS	SB%	GDP	Avg	OBP	Slg
2004	ChC	NL	81	257	79	12	1	6	(3	3)	111	32	23	35	15	0	32	1	4	1	1	1	.50	7	.307	.347	.432
2005	StL	NL	137	528	155	30	3	8	(3	5)	215	64	59	68	26	3	81	7	0	2	8	6	.57	14	.294	.334	.407
2006	KC	AL	134	548	163	32	4	7	(5	2)	224	85	52	69	28	4	69	2	3	5	3	2	.60	12	.297	.331	.409
2007	KC	AL	116	453	137	32	3	6	(4	2)	193	70	51	64	23	2	60	8	0	2	1	2	.33	14	.302	.346	.426
98	Mon	NL	105	396	109	15	1	8	(3	5)	150	51	41	47	21	1	50	9	5	4	11	5	.69	11	.275	.323	.379
98	LAD	NL	51	193	51	6	0	2	(2	0)	63	11	21	17	5	1	23	2	3	3	7	0	1.00	7	.264	.286	.326
13 ML YEARS			1686	6611	1911	367	36	87	(50	37)	2611	900	605	835	337	23	903	99	37	40	129	51	.72	162	.289	.331	.395

Eddie Guardado

Pitches: L **Bats:** R **Pos:** RP-15   **Ht:** 6'0" **Wt:** 227 **Born:** 10/2/1970 **Age:** 37

			HOW MUCH HE PITCHED						WHAT HE GAVE UP											THE RESULTS							
Year	Team	Lg	G	GS	CG	GF	IP	BFP	H	R	ER	HR	SH	SF	HB	TBB	IBB	SO	WP	Bk	W	L	Pct	ShO	Sv-Op	Hld	ERC	ERA
2007	Dayton*	A-	3	0	0	1	3.0	11	2	0	0	0	0	0	0	0	0	3	0	0	0	0	-	0	1--	-	0.91	0.00
2007	Lsville*	AAA	9	0	0	0	8.0	38	11	4	4	2	3	0	0	4	0	3	0	0	0	0	-	0	0--	-	8.06	4.50
1993	Min	AL	19	16	0	2	94.2	426	123	68	65	13	1	3	1	36	2	46	0	0	3	8	.273	0	0-0	0	6.18	6.18
1994	Min	AL	4	4	0	0	17.0	81	26	16	16	3	1	2	0	4	0	8	0	0	0	2	.000	0	0-0	0	7.01	8.47
1995	Min	AL	51	5	0	10	91.1	410	99	54	52	13	6	5	0	45	2	71	5	1	4	9	.308	0	2-5	5	5.20	5.12
1996	Min	AL	83	0	0	17	73.2	313	61	45	43	12	6	4	3	33	4	74	3	0	6	5	.545	0	4-7	18	3.81	5.25
1997	Min	AL	69	0	0	20	46.0	201	45	23	20	7	2	1	2	17	2	54	2	0	0	4	.000	0	1-1	13	4.23	3.91
1998	Min	AL	79	0	0	12	65.2	286	66	34	33	10	3	6	0	28	6	53	2	0	3	1	.750	0	0-4	16	4.42	4.52
1999	Min	AL	63	0	0	13	48.0	197	37	24	24	6	2	1	2	25	4	50	0	0	2	5	.286	0	2-4	15	3.63	4.50
2000	Min	AL	70	0	0	36	61.2	262	55	27	27	14	3	2	1	25	3	52	1	1	7	4	.636	0	9-11	8	4.34	3.94
2001	Min	AL	67	0	0	26	66.2	270	47	27	26	5	5	3	1	23	4	67	4	0	7	1	.875	0	12-14	14	2.13	3.51
2002	Min	AL	68	0	0	62	67.2	270	53	22	22	9	2	2	1	18	2	70	0	0	1	3	.250	0	45-51	0	2.66	2.93
2003	Min	AL	66	0	0	60	65.1	260	50	22	21	7	3	2	0	14	2	60	5	0	3	5	.375	0	41-45	0	2.14	2.89
2004	Sea	AL	41	0	0	35	45.1	176	31	14	14	8	0	1	1	14	0	45	0	0	2	2	.500	0	18-25	0	2.69	2.78
2005	Sea	AL	58	0	0	55	56.1	238	52	23	17	7	3	2	0	15	3	48	1	0	2	3	.400	0	36-41	0	3.12	2.72
2006	2 Tms		43	0	0	26	37.0	166	44	19	16	10	3	1	1	13	2	39	0	0	1	3	.250	0	13-18	2	6.26	3.89
2007	Cin	NL	15	0	0	2	13.2	62	16	11	11	2	0	1	1	4	0	8	0	0	0	0	-	0	0-2	1	5.14	7.24
06	Sea	AL	28	0	0	15	23.0	108	29	14	14	8	3	0	0	11	1	22	0	0	1	3	.250	0	5-8	2	7.78	5.48
06	Cin	NL	15	0	0	11	14.0	58	15	5	2	2	0	1	1	2	1	17	0	0	0	0	-	0	8-10	0	3.98	1.29
15 ML YEARS			796	25	0	376	850.0	3618	805	429	407	126	40	36	14	314	36	745	23	2	41	55	.427	0	183-228	92	3.98	4.31

Vladimir Guerrero

Bats: R **Throws:** R **Pos:** RF-109; DH-41   **Ht:** 6'3" **Wt:** 235 **Born:** 2/9/1976 **Age:** 32

									BATTING											BASERUNNING				AVERAGES		
Year	Team	Lg	G	AB	H	2B	3B	HR	(Hm	Rd)	TB	R	RBI	RC	TBB	IBB	SO	HBP	SH	SF	SB	CS	SB%	GDP	Avg	OBP	Slg
1996	Mon	NL	9	27	5	0	0	1	(0	1)	8	2	1	1	0	0	3	0	0	0	0	0	-	1	.185	.185	.296
1997	Mon	NL	90	325	98	22	2	11	(5	6)	157	44	40	51	19	2	39	7	0	3	3	4	.43	11	.302	.350	.483
1998	Mon	NL	159	623	202	37	7	38	(19	19)	367	108	109	124	42	13	95	7	0	5	11	9	.55	11	.324	.371	.589
1999	Mon	NL	160	610	193	37	5	42	(23	19)	366	102	131	127	55	14	62	7	0	2	14	7	.67	18	.316	.378	.600
2000	Mon	NL	154	571	197	28	11	44	(25	19)	379	101	123	137	58	23	74	8	0	4	9	10	.47	15	.345	.410	.664
2001	Mon	NL	159	599	184	45	4	34	(21	13)	339	107	108	116	60	24	88	9	0	3	37	16	.70	24	.307	.377	.566
2002	Mon	NL	161	614	206	37	2	39	(20	19)	364	106	111	123	84	32	70	6	0	5	40	20	.67	20	.336	.417	.593
2003	Mon	NL	112	394	130	20	3	25	(15	10)	231	71	79	83	63	22	53	6	0	4	9	5	.64	18	.330	.426	.586
2004	LAA	AL	156	612	206	39	2	39	(19	20)	366	124	126	122	52	14	74	8	0	5	15	3	.83	19	.337	.391	.598
2005	LAA	AL	141	520	165	29	2	32	(19	13)	294	95	108	108	61	26	48	8	0	5	13	1	.93	16	.317	.394	.565
2006	LAA	AL	156	607	200	34	1	33	(19	14)	335	92	116	109	50	25	68	4	0	4	15	5	.75	16	.329	.382	.552
2007	LAA	AL	150	574	186	45	1	27	(13	14)	314	89	125	127	71	28	62	9	0	6	2	3	.40	19	.324	.403	.547
12 ML YEARS			1607	6076	1972	373	40	365	(193	172)	3520	1041	1177	1228	615	223	736	79	0	49	168	83	.67	192	.325	.391	.579

Matt Guerrier

Pitches: R **Bats:** R **Pos:** RP-73   **Ht:** 6'3" **Wt:** 193 **Born:** 8/2/1978 **Age:** 29

			HOW MUCH HE PITCHED						WHAT HE GAVE UP											THE RESULTS							
Year	Team	Lg	G	GS	CG	GF	IP	BFP	H	R	ER	HR	SH	SF	HB	TBB	IBB	SO	WP	Bk	W	L	Pct	ShO	Sv-Op	Hld	ERC	ERA
2004	Min	AL	9	2	0	5	19.0	84	22	13	12	5	2	0	1	6	0	11	0	0	0	1	.000	0	0-0	0	6.10	5.68
2005	Min	AL	43	0	0	14	71.2	306	71	29	27	6	4	1	3	24	5	46	3	0	0	3	.000	0	0-0	1	3.71	3.39
2006	Min	AL	39	1	0	13	69.2	300	78	29	26	9	3	4	0	21	0	37	6	0	1	0	1.000	0	1-1	2	4.59	3.36
2007	Min	AL	73	0	0	16	88.0	351	71	23	23	9	0	3	5	21	1	68	6	0	2	4	.333	0	1-4	14	2.70	2.35
4 ML YEARS			164	3	0	48	248.1	1041	242	94	88	29	9	8	9	72	6	162	15	0	3	8	.273	0	2-5	17	3.75	3.19

Carlos Guillen

Bats: B **Throws:** R **Pos:** SS-132; 1B-36; PH-4; DH-3   **Ht:** 6'1" **Wt:** 215 **Born:** 9/30/1975 **Age:** 32

									BATTING											BASERUNNING				AVERAGES		
Year	Team	Lg	G	AB	H	2B	3B	HR	(Hm	Rd)	TB	R	RBI	RC	TBB	IBB	SO	HBP	SH	SF	SB	CS	SB%	GDP	Avg	OBP	Slg
1998	Sea	AL	10	39	13	1	1	0	(0	0)	16	9	5	7	3	0	9	0	0	0	2	0	1.00	0	.333	.381	.410
1999	Sea	AL	5	19	3	0	0	1	(1	0)	6	2	3	1	1	0	6	0	1	0	0	0	-	1	.158	.200	.316
2000	Sea	AL	90	288	74	15	2	7	(3	4)	114	45	42	36	22	0	53	2	7	3	1	3	.25	6	.257	.324	.396
2001	Sea	AL	140	456	118	21	4	5	(2	3)	162	72	53	56	53	0	89	1	7	6	4	1	.80	9	.259	.333	.355
2002	Sea	AL	134	475	124	24	6	9	(4	5)	187	73	56	58	46	4	91	1	3	3	4	5	.44	8	.261	.326	.394
2003	Sea	AL	109	388	107	19	3	7	(4	3)	153	63	52	53	52	2	64	1	5	5	4	4	.50	12	.276	.359	.394
2004	Det	AL	136	522	166	37	10	20	(7	13)	283	97	97	98	52	3	87	2	3	4	12	5	.71	12	.318	.379	.542
2005	Det	AL	87	334	107	15	4	5	(3	2)	145	48	23	39	24	3	45	2	0	1	2	3	.40	9	.320	.368	.434
2006	Det	AL	153	543	174	41	5	19	(10	9)	282	100	85	106	71	10	87	4	0	4	20	9	.69	16	.320	.400	.519
2007	Det	AL	151	564	167	35	9	21	(12	9)	283	86	102	94	55	10	93	3	0	8	13	8	.62	14	.296	.357	.502
10 ML YEARS			1015	3628	1053	208	44	94	(46	48)	1631	595	518	548	385	32	624	16	26	34	62	38	.62	87	.290	.358	.450

Jose Guillen

Bats: R **Throws:** R **Pos:** RF-150; DH-2; PH-1   **Ht:** 6'0" **Wt:** 195 **Born:** 5/17/1976 **Age:** 32

			BATTING																	**BASERUNNING**				**AVERAGES**		
Year	Team	Lg	G	AB	H	2B	3B	HR	(Hm	Rd)	TB	R	RBI	RC	TBB	IBB	SO	HBP	SH	SF	SB	CS	SB%	GDP	Avg	OBP	Slg
1997	Pit	NL	143	498	133	20	5	14	(5	9)	205	58	70	56	17	0	88	8	0	3	1	2	.33	16	.267	.300	.412
1998	Pit	NL	153	573	153	38	2	14	(10	4)	237	60	84	68	21	0	100	6	1	4	3	5	.38	7	.267	.298	.414
1999	2 Tms		87	288	73	16	0	3	(1	2)	98	42	31	28	20	2	57	7	1	2	1	0	1.00	16	.253	.315	.340
2000	TB	AL	105	316	80	16	5	10	(5	5)	136	40	41	43	18	1	65	13	2	0	3	1	.75	6	.253	.320	.430
2001	TB	AL	41	135	37	5	0	3	(0	3)	51	14	11	15	6	2	26	3	0	1	2	3	.40	2	.274	.317	.378
2002	2 Tms	NL	85	240	57	7	0	8	(5	3)	88	25	31	16	14	1	43	3	1	1	4	5	.44	13	.238	.287	.367
2003	2 Tms		136	485	151	28	2	31	(14	17)	276	77	86	86	24	2	95	14	8	3	1	3	.25	16	.311	.359	.569
2004	LAA	AL	148	565	166	28	3	27	(13	14)	281	88	104	98	37	5	92	15	0	3	5	4	.56	14	.294	.352	.497
2005	Was	NL	148	551	156	32	2	24	(3	21)	264	81	76	72	31	6	102	19	1	9	1	1	.50	14	.283	.338	.479
2006	Was	NL	69	241	52	15	1	9	(4	5)	96	28	40	23	15	4	48	7	0	5	1	0	1.00	8	.216	.276	.398
2007	Sea	AL	153	593	172	28	2	23	(12	11)	273	84	99	90	41	2	118	19	0	5	5	1	.83	17	.290	.353	.460
99	Pit	NL	40	120	32	6	0	1	(0	1)	41	18	18	12	10	1	21	0	1	1	1	0	1.00	7	.267	.321	.342
99	TB	NL	47	168	41	10	0	2	(1	1)	57	24	13	16	10	1	36	7	0	1	0	0	-	9	.244	.312	.339
02	Ari	NL	54	131	30	4	0	4	(3	1)	46	13	15	7	7	1	25	2	0	1	3	4	.43	7	.229	.277	.351
02	Cin	NL	31	109	27	3	0	4	(2	2)	42	12	16	9	7	0	18	1	1	0	1	1	.50	6	.248	.299	.385
03	Cin	NL	91	315	106	21	1	23	(10	13)	198	52	63	64	17	1	63	9	6	2	1	3	.25	8	.337	.385	.629
03	Oak	AL	45	170	45	7	1	8	(4	4)	78	25	23	22	7	1	32	5	2	1	0	0	-	8	.265	.311	.459
	11 ML YEARS		1268	4485	1230	233	22	166	(72	94)	2005	597	673	595	244	25	834	114	14	36	27	25	.52	129	.274	.325	.447

Jeremy Guthrie

Pitches: R **Bats:** R **Pos:** SP-26; RP-6   **Ht:** 6'1" **Wt:** 196 **Born:** 4/8/1979 **Age:** 29

			HOW MUCH HE PITCHED						**WHAT HE GAVE UP**										**THE RESULTS**						
Year	Team	Lg	G	GS	CG	GF	IP	BFP	H	R	ER	HR	SH	SF	HB	TBB	IBB	SO	WP	Bk	W	L	Pct	ShO	Sv-Op Hld	ERC	ERA
2004	Cle	AL	6	0	0	2	11.2	49	9	6	6	1	0	0	1	6	0	7	1	0	0	0	-	0	0-0 0	3.58	4.63
2005	Cle	AL	1	0	0	1	6.0	29	9	4	4	2	1	1	0	2	0	3	0	0	0	0	-	0	0-0 0	8.58	6.00
2006	Cle	AL	9	1	0	1	19.1	93	24	15	15	2	0	0	2	15	1	14	3	0	0	0	-	0	0-0 0	7.78	6.98
2007	Bal	AL	32	26	0	3	175.1	723	165	78	72	23	4	6	4	47	2	123	8	1	7	5	.583	0	0-1 0	3.55	3.70
	4 ML YEARS		48	27	0	7	212.1	894	207	103	97	28	5	7	7	70	3	147	12	1	7	5	.583	0	0-1 0	4.03	4.11

Franklin Gutierrez

Bats: R **Throws:** R **Pos:** RF-88; PH-10; LF-9; CF-8; PR-5; DH-1   **Ht:** 6'2" **Wt:** 180 **Born:** 2/21/1983 **Age:** 25

			BATTING																	**BASERUNNING**				**AVERAGES**		
Year	Team	Lg	G	AB	H	2B	3B	HR	(Hm	Rd)	TB	R	RBI	RC	TBB	IBB	SO	HBP	SH	SF	SB	CS	SB%	GDP	Avg	OBP	Slg
2007	Buffalo*	AAA	30	129	44	7	0	4	(-	-)	63	29	16	24	8	0	20	1	0	0	7	3	.70	3	.341	.384	.488
2005	Cle	AL	7	1	0	0	0	0	(0	0)	0	2	0	0	1	0	0	0	0	0	0	0	-	0	.000	.500	.000
2006	Cle	AL	43	136	37	9	0	1	(1	0)	49	21	8	12	3	0	28	0	2	0	0	0	-	4	.272	.288	.360
2007	Cle	AL	100	271	72	13	2	13	(10	3)	128	41	36	36	21	1	77	1	5	3	8	3	.73	7	.266	.318	.472
	3 ML YEARS		150	408	109	22	2	14	(11	3)	177	64	44	48	25	1	105	1	7	3	8	3	.73	11	.267	.309	.434

Juan Gutierrez

Pitches: R **Bats:** R **Pos:** RP-4; SP-3   **Ht:** 6'3" **Wt:** 200 **Born:** 7/14/1983 **Age:** 24

			HOW MUCH HE PITCHED						**WHAT HE GAVE UP**										**THE RESULTS**						
Year	Team	Lg	G	GS	CG	GF	IP	BFP	H	R	ER	HR	SH	SF	HB	TBB	IBB	SO	WP	Bk	W	L	Pct	ShO	Sv-Op Hld	ERC	ERA
2003	Mrtnsvl	R+	16	3	0	4	34.0	162	42	22	18	2	1	4	5	13	1	30	7	1	1	2	.333	0	2-- -	5.45	4.76
2004	Grnsvle	R	13	13	0	0	65.2	294	74	31	27	4	3	2	7	30	0	59	6	0	8	2	.800	0	0-- -	5.29	3.70
2005	Lxngtn	A	22	21	1	1	120.2	511	106	55	43	10	2	6	10	43	0	100	7	2	9	5	.643	0	0-- -	3.44	3.21
2005	Salem	A+	3	2	0	0	12.0	54	10	4	4	1	0	0	0	8	0	9	0	0	1	1	.500	0	0-- -	3.96	3.00
2006	CpChr	AA	20	20	0	0	103.2	438	94	39	35	10	1	2	5	34	0	106	4	0	8	4	.667	0	0-- -	3.43	3.04
2007	RdRck	AAA	26	25	0	0	156.0	665	154	84	72	17	7	4	2	63	4	108	6	1	5	10	.333	0	0-- -	4.15	4.15
2007	Hou	NL	7	3	0	1	21.1	93	25	14	14	3	0	3	0	6	2	16	1	0	1	1	.500	0	0-0 0	4.71	5.91

Angel Guzman

Pitches: R **Bats:** R **Pos:** RP-9; SP-3   **Ht:** 6'3" **Wt:** 195 **Born:** 12/14/1981 **Age:** 26

			HOW MUCH HE PITCHED						**WHAT HE GAVE UP**										**THE RESULTS**						
Year	Team	Lg	G	GS	CG	GF	IP	BFP	H	R	ER	HR	SH	SF	HB	TBB	IBB	SO	WP	Bk	W	L	Pct	ShO	Sv-Op Hld	ERC	ERA
2001	Boise	A-	14	14	0	0	76.2	318	68	27	19	2	2	5	0	19	0	63	2	1	9	1	.900	0	0-- -	2.38	2.23
2002	Lansng	A	9	9	1	0	62.0	0	42	18	13	3	0	0	1	16	0	49	5	1	5	2	.714	0	0-- -	-	1.89
2002	Dytona	A+	16	15	1	0	94.0	412	99	34	25	2	2	4	4	33	1	74	9	2	6	2	.750	0	0-- -	3.73	2.39
2003	WTenn	AA	15	15	0	0	89.2	366	83	30	28	8	3	2	2	26	0	87	3	1	3	3	.500	0	0-- -	3.33	2.81
2004	Dytona	A+	7	7	0	0	30.0	116	27	15	14	2	0	0	1	6	0	40	0	0	3	1	.750	0	0-- -	2.02	4.20
2004	WTenn	AA	4	4	0	0	17.2	74	20	11	11	2	0	0	1	4	0	13	0	0	0	3	.000	0	0-- -	4.31	5.60
2005	Cubs	R	4	4	0	0	12.0	47	10	3	2	0	0	0	1	1	0	17	0	0	0	0	-	0	0-- -	1.79	1.50
2005	Peoria	A	2	2	0	0	6.1	29	10	5	3	1	0	0	1	0	0	7	0	0	0	1	.000	0	0-- -	7.08	4.26
2006	Iowa	AAA	15	15	0	0	75.2	320	72	37	34	5	4	4	2	24	0	77	3	1	4	4	.500	0	0-- -	3.34	4.04
2007	Cubs	R	4	4	0	0	5.0	18	5	1	0	0	0	0	0	1	0	3	0	0	0	1	.000	0	0-- -	0.25	0.00
2007	Iowa	AAA	3	3	0	0	10.1	51	14	14	14	1	0	0	1	6	1	7	0	0	0	2	.000	0	0-- -	7.13	12.19
2006	ChC	NL	15	10	0	1	56.0	272	68	48	46	9	5	3	6	37	1	60	8	1	0	6	.000	0	0-0 0	7.41	7.39
2007	ChC	NL	12	3	0	3	30.1	128	32	12	12	2	1	1	2	9	0	26	3	0	0	1	.000	0	0-1 0	4.10	3.56
	2 ML YEARS		27	13	0	4	86.1	400	100	60	58	11	6	4	8	46	1	86	11	1	0	7	.000	0	0-1 0	6.19	6.05

Cristian Guzman

Bats: B **Throws:** R **Pos:** SS-44; PR-2; PH-1 **Ht:** 6'0" **Wt:** 195 **Born:** 3/21/1978 **Age:** 30

Year	Team	Lg	G	AB	H	2B	3B	HR	(Hm	Rd)	TB	R	RBI	RC	TBB	IBB	SO	HBP	SH	SF	SB	CS	SB%	GDP	Avg	OBP	Slg
1999	Min	AL	131	420	95	12	3	1	(1	0)	116	47	26	29	22	0	90	3	7	4	9	7	.56	6	.226	.267	.276
2000	Min	AL	156	631	156	25	20	8	(3	5)	245	89	54	76	46	1	101	2	7	4	28	10	.74	5	.247	.299	.388
2001	Min	AL	118	493	149	28	14	10	(7	3)	235	80	51	79	21	0	78	5	8	0	25	8	.76	6	.302	.337	.477
2002	Min	AL	148	623	170	31	6	9	(6	3)	240	80	59	63	17	2	79	2	8	6	12	13	.48	12	.273	.292	.385
2003	Min	AL	143	534	143	15	14	3	(1	2)	195	78	53	62	30	0	79	5	12	4	18	9	.67	4	.268	.311	.365
2004	Min	AL	145	576	158	31	4	8	(5	3)	221	84	46	66	30	4	64	1	13	4	10	5	.67	15	.274	.309	.384
2005	Was	NL	142	456	100	19	6	4	(0	4)	143	39	31	26	25	6	76	1	8	2	7	4	.64	12	.219	.260	.314
2007	Was	NL	46	174	57	6	6	2	(1	1)	81	31	14	30	15	1	21	1	0	2	2	0	1.00	1	.328	.380	.466
8 ML YEARS			1029	3907	1028	167	73	45	(24	21)	1476	528	334	431	206	14	588	20	63	26	111	56	.66	61	.263	.302	.378

Freddy Guzman

Bats: B **Throws:** R **Pos:** PR-5; CF-3; LF-1; PH-1 **Ht:** 5'10" **Wt:** 165 **Born:** 1/20/1981 **Age:** 27

Year	Team	Lg	G	AB	H	2B	3B	HR	(Hm	Rd)	TB	R	RBI	RC	TBB	IBB	SO	HBP	SH	SF	SB	CS	SB%	GDP	Avg	OBP	Slg
2007	Okla*	AAA	133	535	144	22	8	4	(-	-)	194	92	34	92	62	1	88	6	1	6	57	14	.80	10	.269	.348	.363
2004	SD	NL	20	76	16	3	0	0	(0	0)	19	8	5	4	3	0	13	1	0	0	5	2	.71	0	.211	.250	.250
2006	Tex	AL	9	7	2	0	0	0	(0	0)	2	1	0	1	1	0	1	1	0	0	0	0	-	0	.286	.444	.286
2007	Tex	AL	8	6	1	0	0	1	(0	1)	4	2	1	0	0	0	2	0	0	0	0	1	.00	0	.167	.167	.667
3 ML YEARS			37	89	19	3	0	1	(0	1)	25	11	6	5	4	0	16	2	0	0	5	3	.63	0	.213	.263	.281

Joel Guzman

Bats: R **Throws:** R **Pos:** 3B-8; SS-3; PH-3; PR-3; 1B-2; DH-2 **Ht:** 6'6" **Wt:** 250 **Born:** 11/24/1984 **Age:** 23

Year	Team	Lg	G	AB	H	2B	3B	HR	(Hm	Rd)	TB	R	RBI	RC	TBB	IBB	SO	HBP	SH	SF	SB	CS	SB%	GDP	Avg	OBP	Slg
2002	Gr Falls	R+	43	151	38	8	2	3	(-	-)	59	19	27	20	18	0	54	0	2	0	5	3	.63	4	.252	.331	.391
2002	Ddgrs	R	10	33	7	2	0	0	(-	-)	9	4	2	3	5	0	8	0	0	0	1	0	1.00	0	.212	.316	.273
2003	SoGA	A	58	217	51	13	0	8	(-	-)	88	33	29	22	9	0	62	0	1	2	4	4	.50	4	.235	.263	.406
2003	VeroB	A+	62	240	59	13	1	5	(-	-)	89	30	24	23	11	0	60	0	1	0	0	4	.00	7	.246	.279	.371
2004	VeroB	A+	87	329	101	22	8	14	(-	-)	181	52	51	62	21	4	78	2	2	3	8	5	.62	8	.307	.349	.550
2004	Jaxnvl	AA	46	182	51	11	3	9	(-	-)	95	26	35	31	13	0	44	1	0	4	1	2	.33	4	.280	.325	.522
2005	Jaxnvl	AA	122	442	127	31	2	16	(-	-)	210	63	75	76	42	3	128	5	0	7	7	3	.70	10	.287	.351	.475
2006	LsVgs	AAA	85	317	94	16	2	11	(-	-)	147	44	55	53	26	1	72	4	1	4	9	5	.64	11	.297	.353	.464
2006	Drham	AAA	25	88	17	5	0	4	(-	-)	34	7	9	7	4	0	23	0	0	0	0	0	-	5	.193	.228	.386
2007	Drham	AAA	110	414	100	17	2	16	(-	-)	169	44	64	50	23	2	117	2	0	6	9	2	.82	14	.242	.281	.408
2006	LAD	NL	8	19	4	0	0	0	(0	0)	4	2	3	3	3	0	2	1	0	0	0	0	-	3	.211	.348	.211
2007	TB	AL	16	37	9	1	2	0	(0	0)	14	5	4	3	2	0	10	0	0	0	0	0	-	1	.243	.282	.378
2 ML YEARS			24	56	13	1	2	0	(0	0)	10	7	7	6	5	0	12	1	0	0	0	0	-	4	.232	.306	.321

Marc Gwyn

Pitches: R **Bats:** R **Pos:** RP-3 **Ht:** 6'3" **Wt:** 215 **Born:** 11/4/1977 **Age:** 30

Year	Team	Lg	G	GS	CG	GF	IP	RFP	H	R	ER	HR	SH	SF	HB	TBB	IBB	SO	WP	Bk	W	L	Pct	ShO	Sv-Op	Hld	ERC	ERA
2000	Vancvr	A	12	2	0	5	28.1	124	29	16	9	0	2	0	4	2	0	31	3	1	2	1	.007	0	1-		2.65	2.86
2001	Mdest	A+	28	25	0	1	140.0	617	137	85	72	9	6	4	9	59	3	101	6	0	3	13	.188	0	0- -	-	3.96	4.63
2002	As	R	5	5	0	0	16.0	67	19	8	5	1	0	0	0	0	0	23	0	0	1	3	.250	0	0- -	-	3.21	2.81
2002	Mdest	A+	8	7	0	1	34.2	163	40	27	23	4	0	3	3	20	0	30	1	1	1	3	.250	0	0- -	-	6.20	5.97
2003	Mdest	A+	32	1	0	21	51.0	218	46	20	18	2	5	1	3	24	4	61	3	0	1	1	.500	0	7- -	-	3.53	3.18
2003	Mdland	AA	9	0	0	0	9.0	36	9	5	5	1	0	0	0	2	0	12	0	0	1	1	.500	0	0- -	-	3.60	5.00
2004	Mdland	AA	44	0	0	27	67.1	279	59	25	22	3	0	0	5	19	1	72	2	1	3	4	.429	0	13- -	-	2.86	2.94
2004	Scrmto	AAA	12	0	0	4	17.0	81	20	16	12	1	0	0	2	8	0	19	1	0	1	0	1.000	0	0- -	-	5.40	6.35
2005	Scrmto	AAA	34	0	0	11	41.2	214	42	28	24	1	2	6	10	37	3	37	8	0	2	2	.500	0	3- -	-	6.09	5.18
2005	Mdland	AA	19	0	0	3	29.0	126	25	9	9	1	0	2	4	17	1	22	4	0	0	1	.000	0	0- -	-	4.15	2.79
2006	Ark	AA	1	0	0	1	1.0	4	1	0	0	0	0	0	0	0	0	1	0	0	0	0	-	0	1- -	-	1.95	0.00
2006	Salt Lk	AAA	50	0	0	22	66.2	295	66	33	27	6	3	1	4	30	0	56	16	0	3	1	.750	0	6- -	-	4.36	3.65
2007	Salt Lk	AAA	47	0	0	36	57.0	247	68	25	23	5	3	1	1	17	2	54	3	0	2	1	.667	0	15- -	-	4.78	3.63
2007	LAA	AL	3	0	0	2	5.1	31	9	5	7	3	0	1	0	5	0	3	1	0	0	0	-	0	1-1	0	14.82	11.81

Tony Gwynn

Bats: L **Throws:** R **Pos:** PH-32; CF-27; RF-10; LF-4; PR-3 **Ht:** 6'0" **Wt:** 190 **Born:** 10/4/1982 **Age:** 25

Year	Team	Lg	G	AB	H	2B	3B	HR	(Hm	Rd)	TB	R	RBI	RC	TBB	IBB	SO	HBP	SH	SF	SB	CS	SB%	GDP	Avg	OBP	Slg
2003	Beloit	A	61	236	66	8	0	1	(-	-)	77	35	33	34	32	0	31	2	4	5	14	2	.88	3	.280	.364	.326
2004	Hntsvl	AA	138	534	130	20	5	2	(-	-)	166	74	37	67	53	0	95	6	4	1	34	16	.68	4	.243	.318	.311
2005	Hntsvl	AA	133	509	138	21	5	1	(-	-)	172	83	41	73	76	1	75	5	9	2	34	15	.69	11	.271	.370	.338
2006	Nashv	AAA	112	447	134	21	5	4	(-	-)	177	84	42	68	42	1	84	2	0	3	30	11	.73	7	.300	.360	.396
2007	Nashv	AAA	32	126	36	3	3	0	(-	-)	45	19	13	15	9	0	14	1	1	1	4	3	.57	2	.286	.336	.357
2006	Mil	NL	32	77	20	2	1	0	(0	0)	24	5	4	5	2	0	15	0	0	1	3	1	.75	2	.260	.275	.312
2007	Mil	NL	69	123	32	3	2	0	(0	0)	39	13	10	16	12	1	24	0	0	0	8	1	.89	0	.260	.326	.317
2 ML YEARS			101	200	52	5	3	0	(0	0)	63	18	14	21	14	1	39	0	0	1	11	2	.85	2	.260	.307	.315

Charlie Haeger

Pitches: R **Bats:** R **Pos:** RP-8 **Ht:** 6'1" **Wt:** 220 **Born:** 9/19/1983 **Age:** 24

Year	Team	Lg	G	GS	CG	GF	IP	BFP	H	R	ER	HR	SH	SF	HB	TBB	IBB	SO	WP	Bk	W	L	Pct	ShO	Sv-Op	Hld	ERC	ERA
2001	WhSox	R	13	4	0	1	31.0	153	44	29	22	2	1	3	1	17	0	17	4	1	0	3	.000	0	0--	-	6.98	6.39
2002	WhSox	R	25	0	0	14	41.0	178	46	25	19	2	2	1	6	13	2	24	1	0	1	4	.200	0	6--	-	4.71	4.17
2004	Bristol	R+	10	10	0	0	57.1	271	70	41	33	6	3	5	10	22	1	23	1	0	1	6	.143	0	0--	-	5.95	5.18
2004	Knapol	A-	5	5	0	0	31.1	137	31	17	7	0	3	4	3	12	0	21	1	0	1	3	.250	0	0--	-	3.59	2.01
2005	WinSa	A+	14	13	0	1	81.2	354	82	33	29	3	3	2	5	40	0	64	2	0	8	2	.800	0	0--	-	4.35	3.20
2005	Brham	AA	13	13	3	0	85.2	374	84	43	36	1	4	1	5	45	1	48	4	0	6	3	.667	2	0--	-	4.10	3.78
2006	Charltt	AAA	26	25	2	1	170.0	716	143	71	58	9	3	3	12	78	3	130	15	0	14	6	.700	0	0--	-	3.41	3.07
2007	Charltt	AAA	24	23	3	0	147.2	637	138	82	67	16	4	8	6	67	0	126	10	0	5	16	.238	0	0--	-	4.17	4.08
2006	CWS	AL	7	1	0	4	18.1	79	12	10	7	0	0	0	0	13	0	19	0	0	1	1	.500	0	1-1	-	2.65	3.44
2007	CWS	AL	8	0	0	5	11.1	59	17	11	9	3	1	1	1	8	2	1	0	0	0	1	.000	0	0-0	1	10.02	7.15
	2 ML YEARS		15	1	0	9	29.2	138	29	21	16	3	1	1	1	21	2	20	0	0	1	2	.333	0	1-1	1	5.15	4.85

Travis Hafner

Bats: L **Throws:** R **Pos:** DH-137; 1B-11; PH-5 **Ht:** 6'3" **Wt:** 240 **Born:** 6/3/1977 **Age:** 31

Year	Team	Lg	G	AB	H	2B	3B	HR	(Hm	Rd)	TB	R	RBI	RC	TBB	IBB	SO	HBP	SH	SF	SB	CS	SB%	GDP	Avg	OBP	Slg
2002	Tex	AL	23	62	15	4	1	1	(0	1)	24	6	6	7	8	1	15	0	0	0	0	1	.00	0	.242	.329	.387
2003	Cle	AL	91	291	74	19	3	14	(7	7)	141	35	40	42	22	2	81	10	0	1	2	1	.67	7	.254	.327	.485
2004	Cle	AL	140	482	150	41	3	28	(7	21)	281	96	109	103	68	7	111	17	0	6	3	2	.60	11	.311	.410	.583
2005	Cle	AL	137	486	148	42	0	33	(14	19)	289	94	108	115	79	7	123	9	0	4	0	0	-	9	.305	.408	.595
2006	Cle	AL	129	454	140	31	1	42	(21	21)	299	100	117	118	100	16	111	7	0	2	0	0	-	10	.308	.439	.659
2007	Cle	AL	152	545	145	25	2	24	(12	12)	246	80	100	94	102	17	115	7	0	5	1	1	.50	15	.266	.385	.451
	6 ML YEARS		672	2320	672	162	10	142	(61	81)	1280	411	480	479	379	50	556	50	0	18	6	5	.55	52	.290	.398	.552

Jerry Hairston

Bats: R **Throws:** R **Pos:** CF-22; LF-21; 2B-16; 3B-10; RF-6; PH-6; PR-5; SS-2 **Ht:** 5'10" **Wt:** 185 **Born:** 5/29/1976 **Age:** 32

Year	Team	Lg	G	AB	H	2B	3B	HR	(Hm	Rd)	TB	R	RBI	RC	TBB	IBB	SO	HBP	SH	SF	SB	CS	SB%	GDP	Avg	OBP	Slg
2007	Frisco*	AA	3	12	2	1	0	1	(-	-)	6	2	2	1	0	0	3	0	0	0	0	0	-	0	.167	.167	.500
2007	Okla*	AAA	4	15	2	0	0	1	(-	-)	5	2	1	1	2	0	1	0	0	0	0	0	-	1	.133	.235	.333
1998	Bal	AL	6	7	0	0	0	0	(0	0)	0	2	0	0	0	0	1	0	0	0	0	0	-	0	.000	.000	.000
1999	Bal	AL	50	175	47	12	1	4	(1	3)	73	26	17	24	11	0	24	3	4	0	9	4	.69	2	.269	.323	.417
2000	Bal	AL	49	180	46	5	0	5	(2	3)	66	27	19	22	21	0	22	6	5	0	8	5	.62	8	.256	.353	.367
2001	Bal	AL	159	532	124	25	5	8	(5	3)	183	63	47	57	44	0	73	13	9	4	29	11	.73	12	.233	.305	.344
2002	Bal	AL	122	426	114	25	3	5	(2	3)	160	55	32	55	34	0	55	7	8	4	21	6	.78	5	.268	.329	.376
2003	Bal	AL	58	218	59	12	2	2	(1	1)	81	25	21	32	23	0	25	6	10	2	14	5	.74	8	.271	.353	.372
2004	Bal	AL	86	287	87	19	1	2	(0	2)	114	43	24	45	29	1	29	8	6	4	13	8	.62	3	.303	.378	.397
2005	ChC	NL	114	380	99	25	2	4	(3	1)	140	51	30	46	31	0	46	12	7	0	8	9	.47	5	.261	.336	.368
2006	2 Tms		101	170	35	6	1	0	(0	0)	43	25	10	9	13	2	34	2	7	0	5	2	.71	5	.206	.270	.253
2007	Tex	AL	73	159	30	7	0	3	(1	2)	46	12	16	12	11	0	24	3	7	4	5	1	.83	5	.189	.249	.289
06	ChC	NL	38	82	17	3	0	0	(0	0)	20	8	4	5	4	2	14	1	5	0	3	0	1.00	1	.207	.253	.244
06	Tex	AL	63	88	18	3	1	0	(0	0)	23	17	6	4	9	0	20	1	2	0	2	2	.50	4	.205	.286	.261
	10 ML YEARS		818	2534	641	136	15	33	(15	18)	906	339	216	302	217	3	333	60	63	18	112	51	.69	53	.253	.324	.358

Scott Hairston

Bats: R **Throws:** R **Pos:** LF-78; PH-29; CF-3; PR-2; DH-1 **Ht:** 6'0" **Wt:** 200 **Born:** 5/25/1980 **Age:** 28

Year	Team	Lg	G	AB	H	2B	3B	HR	(Hm	Rd)	TB	R	RBI	RC	TBB	IBB	SO	HBP	SH	SF	SB	CS	SB%	GDP	Avg	OBP	Slg
2004	Ari	NL	101	339	84	15	6	13	(6	7)	150	39	29	32	21	0	88	1	2	1	3	3	.50	4	.248	.293	.442
2005	Ari	NL	15	20	2	1	0	0	(0	0)	3	0	0	0	0	0	6	0	0	0	0	0	-	1	.100	.100	.150
2006	Ari	NL	9	15	6	2	0	0	(0	0)	8	2	2	2	1	0	5	0	0	0	0	0	-	1	.400	.438	.533
2007	2 Tms		107	263	64	18	2	11	(6	5)	119	37	36	36	26	0	55	1	3	1	2	0	1.00	4	.243	.313	.452
07	Ari	NL	76	176	39	13	1	3	(1	2)	63	21	16	19	19	0	37	1	3	0	2	0	1.00	4	.222	.301	.358
07	SD	NL	31	87	25	5	1	8	(5	3)	56	16	20	17	7	0	18	0	0	1	0	0	-	0	.287	.337	.644
	4 ML YEARS		232	637	156	36	8	24	(12	12)	280	78	67	70	48	0	154	2	5	2	5	3	.63	10	.245	.299	.440

Bill Hall

Bats: R **Throws:** R **Pos:** CF-130; PH-12; PR-1 **Ht:** 6'0" **Wt:** 210 **Born:** 12/28/1979 **Age:** 28

Year	Team	Lg	G	AB	H	2B	3B	HR	(Hm	Rd)	TB	R	RBI	RC	TBB	IBB	SO	HBP	SH	SF	SB	CS	SB%	GDP	Avg	OBP	Slg
2007	Brewrs*	R	2	6	1	0	0	0	(-	-)	1	0	2	0	1	0	1	0	0	1	0	0	-	1	.167	.250	.167
2002	Mil	NL	19	36	7	1	1	1	(0	1)	13	3	5	3	3	0	13	0	0	0	0	1	.00	1	.194	.256	.361
2003	Mil	NL	52	142	37	9	2	5	(2	3)	65	23	20	18	7	0	28	1	4	1	1	2	.33	5	.261	.298	.458
2004	Mil	NL	126	390	93	20	3	9	(5	4)	146	43	53	41	20	1	119	1	2	1	12	6	.67	4	.238	.276	.374
2005	Mil	NL	146	501	146	39	6	17	(12	5)	248	69	62	73	39	2	103	1	2	3	18	6	.75	11	.291	.342	.495
2006	Mil	NL	148	537	145	39	4	35	(18	17)	297	101	85	87	63	6	162	1	3	4	8	9	.47	12	.270	.345	.553
2007	Mil	NL	136	452	115	35	0	14	(10	4)	192	59	63	59	40	1	128	1	3	1	4	5	.44	9	.254	.315	.425
	6 ML YEARS		627	2058	543	143	16	81	(47	34)	961	298	288	281	172	10	553	7	12	17	43	29	.60	42	.264	.320	.467

120

Toby Hall

Bats: R Throws: R Pos: C-37; PH-1   Ht: 6'3" Wt: 240 Born: 10/21/1975 Age: 32

Year	Team	Lg	G	AB	H	2B	3B	HR	(Hm	Rd)	TB	R	RBI	RC	TBB	IBB	SO	HBP	SH	SF	SB	CS	SB%	GDP	Avg	OBP	Slg
2007	Charltt*	AAA	5	19	5	0	0	2	(-	-)	11	3	7	3	2	1	3	0	0	0	0	0	-	1	.263	.333	.579
2000	TB	AL	4	12	2	0	0	1	(0	1)	5	1	1	1	1	0	0	0	0	0	0	0	-	0	.167	.231	.417
2001	TB	AL	49	188	56	16	0	4	(1	3)	84	28	30	25	4	0	16	3	0	1	2	2	.50	5	.298	.321	.447
2002	TB	AL	85	330	85	19	1	6	(2	4)	124	37	42	39	17	3	27	1	2	3	0	1	.00	14	.258	.293	.376
2003	TB	AL	130	463	117	23	0	12	(4	8)	176	50	47	45	23	4	40	7	0	5	0	1	.00	14	.253	.295	.380
2004	TB	AL	119	404	103	21	0	8	(6	2)	148	35	60	42	24	1	41	5	1	7	0	2	.00	20	.255	.300	.366
2005	TB	AL	135	432	124	20	0	5	(1	4)	159	28	48	46	16	1	39	5	3	7	0	0	-	15	.287	.315	.368
2006	2 Tms		85	278	72	17	0	8	(6	2)	113	17	31	25	10	4	22	2	0	4	0	2	.00	10	.259	.286	.406
2007	CWS	AL	38	116	24	4	0	0	(0	0)	28	8	3	3	3	0	12	0	0	1	0	0	-	2	.207	.225	.241
06	TB	AL	64	221	51	13	0	8	(6	2)	88	15	23	18	8	2	17	2	0	3	0	2	.00	8	.231	.261	.398
06	LAD	NL	21	57	21	4	0	0	(0	0)	25	2	8	7	2	2	5	0	0	1	0	0	-	2	.368	.383	.439
8 ML YEARS			645	2223	583	120	1	44	(20	24)	837	204	262	220	90	13	197	23	6	28	2	8	20	80	.262	.297	.377

Roy Halladay

Pitches: R Bats: R Pos: SP-31   Ht: 6'6" Wt: 225 Born: 5/14/1977 Age: 31

			HOW MUCH HE PITCHED						WHAT HE GAVE UP									THE RESULTS						
Year	Team	Lg	G	GS	CG	GF	IP	BFP	H	R	ER	HR	SH	SF	HB	TBB	IBB	SO	WP	Bk	W	L	Pct	ShO	Sv-Op	Hld	ERC	ERA
1998	Tor	AL	2	2	1	0	14.0	53	9	4	3	2	0	0	0	2	0	13	0	0	1	0	1.000	1	0-0	0	1.61	1.93
1999	Tor	AL	36	18	1	2	149.1	668	156	76	65	19	3	4	4	79	1	82	6	0	8	7	.533	1	1-1	2	5.19	3.92
2000	Tor	AL	19	13	0	4	67.2	349	107	87	80	14	2	3	2	42	0	44	6	1	4	7	.364	0	0-0	0	9.70	10.64
2001	Tor	AL	17	16	1	0	105.1	432	97	41	37	3	3	1	1	25	0	96	4	1	5	3	.625	1	0-0	0	2.61	3.16
2002	Tor	AL	34	34	2	0	239.1	993	223	93	78	10	9	2	7	62	6	168	4	1	19	7	.731	1	0-0	0	2.85	2.93
2003	Tor	AL	36	36	9	0	266.0	1071	253	111	96	26	3	2	9	32	1	204	6	1	22	7	.759	2	0-0	0	2.86	3.25
2004	Tor	AL	21	21	1	0	133.0	561	140	66	62	13	4	3	1	39	1	95	2	2	8	8	.500	1	0-0	0	4.00	4.20
2005	Tor	AL	19	19	5	0	141.2	553	118	39	38	11	2	1	7	18	2	108	2	1	12	4	.750	2	0-0	0	2.26	2.41
2006	Tor	AL	32	32	4	0	220.0	876	208	82	78	19	3	5	5	34	5	132	3	0	16	5	.762	0	0-0	0	2.87	3.19
2007	Tor	AL	31	31	7	0	225.1	927	232	101	93	15	2	7	3	48	3	139	4	0	16	7	.696	1	0-0	0	3.37	3.71
10 ML YEARS			247	222	31	6	1561.2	6483	1543	700	630	132	31	28	39	381	19	1081	37	7	111	55	.669	9	1-1	2	3.40	3.63

Cole Hamels

Pitches: L Bats: L Pos: SP-28   Ht: 6'3" Wt: 190 Born: 12/27/1983 Age: 24

			HOW MUCH HE PITCHED						WHAT HE GAVE UP									THE RESULTS						
Year	Team	Lg	G	GS	CG	GF	IP	BFP	H	R	ER	HR	SH	SF	HB	TBB	IBB	SO	WP	Bk	W	L	Pct	ShO	Sv-Op	Hld	ERC	ERA
2003	Lakwd	A	13	13	1	0	74.2	268	32	8	7	0	3	1	3	25	0	115	3	0	6	1	.857	1	0- -	-	1.04	0.84
2003	Clrwtr	A+	5	5	0	0	26.1	115	29	9	8	0	1	2	1	14	0	32	2	0	2	0	.000	0	0- -	-	4.77	2.73
2004	Clrwtr	A+	4	4	0	0	16.0	58	10	2	2	0	1	0	1	4	0	24	1	0	1	0	1.000	0	0- -	-	1.52	1.13
2005	Clrwtr	A+	3	3	0	0	16.0	62	7	5	4	0	1	1	0	7	0	18	4	0	2	0	1.000	0	0- -	-	1.12	2.25
2005	Rdng	AA	3	3	0	0	19.0	77	10	6	5	2	1	0	1	12	0	19	2	0	2	0	1.000	0	0- -	-	2.74	2.37
2006	Lakwd	A	1	1	0	0	5.2	19	3	1	1	1	0	0	0	2	0	3	0	0	0	0	-	0	0- -	-	2.33	1.59
2006	S-WB	AAA	3	3	1	0	23.0	78	10	1	1	0	0	0	0	1	0	36	0	0	2	0	1.000	1	0- -	-	0.49	0.39
2006	Clrwtr	A+	4	4	0	0	20.1	87	16	8	4	0	0	0	0	9	0	29	2	1	1	1	.500	0	0- -	-	2.35	1.77
2006	Phi	NL	23	23	0	0	132.1	558	117	66	60	19	6	8	3	48	4	145	5	0	9	8	.529	0	0-0	0	3.61	4.08
2007	Phi	NL	28	28	2	0	183.1	743	163	72	69	25	5	5	3	43	4	177	5	0	15	5	.750	0	0-0	0	3.12	3.39
2 ML YEARS			51	51	2	0	315.2	1301	280	138	129	44	11	13	6	91	8	322	10	0	24	13	.649	0	0-0	0	3.32	3.68

Josh Hamilton

Bats: L Throws: L Pos: CF-71; RF-10; PH-10; LF-9   Ht: 6'4" Wt: 235 Born: 5/21/1981 Age: 27

									BATTING											BASERUNNING				AVERAGES		
Year	Team	Lg	G	AB	H	2B	3B	HR	(Hm	Rd)	TB	R	RBI	RC	TBB	IBB	SO	HBP	SH	SF	SB	CS	SB%	GDP	Avg	OBP	Slg
1999	Princtn	R+	56	236	82	20	4	10	(-	-)	140	49	48	52	13	0	43	0	1	2	17	3	.85	0	.347	.378	.593
1999	HudVal	A-	16	72	14	3	0	0	(-	-)	17	7	7	2	1	0	14	1	0	1	1	1	.50	2	.194	.213	.236
2000	CtnSC	A	96	391	118	23	3	13	(-	-)	186	62	61	65	27	3	71	2	0	3	14	6	.70	5	.302	.348	.476
2001	CtnSC	A	4	11	4	1	0	1	(-	-)	8	3	2	3	2	0	3	0	0	0	0	0	-	0	.364	.462	.727
2001	Orlndo	AA	23	89	16	5	0	0	(-	-)	21	5	4	4	5	2	22	0	0	1	2	0	1.00	1	.180	.221	.236
2002	Bkrsfld	A+	56	211	64	14	1	9	(-	-)	107	32	44	40	20	3	46	0	1	3	10	1	.91	4	.303	.359	.507
2006	HudVal	A-	15	50	13	3	1	0	(-	-)	18	7	5	5	5	0	11	0	0	0	1	0	1.00	2	.260	.327	.360
2007	Lsvlle	AAA	11	40	14	1	0	4	(-	-)	27	9	8	11	5	0	9	0	0	0	3	0	1.00	0	.350	.422	.675
2007	Cin	NL	90	298	87	17	2	19	(11	8)	165	52	47	58	33	4	65	4	0	2	3	3	.50	6	.292	.368	.554

Jason Hammel

Pitches: R Bats: R Pos: SP-14; RP-10   Ht: 6'6" Wt: 220 Born: 9/2/1982 Age: 25

			HOW MUCH HE PITCHED						WHAT HE GAVE UP									THE RESULTS						
Year	Team	Lg	G	GS	CG	GF	IP	BFP	H	R	ER	HR	SH	SF	HB	TBB	IBB	SO	WP	Bk	W	L	Pct	ShO	Sv-Op	Hld	ERC	ERA
2002	Princtn	R+	2	0	0	1	5.1	22	7	0	0	0	0	0	0	5	0	5	0	0	0	0	-	0	1- -	-	3.64	0.00
2002	HudVal	A-	13	10	0	2	51.2	245	71	41	30	0	0	1	4	14	0	38	3	2	1	5	.167	0	1- -	-	5.10	5.23
2003	CtnSC	A	14	12	1	1	76.2	320	70	32	29	2	3	3	2	27	1	50	4	1	6	2	.750	0	0- -	-	3.03	3.40
2004	CtnSC	A	18	18	0	0	94.2	405	94	54	34	7	5	5	2	27	0	88	8	0	4	7	.364	0	0- -	-	3.43	3.23
2004	Bkrsfld	A+	11	11	0	0	71.1	275	52	18	15	4	3	1	4	20	0	65	3	0	6	2	.750	0	0- -	-	2.27	1.89
2005	Mont	AA	12	12	3	0	81.1	322	70	26	24	5	1	2	2	19	0	76	2	1	8	2	.800	0	0- -	-	2.63	2.66
2005	Drham	AAA	10	10	0	0	54.2	247	57	31	25	8	1	0	3	27	0	48	4	0	3	2	.600	0	0- -	-	5.24	4.12
2006	Drham	AAA	24	24	1	0	127.2	547	133	71	60	11	7	6	7	36	0	117	5	1	5	9	.357	0	0- -	-	3.97	4.23

Year	Team	Lg	G	GS	CG	GF	IP	BFP	H	R	ER	HR	SH	SF	HB	TBB	IBB	SO	WP	Bk	W	L	Pct	ShO	Sv-Op	Hld	ERC	ERA
			HOW MUCH HE PITCHED						**WHAT HE GAVE UP**												**THE RESULTS**						
2007	Drham	AAA	13	13	2	0	76.1	316	61	29	29	3	0	1	4	28	0	75	7	2	4	5	.444	1	0--	-	2.68	3.42
2006	TB	AL	9	9	0	0	44.0	208	61	38	38	7	0	3	1	21	0	32	3	2	0	6	.000	0	0-0	0	7.40	7.77
2007	TB	AL	24	14	0	2	85.0	384	100	58	58	12	2	0	2	40	1	64	3	0	3	5	.375	0	0-0	0	5.86	6.14
	2 ML YEARS		33	23	0	2	129.0	592	161	96	96	19	2	3	3	61	1	96	6	2	3	11	.214	0	0-0	0	6.37	6.70

Robby Hammock

Bats: R Throws: R Pos: PH-15; C-12; LF-5; 3B-4; PR-3; RF-2; 1B-1 **Ht: 5'10" Wt: 185 Born: 5/13/1977 Age: 31**

Year	Team	Lg	G	AB	H	2B	3B	HR	(Hm	Rd)	TB	R	RBI	RC	TBB	IBB	SO	HBP	SH	SF	SB	CS	SB%	GDP	Avg	OBP	Slg
			BATTING																		**BASERUNNING**				**AVERAGES**		
2007	Tucsn*	AAA	67	246	80	17	1	4	(-	-)	111	34	35	50	43	0	34	2	0	2	3	2	.60	7	.325	.427	.451
2003	Ari	NL	65	195	55	10	2	8	(5	3)	93	30	28	28	17	3	44	2	0	2	3	2	.60	5	.282	.343	.477
2004	Ari	NL	62	195	47	16	2	4	(1	3)	79	22	18	14	13	6	39	0	1	1	3	3	.50	9	.241	.287	.405
2006	Ari	NL	1	2	1	1	0	0	(0	0)	2	1	0	0	0	0	0	0	0	0	0	0	.500		.500	.500	1.000
2007	Ari	NL	34	45	11	2	0	0	(0	0)	13	5	0	4	3	0	7	1	0	0	0	0	-	3	.244	.306	.289
	4 ML YEARS		162	437	114	29	4	12	(6	6)	187	58	46	46	33	9	90	3	1	3	6	5	.55	17	.261	.315	.428

Justin Hampson

Pitches: L Bats: L Pos: RP-39 **Ht: 6'1" Wt: 200 Born: 5/24/1980 Age: 28**

Year	Team	Lg	G	GS	CG	GF	IP	BFP	H	R	ER	HR	SH	SF	HB	TBB	IBB	SO	WP	Bk	W	L	Pct	ShO	Sv-Op	Hld	ERC	ERA
			HOW MUCH HE PITCHED						**WHAT HE GAVE UP**												**THE RESULTS**						
2000	PortInd	A-	14	13	0	0	68.2	309	74	43	27	5	3	2	4	27	0	44	1	0	1	4	.444	0	0--	-	4.44	3.54
2001	TriCity	A-	15	15	0	0	81.2	354	84	55	41	5	1	5	4	23	0	63	4	0	4	6	.400	0	0--	-	3.92	4.52
2002	Ashvll	A	27	27	1	0	164.1	710	162	87	70	12	5	2	24	58	1	123	7	1	9	8	.529	0	0--	-	4.25	3.83
2003	Visalia	A+	26	26	1	0	159.0	684	153	73	65	12	3	3	21	51	1	150	2	2	14	7	.667	0	0--	-	3.91	3.68
2003	Tulsa	AA	1	1	0	0	4.0	22	8	6	6	0	0	0	0	3	0	0	0	0	0	1	.000	0	0--	-	11.38	13.50
2004	Tulsa	AA	27	27	1	0	170.1	718	176	82	66	8	13	1	8	63	0	104	5	1	10	9	.526	0	0--	-	4.09	3.49
2005	ColSpr	AAA	27	26	1	0	144.1	672	167	109	96	18	6	3	11	71	0	93	3	2	5	13	.278	0	0--	-	5.83	5.99
2006	ColSpr	AAA	31	13	0	2	121.2	511	121	57	45	10	5	4	5	39	1	95	5	0	8	4	.667	0	0--	-	3.83	3.33
2007	PortInd	AAA	10	0	0	0	12.2	59	12	6	5	3	1	1	1	8	0	12	0	0	1	1	.500	0	0--	-	5.96	3.55
2006	Col	NL	5	1	0	0	12.0	60	19	10	10	3	0	0	1	5	0	9	1	0	1	0	1.000	0	0-1	0	9.41	7.50
2007	SD	NL	39	0	0	12	53.1	219	48	17	16	1	1	1	3	16	4	34	0	0	2	3	.400	0	0-0	4	2.77	2.70
	2 ML YEARS		44	1	0	12	65.1	279	67	27	26	4	1	1	4	21	4	43	1	0	3	3	.500	0	0-1	4	3.82	3.58

Mike Hampton

Pitches: L Bats: R Pos: P **Ht: 5'10" Wt: 195 Born: 9/9/1972 Age: 35**

Year	Team	Lg	G	GS	CG	GF	IP	BFP	H	R	ER	HR	SH	SF	HB	TBB	IBB	SO	WP	Bk	W	L	Pct	ShO	Sv-Op	Hld	ERC	ERA
			HOW MUCH HE PITCHED						**WHAT HE GAVE UP**												**THE RESULTS**						
1993	Sea	AL	13	3	0	2	17.0	95	28	20	18	3	1	1	0	17	3	8	1	1	1	3	.250	0	1-1	2	11.09	9.53
1994	Hou	NL	44	0	0	7	41.1	181	46	19	17	4	0	0	2	16	1	24	5	1	2	1	.667	0	0-1	10	4.88	3.70
1995	Hou	NL	24	24	0	0	150.2	641	141	73	56	13	11	5	4	49	3	115	3	1	9	8	.529	0	0-0	0	3.37	3.35
1996	Hou	NL	27	27	2	0	160.1	691	175	79	64	12	10	3	3	49	1	101	7	2	10	10	.500	1	0-0	0	4.11	3.59
1997	Hou	NL	34	34	7	0	223.0	941	217	105	95	16	11	7	2	77	2	139	6	1	15	10	.600	2	0-0	0	3.56	3.83
1998	Hou	NL	32	32	1	0	211.2	917	227	92	79	18	7	7	5	81	1	137	4	2	11	7	.611	1	0-0	0	4.45	3.36
1999	Hou	NL	34	34	3	0	239.0	979	206	86	77	12	10	9	5	101	2	177	9	0	22	4	.846	2	0-0	0	3.25	2.90
2000	NYM	NL	33	33	3	0	217.2	929	194	89	76	10	11	5	8	99	5	151	10	0	15	10	.600	1	0-0	0	3.44	3.14
2001	Col	NL	32	32	2	0	203.0	904	236	138	122	31	8	6	8	85	7	122	6	0	14	13	.519	1	0-0	0	5.69	5.41
2002	Col	NL	30	30	0	0	178.2	838	228	135	122	24	2	9	7	91	4	74	9	2	7	15	.318	0	0-0	0	6.61	6.15
2003	Atl	NL	31	31	1	0	190.0	823	186	91	81	14	10	5	1	78	4	110	10	1	14	8	.636	0	0-0	0	3.77	3.84
2004	Atl	NL	29	29	1	0	172.1	760	198	86	82	15	8	3	1	65	3	87	3	2	13	9	.591	0	0-0	0	4.76	4.28
2005	Atl	NL	12	12	1	0	69.1	284	74	28	27	5	2	1	0	18	0	27	1	0	5	3	.625	1	0-0	0	3.85	3.50
	13 ML YEARS		375	321	21	9	2074.0	8983	2156	1041	916	177	91	61	46	826	36	1272	74	13	138	101	.577	9	1-2	12	4.28	3.97

Josh Hancock

Pitches: R Bats: R Pos: RP-8 **Ht: 6'3" Wt: 225 Born: 4/11/1978**

Year	Team	Lg	G	GS	CG	GF	IP	BFP	H	R	ER	HR	SH	SF	HB	TBB	IBB	SO	WP	Bk	W	L	Pct	ShO	Sv-Op	Hld	ERC	ERA
			HOW MUCH HE PITCHED						**WHAT HE GAVE UP**												**THE RESULTS**						
2002	Bos	AL	3	1	0	2	7.1	28	5	3	3	1	1	0	0	2	0	6	0	0	0	1	.000	0	0-0	0	2.25	3.68
2003	Phi	NL	2	0	0	0	3.0	11	2	1	1	0	0	0	0	0	0	4	0	0	0	0	-	0	0-0	0	0.91	3.00
2004	2 Tms	NL	16	11	0	2	63.2	293	73	43	36	17	3	2	1	28	2	36	5	0	5	2	.714	0	0-0	0	6.24	5.09
2005	Cin	NL	11	0	0	5	14.0	54	11	4	3	1	0	0	0	1	0	5	0	0	1	0	1.000	0	0-0	0	1.64	1.93
2006	StL	NL	62	0	0	15	77.0	323	70	37	35	9	4	4	1	23	2	50	3	1	3	3	.500	0	1-3	5	3.27	4.09
2007	StL	NL	8	0	0	4	12.2	56	14	6	5	2	2	0	0	5	0	9	1	0	0	1	.000	0	0-0	0	5.06	3.55
	04	Phi	NL	4	2	0	0	9.0	42	13	9	9	3	0	0	0	3	0	5	0	0	0	1	.000	0	0-0	0	8.40	9.00
	04	Cin	NL	12	9	0	2	54.2	251	60	34	27	14	3	2	1	25	2	31	5	0	5	1	.833	0	0-0	0	5.91	4.45
	6 ML YEARS		102	12	0	28	177.2	765	175	94	83	30	10	6	2	59	4	110	9	1	9	7	.563	0	1-3	5	4.14	4.20

Ryan Hanigan

Bats: R Throws: R Pos: C-3; PH-2 **Ht: 6'0" Wt: 195 Born: 8/16/1980 Age: 27**

Year	Team	Lg	G	AB	H	2B	3B	HR	(Hm	Rd)	TB	R	RBI	RC	TBB	IBB	SO	HBP	SH	SF	SB	CS	SB%	GDP	Avg	OBP	Slg
			BATTING																		**BASERUNNING**				**AVERAGES**		
2002	Dayton	A	6	11	3	1	0	0	(-	-)	4	1	0	1	1	0	2	0	0	0	0	0	-	0	.273	.333	.364
2003	Dayton	A	92	311	86	12	0	1	(-	-)	101	43	31	40	40	1	44	4	1	3	3	4	.43	8	.277	.363	.325
2003	Lsvlle	AAA	1	3	1	0	0	0	(-	-)	1	1	0	0	0	0	1	1	1	0	0	0	-	0	.333	.500	.333
2004	Ptomc	A+	119	429	127	21	0	5	(-	-)	163	58	56	65	49	1	51	6	5	9	6	5	.55	12	.296	.369	.380
2005	Chatt	AA	100	333	107	14	1	4	(-	-)	135	45	29	61	50	1	41	5	2	0	4	1	.80	8	.321	.418	.405

Year	Team	Lg	G	AB	H	2B	3B	HR	(Hm	Rd)	TB	R	RBI	RC	TBB	IBB	SO	HBP	SH	SF	SB	CS	SB%	GDP	Avg	OBP	Slg
2006	Chatt	AA	56	126	31	2	0	0	(-	-)	33	17	14	14	19	0	23	2	0	3	0	0	-	1	.246	.347	.262
2006	Lsvlle	AAA	8	13	2	0	0	0	(-	-)	2	2	1	1	6	0	2	0	0	0	0	0	-	0	.154	.421	.154
2007	Chatt	AA	60	197	59	14	1	3	(-	-)	84	30	27	39	41	2	30	3	2	4	0	2	.00	4	.299	.420	.426
2007	Lsvlle	AAA	41	127	32	5	0	1	(-	-)	40	16	9	15	14	2	15	2	6	1	0	0	-	3	.252	.333	.315
2007	Cin	NL	5	10	3	1	0	0	(0	0)	4	3	2	2	1	1	2	0	0	0	0	0	-	0	.300	.364	.400

Jack Hannahan

Bats: L **Throws:** R **Pos:** 3B-41 **Ht:** 6'2" **Wt:** 205 **Born:** 3/4/1980 **Age:** 28

Year	Team	Lg	G	AB	H	2B	3B	HR	(Hm	Rd)	TB	R	RBI	RC	TBB	IBB	SO	HBP	SH	SF	SB	CS	SB%	GDP	Avg	OBP	Slg
2001	Oneont	A-	14	55	16	4	1	0	(-	-)	22	11	8	8	5	0	7	0	0	3	2	1	.67	2	.291	.333	.400
2001	WMich	A	46	170	54	11	0	1	(-	-)	68	24	27	30	26	0	39	1	0	1	4	2	.67	5	.318	.409	.400
2002	Lkland	A+	66	246	67	11	1	6	(-	-)	98	28	42	39	30	2	44	1	0	4	9	3	.75	2	.272	.362	.398
2002	Erie	AA	65	226	54	12	1	3	(-	-)	77	17	20	25	21	0	50	2	0	0	2	1	.67	7	.239	.309	.341
2003	Erie	AA	135	471	121	18	0	9	(-	-)	166	64	45	59	48	6	78	3	5	2	2	0	1.00	13	.257	.328	.352
2004	Erie	AA	108	374	102	21	1	8	(-	-)	149	48	39	59	53	4	60	2	1	1	7	3	.70	9	.273	.365	.398
2005	Erie	AA	7	22	3	0	0	0	(-	-)	3	1	1	0	4	0	8	0	0	0	0	0	-	0	.136	.269	.136
2005	Toledo	AAA	68	238	64	15	0	4	(-	-)	91	31	28	33	25	2	58	3	0	3	6	3	.67	5	.269	.342	.382
2006	Toledo	AAA	119	415	117	27	0	9	(-	-)	171	59	62	70	61	4	114	8	3	7	9	6	.60	5	.282	.379	.412
2007	Toledo	AAA	101	336	99	20	1	13	(-	-)	160	56	63	71	76	1	92	1	0	4	5	5	.50	7	.295	.422	.476
2006	Det	AL	3	9	0	0	0	0	(0	0)	0	0	0	0	1	0	1	0	0	0	0	0	-	0	.000	.100	.000
2007	Oak	AL	41	144	40	12	0	3	(1	2)	61	16	24	23	21	0	39	1	1	2	1	0	1.00	6	.278	.369	.424
2 ML YEARS			44	153	40	12	0	3	(1	2)	61	16	24	23	22	0	40	1	1	2	1	0	1.00	6	.261	.354	.399

Joel Hanrahan

Pitches: R **Bats:** R **Pos:** SP-11; RP-1 **Ht:** 6'3" **Wt:** 215 **Born:** 10/6/1981 **Age:** 26

			HOW MUCH HE PITCHED					WHAT HE GAVE UP											THE RESULTS						
Year	Team	Lg	G	GS	CG	GF	IP	BFP	H	R	ER	HR	SH	SF	HB	TBB	IBB	SO	WP	Bk	W	L	Pct	ShO	Sv-Op Hld	ERC	ERA
2000	Gr Falls	R+	12	11	0	0	55.0	240	49	32	29	4	0	0	5	23	0	40	4	0	3	1	.750	0	0- - -	3.65	4.75
2001	Wilmg	A+	27	26	0	1	144.0	615	136	71	54	13	5	1	11	55	0	116	8	1	9	11	.450	0	0- - -	3.97	3.38
2002	VeroB	A+	25	25	2	0	143.1	608	129	74	67	11	4	7	11	51	1	139	7	1	10	6	.625	1	0- - -	3.49	4.21
2002	Jaxnvl	AA	3	3	0	0	11.0	55	15	14	13	2	0	2	0	7	0	10	0	0	1	1	.500	0	0- - -	7.81	10.64
2003	Jaxnvl	AA	23	23	1	0	133.1	556	117	44	36	5	4	2	7	53	2	130	4	0	10	4	.714	0	0- - -	3.21	2.43
2003	LsVgs	AAA	5	5	0	0	25.0	130	36	28	28	2	1	2	2	20	1	13	2	0	1	2	.333	0	0- - -	8.57	10.08
2004	LsVgs	AAA	25	22	0	1	119.1	548	128	78	67	22	9	7	7	75	0	97	9	0	7	7	.500	0	0- - -	6.45	5.05
2005	VeroB	A+	5	5	0	0	21.1	97	25	15	14	5	0	0	0	11	0	25	2	0	1	0	1.000	0	0- - -	6.69	5.91
2005	Jaxnvl	AA	23	21	0	0	111.2	499	118	71	61	17	6	4	1	55	1	102	9	0	9	8	.529	0	0- - -	5.18	4.92
2006	Jaxnvl	AA	12	12	0	0	66.1	273	49	19	19	4	4	1	3	38	1	67	7	0	7	2	.778	0	0- - -	3.33	2.58
2006	LsVgs	AAA	14	14	0	0	74.1	331	70	47	37	7	5	3	3	39	1	46	3	0	4	3	.571	0	0- - -	4.28	4.48
2007	Clmbo	AAA	15	15	0	0	75.1	330	65	36	31	10	1	1	4	36	0	71	2	0	5	4	.556	0	0- - -	3.98	3.70
2007	Was	NL	12	11	0	0	51.0	247	59	35	34	9	2	1	0	38	0	43	3	0	5	3	.625	0	0-0 0	7.01	6.00

Devern Hansack

Pitches: R **Bats:** R **Pos:** RP-2; SP-1 **Ht:** 6'2" **Wt:** 180 **Born:** 2/5/1978 **Age:** 30

			HOW MUCH HE PITCHED					WHAT HE GAVE UP											THE RESULTS						
Year	Team	Lg	G	GS	CG	GF	IP	BFP	H	R	ER	HR	SH	SF	HB	TBB	IBB	SO	WP	Bk	W	L	Pct	ShO	Sv Op Hld	ERC	ERA
2002	TriCity	A-	12	10	0	0	50.0	207	44	21	20	6	2	3	2	17	0	37	0	1	3	4	.429	0	0- - -	3.52	3.60
2003	Lxngtn	A	22	16	0	0	91.2	397	100	53	46	10	1	3	1	32	0	76	6	1	10	6	.625	0	0- - -	4.53	4.52
2006	Portlnd	AA	31	18	0	8	132.1	555	122	55	48	14	3	4	8	36	4	124	10	0	8	7	.533	0	1- - -	3.36	3.26
2007	Pwtckt	AAA	25	23	0	0	139.2	577	126	62	56	16	2	8	3	40	1	131	7	2	10	7	.588	0	0- - -	3.28	3.61
2006	Bos	AL	2	2	1	0	10.0	36	6	3	3	2	0	0	0	1	0	8	0	0	1	1	.500	1	0-0 0	1.59	2.70
2007	Bos	AL	3	1	0	0	7.2	38	9	5	4	2	0	0	0	5	0	5	0	0	0	1	.000	0	0-0 0	7.11	4.70
2 ML YEARS			5	3	1	0	17.2	74	15	8	7	4	0	0	0	6	0	13	0	0	1	2	.333	1	0-0 0	3.76	3.57

J.A. Happ

Pitches: L **Bats:** L **Pos:** SP-1 **Ht:** 6'6" **Wt:** 200 **Born:** 10/19/1982 **Age:** 25

			HOW MUCH HE PITCHED					WHAT HE GAVE UP											THE RESULTS						
Year	Team	Lg	G	GS	CG	GF	IP	BFP	H	R	ER	HR	SH	SF	HB	TBB	IBB	SO	WP	Bk	W	L	Pct	ShO	Sv-Op Hld	ERC	ERA
2004	Batvia	A-	11	11	0	0	35.2	143	22	8	8	1	1	2	3	18	0	37	0	0	1	2	.333	0	0- - -	2.38	2.02
2005	Lakwd	A	14	12	0	0	72.1	300	57	26	19	3	1	0	5	26	0	70	4	1	4	4	.500	0	0- - -	2.66	2.36
2005	Rdng	AA	1	1	0	0	6.0	23	3	1	1	0	0	1	0	2	0	8	1	0	1	0	1.000	0	0- - -	1.09	1.50
2006	Clrwtr	A+	13	13	0	0	80.0	319	63	35	25	9	4	3	2	19	0	77	1	2	3	7	.300	0	0- - -	2.52	2.81
2006	Rdng	AA	12	12	0	0	74.2	307	58	27	22	2	2	2	3	29	0	81	0	0	6	2	.750	0	0- - -	2.54	2.65
2006	S-WB	AAA	1	1	0	0	6.0	24	3	1	1	1	0	0	1	1	0	4	0	0	1	0	1.000	0	0- - -	1.62	1.50
2007	Ottawa	AAA	24	24	0	0	118.1	515	118	74	66	12	4	4	0	62	1	117	2	1	4	6	.400	0	0- - -	4.63	5.02
2007	Phi	NL	1	1	0	0	4.0	21	7	5	5	3	0	0	0	2	0	5	0	0	0	1	.000	0	0-0 0	15.13	11.25

Aaron Harang

Pitches: R **Bats:** R **Pos:** SP-34 **Ht:** 6'7" **Wt:** 270 **Born:** 5/9/1978 **Age:** 30

			HOW MUCH HE PITCHED					WHAT HE GAVE UP											THE RESULTS						
Year	Team	Lg	G	GS	CG	GF	IP	BFP	H	R	ER	HR	SH	SF	HB	TBB	IBB	SO	WP	Bk	W	L	Pct	ShO	Sv-Op Hld	ERC	ERA
2002	Oak	AL	16	15	0	0	78.1	354	78	44	42	7	3	4	3	45	2	64	1	0	5	4	.556	0	0-0 0	4.76	4.83
2003	2 Tms		16	15	0	1	76.1	327	89	47	45	11	5	1	1	19	0	42	3	1	5	6	.455	0	0-0 0	4.84	5.31
2004	Cin	NL	28	28	1	0	161.0	711	177	90	87	26	13	6	5	53	5	125	7	0	10	9	.526	1	0-0 0	4.81	4.86
2005	Cin	NL	32	32	1	0	211.2	887	217	93	90	22	11	5	8	51	3	163	6	0	11	13	.458	0	0-0 0	3.77	3.83

Year	Team	Lg	G	GS	CG	GF	IP	BFP	H	R	ER	HR	SH	SF	HB	TBB	IBB	SO	WP	Bk	W	L	Pct	ShO	Sv-Op	Hld	ERC	ERA
2006	Cin	NL	36	**35**	**6**	0	234.1	**993**	242	109	98	28	**21**	8	8	56	8	**216**	6	1	**16**	11	.593	2	0-0	0	3.82	3.76
2007	Cin	NL	34	34	2	0	231.2	948	213	100	96	28	4	5	8	52	3	218	**12**	1	16	6	.727	1	0-0	0	3.22	3.73
03	Oak	AL	7	6	0	1	30.1	136	41	19	18	5	2	1	0	9	0	16	0	1	1	3	.250	0	0-0	0	6.32	5.34
03	Cin	NL	9	9	0	0	46.0	191	48	28	27	6	3	0	1	10	0	26	3	0	4	3	.571	0	0-0	0	3.94	5.28
6 ML YEARS			162	159	10	1	993.1	4220	1016	483	458	122	57	29	33	276	21	828	35	3	63	49	.563	4	0-0	0	3.98	4.15

Rich Harden

Pitches: R **Bats:** L **Pos:** SP-4; RP-3 **Ht:** 6'1" **Wt:** 190 **Born:** 11/30/1981 **Age:** 26

Year	Team	Lg	G	GS	CG	GF	IP	BFP	H	R	ER	HR	SH	SF	HB	TBB	IBB	SO	WP	Bk	W	L	Pct	ShO	Sv-Op	Hld	ERC	ERA
2007	Scrmto*	AAA	1	0	0	0	1.0	4	1	0	0	0	0	0	0	0	0	1	0	0	0	0	-	0	0-	-	1.95	0.00
2003	Oak	AL	15	13	0	0	74.2	324	72	38	37	5	2	3	1	40	1	67	6	0	5	4	.556	0	0-0	0	4.28	4.46
2004	Oak	AL	31	31	0	0	189.2	803	171	90	84	16	5	6	3	81	6	167	4	1	11	7	.611	0	0-0	0	3.57	3.99
2005	Oak	AL	22	19	2	0	128.0	514	93	42	36	7	4	2	2	43	0	121	6	0	10	5	.667	1	0-0	1	2.20	2.53
2006	Oak	AL	9	9	0	0	46.2	191	31	22	22	5	0	2	1	26	0	49	0	0	4	0	1.000	0	0-0	0	3.07	4.24
2007	Oak	AL	7	4	0	2	25.2	100	18	7	7	3	0	0	0	11	1	27	0	0	1	2	.333	0	0-0	0	2.80	2.45
5 ML YEARS			84	76	2	2	464.2	1932	385	199	186	36	11	13	7	201	8	431	16	1	31	18	.633	1	0-0	1	3.19	3.60

J.J. Hardy

Bats: R **Throws:** R **Pos:** SS-149; PH-2 **Ht:** 6'2" **Wt:** 190 **Born:** 8/19/1982 **Age:** 25

							BATTING																BASERUNNING				AVERAGES		
Year	Team	Lg	G	AB	H	2B	3B	HR	(Hm	Rd)	TB	R	RBI	RC	TBB	IBB	SO	HBP	SH	SF	SB	CS	SB%	GDP	Avg	OBP	Slg
2005	Mil	NL	124	372	92	22	1	9	(6	3)	143	46	50	49	44	7	48	1	8	2	0	0	-	10	.247	.327	.384
2006	Mil	NL	35	128	31	5	0	5	(4	1)	51	13	14	13	10	0	23	0	1	0	1	1	.50	4	.242	.295	.398
2007	Mil	NL	151	592	164	30	1	26	(15	11)	274	89	80	84	40	1	73	1	4	1	2	3	.40	13	.277	.323	.463
3 ML YEARS			310	1092	287	57	2	40	(25	15)	468	148	144	146	94	8	144	2	12	4	3	4	.43	27	.263	.321	.429

Dan Haren

Pitches: R **Bats:** R **Pos:** SP-34 **Ht:** 6'5" **Wt:** 220 **Born:** 9/17/1980 **Age:** 27

Year	Team	Lg	G	GS	CG	GF	IP	BFP	H	R	ER	HR	SH	SF	HB	TBB	IBB	SO	WP	Bk	W	L	Pct	ShO	Sv-Op	Hld	ERC	ERA
2003	StL	NL	14	14	0	0	72.2	320	84	44	41	9	4	2	5	22	0	43	3	0	3	7	.300	0	0-0	0	5.07	5.08
2004	StL	NL	14	5	0	2	46.0	195	45	23	23	4	4	2	2	17	2	32	1	0	3	3	.500	0	0-0	0	3.91	4.50
2005	Oak	AL	34	34	3	0	217.0	897	212	101	90	26	3	5	6	53	5	163	6	0	14	12	.538	0	0-0	0	3.58	3.73
2006	Oak.	AL	34	**34**	2	0	223.0	930	224	109	102	31	3	3	10	45	6	176	10	0	14	13	.519	0	0-0	0	3.72	4.12
2007	Oak	AL	34	**34**	0	0	222.2	935	214	91	76	24	2	8	3	55	1	192	10	0	15	9	.625	0	0-0	0	3.32	3.07
5 ML YEARS			130	121	5	2	781.1	3277	779	368	332	94	16	20	26	192	14	606	30	0	49	44	.527	0	0-0	0	3.69	3.82

Tim Harikkala

Pitches: R **Bats:** R **Pos:** SP-1 **Ht:** 6'2" **Wt:** 185 **Born:** 7/15/1971 **Age:** 36

Year	Team	Lg	G	GS	CG	GF	IP	BFP	H	R	ER	HR	SH	SF	HB	TBB	IBB	SO	WP	Bk	W	L	Pct	ShO	Sv-Op	Hld	ERC	ERA
2007	ColSpr*	AAA	8	5	0	1	32.2	142	39	17	15	2	0	2	1	11	0	11	2	0	3	1	.750	0	0-	-	4.90	4.13
1995	Sea	AL	1	0	0	1	3.1	18	7	6	6	1	0	0	0	1	0	1	0	0	0	0	-	0	0-0	0	12.43	16.20
1996	Sea	AL	1	1	0	0	4.1	20	4	6	6	1	1	0	1	2	0	1	0	0	0	1	.000	0	0-0	0	5.68	12.46
1999	Bos	AL	7	0	0	2	13.0	58	15	9	9	0	2	0	1	6	1	7	1	0	1	1	.500	0	0-0	0	4.72	6.23
2004	Col	NL	55	0	0	11	62.2	262	55	34	33	10	2	2	1	23	5	30	0	1	6	6	.500	0	0-7	15	3.62	4.74
2005	Oak	AL	8	0	0	5	12.2	56	16	9	9	3	0	0	0	4	0	7	0	0	0	0	-	0	0-0	0	6.40	6.39
2007	Col	NL	1	1	0	0	3.1	19	9	3	3	0	0	0	0	1	0	2	0	0	0	0	-	0	0-0	0	14.52	8.10
6 ML YEARS			73	2	0	19	99.1	433	106	67	66	15	5	2	3	37	6	48	1	1	7	8	.467	0	0-7	15	4.76	5.98

Brendan Harris

Bats: R **Throws:** R **Pos:** SS-87; 2B-47; 3B-4; PH-2; PR-2 **Ht:** 6'1" **Wt:** 200 **Born:** 8/26/1980 **Age:** 27

							BATTING																BASERUNNING				AVERAGES		
Year	Team	Lg	G	AB	H	2B	3B	HR	(Hm	Rd)	TB	R	RBI	RC	TBB	IBB	SO	HBP	SH	SF	SB	CS	SB%	GDP	Avg	OBP	Slg
2004	2 Tms	NL	23	59	10	3	0	1	(0	1)	16	4	3	2	3	0	12	1	0	0	0	0	-	0	.169	.222	.271
2005	Was	NL	4	9	3	1	0	1	(0	1)	7	1	3	3	0	0	0	1	0	0	0	0	-	0	.333	.400	.778
2006	2 Tms	NL	25	42	10	2	0	1	(1	0)	15	5	3	4	4	0	7	1	0	0	0	0	-	2	.238	.319	.357
2007	TB	AL	137	521	149	35	3	12	(5	7)	226	72	59	70	42	1	96	4	8	1	4	1	.80	19	.286	.343	.434
04	ChC	NL	3	9	2	1	0	0	(0	0)	3	0	1	1	1	0	1	0	0	0	0	0	-	0	.222	.300	.333
04	Mon	NL	20	50	8	2	0	1	(0	1)	13	4	2	1	2	0	11	1	0	0	0	0	-	0	.160	.208	.260
06	Was	NL	17	32	8	2	0	0	(0	0)	10	3	2	3	3	0	3	1	0	0	0	0	-	1	.250	.333	.313
06	Cin	NL	8	10	2	0	0	1	(1	0)	5	2	1	1	1	0	4	0	0	0	0	0	-	1	.200	.273	.500
4 ML YEARS			189	631	172	41	3	15	(6	9)	264	82	68	79	49	1	115	7	8	1	4	1	.80	23	.273	.331	.418

Willie Harris

Bats: L **Throws:** R **Pos:** LF-85; CF-20; PH-20; PR-3; 3B-2 **Ht:** 5'9" **Wt:** 170 **Born:** 6/22/1978 **Age:** 30

							BATTING																BASERUNNING				AVERAGES		
Year	Team	Lg	G	AB	H	2B	3B	HR	(Hm	Rd)	TB	R	RBI	RC	TBB	IBB	SO	HBP	SH	SF	SB	CS	SB%	GDP	Avg	OBP	Slg
2007	Rchmd*	AAA	17	58	21	7	2	1	(-	-)	35	17	7	15	8	0	6	3	0	1	7	3	.70	1	.362	.457	.603
2001	Bal	AL	9	24	3	1	0	0	(0	0)	4	3	0	0	0	0	7	0	1	0	0	0	-	0	.125	.125	.167
2002	CWS	AL	49	163	38	4	0	2	(2	0)	48	14	12	15	9	0	21	0	3	2	8	0	1.00	1	.233	.270	.294
2003	CWS	AL	79	137	28	3	1	0	(0	0)	33	19	5	11	10	0	28	0	3	0	12	2	.86	1	.204	.259	.241

Year	Team	Lg	G	AB	H	2B	3B	HR	(Hm	Rd)	TB	R	RBI	RC	TBB	IBB	SO	HBP	SH	SF	SB	CS	SB%	GDP	Avg	OBP	Slg
									BATTING												**BASERUNNING**				**AVERAGES**		
2004	CWS	AL	129	409	107	15	2	2	(2	0)	132	68	27	53	51	0	79	1	7	3	19	7	.73	4	.262	.343	.323
2005	CWS	AL	56	121	31	2	1	1	(1	0)	38	17	8	15	13	0	25	1	4	0	10	3	.77	1	.256	.333	.314
2006	Bos	AL	47	45	7	2	0	0	(0	0)	9	17	1	1	4	0	11	2	0	1	6	3	.67	0	.156	.250	.200
2007	Atl	NL	117	344	93	20	8	2	(1	1)	135	56	32	47	40	0	71	3	1	3	17	11	.61	3	.270	.349	.392
7 ML YEARS			486	1243	307	47	12	7	(6	1)	399	194	85	142	127	0	242	7	19	9	72	26	.73	12	.247	.318	.321

Corey Hart

Bats: R **Throws:** R **Pos:** RF-113; CF-34; PH-16   **Ht:** 6'6" **Wt:** 215 **Born:** 3/24/1982 **Age:** 26

Year	Team	Lg	G	AB	H	2B	3B	HR	(Hm	Rd)	TB	R	RBI	RC	TBB	IBB	SO	HBP	SH	SF	SB	CS	SB%	GDP	Avg	OBP	Slg
									BATTING												**BASERUNNING**				**AVERAGES**		
2004	Mil	NL	1	1	0	0	0	0	(0	0)	0	0	0	0	0	0	1	0	0	0	0	0	-	0	.000	.000	.000
2005	Mil	NL	21	57	11	2	1	2	(2	0)	21	9	7	4	6	0	11	0	0	0	2	0	1.00	6	.193	.270	.368
2006	Mil	NL	87	237	67	13	2	9	(6	3)	111	32	33	30	17	1	50	0	0	2	6	8	.38	7	.283	.328	.468
2007	Mil	NL	140	505	149	33	9	24	(15	9)	272	86	81	94	36	3	99	13	5	7	23	7	.77	6	.295	.353	.539
4 ML YEARS			249	800	227	48	12	35	(23	12)	404	127	121	128	59	4	169	13	5	9	30	15	.67	19	.284	.339	.505

Kevin Hart

Pitches: R **Bats:** R **Pos:** RP-8   **Ht:** 6'4" **Wt:** 215 **Born:** 11/29/1982 **Age:** 25

Year	Team	Lg	G	GS	CG	GF	IP	BFP	H	R	ER	HR	SH	SF	HB	TBB	IBB	SO	WP	Bk	W	L	Pct	ShO	Sv-Op	Hld	ERC	ERA
							HOW MUCH HE PITCHED						**WHAT HE GAVE UP**										**THE RESULTS**					
2004	Abrdn	A-	9	0	0	2	14.1	61	10	7	6	0	0	0	1	7	2	16	2	1	3	0	1.000	0	1--	-	2.13	3.77
2004	Dlmrva	A	4	2	0	0	14.1	63	13	6	6	0	0	1	1	5	0	16	1	0	2	0	1.000	0	0--	-	2.83	3.77
2005	Dlmrva	A	28	28	0	0	152.1	687	170	101	77	9	2	8	12	54	0	164	14	3	9	8	.529	0	0--	-	4.49	4.55
2006	Frdrck	A+	28	27	0	0	148.1	661	149	97	76	18	4	5	10	65	0	122	11	0	6	11	.353	0	0--	-	4.63	4.61
2007	Tenn	AA	18	17	0	0	102.0	431	100	59	48	13	2	4	5	27	2	92	11	1	8	5	.615	0	0--	-	3.77	4.24
2007	Iowa	AAA	9	8	1	0	56.0	240	56	23	22	6	6	3	1	23	0	39	6	0	4	1	.800	0	0--	-	4.30	3.54
2007	ChC	NL	8	0	0	2	11.0	42	7	1	1	0	1	0	0	4	0	13	0	0	0	0	-	0	0-0	0	1.62	0.82

Scott Hatteberg

Bats: L **Throws:** R **Pos:** 1B-96; PH-22; DH-1   **Ht:** 6'1" **Wt:** 210 **Born:** 12/14/1969 **Age:** 38

Year	Team	Lg	G	AB	H	2B	3B	HR	(Hm	Rd)	TB	R	RBI	RC	TBB	IBB	SO	HBP	SH	SF	SB	CS	SB%	GDP	Avg	OBP	Slg
									BATTING												**BASERUNNING**				**AVERAGES**		
1995	Bos	AL	2	2	1	0	0	0	(0	0)	1	1	0	0	0	0	0	0	0	0	0	0	-	1	.500	.500	.500
1996	Bos	AL	10	11	2	1	0	0	(0	0)	3	3	0	1	3	0	2	0	0	0	0	0	-	0	.182	.357	.273
1997	Bos	AL	114	350	97	23	1	10	(5	5)	152	46	44	52	40	2	70	2	2	1	0	1	.00	11	.277	.354	.434
1998	Bos	AL	112	359	99	23	1	12	(4	8)	160	46	43	56	43	3	58	5	0	3	0	0	-	11	.276	.359	.446
1999	Bos	AL	30	80	22	5	0	1	(1	0)	30	12	11	14	18	0	14	1	0	1	0	0	-	3	.275	.410	.375
2000	Bos	AL	92	230	61	15	0	8	(2	6)	100	21	36	36	38	3	39	0	1	2	0	1	.00	8	.265	.367	.435
2001	Bos	AL	94	278	68	19	0	3	(2	1)	96	34	25	32	33	0	20	4	0	1	1	1	.60	7	.245	.332	.345
2002	Oak	AL	136	492	138	22	4	15	(8	7)	213	58	61	77	68	1	56	6	1	1	0	0	-	8	.280	.374	.433
2003	Oak	AL	147	541	137	34	0	12	(6	6)	207	63	61	80	66	0	53	9	3	3	0	1	.00	14	.253	.342	.383
2004	Oak	AL	152	550	156	30	0	15	(8	7)	231	87	82	90	72	5	48	5	3	8	0	0	-	10	.284	.367	.420
2005	Oak	AL	134	464	119	19	0	7	(4	3)	159	52	59	60	51	4	54	4	2	2	0	1	.00	22	.256	.334	.343
2006	Cin	NL	141	456	132	28	0	13	(10	3)	199	62	51	76	74	3	41	3	2	4	2	2	.50	13	.289	.389	.436
2007	Cin	NL	116	361	112	27	1	10	(6	4)	171	50	47	61	49	6	35	3	1	3	0	0	-	8	.310	.394	.474
13 ML YEARS			1280	4174	1144	246	7	106	(56	50)	1722	535	520	635	555	27	490	42	15	20	3	7	.30	117	.274	.363	.413

LaTroy Hawkins

Pitches: R **Bats:** R **Pos:** RP-62   **Ht:** 6'5" **Wt:** 215 **Born:** 12/21/1972 **Age:** 35

Year	Team	Lg	G	GS	CG	GF	IP	BFP	H	R	ER	HR	SH	SF	HB	TBB	IBB	SO	WP	Bk	W	L	Pct	ShO	Sv-Op	Hld	ERC	ERA
							HOW MUCH HE PITCHED						**WHAT HE GAVE UP**										**THE RESULTS**					
2007	ColSpr*	AAA	4	0	0	0	4.0	15	2	1	1	0	0	0	0	2	0	5	0	0	1	0	1.000	0	0--	-	1.51	2.25
1995	Min	AL	6	6	1	0	27.0	131	39	29	26	3	0	3	1	12	0	9	1	1	2	3	.400	0	0-0	0	7.14	8.67
1996	Min	AL	7	6	0	1	26.1	124	42	24	24	8	1	1	0	9	0	24	1	1	1	1	.500	0	0-0	0	9.49	8.20
1997	Min	AL	20	20	0	0	103.1	478	134	71	67	19	2	2	4	47	0	58	6	3	6	12	.333	0	0-0	0	7.01	5.84
1998	Min	AL	33	33	0	0	190.1	840	227	126	111	27	4	10	5	61	1	105	10	2	7	14	.333	0	0-0	0	5.31	5.25
1999	Min	AL	33	33	1	0	174.1	803	238	136	129	29	1	5	1	60	2	103	9	0	10	14	.417	0	0-0	0	6.55	6.66
2000	Min	AL	66	0	0	38	87.2	370	85	34	33	7	4	1	1	32	1	59	6	0	2	5	.286	0	14-14	7	3.70	3.39
2001	Min	AL	62	0	0	51	51.1	248	59	34	34	3	1	4	1	39	3	36	7	0	1	5	.167	0	28-37	1	6.02	5.96
2002	Min	AL	65	0	0	15	80.1	310	63	23	19	5	2	3	0	15	1	63	5	0	6	0	1.000	0	0-3	13	1.99	2.13
2003	Min	AL	74	0	0	12	77.1	310	69	20	16	4	4	1	1	15	1	75	5	0	9	3	.750	0	2-8	28	2.48	1.86
2004	ChC	NL	77	0	0	50	82.0	333	72	27	24	10	6	2	2	14	5	69	2	0	5	4	.556	0	25-34	4	2.66	2.63
2005	2 Tms	NL	66	0	0	21	56.1	247	58	27	24	7	3	1	0	24	3	43	1	0	2	8	.200	0	6-15	15	4.41	3.83
2006	Bal	AL	60	0	0	12	60.1	261	73	30	30	4	1	2	0	15	3	27	2	0	3	2	.600	0	0-4	16	4.37	4.48
2007	Col	AL	62	0	0	10	55.1	225	52	21	21	6	2	1	0	16	1	29	2	0	2	5	.286	0	0-5	18	3.43	3.42
05	ChC	NL	21	0	0	12	19.0	80	18	9	7	4	1	0	0	7	0	13	0	0	1	4	.200	0	4-8	0	4.44	3.32
05	SF	NL	45	0	0	9	37.1	167	40	18	17	3	2	1	0	17	3	30	1	0	1	4	.200	0	2-7	15	4.36	4.10
13 ML YEARS			631	98	2	210	1072.0	4680	1211	602	558	132	31	36	16	359	21	700	57	7	56	76	.424	0	75-120	102	4.77	4.68

Brad Hawpe

Bats: L **Throws:** L **Pos:** RF-142; PH-10 **Ht:** 6'3" **Wt:** 205 **Born:** 6/22/1979 **Age:** 29

Year	Team	Lg	G	AB	H	2B	3B	HR	(Hm	Rd)	TB	R	RBI	RC	TBB	IBB	SO	HBP	SH	SF	SB	CS	SB%	GDP	Avg	OBP	Slg
2004	Col	NL	42	105	26	3	2	3	(1	2)	42	12	9	11	11	3	34	1	0	1	1	1	.50	4	.248	.322	.400
2005	Col	NL	101	305	80	10	3	9	(5	4)	123	38	47	44	43	3	70	0	0	3	2	2	.50	5	.262	.350	.403
2006	Col	NL	150	499	146	33	6	22	(6	16)	257	67	84	85	74	11	123	0	0	2	5	5	.50	8	.293	.383	.515
2007	Col	NL	152	516	150	33	4	29	(19	10)	278	80	116	103	81	11	137	3	1	5	0	2	.00	13	.291	.387	.539
	4 ML YEARS		445	1425	402	79	15	63	(31	32)	700	197	256	243	209	28	364	4	1	11	8	10	.44	30	.282	.373	.491

Nathan Haynes

Bats: L **Throws:** L **Pos:** RF-13; CF-12; PR-9; LF-8; PH-6; DH-3 **Ht:** 5'9" **Wt:** 170 **Born:** 9/7/1979 **Age:** 28

Year	Team	Lg	G	AB	H	2B	3B	HR	(Hm	Rd)	TB	R	RBI	RC	TBB	IBB	SO	HBP	SH	SF	SB	CS	SB%	GDP	Avg	OBP	Slg
1997	As	R	17	54	15	1	0	0	(-	-)	16	8	6	7	7	0	9	2	1	0	5	1	.83	3	.278	.381	.296
1997	SoOre	A-	24	82	23	1	1	0	(-	-)	26	18	9	18	26	0	21	2	0	1	19	3	.86	1	.280	.459	.317
1998	Mdest	A+	125	507	128	13	7	1	(-	-)	158	89	41	57	54	2	139	4	6	2	42	18	.70	10	.252	.328	.312
1999	Visalia	A+	35	145	45	7	1	1	(-	-)	57	28	14	22	17	0	27	3	2	1	12	10	.55	1	.310	.392	.393
1999	Lk Els	A+	26	110	36	5	5	1	(-	-)	54	19	15	21	12	0	19	1	0	1	10	5	.67	2	.327	.395	.491
1999	Erie	AA	5	19	3	1	0	0	(-	-)	4	3	0	2	5	0	5	1	0	0	0	0	-	2	.158	.360	.211
2000	Erie	AA	118	457	116	16	4	6	(-	-)	158	56	43	52	33	0	107	9	8	2	37	20	.65	3	.254	.315	.346
2001	Ark	AA	79	316	98	11	5	5	(-	-)	134	49	23	53	32	2	65	3	2	0	33	15	.69	4	.310	.379	.424
2002	RCuca	A+	11	50	14	0	0	0	(-	-)	14	6	2	6	4	0	8	1	0	0	6	2	.75	0	.280	.345	.280
2002	Salt Lk	AAA	67	283	80	14	6	2	(-	-)	112	37	12	33	12	0	53	1	1	1	10	10	.50	3	.283	.313	.396
2003	Ark	AA	91	372	110	16	10	5	(-	-)	161	59	42	58	34	3	74	2	4	2	27	9	.75	6	.296	.356	.433
2003	Salt Lk	AAA	28	120	26	3	3	1	(-	-)	38	16	7	11	9	1	20	2	0	1	6	0	1.00	2	.217	.280	.317
2004	Fresno	AAA	1	4	1	0	1	0	(-	-)	3	1	0	0	0	0	1	0	0	0	1	0	1.00	0	.250	.250	.750
2005	Giants	R	7	16	4	1	2	0	(-	-)	9	4	1	3	3	0	3	0	0	0	3	0	1.00	1	.250	.368	.563
2006	Ark	AA	52	207	58	14	3	2	(-	-)	84	38	19	30	22	1	49	1	3	1	19	10	.66	5	.280	.351	.406
2006	Salt Lk	AAA	16	57	13	1	2	1	(-	-)	21	7	11	6	4	0	15	1	2	1	3	2	.60	0	.228	.286	.368
2007	Salt Lk	AAA	44	171	66	9	6	4	(-	-)	99	33	32	43	22	2	36	2	3	0	14	7	.67	3	.386	.462	.579
2007	LAA	AL	40	45	12	0	1	0	(0	0)	14	10	1	5	3	0	11	0	0	0	1	2	.33	0	.267	.313	.311

Chase Headley

Bats: B **Throws:** R **Pos:** 3B-5; PH-3 **Ht:** 6'2" **Wt:** 195 **Born:** 5/9/1984 **Age:** 24

Year	Team	Lg	G	AB	H	2B	3B	HR	(Hm	Rd)	TB	R	RBI	RC	TBB	IBB	SO	HBP	SH	SF	SB	CS	SB%	GDP	Avg	OBP	Slg
2005	Eugene	A-	57	220	59	14	3	6	(-	-)	97	29	33	38	34	1	48	4	0	1	1	1	.50	6	.268	.375	.441
2005	FtWyn	A	4	15	3	0	0	0	(-	-)	3	2	1	0	1	0	4	0	0	0	0	0	-	1	.200	.250	.200
2006	Lk Els	A+	129	484	141	33	0	12	(-	-)	210	79	73	86	74	3	96	5	5	3	4	5	.44	10	.291	.389	.434
2007	SnAnt	AA	121	433	143	38	5	20	(-	-)	251	82	78	109	74	7	114	11	0	4	1	0	1.00	7	.330	.437	.580
2007	SD	NL	8	18	4	1	0	0	(0	0)	5	1	0	1	2	0	4	1	0	0	0	0	-	2	.222	.333	.278

Aaron Heilman

Pitches: R **Bats:** R **Pos:** RP-81 **Ht:** 6'5" **Wt:** 227 **Born:** 11/12/1978 **Age:** 29

Year	Team	Lg	HOW MUCH HE PITCHED						WHAT HE GAVE UP											THE RESULTS							
			G	GS	CG	GF	IP	BFP	H	R	ER	HR	SH	SF	HB	TBB	IBB	SO	WP	Bk	W	L	Pct	ShO	Sv-Op Hld	ERC	ERA
2003	NYM	NL	14	13	0	0	65.1	315	79	53	49	13	5	3	3	41	2	51	5	0	2	7	.222	0	0-0 0	7.16	6.75
2004	NYM	NL	5	5	0	0	28.0	119	27	17	17	4	1	0	0	13	0	22	0	0	1	3	.250	0	0-0 0	4.54	5.46
2005	NYM	NL	53	7	1	20	108.0	439	87	40	38	6	4	1	6	37	4	106	1	1	5	3	.625	1	5-6 5	2.74	3.17
2006	NYM	NL	74	0	0	14	87.0	356	73	37	35	5	7	2	3	28	2	73	5	0	4	5	.444	0	0-5 27	2.76	3.62
2007	NYM	NL	81	0	0	28	86.0	352	72	36	29	8	4	2	5	20	1	63	2	0	7	7	.500	0	1-6 22	2.71	3.03
	5 ML YEARS		227	25	1	62	374.1	1581	338	183	168	36	21	8	17	139	9	315	13	1	19	25	.432	1	6-17 54	3.56	4.04

Chris Heintz

Bats: R **Throws:** R **Pos:** C-21; PH-4; PR-2 **Ht:** 6'1" **Wt:** 205 **Born:** 8/6/1974 **Age:** 33

Year	Team	Lg	G	AB	H	2B	3B	HR	(Hm	Rd)	TB	R	RBI	RC	TBB	IBB	SO	HBP	SH	SF	SB	CS	SB%	GDP	Avg	OBP	Slg
2007	Roch*	AAA	48	167	46	8	0	1	(-	-)	57	18	15	20	11	1	32	4	1	1	0	0	-	4	.275	.333	.341
2005	Min	AL	8	25	5	3	0	0	(0	0)	8	1	2	1	1	0	6	0	0	0	0	0	-	0	.200	.231	.320
2006	Min	AL	2	1	0	0	0	0	(0	0)	0	0	0	0	0	0	0	0	0	0	0	0	-	0	.000	.000	.000
2007	Min	AL	24	56	14	0	0	0	(0	0)	14	0	7	7	3	0	12	0	2	0	0	0	-	2	.250	.288	.250
	3 ML YEARS		34	82	19	3	0	0	(0	0)	22	1	9	9	4	0	18	0	2	0	0	0	-	3	.232	.267	.268

Wes Helms

Bats: R **Throws:** R **Pos:** 3B-68; PH-36; 1B-18; PR-1 **Ht:** 6'4" **Wt:** 230 **Born:** 5/12/1976 **Age:** 32

Year	Team	Lg	G	AB	H	2B	3B	HR	(Hm	Rd)	TB	R	RBI	RC	TBB	IBB	SO	HBP	SH	SF	SB	CS	SB%	GDP	Avg	OBP	Slg
1998	Atl	NL	7	13	4	1	0	1	(0	1)	8	2	2	2	0	0	4	0	0	0	0	0	-	0	.308	.308	.615
2000	Atl	NL	6	5	1	0	0	0	(0	0)	1	0	0	0	0	0	2	0	0	0	0	0	-	0	.200	.200	.200
2001	Atl	NL	100	216	48	10	3	10	(4	6)	94	28	36	27	21	2	56	1	0	1	1	1	.50	3	.222	.293	.435
2002	Atl	NL	85	210	51	16	0	6	(4	2)	85	20	22	15	11	2	57	3	1	6	1	1	.50	5	.243	.283	.405
2003	Mil	NL	134	476	124	21	0	23	(16	7)	214	56	67	66	43	3	131	10	0	7	0	1	.00	10	.261	.330	.450
2004	Mil	NL	92	274	72	13	1	4	(3	1)	99	24	28	28	24	1	60	5	1	2	0	1	.00	10	.263	.331	.361

Year Team	Lg	G	AB	H	2B	3B	HR	(Hm	Rd)	TB	R	RBI	RC	TBB	IBB	SO	HBP	SH	SF	SB	CS	SB%	GDP	Avg	OBP	Slg
								BATTING												**BASERUNNING**				**AVERAGES**		
2005 Mil	NL	95	168	50	13	1	4	(2	2)	77	18	24	26	14	0	30	3	0	5	0	1	.00	7	.298	.356	.458
2006 Fla	NL	140	240	79	19	5	10	(4	6)	138	30	47	45	21	1	55	6	6	5	0	4	.00	7	.329	.390	.575
2007 Phi	NL	112	280	69	19	0	5	(3	2)	103	21	39	24	19	2	62	3	2	4	0	0	-	10	.246	.297	.368
9 ML YEARS		771	1882	498	112	10	63	(38	25)	819	199	265	233	153	11	457	31	10	28	2	9	.18	52	.265	.326	.435

Todd Helton

Bats: L Throws: L Pos: 1B-153; DH-1; PH-1   Ht: 6'2" Wt: 210 Born: 8/20/1973 Age: 34

Year Team	Lg	G	AB	H	2B	3B	HR	(Hm	Rd)	TB	R	RBI	RC	TBB	IBB	SO	HBP	SH	SF	SB	CS	SB%	GDP	Avg	OBP	Slg
								BATTING												**BASERUNNING**				**AVERAGES**		
1997 Col	NL	35	93	26	2	1	5	(3	2)	45	13	11	15	8	0	11	0	0	0	0	1	.00	1	.280	.337	.484
1998 Col	NL	152	530	167	37	1	25	(13	12)	281	78	97	101	53	5	54	6	1	5	3	3	.50	15	.315	.380	.530
1999 Col	NL	159	578	185	39	5	35	(23	12)	339	114	113	124	68	6	77	6	0	4	7	6	.54	14	.320	.395	.587
2000 Col	NL	160	580	216	59	2	42	(27	15)	405	138	**147**	**169**	103	22	61	4	0	10	5	3	.03	12	**.372**	**.463**	**.608**
2001 Col	NL	159	587	197	54	2	49	(27	22)	402	132	146	157	98	15	104	4	1	5	7	5	.58	14	.336	.432	.685
2002 Col	NL	156	553	182	39	4	30	(18	12)	319	107	109	127	99	21	91	5	0	10	5	1	.83	10	.329	.429	.577
2003 Col	NL	160	583	209	49	5	33	(23	10)	367	135	117	160	111	21	72	2	0	7	0	4	.00	19	.358	.458	.630
2004 Col	NL	154	547	190	49	2	32	(21	11)	339	115	96	143	127	19	72	3	0	6	3	0	1.00	12	.347	.469	.620
2005 Col	NL	144	509	163	45	2	20	(13	7)	272	92	79	114	106	22	80	9	1	1	3	0	1.00	14	.320	**.445**	.534
2006 Col	NL	145	546	165	40	5	15	(8	7)	260	94	81	118	91	15	64	6	0	6	3	2	.60	10	.302	.404	.476
2007 Col	NL	154	557	178	42	2	17	(9	8)	275	86	91	115	116	16	74	2	0	7	0	1	.00	15	.320	**.434**	.494
11 ML YEARS		1578	5663	1878	455	31	303	(185	118)	3304	1104	1087	1343	980	162	760	48	3	61	36	26	.58	136	.332	.430	.583

Mark Hendrickson

Pitches: L Bats: L Pos: RP-24; SP-15   Ht: 6'9" Wt: 240 Born: 6/23/1974 Age: 34

Year Team	Lg	G	GS	CG	GF	IP	BFP	H	R	ER	HR	SH	SF	HB	TBB	IBB	SO	WP	Bk	W	L	Pct	ShO	Sv-Op	Hld	ERC	ERA
			HOW MUCH HE PITCHED							**WHAT HE GAVE UP**												**THE RESULTS**				
2002 Tor	AL	16	4	0	0	36.2	142	25	11	10	1	2	2	2	12	3	21	0	0	3	0	1.000	0	0-1	1	1.90	2.45
2003 Tor	AL	30	30	1	0	158.1	703	207	111	97	24	1	8	0	40	3	76	4	0	9	9	.500	1	0-0	1	5.64	5.51
2004 TB	AL	32	30	2	1	183.1	803	211	113	98	21	4	5	7	46	5	87	5	2	10	15	.400	1	0-0	0	4.51	4.81
2005 TB	AL	31	31	1	0	178.1	796	227	126	117	24	8	7	2	49	1	89	4	1	11	8	.579	1	0-0	0	5.44	5.90
2006 2 Tms		31	25	1	0	164.2	719	173	87	77	17	5	4	4	62	0	99	6	1	6	15	.286	1	0-0	1	4.38	4.21
2007 LAD	NL	39	15	0	4	122.2	532	142	75	71	15	12	4	1	29	4	92	4	0	4	8	.333	0	0-1	2	4.42	5.21
06 TB	AL	13	13	1	0	89.2	377	81	42	38	10	2	3	2	34	0	51	4	0	4	8	.333	1	0-0	0	3.65	3.81
06 LAD	NL	18	12	0	0	75.0	342	92	45	39	7	3	1	2	28	0	48	2	1	2	7	.222	0	0-0	1	5.29	4.68
6 ML YEARS		179	135	5	5	844.0	3695	985	523	470	102	32	30	16	238	16	464	23	4	43	55	.439	2	0-2	4	4.74	5.01

Sean Henn

Pitches: L Bats: R Pos: RP-28; SP-1   Ht: 6'4" Wt: 225 Born: 4/23/1981 Age: 27

Year Team	Lg	G	GS	CG	GF	IP	BFP	H	R	ER	HR	SH	SF	HB	TBB	IBB	SO	WP	Bk	W	L	Pct	ShO	Sv-Op	Hld	ERC	ERA
			HOW MUCH HE PITCHED							**WHAT HE GAVE UP**												**THE RESULTS**				
2007 S-WB*	AAA	15	3	0	1	31.1	128	26	10	10	1	4	1	0	9	0	29	2	0	1	2	.333	0	0- -	-	2.31	2.87
2005 NYY	AL	3	3	0	0	11.1	61	18	16	14	3	0	0	0	11	0	3	0	0	0	3	.000	0	0-0	0	12.12	11.12
2006 NYY	AL	4	1	0	0	9.1	44	11	5	5	2	0	1	1	5	0	7	0	0	1	0	1.000	0	0-0	0	7.09	4.82
2007 NYY	AL	29	1	0	8	36.2	181	44	32	29	6	1	0	3	27	1	28	1	0	2	2	.500	0	0-0	2	7.47	7.12
3 ML YEARS		36	5	0	8	57.1	286	73	53	48	11	1	1	4	43	1	38	1	0	2	6	.250	0	0-0	2	8.28	7.53

Brad Hennessey

Pitches: R Bats: R Pos: RP-69   Ht: 6'2" Wt: 200 Born: 2/7/1980 Age: 28

Year Team	Lg	G	GS	CG	GF	IP	BFP	H	R	ER	HR	SH	SF	HB	TBB	IBB	SO	WP	Bk	W	L	Pct	ShO	Sv-Op	Hld	ERC	ERA
			HOW MUCH HE PITCHED							**WHAT HE GAVE UP**												**THE RESULTS**				
2004 SF	NL	7	7	0	0	34.1	163	42	24	19	2	4	1	0	15	1	25	1	0	2	2	.500	0	0-0	0	4.91	4.98
2005 SF	NL	21	21	0	0	118.1	521	127	63	61	15	2	3	4	52	3	64	3	1	5	8	.385	0	0-0	0	5.00	4.64
2006 SF	NL	34	12	0	9	99.1	428	92	53	47	12	6	2	10	42	1	42	3	0	5	6	.455	0	1-1	2	4.34	4.26
2007 SF	NL	69	0	0	34	68.1	287	66	26	26	7	4	0	3	23	1	40	2	0	4	5	.444	0	19-24	13	3.87	3.42
4 ML YEARS		131	40	0	43	320.1	1399	327	166	153	36	16	6	17	132	6	171	9	1	16	21	.432	0	20-25	15	4.54	4.30

Clay Hensley

Pitches: R Bats: R Pos: SP-9; RP-4   Ht: 5'11" Wt: 190 Born: 8/31/1979 Age: 28

Year Team	Lg	G	GS	CG	GF	IP	BFP	H	R	ER	HR	SH	SF	HB	TBB	IBB	SO	WP	Bk	W	L	Pct	ShO	Sv-Op	Hld	ERC	ERA
			HOW MUCH HE PITCHED							**WHAT HE GAVE UP**												**THE RESULTS**				
2007 Portlnd*	AAA	13	13	0	0	71.0	345	102	63	53	10	0	1	4	34	0	50	6	0	1	7	.125	0	0- -	-	7.65	6.72
2005 SD	NL	24	1	0	5	47.2	189	33	12	9	0	1	2	0	17	2	28	2	0	1	1	.500	0	0-0	2	1.70	1.70
2006 SD	NL	37	29	1	2	187.0	787	174	82	77	15	10	3	3	76	7	122	3	0	11	12	.478	1	0-1	1	3.64	3.71
2007 SD	NL	13	9	0	1	50.0	238	62	40	38	5	2	1	1	32	2	30	4	1	2	3	.400	0	0-0	0	6.54	6.84
3 ML YEARS		74	39	1	8	284.2	1214	269	134	124	20	13	6	4	125	11	180	9	1	14	16	.467	1	0-1	3	3.75	3.92

Matt Herges

Pitches: R Bats: L Pos: RP-35   Ht: 6'0" Wt: 210 Born: 4/1/1970 Age: 38

Year	Team	Lg	G	GS	CG	GF	IP	BFP	H	R	ER	HR	SH	SF	HB	TBB	IBB	SO	WP	Bk	W	L	Pct	ShO	Sv-Op	Hld	ERC	ERA
2007	ColSpr*	AAA	32	0	0	7	35.1	135	24	6	5	2	0	0	1	10	0	33	0	0	2	1	.667	0	1- -	-	1.94	1.27
1999	LAD	NL	17	0	0	9	24.1	104	24	13	11	5	1	0	1	8	0	18	0	0	0	2	.000	0	0-2	1	4.61	4.07
2000	LAD	NL	59	4	0	17	110.2	461	100	43	39	7	9	4	6	40	5	75	4	0	11	3	.786	0	1-3	4	3.35	3.17
2001	LAD	NL	75	0	0	22	99.1	435	97	39	38	8	4	3	8	46	12	76	2	0	9	8	.529	0	1-8	15	4.20	3.44
2002	Mon	NL	62	0	0	25	64.2	298	80	33	29	10	6	2	2	26	8	50	3	0	2	5	.286	0	6-14	9	5.74	4.04
2003	2 Tms	NL	67	0	0	24	79.0	332	68	27	23	3	2	6	3	29	2	68	1	1	3	2	.600	0	3-6	9	2.87	2.62
2004	SF	NL	70	0	0	43	65.1	301	90	44	38	8	7	4	3	21	4	39	2	0	4	5	.444	0	23-31	5	6.29	5.23
2005	2 Tms	NL	28	0	0	7	29.0	132	35	23	23	6	2	2	1	12	1	9	0	0	1	1	.500	0	0-0	3	6.26	7.14
2006	Fla	NL	66	0	0	21	71.0	328	94	42	34	5	3	1	3	28	5	36	1	0	2	3	.400	0	0-4	9	5.81	4.31
2007	Col	NL	35	0	0	9	48.2	191	34	17	16	4	3	1	0	15	2	30	0	0	5	1	.833	0	0-2	3	2.05	2.96
03	SD	NL	40	0	0	21	44.0	192	40	16	14	2	1	5	2	20	2	40	1	0	2	2	.500	0	3-5	4	3.45	2.86
03	SF	NL	27	0	0	3	35.0	140	28	11	9	1	1	1	1	9	0	28	0	1	1	0	1.000	0	0-1	5	2.18	2.31
05	SF	NL	21	0	0	5	21.0	90	23	11	11	2	2	1	0	7	1	6	0	0	1	1	.500	0	0-0	3	4.29	4.71
05	Ari	NL	7	0	0	2	8.0	42	12	12	12	4	0	1	1	5	0	3	0	0	0	0	-	0	0-0	0	12.23	13.50
9 ML YEARS			479	4	0	177	592.0	2582	622	281	251	56	37	23	27	225	39	401	13	1	37	30	.552	0	34-70	58	4.33	3.82

Jeremy Hermida

Bats: L Throws: R Pos: RF-116; PH-8   Ht: 6'3" Wt: 210 Born: 1/30/1984 Age: 24

Year	Team	Lg	G	AB	H	2B	3B	HR	(Hm	Rd)	TB	R	RBI	RC	TBB	IBB	SO	HBP	SH	SF	SB	CS	SB%	GDP	Avg	OBP	Slg
2007	Jupiter*	A+	3	12	4	0	1	2	(-	-)	12	4	5	4	1	0	4	0	0	0	0	0	-	0	.333	.385	1.000
2007	Albq*	AAA	2	5	1	0	0	0	(-	-)	1	0	2	0	1	0	0	0	0	1	0	0	-	0	.200	.286	.200
2005	Fla	NL	23	41	12	2	0	4	(4	0)	26	9	11	10	6	1	12	0	0	0	2	0	1.00	1	.293	.383	.634
2006	Fla	NL	99	307	77	19	1	5	(3	2)	113	37	28	38	33	3	70	5	2	1	4	1	.80	6	.251	.332	.368
2007	Fla	NL	123	429	127	32	1	18	(8	10)	215	54	63	69	47	2	105	4	1	3	3	4	.43	10	.296	.369	.501
3 ML YEARS			245	777	216	53	2	27	(15	12)	354	100	102	117	86	6	187	9	3	4	9	5	.64	17	.278	.355	.456

Anderson Hernandez

Bats: B Throws: R Pos: PH-3; SS-1; PR-1   Ht: 5'9" Wt: 170 Born: 10/30/1982 Age: 25

Year	Team	Lg	G	AB	H	2B	3B	HR	(Hm	Rd)	TB	R	RBI	RC	TBB	IBB	SO	HBP	SH	SF	SB	CS	SB%	GDP	Avg	OBP	Slg
2007	NewOr*	AAA	128	554	167	28	5	5	(-	-)	220	84	42	76	31	0	82	3	4	5	16	9	.64	8	.301	.339	.397
2005	NYM	NL	6	18	1	0	0	0	(0	0)	1	0	0	1	0	0	1	0	0	0	0	1	.00	0	.056	.105	.056
2006	NYM	NL	25	66	10	1	1	1	(1	0)	16	4	3	0	1	0	12	0	0	0	0	0	-	3	.152	.164	.242
2007	NYM	NL	4	3	1	0	0	0	(1	0)	1	1	0	0	1	0	4	0	0	0	0	0	-	0	.333	.333	.333
3 ML YEARS			35	87	12	1	1	1	(1	0)	18	6	3	0	2	0	17	0	0	0	0	1	.00	3	.138	.157	.207

Felix Hernandez

Pitches: R Bats: R Pos: SP-30   Ht: 6'3" Wt: 230 Born: 4/8/1986 Age: 22

Year	Team	Lg	G	GS	CG	GF	IP	BFP	H	R	ER	HR	SH	SF	HB	TBB	IBB	SO	WP	Bk	W	L	Pct	ShO	Sv-Op	Hld	ERC	ERA
2005	Sea	AL	12	12	0	0	84.1	328	61	26	25	5	1	2	2	23	0	77	3	0	4	4	.500	0	0-0	0	2.08	2.67
2006	Sea	AL	31	31	2	0	191.0	816	195	105	96	23	2	3	6	60	2	176	11	0	12	14	.462	1	0-0	0	4.11	4.52
2007	Sea	AL	30	30	1	0	190.1	808	209	88	83	20	6	1	3	53	4	165	7	1	14	7	.667	1	0-0	0	4.27	3.92
3 ML YEARS			73	73	3	0	465.2	1952	465	219	204	48	9	6	11	136	6	418	21	1	30	25	.545	2	0-0	0	3.78	3.94

Livan Hernandez

Pitches: R Bats: R Pos: SP-33   Ht: 6'2" Wt: 245 Born: 2/20/1975 Age: 33

Year	Team	Lg	G	GS	CG	GF	IP	BFP	H	R	ER	HR	SH	SF	HB	TBB	IBB	SO	WP	Bk	W	L	Pct	ShO	Sv-Op	Hld	ERC	ERA
1996	Fla	NL	1	0	0	0	3.0	13	3	0	0	0	0	0	0	2	0	2	0	0	0	0	-	0	0-0	0	4.60	0.00
1997	Fla	NL	17	17	0	0	96.1	405	81	39	34	5	4	7	3	38	1	72	0	0	9	3	.750	0	0-0	0	2.96	3.18
1998	Fla	NL	33	33	9	0	234.1	1040	265	133	123	37	8	5	6	104	8	162	4	3	10	12	.455	0	0-0	0	5.58	4.72
1999	2 Tms	NL	30	30	2	0	199.2	886	227	110	103	23	7	6	2	76	5	144	2	2	8	12	.400	0	0-0	0	4.88	4.64
2000	SF	NL	33	33	5	0	240.0	1030	254	114	100	22	12	9	4	73	3	165	3	0	17	11	.607	2	0-0	0	4.01	3.75
2001	SF	NL	34	34	2	0	226.2	1008	266	143	132	24	12	12	3	85	7	138	7	0	13	15	.464	0	0-0	0	5.03	5.24
2002	SF	NL	33	33	5	0	216.0	921	233	113	105	19	14	8	4	71	5	134	1	1	12	16	.429	3	0-0	0	4.26	4.38
2003	Mon	NL	33	33	8	0	233.1	967	225	92	83	27	6	4	10	57	3	178	6	1	15	10	.600	0	0-0	0	3.55	3.20
2004	Mon	NL	35	35	9	0	255.0	1053	234	105	102	26	11	4	10	83	9	186	1	0	11	15	.423	2	0-0	0	3.52	3.60
2005	Was	NL	35	35	2	0	246.1	1065	268	116	109	25	15	9	13	84	14	147	3	2	15	10	.600	0	0-0	0	4.54	3.98
2006	2 Tms	NL	34	34	0	0	216.0	959	246	125	116	29	16	8	4	78	6	128	1	0	13	13	.500	0	0-0	0	4.97	4.83
2007	Ari	NL	33	33	1	0	204.1	913	247	116	112	34	17	8	6	79	1	90	3	2	11	11	.500	0	0-0	0	5.94	4.93
99	Fla	NL	20	20	2	0	136.0	612	161	78	72	17	3	4	2	55	3	97	2	1	5	9	.357	0	0-0	0	5.37	4.76
99	SF	NL	10	10	0	0	63.2	274	66	32	31	6	4	2	0	21	2	47	0	1	3	3	.500	0	0-0	0	3.88	4.38
06	Was	NL	24	24	0	0	146.2	661	176	94	87	22	10	7	2	52	4	89	0	0	9	8	.529	0	0-0	0	5.38	5.34
06	Ari	NL	10	10	0	0	69.1	298	70	31	29	7	6	1	2	26	2	39	1	0	4	5	.444	0	0-0	0	4.13	3.76
12 ML YEARS			351	350	43	0	2371.0	10260	2549	1206	1119	271	122	80	65	830	62	1546	31	11	134	128	.511	7	0-0	0	4.51	4.25

Luis Hernandez

Bats: B **Throws:** R **Pos:** SS-23; PR-4; PH-3; 2B-2; LF-1; DH-1 **Ht:** 5'10" **Wt:** 182 **Born:** 6/26/1984 **Age:** 24

Year	Team	Lg	G	AB	H	2B	3B	HR	(Hm	Rd)	TB	R	RBI	RC	TBB	IBB	SO	HBP	SH	SF	SB	CS	SB%	GDP	Avg	OBP	Slg
2002	Braves	R	53	201	51	8	4	0	(-	-)	67	34	20	23	19	0	29	4	1	0	11	6	.65	1	.254	.330	.333
2003	Rome	A	111	337	78	4	1	2	(-	-)	90	27	25	27	24	2	42	2	18	0	7	3	.70	7	.231	.287	.267
2004	MrtlBh	A+	117	402	109	23	4	6	(-	-)	158	49	45	49	16	0	70	5	10	2	8	6	.57	12	.271	.306	.393
2005	Braves	R	1	4	1	0	0	1	(-	-)	4	1	1	1	0	0	2	0	0	0	0	0	-	0	.250	.250	1.000
2005	Missi	AA	122	415	101	12	5	2	(-	-)	129	47	32	43	41	2	56	4	6	3	5	5	.50	11	.243	.315	.311
2006	Missi	AA	104	380	102	12	4	1	(-	-)	125	39	29	39	20	1	46	3	7	3	4	4	.50	8	.268	.308	.329
2006	Rchmd	AAA	19	73	14	4	0	1	(-	-)	21	3	5	3	0	0	8	0	1	0	0	1	1.00	0	.192	.192	.288
2007	Bowie	AA	92	364	88	15	6	0	(-	-)	115	42	37	32	18	0	50	1	6	4	6	5	.55	6	.242	.276	.316
2007	Norfolk	AAA	9	33	9	0	0	0	(-	-)	9	4	3	2	0	0	5	0	1	0	0	0	-	1	.273	.273	.273
2007	Bal	AL	30	69	20	2	0	1	(1	0)	25	5	7	6	1	0	10	0	1	0	2	2	.50	1	.290	.300	.362

Orlando Hernandez

Pitches: R **Bats:** R **Pos:** SP-24; RP-3 **Ht:** 6'2" **Wt:** 220 **Born:** 10/11/1969 **Age:** 38

Year	Team	Lg	G	GS	CG	GF	IP	BFP	H	R	ER	HR	SH	SF	HB	TBB	IBB	SO	WP	Bk	W	L	Pct	ShO	Sv-Op	Hld	ERC	ERA
1998	NYY	AL	21	21	3	0	141.0	574	113	53	49	11	3	5	6	52	1	131	5	2	12	4	.750	1	0-0	0	2.96	3.13
1999	NYY	AL	33	33	2	0	214.1	910	187	108	98	24	3	11	8	87	2	157	4	0	17	9	.654	1	0-0	0	3.60	4.12
2000	NYY	AL	29	29	3	0	195.2	820	186	104	98	34	4	5	6	51	2	141	1	0	12	13	.480	0	0-0	0	3.82	4.51
2001	NYY	AL	17	16	0	0	94.2	414	90	51	51	19	2	2	5	42	1	77	0	0	4	7	.364	0	0-0	0	4.87	4.85
2002	NYY	AL	24	22	0	1	146.0	606	131	63	59	17	1	5	8	36	2	113	8	0	8	5	.615	0	1-1	1	3.20	3.64
2004	NYY	AL	15	15	0	0	84.2	359	73	31	31	9	0	1	5	36	0	84	3	0	8	2	.800	0	0-0	0	3.71	3.30
2005	CWS	AL	24	22	0	1	128.1	568	137	77	73	18	3	5	12	50	1	91	3	2	9	9	.500	0	1-1	1	5.12	5.12
2006	2 Tms	NL	29	29	1	0	162.1	699	155	90	84	22	7	5	12	61	5	164	1	3	11	11	.500	0	0-0	0	4.23	4.66
2007	NYM	NL	27	24	0	0	147.2	608	109	64	61	23	8	3	5	64	4	128	2	0	9	5	.643	0	0-0	0	3.26	3.72
06	Ari	NL	9	9	0	0	45.2	204	52	32	31	8	2	0	4	20	3	52	0	0	2	4	.333	0	0-0	0	6.00	6.11
06	NYM	NL	20	20	1	0	116.2	495	103	58	53	14	5	5	8	41	2	112	1	3	9	7	.563	0	0-0	0	3.60	4.09
	9 ML YEARS		219	211	9	2	1314.2	5558	1181	641	604	177	31	42	67	479	18	1086	27	7	90	65	.581	2	2-2	2	3.79	4.13

Ramon Hernandez

Bats: R **Throws:** R **Pos:** C-104; PH-5; 1B-1 **Ht:** 6'0" **Wt:** 235 **Born:** 5/20/1976 **Age:** 32

Year	Team	Lg	G	AB	H	2B	3B	HR	(Hm	Rd)	TB	R	RBI	RC	TBB	IBB	SO	HBP	SH	SF	SB	CS	SB%	GDP	Avg	OBP	Slg
2007	Abrdn*	A-	2	4	2	1	0	0	(-	-)	3	2	0	2	4	0	0	0	0	0	1	0	1.00	0	.500	.750	.750
2007	Frdrck*	A+	2	6	2	1	0	0	(-	-)	3	0	0	1	0	0	2	1	0	0	0	0	-	0	.333	.429	.500
1999	Oak	AL	40	136	38	7	0	3	(1	2)	54	13	21	20	18	0	11	1	1	2	1	0	1.00	5	.279	.363	.397
2000	Oak	AL	143	419	101	19	0	14	(7	7)	162	52	62	49	38	1	64	7	10	5	1	0	1.00	14	.241	.311	.387
2001	Oak	AL	136	453	115	25	0	15	(5	10)	185	55	60	58	37	3	68	6	9	4	1	1	.50	10	.254	.316	.408
2002	Oak	AL	136	403	94	20	0	7	(3	4)	135	51	42	41	43	1	64	5	3	3	0	0	-	11	.233	.313	.335
2003	Oak	AL	140	483	132	24	1	21	(9	12)	221	70	78	69	33	2	79	12	2	6	0	0	-	14	.273	.331	.458
2004	SD	NL	111	384	106	23	0	18	(10	8)	183	45	63	50	35	0	45	5	4	4	1	0	1.00	16	.276	.341	.477
2005	SD	NL	99	369	107	19	2	12	(5	7)	166	36	58	44	18	0	40	1	1	3	1	0	1.00	14	.290	.322	.450
2006	Bal	AL	144	501	138	29	2	23	(17	6)	240	66	91	82	43	2	79	11	0	5	1	0	1.00	13	.275	.343	.479
2007	Bal	AL	106	364	94	18	0	9	(4	5)	139	40	62	56	36	1	59	6	0	3	1	3	.25	9	.258	.333	.382
	9 ML YEARS		1055	3512	925	184	5	122	(61	61)	1485	428	537	469	301	10	509	54	30	35	7	4	.64	106	.263	.328	.423

Roberto Hernandez

Pitches: R **Bats:** R **Pos:** RP-50 **Ht:** 6'4" **Wt:** 245 **Born:** 11/11/1964 **Age:** 43

Year	Team	Lg	G	GS	CG	GF	IP	BFP	H	R	ER	HR	SH	SF	HB	TBB	IBB	SO	WP	Bk	W	L	Pct	ShO	Sv-Op	Hld	ERC	ERA
2007	LsVgs*	AAA	1	0	0	0	1.0	4	1	0	0	0	0	0	0	0	0	0	0	0	0	0	-	0	0- -		1.95	0.00
1991	CWS	AL	9	3	0	1	15.0	69	18	15	13	1	0	0	0	7	0	6	1	0	1	0	1.000	0	0-0	0	5.19	7.80
1992	CWS	AL	43	0	0	27	71.0	277	45	15	13	4	0	3	4	20	1	68	2	0	7	3	.700	0	12-16	6	1.74	1.65
1993	CWS	AL	70	0	0	67	78.2	314	66	21	20	6	2	2	0	20	1	71	2	0	3	4	.429	0	38-44	0	2.54	2.29
1994	CWS	AL	45	0	0	43	47.2	206	44	29	26	5	0	1	1	19	1	50	1	0	4	4	.500	0	14-20	0	3.66	4.91
1995	CWS	AL	60	0	0	57	59.2	272	63	30	26	9	4	0	3	28	4	84	1	0	3	7	.300	0	32-42	0	5.04	3.92
1996	CWS	AL	72	0	0	61	84.2	355	65	21	18	2	2	2	0	38	5	85	6	0	6	5	.545	0	38-46	0	2.40	1.91
1997	2 Tms		74	0	0	50	80.2	340	67	24	22	7	2	1	1	38	5	82	3	0	10	3	.769	0	31-39	9	3.30	2.45
1998	TB	AL	67	0	0	58	71.1	310	55	33	32	5	4	0	5	41	4	55	1	0	2	6	.250	0	26-35	0	3.43	4.04
1999	TB	AL	72	0	0	66	73.1	321	68	27	25	1	2	3	4	33	1	69	3	0	2	3	.400	0	43-47	0	3.40	3.07
2000	TB	AL	68	0	0	58	73.1	315	76	33	26	9	7	3	3	23	1	61	2	1	4	7	.364	0	32-40	1	4.24	3.19
2001	KC	AL	63	0	0	55	67.2	287	69	34	31	7	1	0	1	26	3	46	6	0	5	6	.455	0	28-34	0	4.23	4.12
2002	KC	AL	53	0	0	42	52.0	227	62	29	25	6	4	1	3	12	2	39	3	0	1	3	.250	0	26-33	0	4.79	4.33
2003	Atl	NL	66	0	0	12	60.0	282	61	36	29	10	4	0	3	43	7	45	0	0	5	3	.625	0	0-4	19	5.95	4.35
2004	Phi	NL	63	0	0	11	56.2	260	66	39	30	9	7	1	1	29	3	44	3	0	3	5	.375	0	0-4	9	5.94	4.76
2005	NYM	NL	67	0	0	20	69.2	291	57	20	20	5	9	2	2	28	4	61	4	0	8	6	.571	0	4-10	18	2.93	2.58
2006	2 Tms	NL	68	0	0	19	63.2	285	61	32	22	5	5	1	1	32	8	40	5	0	3	0	.000	0	2-5	12	3.84	3.11
2007	2 Tms	NL	50	0	0	20	46.1	221	59	37	33	5	3	1	3	25	3	31	7	0	3	3	.500	0	0-1	5	6.48	6.41
97	CWS	AL	46	0	0	43	48.0	203	38	15	13	5	1	1	1	24	4	47	2	0	5	1	.833	0	27-31	0	3.30	2.44
97	SF		28	0	0	32	32.2	137	29	9	9	2	1	0	0	14	1	35	1	0	5	2	.714	0	4-8	9	3.29	2.48
06	Pit	NL	46	0	0	14	43.0	202	46	24	14	3	2	1	0	24	7	33	3	0	0	3	.000	0	2-5	9	4.50	2.93
06	NYM	NL	22	0	0	5	20.2	83	15	8	8	2	3	0	0	8	1	15	2	0	0	0	-	0	0-0	3	2.52	3.48
07	Cle	AL	28	0	0	8	26.0	125	33	21	18	2	1	0	1	16	3	18	4	0	3	1	.750	0	0-1	4	6.31	6.23
07	LAD	NL	22	0	0	12	20.1	96	26	16	15	3	2	1	2	9	0	13	3	0	0	2	.000	0	0-0	1	6.70	6.64
	17 ML YEARS		1010	3	0	667	1071.1	4632	1002	475	411	96	56	21	35	462	53	945	50	1	67	71	.486	0	326-420	79	3.80	3.45

Yoel Hernandez

Pitches: R **Bats:** R **Pos:** RP-14　　　　**Ht:** 6'2" **Wt:** 212 **Born:** 4/15/1980 **Age:** 28

			HOW MUCH HE PITCHED					WHAT HE GAVE UP											THE RESULTS							
Year	Team	Lg	G	GS	CG	GF	IP	BFP	H	R	ER	HR	SH	SF	HB	TBB	IBB	SO	WP	Bk	W	L	Pct	ShO	Sv-Op	Hld	ERC	ERA
2000	Phillies	R	10	9	2	0	60.0	237	39	10	9	2	0	0	7	17	0	46	4	1	4	1	.800	1	0--	-	1.91	1.35
2001	Lakwd	A	25	25	1	0	160.2	700	153	94	62	7	4	7	18	42	1	111	6	2	6	9	.400	0	0--	-	3.21	3.47
2002	Clrwtr	A+	28	28	3	0	170.1	731	176	76	67	6	10	6	12	54	3	116	10	1	7	16	.304	0	0--	-	3.75	3.54
2003	Rdng	AA	43	1	0	22	74.0	349	100	43	35	4	9	4	7	31	3	46	4	0	6	3	.667	0	2--	-	6.22	4.26
2003	S-WB	AAA	2	0	0	0	3.0	14	5	2	2	0	0	0	0	0	0	3	0	0	0	0	-	0	0--	-	5.42	6.00
2004	Rdng	AA	20	0	0	15	31.1	136	24	12	7	0	1	0	2	15	2	33	3	0	1	2	.333	0	6--	-	2.49	2.01
2004	S-WB	AAA	14	2	0	3	30.2	131	38	16	22	4	4	4	2	7	1	18	1	0	0	0	-	0	6--	-	5.41	6.46
2005	Clrwtr	A+	4	0	0	1	5.1	30	8	10	7	1	1	0	1	3	0	7	1	0	1	1	.500	0	0--	-	8.63	11.81
2005	Rdng	AA	9	0	0	2	13.2	60	12	2	2	0	1	0	1	6	2	15	0	0	2	0	1.000	0	0--	-	2.82	1.32
2005	S-WB	AAA	40	0	0	18	53.2	231	51	20	20	5	3	3	4	22	1	50	1	0	6	4	.600	0	3--	-	4.09	3.35
2006	S-WB	AAA	9	0	0	6	10.1	46	11	3	2	0	0	1	0	4	1	8	0	0	1	0	1.000	0	6--	-	3.41	1.74
2007	Ottawa	AAA	22	0	0	14	29.2	135	33	14	13	0	4	0	0	14	4	16	3	0	1	3	.250	0	5--	-	3.92	3.94
2007	Phi	NL	14	0	0	7	15.1	67	20	9	9	2	0	0	0	1	1	13	0	0	0	0	-	0	0-1	0	4.45	5.28

Mike Hessman

Bats: R **Throws:** R **Pos:** 1B-12; 3B-4; PH-3; LF-1　　　　**Ht:** 6'5" **Wt:** 215 **Born:** 3/5/1978 **Age:** 30

					BATTING															BASERUNNING				AVERAGES		
Year	Team	Lg	G	AB	H	2B	3B	HR	(Hm	Rd)	TB	R	RBI	RC	TBB	IBB	SO	HBP	SH	SF	SB	CS	SB%	GDP	Avg	OBP	Slg
2007	Toledo*	AAA	117	422	107	24	2	31	(-	-)	228	71	101	80	64	4	153	6	1	5	6	11	.35	10	.254	.356	.540
2003	Atl	NL	19	21	6	2	0	2	(1	1)	14	2	3	5	1	6	0	0	0	0	0	-	2	.286	.423	.667
2004	Atl	NL	29	69	9	3	0	2	(2	0)	18	8	5	1	1	0	24	1	0	0	0	0	-	0	.130	.155	.261
2007	Det	AL	17	51	12	0	0	4	(3	1)	24	7	12	7	5	0	17	0	0	1	0	0	-	0	.235	.298	.471
	3 ML YEARS		65	141	27	5	0	8	(6	2)	56	17	20	13	11	1	47	1	0	1	0	0	-	2	.191	.253	.397

Aaron Hill

Bats: R **Throws:** R **Pos:** 2B-160; PH-1　　　　**Ht:** 5'11" **Wt:** 195 **Born:** 3/21/1982 **Age:** 26

					BATTING															BASERUNNING				AVERAGES		
Year	Team	Lg	G	AB	H	2B	3B	HR	(Hm	Rd)	TB	R	RBI	RC	TBB	IBB	SO	HBP	SH	SF	SB	CS	SB%	GDP	Avg	OBP	Slg
2005	Tor	AL	105	361	99	25	3	3	(3	0)	139	49	40	50	34	0	41	5	3	4	2	1	.67	5	.274	.342	.385
2006	Tor	AL	155	546	159	28	3	6	(4	2)	211	70	50	68	42	5	66	9	4	5	5	2	.71	15	.291	.349	.386
2007	Tor	AL	160	608	177	47	2	17	(8	9)	279	87	78	88	41	1	102	0	3	5	4	3	.57	21	.291	.333	.459
	3 ML YEARS		420	1515	435	100	8	26	(15	11)	629	206	168	206	117	6	209	14	10	14	11	6	.65	41	.287	.341	.415

Koyie Hill

Bats: B **Throws:** R **Pos:** C-31; PH-5; RF-1; PR-1　　　　**Ht:** 6'0" **Wt:** 190 **Born:** 3/9/1979 **Age:** 29

					BATTING															BASERUNNING				AVERAGES		
Year	Team	Lg	G	AB	H	2B	3B	HR	(Hm	Rd)	TB	R	RBI	RC	TBB	IBB	SO	HBP	SH	SF	SB	CS	SB%	GDP	Avg	OBP	Slg
2007	Iowa*	AAA	47	149	48	16	0	2	(	)	70	22	24	25	11	1	23	0	0	2	1	1	.50	5	.322	.364	.470
2003	LAD	NL	3	3	1	1	0	0	(0	0)	2	0	0	0	0	0	2	0	0	0	0	0	-	0	.333	.333	.667
2004	Ari	NL	13	36	9	1	0	1	(1	0)	13	3	6	5	2	1	6	0	0	0	1	0	1.00	1	.250	.289	.361
2005	Ari	NL	34	78	17	5	0	0	(0	0)	22	6	6	6	11	0	27	0	0	2	0	1	.00	0	.218	.308	.282
2007	ChC	NL	36	93	15	4	0	2	(1	1)	25	7	12	3	8	0	18	1	1	2	0	0	-	4	.161	.231	.269
	4 ML YEARS		86	210	42	11	0	3	(2	1)	62	16	24	14	21	1	53	1	1	4	1	1	.50	5	.200	.271	.295

Rich Hill

Pitches: L **Bats:** L **Pos:** SP-32　　　　**Ht:** 6'5" **Wt:** 205 **Born:** 3/11/1980 **Age:** 28

			HOW MUCH HE PITCHED					WHAT HE GAVE UP											THE RESULTS							
Year	Team	Lg	G	GS	CG	GF	IP	BFP	H	R	ER	HR	SH	SF	HB	TBB	IBB	SO	WP	Bk	W	L	Pct	ShO	Sv-Op	Hld	ERC	ERA
2005	ChC	NL	10	4	0	1	23.2	115	25	24	24	3	1	0	1	17	1	21	0	0	0	2	.000	0	0-0	0	5.81	9.13
2006	ChC	NL	17	16	2	1	99.1	417	83	51	46	16	8	3	2	39	1	90	3	0	6	7	.462	1	0-0	0	3.59	4.17
2007	ChC	NL	32	32	0	0	195.0	812	170	89	85	27	9	4	12	63	3	183	1	1	11	8	.579	0	0-0	0	3.56	3.92
	3 ML YEARS		59	52	2	2	318.0	1344	278	164	155	46	18	7	15	119	5	294	4	1	17	17	.500	1	0-0	0	3.74	4.39

Shawn Hill

Pitches: R **Bats:** R **Pos:** SP-16　　　　**Ht:** 6'2" **Wt:** 180 **Born:** 4/28/1981 **Age:** 27

			HOW MUCH HE PITCHED					WHAT HE GAVE UP											THE RESULTS							
Year	Team	Lg	G	GS	CG	GF	IP	BFP	H	R	ER	HR	SH	SF	HB	TBB	IBB	SO	WP	Bk	W	L	Pct	ShO	Sv-Op	Hld	ERC	ERA
2007	Ptomc*	A+	2	2	0	0	7.0	25	3	1	1	0	0	0	0	1	0	4	1	0	0	0	-	0	0--	-	0.60	1.29
2007	Clmbs*	AAA	1	1	0	0	5.0	18	4	1	1	0	0	0	0	0	0	0	0	0	0	1	.000	0	0--	-	1.34	1.80
2004	Mon	NL	3	3	0	0	9.0	51	17	16	16	1	0	2	1	7	0	10	0	0	1	2	.333	0	0-0	0	12.14	16.00
2006	Was	NL	6	6	0	0	36.2	163	43	20	19	2	2	1	3	12	2	16	1	0	1	3	.250	0	0-0	0	4.70	4.66
2007	Was	NL	16	16	0	0	97.1	399	86	42	37	9	2	1	5	25	2	65	2	0	4	5	.444	0	0-0	0	3.03	3.42
	3 ML YEARS		25	25	0	0	143.0	613	146	78	72	12	4	4	9	44	4	91	3	0	6	10	.375	0	0-0	0	3.93	4.53

Shea Hillenbrand

Bats: R Throws: R Pos: DH-45; 3B-18; 1B-8; PH-4   Ht: 6'1" Wt: 210 Born: 7/27/1975 Age: 32

					BATTING															BASERUNNING				AVERAGES		
Year	Team	Lg	G	AB	H	2B	3B	HR	(Hm	Rd)	TB	R	RBI	RC	TBB	IBB	SO	HBP	SH	SF	SB	CS	SB%	GDP	Avg	OBP	Slg
2007	Portlnd*	AAA	9	34	5	1	0	0	(-	-)	6	2	1	0	1	1	4	0	0	0	0	0	-	2	.147	.171	.176
2007	LsVgs*	AAA	3	13	7	1	0	1	(-	-)	11	3	4	4	0	0	3	0	0	0	0	0	-	0	.538	.538	.846
2001	Bos	AL	139	468	123	20	2	12	(5	7)	183	52	49	49	13	3	61	7	1	4	3	4	.43	12	.263	.291	.391
2002	Bos	AL	156	634	186	43	4	18	(5	13)	291	94	83	88	25	4	95	12	0	5	4	2	.67	18	.293	.330	.459
2003	2 Tms		134	515	144	35	1	20	(11	9)	241	60	97	66	24	4	70	6	0	9	1	0	1.00	22	.280	.314	.468
2004	Ari	NL	148	562	174	36	3	15	(9	6)	261	68	80	82	24	2	49	12	0	6	2	0	1.00	18	.310	.348	.464
2005	Tor	AL	152	594	173	36	2	18	(13	5)	267	91	82	88	26	2	79	22	0	3	5	1	.83	21	.291	.343	.449
2006	Tor	AL	141	530	147	27	1	21	(9	12)	239	73	68	61	21	2	80	9	0	6	1	2	.33	22	.277	.313	.451
2007	2 Tms		73	267	67	5	2	4	(2	2)	88	25	31	23	7	1	30	1	0	3	0	3	.00	9	.251	.270	.330
03	Bos	AL	49	185	56	17	0	3	(0	3)	82	20	38	27	7	1	26	4	0	4	1	0	1.00	9	.303	.335	.443
03	Ari	AL	85	330	88	18	1	17	(11	6)	159	40	59	39	17	3	44	2	0	5	0	0	-	13	.267	.302	.482
06	Tor	AL	81	296	89	15	1	12	(5	7)	142	40	39	38	14	2	40	6	0	3	1	2	.33	15	.301	.342	.480
06	SF	NL	60	234	58	12	0	9	(4	5)	97	33	29	23	7	0	40	3	0	3	0	0	-	7	.248	.275	.415
07	LAA	AL	53	197	50	5	0	3	(1	2)	64	19	22	16	5	0	18	1	0	1	0	2	.00	6	.254	.275	.325
07	LAD	NL	20	70	17	0	2	1	(1	0)	24	6	9	7	2	1	12	0	0	2	0	1	.00	3	.243	.257	.343
	7 ML YEARS		943	3570	1014	202	15	108	(54	54)	1570	463	490	457	140	18	464	69	1	36	16	12	.57	122	.284	.321	.440

Eric Hinske

Bats: L Throws: R Pos: 1B-43; LF-24; PH-14; RF-12; PR-4; DH-3   Ht: 6'2" Wt: 235 Born: 8/5/1977 Age: 30

					BATTING															BASERUNNING				AVERAGES		
Year	Team	Lg	G	AB	H	2B	3B	HR	(Hm	Rd)	TB	R	RBI	RC	TBB	IBB	SO	HBP	SH	SF	SB	CS	SB%	GDP	Avg	OBP	Slg
2002	Tor	AL	151	566	158	38	2	24	(15	9)	272	99	84	103	77	5	138	2	0	5	13	1	.93	12	.279	.365	.481
2003	Tor	AL	124	449	109	45	3	12	(4	8)	196	74	63	66	59	1	104	1	0	5	12	2	.86	11	.243	.329	.437
2004	Tor	AL	155	570	140	23	3	15	(6	9)	214	66	69	60	54	2	109	4	0	6	12	8	.60	14	.246	.312	.375
2005	Tor	AL	147	477	125	31	2	15	(7	8)	205	79	68	71	46	4	121	8	0	6	8	4	.67	8	.262	.333	.430
2006	2 Tms		109	277	75	17	2	13	(7	6)	135	43	34	39	35	2	79	0	0	0	2	2	.50	8	.271	.353	.487
2007	Bos	AL	84	186	38	12	3	6	(4	2)	74	25	21	22	28	2	54	3	0	1	3	0	1.00	7	.204	.317	.398
06	Tor	AL	78	197	52	9	2	12	(6	6)	101	35	29	29	27	2	49	0	0	0	1	1	.50	6	.264	.353	.513
06	Bos	AL	31	80	23	8	0	1	(1	0)	34	8	5	10	8	0	30	0	0	0	1	1	.50	2	.288	.352	.425
	6 ML YEARS		770	2525	645	166	15	85	(43	42)	1096	386	339	361	299	16	605	18	0	23	50	17	.75	60	.255	.336	.434

Jason Hirsh

Pitches: R Bats: R Pos: SP-19   Ht: 6'8" Wt: 250 Born: 2/20/1982 Age: 26

				HOW MUCH HE PITCHED						WHAT HE GAVE UP										THE RESULTS						
Year	Team	Lg	G	GS	CG	GF	IP	BFP	H	R	ER	HR	SH	SF	HB	TBB	IBB	SO	WP	Bk	W	L	Pct	ShO	Sv-Op	Hld	ERC	ERA
2003	TriCity	A-	10	8	0	0	32.1	126	22	10	7	0	0	1	2	7	0	33	1	0	3	1	.750	0	0--	-	1.52	1.95
2004	Salem	A+	26	23	0	1	130.1	557	128	66	58	8	9	7	9	57	0	96	5	0	11	7	.611	0	0--	-	4.24	4.01
2005	CpChr	AA	29	29	1	0	172.1	696	137	63	55	12	4	7	12	42	0	165	7	1	13	8	.619	1	0--	-	2.49	2.87
2006	RdRck	AAA	23	23	1	0	137.1	527	94	37	32	5	3	1	8	51	0	118	2	0	13	2	.867	1	0--	-	2.30	2.10
2007	ColSpr	AAA	3	3	0	0	13.0	58	16	8	7	1	2	0	1	4	0	7	0	0	1	2	.333	0	0--	-	5.23	4.85
2006	Hou	NL	9	9	0	0	44.2	206	48	32	30	11	0	1	3	22	2	29	4	0	3	4	.429	0	0-0	0	6.11	6.04
2007	Col	NL	19	19	1	0	112.1	483	103	63	60	18	6	4	2	48	5	75	5	1	5	7	.417	0	0-0	0	4.12	4.81
	2 ML YEARS		28	28	1	0	157.0	689	151	95	90	29	6	5	5	70	7	104	9	1	8	11	.421	0	0-0	0	4.66	5.16

Luke Hochevar

Pitches: R Bats: R Pos: RP-3; SP-1   Ht: 6'5" Wt: 205 Born: 9/15/1983 Age: 24

				HOW MUCH HE PITCHED						WHAT HE GAVE UP										THE RESULTS						
Year	Team	Lg	G	GS	CG	GF	IP	BFP	H	R	ER	HR	SH	SF	HB	TBB	IBB	SO	WP	Bk	W	L	Pct	ShO	Sv-Op	Hld	ERC	ERA
2006	Burlgtn	A	4	4	0	0	15.1	57	8	3	2	2	0	0	1	2	0	16	1	0	1	0	1.000	0	0--	-	1.32	1.17
2007	Wichta	AA	17	16	0	0	94.0	418	110	62	49	13	1	1	6	26	0	94	6	0	3	6	.333	0	0--	-	5.05	4.69
2007	Omha	AAA	10	10	0	0	58.0	245	53	34	33	11	2	2	3	21	0	44	2	0	1	3	.250	0	0--	-	4.29	5.12
2007	KC	AL	4	1	0	1	12.2	54	11	4	3	1	0	3	1	4	0	5	1	0	0	1	.000	0	0-0	0	3.86	2.13

Jim Hoey

Pitches: R Bats: R Pos: RP-23   Ht: 6'6" Wt: 210 Born: 12/30/1982 Age: 25

				HOW MUCH HE PITCHED						WHAT HE GAVE UP										THE RESULTS						
Year	Team	Lg	G	GS	CG	GF	IP	BFP	H	R	ER	HR	SH	SF	HB	TBB	IBB	SO	WP	Bk	W	L	Pct	ShO	Sv-Op	Hld	ERC	ERA
2003	Bluefld	R+	11	8	0	0	42.0	177	33	19	13	3	0	0	6	19	0	20	2	0	2	3	.400	0	0--	-	3.53	2.79
2004	Abrdn	A-	2	2	0	0	6.2	34	12	8	7	1	0	1	0	1	0	6	0	0	1	0	1.000	0	0--	-	7.91	9.45
2005	Abrdn	A-	9	0	0	2	15.0	67	11	10	8	1	2	1	3	10	0	15	1	0	1	1	.500	0	0--	-	4.17	4.80
2006	Dlmrva	A	27	0	0	23	28.1	113	17	8	8	2	5	1	0	10	0	46	1	0	2	1	.667	0	18--	-	1.68	2.54
2006	Frdrck	A+	14	0	0	14	14.0	63	13	3	1	0	0	0	1	5	0	16	1	0	0	0	-	0	11--	-	2.91	0.64
2006	Bowie	AA	8	0	0	6	9.0	41	9	5	4	1	0	1	0	3	0	11	0	0	0	0	-	0	4--	-	3.59	4.00
2007	Bowie	AA	20	0	0	20	18.2	72	13	0	0	0	2	0	1	4	0	28	0	0	1	0	1.000	0	14--	-	1.57	0.00
2007	Norfolk	AAA	20	0	0	6	27.0	106	15	4	4	1	1	1	1	10	0	41	1	0	2	0	1.000	0	2--	-	1.55	1.33
2006	Bal	AL	12	0	0	2	9.2	49	14	11	11	1	2	2	2	5	0	6	0	1	0	1	.000	0	0-1	4	8.22	10.24
2007	Bal	AL	23	0	0	1	24.2	115	25	21	20	2	0	4	1	18	1	18	1	0	3	4	.429	0	0-3	4	5.43	7.30
	2 ML YEARS		35	0	0	3	34.1	164	39	32	31	3	1	6	3	23	1	24	1	1	3	5	.375	0	0-4	8	6.18	8.13

Trevor Hoffman

Pitches: R Bats: R Pos: RP-61   Ht: 6'0" Wt: 215 Born: 10/13/1967 Age: 40

Year	Team	Lg	G	GS	CG	GF	IP	BFP	H	R	ER	HR	SH	SF	HB	TBB	IBB	SO	WP	Bk	W	L	Pct	ShO	Sv-Op	Hld	ERC	ERA
1993	2 Tms	NL	67	0	0	26	90.0	391	80	43	39	10	4	5	1	39	13	79	5	0	4	6	.400	0	5-8	15	3.40	3.90
1994	SD	NL	47	0	0	41	56.0	225	39	16	16	4	1	2	0	20	6	68	3	0	4	4	.500	0	20-23	1	2.02	2.57
1995	SD	NL	55	0	0	51	53.1	218	48	25	23	10	0	0	0	14	3	52	1	0	7	4	.636	0	31-38	0	3.48	3.88
1996	SD	NL	70	0	0	62	88.0	348	50	23	22	6	2	2	2	31	5	111	2	0	9	5	.643	0	42-49	0	1.58	2.25
1997	SD	NL	70	0	0	59	81.1	322	59	25	24	9	2	1	0	24	4	111	7	0	6	4	.600	0	37-44	0	2.27	2.66
1998	SD	NL	66	0	0	61	73.0	274	41	12	12	2	3	0	1	21	2	86	8	0	4	2	.667	0	**53**-54	0	1.32	1.48
1999	SD	NL	64	0	0	54	67.1	263	48	23	16	5	1	3	0	15	2	73	4	0	2	3	.400	0	40-43	0	1.78	2.14
2000	SD	NL	70	0	0	59	72.1	291	61	29	24	7	3	5	0	11	4	85	4	0	4	7	.364	0	43-**50**	0	2.18	2.99
2001	SD	NL	62	0	0	55	60.1	248	48	25	23	10	2	2	1	21	2	63	3	0	3	4	.429	0	43-46	0	3.20	3.43
2002	SD	NL	61	0	0	52	59.1	245	52	20	18	2	2	2	1	18	2	69	3	0	2	5	.286	0	38-41	0	2.63	2.73
2003	SD	NL	9	0	0	7	9.0	36	7	2	2	1	0	0	0	3	0	11	0	0	0	0	-	0	0-0	0	2.76	2.00
2004	SD	NL	55	0	0	51	54.2	209	42	14	14	5	2	0	0	8	1	53	2	0	3	3	.500	0	41-45	0	1.92	2.30
2005	SD	NL	60	0	0	54	57.2	240	52	23	19	3	2	3	1	12	1	54	1	0	1	6	.143	0	43-46	0	2.49	2.97
2006	SD	NL	65	0	0	50	63.0	248	48	16	15	6	0	0	1	13	1	50	2	0	0	2	.000	0	**46-51**	0	2.14	2.14
2007	SD	NL	61	0	0	50	57.1	235	49	21	19	2	3	2	0	15	5	44	0	0	4	5	.444	0	42-49	0	2.23	2.98
93	Fla	NL	28	0	0	13	35.2	152	24	13	13	5	2	1	0	19	7	26	3	0	2	2	.500	0	2-3	8	2.71	3.28
93	SD	NL	39	0	0	13	54.1	239	56	30	26	5	2	4	1	20	6	53	2	0	2	4	.333	0	3-5	7	3.88	4.31
	15 ML YEARS		882	0	0	732	942.2	3793	724	317	286	82	27	27	8	265	51	1009	45	0	53	60	.469	0	524-587	16	2.28	2.73

Matt Holliday

Bats: R Throws: R Pos: LF-157; DH-1   Ht: 6'4" Wt: 235 Born: 1/15/1980 Age: 28

									BATTING												BASERUNNING				AVERAGES		
Year	Team	Lg	G	AB	H	2B	3B	HR	(Hm	Rd)	TB	R	RBI	RC	TBB	IBB	SO	HBP	SH	SF	SB	CS	SB%	GDP	Avg	OBP	Slg
2004	Col	NL	121	400	116	31	3	14	(10	4)	195	65	57	61	31	0	86	6	1	1	3	3	.50	9	.290	.349	.488
2005	Col	NL	125	479	147	24	7	19	(12	7)	242	68	87	88	36	1	79	7	0	4	14	3	.82	11	.307	.361	.505
2006	Col	NL	155	602	196	45	5	34	(22	12)	353	119	114	112	47	3	110	15	0	3	10	5	.67	22	.326	.387	.586
2007	Col	NL	158	636	**216**	**50**	6	36	(25	11)	**386**	120	**137**	**134**	63	7	126	10	0	4	11	4	.73	23	**.340**	.405	.607
	4 ML YEARS		559	2117	675	150	21	103	(69	34)	1176	372	395	395	177	11	401	38	1	12	38	15	.72	65	.319	.380	.556

Paul Hoover

Bats: R Throws: R Pos: C-2; 1B-1   Ht: 6'1" Wt: 200 Born: 4/14/1976 Age: 32

									BATTING												BASERUNNING				AVERAGES		
Year	Team	Lg	G	AB	H	2B	3B	HR	(Hm	Rd)	TB	R	RBI	RC	TBB	IBB	SO	HBP	SH	SF	SB	CS	SB%	GDP	Avg	OBP	Slg
2007	Mrlns*	R	7	25	11	5	0	0	(-	-)	16	7	4	6	0	0	5	0	0	1	0	0	-	0	.440	.423	.640
2007	Albq*	AAA	31	96	28	7	1	4	(-	-)	49	11	21	16	7	0	18	0	0	2	0	1	.00	3	.292	.333	.510
2001	TB	AL	3	4	1	0	0	0	(0	0)	1	1	0	0	0	0	1	0	0	0	0	0	-	0	.250	.250	.250
2002	TB	AL	5	17	3	0	0	0	(0	0)	3	1	2	1	0	0	5	0	0	0	0	0	-	0	.176	.176	.176
2006	Fla	NL	4	5	2	0	0	0	(0	0)	2	0	1	1	0	0	0	0	0	0	0	0	-	0	.400	.400	.400
2007	Fla	NL	3	8	3	0	0	0	(0	0)	3	1	0	0	0	0	2	0	0	0	0	0	-	0	.375	.375	.375
	4 ML YEARS		15	34	9	0	0	0	(0	0)	9	3	3	2	0	0	8	0	0	0	0	0	-	0	.265	.265	.265

Norris Hopper

Bats: R Throws: R Pos: CF-56; LF-34; PH-31; RF-13; PR-4   Ht: 5'10" Wt: 209 Born: 3/24/1979 Age: 29

									BATTING												BASERUNNING				AVERAGES		
Year	Team	Lg	G	AB	H	2B	3B	HR	(Hm	Rd)	TB	R	RBI	RC	TBB	IBB	SO	HBP	SH	SF	SB	CS	SB%	GDP	Avg	OBP	Slg
1998	Royals	R	40	133	41	2	1	0	(-	-)	45	19	11	19	13	0	12	0	2	1	11	2	.85	1	.308	.365	.338
1999	Royals	R	46	179	46	3	2	0	(-	-)	53	33	13	21	19	0	20	0	2	4	22	6	.79	2	.257	.322	.296
1999	CtnWV	A	5	22	11	0	2	0	(-	-)	15	3	2	6	0	0	1	0	0	0	1	0	1.00	0	.500	.500	.682
2000	CtnWV	A	116	454	127	20	6	0	(-	-)	159	70	29	63	51	0	55	4	4	1	24	10	.71	10	.280	.357	.350
2001	Wilmg	A+	110	389	96	6	2	1	(-	-)	109	38	38	38	32	2	60	5	11	0	16	4	.80	15	.247	.312	.280
2002	Wilmg	A+	125	514	140	12	3	1	(-	-)	161	78	46	57	31	1	55	8	22	2	22	9	.71	15	.272	.323	.313
2003	Wichta	AA	115	424	127	14	2	0	(-	-)	145	56	40	54	27	1	58	4	16	1	24	10	.71	10	.300	.346	.342
2004	Wichta	AA	98	363	101	5	3	0	(-	-)	112	48	40	43	33	0	44	5	10	2	17	7	.71	15	.278	.345	.309
2005	Chatt	AA	116	451	140	15	4	1	(-	-)	166	70	37	63	27	2	38	4	4	1	25	7	.78	12	.310	.354	.368
2006	Chatt	AA	13	46	13	2	1	0	(-	-)	17	7	10	7	6	1	3	0	0	0	3	0	1.00	0	.283	.365	.370
2006	Lsvlle	AAA	98	383	133	11	3	0	(-	-)	150	47	26	60	20	0	25	0	5	2	25	7	.78	7	.347	.378	.392
2007	Srsota	A+	4	17	5	0	0	0	(-	-)	5	1	2	1	0	0	2	0	0	1	0	0	-	1	.294	.294	.294
2007	Lsvlle	AAA	4	15	4	0	0	0	(-	-)	4	2	1	2	1	0	1	1	0	0	2	0	1.00	0	.267	.353	.267
2006	Cin	NL	21	39	14	1	0	1	(1	0)	18	6	5	8	6	0	4	0	1	1	2	2	.50	1	.359	.435	.462
2007	Cin	NL	121	307	101	14	2	0	(0	0)	119	51	14	43	20	1	33	1	6	1	14	6	.70	8	.329	.371	.388
	2 ML YEARS		142	346	115	15	2	1	(1	0)	137	57	19	51	26	1	37	1	7	2	16	8	.67	9	.332	.379	.396

D.J. Houlton

Pitches: R Bats: R Pos: RP-18   Ht: 6'4" Wt: 225 Born: 8/12/1979 Age: 28

Year	Team	Lg	G	GS	CG	GF	IP	BFP	H	R	ER	HR	SH	SF	HB	TBB	IBB	SO	WP	Bk	W	L	Pct	ShO	Sv-Op	Hld	ERC	ERA
2001	Mrtnsvl	R+	13	13	1	0	72.0	290	67	24	20	7	1	2	3	7	0	71	2	0	5	4	.556	0	0--	-	2.68	2.50
2001	Mich	A	1	1	0	0	5.0	23	7	5	3	0	0	0	0	1	0	4	0	0	0	1	.000	0	0--	-	4.69	5.40
2002	Mich	A	35	16	0	7	140.2	577	120	57	49	12	2	2	3	30	0	138	4	0	14	5	.737	0	2--	-	2.52	3.14
2003	RdRck	AA	18	18	1	0	109.0	449	93	45	42	11	4	4	3	28	1	101	2	0	5	4	.556	1	0--	-	2.80	3.47
2003	NewOr	AAA	11	11	0	0	61.2	266	70	39	37	12	1	0	3	19	0	48	3	1	3	4	.429	0	0--	-	5.49	5.40
2004	RdRck	AA	28	28	3	0	159.0	654	141	59	52	14	7	2	12	47	2	159	4	0	12	5	.706	1	0--	-	3.31	2.94
2006	LsVgs	AAA	29	29	1	0	162.1	724	180	115	101	25	3	7	9	60	0	132	3	0	9	11	.450	1	0--	-	5.17	5.60

	HOW MUCH HE PITCHED						WHAT HE GAVE UP												THE RESULTS						
Year Team	Lg	G	GS	CG	GF	IP	BFP	H	R	ER	HR	SH	SF	HB	TBB	IBB	SO	WP	Bk	W	L	Pct	ShO	Sv-Op	Hld	ERC	ERA
2007 LsVgs	AAA	23	19	0	1	106.0	459	106	50	43	12	2	2	5	39	1	92	2	0	6	4	.600	0	0--	-	4.21	3.65
2005 LAD	NL	35	19	0	4	129.0	578	145	79	74	21	11	5	8	52	3	90	2	0	6	9	.400	0	0-0	0	5.51	5.16
2007 LAD	NL	18	0	0	8	28.0	113	28	14	13	5	0	1	0	7	0	21	0	0	0	2	.000	0	0-0	2	4.16	4.18
2 ML YEARS		53	19	0	12	157.0	691	173	93	87	26	11	6	8	59	3	111	2	0	6	11	.353	0	0-0	2	5.27	4.99

J.R. House

Bats: R Throws: R Pos: PH-10; C-9; DH-4; 3B-2; 1B-1   Ht: 6'0" Wt: 212 Born: 11/11/1979 Age: 28

		BATTING																BASERUNNING				AVERAGES		
Year Team	Lg	G	AB	H	2B	3B	HR	(Hm | Rd)	TB	R	RBI	RC	TBB	IBB	SO	HBP	SH	SF	SB	CS	SB%	GDP	Avg	OBP	Slg
2007 Norfolk*	AAA	110	419	125	32	2	11	(- | -)	194	52	66	71	43	4	59	4	0	5	1	5	.17	11	.298	.365	.463
2003 Pit	NL	1	1	1	0	0	0	(0 | 0)	1	0	0	1	0	0	0	0	0	0	0	0	-	0	1.000	1.000	1.000
2004 Pit	NL	5	9	1	1	0	0	(0 | 0)	2	1	0	0	0	0	2	0	0	0	0	0	-	1	.111	.111	.222
2006 Hou	NL	4	9	0	0	0	0	(0 | 0)	0	0	0	0	0	0	2	0	0	0	0	0	-	1	.000	.000	.000
2007 Bal	AL	19	38	8	2	0	3	(2 | 1)	19	5	3	2	1	0	11	2	0	0	0	0	-	0	.211	.268	.500
4 ML YEARS		29	57	10	3	0	3	(2 | 1)	22	6	3	2	1	0	15	2	0	0	0	0	-	2	.175	.217	.386

Ryan Howard

Bats: L Throws: L Pos: 1B-140; PH-4; DH-1   Ht: 6'4" Wt: 256 Born: 11/19/1979 Age: 28

		BATTING																BASERUNNING				AVERAGES		
Year Team	Lg	G	AB	H	2B	3B	HR	(Hm | Rd)	TB	R	RBI	RC	TBB	IBB	SO	HBP	SH	SF	SB	CS	SB%	GDP	Avg	OBP	Slg
2007 Lakwd*	A-	2	6	2	1	0	1	(- | -)	6	1	4	2	2	0	2	0	0	0	0	0	-	1	.333	.500	1.000
2004 Phi	NL	19	39	11	5	0	2	(1 | 1)	22	5	5	7	2	0	13	1	0	0	0	0	-	6	.282	.333	.564
2005 Phi	NL	88	312	90	17	2	22	(11 | 11)	177	52	63	50	33	8	100	1	0	2	0	1	.00	6	.288	.356	.567
2006 Phi	NL	159	581	182	25	1	58	(29 | 29)	383	104	149	138	108	37	181	9	0	6	0	0	-	7	.313	.425	.659
2007 Phi	NL	144	529	142	26	0	47	(23 | 24)	309	94	136	119	107	35	199	5	0	7	1	0	1.00	13	.268	.392	.584
4 ML YEARS		410	1461	425	73	3	129	(64 | 65)	891	255	353	314	250	80	493	16	0	15	1	1	.50	28	.291	.397	.610

J.P. Howell

Pitches: L Bats: L Pos: SP-10   Ht: 6'0" Wt: 180 Born: 4/25/1983 Age: 25

	HOW MUCH HE PITCHED						WHAT HE GAVE UP												THE RESULTS						
Year Team	Lg	G	GS	CG	GF	IP	BFP	H	R	ER	HR	SH	SF	HB	TBB	IBB	SO	WP	Bk	W	L	Pct	ShO	Sv-Op	Hld	ERC	ERA
2007 Drham*	AAA	21	21	1	0	128.0	528	110	63	48	16	5	1	8	34	1	145	7	1	7	8	.467	0	0--	-	3.18	3.38
2005 KC	AL	15	15	0	0	72.2	328	73	55	50	9	3	3	6	39	0	54	7	0	3	5	.375	0	0-0	0	5.18	6.19
2006 TB	AL	8	8	0	0	42.1	187	52	25	24	4	0	2	3	14	0	33	1	0	1	3	.250	0	0-0	0	5.51	5.10
2007 TB	AL	10	10	0	0	51.0	244	69	45	43	8	2	1	3	21	0	49	3	0	1	6	.143	0	0-0	0	6.84	7.59
3 ML YEARS		33	33	0	0	166.0	759	194	125	117	21	5	6	12	74	0	136	11	0	5	14	.263	0	0-0	0	5.76	6.34

Bob Howry

Pitches: R Bats: L Pos: RP-78   Ht: 6'5" Wt: 220 Born: 8/4/1973 Age: 34

	HOW MUCH HE PITCHED						WHAT HE GAVE UP												THE RESULTS						
Year Team	Lg	G	GS	CG	GF	IP	BFP	H	R	ER	HR	SH	SF	HB	TBB	IBB	SO	WP	Bk	W	L	Pct	ShO	Sv-Op	Hld	ERC	ERA
1998 CWS	AL	44	0	0	15	54.1	217	37	20	19	7	2	3	2	19	2	51	2	0	0	3	.000	0	9-11	19	2.50	3.15
1999 CWS	AL	69	0	0	54	67.2	298	58	34	27	8	3	1	3	38	3	80	3	1	5	3	.625	0	28-34	1	4.11	3.59
2000 CWS	AL	65	0	0	29	71.0	289	54	26	25	6	2	4	4	29	2	60	2	0	2	4	.333	0	7-12	14	2.96	3.17
2001 CWS	AL	69	0	0	23	78.2	346	85	41	41	11	4	3	4	30	9	64	6	0	4	5	.444	0	5-11	21	4.78	4.69
2002 2 Tms		67	0	0	26	68.2	292	67	37	32	9	4	6	5	21	4	45	2	0	3	5	.375	0	0-1	15	4.00	4.19
2003 Bos	AL	4	0	0	3	4.1	27	11	6	6	1	0	1	0	3	1	4	0	0	0	0	-	0	0-1	0	16.51	12.46
2004 Cle	AL	37	0	0	6	42.2	178	37	14	13	5	1	1	2	12	0	39	0	0	4	2	.667	0	0-2	8	3.15	2.74
2005 Cle	AL	79	0	0	24	73.0	277	49	23	20	4	3	2	0	16	1	48	0	0	7	4	.636	0	3-5	29	1.58	2.47
2006 ChC	AL	84	0	0	26	76.2	314	70	28	27	8	5	3	1	17	4	71	1	0	4	5	.444	0	5-9	21	3.03	3.17
2007 ChC	NL	78	0	0	32	81.1	336	76	31	30	8	4	1	2	19	3	72	1	0	6	7	.462	0	8-12	22	3.10	3.32
02 CWS	AL	47	0	0	17	50.2	209	45	22	22	7	1	4	3	17	2	31	1	0	2	2	.500	0	0-0	10	3.72	3.91
02 Bos	AL	20	0	0	9	18.0	83	22	15	10	2	3	2	2	4	2	14	1	0	1	3	.250	0	0-1	5	4.79	5.00
10 ML YEARS		596	0	0	238	618.1	2574	544	260	240	67	28	25	25	204	29	534	17	1	35	38	.479	0	65-98	150	3.30	3.49

Chin-Lung Hu

Bats: R Throws: R Pos: SS-10; PH-1; PR-1   Ht: 5'11" Wt: 190 Born: 2/2/1984 Age: 24

		BATTING																BASERUNNING				AVERAGES		
Year Team	Lg	G	AB	H	2B	3B	HR	(Hm | Rd)	TB	R	RBI	RC	TBB	IBB	SO	HBP	SH	SF	SB	CS	SB%	GDP	Avg	OBP	Slg
2003 Ogden	R+	53	220	67	9	5	3	(- | -)	95	34	23	32	14	0	33	0	4	2	5	4	.56	2	.305	.343	.432
2004 Clmbs	A	84	332	99	15	4	6	(- | -)	140	58	25	50	20	0	50	3	11	2	17	7	.71	7	.298	.342	.422
2004 VeroB	A+	20	75	23	4	1	0	(- | -)	29	12	10	10	5	0	6	0	3	0	3	1	.75	1	.307	.350	.387
2005 VeroB	A+	116	470	147	29	1	8	(- | -)	202	80	56	73	19	1	40	7	7	2	23	6	.79	6	.313	.347	.430
2006 Jaxnvl	AA	125	488	124	20	2	5	(- | -)	163	71	34	58	49	1	63	4	13	2	11	5	.69	10	.254	.334	.334
2007 Jaxnvl	AA	82	325	107	30	5	6	(- | -)	165	56	34	63	26	1	33	1	3	1	12	4	.75	5	.329	.380	.508
2007 LsVgs	AAA	45	192	61	10	1	8	(- | -)	97	33	28	31	6	0	18	0	1	1	3	4	.43	5	.318	.337	.505
2007 LAD	NL	12	29	7	0	1	2	(2 | 0)	15	5	5	5	0	0	8	0	2	0	0	0	-	0	.241	.241	.517

Jon Huber

Pitches: R **Bats:** R **Pos:** RP-9   **Ht:** 6'2" **Wt:** 195 **Born:** 7/7/1981 **Age:** 26

			HOW MUCH HE PITCHED						WHAT HE GAVE UP												THE RESULTS						
Year	Team	Lg	G	GS	CG	GF	IP	BFP	H	R	ER	HR	SH	SF	HB	TBB	IBB	SO	WP	Bk	W	L	Pct	ShO	Sv-Op	Hld	ERC	ERA
2000	Padres	R	14	10	0	0	45.0	223	54	49	33	1	3	3	1	32	0	39	6	0	1	4	.200	0	0--	-	5.78	6.60
2001	Idaho	R+	15	15	0	0	73.0	344	77	61	49	7	4	4	7	48	0	75	10	0	5	9	.357	0	0--	-	5.77	6.04
2002	FtWyn	A	28	26	2	0	146.0	659	168	99	83	7	6	11	7	59	0	86	11	3	8	12	.400	0	0--	-	4.73	5.12
2003	FtWyn	A	7	7	0	0	38.1	157	31	18	16	2	1	4	4	11	0	34	0	0	1	1	.500	0	0--	-	2.74	3.76
2003	Lk Els	A+	12	11	0	0	57.1	265	69	41	33	2	1	2	1	31	1	43	2	1	3	5	.375	0	0--	-	5.38	5.18
2004	Lk Els	A+	20	20	0	0	107.0	466	107	53	44	9	5	4	4	44	0	100	7	0	8	6	.571	0	0--	-	4.15	3.70
2004	InldEm	A+	7	5	0	1	32.1	157	42	24	22	4	0	1	3	14	0	38	0	0	4	1	.800	0	0--	-	6.37	6.12
2005	SnAnt	AA	26	26	1	0	148.0	640	159	87	78	11	4	3	6	49	1	112	7	2	7	8	.467	1	0--	-	4.21	4.74
2006	SnAnt	AA	21	0	0	21	24.0	105	30	13	13	0	2	3	1	4	1	19	0	0	0	3	.000	0	11--	-	3.91	4.88
2006	Tacom	AAA	29	0	0	24	61.1	179	46	14	12	3	0	2	3	10	0	38	4	0	3	1	.750	0	12--	-	4.18	2.61
2007	Tacom	AAA	24	1	0	9	33.2	155	43	33	28	5	1	4	2	9	0	28	4	0	1	4	.200	0	5--	-	5.62	7.49
2006	Sea	AL	16	0	0	4	16.2	66	10	3	2	0	2	0	0	6	1	11	0	0	2	1	.667	0	0-0	6	1.37	1.08
2007	Sea	AL	9	0	0	3	11.1	47	13	6	6	1	0	0	0	4	0	8	0	0	0	0	-	0	0-0	3	4.96	4.76
	2 ML YEARS		25	0	0	7	28.0	113	23	9	8	1	2	0	0	10	1	19	0	0	2	1	.667	0	0-0	9	2.55	2.57

Justin Huber

Bats: R **Throws:** R **Pos:** LF-3; PR-3; DH-2; PH-1   **Ht:** 6'2" **Wt:** 205 **Born:** 7/1/1982 **Age:** 25

						BATTING																BASERUNNING				AVERAGES		
Year	Team	Lg	G	AB	H	2B	3B	HR	(Hm	Rd)	TB	R	RBI	RC	TBB	IBB	SO	HBP	SH	SF		SB	CS	SB%	GDP	Avg	OBP	Slg
2007	Royals*	R	7	25	9	4	0	2	(-	-)	19	4	7	7	2	0	4	1	0	1		0	0	-	0	.360	.414	.760
2007	Omha*	AAA	77	286	79	13	1	18	(-	-)	148	39	68	51	20	2	48	8	0	4		1	0	1.00	12	.276	.336	.517
2005	KC	AL	25	78	17	3	0	0	(0	0)	20	6	6	4	5	0	20	1	0	1		0	0	-	1	.218	.271	.256
2006	KC	AL	5	10	2	1	0	0	(0	0)	3	1	1	1	1	0	4	0	0	0		1	0	1.00	0	.200	.273	.300
2007	KC	AL	8	10	1	0	0	0	(0	0)	1	2	0	0	0	0	2	0	0	0		0	0	-	0	.100	.100	.100
	3 ML YEARS		38	98	20	4	0	0	(0	0)	24	9	7	5	6	0	26	1	0	1		1	0	1.00	1	.204	.255	.245

Luke Hudson

Pitches: R **Bats:** R **Pos:** SP-1   **Ht:** 6'3" **Wt:** 205 **Born:** 5/2/1977 **Age:** 31

					HOW MUCH HE PITCHED				WHAT HE GAVE UP												THE RESULTS						
Year	Team	Lg	G	GS	CG	GF	IP	BFP	H	R	ER	HR	SH	SF	HB	TBB	IBB	SO	WP	Bk	W	L	Pct	ShO	Sv-Op	Hld	ERC	ERA
2007	Wichta*	AA	2	2	0	0	7.1	34	8	5	3	1	0	0	1	2	0	12	0	0	0	1	.000	0	0--	-	4.63	3.68
2007	Omha*	AAA	2	2	0	0	9.0	43	11	7	5	2	0	0	0	4	0	14	0	0	0	1	.000	0	0--	-	6.21	5.00
2002	Cin	NL	3	0	0	0	6.0	28	5	5	3	1	0	0	0	6	0	7	2	0	0	0	-	0	0-0	1	6.15	4.50
2004	Cin	NL	9	9	0	0	48.1	204	36	16	13	3	2	2	2	25	1	38	5	0	4	2	.667	0	0-0	0	3.01	2.42
2005	Cin	NL	19	16	0	1	84.2	380	83	62	60	14	5	4	11	50	2	53	5	0	6	9	.400	0	0-0	0	5.88	6.38
2006	KC	AL	26	15	0	1	102.0	440	109	62	58	7	0	3	4	38	1	64	6	0	7	6	.538	0	0-1	1	4.34	5.12
2007	KC	AL	1	1	0	0	2.0	13	2	5	4	1	0	0	0	4	0	0	0	0	1	0	1.000	0	0-0	0	13.81	18.00
	5 ML YEARS		58	41	0	2	243.0	1065	235	150	138	26	7	9	17	123	4	162	18	0	17	18	.486	0	0-1	2	4.68	5.11

Orlando Hudson

Bats: B **Throws:** R **Pos:** 2B-137; PH-2; DH-1   **Ht:** 6'0" **Wt:** 185 **Born:** 12/12/1977 **Age:** 30

						BATTING																BASERUNNING				AVERAGES		
Year	Team	Lg	G	AB	H	2B	3B	HR	(Hm	Rd)	TB	R	RBI	RC	TBB	IBB	SO	HBP	SH	SF		SB	CS	SB%	GDP	Avg	OBP	Slg
2002	Tor	AL	54	192	53	10	5	4	(2	2)	85	20	23	30	11	0	27	2	0	2		0	1	.00	6	.276	.319	.443
2003	Tor	AL	142	474	127	21	6	9	(5	4)	187	54	57	64	39	1	87	5	0	3		5	4	.56	13	.268	.328	.395
2004	Tor	AL	135	489	132	32	7	12	(5	7)	214	73	58	71	51	0	98	4	3	4		7	3	.70	12	.270	.341	.438
2005	Tor	AL	131	461	125	25	5	10	(4	6)	190	62	63	59	30	1	65	3	0	7		7	1	.88	10	.271	.315	.412
2006	Ari	NL	157	579	166	34	9	15	(7	8)	263	87	67	89	61	5	78	2	4	4		9	6	.60	17	.287	.354	.454
2007	Ari	NL	139	517	152	28	9	10	(7	3)	228	69	63	82	70	1	87	2	5	7		10	2	.83	21	.294	.376	.441
	6 ML YEARS		758	2712	755	150	41	60	(30	30)	1167	365	331	395	262	8	442	18	12	27		38	17	.69	79	.278	.343	.430

Tim Hudson

Pitches: R **Bats:** R **Pos:** SP-34   **Ht:** 6'1" **Wt:** 170 **Born:** 7/14/1975 **Age:** 32

					HOW MUCH HE PITCHED				WHAT HE GAVE UP												THE RESULTS						
Year	Team	Lg	G	GS	CG	GF	IP	BFP	H	R	ER	HR	SH	SF	HB	TBB	IBB	SO	WP	Bk	W	L	Pct	ShO	Sv-Op	Hld	ERC	ERA
1999	Oak	AL	21	21	1	0	136.1	580	121	56	49	8	1	2	4	62	2	132	6	0	11	2	.846	0	0-0	0	3.50	3.23
2000	Oak	AL	32	32	2	0	202.1	847	169	100	93	24	5	7	7	82	5	169	7	0	20	6	.769	2	0-0	0	3.43	4.14
2001	Oak	AL	35	35	3	0	235.0	980	216	100	88	20	12	8	6	71	5	181	9	1	18	9	.667	2	0-0	0	3.22	3.37
2002	Oak	AL	34	34	4	0	238.1	983	237	87	79	19	6	5	8	62	9	152	7	1	15	9	.625	2	0-0	0	3.51	2.98
2003	Oak	AL	34	34	3	0	240.0	967	197	84	72	15	11	2	10	61	9	162	6	0	16	7	.696	2	0-0	0	2.47	2.70
2004	Oak	AL	27	27	3	0	188.2	793	194	82	74	8	7	4	12	44	3	103	4	1	12	6	.667	2	0-0	0	3.44	3.53
2005	Atl	NL	29	29	2	0	192.0	817	194	79	75	20	9	1	9	65	5	115	4	0	14	9	.609	0	0-0	0	4.12	3.52
2006	Atl	NL	35	35	2	0	218.1	959	235	129	118	25	8	3	9	79	10	141	7	0	13	12	.520	1	0-0	0	4.54	4.86
2007	Atl	NL	34	34	1	0	224.1	925	221	87	83	10	11	6	8	53	8	132	5	2	16	10	.615	1	0-0	0	3.12	3.33
	9 ML YEARS		281	281	21	0	1875.1	7851	1784	804	731	149	70	38	73	579	56	1287	55	5	135	70	.659	10	0-0	0	3.45	3.51

Aubrey Huff

Bats: L **Throws:** R **Pos:** DH-80; 1B-51; 3B-15; PH-8   **Ht:** 6'4" **Wt:** 230 **Born:** 12/20/1976 **Age:** 31

Year	Team	Lg	G	AB	H	2B	3B	HR	(Hm	Rd)	TB	R	RBI	RC	TBB	IBB	SO	HBP	SH	SF	SB	CS	SB%	GDP	Avg	OBP	Slg
2000	TB	AL	39	122	35	7	0	4	(3	1)	54	12	14	15	5	1	18	1	0	1	0	0	-	6	.287	.318	.443
2001	TB	AL	111	411	102	25	1	8	(5	3)	153	42	45	37	23	2	72	0	0	0	1	3	.25	18	.248	.288	.372
2002	TB	AL	113	454	142	25	0	23	(17	6)	236	67	59	66	37	7	55	1	0	2	4	1	.80	17	.313	.364	.520
2003	TB	AL	162	636	198	47	3	34	(15	19)	353	91	107	112	53	17	80	8	0	9	2	3	.40	19	.311	.367	.555
2004	IB	AL	157	600	178	27	2	29	(16	13)	296	92	104	96	56	6	74	6	0	5	5	1	.83	9	.297	.360	.493
2005	TB	AL	154	575	150	26	2	22	(9	13)	246	70	92	77	49	13	88	5	0	7	8	7	.53	12	.261	.321	.428
2006	2 Tms		131	454	121	25	2	21	(9	12)	213	57	66	55	50	6	64	7	0	6	0	0	-	11	.267	.344	.469
2007	Bal	AL	151	550	154	34	5	15	(8	7)	243	68	72	79	48	2	87	1	0	4	1	1	.50	13	.280	.337	.442
06	TB	AL	63	230	65	15	1	8	(4	4)	106	26	28	28	24	3	25	0	0	2	0	0	-	4	.283	.348	.461
06	Hou	NL	68	224	56	10	1	13	(5	8)	107	31	38	27	26	3	39	7	0	4	0	0	-	7	.250	.341	.478
8 ML YEARS			1018	3802	1080	216	15	156	(82	74)	1794	499	559	537	321	54	538	29	0	34	21	16	.57	105	.284	.342	.472

Phil Hughes

Pitches: R **Bats:** R **Pos:** SP-13   **Ht:** 6'5" **Wt:** 220 **Born:** 6/24/1986 **Age:** 22

			HOW MUCH HE PITCHED					WHAT HE GAVE UP										THE RESULTS						
Year	Team	Lg	G	GS	CG	GF	IP	BFP	H	R	ER	HR	SH	SF	HB	TBB	IBB	SO	WP	Bk	W	L	Pct	ShO	Sv-Op Hld	ERC	ERA
2004	Yanks	R	3	3	0	0	5.0	18	4	0	0	0	0	0	0	0	0	8	0	0	0	0	-	0	0-- -	1.34	0.00
2005	CtnSC	A	12	12	1	0	68.2	265	46	19	15	1	2	4	3	16	0	72	3	0	7	1	.875	0	0-- -	1.55	1.97
2005	Tampa	A+	5	4	0	0	17.2	65	8	6	6	0	1	0	3	4	0	21	0	0	2	0	1.000	0	0-- -	1.13	3.06
2006	Tampa	A+	5	5	0	0	30.0	110	19	7	6	0	0	0	1	2	0	30	0	0	3	2	.400	0	0-- -	1.03	1.80
2006	Trntn	AA	21	21	0	0	116.0	448	73	30	29	5	4	2	2	32	0	138	5	0	10	3	.769	0	0-- -	1.57	2.25
2007	Tampa	A+	1	1	0	0	2.0	8	0	1	0	0	0	0	0	2	0	3	0	0	0	0	-	0	0-- -	0.95	0.00
2007	S-WB	AAA	5	5	0	0	28.2	106	16	7	7	0	1	0	1	8	0	28	2	0	4	1	.800	0	0-- -	1.27	2.20
2007	Trntn	AA	2	2	0	0	7.0	27	5	1	1	0	0	0	0	2	0	11	0	0	0	0	-	0	0-- -	1.68	1.29
2007	NYY	AL	13	13	0	0	72.2	306	64	39	36	8	2	1	2	29	0	58	4	0	5	3	.625	0	0-0 0	3.61	4.46

Eric Hull

Pitches: R **Bats:** R **Pos:** RP-5   **Ht:** 5'11" **Wt:** 185 **Born:** 12/3/1979 **Age:** 28

			HOW MUCH HE PITCHED					WHAT HE GAVE UP										THE RESULTS						
Year	Team	Lg	G	GS	CG	GF	IP	BFP	H	R	ER	HR	SH	SF	HB	TBB	IBB	SO	WP	Bk	W	L	Pct	ShO	Sv-Op Hld	ERC	ERA
2002	SoGA	A	13	0	0	5	22.0	89	22	6	5	1	1	1	0	6	0	13	0	0	1	0	1.000	0	1-- -	3.35	2.05
2002	Gr Falls	R+	11	0	0	9	11.2	41	4	1	0	0	0	0	0	4	0	17	0	0	1	0	.000	0	5-- -	0.76	0.00
2003	VeroB	A+	31	14	1	3	110.2	440	82	37	33	9	4	7	1	40	0	105	7	0	3	5	.375	0	1-- -	2.54	2.68
2004	VeroB	A+	9	9	0	0	51.2	201	48	25	24	3	2	2	1	8	0	49	3	0	3	1	.750	0	0-- -	2.70	4.18
2004	Jaxnvl	AA	21	8	0	2	60.1	268	70	29	28	5	6	1	1	26	3	39	3	0	4	3	.571	0	0-- -	5.05	4.18
2005	Jaxnvl	AA	27	18	1	4	116.1	496	105	50	43	9	5	2	2	44	1	117	6	0	7	7	.500	1	3-- -	3.31	3.33
2005	LsVgs	AAA	2	2	0	0	8.0	41	9	11	7	0	1	0	0	8	1	7	0	0	1	0	1.000	0	0-- -	5.96	7.88
2006	LsVgs	AAA	44	2	0	12	73.0	313	54	39	34	6	1	3	5	43	2	78	5	0	2	4	.333	0	2-- -	3.49	4.19
2007	LsVgs	AAA	49	0	0	30	65.2	272	59	22	20	3	0	1	0	26	4	81	5	0	4	3	.571	0	11-- -	3.10	2.74
2007	LAD	NL	5	0	0	3	6.2	27	4	3	3	0	1	0	0	3	0	5	0	0	0	0	-	0	0-0 0	1.61	4.05

Philip Humber

Pitches: R **Bats:** R **Pos:** RP-2; SP-1   **Ht:** 6'4" **Wt:** 210 **Born:** 12/21/1982 **Age:** 25

			HOW MUCH HE PITCHED					WHAT HE GAVE UP										THE RESULTS						
Year	Team	Lg	G	GS	CG	GF	IP	BFP	H	R	ER	HR	SH	SF	HB	TBB	IBB	SO	WP	Bk	W	L	Pct	ShO	Sv-Op Hld	ERC	ERA
2005	StLuci	A+	14	14	0	0	70.1	301	74	41	39	6	1	3	8	18	0	65	2	0	2	6	.250	0	0-- -	4.20	4.99
2005	Bnghtn	AA	1	1	0	0	4.0	18	4	3	3	0	0	0	0	2	0	2	0	0	0	1	.000	0	0-- -	3.63	6.75
2006	Mets	R	1	1	0	0	4.0	20	7	3	3	0	0	0	1	1	0	7	1	0	0	0	-	0	0-- -	8.49	6.75
2006	StLuci	A+	7	7	0	0	38.0	151	24	12	10	4	2	2	3	9	0	36	1	0	3	1	.750	0	0-- -	1.88	2.37
2006	Bnghtn	AA	6	6	0	0	34.1	141	25	12	11	4	1	1	2	10	0	36	0	0	2	2	.500	0	0-- -	2.50	2.88
2007	NewOr	AAA	25	25	0	0	139.0	586	129	70	66	21	4	0	9	44	0	120	6	1	11	9	.550	0	0-- -	3.97	4.27
2006	NYM	NL	2	0	0	1	2.0	7	0	0	0	0	0	0	0	1	0	2	0	0	0	0	-	0	0-0 0	0.27	0.00
2007	NYM	NL	3	1	0	2	7.0	32	9	6	6	1	0	0	0	2	0	2	0	0	0	0	-	0	0-0 0	5.46	7.71
2 ML YEARS			5	1	0	3	9.0	39	9	6	6	1	0	0	0	3	0	4	0	0	0	0	-	0	0-0 0	3.80	6.00

Torii Hunter

Bats: R **Throws:** R **Pos:** CF-155; DH-3; PH-2   **Ht:** 6'2" **Wt:** 225 **Born:** 7/18/1975 **Age:** 32

Year	Team	Lg	G	AB	H	2B	3B	HR	(Hm	Rd)	TB	R	RBI	RC	TBB	IBB	SO	HBP	SH	SF	SB	CS	SB%	GDP	Avg	OBP	Slg
1997	Min	AL	1	0	0	0	0	0	(0	0)	0	0	0	0	0	0	0	0	0	0	0	0	-	0	-	-	-
1998	Min	AL	6	17	4	1	0	0	(0	0)	5	0	2	1	2	0	6	0	0	0	0	1	.00	1	.235	.316	.294
1999	Min	AL	135	384	98	17	2	9	(2	7)	146	52	35	44	26	1	72	6	1	5	10	6	.63	9	.255	.309	.380
2000	Min	AL	99	336	94	14	7	5	(4	1)	137	44	44	39	18	2	68	2	0	2	4	3	.57	13	.280	.318	.408
2001	Min	AL	148	564	147	32	5	27	(13	14)	270	82	92	79	29	0	125	8	1	1	9	6	.60	12	.261	.306	.479
2002	Min	AL	148	561	162	37	4	29	(13	16)	294	89	94	85	35	3	118	5	0	3	23	8	.74	17	.289	.334	.524
2003	Min	AL	154	581	145	31	4	26	(12	14)	262	83	102	76	50	7	106	5	0	6	6	7	.46	15	.250	.312	.451
2004	Min	AL	138	520	141	37	4	23	(9	14)	247	79	81	69	40	4	101	7	0	2	21	7	.75	23	.271	.330	.475
2005	Min	AL	98	372	100	24	1	14	(6	8)	168	63	56	53	34	3	65	6	0	4	23	7	.77	8	.269	.337	.452
2006	Min	AL	147	557	155	21	2	31	(15	16)	273	86	98	81	45	2	108	5	0	4	12	6	.67	19	.278	.336	.490
2007	Min	AL	160	600	172	45	1	28	(11	17)	303	94	107	99	40	10	101	5	0	5	18	9	.67	17	.287	.334	.505
11 ML YEARS			1234	4492	1218	259	26	192	(85	107)	2105	672	711	626	319	32	870	49	2	32	126	60	.68	134	.271	.324	.469

Chris Iannetta

Bats: R **Throws:** R **Pos:** C-60; PH-9   **Ht:** 6'0" **Wt:** 225 **Born:** 4/8/1983 **Age:** 25

Year	Team	Lg	G	AB	H	2B	3B	HR	(Hm	Rd)	TB	R	RBI	RC	TBB	IBB	SO	HBP	SH	SF	SB	CS	SB%	GDP	Avg	OBP	Slg
2004	Ashvll	A	36	121	38	5	1	5	(-	-)	60	23	17	28	27	0	29	4	0	0	0	1	.00	3	.314	.454	.496
2005	Mdest	A+	74	261	72	17	3	11	(-	-)	128	51	58	50	45	1	61	2	0	4	1	2	.33	9	.276	.381	.490
2005	Tulsa	AA	19	60	14	3	1	2	(-	-)	25	7	11	8	8	0	15	1	0	1	0	0	-	5	.233	.329	.417
2006	Tulsa	AA	44	156	50	10	2	11	(-	-)	97	38	26	39	24	0	26	3	1	1	1	0	1.00	3	.321	.418	.622
2006	ColSpr	AAA	47	151	53	11	2	3	(-	-)	77	23	22	35	24	0	29	3	1	1	0	0	-	9	.351	.447	.510
2007	ColSpr	AAA	16	54	16	3	0	1	(-	-)	22	8	7	9	7	0	6	2	0	0	0	0	-	4	.296	.397	.407
2006	Col	NL	21	77	20	4	0	2	(0	2)	30	12	10	9	13	2	17	1	1	1	0	1	.00	1	.260	.370	.390
2007	Col	NL	67	197	43	8	3	4	(1	3)	69	22	27	27	29	3	58	5	1	2	0	0	-	3	.218	.330	.350
2 ML YEARS			88	274	63	12	3	6	(1	5)	99	34	37	36	42	5	75	6	2	3	0	1	.00	4	.230	.342	.361

Raul Ibanez

Bats: L **Throws:** R **Pos:** LF-131; DH-13; PH-5   **Ht:** 6'2" **Wt:** 220 **Born:** 6/2/1972 **Age:** 36

Year	Team	Lg	G	AB	H	2B	3B	HR	(Hm	Rd)	TB	R	RBI	RC	TBB	IBB	SO	HBP	SH	SF	SB	CS	SB%	GDP	Avg	OBP	Slg
1996	Sea	AL	4	5	0	0	0	0	(0	0)	0	0	0	0	0	0	1	1	0	0	0	0	-	0	.000	.167	.000
1997	Sea	AL	11	26	4	0	1	1	(1	0)	9	3	4	1	0	0	6	0	0	0	0	0	-	0	.154	.154	.346
1998	Sea	AL	37	98	25	7	1	2	(1	1)	40	12	12	10	5	0	22	0	0	0	0	0	-	0	.255	.291	.408
1999	Sea	AL	87	209	54	7	0	9	(3	6)	88	23	27	28	17	1	32	0	0	1	5	1	.83	4	.258	.313	.421
2000	Sea	AL	92	140	32	8	0	2	(2	0)	46	21	15	15	14	1	25	1	0	1	2	0	1.00	1	.229	.301	.329
2001	KC	AL	104	279	78	11	5	13	(5	8)	138	44	54	46	32	2	51	0	1	4	5	3	.63	11	.280	.353	.495
2002	KC	AL	137	497	146	37	6	24	(14	10)	267	70	103	89	40	5	76	2	1	4	5	3	.63	11	.294	.346	.537
2003	KC	AL	157	610	179	33	5	18	(8	10)	276	95	90	91	49	5	81	3	1	10	8	4	.67	10	.294	.345	.454
2004	Sea	AL	123	481	146	31	1	16	(9	7)	227	67	62	67	36	5	72	3	0	4	1	2	.33	10	.304	.353	.472
2005	Sea	AL	162	614	172	32	2	20	(9	11)	268	92	89	99	71	6	99	2	0	3	9	4	.69	12	.280	.355	.436
2006	Sea	AL	159	626	181	33	5	33	(17	16)	323	103	123	114	65	15	115	1	0	7	2	4	.33	13	.289	.353	.516
2007	Sea	AL	149	573	167	35	5	21	(7	14)	275	80	105	101	53	4	97	3	0	7	0	0	-	14	.291	.351	.480
12 ML YEARS			1222	4156	1184	234	31	159	(76	83)	1957	610	684	661	382	44	677	16	2	38	32	20	.62	85	.285	.345	.471

Kei Igawa

Pitches: L **Bats:** L **Pos:** SP-12; RP-2   **Ht:** 6'1" **Wt:** 212 **Born:** 7/13/1979 **Age:** 28

Year	Team	Lg	G	GS	CG	GF	IP	BFP	H	R	ER	HR	SH	SF	HB	TBB	IBB	SO	WP	Bk	W	L	Pct	ShO	Sv-Op	Hld	ERC	ERA
1999	Hnshn	Jap	7	3	0	1	15.1	80	23	11	11	1	-	-	1	13	-	14	0	0	1	1	.500	0	0- -	-	9.21	6.46
2000	Hnshn	Jap	9	5	0	1	39.1	172	36	19	19	5	-	0	0	19	-	37	7	0	1	3	.250	0	0- -	-	4.05	4.35
2001	Hnshn	Jap	29	28	3	0	192.0	829	174	76	57	11	-	-	3	89	-	171	6	0	9	13	.409	2	0- -	-	3.54	2.67
2002	Hnshn	Jap	31	29	8	2	209.2	830	163	63	58	15	-	-	7	53	-	206	8	0	14	9	.609	4	0- -	-	2.35	2.49
2003	Hnshn	Jap	29	29	8	0	206.0	839	184	72	64	15	0	0	3	58	3	179	5	0	20	5	.800	2	0- -	-	2.94	2.80
2004	Hnshn	Jap	29	29	6	0	200.1	840	190	95	83	29	11	2	6	54	0	228	5	0	14	11	.560	3	0- -	-	3.67	3.73
2005	Hnshn	Jap	27	27	2	0	172.1	778	199	91	74	23	-	-	1	60	-	145	4	0	13	9	.591	1	0- -	-	4.90	3.86
2006	Hnshn	Jap	28	28	7	0	200.0	820	174	77	69	17	-	-	6	46	-	184	4	0	13	9	.591	2	0- -	-	2.73	3.11
2007	Tampa	A+	2	2	0	0	9.0	37	7	4	2	0	0	0	0	3	0	6	0	0	1	1	.500	0	0- -	-	2.01	2.00
2007	S-WB	AAA	11	11	0	0	68.1	282	68	30	28	10	2	1	2	15	0	71	0	1	5	4	.556	0	0- -	-	3.80	3.69
2007	NYY	AL	14	12	0	0	67.2	313	76	48	47	15	0	0	4	37	1	53	5	1	2	3	.400	0	0-0	0	6.60	6.25

Tadahito Iguchi

Bats: R **Throws:** R **Pos:** 2B-121; PH-14   **Ht:** 5'10" **Wt:** 200 **Born:** 12/4/1974 **Age:** 33

Year	Team	Lg	G	AB	H	2B	3B	HR	(Hm	Rd)	TB	R	RBI	RC	TBB	IBB	SO	HBP	SH	SF	SB	CS	SB%	GDP	Avg	OBP	Slg
2005	CWS	AL	135	511	142	25	6	15	(7	8)	224	74	71	74	47	0	114	6	11	6	15	5	.75	16	.278	.342	.438
2006	CWS	AL	138	555	156	24	0	18	(12	6)	234	97	67	87	59	0	110	3	8	2	11	5	.69	7	.281	.352	.422
2007	2 Tms		135	465	124	27	4	9	(6	3)	186	67	43	68	57	1	88	3	2	6	14	2	.88	6	.267	.347	.400
07	CWS	AL	90	327	82	17	4	6	(4	2)	125	45	31	46	44	1	65	2	1	3	8	1	.89	5	.251	.340	.382
07	Phi	NL	45	138	42	10	0	3	(2	1)	61	22	12	22	13	0	23	1	1	3	6	1	.86	1	.304	.361	.442
3 ML YEARS			408	1531	422	76	10	42	(25	17)	644	238	181	229	163	1	312	12	21	14	40	12	.77	29	.276	.347	.421

Omar Infante

Bats: R **Throws:** R **Pos:** 2B-20; SS-14; CF-12; 3B-9; PH-8; RF-6; PR-5; DH-2; LF-1   **Ht:** 6'0" **Wt:** 180 **Born:** 12/26/1981 **Age:** 26

Year	Team	Lg	G	AB	H	2B	3B	HR	(Hm	Rd)	TB	R	RBI	RC	TBB	IBB	SO	HBP	SH	SF	SB	CS	SB%	GDP	Avg	OBP	Slg
2007	Toledo*	AAA	10	38	14	2	0	0	(-	-)	16	3	4	7	4	0	2	0	0	1	1	0	1.00	0	.368	.419	.421
2002	Det	AL	18	72	24	3	0	1	(0	1)	30	4	6	12	3	0	10	0	0	0	1	0	.00	0	.333	.360	.417
2003	Det	AL	69	221	49	6	1	0	(0	0)	57	24	8	16	18	0	37	0	3	2	6	3	.67	1	.222	.278	.258
2004	Det	AL	142	503	133	27	9	16	(7	9)	226	69	55	69	40	3	112	1	7	5	13	7	.65	4	.264	.317	.449
2005	Det	AL	121	406	90	28	2	9	(3	6)	149	36	43	38	16	0	73	2	8	2	8	0	1.00	5	.222	.254	.367
2006	Det	AL	78	224	62	11	4	4	(0	4)	93	35	25	26	14	0	45	3	2	2	3	2	.60	5	.277	.325	.415
2007	Det	AL	66	166	45	6	1	2	(0	2)	59	24	17	23	9	0	29	0	2	1	4	1	.80	4	.271	.307	.355
6 ML YEARS			494	1592	403	81	17	32	(10	22)	614	192	154	184	100	3	306	6	22	12	34	14	.71	19	.253	.298	.386

Brandon Inge

Bats: R Throws: R Pos: 3B-150; PR-1   Ht: 5'11" Wt: 190 Born: 5/19/1977 Age: 31

							BATTING																BASERUNNING				AVERAGES		
Year	Team	Lg	G	AB	H	2B	3B	HR	(Hm	0)	TB	R	RBI	RC	TBB	IBB	SO	HBP	SH	SF	SB	CS	SB%	GDP	Avg	OBP	Slg
2001	Det	AL	79	189	34	11	0	0	(0	0)	45	13	15	6	9	0	41	0	2	2	1	4	.20	2	.180	.215	.238
2002	Det	AL	95	321	65	15	3	7	(3	4)	107	27	24	24	24	0	101	4	1	1	3	3	.25	7	.202	.266	.333
2003	Det	AL	104	330	67	15	3	8	(4	4)	112	32	30	23	24	0	79	5	4	3	4	4	.50	8	.203	.265	.339
2004	Det	AL	131	408	117	15	7	13	(9	4)	185	43	64	63	32	0	72	4	8	6	5	4	.56	4	.287	.340	.453
2005	Det	AL	160	616	161	31	9	16	(10	6)	258	75	72	82	63	1	140	4	6	6	7	6	.54	14	.261	.330	.419
2006	Det	AL	159	542	137	29	2	27	(12	15)	251	83	83	79	43	2	128	7	4	5	7	4	.64	12	.253	.313	.463
2007	Det	AL	151	508	120	25	2	14	(9	5)	191	64	71	65	47	5	150	11	7	4	9	2	.82	8	.236	.312	.376
	7 ML YEARS		879	2914	701	141	26	85	(47	38)	1149	337	359	342	242	8	711	34	32	27	34	27	.56	55	.241	.304	.394

Joe Inglett

Bats: L Throws: R Pos: 3B-1; DH-1; PR-1   Ht: 5'10" Wt: 180 Born: 6/29/1978 Age: 30

							BATTING																BASERUNNING				AVERAGES		
Year	Team	Lg	G	AB	H	2B	3B	HR	(Hm	Rd)	TB	R	RBI	RC	TBB	IBB	SO	HBP	SH	SF	SB	CS	SB%	GDP	Avg	OBP	Slg
2000	MhVlly	A-	56	202	58	12	4	2	(-	-)	84	37	37	34	31	1	30	5	0	0	4	5	.44	1	.287	.395	.416
2001	Clmbs	A	62	237	71	9	2	2	(-	-)	90	33	33	34	24	0	22	0	0	2	5	3	.63	7	.300	.361	.380
2002	Clmbs	A	60	235	73	18	5	2	(-	-)	107	44	46	43	28	1	25	4	1	3	5	3	.63	5	.311	.389	.455
2002	Knstn	A+	66	238	67	12	0	0	(-	-)	79	24	29	32	29	3	38	2	0	2	5	2	.71	3	.282	.362	.332
2003	Knstn	A+	28	85	28	10	1	0	(-	-)	40	21	15	20	20	0	14	1	0	2	1	0	1.00	2	.329	.454	.471
2003	Akron	AA	71	276	78	16	1	4	(-	-)	108	41	25	44	37	0	36	6	1	2	1	2	.33	8	.283	.377	.391
2004	Akron	AA	66	266	85	19	7	1	(-	-)	121	49	20	47	31	2	28	1	2	0	3	5	.38	1	.320	.393	.455
2005	Buffalo	AAA	95	327	108	20	9	2	(-	-)	152	57	40	58	17	1	41	9	10	3	13	6	.68	7	.330	.376	.465
2006	Akron	AA	18	64	33	9	0	3	(-	-)	51	20	9	25	11	0	4	0	2	0	7	3	.70	0	.516	.587	.797
2006	Buffalo	AAA	40	157	47	7	2	1	(-	-)	61	21	13	23	13	0	24	2	8	1	3	2	.60	6	.299	.358	.389
2007	Buffalo	AAA	107	392	99	15	9	4	(-	-)	144	45	57	48	40	3	62	7	9	7	7	12	.37	4	.253	.327	.367
2006	Cle	AL	64	201	57	8	3	2	(1	1)	77	26	21	28	14	0	39	1	5	1	5	1	.83	1	.284	.332	.383
2007	Tor	AL	2	5	3	0	1	0	(0	0)	5	0	2	3	0	0	0	0	0	0	1	0	1.00	0	.600	.600	1.000
	2 ML YEARS		66	206	60	8	4	2	(1	1)	82	26	23	31	14	0	39	1	5	1	6	1	.86	1	.291	.338	.398

Jason Isringhausen

Pitches: R Bats: R Pos: RP-63   Ht: 6'3" Wt: 230 Born: 9/7/1972 Age: 35

			HOW MUCH HE PITCHED					WHAT HE GAVE UP												THE RESULTS						
Year	Team	Lg	G	GS	CG	GF	IP	BFP	H	R	ER	HR	SH	SF	HB	TBB	IBB	SO	WP	Bk	W	L	Pct	ShO	Sv-Op	Hld	ERC	ERA
1995	NYM	NL	14	14	1	0	93.0	385	88	29	29	6	3	3	2	31	2	55	4	1	9	2	.818	0	0-0	0	3.40	2.81
1996	NYM	NL	27	27	2	0	171.2	766	190	103	91	13	7	9	8	73	5	114	14	0	6	14	.300	1	0-0	0	4.75	4.77
1997	NYM	NL	6	6	0	0	29.2	145	40	27	25	3	1	2	1	22	0	25	3	0	2	2	.500	0	0-0	0	7.99	7.58
1999	2 Tms		33	5	0	20	64.2	286	64	35	34	9	0	1	2	34	4	51	4	0	1	4	.200	0	9-9	0	4.86	4.73
2000	Oak	Al	66	0	0	57	69.0	304	67	34	29	6	2	1	3	32	5	57	5	1	6	4	.600	0	33-40	0	4.09	3.78
2001	Oak	AL	65	0	0	54	71.1	293	54	24	21	5	0	1	0	23	5	74	2	0	4	3	.571	0	34-43	0	2.18	2.65
2002	StL	NL	60	0	0	51	65.1	257	46	22	18	0	4	3	1	18	1	68	0	0	3	2	.600	0	32-37	0	1.01	2.48
2003	StL	NL	40	0	0	31	42.0	174	31	14	11	2	1	0	0	18	1	41	6	0	1	0	.000	0	22-25	1	2.40	2.36
2004	StL	NL	74	0	0	66	75.1	308	55	27	24	5	6	1	2	23	4	71	1	0	4	2	.667	0	47-54	0	2.09	2.87
2005	StL	NL	63	0	0	52	59.0	245	43	14	14	4	3	1	1	27	5	51	2	0	1	2	.333	0	39-43	1	2.56	2.14
2006	StL	NL	59	0	0	51	58.1	257	47	25	23	10	1	3	3	38	3	52	3	0	4	4	.333	0	33-43	0	4.63	3.55
2007	StL	NL	63	0	0	54	65.1	267	42	21	18	4	1	1	2	28	3	54	3	0	4	0	1.000	0	32-34	0	2.11	2.48
99	NYM	NL	13	5	0	2	39.1	179	43	29	20	7	0	1	1	22	2	31	2	0	1	3	.250	0	1-1	0	5.93	6.41
99	Oak	AL	20	0	0	18	25.1	107	21	6	2	0	0	1	1	12	2	20	2	0	0	1	.000	0	8-8	0	3.33	2.13
	12 ML YEARS		570	52	3	436	864.2	3687	767	375	337	67	32	26	25	367	38	713	47	2	44	44	.500	1	281-328	2	3.43	3.51

Akinori Iwamura

Bats: L Throws: R Pos: 3B-120; 2B-1; DH-1; PH-1   Ht: 5'9" Wt: 176 Born: 2/9/1979 Age: 29

							BATTING																BASERUNNING				AVERAGES		
Year	Team	Lg	G	AB	H	2B	3B	HR	(Hm	Rd)	TB	R	RBI	RC	TBB	IBB	SO	HBP	SH	SF	SB	CS	SB%	GDP	Avg	OBP	Slg
1998	Yakult	Jap	1	3	0	0	0	0	(-	-)	0	0	0	0	0	-	2	0	0	0	0	0	-	0	.000	.000	.000
1999	Yakult	Jap	83	252	74	11	4	11	(-	-)	126	28	35	44	18	-	46	1	0	2	7	1	.88	2	.294	.341	.500
2000	Yakult	Jap	130	436	121	13	9	18	(-	-)	206	67	66	74	39	-	103	4	9	1	13	1	.93	7	.278	.342	.472
2001	Yakult	Jap	136	520	149	24	4	19	(-	-)	238	79	81	80	32	-	111	3	5	4	15	6	.71	6	.287	.329	.458
2002	Yakult	Jap	140	510	163	35	2	23	(-	-)	271	67	75	104	58	6	114	3	2	4	5	4	.56	10	.320	.390	.531
2003	Yakult	Jap	60	232	61	6	2	12	(-	-)	107	43	31	36	22	3	55	1	2	1	5	1	.83	3	.263	.328	.461
2004	Yakult	Jap	138	533	160	19	0	44	(-	-)	311	99	103	117	70	3	173	4	0	4	8	3	.73	5	.300	.383	.583
2005	Yakult	Jap	144	548	175	31	4	30	(-	-)	304	83	102	114	63	-	146	2	0	5	6	3	.67	2	.319	.388	.555
2006	Yakult	Jap	145	546	170	27	2	32	(-	-)	297	84	77	113	67	-	128	1	1	3	8	1	.89	5	.311	.386	.544
2007	TB	AL	123	491	140	21	10	7	(4	3)	202	82	34	68	58	0	114	1	4	5	12	8	.60	2	.285	.359	.411

Cesar Izturis

Bats: B Throws: R Pos: SS-90; PH-16; 3B-11; PR-3   Ht: 5'9" Wt: 189 Born: 2/10/1980 Age: 28

							BATTING																BASERUNNING				AVERAGES		
Year	Team	Lg	G	AB	H	2B	3B	HR	(Hm	Rd)	TB	R	RBI	RC	TBB	IBB	SO	HBP	SH	SF	SB	CS	SB%	GDP	Avg	OBP	Slg
2001	Tor	AL	46	134	36	6	2	2	(1	1)	52	19	9	16	2	0	15	0	4	0	8	1	.89	0	.269	.279	.388
2002	LAD	NL	135	439	102	24	2	1	(0	1)	133	43	31	26	14	1	39	0	10	5	7	7	.50	12	.232	.253	.303
2003	LAD	NL	158	558	140	21	6	1	(0	1)	176	47	40	42	25	8	70	0	7	3	10	5	.67	8	.251	.282	.315
2004	LAD	NL	159	670	193	32	9	4	(1	3)	255	90	62	95	43	2	70	0	12	3	25	9	.74	6	.288	.330	.381
2005	LAD	NL	106	444	114	19	2	2	(1	1)	143	48	31	37	25	1	51	4	4	1	8	8	.50	11	.257	.302	.322
2006	2 Tms	NL	54	192	47	9	1	1	(1	0)	61	14	18	14	12	3	14	2	1	1	2	10	.20	4	.245	.295	.318
2007	2 Tms	NL	110	314	81	14	2	0	(0	0)	99	31	16	27	19	2	19	1	3	0	3	3	.50	7	.258	.302	.315

137

Year	Team	Lg	G	AB	H	2B	3B	HR	(Hm	Rd)	TB	R	RBI	RC	TBB	IBB	SO	HBP	SH	SF	SB	CS	SB%	GDP	Avg	OBP	Slg
									BATTING												BASERUNNING				AVERAGES		
06	LAD	NL	32	119	30	7	1	1	(1	0)	42	10	12	10	7	3	6	2	0	1	1	3	.25	.	.252	.302	.353
06	ChC	NL	22	73	17	2	0	0	(0	0)	19	4	6	4	5	0	8	0	1	0	0	1	.00	3	.233	.282	.260
07	ChC	NL	65	191	47	11	0	0	(0	0)	58	15	8	13	13	2	16	1	2	0	3	0	1.00	6	.246	.298	.304
07	Pit	NL	45	123	34	3	2	0	(0	0)	41	16	8	14	6	0	3	0	1	0	0	3	.00	1	.276	.310	.333
7 ML YEARS			768	2751	713	125	24	11	(4	7)	919	292	207	257	140	17	278	7	41	13	62	37	.63	48	.259	.295	.334

Maicer Izturis

Bats: B Throws: R Pos: 3B-53; 2B-40; PH-8; SS-3; DH-3   Ht: 5'8" Wt: 165 Born: 9/12/1980 Age: 27

Year	Team	Lg	G	AB	H	2B	3B	HR	(Hm	Rd)	TB	R	RBI	RC	TBB	IBB	SO	HBP	SH	SF	SB	CS	SB%	GDP	Avg	OBP	Slg
									BATTING												BASERUNNING				AVERAGES		
2007	RCuca*	A+	7	22	7	1	0	0	(-	-)	8	5	3	4	6	0	3	0	0	1	0	0	-	0	.318	.448	.364
2007	Salt Lk*	AAA	5	17	6	1	0	0	(-	-)	7	3	0	2	3	1	2	0	0	0	0	2	.00	0	.353	.450	.412
2004	Mon	NL	32	107	22	5	2	1	(1	0)	34	10	4	8	10	1	20	2	2	0	4	0	1.00	1	.206	.286	.318
2005	LAA	AL	77	191	47	8	4	1	(0	1)	66	18	15	25	17	2	21	0	1	1	9	3	.75	5	.246	.306	.346
2006	LAA	AL	104	352	103	21	3	5	(1	4)	145	64	44	56	38	1	35	3	5	1	14	6	.70	7	.293	.365	.412
2007	LAA	AL	102	336	97	17	2	6	(4	2)	136	47	51	65	33	2	39	0	1	4	7	1	.88	4	.289	.349	.405
4 ML YEARS			315	986	269	51	11	13	(6	7)	381	139	114	154	98	6	115	5	9	6	34	10	.77	17	.273	.340	.386

Conor Jackson

Bats: R Throws: R Pos: 1B-108; PH-19; DH-3; 3B-2; LF-2   Ht: 6'2" Wt: 225 Born: 5/7/1982 Age: 26

Year	Team	Lg	G	AB	H	2B	3B	HR	(Hm	Rd)	TB	R	RBI	RC	TBB	IBB	SO	HBP	SH	SF	SB	CS	SB%	GDP	Avg	OBP	Slg
									BATTING												BASERUNNING				AVERAGES		
2005	Ari	NL	40	85	17	3	0	2	(2	0)	26	8	8	6	12	0	11	1	0	1	0	0	-	6	.200	.303	.306
2006	Ari	NL	140	485	141	26	1	15	(8	7)	214	75	79	77	54	2	73	9	1	7	1	0	1.00	18	.291	.368	.441
2007	Ari	NL	130	415	118	29	1	15	(8	7)	194	56	60	67	53	2	50	4	2	3	2	2	.50	8	.284	.368	.467
3 ML YEARS			310	985	276	58	2	32	(18	14)	434	139	147	150	119	4	134	14	3	11	3	2	.60	32	.280	.362	.441

Edwin Jackson

Pitches: R Bats: R Pos: SP-31; RP-1   Ht: 6'3" Wt: 210 Born: 9/9/1983 Age: 24

Year	Team	Lg	G	GS	CG	GF	IP	BFP	H	R	ER	HR	SH	SF	HB	TBB	IBB	SO	WP	Bk	W	L	Pct	ShO	Sv-Op	Hld	ERC	ERA
			HOW MUCH HE PITCHED						WHAT HE GAVE UP												THE RESULTS							
2003	LAD	NL	4	3	0	0	22.0	91	17	6	6	2	1	1	1	11	1	19	3	0	2	1	.667	0	0-0	0	3.36	2.45
2004	LAD	NL	8	5	0	1	24.2	113	31	20	20	7	1	0	0	11	1	16	0	0	2	1	.667	0	0-0	0	7.21	7.30
2005	LAD	NL	7	6	0	0	28.2	134	31	22	20	2	0	2	1	17	0	13	2	1	2	2	.500	0	0-0	0	5.13	6.28
2006	TB	AL	23	1	0	7	36.1	174	42	27	22	2	2	2	1	25	0	27	3	1	0	0	-	0	0-0	0	5.86	5.45
2007	TB	AL	32	31	1	0	161.0	755	195	116	103	19	5	6	4	88	3	128	7	1	5	15	.250	1	0-0	0	6.11	5.76
5 ML YEARS			74	46	1	8	272.2	1267	316	191	171	32	9	11	7	152	5	203	15	3	11	19	.367	1	0-0	0	5.84	5.64

Mike Jacobs

Bats: L Throws: R Pos: 1B-108; PH-8   Ht: 6'3" Wt: 215 Born: 10/30/1980 Age: 27

Year	Team	Lg	G	AB	H	2B	3B	HR	(Hm	Rd)	TB	R	RBI	RC	TBB	IBB	SO	HBP	SH	SF	SB	CS	SB%	GDP	Avg	OBP	Slg
									BATTING												BASERUNNING				AVERAGES		
2007	Jupiter*	A+	3	12	2	0	0	1	(-	-)	5	2	3	1	1	0	2	0	0	0	0	0	-	0	.167	.231	.417
2007	Carlina*	AA	4	10	3	0	0	1	(-	-)	6	1	2	1	0	0	3	0	0	0	0	0	-	0	.300	.300	.600
2005	NYM	NL	30	100	31	7	0	11	(6	5)	71	19	23	21	10	0	22	1	0	1	0	0	-	5	.310	.375	.710
2006	Fla	NL	136	469	123	37	1	20	(12	8)	222	54	77	66	45	2	105	1	0	5	3	0	1.00	16	.262	.325	.473
2007	Fla	NL	114	426	113	27	2	17	(10	7)	195	57	54	51	31	3	101	2	0	1	1	2	.33	12	.265	.317	.458
3 ML YEARS			280	995	267	71	3	48	(28	20)	488	130	154	138	86	5	228	4	0	7	4	2	.67	33	.268	.327	.490

Chuck James

Pitches: L Bats: L Pos: SP-30   Ht: 6'0" Wt: 170 Born: 11/9/1981 Age: 26

Year	Team	Lg	G	GS	CG	GF	IP	BFP	H	R	ER	HR	SH	SF	HB	TBB	IBB	SO	WP	Bk	W	L	Pct	ShO	Sv-Op	Hld	ERC	ERA
			HOW MUCH HE PITCHED						WHAT HE GAVE UP												THE RESULTS							
2005	Atl	NL	2	0	0	0	5.2	23	4	1	1	0	0	0	0	3	0	5	1	0	0	0	-	0	0-0	0	2.41	1.59
2006	Atl	NL	25	18	0	0	119.0	504	101	54	50	20	8	7	6	47	2	91	2	0	11	4	.733	0	0-0	0	3.84	3.78
2007	Atl	NL	30	30	0	0	161.1	691	164	77	76	32	9	4	1	58	5	116	1	1	11	10	.524	0	0-0	0	4.69	4.24
3 ML YEARS			57	48	0	0	286.0	1218	269	132	127	52	17	11	7	108	7	212	4	1	22	14	.611	0	0-0	0	4.28	4.00

Casey Janssen

Pitches: R Bats: R Pos: RP-70   Ht: 6'4" Wt: 205 Born: 9/17/1981 Age: 26

Year	Team	Lg	G	GS	CG	GF	IP	BFP	H	R	ER	HR	SH	SF	HB	TBB	IBB	SO	WP	Bk	W	L	Pct	ShO	Sv-Op	Hld	ERC	ERA
			HOW MUCH HE PITCHED						WHAT HE GAVE UP												THE RESULTS							
2004	Auburn	A-	10	10	0	0	51.2	208	47	21	20	2	0	0	2	10	0	45	2	0	3	1	.750	0	0--	-	2.61	3.48
2005	Lansng	A	7	7	0	0	46.0	163	27	8	7	0	0	3	1	4	0	38	1	0	4	0	1.000	0	0--	-	0.95	1.37
2005	Dnedin	A+	10	10	0	0	59.2	228	46	16	15	2	1	1	2	12	0	51	1	0	6	1	.857	0	0--	-	1.98	2.26
2005	NHam	AA	9	9	0	0	43.0	177	49	26	14	3	1	0	2	4	0	47	2	0	3	3	.500	0	0--	-	3.69	2.93
2006	Syrcse	AAA	9	9	0	0	42.2	178	47	23	23	3	1	1	2	8	0	32	2	0	1	5	.167	0	0--	-	3.86	4.85
2006	Tor	AL	19	17	0	1	94.0	407	103	58	53	12	2	2	7	21	3	44	3	2	6	10	.375	0	0-0	0	4.32	5.07
2007	Tor	AL	70	0	0	21	72.2	297	67	22	19	4	0	3	3	20	2	39	4	0	2	3	.400	0	6-11	24	3.06	2.35
2 ML YEARS			89	17	0	22	166.2	704	170	80	72	16	2	5	10	41	5	83	7	2	8	13	.381	0	6-11	24	3.76	3.89

Geoff Jenkins

Bats: L **Throws:** R **Pos:** LF-121; PH-14   **Ht:** 6'1" **Wt:** 210 **Born:** 7/21/1974 **Age:** 33

Year	Team	Lg	G	AB	H	2B	3B	HR	(Hm	Rd)	TB	R	RBI	RC	TBB	IBB	SO	HBP	SH	SF	SB	CS	SB%	GDP	Avg	OBP	Slg
1998	Mil	NL	84	262	60	12	1	9	(4	5)	101	33	28	26	20	4	61	2	0	1	1	3	.25	7	.229	.288	.385
1999	Mil	NL	135	447	140	43	3	21	(10	11)	252	70	82	88	35	7	87	7	3	1	5	1	.83	10	.313	.371	.564
2000	Mil	NL	135	512	155	36	4	34	(15	19)	301	100	94	104	33	6	135	15	0	4	11	1	.92	9	.303	.360	.588
2001	Mil	NL	105	397	105	21	1	20	(11	9)	188	60	63	60	36	7	120	8	0	5	4	2	.67	11	.264	.334	.474
2002	Mil	NL	67	243	59	17	1	10	(4	6)	108	35	29	28	22	1	60	6	0	1	1	2	.33	8	.243	.320	.444
2003	Mil	NL	124	487	144	30	2	28	(16	12)	262	81	95	90	58	10	120	6	0	3	0	0	-	12	.296	.375	.538
2004	Mil	NL	157	617	163	36	6	27	(13	14)	292	88	93	76	46	10	152	12	0	6	3	1	.75	19	.264	.325	.473
2005	Mil	NL	148	538	157	42	1	25	(10	15)	276	87	86	87	56	9	138	19	0	5	0	0	-	9	.292	.375	.513
2006	Mil	NL	147	484	131	26	1	17	(8	9)	210	62	70	76	56	8	129	11	0	4	4	1	.80	9	.271	.357	.434
2007	Mil	NL	132	420	107	24	2	21	(11	10)	198	45	64	60	32	10	116	9	0	3	2	2	.50	9	.255	.319	.471
10 ML YEARS			1234	4407	1221	287	22	212	(102	110)	2188	661	704	695	394	72	1118	95	3	33	31	13	.70	107	.277	.347	.496

Bobby Jenks

Pitches: R **Bats:** R **Pos:** RP-66   **Ht:** 6'3" **Wt:** 275 **Born:** 3/14/1981 **Age:** 27

Year	Team	Lg	G	GS	CG	GF	IP	BFP	H	R	ER	HR	SH	SF	HB	TBB	IBB	SO	WP	Bk	W	L	Pct	ShO	Sv-Op	Hld	ERC	ERA
2005	CWS	AL	32	0	0	18	39.1	168	34	15	12	3	1	1	3	15	3	50	4	0	1	1	.500	0	6-8	3	3.02	2.75
2006	CWS	AL	67	0	0	58	69.2	300	66	32	31	5	4	2	2	31	10	80	3	0	3	4	.429	0	41-45	0	3.65	4.00
2007	CWS	AL	66	0	0	62	65.0	249	45	20	20	2	5	3	1	13	4	56	4	0	3	5	.375	0	40-46	0	1.49	2.77
3 ML YEARS			165	0	0	138	174.0	717	145	67	63	10	10	5	4	59	17	186	11	0	7	10	.412	0	87-99	3	2.62	3.26

Jason Jennings

Pitches: R **Bats:** L **Pos:** SP-18; RP-1   **Ht:** 6'2" **Wt:** 235 **Born:** 7/17/1978 **Age:** 29

Year	Team	Lg	G	GS	CG	GF	IP	BFP	H	R	ER	HR	SH	SF	HB	TBB	IBB	SO	WP	Bk	W	L	Pct	ShO	Sv-Op	Hld	ERC	ERA
2007	CpChr*	AA	1	1	0	0	5.0	17	3	0	0	0	0	0	0	1	0	2	0	0	0	0	-	0	0--	-	1.24	0.00
2007	RdRck*	AAA	1	1	0	0	3.1	18	3	4	4	0	0	1	0	5	0	2	0	0	0	0	-	0	0--	-	6.82	10.80
2001	Col	NL	7	7	1	0	39.1	174	42	21	20	2	1	1	1	19	0	26	1	0	4	1	.800	1	0-0	0	4.58	4.58
2002	Col	NL	32	32	0	0	185.1	808	201	102	93	26	9	3	8	70	2	127	10	0	16	8	.667	0	0-0	0	4.98	4.52
2003	Col	NL	32	32	1	0	181.1	820	212	115	103	20	11	6	5	88	7	119	7	0	12	13	.480	0	0-0	0	5.60	5.11
2004	Col	NL	33	33	0	0	201.0	925	241	125	123	27	9	3	7	101	14	133	6	1	11	12	.478	0	0-0	0	5.99	5.51
2005	Col	NL	20	20	1	0	122.0	551	130	73	68	11	6	3	5	62	4	75	8	0	6	9	.400	0	0-0	0	4.91	5.02
2006	Col	NL	32	32	3	0	212.0	902	206	94	89	17	8	6	3	85	7	142	10	0	9	13	.409	2	0-0	0	3.83	3.78
2007	Hou	NL	19	18	0	0	99.0	445	119	73	71	19	6	7	2	34	2	71	5	0	2	9	.182	0	0-0	0	5.72	6.45
7 ML YEARS			175	174	6	0	1040.0	4625	1151	603	567	122	50	29	31	459	36	693	47	1	60	65	.480	3	0-0	0	5.08	4.91

Derek Jeter

Bats: R **Throws:** R **Pos:** SS-156; PH-2   **Ht:** 6'3" **Wt:** 195 **Born:** 6/26/1974 **Age:** 34

Year	Team	Lg	G	AB	H	2B	3B	HR	(Hm	Rd)	TB	R	RBI	RC	TBB	IBB	SO	HBP	SH	SF	SB	CS	SB%	GDP	Avg	OBP	Slg
1995	NYY	AL	15	48	12	4	1	0	(0	0)	18	5	7	5	3	0	11	0	0	0	0	0	-	0	.250	.294	.375
1996	NYY	AL	157	582	183	25	6	10	(3	7)	250	104	78	92	48	1	102	9	6	9	14	7	.67	13	.314	.370	.430
1997	NYY	AL	159	654	190	31	7	10	(5	5)	265	116	70	99	74	0	125	10	8	2	23	12	.66	14	.291	.370	.405
1998	NYY	AL	149	626	203	25	8	19	(9	10)	301	127	84	115	57	1	119	5	3	3	30	6	.83	13	.324	.304	.481
1999	NYY	AL	158	627	219	37	9	24	(15	9)	346	134	102	146	91	5	116	12	3	6	19	8	.70	12	.349	.438	.552
2000	NYY	AL	148	593	201	31	4	15	(8	7)	285	119	73	118	68	4	99	12	3	3	22	4	.85	14	.339	.416	.481
2001	NYY	AL	150	614	191	35	3	21	(13	8)	295	110	74	112	56	7	99	10	5	1	27	3	.90	13	.311	.377	.480
2002	NYY	AL	157	644	191	26	0	18	(8	10)	271	124	75	108	73	2	114	7	3	3	32	3	.91	14	.297	.373	.421
2003	NYY	AL	119	482	156	25	3	10	(7	3)	217	87	52	86	43	2	88	13	1	5	11	5	.69	10	.324	.393	.450
2004	NYY	AL	154	643	188	44	1	23	(11	12)	303	111	78	100	46	1	99	14	16	2	23	4	.85	19	.292	.352	.471
2005	NYY	AL	159	654	202	25	5	19	(12	7)	294	122	70	105	77	3	117	11	7	3	14	5	.74	15	.309	.389	.450
2006	NYY	AL	154	623	214	39	3	14	(8	6)	301	118	97	132	69	4	102	12	7	4	34	5	.87	13	.343	.417	.483
2007	NYY	AL	156	639	206	39	4	12	(4	8)	289	102	73	112	56	3	100	14	3	2	15	8	.65	21	.322	.388	.452
13 ML YEARS			1835	7429	2356	386	54	195	(103	92)	3435	1379	933	1330	761	29	1291	129	67	39	264	70	.79	171	.317	.388	.462

D'Angelo Jimenez

Bats: B **Throws:** R **Pos:** PH-51; SS-11; 2B-10; 3B-1; PR-1   **Ht:** 6'0" **Wt:** 190 **Born:** 12/21/1977 **Age:** 30

Year	Team	Lg	G	AB	H	2B	3B	HR	(Hm	Rd)	TB	R	RBI	RC	TBB	IBB	SO	HBP	SH	SF	SB	CS	SB%	GDP	Avg	OBP	Slg
2007	Clmbs*	AAA	50	171	63	13	2	7	(-	-)	101	28	25	45	31	2	19	0	0	2	2	2	.50	3	.368	.461	.591
1999	NYY	AL	7	20	8	2	0	0	(0	0)	10	3	4	5	3	0	4	0	0	0	0	0	-	0	.400	.478	.500
2001	SD	NL	86	308	85	19	0	3	(2	1)	113	45	33	39	39	4	68	0	0	2	2	3	.40	9	.276	.355	.367
2002	2 Tms		114	429	108	15	7	4	(3	1)	149	61	44	54	50	1	73	1	0	2	6	3	.67	11	.252	.330	.347
2003	2 Tms		146	561	153	24	7	14	(6	8)	233	69	57	78	66	1	89	2	6	4	11	7	.61	7	.273	.349	.415
2004	Cin	NL	152	563	152	28	3	12	(6	6)	222	76	67	87	82	1	99	2	3	2	13	7	.65	15	.270	.364	.394
2005	Cin	NL	35	105	24	7	0	0	(0	0)	31	14	5	10	14	0	23	0	0	0	2	1	.67	1	.229	.319	.295
2006	2 Tms	AL	28	71	13	3	0	1	(0	1)	19	8	7	7	16	2	13	0	1	0	0	0	-	3	.183	.333	.268
2007	Was	NL	73	102	25	7	0	2	(2	0)	38	14	10	16	21	0	22	1	4	0	2	1	.67	3	.245	.379	.373
02	SD	NL	87	321	77	11	4	3	(2	1)	105	39	33	34	34	1	63	0	0	2	4	2	.67	10	.240	.311	.327
02	CWS	AL	27	108	31	4	3	1	(1	0)	44	22	11	20	16	0	10	1	0	0	2	1	.67	1	.287	.384	.407
03	CWS	AL	73	271	69	11	5	7	(3	4)	111	35	26	35	32	1	46	0	4	1	4	3	.57	3	.255	.332	.410

Year	Team	Lg	G	AB	H	2B	3B	HR	(Hm	Rd)	TB	R	RBI	RC	TBB	IBB	SO	HBP	SH	SF	SB	CS	SB%	GDP	Avg	OBP	Slg
									BATTING												BASERUNNING				AVERAGES		
03	Cin	NL	73	290	84	13	2	7	(3	4)	122	34	31	43	34	0	43	2	2	3	7	4	.64	4	.290	.365	.421
06	Tex	AL	20	57	12	3	0	1	(0	1)	18	7	8	7	10	0	6	0	1	0	0	0	-	2	.211	.328	.316
06	Oak	AL	8	14	1	0	0	0	(0	0)	1	1	0	0	6	2	7	0	0	0	0	0	-	1	.071	.350	.071
	8 ML YEARS		641	2159	568	105	17	36	(19	17)	815	290	228	296	291	9	391	6	14	10	36	22	.62	49	.263	.351	.377

Kelvin Jimenez

Pitches: R Bats: R Pos: RP-34   **Ht: 6'2" Wt: 195 Born: 10/27/1980 Age: 27**

Year	Team	Lg	G	GS	CG	GF	IP	BFP	H	R	ER	HR	SH	SF	HB	TBB	IBB	SO	WP	Bk	W	L	Pct	ShO	Sv-Op	Hld	ERC	ERA
			HOW MUCH HE PITCHED						WHAT HE GAVE UP												THE RESULTS							
2001	Pulaski	R+	4	4	0	0	14.1	73	24	14	10	2	0	1	4	4	0	10	1	0	0	3	.000	0	0--	-	8.04	6.28
2001	Rngrs	R	9	6	1	1	45.2	183	36	19	13	2	1	3	2	9	0	51	2	0	3	3	.500	1	1--	-	2.03	2.56
2002	Savann	A	29	16	0	8	121.0	524	122	63	43	9	7	1	7	37	2	116	4	0	5	10	.333	0	0--	-	3.72	3.20
2003	Stcktn	A+	34	18	0	4	131.1	565	135	81	69	14	2	3	9	43	1	101	11	2	6	5	.545	0	2--	-	4.28	4.73
2004	Frisco	AA	26	21	0	0	129.0	584	135	76	65	13	6	6	7	67	1	101	12	1	3	5	.375	0	0--	-	5.02	4.53
2005	Frisco	AA	6	0	0	3	13.0	60	12	5	5	0	1	1	2	6	0	12	2	0	0	0	-	0	2--	-	3.57	3.46
2005	Okla	AAA	37	5	0	11	79.1	345	79	40	32	6	3	3	4	33	3	64	4	1	4	6	.400	0	3--	-	4.09	3.63
2006	Okla	AAA	26	0	0	4	38.0	179	40	22	22	4	1	2	1	24	1	40	6	0	4	2	.667	0	1--	-	5.28	5.21
2007	Memp	AAA	30	0	0	8	39.2	174	46	16	12	2	1	2	1	11	4	34	2	1	2	3	.400	0	1--	-	4.03	2.72
2007	StL	NL	34	0	0	15	42.0	198	56	36	35	2	1	1	4	17	1	24	0	0	3	0	1.000	0	0-0	1	5.99	7.50

Ubaldo Jimenez

Pitches: R Bats: R Pos: SP-15   **Ht: 6'4" Wt: 200 Born: 1/22/1984 Age: 24**

Year	Team	Lg	G	GS	CG	GF	IP	BFP	H	R	ER	HR	SH	SF	HB	TBB	IBB	SO	WP	Bk	W	L	Pct	ShO	Sv-Op	Hld	ERC	ERA
			HOW MUCH HE PITCHED						WHAT HE GAVE UP												THE RESULTS							
2002	Casper	R+	14	14	0	0	62.0	288	72	46	45	6	1	3	5	29	1	65	2	3	3	5	.375	0	0--	-	5.51	6.53
2003	Ashvll	A	27	27	0	0	153.2	646	129	67	59	11	2	1	14	67	0	138	9	0	10	6	.625	0	0--	-	3.56	3.46
2003	Visalia	A+	1	0	0	1	5.0	18	3	0	0	0	0	0	0	1	0	7	0	0	1	0	1.000	0	0--	-	1.17	0.00
2004	Visalia	A+	9	9	1	0	44.1	176	29	15	11	2	1	2	3	12	0	61	1	0	4	1	.800	0	0--	-	1.65	2.23
2005	Mdest	A+	14	14	0	0	72.1	319	61	35	32	5	0	1	5	40	1	78	4	0	5	3	.625	0	0--	-	3.78	3.98
2005	Tulsa	AA	12	11	0	0	63.0	279	58	40	38	12	0	5	4	31	0	53	7	0	2	5	.286	0	0--	-	4.85	5.43
2006	Tulsa	AA	13	13	1	0	73.1	299	49	21	20	2	2	1	4	40	1	86	3	1	9	2	.818	1	0--	-	2.63	2.45
2006	ColSpr	AAA	13	13	0	0	78.1	349	74	49	44	7	1	3	7	43	1	64	10	1	5	2	.714	0	0--	-	4.63	5.06
2007	ColSpr	AAA	19	19	1	0	103.0	467	110	74	67	9	4	4	3	62	0	89	11	0	8	5	.615	0	0--	-	5.37	5.85
2006	Col	NL	2	1	0	0	7.2	30	5	4	3	1	0	0	0	3	0	3	0	0	0	0	-	0	0-0	-	2.48	3.52
2007	Col	NL	15	15	0	0	82.0	354	70	46	39	10	3	1	6	37	4	68	3	0	4	4	.500	0	0-0	0	3.80	4.28
	2 ML YEARS		17	16	0	0	89.2	384	75	50	42	11	3	1	6	40	4	71	3	0	4	4	.500	0	0-0	0	3.68	4.22

Charlton Jimerson

Bats: R Throws: R Pos: PR-7; RF-2; DH-2; CF-1; PH-1   **Ht: 6'3" Wt: 210 Born: 9/22/1979 Age: 28**

Year	Team	Lg	G	AB	H	2B	3B	HR	(Hm	Rd)	TB	R	RBI	RC	TBB	IBB	SO	HBP	SH	SF	SB	CS	SB%	GDP	Avg	OBP	Slg
									BATTING												BASERUNNING				AVERAGES		
2007	WTenn*	AA	82	322	89	18	3	23	(-	-)	182	54	74	64	29	2	117	6	3	1	30	9	.77	4	.276	.346	.565
2007	Tacom*	AAA	17	65	20	4	1	2	(-	-)	32	7	7	11	5	0	22	0	1	0	5	1	.83	0	.308	.357	.492
2005	Hou	NL	1	0	0	0	0	0	(0	0)	0	0	0	0	0	0	0	0	0	0	0	0	-	0	-	-	-
2006	Hou	NL	17	6	2	0	0	1	(0	1)	5	2	1	1	0	0	3	0	0	0	2	0	1.00	0	.333	.333	.833
2007	Sea	AL	11	2	2	0	0	1	(1	0)	5	5	1	2	0	0	0	0	0	0	2	0	1.00	0	1.000	1.000	2.500
	3 ML YEARS		29	8	4	0	0	2	(1	1)	10	7	2	3	0	0	3	0	0	0	4	0	1.00	0	.500	.500	1.250

Kenji Johjima

Bats: R Throws: R Pos: C-133; PH-4   **Ht: 6'0" Wt: 198 Born: 6/8/1976 Age: 32**

Year	Team	Lg	G	AB	H	2B	3B	HR	(Hm	Rd)	TB	R	RBI	RC	TBB	IBB	SO	HBP	SH	SF	SB	CS	SB%	GDP	Avg	OBP	Slg
									BATTING												BASERUNNING				AVERAGES		
1995	Fk Dai	Jap	12	12	2	0	0	0	(-	-)	2	2	1	0	1	-	4	0	0	0	0	0	-	0	.167	.231	.167
1996	Fk Dai	Jap	17	58	14	2	0	4	(-	-)	28	5	9	8	3	-	9	1	0	0	1	0	1.00	1	.241	.290	.483
1997	Fk Dai	Jap	120	432	133	24	2	15	(-	-)	206	49	68	72	22	-	62	5	4	7	6	2	.75	15	.308	.343	.477
1998	Fk Dai	Jap	122	395	99	19	0	16	(-	-)	166	53	58	54	27	-	67	8	6	4	5	2	.71	18	.251	.309	.420
1999	Fk Dai	Jap	135	493	151	33	1	17	(-	-)	237	65	77	85	31	-	61	8	6	1	6	2	.75	13	.306	.356	.481
2000	Fk Dai	Jap	84	303	94	22	2	9	(-	-)	147	38	50	57	27	-	48	6	5	1	10	2	.83	13	.310	.377	.485
2001	Fk Dai	Jap	140	534	138	18	0	31	(-	-)	249	63	95	78	31	-	55	6	5	2	9	4	.69	17	.258	.305	.466
2002	Fk Dai	Jap	115	416	122	18	0	25	(-	-)	215	60	74	75	30	5	41	8	3	6	8	7	.53	11	.293	.348	.517
2003	Fk Dai	Jap	140	551	182	39	2	34	(-	-)	327	101	119	128	53	10	50	15	2	7	9	4	.69	22	.330	.399	.593
2004	Fk Dai	Jap	116	426	144	25	1	36	(-	-)	279	91	91	113	49	5	45	22	0	1	6	5	.55	16	.338	.432	.655
2005	Fk Dai	Jap	116	411	127	22	4	24	(-	-)	229	70	57	86	33	4	32	17	0	3	3	4	.43	19	.309	.381	.557
2006	Sea	AL	144	506	147	25	1	18	(6	12)	228	61	76	79	20	1	46	13	0	3	3	1	.75	15	.291	.332	.451
2007	Sea	AL	135	485	139	29	0	14	(8	6)	210	52	61	55	15	0	41	11	0	2	0	2	.00	22	.287	.322	.433
	2 ML YEARS		279	991	286	54	1	32	(14	18)	438	113	137	134	35	1	87	24	0	5	3	3	.50	37	.289	.327	.442

Ben Johnson

Bats: R Throws: R Pos: LF-5; RF-4   **Ht: 6'1" Wt: 220 Born: 6/18/1981 Age: 27**

Year	Team	Lg	G	AB	H	2B	3B	HR	(Hm	Rd)	TB	R	RBI	RC	TBB	IBB	SO	HBP	SH	SF	SB	CS	SB%	GDP	Avg	OBP	Slg
									BATTING												BASERUNNING				AVERAGES		
2007	NewOr*	AAA	53	188	51	10	0	2	(-	-)	67	26	12	27	25	0	36	3	1	1	3	1	.75	6	.271	.364	.356

140

Year	Team	Lg	G	AB	H	2B	3B	HR	(Hm	Rd)	TB	R	RBI	RC	TBB	IBB	SO	HBP	SH	SF	SB	CS	SB%	GDP	Avg	OBP	Slg
2005	SD	NL	31	75	16	8	1	3	(1	2)	35	10	13	8	11	1	23	0	1	1	0	2	.00	4	.213	.310	.467
2006	SD	NL	58	120	30	5	2	4	(4	0)	51	19	12	10	14	2	36	1	0	0	3	0	1.00	3	.250	.333	.425
2007	NYM	NL	9	27	5	1	0	0	(0	0)	6	2	1	0	2	0	11	0	0	1	0	0	-	0	.185	.233	.222
3 ML YEARS			98	222	51	14	3	7	(5	2)	92	31	26	18	27	3	70	1	1	2	3	2	.60	7	.230	.313	.414

Dan Johnson

Bats: L Throws: R Pos: 1B-97; DH-17; PH-3 Ht: 6'2" Wt: 226 Born: 8/10/1979 Age: 28

Year	Team	Lg	G	AB	H	2B	3B	HR	(Hm	Rd)	TB	R	RBI	RC	TBB	IBB	SO	HBP	SH	SF	SB	CS	SB%	GDP	Avg	OBP	Slg
2007	Scrmto*	AAA	2	5	3	0	0	1	(-	-)	6	1	3	3	3	0	0	0	0	0	0	0	-	0	.600	.750	1.200
2005	Oak	AL	109	375	103	21	0	15	(2	13)	169	54	58	56	50	1	52	1	0	8	0	1	.00	11	.275	.355	.451
2006	Oak	AL	91	286	67	13	1	9	(4	5)	109	30	37	33	40	2	45	0	0	5	0	0	-	6	.234	.323	.381
2007	Oak	AL	117	416	98	20	1	18	(9	9)	174	53	62	58	72	4	77	3	0	4	0	0	-	12	.236	.349	.418
3 ML YEARS			317	1077	268	54	2	42	(15	27)	452	137	157	147	162	7	174	4	0	17	0	1	.00	29	.249	.344	.420

Jim Johnson

Pitches: R Bats: R Pos: RP-1 Ht: 6'5" Wt: 245 Born: 6/27/1983 Age: 25

			HOW MUCH HE PITCHED						WHAT HE GAVE UP											THE RESULTS							
Year	Team	Lg	G	GS	CG	GF	IP	BFP	H	R	ER	HR	SH	SF	HB	TBB	IBB	SO	WP	Bk	W	L	Pct	ShO	Sv-Op	Hld	ERC	ERA
2001	Orioles	R	7	4	0	0	18.2	81	17	10	8	3	1	0	2	7	1	19	1	0	0	1	.000	0	0--	-	4.21	3.86
2002	Bluefld	R+	11	9	0	0	55.2	231	52	36	27	5	2	2	3	16	2	36	1	1	4	2	.667	0	0--	-	3.41	4.37
2003	Bluefld	R+	11	11	0	0	51.1	237	62	24	21	2	0	2	4	18	0	46	4	1	3	2	.600	0	0--	-	4.81	3.68
2004	Dlmrva	A	20	17	0	1	106.2	443	97	44	39	9	5	5	9	30	1	93	6	0	8	7	.533	0	0--	-	3.37	3.29
2004	Frdrck	A+	1	1	0	0	3.0	15	6	4	3	0	2	0	1	6	1	10	1	0	0	0	-	0	0--	-	9.61	9.00
2005	Frdrck	A+	28	27	2	1	159.2	685	139	77	62	11	4	1	19	64	2	168	5	1	12	9	.571	0	1--	-	3.60	3.49
2005	Bowie	AA	1	1	0	0	7.0	25	3	0	0	0	1	0	1	2	0	6	0	0	0	0	-	0	0--	-	1.16	0.00
2006	Bowie	AA	27	26	0	0	156.0	690	165	80	77	13	4	3	11	57	1	124	6	0	13	6	.684	0	0--	-	4.38	4.44
2007	Norfolk	AAA	26	25	2	0	148.0	657	164	79	67	15	5	2	12	48	2	109	6	0	6	12	.333	0	0--	-	4.67	4.07
2006	Bal	AL	1	1	0	0	3.0	21	9	8	8	1	0	1	1	3	0	0	0	0	0	1	.000	0	0-0	0	26.81	24.00
2007	Bal	AL	1	0	0	1	2.0	11	3	2	2	0	0	1	0	2	0	1	0	0	0	0	-	0	0-0	0	8.58	9.00
2 ML YEARS			2	1	0	1	5.0	32	12	10	10	1	0	2	1	5	0	1	0	0	0	1	.000	0	0-0	0	18.89	18.00

Josh Johnson

Pitches: R Bats: L Pos: SP-4 Ht: 6'7" Wt: 230 Born: 1/31/1984 Age: 24

			HOW MUCH HE PITCHED						WHAT HE GAVE UP											THE RESULTS							
Year	Team	Lg	G	GS	CG	GF	IP	BFP	H	R	ER	HR	SH	SF	HB	TBB	IBB	SO	WP	Bk	W	L	Pct	ShO	Sv-Op	Hld	ERC	ERA
2007	Jupiter*	A+	3	3	0	0	11.1	41	9	2	1	0	0	0	0	0	0	13	1	0	0	0	-	0	0--	-	1.31	0.79
2007	Carlina*	AA	2	2	0	0	10.1	44	8	2	2	0	2	0	0	5	0	9	0	0	0	0	-	0	0--	-	2.46	1.74
2005	Fla	NL	4	1	0	0	12.1	55	11	5	5	0	1	0	1	10	0	10	0	0	0	0	-	0	0-0	0	4.82	3.65
2006	Fla	NL	31	24	0	1	157.0	659	136	63	54	14	11	0	4	68	6	133	3	1	12	7	.632	0	0-1	0	3.48	3.10
2007	Fla	NL	4	4	0	0	15.2	82	26	17	13	1	2	1	0	12	3	14	1	0	0	3	.000	0	0-0	0	9.16	7.47
3 ML YEARS			39	29	0	1	185.0	796	173	85	72	15	14	1	5	90	9	157	4	1	12	10	.545	0	0-1	0	3.99	3.50

Kelly Johnson

Bats: L Throws: R Pos: 2B-133; PH-16; PR-1 Ht: 6'1" Wt: 205 Born: 2/22/1982 Age: 26

Year	Team	Lg	G	AB	H	2B	3B	HR	(Hm	Rd)	TB	R	RBI	RC	TBB	IBB	SO	HBP	SH	SF	SB	CS	SB%	GDP	Avg	OBP	Slg
2000	Braves	R	53	193	52	12	3	4	(-	-)	82	27	29	30	24	0	45	0	1	1	6	1	.86	4	.269	.349	.425
2001	Macon	A	124	415	120	22	1	23	(-	-)	213	75	66	91	71	7	111	10	1	1	25	6	.81	4	.289	.404	.513
2002	MrtlBh	A+	126	482	123	21	5	12	(-	-)	190	62	49	62	51	0	105	1	2	4	12	15	.44	5	.255	.325	.394
2003	Braves	R	6	26	10	1	1	1	(-	-)	16	10	3	6	3	1	4	1	0	0	1	1	.50	2	.385	.467	.615
2003	Grnville	AA	98	334	92	22	5	6	(-	-)	142	46	45	51	35	3	81	0	3	5	10	3	.77	4	.275	.340	.425
2004	Grnville	AA	135	479	135	35	3	16	(-	-)	224	70	50	78	49	2	102	3	0	3	9	9	.50	5	.282	.350	.468
2005	Rchmd	AAA	44	155	48	12	3	8	(-	-)	90	35	22	40	34	7	22	2	0	1	7	1	.88	3	.310	.438	.581
2006	Rome	A	5	19	9	2	1	1	(-	-)	16	5	3	7	4	0	3	1	0	0	2	2	.50	0	.474	.583	.842
2006	Rchmd	AAA	10	39	13	4	0	1	(-	-)	20	3	7	9	6	1	6	1	0	1	1	0	1.00	0	.333	.426	.513
2005	Atl	NL	87	290	70	12	3	9	(2	7)	115	46	40	41	40	1	75	1	2	1	2	1	.67	11	.241	.334	.397
2007	Atl	NL	147	521	144	26	10	16	(5	11)	238	91	68	87	79	3	117	4	2	2	9	5	.64	8	.276	.375	.457
2 ML YEARS			234	811	214	38	13	25	(7	18)	353	137	108	128	119	4	192	5	4	3	11	6	.65	19	.264	.360	.435

Nick Johnson

Bats: L Throws: L Pos: 1B Ht: 6'3" Wt: 225 Born: 9/19/1978 Age: 29

Year	Team	Lg	G	AB	H	2B	3B	HR	(Hm	Rd)	TB	R	RBI	RC	TBB	IBB	SO	HBP	SH	SF	SB	CS	SB%	GDP	Avg	OBP	Slg
2001	NYY	AL	23	67	13	2	0	2	(1	1)	21	6	8	6	7	0	15	4	0	0	0	0	-	3	.194	.308	.313
2002	NYY	AL	129	378	92	15	0	15	(7	8)	152	56	58	59	48	5	98	12	3	0	1	3	.25	11	.243	.347	.402
2003	NYY	AL	96	324	92	19	0	14	(8	6)	153	60	47	65	70	4	57	8	3	1	5	2	.71	9	.284	.422	.472
2004	Mon	NL	73	251	63	16	0	7	(4	3)	100	35	33	36	40	2	58	3	0	1	6	3	.67	5	.251	.359	.398
2005	Was	NL	131	453	131	35	3	15	(7	8)	217	66	74	83	80	8	87	12	0	2	3	8	.27	15	.289	.408	.479
2006	Was	NL	147	500	145	46	0	23	(10	13)	260	100	77	104	110	15	99	13	2	3	10	3	.77	12	.290	.428	.520
6 ML YEARS			599	1973	536	133	3	76	(37	39)	903	323	297	353	355	34	414	52	8	7	25	19	.57	55	.272	.395	.458

Randy Johnson

Pitches: L **Bats:** R **Pos:** SP-10   **Ht:** 6'10" **Wt:** 230 **Born:** 9/10/1963 **Age:** 44

Year	Team	Lg	G	GS	CG	GF	IP	BFP	H	R	ER	HR	SH	SF	HB	TBB	IBB	SO	WP	Bk	W	L	Pct	ShO	Sv-Op	Hld	ERC	ERA
2007	Visal*	A+	1	1	0	0	6.0	22	4	2	2	0	0	0	0	0	0	4	0	0	0	0	—	0	0--	-	0.91	3.00
2007	Tuc*	AAA	2	2	0	0	12.0	49	14	5	4	1	0	1	0	2	0	10	1	0	1	0	1.000	0	0--	-	4.14	3.00
1988	Mon	NL	4	4	1	0	26.0	109	23	8	7	3	0	0	0	7	0	25	3	0	3	0	1.000	0	0-0	0	2.96	2.42
1989	2 Tms		29	28	2	1	160.2	715	147	100	86	13	10	13	3	96	2	130	7	7	7	13	.350	0	0-0	0	4.26	4.82
1990	Sea	AL	33	33	5	0	219.2	944	174	103	89	26	7	6	5	120	2	194	4	2	14	11	.560	2	0-0	0	3.68	3.65
1991	Sea	AL	33	33	2	0	201.1	889	151	96	89	15	9	8	12	152	0	228	12	2	13	10	.565	1	0-0	0	4.15	3.98
1992	Sea	AL	31	31	6	0	210.1	922	154	104	88	13	3	8	18	144	1	241	13	1	12	14	.462	2	0-0	0	3.75	3.77
1993	Sea	AL	35	34	10	1	255.1	1043	185	97	92	22	8	7	16	99	1	308	8	2	19	8	.704	3	1-1	0	2.73	3.24
1994	Sea	AL	23	23	9	0	172.0	694	132	65	61	14	3	1	6	72	2	204	5	0	13	6	.684	4	0-0	0	2.99	3.19
1995	Sea	AL	30	30	6	0	214.1	866	159	65	59	12	2	1	6	65	1	294	5	2	18	2	.900	3	0-0	0	2.18	2.48
1996	Sea	AL	14	8	0	2	61.1	256	48	27	25	8	1	0	2	25	0	85	1	5	5	0	1.000	0	1-2	0	3.24	3.67
1997	Sea	AL	30	29	5	0	213.0	850	147	60	54	20	4	1	10	77	2	291	4	0	20	4	.833	2	0-0	0	2.47	2.28
1998	2 Tms		34	34	10	0	244.1	1014	203	102	89	23	5	2	14	86	1	329	7	2	19	11	.633	6	0-0	0	3.16	3.28
1999	Ari	NL	35	35	12	0	271.2	1079	207	86	75	30	4	3	9	70	3	364	4	2	17	9	.654	2	0-0	0	2.49	2.48
2000	Ari	NL	35	35	8	0	248.2	1001	202	89	73	23	14	5	6	76	1	347	5	2	19	7	.731	3	0-0	0	2.80	2.64
2001	Ari	NL	35	34	3	1	249.2	994	181	74	69	19	10	5	18	71	2	372	8	1	21	6	.778	2	0-0	0	2.35	2.49
2002	Ari	NL	35	35	8	0	260.0	1035	197	78	67	26	4	2	13	71	1	334	3	2	24	5	.828	4	0-0	0	2.54	2.32
2003	Ari	NL	18	18	1	0	114.0	489	125	61	54	16	4	3	8	27	3	125	1	1	6	8	.429	1	0-0	0	4.52	4.26
2004	Ari	NL	35	35	4	0	245.2	964	177	88	71	18	7	5	10	44	1	290	3	1	16	14	.533	2	0-0	0	1.82	2.60
2005	NYY	AL	34	34	4	0	225.2	920	207	102	95	32	5	5	12	47	2	211	3	1	17	8	.680	0	0-0	0	3.38	3.79
2006	NYY	AL	33	33	2	0	205.0	860	194	125	114	28	6	7	10	60	1	172	3	2	17	11	.607	0	0-0	0	3.80	5.00
2007	Ari	NL	10	10	0	0	56.2	233	52	26	24	7	4	0	4	13	3	72	1	0	4	3	.571	0	0-0	0	3.34	3.81
89	Mon	NL	7	6	0	1	29.2	143	29	25	22	2	3	4	0	26	1	26	2	2	0	4	.000	0	0-0	0	5.42	6.67
89	Sea	AL	22	22	2	0	131.0	572	118	75	64	11	7	9	3	70	1	104	5	5	7	9	.438	0	0-0	0	4.01	4.40
98	Sea	AL	23	23	6	0	160.0	685	146	90	77	19	5	1	11	60	0	213	7	2	9	10	.474	2	0-0	0	3.88	4.33
98	Hou	NL	11	11	4	0	84.1	329	57	12	12	4	0	1	3	26	1	116	0	0	10	1	.909	4	0-0	0	1.93	1.28
20 ML YEARS			566	556	98	5	3855.1	15877	3065	1556	1381	368	110	82	182	1422	29	4616	102	31	284	150	.654	37	2-3	0	3.01	3.22

Reed Johnson

Bats: R **Throws:** R **Pos:** LF-70; RF-8; PH-3; CF-1; DH-1; PR-1   **Ht:** 5'10" **Wt:** 180 **Born:** 12/8/1976 **Age:** 31

Year	Team	Lg	G	AB	H	2B	3B	HR	(Hm	Rd)	TB	R	RBI	RC	TBB	IBB	SO	HBP	SH	SF	SB	CS	SB%	GDP	Avg	OBP	Slg
2007	Dnedin*	A+	4	12	4	1	0	1	(-	-)	8	1	1	3	2	0	4	0	0	0	0	0	-	0	.333	.429	.667
2007	Syrcse*	AAA	2	8	3	0	0	0	(-	-)	3	1	1	1	0	0	1	1	0	0	0	0	-	0	.375	.444	.375
2003	Tor	AL	114	412	121	21	2	10	(6	4)	176	79	52	64	20	1	67	20	1	4	5	3	.63	10	.294	.353	.427
2004	Tor	AL	141	537	145	25	2	10	(8	2)	204	68	61	65	28	2	98	12	3	2	6	3	.67	17	.270	.320	.380
2005	Tor	AL	142	398	107	21	6	8	(4	4)	164	55	58	57	22	1	82	16	2	1	5	6	.45	8	.269	.332	.412
2006	Tor	AL	134	461	147	34	2	12	(4	8)	221	86	49	76	33	4	81	21	1	1	8	2	.80	9	.319	.390	.479
2007	Tor	AL	79	275	65	13	2	2	(1	1)	88	31	14	24	16	0	56	11	5	0	4	2	.67	7	.236	.305	.320
5 ML YEARS			610	2083	585	114	14	42	(23	19)	853	319	234	286	119	8	384	80	12	8	28	16	.64	51	.281	.342	.410

Rob Johnson

Bats: R **Throws:** R **Pos:** C-4; PR-2   **Ht:** 6'1" **Wt:** 200 **Born:** 7/22/1983 **Age:** 24

Year	Team	Lg	G	AB	H	2B	3B	HR	(Hm	Rd)	TB	R	RBI	RC	TBB	IBB	SO	HBP	SH	SF	SB	CS	SB%	GDP	Avg	OBP	Slg
2004	Everett	A-	20	77	18	3	1	1	(-	-)	26	17	7	8	4	0	10	2	0	1	6	2	.75	1	.234	.286	.338
2004	Ms	R	8	27	6	1	0	0	(-	-)	7	4	1	2	3	0	7	1	0	0	1	1	.50	1	.222	.323	.259
2005	Wisc	A	77	305	83	19	1	9	(-	-)	131	41	51	44	20	0	31	3	3	4	10	3	.77	8	.272	.319	.430
2005	InldEm	A+	19	70	22	3	0	2	(-	-)	31	15	12	13	10	0	14	0	2	4	2	0	1.00	1	.314	.381	.443
2006	Tacom	AAA	97	337	78	9	4	4	(-	-)	107	28	33	27	13	1	74	1	6	2	14	7	.67	9	.231	.261	.318
2007	Tacom	AAA	112	422	113	26	0	6	(-	-)	157	57	40	53	39	2	62	1	3	0	7	7	.50	11	.268	.331	.372
2007	Sea	AL	6	3	1	0	0	0	(0	0)	1	1	0	0	0	0	0	0	0	0	1	0	1.00	0	.333	.333	.333

Tyler Johnson

Pitches: L **Bats:** B **Pos:** RP-55   **Ht:** 6'2" **Wt:** 205 **Born:** 6/7/1981 **Age:** 27

Year	Team	Lg	G	GS	CG	GF	IP	BFP	H	R	ER	HR	SH	SF	HB	TBB	IBB	SO	WP	Bk	W	L	Pct	ShO	Sv-Op	Hld	ERC	ERA
2007	Memp*	AAA	1	0	0	0	1.0	3	0	0	0	0	0	0	0	0	0	1	0	0	0	0	—	0	0--	-	0.00	0.00
2007	Sprgfld*	AA	3	1	0	0	3.0	12	2	1	1	0	0	0	0	2	0	3	0	0	0	0	—	0	0--	-	2.79	3.00
2005	StL	NL	5	0	0	1	2.2	13	3	0	0	0	0	0	0	3	0	4	0	0	0	0	—	0	0-1	1	7.28	0.00
2006	StL	NL	56	0	0	12	36.1	164	33	21	20	5	1	1	4	23	2	37	2	0	2	4	.333	0	0-2	11	5.16	4.95
2007	StL	NL	55	0	0	6	38.0	164	31	18	17	4	1	1	3	16	2	24	2	0	1	1	.500	0	0-1	5	3.33	4.03
3 ML YEARS			116	0	0	19	77.0	341	67	39	37	9	2	2	7	42	4	65	4	0	3	5	.375	0	0-4	17	4.29	4.32

Adam Jones

Bats: R **Throws:** R **Pos:** LF-26; CF-7; PR-7; RF-6; PH-4   **Ht:** 6'2" **Wt:** 200 **Born:** 8/1/1985 **Age:** 22

Year	Team	Lg	G	AB	H	2B	3B	HR	(Hm	Rd)	TB	R	RBI	RC	TBB	IBB	SO	HBP	SH	SF	SB	CS	SB%	GDP	Avg	OBP	Slg
2003	Ms	R	28	109	31	5	1	0	(-	-)	38	18	8	16	5	0	19	10	3	1	5	1	.83	1	.284	.368	.349
2003	Everett	A-	3	13	6	1	0	0	(-	-)	7	2	4	3	1	0	3	0	0	1	0	0	-	1	.462	.467	.538
2004	Wisc	A	130	510	136	23	7	11	(-	-)	206	76	72	67	33	0	124	5	4	7	8	4	.67	13	.267	.314	.404
2005	InldEm	A+	68	271	80	20	5	8	(-	-)	134	43	46	50	29	0	64	8	2	5	4	5	.44	4	.295	.374	.494
2005	SnAnt	AA	63	228	68	10	3	7	(-	-)	105	33	20	39	22	1	48	3	2	2	9	4	.69	4	.298	.365	.461
2006	Tacom	AAA	96	380	109	19	4	16	(-	-)	184	69	62	65	28	1	78	6	1	1	13	4	.76	12	.287	.345	.484

BATTING														BASERUNNING				AVERAGES		
Year Team	Lg	G	AB	H	2B	3B	HR	(Hm Rd)	TB	R	RBI	RC	TBB	IBB	SO	HBP	SH	SF	SB	CS	SB%	GDP	Avg	OBP	Slg
2007 Tacom	AAA	101	420	132	27	6	25	(- -)	246	75	84	90	36	1	106	11	0	2	8	7	.53	7	.314	.382	.586
2006 Sea	AL	32	74	16	4	0	1	(0 1)	23	6	8	4	2	0	22	0	0	0	3	1	.75	3	.216	.237	.311
2007 Sea	AL	41	65	16	2	1	2	(1 1)	26	16	4	5	4	0	21	1	1	0	2	1	.67	0	.246	.300	.400
2 ML YEARS		73	139	32	6	1	3	(1 2)	49	22	12	9	6	0	43	1	1	0	5	2	.71	3	.230	.267	.353

Andruw Jones

Bats: R **Throws:** R **Pos:** CF-154   **Ht:** 6'1" **Wt:** 210 **Born:** 4/23/1977 **Age:** 31

BATTING														BASERUNNING				AVERAGES		
Year Team	Lg	G	AB	H	2B	3B	HR	(Hm Rd)	TB	R	RBI	RC	TBB	IBB	SO	HBP	SH	SF	SB	CS	SB%	GDP	Avg	OBP	Slg
1996 Atl	NL	31	106	23	7	1	5	(3 2)	47	11	13	13	7	0	29	0	0	0	3	0	1.00	1	.217	.265	.443
1997 Atl	NL	153	399	92	18	1	18	(5 13)	166	60	70	54	56	2	107	4	5	3	20	11	.65	11	.231	.329	.416
1998 Atl	NL	159	582	158	33	8	31	(16 15)	300	89	90	97	40	8	129	4	1	4	27	4	.87	10	.271	.321	.515
1999 Atl	NL	162	592	163	35	5	26	(10 16)	286	97	84	103	76	11	103	9	0	2	24	12	.67	12	.275	.365	.483
2000 Atl	NL	161	656	199	36	6	36	(15 21)	355	122	104	127	59	0	100	9	0	5	21	6	.78	12	.303	.366	.541
2001 Atl	NL	161	625	157	25	2	34	(16 18)	288	104	104	90	56	3	142	9	0	9	11	4	.73	10	.251	.312	.461
2002 Atl	NL	154	560	148	34	0	35	(18 17)	287	91	94	94	83	4	135	10	0	6	8	3	.73	14	.264	.366	.513
2003 Atl	NL	156	595	165	28	2	36	(16 20)	305	101	116	92	53	2	125	5	0	6	4	3	.57	18	.277	.338	.513
2004 Atl	NL	154	570	149	34	4	29	(13 16)	278	85	91	75	71	9	147	3	0	2	6	6	.50	24	.261	.345	.488
2005 Atl	NL	160	586	154	24	3	51	(21 30)	337	95	128	91	64	13	112	15	0	7	5	3	.63	19	.263	.347	.575
2006 Atl	NL	156	565	148	29	0	41	(19 22)	300	107	129	108	82	9	127	13	0	9	4	1	.80	13	.262	.363	.531
2007 Atl	NL	154	572	127	27	2	26	(16 10)	236	83	94	71	70	4	138	8	0	9	5	2	.71	16	.222	.311	.413
12 ML YEARS		1761	6408	1683	330	34	368	(168 200)	3185	1045	1117	1015	717	65	1394	83	6	62	138	55	.72	160	.263	.342	.497

Brandon Jones

Bats: L **Throws:** R **Pos:** LF-5   **Ht:** 6'2" **Wt:** 195 **Born:** 12/10/1983 **Age:** 24

BATTING														BASERUNNING				AVERAGES		
Year Team	Lg	G	AB	H	2B	3B	HR	(Hm Rd)	TB	R	RBI	RC	TBB	IBB	SO	HBP	SH	SF	SB	CS	SB%	GDP	Avg	OBP	Slg
2004 Danvle	R	57	209	62	6	5	3	(- -)	87	35	33	33	23	0	33	1	0	2	4	2	.67	5	.297	.366	.416
2005 Braves	R	2	8	1	0	0	0	(- -)	1	0	2	0	0	0	2	0	0	0	0	1	.00	0	.125	.125	.125
2005 Danvle	R	2	7	2	0	0	0	(- -)	2	0	1	0	1	0	1	0	0	0	0	0	-	0	.286	.375	.286
2005 Rome	A	43	156	48	12	3	8	(- -)	90	37	27	38	29	0	29	3	0	1	4	1	.80	3	.308	.423	.577
2005 MrtlBh	A+	17	60	21	4	0	0	(- -)	25	7	5	11	9	0	9	1	0	1	0	1	.00	1	.350	.437	.417
2006 MrtlBh	A+	59	226	58	10	3	7	(- -)	95	27	35	32	25	6	49	1	0	3	11	6	.65	6	.257	.329	.420
2006 Missi	AA	48	176	48	9	3	7	(- -)	84	18	25	28	15	1	38	0	1	2	4	2	.67	3	.273	.326	.477
2007 Missi	AA	94	365	107	21	6	15	(- -)	185	58	74	69	44	2	84	3	0	6	12	7	.63	6	.293	.368	.507
2007 Rchmd	AAA	44	170	51	12	1	4	(- -)	77	26	26	29	17	2	36	1	1	2	5	0	1.00	4	.300	.363	.453
2007 Atl	NL	5	19	3	1	0	0	(0 0)	4	0	4	1	0	0	8	1	0	1	0	0	-	0	.158	.190	.211

Chipper Jones

Bats: B **Throws:** R **Pos:** 3B-126; DH-6; PH-2; SS-1   **Ht:** 6'4" **Wt:** 210 **Born:** 4/24/1972 **Age:** 36

BATTING														BASERUNNING				AVERAGES		
Year Team	Lg	G	AB	H	2B	3B	HR	(Hm Rd)	TB	R	RBI	RC	TBB	IBB	SO	HBP	SH	SF	SB	CS	SB%	GDP	Avg	OBP	Slg
1993 Atl	NL	8	3	2	1	0	0	(0 0)	3	2	0	2	1	0	1	0	0	0	0	0	-	0	.667	.750	1.000
1995 Atl	NL	140	524	139	22	3	23	(15 8)	236	87	86	84	73	1	99	0	1	4	8	4	.67	10	.265	.353	.450
1996 Atl	NL	157	598	185	32	5	30	(18 12)	317	114	110	123	87	0	88	0	1	7	14	1	.93	14	.309	.393	.530
1997 Atl	NL	157	597	170	41	3	21	(7 14)	286	100	111	104	76	8	88	0	0	6	20	5	.80	19	.295	.371	.479
1998 Atl	NL	160	601	188	29	5	34	(17 17)	329	123	107	129	96	1	93	1	1	8	16	6	.73	17	.313	.404	.547
1999 Atl	NL	157	567	181	41	1	45	(25 20)	359	116	110	150	126	18	94	2	0	6	25	3	.89	20	.319	.441	.633
2000 Atl	NL	156	579	180	38	1	36	(18 18)	328	118	111	128	95	10	64	2	0	10	14	7	.67	14	.311	.404	.566
2001 Atl	NL	159	572	189	33	5	38	(19 19)	346	113	102	136	98	20	82	2	0	5	9	10	.47	13	.330	.427	.605
2002 Atl	NL	158	548	179	35	1	26	(17 9)	294	90	100	119	107	23	89	2	0	5	8	2	.80	18	.327	.435	.536
2003 Atl	NL	153	555	169	33	2	27	(16 11)	287	103	106	110	94	13	83	1	0	6	2	2	.50	10	.305	.402	.517
2004 Atl	NL	137	472	117	20	1	30	(19 11)	229	69	96	82	84	8	96	4	0	7	2	0	1.00	14	.248	.362	.485
2005 Atl	NL	109	358	106	30	0	21	(9 12)	199	66	72	78	72	5	56	0	0	2	5	1	.83	9	.296	.412	.556
2006 Atl	NL	110	411	133	28	3	26	(12 14)	245	87	86	94	61	4	73	1	0	4	6	1	.86	12	.324	.409	.596
2007 Atl	NL	134	513	173	42	4	29	(14 15)	310	108	102	110	82	10	75	0	0	5	5	1	.83	21	.337	.425	.604
14 ML YEARS		1895	6898	2117	425	34	386	(206 180)	3768	1296	1299	1449	1152	121	1081	15	3	75	134	43	.76	191	.307	.403	.546

Garrett Jones

Bats: L **Throws:** L **Pos:** DH-12; 1B-8; LF-5; PH-5; RF-1   **Ht:** 6'4" **Wt:** 227 **Born:** 6/21/1981 **Age:** 27

BATTING														BASERUNNING				AVERAGES		
Year Team	Lg	G	AB	H	2B	3B	HR	(Hm Rd)	TB	R	RBI	RC	TBB	IBB	SO	HBP	SH	SF	SB	CS	SB%	GDP	Avg	OBP	Slg
1999 Braves	R	46	170	41	3	0	3	(- -)	53	17	18	16	16	0	47	1	0	1	1	2	.33	1	.241	.309	.312
2000 Danvle	R	40	138	24	7	2	0	(- -)	35	12	16	6	13	0	55	0	0	2	0	3	.00	2	.174	.242	.254
2001 Danvle	R	40	149	43	11	0	3	(- -)	63	13	23	20	9	0	58	1	0	0	0	1	.00	0	.289	.333	.423
2002 QuadC	A	63	223	45	8	0	10	(- -)	83	21	32	19	11	1	82	0	3	1	3	1	.75	5	.202	.238	.372
2003 FtMyrs	A+	117	404	89	12	5	18	(- -)	165	52	67	47	32	1	98	2	3	2	5	4	.56	8	.220	.280	.408
2004 FtMyrs	A+	19	66	16	5	0	1	(- -)	24	6	6	7	4	2	19	0	0	0	2	0	1.00	0	.242	.286	.364
2004 NwBrit	AA	122	450	140	33	2	30	(- -)	267	68	92	93	28	0	98	7	1	7	10	4	.71	5	.311	.356	.593
2005 Roch	AAA	134	488	119	22	2	24	(- -)	217	71	72	66	36	4	109	1	1	1	5	1	.83	5	.244	.297	.445
2006 Roch	AAA	140	525	125	32	3	21	(- -)	226	72	92	70	49	3	121	2	0	6	3	4	.43	8	.238	.302	.430
2007 Roch	AAA	107	400	112	32	3	13	(- -)	189	57	70	65	32	4	83	5	0	9	2	2	.50	4	.280	.334	.473
2007 Min	AL	31	77	16	2	1	2	(1 1)	26	7	5	3	6	0	20	0	0	1	1	1	.50	2	.208	.262	.338

Greg Jones

Pitches: R **Bats:** R **Pos:** RP-9   **Ht:** 6'2" **Wt:** 205 **Born:** 11/15/1976 **Age:** 31

Year	Team	Lg	G	GS	CG	GF	IP	BFP	H	R	ER	HR	SH	SF	HB	TBB	IBB	SO	WP	Bk	W	L	Pct	ShO	Sv-Op	Hld	ERC	ERA
2007	Salt Lk*	AAA	36	0	0	19	53.2	233	68	34	30	7	3	2	2	14	0	39	3	1	4	2	.667	0	3- -	-	5.61	5.03
2003	LAA	AL	18	0	0	7	27.2	127	29	15	15	3	0	0	2	14	0	28	5	0	0	0	-	0	0-0	2	5.05	4.88
2005	LAA	AL	6	0	0	6	5.1	24	7	4	4	2	0	0	0	2	0	6	0	0	0	0	-	0	0-0	0	8.19	6.75
2006	LAA	AL	5	0	0	2	6.0	28	8	5	4	1	0	3	0	2	0	1	0	0	0	0	-	0	0-0	0	6.14	6.00
2007	LAA	AL	9	0	0	8	8.2	42	10	6	6	2	0	0	1	5	0	5	1	0	0	0	-	0	0-0	0	7.12	6.23
4 ML YEARS			38	0	0	23	47.2	221	54	30	29	8	0	3	3	23	0	40	6	0	0	0	-	0	0-0	2	5.89	5.48

Jacque Jones

Bats: L **Throws:** L **Pos:** CF-84; RF-67; PH-12; LF-2; PR-2; DH-1   **Ht:** 5'10" **Wt:** 200 **Born:** 4/25/1975 **Age:** 33

Year	Team	Lg	G	AB	H	2B	3B	HR	(Hm	Rd)	TB	R	RBI	RC	TBB	IBB	SO	HBP	SH	SF	SB	CS	SB%	GDP	Avg	OBP	Slg
1999	Min	AL	95	322	93	24	2	9	(5	4)	148	54	44	46	17	1	63	4	1	3	3	4	.43	7	.289	.329	.460
2000	Min	AL	154	523	149	26	5	19	(11	8)	242	66	76	70	26	4	111	0	1	0	7	5	.58	17	.285	.319	.463
2001	Min	AL	149	475	131	25	0	14	(5	9)	198	57	49	63	39	2	92	3	2	0	12	9	.57	10	.276	.335	.417
2002	Min	AL	149	577	173	37	2	27	(6	21)	295	96	85	100	37	2	129	2	4	6	6	7	.46	8	.300	.341	.511
2003	Min	AL	136	517	157	33	1	16	(7	9)	240	76	69	73	21	2	105	4	1	5	13	1	.93	10	.304	.333	.464
2004	Min	AL	151	555	141	22	1	24	(9	15)	237	69	80	73	40	2	117	10	2	1	13	10	.57	12	.254	.315	.427
2005	Min	AL	142	523	130	22	4	23	(9	14)	229	74	73	72	51	12	120	5	2	4	13	4	.76	17	.249	.319	.438
2006	ChC	NL	149	533	152	31	1	27	(12	15)	266	73	81	82	35	6	116	5	2	2	9	1	.90	17	.285	.334	.499
2007	ChC	NL	135	453	129	33	2	5	(3	2)	181	52	66	62	34	5	70	2	3	3	6	3	.67	15	.285	.335	.400
9 ML YEARS			1260	4478	1255	253	18	164	(67	97)	2036	617	623	641	300	36	923	35	18	24	82	44	.65	113	.280	.329	.455

Todd Jones

Pitches: R **Bats:** B **Pos:** RP-63   **Ht:** 6'3" **Wt:** 230 **Born:** 4/24/1968 **Age:** 40

Year	Team	Lg	G	GS	CG	GF	IP	BFP	H	R	ER	HR	SH	SF	HB	TBB	IBB	SO	WP	Bk	W	L	Pct	ShO	Sv-Op	Hld	ERC	ERA
1993	Hou	NL	27	0	0	8	37.1	150	28	14	13	4	2	1	1	15	2	25	1	1	1	2	.333	0	2-3	6	2.90	3.13
1994	Hou	NL	48	0	0	20	72.2	288	52	23	22	3	3	1	1	26	4	63	1	0	5	2	.714	0	5-9	8	2.10	2.72
1995	Hou	NL	68	0	0	40	99.2	442	89	38	34	8	5	4	6	52	17	96	5	0	6	5	.545	0	15-20	8	3.70	3.07
1996	Hou	NL	51	0	0	37	57.1	263	61	30	28	5	2	1	5	32	6	44	3	0	6	3	.667	0	17-23	1	5.16	4.40
1997	Det	AL	68	0	0	51	70.0	301	60	29	24	3	1	4	1	35	2	70	7	0	5	4	.556	0	31-36	5	3.27	3.09
1998	Det	AL	65	0	0	53	63.1	279	58	38	35	7	2	6	2	36	4	57	5	0	1	4	.200	0	28-32	0	4.37	4.97
1999	Det	AL	65	0	0	62	66.1	287	64	30	28	7	3	1	1	35	1	64	2	0	4	4	.500	0	30-35	0	4.55	3.80
2000	Det	AL	67	0	0	60	64.0	271	67	28	25	6	1	1	1	25	1	67	2	0	2	4	.333	0	42-46	0	4.43	3.52
2001	2 Tms	AL	69	0	0	36	68.0	314	87	39	32	9	3	3	0	29	1	54	3	0	5	5	.500	0	13-21	10	6.03	4.24
2002	Col	NL	79	0	0	20	82.1	352	84	43	43	10	6	3	3	28	3	73	1	0	1	4	.200	0	1-3	30	4.22	4.70
2003	2 Tms	NL	59	1	0	14	68.2	326	93	58	54	10	3	3	1	31	2	59	0	0	3	5	.375	0	0-5	4	6.73	7.08
2004	2 Tms	NL	78	0	0	16	82.1	358	84	39	38	7	5	6	6	33	5	59	2	0	11	5	.688	0	2-8	27	4.32	4.15
2005	Fla	NL	68	0	0	55	73.0	289	61	19	17	2	6	1	3	14	2	62	2	0	1	5	.167	0	40-45	1	2.15	2.10
2006	Det	AL	62	0	0	56	64.0	272	70	31	28	4	3	1	3	11	3	28	2	0	2	6	.250	0	37-43	0	3.53	3.94
2007	Det	AL	63	0	0	54	61.1	265	64	29	29	3	2	0	0	23	6	33	3	0	1	4	.200	0	38-44	0	3.70	4.26
01	Det	AL	45	0	0	28	48.2	225	60	31	25	6	2	3	0	22	1	39	3	0	4	5	.444	0	11-17	3	5.74	4.62
01	Min	AL	24	0	0	8	19.1	89	27	8	7	3	1	0	0	7	0	15	0	0	1	0	1.000	0	2-4	7	6.80	3.26
03	Col	NL	33	1	0	7	39.1	193	61	39	36	8	3	2	1	18	0	28	0	0	1	4	.200	0	0-5	3	8.77	8.24
03	Bos	AL	26	0	0	7	29.1	133	32	19	18	2	0	1	0	13	2	31	0	0	2	1	.667	0	0-0	1	4.30	5.52
04	Cin	NL	51	0	0	10	57.0	235	49	25	24	4	2	5	1	25	2	37	2	0	8	2	.800	0	1-6	22	3.37	3.79
04	Phi	NL	27	0	0	6	25.1	123	35	14	14	3	3	1	5	8	3	22	0	0	3	3	.500	0	1-2	5	6.65	4.97
15 ML YEARS			937	1	0	582	1030.1	4457	1022	488	450	88	47	36	34	425	59	854	39	1	54	62	.466	0	301-373	100	4.03	3.93

Ryan Jorgensen

Bats: R **Throws:** R **Pos:** C-4   **Ht:** 6'2" **Wt:** 220 **Born:** 5/4/1979 **Age:** 29

Year	Team	Lg	G	AB	H	2B	3B	HR	(Hm	Rd)	TB	R	RBI	RC	TBB	IBB	SO	HBP	SH	SF	SB	CS	SB%	GDP	Avg	OBP	Slg
2000	Eugene	A-	41	130	39	10	2	1	(-	-)	56	17	23	21	17	0	27	1	2	2	2	4	.33	1	.300	.380	.431
2001	Dytona	A+	54	188	53	12	1	6	(-	-)	91	24	29	33	23	0	39	2	0	0	1	3	.25	6	.282	.366	.484
2001	WTenn	AA	32	109	13	4	0	2	(-	-)	23	8	7	3	11	0	38	0	0	3	0	0	-	5	.119	.195	.211
2002	Jupiter	A+	60	223	58	16	0	3	(-	-)	83	26	35	30	24	0	38	1	3	0	4	1	.80	4	.260	.335	.372
2002	Portlnd	AA	41	144	32	4	0	2	(-	-)	42	15	14	12	12	0	33	1	0	1	3	1	.75	3	.222	.287	.292
2003	Carlina	AA	67	211	51	16	0	6	(-	-)	85	28	34	31	30	2	53	2	0	3	1	0	1.00	2	.242	.337	.403
2004	Albq	AAA	61	201	52	11	0	8	(-	-)	87	20	29	25	9	0	51	0	1	1	0	0	-	7	.259	.289	.433
2005	Albq	AAA	53	137	27	5	0	2	(-	-)	38	20	11	13	21	3	46	1	2	0	1	0	1.00	1	.197	.308	.277
2006	Lsvlle	AAA	74	230	49	9	0	8	(-	-)	82	25	30	28	31	5	57	4	2	2	1	0	1.00	4	.213	.315	.357
2007	Lsvlle	AAA	73	249	59	16	0	2	(-	-)	81	29	26	25	21	0	52	0	5	4	1	0	1.00	10	.237	.292	.325
2005	Fla	NL	4	4	0	0	0	0	(0	0)	0	0	0	0	0	0	3	0	0	0	0	0	-	0	.000	.000	.000
2007	Cin	NL	4	15	3	0	0	2	(1	1)	9	3	6	4	0	0	5	0	0	0	0	0	-	0	.200	.200	.600
2 ML YEARS			8	19	3	0	0	2	(1	1)	9	3	6	4	0	0	8	0	0	0	0	0	-	0	.158	.158	.474

Jorge Julio

Pitches: R **Bats:** R **Pos:** RP-68 — **Ht:** 6'1" **Wt:** 225 **Born:** 3/3/1979 **Age:** 29

Year	Team	Lg	G	GS	CG	GF	IP	BFP	H	R	ER	HR	SH	SF	HB	TBB	IBB	SO	WP	Bk	W	L	Pct	ShO	Sv-Op	Hld	ERC	ERA
2007	Jupiter*	A+	2	2	0	0	5.0	28	11	7	2	0	0	0	0	1	0	6	0	0	0	1	.000	0	0--	-	9.35	3.60
2001	Bal	AL	18	0	0	8	21.1	99	25	13	9	2	2	0	1	9	0	22	1	0	1	1	.500	0	0-1	3	5.17	3.80
2002	Bal	AL	67	0	0	61	68.0	289	55	22	15	5	1	1	2	27	3	55	8	0	5	6	.455	0	25-31	1	2.83	1.99
2003	Bal	Al	64	0	0	51	61.2	273	60	36	30	10	2	1	2	34	4	52	0	0	0	7	.000	0	36-44	2	5.05	4.38
2004	Bal	AL	65	0	0	50	69.0	306	59	35	35	11	2	3	3	39	4	70	7	0	2	5	.286	0	22-26	2	4.35	4.57
2005	Bal	AL	67	0	0	19	71.2	313	76	50	47	14	1	3	2	24	4	58	10	0	3	5	.375	0	0-2	12	4.82	5.90
2006	2 Tms	NL	62	0	0	44	66.0	285	52	35	31	10	1	0	1	35	2	88	9	0	2	4	.333	0	16-20	1	3.72	4.23
2007	2 Tms	NL	68	0	0	14	62.0	280	68	39	36	8	2	4	3	31	2	56	6	1	0	5	.000	0	0-7	17	5.44	5.23
06	NYM	NL	18	0	0	12	21.1	96	21	15	12	4	0	0	1	10	1	33	2	0	1	2	.333	0	1-1	0	4.90	5.06
06	Ari	NL	44	0	0	32	44.2	189	31	20	19	6	1	0	0	25	1	55	7	0	1	2	.333	0	15-19	1	3.18	3.83
07	Fla	NL	10	0	0	5	9.1	59	18	14	13	2	1	0	2	11	1	6	1	1	0	2	.000	0	0-2	1	15.51	12.54
07	Col	NL	58	0	0	9	52.2	221	50	25	23	6	1	4	1	20	1	50	5	0	0	3	.000	0	0-5	16	3.93	3.93
	7 ML YEARS		411	0	0	247	419.2	1845	395	230	203	60	11	12	14	199	19	401	41	1	13	33	.283	0	99-131	38	4.36	4.35

Jair Jurrjens

Pitches: R **Bats:** R **Pos:** SP-7 — **Ht:** 6'1" **Wt:** 160 **Born:** 1/29/1986 **Age:** 22

Year	Team	Lg	G	GS	CG	GF	IP	BFP	H	R	ER	HR	SH	SF	HB	TBB	IBB	SO	WP	Bk	W	L	Pct	ShO	Sv-Op	Hld	ERC	ERA
2003	Tigers	R	7	2	0	3	28.0	121	33	16	10	3	1	0	4	3	0	20	0	0	2	1	.667	0	0--	-	4.55	3.21
2004	Tigers	R	6	6	2	1	39.2	158	25	16	10	2	1	0	1	10	1	39	4	0	4	2	.667	1	0--	-	1.49	2.27
2004	Oneont	A-	7	7	0	0	39.0	178	50	25	23	0	0	2	3	10	1	31	5	1	1	5	.167	0	0--	-	4.55	5.31
2005	WMich	A	26	26	0	0	142.2	586	132	62	54	5	3	4	6	36	0	108	12	3	12	6	.667	0	0--	-	2.87	3.41
2006	Lkland	A+	12	12	0	0	73.2	281	53	23	17	4	1	0	2	10	0	59	3	0	5	0	1.000	0	0--	-	1.60	2.08
2006	Erie	AA	12	12	0	0	67.0	283	71	30	25	7	2	0	4	21	2	53	4	0	3	5	.571	0	0--	-	4.42	3.36
2007	Erie	AA	19	19	1	0	112.2	470	112	43	40	7	1	1	1	31	3	94	9	1	7	5	.583	1	0--	-	3.32	3.20
2007	Det	AL	7	7	0	0	30.2	122	24	16	16	4	0	1	1	11	0	13	2	0	3	1	.750	0	0-0	0	3.19	4.70

Jeff Karstens

Pitches: R **Bats:** R **Pos:** RP-4; SP-3 — **Ht:** 6'3" **Wt:** 185 **Born:** 9/24/1982 **Age:** 25

Year	Team	Lg	G	GS	CG	GF	IP	BFP	H	R	ER	HR	SH	SF	HB	TBB	IBB	SO	WP	Bk	W	L	Pct	ShO	Sv-Op	Hld	ERC	ERA
2003	StlIsInd	A-	14	10	0	2	67.1	275	63	22	19	2	6	5	2	16	1	53	3	0	4	2	.667	0	0--	-	2.78	2.54
2004	Tampa	A+	24	24	1	0	138.2	582	151	70	62	11	7	8	4	31	3	116	2	1	6	9	.400	1	0--	-	3.87	4.02
2005	Trntn	AA	28	27	0	0	169.0	742	192	91	78	16	3	5	3	42	1	147	8	1	12	11	.522	0	0--	-	4.17	4.15
2006	Trntn	AA	11	11	0	0	74.0	296	54	20	19	4	2	3	3	14	1	67	5	0	6	0	1.000	0	0--	-	1.75	2.31
2006	Clmbs	AAA	14	14	1	0	73.2	326	80	42	35	9	1	3	1	30	1	48	1	1	5	5	.500	0	0--	-	4.77	4.28
2007	Yanks	R	1	1	0	0	3.1	15	3	0	0	0	0	0	0	1	0	2	0	0	0	0	-	0	0--	-	2.26	0.00
2007	StlIsInd	A-	1	1	0	0	5.0	19	4	1	1	1	0	0	0	0	0	8	0	0	1	0	1.000	0	0--	-	2.06	1.80
2007	Tampa	A+	1	1	0	0	4.0	16	3	0	0	0	0	0	0	1	0	5	0	0	1	0	1.000	0	0--	-	1.65	0.00
2007	Trntn	AA	1	1	0	0	5.0	20	4	1	1	0	0	0	0	2	0	5	0	0	1	0	1.000	0	0--	-	2.46	1.80
2007	S-WB	AAA	6	5	0	0	31.0	124	25	6	6	2	0	1	0	9	0	27	4	0	3	0	1.000	0	0--	-	2.45	1.74
2006	NYY	AL	8	6	0	2	42.2	179	40	20	18	6	0	2	1	11	2	16	3	1	2	1	.667	0	0-0	0	3.42	3.80
2007	NYY	AL	7	3	0	2	14.2	80	27	21	18	4	2	1	0	9	0	5	2	0	1	4	.200	0	0-0	0	11.86	11.05
	2 ML YEARS		15	9	0	4	57.1	259	67	41	36	10	2	3	1	20	2	21	5	1	3	5	.375	0	0-0	0	5.30	5.65

Matt Kata

Bats: B **Throws:** R **Pos:** PH-32; 3B-17; 2B-12; LF-12; SS-9; 1B-4; DH-3; PR-3; RF-1 — **Ht:** 6'1" **Wt:** 185 **Born:** 3/14/1978 **Age:** 30

Year	Team	Lg	G	AB	H	2B	3B	HR	(Hm	Rd)	TB	R	RBI	RC	TBB	IBB	SO	HBP	SH	SF	SB	CS	SB%	GDP	Avg	OBP	Slg
2007	Indy*	AAA	19	72	20	5	1	2	(-	-)	33	12	5	11	7	3	8	0	1	1	2	1	.67	2	.278	.338	.458
2003	Ari	NL	78	288	74	16	5	7	(3	4)	121	42	29	40	25	0	53	1	5	3	3	2	.60	4	.257	.315	.420
2004	Ari	NL	42	162	40	9	2	2	(1	1)	59	17	13	19	13	2	29	0	1	1	4	1	.80	1	.247	.301	.364
2005	2 Tms	NL	40	37	7	2	1	0	(0	0)	11	7	0	2	5	0	6	0	2	0	0	1	.00	0	.189	.286	.297
2007	2 Tms		78	158	35	9	1	3	(2	1)	55	21	16	14	5	0	33	2	2	0	1	0	1.00	3	.222	.255	.348
05	Ari	NL	30	31	6	2	1	0	(0	0)	10	6	0	2	5	0	4	0	2	0	0	1	.00	0	.194	.306	.323
05	Phi	NL	10	6	1	0	0	0	(0	0)	1	1	0	0	0	0	2	0	0	0	0	0	-	0	.167	.167	.167
07	Tex	AL	31	70	13	2	0	2	(1	1)	21	12	6	5	5	0	18	1	1	0	1	0	1.00	0	.186	.250	.300
07	Pit	NL	47	88	22	7	1	1	(1	0)	34	9	10	9	0	0	15	1	1	0	0	0	-	3	.250	.258	.386
	4 ML YEARS		238	645	156	36	9	12	(6	6)	246	87	58	75	48	2	121	3	10	4	8	4	.67	8	.242	.296	.381

Scott Kazmir

Pitches: L **Bats:** L **Pos:** SP-34 — **Ht:** 6'0" **Wt:** 190 **Born:** 1/24/1984 **Age:** 24

Year	Team	Lg	G	GS	CG	GF	IP	BFP	H	R	ER	HR	SH	SF	HB	TBB	IBB	SO	WP	Bk	W	L	Pct	ShO	Sv-Op	Hld	ERC	ERA
2004	TB	AL	8	7	0	0	33.1	152	33	22	21	4	0	0	2	21	0	41	3	0	2	3	.400	0	0-0	0	5.36	5.67
2005	TB	AL	32	32	0	0	186.0	818	172	90	78	12	6	9	10	100	3	174	7	1	10	9	.526	0	0-0	0	4.13	3.77
2006	TB	AL	24	24	1	0	144.2	610	132	59	52	15	0	5	2	53	3	163	6	0	10	8	.556	1	0-0	0	3.47	3.24
2007	TB	AL	34	34	0	0	206.2	887	196	91	80	18	6	3	7	89	1	239	10	0	13	9	.591	0	0-0	0	3.97	3.48
	4 ML YEARS		98	97	1	0	570.2	2467	533	262	231	49	12	17	21	262	7	617	26	1	35	29	.547	1	0-0	0	3.98	3.64

Austin Kearns

Bats: R Throws: R Pos: RF-158; CF-6; PH-2   Ht: 6'4" Wt: 225 Born: 5/20/1980 Age: 28

										BATTING												BASERUNNING				AVERAGES		
Year	Team	Lg	G	AB	H	2B	3B	HR	(Hm	Rd)	TB	R	RBI	RC	TBB	IBB	SO	HBP	SH	SF	SB	CS	SB%	GDP	Avg	OBP	Slg
2002	Cin	NL	107	372	117	24	3	13	(7	6)	186	66	56	70	54	3	81	6	0	3	6	3	.67	11	.315	.407	.500
2003	Cin	NL	82	292	77	11	0	15	(8	7)	133	39	58	52	41	1	68	5	0	0	5	2	.71	7	.264	.364	.455
2004	Cin	NL	64	217	50	10	2	9	(3	6)	91	28	32	26	28	0	71	1	0	0	2	1	.67	8	.230	.321	.419
2005	Cin	NL	112	387	93	26	1	18	(9	9)	175	62	67	55	48	2	107	8	0	5	0	0	-	8	.240	.333	.452
2006	2 Tms	NL	150	537	142	33	2	24	(12	12)	251	86	86	81	76	4	135	10	1	5	9	4	.69	18	.264	.363	.467
2007	Was	NL	161	587	156	35	1	16	(8	8)	241	84	74	87	71	5	106	12	0	4	2	2	.50	13	.266	.355	.411
06	Cin	NL	87	325	89	21	1	16	(8	8)	160	53	50	46	35	2	85	5	0	3	7	1	.88	14	.274	.351	.492
06	Was	NL	63	212	53	12	1	8	(4	4)	91	33	36	35	41	2	50	5	1	2	2	3	.40	4	.250	.381	.429
6 ML YEARS			676	2392	635	139	9	95	(47	48)	1077	365	373	371	318	15	568	42	1	17	24	12	.67	65	.265	.359	.450

Randy Keisler

Pitches: L Bats: L Pos: SP-3; RP-1   Ht: 6'2" Wt: 200 Born: 2/24/1976 Age: 32

			HOW MUCH HE PITCHED						WHAT HE GAVE UP										THE RESULTS						
Year	Team	Lg	G	GS	CG	GF	IP	BFP	H	R	ER	HR	SH	SF	HB	TBB	IBB	SO	WP	Bk	W	L	Pct	ShO	Sv-Op	Hld	ERC	ERA
2007	Memp*	AAA	25	24	1	0	156.0	678	178	90	83	19	8	4	6	51	1	102	7	0	8	11	.421	0	0- -	-	4.97	4.79
2000	NYY	AL	4	1	0	0	10.2	52	16	14	14	1	0	0	0	8	0	6	0	0	1	0	1.000	0	0-0	0	9.10	11.81
2001	NYY	AL	10	10	0	0	50.2	236	52	36	35	12	0	0	0	34	0	36	0	0	1	2	.333	0	0-0	0	6.33	6.22
2003	SD	NL	2	2	0	0	6.0	33	7	9	8	3	0	1	1	7	0	5	0	1	0	1	.000	0	0-0	0	12.82	12.00
2005	Cin	NL	24	4	0	7	56.0	262	64	45	39	10	1	1	1	28	2	43	2	0	2	1	.667	0	0-0	0	5.77	6.27
2006	Oak	AL	11	0	0	2	10.0	42	14	5	5	3	0	0	0	2	1	5	0	0	0	0	-	0	0-0	1	7.51	4.50
2007	StL	NL	4	3	0	1	17.1	77	21	12	10	3	2	2	0	5	0	5	0	0	0	0	-	0	0-0	0	5.33	5.19
6 ML YEARS			55	20	0	10	150.2	702	174	121	111	32	3	4	2	84	3	100	2	1	4	4	.500	0	0-0	1	6.50	6.63

Don Kelly

Bats: L Throws: R Pos: PH-19; SS-5; 2B-3; LF-1; RF-1   Ht: 6'4" Wt: 190 Born: 2/15/1980 Age: 28

										BATTING												BASERUNNING				AVERAGES		
Year	Team	Lg	G	AB	H	2B	3B	HR	(Hm	Rd)	TB	R	RBI	RC	TBB	IBB	SO	HBP	SH	SF	SB	CS	SB%	GDP	Avg	OBP	Slg
2001	Oneont	A-	67	262	75	8	3	0	(-	-)	89	41	25	33	25	1	16	0	2	3	8	5	.62	6	.286	.345	.340
2002	WMich	A	128	455	130	21	5	1	(-	-)	164	72	59	66	59	1	40	3	2	5	9	6	.60	11	.286	.368	.360
2003	Lkland	A+	87	303	96	17	4	1	(-	-)	124	48	38	56	45	1	25	1	1	5	15	2	.88	4	.317	.401	.409
2003	Erie	AA	22	83	22	5	1	1	(-	-)	32	14	13	13	15	0	9	0	3	0	0	0	-	2	.265	.378	.386
2004	Erie	AA	28	101	23	6	2	0	(-	-)	33	17	9	12	15	0	13	1	1	1	3	1	.75	4	.228	.331	.327
2004	Tigers	R	3	10	4	0	0	0	(-	-)	4	2	0	1	0	0	2	0	0	0	1	0	1.00	0	.400	.400	.400
2005	Erie	AA	82	328	112	22	3	9	(-	-)	167	54	54	69	36	5	43	1	0	6	10	2	.83	6	.341	.402	.509
2005	Toledo	AAA	43	160	40	8	0	1	(-	-)	51	22	13	17	13	0	15	0	3	0	8	2	.80	2	.250	.306	.319
2006	Toledo	AAA	66	237	54	14	3	0	(-	-)	74	23	19	25	24	0	32	2	4	0	18	7	.72	3	.228	.304	.312
2006	Erie	AA	58	207	57	11	1	0	(-	-)	70	30	24	28	27	0	23	1	0	5	5	3	.63	5	.275	.354	.338
2007	Indy	AAA	52	150	37	5	2	0	(-	-)	46	20	11	17	18	0	17	2	4	0	6	4	.60	4	.247	.335	.307
2007	Pit	NL	25	27	4	0	0	0	(0	0)	4	2	0	1	3	0	3	2	0	0	0	0	-	1	.148	.281	.148

Matt Kemp

Bats: R Throws: R Pos: RF-88; PH-10; CF-6; PR-5   Ht: 6'2" Wt: 230 Born: 9/23/1984 Age: 23

										BATTING												BASERUNNING				AVERAGES		
Year	Team	Lg	G	AB	H	2B	3B	HR	(Hm	Rd)	TB	R	RBI	RC	TBB	IBB	SO	HBP	SH	SF	SB	CS	SB%	GDP	Avg	OBP	Slg
2003	Ddgrs	R	42	159	43	5	2	1	(-	-)	55	11	17	16	7	1	25	0	0	2	2	1	.67	1	.270	.298	.346
2004	Clmbs	A	111	423	122	22	8	17	(-	-)	211	67	66	69	24	1	100	5	1	5	8	7	.53	10	.288	.330	.499
2004	VeroB	A+	11	37	13	5	0	1	(-	-)	21	5	9	8	4	0	12	0	0	1	2	1	.67	0	.351	.405	.568
2005	VeroB	A+	109	418	128	21	4	27	(-	-)	238	76	90	84	25	2	92	5	1	5	23	6	.79	8	.306	.349	.569
2006	Jaxnvl	AA	48	199	65	15	2	7	(-	-)	105	38	34	43	20	4	38	5	0	0	11	2	.85	10	.327	.402	.528
2006	LsVgs	AAA	44	182	67	14	6	3	(-	-)	102	37	36	43	17	0	26	2	1	0	14	3	.82	4	.368	.428	.560
2007	LsVgs	AAA	39	161	53	16	3	4	(-	-)	87	32	20	32	10	0	26	2	0	1	9	2	.82	3	.329	.374	.540
2006	LAD	NL	52	154	39	7	1	7	(4	3)	69	30	23	20	9	1	53	0	0	3	6	0	1.00	1	.253	.289	.448
2007	LAD	NL	98	292	100	12	5	10	(9	1)	152	47	42	49	16	0	66	0	0	3	10	5	.67	6	.342	.373	.521
2 ML YEARS			150	446	139	19	6	17	(13	4)	221	77	65	69	25	1	119	0	0	6	16	5	.76	7	.312	.344	.496

Jason Kendall

Bats: R Throws: R Pos: C-132; PH-5; LF-2   Ht: 6'0" Wt: 204 Born: 6/26/1974 Age: 34

										BATTING												BASERUNNING				AVERAGES		
Year	Team	Lg	G	AB	H	2B	3B	HR	(Hm	Rd)	TB	R	RBI	RC	TBB	IBB	SO	HBP	SH	SF	SB	CS	SB%	GDP	Avg	OBP	Slg
1996	Pit	NL	130	414	124	23	5	3	(2	1)	166	54	42	63	35	11	30	15	3	4	5	2	.71	7	.300	.372	.401
1997	Pit	NL	144	486	143	36	4	8	(5	3)	211	71	49	86	49	2	53	31	1	5	18	6	.75	11	.294	.391	.434
1998	Pit	NL	149	535	175	36	3	12	(6	6)	253	95	75	110	51	3	51	31	2	8	26	5	.84	6	.327	.411	.473
1999	Pit	NL	78	280	93	20	3	8	(5	3)	143	61	41	63	38	3	32	12	0	4	22	3	.88	8	.332	.428	.511
2000	Pit	NL	152	579	185	33	6	14	(7	7)	272	112	58	112	79	3	79	15	1	4	22	12	.65	13	.320	.412	.470
2001	Pit	NL	157	606	161	22	2	10	(3	7)	217	84	53	68	44	4	48	20	0	2	13	14	.48	18	.266	.335	.358
2002	Pit	NL	145	545	154	25	3	3	(1	2)	194	59	44	66	49	1	29	9	0	2	15	8	.65	11	.283	.350	.356
2003	Pit	NL	150	587	191	29	3	6	(3	3)	244	84	58	97	49	3	40	25	1	3	8	7	.53	9	.325	.399	.416
2004	Pit	NL	147	574	183	32	0	3	(2	1)	224	86	51	95	60	2	41	19	1	4	11	8	.58	12	.319	.399	.390
2005	Oak	AL	150	601	163	28	1	0	(0	0)	193	70	53	79	50	0	39	20	0	5	8	3	.73	26	.271	.345	.321
2006	Oak	AL	143	552	163	23	0	1	(1	0)	189	76	50	80	53	2	54	12	4	5	11	5	.69	19	.295	.367	.342
2007	2 Tms	NL	137	466	113	20	1	3	(1	2)	144	45	41	43	31	2	42	9	5	3	3	4	.43	8	.242	.301	.309
07	Oak	AL	80	292	66	10	0	2	(0	2)	82	24	22	18	12	0	27	3	2	3	3	1	.75	7	.226	.261	.281
07	ChC	NL	57	174	47	10	1	1	(1	0)	62	21	19	25	19	2	15	6	3	0	0	3	.00	1	.270	.362	.356
12 ML YEARS			1682	6225	1848	327	31	71	(36	35)	2450	897	615	962	588	36	538	218	18	49	162	77	.68	148	.297	.375	.394

Howie Kendrick

Bats: R Throws: R Pos: 2B-86; DH-1; PH-1   Ht: 5'10" Wt: 200 Born: 7/12/1983 Age: 24

									BATTING												BASERUNNING				AVERAGES		
Year	Team	Lg	G	AB	H	2B	3B	HR	(Hm	Rd)	TB	R	RBI	RC	TBB	IBB	SO	HBP	SH	SF	SB	CS	SB%	GDP	Avg	OBP	Slg
2002	Angels	R	42	157	50	6	4	0	(-	-)	64	24	13	24	7	0	11	6	1	1	12	6	.67	2	.318	.368	.408
2003	Provo	R+	63	234	86	20	3	3	(-	-)	121	65	36	53	24	1	28	6	3	3	8	3	.73	5	.368	.434	.517
2004	Angels	R	3	12	3	1	0	0	(-	-)	4	1	0	1	1	0	0	0	0	0	2	0	1.00	0	.250	.308	.333
2004	CRpds	A	75	313	115	24	6	10	(-	-)	181	66	49	69	12	2	41	6	3	3	15	6	.71	2	.367	.398	.578
2005	RCuca	A+	63	279	107	23	6	12	(-	-)	178	69	47	70	14	0	42	7	0	4	13	4	.76	5	.384	.421	.638
2005	Ark	AA	46	190	65	20	2	7	(-	-)	110	35	42	41	6	0	20	7	0	1	12	4	.75	7	.342	.382	.579
2006	Salt Lk	AAA	69	290	107	25	6	13	(-	-)	183	57	62	70	12	1	48	8	1	1	11	3	.79	2	.369	.408	.631
2007	RCuca	A+	1	4	1	0	0	0	(-	-)	1	0	0	0	0	0	0	0	0	0	0	0	-	0	.250	.250	.250
2007	Salt Lk	AAA	13	50	15	1	0	3	(-	-)	25	9	11	8	1	0	9	2	0	1	1	0	1.00	0	.300	.333	.500
2006	LAA	AL	72	267	76	21	1	4	(2	2)	111	25	30	32	9	2	44	4	0	3	6	0	1.00	5	.285	.314	.416
2007	LAA	AL	88	338	109	24	2	5	(3	2)	152	55	39	41	9	2	61	4	1	1	5	4	.56	15	.322	.347	.450
2 ML YEARS			160	605	185	45	3	9	(5	4)	263	80	69	73	18	4	106	8	1	4	11	4	.73	20	.306	.332	.435

Kyle Kendrick

Pitches: R Bats: R Pos: SP-20   Ht: 6'3" Wt: 190 Born: 8/26/1984 Age: 23

			HOW MUCH HE PITCHED						WHAT HE GAVE UP												THE RESULTS						
Year	Team	Lg	G	GS	CG	GF	IP	BFP	H	R	ER	HR	SH	SF	HB	TBB	IBB	SO	WP	Bk	W	L	Pct	ShO	Sv-Op	Hld	ERC	ERA
2003	Phillies	R	9	5	0	0	31.1	145	40	24	19	3	1	0		12	0	26	2	0		.000	0	0--	-	5.49	5.46
2004	Lakwd	A	15	15	0	0	66.2	318	85	56	45	9	6	4		33	0	36	4	0	3	8	.273	0	0--	-	6.92	6.08
2004	Batvia	A-	13	12	0	0	70.2	317	94	52	43	6	3	6	5	18	1	53	1	1	2	8	.200	0	0--	-	5.64	5.48
2005	Lakwd	A	5	5	0	0	22.2	117	38	24	23	2	0	2	2	10	0	11	1	0	0	3	.000	0	0--	-	8.61	9.13
2005	Clrwtr	A+	1	1	0	0	4.0	18	5	1	0	0	0	0	1	2	0	1	0	0	0	1	.000	0	0--	-	6.70	0.00
2005	Batvia	AA	14	14	1	0	91.1	391	94	49	38	7	5	1	4	22	0	70	2	1	5	4	.556	0	0--	-	3.57	3.74
2006	Lakwd	A	7	7	0	0	46.0	188	34	14	11	0	0	1	1	15	0	54	0	0	3	2	.600	0	0--	-	1.88	2.15
2006	Clrwtr	A+	21	20	2	0	130.0	533	117	59	51	15	4	2	3	37	0	79	1	0	9	7	.563	1	0--	-	3.31	3.53
2007	Rdng	AA	12	12	1	0	81.1	337	82	38	29	3	4	3	2	18	0	50	2	0	4	7	.364	0	0--	-	3.13	3.21
2007	Phi	NL	20	20	0	0	121.0	499	129	53	52	16	4	2	7	25	3	49	0	0	10	4	.714	0	0-0	0	4.23	3.87

Adam Kennedy

Bats: L Throws: R Pos: 2B-79; PH-8; SS-1; RF-1   Ht: 6'1" Wt: 195 Born: 1/10/1976 Age: 32

									BATTING												BASERUNNING				AVERAGES		
Year	Team	Lg	G	AB	H	2B	3B	HR	(Hm	Rd)	TB	R	RBI	RC	TBB	IBB	SO	HBP	SH	SF	SB	CS	SB%	GDP	Avg	OBP	Slg
1999	StL	NL	33	102	26	10	1	1	(1	0)	41	12	16	12	3	0	8	2	1	2	0	1	.00	1	.255	.284	.402
2000	LAA	AL	156	598	159	33	11	9	(7	2)	241	82	72	72	28	5	73	3	8	4	22	8	.73	10	.266	.300	.403
2001	LAA	AL	137	478	129	25	3	6	(4	2)	178	48	40	57	27	3	71	11	7	9	12	7	.63	7	.270	.318	.372
2002	LAA	AL	144	474	148	32	6	7	(6	1)	213	65	52	70	19	1	80	7	5	4	17	4	.81	5	.312	.345	.449
2003	LAA	AL	143	449	121	17	1	13	(8	5)	179	71	49	61	45	4	73	9	2	5	22	9	.71	7	.269	.344	.399
2004	LAA	AL	144	408	130	20	5	10	(5	5)	190	70	40	00	41	7	02	10	0	2	16	5	.76	10	.278	.361	.406
2005	LAA	AL	129	416	125	23	0	2	(1	1)	154	49	37	62	29	1	64	7	5	3	19	4	.83	5	.300	.354	.370
2006	LAA	AL	139	451	123	26	6	4	(3	1)	173	50	55	62	39	5	72	5	3	5	16	10	.62	15	.273	.334	.384
2007	StL	NL	87	279	61	9	1	3	(0	3)	81	27	18	19	22	6	33	3	1	1	6	2	.75	9	.219	.282	.290
9 ML YEARS			1112	3715	1022	195	34	55	(35	20)	1450	474	387	475	253	32	566	60	41	35	129	50	.72	69	.275	.329	.390

Ian Kennedy

Pitches: R Bats: R Pos: SP-3   Ht: 6'0" Wt: 190 Born: 12/19/1984 Age: 23

			HOW MUCH HE PITCHED						WHAT HE GAVE UP												THE RESULTS						
Year	Team	Lg	G	GS	CG	GF	IP	BFP	H	R	ER	HR	SH	SF	HB	TBB	IBB	SO	WP	Bk	W	L	Pct	ShO	Sv-Op	Hld	ERC	ERA
2006	StIslnd	A-	1	1	0	0	2.2	12	2	0	0	0	0	0	0	2	0	2	0	0	0	0	-	0	0--	-	3.21	0.00
2007	Tampa	A+	11	10	1	0	63.0	250	39	9	9	2	1	1	1	22	0	72	1	0	6	1	.857	0	0--	-	1.63	1.29
2007	Trntn	AA	9	9	0	0	48.2	186	27	14	14	2	1	0	2	17	0	57	2	0	5	1	.833	0	0--	-	1.57	2.59
2007	S-WB	AAA	6	6	0	0	34.2	137	25	8	8	2	1	0	3	11	1	34	0	0	1	1	.500	0	0--	-	2.40	2.08
2007	NYY	AL	3	3	0	0	19.0	77	13	6	4	1	0	0	0	9	0	15	0	0	1	0	1.000	0	0-0	0	2.42	1.89

Joe Kennedy

Pitches: L Bats: R Pos: RP-23; SP-16   Ht: 6'4" Wt: 252 Born: 5/24/1979 Age: 29

			HOW MUCH HE PITCHED						WHAT HE GAVE UP												THE RESULTS						
Year	Team	Lg	G	GS	CG	GF	IP	BFP	H	R	ER	HR	SH	SF	HB	TBB	IBB	SO	WP	Bk	W	L	Pct	ShO	Sv-Op	Hld	ERC	ERA
2007	Syrcse*	AAA	2	0	0	0	2.2	11	2	0	0	0	0	0	0	1	0	3	0	0	0	0	-	0	0--	-	2.01	0.00
2001	TB	AL	20	20	0	0	117.2	498	122	63	58	16	2	5	3	34	0	78	5	1	7	8	.467	0	0-0	0	4.23	4.44
2002	TB	AL	30	30	5	0	196.2	840	204	114	99	23	2	9	16	55	0	109	4	0	8	11	.421	1	0-0	0	4.29	4.53
2003	TB	AL	32	22	1	7	133.2	619	167	101	91	19	1	8	11	47	1	77	3	1	3	12	.200	1	1-2	1	5.92	6.13
2004	Col	NL	27	27	1	0	162.1	705	163	68	66	17	9	6	8	67	12	117	5	0	9	7	.563	0	0-0	0	4.29	3.66
2005	2 Tms		35	24	0	3	152.2	704	192	114	102	20	4	6	7	64	6	97	4	1	8	13	.381	0	0-2	0	6.04	6.01
2006	Oak	AL	39	0	0	8	35.0	148	34	10	9	1	0	0	1	13	3	29	2	0	4	1	.800	0	1-3	14	3.32	2.31
2007	3 Tms		39	16	0	6	110.2	501	119	66	59	9	6	9	9	55	1	51	9	0	4	9	.308	0	0-1	3	5.09	4.80
05	Col	NL	16	16	0	0	92.0	442	128	81	72	12	4	5	6	44	4	52	7	1	4	8	.333	0	0 0	0	7.24	7.04
05	Col	NL	19	8	0	3	60.2	262	64	33	30	8	0	1	1	20	2	45	1	0	4	5	.444	0	0-2	0	4.33	4.45
07	Oak	AL	27	16	0	4	101.0	450	109	53	49	9	6	7	5	48	1	42	7	0	3	9	.250	0	0-1	0	4.99	4.37
07	Ari	NL	3	0	0	0	2.2	19	4	7	6	0	0	1	4	2	0	1	2	0	0	0	-	0	0-0	1	13.34	20.25
07	Tor	AL	9	0	0	2	7.0	32	6	6	4	0	0	1	0	5	0	8	0	0	1	0	1.000	0	0-0	2	3.64	5.14
7 ML YEARS			222	139	7	24	908.2	4015	1001	536	484	105	24	43	55	335	23	558	36	3	43	61	.413	2	2-8	18	4.86	4.79

Logan Kensing

Pitches: R **Bats:** R **Pos:** RP-9 **Ht:** 6'1" **Wt:** 185 **Born:** 7/3/1982 **Age:** 25

Year	Team	Lg	G	GS	CG	GF	IP	BFP	H	R	ER	HR	SH	SF	HB	TBB	IBB	SO	WP	Bk	W	L	Pct	ShO	Sv-Op	Hld	ERC	ERA
2007	Mrlns*	R	3	2	0	0	3.0	9	0	0	0	0	0	0	0	0	0	5	0	0	0	0	-	0	0--	-	0.00	0.00
2007	Jupiter*	A+	1	0	0	0	0.2	6	4	2	2	1	0	0	0	0	0	2	0	0	0	0	-	0	0--	-	61.64	27.00
2007	Carlina*	AA	3	0	0	0	3.0	12	2	1	1	0	0	0	0	1	0	6	0	0	0	0	-	0	0--	-	1.57	3.00
2007	Albq*	AAA	8	0	0	3	9.0	40	7	4	4	0	0	0	0	7	1	8	0	0	0	1	.000	0	0--	-	3.35	4.00
2004	Fla	NL	5	3	0	2	13.2	66	19	15	15	5	0	1	1	9	0	7	2	0	0	3	.000	0	0-0	0	10.74	9.88
2005	Fla	NL	3	0	0	0	5.2	31	11	7	7	2	0	1	0	3	0	4	0	0	0	0	-	0	0-0	1	12.96	11.12
2006	Fla	NL	37	0	0	10	37.2	161	30	19	19	6	3	0	3	19	2	45	0	0	1	3	.250	0	1-7	14	4.02	4.54
2007	Fla	NL	9	0	0	0	13.1	59	11	2	2	0	1	0	2	7	2	13	0	0	3	0	1.000	0	0-0	0	3.15	1.35
	4 ML YEARS		54	3	0	12	70.1	317	71	43	43	13	4	2	6	38	4	69	2	0	4	6	.400	0	1-7	15	5.64	5.50

Jeff Kent

Bats: R **Throws:** R **Pos:** 2B-133; PH-4 **Ht:** 6'2" **Wt:** 210 **Born:** 3/7/1968 **Age:** 40

Year	Team	Lg	G	AB	H	2B	3B	HR	(Hm	Rd)	TB	R	RBI	RC	TBB	IBB	SO	HBP	SH	SF	SB	CS	SB%	GDP	Avg	OBP	Slg
1992	2 Tms		102	305	73	21	2	11	(4	7)	131	52	50	40	27	0	76	7	0	4	2	3	.40	5	.239	.312	.430
1993	NYM	NL	140	496	134	24	0	21	(9	12)	221	65	80	68	30	2	88	8	6	4	4	4	.50	11	.270	.320	.446
1994	NYM	NL	107	415	121	24	5	14	(10	4)	197	53	68	64	23	3	84	10	1	3	1	4	.20	7	.292	.341	.475
1995	NYM	NL	125	472	131	22	3	20	(11	9)	219	65	65	69	29	3	89	8	1	4	3	3	.50	9	.278	.327	.464
1996	2 Tms		128	437	124	27	1	12	(4	8)	189	61	55	61	31	1	78	2	1	6	6	4	.60	8	.284	.330	.432
1997	SF	NL	155	580	145	38	2	29	(13	16)	274	90	121	86	48	6	133	13	0	10	11	3	.79	14	.250	.316	.472
1998	SF	NL	137	526	156	37	3	31	(17	14)	292	94	128	100	48	4	110	9	1	10	9	4	.69	16	.297	.359	.555
1999	SF	NL	138	511	148	40	2	23	(11	12)	261	86	101	93	61	3	112	5	0	8	13	6	.68	12	.290	.366	.511
2000	SF	NL	159	587	196	41	7	33	(14	19)	350	114	125	138	90	6	107	9	0	9	12	9	.57	17	.334	.424	.596
2001	SF	NL	159	607	181	49	6	22	(8	14)	308	84	106	112	65	4	96	11	0	13	7	6	.54	11	.298	.369	.507
2002	SF	NL	152	623	195	42	2	37	(11	26)	352	102	108	105	52	3	101	4	0	3	5	1	.83	20	.313	.368	.565
2003	Hou	NL	130	505	150	39	1	22	(9	13)	257	77	93	92	39	2	85	5	0	3	6	2	.75	13	.297	.351	.509
2004	Hou	NL	145	540	156	34	8	27	(14	13)	287	96	107	87	49	3	96	6	0	11	7	3	.70	23	.289	.348	.531
2005	LAD	NL	149	553	160	36	0	29	(15	14)	283	100	105	105	72	8	85	8	0	4	6	2	.75	19	.289	.377	.512
2006	LAD	NL	115	407	119	27	3	14	(10	4)	194	61	68	71	55	8	69	8	0	3	1	2	.33	9	.292	.385	.477
2007	LAD	NL	136	494	149	36	1	20	(9	11)	247	78	79	75	57	4	61	5	0	6	1	3	.25	17	.302	.375	.500
92	Tor	AL	65	192	46	13	1	8	(2	6)	85	36	35	28	20	0	47	6	0	4	2	1	.67	3	.240	.324	.443
92	NYM	NL	37	113	27	8	1	3	(2	1)	46	16	15	12	7	0	29	1	0	0	0	2	.00	2	.239	.289	.407
96	NYM	NL	89	335	97	20	1	9	(2	7)	146	45	39	46	21	1	56	1	1	3	4	3	.57	7	.290	.331	.436
96	Cle	AL	39	102	27	7	0	3	(2	1)	43	16	16	15	10	0	22	1	0	3	2	1	.67	1	.265	.328	.422
	16 ML YEARS		2177	8058	2338	537	46	365	(169	196)	4062	1278	1459	1366	776	60	1470	118	10	101	94	59	.61	211	.290	.357	.504

Bobby Keppel

Pitches: R **Bats:** R **Pos:** RP-4 **Ht:** 6'5" **Wt:** 205 **Born:** 6/11/1982 **Age:** 26

Year	Team	Lg	G	GS	CG	GF	IP	BFP	H	R	ER	HR	SH	SF	HB	TBB	IBB	SO	WP	Bk	W	L	Pct	ShO	Sv-Op	Hld	ERC	ERA
2000	Kngspt	R+	8	6	0	0	29.0	136	31	22	22	1	0	0	4	13	0	29	6	0	1	2	.333	0	0--	-	4.54	6.83
2001	CptCty	A	26	20	1	3	124.1	516	118	58	43	6	2	2	14	25	1	87	7	0	6	7	.462	0	0--	-	3.13	3.11
2002	StLuci	A+	27	26	0	0	152.0	656	162	83	73	13	5	7	16	43	0	109	12	1	9	7	.563	0	0--	-	4.34	4.32
2003	Bnghtn	AA	18	17	2	0	94.2	388	92	36	32	6	5	1	6	27	0	46	3	1	7	4	.636	2	0--	-	3.60	3.04
2003	Bklyn	A-	3	3	0	0	14.1	57	10	5	4	0	0	0	2	2	0	13	0	0	2	0	1.000	0	0--	-	1.55	2.51
2004	StLuci	A+	2	2	0	0	10.0	37	7	2	1	0	0	0	2	0	0	6	0	0	1	1	.500	0	0--	-	1.47	0.90
2004	Norfolk	AAA	17	16	1	0	93.2	402	111	51	49	8	8	6	9	22	1	42	2	1	3	7	.300	0	0--	-	4.88	4.71
2005	Norfolk	AAA	5	5	0	0	27.1	112	24	11	10	0	0	0	4	6	0	19	1	0	2	1	.667	0	0--	-	2.68	3.29
2006	Omha	AAA	25	14	0	2	98.1	432	126	73	62	12	2	4	1	28	1	43	8	1	6	7	.462	0	1--	-	5.54	5.67
2007	ColSpr	AAA	26	23	0	0	138.0	620	162	95	84	14	3	3	10	60	1	64	6	1	8	10	.444	0	0--	-	5.63	5.48
2006	KC	AL	8	6	0	0	34.1	157	45	21	21	6	1	2	1	15	2	20	0	0	0	4	.000	0	0-0	0	6.85	5.50
2007	Col	NL	4	0	0	1	4.0	20	6	5	5	1	0	0	0	3	0	1	0	0	0	0	-	0	0-0	0	10.40	11.25
	2 ML YEARS		12	6	0	1	38.1	177	51	26	26	7	1	2	1	18	2	21	0	0	0	4	.000	0	0-0	0	7.20	6.10

Jeff Keppinger

Bats: R **Throws:** R **Pos:** SS-47; 3B-13; PH-7; 2B-3; 1B-1; LF-1; RF-1 **Ht:** 6'0" **Wt:** 180 **Born:** 4/21/1980 **Age:** 28

Year	Team	Lg	G	AB	H	2B	3B	HR	(Hm	Rd)	TB	R	RBI	RC	TBB	IBB	SO	HBP	SH	SF	SB	CS	SB%	GDP	Avg	OBP	Slg
2007	Srsota*	A+	3	12	4	2	0	0	(-	-)	6	1	1	1	0	0	0	0	0	1	0	1	.00	0	.333	.308	.500
2007	Lsvlle*	AAA	57	228	84	15	1	2	(-	-)	107	31	18	46	23	1	14	1	6	3	1	1	.50	2	.368	.424	.469
2004	NYM	NL	33	116	33	2	0	3	(3	0)	44	9	9	12	6	0	7	0	0	1	2	1	.67	6	.284	.317	.379
2006	KC	AL	22	60	16	2	0	2	(0	2)	24	11	8	8	5	1	6	0	2	0	0	0	-	2	.267	.323	.400
2007	Cin	NL	67	241	80	16	2	5	(2	3)	115	39	32	42	24	0	12	4	6	1	2	1	.67	11	.332	.400	.477
	3 ML YEARS		122	417	129	20	2	10	(5	5)	183	59	49	62	35	1	25	4	8	2	4	2	.67	19	.309	.367	.439

Bobby Kielty

Bats: B **Throws:** R **Pos:** RF-17; LF-12; PH-4; PR-2; CF-1; DH-1 **Ht:** 6'1" **Wt:** 225 **Born:** 8/5/1976 **Age:** 31

Year	Team	Lg	G	AB	H	2B	3B	HR	(Hm	Rd)	TB	R	RBI	RC	TBB	IBB	SO	HBP	SH	SF	SB	CS	SB%	GDP	Avg	OBP	Slg
2007	Scrmto*	AAA	9	33	13	4	0	0	(-	-)	17	6	1	7	4	0	7	0	0	0	0	0	-	1	.394	.459	.515
2007	Pwtckt*	AAA	10	38	9	1	0	2	(-	-)	16	7	5	5	5	0	14	0	0	0	0	0	-	0	.237	.326	.421
2001	Min	AL	37	104	26	8	0	2	(1	1)	40	8	14	13	8	2	25	1	0	5	3	0	1.00	2	.250	.297	.385
2002	Min	AL	112	289	84	14	3	12	(8	4)	140	49	46	59	52	4	66	5	0	4	4	1	.80	4	.291	.405	.484
2003	2 Tms	AL	137	427	104	26	1	13	(6	7)	171	71	57	68	71	6	92	7	0	4	8	3	.73	11	.244	.358	.400

148

		BATTING																	BASERUNNING				AVERAGES		
Year	Team	Lg	G	AB	H	2B	3B	HR	(Hm	Rd)	TB	R	RBI	RC	TBB	IBB	SO	HBP	SH	SF	SB	CS	SB%	GDP	Avg	OBP	Slg
2004	Oak	AL	83	238	51	14	1	7	(6	1)	88	29	31	29	35	0	47	3	1	1	1	0	1.00	5	.214	.321	.370
2005	Oak	AL	116	377	99	20	0	10	(6	4)	149	55	57	53	50	3	67	2	2	2	3	2	.60	14	.263	.350	.395
2006	Oak	AL	81	270	73	20	1	8	(5	3)	119	35	36	40	22	0	49	2	2	1	2	0	1.00	9	.270	.329	.441
2007	2 Tms	AL	33	87	19	3	0	1	(0	1)	25	10	12	7	8	0	26	2	0	4	0	0	-	4	.218	.287	.287
03	Min	AL	75	238	60	13	0	9	(4	5)	100	40	32	41	42	2	56	3	0	1	6	2	.75	5	.252	.370	.420
03	Tor	AL	62	189	44	13	1	4	(2	2)	71	31	25	27	29	4	36	4	0	3	2	1	.67	6	.233	.342	.376
07	Oak	AL	13	35	7	1	0	0	(0	0)	8	4	3	2	3	0	9	1	0	1	0	0	-	1	.200	.275	.229
07	Bos	AL	20	52	12	2	0	1	(0	1)	17	6	9	5	5	0	17	1	0	3	0	0	-	3	.231	.295	.327
	7 ML YEARS		599	1792	456	105	6	53	(32	21)	732	257	253	269	246	15	372	22	5	19	21	6	.78	49	.254	.348	.408

Byung-Hyun Kim

Pitches: R Bats: R Pos: SP-22; RP-6   Ht: 5'9" Wt: 175 Born: 1/19/1979 Age: 29

			HOW MUCH HE PITCHED						WHAT HE GAVE UP											THE RESULTS						
Year	Team	Lg	G	GS	CG	GF	IP	BFP	H	R	ER	HR	SH	SF	HB	TBB	IBB	SO	WP	Bk	W	L	Pct	ShO	Sv-Op	Hld	ERC	ERA
2007	ColSpr*	AAA	5	5	0	0	24.1	104	21	10	8	2	1	2	0	11	0	31	2	0	1	1	.500	0	0- -	-	3.37	2.96
1999	Ari	NL	25	0	0	10	27.1	121	20	15	14	2	1	0	5	20	2	31	4	1	1	2	.333	0	1-4	3	4.35	4.61
2000	Ari	NL	61	1	0	30	70.2	320	52	39	35	9	2	3	9	46	5	111	3	2	6	6	.500	0	14-20	5	4.04	4.46
2001	Ari	NL	78	0	0	44	98.0	392	58	32	32	10	5	0	8	44	3	113	5	1	5	6	.455	0	19-23	11	2.45	2.94
2002	Ari	NL	72	0	0	66	84.0	343	64	20	19	5	1	2	6	26	2	92	2	0	8	3	.727	0	36-42	0	2.45	2.04
2003	2 Tms		56	12	0	35	122.1	517	104	55	45	12	6	2	12	33	3	102	1	0	9	10	.474	0	16-19	1	3.02	3.31
2004	Bos	AL	7	3	0	2	17.1	77	17	15	12	1	0	2	2	7	1	6	1	0	2	1	.667	0	0-0	0	3.98	6.23
2005	Col	NL	40	22	0	3	148.0	667	156	82	80	17	8	7	14	71	8	115	11	1	5	12	.294	0	0-2	1	5.13	4.86
2006	Col	NL	27	27	0	0	155.0	689	179	103	96	18	8	5	8	61	8	129	5	1	8	12	.400	0	0-0	0	5.25	5.57
2007	3 Tms		28	22	0	4	118.1	562	131	90	80	20	4	6	16	68	3	107	4	1	10	8	.556	0	0-0	0	6.44	6.08
03	Ari	NL	7	7	0	0	43.0	181	34	17	17	6	3	0	4	15	0	33	0	0	1	5	.167	0	0-0	0	3.32	3.56
03	Bos	AL	49	5	0	35	79.1	336	70	38	28	6	3	2	8	18	3	69	1	0	8	5	.615	0	16-19	1	2.87	3.18
07	Col	NL	3	1	0	2	6.0	29	6	7	7	2	0	3	1	4	0	2	0	0	1	2	.333	0	0-0	0	7.63	10.50
07	Fla	NL	23	19	0	2	109.2	511	114	74	66	17	3	3	14	62	3	102	4	1	9	5	.643	0	0-0	0	5.84	5.42
07	Ari	NL	2	2	0	0	2.2	22	11	9	7	1	1	0	1	2	0	3	0	0	0	1	.000	0	0-0	0	34.68	23.63
	9 ML YEARS		394	87	0	194	841.0	3688	781	451	413	94	35	27	80	376	35	806	36	7	54	60	.474	0	86-110	21	4.24	4.42

Ray King

Pitches: L Bats: L Pos: RP-67   Ht: 6'1" Wt: 240 Born: 1/15/1974 Age: 34

			HOW MUCH HE PITCHED						WHAT HE GAVE UP											THE RESULTS						
Year	Team	Lg	G	GS	CG	GF	IP	BFP	H	R	ER	HR	SH	SF	HB	TBB	IBB	SO	WP	Bk	W	L	Pct	ShO	Sv-Op	Hld	ERC	ERA
2007	Hrsbrg*	AA	1	1	0	0	1.1	5	0	0	0	0	0	0	0	1	0	1	0	0	0	0	-	0	0- -	-	0.57	0.00
1999	ChC	NL	10	0	0	0	10.2	50	11	8	7	2	1	0	1	10	0	5	1	0	0	0	-	0	0-0	2	8.10	5.91
2000	Mil	NL	36	0	0	8	28.2	111	18	7	4	1	0	1	0	10	1	19	1	0	3	2	.600	0	0-1	5	1.64	1.26
2001	Mil	NL	82	0	0	19	55.0	234	49	22	22	5	3	2	1	25	7	49	2	0	0	4	.000	0	1-4	18	3.51	3.60
2002	Mil	NL	76	0	0	15	65.0	273	61	24	22	5	5	2	3	24	6	50	0	1	3	2	.600	0	0-1	15	3.55	3.05
2003	All	NL	80	0	0	9	59.0	247	46	30	23	3	1	2	1	27	2	43	4	0	3	4	.429	0	0-1	18	2.79	3.51
2004	StL	NL	86	0	0	9	62.0	248	43	19	18	1	2	1	3	24	0	40	2	0	5	2	.714	0	0-1	31	2.13	2.61
2005	StL	NL	77	0	0	18	40.0	177	46	17	15	4	0	1	3	16	0	23	1	0	4	4	.500	0	0-6	15	5.37	3.38
2006	Col	NL	67	0	0	7	44.2	199	56	26	22	6	3	3	2	20	0	23	3	0	1	4	.200	0	1-2	15	6.51	4.43
2007	2 Tms		67	0	0	10	39.2	175	37	21	21	6	1	2	2	21	1	25	2	0	1	1	.500	0	0-0	11	4.75	4.76
07	Was	NL	55	0	0	7	33.2	149	31	17	17	5	1	2	2	18	1	18	2	0	1	1	.500	0	0-0	10	4.70	4.54
07	Mil	NL	12	0	0	3	6.0	26	6	4	4	1	0	0	0	3	0	7	0	0	0	0	-	0	0-0	1	5.06	6.00
	9 ML YEARS		581	0	0	95	404.2	1714	367	174	154	33	16	14	16	177	17	277	16	1	20	23	.465	0	2-16	131	3.72	3.43

Josh Kinney

Pitches: R Bats: R Pos: P   Ht: 6'1" Wt: 195 Born: 3/31/1979 Age: 29

			HOW MUCH HE PITCHED						WHAT HE GAVE UP											THE RESULTS						
Year	Team	Lg	G	GS	CG	GF	IP	BFP	H	R	ER	HR	SH	SF	HB	TBB	IBB	SO	WP	Bk	W	L	Pct	ShO	Sv-Op	Hld	ERC	ERA
2001	NewJrs	A-	3	0	0	0	5.2	18	2	0	0	0	0	0	0	0	0	5	0	0	2	0	1.000	0	0- -	-	0.30	0.00
2001	Peoria	A	27	0	0	5	41.0	192	47	24	20	1	4	2	7	15	0	35	4	1	1	4	.200	0	0- -	-	4.75	4.39
2002	Ptomc	A+	44	0	0	28	55.0	239	52	21	14	2	2	1	3	23	1	42	6	0	1	3	.250	0	7- -	-	3.55	2.29
2003	PlmBh	A+	31	0	0	10	41.1	167	38	7	7	0	2	0	0	10	4	35	5	0	3	0	1.000	0	3- -	-	2.31	1.52
2003	Tenn	AA	29	0	0	12	39.2	147	19	4	3	2	1	0	0	12	0	48	1	0	2	1	.667	0	2- -	1	1.18	0.68
2004	Tenn	AA	50	0	0	25	55.2	270	67	40	34	6	0	3	3	34	0	48	6	0	3	8	.273	0	4- -	-	6.30	5.50
2004	PlmBh	A+	7	0	0	7	8.1	39	8	6	4	1	0	0	1	6	2	12	0	0	1	0	1.000	0	0- -	-	5.33	4.32
2005	Sprgfld	AA	32	0	0	22	42.0	165	28	9	6	2	0	2	1	12	0	42	1	0	5	2	.714	0	11- -	1	1.67	1.29
2005	Memp	AAA	26	0	0	8	25.2	135	40	21	21	4	0	1	2	19	1	25	4	0	1	2	.333	0	0- -	-	9.84	7.36
2006	Memp	AAA	51	0	0	17	71.0	286	46	16	12	2	4	1	5	29	4	76	12	0	2	2	.500	0	3- -	-	2.03	1.52
2006	StL	NL	21	0	0	4	25.0	99	17	9	9	3	0	0	1	8	0	22	0	0	0	0	-	0	0-0	2	2.40	3.24

Ian Kinsler

Bats: R Throws: R Pos: 2B-130; PH-1   Ht: 6'0" Wt: 200 Born: 6/22/1982 Age: 26

			BATTING																	BASERUNNING				AVERAGES		
Year	Team	Lg	G	AB	H	2B	3B	HR	(Hm	Rd)	TB	R	RBI	RC	TBB	IBB	SO	HBP	SH	SF	SB	CS	SB%	GDP	Avg	OBP	Slg
2003	Spkane	A-	51	188	52	10	6	1	(-	-)	77	32	15	30	20	0	34	4	0	4	11	3	.79	5	.277	.352	.410
2004	Clinton	A	59	224	90	30	1	11	(-	-)	155	52	52	66	25	3	36	3	1	2	16	5	.76	7	.402	.465	.692
2004	Frisco	AA	71	277	83	21	4	9	(-	-)	133	51	46	55	32	1	47	15	1	1	7	4	.64	5	.300	.400	.480
2005	Okla	AAA	131	530	145	28	2	23	(-	-)	246	102	94	90	53	0	89	9	2	3	19	5	.79	21	.274	.348	.464
2006	Okla	AAA	10	39	10	3	0	2	(-	-)	19	7	6	5	2	0	5	0	0	0	1	1	.50	1	.256	.293	.487

Year	Team	Lg	G	AB	H	2B	3B	HR	(Hm	Rd)	TB	R	RBI	RC	TBB	IBB	SO	HBP	SH	SF	SB	CS	SB%	GDP	Avg	OBP	Slg
2007	Okla	AAA	3	13	5	0	0	0	(-	-)	5	1	3	2	0	0	1	0	0	1	2	0	1.00	0	.385	.357	.385
2006	Tex	AL	120	423	121	27	1	14	(10	4)	192	65	55	65	40	1	64	3	1	7	11	4	.73	12	.286	.347	.454
2007	Tex	AL	130	483	127	22	2	20	(12	8)	213	96	61	79	62	2	83	9	8	4	23	2	.92	14	.263	.355	.441
2 ML YEARS			250	906	248	49	3	34	(22	12)	405	161	116	144	102	3	147	12	9	11	34	6	.85	26	.274	.351	.447

Ryan Klesko

Bats: L **Throws:** L **Pos:** 1B-100; PH-19; LF-2; RF-1   **Ht:** 6'3" **Wt:** 220 **Born:** 6/12/1971 **Age:** 37

Year	Team	Lg	G	AB	H	2B	3B	HR	(Hm	Rd)	TB	R	RBI	RC	TBB	IBB	SO	HBP	SH	SF	SB	CS	SB%	GDP	Avg	OBP	Slg
1992	Atl	NL	13	14	0	0	0	0	(0	0)	0	0	1	0	0	0	5	1	0	0	0	0	-	0	.000	.067	.000
1993	Atl	NL	22	17	6	1	0	2	(2	0)	13	3	5	5	3	1	4	0	0	0	0	0	-	0	.353	.450	.765
1994	Atl	NL	92	245	68	13	3	17	(7	10)	138	42	47	45	26	3	48	1	0	4	1	0	1.00	8	.278	.344	.563
1995	Atl	NL	107	329	102	25	2	23	(15	8)	200	48	70	73	47	10	72	2	0	3	5	4	.56	8	.310	.396	.608
1996	Atl	NL	153	528	149	21	4	34	(20	14)	280	90	93	99	68	10	129	2	0	4	6	3	.67	10	.282	.364	.530
1997	Atl	NL	143	467	122	23	6	24	(10	14)	229	67	84	73	48	5	130	4	1	2	4	4	.50	12	.261	.334	.490
1998	Atl	NL	129	427	117	29	1	18	(8	10)	202	69	70	72	56	5	66	3	0	4	5	3	.63	9	.274	.359	.473
1999	Atl	NL	133	404	120	28	2	21	(12	9)	215	55	80	80	53	8	69	2	0	7	5	2	.71	6	.297	.376	.532
2000	SD	NL	145	494	140	33	2	26	(9	17)	255	88	92	101	91	9	81	1	0	4	23	7	.77	10	.283	.393	.516
2001	SD	NL	146	538	154	34	6	30	(15	15)	290	105	113	111	88	7	89	3	0	9	23	4	.85	16	.286	.384	.539
2002	SD	NL	146	540	162	39	1	29	(11	18)	290	90	95	111	76	11	86	4	1	4	6	2	.75	7	.300	.388	.537
2003	SD	NL	121	397	100	18	0	21	(8	13)	181	47	67	59	65	5	83	3	0	9	2	5	.29	11	.252	.354	.456
2004	SD	NL	127	402	117	32	2	9	(3	6)	180	58	66	76	73	6	67	1	1	3	3	2	.60	8	.291	.399	.448
2005	SD	NL	137	443	110	19	1	18	(10	8)	185	61	58	64	75	2	80	1	0	1	3	4	.43	6	.248	.358	.418
2006	SD	NL	6	4	3	1	0	0	(0	0)	4	0	2	3	2	0	0	0	0	0	0	0	-	0	.750	.833	1.000
2007	SF	NL	116	362	94	27	3	6	(3	3)	145	51	44	44	46	2	68	1	1	1	5	1	.83	14	.260	.344	.401
16 ML YEARS			1736	5611	1564	343	33	278	(133	145)	2807	874	987	1016	817	84	1077	29	4	55	91	41	.69	125	.279	.370	.500

Steve Kline

Pitches: L **Bats:** R **Pos:** RP-68   **Ht:** 6'1" **Wt:** 210 **Born:** 8/22/1972 **Age:** 35

Year	Team	Lg	G	GS	CG	GF	IP	BFP	H	R	ER	HR	SH	SF	HB	TBB	IBB	SO	WP	Bk	W	L	Pct	ShO	Sv-Op	Hld	ERC	ERA
1997	2 Tms		46	1	0	7	52.2	248	73	37	35	10	4	2	2	23	4	37	4	1	4	4	.500	0	0-3	5	7.39	5.98
1998	Mon	NL	78	0	0	18	71.2	319	62	25	22	4	1	2	3	41	7	76	5	0	3	6	.333	0	1-2	18	3.60	2.76
1999	Mon	NL	82	0	0	18	69.2	297	56	32	29	8	3	1	3	33	6	69	2	0	7	4	.636	0	0-2	16	3.40	3.75
2000	Mon	NL	83	0	0	42	82.1	349	88	36	32	8	2	1	3	27	2	64	4	0	1	5	.167	0	14-18	12	4.37	3.50
2001	StL	NL	89	0	0	26	75.0	303	53	16	15	3	4	5	4	29	7	54	1	0	3	3	.500	0	9-10	17	2.20	1.80
2002	StL	NL	66	0	0	17	58.1	241	54	23	22	3	2	2	1	21	2	41	1	0	2	1	.667	0	6-8	21	3.28	3.39
2003	StL	NL	78	0	0	22	63.2	274	56	29	27	5	3	2	3	30	5	31	2	0	5	5	.500	0	3-7	18	3.59	3.82
2004	StL	NL	67	0	0	22	50.1	202	37	12	10	3	3	1	4	17	4	35	1	0	2	2	.500	0	3-4	15	2.43	1.79
2005	Bal	AL	67	0	0	23	61.0	264	59	34	29	11	2	2	0	30	5	36	4	3	2	4	.333	0	0-3	9	4.75	4.28
2006	SF	NL	72	0	0	17	51.2	227	53	24	21	3	6	1	1	26	3	33	1	0	4	3	.571	0	1-1	18	4.35	3.66
2007	SF	NL	68	0	0	19	46.0	216	58	25	24	2	3	0	2	18	3	17	1	0	1	2	.333	0	2-4	9	5.03	4.70
97	Cle	AL	20	1	0	0	26.1	130	42	19	17	6	1	0	1	13	1	17	3	1	3	1	.750	0	0-2	4	9.58	5.81
97	Mon	NL	26	0	0	7	26.1	118	31	18	18	4	3	2	1	10	3	20	1	0	1	3	.250	0	0-1	1	5.39	6.15
11 ML YEARS			796	1	0	231	682.1	2940	649	293	266	60	33	19	26	295	48	493	26	4	34	39	.466	0	39-62	158	3.90	3.51

Jon Knott

Bats: R **Throws:** R **Pos:** DH-3; LF-2; PH-2   **Ht:** 6'3" **Wt:** 233 **Born:** 8/4/1978 **Age:** 29

Year	Team	Lg	G	AB	H	2B	3B	HR	(Hm	Rd)	TB	R	RBI	RC	TBB	IBB	SO	HBP	SH	SF	SB	CS	SB%	GDP	Avg	OBP	Slg
2007	Norfolk*	AAA	87	288	72	15	2	13	(-	-)	130	42	34	49	48	0	80	1	0	3	4	2	.67	5	.250	.356	.451
2004	SD	NL	9	14	3	2	0	0	(0	0)	5	1	1	1	1	0	5	0	0	0	0	0	-	0	.214	.267	.357
2006	SD	NL	3	3	0	0	0	0	(0	0)	0	0	0	0	0	0	1	0	0	0	0	0	-	0	.000	.000	.000
2007	Bal	AL	7	14	3	0	0	1	(0	1)	6	3	4	4	4	0	3	0	0	1	0	0	-	1	.214	.368	.429
3 ML YEARS			19	31	6	2	0	1	(0	1)	11	4	5	5	5	0	9	0	0	1	0	0	-	1	.194	.297	.355

Dan Kolb

Pitches: R **Bats:** R **Pos:** RP-3   **Ht:** 6'4" **Wt:** 210 **Born:** 3/29/1975 **Age:** 33

Year	Team	Lg	G	GS	CG	GF	IP	BFP	H	R	ER	HR	SH	SF	HB	TBB	IBB	SO	WP	Bk	W	L	Pct	ShO	Sv-Op	Hld	ERC	ERA
2007	Indy*	AAA	18	0	0	12	20.0	88	19	7	7	0	0	0	3	8	0	16	2	0	2	1	.667	0	4--	-	3.64	3.15
1999	Tex	AL	16	0	0	6	31.0	139	33	18	16	2	0	1	0	15	0	15	2	0	2	1	.667	0	0-0	0	4.63	4.65
2000	Tex	AL	1	0	0	0	0.2	9	5	5	5	0	0	1	0	2	0	0	0	0	0	0	-	0	0-0	0	69.84	67.50
2001	Tex	AL	17	0	0	1	15.1	70	15	8	8	2	1	1	0	10	1	15	3	0	0	0	-	0	0-0	7	5.03	4.70
2002	Tex	AL	34	0	0	14	32.0	145	27	17	15	1	1	2	1	22	2	20	6	0	3	6	.333	0	1-4	2	3.74	4.22
2003	Mil	NL	37	0	0	25	41.1	175	34	10	9	2	1	0	1	19	3	39	1	0	1	2	.333	0	21-23	4	2.96	1.96
2004	Mil	NL	64	0	0	48	57.1	236	50	22	19	3	3	1	3	15	1	21	2	0	0	4	.000	0	39-44	1	2.73	2.98
2005	Atl	NL	65	0	0	34	57.2	270	78	39	38	5	2	1	1	29	5	39	5	0	3	8	.273	0	11-18	6	6.52	5.93
2006	Mil	NL	53	0	0	18	48.1	213	53	28	26	4	1	3	1	20	1	26	5	0	2	2	.500	0	1-3	6	4.63	4.84
2007	Pit	NL	3	0	0	1	3.0	16	6	3	3	1	0	1	0	2	1	2	0	0	0	0	-	0	0-0	0	14.00	9.00
9 ML YEARS			290	0	0	147	286.2	1273	301	150	139	20	9	10	8	134	14	177	24	0	11	23	.324	0	73-92	26	4.43	4.36

Shane Komine

Pitches: R **Bats:** R **Pos:** RP-2   **Ht:** 5'9" **Wt:** 180 **Born:** 10/18/1980 **Age:** 27

Year	Team	Lg	G	GS	CG	GF	IP	BFP	H	R	ER	HR	SH	SF	HB	TBB	IBB	SO	WP	Bk	W	L	Pct	ShO	Sv-Op	Hld	ERC	ERA
2002	Visalia	A+	18	0	0	2	25.2	120	23	20	17	2	3	0	1	20	3	22	3	0	1	3	.250	0	0--	-	4.67	5.96
2003	Kane	A	8	8	1	0	54.1	216	45	12	11	1	0	3	2	9	0	50	0	1	6	0	1.000	1	0--	-	1.97	1.82
2003	Mdland	AA	19	18	1	0	103.1	442	108	51	43	6	5	6	1	30	2	75	4	1	4	6	.400	1	0--	-	3.59	3.75
2004	Mdland	AA	17	17	0	0	94.1	409	103	56	50	10	5	5	3	28	0	65	6	1	4	5	.444	0	0--	-	4.34	4.77
2005	As	R	4	4	0	0	8.1	42	10	10	9	0	0	1	1	7	0	11	1	2	0	1	.000	0	0--	-	6.68	9.72
2005	Stcktn	A+	2	2	0	0	8.2	39	10	4	4	0	0	0	2	3	0	11	3	0	0	0	-	0	0--	-	5.02	4.15
2005	Mdland	AA	5	5	0	0	31.1	128	27	12	11	5	0	0	2	7	0	33	1	0	2	1	.667	0	0--	-	3.27	3.16
2006	Scrmto	AAA	24	22	1	0	140.0	591	145	67	63	13	2	2	6	38	2	116	11	1	11	8	.579	1	0--	-	3.91	4.05
2007	Scrmto	AAA	23	23	0	0	133.0	569	143	76	72	21	5	4	4	46	3	99	9	1	5	12	.294	0	0--	-	4.89	4.87
2006	Oak	AL	2	2	0	0	9.0	45	10	5	5	3	0	0	0	8	1	1	0	0	0	0	-	0	0-0	0	8.41	5.00
2007	Oak	AL	2	0	0	1	7.2	31	6	4	4	2	0	1	1	1	0	1	0	0	0	0	-	0	0-0	0	3.29	4.70
	2 ML YEARS		4	2	0	1	16.2	76	16	9	9	5	0	1	1	9	1	2	0	0	0	0	-	0	0-0	0	5.93	4.86

Paul Konerko

Bats: R **Throws:** R **Pos:** 1B-141; DH-10   **Ht:** 6'2" **Wt:** 215 **Born:** 3/5/1976 **Age:** 32

Year	Team	Lg	G	AB	H	2B	3B	HR	(Hm	Rd)	TB	R	RBI	RC	TBB	IBB	SO	HBP	SH	SF	SB	CS	SB%	GDP	Avg	OBP	Slg
1997	LAD	NL	6	7	1	0	0	0	(0	0)	1	0	0	0	1	0	2	0	0	0	0	0	-	1	.143	.250	.143
1998	2 Tms	NL	75	217	47	4	0	7	(2	5)	72	21	29	17	16	0	40	3	0	3	0	1	.00	10	.217	.276	.332
1999	CWS	AL	142	513	151	31	4	24	(18	6)	262	71	81	86	45	0	68	2	1	3	1	0	1.00	19	.294	.352	.511
2000	CWS	AL	143	524	156	31	1	21	(10	11)	252	84	97	86	47	0	72	10	0	5	1	0	1.00	12	.298	.363	.481
2001	CWS	AL	156	582	164	35	4	32	(19	13)	295	92	99	99	54	6	89	9	0	5	1	0	1.00	17	.282	.349	.507
2002	CWS	AL	151	570	173	30	0	27	(13	14)	284	81	104	96	44	2	72	9	0	7	0	0	-	17	.304	.359	.498
2003	CWS	AL	137	444	104	19	0	18	(9	9)	177	49	65	42	43	7	50	4	0	4	0	0	-	28	.234	.305	.399
2004	CWS	AL	155	563	156	22	0	41	(29	12)	301	84	117	106	69	5	107	6	0	5	1	0	1.00	23	.277	.359	.535
2005	CWS	AL	158	575	163	24	0	40	(23	17)	307	98	100	106	81	10	109	5	0	3	0	0	-	9	.283	.375	.534
2006	CWS	AL	152	566	177	30	0	35	(21	14)	312	97	113	110	60	3	104	8	0	9	1	0	1.00	25	.313	.381	.551
2007	CWS	AL	151	549	142	34	0	31	(17	14)	269	71	90	88	78	9	102	3	0	6	0	1	.00	21	.259	.351	.490
98	LAD	NL	49	144	31	1	0	4	(1	2)	44	14	16	10	10	0	30	2	0	2	0	1	.00	5	.215	.272	.306
98	Cin	NL	26	73	16	3	0	3	(0	3)	28	7	13	7	6	0	10	1	0	1	0	0	-	5	.219	.284	.384
	11 ML YEARS		1426	5110	1434	260	5	276	(159	117)	2532	748	895	836	538	42	815	59	1	50	5	2	.71	192	.281	.353	.495

Mike Koplove

Pitches: R **Bats:** R **Pos:** RP-5   **Ht:** 5'11" **Wt:** 175 **Born:** 8/30/1976 **Age:** 31

Year	Team	Lg	G	GS	CG	GF	IP	BFP	H	R	ER	HR	SH	SF	HB	TBB	IBB	SO	WP	Bk	W	L	Pct	ShO	Sv-Op	Hld	ERC	ERA
2007	Buffalo*	AAA	51	0	0	28	54.0	226	49	16	15	3	1	0	1	22	0	44	2	1	4	2	.667	0	14--	-	3.42	2.50
2001	Ari	NL	9	0	0	1	10.0	50	8	7	4	1	1	0	2	9	1	14	1	0	1	0	1.000	0	0-0	1	6.26	3.60
2002	Ari	NL	55	0	0	15	61.2	249	47	24	23	2	4	1	0	23	4	46	1	0	6	1	.857	0	0-0	10	2.23	3.36
2003	Ari	NL	31	0	0	5	37.2	157	31	11	9	3	2	2	5	10	1	27	1	0	3	0	1.000	0	0-1	5	2.93	2.15
2004	Ari	NL	76	0	0	24	86.2	371	86	42	39	7	8	1	5	37	10	55	4	0	4	4	.500	0	2-8	19	4.14	4.05
2005	Ari	NL	44	0	0	11	49.2	217	48	31	28	6	1	3	6	20	3	28	1	1	2	1	.667	0	0-2	9	4.45	5.07
2006	Ari	NL	2	0	0	0	3.0	15	5	1	1	0	1	0	0	2	0	1	0	0	0	0	-	0	0-0	0	8.83	3.00
2007	Cle	AL	5	0	0	4	6.0	26	6	4	4	0	0	0	1	2	0	4	0	0	0	0	-	0	0-0	0	3.79	6.00
	7 ML YEARS		222	0	0	60	254.2	1085	231	120	108	19	17	7	19	103	19	175	8	1	15	7	.682	0	2-11	44	3.60	3.82

John Koronka

Pitches: L **Bats:** L **Pos:** SP-2   **Ht:** 6'1" **Wt:** 180 **Born:** 7/3/1980 **Age:** 27

Year	Team	Lg	G	GS	CG	GF	IP	BFP	H	R	ER	HR	SH	SF	HB	TBB	IBB	SO	WP	Bk	W	L	Pct	ShO	Sv-Op	Hld	ERC	ERA
2007	Okla*	AAA	14	14	0	0	83.2	369	88	45	41	9	4	6	1	37	0	53	4	0	6	4	.600	0	0--	-	4.64	4.41
2007	Buffalo*	AAA	9	9	0	0	48.1	217	62	25	19	2	0	0	1	17	0	29	2	0	3	3	.500	1	0--	-	5.22	3.54
2005	ChC	NL	4	3	0	1	15.2	76	19	13	13	2	1	0	0	8	0	10	1	2	1	2	.333	0	0-0	0	5.68	7.47
2006	Tex	AL	23	23	0	0	125.0	554	145	80	79	17	1	7	5	47	2	61	4	1	7	7	.500	0	0-0	0	5.37	5.69
2007	Tex	AL	2	2	0	0	10.1	52	16	9	9	0	2	1	1	5	0	2	0	0	0	2	.000	0	0-0	0	7.26	7.84
	3 ML YEARS		29	28	0	1	151.0	682	180	102	101	19	4	8	6	60	2	73	5	3	8	11	.421	0	0-0	0	5.53	6.02

Joe Koshansky

Bats: L **Throws:** L **Pos:** PH-14; 1B-3; PR-1   **Ht:** 6'4" **Wt:** 225 **Born:** 5/26/1982 **Age:** 26

Year	Team	Lg	G	AB	H	2B	3B	HR	(Hm	Rd)	TB	R	RBI	RC	TBB	IBB	SO	HBP	SH	SF	SB	CS	SB%	GDP	Avg	OBP	Slg
2004	TriCity	A-	66	239	56	18	0	12	(-	-)	110	41	43	38	31	1	84	4	2	2	1	0	1.00	4	.234	.330	.460
2005	Ashvll	A	120	453	132	31	1	36	(-	-)	273	92	103	100	53	7	122	11	0	8	6	6	.50	14	.291	.373	.603
2005	Tulsa	AA	12	45	12	3	0	2	(-	-)	21	5	12	6	2	0	15	0	0	1	0	0	-	0	.267	.292	.467
2006	Tulsa	AA	132	500	142	28	0	31	(-	-)	263	84	109	98	64	5	134	6	1	2	3	2	.60	12	.284	.371	.526
2007	ColSpr	AAA	136	498	147	30	2	21	(-	-)	244	79	99	94	67	4	128	2	0	2	4	3	.57	14	.295	.380	.490
2007	Col	NL	17	12	1	1	0	0	(0	0)	2	0	2	1	2	0	5	0	0	1	0	0	-	0	.083	.200	.167

Casey Kotchman

Bats: L **Throws:** L **Pos:** 1B-130; PH-15; DH-1   **Ht:** 6'3" **Wt:** 215 **Born:** 2/22/1983 **Age:** 25

							BATTING														BASERUNNING				AVERAGES		
Year	Team	Lg	G	AB	H	2B	3B	HR	(Hm	Rd)	TB	R	RBI	RC	TBB	IBB	SO	HBP	SH	SF	SB	CS	SB%	GDP	Avg	OBP	Slg
2004	LAA	AL	38	116	26	6	0	0	(0	0)	32	7	15	14	7	3	11	4	0	1	3	0	1.00	5	.224	.289	.276
2005	LAA	AL	47	126	35	5	0	7	(5	2)	61	16	22	21	15	0	18	0	1	1	1	1	.50	3	.278	.352	.484
2006	LAA	AL	29	79	12	2	0	1	(0	1)	17	6	6	1	7	0	13	0	2	0	0	1	.00	2	.152	.221	.215
2007	LAA	AL	137	443	131	37	3	11	(5	6)	207	64	68	74	53	1	43	4	3	5	2	4	.33	17	.296	.372	.467
	4 ML YEARS		251	764	204	50	3	19	(10	9)	317	93	111	110	82	4	85	8	6	7	6	6	.50	25	.267	.341	.415

Mark Kotsay

Bats: L **Throws:** L **Pos:** CF-56   **Ht:** 6'0" **Wt:** 204 **Born:** 12/2/1975 **Age:** 32

							BATTING														BASERUNNING				AVERAGES		
Year	Team	Lg	G	AB	H	2B	3B	HR	(Hm	Rd)	TB	R	RBI	RC	TBB	IBB	SO	HBP	SH	SF	SB	CS	SB%	GDP	Avg	OBP	Slg
2007	Scrmto*	AAA	10	37	10	1	0	0	(-	-)	11	2	2	5	7	0	1	0	0	0	2	0	1.00	1	.270	.386	.297
1997	Fla	NL	14	52	10	1	1	0	(0	0)	13	5	4	3	4	0	7	0	1	0	3	0	1.00	1	.192	.250	.250
1998	Fla	NL	154	578	161	25	7	11	(5	6)	233	72	68	70	34	2	61	1	7	3	10	5	.67	17	.279	.318	.403
1999	Fla	NL	148	495	134	23	9	8	(5	3)	199	57	50	58	29	5	50	0	2	9	7	6	.54	11	.271	.306	.402
2000	Fla	NL	152	530	158	31	5	12	(5	7)	235	87	57	78	42	2	46	0	2	4	19	9	.68	17	.298	.347	.443
2001	SD	NL	119	406	118	29	2	10	(3	7)	179	67	58	65	48	1	58	2	1	3	13	5	.72	11	.291	.366	.441
2002	SD	NL	153	578	169	27	7	17	(11	6)	261	82	61	92	59	0	89	3	2	4	11	9	.55	10	.292	.359	.452
2003	SD	NL	128	482	128	28	4	7	(1	6)	185	64	38	59	56	3	82	1	1	1	6	3	.67	8	.266	.343	.384
2004	Oak	AL	148	606	190	37	3	15	(9	6)	278	78	63	94	55	5	70	2	5	5	8	5	.62	6	.314	.370	.459
2005	Oak	AL	139	582	163	35	1	15	(4	11)	245	75	82	86	40	3	51	1	2	4	5	5	.50	13	.280	.325	.421
2006	Oak	AL	129	502	138	29	3	7	(1	6)	194	57	59	63	44	1	55	0	2	4	6	3	.67	18	.275	.332	.386
2007	Oak	AL	56	206	44	14	0	1	(0	1)	61	20	20	19	19	3	20	0	0	1	1	1	.50	4	.214	.279	.296
	11 ML YEARS		1340	5017	1413	279	41	103	(44	59)	2083	664	560	687	430	25	589	12	27	40	89	51	.64	116	.282	.337	.415

Kevin Kouzmanoff

Bats: R **Throws:** R **Pos:** 3B-136; PH-12   **Ht:** 6'1" **Wt:** 210 **Born:** 7/25/1981 **Age:** 26

							BATTING														BASERUNNING				AVERAGES		
Year	Team	Lg	G	AB	H	2B	3B	HR	(Hm	Rd)	TB	R	RBI	RC	TBB	IBB	SO	HBP	SH	SF	SB	CS	SB%	GDP	Avg	OBP	Slg
2003	MhVlly	A-	54	206	56	8	1	8	(-	-)	90	31	33	32	21	1	36	3	0	4	2	1	.67	6	.272	.342	.437
2004	Lk Cty	A	123	473	156	35	5	16	(-	-)	249	74	87	97	44	0	75	9	0	5	5	4	.56	17	.330	.394	.526
2004	Akron	AA	7	24	5	1	1	1	(-	-)	11	3	6	3	2	0	5	0	0	1	0	0	-	0	.208	.259	.458
2005	Knstn	A+	68	254	86	20	4	12	(-	-)	150	47	58	58	24	1	51	5	0	4	1	0	.75	6	.339	.401	.591
2005	MhVlly	A-	3	7	1	0	0	0	(-	-)	1	0	0	0	1	0	2	0	0	0	0	0	-	0	.143	.250	.143
2006	Akron	AA	67	244	95	19	1	15	(-	-)	161	46	55	66	23	6	34	6	0	3	2	3	.40	5	.389	.449	.660
2006	Buffalo	AAA	27	102	36	9	0	7	(-	-)	66	22	20	25	10	0	12	1	0	2	1	1	.67	1	.353	.409	.647
2006	Cle	AL	16	56	12	2	0	3	(0	3)	23	4	11	7	5	0	12	0	0	0	0	0	-	3	.214	.279	.411
2007	SD	NL	145	484	133	30	2	18	(5	13)	221	57	74	69	32	2	94	10	2	6	1	0	1.00	9	.275	.329	.457
	2 ML YEARS		161	540	145	32	2	21	(5	16)	244	61	85	76	37	2	106	10	2	6	1	0	1.00	12	.269	.324	.452

Marc Kroon

Pitches: R **Bats:** R **Pos:** P   **Ht:** 6'2" **Wt:** 190 **Born:** 4/2/1973 **Age:** 35

			HOW MUCH HE PITCHED						WHAT HE GAVE UP										THE RESULTS						
Year	Team	Lg	G	GS	CG	GF	IP	BFP	H	R	ER	HR	SH	SF	HB	TBB	IBB	SO	WP	Bk	W	L	Pct	ShO	Sv-Op Hld	ERC	ERA
2007	Yokha*	Jap	40	0	0	37	37.1	155	31	12	11	3	-	-	1	12	-	56	5	0	3	1	.750	0	27- - -	2.81	2.65
1995	SD	NL	2	0	0	1	1.2	7	1	2	2	0	0	0	0	2	0	2	0	0	0	1	.000	0	0-0 0	4.62	10.80
1997	SD	NL	12	0	0	2	11.1	56	14	9	9	2	0	0	1	5	0	12	1	0	0	1	.000	0	0-0 1	6.21	7.15
1998	2 Tms	NL	6	0	0	4	7.2	38	7	8	8	0	0	0	1	9	0	6	2	1	0	0	-	0	0-0 0	6.49	9.39
2004	Col	NL	6	0	0	1	6.0	32	7	4	4	1	1	1	0	10	0	3	1	0	0	0	-	0	0-0 0	12.08	6.00
98	SD	NL	2	0	0	2	2.1	8	0	0	0	0	0	0	0	1	0	2	0	0	0	0	-	0	0-0 0	0.20	0.00
98	Cin	NL	4	0	0	2	5.1	30	7	8	8	0	0	0	1	8	0	4	2	1	0	0	-	0	0-0 0	11.01	13.50
	4 ML YEARS		26	0	0	8	26.2	133	29	23	23	3	1	1	2	26	0	23	4	1	0	2	.000	0	0-0 1	7.45	7.76

Jason Kubel

Bats: L **Throws:** R **Pos:** LF-84; DH-35; PH-11; PR-1   **Ht:** 6'0" **Wt:** 210 **Born:** 5/25/1982 **Age:** 26

							BATTING														BASERUNNING				AVERAGES		
Year	Team	Lg	G	AB	H	2B	3B	HR	(Hm	Rd)	TB	R	RBI	RC	TBB	IBB	SO	HBP	SH	SF	SB	CS	SB%	GDP	Avg	OBP	Slg
2004	Min	AL	23	60	18	2	0	2	(0	2)	26	10	7	13	6	0	9	0	0	1	1	1	.50	0	.300	.358	.433
2006	Min	AL	73	220	53	8	0	8	(3	5)	85	23	26	20	12	0	45	0	2	1	2	0	1.00	13	.241	.279	.386
2007	Min	AL	128	418	114	31	2	13	(6	7)	188	49	65	64	41	2	79	1	1	5	5	0	1.00	9	.273	.335	.450
	3 ML YEARS		224	698	185	41	2	23	(9	14)	299	82	98	97	59	2	133	1	3	7	8	1	.89	22	.265	.320	.428

Hong-Chih Kuo

Pitches: L **Bats:** L **Pos:** SP-6; RP-2   **Ht:** 6'1" **Wt:** 235 **Born:** 7/23/1981 **Age:** 26

			HOW MUCH HE PITCHED						WHAT HE GAVE UP										THE RESULTS						
Year	Team	Lg	G	GS	CG	GF	IP	BFP	H	R	ER	HR	SH	SF	HB	TBB	IBB	SO	WP	Bk	W	L	Pct	ShO	Sv-Op Hld	ERC	ERA
2007	LsVgs*	AAA	7	5	0	1	20.0	83	18	9	8	2	0	0	1	8	0	28	0	0	0	1	.000	0	0- - -	3.84	3.60
2005	LAD	NL	9	0	0	5	5.1	26	5	4	4	1	0	0	0	5	1	10	0	1	0	0	-	0	0-1 3	6.10	6.75
2006	LAD	NL	28	5	0	6	59.2	258	54	30	28	3	2	1	1	33	5	71	2	0	1	5	.167	0	0-0 2	3.76	4.22
2007	LAD	NL	8	6	0	1	30.1	140	35	26	25	3	1	1	1	14	0	27	1	0	1	4	.200	0	0-0 0	5.25	7.42
	3 ML YEARS		45	11	0	7	95.1	424	94	60	57	7	3	2	2	52	6	108	3	1	2	10	.167	0	0-1 5	4.35	5.38

Masumi Kuwata

Pitches: R **Bats:** R **Pos:** RP-19 **Ht:** 5'10" **Wt:** 185 **Born:** 4/1/1968 **Age:** 40

Year	Team	Lg	G	GS	CG	GF	IP	BFP	H	R	ER	HR	SH	SF	HB	TBB	IBB	SO	WP	Bk	W	L	Pct	ShO	Sv-Op	Hld	ERC	ERA
1986	Yomiuri	Jap	15	12	1	0	61.1	261	64	36	35	13	-	-	1	17	-	57	2	0	2	1	.667	0	0--	-	4.66	5.14
1987	Yomiuri	Jap	28	27	14	0	207.2	823	177	59	50	16	-	-	5	43	-	151	1	0	15	6	.714	2	0--	-	2.56	2.17
1988	Yomiuri	Jap	27	27	5	0	198.1	806	174	80	75	19	-	-	5	53	-	139	4	0	10	11	.476	1	0--	-	3.01	3.40
1989	Yomiuri	Jap	30	30	20	0	249.0	995	214	77	72	18	-	-	9	54	-	155	6	1	17	9	.654	5	0--	-	2.64	2.60
1990	Yomiuri	Jap	23	22	17	1	186.1	748	161	58	52	12	-	-	1	40	-	115	2	1	14	7	.667	2	0--	-	2.47	2.51
1991	Yomiuri	Jap	28	27	17	1	227.2	934	192	89	80	17	-	-	5	58	-	175	8	0	16	8	.667	3	1--	-	2.58	3.16
1992	Yomiuri	Jap	29	29	11	0	210.1	912	235	112	103	24	-	-	5	64	-	152	9	1	10	14	.417	3	0--	-	4.57	4.41
1993	Yomiuri	Jap	26	26	8	0	178.0	745	162	85	79	15	-	-	6	61	-	158	5	0	8	15	.348	1	0--	-	3.40	3.99
1994	Yomiuri	Jap	28	27	10	1	207.1	836	175	65	58	16	-	-	4	51	-	185	6	0	14	11	.560	1	1--	-	2.61	2.52
1995	Yomiuri	Jap	9	9	3	0	65.1	265	53	22	18	2	-	-	2	18	-	61	2	0	3	3	.500	1	0--	-	2.30	2.48
1997	Yomiuri	Jap	26	26	0	0	141.0	580	127	68	59	15	-	-	5	37	-	104	1	0	10	7	.588	0	0--	-	3.20	3.77
1998	Yomiuri	Jap	27	27	7	0	181.0	779	197	88	82	17	-	-	6	46	-	116	4	1	16	5	.762	1	0--	-	4.06	4.08
1999	Yomiuri	Jap	32	22	2	9	141.2	608	137	69	64	17	-	-	4	57	-	100	6	1	8	9	.471	0	5--	-	4.17	4.07
2000	Yomiuri	Jap	30	10	0	16	86.0	385	103	43	43	6	-	-	3	28	-	49	0	1	5	8	.385	0	2--	-	4.80	4.50
2001	Yomiuri	Jap	16	8	0	6	50.1	226	56	29	27	4	8	2	0	19	4	31	0	0	4	5	.444	0	2--	-	4.23	4.83
2002	Yomiuri	Jap	23	23	3	0	158.1	640	138	51	39	13	-	-	3	38	-	108	3	0	12	6	.667	1	0--	-	2.76	2.22
2003	Yomiuri	Jap	14	13	0	0	71.1	314	92	48	47	13	-	-	3	16	1	46	1	1	5	3	.625	0	0--	-	5.89	5.93
2004	Yomiuri	Jap	16	16	0	0	79.1	357	100	58	57	16	4	7	4	28	1	39	4	0	3	5	.375	0	0--	-	6.49	6.47
2005	Yomiuri	Jap	12	12	0	0	49.2	238	65	43	40	7	4	1	5	23	2	34	4	0	0	7	.000	0	0--	-	6.82	7.25
2006	Yomiuri	Jap	3	3	0	0	11.2	55	19	11	9	4	0	1	0	1	0	5	0	0	1	1	.500	0	0--	-	8.29	6.94
2007	Indy	AAA	3	0	0	0	4.1	15	3	0	0	0	0	0	0	0	0	3	0	0	0	0	-	0	0--	-	1.04	0.00
2007	Pit	NL	19	0	0	3	21.0	103	25	23	22	6	1	3	1	15	4	12	0	0	0	1	.000	0	0-0	3	7.85	9.43

John Lackey

Pitches: R **Bats:** R **Pos:** SP-33 **Ht:** 6'6" **Wt:** 245 **Born:** 10/23/1978 **Age:** 29

Year	Team	Lg	G	GS	CG	GF	IP	BFP	H	R	ER	HR	SH	SF	HB	TBB	IBB	SO	WP	Bk	W	L	Pct	ShO	Sv-Op	Hld	ERC	ERA
2002	LAA	AL	18	18	1	0	108.1	465	113	52	44	10	0	4	4	33	0	69	7	2	9	4	.692	0	0-0	0	4.03	3.66
2003	LAA	AL	33	33	2	0	204.0	885	223	117	105	31	2	6	10	66	4	151	11	1	10	16	.385	2	0-0	0	4.88	4.63
2004	LAA	AL	33	32	1	0	198.1	855	215	108	103	22	9	4	8	60	4	144	11	1	14	13	.519	1	0-0	0	4.39	4.67
2005	LAA	AL	33	33	1	0	209.0	892	208	85	80	13	1	2	11	71	3	199	18	0	14	5	.737	0	0-0	0	3.76	3.44
2006	LAA	AL	33	33	3	0	217.2	922	203	98	86	14	8	6	9	72	4	190	16	0	13	11	.542	2	0-0	0	3.31	3.56
2007	LAA	AL	33	33	2	0	224.0	929	219	87	75	18	1	1	12	52	2	179	9	1	19	9	.679	2	0-0	0	3.40	**3.01**
	6 ML YEARS		183	182	10	0	1161.1	4948	1181	547	493	108	21	23	54	354	17	932	72	5	79	58	.577	7	0-0	0	3.92	3.82

Aaron Laffey

Pitches: L **Bats:** L **Pos:** SP-9 **Ht:** 6'0" **Wt:** 185 **Born:** 4/15/1985 **Age:** 23

Year	Team	Lg	G	GS	CG	GF	IP	BFP	H	R	ER	HR	SH	SF	HB	TBB	IBB	SO	WP	Bk	W	L	Pct	ShO	Sv-Op	Hld	ERC	ERA
2003	Burlgtn	A	9	4	0	1	34.0	143	22	13	11	0	0	1	7	15	0	46	4	1	3	1	.750	0	0--	-	2.44	2.91
2004	Lk Cty	A	19	15	0	2	73.0	346	79	58	53	6	3	3	8	44	0	67	3	1	3	7	.300	0	1--	-	5.60	6.53
2004	MhVlly	A-	8	8	0	0	43.2	180	38	15	6	1	1	1	2	10	0	30	2	0	3	1	.750	0	0--	-	2.39	1.24
2005	Lk Cty	A	25	23	1	2	142.1	581	123	62	51	5	9	1	4	52	0	69	2	2	7	7	.500	1	1--	-	2.97	3.22
2005	Akron	AA	1	1	0	0	5.0	24	8	2	2	0	0	0	0	2	0	6	1	0	1	0	1.000	0	0--	-	6.98	3.60
2006	Knstn	A+	10	4	1	2	41.1	170	38	16	10	0	3	0	3	6	0	24	2	0	4	1	.800	1	1--	-	2.30	2.18
2006	Akron	AA	19	19	0	0	112.1	476	121	50	44	9	8	3	8	33	0	61	4	0	8	3	.727	0	0--	-	4.35	3.53
2007	Akron	AA	6	6	0	0	35.0	141	29	13	9	2	1	1	3	7	0	24	0	0	4	1	.800	0	0--	-	2.49	2.31
2007	Buffalo	AAA	16	15	2	0	96.1	395	89	36	33	5	2	0	3	23	0	75	0	1	9	3	.750	1	0--	-	2.87	3.08
2007	Cle	AL	9	9	0	0	49.1	207	54	26	25	2	1	2	4	12	0	25	2	1	4	2	.667	0	0-0	0	4.02	4.56

Pete LaForest

Bats: L **Throws:** R **Pos:** PH-16; C-7; 1B-1 **Ht:** 6'2" **Wt:** 208 **Born:** 1/27/1978 **Age:** 30

Year	Team	Lg	G	AB	H	2B	3B	HR	(Hm	Rd)	TB	R	RBI	RC	TBB	IBB	SO	HBP	SH	SF	SB	CS	SB%	GDP	Avg	OBP	Slg
2007	Portlnd*	AAA	86	296	68	6	0	29	(-	-)	161	53	72	58	54	2	92	1	0	3	2	0	1.00	9	.230	.347	.544
2003	TB	AL	19	48	8	2	0	0	(0	0)	10	0	6	1	1	0	14	1	0	1	0	0	-	0	.167	.196	.208
2005	TB	AL	25	64	11	3	0	1	(1	0)	17	5	4	2	6	1	23	0	0	0	0	1	.00	2	.172	.243	.266
2007	2 Tms		24	36	10	1	0	1	(1	0)	14	9	4	6	7	1	12	0	0	0	0	0	-	1	.278	.395	.389
07	SD	NL	10	25	9	1	0	1	(1	0)	13	7	3	6	5	1	8	0	0	0	0	0	-	0	.360	.467	.520
07	Phi	NL	14	11	1	0	0	0	(0	0)	1	2	1	0	2	0	4	0	0	0	0	0	-	1	.091	.231	.091
	3 ML YEARS		68	148	29	6	0	2	(2	0)	41	14	14	9	14	2	49	1	0	1	0	1	.00	4	.196	.268	.277

Gerald Laird

Bats: R **Throws:** R **Pos:** C-119; PH-3; LF-1 **Ht:** 6'1" **Wt:** 225 **Born:** 11/13/1979 **Age:** 28

Year	Team	Lg	G	AB	H	2B	3B	HR	(Hm	Rd)	TB	R	RBI	RC	TBB	IBB	SO	HBP	SH	SF	SB	CS	SB%	GDP	Avg	OBP	Slg
2003	Tex	AL	19	44	12	2	1	1	(0	1)	19	9	4	5	5	0	11	1	0	0	0	0	-	2	.273	.360	.432
2004	Tex	AL	49	147	33	6	0	1	(1	0)	42	20	16	11	12	0	35	2	4	3	0	1	.00	5	.224	.287	.286
2005	Tex	AL	13	40	9	2	0	1	(0	1)	14	7	4	4	2	0	7	0	0	0	0	0	-	1	.225	.262	.350
2006	Tex	AL	78	243	72	20	1	7	(4	3)	115	46	22	24	12	0	54	2	1	2	3	1	.75	7	.296	.332	.473
2007	Tex	AL	120	407	91	18	3	9	(6	3)	142	48	47	45	30	1	103	2	5	4	6	2	.75	3	.224	.278	.349
	5 ML YEARS		279	881	217	48	5	19	(10	9)	332	130	93	89	61	1	210	7	10	9	9	4	.69	18	.246	.297	.377

Mike Lamb

Bats: L **Throws:** R **Pos:** 3B-58; PH-45; 1B-43; RF-1   **Ht:** 6'1" **Wt:** 200 **Born:** 8/9/1975 **Age:** 32

								BATTING												BASERUNNING				AVERAGES		
Year	Team	Lg	G	AB	H	2B	3B	HR	(Hm | Rd)	TB	R	RBI	RC	TBB	IBB	SO	HBP	SH	SF	SB	CS	SB%	GDP	Avg	OBP	Slg
2000	Tex	AL	138	493	137	25	2	6	(4 | 2)	184	65	47	59	34	6	60	4	5	2	0	2	.00	10	.278	.328	.373
2001	Tex	AL	76	284	87	18	0	4	(1 | 3)	117	42	35	40	14	1	27	5	1	2	2	1	.67	6	.306	.348	.412
2002	Tex	AL	115	314	89	13	0	9	(7 | 2)	129	54	33	46	33	5	48	3	2	3	0	0	-	7	.283	.354	.411
2003	Tex	AL	28	38	5	0	0	0	(0 | 0)	5	3	2	0	2	0	7	1	0	1	1	0	1.00	1	.132	.190	.132
2004	Hou	NL	112	278	80	14	3	14	(8 | 6)	142	38	58	51	31	3	63	0	0	3	1	1	.50	4	.288	.356	.511
2005	Hou	NL	125	322	76	13	5	12	(4 | 8)	135	41	53	38	22	1	65	1	0	4	1	1	.50	10	.236	.284	.419
2006	Hou	NL	126	381	117	22	3	12	(5 | 7)	181	70	45	52	35	6	55	0	0	5	2	4	.33	10	.307	.361	.475
2007	Hou	NL	124	311	90	14	2	11	(5 | 6)	141	45	40	48	36	5	45	3	1	2	0	0	-	5	.289	.366	.453
8 ML YEARS			844	2421	681	119	15	68	(34 | 34)	1034	358	313	334	207	27	370	17	9	22	7	9	.44	53	.281	.339	.427

Jason Lane

Bats: R **Throws:** L **Pos:** CF-37; RF-19; PH-16; LF-4; PR-1   **Ht:** 6'2" **Wt:** 220 **Born:** 12/22/1976 **Age:** 31

								BATTING												BASERUNNING				AVERAGES		
Year	Team	Lg	G	AB	H	2B	3B	HR	(Hm | Rd)	TB	R	RBI	RC	TBB	IBB	SO	HBP	SH	SF	SB	CS	SB%	GDP	Avg	OBP	Slg
2007	RdRck*	AAA	50	185	59	15	0	9	(- | -)	101	37	41	40	23	1	26	2	0	4	2	1	.67	4	.319	.393	.546
2002	Hou	NL	44	69	20	3	1	4	(2 | 2)	37	12	10	11	10	1	12	0	0	1	1	1	.50	0	.290	.375	.536
2003	Hou	NL	18	27	8	2	0	4	(4 | 0)	22	5	10	6	0	0	2	0	0	0	0	0	-	0	.296	.296	.815
2004	Hou	NL	107	136	37	10	2	4	(4 | 0)	63	21	19	23	16	0	33	1	1	2	1	0	1.00	2	.272	.348	.463
2005	Hou	NL	145	517	138	34	4	26	(14 | 12)	258	65	78	72	32	1	105	7	0	5	6	2	.75	10	.267	.316	.499
2006	Hou	NL	112	288	58	10	0	15	(8 | 7)	113	44	45	39	49	0	75	2	2	4	1	2	.33	6	.201	.318	.392
2007	2 Tms	NL	71	171	30	5	0	8	(2 | 6)	59	18	27	16	16	0	31	3	1	3	1	1	.50	4	.175	.254	.345
07	Hou	NL	68	169	30	5	0	8	(2 | 6)	59	18	27	16	16	0	30	3	1	3	1	1	.50	4	.178	.257	.349
07	SD	NL	3	2	0	0	0	0	(0 | 0)	0	0	0	0	0	0	1	0	0	0	0	0	-	0	.000	.000	.000
6 ML YEARS			497	1208	291	64	7	61	(34 | 27)	552	165	189	167	123	2	258	13	4	15	10	6	.63	22	.241	.314	.457

Ryan Langerhans

Bats: L **Throws:** L **Pos:** LF-66; CF-40; PH-29; RF-7; PR-7   **Ht:** 6'3" **Wt:** 205 **Born:** 2/20/1980 **Age:** 28

								BATTING												BASERUNNING				AVERAGES		
Year	Team	Lg	G	AB	H	2B	3B	HR	(Hm | Rd)	TB	R	RBI	RC	TBB	IBB	SO	HBP	SH	SF	SB	CS	SB%	GDP	Avg	OBP	Slg
2007	Clmbs*	AAA	14	51	14	3	0	1	(- | -)	20	11	2	7	6	0	15	0	2	0	1	0	1.00	1	.275	.351	.392
2002	Atl	NL	1	1	0	0	0	0	(0 | 0)	0	0	0	0	0	0	0	0	0	0	0	0	-	0	.000	.000	.000
2003	Atl	NL	16	15	4	0	0	0	(0 | 0)	4	2	0	1	0	0	6	0	0	0	0	0	-	1	.267	.267	.267
2005	Atl	NL	128	326	87	22	3	8	(3 | 5)	139	48	42	53	37	3	75	5	2	3	0	2	.00	3	.267	.348	.426
2006	Atl	NL	131	315	76	16	3	7	(3 | 4)	119	46	28	45	50	8	91	3	0	1	1	2	.33	9	.241	.350	.378
2007	3 Tms	NL	125	210	35	7	2	6	(1 | 5)	64	27	23	22	29	2	81	2	1	2	3	1	.75	4	.167	.272	.305
07	Atl	NL	20	44	3	1	0	0	(0 | 0)	4	3	1	0	6	1	16	1	0	1	0	1	.00	0	.068	.192	.091
07	Oak	AL	2	4	0	0	0	0	(0 | 0)	0	0	0	0	1	0	2	0	0	0	0	0	-	0	.000	.200	.000
07	Was	NL	103	162	32	6	2	6	(1 | 5)	60	24	22	22	22	1	63	1	1	1	3	0	1.00	1	.198	.296	.370
5 ML YEARS			401	867	202	45	8	21	(7 | 14)	326	123	93	121	116	13	253	10	3	6	4	5	.44	16	.233	.328	.376

John Lannan

Pitches: L **Bats:** L **Pos:** SP-6   **Ht:** 6'5" **Wt:** 200 **Born:** 9/27/1984 **Age:** 23

			HOW MUCH HE PITCHED						WHAT HE GAVE UP										THE RESULTS						
Year	Team	Lg	G	GS	CG	GF	IP	BFP	H	R	ER	HR	SH	SF	HB	TBB	IBB	SO	WP	Bk	W	L	Pct	ShO	Sv-Op	Hld	ERC	ERA
2005	Vrmnt	A-	14	11	0	1	63.1	296	74	46	37	7	0	3	4	31	0	41	5	3	3	5	.375	0	0- -	-	5.43	5.26
2006	Savann	A	27	25	1	1	138.0	613	149	83	73	11	4	8	6	54	0	114	4	0	6	8	.429	1	0- -	-	4.49	4.76
2007	Ptomc	A+	8	8	0	0	50.2	198	31	13	12	3	1	0	0	15	0	35	1	0	6	0	1.000	0	0- -	-	1.56	2.13
2007	Hrsbrg	AA	6	5	0	0	36.0	149	31	14	13	2	0	0	1	15	1	20	0	0	3	2	.600	0	0- -	-	3.22	3.25
2007	Clmbs	AAA	7	6	0	1	38.0	155	30	8	7	1	0	0	2	12	0	19	1	0	3	1	.750	0	0- -	-	2.38	1.66
2007	Was	NL	6	6	0	0	34.2	153	36	17	16	3	2	0	2	17	1	10	1	0	2	2	.500	0	0-0	0	4.82	4.15

Juan Lara

Pitches: L **Bats:** R **Pos:** RP-1   **Ht:** 6'2" **Wt:** 190 **Born:** 1/26/1981 **Age:** 27

			HOW MUCH HE PITCHED						WHAT HE GAVE UP										THE RESULTS						
Year	Team	Lg	G	GS	CG	GF	IP	BFP	H	R	ER	HR	SH	SF	HB	TBB	IBB	SO	WP	Bk	W	L	Pct	ShO	Sv-Op	Hld	ERC	ERA
2002	Burlgtn	R	14	14	0	0	65.0	283	67	42	36	4	3	1	7	28	0	50	0	2	2	6	.250	0	0- -	-	4.64	4.98
2003	Lk Cty	A	16	3	0	6	45.0	215	51	31	25	7	1	2	3	26	0	37	6	1	1	4	.200	0	1- -	-	6.16	5.00
2003	MhVlly	A-	12	12	0	0	61.2	261	54	29	24	4	4	1	8	18	1	54	6	0	3	3	.500	0	0- -	-	3.20	3.50
2004	Knstn	A+	35	8	0	12	84.1	393	106	60	53	6	3	3	4	38	1	74	6	2	4	3	.571	0	1- -	-	5.71	5.66
2005	Knstn	A+	26	0	0	7	42.1	180	40	22	19	4	1	0	0	15	0	46	6	0	0	1	.000	0	0- -	-	3.52	4.04
2005	Akron	AA	18	0	0	8	23.2	112	27	15	12	1	2	2	1	14	3	16	3	1	1	2	.333	0	5- -	-	5.05	4.56
2006	Akron	AA	40	0	0	17	46.2	197	32	14	14	2	5	0	2	21	1	48	0	0	4	2	.667	0	7- -	-	2.29	2.70
2006	Buffalo	AAA	13	0	0	6	15.0	65	17	6	5	1	0	0	1	3	0	15	1	0	1	1	.500	0	1- -	-	4.03	3.00
2007	Buffalo	AAA	52	0	0	19	58.0	254	53	28	25	3	5	3	3	27	6	50	4	0	4	3	.571	0	2- -	-	3.49	3.88
2007	Akron	AA	2	0	0	0	1.1	6	1	0	0	0	0	0	0	0	0	2	0	0	0	0	-	0	0- -	-	0.94	0.00
2006	Cle	AL	9	0	0	1	5.0	19	4	2	1	0	0	0	0	1	0	2	0	0	0	0	-	0	0-1	0	1.82	1.80
2007	Cle	AL	1	0	0	1	1.1	7	2	2	2	1	0	0	0	1	0	2	0	0	0	0	-	0	0-0	0	14.59	13.50
2 ML YEARS			10	0	0	2	6.1	26	6	4	3	1	0	0	0	2	0	4	0	0	0	0	-	0	0-1	0	3.93	4.26

Adam LaRoche

Bats: L **Throws:** L **Pos:** 1B-151; PH-1   **Ht:** 6'3" **Wt:** 205 **Born:** 11/6/1979 **Age:** 28

Year	Team	Lg	G	AB	H	2B	3B	HR	(Hm	Rd)	TB	R	RBI	RC	TBB	IBB	SO	HBP	SH	SF	SB	CS	SB%	GDP	Avg	OBP	Slg
2004	Atl	NL	110	324	90	27	1	13	(7	6)	158	45	45	43	27	1	78	1	2	2	0	0	-	10	.278	.333	.488
2005	Atl	NL	141	451	117	28	0	20	(11	9)	205	53	78	63	39	7	87	4	2	6	0	2	.00	15	.259	.320	.455
2006	Atl	NL	149	492	140	38	1	32	(11	21)	276	89	90	83	55	5	128	2	1	7	0	2	.00	9	.285	.354	.561
2007	Pit	NL	152	563	153	42	0	21	(10	11)	258	71	88	84	62	5	131	3	0	4	1	1	.50	18	.272	.345	.458
	4 ML YEARS		552	1830	500	135	2	86	(39	47)	897	258	301	273	183	18	424	10	5	19	1	5	.17	52	.273	.339	.490

Andy LaRoche

Bats: R **Throws:** R **Pos:** 3B-30; PH-4; LF-1   **Ht:** 6'1" **Wt:** 220 **Born:** 9/13/1983 **Age:** 24

Year	Team	Lg	G	AB	H	2B	3B	HR	(Hm	Rd)	TB	R	RBI	RC	TBB	IBB	SO	HBP	SH	SF	SB	CS	SB%	GDP	Avg	OBP	Slg
2003	Ogden	R+	6	19	4	1	0	0	(-	-)	5	1	5	1	1	0	4	0	0	1	0	0	-	0	.211	.238	.263
2004	Clmbs	A	65	244	69	20	0	13	(-	-)	128	52	42	49	29	1	30	8	2	2	12	5	.71	6	.283	.375	.525
2004	VeroB	A+	62	219	52	13	0	10	(-	-)	95	26	34	28	17	0	42	2	2	3	2	3	.40	1	.237	.295	.434
2005	VeroB	A+	63	249	83	14	1	21	(-	-)	162	54	51	59	19	3	38	1	0	2	6	1	.86	6	.333	.380	.651
2005	Jaxnvl	AA	64	227	62	12	0	9	(-	-)	101	41	43	39	32	2	54	3	0	2	2	1	.67	9	.273	.367	.445
2006	Jaxnvl	AA	62	230	71	13	0	9	(-	-)	111	42	46	49	41	1	32	4	0	2	6	3	.67	2	.309	.419	.483
2006	LsVgs	AAA	55	202	65	14	1	10	(-	-)	111	35	35	43	25	0	32	2	0	1	3	2	.60	7	.322	.400	.550
2007	LsVgs	AAA	73	265	82	18	1	18	(-	-)	156	55	48	61	39	0	42	3	0	4	2	2	.50	8	.309	.399	.589
2007	LAD	NL	35	93	21	5	0	1	(0	1)	29	16	10	12	20	5	24	1	0	1	2	1	.67	1	.226	.365	.312

Jason LaRue

Bats: R **Throws:** R **Pos:** C-65; 3B-1   **Ht:** 5'11" **Wt:** 205 **Born:** 3/19/1974 **Age:** 34

Year	Team	Lg	G	AB	H	2B	3B	HR	(Hm	Rd)	TB	R	RBI	RC	TBB	IBB	SO	HBP	SH	SF	SB	CS	SB%	GDP	Avg	OBP	Slg
2007	Omha*	AAA	4	12	1	1	0	0	(-	-)	2	2	0	0	0	0	3	2	1	0	0	0	-	0	.083	.214	.167
1999	Cin	NL	36	90	19	7	0	3	(1	2)	35	12	10	10	11	1	32	2	0	0	4	1	.80	4	.211	.311	.389
2000	Cin	NL	31	98	23	3	0	5	(1	4)	41	12	12	12	5	2	19	4	0	0	0	0	-	1	.235	.299	.418
2001	Cin	NL	121	364	86	21	2	12	(3	9)	147	39	43	42	27	4	106	9	1	2	3	3	.50	11	.236	.303	.404
2002	Cin	NL	113	353	88	17	1	12	(5	7)	143	42	52	44	27	6	117	13	2	2	1	2	.33	13	.249	.324	.405
2003	Cin	NL	118	379	87	23	1	16	(12	4)	160	52	50	47	33	4	111	20	1	4	3	3	.50	9	.230	.321	.422
2004	Cin	NL	114	390	98	24	2	14	(3	11)	168	46	55	53	26	5	108	24	2	3	0	2	.00	7	.251	.334	.431
2005	Cin	NL	110	361	94	27	0	14	(6	8)	163	38	60	63	41	7	101	13	5	2	0	0	-	8	.260	.355	.452
2006	Cin	NL	72	191	37	5	0	8	(5	3)	66	22	21	17	27	9	51	8	3	1	1	0	1.00	3	.194	.317	.346
2007	KC	AL	66	169	25	9	0	4	(2	2)	46	14	13	7	17	0	66	4	3	2	1	0	1.00	5	.148	.240	.272
	9 ML YEARS		781	2395	557	136	6	88	(38	50)	969	277	316	295	214	38	711	97	17	16	13	11	.54	62	.233	.319	.405

Brian Lawrence

Pitches: R **Bats:** R **Pos:** SP-6   **Ht:** 6'0" **Wt:** 195 **Born:** 5/14/1976 **Age:** 32

Year	Team	Lg	G	GS	CG	GF	IP	BFP	H	R	ER	HR	SH	SF	HB	TBB	IBB	SO	WP	Bk	W	L	Pct	ShO	Sv-Op	Hld	ERC	ERA
2007	ColSpr*	AAA	3	3	1	0	19.2	91	32	14	19	3	1	0	0	5	0	10	0	0	0	2	.000	0	0- -	-	7.98	8.69
2007	NewOr*	AAA	13	13	1	0	85.0	343	88	38	36	6	3	5	1	9	0	57	0	0	8	3	.727	0	0- -	-	3.03	3.81
2001	SD	NL	27	15	1	5	114.2	484	107	53	44	10	4	3	5	34	5	84	1	0	5	5	.500	0	0-0	0	3.30	3.45
2002	SD	NL	35	31	2	0	210.0	894	230	97	86	16	8	4	11	52	6	149	2	1	12	12	.500	2	0-0	1	4.05	3.69
2003	SD	NL	33	33	1	0	210.2	884	206	106	98	27	11	6	11	57	8	116	4	0	10	15	.400	0	0-0	0	3.81	4.19
2004	SD	NL	34	34	2	0	203.0	870	226	101	93	26	11	9	7	55	7	121	2	0	15	14	.517	1	0-0	0	4.53	4.12
2005	SD	NL	33	33	1	0	195.2	852	211	106	105	18	3	7	11	57	7	109	3	1	7	15	.318	0	0-0	0	4.17	4.83
2007	NYM	NL	6	6	0	0	29.0	139	43	22	22	4	1	0	1	13	1	18	1	0	1	2	.333	0	0-0	0	7.72	6.83
	6 ML YEARS		168	152	7	5	963.0	4123	1023	485	448	101	38	29	46	268	34	597	13	2	50	63	.442	3	0-0	1	4.13	4.19

Brandon League

Pitches: R **Bats:** R **Pos:** RP-14   **Ht:** 6'3" **Wt:** 192 **Born:** 3/16/1983 **Age:** 25

Year	Team	Lg	G	GS	CG	GF	IP	BFP	H	R	ER	HR	SH	SF	HB	TBB	IBB	SO	WP	Bk	W	L	Pct	ShO	Sv-Op	Hld	ERC	ERA
2007	B Jays*	R	1	1	0	0	1.0	3	1	0	0	0	0	0	0	0	0	1	0	0	0	0	-	0	0- -	-	2.79	0.00
2007	Dnedin*	A+	4	0	0	1	6.0	26	5	3	3	1	0	0	0	2	0	6	0	0	0	1	.000	0	0- -	-	3.13	4.50
2007	NHam*	AA	6	0	0	1	7.2	34	5	3	3	0	0	0	0	7	0	7	2	0	1	1	.500	0	0- -	-	3.38	3.52
2007	Syrcse*	AAA	11	0	0	0	12.0	57	12	9	4	0	1	1	4	6	0	10	3	0	0	0	-	0	0- -	-	4.94	3.00
2004	Tor	AL	3	0	0	0	4.2	18	3	0	0	0	0	0	0	1	0	2	0	0	1	0	1.000	0	0-0	1	1.26	0.00
2005	Tor	AL	20	0	0	4	35.2	162	42	27	26	8	0	1	2	20	1	17	5	0	1	0	1.000	0	0-0	1	7.24	6.56
2006	Tor	AL	33	0	0	8	42.2	173	34	17	12	3	2	0	3	9	2	29	0	0	1	2	.333	0	1-4	12	2.30	2.53
2007	Tor	AL	14	0	0	2	11.2	58	19	8	8	1	0	1	0	7	0	7	3	0	0	0	-	0	0-1	0	8.98	6.17
	4 ML YEARS		70	0	0	14	94.2	411	98	52	46	12	2	2	5	37	3	55	8	0	3	2	.600	0	1-5	14	4.64	4.37

Matthew LeCroy

Bats: R **Throws:** R **Pos:** C-4; DH-2; PH-2; 1B-1   **Ht:** 6'2" **Wt:** 230 **Born:** 12/13/1975 **Age:** 32

Year	Team	Lg	G	AB	H	2B	3B	HR	(Hm	Rd)	TB	R	RBI	RC	TBB	IBB	SO	HBP	SH	SF	SB	CS	SB%	GDP	Avg	OBP	Slg
2007	Roch*	AAA	80	247	48	12	0	3	(-	-)	69	12	25	21	26	1	48	5	0	3	0	0	-	10	.194	.281	.279
2000	Min	AL	56	167	29	10	0	5	(2	3)	54	18	17	12	17	2	38	2	1	3	0	0	-	6	.174	.254	.323
2001	Min	AL	15	40	17	5	0	3	(0	3)	31	6	12	11	0	0	8	1	0	1	0	0	-	0	.425	.429	.775
2002	Min	AL	63	181	47	11	1	7	(2	5)	81	19	27	24	13	1	38	0	0	2	0	2	.00	5	.260	.306	.448

Year	Team	Lg	G	AB	H	2B	3B	HR	(Hm	Rd)	TB	R	RBI	RC	TBB	IBB	SO	HBP	SH	SF	SB	CS	SB%	GDP	Avg	OBP	Slg
2003	Min	AL	107	345	99	19	0	17	(9	8)	169	39	64	60	25	1	82	4	0	0	0	1	.00	8	.287	.342	.490
2004	Min	AL	88	264	71	14	0	9	(5	4)	112	25	39	32	16	0	60	5	0	2	0	0	-	7	.269	.321	.424
2005	Min	AL	101	304	79	5	0	17	(10	7)	135	33	50	48	41	2	85	4	0	1	0	0	-	7	.260	.354	.444
2006	Was	NL	39	67	16	3	0	2	(0	2)	25	5	9	9	11	0	17	1	0	1	0	0	-	2	.239	.350	.373
2007	Min	AL	7	20	3	1	0	0	(0	0)	4	1	0	0	0	0	4	0	0	0	0	0	-	1	.150	.150	.200
8 ML YEARS			476	1388	361	68	1	60	(28	32)	611	146	218	196	123	6	332	17	1	10	0	4	.00	36	.260	.326	.440

Ricky Ledee

Bats: L Throws: L Pos: LF-11; PH-8   Ht: 6'1" Wt: 225 Born: 11/22/1973 Age: 34

Year	Team	Lg	G	AB	H	2B	3B	HR	(Hm	Rd)	TB	R	RBI	RC	TBB	IBB	SO	HBP	SH	SF	SB	CS	SB%	GDP	Avg	OBP	Slg
2007	NewOr*	AAA	86	290	76	11	1	11	(-	-)	122	37	64	42	30	4	63	2	0	3	0	0	-	4	.262	.332	.421
1998	NYY	AL	42	79	19	5	2	1	(0	1)	31	13	12	9	7	0	29	0	0	1	1	1	.75	1	.241	.299	.392
1999	NYY	AL	88	250	69	13	5	9	(4	5)	119	45	40	41	28	5	73	0	0	2	4	3	.57	2	.276	.346	.476
2000	3 Tms	AL	137	467	110	19	5	13	(6	7)	178	59	77	56	59	4	98	2	0	3	13	6	.68	17	.236	.322	.381
2001	Tex	AL	78	242	56	21	1	2	(1	1)	85	33	36	26	23	0	58	3	1	3	3	3	.50	3	.231	.303	.351
2002	Phi	NL	96	203	46	13	1	8	(4	4)	85	33	23	24	35	0	50	1	1	1	1	2	.33	3	.227	.342	.419
2003	Phi	NL	121	255	63	15	2	13	(6	7)	121	37	46	36	34	5	59	0	1	1	0	0	-	4	.247	.334	.475
2004	2 Tms	NL	104	176	41	9	0	7	(3	4)	71	25	30	24	27	2	47	1	0	1	3	0	1.00	6	.233	.337	.403
2005	LAD	NL	102	237	66	16	1	7	(5	2)	105	31	39	34	20	1	55	3	0	6	0	0	-	5	.278	.335	.443
2006	2 Tms	NL	70	85	16	6	0	2	(1	1)	28	8	9	5	6	0	16	0	0	1	1	0	1.00	3	.188	.242	.329
2007	NYM	NL	17	36	8	3	0	1	(1	0)	14	6	6	6	5	1	10	0	1	1	1	0	1.00	0	.222	.310	.389
00	NYY	AL	62	191	46	11	1	7	(2	5)	80	23	31	26	26	2	39	1	0	2	7	3	.70	7	.241	.332	.419
00	Cle	AL	17	63	14	2	1	2	(2	0)	24	13	8	7	8	0	9	0	0	0	0	0	-	3	.222	.310	.381
00	Tex	AL	58	213	50	6	3	4	(2	2)	74	23	38	23	25	2	50	1	0	1	6	3	.67	7	.235	.317	.347
04	Phi	NL	73	123	35	7	0	7	(3	4)	63	19	26	23	22	2	27	0	0	1	2	0	1.00	5	.285	.393	.512
04	SF	NL	31	53	6	2	0	0	(0	0)	8	6	4	1	5	0	20	1	0	1	1	0	1.00	1	.113	.200	.151
06	LAD	NL	43	53	13	5	0	1	(0	1)	21	4	8	5	2	0	10	0	0	0	1	0	1.00	3	.245	.273	.396
06	NYM	NL	27	32	3	1	0	1	(1	0)	7	4	1	0	4	0	6	0	0	0	0	0	-	0	.094	.194	.219
10 ML YEARS			855	2030	494	120	17	63	(31	32)	837	290	318	261	244	18	495	10	4	19	29	15	.66	44	.243	.325	.412

Wil Ledezma

Pitches: L Bats: L Pos: RP-43; SP-1   Ht: 6'4" Wt: 210 Born: 1/21/1981 Age: 27

Year	Team	Lg	G	GS	CG	GF	IP	BFP	H	R	ER	HR	SH	SF	HB	TBB	IBB	SO	WP	Bk	W	L	Pct	ShO	Sv-Op	Hld	ERC	ERA
2003	Det	AL	34	8	0	13	84.0	376	99	55	54	12	1	4	3	35	3	49	2	0	3	7	.300	0	0-1	1	5.67	5.79
2004	Det	AL	15	8	0	1	53.1	225	55	28	26	3	0	3	2	18	0	29	3	1	4	3	.571	0	0-1	0	3.94	4.39
2005	Det	AL	10	10	0	0	49.2	234	61	46	39	10	3	4	2	24	0	30	2	2	2	4	.333	0	0-0	0	6.66	7.07
2006	Det	AL	24	7	0	2	60.1	264	60	28	24	5	2	1	2	23	0	39	2	0	3	3	.500	0	0-1	2	3.92	3.58
2007	3 Tms	NL	44	1	0	13	59.1	280	70	42	37	7	2	3	0	38	4	47	3	2	3	3	.500	0	0-2	4	6.13	5.61
07	Det	AL	23	0	0	5	35.2	166	38	21	19	4	2	1	0	26	2	24	3	2	3	1	.750	0	0-2	2	5.83	4.79
07	Atl	NL	12	0	0	4	9.1	45	12	10	8	1	0	1	0	4	0	7	0	0	0	0	.000	0	0-0	2	5.64	7.71
07	SD	NL	9	1	0	4	14.1	69	20	11	10	2	0	1	0	8	2	16	0	0	0	0	-	0	0-0	0	7.23	6.28
5 ML YEARS			127	34	0	29	306.2	1379	345	199	180	37	8	15	9	138	7	194	12	5	15	20	.429	0	0-5	7	5.24	5.28

Carlos Lee

Bats: R Throws: R Pos: LF-157; DH-3; PH-2   Ht: 6'2" Wt: 240 Born: 6/20/1976 Age: 32

Year	Team	Lg	G	AB	H	2B	3B	HR	(Hm	Rd)	TB	R	RBI	RC	TBB	IBB	SO	HBP	SH	SF	SB	CS	SB%	GDP	Avg	OBP	Slg
1999	CWS	AL	127	492	144	32	2	16	(10	6)	228	66	84	68	13	0	72	4	1	7	4	2	.67	11	.293	.312	.463
2000	CWS	AL	152	572	172	29	2	24	(12	12)	277	107	92	91	38	1	94	3	1	5	13	4	.76	11	.301	.345	.484
2001	CWS	AL	150	558	150	33	3	24	(12	12)	261	75	84	81	38	2	85	6	1	2	17	7	.71	15	.269	.321	.468
2002	CWS	AL	140	492	130	26	2	26	(14	12)	238	82	80	86	75	4	73	2	0	7	1	4	.20	5	.264	.359	.484
2003	CWS	AL	158	623	181	35	1	31	(18	13)	311	100	113	105	37	2	91	4	0	7	18	4	.82	20	.291	.331	.499
2004	CWS	AL	153	591	180	37	0	31	(17	14)	310	103	99	112	54	3	86	7	0	6	11	5	.69	10	.305	.366	.525
2005	Mil	NL	162	618	164	41	0	32	(15	17)	301	85	114	98	57	7	87	2	0	11	13	4	.76	8	.265	.324	.487
2006	2 Tms	NL	161	624	187	37	1	37	(15	22)	337	102	116	113	58	6	65	2	0	11	19	2	.90	22	.300	.355	.540
2007	Hou	NL	162	627	190	43	1	32	(17	15)	331	93	119	104	53	10	63	4	0	13	10	5	.67	27	.303	.354	.528
06	Mil	NL	102	388	111	18	0	28	(10	18)	213	60	81	75	38	4	39	2	0	7	12	2	.86	13	.286	.347	.549
06	Tex	AL	59	236	76	19	1	9	(5	4)	124	42	35	38	20	2	26	0	0	4	7	0	1.00	9	.322	.369	.525
9 ML YEARS			1365	5197	1498	313	12	253	(130	123)	2594	813	901	858	423	35	716	34	3	69	106	37	.74	135	.288	.342	.499

Cliff Lee

Pitches: L Bats: L Pos: SP-16; RP-4   Ht: 6'3" Wt: 190 Born: 8/30/1978 Age: 29

Year	Team	Lg	G	GS	CG	GF	IP	BFP	H	R	ER	HR	SH	SF	HB	TBB	IBB	SO	WP	Bk	W	L	Pct	ShO	Sv-Op	Hld	ERC	ERA
2007	Knstn*	A+	1	1	0	0	2.0	7	1	0	0	0	0	0	0	0	0	4	0	0	0	0	-	0	0--	-	0.54	0.00
2007	Akron*	AA	1	1	0	0	5.0	19	2	0	0	0	0	0	0	1	0	7	0	0	1	0	1.000	0	0--	-	0.60	0.00
2007	Buffalo*	AAA	8	8	0	0	41.0	183	32	17	16	1	2	0	1	25	0	50	3	0	1	3	.250	0	0--	-	3.11	3.51
2002	Cle	AL	2	2	0	0	10.1	44	6	2	2	1	0	0	0	8	1	6	0	1	0	1	.000	0	0-0	0	2.38	1.74
2003	Cle	AL	9	9	0	0	52.1	210	41	28	21	7	1	1	2	20	1	44	3	0	3	3	.500	0	0-0	0	3.29	3.61
2004	Cle	AL	33	33	0	0	179.0	802	188	113	108	30	2	6	11	81	1	161	6	0	14	8	.636	0	0-0	0	5.31	5.43
2005	Cle	AL	32	32	1	0	202.0	838	194	91	85	22	5	7	0	52	1	143	4	0	18	5	.783	0	0-0	0	3.35	3.79
2006	Cle	AL	33	33	1	0	200.2	882	224	114	98	29	3	6	8	58	3	129	3	0	14	11	.560	0	0-0	0	4.69	4.40
2007	Cle	AL	20	16	1	1	97.1	443	112	73	68	17	3	2	7	36	1	66	5	0	5	8	.385	0	0-0	0	5.59	6.29
6 ML YEARS			129	125	3	1	741.2	3219	765	421	382	105	15	22	28	255	8	549	21	1	54	36	.600	0	0-0	0	4.44	4.64

Derrek Lee

Bats: R Throws: R Pos: 1B-147; PH-2; DH-1   Ht: 6'5" Wt: 245 Born: 9/6/1975 Age: 32

							BATTING													BASERUNNING				AVERAGES		
Year	Team	Lg	G	AB	H	2B	3B	HR	(Hm | Rd)	TB	R	RBI	RC	TBB	IBB	SO	HBP	SH	SF	SB	CS	SB%	GDP	Avg	OBP	Slg
1997	SD	NL	22	54	14	3	0	1	(0 | 1)	20	9	4	8	9	0	24	0	0	0	0	0	-	1	.259	.365	.370
1998	Fla	NL	141	454	106	29	1	17	(4 | 13)	188	62	74	59	47	1	120	10	0	2	5	2	.71	12	.233	.318	.414
1999	Fla	NL	70	218	45	9	1	5	(0 | 5)	71	21	20	18	17	1	70	0	0	1	2	1	.67	3	.206	.263	.326
2000	Fla	NL	158	477	134	18	3	28	(9 | 19)	242	70	70	84	63	6	123	4	0	2	0	3	.00	14	.281	.368	.507
2001	Fla	NL	158	561	158	37	4	21	(8 | 13)	266	83	75	88	50	1	126	8	0	6	4	2	.67	18	.282	.346	.474
2002	Fla	NL	162	581	157	35	7	27	(9 | 18)	287	95	86	96	98	8	164	5	0	4	19	9	.68	14	.270	.378	.494
2003	Fla	NL	155	539	146	31	2	31	(11 | 20)	274	91	92	99	88	7	131	10	0	6	21	8	.72	9	.271	.379	.508
2004	ChC	NL	161	605	168	39	1	32	(18 | 14)	305	90	98	101	68	4	128	8	2	5	12	5	.71	14	.278	.356	.504
2005	ChC	NL	158	594	199	50	3	46	(24 | 22)	393	120	107	135	85	23	109	5	0	7	15	3	.83	12	.335	.418	.662
2006	ChC	NL	50	175	50	9	0	8	(5 | 3)	83	30	30	27	25	1	41	0	0	4	8	4	.67	1	.286	.368	.474
2007	ChC	NL	150	567	180	43	1	22	(16 | 6)	291	91	82	108	71	8	114	9	0	3	6	5	.55	15	.317	.400	.513
11 ML YEARS			1385	4825	1357	303	23	238	(104 | 134)	2420	762	738	823	621	60	1150	59	2	40	92	42	.69	123	.281	.367	.502

Jon Leicester

Pitches: R Bats: R Pos: SP-5; RP-5   Ht: 6'3" Wt: 221 Born: 2/7/1979 Age: 29

			HOW MUCH HE PITCHED						WHAT HE GAVE UP										THE RESULTS							
Year	Team	Lg	G	GS	CG	GF	IP	BFP	H	R	ER	HR	SH	SF	HB	TBB	IBB	SO	WP	Bk	W	L	Pct	ShO	Sv-Op	Hld	ERC	ERA
2007	Orioles*	R	2	2	0	0	4.0	17	3	1	1	0	0	0	0	2	0	7	1	0	0	0	-	0	0--	-	2.40	2.25
2007	Abrdn*	A-	2	2	0	0	5.2	24	7	2	2	0	0	0	0	2	0	6	0	0	0	0	-	0	0--	-	4.76	3.18
2007	Norfolk*	AAA	13	11	0	2	65.0	258	48	22	16	5	2	3	5	22	1	54	2	0	3	3	.500	0	0--	-	2.68	2.22
2004	ChC	NL	32	0	0	6	41.2	175	40	20	18	7	2	2	0	15	0	35	0	0	5	1	.833	0	0-2	5	4.20	3.89
2005	ChC	NL	6	1	0	2	9.0	46	11	10	9	2	1	0	2	9	0	7	1	0	0	2	.000	0	0-0	0	10.60	9.00
2007	Bal	AL	10	5	1	1	32.0	145	36	27	27	3	1	1	3	13	0	16	1	0	2	3	.400	0	0-0	0	5.14	7.59
3 ML YEARS			48	6	1	9	82.2	366	87	57	54	12	4	3	5	37	0	58	2	0	7	6	.538	0	0-2	5	5.20	5.88

Anthony Lerew

Pitches: R Bats: L Pos: SP-3   Ht: 6'3" Wt: 220 Born: 10/28/1982 Age: 25

			HOW MUCH HE PITCHED						WHAT HE GAVE UP										THE RESULTS							
Year	Team	Lg	G	GS	CG	GF	IP	BFP	H	R	ER	HR	SH	SF	HB	TBB	IBB	SO	WP	Bk	W	L	Pct	ShO	Sv-Op	Hld	ERC	ERA
2007	Rchmd*	AAA	5	5	0	0	26.1	107	20	5	4	0	1	0	3	8	0	15	1	0	1	0	1.000	0	0--	-	2.26	1.37
2005	Atl	NL	7	0	0	4	8.0	37	9	5	5	1	1	0	0	5	2	5	0	0	0	0	-	0	0-1	0	5.47	5.63
2006	Atl	NL	1	0	0	0	2.0	15	5	5	5	0	0	0	1	3	0	1	0	0	0	0	-	0	0-0	0	20.57	22.50
2007	Atl	NL	3	3	0	0	11.2	57	14	10	10	4	3	0	0	7	1	9	1	0	0	2	.000	0	0-0	0	7.62	7.71
3 ML YEARS			11	3	0	4	21.2	109	28	20	20	5	4	0	1	15	3	15	1	0	0	2	.000	0	0-1	0	7.95	8.31

Jon Lester

Pitches: L Bats: L Pos: SP-11; RP-1   Ht: 6'2" Wt: 190 Born: 1/7/1984 Age: 24

			HOW MUCH HE PITCHED						WHAT HE GAVE UP										THE RESULTS							
Year	Team	Lg	G	GS	CG	GF	IP	BFP	H	R	ER	HR	SH	SF	HB	TBB	IBB	SO	WP	Bk	W	L	Pct	ShO	Sv-Op	Hld	ERC	ERA
2002	RedSx	R	1	1	0	0	0.2	8	5	6	1	0	0	0	0	1	0	1	0	0	0	1	.000	0	0--	-	61.66	13.50
2003	Augsta	A	24	21	0	2	106.0	452	102	54	43	7	6	4	8	44	0	71	2	0	6	9	.400	0	0--	-	4.07	3.65
2004	Srsota	A+	21	20	0	0	90.1	390	82	46	43	2	0	0	3	37	0	97	1	1	7	6	.538	0	0--	-	3.14	4.28
2004	RedSx	R	1	1	0	0	1.0	6	0	0	0	0	0	0	0	2	0	1	1	0	0	0	-	0	0--	-	3.47	0.00
2005	Portlnd	AA	26	26	3	0	148.1	603	114	52	43	10	6	4	4	57	3	163	10	1	11	6	.647	1	0--	-	2.68	2.61
2006	Pwtckt	AAA	11	11	0	0	46.2	207	43	17	14	5	2	1	0	25	0	43	0	0	3	4	.429	0	0--	-	4.14	2.70
2007	Grnville	A-	3	3	0	0	13.0	51	11	3	3	2	1	0	0	2	0	15	0	0	0	0	-	0	0--	-	2.67	2.08
2007	Pwtckt	AAA	14	14	2	0	71.2	306	67	32	31	4	3	1	3	31	0	51	4	0	4	5	.444	0	0--	-	3.74	3.89
2007	Portlnd	AA	1	1	0	0	6.0	27	5	1	1	0	0	0	0	4	0	4	0	0	1	0	1.000	0	0--	-	3.35	1.50
2006	Bos	AL	15	15	0	0	81.1	367	91	43	43	7	2	8	5	43	1	60	5	0	7	2	.778	0	0-0	0	5.52	4.76
2007	Bos	AL	12	11	0	0	63.0	275	61	33	32	10	1	5	1	31	0	50	1	0	4	0	1.000	0	0-0	0	4.78	4.57
2 ML YEARS			27	26	0	0	144.1	642	152	76	75	17	3	13	6	74	1	110	6	0	11	2	.846	0	0-0	0	5.20	4.68

Colby Lewis

Pitches: R Bats: R Pos: RP-25; SP-1   Ht: 6'4" Wt: 230 Born: 8/2/1979 Age: 28

			HOW MUCH HE PITCHED						WHAT HE GAVE UP										THE RESULTS							
Year	Team	Lg	G	GS	CG	GF	IP	BFP	H	R	ER	HR	SH	SF	HB	TBB	IBB	SO	WP	Bk	W	L	Pct	ShO	Sv-Op	Hld	ERC	ERA
2007	Scrmto*	AAA	15	15	0	0	95.2	375	70	24	20	8	1	3	1	23	0	97	1	0	8	3	.727	0	0--	-	2.06	1.88
2002	Tex	AL	15	4	0	4	34.1	168	42	26	24	4	2	0	2	26	2	28	3	1	1	3	.250	0	0-2	1	7.22	6.29
2003	Tex	AL	26	26	0	0	127.0	594	163	104	103	23	2	2	5	70	1	88	5	0	10	9	.526	0	0-0	0	7.38	7.30
2004	Tex	AL	3	3	0	0	15.1	71	13	7	7	1	0	0	1	13	0	11	0	0	1	1	.500	0	0-0	0	4.98	4.11
2006	Det	AL	2	0	0	1	3.0	18	8	1	1	1	0	0	0	1	0	5	0	0	0	0	-	0	0-0	0	17.35	3.00
2007	Oak	AL	26	1	0	8	37.2	170	44	28	27	7	1	2	3	14	3	23	1	1	0	2	.000	0	0-1	3	5.79	6.45
5 ML YEARS			72	34	0	13	217.1	1021	270	166	162	36	5	4	11	124	6	155	9	2	12	15	.444	0	0-3	4	7.03	6.71

Fred Lewis

Bats: L Throws: R Pos: RF-27; LF-24; PR-9; PH-7; CF-5   Ht: 6'2" Wt: 190 Born: 12/9/1980 Age: 27

							BATTING													BASERUNNING				AVERAGES		
Year	Team	Lg	G	AB	H	2B	3B	HR	(Hm	Rd)	TB	R	RBI	RC	TBB	IBB	SO	HBP	SH	SF	SB	CS	SB%	GDP	Avg	OBP	Slg
2002	SlmKzr	A-	58	239	77	9	3	1	(-	-)	95	43	23	39	26	1	58	3	1	0	9	6	.60	1	.322	.396	.397
2003	Hgrstn	A	114	420	105	17	8	1	(-	-)	141	61	27	58	68	1	112	6	6	2	30	15	.67	5	.250	.361	.336
2004	SnJos	A+	115	439	132	20	11	8	(-	-)	198	88	57	92	84	1	109	12	3	3	33	14	.70	5	.301	.424	.451
2004	Fresno	AAA	6	23	7	1	0	1	(-	-)	11	3	2	4	5	0	5	0	1	0	1	1	.50	1	.304	.429	.478

Year	Team	Lg	G	AB	H	2B	3B	HR	(Hm	Rd)	TB	R	RBI	RC	TBB	IBB	SO	HBP	SH	SF	SB	CS	SB%	GDP	Avg	OBP	Slg
									BATTING												BASERUNNING				AVERAGES		
2005	Nrwich	AA	137	512	140	28	7	7	(-	-)	203	79	47	79	69	2	124	3	6	4	30	13	.70	9	.273	.361	.396
2006	Fresno	AAA	120	439	121	20	11	12	(-	-)	199	85	56	79	68	2	105	4	2	4	18	8	.69	13	.276	.375	.453
2007	SnJos	A+	7	23	5	0	1	2	(-	-)	13	5	6	4	5	1	8	1	0	1	2	2	.50	2	.217	.367	.565
2007	Fresno	AAA	42	171	50	8	6	8	(-	-)	94	31	32	35	19	0	36	1	1	0	9	1	.90	2	.292	.366	.550
2006	SF	NL	13	11	5	1	0	0	(0	0)	6	5	2	4	0	0	3	0	0	0	0	0	-	0	.455	.455	.545
2007	SF	NL	58	157	45	6	2	3	(0	3)	64	34	19	27	19	0	32	3	1	0	5	1	.83	4	.287	.374	.408
2 ML YEARS			71	168	50	7	2	3	(0	3)	70	39	21	31	19	0	35	3	1	0	5	1	.83	4	.298	.379	.417

Jensen Lewis

Pitches: R Bats: R Pos: RP-26 **Ht: 6'3" Wt: 195 Born: 5/16/1984 Age: 24**

Year	Team	Lg	G	GS	CG	GF	IP	BFP	H	R	ER	HR	SH	SF	HB	TBB	IBB	SO	WP	Bk	W	L	Pct	ShO	Sv-Op	Hld	ERC	ERA
				HOW MUCH HE PITCHED								WHAT HE GAVE UP											THE RESULTS				
2005	Nrwich	A-	13	11	0	0	59.0	249	58	24	21	6	2	1	6	11	0	59	2	0	4	2	.667	0	0--	-	3.53	3.20
2006	Knstn	A+	21	20	0	0	108.1	460	110	59	48	11	0	1	9	29	0	94	5	0	7	6	.538	0	0--	-	4.01	3.99
2006	Akron	AA	7	7	0	0	39.1	170	41	24	17	4	1	1	4	12	0	44	0	0	1	2	.333	0	0--	-	4.39	3.89
2007	Akron	AA	24	0	0	12	39.0	154	27	12	8	2	0	2	1	13	1	49	1	0	2	0	1.000	0	1--	-	2.04	1.85
2007	Buffalo	AAA	10	0	0	2	13.0	48	5	2	2	1	0	1	0	4	0	12	0	0	1	0	1.000	0	1--	-	1.00	1.38
2007	Cle	AL	26	0	0	5	29.1	125	26	8	7	1	2	1	1	10	1	34	1	0	1	1	.500	0	0-0	5	2.81	2.15

Brad Lidge

Pitches: R Bats: R Pos: RP-66 **Ht: 6'5" Wt: 210 Born: 12/23/1976 Age: 31**

Year	Team	Lg	G	GS	CG	GF	IP	BFP	H	R	ER	HR	SH	SF	HB	TBB	IBB	SO	WP	Bk	W	L	Pct	ShO	Sv-Op	Hld	ERC	ERA
				HOW MUCH HE PITCHED								WHAT HE GAVE UP											THE RESULTS				
2007	CpChr*	AA	1	1	0	0	1.0	3	0	0	0	0	0	0	0	0	0	0	0	0	0	0	-	0	0--	-	0.00	0.00
2002	Hou	NL	6	1	0	2	8.2	48	12	6	6	0	1	0	2	9	1	12	0	0	1	0	1.000	0	0-0	0	8.90	6.23
2003	Hou	NL	78	0	0	9	85.0	349	60	36	34	6	2	3	5	42	7	97	4	1	6	3	.667	0	1-6	28	2.82	3.60
2004	Hou	NL	80	0	0	44	94.2	369	57	21	20	8	3	2	6	30	5	157	3	1	6	5	.545	0	29-33	17	1.85	1.90
2005	Hou	NL	70	0	0	65	70.2	291	58	21	18	5	4	1	3	23	1	103	8	0	4	4	.500	0	42-46	0	2.79	2.29
2006	Hou	NL	78	0	0	52	75.0	340	69	47	44	10	6	2	6	36	4	104	11	0	1	5	.167	0	32-38	6	4.25	5.28
2007	Hou	NL	66	0	0	34	67.0	287	54	29	25	9	5	1	4	30	4	88	6	0	5	3	.625	0	19-27	7	3.52	3.36
6 ML YEARS			378	1	0	206	401.0	1684	310	160	147	38	21	9	26	170	22	561	32	2	23	20	.535	0	123-150	58	3.06	3.30

Jon Lieber

Pitches: R Bats: L Pos: SP-12; RP-2 **Ht: 6'2" Wt: 240 Born: 4/2/1970 Age: 38**

Year	Team	Lg	G	GS	CG	GF	IP	BFP	H	R	ER	HR	SH	SF	HB	TBB	IBB	SO	WP	Bk	W	L	Pct	ShO	Sv-Op	Hld	ERC	ERA
				HOW MUCH HE PITCHED								WHAT HE GAVE UP											THE RESULTS				
2007	Clrwtr*	A+	1	1	0	0	2.2	16	4	2	1	0	0	0	0	0	0	4	0	0	0	0	-	0	0--	-	3.21	3.38
1994	Pit	NL	17	17	1	0	108.2	460	116	62	45	12	3	3	1	25	3	71	2	3	6	7	.462	0	0-0	0	3.83	3.73
1995	Pit	NL	21	12	0	3	72.2	327	103	56	51	7	5	6	4	14	0	45	3	0	4	7	.364	0	0-1	3	5.96	6.32
1996	Plt	NL	51	15	0	6	142.0	600	156	70	63	19	7	2	3	28	2	94	0	0	9	5	.643	0	1-4	9	4.12	3.99
1997	Pit	NL	33	32	1	0	188.1	799	193	102	94	23	6	7	1	51	8	160	3	1	11	14	.440	0	0-0	0	3.78	4.49
1998	Pit	NL	29	28	2	1	171.0	731	182	93	78	23	7	4	3	40	4	138	0	3	8	14	.364	0	1-1	0	4.00	4.11
1999	ChC	NL	31	31	3	0	203.1	875	226	107	92	28	7	11	4	46	6	186	2	2	10	11	.476	1	0-0	0	4.19	4.07
2000	ChC	NL	35	35	6	0	251.0	1047	248	130	123	36	9	7	10	54	3	192	2	2	12	11	.522	1	0-0	0	3.70	4.41
2001	ChC	NL	34	34	5	0	232.1	958	226	104	98	25	13	9	7	41	4	148	4	1	20	6	.769	1	0-0	0	3.19	3.80
2002	ChC	NL	21	21	3	0	141.0	582	153	64	58	15	10	6	1	12	2	87	0	0	6	8	.429	0	0-0	0	3.33	3.70
2004	NYY	AL	27	27	0	0	176.2	749	216	95	85	20	3	7	2	18	2	102	7	0	14	8	.636	0	0-0	0	4.26	4.33
2005	Phi	NL	35	35	1	0	218.1	912	223	107	102	33	13	5	5	41	6	149	3	0	17	13	.567	0	0-0	0	3.72	4.20
2006	Phi	NL	27	27	2	0	168.0	714	196	100	92	27	6	4	6	24	3	100	3	0	9	11	.450	0	0-0	0	4.53	4.93
2007	Phi	NL	14	12	1	1	78.0	342	91	44	41	7	2	4	3	22	5	54	1	1	3	6	.333	1	0-0	0	4.53	4.73
13 ML YEARS			375	326	25	11	2151.1	9096	2329	1134	1022	275	91	75	47	416	48	1526	30	13	129	121	.516	5	2-6	12	3.94	4.28

Mike Lieberthal

Bats: R Throws: R Pos: C-31; PH-10; DH-1 **Ht: 6'0" Wt: 195 Born: 1/18/1972 Age: 36**

Year	Team	Lg	G	AB	H	2B	3B	HR	(Hm	Rd)	TB	R	RBI	RC	TBB	IBB	SO	HBP	SH	SF	SB	CS	SB%	GDP	Avg	OBP	Slg
									BATTING												BASERUNNING				AVERAGES		
1994	Phi	NL	24	79	21	3	1	1	(1	0)	29	6	5	8	3	0	5	1	1	0	0	0	-	4	.266	.301	.367
1995	Phi	NL	16	47	12	2	0	0	(0	0)	14	1	4	5	5	0	5	0	2	0	0	0	-	4	.255	.327	.298
1996	Phi	NL	50	166	42	8	0	7	(4	3)	71	21	23	21	10	0	30	2	0	4	0	0	-	4	.253	.297	.428
1997	Phi	NL	134	455	112	27	1	20	(11	9)	201	59	77	62	44	1	76	4	0	7	3	4	.43	10	.246	.314	.442
1998	Phi	NL	86	313	80	15	3	8	(5	3)	125	39	45	39	17	1	44	7	0	5	2	1	.67	4	.256	.304	.399
1999	Phi	NL	145	510	153	33	1	31	(10	21)	281	84	96	96	44	7	86	11	1	8	0	0	-	15	.300	.363	.551
2000	Phi	NL	108	389	108	30	0	15	(8	7)	183	55	71	62	40	3	53	6	0	3	2	0	1.00	12	.278	.352	.470
2001	Phi	NL	34	121	28	8	0	2	(0	2)	42	21	11	13	12	2	21	3	0	0	0	0	-	2	.231	.316	.347
2002	Phi	NL	130	476	133	29	2	15	(7	8)	211	46	52	56	38	2	58	14	0	2	0	1	.00	16	.279	.349	.443
2003	Phi	NL	131	508	159	30	1	13	(6	7)	230	68	81	81	38	2	59	12	0	3	0	0	-	14	.313	.373	.453
2004	Phi	NL	131	476	129	31	1	17	(8	9)	213	58	61	49	37	2	69	11	1	4	1	1	.50	19	.271	.335	.447
2005	Phi	NL	118	392	103	25	0	12	(6	6)	164	48	47	49	35	14	35	11	0	5	0	0	-	6	.263	.336	.418
2006	Phi	NL	67	209	57	14	0	9	(5	4)	98	22	36	28	8	0	19	6	5	2	0	0	-	12	.273	.316	.469
2007	LAD	NL	38	77	18	2	0	0	(0	0)	20	6	1	5	4	0	11	1	0	0	0	0	-	2	.234	.280	.260
14 ML YEARS			1212	4218	1155	257	10	150	(71	79)	1882	534	610	574	335	34	571	89	10	43	8	7	.53	114	.274	.337	.446

Ted Lilly

Pitches: L **Bats:** L **Pos:** SP-34   **Ht:** 6'1" **Wt:** 190 **Born:** 1/4/1976 **Age:** 32

Year	Team	Lg	G	GS	CG	GF	IP	BFP	H	R	ER	HR	SH	SF	HB	TBB	IBB	SO	WP	Bk	W	L	Pct	ShO	Sv-Op	Hld	ERC	ERA
1999	Mon	NL	9	3	0	1	23.2	110	30	20	20	7	0	1	3	9	0	28	1	0	0	1	.000	0	0-0	0	7.76	7.61
2000	NYY	AL	7	0	0	1	8.0	39	8	6	5	1	0	0	0	5	0	11	1	1	0	0	-	0	0-0	0	4.76	5.63
2001	NYY	AL	26	21	0	2	120.2	537	126	81	72	20	2	5	7	51	1	112	9	2	5	6	.455	0	0-0	0	5.10	5.37
2002	2 Tms		22	16	2	1	100.0	413	80	43	41	15	0	3	6	31	3	77	6	1	5	7	.417	1	0-0	0	3.14	3.69
2003	Oak	AL	32	31	0	0	178.1	773	179	92	86	24	3	4	5	58	3	147	5	4	12	10	.545	0	0-0	0	4.06	4.34
2004	Tor	AL	32	32	2	0	197.1	845	171	92	89	26	3	3	6	89	2	168	6	4	12	10	.545	1	0-0	0	3.84	4.06
2005	Tor	AL	25	25	0	0	126.1	566	135	79	78	23	3	5	3	58	1	96	2	2	10	11	.476	0	0-0	0	5.38	5.56
2006	Tor	AL	32	32	0	0	181.2	797	179	98	87	28	4	2	4	81	6	160	7	4	15	13	.536	0	0-0	0	4.57	4.31
2007	ChC	NL	34	34	0	0	207.0	847	181	91	88	28	11	9	3	55	2	174	7	0	15	8	.652	0	0-0	0	3.14	3.83
02	NYY	AL	16	11	2	1	76.2	314	57	31	29	10	0	3	5	24	3	59	6	0	3	6	.333	1	0-0	0	2.74	3.40
02	Oak	AL	6	5	0	0	23.1	99	23	12	12	5	0	0	1	7	0	18	0	1	2	1	.667	0	0-0	0	4.56	4.63
	9 ML YEARS		219	194	4	5	1143.0	4927	1089	602	566	172	26	32	37	437	18	973	44	18	74	66	.529	2	0-0	0	4.17	4.46

Tim Lincecum

Pitches: R **Bats:** L **Pos:** SP-24   **Ht:** 5'11" **Wt:** 170 **Born:** 6/15/1984 **Age:** 24

Year	Team	Lg	G	GS	CG	GF	IP	BFP	H	R	ER	HR	SH	SF	HB	TBB	IBB	SO	WP	Bk	W	L	Pct	ShO	Sv-Op	Hld	ERC	ERA
2006	SlmKzr	A-	2	2	0	0	4.0	14	1	0	0	0	0	0	0	0	0	10	1	0	0	0	-	0	0--	-	0.13	0.00
2006	SnJos	A+	6	6	0	0	27.2	108	13	7	6	3	0	0	0	12	0	48	2	0	2	0	1.000	0	0--	-	1.61	1.95
2007	Fresno	AAA	5	5	0	0	31.0	114	12	1	1	0	0	1	1	11	0	46	1	0	4	0	1.000	0	0--	-	0.92	0.29
2007	SF	NL	24	24	0	0	146.1	618	122	70	65	12	5	7	2	65	5	150	10	0	7	5	.583	0	0-0	0	3.21	4.00

Adam Lind

Bats: L **Throws:** L **Pos:** LF-80; PH-12   **Ht:** 6'2" **Wt:** 195 **Born:** 7/17/1983 **Age:** 24

Year	Team	Lg	G	AB	H	2B	3B	HR	(Hm	Rd)	TB	R	RBI	RC	TBB	IBB	SO	HBP	SH	SF	SB	CS	SB%	GDP	Avg	OBP	Slg
2004	Auburn	A-	70	266	83	23	0	7	(-	-)	127	43	50	48	24	0	36	2	1	2	1	0	1.00	7	.312	.371	.477
2005	Dnedin	A+	126	495	155	42	4	12	(-	-)	241	80	84	92	49	7	77	4	0	6	2	1	.67	12	.313	.375	.487
2006	NHam	AA	91	348	108	24	0	19	(-	-)	189	43	71	66	25	2	87	2	0	3	2	1	.67	5	.310	.357	.543
2006	Syrcse	AAA	34	109	43	7	0	5	(-	-)	65	20	18	32	23	5	18	2	0	1	1	0	1.00	2	.394	.496	.596
2007	Syrcse	AAA	46	174	52	8	2	6	(-	-)	82	20	28	29	14	3	42	1	0	1	0	0	-	2	.299	.353	.471
2006	Tor	AL	18	60	22	8	0	2	(0	2)	36	8	8	13	5	0	12	0	0	0	0	0	-	0	.367	.415	.600
2007	Tor	AL	89	290	69	14	0	11	(10	1)	116	34	46	38	16	0	65	1	2	2	1	2	.33	7	.238	.278	.400
	2 ML YEARS		107	350	91	22	0	13	(10	3)	152	42	54	51	21	0	77	1	2	2	1	2	.33	7	.260	.302	.434

Todd Linden

Bats: B **Throws:** R **Pos:** PH-60; LF-37; CF-13; RF-11; PR-9   **Ht:** 6'3" **Wt:** 220 **Born:** 6/30/1980 **Age:** 28

Year	Team	Lg	G	AB	H	2B	3B	HR	(Hm	Rd)	TB	R	RBI	RC	TBB	IBB	SO	HBP	SH	SF	SB	CS	SB%	GDP	Avg	OBP	Slg
2007	Alba*	AAA	14	48	18	3	1	1	(-	-)	26	10	10	11	8	0	12	1	0	0	0	1	.00	0	.375	.474	.542
2003	SF	NL	18	38	8	1	0	1	(0	1)	12	2	6	5	1	0	8	0	0	0	0	0	-	2	.211	.231	.316
2004	SF	NL	16	32	5	1	0	0	(0	0)	6	6	1	1	5	0	7	1	2	0	0	0	-	0	.156	.289	.188
2005	SF	NL	60	171	37	8	0	4	(2	2)	57	20	13	12	10	0	54	5	1	0	3	0	1.00	5	.216	.280	.333
2006	SF	NL	61	77	21	4	2	2	(0	2)	35	15	5	10	9	0	20	1	2	0	1	0	1.00	2	.273	.356	.455
2007	2 Tms	NL	115	184	45	8	1	1	(0	1)	58	21	11	21	19	1	59	1	0	0	4	0	1.00	4	.245	.319	.315
07	SF	NL	30	55	10	1	0	0	(0	0)	11	6	3	4	5	1	23	0	0	0	0	0	-	0	.182	.250	.200
07	Fla	NL	85	129	35	7	1	1	(0	1)	47	15	8	17	14	0	36	1	0	0	4	0	1.00	4	.271	.347	.364
	5 ML YEARS		270	502	116	22	3	8	(2	6)	168	64	36	49	44	1	148	8	5	0	8	0	1.00	13	.231	.303	.335

Matt Lindstrom

Pitches: R **Bats:** R **Pos:** RP-71   **Ht:** 6'4" **Wt:** 205 **Born:** 2/11/1980 **Age:** 28

Year	Team	Lg	G	GS	CG	GF	IP	BFP	H	R	ER	HR	SH	SF	HB	TBB	IBB	SO	WP	Bk	W	L	Pct	ShO	Sv-Op	Hld	ERC	ERA
2002	Kngspt	R+	12	11	0	0	48.1	228	56	45	26	6	1	4	2	21	0	39	4	1	0	6	.000	0	0--	-	5.25	4.84
2003	CptCty	A	12	11	0	0	56.2	237	46	21	18	2	0	1	1	33	0	50	6	3	2	3	.400	0	0--	-	3.48	2.86
2003	Bklyn	A-	14	14	0	0	65.1	280	61	28	25	2	0	2	7	27	0	52	6	0	7	3	.700	0	0--	-	3.74	3.44
2004	CptCty	A	13	12	0	0	56.0	222	47	26	20	3	1	3	4	10	0	64	7	0	3	2	.600	0	0--	-	2.43	3.21
2004	StLuci	A+	14	14	1	0	79.2	329	83	44	33	5	6	6	3	20	0	50	4	0	5	5	.500	0	0--	-	3.73	3.73
2005	Bnghtn	AA	35	10	0	11	73.1	366	90	61	44	11	3	4	5	55	2	58	11	1	2	5	.286	0	0--	-	7.48	5.40
2006	StLuci	A+	11	0	0	5	18.0	75	14	7	5	2	1	0	0	7	0	16	1	0	1	0	1.000	0	2--	-	2.86	2.50
2006	Bnghtn	AA	35	0	0	22	40.2	179	42	19	17	2	0	2	5	14	1	54	3	2	2	4	.333	0	11--	-	4.11	3.76
2007	Fla	NL	71	0	0	11	67.0	284	66	27	23	2	3	1	3	21	4	62	5	0	3	4	.429	0	0-2	19	3.26	3.09

Scott Linebrink

Pitches: R **Bats:** R **Pos:** RP-71   **Ht:** 6'2" **Wt:** 200 **Born:** 8/4/1976 **Age:** 31

Year	Team	Lg	G	GS	CG	GF	IP	BFP	H	R	ER	HR	SH	SF	HB	TBB	IBB	SO	WP	Bk	W	L	Pct	ShO	Sv-Op	Hld	ERC	ERA
2000	2 Tms	NL	11	0	0	4	12.0	63	18	8	8	4	0	0	3	8	0	6	0	0	0	0	-	0	0-0	0	11.88	6.00
2001	Hou	NL	9	0	0	2	10.1	44	6	4	3	0	1	1	2	6	0	9	1	0	0	0	-	0	0-0	0	2.54	2.61
2002	Hou	NL	22	0	0	4	24.1	120	31	21	19	2	0	2	1	13	4	24	0	0	0	0	-	0	0-0	1	5.70	7.03
2003	2 Tms	NL	52	6	0	8	92.1	397	93	37	34	9	4	6	6	36	4	68	11	0	3	2	.600	0	0-0	6	4.32	3.31
2004	SD	NL	73	0	0	7	84.0	326	61	22	20	8	2	3	3	26	2	83	3	0	7	3	.700	0	0-5	28	2.48	2.14

Year	Team	Lg	HOW MUCH HE PITCHED						WHAT HE GAVE UP												THE RESULTS							
			G	GS	CG	GF	IP	BFP	H	R	ER	HR	SH	SF	HB	TBB	IBB	SO	WP	Bk	W	L	Pct	ShO	Sv-Op	Hld	ERC	ERA
2005	SD	NL	73	0	0	17	73.2	288	55	17	15	4	2	0	0	23	4	70	3	0	8	1	.889	0	1-6	26	2.15	1.83
2006	SD	NL	73	0	0	11	75.2	314	70	31	30	9	1	2	1	22	3	68	2	0	7	4	.636	0	2-11	36	3.36	3.57
2007	2 Tms	NL	71	0	0	11	70.1	295	68	33	29	12	0	0	1	25	3	50	6	0	5	6	.455	0	1-8	21	4.26	3.71
00	SF	NL	3	0	0	1	2.1	16	7	3	3	1	0	0	0	2	0	0	0	0	0	0	-	0	0-0	0	24.13	11.57
00	Hou	NL	8	0	0	3	9.2	47	11	5	5	3	0	0	3	6	0	6	0	0	0	0	-	0	0-0	0	9.21	4.66
03	Hou	NL	9	6	0	2	31.2	140	38	15	15	4	2	1	3	14	1	17	5	0	1	1	.500	0	0-0	0	6.27	4.26
03	SD	NL	43	0	0	6	60.2	257	55	22	19	5	2	5	3	22	3	51	6	0	2	1	.667	0	0-0	6	3.41	2.82
07	SD	NL	44	0	0	7	45.0	186	41	19	19	9	0	0	1	14	1	25	4	0	3	3	.500	0	1-7	15	3.99	3.80
07	Mil	NL	27	0	0	4	25.1	109	27	14	10	3	0	0	0	11	2	25	2	0	2	3	.400	0	0-1	6	4.71	3.55
	8 ML YEARS		384	6	0	64	442.2	1847	402	173	158	48	10	14	17	159	20	378	26	0	30	16	.652	0	4-30	118	3.60	3.21

Francisco Liriano

Pitches: L **Bats:** L **Pos:** P   **Ht:** 6'2" **Wt:** 200 **Born:** 10/26/1983 **Age:** 24

Year	Team	Lg	HOW MUCH HE PITCHED						WHAT HE GAVE UP												THE RESULTS							
			G	GS	CG	GF	IP	BFP	H	R	ER	HR	SH	SF	HB	TBB	IBB	SO	WP	Bk	W	L	Pct	ShO	Sv-Op	Hld	ERC	ERA
2001	Giants	R	13	12	0	0	62.0	261	51	26	25	3	1	0	1	24	0	67	6	3	5	4	.556	0	0--	-	2.75	3.63
2001	SlmKzr	A-	2	2	0	0	9.0	35	7	5	5	2	0	0	0	1	0	12	0	0	0	0	-	0	0--	-	2.47	5.00
2002	Hgrstn	A	16	16	0	0	80.0	332	61	45	31	6	4	3	0	31	0	85	4	0	3	6	.333	0	0--	-	2.56	3.49
2003	SnJos	A+	1	1	0	0	0.2	9	5	4	4	0	3	1	0	2	0	0	1	0	0	1	.000	0	0--	-	69.84	54.00
2003	Giants	R	4	4	0	0	8.1	36	5	4	4	1	0	0	0	6	0	9	1	1	0	1	.000	0	0--	-	3.20	4.32
2004	FtMyrs	A+	21	21	0	0	117.0	512	118	56	52	6	4	1	0	43	2	125	6	2	6	7	.462	0	0--	-	3.54	4.00
2004	NwBrit	AA	7	7	0	0	39.2	181	45	14	14	4	3	1	2	17	0	49	3	0	3	2	.600	0	0--	-	5.11	3.18
2005	NwBrit	AA	13	13	0	0	76.2	326	70	36	31	6	0	0	2	26	0	92	3	1	3	5	.375	0	0--	-	3.27	3.64
2005	Roch	AAA	14	14	0	0	91.0	353	56	25	18	4	0	2	0	24	0	112	2	1	9	2	.818	0	0--	-	1.44	1.78
2005	Min	AL	6	4	0	2	23.2	93	19	15	15	4	0	0	0	7	0	33	0	0	1	2	.333	0	0-0	0	3.15	5.70
2006	Min	AL	28	16	0	2	121.0	473	89	31	29	9	4	2	1	32	0	144	9	1	12	3	.800	0	1-1	1	2.12	2.16
	2 ML YEARS		34	20	0	4	144.2	566	108	46	44	13	4	2	1	39	0	177	9	1	13	5	.722	0	1-1	1	2.28	2.74

Jesse Litsch

Pitches: R **Bats:** R **Pos:** SP-20   **Ht:** 6'1" **Wt:** 175 **Born:** 3/9/1985 **Age:** 23

Year	Team	Lg	HOW MUCH HE PITCHED						WHAT HE GAVE UP												THE RESULTS							
			G	GS	CG	GF	IP	BFP	H	R	ER	HR	SH	SF	HB	TBB	IBB	SO	WP	Bk	W	L	Pct	ShO	Sv-Op	Hld	ERC	ERA
2005	Pulaski	R+	11	11	0	0	65.2	255	51	22	20	6	0	0	4	10	0	67	2	1	5	1	.833	0	0--	-	2.22	2.74
2005	Auburn	A-	4	3	0	0	10.0	50	11	9	4	0	1	2	0	6	0	7	1	0	0	1	.000	0	0--	-	4.23	3.60
2006	Dnedin	A+	16	15	2	0	89.1	367	94	39	35	5	1	1	5	8	0	81	5	0	6	6	.500	1	0--	-	3.10	3.53
2006	NHam	AA	12	12	1	0	69.1	298	85	44	39	6	1	3	6	13	0	54	3	0	3	4	.429	0	0--	-	4.89	5.06
2007	NHam	AA	10	10	1	0	61.1	252	51	24	16	5	1	0	4	14	0	46	2	0	7	2	.778	0	0--	-	2.62	2.35
2007	Syrcse	AAA	2	2	0	0	15.0	58	12	3	3	0	1	1	0	3	0	10	0	0	1	0	1.000	0	0--	-	1.78	1.80
2007	Tor	AL	20	20	0	0	111.0	478	116	56	47	14	3	3	7	36	2	50	2	0	7	9	.438	0	0-0	-	4.48	3.81

Wes Littleton

Pitches: R **Bats:** R **Pos:** RP-35   **Ht:** 6'2" **Wt:** 210 **Born:** 9/2/1982 **Age:** 25

Year	Team	Lg	HOW MUCH HE PITCHED						WHAT HE GAVE UP												THE RESULTS							
			G	GS	CG	GF	IP	BFP	H	R	ER	HR	SH	SF	HB	TBB	IBB	SO	WP	Bk	W	L	Pct	ShO	Sv-Op	Hld	ERC	ERA
2003	Spkane	A-	12	8	0	2	52.0	192	36	9	9	2	1	0	1	8	0	47	2	1	6	0	1.000	0	0--	-	1.53	1.56
2004	Stcktn	A+	30	23	0	1	141.0	600	139	76	65	7	8	15	11	56	0	72	14	0	8	10	.444	0	0--	-	4.04	4.15
2005	Frisco	AA	48	0	0	27	81.2	369	93	37	36	9	2	4	3	24	7	71	3	1	2	3	.400	0	3--	-	4.35	3.97
2006	Frisco	AA	17	0	0	6	27.1	104	13	3	2	1	0	0	2	7	0	25	1	0	3	0	1.000	0	3--	-	1.15	0.66
2006	Okla	AAA	13	0	0	6	16.2	66	14	4	4	3	1	0	0	5	0	15	0	0	4	1	.800	0	2--	-	3.45	2.16
2007	Okla	AAA	23	0	0	13	32.1	130	31	19	18	5	1	1	0	8	0	21	0	0	1	0	1.000	0	2--	-	3.73	5.01
2006	Tex	AL	33	0	0	6	36.1	138	23	7	7	2	0	1	2	13	0	17	0	0	2	1	.667	0	1-1	7	2.10	1.73
2007	Tex	AL	35	0	0	11	48.0	205	48	23	23	6	0	3	3	16	1	24	1	0	3	2	.600	0	2-3	2	4.24	4.31
	2 ML YEARS		68	0	0	17	84.1	343	71	30	30	8	0	4	5	29	1	41	1	0	5	3	.625	0	3-4	9	3.27	3.20

Bobby Livingston

Pitches: L **Bats:** L **Pos:** SP-10   **Ht:** 6'3" **Wt:** 206 **Born:** 9/3/1982 **Age:** 25

Year	Team	Lg	HOW MUCH HE PITCHED						WHAT HE GAVE UP												THE RESULTS							
			G	GS	CG	GF	IP	BFP	H	R	ER	HR	SH	SF	HB	TBB	IBB	SO	WP	Bk	W	L	Pct	ShO	Sv-Op	Hld	ERC	ERA
2002	Everett	A-	15	14	0	1	80.1	338	80	33	27	2	1	2	7	14	0	76	4	2	6	5	.545	0	0--	-	2.99	3.02
2003	Wisc	A	26	26	1	0	178.0	733	176	72	54	10	7	7	12	28	0	105	1	3	15	7	.682	0	0--	-	3.07	2.73
2004	InldEm	A+	28	27	1	0	186.2	762	187	90	74	15	8	4	7	30	0	141	4	0	12	6	.667	1	0--	-	3.21	3.57
2005	SnAnt	AA	18	18	0	0	116.1	467	103	45	37	7	7	5	2	27	0	78	2	1	8	4	.667	0	0--	-	2.68	2.86
2005	Tacom	AAA	10	10	0	0	51.2	224	53	31	27	2	3	1	1	15	0	41	1	0	6	2	.750	0	0--	-	3.36	4.70
2006	Tacom	AAA	23	22	0	1	135.1	583	165	74	69	18	1	9	2	36	2	69	2	2	8	11	.421	0	0--	-	5.19	4.59
2007	Lsvlle	AAA	17	16	1	0	104.1	440	123	47	44	7	8	3	1	17	1	63	1	2	3	4	.429	0	0--	-	3.97	3.80
2006	Sea	AL	3	0	0	1	5.0	32	9	10	10	2	0	0	2	6	1	3	0	0	0	0	-	0	0-0	0	17.47	18.00
2007	Cin	NL	10	10	0	0	56.1	250	77	35	33	8	4	0	1	8	0	27	2	1	3	3	.500	0	0-0	0	5.52	5.27
	2 ML YEARS		13	10	0	1	61.1	282	86	45	43	10	4	0	3	14	1	30	2	1	3	3	.500	0	0-0	0	6.38	6.31

Radhames Liz

Pitches: R **Bats:** R **Pos:** RP-5; SP-4   **Ht:** 6'2" **Wt:** 185 **Born:** 6/10/1983 **Age:** 25

			HOW MUCH HE PITCHED						WHAT HE GAVE UP										THE RESULTS						
Year	Team	Lg	G	GS	CG	GF	IP	BFP	H	R	ER	HR	SH	SF	HB	TBB	IBB	SO	WP	Bk	W	L	Pct	ShO	Sv-Op Hld	ERC	ERA
2005	Dlmrva	A	10	10	0	0	38.1	170	33	23	19	2	2	1	1	23	0	55	5	0	2	3	.400	0	0-- -	3.78	4.46
2005	Abrdn	A-	11	11	0	0	56.0	214	36	14	11	1	2	0	2	19	0	82	4	3	5	4	.556	0	0-- -	1.77	1.77
2006	Frdrck	A+	16	16	0	0	83.0	341	57	32	26	8	0	1	5	44	0	95	2	0	6	5	.545	0	0-- -	3.17	2.82
2006	Bowie	AA	10	10	0	0	50.1	230	55	31	30	9	1	0	2	31	1	54	4	0	3	1	.750	0	0-- -	6.37	5.36
2007	Bowie	AA	25	25	2	0	137.0	584	101	60	49	13	3	3	12	70	0	161	11	0	11	4	.733	1	0-- -	3.36	3.22
2007	Bal	AL	9	4	0	5	24.2	122	25	21	19	3	1	1	1	23	1	24	3	0	0	2	.000	0	0-0 0	6.49	6.93

Paul Lo Duca

Bats: R **Throws:** R **Pos:** C-113; DH-3; PH-3   **Ht:** 5'10" **Wt:** 205 **Born:** 4/12/1972 **Age:** 36

			BATTING																	BASERUNNING				AVERAGES		
Year	Team	Lg	G	AB	H	2B	3B	HR	(Hm	Rd)	TB	R	RBI	RC	TBB	IBB	SO	HBP	SH	SF	SB	CS	SB%	GDP	Avg	OBP	Slg
2007	Bklyn*	A-	2	5	2	0	0	1	(-	-)	5	1	2	2	1	0	2	1	0	0	0	0	-	0	.400	.571	1.000
2007	Bnghtn*	AA	1	3	1	0	0	0	(-	-)	1	0	0	0	0	0	1	0	0	0	0	0	-	0	.333	.333	.333
1998	LAD	NL	6	14	4	1	0	0	(0	0)	5	2	1	1	0	0	1	0	0	0	0	0	-	0	.286	.286	.357
1999	LAD	NL	36	95	22	1	0	3	(1	2)	32	11	11	9	10	4	9	2	1	2	1	2	.33	3	.232	.312	.337
2000	LAD	NL	34	65	16	2	0	2	(0	2)	24	6	8	6	6	0	8	0	2	2	0	2	.00	2	.246	.301	.369
2001	LAD	NL	125	460	147	28	0	25	(11	14)	250	71	90	89	39	2	30	6	5	9	2	4	.33	11	.320	.374	.543
2002	LAD	NL	149	580	163	38	1	10	(5	5)	233	74	64	73	34	2	31	10	4	4	3	1	.75	20	.281	.330	.402
2003	LAD	NL	147	568	155	34	2	7	(4	3)	214	64	52	67	44	6	54	10	7	1	0	2	.00	21	.273	.335	.377
2004	2 Tms	NL	143	535	153	29	2	13	(8	5)	225	68	80	78	36	0	49	9	8	6	4	5	.44	22	.286	.334	.421
2005	Fla	NL	132	445	126	23	1	6	(2	4)	169	45	57	50	34	5	31	4	5	8	4	3	.57	16	.283	.334	.380
2006	NYM	NL	124	512	163	39	1	5	(2	3)	219	80	49	71	24	0	38	6	7	2	3	0	1.00	15	.318	.355	.428
2007	NYM	NL	119	445	121	18	1	9	(3	6)	168	46	54	48	24	4	33	6	3	10	2	0	1.00	18	.272	.311	.378
04	LAD	NL	91	349	105	18	1	10	(6	4)	155	41	49	51	22	0	27	6	2	2	2	4	.33	15	.301	.351	.444
04	Fla	NL	52	186	48	11	1	3	(2	1)	70	27	31	27	14	0	22	3	6	4	2	1	.67	7	.258	.314	.376
10 ML YEARS			1015	3719	1070	213	8	80	(36	44)	1539	467	466	492	251	23	284	53	42	44	19	19	.50	128	.288	.338	.414

Esteban Loaiza

Pitches: R **Bats:** R **Pos:** SP-7   **Ht:** 6'2" **Wt:** 228 **Born:** 12/31/1971 **Age:** 36

			HOW MUCH HE PITCHED						WHAT HE GAVE UP										THE RESULTS						
Year	Team	Lg	G	GS	CG	GF	IP	BFP	H	R	ER	HR	SH	SF	HB	TBB	IBB	SO	WP	Bk	W	L	Pct	ShO	Sv-Op Hld	ERC	ERA
2007	Scrmto*	AAA	6	6	0	0	28.0	118	35	13	12	3	1	1	0	4	0	13	1	0	2	1	.667	0	0-- -	4.61	3.86
1995	Pit	NL	32	31	1	0	172.2	762	205	115	99	21	10	9	5	55	3	85	6	1	8	9	.471	0	0-0 0	5.10	5.16
1996	Pit	NL	10	10	1	0	52.2	236	65	32	29	11	3	1	2	19	2	32	0	0	2	3	.400	1	0-0 0	6.30	4.96
1997	Pit	NL	33	32	1	0	196.1	851	214	99	90	17	10	7	12	56	9	122	2	3	11	11	.500	0	0-0 0	4.20	4.13
1998	2 Tms		35	28	1	3	171.0	751	199	107	98	28	7	12	5	52	4	108	4	2	9	11	.450	0	0-1 0	5.19	5.16
1999	Tex	Al	30	15	0	4	120.1	517	128	65	61	10	7	4	0	40	2	77	2	0	9	5	.643	0	0-0 0	4.03	4.56
2000	2 Tms		34	31	1	0	199.1	871	228	112	101	29	4	5	13	57	1	137	1	0	10	13	.435	1	1 1 0	5.07	4.56
2001	Tor	AL	36	30	1	1	190.0	837	239	113	106	27	6	4	9	40	1	110	1	1	11	11	.500	1	0-0 0	5.30	5.02
2002	Tor	AL	25	25	3	0	151.1	670	192	102	96	18	1	6	4	38	3	87	1	0	9	10	.474	1	0-0 0	5.26	5.71
2003	CWS	AL	34	34	1	0	226.1	922	196	75	73	17	7	6	10	56	2	207	3	1	21	9	.700	1	0-0 0	2.79	2.90
2004	2 Tms	AL	31	27	2	1	183.0	818	217	124	116	32	1	10	3	71	4	117	4	0	10	7	.588	0	0-0 0	5.72	5.70
2005	Was	AL	34	34	0	0	217.0	912	227	93	91	18	9	3	5	55	3	173	6	0	12	10	.545	0	0-0 0	3.74	3.77
2006	Oak	AL	26	26	2	0	154.2	679	179	92	84	17	5	8	5	40	3	97	2	0	11	9	.550	1	0-0 0	4.53	4.89
2007	2 Tms		7	7	0	0	37.1	164	36	24	24	10	3	1	1	20	1	20	0	1	2	4	.333	0	0-0 0	5.79	5.79
98	Pit	NL	21	14	0	3	91.2	394	96	50	46	13	5	7	3	30	1	53	1	2	6	5	.545	0	0-1 0	4.48	4.52
98	Tex	AL	14	14	1	0	79.1	357	103	57	52	15	2	5	2	22	3	55	3	0	3	6	.333	0	0-0 0	6.04	5.90
00	Tex	AL	20	17	0	2	107.1	480	133	67	64	21	2	4	3	31	1	75	1	0	5	6	.455	0	1-1 0	5.81	5.37
00	Tor	AL	14	14	1	0	92.0	391	95	45	37	8	2	1	10	26	0	62	0	0	5	7	.417	1	0-0 0	4.22	3.62
04	CWS	AL	21	21	2	0	140.2	604	156	81	76	23	1	5	1	45	3	83	2	0	9	5	.643	0	0-0 0	4.89	4.86
04	NYY	AL	10	6	0	1	42.1	214	61	43	40	9	0	5	2	26	2	34	2	0	1	2	.333	0	0-0 0	8.70	8.50
07	Oak	AL	2	2	0	0	14.2	56	10	3	3	1	0	0	0	4	0	5	0	0	1	0	1.000	0	0-0 0	1.87	1.84
07	LAD	NL	5	5	0	0	22.2	108	26	21	21	9	3	1	1	16	1	15	0	1	1	4	.200	0	0-0 0	8.92	8.34
13 ML YEARS			367	330	14	11	2072.0	8990	2325	1153	1068	255	73	76	74	599	39	1372	32	9	125	112	.527	6	1-2 0	4.62	4.64

Kameron Loe

Pitches: R **Bats:** R **Pos:** SP-23; RP-5   **Ht:** 6'7" **Wt:** 240 **Born:** 9/10/1981 **Age:** 26

			HOW MUCH HE PITCHED						WHAT HE GAVE UP										THE RESULTS						
Year	Team	Lg	G	GS	CG	GF	IP	BFP	H	R	ER	HR	SH	SF	HB	TBB	IBB	SO	WP	Bk	W	L	Pct	ShO	Sv-Op Hld	ERC	ERA
2007	Frisco*	AA	1	1	0	0	3.0	15	1	3	2	0	0	0	0	5	0	1	0	0	0	0	-	0	0-- -	4.14	6.00
2004	Tex	AL	2	1	0	0	6.2	29	6	5	4	0	0	0	1	6	0	3	0	0	0	0	-	0	0-0 0	5.87	5.40
2005	Tex	AL	48	8	0	13	92.0	392	89	43	35	7	5	1	2	31	6	45	2	0	9	6	.600	0	1-4 4	3.45	3.42
2006	Tex	AL	15	15	1	0	78.1	358	105	54	51	10	1	3	1	22	0	34	3	0	3	6	.333	1	0-0 0	5.79	5.86
2007	Tex	AL	28	23	0	0	136.0	615	162	96	81	13	1	5	4	56	6	78	6	0	6	11	.353	0	0-0 0	5.24	5.36
4 ML YEARS			93	47	1	13	313.0	1394	362	198	171	30	7	9	8	115	12	160	11	0	18	23	.439	1	1-4 4	4.84	4.92

Adam Loewen

Pitches: L **Bats:** L **Pos:** SP-6   **Ht:** 6'6" **Wt:** 235 **Born:** 4/9/1984 **Age:** 24

			HOW MUCH HE PITCHED						WHAT HE GAVE UP										THE RESULTS						
Year	Team	Lg	G	GS	CG	GF	IP	BFP	H	R	ER	HR	SH	SF	HB	TBB	IBB	SO	WP	Bk	W	L	Pct	ShO	Sv-Op Hld	ERC	ERA
2003	Abrdn	A-	7	7	0	0	23.1	91	13	7	7	0	0	0	4	9	0	25	2	0	0	2	.000	0	0-- -	1.84	2.70
2004	Dlmrva	A	20	19	1	0	85.1	376	77	47	39	3	2	4	4	58	0	82	8	4	4	5	.444	0	0-- -	4.43	4.11
2004	Frdrck	A+	2	2	1	0	8.0	37	7	6	6	2	1	0	0	9	0	3	0	0	0	2	.000	0	0-- -	8.07	6.75
2005	Frdrck	A+	28	27	1	0	142.0	631	130	77	65	8	4	1	14	86	0	146	15	1	10	8	.556	0	0-- -	4.54	4.12

Year	Team	Lg	G	GS	CG	GF	IP	BFP	H	R	ER	HR	SH	SF	HB	TBB	IBB	SO	WP	Bk	W	L	Pct	ShO	Sv-Op	Hld	ERC	ERA
2006	Bowie	AA	9	8	0	0	49.2	215	46	17	15	3	2	1	2	26	0	55	6	2	4	2	.667	0	0--	-	4.08	2.72
2006	Ottawa	AAA	3	3	0	0	21.1	73	10	3	3	0	0	0	0	3	0	21	1	0	2	0	1.000	0	0--	-	0.72	1.27
2006	Bal	AL	22	19	0	1	112.1	504	111	72	67	8	1	4	8	62	0	98	3	1	6	6	.500	0	0-0	1	4.70	5.37
2007	Bal	AL	6	6	0	0	30.1	143	27	14	12	1	1	0	3	26	0	21	2	1	2	0	1.000	0	0-0	0	5.11	3.56
2 ML YEARS			28	25	0	1	142.2	647	138	86	79	9	2	4	11	88	0	120	4	2	8	6	.571	0	0-0	1	4.79	4.98

Kenny Lofton

Bats: L **Throws:** L **Pos:** CF-83; LF-50; PH-11; PR-1 **Ht:** 5'11" **Wt:** 190 **Born:** 5/31/1967 **Age:** 41

Year	Team	Lg	G	AB	H	2B	3B	HR	(Hm	Rd)	TB	R	RBI	RC	TBB	IBB	SO	HBP	SH	SF	SB	CS	SB%	GDP	Avg	OBP	Slg
1991	Hou	NL	20	74	15	1	0	0	(0	0)	16	9	0	4	5	0	19	0	0	0	2	1	.67	0	.203	.253	.216
1992	Cle	AL	148	576	164	15	8	5	(3	2)	210	96	42	88	68	3	54	2	4	1	66	12	.85	7	.285	.362	.365
1993	Cle	AL	148	569	185	28	8	1	(1	0)	232	116	42	107	81	6	83	1	2	4	70	14	.83	8	.325	.408	.408
1994	Cle	AL	112	459	160	32	9	12	(10	2)	246	105	57	105	52	5	56	2	4	6	60	12	.83	5	.349	.412	.536
1995	Cle	AL	118	481	149	22	13	7	(5	2)	218	93	53	83	40	6	49	1	4	3	54	15	.78	6	.310	.362	.453
1996	Cle	AL	154	662	210	35	4	14	(7	7)	295	132	67	118	61	3	82	0	7	6	75	17	.82	7	.317	.372	.446
1997	Atl	NL	122	493	164	20	6	5	(3	2)	211	90	48	84	64	5	83	2	2	3	27	20	.57	10	.333	.409	.428
1998	Cle	AL	154	600	169	31	6	12	(6	6)	248	101	64	103	87	1	80	2	3	6	54	10	.84	7	.282	.371	.413
1999	Cle	AL	120	465	140	28	6	7	(1	6)	201	110	39	89	79	2	84	6	5	5	25	6	.81	6	.301	.405	.432
2000	Cle	AL	137	543	151	23	5	15	(10	5)	229	107	73	91	79	3	72	4	6	8	30	7	.81	11	.278	.369	.422
2001	Cle	AL	133	517	135	21	4	14	(9	5)	206	91	66	67	47	1	69	2	5	5	16	8	.67	8	.261	.322	.398
2002	2 Tms		139	532	139	30	9	11	(3	8)	220	98	51	83	72	0	73	1	5	1	29	11	.73	1	.261	.350	.414
2003	2 Tms	NL	140	547	162	32	8	3	(5	7)	246	97	46	79	46	3	51	4	7	6	30	9	.77	6	.296	.352	.450
2004	NYY	AL	83	276	76	10	7	3	(2	1)	109	51	18	36	31	1	27	1	1	4	7	3	.70	4	.275	.346	.395
2005	Phi	NL	110	367	123	15	5	2	(1	1)	154	67	36	62	32	2	41	2	5	0	22	3	.88	3	.335	.392	.420
2006	LAD	NL	129	469	141	15	12	3	(1	2)	189	79	41	68	45	1	42	0	6	2	32	5	.86	16	.301	.360	.403
2007	2 Tms	AL	136	490	145	25	6	7	(6	1)	203	86	38	77	56	1	51	2	6	5	23	7	.77	6	.296	.367	.414
02	CWS	AL	93	352	91	20	6	8	(3	5)	147	68	42	57	49	0	51	0	4	1	22	8	.73	0	.259	.348	.418
02	SF	NL	46	180	48	10	3	3	(0	3)	72	30	9	26	23	0	22	1	1	0	7	3	.70	1	.267	.353	.406
03	Pit	NL	84	339	94	19	4	9	(4	5)	148	58	26	42	28	1	29	2	2	3	18	5	.78	2	.277	.333	.437
03	ChC	NL	56	208	68	13	4	3	(1	2)	98	39	20	37	18	2	22	2	5	3	12	4	.75	4	.327	.381	.471
07	Tex	AL	84	317	96	16	3	7	(6	1)	139	62	23	54	39	1	28	2	2	3	21	4	.84	5	.303	.380	.438
07	Cle	AL	52	173	49	9	3	0	(0	0)	64	24	15	23	17	0	23	0	4	2	2	3	.40	1	.283	.344	.370
17 ML YEARS			2103	8120	2428	383	116	130	(73	57)	3433	1528	781	1344	945	43	1016	32	72	65	622	160	.80	111	.299	.372	.423

Boone Logan

Pitches: L **Bats:** R **Pos:** RP-68 **Ht:** 6'5" **Wt:** 200 **Born:** 8/13/1984 **Age:** 23

Year	Team	Lg	G	GS	CG	GF	IP	BFP	H	R	ER	HR	SH	SF	HB	TBB	IBB	SO	WP	Bk	W	L	Pct	ShO	Sv-Op	Hld	ERC	ERA
2003	Gr Falls	R+	16	14	0	0	67.0	321	76	60	49	4	3	4	11	31	0	48	8	1	3	3	.500	0	0--	-	5.28	6.58
2004	Gr Falls	R+	18	9	0	2	64.1	297	74	48	40	7	2	2	4	31	0	48	8	2	3	7	.300	0	1--	-	5.57	5.60
2005	Gr Falls	R+	21	0	0	5	35.1	141	34	15	13	1	0	2	3	4	0	29	4	0	1	1	.500	0	2--	-	2.72	3.31
2005	WinSa	A+	4	0	0	1	5.1	27	7	3	3	2	0	1	0	4	0	5	0	0	0	0	-	0	0--	-	9.71	5.06
2006	Charltt	AAA	38	0	0	24	42.2	181	35	18	16	1	1	1	9	12	3	57	3	0	3	1	.750	0	11--	-	2.81	3.38
2007	Charltt	AAA	4	0	0	2	8.1	37	8	2	2	1	1	0	0	4	2	11	0	0	0	1	.000	0	1--	-	3.82	2.16
2006	CWS	AL	21	0	0	4	17.1	93	21	18	16	2	1	1	3	15	2	15	1	0	0	0	-	0	1-2	2	7.56	8.31
2007	CWS	AL	68	0	0	13	50.2	226	59	30	28	7	2	6	0	20	3	35	2	0	2	1	.667	0	0-2	11	5.18	4.97
2 ML YEARS			89	0	0	17	68.0	319	80	48	44	9	3	7	3	35	5	50	3	0	2	1	.667	0	1-4	13	5.80	5.82

Nook Logan

Bats: R **Throws:** R **Pos:** CF-111; PH-10; PR-7 **Ht:** 6'2" **Wt:** 180 **Born:** 11/28/1979 **Age:** 28

Year	Team	Lg	G	AB	H	2B	3B	HR	(Hm	Rd)	TB	R	RBI	RC	TBB	IBB	SO	HBP	SH	SF	SB	CS	SB%	GDP	Avg	OBP	Slg
2004	Det	AL	47	133	37	5	2	0	(0	0)	46	12	10	15	13	0	24	0	5	1	8	2	.80	1	.278	.340	.346
2005	Det	AL	129	322	83	12	5	1	(0	1)	108	40	17	33	21	3	52	1	12	0	23	6	.79	5	.258	.305	.335
2006	Was	NL	27	90	27	3	1	1	(0	1)	35	13	8	10	6	1	20	0	1	2	2	1	.67	0	.300	.337	.389
2007	Was	NL	118	325	86	18	4	0	(0	0)	112	39	21	33	19	1	86	0	5	1	23	5	.82	9	.265	.304	.345
4 ML YEARS			321	870	233	38	12	2	(0	2)	301	111	56	91	59	5	182	1	23	4	56	14	.80	15	.268	.314	.346

Kyle Lohse

Pitches: R **Bats:** R **Pos:** SP-32; RP-2 **Ht:** 6'2" **Wt:** 209 **Born:** 10/4/1978 **Age:** 29

Year	Team	Lg	G	GS	CG	GF	IP	BFP	H	R	ER	HR	SH	SF	HB	TBB	IBB	SO	WP	Bk	W	L	Pct	ShO	Sv-Op	Hld	ERC	ERA
2001	Min	AL	19	16	0	2	90.1	402	102	60	57	16	1	5	8	29	0	64	5	0	4	7	.364	0	0-0	0	5.43	5.68
2002	Min	AL	32	31	1	0	180.2	783	181	92	85	26	3	3	9	70	2	124	8	0	13	8	.619	1	0-1	0	4.55	4.23
2003	Min	AL	33	33	2	0	201.0	850	211	107	103	28	8	5	5	45	1	130	10	1	14	11	.560	1	0-0	0	4.00	4.61
2004	Min	AL	35	34	1	1	194.0	883	240	128	115	28	5	7	7	76	5	111	6	0	9	13	.409	0	0-0	0	5.89	5.34
2005	Min	AL	31	30	0	1	178.2	769	211	85	83	22	3	7	9	44	5	86	4	1	9	13	.409	0	0-0	0	4.91	4.18
2006	2 Tms		34	19	0	6	126.2	567	150	83	82	15	8	5	6	44	4	97	3	1	5	10	.333	0	0-0	0	5.20	5.83
2007	2 Tms	NL	34	32	2	0	192.2	829	207	100	99	22	14	4	12	57	3	122	3	0	9	12	.429	1	0-0	0	4.45	4.62
06	Min	AL	22	8	0	5	63.2	295	80	50	50	8	1	3	6	25	2	46	1	1	2	5	.286	0	0-0	0	6.10	7.07
06	Cin	NL	12	11	0	1	63.0	272	70	33	32	7	7	2	0	19	2	51	2	0	3	5	.375	0	0-0	0	4.34	4.57
07	Cin	NL	21	21	2	0	131.2	561	143	67	67	16	8	4	6	33	1	80	3	0	6	12	.333	1	0-0	0	4.32	4.58
07	Phi	NL	13	11	0	0	61.0	268	64	33	32	6	6	0	6	24	2	42	0	0	3	0	1.000	0	0-0	0	4.71	4.72
7 ML YEARS			218	195	6	10	1164.0	5083	1302	664	624	157	42	36	56	365	20	734	39	3	63	74	.460	4	0-1	0	4.85	4.82

James Loney

Bats: L **Throws:** L **Pos:** 1B-93; PH-6; RF-1   **Ht:** 6'3" **Wt:** 220 **Born:** 5/7/1984 **Age:** 24

								BATTING												BASERUNNING				AVERAGES		
Year	Team	Lg	G	AB	H	2B	3B	HR	(Hm | Rd)	TB	R	RBI	RC	TBB	IBB	SO	HBP	SH	SF	SB	CS	SB%	GDP	Avg	OBP	Slg
2002	Gr Falls	R+	47	170	63	22	3	5	(- | -)	106	33	30	45	25	1	18	2	0	0	5	4	.56	4	.371	.457	.624
2002	VeroB	A+	17	67	20	6	0	0	(- | -)	26	6	5	9	6	0	10	0	1	0	0	0	-	2	.299	.356	.388
2003	VeroB	A+	125	468	129	31	3	7	(- | -)	187	64	46	66	43	5	80	1	3	1	9	4	.69	13	.276	.337	.400
2004	Jaxnvl	AA	104	395	94	19	2	4	(- | -)	129	39	35	43	42	6	75	3	0	2	5	5	.50	7	.238	.314	.327
2005	Jaxnvl	AA	138	504	143	31	2	11	(- | -)	211	74	65	78	59	8	87	2	1	6	1	4	.20	13	.284	.357	.419
2006	LsVgs	AAA	98	366	139	33	2	8	(- | -)	200	64	67	82	32	7	34	2	0	6	9	5	.64	11	.380	.426	.546
2007	LsVgs	AAA	58	233	65	19	1	1	(- | -)	89	28	32	32	25	3	48	0	0	3	2	1	.67	8	.279	.345	.382
2006	LAD	NL	48	102	29	6	5	4	(1 | 3)	57	20	18	17	8	1	10	1	0	0	1	0	1.00	8	.284	.342	.559
2007	LAD	NL	96	344	114	18	4	15	(5 | 10)	185	41	67	71	28	5	48	1	0	2	0	1	.00	6	.331	.381	.538
	2 ML YEARS		144	446	143	24	9	19	(6 | 13)	242	61	85	88	36	6	58	2	0	2	1	1	.50	14	.321	.372	.543

Braden Looper

Pitches: R **Bats:** R **Pos:** SP-30; RP-1   **Ht:** 6'3" **Wt:** 235 **Born:** 10/28/1974 **Age:** 33

			HOW MUCH HE PITCHED					WHAT HE GAVE UP										THE RESULTS						
Year	Team	Lg	G	GS	CG	GF	IP	BFP	H	R	ER	HR	SH	SF	HB	TBB	IBB	SO	WP	Bk	W	L	Pct	ShO	Sv-Op	Hld	ERC	ERA
1998	StL	NL	4	0	0	3	3.1	16	5	4	2	1	0	1	0	1	0	4	1	0	0	1	.000	0	0-2	0	8.14	5.40
1999	Fla	NL	72	0	0	22	83.0	370	96	43	35	7	5	5	1	31	6	50	2	2	3	3	.500	0	0-4	8	4.65	3.80
2000	Fla	NL	73	0	0	23	67.1	311	71	41	33	3	3	2	5	36	6	29	5	0	5	1	.833	0	2-5	18	4.55	4.41
2001	Fla	NL	71	0	0	21	71.0	295	63	28	28	8	0	3	2	30	3	52	0	0	3	3	.500	0	3-6	16	3.77	3.55
2002	Fla	NL	78	0	0	40	86.0	349	73	31	30	8	3	0	1	28	3	55	1	0	2	5	.286	0	13-16	16	2.98	3.14
2003	Fla	NL	74	0	0	64	80.2	347	82	34	33	4	3	3	1	29	1	56	2	0	6	4	.600	0	28-34	3	3.67	3.68
2004	NYM	NL	71	0	0	60	83.1	346	86	28	25	5	2	2	3	16	3	60	1	0	2	5	.286	0	29-34	0	3.28	2.70
2005	NYM	NL	60	0	0	54	59.1	271	65	31	26	7	4	0	5	22	3	27	1	0	4	7	.364	0	28-36	0	4.75	3.94
2006	StL	NL	69	0	0	28	73.1	308	76	30	29	3	7	5	2	20	5	41	0	0	9	3	.750	0	0-2	15	3.41	3.56
2007	StL	NL	31	30	0	0	175.0	746	183	100	96	22	4	6	4	51	2	87	0	3	12	12	.500	0	0-0	0	4.16	4.94
	10 ML YEARS		603	30	0	315	782.1	3359	800	370	337	68	31	27	24	264	32	461	13	5	46	44	.511	0	103-139	73	3.92	3.88

Aquilino Lopez

Pitches: R **Bats:** R **Pos:** RP-10   **Ht:** 6'3" **Wt:** 187 **Born:** 4/21/1975 **Age:** 33

			HOW MUCH HE PITCHED					WHAT HE GAVE UP										THE RESULTS						
Year	Team	Lg	G	GS	CG	GF	IP	BFP	H	R	ER	HR	SH	SF	HB	TBB	IBB	SO	WP	Bk	W	L	Pct	ShO	Sv-Op	Hld	ERC	ERA
2007	Toledo*	AAA	48	0	0	45	53.2	216	46	18	14	5	2	0	0	11	3	58	0	0	3	5	.375	0	26- -	-	2.45	2.35
2003	Tor	AL	72	0	0	34	73.2	316	58	31	28	5	2	2	5	34	5	64	2	1	1	3	.250	0	14-16	16	3.04	3.42
2004	Tor	AL	18	0	0	6	21.0	95	21	15	14	5	0	1	2	13	3	13	0	0	1	1	.500	0	0-0	3	6.32	6.00
2005	2 Tms	NL	11	0	0	5	16.2	72	16	5	4	2	1	0	0	7	1	22	1	0	0	1	.000	0	0-0	0	3.95	2.16
2007	Det	AL	10	0	0	6	17.1	76	18	10	10	2	0	2	2	6	0	7	0	0	0	0	-	0	1-1	1	4.68	5.19
05	Col	NL	1	0	0	0	4.0	15	3	1	1	0	0	0	0	0	0	6	0	0	0	0	-	0	0-0	0	1.13	2.25
05	Phi	NL	10	0	0	5	12.2	57	13	4	3	2	1	0	0	7	1	16	1	0	0	1	.000	0	0-0	0	5.12	2.13
	4 ML YEARS		111	0	0	51	128.2	559	113	61	56	14	3	5	9	60	9	106	3	1	2	5	.286	0	15-17	20	3.86	3.92

Felipe Lopez

Bats: B **Throws:** R **Pos:** SS-111; 2B-43; PH-3   **Ht:** 6'1" **Wt:** 185 **Born:** 5/12/1980 **Age:** 28

								BATTING												BASERUNNING				AVERAGES		
Year	Team	Lg	G	AB	H	2B	3B	HR	(Hm	Rd)	TB	R	RBI	RC	TBB	IBB	SO	HBP	SH	SF	SB	CS	SB%	GDP	Avg	OBP	Slg
2001	Tor	AL	49	177	46	5	4	5	(3	2)	74	21	23	22	12	1	39	0	1	2	4	3	.57	2	.260	.304	.418
2002	Tor	AL	85	282	64	15	3	8	(5	3)	109	35	34	32	23	1	90	1	2	1	5	4	.56	4	.227	.287	.387
2003	Cin	NL	59	197	42	7	2	2	(0	2)	59	28	13	21	28	1	59	1	2	1	8	5	.62	2	.213	.313	.299
2004	Cin	NL	79	264	64	18	2	7	(3	4)	107	35	31	34	25	0	81	3	2	1	1	1	.50	1	.242	.314	.405
2005	Cin	NL	148	580	169	34	5	23	(16	7)	282	97	85	95	57	2	111	1	3	7	15	7	.68	8	.291	.352	.486
2006	2 Tms	NL	156	617	169	27	3	11	(5	6)	235	98	52	84	81	1	126	2	11	3	44	12	.79	9	.274	.358	.381
2007	Was	NL	154	603	148	25	6	9	(2	7)	212	70	50	63	53	1	109	4	5	6	24	9	.73	11	.245	.308	.352
06	Cin	NL	85	343	92	14	1	9	(5	4)	135	55	30	48	47	1	66	0	3	1	23	6	.79	6	.268	.355	.394
06	Was	NL	71	274	77	13	2	2	(0	2)	100	43	22	36	34	0	60	2	8	2	21	6	.78	3	.281	.362	.365
	7 ML YEARS		730	2720	702	131	25	65	(34	31)	1078	384	288	351	279	7	615	12	26	21	101	41	.71	37	.258	.328	.396

Javier Lopez

Pitches: L **Bats:** L **Pos:** RP-61   **Ht:** 6'4" **Wt:** 185 **Born:** 7/11/1977 **Age:** 30

			HOW MUCH HE PITCHED					WHAT HE GAVE UP										THE RESULTS						
Year	Team	Lg	G	GS	CG	GF	IP	BFP	H	R	ER	HR	SH	SF	HB	TBB	IBB	SO	WP	Bk	W	L	Pct	ShO	Sv-Op	Hld	ERC	ERA
2007	Pwtckt*	AAA	17	0	0	4	16.2	76	19	7	7	0	1	2	2	8	1	15	1	1	2	1	.667	0	0- -	-	4.85	3.78
2003	Col	NL	75	0	0	7	58.1	242	58	25	24	5	1	0	4	12	2	40	1	3	4	1	.800	0	1-2	15	3.44	3.70
2004	Col	NL	64	0	0	10	40.2	187	45	34	34	1	1	0	3	26	4	20	3	0	1	2	.333	0	0-1	12	5.28	7.52
2005	2 Tms	NL	32	0	0	6	16.1	87	26	20	20	2	1	0	1	11	3	12	0	0	1	1	.500	0	2-4	6	8.82	11.02
2006	Bos	AL	27	0	0	8	16.2	69	13	10	5	1	0	1	2	11	1	11	0	0	1	0	1.000	0	1-1	6	3.96	2.70
2007	Bos	AL	61	0	0	11	40.2	174	36	16	14	2	1	1	4	18	2	26	1	0	2	1	.667	0	0-2	13	3.59	3.10
05	Col	NL	3	0	0	1	2.0	13	7	5	5	0	0	0	0	4	1	1	0	0	0	0	-	0	0-1	0	18.39	22.50
05	Ari	NL	29	0	0	5	14.1	74	19	15	15	2	1	0	1	11	3	11	0	0	1	1	.500	0	2-3	6	7.63	9.42
	5 ML YEARS		259	0	0	46	172.2	759	178	105	97	11	4	2	14	77	12	109	5	3	9	5	.643	0	4-10	52	4.43	5.06

Jose Lopez

Bats: R **Throws:** R **Pos:** 2B-146; 3B-3; PR-3; PH-1   **Ht:** 6'0" **Wt:** 200 **Born:** 11/24/1983 **Age:** 24

Year	Team	Lg	G	AB	H	2B	3B	HR	(Hm	Rd)	TB	R	RBI	RC	TBB	IBB	SO	HBP	SH	SF	SB	CS	SB%	GDP	Avg	OBP	Slg
2004	Sea	AL	57	207	48	13	0	5	(4	1)	76	28	22	20	8	0	31	1	1	1	0	1	.00	1	.232	.263	.367
2005	Sea	AL	54	190	47	19	0	2	(1	1)	72	18	25	24	6	0	25	4	1	2	4	2	.67	5	.247	.282	.379
2006	Sea	AL	151	603	170	28	8	10	(4	6)	244	78	79	84	26	1	80	9	12	5	5	2	.71	17	.282	.319	.405
2007	Sea	AL	149	524	132	17	2	11	(5	6)	186	58	62	52	20	0	64	5	9	3	2	3	.40	16	.252	.284	.355
	4 ML YEARS		411	1524	397	77	10	28	(14	14)	578	182	188	180	60	1	200	19	23	11	11	8	.58	39	.260	.295	.379

Pedro Lopez

Bats: R **Throws:** R **Pos:** SS-12; 2B-1; PR-1   **Ht:** 6'1" **Wt:** 160 **Born:** 4/28/1984 **Age:** 24

Year	Team	Lg	G	AB	H	2B	3B	HR	(Hm	Rd)	TB	R	RBI	RC	TBB	IBB	SO	HBP	SH	SF	SB	CS	SB%	GDP	Avg	OBP	Slg
2001	WhSox	R	50	199	62	11	3	1	(-	-)	82	26	19	30	16	0	24	0	3	2	12	6	.67	4	.312	.359	.412
2002	Bristol	R+	63	260	83	11	0	0	(-	-)	94	42	35	38	20	0	27	1	17	0	22	8	.73	3	.319	.370	.362
2003	Knapol	A-	109	390	103	23	0	0	(-	-)	126	40	33	41	26	1	43	3	16	2	24	14	.63	8	.264	.314	.323
2003	WinSa	A+	4	13	3	0	0	0	(-	-)	3	1	0	1	0	0	0	0	0	0	0	0	-	0	.231	.286	.231
2004	WinSa	A+	111	430	124	13	0	4	(-	-)	149	62	35	51	23	0	35	4	16	3	12	9	.57	3	.288	.328	.347
2004	Brham	AA	7	23	5	0	1	0	(-	-)	7	3	0	3	5	0	2	1	2	0	2	0	1.00	0	.217	.379	.304
2005	Brham	AA	68	239	57	7	1	3	(-	-)	75	26	24	22	13	0	29	4	13	2	0	2	.00	9	.238	.287	.314
2005	Charltt	AAA	55	188	38	6	0	3	(-	-)	53	14	17	12	7	0	24	2	9	2	1	1	.50	4	.202	.236	.282
2006	Brham	AA	65	258	83	15	2	5	(-	-)	117	30	34	41	16	1	32	1	5	4	3	6	.33	7	.322	.358	.453
2006	Charltt	AAA	59	208	57	12	0	5	(-	-)	84	32	24	28	11	1	28	3	6	0	4	0	1.00	5	.274	.320	.404
2007	Charltt	AAA	41	161	39	7	0	2	(-	-)	52	20	11	16	15	0	26	0	5	0	1	3	.25	5	.242	.307	.323
2007	Lsvlle	AAA	34	124	42	6	1	1	(-	-)	53	20	17	22	13	1	12	0	4	2	3	0	1.00	2	.339	.396	.427
2005	CWS	AL	2	7	2	0	0	0	(0	0)	2	1	2	2	0	0	1	0	1	0	0	0	-	0	.286	.286	.286
2007	Cin	NL	14	45	8	2	0	0	(0	0)	10	1	0	0	1	0	10	1	0	0	0	0	-	0	.178	.213	.222
	2 ML YEARS		16	52	10	2	0	0	(0	0)	12	2	2	2	1	0	11	1	1	0	0	0	-	0	.192	.222	.231

Rodrigo Lopez

Pitches: R **Bats:** R **Pos:** SP-14   **Ht:** 6'1" **Wt:** 185 **Born:** 12/14/1975 **Age:** 32

Year	Team	Lg	G	GS	CG	GF	IP	BFP	H	R	ER	HR	SH	SF	HB	TBB	IBB	SO	WP	Bk	W	L	Pct	ShO	Sv-Op	Hld	ERC	ERA
2007	ColSpr*	AAA	2	2	0	0	11.1	40	4	3	3	0	0	0	0	3	0	4	0	0	1	0	1.000	0	0- -	-	0.64	2.38
2000	SD	NL	6	6	0	0	24.2	120	40	24	24	5	0	1	0	13	0	17	0	0	0	3	.000	0	0-0	0	9.78	8.76
2002	Bal	AL	33	28	1	0	196.2	809	172	83	78	23	2	4	5	62	4	136	2	1	15	9	.625	0	0-0	0	3.27	3.57
2003	Bal	AL	26	26	3	0	147.0	663	188	101	95	24	3	7	10	43	6	103	2	1	7	10	.412	1	0-0	0	6.00	5.82
2004	Bal	AL	37	23	1	3	170.2	714	164	71	68	21	5	2	2	54	2	121	4	1	14	9	.609	1	0-1	4	3.74	3.59
2005	Bal	AL	35	35	0	0	209.1	918	232	126	114	28	3	5	7	63	1	118	5	1	15	12	.556	0	0-0	0	4.62	4.90
2006	Bal	AL	36	29	0	2	189.0	847	234	129	124	32	5	5	4	59	2	136	6	1	9	18	.333	0	0-0	0	5.68	5.90
2007	Col	NL	14	14	0	0	79.1	333	83	43	39	11	3	5	0	21	6	43	0	0	5	4	.556	0	0-0	0	3.97	4.42
	7 ML YEARS		187	161	5	5	1016.2	4404	1113	577	542	144	21	29	28	315	21	674	19	5	65	65	.500	2	0-1	4	4.64	4.80

Mark Loretta

Bats: R **Throws:** R **Pos:** SS-72; 2B-49; 1B-24; 3B-23; PH-16; DH-1   **Ht:** 6'0" **Wt:** 185 **Born:** 8/14/1971 **Age:** 36

Year	Team	Lg	G	AB	H	2B	3B	HR	(Hm	Rd)	TB	R	RBI	RC	TBB	IBB	SO	HBP	SH	SF	SB	CS	SB%	GDP	Avg	OBP	Slg
1995	Mil	AL	19	50	13	3	0	1	(0	1)	19	13	3	6	4	0	7	1	1	0	1	1	.50	1	.260	.327	.380
1996	Mil	AL	73	154	43	3	0	1	(0	1)	49	20	13	16	14	0	15	0	2	0	2	1	.67	7	.279	.339	.318
1997	Mil	AL	132	418	120	17	5	5	(2	3)	162	56	47	56	47	2	60	2	5	10	5	5	.50	15	.287	.354	.388
1998	Mil	NL	140	434	137	29	0	6	(3	3)	184	55	54	68	42	1	47	7	4	4	9	6	.60	14	.316	.382	.424
1999	Mil	NL	153	587	170	34	5	5	(3	2)	229	93	67	82	52	1	59	10	9	6	4	1	.80	14	.290	.354	.390
2000	Mil	NL	91	352	99	21	1	7	(3	4)	143	49	40	48	37	2	38	1	8	1	0	3	.00	9	.281	.350	.406
2001	Mil	NL	102	384	111	14	2	2	(0	2)	135	40	29	48	28	0	46	7	7	3	1	2	.33	6	.289	.346	.352
2002	2 Tms	NL	107	283	86	18	0	4	(2	2)	116	33	27	50	32	1	37	5	6	3	1	1	.50	7	.304	.381	.410
2003	SD	NL	154	589	185	28	4	13	(10	3)	260	74	72	93	54	2	62	3	3	4	5	4	.56	17	.314	.372	.441
2004	SD	NL	154	620	208	47	2	16	(11	5)	307	108	76	112	58	3	45	9	4	16	5	3	.63	10	.335	.391	.495
2005	SD	NL	105	404	113	16	1	3	(1	2)	140	54	38	53	45	4	34	8	2	4	8	4	.67	11	.280	.360	.347
2006	Bos	AL	155	635	181	33	0	5	(4	1)	229	75	59	80	49	1	63	12	2	5	4	1	.80	16	.285	.345	.361
2007	Hou	NL	133	460	132	23	2	4	(4	0)	171	52	41	60	44	0	41	3	3	1	1	2	.33	15	.287	.352	.372
02	Mil	NL	86	217	58	14	0	2	(1	1)	78	23	19	33	23	1	32	5	6	1	0	0	-	6	.267	.350	.359
02	Hou	NL	21	66	28	4	0	2	(1	1)	38	10	8	17	9	0	5	0	0	2	1	1	.50	1	.424	.481	.576
	13 ML YEARS		1518	5370	1598	286	22	72	(42	30)	2144	722	566	772	506	17	554	68	56	57	46	34	.58	142	.298	.362	.399

Derek Lowe

Pitches: R **Bats:** R **Pos:** SP-32; RP-1   **Ht:** 6'6" **Wt:** 230 **Born:** 6/1/1973 **Age:** 35

Year	Team	Lg	G	GS	CG	GF	IP	BFP	H	R	ER	HR	SH	SF	HB	TBB	IBB	SO	WP	Bk	W	L	Pct	ShO	Sv-Op	Hld	ERC	ERA
1997	2 Tms	AL	20	9	0	1	69.0	298	74	49	47	11	4	2	4	23	3	52	2	0	2	6	.250	0	0-2	1	4.88	6.13
1998	Bos	AL	63	10	0	8	123.0	527	126	65	55	5	4	5	4	42	5	77	8	0	3	9	.250	0	4-9	12	3.64	4.02
1999	Bos	AL	74	0	0	32	109.1	436	84	35	32	7	1	2	4	25	1	80	1	0	6	3	.667	0	15-20	22	2.14	2.63
2000	Bos	AL	74	0	0	64	91.1	379	90	27	26	6	4	1	2	22	5	79	2	1	4	4	.500	0	42-47	0	3.17	2.56
2001	Bos	AL	67	3	0	50	91.2	404	103	39	36	7	5	1	5	29	9	82	4	0	5	10	.333	0	24-30	4	4.31	3.53
2002	Bos	AL	32	32	1	0	219.2	854	166	65	63	12	5	2	12	48	0	127	5	0	21	8	.724	1	0-0	0	2.13	2.58
2003	Bos	AL	33	33	1	0	203.1	886	216	113	101	17	3	5	11	72	4	110	3	0	17	7	.708	0	0-0	0	4.32	4.47
2004	Bos	AL	33	33	0	0	182.2	839	224	138	110	15	8	4	8	71	2	105	3	0	14	12	.538	0	0-0	0	5.31	5.42
2005	LAD	NL	35	35	2	0	222.0	934	223	113	89	28	12	5	5	55	1	146	3	2	12	15	.444	2	0-0	0	3.75	3.61

			HOW MUCH HE PITCHED						WHAT HE GAVE UP										THE RESULTS						
Year	Team	Lg	G	GS	CG	GF	IP	BFP	H	R	ER	HR	SH	SF	HB	TBB	IBB	SO	WP	Bk	W	L	Pct	ShO	Sv-Op	Hld	ERC	ERA
2006	LAD	NL	35	34	1	1	218.0	913	221	97	88	14	7	2	5	55	2	123	3	2	16	8	.667	0	0-0	0	3.42	3.63
2007	LAD	NL	33	32	3	0	199.1	831	194	100	86	20	6	2	1	59	2	147	3	1	12	14	.462	0	0-0	1	3.55	3.88
97	Sea	AL	12	9	0	1	53.0	234	59	43	41	11	2	1	2	20	2	39	2	0	2	4	.333	0	0-0	0	5.55	6.96
97	Bos	AL	8	0	0	0	16.0	64	15	6	6	0	2	1	2	3	1	13	0	0	0	2	.000	0	0-2	1	2.78	3.38
11 ML YEARS			499	221	8	156	1729.1	7301	1721	841	733	142	59	31	61	501	34	1128	37	6	112	96	.538	3	85-108	40	3.61	3.81

Mark Lowe

Pitches: R **Bats:** R **Pos:** RP-4   **Ht:** 6'3" **Wt:** 190 **Born:** 6/7/1983 **Age:** 25

			HOW MUCH HE PITCHED						WHAT HE GAVE UP										THE RESULTS						
Year	Team	Lg	G	GS	CG	GF	IP	BFP	H	R	ER	HR	SH	SF	HB	TBB	IBB	SO	WP	Bk	W	L	Pct	ShO	Sv-Op	Hld	ERC	ERA
2004	Everett	A-	18	3	0	12	38.1	173	42	22	21	4	2	1	4	14	0	38	2	1	1	2	.333	0	7- --		4.88	4.93
2005	Wisc	A	22	22	0	0	103.2	468	107	72	63	12	1	2	11	49	0	72	5	0	6	6	.500	0	0- --		5.09	5.47
2006	InldEm	A+	13	2	0	5	29.1	118	14	10	6	0	0	0	1	11	0	46	1	1	1	0	1.000	0	2- --		1.13	1.84
2006	SnAnt	AA	11	0	0	9	16.2	63	14	4	4	1	0	0	0	3	0	14	0	0	0	2	.000	0	4- --		2.32	2.16
2007	Everett	A-	1	1	0	0	1.0	3	0	0	0	0	0	0	0	0	0	0	0	0	0	0	-	0	0- --		0.00	0.00
2007	WTenn	AA	3	1	0	0	2.2	11	2	1	1	0	0	0	0	2	0	1	0	0	0	0	-	0	0- --		3.56	3.38
2007	Tacom	AAA	7	3	0	0	6.1	34	12	4	4	1	0	0	0	3	0	5	0	0	0	0	-	0	0- --		10.43	5.68
2006	Sea	AL	15	0	0	3	18.2	75	12	4	4	1	1	0	2	9	1	20	1	0	1	0	1.000	0	0-0	7	2.61	1.93
2007	Sea	AL	4	0	0	1	2.2	13	2	2	2	1	0	0	0	3	0	3	0	0	0	0	-	0	0-0	1	7.69	6.75
2 ML YEARS			19	0	0	4	21.1	88	14	6	6	2	1	0	2	12	1	23	1	0	1	0	1.000	0	0-0	8	3.17	2.53

Mike Lowell

Bats: R **Throws:** R **Pos:** 3B-154; PH-3   **Ht:** 6'3" **Wt:** 210 **Born:** 2/24/1974 **Age:** 34

			BATTING																BASERUNNING				AVERAGES		
Year	Team	Lg	G	AB	H	2B	3B	HR	(Hm | Rd)	TB	R	RBI	RC	TBB	IBB	SO	HBP	SH	SF	SB	CS	SB%	GDP	Avg	OBP	Slg
1998	NYY	AL	8	15	4	0	0	0	(0)	4)	4	1	0	1	0	0	1	0	0	0	0	0	-	0	.267	.267	.267
1999	Fla	NL	97	308	78	15	0	12	(7 | 5)	129	32	47	40	26	1	69	5	0	5	0	0	-	8	.253	.317	.419
2000	Fla	NL	140	508	137	38	0	22	(11 | 11)	241	73	91	86	54	4	75	9	0	11	4	0	1.00	4	.270	.344	.474
2001	Fla	NL	146	551	156	37	0	18	(12 | 6)	247	65	100	84	43	3	79	10	0	10	1	2	.33	9	.283	.340	.448
2002	Fla	NL	160	597	165	44	0	24	(13 | 11)	281	88	92	84	65	5	92	4	0	11	4	3	.57	16	.276	.346	.471
2003	Fla	NL	130	492	136	27	1	32	(14 | 18)	261	76	105	88	56	6	78	3	0	6	3	1	.75	14	.276	.350	.530
2004	Fla	NL	158	598	175	44	1	27	(14 | 13)	302	87	85	96	64	8	77	6	0	3	5	1	.83	17	.293	.365	.505
2005	Fla	NL	150	500	118	36	1	8	(5 | 3)	180	56	58	46	46	1	58	2	1	9	4	0	1.00	14	.236	.298	.360
2006	Bos	AL	153	573	163	47	1	20	(9 | 11)	272	79	80	77	47	5	61	4	0	7	2	2	.50	22	.284	.339	.475
2007	Bos	AL	154	589	191	37	2	21	(14 | 7)	295	79	120	106	53	4	71	3	0	8	3	2	.60	19	.324	.378	.501
10 ML YEARS			1296	4731	1323	325	6	184	(99 | 85)	2212	636	778	708	454	37	661	46	1	70	26	11	.70	123	.280	.344	.468

Noah Lowry

Pitches: L **Bats:** R **Pos:** SP-26   **Ht:** 6'2" **Wt:** 205 **Born:** 10/10/1980 **Age:** 27

			HOW MUCH HE PITCHED						WHAT HE GAVE UP										THE RESULTS						
Year	Team	Lg	G	GS	CG	GF	IP	BFP	H	R	ER	HR	SH	SF	HB	TBB	IBB	SO	WP	Bk	W	L	Pct	ShO	Sv-Op	Hld	ERC	ERA
2003	SF	NL	4	0	0	3	6.1	24	1	0	0	0	0	0	1	2	0	5	0	0	0	0	-	0	0-0	0	0.50	0.00
2004	SF	NL	16	14	2	0	92.0	383	91	41	39	10	2	1	0	28	1	72	2	0	6	0	1.000	1	0-0	0	3.73	3.82
2005	SF	NL	33	33	0	0	204.2	875	193	92	86	21	13	3	7	76	1	172	2	0	13	13	.500	1	0-0	0	3.78	3.78
2006	SF	NL	27	27	1	0	159.1	689	166	89	84	21	11	7	6	56	2	84	2	1	7	10	.412	1	0-0	0	4.49	4.74
2007	SF	NL	26	26	1	0	156.0	694	155	70	68	12	14	4	5	87	2	87	5	0	14	8	.636	0	0-0	0	4.63	3.92
5 ML YEARS			106	100	4	3	618.1	2665	606	298	277	64	40	15	19	249	6	420	11	1	40	31	.563	2	0-0	0	4.12	4.03

Donny Lucy

Bats: R **Throws:** R **Pos:** C-5; PH-4; DH-2   **Ht:** 6'3" **Wt:** 210 **Born:** 8/8/1982 **Age:** 25

			BATTING																BASERUNNING				AVERAGES		
Year	Team	Lg	G	AB	H	2B	3B	HR	(Hm | Rd)	TB	R	RBI	RC	TBB	IBB	SO	HBP	SH	SF	SB	CS	SB%	GDP	Avg	OBP	Slg
2004	Gr Falls	R+	50	176	42	7	1	1	(- | -)	54	19	26	20	17	0	36	3	5	3	13	1	.93	4	.239	.312	.307
2005	Knapol	A-	54	178	47	5	0	1	(- | -)	55	25	22	22	21	0	41	5	4	3	6	3	.67	4	.264	.353	.309
2006	WinSa	A+	97	332	87	17	1	7	(- | -)	127	48	32	47	33	0	67	8	6	2	12	3	.80	8	.262	.341	.383
2006	Brham	AA	18	60	17	1	0	0	(- | -)	18	2	3	7	4	1	15	3	2	0	1	0	1.00	5	.283	.358	.300
2007	Brham	AA	87	290	78	17	0	6	(- | -)	113	42	27	43	30	0	59	3	2	1	14	1	.93	7	.269	.343	.390
2007	Charltt	AAA	19	75	15	3	0	0	(- | -)	18	5	3	3	3	0	25	0	0	0	0	0	-	3	.200	.231	.240
2007	CWS	AL	8	15	3	0	0	0	(0 | 0)	3	0	0	0	0	0	6	0	0	0	0	0	-	0	.200	.200	.200

Ryan Ludwick

Bats: R **Throws:** L **Pos:** LF-49; RF-41; PH-41; CF-6   **Ht:** 6'3" **Wt:** 220 **Born:** 7/13/1978 **Age:** 29

			BATTING																BASERUNNING				AVERAGES		
Year	Team	Lg	G	AB	H	2B	3B	HR	(Hm | Rd)	TB	R	RBI	RC	TBB	IBB	SO	HBP	SH	SF	SB	CS	SB%	GDP	Avg	OBP	Slg
2007	Memp*	AAA	29	106	36	8	0	8	(- | -)	68	27	36	25	10	1	20	0	0	5	1	1	.50	2	.340	.380	.642
2002	Tex	AL	23	81	19	6	0	1	(1 | 0)	28	10	9	6	7	0	24	0	0	0	2	1	.67	4	.235	.295	.346
2003	2 Tms	AL	47	162	40	8	1	7	(2 | 5)	71	17	26	28	12	1	48	0	1	0	2	0	1.00	1	.247	.299	.438
2004	Cle	AL	15	50	11	2	0	2	(0 | 2)	19	3	4	4	2	0	14	2	0	0	0	0	-	1	.220	.278	.380
2005	Cle	AL	19	41	9	0	0	4	(3 | 1)	21	8	5	3	7	0	13	0	0	0	0	1	.00	1	.220	.333	.512
2007	StL	NL	120	303	81	22	0	14	(7 | 7)	145	42	52	45	26	1	72	7	3	0	4	4	.50	1	.267	.339	.479
03	Tex	AL	8	26	4	1	0	0	(0 | 0)	5	3	0	1	4	0	9	0	0	0	0	0	-	0	.154	.267	.192
03	Cle	AL	39	136	36	7	1	7	(2 | 5)	66	14	26	27	8	1	39	0	1	0	2	0	1.00	1	.265	.306	.485
5 ML YEARS			224	637	160	38	1	28	(13 | 15)	284	80	96	86	54	2	171	9	4	0	8	6	.57	7	.251	.319	.446

Julio Lugo

Bats: R **Throws:** R **Pos:** SS-145; PR-6; DH-1; PH-1   **Ht:** 6'1" **Wt:** 175 **Born:** 11/16/1975 **Age:** 32

Year	Team	Lg	G	AB	H	2B	3B	HR	(Hm	Rd)	TB	R	RBI	RC	TBB	IBB	SO	HBP	SH	SF	SB	CS	SB%	GDP	Avg	OBP	Slg
2000	Hou	NL	116	420	119	22	5	10	(6	4)	181	78	40	62	37	0	93	4	3	1	22	9	.71	9	.283	.346	.431
2001	Hou	NL	140	513	135	20	3	10	(6	4)	191	93	37	63	46	0	116	5	15	7	12	11	.52	7	.263	.326	.372
2002	Hou	NL	88	322	84	15	1	8	(6	2)	125	45	35	43	28	3	74	2	4	2	9	3	.75	6	.261	.322	.388
2003	2 Tms		139	498	135	16	4	15	(5	10)	204	64	55	68	44	1	100	4	7	3	12	4	.75	7	.271	.333	.410
2004	TB	AL	157	581	160	41	4	7	(3	4)	230	83	75	86	54	0	106	5	7	8	21	5	.81	8	.275	.338	.396
2005	TB	AL	158	616	182	36	6	6	(0	6)	248	89	57	94	61	0	72	6	1	3	39	11	.78	5	.295	.362	.403
2006	2 Tms		122	435	121	22	2	12	(7	5)	183	69	37	61	39	0	76	4	5	3	24	9	.73	9	.278	.341	.421
2007	Bos	AL	147	570	135	36	2	8	(2	6)	199	71	73	65	48	0	82	0	8	4	33	6	.85	9	.237	.294	.349
03	Hou	NL	22	65	16	3	0	0	(0	0)	19	6	2	7	9	1	12	0	0	0	2	1	.67	2	.246	.338	.292
03	TB	AL	117	433	119	13	4	15	(5	10)	185	58	53	61	35	0	88	4	7	3	10	3	.77	5	.275	.333	.427
06	TB	AL	73	289	89	17	1	12	(7	5)	144	53	27	52	27	0	47	3	3	0	18	4	.82	7	.308	.373	.498
06	LAD	NL	49	146	32	5	1	0	(0	0)	39	16	10	9	12	0	29	1	2	3	6	5	.55	2	.219	.278	.267
8 ML YEARS			1067	3955	1071	208	27	76	(35	41)	1561	592	409	542	357	4	719	30	52	32	172	58	.75	60	.271	.333	.395

Ruddy Lugo

Pitches: R **Bats:** R **Pos:** RP-38   **Ht:** 6'0" **Wt:** 215 **Born:** 5/22/1980 **Age:** 28

Year	Team	Lg	G	GS	CG	GF	IP	BFP	H	R	ER	HR	SH	SF	HB	TBB	IBB	SO	WP	Bk	W	L	Pct	ShO	Sv-Op	Hld	ERC	ERA
1999	Ogden	R+	6	6	0	0	24.0	117	35	23	21	2	1	0	1	12	0	26	1	0	1	2	.333	0	0--	-	7.33	7.88
2000	Ogden	R+	16	16	1	0	91.2	397	82	48	35	7	3	6	12	52	1	88	7	0	5	5	.500	0	0--	-	4.64	3.44
2001	Beloit	A	10	0	0	8	15.0	60	10	1	1	0	1	0	1	6	0	20	0	0	1	0	1.000	0	5--	-	2.01	0.60
2001	Wilmg	A+	16	0	0	7	31.0	133	29	14	13	2	2	4	2	13	0	23	2	0	0	2	.000	0	2--	-	3.83	3.77
2002	VeroB	A+	22	9	1	6	87.0	347	68	28	23	5	1	3	3	26	0	77	7	0	8	2	.800	1	1--	-	2.46	2.38
2002	Jaxnvl	AA	11	2	0	2	33.1	144	34	15	15	3	4	0	3	13	5	23	4	0	3	1	.750	0	1--	-	4.26	4.05
2003	RdRck	AA	41	15	1	10	118.1	539	133	93	79	12	6	6	5	53	5	112	3	0	4	15	.211	0	1--	-	5.03	6.01
2004	Jupiter	A+	31	0	0	28	39.2	180	42	31	23	4	0	0	4	15	4	33	3	0	1	7	.125	0	11--	-	4.44	5.22
2004	Carlina	AA	8	1	0	2	14.2	67	16	10	8	3	0	1	1	9	0	6	0	0	0	1	.000	0	0--	-	6.77	4.91
2005	Visalia	A+	1	0	0	1	2.0	13	7	4	3	0	0	0	0	1	0	0	0	0	0	0	-	0	0--	-	22.64	13.50
2005	Mont	AA	26	0	0	13	40.1	172	25	12	5	1	0	0	1	23	0	48	8	0	1	1	.500	0	2--	-	2.22	1.12
2006	Visalia	A+	4	0	0	1	4.0	21	6	4	3	0	0	0	0	2	0	5	0	0	0	0	-	0	1--	-	6.14	6.75
2007	Drham	AAA	11	0	0	5	14.2	65	12	5	3	0	1	0	0	11	1	7	1	0	2	1	.667	0	0--	-	3.87	1.84
2007	Scrmto	AAA	17	0	0	15	20.0	70	5	1	1	0	1	0	0	7	0	22	1	0	3	0	1.000	0	10--	-	0.55	0.45
2006	TB	AL	64	0	0	24	85.0	363	75	39	36	4	1	7	5	37	0	48	3	0	2	4	.333	0	0-0	8	3.44	3.81
2007	2 Tms		38	0	0	14	48.1	228	48	29	29	3	3	2	2	37	6	34	2	0	6	0	1.000	0	0-2	1	5.08	5.40
07	TB	AL	11	0	0	4	10.2	61	17	11	11	2	1	0	0	13	2	8	1	0	2	0	1.000	0	0-2	0	11.90	9.28
07	Oak	AL	27	0	0	10	37.2	167	31	18	18	1	2	2	2	24	4	26	1	0	4	0	1.000	0	0-0	1	3.47	4.30
2 ML YEARS			102	0	0	38	133.1	591	123	68	65	7	4	9	7	74	6	82	5	0	8	4	.667	0	0-2	9	4.02	4.39

Hector Luna

Bats: R **Throws:** R **Pos:** 3B-15; PR-5; DH-3; PH-3; 1B-2; RF-1   **Ht:** 6'1" **Wt:** 190 **Born:** 2/1/1980 **Age:** 28

Year	Team	Lg	G	AB	H	2B	3B	HR	(Hm	Rd)	TB	R	RBI	RC	TBB	IBB	SO	HBP	SH	SF	SB	CS	SB%	GDP	Avg	OBP	Slg
2007	Buffalo*	AAA	83	323	81	18	0	6	(-	-)	117	39	35	35	21	0	48	2	0	4	4	4	.50	7	.251	.297	.362
2007	Syrcse*	AAA	18	67	23	7	1	2	(-	-)	38	15	8	16	9	0	14	3	0	0	0	0	-	0	.343	.443	.567
2004	StL	NL	83	173	43	7	2	3	(1	2)	63	25	22	20	13	0	37	2	1	3	6	3	.67	2	.249	.304	.364
2005	StL	NL	64	137	39	10	2	1	(0	1)	56	26	18	19	9	0	25	4	2	1	10	2	.83	4	.285	.344	.409
2006	2 Tms		113	350	100	21	2	6	(1	5)	143	41	38	46	27	1	60	1	0	1	5	4	.56	7	.286	.338	.409
2007	Tor	AL	22	42	7	0	0	1	(1	0)	10	5	4	1	2	0	10	1	0	1	2	0	1.00	0	.167	.217	.238
06	StL	NL	76	223	65	14	1	4	(1	3)	93	27	21	32	21	1	34	1	0	0	5	3	.63	3	.291	.355	.417
06	Cle	AL	37	127	35	7	1	2	(0	2)	50	14	17	14	6	0	26	0	0	1	0	1	.00	4	.276	.306	.394
4 ML YEARS			282	702	189	38	6	11	(3	8)	272	97	82	86	51	1	132	8	3	6	23	9	.72	13	.269	.323	.387

Brandon Lyon

Pitches: R **Bats:** R **Pos:** RP-73   **Ht:** 6'1" **Wt:** 195 **Born:** 8/10/1979 **Age:** 28

Year	Team	Lg	G	GS	CG	GF	IP	BFP	H	R	ER	HR	SH	SF	HB	TBB	IBB	SO	WP	Bk	W	L	Pct	ShO	Sv-Op	Hld	ERC	ERA
2001	Tor	AL	11	11	0	0	63.0	261	63	31	30	6	2	6	1	15	0	35	0	1	5	4	.556	0	0-0	0	3.50	4.29
2002	Tor	AL	15	10	0	0	62.0	279	78	47	45	14	3	2	2	19	2	30	2	0	1	4	.200	0	0-1	0	6.24	6.53
2003	Bos	AL	49	0	0	31	59.0	273	73	33	27	6	1	4	2	19	5	50	0	0	4	6	.400	0	9-12	2	4.96	4.12
2005	Ari	NL	32	0	0	22	29.1	144	44	25	21	6	2	1	2	10	2	17	1	1	0	2	.000	0	14-15	1	7.72	6.44
2006	Ari	NL	68	0	0	22	69.1	293	68	32	30	7	3	4	0	22	7	46	1	0	2	4	.333	0	0-7	23	3.49	3.89
2007	Ari	NL	73	0	0	20	74.0	307	70	25	22	2	3	2	1	22	2	40	3	1	6	4	.600	0	2-5	35	2.93	2.68
6 ML YEARS			248	21	0	95	356.2	1557	396	193	175	41	14	19	8	107	18	218	7	3	18	24	.429	0	25-40	61	4.38	4.42

John Mabry

Bats: L **Throws:** R **Pos:** PH-23; 3B-4; LF-1   **Ht:** 6'4" **Wt:** 210 **Born:** 10/17/1970 **Age:** 37

Year	Team	Lg	G	AB	H	2B	3B	HR	(Hm	Rd)	TB	R	RBI	RC	TBB	IBB	SO	HBP	SH	SF	SB	CS	SB%	GDP	Avg	OBP	Slg
1994	StL	NL	6	23	7	3	0	0	(0	0)	10	2	3	4	2	0	4	0	0	0	0	0	-	0	.304	.360	.435
1995	StL	NL	129	388	119	21	1	5	(2	3)	157	35	41	53	24	5	45	2	0	4	0	3	.00	6	.307	.347	.405
1996	StL	NL	151	543	161	30	2	13	(3	10)	234	63	74	74	37	11	84	3	3	5	3	2	.60	21	.297	.342	.431
1997	StL	NL	116	388	110	19	0	5	(1	4)	144	40	36	49	39	9	77	3	2	2	0	1	.00	11	.284	.352	.371
1998	StL	NL	142	377	94	22	0	9	(4	5)	143	41	46	42	30	6	76	1	3	2	0	2	.00	6	.249	.305	.379
1999	Sea	AL	87	262	64	14	0	9	(5	4)	105	34	33	30	20	1	60	0	2	1	2	1	.67	6	.244	.297	.401

Year	Team	Lg	G	AB	H	2B	3B	HR	(Hm	Rd)	TB	R	RBI	RC	TBB	IBB	SO	HBP	SH	SF	SB	CS	SB%	GDP	Avg	OBP	Slg
2000	2 Tms		95	226	53	13	0	8	(3	5)	90	35	32	25	15	0	69	2	0	1	0	1	.00	4	.235	.287	.398
2001	2 Tms	NL	87	154	32	7	0	6	(2	4)	57	14	20	16	13	1	46	5	0	2	1	0	1.00	6	.208	.287	.370
2002	2 Tms		110	214	59	13	1	11	(8	3)	107	28	43	34	15	2	42	1	0	4	1	1	.50	7	.276	.321	.500
2003	Sea	AL	64	104	22	6	0	3	(1	2)	37	12	16	11	15	2	21	3	0	0	0	0	-	3	.212	.328	.356
2004	StL	NL	87	240	71	11	0	13	(7	6)	121	32	40	37	26	5	63	1	5	3	0	1	.00	6	.296	.363	.504
2005	StL	NL	112	246	59	15	1	8	(2	6)	100	26	32	25	20	1	63	0	6	2	0	0	-	6	.240	.295	.407
2006	ChC	NL	107	210	43	8	1	5	(2	3)	68	16	25	24	23	0	57	1	0	3	0	0	-	5	.205	.283	.324
2007	Col		28	34	4	1	0	1	(0	1)	8	4	5	2	5	0	10	0	0	0	0	0	-	0	.118	.231	.235
00	Sea	AL	47	103	25	5	0	1	(0	1)	33	18	7	11	10	0	31	2	0	0	0	1	.00	1	.243	.322	.320
00	SD	NL	48	123	28	8	0	7	(3	4)	57	17	25	14	5	0	38	0	0	1	0	0	-	3	.228	.256	.463
01	StL	NL	5	7	0	0	0	0	(0	0)	0	0	0	0	0	0	2	0	0	0	0	0	-	0	.000	.000	.000
01	Fla	NL	82	147	32	7	0	6	(2	4)	57	14	20	16	13	1	44	5	0	2	1	0	1.00	6	.218	.299	.388
02	Phi	NL	21	21	6	0	0	0	(0	0)	6	1	3	3	1	1	5	0	0	1	0	0	-	0	.286	.304	.286
02	Oak	AL	89	193	53	13	1	11	(8	3)	101	27	40	31	14	1	37	1	0	3	1	1	.50	7	.275	.322	.523
14 ML YEARS			1321	3409	090	183	6	06	(44	52)	1381	382	446	426	284	43	717	22	21	29	7	12	.37	88	.263	.322	.405

Mike MacDougal

Pitches: R Bats: B Pos: RP-54   Ht: 6'3" Wt: 180 Born: 3/5/1977 Age: 31

			HOW MUCH HE PITCHED				WHAT HE GAVE UP													THE RESULTS						
Year	Team	Lg	G	GS	CG	GF	IP	BFP	H	R	ER	HR	SH	SF	HB	TBB	IBB	SO	WP	Bk	W	L	Pct	ShO	Sv-Op	Hld	ERC	ERA
2007	Charltt*	AAA	8	0	0	2	8.2	35	7	1	0	0	1	0	0	2	0	11	0	0	2	0	1.000	0	0- -	-	1.83	0.00
2001	KC	AL	3	3	0	0	15.1	67	18	10	8	2	0	0	1	4	0	7	3	0	1	1	.500	0	0-0	0	5.04	4.70
2002	KC	AL	6	0	0	1	9.0	38	5	5	5	0	0	0	0	7	1	10	1	0	0	0	-	0	0-0	0	2.26	5.00
2003	KC	AL	68	0	0	61	64.0	285	64	36	29	4	3	2	8	32	0	57	6	0	3	5	.375	0	27-35	1	4.76	4.08
2004	KC	AL	13	0	0	8	11.1	61	16	8	7	2	0	0	1	9	0	14	2	0	1	1	.500	0	1-3	0	9.04	5.56
2005	KC	AL	68	0	0	53	70.1	298	69	32	26	6	1	1	3	24	2	72	6	1	5	6	.455	0	21-25	0	3.80	3.33
2006	2 Tms	AL	29	0	0	7	29.0	110	21	5	5	1	1	0	1	6	0	21	1	0	1	1	.500	0	1-2	11	1.80	1.55
2007	CWS	AL	54	0	0	8	42.1	208	50	37	32	3	0	1	2	33	3	39	8	0	2	5	.286	0	0-3	19	6.49	6.80
06	KC	AL	4	0	0	3	4.0	13	2	0	0	0	0	0	0	0	0	2	0	0	0	0	-	0	1-1	0	0.58	0.00
06	CWS	AL	25	0	0	4	25.0	97	19	5	5	1	1	0	1	6	0	19	1	0	1	1	.500	0	0-1	11	2.10	1.80
7 ML YEARS			241	3	0	138	241.1	1067	243	133	112	18	5	4	16	115	6	220	27	1	13	20	.394	0	50-68	31	4.48	4.18

Drew Macias

Bats: L Throws: L Pos: PR-1   Ht: 6'3" Wt: 175 Born: 3/7/1983 Age: 25

Year	Team	Lg	G	AB	H	2B	3B	HR	(Hm	Rd)	TB	R	RBI	RC	TBB	IBB	SO	HBP	SH	SF	SB	CS	SB%	GDP	Avg	OBP	Slg
2003	Idaho	R+	61	239	60	10	4	2	(-	-)	84	41	13	30	19	1	32	5	6	1	15	4	.79	8	.251	.318	.351
2003	FtWyn	A	1	2	0	0	0	0	(-	-)	0	0	0	0	0	0	1	0	1	0	0	0	-	1	.000	.000	.000
2004	FtWyn	A	129	478	127	18	5	8	(-	-)	179	60	55	64	49	1	68	8	4	6	16	14	.53	7	.266	.340	.374
2005	Lk Els	A+	128	492	142	23	6	6	(-	-)	195	79	66	70	46	3	78	6	5	2	15	15	.50	7	.289	.355	.396
2006	Mobile	AA	134	430	110	20	3	7	(-	-)	157	43	46	52	44	3	94	8	1	3	4	12	.25	5	.256	.334	.365
2007	SnAnt	AA	100	331	83	15	5	8	(-	-)	132	43	50	49	51	3	53	5	0	4	5	8	.38	6	.251	.355	.399
2007	Portlnd	AAA	31	110	31	6	1	2	(-	-)	45	14	11	19	21	0	25	0	0	0	3	1	.75	0	.282	.397	.409
2007	SD	NL	1	0	0	0	0	0	(0	0)	0	1	0	0	0	0	0	0	0	0	0	0	-	0	-	-	-

Rob Mackowiak

Bats: L Throws: R Pos: LF-65; PH-28; RF-24; DH-7; 1B-5, PR-2; 3D-1; CF-1   Ht: 5'11" Wt: 193 Born: 6/20/1976 Age: 32

Year	Team	Lg	G	AB	H	2B	3B	HR	(Hm	Rd)	TB	R	RBI	RC	TBB	IBB	SO	HBP	SH	SF	SB	CS	SB%	GDP	Avg	OBP	Slg
2001	Pit	NL	83	214	57	15	2	4	(3	1)	88	30	21	28	15	5	52	3	2	3	4	3	.57	3	.266	.319	.411
2002	Pit	NL	136	385	94	22	0	16	(9	7)	164	57	48	57	42	5	120	7	3	2	9	3	.75	0	.244	.328	.426
2003	Pit	NL	77	174	47	4	4	6	(1	5)	77	20	19	27	15	2	53	4	0	0	6	0	1.00	1	.270	.342	.443
2004	Pit	NL	155	491	121	22	6	17	(11	6)	206	65	75	73	50	2	114	6	1	7	13	4	.76	3	.246	.319	.420
2005	Pit	NL	142	463	126	21	3	9	(7	2)	180	57	58	59	43	4	100	3	2	1	8	4	.67	7	.272	.337	.389
2006	CWS	AL	112	255	74	12	1	5	(2	3)	103	31	23	35	28	3	59	3	2	2	5	2	.71	1	.290	.365	.404
2007	2 Tms	NL	113	293	77	14	2	6	(4	2)	113	40	38	37	26	1	71	8	0	2	4	1	.80	7	.263	.337	.386
07	CWS	AL	85	237	66	11	2	6	(4	2)	99	34	36	37	23	1	53	6	0	2	3	1	.75	5	.278	.354	.418
07	SD	NL	28	56	11	3	0	0	(0	0)	14	6	2	0	3	0	18	2	0	0	1	0	1.00	2	.196	.262	.250
7 ML YEARS			818	2275	596	110	18	63	(37	26)	931	300	282	316	219	22	569	34	10	17	49	17	.74	22	.262	.334	.409

Greg Maddux

Pitches: R Bats: R Pos: SP-34   Ht: 6'0" Wt: 180 Born: 4/14/1966 Age: 42

			HOW MUCH HE PITCHED				WHAT HE GAVE UP													THE RESULTS						
Year	Team	Lg	G	GS	CG	GF	IP	BFP	H	R	ER	HR	SH	SF	HB	TBB	IBB	SO	WP	Bk	W	L	Pct	ShO	Sv-Op	Hld	ERC	ERA
1986	ChC	NL	6	5	1	1	31.0	144	44	20	19	3	1	0	1	11	2	20	2	0	2	4	.333	0	0-0	0	6.45	5.52
1987	ChC	NL	30	27	1	2	155.2	701	181	111	97	17	7	1	4	74	13	101	4	7	6	14	.300	1	0-0	0	5.42	5.61
1988	ChC	NL	34	34	9	0	249.0	1047	230	97	88	13	11	2	9	81	16	140	3	6	18	8	.692	3	0-0	0	3.09	3.18
1989	ChC	NL	35	35	7	0	238.1	1002	222	90	78	13	18	6	6	82	13	135	5	3	19	12	.613	1	0-0	0	3.20	2.95
1990	ChC	NL	35	35	8	0	237.0	1011	242	116	91	11	18	5	4	71	10	144	3	3	15	15	.500	2	0-0	0	3.41	3.46
1991	ChC	NL	37	37	7	0	263.0	1070	232	113	98	18	16	3	6	66	9	198	6	3	15	11	.577	2	0-0	0	2.73	3.35
1992	ChC	NL	35	35	9	0	268.0	1061	201	68	65	7	15	3	14	70	7	199	5	0	20	11	.645	4	0-0	0	2.01	2.18
1993	Atl	NL	36	36	8	0	267.0	1064	228	85	70	14	15	7	6	52	7	197	5	1	20	10	.667	1	0-0	0	2.32	2.36
1994	Atl	NL	25	25	10	0	202.0	774	150	44	35	4	6	5	6	31	3	156	3	1	16	6	.727	3	0-0	0	1.59	1.56
1995	Atl	NL	28	28	10	0	209.2	785	147	39	38	8	9	1	4	23	3	181	1	0	19	2	.905	3	0-0	0	1.41	1.63
1996	Atl	NL	35	35	5	0	245.0	989	225	85	74	11	8	3	5	28	11	172	4	0	15	11	.577	1	0-0	0	2.22	2.72
1997	Atl	NL	33	33	5	0	232.2	893	200	58	57	9	11	7	6	20	6	177	0	0	19	4	.826	2	0-0	0	1.95	2.20
1998	Atl	NL	34	34	9	0	251.0	987	201	75	62	13	15	5	7	45	10	204	4	0	18	9	.667	5	0-0	0	2.01	2.22

Year	Team	Lg	G	GS	CG	GF	IP	BFP	H	R	ER	HR	SH	SF	HB	TBB	IBB	SO	WP	Bk	W	L	Pct	ShO	Sv-Op	Hld	ERC	ERA
1999	Atl	NL	33	33	4	0	219.1	940	258	103	87	16	15	5	4	37	8	136	1	0	19	9	.679	0	0-0	0	3.95	3.57
2000	Atl	NL	35	35	6	0	249.1	1012	225	91	83	19	8	5	10	42	12	190	1	2	19	9	.679	3	0-0	0	2.60	3.00
2001	Atl	NL	34	34	3	0	233.0	927	220	86	79	20	12	11	7	27	10	173	2	0	17	11	.607	3	0-0	0	2.70	3.05
2002	Atl	NL	34	34	0	0	199.1	820	194	67	58	14	13	4	4	45	7	118	1	0	16	6	.727	0	0-0	0	3.11	2.62
2003	Atl	NL	36	36	1	0	218.1	901	225	112	96	24	10	9	8	33	7	124	3	0	16	11	.593	0	0-0	0	3.44	3.96
2004	ChC	NL	33	33	2	0	212.2	872	218	103	95	35	12	8	9	33	4	151	2	0	16	11	.593	1	0-0	0	3.86	4.02
2005	ChC	NL	35	35	3	0	225.0	936	239	112	106	29	19	6	7	36	4	136	8	0	13	15	.464	0	0-0	0	3.77	4.24
2006	2 Tms	NL	34	34	0	0	210.0	862	219	109	98	20	11	5	0	37	7	117	0	0	15	14	.517	0	0-0	0	3.39	4.20
2007	SD	NL	34	34	1	0	198.0	830	221	92	91	14	15	8	6	25	3	104	5	0	14	11	.560	0	0-0	0	3.54	4.14
06	ChC	NL	22	22	0	0	136.1	572	153	78	71	14	7	3	0	23	3	81	0	0	9	11	.450	0	0-0	0	3.83	4.69
06	LAD	NL	12	12	0	0	73.2	290	66	31	27	6	4	2	0	14	4	36	0	0	6	3	.667	0	0-0	0	2.61	3.30
22 ML YEARS			711	707	109	3	4814.1	19617	4522	1876	1665	332	265	111	131	969	172	3273	68	26	347	214	.619	35	0-0	0	2.86	3.11

Ryan Madson

Pitches: R Bats: L Pos: RP-38

Ht: 6'6" Wt: 200 Born: 8/28/1980 Age: 27

Year	Team	Lg	G	GS	CG	GF	IP	BFP	H	R	ER	HR	SH	SF	HB	TBB	IBB	SO	WP	Bk	W	L	Pct	ShO	Sv-Op	Hld	ERC	ERA
2007	Rdng*	AA	2	0	0	1	3.0	11	3	0	0	0	0	0	0	4	0	0	0	0	0	0	-	0	0--	-	2.18	0.00
2003	Phi	NL	1	0	0	0	2.0	6	0	0	0	0	0	0	0	0	0	0	0	0	0	0	-	0	0-0	0	0.00	0.00
2004	Phi	NL	52	1	0	14	77.0	312	68	23	20	6	1	1	5	19	4	55	7	0	9	3	.750	0	1-2	7	2.95	2.34
2005	Phi	NL	78	0	0	10	87.0	365	84	44	40	11	5	5	6	25	6	79	6	1	6	5	.545	0	0-7	32	3.83	4.14
2006	Phi	NL	50	17	0	8	134.1	620	176	92	85	20	9	3	10	50	4	99	12	0	11	9	.550	0	2-4	6	6.50	5.69
2007	Phi	NL	38	0	0	9	56.0	237	48	19	19	5	2	2	2	23	4	43	2	2	2	2	.500	0	1-2	7	3.28	3.05
5 ML YEARS			219	18	0	41	356.1	1540	376	178	164	42	17	11	23	117	18	276	27	3	28	19	.596	0	4-15	52	4.44	4.14

Kevin Mahar

Bats: R Throws: R Pos: CF-5; RF-2

Ht: 6'5" Wt: 220 Born: 6/8/1981 Age: 27

Year	Team	Lg	G	AB	H	2B	3B	HR	(Hm	Rd)	TB	R	RBI	RC	TBB	IBB	SO	HBP	SH	SF	SB	CS	SB%	GDP	Avg	OBP	Slg
2004	Spkane	A-	38	152	48	9	0	6	(-	-)	75	26	22	29	12	0	38	4	0	1	5	1	1.00	0	.316	.379	.493
2004	Rngrs	R	27	100	28	5	1	5	(-	-)	50	20	18	19	9	0	28	3	0	3	7	1	.88	0	.280	.348	.500
2005	Bkrsfld	A+	110	447	141	27	4	17	(-	-)	227	98	63	90	47	2	109	15	0	4	17	10	.63	10	.315	.396	.508
2006	Frisco	AA	127	505	135	38	2	20	(-	-)	237	82	82	77	33	1	110	8	7	5	13	7	.65	12	.267	.319	.469
2007	Frisco	AA	25	91	22	2	1	3	(-	-)	35	14	14	14	11	0	23	6	0	0	3	0	1.00	2	.242	.361	.385
2007	Okla	AAA	99	391	108	22	2	6	(-	-)	152	53	37	47	14	0	98	2	1	2	4	1	.80	5	.276	.303	.389
2007	Tex	AL	7	18	3	1	0	0	(0	0)	4	2	1	0	0	0	7	0	0	0	0	0	-	1	.167	.167	.222

Ron Mahay

Pitches: L Bats: L Pos: RP-58

Ht: 6'2" Wt: 190 Born: 6/28/1971 Age: 37

Year	Team	Lg	G	GS	CG	GF	IP	BFP	H	R	ER	HR	SH	SF	HB	TBB	IBB	SO	WP	Bk	W	L	Pct	ShO	Sv-Op	Hld	ERC	ERA
2007	Frisco*	AA	3	0	0	1	4.2	20	5	2	0	0	0	0	0	1	0	4	0	0	0	0	-	0	0--	-	3.00	0.00
2007	Okla*	AAA	4	0	0	1	5.2	32	10	8	7	1	0	1	0	4	0	5	1	0	0	1	.000	0	0--	-	10.46	11.12
1997	Bos	AL	28	0	0	7	25.0	105	19	7	7	3	1	0	0	11	0	22	3	0	3	1	.750	0	0-2	5	3.01	2.52
1998	Bos	AL	29	0	0	6	26.0	120	26	16	10	2	0	4	2	15	1	14	3	0	1	1	.500	0	1-2	7	4.76	3.46
1999	Oak	AL	6	1	0	2	19.1	68	8	4	4	2	0	0	0	3	0	15	0	0	2	0	1.000	0	1-1	0	0.88	1.86
2000	2 Tms	AL	23	2	0	7	41.1	199	57	35	33	10	1	2	0	25	1	32	4	0	1	1	.500	0	0-0	2	8.55	7.19
2001	ChC	NL	17	0	0	4	20.2	86	14	6	6	4	0	0	0	15	1	24	1	0	0	0	-	0	0-0	2	4.32	2.61
2002	ChC	NL	11	0	0	1	14.2	65	13	14	14	6	0	0	0	8	0	14	0	0	2	0	1.000	0	0-0	6	6.11	8.59
2003	Tex	AL	35	0	0	5	45.1	189	33	19	16	3	0	0	0	20	7	38	4	0	3	3	.500	0	0-3	9	2.31	3.18
2004	Tex	AL	60	0	0	12	67.0	290	60	23	19	5	4	0	2	29	5	54	2	0	3	0	1.000	0	0-2	14	3.39	2.55
2005	Tex	AL	30	0	0	9	35.2	167	47	28	27	8	0	1	0	16	1	30	2	0	0	2	.000	0	1-1	6	7.10	6.81
2006	Tex	AL	62	0	0	14	57.0	246	54	30	25	7	1	1	0	28	2	56	1	0	1	3	.250	0	0-1	9	4.28	3.95
2007	2 Tms	AL	58	0	0	8	67.0	281	52	20	19	4	3	2	1	37	2	55	1	1	3	0	1.000	0	1-2	7	3.23	2.55
00	Oak	AL	5	2	0	1	16.0	82	26	18	16	4	1	1	0	9	0	5	2	0	0	1	1.000	0	0-0	0	9.97	9.00
00	Fla	NL	18	0	0	6	25.1	117	31	17	17	6	0	1	0	16	1	27	2	0	1	0	1.000	0	0-0	2	7.67	6.04
07	Tex	AL	28	0	0	8	39.0	164	33	12	12	3	1	1	1	21	0	32	0	1	2	0	1.000	0	1-1	6	3.81	2.77
07	Atl	NL	30	0	0	0	28.0	117	19	8	7	1	2	1	0	16	2	23	1	0	1	0	1.000	0	0-1	6	2.47	2.25
11 ML YEARS			359	3	0	75	419.0	1816	383	202	180	54	10	10	5	207	20	354	21	1	19	10	.655	0	4-14	61	4.14	3.87

Paul Maholm

Pitches: L Bats: L Pos: SP-29

Ht: 6'2" Wt: 230 Born: 6/25/1982 Age: 26

Year	Team	Lg	G	GS	CG	GF	IP	BFP	H	R	ER	HR	SH	SF	HB	TBB	IBB	SO	WP	Bk	W	L	Pct	ShO	Sv-Op	Hld	ERC	ERA
2005	Pit	NL	6	6	0	0	41.1	168	31	10	10	2	0	0	3	17	0	26	0	0	3	1	.750	0	0-0	0	2.79	2.18
2006	Pit	NL	30	30	0	0	176.0	788	202	98	93	19	7	4	12	81	6	117	3	1	8	10	.444	0	0-0	0	5.58	4.76
2007	Pit	NL	29	29	2	0	177.2	765	204	110	99	22	13	6	6	49	3	105	5	0	10	15	.400	1	0-0	0	4.77	5.02
3 ML YEARS			65	65	2	0	395.0	1721	437	218	202	43	20	10	21	147	9	248	8	1	21	26	.447	1	0-0	0	4.90	4.60

John Maine

Pitches: R Bats: R Pos: SP-32   Ht: 6'4" Wt: 200 Born: 5/8/1981 Age: 27

			HOW MUCH HE PITCHED					WHAT HE GAVE UP												THE RESULTS						
Year	Team	Lg	G	GS	CG	GF	IP	BFP	H	R	ER	HR	SH	SF	HB	TBB	IBB	SO	WP	Bk	W	L	Pct	ShO	Sv-Op	Hld	ERC	ERA
2004	Bal	AL	1	1	0	0	3.2	19	7	4	4	1	0	0	0	3	0	1	1	0	0	1	.000	0	0-0	0	14.87	9.82
2005	Bal	AL	10	8	0	1	40.0	184	39	30	28	8	0	2	1	24	0	24	0	1	2	3	.400	0	0-0	0	5.47	6.30
2006	NYM	NL	16	15	1	1	90.0	365	69	40	36	15	3	1	2	33	1	71	3	0	6	5	.545	1	0-0	0	3.22	3.60
2007	NYM	NL	32	32	1	0	191.0	810	168	90	83	23	11	4	5	75	3	180	2	0	15	10	.600	1	0-0	0	3.58	3.91
	4 ML YEARS		59	56	2	2	324.2	1378	283	164	151	47	14	7	8	135	4	276	6	1	23	19	.548	2	0-0	0	3.80	4.19

Gary Majewski

Pitches: R Bats: R Pos: RP-32   Ht: 6'1" Wt: 215 Born: 2/26/1980 Age: 28

			HOW MUCH HE PITCHED					WHAT HE GAVE UP												THE RESULTS						
Year	Team	Lg	G	GS	CG	GF	IP	BFP	H	R	ER	HR	SH	SF	HB	TBB	IBB	SO	WP	Bk	W	L	Pct	ShO	Sv-Op	Hld	ERC	ERA
2007	Lsvlle*	AAA	38	0	0	13	30.2	156	33	17	17	2	0	2	1	15	1	30	1	0	1	1	.500	0	4- -	1	3.11	3.96
2004	Mon	NL	16	0	0	7	21.0	95	28	15	9	2	1	1	2	5	1	12	0	0	0	1	.000	0	1-2	0	5.68	3.86
2005	Was	NL	79	0	0	24	86.0	376	80	32	28	2	5	4	7	37	6	50	1	0	4	4	.500	0	1-5	24	3.43	2.93
2006	2 Tms	NL	65	0	0	21	70.1	316	79	38	36	5	1	3	4	29	3	43	6	0	4	4	.500	0	0-7	8	4.76	4.61
2007	Cin	NL	32	0	0	3	23.0	113	43	22	21	3	0	0	2	3	1	10	0	0	0	4	.000	0	0-3	6	9.01	8.22
	06 Was	NL	46	0	0	14	55.1	237	49	24	22	4	1	0	1	25	1	34	6	0	3	2	.600	0	0-5	6	3.48	3.58
	06 Cin	NL	19	0	0	7	15.0	79	30	14	14	1	0	3	3	4	2	9	0	0	1	2	.333	0	0-2	2	10.33	8.40
	4 ML YEARS		192	0	0	55	200.1	900	230	107	94	12	7	8	15	74	11	115	7	0	8	13	.381	0	2-17	38	4.69	4.22

Carlos Maldonado

Bats: R Throws: R Pos: C-13   Ht: 6'1" Wt: 245 Born: 1/3/1979 Age: 29

			BATTING																				BASERUNNING				AVERAGES		
Year	Team	Lg	G	AB	H	2B	3B	HR	(Hm	Rd)	TB	R	RBI	RC	TBB	IBB	SO	HBP	SH	SF	SB	CS	SB%	GDP	Avg	OBP	Slg
1996	Ms	R	29	100	22	0	0	2	(-	-)	28	10	18	7	6	0	10	1	1	4	0	1	.00	7	.220	.261	.280
1997	Wisc	A	97	316	60	8	2	0	(-	-)	72	15	25	15	17	1	33	3	8	3	2	3	.40	8	.190	.236	.228
1998	Wisc	A	7	23	4	0	0	0	(-	-)	4	4	1	0	2	0	1	0	0	0	0	0	-	1	.174	.240	.174
1998	Everett	A-	42	150	43	10	0	5	(-	-)	68	19	24	23	10	0	17	2	0	2	1	0	1.00	5	.287	.335	.453
1998	Tacom	AAA	3	9	0	0	0	0	(-	-)	0	0	0	0	0	0	1	0	0	0	0	0	-	0	.000	.000	.000
1999	Wisc	A	92	302	93	13	0	0	(-	-)	106	35	33	45	43	1	32	0	2	2	4	6	.40	10	.308	.392	.351
2000	RdRck	AA	116	423	114	24	2	5	(-	-)	157	46	52	54	35	3	71	5	5	6	5	4	.56	15	.270	.328	.371
2001	RdRck	AA	76	262	75	14	0	4	(-	-)	101	29	33	38	27	0	55	3	0	3	1	2	.33	11	.286	.356	.385
2002	NewOr	AAA	12	29	5	0	0	0	(-	-)	5	1	2	0	1	0	7	0	0	0	0	0	-	0	.172	.200	.172
2002	RdRck	AA	47	123	31	8	0	4	(-	-)	51	13	20	20	22	0	23	0	0	3	0	0	-	3	.252	.356	.415
2003	Brham	AA	120	408	107	24	1	6	(-	-)	151	50	63	55	43	1	50	6	3	9	1	1	.50	12	.262	.335	.370
2004	Brham	AA	108	388	103	30	1	12	(-	-)	171	48	68	63	52	1	81	3	1	4	0	3	.00	10	.265	.353	.441
2005	Altna	AA	82	278	70	14	0	7	(-	-)	105	27	34	38	35	0	63	2	5	1	0	1	.00	10	.252	.339	.378
2006	Altna	AA	5	18	5	2	0	0	(-	-)	7	1	0	1	0	0	6	0	0	0	0	0	-	0	.278	.278	.389
2006	Indy	AAA	103	336	95	18	0	6	(-	-)	131	37	47	50	36	3	67	3	5	4	2	0	1.00	11	.283	.354	.390
2007	Altna	AA	3	6	0	0	0	0	(-	-)	0	0	0	0	0	0	1	0	0	0	0	0	-	1	.000	.000	.000
2007	Indy	AAA	46	137	30	4	0	1	(-	-)	37	14	19	14	20	0	27	2	4	1	0	0	-	0	.219	.325	.270
2006	Pit	NL	8	19	2	0	0	0	(0	0)	2	0	0	0	1	1	10	0	0	0	1	0	1.00	0	.105	.150	.105
2007	Pit	NL	13	24	5	1	0	2	(0	2)	12	2	4	2	5	2	8	0	0	1	0	0	-	2	.208	.333	.500
	2 ML YEARS		21	43	7	1	0	2	(0	2)	14	2	4	2	6	3	18	0	0	1	1	0	1.00	2	.163	.260	.326

Shaun Marcum

Pitches: R Bats: R Pos: SP-25; RP-13   Ht: 6'0" Wt: 180 Born: 12/14/1981 Age: 26

			HOW MUCH HE PITCHED					WHAT HE GAVE UP												THE RESULTS						
Year	Team	Lg	G	GS	CG	GF	IP	BFP	H	R	ER	HR	SH	SF	HB	TBB	IBB	SO	WP	Bk	W	L	Pct	ShO	Sv-Op	Hld	ERC	ERA
2005	Tor	AL	5	0	0	3	8.0	32	6	0	0	0	0	0	0	4	0	4	0	0	0	0	-	0	0-0	0	2.58	0.00
2006	Tor	AL	21	14	0	3	78.1	357	87	44	44	14	1	2	4	38	3	65	1	0	3	4	.429	0	0-0	0	5.80	5.06
2007	Tor	AL	38	25	0	6	159.0	660	149	76	73	27	3	3	5	49	1	122	1	0	12	6	.667	0	1-2	1	4.00	4.13
	3 ML YEARS		64	39	0	12	245.1	1049	242	120	117	41	4	5	9	91	4	191	2	0	15	10	.600	0	1-2	1	4.51	4.29

Nick Markakis

Bats: L Throws: L Pos: RF-161; PR-1   Ht: 6'2" Wt: 214 Born: 11/17/1983 Age: 24

			BATTING																				BASERUNNING				AVERAGES		
Year	Team	Lg	G	AB	H	2B	3B	HR	(Hm	Rd)	TB	R	RBI	RC	TBB	IBB	SO	HBP	SH	SF	SB	CS	SB%	GDP	Avg	OBP	Slg
2003	Abrdn	A-	59	205	58	14	3	1	(-	-)	81	22	28	33	30	1	33	1	1	3	13	5	.72	6	.283	.372	.395
2004	Dlmrva	A	96	355	106	22	3	11	(-	-)	167	57	64	65	42	1	66	2	2	5	12	3	.80	6	.299	.371	.470
2005	Frdrck	A+	91	350	105	25	1	12	(-	-)	168	59	62	65	43	4	65	4	0	1	2	1	.67	6	.300	.379	.480
2005	Bowie	AA	33	124	42	16	2	3	(-	-)	71	19	30	28	18	0	30	0	0	1	0	1	.00	5	.339	.420	.573
2006	Bal	AL	147	491	143	25	2	16	(9	7)	220	72	62	67	43	3	72	3	3	2	2	0	1.00	15	.291	.351	.448
2007	Bal	AL	161	637	191	43	3	23	(15	8)	309	97	112	103	61	5	112	5	1	6	18	6	.75	22	.300	.362	.485
	2 ML YEARS		308	1128	334	68	5	39	(24	15)	529	169	174	170	104	8	184	8	4	8	20	6	.77	37	.296	.357	.469

Carlos Marmol

Pitches: R Bats: R Pos: RP-59

Ht: 6'2" Wt: 180 Born: 10/14/1982 Age: 25

Year Team	Lg	G	GS	CG	GF	IP	BFP	H	R	ER	HR	SH	SF	HB	TBB	IBB	SO	WP	Bk	W	L	Pct	ShO	Sv-Op	Hld	ERC	ERA
2002 Cubs	R	1	0	0	1	1.0	5	1	0	0	0	0	0	0	1	0	1	0	1	0	0	-	0	0--	-	5.48	0.00
2003 Cubs	R	14	9	0	0	62.1	288	54	38	29	5	2	2	7	37	0	74	6	2	3	5	.375	0	0--	-	4.21	4.19
2004 Lansng	A	26	24	0	1	154.2	635	131	64	55	15	9	6	14	53	0	154	5	2	14	8	.636	0	0--	-	3.44	3.20
2005 Dytona	A+	13	13	0	0	72.1	315	60	30	24	7	1	1	3	37	1	71	5	1	6	2	.750	0	0--	-	3.63	2.99
2005 WTenn	AA	14	14	0	0	81.1	349	70	33	33	10	6	2	8	40	0	70	1	1	3	4	.429	0	0--	-	4.28	3.65
2006 WTenn	AA	11	11	0	0	58.0	234	42	18	15	1	4	1	1	25	0	67	3	1	3	2	.600	0	0--	-	2.32	2.33
2006 Iowa	AAA	2	0	0	0	3.0	13	4	3	3	0	0	0	0	1	0	1	0	0	0	0	-	0	0--	-	5.24	9.00
2007 Iowa	AAA	8	7	0	0	41.0	173	30	18	18	4	3	3	8	12	0	48	4	0	4	1	.800	0	0--	-	2.90	3.95
2006 ChC	NL	19	13	0	1	77.0	356	71	54	52	14	6	2	5	59	2	59	3	1	5	7	.417	0	0-0	0	6.01	6.08
2007 ChC	NL	59	0	0	6	69.1	285	41	11	11	3	1	2	4	35	3	96	5	1	5	1	.833	0	1-2	16	2.11	1.43
2 ML YEARS		78	13	0	7	146.1	641	112	65	63	17	7	4	9	94	5	155	8	2	10	8	.556	0	1-2	16	4.01	3.87

Mike Maroth

Pitches: L Bats: L Pos: SP-20; RP-7

Ht: 6'0" Wt: 190 Born: 8/17/1977 Age: 30

Year Team	Lg	G	GS	CG	GF	IP	BFP	H	R	ER	HR	SH	SF	HB	TBB	IBB	SO	WP	Bk	W	L	Pct	ShO	Sv-Op	Hld	ERC	ERA
2007 Memp*	AAA	2	1	0	0	4.1	20	5	4	4	1	0	0	0	3	0	4	0	0	1	0	1.000	0	0--	-	7.50	8.31
2002 Det	AL	21	21	0	0	128.2	538	136	68	64	7	5	3	2	36	1	58	4	0	6	10	.375	0	0-0	0	3.73	4.48
2003 Det	AL	33	33	1	0	193.1	847	231	131	123	34	4	8	8	50	2	87	7	0	9	21	.300	0	0-0	0	5.36	5.73
2004 Det	AL	33	33	2	0	217.0	928	244	112	104	25	11	4	7	59	1	108	10	1	11	13	.458	1	0-0	0	4.57	4.31
2005 Det	AL	34	34	0	0	209.0	889	235	123	110	30	3	11	9	51	1	115	5	0	14	14	.500	0	0-0	0	4.71	4.74
2006 Det	AL	13	9	0	2	53.2	234	64	26	25	11	0	0	1	16	1	24	0	0	5	2	.714	0	0-0	0	5.67	4.19
2007 2 Tms		27	20	0	2	116.1	549	168	103	89	26	4	6	5	50	1	51	2	0	5	7	.417	0	0-0	0	8.28	6.89
07 Det	AL	13	13	0	0	78.1	346	97	47	44	15	2	4	3	33	0	28	1	0	5	2	.714	0	0-0	0	6.73	5.06
07 StL	NL	14	7	0	2	38.0	203	71	56	45	11	2	2	2	17	1	23	1	0	0	5	.000	0	0-0	0	11.65	10.66
6 ML YEARS		161	150	3	4	918.0	3985	1078	563	515	133	31	32	32	262	7	443	28	1	50	67	.427	1	0-0	0	5.14	5.05

Jason Marquis

Pitches: R Bats: L Pos: SP-33; RP-1

Ht: 6'1" Wt: 210 Born: 8/21/1978 Age: 29

Year Team	Lg	G	GS	CG	GF	IP	BFP	H	R	ER	HR	SH	SF	HB	TBB	IBB	SO	WP	Bk	W	L	Pct	ShO	Sv-Op	Hld	ERC	ERA
2000 Atl	NL	15	0	0	7	23.1	103	23	16	13	4	1	1	1	12	1	17	1	0	1	0	1.000	0	0-1	1	5.13	5.01
2001 Atl	NL	38	16	0	9	129.1	556	113	62	50	14	6	5	4	59	4	98	1	2	5	6	.455	0	0-2	2	3.70	3.48
2002 Atl	NL	22	22	0	0	114.1	507	127	66	64	19	4	3	3	49	3	84	4	0	8	9	.471	0	0-0	0	5.43	5.04
2003 Atl	NL	21	2	0	10	40.2	182	43	27	25	3	0	3	2	18	2	19	2	0	0	0	-	0	1-1	0	4.45	5.53
2004 StL	NL	32	32	0	0	201.1	874	215	90	83	26	5	6	10	70	1	138	6	0	15	7	.682	0	0-0	0	4.69	3.71
2005 StL	NL	33	32	3	0	207.0	868	206	110	95	29	4	3	5	69	2	100	10	3	13	14	.481	1	0-0	0	4.23	4.13
2006 StL	NL	33	33	0	0	194.1	870	221	136	130	35	12	3	16	75	2	96	2	1	14	16	.467	0	0-0	0	5.79	6.02
2007 ChC	NL	34	33	1	0	191.2	846	190	111	98	22	13	1	13	76	6	109	3	0	12	9	.571	0	0-0	0	4.28	4.60
8 ML YEARS		228	170	4	26	1102.0	4806	1138	618	558	152	45	25	54	428	21	661	29	6	68	61	.527	2	1-4	3	4.67	4.56

Jay Marshall

Pitches: L Bats: L Pos: RP-51

Ht: 6'5" Wt: 185 Born: 2/25/1983 Age: 25

Year Team	Lg	G	GS	CG	GF	IP	BFP	H	R	ER	HR	SH	SF	HB	TBB	IBB	SO	WP	Bk	W	L	Pct	ShO	Sv-Op	Hld	ERC	ERA
2003 Bristol	R+	10	10	0	0	41.1	173	38	15	12	3	0	0	4	13	0	42	2	0	2	0	1.000	0	0--	-	3.54	2.61
2004 Bristol	R+	11	11	0	0	57.2	241	63	31	23	8	4	2	2	8	1	52	4	1	1	6	.143	0	0--	-	3.93	3.59
2004 Gr Falls	R+	4	2	0	1	15.2	69	19	9	6	2	0	0	0	6	0	17	0	0	2	0	1.000	0	0--	-	5.57	3.45
2005 Gr Falls	R+	29	0	0	16	43.1	174	35	20	13	3	0	1	3	7	0	43	1	0	2	0	1.000	0	6--	-	2.23	2.70
2006 WinSa	A+	58	0	0	16	62.0	234	46	11	7	2	5	0	2	8	0	44	2	1	5	1	.833	0	4--	-	1.61	1.02
2007 Oak	AL	51	0	0	15	42.0	198	50	33	30	3	3	1	4	22	6	18	2	0	1	2	.333	0	0-2	9	5.56	6.43

Sean Marshall

Pitches: L Bats: L Pos: SP-19; RP-2

Ht: 6'7" Wt: 205 Born: 8/30/1982 Age: 25

Year Team	Lg	G	GS	CG	GF	IP	BFP	H	R	ER	HR	SH	SF	HB	TBB	IBB	SO	WP	Bk	W	L	Pct	ShO	Sv-Op	Hld	ERC	ERA
2003 Boise	A-	14	14	0	0	73.2	66	66	31	21	1	3	5	5	23	0	88	8	0	5	6	.455	0	0--	-	15.42	2.57
2003 Lansng	A	1	1	0	0	7.0	26	5	1	0	0	0	0	0	0	0	11	0	0	1	0	1.000	0	0--	-	1.04	0.00
2004 Lansng	A	7	7	1	0	48.2	175	29	7	6	1	2	0	0	4	0	51	4	0	2	0	1.000	1	0--	-	0.97	1.11
2004 WTenn	AA	6	6	0	0	29.0	131	36	20	19	2	2	2	2	12	0	23	3	0	2	2	.500	0	0--	-	5.71	5.90
2005 Dytona	A+	12	12	1	0	69.0	296	63	24	21	7	1	0	1	26	0	61	7	1	4	4	.500	0	0--	-	3.51	2.74
2005 WTenn	AA	4	4	0	0	25.0	96	16	7	7	1	1	0	1	5	0	24	2	1	0	1	.000	0	0--	-	1.46	2.52
2006 Iowa	AAA	4	4	0	0	21.2	92	17	10	8	1	1	0	0	14	0	21	5	0	0	2	.000	0	0--	-	3.54	3.32
2007 Dytona	A+	1	1	0	0	6.0	24	7	2	2	1	0	0	0	1	0	4	1	0	1	0	1.000	0	0--	-	4.85	3.00
2007 Iowa	AAA	4	4	0	0	24.2	97	16	6	5	2	0	0	0	8	0	15	2	0	2	0	1.000	0	0--	-	2.11	1.82
2006 ChC	NL	24	24	0	0	125.2	563	132	85	78	20	7	1	7	59	3	77	6	0	6	9	.400	0	0-0	0	5.27	5.59
2007 ChC	NL	21	19	0	0	103.1	446	107	52	45	13	7	2	1	35	3	67	4	0	7	8	.467	0	0-0	0	4.18	3.92
2 ML YEARS		45	43	0	0	229.0	1009	239	137	123	33	14	3	8	94	6	144	10	0	13	17	.433	0	0-0	0	4.77	4.83

Andy Marte

Bats: R Throws: R Pos: 3B-19; PH-1   Ht: 6'1" Wt: 190 Born: 10/21/1983 Age: 24

Year	Team	Lg	G	AB	H	2B	3B	HR	(Hm	Rd)	TB	R	RBI	RC	TBB	IBB	SO	HBP	SH	SF	SB	CS	SB%	GDP	Avg	OBP	Slg
2007	Buffalo*	AAA	96	352	94	17	1	16	(-	-)	161	47	60	51	21	2	64	2	0	4	0	0	-	13	.267	.309	.457
2005	Atl	NL	24	57	8	2	1	0	(0	0)	12	3	4	1	7	0	13	0	0	2	0	1	.00	1	.140	.227	.211
2006	Cle	AL	50	164	37	15	1	5	(3	2)	69	20	23	21	13	0	38	1	0	0	0	0	-	3	.226	.287	.421
2007	Cle	AL	20	57	11	4	0	1	(0	1)	18	3	8	4	2	0	9	1	0	0	0	0	-	0	.193	.233	.316
	3 ML YEARS		94	278	56	21	2	6	(3	3)	99	26	35	26	22	0	60	2	0	2	0	1	.00	5	.201	.263	.356

Damaso Marte

Pitches: L Bats: L Pos: RP-65   Ht: 6'2" Wt: 210 Born: 2/14/1975 Age: 33

Year	Team	Lg	G	GS	CG	GF	IP	BFP	H	R	ER	HR	SH	SF	HB	TBB	IBB	SO	WP	Bk	W	L	Pct	ShO	Sv-Op	Hld	ERC	ERA
1999	Sea	AL	5	0	0	2	8.2	47	16	9	9	3	0	0	0	6	0	3	0	0	0	1	.000	0	0-0	0	13.32	9.35
2001	Pit	NL	23	0	0	4	36.1	154	34	21	19	5	1	2	3	12	3	39	1	0	0	1	.000	0	0-0	1	3.93	4.71
2002	CWS	AL	68	0	0	22	60.1	240	44	19	19	5	1	1	4	18	2	72	3	1	1	1	.500	0	10-12	14	2.42	2.83
2003	CWS	AL	71	0	0	25	79.2	314	50	16	14	3	3	3	3	34	6	87	1	0	4	2	.667	0	11-18	14	1.96	1.58
2004	CWS	AL	74	0	0	24	73.2	303	56	28	28	10	2	6	3	34	4	68	3	0	6	5	.545	0	6-12	21	3.39	3.42
2005	CWS	AL	66	0	0	15	45.1	213	45	21	19	5	1	0	3	33	4	54	1	1	3	4	.429	0	4-8	22	5.51	3.77
2006	Pit	NL	75	0	0	15	58.1	255	51	30	24	5	8	3	4	31	6	63	3	1	1	7	.125	0	0-4	13	3.88	3.70
2007	Pit	NL	65	0	0	11	45.1	182	32	14	12	2	0	2	2	18	1	51	0	1	2	0	1.000	0	0-0	15	2.35	2.38
	8 ML YEARS		447	0	0	118	407.2	1708	328	158	144	38	16	17	22	186	26	437	12	4	17	21	.447	0	31-54	99	3.33	3.18

Russell Martin

Bats: R Throws: R Pos: C-145; PH-4; DH-2   Ht: 5'10" Wt: 210 Born: 2/15/1983 Age: 25

Year	Team	Lg	G	AB	H	2B	3B	HR	(Hm	Rd)	TB	R	RBI	RC	TBB	IBB	SO	HBP	SH	SF	SB	CS	SB%	GDP	Avg	OBP	Slg
2002	Ddgrs	R	41	126	36	3	3	0	(-	-)	45	22	10	22	23	0	18	4	2	0	7	1	.88	4	.286	.412	.357
2003	SoGA	A	25	98	28	4	1	3	(-	-)	43	15	14	15	9	0	11	0	1	1	5	2	.71	1	.286	.343	.439
2003	Ogden	R+	52	188	51	13	0	6	(-	-)	82	25	36	32	26	1	26	4	2	2	3	1	.75	6	.271	.368	.436
2004	VeroB	A+	122	416	104	24	1	15	(-	-)	175	74	64	71	71	1	54	10	0	8	9	5	.64	10	.250	.366	.421
2005	Jaxnvl	AA	129	409	127	17	1	9	(-	-)	173	83	61	82	78	0	69	10	5	3	15	7	.68	14	.311	.430	.423
2006	LsVgs	AAA	23	74	22	9	0	0	(-	-)	31	14	9	12	13	0	11	0	1	3	0	2	.00	1	.297	.389	.419
2006	LAD	NL	121	415	117	26	4	10	(8	2)	181	65	65	58	45	8	57	4	1	3	10	5	.67	17	.282	.355	.436
2007	LAD	NL	151	540	158	32	3	19	(8	11)	253	87	87	84	67	1	89	7	0	6	21	9	.70	16	.293	.374	.469
	2 ML YEARS		272	955	275	58	7	29	(16	13)	434	152	152	142	112	9	146	11	1	9	31	14	.69	33	.288	.366	.454

Tom Martin

Pitches: L Bats: L Pos: RP-26   Ht: 6'1" Wt: 205 Born: 5/21/1970 Age: 38

Year	Team	Lg	G	GS	CG	GF	IP	BFP	H	R	ER	HR	SH	SF	HB	TBB	IBB	SO	WP	Bk	W	L	Pct	ShO	Sv-Op	Hld	ERC	ERA
2007	ColSpr*	AAA	5	0	0	0	5.0	22	6	4	4	2	0	0	0	1	0	4	0	0	0	0	-	0	0--	-	6.40	7.20
1997	Hou	NL	55	0	0	18	56.0	236	52	13	13	2	6	1	1	23	2	36	3	0	5	3	.625	0	2-3	7	3.34	2.09
1998	Cle	AL	14	0	0	1	14.2	85	29	21	21	3	1	1	0	12	0	9	2	0	1	1	.500	0	0-0	3	13.19	12.89
1999	Cle	AL	6	0	0	0	9.1	44	13	9	9	2	0	1	0	3	1	8	0	0	0	1	.000	0	0-0	0	6.64	8.68
2000	Cle	AL	31	0	0	7	33.1	143	32	16	15	3	0	1	1	15	2	21	1	0	1	0	1.000	0	0-0	0	4.05	4.05
2001	NYM	NL	14	0	0	2	17.0	85	23	22	19	4	1	1	1	10	2	12	0	0	1	0	1.000	0	0 0	1	8.02	10.06
2002	TB	AL	2	0	0	2	1.2	11	5	3	3	0	0	0	0	1	0	1	0	0	0	0	-	0	0-0	0	17.54	16.20
2003	LAD	NL	80	0	0	13	51.0	210	36	21	20	6	0	2	2	24	4	51	1	0	1	2	.333	0	0-1	28	2.94	3.53
2004	2 Tms	NL	76	0	0	11	45.1	204	49	20	20	7	5	4	3	19	3	30	1	0	0	2	.000	0	1-4	12	5.14	3.97
2005	Atl	NL	4	0	0	1	2.1	14	6	5	5	1	0	0	0	2	0	0	0	0	0	0	-	0	0-0	0	22.06	19.29
2006	Col	NL	68	0	0	9	60.1	266	62	37	34	4	1	1	4	25	5	46	1	0	2	0	1.000	0	0-1	11	4.16	5.07
2007	Col	NL	26	0	0	7	25.2	117	32	14	14	4	1	0	1	9	0	10	0	1	0	0	-	0	0-0	2	5.87	4.91
04	LAD	NL	47	0	0	9	28.1	132	32	13	13	3	3	2	3	14	1	18	1	0	0	1	.000	0	1-1	5	5.58	4.13
04	Atl	NL	29	0	0	2	17.0	72	17	7	7	4	2	2	0	5	2	12	0	0	0	1	.000	0	0-3	7	4.36	3.71
	11 ML YEARS		376	0	0	71	316.2	1415	339	181	173	36	15	12	13	143	19	224	9	1	11	9	.550	0	3-9	64	4.84	4.92

Carlos Martinez

Pitches: R Bats: R Pos: RP-2   Ht: 6'3" Wt: 200 Born: 5/26/1982 Age: 26

Year	Team	Lg	G	GS	CG	GF	IP	BFP	H	R	ER	HR	SH	SF	HB	TBB	IBB	SO	WP	Bk	W	L	Pct	ShO	Sv-Op	Hld	ERC	ERA
2002	Mrlns	R	22	0	0	19	32.1	130	26	8	4	1	3	1	0	6	0	23	2	0	1	2	.333	0	7--	-	1.83	1.11
2003	Mrlns	R	3	0	0	3	6.1	20	1	0	0	0	0	0	0	1	0	2	0	0	1	0	1.000	0	1--	-	0.18	0.00
2003	Jmstwn	A-	1	0	0	1	1.2	9	2	1	1	0	0	0	0	1	0	4	1	0	0	0	-	0	0--	-	4.47	5.40
2003	Grnsbr	A	15	0	0	5	18.1	80	18	7	6	1	1	1	2	4	0	15	0	0	0	3	.000	0	1--	-	3.26	2.95
2004	Grnsbr	A	40	0	0	21	48.1	203	43	21	17	8	0	0	1	12	0	37	2	1	2	3	.400	0	6--	-	3.29	3.17
2005	Jupiter	A+	47	0	0	37	60.2	257	52	25	21	5	3	2	3	22	1	65	1	0	4	5	.444	0	22--	-	3.16	3.12
2005	Albq	AAA	2	0	0	0	2.0	10	4	2	2	1	0	0	0	0	0	0	0	0	0	0	-	0	0--	-	11.88	9.00
2005	Carlina	AA	1	0	0	1	1.0	5	1	1	1	0	0	0	0	1	0	0	0	0	0	0	-	0	1--	-	5.48	9.00
2006	Jupiter	A+	2	1	0	0	2.0	8	0	0	0	0	0	0	0	1	0	0	0	0	0	0	-	0	0--	-	0.24	0.00
2007	Jupiter	A+	2	0	0	0	2.0	9	3	1	1	0	0	0	0	0	0	2	0	0	0	0	-	0	0--	-	8.13	4.50
2007	Carlina	AA	19	0	0	7	21.1	93	21	12	8	2	1	0	2	5	0	18	4	0	1	1	.500	0	0--	-	3.54	3.38
2007	Albq	AAA	3	0	0	1	1.1	9	3	1	1	0	0	0	1	1	0	2	0	0	0	0	-	0	0--	-	16.21	6.75
2006	Fla	NL	12	0	0	4	10.1	44	9	2	2	0	0	2	0	6	0	11	0	0	0	1	.000	0	0-0	5	3.42	1.74
2007	Fla	NL	2	0	0	1	2.2	13	4	4	4	3	0	0	0	1	0	2	0	0	0	0	-	0	0-0	0	15.48	13.50
	2 ML YEARS		14	0	0	5	13.0	57	13	6	6	3	0	2	0	7	0	13	0	0	0	1	.000	0	0-0	5	5.70	4.15

Pedro Martinez

Pitches: R Bats: R Pos: SP-5   Ht: 5'11" Wt: 193 Born: 10/25/1971 Age: 36

Year	Team	Lg	G	GS	CG	GF	IP	BFP	H	R	ER	HR	SH	SF	HB	TBB	IBB	SO	WP	Bk	W	L	Pct	ShO	Sv-Op	Hld	ERC	ERA
2007	Mets*	R	1	1	0	0	4.0	16	3	3	3	1	0	0	0	1	0	4	0	0	0	0	-	0	0--	-	3.01	6.75
2007	StLuci*	A+	3	3	0	0	14.0	63	13	8	5	2	1	0	1	3	-	13	1	0	1	1	.500	0	0--	-	3.19	3.21
1992	LAD	NL	2	1	0	1	8.0	31	6	2	2	0	0	0	0	1	0	8	0	0	0	1	.000	0	0-0	0	1.38	2.25
1993	LAD	NL	65	2	0	20	107.0	444	76	34	31	5	0	5	4	57	4	119	3	1	10	5	.667	0	2-3	14	2.79	2.61
1994	Mon	NL	24	23	1	1	144.2	584	115	58	55	11	2	3	11	45	3	142	6	0	11	5	.688	1	1-1	0	2.81	3.42
1995	Mon	NL	30	30	2	0	194.2	784	158	79	76	21	7	3	11	66	1	174	5	2	14	10	.583	2	0-0	0	3.19	3.51
1996	Mon	NL	33	33	4	0	216.2	901	189	100	89	19	9	6	3	70	3	222	6	0	13	10	.565	1	0-0	0	3.02	3.70
1997	Mon	NL	31	31	13	0	241.1	947	158	65	51	16	9	1	9	67	5	305	3	1	17	8	.680	4	0-0	0	1.79	1.90
1998	Bos	AL	33	33	3	0	233.2	951	188	82	75	26	4	7	8	67	3	251	9	0	19	7	.731	2	0-0	0	2.78	2.89
1999	Bos	AL	31	29	5	1	213.1	835	160	56	49	9	3	6	9	37	1	313	6	0	23	4	.852	1	0-0	0	1.79	2.07
2000	Bos	AL	29	29	7	0	217.0	817	128	44	42	17	2	1	14	32	0	284	1	0	18	6	.750	4	0-0	0	1.39	1.74
2001	Bos	AL	18	18	1	0	116.2	456	84	33	31	5	2	0	6	25	0	163	4	0	7	3	.700	0	0-0	0	1.84	2.39
2002	Bos	AL	30	30	2	0	199.1	787	144	62	50	13	2	4	15	40	1	239	3	0	20	4	.833	0	0-0	0	1.98	2.26
2003	Bos	AL	29	29	3	0	186.2	749	147	52	46	7	4	4	9	47	0	206	5	0	14	4	.778	0	0-0	0	2.22	2.22
2004	Bos	AL	33	33	1	0	217.0	903	193	99	94	26	5	9	16	61	0	227	2	0	16	9	.640	1	0-0	0	3.44	3.90
2005	NYM	NL	31	31	4	0	217.0	843	159	69	68	19	9	2	4	47	3	208	4	0	15	8	.652	1	0-0	0	2.03	2.82
2006	NYM	NL	23	23	0	0	132.2	550	108	72	66	19	6	5	10	39	2	137	2	1	9	8	.529	0	0-0	0	3.18	4.48
2007	NYM	NL	5	5	0	0	28.0	128	33	11	8	0	1	2	2	7	1	32	1	0	3	1	.750	0	0-0	0	3.80	2.57
16 ML YEARS			447	380	46	23	2673.2	10710	2046	918	833	213	65	58	131	708	27	3030	60	5	209	93	.692	17	3-4	14	2.40	2.80

Ramon Martinez

Bats: R Throws: R Pos: 2B-36; 3B-17; PH-10; SS-8; PR-7; 1B-1   Ht: 6'0" Wt: 190 Born: 10/10/1972 Age: 35

Year	Team	Lg	G	AB	H	2B	3B	HR	(Hm	Rd)	TB	R	RBI	RC	TBB	IBB	SO	HBP	SH	SF	SB	CS	SB%	GDP	Avg	OBP	Slg
2007	LsVgs*	AAA	6	14	5	1	0	0	(-	-)	6	6	2	3	4	0	1	0	0	0	0	0	-	2	.357	.500	.429
1998	SF	NL	19	19	6	1	0	0	(0	0)	7	4	0	4	4	0	2	0	1	0	0	0	-	-	.316	.435	.368
1999	SF	NL	61	144	38	6	0	5	(3	2)	59	21	19	19	14	0	17	0	6	1	1	2	.33	2	.264	.327	.410
2000	SF	NL	88	189	57	13	2	6	(4	2)	92	30	25	31	15	1	22	1	4	1	3	2	.60	6	.302	.354	.487
2001	SF	NL	128	391	99	18	3	5	(1	4)	138	48	37	44	38	6	52	5	6	6	1	2	.33	11	.253	.323	.353
2002	SF	NL	72	181	49	10	2	4	(4	0)	75	26	25	33	14	2	26	4	0	1	2	0	1.00	1	.271	.335	.414
2003	ChC	NL	108	293	83	16	1	3	(1	2)	110	30	34	34	24	1	50	2	6	8	0	1	.00	8	.283	.333	.375
2004	ChC	NL	102	260	64	15	1	3	(1	2)	90	22	30	28	26	3	40	1	7	4	1	0	1.00	5	.246	.313	.346
2005	2 Tms		52	112	31	3	0	1	(1	0)	37	11	14	14	6	0	11	1	4	4	0	0	-	4	.277	.309	.330
2006	LAD	NL	82	176	49	7	1	2	(1	1)	64	20	24	22	15	1	20	1	2	0	0	0	-	9	.278	.339	.364
2007	LAD	NL	67	129	25	4	0	0	(0	0)	29	10	27	11	11	0	15	0	2	5	1	0	1.00	1	.194	.248	.225
05	Det	AL	19	56	15	1	0	0	(0	0)	16	4	5	7	3	0	4	0	2	1	0	0	-	1	.268	.300	.286
05	Phi	NL	33	56	16	2	0	1	(1	0)	21	7	9	7	3	0	7	1	2	3	0	0	-	3	.286	.317	.375
10 ML YEARS			779	1894	501	93	10	29	(18	11)	701	222	235	240	167	14	255	15	38	30	9	7	.56	44	.265	.324	.370

Victor Martinez

Bats: B Throws: R Pos: C-121; 1B-30; DH-3; PH-2   Ht: 6'2" Wt: 195 Born: 12/23/1978 Age: 29

Year	Team	Lg	G	AB	H	2B	3B	HR	(Hm	Rd)	TB	R	RBI	RC	TBB	IBB	SO	HBP	SH	SF	SB	CS	SB%	GDP	Avg	OBP	Slg
2002	Cle	AL	12	32	9	1	0	1	(1	0)	13	2	5	5	3	0	2	0	0	1	0	0	-	1	.281	.333	.406
2003	Cle	AL	49	159	46	4	0	1	(0	1)	53	15	16	17	13	0	21	1	0	1	1	1	.50	8	.289	.345	.333
2004	Cle	AL	141	520	147	38	1	23	(8	15)	256	77	108	90	60	11	69	5	0	6	0	1	.00	16	.283	.359	.492
2005	Cle	AL	147	547	167	33	0	20	(10	10)	260	73	80	90	63	9	78	5	0	7	0	1	.00	16	.305	.378	.475
2006	Cle	AL	153	572	181	37	0	16	(4	12)	266	82	93	96	71	8	78	3	0	6	0	0	-	27	.316	.391	.465
2007	Cle	AL	147	562	169	40	0	25	(12	13)	284	78	114	108	62	12	76	10	0	11	0	0	-	19	.301	.374	.505
6 ML YEARS			649	2392	719	153	1	86	(35	51)	1132	327	416	406	272	40	324	24	0	32	1	3	.25	87	.301	.373	.473

Nick Masset

Pitches: R Bats: R Pos: RP-26; SP-1   Ht: 6'4" Wt: 235 Born: 5/17/1982 Age: 26

Year	Team	Lg	G	GS	CG	GF	IP	BFP	H	R	ER	HR	SH	SF	HB	TBB	IBB	SO	WP	Bk	W	L	Pct	ShO	Sv-Op	Hld	ERC	ERA
2001	Rngrs	R	15	14	0	0	31.0	131	34	21	15	2	0	1	2	7	0	32	1	0	0	6	.000	0	0--	-	4.00	4.35
2002	Savann	A	33	16	0	4	120.1	539	129	75	61	11	4	9	9	47	1	93	11	1	5	8	.385	0	0--	-	4.62	4.56
2003	Clinton	A	30	20	0	6	123.2	557	144	75	56	7	6	6	9	43	0	63	8	3	7	7	.500	0	2--	-	4.74	4.08
2004	Stcktn	A+	16	11	0	0	77.0	323	71	38	30	6	2	3	6	19	0	43	4	0	6	5	.545	0	0--	-	3.19	3.51
2004	Frisco	AA	2	1	0	0	10.0	37	8	2	2	0	0	1	2	4	0	4	0	0	1	0	1.000	0	0--	-	3.63	1.80
2005	Frisco	AA	29	27	1	1	157.1	706	197	124	108	19	3	4	9	61	1	105	9	2	7	12	.368	0	0--	-	6.04	6.18
2006	Frisco	AA	8	8	0	0	48.0	203	38	16	11	0	3	0	2	20	0	40	4	1	2	2	.500	0	0--	-	2.47	2.06
2006	Okla	AAA	24	7	1	8	67.1	306	79	48	36	4	3	2	3	28	1	65	3	0	4	5	.444	0	3--	-	4.96	4.81
2007	Charltt	AAA	11	9	0	1	45.1	191	51	26	23	6	0	2	1	9	0	33	0	1	0	4	.000	0	0--	-	4.34	4.57
2006	Tex	AL	8	0	0	7	8.2	36	9	4	4	0	0	2	2	2	0	4	0	0	0	0	-	0	0-0	0	4.05	4.15
2007	CWS	AL	27	1	0	4	39.1	193	52	33	31	2	1	3	2	26	5	21	4	0	2	3	.400	0	0-1	2	6.63	7.09
2 ML YEARS			35	1	0	11	48.0	229	61	37	35	2	1	5	4	28	5	25	4	0	2	3	.400	0	0-1	2	6.15	6.56

Tom Mastny

Pitches: R **Bats:** R **Pos:** RP-51 **Ht:** 6'6" **Wt:** 220 **Born:** 2/4/1981 **Age:** 27

		HOW MUCH HE PITCHED						WHAT HE GAVE UP											THE RESULTS					
Year	Team	Lg	G	GS	CG	GF	IP	BFP	H	R	ER	HR	SH	SF	HB	TBB	IBB	SO	WP	Bk	W	L	Pct	ShO	Sv-Op Hld	ERC	ERA
2003	Auburn	A-	14	14	0	0	63.2	251	56	19	16	1	0	0	3	12	0	68	2	1	8	0	1.000	0	0-- -	2.37	2.26
2004	CtnWV	A	27	27	0	0	149.0	592	123	44	36	4	9	5	3	41	0	141	7	0	10	3	.769	0	0-- -	2.37	2.17
2005	Knstn	A+	29	11	0	0	88.0	367	78	28	23	4	6	1	5	26	0	94	2	0	7	3	.700	0	2-- -	2.91	2.35
2005	Akron	AA	5	3	0	1	20.2	87	18	7	5	0	0	0	2	5	0	18	1	0	1	1	.500	0	0-- -	2.45	2.18
2006	Akron	AA	12	1	0	6	24.2	100	15	5	3	0	1	1	1	8	1	30	1	0	1	0	1.000	0	1-- -	1.39	1.09
2006	Buffalo	AAA	24	0	0	7	38.0	158	25	11	11	0	2	0	4	16	2	46	2	0	2	1	.667	0	0-- -	2.00	2.61
2006	Cle	AL	15	0	0	12	16.1	73	17	10	10	1	1	2	1	8	1	14	0	0	0	1	.000	0	5-7 0	4.53	5.51
2007	Cle	AL	51	0	0	18	57.2	262	63	30	30	6	3	2	2	32	9	52	5	0	7	2	.778	0	0-0 7	5.16	4.68
	2 ML YEARS		66	0	0	30	74.0	335	80	40	40	7	4	4	3	40	10	66	5	0	7	3	.700	0	5-7 7	5.02	4.86

Julio Mateo

Pitches: R **Bats:** R **Pos:** RP-9 **Ht:** 6'0" **Wt:** 222 **Born:** 8/2/1977 **Age:** 30

		HOW MUCH HE PITCHED						WHAT HE GAVE UP											THE RESULTS					
Year	Team	Lg	G	GS	CG	GF	IP	BFP	H	R	ER	HR	SH	SF	HB	TBB	IBB	SO	WP	Bk	W	L	Pct	ShO	Sv-Op Hld	ERC	ERA
2007	Tacom*	AAA	24	0	0	20	34.2	129	25	4	3	3	1	0	1	2	1	29	1	0	3	1	.750	0	12-- -	1.54	0.78
2007	Rdng*	AA	11	0	0	10	16.0	61	14	5	5	2	1	0	0	1	0	14	0	0	1	0	1.000	0	3-- -	2.36	2.81
2002	Sea	AL	12	0	0	7	21.0	94	20	10	10	2	0	0	1	12	0	15	1	0	0	0	-	0	0-0 2	4.63	4.29
2003	Sea	AL	50	0	0	17	85.2	338	69	32	30	14	2	4	5	13	1	71	1	1	4	0	1.000	0	1-1 2	2.71	3.15
2004	Sea	AL	45	0	0	9	57.2	248	56	30	30	11	0	4	5	16	3	43	2	0	1	2	.333	0	1-4 6	4.26	4.68
2005	Sea	AL	55	1	0	7	88.1	364	79	32	30	12	5	2	7	17	6	52	1	0	3	6	.333	0	0-2 8	3.12	3.06
2006	Sea	AL	48	0	0	13	53.2	241	62	27	25	6	2	5	3	22	8	31	1	0	9	4	.692	0	0-3 7	5.10	4.19
2007	Sea	AL	9	0	0	1	12.0	52	12	5	5	0	0	0	0	5	1	4	0	0	1	0	1.000	0	0-2 0	3.28	3.75
	6 ML YEARS		219	1	0	54	318.1	1337	298	136	130	45	9	15	21	85	19	216	6	1	18	12	.600	0	2-12 25	3.64	3.68

Scott Mathieson

Pitches: R **Bats:** R **Pos:** P **Ht:** 6'3" **Wt:** 190 **Born:** 2/27/1984 **Age:** 24

		HOW MUCH HE PITCHED						WHAT HE GAVE UP											THE RESULTS					
Year	Team	Lg	G	GS	CG	GF	IP	BFP	H	R	ER	HR	SH	SF	HB	TBB	IBB	SO	WP	Bk	W	L	Pct	ShO	Sv-Op Hld	ERC	ERA
2002	Phillies	R	7	2	0	1	16.2	81	24	11	10	0	1	1	2	6	0	14	0	1	0	2	.000	0	0-- -	6.11	5.40
2003	Phillies	R	11	11	0	0	58.2	257	59	42	36	5	1	3	1	13	0	51	4	0	2	7	.222	0	0-- -	3.19	5.52
2003	Batvia	A-	2	0	0	1	6.0	18	0	0	0	0	0	0	0	0	0	7	0	0	0	0	-	0	1-- -	0.00	0.00
2004	Lakwd	A	25	25	1	0	131.1	572	130	73	63	7	0	7	9	50	0	112	9	0	8	9	.471	0	0-- -	3.86	4.32
2005	Clrwtr	A+	23	23	1	0	121.2	508	111	62	56	17	4	5	5	34	0	118	7	0	3	8	.273	0	0-- -	3.53	4.14
2006	Rdng	AA	14	14	0	0	92.2	375	73	35	33	8	3	5	7	29	1	99	1	0	7	2	.778	0	0-- -	2.85	3.21
2006	S-WB	AAA	5	5	0	0	34.1	138	26	16	15	2	1	1	1	10	0	36	3	0	3	1	.750	0	0-- -	2.26	3.93
2007	Phillies	R+	2	2	0	0	2.0	6	0	0	0	0	0	0	0	1	0	3	0	0	0	0	-	0	0-- -	0.32	0.00
2007	Clrwtr	A+	3	2	0	1	4.0	17	3	3	2	0	0	0	0	3	0	5	1	0	0	0	-	0	0-- -	3.44	4.50
2007	Rdng	AA	2	2	0	0	2.0	11	3	3	2	1	0	0	0	2	0	1	0	0	0	0	-	0	0-- -	13.58	9.00
2006	Phi	NL	9	8	0	0	37.1	177	48	36	31	8	6	1	1	16	1	28	2	1	1	4	.200	0	0-0 0	6.71	7.47

Jeff Mathis

Bats: R **Throws:** R **Pos:** C-57; PH-2; PR-1 **Ht:** 6'0" **Wt:** 200 **Born:** 3/31/1983 **Age:** 25

			BATTING															BASERUNNING				AVERAGES		
Year	Team	Lg	G	AB	H	2B	3B	HR	(Hm | Rd)	TB	R	RBI	RC	TBB	IBB	SO	HBP	SH	SF	SB	CS	SB%	GDP	Avg	OBP	Slg
2007	Salt Lk*	AAA	66	260	61	14	2	5	(- | -)	94	39	26	29	17	0	45	2	2	2	3	1	.75	8	.244	.295	.376
2005	LAA	AL	5	3	1	0	0	0	(0 | 0)	1	1	0	0	0	0	1	0	0	0	0	0	-	0	.333	.333	.333
2006	LAA	AL	23	55	8	2	0	2	(1 | 1)	16	9	6	4	7	1	14	0	0	1	0	0	-	0	.145	.238	.291
2007	LAA	AL	59	171	36	12	0	4	(3 | 1)	60	24	23	13	15	0	49	2	3	4	0	1	.00	3	.211	.276	.351
	3 ML YEARS		87	229	45	14	0	6	(4 | 2)	77	34	29	17	22	1	64	2	3	5	0	1	.00	3	.197	.267	.336

Hideki Matsui

Bats: L **Throws:** R **Pos:** LF-112; DH-32 **Ht:** 6'2" **Wt:** 210 **Born:** 6/12/1974 **Age:** 34

			BATTING															BASERUNNING				AVERAGES		
Year	Team	Lg	G	AB	H	2B	3B	HR	(Hm | Rd)	TB	R	RBI	RC	TBB	IBB	SO	HBP	SH	SF	SB	CS	SB%	GDP	Avg	OBP	Slg
2007	Tampa*	A+	2	6	2	0	0	0	(- | -)	2	1	0	0	0	0	0	0	0	0	0	0	-	2	.333	.333	.333
2003	NYY	AL	163	623	179	42	1	16	(9 | 7)	271	82	106	96	63	5	86	3	0	6	2	2	.50	25	.287	.353	.435
2004	NYY	AL	162	584	174	34	2	31	(18 | 13)	305	109	108	117	88	2	103	3	0	5	3	0	1.00	11	.298	.390	.522
2005	NYY	AL	162	629	192	45	3	23	(15 | 8)	312	108	116	109	63	7	78	3	0	8	2	2	.50	16	.305	.367	.496
2006	NYY	AL	51	172	52	9	0	8	(1 | 7)	85	32	29	30	27	2	23	0	0	2	1	0	1.00	6	.302	.393	.494
2007	NYY	AL	143	547	156	28	4	25	(16 | 9)	267	100	103	91	73	2	73	3	0	10	4	2	.67	9	.285	.367	.488
	5 ML YEARS		681	2555	753	158	10	103	(59 | 44)	1240	431	462	443	314	18	363	12	0	31	12	6	.67	67	.295	.371	.485

Kaz Matsui

Bats: B **Throws:** R **Pos:** 2B-102; PH-3; PR-2 **Ht:** 5'10" **Wt:** 185 **Born:** 10/23/1975 **Age:** 32

			BATTING															BASERUNNING				AVERAGES		
Year	Team	Lg	G	AB	H	2B	3B	HR	(Hm | Rd)	TB	R	RBI	RC	TBB	IBB	SO	HBP	SH	SF	SB	CS	SB%	GDP	Avg	OBP	Slg
2007	ColSpr*	AAA	2	6	3	0	0	0	(- | -)	3	1	0	1	2	0	0	0	0	0	1	1	.50	0	.500	.625	.500
2004	NYM	NL	114	460	125	32	2	7	(4 | 3)	182	65	44	63	40	4	97	2	5	2	14	3	.82	3	.272	.331	.396
2005	NYM	NL	87	267	68	9	4	3	(1 | 2)	94	31	24	27	14	1	43	5	5	4	6	1	.86	2	.255	.300	.352
2006	2 Tms	NL	70	243	65	12	3	3	(0 | 3)	92	32	26	28	16	1	46	0	4	2	10	1	.91	1	.267	.310	.379

								BATTING													BASERUNNING				AVERAGES		
Year Team	Lg	G	AB	H	2B	3B	HR	(Hm	Rd)	TB	R	RBI	RC	TBB	IBB	SO	HBP	SH	SF	SB	CS	SB%	GDP	Avg	OBP	Slg
2007 Col	NL	104	410	118	24	6	4	(4	0)	166	84	37	61	34	1	69	0	8	1	32	4	.89	1	.288	.342	.405
06 NYM	NL	38	130	26	6	0	1	(0	1)	35	10	7	5	6	1	19	0	3	0	2	0	1.00	1	.200	.235	.269
06 Col	NL	32	113	39	6	3	2	(0	2)	57	22	19	23	10	0	27	0	1	2	8	1	.89	0	.345	.392	.504
4 ML YEARS		375	1380	376	77	15	17	(9	8)	534	212	131	179	104	7	255	7	22	9	62	9	.87	7	.272	.325	.387

Daisuke Matsuzaka

Pitches: R **Bats:** R **Pos:** SP-32 **Ht:** 6'0" **Wt:** 190 **Born:** 9/13/1980 **Age:** 27

		HOW MUCH HE PITCHED						WHAT HE GAVE UP												THE RESULTS							
Year Team	Lg	G	GS	CG	GF	IP	BFP	H	R	ER	HR	SH	SF	HB	TBB	IBB	SO	WP	Bk	W	L	Pct	ShO	Sv-Op	Hld	ERC	ERA
1999 Seibu	Jap	25	24	6	1	180.0	743	124	55	52	14	-	-	8	87	-	151	5	2	16	5	.762	2	0--	-	2.77	2.60
2000 Seibu	Jap	27	24	6	2	167.2	727	132	85	74	12	-	-	4	95	-	144	2	0	14	7	.667	2	1--	-	3.40	3.97
2001 Seibu	Jap	33	32	12	1	240.1	1004	184	104	96	27	-	-	8	117	-	214	9	1	15	15	.500	2	0--	-	3.38	3.60
2002 Seibu	Jap	14	11	2	0	73.1	302	60	30	30	13	-	-	7	15	-	78	2	1	6	2	.750	0	0--	-	3.14	3.68
2003 Seibu	Jap	29	27	8	1	194.0	801	165	71	61	13	-	-	9	63	3	215	4	0	16	7	.696	2	0--	-	2.94	2.83
2004 Seibu	Jap	23	19	10	0	146.0	601	127	50	47	7	8	6	6	42	0	127	5	0	10	6	.625	5	0--	-	2.78	2.90
2005 Seibu	Jap	28	28	15	0	215.0	868	172	63	55	13	11	1	10	49	0	226	9	0	14	13	.519	3	0--	-	2.30	2.30
2006 Seibu	Jap	25	25	13	0	186.1	722	138	50	44	13	10	6	3	34	0	200	5	0	17	5	.773	2	0--	-	1.86	2.13
2007 Bos	AL	32	32	1	0	204.2	874	191	100	100	25	3	2	13	80	1	201	5	0	15	12	.556	0	0-0	-	4.10	4.40

Gary Matthews Jr.

Bats: B **Throws:** R **Pos:** CF-135; DH-4; PH-1; PR-1 **Ht:** 6'3" **Wt:** 225 **Born:** 8/25/1974 **Age:** 33

								BATTING													BASERUNNING				AVERAGES		
Year Team	Lg	G	AB	H	2B	3B	HR	(Hm	Rd)	TB	R	RBI	RC	TBB	IBB	SO	HBP	SH	SF	SB	CS	SB%	GDP	Avg	OBP	Slg
1999 SD	NL	23	36	8	0	0	0	(0	0)	8	4	7	4	9	0	9	0	0	0	2	0	1.00	1	.222	.378	.222
2000 ChC	NL	80	158	30	1	2	4	(2	2)	47	24	14	13	15	1	28	1	1	0	3	0	1.00	2	.190	.264	.297
2001 2 Tms	NL	152	405	92	15	2	14	(4	10)	153	63	44	51	60	2	100	1	5	1	8	5	.62	8	.227	.328	.378
2002 2 Tms		111	345	95	25	3	7	(6	1)	147	54	38	55	43	1	69	1	5	4	15	5	.75	4	.275	.354	.426
2003 2 Tms		144	468	116	31	2	6	(3	3)	169	71	42	51	43	0	95	2	0	0	12	8	.60	8	.248	.314	.361
2004 Tex	AL	87	280	77	17	1	11	(7	4)	129	37	36	48	33	5	64	1	0	3	5	1	.83	1	.275	.350	.461
2005 Tex	AL	131	475	121	25	5	17	(8	9)	207	72	55	63	47	1	90	0	1	3	2	2	.82	11	.255	.320	.436
2006 Tex	AL	147	620	194	44	6	19	(11	8)	307	102	79	109	58	5	99	4	0	8	10	7	.59	8	.313	.371	.495
2007 LAA	AL	140	516	130	26	3	18	(7	11)	216	79	72	66	55	6	102	2	0	6	18	4	.82	12	.252	.323	.419
01 ChC	NL	106	258	56	9	1	9	(2	7)	94	41	30	31	38	2	55	1	5	0	5	3	.63	4	.217	.320	.364
01 Pit	NL	46	147	36	6	1	5	(2	3)	59	22	14	20	22	0	45	0	0	1	3	2	.60	4	.245	.341	.401
02 NYM	NL	2	1	0	0	0	0	(0	0)	0	0	0	0	0	0	0	0	0	0	0	0	-	0	.000	.000	.000
02 Bal	AL	109	344	95	25	3	7	(6	1)	147	54	38	55	43	1	69	1	5	4	15	5	.75	4	.276	.355	.427
03 Bal	AL	41	162	33	12	1	2	(2	0)	53	21	20	15	9	0	29	1	0	0	0	3	.00	4	.204	.250	.327
03 SD	NL	103	306	83	19	1	4	(1	3)	116	50	22	36	34	0	66	1	0	0	12	5	.71	4	.271	.346	.379
9 ML YEARS		1015	3303	863	184	24	96	(48	48)	1383	506	387	460	363	21	656	12	12	25	82	32	.72	55	.261	.334	.419

Joe Mauer

Bats: L **Throws:** R **Pos:** C-91; DH-19; PH-3 **Ht:** 6'5" **Wt:** 215 **Born:** 4/19/1983 **Age:** 25

								BATTING													BASERUNNING				AVERAGES		
Year Team	Lg	G	AB	H	2B	3B	HR	(Hm	Rd)	TB	R	RBI	RC	TBB	IBB	SO	HBP	SH	SF	SB	CS	SB%	GDP	Avg	OBP	Slg
2007 FtMyrs*	A+	1	3	0	0	0	0	(-	-)	0	0	0	0	1	0	0	0	0	0	0	0	-	0	.000	.250	.000
2004 Min	AL	35	107	33	8	1	6	(4	2)	61	18	17	21	11	0	14	1	0	3	1	0	1.00	9	.308	.369	.570
2005 Min	AL	131	489	144	26	2	9	(4	5)	201	61	55	78	61	12	64	1	0	9	13	1	.93	9	.294	.372	.411
2006 Min	AL	140	521	181	36	4	13	(3	10)	264	86	84	103	79	21	54	1	0	7	8	3	.73	24	**.347**	.429	.507
2007 Min	AL	109	406	119	27	3	7	(2	5)	173	62	60	69	57	10	51	3	2	3	7	1	.88	11	.293	.382	.426
4 ML YEARS		415	1523	477	97	10	35	(13	22)	699	227	216	271	208	43	183	6	2	16	29	5	.85	45	.313	.394	.459

Justin Maxwell

Bats: R **Throws:** R **Pos:** PH-6; CF-5; PR-3; LF-1 **Ht:** 6'5" **Wt:** 225 **Born:** 11/6/1983 **Age:** 24

								BATTING													BASERUNNING				AVERAGES		
Year Team	Lg	G	AB	H	2B	3B	HR	(Hm	Rd)	TB	R	RBI	RC	TBB	IBB	SO	HBP	SH	SF	SB	CS	SB%	GDP	Avg	OBP	Slg
2006 Savann	A	17	58	10	2	2	1	(-	-)	19	8	7	6	8	0	23	2	0	1	1	0	1.00	1	.172	.294	.328
2006 Vrmnt	A-	74	271	73	11	3	4	(-	-)	102	36	33	39	27	0	61	6	0	2	20	5	.80	3	.269	.346	.376
2007 Hgrstn	A-	56	209	63	12	2	14	(-	-)	121	51	40	47	26	0	57	6	0	3	14	3	.82	0	.301	.389	.579
2007 Ptomc	A+	58	228	60	13	0	13	(-	-)	112	35	43	41	24	0	65	4	0	4	21	5	.81	7	.263	.338	.491
2007 Was	NL	15	26	7	0	0	2	(0	2)	13	5	5	4	1	0	8	0	0	0	0	0	-	0	.269	.296	.500

Cameron Maybin

Bats: R **Throws:** R **Pos:** LF-10; PR-8; CF-5; PH-4; DH-2 **Ht:** 6'4" **Wt:** 205 **Born:** 4/4/1987 **Age:** 21

								BATTING													BASERUNNING				AVERAGES		
Year Team	Lg	G	AB	H	2B	3B	HR	(Hm	Rd)	TB	R	RBI	RC	TBB	IBB	SO	HBP	SH	SF	SB	CS	SB%	GDP	Avg	OBP	Slg
2006 WMich	A	101	385	117	20	6	9	(-	-)	176	59	69	73	50	3	116	5	0	5	27	7	.79	9	.304	.387	.457
2007 Tigers	R	2	7	4	0	0	0	(-	-)	4	1	1	2	2	0	2	0	0	0	0	0	-	0	.571	.667	.571
2007 Lkland	A+	83	296	90	14	5	10	(-	-)	144	58	44	61	43	0	83	4	1	6	25	6	.81	5	.304	.393	.486
2007 Erie	AA	6	20	8	1	0	4	(-	-)	21	9	8	9	6	0	6	0	0	0	0	0	-	1	.400	.538	1.050
2007 Det	AL	24	49	7	3	0	1	(0	1)	13	8	2	2	3	0	21	1	0	0	5	0	1.00	0	.143	.208	.265

Paul McAnulty

Bats: L Throws: R Pos: PH-11; RF-5; LF-4　　　　Ht: 5'10" Wt: 220 Born: 2/24/1981 Age: 27

Year Team	Lg	G	AB	H	2B	3B	HR	(Hm	Rd)	TB	R	RBI	RC	TBB	IBB	SO	HBP	SH	SF	SB	CS	SB%	GDP	Avg	OBP	Slg
2007 Padres*	R	6	15	6	1	0	0	(-	-)	7	2	4	3	2	0	2	0	0	0	0	0	-	0	.400	.471	.467
2007 Portlnd*	AAA	63	233	61	12	1	4	(-	-)	87	25	31	31	29	2	47	2	0	1	0	2	.00	2	.262	.347	.373
2005 SD	NL	22	24	5	0	0	0	(0	0)	5	4	0	1	3	1	7	1	1	0	1	0	1.00	0	.208	.321	.208
2006 SD	NL	16	13	3	1	0	1	(1	0)	7	3	3	3	2	0	4	0	0	0	0	0	-	0	.231	.333	.538
2007 SD	NL	20	40	8	1	0	1	(0	1)	12	5	5	3	3	1	10	0	0	0	0	0	-	0	.200	.256	.300
3 ML YEARS		58	77	16	2	0	2	(1	1)	24	12	8	7	8	2	21	1	1	0	1	0	1.00	0	.208	.291	.312

Marcus McBeth

Pitches: R Bats: R Pos: RP-23　　　　Ht: 6'2" Wt: 195 Born: 8/23/1980 Age: 27

Year Team	Lg	G	GS	CG	GF	IP	BFP	H	R	ER	HR	SH	SF	HB	TBB	IBB	SO	WP	Bk	W	L	Pct	ShO	Sv-Op	Hld	ERC	ERA
2005 Kane	A	16	0	0	11	19.2	91	20	11	11	2	0	2	0	13	0	21	4	0	1	2	.333	0	1--	-	5.17	5.03
2005 As	R	8	0	0	8	10.0	41	5	2	1	1	2	0	0	5	0	13	0	0	1	0	1.000	0	4--	-	1.82	0.90
2005 Stcktn	A+	2	0	0	1	2.2	11	1	0	0	0	0	0	1	2	0	3	0	0	0	0	-	0	0--	-	2.87	0.00
2006 Stckn	A+	8	0	0	8	8.2	29	1	0	0	0	0	0	0	2	0	14	0	0	0	0	-	0	7--	-	0.18	0.00
2006 Scrmto	AAA	6	0	0	1	7.1	36	7	9	9	3	0	0	1	6	0	7	2	0	0	1	.000	0	0--	-	8.54	11.05
2006 Mdland	AA	45	0	0	39	54.1	229	43	16	15	4	6	1	0	20	1	65	9	0	3	2	.600	0	25--	-	2.56	2.48
2007 Scrmto	AAA	8	0	0	10	10.0	40	7	3	2	2	1	0	1	3	0	6	0	0	1	0	1.000	0	5--	-	3.14	1.80
2007 Lsvlle	AAA	30	0	0	23	31.2	138	33	12	9	2	1	1	2	7	0	29	3	0	1	1	.500	0	12--	-	3.49	2.56
2007 Cin	NL	23	0	0	7	19.2	88	22	13	13	2	2	1	1	7	1	17	2	0	3	2	.600	0	0-2	3	4.65	5.95

Macay McBride

Pitches: L Bats: L Pos: RP-38　　　　Ht: 5'11" Wt: 210 Born: 10/24/1982 Age: 25

Year Team	Lg	G	GS	CG	GF	IP	BFP	H	R	ER	HR	SH	SF	HB	TBB	IBB	SO	WP	Bk	W	L	Pct	ShO	Sv-Op	Hld	ERC	ERA
2007 Rchmd	AAA	7	5	0	0	23.0	104	26	10	7	3	0	1	1	7	0	24	0	0	1	2	.333	0	0--	-	4.67	2.74
2007 Toledo*	AAA	5	0	0	2	8.0	35	9	4	3	1	0	1	0	5	0	6	0	0	1	0	1.000	0	0--	-	6.32	3.38
2005 Atl	NL	23	0	0	4	14.0	68	18	11	9	0	1	1	0	7	0	22	2	0	1	0	1.000	0	1-1	6	5.12	5.79
2006 Atl	NL	71	0	0	13	56.2	249	53	28	23	2	2	0	1	32	4	46	3	0	4	1	.800	0	1-2	10	3.85	3.65
2007 2 Tms		38	0	0	5	32.2	156	33	21	18	4	1	0	2	25	0	30	2	0	1	1	.500	0	0-0	4	5.98	4.96
07 Atl	NL	18	0	0	4	15.0	75	14	9	6	1	0	0	0	15	0	17	1	0	1	0	1.000	0	0-0	4	5.93	3.60
07 Det	AL	20	0	0	1	17.2	81	19	12	12	3	1	0	1	10	0	13	1	0	0	1	.000	0	0-0	4	5.99	6.11
3 ML YEARS		132	0	0	22	103.1	473	104	60	50	6	4	1	3	64	4	98	7	0	6	2	.750	0	2-3	20	4.67	4.35

Brian McCann

Bats: L Throws: R Pos: C-132; PH-8　　　　Ht: 6'3" Wt: 210 Born: 2/20/1984 Age: 24

Year Team	Lg	G	AB	H	2B	3B	HR	(Hm	Rd)	TB	R	RBI	RC	TBB	IBB	SO	HBP	SH	SF	SB	CS	SB%	GDP	Avg	OBP	Slg
2005 Atl	NL	59	180	50	7	0	5	(2	3)	72	20	23	25	18	5	26	1	4	1	1	1	.50	5	.278	.345	.400
2006 Atl	NL	130	442	147	34	0	24	(10	14)	253	61	93	94	41	8	54	3	0	6	2	0	1.00	12	.333	.388	.572
2007 Atl	NL	139	504	136	38	0	18	(6	12)	228	51	92	68	35	7	74	5	2	6	0	1	.00	19	.270	.320	.452
3 ML YEARS		328	1126	333	79	0	47	(18	29)	553	132	208	187	94	20	154	9	6	13	3	2	.60	36	.296	.351	.491

Brandon McCarthy

Pitches: R Bats: R Pos: SP-22; RP-1　　　　Ht: 6'7" Wt: 200 Born: 7/7/1983 Age: 24

Year Team	Lg	G	GS	CG	GF	IP	BFP	H	R	ER	HR	SH	SF	HB	TBB	IBB	SO	WP	Bk	W	L	Pct	ShO	Sv-Op	Hld	ERC	ERA
2007 Okla*	AAA	1	1	0	0	4.1	16	3	0	0	0	0	0	0	0	0	6	0	0	0	0	-	0	0--	-	0.98	0.00
2005 CWS	AL	12	10	0	0	67.0	277	62	30	30	13	1	1	2	17	0	48	1	1	3	2	.600	0	0-0	0	3.83	4.03
2006 CWS	AL	53	2	0	13	84.2	354	77	44	44	17	3	1	0	33	9	69	5	0	4	7	.364	0	0-1	11	4.10	4.68
2007 Tex	AL	23	22	0	0	101.2	459	111	62	55	9	3	5	3	48	0	59	4	1	5	10	.333	0	0-0	0	4.89	4.87
3 ML YEARS		88	34	0	13	253.1	1090	250	136	129	39	7	7	5	98	9	176	10	2	12	19	.387	0	0-1	11	4.35	4.58

Scott McClain

Bats: R Throws: R Pos: PH-6; 1B-3　　　　Ht: 6'4" Wt: 220 Born: 5/19/1972 Age: 36

Year Team	Lg	G	AB	H	2B	3B	HR	(Hm	Rd)	TB	R	RBI	RC	TBB	IBB	SO	HBP	SH	SF	SB	CS	SB%	GDP	Avg	OBP	Slg
2007 Fresno*	AAA	132	468	125	24	0	31	(-	-)	242	69	100	86	59	2	98	2	0	4	1	2	.33	11	.267	.349	.517
1998 TB	AL	9	20	2	0	0	0	(-	-)	2	2	0	0	2	0	6	1	0	0	0	0	-	0	.100	.217	.100
2005 ChC	NL	13	14	2	1	0	0	(0	0)	3	1	1	0	2	0	2	0	0	0	0	0	-	1	.143	.250	.214
2007 SF	NL	8	11	2	0	0	0	(0	0)	2	1	0	0	0	0	2	0	0	0	0	0	-	0	.182	.182	.182
3 ML YEARS		30	45	6	1	0	0	(0	0)	7	4	1	0	4	0	10	1	0	0	0	0	-	1	.133	.220	.156

Zach McClellan

Pitches: R Bats: R Pos: RP-12　　　　Ht: 6'5" Wt: 190 Born: 11/25/1978 Age: 29

Year Team	Lg	G	GS	CG	GF	IP	BFP	H	R	ER	HR	SH	SF	HB	TBB	IBB	SO	WP	Bk	W	L	Pct	ShO	Sv-Op	Hld	ERC	ERA
2000 Spkane	A-	13	13	0	0	55.1	244	52	24	22	1	2	2	4	29	0	46	3	1	2	3	.400	0	0--	-	3.92	3.58
2001 Burlgtn	A	24	22	0	0	127.0	554	142	79	64	5	2	3	6	36	0	87	7	0	5	10	.333	0	0--	-	4.01	4.54
2002 Wilmg	A+	28	27	0	0	145.1	629	162	76	65	8	7	8	6	43	0	75	4	1	7	9	.438	0	0--	-	4.17	4.03
2003 Wilmg	A+	30	23	1	0	133.0	529	101	51	42	6	4	5	5	39	1	100	5	0	8	8	.500	1	0--	-	2.25	2.84

			HOW MUCH HE PITCHED						WHAT HE GAVE UP													THE RESULTS							
Year	Team	Lg	G	GS	CG	GF	IP	BFP	H	R	ER	HR	SH	SF	HB	TBB	IBB	SO	WP	Bk	W	L	Pct	ShO	Sv-Op	Hld	ERC	ERA
2004	Tulsa	AA	26	23	1	1	138.2	593	145	69	64	17	8	6	10	36	0	111	5	1	4	7	.364	0	1- -	-	4.23	4.15
2005	ColSpr	AAA	44	2	0	9	71.0	323	90	48	47	10	2	2	3	26	2	67	3	0	3	3	.500	0	0- -	-	5.98	5.96
2006	ColSpr	AAA	54	0	0	17	64.2	292	77	33	30	3	3	1	1	29	3	49	5	1	4	3	.571	0	3- -	-	4.97	4.18
2007	ColSpr	AAA	3	0	0	0	4.0	14	2	0	0	0	0	0	0	0	0	3	1	0	1	0	1.000	0	0- -	-	0.54	0.00
2007	Col	NL	12	0	0	1	14.0	63	20	9	9	0	0	1	0	5	2	13	0	0	1	0	1.000	0	0-1	0	5.57	5.79

Seth McClung

Pitches: R **Bats:** R **Pos:** RP-14   **Ht:** 6'6" **Wt:** 260 **Born:** 2/7/1981 **Age:** 27

			HOW MUCH HE PITCHED						WHAT HE GAVE UP													THE RESULTS							
Year	Team	Lg	G	GS	CG	GF	IP	BFP	H	R	ER	HR	SH	SF	HB	TBB	IBB	SO	WP	Bk	W	L	Pct	ShO	Sv-Op	Hld	ERC	ERA
2007	Drham*	AAA	40	0	0	15	58.2	256	38	18	13	3	1	2	4	43	0	68	3	1	1	5	.167	0	5- -	-	3.32	1.99
2007	Nashv*	AAA	5	3	0	0	19.0	74	14	3	3	2	1	0	0	5	0	25	0	0	2	0	1.000	0	0- -	-	2.28	1.42
2003	TB	AL	12	5	0	2	38.2	167	33	23	23	6	1	1	3	25	1	25	2	0	4	1	.800	0	0-0	1	5.11	5.35
2005	TB	AL	34	17	0	3	109.1	500	106	85	80	20	0	5	7	62	1	92	6	0	7	11	.389	0	0-1	2	5.36	6.59
2006	TB	AL	39	15	0	20	103.0	489	120	77	72	14	1	9	3	68	5	59	7	0	6	12	.333	0	6-7	0	6.44	6.29
2007	Mil	NL	14	0	0	1	12.0	51	11	9	5	0	0	1	1	5	0	11	0	0	0	1	.000	0	0-0	0	3.35	3.75
4 ML YEARS			99	37	0	26	263.0	1207	270	194	180	40	2	16	14	160	7	187	15	0	17	25	.405	0	6-8	3	5.64	6.16

Darnell McDonald

Bats: R **Throws:** R **Pos:** RF-3; PH-1   **Ht:** 5'11" **Wt:** 210 **Born:** 11/17/1978 **Age:** 29

			BATTING																	BASERUNNING				AVERAGES		
Year	Team	Lg	G	AB	H	2B	3B	HR	(Hm	Rd)	TB	R	RBI	RC	TBB	IBB	SO	HBP	SH	SF	SB	CS	SB%	GDP	Avg	OBP	Slg
1998	Dlmrva	A	134	528	138	24	5	6	(-	-)	190	87	44	61	33	0	117	5	4	5	35	11	.76	5	.261	.308	.360
1998	Frdrck	A+	4	18	4	2	0	1	(-	-)	9	3	2	3	3	0	6	0	0	0	2	0	1.00	1	.222	.333	.500
1999	Frdrck	A+	130	507	135	23	5	6	(-	-)	186	81	73	68	61	0	92	5	7	7	26	9	.74	13	.266	.347	.367
2000	Bowie	AA	116	459	111	13	5	6	(-	-)	152	59	43	45	29	0	87	4	6	4	11	4	.73	7	.242	.290	.331
2001	Bowie	AA	30	117	33	7	1	3	(-	-)	51	16	21	16	9	0	28	1	0	1	3	3	.50	1	.282	.336	.436
2001	Roch	AAA	104	391	93	19	2	2	(-	-)	122	37	35	33	29	0	75	1	2	2	13	9	.59	8	.238	.291	.312
2002	Bowie	AA	37	144	42	9	1	4	(-	-)	65	21	15	26	22	0	27	2	0	0	9	3	.75	1	.292	.393	.451
2002	Roch	AAA	91	332	96	21	6	6	(-	-)	147	43	35	51	32	0	78	2	1	2	11	3	.79	8	.289	.353	.443
2003	Ottawa	AAA	40	152	45	7	1	0	(-	-)	54	19	20	20	18	0	27	1	1	0	5	7	.42	3	.296	.374	.355
2004	Ottawa	AAA	107	410	96	32	1	7	(-	-)	151	44	44	40	34	0	100	3	2	5	12	6	.67	12	.234	.294	.368
2005	Buffalo	AAA	26	74	20	7	0	1	(-	-)	30	11	4	10	7	0	19	2	0	0	0	1	.00	0	.270	.349	.405
2005	Drham	AAA	73	285	81	13	2	12	(-	-)	134	45	34	56	20	0	62	1	0	0	7	0	1.00	0	.284	.333	.470
2006	Drham	AAA	136	538	157	33	1	14	(-	-)	234	80	57	86	47	3	115	4	4	3	30	12	.71	10	.292	.351	.435
2007	Clmbs	AAA	73	267	84	17	4	2	(-	-)	115	39	41	47	31	3	64	1	0	5	14	5	.74	4	.315	.382	.431
2007	Roch	AAA	61	224	62	12	2	5	(-	-)	93	32	32	36	19	2	35	4	1	4	19	2	.90	5	.277	.339	.415
2004	Bal	AL	17	32	5	1	0	0	(0	0)	6	3	1	2	2	0	6	0	0	0	1	0	1.00	0	.156	.206	.188
2007	Min	AL	4	10	1	0	0	0	(0	0)	1	0	0	0	1	0	3	0	0	0	0	0	-	0	.100	.182	.100
2 ML YEARS			21	42	6	1	0	0	(0	0)	7	3	1	2	3	0	9	0	0	0	1	0	1.00	0	.143	.200	.167

John McDonald

Bats: R **Throws:** R **Pos:** SS-103; 3B-15; PR-8; PH-4   **Ht:** 5'11" **Wt:** 185 **Born:** 9/24/1974 **Age:** 33

			BATTING																	BASERUNNING				AVERAGES		
Year	Team	Lg	G	AB	H	2B	3B	HR	(Hm	Rd)	TB	R	RBI	RC	TBB	IBB	SO	HBP	SH	SF	SB	CS	SB%	GDP	Avg	OBP	Slg
1999	Cle	AL	18	21	7	0	0	0	(0	0)	7	2	0	1	0	0	3	0	0	0	0	1	.00	2	.333	.333	.333
2000	Cle	AL	9	9	4	0	0	0	(0	0)	4	0	0	2	0	0	1	0	0	0	0	0	-	0	.444	.444	.444
2001	Cle	AL	17	22	2	1	0	0	(0	0)	3	1	0	0	1	0	7	1	1	0	0	0	-	0	.091	.167	.136
2002	Cle	AL	93	264	66	11	3	1	(0	1)	86	35	12	24	10	0	50	5	7	2	3	0	1.00	4	.250	.288	.326
2003	Cle	AL	82	214	46	9	1	1	(0	1)	60	21	14	18	11	0	31	2	4	2	3	3	.50	4	.215	.258	.280
2004	Cle	AL	66	93	19	5	1	2	(0	2)	32	17	7	6	4	0	11	0	3	0	0	0	-	2	.204	.237	.344
2005	2 Tms	AL	68	166	46	6	1	0	(0	0)	54	18	16	19	11	0	24	2	3	2	6	1	.86	6	.277	.326	.325
2006	Tor	AL	104	260	58	7	3	3	(1	2)	80	35	23	20	16	0	41	2	6	2	7	2	.78	4	.223	.271	.308
2007	Tor	AL	123	327	82	20	2	1	(1	0)	109	32	31	35	11	0	48	2	12	1	7	2	.78	4	.251	.279	.333
05	Tor	AL	37	93	27	3	0	0	(0	0)	30	8	12	13	6	0	12	2	3	2	5	0	1.00	3	.290	.340	.323
05	Det	AL	31	73	19	3	1	0	(0	0)	24	10	4	6	5	0	12	0	0	0	1	1	.50	3	.260	.308	.329
9 ML YEARS			580	1376	330	59	11	8	(2	6)	435	161	103	125	64	0	216	14	36	9	26	9	.74	30	.240	.279	.316

Dustin McGowan

Pitches: R **Bats:** R **Pos:** SP-27   **Ht:** 6'3" **Wt:** 220 **Born:** 3/24/1982 **Age:** 26

			HOW MUCH HE PITCHED						WHAT HE GAVE UP													THE RESULTS							
Year	Team	Lg	G	GS	CG	GF	IP	BFP	H	R	ER	HR	SH	SF	HB	TBB	IBB	SO	WP	Bk	W	L	Pct	ShO	Sv-Op	Hld	ERC	ERA
2007	Syrcse	AAA	5	5	0	0	22.0	89	16	6	4	0	1	2	0	9	0	29	2	0	0	2	.000	0	0- -	-	2.07	1.64
2005	Tor	AL	13	7	0	2	45.1	205	49	34	32	7	0	4	7	17	0	34	7	0	1	3	.250	0	0-0	1	5.47	6.35
2006	Tor	AL	16	3	0	3	27.1	143	35	27	22	2	0	1	2	25	2	22	3	1	1	2	.333	0	0-1	1	7.72	7.24
2007	Tor	AL	27	27	2	0	169.2	705	146	80	77	14	0	6	2	61	3	144	13	0	12	10	.545	1	0-0	0	3.07	4.08
3 ML YEARS			56	37	2	5	242.1	1053	230	141	131	23	0	11	11	103	5	200	23	1	14	15	.483	1	0-1	2	3.98	4.87

176

Marty McLeary

Pitches: R Bats: R Pos: RP-4
Ht: 6'3" Wt: 225 Born: 10/26/1974 Age: 33

			HOW MUCH HE PITCHED						WHAT HE GAVE UP										THE RESULTS						
Year	Team	Lg	G	GS	CG	GF	IP	BFP	H	R	ER	HR	SH	SF	HB	TBB	IBB	SO	WP	Bk	W	L	Pct	ShO	Sv-Op	Hld	ERC	ERA
2007	Indy*	AAA	24	24	0	0	122.2	541	127	71	63	13	8	5	2	53	1	95	4	1	5	8	.385	0	0- -	-	4.47	4.62
2004	SD	NL	3	0	0	2	3.2	20	7	6	6	2	1	1	0	2	0	4	0	0	0	0	-	0	0-0	0	14.71	14.73
2006	Pit	NL	5	2	0	1	17.2	73	17	5	4	1	0	1	0	6	1	8	1	0	2	0	1.000	0	0-0	0	3.33	2.04
2007	Pit	NL	4	0	0	0	7.2	34	9	8	7	4	0	0	0	2	0	5	0	0	0	0	-	0	0-1	0	7.39	8.22
	3 ML YEARS		12	2	0	3	29.0	127	33	19	17	7	1	2	0	10	1	17	1	0	2	0	1.000	0	0-1	0	5.64	5.28

Mark McLemore

Pitches: L Bats: L Pos: RP-29
Ht: 6'2" Wt: 220 Born: 10/9/1980 Age: 27

			HOW MUCH HE PITCHED						WHAT HE GAVE UP										THE RESULTS						
Year	Team	Lg	G	GS	CG	GF	IP	BFP	H	R	ER	HR	SH	SF	HB	TBB	IBB	SO	WP	Bk	W	L	Pct	ShO	Sv-Op	Hld	ERC	ERA
2002	Mrtnsvl	R+	4	2	0	0	10.0	44	9	3	2	0	0	1	0	5	0	11	0	0	0	1	.000	0	0- -	-	3.12	1.80
2002	TriCity	A-	9	6	0	1	23.0	124	42	37	36	2	0	0	0	17	0	16	3	0	1	5	.167	0	0- -	-	10.86	14.09
2003	Lxngtn	A	36	7	0	9	92.1	420	84	57	47	4	6	8	6	55	5	101	6	0	2	11	.154	0	0- -	-	3.98	4.58
2004	Salem	A+	37	14	1	13	93.1	400	80	38	38	8	4	2	4	44	2	79	2	1	7	7	.500	0	6- -	-	3.60	3.66
2005	CpChr	AAA	15	15	1	0	73.2	310	59	34	23	5	3	0	2	34	0	65	1	0	5	6	.455	0	0- -	-	3.12	2.81
2006	RdRck	AAA	21	9	0	0	57.2	259	48	27	18	5	3	2	6	38	0	52	0	0	2	3	.400	0	0- -	-	4.46	2.81
2007	RdRck	AAA	21	9	0	1	52.0	227	34	20	16	2	3	1	4	35	1	52	2	0	0	1	.000	0	0- -	-	3.01	2.77
2007	Hou	NL	29	0	0	9	35.0	161	38	17	15	5	0	1	1	18	2	35	2	0	3	0	1.000	0	0-2	1	5.28	3.86

Nate McLouth

Bats: L Throws: R Pos: CF-66; PH-50; LF-24; RF-18; PR-3
Ht: 5'11" Wt: 185 Born: 10/28/1981 Age: 26

			BATTING																	BASERUNNING				AVERAGES		
Year	Team	Lg	G	AB	H	2B	3B	HR	(Hm	Rd)	TB	R	RBI	RC	TBB	IBB	SO	HBP	SH	SF	SB	CS	SB%	GDP	Avg	OBP	Slg
2005	Pit	NL	41	109	28	6	0	5	(2	3)	49	20	12	9	3	0	20	5	2	1	2	0	1.00	3	.257	.305	.450
2006	Pit	NL	106	270	63	16	2	7	(3	4)	104	50	16	25	18	0	59	5	3	1	10	1	.91	7	.233	.293	.385
2007	Pit	NL	137	329	85	21	3	13	(5	8)	151	62	38	52	39	2	77	9	3	2	22	1	**.96**	2	.258	.351	.459
	3 ML YEARS		284	708	176	43	5	25	(10	15)	304	132	66	86	60	2	156	19	8	4	34	2	.94	12	.249	.322	.429

Dallas McPherson

Bats: L Throws: R Pos: 3B
Ht: 6'4" Wt: 230 Born: 7/23/1980 Age: 27

			BATTING																	BASERUNNING				AVERAGES		
Year	Team	Lg	G	AB	H	2B	3B	HR	(Hm	Rd)	TB	R	RBI	RC	TBB	IBB	SO	HBP	SH	SF	SB	CS	SB%	GDP	Avg	OBP	Slg
2004	LAA	AL	16	40	9	1	0	3	(2	1)	19	5	6	5	3	0	17	0	0	0	1	0	1.00	0	.225	.279	.475
2005	LAA	AL	61	205	50	14	2	8	(6	2)	92	29	26	28	14	0	64	1	0	0	3	3	.50	5	.244	.295	.449
2006	LAA	AL	40	115	30	4	0	7	(3	4)	55	16	13	16	6	0	40	0	0	0	1	0	1.00	3	.261	.298	.478
	3 ML YEARS		117	360	89	19	2	18	(11	7)	166	50	45	49	23	0	121	1	0	0	5	3	.63	8	.247	.294	.461

Gil Meche

Pitches: R Bats: R Pos: SP-34
Ht: 6'3" Wt: 220 Born: 9/8/1978 Age: 29

			HOW MUCH HE PITCHED						WHAT HE GAVE UP										THE RESULTS						
Year	Team	Lg	G	GS	CG	GF	IP	BFP	H	R	ER	HR	SH	SF	HB	TBB	IBB	SO	WP	Bk	W	L	Pct	ShO	Sv-Op	Hld	ERC	ERA
1999	Sea	AL	16	15	0	0	85.2	375	73	48	45	9	5	3	2	57	1	47	1	0	8	4	.667	0	0-0	0	4.47	4.73
2000	Sea	AL	15	15	1	0	85.2	363	75	37	36	7	5	4	1	40	0	60	2	0	4	4	.500	1	0-0	0	3.60	3.78
2003	Sea	AL	32	32	1	0	186.1	785	187	97	95	30	3	5	3	63	2	130	7	0	15	13	.536	0	0-0	0	4.39	4.59
2004	Sea	AL	23	23	1	0	127.2	565	139	73	71	21	1	3	5	47	0	99	4	0	7	7	.500	1	0-0	0	5.06	5.01
2005	Sea	AL	29	26	0	2	143.1	638	153	92	81	18	1	5	2	72	1	83	4	0	10	8	.556	0	0-0	0	5.15	5.09
2006	Sea	AL	32	32	0	0	186.2	811	183	106	93	24	3	2	8	84	2	156	4	2	11	8	.579	0	0-0	0	4.56	4.48
2007	KC	AL	34	**34**	1	0	216.0	906	218	98	88	22	5	7	3	62	2	156	3	0	9	13	.409	0	0-0	0	3.77	3.67
	7 ML YEARS		181	177	5	2	1031.1	4443	1028	551	509	131	23	29	24	425	8	731	25	2	64	57	.529	2	0-0	0	4.42	4.44

Brandon Medders

Pitches: R Bats: R Pos: RP-30
Ht: 6'1" Wt: 190 Born: 1/26/1980 Age: 28

			HOW MUCH HE PITCHED						WHAT HE GAVE UP										THE RESULTS						
Year	Team	Lg	G	GS	CG	GF	IP	BFP	H	R	ER	HR	SH	SF	HB	TBB	IBB	SO	WP	Bk	W	L	Pct	ShO	Sv-Op	Hld	ERC	ERA
2007	Tucsn*	AAA	35	0	0	16	48.0	220	55	28	25	3	1	2	1	24	2	38	8	0	5	3	.625	0	5- -	-	5.01	4.69
2005	Ari	NL	27	0	0	10	30.1	122	21	6	6	2	0	2	1	11	0	31	1	0	4	1	.800	0	0-0	2	2.25	1.78
2006	Ari	NL	60	0	0	13	71.2	316	76	37	29	5	3	2	2	28	3	47	2	0	5	3	.625	0	0-1	10	4.17	3.64
2007	Ari	NL	30	0	0	7	29.1	128	30	16	14	9	1	0	1	16	0	23	1	0	1	2	.333	0	0-1	1	6.76	4.30
	3 ML YEARS		117	0	0	30	131.1	566	127	59	49	16	4	4	4	55	3	101	4	0	10	6	.625	0	0-2	13	4.22	3.36

Adam Melhuse

Bats: B Throws: R Pos: C-25; 3B-6; PH-5; DH-1; PR-1
Ht: 6'2" Wt: 208 Born: 3/27/1972 Age: 36

			BATTING																	BASERUNNING				AVERAGES		
Year	Team	Lg	G	AB	H	2B	3B	HR	(Hm	Rd)	TB	R	RBI	RC	TBB	IBB	SO	HBP	SH	SF	SB	CS	SB%	GDP	Avg	OBP	Slg
2007	Scrmto*	AAA	2	8	3	2	0	0	(-	-)	5	0	0	1	0	0	3	0	0	0	0	0	-	0	.375	.375	.625
2000	2 Tms	NL	24	24	4	0	1	0	(0	0)	6	3	4	2	3	0	6	0	0	0	0	0	-	1	.167	.259	.250
2001	Col	NL	40	71	13	2	0	1	(0	1)	18	5	8	4	6	0	18	0	0	2	1	0	1.00	3	.183	.241	.254
2003	Oak	AL	40	77	23	7	0	5	(2	3)	45	13	14	15	9	0	19	0	0	0	0	0	-	2	.299	.372	.584
2004	Oak	AL	69	214	55	11	0	11	(3	8)	99	23	31	21	16	1	47	0	1	0	0	1	.00	4	.257	.309	.463
2005	Oak	AL	39	97	24	7	0	2	(1	1)	37	11	12	12	5	0	28	0	0	1	0	0	-	0	.247	.284	.381
2006	Oak	AL	49	128	28	8	0	4	(2	2)	48	10	18	16	9	1	34	1	0	1	0	1	.00	6	.219	.273	.375

Year	Team	Lg	G	AB	H	2B	3B	HR	(Hm	Rd)	TB	R	RBI	RC	TBB	IBB	SO	HBP	SH	SF	SB	CS	SB%	GDP	Avg	OBP	Slg
2007	2 Tms	AL	35	94	20	4	0	1	(1	0)	27	8	9	9	7	0	26	1	1	0	0	0	-	3	.213	.275	.287
00	LAD	NL	1	1	0	0	0	0	(0	0)	0	0	0	0	0	0	1	0	0	0	0	0	-	0	.000	.000	.000
00	Col	NL	23	23	4	0	1	0	(0	0)	6	3	4	2	3	0	5	0	0	0	0	0	-	1	.174	.269	.261
07	Oak	AL	12	26	6	1	0	0	(0	0)	7	2	2	3	4	0	8	0	0	0	0	0	-	0	.231	.333	.269
07	Tex	AL	23	68	14	3	0	1	(1	0)	20	6	7	6	3	0	18	1	1	0	0	0	-	3	.206	.250	.294
7 ML YEARS			296	705	167	39	1	24	(9	15)	280	73	96	73	55	2	178	2	2	3	1	2	.33	19	.237	.293	.397

Kevin Melillo

Bats: L Throws: R Pos: PH-1   **Ht: 5'10" Wt: 195 Born: 5/14/1982 Age: 26**

									BATTING												BASERUNNING				AVERAGES		
Year	Team	Lg	G	AB	H	2B	3B	HR	(Hm	Rd)	TB	R	RBI	RC	TBB	IBB	SO	HBP	SH	SF	SB	CS	SB%	GDP	Avg	OBP	Slg
2004	Vancvr	A-	22	94	32	11	2	2	(-	-)	53	22	21	22	11	0	16	3	0	1	2	1	.67	1	.340	.422	.564
2005	Kane	A	78	280	80	18	3	8	(-	-)	128	47	36	56	53	1	40	3	1	5	10	4	.71	5	.286	.399	.457
2005	Stcktn	A+	22	90	36	7	1	9	(-	-)	72	21	23	30	12	0	18	1	0	1	2	0	1.00	1	.400	.471	.800
2005	Mdland	AA	35	131	37	10	0	7	(-	-)	68	33	34	25	14	0	23	0	0	2	9	2	.82	4	.282	.347	.519
2006	Mdland	AA	136	500	140	31	3	12	(-	-)	213	73	73	83	68	3	97	4	3	6	14	7	.67	11	.280	.367	.426
2007	Scrmto	AAA	98	382	100	27	6	10	(-	-)	169	63	55	62	54	1	100	2	4	1	8	7	.53	3	.262	.355	.442
2007	Oak	AL	1	0	0	0	0	0	(0	0)	0	0	0	0	1	0	0	0	0	0	0	0	-	0	-	1.000	-

Jonathan Meloan

Pitches: R Bats: R Pos: RP-5   **Ht: 6'3" Wt: 230 Born: 7/11/1984 Age: 23**

				HOW MUCH HE PITCHED							WHAT HE GAVE UP											THE RESULTS						
Year	Team	Lg	G	GS	CG	GF	IP	BFP	H	R	ER	HR	SH	SF	HB	TBB	IBB	SO	WP	Bk	W	L	Pct	ShO	Sv-Op	Hld	ERC	ERA
2005	Ogden	R+	16	6	0	5	39.0	166	30	16	16	4	1	2	2	18	0	54	6	1	0	2	.000	0	1--	-	3.23	3.69
2006	Clmbs	A	12	0	0	7	23.1	84	9	5	4	2	0	1	0	7	0	41	0	0	1	1	.500	0	1--	-	1.04	1.54
2006	Jaxnvl	AA	5	0	0	0	10.2	40	3	2	2	1	0	0	0	5	0	23	0	0	1	0	1.000	0	0--	-	1.69	1.69
2006	VeroB	A+	4	3	0	0	18.0	73	15	6	5	2	0	0	1	4	0	27	2	0	1	0	1.000	0	0--	-	2.79	2.50
2007	Jaxnvl	AA	35	0	0	33	45.1	176	24	13	11	3	0	1	2	18	0	70	3	0	5	2	.714	0	19--	-	1.69	2.18
2007	LsVgs	AAA	14	0	0	4	21.1	87	12	5	4	2	0	1	1	9	0	21	1	0	2	0	1.000	0	1--	-	1.99	1.69
2007	LAD	NL	5	0	0	3	7.1	38	8	9	9	1	1	0	1	8	0	7	0	0	0	0	-	0	0-0	0	8.45	11.05

Kevin Mench

Bats: R Throws: R Pos: LF-51; RF-33; PH-30   **Ht: 6'0" Wt: 215 Born: 1/7/1978 Age: 30**

									BATTING												BASERUNNING				AVERAGES		
Year	Team	Lg	G	AB	H	2B	3B	HR	(Hm	Rd)	TB	R	RBI	RC	TBB	IBB	SO	HBP	SH	SF	SB	CS	SB%	GDP	Avg	OBP	Slg
2002	Tex	AL	110	366	95	20	2	15	(8	7)	164	52	60	59	31	0	83	8	2	5	1	1	.50	4	.260	.327	.448
2003	Tex	AL	38	125	40	12	0	2	(1	1)	58	15	11	23	10	0	17	3	0	1	1	1	.50	2	.320	.381	.464
2004	Tex	AL	125	438	122	30	3	26	(14	12)	236	69	71	72	33	2	63	6	0	4	0	0	-	6	.279	.335	.539
2005	Tex	AL	150	557	147	33	3	25	(13	12)	261	71	73	75	50	4	68	5	0	3	4	3	.57	6	.264	.328	.469
2006	2 Tms		127	446	120	24	2	13	(9	4)	187	45	68	57	27	5	59	4	0	5	1	0	1.00	8	.269	.313	.419
2007	Mil	NL	101	288	77	20	3	8	(3	5)	127	39	37	42	16	2	21	1	0	3	3	1	.75	3	.267	.305	.441
06	Tex	AL	87	320	91	18	1	12	(8	4)	147	36	50	48	23	5	42	4	0	2	1	0	1.00	4	.284	.338	.459
06	Mil	NL	40	126	29	6	1	1	(1	0)	40	9	18	9	4	0	17	0	0	3	0	0	-	4	.230	.248	.317
6 ML YEARS			651	2220	601	139	13	89	(48	41)	1033	291	320	328	167	13	311	27	2	21	10	6	.63	29	.271	.326	.465

Luis Mendoza

Pitches: R Bats: R Pos: SP-3; RP-3   **Ht: 6'3" Wt: 180 Born: 10/31/1983 Age: 24**

				HOW MUCH HE PITCHED							WHAT HE GAVE UP											THE RESULTS						
Year	Team	Lg	G	GS	CG	GF	IP	BFP	H	R	ER	HR	SH	SF	HB	TBB	IBB	SO	WP	Bk	W	L	Pct	ShO	Sv-Op	Hld	ERC	ERA
2002	RedSx	R	13	10	0	2	57.2	245	76	36	27	3	2	1	3	8	0	21	4	0	3	4	.429	0	1--	-	4.89	4.21
2003	Augsta	A-	13	11	0	0	59.2	241	46	19	15	1	2	1	5	14	0	29	2	0	3	3	.500	0	0--	-	2.06	2.26
2003	RedSx	R	2	2	0	0	5.0	19	4	0	0	0	0	0	1	0	0	3	0	0	0	0	-	0	0--	-	1.82	0.00
2004	Srsota	A+	25	25	1	0	137.0	596	133	76	57	12	6	8	6	54	5	51	10	0	8	7	.533	0	0--	-	3.88	3.74
2005	Wilmg	A+	23	22	1	1	119.1	539	145	91	84	17	5	8	7	36	0	60	8	0	4	9	.308	0	0--	-	5.43	6.34
2005	Lk Els	A+	2	2	0	0	10.2	51	18	14	11	1	1	0	0	4	0	3	1	0	0	1	.000	0	0--	-	8.46	9.28
2006	Wilmg	A+	13	13	0	0	63.0	270	67	26	22	4	0	2	3	14	-	46	6	0	5	4	.556	0	0--	-	3.62	3.14
2006	Portlnd	AA	9	9	0	0	48.0	226	73	35	34	4	4	0	3	14	1	29	3	1	1	5	.167	0	0--	-	6.93	6.38
2006	Frisco	AA	7	7	0	0	38.1	181	55	33	33	2	0	3	2	11	0	21	7	0	2	4	.333	0	0--	-	5.93	7.75
2007	Frisco	AA	26	25	3	1	148.2	633	145	75	65	11	4	3	10	48	0	93	10	1	15	4	.789	1	0--	-	3.74	3.93
2007	Tex	AL	6	3	0	2	16.0	64	13	4	4	1	0	2	2	4	0	7	0	0	1	0	1.000	0	0-0	0	2.83	2.25

Cla Meredith

Pitches: R Bats: R Pos: RP-80   **Ht: 6'0" Wt: 180 Born: 6/4/1983 Age: 25**

				HOW MUCH HE PITCHED							WHAT HE GAVE UP											THE RESULTS						
Year	Team	Lg	G	GS	CG	GF	IP	BFP	H	R	ER	HR	SH	SF	HB	TBB	IBB	SO	WP	Bk	W	L	Pct	ShO	Sv-Op	Hld	ERC	ERA
2005	Bos	AL	3	0	0	0	2.1	18	6	7	7	1	0	0	1	4	0	0	1	0	0	0	-	0	0-0	0	27.60	27.00
2006	SD	NL	45	0	0	11	50.2	185	30	6	6	3	1	0	2	6	3	37	0	2	5	1	.833	0	0-2	16	1.19	1.07
2007	SD	NL	80	0	0	18	79.2	342	94	38	31	6	1	3	3	17	4	59	3	1	5	6	.455	0	0-5	10	4.28	3.50
3 ML YEARS			128	0	0	29	132.2	545	130	51	44	10	2	3	6	27	7	96	4	3	10	7	.588	0	0-7	26	3.18	2.98

Jose Mesa

Pitches: R Bats: R Pos: RP-56   **Ht: 6'3" Wt: 235 Born: 5/22/1966 Age: 42**

Year	Team	Lg	G	GS	CG	GF	IP	BFP	H	R	ER	HR	SH	SF	HB	TBB	IBB	SO	WP	Bk	W	L	Pct	ShO	Sv-Op	Hld	ERC	ERA
2007	Tol*	AAA	1	1	0	0	2.0	8	2	0	0	0	0	0	0	1	0	0	1	0	0	0	-	0	0- -	1	1.95	0.00
1987	Bal	AL	6	5	0	0	31.1	143	38	23	21	7	0	0	0	15	0	17	4	0	1	3	.250	0	0-0	1	6.67	6.03
1990	Bal	AL	7	7	0	0	46.2	202	37	20	20	2	2	2	1	27	2	24	1	1	3	2	.600	0	0-0	0	3.21	3.86
1991	Bal	AL	23	23	2	0	123.2	566	151	86	82	11	5	4	3	62	2	64	3	0	6	11	.353	1	0-0	0	5.85	5.97
1992	2 Tms	AL	28	27	1	1	160.2	700	169	86	82	14	2	5	4	70	1	62	2	0	7	12	.368	1	0-0	0	4.57	4.59
1993	Cle	AL	34	33	3	0	208.2	897	232	122	114	21	9	9	7	62	2	118	8	2	10	12	.455	0	0-0	0	4.48	4.92
1994	Cle	AL	51	0	0	22	73.0	315	71	33	31	3	3	4	3	26	7	63	3	0	7	5	.583	0	2-6	8	3.31	3.82
1995	Cle	AL	62	0	0	57	64.0	250	49	9	8	3	4	2	0	17	2	58	5	0	3	0	1.000	0	46-48	0	2.06	1.13
1996	Cle	AL	69	0	0	60	72.1	304	69	32	30	6	2	2	3	28	4	64	4	0	2	7	.222	0	39-44	0	3.81	3.73
1997	Cle	AL	66	0	0	38	82.1	356	83	28	22	7	2	2	3	28	3	69	1	0	4	4	.500	0	16-21	9	3.83	2.40
1998	2 Tms		76	0	0	36	84.2	383	91	50	43	8	6	2	4	38	5	63	10	0	8	7	.533	0	1-4	13	4.68	4.57
1999	Sea	AL	68	0	0	60	68.2	325	84	42	38	11	2	4	4	40	4	47	7	0	3	6	.333	0	33-38	1	6.83	4.98
2000	Sea	AL	66	0	0	29	80.2	372	09	48	48	11	2	6	5	41	0	84	3	0	4	6	.400	0	1-3	11	5.60	5.36
2001	Phi	NL	71	0	0	59	69.1	291	65	26	18	4	2	3	2	20	2	59	2	1	3	3	.500	0	42-46	1	3.07	2.34
2002	Phi	NL	74	0	0	64	75.2	331	65	26	25	5	6	1	4	39	7	64	9	0	4	6	.400	0	45-54	0	3.51	2.97
2003	Phi	NL	61	0	0	47	58.0	273	71	44	42	7	1	0	1	31	2	45	3	0	5	7	.417	0	24-28	2	6.07	6.52
2004	Pit	NL	70	0	0	65	69.1	295	78	26	25	6	4	2	1	20	3	37	1	0	5	2	.714	0	43-48	0	4.31	3.25
2005	Pit	NL	55	0	0	48	56.2	257	61	30	30	7	8	6	3	26	3	37	2	0	2	8	.200	0	27-34	1	4.99	4.76
2006	Col	NL	79	0	0	26	72.1	315	73	32	31	9	2	2	5	36	6	39	4	1	1	5	.167	0	1-8	19	4.98	3.86
2007	2 Tms		56	0	0	21	50.2	229	53	48	40	9	2	6	2	25	2	29	3	0	2	3	.400	0	1-1	7	5.35	7.11
92	Bal	AL	13	12	0	1	67.2	300	77	41	39	9	0	3	2	27	1	22	2	0	3	8	.273	0	0-0	0	5.25	5.19
92	Cle	AL	15	15	1	0	93.0	400	92	45	43	5	2	2	2	43	0	40	0	0	4	4	.500	1	0-0	0	4.09	4.16
98	Cle	AL	44	0	0	18	54.0	244	61	36	31	7	2	2	4	20	3	35	2	0	3	4	.429	0	1-3	7	5.07	5.17
98	SF	NL	32	0	0	18	30.2	139	30	14	12	1	4	0	0	18	2	28	8	0	5	3	.625	0	0-1	6	3.99	3.52
07	Det	AL	16	0	0	8	11.2	59	19	16	16	3	0	1	0	6	0	9	0	0	1	1	.500	0	0-0	3	9.87	12.34
07	Phi	NL	40	0	0	13	39.0	170	34	32	24	6	2	5	2	19	2	20	3	0	1	2	.333	0	1-1	4	4.16	5.54
	19 ML YEARS		1022	95	6	633	1548.2	6804	1629	811	750	151	64	62	55	651	57	1038	75	5	80	109	.423	2	321-383	73	4.53	4.36

Randy Messenger

Pitches: R Bats: R Pos: RP-60   **Ht: 6'6" Wt: 240 Born: 8/13/1981 Age: 26**

Year	Team	Lg	G	GS	CG	GF	IP	BFP	H	R	ER	HR	SH	SF	HB	TBB	IBB	SO	WP	Bk	W	L	Pct	ShO	Sv-Op	Hld	ERC	ERA
2005	Fla	NL	29	0	0	8	37.0	178	39	22	22	5	2	3	0	30	7	29	1	0	0	0	-	0	0-0	2	5.91	5.35
2006	Fla	NL	59	0	0	10	60.1	275	72	42	38	8	5	2	1	24	2	45	3	0	2	7	.222	0	0-1	9	5.38	5.67
2007	2 Tms		60	0	0	21	64.1	291	85	30	30	4	6	5	1	21	5	34	1	0	2	4	.333	0	1-5	11	5.32	4.20
07	Fla	NL	23	0	0	8	23.2	103	27	7	7	0	4	1	0	9	2	12	0	0	1	1	.500	0	0-0	6	3.97	2.66
07	SF	NL	37	0	0	13	40.2	188	58	23	23	4	2	4	1	12	3	22	1	0	1	3	.250	0	1-5	5	6.14	5.09
	3 ML YEARS		148	0	0	39	161.2	744	196	94	90	17	13	10	2	75	14	108	5	0	4	11	.267	0	1-6	22	5.48	5.01

Travis Metcalf

Bats: R Throws: R Pos: 3B-55; PH-2; PR-1   **Ht: 6'3" Wt: 215 Born: 8/17/1982 Age: 25**

Year	Team	Lg	G	AB	H	2B	3B	HR	(Hm	Rd)	TB	R	RBI	RC	TBB	IBB	SO	HBP	SH	SF	SB	CS	SB%	GDP	Avg	OBP	Slg
2004	Spkane	A-	72	290	78	21	1	15	(-	-)	146	48	62	52	37	1	74	3	1	4	1	2	.33	6	.269	.351	.503
2005	Bkrsfld	A+	132	505	147	32	7	22	(-	-)	259	80	94	94	49	0	129	6	1	6	0	2	.80	14	.291	.358	.513
2006	Frisco	AA	121	425	94	16	2	8	(-	-)	138	51	37	43	45	2	112	3	0	4	9	7	.56	9	.221	.298	.325
2007	Frisco	AA	55	200	56	18	0	7	(-	-)	95	38	34	34	21	2	44	1	0	4	2	1	.67	3	.280	.345	.475
2007	Okla	AAA	18	61	9	3	0	0	(-	-)	12	2	6	6	7	0	17	0	0	1	0	0	-	3	.148	.232	.197
2007	Tex	AL	57	161	41	12	1	5	(1	4)	70	25	21	20	13	0	41	0	5	2	0	1	.00	6	.255	.307	.435

Dan Meyer

Pitches: L Bats: R Pos: SP-3; RP-3   **Ht: 6'3" Wt: 210 Born: 7/3/1981 Age: 26**

Year	Team	Lg	G	GS	CG	GF	IP	BFP	H	R	ER	HR	SH	SF	HB	TBB	IBB	SO	WP	Bk	W	L	Pct	ShO	Sv-Op	Hld	ERC	ERA
2002	Danvle	R	13	13	1	0	65.2	262	47	22	20	4	2	0	5	18	0	77	4	0	3	3	.500	0	0- -	-	2.19	2.74
2003	Rome	A	15	15	0	0	81.2	330	76	35	26	6	2	1	6	15	1	95	7	0	4	4	.500	0	0- -	-	3.03	2.87
2003	MrtlBh	A+	13	13	0	0	78.1	315	69	29	25	7	1	2	3	17	1	63	1	0	3	6	.333	0	0- -	-	2.84	2.87
2004	Grnville	AA	14	13	0	0	65.0	253	50	17	16	1	4	1	4	12	0	86	2	0	6	3	.667	0	0- -	-	1.87	2.22
2004	Rchmd	AAA	12	11	0	1	61.1	263	62	23	19	6	6	1	1	25	1	60	2	1	3	3	.500	0	0- -	-	4.25	2.79
2005	Scrmto	AAA	19	17	0	0	89.0	411	101	64	53	15	2	2	2	43	0	63	2	0	2	8	.200	0	0- -	-	5.71	5.36
2006	Scrmto	AAA	10	10	0	0	49.2	226	63	34	28	10	2	2	2	20	0	29	4	0	3	3	.500	0	0- -	-	6.74	5.07
2007	Mdland	AA	1	1	0	0	4.0	18	5	3	3	2	0	0	0	4	0	2	1	0	0	0	-	0	0- -	-	13.74	6.75
2007	Scrmto	AAA	21	21	0	0	115.1	483	103	44	42	12	3	5	1	51	4	105	8	0	8	2	.800	0	0- -	-	3.73	3.28
2004	Atl	NL	2	0	0	1	2.0	8	2	0	0	0	0	0	0	1	1	1	0	0	0	0	-	0	0-0	0	3.21	0.00
2007	Oak	AL	6	3	0	2	16.1	79	20	19	16	2	1	1	0	9	0	11	3	0	0	2	.000	0	0-0	0	5.97	8.82
	2 ML YEARS		8	3	0	3	18.1	87	22	19	16	2	1	1	0	10	1	12	3	0	0	2	.000	0	0-0	0	5.67	7.85

179

Jason Michaels

Bats: R **Throws:** R **Pos:** LF-74; RF-27; PH-25; PR-8; DH-2; CF-1   **Ht:** 6'0" **Wt:** 205 **Born:** 5/4/1976 **Age:** 32

Year	Team	Lg	G	AB	H	2B	3B	HR	(Hm	Rd)	TB	R	RBI	RC	TBB	IBB	SO	HBP	SH	SF	SB	CS	SB%	GDP	Avg	OBP	Slg
2001	Phi	NL	6	6	1	0	0	0	(0	0)	1	0	1	0	0	0	2	0	0	0	0	0	-	0	.167	.167	.167
2002	Phi	NL	81	105	28	10	3	2	(0	2)	50	16	11	14	13	1	33	1	0	2	1	1	.50	1	.267	.347	.476
2003	Phi	NL	76	109	36	11	0	5	(1	4)	62	20	17	19	15	1	22	1	0	0	0	0	-	3	.330	.416	.569
2004	Phi	NL	115	299	82	12	0	10	(5	5)	124	44	40	47	42	1	80	2	0	3	2	2	.50	3	.274	.364	.415
2005	Phi	NL	105	289	88	16	2	4	(1	3)	120	54	31	47	44	1	45	4	2	4	3	3	.50	3	.304	.399	.415
2006	Cle	AL	123	494	132	32	1	9	(4	5)	193	77	55	62	43	0	101	3	2	6	9	5	.64	6	.267	.326	.391
2007	Cle	AL	105	267	72	11	1	7	(5	2)	106	43	39	37	20	1	50	3	2	3	3	4	.43	3	.270	.324	.397
	7 ML YEARS		611	1569	439	92	7	37	(16	21)	656	254	194	226	177	5	333	14	6	18	18	15	.55	19	.280	.354	.418

Doug Mientkiewicz

Bats: L **Throws:** R **Pos:** 1B-70; PH-7; PR-1   **Ht:** 6'2" **Wt:** 210 **Born:** 6/19/1974 **Age:** 34

Year	Team	Lg	G	AB	H	2B	3B	HR	(Hm	Rd)	TB	R	RBI	RC	TBB	IBB	SO	HBP	SH	SF	SB	CS	SB%	GDP	Avg	OBP	Slg
2007	Tampa*	A+	5	14	6	3	0	0	(-	-)	9	4	8	4	3	0	1	0	0	0	0	0	-	0	.429	.529	.643
2007	S-WB*	AAA	5	21	8	3	0	1	(-	-)	14	5	7	5	1	0	2	0	0	1	0	0	-	0	.381	.391	.667
1998	Min	AL	8	25	5	1	0	0	(0	0)	6	1	2	2	4	0	3	0	0	0	1	1	.50	0	.200	.310	.240
1999	Min	AL	118	327	75	21	3	2	(0	2)	108	34	32	34	43	3	51	4	3	2	1	1	.50	13	.229	.324	.330
2000	Min	AL	3	14	6	0	0	0	(0	0)	6	0	4	2	0	0	0	0	0	1	0	0	-	1	.429	.400	.429
2001	Min	AL	151	543	166	39	1	15	(11	4)	252	77	74	96	67	6	92	9	0	7	2	6	.25	10	.306	.387	.464
2002	Min	AL	143	467	122	29	1	10	(6	4)	183	60	64	76	74	8	69	6	0	7	1	2	.33	7	.261	.365	.392
2003	Min	AL	142	487	146	38	1	11	(6	5)	219	67	65	89	74	4	55	5	2	6	4	1	.80	9	.300	.393	.450
2004	2 Tms	AL	127	391	93	24	1	6	(1	5)	137	47	35	46	48	2	56	4	2	2	2	3	.40	12	.238	.326	.350
2005	NYM	NL	87	275	66	13	0	11	(3	8)	112	36	29	28	32	7	39	2	2	2	0	1	.00	11	.240	.322	.407
2006	KC	AL	91	314	89	24	2	4	(1	3)	129	37	43	48	35	1	50	5	1	5	3	0	1.00	6	.283	.359	.411
2007	NYY	AL	72	166	46	12	0	5	(4	1)	73	26	24	25	16	0	23	3	6	1	0	0	-	3	.277	.349	.440
04	Min	AL	78	284	70	18	0	5	(1	4)	103	34	25	34	38	2	38	3	2	1	2	2	.50	9	.246	.340	.363
04	Bos	AL	49	107	23	6	1	1	(0	1)	34	13	10	12	10	0	18	1	0	1	0	1	.00	3	.215	.286	.318
	10 ML YEARS		942	3009	814	201	9	64	(32	32)	1225	385	372	446	393	31	438	38	16	33	14	15	.48	72	.271	.358	.407

Aaron Miles

Bats: B **Throws:** R **Pos:** 2B-85; SS-40; PH-19; 3B-3; LF-1   **Ht:** 5'8" **Wt:** 185 **Born:** 12/15/1976 **Age:** 31

Year	Team	Lg	G	AB	H	2B	3B	HR	(Hm	Rd)	TB	R	RBI	RC	TBB	IBB	SO	HBP	SH	SF	SB	CS	SB%	GDP	Avg	OBP	Slg
2003	CWS	AL	8	12	4	3	0	0	(0	0)	7	3	2	3	0	0	0	0	0	0	0	0	-	0	.333	.333	.583
2004	Col	NL	134	522	153	15	3	6	(4	2)	192	75	47	70	29	0	53	2	7	6	12	7	.63	12	.293	.329	.368
2005	Col	NL	99	324	91	12	3	2	(0	2)	115	37	28	42	8	1	38	4	10	1	4	2	.67	6	.281	.306	.355
2006	StL	NL	135	426	112	20	5	2	(1	1)	148	48	30	49	38	9	42	2	2	3	2	1	.67	8	.263	.324	.347
2007	StL	NL	133	414	120	16	1	2	(0	2)	144	55	32	49	25	1	40	1	4	5	2	1	.67	11	.290	.328	.348
	5 ML YEARS		509	1698	480	66	12	12	(5	7)	606	218	139	213	100	11	173	9	23	15	20	11	.65	37	.283	.323	.357

Kevin Millar

Bats: R **Throws:** R **Pos:** 1B-101; DH-34; PH-6; LF-3   **Ht:** 6'0" **Wt:** 215 **Born:** 9/24/1971 **Age:** 36

Year	Team	Lg	G	AB	H	2B	3B	HR	(Hm	Rd)	TB	R	RBI	RC	TBB	IBB	SO	HBP	SH	SF	SB	CS	SB%	GDP	Avg	OBP	Slg
1998	Fla	NL	2	2	1	0	0	0	(0	0)	1	1	0	1	1	0	0	0	0	0	0	0	-	0	.500	.667	.500
1999	Fla	NL	105	351	100	17	4	9	(3	6)	152	48	67	57	40	2	64	7	1	8	1	0	1.00	7	.285	.362	.433
2000	Fla	NL	123	259	67	14	3	14	(6	8)	129	36	42	47	36	0	47	8	0	2	0	0	-	5	.259	.364	.498
2001	Fla	NL	144	449	141	39	5	20	(13	7)	250	62	85	89	39	2	70	5	0	2	0	0	-	8	.314	.374	.557
2002	Fla	NL	126	438	134	41	0	16	(11	5)	223	58	57	63	40	0	74	5	0	6	0	2	.00	15	.306	.366	.509
2003	Bos	AL	148	544	150	30	1	25	(10	15)	257	83	96	87	60	5	108	5	0	9	3	2	.60	14	.276	.348	.472
2004	Bos	AL	150	508	151	36	0	18	(12	6)	241	74	74	90	57	0	91	17	0	6	1	1	.50	16	.297	.383	.474
2005	Bos	AL	134	449	122	28	1	9	(8	1)	179	57	50	58	54	0	74	8	0	8	0	1	.00	12	.272	.355	.399
2006	Bal	AL	132	430	117	26	0	15	(7	8)	188	64	64	67	59	3	74	12	0	2	1	1	.50	14	.272	.374	.437
2007	Bal	AL	140	476	121	26	1	17	(12	5)	200	63	63	71	76	2	94	8	0	2	1	1	.50	8	.254	.365	.420
	10 ML YEARS		1204	3906	1104	257	15	143	(82	61)	1820	546	598	630	462	14	696	75	1	45	7	8	.47	99	.283	.366	.466

Lastings Milledge

Bats: R **Throws:** R **Pos:** RF-28; CF-14; LF-11; PH-9; PR-1   **Ht:** 6'0" **Wt:** 203 **Born:** 4/5/1985 **Age:** 23

Year	Team	Lg	G	AB	H	2B	3B	HR	(Hm	Rd)	TB	R	RBI	RC	TBB	IBB	SO	HBP	SH	SF	SB	CS	SB%	GDP	Avg	OBP	Slg
2003	Kngspt	R+	7	26	6	2	0	0	(-	-)	8	4	2	4	3	0	4	1	0	1	5	1	.83	0	.231	.323	.308
2004	CptCty	A	65	261	88	22	1	13	(-	-)	151	66	58	60	17	1	53	12	1	3	23	6	.79	3	.337	.399	.579
2004	StLuci	A+	22	81	19	6	2	2	(-	-)	35	6	8	11	9	0	21	1	2	0	3	2	.60	3	.235	.319	.432
2005	StLuci	A+	62	232	70	15	0	4	(-	-)	97	48	22	38	19	1	41	13	4	1	18	13	.58	5	.302	.385	.418
2005	Bnghtn	AA	48	193	65	17	0	4	(-	-)	94	33	24	36	14	1	47	4	2	1	11	5	.69	1	.337	.392	.487
2006	Norfolk	AAA	84	307	85	21	4	7	(-	-)	135	52	36	55	43	1	67	14	1	2	13	10	.57	1	.277	.388	.440
2007	Mets	R	2	7	1	1	0	0	(-	-)	2	1	0	0	1	0	2	1	0	0	0	1	.00	1	.143	.333	.286
2007	StLuci	A+	1	4	1	0	0	0	(-	-)	1	2	0	0	1	0	0	0	0	0	0	0	-	0	.250	.400	.250
2007	NewOr	AAA	11	39	13	1	0	1	(-	-)	17	9	5	7	2	0	12	1	0	1	5	0	1.00	1	.333	.372	.436
2007	Bnghtn	AA	5	23	10	1	1	3	(-	-)	22	7	8	8	0	0	4	1	0	0	1	0	1.00	0	.435	.458	.957
2006	NYM	NL	56	166	40	7	2	4	(2	2)	63	14	22	21	12	4	39	5	1	1	1	2	.33	4	.241	.310	.380
2007	NYM	NL	59	184	50	9	1	7	(6	1)	82	27	29	27	13	2	42	7	1	1	3	2	.60	5	.272	.341	.446
	2 ML YEARS		115	350	90	16	3	11	(8	3)	145	41	51	48	25	6	81	12	2	2	4	4	.50	9	.257	.326	.414

Andrew Miller

Pitches: L Bats: L Pos: SP-13   Ht: 6'6" Wt: 210 Born: 5/21/1985 Age: 23

			HOW MUCH HE PITCHED					WHAT HE GAVE UP										THE RESULTS							
Year	Team	Lg	G	GS	CG	GF	IP	BFP	H	R	ER	HR	SH	SF	HB	TBB	IBB	SO	WP	Bk	W	L	Pct	ShO	Sv-Op	Hld	ERC	ERA
2006	Lkland	A+	3	0	0	0	5.0	19	2	0	0	0	0	0	1	1	0	9	1	0	0	0	-	0	0- -	-	0.95	0.00
2007	Lkland	A+	9	7	2	0	43.1	190	45	21	16	1	0	0	3	16	0	29	3	0	1	4	.200	1	0- -	-	3.87	3.32
2007	Erie	AA	4	4	0	0	30.2	116	22	3	3	2	1	0	4	5	0	24	2	0	2	0	1.000	0	0- -	-	2.15	0.88
2007	Toledo	AAA	2	2	0	0	6.0	29	6	6	6	0	0	0	0	5	0	9	1	0	0	0	-	0	0- -	-	4.85	9.00
2006	Det	AL	8	0	0	3	10.1	51	8	9	7	0	0	0	2	10	0	6	1	0	0	1	.000	0	0-0	1	4.79	6.10
2007	Det	AL	13	13	0	0	64.0	309	73	43	40	8	3	1	7	39	0	56	4	1	5	5	.500	0	0-0	0	6.31	5.63
2 ML YEARS			21	13	0	3	74.1	360	81	52	47	8	3	1	9	49	0	62	5	1	5	6	.455	0	0-0	1	6.10	5.69

Corky Miller

Bats: R Throws: R Pos: C-11; PH-1   Ht: 6'1" Wt: 245 Born: 3/18/1976 Age: 32

								BATTING												BASERUNNING				AVERAGES		
Year	Team	Lg	G	AB	H	2B	3B	HR	(Hm	Rd)	TB	R	RBI	RC	TBB	IBB	SO	HBP	SH	SF	SB	CS	SB%	GDP	Avg	OBP	Slg
2007	Rchmd*	AAA	65	181	38	8	0	4	(-	-)	58	12	25	24	25	1	26	13	0	3	4	0	1.00	9	.210	.342	.320
2001	Cin	NL	17	49	9	2	0	3	(1	2)	20	5	7	6	4	0	16	2	0	2	1	0	1.00	1	.184	.263	.408
2002	Cin	NL	39	114	29	10	0	3	(2	1)	48	9	15	15	9	2	20	4	1	1	0	0	-	7	.254	.328	.421
2003	Cin	NL	14	30	8	0	0	0	(0	0)	8	4	1	5	5	0	7	2	0	1	0	0	-	1	.267	.395	.267
2004	Cin	NL	13	39	1	0	0	0	(0	0)	1	2	3	0	6	0	12	3	0	1	0	0	-	3	.026	.204	.026
2005	Min	AL	5	12	0	0	0	0	(0	0)	0	0	0	0	0	0	2	0	0	0	0	0	-	0	.000	.000	.000
2006	Bos	AL	1	4	0	0	0	0	(0	0)	0	0	0	0	0	0	1	0	0	0	0	0	-	0	.000	.000	.000
2007	Atl	NL	12	27	7	2	0	1	(0	1)	12	3	4	4	1	0	5	1	0	0	0	0	-	1	.259	.310	.444
7 ML YEARS			101	275	54	14	0	7	(3	4)	89	23	30	30	25	2	63	12	1	5	1	0	1.00	13	.196	.287	.324

Damian Miller

Bats: R Throws: R Pos: C-56; 1B-1; PH-1   Ht: 6'3" Wt: 220 Born: 10/13/1969 Age: 38

								BATTING												BASERUNNING				AVERAGES		
Year	Team	Lg	G	AB	H	2B	3B	HR	(Hm	Rd)	TB	R	RBI	RC	TBB	IBB	SO	HBP	SH	SF	SB	CS	SB%	GDP	Avg	OBP	Slg
1997	Min	AL	25	66	18	1	0	2	(1	1)	25	5	13	7	2	0	12	0	0	3	0	0	-	2	.273	.282	.379
1998	Ari	NL	57	168	48	14	2	3	(2	1)	75	17	14	25	11	2	43	2	2	0	1	0	1.00	2	.286	.337	.446
1999	Ari	NL	86	296	80	19	0	11	(3	8)	132	35	47	40	19	3	78	2	0	3	0	0	-	7	.270	.316	.446
2000	Ari	NL	100	324	89	24	0	10	(6	4)	143	43	44	49	36	4	74	1	1	2	2	2	.50	6	.275	.347	.441
2001	Ari	NL	123	380	103	19	0	13	(9	4)	161	45	47	52	35	9	80	4	4	2	0	1	.00	9	.271	.337	.424
2002	Ari	NL	101	297	74	22	0	11	(4	7)	129	40	42	35	38	5	88	3	2	0	0	0	-	14	.249	.340	.434
2003	ChC	NL	114	352	82	19	1	9	(6	3)	130	34	36	36	39	6	91	1	7	1	1	0	1.00	15	.233	.310	.369
2004	Oak	AL	110	397	108	25	0	9	(5	4)	160	39	58	54	39	0	87	2	2	2	0	1	.00	19	.272	.339	.403
2005	Mil	NL	114	385	105	25	1	9	(3	6)	159	50	43	39	37	6	94	4	2	3	0	1	.00	16	.273	.340	.413
2006	Mil	NL	101	331	83	28	0	6	(5	1)	129	34	38	38	33	7	86	4	3	5	0	0	-	11	.251	.322	.390
2007	Mil	NL	58	186	44	9	0	4	(1	3)	65	19	24	17	14	0	39	3	0	3	1	0	1.00	8	.237	.296	.349
11 ML YEARS			989	3182	834	205	4	87	(45	42)	1308	361	406	392	303	42	772	26	23	24	5	5	.50	109	.262	.329	.411

Jason Miller

Pitches: L Bats: L Pos: RP-4   Ht: 6'1" Wt: 195 Born: 7/20/1982 Age: 25

			HOW MUCH HE PITCHED					WHAT HE GAVE UP										THE RESULTS							
Year	Team	Lg	G	GS	CG	GF	IP	BFP	H	R	ER	HR	SH	SF	HB	TBB	IBB	SO	WP	Bk	W	L	Pct	ShO	Sv-Op	Hld	ERC	ERA
2000	Twins	R	2	1	0	0	4.0	15	2	1	0	0	1	0	0	0	0	3	0	0	0	0	-	0	0- -	-	0.50	0.00
2000	Elizab	R+	9	5	0	0	26.0	104	23	16	13	7	0	1	1	5	0	22	0	1	2	1	.667	0	0- -	-	3.89	4.50
2001	Elizab	R+	12	11	1	0	53.1	228	46	26	24	4	1	3	4	19	0	66	3	1	4	3	.571	0	0- -	-	3.22	4.05
2002	QuadC	A	23	8	0	6	65.1	270	55	23	17	7	0	0	2	22	0	71	2	0	2	2	.500	0	0- -	-	3.15	2.34
2003	QuadC	A	13	12	0	0	68.2	285	67	25	18	4	4	2	4	21	0	50	4	0	5	1	.833	0	0- -	-	3.61	2.36
2003	FtMyrs	A+	13	10	0	1	51.0	224	60	30	24	3	1	1	1	21	0	39	3	0	3	4	.429	0	0- -	-	5.04	4.24
2004	FtMyrs	A+	19	0	0	5	29.1	116	16	5	5	2	0	0	1	11	1	40	1	0	1	0	1.000	0	1- -	-	1.61	1.53
2004	NwBrit	AA	33	1	0	7	40.0	174	33	19	19	2	0	0	2	21	1	42	2	2	0	2	.000	0	2- -	-	3.36	4.28
2005	NwBrit	AA	25	0	0	10	48.2	204	34	17	15	5	3	1	0	22	2	56	1	0	1	2	.333	0	4- -	-	2.56	2.77
2005	Roch	AAA	13	0	0	3	26.0	121	28	14	11	4	0	1	0	17	0	27	2	0	2	0	1.000	0	0- -	-	5.95	3.81
2006	Roch	AAA	32	15	1	8	99.1	425	101	48	42	10	1	3	3	36	1	87	4	1	3	8	.273	1	1- -	-	4.17	3.81
2007	Roch	AAA	31	10	0	7	75.1	323	84	35	33	10	5	3	0	24	4	37	0	0	1	5	.167	0	0- -	-	4.61	3.94
2007	Min	AL	4	0	0	1	4.0	22	7	8	8	2	0	0	0	3	1	2	0	0	0	0	-	0	0-0	0	13.58	18.00

Justin Miller

Pitches: R Bats: R Pos: RP-62   Ht: 6'2" Wt: 200 Born: 8/27/1977 Age: 30

			HOW MUCH HE PITCHED					WHAT HE GAVE UP										THE RESULTS							
Year	Team	Lg	G	GS	CG	GF	IP	BFP	H	R	ER	HR	SH	SF	HB	TBB	IBB	SO	WP	Bk	W	L	Pct	ShO	Sv-Op	Hld	ERC	ERA
2007	Ottawa*	AAA	3	0	0	2	2.1	13	4	1	1	0	0	0	0	3	0	2	0	0	0	0	-	0	0- -	-	12.21	3.86
2007	Albq*	AAA	11	0	0	11	12.0	50	9	3	2	0	0	0	0	4	0	20	1	0	0	0	-	0	6- -	-	1.84	1.50
2002	Tor	AL	25	18	0	2	102.1	469	103	70	63	17	6	1	11	66	2	68	6	0	9	5	.643	0	0-0	1	5.73	5.54
2004	Tor	AL	19	15	0	0	81.2	375	101	58	55	14	2	6	5	42	3	47	3	1	3	4	.429	0	0-0	0	6.91	6.06
2005	Tor	AL	1	0	0	0	2.1	12	5	4	4	3	0	0	0	0	0	2	0	0	0	0	-	0	0-0	0	20.19	15.43
2007	Fla	NL	62	0	0	10	61.2	259	53	27	25	5	3	0	0	24	6	74	4	1	5	0	1.000	0	0-3	17	2.98	3.65
4 ML YEARS			107	33	0	12	248.0	1115	262	159	147	34	6	12	16	132	11	191	13	2	17	9	.654	0	0-3	18	5.48	5.33

Matt Miller

Pitches: R **Bats:** R **Pos:** RP-2 **Ht:** 6'3" **Wt:** 215 **Born:** 11/23/1971 **Age:** 36

Year	Team	Lg	G	GS	CG	GF	IP	BFP	H	R	ER	HR	SH	SF	HB	TBB	IBB	SO	WP	Bk	W	L	Pct	ShO	Sv-Op	Hld	ERC	ERA
2007	Buffalo*	AAA	38	0	0	13	37.1	156	25	16	12	4	8	0	2	21	2	36	1	0	0	1	.000	0	1- -	1	3.11	2.89
2003	Col	NL	4	0	0	2	4.1	18	5	1	1	0	0	0	0	2	0	5	0	0	0	0	-	0	0-0	0	4.86	2.08
2004	Cle	AL	57	0	0	13	55.1	226	42	22	19	1	2	1	6	23	8	55	1	1	4	1	.800	0	1-2	7	2.56	3.09
2005	Cle	AL	23	0	0	4	29.2	118	22	6	6	1	0	1	3	10	3	23	1	1	0	1	.000	0	1-2	4	2.37	1.82
2006	Cle	AL	14	0	0	3	15.2	65	11	6	6	2	0	2	2	9	0	12	0	0	1	0	1.000	0	0-0	1	3.98	3.45
2007	Cle	AL	2	0	0	2	1.0	5	2	0	0	0	0	0	0	0	0	0	0	0	0	0	-	0	0-0	0	7.48	0.00
	5 ML YEARS		100	0	0	24	106.0	432	82	35	32	4	2	4	11	44	11	95	2	2	6	1	.857	0	2-4	12	2.83	2.72

Trever Miller

Pitches: L **Bats:** R **Pos:** RP-76 **Ht:** 6'3" **Wt:** 200 **Born:** 5/29/1973 **Age:** 35

Year	Team	Lg	G	GS	CG	GF	IP	BFP	H	R	ER	HR	SH	SF	HB	TBB	IBB	SO	WP	Bk	W	L	Pct	ShO	Sv-Op	Hld	ERC	ERA
1996	Det	AL	5	4	0	0	16.2	88	28	17	17	3	2	2	2	9	0	8	0	0	0	4	.000	0	0-0	0	10.15	9.18
1998	Hou	NL	37	1	0	15	53.1	235	57	21	18	4	0	0	1	20	1	30	1	0	2	0	1.000	0	1-2	1	4.18	3.04
1999	Hou	NL	47	0	0	11	49.2	232	58	29	28	6	2	2	5	29	1	37	4	0	3	2	.600	0	1-1	4	6.48	5.07
2000	2 Tms	NL	16	0	0	2	16.1	90	27	22	19	3	1	1	2	12	1	11	1	0	0	0	-	0	0-0	0	10.68	10.47
2003	Tor	AL	79	0	0	18	52.2	233	46	30	27	7	1	0	5	28	3	44	2	0	2	2	.500	0	3-4	16	4.38	4.61
2004	TB	AL	60	0	0	15	49.0	208	48	21	17	3	3	0	3	15	4	43	2	0	1	1	.500	0	1-3	9	3.45	3.12
2005	TB	AL	61	0	0	13	44.1	206	45	23	20	4	3	5	7	29	6	35	2	0	2	2	.500	0	0-3	11	5.57	4.06
2006	Hou	NL	70	0	0	14	50.2	207	42	17	17	7	1	2	4	13	2	56	1	0	2	3	.400	0	1-3	12	3.11	3.02
2007	Hou	NL	76	0	0	12	46.1	211	45	26	25	6	3	0	4	23	6	46	1	0	0	0	-	0	1-3	12	4.52	4.86
00	Phi	NL	14	0	0	2	14.0	72	19	16	13	3	1	1	1	9	1	10	1	0	0	0	-	0	0-0	0	8.14	8.36
00	LAD	NL	2	0	0	0	2.1	18	8	6	6	0	0	0	1	3	0	1	0	0	0	0	-	0	0-0	0	28.18	23.14
	9 ML YEARS		451	5	0	100	379.0	1710	396	206	188	43	16	12	33	178	24	310	14	0	12	14	.462	0	8-19	65	4.94	4.46

Wade Miller

Pitches: R **Bats:** R **Pos:** SP-3 **Ht:** 6'2" **Wt:** 210 **Born:** 9/13/1976 **Age:** 31

Year	Team	Lg	G	GS	CG	GF	IP	BFP	H	R	ER	HR	SH	SF	HB	TBB	IBB	SO	WP	Bk	W	L	Pct	ShO	Sv-Op	Hld	ERC	ERA
2007	Peoria*	A	1	1	0	0	3.0	13	4	2	2	0	0	1	0	0	0	5	0	0	0	0	-	0	0- -		3.56	6.00
2007	Tenn*	AA	2	1	0	0	8.2	42	13	10	10	1	0	1	0	4	0	7	0	0	0	1	.000	0	0- -		7.51	10.38
2007	Iowa*	AAA	3	3	0	0	14.0	60	12	5	5	0	2	1	0	6	0	12	1	0	0	1	.000	0	0- -		2.67	3.21
1999	Hou	NL	5	1	0	2	10.1	52	17	11	11	4	0	0	0	5	0	8	0	0	0	1	.000	0	0-0	0	11.07	9.58
2000	Hou	NL	16	16	2	0	105.0	453	104	66	60	14	3	1	3	42	1	89	1	0	6	6	.500	0			4.37	5.14
2001	Hou	NL	32	32	1	0	212.0	873	183	91	80	31	7	5	4	76	3	183	8	0	16	8	.667	0			3.57	3.40
2002	Hou	NL	26	26	1	0	164.2	688	151	63	60	14	8	5	6	62	9	144	4	0	15	4	.789	1			3.54	3.28
2003	Hou	NL	33	33	1	0	187.1	797	168	96	86	17	8	7	10	77	1	161	4	0	14	13	.519	0			3.70	4.13
2004	Hou	NL	15	15	0	0	88.2	383	76	35	33	11	5	1	0	44	0	74	1	0	7	7	.500	0			3.78	3.35
2005	Bos	AL	16	16	0	0	91.0	414	96	53	50	8	1	4	3	47	0	64	6	0	4	4	.500	0			4.84	4.95
2006	ChC	NL	5	5	0	0	21.2	103	19	12	11	4	2	0	1	18	1	20	1	0	0	2	.000	0			5.73	4.57
2007	ChC	NL	3	3	0	0	13.2	70	24	16	16	5	1	0	0	6	0	6	0	0	0	1	.000	0			11.40	10.54
	9 ML YEARS		151	147	5	2	894.1	3833	838	443	407	108	35	23	27	377	15	749	25	0	62	46	.574	1	0-0	0	4.06	4.10

Kevin Millwood

Pitches: R **Bats:** R **Pos:** SP-31 **Ht:** 6'4" **Wt:** 230 **Born:** 12/24/1974 **Age:** 33

Year	Team	Lg	G	GS	CG	GF	IP	BFP	H	R	ER	HR	SH	SF	HB	TBB	IBB	SO	WP	Bk	W	L	Pct	ShO	Sv-Op	Hld	ERC	ERA
2007	Frisco*	AA	1	1	0	0	5.0	17	1	0	0	0	0	0	0	1	0	3	0	0	0	0	-	0	0- -	-	0.27	0.00
1997	Atl	NL	12	8	0	2	51.1	227	55	26	23	1	3	5	2	21	1	42	1	0	5	3	.625	0	0-0	0	4.03	4.03
1998	Atl	NL	31	29	3	1	174.1	748	175	86	79	18	8	3	3	56	3	163	6	1	17	8	.680	1	0-0	1	3.81	4.08
1999	Atl	NL	33	33	2	0	228.0	906	168	80	68	24	9	3	4	59	2	205	5	0	18	7	.720	0	0-0	0	2.26	2.68
2000	Atl	NL	36	35	0	0	212.2	903	213	115	110	26	8	5	3	62	2	168	4	0	10	13	.435	0	0-0	0	3.83	4.66
2001	Atl	NL	21	21	0	0	121.0	515	121	66	58	20	7	2	1	40	6	84	5	1	7	7	.500	0	0-0	0	4.20	4.31
2002	Atl	NL	35	34	1	0	217.0	895	186	83	78	16	9	4	8	65	7	178	4	0	18	8	.692	1	0-0	0	2.85	3.24
2003	Phi	NL	35	35	5	0	222.0	930	210	103	99	19	12	5	4	68	6	169	2	0	14	12	.538	3	0-0	0	3.35	4.01
2004	Phi	NL	25	25	0	0	141.0	628	155	81	76	14	11	2	7	51	5	125	4	0	9	6	.600	0	0-0	0	4.57	4.85
2005	Cle	AL	30	30	1	0	192.0	799	182	72	61	20	6	4	4	52	0	146	2	0	9	11	.450	0	0-0	0	3.40	2.86
2006	Tex	AL	34	34	2	0	215.0	907	228	114	108	23	8	3	4	53	4	157	6	0	16	12	.571	0	0-0	0	3.92	4.52
2007	Tex	AL	31	31	0	0	172.2	788	213	111	99	19	1	4	8	67	2	123	4	0	10	14	.417	0	0-0	0	5.64	5.16
	11 ML YEARS		323	315	14	3	1947.0	8246	1906	937	859	200	82	40	48	594	38	1560	43	2	133	101	.568	5	0-0	1	3.66	3.97

Eric Milton

Pitches: L **Bats:** L **Pos:** SP-6 **Ht:** 6'3" **Wt:** 218 **Born:** 8/4/1975 **Age:** 32

Year	Team	Lg	G	GS	CG	GF	IP	BFP	H	R	ER	HR	SH	SF	HB	TBB	IBB	SO	WP	Bk	W	L	Pct	ShO	Sv-Op	Hld	ERC	ERA
1998	Min	AL	32	32	1	0	172.1	772	195	113	108	25	2	6	2	70	0	107	1	0	8	14	.364	0	0-0	0	5.21	5.64
1999	Min	AL	34	34	4	0	206.1	858	190	111	103	28	3	6	3	63	2	163	2	0	7	11	.389	2	0-0	0	3.56	4.49
2000	Min	AL	33	33	0	0	200.0	849	205	123	108	35	4	6	7	44	0	160	5	0	13	10	.565	0	0-0	0	4.09	4.86
2001	Min	AL	35	34	2	0	220.2	944	222	109	106	35	8	6	5	61	0	157	2	0	15	7	.682	1	0-0	0	4.05	4.32
2002	Min	AL	29	29	2	0	171.0	707	173	96	92	24	0	4	3	30	0	121	4	0	13	9	.591	1	0-0	0	3.59	4.84
2003	Min	AL	3	3	0	0	17.0	66	15	5	5	2	0	1	0	1	0	7	0	0	0	1	.000	0	0-0	0	2.29	2.65
2004	Phi	NL	34	34	0	0	201.0	862	196	110	106	43	11	6	1	75	6	161	3	0	14	6	.700	0	0-0	0	4.57	4.75

Year	Team	Lg	G	GS	CG	GF	IP	BFP	H	R	ER	HR	SH	SF	HB	TBB	IBB	SO	WP	Bk	W	L	Pct	ShO	Sv-Op	Hld	ERC	ERA
2005	Cin	NL	34	34	0	0	186.1	855	237	141	134	40	6	6	7	52	2	123	8	0	8	15	.348	0	0-0	0	6.03	6.47
2006	Cin	NL	26	26	0	0	152.2	662	163	94	88	29	6	3	5	42	4	90	2	0	8	8	.500	0	0-0	0	4.62	5.19
2007	Cin	NL	6	6	0	0	31.1	143	39	21	18	4	3	0	0	9	0	18	2	0	0	4	.000	0	0-0	0	5.07	5.17
10 ML YEARS			266	265	9	0	1558.2	6718	1635	923	868	265	43	44	33	447	14	1107	29	0	87	84	.509	4	0-0	0	4.41	5.01

Zach Miner

Pitches: R **Bats:** R **Pos:** RP-33; SP-1 **Ht:** 6'3" **Wt:** 200 **Born:** 3/12/1982 **Age:** 26

Year	Team	Lg	G	GS	CG	GF	IP	BFP	H	R	ER	HR	SH	SF	HB	TBB	IBB	SO	WP	Bk	W	L	Pct	ShO	Sv-Op	Hld	ERC	ERA
2001	Jmstwn	A-	15	15	0	0	90.2	358	76	26	19	6	2	0	4	16	0	68	4	1	3	4	.429	0	0--	-	2.39	1.89
2002	Macon	A	29	28	1	0	159.0	663	143	73	58	10	6	5	12	51	1	131	9	1	8	9	.471	1	0--	-	3.29	3.28
2003	MrtlBh	A+	27	27	2	0	153.2	652	150	74	63	10	6	5	7	61	1	88	4	1	6	10	.375	0	0--	-	3.93	3.69
2004	Grnville	AA	27	22	1	1	129.1	552	132	87	75	14	9	9	5	55	0	111	1	1	6	10	.375	0	0--	-	4.65	5.22
2005	Missi	AA	4	2	0	1	16.2	73	21	10	8	0	0	1	0	5	0	18	2	0	0	1	.000	0	1--	-	4.49	4.32
2005	Rchmd	AAA	17	17	0	0	89.1	402	97	47	42	6	1	1	2	45	1	63	3	0	1	7	.125	0	0--	-	4.81	4.23
2005	Toledo	AAA	6	6	0	0	34.1	147	28	10	9	4	2	1	2	20	0	20	0	0	3	1	.750	0	0--	-	4.20	2.36
2006	Toledo	AAA	9	9	1	0	51.0	206	43	18	16	2	0	0	0	21	0	40	1	0	6	0	1.000	0	0--	-	2.99	2.82
2007	Toledo	AAA	11	8	0	0	51.2	215	43	30	28	4	0	2	2	22	0	33	1	0	1	4	.200	0	0--	-	3.31	4.88
2007	Erie	AA	2	0	0	1	2.0	11	4	1	1	0	0	0	0	1	0	2	1	0	0	0	-	0	0--	-	9.72	4.50
2006	Det	AL	27	16	1	4	93.0	398	100	53	50	11	2	2	0	32	1	59	1	0	7	6	.538	0	0-0	-	4.44	4.84
2007	Det	AL	34	1	0	8	53.2	232	56	22	18	3	4	1	0	22	4	34	1	0	3	4	.429	0	0-2	9	3.95	3.02
2 ML YEARS			61	17	1	12	146.2	630	156	75	68	14	6	3	0	54	5	93	2	0	10	10	.500	0	0-2	10	4.26	4.17

Doug Mirabelli

Bats: R **Throws:** R **Pos:** C-46; PH-5; DH-2 **Ht:** 6'1" **Wt:** 220 **Born:** 10/18/1970 **Age:** 37

Year	Team	Lg	G	AB	H	2B	3B	HR	(Hm	Rd)	TB	R	RBI	RC	TBB	IBB	SO	HBP	SH	SF	SB	CS	SB%	GDP	Avg	OBP	Slg
1996	SF	NL	9	18	4	1	0	0	(0	0)	5	2	1	2	3	0	4	0	0	0	0	0	-	0	.222	.333	.278
1997	SF	NL	6	7	1	0	0	0	(0	0)	1	0	0	0	1	0	3	0	0	0	0	0	-	0	.143	.250	.143
1998	SF	NL	10	17	4	2	0	1	(1	0)	9	2	4	3	2	0	6	0	0	0	0	0	-	0	.235	.316	.529
1999	SF	NL	33	87	22	6	0	1	(1	0)	31	10	10	10	9	2	25	1	0	1	0	0	-	1	.253	.327	.356
2000	SF	NL	82	230	53	10	2	6	(2	4)	85	23	28	30	36	2	57	2	3	2	1	0	1.00	6	.230	.337	.370
2001	2 Tms	AL	77	190	43	10	0	11	(5	6)	86	20	29	29	27	2	57	4	1	2	0	0	-	3	.226	.332	.453
2002	Bos	AL	57	151	34	7	0	7	(5	2)	62	17	25	19	17	0	33	3	0	2	0	0	-	6	.225	.312	411
2003	Bos	AL	62	163	42	13	0	6	(3	3)	73	23	18	15	11	0	36	1	0	1	0	0	-	3	.258	.307	.448
2004	Bos	AL	59	160	45	12	0	9	(3	6)	84	27	32	32	19	0	46	3	0	0	0	0	-	5	.281	.368	.525
2005	Bos	AL	50	136	31	7	0	6	(4	2)	56	16	18	19	14	0	48	2	0	0	2	0	1.00	2	.228	.309	.412
2006	2 Tms		73	183	35	7	0	6	(3	3)	60	13	25	17	15	0	59	4	0	0	0	0	-	2	.191	.267	.328
2007	Bos	AL	48	114	23	3	0	5	(2	3)	41	9	16	11	11	0	41	1	1	0	0	0	-	4	.202	.278	.360
01	Tex	AL	23	49	5	2	0	2	(1	1)	13	4	3	3	10	0	21	0	0	0	0	0	-	1	.102	.254	.265
01	Bos	AL	54	141	38	8	0	9	(4	5)	73	16	20	26	17	2	36	4	1	2	0	0	-	2	.270	.360	.518
06	SD	NL	14	22	4	1	0	0	(0	0)	5	1	0	1	4	0	5	0	0	0	0	0	-	0	.182	.308	.227
06	Bos	AL	59	161	31	6	0	6	(3	3)	55	12	25	16	11	0	54	4	0	0	0	0	-	2	.193	.261	.342
12 ML YEARS			566	1456	337	78	2	58	(29	29)	593	162	206	187	165	5	415	21	5	8	3	0	1.00	32	.231	.317	.407

Pat Misch

Pitches: L **Bats:** R **Pos:** RP-14; SP-4 **Ht:** 6'2" **Wt:** 170 **Born:** 8/18/1981 **Age:** 26

Year	Team	Lg	G	GS	CG	GF	IP	BFP	H	R	ER	HR	SH	SF	HB	TBB	IBB	SO	WP	Bk	W	L	Pct	ShO	Sv-Op	Hld	ERC	ERA
2003	SlmKzr	A-	14	14	0	0	86.0	350	78	33	21	3	3	4	7	20	0	61	1	0	7	5	.583	0	0--	-	2.88	2.20
2004	Nrwich	AA	26	26	4	0	159.0	623	138	61	54	13	10	6	3	35	0	123	4	1	7	6	.538	3	0--	-	2.75	3.06
2005	Fresno	AAA	19	19	1	0	102.0	476	135	80	72	18	11	4	6	40	0	69	2	1	3	9	.250	0	0--	-	6.84	6.35
2005	Nrwich	AA	9	9	1	0	61.1	248	63	25	24	7	3	2	1	7	0	43	0	0	4	2	.667	0	0--	-	3.46	3.52
2006	Conn	AA	18	17	0	0	103.2	420	95	32	26	7	1	2	8	24	0	79	0	1	5	4	.556	0	0--	-	3.14	2.26
2006	Fresno	AAA	10	10	1	0	65.0	275	74	32	29	7	5	2	0	11	0	57	1	1	4	2	.667	0	0--	-	3.97	4.02
2007	Fresno	AAA	34	3	0	4	66.2	265	54	24	22	4	3	3	2	19	0	74	3	0	2	5	.286	0	1--	-	2.57	2.97
2006	SF	NL	1	0	0	0	1.0	5	2	0	0	0	0	0	0	0	0	1	0	0	0	0	-	0	0-0	-	7.48	0.00
2007	SF	NL	18	4	0	2	40.1	176	47	21	19	3	1	2	2	12	2	26	0	0	0	4	.000	0	0-0	2	4.59	4.24
2 ML YEARS			19	4	0	2	41.1	181	49	21	19	3	1	2	2	12	2	27	0	0	0	4	.000	0	0-0	2	4.65	4.14

Sergio Mitre

Pitches: R **Bats:** R **Pos:** SP-27 **Ht:** 6'3" **Wt:** 225 **Born:** 2/16/1981 **Age:** 27

Year	Team	Lg	G	GS	CG	GF	IP	BFP	H	R	ER	HR	SH	SF	HB	TBB	IBB	SO	WP	Bk	W	L	Pct	ShO	Sv-Op	Hld	ERC	ERA
2007	Jupiter*	A+	2	2	0	0	9.0	34	5	1	1	0	0	0	0	0	0	4	0	0	2	0	1.000	0	0--	-	0.62	1.00
2003	ChC	NL	3	2	0	1	8.2	43	15	8	8	1	0	1	0	4	1	3	0	0	0	1	.000	0	0-0	0	9.02	8.31
2004	ChC	NL	12	9	0	2	51.2	244	71	38	38	6	3	0	4	20	1	37	5	1	2	4	.333	0	0-0	2	6.69	6.62
2005	ChC	NL	21	7	1	7	60.1	268	62	37	36	11	1	3	3	23	2	37	5	0	2	5	.286	1	0-0	0	4.81	5.37
2006	Fla	NL	15	7	0	3	41.0	189	44	28	26	7	2	1	6	20	3	31	1	0	1	5	.167	0	0-1	2	5.87	5.71
2007	Fla	NL	27	27	0	0	149.0	662	180	88	77	9	6	10	10	41	3	80	6	0	5	8	.385	0	0-0	0	4.71	4.65
5 ML YEARS			78	52	1	13	310.2	1406	372	199	185	34	12	15	23	108	10	188	17	1	10	23	.303	1	0-1	2	5.31	5.36

Brian Moehler

Pitches: R **Bats:** R **Pos:** RP-42   **Ht:** 6'3" **Wt:** 235 **Born:** 12/31/1971 **Age:** 36

		HOW MUCH HE PITCHED						WHAT HE GAVE UP											THE RESULTS							
Year	Team	Lg	G	GS	CG	GF	IP	BFP	H	R	ER	HR	SH	SF	HB	TBB	IBB	SO	WP	Bk	W	L	Pct	ShO	Sv-Op	Hld	ERC	ERA
1996	Det	AL	2	2	0	0	10.1	51	11	10	5	1	1	0	0	8	1	2	1	0	0	1	.000	0	0-0	0	5.49	4.35
1997	Det	AL	31	31	2	0	175.1	770	198	97	91	22	1	8	5	61	1	97	3	0	11	12	.478	1	0-0	0	4.92	4.67
1998	Det	AL	33	33	4	0	221.1	912	220	103	96	30	3	3	2	56	1	123	4	0	14	13	.519	3	0-0	0	3.79	3.90
1999	Det	AL	32	32	2	0	196.1	859	229	116	110	22	8	5	7	59	5	106	4	0	10	16	.385	2	0-0	0	4.85	5.04
2000	Det	AL	29	29	2	0	178.0	776	222	99	89	20	3	4	2	40	0	103	2	1	12	9	.571	0	0-0	0	4.95	4.50
2001	Det	AL	1	1	0	0	8.0	30	6	3	3	0	0	0	0	1	0	2	0	0	0	0	-	0	0-0	0	1.43	3.38
2002	2 Tms		13	12	0	0	63.0	278	78	39	34	11	4	2	1	13	0	31	0	0	3	5	.375	0	0-0	0	5.20	4.86
2003	Hou	NL	3	3	0	0	13.2	66	22	12	12	4	1	1	0	6	0	5	0	0	0	0	-	0	0-0	0	9.97	7.90
2005	Fla	NL	37	25	0	4	158.1	696	198	82	80	16	13	4	5	42	9	95	1	0	6	12	.333	0	0-0	1	5.07	4.55
2006	Fla	NL	29	21	0	2	122.0	556	164	95	89	19	7	2	5	38	3	58	2	1	7	11	.389	0	0-1	0	6.36	6.57
2007	Hou	NL	42	0	0	29	59.2	257	67	29	27	8	1	1	0	17	3	36	1	0	1	4	.200	0	1-1	1	4.48	4.07
	02 Det	AL	3	3	0	0	19.2	77	17	5	5	3	1	1	0	2	0	13	0	0	1	1	.500	0	0-0	0	2.54	2.29
	02 Cin	NL	10	9	0	0	43.1	201	61	34	29	8	3	1	1	11	0	18	0	0	2	4	.333	0	0-0	0	6.56	6.02
11 ML YEARS			252	189	10	35	1206.0	5251	1415	685	636	153	42	30	27	341	23	658	18	2	64	83	.435	6	1-2	2	4.88	4.75

Chad Moeller

Bats: R **Throws:** R **Pos:** C-24; PH-15   **Ht:** 6'3" **Wt:** 215 **Born:** 2/18/1975 **Age:** 33

					BATTING																	BASERUNNING				AVERAGES		
Year	Team	Lg	G	AB	H	2B	3B	HR	(Hm	Rd)	TB	R	RBI	RC	TBB	IBB	SO	HBP	SH	SF	SB	CS	SB%	GDP	Avg	OBP	Slg
2007	Lsvlle*	AAA	16	48	12	5	0	3	(-	-)	26	5	10	8	4	1	12	0	0	0	0	0	-	2	.250	.308	.542
2007	LsVgs*	AAA	12	37	12	1	0	1	(-	-)	16	3	6	8	9	0	8	1	0	0	0	0	-	3	.324	.468	.432
2000	Min	AL	48	128	27	3	1	1	(1	0)	35	13	9	8	9	0	33	0	1	1	1	0	1.00	3	.211	.261	.273
2001	Ari	NL	25	56	13	0	1	1	(1	0)	18	8	2	5	6	1	12	0	1	0	0	0	-	2	.232	.306	.321
2002	Ari	NL	37	105	30	11	1	2	(2	0)	49	10	16	17	17	3	23	0	1	0	0	1	.00	1	.286	.385	.467
2003	Ari	NL	78	239	64	17	1	7	(2	5)	104	29	29	28	23	11	59	2	3	2	1	2	.33	7	.268	.335	.435
2004	Mil	NL	101	317	66	13	1	5	(3	2)	96	25	27	14	21	1	74	4	6	1	0	1	.00	12	.208	.265	.303
2005	Mil	NL	66	199	41	9	1	7	(5	2)	73	23	23	14	13	1	48	1	2	1	0	0	-	3	.206	.257	.367
2006	Mil	NL	29	98	18	3	0	2	(2	0)	27	9	5	3	4	0	26	2	0	0	0	0	-	3	.184	.231	.276
2007	2 Tms		37	56	9	1	0	1	(1	0)	13	8	2	0	0	0	18	1	1	0	0	0	-	2	.161	.175	.232
	07 Cin	NL	30	48	8	1	0	1	(1	0)	12	6	2	0	0	0	17	0	1	0	0	0	-	1	.167	.167	.250
	07 LAD	NL	7	8	1	0	0	0	(0	0)	1	2	0	0	0	0	1	1	0	0	0	0	-	1	.125	.222	.125
8 ML YEARS			421	1198	268	57	6	26	(17	9)	415	125	113	89	93	17	293	10	15	5	2	4	.33	45	.224	.284	.346

Dustan Mohr

Bats: R **Throws:** R **Pos:** LF-3; PR-2; CF-1; RF-1   **Ht:** 6'1" **Wt:** 210 **Born:** 6/19/1976 **Age:** 32

					BATTING																	BASERUNNING				AVERAGES		
Year	Team	Lg	G	AB	H	2B	3B	HR	(Hm	Rd)	TB	R	RBI	RC	TBB	IBB	SO	HBP	SH	SF	SB	CS	SB%	GDP	Avg	OBP	Slg
2007	Drham*	AAA	58	201	46	15	0	9	(-	-)	88	25	24	26	18	2	79	2	0	0	1	1	.50	3	.229	.299	.438
2001	Min	AL	20	51	12	2	0	0	(0	0)	14	6	4	4	5	0	17	0	0	1	1	1	.50	2	.235	.298	.275
2002	Min	AL	120	383	100	23	2	12	(3	9)	166	55	45	51	31	3	86	1	2	0	6	3	.67	5	.261	.325	.433
2003	Min	AL	121	348	87	22	0	10	(4	6)	139	50	36	37	33	0	106	1	2	3	5	2	.71	10	.250	.314	.399
2004	SF	NL	117	263	72	20	1	7	(3	4)	115	52	28	43	46	3	64	8	4	3	0	3	.00	5	.274	.394	.437
2005	Col	NL	98	266	57	10	3	17	(13	4)	124	34	38	27	23	2	94	2	0	2	1	2	.33	3	.214	.280	.466
2006	Bos	AL	21	40	7	1	0	2	(2	0)	14	5	3	2	3	0	20	0	0	0	0	0	-	0	.175	.233	.350
2007	TB	AL	7	16	2	0	0	1	(0	1)	5	1	2	0	0	0	6	0	0	0	0	1	.00	0	.125	.125	.313
7 ML YEARS			504	1367	340	78	6	49	(25	24)	577	203	156	164	141	8	393	12	8	9	13	12	.52	23	.249	.322	.422

Bengie Molina

Bats: R **Throws:** R **Pos:** C-129; PH-7   **Ht:** 5'11" **Wt:** 225 **Born:** 7/20/1974 **Age:** 33

					BATTING																	BASERUNNING				AVERAGES		
Year	Team	Lg	G	AB	H	2B	3B	HR	(Hm	Rd)	TB	R	RBI	RC	TBB	IBB	SO	HBP	SH	SF	SB	CS	SB%	GDP	Avg	OBP	Slg
1998	LAA	AL	2	1	0	0	0	0	(0	0)	0	0	0	0	0	0	0	0	0	0	0	0	-	0	.000	.000	.000
1999	LAA	AL	31	101	26	5	0	1	(0	1)	34	8	10	9	6	0	6	2	0	0	0	1	.00	5	.257	.312	.337
2000	LAA	AL	130	473	133	20	2	14	(11	3)	199	59	71	60	23	0	33	6	4	7	1	0	1.00	17	.281	.318	.421
2001	LAA	AL	96	325	85	11	0	6	(6	0)	114	31	40	34	16	3	51	6	3	2	0	1	.00	8	.262	.309	.351
2002	LAA	AL	122	428	105	18	0	5	(2	3)	138	34	47	33	15	3	34	4	6	6	0	0	-	15	.245	.274	.322
2003	LAA	AL	119	409	115	24	0	14	(7	7)	181	37	71	57	13	2	31	2	2	4	1	1	.50	17	.281	.304	.443
2004	LAA	AL	97	337	93	13	0	10	(5	5)	136	36	54	44	18	1	35	2	2	4	0	1	.00	18	.276	.313	.404
2005	LAA	AL	119	410	121	17	0	15	(8	7)	183	45	69	53	27	2	41	1	5	6	0	2	.00	14	.295	.336	.446
2006	Tor	AL	117	433	123	20	1	19	(12	7)	202	44	57	58	19	1	47	4	0	2	1	1	.50	15	.284	.319	.467
2007	SF	NL	134	497	137	19	1	19	(9	10)	215	38	81	64	15	2	53	2	1	2	0	0	-	13	.276	.298	.433
10 ML YEARS			967	3414	938	147	4	103	(60	43)	1402	332	500	412	152	14	331	31	22	35	3	7	.30	122	.275	.309	.411

Gustavo Molina

Bats: R **Throws:** R **Pos:** C-16; PH-2   **Ht:** 6'0" **Wt:** 220 **Born:** 2/24/1982 **Age:** 26

					BATTING																	BASERUNNING				AVERAGES		
Year	Team	Lg	G	AB	H	2B	3B	HR	(Hm	Rd)	TB	R	RBI	RC	TBB	IBB	SO	HBP	SH	SF	SB	CS	SB%	GDP	Avg	OBP	Slg
2000	WhSox	R	31	115	28	10	0	1	(-	-)	41	15	22	15	13	0	13	2	1	3	3	1	.75	0	.243	.323	.357
2001	Bristol	R+	46	166	47	9	0	2	(-	-)	62	18	24	22	9	1	26	5	1	3	3	1	.75	2	.283	.333	.373
2002	Knapol	A	94	310	70	13	1	2	(-	-)	91	37	34	31	27	1	61	9	7	6	7	2	.78	6	.226	.301	.294
2003	Knapol	A	96	315	72	15	1	5	(-	-)	104	30	41	31	17	0	56	9	8	1	5	3	.63	4	.229	.287	.330
2004	Knapol	A	37	105	17	3	0	4	(-	-)	32	16	17	9	12	0	24	4	3	0	2	1	.67	6	.162	.273	.305
2004	WinSa	A+	25	77	22	6	0	3	(-	-)	37	10	14	12	5	0	16	1	1	1	0	0	-	0	.286	.333	.481
2005	WinSa	A+	109	345	90	20	1	11	(-	-)	145	38	41	49	30	0	47	6	8	3	1	2	.33	16	.261	.328	.420

Year	Team	Lg	G	AB	H	2B	3B	HR	(Hm	Rd)	TB	R	RBI	RC	TBB	IBB	SO	HBP	SH	SF	SB	CS	SB%	GDP	Avg	OBP	Slg
2006	Brham	AA	103	344	78	14	0	7	(-	-)	113	26	34	32	25	0	65	4	8	1	5	6	.45	8	.227	.286	.328
2006	Charltt	AAA	10	30	5	0	0	0	(-	-)	5	0	0	0	1	0	5	0	0	0	0	0	-	3	.167	.194	.167
2007	Charltt	AAA	43	139	29	4	0	2	(-	-)	39	13	9	9	9	0	27	2	5	1	0	2	.00	0	.209	.265	.281
2007	Bowie	AA	22	77	28	4	0	0	(-	-)	32	5	6	12	3	0	9	0	0	0	0	0	-	3	.364	.388	.416
2007	2 Tms	AL	17	27	3	1	0	0	(0	0)	4	1	1	1	1	0	7	0	1	1	0	0	-	0	.111	.138	.148
07	CWS	AL	10	18	1	0	0	0	(0	0)	1	0	1	0	1	0	4	0	1	1	0	0	-	0	.056	.100	.056
07	Bal	AL	7	9	2	1	0	0	(0	0)	3	1	0	1	0	0	3	0	0	0	0	0	-	0	.222	.222	.333

Jose Molina

Bats: R **Throws:** R **Pos:** C-69; PH-1   **Ht:** 6'2" **Wt:** 245 **Born:** 6/3/1975 **Age:** 33

Year	Team	Lg	G	AB	H	2B	3B	HR	(Hm	Rd)	TB	R	RBI	RC	TBB	IBB	SO	HBP	SH	SF	SB	CS	SB%	GDP	Avg	OBP	Slg
1999	ChC	NL	10	19	5	1	0	0	(0	0)	6	3	1	2	2	1	4	0	0	0	0	0	-	0	.263	.333	.316
2001	LAA	AL	15	37	10	3	0	2	(0	2)	19	8	4	6	3	0	8	0	2	0	0	0	-	2	.270	.325	.514
2002	LAA	AL	29	70	19	3	0	0	(0	0)	22	5	5	4	5	0	15	0	4	2	0	2	.00	2	.271	.312	.314
2003	LAA	AL	53	114	21	4	0	0	(0	0)	25	12	6	5	1	0	26	3	4	1	0	0	-	1	.184	.210	.219
2004	LAA	AL	73	203	53	10	2	3	(1	2)	76	26	25	19	10	0	52	0	5	0	4	1	.80	6	.261	.296	.374
2005	LAA	AL	75	184	42	4	0	6	(2	4)	64	14	25	19	13	0	41	2	4	0	2	0	1.00	5	.228	.286	.348
2006	LAA	AL	78	225	54	17	0	4	(0	4)	83	18	22	21	9	0	49	2	7	2	1	0	1.00	6	.240	.273	.369
2007	2 Tms	AL	69	191	49	13	0	1	(1	0)	65	18	19	20	5	0	43	0	5	1	2	1	.67	4	.257	.274	.340
07	LAA	AL	40	125	28	8	0	0	(0	0)	36	9	10	9	3	0	30	0	3	0	2	1	.67	3	.224	.242	.288
07	NYY	AL	29	66	21	5	0	1	(1	0)	29	9	9	11	2	0	13	0	2	1	0	0	-	1	.318	.333	.439
	8 ML YEARS		402	1043	253	55	2	16	(4	12)	360	104	107	96	48	1	238	7	31	6	9	4	.69	26	.243	.279	.345

Yadier Molina

Bats: R **Throws:** R **Pos:** C-107; PH-5; 1B-1   **Ht:** 5'11" **Wt:** 220 **Born:** 7/13/1982 **Age:** 25

Year	Team	Lg	G	AB	H	2B	3B	HR	(Hm	Rd)	TB	R	RBI	RC	TBB	IBB	SO	HBP	SH	SF	SB	CS	SB%	GDP	Avg	OBP	Slg
2004	StL	NL	51	135	36	6	0	2	(1	1)	48	12	15	15	13	3	20	0	2	1	0	1	.00	4	.267	.329	.356
2005	StL	NL	114	385	97	15	1	8	(6	2)	138	36	49	46	23	3	30	2	8	3	2	3	.40	10	.252	.295	.358
2006	StL	NL	129	417	90	26	0	6	(2	4)	134	29	49	35	26	2	41	8	8	2	1	2	.33	15	.216	.274	.321
2007	StL	NL	111	353	97	15	0	6	(4	2)	130	30	40	38	34	5	43	3	2	4	1	1	.50	18	.275	.340	.368
	4 ML YEARS		405	1290	320	62	1	22	(13	9)	450	107	153	134	96	13	134	13	20	10	4	7	.36	47	.248	.304	.349

Craig Monroe

Bats: R **Throws:** R **Pos:** LF-102; PH-12; RF-9; CF-7; DH-1; PR-1   **Ht:** 6'1" **Wt:** 205 **Born:** 2/27/1977 **Age:** 31

Year	Team	Lg	G	AB	H	2B	3B	HR	(Hm	Rd)	TB	R	RBI	RC	TBB	IBB	SO	HBP	SH	SF	SB	CS	SB%	GDP	Avg	OBP	Slg
2001	Tex	AL	27	52	11	1	0	2	(1	1)	18	8	5	6	6	0	18	0	0	0	2	0	1.00	1	.212	.293	.346
2002	Det	AL	13	25	3	1	0	1	(1	0)	7	3	1	4	0	0	5	1	0	0	0	2	.00	1	.120	.154	.280
2003	Det	AL	128	425	102	18	1	23	(10	13)	191	51	70	61	27	2	89	2	1	3	4	2	.67	10	.240	.287	.449
2004	Det	AL	128	447	131	27	3	18	(9	9)	218	65	72	66	29	1	79	2	0	3	3	4	.43	8	.293	.337	.488
2005	Det	AL	157	567	157	30	3	20	(9	11)	253	69	89	77	40	4	95	3	1	12	8	3	.73	16	.277	.322	.446
2006	Det	AL	147	541	138	35	2	28	(12	16)	261	89	92	76	37	3	126	1	0	6	2	2	.50	14	.255	.301	.482
2007	2 Tms		122	392	86	23	0	12	(5	7)	145	53	59	36	26	0	107	2	1	6	0	4	.00	13	.219	.268	.370
07	Det	AL	99	343	76	19	0	11	(5	6)	128	47	55	32	20	0	94	2	1	6	0	3	.00	10	.222	.264	.373
07	ChC	NL	23	49	10	4	0	1	(0	1)	17	6	4	4	6	0	13	0	0	0	0	1	.00	3	.204	.291	.347
	7 ML YEARS		722	2449	628	135	9	104	(46	58)	1093	338	388	322	165	10	519	11	3	30	19	17	.53	63	.256	.303	.446

Miguel Montero

Bats: L **Throws:** R **Pos:** C-73; PH-24   **Ht:** 5'11" **Wt:** 195 **Born:** 7/9/1983 **Age:** 24

Year	Team	Lg	G	AB	H	2B	3B	HR	(Hm	Rd)	TB	R	RBI	RC	TBB	IBB	SO	HBP	SH	SF	SB	CS	SB%	GDP	Avg	OBP	Slg
2002	Msoula	R+	50	152	40	10	1	3	(-	-)	61	21	14	22	17	0	26	3	1	3	2	1	.67	5	.263	.343	.401
2003	Msoula	R+	59	196	59	10	2	4	(-	-)	85	24	32	30	9	2	15	8	0	3	2	3	.40	6	.301	.352	.434
2004	Sbend	A	115	403	106	22	2	11	(-	-)	165	47	59	58	36	0	74	6	0	4	8	2	.80	5	.263	.330	.409
2005	Lancst	A+	85	355	124	24	1	24	(-	-)	222	73	82	85	26	0	52	10	2	6	1	2	.33	5	.349	.403	.625
2005	Tenn	AA	30	108	27	1	2	2	(-	-)	38	13	13	12	7	0	26	3	1	1	1	0	1.00	2	.250	.311	.352
2006	Tenn	AA	81	289	78	18	0	10	(-	-)	126	24	46	47	39	3	44	5	0	4	0	3	.00	3	.270	.362	.436
2006	Tucsn	AAA	36	134	43	5	0	7	(-	-)	69	21	29	27	14	0	21	4	0	2	1	1	.50	4	.321	.396	.515
2006	Ari	NL	6	16	4	1	0	0	(0	0)	5	0	3	2	1	0	3	0	0	0	0	0	-	0	.250	.294	.313
2007	Ari	NL	84	214	48	7	0	10	(7	3)	85	30	37	19	20	2	35	3	1	6	0	0	-	7	.224	.292	.397
	2 ML YEARS		90	230	52	8	0	10	(7	3)	90	30	40	21	21	2	38	3	1	6	0	0	-	7	.226	.292	.391

Scott Moore

Bats: L **Throws:** R **Pos:** 3B-12; 1B-4; PH-3; LF-1   **Ht:** 6'2" **Wt:** 195 **Born:** 11/17/1983 **Age:** 24

Year	Team	Lg	G	AB	H	2B	3B	HR	(Hm	Rd)	TB	R	RBI	RC	TBB	IBB	SO	HBP	SH	SF	SB	CS	SB%	GDP	Avg	OBP	Slg
2002	Tigers	R	40	133	39	6	2	4	(-	-)	61	18	25	21	10	1	31	3	0	3	1	2	.33	2	.293	.349	.459
2003	WMich	A	107	372	89	16	6	6	(-	-)	135	40	45	45	41	0	110	7	0	1	2	4	.33	9	.239	.325	.363
2004	Lkland	A+	118	391	87	13	4	14	(-	-)	150	52	56	51	49	1	125	10	0	3	2	4	.33	10	.223	.322	.384
2005	Dytona	A+	128	466	131	31	2	20	(-	-)	226	77	82	85	55	4	134	6	0	9	22	7	.76	7	.281	.358	.485
2006	WTenn	AA	132	463	128	28	0	22	(-	-)	222	52	75	82	55	7	126	8	1	5	12	7	.63	7	.276	.360	.479
2006	Iowa	AAA	1	4	1	0	0	0	(-	-)	2	1	0	0	0	0	1	0	0	0	0	0	-	0	.250	.250	.500
2007	Iowa	AAA	103	321	85	19	4	19	(-	-)	169	61	69	64	48	1	100	9	1	3	4	3	.57	5	.265	.373	.526

Year Team	Lg	G	AB	H	2B	3B	HR	(Hm	Rd)	TB	R	RBI	RC	TBB	IBB	SO	HBP	SH	SF	SB	CS	SB%	GDP	Avg	OBP	Slg
																								BATTING									**BASERUNNING**			**AVERAGES**		
2006 ChC	NL	16	38	10	2	0	2	(1	1)	18	6	5	5	2	0	10	1	1	0	0	0	-	1	.263	.317	.474
2007 2 Tms		19	52	12	2	0	1	(1	0)	17	2	11	6	1	0	17	0	0	2	0	1	.00	1	.231	.236	.327
07 ChC	NL	2	5	0	0	0	0	(0	0)	0	0	0	0	0	0	2	0	0	0	0	0	-	0	.000	.000	.000
07 Bal	AL	17	47	12	2	0	1	(1	0)	17	2	11	6	1	0	15	0	0	2	0	1	.00	1	.255	.260	.362
2 ML YEARS		35	90	22	4	0	3	(2	1)	35	8	16	11	3	0	27	1	1	2	0	1	.00	2	.244	.271	.389

Melvin Mora

Bats: R **Throws:** R **Pos:** 3B-120; PH-4; DH-2   **Ht:** 5'11" **Wt:** 200 **Born:** 2/2/1972 **Age:** 36

Year Team	Lg	G	AB	H	2B	3B	HR	(Hm	Rd)	TB	R	RBI	RC	TBB	IBB	SO	HBP	SH	SF	SB	CS	SB%	GDP	Avg	OBP	Slg
2007 Orioles*	R	2	7	2	1	0	0	(-	-)	3	1	1	0	0	0	1	0	0	0	0	0	-	0	.286	.286	.429
1999 NYM	NL	66	31	5	0	0	0	(0	0)	5	6	1	2	4	0	7	1	3	0	2	1	.67	0	.161	.278	.161
2000 2 Tms		132	414	114	22	5	8	(5	3)	170	60	47	56	35	3	80	6	4	5	12	11	.52	5	.275	.337	.411
2001 Bal	AL	128	436	109	28	0	7	(6	1)	158	49	48	55	41	2	91	14	5	7	11	4	.73	6	.250	.329	.362
2002 Bal	AL	149	557	130	30	4	19	(8	11)	225	86	64	78	70	2	108	20	1	4	16	10	.62	7	.233	.338	.404
2003 Bal	AL	96	344	109	17	1	15	(8	7)	173	68	48	67	49	0	71	12	6	2	6	3	.67	3	.317	.418	.503
2004 Bal	AL	140	550	187	41	0	27	(15	12)	309	111	104	115	66	0	95	11	6	3	11	6	.65	10	.340	.419	.562
2005 Bal	AL	149	593	168	30	1	27	(13	14)	281	86	88	88	50	0	112	10	8	3	7	4	.64	9	.283	.348	.474
2006 Bal	AL	155	624	171	25	0	16	(8	8)	244	96	83	93	54	1	99	14	6	7	11	1	.92	9	.274	.342	.391
2007 Bal	AL	126	467	128	23	1	14	(7	7)	195	67	58	61	47	3	83	3	5	5	9	3	.75	22	.274	.341	.418
00 NYM	NL	79	215	56	13	2	6	(4	2)	91	35	30	29	18	3	48	2	2	5	7	3	.70	3	.260	.317	.423
00 Bal	AL	53	199	58	9	3	2	(1	1)	79	25	17	27	17	0	32	4	2	0	5	8	.38	2	.291	.359	.397
9 ML YEARS		1141	4016	1121	216	12	133	(70	63)	1760	629	541	615	416	11	746	91	44	36	85	43	.66	71	.279	.357	.438

Franklin Morales

Pitches: L **Bats:** L **Pos:** SP-8   **Ht:** 6'0" **Wt:** 170 **Born:** 1/24/1986 **Age:** 22

		HOW MUCH HE PITCHED						**WHAT HE GAVE UP**										**THE RESULTS**							
Year Team	Lg	G	GS	CG	GF	IP	BFP	H	R	ER	HR	SH	SF	HB	TBB	IBB	SO	WP	Bk	W	L	Pct	ShO	Sv-Op	Hld	ERC	ERA
2004 Casper	R+	15	15	1	0	65.0	320	92	61	55	8	2	2	5	39	0	82	7	4	6	4	.600	1	0--	-	8.09	7.62
2005 Ashvll	A	21	15	0	3	96.1	399	73	40	33	6	1	1	8	48	0	108	7	7	8	4	.667	0	1--	-	3.29	3.08
2006 Mdest	A+	27	26	0	0	154.0	671	126	77	63	9	3	2	11	80	0	179	24	10	10	9	.526	0	0--	-	3.75	3.68
2007 Tulsa	AA	17	17	1	0	95.2	401	77	41	37	8	4	3	8	45	0	77	6	2	8	4	.429	0	0--	-	3.56	3.48
2007 ColSpr	AAA	3	3	0	0	17.0	75	20	8	7	1	0	0	0	13	1	16	3	0	2	0	1.000	0	0--	-	6.78	3.71
2007 Col	NL	8	8	0	0	39.1	163	34	15	15	2	4	2	2	14	1	26	0	0	3	2	.600	0	0-0	0	3.04	3.43

Jose Morales

Bats: B **Throws:** R **Pos:** C-1   **Ht:** 5'11" **Wt:** 190 **Born:** 2/20/1983 **Age:** 25

Year Team	Lg	G	AB	H	2B	3B	HR	(Hm	Rd)	TB	R	RBI	RC	TBB	IBB	SO	HBP	SH	SF	SB	CS	SB%	GDP	Avg	OBP	Slg
2001 Twins	R	35	117	29	6	2	0	(-	-)	39	13	18	12	6	0	26	2	2	0	4	1	.80	1	.248	.296	.333
2002 Twins	R	53	175	54	7	2	0	(-	-)	65	25	28	24	7	0	28	5	2	3	3	1	.75	5	.309	.347	.371
2003 FtMyrs	A+	12	42	15	3	1	0	(-	-)	20	6	2	6	1	1	5	0	0	0	0	2	.00	1	.357	.372	.476
2003 QuadC	A	48	170	46	10	1	2	(-	-)	64	14	25	19	5	0	32	3	3	1	0	1	.00	6	.271	.302	.376
2004 FtMyrs	A+	91	331	95	13	4	4	(-	-)	128	30	46	45	29	3	77	0	0	5	0	1	.00	5	.287	.340	.387
2005 NwBrit	AA	7	20	5	1	0	0	(-	-)	6	1	0	1	1	0	3	0	0	0	0	0	-	3	.250	.286	.300
2006 NwBrit	AA	80	251	53	14	1	3	(-	-)	78	23	26	22	19	0	56	5	3	4	2	1	.67	11	.211	.276	.311
2006 Roch	AAA	2	7	1	0	0	0	(-	-)	1	0	0	0	0	0	0	0	0	0	0	0	-	0	.143	.143	.143
2007 Roch	AAA	108	376	117	25	1	2	(-	-)	150	42	37	56	30	5	44	3	1	1	1	4	.20	13	.311	.366	.399
2007 Min	AL	1	3	3	1	0	0	(0	0)	4	1	0	2	0	0	0	0	0	0	0	0	-	0	1.000	1.000	1.333

Kendry Morales

Bats: B **Throws:** R **Pos:** 1B-19; DH-15; PH-8; RF-6   **Ht:** 6'1" **Wt:** 225 **Born:** 6/20/1983 **Age:** 25

Year Team	Lg	G	AB	H	2B	3B	HR	(Hm	Rd)	TB	R	RBI	RC	TBB	IBB	SO	HBP	SH	SF	SB	CS	SB%	GDP	Avg	OBP	Slg
2005 RCuca	A+	22	90	31	3	0	5	(-	-)	49	18	17	19	6	0	11	3	0	1	0	0	-	3	.344	.400	.544
2005 Ark	AA	74	281	86	12	0	17	(-	-)	149	47	54	51	17	1	43	2	0	1	2	0	1.00	6	.306	.349	.530
2006 Salt Lk	AAA	66	256	82	13	1	12	(-	-)	133	41	52	45	14	0	40	2	0	1	0	3	.00	6	.320	.359	.520
2007 Salt Lk	AAA	64	255	87	20	1	5	(-	-)	124	42	37	46	15	1	30	4	0	1	0	2	.00	6	.341	.385	.486
2006 LAA	AL	57	197	46	10	1	5	(1	4)	73	21	22	19	17	1	28	0	0	1	1	1	.50	11	.234	.293	.371
2007 LAA	AL	43	119	35	10	0	4	(2	2)	57	12	15	15	6	2	21	1	0	0	1	1	.00	5	.294	.333	.479
2 ML YEARS		100	316	81	20	1	9	(3	6)	130	33	37	34	23	3	49	1	0	1	2	2	.33	16	.256	.308	.411

Nyjer Morgan

Bats: L **Throws:** L **Pos:** CF-28; PH-1   **Ht:** 6'0" **Wt:** 172 **Born:** 7/2/1980 **Age:** 27

Year Team	Lg	G	AB	H	2B	3B	HR	(Hm	Rd)	TB	R	RBI	RC	TBB	IBB	SO	HBP	SH	SF	SB	CS	SB%	GDP	Avg	OBP	Slg
2003 Wmspt	A-	72	268	92	7	4	0	(-	-)	107	49	23	50	33	1	44	13	10	0	26	17	.60	2	.343	.439	.399
2004 Hickory	A	134	514	131	16	7	4	(-	-)	173	83	41	75	53	2	120	33	10	6	55	16	.77	1	.255	.358	.337
2005 Lynbrg	A+	60	252	72	12	3	0	(-	-)	90	36	24	32	11	0	40	7	3	4	24	10	.71	0	.286	.328	.357
2006 Lynbrg	A+	61	228	69	7	3	0	(-	-)	82	43	22	39	20	1	40	15	7	4	38	11	.78	1	.303	.390	.360
2006 Altna	AA	56	219	67	6	5	1	(-	-)	86	39	10	32	15	0	28	3	7	0	21	11	.66	2	.306	.359	.393
2007 Pirates	R	4	13	4	0	0	1	(-	-)	7	3	1	3	2	0	3	1	0	0	0	0	-	0	.308	.438	.538
2007 Indy	AAA	44	164	50	4	2	0	(-	-)	58	30	10	25	15	1	28	3	2	0	26	7	.79	1	.305	.374	.354
2007 Pit	NL	28	107	32	3	4	1	(1	0)	46	15	7	18	9	0	19	1	1	0	7	3	.70	0	.299	.359	.430

Juan Morillo

Pitches: R Bats: R Pos: RP-4 Ht: 6'3" Wt: 190 **Born:** 11/5/1983 **Age:** 24

Year	Team	Lg	G	GS	CG	GF	IP	BFP	H	R	ER	HR	SH	SF	HB	TBB	IBB	SO	WP	Bk	W	L	Pct	ShO	Sv-Op Hld	ERC	ERA
2003	Casper	R+	15	15	0	0	64.0	320	85	73	42	6	4	4	5	40	0	44	7	0	1	6	.143	0	0- - -	7.14	5.91
2004	TriCity	A-	14	14	0	0	66.1	295	56	34	22	0	1	1	4	41	0	73	3	0	3	2	.600	0	0- - -	3.52	2.98
2005	Ashvll	A	7	7	0	0	33.2	154	40	24	17	2	0	0	1	13	0	43	3	0	1	3	.250	0	0- - -	4.82	4.54
2005	Mdest	A+	20	20	0	0	112.1	509	107	69	55	10	3	2	8	65	0	101	13	1	6	5	.545	0	0- - -	4.68	4.41
2006	Tulsa	AA	27	27	1	0	140.1	618	128	82	72	13	11	3	8	80	1	132	12	0	12	8	.600	0	0- - -	4.45	4.62
2007	Tulsa	AA	46	0	0	12	57.1	242	44	19	15	2	1	1	3	27	0	59	4	0	6	4	.600	0	0- - -	2.84	2.35
2007	ColSpr	AAA	7	0	0	1	9.2	39	7	4	4	0	0	0	0	4	0	12	2	0	0	1	.000	0	0- - -	2.08	3.72
2006	Col	NL	1	1	0	0	4.0	24	8	7	7	3	1	0	1	3	0	4	0	0	0	0	-	0	0-0	0	20.26	15.75
2007	Col	NL	4	0	0	1	3.2	16	3	4	4	1	0	0	1	1	0	3	0	0	0	0	-	0	0-0	0	4.74	9.82
	2 ML YEARS		5	1	0	1	7.2	40	11	11	11	4	1	0	2	4	0	7	0	0	0	0	-	0	0-0	0	12.12	12.91

Justin Morneau

Bats: L Throws: R Pos: 1B-143; DH-14 Ht: 6'4" Wt: 223 **Born:** 5/15/1981 **Age:** 27

								BATTING														BASERUNNING				AVERAGES		
Year	Team	Lg	G	AB	H	2B	3B	HR	(Hm	Rd)	TB	R	RBI	RC	TBB	IBB	SO	HBP	SH	SF	SB	CS	SB%	GDP	Avg	OBP	Slg
2003	Min	AL	40	106	24	4	0	4	(1	3)	40	14	16	11	9	1	30	0	0	0	0	0	-	4	.226	.287	.377
2004	Min	AL	74	280	76	17	0	19	(9	10)	150	39	58	48	28	8	54	2	0	2	0	0	-	4	.271	.340	.536
2005	Min	AL	141	490	117	23	4	22	(9	13)	214	62	79	58	44	8	94	4	0	5	0	2	.00	12	.239	.304	.437
2006	Min	AL	157	592	190	37	1	34	(17	17)	331	97	130	118	53	9	93	5	0	11	3	3	.50	10	.321	.375	.559
2007	Min	AL	157	590	160	31	3	31	(15	16)	290	84	111	95	64	11	91	5	0	9	1	1	.50	17	.271	.343	.492
	5 ML YEARS		569	2058	567	112	8	110	(51	59)	1025	296	394	330	198	37	362	16	0	27	4	6	.40	47	.276	.340	.498

Matt Morris

Pitches: R Bats: R Pos: SP-32 Ht: 6'5" Wt: 215 **Born:** 8/9/1974 **Age:** 33

Year	Team	Lg	G	GS	CG	GF	IP	BFP	H	R	ER	HR	SH	SF	HB	TBB	IBB	SO	WP	Bk	W	L	Pct	ShO	Sv-Op Hld	ERC	ERA
1997	StL	NL	33	33	3	0	217.0	900	208	88	77	12	11	7	7	69	2	149	5	3	12	9	.571	0	0-0	0	3.41	3.19
1998	StL	NL	17	17	2	0	113.2	468	101	37	32	8	6	1	3	42	6	79	3	0	7	5	.583	1	0-0	0	3.25	2.53
2000	StL	NL	31	0	0	12	53.0	226	53	22	21	3	3	1	2	17	1	34	0	0	3	3	.500	0	4-7	7	3.58	3.57
2001	StL	NL	34	34	2	0	216.1	909	218	86	76	13	14	5	13	54	3	185	5	1	22	8	.733	1	0-0	0	3.50	3.16
2002	StL	NL	32	32	1	0	210.1	890	210	86	80	16	7	8	6	64	3	171	3	0	17	9	.654	1	0-0	0	3.63	3.42
2003	StL	NL	27	27	5	0	172.1	703	164	76	72	20	5	3	4	39	1	120	3	0	11	8	.579	3	0-0	0	3.37	3.76
2004	StL	NL	32	32	3	0	202.0	850	205	116	106	35	13	5	6	56	3	131	3	1	15	10	.600	2	0-0	0	4.30	4.72
2005	StL	NL	31	31	2	0	192.2	818	209	101	88	22	10	5	8	37	3	117	1	1	14	10	.583	0	0-0	0	3.95	4.11
2006	SF	NL	33	33	2	0	207.2	903	218	123	115	22	9	5	14	63	9	117	1	3	10	15	.400	0	0-0	0	4.19	4.98
2007	2 Tms	NL	32	32	3	0	198.2	884	240	123	108	18	10	8	9	61	4	102	4	0	10	11	.476	0	0-0	0	4.98	4.89
07	SF	NL	21	21	3	0	136.2	603	162	79	66	12	5	6	5	39	3	73	1	0	7	7	.500	0	0-0	0	4.69	4.35
07	Pit	NL	11	11	0	0	62.0	281	78	44	42	6	5	2	4	22	1	29	3	0	3	4	.429	0	0-0	0	5.66	6.10
	10 ML YEARS		302	271	23	12	1783.2	7551	1826	858	776	160	00	40	72	502	35	1205	28	9	121	88	.579	8	4-7	7	3.86	3.91

Brandon Morrow

Pitches: R Bats: R Pos: RP-60 Ht: 6'3" Wt: 190 **Born:** 7/26/1984 **Age:** 23

Year	Team	Lg	G	GS	CG	GF	IP	BFP	H	R	ER	HR	SH	SF	HB	TBB	IBB	SO	WP	Bk	W	L	Pct	ShO	Sv-Op Hld	ERC	ERA
2000	Ms	R	7	4	0	0	13.0	53	10	4	4	0	0	0	0	9	0	13	3	0	0	2	.000	0	0- - -	3.46	2.77
2006	InldEm	A+	1	1	0	0	3.0	9	0	0	0	0	0	0	0	0	0	4	0	0	0	0	-	0	0- - -	0.00	0.00
2007	Sea	AL	60	0	0	18	63.1	289	56	29	29	3	4	4	1	50	5	66	4	0	3	4	.429	0	0-2	18	4.47	4.12

Mike Morse

Bats: R Throws: R Pos: 1B-5; 3B-3; SS-1; RF-1; PH-1 Ht: 6'4" Wt: 225 **Born:** 3/22/1982 **Age:** 26

								BATTING														BASERUNNING				AVERAGES		
Year	Team	Lg	G	AB	H	2B	3B	HR	(Hm	Rd)	TB	R	RBI	RC	TBB	IBB	SO	HBP	SH	SF	SB	CS	SB%	GDP	Avg	OBP	Slg
2007	Ms*	R	5	15	3	1	0	0	(-	-)	4	2	2	1	3	0	0	0	0	0	0	1	.00	2	.200	.333	.267
2007	Tacom*	AAA	76	291	90	26	0	6	(-	-)	134	48	39	50	26	2	47	3	1	3	5	3	.63	15	.309	.368	.460
2005	Sea	AL	72	230	64	10	1	3	(3	0)	85	27	23	28	18	0	50	8	0	2	3	1	.75	9	.278	.349	.370
2006	Sea	AL	21	43	16	5	0	0	(0	0)	21	5	11	9	3	0	7	0	0	2	1	0	1.00	2	.372	.396	.488
2007	Sea	AL	9	18	8	2	0	0	(0	0)	10	1	3	6	1	0	4	1	0	0	0	0	-	0	.444	.500	.556
	3 ML YEARS		102	291	88	17	1	3	(3	0)	116	33	37	43	22	0	61	9	0	4	4	1	.80	11	.302	.365	.399

Colt Morton

Bats: R Throws: R Pos: PH-1 Ht: 6'5" Wt: 230 **Born:** 4/10/1982 **Age:** 26

								BATTING														BASERUNNING				AVERAGES		
Year	Team	Lg	G	AB	H	2B	3B	HR	(Hm	Rd)	TB	R	RBI	RC	TBB	IBB	SO	HBP	SH	SF	SB	CS	SB%	GDP	Avg	OBP	Slg
2003	Eugene	A-	25	97	27	6	0	7	(-	-)	54	14	20	18	10	0	29	0	0	0	0	0	-	1	.278	.346	.557
2003	FtWyn	A	22	76	13	4	0	2	(-	-)	23	5	7	4	5	1	28	0	0	0	0	0	-	2	.171	.222	.303
2004	FtWyn	A	36	127	19	5	1	4	(-	-)	38	10	11	10	16	0	45	3	0	0	0	0	-	0	.150	.260	.299
2004	Eugene	A-	66	243	58	13	0	17	(-	-)	122	43	45	43	33	1	75	6	0	3	2	0	1.00	3	.239	.340	.502
2004	Mobile	AA	1	3	1	0	0	1	(-	-)	4	1	1	1	1	0	0	0	0	0	0	0	-	0	.333	.500	1.333
2005	FtWyn	A	63	222	58	15	0	10	(-	-)	103	27	46	40	35	1	57	3	0	5	0	0	-	4	.261	.362	.464
2005	Lk Els	A+	26	96	31	4	0	9	(-	-)	62	19	19	24	14	0	30	1	0	2	0	1	.00	1	.323	.407	.646
2006	Lk Els	A+	53	176	40	15	0	5	(-	-)	70	30	22	29	36	0	44	7	0	3	0	1	.00	7	.227	.374	.398
2006	Mobile	AA	41	139	37	10	0	6	(-	-)	65	15	21	21	11	0	44	2	0	0	0	0	-	2	.266	.329	.468

187

			BATTING																		BASERUNNING				AVERAGES		
Year	Team	Lg	G	AB	H	2B	3B	HR	(Hm	Rd)	TB	R	RBI	RC	TBB	IBB	SO	HBP	SH	SF	SB	CS	SB%	GDP	Avg	OBP	Slg
2007	Padres	R	11	31	9	4	0	0	(-	-)	13	9	8	5	5	0	11	1	0	4	0	0	-	0	.290	.366	.419
2007	Lk Els	A+	6	24	12	7	0	3	(-	-)	28	5	8	12	4	0	3	2	0	0	0	0	-	0	.500	.600	1.167
2007	SnAnt	AA	29	94	25	3	0	6	(-	-)	46	17	19	18	15	1	34	4	1	2	0	0	-	0	.266	.383	.489
2007	SD	NL	1	1	0	0	0	0	(0	0)	0	0	0	0	0	0	0	0	0	0	0	0	-	0	.000	.000	.000

Dustin Moseley

Pitches: R **Bats:** R **Pos:** RP-38; SP-8   **Ht:** 6'4" **Wt:** 215 **Born:** 12/26/1981 **Age:** 26

			HOW MUCH HE PITCHED						WHAT HE GAVE UP										THE RESULTS						
Year	Team	Lg	G	GS	CG	GF	IP	BFP	H	R	ER	HR	SH	SF	HB	TBB	IBB	SO	WP	Bk	W	L	Pct	ShO	Sv-Op	Hld	ERC	ERA
2001	Dayton	A	25	25	0	0	148.0	638	158	83	69	10	4	1	8	42	0	108	3	2	10	8	.556	0	0--	-	3.98	4.20
2002	Stcktn	A+	14	14	2	0	88.2	350	60	28	27	3	2	0	8	21	0	80	2	3	6	3	.667	2	0--	-	1.78	2.74
2002	Chatt	AA	13	13	0	0	80.2	361	91	47	37	5	6	3	4	37	0	52	2	0	5	6	.455	0	0--	-	5.02	4.13
2003	Chatt	AA	18	18	0	0	112.2	480	116	55	48	10	3	3	7	28	0	73	2	0	5	6	.455	0	0--	-	3.80	3.83
2003	Lsvlle	AAA	8	8	0	0	50.0	207	46	19	15	5	1	3	1	14	0	27	2	1	2	3	.400	0	0--	-	3.26	2.70
2004	Chatt	AA	8	8	0	0	47.1	181	33	16	14	4	1	1	2	10	0	40	0	3	3	2	.600	0	0--	-	1.96	2.66
2004	Lsvlle	AAA	12	12	0	0	71.2	312	78	38	37	7	4	5	4	34	0	48	2	0	2	4	.333	0	0--	-	5.30	4.65
2005	Salt Lk	AAA	17	17	0	0	82.1	371	102	51	46	11	1	8	5	30	1	38	1	2	4	6	.400	0	0--	-	5.89	5.03
2006	Salt Lk	AAA	26	26	3	0	149.2	646	164	89	78	18	3	5	8	51	0	114	7	2	13	8	.619	0	0--	-	4.84	4.69
2006	LAA	AL	3	2	0	1	11.0	54	22	11	11	3	0	1	0	2	0	3	0	0	1	0	1.000	0	0-0	0	11.45	9.00
2007	LAA	AL	46	8	0	13	92.0	383	97	45	45	7	1	2	3	27	3	50	6	1	4	3	.571	0	0-0	4	4.00	4.40
	2 ML YEARS		49	10	0	14	103.0	437	119	56	56	10	1	3	3	29	3	53	6	1	5	3	.625	0	0-0	4	4.68	4.89

Brandon Moss

Bats: L **Throws:** R **Pos:** LF-13; RF-4; PR-3; PH-2   **Ht:** 6'0" **Wt:** 205 **Born:** 9/16/1983 **Age:** 24

			BATTING																		BASERUNNING				AVERAGES		
Year	Team	Lg	G	AB	H	2B	3B	HR	(Hm	Rd)	TB	R	RBI	RC	TBB	IBB	SO	HBP	SH	SF	SB	CS	SB%	GDP	Avg	OBP	Slg
2002	RedSx	R	42	113	23	6	2	0	(-	-)	33	10	6	10	13	0	40	2	1	1	1	2	.33	2	.204	.295	.292
2003	Lowell	A-	65	228	54	15	4	7	(-	-)	98	29	34	29	15	0	53	4	0	5	7	5	.58	1	.237	.290	.430
2004	Augsta	A	109	433	147	25	6	13	(-	-)	223	66	101	90	46	4	75	4	0	7	19	8	.70	8	.339	.402	.515
2004	Srsota	A+	23	83	35	2	1	2	(-	-)	45	16	10	20	7	2	15	0	0	1	2	0	1.00	1	.422	.462	.542
2005	Portlnd	AA	135	503	136	31	4	16	(-	-)	223	87	61	79	53	6	129	3	1	8	6	3	.67	6	.270	.339	.443
2006	Portlnd	AA	133	508	145	36	3	12	(-	-)	223	76	83	82	56	5	108	3	2	4	8	5	.62	13	.285	.357	.439
2007	Pwtckt	AAA	133	493	139	41	2	16	(-	-)	232	66	78	85	61	3	148	3	0	2	3	5	.38	7	.282	.363	.471
2007	Bos	AL	15	25	7	2	1	0	(0	0)	11	6	1	3	4	0	6	0	0	0	0	0	-	1	.280	.379	.440

Guillermo Mota

Pitches: R **Bats:** R **Pos:** RP-52   **Ht:** 6'6" **Wt:** 210 **Born:** 7/25/1973 **Age:** 34

			HOW MUCH HE PITCHED						WHAT HE GAVE UP										THE RESULTS						
Year	Team	Lg	G	GS	CG	GF	IP	BFP	H	R	ER	HR	SH	SF	HB	TBB	IBB	SO	WP	Bk	W	L	Pct	ShO	Sv-Op	Hld	ERC	ERA
2007	NewOr*	AAA	7	0	0	3	7.2	38	11	6	6	1	0	1	0	5	0	7	1	0	0	1	.000	0	0--	-	8.10	7.04
1999	Mon	NL	51	0	0	18	55.1	243	54	24	18	5	3	3	2	25	3	27	1	1	2	4	.333	0	0-1	3	4.10	2.93
2000	Mon	NL	29	0	0	7	30.0	126	27	21	20	3	1	1	2	12	0	24	1	1	2	2	.500	0	0-0	5	3.86	6.00
2001	Mon	NL	53	0	0	12	49.2	212	51	30	29	9	3	2	1	18	1	31	1	0	1	3	.250	0	0-3	12	4.77	5.26
2002	LAD	NL	43	0	0	11	60.2	256	45	30	28	4	3	1	2	27	6	49	3	0	1	3	.250	0	0-1	4	2.57	4.15
2003	LAD	NL	76	0	0	18	105.0	410	78	23	23	7	3	1	1	26	4	99	0	0	6	3	.667	0	1-3	13	2.01	1.97
2004	2 Tms	NL	78	0	0	18	96.2	393	75	33	33	8	5	3	4	37	6	85	5	0	9	8	.529	0	4-8	30	2.82	3.07
2005	Fla	NL	56	0	0	24	67.0	293	65	38	35	5	1	3	1	32	7	60	4	0	2	2	.500	0	2-4	14	3.90	4.70
2006	2 Tms	NL	52	0	0	17	55.2	241	55	29	28	11	0	3	0	24	4	46	2	0	4	3	.571	0	0-0	9	4.71	4.53
2007	NYM	NL	52	0	0	10	59.1	261	63	39	38	8	2	0	2	18	2	47	2	0	2	2	.500	0	0-3	6	4.26	5.76
04	LAD	NL	52	0	0	11	63.0	259	51	15	15	4	4	2	2	27	5	52	5	0	8	4	.667	0	1-1	17	2.98	2.14
04	Fla	NL	26	0	0	7	33.2	134	24	18	18	4	1	1	2	10	1	33	0	0	1	4	.200	0	3-7	13	2.51	4.81
06	Cle	AL	34	0	0	13	37.2	173	45	27	26	9	0	3	0	19	3	27	2	0	1	3	.250	0	0-0	5	6.62	6.21
06	NYM	NL	18	0	0	4	18.0	68	10	2	2	2	0	0	0	5	1	19	0	0	3	0	1.000	0	0-0	4	1.51	1.00
	9 ML YEARS		490	0	0	135	579.1	2435	513	267	252	60	21	17	15	219	33	468	19	2	28	29	.491	0	7-23	96	3.41	3.91

Jamie Moyer

Pitches: L **Bats:** L **Pos:** SP-33   **Ht:** 6'0" **Wt:** 185 **Born:** 11/18/1962 **Age:** 45

			HOW MUCH HE PITCHED						WHAT HE GAVE UP										THE RESULTS						
Year	Team	Lg	G	GS	CG	GF	IP	BFP	H	R	ER	HR	SH	SF	HB	TBB	IBB	SO	WP	Bk	W	L	Pct	ShO	Sv-Op	Hld	ERC	ERA
1986	ChC	NL	16	16	1	0	87.1	395	107	52	49	10	3	3	3	42	1	45	3	3	7	4	.636	1	0-0	0	6.13	5.05
1987	ChC	NL	35	33	1	1	201.0	899	210	127	114	28	14	7	5	97	9	147	11	2	12	15	.444	0	0-0	0	4.96	5.10
1988	ChC	NL	34	30	3	1	202.0	855	212	84	78	20	14	4	4	55	7	121	4	0	9	15	.375	1	0-2	0	3.89	3.48
1989	Tex	AL	15	15	1	0	76.0	337	84	51	41	10	1	4	2	33	0	44	1	0	4	9	.308	0	0-0	0	5.20	4.86
1990	Tex	AL	33	10	1	6	102.1	447	115	59	53	6	1	7	4	39	4	58	1	0	2	6	.250	0	0-0	1	4.57	4.66
1991	StL	NL	8	7	0	1	31.1	142	38	21	20	5	4	2	1	16	0	20	2	1	0	5	.000	0	0-0	0	6.58	5.74
1993	Bal	AL	25	25	3	0	152.0	630	154	63	58	11	3	1	6	38	2	90	1	1	12	9	.571	1	0-0	0	3.58	3.43
1994	Bal	AL	23	23	0	0	149.0	631	158	81	79	23	5	2	2	38	3	87	1	0	5	7	.417	0	0-0	0	4.24	4.77
1995	Bal	AL	27	18	0	3	115.2	483	117	70	67	18	5	3	3	30	0	65	0	0	8	6	.571	0	0-0	0	4.11	5.21
1996	2 Tms	AL	34	21	0	1	160.2	703	177	86	71	23	7	6	7	46	5	79	3	1	13	3	.813	0	0-0	0	4.42	3.98
1997	Sea	AL	30	30	2	0	188.2	787	187	82	81	21	7	6	7	43	2	113	3	0	17	5	.773	0	0-0	0	3.56	3.86
1998	Sea	AL	34	34	4	0	234.1	974	234	99	92	23	4	3	10	42	4	158	3	1	15	9	.625	3	0-0	0	3.34	3.53
1999	Sea	AL	32	32	4	0	228.0	945	235	108	98	23	6	2	9	48	1	137	3	0	14	8	.636	0	0-0	0	3.71	3.87
2000	Sea	AL	26	26	0	0	154.0	678	173	103	93	22	3	3	9	53	2	98	4	1	13	10	.565	0	0-0	0	4.91	5.49
2001	Sea	AL	33	33	1	0	209.2	851	187	84	80	24	5	11	10	44	4	119	1	0	20	6	.769	0	0-0	0	3.03	3.43
2002	Sea	AL	34	34	4	0	230.2	931	199	89	85	28	5	7	9	50	4	147	3	0	13	8	.619	2	0-0	0	2.89	3.32
2003	Sea	AL	33	33	1	0	215.0	897	199	83	78	19	7	6	8	66	3	129	0	1	21	7	.750	0	0-0	0	3.37	3.27
2004	Sea	AL	34	33	1	1	202.0	888	217	127	117	44	9	6	11	63	2	125	1	0	7	13	.350	0	0-0	0	5.13	5.21

Year	Team	Lg		HOW MUCH HE PITCHED							WHAT HE GAVE UP														THE RESULTS						
			G	GS	CG	GF	IP	BFP	H	R	ER	HR	SH	SF	HB	TBB	IBB	SO	WP	Bk	W	L	Pct	ShO	Sv-Op	Hld	ERC	ERA
2005	Sea	AL	32	32	1	0	200.0	868	225	99	95	23	6	8	6	52	2	102	3	0	13	7	.650	0	0-0	0	4.46	4.28
2006	2 Tms		33	33	2	0	211.1	894	228	110	101	33	5	9	5	51	5	108	3	1	11	14	.440	1	0-0	0	4.36	4.30
2007	Phi	NL	33	33	1	0	199.1	867	222	118	111	30	11	5	5	66	3	133	2	0	14	12	.538	0	0-0	0	4.92	5.01
96	Bos	AL	23	10	0	1	90.0	405	111	50	45	14	4	3	1	27	2	50	2	1	7	1	.875	0	0-0	1	5.37	4.50
96	Sea	AL	11	11	0	0	70.2	298	66	36	26	9	3	3	1	19	3	29	1	0	6	2	.750	0	0-0	0	3.31	3.31
06	Sea	AL	25	25	2	0	160.0	685	179	85	78	25	3	7	3	44	3	82	3	1	6	12	.333	1	0-0	0	4.74	4.39
06	Phi	NL	8	8	0	0	51.1	209	49	25	23	8	2	2	2	7	2	26	0	0	5	2	.714	0	0-0	0	3.24	4.03
21 ML YEARS			604	551	31	14	3550.1	15102	3677	1796	1662	444	124	90	117	1012	62	2125	53	11	230	178	.564	9	0-2	2	4.11	4.21

Peter Moylan

Pitches: R **Bats:** R **Pos:** RP-80 **Ht:** 6'3" **Wt:** 200 **Born:** 12/2/1978 **Age:** 29

Year	Team	Lg		HOW MUCH HE PITCHED							WHAT HE GAVE UP														THE RESULTS						
			G	GS	CG	GF	IP	BFP	H	R	ER	HR	SH	SF	HB	TBB	IBB	SO	WP	Bk	W	L	Pct	ShO	Sv-Op	Hld	ERC	FRA
1996	Twins	R	13	0	0	4	28.2	128	34	16	13	3	1	2	3	9	0	16	4	0	1	1	.500	0	1--	-	5.31	4.08
1997	Twins	R	12	7	0	2	40.0	178	46	21	18	0	0	1	4	10	0	40	3	0	4	2	.667	0	0--	-	3.93	4.05
2006	Rchmd	AAA	35	0	0	11	56.2	275	61	43	40	4	4	1	8	38	6	54	6	0	1	7	.125	0	1--	-	5.64	6.35
2007	Rchmd	AAA	2	0	0	2	2.0	8	0	0	0	0	0	0	0	1	0	3	0	0	0	0	-	0	1--	-	0.24	0.00
2006	Atl	NL	15	0	0	5	15.0	68	18	8	8	1	1	0	0	5	1	14	0	0	0	0	-	0	0-0	0	4.47	4.80
2007	Atl	NL	80	0	0	16	90.0	359	65	27	18	6	4	4	7	31	12	63	2	0	5	3	.625	0	1-2	8	2.36	1.80
2 ML YEARS			95	0	0	21	105.0	427	83	35	26	7	5	4	7	36	13	77	2	0	5	3	.625	0	1-2	8	2.64	2.23

Edward Mujica

Pitches: R **Bats:** R **Pos:** RP-10 **Ht:** 6'2" **Wt:** 220 **Born:** 5/10/1984 **Age:** 24

Year	Team	Lg		HOW MUCH HE PITCHED							WHAT HE GAVE UP														THE RESULTS						
			G	GS	CG	GF	IP	BFP	H	R	ER	HR	SH	SF	HB	TBB	IBB	SO	WP	Bk	W	L	Pct	ShO	Sv-Op	Hld	ERC	ERA
2003	Burlgtn	A	14	10	0	3	55.2	231	57	31	27	3	2	1	1	20	0	41	2	1	2	6	.250	0	0--	-	3.96	4.37
2004	Lk Cty	A	26	19	1	3	124.0	525	130	77	64	18	5	7	13	32	1	89	6	4	7	7	.500	0	2--	-	4.61	4.65
2005	Knstn	A+	25	0	0	25	26.0	96	17	6	6	3	1	0	1	2	0	32	1	0	1	0	1.000	0	14--	-	1.51	2.08
2005	Akron	AA	27	0	0	18	34.1	141	36	11	11	2	4	0	0	5	0	33	3	1	2	1	.667	0	10--	-	3.09	2.88
2006	Akron	AA	12	0	0	10	19.0	77	11	1	0	0	2	0	1	9	1	17	1	0	1	0	1.000	0	8--	-	1.68	0.00
2006	Buffalo	AAA	22	0	0	16	32.2	130	31	10	9	1	4	0	1	5	0	29	1	0	3	1	.750	0	5--	-	2.61	2.48
2007	Buffalo	AAA	34	0	0	27	37.2	154	35	22	21	4	1	2	1	9	1	44	1	1	2	1	.667	0	14--	-	3.20	5.02
2006	Cle	AL	10	0	0	2	18.1	78	25	6	6	1	0	2	1	0	0	12	0	0	0	1	.000	0	0-0	0	4.50	2.95
2007	Cle	AL	10	0	0	5	13.0	60	19	12	12	3	0	1	0	2	0	7	0	0	0	0	-	0	0-0	0	6.63	8.31
2 ML YEARS			20	0	0	7	31.1	138	44	18	18	4	0	3	1	2	0	19	0	0	0	1	.000	0	0-0	0	5.37	5.17

Mark Mulder

Pitches: L **Bats:** L **Pos:** SP-3 **Ht:** 6'6" **Wt:** 215 **Born:** 8/5/1977 **Age:** 30

Year	Team	Lg		HOW MUCH HE PITCHED							WHAT HE GAVE UP														THE RESULTS						
			G	GS	CG	GF	IP	BFP	H	R	ER	HR	SH	SF	HB	TBB	IBB	SO	WP	Bk	W	L	Pct	ShO	Sv-Op	Hld	ERC	ERA
2007	PlmBh*	A+	3	3	0	0	9.1	40	7	6	2	0	0	0	0	3	0	5	1	0	0	2	.000	0	0--	-	1.73	1.93
2007	Memp*	AAA	1	1	0	0	5.0	21	5	2	2	1	1	0	0	2	0	4	0	0	0	0	-	0	0--	-	4.93	3.60
2000	Oak	AL	27	27	0	0	154.0	705	191	106	93	22	3	8	4	69	3	88	6	0	9	10	.474	0	0-0	0	6.14	5.44
2001	Oak	AL	34	34	6	0	229.1	927	214	92	88	16	8	3	5	51	4	153	4	0	21	8	.724	4	0-0	0	2.95	3.45
2002	Oak	AL	30	30	2	0	207.1	862	182	88	80	21	6	4	11	55	3	159	7	1	19	7	.731	1	0-0	0	3.06	3.47
2003	Oak	AL	26	26	9	0	186.2	747	180	66	65	15	7	2	2	40	2	128	7	0	15	9	.625	2	0-0	0	3.17	3.13
2004	Oak	AL	33	33	5	0	225.2	952	223	119	111	25	7	6	12	83	1	140	10	0	17	8	.680	1	0-0	0	4.27	4.43
2005	StL	NL	32	32	3	0	205.0	868	212	90	83	19	9	4	9	70	1	111	9	0	16	8	.667	2	0-0	0	4.25	3.64
2006	StL	NL	17	17	0	0	93.1	430	124	77	74	19	10	1	5	35	1	50	3	0	6	7	.462	0	0-0	0	7.04	7.14
2007	StL	NL	3	3	0	0	11.0	59	22	17	15	4	1	0	1	7	0	3	0	0	0	3	.000	0	0-0	0	15.59	12.27
8 ML YEARS			202	202	25	0	1312.1	5550	1348	655	609	141	51	28	49	410	15	832	46	1	103	60	.632	10	0-0	0	4.13	4.18

Carlos Muniz

Pitches: R **Bats:** R **Pos:** RP-2 **Ht:** 6'1" **Wt:** 180 **Born:** 3/12/1981 **Age:** 27

Year	Team	Lg		HOW MUCH HE PITCHED							WHAT HE GAVE UP														THE RESULTS						
			G	GS	CG	GF	IP	BFP	H	R	ER	HR	SH	SF	HB	TBB	IBB	SO	WP	Bk	W	L	Pct	ShO	Sv-Op	Hld	ERC	ERA
2003	Bklyn	A-	19	0	0	15	20.0	73	12	1	1	1	1	0	0	5	2	23	3	0	0	0	-	0	13--	-	1.38	0.45
2004	CptCty	A	16	0	0	14	21.0	84	11	10	10	1	0	0	3	8	0	19	0	0	4	0	1.000	0	7--	-	1.78	4.29
2004	Bklyn	A-	12	0	0	11	14.2	62	14	8	5	1	0	0	1	3	2	20	2	0	3	2	.600	0	3--	-	2.86	3.07
2005	Hgrstn	A	30	0	0	26	37.2	169	37	22	20	6	3	1	2	19	0	43	1	2	3	4	.429	0	14--	-	5.00	4.78
2005	Mets	R	2	0	0	1	1.2	11	6	4	3	0	0	0	0	0	0	0	0	0	0	1	.000	0	0--	-	19.18	16.20
2005	StLuci	A+	14	0	0	3	17.0	73	13	11	11	3	1	1	0	9	0	19	1	0	1	3	.250	0	0--	-	3.73	5.82
2006	StLuci	A+	48	0	0	44	49.2	208	39	21	17	5	2	3	2	18	0	45	1	0	4	3	.571	0	31--	-	2.88	3.08
2007	Bnghtn	AA	44	0	0	36	58.2	241	43	20	16	2	3	1	2	17	5	62	2	0	2	4	.333	0	23--	-	1.84	2.45
2007	NewOr	AAA	3	0	0	1	5.2	22	4	0	0	0	0	0	0	1	0	4	0	0	0	0	-	0	0--	-	1.36	0.00
2007	NYM	NL	2	0	0	1	2.1	10	1	2	2	0	0	0	0	2	0	2	0	0	0	0	-	0	0-0	0	2.03	7.71

Arnie Munoz

Pitches: L **Bats:** L **Pos:** RP-13 **Ht:** 5'9" **Wt:** 170 **Born:** 6/21/1982 **Age:** 26

Year	Team	Lg		HOW MUCH HE PITCHED							WHAT HE GAVE UP														THE RESULTS						
			G	GS	CG	GF	IP	BFP	H	R	ER	HR	SH	SF	HB	TBB	IBB	SO	WP	Bk	W	L	Pct	ShO	Sv-Op	Hld	ERC	ERA
1999	WhSox	R	14	0	0	7	12.0	61	13	10	7	1	0	0	2	8	0	12	1	1	0	2	.000	0	1--	-	5.82	5.25
2000	Burlgtn	A	22	0	0	8	38.1	185	45	34	29	2	1	0	6	25	0	44	7	5	2	3	.400	0	0--	-	6.43	6.81
2001	Knapol	A-	60	0	0	30	79.2	310	41	24	22	2	2	4	7	42	1	115	8	4	6	3	.667	0	12--	-	1.97	2.49
2002	Brham	AA	51	0	0	18	72.1	306	62	29	21	6	5	3	1	29	0	78	5	2	6	0	1.000	0	6--	-	3.21	2.61

		HOW MUCH HE PITCHED						WHAT HE GAVE UP											THE RESULTS						
Year	Team	Lg	G	GS	CG	GF	IP	BFP	H	R	ER	HR	SH	SF	HB	TBB	IBB	SO	WP	Bk	W	L	Pct	ShO	Sv-Op	Hld	ERC	ERA
2003	Charltt	AAA	49	0	0	17	55.0	238	52	35	29	7	3	0	3	27	2	63	7	1	4	3	.571	0	6--	-	4.56	4.75
2004	Brham	AA	13	13	0	0	74.2	293	52	24	17	1	2	3	4	22	3	68	3	2	7	2	.778	0	0--	-	1.80	2.05
2004	Charltt	AAA	13	13	0	0	69.2	316	81	48	44	11	3	2	2	29	0	60	6	2	2	6	.250	0	0--	-	5.61	5.68
2005	Charltt	AAA	40	18	0	7	132.2	608	150	79	63	16	3	5	5	60	2	109	9	3	8	14	.364	0	1--	-	5.24	4.27
2006	Brham	AA	26	2	0	5	46.0	189	38	20	19	4	2	2	2	14	0	48	4	4	2	4	.333	0	2--	-	2.86	3.72
2006	Brham	AA	7	0	0	2	6.1	36	10	10	10	1	0	0	1	7	1	5	3	0	0	1	.000	0	0--	-	11.90	14.21
2007	Clmbs	AAA	54	0	0	17	52.2	219	46	17	15	5	0	0	0	18	1	46	7	0	3	1	.750	0	0--	-	3.09	2.56
2004	CWS	AL	11	1	0	3	14.1	75	20	16	16	4	1	2	1	12	1	11	2	0	0	1	.000	0	0-0	0	10.17	10.05
2007	Was	NL	13	0	0	0	5.1	32	6	4	4	2	1	0	2	7	1	3	0	0	0	0		0	0-1	4	12.15	6.75
	2 ML YEARS		24	1	0	3	19.2	107	26	20	20	6	2	2	3	19	2	14	2	0	0	1	.000	0	0-1	4	10.71	9.15

Eric Munson

Bats: L **Throws:** R **Pos:** C-43; 1B-5; PH-5   **Ht:** 6'3" **Wt:** 220 **Born:** 10/3/1977 **Age:** 30

								BATTING												BASERUNNING				AVERAGES		
Year	Team	Lg	G	AB	H	2B	3B	HR	(Hm	Rd)	TB	R	RBI	RC	TBB	IBB	SO	HBP	SH	SF	SB	CS	SB%	GDP	Avg	OBP	Slg
2007	RdRck*	AAA	50	173	49	18	0	7	(-	-)	88	28	26	33	24	1	34	1	0	3	1	1	.50	1	.283	.368	.509
2000	Det	AL	3	5	0	0	0	0	(0	0)	0	0	1	0	0	0	1	0	0	0	0	0	-	0	.000	.000	.000
2001	Det	AL	17	66	10	3	1	1	(1	0)	18	4	6	2	3	0	21	0	0	0	0	1	.00	2	.152	.188	.273
2002	Det	AL	18	59	11	0	0	2	(0	2)	17	3	5	3	6	0	11	1	0	1	0	0	-	1	.186	.269	.288
2003	Det	AL	99	313	75	9	0	18	(7	11)	138	28	50	45	35	1	61	1	1	7	3	0	1.00	4	.240	.312	.441
2004	Det	AL	109	321	68	14	2	19	(13	6)	143	36	49	48	29	3	90	6	1	0	1	1	.50	1	.212	.289	.445
2005	TB	AL	11	18	3	1	0	0	(0	0)	4	2	2	2	4	0	3	1	0	1	0	0	-	2	.167	.333	.222
2006	Hou	NL	53	141	28	6	0	5	(2	3)	49	10	19	12	11	1	32	3	0	1	0	0	-	2	.199	.269	.348
2007	Hou	NL	50	132	31	4	0	4	(3	1)	47	14	15	10	16	1	15	0	0	2	0	0	-	8	.235	.313	.356
	8 ML YEARS		360	1055	226	37	3	49	(26	23)	416	97	147	122	104	6	234	12	2	12	4	2	.67	20	.214	.289	.394

Scott Munter

Pitches: R **Bats:** R **Pos:** RP-12   **Ht:** 6'6" **Wt:** 260 **Born:** 3/7/1980 **Age:** 28

			HOW MUCH HE PITCHED						WHAT HE GAVE UP											THE RESULTS						
Year	Team	Lg	G	GS	CG	GF	IP	BFP	H	R	ER	HR	SH	SF	HB	TBB	IBB	SO	WP	Bk	W	L	Pct	ShO	Sv-Op	Hld	ERC	ERA
2007	Fresno*	AAA	48	0	0	16	58.1	252	62	28	27	3	2	2	2	24	0	14	2	0	1	6	.143	0	1--	-	4.35	4.17
2005	SF	NL	45	0	0	7	38.2	159	40	15	11	1	2	1	1	12	1	11	1	0	2	0	1.000	0	0-3	12	3.62	2.56
2006	SF	NL	27	0	0	11	22.2	110	30	22	22	1	7	1	2	18	2	7	0	0	1	1	.000	0	0-0	5	7.75	8.74
2007	SF	NL	12	0	0	5	10.2	46	14	5	5	0	2	2	0	4	0	4	0	0	1	1	.500	0	0-0	0	5.34	4.22
	3 ML YEARS		84	0	0	23	72.0	315	84	42	38	2	11	4	3	34	3	22	1	0	3	2	.600	0	0-3	17	5.09	4.75

Bill Murphy

Pitches: L **Bats:** L **Pos:** RP-10   **Ht:** 5'11" **Wt:** 215 **Born:** 5/9/1981 **Age:** 27

			HOW MUCH HE PITCHED						WHAT HE GAVE UP											THE RESULTS						
Year	Team	Lg	G	GS	CG	GF	IP	BFP	H	R	ER	HR	SH	SF	HB	TBB	IBB	SO	WP	Bk	W	L	Pct	ShO	Sv-Op	Hld	ERC	ERA
2002	Vancvr	A-	13	9	0	0	41.1	187	28	23	21	2	1	3	2	35	0	46	4	0	1	4	.200	0	0--	-	3.75	4.57
2003	Kane	A	14	14	1	0	92.0	363	61	27	23	5	1	4	2	32	0	87	1	3	7	4	.636	1	0--	-	1.98	2.25
2003	Mdland	AA	11	11	0	0	55.0	233	44	25	25	4	1	3	3	26	1	34	1	3	3	3	.500	0	0--	-	3.26	4.09
2004	Carlina	AA	20	20	0	0	103.2	438	80	48	47	17	6	8	3	59	1	113	4	2	6	4	.600	0	0--	-	4.09	4.08
2004	ElPaso	AA	6	6	0	0	31.0	141	41	28	23	6	0	2	1	17	0	24	2	1	3	3	.500	0	0--	-	8.01	6.68
2005	Tucsn	AAA	23	21	0	0	121.0	570	135	81	76	14	6	4	7	78	0	87	7	1	6	8	.429	0	0--	-	6.12	5.65
2006	Tenn	AA	5	4	0	0	21.0	93	22	13	13	2	2	0	1	9	0	26	0	0	1	0	1.000	0	0--	-	4.61	5.57
2006	Tucsn	AAA	37	9	0	5	80.2	358	86	53	50	5	6	5	1	38	0	72	3	2	5	4	.556	0	0--	-	4.51	5.58
2007	Tucsn	AAA	54	9	0	13	100.1	435	93	53	41	10	3	2	9	43	0	102	9	1	3	3	.500	0	1--	-	4.15	3.68
2007	Ari	NL	10	0	0	2	6.1	34	9	4	4	0	0	0	1	7	2	2	0	0	0	0	-	0	0-0	1	8.97	5.68

David Murphy

Bats: L **Throws:** L **Pos:** LF-32; RF-15; CF-10; PR-3; PH-1   **Ht:** 6'4" **Wt:** 192 **Born:** 10/18/1981 **Age:** 26

								BATTING												BASERUNNING				AVERAGES		
Year	Team	Lg	G	AB	H	2B	3B	HR	(Hm	Rd)	TB	R	RBI	RC	TBB	IBB	SO	HBP	SH	SF	SB	CS	SB%	GDP	Avg	OBP	Slg
2003	Srsota	A+	45	153	37	5	1	1	(-	-)	47	18	18	17	20	1	33	0	0	5	6	2	.75	3	.242	.329	.307
2003	Lowell	A-	21	78	27	4	0	0	(-	-)	31	13	13	16	16	2	9	0	0	1	4	1	.80	1	.346	.453	.397
2004	RedSx	R	5	18	5	1	0	0	(-	-)	6	3	1	2	1	0	2	0	0	0	1	0	1.00	1	.278	.316	.333
2004	Srsota	A+	73	272	71	11	0	4	(-	-)	94	35	38	30	25	4	46	0	0	0	3	5	.38	5	.261	.323	.346
2005	Portlnd	AA	135	484	133	25	4	14	(-	-)	208	71	75	73	46	3	83	1	1	3	13	6	.68	11	.275	.337	.430
2006	Portlnd	AA	42	172	47	17	1	3	(-	-)	75	22	25	24	11	0	29	0	0	1	4	2	.67	3	.273	.315	.436
2006	Pwtckt	AAA	84	318	85	23	5	8	(-	-)	142	45	44	52	45	8	53	0	0	3	3	3	.50	13	.267	.355	.447
2007	Pwtckt	AAA	100	400	112	20	5	9	(-	-)	169	50	48	62	41	2	68	1	0	2	8	1	.89	8	.280	.347	.423
2007	Okla	AAA	2	7	2	0	0	0	(-	-)	2	0	0	0	0	0	3	0	0	0	0	1	.00	0	.286	.286	.286
2006	Bos	AL	20	22	5	1	0	1	(0	1)	9	4	2	2	4	0	4	0	0	0	0	0	-	1	.227	.346	.409
2007	2 Tms	AL	46	105	36	12	2	2	(1	1)	58	17	14	23	7	0	20	0	0	0	0	0	-	1	.343	.384	.552
07	Bos	AL	3	2	1	0	0	0	(0	0)	3	1	0	1	0	0	1	0	0	0	0	0	-	0	.500	.500	1.500
07	Tex	AL	43	103	35	12	1	2	(1	1)	55	16	14	22	7	0	19	0	0	0	0	0	-	1	.340	.382	.534
	2 ML YEARS		66	127	41	13	2	3	(1	2)	67	21	16	25	11	0	24	0	0	0	0	0	-	2	.323	.377	.528

Donnie Murphy

Bats: R **Throws:** R **Pos:** SS-31; PH-5; PR-4; 2B-2; 3B-1; DH-1   **Ht:** 5'10" **Wt:** 185 **Born:** 3/10/1983 **Age:** 25

							BATTING													BASERUNNING				AVERAGES		
Year	Team	Lg	G	AB	H	2B	3B	HR	(Hm | Rd)	TB	R	RBI	RC	TBB	IBB	SO	HBP	SH	SF	SB	CS	SB%	GDP	Avg	OBP	Slg
2007	Scrmto*	AAA	45	175	57	19	2	3	(- | -)	89	31	22	34	17	2	44	2	3	2	4	2	.67	4	.326	.388	.509
2004	KC	AL	7	27	5	3	0	0	(0 | 0)	8	1	3	2	0	0	7	0	0	0	1	0	1.00	1	.185	.185	.296
2005	KC	AL	32	77	12	5	0	1	(0 | 1)	20	4	8	1	9	0	23	0	1	1	0	1	.00	3	.156	.241	.260
2007	Oak	AL	42	118	26	8	0	6	(2 | 4)	52	21	21	16	10	0	35	2	1	1	1	0	1.00	3	.220	.290	.441
	3 ML YEARS		81	222	43	16	0	7	(2 | 5)	80	26	32	19	19	0	65	2	2	2	2	1	.67	7	.194	.261	.360

Tommy Murphy

Bats: B **Throws:** R **Pos:** RF-9; LF-5; PH-3; PR-3; CF-2; DH-1   **Ht:** 6'0" **Wt:** 190 **Born:** 8/27/1979 **Age:** 28

							BATTING													BASERUNNING				AVERAGES		
Year	Team	Lg	G	AB	H	2B	3B	HR	(Hm | Rd)	TB	R	RBI	RC	TBB	IBB	SO	HBP	SH	SF	SB	CS	SB%	GDP	Avg	OBP	Slg
2000	Boise	A-	55	213	48	18	1	2	(- | -)	74	38	25	22	15	0	52	5	1	1	14	7	.67	1	.225	.291	.347
2001	CRpds	A	74	280	57	15	3	4	(- | -)	90	32	31	21	16	1	94	6	6	3	7	10	.41	5	.204	.259	.321
2001	RCuca	A+	50	200	38	8	0	0	(- | -)	46	16	11	7	5	0	69	1	1	0	7	3	.70	1	.190	.214	.230
2002	CRpds	A	128	485	131	20	2	3	(- | -)	164	72	48	58	40	0	115	1	7	5	31	11	.74	8	.270	.324	.338
2003	RCuca	A+	132	565	151	25	6	11	(- | -)	221	74	43	71	31	0	138	8	7	3	24	12	.67	7	.267	.313	.391
2004	Ark	AA	129	477	124	24	6	7	(- | -)	181	77	45	62	36	1	113	1	9	5	27	5	.84	9	.260	.310	.379
2005	Ark	AA	135	500	144	24	11	17	(- | -)	241	85	76	86	43	2	97	5	2	7	26	12	.68	11	.288	.346	.482
2006	Salt Lk	AAA	73	285	86	16	3	7	(- | -)	129	43	36	42	19	2	62	3	2	1	6	13	.32	1	.302	.351	.453
2007	Salt Lk	AAA	80	307	83	18	6	4	(- | -)	125	36	32	41	23	0	67	2	3	2	15	10	.60	4	.270	.323	.407
2006	LAA	AL	48	70	16	4	1	1	(1 | 0)	25	12	6	7	5	0	21	0	1	1	4	1	.80	0	.229	.276	.357
2007	LAA	AL	20	38	7	1	0	0	(0 | 0)	8	2	2	0	0	0	9	1	0	0	0	0	-	1	.184	.205	.211
	2 ML YEARS		68	108	23	5	1	1	(1 | 0)	33	14	8	7	5	0	30	1	1	1	4	1	.80	1	.213	.252	.306

A.J. Murray

Pitches: L **Bats:** B **Pos:** RP-12; SP-2   **Ht:** 6'3" **Wt:** 220 **Born:** 3/17/1982 **Age:** 26

			HOW MUCH HE PITCHED					WHAT HE GAVE UP											THE RESULTS						
Year	Team	Lg	G	GS	CG	GF	IP	BFP	H	R	ER	HR	SH	SF	HB	TBB	IBB	SO	WP	Bk	W	L	Pct	ShO	Sv-Op	Hld	ERC	ERA
2001	Rngrs	R	12	8	0	2	53.1	207	48	15	11	1	1	1	1	10	2	45	4	1	3	3	.500	0	0- -	-	2.38	1.86
2002	Savann	A	14	8	0	2	62.2	255	63	22	20	0	2	6	0	14	0	51	5	0	5	3	.625	0	0- -	-	2.83	2.87
2002	Charltt	A+	19	14	0	3	83.1	339	77	31	28	4	1	1	0	20	0	68	3	1	3	3	.500	0	2- -	-	2.75	3.02
2003	Frisco	AA	27	25	0	1	144.0	611	134	68	58	13	5	12	4	63	2	90	9	0	10	4	.714	0	0	-	3.92	3.63
2005	Brisfld	A+	14	11	0	0	60.0	266	75	38	35	6	0	2	2	13	0	64	2	0	2	5	.286	0	0- -	-	4.86	5.25
2005	Frisco	AA	11	10	0	0	58.0	239	62	27	21	3	1	4	1	15	0	49	1	0	4	4	.500	0	0- -	-	3.77	3.26
2005	Okla	AAA	2	2	0	0	10.0	42	11	7	7	4	0	0	0	2	0	11	0	0	1	0	1.000	0	0- -	-	5.90	6.30
2007	Okla	AAA	41	1	0	21	52.2	221	42	19	18	2	3	1	2	25	0	51	1	0	3	3	.500	0	5- -	-	3.01	3.08
2007	Tex	AL	14	2	0	6	28.0	123	25	15	14	6	1	1	0	15	1	18	0	0	1	2	.333	0	0-0	0	4.71	4.50

Matt Murton

Bats: R **Throws:** R **Pos:** RF-41; PH-34; LF-28; CF-1   **Ht:** 6'1" **Wt:** 220 **Born:** 10/3/1981 **Age:** 26

							BATTING													BASERUNNING				AVERAGES		
Year	Team	Lg	G	AB	H	2B	3B	HR	(Hm | Rd)	TB	R	RBI	RC	TBB	IBB	SO	HBP	SH	SF	SB	CS	SB%	GDP	Avg	OBP	Slg
2007	Iowa*	AAA	39	151	49	16	1	6	(- | -)	85	30	27	33	18	1	18	2	0	1	1	0	1.00	8	.325	.401	.563
2005	ChC	NL	51	140	45	3	2	7	(2 | 5)	73	19	14	19	16	4	22	0	2	2	2	1	.67	4	.321	.386	.521
2006	ChC	NL	144	455	135	22	3	13	(7 | 6)	202	70	62	60	45	1	62	5	1	2	5	2	.71	16	.297	.365	.444
2007	ChC	NL	94	235	66	13	0	8	(2 | 6)	103	35	22	28	26	0	39	0	0	0	1	0	1.00	4	.281	.352	.438
	3 ML YEARS		289	830	246	38	5	28	(11 | 17)	378	124	98	115	87	5	123	5	3	4	8	3	.73	24	.296	.365	.455

Neal Musser

Pitches: L **Bats:** L **Pos:** RP-17   **Ht:** 6'1" **Wt:** 235 **Born:** 8/25/1980 **Age:** 27

			HOW MUCH HE PITCHED					WHAT HE GAVE UP											THE RESULTS						
Year	Team	Lg	G	GS	CG	GF	IP	BFP	H	R	ER	HR	SH	SF	HB	TBB	IBB	SO	WP	Bk	W	L	Pct	ShO	Sv-Op	Hld	ERC	ERA
1999	Mets	R	8	7	0	0	31.1	134	26	13	7	1	0	0	0	18	0	22	4	0	2	1	.667	0	0- -	-	3.36	2.01
2000	Kngspt	R+	7	7	0	0	34.1	138	33	10	8	1	0	0	1	6	0	21	3	0	3	2	.600	0	0- -	-	2.72	2.10
2001	Clmbia	A	17	17	1	0	95.0	387	86	38	30	3	4	3	3	18	0	98	8	1	7	4	.636	0	0- -	-	2.46	2.84
2001	StLuci	A+	9	9	0	0	45.2	201	45	24	18	2	0	2	5	19	0	40	2	0	3	4	.429	0	0- -	-	4.08	3.55
2002	StLuci	A+	4	4	0	0	19.0	80	20	4	3	1	0	1	1	5	0	12	1	0	2	0	1.000	0	0- -	-	3.77	1.42
2002	Bklyn	A-	4	4	0	0	13.0	49	7	2	1	0	0	0	1	5	0	12	0	0	0	0	-	0	0- -	-	1.54	0.69
2003	StLuci	A+	7	6	0	0	34.2	155	41	20	18	5	1	1	3	9	0	16	1	1	3	0	1.000	0	0- -	-	5.19	4.67
2003	Bnghtn	AA	20	20	0	0	100.1	436	108	57	51	9	4	4	6	39	0	76	5	1	5	9	.357	0	0- -	-	4.72	4.57
2004	Bnghtn	AA	19	19	0	0	108.1	458	103	52	41	7	8	5	4	40	0	70	3	1	9	6	.600	0	0- -	-	3.62	3.41
2004	Norfolk	AAA	7	7	0	0	36.0	161	39	30	25	4	5	5	0	17	2	24	3	0	2	4	.333	0	0- -	-	4.81	6.25
2005	Norfolk	AAA	24	24	0	0	123.2	561	141	75	69	12	6	6	9	52	0	89	7	1	6	11	.353	0	0- -	-	5.23	5.02
2006	Tucsn	AAA	8	7	0	0	36.1	174	44	26	22	4	1	0	5	24	0	18	6	0	1	3	.250	0	0- -	-	7.25	5.45
2006	Omha	AAA	2	2	0	0	9.2	38	7	2	2	2	0	0	0	3	0	6	0	0	1	0	1.000	0	0	-	2.96	1.86
2006	Wichta	AA	18	11	0	3	83.2	372	80	53	46	12	2	3	5	48	3	67	6	1	6	3	.667	0	2- -	-	5.08	4.95
2007	Omha	AAA	32	0	0	20	55.1	204	32	5	3	1	2	3	3	11	0	47	4	0	4	1	.800	0	8- -	-	1.27	0.49
2007	KC	AL	17	0	0	3	24.2	116	32	13	12	5	0	0	0	14	3	19	2	0	0	1	.000	0	0-0	1	7.27	4.38

Mike Mussina

Pitches: R Bats: L Pos: SP-27; RP-1   Ht: 6'2" Wt: 190 Born: 12/8/1968 Age: 39

			HOW MUCH HE PITCHED						WHAT HE GAVE UP										THE RESULTS						
Year	Team	Lg	G	GS	CG	GF	IP	BFP	H	R	ER	HR	SH	SF	HB	TBB	IBB	SO	WP	Bk	W	L	Pct	ShO	Sv-Op	Hld	ERC	ERA
1991	Bal	AL	12	12	2	0	87.2	349	77	31	28	7	3	2	1	21	0	52	3	1	4	5	.444	0	0-0	0	2.80	2.87
1992	Bal	AL	32	32	8	0	241.0	957	212	70	68	16	13	6	2	48	2	130	6	0	18	5	.783	4	0-0	0	2.54	2.54
1993	Bal	AL	25	25	3	0	167.2	693	163	84	83	20	6	4	3	44	2	117	5	0	14	6	.700	2	0-0	0	3.61	4.46
1994	Bal	AL	24	24	3	0	176.1	712	163	63	60	19	3	9	1	42	1	99	0	0	16	5	.762	0	0-0	0	3.16	3.06
1995	Bal	AL	32	32	7	0	221.2	882	187	86	81	24	2	2	1	50	4	158	2	0	19	9	.679	4	0-0	0	2.66	3.29
1996	Bal	AL	36	36	4	0	243.1	1039	264	137	130	31	4	4	3	69	0	204	3	0	19	11	.633	1	0-0	0	4.36	4.81
1997	Bal	AL	33	33	4	0	224.2	905	197	87	80	27	3	2	3	54	3	218	5	0	15	8	.652	1	0-0	0	3.00	3.20
1998	Bal	AL	29	29	4	0	206.1	835	189	85	80	22	6	3	4	41	3	175	10	0	13	10	.565	2	0-0	0	2.96	3.49
1999	Bal	AL	31	31	4	0	203.1	842	207	88	79	16	9	7	1	52	0	172	2	0	18	7	.720	0	0-0	0	3.54	3.50
2000	Bal	AL	34	34	6	0	237.2	987	236	105	100	28	8	6	3	46	0	210	3	0	11	15	.423	1	0-0	0	3.37	3.79
2001	NYY	AL	34	34	4	0	228.2	909	202	87	80	20	5	6	4	42	2	214	6	0	17	11	.607	3	0-0	0	2.65	3.15
2002	NYY	AL	33	33	2	0	215.2	886	208	103	97	27	5	5	5	48	1	182	7	0	18	10	.643	2	0-0	0	3.46	4.05
2003	NYY	AL	31	31	2	0	214.2	855	192	86	81	21	1	4	3	40	4	195	4	0	17	8	.680	1	0-0	0	2.75	3.40
2004	NYY	AL	27	27	1	0	164.2	697	178	91	84	22	5	4	2	40	1	132	5	0	12	9	.571	0	0-0	0	4.19	4.59
2005	NYY	AL	30	30	2	0	179.2	766	199	93	88	23	6	4	7	47	0	142	2	0	13	8	.619	2	0-0	0	4.55	4.41
2006	NYY	AL	32	32	1	0	197.1	804	184	88	77	22	1	1	5	35	1	172	3	0	15	7	.682	0	0-0	0	3.01	3.51
2007	NYY	AL	28	27	0	0	152.0	656	188	90	87	14	6	6	4	35	2	91	1	0	11	10	.524	0	0-0	0	4.87	5.15
17 ML YEARS			503	502	57	0	3362.1	13774	3246	1474	1383	359	86	75	52	754	26	2663	67	1	250	144	.635	23	0-0	0	3.33	3.70

Brett Myers

Pitches: R Bats: R Pos: RP-48; SP-3   Ht: 6'4" Wt: 238 Born: 8/17/1980 Age: 27

			HOW MUCH HE PITCHED						WHAT HE GAVE UP										THE RESULTS						
Year	Team	Lg	G	GS	CG	GF	IP	BFP	H	R	ER	HR	SH	SF	HB	TBB	IBB	SO	WP	Bk	W	L	Pct	ShO	Sv-Op	Hld	ERC	ERA
2007	Clrwtr*	A+	3	3	0	0	3.1	12	2	0	0	0	0	0	1	0	4	0	0	0	0	-	0	0--	-	1.41	0.00
2002	Phi	NL	12	12	1	0	72.0	307	73	38	34	11	6	2	6	29	1	34	2	1	4	5	.444	0	0-0	0	5.04	4.25
2003	Phi	NL	32	32	1	0	193.0	848	205	99	95	20	6	3	9	76	4	143	9	0	14	9	.609	1	0-0	0	4.56	4.43
2004	Phi	NL	32	31	1	1	176.0	778	196	113	108	31	9	3	6	62	4	116	5	0	11	11	.500	1	0-0	0	5.17	5.52
2005	Phi	NL	34	34	2	0	215.1	905	193	94	89	31	9	3	11	68	2	208	4	4	13	8	.619	0	0-0	0	3.64	3.72
2006	Phi	NL	31	31	1	0	198.0	833	194	93	86	29	7	4	3	63	3	189	3	0	12	7	.632	0	0-0	0	4.02	3.91
2007	Phi	NL	51	3	0	37	68.2	293	61	33	33	9	3	1	1	27	1	83	5	0	5	7	.417	0	21-24	3	3.63	4.33
6 ML YEARS			192	143	6	38	923.0	3964	922	470	445	131	40	16	36	325	19	773	28	5	59	47	.557	2	21-24	3	4.30	4.34

Mike Myers

Pitches: L Bats: L Pos: RP-72   Ht: 6'3" Wt: 225 Born: 6/26/1969 Age: 39

			HOW MUCH HE PITCHED						WHAT HE GAVE UP										THE RESULTS						
Year	Team	Lg	G	GS	CG	GF	IP	BFP	H	R	ER	HR	SH	SF	HB	TBB	IBB	SO	WP	Bk	W	L	Pct	ShO	Sv-Op	Hld	ERC	ERA
1995	2 Tms		13	0	0	5	8.1	42	11	7	7	1	0	1	2	7	0	4	0	0	1	0	1.000	0	0-1	1	9.61	7.56
1996	Det	AL	83	0	0	25	64.2	298	70	41	36	6	2	1	4	34	8	69	2	0	1	5	.167	0	6-8	17	4.97	5.01
1997	Det	AL	88	0	0	23	53.2	246	58	36	34	12	4	3	2	25	2	50	0	0	0	4	.000	0	2-5	18	5.70	5.70
1998	Mil	NL	70	0	0	14	50.0	211	44	19	15	5	4	2	6	22	1	40	2	1	2	2	.500	0	1-3	23	4.14	2.70
1999	Mil	NL	71	0	0	14	41.1	179	46	24	24	7	5	0	3	13	1	35	1	0	2	1	.667	0	0-3	14	5.24	5.23
2000	Col	NL	78	0	0	22	45.1	177	24	10	10	2	1	0	2	24	3	41	1	0	0	1	.000	0	1-2	15	1.94	1.99
2001	Col	NL	73	0	0	14	40.0	169	32	17	16	2	1	1	1	24	7	36	0	0	2	3	.400	0	0-2	10	3.29	3.60
2002	Ari	NL	69	0	0	17	37.0	171	39	18	18	2	3	1	4	17	0	31	0	0	4	3	.571	0	4-9	17	5.13	4.38
2003	Ari	NL	64	0	0	17	36.1	172	38	23	23	4	1	0	5	21	1	21	1	0	0	1	.000	0	0-3	6	5.54	5.70
2004	2 Tms	AL	75	0	0	15	42.2	192	45	22	22	5	2	1	2	23	5	32	2	0	5	1	.833	0	0-0	10	5.11	4.64
2005	Bos	AL	65	0	0	11	37.1	151	30	14	13	3	1	1	2	13	2	21	0	0	3	1	.750	0	0-1	9	2.90	3.13
2006	NYY	AL	62	0	0	6	30.2	132	29	14	11	3	0	0	3	10	1	22	1	0	1	2	.333	0	0-1	18	3.78	3.23
2007	2 Tms	AL	72	0	0	14	54.1	245	59	33	29	6	2	4	3	23	2	27	0	1	4	0	1.000	0	0-3	6	4.84	4.80
95	Fla	NL	2	0	0	2	2.0	9	1	0	0	0	0	0	0	3	0	0	0	0	0	0	-	0	0-0	0	5.03	0.00
95	Det	AL	11	0	0	3	6.1	33	10	7	7	1	0	1	2	4	0	4	0	0	1	0	1.000	0	0-1	1	11.13	9.95
04	Sea	AL	50	0	0	10	27.2	126	29	15	15	3	2	1	2	17	4	23	1	0	4	1	.800	0	0-0	8	5.40	4.88
04	Bos	AL	25	0	0	5	15.0	66	16	7	7	2	0	0	0	6	1	9	1	0	1	0	1.000	0	0-0	2	4.55	4.20
07	NYY	AL	55	0	0	11	40.2	175	38	14	12	3	1	2	2	16	0	21	0	1	3	0	1.000	0	0-2	4	3.68	2.66
07	CWS	AL	17	0	0	3	13.2	70	21	19	17	3	1	2	1	7	2	6	0	0	1	0	1.000	0	0-1	2	8.76	11.20
13 ML YEARS			883	0	0	195	541.2	2385	525	278	258	58	26	15	43	256	33	429	10	2	25	24	.510	0	14-41	164	4.47	4.29

Brian Myrow

Bats: L Throws: R Pos: PH-12   Ht: 5'11" Wt: 190 Born: 9/4/1976 Age: 31

			BATTING																		BASERUNNING				AVERAGES		
Year	Team	Lg	G	AB	H	2B	3B	HR	(Hm	Rd)	TB	R	RBI	RC	TBB	IBB	SO	HBP	SH	SF	SB	CS	SB%	GDP	Avg	OBP	Slg
2001	Tampa	A+	48	149	38	11	1	3	(-	-)	60	30	28	28	32	0	29	5	4	2	5	1	.83	4	.255	.399	.403
2002	Tampa	A+	61	225	63	12	1	5	(-	-)	92	29	40	42	42	2	45	9	0	3	0	0	-	4	.280	.409	.409
2002	Nrwich	AA	61	188	57	16	0	3	(-	-)	82	37	30	41	41	1	42	6	0	1	5	0	1.00	4	.303	.441	.436
2003	Trntn	AA	137	461	141	31	8	18	(-	-)	242	99	78	114	107	8	113	16	1	6	6	3	.67	3	.306	.447	.525
2004	Clmbs	AAA	47	164	44	12	3	3	(-	-)	71	28	15	26	23	2	37	2	2	0	3	4	.43	4	.268	.365	.433
2004	LsVgs	AAA	50	153	55	15	2	6	(-	-)	92	29	29	38	21	2	47	4	0	2	2	3	.40	2	.359	.444	.601
2005	LsVgs	AAA	121	393	111	28	5	22	(-	-)	215	83	73	90	74	3	83	10	0	5	4	2	.67	4	.282	.405	.547
2006	Portlnd	AAA	20	63	17	5	0	0	(-	-)	22	3	6	6	3	0	17	0	0	1	0	0	-	1	.270	.299	.349
2007	Portlnd	AAA	107	347	123	31	4	13	(-	-)	201	61	73	87	56	1	74	0	0	8	1	0	1.00	6	.354	.440	.579
2005	LAD	NL	19	20	4	1	0	0	(0	0)	5	2	0	3	5	0	8	0	0	0	0	0	-	0	.200	.360	.250
2007	SD	NL	12	10	1	1	0	0	(0	0)	2	0	1	1	1	0	4	1	0	0	0	0	-	1	.100	.250	.200
2 ML YEARS			31	30	5	2	0	0	(0	0)	7	2	1	4	6	0	12	1	0	0	0	0	-	1	.167	.324	.233

192

Xavier Nady

Bats: R Throws: R Pos: RF-94; PH-12; CF-11; LF-10; DH-4   Ht: 6'2" Wt: 210 Born: 11/14/1978 Age: 29

							BATTING													BASERUNNING				AVERAGES		
Year	Team	Lg	G	AB	H	2B	3B	HR	(Hm | Rd)	TB	R	RBI	RC	TBB	IBB	SO	HBP	SH	SF	SB	CS	SB%	GDP	Avg	OBP	Slg
2000	SD	NL	1	1	1	0	0	0	(0 | 0)	1	1	0	1	0	0	0	0	0	0	0	0	-	0	1.000	1.000	1.000
2003	SD	NL	110	371	99	17	1	9	(5 | 4)	145	50	39	39	24	0	74	6	2	1	6	2	.75	14	.267	.321	.391
2004	SD	NL	34	77	19	4	0	3	(1 | 2)	32	7	9	8	5	0	13	1	1	0	0	0	-	4	.247	.301	.416
2005	SD	NL	124	326	85	15	2	13	(5 | 8)	143	40	43	37	22	1	67	7	1	0	2	1	.67	5	.261	.321	.439
2006	2 Tms	NL	130	468	131	28	1	17	(10 | 7)	212	57	63	62	30	7	85	11	2	1	3	3	.50	12	.280	.337	.453
2007	Pit	NL	125	431	120	23	1	20	(7 | 13)	205	55	72	60	23	2	101	12	0	4	3	1	.75	16	.278	.330	.476
06	NYM	NL	75	265	70	15	1	14	(10 | 4)	129	37	40	35	19	4	51	6	1	1	2	1	.67	7	.264	.326	.487
06	Pit	NL	55	203	61	13	0	3	(0 | 3)	83	20	23	27	11	3	34	5	1	0	1	2	.33	5	.300	.352	.409
	6 ML YEARS		524	1674	455	87	5	62	(28 | 34)	738	210	226	207	104	10	340	37	6	6	14	7	.67	51	.272	.327	.441

Mike Napoli

Bats: R Throws: R Pos: C-75; PH-1; PR-1   Ht: 6'0" Wt: 210 Born: 10/31/1981 Age: 26

							BATTING													BASERUNNING				AVERAGES		
Year	Team	Lg	G	AB	H	2B	3B	HR	(Hm	Rd)	TB	R	RBI	RC	TBB	IBB	SO	HBP	SH	SF	SB	CS	SB%	GDP	Avg	OBP	Slg
2000	Butte	R+	10	26	6	2	0	0	(-	-)	8	3	3	4	8	1	8	0	1	1	1	0	1.00	2	.231	.400	.308
2001	RCuca	A+	7	20	4	0	0	1	(-	-)	7	3	4	3	8	0	11	0	0	0	0	0	-	0	.200	.429	.350
2001	CRpds	A	43	155	36	10	1	5	(-	-)	63	23	18	23	24	0	54	2	1	1	3	2	.60	1	.232	.341	.406
2002	CRpds	A	106	362	91	19	1	10	(-	-)	142	57	50	56	62	1	104	4	0	6	6	5	.55	9	.251	.362	.392
2003	RCuca	A+	47	165	44	10	1	4	(-	-)	68	28	26	28	23	1	32	4	0	3	5	0	1.00	3	.267	.364	.412
2004	RCuca	A+	132	482	136	29	4	29	(-	-)	260	94	118	105	88	5	166	5	1	8	9	5	.64	6	.282	.393	.539
2005	Ark	AA	131	439	104	22	2	31	(-	-)	223	96	99	88	88	1	140	9	0	5	12	4	.75	8	.237	.372	.508
2006	Salt Lk	AAA	21	78	19	6	0	3	(-	-)	34	12	10	12	8	0	29	4	0	0	1	1	.50	0	.244	.344	.436
2006	LAA	AL	99	268	61	13	0	16	(10	6)	122	47	42	40	51	0	90	5	0	1	2	3	.40	2	.228	.360	.455
2007	LAA	AL	75	219	54	11	1	10	(5	5)	97	40	34	35	33	2	63	5	1	5	5	2	.71	5	.247	.351	.443
	2 ML YEARS		174	487	115	24	1	26	(15	11)	219	87	76	75	84	2	153	10	1	6	7	5	.58	7	.236	.356	.450

Joe Nathan

Pitches: R Bats: R Pos: RP-68   Ht: 6'4" Wt: 220 Born: 11/22/1974 Age: 33

			HOW MUCH HE PITCHED						WHAT HE GAVE UP										THE RESULTS						
Year	Team	Lg	G	GS	CG	GF	IP	BFP	H	R	ER	HR	SH	SF	HB	TBB	IBB	SO	WP	Bk	W	L	Pct	ShO	Sv-Op	Hld	ERC	ERA
1999	SF	NL	19	14	0	2	90.1	395	84	45	42	17	2	0	1	46	0	54	2	0	7	4	.636	0	1-1	0	4.78	4.18
2000	SF	NL	20	15	0	0	93.1	426	89	63	54	12	5	5	4	63	4	61	5	0	5	2	.714	0	0-1	0	5.23	5.21
2002	SF	NL	4	0	0	3	3.2	12	1	0	0	0	0	0	0	0	0	2	0	0	0	0	-	0	0-0	0	0.17	0.00
2003	SF	NL	78	0	0	9	79.0	316	51	26	26	7	2	4	3	33	3	83	4	1	12	4	.750	0	0-3	20	2.34	2.96
2004	Min	AL	73	0	0	63	72.1	284	48	14	13	3	2	0	2	23	3	89	5	0	1	2	.333	0	44-47	0	1.78	1.62
2005	Min	AL	69	0	0	58	70.0	276	46	22	21	5	1	2	0	22	1	94	2	0	7	4	.636	0	43-48	0	1.83	2.70
2006	Min	AL	64	0	0	61	68.1	262	38	12	12	3	3	2	1	16	4	95	3	0	7	0	1.000	0	36-38	0	1.18	1.58
2007	Min	AL	68	0	0	60	71.2	282	54	15	15	4	2	2	1	19	2	77	3	0	4	3	.667	0	37-41	0	2.08	1.88
	8 ML YEARS		395	29	0	256	548.2	2253	411	197	183	51	17	15	12	222	17	555	24	1	43	18	.705	0	161-179	20	2.75	3.00

Dioner Navarro

Bats: B Throws: R Pos: C-112; PH-8   Ht: 5'9" Wt: 205 Born: 2/9/1984 Age: 24

							BATTING													BASERUNNING				AVERAGES		
Year	Team	Lg	G	AB	H	2B	3B	HR	(Hm	Rd)	TB	R	RBI	RC	TBB	IBB	SO	HBP	SH	SF	SB	CS	SB%	GDP	Avg	OBP	Slg
2004	NYY	AL	5	7	3	0	0	0	(0	0)	3	2	1	1	0	0	0	0	0	0	0	0	-	1	.429	.429	.429
2005	LAD	NL	50	176	48	9	0	3	(3	0)	66	21	14	18	20	1	21	2	1	0	0	0	-	3	.273	.354	.375
2006	2 Tms	NL	81	268	68	9	0	6	(4	2)	95	28	28	27	31	6	51	1	1	1	2	1	.67	7	.254	.332	.354
2007	TB	AL	119	388	88	19	2	9	(5	4)	138	46	44	35	33	3	67	1	7	5	3	1	.75	11	.227	.286	.356
06	LAD	NL	25	75	21	2	0	2	(1	1)	29	5	8	8	11	4	18	0	0	0	1	0	1.00	1	.280	.372	.387
06	TB	AL	56	193	47	7	0	4	(3	1)	66	23	20	19	20	2	33	1	1	1	1	1	.50	6	.244	.316	.342
	4 ML YEARS		255	839	207	37	2	18	(12	6)	302	97	87	81	84	10	139	4	9	6	5	2	.71	22	.247	.316	.360

Joe Nelson

Pitches: R Bats: R Pos: P   Ht: 6'1" Wt: 210 Born: 10/25/1974 Age: 33

			HOW MUCH HE PITCHED						WHAT HE GAVE UP										THE RESULTS						
Year	Team	Lg	G	GS	CG	GF	IP	BFP	H	R	ER	HR	SH	SF	HB	TBB	IBB	SO	WP	Bk	W	L	Pct	ShO	Sv-Op	Hld	ERC	ERA
2001	Atl	NL	2	0	0	0	2.0	16	7	9	8	1	0	1	1	2	0	0	0	0	0	0	-	0	0-0	0	33.03	36.00
2004	Bos	AL	3	0	0	1	2.2	17	4	5	5	0	1	0	2	3	0	5	0	0	0	0	-	0	0-0	0	12.43	16.88
2006	KC	AL	43	0	0	20	44.2	193	37	22	22	5	3	1	1	24	4	44	1	0	1	1	.500	0	9-10	5	3.67	4.43
	3 ML YEARS		48	0	0	21	49.1	226	48	36	35	6	4	2	4	29	4	49	1	0	1	1	.500	0	9-10	5	4.97	6.39

Pat Neshek

Pitches: R Bats: B Pos: RP-74   Ht: 6'3" Wt: 205 Born: 9/4/1980 Age: 27

			HOW MUCH HE PITCHED						WHAT HE GAVE UP										THE RESULTS						
Year	Team	Lg	G	GS	CG	GF	IP	BFP	H	R	ER	HR	SH	SF	HB	TBB	IBB	SO	WP	Bk	W	L	Pct	ShO	Sv-Op	Hld	ERC	ERA
2002	Elizab	R+	23	0	0	22	27.1	102	13	6	3	0	1	0	2	6	0	41	1	0	0	2	.000	0	15--	-	0.97	0.99
2003	QuadC	A	28	0	0	24	34.1	136	20	3	2	0	3	0	1	11	2	53	1	0	3	2	.600	0	14--	-	1.29	0.52
2003	FtMyrs	A+	20	0	0	15	29.1	117	22	8	7	2	1	0	1	6	1	29	0	1	4	1	.800	0	2--	-	1.94	2.15
2003	NwBrit	AA	5	1	0	2	7.2	34	7	5	5	2	0	0	1	3	0	5	0	0	1	1	.500	0	1--	-	5.12	5.87
2004	NwBrit	AA	26	0	0	15	35.1	158	34	15	15	2	1	0	1	18	5	38	1	0	2	1	.667	0	2--	-	3.77	3.82
2004	FtMyrs	A+	16	0	0	15	18.1	73	16	7	6	2	0	0	0	2	0	19	0	0	1	0	1.000	0	10--	-	2.33	2.95
2005	NwBrit	AA	55	0	0	48	82.1	335	69	25	20	9	4	2	2	21	3	95	3	0	6	4	.600	0	24--	-	2.75	2.19

Year	Team	Lg	G	GS	CG	GF	IP	BFP	H	R	ER	HR	SH	SF	HB	TBB	IBB	SO	WP	Bk	W	L	Pct	ShO	Sv-Op	Hld	ERC	ERA
2006	Roch	AAA	33	0	0	23	60.0	234	41	13	13	7	2	0	1	14	4	87	2	0	6	2	.750	0	14--	-	1.92	1.95
2006	Min	AL	32	0	0	3	37.0	138	23	9	9	6	0	1	0	6	0	53	0	0	4	2	.667	0	0-2	10	1.68	2.19
2007	Min	AL	74	0	0	20	70.1	278	44	25	23	7	4	5	2	27	5	74	2	0	7	2	.778	0	0-3	15	2.12	2.94
2 ML YEARS			106	0	0	23	107.1	416	67	34	32	13	4	6	2	33	5	127	2	0	11	4	.733	0	0-5	25	1.98	2.68

David Newhan

Bats: L **Throws:** R **Pos:** PH-46; LF-8; 2B-1; 3B-1; PR-1 **Ht:** 5'10" **Wt:** 170 **Born:** 9/7/1973 **Age:** 34

Year	Team	Lg	G	AB	H	2B	3B	HR	(Hm	Rd)	TB	R	RBI	RC	TBB	IBB	SO	HBP	SH	SF	SB	CS	SB%	GDP	Avg	OBP	Slg
2007	NewOr*	AAA	44	173	60	12	3	7	(-	-)	99	27	30	39	20	3	28	1	0	2	7	4	.64	4	.347	.413	.572
1999	SD	NL	32	43	6	1	0	2	(1	1)	13	7	6	1	1	0	11	0	0	0	2	1	.67	0	.140	.159	.302
2000	2 Tms	NL	24	37	6	1	0	1	(1	0)	10	8	2	2	8	1	13	0	0	0	0	0	-	2	.162	.311	.270
2001	Phi	NL	7	6	2	1	0	0	(0	0)	3	2	1	1	1	0	0	0	0	1	0	0	-	0	.333	.375	.500
2004	Bal	AL	95	373	116	15	7	8	(3	5)	169	66	54	70	27	0	72	4	5	3	11	1	.92	4	.311	.361	.453
2005	Bal	AL	96	218	44	9	0	5	(1	4)	68	31	21	19	22	1	45	2	5	2	9	2	.82	2	.202	.279	.312
2006	Bal	AL	39	131	33	4	0	4	(3	1)	49	14	18	10	7	1	22	2	0	3	4	2	.67	4	.252	.294	.374
2007	NYM	NL	56	74	15	1	1	1	(1	0)	21	9	6	8	8	0	19	1	0	0	2	0	1.00	1	.203	.289	.284
00	SD	NL	14	20	3	1	0	1	(1	0)	7	5	2	2	6	1	7	0	0	0	0	0	-	0	.150	.346	.350
00	Phi	NL	10	17	3	0	0	0	(0	0)	3	3	0	0	2	0	6	0	0	0	0	0	-	2	.176	.263	.176
7 ML YEARS			349	882	222	32	8	21	(10	11)	333	137	108	111	74	3	182	9	10	9	28	6	.82	13	.252	.313	.378

Josh Newman

Pitches: L **Bats:** L **Pos:** RP-2 **Ht:** 6'1" **Wt:** 200 **Born:** 6/11/1982 **Age:** 26

Year	Team	Lg	G	GS	CG	GF	IP	BFP	H	R	ER	HR	SH	SF	HB	TBB	IBB	SO	WP	Bk	W	L	Pct	ShO	Sv-Op	Hld	ERC	ERA
2004	Casper	R+	27	0	0	8	33.2	139	30	17	13	2	0	0	0	8	0	46	1	0	1	2	.333	0	1--	-	2.57	3.48
2005	Mdest	A+	41	0	0	16	63.1	268	45	22	22	5	1	0	0	40	0	99	2	0	5	2	.714	0	0--	-	3.27	3.13
2006	Tulsa	AA	62	0	0	22	77.0	303	56	27	27	8	1	1	3	24	1	77	2	0	9	5	.643	0	2--	-	2.53	3.16
2007	ColSpr	AAA	55	0	0	14	62.0	288	73	34	28	3	2	2	4	30	1	49	4	0	3	2	.600	0	0--	-	5.23	4.06
2007	Col	NL	2	0	0	2	2.0	8	2	1	1	0	0	0	0	0	0	3	1	0	0	0	-	0	0-0	0	1.95	4.50

Lance Niekro

Bats: R **Throws:** R **Pos:** PH-8; 1B-3 **Ht:** 6'3" **Wt:** 225 **Born:** 1/29/1979 **Age:** 29

Year	Team	Lg	G	AB	H	2B	3B	HR	(Hm	Rd)	TB	R	RBI	RC	TBB	IBB	SO	HBP	SH	SF	SB	CS	SB%	GDP	Avg	OBP	Slg
2007	Fresno*	AAA	47	143	43	8	2	5	(-	-)	70	21	20	24	12	0	32	1	0	2	0	1	.00	6	.301	.354	.490
2003	SF	NL	5	5	1	1	0	0	(0	0)	2	2	2	1	0	0	1	0	0	0	0	0	-	0	.200	.200	.400
2005	SF	NL	113	278	70	16	3	12	(5	7)	128	32	46	35	17	0	53	2	0	5	0	2	.00	11	.252	.295	.460
2006	SF	NL	66	199	49	9	2	5	(3	2)	77	27	31	22	11	0	32	0	0	0	0	0	-	7	.246	.286	.387
2007	SF	NL	11	17	3	0	0	0	(0	0)	3	0	0	0	1	0	5	0	0	0	0	0	-	1	.176	.222	.176
4 ML YEARS			195	499	123	26	5	17	(8	9)	210	61	79	58	29	0	91	2	0	5	0	2	.00	19	.246	.288	.421

Fernando Nieve

Pitches: R **Bats:** R **Pos:** P **Ht:** 6'0" **Wt:** 195 **Born:** 7/15/1982 **Age:** 25

Year	Team	Lg	G	GS	CG	GF	IP	BFP	H	R	ER	HR	SH	SF	HB	TBB	IBB	SO	WP	Bk	W	L	Pct	ShO	Sv-Op	Hld	ERC	ERA
2001	Mrtnsvl	R+	12	8	1	0	38.0	161	27	20	16	2	0	0	3	21	0	49	3	1	4	2	.667	0	0--	-	3.08	3.79
2002	Mrtnsvl	R+	13	13	0	0	67.2	280	46	23	18	5	1	2	2	27	0	60	1	0	4	1	.800	0	0--	-	2.28	2.39
2002	Lxngtn	A	1	1	0	0	3.0	18	6	5	2	0	0	0	1	0	0	2	0	0	0	1	.000	0	0--	-	7.91	6.00
2003	Lxngtn	A	28	28	1	0	150.1	638	133	69	61	10	4	8	0	65	0	144	7	1	14	9	.609	0	0--	-	3.33	3.65
2004	Salem	A+	24	24	2	0	149.0	599	136	52	49	9	10	6	1	40	0	117	5	0	10	6	.625	2	0--	-	2.95	2.96
2004	RdRck	AAA	3	3	0	0	17.1	69	12	4	3	0	1	0	1	8	0	17	0	0	2	0	1.000	0	0--	-	2.35	1.56
2005	CpChr	AAA	14	14	0	0	85.0	341	62	27	25	7	2	3	3	29	0	96	4	0	4	3	.571	0	0--	-	2.48	2.65
2005	RdRck	AAA	13	13	2	0	82.0	372	92	45	44	10	2	5	5	33	2	75	3	0	4	4	.500	2	0--	-	5.09	4.83
2006	RdRck	AAA	4	0	0	2	5.1	19	2	0	0	0	0	0	0	0	0	7	0	0	0	0	-	0	2--	-	0.30	0.00
2007	RdRck	AAA	5	5	0	0	21.2	105	30	19	15	1	0	2	1	15	1	13	2	0	1	3	.250	0	0--	-	7.51	6.23
2006	Hou	NL	40	11	0	11	96.1	411	87	46	45	18	5	3	2	41	5	70	1	0	3	3	.500	0	0-0	-	4.24	4.20

Wil Nieves

Bats: R **Throws:** R **Pos:** C-25; 1B-1; PH-1 **Ht:** 5'11" **Wt:** 190 **Born:** 9/25/1977 **Age:** 30

Year	Team	Lg	G	AB	H	2B	3B	HR	(Hm	Rd)	TB	R	RBI	RC	TBB	IBB	SO	HBP	SH	SF	SB	CS	SB%	GDP	Avg	OBP	Slg
2007	S-WB*	AAA	27	90	23	1	2	1	(-	-)	31	5	8	10	6	0	10	1	0	1	1	0	1.00	2	.256	.306	.344
2002	SD	NL	28	72	13	3	1	0	(0	0)	18	2	3	4	4	4	15	0	0	0	1	0	1.00	1	.181	.224	.250
2005	NYY	AL	3	4	0	0	0	0	(0	0)	0	0	0	0	0	0	1	0	0	0	0	0	-	0	.000	.000	.000
2006	NYY	AL	6	6	0	0	0	0	(0	0)	0	0	0	0	0	0	1	0	0	0	0	0	-	0	.000	.000	.000
2007	NYY	AL	26	61	10	4	0	0	(0	0)	14	6	8	4	2	0	9	0	3	0	0	0	-	3	.164	.190	.230
4 ML YEARS			63	143	23	7	1	0	(0	0)	32	8	11	8	6	4	26	0	3	0	1	0	1.00	4	.161	.195	.224

Dustin Nippert

Pitches: R **Bats:** R **Pos:** RP-36   **Ht:** 6'8" **Wt:** 225 **Born:** 5/6/1981 **Age:** 27

			HOW MUCH HE PITCHED							WHAT HE GAVE UP									THE RESULTS						
Year	Team	Lg	G	GS	CG	GF	IP	BFP	H	R	ER	HR	SH	SF	HB	TBB	IBB	SO	WP	Bk	W	L	Pct	ShO	Sv-Op Hld	ERC	ERA
2007	Tucsn*	AAA	10	8	0	0	36.0	147	23	19	19	3	2	0	0	23	0	46	6	0	0	3	.000	0	0- - -	3.03	4.75
2005	Ari	NL	3	3	0	0	14.2	68	10	9	9	1	0	0	1	13	0	11	1	0	1	0	1.000	0	0-0 0	4.09	5.52
2006	Ari	NL	2	2	0	0	10.0	51	15	13	13	5	1	0	0	7	0	9	0	0	0	2	.000	0	0-0 0	12.21	11.70
2007	Ari	NL	36	0	0	8	45.1	196	48	30	28	5	0	0	0	16	1	38	4	0	1	1	.500	0	0-0 2	4.25	5.56
	3 ML YEARS		41	5	0	8	70.0	315	73	52	50	11	1	0	1	36	1	58	5	0	2	3	.400	0	0-0 2	5.21	6.43

Laynce Nix

Bats: L **Throws:** L **Pos:** PH-8; CF-4; LF-1   **Ht:** 6'0" **Wt:** 200 **Born:** 10/30/1980 **Age:** 27

			BATTING																BASERUNNING				AVERAGES		
Year	Team	Lg	G	AB	H	2B	3B	HR	(Hm | Rd)	TB	R	RBI	RC	TBB	IBB	SO	HBP	SH	SF	SB	CS	SB%	GDP	Avg	OBP	Slg
2007	Hntsvl*	AA	4	11	4	1	0	1	(- | -)	8	2	6	3	1	0	2	0	0	0	0	0	-	1	.364	.417	.727
2007	Nashv*	AAA	95	347	93	20	1	24	(- | -)	187	60	74	63	31	3	104	3	0	5	5	0	1.00	4	.268	.329	.539
2003	Tex	AL	53	184	47	10	0	8	(7 | 1)	81	25	30	25	9	0	53	0	1	1	3	0	1.00	5	.255	.289	.440
2004	Tex	AL	115	371	92	20	4	14	(9 | 5)	162	58	46	44	23	4	113	2	1	3	1	1	.50	6	.248	.293	.437
2005	Tex	AL	63	229	55	12	3	6	(3 | 3)	91	28	32	26	9	3	45	0	0	2	2	0	1.00	3	.240	.267	.397
2006	2 Tms		19	67	11	2	0	1	(1 | 0)	16	3	10	3	0	0	28	2	0	1	0	0	-	1	.164	.186	.239
2007	Mil	NL	10	12	0	0	0	0	(0 | 0)	0	0	0	0	0	0	4	0	0	0	0	0	-	0	.000	.000	.000
06	Tex	AL	9	32	3	1	0	0	(0 | 0)	4	1	4	0	0	0	17	1	0	1	0	0	-	0	.094	.118	.125
06	Mil	NL	10	35	8	1	0	1	(1 | 0)	12	2	6	3	0	0	11	1	0	0	0	0	-	1	.229	.250	.343
	5 ML YEARS		260	863	205	44	7	29	(20 | 9)	350	114	118	98	41	7	243	4	2	7	6	1	.86	11	.238	.273	.406

Trot Nixon

Bats: L **Throws:** L **Pos:** RF-87; PH-11; DH-5   **Ht:** 6'0" **Wt:** 210 **Born:** 4/11/1974 **Age:** 34

			BATTING																BASERUNNING				AVERAGES		
Year	Team	Lg	G	AB	H	2B	3B	HR	(Hm | Rd)	TB	R	RBI	RC	TBB	IBB	SO	HBP	SH	SF	SB	CS	SB%	GDP	Avg	OBP	Slg
1996	Bos	AL	2	4	2	1	0	0	(0 | 0)	3	2	0	1	0	0	1	0	0	0	1	0	1.00	0	.500	.500	.750
1998	Bos	AL	13	27	7	1	0	0	(0 | 0)	8	3	0	2	1	0	3	0	0	0	0	0	-	0	.259	.286	.296
1999	Bos	AL	124	381	103	22	5	15	(3 | 12)	180	67	52	66	53	1	75	3	2	8	3	1	.75	7	.270	.357	.472
2000	Bos	AL	123	427	118	27	8	12	(4 | 8)	197	66	60	74	63	2	85	2	5	5	8	1	.89	11	.276	.368	.461
2001	Bos	AL	148	535	150	31	4	27	(14 | 13)	270	100	88	102	79	1	113	7	6	6	7	4	.64	8	.280	.376	.505
2002	Bos	AL	152	532	136	36	3	24	(8 | 16)	250	81	94	85	65	2	109	5	3	7	4	2	.07	7	.256	.330	.470
2003	Bos	AL	134	441	135	24	6	28	(10 | 18)	255	81	87	90	65	4	96	3	1	3	4	2	.67	3	.306	.396	.578
2004	Bos	AL	48	149	47	9	1	6	(3 | 3)	76	24	23	24	15	1	24	1	0	2	0	0	-	3	.315	.377	.510
2005	Bos	AL	124	408	112	29	1	13	(5 | 8)	182	64	67	70	53	3	59	3	0	6	2	1	.67	7	.275	.357	.446
2006	Bos	AL	114	381	102	24	0	8	(1 | 7)	150	59	52	55	60	1	56	7	0	5	0	2	.00	10	.268	.373	.394
2007	Cle	AL	99	307	77	17	0	3	(2 | 1)	103	30	31	34	44	7	59	0	0	3	0	0	-	9	.251	.342	.336
	11 ML YEARS		1081	3592	989	221	28	136	(50 | 86)	1674	577	554	603	498	22	680	31	17	45	29	13	.69	65	.275	.364	.466

Ricky Nolasco

Pitches: R **Bats:** R **Pos:** SP-4; RP-1   **Ht:** 6'2" **Wt:** 220 **Born:** 12/13/1982 **Age:** 25

			HOW MUCH HE PITCHED							WHAT HE GAVE UP									THE RESULTS						
Year	Team	Lg	G	GS	CG	GF	IP	BFP	H	R	ER	HR	SH	SF	HB	TBB	IBB	SO	WP	Bk	W	L	Pct	ShO	Sv-Op Hld	ERC	ERA
2001	Cubs	R	5	4	0	0	18.0	69	11	3	3	0	0	0	1	5	0	23	1	0	1	0	1.000	0	0- - -	1.45	1.50
2002	Boise	A-	15	1	5	0	90.2	379	72	32	25	1	8	1	9	25	0	92	5	0	7	2	.778	0	0- - -	2.27	2.48
2003	Dytona	A+	26	26	1	0	149.0	620	129	58	49	7	5	4	8	48	0	136	12	1	11	5	.688	0	0- - -	2.91	2.96
2004	WTenn	AA	19	19	0	0	107.0	454	104	50	44	13	7	4	6	37	3	115	5	1	6	4	.600	0	0- - -	4.08	3.70
2004	Iowa	AAA	9	9	0	0	40.2	173	68	42	42	7	4	3	5	16	1	28	2	0	2	3	.400	0	0- - -	11.31	9.30
2005	WTenn	AA	27	27	1	0	161.2	687	151	57	52	13	11	2	11	46	1	173	4	2	14	3	.824	0	0- - -	3.35	2.89
2007	Mrlns	R	2	2	0	0	3.1	14	4	2	1	0	0	0	0	0	0	8	0	0	0	0	-	0	0- - -	2.89	2.70
2007	Jupiter	A+	5	3	0	0	12.0	48	10	3	1	0	1	0	0	1	0	9	1	0	1	1	.500	0	0- - -	1.51	0.75
2007	Carlina	AA	1	1	0	0	3.0	13	2	3	2	0	1	0	1	1	0	2	0	0	0	1	.000	0	0- - -	1.45	6.00
2007	Albq	AAA	4	4	0	0	15.1	81	29	26	24	6	0	1	2	4	0	15	2	0	0	2	.000	0	0- - -	12.23	14.09
2006	Fla	NL	35	22	0	0	140.0	613	157	86	75	20	8	6	10	41	5	99	7	0	11	11	.500	0	0-0 2	4.89	4.82
2007	Fla	NL	5	4	0	0	21.1	99	26	16	13	3	3	5	1	9	2	11	1	0	1	2	.333	0	0-0 0	5.71	5.48
	2 ML YEARS		40	26	0	0	161.1	712	183	102	88	23	11	11	11	50	7	110	8	0	12	13	.480	0	0-0 2	5.00	4.91

Greg Norton

Bats: B **Throws:** R **Pos:** DH-52; PH-20; RF-6; 1B-3; LF-3   **Ht:** 6'1" **Wt:** 205 **Born:** 7/6/1972 **Age:** 35

			BATTING																BASERUNNING				AVERAGES		
Year	Team	Lg	G	AB	H	2B	3B	HR	(Hm | Rd)	TB	R	RBI	RC	TBB	IBB	SO	HBP	SH	SF	SB	CS	SB%	GDP	Avg	OBP	Slg
2007	Mont*	AA	7	25	7	2	0	0	(- | -)	9	2	4	4	5	0	4	1	0	0	0	0	-	4	.280	.419	.360
1996	CWS	AL	11	23	5	0	0	2	(0 | 2)	11	4	3	3	4	0	6	0	0	0	0	1	.00	0	.217	.333	.478
1997	CWS	AL	18	34	9	2	2	0	(0 | 0)	15	5	1	5	2	0	8	0	1	0	0	0	-	0	.265	.306	.441
1998	CWS	AL	105	299	71	17	2	9	(6 | 3)	119	38	36	33	26	1	77	2	1	2	3	3	.50	11	.237	.301	.398
1999	CWS	AL	132	436	111	26	0	16	(5 | 11)	185	62	50	66	69	3	93	2	1	2	4	4	.50	11	.255	.358	.424
2000	CWS	AL	71	201	49	6	1	6	(4 | 2)	75	25	28	27	26	0	47	2	0	2	1	0	1.00	2	.244	.333	.373
2001	Col	NL	117	225	60	13	2	13	(7 | 6)	116	30	40	36	19	2	65	0	0	2	1	0	1.00	6	.267	.321	.516
2002	Col	NL	113	168	37	8	1	7	(3 | 4)	68	19	37	22	24	0	52	0	1	2	2	3	.40	4	.220	.314	.405
2003	Col	NL	114	179	47	15	0	6	(2 | 4)	80	19	31	26	16	0	47	1	0	1	2	1	.67	5	.263	.325	.447
2004	Det	AL	41	86	15	1	0	2	(1 | 1)	22	9	2	1	12	1	21	0	1	0	0	0	-	3	.174	.276	.256
2006	TB	AL	98	294	87	15	0	17	(9 | 8)	153	47	45	53	35	2	69	3	1	2	1	5	.17	2	.296	.374	.520
2007	TB	AL	75	202	49	9	0	4	(2 | 2)	70	25	23	28	37	3	55	0	0	1	1	1	.50	1	.243	.358	.347
	11 ML YEARS		895	2147	540	112	8	82	(39 | 43)	914	283	296	300	270	12	540	10	6	14	15	18	.45	44	.252	.336	.426

Abraham Nunez

Bats: B **Throws:** R **Pos:** 3B-113; PH-26; SS-8; 2B-5; PR-5 **Ht:** 5'11" **Wt:** 201 **Born:** 3/16/1976 **Age:** 32

Year	Team	Lg	G	AB	H	2B	3B	HR	(Hm	Rd)	TB	R	RBI	RC	TBB	IBB	SO	HBP	SH	SF	SB	CS	SB%	GDP	Avg	OBP	Slg
1997	Pit	NL	19	40	9	2	2	0	(0	1)	15	3	6	4	3	0	10	1	0	1	1	0	1.00	1	.225	.289	.375
1998	Pit	NL	24	52	10	2	0	1	(0	1)	15	6	2	6	12	0	14	0	3	0	4	2	.67	1	.192	.344	.288
1999	Pit	NL	90	259	57	8	0	0	(0	0)	65	25	17	22	28	0	54	1	13	0	9	1	.90	2	.220	.299	.251
2000	Pit	NL	40	91	20	1	0	1	(0	1)	24	10	8	6	8	1	14	0	0	0	0	0	-	3	.220	.283	.264
2001	Pit	NL	115	301	79	11	4	1	(0	1)	101	30	21	36	28	1	53	1	4	1	8	2	.80	0	.262	.326	.336
2002	Pit	NL	112	253	59	14	1	2	(2	0)	81	28	15	25	27	1	44	2	3	1	3	4	.43	2	.233	.311	.320
2003	Pit	NL	118	311	77	8	7	4	(2	2)	111	37	35	28	26	1	53	3	9	2	9	3	.75	4	.248	.310	.357
2004	Pit	NL	112	182	43	9	0	2	(1	1)	58	17	13	12	10	0	36	0	4	0	1	3	.25	8	.236	.275	.319
2005	StL	NL	139	421	120	13	2	5	(3	2)	152	64	44	54	37	4	63	0	9	0	0	1	.00	6	.285	.343	.361
2006	Phi	NL	123	322	68	10	2	2	(2	0)	88	42	32	27	41	8	58	2	3	1	1	0	1.00	7	.211	.303	.273
2007	Phi	NL	136	252	59	10	1	0	(0	0)	71	24	16	21	30	5	48	1	4	0	2	0	1.00	10	.234	.318	.282
11 ML YEARS			1028	2484	601	88	19	18	(10	8)	781	286	209	241	250	21	447	11	50	7	38	16	.70	48	.242	.313	.314

Leo Nunez

Pitches: R **Bats:** R **Pos:** RP-7; SP-6 **Ht:** 6'1" **Wt:** 175 **Born:** 8/14/1983 **Age:** 24

Year	Team	Lg	G	GS	CG	GF	IP	BFP	H	R	ER	HR	SH	SF	HB	TBB	IBB	SO	WP	Bk	W	L	Pct	ShO	Sv-Op	Hld	ERC	ERA
2007	Wichta*	AA	6	5	0	0	20.2	75	10	2	2	1	0	0	1	6	0	13	0	0	1	0	1.000	0	0--	-	1.30	0.87
2007	Omha*	AAA	5	4	0	0	23.0	89	16	7	7	3	1	0	0	4	1	19	2	0	1	2	.333	0	0--	-	1.80	2.74
2005	KC	AL	41	0	0	10	53.2	246	73	45	45	9	1	2	3	18	2	32	1	0	3	2	.600	0	0-1	2	6.76	7.55
2006	KC	AL	7	0	0	5	13.1	58	15	7	7	2	0	1	2	5	0	7	0	0	0	0	-	0	0-0	0	5.98	4.73
2007	KC	AL	13	6	0	2	43.2	182	44	21	19	8	0	2	0	10	0	37	1	0	2	4	.333	0	0-0	1	3.98	3.92
3 ML YEARS			61	6	0	17	110.2	486	132	73	71	19	1	5	5	33	2	76	2	0	5	6	.455	0	0-1	3	5.53	5.77

Wes Obermueller

Pitches: R **Bats:** R **Pos:** RP-11; SP-7 **Ht:** 6'2" **Wt:** 190 **Born:** 12/22/1976 **Age:** 31

Year	Team	Lg	G	GS	CG	GF	IP	BFP	H	R	ER	HR	SH	SF	HB	TBB	IBB	SO	WP	Bk	W	L	Pct	ShO	Sv-Op	Hld	ERC	ERA
2007	Albq*	AAA	11	11	0	0	63.1	281	67	36	32	6	2	3	2	27	0	45	5	0	4	1	.800	0	0--	-	4.57	4.55
2002	KC	AL	2	2	0	0	7.2	39	14	10	10	3	0	0	0	2	0	5	0	0	0	2	.000	0	0-0	0	11.04	11.74
2003	Mil	NL	12	11	0	0	65.2	303	81	40	37	10	1	2	6	25	2	34	5	0	2	5	.286	0	0-0	0	6.08	5.07
2004	Mil	NL	25	20	1	1	118.0	529	138	80	76	15	4	5	3	42	0	59	4	0	6	8	.429	1	0-0	0	5.14	5.80
2005	Mil	NL	23	8	0	4	65.0	305	74	41	38	7	4	4	5	36	2	33	3	0	1	4	.200	0	0-0	0	5.79	5.26
2007	Fla	NL	18	7	0	4	59.0	278	72	49	43	7	0	3	4	36	5	35	2	0	2	3	.400	0	0-0	0	6.64	6.56
5 ML YEARS			80	48	1	9	315.1	1454	379	220	204	42	9	14	18	141	9	166	14	0	11	22	.333	1	0-0	0	5.88	5.82

Eric O'Flaherty

Pitches: L **Bats:** L **Pos:** RP-56 **Ht:** 6'2" **Wt:** 195 **Born:** 2/5/1985 **Age:** 23

Year	Team	Lg	G	GS	CG	GF	IP	BFP	H	R	ER	HR	SH	SF	HB	TBB	IBB	SO	WP	Bk	W	L	Pct	ShO	Sv-Op	Hld	ERC	ERA
2003	Ms	R	13	1	0	5	27.2	110	17	10	6	1	2	1	2	7	1	20	0	0	3	0	1.000	0	0--	-	1.49	1.95
2003	Everett	A-	3	1	0	0	10.2	41	8	5	4	1	0	2	2	3	0	7	1	0	1	0	1.000	0	0--	-	3.23	3.38
2004	Wisc	A	12	10	0	0	57.1	274	83	43	39	3	4	3	3	23	1	38	12	0	3	3	.500	0	0-0	0	6.56	6.12
2005	Wisc	A	45	0	0	31	69.2	305	73	35	29	2	3	0	3	30	1	51	7	1	4	4	.500	0	13--	4	4.12	3.75
2006	InldEm	A+	16	0	0	4	31.1	118	36	15	15	1	2	1	2	7	0	34	0	0	0	1	.000	0	1--	-	4.84	4.31
2006	SnAnt	AA	25	0	0	14	39.1	171	45	10	5	0	2	0	4	15	1	36	0	2	2	2	.500	0	7--	7	4.61	1.14
2006	Tacom	AAA	2	0	0	0	3.2	15	3	0	0	0	0	0	0	1	0	4	0	0	0	0	1.000	0	0--	0	2.00	0.00
2007	Tacom	AAA	6	0	0	3	8.0	34	5	1	1	0	1	0	1	4	0	8	1	0	0	0	-	0	3--	1	2.21	1.13
2006	Sea	AL	15	0	0	5	11.0	57	18	9	5	2	1	0	0	6	3	6	2	0	0	0	-	0	0-0	1	8.63	4.09
2007	Sea	AL	56	0	0	9	52.1	221	45	26	26	1	0	2	5	20	1	36	4	1	7	1	.875	0	0-1	4	3.04	4.47
2 ML YEARS			71	0	0	14	63.1	278	63	35	31	3	1	2	5	26	4	42	6	1	7	1	.875	0	0-1	5	3.90	4.41

Tomo Ohka

Pitches: R **Bats:** R **Pos:** SP-10 **Ht:** 6'1" **Wt:** 200 **Born:** 3/18/1976 **Age:** 32

Year	Team	Lg	G	GS	CG	GF	IP	BFP	H	R	ER	HR	SH	SF	HB	TBB	IBB	SO	WP	Bk	W	L	Pct	ShO	Sv-Op	Hld	ERC	ERA
2007	Memp*	AAA	3	3	0	0	18.1	81	27	15	14	2	1	2	0	3	0	7	0	0	0	2	.000	0	0--	-	6.12	6.87
2007	Tacom*	AAA	4	4	0	0	22.2	110	38	26	26	6	0	0	2	9	0	9	0	0	0	3	.000	0	0--	-	10.63	10.32
1999	Bos	AL	8	2	0	3	13.0	65	21	12	9	2	0	1	0	6	0	8	0	0	1	2	.333	0	0-0	0	8.56	6.23
2000	Bos	AL	13	12	0	0	69.1	297	70	25	24	7	1	2	2	26	0	40	3	0	3	6	.333	0	0-0	0	4.19	3.12
2001	2 Tms		22	21	0	1	107.0	469	134	70	65	15	2	2	3	29	0	68	2	1	3	9	.250	0	0-0	0	5.52	5.47
2002	Mon	NL	32	31	2	1	192.2	806	194	83	68	19	13	6	7	45	7	118	2	1	13	8	.619	0	0-0	0	3.55	3.18
2003	Mon	NL	34	34	2	0	199.0	864	233	106	92	24	8	3	9	45	11	118	8	0	10	12	.455	0	0-0	0	4.59	4.16
2004	Mon	NL	15	15	0	0	84.2	367	98	40	32	11	4	2	1	20	1	38	3	0	3	7	.300	0	0-0	0	4.53	3.40
2005	2 Tms		32	29	1	0	180.1	774	189	88	81	22	7	4	3	55	5	98	8	0	11	9	.550	1	0-0	0	4.13	4.04
2006	Mil	NL	18	18	0	0	97.0	421	98	58	52	12	8	4	5	35	1	50	0	0	4	5	.444	0	0-0	0	4.32	4.82
2007	Tor	AL	10	10	0	0	56.0	251	68	39	36	11	1	1	0	22	1	21	2	0	2	5	.286	0	0-0	0	5.90	5.79
01	Bos	AL	12	11	0	1	52.1	241	69	40	36	7	1	1	2	19	0	37	1	1	2	5	.286	0	0-0	0	6.24	6.19
01	Mon	NL	10	10	0	0	54.2	228	65	30	29	8	1	1	1	10	0	31	1	0	1	4	.200	0	0-0	0	4.83	4.77
05	Was	NL	10	9	0	0	54.0	231	44	23	20	6	6	1	1	27	1	17	3	0	4	3	.571	0	0-0	0	3.54	3.33
05	Mil	NL	22	20	1	0	126.1	543	145	65	61	16	1	3	2	28	4	81	5	0	7	6	.538	1	0-0	0	4.39	4.35
9 ML YEARS			184	172	5	6	999.0	4314	1105	521	459	122	44	25	30	283	26	559	32	2	50	63	.442	1	0-0	0	4.45	4.14

Ross Ohlendorf

Pitches: R **Bats:** R **Pos:** RP-6   **Ht:** 6'4" **Wt:** 235 **Born:** 8/8/1982 **Age:** 25

	HOW MUCH HE PITCHED						WHAT HE GAVE UP												THE RESULTS							
Year Team	Lg	G	GS	CG	GF	IP	BFP	H	R	ER	HR	SH	SF	HB	TBB	IBB	SO	WP	Bk	W	L	Pct	ShO	Sv-Op	Hld	ERC	ERA
2004 Yakima	A-	7	7	0	0	29.0	128	22	14	9	1	0	0	4	19	0	28	9	0	2	3	.400	0	0- -	-	3.79	2.79
2005 Sbend	A	27	26	1	1	157.0	699	181	97	79	10	4	4	10	48	0	144	9	0	11	10	.524	1	0- -	-	4.52	4.53
2006 Tenn	AA	27	27	4	0	177.2	713	180	70	65	13	8	2	8	29	2	125	16	1	10	8	.556	2	0- -	-	3.33	3.29
2006 Tucsn	AAA	1	1	0	0	5.0	21	6	1	1	0	0	0	1	0	0	4	0	0	0	0	-	0	0- -	-	3.80	1.80
2007 Yanks	R	4	4	0	0	16.0	62	13	8	7	2	0	0	3	1	0	17	1	0	1	1	.500	0	0- -	-	2.78	3.94
2007 S-WB	AAA	22	9	0	1	68.1	308	89	41	39	7	2	3	2	24	2	49	4	1	3	4	.429	0	0- -	-	5.83	5.14
2007 NYY	AL	6	0	0	3	6.1	26	5	2	2	1	0	0	0	2	0	9	0	0	0	0	-	0	0-0	1	2.94	2.84

Will Ohman

Pitches: L **Bats:** L **Pos:** RP-56   **Ht:** 6'2" **Wt:** 203 **Born:** 8/13/1977 **Age:** 30

	HOW MUCH HE PITCHED						WHAT HE GAVE UP												THE RESULTS							
Year Team	Lg	G	GS	CG	GF	IP	BFP	H	R	ER	HR	SH	SF	HB	TBB	IBB	SO	WP	Bk	W	L	Pct	ShO	Sv-Op	Hld	ERC	ERA
2007 Iowa*	AAA	9	0	0	1	6.2	32	7	2	2	0	3	0	0	5	0	9	1	0	0	0	-	0	0- -	-	4.82	2.70
2000 ChC	NL	6	0	0	2	3.1	17	4	3	3	0	0	0	0	4	1	2	1	0	1	0	1.000	0	0-0	1	7.25	8.10
2001 ChC	NL	11	0	0	0	11.2	54	14	10	10	2	0	0	0	6	0	12	2	0	1	0	1.000	0	0-0	-	6.26	7.71
2005 ChC	NL	69	0	0	13	43.1	187	32	14	14	6	1	0	3	24	3	45	6	1	2	2	.500	0	0-3	13	3.62	2.91
2006 ChC	NL	78	0	0	14	65.1	286	51	30	30	6	0	2	5	34	2	74	4	0	1	1	.500	0	0-0	9	3.44	4.13
2007 ChC	NL	56	0	0	11	36.1	168	42	20	20	3	2	0	1	16	4	33	2	0	2	4	.333	0	1-1	12	4.79	4.95
5 ML YEARS		220	0	0	40	160.0	712	143	77	77	17	3	2	9	84	10	166	15	1	6	8	.429	0	1-4	36	4.06	4.33

Augie Ojeda

Bats: B **Throws:** R **Pos:** 2B-26; PH-16; SS-12; 3B-7; PR-1   **Ht:** 5'8" **Wt:** 170 **Born:** 12/20/1974 **Age:** 33

	BATTING																			BASERUNNING				AVERAGES		
Year Team	Lg	G	AB	H	2B	3B	HR	(Hm	Rd)	TB	R	RBI	RC	TBB	IBB	SO	HBP	SH	SF	SB	CS	SB%	GDP	Avg	OBP	Slg
2007 Tucsn*	AAA	32	97	31	7	0	0	(-	-)	38	19	17	16	10	0	11	3	4	2	1	0	1.00	6	.320	.393	.392
2000 ChC	NL	28	77	17	3	1	2	(1	1)	28	10	8	9	10	1	9	0	1	1	0	1	.00	1	.221	.307	.364
2001 ChC	NL	78	144	29	5	1	1	(1	0)	39	16	12	10	12	1	20	2	2	2	1	0	1.00	2	.201	.269	.271
2002 ChC	NL	30	70	13	4	0	0	(0	0)	17	4	4	4	5	0	5	1	4	1	1	0	1.00	2	.186	.247	.243
2003 ChC	NL	12	25	3	0	0	0	(0	0)	3	2	0	0	1	1	5	1	0	0	0	0	-	1	.120	.185	.120
2004 Min	AL	30	59	20	1	0	2	(0	2)	27	16	7	11	10	0	3	0	2	1	1	1	.50	2	.339	.429	.458
2007 Ari	NL	57	113	31	2	2	1	(0	1)	40	16	12	16	15	3	13	0	2	2	1	0	1.00	1	.274	.354	.354
6 ML YEARS		235	488	113	15	4	6	(2	4)	154	64	43	50	53	6	55	4	11	7	4	2	.67	7	.232	.308	.316

Hideki Okajima

Pitches: L **Bats:** L **Pos:** RP-66   **Ht:** 6'1" **Wt:** 194 **Born:** 12/25/1975 **Age:** 32

	HOW MUCH HE PITCHED						WHAT HE GAVE UP												THE RESULTS							
Year Team	Lg	G	GS	CG	GF	IP	BFP	H	R	ER	HR	SH	SF	HB	TBB	IBB	SO	WP	Bk	W	L	Pct	ShO	Sv-Op	Hld	ERC	ERA
1995 Yomiuri	Jap	1	1	0	0	5.0	20	5	1	1	0	-	-	0	2	0	9	0	0	0	0	-	0	0- -	-	3.66	1.80
1996 Yomiuri	Jap	5	1	0	2	12.2	60	13	2	1	0	-	-	1	9	0	8	1	0	1	0	1.000	0	0- -	-	4.92	0.71
1997 Yomiuri	Jap	25	21	2	2	109.1	477	92	47	42	7	-	-	4	59	0	102	3	0	4	9	.308	1	0- -	-	3.59	3.46
1998 Yomiuri	Jap	14	12	0	2	62.1	273	61	31	30	7	-	-	2	32	0	54	3	1	3	6	.333	0	0- -	-	4.68	4.33
1999 Yomiuri	Jap	37	3	0	9	69.2	275	42	25	23	6	-	-	3	28	0	77	3	0	4	1	.800	0	0- -	-	2.15	2.97
2000 Yomiuri	Jap	56	0	0	26	72.1	300	53	26	25	4	-	-	2	31	0	102	5	0	5	4	.556	0	7- -	-	2.56	3.11
2001 Yomiuri	Jap	58	0	0	43	62.0	281	62	21	19	5	9	2	2	39	6	70	2	0	2	1	.667	0	25- -	-	4.82	2.76
2002 Yomiuri	Jap	52	0	0	13	55.2	231	42	21	21	8	-	-	3	22	0	58	4	0	6	3	.667	0	0- -	-	3.21	3.40
2003 Yomiuri	Jap	41	0	0	7	38.2	177	45	22	21	6	-	-	1	20	3	29	1	0	2	3	.400	0	0- -	-	5.95	4.89
2004 Yomiuri	Jap	53	0	0	21	46.2	192	33	16	16	5	0	0	1	20	1	53	2	0	4	3	.571	0	5- -	-	2.71	3.09
2005 Yomiuri	Jap	42	0	0	18	53.0	231	55	31	28	10	2	3	4	19	0	56	1	0	1	0	1.000	0	0- -	-	5.10	4.75
2006 HNHF	Jap	55	0	0	13	54.2	220	46	14	13	5	3	2	1	14	2	63	6	0	2	2	.500	0	4- -	-	2.68	2.14
2007 Bos	AL	66	0	0	13	69.0	272	50	17	17	6	5	1	1	17	2	63	0	0	3	2	.600	0	5-7	27	2.03	2.22

Darren Oliver

Pitches: L **Bats:** R **Pos:** RP-61   **Ht:** 6'2" **Wt:** 200 **Born:** 10/6/1970 **Age:** 37

	HOW MUCH HE PITCHED						WHAT HE GAVE UP												THE RESULTS							
Year Team	Lg	G	GS	CG	GF	IP	BFP	H	R	ER	HR	SH	SF	HB	TBB	IBB	SO	WP	Bk	W	L	Pct	ShO	Sv-Op	Hld	ERC	ERA
1993 Tex	AL	2	0	0	0	3.1	14	2	1	1	1	0	0	0	1	1	4	0	0	0	0	-	0	0-0	0	2.15	2.70
1994 Tex	AL	43	0	0	10	50.0	226	40	24	19	4	6	0	6	35	4	50	2	2	4	0	1.000	0	2-3	9	4.29	3.42
1995 Tex	AL	17	7	0	2	49.0	222	47	25	23	3	5	1	1	32	1	39	4	0	4	2	.667	0	0-0	0	4.59	4.22
1996 Tex	AL	30	30	1	0	173.2	777	190	97	90	20	2	7	10	76	3	112	5	1	14	6	.700	1	0-0	0	5.10	4.66
1997 Tex	AL	32	32	3	0	201.1	887	213	111	94	29	2	5	11	82	3	104	7	0	13	12	.520	1	0-0	0	4.98	4.20
1998 2 Tms		29	29	2	0	160.1	749	204	115	102	18	8	8	10	66	2	87	7	4	10	11	.476	0	0-0	0	6.01	5.73
1999 StL	NL	30	30	2	0	196.1	842	197	96	93	16	11	4	11	74	4	119	6	2	9	9	.500	1	0-0	0	4.11	4.26
2000 Tex	AL	21	21	0	0	108.0	501	151	95	89	16	5	4	4	42	3	49	4	1	2	9	.182	0	0-0	0	7.04	7.42
2001 Tex	AL	28	28	1	0	154.0	696	189	109	103	23	1	5	6	65	0	104	8	2	11	11	.500	0	0-0	0	6.14	6.02
2002 Bos	AL	14	9	1	0	58.0	258	70	30	30	7	1	3	6	27	0	32	1	0	4	5	.444	0	0-0	0	6.49	4.66
2003 Col	NL	33	32	1	0	180.1	786	201	108	101	21	4	5	8	61	3	88	0	0	13	11	.542	0	0-0	0	4.80	5.04
2004 2 Tms		27	10	0	5	72.2	314	87	50	48	14	4	3	1	21	1	46	1	0	3	3	.500	0	0-0	0	5.59	5.94
2006 NYM	NL	45	0	0	10	81.0	333	70	33	31	13	2	4	3	21	2	60	1	0	4	1	.800	0	0-0	3	3.27	3.44
2007 LAA	AL	61	0	0	20	64.1	273	58	31	27	5	2	4	1	23	2	51	1	1	3	1	.750	0	0-0	8	3.19	3.78
98 Tex	AL	19	19	2	0	103.1	493	140	84	75	11	3	6	10	43	1	58	6	1	6	7	.462	0	0-0	0	6.68	6.53
98 StL	NL	10	10	0	0	57.0	256	64	31	27	7	5	2	0	23	1	29	1	3	4	4	.500	0	0-0	0	4.85	4.26
04 Fla	NL	18	8	0	3	58.2	260	75	44	42	13	4	3	1	17	1	33	1	0	2	3	.400	0	0-0	0	6.30	6.44
04 Hou	NL	9	2	0	2	14.0	54	12	6	6	1	0	0	0	4	0	13	0	0	1	0	1.000	0	0-0	0	2.89	3.86
14 ML YEARS		412	228	11	47	1552.1	6878	1719	925	851	190	53	53	78	626	29	945	47	13	94	81	.537	4	2-3	20	5.08	4.93

Miguel Olivo

Bats: R **Throws:** R **Pos:** C-119; PH-8
Ht: 6'0" **Wt:** 220 **Born:** 7/15/1978 **Age:** 29

Year	Team	Lg	G	AB	H	2B	3B	HR	(Hm	Rd)	TB	R	RBI	RC	TBB	IBB	SO	HBP	SH	SF	SB	CS	SB%	GDP	Avg	OBP	Slg
2002	CWS	AL	6	19	4	1	0	1	(0	1)	8	2	5	4	2	0	5	0	0	0	0	0	-	1	.211	.286	.421
2003	CWS	AL	114	317	75	19	1	6	(4	2)	114	37	27	32	19	0	80	4	4	2	6	4	.60	3	.237	.287	.360
2004	2 Tms	AL	96	301	70	15	4	13	(8	5)	132	46	40	33	20	2	84	3	4	1	7	6	.54	4	.233	.286	.439
2005	2 Tms	AL	91	267	58	11	1	9	(5	4)	98	30	34	23	8	2	80	3	1	2	7	2	.78	5	.217	.246	.367
2006	Fla	NL	127	430	113	22	3	16	(7	9)	189	52	58	49	9	4	103	7	3	3	2	3	.40	9	.263	.287	.440
2007	Fla	NL	122	452	107	20	4	16	(11	5)	183	43	60	43	14	2	123	2	0	1	3	2	.60	13	.237	.262	.405
04	CWS	AL	46	141	38	7	2	7	(4	3)	70	21	26	21	10	1	29	0	4	1	5	4	.56	2	.270	.316	.496
04	Sea	AL	50	160	32	8	2	6	(4	2)	62	25	14	12	10	1	55	3	0	0	2	2	.50	2	.200	.260	.388
05	Sea	AL	54	152	23	4	0	5	(4	1)	42	14	18	6	4	0	49	0	0	1	1	1	.50	3	.151	.172	.276
05	SD	NL	37	115	35	7	1	4	(1	3)	56	16	16	17	4	2	31	3	1	1	6	1	.86	4	.304	.341	.487
6 ML YEARS			556	1786	427	88	13	61	(35	26)	724	210	224	184	72	10	475	19	12	9	25	17	.60	37	.239	.275	.405

Ray Olmedo

Bats: B **Throws:** R **Pos:** SS-24; PH-3; 3B-2; PR-1
Ht: 5'11" **Wt:** 172 **Born:** 5/31/1981 **Age:** 27

Year	Team	Lg	G	AB	H	2B	3B	HR	(Hm	Rd)	TB	R	RBI	RC	TBB	IBB	SO	HBP	SH	SF	SB	CS	SB%	GDP	Avg	OBP	Slg
2007	Syrcse*	AAA	97	328	95	12	1	1	(-	-)	112	32	26	41	28	0	53	1	14	2	7	5	.58	9	.290	.345	.341
2003	Cin	NL	79	230	55	6	1	0	(0	0)	63	24	17	19	13	0	46	0	7	0	1	1	.50	4	.239	.280	.274
2004	Cin	NL	8	1	0	0	0	0	(0	0)	0	0	0	0	1	0	0	0	0	0	0	0	-	0	.000	.500	.000
2005	Cin	NL	54	77	17	4	1	1	(1	0)	26	10	4	6	6	0	22	1	3	1	4	0	1.00	1	.221	.282	.338
2006	Cin	NL	30	44	9	2	0	1	(0	1)	14	5	4	4	4	0	4	0	0	0	1	0	1.00	1	.205	.271	.318
2007	Tor	AL	27	51	11	4	0	0	(0	0)	15	6	1	2	2	0	9	0	1	0	0	0	-	1	.216	.245	.294
5 ML YEARS			198	403	92	16	2	2	(1	1)	118	45	26	31	26	0	81	1	11	1	6	1	.86	6	.228	.276	.293

Scott Olsen

Pitches: L **Bats:** L **Pos:** SP-33
Ht: 6'5" **Wt:** 215 **Born:** 1/12/1984 **Age:** 24

Year	Team	Lg	G	GS	CG	GF	IP	BFP	H	R	ER	HR	SH	SF	HB	TBB	IBB	SO	WP	Bk	W	L	Pct	ShO	Sv-Op	Hld	ERC	ERA
2005	Fla	NL	5	4	0	0	20.1	91	21	13	9	5	0	0	0	10	0	21	1	0	1	1	.500	0	0-0	0	5.66	3.98
2006	Fla	NL	31	31	0	0	180.2	761	160	94	81	23	7	2	7	75	1	166	8	0	12	10	.545	0	0-0	0	3.88	4.04
2007	Fla	NL	33	33	0	0	176.2	826	226	134	114	29	14	8	1	85	4	133	8	0	10	15	.400	0	0-0	0	6.54	5.81
3 ML YEARS			69	68	0	0	377.2	1678	407	241	204	57	21	10	8	170	5	320	17	0	23	26	.469	0	0-0	0	5.18	4.86

Garrett Olson

Pitches: L **Bats:** R **Pos:** SP-7
Ht: 6'1" **Wt:** 200 **Born:** 10/18/1983 **Age:** 24

Year	Team	Lg	G	GS	CG	GF	IP	BFP	H	R	ER	HR	SH	SF	HB	TBB	IBB	SO	WP	Bk	W	L	Pct	ShO	Sv-Op	Hld	ERC	ERA
2005	Abrdn	A-	11	6	0	2	40.0	153	22	7	7	1	4	0	2	13	0	40	1	0	2	1	.667	0	1--	-	1.45	1.58
2005	Frdrck	A+	3	3	0	0	14.1	61	10	5	5	0	0	0	2	7	0	19	1	0	0	-	-	0	0--	-	2.61	3.14
2006	Frdrck	A+	14	14	0	0	81.1	342	81	32	25	7	3	5	10	19	0	77	2	0	4	4	.500	0	0--	-	3.85	2.77
2006	Bowie	AA	14	14	0	0	84.1	357	78	33	32	5	4	3	6	31	0	86	4	1	6	5	.545	0	0--	-	3.57	3.42
2007	Norfolk	AAA	22	22	1	0	128.0	510	95	49	45	13	4	5	5	39	0	120	1	0	9	7	.563	0	0--	-	2.55	3.16
2007	Bal	AL	7	7	0	0	32.1	162	42	28	28	4	0	3	2	28	1	28	1	1	1	3	.250	0	0-0	0	8.46	7.79

Magglio Ordonez

Bats: R **Throws:** R **Pos:** RF-143; DH-14; PH-1
Ht: 6'0" **Wt:** 215 **Born:** 1/28/1974 **Age:** 34

Year	Team	Lg	G	AB	H	2B	3B	HR	(Hm	Rd)	TB	R	RBI	RC	TBB	IBB	SO	HBP	SH	SF	SB	CS	SB%	GDP	Avg	OBP	Slg
1997	CWS	AL	21	69	22	6	0	4	(2	2)	40	12	11	12	2	0	8	0	1	0	1	2	.33	1	.319	.338	.580
1998	CWS	AL	145	535	151	25	2	14	(8	6)	222	70	65	67	28	1	53	9	2	4	7	7	.56	19	.282	.326	.415
1999	CWS	AL	157	624	188	34	3	30	(16	14)	318	100	117	102	47	4	64	1	0	5	13	6	.68	24	.301	.349	.510
2000	CWS	AL	153	588	185	34	3	32	(21	11)	321	102	126	112	60	3	64	2	0	15	18	4	.82	28	.315	.371	.546
2001	CWS	AL	160	593	181	40	1	31	(17	14)	316	97	113	117	70	7	70	5	0	3	25	7	.78	14	.305	.382	.533
2002	CWS	AL	153	590	189	47	1	38	(24	14)	352	116	135	119	53	2	77	7	0	3	7	5	.58	21	.320	.381	.597
2003	CWS	AL	160	606	192	46	3	29	(17	12)	331	95	99	109	57	1	73	7	0	4	9	5	.64	20	.317	.380	.546
2004	CWS	AL	52	202	59	8	2	9	(4	5)	98	32	37	39	16	2	22	3	0	1	0	2	.00	4	.292	.351	.485
2005	Det	AL	82	305	92	17	0	8	(2	6)	133	38	46	51	30	1	35	1	0	7	0	0	-	8	.302	.359	.436
2006	Det	AL	155	593	177	32	1	24	(8	16)	283	82	104	97	45	3	87	4	0	4	1	4	.20	13	.298	.350	.477
2007	Det	AL	157	595	216	54	0	28	(17	11)	354	117	139	146	76	8	79	2	0	5	4	1	.80	20	.363	.434	.595
11 ML YEARS			1395	5300	1652	343	16	247	(136	111)	2768	861	992	971	484	32	632	41	3	51	87	43	.67	172	.312	.370	.522

Pete Orr

Bats: L **Throws:** R **Pos:** PH-32; 3B-14; PR-11; 2B-4; LF-1
Ht: 6'1" **Wt:** 185 **Born:** 6/8/1979 **Age:** 29

Year	Team	Lg	G	AB	H	2B	3B	HR	(Hm	Rd)	TB	R	RBI	RC	TBB	IBB	SO	HBP	SH	SF	SB	CS	SB%	GDP	Avg	OBP	Slg
2007	Rchmd*	AAA	43	154	37	6	4	1	(-	-)	54	26	8	17	14	1	39	1	0	0	7	3	.70	1	.240	.308	.351
2005	Atl	NL	112	150	45	8	1	1	(0	1)	58	32	8	18	6	0	23	1	5	0	7	1	.88	2	.300	.331	.387
2006	Atl	NL	102	154	39	3	4	1	(1	0)	53	22	8	16	5	1	30	0	5	0	2	4	.33	1	.253	.277	.344
2007	Atl	NL	57	65	13	1	0	0	(0	0)	14	11	2	3	3	0	14	0	1	0	1	0	1.00	1	.200	.235	.215
3 ML YEARS			271	369	97	12	5	2	(1	1)	125	65	18	37	14	1	67	1	11	0	10	5	.67	4	.263	.292	.339

David Ortiz

Bats: L **Throws:** L **Pos:** DH-140; 1B-7; PH-2   **Ht:** 6'4" **Wt:** 230 **Born:** 11/18/1975 **Age:** 32

								BATTING													BASERUNNING				AVERAGES		
Year	Team	Lg	G	AB	H	2B	3B	HR	(Hm	Rd)	TB	R	RBI	RC	TBB	IBB	SO	HBP	SH	SF	SB	CS	SB%	GDP	Avg	OBP	Slg
1997	Min	AL	15	49	16	3	0	1	(0	1)	22	10	6	7	2	0	19	0	0	0	0	0	-	1	.327	.353	.449
1998	Min	AL	86	278	77	20	0	9	(2	7)	124	47	46	46	39	3	72	5	0	4	1	0	1.00	8	.277	.371	.446
1999	Min	AL	10	20	0	0	0	0	(0	0)	0	1	0	0	5	0	12	0	0	0	0	0	-	2	.000	.200	.000
2000	Min	AL	130	415	117	36	1	10	(7	3)	185	59	63	66	57	2	81	0	0	6	1	0	1.00	13	.282	.364	.446
2001	Min	AL	89	303	71	17	1	18	(6	12)	144	46	48	46	40	8	68	1	1	2	1	0	1.00	6	.234	.324	.475
2002	Min	AL	125	412	112	32	1	20	(5	15)	206	52	75	62	43	0	87	3	0	8	1	2	.33	5	.272	.339	.500
2003	Bos	AL	128	448	129	39	2	31	(17	14)	265	79	101	80	58	8	83	1	0	2	0	0	-	9	.288	.369	.592
2004	Bos	AL	150	582	175	47	3	41	(17	24)	351	94	139	127	75	8	133	4	0	8	0	0	-	12	.301	.380	.603
2005	Bos	AL	159	601	180	40	1	47	(20	27)	363	119	148	137	102	9	124	1	0	9	1	0	1.00	13	.300	.397	.604
2006	Bos	AL	151	558	160	29	2	54	(22	32)	355	115	137	129	119	23	117	4	0	5	1	0	1.00	12	.287	.413	.636
2007	Bos	AL	149	549	182	52	1	35	(16	19)	341	116	117	138	111	12	103	4	0	3	3	1	.75	16	.332	.445	.621
11 ML YEARS			1192	4215	1219	315	12	266	(112	154)	2356	738	880	838	651	73	899	23	1	47	9	3	.75	97	.289	.384	.559

Ramon Ortiz

Pitches: R **Bats:** R **Pos:** RP-28; SP-10   **Ht:** 6'0" **Wt:** 175 **Born:** 5/23/1973 **Age:** 35

			HOW MUCH HE PITCHED						WHAT HE GAVE UP										THE RESULTS						
Year	Team	Lg	G	GS	CG	GF	IP	BFP	H	R	ER	HR	SH	SF	HB	TBB	IBB	SO	WP	Bk	W	L	Pct	ShO	Sv-Op	Hld	ERC	ERA
1999	LAA	AL	9	9	0	0	48.1	218	50	35	35	7	0	2	2	25	0	44	2	2	2	3	.400	0	0-0	0	5.23	6.52
2000	LAA	AL	18	18	2	0	111.1	472	96	69	63	18	4	4	2	55	0	73	7	4	8	6	.571	0	0-0	0	4.24	5.09
2001	LAA	AL	32	32	2	0	208.2	916	223	114	101	25	9	6	12	76	6	135	7	0	13	11	.542	0	0-0	0	4.65	4.36
2002	LAA	AL	32	32	4	0	217.1	896	188	97	91	40	2	5	5	68	0	162	7	3	15	9	.625	1	0-0	0	3.64	3.77
2003	LAA	AL	32	32	1	0	180.0	814	209	121	104	28	3	7	12	63	0	94	4	0	16	13	.552	0	0-0	0	5.44	5.20
2004	LAA	AL	34	14	0	13	128.0	543	139	64	63	18	2	3	4	38	4	82	5	3	5	7	.417	0	0-0	0	4.61	4.43
2005	Cin	NL	30	30	1	0	171.1	755	206	110	102	34	7	8	7	51	1	96	4	1	9	11	.450	0	0-0	0	5.78	5.36
2006	Was	NL	33	33	0	0	190.2	871	230	127	118	31	10	4	18	64	14	104	4	3	11	16	.407	0	0-0	0	5.71	5.57
2007	2 Tms		38	10	0	15	104.0	459	127	65	63	16	1	5	6	22	1	51	2	1	5	4	.556	0	0-0	0	5.17	5.45
07	Min	AL	28	10	0	11	91.0	400	112	54	52	12	0	4	5	15	1	44	2	1	4	4	.500	0	0-0	0	4.83	5.14
07	Col	NL	10	0	0	4	13.0	59	15	11	11	4	1	1	1	7	0	7	0	0	1	0	1.000	0	0-0	0	7.81	7.62
9 ML YEARS			258	210	10	28	1359.2	5944	1468	802	740	217	38	44	68	462	26	841	42	17	84	80	.512	1	0-0	0	4.90	4.90

Russ Ortiz

Pitches: R **Bats:** R **Pos:** SP-8; RP-4   **Ht:** 6'1" **Wt:** 220 **Born:** 6/5/1974 **Age:** 34

			HOW MUCH HE PITCHED						WHAT HE GAVE UP										THE RESULTS						
Year	Team	Lg	G	GS	CG	GF	IP	BFP	H	R	ER	HR	SH	SF	HB	TBB	IBB	SO	WP	Bk	W	L	Pct	ShO	Sv-Op	Hld	ERC	ERA
2007	SnJos*	A+	1	1	0	0	4.0	16	2	2	0	0	1	0	1	1	0	5	0	0	0	0	-	0	0--	-	0.88	0.00
2007	Fresno*	AAA	5	3	0	0	16.2	66	16	7	6	1	0	0	0	2	0	12	2	0	1	1	.500	0	0--	-	2.60	3.24
1998	SF	NL	22	13	0	3	88.1	394	80	51	40	11	6	4	4	46	1	76	3	0	4	4	.500	0	0 0	1	5.06	4.00
1999	SF	NL	33	33	3	0	207.2	922	189	109	88	24	11	6	6	125	5	164	13	0	18	9	.667	0	0-0	0	4.56	3.81
2000	SF	NL	33	32	0	0	195.2	871	192	117	109	28	10	6	7	112	1	167	6	0	14	12	.538	0	0-0	0	5.17	5.01
2001	SF	NL	33	33	1	0	218.2	911	187	90	80	13	10	4	0	91	3	169	8	1	17	9	.654	1	0-0	0	3.08	3.29
2002	SF	NL	33	33	2	0	214.1	911	191	89	86	15	15	6	4	94	5	137	5	0	14	10	.583	0	0-0	0	3.46	3.61
2003	Atl	NL	34	34	1	0	212.1	912	177	101	90	17	6	7	4	102	7	149	5	0	21	7	.750	1	0-0	0	3.32	3.81
2004	Atl	NL	34	34	2	0	204.2	896	197	98	94	23	10	7	3	112	7	143	4	1	15	9	.625	1	0-0	0	4.60	4.13
2005	Ari	NL	22	22	0	0	115.0	551	147	92	88	18	5	8	4	65	3	46	5	0	5	11	.313	0	0 0	0	6.96	6.89
2006	2 Tms		26	11	0	5	63.0	303	86	60	57	18	1	1	3	40	1	44	2	0	0	8	.000	0	0-0	0	9.39	8.14
2007	SF	NL	12	8	0	1	49.0	223	57	32	30	4	3	1	6	20	1	27	0	0	2	3	.400	0	0-0	0	5.42	5.51
06	Ari	NL	6	6	0	0	22.2	113	27	21	19	3	1	0	1	22	1	21	0	0	0	5	.000	0	0-0	0	8.19	7.54
06	Bal	AL	20	5	0	5	40.1	190	59	39	38	15	0	1	2	18	0	23	2	0	0	3	.000	0	0-0	0	9.99	8.48
10 ML YEARS			282	253	9	9	1568.2	6894	1513	839	771	171	76	50	41	807	34	1121	53	2	110	82	.573	3	0-0	1	4.48	4.42

Dan Ortmeier

Bats: B **Throws:** R **Pos:** 1B-22; LF-22; RF-13; PH-9; PR-6; CF-1   **Ht:** 6'4" **Wt:** 215 **Born:** 5/11/1981 **Age:** 27

								BATTING													BASERUNNING				AVERAGES		
Year	Team	Lg	G	AB	H	2B	3B	HR	(Hm	Rd)	TB	R	RBI	RC	TBB	IBB	SO	HBP	SH	SF	SB	CS	SB%	GDP	Avg	OBP	Slg
2007	Fresno*	AAA	79	305	80	19	1	10	(-	-)	131	39	54	48	27	1	63	7	0	3	16	2	.89	6	.262	.333	.430
2005	SF	NL	15	22	3	0	0	0	(0	0)	3	1	1	1	3	0	5	1	0	0	1	0	1.00	0	.136	.269	.136
2006	SF	NL	9	12	3	1	0	0	(0	0)	4	0	2	2	0	0	4	0	0	0	0	0	-	0	.250	.250	.333
2007	SF	NL	62	157	45	7	4	6	(1	5)	78	20	16	20	7	1	41	1	0	2	2	1	.67	2	.287	.317	.497
3 ML YEARS			86	191	51	8	4	6	(1	5)	85	21	19	23	10	1	50	2	0	2	3	1	.75	4	.267	.307	.445

Chad Orvella

Pitches: R **Bats:** R **Pos:** RP-10   **Ht:** 5'11" **Wt:** 195 **Born:** 10/1/1980 **Age:** 27

			HOW MUCH HE PITCHED						WHAT HE GAVE UP										THE RESULTS						
Year	Team	Lg	G	GS	CG	GF	IP	BFP	H	R	ER	HR	SH	SF	HB	TBB	IBB	SO	WP	Bk	W	L	Pct	ShO	Sv-Op	Hld	ERC	ERA
2007	Drham*	AAA	42	0	0	32	52.0	215	39	20	18	6	3	0	2	19	3	53	2	0	3	3	.500	0	20		2.74	3.12
2005	TB	AL	37	0	0	9	50.0	220	47	26	20	4	1	4	1	23	2	43	0	0	3	3	.500	0	1-2	14	3.77	3.60
2006	TB	AL	22	0	0	5	24.1	130	36	23	20	6	2	1	3	20	0	17	1	0	1	5	.167	0	0-3	1	10.81	7.40
2007	TB	AL	10	0	0	0	8.0	56	18	16	13	3	0	0	1	10	1	6	0	1	0	2	.000	0	0-0	0	18.69	14.63
3 ML YEARS			69	0	0	14	82.1	406	101	65	53	13	3	5	5	53	3	66	1	1	4	10	.286	0	1-5	15	6.95	5.79

Franquelis Osoria

Pitches: R **Bats:** R **Pos:** RP-25 **Ht:** 6'0" **Wt:** 210 **Born:** 9/12/1981 **Age:** 26

			HOW MUCH HE PITCHED						WHAT HE GAVE UP												THE RESULTS							
Year	Team	Lg	G	GS	CG	GF	IP	BFP	H	R	ER	HR	SH	SF	HB	TBB	IBB	SO	WP	Bk	W	L	Pct	ShO	Sv-Op	Hld	ERC	ERA
2007	Indy*	AAA	39	0	0	27	54.2	239	51	22	16	3	4	3	8	19	7	33	1	0	2	5	.286	0	11--	-	3.50	2.63
2005	LAD	NL	24	0	0	6	29.2	122	28	14	13	3	3	0	3	8	0	15	0	0	0	2	.000	0	0-2	3	3.78	3.94
2006	LAD	NL	12	0	0	1	17.2	86	27	14	14	4	1	0	1	9	1	13	0	0	0	2	.000	0	0-0	0	9.30	7.13
2007	Pit	NL	25	0	0	3	28.1	126	33	16	15	3	0	0	4	8	2	13	2	0	0	2	.000	0	0-0	4	5.09	4.76
	3 ML YEARS		61	0	0	10	75.2	334	88	44	42	10	4	0	8	25	3	41	2	0	0	6	.000	0	0-2	7	5.45	5.00

Roy Oswalt

Pitches: R **Bats:** R **Pos:** SP-32; RP-1 **Ht:** 6'0" **Wt:** 185 **Born:** 8/29/1977 **Age:** 30

			HOW MUCH HE PITCHED						WHAT HE GAVE UP												THE RESULTS							
Year	Team	Lg	G	GS	CG	GF	IP	BFP	H	R	ER	HR	SH	SF	HB	TBB	IBB	SO	WP	Bk	W	L	Pct	ShO	Sv-Op	Hld	ERC	ERA
2001	Hou	NL	28	20	3	4	141.2	575	126	48	43	14	4	4	6	24	2	144	0	0	14	3	.824	1	0-0	0	2.68	2.73
2002	Hou	NL	35	34	0	0	233.0	956	215	86	78	17	12	7	5	62	4	208	3	0	19	9	.679	0	0-0	0	3.05	3.01
2003	Hou	NL	21	21	0	0	127.1	514	116	48	42	15	7	1	5	29	0	108	1	0	10	5	.667	0	0-0	0	3.26	2.97
2004	Hou	NL	36	35	2	0	237.0	983	233	100	92	17	11	4	11	62	5	206	5	1	20	10	.667	2	0-0	0	3.46	3.49
2005	Hou	NL	35	35	4	0	241.2	1002	243	85	79	18	12	7	8	48	3	184	5	1	20	12	.625	1	0-0	0	3.27	2.94
2006	Hou	NL	33	32	2	1	220.2	896	220	76	73	18	12	4	6	38	4	166	1	1	15	8	.652	0	0-0	0	3.19	2.98
2007	Hou	NL	33	32	1	0	212.0	910	221	80	75	14	6	4	7	60	6	154	1	1	14	7	.667	0	0-0	1	3.68	3.18
	7 ML YEARS		221	209	12	5	1413.1	5836	1374	523	482	112	64	31	48	323	24	1170	16	4	112	54	.675	4	0-0	1	3.25	3.07

Akinori Otsuka

Pitches: R **Bats:** R **Pos:** RP-34 **Ht:** 6'0" **Wt:** 210 **Born:** 1/13/1972 **Age:** 36

			HOW MUCH HE PITCHED						WHAT HE GAVE UP												THE RESULTS							
Year	Team	Lg	G	GS	CG	GF	IP	BFP	H	R	ER	HR	SH	SF	HB	TBB	IBB	SO	WP	Bk	W	L	Pct	ShO	Sv-Op	Hld	ERC	ERA
2004	SD	NL	73	0	0	18	77.1	312	56	16	15	6	4	0	6	26	6	87	0	0	7	2	.778	0	2-7	34	2.14	1.75
2005	SD	NL	66	0	0	17	62.2	276	55	28	25	3	5	0	2	34	8	60	1	0	2	8	.200	0	1-7	22	3.44	3.59
2006	Tex	AL	63	0	0	48	59.2	232	53	17	14	3	0	1	0	11	0	47	3	0	2	4	.333	0	32-36	7	2.46	2.11
2007	Tex	AL	34	0	0	13	32.1	131	26	10	9	0	1	2	0	9	1	23	0	0	2	1	.667	0	4-7	11	1.93	2.51
	4 ML YEARS		236	0	0	96	232.0	951	190	71	63	12	10	3	2	80	15	217	4	0	13	15	.464	0	39-57	74	2.54	2.44

Lyle Overbay

Bats: L **Throws:** L **Pos:** 1B-119; PH-8; DH-1 **Ht:** 6'2" **Wt:** 236 **Born:** 1/28/1977 **Age:** 31

			BATTING																			BASERUNNING				AVERAGES		
Year	Team	Lg	G	AB	H	2B	3B	HR	(Hm	Rd)	TB	R	RBI	RC	TBB	IBB	SO	HBP	SH	SF		SB	CS	SB%	GDP	Avg	OBP	Slg
2007	NHam*	AA	4	15	4	1	0	1	(-	-)	8	2	5	3	3	0	3	0	0	0		0	0	-	1	.267	.389	.533
2001	Ari	NL	2	2	1	0	0	0	(0	0)	1	0	0	0	0	0	1	0	0	0		0	0	-	0	.500	.500	.500
2002	Ari	NL	10	10	1	0	0	0	(0	0)	1	0	1	0	0	0	5	0	0	0		0	0	-	0	.100	.100	.100
2003	Ari	NL	86	254	70	20	0	4	(2	2)	102	23	28	34	35	7	67	2	0	2		1	0	1.00	8	.276	.365	.402
2004	Mil	NL	159	579	174	53	1	16	(6	10)	277	83	87	94	81	9	128	2	0	6		2	1	.67	11	.301	.385	.478
2005	Mil	NL	158	537	148	34	1	19	(10	9)	241	80	72	84	78	8	98	2	1	4		1	0	1.00	17	.276	.367	.449
2006	Tor	AL	157	581	181	46	1	22	(17	5)	295	82	92	89	55	7	96	2	0	2		5	3	.63	19	.312	.372	.508
2007	Tor	AL	122	425	102	30	2	10	(6	4)	166	49	44	45	47	4	78	1	0	3		2	0	1.00	17	.240	.315	.391
	7 ML YEARS		694	2388	677	183	5	71	(41	30)	1083	317	324	346	296	35	473	9	1	17		11	4	.73	67	.284	.362	.454

Henry Owens

Pitches: R **Bats:** R **Pos:** RP-22 **Ht:** 6'3" **Wt:** 230 **Born:** 4/23/1979 **Age:** 29

			HOW MUCH HE PITCHED						WHAT HE GAVE UP												THE RESULTS							
Year	Team	Lg	G	GS	CG	GF	IP	BFP	H	R	ER	HR	SH	SF	HB	TBB	IBB	SO	WP	Bk	W	L	Pct	ShO	Sv-Op	Hld	ERC	ERA
2001	Pirates	R	6	0	0	5	7.0	28	5	1	1	0	0	0	0	2	0	8	0	0	1	0	1.000	0	1--	-	1.62	1.29
2002	Wmspt	A-	23	0	0	15	44.2	177	23	18	13	4	0	1	3	16	0	63	8	0	0	3	.000	0	7--	-	1.65	2.62
2003	Hickory	A	22	0	0	17	34.0	143	21	14	11	1	1	0	6	17	0	52	7	0	2	1	.667	0	5--	-	2.60	2.91
2003	Lynbrg	A+	13	0	0	11	14.2	65	9	6	4	0	2	0	1	11	0	21	0	0	1	2	.333	0	5--	-	2.77	2.45
2004	Lynbrg	A+	39	0	0	27	54.2	240	46	26	26	4	0	0	4	26	1	49	10	0	3	4	.429	0	4--	-	3.47	4.28
2005	StLuci	A+	38	1	0	16	54.1	240	49	29	19	2	0	1	5	24	2	74	7	0	2	5	.286	0	4--	-	3.46	3.15
2006	Bnghtn	AA	37	0	0	36	40.0	154	19	9	7	1	1	0	3	10	1	74	5	0	2	2	.500	0	20--	-	1.07	1.58
2007	Jupiter	A+	3	0	0	0	3.0	10	1	0	0	0	0	0	0	0	0	5	1	0	1	0	1.000	0	0--	-	0.25	0.00
2006	NYM	NL	3	0	0	1	4.0	19	4	4	4	0	0	1	0	4	0	2	0	0	0	0	-	0	0-0	0	5.79	9.00
2007	Fla	NL	22	0	0	10	23.0	98	19	7	5	3	0	0	0	10	1	16	2	0	2	0	1.000	0	4-5	5	3.33	1.96
	2 ML YEARS		25	0	0	11	27.0	117	23	11	9	3	0	1	0	14	1	18	2	0	2	0	1.000	0	4-5	5	3.69	3.00

Jerry Owens

Bats: L **Throws:** L **Pos:** CF-84; LF-11; PH-7; DH-1; PR-1 **Ht:** 6'3" **Wt:** 190 **Born:** 2/16/1981 **Age:** 27

			BATTING																			BASERUNNING				AVERAGES		
Year	Team	Lg	G	AB	H	2B	3B	HR	(Hm	Rd)	TB	R	RBI	RC	TBB	IBB	SO	HBP	SH	SF		SB	CS	SB%	GDP	Avg	OBP	Slg
2003	Vrmnt	A-	2	8	1	0	0	0	(-	-)	1	0	0	0	0	0	0	0	0	0		1	0	1.00	0	.125	.125	.125
2004	Savann	A	108	418	122	17	2	1	(-	-)	146	69	37	59	46	1	59	3	1	2		30	13	.70	3	.292	.365	.349
2005	Brham	AA	130	522	173	21	6	2	(-	-)	212	99	52	87	52	4	72	2	9	2		38	20	.66	5	.331	.393	.406
2006	Charltt	AAA	112	439	115	15	5	4	(-	-)	152	75	48	57	45	2	61	1	5	3		40	12	.77	5	.262	.330	.346
2007	Charltt	AAA	59	232	66	10	4	3	(-	-)	85	39	21	35	29	3	37	1	1	4		23	4	.85	5	.284	.361	.366
2006	CWS	AL	12	9	3	1	0	0	(0	0)	4	4	0	1	0	0	2	0	0	0		1	0	1.00	0	.333	.333	.444
2007	CWS	AL	93	356	95	9	2	1	(1	0)	111	44	17	41	27	0	63	3	3	0		32	8	.80	5	.267	.324	.312
	2 ML YEARS		105	365	98	10	2	1	(1	0)	115	48	17	42	27	0	65	3	3	0		33	8	.80	5	.268	.324	.315

Micah Owings

Pitches: R Bats: R Pos: SP-27; RP-2 Ht: 6'5" Wt: 220 Born: 9/28/1982 Age: 25

		HOW MUCH HE PITCHED						WHAT HE GAVE UP										THE RESULTS						
Year	Team	Lg	G	GS	CG	GF	IP	BFP	H	R	ER	HR	SH	SF	HB	TBB	IBB	SO	WP	Bk	W	L	Pct	ShO	Sv-Op Hld	ERC	ERA
2005	Lancst	A+	16	0	0	1	22.0	83	17	6	6	0	1	1	0	4	0	30	0	0	1	1	.500	0	0- - -	1.65	2.45
2006	Tenn	AA	12	12	0	0	74.1	297	66	24	24	4	4	2	6	17	2	69	2	0	6	2	.750	0	0- - -	2.90	2.91
2006	Tucsn	AAA	15	15	1	0	87.2	381	96	40	36	4	6	5	5	34	0	61	5	0	10	0	1.000	0	0- - -	4.49	3.70
2007	Tucsn	AAA	1	1	0	0	5.0	18	4	0	0	0	1	0	0	1	0	7	0	0	0	0	-	0	0- - -	1.95	0.00
2007	Ari	NL	29	27	2	0	152.2	651	146	81	73	20	7	3	14	50	2	106	5	0	8	8	.500	1	0-0 0	4.13	4.30

Pablo Ozuna

Bats: R Throws: R Pos: 3B-9; LF-7; DH-7; PR-4; 2B-3; PH-2; SS-1 Ht: 5'11" Wt: 190 Born: 8/25/1974 Age: 33

			BATTING																BASERUNNING				AVERAGES		
Year	Team	Lg	G	AB	H	2B	3B	HR	(Hm | Rd)	TB	R	RBI	RC	TBR	IBB	SO	HDP	SH	SF	SB	CS	SB%	GDP	Avg	OBP	Slg
2000	Fla	NL	14	24	8	1	0	0	(0 | 0)	9	2	0	3	0	0	2	0	2	0	1	0	1.00	0	.333	.333	.375
2002	Fla	NL	34	47	13	2	2	0	(0 | 0)	19	4	3	4	1	0	3	1	0	1	1	1	.50	2	.277	.300	.404
2003	Col	NL	17	40	8	1	0	0	(0 | 0)	9	5	2	4	2	0	6	2	1	0	3	0	1.00	1	.200	.273	.225
2005	CWS	AL	70	203	56	7	2	0	(0 | 0)	67	27	11	20	7	0	26	4	3	0	14	7	.67	5	.276	.313	.330
2006	CWS	AL	79	189	62	12	2	2	(2 | 0)	84	25	17	30	7	0	16	4	3	0	6	6	.50	3	.328	.365	.444
2007	CWS	AL	27	78	19	3	0	0	(0 | 0)	22	9	3	5	3	0	9	1	3	0	3	0	1.00	1	.244	.280	.282
6 ML YEARS			241	581	166	26	6	2	(2 | 0)	210	72	36	66	20	0	62	12	12	1	28	14	.67	12	.286	.322	.361

Vicente Padilla

Pitches: R Bats: R Pos: SP-23 Ht: 6'2" Wt: 220 Born: 9/27/1977 Age: 30

			HOW MUCH HE PITCHED						WHAT HE GAVE UP										THE RESULTS						
Year	Team	Lg	G	GS	CG	GF	IP	BFP	H	R	ER	HR	SH	SF	HB	TBB	IBB	SO	WP	Bk	W	L	Pct	ShO	Sv-Op Hld	ERC	ERA
2007	Frisco*	AA	5	5	0	0	11.0	51	11	7	7	1	1	0	0	8	0	11	1	0	0	1	.000	0	0- - -	5.30	5.73
1999	Ari	NL	5	0	0	2	2.2	19	7	5	5	1	1	0	0	3	0	0	0	0	0	1	.000	0	0-1 1	20.65	16.88
2000	2 Tms	NL	55	0	0	16	65.1	291	72	33	27	3	5	3	1	28	7	51	1	0	4	7	.364	0	2-7 15	4.22	3.72
2001	Phi	NL	23	0	0	5	34.0	144	36	18	16	1	0	0	0	12	0	29	1	0	3	1	.750	0	0-3 1	3.80	4.24
2002	Phi	NL	32	32	1	0	206.0	862	198	83	75	16	10	3	15	53	5	128	6	2	14	11	.560	1	0-0 0	3.42	3.28
2003	Phi	NL	32	32	1	0	208.2	876	196	94	84	22	11	7	16	62	4	133	3	2	14	12	.538	1	0-0 0	3.68	3.62
2004	Phi	NL	20	20	0	0	115.1	503	119	63	58	16	7	5	10	36	6	82	2	0	7	7	.500	0	0-0 0	4.42	4.53
2005	Phi	NL	27	27	0	0	147.0	654	146	79	77	22	7	3	8	74	9	103	1	0	9	12	.429	0	0-0 0	4.94	4.71
2006	Tex	AL	33	33	0	0	200.0	872	206	108	100	21	6	6	17	70	2	156	4	2	15	10	.600	0	0-0 0	4.41	4.50
2007	Tex	AL	23	23	0	0	120.1	553	146	88	77	16	3	2	9	50	1	71	2	0	6	10	.375	0	0-0 0	5.95	5.76
00	Ari	NL	27	0	0	12	35.0	143	32	10	9	0	0	1	0	10	2	30	0	0	2	1	.667	0	0-1 7	2.48	2.31
00	Phi	NL	28	0	0	4	30.1	148	40	23	18	3	5	2	1	18	5	21	1	0	2	6	.250	0	2-6 8	6.52	5.34
9 ML YEARS			250	167	2	23	1099.1	4774	1126	571	519	118	50	29	76	388	34	753	20	6	72	71	.503	2	2-11 17	4.31	4.25

Angel Pagan

Bats: B Throws: R Pos: CF-34; RF-29; PH-16; PR-9; LF-2 Ht: 6'1" Wt: 180 Born: 7/2/1981 Age: 26

			BATTING																BASERUNNING				AVERAGES		
Year	Team	Lg	G	AB	H	2B	3B	HR	(Hm | Rd)	TB	R	RBI	RC	TBB	IBB	SO	HBP	SH	SF	SB	CS	SB%	GDP	Avg	OBP	Slg
2000	Kngspt	R+	19	72	26	5	1	0	(- | -)	33	13	8	14	6	0	8	0	0	0	6	1	.86	1	.361	.410	.458
2001	Clmbia	A	15	57	17	1	1	0	(- | -)	20	4	5	7	6	0	5	0	1	0	3	2	.60	3	.298	.365	.351
2001	Bklyn	A-	62	238	75	10	2	0	(- | -)	89	46	15	36	22	0	30	7	3	1	30	18	.63	1	.315	.388	.374
2002	Clmbia	A	108	458	128	14	5	1	(- | -)	155	79	36	54	32	0	87	0	4	3	52	21	.71	1	.279	.325	.338
2002	StLuci	A+	16	67	23	2	1	1	(- | -)	30	12	7	13	7	1	9	0	1	0	10	2	.83	5	.343	.405	.448
2003	StLuci	A+	113	441	110	15	5	1	(- | -)	138	64	33	46	35	1	80	2	11	1	35	15	.70	5	.249	.307	.313
2004	Bnghtn	AA	112	449	129	25	8	4	(- | -)	182	71	63	69	42	0	96	1	4	5	29	5	.85	6	.287	.346	.405
2004	Norfolk	AAA	12	45	13	3	3	0	(- | -)	22	13	1	8	4	0	8	0	0	0	4	1	.80	0	.289	.347	.489
2005	Norfolk	AAA	129	516	140	20	10	8	(- | -)	204	69	40	71	49	2	111	1	9	4	27	15	.64	7	.271	.333	.395
2006	Cubs	R	3	9	1	0	0	0	(- | -)	1	1	0	0	2	0	3	0	0	0	1	0	1.00	0	.111	.273	.111
2006	Iowa	AAA	4	15	4	1	0	0	(- | -)	5	2	1	1	1	0	4	0	0	0	1	0	1.00	0	.267	.313	.333
2007	Iowa	AAA	33	116	29	4	3	3	(- | -)	48	18	9	16	10	1	20	0	1	0	6	1	.86	1	.250	.310	.414
2006	ChC	NL	77	170	42	6	2	5	(4 | 1)	67	28	18	21	15	0	28	0	1	1	4	2	.67	1	.247	.306	.394
2007	ChC	NL	71	148	39	10	2	4	(3 | 1)	65	21	21	23	10	0	32	0	1	2	4	1	.80	0	.264	.306	.439
2 ML YEARS			148	318	81	16	4	9	(7 | 2)	132	49	39	44	25	0	60	0	2	3	8	3	.73	3	.255	.306	.415

Orlando Palmeiro

Bats: L Throws: L Pos: PH-87; RF-16; LF-11 Ht: 5'11" Wt: 185 Born: 1/19/1969 Age: 39

			BATTING																BASERUNNING				AVERAGES		
Year	Team	Lg	G	AB	H	2B	3B	HR	(Hm | Rd)	TB	R	RBI	RC	TBB	IBB	SO	HBP	SH	SF	SB	CS	SB%	GDP	Avg	OBP	Slg
1995	LAA	AL	15	20	7	0	0	0	(0 | 0)	7	3	1	3	1	0	1	0	0	0	0	0	-	0	.350	.381	.350
1996	LAA	AL	50	87	25	6	1	0	(0 | 0)	33	6	6	12	8	1	13	2	1	0	0	1	.00	1	.287	.361	.379
1997	LAA	AL	74	134	29	2	2	0	(0 | 0)	35	19	8	10	17	1	11	1	3	1	2	2	.50	4	.216	.307	.261
1998	LAA	AL	75	165	53	7	2	0	(0 | 0)	64	28	21	26	20	1	11	0	7	0	5	4	.56	2	.321	.395	.388
1999	LAA	AL	109	317	88	12	1	1	(0 | 1)	105	46	23	41	39	1	30	6	6	3	5	5	.50	4	.278	.364	.331
2000	LAA	AL	108	243	73	20	2	0	(0 | 0)	97	38	25	42	38	0	20	2	10	3	4	1	.80	4	.300	.395	.399
2001	LAA	AL	104	230	56	10	1	2	(0 | 2)	74	29	23	25	25	2	24	3	7	5	6	6	.50	3	.243	.319	.322
2002	LAA	AL	110	263	79	12	1	0	(0 | 0)	93	35	31	39	30	1	22	0	4	3	7	2	.78	7	.300	.368	.354
2003	StL	NL	141	317	86	13	1	3	(1 | 2)	110	37	33	37	32	3	31	2	7	6	3	3	.50	1	.271	.336	.347
2004	Hou	NL	102	133	32	5	0	3	(1 | 2)	46	19	12	18	18	1	19	1	3	0	2	1	.67	1	.241	.344	.346
2005	Hou	NL	114	204	58	17	2	3	(1 | 2)	88	22	20	29	15	1	23	4	5	3	3	1	.75	4	.284	.341	.431
2006	Hou	NL	103	119	30	6	1	0	(0 | 0)	38	12	17	13	6	0	17	1	2	0	0	1	.00	1	.252	.294	.319
2007	Hou	NL	101	103	24	3	0	0	(0 | 0)	27	12	6	12	16	1	8	1	2	0	0	1	.00	2	.233	.342	.262
13 ML YEARS			1206	2335	640	113	14	12	(3 | 9)	817	306	226	307	265	13	230	25	56	24	37	28	.57	35	.274	.351	.350

201

Jonathan Papelbon

Pitches: R **Bats:** R **Pos:** RP-59

Ht: 6'4" **Wt:** 230 **Born:** 11/23/1980 **Age:** 27

Year	Team	Lg	G	GS	CG	GF	IP	BFP	H	R	ER	HR	SH	SF	HB	TBB	IBB	SO	WP	Bk	W	L	Pct	ShO	Sv-Op	Hld	ERC	ERA
2005	Bos	AL	17	3	0	4	34.0	148	33	11	10	4	1	0	3	17	2	34	1	0	3	1	.750	0	0-1	4	4.82	2.65
2006	Bos	AL	59	0	0	49	68.1	257	40	8	7	3	1	2	1	13	2	75	2	0	4	2	.667	0	35-41	1	1.22	0.92
2007	Bos	AL	59	0	0	53	58.1	224	30	12	12	5	0	0	4	15	0	84	0	0	1	3	.250	0	37-40	2	1.43	1.85
	3 ML YEARS		135	3	0	106	160.2	629	103	31	29	12	2	2	8	45	4	193	3	0	8	6	.571	0	72-82	7	1.83	1.62

Chan Ho Park

Pitches: R **Bats:** R **Pos:** SP-1

Ht: 6'2" **Wt:** 210 **Born:** 6/30/1973 **Age:** 35

Year	Team	Lg	G	GS	CG	GF	IP	BFP	H	R	ER	HR	SH	SF	HB	TBB	IBB	SO	WP	Bk	W	L	Pct	ShO	Sv-Op	Hld	ERC	ERA
2007	NewOr*	AAA	9	9	0	0	51.2	228	64	34	32	9	0	1	2	16	0	49	2	0	4	4	.500	0	0- -	-	5.93	5.57
2007	RdRck*	AAA	15	15	0	0	84.0	376	100	70	58	18	4	3	3	24	1	70	5	0	2	10	.167	0	0- -	-	5.60	6.21
1994	LAD	NL	2	0	0	1	4.0	23	5	5	5	1	0	0	1	5	0	6	0	0	0	0	-	0	0-0	0	11.69	11.25
1995	LAD	NL	2	1	0	0	4.0	16	2	2	2	1	0	0	0	2	0	7	0	1	0	0	-	0	0-0	0	2.70	4.50
1996	LAD	NL	48	10	0	7	108.2	477	82	48	44	7	8	1	4	71	3	119	4	3	5	5	.500	0	0-0	4	3.50	3.64
1997	LAD	NL	32	29	2	1	192.0	792	149	80	72	24	9	5	8	70	1	166	4	1	14	8	.636	0	0-0	0	3.04	3.38
1998	LAD	NL	34	34	2	0	220.2	946	199	101	91	16	11	**10**	11	97	1	191	6	2	15	9	.625	0	0-0	0	3.69	3.71
1999	LAD	NL	33	33	0	0	194.1	883	208	120	113	31	10	5	14	100	4	174	11	1	13	11	.542	0	0-0	0	5.68	5.23
2000	LAD	NL	34	34	3	0	226.0	963	173	92	82	21	12	5	12	124	4	217	13	0	18	10	.643	1	0-0	0	3.51	3.27
2001	LAD	NL	36	**35**	2	0	234.0	981	183	98	91	23	16	7	**20**	91	1	218	3	**3**	15	11	.577	1	0-0	0	3.15	3.50
2002	Tex	AL	25	25	0	0	145.2	666	154	95	93	20	4	3	**17**	78	2	121	9	0	9	8	.529	0	0-0	0	5.75	5.75
2003	Tex	AL	7	7	0	0	29.2	146	34	26	25	5	1	3	6	25	0	16	1	1	1	3	.250	0	0-0	0	8.56	7.58
2004	Tex	AL	16	16	0	0	95.2	428	105	63	58	22	4	4	13	33	0	63	1	1	4	7	.364	0	0-0	0	5.97	5.46
2005	2 Tms		30	29	0	0	155.1	715	180	103	99	11	7	3	10	80	1	113	6	0	12	8	.600	0	0-0	0	5.52	5.74
2006	SD	NL	24	21	1	0	136.2	606	146	81	73	20	10	4	10	44	7	96	5	0	7	7	.500	1	0-0	0	4.62	4.81
2007	NYM	NL	1	1	0	0	4.0	20	6	7	7	2	0	0	0	2	0	4	1	0	0	1	.000	0	0-0	0	10.88	15.75
05	Tex	AL	20	20	0	0	109.2	502	130	70	69	8	5	2	6	54	1	80	3	0	8	5	.615	0	0-0	0	5.58	5.66
05	SD	NL	10	9	0	0	45.2	213	50	33	30	3	2	1	4	26	0	33	3	0	4	3	.571	0	0-0	0	5.36	5.91
	14 ML YEARS		324	275	10	9	1750.2	7662	1626	921	855	204	92	50	126	822	24	1511	64	13	113	88	.562	3	0-0	4	4.33	4.40

Chad Paronto

Pitches: R **Bats:** R **Pos:** RP-41

Ht: 6'5" **Wt:** 250 **Born:** 7/28/1975 **Age:** 32

Year	Team	Lg	G	GS	CG	GF	IP	BFP	H	R	ER	HR	SH	SF	HB	TBB	IBB	SO	WP	Bk	W	L	Pct	ShO	Sv-Op	Hld	ERC	ERA
2007	Rchmd*	AAA	11	0	0	4	16.2	73	18	8	7	1	2	0	2	4	0	11	0	0	0	0	-	0	2- -	-	4.04	3.78
2001	Bal	AL	24	0	0	9	27.0	128	33	24	15	5	1	1	1	11	0	16	1	0	1	3	.250	0	0-1	5	5.98	5.00
2002	Cle	AL	29	0	0	11	35.2	154	34	19	16	3	0	4	2	11	1	23	2	0	0	2	.000	0	0-0	4	3.45	4.04
2003	Cle	AL	6	0	0	5	6.2	29	7	8	7	1	1	1	0	3	0	6	0	0	0	2	.000	0	0-0	0	5.00	9.45
2006	Atl	NL	65	0	0	11	56.2	237	53	23	20	5	4	1	3	19	3	41	3	0	2	3	.400	0	0-2	8	3.56	3.18
2007	Atl	NL	41	0	0	12	40.1	180	47	20	16	1	2	3	3	19	5	14	2	0	3	1	.750	0	1-2	2	4.95	3.57
	5 ML YEARS		165	0	0	48	166.1	728	174	94	74	15	8	10	9	63	9	100	8	0	6	11	.353	0	1-5	15	4.31	4.00

Manny Parra

Pitches: L **Bats:** L **Pos:** RP-7; SP-2

Ht: 6'3" **Wt:** 200 **Born:** 10/30/1982 **Age:** 25

Year	Team	Lg	G	GS	CG	GF	IP	BFP	H	R	ER	HR	SH	SF	HB	TBB	IBB	SO	WP	Bk	W	L	Pct	ShO	Sv-Op	Hld	ERC	ERA
2002	Brewrs	R	1	1	0	0	2.0	7	1	1	1	0	0	0	0	0	0	4	0	0	0	0	-	0	0- -	-	1.73	4.50
2002	Ogden	R+	11	10	0	0	47.2	213	59	30	17	3	0	1	4	10	0	51	5	0	3	1	.750	0	0- -	-	4.69	3.21
2003	Beloit	A	23	23	1	0	138.2	551	127	50	42	9	5	0	0	24	0	117	6	3	11	2	.846	0	0- -	-	2.59	2.73
2004	Hi Dsrt	A+	13	13	1	0	67.1	295	76	41	26	3	6	6	2	19	0	64	3	1	5	2	.714	1	0- -	-	4.01	3.48
2004	Hntsvl	AA	3	3	0	0	6.0	23	5	3	2	0	0	0	0	0	0	10	1	0	1	0	1.000	0	0- -	-	1.37	3.00
2005	Hntsvl	AA	16	16	0	0	91.0	404	111	47	40	4	5	1	2	21	0	85	7	3	5	6	.455	0	0- -	-	4.25	3.96
2006	BrvdCt	A+	15	14	0	0	54.2	239	47	29	18	4	3	1	3	32	0	61	1	0	1	3	.250	0	0- -	-	4.06	2.96
2006	Hntsvl	AA	6	6	0	0	31.1	125	26	13	10	0	1	2	2	8	0	29	1	0	3	0	1.000	0	0- -	-	2.31	2.87
2007	Hntsvl	AA	13	13	0	0	80.2	334	70	28	24	2	3	3	3	26	1	81	2	2	7	3	.700	0	0- -	-	2.71	2.68
2007	Nashv	AAA	4	4	1	0	26.0	101	15	6	5	1	5	0	2	7	0	25	1	0	1	1	.750	1	0- -	-	1.50	1.73
2007	Mil	NL	9	2	0	3	26.1	116	25	13	11	1	1	3	2	12	0	26	1	0	0	1	.000	0	0-0	1	3.83	3.76

John Parrish

Pitches: L **Bats:** L **Pos:** RP-53

Ht: 5'11" **Wt:** 208 **Born:** 11/26/1977 **Age:** 30

Year	Team	Lg	G	GS	CG	GF	IP	BFP	H	R	ER	HR	SH	SF	HB	TBB	IBB	SO	WP	Bk	W	L	Pct	ShO	Sv-Op	Hld	ERC	ERA
2007	Tacom*	AAA	3	0	0	0	4.1	24	8	7	7	1	0	1	0	4	0	4	0	0	1	0	1.000	0	0- -	-	13.58	14.54
2000	Bal	AL	8	8	0	0	36.1	180	40	32	29	6	0	0	0	35	0	28	0	0	2	4	.333	0	0-0	0	7.59	7.18
2001	Bal	AL	16	1	0	0	22.0	107	22	17	15	5	0	0	0	17	0	20	0	0	1	2	.333	0	0-0	0	6.34	6.14
2003	Bal	AL	14	0	0	2	23.2	93	17	7	5	2	0	1	1	8	2	15	2	0	0	1	.000	0	0-2	1	2.39	1.90
2004	Bal	AL	56	1	0	17	78.0	353	68	39	30	4	3	6	3	55	6	71	6	0	6	3	.667	0	1-1	2	4.17	3.46
2005	Bal	AL	14	0	0	2	17.1	86	19	6	6	1	1	0	0	17	1	25	6	0	1	0	1.000	0	0-0	1	6.53	3.12
2007	2 Tms	AL	53	0	0	14	52.0	254	63	34	33	2	1	1	2	37	4	41	3	0	2	2	.500	0	0-2	10	6.03	5.71
07	Bal	AL	45	0	0	9	41.2	199	41	26	25	2	0	1	2	33	4	36	2	0	2	2	.500	0	0-2	9	5.65	5.40
07	Sea	AL	8	0	0	5	10.1	55	22	8	8	0	1	0	0	4	0	5	1	0	0	0	-	0	0-0	1	10.48	6.97
	6 ML YEARS		161	10	0	35	229.1	1073	229	135	118	20	5	8	6	169	13	200	17	0	12	12	.500	0	1-5	14	5.28	4.63

Corey Patterson

Bats: L Throws: R Pos: CF-132; PR-5; PH-2   Ht: 5'9" Wt: 175 Born: 8/13/1979 Age: 28

Year	Team	Lg	G	AB	H	2B	3B	HR	(Hm	Rd)	TB	R	RBI	RC	TBB	IBB	SO	HBP	SH	SF	SB	CS	SB%	GDP	Avg	OBP	Slg
									BATTING												**BASERUNNING**				**AVERAGES**		
2000	ChC	NL	11	42	7	1	0	2	(1	1)	14	9	2	3	3	0	14	1	1	0	1	1	.50	0	.167	.239	.333
2001	ChC	NL	59	131	29	3	0	4	(1	3)	44	26	14	13	6	0	33	3	2	3	4	0	1.00	1	.221	.266	.336
2002	ChC	NL	153	592	150	30	5	14	(7	7)	232	71	54	61	19	1	142	8	4	5	18	3	.86	8	.253	.284	.392
2003	ChC	NL	83	329	98	17	7	13	(7	6)	168	49	55	55	15	2	77	1	0	2	16	5	.76	5	.298	.329	.511
2004	ChC	NL	157	631	168	33	6	24	(14	10)	285	91	72	87	45	7	168	5	5	1	32	9	.78	7	.266	.320	.452
2005	ChC	NL	126	451	97	15	3	13	(9	4)	157	47	34	32	23	3	118	1	5	1	15	5	.75	5	.215	.254	.348
2006	Bal	AL	135	463	128	19	5	16	(9	7)	205	75	53	66	21	5	94	5	8	1	45	9	.83	0	.276	.314	.443
2007	Bal	AL	132	461	124	26	2	8	(5	3)	178	65	45	51	21	1	65	4	**13**	4	37	9	.80	3	.269	.304	.386
	8 ML YEARS		856	3100	801	144	28	94	(53	41)	1283	433	329	368	153	19	711	28	38	17	168	41	.80	29	.258	.298	.414

Eric Patterson

Bats: L Throws: R Pos: PH-5; LF-2   Ht: 5'11" Wt: 170 Born: 4/8/1983 Age: 25

Year	Team	Lg	G	AB	H	2B	3B	HR	(Hm	Rd)	TB	R	RBI	RC	TBB	IBB	SO	HBP	SH	SF	SB	CS	SB%	GDP	Avg	OBP	Slg
									BATTING												**BASERUNNING**				**AVERAGES**		
2005	Peoria	A	110	432	144	26	11	13	(-	-)	231	90	71	97	53	3	94	4	4	7	40	11	.78	7	.333	.405	.535
2005	WTenn	AA	9	30	6	2	0	0	(-	-)	8	5	2	3	6	0	7	0	0	1	3	2	.60	0	.200	.324	.267
2006	WTenn	AA	121	441	116	22	9	8	(-	-)	180	66	48	65	46	2	89	1	7	6	38	12	.76	2	.263	.330	.408
2006	Iowa	AAA	17	67	24	1	1	2	(-	-)	33	14	12	15	6	0	9	0	0	3	8	0	1.00	2	.358	.395	.493
2007	Iowa	AAA	128	516	153	28	6	14	(-	-)	235	94	65	89	54	2	85	2	4	6	24	9	.73	4	.297	.362	.455
2007	ChC	NL	7	8	2	1	0	0	(0	0)	3	0	0	0	0	0	3	0	1	0	0	0	-	0	.250	.250	.375

John Patterson

Pitches: R Bats: R Pos: SP-7   Ht: 6'6" Wt: 211 Born: 1/30/1978 Age: 30

Year	Team	Lg	G	GS	CG	GF	IP	BFP	H	R	ER	HR	SH	SF	HB	TBB	IBB	SO	WP	Bk	W	L	Pct	ShO	Sv-Op	Hld	ERC	ERA
				HOW MUCH HE PITCHED								**WHAT HE GAVE UP**										**THE RESULTS**					
2007	Ptomc*	A+	2	2	0	0	5.1	26	6	4	4	2	1	0	0	5	0	2	1	0	0	0	-	0	0- -	-	9.71	6.75
2002	Ari	NL	7	5	0	1	30.2	123	27	11	11	7	0	0	1	7	0	31	2	0	2	0	1.000	0	0-0	0	3.76	3.23
2003	Ari	NL	16	8	0	3	55.0	252	61	39	37	7	1	2	2	30	5	43	4	0	1	4	.200	0	1-1	0	5.50	6.05
2004	Mon	NL	19	19	0	0	98.1	445	100	58	55	18	4	2	8	46	4	99	0	0	4	7	.364	0	0-0	0	5.26	5.03
2005	Was	NL	31	31	2	0	198.1	817	172	71	69	19	5	4	5	65	11	185	9	1	9	7	.563	1	0-0	0	3.09	3.13
2006	Was	NL	8	8	0	0	40.2	170	36	21	20	4	2	4	3	9	1	42	0	0	1	2	.333	0	0-0	0	2.95	4.43
2007	Was	NL	7	7	0	0	31.1	152	39	26	26	5	3	1	0	22	1	15	4	0	1	5	.167	0	0-0	0	7.23	7.47
	6 ML YEARS		88	78	2	4	454.1	1959	435	226	218	60	15	13	19	179	22	415	19	1	18	25	.419	1	1-1	0	4.12	4.32

Troy Patton

Pitches: L Bats: B Pos: SP-2; RP-1   Ht: 6'1" Wt: 185 Born: 9/3/1985 Age: 22

Year	Team	Lg	G	GS	CG	GF	IP	BFP	H	R	ER	HR	SH	SF	HB	TBB	IBB	SO	WP	Bk	W	L	Pct	ShO	Sv-Op	Hld	ERC	ERA
				HOW MUCH HE PITCHED								**WHAT HE GAVE UP**										**THE RESULTS**					
2004	Grnsvle	R	6	6	0	0	28.0	111	23	8	6	1	0	3	1	5	0	32	0	0	2	2	.500	0	0- -	-	2.08	1.93
2005	Lxngtn	A	15	15	0	0	78.2	310	59	24	17	3	4	0	5	20	0	94	0	0	5	2	.714	0	0- -	-	2.14	1.94
2005	Salem	A+	10	9	0	0	41.0	162	34	12	12	2	0	2	2	8	0	38	1	0	1	4	.200	0	0- -	-	2.33	2.63
2006	Salem	A+	19	19	1	0	101.1	435	92	49	33	4	6	4	5	37	0	102	3	0	7	7	.500	0	0- -	-	3.16	2.93
2006	CpChr	AA	8	8	0	0	45.1	195	48	26	22	6	2	1	2	13	0	37	3	0	2	5	.286	0	0- -	-	4.36	4.37
2007	CpChr	AA	16	16	0	0	102.1	437	96	38	34	10	5	1	9	33	1	69	2	0	6	6	.500	0	0- -	-	3.73	2.99
2007	RdRck	AAA	8	8	0	0	49.0	200	44	26	25	5	4	3	3	11	0	25	0	0	4	2	.667	0	0- -	-	3.13	4.59
2007	Hou	NL	3	2	0	1	12.2	54	10	6	5	3	1	0	2	4	0	8	0	0	0	2	.000	0	0-0	0	4.04	3.55

Josh Paul

Bats: R Throws: R Pos: C-35; PR-3; PH-2   Ht: 6'1" Wt: 210 Born: 5/19/1975 Age: 33

Year	Team	Lg	G	AB	H	2B	3B	HR	(Hm	Rd)	TB	R	RBI	RC	TBB	IBB	SO	HBP	SH	SF	SB	CS	SB%	GDP	Avg	OBP	Slg
									BATTING												**BASERUNNING**				**AVERAGES**		
2007	VeroB*	A+	7	25	4	0	0	0	(-	-)	4	3	1	0	0	0	2	0	0	1	0	0	-	2	.160	.154	.160
2007	Mont*	AA	3	10	4	0	0	0	(-	-)	4	2	2	2	4	0	2	0	0	0	0	0	-	0	.400	.571	.400
1999	CWS	AL	6	18	4	1	0	0	(0	0)	5	2	1	1	0	0	4	0	0	0	0	0	-	0	.222	.222	.278
2000	CWS	AL	36	71	20	3	2	1	(1	0)	30	15	8	9	5	0	17	1	2	0	1	0	1.00	3	.282	.338	.423
2001	CWS	AL	57	139	37	11	0	3	(0	3)	57	20	18	19	13	0	25	0	1	1	6	2	.75	3	.266	.327	.410
2002	CWS	AL	33	104	25	4	0	0	(0	0)	29	11	11	12	9	0	22	1	2	2	2	0	1.00	1	.240	.302	.279
2003	2 Tms		16	23	6	0	0	0	(0	0)	6	6	4	5	3	0	6	0	1	0	0	0	-	0	.261	.346	.261
2004	LAA	AL	46	70	17	3	0	2	(0	2)	26	11	10	9	7	0	17	0	3	1	2	1	.67	2	.243	.308	.371
2005	LAA	AL	34	37	7	1	0	2	(2	0)	14	4	4	3	2	0	9	0	1	0	0	0	-	0	.189	.231	.378
2006	TB	AL	58	146	38	9	0	1	(0	1)	50	15	8	16	14	0	39	1	3	1	1	2	.33	2	.260	.327	.342
2007	TB	AL	35	105	20	3	0	1	(1	0)	26	8	9	7	6	0	30	4	0	1	1	0	1.00	1	.190	.234	.248
	03 CWS	AL	13	17	6	0	0	0	(0	0)	6	6	4	5	3	0	3	0	0	0	0	0	-	0	.353	.450	.353
	03 ChC	NL	3	6	0	0	0	0	(0	0)	0	0	0	0	0	0	3	0	1	0	0	0	-	0	.000	.000	.000
	9 ML YEARS		321	713	174	35	2	10	(4	6)	243	92	73	81	59	0	169	3	17	5	13	5	.72	13	.244	.303	.341

Felipe Paulino

Pitches: R **Bats:** R **Pos:** SP-3; RP-2   **Ht:** 6'2" **Wt:** 180 **Born:** 10/5/1983 **Age:** 24

			HOW MUCH HE PITCHED					WHAT HE GAVE UP													THE RESULTS							
Year	Team	Lg	G	GS	CG	GF	IP	BFP	H	R	ER	HR	SH	SF	HB	TBB	IBB	SO	WP	Bk	W	L	Pct	ShO	Sv-Op	Hld	ERC	ERA
2003	Mrtnsvl	R+	16	0	0	6	25.2	126	23	20	16	0	0	1	8	19	0	27	8	0	2	2	.500	0	1--	-	5.12	5.61
2004	Grnsvle	R	10	10	0	0	32.0	149	30	30	27	4	0	1	4	22	0	37	6	0	1	3	.250	0	0--	-	5.55	7.59
2005	TriCity	A-	13	2	0	10	30.2	126	21	15	13	2	1	0	3	11	0	34	8	0	2	2	.500	0	1--	-	2.39	3.82
2005	Lxngtn	A	7	5	0	0	24.1	100	21	8	5	2	3	1	0	6	0	30	2	0	1	1	.500	0	0--	-	2.61	1.85
2006	Salem	A+	27	26	0	0	126.1	546	119	67	61	13	2	2	7	59	0	91	9	0	9	7	.563	0	0--	-	4.31	4.35
2007	CpChr	AA	22	21	0	0	112.0	488	103	55	45	6	0	4	3	49	0	110	7	1	4	5	.444	0	0--	-	3.49	3.62
2007	Hou	NL	5	3	0	0	19.0	85	22	15	15	5	2	0	0	7	1	11	1	0	2	1	.667	0	0-0	0	5.93	7.11

Ronny Paulino

Bats: R **Throws:** R **Pos:** C-129; PH-5   **Ht:** 6'2" **Wt:** 265 **Born:** 4/21/1981 **Age:** 27

								BATTING														BASERUNNING				AVERAGES		
Year	Team	Lg	G	AB	H	2B	3B	HR	(Hm	Rd)	TB	R	RBI	RC	TBB	IBB	SO	HBP	SH	SF	SB	CS	SB%	GDP	Avg	OBP	Slg
2005	Pit	NL	2	4	2	0	0	0	(0	0)	2	1	0	1	1	0	0	0	0	0	0	0	-	0	.500	.600	.500
2006	Pit	NL	129	442	137	19	0	6	(2	4)	174	37	55	60	34	5	79	2	1	2	0	0	-	17	.310	.360	.394
2007	Pit	NL	133	457	120	25	0	11	(7	4)	178	56	55	49	33	0	79	2	0	2	2	2	.50	14	.263	.314	.389
	3 ML YEARS		264	903	259	44	0	17	(9	8)	354	94	110	110	68	5	158	4	1	4	2	2	.50	31	.287	.338	.392

Carl Pavano

Pitches: R **Bats:** R **Pos:** SP-2   **Ht:** 6'5" **Wt:** 241 **Born:** 1/8/1976 **Age:** 32

					HOW MUCH HE PITCHED					WHAT HE GAVE UP											THE RESULTS							
Year	Team	Lg	G	GS	CG	GF	IP	BFP	H	R	ER	HR	SH	SF	HB	TBB	IBB	SO	WP	Bk	W	L	Pct	ShO	Sv-Op	Hld	ERC	ERA
1998	Mon	NL	24	23	0	0	134.2	580	130	70	63	18	5	6	8	43	1	83	1	0	6	9	.400	0	0-0	0	3.97	4.21
1999	Mon	NL	19	18	1	0	104.0	457	117	66	65	8	5	2	4	35	1	70	1	3	6	8	.429	1	0-0	0	4.51	5.63
2000	Mon	NL	15	15	0	0	97.0	408	89	40	33	8	4	3	8	34	1	64	1	1	8	4	.667	0	0-0	0	3.67	3.06
2001	Mon	NL	8	8	0	0	42.2	199	59	33	30	7	2	1	2	16	1	36	0	1	1	6	.143	0	0-0	0	6.99	6.33
2002	2 Tms	NL	37	22	0	2	136.0	619	174	88	78	19	4	4	10	45	8	92	3	2	6	10	.375	0	0-0	0	5.98	5.16
2003	Fla	NL	33	32	2	1	201.0	846	204	99	96	19	9	10	7	49	10	133	3	2	12	13	.480	0	0-0	0	3.57	4.30
2004	Fla	NL	31	31	2	0	222.1	909	212	80	74	16	7	4	11	49	13	139	2	3	18	8	.692	2	0-0	0	3.10	3.00
2005	NYY	AL	17	17	1	0	100.0	442	129	66	53	17	4	3	8	18	1	56	2	1	4	6	.400	1	0-0	0	5.74	4.77
2007	NYY	AL	2	2	0	0	11.1	46	12	7	6	1	0	0	0	2	0	4	0	0	1	0	1.000	0	0-0	0	3.54	4.76
02	Mon	NL	15	14	0	0	74.1	350	98	55	52	14	2	2	7	31	5	51	2	1	3	8	.273	0	0-0	0	7.07	6.30
02	Fla	NL	22	8	0	2	61.2	269	76	33	26	5	2	2	3	14	3	41	1	1	3	2	.600	0	0-0	0	4.74	3.79
	9 ML YEARS		186	168	6	3	1049.0	4506	1126	549	498	113	40	33	58	291	36	677	13	13	62	64	.492	4	0-0	0	4.24	4.27

Jay Payton

Bats: R **Throws:** R **Pos:** LF-123; CF-17; RF-6; PH-6; PR-1   **Ht:** 5'10" **Wt:** 207 **Born:** 11/22/1972 **Age:** 35

									BATTING													BASERUNNING				AVERAGES		
Year	Team	Lg	G	AB	H	2B	3B	HR	(Hm	Rd)	TB	R	RBI	RC	TBB	IBB	SO	HBP	SH	SF	SB	CS	SB%	GDP	Avg	OBP	Slg
2007	Norfolk*	AAA	2	8	2	1	0	0	(-	-)	3	3	0	1	1	0	1	0	0	0	0	0	-	0	.250	.333	.375
1998	NYM	NL	15	22	7	1	0	0	(0	0)	8	2	0	3	1	0	4	0	0	0	0	0	-	0	.318	.348	.364
1999	NYM	NL	13	8	2	1	0	0	(0	0)	3	1	1	0	0	0	2	1	0	0	0	0	-	0	.250	.333	.375
2000	NYM	NL	149	488	142	23	1	17	(9	8)	218	63	62	68	30	0	60	3	0	8	5	11	.31	9	.291	.331	.447
2001	NYM	NL	104	361	92	16	1	8	(6	2)	134	44	34	37	18	1	52	5	0	2	4	3	.57	11	.255	.298	.371
2002	2 Tms	NL	134	445	135	20	7	16	(9	7)	217	69	59	71	29	0	54	4	2	1	7	4	.64	11	.303	.351	.488
2003	Col	NL	157	600	181	32	5	28	(13	15)	307	93	89	95	43	3	77	7	5	3	6	4	.60	27	.302	.354	.512
2004	SD	NL	143	458	119	17	4	8	(0	8)	168	57	55	61	43	2	56	4	2	4	2	0	1.00	12	.260	.326	.367
2005	2 Tms	AL	124	408	109	16	1	18	(11	7)	181	62	63	56	24	2	47	0	0	3	0	1	.00	8	.267	.306	.444
2006	Oak	AL	142	557	165	32	3	10	(5	5)	233	78	59	76	22	1	52	4	0	5	8	4	.67	12	.296	.325	.418
2007	Bal	AL	131	434	111	21	5	7	(6	1)	163	48	58	49	22	0	42	3	5	6	5	2	.71	9	.256	.292	.376
02	NYM	NL	87	275	78	6	3	8	(4	4)	114	33	31	38	21	0	34	1	2	1	4	1	.80	8	.284	.336	.415
02	Col	NL	47	170	57	14	4	8	(5	3)	103	36	28	33	8	0	20	3	0	0	3	3	.50	3	.335	.376	.606
05	Bos	AL	55	133	35	7	0	5	(2	3)	57	24	21	16	10	0	14	0	0	1	0	0	-	4	.263	.313	.429
05	Oak	AL	69	275	74	9	1	13	(9	4)	124	38	42	40	14	2	33	0	0	2	0	1	.00	4	.269	.302	.451
	10 ML YEARS		1112	3781	1063	179	27	112	(59	53)	1632	517	480	516	232	9	446	31	14	32	38	31	.55	99	.281	.325	.432

Steve Pearce

Bats: R **Throws:** R **Pos:** RF-18; PH-4; 1B-2   **Ht:** 5'11" **Wt:** 210 **Born:** 4/13/1983 **Age:** 25

									BATTING													BASERUNNING				AVERAGES		
Year	Team	Lg	G	AB	H	2B	3B	HR	(Hm	Rd)	TB	R	RBI	RC	TBB	IBB	SO	HBP	SH	SF	SB	CS	SB%	GDP	Avg	OBP	Slg
2005	Wmspt	A-	72	272	82	26	0	7	(-	-)	129	48	52	49	35	0	43	2	0	3	2	4	.33	9	.301	.381	.474
2006	Hickory	A	41	160	46	13	1	12	(-	-)	97	35	38	33	15	1	32	4	0	0	1	3	.25	3	.288	.363	.606
2006	Lynbrg	A+	90	328	87	27	1	14	(-	-)	158	48	60	56	34	0	65	10	1	4	7	5	.58	9	.265	.348	.482
2007	Lynbrg	A+	19	75	26	4	1	11	(-	-)	65	19	24	24	8	0	13	1	0	1	2	0	1.00	1	.347	.412	.867
2007	Altna	AA	81	290	97	27	2	14	(-	-)	170	57	72	68	33	0	45	4	0	8	7	2	.78	10	.334	.400	.586
2007	Indy	AAA	34	122	39	9	1	6	(-	-)	68	18	17	25	6	0	12	3	0	0	5	0	1.00	2	.320	.366	.557
2007	Pit	NL	23	68	20	5	1	0	(0	0)	27	13	6	9	5	0	12	0	0	0	2	1	.67	2	.294	.342	.397

Jake Peavy

Pitches: R **Bats:** R **Pos:** SP-34　　　　　　　　　　**Ht:** 6'1" **Wt:** 182 **Born:** 5/31/1981 **Age:** 27

Year	Team	Lg	G	GS	CG	GF	IP	BFP	H	R	ER	HR	SH	SF	HB	TBB	IBB	SO	WP	Bk	W	L	Pct	ShO	Sv-Op	Hld	ERC	ERA
2002	SD	NL	17	17	0	0	97.2	430	106	54	49	11	5	2	3	33	4	90	4	1	6	7	.462	0	0-0	0	4.41	4.52
2003	SD	NL	32	32	0	0	194.2	827	173	94	89	33	7	5	6	82	3	156	2	0	12	11	.522	0	0-0	0	4.13	4.11
2004	SD	NL	27	27	0	0	166.1	694	146	49	42	13	5	6	11	53	4	173	1	1	15	6	.714	0	0-0	0	3.18	**2.27**
2005	SD	NL	30	30	3	0	203.0	812	162	70	65	18	4	5	7	50	3	**216**	3	1	13	7	.650	3	0-0	0	2.49	2.88
2006	SD	NL	32	32	2	0	202.1	846	187	93	92	23	5	1	6	62	11	215	4	0	11	14	.440	0	0-0	0	3.42	4.09
2007	SD	NL	34	34	0	0	223.1	898	169	67	63	13	5	7	6	68	5	**240**	4	0	**19**	6	.760	0	0-0	0	**2.27**	2.54
6 ML YEARS			172	172	5	0	1087.1	4507	943	427	400	111	31	26	39	348	30	1090	18	3	76	51	.598	3	0-0	0	3.16	3.31

Dustin Pedroia

Bats: R **Throws:** R **Pos:** 2B-137; PH-3; DH-1　　　　　　**Ht:** 5'9" **Wt:** 180 **Born:** 8/17/1983 **Age:** 24

Year	Team	Lg	G	AB	H	2B	3B	HR	(Hm	Rd)	TB	R	RBI	RC	TBB	IBB	SO	HBP	SH	SF	SB	CS	SB%	GDP	Avg	OBP	Slg
2004	Augsta	A	12	50	20	5	0	1	(-	-)	28	11	5	13	6	0	3	1	0	0	2	0	1.00	1	.400	.474	.560
2004	Srsota	A+	30	107	36	8	3	2	(-	-)	56	23	14	23	13	0	4	4	1	3	0	2	.00	3	.336	.417	.523
2005	Portlnd	AA	66	256	83	19	2	8	(-	-)	130	39	40	54	34	2	26	4	2	2	7	3	.70	7	.324	.409	.508
2005	Pwtckt	AAA	51	204	52	9	1	5	(-	-)	78	39	24	31	24	0	17	9	1	2	1	0	1.00	6	.255	.356	.382
2006	Pwtckt	AAA	111	423	129	30	3	5	(-	-)	180	55	50	72	48	0	27	9	9	4	1	4	.20	9	.305	.384	.426
2006	Bos	AL	31	89	17	4	0	2	(1	1)	27	5	7	3	7	0	7	1	1	0	0	1	.00	1	.191	.258	.303
2007	Bos	AL	139	520	165	39	1	8	(5	3)	230	86	50	79	47	1	42	7	5	2	7	1	.88	8	.317	.380	.442
2 ML YEARS			170	609	182	43	1	10	(6	4)	257	91	57	82	54	1	49	8	6	2	7	2	.78	9	.299	.363	.422

Jailen Peguero

Pitches: R **Bats:** R **Pos:** RP-18　　　　　　　　　　**Ht:** 6'0" **Wt:** 195 **Born:** 1/4/1981 **Age:** 27

Year	Team	Lg	G	GS	CG	GF	IP	BFP	H	R	ER	HR	SH	SF	HB	TBB	IBB	SO	WP	Bk	W	L	Pct	ShO	Sv-Op	Hld	ERC	ERA
2002	TriCity	A-	25	3	0	14	49.2	208	49	20	19	3	1	2	0	17	1	42	6	0	1	1	.500	0	6--	-	3.52	3.44
2003	Lxngtn	A	31	21	0	5	146.0	609	110	74	59	11	2	6	8	69	1	111	10	0	5	13	.278	0	1--	-	3.08	3.64
2004	Salem	A+	51	1	0	31	86.0	384	93	51	37	7	0	0	4	32	3	79	5	1	5	6	.455	0	8--	-	4.34	3.87
2005	CpChr	AA	50	0	0	36	64.1	280	62	25	21	3	4	3	4	25	5	63	2	0	2	2	.500	0	12--	-	3.53	2.94
2006	CpChr	AA	27	0	0	26	30.2	149	18	4	3	0	1	1	6	16	0	48	2	0	2	0	1.000	0	14--	-	1.52	0.70
2006	RdRck	AAA	21	0	0	6	36.1	162	34	18	14	3	2	2	1	18	2	30	4	1	1	2	.333	0	1--	-	3.88	3.47
2007	Tucsn	AAA	53	0	0	22	66.2	268	47	19	14	5	4	2	2	26	1	68	3	0	6	2	.750	0	4--	-	2.46	1.89
2007	Ari	NL	18	0	0	6	14.2	71	17	15	15	2	1	1	1	13	1	9	1	0	1	0	1.000	0	0-0	3	7.79	9.20

Mike Pelfrey

Pitches: R **Bats:** R **Pos:** SP-13; RP-2　　　　　　　　**Ht:** 6'7" **Wt:** 216 **Born:** 1/14/1984 **Age:** 24

Year	Team	Lg	G	GS	CG	GF	IP	BFP	H	R	ER	HR	SH	SF	HB	TBB	IBB	SO	WP	Bk	W	L	Pct	ShO	Sv-Op	Hld	ERC	ERA
2006	StLuci	A+	4	4	0	0	22.0	80	17	5	4	1	0	1	1	2	0	26	3	0	2	1	.667	0	0--	-	1.80	1.64
2006	Bnghtn	AA	12	12	0	0	66.1	280	60	23	20	2	2	2	4	26	1	77	2	0	4	2	.667	0	0--	-	3.28	2.71
2006	Norfolk	AAA	2	2	0	0	8.0	32	4	2	2	1	0	0	0	5	0	6	0	0	1	0	1.000	0	0--	-	2.51	2.25
2007	StLuci	A+	1	1	0	0	6.0	25	5	3	2	1	0	0	2	3	0	2	0	0	0	0	-	0	0	-	6.04	3.00
2007	NewOr	AAA	14	14	0	0	74.0	323	74	35	33	2	2	5	6	26	0	56	2	0	3	6	.333	0	0--	-	4.04	4.01
2006	NYM	NL	4	4	0	0	21.1	99	25	14	13	1	1	1	3	12	0	13	2	0	2	1	.667	0	0-0	0	6.05	5.48
2007	NYM	NL	15	13	0	0	72.2	342	85	47	45	6	6	3	9	39	1	45	3	0	3	8	.273	0	0-0	0	5.99	5.57
2 ML YEARS			19	17	0	0	94.0	441	110	61	58	7	7	4	12	51	1	58	5	0	5	9	.357	0	0-0	0	6.00	5.55

Brayan Pena

Bats: B **Throws:** R **Pos:** C-10; PH-8; PR-1　　　　　　**Ht:** 5'11" **Wt:** 220 **Born:** 1/7/1982 **Age:** 26

Year	Team	Lg	G	AB	H	2B	3B	HR	(Hm	Rd)	TB	R	RBI	RC	TBB	IBB	SO	HBP	SH	SF	SB	CS	SB%	GDP	Avg	OBP	Slg
2007	Rchmd*	AAA	94	345	104	20	2	6	(-	-)	146	42	48	49	19	3	38	2	3	1	5	7	.42	11	.301	.341	.423
2005	Atl	NL	18	39	7	2	0	0	(0	0)	9	2	4	0	1	1	7	0	0	0	0	0	-	1	.179	.200	.231
2006	Atl	NL	23	41	11	2	0	1	(0	1)	16	9	5	4	2	0	5	0	0	0	0	0	-	2	.268	.302	.390
2007	Atl	NL	16	33	7	0	0	1	(1	0)	10	2	3	0	0	0	3	0	0	0	0	1	.00	2	.212	.212	.303
3 ML YEARS			57	113	25	4	0	2	(1	1)	35	13	12	4	3	1	15	0	0	0	0	1	.00	5	.221	.241	.310

Carlos Pena

Bats: L **Throws:** L **Pos:** 1B-144; DH-3; PH-2　　　　　　**Ht:** 6'2" **Wt:** 215 **Born:** 5/17/1978 **Age:** 30

Year	Team	Lg	G	AB	H	2B	3B	HR	(Hm	Rd)	TB	R	RBI	RC	TBB	IBB	SO	HBP	SH	SF	SB	CS	SB%	GDP	Avg	OBP	Slg
2001	Tex	AL	22	62	16	4	1	3	(2	1)	31	6	12	11	10	0	17	0	0	0	0	0	-	1	.258	.361	.500
2002	2 Tms	AL	115	397	96	17	4	19	(10	9)	178	43	52	56	41	0	111	3	0	2	2	2	.50	7	.242	.316	.448
2003	Det	AL	131	452	112	21	6	18	(8	10)	199	51	50	61	53	1	123	6	1	4	4	5	.44	6	.248	.332	.440
2004	Det	AL	142	481	116	22	4	27	(10	17)	227	89	82	73	70	2	146	3	2	5	7	1	.88	11	.241	.338	.472
2005	Det	AL	79	260	61	9	0	18	(14	4)	124	37	44	40	31	2	95	4	0	0	0	1	.00	3	.235	.325	.477
2006	Det	AL	18	33	9	2	0	1	(1 | 0)	14	3	3	4	3	4	0	10	0	0	0	0	0	-	1	.273	.351	.424
2007	TB	AL	148	490	138	29	1	46	(23	23)	307	99	121	114	103	10	142	10	1	8	1	0	1.00	5	.282	.411	.627
02	Oak	AL	40	124	27	4	0	7	(5	2)	52	12	16	17	15	0	38	1	0	1	0	0	-	2	.218	.305	.419
02	Det	AL	75	273	69	13	4	12	(5	7)	126	31	36	39	26	0	73	2	0	1	2	2	.50	5	.253	.321	.462
7 ML YEARS			655	2175	548	104	16	132	(68	64)	1080	328	364	358	312	15	644	26	4	19	14	9	.61	36	.252	.350	.497

Tony Pena

Pitches: R Bats: R Pos: RP-75   Ht: 6'1" Wt: 220 Born: 1/9/1982 Age: 26

			HOW MUCH HE PITCHED						WHAT HE GAVE UP											THE RESULTS						
Year	Team	Lg	G	GS	CG	GF	IP	BFP	H	R	ER	HR	SH	SF	HB	TBB	IBB	SO	WP	Bk	W	L	Pct	ShO	Sv-Op	Hld	ERC	ERA
2002	Msoula	R+	4	4	0	0	20.0	89	26	15	14	1	1	1	3	3	0	14	4	1	1	2	.333	0	0--	-	4.68	6.30
2003	Sbend	A	27	27	0	0	160.1	652	149	59	51	4	1	1	7	30	0	119	8	4	9	5	.643	0	0--	-	2.59	2.86
2004	ElPaso	A	7	7	0	0	43.0	174	47	27	26	4	0	0	1	5	0	36	0	0	3	3	.500	0	0--	-	3.62	5.44
2005	Tenn	AA	25	25	2	0	148.1	651	165	86	73	17	4	4	10	40	1	95	5	0	7	13	.350	1	0--	-	4.52	4.43
2006	Tenn	AA	17	0	0	3	20.1	35	18	2	2	0	1	0	1	5	0	17	1	0	2	0	1.000	0	6--	-	6.56	0.89
2006	Tucsn	AAA	24	0	0	17	26.1	81	17	6	5	1	1	0	2	2	0	21	1	0	3	1	.750	0	7--	-	1.57	1.71
2006	Ari	NL	25	0	0	6	30.2	135	36	21	19	6	2	1	0	8	0	21	1	0	3	4	.429	0	1-1	2	5.12	5.58
2007	Ari	NL	75	0	0	13	85.1	344	63	36	31	8	1	3	5	31	4	63	3	1	5	4	.556	0	2-5	30	2.71	3.27
	2 ML YEARS		100	0	0	19	116.0	479	99	57	50	14	3	4	5	39	4	84	4	1	8	8	.500	0	3-6	32	3.31	3.88

Tony F Pena

Bats: R Throws: R Pos: SS-150; 2B-1; DH-1; PH-1; PR-1   Ht: 6'2" Wt: 180 Born: 3/23/1981 Age: 27

									BATTING												BASERUNNING				AVERAGES		
Year	Team	Lg	G	AB	H	2B	3B	HR	(Hm	Rd)	TB	R	RBI	RC	TBB	IBB	SO	HBP	SH	SF	SB	CS	SB%	GDP	Avg	OBP	Slg
2000	Danvle	R	55	215	46	5	0	2	(-	-)	57	22	20	12	5	0	53	0	2	2	6	2	.75	8	.214	.230	.265
2001	Jmstwn	A-	72	264	65	12	2	0	(-	-)	81	26	18	22	10	0	48	2	3	1	8	6	.57	7	.246	.278	.307
2002	Macon	A	118	405	101	9	5	2	(-	-)	126	42	36	32	14	0	68	5	8	2	11	15	.42	6	.249	.282	.311
2003	MrtlBh	A+	120	405	105	14	1	4	(-	-)	133	43	30	40	24	1	82	2	7	0	17	12	.59	9	.259	.304	.328
2004	Grnville	AA	130	495	126	22	0	11	(-	-)	181	65	34	51	16	0	108	4	9	3	25	13	.66	6	.255	.282	.366
2005	Rchmd	AAA	138	490	122	25	4	5	(-	-)	170	49	40	47	21	0	113	5	6	4	17	15	.53	7	.249	.285	.347
2006	Rchmd	AAA	81	298	84	12	4	1	(-	-)	107	38	23	35	12	1	56	2	5	2	12	3	.80	6	.282	.312	.359
2006	Atl	NL	40	44	10	2	0	1	(1	0)	15	12	3	3	2	1	10	0	0	0	0	0	-	1	.227	.261	.341
2007	KC	AL	152	509	136	25	7	2	(1	1)	181	58	47	48	10	0	78	4	8	5	5	6	.45	13	.267	.284	.356
	2 ML YEARS		192	553	146	27	7	3	(2	1)	196	70	50	51	12	1	88	4	8	5	5	6	.45	14	.264	.282	.354

Wily Mo Pena

Bats: R Throws: R Pos: LF-55; RF-37; PH-14; CF-12; PR-4; DH-2   Ht: 6'3" Wt: 245 Born: 1/23/1982 Age: 26

									BATTING												BASERUNNING				AVERAGES		
Year	Team	Lg	G	AB	H	2B	3B	HR	(Hm	Rd)	TB	R	RBI	RC	TBB	IBB	SO	HBP	SH	SF	SB	CS	SB%	GDP	Avg	OBP	Slg
2002	Cin	NL	13	18	4	0	0	1	(1	0)	7	1	1	1	0	0	11	0	0	0	0	0	-	0	.222	.222	.389
2003	Cin	NL	80	165	36	6	1	5	(1	4)	59	20	16	14	12	2	53	3	1	0	3	2	.60	2	.218	.283	.358
2004	Cin	NL	110	336	87	10	1	26	(13	13)	177	45	66	54	22	1	108	6	0	0	5	2	.71	7	.259	.316	.527
2005	Cin	NL	99	311	79	17	0	19	(11	8)	153	42	51	40	20	0	116	3	0	1	2	1	.67	7	.254	.304	.492
2006	Bos	AL	84	276	83	15	2	11	(5	6)	135	36	42	39	20	0	90	3	0	5	0	1	.00	5	.301	.349	.489
2007	2 Tms		110	289	73	13	1	13	(3	10)	127	42	39	31	22	2	94	6	0	0	2	1	.67	9	.253	.319	.439
07	Bos	AL	73	156	34	9	1	5	(1	4)	60	18	17	11	14	0	58	2	0	0	0	1	.00	5	.218	.291	.385
07	Was	NL	37	133	39	4	0	8	(2	6)	67	24	22	20	8	2	36	4	0	0	2	0	1.00	2	.293	.352	.504
	6 ML YEARS		496	1395	362	61	5	75	(34	41)	658	186	215	179	96	5	472	21	1	6	12	7	.63	30	.259	.316	.472

Hunter Pence

Bats: R Throws: R Pos: CF-95; RF-14   Ht: 6'4" Wt: 210 Born: 4/13/1983 Age: 25

									BATTING												BASERUNNING				AVERAGES		
Year	Team	Lg	G	AB	H	2B	3B	HR	(Hm	Rd)	TB	R	RBI	RC	TBB	IBB	SO	HBP	SH	SF	SB	CS	SB%	GDP	Avg	OBP	Slg
2004	TriCity	A-	51	199	59	18	1	8	(-	-)	103	36	37	37	23	1	30	1	0	2	8	5	.38	4	.296	.369	.518
2005	Lxngtn	A	80	302	102	14	3	25	(-	-)	197	59	60	77	38	2	53	1	0	0	8	3	.73	2	.338	.413	.652
2005	Salem	A+	41	151	46	8	1	6	(-	-)	74	24	30	27	18	0	37	0	0	2	1	2	.33	6	.305	.374	.490
2006	CpChr	AA	136	523	148	31	8	28	(-	-)	279	97	95	102	60	6	109	3	1	5	17	4	.81	11	.283	.357	.533
2007	RdRck	AAA	25	95	31	11	1	3	(-	-)	53	17	21	20	10	0	15	0	0	1	2	0	1.00	4	.326	.387	.558
2007	Hou	NL	108	456	147	30	9	17	(7	10)	246	57	69	77	26	0	95	1	0	1	11	5	.69	10	.322	.360	.539

Hayden Penn

Pitches: R Bats: R Pos: P   Ht: 6'3" Wt: 195 Born: 10/13/1984 Age: 23

						HOW MUCH HE PITCHED						WHAT HE GAVE UP										THE RESULTS						
Year	Team	Lg	G	GS	CG	GF	IP	BFP	H	R	ER	HR	SH	SF	HB	TBB	IBB	SO	WP	Bk	W	L	Pct	ShO	Sv-Op	Hld	ERC	ERA
2003	Orioles	R	1	1	0	0	3.1	13	3	1	1	0	0	1	0	1	0	4	0	0	0	0	-	0	0--	-	2.69	2.70
2003	Bluefld	R+	12	11	0	0	52.1	230	58	27	25	4	2	0	4	19	0	38	3	0	1	4	.200	0	0--	-	4.74	4.30
2004	Dlmrva	A	13	6	0	2	43.1	174	30	18	16	4	2	1	3	19	1	41	4	0	4	1	.800	0	1--	-	2.86	3.32
2004	Frdrck	A+	13	13	0	0	73.1	287	59	33	31	7	1	1	2	20	0	61	1	0	6	5	.545	0	0--	-	2.74	3.80
2004	Bowie	AA	4	4	0	0	20.1	89	22	12	11	0	0	0	1	9	0	20	0	0	3	0	1.000	0	0--	-	4.24	4.87
2005	Bowie	AA	20	19	1	0	110.1	469	101	51	47	11	1	8	1	37	0	120	6	0	7	6	.538	0	0--	-	3.33	3.83
2006	Ottawa	AAA	14	14	2	0	87.2	351	71	25	22	5	1	2	0	27	1	85	2	0	7	4	.636	1	0--	-	2.48	2.26
2006	Bowie	AA	1	1	0	0	2.0	10	3	2	2	1	0	0	0	2	0	1	0	0	0	0	-	0	0--	-	15.00	9.00
2007	Orioles	R	5	5	0	0	15.0	68	17	6	4	0	0	0	3	4	0	17	1	0	0	0	-	0	0--	-	4.29	2.40
2007	Abrdn	A-	1	1	0	0	4.0	19	4	4	2	1	0	0	0	2	0	5	0	0	0	1	.000	0	0--	-	5.15	4.50
2007	Norfolk	AAA	4	4	0	0	21.0	91	26	12	12	2	0	1	1	5	0	20	3	0	2	1	.667	0	0--	-	5.06	5.14
2005	Bal	AL	8	8	0	0	38.1	178	46	30	27	6	0	0	1	21	3	18	3	1	3	2	.600	0	0-0	0	6.17	6.34
2006	Bal	AL	6	6	0	0	19.2	112	38	33	33	8	0	0	2	13	0	8	0	0	0	4	.000	0	0-0	0	14.68	15.10
	2 ML YEARS		14	14	0	0	58.0	290	84	63	60	14	1	0	3	34	3	26	3	1	3	6	.333	0	0-0	0	8.85	9.31

Brad Penny

Pitches: R **Bats:** R **Pos:** SP-33   **Ht:** 6'4" **Wt:** 260 **Born:** 5/24/1978 **Age:** 30

Year	Team	Lg	G	GS	CG	GF	IP	BFP	H	R	ER	HR	SH	SF	HB	TBB	IBB	SO	WP	Bk	W	L	Pct	ShO	Sv-Op	Hld	ERC	ERA
2000	Fla	NL	23	22	0	0	119.2	529	120	70	64	13	6	2	5	60	4	80	4	1	8	7	.533	0	0-0	0	4.70	4.81
2001	Fla	NL	31	31	1	0	205.0	833	183	92	84	15	8	2	7	54	3	154	2	0	10	10	.500	1	0-0	0	2.96	3.69
2002	Fla	NL	24	24	1	0	129.1	574	148	76	67	18	6	4	1	50	7	93	4	0	8	7	.533	1	0-0	0	5.08	4.66
2003	Fla	NL	32	32	0	0	196.1	811	195	96	90	21	7	5	3	56	6	138	3	4	14	10	.583	0	0-0	0	3.73	4.13
2004	2 Tms	NL	24	24	0	0	143.0	590	130	55	50	12	3	3	3	45	6	111	5	0	9	10	.474	0	0-0	0	3.20	3.15
2005	LAD	NL	29	29	1	0	175.1	738	185	78	76	17	7	1	3	41	2	122	3	0	7	9	.438	0	0-0	0	3.77	3.90
2006	LAD	NL	34	33	0	0	189.0	813	206	94	91	19	8	3	9	54	4	148	6	0	16	9	.640	0	0-0	1	4.32	4.33
2007	LAD	NL	33	33	0	0	208.0	865	199	75	70	9	13	9	5	73	2	135	6	0	16	4	.800	0	0-0	0	3.41	3.03
04	Fla	NL	21	21	0	0	131.1	545	124	50	46	10	3	3	3	39	6	105	5	0	8	8	.500	0	0-0	0	3.26	3.15
04	LAD	NL	3	3	0	0	11.2	45	6	5	4	2	0	0	0	6	0	6	0	0	1	2	.333	0	0-0	0	2.51	3.09
8 ML YEARS			230	228	3	0	1365.2	5753	1366	636	592	124	58	20	36	433	34	901	33	5	88	66	.571	2	0-0	1	3.80	3.90

Jhonny Peralta

Bats: R **Throws:** R **Pos:** SS-152; PH-2   **Ht:** 6'1" **Wt:** 195 **Born:** 5/28/1982 **Age:** 26

Year	Team	Lg	G	AB	H	2B	3B	HR	(Hm	Rd)	TB	R	RBI	RC	TBB	IBB	SO	HBP	SH	SF	SB	CS	SB%	GDP	Avg	OBP	Slg
2003	Cle	AL	77	242	55	10	1	4	(3	1)	79	24	21	24	20	0	65	4	2	2	1	3	.25	5	.227	.295	.326
2004	Cle	AL	8	25	6	1	0	0	(0	0)	7	2	2	2	3	0	6	0	0	0	0	1	.00	0	.240	.321	.280
2005	Cle	AL	141	504	147	35	4	24	(14	10)	262	82	78	87	58	3	128	3	1	4	0	2	.00	12	.292	.366	.520
2006	Cle	AL	149	569	146	28	3	13	(7	6)	219	84	68	66	56	0	152	1	3	3	0	1	.00	19	.257	.323	.385
2007	Cle	AL	152	574	155	27	1	21	(16	5)	247	87	72	85	61	2	146	4	1	7	4	4	.50	12	.270	.341	.430
5 ML YEARS			527	1914	509	101	9	62	(40	22)	814	279	241	264	198	5	497	12	7	16	5	11	.31	48	.266	.336	.425

Joel Peralta

Pitches: R **Bats:** R **Pos:** RP-62   **Ht:** 5'11" **Wt:** 190 **Born:** 3/23/1976 **Age:** 32

Year	Team	Lg	G	GS	CG	GF	IP	BFP	H	R	ER	HR	SH	SF	HB	TBB	IBB	SO	WP	Bk	W	L	Pct	ShO	Sv-Op	Hld	ERC	ERA
2005	LAA	AL	28	0	0	10	34.2	145	28	15	15	6	2	1	0	14	2	30	2	0	1	0	1.000	0	0-0	0	3.40	3.89
2006	KC	AL	64	0	0	21	73.2	304	74	37	36	10	1	3	2	17	2	57	5	0	1	3	.250	0	1-3	17	3.80	4.40
2007	KC	AL	62	0	0	18	87.2	366	93	39	37	9	2	4	2	19	5	66	2	0	1	3	.250	0	1-5	5	3.75	3.80
3 ML YEARS			154	0	0	49	196.0	815	195	91	88	25	5	8	4	50	9	153	9	0	3	6	.333	0	2-8	24	3.71	4.04

Troy Percival

Pitches: R **Bats:** R **Pos:** RP-33; SP-1   **Ht:** 6'3" **Wt:** 240 **Born:** 8/9/1969 **Age:** 38

Year	Team	Lg	G	GS	CG	GF	IP	BFP	H	R	ER	HR	SH	SF	HB	TBB	IBB	SO	WP	Bk	W	L	Pct	ShO	Sv-Op	Hld	ERC	ERA
2007	Mem*	AAA	6	0	0	1	6.2	30	4	1	1	0	0	0	1	5	0	9	0	0	0	0	-	0	0- -	-	2.96	1.35
1995	LAA	AL	62	0	0	16	74.0	284	37	19	16	6	4	1	1	26	2	94	2	2	3	2	.600	0	3-6	29	1.44	1.95
1996	LAA	AL	62	0	0	52	74.0	291	38	20	19	8	2	1	2	31	4	100	2	0	0	2	.000	0	36-39	2	1.76	2.31
1997	LAA	AL	55	0	0	46	52.0	224	40	20	20	6	1	2	4	22	2	72	5	0	5	5	.500	0	27-31	0	3.15	3.46
1998	LAA	AL	67	0	0	60	66.2	285	45	31	27	5	3	2	3	37	4	87	3	0	2	7	.222	0	42-48	0	2.74	3.65
1999	LAA	AL	60	0	0	50	57.0	230	38	24	24	9	0	1	3	22	0	58	3	0	4	6	.400	0	31-39	0	2.83	3.79
2000	LAA	AL	54	0	0	45	50.0	221	42	27	25	7	3	2	1	30	4	49	1	0	5	5	.500	0	32-42	0	4.24	4.50
2001	LAA	AL	57	0	0	50	57.2	230	39	19	17	3	1	0	2	18	1	71	2	0	4	2	.667	0	39-42	0	1.90	2.65
2002	LAA	AL	58	0	0	56	56.1	228	38	12	12	5	0	1	0	25	1	68	5	0	4	1	.800	0	40-44	0	2.45	1.92
2003	LAA	AL	52	0	0	49	49.1	206	33	22	19	7	0	1	3	23	1	48	1	0	0	5	.000	0	33-37	0	2.99	3.47
2004	LAA	AL	52	0	0	48	49.2	211	43	19	16	7	0	2	3	19	3	33	2	0	2	3	.400	0	33-38	0	3.67	2.90
2005	Det	AL	26	0	0	23	25.0	107	19	16	16	7	1	1	2	11	3	20	0	0	1	3	.250	0	8-11	0	4.17	5.76
2007	StL	NL	34	1	0	9	40.0	150	24	8	8	3	0	0	0	10	0	36	2	0	3	0	1.000	0	0-0	3	1.52	1.80
12 ML YEARS			639	1	0	498	651.2	2669	436	237	219	73	15	14	25	274	25	736	28	2	33	41	.446	0	324-377	34	2.55	3.02

Juan Perez

Pitches: L **Bats:** R **Pos:** RP-17   **Ht:** 6'0" **Wt:** 175 **Born:** 9/3/1978 **Age:** 29

Year	Team	Lg	G	GS	CG	GF	IP	BFP	H	R	ER	HR	SH	SF	HB	TBB	IBB	SO	WP	Bk	W	L	Pct	ShO	Sv-Op	Hld	ERC	ERA
2000	RedSx	R	9	5	0	2	34.1	139	24	12	9	2	0	0	1	13	0	43	0	0	3	1	.750	0	1- -	-	2.27	2.36
2001	Augsta	A	26	25	0	1	125.2	525	118	69	50	14	2	7	3	42	0	113	9	0	8	8	.500	0	0- -	-	3.69	3.58
2002	Srsota	A+	16	14	0	0	66.2	286	71	34	28	4	2	4	2	19	0	39	4	0	0	6	.000	0	0- -	-	3.82	3.78
2003	Srsota	A+	33	0	0	24	38.0	165	34	15	10	0	2	3	0	12	2	37	4	0	3	4	.429	0	18- -	-	2.32	2.37
2003	Portlnd	AA	18	0	0	6	30.2	136	37	19	13	4	1	3	0	11	1	24	2	0	3	3	.500	0	- -	-	5.31	3.82
2004	Portlnd	AA	46	0	0	18	78.1	345	72	46	36	12	1	1	2	37	5	79	7	0	5	1	.833	0	6- -	-	4.20	4.14
2005	Pwtckt	AAA	40	1	0	18	62.0	274	61	31	31	7	5	1	5	29	0	74	5	2	4	5	.444	0	1- -	-	4.69	4.50
2006	Norfolk	AAA	43	0	0	12	63.0	284	65	24	20	4	2	2	2	34	0	55	4	0	0	1	.000	0	0- -	-	4.65	2.86
2006	Indy	AAA	4	0	0	0	7.0	30	3	0	0	0	0	0	0	3	1	6	0	0	0	0	-	0	0- -	-	0.86	0.00
2007	Indy	AAA	40	0	0	13	55.2	242	52	31	29	5	2	0	1	25	2	63	7	1	3	2	.600	0	2- -	-	3.80	4.69
2006	Pit	NL	7	0	0	0	3.1	17	5	3	3	1	0	1	0	1	0	3	0	0	0	1	.000	0	0-0	0	11.77	8.10
2007	Pit	NL	17	0	0	4	12.1	57	14	7	6	2	0	0	0	8	0	10	1	0	0	0	-	0	0-0	0	6.48	4.38
2 ML YEARS			24	0	0	4	15.2	74	19	10	9	3	0	1	0	9	0	13	1	0	0	1	.000	0	0-0	0	7.52	5.17

Neifi Perez

Bats: B **Throws:** R **Pos:** SS-24; 2B-7; 3B-3; PR-2; PH-1 **Ht:** 6'0" **Wt:** 175 **Born:** 6/2/1973 **Age:** 35

Year	Team	Lg	G	AB	H	2B	3B	HR	(Hm	Rd)	TB	R	RBI	RC	TBB	IBB	SO	HBP	SH	SF	SB	CS	SB%	GDP	Avg	OBP	Slg
1996	Col	NL	17	45	7	2	0	0	(0	0)	9	4	3	0	0	0	8	0	1	0	2	2	.50	2	.156	.156	.200
1997	Col	NL	83	313	91	13	10	5	(3	2)	139	46	31	46	21	4	43	1	5	4	4	3	.57	3	.291	.333	.444
1998	Col	NL	162	647	177	25	9	9	(6	3)	247	80	59	77	38	0	70	1	22	4	5	6	.45	8	.274	.313	.382
1999	Col	NL	157	690	193	27	11	12	(8	4)	278	108	70	87	28	0	54	1	9	4	13	5	.72	4	.280	.307	.403
2000	Col	NL	162	651	187	39	11	10	(7	3)	278	92	71	85	30	6	63	0	7	11	3	6	.33	9	.287	.314	.427
2001	2 Tms		136	581	162	26	9	8	(7	1)	230	83	59	69	26	1	68	1	11	4	9	6	.60	10	.279	.309	.396
2002	KC	AL	145	554	131	20	4	3	(1	2)	168	65	37	37	20	2	53	0	5	6	8	9	.47	11	.236	.260	.303
2003	SF	NL	120	328	84	19	4	1	(1	0)	114	27	31	29	14	3	23	0	9	2	3	2	.60	9	.256	.285	.348
2004	2 Tms		126	381	97	17	1	4	(2	2)	128	40	39	39	24	3	41	0	11	4	1	1	.50	8	.255	.296	.336
2005	ChC	NL	154	572	157	33	1	9	(4	5)	219	59	54	58	18	3	47	3	12	4	8	4	.67	22	.274	.298	.383
2006	2 Tms		108	301	73	14	1	2	(1	1)	95	31	29	27	8	2	25	0	4	3	1	1	.50	5	.243	.260	.316
2007	Det	AL	33	64	11	3	0	1	(0	1)	17	5	6	4	4	0	8	0	3	0	0	0	-	2	.172	.221	.266
01	Col	NL	87	382	114	19	8	7	(7	0)	170	65	47	53	16	1	49	0	4	1	6	2	.75	8	.298	.326	.445
01	KC	AL	49	199	48	7	1	1	(0	1)	60	18	12	16	10	0	19	1	7	3	3	4	.43	2	.241	.277	.302
04	SF	NL	103	319	74	12	1	2	(0	2)	94	28	33	26	21	3	35	0	9	4	0	1	.00	7	.232	.276	.295
04	ChC	NL	23	62	23	5	0	2	(2	0)	34	12	6	13	3	0	6	0	2	0	1	0	1.00	1	.371	.400	.548
06	Chc	NL	87	236	60	13	1	2	(1	1)	81	27	24	24	5	2	21	0	2	3	0	1	.00	3	.254	.266	.343
06	Det	AL	21	65	13	1	0	0	(0	0)	14	4	5	3	3	0	4	0	2	0	1	0	1.00	2	.200	.235	.215
12 ML YEARS			1403	5127	1370	238	61	64	(40	24)	1922	640	489	558	231	24	503	7	99	46	57	45	.56	93	.267	.297	.375

Odalis Perez

Pitches: L **Bats:** L **Pos:** SP-26 **Ht:** 6'0" **Wt:** 225 **Born:** 6/11/1977 **Age:** 31

Year	Team	Lg	G	GS	CG	GF	IP	BFP	H	R	ER	HR	SH	SF	HB	TBB	IBB	SO	WP	Bk	W	L	Pct	ShO	Sv-Op	Hld	ERC	ERA
1998	Atl	NL	10	0	0	0	10.2	45	10	5	5	1	0	0	0	4	0	5	0	0	0	1	.000	0	0-1	5	3.60	4.22
1999	Atl	NL	18	17	0	0	93.0	424	100	65	62	12	3	4	1	53	2	82	5	3	4	6	.400	0	0-0	0	5.42	6.00
2001	Atl	NL	24	16	0	1	95.1	418	108	55	52	7	3	3	1	39	0	71	2	3	7	8	.467	0	0-0	0	4.79	4.91
2002	LAD	NL	32	32	4	0	222.1	869	182	76	74	21	13	7	4	38	5	155	2	3	15	10	.600	2	0-0	0	2.31	3.00
2003	LAD	NL	30	30	0	0	185.1	772	191	98	93	28	5	3	3	46	4	141	2	1	12	12	.500	0	0-0	0	4.07	4.52
2004	LAD	NL	31	31	0	0	196.1	787	180	76	71	26	16	3	3	44	4	128	2	2	7	6	.538	0	0-0	0	3.26	3.25
2005	LAD	NL	19	19	0	0	108.2	453	109	59	55	13	8	1	0	28	2	74	3	0	7	8	.467	0	0-0	0	3.65	4.56
2006	2 Tms		32	20	0	6	126.1	573	169	93	87	18	4	7	3	31	2	81	6	2	6	8	.429	0	0-1	0	5.77	6.20
2007	KC	AL	26	26	0	0	137.1	626	178	90	85	14	6	7	4	50	5	64	3	0	8	11	.421	0	0-0	0	5.77	5.57
06	SD	NL	20	8	0	6	59.1	275	89	49	45	9	1	2	2	13	1	33	4	1	4	4	.500	0	0-0	0	6.85	6.83
06	KC	AL	12	12	0	0	67.0	298	80	44	42	9	3	5	1	18	1	48	2	1	2	4	.333	0	0-0	0	4.86	5.64
9 ML YEARS			222	191	4	7	1175.1	4967	1227	617	584	140	58	35	19	333	24	801	25	14	66	70	.485	2	0-2	5	4.06	4.47

Oliver Perez

Pitches: L **Bats:** L **Pos:** SP-29 **Ht:** 6'3" **Wt:** 217 **Born:** 8/15/1981 **Age:** 26

Year	Team	Lg	G	GS	CG	GF	IP	BFP	H	R	ER	HR	SH	SF	HB	TBB	IBB	SO	WP	Bk	W	L	Pct	ShO	Sv-Op	Hld	ERC	ERA
2007	Mets*	R	1	1	0	0	4.0	15	2	0	0	0	0	0	1	0	0	7	0	0	0	0	-	0	0--	-	0.94	0.00
2002	SD	NL	16	15	0	0	90.0	387	71	37	35	13	5	3	5	48	1	94	3	0	4	5	.444	0	0-0	0	3.93	3.50
2003	2 Tms		24	24	0	0	126.2	579	129	80	77	22	5	2	4	77	3	141	7	1	4	10	.286	0	0-0	0	5.66	5.47
2004	Pit	NL	30	30	2	0	196.0	805	145	71	65	22	9	5	9	81	2	239	2	1	12	10	.545	1	0-0	0	2.99	2.98
2005	Pit	NL	20	20	0	0	103.0	471	102	68	67	23	5	4	6	70	1	97	3	0	7	5	.583	0	0-0	0	6.44	5.85
2006	2 Tms		22	22	1	0	112.2	529	129	90	82	20	5	10	6	68	0	102	5	1	3	13	.188	0	0-0	0	6.62	6.55
2007	NYM	NL	29	29	0	0	177.0	765	153	90	70	22	4	7	7	79	1	174	6	0	15	10	.600	0	0-0	0	3.76	3.56
03	SD	NL	19	19	0	0	103.2	473	103	65	62	20	4	2	3	65	2	117	6	1	4	7	.364	0	0-0	0	5.74	5.38
03	Pit	NL	5	5	0	0	23.0	106	26	15	15	2	1	0	1	12	1	24	1	0	0	3	.000	0	0-0	0	5.29	5.87
06	Pit	NL	15	15	0	0	76.0	364	88	64	56	13	5	8	3	51	0	61	4	1	2	10	.167	0	0-0	0	6.85	6.63
06	NYM	NL	7	7	1	0	36.2	165	41	26	26	7	0	2	3	17	0	41	1	0	1	3	.250	0	0-0	0	6.16	6.38
6 ML YEARS			141	140	3	0	805.1	3536	729	436	396	122	33	31	37	423	8	847	26	3	45	53	.459	2	0-0	0	4.57	4.43

Rafael Perez

Pitches: L **Bats:** L **Pos:** RP-44 **Ht:** 6'3" **Wt:** 185 **Born:** 5/15/1982 **Age:** 26

Year	Team	Lg	G	GS	CG	GF	IP	BFP	H	R	ER	HR	SH	SF	HB	TBB	IBB	SO	WP	Bk	W	L	Pct	ShO	Sv-Op	Hld	ERC	ERA
2003	Burlgtn	R+	13	12	0	0	69.0	277	56	23	13	1	2	0	5	16	0	63	4	0	9	3	.750	0	0--	-	2.22	1.70
2004	Lk Cty	A	23	22	0	0	115.0	503	121	75	62	9	7	4	8	47	0	99	12	3	7	6	.538	0	0--	-	4.59	4.85
2004	Knstn	A+	1	1	0	0	4.2	25	10	6	6	1	0	0	0	2	1	3	0	0	0	0	-	0	0--	-	12.56	11.57
2005	Knstn	A+	14	14	0	0	77.2	315	54	33	29	6	0	2	2	32	0	48	7	0	8	5	.615	0	0--	-	2.48	3.36
2005	Akron	AA	15	8	0	3	66.2	268	53	22	13	5	4	3	2	12	0	46	3	0	4	3	.571	0	1--	-	2.11	1.76
2006	Akron	AA	12	12	1	0	67.1	274	53	25	21	3	3	3	3	22	1	53	7	0	4	5	.444	1	0--	-	2.48	2.81
2006	Buffalo	AAA	13	0	0	4	27.1	112	20	11	8	0	3	0	2	8	1	33	6	0	0	3	.000	0	0--	-	1.85	2.63
2007	Buffalo	AAA	8	7	0	1	46.2	196	52	27	19	3	3	3	1	11	0	31	2	0	3	3	.500	0	0--	-	4.12	3.66
2006	Cle	AL	18	0	0	5	12.1	56	10	6	6	2	1	0	0	6	1	15	4	1	0	0	-	0	0-1	1	3.37	4.38
2007	Cle	AL	44	0	0	11	60.2	236	41	15	12	5	1	1	0	15	2	62	4	0	1	2	.333	0	1-2	12	1.74	1.78
2 ML YEARS			62	0	0	16	73.0	292	51	21	18	7	2	1	0	21	3	77	8	1	1	2	.333	0	1-3	13	2.00	2.22

Timo Perez

Bats: L **Throws:** L **Pos:** LF-21; PH-5; RF-4; DH-2; PR-1   **Ht:** 5'9" **Wt:** 180 **Born:** 4/8/1975 **Age:** 33

Year	Team	Lg	G	AB	H	2B	3B	HR	(Hm	Rd)	TB	R	RBI	RC	TBB	IBB	SO	HBP	SH	SF	SB	CS	SB%	GDP	Avg	OBP	Slg
2007	Toledo*	AAA	122	489	151	39	1	13	(-	-)	231	76	69	84	35	4	47	4	7	5	13	6	.68	15	.309	.356	.472
2000	NYM	NL	24	49	14	4	1	1	(0	1)	23	11	3	8	3	0	5	1	0	1	1	1	.50	0	.286	.333	.469
2001	NYM	NL	85	239	59	9	1	5	(2	3)	85	26	22	23	12	0	25	2	6	1	6	14	.1	1	.247	.287	.356
2002	NYM	NL	136	444	131	27	6	8	(3	5)	194	52	47	63	23	2	36	2	10	2	10	6	.63	10	.295	.331	.437
2003	NYM	NL	127	346	93	21	0	4	(1	3)	126	32	42	37	18	1	29	2	7	9	5	6	.45	5	.269	.301	.364
2004	CWS	AL	103	293	72	12	0	5	(2	3)	99	38	40	39	15	0	29	2	9	2	3	1	.75	9	.246	.285	.338
2005	CWS	AL	76	179	39	8	0	2	(1	1)	53	13	15	13	12	1	25	0	4	1	2	2	.50	3	.218	.266	.296
2006	StL	NL	23	31	6	1	0	1	(0	1)	10	3	3	3	3	1	4	1	0	0	0	0	-	0	.194	.286	.323
2007	Det	AL	29	90	35	9	2	0	(0	0)	48	12	13	17	6	0	6	0	0	0	1	1	.50	5	.389	.427	.533
	8 ML YEARS		603	1671	449	91	10	26	(9	17)	638	187	185	203	92	5	159	10	36	16	23	23	.50	33	.269	.308	.382

Glen Perkins

Pitches: L **Bats:** L **Pos:** RP-19   **Ht:** 5'11" **Wt:** 200 **Born:** 3/2/1983 **Age:** 25

Year	Team	Lg	G	GS	CG	GF	IP	BFP	H	R	ER	HR	SH	SF	HB	TBB	IBB	SO	WP	Bk	W	L	Pct	ShO	Sv-Op	Hld	ERC	ERA
2004	Elizab	R+	3	3	0	0	12.0	50	8	3	3	0	1	2	0	4	0	22	0	0	1	0	1.000	0	0--	-	1.51	2.25
2004	QuadC	A	9	9	0	0	48.1	183	33	9	7	2	6	1	3	12	0	49	0	0	2	1	.667	0	0--	-	1.89	1.30
2005	FtMyrs	A+	10	9	2	0	55.0	218	41	14	13	2	1	3	1	13	0	66	2	0	3	2	.600	1	0--	-	1.86	2.13
2005	NwBrit	AA	14	14	0	0	79.0	352	80	45	43	4	3	2	8	35	1	67	3	1	4	4	.500	0	0--	-	4.32	4.90
2006	NwBrit	AA	23	23	2	0	117.1	503	109	60	51	11	1	3	6	45	0	131	3	1	4	11	.267	1	0--	-	3.76	3.91
2006	Roch	AAA	1	1	0	0	4.1	23	6	1	1	0	0	0	0	5	0	3	0	0	1	0	1.000	0	0--	-	8.88	2.08
2007	Twins	R	3	3	0	0	5.0	21	3	1	1	0	0	0	1	2	0	6	1	0	0	0	-	0	0--	-	2.03	1.80
2007	FtMyrs	A+	1	1	0	0	1.0	6	3	3	3	1	0	0	0	0	0	1	0	0	0	0	-	0	0--	-	25.51	27.00
2007	Roch	AAA	1	1	0	0	6.0	20	2	1	1	1	0	0	0	1	0	2	0	0	0	0	-	0	0--	-	0.88	1.50
2007	NwBrit	AA	3	3	0	0	7.1	39	11	9	9	1	0	0	0	7	0	7	2	0	0	2	.000	0	0--	-	14.16	11.05
2006	Min	AL	4	0	0	1	5.2	20	3	1	1	0	0	0	0	0	0	6	0	0	0	0	-	0	0-0	1	0.60	1.59
2007	Min	AL	19	0	0	3	28.2	115	23	10	10	2	1	1	2	12	0	20	2	0	0	0	-	0	0-0	3	3.32	3.14
	2 ML YEARS		23	0	0	4	34.1	135	26	11	11	2	1	1	2	12	0	26	2	0	0	0	-	0	0-0	4	2.68	2.88

Yusmeiro Petit

Pitches: R **Bats:** R **Pos:** SP-10; RP-4   **Ht:** 6'0" **Wt:** 230 **Born:** 11/22/1984 **Age:** 23

Year	Team	Lg	G	GS	CG	GF	IP	BFP	H	R	ER	HR	SH	SF	HB	TBB	IBB	SO	WP	Bk	W	L	Pct	ShO	Sv-Op	Hld	ERC	ERA
2003	Kngspt	R+	12	12	0	0	62.0	230	47	19	16	2	1	2	4	8	0	65	1	0	3	3	.500	0	0--	-	1.83	2.32
2003	Bklyn	A-	2	2	0	0	12.1	45	5	3	3	0	0	0	1	2	0	20	0	0	1	0	1.000	0	0--	-	0.71	2.19
2004	CptCty	A	15	15	0	0	83.0	319	47	29	22	8	2	1	4	22	0	122	4	0	9	2	.818	0	0--	-	1.61	2.39
2004	StLuci	A+	9	9	1	0	44.1	177	27	9	6	0	4	1	3	14	1	62	0	1	2	3	.400	1	0--	-	1.48	1.22
2004	Bnghtn	AA	2	2	0	0	12.0	49	10	6	6	1	0	1	0	5	0	16	0	0	1	1	.500	0	0--	-	2.65	4.50
2005	Bnghtn	AA	21	21	2	0	117.2	456	90	41	38	15	3	2	2	18	1	130	0	0	9	3	.750	0	0--	-	2.17	2.91
2005	Norfolk	AAA	3	3	0	0	14.2	71	24	16	15	5	1	0	0	6	0	14	0	0	0	3	.000	0	0--	-	10.43	9.20
2006	Albq	AAA	17	17	0	0	96.2	404	101	53	46	14	4	2	1	20	1	68	2	0	4	6	.400	0	0--	-	3.89	4.28
2007	Tucsn	AAA	17	17	0	0	93.2	397	83	47	42	11	4	4	1	38	0	60	5	1	8	4	.667	0	0--	-	3.62	4.04
2006	Fla	NL	15	1	0	5	26.1	129	46	28	28	7	1	1	0	9	1	20	0	0	1	1	.500	0	0-0	0	10.07	9.57
2007	Ari	NL	14	10	0	2	57.0	243	58	30	29	12	1	1	0	18	1	40	0	1	3	4	.429	0	0-0	0	4.50	4.58
	2 ML YEARS		29	11	0	7	83.1	372	104	58	57	19	2	2	0	27	2	60	0	1	4	5	.444	0	0-0	0	6.16	6.16

Billy Petrick

Pitches: R **Bats:** R **Pos:** RP-8   **Ht:** 6'6" **Wt:** 240 **Born:** 4/29/1984 **Age:** 24

Year	Team	Lg	G	GS	CG	GF	IP	BFP	H	R	ER	HR	SH	SF	HB	TBB	IBB	SO	WP	Bk	W	L	Pct	ShO	Sv-Op	Hld	ERC	ERA
2002	Cubs	R	6	6	0	0	31.2	120	21	8	6	0	0	0	3	6	0	35	0	0	2	1	.667	0	0--	-	1.52	1.71
2003	Boise	A-	14	14	0	0	64.1	286	60	49	34	4	1	1	6	27	2	64	1	0	2	5	.286	0	0--	-	3.72	4.76
2004	Lansng	A	26	24	0	1	146.2	611	149	66	57	3	8	10	10	43	1	113	6	1	13	7	.650	0	0--	-	3.56	3.50
2005	Dytona	A+	9	9	0	0	37.0	172	39	23	23	0	4	0	7	19	0	25	3	0	1	4	.200	0	0--	-	4.78	5.59
2006	Boise	A-	7	7	0	0	36.1	156	37	10	9	0	0	2	4	12	0	28	2	0	5	0	1.000	0	0--	-	3.67	2.23
2006	Dytona	A+	3	3	0	0	16.1	74	24	11	11	3	0	0	2	2	0	9	0	0	2	.333	-	0	0--	-	7.02	6.06
2007	Dytona	A+	6	0	0	3	11.2	49	12	4	4	0	0	1	1	2	0	10	0	0	0	1	.000	0	0--	-	3.00	3.09
2007	Tenn	AA	18	0	0	4	30.1	121	22	10	8	3	0	2	2	8	0	33	2	0	1	1	.500	0	2--	-	2.38	2.37
2007	Iowa	AAA	9	0	0	1	12.1	55	17	8	7	3	2	0	3	2	0	7	0	0	1	1	.500	0	0--	-	7.94	5.11
2007	ChC	NL	8	0	0	1	9.2	42	8	8	8	3	0	0	0	7	0	6	0	0	0	0	-	0	0-0	1	6.15	7.45

Andy Pettitte

Pitches: L **Bats:** L **Pos:** SP-34; RP-2   **Ht:** 6'5" **Wt:** 225 **Born:** 6/15/1972 **Age:** 36

Year	Team	Lg	G	GS	CG	GF	IP	BFP	H	R	ER	HR	SH	SF	HB	TBB	IBB	SO	WP	Bk	W	L	Pct	ShO	Sv-Op	Hld	ERC	ERA
1995	NYY	AL	31	26	3	1	175.0	745	183	86	81	15	4	5	1	63	3	114	8	1	12	9	.571	0	0-0	0	4.13	4.17
1996	NYY	AL	35	34	2	1	221.0	929	229	105	95	23	7	3	3	72	2	162	6	1	21	8	.724	0	0-0	0	4.14	3.87
1997	NYY	AL	35	35	4	0	240.1	986	233	86	77	7	6	2	3	65	0	166	7	0	18	7	.720	1	0-0	0	3.05	2.88
1998	NYY	AL	33	32	5	0	216.1	932	226	110	102	20	6	7	6	87	1	146	6	0	16	11	.593	0	0-0	0	4.46	4.24
1999	NYY	AL	31	31	0	0	191.2	851	216	105	100	20	6	6	3	89	3	121	3	1	14	11	.560	0	0-0	0	5.22	4.70
2000	NYY	AL	32	32	3	0	204.2	903	219	111	99	17	7	4	4	80	4	125	2	3	19	9	.679	1	0-0	0	4.32	4.35
2001	NYY	AL	31	31	2	0	200.2	858	224	103	89	14	8	7	6	41	3	164	2	2	15	10	.600	0	0-0	0	3.82	3.99
2002	NYY	AL	22	22	3	0	134.2	570	144	58	49	6	3	2	4	32	2	97	2	1	13	5	.722	0	0-0	0	3.55	3.27
2003	NYY	AL	33	33	1	0	208.1	896	227	109	93	21	3	5	1	50	3	180	5	0	21	8	.724	0	0-0	0	3.89	4.02

Year	Team	Lg	G	GS	CG	GF	IP	BFP	H	R	ER	HR	SH	SF	HB	TBB	IBB	SO	WP	Bk	W	L	Pct	ShO	Sv-Op	Hld	ERC	ERA
							HOW MUCH HE PITCHED						**WHAT HE GAVE UP**													**THE RESULTS**			
2004	Hou	NL	15	15	0	0	83.0	346	71	37	36	8	1	0	0	31	2	79	4	0	6	4	.600	0	0-0	0	3.12	3.90
2005	Hou	NL	33	33	0	0	222.1	875	188	66	59	17	10	4	3	41	0	171	2	0	17	9	.654	0	0-0	0	2.40	2.39
2006	Hou	NL	36	35	2	1	214.1	929	238	114	100	27	14	5	2	70	9	178	2	1	14	13	.519	1	0-0	0	4.58	4.20
2007	NYY	AL	36	34	0	0	215.1	916	238	106	97	16	5	9	1	69	1	141	3	0	15	9	.625	0	0-0	0	4.27	4.05
	13 ML YEARS		403	393	25	3	2527.2	10736	2636	1196	1077	211	82	59	37	790	33	1844	51	10	201	113	.640	4	0-0	1	3.92	3.83

Josh Phelps

Bats: R **Throws:** R **Pos:** 1B-51; PH-48; DH-5; C-4; PR-1   **Ht:** 6'3" **Wt:** 225 **Born:** 5/12/1978 **Age:** 30

Year	Team	Lg	G	AB	H	2B	3B	HR	(Hm	Rd)	TB	R	RBI	RC	TBB	IBB	SO	HBP	SH	SF	SB	CS	SB%	GDP	Avg	OBP	Slg
									BATTING													**BASERUNNING**				**AVERAGES**		
2000	Tor	AL	1	1	0	0	0	0	(0	0)	0	0	0	0	0	0	1	0	0	0	0	0	-	0	.000	.000	.000
2001	Tor	AL	8	12	0	0	0	0	(0	0)	0	3	1	0	2	0	5	0	0	0	1	0	1.00	1	.000	.143	.000
2002	Tor	AL	74	265	82	20	1	15	(6	9)	149	41	58	52	19	0	82	3	0	0	0	0	-	5	.309	.362	.562
2003	Tor	AL	119	396	106	18	1	20	(11	9)	186	57	66	65	39	3	115	17	0	1	1	2	.33	12	.268	.358	.470
2004	2 Tms		103	371	93	19	2	17	(9	8)	167	51	61	50	22	2	93	7	0	1	0	0	-	13	.251	.304	.450
2005	TB	AL	47	158	42	10	0	5	(4	1)	67	21	26	23	12	1	48	4	0	3	0	0	-	6	.266	.328	.424
2007	2 Tms		94	157	48	6	2	7	(2	5)	79	21	31	26	20	0	42	5	0	1	0	0	-	6	.306	.399	.503
04	NYY	AL	79	295	70	13	2	12	(7	5)	123	38	51	40	18	2	73	7	0	1	0	0	-	9	.237	.296	.417
04	Cle	AL	24	76	23	6	0	5	(2	3)	44	13	10	10	4	0	20	0	0	0	0	0	-	4	.303	.338	.579
07	NYY	AL	36	80	21	2	0	2	(1	1)	29	8	12	8	6	0	19	2	0	0	0	0	-	5	.263	.330	.363
07	Pit	NL	58	77	27	4	2	5	(1	4)	50	13	19	18	14	0	23	3	0	1	0	0	-	1	.351	.463	.649
	7 ML YEARS		446	1360	371	73	6	64	(32	32)	648	194	243	216	114	6	386	36	0	6	2	2	.50	42	.273	.344	.476

Andy Phillips

Bats: R **Throws:** R **Pos:** 1B-57; 3B-9; PH-4; 2B-1; PR-1   **Ht:** 6'0" **Wt:** 210 **Born:** 4/6/1977 **Age:** 31

Year	Team	Lg	G	AB	H	2B	3B	HR	(Hm	Rd)	TB	R	RBI	RC	TBB	IBB	SO	HBP	SH	SF	SB	CS	SB%	GDP	Avg	OBP	Slg
									BATTING													**BASERUNNING**				**AVERAGES**		
2007	S-WB*	AAA	65	249	75	11	2	11	(-	-)	123	37	36	47	32	2	43	1	0	1	2	1	.67	6	.301	.382	.494
2004	NYY	AL	5	8	2	0	0	1	(0	1)	5	1	2	1	0	0	1	0	0	0	0	0	-	1	.250	.250	.625
2005	NYY	AL	27	40	6	4	0	1	(1	0)	13	7	4	2	1	0	13	0	0	0	0	0	-	1	.150	.171	.325
2006	NYY	AL	110	246	59	11	3	7	(5	2)	97	30	29	22	15	0	56	0	0	2	3	2	.60	9	.240	.281	.394
2007	NYY	AL	61	185	54	7	1	2	(1	1)	69	27	25	23	12	0	26	2	6	2	0	3	.00	5	.292	.338	.373
	4 ML YEARS		203	479	121	22	4	11	(7	4)	184	65	60	48	28	0	96	2	6	4	3	5	.38	16	.253	.294	.384

Brandon Phillips

Bats: R **Throws:** R **Pos:** 2B-156; PH-3; SS-1   **Ht:** 6'0" **Wt:** 195 **Born:** 6/28/1981 **Age:** 27

Year	Team	Lg	G	AB	H	2B	3B	HR	(Hm	Rd)	TB	R	RBI	RC	TBB	IBB	SO	HBP	SH	SF	SB	CS	SB%	GDP	Avg	OBP	Slg
									BATTING													**BASERUNNING**				**AVERAGES**		
2002	Cle	AL	11	31	8	3	1	0	(0	0)	13	5	4	5	3	0	6	1	1	0	0	0	-	0	.258	.343	.419
2003	Cle	AL	112	370	77	18	1	6	(3	3)	115	36	33	22	14	0	77	3	5	1	4	5	.44	12	.208	.242	.311
2004	Cle	AL	6	22	4	2	0	0	(0	0)	6	1	1	0	2	0	5	0	0	0	0	2	.00	1	.182	.250	.273
2005	Cle	AL	6	9	0	0	0	0	(0	0)	0	1	0	0	0	0	4	0	0	0	0	0	-	0	.000	.000	.000
2006	Cin	NL	149	536	148	28	1	17	(9	8)	229	65	75	74	35	3	88	6	4	6	25	2	.93	19	.276	.324	.427
2007	Cin	NL	158	650	187	26	6	30	(17	13)	315	107	94	88	33	4	109	12	2	5	32	8	.80	26	.288	.331	.485
	6 ML YEARS		442	1618	424	77	9	53	(29	24)	678	215	207	189	87	7	289	22	12	12	61	17	.78	58	.262	.306	.419

Heath Phillips

Pitches: L **Bats:** L **Pos:** RP-6   **Ht:** 6'3" **Wt:** 205 **Born:** 3/24/1982 **Age:** 26

Year	Team	Lg	G	GS	CG	GF	IP	BFP	H	R	ER	HR	SH	SF	HB	TBB	IBB	SO	WP	Bk	W	L	Pct	ShO	Sv-Op	Hld	ERC	ERA
								HOW MUCH HE PITCHED						**WHAT HE GAVE UP**													**THE RESULTS**			
2001	Knapol	A	14	12	1	1	71.2	304	74	36	29	1	5	6	7	18	1	54	1	1	2	7	.222	0	0- -	-	3.47	3.64
2002	WinSa	A+	28	28	5	0	179.0	748	184	82	70	17	4	3	3	50	5	112	6	2	6	16	.273	3	0- -	-	3.80	3.52
2003	Knapol	A	3	3	0	0	21.0	79	13	4	4	1	1	0	0	5	0	11	0	0	2	0	1.000	0	0- -	-	1.45	1.71
2003	Brham	AA	1	1	0	0	6.0	31	14	8	7	1	0	0	0	1	0	5	0	0	1	0	.000	0	0- -	-	12.97	10.50
2003	WinSa	A+	13	13	0	0	75.1	311	84	37	30	6	7	6	0	7	0	51	1	1	2	7	.222	0	0- -	-	3.37	3.58
2004	Brham	AA	27	26	0	1	154.1	649	179	78	69	12	5	12	4	36	3	107	5	2	12	10	.545	0	0- -	-	4.36	4.02
2005	Charltt	AAA	5	5	0	0	21.2	102	29	22	20	10	1	0	1	13	0	16	1	0	3	0	.000	0	0- -	-	10.76	8.31
2005	Brham	AA	22	21	2	0	135.0	567	161	64	61	12	5	5	3	30	2	78	3	1	9	5	.643	0	0- -	-	4.61	4.07
2006	Charltt	AAA	25	24	2	0	155.0	633	152	62	51	12	6	6	5	39	2	102	2	4	13	5	.722	0	0- -	-	3.44	2.96
2007	Charltt	AAA	28	28	1	0	173.2	756	198	90	83	23	3	2	3	56	1	108	3	0	13	7	.650	0	0- -	-	4.90	4.30
2007	CWS	AL	6	0	0	5	7.1	34	10	3	3	1	0	0	0	4	1	2	0	0	1	1	.500	0	0-0	0	7.17	3.68

Jason Phillips

Bats: R **Throws:** R **Pos:** C-49; 1B-4; PH-3   **Ht:** 6'1" **Wt:** 220 **Born:** 9/27/1976 **Age:** 31

Year	Team	Lg	G	AB	H	2B	3B	HR	(Hm	Rd)	TB	R	RBI	RC	TBB	IBB	SO	HBP	SH	SF	SB	CS	SB%	GDP	Avg	OBP	Slg
									BATTING													**BASERUNNING**				**AVERAGES**		
2007	Albq*	AAA	8	27	5	0	0	0	(-	-)	5	2	2	0	0	0	2	0	0	1	0	0	-	1	.185	.179	.185
2001	NYM	NL	6	7	1	1	0	0	(0	0)	2	2	0	0	0	0	1	0	0	0	0	0	-	0	.143	.143	.286
2002	NYM	NL	11	19	7	0	0	1	(0	1)	10	4	3	3	1	0	1	1	0	0	0	0	-	1	.368	.409	.526
2003	NYM	NL	119	403	120	25	0	11	(7	4)	178	45	58	65	39	3	50	10	0	1	0	1	.00	21	.298	.373	.442
2004	NYM	NL	128	362	79	18	0	7	(2	5)	118	34	34	30	35	4	42	8	2	5	0	1	.00	11	.218	.298	.326
2005	LAD	NL	121	399	95	20	0	10	(6	4)	145	38	55	42	25	4	50	4	2	4	0	1	.00	16	.238	.287	.363
2006	Tor	AL	25	48	12	6	0	0	(0	0)	18	4	6	3	1	0	5	1	0	0	0	0	-	2	.250	.275	.375
2007	Tor	AL	55	144	30	7	0	1	(0	1)	40	11	12	10	10	0	21	2	2	0	0	1	.00	5	.208	.269	.278
	7 ML YEARS		465	1382	344	77	0	30	(15	15)	511	138	168	153	111	11	170	26	6	12	0	5	.00	56	.249	.314	.370

Paul Phillips

Bats: R **Throws:** R **Pos:** C-7; 1B-1; PR-1   **Ht:** 5'11" **Wt:** 205 **Born:** 4/15/1977 **Age:** 31

Year	Team	Lg	G	AB	H	2B	3B	HR	(Hm	Rd)	TB	R	RBI	RC	TBB	IBB	SO	HBP	SH	SF	SB	CS	SB%	GDP	Avg	OBP	Slg
2007	Omha*	AAA	58	202	48	7	0	2	(-	-)	61	21	14	19	17	1	25	0	3	2	0	0	-	4	.238	.294	.302
2004	KC	AL	4	5	1	0	0	0	(0	0)	1	2	0	0	0	0	1	1	0	0	0	0	-	0	.200	.333	.200
2005	KC	AL	23	67	18	4	1	1	(0	1)	27	6	9	8	0	0	5	0	0	0	0	0	-	4	.269	.269	.403
2006	KC	AL	23	65	18	3	0	1	(0	1)	24	8	5	8	1	0	8	0	2	1	0	0	-	0	.277	.284	.369
2007	KC	AL	8	14	2	1	0	0	(0	0)	3	2	2	1	1	0	1	0	0	0	0	0	-	1	.143	.200	.214
4 ML YEARS			58	151	39	8	1	2	(0	2)	55	18	16	17	2	0	15	1	2	1	0	0	-	5	.258	.271	.364

Mike Piazza

Bats: R **Throws:** R **Pos:** DH-73; PH-12   **Ht:** 6'3" **Wt:** 215 **Born:** 9/4/1968 **Age:** 39

Year	Team	Lg	G	AB	H	2B	3B	HR	(Hm	Rd)	TB	R	RBI	RC	TBB	IBB	SO	HBP	SH	SF	SB	CS	SB%	GDP	Avg	OBP	Slg
2007	Stcktn*	A+	3	9	3	0	0	2	(-	-)	9	2	4	3	2	0	3	0	0	0	0	0	-	0	.333	.455	1.000
2007	Scrmto*	AAA	3	17	7	2	0	0	(-	-)	9	1	1	3	0	0	3	0	0	0	0	0	-	0	.412	.412	.529
1992	LAD	NL	21	69	16	3	0	1	(1	0)	22	5	7	6	4	0	12	1	0	0	0	0	-	1	.232	.284	.319
1993	LAD	NL	149	547	174	24	2	35	(21	14)	307	81	112	107	46	6	86	3	0	6	3	4	.43	10	.318	.370	.561
1994	LAD	NL	107	405	129	18	0	24	(13	11)	219	64	92	74	33	10	65	1	0	2	1	3	.25	11	.319	.370	.541
1995	LAD	NL	112	434	150	17	0	32	(9	23)	263	82	93	96	39	10	80	1	0	1	1	0	1.00	10	.346	.400	.606
1996	LAD	NL	148	547	184	16	0	36	(14	22)	308	87	105	117	81	21	93	1	0	2	0	3	.00	21	.336	.422	.563
1997	LAD	NL	152	556	201	32	1	40	(22	18)	355	104	124	137	69	11	77	3	0	5	5	1	.83	19	.362	.431	.638
1998	3 Tms	NL	151	561	184	38	1	32	(15	17)	320	88	111	116	58	14	80	2	0	5	1	0	1.00	15	.328	.390	.570
1999	NYM	NL	141	534	162	25	0	40	(18	22)	307	100	124	99	51	11	70	1	0	7	2	2	.50	27	.303	.361	.575
2000	NYM	NL	136	482	156	26	0	38	(17	21)	296	90	113	107	58	10	69	3	0	2	4	2	.67	15	.324	.398	.614
2001	NYM	NL	141	503	151	29	0	36	(16	20)	288	81	94	100	67	19	87	2	0	1	0	2	.00	20	.300	.384	.573
2002	NYM	NL	135	478	134	23	2	33	(12	21)	260	69	98	82	57	9	82	3	0	3	0	3	.00	26	.280	.359	.544
2003	NYM	NL	68	234	67	13	0	11	(4	7)	113	37	34	42	35	3	40	1	0	3	0	0	-	11	.286	.377	.483
2004	NYM	NL	129	455	121	21	0	20	(12	8)	202	47	54	63	68	14	78	2	0	3	0	0	-	14	.266	.362	.444
2005	NYM	NL	113	398	100	23	0	19	(9	10)	180	41	62	55	41	6	67	3	0	0	0	0	-	7	.251	.326	.452
2006	SD	NL	126	399	113	19	1	22	(10	12)	200	39	68	56	34	2	66	3	0	3	0	0	-	13	.283	.342	.501
2007	Oak	AL	83	309	85	17	1	8	(2	6)	128	33	44	37	18	0	61	0	0	2	0	0	-	9	.275	.313	.414
98	LAD	NL	37	149	42	5	0	9	(5	4)	74	20	30	23	11	4	27	0	0	1	0	0	-	3	.282	.329	.497
98	Fla	NL	5	18	5	0	1	0	(0	0)	7	1	5	2	0	0	0	0	0	1	0	0	-	0	.278	.263	.389
90	NYM	NL	109	394	137	33	0	23	(10	13)	239	67	76	91	47	10	53	2	0	3	1	0	1.00	12	.348	.417	.607
16 ML YEARS			1912	6911	2127	344	8	427	(195	232)	3768	1048	1335	1294	759	146	1113	30	0	45	17	20	.46	229	.308	.377	.545

Felix Pie

Bats: L **Throws:** L **Pos:** CF-80; PR-17; PH-5; LF-2   **Ht:** 6'2" **Wt:** 170 **Born:** 2/8/1985 **Age:** 23

Year	Team	Lg	G	AB	H	2B	3B	HR	(Hm	Rd)	TB	R	RBI	RC	TBB	IBB	SO	HBP	SH	SF	SB	CS	SB%	GDP	Avg	OBP	Slg
2002	Cubs	R	55	218	70	16	13	4	(-	-)	124	42	37	47	21	1	47	4	1	4	17	8	.68	1	.321	.385	.569
2002	Boise	A-	2	8	1	0	0	0	(-	-)	2	1	1	0	1	0	1	0	0	0	0	0	-	0	.125	.222	.250
2003	Lansng	A	124	505	144	22	9	4	(-	-)	196	72	47	69	41	2	98	6	3	0	19	13	.59	3	.285	.346	.388
2004	Dytona	A+	106	415	125	17	10	8	(-	-)	186	79	47	70	39	2	113	5	7	5	32	16	.67	5	.301	.364	.448
2005	WTenn	AA	59	240	73	17	5	11	(-	-)	133	40	25	45	16	1	53	2	1	3	13	8	.62	0	.304	.349	.554
2006	Iowa	AAA	141	559	158	33	8	15	(-	-)	252	78	57	87	46	3	126	5	10	3	17	11	.61	11	.283	.341	.451
2007	Iowa	AAA	55	229	83	9	5	9	(-	-)	129	51	43	49	19	1	40	0	1	1	9	6	.60	3	.362	.410	.563
2007	ChC	NL	87	177	38	9	3	2	(0	2)	59	26	20	21	14	0	43	0	2	1	8	1	.89	0	.215	.271	.333

Juan Pierre

Bats: L **Throws:** L **Pos:** CF-162   **Ht:** 5'11" **Wt:** 180 **Born:** 8/14/1977 **Age:** 30

Year	Team	Lg	G	AB	H	2B	3B	HR	(Hm	Rd)	TB	R	RBI	RC	TBB	IBB	SO	HBP	SH	SF	SB	CS	SB%	GDP	Avg	OBP	Slg
2000	Col	NL	51	200	62	2	0	0	(0	0)	64	26	20	23	13	0	15	1	4	1	7	6	.54	2	.310	.353	.320
2001	Col	NL	156	617	202	26	11	2	(0	2)	256	108	55	101	41	1	29	10	14	1	46	17	.73	6	.327	.378	.415
2002	Col	NL	152	592	170	20	5	1	(0	1)	203	90	35	79	31	0	52	9	8	0	47	12	.80	7	.287	.332	.343
2003	Fla	NL	162	668	204	28	7	1	(1	0)	249	100	41	92	55	1	35	5	15	3	65	20	.76	9	.305	.361	.373
2004	Fla	NL	162	678	221	22	12	3	(1	2)	276	100	49	101	45	1	35	8	15	2	45	24	.65	9	.326	.374	.407
2005	Fla	NL	162	656	181	19	13	2	(1	1)	232	96	47	76	41	1	45	9	10	2	57	17	.77	10	.276	.326	.354
2006	ChC	NL	162	699	204	32	13	3	(1	2)	271	87	40	84	32	0	38	8	10	1	58	20	.74	6	.292	.330	.388
2007	LAD	NL	162	668	196	24	8	0	(0	0)	236	96	41	75	33	0	37	6	20	2	64	15	.81	10	.293	.331	.353
8 ML YEARS			1169	4778	1440	173	69	12	(4	8)	1787	703	328	631	291	4	286	56	96	12	389	131	.75	59	.301	.348	.374

A.J. Pierzynski

Bats: L **Throws:** R **Pos:** C-130; PH-18   **Ht:** 6'3" **Wt:** 240 **Born:** 12/30/1976 **Age:** 31

Year	Team	Lg	G	AB	H	2B	3B	HR	(Hm	Rd)	TB	R	RBI	RC	TBB	IBB	SO	HBP	SH	SF	SB	CS	SB%	GDP	Avg	OBP	Slg
1998	Min	AL	7	10	3	0	0	0	(0	0)	3	1	1	2	1	0	2	1	0	1	0	0	-	0	.300	.385	.300
1999	Min	AL	9	22	6	2	0	0	(0	0)	8	3	3	3	1	0	4	1	0	0	0	0	-	0	.273	.333	.364
2000	Min	AL	33	88	27	5	1	2	(1	1)	40	12	11	14	5	0	14	2	0	1	1	0	1.00	1	.307	.354	.455
2001	Min	AL	114	381	110	33	2	7	(3	4)	168	51	55	50	16	4	57	4	1	3	1	7	.13	7	.289	.322	.441
2002	Min	AL	130	440	132	31	6	6	(2	4)	193	54	49	60	13	1	61	11	2	3	1	2	.33	14	.300	.334	.439
2003	Min	AL	137	487	152	35	3	11	(6	5)	226	63	74	80	24	12	55	15	2	5	3	1	.75	13	.312	.360	.464
2004	SF	NL	131	471	128	28	2	11	(3	8)	193	45	77	58	19	4	27	15	2	3	0	1	.00	27	.272	.319	.410

Year	Team	Lg	G	AB	H	2B	3B	HR	(Hm	Rd)	TB	R	RBI	RC	TBB	IBB	SO	HBP	SH	SF	SB	CS	SB%	GDP	Avg	OBP	Slg
									BATTING												**BASERUNNING**				**AVERAGES**		
2005	CWS	AL	128	460	118	21	0	18	(12	6)	193	61	56	55	23	5	68	12	1	1	0	2	.00	13	.257	.308	.420
2006	CWS	AL	140	509	150	24	0	16	(9	7)	222	65	64	68	22	6	72	8	3	1	1	0	1.00	10	.295	.333	.436
2007	CWS	AL	136	472	124	24	0	14	(8	6)	190	54	50	49	25	5	66	8	1	3	1	1	.50	21	.263	.309	.403
10 ML YEARS			965	3340	950	203	14	85	(44	41)	1436	409	440	439	149	37	426	77	12	21	8	14	.36	106	.284	.328	.430

Carmen Pignatiello

Pitches: L **Bats:** R **Pos:** RP-4   **Ht:** 6'0" **Wt:** 205 **Born:** 9/12/1982 **Age:** 25

Year	Team	Lg	G	GS	CG	GF	IP	BFP	H	R	ER	HR	SH	SF	HB	TBB	IBB	SO	WP	Bk	W	L	Pct	ShO	Sv-Op	Hld	ERC	ERA
				HOW MUCH HE PITCHED						**WHAT HE GAVE UP**												**THE RESULTS**					
2000	Cubs	R	9	3	0	1	36.1	169	48	26	18	1	1	1	1	13	0	32	1	2	4	1	.800	0	0--	-	5.25	4.46
2001	Boise	A-	16	12	0	3	78.0	337	70	37	26	2	4	1	6	22	0	83	6	0	7	3	.700	0	1--	-	2.75	3.00
2002	Lansng	A	27	27	1	0	167.1	702	152	76	59	10	7	5	6	51	0	139	4	1	9	11	.450	0	0--	-	3.06	3.17
2003	Dytona	A+	26	26	1	0	156.1	674	144	87	76	13	5	3	13	55	0	140	7	2	8	11	.421	0	0--	-	3.62	4.38
2003	WTenn	AA	1	1	0	0	6.0	22	3	1	1	1	0	0	0	2	0	11	0	0	1	0	1.000	0	0--	-	1.80	1.50
2004	WTenn	AA	27	27	1	0	148.0	637	167	89	75	16	16	7	9	39	1	137	5	0	9	7	.563	0	0--	-	4.61	4.56
2005	WTenn	AA	16	10	0	1	80.2	329	68	26	24	3	5	1	2	28	1	77	3	0	5	4	.556	0	0--	-	2.75	2.68
2005	Iowa	AAA	22	5	0	6	47.1	213	52	34	29	6	1	0	2	20	2	43	2	0	1	5	.167	0	0--	-	4.98	5.51
2006	WTenn	AA	38	1	0	8	60.1	254	52	19	18	3	2	1	5	19	1	74	6	0	3	1	.750	0	0--	-	2.93	2.69
2006	Iowa	AAA	8	0	0	1	6.2	28	7	4	2	0	0	0	0	2	0	4	1	0	0	0	-	0	0--	-	3.32	2.70
2007	Tenn	AA	5	0	0	2	6.2	27	2	2	0	0	0	0	0	2	0	6	0	0	1	0	1.000	0	0--	-	0.50	0.00
2007	Iowa	AAA	45	0	0	11	49.0	205	40	20	15	5	3	0	1	16	0	44	2	0	1	0	1.000	0	2--	-	2.83	2.76
2007	ChC	NL	4	0	0	0	2.0	8	3	1	1	1	0	0	0	0	0	3	0	0	0	0	-	0	0-0	1	9.22	4.50

Joel Pineiro

Pitches: R **Bats:** R **Pos:** RP-31; SP-11   **Ht:** 6'1" **Wt:** 200 **Born:** 9/25/1978 **Age:** 29

Year	Team	Lg	G	GS	CG	GF	IP	BFP	H	R	ER	HR	SH	SF	HB	TBB	IBB	SO	WP	Bk	W	L	Pct	ShO	Sv-Op	Hld	ERC	ERA
				HOW MUCH HE PITCHED						**WHAT HE GAVE UP**												**THE RESULTS**					
2007	Lowell*	A-	1	1	0	0	1.0	3	0	0	0	0	0	0	0	0	0	2	0	0	0	0	-	0	0--	-	0.00	0.00
2007	Pwtckt*	AAA	2	2	0	0	8.0	28	3	2	2	0	0	0	0	4	0	3	1	0	0	0	-	0	0--	-	1.18	2.25
2000	Sea	AL	8	1	0	5	19.1	94	25	13	12	3	0	2	0	13	0	10	0	0	1	0	1.000	0	0-0	0	7.44	5.59
2001	Sea	AL	17	11	0	1	75.1	289	50	24	17	2	1	2	3	21	0	56	2	0	6	2	.750	0	0-0	2	1.71	2.03
2002	Sea	AL	37	28	2	4	194.1	812	189	75	70	24	5	7	7	54	1	136	8	0	14	7	.667	1	0-0	3	3.77	3.24
2003	Sea	AL	32	32	3	0	211.2	890	192	94	89	19	3	9	6	76	3	151	5	0	16	11	.593	2	0-0	0	3.43	3.78
2004	Sea	AL	21	21	1	0	140.2	596	144	77	73	21	1	5	4	43	1	111	4	0	6	11	.353	0	0-0	0	4.32	4.67
2005	Sea	AL	30	30	2	0	189.0	822	224	118	118	23	5	7	6	56	4	107	7	1	7	11	.389	0	0-0	0	5.05	5.62
2006	Sea	AL	40	25	1	6	165.2	753	209	123	117	23	1	6	10	64	13	87	4	1	8	13	.381	0	1-2	4	6.05	6.36
2007	2 Tms		42	11	0	15	97.2	419	110	49	47	14	3	1	2	26	0	60	3	0	7	5	.583	0	0-0	1	4.68	4.33
07	Bos	AL	31	0	0	15	34.0	157	41	20	19	3	1	1	1	14	0	20	3	0	1	1	.500	0	0-0	1	5.25	5.03
07	StL	NL	11	11	0	0	63.2	262	69	29	28	11	2	0	1	12	0	40	0	0	6	4	.600	0	0-0	0	4.36	3.96
8 ML YEARS			227	159	9	31	1093.2	4675	1143	573	543	129	19	39	38	353	22	718	33	2	65	60	.520	3	1-2	10	4.30	4.47

Renyel Pinto

Pitches: L **Bats:** L **Pos:** RP-57   **Ht:** 6'4" **Wt:** 195 **Born:** 7/8/1982 **Age:** 25

Year	Team	Lg	G	GS	CG	GF	IP	BFP	H	R	ER	HR	SH	SF	HB	TBB	IBB	SO	WP	Bk	W	L	Pct	ShO	Sv-Op	Hld	ERC	ERA
				HOW MUCH HE PITCHED						**WHAT HE GAVE UP**												**THE RESULTS**					
2000	Cubs	R	9	4	0	0	30.0	152	42	29	21	3	2	0	5	16	0	23	6	3	0	2	.000	0	0--	-	7.65	6.30
2001	Lansng	A	20	20	1	0	88.0	393	94	64	51	9	4	4	3	44	1	69	5	3	4	8	.333	0	0--	-	5.04	5.22
2002	Dytona	A+	7	7	0	0	32.2	149	45	23	20	5	1	1	3	11	0	24	3	2	3	3	.500	0	0--	-	7.11	5.51
2002	Lansng	A	17	16	0	0	98.0	400	79	39	36	9	4	6	8	28	0	92	3	0	7	5	.583	0	0--	-	2.88	3.31
2003	Dytona	A+	20	19	0	0	114.2	476	91	47	41	4	6	4	9	45	1	104	6	3	8	3	.273	0	0--	-	2.81	3.22
2004	WTenn	AA	25	25	0	0	141.2	587	107	50	46	10	8	5	6	72	0	179	9	1	11	8	.579	0	0--	-	3.20	2.92
2004	Iowa	AAA	2	2	0	0	9.1	43	9	9	8	2	0	0	0	8	0	9	1	0	1	1	.500	0	0--	-	6.84	7.71
2005	Iowa	AAA	6	6	0	0	22.2	121	31	30	24	3	4	2	2	24	0	24	0	0	1	2	.333	0	0--	-	10.01	9.53
2005	WTenn	AA	22	21	1	0	129.2	528	101	43	39	3	5	2	9	58	0	123	3	0	10	3	.769	1	0--	-	2.92	2.71
2006	Albq	AAA	18	18	1	0	95.1	418	82	40	36	8	4	1	13	47	1	96	7	0	8	2	.800	0	0--	-	4.06	3.40
2006	Fla	NL	27	0	0	7	29.2	135	20	12	10	3	0	1	2	27	0	36	4	0	0	0	-	0	1-3	4	4.33	3.03
2007	Fla	NL	57	0	0	4	58.2	242	45	25	24	7	1	3	3	32	2	56	2	0	2	4	.333	0	1-6	16	3.79	3.68
2 ML YEARS			84	0	0	11	88.1	377	65	37	34	10	1	4	4	59	2	92	6	0	2	4	.333	0	2-7	19	3.98	3.46

Scott Podsednik

Bats: L **Throws:** L **Pos:** LF-55; PR-4; CF-3; DH-2; PH-2   **Ht:** 6'1" **Wt:** 190 **Born:** 3/18/1976 **Age:** 32

Year	Team	Lg	G	AB	H	2B	3B	HR	(Hm	Rd)	TB	R	RBI	RC	TBB	IBB	SO	HBP	SH	SF	SB	CS	SB%	GDP	Avg	OBP	Slg
									BATTING												**BASERUNNING**				**AVERAGES**		
2007	Charltt*	AAA	20	73	21	5	0	1	(-	-)	29	12	6	11	10	0	15	2	0	2	2	3	.40	1	.288	.379	.397
2001	Sea	AL	5	6	1	0	1	0	(0	0)	3	1	3	0	0	0	1	0	0	0	0	0	-	1	.167	.167	.500
2002	Sea	AL	14	20	4	0	0	1	(0	1)	7	2	5	3	4	0	6	0	0	1	0	0	-	1	.200	.320	.350
2003	Mil	NL	154	558	175	29	8	9	(7	2)	247	100	58	101	56	2	91	4	8	2	43	10	.81	11	.314	.379	.443
2004	Mil	NL	154	640	156	27	7	12	(3	9)	233	85	39	76	58	2	105	7	6	1	70	13	.84	7	.244	.313	.364
2005	CWS	AL	129	507	147	28	1	0	(0	0)	177	80	25	64	47	0	75	3	6	5	59	23	.72	7	.290	.351	.349
2006	CWS	AL	139	524	137	27	6	3	(2	1)	185	86	45	65	54	1	96	2	8	4	40	19	.68	7	.261	.330	.353
2007	CWS	AL	62	214	52	13	4	2	(1	1)	79	30	11	17	13	0	36	4	4	0	12	5	.71	9	.243	.299	.369
7 ML YEARS			657	2469	672	124	27	27	(13	14)	931	384	186	326	232	5	410	20	32	13	224	70	.76	43	.272	.338	.377

Placido Polanco

Bats: R **Throws:** R **Pos:** 2B-141; PH-2; DH-1 **Ht:** 5'10" **Wt:** 195 **Born:** 10/10/1975 **Age:** 32

Year	Team	Lg	G	AB	H	2B	3B	HR	(Hm	Rd)	TB	R	RBI	RC	TBB	IBB	SO	HBP	SH	SF	SB	CS	SB%	GDP	Avg	OBP	Slg
1998	StL	NL	45	114	29	3	2	1	(1	0)	39	10	11	12	5	0	9	1	2	0	2	0	1.00	1	.254	.292	.342
1999	StL	NL	88	220	61	9	3	1	(0	1)	79	24	19	23	15	1	24	0	3	2	1	3	.25	7	.277	.321	.359
2000	StL	NL	118	323	102	12	3	5	(2	3)	135	50	39	44	16	0	26	1	7	3	4	4	.50	8	.316	.347	.418
2001	StL	NL	144	564	173	20	4	3	(1	2)	216	87	38	70	25	0	43	6	14	1	12	3	.80	22	.307	.342	.383
2002	2 Tms	NL	147	548	158	32	2	9	(8	1)	221	75	49	64	26	1	41	8	13	0	5	3	.63	15	.288	.330	.403
2003	Phi	NL	122	492	142	30	3	14	(7	7)	220	87	63	74	42	1	38	8	8	4	14	2	.88	16	.289	.352	.447
2004	Phi	NL	126	503	150	21	0	17	(10	7)	222	74	55	71	27	0	39	12	7	6	7	4	.64	13	.298	.345	.441
2005	2 Tms		129	501	166	27	2	9	(6	3)	224	84	56	86	33	0	25	11	2	4	4	3	.57	12	.331	.383	.447
2006	Det	AL	110	461	136	18	1	4	(2	2)	168	58	52	65	17	0	27	7	8	2	1	2	.33	18	.295	.329	.364
2007	Det	AL	142	587	200	36	3	9	(7	2)	269	105	67	100	37	3	30	11	2	4	7	3	.70	9	.341	.388	.458
02	StL	NL	94	342	97	19	1	5	(5	0)	133	47	27	38	12	1	27	4	9	0	3	1	.75	12	.284	.316	.389
02	Phi	NL	53	206	61	13	1	4	(3	1)	88	28	22	26	14	0	14	4	4	0	2	2	.50	3	.296	.353	.427
05	Phi	NL	43	158	50	7	0	3	(2	1)	66	26	20	26	12	0	9	3	0	0	0	0	-	3	.316	.376	.418
05	Det	AL	86	343	116	20	2	6	(4	2)	158	58	36	60	21	0	16	8	2	4	4	3	.57	9	.338	.386	.461
10 ML YEARS			1171	4313	1317	214	23	72	(44	28)	1793	654	449	609	243	6	302	65	66	26	57	27	.68	121	.305	.350	.416

Sidney Ponson

Pitches: R **Bats:** R **Pos:** SP-7 **Ht:** 6'1" **Wt:** 258 **Born:** 11/2/1976 **Age:** 31

Year	Team	Lg	G	GS	CG	GF	IP	BFP	H	R	ER	HR	SH	SF	HB	TBB	IBB	SO	WP	Bk	W	L	Pct	ShO	Sv-Op	Hld	ERC	ERA
1998	Bal	AL	31	20	0	5	135.0	588	157	82	79	19	3	4	3	42	2	85	4	1	8	9	.471	0	1-2	0	5.07	5.27
1999	Bal	AL	32	32	6	0	210.0	897	227	118	110	35	4	7	1	80	2	112	4	0	12	12	.500	0	0-0	0	5.08	4.71
2000	Bal	AL	32	32	6	0	222.0	953	223	125	119	30	3	3	1	83	0	152	5	0	9	13	.409	1	0-0	0	4.26	4.82
2001	Bal	AL	23	23	3	0	138.1	605	161	83	76	21	3	2	6	37	0	84	2	0	5	10	.333	1	0-0	0	5.04	4.94
2002	Bal	AL	28	28	3	0	176.0	736	172	84	80	26	2	3	2	63	1	120	3	0	7	9	.438	0	0-0	0	4.24	4.09
2003	2 Tms		31	31	4	0	216.0	898	211	94	90	16	6	5	5	61	5	134	9	0	17	12	.586	0	0-0	0	3.41	3.75
2004	Bal	AL	33	33	5	0	215.2	954	265	136	127	23	6	3	8	69	3	115	8	2	11	15	.423	2	0-0	0	5.33	5.30
2005	Bal	AL	23	23	1	0	130.1	595	177	97	90	16	2	8	3	48	1	68	10	0	7	11	.389	0	0-0	0	6.45	6.21
2006	2 Tms		19	16	0	1	85.0	384	108	62	59	10	4	0	4	36	1	48	2	0	4	5	.444	0	0-0	0	6.25	6.25
2007	Min	AL	7	7	0	0	37.2	181	54	31	29	7	0	0	3	17	1	23	0	0	2	5	.286	0	0-0	0	8.04	6.93
03	Bal	AL	21	21	4	0	148.0	622	147	65	62	10	2	3	4	43	2	100	6	0	14	6	.700	0	0-0	0	3.50	3.77
03	SF	NL	10	10	0	0	68.0	276	64	29	28	6	4	2	1	18	3	34	3	0	3	6	.333	0	0-0	0	3.23	3.71
06	StL	NL	14	13	0	0	68.2	303	82	42	40	7	4	0	4	29	1	33	2	0	4	4	.500	0	0-0	0	5.74	5.24
06	NYY	AL	5	3	0	1	16.1	81	26	20	19	3	0	0	0	7	0	15	0	0	0	1	.000	0	0-0	0	8.48	10.47
10 ML YEARS			259	245	28	6	1566.0	6791	1755	912	859	203	33	35	36	536	16	941	47	3	82	101	.448	4	1-2	0	4.89	4.94

Jorge Posada

Bats: B **Throws:** R **Pos:** C-138; PH-13; DH-5; 1B-1 **Ht:** 6'2" **Wt:** 205 **Born:** 8/17/1971 **Age:** 36

Year	Team	Lg	G	AB	H	2B	3B	HR	(Hm	Rd)	TB	R	RBI	RC	TBB	IBB	SO	HBP	SH	SF	SB	CS	SB%	GDP	Avg	OBP	Slg
1995	NYY	AL	1	0	0	0	0	0	(0	0)	0	0	0	0	0	0	0	0	0	0	0	0	-	0			
1996	NYY	AL	8	14	1	0	0	0	(0	0)	1	1	0	0	1	0	6	0	0	0	0	0	-	1	.071	.133	.071
1997	NYY	AL	60	188	47	12	0	6	(2	4)	77	29	25	29	30	2	33	3	1	2	1	2	.33	2	.250	.359	.410
1998	NYY	AL	111	358	96	23	0	17	(6	11)	170	56	63	56	47	7	92	0	1	0	0	1	.00	10	.268	.350	.475
1999	NYY	AL	112	379	90	19	2	12	(4	8)	152	50	57	52	53	2	91	3	0	2	1	0	1.00	9	.245	.341	.401
2000	NYY	AL	151	505	145	35	1	28	(18	10)	266	92	86	110	107	10	151	8	0	4	2	2	.50	11	.287	.417	.527
2001	NYY	AL	138	484	134	28	1	22	(14	8)	230	59	95	80	62	10	132	6	0	5	2	6	.25	10	.277	.363	.475
2002	NYY	AL	143	511	137	40	1	20	(12	8)	239	79	99	92	81	9	143	3	0	3	1	0	1.00	23	.268	.370	.468
2003	NYY	AL	142	481	135	24	0	30	(15	15)	249	83	101	98	93	6	110	10	0	4	2	4	.33	13	.281	.405	.518
2004	NYY	AL	137	449	122	31	0	21	(11	10)	216	72	81	78	88	5	92	9	0	1	1	3	.25	24	.272	.400	.481
2005	NYY	AL	142	474	124	23	0	19	(11	8)	204	67	71	71	66	5	94	2	0	4	1	0	1.00	8	.262	.352	.430
2006	NYY	AL	143	465	129	27	2	23	(11	12)	229	65	93	89	64	1	97	11	0	5	3	0	1.00	10	.277	.374	.492
2007	NYY	AL	144	506	171	42	1	20	(11	9)	275	91	90	99	74	7	98	6	0	3	2	0	1.00	18	.338	.426	.543
13 ML YEARS			1432	4814	1334	304	8	218	(115	103)	2308	744	861	854	766	64	1139	61	1	37	16	18	.47	143	.277	.381	.479

Martin Prado

Bats: R **Throws:** R **Pos:** PH-12; 2B-10; 3B-9 **Ht:** 6'1" **Wt:** 190 **Born:** 10/27/1983 **Age:** 24

Year	Team	Lg	G	AB	H	2B	3B	HR	(Hm	Rd)	TB	R	RBI	RC	TBB	IBB	SO	HBP	SH	SF	SB	CS	SB%	GDP	Avg	OBP	Slg
2003	Braves	R	59	220	63	2	6	0	(-	-)	77	28	23	28	24	0	30	1	5	1	9	9	.50	4	.286	.358	.350
2004	Rome	A	107	429	135	25	6	3	(-	-)	181	68	38	66	30	0	47	3	4	1	14	10	.58	10	.315	.363	.422
2005	MrtlBh	A+	75	297	91	13	3	4	(-	-)	122	44	34	44	24	0	48	0	0	5	9	6	.60	7	.306	.353	.411
2005	Missi	AA	39	143	40	7	1	1	(-	-)	52	17	11	19	17	1	17	0	1	1	3	3	.50	5	.280	.354	.364
2006	Missi	AA	43	176	49	6	2	1	(-	-)	62	17	15	21	14	0	35	0	0	1	2	2	.50	4	.278	.330	.352
2006	Rchmd	AAA	60	241	68	12	1	2	(-	-)	88	30	23	28	12	0	28	0	2	2	2	2	.50	8	.282	.314	.365
2007	Rchmd	AAA	103	395	125	23	3	4	(-	-)	166	61	41	64	34	1	41	4	7	3	5	4	.56	9	.316	.374	.420
2006	Atl	NL	24	42	11	1	1	1	(1	0)	17	3	9	9	5	0	7	0	2	0	0	0	-	0	.262	.340	.405
2007	Atl	NL	28	59	17	3	0	0	(0	0)	20	5	2	6	3	0	6	0	0	0	0	0	-	0	.288	.323	.339
2 ML YEARS			52	101	28	4	1	1	(1	0)	37	8	11	15	8	0	13	0	2	0	0	0	-	2	.277	.330	.366

Bret Prinz

Pitches: R **Bats:** R **Pos:** RP-4   **Ht:** 6'2" **Wt:** 215 **Born:** 6/15/1977 **Age:** 31

Year	Team	Lg	G	GS	CG	GF	IP	BFP	H	R	ER	HR	SH	SF	HB	TBB	IBB	SO	WP	Bk	W	L	Pct	ShO	Sv-Op	Hld	ERC	ERA
2007	Charltt*	AAA	15	0	0	6	16.0	67	10	2	1	0	1	0	1	9	1	16	1	0	0	1	.000	0	1--	-	2.16	0.56
2007	Iowa*	AAA	8	0	0	2	14.0	65	15	10	8	3	1	4	3	6	0	15	0	0	1	1	.500	0	0--	-	6.35	5.14
2007	Indy*	AAA	14	0	0	10	14.0	59	13	2	2	0	0	1	0	7	1	15	1	0	0	0	-	0	6--	-	3.34	1.29
2001	Ari	NL	46	0	0	26	41.0	174	33	13	12	4	3	1	1	19	1	27	1	1	4	1	.800	0	9-12	6	3.27	2.63
2002	Ari	NL	20	0	0	5	13.1	71	23	14	14	1	2	1	1	10	1	10	3	0	0	2	.000	0	0-2	5	10.34	9.45
2003	2 Tms		3	0	0	2	3.0	20	7	4	4	1	0	0	0	4	2	3	0	0	0	0	-	0	0-0	0	18.22	12.00
2004	NYY	AL	26	0	0	10	28.1	124	28	17	16	5	0	1	1	14	0	22	2	0	1	0	1.000	0	0-0	1	5.16	5.08
2005	LAA	AL	3	0	0	2	3.0	14	4	1	1	1	0	0	0	1	0	1	0	0	0	1	.000	0	0-0	0	7.44	3.00
2007	CWS	AL	4	0	0	1	3.1	16	4	3	3	1	0	0	0	2	1	1	0	0	0	0	-	0	0-0	0	7.00	8.10
03	Ari	NL	1	0	0	0	1.0	5	1	0	0	0	0	0	0	1	1	1	0	0	0	0	-	0	0-0	0	3.46	0.00
03	NYY	AL	2	0	0	2	2.0	15	6	4	4	1	0	0	0	3	1	2	0	0	0	0	-	0	0-0	0	27.15	18.00
	6 ML YEARS		102	0	0	46	92.0	419	99	52	50	13	5	3	3	50	5	64	6	1	5	4	.556	0	9-14	12	5.45	4.89

Mark Prior

Pitches: R **Bats:** R **Pos:** P   **Ht:** 6'5" **Wt:** 230 **Born:** 9/7/1980 **Age:** 27

Year	Team	Lg	G	GS	CG	GF	IP	BFP	H	R	ER	HR	SH	SF	HB	TBB	IBB	SO	WP	Bk	W	L	Pct	ShO	Sv-Op	Hld	ERC	ERA
2002	ChC	NL	19	19	1	0	116.2	486	98	45	43	14	3	4	7	38	0	147	1	0	6	6	.500	0	0-0	0	3.27	3.32
2003	ChC	NL	30	30	3	0	211.1	863	183	67	57	15	9	2	9	50	4	245	9	0	18	6	.750	1	0-0	0	2.69	2.43
2004	ChC	NL	21	21	0	0	118.2	510	112	53	53	14	8	4	3	48	2	139	2	1	6	4	.600	0	0-0	0	3.97	4.02
2005	ChC	NL	27	27	1	0	166.2	701	143	73	68	25	5	3	4	59	2	188	4	1	11	7	.611	0	0-0	0	3.49	3.67
2006	ChC	NL	9	9	0	0	43.2	211	46	39	35	9	2	2	8	28	2	38	5	0	1	6	.143	0	0-0	0	6.84	7.21
	5 ML YEARS		106	106	5	0	657.0	2771	582	277	256	77	27	15	31	223	10	757	21	2	42	29	.592	1	0-0	0	3.47	3.51

Scott Proctor

Pitches: R **Bats:** R **Pos:** RP-83   **Ht:** 6'1" **Wt:** 195 **Born:** 1/2/1977 **Age:** 31

Year	Team	Lg	G	GS	CG	GF	IP	BFP	H	R	ER	HR	SH	SF	HB	TBB	IBB	SO	WP	Bk	W	L	Pct	ShO	Sv-Op	Hld	ERC	ERA
2004	NYY	AL	26	0	0	12	25.0	118	29	18	15	5	0	2	0	14	0	21	1	1	2	1	.667	0	0-0	2	6.32	5.40
2005	NYY	AL	29	1	0	11	44.2	199	46	32	30	10	0	1	2	17	4	36	4	1	1	0	1.000	0	0-0	0	4.98	6.04
2006	NYY	AL	83	0	0	12	102.1	426	89	41	40	12	2	6	2	33	6	89	2	0	6	4	.600	0	1-8	26	3.15	3.52
2007	2 Tms		83	0	0	14	86.1	382	78	41	35	12	3	7	6	44	4	64	5	1	5	5	.500	0	0-6	18	4.41	3.65
07	NYY	AL	52	0	0	10	54.1	245	53	27	23	8	1	6	3	29	3	37	3	0	2	5	.286	0	0-4	11	4.90	3.81
07	LAD	NL	31	0	0	4	32.0	137	25	14	12	4	2	1	3	15	1	27	2	1	3	0	1.000	0	0-2	7	3.61	3.38
	4 ML YEARS		221	1	0	49	258.1	1125	242	132	120	39	5	16	10	108	14	210	12	3	14	10	.583	0	1-14	46	4.16	4.18

Albert Pujols

Bats: R **Throws:** R **Pos:** 1B-154; PH-4   **Ht:** 6'3" **Wt:** 230 **Born:** 1/16/1980 **Age:** 28

Year	Team	Lg	G	AB	H	2B	3B	HR	(Hm	Rd)	TB	R	RBI	RC	TBB	IBB	SO	HBP	SH	SF	SB	CS	SB%	GDP	Avg	OBP	Slg
2001	StL	NL	161	590	194	47	4	37	(18	19)	360	112	130	132	69	6	93	9	1	7	1	3	.25	21	.329	.403	.610
2002	StL	NL	157	590	185	40	2	34	(14	20)	331	118	127	121	72	13	69	9	0	4	2	4	.33	20	.314	.394	.561
2003	StL	NL	157	591	212	51	1	43	(21	22)	394	137	124	160	79	12	65	10	0	5	5	1	.83	13	.359	.439	.667
2004	StL	NL	154	592	196	51	2	46	(18	28)	389	133	123	143	84	12	52	7	0	9	5	5	.50	21	.331	.415	.657
2005	StL	NL	161	591	195	38	2	41	(23	18)	360	129	117	139	97	27	65	9	0	3	16	2	.89	19	.330	.430	.609
2006	StL	NL	143	535	177	33	1	49	(24	25)	359	119	137	146	92	28	50	4	0	3	7	2	.78	20	.331	.431	.671
2007	StL	NL	158	565	185	38	1	32	(12	20)	321	99	103	118	99	22	58	7	0	8	2	6	.25	27	.327	.429	.568
	7 ML YEARS		1091	4054	1344	298	13	282	(130	152)	2514	847	861	959	592	120	452	55	1	39	38	23	.62	141	.332	.420	.620

Nick Punto

Bats: B **Throws:** R **Pos:** 3B-108; SS-27; 2B-25; PR-3; PH-1   **Ht:** 5'9" **Wt:** 186 **Born:** 11/8/1977 **Age:** 30

Year	Team	Lg	G	AB	H	2B	3B	HR	(Hm	Rd)	TB	R	RBI	RC	TBB	IBB	SO	HBP	SH	SF	SB	CS	SB%	GDP	Avg	OBP	Slg
2001	Phi	NL	4	5	2	0	0	0	(0	0)	2	0	0	1	0	0	0	0	0	0	0	0	-	0	.400	.400	.400
2002	Phi	NL	9	6	1	0	0	0	(0	0)	1	0	0	0	0	0	3	0	1	0	0	0	-	0	.167	.167	.167
2003	Phi	NL	64	92	20	2	0	1	(0	1)	25	14	4	7	7	1	22	0	0	0	2	1	.67	0	.217	.273	.272
2004	Min	AL	38	91	23	0	0	2	(2	0)	29	17	12	15	12	0	19	0	0	0	6	0	1.00	2	.253	.340	.319
2005	Min	AL	112	394	94	18	4	4	(3	1)	132	45	26	35	36	0	86	0	7	2	13	8	.62	9	.239	.301	.335
2006	Min	AL	135	459	133	21	7	1	(0	1)	171	73	45	59	47	0	68	1	10	7	17	5	.77	8	.290	.352	.373
2007	Min	AL	150	472	99	18	4	1	(0	1)	128	53	25	37	55	1	90	0	6	3	16	6	.73	7	.210	.291	.271
	7 ML YEARS		512	1519	372	59	15	9	(5	4)	488	202	112	154	157	2	288	1	24	12	54	20	.73	26	.245	.314	.321

Danny Putnam

Bats: L **Throws:** L **Pos:** CF-6; RF-5; LF-1; PR-1   **Ht:** 5'10" **Wt:** 200 **Born:** 9/17/1982 **Age:** 25

Year	Team	Lg	G	AB	H	2B	3B	HR	(Hm	Rd)	TB	R	RBI	RC	TBB	IBB	SO	HBP	SH	SF	SB	CS	SB%	GDP	Avg	OBP	Slg
2004	Vancvr	A	11	38	11	2	0	2	(-	-)	19	10	3	10	14	1	8	0	0	0	1	0	1.00	2	.289	.481	.500
2004	Kane	A	49	160	35	5	2	7	(-	-)	65	29	27	25	29	1	40	3	1	1	0	0	-	11	.219	.347	.406
2005	Stcktn	A+	131	514	158	37	3	15	(-	-)	246	97	100	98	66	1	92	6	1	7	3	3	.25	13	.307	.388	.479
2006	Mdland	AA	60	225	55	13	2	8	(-	-)	96	33	37	32	23	0	37	2	2	2	2	1	.67	4	.244	.317	.427
2006	As	R	6	18	5	1	0	0	(-	-)	6	2	2	3	6	0	2	0	0	0	0	0	-	0	.278	.458	.333
2006	Stcktn	A+	10	40	15	2	0	1	(-	-)	20	7	9	9	6	0	8	0	0	0	0	0	-	0	.375	.457	.500

Year	Team	Lg	G	AB	H	2B	3B	HR	(Hm	Rd)	TB	R	RBI	RC	TBB	IBB	SO	HBP	SH	SF	SB	CS	SB%	GDP	Avg	OBP	Slg
2007	Mdland	AA	13	52	17	7	1	2	(-	-)	32	9	15	11	5	0	4	0	0	0	1	2	.33	2	.327	.386	.615
2007	As	R	6	19	6	0	0	1	(-	-)	9	2	1	3	2	0	3	0	0	0	0	0	-	0	.316	.381	.474
2007	Stcktn	A+	3	14	4	1	0	1	(-	-)	8	3	5	2	0	0	0	0	0	0	0	0	-	1	.286	.286	.571
2007	Scrmto	AAA	51	171	37	11	1	1	(-	-)	53	14	17	16	17	1	41	4	1	0	2	2	.50	0	.216	.302	.310
2007	Oak	AL	11	28	6	0	0	1	(0	1)	9	3	2	1	3	0	11	0	0	0	0	0	-	0	.214	.290	.321

J.J. Putz

Pitches: R Bats: R Pos: RP-68   Ht: 6'5" Wt: 250 Born: 2/22/1977 Age: 31

			HOW MUCH HE PITCHED					WHAT HE GAVE UP										THE RESULTS							
Year	Team	Lg	G	GS	CG	GF	IP	BFP	H	R	ER	HR	SH	SF	HB	TBB	IBB	SO	WP	Bk	W	L	Pct	ShO	Sv-Op	Hld	ERC	ERA
2003	Sea	AL	3	0	0	0	3.2	18	4	2	2	0	0	0	0	3	0	3	0	0	0	0	-	0	0-0	0	5.31	4.91
2004	Sea	AL	54	0	0	30	63.0	275	66	35	33	10	3	2	5	24	4	47	1	0	0	3	.000	0	9-13	3	4.97	4.71
2005	Sea	AL	64	0	0	20	60.0	259	58	27	24	8	3	3	2	23	2	45	2	0	6	5	.545	0	1-4	21	4.11	3.60
2006	Sea	AL	72	0	0	57	78.1	303	59	20	20	4	1	2	2	13	1	104	1	0	4	1	.800	0	36-43	5	1.78	2.30
2007	Sea	AL	68	0	0	65	71.2	260	37	11	11	6	2	1	2	13	0	82	3	0	6	1	.857	0	40-42	0	1.21	1.38
5 ML YEARS			261	0	0	172	276.2	1115	224	95	90	28	9	8	11	76	7	281	7	0	16	10	.615	0	86-102	29	2.74	2.93

Chad Qualls

Pitches: R Bats: R Pos: RP-79   Ht: 6'5" Wt: 225 Born: 8/17/1978 Age: 29

			HOW MUCH HE PITCHED					WHAT HE GAVE UP										THE RESULTS							
Year	Team	Lg	G	GS	CG	GF	IP	BFP	H	R	ER	HR	SH	SF	HB	TBB	IBB	SO	WP	Bk	W	L	Pct	ShO	Sv-Op	Hld	ERC	ERA
2004	Hou	NL	25	0	0	4	33.0	141	34	13	13	3	0	1	4	8	1	24	0	0	4	0	1.000	0	1-2	9	4.02	3.55
2005	Hou	NL	77	0	0	19	79.2	329	73	33	29	7	4	3	6	23	2	60	1	0	6	4	.600	0	0-0	22	3.42	3.28
2006	Hou	NL	81	0	0	13	88.2	356	76	38	37	10	4	4	6	28	6	56	0	0	7	3	.700	0	0-6	23	3.36	3.76
2007	Hou	NL	79	0	0	16	82.2	345	84	29	28	10	6	2	3	25	5	78	2	0	6	5	.545	0	5-10	21	4.07	3.05
4 ML YEARS			262	0	0	52	284.0	1171	267	113	107	30	14	10	19	84	14	218	3	0	23	12	.657	0	6-18	75	3.66	3.39

Carlos Quentin

Bats: R Throws: R Pos: RF-75; PH-6; LF-3   Ht: 6'1" Wt: 220 Born: 8/28/1982 Age: 25

			BATTING																	BASERUNNING				AVERAGES		
Year	Team	Lg	G	AB	H	2B	3B	HR	(Hm	Rd)	TB	R	RBI	RC	TBB	IBB	SO	HBP	SH	SF	SB	CS	SB%	GDP	Avg	OBP	Slg
2004	Lancst	A+	65	242	75	14	1	15	(-	-)	136	64	51	60	25	1	33	27	0	3	5	1	.83	10	.310	.428	.562
2004	ElPaso	AA	60	210	75	19	0	6	(-	-)	112	39	38	47	18	1	23	16	0	2	0	6	.00	6	.357	.443	.533
2005	Tucsn	AAA	136	452	136	28	4	21	(-	-)	235	98	89	106	72	0	71	29	0	8	9	1	.90	14	.301	.422	.520
2006	Tucsn	AAA	85	318	92	30	3	9	(-	-)	155	66	52	71	45	1	46	31	0	2	5	0	1.00	13	.289	.424	.487
2007	Tucsn	AAA	33	115	40	12	1	4	(-	-)	66	30	27	27	9	1	14	9	0	2	1	0	1.00	2	.348	.430	.574
2006	Ari	NL	57	166	42	13	3	9	(3	6)	88	23	32	29	15	2	34	8	1	1	1	0	1.00	6	.253	.342	.530
2007	Ari	NL	81	229	49	16	0	5	(5	0)	80	29	31	27	18	1	54	11	1	4	2	2	.50	5	.214	.298	.349
2 ML YEARS			138	395	91	29	3	14	(8	6)	168	52	63	56	33	3	88	19	2	5	3	2	.60	11	.230	.316	.425

Robb Quinlan

Bats: R Throws: R Pos: 1B-34; LF-16; PH-15; 3B-10; DH-7; RF-6; PR-2   Ht: 6'1" Wt: 215 Born: 3/17/1977 Age: 31

			BATTING																	BASERUNNING				AVERAGES		
Year	Team	Lg	G	AB	H	2B	3B	HR	(Hm	Rd)	TB	R	RBI	RC	TBB	IBB	SO	HBP	SH	SF	SB	CS	SB%	GDP	Avg	OBP	Slg
2003	LAA	AL	38	94	27	4	2	0	(0	0)	35	13	4	8	6	0	16	0	1	0	1	2	.33	3	.287	.330	.372
2004	LAA	AL	56	160	55	14	0	5	(3	2)	84	23	23	33	14	0	26	2	0	1	3	1	.75	1	.344	.401	.525
2005	LAA	AL	54	134	31	8	0	5	(3	2)	54	17	14	11	7	0	26	1	0	1	0	1	.00	4	.231	.273	.403
2006	LAA	AL	86	234	75	11	1	9	(3	6)	115	28	32	36	7	1	28	2	0	1	2	1	.67	6	.321	.344	.491
2007	LAA	AL	79	178	44	9	0	3	(1	2)	62	21	21	15	14	1	27	1	0	1	3	2	.60	6	.247	.304	.348
5 ML YEARS			313	800	232	46	3	22	(10	12)	350	102	94	103	48	2	123	6	1	4	9	7	.56	20	.290	.333	.438

Omar Quintanilla

Bats: L Throws: R Pos: 2B-25; PH-4; SS-2; PR-1   Ht: 5'9" Wt: 190 Born: 10/24/1981 Age: 26

			BATTING																	BASERUNNING				AVERAGES		
Year	Team	Lg	G	AB	H	2B	3B	HR	(Hm	Rd)	TB	R	RBI	RC	TBB	IBB	SO	HBP	SH	SF	SB	CS	SB%	GDP	Avg	OBP	Slg
2007	ColSpr*	AAA	98	348	111	30	4	3	(-	-)	158	54	43	62	31	0	65	5	6	3	2	1	.75	8	.319	.380	.454
2005	Col	NL	39	128	28	1	1	0	(0	0)	31	16	7	9	9	0	15	0	6	0	2	1	.67	3	.219	.270	.242
2006	Col	NL	11	34	6	1	1	0	(0	0)	9	3	3	2	3	1	9	0	1	0	1	1	.50	1	.176	.243	.265
2007	Col	NL	27	70	16	4	0	0	(0	0)	20	6	5	6	5	0	15	0	0	0	0	0	-	3	.229	.280	.286
3 ML YEARS			77	232	50	6	2	0	(0	0)	60	25	15	17	17	1	39	0	7	0	3	2	.60	7	.216	.269	.259

Humberto Quintero

Bats: R Throws: R Pos: C-26; PH-3   Ht: 5'9" Wt: 215 Born: 8/8/1979 Age: 28

			BATTING																	BASERUNNING				AVERAGES		
Year	Team	Lg	G	AB	H	2B	3B	HR	(Hm	Rd)	TB	R	RBI	RC	TBB	IBB	SO	HBP	SH	SF	SB	CS	SB%	GDP	Avg	OBP	Slg
2007	RdRck*	AAA	53	177	59	12	1	5	(-	-)	88	22	22	29	4	0	21	2	5	0	0	2	.00	4	.333	.355	.497
2003	SD	NL	12	23	5	0	0	0	(0	0)	5	1	2	2	1	1	6	0	0	0	0	0	-	0	.217	.250	.217
2004	SD	NL	23	72	18	3	0	2	(1	1)	27	7	10	6	5	0	16	0	0	1	0	2	.00	5	.250	.295	.375
2005	Hou	NL	18	54	10	1	0	1	(1	0)	14	6	8	2	1	1	10	0	2	0	0	0	-	3	.185	.200	.259
2006	Hou	NL	11	21	7	2	0	0	(0	0)	9	2	2	1	1	0	3	0	0	0	0	0	-	2	.333	.364	.429
2007	Hou	NL	29	53	12	2	0	0	(2	0)	14	2	1	3	2	1	13	2	0	0	0	0	-	2	.226	.281	.264
5 ML YEARS			93	223	52	8	0	3	(2	1)	69	18	23	14	10	3	48	2	2	1	0	2	.00	12	.233	.271	.309

Guillermo Quiroz

Bats: R **Throws:** R **Pos:** C-8; PH-1   **Ht:** 6'1" **Wt:** 200 **Born:** 11/29/1981 **Age:** 26

Year	Team	Lg	G	AB	H	2B	3B	HR	(Hm	Rd)	TB	R	RBI	RC	TBB	IBB	SO	HBP	SH	SF	SB	CS	SB%	GDP	Avg	OBP	Slg
2007	Okla*	AAA	71	259	69	16	0	6	(-	-)	103	22	33	32	15	1	52	1	1	2	1	0	1.00	10	.266	.307	.398
2004	Tor	AL	17	52	11	2	0	0	(0	0)	13	2	6	4	2	0	8	2	0	1	1	0	1.00	1	.212	.263	.250
2005	Tor	AL	12	36	7	2	0	0	(0	0)	9	3	4	3	2	0	13	1	0	0	0	0	-	0	.194	.256	.250
2006	Sea	AL	1	2	0	0	0	0	(0	0)	0	0	0	0	0	0	2	0	0	0	0	0	-	0	.000	.000	.000
2007	Tex	AL	9	10	4	1	0	0	(0	0)	5	1	2	3	1	0	2	0	0	0	0	0	-	0	.400	.455	.500
	4 ML YEARS		39	100	22	5	0	0	(0	0)	27	6	12	10	5	0	25	3	0	1	1	0	1.00	1	.220	.275	.270

Josh Rabe

Bats: R **Throws:** R **Pos:** LF-7; DH-4; RF-2; PH-2; PR-2   **Ht:** 6'3" **Wt:** 215 **Born:** 10/15/1978 **Age:** 29

Year	Team	Lg	G	AB	H	2B	3B	HR	(Hm	Rd)	TB	R	RBI	RC	TBB	IBB	SO	HBP	SH	SF	SB	CS	SB%	GDP	Avg	OBP	Slg
2000	Elizab	R+	44	154	34	5	0	3	(-	-)	48	33	11	19	25	0	34	4	0	0	2	0	1.00	6	.221	.344	.312
2001	QuadC	A	119	397	112	25	3	6	(-	-)	161	58	44	57	32	0	64	8	4	3	9	7	.56	9	.282	.345	.406
2002	FtMyrs	A+	85	297	101	23	2	5	(-	-)	143	60	40	64	44	2	36	3	2	3	16	4	.80	10	.340	.427	.481
2002	NwBrit	AA	46	183	43	10	0	1	(-	-)	56	21	18	16	10	0	30	2	1	0	4	1	.80	5	.235	.282	.306
2003	NwBrit	AA	94	366	111	15	2	11	(-	-)	163	63	72	63	30	1	63	6	0	5	19	3	.86	10	.303	.361	.445
2003	Roch	AAA	38	131	31	6	0	5	(-	-)	52	15	11	16	11	0	22	1	1	0	2	1	.67	7	.237	.301	.397
2004	Roch	AAA	122	429	113	27	0	7	(-	-)	161	54	45	60	40	3	76	6	3	3	26	5	.84	9	.263	.333	.375
2005	Roch	AAA	90	285	68	17	0	11	(-	-)	118	50	49	39	29	0	57	3	2	2	5	2	.71	7	.239	.313	.414
2006	Roch	AAA	93	355	106	20	1	6	(-	-)	146	51	47	56	35	1	37	3	0	5	7	4	.64	5	.299	.362	.411
2007	Roch	AAA	5	20	6	1	0	1	(-	-)	10	3	6	4	4	0	3	0	0	0	0	0	-	0	.300	.417	.500
2006	Min	AL	24	49	14	1	0	3	(2	1)	24	8	7	6	2	0	11	0	0	0	0	1	.00	3	.286	.314	.490
2007	Min	AL	14	31	6	0	0	0	(0	0)	6	2	2	1	0	0	7	0	0	0	0	0	-	0	.194	.194	.194
	2 ML YEARS		38	80	20	1	0	3	(2	1)	30	10	9	7	2	0	18	0	0	0	0	1	.00	3	.250	.268	.375

Mike Rabelo

Bats: B **Throws:** R **Pos:** C-49; PH-3; DH-1; PR-1   **Ht:** 6'1" **Wt:** 200 **Born:** 1/17/1980 **Age:** 28

Year	Team	Lg	G	AB	H	2B	3B	HR	(Hm	Rd)	TB	R	RBI	RC	TBB	IBB	SO	HBP	SH	SF	SB	CS	SB%	GDP	Avg	OBP	Slg
2001	Oneont	A-	53	194	63	4	2	0	(-	-)	71	27	32	31	23	0	45	4	0	1	1	2	.33	4	.325	.405	.366
2002	WMich	A	123	410	80	13	1	2	(-	-)	101	42	41	30	42	0	91	8	5	2	3	1	.75	21	.195	.281	.246
2003	WMich	A	123	394	108	16	0	5	(-	-)	139	41	40	49	31	3	62	3	5	5	9	4	.69	13	.274	.328	.353
2004	Lkland	A+	92	327	94	20	2	0	(-	-)	118	36	38	43	25	1	56	7	1	2	3	2	.60	9	.287	.349	.361
2004	Erie	AA	5	20	2	0	0	0	(-	-)	2	0	2	0	1	0	4	1	0	0	0	0	-	0	.100	.182	.100
2005	Erie	AA	77	282	77	18	1	2	(-	-)	103	33	26	36	18	1	42	9	3	2	0	1	.00	6	.273	.334	.365
2006	Erie	AA	62	213	59	13	1	6	(-	-)	92	31	28	34	19	0	38	9	1	0	2	1	.67	7	.277	.361	.432
2006	Toledo	AAA	38	137	37	12	0	3	(-	-)	58	19	22	20	11	0	33	3	0	2	1	1	.50	3	.270	.333	.423
2006	Det	AL	1	1	0	0	0	0	(0	0)	0	0	0	0	0	0	1	0	0	0	0	0	-	0	.000	.000	.000
2007	Det	AL	51	168	43	10	2	1	(0	1)	60	14	18	16	6	0	41	5	5	1	0	0	-	4	.256	.300	.357
	2 ML YEARS		52	169	43	10	2	1	(0	1)	60	14	18	16	6	0	42	5	5	1	0	0	-	4	.254	.298	.355

Ryan Raburn

Bats: R **Throws:** R **Pos:** RF-16; CF-13; 2B-10; LF-10; PH-6; 3B-3; PR-1   **Ht:** 6'0" **Wt:** 185 **Born:** 4/17/1981 **Age:** 27

Year	Team	Lg	G	AB	H	2B	3B	HR	(Hm	Rd)	TB	R	RBI	RC	TBB	IBB	SO	HBP	SH	SF	SB	CS	SB%	GDP	Avg	OBP	Slg
2001	Tigers	R	19	58	9	2	0	1	(-	-)	14	4	5	4	9	1	19	3	0	0	2	1	.67	0	.155	.300	.241
2001	Oneont	A-	44	171	62	17	8	8	(-	-)	119	25	42	40	17	1	42	0	0	1	1	3	.25	7	.363	.418	.696
2002	Tigers	R	8	30	9	3	1	1	(-	-)	17	4	5	5	3	0	7	0	0	0	0	0	-	2	.300	.364	.567
2002	WMich	A	40	150	33	10	1	6	(-	-)	63	27	28	18	16	1	46	4	0	3	0	2	.00	4	.220	.306	.420
2003	WMich	A	16	57	20	7	0	3	(-	-)	36	14	12	13	6	0	14	2	0	0	1	1	.50	0	.351	.431	.632
2003	Lkland	A+	95	325	72	14	3	12	(-	-)	128	52	56	44	45	0	89	10	0	2	2	1	.67	5	.222	.332	.394
2004	Lkland	A+	3	11	3	1	0	1	(-	-)	7	1	3	2	1	0	6	0	0	0	0	0	-	0	.273	.333	.636
2004	Erie	AA	98	366	110	29	4	16	(-	-)	195	66	63	72	47	1	96	7	1	1	3	0	1.00	9	.301	.390	.533
2005	Toledo	AAA	130	471	119	22	4	19	(-	-)	206	62	64	69	45	2	109	5	1	4	8	3	.73	12	.253	.323	.437
2006	Toledo	AAA	118	451	124	29	4	20	(-	-)	221	68	79	81	51	1	120	5	1	4	16	4	.80	9	.275	.352	.490
2007	Toledo	AAA	85	315	92	21	3	17	(-	-)	170	60	64	69	51	3	73	4	0	3	12	4	.75	8	.292	.394	.540
2004	Det	AL	12	29	4	1	0	0	(0	0)	5	4	1	1	2	0	15	0	0	0	1	0	1.00	0	.138	.194	.172
2007	Det	AL	49	138	42	12	2	4	(2	2)	70	28	27	21	8	1	33	0	1	1	3	0	1.00	7	.304	.340	.507
	2 ML YEARS		61	167	46	13	2	4	(2	2)	75	32	28	22	10	1	48	0	1	1	4	0	1.00	7	.275	.315	.449

Aaron Rakers

Pitches: R **Bats:** R **Pos:** RP-1   **Ht:** 6'3" **Wt:** 229 **Born:** 1/22/1977 **Age:** 31

	HOW MUCH HE PITCHED							WHAT HE GAVE UP												THE RESULTS						
Year	Team	Lg	G	GS	CG	GF	IP	BFP	H	R	ER	HR	SH	SF	HB	TBB	IBB	SO	WP	Bk	W	L	Pct	ShO	Sv-Op	Hld	ERC	ERA
2007	Portlnd*	AAA	61	0	0	18	79.0	352	101	50	50	17	1	5	2	20	3	58	4	1	4	5	.444	0	0- -	-	6.01	5.70
2004	Bal	AL	3	0	0	1	4.1	19	5	2	2	0	0	0	0	1	0	3	0	0	0	0	-	0	0-0	0	3.47	4.15
2005	Bal	AL	10	0	0	1	13.2	55	11	5	5	3	0	2	0	3	0	11	0	0	1	0	1.000	0	0-0	1	3.01	3.29
2007	SD	NL	1	0	0	1	1.0	4	1	0	0	0	0	0	0	0	0	0	0	0	0	0	-	0	0-0	0	1.95	0.00
	3 ML YEARS		14	0	0	3	19.0	78	17	7	7	3	0	2	0	4	0	14	0	0	1	0	1.000	0	0-0	1	3.08	3.32

Aramis Ramirez

Bats: R **Throws:** R **Pos:** 3B-126; DH-3; PH-3   **Ht:** 6'1" **Wt:** 215 **Born:** 6/25/1978 **Age:** 30

Year	Team	Lg	G	AB	H	2B	3B	HR	(Hm	Rd)	TB	R	RBI	RC	TBB	IBB	SO	HBP	SH	SF	SB	CS	SB%	GDP	Avg	OBP	Slg
1998	Pit	NL	72	251	59	9	1	6	(3	3)	88	23	24	26	18	0	72	4	1	1	0	1	.00	3	.235	.296	.351
1999	Pit	NL	18	56	10	2	1	0	(0	0)	14	2	7	4	6	0	9	0	1	1	0	0	-	0	.179	.254	.250
2000	Pit	NL	73	254	65	15	2	6	(4	2)	102	19	35	28	10	0	36	5	1	4	0	0	-	9	.256	.293	.402
2001	Pit	NL	158	603	181	40	0	34	(16	18)	323	83	112	108	40	4	100	8	0	4	5	4	.56	9	.300	.350	.536
2002	Pit	NL	142	522	122	26	0	18	(7	11)	202	51	71	49	29	3	95	8	0	11	2	0	1.00	17	.234	.279	.387
2003	2 Tms	NL	159	607	165	32	2	27	(10	17)	282	75	106	88	42	3	99	10	0	11	2	2	.50	21	.272	.324	.465
2004	ChC	NL	145	547	174	32	1	36	(22	14)	316	99	103	100	49	6	62	3	0	7	0	2	.00	25	.318	.373	.578
2005	ChC	NL	123	463	140	30	0	31	(11	20)	263	72	92	79	35	4	60	6	0	2	0	1	.00	15	.302	.358	.568
2006	ChC	NL	157	594	173	38	4	38	(14	24)	333	93	119	109	50	4	63	9	0	7	2	1	.67	15	.291	.352	.561
2007	ChC	NL	132	506	157	35	4	26	(17	9)	278	72	101	95	43	8	66	4	0	5	0	0	-	13	.310	.366	.549
03	Pit	NL	96	375	105	25	1	12	(6	6)	168	44	67	49	25	3	68	7	0	8	1	1	.50	17	.280	.330	.448
03	ChC	NL	63	232	60	7	1	15	(4	11)	114	31	39	39	17	0	31	3	0	3	1	1	.50	4	.259	.314	.491
10 ML YEARS			1179	4403	1246	259	15	222	(104	118)	2201	589	770	686	322	32	662	57	3	53	11	11	.50	127	.283	.336	.500

Edwar Ramirez

Pitches: R **Bats:** R **Pos:** RP-21   **Ht:** 6'3" **Wt:** 150 **Born:** 3/28/1981 **Age:** 27

			HOW MUCH HE PITCHED					WHAT HE GAVE UP											THE RESULTS						
Year	Team	Lg	G	GS	CG	GF	IP	BFP	H	R	ER	HR	SH	SF	HB	TBB	IBB	SO	WP	Bk	W	L	Pct	ShO	Sv-Op	Hld	ERC	ERA
2002	Angels	R	13	7	0	1	46.1	197	47	22	19	1	0	1	4	13	0	45	1	0	2	5	.286	0	0--	-	3.51	3.69
2002	Provo	R+	2	1	0	0	9.2	47	14	10	10	0	0	2	3	4	0	4	2	0	1	0	1.000	0	0--	-	7.58	9.31
2003	RCuca	A+	4	4	0	0	16.2	83	29	16	15	5	1	0	0	7	0	9	1	0	0	2	.000	0	0--	-	10.81	8.10
2003	CRpds	A	6	1	0	0	19.0	83	17	7	7	2	0	1	1	8	0	15	1	0	1	1	.500	0	0--	-	3.73	3.32
2005	Salt Lk	AAA	1	0	0	0	2.0	6	0	0	0	0	0	0	0	0	0	2	0	0	0	0	-	0	0--	-	0.00	0.00
2006	Tampa	A+	19	0	0	12	30.2	112	14	4	4	0	0	0	1	6	0	47	2	0	4	1	.800	0	3--	-	0.81	1.17
2007	Trntn	AA	9	0	0	3	16.2	67	6	1	1	1	0	0	1	8	1	33	1	0	3	0	1.000	0	1--	-	1.24	0.54
2007	S-WB	AAA	25	0	0	10	40.0	153	20	4	4	0	2	0	3	14	0	69	3	1	1	0	1.000	0	6--	-	1.30	0.90
2007	NYY	AL	21	0	0	5	21.0	103	24	19	19	6	1	1	3	14	2	31	4	0	1	1	.500	0	1-3	3	7.95	8.14

Elizardo Ramirez

Pitches: R **Bats:** B **Pos:** SP-3; RP-1   **Ht:** 6'0" **Wt:** 190 **Born:** 1/28/1983 **Age:** 25

			HOW MUCH HE PITCHED					WHAT HE GAVE UP											THE RESULTS						
Year	Team	Lg	G	GS	CG	GF	IP	BFP	H	R	ER	HR	SH	SF	HB	TBB	IBB	SO	WP	Bk	W	L	Pct	ShO	Sv-Op	Hld	ERC	ERA
2007	Lsvlle*	AAA	12	12	0	0	65.0	282	71	28	27	4	4	1	4	19	0	44	1	3	4	3	.571	0	0--	-	4.15	3.74
2004	Phi	NL	7	0	0	5	15.0	67	17	8	8	3	0	1	1	5	1	9	1	0	0	0	-	0	0-0	0	5.44	4.80
2005	Cin	NL	6	4	0	1	22.1	110	33	22	21	5	2	0	2	10	2	9	2	0	0	3	.000	0	0-0	0	8.45	8.46
2006	Cin	NL	21	19	0	1	104.0	465	123	70	62	14	5	3	8	29	2	69	0	3	4	9	.308	0	0-0	0	5.13	5.37
2007	Cin	NL	4	3	0	0	16.1	73	20	14	14	5	1	0	0	8	0	8	0	0	0	2	.000	0	0-0	0	7.69	7.71
4 ML YEARS			38	26	0	7	157.2	715	193	114	105	27	8	4	11	52	5	95	3	3	4	14	.222	0	0-0	-	5.86	5.99

Erasmo Ramirez

Pitches: L **Bats:** L **Pos:** RP-7   **Ht:** 6'0" **Wt:** 190 **Born:** 4/29/1976 **Age:** 32

			HOW MUCH HE PITCHED					WHAT HE GAVE UP											THE RESULTS						
Year	Team	Lg	G	GS	CG	GF	IP	BFP	H	R	ER	HR	SH	SF	HB	TBB	IBB	SO	WP	Bk	W	L	Pct	ShO	Sv-Op	Hld	ERC	ERA
2007	Scrmto*	AAA	19	0	0	5	21.1	86	20	4	4	0	2	0	0	2	0	11	0	0	3	0	1.000	0	2--	-	1.97	1.69
2007	Albq*	AAA	22	0	0	3	21.2	92	27	10	9	3	0	1	1	4	0	10	0	0	2	1	.667	0	1--	-	5.26	3.74
2003	Tex	AL	34	0	0	9	49.0	200	46	21	21	4	2	2	4	9	0	28	1	0	3	1	.750	0	0-1	2	3.15	3.86
2004	Tex	AL	34	0	0	6	35.2	148	34	19	17	5	2	1	3	7	1	21	1	0	5	3	.625	0	0-2	3	3.58	4.29
2005	Tex	AL	16	0	0	4	23.0	96	24	10	10	3	3	0	2	3	0	6	0	0	0	0	-	0	0-1	0	3.81	3.91
2007	2 Tms		7	0	0	3	6.1	29	7	2	2	0	1	0	0	3	0	1	0	0	0	0	-	0	0-0	0	4.09	2.84
07	Oak	AL	3	0	0	2	3.0	12	3	0	0	0	0	0	0	1	0	0	0	0	0	0	-	0	0-0	0	3.35	0.00
07	Fla	NL	4	0	0	1	3.1	17	4	2	2	0	1	0	0	2	0	1	0	0	0	0	-	0	0-0	0	4.76	5.40
4 ML YEARS			91	0	0	22	114.0	473	111	52	50	12	8	3	9	22	1	56	2	0	8	4	.667	0	0-4	5	3.47	3.95

Hanley Ramirez

Bats: R **Throws:** R **Pos:** SS-151; PH-3; DH-1   **Ht:** 6'3" **Wt:** 200 **Born:** 12/23/1983 **Age:** 24

Year	Team	Lg	G	AB	H	2B	3B	HR	(Hm	Rd)	TB	R	RBI	RC	TBB	IBB	SO	HBP	SH	SF	SB	CS	SB%	GDP	Avg	OBP	Slg
2005	Bos	AL	2	2	0	0	0	0	(0	0)	0	0	0	0	0	0	0	0	0	0	0	0	-	0	.000	.000	.000
2006	Fla	NL	158	633	185	46	11	17	(9	8)	304	119	59	101	56	0	128	4	5	2	51	15	.77	7	.292	.353	.480
2007	Fla	NL	154	639	212	48	6	29	(15	14)	359	125	81	115	52	3	95	7	4	4	51	14	.78	10	.332	.386	.562
3 ML YEARS			314	1274	397	94	17	46	(24	22)	663	244	140	216	108	3	225	11	9	6	102	29	.78	17	.312	.369	.520

Horacio Ramirez

Pitches: L **Bats:** L **Pos:** SP-20   **Ht:** 6'1" **Wt:** 210 **Born:** 11/24/1979 **Age:** 28

			HOW MUCH HE PITCHED					WHAT HE GAVE UP											THE RESULTS						
Year	Team	Lg	G	GS	CG	GF	IP	BFP	H	R	ER	HR	SH	SF	HB	TBB	IBB	SO	WP	Bk	W	L	Pct	ShO	Sv-Op	Hld	ERC	ERA
2007	Tacom*	AAA	2	2	0	0	10.0	40	7	7	7	3	0	1	0	3	0	5	0	0	1	0	1.000	0	0--	-	3.23	6.30
2007	Ms*	R	1	1	0	0	7.0	29	9	1	0	0	0	0	0	0	0	4	0	1	1	0	1.000	0	0--	-	3.45	0.00
2003	Atl	NL	29	29	1	0	182.1	781	181	91	81	21	12	3	6	72	10	100	5	1	12	4	.750	0	0-0	0	4.21	4.00
2004	Atl	NL	10	9	1	0	60.1	259	51	24	16	7	2	1	0	30	5	31	0	2	2	4	.333	0	0-0	0	3.55	2.39

Year	Team	Lg	G	GS	CG	GF	IP	BFP	H	R	ER	HR	SH	SF	HB	TBB	IBB	SO	WP	Bk	W	L	Pct	ShO	Sv-Op	Hld	ERC	ERA
			HOW MUCH HE PITCHED						WHAT HE GAVE UP												THE RESULTS							
2005	Atl	NL	33	32	1	0	202.1	847	214	108	104	31	13	5	2	67	1	80	4	1	11	9	.550	1	0-0	0	4.66	4.63
2006	Atl	NL	14	14	0	0	76.1	337	85	42	38	6	3	3	4	31	2	37	0	1	5	5	.500	0	0-0	0	4.82	4.48
2007	Sea	AL	20	20	0	0	98.0	459	139	86	78	13	1	1	2	42	1	40	1	0	8	7	.533	0	0-0	0	7.17	7.16
	5 ML YEARS		106	104	3	0	619.1	2683	670	351	317	78	31	13	14	242	22	288	10	5	38	29	.567	1	0-0	0	4.81	4.61

Manny Ramirez

Bats: R **Throws:** R **Pos:** LF-120; DH-11; PH-2   **Ht:** 6'0" **Wt:** 200 **Born:** 5/30/1972 **Age:** 36

Year	Team	Lg	G	AB	H	2B	3B	HR	(Hm	Rd)	TB	R	RBI	RC	TBB	IBB	SO	HBP	SH	SF	SB	CS	SB%	GDP	Avg	OBP	Slg
			BATTING																		BASERUNNING				AVERAGES		
1993	Cle	AL	22	53	9	1	0	2	(0	2)	16	5	5	2	2	0	8	0	0	0	0	0	-	3	.170	.200	.302
1994	Cle	AL	91	290	78	22	0	17	(9	8)	151	51	60	53	42	4	72	0	0	4	4	2	.67	6	.269	.357	.521
1995	Cle	AL	137	484	149	26	1	31	(12	19)	270	85	107	103	75	6	112	5	2	5	6	6	.50	13	.308	.402	.558
1996	Cle	AL	152	550	170	45	3	33	(19	14)	320	94	112	120	85	8	104	3	0	9	8	5	.62	18	.309	.399	.582
1997	Cle	AL	150	561	184	40	0	26	(14	12)	302	99	88	117	79	5	115	7	0	4	2	3	.40	19	.328	.415	.538
1998	Cle	AL	150	571	168	35	2	45	(25	20)	342	108	145	121	76	6	121	6	0	10	5	3	.63	18	.294	.377	.599
1999	Cle	AL	147	522	174	34	3	44	(21	23)	346	131	**165**	**141**	96	9	131	13	0	9	2	4	.33	12	.333	.442	**.663**
2000	Cle	AL	118	439	154	34	2	38	(22	16)	306	92	122	127	86	9	117	3	0	4	1	1	.50	9	.351	.457	**.697**
2001	Bos	AL	142	529	162	33	2	41	(21	20)	322	93	125	122	81	**25**	147	8	0	2	0	1	.00	9	.306	.405	.609
2002	Bos	AL	120	436	152	31	0	33	(18	15)	282	84	107	125	73	14	85	8	0	1	0	0	-	13	**.349**	**.450**	.647
2003	Bos	AL	154	569	185	36	1	37	(18	19)	334	117	104	128	97	**28**	94	8	0	5	3	1	.75	22	.325	**.427**	.587
2004	Bos	AL	152	568	175	44	0	**43**	(23	20)	348	108	130	124	82	15	124	6	0	7	2	4	.33	17	.308	.397	**.613**
2005	Bos	AL	152	554	162	30	1	45	(22	23)	329	112	144	134	80	9	119	10	0	6	1	0	1.00	20	.292	.388	.594
2006	Bos	AL	130	449	144	27	1	35	(16	19)	278	79	102	114	100	16	102	1	0	8	0	1	.00	13	.321	**.439**	.619
2007	Bos	AL	133	483	143	33	1	20	(10	10)	238	84	88	78	71	13	92	7	0	8	0	0	-	21	.296	.388	.493
	15 ML YEARS		1950	7058	2209	471	17	490	(250	240)	4184	1342	1604	1609	1125	167	1543	85	2	82	34	31	.52	213	.313	.409	.593

Ramon Ramirez

Pitches: R **Bats:** R **Pos:** RP-22   **Ht:** 5'11" **Wt:** 190 **Born:** 8/31/1981 **Age:** 26

Year	Team	Lg	G	GS	CG	GF	IP	BFP	H	R	ER	HR	SH	SF	HB	TBB	IBB	SO	WP	Bk	W	L	Pct	ShO	Sv-Op	Hld	ERC	ERA
			HOW MUCH HE PITCHED						WHAT HE GAVE UP												THE RESULTS							
2003	Tampa	A+	14	14	0	0	74.1	327	88	47	43	7	1	2	2	20	2	70	3	1	2	8	.200	0	0- -	-	4.60	5.21
2003	Trntn	AA	4	3	0	0	21.1	88	18	8	4	3	0	1	0	8	1	21	0	1	1	1	.500	0	0- -	-	3.35	1.69
2003	Clmbs	AAA	2	1	0	0	6.0	25	5	5	3	1	0	0	0	1	0	5	0	0	0	1	.000	0	0- -	-	2.53	4.50
2004	Clmbs	AAA	4	4	0	0	18.0	87	25	19	17	3	0	3	0	8	1	17	1	0	0	3	.000	0	0- -	-	6.87	8.50
2004	Trntn	AA	18	18	2	0	115.0	485	116	60	59	11	6	4	3	32	0	128	9	3	4	6	.400	0	0- -	-	3.73	4.62
2005	Clmbs	AAA	6	6	0	0	27.0	115	32	16	16	3	0	0	1	9	0	26	1	0	1	3	.250	0	0- -	-	5.37	5.33
2005	Trntn	AA	15	15	0	0	89.0	375	79	44	38	10	1	3	1	35	0	82	4	1	6	5	.545	0	0- -	-	3.56	3.84
2005	Tulsa	AA	9	3	0	2	25.1	110	27	17	15	6	1	1	1	8	0	23	3	0	2	1	.667	0	0- -	-	5.24	5.33
2006	ColSpr	AAA	1	0	0	1	1.0	3	0	0	0	0	0	0	0	0	0	1	0	0	0	0	-	0	0- -	-	0.00	0.00
2007	ColSpr	AAA	25	0	0	2	27.2	116	18	10	7	2	1	0	0	16	0	35	1	0	4	0	1.000	0	0- -	-	2.68	2.28
2006	Col	NL	61	0	0	14	67.2	285	58	28	26	5	2	3	1	27	3	61	2	0	4	3	.571	0	0-2	10	3.09	3.46
2007	Col	NL	22	0	0	5	17.1	78	21	16	16	2	2	2	1	6	2	15	2	0	2	2	.500	0	0-0	3	5.24	8.31
	2 ML YEARS		83	0	0	19	85.0	363	79	44	42	7	4	5	2	33	5	76	4	0	6	5	.545	0	0-2	13	3.50	4.45

Stephen Randolph

Pitches: L **Bats:** L **Pos:** RP-14   **Ht:** 6'3" **Wt:** 205 **Born:** 5/1/1974 **Age:** 34

Year	Team	Lg	G	GS	CG	GF	IP	BFP	H	R	ER	HR	SH	SF	HB	TBB	IBB	SO	WP	Bk	W	L	Pct	ShO	Sv-Op	Hld	ERC	ERA
			HOW MUCH HE PITCHED						WHAT HE GAVE UP												THE RESULTS							
2007	RdRck*	AAA	31	0	0	20	52.0	199	23	14	11	5	0	2	2	22	0	78	3	0	10	2	.833	0	4- -	-	1.57	1.90
2003	Ari	NL	50	0	0	9	60.0	271	50	28	27	7	5	0	2	43	3	50	4	2	8	1	.889	0	0-0	2	4.51	4.05
2004	Ari	NL	45	6	0	5	81.2	393	73	56	50	11	2	4	1	76	2	62	3	0	2	5	.286	0	0-0	2	5.77	5.51
2007	Hou	NL	14	0	0	4	13.1	78	21	19	18	4	1	1	1	17	2	22	2	0	0	1	.000	0	0-0	0	13.68	12.15
	3 ML YEARS		109	6	0	18	155.0	742	144	103	95	22	8	5	4	136	7	134	9	2	10	7	.588	0	0-0	4	5.86	5.52

Cody Ransom

Bats: R **Throws:** R **Pos:** SS-12; PH-4; 2B-3; 3B-2   **Ht:** 6'2" **Wt:** 205 **Born:** 2/17/1976 **Age:** 32

Year	Team	Lg	G	AB	H	2B	3B	HR	(Hm	Rd)	TB	R	RBI	RC	TBB	IBB	SO	HBP	SH	SF	SB	CS	SB%	GDP	Avg	OBP	Slg
			BATTING																		BASERUNNING				AVERAGES		
2007	RdRck*	AAA	135	503	131	35	0	28	(-	-)	250	75	90	87	52	2	131	4	1	3	21	5	.81	9	.260	.333	.497
2001	SF	NL	9	7	0	0	0	0	(0	0)	0	1	0	0	0	0	5	0	0	0	0	0	-	0	.000	.000	.000
2002	SF	NL	7	3	2	0	0	0	(0	0)	2	2	1	1	1	1	1	0	0	0	0	0	-	0	.667	.750	.667
2003	SF	NL	20	27	6	1	0	1	(1	0)	10	7	1	1	1	0	11	0	0	0	0	0	-	0	.222	.250	.370
2004	SF	NL	78	68	17	6	0	1	(0	1)	26	13	11	9	6	0	20	1	3	0	2	2	.50	2	.250	.320	.382
2007	Hou	NL	19	35	8	2	0	1	(1	0)	13	9	3	6	9	1	9	2	0	0	0	0	-	1	.229	.413	.371
	5 ML YEARS		133	140	33	9	0	3	(2	1)	51	32	16	17	17	2	46	3	3	0	2	2	.50	3	.236	.331	.364

Clay Rapada

Pitches: L **Bats:** R **Pos:** RP-5   **Ht:** 6'5" **Wt:** 200 **Born:** 3/9/1981 **Age:** 27

Year	Team	Lg	G	GS	CG	GF	IP	BFP	H	R	ER	HR	SH	SF	HB	TBB	IBB	SO	WP	Bk	W	L	Pct	ShO	Sv-Op	Hld	ERC	ERA
			HOW MUCH HE PITCHED						WHAT HE GAVE UP												THE RESULTS							
2002	Boise	A-	12	0	0	2	18.0	85	18	7	3	0	2	3	3	8	0	12	0	0	0	0	-	0	1- -	-	3.92	1.50
2003	Boise	A-	1	0	0	0	3.0	12	2	0	0	1	0	1	0	1	0	3	0	0	0	0	-	0	0- -	-	1.57	0.00
2003	Lansng	A	21	4	0	2	42.1	193	46	29	25	3	0	3	3	19	0	24	1	0	1	2	.333	0	0- -	-	4.76	5.31
2004	Lansng	A	57	0	0	18	85.0	353	65	30	22	2	0	0	4	30	4	91	4	0	6	6	.500	0	3- -	-	2.24	2.33
2005	Dytona	A+	27	0	0	12	42.1	186	40	21	18	2	4	0	3	16	0	61	2	2	1	3	.250	0	5- -	-	3.50	3.83

Year Team	Lg	HOW MUCH HE PITCHED						WHAT HE GAVE UP												THE RESULTS							
		G	GS	CG	GF	IP	BFP	H	R	ER	HR	SH	SF	HB	TBB	IBB	SO	WP	Bk	W	L	Pct	ShO	Sv-Op	Hld	ERC	ERA
2006 WTenn	AA	33	0	0	28	43.2	169	30	7	4	1	1	0	2	10	2	45	0	0	3	2	.600	0	21--	-	1.60	0.82
2006 Iowa	AAA	28	0	0	5	23.2	109	27	8	8	0	3	2	2	15	1	21	3	1	3	2	.600	0	0--	-	5.44	3.04
2007 Iowa	AAA	55	0	0	39	65.1	234	55	24	22	4	0	4	3	25	3	50	2	0	7	2	.778	0	17--	-	4.36	3.58
2007 Toledo	AAA	2	0	0	0	2.1	13	5	3	3	0	0	0	0	1	0	3	2	0	0	0	-	0	0--	-	10.38	11.57
2007 2 Tms		5	0	0	2	2.2	13	3	3	3	2	0	0	0	2	0	4	2	0	0	0	-	0	0-0	0	11.59	10.13
07 ChC	NL	1	0	0	0	0.1	1	0	0	0	0	0	0	0	0	0	0	0	0	0	0	-	0	0-0	0	0.00	0.00
07 Det	AL	4	0	0	2	2.1	12	3	3	3	2	0	0	0	2	0	4	2	0	0	0	-	0	0-0	0	14.48	11.57

Darrell Rasner

Pitches: R Bats: R Pos: SP-6　　　　　　**Ht: 6'3" Wt: 210 Born: 1/13/1981 Age: 27**

Year Team	Lg	HOW MUCH HE PITCHED						WHAT HE GAVE UP												THE RESULTS							
		G	GS	CG	GF	IP	BFP	H	R	ER	HR	SH	SF	HB	TBB	IBB	SO	WP	Bk	W	L	Pct	ShO	Sv-Op	Hld	ERC	ERA
2007 S-WB*	AAA	2	1	0	2	8.0	31	5	0	0	0	0	0	2	0	3	0	0		1	0	1.000	0	0--	-	1.28	0.00
2007 StsInd*	A-	2	2	0	0	7.0	33	8	4	4	1	0	0	1	3	0	3	0	0	0	0	-	0	0--	-	5.81	5.14
2005 Was	NL	5	1	0	1	7.1	31	5	3	3	0	1	0	2	2	1	4	0	0	0	0	.000	0	0-0	0	2.03	3.68
2006 NYY	AL	6	3	0	1	20.1	83	18	10	10	2	1	0	1	5	0	11	1	0	3	1	.750	0	0-0	0	3.07	4.43
2007 NYY	AL	6	6	0	0	24.2	111	29	14	11	4	0	1	2	8	0	11	0	0	1	3	.250	0	0-0	0	5.56	4.01
3 ML YEARS		17	10	0	2	52.1	225	52	27	24	6	2	1	5	15	1	26	1	0	4	5	.444	0	0-0	0	4.03	4.13

Jon Rauch

Pitches: R Bats: R Pos: RP-88　　　　　　**Ht: 6'11" Wt: 251 Born: 9/27/1978 Age: 29**

Year Team	Lg	HOW MUCH HE PITCHED						WHAT HE GAVE UP												THE RESULTS							
		G	GS	CG	GF	IP	BFP	H	R	ER	HR	SH	SF	HB	TBB	IBB	SO	WP	Bk	W	L	Pct	ShO	Sv-Op	Hld	ERC	ERA
2002 CWS	AL	8	6	0	1	28.2	130	28	26	21	7	0	1	2	14	2	19	1	1	2	1	.667	0	0-0	0	5.41	6.59
2004 2 Tms		11	4	0	1	32.0	131	30	10	10	1	2	1	0	11	2	22	2	0	4	1	.800	0	0-0	0	3.05	2.81
2005 Was	NL	15	1	0	4	30.0	124	24	12	12	3	1	1	1	11	2	23	2	0	2	4	.333	0	0-0	0	2.90	3.60
2006 Was	NL	85	0	0	19	91.1	383	78	37	34	13	1	6	2	36	6	86	4	1	4	5	.444	0	2-5	18	3.52	3.35
2007 Was	NL	88	0	0	26	87.1	354	75	37	35	7	2	5	0	21	4	71	2	0	8	4	.667	0	4-10	33	2.53	3.61
04 CWS	AL	2	2	0	0	8.2	43	16	6	6	0	1	1	0	4	0	4	1	0	1	1	.500	0	0-0	0	9.15	6.23
04 Mon	NL	9	2	0	1	23.1	88	14	4	4	1	1	0	0	7	2	18	1	0	3	0	1.000	0	0-0	0	1.44	1.54
5 ML YEARS		207	11	0	51	269.1	1122	235	122	112	31	6	14	5	93	16	221	11	2	20	15	.571	0	6-15	51	3.25	3.74

Chris Ray

Pitches: R Bats: R Pos: RP-43　　　　　　**Ht: 6'3" Wt: 214 Born: 1/12/1982 Age: 26**

Year Team	Lg	HOW MUCH HE PITCHED						WHAT HE GAVE UP												THE RESULTS							
		G	GS	CG	GF	IP	BFP	H	R	ER	HR	SH	SF	HB	TBB	IBB	SO	WP	Bk	W	L	Pct	ShO	Sv-Op	Hld	ERC	ERA
2005 Bal	AL	41	0	0	8	40.2	174	34	15	12	5	1	1	1	18	3	43	0	1	1	3	.250	0	0-4	8	3.43	2.66
2006 Bal	AL	61	0	0	56	66.0	267	45	22	20	10	2	4	1	27	2	51	2	0	4	4	.500	0	33 38	0	2.77	2.73
2007 Bal	AL	43	0	0	37	42.2	179	35	22	21	5	0	1	2	18	2	44	1	0	5	6	.455	0	16-20	0	3.42	4.43
3 ML YEARS		145	0	0	101	149.1	620	114	59	53	20	3	6	4	63	7	138	3	1	10	13	.435	0	49-62	8	3.13	3.19

Tim Redding

Pitches: R Bats: R Pos: SP-15　　　　　　**Ht: 6'0" Wt: 195 Born: 2/12/1978 Age: 30**

Year Team	Lg	HOW MUCH HE PITCHED						WHAT HE GAVE UP												THE RESULTS							
		G	GS	CG	GF	IP	BFP	H	R	ER	HR	SH	SF	HB	TBB	IBB	SO	WP	Bk	W	L	Pct	ShO	Sv-Op	Hld	ERC	ERA
2007 Clmbs*	AAA	17	16	0	0	89.2	389	110	58	53	9	1	2	0	24	1	63	3	0	9	5	.643	0	0--	-	4.89	5.32
2001 Hou	NL	13	9	0	1	55.2	249	62	38	34	11	2	3	3	24	0	55	2	0	3	1	.750	0	0-0	0	5.87	5.50
2002 Hou	NL	18	14	0	1	73.1	325	78	49	44	10	4	3	0	35	3	63	5	1	3	6	.333	0	0-0	0	4.96	5.40
2003 Hou	NL	33	32	0	0	176.0	769	179	85	72	16	7	3	7	65	4	116	3	0	10	14	.417	0	0-0	0	4.07	3.68
2004 Hou	NL	27	17	0	2	100.2	465	125	73	64	15	10	3	5	43	3	56	2	0	5	7	.417	0	0-0	0	6.14	5.72
2005 2 Tms		10	7	0	0	30.2	154	44	41	36	7	3	3	2	17	1	19	1	0	0	6	.000	0	0-0	0	8.60	10.57
2007 Was	NL	15	15	0	0	84.0	366	84	35	34	10	6	1	4	38	4	47	1	1	3	6	.333	0	0-0	0	4.59	3.64
05 SD	NL	9	6	0	0	29.2	143	40	35	30	7	3	3	2	13	1	17	1	0	0	5	.000	0	0-0	0	7.56	9.10
05 NYY	AL	1	1	0	0	1.0	11	4	6	6	0	0	0	0	4	0	2	0	0	0	1	.000	0	0-0	0	43.35	54.00
6 ML YEARS		116	94	0	4	520.1	2328	572	321	284	69	32	16	21	222	15	356	14	2	24	40	.375	0	0-0	0	5.10	4.91

Mark Redman

Pitches: L Bats: L Pos: SP-8; RP-3　　　　　　**Ht: 6'5" Wt: 245 Born: 1/5/1974 Age: 34**

Year Team	Lg	HOW MUCH HE PITCHED						WHAT HE GAVE UP												THE RESULTS							
		G	GS	CG	GF	IP	BFP	H	R	ER	HR	SH	SF	HB	TBB	IBB	SO	WP	Bk	W	L	Pct	ShO	Sv-Op	Hld	ERC	ERA
2007 Rchmd*	AAA	1	1	0	0	5.2	23	5	0	0	0	0	0	1	2	0	6	0	0	1	0	1.000	0	0--	-	3.45	0.00
2007 Okla*	AAA	9	9	1	0	55.2	249	62	34	33	3	4	2	0	21	1	28	1	0	2	4	.333	0	0--	-	5.15	5.34
2007 Syrcse*	AAA	4	4	0	0	19.1	95	26	18	11	3	0	1	1	12	1	10	2	0	0	2	.000	0	0--	-	7.67	5.12
2007 Tulsa*	AA	1	1	0	0	5.0	22	5	5	5	2	0	0	0	2	0	7	0	0	0	0	-	0	0--	-	6.08	9.00
2007 ColSpr*	AAA	2	2	0	0	12.1	52	17	4	4	1	0	0	0	4	0	5	2	1	0	0	-	0	0--	-	6.42	2.92
1999 Min	AL	5	1	0	0	12.2	65	17	13	12	3	0	1	0	7	0	11	0	0	1	0	1.000	0	0-0	0	7.86	8.53
2000 Min	AL	32	24	0	3	151.1	651	168	81	80	22	3	2	3	45	0	117	6	0	12	9	.571	0	0-0	0	4.73	4.76
2001 2 Tms	AL	11	11	0	0	58.0	261	68	32	29	7	2	0	1	23	0	33	6	0	2	6	.250	0	0-0	0	5.26	4.50
2002 Det	AL	30	30	3	0	203.0	858	211	107	95	15	5	8	6	51	2	109	11	1	8	15	.348	0	0-0	0	3.64	4.21
2003 Fla	NL	29	29	3	0	190.2	802	172	82	76	16	10	5	5	61	3	151	8	2	14	9	.609	0	0-0	0	3.17	3.59
2004 Oak	AL	32	32	2	0	191.0	832	218	110	100	28	5	7	6	68	6	102	6	1	11	12	.478	0	0-0	0	5.23	4.71
2005 Pit	NL	30	30	2	0	178.1	751	188	100	97	18	11	5	2	56	3	101	7	3	5	15	.250	1	0-0	0	4.15	4.90
2006 KC	AL	29	29	2	0	167.0	740	202	110	106	19	6	4	8	63	1	76	12	2	11	10	.524	0	0-0	0	5.63	5.71
2007 2 Tms	NL	11	8	0	0	41.1	200	59	37	35	6	0	2	2	17	2	27	1	1	4	3	.333	0	0-0	0	7.09	7.62
01 Min	AL	9	9	0	0	49.0	219	57	26	23	6	1	0	0	19	0	29	6	0	2	4	.333	0	0-0	0	5.11	4.22

HOW MUCH HE PITCHED							WHAT HE GAVE UP												THE RESULTS							
Year	Team	Lg	G	GS	CG	GF	IP	BFP	H	R	ER	HR	SH	SF	HB	TBB	IBB	SO	WP	Bk	W	L	Pct	ShO	Sv-Op	Hld	ERC	ERA
01	Det	AL	2	2	0	0	9.0	42	11	6	6	1	1	0	1	4	0	4	0	0	0	2	.000	0	0-0	0	6.12	6.00
07	Atl	NL	6	5	0	0	21.2	116	38	29	28	4	0	2	2	11	2	13	1	0	0	4	.000	0	0-0	0	10.10	11.63
07	Col	NL	5	3	0	0	19.2	84	21	8	7	2	0	0	0	6	0	14	0	1	2	0	1.000	0	0-0	0	4.10	3.20
9 ML YEARS			209	194	12	3	1193.1	5160	1303	672	630	134	42	33	34	391	17	727	57	10	66	80	.452	2	0-0	0	4.52	4.75

Tike Redman

Bats: L **Throws:** L **Pos:** CF-28; LF-9; PH-5; PR-1   **Ht:** 5'11" **Wt:** 175 **Born:** 3/10/1977 **Age:** 31

			BATTING																BASERUNNING				AVERAGES		
Year	Team	Lg	G	AB	H	2B	3B	HR	(Hm | Rd)	TB	R	RBI	RC	TBB	IBB	SO	HBP	SH	SF	SB	CS	SB%	GDP	Avg	OBP	Slg
2007	Norfolk*	AAA	80	296	90	15	6	2	(- | -)	123	53	27	50	32	0	24	2	3	3	25	8	.76	3	.304	.372	.416
2000	Pit	NL	9	18	6	1	0	1	(0 | 1)	10	2	1	4	1	0	7	0	0	0	1	0	1.00	0	.333	.368	.556
2001	Pit	NL	37	125	28	4	1	1	(1 | 0)	37	8	4	8	4	0	25	0	0	1	3	5	.38	2	.224	.246	.296
2003	Pit	NL	56	230	76	16	5	3	(2 | 1)	111	36	19	41	14	0	18	2	2	0	7	3	.70	1	.330	.374	.483
2004	Pit	NL	155	546	153	19	4	8	(5 | 3)	204	65	51	61	23	2	52	3	4	5	18	6	.75	6	.280	.310	.374
2005	Pit	NL	135	319	80	12	4	2	(1 | 1)	106	33	26	31	19	0	27	1	2	3	4	1	.80	8	.251	.292	.332
2007	Bal	AL	40	132	42	9	2	2	(2 | 0)	61	23	16	21	5	0	18	0	1	1	7	1	.88	2	.318	.341	.462
6 ML YEARS			432	1370	385	61	16	17	(11 | 6)	529	167	117	166	66	2	147	6	9	10	40	16	.71	19	.281	.315	.386

Mike Redmond

Bats: R **Throws:** R **Pos:** C-56; DH-18; PH-9; PR-1   **Ht:** 5'11" **Wt:** 202 **Born:** 5/5/1971 **Age:** 37

			BATTING																BASERUNNING				AVERAGES		
Year	Team	Lg	G	AB	H	2B	3B	HR	(Hm | Rd)	TB	R	RBI	RC	TBB	IBB	SO	HBP	SH	SF	SB	CS	SB%	GDP	Avg	OBP	Slg
1998	Fla	NL	37	118	39	9	0	2	(1 | 1)	54	10	12	18	5	2	16	2	4	0	0	0	-	6	.331	.368	.458
1999	Fla	NL	84	242	73	9	0	1	(0 | 1)	85	22	27	33	26	2	34	5	5	0	0	0	-	8	.302	.381	.351
2000	Fla	NL	87	210	53	8	1	0	(0 | 0)	63	17	15	20	13	3	19	8	1	3	0	0	-	2	.252	.316	.300
2001	Fla	NL	48	141	44	4	0	4	(3 | 1)	60	19	14	21	13	4	13	2	1	1	0	0	-	6	.312	.376	.426
2002	Fla	NL	89	256	78	15	0	2	(1 | 1)	99	19	28	37	21	8	34	8	2	3	0	2	.00	4	.305	.372	.387
2003	Fla	NL	59	125	30	7	1	0	(0 | 0)	39	12	11	10	7	0	16	5	2	2	0	0	-	2	.240	.302	.312
2004	Fla	NL	81	246	63	15	0	2	(0 | 2)	84	19	25	27	14	0	28	8	3	2	1	0	1.00	10	.256	.315	.341
2005	Min	AL	45	148	46	9	0	1	(1 | 0)	58	17	26	23	6	0	14	3	2	0	0	0	-	9	.311	.350	.392
2006	Min	AL	47	179	61	13	0	0	(0 | 0)	74	20	23	22	4	0	18	4	1	2	0	0	-	9	.341	.365	.413
2007	Min	AL	82	272	80	13	0	1	(1 | 0)	96	23	38	38	18	3	23	5	0	3	0	0	-	9	.294	.346	.353
10 ML YEARS			659	1937	567	102	2	13	(6 | 7)	712	178	219	249	127	22	215	50	21	16	1	2	.33	68	.293	.349	.368

Eric Reed

Bats: L **Throws:** L **Pos:** PH-14; CF-4; PR-2   **Ht:** 6'0" **Wt:** 170 **Born:** 12/2/1980 **Age:** 27

			BATTING																BASERUNNING				AVERAGES		
Year	Team	Lg	G	AB	H	2B	3B	HR	(Hm | Rd)	TB	R	RBI	RC	TBB	IBB	SO	HBP	SH	SF	SB	CS	SB%	GDP	Avg	OBP	Slg
2002	Jmstwn	A-	60	250	77	5	1	0	(- | -)	84	35	17	31	17	1	30	0	1	3	19	10	.66	3	.308	.348	.336
2002	Kane	A	12	50	18	1	0	0	(- | -)	19	11	2	8	3	0	11	0	2	0	7	1	.88	1	.360	.396	.380
2003	Jupiter	A+	134	514	154	15	8	0	(- | -)	185	86	25	76	52	4	83	3	19	0	53	18	.75	4	.300	.367	.360
2004	Carlina	AA	55	222	68	9	6	3	(- | -)	98	32	14	36	14	1	55	0	1	2	24	6	.80	2	.306	.345	.441
2005	Carlina	AA	71	271	69	9	1	0	(- | -)	81	35	15	27	17	1	62	4	3	3	23	8	.74	2	.255	.305	.299
2005	Albq	AAA	39	171	53	5	4	1	(- | -)	69	19	20	24	3	0	31	4	2	1	17	7	.71	1	.310	.335	.404
2006	Albq	AAA	95	390	118	20	9	5	(- | -)	171	68	39	60	24	1	94	2	1	3	20	9	.69	7	.303	.344	.438
2007	Albq	AAA	95	303	86	10	12	0	(- | -)	120	54	20	44	17	0	59	2	7	4	30	3	.91	1	.284	.322	.396
2006	Fla	NL	42	41	4	0	0	0	(0 | 0)	4	6	0	0	2	1	10	2	2	0	3	1	.75	1	.098	.178	.098
2007	Fla	NL	18	20	2	0	0	0	(0 | 0)	2	3	0	0	1	0	6	0	0	0	1	0	1.00	0	.100	.143	.100
2 ML YEARS			60	61	6	0	0	0	(0 | 0)	6	9	0	0	3	1	16	2	2	0	4	1	.80	1	.098	.167	.098

Jeremy Reed

Bats: L **Throws:** L **Pos:** PH-11; LF-3; RF-1; DH-1   **Ht:** 6'0" **Wt:** 200 **Born:** 6/15/1981 **Age:** 27

			BATTING																BASERUNNING				AVERAGES		
Year	Team	Lg	G	AB	H	2B	3B	HR	(Hm | Rd)	TB	R	RBI	RC	TBB	IBB	SO	HBP	SH	SF	SB	CS	SB%	GDP	Avg	OBP	Slg
2007	Tacom*	AAA	135	563	168	37	5	13	(- | -)	254	92	63	91	47	1	73	3	10	5	14	9	.61	11	.298	.353	.451
2004	Sea	AL	18	58	23	4	0	0	(0 | 0)	27	11	5	11	7	1	4	1	0	0	3	1	.75	2	.397	.470	.466
2005	Sea	AL	141	488	124	33	3	3	(0 | 3)	172	61	45	49	48	1	74	2	4	2	12	11	.52	10	.254	.322	.352
2006	Sea	AL	67	212	46	6	5	6	(1 | 5)	80	27	17	13	11	1	31	2	2	2	2	3	.40	5	.217	.260	.377
2007	Sea	AL	13	17	3	0	1	0	(0 | 0)	5	2	0	0	0	0	3	0	0	0	0	0	-	0	.176	.176	.294
4 ML YEARS			239	775	196	43	9	9	(1 | 8)	284	101	67	73	66	3	112	5	6	4	17	15	.53	17	.253	.314	.366

Chris Reitsma

Pitches: R **Bats:** R **Pos:** RP-26   **Ht:** 6'5" **Wt:** 235 **Born:** 12/31/1977 **Age:** 30

HOW MUCH HE PITCHED								WHAT HE GAVE UP												THE RESULTS							
Year	Team	Lg	G	GS	CG	GF	IP	BFP	H	R	ER	HR	SH	SF	HB	TBB	IBB	SO	WP	Bk	W	L	Pct	ShO	Sv-Op	Hld	ERC	ERA
2007	Tacom*	AAA	2	1	0	0	3.0	10	1	0	0	0	0	0	0	0	0	2	0	0	0	0	-	0	0--	-	0.25	0.00
2001	Cin	NL	36	29	0	1	182.0	800	209	121	107	23	13	8	5	49	6	96	5	0	7	15	.318	0	0-0	1	4.59	5.29
2002	Cin	NL	32	21	1	6	138.1	598	144	73	56	17	4	4	5	45	5	84	4	0	6	12	.333	1	0-0	0	4.24	3.64
2003	Cin	NL	57	3	0	36	84.0	351	92	41	40	14	4	1	0	19	6	53	2	0	9	5	.643	0	12-18	3	4.33	4.29
2004	Atl	NL	84	0	0	12	79.2	344	89	38	36	9	2	6	3	20	3	60	1	0	6	4	.600	0	2-9	31	4.32	4.07
2005	Atl	NL	76	0	0	37	73.1	307	79	32	32	3	1	2	0	14	3	42	2	0	3	6	.333	0	15-24	13	3.22	3.93
2006	Atl	NL	27	0	0	16	28.0	142	46	27	27	7	3	1	3	8	3	13	0	0	1	2	.333	0	8-12	3	8.85	8.68
2007	Sea	AL	26	0	0	6	23.2	115	37	22	20	3	2	1	0	9	1	11	4	0	0	2	.000	0	0-1	6	7.52	7.61
7 ML YEARS			338	53	1	114	609.0	2657	696	354	318	76	29	23	16	164	27	359	18	0	32	46	.410	1	37-64	57	4.55	4.70

Desi Relaford

Bats: B **Throws:** R **Pos:** 2B-12; LF-2; PH-2; PR-1   **Ht:** 5'9" **Wt:** 185 **Born:** 9/16/1973 **Age:** 34

							BATTING													BASERUNNING				AVERAGES		
Year	Team	Lg	G	AB	H	2B	3B	HR	(Hm | Rd)	TB	R	RBI	RC	TBB	IBB	SO	HBP	SH	SF	SB	CS	SB%	GDP	Avg	OBP	Slg
2007	Okla*	AAA	88	316	84	17	2	6	(- | -)	123	45	52	48	41	0	54	3	2	2	6	0	1.00	11	.266	.354	.389
1996	Phi	NL	15	40	7	2	0	0	(0 | 0)	9	2	1	2	3	0	9	0	1	0	1	0	1.00	1	.175	.233	.225
1997	Phi	NL	15	38	7	1	2	0	(0 | 0)	12	3	6	4	5	0	6	0	1	0	3	0	1.00	0	.184	.279	.316
1998	Phi	NL	142	494	121	25	3	5	(4 | 1)	167	45	41	48	33	4	87	3	10	6	9	5	.64	9	.245	.293	.338
1999	Phi	NL	65	211	51	11	2	1	(0 | 1)	69	31	26	22	19	2	34	6	6	0	4	3	.57	5	.242	.322	.327
2000	2 Tms		128	410	88	14	3	5	(0 | 5)	123	55	46	51	75	7	71	12	3	2	13	0	1.00	10	.215	.351	.300
2001	NYM	NL	120	301	91	27	0	8	(4 | 4)	142	43	36	52	27	1	65	5	2	5	13	5	.72	4	.302	.364	.472
2002	Sea	AL	112	329	88	13	2	6	(1 | 5)	123	55	43	43	33	2	51	6	1	7	10	3	.77	6	.267	.339	.374
2003	KC	AL	141	500	127	27	5	8	(5 | 3)	188	70	59	68	40	1	70	6	8	3	20	4	.83	10	.254	.315	.376
2004	KC	AL	114	380	84	14	0	6	(2 | 4)	116	45	34	37	34	3	56	8	4	4	5	4	.56	10	.221	.296	.305
2005	Col	NL	73	210	47	13	2	1	(0 | 1)	67	24	16	19	22	2	42	4	1	1	3	3	.50	1	.224	.308	.319
2007	Tex	AL	14	26	3	0	0	0	(0 | 0)	3	2	0	0	2	0	6	0	0	0	0	1	.00	2	.115	.179	.115
00	Phi	NL	83	253	56	12	3	3	(0 | 3)	83	29	30	34	48	7	45	9	2	1	5	0	1.00	7	.221	.363	.328
00	SD	NL	45	157	32	2	0	2	(0 | 2)	40	26	16	17	27	0	26	3	1	1	8	0	1.00	3	.204	.330	.255
	11 ML YEARS		939	2939	714	147	19	40	(16 | 24)	1019	375	308	346	293	22	497	50	37	28	81	28	.74	58	.243	.319	.347

Edgar Renteria

Bats: R **Throws:** R **Pos:** SS-122; PH-2   **Ht:** 6'1" **Wt:** 200 **Born:** 8/7/1975 **Age:** 32

							BATTING													BASERUNNING				AVERAGES		
Year	Team	Lg	G	AB	H	2B	3B	HR	(Hm | Rd)	TB	R	RBI	RC	TBB	IBB	SO	HBP	SH	SF	SB	CS	SB%	GDP	Avg	OBP	Slg
1996	Fla	NL	106	431	133	18	3	5	(2 | 3)	172	68	31	62	33	0	68	2	2	3	16	2	.89	12	.309	.358	.399
1997	Fla	NL	154	617	171	21	3	4	(3 | 1)	210	90	52	68	45	1	108	4	19	6	32	15	.68	17	.277	.327	.340
1998	Fla	NL	133	517	146	18	2	3	(2 | 1)	177	79	31	61	48	1	78	4	9	2	41	22	.65	13	.282	.347	.342
1999	StL	NL	154	585	161	36	2	11	(6 | 5)	234	92	63	81	53	0	82	2	6	7	37	8	.82	16	.275	.334	.400
2000	StL	NL	150	562	156	32	1	16	(4 | 12)	238	94	76	80	63	3	77	1	8	9	21	13	.62	19	.278	.346	.423
2001	StL	NL	141	493	128	19	3	10	(3 | 7)	183	54	57	57	39	4	73	3	8	6	17	4	.81	15	.260	.314	.371
2002	StL	NL	152	544	166	36	2	11	(4 | 7)	239	77	83	94	49	7	57	4	7	5	22	7	.76	17	.305	.364	.439
2003	StL	NL	157	587	194	47	1	13	(4 | 9)	282	96	100	103	65	12	54	1	3	7	34	7	.83	21	.330	.394	.480
2004	StL	NL	149	586	168	37	0	10	(7 | 3)	235	84	72	74	39	5	78	1	6	10	17	11	.61	14	.287	.327	.401
2005	Bos	AL	153	623	172	36	4	8	(3 | 5)	240	100	70	82	55	0	100	3	6	5	9	4	.69	15	.276	.335	.385
2006	Atl	NL	149	598	175	40	2	14	(4 | 10)	261	100	70	89	62	0	89	3	8	2	17	6	.74	17	.293	.361	.436
2007	Atl	NL	124	494	164	30	1	12	(5 | 7)	232	87	57	82	46	0	77	1	2	0	11	2	.85	14	.332	.390	.470
	12 ML YEARS		1722	6637	1934	370	24	117	(47 | 70)	2703	1021	762	933	597	33	941	29	84	62	274	101	.73	190	.291	.349	.407

Jason Repko

Bats: R **Throws:** R **Pos:** OF   **Ht:** 5'10" **Wt:** 190 **Born:** 12/27/1980 **Age:** 27

							BATTING													BASERUNNING				AVERAGES		
Year	Team	Lg	G	AB	H	2B	3B	HR	(Hm | Rd)	TB	R	RBI	RC	TBB	IBB	SO	HBP	SH	SF	SB	CS	SB%	GDP	Avg	OBP	Slg
1999	Gr Falls	R+	49	207	63	9	9	8	(- | -)	114	51	32	42	21	0	43	3	1	1	12	5	.71	1	.304	.375	.551
2000	Yakima	A-	8	17	5	2	0	0	(- | -)	7	3	1	2	1	0	7	0	0	0	0	0	-	0	.294	.333	.412
2001	Wilmg	A	88	337	74	17	4	4	(- | -)	111	36	32	29	15	0	68	3	6	3	17	8	.68	2	.220	.257	.329
2002	VeroB	A+	120	470	128	29	5	9	(- | -)	194	73	53	64	25	1	92	8	8	2	29	13	.69	3	.272	.319	.413
2003	Jaxnvl	AA	119	416	100	14	5	10	(- | -)	154	62	23	53	42	0	89	6	9	3	21	8	.72	1	.240	.317	.370
2004	Jaxnvl	AA	46	189	55	11	2	6	(- | -)	88	26	19	30	13	1	43	2	2	1	10	5	.67	1	.291	.341	.466
2004	LsVgs	AAA	75	302	94	26	4	7	(- | -)	149	55	41	53	18	2	57	3	2	1	13	5	.72	4	.311	.355	.493
2005	LsVgs	AAA	8	31	12	0	0	3	(- | -)	21	6	6	7	0	0	4	0	1	0	1	0	1.00	0	.387	.387	.677
2006	LsVgs	AAA	9	29	8	2	0	0	(- | -)	10	2	2	4	3	0	6	2	0	0	1	0	1.00	1	.276	.382	.345
2005	LAD	NL	129	276	61	15	3	8	(4 | 4)	106	43	30	28	16	1	80	7	2	0	5	0	1.00	7	.221	.281	.384
2006	LAD	NL	69	130	33	5	1	3	(1 | 2)	49	21	16	21	15	1	24	3	2	0	10	4	.71	2	.254	.345	.377
	2 ML YEARS		198	406	94	20	4	11	(5 | 6)	155	64	46	49	31	2	104	10	4	0	15	4	.79	9	.232	.302	.382

Chris Resop

Pitches: R **Bats:** R **Pos:** RP-4   **Ht:** 6'3" **Wt:** 215 **Born:** 11/4/1982 **Age:** 25

			HOW MUCH HE PITCHED						WHAT HE GAVE UP										THE RESULTS						
Year	Team	Lg	G	GS	CG	GF	IP	BFP	H	R	ER	HR	SH	SF	HB	TBB	IBB	SO	WP	Bk	W	L	Pct	ShO	Sv-Op	Hld	ERC	ERA
2007	Salt Lk*	AAA	27	0	0	7	45.1	200	50	26	23	4	2	1	0	16	0	39	1	0	1	3	.250	0	0--	-	4.33	4.57
2005	Fla	NL	15	0	0	6	17.0	80	22	16	16	1	0	2	1	9	0	15	3	0	2	0	1.000	0	0-0	0	6.35	8.47
2006	Fla	NL	22	0	0	10	21.1	101	26	9	8	1	0	0	1	16	5	10	0	0	1	2	.333	0	0-1	2	6.30	3.38
2007	LAA	AL	4	0	0	3	4.1	17	4	2	2	1	2	1	0	1	0	2	0	0	0	0	-	0	0-0	0	4.00	4.15
	3 ML YEARS		41	0	0	19	42.2	198	52	27	26	3	2	3	2	26	5	27	3	0	3	2	.600	0	0-1	2	6.11	5.48

Mike Restovich

Bats: R **Throws:** R **Pos:** PH-7; LF-6; RF-2   **Ht:** 6'4" **Wt:** 250 **Born:** 1/3/1979 **Age:** 29

							BATTING													BASERUNNING				AVERAGES		
Year	Team	Lg	G	AB	H	2B	3B	HR	(Hm | Rd)	TB	R	RBI	RC	TBB	IBB	SO	HBP	SH	SF	SB	CS	SB%	GDP	Avg	OBP	Slg
2007	Clmbs*	AAA	97	356	96	19	2	20	(- | -)	179	42	58	60	33	1	108	1	1	2	3	2	.60	12	.270	.332	.503
2002	Min	AL	8	13	4	0	0	1	(0 | 1)	7	3	1	0	1	0	4	0	0	0	1	0	1.00	2	.308	.357	.538
2003	Min	AL	24	53	15	3	2	0	(0 | 0)	22	10	4	8	10	0	12	1	0	0	0	0	-	3	.283	.406	.415
2004	Min	AL	29	47	12	3	0	2	(1 | 1)	21	9	6	6	4	0	10	0	0	0	0	0	-	0	.255	.314	.447
2005	2 Tms	NL	66	115	27	5	1	3	(1 | 2)	43	15	8	10	11	0	29	0	0	0	0	0	-	5	.235	.302	.374
2006	ChC	NL	10	12	2	1	0	0	(0 | 0)	3	0	1	1	1	0	5	0	0	0	0	0	-	0	.167	.231	.250

BATTING

Year	Team	Lg	G	AB	H	2B	3B	HR	(Hm	Rd)	TB	R	RBI	RC	TBB	IBB	SO	HBP	SH	SF	SB	CS	SB%	GDP	Avg	OBP	Slg
2007	Was	NL	15	28	4	1	0	0	(0	0)	5	0	1	0	1	0	8	0	0	0	0	0	-	0	.143	.172	.179
05	Col	NL	14	31	9	2	0	1	(1	0)	14	5	3	5	3	0	5	0	0	0	0	0	-	2	.290	.353	.452
05	Pit	NL	52	84	18	3	1	2	(0	2)	29	10	5	5	8	0	24	0	0	0	0	0	-	3	.214	.283	.345
	6 ML YEARS		152	268	64	13	3	6	(2	4)	101	37	21	25	28	0	68	1	0	0	1	0	1.00	10	.239	.313	.377

Al Reyes

Pitches: R **Bats:** R **Pos:** RP-61   **Ht:** 6'1" **Wt:** 230 **Born:** 4/10/1970 **Age:** 38

| | | | HOW MUCH HE PITCHED | | | | | | WHAT HE GAVE UP | | | | | | | | | | | THE RESULTS | | | | | | |
Year	Team	Lg	G	GS	CG	GF	IP	BFP	H	R	ER	HR	SH	SF	HB	TBB	IBB	SO	WP	Bk	W	L	Pct	ShO	Sv-Op	Hld	ERC	ERA
2007	VeroB*	A+	1	1	0	0	1.0	5	2	1	1	1	0	0	0	0	0	1	0	0	0	0	-	0	0--	-	16.28	9.00
1995	Mil	AL	27	0	0	13	33.1	138	19	9	9	3	1	2	3	18	2	29	0	0	1	1	.500	0	1-1	4	2.51	2.43
1996	Mil	AL	5	0	0	2	5.2	27	8	5	5	1	0	0	0	2	0	2	2	0	1	0	1.000	0	0-0	0	6.79	7.94
1997	Mil	AL	19	0	0	7	29.2	131	32	19	18	4	2	0	3	9	0	28	1	0	1	2	.333	0	1-1	1	4.76	5.46
1998	Mil	NL	50	0	0	13	57.0	253	55	26	25	9	2	1	2	31	1	58	2	0	5	1	.833	0	0-1	10	5.01	3.95
1999	2 Tms		53	0	0	12	65.2	287	50	33	33	9	4	3	6	41	3	67	3	0	4	3	.571	0	0-4	6	4.19	4.52
2000	2 Tms		19	0	0	6	19.2	86	15	10	10	2	1	2	0	12	1	18	0	0	1	0	1.000	0	0-1	3	3.43	4.58
2001	LAD	NL	19	0	0	9	25.2	120	28	13	11	3	0	2	1	13	1	23	0	1	2	1	.667	0	1-2	0	5.07	3.86
2002	Pit	NL	15	0	0	6	17.0	67	9	5	5	1	1	1	2	7	0	21	1	0	0	0	-	0	0-1	3	1.93	2.65
2003	NYY	AL	13	0	0	2	17.0	73	13	7	6	1	0	0	0	9	1	9	1	0	0	0	-	0	0-1	0	2.86	3.18
2004	StL	NL	12	2	0	4	12.0	41	3	1	1	0	2	0	0	2	0	11	0	0	0	0	-	0	0-0	0	0.31	0.75
2005	StL	NL	65	0	0	18	62.2	244	38	15	15	5	3	1	5	20	2	67	1	0	4	2	.667	0	3-3	16	1.94	2.15
2007	TB	AL	61	0	0	52	60.2	254	49	35	33	13	1	2	2	21	1	70	1	0	2	4	.333	0	26-30	0	3.60	4.90
99	Mil	NL	26	0	0	6	36.0	161	27	17	17	5	1	1	3	25	1	39	2	0	2	0	1.000	0	0-1	2	4.35	4.25
99	Bal	AL	27	0	0	6	29.2	126	23	16	16	4	3	2	3	16	2	28	1	0	2	3	.400	0	0-3	4	3.99	4.85
00	Bal	AL	13	0	0	2	13.0	62	13	10	10	2	1	2	0	11	1	10	0	0	1	0	1.000	0	0-1	2	6.14	6.92
00	LAD	NL	6	0	0	4	6.2	24	2	0	0	0	0	0	0	1	0	8	0	0	0	0	-	0	0-0	1	0.35	0.00
	12 ML YEARS		358	2	0	144	406.0	1721	319	178	171	51	17	14	24	185	12	403	12	1	21	14	.600	0	32-45	43	3.46	3.79

Anthony Reyes

Pitches: R **Bats:** R **Pos:** SP-20; RP-2   **Ht:** 6'2" **Wt:** 230 **Born:** 10/16/1981 **Age:** 26

| | | | HOW MUCH HE PITCHED | | | | | | WHAT HE GAVE UP | | | | | | | | | | | THE RESULTS | | | | | | |
Year	Team	Lg	G	GS	CG	GF	IP	BFP	H	R	ER	HR	SH	SF	HB	TBB	IBB	SO	WP	Bk	W	L	Pct	ShO	Sv-Op	Hld	ERC	ERA
2007	Memp*	AAA	6	6	1	0	36.2	142	27	12	12	4	3	1	2	11	0	32	1	0	1	1	.500	0	0--	-	2.70	2.95
2005	StL	NL	4	1	0	0	13.1	51	6	4	4	2	1	0	0	4	1	12	2	0	1	1	.500	0	0-0	0	1.32	2.70
2006	StL	NL	17	17	1	0	85.1	370	84	48	48	17	5	3	7	34	0	72	2	0	5	8	.385	0	0-0	0	5.08	5.06
2007	StL	NL	22	20	1	1	107.1	474	108	77	72	16	1	7	9	43	0	74	1	2	2	14	.125	0	0-0	0	4.78	6.04
	3 ML YEARS		43	38	2	1	206.0	895	198	129	124	35	7	11	16	81	1	158	5	2	8	23	.258	0	0-0	0	4.63	5.42

Dennys Reyes

Pitches: L **Bats:** R **Pos:** RP-50   **Ht:** 6'3" **Wt:** 245 **Born:** 4/19/1977 **Age:** 31

| | | | HOW MUCH HE PITCHED | | | | | | WHAT HE GAVE UP | | | | | | | | | | | THE RESULTS | | | | | | |
Year	Team	Lg	G	GS	CG	GF	IP	BFP	H	R	ER	HR	SH	SF	HB	TBB	IBB	SO	WP	Bk	W	L	Pct	ShO	Sv-Op	Hld	ERC	ERA
1997	LAD	NL	14	5	0	0	47.0	207	51	21	20	4	5	1	1	18	3	36	2	1	2	3	.400	0	0-0	0	4.34	3.83
1998	2 Tms	NL	19	10	0	4	67.1	300	62	36	34	3	7	2	1	47	5	77	6	1	3	5	.375	0	0-0	0	4.37	4.54
1999	Cin	NL	65	1	0	12	61.2	277	53	30	26	5	4	3	0	39	1	72	5	1	2	2	.500	0	2-3	14	4.16	3.79
2000	Cin	NL	62	0	0	15	43.2	200	43	31	22	5	3	3	1	29	0	36	5	0	2	1	.667	0	0-1	10	5.24	4.53
2001	Cin	NL	35	6	0	2	53.0	246	51	35	29	5	2	2	1	35	1	52	5	0	2	6	.250	0	0-0	4	4.77	4.92
2002	2 Tms	NL	58	5	0	15	82.2	378	98	52	49	10	3	2	0	45	4	59	10	1	4	4	.500	0	0-0	4	5.90	5.33
2003	2 Tms	NL	15	0	0	4	12.2	63	15	16	15	2	1	2	0	10	1	16	5	0	0	0	-	0	0-0	2	6.96	10.66
2004	KC	AL	40	12	0	5	108.0	483	114	64	57	12	7	5	4	50	3	91	6	2	4	8	.333	0	0-1	5	4.81	4.75
2005	SD	NL	36	1	0	9	43.2	215	57	30	25	3	1	0	1	32	2	35	3	1	3	2	.600	0	0-1	0	7.06	5.15
2006	Min	AL	66	0	0	8	50.2	194	35	8	5	3	1	0	0	15	2	49	4	0	5	0	1.000	0	0-1	16	1.90	0.89
2007	Min	AL	50	0	0	7	29.1	139	34	14	13	1	3	3	2	21	1	21	4	0	2	1	.667	0	0-0	8	6.08	3.99
98	LAD	NL	11	3	0	4	28.2	130	27	17	15	1	3	1	0	20	4	33	1	1	0	4	.000	0	0-0	0	4.16	4.71
98	Cin	NL	8	7	0	0	38.2	170	35	19	19	2	4	1	1	27	1	44	5	0	3	1	.750	0	0-0	0	4.54	4.42
02	Col	NL	43	0	0	13	40.1	182	43	19	19	1	2	2	0	24	3	30	4	0	0	0	1.000	0	0-0	4	4.55	4.24
02	Tex	AL	15	5	0	2	42.1	196	55	33	30	9	1	0	0	21	1	29	6	1	4	3	.571	0	0-0	0	7.24	6.38
03	Pit	NL	12	0	0	4	10.1	50	10	13	12	1	1	2	0	9	1	11	5	0	0	0	-	0	0-0	2	5.43	10.45
03	Ari	NL	3	0	0	0	2.1	13	5	3	3	1	0	0	0	1	0	5	0	0	0	0	-	0	0-0	0	14.73	11.57
	11 ML YEARS		460	40	0	81	599.2	2702	613	337	295	53	37	23	14	341	23	544	55	7	29	32	.475	0	2-7	65	4.82	4.43

Jo-Jo Reyes

Pitches: L **Bats:** L **Pos:** SP-10; RP-1   **Ht:** 6'2" **Wt:** 230 **Born:** 11/20/1984 **Age:** 23

| | | | HOW MUCH HE PITCHED | | | | | | WHAT HE GAVE UP | | | | | | | | | | | THE RESULTS | | | | | | |
Year	Team	Lg	G	GS	CG	GF	IP	BFP	H	R	ER	HR	SH	SF	HB	TBB	IBB	SO	WP	Bk	W	L	Pct	ShO	Sv-Op	Hld	ERC	ERA
2003	Braves	R	11	10	0	0	45.2	181	34	16	13	1	0	0	1	14	0	55	3	0	5	3	.625	0	0--	-	2.04	2.56
2004	Rome	A	15	14	1	1	74.1	328	84	49	44	10	7	4	2	25	2	71	3	3	2	4	.333	0	0--	-	4.86	5.33
2005	Braves	R	3	2	0	0	5.1	23	6	2	1	0	0	0	0	1	0	6	0	0	0	0	-	0	0--	-	3.17	1.69
2005	Danvle	R	9	8	0	0	43.1	170	37	18	17	3	1	1	0	6	0	27	2	1	3	0	1.000	0	0--	-	2.17	3.53
2006	Rome	A	13	13	1	0	75.1	311	62	26	25	5	1	2	7	25	0	84	5	0	8	1	.889	0	0--	-	3.03	2.99
2006	MrtlBh	A+	14	14	0	0	65.2	281	52	36	30	0	3	3	3	36	0	58	1	0	4	4	.500	0	0--	-	2.99	4.11
2007	Missi	AA	13	13	0	0	73.1	308	63	31	29	5	2	5	3	35	0	71	0	0	8	1	.889	0	0--	-	3.62	3.56
2007	Rchmd	AAA	6	6	0	0	36.0	143	25	7	4	2	1	0	0	12	0	39	0	0	4	0	1.000	0	0--	-	2.00	1.00
2007	Atl	NL	11	10	0	0	50.2	230	55	39	35	9	5	2	1	30	2	27	1	0	2	2	.500	0	0-0	0	6.06	6.22

Jose Reyes

Bats: B Throws: R Pos: SS-160   Ht: 6'1" Wt: 200 Born: 6/11/1983 Age: 25

								BATTING												BASERUNNING				AVERAGES		
Year	Team	Lg	G	AB	H	2B	3B	HR	(Hm Rd)	TB	R	RBI	RC	TBB	IBB	SO	HBP	SH	SF	SB	CS	SB%	GDP	Avg	OBP	Slg
2003	NYM	NL	69	274	84	12	4	5	(1 4)	119	47	32	36	13	0	36	0	2	3	13	3	.81	1	.307	.334	.434
2004	NYM	NL	53	220	56	16	2	2	(1 1)	82	33	14	25	5	0	31	0	4	0	19	2	.90	1	.255	.271	.373
2005	NYM	NL	161	696	190	24	17	7	(2 5)	269	99	58	84	27	0	78	2	4	4	60	15	.80	7	.273	.300	.386
2006	NYM	NL	153	647	194	30	17	19	(9 10)	315	122	81	121	53	6	81	1	2	0	64	17	.79	6	.300	.354	.487
2007	NYM	NL	160	681	191	36	12	12	(7 5)	287	119	57	99	77	13	78	1	5	1	78	21	.79	6	.280	.354	.421
5 ML YEARS			596	2518	715	118	52	45	(20 25)	1072	420	242	375	175	19	304	4	17	8	234	58	.80	21	.284	.330	.426

Mark Reynolds

Bats: R Throws: R Pos: 3B 104; PH-9; 2B-2; RF-2   Ht: 6'1" Wt: 200 Born: 8/3/1983 Age: 24

								BATTING												BASERUNNING				AVERAGES		
Year	Team	Lg	G	AB	H	2B	3B	HR	(Hm Rd)	TB	R	RBI	RC	TBB	IBB	SO	HBP	SH	SF	SB	CS	SB%	GDP	Avg	OBP	Slg
2004	Yakima	A-	64	234	64	19	1	12	(- -)	121	58	41	46	25	3	65	13	3	2	4	1	.80	3	.274	.372	.517
2004	Sbend	A	4	15	1	1	0	0	(- -)	2	0	0	0	1	0	5	0	0	0	0	0	-	0	.067	.125	.133
2004	Lancst	A+	4	12	1	0	0	0	(- -)	1	1	1	0	0	0	4	0	0	0	0	0	-	0	.083	.083	.083
2005	Sbend	A	118	434	110	26	2	19	(- -)	197	65	76	65	37	2	107	6	5	2	4	1	.80	7	.253	.319	.454
2006	Lancst	A+	76	273	92	18	2	23	(- -)	183	64	77	73	41	1	72	3	0	5	1	1	.50	3	.337	.422	.670
2006	Tenn	AA	30	114	31	7	0	8	(- -)	62	23	21	21	11	0	37	2	0	0	0	1	.00	1	.272	.346	.544
2007	Mobile	AA	37	134	41	9	2	6	(- -)	72	28	21	28	20	2	32	0	0	1	3	1	.75	6	.306	.394	.537
2007	Ari	NL	111	366	102	20	4	17	(7 10)	181	62	62	62	37	4	129	5	1	5	0	1	.00	5	.279	.349	.495

John Rheinecker

Pitches: L Bats: L Pos: RP-16; SP-7   Ht: 6'2" Wt: 230 Born: 5/29/1979 Age: 29

			HOW MUCH HE PITCHED						WHAT HE GAVE UP												THE RESULTS							
Year	Team	Lg	G	GS	CG	GF	IP	BFP	H	R	ER	HR	SH	SF	HB	TBB	IBB	SO	WP	Bk	W	L	Pct	ShO	Sv-Op	Hld	ERC	ERA
2001	Vancvr	A-	6	5	0	0	22.2	86	13	5	4	0	1	0	0	4	0	17	1	0	0	1	.000	0	0- -	-	0.99	1.59
2001	Mdest	A+	2	2	0	0	10.0	45	10	7	7	1	1	0	0	5	1	5	1	0	0	1	.000	0	0- -	-	4.20	6.30
2002	Visalia	A+	9	9	0	0	50.2	203	41	16	13	2	0	0	3	10	0	62	1	0	3	0	1.000	0	0- -	-	2.18	2.31
2002	Mdland	AA	20	20	1	0	128.0	540	137	63	48	7	3	6	7	24	1	100	6	1	7	7	.500	1	0- -	-	3.53	3.38
2003	Mdland	AA	23	23	1	0	142.1	640	186	90	75	13	3	4	7	32	1	89	3	1	9	6	.600	1	0- -	-	5.24	4.74
2003	Scrmto	AAA	6	6	0	0	38.0	171	47	19	16	1	0	2	2	12	1	26	0	1	2	1	1.000	0	0- -	-	4.70	3.79
2004	Scrmto	AAA	28	27	0	1	172.1	757	192	102	85	22	9	5	15	51	3	129	8	0	11	9	.550	0	0- -	-	4.84	4.44
2005	Scrmto	AAA	7	7	0	0	45.2	179	29	15	9	0	0	2	3	14	0	24	0	0	4	0	1.000	0	0- -	-	1.59	1.77
2006	Okla	AAA	15	15	2	0	93.0	378	93	33	26	5	2	0	2	24	0	68	3	0	4	5	.444	2	0- -	-	3.42	2.52
2007	Okla	AAA	9	9	0	0	58.0	235	59	26	23	4	2	2	1	12	0	30	1	0	4	2	.667	0	0- -	-	3.38	3.57
2006	Tex	AL	21	13	0	0	70.2	322	104	46	46	6	1	1	3	19	0	28	0	0	4	6	.400	0	0-0	1	6.57	5.86
2007	Tox	AL	23	7	0	0	50.1	239	61	38	30	9	1	1	2	28	2	40	3	0	4	3	.571	0	0-0	2	6.64	5.36
2 ML YEARS			44	20	0	2	121.0	561	165	84	76	15	2	2	5	47	2	68	3	0	8	9	.471	0	0-0	3	6.60	5.65

Danny Richar

Bats: L Throws: R Pos: 2B-56; PR-1   Ht: 6'0" Wt: 170 Born: 6/9/1983 Age: 25

								BATTING												BASERUNNING				AVERAGES		
Year	Team	Lg	G	AB	H	2B	3B	HR	(Hm Rd)	TB	R	RBI	RC	TBB	IBB	SO	HBP	SH	SF	SB	CS	SB%	GDP	Avg	OBP	Slg
2002	Lancst	A+	85	251	58	7	1	1	(- -)	70	27	17	18	12	0	49	3	10	0	4	5	.44	2	.231	.274	.279
2002	Yakima	A-	25	88	20	5	1	0	(- -)	27	7	9	6	6	0	21	0	1	1	0	3	.00	2	.227	.274	.307
2003	Lancst	A+	123	405	123	19	9	1	(- -)	163	51	42	54	14	0	70	3	10	1	6	3	.67	10	.304	.331	.402
2004	ElPaso	AA	26	82	17	3	0	0	(- -)	20	6	5	6	7	0	17	2	0	0	2	0	1.00	0	.207	.286	.244
2004	Lancst	A+	96	383	108	13	4	6	(- -)	147	51	44	48	16	0	78	2	13	3	22	8	.73	2	.282	.312	.384
2005	Lancst	A+	121	454	136	32	8	20	(- -)	244	78	79	85	32	0	64	3	10	4	9	3	.75	10	.300	.347	.537
2006	Tenn	AA	129	480	140	25	5	8	(- -)	199	79	42	77	52	2	77	3	6	7	15	5	.75	2	.292	.360	.415
2007	Tucsn	AAA	66	265	75	19	4	8	(- -)	126	39	46	43	27	2	47	0	3	2	3	5	.38	2	.283	.347	.475
2007	Charltt	AAA	32	133	46	5	4	5	(- -)	74	21	15	29	10	2	24	2	0	0	4	0	1.00	4	.346	.400	.556
2007	CWS	AL	56	187	43	9	3	6	(3 3)	76	30	15	21	16	0	33	0	2	1	1	3	.25	5	.230	.289	.406

Jeff Ridgway

Pitches: L Bats: R Pos: RP-3   Ht: 6'3" Wt: 190 Born: 8/17/1980 Age: 27

			HOW MUCH HE PITCHED						WHAT HE GAVE UP												THE RESULTS							
Year	Team	Lg	G	GS	CG	GF	IP	BFP	H	R	ER	HR	SH	SF	HB	TBB	IBB	SO	WP	Bk	W	L	Pct	ShO	Sv-Op	Hld	ERC	ERA
2000	Princtn	R+	12	12	0	0	54.2	237	47	24	15	2	0	2	1	30	0	60	6	0	3	4	.429	0	0- -	-	3.49	2.47
2001	CtnSC	A	22	22	0	0	104.0	458	110	55	47	4	2	2	9	42	0	71	11	0	7	8	.467	0	0- -	-	4.34	4.07
2003	CtnSC	A	24	19	0	1	99.1	444	102	63	46	2	7	4	12	41	0	74	5	1	5	8	.385	0	0- -	-	4.14	4.17
2004	Bkrsfld	A+	15	1	0	1	35.0	155	32	17	9	0	1	0	2	19	1	27	3	0	2	3	.400	0	1- -	-	3.57	2.31
2005	Visalia	A+	24	0	0	9	45.0	218	43	31	26	2	7	5	3	36	0	56	7	0	3	4	.429	0	0- -	-	5.06	5.20
2006	Mont	AA	16	0	0	4	19.1	79	10	5	5	1	4	0	2	7	0	29	1	0	1	0	1.000	0	2- -	-	1.57	2.33
2006	Drham	AAA	34	0	0	9	38.2	166	35	15	13	3	2	2	2	13	0	38	2	0	1	4	.200	0	0- -	-	3.28	3.03
2007	Drham	AAA	54	0	0	15	64.2	275	54	25	22	8	4	2	2	30	1	67	4	0	2	3	.400	0	4- -	-	3.67	3.06
2007	TB	AL	3	0	0	0	0.1	10	7	7	7	1	0	0	1	1	0	0	0	0	0	0	-	0	0-0	0	276.0	189.0

Shawn Riggans

Bats: R **Throws:** R **Pos:** C-3   **Ht:** 6'2" **Wt:** 210 **Born:** 7/25/1980 **Age:** 27

Year	Team	Lg	G	AB	H	2B	3B	HR	(Hm	Rd)	TB	R	RBI	RC	TBB	IBB	SO	HBP	SH	SF	SB	CS	SB%	GDP	Avg	OBP	Slg
2001	Princtn	R+	15	58	20	4	0	6	(-	-)	48	15	17	18	9	0	18	0	0	0	1	0	1.00	0	.345	.433	.828
2002	HudVal	A-	73	266	70	13	0	9	(-	-)	110	34	48	39	32	1	72	1	2	1	2	2	.50	0	.263	.343	.414
2003	CtnSC	A	68	232	65	17	0	3	(-	-)	91	33	34	32	19	0	35	4	1	4	3	4	.43	8	.280	.340	.392
2003	Orlndo	AA	22	62	17	6	0	1	(-	-)	26	7	11	8	4	0	14	1	0	2	0	0	-	0	.274	.319	.419
2004	Bkrsfld	A+	34	127	44	11	0	5	(-	-)	70	20	22	28	15	0	23	1	0	1	0	1	.00	3	.346	.417	.551
2004	Mont	AA	10	36	8	1	0	2	(-	-)	15	3	7	4	2	0	14	1	0	0	0	0	-	2	.222	.282	.417
2005	Mont	AA	89	313	97	21	0	8	(-	-)	142	40	53	53	26	0	69	4	2	5	1	2	.33	11	.310	.365	.454
2006	Drham	AAA	115	417	122	26	2	11	(-	-)	185	43	54	64	27	1	88	5	2	2	2	2	.50	11	.293	.341	.444
2007	VeroB	A+	8	30	9	2	0	0	(-	-)	11	3	5	3	1	0	5	0	0	0	0	0	-	0	.300	.323	.367
2007	Drham	AAA	33	121	34	9	1	4	(-	-)	57	10	16	18	4	0	30	6	1	1	0	3	.00	6	.281	.333	.471
2006	TB	AL	10	29	5	1	0	0	(0	0)	6	3	1	0	4	0	7	0	0	0	0	0	-	1	.172	.273	.207
2007	TB	AL	3	10	1	0	0	0	(0	0)	1	1	2	0	0	0	1	0	0	0	0	0	-	1	.100	.100	.100
	2 ML YEARS		13	39	6	1	0	0	(0	0)	7	4	3	0	4	0	8	0	0	0	0	0	-	2	.154	.233	.179

Juan Rincon

Pitches: R **Bats:** R **Pos:** RP-63   **Ht:** 5'11" **Wt:** 210 **Born:** 1/23/1979 **Age:** 29

			HOW MUCH HE PITCHED						WHAT HE GAVE UP										THE RESULTS							
Year	Team	Lg	G	GS	CG	GF	IP	BFP	H	R	ER	HR	SH	SF	HB	TBB	IBB	SO	WP	Bk	W	L	Pct	ShO	Sv-Op	Hld	ERC	ERA
2001	Min	AL	4	0	0	1	5.2	28	7	5	4	1	1	0	0	5	0	4	0	0	0	0	-	0	0-0	0	8.33	6.35
2002	Min	AL	10	3	0	0	31.2	135	44	23	20	5	0	1	0	9	0	21	2	0	0	2	.000	0	0-1	0	7.62	6.28
2003	Min	AL	58	0	0	20	85.2	370	74	38	35	5	2	5	4	38	7	63	7	0	5	6	.455	0	0-1	5	3.21	3.68
2004	Min	AL	77	0	0	18	82.0	327	52	27	24	5	3	3	2	32	1	106	2	0	11	6	.647	0	2-6	16	2.00	2.63
2005	Min	AL	75	0	0	18	77.0	319	63	26	21	2	4	1	3	30	3	84	5	1	6	6	.500	0	0-5	25	2.68	2.45
2006	Min	AL	75	0	0	22	74.1	315	76	30	24	2	5	1	3	24	3	65	2	0	3	1	.750	0	1-3	26	3.53	2.91
2007	Min	AL	63	0	0	16	59.2	272	65	38	34	9	2	1	3	28	3	49	4	0	3	3	.500	0	0-2	14	5.31	5.13
	7 ML YEARS		362	3	0	95	413.0	1766	381	187	162	29	17	12	15	166	17	392	22	1	28	24	.538	0	3-18	86	3.52	3.53

Royce Ring

Pitches: L **Bats:** L **Pos:** RP-26   **Ht:** 6'0" **Wt:** 220 **Born:** 12/21/1980 **Age:** 27

			HOW MUCH HE PITCHED						WHAT HE GAVE UP										THE RESULTS							
Year	Team	Lg	G	GS	CG	GF	IP	BFP	H	R	ER	HR	SH	SF	HB	TBB	IBB	SO	WP	Bk	W	L	Pct	ShO	Sv-Op	Hld	ERC	ERA
2007	Portlnd*	AAA	27	0	0	6	31.2	129	22	8	7	0	1	0	0	11	1	44	1	0	4	0	1.000	0	1--	-	1.65	1.99
2007	Rchmd*	AAA	15	0	0	3	12.2	61	17	9	8	2	1	1	1	7	1	14	1	0	1	2	.333	0	1--	-	7.53	5.68
2005	NYM	NL	15	0	0	2	10.2	51	10	6	6	0	1	0	0	10	1	8	0	0	0	2	.000	0	0-0	3	4.80	5.06
2006	NYM	NL	11	0	0	2	12.2	48	7	3	3	2	0	0	0	3	0	8	0	0	0	0	-	0	0-0	2	1.60	2.13
2007	2 Tms	NL	26	0	0	7	20.0	88	13	8	6	1	0	1	0	17	2	21	2	0	1	0	1.000	0	0-0	0	3.33	2.70
07	SD	NL	15	0	0	4	15.0	69	11	8	6	1	0	0	0	14	2	17	2	0	1	0	1.000	0	0-0	0	4.10	3.60
07	Atl	NL	11	0	0	3	5.0	19	2	0	0	0	0	1	0	3	0	4	0	0	0	0	-	0	0-0	0	1.39	0.00
	3 ML YEARS		52	0	0	11	43.1	187	30	17	15	3	1	1	0	30	3	37	2	0	1	2	.333	0	0-0	5	3.17	3.12

Alex Rios

Bats: R **Throws:** R **Pos:** RF-147; CF-22; PH-2   **Ht:** 6'5" **Wt:** 194 **Born:** 2/18/1981 **Age:** 27

Year	Team	Lg	G	AB	H	2B	3B	HR	(Hm	Rd)	TB	R	RBI	RC	TBB	IBB	SO	HBP	SH	SF	SB	CS	SB%	GDP	Avg	OBP	Slg
2004	Tor	AL	111	426	122	24	7	1	(0	1)	163	55	28	49	31	0	84	2	1	0	15	3	.83	14	.286	.338	.383
2005	Tor	AL	146	481	126	23	6	10	(5	5)	191	71	59	56	28	1	101	5	0	5	14	9	.61	14	.262	.306	.397
2006	Tor	AL	128	450	136	33	6	17	(12	5)	232	68	82	83	35	1	89	3	0	10	15	6	.71	10	.302	.349	.516
2007	Tor	AL	161	643	191	43	7	24	(13	11)	320	114	85	105	55	3	103	6	0	7	17	4	.81	9	.297	.354	.498
	4 ML YEARS		546	2000	575	123	26	52	(30	22)	906	308	254	293	149	5	377	16	1	22	61	22	.73	47	.288	.338	.453

David Riske

Pitches: R **Bats:** R **Pos:** RP-65   **Ht:** 6'2" **Wt:** 180 **Born:** 10/23/1976 **Age:** 31

			HOW MUCH HE PITCHED						WHAT HE GAVE UP										THE RESULTS							
Year	Team	Lg	G	GS	CG	GF	IP	BFP	H	R	ER	HR	SH	SF	HB	TBB	IBB	SO	WP	Bk	W	L	Pct	ShO	Sv-Op	Hld	ERC	ERA
1999	Cle	AL	12	0	0	3	14.0	68	20	15	13	2	1	1	0	6	0	16	0	0	1	1	.500	0	0-1	0	6.96	8.36
2001	Cle	AL	26	0	0	6	27.1	118	20	7	6	3	0	1	2	18	3	29	1	0	2	0	1.000	0	1-1	3	3.81	1.98
2002	Cle	AL	51	0	0	17	51.1	237	49	32	30	8	4	3	4	35	4	65	1	0	2	2	.500	0	1-1	5	5.55	5.26
2003	Cle	AL	68	0	0	24	74.2	293	52	21	19	9	4	1	3	20	3	82	1	0	2	2	.500	0	8-13	17	2.26	2.29
2004	Cle	AL	72	0	0	27	77.1	336	69	32	32	11	3	2	2	41	4	78	3	0	7	3	.700	0	5-12	9	4.32	3.72
2005	Cle	AL	58	0	0	33	72.2	288	55	28	25	11	3	1	4	15	0	48	0	0	3	4	.429	0	1-1	0	2.59	3.10
2006	2 Tms	AL	41	0	0	12	44.0	189	40	20	19	6	1	2	3	17	1	28	0	0	1	2	.333	0	0-1	3	3.98	3.89
2007	KC	AL	65	0	0	27	69.2	289	61	19	19	8	4	3	1	27	4	52	0	0	1	4	.200	0	4-8	16	3.46	2.45
06	Bos	AL	8	0	0	2	9.2	42	8	4	4	2	1	0	2	3	0	5	0	0	0	1	.000	0	0-0	0	4.23	3.72
06	CWS	AL	33	0	0	10	34.1	147	32	16	15	4	0	2	1	14	1	23	0	0	1	1	.500	0	0-1	3	3.91	3.93
	8 ML YEARS		393	0	0	149	431.0	1818	366	174	163	58	20	14	19	179	19	398	6	0	19	18	.514	0	20-38	52	3.66	3.40

Luis Rivas

Bats: R Throws: R Pos: 2B-2; SS-1; PH-1; PR-1   Ht: 5'11" Wt: 190 Born: 8/30/1979 Age: 28

									BATTING													BASERUNNING				AVERAGES		
Year	Team	Lg	G	AB	H	2B	3B	HR	(Hm	Rd)	TB	R	RBI	RC	TBB	IBB	SO	HBP	SH	SF		SB	CS	SB%	GDP	Avg	OBP	Slg
2007	Buffalo*	AAA	105	410	108	17	3	11	(-	-)	164	58	43	59	42	1	69	7	4	2		13	7	.65	15	.263	.341	.400
2000	Min	AL	16	58	18	4	1	0	(0	0)	24	8	6	8	2	0	4	0	2	2		2	0	1.00	2	.310	.323	.414
2001	Min	AL	153	563	150	21	6	7	(3	4)	204	70	47	65	40	0	99	6	5	5		31	11	.74	15	.266	.319	.362
2002	Min	AL	93	316	81	23	4	4	(2	2)	124	46	35	35	19	2	51	3	8	0		9	4	.69	12	.256	.305	.392
2003	Min	AL	135	475	123	16	9	8	(4	4)	181	69	43	46	30	0	65	5	8	3		17	7	.71	20	.259	.308	.381
2004	Min	AL	109	336	86	19	5	10	(4	6)	145	44	34	34	13	0	53	1	5	3		15	1	.94	8	.256	.283	.432
2005	Min	AL	59	136	35	3	1	1	(0	1)	43	21	12	16	9	0	17	2	0	1		4	0	1.00	2	.257	.311	.316
2007	Cle	AL	4	11	3	0	1	0	(0	1)	8	3	4	2	0	0	0	0	0	0		0	0	-	0	.273	.273	.727
	7 ML YEARS		569	1895	496	86	27	31	(13	18)	729	261	181	206	113	2	289	17	28	14		78	23	.77	59	.262	.307	.385

Juan Rivera

Bats: R Throws: R Pos: RF-7; DH-4; LF-2; PH-2   Ht: 6'2" Wt: 225 Born: 7/3/1978 Age: 29

									BATTING													BASERUNNING				AVERAGES		
Year	Team	Lg	G	AB	H	2B	3B	HR	(Hm	Rd)	TB	R	RBI	RC	TBB	IBB	SO	HBP	SH	SF		SB	CS	SB%	GDP	Avg	OBP	Slg
2007	RCuca*	A+	3	10	4	1	0	0	(-	-)	5	3	2	1	0	0	2	0	0	0		0	0	-	0	.400	.400	.500
2007	Salt Lk*	AAA	15	61	16	8	0	0	(-	-)	24	4	17	7	3	0	6	0	0	1		0	0	-	8	.262	.292	.393
2001	NYY	AL	3	4	0	0	0	0	(0	0)	0	0	0	0	0	0	0	0	0	0		0	0	-	0	.000	.000	.000
2002	NYY	AL	28	83	22	5	0	1	(0	1)	30	9	6	8	6	0	10	0	1	1		1	1	.50	4	.265	.311	.361
2003	NYY	AL	57	173	46	14	0	7	(4	3)	81	22	26	23	10	1	27	0	1	1		0	0	-	8	.266	.304	.468
2004	Mon	NL	134	391	120	24	1	12	(6	6)	182	48	49	60	34	7	45	1	0	0		6	2	.75	11	.307	.364	.465
2005	LAA	AL	106	350	95	17	1	15	(8	7)	159	46	59	49	23	0	44	0	2	1		1	9	.10	15	.271	.316	.454
2006	LAA	AL	124	448	139	27	0	23	(12	11)	235	65	85	80	33	0	59	7	0	6		0	4	.00	14	.310	.362	.525
2007	LAA	AL	14	43	12	1	0	2	(1	1)	19	3	8	5	1	0	4	0	0	0		0	0	-	5	.279	.295	.442
	7 ML YEARS		466	1492	434	88	2	60	(31	29)	706	193	233	225	107	8	189	8	4	9		8	16	.33	57	.291	.340	.473

Mariano Rivera

Pitches: R Bats: R Pos: RP-67   Ht: 6'2" Wt: 185 Born: 11/29/1969 Age: 38

			HOW MUCH HE PITCHED						WHAT HE GAVE UP												THE RESULTS							
Year	Team	Lg	G	GS	CG	GF	IP	BFP	H	R	ER	HR	SH	SF	HB	TBB	IBB	SO	WP	Bk	W	L	Pct	ShO	Sv-Op	Hld	ERC	ERA
1995	NYY	AL	19	10	0	2	67.0	301	71	43	41	11	0	2	2	30	0	51	0	1	5	3	.625	0	0-1	0	5.14	5.51
1996	NYY	AL	61	0	0	14	107.2	425	73	25	25	1	2	1	2	34	3	130	1	0	8	3	.727	0	5-8	27	1.65	2.09
1997	NYY	AL	66	0	0	56	71.2	301	65	17	15	5	3	4	0	20	6	68	2	0	6	4	.600	0	43-52	0	2.73	1.88
1998	NYY	AL	54	0	0	49	61.1	246	48	13	13	3	2	3	1	17	1	36	0	0	3	0	1.000	0	36-41	0	2.21	1.91
1999	NYY	AL	66	0	0	63	69.0	268	43	15	14	2	0	2	3	18	3	52	2	1	4	3	.571	0	45-49	0	1.47	1.83
2000	NYY	AL	66	0	0	61	75.2	311	58	26	24	4	5	2	0	25	3	58	2	0	7	4	.636	0	36-41	0	2.20	2.85
2001	NYY	AL	71	0	0	66	80.2	310	61	24	21	5	4	1	0	12	2	83	1	0	4	6	.400	0	50-57	0	1.74	2.34
2002	NYY	AL	45	0	0	37	46.0	187	35	16	14	3	2	0	2	11	2	41	1	1	1	4	.200	0	28-32	2	2.08	2.74
2003	NYY	AL	64	0	0	57	70.2	277	61	15	13	3	1	2	4	10	1	63	0	0	5	2	.714	0	40-46	0	2.29	1.66
2004	NYY	AL	74	0	0	69	78.2	316	65	17	17	3	2	0	5	20	3	66	0	0	4	2	.667	0	53-57	0	2.45	1.94
2005	NYY	AL	71	0	0	67	78.1	306	50	18	12	2	0	1	4	18	0	80	0	0	7	4	.636	0	43-47	0	1.48	1.38
2006	NYY	AL	63	0	0	59	75.0	293	61	16	15	3	1	2	5	11	4	55	0	0	5	5	.500	0	34-37	0	2.03	1.80
2007	NYY	AL	67	0	0	59	71.1	295	68	25	25	4	1	1	6	12	2	74	1	0	3	4	.429	0	30-34	0	2.92	3.15
	13 ML YEARS		787	10	0	659	953.0	3836	759	270	249	49	23	21	35	238	30	857	10	3	62	44	.585	0	443-502	29	2.24	2.35

Mike Rivera

Bats: R Throws: R Pos: C-11; PH-1   Ht: 6'0" Wt: 210 Born: 9/8/1976 Age: 31

									BATTING													BASERUNNING				AVERAGES		
Year	Team	Lg	G	AB	H	2B	3B	HR	(Hm	Rd)	TB	R	RBI	RC	TBB	IBB	SO	HBP	SH	SF		SB	CS	SB%	GDP	Avg	OBP	Slg
2007	Nashv*	AAA	96	349	75	15	0	19	(-	-)	147	37	46	40	24	3	71	4	0	5		5	5	.50	18	.215	.270	.421
2001	Det	AL	4	12	4	2	0	0	(0	0)	6	2	1	2	0	0	2	0	0	0		0	0	-	0	.333	.333	.500
2002	Det	AL	39	132	30	8	1	1	(0	1)	43	11	11	8	4	0	35	1	0	1		0	0	-	5	.227	.254	.326
2003	SD	NL	19	53	9	1	0	1	(0	1)	13	2	2	0	5	0	11	0	0	0		0	0	-	4	.170	.241	.245
2006	Mil	NL	46	142	38	9	0	6	(3	3)	65	16	24	19	10	5	21	3	1	2		0	0	-	0	.268	.325	.458
2007	Mil	NL	11	13	3	0	0	2	(1	1)	9	2	3	2	1	0	3	0	1	0		0	0	-	0	.231	.286	.692
	5 ML YEARS		119	352	84	20	1	10	(4	6)	136	33	41	31	20	5	72	4	2	3		0	0	-	12	.239	.285	.386

Saul Rivera

Pitches: R Bats: L Pos: RP-85   Ht: 5'11" Wt: 155 Born: 12/7/1977 Age: 30

			HOW MUCH HE PITCHED						WHAT HE GAVE UP												THE RESULTS							
Year	Team	Lg	G	GS	CG	GF	IP	BFP	H	R	ER	HR	SH	SF	HB	TBB	IBB	SO	WP	Bk	W	L	Pct	ShO	Sv-Op	Hld	ERC	ERA
1998	Elizab	R+	23	0	0	21	36.0	147	19	10	9	4	2	0	0	19	2	65	1	0	3	3	.500	0	7--	-	2.06	2.25
1999	QuadC	A	60	0	0	54	69.2	283	42	12	11	0	2	0	0	36	5	102	2	0	4	1	.800	0	23--	-	1.73	1.42
2000	FtMyrs	A+	29	0	0	22	37.2	166	34	15	15	0	2	0	0	19	3	45	6	1	8	1	.889	0	5--	-	3.02	3.58
2000	NwBrit	AA	22	0	0	7	37.0	163	28	16	16	0	2	1	2	22	0	47	8	0	1	0	1.000	0	0--	-	2.91	3.89
2001	NwBrit	AA	33	0	0	27	42.2	181	35	16	15	3	2	1	1	18	1	55	1	0	5	2	.714	0	13--	-	3.00	3.16
2001	Twins	R	3	0	0	0	3.0	13	2	0	0	0	0	0	0	1	0	4	0	0	0	0	-	0	0--	-	1.45	0.00
2002	Bnghtn	AA	30	0	0	24	38.2	165	25	18	13	2	1	3	1	23	2	32	1	0	2	3	.400	0	13--	-	2.56	3.03
2002	Hrsbrg	AA	15	0	0	9	19.0	89	21	8	7	0	3	0	4	9	1	15	2	1	0	2	.000	0	3--	-	4.90	3.32
2004	Hrsbrg	AA	18	0	0	12	21.0	101	27	22	18	0	6	1	0	12	2	15	1	1	0	2	.000	0	3--	-	6.85	7.71
2004	Hntsvl	AA	26	0	0	10	33.1	146	30	11	6	1	0	0	0	16	1	25	0	0	0	1	.667	0	1--	-	3.21	1.62
2005	Hrsbrg	AA	40	0	0	29	76.2	326	72	30	21	3	7	0	3	20	6	70	3	0	3	3	.500	0	9--	-	2.77	2.47
2006	NewOr	AAA	12	2	0	3	28.1	125	25	7	5	1	3	0	4	12	1	25	4	0	1	1	.500	0	1--	-	3.48	1.59

Year Team	Lg		G	GS	CG	GF	IP	BFP	H	R	ER	HR	SH	SF	HB	TBB	IBB	SO	WP	Bk	W	L	Pct	ShO	Sv-Op	Hld	ERC	ERA
			HOW MUCH HE PITCHED						**WHAT HE GAVE UP**												**THE RESULTS**							
2007 Clmbs	AAA		1	0	0	1	0.2	4	2	1	1	0	1	0	0	0	0	0	0	0	0	1	.000	0	0--	-	14.52	13.50
2006 Was	NL		54	0	0	16	60.1	277	59	28	23	4	4	1	4	32	6	41	3	0	3	0	1.000	0	1-3	9	4.17	3.43
2007 Was	NL		85	0	0	17	93.0	398	88	39	38	1	5	4	2	42	4	64	4	0	4	6	.400	0	3-5	19	3.39	3.68
2 ML YEARS			139	0	0	33	153.1	675	147	67	61	5	9	5	6	74	10	105	7	0	7	6	.538	0	4-8	28	3.70	3.58

Chris Roberson

Bats: B **Throws:** R **Pos:** RF-16; PR-9; PH-5; CF-2; LF-1   **Ht:** 6'2" **Wt:** 180 **Born:** 8/23/1979 **Age:** 28

Year Team	Lg	G	AB	H	2B	3B	HR	(Hm	Rd)	TB	R	RBI	RC	TBB	IBB	SO	HBP	SH	SF	SB	CS	SB%	GDP	Avg	OBP	Slg
								BATTING												**BASERUNNING**				**AVERAGES**		
2001 Phillies	R	38	133	33	8	1	0	(-	-)	43	17	13	16	16	0	30	2	5	1	6	2	.75	3	.248	.336	.323
2002 Batvia	A-	62	214	59	8	3	2	(-	-)	79	29	24	33	26	0	51	10	1	2	17	8	.68	2	.276	.377	.369
2003 Lakwd	A	132	470	110	19	5	2	(-	-)	145	64	32	59	57	1	108	12	8	1	59	16	.79	9	.234	.331	.309
2004 Clrwtr	A+	83	313	96	13	6	9	(-	-)	148	52	38	53	27	0	71	5	0	0	16	12	.57	5	.307	.371	.473
2005 Rdng	AA	139	553	172	24	8	15	(-	-)	257	90	70	96	40	2	112	9	5	4	34	14	.71	6	.311	.365	.465
2006 S-WB	AAA	74	284	83	14	2	1	(-	-)	104	44	17	40	23	0	57	3	4	2	25	9	.74	7	.292	.349	.366
2007 Ottawa	AAA	113	463	123	21	3	4	(-	-)	162	64	48	54	31	1	57	3	7	5	19	9	.68	7	.266	.313	.350
2006 Phi	NL	57	41	8	0	1	0	(0	0)	10	9	1	2	0	0	9	1	1	0	3	0	1.00	0	.195	.214	.244
2007 Phi	NL	28	28	8	0	0	0	(0	0)	8	6	1	3	1	0	4	0	0	0	2	0	1.00	0	.286	.310	.286
2 ML YEARS		85	69	16	0	1	0	(0	0)	18	15	2	5	1	0	13	1	1	0	5	0	1.00	0	.232	.254	.261

Brian Roberts

Bats: B **Throws:** R **Pos:** 2B-154; PH-4   **Ht:** 5'9" **Wt:** 175 **Born:** 10/9/1977 **Age:** 30

Year Team	Lg	G	AB	H	2B	3B	HR	(Hm	Rd)	TB	R	RBI	RC	TBB	IBB	SO	HBP	SH	SF	SB	CS	SB%	GDP	Avg	OBP	Slg
								BATTING												**BASERUNNING**				**AVERAGES**		
2001 Bal	AL	75	273	69	12	3	2	(0	2)	93	42	17	27	13	0	36	0	3	3	12	3	.80	3	.253	.284	.341
2002 Bal	AL	38	128	29	6	0	1	(1	0)	38	18	11	12	15	0	21	1	3	2	9	2	.82	3	.227	.308	.297
2003 Bal	AL	112	460	124	22	4	5	(3	2)	169	65	41	62	46	1	58	1	4	1	23	6	.79	9	.270	.337	.367
2004 Bal	AL	159	641	175	50	2	4	(0	4)	241	107	53	91	71	1	95	1	15	6	29	12	.71	3	.273	.344	.376
2005 Bal	AL	143	561	176	45	7	18	(9	9)	289	92	73	106	67	5	83	3	5	4	27	10	.73	6	.314	.387	.515
2006 Bal	AL	138	563	161	34	3	10	(6	4)	231	85	55	74	55	4	66	0	6	5	36	7	.84	16	.286	.347	.410
2007 Bal	AL	156	621	180	42	5	12	(6	6)	268	103	57	105	89	6	99	0	2	4	50	7	.88	8	.290	.377	.432
7 ML YEARS		821	3247	914	211	24	52	(25	27)	1329	512	307	477	356	17	458	6	38	25	186	47	.80	48	.281	.351	.409

Dave Roberts

Bats: L **Throws:** L **Pos:** CF-92; LF-20; PH-10; PR-5   **Ht:** 5'10" **Wt:** 180 **Born:** 5/31/1972 **Age:** 36

Year Team	Lg	G	AB	H	2B	3B	HR	(Hm	Rd)	TB	R	RBI	RC	TBB	IBB	SO	HBP	SH	SF	SB	CS	SB%	GDP	Avg	OBP	Slg
								BATTING												**BASERUNNING**				**AVERAGES**		
2007 Fresno*	AAA	2	7	1	0	0	0	(-	-)	1	1	0	0	1	0	2	0	0	0	0	0	-	0	.143	.250	.143
1999 Cle	AL	41	143	34	4	0	2	(1	1)	44	26	12	14	9	0	16	0	3	1	11	3	.79	0	.238	.281	.308
2000 Cle	AL	19	10	2	0	0	0	(0	0)	2	1	0	1	2	0	2	0	1	0	1	1	.50	0	.200	.333	.200
2001 Cle	AL	15	12	4	1	0	0	(0	0)	5	3	2	2	1	0	2	0	0	0	1	0	1.00	0	.333	.385	.417
2002 LAD	NL	127	422	117	14	7	3	(0	3)	154	63	34	67	48	0	51	2	6	1	45	10	.82	1	.277	.353	.365
2003 LAD	NL	107	388	97	6	5	2	(1	1)	119	56	16	43	43	1	39	4	5	0	40	14	.74	0	.250	.331	.307
2004 2 Tms		113	319	81	14	7	4	(2	2)	121	64	35	52	38	0	48	5	3	6	38	3	.93	4	.254	.337	.379
2005 SD	NL	115	411	113	19	10	8	(5	3)	176	65	38	59	53	3	59	1	11	4	23	12	.66	9	.275	.356	.428
2006 SD	NL	129	499	146	18	13	2	(1	1)	196	80	44	81	51	2	61	4	7	5	49	6	.89	5	.293	.360	.393
2007 SF	NL	114	396	103	17	9	2	(1	1)	144	61	23	51	42	1	66	0	4	0	31	5	.86	4	.260	.331	.364
04 LAD	NL	68	233	59	4	7	2	(1	1)	83	45	21	41	28	0	31	4	2	3	33	1	.97	2	.253	.340	.356
04 Bos	AL	45	86	22	10	0	2	(1	1)	38	19	14	11	10	0	17	1	1	3	5	2	.71	2	.256	.330	.442
9 ML YEARS		780	2600	697	93	51	23	(11	12)	961	419	204	370	287	7	344	16	40	17	238	55	.81	23	.268	.342	.370

Ryan Roberts

Bats: R **Throws:** R **Pos:** 3B-3; PH-2; 2B-1; LF-1; DH-1; PR-1   **Ht:** 5'11" **Wt:** 190 **Born:** 9/19/1980 **Age:** 27

Year Team	Lg	G	AB	H	2B	3B	HR	(Hm	Rd)	TB	R	RBI	RC	TBB	IBB	SO	HBP	SH	SF	SB	CS	SB%	GDP	Avg	OBP	Slg
								BATTING												**BASERUNNING**				**AVERAGES**		
2003 Auburn	A-	66	248	69	10	3	8	(-	-)	109	52	36	43	35	0	63	4	0	2	7	3	.70	10	.278	.374	.440
2004 CtnWV	A	64	226	64	9	0	13	(-	-)	112	38	39	53	55	1	50	9	0	1	0	0	-	6	.283	.440	.496
2004 Dnedin	A+	59	205	49	1	1	7	(-	-)	73	29	25	28	36	2	51	1	0	4	0	3	.00	8	.239	.350	.356
2005 Dnedin	A+	42	164	47	9	0	9	(-	-)	83	33	35	33	24	0	27	2	0	2	6	1	.86	5	.287	.380	.506
2005 NHam	AA	92	338	92	19	3	15	(-	-)	162	54	44	64	55	5	94	4	1	1	5	1	.83	6	.272	.379	.479
2006 Syrcse	AAA	98	362	99	28	1	10	(-	-)	159	44	49	54	30	0	86	2	6	3	5	3	.63	5	.273	.330	.439
2007 Syrcse	AAA	100	337	84	16	1	12	(-	-)	138	46	47	52	55	1	85	2	2	3	1	2	.33	13	.249	.355	.409
2006 Tor	AL	9	13	1	0	0	1	(0	1)	4	1	1	0	1	0	4	0	0	0	0	0	-	1	.077	.143	.308
2007 Tor	AL	8	13	1	0	0	0	(0	0)	1	2	0	0	2	0	7	1	0	0	0	0	-	0	.077	.250	.077
2 ML YEARS		17	26	2	0	0	1	(0	1)	5	3	1	0	3	0	11	1	0	0	0	0	-	1	.077	.200	.192

Connor Robertson

Pitches: R **Bats:** R **Pos:** RP-3   **Ht:** 6'2" **Wt:** 225 **Born:** 9/10/1981 **Age:** 26

Year Team	Lg	G	GS	CG	GF	IP	BFP	H	R	ER	HR	SH	SF	HB	TBB	IBB	SO	WP	Bk	W	L	Pct	ShO	Sv-Op	Hld	ERC	ERA
		HOW MUCH HE PITCHED						**WHAT HE GAVE UP**												**THE RESULTS**							
2004 As	R	25	0	0	22	29.1	120	17	8	3	2	0	2	2	8	0	46	0	0	2	2	.500	0	13--	-	1.53	0.92
2004 Vancvr	A	3	0	0	2	5.0	21	4	2	2	1	0	0	0	2	0	5	0	0	0	0	-	0	0--	-	3.57	3.60
2005 Kane	A	20	0	0	6	27.2	118	23	10	9	0	2	0	3	14	0	47	3	1	2	2	.500	0	1--	-	3.32	2.93
2005 Scrmto	AAA	3	0	0	1	5.0	22	2	1	1	0	1	0	1	3	1	5	0	0	0	0	-	0	1--	-	1.44	1.80
2005 Stcktn	A+	32	0	0	7	42.1	189	37	17	13	1	1	1	2	23	0	68	4	0	5	2	.714	0	1--	-	3.47	2.76

Year	Team	Lg	G	GS	CG	GF	IP	BFP	H	R	ER	HR	SH	SF	HB	TBB	IBB	SO	WP	Bk	W	L	Pct	ShO	Sv-Op	Hld	ERC	ERA
2006	Mdland	AA	55	0	0	19	83.2	325	73	28	26	1	2	1	2	22	2	97	2	0	7	2	.778	0	6--	-	2.53	2.80
2007	As	R	1	0	0	0	1.0	3	0	0	0	0	0	0	0	0	0	2	0	0	1	0	1.000	0	0--	-	0.00	0.00
2007	Scrmto	AAA	31	0	0	10	39.1	175	43	25	19	3	0	1	1	21	0	40	6	0	4	1	.800	0	2--	-	5.19	4.35
2007	Oak	AL	3	0	0	0	2.0	15	6	4	4	0	0	1	1	2	1	2	0	0	0	0	-	0	0-0	0	20.56	18.00

Nate Robertson

Pitches: L Bats: R Pos: SP-30 **Ht: 6'2" Wt: 225 Born: 9/3/1977 Age: 30**

Year	Team	Lg	G	GS	CG	GF	IP	BFP	H	R	ER	HR	SH	SF	HB	TBB	IBB	SO	WP	Bk	W	L	Pct	ShO	Sv-Op	Hld	ERC	ERA
2007	Erie*	AA	1	1	0	0	6.0	19	0	0	0	0	0	0	0	1	0	6	0	0	1	0	1.000	0	0--	-	0.03	0.00
2002	Fla	NL	6	1	0	1	8.1	46	15	11	11	3	0	0	2	4	1	3	0	0	0	1	.000	0	0-0	0	12.69	11.88
2003	Det	AL	8	8	0	0	44.2	203	55	27	27	6	0	0	0	23	2	33	3	0	1	2	.333	0	0-0	0	6.24	5.44
2004	Det	AL	34	32	1	1	196.2	852	210	116	107	30	12	4	4	66	1	155	5	1	12	10	.545	0	1-1	0	4.65	4.90
2005	Det	AL	32	32	2	0	196.2	846	202	113	98	28	3	11	7	65	2	122	6	1	7	16	.304	0	0-0	0	4.38	4.48
2006	Det	AL	32	32	1	0	208.2	881	206	98	89	29	4	7	8	67	2	137	6	0	13	13	.500	0	0-0	0	4.14	3.84
2007	Det	AL	30	30	0	0	177.2	781	199	98	94	22	5	6	3	63	2	119	5	1	9	13	.409	0	0-0	0	4.80	4.76
	6 ML YEARS		142	135	4	2	832.2	3609	887	463	426	118	24	28	24	288	10	569	25	3	42	55	.433	0	1-1	0	4.64	4.60

Oscar Robles

Bats: L Throws: R Pos: PH-15; 2B-8; 3B-4 **Ht: 5'10" Wt: 185 Born: 4/9/1976 Age: 32**

								BATTING												BASERUNNING				AVERAGES		
Year	Team	Lg	G	AB	H	2B	3B	HR	(Hm | Rd)	TB	R	RBI	RC	TBB	IBB	SO	HBP	SH	SF	SB	CS	SB%	GDP	Avg	OBP	Slg
2007	Portlnd*	AAA	28	102	29	5	3	0	(- | -)	40	9	11	13	8	0	9	0	1	2	0	1	.00	3	.284	.330	.392
2005	LAD	NL	110	364	99	18	1	5	(2 | 3)	134	44	34	41	31	0	33	2	1	1	0	8	.00	8	.272	.332	.368
2006	LAD	NL	29	33	5	0	1	0	(0 | 0)	7	6	0	1	5	0	5	0	1	0	0	0	-	0	.152	.263	.212
2007	SD	NL	24	26	6	0	0	0	(0 | 0)	6	0	2	4	2	1	4	0	5	0	0	0	-	0	.231	.286	.231
	3 ML YEARS		163	423	110	18	2	5	(2 | 3)	147	50	36	46	38	1	42	2	7	1	0	8	.00	8	.260	.323	.348

Fernando Rodney

Pitches: R Bats: R Pos: RP-48 **Ht: 5'11" Wt: 220 Born: 3/18/1977 Age: 31**

Year	Team	Lg	G	GS	CG	GF	IP	BFP	H	R	ER	HR	SH	SF	HB	TBB	IBB	SO	WP	Bk	W	L	Pct	ShO	Sv-Op	Hld	ERC	ERA
2007	Toledo*	AAA	4	0	0	0	3.0	15	4	0	0	0	0	0	0	2	0	4	0	0	0	0	-	0	0--	-	6.15	0.00
2002	Det	AL	20	0	0	10	18.0	89	25	15	12	2	2	1	0	10	2	10	0	1	1	3	.250	0	0-4	0	6.77	6.00
2003	Det	AL	27	0	0	11	29.2	143	35	20	20	2	3	3	1	17	1	33	0	0	1	3	.250	0	3-6	3	5.46	6.07
2005	Det	AL	39	0	0	26	44.0	185	39	14	14	5	2	0	2	17	3	42	2	0	2	3	.400	0	9-15	3	3.59	2.86
2006	Det	AL	63	0	0	30	71.2	304	51	36	28	6	2	0	8	34	4	66	3	0	7	4	.636	0	7-11	18	3.01	3.52
2007	Det	AL	48	0	0	12	50.2	223	46	27	24	5	4	2	3	21	0	54	4	0	2	6	.250	0	1-3	12	3.74	4.26
	5 ML YEARS		197	0	0	89	214.0	944	196	112	98	20	13	6	14	99	10	204	9	1	13	19	.406	0	20-39	36	3.92	4.12

Alex Rodriguez

Bats: R Throws: R Pos: 3B-154; DH-4 **Ht: 6'3" Wt: 225 Born: 7/27/1975 Age: 32**

								BATTING												BASERUNNING				AVERAGES		
Year	Team	Lg	G	AB	H	2B	3B	HR	(Hm	Rd)	TB	R	RBI	RC	TBB	IBB	SO	HBP	SH	SF	SB	CS	SB%	GDP	Avg	OBP	Slg
1994	Sea	AL	17	54	11	0	0	0	(0	0)	11	4	2	3	3	0	20	0	1	1	3	0	1.00	0	.204	.241	.204
1995	Sea	AL	48	142	33	6	2	5	(1	4)	58	15	19	15	6	0	42	0	1	0	4	2	.67	0	.232	.264	.408
1996	Sea	AL	146	601	215	54	1	36	(18	18)	379	141	123	144	59	4	104	4	6	7	15	4	.79	15	.358	.414	.631
1997	Sea	AL	141	587	176	40	3	23	(16	7)	291	100	84	100	41	1	99	5	4	1	29	6	.83	14	.300	.350	.496
1998	Sea	AL	161	686	213	35	5	42	(18	24)	384	123	124	135	45	0	121	10	3	4	46	13	.78	12	.310	.360	.560
1999	Sea	AL	129	502	143	25	0	42	(20	22)	294	110	111	102	56	2	109	5	1	8	21	7	.75	12	.285	.357	.586
2000	Sea	AL	148	554	175	34	2	41	(13	28)	336	134	132	138	100	5	121	7	0	11	15	4	.79	10	.316	.420	.606
2001	Tex	AL	162	632	201	34	1	52	(26	26)	393	133	135	148	75	6	131	16	0	9	18	3	.86	17	.318	.399	.622
2002	Tex	AL	162	624	187	27	2	57	(34	23)	389	125	142	152	87	12	122	10	0	4	9	4	.69	14	.300	.392	.623
2003	Tex	AL	161	607	181	30	6	47	(26	21)	364	124	118	131	87	10	126	15	0	6	17	3	.85	14	.298	.396	.600
2004	NYY	AL	155	601	172	24	2	36	(17	19)	308	112	106	112	80	6	131	10	0	7	28	4	.88	18	.286	.375	.512
2005	NYY	AL	162	605	194	29	1	48	(26	22)	369	124	130	137	91	8	139	16	0	3	21	6	.78	8	.321	.421	.610
2006	NYY	AL	154	572	166	26	1	35	(20	15)	299	113	121	112	90	8	139	8	0	4	15	4	.79	22	.290	.392	.523
2007	NYY	AL	158	583	183	31	0	54	(26	28)	376	143	156	159	95	11	120	21	0	9	24	4	.86	15	.314	.422	.645
	14 ML YEARS		1904	7350	2250	395	26	518	(261	257)	4251	1501	1503	1588	915	70	1524	127	16	74	265	64	.81	173	.306	.389	.578

Francisco Rodriguez

Pitches: R Bats: R Pos: RP-64 **Ht: 6'0" Wt: 195 Born: 1/7/1982 Age: 26**

Year	Team	Lg	G	GS	CG	GF	IP	BFP	H	R	ER	HR	SH	SF	HB	TBB	IBB	SO	WP	Bk	W	L	Pct	ShO	Sv-Op	Hld	ERC	ERA
2002	LAA	AL	5	0	0	4	5.2	21	3	0	0	0	0	1	2	1	1	13	0	0	0	0	-	0	0-0	0	1.52	0.00
2003	LAA	AL	59	0	0	23	86.0	334	50	30	29	12	2	4	2	35	5	95	7	0	8	3	.727	0	2-6	7	2.25	3.03
2004	LAA	AL	69	0	0	29	84.0	335	51	21	17	2	2	1	4	33	1	123	5	0	4	1	.800	0	12-19	27	1.64	1.82
2005	LAA	AL	66	0	0	58	67.1	279	45	20	20	7	1	1	0	32	3	91	8	0	2	5	.286	0	45-50	0	2.52	2.67
2006	LAA	AL	69	0	0	58	73.0	296	52	16	14	6	3	0	1	28	5	98	10	0	2	3	.400	0	47-51	0	2.35	1.73
2007	LAA	AL	64	0	0	56	67.1	285	50	22	21	3	1	4	1	34	0	90	7	1	5	2	.714	0	40-46	0	2.74	2.81
	6 ML YEARS		332	0	0	228	383.1	1550	251	109	101	30	9	10	6	164	15	510	37	1	21	14	.600	0	146-172	34	2.25	2.37

Guillermo Rodriquez

Bats: R Throws: R Pos: C-33; PH-8; PR-3 Ht: 5'11" Wt: 195 Born: 5/15/1978 Age: 30

Year	Team	Lg	G	AB	H	2B	3B	HR	(Hm	Rd)	TB	R	RBI	RC	TBB	IBB	SO	HBP	SH	SF	SB	CS	SB%	GDP	Avg	OBP	Slg
1996	Bllghm	A-	3	4	0	0	0	0	(-	-)	0	1	0	0	0	0	1	0	0	0	0	0	-		.000	.000	.000
1997	SlmKzr	A-	11	39	9	3	0	0	(-	-)	12	3	3	3	5	0	12	0	0	0	0	1	.00	1	.231	.318	.308
1997	SnJos	A+	13	27	4	3	1	0	(-	-)	9	2	2	1	0	0	9	0	2	0	0	0	-	1	.148	.148	.333
1998	SlmKzr	A-	1	4	1	0	0	0	(-	-)	1	0	0	0	0	0	1	0	0	0	0	1	.00	0	.250	.250	.250
1998	SnJos	A+	1	1	0	0	0	0	(-	-)	0	0	0	0	0	0	0	0	0	0	0	0	-	0	.000	.000	.000
1999	Bkrsfld	A+	41	93	27	5	0	1	(-	-)	35	10	11	13	3	0	18	4	3	2	4	0	1.00	2	.290	.333	.376
1999	SlmKzr	A-	33	114	29	5	0	6	(-	-)	52	16	34	16	9	1	28	3	0	0	1	3	.25	2	.254	.325	.456
2000	Bkrsfld	A+	118	437	105	27	1	10	(-	-)	164	63	58	53	30	0	101	13	4	3	20	8	.71	11	.240	.306	.375
2001	Shreve	AA	65	216	44	7	0	5	(-	-)	66	21	25	17	8	0	40	6	5	3	3	0	1.00	5	.204	.249	.306
2001	SnJos	A+	35	126	34	10	0	2	(-	-)	50	18	21	18	9	0	26	8	4	1	2	2	.50	4	.270	.354	.397
2002	SnJos	A+	42	152	55	15	1	1	(-	-)	75	24	20	29	10	0	26	1	1	0	2	1	.67	4	.362	.405	.493
2002	Fresno	AAA	32	115	27	5	0	2	(-	-)	38	9	8	11	6	0	23	5	1	1	0	1	.00	4	.235	.299	.330
2002	Shreve	AA	13	41	11	1	1	1	(-	-)	17	4	6	5	4	0	10	1	0	0	1	2	.33	0	.268	.348	.415
2003	Fresno	AAA	78	239	66	8	4	5	(-	-)	97	31	36	33	14	0	25	5	1	1	1	0	1.00	9	.276	.328	.406
2004	Toledo	AAA	73	219	41	8	2	7	(-	-)	74	17	21	18	14	0	45	3	3	2	2	2	.50	6	.187	.244	.338
2005	SnJos	A+	67	209	57	14	3	9	(-	-)	104	36	43	36	12	0	50	10	3	7	5	1	.83	5	.273	.332	.498
2005	Nrwich	AA	6	15	4	1	0	0	(-	-)	5	1	1	2	3	0	4	1	0	0	0	0	-	0	.267	.400	.333
2006	Fresno	AAA	40	127	28	8	1	8	(-	-)	62	20	16	19	12	0	25	4	0	2	0	1	.00	3	.220	.303	.488
2006	SnJos	A+	26	77	28	6	1	5	(-	-)	51	20	21	22	10	0	12	3	0	1	2	0	1.00	6	.364	.451	.662
2007	Fresno	AAA	33	103	25	6	0	1	(-	-)	34	15	16	12	11	1	8	1	3	1	1	0	1.00	3	.243	.319	.330
2007	SF	NL	39	87	22	6	0	1	(1	0)	31	10	14	13	10	0	17	0	0	1	0	1	.00	3	.253	.327	.356

Ivan Rodriguez

Bats: R Throws: R Pos: C-127; PH-4; DH-1; PR-1 Ht: 5'9" Wt: 190 Born: 11/30/1971 Age: 36

Year	Team	Lg	G	AB	H	2B	3B	HR	(Hm	Rd)	TB	R	RBI	RC	TBB	IBB	SO	HBP	SH	SF	SB	CS	SB%	GDP	Avg	OBP	Slg
1991	Tex	AL	88	280	74	16	0	3	(3	0)	99	24	27	23	5	0	42	0	2	1	0	1	.00	10	.264	.276	.354
1992	Tex	AL	123	420	109	16	1	8	(4	4)	151	39	37	41	24	2	73	1	7	2	0	0	-	15	.260	.300	.360
1993	Tex	AL	137	473	129	28	4	10	(7	3)	195	56	66	57	29	3	70	4	5	8	8	7	.53	16	.273	.315	.412
1994	Tex	AL	99	363	108	19	1	16	(7	9)	177	56	57	61	31	5	42	7	0	4	6	3	.67	10	.298	.360	.488
1995	Tex	AL	130	492	149	32	2	12	(5	7)	221	56	67	68	16	2	48	4	0	5	0	2	.00	11	.303	.327	.449
1996	Tex	AL	153	639	192	47	3	19	(10	9)	302	116	86	99	38	7	55	4	0	4	5	0	1.00	15	.300	.342	.473
1997	Tex	AL	150	597	187	34	4	20	(12	8)	289	98	77	98	38	7	89	8	1	4	7	3	.70	18	.313	.360	.484
1998	Tex	AL	145	579	186	40	4	21	(12	9)	297	88	91	100	32	4	88	3	0	3	9	0	1.00	18	.321	.358	.513
1999	Tex	AL	144	600	199	29	1	35	(12	23)	335	116	113	104	24	2	64	1	0	5	25	12	.68	31	.332	.356	.558
2000	Tex	AL	91	363	126	27	4	27	(16	11)	242	66	83	78	19	5	48	1	0	6	5	5	.50	17	.347	.375	.667
2001	Tex	AL	111	442	136	24	2	25	(16	9)	239	70	65	77	23	3	73	4	0	1	10	3	.77	13	.308	.347	.541
2002	Tex	AL	108	408	128	32	2	19	(15	4)	221	67	60	63	25	2	71	2	1	4	5	4	.56	13	.314	.353	.542
2003	Fla	NL	144	511	152	36	3	16	(8	8)	242	90	85	91	55	6	92	6	1	5	10	6	.63	18	.297	.369	.474
2004	Det	AL	135	527	176	32	2	19	(7	12)	269	72	86	98	41	6	91	3	0	4	7	4	.64	15	.334	.383	.510
2005	Det	AL	129	504	139	33	5	14	(8	6)	224	71	50	44	11	2	93	2	1	7	7	3	.70	19	.276	.290	.444
2006	Det	AL	136	547	164	28	4	13	(5	8)	239	74	69	82	26	4	86	1	4	2	8	3	.73	16	.300	.332	.437
2007	Det	AL	129	502	141	31	3	11	(4	7)	211	50	63	55	9	1	96	1	1	2	2	2	.50	16	.281	.294	.420
17 ML YEARS			2152	8247	2495	504	45	288	(151	137)	3953	1209	1182	1239	446	61	1221	52	23	67	114	58	.66	271	.303	.340	.479

Luis Rodriguez

Bats: B Throws: R Pos: 3B-38; 2B-21; PH-14; 1B-3; DH-3; PR-2 Ht: 5'9" Wt: 188 Born: 6/27/1980 Age: 28

Year	Team	Lg	G	AB	H	2B	3B	HR	(Hm	Rd)	TB	R	RBI	RC	TBB	IBB	SO	HBP	SH	SF	SB	CS	SB%	GDP	Avg	OBP	Slg
2007	Roch*	AAA	6	19	8	1	0	0	(-	-)	9	3	1	4	4	0	2	0	0	0	0	0	-	0	.421	.522	.474
2005	Min	AL	79	175	47	10	2	2	(1	1)	67	21	20	27	18	0	23	1	6	3	2	2	.50	4	.269	.335	.383
2006	Min	AL	59	115	27	4	0	2	(1	1)	37	11	6	8	14	1	16	0	2	1	0	0	-	3	.235	.315	.322
2007	Min	AL	68	155	34	5	1	2	(1	1)	47	18	12	11	12	0	14	2	2	2	1	0	1.00	8	.219	.281	.303
3 ML YEARS			206	445	108	19	3	6	(3	3)	151	50	38	46	44	1	53	3	10	6	3	2	.60	15	.243	.311	.339

Wandy Rodriguez

Pitches: L Bats: B Pos: SP-31 Ht: 5'11" Wt: 160 Born: 1/18/1979 Age: 29

Year	Team	Lg	G	GS	CG	GF	IP	BFP	H	R	ER	HR	SH	SF	HB	TBB	IBB	SO	WP	Bk	W	L	Pct	ShO	Sv-Op	Hld	ERC	ERA
2005	Hou	NL	25	22	0	0	128.2	560	135	82	79	19	3	3	8	53	2	80	3	3	10	10	.500	0	0-0	0	5.08	5.53
2006	Hou	NL	30	24	0	1	135.2	611	154	96	85	17	7	4	6	63	7	98	6	0	9	10	.474	0	0-0	0	5.45	5.64
2007	Hou	NL	31	31	1	0	182.2	782	179	102	93	22	6	4	5	62	2	158	3	0	9	13	.409	1	0-0	0	3.94	4.58
3 ML YEARS			86	77	1	1	447.0	1953	468	280	257	58	16	11	19	178	11	336	12	3	28	33	.459	1	0-0	0	4.71	5.17

Brian Rogers

Pitches: R Bats: R Pos: RP-3 Ht: 6'4" Wt: 188 Born: 7/17/1982 Age: 25

Year	Team	Lg	G	GS	CG	GF	IP	BFP	H	R	ER	HR	SH	SF	HB	TBB	IBB	SO	WP	Bk	W	L	Pct	ShO	Sv-Op	Hld	ERC	ERA
2003	Oneont	A-	12	12	0	0	56.2	237	49	23	21	2	2	3	18	0	66	1	0	3	2	.600	0	0--	-	2.79	3.34
2004	WMich	A	25	25	0	0	142.1	627	163	76	72	9	6	11	10	44	1	120	8	0	6	8	.429	0	0--	-	4.55	4.55
2005	Lkland	A+	52	1	0	10	65.2	269	50	16	15	2	1	2	3	21	1	65	6	0	4	1	.800	0	2--	-	2.22	2.06
2006	Altna	AA	2	0	0	1	4.0	15	2	0	0	0	1	0	0	2	1	5	0	0	0	0			1--	-	1.26	0.00
2006	Erie	AA	37	0	0	10	64.0	250	49	19	17	7	1	1	1	14	1	69	3	0	3	2	.600	0	1--	-	2.31	2.39
2006	Indy	AAA	7	0	0	3	8.1	27	2	1	1	1	0	0	0	1	0	8	1	0	1	1	.500	0	1--	-	0.47	1.08

			HOW MUCH HE PITCHED						WHAT HE GAVE UP													THE RESULTS							
Year	Team	Lg	G	GS	CG	GF	IP	BFP	H	R	ER	HR	SH	SF	HB	TBB	IBB	SO	WP	Bk	W	L	Pct	ShO	Sv-Op	Hld	ERC	ERA
2007	Indy	AAA	48	0	0	13	65.0	272	50	23	22	1	3	1	1	32	2	65	9	0	2	1	.667	0	2--	-	2.64	3.05
2006	Pit	NL	10	0	0	4	8.2	38	11	8	8	2	1	0	1	2	0	7	1	0	0	0	-	0	0-0	0	6.65	8.31
2007	Pit	NL	3	0	0	1	2.0	9	3	3	3	2	1	1	0	1	0	1	0	0	0	0	-	0	0-0	0	17.03	13.50
	2 ML YEARS		13	0	0	5	10.2	47	14	11	11	4	2	1	1	3	0	8	1	0	0	0	-	0	0-0	0	8.37	9.28

Kenny Rogers

Pitches: L Bats: L Pos: SP-11   **Ht: 6'1" Wt: 190 Born: 11/10/1964 Age: 43**

			HOW MUCH HE PITCHED						WHAT HE GAVE UP													THE RESULTS							
Year	Team	Lg	G	GS	CG	GF	IP	BFP	H	R	ER	HR	SH	SF	HB	TBB	IBB	SO	WP	Bk	W	L	Pct	ShO	Sv-Op	Hld	ERC	ERA
2007	WMich*	A-	1	1	0	0	5.0	23	7	3	1	0	0	0	0	2	0	4	1	0	0	1	.000	0	0--	-	5.74	1.80
2007	Toledo*	AAA	1	1	0	0	3.2	13	3	0	0	0	0	0	0	0	0	2	0	0	0	0	-	0	0--	-	1.42	0.00
1989	Tex	AL	73	0	0	24	73.2	314	60	28	24	2	6	3	4	42	9	63	6	0	3	4	.429	0	2-5	15	3.26	2.93
1990	Tex	AL	69	3	0	46	97.2	428	93	40	34	6	7	4	1	42	5	74	5	0	10	6	.625	0	15-23	6	3.53	3.13
1991	Tex	AL	63	9	0	20	109.2	511	121	80	66	14	9	5	6	61	7	73	3	1	10	10	.500	0	5-6	11	5.57	5.42
1992	Tex	AL	81	0	0	38	78.2	337	80	32	27	7	4	1	0	26	8	70	4	1	3	6	.333	0	6-10	16	3.63	3.09
1993	Tex	AL	35	33	5	0	208.1	885	210	108	95	18	7	5	4	71	2	140	6	5	16	10	.615	0	0-0	1	3.88	4.10
1994	Tex	AL	24	24	6	0	167.1	714	169	93	83	24	3	6	3	52	1	120	3	1	11	8	.579	2	0-0	0	4.12	4.46
1995	Tex	AL	31	31	3	0	208.0	877	192	87	78	26	3	5	2	76	1	140	8	1	17	7	.708	1	0-0	0	3.72	3.38
1996	NYY	AL	30	30	2	0	179.0	786	179	97	93	16	6	3	8	83	2	92	5	0	12	8	.600	1	0-0	0	4.43	4.68
1997	NYY	AL	31	22	1	4	145.0	651	161	100	91	18	2	4	7	62	1	78	2	2	6	7	.462	0	0-0	1	5.18	5.65
1998	Oak	AL	34	34	7	0	238.2	970	215	96	84	19	4	5	7	67	0	138	5	2	16	8	.667	1	0-0	0	3.13	3.17
1999	2 Tms		31	31	5	0	195.1	845	206	101	91	16	7	7	13	69	1	126	4	1	10	4	.714	1	0-0	0	4.38	4.19
2000	Tex	AL	34	34	2	0	227.1	**998**	257	126	115	20	3	4	11	78	2	127	1	1	13	13	.500	0	0-0	0	4.72	4.55
2001	Tex	AL	20	20	0	0	120.2	552	150	88	83	18	1	6	8	49	2	74	4	1	5	7	.417	0	0-0	0	6.22	6.19
2002	Tex	AL	33	33	2	0	210.2	892	212	101	90	21	3	1	6	70	1	107	5	1	13	8	.619	1	0-0	0	3.99	3.84
2003	Min	AL	33	31	0	0	195.0	851	227	108	99	22	9	3	11	50	5	116	6	**4**	13	8	.619	0	0-0	0	4.73	4.57
2004	Tex	AL	35	**35**	2	0	211.2	935	248	117	112	24	7	4	9	66	0	126	2	1	18	9	.667	1	0-0	0	4.99	4.76
2005	Tex	AL	30	30	1	0	195.1	828	205	86	75	15	5	6	8	53	1	87	0	0	14	8	.636	1	0-0	0	3.87	3.46
2006	Det	AL	34	33	0	1	204.0	849	195	97	87	23	1	7	9	62	2	99	5	0	17	8	.680	0	0-0	0	3.76	3.84
2007	Det	AL	11	11	0	0	63.0	275	65	36	31	8	0	3	1	25	0	36	1	0	3	4	.429	0	0-0	0	4.48	4.43
99	Oak	AL	19	19	3	0	119.1	528	135	66	57	8	4	6	9	41	0	68	3	1	5	3	.625	0	0-0	0	4.68	4.30
99	NYM	NL	12	12	2	0	76.0	317	71	35	34	8	3	1	4	28	1	58	1	0	5	1	.833	1	0-0	0	3.91	4.03
	19 ML YEARS		732	444	36	133	3129.0	13498	3245	1621	1458	317	87	82	118	1104	50	1886	75	22	210	143	.595	9	28-44	50	4.25	4.19

Scott Rolen

Bats: R Throws: R Pos: 3D-112   **Ht: 6'4" Wt: 240 Born: 4/4/1975 Age: 33**

					BATTING																		BASERUNNING				AVERAGES		
Year	Team	Lg	G	AB	H	2B	3B	HR	(Hm	Rd)	TB	R	RBI	RC	TBB	IBD	SO	HBP	SH	SF	SB	CS	SB%	GDP	Avg	OBP	Slg
1996	Phi	NL	37	130	33	7	0	4	(2	2)	52	10	18	16	13	0	27	1	0	2	0	2	.00	4	.254	.322	.400
1997	Phi	NL	156	561	159	35	3	21	(11	10)	263	93	92	103	76	4	138	13	0	7	16	6	.73	6	.283	.377	.469
1998	Phi	NL	160	601	174	45	4	31	(19	12)	320	120	110	124	93	6	141	11	0	6	14	7	.67	10	.290	.391	.532
1999	Phi	NL	112	421	113	28	1	26	(9	17)	221	74	77	83	67	2	114	3	0	6	12	2	.86	8	.268	.368	.525
2000	Phi	NL	128	483	144	32	6	26	(12	14)	266	88	89	97	51	9	99	5	0	2	8	1	.89	4	.298	.370	.551
2001	Phi	NL	151	554	160	39	1	25	(12	13)	276	96	107	108	74	6	127	13	0	12	16	5	.76	6	.289	.378	.498
2002	2 Tms	NL	155	580	154	29	8	31	(14	17)	292	89	110	98	72	4	102	12	0	3	8	4	.67	22	.266	.357	.503
2003	StL	NL	154	559	160	49	1	28	(12	16)	295	98	104	104	82	5	104	9	0	7	13	3	.81	19	.286	.382	.528
2004	StL	NL	142	500	157	34	4	34	(10	24)	299	109	124	124	72	5	92	13	1	7	4	3	.57	8	.314	.409	.598
2005	StL	NL	56	196	46	12	1	5	(2	3)	75	28	28	22	25	1	28	1	0	1	1	2	.33	3	.235	.323	.383
2006	StL	NL	142	521	154	48	1	22	(12	10)	270	94	95	89	56	7	69	9	0	8	7	4	.64	10	.296	.369	.518
2007	StL	NL	112	392	104	24	2	8	(4	4)	156	55	58	47	32	2	56	5	0	7	5	3	.63	13	.265	.331	.398
02	Phi	NL	100	375	97	21	4	17	(8	9)	177	52	66	60	52	2	68	8	0	3	5	2	.71	12	.259	.358	.472
02	StL	NL	55	205	57	8	4	14	(6	8)	115	37	44	38	20	2	34	4	0	0	3	2	.60	10	.278	.354	.561
	12 ML YEARS		1505	5498	1558	380	32	261	(119	142)	2785	954	1012	1015	718	51	1097	95	1	68	104	42	.71	113	.283	.372	.507

Jimmy Rollins

Bats: B Throws: R Pos: SS-162   **Ht: 5'8" Wt: 174 Born: 11/27/1978 Age: 29**

					BATTING																		BASERUNNING				AVERAGES		
Year	Team	Lg	G	AB	H	2B	3B	HR	(Hm	Rd)	TB	R	RBI	RC	TBB	IBD	SO	HBP	SH	SF	SB	CS	SB%	GDP	Avg	OBP	Slg
2000	Phi	NL	14	53	17	1	1	0	(0	0)	20	5	5	8	2	0	7	0	0	0	3	0	1.00	0	.321	.345	.377
2001	Phi	NL	158	**656**	180	29	**12**	14	(8	6)	275	97	54	96	48	2	108	2	9	5	46	8	.85	5	.274	.323	.419
2002	Phi	NL	154	**637**	156	33	**10**	11	(3	8)	242	82	60	72	54	3	103	4	6	4	31	13	.70	14	.245	.306	.380
2003	Phi	NL	156	628	165	42	6	8	(5	3)	243	85	62	76	54	4	113	0	5	2	20	12	.63	9	.263	.320	.387
2004	Phi	NL	154	657	190	43	**12**	14	(8	6)	299	119	73	108	57	3	73	3	6	2	30	9	.77	4	.289	.348	.455
2005	Phi	NL	158	677	196	38	11	12	(5	7)	292	115	54	100	47	8	71	4	2	2	41	6	.87	9	.290	.338	.431
2006	Phi	NL	158	689	191	45	9	25	(15	10)	329	127	83	114	57	5	80	5	0	7	36	4	.90	12	.277	.334	.478
2007	Phi	NL	162	**716**	212	38	**20**	30	(18	12)	380	**139**	94	124	49	5	85	7	0	6	41	6	.87	11	.296	.344	.531
	8 ML YEARS		1114	4713	1307	269	81	114	(62	52)	2080	769	485	698	368	27	640	25	28	28	248	58	.81	64	.277	.331	.441

J.C. Romero

Pitches: L Bats: B Pos: RP-74   **Ht: 5'11" Wt: 205 Born: 6/4/1976 Age: 32**

			HOW MUCH HE PITCHED						WHAT HE GAVE UP													THE RESULTS							
Year	Team	Lg	G	GS	CG	GF	IP	BFP	H	R	ER	HR	SH	SF	HB	TBB	IBB	SO	WP	Bk	W	L	Pct	ShO	Sv-Op	Hld	ERC	ERA
1999	Min	AL	5	0	0	3	9.2	39	13	4	4	0	0	0	0	4	0	4	0	0	0	0	-	0	0-0	0	3.95	3.72
2000	Min	AL	12	11	0	0	57.2	268	72	51	45	8	4	2	1	30	0	50	2	1	2	7	.222	0	0-0	0	6.48	7.02
2001	Min	AL	14	11	0	1	65.0	286	71	48	45	10	3	2	1	24	1	39	1	0	1	4	.200	0	0-0	0	4.89	6.23
2002	Min	AL	81	0	0	15	81.0	332	62	17	17	3	1	0	4	36	4	76	9	0	9	2	.818	0	1-5	33	2.74	1.89
2003	Min	AL	73	0	0	17	63.0	295	66	37	35	7	4	0	6	42	7	50	9	2	2	0	1.000	0	0-4	22	5.72	5.00

Year	Team	Lg	G	GS	CG	GF	IP	BFP	H	R	ER	HR	SH	SF	HB	TBB	IBB	SO	WP	Bk	W	L	Pct	ShO	Sv-Op	Hld	ERC	ERA
			HOW MUCH HE PITCHED						WHAT HE GAVE UP												THE RESULTS						
2004	Min	AL	74	0	0	12	74.1	319	61	32	29	4	3	1	5	38	6	69	5	0	7	4	.636	0	1-8	16	3.33	3.51
2005	Min	AL	68	0	0	11	57.0	264	50	26	22	6	5	1	6	39	8	48	1	1	4	3	.571	0	0-1	11	4.62	3.47
2006	LAA	AL	65	0	0	16	48.1	226	57	40	36	3	1	5	1	28	2	31	1	0	1	2	.333	0	0-1	7	5.54	6.57
2007	2 Tms		74	0	0	10	56.1	237	39	12	12	3	1	1	2	40	5	42	4	0	2	2	.500	0	1-2	24	3.35	1.92
07	Bos	AL	23	0	0	5	20.0	94	24	7	7	2	0	1	0	15	3	11	0	0	1	0	1.000	0	1-1	2	6.61	3.15
07	Phi	NL	51	0	0	5	36.1	143	15	5	5	1	1	0	2	25	2	31	4	0	1	2	.333	0	0-1	22	1.86	1.24
	9 ML YEARS		466	22	0	85	512.1	2266	491	267	245	44	22	12	26	277	33	409	32	4	28	24	.538	0	3-21	113	4.41	4.30

Francisco Rosario

Pitches: R **Bats:** R **Pos:** RP-23   **Ht:** 6'0" **Wt:** 197 **Born:** 9/28/1980 **Age:** 27

Year	Team	Lg	G	GS	CG	GF	IP	BFP	H	R	ER	HR	SH	SF	HB	TBB	IBB	SO	WP	Bk	W	L	Pct	ShO	Sv-Op	Hld	ERC	ERA
			HOW MUCH HE PITCHED						WHAT HE GAVE UP												THE RESULTS						
2001	MdHat	R+	16	15	0	0	75.2	344	79	61	47	6	4	1	4	38	0	55	6	6	3	7	.300	0	0--	-	5.28	5.59
2002	CtnWV	A	13	13	1	0	66.2	265	50	22	19	5	2	2	4	14	0	78	2	0	6	1	.857	0	0--	-	2.15	2.57
2002	Dnedin	A+	13	12	0	0	63.0	248	33	10	9	3	1	1	3	25	0	65	1	2	3	3	.500	0	0--	-	1.58	1.29
2004	Dnedin	A+	6	6	0	0	17.1	80	16	12	9	2	0	2	0	11	0	16	1	0	1	1	.500	0	0--	-	4.51	4.67
2004	NHam	AA	12	10	0	0	48.0	199	48	25	23	6	1	3	2	16	0	45	1	0	2	4	.333	0	0--	-	4.31	4.31
2005	Syrcse	AAA	30	18	0	4	116.1	489	111	59	51	16	5	1	10	42	1	80	5	1	2	7	.222	0	2--	-	4.38	3.95
2006	Syrcse	AAA	14	8	0	2	42.0	168	29	14	13	2	1	1	5	13	0	50	2	0	0	3	.000	0	1--	-	2.28	2.79
2007	Clrwtr	A+	6	5	0	0	13.1	56	9	6	6	1	0	1	2	5	16	0	0	0		0	0	-	0	0--	-	1.08	4.05
2006	Tor	AL	17	1	0	4	23.0	108	24	17	17	4	0	0	1	16	2	21	3	0	1	2	.333	0	0-0	1	6.12	6.65
2007	Phi	NL	23	0	0	10	26.1	127	34	16	16	3	2	2	4	13	1	25	1	0	0	3	.000	0	1-1	1	6.89	5.47
	2 ML YEARS		40	1	0	14	49.1	235	58	33	33	7	2	2	5	29	3	46	4	0	1	5	.167	0	1-1	2	6.53	6.02

Cody Ross

Bats: R **Throws:** L **Pos:** CF-36; RF-19; PH-11; LF-8; PR-2   **Ht:** 5'9" **Wt:** 205 **Born:** 12/23/1980 **Age:** 27

Year	Team	Lg	G	AB	H	2B	3B	HR	(Hm	Rd)	TB	R	RBI	RC	TBB	IBB	SO	HBP	SH	SF	SB	CS	SB%	GDP	Avg	OBP	Slg
			BATTING																		BASERUNNING				AVERAGES		
2007	Jupiter*	A+	7	23	6	1	0	2	(-	-)	13	2	3	3	1	0	6	0	0	0	0	0	-	0	.261	.292	.565
2003	Det	AL	6	19	4	1	0	1	(1	0)	8	1	5	4	1	0	7	1	1	0	0	0	-	0	.211	.286	.421
2005	LAD	NL	14	25	4	1	0	0	(0	0)	5	1	1	0	1	0	10	0	0	0	0	0	-	1	.160	.192	.200
2006	3 Tms	NL	101	269	61	12	2	13	(6	7)	116	34	46	36	22	0	65	4	1	2	1	1	.50	8	.227	.293	.431
2007	Fla	NL	66	173	58	19	0	12	(8	4)	113	35	39	42	20	3	38	3	0	1	3	0	1.00	2	.335	.411	.653
06	LAD	NL	8	14	7	1	1	2	(0	2)	16	4	9	6	0	0	2	0	0	0	1	0	1.00	0	.500	.500	1.143
06	Cin	NL	2	5	1	0	0	0	(0	0)	1	0	0	1	0	0	2	0	0	0	0	0	-	0	.200	.200	.200
06	Fla	NL	91	250	53	11	1	11	(6	5)	99	30	37	29	22	0	61	4	1	2	0	1	.00	8	.212	.284	.396
	4 ML YEARS		187	486	127	33	2	26	(15	11)	242	71	91	82	44	3	116	8	2	3	3	1	.75	11	.261	.331	.498

Dave Ross

Bats: R **Throws:** R **Pos:** C-108; PH-6   **Ht:** 6'2" **Wt:** 238 **Born:** 3/19/1977 **Age:** 31

Year	Team	Lg	G	AB	H	2B	3B	HR	(Hm	Rd)	TB	R	RBI	RC	TBB	IBB	SO	HBP	SH	SF	SB	CS	SB%	GDP	Avg	OBP	Slg
			BATTING																		BASERUNNING				AVERAGES		
2007	Lsville*	AAA	3	9	2	1	0	0	(-	-)	3	0	0	1	1	0	1	1	0	0	0	0	-	1	.222	.364	.333
2002	LAD	NL	8	10	2	1	0	1	(0	1)	6	2	2	2	2	0	4	1	0	0	0	0	-	0	.200	.385	.600
2003	LAD	NL	40	124	32	7	0	10	(5	5)	69	19	18	18	13	0	42	2	0	1	0	0	-	4	.258	.336	.556
2004	LAD	NL	70	165	28	3	1	5	(2	3)	48	13	15	11	15	1	62	5	0	5	0	0	-	3	.170	.253	.291
2005	2 Tms	NL	51	125	30	8	1	3	(2	1)	49	11	15	13	6	0	28	2	2	3	0	0	-	3	.240	.279	.392
2006	Cin	NL	90	247	63	15	1	21	(13	8)	143	37	52	43	37	7	75	3	4	5	0	0	-	4	.255	.353	.579
2007	Cin	NL	112	311	63	10	0	17	(12	5)	124	32	39	27	30	4	92	0	5	2	0	0	-	9	.203	.271	.399
05	Pit	NL	40	108	24	8	0	3	(2	1)	41	9	15	9	6	0	24	1	1	3	0	0	-	3	.222	.263	.380
05	SD	NL	11	17	6	0	1	0	(0	0)	8	2	0	4	0	0	4	1	1	0	0	0	-	0	.353	.389	.471
	6 ML YEARS		371	982	218	44	3	57	(34	23)	439	114	141	114	103	12	303	13	11	16	0	0	-	23	.222	.300	.447

Vinny Rottino

Bats: R **Throws:** R **Pos:** PH-6; 1B-1; LF-1   **Ht:** 6'0" **Wt:** 208 **Born:** 4/7/1980 **Age:** 28

Year	Team	Lg	G	AB	H	2B	3B	HR	(Hm	Rd)	TB	R	RBI	RC	TBB	IBB	SO	HBP	SH	SF	SB	CS	SB%	GDP	Avg	OBP	Slg
			BATTING																		BASERUNNING				AVERAGES		
2003	Helena	R+	64	222	69	10	0	1	(-	-)	82	42	20	37	28	1	25	8	1	2	5	2	.71	4	.311	.404	.369
2004	Beloit	A	140	529	161	25	9	17	(-	-)	255	78	124	92	40	3	71	4	1	10	5	1	.83	12	.304	.352	.482
2005	Hntsvl	AA	120	469	139	20	6	6	(-	-)	189	63	52	69	40	1	68	2	0	5	2	1	.67	14	.296	.351	.403
2005	Nashv	AAA	9	29	10	1	0	1	(-	-)	14	4	2	5	3	0	6	0	0	0	0	1	.00	1	.345	.406	.483
2006	Nashv	AAA	117	398	125	25	2	7	(-	-)	175	55	42	69	40	2	74	5	4	5	12	7	.63	9	.314	.379	.440
2007	Nashv	AAA	107	377	109	17	3	12	(-	-)	168	59	53	63	37	0	58	9	3	4	15	9	.63	4	.289	.363	.446
2006	Mil	NL	9	14	3	1	0	0	(0	0)	4	1	1	1	1	0	2	0	0	0	1	0	1.00	0	.214	.267	.286
2007	Mil	NL	8	9	2	1	0	0	(0	0)	3	0	3	2	0	0	1	0	0	0	0	0	-	0	.222	.222	.333
	2 ML YEARS		17	23	5	2	0	0	(0	0)	7	1	4	3	1	0	3	0	0	0	1	0	1.00	0	.217	.250	.304

Mike Rouse

Bats: L **Throws:** R **Pos:** 2B-14; 3B-14; SS-11; PH-5; PR-5; DH-1   **Ht:** 5'11" **Wt:** 190 **Born:** 4/25/1980 **Age:** 28

Year	Team	Lg	G	AB	H	2B	3B	HR	(Hm	Rd)	TB	R	RBI	RC	TBB	IBB	SO	HBP	SH	SF	SB	CS	SB%	GDP	Avg	OBP	Slg
			BATTING																		BASERUNNING				AVERAGES		
2001	Dnedin	A+	48	180	49	17	2	5	(-	-)	85	27	24	28	13	0	45	2	6	1	3	1	.75	2	.272	.327	.472
2002	Tenn	AA	71	231	60	11	0	9	(-	-)	98	35	43	35	29	1	47	2	4	4	7	6	.54	3	.260	.342	.424
2003	Mdland	AA	129	457	137	33	3	3	(-	-)	185	75	53	80	63	2	83	9	13	4	2	1	.78	16	.300	.392	.405
2003	Scrmto	AAA	2	7	3	0	0	0	(-	-)	3	2	1	1	0	0	0	0	0	0	0	0	-	0	.429	.429	.429

Year	Team	Lg	G	AB	H	2B	3B	HR	(Hm	Rd)	TB	R	RBI	RC	TBB	IBB	SO	HBP	SH	SF	SB	CS	SB%	GDP	Avg	OBP	Slg
2004	Scrmto	AAA	99	323	89	11	2	10	(-	-)	134	53	40	54	50	0	68	5	11	2	0	4	.00	5	.276	.379	.415
2005	Scrmto	AAA	130	469	126	30	3	7	(-	-)	183	69	72	70	59	0	115	7	17	2	2	4	.33	6	.269	.358	.390
2006	Scrmto	AAA	99	345	89	21	1	6	(-	-)	130	59	47	49	42	0	67	6	3	2	4	1	.80	8	.258	.347	.377
2007	Buffalo	AAA	20	65	18	4	1	0	(-	-)	24	11	3	9	9	0	8	1	3	1	1	1	.50	1	.277	.368	.369
2006	Oak	AL	8	24	7	3	0	0	(0	0)	10	2	2	3	1	0	4	1	0	0	1	0	1.00	1	.292	.346	.417
2007	Cle	AL	41	67	8	1	0	0	(0	0)	9	7	4	0	7	1	20	0	1	1	1	1	.50	0	.119	.200	.134
2 ML YEARS			49	91	15	4	0	0	(0	0)	19	9	6	3	8	1	24	1	1	1	2	1	.67	1	.165	.238	.209

Aaron Rowand

Bats: R **Throws:** R **Pos:** CF-161; PH-2   **Ht:** 6'0" **Wt:** 200 **Born:** 8/29/1977 **Age:** 30

Year	Team	Lg	G	AB	H	2B	3B	HR	(Hm	Rd)	TB	R	RBI	RC	TBB	IBB	SO	HBP	SH	SF	SB	CS	SB%	GDP	Avg	OBP	Slg
2001	CWS	AL	63	123	36	5	0	4	(3	1)	53	21	20	22	15	0	28	4	5	1	5	1	.83	2	.293	.385	.431
2002	CWS	AL	126	302	78	16	2	7	(5	2)	119	41	29	37	12	1	54	6	9	2	0	1	.00	8	.258	.298	.394
2003	CWS	AL	93	157	45	8	0	6	(5	1)	71	22	24	28	7	0	21	3	2	1	0	0	-	1	.287	.327	.452
2004	CWS	AL	140	487	151	38	2	24	(12	12)	265	94	69	92	30	1	91	10	5	2	17	5	.77	5	.310	.361	.544
2005	CWS	AL	157	578	156	30	5	13	(8	5)	235	77	69	78	32	3	116	21	5	4	16	5	.76	17	.270	.329	.407
2006	Phi	NL	109	405	106	24	3	12	(6	6)	172	59	47	47	18	2	76	18	2	4	10	4	.71	13	.262	.321	.425
2007	Phi	NL	161	612	189	45	4	27	(17	10)	315	105	89	100	47	3	119	19	2	4	6	3	.67	18	.309	.374	.515
7 ML YEARS			849	2664	761	166	12	93	(56	37)	1230	419	347	404	161	10	505	81	30	16	54	19	.74	64	.286	.343	.462

Ryan Rowland-Smith

Pitches: L **Bats:** L **Pos:** RP-26   **Ht:** 6'3" **Wt:** 205 **Born:** 1/26/1983 **Age:** 25

Year	Team	Lg	G	GS	CG	GF	IP	BFP	H	R	ER	HR	SH	SF	HB	TBB	IBB	SO	WP	Bk	W	L	Pct	ShO	Sv-Op Hld	ERC	ERA
2001	Ms	R	17	0	0	10	33.1	128	25	11	11	1	1	0	2	9	1	39	0	0	1	1	.500	0	5-- -	2.17	2.97
2002	Wisc	A	12	8	0	2	41.1	198	50	39	31	7	2	1	3	19	0	38	1	4	1	2	.333	0	0-- -	6.19	6.75
2002	Everett	A-	18	6	0	5	61.2	267	58	22	19	2	3	2	4	22	0	58	4	3	4	1	.800	0	2-- -	3.31	2.77
2003	Wisc	A	13	0	0	5	32.1	141	22	13	4	0	2	1	3	14	0	37	0	0	3	0	1.000	0	1-- -	2.06	1.11
2003	InldEm	A+	15	0	0	3	19.2	80	12	9	7	0	0	3	3	8	0	15	0	1	1	0	1.000	0	0-- -	2.01	3.20
2004	InldEm	A+	29	12	0	4	99.2	425	107	50	42	10	4	3	3	30	0	119	5	1	5	3	.625	0	3-- -	4.27	3.79
2005	SnAnt	AA	33	17	0	4	122.0	537	134	72	59	7	5	6	5	51	0	102	15	2	6	7	.462	0	0-- -	4.61	4.35
2006	InldEm	A+	7	0	0	1	6.1	31	8	7	4	1	2	1	0	2	0	9	1	0	1	0	1.000	0	0-- -	5.17	5.68
2006	SnAnt	AA	23	1	0	9	41.1	182	38	18	13	2	4	1	1	18	1	48	2	0	1	3	.250	0	4-- -	3.36	2.83
2007	Tacom	AAA	25	0	0	7	41.2	183	35	20	17	2	2	1	3	22	1	50	1	0	3	4	.429	0	0-- -	3.51	3.67
2007	Sea	AL	26	0	0	6	38.2	168	39	19	17	4	1	4	2	15	1	42	0	0	1	0	1.000	0	0-0 3	4.27	3.96

Justin Ruggiano

Bats: R **Throws:** R **Pos:** CF-3; PR-2; LF-1; RF-1; PH-1   **Ht:** 6'2" **Wt:** 205 **Born:** 4/12/1082 **Age:** 26

Year	Team	Lg	G	AB	H	2B	3B	HR	(Hm	Rd)	TB	R	RBI	RC	TBB	IBB	SO	HBP	SH	SF	SB	CS	SB%	GDP	Avg	OBP	Slg
2004	Ogden	R+	46	155	51	12	0	7	(-	-)	84	26	36	37	23	0	38	6	0	3	6	1	.86	7	.329	.428	.542
2005	VeroB	A+	71	242	75	15	4	9	(-	-)	125	47	37	51	28	2	65	9	0	1	16	5	.76	6	.310	.400	.517
2005	Jaxnvl	AA	53	161	55	10	1	6	(-	-)	85	23	29	35	17	0	56	6	0	1	8	3	.73	1	.342	.422	.528
2006	Jaxnvl	AA	89	292	76	19	3	9	(-	-)	128	51	45	50	46	3	74	5	0	3	10	5	.67	6	.260	.367	.438
2006	Mont	AA	31	108	36	14	3	4	(-	-)	68	25	27	28	19	0	29	2	1	0	4	4	.50	3	.333	.442	.630
2007	Drham	AAA	127	482	149	29	2	20	(-	-)	242	78	73	94	53	2	151	8	2	1	26	11	.70	5	.309	.386	.502
2007	TB	AL	7	14	3	0	0	0	(0	0)	3	2	3	1	1	0	5	0	0	0	0	0	-	0	.214	.267	.214

Carlos Ruiz

Bats: R **Throws:** R **Pos:** C-111; PH-6; PR-1   **Ht:** 5'10" **Wt:** 202 **Born:** 1/22/1979 **Age:** 29

Year	Team	Lg	G	AB	H	2B	3B	HR	(Hm	Rd)	TB	R	RBI	RC	TBB	IBB	SO	HBP	SH	SF	SB	CS	SB%	GDP	Avg	OBP	Slg
2000	Phillies	R	38	130	36	7	1	1	(-	-)	48	11	22	17	9	0	9	2	0	2	3	0	1.00	5	.277	.329	.369
2001	Lakwd	A	73	249	65	14	3	4	(-	-)	97	21	32	28	10	0	27	1	1	2	5	4	.56	5	.261	.290	.390
2002	Clrwtr	A+	92	342	73	18	3	5	(-	-)	112	35	32	30	18	1	30	6	2	1	3	1	.75	16	.213	.264	.327
2003	Clrwtr	A+	15	54	17	0	0	2	(-	-)	23	5	9	7	2	0	5	0	0	2	2	2	.50	5	.315	.339	.426
2003	Rdng	AA	52	169	45	6	0	2	(-	-)	57	22	16	19	12	0	15	3	1	3	1	1	.50	10	.266	.321	.337
2004	Rdng	AA	101	349	99	15	2	17	(-	-)	169	45	50	58	22	1	37	8	1	3	8	4	.67	15	.284	.338	.484
2005	S-WB	AAA	100	347	104	25	9	4	(-	-)	159	50	40	57	30	2	48	3	1	7	4	5	.44	14	.300	.354	.458
2006	S-WB	AAA	100	368	113	25	0	16	(-	-)	186	56	69	73	42	6	56	9	1	3	4	3	.57	13	.307	.389	.505
2006	Phi	NL	27	69	18	1	1	3	(2	1)	30	5	10	10	5	2	8	1	2	1	0	0	-	3	.261	.316	.435
2007	Phi	NL	115	374	97	29	2	6	(4	2)	148	42	54	49	42	10	49	5	5	3	6	1	.86	17	.259	.340	.396
2 ML YEARS			142	443	115	30	3	9	(6	3)	178	47	64	59	47	12	57	6	7	4	6	1	.86	20	.260	.336	.402

B.J. Ryan

Pitches: L **Bats:** L **Pos:** RP-5   **Ht:** 6'6" **Wt:** 260 **Born:** 12/28/1975 **Age:** 32

Year	Team	Lg	G	GS	CG	GF	IP	BFP	H	R	ER	HR	SH	SF	HB	TBB	IBB	SO	WP	Bk	W	L	Pct	ShO	Sv-Op Hld	ERC	ERA
1999	2 Tms		14	0	0	3	20.1	82	13	7	7	0	0	1	0	13	1	29	1	0	1	0	1.000	0	0-0 0	2.42	3.10
2000	Bal	AL	42	0	0	9	42.2	193	36	29	28	7	1	1	0	31	1	41	2	1	2	3	.400	0	0-3 7	4.87	5.91
2001	Bal	AL	61	0	0	9	53.0	237	47	31	25	6	1	2	2	30	4	54	0	0	2	4	.333	0	2-4 14	4.13	4.25
2002	Bal	AL	67	0	0	13	57.2	252	51	31	30	7	3	0	4	33	4	56	4	0	2	1	.667	0	1-2 12	4.48	4.68
2003	Bal	AL	76	0	0	19	50.1	219	42	19	19	1	1	3	3	27	0	63	2	0	4	1	.800	0	0-2 19	3.33	3.40
2004	Bal	AL	76	0	0	19	87.0	361	64	24	22	4	3	2	1	35	9	122	0	0	4	6	.400	0	3-7 21	2.20	2.28

(continued)

Year	Team	Lg	G	GS	CG	GF	IP	BFP	H	R	ER	HR	SH	SF	HB	TBB	IBB	SO	WP	Bk	W	L	Pct	ShO	Sv-Op	Hld	ERC	ERA
2005	Bal	AL	69	0	0	61	70.1	£50	54	20	19	4	1	1	2	26	2	100	5	0	1	4	.200	0	36-41	0	2.50	2.43
2006	Tor	AL	65	0	0	57	72.1	270	42	12	11	3	1	1	0	20	1	86	4	0	2	2	.500	0	38-42	1	1.39	1.37
2007	Tor	AL	5	0	0	4	4.1	25	7	7	6	1	0	0	0	4	0	3	0	0	0	2	.000	0	3-5	0	10.86	12.46
99	Cin	NL	1	0	0	0	2.0	9	4	1	1	0	0	0	0	1	0	1	0	0	0	0	-	0	0-0	0	12.01	4.50
99	Bal	AL	13	0	0	3	18.1	73	9	6	6	0	0	1	0	12	1	28	1	0	1	0	1.000	0	0-0	0	1.73	2.95
9 ML YEARS			475	0	0	192	458.0	1929	356	180	167	33	11	11	12	219	22	554	18	1	18	23	.439	0	83-106	74	3.00	3.28

Brendan Ryan

Bats: R **Throws:** R **Pos:** SS-28; 3B-24; 2B-17; PH-13; PR-1
Ht: 6'2" **Wt:** 195 **Born:** 3/26/1982 **Age:** 26

Year	Team	Lg	G	AB	H	2B	3B	HR	(Hm	Rd)	TB	R	RBI	RC	TBB	IBB	SO	HBP	SH	SF	SB	CS	SB%	GDP	Avg	OBP	Slg
2003	NewJrs	A-	53	193	60	14	4	0	(-	-)	82	20	13	31	14	1	25	3	1	2	11	3	.79	4	.311	.363	.425
2004	Peoria	A	105	426	137	21	4	2	(-	-)	172	72	59	67	24	2	42	4	9	9	30	7	.81	13	.322	.356	.404
2005	PlmBh	A+	49	188	57	17	0	1	(-	-)	77	29	16	29	15	0	20	0	4	0	8	1	.89	4	.303	.355	.410
2005	Sprgfld	AA	43	154	42	8	1	2	(-	-)	58	28	9	22	15	0	19	2	2	1	7	0	1.00	3	.273	.343	.377
2006	StCol	A	8	34	8	0	0	0	(-	-)	8	5	3	2	3	0	4	0	1	2	1	0	1.00	0	.235	.282	.235
2006	Sprgfld	AA	10	43	13	1	0	0	(-	-)	14	6	3	5	3	0	6	0	1	0	1	1	.50	2	.302	.348	.326
2006	PlmBh	A+	3	14	6	1	0	0	(-	-)	7	2	1	2	0	0	2	0	0	0	1	0	1.00	1	.429	.429	.500
2006	Memp	AAA	7	26	4	0	0	1	(-	-)	7	4	6	1	1	0	3	0	0	0	1	0	1.00	1	.154	.185	.269
2007	Memp	AAA	81	321	87	8	5	1	(-	-)	108	55	15	38	25	0	39	2	2	1	17	6	.74	6	.271	.327	.336
2007	StL	NL	67	180	52	9	0	4	(2	2)	73	30	12	21	15	0	19	1	3	0	7	0	1.00	3	.289	.347	.406

Jae Kuk Ryu

Pitches: R **Bats:** R **Pos:** RP-17
Ht: 6'3" **Wt:** 223 **Born:** 5/30/1983 **Age:** 25

Year	Team	Lg	G	GS	CG	GF	IP	BFP	H	R	ER	HR	SH	SF	HB	TBB	IBB	SO	WP	Bk	W	L	Pct	ShO	Sv-Op	Hld	ERC	ERA
2001	Cubs	R	4	3	0	0	14.2	61	11	2	1	0	0	0	0	5	0	20	2	0	1	0	1.000	0	0- -		1.87	0.61
2002	Boise	A-	10	10	0	0	53.0	234	45	28	21	1	1	2	4	25	0	56	8	1	6	1	.857	0	0- -		3.14	3.57
2002	Lansng	A	5	4	0	0	19.0	91	26	16	15	1	3	0	2	8	0	21	5	0	1	2	.333	0	0- -		6.39	7.11
2003	Dytona	A+	4	4	0	0	20.2	79	14	14	7	1	1	0	2	11	0	22	2	0	0	1	.000	0	0- -		3.21	3.05
2003	Lansng	A	11	11	0	0	72.0	292	59	19	14	2	2	4	5	19	0	57	10	1	6	1	.857	0	0- -		2.43	1.75
2003	WTenn	AA	11	11	1	0	58.0	261	63	37	35	3	4	2	5	25	0	45	2	1	2	5	.286	0	0- -		4.66	5.43
2004	Cubs	R	2	2	0	0	4.0	16	4	2	2	1	0	0	0	0	0	5	0	0	0	0	-	0	0- -		3.33	4.50
2004	Boise	A-	5	0	0	0	7.0	33	7	3	2	0	0	0	0	5	0	7	4	0	0	2	.000	0	0- -		4.40	2.57
2004	WTenn	AA	14	0	0	1	18.1	88	22	8	6	0	0	0	1	10	3	19	2	0	1	0	1.000	0	0- -		4.79	2.95
2004	Iowa	AAA	1	0	0	0	0.2	5	2	4	3	1	0	0	0	1	0	0	0	0	0	0	-	0	0- -		41.86	40.50
2005	WTenn	AA	27	27	1	0	169.2	686	154	67	63	12	15	4	6	49	1	133	9	0	11	8	.579	1	0- -		3.18	3.34
2006	Iowa	AAA	24	23	1	0	139.1	582	123	54	50	12	4	3	4	51	1	114	8	0	8	8	.500	0	0- -		3.33	3.23
2007	Drham	AAA	14	14	1	0	71.1	297	67	36	32	5	0	0	1	21	0	67	5	0	5	4	.556	0	0- -		3.20	4.04
2006	ChC	NL	10	1	0	4	15.0	77	23	14	14	7	3	0	2	6	1	17	1	0	0	1	.000	0	0-0	0	10.72	8.40
2007	TB	AL	17	0	0	7	23.1	110	31	19	19	2	0	0	4	11	0	14	2	0	1	2	.333	0	0-1	1	7.17	7.33
2 ML YEARS			27	1	0	11	38.1	187	54	33	33	9	3	0	6	17	1	31	3	0	1	3	.250	0	0-1	1	8.59	7.75

Kirk Saarloos

Pitches: R **Bats:** R **Pos:** RP-31; SP-3
Ht: 6'0" **Wt:** 185 **Born:** 5/23/1979 **Age:** 29

Year	Team	Lg	G	GS	CG	GF	IP	BFP	H	R	ER	HR	SH	SF	HB	TBB	IBB	SO	WP	Bk	W	L	Pct	ShO	Sv-Op	Hld	ERC	ERA
2007	Lsvlle*	AAA	18	5	0	5	41.0	175	47	19	18	3	0	2	0	9	0	28	0	0	0	2	.000	0	0- -		4.00	3.95
2002	Hou	NL	17	17	1	0	85.1	372	100	59	57	12	5	2	6	27	5	54	1	0	6	7	.462	1	0-0	0	5.35	6.01
2003	Hou	NL	36	4	0	11	49.1	218	55	31	27	4	1	1	3	17	3	43	0	0	2	1	.667	0	0-0	4	4.51	4.93
2004	Oak	AL	6	5	0	1	24.1	112	27	13	12	4	2	1	2	12	0	10	0	0	2	1	.667	0	0-0	0	5.91	4.44
2005	Oak	AL	29	27	2	0	159.2	682	170	75	74	11	3	3	11	54	8	53	1	0	10	9	.526	1	0-0	0	4.27	4.17
2006	Oak	AL	35	16	0	7	121.1	548	149	70	64	19	2	6	3	53	3	52	3	0	7	7	.500	0	2-3	6	6.17	4.75
2007	Cin	NL	34	3	0	7	42.2	201	54	36	34	8	2	0	3	19	1	27	1	0	1	5	.167	0	0-1	0	6.75	7.17
6 ML YEARS			157	72	3	26	482.2	2133	555	284	268	58	15	13	28	182	20	239	6	0	28	30	.483	2	2-4	8	5.24	5.00

C.C. Sabathia

Pitches: L **Bats:** L **Pos:** SP-34
Ht: 6'7" **Wt:** 290 **Born:** 7/21/1980 **Age:** 27

Year	Team	Lg	G	GS	CG	GF	IP	BFP	H	R	ER	HR	SH	SF	HB	TBB	IBB	SO	WP	Bk	W	L	Pct	ShO	Sv-Op	Hld	ERC	ERA
2001	Cle	AL	33	33	0	0	180.1	763	149	93	88	19	3	5	7	95	1	171	7	3	17	5	.773	0	0-0	0	3.86	4.39
2002	Cle	AL	33	33	2	0	210.0	891	198	109	102	17	5	10	4	88	2	149	6	3	13	11	.542	0	0-0	0	3.74	4.37
2003	Cle	AL	30	30	2	0	197.2	832	190	85	79	19	10	4	6	66	3	141	4	2	13	9	.591	1	0-0	0	3.70	3.60
2004	Cle	AL	30	30	1	0	188.0	787	176	90	86	20	3	6	7	72	3	139	1	1	11	10	.524	1	0-0	0	3.91	4.12
2005	Cle	AL	31	31	1	0	196.2	823	185	92	86	19	6	3	7	62	1	161	7	0	15	10	.600	0	0-0	0	3.55	4.03
2006	Cle	AL	28	28	6	0	192.2	802	182	83	69	17	8	5	7	44	3	172	3	0	12	11	.522	2	0-0	0	3.13	3.22
2007	Cle	AL	34	34	4	0	241.0	975	238	94	86	20	6	6	8	37	1	209	1	0	19	7	.731	1	0-0	0	3.12	3.21
7 ML YEARS			219	219	16	0	1406.1	5873	1318	646	598	131	41	39	43	464	14	1142	29	9	100	63	.613	5	0-0	0	3.55	3.83

Donnie Sadler

Bats: R Throws: R Pos: 2B-1   Ht: 5'6" Wt: 175 Born: 6/17/1975 Age: 33

			BATTING																	BASERUNNING				AVERAGES		
Year	Team	Lg	G	AB	H	2B	3B	HR	(Hm Rd)	TB	R	RBI	RC	TBB	IBB	SO	HBP	SH	SF	SB	CS	SB%	GDP	Avg	OBP	Slg
2007	Tucsn*	AAA	52	112	24	1	5	2	(- -)	41	19	17	17	22	2	26	1	2	0	5	0	1.00	0	.214	.348	.366
1998	Bos	AL	58	124	28	4	4	3	(0 3)	49	21	15	15	6	0	28	3	5	1	4	0	1.00	1	.226	.276	.395
1999	Bos	AL	49	107	30	5	1	0	(0 0)	37	18	4	12	5	0	20	0	3	0	2	1	.67	1	.280	.313	.346
2000	Bos	AL	49	99	22	5	0	1	(0 1)	30	14	10	8	5	0	18	1	5	2	3	1	.75	1	.222	.262	.303
2001	2 Tms		93	185	30	6	0	1	(0 1)	39	28	5	8	18	0	37	2	5	1	7	4	.64	3	.162	.243	.211
2002	2 Tms		73	98	16	2	1	0	(0 0)	20	16	7	4	7	0	19	2	1	1	5	3	.63	1	.163	.231	.204
2003	Tex	AL	77	131	26	5	2	1	(0 1)	38	27	5	10	13	0	34	2	2	2	4	3	.57	1	.198	.277	.290
2004	Ari	NL	18	23	3	2	0	0	(0 0)	5	1	0	0	1	0	7	0	0	0	0	0	-	0	.130	.167	.217
2007	Ari	NL	1	1	0	0	0	0	(0 0)	0	0	0	0	0	0	0	0	0	0	0	0	-	0	.000	.000	.000
01	Cin	NL	39	84	17	3	0	1	(0 1)	23	9	3	5	9	0	20	0	2	0	3	3	.50	3	.202	.280	.274
01	KC	AL	54	101	13	3	0	0	(0 0)	16	19	2	3	9	0	17	2	3	1	4	1	.80	0	.129	.212	.158
02	KC	AL	35	68	13	1	1	0	(0 0)	16	10	5	4	4	0	12	0	0	1	3	1	.75	0	.191	.233	.235
02	Tex	AL	38	30	3	1	0	0	(0 0)	4	6	2	0	3	0	7	2	1	0	2	2	.50	1	.100	.229	.133
8 ML YEARS			418	768	155	29	8	6	(0 6)	218	125	46	57	55	0	163	10	21	7	25	12	.68	8	.202	.262	.284

Olmedo Saenz

Bats: R Throws: R Pos: PH-75; 1B-13; DH-5; 3B-3   Ht: 6'1" Wt: 230 Born: 10/8/1970 Age: 37

			BATTING																	BASERUNNING				AVERAGES		
Year	Team	Lg	G	AB	H	2B	3B	HR	(Hm Rd)	TB	R	RBI	RC	TBB	IBB	SO	HBP	SH	SF	SB	CS	SB%	GDP	Avg	OBP	Slg
1994	CWS	AL	5	14	2	0	1	0	(0 0)	4	2	0	0	0	0	5	0	1	0	0	0	-	1	.143	.143	.286
1999	Oak	AL	97	255	70	18	0	11	(8 3)	121	41	41	44	22	1	47	15	0	3	1	1	.50	6	.275	.363	.475
2000	Oak	AL	76	214	67	12	2	9	(3 6)	110	40	33	42	25	2	40	7	0	1	1	0	1.00	6	.313	.401	.514
2001	Oak	AL	106	305	67	21	1	9	(6 3)	117	33	32	32	19	1	64	13	1	3	0	1	.00	9	.220	.291	.384
2002	Oak	AL	68	156	43	10	1	6	(3 3)	73	15	18	23	13	1	31	7	0	2	1	1	.50	2	.276	.354	.468
2004	LAD	NL	77	111	31	1	0	8	(3 5)	56	17	22	18	12	1	33	2	0	3	0	0	-	4	.279	.352	.505
2005	LAD	NL	109	319	84	24	0	15	(9 6)	153	39	63	50	27	1	63	3	0	2	0	1	.00	12	.263	.325	.480
2006	LAD	NL	103	179	53	15	0	11	(6 5)	101	30	48	33	14	1	47	7	0	4	0	0	-	4	.296	.363	.564
2007	LAD	NL	92	110	21	5	0	4	(2 2)	38	9	18	9	16	0	25	2	0	4	0	0	-	5	.191	.295	.345
9 ML YEARS			733	1663	438	106	5	73	(40 33)	773	226	275	251	148	8	355	56	2	22	3	4	.43	49	.263	.340	.465

Takashi Saito

Pitches: R Bats: R Pos: RP-63   Ht: 6'2" Wt: 200 Born: 2/14/1970 Age: 38

			HOW MUCH HE PITCHED						WHAT HE GAVE UP												THE RESULTS							
Year	Team	Lg	G	GS	CG	GF	IP	BFP	H	R	ER	HR	SH	SF	HB	TBB	IBB	SO	WP	Bk	W	L	Pct	ShO	Sv-Op	Hld	ERC	ERA
1992	Yokha	Jap	6	2	0	1	16.0	76	18	16	15	2	-	-	0	10	-	21	2	0	0	2	.000	0	0--	-	5.78	8.44
1993	Yokha	Jap	29	21	2	1	149.0	627	127	66	63	15	-	-	6	61	-	125	7	0	8	10	.444	0	0--	-	3.48	3.81
1994	Yokha	Jap	28	20	7	0	181.0	769	175	70	63	5	-	-	8	69	-	169	2	0	9	12	.429	3	0--	-	3.53	3.13
1995	Yokha	Jap	26	24	2	0	162.0	682	166	79	71	13	-	-	6	45	-	132	1	0	8	9	.471	0	0--	-	3.78	3.94
1996	Yokha	Jap	28	16	11	0	196.2	801	157	80	72	31	-	-	11	63	-	206	4	1	10	10	.500	2	0--	-	3.30	3.29
1998	Yokha	Jap	34	17	1	4	143.2	572	131	49	47	9	-	-	2	23	-	101	2	0	13	5	.722	0	1--	-	2.55	2.94
1999	Yokha	Jap	26	21	5	0	184.2	754	178	83	81	32	-	-	6	31	-	125	1	1	14	3	.824	2	0--	-	3.58	3.95
2000	Yokha	Jap	19	18	1	0	115.2	493	123	74	71	17	-	-	3	36	-	97	1	0	6	10	.375	1	0--	-	4.57	5.52
2001	Yokha	Jap	50	0	0	43	64.0	251	51	12	12	6	-	-	0	14	-	60	0	0	7	1	.875	0	27--	-	2.33	1.69
2002	Yokha	Jap	39	0	0	34	47.2	197	37	17	13	5	-	-	4	15	-	46	0	0	1	2	.333	0	20--	-	2.88	2.45
2003	Yokha	Jap	17	16	1	0	103.1	439	103	59	48	12	-	-	9	22	1	72	1	0	6	7	.462	0	0--	-	3.98	4.18
2004	Yokha	Jap	16	7	0	3	44.1	211	64	41	38	12	2	3	2	13	0	37	1	1	2	5	.286	0	0--	-	7.74	7.71
2005	Yokha	Jap	21	16	0	1	106.0	458	111	50	45	12	10	3	7	29	1	93	2	0	3	4	.429	0	0--	-	4.15	3.82
2006	LAD	NL	72	0	0	48	78.1	303	48	19	18	3	3	4	2	23	3	107	2	0	6	2	.750	0	24-26	7	1.52	2.07
2007	LAD	NL	63	0	0	55	64.1	234	33	10	10	5	0	0	3	13	0	78	0	0	2	1	.667	0	39-43	1	1.28	1.40
2 ML YEARS			135	0	0	103	142.2	537	81	29	28	8	3	4	5	36	3	185	2	0	8	3	.727	0	63-69	8	1.41	1.77

Juan Salas

Pitches: R Bats: R Pos: RP-34   Ht: 6'2" Wt: 230 Born: 11/7/1978 Age: 29

			HOW MUCH HE PITCHED						WHAT HE GAVE UP												THE RESULTS							
Year	Team	Lg	G	GS	CG	GF	IP	BFP	H	R	ER	HR	SH	SF	HB	TBB	IBB	SO	WP	Bk	W	L	Pct	ShO	Sv-Op	Hld	ERC	ERA
2004	Princtn	R+	8	0	0	3	9.1	44	10	7	5	2	0	0	0	6	1	6	0	1	1	0	1.000	0	0--	-	6.05	4.82
2005	Visalia	A+	25	0	0	11	38.1	164	30	19	15	6	2	1	5	18	1	47	6	1	2	1	.667	0	1--	-	4.03	3.52
2005	Mont	AA	15	0	0	6	22.0	104	25	12	9	2	0	1	2	12	0	18	5	1	1	0	1.000	0	0--	-	5.68	3.68
2006	Mont	AA	23	0	0	22	34.2	133	13	4	0	0	0	0	1	14	0	52	0	0	3	0	1.000	0	14--	-	0.94	0.00
2006	Drham	AAA	27	0	0	10	28.2	113	15	5	5	3	0	0	1	11	0	33	1	0	1	1	.500	0	3--	-	1.75	1.57
2007	Mont	AA	2	0	0	1	1.1	10	4	4	4	0	0	0	0	2	0	2	0	0	1	0	1.000	0	1--	-	22.07	27.00
2007	Drham	AAA	7	0	0	1	8.2	34	5	2	2	0	0	0	0	3	1	12	4	1	1	0	1.000	0	1--	-	1.33	2.08
2006	TB	AL	8	0	0	2	10.0	48	13	7	6	1	0	1	0	3	0	8	3	0	0	0	-	0	0-1	1	5.03	5.40
2007	TB	AL	34	0	0	10	36.1	168	36	19	15	7	1	0	5	17	0	26	3	0	1	1	.500	0	0-1	2	5.39	3.72
2 ML YEARS			42	0	0	12	46.1	216	49	26	21	8	1	1	5	20	0	34	6	0	1	1	.500	0	0 2	3	5.31	4.08

Jeff Salazar

Bats: L Throws: L Pos: RF-27; PH-11; LF-6; CF-1   Ht: 6'0" Wt: 190 Born: 11/24/1980 Age: 27

			BATTING																	BASERUNNING				AVERAGES		
Year	Team	Lg	G	AB	H	2B	3B	HR	(Hm Rd)	TB	R	RBI	RC	TBB	IBB	SO	HBP	SH	SF	SB	CS	SB%	GDP	Avg	OBP	Slg
2002	TriCity	A-	72	268	63	5	4	4	(- -)	88	38	21	35	47	0	43	2	9	2	10	6	.63	2	.235	.351	.328
2003	Ashvll	A	129	486	138	23	4	29	(- -)	256	109	98	102	77	8	74	7	4	4	28	14	.67	5	.284	.387	.527
2003	Visalia	A+	1	5	0	0	0	0	(- -)	0	1	0	0	0	0	0	0	0	0	0	0	-	0	.000	.000	.000
2004	Visalia	A+	75	314	109	18	9	13	(- -)	184	79	44	77	38	3	33	2	2	2	17	2	.89	4	.347	.419	.586

					BATTING																BASERUNNING				AVERAGES		
Year	Team	Lg	G	AB	H	2B	3B	HR	(Hm | Rd)	TB	R	RBI	RC	TBB	IBB	SO	HBP	SH	SF		SB	CS	SB%	GDP		Avg	OBP	Slg
2004	Tulsa	AA	58	224	50	13	?	1	(- | -)	70	39	17	27	35	0	31	2	7	2		10	3	.77	1		.223	.331	.313
2005	Tulsa	AA	65	266	74	13	2	6	(- | -)	109	47	35	45	44	4	49	2	4	3		12	8	.60	1		.278	.381	.410
2005	ColSpr	AAA	59	236	62	17	3	6	(- | -)	103	42	26	38	32	0	58	0	3	1		5	2	.71	1		.263	.349	.436
2006	ColSpr	AAA	85	328	87	14	7	9	(- | -)	142	62	39	54	46	1	64	2	3	2		12	5	.71	0		.265	.357	.433
2007	Tucsn	AAA	108	400	119	31	9	10	(- | -)	198	75	67	80	56	1	56	5	2	7		17	5	.77	5		.298	.385	.495
2006	Col	NL	19	53	15	4	0	1	(1 | 0)	22	13	8	11	11	2	16	1	1	1		2	0	1.00	0		.283	.409	.415
2007	Ari	NL	38	94	26	6	1	1	(0 | 1)	37	13	10	16	9	0	19	0	0	0		2	0	1.00	1		.277	.340	.394
	2 ML YEARS		57	147	41	10	1	2	(1 | 1)	59	26	18	27	20	2	35	1	1	1		4	0	1.00	1		.279	.367	.401

Brad Salmon

Pitches: R **Bats:** L **Pos:** RP-26

Ht: 6'3" **Wt:** 230 **Born:** 1/3/1980 **Age:** 28

				HOW MUCH HE PITCHED				WHAT HE GAVE UP													THE RESULTS						
Year	Team	Lg	G	GS	CG	GF	IP	BFP	H	R	ER	HR	SH	SF	HB	TBB	IBB	SO	WP	Bk	W	L	Pct	ShO	Sv-Op	Hld	ERC	ERA
1999	Billings	R+	16	6	0	2	49.1	239	67	46	41	2	2	4	6	19	1	43	2	3	2	2	.500	0	1--	-	5.98	7.48
2000	Clinton	A	22	22	1	0	123.2	538	134	71	59	4	3	4	2	46	0	119	11	0	7	5	.583	0	0--	-	4.03	4.29
2001	Mudvle	A+	33	18	1	8	135.1	587	132	75	61	10	5	3	6	51	0	110	11	0	5	8	.385	0	0--	-	3.80	4.06
2002	Dayton	A	29	27	1	0	159.1	698	165	94	79	9	2	0	16	48	2	117	7	0	12	9	.571	1	0--	-	3.91	4.46
2003	Ptomc	A+	32	1	0	12	49.1	221	55	27	25	4	8	1	0	18	4	53	3	0	3	2	.600	0	1--	-	4.20	4.56
2003	Chatt	AA	10	1	0	5	24.2	107	27	14	14	2	0	0	1	9	0	21	0	1	4	0	1.000	0	1--	-	4.57	5.11
2004	Chatt	AA	39	1	0	20	65.1	288	68	35	31	3	3	1	2	22	2	53	2	0	4	2	.667	0	3--	-	3.65	4.27
2004	Ptomc	A+	5	1	0	0	16.2	66	12	1	1	0	0	0	1	3	0	16	0	0	1	0	1.000	0	0--	-	1.54	0.54
2005	Chatt	AA	38	0	0	13	71.2	304	64	31	27	3	8	1	3	30	2	70	7	0	3	8	.273	0	4--	-	3.29	3.39
2005	Lsvlle	AAA	9	0	0	3	16.1	67	13	6	6	2	0	0	0	5	1	8	0	0	0	0	-	0	0--	-	2.64	3.31
2006	Chatt	AA	16	0	0	4	23.1	103	18	7	7	0	2	1	0	16	0	24	1	0	2	1	.667	0	0--	-	3.14	2.70
2006	Lsvlle	AAA	39	0	0	10	57.2	232	36	18	15	3	5	2	2	27	0	72	6	0	5	1	.833	0	2--	-	2.23	2.34
2007	Lsvlle	AAA	37	0	0	14	43.0	186	41	19	18	3	0	2	5	17	0	40	4	0	2	2	.500	0	3--	-	4.08	3.77
2007	Cin	NL	26	0	0	9	24.0	101	22	11	11	3	0	0	1	10	1	22	2	0	1	0	.000	0	0-1	0	4.03	4.13

Jarrod Saltalamacchia

Bats: B **Throws:** R **Pos:** C-47; 1B-38; PH-11; DH-2

Ht: 6'4" **Wt:** 195 **Born:** 5/2/1985 **Age:** 23

					BATTING																BASERUNNING				AVERAGES		
Year	Team	Lg	G	AB	H	2B	3B	HR	(Hm | Rd)	TB	R	RBI	RC	TBB	IBB	SO	HBP	SH	SF		SB	CS	SB%	GDP		Avg	OBP	Slg
2003	Braves	R	46	134	32	11	2	2	(- | -)	53	23	14	22	28	0	33	3	0	0		0	0	-	0		.239	.382	.396
2004	Rome	A	91	323	88	19	2	10	(- | -)	141	42	51	51	34	2	83	5	1	3		1	0	1.00	6		.272	.348	.437
2005	MrtlBh	A+	129	459	144	35	1	19	(- | -)	238	70	81	95	57	11	99	7	1	5		4	2	.67	14		.314	.394	.519
2006	Missi	AA	92	313	72	18	1	9	(- | -)	119	30	39	46	55	5	71	6	0	3		0	1	.00	1		.230	.353	.380
2007	Missi	AA	22	81	25	7	0	6	(- | -)	50	18	13	20	13	1	17	0	0	0		2	0	1.00	1		.309	.404	.617
2007	2 Tms		93	308	82	13	1	11	(6 | 5)	130	39	33	32	19	1	75	1	0	1		0	0	-	8		.266	.310	.422
07	Atl	NL	47	141	40	6	0	4	(4 | 0)	58	11	12	13	10	1	28	1	0	1		0	0	-	4		.284	.333	.411
07	Tex	AL	46	167	42	7	1	7	(2 | 5)	72	28	21	19	9	0	47	0	0	0		0	0	-	4		.251	.290	.431

Clint Sammons

Bats: R **Throws:** R **Pos:** C-2

Ht: 6'0" **Wt:** 200 **Born:** 5/15/1983 **Age:** 25

					BATTING																BASERUNNING				AVERAGES		
Year	Team	Lg	G	AB	H	2B	3B	HR	(Hm | Rd)	TB	R	RBI	RC	TBB	IBB	SO	HBP	SH	SF		SB	CS	SB%	GDP		Avg	OBP	Slg
2004	Danvle	R	40	132	38	7	2	0	(- | -)	49	19	17	20	18	1	26	0	1	2		5	1	.83	3		.288	.368	.371
2005	Rome	A	121	427	122	29	0	4	(- | -)	163	60	62	66	55	0	66	5	0	7		4	1	.80	15		.286	.368	.382
2006	MrtlBh	A+	103	360	93	21	0	8	(- | -)	138	36	56	47	32	1	65	5	4	6		4	4	.50	7		.258	.323	.383
2007	MrtlBh	A+	23	78	21	6	0	4	(- | -)	39	13	13	14	10	0	14	2	0	1		1	1	.50	0		.269	.363	.500
2007	Missi	AA	83	296	72	10	0	5	(- | -)	97	27	36	31	26	0	72	1	2	3		1	1	.50	5		.243	.304	.328
2007	Atl	NL	2	3	2	1	0	0	(0 | 0)	3	0	0	1	0	0	0	0	0	0		0	0	-	1		.667	.667	1.000

Chris Sampson

Pitches: R **Bats:** R **Pos:** SP-19; RP-5

Ht: 6'1" **Wt:** 190 **Born:** 5/23/1978 **Age:** 30

				HOW MUCH HE PITCHED				WHAT HE GAVE UP													THE RESULTS						
Year	Team	Lg	G	GS	CG	GF	IP	BFP	H	R	ER	HR	SH	SF	HB	TBB	IBB	SO	WP	Bk	W	L	Pct	ShO	Sv-Op	Hld	ERC	ERA
2003	Lxngtn	A	22	14	0	2	81.0	332	66	17	13	2	1	0	5	14	0	66	0	0	4	3	.571	0	1--	-	1.98	1.44
2003	Salem	A+	3	0	0	5	10.2	51	14	8	7	0	2	0	1	5	2	6	0	0	1	1	.500	0	1--	-	5.36	5.91
2004	Salem	A+	27	27	2	0	151.2	626	179	72	64	8	6	8	9	26	0	101	2	0	7	11	.389	2	0--	-	4.29	3.80
2004	RdRck	AA	1	0	0	0	2.0	9	3	0	0	0	0	0	0	0	0	1	0	0	0	0	-	0	0--	-	4.47	0.00
2005	CpChr	AA	32	19	2	9	150.0	618	147	67	52	11	4	4	4	19	2	92	2	0	4	12	.250	1	4--	-	2.79	3.12
2006	RdRck	AAA	27	18	2	8	125.2	501	110	48	35	12	7	5	3	14	0	68	2	0	12	3	.800	0	4--	-	2.38	2.51
2007	RdRck	AAA	2	0	0	1	3.0	13	3	0	0	0	0	0	0	0	1	0	0	0	1	0	1.000	0	0--	-	3.95	0.00
2006	Hou	NL	12	3	0	0	34.0	130	25	10	8	3	1	1	1	5	1	15	0	0	2	1	.667	0	0-0	-	1.84	2.12
2007	Hou	NL	24	19	0	2	121.2	522	138	64	62	20	6	6	7	30	2	51	3	0	7	8	.467	0	0-0	-	4.96	4.59
	2 ML YEARS		36	22	0	2	155.2	652	163	74	70	23	7	7	8	35	3	66	3	0	9	9	.500	0	0-0	-	4.20	4.05

Brian Sanches

Pitches: R **Bats:** R **Pos:** RP-12

Ht: 6'0" **Wt:** 190 **Born:** 8/8/1978 **Age:** 29

				HOW MUCH HE PITCHED				WHAT HE GAVE UP													THE RESULTS						
Year	Team	Lg	G	GS	CG	GF	IP	BFP	H	R	ER	HR	SH	SF	HB	TBB	IBB	SO	WP	Bk	W	L	Pct	ShO	Sv-Op	Hld	ERC	ERA
1999	Spkane	A-	9	9	0	0	34.0	146	32	19	18	2	0	0	1	12	0	51	0	0	1	1	.500	0	0--	-	3.35	4.76
2000	Wilmg	A	28	27	2	0	158.0	665	132	77	62	9	5	7	15	69	0	122	11	3	6	12	.333	1	0--	-	3.45	3.53
2001	Wichta	AA	29	21	0	3	134.0	610	152	96	89	12	7	3	13	61	4	95	12	1	7	9	.438	0	0--	-	5.37	5.98
2002	Wichta	AA	33	15	0	7	116.2	498	111	60	57	8	5	3	6	43	5	101	7	1	10	6	.625	0	0--	-	3.61	4.40

Year	Team	Lg	G	GS	CG	GF	IP	BFP	H	R	ER	HR	SH	SF	HB	TBB	IBB	SO	WP	Bk	W	L	Pct	ShO	Sv-Op	Hld	ERC	ERA
2003	Wichta	AA	38	6	0	13	85.0	351	84	38	30	8	4	4	3	17	2	72	3	2	1	5	.167	0	2--	-	3.31	3.18
2004	Rdng	AA	41	6	0	14	69.2	292	55	22	21	10	2	1	3	25	1	60	1	0	4	2	.667	0	3--	-	3.15	2.71
2004	S-WB	AAA	4	0	0	1	6.0	30	9	5	5	1	0	0	0	3	0	4	0	0	0	0	-	0	0--	-	7.95	7.50
2005	S-WB	AAA	51	2	0	13	83.0	352	81	36	34	9	1	4	9	27	2	75	1	0	5	3	.625	0	1--	-	4.18	3.69
2006	S-WB	AAA	36	0	0	28	43.2	164	24	9	9	2	2	2	1	13	1	52	1	1	3	2	.600	0	19--	-	1.40	1.85
2007	Ottawa	AAA	36	1	0	29	47.1	203	56	29	25	5	2	0	1	8	1	52	6	0	2	3	.400	0	16--	-	4.26	4.75
2006	Phi	NL	18	0	0	5	21.1	98	23	14	14	5	0	0	0	13	3	22	0	1	0	0	-	0	0-0	0	6.18	5.91
2007	Phi	NL	12	0	0	4	14.2	68	13	11	9	6	1	0	1	12	2	9	1	0	1	1	.500	0	0-0	1	7.73	5.52
2 ML YEARS			30	0	0	9	36.0	166	36	25	23	11	1	0	1	25	5	31	1	1	1	1	.500	0	0-0	1	6.80	5.75

Anibal Sanchez

Pitches: R Bats: R Pos: SP-6   Ht: 6'0" Wt: 180 Born: 2/27/1984 Age: 24

Year	Team	Lg	G	GS	CG	GF	IP	BFP	H	R	ER	HR	SH	SF	HB	TBB	IBB	SO	WP	Bk	W	L	Pct	ShO	Sv-Op	Hld	ERC	ERA
2004	Lowell	A-	15	15	0	0	76.1	310	43	24	15	3	3	4	6	29	0	101	2	1	3	4	.429	0	0--	-	1.67	1.77
2005	Wilmg	A+	14	14	0	0	78.2	313	53	25	21	7	0	5	3	24	0	95	5	0	6	1	.857	0	2--	-	2.11	2.40
2005	Portlnd	AA	11	11	0	0	57.1	241	53	28	22	5	1	2	5	16	2	63	4	1	3	5	.375	0	0--	-	3.40	3.45
2006	Carlna	AA	15	15	2	0	85.2	366	82	41	30	7	3	0	2	27	1	92	4	0	6	3	.333	1	0--	-	3.40	3.15
2006	Fla	NL	18	17	2	0	114.1	469	90	39	36	9	3	1	4	46	1	72	4	1	10	3	.769	1	0-0	0	2.96	2.83
2007	Fla	NL	6	6	0	0	30.0	151	43	17	16	3	2	2	2	19	1	14	3	0	2	1	.667	0	0-0	0	7.90	4.80
2 ML YEARS			24	23	2	0	144.1	620	133	56	52	12	5	3	6	65	2	86	7	1	12	4	.750	1	0-0	0	3.88	3.24

Duaner Sanchez

Pitches: R Bats: R Pos: P   Ht: 6'2" Wt: 210 Born: 10/14/1979 Age: 28

Year	Team	Lg	G	GS	CG	GF	IP	BFP	H	R	ER	HR	SH	SF	HB	TBB	IBB	SO	WP	Bk	W	L	Pct	ShO	Sv-Op	Hld	ERC	ERA
2002	2 Tms	NL	9	0	0	5	6.0	31	6	6	6	2	0	0	0	7	0	6	0	0	0	0	-	0	0-1	1	9.19	9.00
2003	Pit	NL	6	0	0	2	6.0	34	15	11	11	2	0	1	2	1	0	3	0	0	1	0	1.000	0	0-0	0	17.96	16.50
2004	LAD	NL	67	0	0	27	80.0	342	81	34	30	9	2	3	6	27	2	44	6	0	3	1	.750	0	0-1	4	4.31	3.38
2005	LAD	NI	79	0	0	31	82.0	353	75	36	34	8	10	1	3	36	6	71	7	1	4	7	.364	0	8-12	13	3.76	3.73
2006	NYM	NL	49	0	0	15	55.1	229	43	19	16	3	4	4	4	24	6	44	1	0	5	1	.833	0	0-1	14	2.85	2.60
02	Ari	NL	6	0	0	3	3.2	19	3	2	2	1	0	0	0	5	0	4	0	0	0	0	-	0	0-1	1	8.32	4.91
02	Pit	NL	3	0	0	2	2.1	12	3	4	4	1	0	0	0	2	0	2	0	0	0	0	-	0	0-0	0	10.55	15.43
5 ML YEARS			210	0	0	80	229.1	989	220	106	97	24	16	9	15	95	14	168	14	1	13	9	.591	0	8-15	32	4.13	3.81

Freddy Sanchez

Bats: R Throws: R Pos: 2B-146; SS-1, DH-1   Ht: 5'10" Wt: 187 Born: 12/21/1977 Age: 30

Year	Team	Lg	G	AB	H	2B	3B	HR	(Hm	Rd)	TB	R	RBI	RC	TBB	IBB	SO	HBP	SH	SF	SB	CS	SB%	GDP	Avg	OBP	Slg
2007	Indy*	AAA	1	2	1	1	0	0	(-	-)	2	1	0	1	2	0	0	0	0	0	0	0	-	0	.500	.750	1.000
2002	Bos	AL	12	16	3	0	0	0	(0	0)	3	3	2	1	2	0	3	0	0	0	0	0	-	0	.188	.278	.188
2003	Bos	AL	20	34	8	2	0	0	(0	0)	10	6	2	1	0	0	8	0	0	0	0	0	-	0	.235	.235	.294
2004	Pit	NL	9	19	3	0	0	0	(0	0)	3	2	2	2	0	0	3	0	1	0	0	0	-	0	.158	.158	.158
2005	Pit	NL	132	453	132	26	4	5	(3	2)	181	54	35	57	27	1	36	5	4	3	2	2	.50	6	.291	.336	.400
2006	Pit	NL	157	582	200	53	2	6	(2	4)	275	85	85	101	31	6	52	7	3	9	3	2	.60	12	.344	.378	.473
2007	Pit	NL	147	602	183	42	4	11	(5	6)	266	77	81	94	32	2	76	8	2	9	0	1	.00	13	.304	.343	.442
6 ML YEARS			477	1706	529	123	10	22	(10	12)	738	227	207	256	92	9	178	20	10	21	5	5	.50	31	.310	.349	.433

Jonathan Sanchez

Pitches: L Bats: L Pos: RP-29; SP-4   Ht: 6'2" Wt: 180 Born: 11/19/1982 Age: 25

Year	Team	Lg	G	GS	CG	GF	IP	BFP	H	R	ER	HR	SH	SF	HB	TBB	IBB	SO	WP	Bk	W	L	Pct	ShO	Sv-Op	Hld	ERC	ERA
2004	Giants	R	9	3	0	3	26.0	109	22	9	8	0	0	1	2	9	1	27	1	0	5	0	1.000	0	1--	-	2.60	2.77
2004	SlmKzr	A-	6	6	0	0	21.1	102	16	13	12	3	2	1	1	19	0	34	0	1	1	1	.667	0	0--	-	4.62	4.84
2005	Augsta	A	25	25	0	0	125.2	538	122	59	57	8	3	5	7	39	0	166	7	0	5	7	.417	0	0--	-	3.50	4.08
2006	Conn	AA	13	3	0	4	31.1	116	14	7	4	0	2	1	2	9	0	46	2	0	2	1	.667	0	2--	-	1.01	1.15
2006	Fresno	AAA	6	6	0	0	23.2	97	13	10	10	1	0	2	2	13	0	28	1	0	2	2	.500	0	0--	-	2.22	3.80
2007	SnJos	A+	2	2	0	0	3.0	9	0	0	0	0	0	0	0	1	0	5	0	0	0	0	-	0	0--	-	0.14	0.00
2007	Fresno	AAA	6	3	0	0	20.2	84	15	5	5	0	0	0	0	8	0	27	3	0	0	0	-	0	0--	-	1.97	2.18
2006	SF	NL	27	4	0	4	40.0	185	39	26	22	2	0	2	4	23	0	33	2	0	3	1	.750	0	0-0	5	4.54	4.95
2007	SF	NL	33	4	0	8	52.0	238	57	34	34	8	2	2	5	28	1	62	4	0	1	5	.167	0	0-0	2	6.06	5.88
2 ML YEARS			60	8	0	12	92.0	423	96	60	56	10	2	4	9	51	1	95	6	0	4	6	.400	0	0-0	7	5.38	5.48

Romulo Sanchez

Pitches: R Bats: R Pos: RP-16   Ht: 6'5" Wt: 243 Born: 4/28/1984 Age: 24

Year	Team	Lg	G	GS	CG	GF	IP	BFP	H	R	ER	HR	SH	SF	HB	TBB	IBB	SO	WP	Bk	W	L	Pct	ShO	Sv-Op	Hld	ERC	ERA
2005	Pirates	R	2	1	0	0	10.0	38	7	2	2	1	0	0	0	4	0	7	0	0	1	0	1.000	0	0--	-	2.70	1.80
2005	Altna	AA	2	2	0	0	10.0	44	11	4	4	2	0	1	0	4	0	5	1	0	1	0	1.000	0	0--	-	5.40	3.60
2005	Hickory	A	10	10	0	0	53.2	235	59	34	28	5	3	1	10	19	0	24	4	1	3	3	.500	0	0--	-	5.37	4.70
2006	Hickory	A	21	3	0	12	40.2	198	51	36	32	4	1	3	6	18	0	28	6	1	0	3	.000	0	4--	-	6.16	7.08
2006	Altna	AA	8	0	0	4	9.0	41	8	5	5	1	0	0	0	8	0	5	0	0	0	0	-	0	0--	-	5.63	5.00
2006	Lynbrg	A+	8	0	0	7	8.2	38	7	1	1	0	0	0	1	4	0	6	0	0	0	0	-	0	1--	-	2.92	1.04
2007	Altna	AA	40	0	0	16	57.2	236	43	24	18	8	2	3	3	17	2	52	5	1	6	3	.667	0	1--	-	2.68	2.81
2007	Pit	NL	16	0	0	7	18.0	73	16	10	10	2	0	1	1	8	0	11	1	0	1	0	1.000	0	0-0	2	4.20	5.00

Reggie Sanders

Bats: R **Throws:** R **Pos:** LF-9; RF-9; DH-7; PH-2; PR-2   **Ht:** 6'1 **Wt:** 200 **Born:** 12/1/1967 **Age:** 40

									BATTING													BASERUNNING				AVERAGES		
Year	Team	Lg	G	AB	H	2B	3B	HR	(Hm	Rd)	TB	R	RBI	RC	TBB	IBB	SO	HBP	SH	SF		SB	CS	SB%	GDP	Avg	OBP	Slg
1991	Cin	NL	9	40	8	0	0	1	(0	1)	11	6	3	1	0	0	9	0	0	0		1	1	.50	1	.200	.200	.275
1992	Cin	NL	116	385	104	26	6	12	(6	6)	178	62	36	64	48	2	98	4	0	1		16	7	.70	6	.270	.356	.462
1993	Cin	NL	138	496	136	16	4	20	(8	12)	220	90	83	76	51	7	118	5	3	8		27	10	.73	10	.274	.343	.444
1994	Cin	NL	107	400	105	20	8	17	(10	7)	192	66	62	65	41	1	114	2	1	3		21	9	.70	2	.263	.332	.480
1995	Cin	NL	133	484	148	36	6	28	(9	19)	280	91	99	109	69	4	122	8	0	6		36	12	.75	9	.306	.397	.579
1996	Cin	NL	81	287	72	17	1	14	(7	7)	133	49	33	47	44	4	86	2	0	1		24	8	.75	8	.251	.353	.463
1997	Cin	NL	86	312	79	19	2	19	(11	8)	159	52	56	53	42	3	93	3	1	0		13	7	.65	9	.253	.347	.510
1998	Cin	NL	135	481	129	18	6	14	(7	7)	201	83	59	69	51	2	137	7	4	2		20	9	.69	10	.268	.346	.418
1999	SD	NL	133	478	136	24	7	26	(11	15)	252	92	72	94	65	1	108	6	0	1		36	13	.73	10	.285	.376	.527
2000	Atl	NL	103	340	79	23	1	11	(4	7)	137	43	37	42	32	2	78	2	3	0		21	4	.84	9	.232	.302	.403
2001	Ari	NL	126	441	116	21	3	33	(19	14)	242	84	90	80	46	7	126	5	1	3		14	10	.58	2	.263	.337	.549
2002	SF	NL	140	505	126	23	6	23	(12	11)	230	75	85	65	47	3	121	12	0	7		18	6	.75	10	.250	.324	.455
2003	Pit	NL	130	453	129	27	4	31	(17	14)	257	74	87	78	38	4	110	5	0	2		15	5	.75	10	.285	.345	.567
2004	StL	NL	135	446	116	27	3	22	(8	14)	215	64	67	65	33	5	118	4	1	3		21	5	.81	5	.260	.315	.482
2005	StL	NL	93	295	80	14	2	21	(14	7)	161	49	54	49	28	1	75	4	0	2		14	1	.93	8	.271	.340	.546
2006	KC	AL	88	325	80	23	1	11	(7	4)	138	45	49	40	28	3	86	1	0	4		7	7	.50	10	.246	.304	.425
2007	KC	AL	24	73	23	7	0	2	(2	0)	36	12	11	14	11	0	15	1	0	0		0	1	.00	2	.315	.412	.493
17 ML YEARS			1777	6241	1666	341	60	305	(152	153)	3042	1037	983	1011	674	49	1614	71	14	43		304	115	.73	121	.267	.343	.487

Ervin Santana

Pitches: R **Bats:** R **Pos:** SP-26; RP-2   **Ht:** 6'2" **Wt:** 185 **Born:** 12/12/1982 **Age:** 25

			HOW MUCH HE PITCHED						WHAT HE GAVE UP												THE RESULTS						
Year	Team	Lg	G	GS	CG	GF	IP	BFP	H	R	ER	HR	SH	SF	HB	TBB	IBB	SO	WP	Bk		W	L	Pct	ShO	Sv-Op	Hld	ERC	ERA
2007	Salt Lk*	AAA	5	5	0	0	32.1	144	39	19	18	4	2	1	3	10	0	32	1	0		2	1	.667	0	0- -	-	5.53	5.01
2005	LAA	AL	23	23	1	0	133.2	585	139	73	69	17	1	4	8	47	2	99	4	0		12	8	.600	1	0-0	0	4.51	4.65
2006	LAA	AL	33	33	0	0	204.0	846	181	106	97	21	4	10	11	70	2	141	10	2		16	8	.667	0	0-0	0	3.51	4.28
2007	LAA	AL	28	26	0	1	150.0	675	174	103	96	26	3	2	8	58	3	126	7	0		7	14	.333	0	0-0	0	5.69	5.76
3 ML YEARS			84	82	1	1	487.2	2104	494	282	262	64	8	16	27	175	7	366	21	2		35	30	.538	1	0-0	0	4.43	4.84

Johan Santana

Pitches: L **Bats:** L **Pos:** SP-33   **Ht:** 6'0" **Wt:** 208 **Born:** 3/13/1979 **Age:** 29

			HOW MUCH HE PITCHED						WHAT HE GAVE UP												THE RESULTS						
Year	Team	Lg	G	GS	CG	GF	IP	BFP	H	R	ER	HR	SH	SF	HB	TBB	IBB	SO	WP	Bk		W	L	Pct	ShO	Sv-Op	Hld	ERC	ERA
2000	Min	AL	30	5	0	9	86.0	398	102	64	62	11	1	3	2	54	0	64	5	2		2	3	.400	0	0-0	0	6.59	6.49
2001	Min	AL	15	4	0	5	43.2	195	50	25	23	6	2	3	3	16	0	28	3	0		1	0	1.000	0	0-0	0	5.36	4.74
2002	Min	AL	27	14	0	2	108.1	452	84	41	36	7	3	3	1	49	0	137	15	2		8	6	.571	0	1-1	3	2.86	2.99
2003	Min	AL	45	18	0	7	158.1	644	127	56	54	17	2	4	3	47	1	169	6	2		12	3	.800	0	0-0	5	2.73	3.07
2004	Min	AL	34	34	1	0	228.0	801	156	70	66	24	3	3	9	54	0	265	7	0		20	6	.769	1	0-0	0	2.07	2.61
2005	Min	AL	33	33	3	0	231.2	910	180	77	74	22	6	2	1	45	1	238	8	0		16	7	.696	2	0-0	0	2.14	2.87
2006	Min	AL	34	34	1	0	233.2	923	186	79	72	24	6	4	4	47	0	245	4	1		19	6	.760	0	0-0	0	2.36	2.77
2007	Min	AL	33	33	1	0	219.0	878	183	88	81	33	4	4	4	52	0	235	7	1		15	13	.536	1	0-0	0	2.98	3.33
8 ML YEARS			251	175	6	23	1308.2	5281	1068	500	468	144	27	26	27	364	2	1381	55	8		93	44	.679	4	1-1	8	2.79	3.22

Ramon Santiago

Bats: B **Throws:** R **Pos:** SS-31; PR-6   **Ht:** 5'11" **Wt:** 175 **Born:** 8/31/1979 **Age:** 28

									BATTING													BASERUNNING				AVERAGES		
Year	Team	Lg	G	AB	H	2B	3B	HR	(Hm	Rd)	TB	R	RBI	RC	TBB	IBB	SO	HBP	SH	SF		SB	CS	SB%	GDP	Avg	OBP	Slg
2007	Toledo*	AAA	91	365	96	19	4	3	(-	-)	132	40	30	40	16	0	61	9	11	1		8	9	.47	8	.263	.309	.362
2002	Det	AL	65	222	54	5	5	4	(3	1)	81	33	20	23	13	0	48	8	4	2		8	5	.62	2	.243	.306	.365
2003	Det	AL	141	444	100	18	1	2	(1	1)	126	41	29	38	33	0	66	10	18	2		10	4	.71	9	.225	.292	.284
2004	Sea	AL	19	39	7	1	0	0	(0	0)	8	8	2	1	3	0	3	1	2	0		0	0	-	1	.179	.256	.205
2005	Sea	AL	8	8	1	0	0	0	(0	0)	1	2	0	1	1	0	2	3	1	0		0	0	-	0	.125	.417	.125
2006	Det	AL	43	80	18	1	1	0	(0	0)	21	9	3	3	1	0	14	1	4	0		2	0	1.00	0	.225	.244	.263
2007	Det	AL	32	67	19	5	1	0	(0	0)	26	10	7	11	1	0	10	3	3	0		3	0	1.00	0	.284	.324	.388
6 ML YEARS			308	860	199	30	8	6	(4	2)	263	103	61	77	52	0	143	26	32	4		23	9	.72	13	.231	.294	.306

Victor Santos

Pitches: R **Bats:** R **Pos:** RP-33; SP-3   **Ht:** 6'2" **Wt:** 205 **Born:** 10/2/1976 **Age:** 31

			HOW MUCH HE PITCHED						WHAT HE GAVE UP												THE RESULTS						
Year	Team	Lg	G	GS	CG	GF	IP	BFP	H	R	ER	HR	SH	SF	HB	TBB	IBB	SO	WP	Bk		W	L	Pct	ShO	Sv-Op	Hld	ERC	ERA
2007	Lsvlle*	AAA	8	4	0	1	24.1	101	24	6	3	1	1	1	5	0	15	1	0		1	1	.500	0	0- -	-	3.02	1.11
2001	Det	AL	33	7	0	6	76.1	335	62	33	28	9	1	3	3	49	4	52	0	0		2	2	.500	0	0-0	2	4.18	3.30
2002	Col	NL	24	2	0	6	26.0	140	41	30	30	3	3	1	0	22	3	25	2	0		0	4	.000	0	0-0	1	9.37	10.38
2003	Tex	AL	8	4	0	2	25.2	117	29	21	20	5	1	1	1	16	1	15	0	0		0	2	.000	0	0-0	0	6.82	7.01
2004	Mil	NL	31	28	0	2	154.0	684	169	95	85	18	6	7	4	57	5	115	2	1		11	12	.478	0	0-0	0	4.73	4.97
2005	Mil	NL	29	24	1	2	141.2	640	153	87	72	20	5	1	5	60	8	89	7	0		4	13	.235	0	0-0	0	4.89	4.57
2006	Pit	NL	25	19	0	3	115.1	522	150	80	73	16	5	4	4	42	3	81	5	0		5	9	.357	0	0-0	0	6.20	5.70
2007	2 Tms		36	3	0	12	63.1	284	71	41	41	15	4	4	3	33	6	48	3	0		1	6	.143	0	0-0	5	6.55	5.83
07	Cin	NL	32	0	0	12	49.0	216	51	28	28	10	3	3	2	23	5	44	2	0		1	4	.200	0	0-0	5	5.42	5.14
07	Bal	AL	4	3	0	0	14.1	68	20	13	13	5	1	1	1	10	1	4	1	0		0	2	.000	0	0-0	0	10.93	8.16
7 ML YEARS			186	87	1	33	602.1	2722	675	387	349	86	25	21	23	279	30	425	19	1		23	48	.324	0	0-0	5	5.43	5.21

Bronson Sardinha

Bats: L **Throws:** R **Pos:** PR-6; RF-4; 3B-1; LF-1   **Ht:** 6'1" **Wt:** 195 **Born:** 4/6/1983 **Age:** 25

Year	Team	Lg	G	AB	H	2B	3B	HR	(Hm	Rd)	TB	R	RBI	RC	TBB	IBB	SO	HBP	SH	SF	SB	CS	SB%	GDP	Avg	OBP	Slg
2001	Yanks	R	55	188	57	14	3	4	(-	-)	89	42	27	38	28	2	51	3	1	2	11	2	.85	6	.303	.398	.473
2002	Grnsbr	A	93	342	90	13	0	12	(-	-)	139	49	44	50	34	2	78	6	0	7	15	6	.71	6	.263	.334	.406
2002	StIsInd	A-	36	124	40	8	0	4	(-	-)	60	25	16	27	24	2	38	1	0	1	4	1	.80	3	.323	.433	.484
2003	Tampa	A+	59	212	41	8	2	1	(-	-)	56	23	17	17	24	0	57	2	0	2	8	2	.80	3	.193	.279	.264
2003	Btl Crk	A	71	269	74	16	0	8	(-	-)	114	54	41	46	40	2	40	5	0	4	5	3	.63	5	.275	.374	.424
2004	Tampa	A+	63	248	78	12	2	2	(-	-)	100	37	33	42	29	3	39	3	0	3	9	2	.82	3	.315	.389	.403
2004	Trntn	AA	72	266	71	11	1	6	(-	-)	102	37	29	22	37	3	65	0	0	0	4	1	.80	8	.267	.356	.383
2005	Trntn	AA	133	503	130	30	2	12	(-	-)	200	63	68	72	55	1	115	7	1	3	11	3	.79	14	.258	.338	.398
2006	Trntn	AA	86	334	85	10	1	10	(-	-)	127	47	40	43	34	2	78	2	0	3	0	2	.00	7	.254	.324	.380
2006	Clmbs	AAA	52	185	53	10	5	6	(-	-)	91	27	27	34	23	2	36	1	0	2	3	2	.60	4	.286	.365	.492
2007	S-WB	AAA	109	388	86	21	5	11	(-	-)	150	48	56	49	46	2	77	2	1	2	10	3	.77	12	.222	.306	.387
2007	Trntn	AA	15	56	24	3	1	4	(-	-)	41	14	18	18	7	1	10	0	0	1	3	0	1.00	0	.429	.484	.732
2007	NYY	AL	10	9	3	0	0	0	(0	0)	3	6	2	2	2	0	1	0	0	1	0	0	-	2	.333	.417	.333

Dennis Sarfate

Pitches: R **Bats:** R **Pos:** RP-7   **Ht:** 6'4" **Wt:** 210 **Born:** 4/9/1981 **Age:** 27

Year	Team	Lg	G	GS	CG	GF	IP	BFP	H	R	ER	HR	SH	SF	HB	TBB	IBB	SO	WP	Bk	W	L	Pct	ShO	Sv-Op	Hld	ERC	ERA
2001	Ogden	R+	9	4	0	1	23.1	100	20	13	12	4	1	0	2	10	0	32	2	0	1	2	.333	0	1--	-	4.23	4.63
2002	Brewrs	R	5	5	0	0	14.0	56	6	4	4	0	0	0	1	7	0	22	0	2	0	0	-	0	0--	-	1.35	2.57
2002	Ogden	R+	1	0	0	0	1.0	6	2	1	1	0	0	0	0	1	0	2	0	0	0	0	-	0	0--	-	12.01	9.00
2003	Beloit	A	26	26	0	0	139.2	581	114	50	44	11	4	5	3	66	0	140	5	2	12	2	.857	0	0--	-	3.35	2.84
2004	Hntsvl	AA	28	25	0	2	129.0	566	128	71	58	12	10	8	9	78	0	113	6	2	7	12	.368	0	0--	-	5.30	4.05
2005	Hntsvl	AA	24	24	1	0	130.0	567	120	65	56	13	5	4	10	59	1	110	11	1	9	9	.500	0	0--	-	4.14	3.88
2005	Nashv	AAA	2	1	0	1	12.0	46	6	3	3	1	0	1	1	4	0	10	0	0	0	1	.000	0	0--	-	1.61	2.25
2006	Nashv	AAA	34	21	0	7	125.0	565	125	63	51	7	7	3	6	78	0	117	10	0	10	7	.588	0	0--	-	4.87	3.67
2007	Nashv	AAA	45	1	0	23	61.2	285	61	35	31	6	6	2	4	47	2	68	3	0	2	7	.222	0	4--	-	5.76	4.52
2006	Mil	NL	8	0	0	5	8.1	38	9	4	4	0	0	0	0	4	1	11	2	0	0	0	-	0	0-0	0	3.77	4.32
2007	Hou	NL	7	0	0	1	8.1	31	5	1	1	0	0	1	0	1	0	14	0	0	0	1	1.000	0	0-0	3	0.96	1.08
	2 ML YEARS		15	0	0	6	16.2	69	14	5	5	0	0	1	0	5	1	25	2	0	1	0	1.000	0	0-0	3	2.10	2.70

Joe Saunders

Pitches: L **Bats:** L **Pos:** SP-18   **Ht:** 6'3" **Wt:** 210 **Born:** 6/16/1981 **Age:** 27

Year	Team	Lg	G	GS	CG	GF	IP	BFP	H	R	ER	HR	SH	SF	HB	TBB	IBB	SO	WP	Bk	W	L	Pct	ShO	Sv-Op	Hld	ERC	ERA
2007	Salt Lk*	AAA	14	14	0	0	86.1	367	89	53	49	10	2	2	1	20	0	84	6	0	4	7	.364	0	0--	-	3.68	5.11
2005	LAA	AL	2	2	0	0	9.1	41	10	8	8	3	0	0	0	4	0	4	1	0	0	0	-	0	0-0	0	6.27	7.71
2006	LAA	AL	13	13	0	0	70.2	302	71	42	37	6	1	2	1	29	1	51	2	1	7	3	.700	0	0-0	0	4.13	4.71
2007	LAA	AL	18	18	0	0	107.1	473	129	56	53	11	0	5	1	34	1	69	3	0	8	5	.615	0	0-0	0	4.96	4.44
	3 ML YEARS		33	33	0	0	187.1	816	210	106	98	20	1	7	2	67	2	124	6	1	15	8	.652	0	0-0	0	4.71	4.71

Nate Schierholtz

Bats: L **Throws:** R **Pos:** RF-30; PH-11   **Ht:** 6'2" **Wt:** 215 **Born:** 2/15/1984 **Age:** 24

Year	Team	Lg	G	AB	H	2B	3B	HR	(Hm	Rd)	TB	R	RBI	RC	TBB	IBB	SO	HBP	SH	SF	SB	CS	SB%	GDP	Avg	OBP	Slg
2003	Giants	R	11	45	18	0	2	0	(-	-)	22	5	5	10	3	0	8	1	0	0	4	0	1.00	0	.400	.449	.489
2003	SlmKzr	A-	35	124	38	6	2	3	(-	-)	57	23	29	22	12	1	15	5	0	3	0	1	.00	1	.306	.382	.460
2004	Hgrstn	A	58	233	69	22	0	15	(-	-)	136	41	53	47	18	3	52	4	0	3	1	0	1.00	4	.296	.353	.584
2004	SnJos	A+	62	258	76	18	9	3	(-	-)	121	39	31	41	15	1	41	3	3	2	3	1	.75	6	.295	.338	.469
2005	SnJos	A+	128	502	160	37	8	15	(-	-)	258	83	86	91	32	0	132	6	3	5	5	7	.42	10	.319	.363	.514
2006	Conn	AA	125	470	127	25	7	14	(-	-)	208	55	54	69	27	8	81	12	0	1	8	3	.73	11	.270	.325	.443
2007	Fresno	AAA	110	411	137	31	7	16	(-	-)	230	67	68	82	17	3	58	7	1	4	10	4	.71	8	.333	.367	.560
2007	SF	NL	39	112	34	5	3	0	(0	0)	45	9	10	14	2	0	19	1	0	2	3	1	.75	0	.304	.316	.402

Curt Schilling

Pitches: R **Bats:** R **Pos:** SP-24   **Ht:** 6'5" **Wt:** 235 **Born:** 11/14/1966 **Age:** 41

Year	Team	Lg	G	GS	CG	GF	IP	BFP	H	R	ER	HR	SH	SF	HB	TBB	IBB	SO	WP	Bk	W	L	Pct	ShO	Sv-Op	Hld	ERC	ERA
2007	Pwtckt*	AAA	3	3	0	0	15.0	52	8	0	0	1	0	0	0	0	0	18	0	0	0	0	-	0	0--	-	0.62	0.00
1988	Bal	AL	4	4	0	0	14.2	76	22	19	16	3	0	3	1	10	1	4	2	0	0	3	.000	0	0-0	0	9.43	9.82
1989	Bal	AL	5	1	0	0	8.2	38	10	6	6	2	0	0	0	3	0	6	1	0	0	1	.000	0	0-0	0	5.74	6.23
1990	Bal	AL	35	0	0	16	46.0	191	38	13	13	1	2	4	0	19	0	32	0	0	1	2	.333	0	3-9	5	2.68	2.54
1991	Hou	NL	56	0	0	34	75.2	336	79	35	32	2	5	1	0	39	7	71	4	1	3	5	.375	0	8-11	5	4.08	3.81
1992	Phi	NL	42	26	10	10	226.1	895	165	67	59	11	7	8	1	59	4	147	4	0	14	11	.560	4	2-3	0	1.86	2.35
1993	Phi	NL	34	34	7	0	235.1	982	234	114	105	23	9	7	4	57	6	186	9	3	16	7	.696	2	0-0	0	3.44	4.02
1994	Phi	NL	13	13	1	0	82.1	360	87	42	41	10	4	2	0	28	3	58	3	1	2	8	.200	0	0-0	0	4.36	4.48
1995	Phi	NL	17	17	1	0	116.0	473	96	52	46	12	5	2	3	26	2	114	0	1	7	5	.583	0	0-0	0	2.55	3.57
1996	Phi	NL	26	26	8	0	183.1	732	149	69	65	16	6	4	3	50	5	182	5	0	9	10	.474	2	0-0	0	2.59	3.19
1997	Phi	NL	35	35	7	0	254.1	1009	208	96	84	25	8	8	5	58	3	319	5	1	17	11	.607	2	0-0	0	2.55	2.97
1998	Phi	NL	35	35	15	0	268.2	1089	236	101	97	23	14	7	6	61	3	300	12	0	15	14	.517	2	0-0	0	2.75	3.25
1999	Phi	NL	24	24	8	0	180.1	735	159	74	71	25	11	3	6	44	0	152	4	0	15	6	.714	1	0-0	0	3.20	3.54
2000	2 Tms	NL	29	29	8	0	210.1	862	204	90	89	27	11	4	1	45	4	168	4	0	11	12	.478	2	0-0	0	3.38	3.81
2001	Ari	NL	35	35	6	0	256.2	1021	237	86	85	37	8	5	1	39	0	293	4	0	22	6	.786	1	0-0	0	3.03	2.98
2002	Ari	NL	36	35	5	0	259.1	1017	218	95	93	29	4	3	3	33	1	316	6	0	23	7	.767	1	0-0	0	2.33	3.23

Year	Team	Lg	G	GS	CG	GF	IP	BFP	H	R	ER	HR	SH	SF	HB	TBB	IBB	SO	WP	Bk	W	L	Pct	ShO	Sv-Op	Hld	ERC	ERA
2003	Ari	NL	24	24	3	0	168.0	673	144	58	55	17	11	1	3	32	2	194	4	0	8	9	.471	2	0-0	0	2.59	2.95
2004	Bos	AL	32	32	3	0	226.2	910	206	84	82	23	3	6	5	35	0	203	3	0	**21**	6	**.778**	0	0-0	0	2.75	3.26
2005	Bos	AL	32	11	0	21	93.1	418	121	59	59	12	3	5	3	22	0	87	1	1	8	8	.500	0	9-11	0	5.45	5.69
2006	Bos	AL	31	31	0	0	204.0	834	220	90	90	28	5	2	3	28	1	183	1	0	15	7	.682	0	0-0	0	3.83	3.97
2007	Bos	AL	24	24	1	0	151.0	633	165	68	65	21	4	3	2	23	1	101	0	0	9	8	.529	1	0-0	0	3.90	3.87
00	Phi	NL	16	16	4	0	112.2	474	110	49	49	17	5	1	1	32	4	96	4	0	6	6	.500	1	0-0	0	3.79	3.91
00	Ari	NL	13	13	4	0	97.2	388	94	41	40	10	6	3	0	13	0	72	0	0	5	6	.455	1	0-0	0	2.91	3.69
20 ML YEARS			569	436	83	81	3261.0	13284	2998	1318	1253	347	122	77	52	711	43	3116	72	8	216	146	.597	20	22-34	10	3.03	3.46

Jason Schmidt

Pitches: R Bats: R Pos: SP-6

Ht: 6'5" Wt: 210 Born: 1/29/1973 Age: 35

Year	Team	Lg	G	GS	CG	GF	IP	BFP	H	R	ER	HR	SH	SF	HB	TBB	IBB	SO	WP	Bk	W	L	Pct	ShO	Sv-Op	Hld	ERC	ERA
2007	InldEm*	A+	1	1	0	0	6.0	20	2	0	0	0	0	0	0	1	0	7	0	0	0	0	-	0	0--	-	0.47	0.00
1995	Atl	NL	9	2	0	1	25.0	119	27	17	16	2	2	4	1	18	3	19	1	0	2	2	.500	0	0-1	0	5.56	5.76
1996	2 Tms	NL	19	17	1	0	96.1	445	108	67	61	10	4	9	2	53	0	74	8	1	5	6	.455	0	0-0	0	5.46	5.70
1997	Pit	NL	32	32	2	0	187.2	825	193	106	96	16	10	3	6	76	2	136	8	0	10	9	.526	0	0-0	0	4.31	4.60
1998	Pit	NL	33	33	0	0	214.1	916	228	106	97	24	10	3	4	71	3	158	**15**	1	11	14	.440	0	0-0	0	4.35	4.07
1999	Pit	NL	33	33	2	0	212.2	937	219	110	99	24	7	7	3	85	4	148	6	**4**	13	11	.542	0	0-0	0	4.30	4.19
2000	Pit	NL	11	11	0	0	63.1	295	71	43	38	6	1	2	1	41	2	51	1	0	2	5	.286	0	0-0	0	5.77	5.40
2001	2 Tms	NL	25	25	1	0	150.1	641	138	75	68	13	5	3	7	61	3	142	8	1	13	7	.650	0	0-0	0	3.72	4.06
2002	SF	NL	29	29	2	0	185.1	769	148	78	71	15	11	5	2	73	1	196	12	0	13	8	.619	2	0-0	0	2.87	3.45
2003	SF	NL	29	29	5	0	207.2	819	152	56	54	14	6	3	5	46	1	208	7	1	17	5	**.773**	**3**	0-0	0	**1.93**	**2.34**
2004	SF	NL	32	32	4	0	225.0	907	165	84	80	18	7	3	3	77	3	251	7	1	18	7	.720	**3**	0-0	0	2.37	3.20
2005	SF	NL	29	29	0	0	172.0	757	160	90	84	16	8	8	5	85	4	165	7	1	12	7	.632	0	0-0	0	4.04	4.40
2006	SF	NL	32	32	3	0	213.1	894	189	94	85	21	7	7	6	80	6	180	11	1	11	9	.550	1	0-0	0	3.43	3.59
2007	LAD	NL	6	6	0	0	25.2	125	32	20	18	4	2	0	1	14	2	22	2	0	1	4	.200	0	0-0	0	6.40	6.31
96	Atl	NL	13	11	0	0	58.2	274	69	48	44	8	3	6	0	32	0	48	5	1	3	4	.429	0	0-0	0	5.92	6.75
96	Pit	NL	6	6	1	0	37.2	171	39	19	17	2	1	3	2	21	0	26	3	0	2	2	.500	0	0-0	0	4.75	4.06
01	Pit	NL	14	14	1	0	84.0	357	81	46	43	11	3	2	7	28	2	77	3	1	6	6	.500	0	0-0	0	4.17	4.61
01	SF	NL	11	11	0	0	66.1	284	57	29	25	2	2	1	0	33	1	65	5	0	7	1	.875	0	0-0	0	3.16	3.39
13 ML YEARS			319	310	20	1	1978.2	8449	1830	946	867	183	80	57	49	780	34	1750	93	11	128	94	.577	9	0-1	0	3.64	3.94

Brian Schneider

Bats: L Throws: R Pos: C-122; PH-7; 1B-1

Ht: 6'1" Wt: 196 Born: 11/26/1976 Age: 31

Year	Team	Lg	G	AB	H	2B	3B	HR	(Hm	Rd)	TB	R	RBI	RC	TBB	IBB	SO	HBP	SH	SF	SB	CS	SB%	GDP	Avg	OBP	Slg
2000	Mon	NL	45	115	27	6	0	0	(0	0)	33	6	11	8	7	2	24	0	0	1	0	1	.00	1	.235	.276	.287
2001	Mon	NL	27	41	13	3	0	1	(1	0)	19	4	6	8	6	1	3	0	0	1	0	0	-	0	.317	.396	.463
2002	Mon	NL	73	207	57	19	2	5	(3	2)	95	21	29	29	21	8	41	0	2	2	1	2	.33	7	.275	.339	.459
2003	Mon	NL	108	335	77	26	1	9	(9	0)	132	34	46	36	37	8	75	2	1	2	0	2	.00	12	.230	.309	.394
2004	Mon	NL	135	436	112	20	3	12	(5	7)	174	40	49	52	42	10	63	3	5	2	0	1	.00	6	.257	.325	.399
2005	Was	NL	116	369	99	20	1	10	(5	5)	151	38	44	48	29	7	48	6	2	2	1	0	1.00	10	.268	.330	.409
2006	Was	NL	124	410	105	18	0	4	(3	1)	135	30	55	45	38	10	67	2	2	3	2	2	.50	14	.256	.320	.329
2007	Was	NL	129	408	96	21	1	6	(2	4)	137	33	54	41	56	7	56	2	4	7	0	0	-	15	.235	.326	.336
8 ML YEARS			757	2321	586	133	8	47	(28	19)	876	206	294	267	236	53	377	15	16	20	4	8	.33	67	.252	.323	.377

Scott Schoeneweis

Pitches: L Bats: L Pos: RP-70

Ht: 6'0" Wt: 190 Born: 10/2/1973 Age: 34

Year	Team	Lg	G	GS	CG	GF	IP	BFP	H	R	ER	HR	SH	SF	HB	TBB	IBB	SO	WP	Bk	W	L	Pct	ShO	Sv-Op	Hld	ERC	ERA
1999	LAA	AL	31	0	0	6	39.1	175	47	24	24	4	0	1	0	14	1	22	1	0	1	1	.500	0	0-0	3	4.99	5.49
2000	LAA	AL	27	27	1	0	170.0	742	183	112	103	21	2	5	6	67	2	78	4	3	7	10	.412	1	0-0	0	4.84	5.45
2001	LAA	AL	32	32	1	0	205.1	910	227	122	116	21	3	8	14	77	2	104	4	1	10	11	.476	0	0-0	0	4.87	5.08
2002	LAA	AL	54	15	0	4	118.0	510	119	68	64	17	1	5	5	49	4	65	1	1	9	8	.529	0	1-4	11	4.68	4.88
2003	2 Tms	AL	59	0	0	19	64.2	276	63	35	30	3	2	4	4	19	5	56	3	0	3	2	.600	0	0-2	4	3.25	4.18
2004	CWS	AL	20	19	0	0	112.2	500	129	74	70	17	3	2	3	49	0	69	3	0	6	9	.400	0	0-0	0	5.65	5.59
2005	Tor	AL	80	0	0	15	57.0	250	54	23	21	2	1	0	4	25	5	43	2	0	3	4	.429	0	1-4	21	3.56	3.32
2006	2 Tms	AL	71	0	0	16	51.2	221	48	28	28	4	1	2	3	24	6	29	3	0	4	2	.667	0	4-6	19	3.79	4.88
2007	NYM	NL	70	0	0	17	59.0	265	62	36	33	8	4	1	3	28	5	41	3	1	0	2	.000	0	2-3	11	4.97	5.03
03	LAA	AL	39	0	0	12	38.2	163	37	19	17	2	1	1	3	10	3	29	1	0	1	1	.500	0	0-1	4	3.14	3.96
03	CWS	AL	20	0	0	7	26.0	113	26	16	13	1	1	3	1	9	2	27	2	0	2	1	.667	0	0-1	0	3.41	4.50
06	Tor	AL	55	0	0	8	37.1	161	39	27	27	3	1	1	0	16	5	18	2	0	1	0	.500	0	1-3	18	4.27	6.51
06	Cin	NL	16	0	0	8	14.1	60	9	1	1	1	0	1	0	8	1	11	1	0	2	0	1.000	0	3-3	1	2.64	0.63
9 ML YEARS			444	93	2	77	877.2	3849	932	525	489	97	17	23	41	352	30	507	24	6	43	49	.467	1	8-19	69	4.67	5.01

Chris Schroder

Pitches: R Bats: R Pos: RP-37

Ht: 6'3" Wt: 210 Born: 8/20/1978 Age: 29

Year	Team	Lg	G	GS	CG	GF	IP	BFP	H	R	ER	HR	SH	SF	HB	TBB	IBB	SO	WP	Bk	W	L	Pct	ShO	Sv-Op	Hld	ERC	ERA
2001	Vrmnt	A-	11	0	0	7	12.0	48	8	2	2	1	0	0	0	5	0	18	0	0	0	0	-	0	2--	-	2.32	1.50
2001	Jupiter	A+	10	0	0	2	15.2	64	12	5	4	1	0	0	0	4	0	20	4	0	1	0	1.000	0	0--	-	2.04	2.30
2002	Clinton	A	22	0	0	20	27.1	113	15	7	5	1	1	0	2	14	1	42	1	0	1	3	.250	0	10--	-	1.93	1.65
2002	BrvdCt	A+	23	0	0	21	29.2	118	13	6	5	2	0	1	0	19	1	36	2	0	2	2	.500	0	5--	-	1.87	1.52
2003	Hrsbrg	AA	49	0	0	22	82.1	353	68	29	26	5	6	4	2	47	1	81	1	0	9	2	.818	0	4--	-	3.61	2.84
2004	Hrsbrg	AA	32	0	0	22	48.1	205	39	13	13	3	0	0	5	17	2	51	2	0	2	2	.500	0	11--	-	2.88	2.42
2004	Edmtn	AAA	17	1	0	5	26.2	120	24	13	13	3	0	0	1	15	0	32	2	0	2	1	.667	0	0--	-	4.29	4.39

Year	Team	Lg	G	GS	CG	GF	IP	BFP	H	R	ER	HR	SH	SF	HB	TBB	IBB	SO	WP	Bk	W	L	Pct	ShO	Sv-Op	Hld	ERC	ERA
			HOW MUCH HE PITCHED						**WHAT HE GAVE UP**												**THE RESULTS**							
2005	Hrsbrg	AA	16	0	0	5	23.0	100	20	13	12	4	3	1	1	11	3	28	1	0	2	3	.400	0	0- -	-	4.09	4.70
2005	NewOr	AAA	19	0	0	8	23.0	106	21	21	20	6	2	0	4	15	1	29	1	1	2	0	1.000	0	4- -	-	6.56	7.83
2005	Nats	R	1	0	0	0	1.0	5	2	1	1	0	0	0	0	0	0	3	0	0	0	0	-	0	0- -	-	7.48	9.00
2005	Ptomc	A+	5	0	0	2	7.0	32	7	3	0	0	0	1	1	2	0	10	0	0	0	0	-	0	1- -	-	3.26	0.00
2006	Hrsbrg	AA	9	0	0	3	14.1	66	18	9	8	2	0	0	0	6	2	13	3	0	2	0	1.000	0	1- -	-	5.66	5.02
2006	NewOr	AAA	28	0	0	5	47.1	188	25	9	8	2	2	1	3	16	1	60	2	0	2	1	.667	0	1- -	-	1.43	1.52
2007	Clmbs	AAA	26	0	0	7	33.0	137	23	8	6	0	3	0	2	17	3	45	4	1	2	2	.500	0	1- -	-	2.34	1.64
2006	Was	NL	21	0	0	3	28.1	127	23	21	20	7	1	3	5	15	3	39	0	0	0	2	.000	0	0-1	1	5.07	6.35
2007	Was	NL	37	0	0	8	45.1	192	36	19	16	2	2	0	2	15	1	43	0	0	2	3	.400	0	0-0	1	2.40	3.18
	2 ML YEARS		58	0	0	11	73.2	319	59	40	36	9	3	3	7	30	4	82	0	0	2	5	.286	0	0-1	2	3.35	4.40

Mike Schultz

Pitches: R Bats: R Pos: RP-1 Ht: 6'7" Wt: 220 Born: 11/28/1979 Age: 28

Year	Team	Lg	G	GS	CG	GF	IP	BFP	H	R	ER	HR	SH	SF	HB	TBB	IBB	SO	WP	Bk	W	L	Pct	ShO	Sv-Op	Hld	ERC	ERA
			HOW MUCH HE PITCHED						**WHAT HE GAVE UP**												**THE RESULTS**							
2000	DBcks	R	2	0	0	0	2.2	17	7	7	2	1	0	1	1	1	0	2	0	0	0	0	.000	0	0- -	-	19.78	6.75
2000	Hi Dsrt	A+	7	7	0	0	22.1	90	15	9	9	2	0	1	0	11	0	16	1	0	1	2	.333	0	0- -	-	2.68	3.63
2003	Yakima	A-	5	5	0	0	28.2	120	21	16	15	2	1	2	2	10	0	27	0	1	1	0	1.000	0	0- -	-	2.47	4.71
2003	Lancst	A+	9	9	0	0	44.1	198	57	27	23	5	2	3	2	20	0	32	2	0	2	2	.500	0	0- -	-	6.58	4.67
2004	Tucsn	AAA	7	0	0	1	9.0	44	12	7	5	1	0	0	0	5	0	4	1	0	0	1	.000	0	0- -	-	6.64	5.00
2004	Lancst	A+	13	0	0	5	18.0	88	19	13	6	0	0	0	2	13	1	18	3	0	1	1	.500	0	2- -	-	5.05	3.00
2004	ElPaso	AA	12	0	0	7	13.2	70	16	7	7	0	0	0	0	13	0	14	2	0	0	0	-	0	1- -	-	6.30	4.61
2005	Tenn	AA	63	0	0	26	65.1	294	69	31	25	3	7	3	0	41	4	68	10	0	4	6	.400	0	6- -	-	4.86	3.44
2006	Tenn	AA	9	0	0	7	11.2	41	4	2	2	0	0	0	0	4	0	7	0	0	1	0	1.000	0	3- -	-	0.76	1.54
2006	Tucsn	AAA	49	0	0	22	53.2	236	58	22	21	1	1	0	2	19	1	41	4	0	2	4	.333	0	4- -	-	3.84	3.52
2007	Tucsn	AAA	54	1	0	15	77.0	337	84	38	34	4	4	1	3	35	1	50	12	0	4	5	.444	0	4- -	-	4.70	3.97
2007	Ari	NL	1	0	0	1	1.0	3	1	0	0	0	0	0	0	0	0	1	0	0	0	0	-	0	0-0	0	2.79	0.00

Skip Schumaker

Bats: L Throws: R Pos: PH-47; RF-26; LF-23; CF-15 Ht: 5'10" Wt: 195 Born: 2/3/1980 Age: 28

Year	Team	Lg	G	AB	H	2B	3B	HR	(Hm	Rd)	TB	R	RBI	RC	TBB	IBB	SO	HBP	SH	SF	SB	CS	SB%	GDP	Avg	OBP	Slg
			BATTING																		**BASERUNNING**				**AVERAGES**		
2007	Memp*	AAA	59	232	71	16	0	7	(-	-)	108	34	31	41	27	1	37	2	2	1	2	3	.40	4	.306	.382	.466
2005	StL	NL	27	24	6	1	0	0	(0	0)	7	9	1	2	2	0	2	0	0	0	1	0	1.00	1	.250	.308	.292
2006	StL	NL	28	54	10	1	0	1	(0	1)	14	3	2	2	5	1	6	0	1	0	2	1	.67	1	.185	.254	.259
2007	StL	NL	88	177	59	12	2	2	(1	1)	81	19	19	30	8	0	20	0	1	2	1	1	.50	5	.333	.358	.458
	3 ML YEARS		143	255	75	14	2	3	(1	2)	102	31	22	34	15	1	28	0	2	2	4	2	.67	6	.294	.331	.400

Luke Scott

Bats: L Throws: R Pos: RF-101; PH-28; LF-5; CF-3 Ht: 6'0" Wt: 210 Born: 6/25/1978 Age: 30

Year	Team	Lg	G	AB	H	2B	3B	HR	(Hm	Rd)	TB	R	RBI	RC	TBB	IBB	SO	HBP	SH	SF	SB	CS	SB%	GDP	Avg	OBP	Slg
			BATTING																		**BASERUNNING**				**AVERAGES**		
2005	Hou	NL	34	80	15	4	2	0	(0	0)	23	6	4	6	9	1	23	0	0	0	1	1	.50	0	.188	.270	.288
2006	Hou	NL	65	214	72	19	6	10	(8	2)	133	31	37	40	30	4	43	4	0	1	2	1	.67	2	.336	.426	.621
2007	Hou	NL	132	369	94	28	5	18	(8	10)	186	49	64	55	53	4	95	2	0	1	3	1	.76	8	.255	.351	.504
	3 ML YEARS		231	663	181	51	13	28	(16	12)	342	86	105	109	92	9	161	6	0	2	6	3	.67	10	.273	.366	.516

Marco Scutaro

Bats: R Throws: R Pos: SS-43; 3B-36; 2B-13; PH-8; LF-6; RF-4; PR-2 Ht: 5'10" Wt: 186 Born: 10/30/1975 Age: 32

Year	Team	Lg	G	AB	H	2B	3B	HR	(Hm	Rd)	TB	R	RBI	RC	TBB	IBB	SO	HBP	SH	SF	SB	CS	SB%	GDP	Avg	OBP	Slg
			BATTING																		**BASERUNNING**				**AVERAGES**		
2002	NYM	NL	27	36	8	0	1	1	(1	0)	13	2	6	2	0	0	11	0	1	1	0	1	.00	1	.222	.216	.361
2003	NYM	NL	48	75	16	4	0	2	(0	2)	26	10	6	10	13	2	14	1	1	1	2	0	1.00	1	.213	.333	.347
2004	Oak	AL	137	455	124	32	1	7	(6	1)	179	50	43	48	16	1	58	0	5	1	0	0	-	9	.273	.297	.393
2005	Oak	AL	118	381	94	22	3	9	(5	4)	149	48	37	45	36	1	48	0	4	2	5	2	.71	6	.247	.310	.391
2006	Oak	AL	117	365	97	21	6	5	(1	4)	145	52	41	47	50	0	66	0	3	5	5	1	.83	16	.266	.350	.397
2007	Oak	AL	104	338	88	13	0	7	(2	5)	122	49	41	42	35	1	40	2	2	2	2	1	.67	13	.260	.332	.361
	6 ML YEARS		551	1650	427	92	11	31	(15	16)	634	211	174	194	150	5	237	3	16	12	14	5	.74	46	.259	.320	.384

Rudy Seanez

Pitches: R Bats: R Pos: RP-73 Ht: 5'11" Wt: 225 Born: 10/20/1968 Age: 39

Year	Team	Lg	G	GS	CG	GF	IP	BFP	H	R	ER	HR	SH	SF	HB	TBB	IBB	SO	WP	Bk	W	L	Pct	ShO	Sv-Op	Hld	ERC	ERA
			HOW MUCH HE PITCHED						**WHAT HE GAVE UP**												**THE RESULTS**							
1989	Cle	AL	5	0	0	2	5.0	20	1	2	2	0	0	2	0	4	1	7	1	1	0	0	-	0	0-0	0	0.94	3.60
1990	Cle	AL	24	0	0	12	27.1	127	22	17	17	2	0	1	1	25	1	24	5	0	2	1	.667	0	0-0	3	4.85	5.60
1991	Cle	AL	5	0	0	0	5.0	33	10	12	9	2	0	0	0	7	0	7	2	0	0	0	-	0	0-1	0	17.96	16.20
1993	SD	NL	3	0	0	3	3.1	20	8	6	5	1	1	0	0	2	0	1	0	0	0	0	-	0	0-0	0	16.31	13.50
1994	LAD	NL	17	0	0	6	23.2	104	24	7	7	2	4	2	1	9	1	18	3	0	1	1	.500	0	0-1	1	4.01	2.66
1995	LAD	NL	37	0	0	12	34.2	159	39	27	26	5	3	0	1	18	3	29	0	0	1	3	.250	0	3-4	6	5.57	6.75
1998	Atl	NL	34	0	0	8	36.0	148	25	13	11	2	1	2	1	16	0	50	2	0	4	1	.800	0	2-4	8	2.44	2.75
1999	Atl	NL	56	0	0	13	53.2	225	47	21	20	3	0	2	1	21	1	41	3	0	6	1	.857	0	3-8	18	3.12	3.35
2000	Atl	NL	23	0	0	8	21.0	89	15	11	10	3	1	0	1	9	1	20	0	0	2	4	.333	0	2-3	6	2.95	4.29
2001	2 Tms	NL	38	0	0	8	36.0	150	23	12	11	4	0	1	1	19	0	41	4	0	0	2	.000	0	1-3	9	2.78	2.75
2002	Tex	AL	33	0	0	4	33.0	150	28	25	21	5	3	1	0	24	1	40	6	0	1	3	.250	0	0-4	10	4.77	5.73
2003	Bos	AL	9	0	0	4	8.2	44	11	7	6	2	0	1	0	6	1	9	3	0	0	0	.000	0	0-1	0	7.45	6.23

Year	Team	Lg	G	GS	CG	GF	IP	BFP	H	R	ER	HR	SH	SF	HB	TBB	IBB	SO	WP	Bk	W	L	Pct	ShO	Sv-Op	Hld	ERC	ERA
2004	2 Tms		39	0	0	15	46.0	100	38	17	17	3	0	3	0	19	3	46	4	0	3	2	.600	0	0-2	4	2.96	3.33
2005	SD	NL	57	0	0	9	60.1	248	49	19	18	4	2	1	2	22	4	84	4	0	7	1	.875	0	0-2	11	2.76	2.69
2006	2 Tms		49	0	0	22	53.0	249	58	32	29	8	0	1	1	32	4	54	7	0	3	3	.500	0	0-2	3	5.68	4.92
2007	LAD	NL	73	0	0	19	76.0	329	78	33	32	10	2	3	4	27	3	73	2	0	6	3	.667	0	1-3	4	4.43	3.79
01	SD	NL	26	0	0	8	24.0	102	15	8	7	3	0	1		15	0	24	1	0	0	2	.000	0	1-3	5	3.21	2.63
01	Atl	NL	12	0	0	0	12.0	48	8	4	4	1	0	0	0	4	0	17	3	0	0	0	-	0	0-0	4	1.99	3.00
04	KC	AL	16	0	0	7	23.0	100	21	10	10	0	0	3	0	11	2	21	3	0	0	1	.000	0	0-1	1	3.01	3.91
04	Fla	NL	23	0	0	8	23.0	93	18	7	7	3	0	0	0	8	1	25	1	0	3	1	.750	0	0-1	3	2.87	2.74
06	Bos	AL	41	0	0	16	46.2	216	51	28	25	6	0	1	1	26	1	48	7	0	2	1	.667	0	0-1	3	5.44	4.82
06	SD	NL	8	0	0	6	6.1	33	7	4	4	2	0	0	0	6	3	6	0	0	1	2	.333	0	0-1	0	7.49	5.68
16 ML YEARS			502	0	0	145	522.2	2288	477	261	241	56	17	20	14	260	24	544	46	1	36	26	.581	0	12-38	83	4.02	4.15

Bobby Seay

Pitches: L **Bats:** L **Pos:** RP-58   **Ht:** 6'2" **Wt:** 235 **Born:** 6/20/1978 **Age:** 30

Year	Team	Lg	G	GS	CG	GF	IP	BFP	H	R	ER	HR	SH	SF	HB	TBB	IBB	SO	WP	Bk	W	L	Pct	ShO	Sv-Op	Hld	ERC	ERA
2001	TB	AL	12	0	0	4	13.0	58	13	11	9	3	2	0	1	5	1	12	1	0	1	1	.500	0	0-0	0	5.03	6.23
2003	TB	AL	12	0	0	2	9.0	39	7	3	3	0	0	2	0	6	0	5	0	0	0	0	-	0	0-1	0	3.17	3.00
2004	TB	AL	21	0	0	6	22.2	95	21	6	6	2	0	0	2	5	1	17	1	0	0	0	-	0	0-0	0	3.15	2.38
2005	Col	NL	17	0	0	5	11.2	58	18	11	11	3	1	0	0	8	1	11	0	1	0	0	-	0	0-1	1	10.28	8.49
2006	Det	AL	14	0	0	6	15.1	71	14	11	11	1	1	1	3	9	1	12	0	0	0	0	-	0	0-0	0	4.65	6.46
2007	Det	AL	58	0	0	19	46.1	189	38	12	12	1	2	2	2	15	4	38	1	1	3	0	1.000	0	1-2	10	2.39	2.33
6 ML YEARS			134	0	0	42	118.0	510	111	54	52	10	6	5	8	48	8	95	3	2	4	1	.800	0	1-4	11	3.82	3.97

Chris Seddon

Pitches: L **Bats:** L **Pos:** SP-4; RP-3   **Ht:** 6'3" **Wt:** 220 **Born:** 10/13/1983 **Age:** 24

Year	Team	Lg	G	GS	CG	GF	IP	BFP	H	R	ER	HR	SH	SF	HB	TBB	IBB	SO	WP	Bk	W	L	Pct	ShO	Sv-Op	Hld	ERC	ERA
2001	Princtn	R	4	2	0	1	12.1	56	15	7	7	2	0	0	0	6	0	18	0	0	1	2	.333	0	0--	-	6.28	5.11
2002	CtnSC	A	26	20	0	2	117.0	507	93	63	47	7	2	3	6	68	0	88	10	0	6	8	.429	0	1--	-	3.56	3.62
2003	Bkrsfld	A+	26	26	0	0	133.1	595	147	93	74	12	2	6	7	54	0	95	7	1	9	11	.450	0	0--	-	4.81	5.00
2004	Bkrsfld	A+	7	7	0	0	41.1	156	30	4	3	0	1	0	2	8	0	41	2	1	5	0	1.000	0	0--	-	1.64	0.65
2004	Mont	AA	21	21	1	0	119.0	516	129	67	58	19	5	6	6	44	0	102	5	0	9	10	.474	0	0--	-	5.17	4.39
2005	Mont	AA	10	10	0	0	52.1	231	58	31	28	4	5	1	1	20	0	46	4	0	6	1	.857	0	0--	-	4.52	4.82
2005	Drham	AAA	19	19	0	0	95.2	453	114	74	58	11	1	9	13	43	0	70	7	5	4	9	.308	0	0--	-	5.99	5.46
2006	Drham	AAA	28	28	1	0	154.1	668	168	92	81	20	5	5	5	46	2	108	2	0	9	9	.500	0	0--	-	4.49	4.72
2007	Mont	AA	12	12	0	0	71.0	292	71	40	39	7	2	4	4	23	1	40	4	0	3	4	.429	0	0--	-	4.16	4.94
2007	Carlina	AA	14	14	0	0	68.2	289	65	37	33	6	5	0	1	25	1	58	2	0	3	6	.333	0	0--	-	3.62	4.33
2007	Fla	NL	7	4	0	1	17.1	91	29	19	17	2	1	1	1	5	0	10	0	0	0	2	.000	0	0-0	0	7.56	8.83

Zack Segovia

Pitches: R **Bats:** R **Pos:** SP-1   **Ht:** 6'2" **Wt:** 244 **Born:** 4/11/1983 **Age:** 25

Year	Team	Lg	G	GS	CG	GF	IP	BFP	H	R	ER	HR	SH	SF	HB	TBB	IBB	SO	WP	Bk	W	L	Pct	ShO	Sv-Op	Hld	ERC	ERA
2002	Phillies	R	8	8	0	0	34.1	128	21	11	8	0	1	0	3	3	0	30	1	0	3	2	.600	0	0--	-	1.11	2.10
2003	Lakwd	A	11	10	0	0	49.2	225	63	25	22	2	2	2	2	14	1	27	2	0	1	5	.167	0	0--	-	4.76	3.99
2003	Clrwtr	A+	5	4	0	0	9.0	35	8	5	4	0	0	0	1	0	0	6	0	0	0	1	.000	0	0--	-	1.88	4.00
2005	Clrwtr	A+	27	27	0	0	144.2	654	168	98	89	18	5	6	17	48	0	83	9	1	4	14	.222	0	0--	-	5.38	5.54
2006	Clrwtr	A+	7	7	0	0	49.1	193	39	14	12	2	0	0	5	12	0	41	1	0	5	1	.833	0	0--	-	2.51	2.19
2006	Rdng	AA	17	16	3	0	107.0	437	90	45	37	8	4	2	8	24	2	75	5	0	11	5	.688	1	0--	-	2.65	3.11
2007	Ottawa	AAA	13	13	1	0	77.1	348	99	55	52	8	2	2	2	28	0	22	4	0	1	9	.100	0	0--	-	5.78	6.05
2007	Rdng	AA	10	10	0	0	57.2	258	65	34	31	4	4	3	5	22	0	30	1	0	5	3	.625	0	0--	-	4.87	4.84
2007	Phi	NL	1	1	0	0	5.0	23	8	5	5	1	1	0	1	1	1	2	0	0	0	1	.000	0	0-0	0	7.45	9.00

Aaron Sele

Pitches: R **Bats:** R **Pos:** RP-34   **Ht:** 6'3" **Wt:** 220 **Born:** 6/25/1970 **Age:** 38

Year	Team	Lg	G	GS	CG	GF	IP	BFP	H	R	ER	HR	SH	SF	HB	TBB	IBB	SO	WP	Bk	W	L	Pct	ShO	Sv-Op	Hld	ERC	ERA
1993	Bos	AL	18	18	0	0	111.2	484	100	42	34	5	2	5	7	48	2	93	5	0	7	2	.778	0	0-0	0	3.40	2.74
1994	Bos	AL	22	22	2	0	143.1	615	140	68	61	13	4	5	9	60	2	105	4	0	8	7	.533	0	0-0	0	4.26	3.83
1995	Bos	AL	6	6	0	0	32.1	146	32	14	11	3	1	1	3	14	0	21	3	0	3	1	.750	0	0-0	0	4.35	3.06
1996	Bos	AL	29	29	1	0	157.1	722	192	110	93	14	6	7	8	67	2	137	2	0	7	11	.389	0	0-0	0	5.56	5.32
1997	Bos	AL	33	33	1	0	177.1	810	196	115	106	25	5	7	15	80	4	122	7	0	13	12	.520	0	0-0	0	5.47	5.38
1998	Tex	AL	33	33	3	0	212.2	954	239	116	100	14	5	7	13	84	6	167	4	0	19	11	.633	2	0-0	0	4.69	4.23
1999	Tex	AL	33	33	2	0	205.0	920	244	115	109	21	1	3	12	70	3	186	4	0	18	9	.667	2	0-0	0	5.17	4.79
2000	Sea	AL	34	34	2	0	211.2	908	221	110	106	17	5	8	5	74	7	137	5	0	17	10	.630	2	0-0	0	4.06	4.51
2001	Sea	AL	34	33	2	0	215.0	899	216	93	86	25	5	9	7	51	2	114	1	0	15	5	.750	1	0-0	0	3.70	3.60
2002	LAA	AL	26	26	1	0	160.0	706	190	92	87	21	5	10	7	49	2	82	5	0	8	9	.471	1	0-0	0	5.20	4.89
2003	LAA	AL	25	25	0	0	121.2	553	135	82	78	17	2	5	12	58	1	53	5	0	7	11	.389	0	0-0	0	5.77	5.77
2004	LAA	AL	28	24	0	1	132.0	593	163	84	74	16	8	3	8	51	2	51	4	2	9	4	.692	0	0-0	0	5.77	5.05
2005	Sea	AL	21	21	0	0	116.0	523	147	76	73	18	1	9	5	41	2	53	2	0	6	12	.333	1	0-0	0	6.11	5.66
2006	LAD	NL	28	15	0	4	103.1	451	120	57	52	11	4	1	2	30	2	57	3	0	8	6	.571	0	0-1	0	4.66	4.53
2007	NYM	NL	34	0	0	10	53.2	250	78	34	32	5	4	5	2	21	2	29	0	0	3	2	.600	0	0-0	1	6.97	5.37
15 ML YEARS			404	352	15	15	2153.0	9534	2413	1208	1102	225	53	90	112	798	39	1407	54	2	148	112	.569	9	0-1	1	4.88	4.61

Jae Seo

Pitches: R **Bats:** R **Pos:** SP-10; RP-1   **Ht:** 6'0" **Wt:** 225 **Born:** 5/24/1977 **Age:** 31

			HOW MUCH HE PITCHED							WHAT HE GAVE UP											THE RESULTS							
Year	Team	Lg	G	GS	CG	GF	IP	BFP	H	R	ER	HR	SH	SF	HB	TBB	IBB	SO	WP	Bk	W	L	Pct	ShO	Sv-Op	Hld	ERC	ERA
2007	Drham*	AAA	17	16	0	0	97.2	390	98	42	40	8	3	1	3	14	0	64	1	1	9	4	.692	0	0- -	-	3.20	3.69
2002	NYM	NL	1	0	0	1	1.0	3	0	0	0	0	0	0	0	0	0	1	0	0	0	0	-	0	0-0	0	0.00	0.00
2003	NYM	NL	32	31	0	0	188.1	806	193	94	80	18	8	4	6	46	11	110	2	0	9	12	.429	0	0-0	0	3.54	3.82
2004	NYM	NL	24	21	0	1	117.2	512	133	67	64	17	12	3	2	50	7	54	0	1	5	10	.333	0	0-0	0	5.39	4.90
2005	NYM	NL	14	14	1	0	90.1	363	84	26	26	9	9	3	1	16	0	59	2	0	8	2	.800	0	0-0	0	2.91	2.59
2006	2 Tms		36	26	0	5	157.0	707	197	101	93	31	6	8	4	56	4	88	5	1	3	12	.200	0	0-0	1	6.26	5.33
2007	TB	AL	11	10	0	1	52.0	248	84	53	47	11	1	1	4	16	1	28	1	0	3	4	.429	0	0-0	0	8.97	8.13
06	LAD	NL	19	10	0	5	67.0	296	75	45	43	14	3	3	1	25	1	49	1	1	2	4	.333	0	0-0	0	5.49	5.78
06	TB	AL	17	16	0	0	90.0	411	122	56	50	17	3	5	3	31	3	39	4	0	1	8	.111	0	0-0	1	6.85	5.00
	6 ML YEARS		118	102	1	8	606.1	2639	691	341	310	86	36	19	17	184	23	340	10	2	28	40	.412	0	0-0	1	4.87	4.60

Dan Serafini

Pitches: L **Bats:** B **Pos:** RP-3   **Ht:** 6'1" **Wt:** 190 **Born:** 1/25/1974 **Age:** 34

			HOW MUCH HE PITCHED							WHAT HE GAVE UP											THE RESULTS							
Year	Team	Lg	G	GS	CG	GF	IP	BFP	H	R	ER	HR	SH	SF	HB	TBB	IBB	SO	WP	Bk	W	L	Pct	ShO	Sv-Op	Hld	ERC	ERA
2007	ColSpr*	AAA	11	3	0	4	20.2	85	18	8	8	0	0	0	1	9	0	12	0	0	0	1	.000	0	1- -	0	3.13	3.48
1996	Min	AL	1	1	0	0	4.1	23	7	5	5	1	0	0	0	2	0	1	0	0	0	1	.000	0	0-0	0	8.69	10.38
1997	Min	AL	6	4	1	1	26.1	111	27	11	10	1	0	0	1	11	0	15	1	0	2	1	.667	0	0-0	0	4.16	3.42
1998	Min	AL	28	9	0	3	75.0	345	95	58	54	10	0	0	1	29	0	46	2	0	7	4	.636	0	0-0	0	5.85	6.48
1999	ChC	NL	42	4	0	8	62.1	302	86	51	48	9	0	0	1	32	0	17	3	0	3	2	.600	0	1-0	0	7.21	6.93
2000	2 Tms		14	11	0	1	65.1	300	79	41	40	11	0	0	4	28	0	35	3	0	2	5	.286	0	0-0	0	6.22	5.51
2003	Cin	NL	10	4	0	2	30.0	141	41	23	18	5	3	2	0	14	1	13	1	0	1	3	.250	0	0-0	0	7.08	5.40
2007	Col	NL	3	0	0	0	0.1	4	0	2	2	0	0	0	1	2	0	0	0	0	0	0	-	0	0-0	0	33.46	54.00
00	SD	NL	3	0	0	0	3.0	20	9	6	6	2	0	0	0	2	0	3	1	0	0	0	-	0	0-0	0	25.94	18.00
00	Pit	NL	11	11	0	1	62.1	280	70	35	34	9	0	0	4	26	0	32	2	0	2	5	.286	0	0-0	0	5.47	4.91
	7 ML YEARS		104	33	1	15	263.2	1226	335	191	177	37	3	2	8	118	1	127	10	1	15	16	.484	0	1-0	0	6.30	6.04

Richie Sexson

Bats: R **Throws:** R **Pos:** 1B-116; DH-3, PH-3   **Ht:** 6'8" **Wt:** 237 **Born:** 12/29/1974 **Age:** 33

			BATTING																		BASERUNNING				AVERAGES		
Year	Team	Lg	G	AB	H	2B	3B	HR	(Hm	Rd)	TB	R	RBI	RC	TBB	IBB	SO	HBP	SH	SF	SB	CS	SB%	GDP	Avg	OBP	Slg
1997	Cle	AL	5	11	3	0	0	0	(0	0)	3	1	0	0	0	0	2	0	0	0	0	0	-	2	.273	.273	.273
1998	Cle	AL	49	174	54	14	1	11	(9	2)	103	28	35	33	6	0	42	3	0	0	1	1	.50	3	.310	.344	.592
1999	Cle	AL	134	479	122	17	7	31	(18	13)	246	72	116	70	34	0	117	4	0	8	3	3	.50	19	.255	.305	.514
2000	2 Tms		148	537	146	30	1	30	(15	15)	268	89	91	91	59	2	159	7	0	4	2	0	1.00	11	.272	.349	.499
2001	Mil	NL	158	598	162	24	3	45	(28	17)	327	94	125	103	60	5	178	6	0	3	2	4	.33	20	.271	.342	.547
2002	Mil	NL	157	570	159	37	2	29	(13	16)	287	86	102	98	70	7	136	8	0	4	0	0	-	17	.279	.363	.504
2003	Mil	NL	162	606	165	28	2	45	(23	22)	332	97	124	116	98	7	151	9	0	5	2	3	.40	18	.272	.379	.548
2004	Ari	NL	23	90	21	4	0	9	(6	3)	52	20	23	18	14	0	21	0	0	0	0	0	-	2	.233	.337	.578
2005	Sea	AL	156	558	147	36	1	39	(21	18)	302	99	121	117	89	4	167	6	0	3	1	1	.50	14	.263	.369	.541
2006	Sea	AL	158	591	156	40	0	34	(17	17)	298	75	107	92	64	5	154	4	0	4	1	1	.50	17	.264	.338	.504
2007	Sea	AL	121	434	89	21	0	21	(12	9)	173	58	63	46	51	1	100	5	0	1	1	0	1.00	12	.205	.295	.399
00	Cle	AL	91	324	83	16	1	16	(8	8)	149	46	44	45	25	0	96	4	0	3	1	0	1.00	8	.256	.315	.460
00	Mil	NL	57	213	63	14	0	14	(7	7)	119	44	47	46	34	2	63	3	0	1	1	0	1.00	3	.296	.398	.559
	11 ML YEARS		1271	4648	1224	251	17	294	(162	132)	2391	719	907	784	545	31	1227	52	0	32	13	13	.50	135	.263	.345	.514

Josh Sharpless

Pitches: R **Bats:** R **Pos:** RP-6   **Ht:** 6'5" **Wt:** 242 **Born:** 1/26/1981 **Age:** 27

			HOW MUCH HE PITCHED							WHAT HE GAVE UP											THE RESULTS							
Year	Team	Lg	G	GS	CG	GF	IP	BFP	H	R	ER	HR	SH	SF	HB	TBB	IBB	SO	WP	Bk	W	L	Pct	ShO	Sv-Op	Hld	ERC	ERA
2003	Wmspt	A-	22	0	0	9	31.1	130	19	9	9	2	1	0	2	17	0	45	0	0	1	1	.500	0	5- -	-	2.53	2.59
2004	Hickory	A	44	0	0	21	74.1	323	42	28	25	4	0	0	3	55	2	109	8	0	6	2	.750	0	4- -	-	2.74	3.03
2005	Lynbrg	A+	17	0	0	9	27.0	97	7	1	0	0	0	0	0	11	0	46	0	0	3	0	1.000	0	5- -	-	0.65	0.00
2005	Altna	AA	7	0	0	2	9.1	39	6	3	3	0	0	1	0	3	0	13	1	0	1	0	1.000	0	0- -	-	1.40	2.89
2006	Altna	AA	14	0	0	11	21.0	80	8	2	2	0	1	0	0	9	0	30	0	0	2	0	1.000	0	8- -	-	0.95	0.86
2006	Indy	AAA	23	0	0	9	33.0	146	32	11	9	1	1	2	0	15	2	30	3	0	1	1	.500	0	1- -	-	3.43	2.45
2007	Indy	AAA	43	0	0	17	64.1	288	61	36	31	10	2	2	0	39	2	69	9	0	1	5	.167	0	3- -	-	4.94	4.34
2006	Pit	NL	14	0	0	3	12.0	53	7	2	2	0	1	1	0	11	1	7	2	0	0	0	-	0	0-0	2	2.86	1.50
2007	Pit	NL	6	0	0	2	4.1	21	7	6	6	3	1	0	0	1	0	1	0	0	0	1	.000	0	0-0	0	11.87	12.46
	2 ML YEARS		20	0	0	5	16.1	74	14	8	8	3	2	1	0	12	1	8	2	0	0	1	.000	0	0-0	2	5.08	4.41

Ryan Shealy

Bats: R **Throws:** R **Pos:** 1B-52; PH-1   **Ht:** 6'5" **Wt:** 240 **Born:** 8/29/1979 **Age:** 28

			BATTING																		BASERUNNING				AVERAGES		
Year	Team	Lg	G	AB	H	2B	3B	HR	(Hm	Rd)	TB	R	RBI	RC	TBB	IBB	SO	HBP	SH	SF	SB	CS	SB%	GDP	Avg	OBP	Slg
2007	Omha*	AAA	34	122	32	7	0	7	(-	-)	60	14	24	21	15	0	28	1	0	1	0	0	-	4	.262	.345	.492
2005	Col	NL	36	91	30	7	0	2	(0	2)	43	14	16	14	13	0	22	0	0	0	1	0	1.00	6	.330	.413	.473
2006	2 Tms		56	202	56	12	1	7	(5	2)	91	31	37	32	15	1	54	2	0	0	1	1	.50	5	.277	.333	.450
2007	KC	AL	52	172	38	6	0	3	(0	3)	53	18	21	15	13	0	53	3	0	1	0	0	-	4	.221	.286	.308
06	Col	NL	5	9	2	2	0	0	(0	0)	4	2	1	0	0	0	4	0	0	0	0	0	-	0	.222	.222	.444
06	KC	AL	51	193	54	10	1	7	(5	2)	87	29	36	32	15	1	50	2	0	0	1	1	.50	5	.280	.338	.451
	3 ML YEARS		144	465	124	25	1	12	(5	7)	187	63	74	61	41	1	129	5	0	1	2	1	.67	15	.267	.332	.402

Tom Shearn

Pitches: R **Bats:** R **Pos:** SP-6; RP-1   **Ht:** 6'4" **Wt:** 230 **Born:** 8/28/1977 **Age:** 30

Year	Team	Lg	G	GS	CG	GF	IP	BFP	H	R	ER	HR	SH	SF	HB	TBB	IBB	SO	WP	Bk	W	L	Pct	ShO	Sv-Op	Hld	ERC	ERA
1996	Astros	R	17	3	0	3	41.2	162	34	13	8	2	1	2	2	10	0	43	2	1	5	2	.714	0	0- -	-	2.48	1.73
1997	Auburn	A-	14	14	2	0	82.1	349	79	42	32	4	1	4	9	26	3	59	7	1	4	6	.400	2	0- -	-	3.58	3.50
1998	QuadC	A	21	21	2	0	120.0	487	88	38	30	8	4	0	6	52	1	93	3	0	7	7	.500	1	0- -	-	2.81	2.25
1999	Kissim	A+	24	24	0	0	145.1	624	144	75	63	11	5	5	4	53	2	107	15	1	10	6	.625	0	0- -	-	3.80	3.90
2000	RdRck	AA	25	23	0	0	136.1	602	134	79	71	14	4	5	8	67	1	102	7	0	9	6	.600	0	0- -	-	4.60	4.69
2001	RdRck	AA	43	8	0	7	110.0	470	94	54	47	7	5	5	7	51	0	136	10	0	5	6	.455	0	1- -	-	3.53	3.85
2002	NewOr	AAA	57	0	0	27	83.1	360	77	29	27	7	5	2	4	41	6	80	7	0	4	6	.400	0	8- -	-	4.01	2.92
2004	Chatt	AA	37	0	0	22	61.1	269	56	34	30	9	1	0	2	27	0	67	8	0	6	4	.600	0	5- -	-	4.11	4.40
2004	Lsvlle	AAA	11	0	0	2	17.2	68	10	6	5	1	1	1	0	6	0	12	0	0	1	0	1.000	0	0- -	-	1.53	2.55
2005	Lsvlle	AAA	44	9	0	9	93.0	401	83	50	44	11	1	1	3	44	1	93	6	0	4	5	.444	0	1- -	-	4.00	4.26
2006	Lsvlle	AAA	32	14	0	3	96.1	404	83	37	27	10	5	1	2	42	2	79	8	0	9	4	.692	0	0- -	-	3.57	2.52
2006	Chatt	AA	1	0	0	0	2.1	12	4	2	2	0	0	0	1	1	0	4	0	0	0	0	-	0	0- -	-	7.52	7.71
2007	Lsvlle	AAA	26	24	0	0	143.2	619	153	72	67	9	4	6	3	51	0	109	11	1	7	10	.412	0	0- -	-	4.11	4.20
2007	Cin	NL	7	6	0	0	32.2	137	32	18	18	8	1	1	0	13	0	16	1	0	3	0	1.000	0	0-0	0	5.10	4.96

Ben Sheets

Pitches: R **Bats:** R **Pos:** SP-24   **Ht:** 6'1" **Wt:** 220 **Born:** 7/18/1978 **Age:** 29

Year	Team	Lg	G	GS	CG	GF	IP	BFP	H	R	ER	HR	SH	SF	HB	TBB	IBB	SO	WP	Bk	W	L	Pct	ShO	Sv-Op	Hld	ERC	ERA
2001	Mil	NL	25	25	1	0	151.1	653	166	89	80	23	8	5	5	48	6	94	3	0	11	10	.524	1	0-0	0	4.78	4.76
2002	Mil	NL	34	34	1	0	216.2	934	237	105	100	21	10	0	10	70	10	170	9	0	11	16	.407	0	0-0	0	4.45	4.15
2003	Mil	NL	34	34	1	0	220.2	931	232	122	109	29	11	6	6	43	2	157	7	0	11	13	.458	0	0-0	0	3.83	4.45
2004	Mil	NL	34	34	5	0	237.0	937	201	85	71	25	6	4	4	32	1	264	8	1	12	14	.462	0	0-0	0	2.37	2.70
2005	Mil	NL	22	22	3	0	156.2	633	142	66	58	19	6	2	2	25	1	141	7	0	10	9	.526	0	0-0	0	2.81	3.33
2006	Mil	NL	17	17	0	0	106.0	430	105	47	45	9	6	5	2	11	1	116	3	0	6	7	.462	0	0-0	0	2.84	3.82
2007	Mil	NL	24	24	2	0	141.1	592	138	62	60	17	4	5	1	37	2	106	4	0	12	5	.706	0	0-0	0	3.53	3.82
	7 ML YEARS		190	190	13	0	1229.2	5110	1221	576	523	143	51	27	30	266	23	1048	41	1	73	74	.497	1	0-0	0	3.49	3.83

Gary Sheffield

Bats: R **Throws:** R **Pos:** DH-119; LF-7; RF-7; PH-2   **Ht:** 6'0" **Wt:** 215 **Born:** 11/18/1968 **Age:** 39

Year	Team	Lg	G	AB	H	2B	3B	HR	(Hm	Rd)	TB	R	RBI	RC	TBB	IBB	SO	HBP	SH	SF	SB	CS	SB%	GDP	Avg	OBP	Slg
1988	Mil	AL	24	80	19	1	0	4	(1	3)	32	12	12	8	7	0	7	0	1	1	3	1	.75	5	.238	.295	.400
1989	Mil	AL	95	368	91	18	0	5	(2	3)	124	34	32	38	27	0	33	4	3	3	10	6	.63	4	.247	.303	.337
1990	Mil	AL	125	487	143	30	1	10	(3	7)	205	67	67	73	44	1	41	3	4	9	25	10	.71	11	.294	.350	.421
1991	Mil	AL	50	175	34	12	2	2	(2	0)	56	25	22	15	19	1	15	3	1	5	5	5	.50	3	.194	.277	.320
1992	SD	NL	146	557	184	34	3	33	(23	10)	323	87	100	113	48	5	40	6	0	7	5	6	.45	19	.330	.385	.580
1993	2 Tms	NL	140	494	145	20	5	20	(10	10)	235	67	73	84	47	6	64	9	0	7	17	5	.77	11	.294	.361	.476
1994	Fla	NL	87	322	89	16	1	27	(15	12)	188	61	78	68	51	11	50	0	0	5	12	6	.67	10	.276	.380	.584
1995	Fla	NL	63	213	69	8	0	16	(4	12)	125	46	46	60	55	8	45	4	0	2	19	4	.83	3	.324	.467	.587
1996	Fla	NL	161	519	163	33	1	42	(19	23)	324	118	120	144	142	19	66	10	0	6	16	9	.64	16	.314	.465	.624
1997	Fla	NL	135	444	111	22	1	21	(13	8)	198	86	71	92	121	11	79	15	0	2	11	7	.61	7	.250	.424	.446
1998	2 Tms	NL	130	437	132	27	2	22	(11	11)	229	73	85	102	95	12	46	8	0	9	22	7	.76	7	.302	.428	.524
1999	LAD	NL	152	549	165	20	0	34	(15	19)	287	103	101	118	101	4	64	4	0	9	11	5	.69	10	.301	.407	.523
2000	LAD	NL	141	501	163	24	3	43	(23	20)	322	105	109	131	101	7	71	4	0	6	4	6	.40	13	.325	.438	.643
2001	LAD	NL	143	515	160	28	2	36	(16	20)	300	98	100	120	94	13	67	4	0	5	10	4	.71	12	.311	.417	.583
2002	Atl	NL	135	492	151	26	0	25	(10	15)	252	82	84	102	72	2	53	11	0	4	12	2	.86	16	.307	.404	.512
2003	Atl	NL	155	576	190	37	2	39	(20	19)	348	126	132	134	86	6	55	8	0	8	18	4	.82	16	.330	.419	.604
2004	NYY	AL	154	573	166	30	1	36	(19	17)	306	117	121	123	92	7	83	11	0	8	5	6	.45	16	.290	.393	.534
2005	NYY	AL	154	584	170	27	0	34	(19	15)	299	104	123	130	78	7	76	8	0	5	10	2	.83	11	.291	.379	.512
2006	NYY	AL	39	151	45	5	0	6	(5	1)	68	22	25	21	13	2	16	1	0	1	5	1	.83	6	.298	.355	.450
2007	Det	AL	133	494	131	20	1	25	(14	11)	228	107	75	90	84	2	71	9	0	6	22	5	.81	10	.265	.378	.462
93	SD	NL	68	258	76	12	2	10	(6	4)	122	34	36	40	18	0	30	3	0	3	5	1	.83	9	.295	.344	.473
93	Fla	NL	72	236	69	8	3	10	(4	6)	113	33	37	44	29	6	34	6	0	4	12	4	.75	2	.292	.378	.479
98	Fla	NL	40	136	37	11	1	6	(6	0)	68	21	28	27	26	1	16	2	0	2	4	2	.67	3	.272	.392	.500
98	LAD	NL	90	301	95	16	1	16	(5	11)	161	52	57	75	69	11	30	6	0	7	18	5	.78	4	.316	.444	.535
	20 ML YEARS		2362	8531	2521	438	25	480	(244	236)	4449	1540	1576	1766	1377	124	1042	128	9	108	242	101	.71	206	.296	.397	.522

George Sherrill

Pitches: L **Bats:** L **Pos:** RP-73   **Ht:** 6'0" **Wt:** 225 **Born:** 4/19/1977 **Age:** 31

Year	Team	Lg	G	GS	CG	GF	IP	BFP	H	R	ER	HR	SH	SF	HB	TBB	IBB	SO	WP	Bk	W	L	Pct	ShO	Sv-Op	Hld	ERC	ERA
2004	Sea	AL	21	0	0	4	23.2	104	24	12	10	3	0	1	1	9	1	16	4	1	2	1	.667	0	0-0	3	4.31	3.80
2005	Sea	AL	29	0	0	2	19.0	77	13	12	11	3	1	1	1	7	2	24	0	0	4	3	.571	0	0-0	9	2.70	5.21
2006	Sea	AL	72	0	0	6	40.0	174	30	19	19	0	4	2	0	27	4	42	0	0	2	4	.333	0	1-1	17	2.86	4.28
2007	Sea	AL	73	0	0	16	45.2	182	28	12	12	4	4	4	1	17	1	56	1	1	2	0	1.000	0	3-7	22	1.96	2.36
	4 ML YEARS		195	0	0	28	128.1	537	95	55	52	10	9	8	3	60	8	138	5	2	10	8	.556	0	4-8	51	2.77	3.65

James Shields

Pitches: R Bats: R Pos: SP-31   Ht: 6'4" Wt: 215 Born: 12/20/1981 Age: 26

		HOW MUCH HE PITCHED						WHAT HE GAVE UP												THE RESULTS							
Year Team	Lg	G	GS	CG	GF	IP	BFP	H	R	ER	HR	SH	SF	HB	TBB	IBB	SO	WP	Bk	W	L	Pct	ShO	Sv-Op	Hld	ERC	ERA
2001 HudVal	A-	5	5	0	0	27.1	113	27	8	7	1	1	0	1	5	0	25	1	1	2	1	.667	0	0- -	-	2.90	2.30
2001 CtnSC	A	10	10	2	0	71.1	284	63	24	21	7	3	2	2	10	0	60	2	1	4	5	.444	1	0- -	-	2.58	2.65
2003 Bkrsfld	A+	26	24	0	1	143.2	632	161	85	71	19	3	2	12	38	0	119	6	4	10	10	.500	0	1- -	-	4.76	4.45
2004 Mont	AA	4	4	0	0	18.1	84	24	16	16	4	3	0	0	8	0	14	0	0	0	3	.000	0	0- -	-	7.12	7.85
2004 Bkrsfld	A+	20	20	1	0	117.0	488	119	61	55	13	4	5	9	33	0	92	6	0	8	5	.615	1	0- -	-	4.22	4.23
2005 Mont	AA	17	16	0	1	109.1	434	95	36	34	6	5	2	6	31	0	104	7	0	7	5	.583	0	0- -	-	2.98	2.80
2005 Drham	AAA	1	1	0	0	6.0	29	9	4	4	0	0	0	0	3	0	6	1	0	1	0	1.000	0	0- -	-	6.72	6.00
2006 Drham	AAA	10	10	0	0	61.1	241	60	24	18	3	3	1	2	6	0	64	4	1	3	2	.600	0	0- -	-	2.70	2.64
2006 TB	AL	21	21	1	0	124.2	540	141	69	67	18	4	3	5	38	5	104	9	0	6	8	.429	0	0-0	0	4.92	4.84
2007 TB	AL	31	31	1	0	215.0	874	202	98	92	28	4	5	10	36	0	184	9	0	12	8	.600	0	0-0	0	3.24	3.85
2 ML YEARS		52	52	2	0	339.2	1414	343	167	159	46	8	8	15	74	5	288	18	0	18	16	.529	0	0-0	0	3.83	4.21

Scot Shields

Pitches: R Bats: R Pos: RP-71   Ht: 6'1" Wt: 180 Born: 7/22/1975 Age: 32

		HOW MUCH HE PITCHED						WHAT HE GAVE UP												THE RESULTS							
Year Team	Lg	G	GS	CG	GF	IP	BFP	H	R	ER	HR	SH	SF	HB	TBB	IBB	SO	WP	Bk	W	L	Pct	ShO	Sv-Op	Hld	ERC	ERA
2001 LAA	AL	8	0	0	6	11.0	48	8	1	0	0	0	0	1	7	0	7	2	0	0	0	-	0	0-0	0	3.10	0.00
2002 LAA	AL	29	1	0	13	49.0	188	31	13	12	4	1	0	1	21	1	30	3	0	5	3	.625	0	0-0	0	2.35	2.20
2003 LAA	AL	44	13	0	5	148.1	609	138	56	47	12	3	4	5	38	6	111	4	0	5	6	.455	0	1-1	3	3.12	2.85
2004 LAA	AL	60	0	0	12	105.1	454	97	42	39	6	2	2	3	40	5	109	4	0	8	2	.800	0	4-7	17	3.24	3.33
2005 LAA	AL	78	0	0	21	91.2	375	66	33	28	5	4	3	2	37	2	98	12	0	10	11	.476	0	7-13	33	2.37	2.75
2006 LAA	AL	74	0	0	13	87.2	351	70	30	28	8	3	1	1	24	4	84	8	0	7	7	.500	0	2-8	31	2.48	2.87
2007 LAA	AL	71	0	0	13	77.0	320	62	36	33	7	0	1	4	33	0	77	6	0	4	5	.444	0	2-8	31	3.31	3.86
7 ML YEARS		364	14	0	83	570.0	2345	472	211	187	42	13	11	17	200	18	516	39	0	39	34	.534	0	16-37	118	2.88	2.95

Kelly Shoppach

Bats: R Throws: R Pos: C-58; PH-2   Ht: 6'0" Wt: 220 Born: 4/29/1980 Age: 28

		BATTING																	BASERUNNING				AVERAGES		
Year Team	Lg	G	AB	H	2B	3B	HR	(Hm	Rd)	TB	R	RBI	RC	TBB	IBB	SO	HBP	SH	SF	SB	CS	SB%	GDP	Avg	OBP	Slg
2005 Bos	AL	9	15	0	0	0	0	(0	0)	0	1	0	0	0	0	7	1	0	0	0	0	-	0	.000	.063	.000
2006 Cle	AL	41	110	27	6	0	3	(2	1)	42	7	16	13	8	0	45	0	2	0	0	0	-	2	.245	.297	.382
2007 Cle	AL	59	161	42	13	0	7	(4	3)	76	26	30	24	11	0	56	1	3	1	0	0	-	2	.261	.310	.472
3 ML YEARS		109	286	69	19	0	10	(6	4)	118	34	46	37	19	0	108	2	5	1	0	0	-	4	.241	.292	.413

Brian Shouse

Pitches: L Bats: L Pos: RP-73   Ht: 5'11" Wt: 190 Born: 9/26/1968 Age: 39

		HOW MUCH HE PITCHED						WHAT HE GAVE UP												THE RESULTS							
Year Team	Lg	G	GS	CG	GF	IP	BFP	H	R	ER	HR	SH	SF	HB	TBB	IBB	SO	WP	Bk	W	L	Pct	ShO	Sv-Op	Hld	ERC	ERA
1993 Pit	NL	6	0	0	1	4.0	22	7	4	4	1	0	1	0	2	0	3	1	0	0	0	-	0	0-0	0	9.92	9.00
1998 Bos	AL	7	0	0	4	8.0	36	9	5	5	2	0	0	0	4	0	5	0	0	0	1	.000	0	0-0	1	6.42	5.63
2002 KC	AL	23	0	0	7	14.2	71	15	10	10	3	1	1	2	9	1	11	2	0	0	0	-	0	0-0	2	6.11	6.14
2003 Tex	AL	62	0	0	14	61.0	253	62	24	21	1	3	0	4	14	6	40	0	0	0	1	.000	0	1-1	10	3.10	3.10
2004 Tex	AL	53	0	0	14	44.1	184	36	12	11	3	2	2	1	18	3	34	0	0	2	0	1.000	0	0-0	12	2.87	2.23
2005 Tex	AL	64	0	0	12	53.1	233	55	37	31	7	2	3	3	18	4	35	2	0	3	2	.600	0	0-2	11	4.29	5.23
2006 2 Tms		65	0	0	10	38.1	174	40	18	17	4	1	1	6	18	5	23	0	0	1	3	.250	0	2-5	15	5.06	3.99
2007 Mil	NL	73	0	0	13	47.2	201	46	19	16	0	4	2	2	14	5	32	0	1	1	1	.500	0	1-4	21	2.79	3.02
06 Tex	AL	6	0	0	2	4.1	20	6	2	2	1	0	0	0	1	1	3	0	0	0	0	-	0	0-1	1	6.09	4.15
06 Mil	NL	59	0	0	8	34.0	154	34	16	15	3	1	1	6	17	4	20	0	0	1	3	.250	0	2-4	14	4.92	3.97
8 ML YEARS		353	0	0	75	271.1	1174	270	129	115	21	13	10	18	97	24	183	5	1	7	8	.467	0	4-12	72	3.83	3.81

Paul Shuey

Pitches: R Bats: R Pos: RP-25   Ht: 6'3" Wt: 215 Born: 9/16/1970 Age: 37

		HOW MUCH HE PITCHED						WHAT HE GAVE UP												THE RESULTS							
Year Team	Lg	G	GS	CG	GF	IP	BFP	H	R	ER	HR	SH	SF	HB	TBB	IBB	SO	WP	Bk	W	L	Pct	ShO	Sv-Op	Hld	ERC	ERA
2007 Bowie*	AA	1	1	0	0	1.0	3	0	0	0	0	0	0	0	0	0	0	0	0	0	0	-	0	0- -	-	0.00	0.00
2007 Norfolk*	AAA	21	0	0	6	23.0	107	30	14	11	2	1	1	0	9	0	24	2	0	0	0	-	0	1- -	-	5.63	4.30
1994 Cle	AL	14	0	0	11	11.2	62	14	11	11	1	0	0	0	12	1	16	4	0	0	1	.000	0	5-5	1	7.28	8.49
1995 Cle	AL	7	0	0	3	6.1	28	5	4	3	0	2	0	0	5	0	5	1	0	0	2	.000	0	0-0	0	3.70	4.26
1996 Cle	AL	42	0	0	18	53.2	225	45	19	17	6	1	3	0	26	3	44	3	1	5	2	.714	0	4-7	7	3.56	2.85
1997 Cle	AL	40	0	0	16	45.0	212	52	31	31	5	4	2	1	28	3	46	2	0	4	2	.667	0	2-3	4	5.92	6.20
1998 Cle	AL	43	0	0	16	51.0	222	44	19	17	6	2	0	3	25	5	58	3	0	5	4	.556	0	2-5	12	3.83	3.00
1999 Cle	AL	72	0	0	20	81.2	351	68	37	32	8	4	1	4	40	7	103	8	0	8	5	.615	0	6-12	19	3.36	3.53
2000 Cle	AL	57	0	0	12	63.2	270	51	25	24	4	1	3	3	30	3	69	0	0	4	2	.667	0	0-5	28	3.11	3.39
2001 Cle	AL	47	0	0	11	54.1	244	53	25	17	1	4	2	1	26	5	70	6	0	5	3	.625	0	2-5	9	3.46	2.82
2002 2 Tms		67	0	0	18	68.0	288	56	29	25	3	1	2	1	31	2	63	3	0	8	2	.800	0	1-5	19	2.95	3.31
2003 LAD	NL	62	0	0	18	69.0	281	50	24	23	6	2	0	4	33	3	60	3	0	6	4	.600	0	0-1	10	3.06	3.00
2007 Bal	AL	25	0	0	5	25.2	126	32	28	28	3	1	0	0	21	0	22	3	0	0	1	-	0	1-1	6	7.85	9.82
02 Cle	AL	39	0	0	12	37.1	150	31	11	10	1	1	1	0	10	1	39	2	0	3	0	1.000	0	0-2	12	2.21	2.41
02 LAD	NL	28	0	0	6	30.2	138	25	18	15	2	0	1	1	21	1	24	1	0	5	2	.714	0	1-3	7	3.89	4.40
11 ML YEARS		476	0	0	156	530.0	2309	471	252	228	43	22	13	14	277	32	556	36	1	45	28	.616	0	23-49	115	3.79	3.87

Carlos Silva

Pitches: R Bats: R Pos: SP-33　　　　　Ht: 6'4" Wt: 246 Born: 4/23/1979 Age: 20

Year	Team	Lg	G	GS	CG	GF	IP	BFP	H	R	ER	HR	SH	SF	HB	TBB	IBB	SO	WP	Bk	W	L	Pct	ShO	Sv-Op	Hld	ERC	ERA
2002	Phi	NL	68	0	0	21	84.0	350	88	34	30	4	9	3	4	22	6	41	3	0	5	0	1.000	0	1-5	8	3.60	3.21
2003	Phi	NL	62	1	0	15	87.1	381	92	43	43	7	6	1	8	37	5	48	12	1	3	1	.750	0	1-3	4	4.71	4.43
2004	Min	AL	33	33	1	0	203.0	869	255	100	95	23	6	0	5	35	2	76	5	1	14	8	.636	1	0-0	0	4.89	4.21
2005	Min	AL	27	27	2	0	188.1	749	212	83	72	25	2	5	3	9	2	71	0	0	9	8	.529	0	0-0	0	3.78	3.44
2006	Min	AL	36	31	0	2	180.1	811	246	130	119	38	6	7	7	32	4	70	1	0	11	15	.423	0	0-0	2	6.23	5.94
2007	Min	AL	33	33	2	0	202.0	848	229	99	94	20	6	5	4	36	2	89	4	1	13	14	.481	1	0-0	0	4.05	4.19
6 ML YEARS			259	125	5	38	945.0	4008	1122	489	453	117	35	21	31	171	21	395	25	3	55	46	.545	2	2-8	14	4.60	4.31

Jason Simontacchi

Pitches: R Bats: R Pos: SP-13　　　　　Ht: 6'2" Wt: 190 Born: 11/13/1973 Age: 34

Year	Team	Lg	G	GS	CG	GF	IP	BFP	H	R	ER	HR	SH	SF	HB	TBB	IBB	SO	WP	Bk	W	L	Pct	ShO	Sv-Op	Hld	ERC	ERA
2007	Clmbs*	AAA	2	2	0	0	10.2	47	17	7	7	0	1	0	1	1	0	3	0	0	0	1	.000	0	0--	-	6.30	5.91
2002	StL	NL	24	24	0	0	143.1	600	134	68	64	18	6	4	6	54	4	72	1	0	11	5	.688	0	0-0	0	4.01	4.02
2003	StL	NL	46	16	1	7	126.1	563	153	82	78	21	2	4	5	41	0	74	4	0	9	5	.643	0	1-3	7	5.68	5.56
2004	StL	NL	13	0	0	6	15.1	67	17	10	9	5	2	1	1	7	0	3	0	0	0	0	-	0	0-0	0	7.26	5.28
2007	Was	NL	13	13	0	0	70.2	322	95	53	50	13	4	4	3	23	4	42	1	0	6	7	.462	0	0-0	0	6.63	6.37
4 ML YEARS			96	53	1	13	355.2	1552	399	213	201	57	14	13	15	125	8	191	6	0	26	17	.605	0	1-3	7	5.23	5.09

Andy Sisco

Pitches: L Bats: L Pos: RP-19　　　　　Ht: 6'10" Wt: 270 Born: 1/13/1983 Age: 25

Year	Team	Lg	G	GS	CG	GF	IP	BFP	H	R	ER	HR	SH	SF	HB	TBB	IBB	SO	WP	Bk	W	L	Pct	ShO	Sv-Op	Hld	ERC	ERA
2007	Charltt*	AAA	23	15	0	3	78.2	345	76	43	38	10	3	2	3	44	1	76	6	0	3	6	.333	0	0--	-	4.95	4.35
2005	KC	AL	67	0	0	13	75.1	329	68	27	26	6	2	3	2	42	4	76	2	0	2	5	.286	0	0-5	14	4.04	3.11
2006	KC	AL	65	0	0	16	58.1	278	66	47	46	8	4	5	1	40	6	52	4	0	1	3	.250	0	1-5	5	6.14	7.10
2007	CWS	AL	19	0	0	6	14.0	74	19	13	13	2	0	0	1	11	0	13	3	0	1	0	1.000	0	0-0	4	8.28	8.36
3 ML YEARS			151	0	0	35	147.2	681	153	87	85	16	6	8	4	93	10	141	9	0	3	9	.250	0	1-10	23	5.23	5.18

Grady Sizemore

Bats: L Throws: L Pos: CF-160; PH-2; DH-1; PR-1　　　　　Ht: 6'2" Wt: 200 Born: 8/2/1982 Age: 25

Year	Team	Lg	G	AB	H	2B	3B	HR	(Hm	Rd)	TB	R	RBI	RC	TBB	IBB	SO	HBP	SH	SF	SB	CS	SB%	GDP	Avg	OBP	Slg
2004	Cle	AL	43	138	34	6	2	4	(2	2)	56	15	24	21	14	0	34	5	0	2	2	0	1.00	0	.246	.333	.406
2005	Cle	AL	158	640	185	37	11	22	(10	12)	310	111	81	101	52	1	132	7	5	2	22	10	.69	17	.289	.348	.484
2006	Cle	AL	162	655	190	53	11	28	(14	14)	349	134	76	121	78	8	153	13	1	4	22	6	.79	2	.290	.375	.533
2007	Cle	AL	162	628	174	34	5	24	(11	13)	290	118	78	123	101	9	155	17	0	2	33	10	.77	3	.277	.390	.462
4 ML YEARS			525	2061	583	130	29	78	(37	41)	1005	378	259	366	245	18	474	42	6	10	79	26	.75	22	.283	.369	.488

Doug Slaten

Pitches: L Bats: L Pos: RP-61　　　　　Ht: 6'5" Wt: 200 Born: 2/4/1980 Age: 28

Year	Team	Lg	G	GS	CG	GF	IP	BFP	H	R	ER	HR	SH	SF	HB	TBB	IBB	SO	WP	Bk	W	L	Pct	ShO	Sv-Op	Hld	ERC	ERA
2000	DBcks	R	9	4	0	3	9.1	40	7	1	1	0	0	0	2	3	0	7	0	0	0	0	-	0	0--	-	2.51	0.96
2001	Lancst	A+	28	27	1	0	157.2	723	207	105	84	16	5	5	4	45	3	110	6	5	9	8	.529	0	0--	-	5.42	4.79
2002	Lancst	A+	8	8	0	0	35.0	183	59	43	35	4	1	3	3	12	0	23	5	3	1	6	.143	0	0--	-	8.18	9.00
2002	Sbend	A	7	0	0	2	14.1	63	18	8	7	0	1	0	0	4	0	5	1	0	0	0	-	0	0--	-	4.34	4.40
2003	Lancst	A+	32	19	0	3	119.1	555	156	94	80	13	3	1	10	47	0	78	4	3	6	7	.462	0	0--	-	6.33	6.03
2004	ElPaso	AA	11	0	0	2	9.0	53	16	13	10	1	1	1	0	10	0	6	0	0	0	1	.000	0	0--	-	12.15	10.00
2004	Sbend	A	36	0	0	16	44.0	191	44	13	11	2	0	0	2	13	1	40	3	0	5	2	.714	0	5--	-	3.35	2.25
2005	Tenn	AA	58	0	0	6	61.1	270	61	45	29	2	5	3	3	26	0	72	3	2	2	2	.500	0	1--	-	3.81	4.26
2006	Tenn	AA	40	0	0	24	43.0	168	31	12	9	1	2	2	1	15	0	59	3	0	2	3	.400	0	8--	-	2.14	1.88
2006	Tucsn	AAA	18	0	0	6	20.0	77	10	2	1	0	2	2	0	7	0	21	0	0	2	1	.667	0	2--	-	1.12	0.45
2006	Ari	NL	9	0	0	0	5.2	21	3	0	0	0	1	0	0	2	1	3	0	0	0	0	-	0	0-0	2	1.11	0.00
2007	Ari	NL	61	0	0	13	36.1	163	41	15	11	4	0	0	0	14	0	28	3	0	3	2	.600	0	0-1	7	4.74	2.72
2 ML YEARS			70	0	0	13	42.0	184	44	15	11	4	1	0	0	16	1	31	3	0	3	2	.600	0	0-1	9	4.14	2.36

Terrmel Sledge

Bats: L Throws: L Pos: LF-54; PH-44; RF-6; PR-2　　　　　Ht: 6'0" Wt: 185 Born: 3/18/1977 Age: 31

Year	Team	Lg	G	AB	H	2B	3B	HR	(Hm	Rd)	TB	R	RBI	RC	TBB	IBB	SO	HBP	SH	SF	SB	CS	SB%	GDP	Avg	OBP	Slg
2007	Portlnd*	AAA	8	27	10	2	0	1	(-	-)	15	5	3	6	3	0	3	0	1	0	1	0	1.00	1	.370	.433	.556
2004	Mon	NL	133	398	107	20	6	15	(6	9)	184	45	62	66	40	4	66	1	6	1	3	3	.50	2	.269	.336	.462
2005	Was	NL	20	37	9	0	1	1	(0	1)	14	7	8	4	7	1	8	0	0	2	2	1	.67	3	.243	.348	.378
2006	SD	NL	38	70	16	3	0	2	(2	0)	25	7	7	6	8	0	17	0	0	1	0	0	-	1	.229	.308	.357
2007	SD	NL	100	200	42	9	0	7	(3	4)	72	22	23	21	27	2	60	3	1	2	1	2	.33	7	.210	.310	.360
4 ML YEARS			291	705	174	32	7	25	(9	16)	295	81	100	97	82	7	151	4	7	5	6	6	.50	13	.247	.327	.418

Kevin Slowey

Pitches: R Bats: R Pos: SP-11; RP-2   Ht: 6'3" Wt: 197 Born: 5/4/1984 Age: 24

		HOW MUCH HE PITCHED						WHAT HE GAVE UP												THE RESULTS							
Year	Team	Lg	G	GS	CG	GF	IP	BFP	H	R	ER	HR	SH	SF	HB	TBB	IBB	SO	WP	Bk	W	L	Pct	ShO	Sv-Op	Hld	ERC	ERA
2005	Elizab	R+	4	0	0	2	7.2	25	2	1	1	1	0	0	0	0	0	15	0	0	0	0	-	0	1--	-	0.33	1.17
2005	Beloit	A	13	9	1	2	64.1	243	42	18	16	4	1	2	2	8	0	69	0	0	3	2	.600	1	0--	-	1.40	2.24
2006	FtMyrs	A+	14	14	0	0	89.2	333	52	19	10	2	1	1	4	9	0	99	0	0	4	2	.667	0	0--	-	1.03	1.00
2006	NwBrit	AA	9	9	1	0	59.1	242	50	23	21	6	1	2	2	13	0	52	0	0	4	3	.571	0	0--	-	2.65	3.19
2007	Roch	AAA	20	20	5	0	133.2	523	110	31	28	4	8	1	3	18	0	107	1	1	10	5	.667	1	0--	-	1.88	1.89
2007	Min	AL	13	11	0	0	66.2	297	82	39	35	16	0	1	0	11	0	47	3	0	4	1	.800	0	0-0	0	5.22	4.73

Jason Smith

Bats: l Throws: R Pos: SS-24; PH-20; 3B-19; 2B-7; PR-6; DH-5; 1B-3   Ht: 6'3" Wt: 200 Born: 7/24/1977 Age: 30

								BATTING													BASERUNNING				AVERAGES		
Year	Team	Lg	G	AB	H	2B	3B	HR	(Hm	Rd)	TB	R	RBI	RC	TBB	IBB	SO	HBP	SH	SF	SB	CS	SB%	GDP	Avg	OBP	Slg
2007	Visalia*	A+	3	9	4	0	0	1	(-	-)	7	4	5	3	2	0	1	1	0	0	0	0	-	0	.444	.583	.778
2007	Tucsn*	AAA	14	54	17	3	1	3	(-	-)	31	9	10	9	0	0	17	1	0	2	0	2	.00	1	.315	.316	.574
2001	ChC	NL	2	1	0	0	0	0	(0	0)	0	0	0	0	0	0	1	0	0	0	0	0	-	0	.000	.000	.000
2002	TB	AL	26	65	13	1	2	1	(0	1)	21	9	6	5	2	0	24	0	2	0	3	0	1.00	0	.200	.224	.323
2003	TB	AL	1	4	1	0	0	0	(0	0)	1	0	0	0	0	0	0	0	0	0	0	0	-	0	.250	.250	.250
2004	Det	AL	61	155	37	7	4	5	(0	5)	67	20	19	13	8	0	37	1	5	0	1	2	.33	0	.239	.280	.432
2005	Det	AL	27	58	11	1	2	0	(0	0)	16	4	2	4	0	0	16	1	4	0	2	1	.67	0	.190	.203	.276
2006	Col	NL	49	99	26	1	0	5	(1	4)	42	9	13	15	7	1	29	2	0	0	3	0	1.00	1	.263	.324	.424
2007	3 Tms		69	141	28	3	2	6	(0	6)	53	16	18	11	6	0	53	1	0	1	0	0	-	2	.199	.235	.376
07	Tor	AL	27	52	11	1	1	0	(0	0)	14	7	4	3	3	0	22	1	0	0	0	0	-	0	.212	.268	.269
07	Ari	NL	2	4	1	0	0	0	(0	0)	1	0	0	0	0	0	2	0	0	0	0	0	-	0	.250	.250	.250
07	KC	AL	40	85	16	2	1	6	(0	6)	38	9	14	8	3	0	29	0	0	1	0	0	-	2	.188	.213	.447
7 ML YEARS			235	523	116	13	10	17	(1	16)	200	58	58	48	23	1	160	5	11	1	9	3	.75	3	.222	.261	.382

Joe Smith

Pitches: R Bats: R Pos: RP-54   Ht: 6'2" Wt: 213 Born: 3/22/1984 Age: 24

			HOW MUCH HE PITCHED						WHAT HE GAVE UP												THE RESULTS							
Year	Team	Lg	G	GS	CG	GF	IP	BFP	H	R	ER	HR	SH	SF	HB	TBB	IBB	SO	WP	Bk	W	L	Pct	ShO	Sv-Op	Hld	ERC	ERA
2006	Bklyn	A-	17	0	0	15	20.0	78	10	3	1	0	0	0	4	3	0	28	2	0	0	1	.000	0	9--	-	1.11	0.45
2006	Bnghtn	AA	10	0	0	5	12.2	59	12	8	8	1	2	0	1	11	1	12	1	0	0	2	.000	0	0--	-	5.80	5.68
2007	NewOr	AAA	8	0	0	4	9.0	35	7	3	2	0	0	1	0	4	0	5	0	0	0	0	-	0	2--	-	2.60	2.00
2007	NYM	NL	54	0	0	14	44.1	205	48	18	17	3	2	0	7	21	4	45	2	0	3	2	.600	0	0-0	10	5.04	3.45

Matt Smith

Pitches: L Bats: L Pos: RP-9   Ht: 6'4" Wt: 215 Born: 6/15/1979 Age: 29

			HOW MUCH HE PITCHED						WHAT HE GAVE UP												THE RESULTS							
Year	Team	Lg	G	GS	CG	GF	IP	BFP	H	R	ER	HR	SH	SF	HB	TBB	IBB	SO	WP	Bk	W	L	Pct	ShO	Sv-Op	Hld	ERC	ERA
2000	StsIsnd	A-	14	14	0	0	75.2	308	74	32	20	1	3	0	2	20	0	59	4	0	5	4	.556	0	0--	-	3.05	2.38
2001	Grnsbr	A	16	16	1	0	97.1	389	69	37	28	1	3	1	3	32	0	116	8	0	5	3	.625	1	0--	-	1.89	2.59
2001	Tampa	A+	11	11	0	0	68.1	276	54	21	17	2	1	1	1	22	0	71	4	4	6	2	.750	0	0--	-	2.31	2.24
2002	Nrwich	AA	17	17	0	0	80.1	419	112	63	54	8	3	3	9	37	0	70	11	0	3	8	.273	0	0--	-	5.91	5.44
2002	Tampa	A+	8	6	0	1	27.1	133	37	23	20	1	0	4	0	17	0	20	2	0	0	4	.000	0	0--	-	6.56	6.59
2003	Tampa	A+	6	6	0	0	32.1	131	20	11	8	0	0	4	1	12	0	25	1	0	2	3	.400	0	0--	-	1.56	2.23
2003	Trntn	AA	9	9	0	0	50.2	226	57	29	24	6	1	3	2	24	0	36	0	0	2	3	.400	0	0--	-	5.50	4.26
2004	Trntn	AA	14	11	0	0	61.2	271	67	34	34	5	2	2	1	31	1	56	3	0	4	4	.500	0	0--	-	5.01	4.96
2005	Clmbs	AAA	25	0	0	7	27.2	122	24	9	8	3	1	0	3	13	1	33	0	0	2	0	1.000	0	1--	-	3.98	2.60
2005	Trntn	AA	22	4	0	5	54.2	228	46	24	17	2	2	2	0	23	0	59	3	1	3	4	.429	0	2--	-	2.89	2.80
2006	Clmbs	AAA	24	0	0	5	26.0	111	27	9	6	3	1	0	1	8	1	22	1	0	0	1	.000	0	0--	-	4.15	2.08
2006	S-WB	AAA	9	0	0	6	9.0	40	5	2	2	1	2	0	1	6	0	6	0	0	0	0	-	0	4--	-	3.02	2.00
2006	Clrwtr	A+	2	0	0	1	2.0	6	0	0	0	0	0	0	0	0	0	6	0	0	0	0	-	0	0--	-	0.00	0.00
2007	Ottawa	AAA	16	0	0	5	17.1	71	13	5	5	2	1	1	0	7	0	16	0	0	2	1	.667	0	1--	-	2.85	2.60
2006	2 Tms		26	0	0	9	20.2	77	7	2	2	0	0	0	1	12	1	21	0	0	0	1	.000	0	0-0	6	1.13	0.87
2007	Phi	NL	9	0	0	0	4.0	27	4	5	5	0	0	0	0	11	1	1	1	0	0	0	-	0	0-0	3	12.02	11.25
06	NYY	AL	12	0	0	6	12.0	46	4	0	0	0	0	0	0	8	1	9	0	0	0	0	-	0	0-0	0	1.23	0.00
06	Phi	NL	14	0	0	3	8.2	31	3	2	2	0	0	0	1	4	0	12	0	0	0	1	.000	0	0-0	6	0.98	2.08
2 ML YEARS			35	0	0	9	24.2	104	11	7	7	0	0	0	1	23	2	22	1	0	0	1	.000	0	0-0	9	2.31	2.55

Seth Smith

Bats: L Throws: L Pos: PH-7; RF-1   Ht: 6'3" Wt: 215 Born: 9/30/1982 Age: 25

								BATTING													BASERUNNING				AVERAGES		
Year	Team	Lg	G	AB	H	2B	3B	HR	(Hm	Rd)	TB	R	RBI	RC	TBB	IBB	SO	HBP	SH	SF	SB	CS	SB%	GDP	Avg	OBP	Slg
2004	Casper	R+	56	233	86	21	3	9	(-	-)	140	46	61	58	25	0	47	0	0	2	9	1	.90	7	.369	.427	.601
2004	TriCity	A-	9	27	7	1	1	2	(-	-)	16	6	5	4	1	1	3	0	0	1	0	0	-	1	.259	.276	.593
2005	Mdest	A+	129	533	160	45	6	9	(-	-)	244	87	72	87	44	1	115	1	4	3	5	3	.63	16	.300	.353	.458
2006	Tulsa	AA	130	524	154	46	4	15	(-	-)	253	79	71	92	51	1	74	4	3	0	4	4	.50	7	.294	.361	.483
2007	ColSpr	AAA	129	451	143	32	6	17	(-	-)	238	68	82	90	39	0	73	10	1	4	7	3	.70	10	.317	.381	.528
2007	Col	NL	7	8	5	0	1	0	(0	0)	7	4	0	3	0	0	1	0	0	0	0	0	-	0	.625	.625	.875

John Smoltz

Pitches: R **Bats:** R **Pos:** SP-32   **Ht:** 6'3" **Wt:** 220 **Born:** 5/15/1967 **Age:** 41

			HOW MUCH HE PITCHED						WHAT HE GAVE UP										THE RESULTS							
Year	Team	Lg	G	GS	CG	GF	IP	BFP	H	R	ER	HR	SH	SF	HB	TBB	IBB	SO	WP	Bk	W	L	Pct	ShO	Sv-Op Hld	ERC	ERA
1988	Atl	NL	12	12	0	0	64.0	297	74	40	39	10	2	0	2	33	4	37	2	1	2	7	.222	0	0-0 0	5.86	5.48
1989	Atl	NL	29	29	5	0	208.0	847	160	79	68	15	10	7	2	72	2	168	8	3	12	11	.522	0	0-0 0	2.50	2.94
1990	Atl	NL	34	34	6	0	231.1	966	206	109	99	20	9	8	1	90	3	170	14	3	14	11	.560	2	0-0 0	3.37	3.85
1991	Atl	NL	36	36	5	0	229.2	947	206	101	97	16	9	9	3	77	1	148	20	2	14	13	.519	0	0-0 0	3.15	3.80
1992	Atl	NL	35	35	9	0	246.2	1021	206	90	78	17	7	8	5	80	5	215	17	1	15	12	.556	3	0-0 0	2.73	2.85
1993	Atl	NL	35	35	3	0	243.2	1028	208	104	98	23	13	4	6	100	12	208	13	1	15	11	.577	1	0-0 0	3.29	3.62
1994	Atl	NL	21	21	1	0	134.2	568	120	69	62	15	7	6	4	48	4	113	7	0	6	10	.375	0	0-0 0	3.44	4.14
1995	Atl	NL	29	29	2	0	192.2	808	166	76	68	15	13	5	4	72	8	193	13	0	12	7	.632	1	0-0 0	3.08	3.18
1996	Atl	NL	35	35	6	0	253.2	995	199	93	83	19	12	4	2	55	3	276	10	1	24	8	.750	2	0-0 0	2.17	2.94
1997	Atl	NL	35	35	7	0	256.0	1043	234	97	86	21	10	3	1	63	9	241	10	1	15	12	.556	2	0-0 0	2.89	3.02
1998	Atl	NL	26	26	2	0	167.2	681	145	58	54	10	4	2	4	44	2	173	3	1	17	3	.850	2	0-0 0	2.67	2.90
1999	Atl	NL	29	29	1	0	186.1	746	168	70	66	14	10	5	4	40	2	156	2	0	11	8	.579	1	0-0 0	2.81	3.19
2001	Atl	NL	36	5	0	20	59.0	238	53	24	22	7	1	2	2	10	2	57	0	0	3	3	.500	0	10-11 5	2.85	3.36
2002	Atl	NL	75	0	0	68	80.1	314	59	30	29	4	2	1	0	24	1	85	1	1	3	2	.600	0	55-59 0	2.06	3.25
2003	Atl	NL	62	0	0	55	64.1	244	48	9	8	2	0	1	0	8	1	73	2	0	0	2	.000	0	45-49 0	1.50	1.12
2004	Atl	NL	73	0	0	61	81.2	323	75	25	25	8	4	0	0	13	2	85	6	0	0	1	.000	0	44-49 0	2.73	2.76
2005	Atl	NL	33	33	3	0	229.2	931	210	83	78	18	10	3	1	53	7	169	2	1	14	7	.667	1	0-0 0	2.83	3.06
2006	Atl	NL	35	35	3	0	232.0	960	221	93	90	23	4	10	3	55	4	211	5	0	16	9	.640	1	0-0 0	3.32	3.49
2007	Atl	NL	32	32	0	0	205.2	853	196	78	71	18	10	5	4	47	9	197	8	0	14	8	.636	0	0-0 0	3.07	3.11
19 ML YEARS			702	461	53	204	3367.0	13810	2954	1328	1221	275	137	83	54	984	81	2975	143	16	207	145	.588	16	154-168 5	2.92	3.26

Ian Snell

Pitches: R **Bats:** R **Pos:** SP-32   **Ht:** 5'11" **Wt:** 190 **Born:** 10/30/1981 **Age:** 26

			HOW MUCH HE PITCHED						WHAT HE GAVE UP										THE RESULTS							
Year	Team	Lg	G	GS	CG	GF	IP	BFP	H	R	ER	HR	SH	SF	HB	TBB	IBB	SO	WP	Bk	W	L	Pct	ShO	Sv-Op Hld	ERC	ERA
2004	Pit	NL	3	1	0	1	12.0	56	14	10	10	2	0	0	0	9	0	9	0	0	1	0	.000	0	0-0 0	7.31	7.50
2005	Pit	NL	15	5	0	2	42.0	189	43	25	24	5	2	1	1	24	3	34	4	0	1	2	.333	0	0-0 1	5.03	5.14
2006	Pit	NL	32	32	0	0	186.0	813	198	104	98	29	16	6	2	74	4	169	8	0	14	11	.560	0	0-0 0	4.86	4.74
2007	Pit	NL	32	32	1	0	208.0	882	209	94	87	22	6	7	8	68	4	177	12	0	9	12	.429	0	0-0 0	4.02	3.76
4 ML YEARS			82	70	1	3	448.0	1940	464	233	219	58	24	14	11	175	11	389	24	0	24	26	.480	0	0-0 1	4.54	4.40

Chris Snelling

Bats: L **Throws:** L **Pos:** LF-21; CF-5; PH-5   **Ht:** 5'10" **Wt:** 205 **Born:** 12/3/1981 **Age:** 26

			BATTING																	BASERUNNING				AVERAGES		
Year	Team	Lg	G	AB	H	2B	3B	HR	(Hm	Rd)	TB	R	RBI	RC	TBB	IBB	SO	HBP	SH	SF	SB	CS	SB%	GDP	Avg	OBP	Slg
2007	Scrmto*	AAA	6	19	3	0	0	0	(-	-)	3	1	2	1	3	0	6	1	0	0	0	0	-	0	.158	.304	.158
2002	Sea	AL	8	27	4	0	0	1	(0	1)	7	2	3	3	2	0	4	0	0	0	0	0	-	2	.148	.207	.259
2005	Sea	AL	15	29	8	2	0	1	(1	0)	13	4	1	3	5	0	2	0	1	0	0	2	.00	0	.276	.382	.448
2006	Sea	AL	36	96	24	6	1	3	(2	1)	41	14	8	11	13	0	38	4	5	1	2	1	.67	0	.250	.360	.427
2007	2 Tms		30	69	17	1	1	1	(0	1)	23	10	7	10	14	1	15	3	0	0	0	1	.00	1	.246	.395	.333
07	Was	NL	24	49	10	1	1	1	(0	1)	16	6	7	6	9	1	11	3	0	0	0	1	.00	1	.204	.361	.327
07	Oak	AL	6	20	7	0	0	0	(0	0)	7	4	0	4	5	0	4	0	0	0	0	0	-	0	.350	.480	.350
4 ML YEARS			89	221	53	9	2	6	(3	3)	84	30	19	27	34	1	59	7	6	1	2	4	.33	3	.240	.357	.380

Chris Snyder

Bats: R **Throws:** R **Pos:** C-106; PH-4; 1B-2; LF-1   **Ht:** 6'3" **Wt:** 230 **Born:** 2/12/1981 **Age:** 27

			BATTING																	BASERUNNING				AVERAGES		
Year	Team	Lg	G	AB	H	2B	3B	HR	(Hm	Rd)	TB	R	RBI	RC	TBB	IBB	SO	HBP	SH	SF	SB	CS	SB%	GDP	Avg	OBP	Slg
2004	Ari	NL	29	96	23	6	0	5	(1	4)	44	10	15	11	13	1	25	0	0	1	0	0	-	0	.240	.327	.458
2005	Ari	NL	115	326	66	14	0	6	(2	4)	98	24	28	25	40	5	87	4	3	0	0	1	.00	6	.202	.297	.301
2006	Ari	NL	61	184	51	9	0	6	(4	2)	78	19	32	27	22	4	39	1	1	5	0	0	-	5	.277	.349	.424
2007	Ari	NL	110	326	82	20	0	13	(4	9)	141	37	47	48	40	3	67	7	3	4	0	1	.00	9	.252	.342	.433
4 ML YEARS			315	932	222	49	0	30	(11	19)	361	90	122	111	115	13	218	12	7	10	0	2	.00	20	.238	.326	.387

Kyle Snyder

Pitches: R **Bats:** B **Pos:** RP-46   **Ht:** 6'8" **Wt:** 215 **Born:** 9/9/1977 **Age:** 30

			HOW MUCH HE PITCHED						WHAT HE GAVE UP										THE RESULTS							
Year	Team	Lg	G	GS	CG	GF	IP	BFP	H	R	ER	HR	SH	SF	HB	TBB	IBB	SO	WP	Bk	W	L	Pct	ShO	Sv-Op Hld	ERC	ERA
2003	KC	AL	15	15	0	0	85.1	364	94	52	49	11	0	9	2	21	3	39	4	0	1	6	.143	0	0-0 0	4.29	5.17
2005	KC	AL	13	3	0	4	36.0	169	55	29	27	3	0	2	1	10	1	19	1	0	1	3	.250	0	0-0 0	6.70	6.75
2006	2 Tms		17	11	0	3	60.1	287	87	51	44	12	0	2	2	20	3	57	3	0	4	5	.444	0	0-0 1	7.21	6.56
2007	Bos	AL	46	0	0	17	54.1	242	45	29	23	7	1	1	6	32	2	41	4	0	2	3	.400	0	0-0 1	4.41	3.81
06	KC	AL	1	1	0	0	2.0	19	10	9	5	1	0	0	0	1	0	2	0	0	0	0	-	0	0-0 0	36.36	22.50
06	Bos	AL	16	10	0	3	58.1	268	77	42	39	11	0	2	2	19	3	55	3	0	4	5	.444	0	0-0 1	6.38	6.02
4 ML YEARS			91	29	0	24	236.0	1062	281	161	143	33	1	14	11	83	9	156	12	0	8	17	.320	0	0-0 2	5.39	5.45

246

Andy Sonnanstine

Pitches: R Bats: L Pos: SP-22   Ht: 6'3" Wt: 185 Born: 3/18/1983 Age: 25

		HOW MUCH HE PITCHED						WHAT HE GAVE UP												THE RESULTS							
Year	Team	Lg	G	GS	CG	GF	IP	BFP	H	R	ER	HR	SH	SF	TIB	TBB	IBB	SO	WP	Bk	W	L	Pct	ShO	Sv-Op	Hld	ERC	FRA
2004	HudVal	A-	9	2	0	1	27.0	105	18	4	3	0	1	0	0	3	0	24	0	0	3	1	.750	0	1- -	-	1.09	1.00
2004	CtnSC	A	8	5	0	1	30.2	116	18	5	2	0	1	0	0	7	0	42	0	0	2	0	1.000	0	0- -	-	1.14	0.59
2005	SWMch	A	18	18	1	0	116.2	461	103	42	33	10	2	2	2	11	0	103	5	0	10	4	.714	0	0- -	-	2.29	2.55
2005	Visalia	A+	10	10	0	0	64.0	266	71	29	27	5	0	2	1	7	0	75	2	0	4	1	.800	0	0- -	-	3.45	3.80
2006	Mont	AA	28	28	4	0	185.2	721	151	63	55	15	3	4	5	34	1	152	3	0	15	8	.652	4	0- -	-	2.33	2.67
2007	Drham	AAA	11	11	0	0	71.0	283	60	24	21	8	3	1	2	13	0	66	2	0	4	4	.600	0	0- -	-	2.63	2.66
2007	TB	AL	22	22	0	0	130.2	554	151	87	85	18	3	5	5	26	2	97	2	0	6	10	.375	0	0-0	0	4.62	5.85

Joakim Soria

Pitches: R Bats: R Pos: RP 62   Ht: 6'3" Wt: 185 Born: 5/18/1984 Age: 24

		HOW MUCH HE PITCHED						WHAT HE GAVE UP												THE RESULTS							
Year	Team	Lg	G	GS	CG	GF	IP	BFP	H	R	ER	HR	SH	SF	HB	TBB	IBB	SO	WP	Bk	W	L	Pct	ShO	Sv-Op	Hld	ERC	ERA
2002	Ddgrs	R	4	0	0	2	5.0	21	6	2	2	0	0	0	0	0	0	6	0	0	0	0	-	0	0- -	-	2.89	3.60
2006	FtWyn	A	7	0	0	2	11.2	40	5	3	3	1	0	0	0	2	0	11	0	0	1	0	1.000	0	0- -	-	0.93	2.31
2007	KC	AL	62	0	0	38	69.0	270	46	20	19	3	1	3	1	19	3	75	2	0	2	3	.400	0	17-21	9	1.63	2.48

Alfonso Soriano

Bats: R Throws: R Pos: LF-122; CF-12; 2B-1; PH-1   Ht: 6'1" Wt: 180 Born: 1/7/1976 Age: 32

								BATTING											BASERUNNING				AVERAGES		
Year	Team	Lg	G	AB	H	2B	3B	HR	(Hm Rd)	TB	R	RBI	RC	TBB	IBB	SO	HBP	SH	SF	SB	CS	SB%	GDP	Avg	OBP	Slg
1999	NYY	AL	9	8	1	0	0	1	(1 0)	4	2	1	0	0	0	3	0	0	0	0	1	.00	0	.125	.125	.500
2000	NYY	AL	22	50	9	3	0	2	(0 2)	18	5	3	4	1	0	15	0	2	0	2	1	1.00	0	.180	.196	.360
2001	NYY	AL	158	574	154	34	3	18	(8 10)	248	77	73	77	29	0	125	3	3	5	43	14	.75	7	.268	.304	.432
2002	NYY	AL	156	696	209	51	2	39	(17 22)	381	128	102	121	23	1	157	14	1	7	41	13	.76	8	.300	.332	.547
2003	NYY	AL	156	682	198	36	5	38	(15 23)	358	114	91	110	38	7	130	12	0	2	35	8	.81	8	.290	.338	.525
2004	Tex	AL	145	608	170	32	4	28	(12 16)	294	77	91	90	33	4	121	10	0	7	18	5	.78	7	.280	.324	.484
2005	Tex	AL	156	637	171	43	2	36	(25 11)	326	102	104	93	33	3	125	7	0	5	30	2	.94	6	.268	.309	.512
2006	Was	NL	159	647	179	41	2	46	(24 22)	362	119	95	114	67	16	160	9	2	3	41	17	.71	3	.277	.351	.560
2007	ChC	NL	135	579	173	42	5	33	(13 20)	324	97	70	91	31	4	130	4	0	3	19	6	.76	9	.299	.337	.560
9 ML YEARS			1096	4481	1264	282	23	241	(115 126)	2315	721	630	700	255	35	966	59	8	32	229	66	.78	48	.282	.327	.517

Rafael Soriano

Pitches: R Bats: R Pos: RP-71   Ht: 6'1" Wt: 220 Born: 12/19/1979 Age: 28

		HOW MUCH HE PITCHED						WHAT HE GAVE UP												THE RESULTS							
Year	Team	Lg	G	GS	CG	GF	IP	BFP	H	R	ER	HR	SH	SF	HB	TBB	IBB	SO	WP	Bk	W	L	Pct	ShO	Sv-Op	Hld	ERC	ERA
2002	Sea	AL	10	8	0	1	47.1	202	45	25	24	8	1	0	0	16	1	32	2	0	0	3	.000	0	1-1	0	3.03	4.66
2003	Sea	AL	40	0	0	12	53.0	201	30	9	9	2	0	1	3	12	1	68	0	0	3	0	1.000	0	1-2	5	1.32	1.53
2004	Sea	AL	6	0	0	0	3.1	23	9	6	5	0	0	0	0	3	0	3	0	0	0	3	.000	0	0-1	0	15.97	13.50
2005	Sea	AL	7	0	0	4	7.1	30	6	2	2	0	0	1	1	1	0	9	0	0	0	0	-	0	0-0	1	2.00	2.45
2006	Sea	AL	53	0	0	14	60.0	241	44	15	15	6	1	1	2	21	0	65	2	0	1	2	.333	0	2-6	18	2.64	2.25
2007	Atl	NL	71	0	0	28	72.0	276	47	26	24	12	0	0	2	15	2	70	0	0	3	3	.500	0	9-12	19	2.05	3.00
6 ML YEARS			187	8	0	59	243.0	973	181	83	79	28	2	3	8	68	4	247	4	0	7	11	.389	0	13-22	43	2.48	2.93

Jorge Sosa

Pitches: R Bats: R Pos: RP-28; SP-14   Ht: 6'2" Wt: 210 Born: 4/28/1977 Age: 31

		HOW MUCH HE PITCHED						WHAT HE GAVE UP												THE RESULTS							
Year	Team	Lg	G	GS	CG	GF	IP	BFP	H	R	ER	HR	SH	SF	HB	TBB	IBB	SO	WP	Bk	W	L	Pct	ShO	Sv-Op	Hld	ERC	ERA
2007	NewOr*	AAA	5	5	0	0	32.0	124	29	6	4	1	2	2	0	4	0	29	0	0	4	0	1.000	0	0- -	-	2.21	1.13
2002	TB	AL	31	14	0	10	99.1	434	88	63	61	16	0	5	2	54	0	48	5	0	2	7	.222	0	0-0	1	4.51	5.53
2003	TB	AL	29	19	1	4	128.2	566	137	71	66	14	4	6	4	60	4	72	8	1	5	12	.294	1	0-0	0	4.93	4.62
2004	TB	AL	43	8	0	6	99.1	447	100	67	61	17	2	4	1	54	3	94	2	0	4	7	.364	0	1-1	6	5.17	5.53
2005	Atl	NL	44	20	0	5	134.0	577	122	42	38	12	5	2	0	64	8	85	3	0	13	3	.813	0	0-0	4	3.70	2.55
2006	2 Tms	NL	45	13	0	12	118.0	524	138	79	71	30	7	4	1	40	6	75	2	0	3	11	.214	0	4-7	0	5.88	5.42
2007	NYM	NL	42	14	0	2	112.2	481	109	58	56	10	10	3	0	41	2	69	0	0	9	8	.529	0	0-2	9	3.63	4.47
06	Atl	NL	26	13	0	8	87.1	394	105	61	53	20	5	4	1	32	5	58	2	0	3	10	.231	0	3-6	0	6.00	5.46
06	StL	NL	19	0	0	4	30.2	130	33	18	18	10	2	0	0	8	1	17	0	0	0	1	.000	0	1-1	0	5.48	5.28
6 ML YEARS			234	88	1	39	692.0	3029	694	380	353	99	28	23	8	313	23	443	20	1	36	48	.429	1	5-10	20	4.60	4.59

Sammy Sosa

Bats: R Throws: R Pos: DH-88; RF-16; PH-11   Ht: 6'0" Wt: 225 Born: 11/12/1968 Age: 39

								BATTING											BASERUNNING				AVERAGES		
Year	Team	Lg	G	AB	H	2B	3B	HR	(Hm Rd)	TB	R	RBI	RC	TBB	IBB	SO	HBP	SH	SF	SB	CS	SB%	GDP	Avg	OBP	Slg
1989	2 Tms	AL	58	183	47	8	0	4	(1 3)	67	27	13	18	11	2	47	2	5	2	7	5	.58	6	.257	.303	.366
1990	CWS	AL	153	532	124	26	10	15	(10 5)	215	72	70	59	33	4	150	6	2	6	32	16	.67	10	.233	.282	.404
1991	CWS	AL	116	316	64	10	1	10	(3 7)	106	39	33	23	14	2	98	2	5	1	13	6	.68	5	.203	.240	.335
1992	ChC	NL	67	262	68	7	2	8	(4 4)	103	41	25	33	19	1	63	4	4	2	15	7	.68	4	.260	.317	.393
1993	ChC	NL	159	598	156	25	5	33	(23 10)	290	92	93	88	38	6	135	4	0	1	36	11	.77	14	.261	.309	.485
1994	ChC	NL	105	426	128	17	6	25	(11 14)	232	59	70	75	25	1	92	2	1	4	22	13	.63	7	.300	.339	.545
1995	ChC	NL	144	564	151	17	3	36	(19 17)	282	89	119	98	58	11	134	5	0	8	34	7	.83	8	.268	.340	.500
1996	ChC	NL	124	498	136	21	2	40	(26 14)	281	84	100	87	34	6	134	5	0	4	18	5	.78	14	.273	.323	.564
1997	ChC	NL	162	642	161	31	4	36	(25 11)	308	90	119	88	45	9	174	2	0	5	22	12	.65	16	.251	.300	.480
1998	ChC	NL	159	643	198	20	0	66	(35 31)	416	134	158	142	73	14	171	1	0	5	18	9	.67	20	.308	.377	.647

Year	Team	Lg	G	AB	H	2B	3B	HR	(Hm	Rd)	TB	R	RBI	RC	TBB	IBB	SO	HBP	SH	SF	SB	CS	SB%	GDP	Avg	OBP	Slg
																									BATTING — BASERUNNING — AVERAGES		
1999	ChC	NL	**162**	625	180	24	2	63	(33	**30)**	397	114	141	134	78	8	**171**	3	0	6	7	8	.47	17	.288	.367	.635
2000	ChC	NL	156	604	193	38	1	50	(22	28)	393	106	120	111	91	10	100	2	0	8	1	4	.04	12	.320	.406	.634
2001	ChC	NL	160	577	189	34	5	64	(34	30)	425	146	160	170	116	37	153	6	0	12	0	2	.00	6	.328	.437	.737
2002	ChC	NL	150	556	160	19	2	49	(24	25)	330	122	108	121	103	15	144	3	0	4	2	0	1.00	14	.288	.399	.594
2003	ChC	NL	137	517	144	22	0	40	(19	21)	286	99	103	94	62	9	143	5	0	5	0	1	.00	14	.279	.358	.553
2004	ChC	NL	126	478	121	21	0	35	(18	17)	247	69	80	68	56	4	133	2	0	3	0	0	-	9	.253	.332	.517
2005	Bal	AL	102	380	84	15	1	14	(4	10)	143	39	45	36	39	3	84	2	0	3	1	1	.50	15	.221	.295	.376
2007	Tex	AL	114	412	104	24	1	21	(10	11)	193	53	92	69	34	3	112	3	0	5	0	0	-	11	.252	.311	.468
89	Tex	AL	25	84	20	3	0	1	(0	1)	26	8	3	4	0	0	20	0	4	0	0	2	.00	3	.238	.238	.310
89	CWS	AL	33	99	27	5	0	3	(1	2)	41	19	10	14	11	2	27	2	1	2	7	3	.70	3	.273	.351	.414
18 ML YEARS			2354	8813	2408	379	45	609	(321	288)	4704	1475	1667	1547	929	154	2306	59	17	78	234	107	.69	202	.273	.344	.534

Geovany Soto

Bats: R **Throws:** R **Pos:** C-16; PH-2   **Ht:** 6'1" **Wt:** 230 **Born:** 1/20/1983 **Age:** 25

Year	Team	Lg	G	AB	H	2B	3B	HR	(Hm	Rd)	TB	R	RBI	RC	TBB	IBB	SO	HBP	SH	SF	SB	CS	SB%	GDP	Avg	OBP	Slg
2007	Iowa*	AAA	110	385	136	31	3	26	(-	-)	251	75	109	101	53	0	94	1	1	9	0	0	-	12	.353	.424	.652
2005	ChC	NL	1	1	0	0	0	0	(0	0)	0	0	0	0	0	0	0	0	0	0	0	0	-	0	.000	.000	.000
2006	ChC	NL	11	25	5	1	0	0	(0	0)	6	1	2	0	0	0	5	1	0	0	0	0	-	0	.200	.231	.240
2007	ChC	NL	18	54	21	6	0	3	(2	1)	36	12	8	13	5	0	14	0	0	1	0	0	-	1	.389	.433	.667
3 ML YEARS			30	80	26	7	0	3	(2	1)	42	13	10	13	5	0	19	1	0	1	0	0	-	1	.325	.368	.525

Jeremy Sowers

Pitches: L **Bats:** L **Pos:** SP-13   **Ht:** 6'1" **Wt:** 180 **Born:** 5/17/1983 **Age:** 25

Year	Team	Lg	G	GS	CG	GF	IP	BFP	H	R	ER	HR	SH	SF	HB	TBB	IBB	SO	WP	Bk	W	L	Pct	ShO	Sv-Op	Hld	ERC	ERA
2005	Knstn	A+	13	13	0	0	71.1	292	60	25	22	5	0	1	0	19	0	75	4	0	8	3	.727	0	0- -	-	2.51	2.78
2005	Akron	AA	13	13	0	0	82.1	323	74	25	19	8	2	2	3	9	1	70	2	0	5	1	.833	0	0- -	-	2.59	2.08
2005	Buffalo	AAA	1	1	0	0	5.2	25	7	1	1	0	0	0	0	1	0	4	1	0	1	0	1.000	0	0- -	-	3.70	1.59
2006	Buffalo	AAA	15	15	2	0	97.1	383	78	20	15	1	4	1	1	29	1	54	2	0	9	1	.900	2	0- -	-	2.20	1.39
2007	Buffalo	AAA	15	15	1	0	96.2	430	112	56	44	6	8	5	4	24	0	61	1	1	4	5	.444	0	0- -	-	4.15	4.10
2006	Cle	AL	14	14	2	0	88.1	360	85	36	35	10	1	0	2	20	1	35	1	0	7	4	.636	2	0-0	0	3.41	3.57
2007	Cle	AL	13	13	0	0	67.1	303	84	49	48	10	0	5	4	21	2	24	3	0	1	6	.143	0	0-0	0	5.75	6.42
2 ML YEARS			27	27	2	0	155.2	663	169	85	83	20	1	5	6	41	3	59	4	0	8	10	.444	2	0-0	0	4.38	4.80

Justin Speier

Pitches: R **Bats:** R **Pos:** RP-51   **Ht:** 6'4" **Wt:** 205 **Born:** 11/6/1973 **Age:** 34

Year	Team	Lg	G	GS	CG	GF	IP	BFP	H	R	ER	HR	SH	SF	HB	TBB	IBB	SO	WP	Bk	W	L	Pct	ShO	Sv-Op	Hld	ERC	ERA
2007	Angels*	R	2	2	0	0	3.0	9	1	0	0	0	0	0	0	0	0	3	0	0	0	0	-	0	0- -	-	0.28	0.00
2007	RCuca*	A+	8	3	0	0	9.0	40	10	3	3	1	1	0	0	5	0	7	1	1	1	0	1.000	0	0- -	-	5.59	3.00
1998	2 Tms	NL	19	0	0	10	20.2	99	27	20	20	7	2	1	0	13	1	17	3	0	0	3	.000	0	0-1	1	8.94	8.71
1999	Atl	NL	19	0	0	8	28.2	127	28	18	18	8	0	1	0	13	1	22	0	0	0	0	-	0	0-0	0	5.27	5.65
2000	Cle	AL	47	0	0	12	68.1	290	57	27	25	9	2	4	4	28	3	69	7	1	5	2	.714	0	0-1	6	3.56	3.29
2001	2 Tms		54	0	0	10	76.2	324	71	40	39	13	2	7	4	20	3	62	6	1	6	3	.667	0	0-1	4	3.93	4.58
2002	Col	NL	63	0	0	7	62.1	259	51	31	30	9	0	1	3	19	4	47	1	2	5	1	.833	0	1-4	18	3.06	4.33
2003	Col	NL	72	0	0	31	73.1	319	73	37	33	11	1	4	7	23	6	66	0	0	3	1	.750	0	9-12	12	4.27	4.05
2004	Tor	AL	62	0	0	32	69.0	294	61	32	30	8	6	3	5	25	6	52	4	0	3	8	.273	0	7-11	7	3.52	3.91
2005	Tor	AL	65	0	0	36	66.2	264	48	20	19	10	4	0	3	15	2	56	1	1	3	2	.600	0	0-4	11	2.38	2.57
2006	Tor	AL	58	0	0	8	51.1	222	47	18	17	5	0	0	1	21	3	55	4	0	2	0	1.000	0	0-3	25	3.55	2.98
2007	LAA	AL	51	0	0	9	50.0	198	36	17	16	6	2	2	4	12	1	47	2	0	2	3	.400	0	0-1	24	2.43	2.88
98	ChC	NL	1	0	0	0	1.1	7	2	2	2	0	0	0	0	1	0	2	1	0	0	0	-	0	0-0	0	7.52	13.50
98	Fla	NL	18	0	0	10	19.1	92	25	18	18	7	2	1	0	12	1	15	2	0	0	3	.000	0	0-1	1	9.02	8.38
01	Cle	AL	12	0	0	2	20.2	96	24	16	16	5	0	3	3	8	0	15	2	0	2	0	1.000	0	0-0	0	6.61	6.97
01	Col	NL	42	0	0	8	56.0	228	47	24	23	8	2	4	1	12	3	47	4	1	4	3	.571	0	0-1	4	3.04	3.70
10 ML YEARS			510	0	0	163	567.0	2396	499	260	247	86	19	23	35	189	30	493	28	5	29	23	.558	0	17-38	108	3.64	3.92

Ryan Speier

Pitches: R **Bats:** R **Pos:** RP-20   **Ht:** 6'7" **Wt:** 210 **Born:** 7/24/1979 **Age:** 28

Year	Team	Lg	G	GS	CG	GF	IP	BFP	H	R	ER	HR	SH	SF	HB	TBB	IBB	SO	WP	Bk	W	L	Pct	ShO	Sv-Op	Hld	ERC	ERA
2001	Casper	R+	17	0	0	8	25.2	106	19	12	9	2	1	0	2	9	4	24	2	0	1	2	.333	0	1- -	-	2.42	3.16
2002	Salem	A+	24	0	0	14	32.0	142	35	21	14	0	6	0	2	11	2	33	2	0	2	2	.500	0	4- -	-	3.74	3.94
2002	Ashvll	A	28	0	0	6	36.2	155	32	21	16	3	2	1	1	13	1	39	5	0	3	1	.750	0	1- -	-	3.11	3.93
2003	Visalia	A+	56	0	0	43	58.2	243	50	14	10	2	5	7	6	17	2	73	2	0	4	2	.667	0	18- -	-	2.78	1.53
2004	Tulsa	AA	62	0	0	59	62.1	246	33	14	14	3	0	0	3	26	1	71	4	1	3	1	.750	0	37- -	-	1.63	2.02
2005	ColSpr	AAA	45	0	0	22	52.1	245	70	30	29	2	4	0	8	18	0	45	6	0	2	2	.500	0	6- -	-	6.02	4.99
2007	ColSpr	AAA	50	0	0	47	49.1	217	47	26	24	3	2	2	4	23	2	40	5	1	1	4	.200	0	33- -	-	4.03	4.38
2005	Col	NL	22	0	0	10	24.2	111	26	12	10	0	2	1	1	13	0	10	2	0	2	1	.667	0	0-1	2	4.29	3.65
2007	Col	NL	20	0	0	5	18.0	77	20	8	8	1	1	0	1	8	1	13	2	1	3	1	.750	0	0-1	2	4.95	4.00
2 ML YEARS			42	0	0	15	42.2	188	46	20	18	1	3	1	2	21	1	23	4	1	5	2	.714	0	0-2	4	4.56	3.80

248

Levale Speigner

Pitches: R **Bats:** R **Pos:** RP-13; SP-6   **Ht:** 5'11" **Wt:** 175 **Born:** 9/24/1980 **Age:** 27

			HOW MUCH HE PITCHED						WHAT HE GAVE UP												THE RESULTS							
Year	Team	Lg	G	GS	CG	GF	IP	BFP	H	R	ER	HR	SH	SF	HB	TBB	IBB	SO	WP	Bk	W	L	Pct	ShO	Sv-Op	Hld	ERC	ERA
2003	Elizab	R+	22	0	0	19	29.2	122	31	13	13	1	0	0	1	4	0	35	2	0	5	2	.714	0	4--	-	3.01	3.94
2004	QuadC	A	22	0	0	15	31.2	144	27	14	10	1	1	1	2	15	4	29	3	0	2	2	.500	0	9--	-	2.90	2.84
2004	FtMyrs	A+	22	1	0	7	73.1	201	46	15	9	3	1	0	2	14	1	49	3	0	4	3	.571	0	2--	-	1.98	1.10
2005	NwBrit	AA	23	23	2	0	143.2	605	149	75	66	14	5	2	12	28	1	94	1	1	6	10	.375	1	0--	-	3.79	4.13
2005	Roch	AAA	2	1	0	0	7.1	38	14	7	6	0	1	2	0	1	0	5	0	0	0	1	.000	0	0--	-	7.29	7.36
2006	NwBrit	AA	40	0	0	31	58.0	252	61	27	21	5	4	2	3	14	1	37	0	0	3	2	.600	0	13--	-	3.73	3.26
2006	Roch	AAA	9	0	0	4	12.2	60	16	7	7	1	1	0	0	5	1	8	0	0	1	1	.500	0	1--	-	5.05	4.97
2007	Clmbs	AAA	17	6	0	1	49.0	230	63	30	27	1	2	4	1	20	1	33	1	0	3	4	.429	0	0--	-	5.08	4.96
2007	Was	NL	19	6	0	3	40.0	198	58	39	39	4	2	3	0	23	1	19	1	0	2	3	.400	0	0-0	0	7.38	8.78

Scott Spiezio

Bats: B **Throws:** R **Pos:** 3B-27; PH-27; RF-15; 1B-9; DH-6; 2B-5; LF-3   **Ht:** 6'2" **Wt:** 215 **Born:** 9/21/1972 **Age:** 35

					BATTING																BASERUNNING				AVERAGES		
Year	Team	Lg	G	AB	H	2B	3B	HR	(Hm	Rd)	TB	R	RBI	RC	TBB	IBB	SO	HBP	SH	SF	SB	CS	SB%	GDP	Avg	OBP	Slg
1996	Oak	AL	9	29	9	2	0	2	(1	1)	17	6	8	6	4	1	4	0	2	0	0	1	.00	0	.310	.394	.586
1997	Oak	AL	147	538	131	28	4	14	(6	8)	209	58	65	61	44	2	75	1	3	4	9	3	.75	13	.243	.300	.388
1998	Oak	AL	114	406	105	19	1	9	(6	3)	153	54	50	50	44	3	56	2	7	2	1	3	.25	10	.259	.333	.377
1999	Oak	AL	89	247	60	24	0	8	(3	5)	108	31	33	35	29	3	36	2	1	3	0	0	-	5	.243	.324	.437
2000	LAA	AL	123	297	72	11	2	17	(10	7)	138	47	49	47	40	2	56	3	1	4	1	2	.33	5	.242	.334	.465
2001	LAA	AL	139	457	124	29	4	13	(8	5)	200	57	54	65	34	4	65	5	3	4	5	2	.71	6	.271	.326	.438
2002	LAA	AL	153	491	140	34	2	12	(7	5)	214	80	82	86	67	7	52	4	3	6	6	7	.46	12	.285	.371	.436
2003	LAA	AL	158	521	138	36	7	16	(7	9)	236	69	83	72	46	8	66	5	2	7	6	3	.67	12	.265	.326	.453
2004	Sea	AL	112	367	79	12	3	10	(5	5)	127	38	41	31	36	2	60	4	2	6	4	1	.80	7	.215	.288	.346
2005	Sea	AL	29	47	3	1	0	1	(0	1)	7	2	1	0	4	0	18	0	0	0	0	0	-	1	.064	.137	.149
2006	StL	NL	119	276	75	15	4	13	(4	9)	137	44	52	52	37	1	66	5	1	2	1	0	1.00	5	.272	.366	.496
2007	StL	NL	81	223	60	14	0	4	(2	2)	86	31	31	32	27	2	40	4	0	3	0	1	.00	5	.269	.354	.386
12 ML YEARS			1273	3899	996	225	27	119	(59	60)	1632	517	549	537	412	35	594	35	25	41	33	23	.59	77	.255	.329	.419

Ryan Spilborghs

Bats: R **Throws:** R **Pos:** CF-46; PH-34; RF-20; LF-15; DH-2   **Ht:** 6'1" **Wt:** 190 **Born:** 9/5/1979 **Age:** 28

					BATTING																BASERUNNING				AVERAGES		
Year	Team	Lg	G	AB	H	2B	3B	HR	(Hm	Rd)	TB	R	RBI	RC	TBB	IBB	SO	HBP	SH	SF	SB	CS	SB%	GDP	Avg	OBP	Slg
2007	ColSpr*	AAA	34	124	39	7	1	5	(-	-)	63	25	17	25	18	0	19	1	1	1	4	3	.57	4	.315	.403	.508
2005	Col	NL	1	4	2	0	0	0	(0	0)	2	0	1	1	0	0	1	0	0	0	0	0	-	0	.500	.500	.500
2006	Col	NL	67	167	48	6	3	4	(3	1)	72	26	21	22	14	0	30	0	2	3	5	2	.71	7	.287	.337	.431
2007	Col	NL	97	264	79	14	1	11	(5	6)	128	40	51	48	28	1	45	2	0	6	4	1	.80	5	.299	.363	.485
3 ML YEARS			165	435	129	20	4	15	(8	7)	202	66	73	71	42	1	76	2	2	9	9	3	.75	12	.297	.355	.464

Russ Springer

Pitches: R **Bats:** R **Pos:** RP-76   **Ht:** 6'4" **Wt:** 225 **Born:** 11/7/1968 **Age:** 39

				HOW MUCH HE PITCHED						WHAT HE GAVE UP											THE RESULTS							
Year	Team	Lg	G	GS	CG	GF	IP	BFP	H	R	ER	HR	SH	SF	HB	TBB	IBB	SO	WP	Bk	W	L	Pct	ShO	Sv-Op	Hld	ERC	ERA
1992	NYY	AL	14	0	0	5	16.0	75	18	11	11	0	0	0	1	10	0	12	0	0	0	0	-	0	0-0	2	5.15	6.19
1993	LAA	AL	14	9	1	3	60.0	278	73	48	48	11	1	1	3	32	1	31	6	0	1	6	.143	0	0-0	0	6.87	7.20
1994	LAA	AL	18	5	0	6	45.2	198	53	28	28	9	1	1	0	14	0	28	2	0	2	2	.500	0	2-3	1	5.38	5.52
1995	2 Tms		33	6	0	6	78.1	350	82	48	46	16	2	2	7	35	4	70	2	0	1	2	.333	0	1-2	0	5.63	5.29
1996	Phi	NL	51	7	0	12	96.2	437	106	60	50	12	5	3	1	38	6	94	5	0	3	10	.231	0	0-3	6	4.57	4.66
1997	Hou	NL	54	0	0	13	55.1	241	48	28	26	4	1	2	4	27	2	74	4	0	3	3	.500	0	3-7	9	3.69	4.23
1998	2 Tms	NL	48	0	0	14	52.2	232	51	26	24	4	2	1	1	30	4	56	5	0	5	4	.556	0	0-4	7	4.38	4.10
1999	Atl	NL	49	0	0	8	47.1	194	31	20	18	5	0	2	2	22	2	49	0	0	2	1	.667	0	1-1	8	2.63	3.42
2000	Ari	NL	52	0	0	10	62.0	282	63	36	35	11	2	3	2	34	6	59	3	0	2	4	.333	0	0-2	3	5.25	5.08
2001	Ari	NL	18	0	0	9	17.2	79	20	16	14	5	1	1	0	4	0	12	2	0	0	0	-	0	1-1	2	5.13	7.13
2003	StL	NL	17	0	0	4	17.1	77	19	16	16	8	0	0	1	6	0	11	1	0	1	1	.500	0	0-1	5	7.27	8.31
2004	Hou	NL	16	0	0	3	13.2	62	15	4	4	1	0	1	1	6	0	9	2	0	1	0	1.000	0	0-0	5	4.84	2.63
2005	Hou	NL	62	0	0	11	59.0	246	49	34	31	9	4	0	3	21	3	54	2	0	4	4	.500	0	0-3	10	3.45	4.73
2006	Hou	NL	72	0	0	17	59.2	240	46	23	23	10	2	0	4	16	1	46	2	0	1	1	.500	0	0-0	9	3.03	3.47
2007	StL	NL	76	0	0	18	66.0	257	41	18	16	3	3	6	3	19	1	66	1	0	8	1	.889	0	0-2	11	1.63	2.18
95	LAA	AL	19	6	0	3	51.2	238	60	37	35	11	1	0	5	25	1	38	1	0	1	2	.333	0	1-2	0	6.69	6.10
95	Phi	NL	14	0	0	3	26.2	112	22	11	11	5	1	2	2	10	3	32	1	0	0	0	-	0	0-0	0	3.73	3.71
98	Ari	NL	26	0	0	13	32.2	140	29	16	15	4	0	0	1	14	1	37	3	0	4	3	.571	0	0-3	1	3.77	4.13
98	Atl	NL	22	0	0	1	20.0	92	22	10	9	0	2	1	0	16	3	19	2	0	1	1	.500	0	0-1	6	5.36	4.05
15 ML YEARS			594	27	1	139	747.1	3248	715	416	390	108	21	23	33	314	30	671	37	0	33	40	.452	0	8-29	78	4.32	4.70

Chris Spurling

Pitches: R **Bats:** R **Pos:** RP-49   **Ht:** 6'6" **Wt:** 240 **Born:** 6/28/1977 **Age:** 31

				HOW MUCH HE PITCHED						WHAT HE GAVE UP											THE RESULTS							
Year	Team	Lg	G	GS	CG	GF	IP	BFP	H	R	ER	HR	SH	SF	HB	TBB	IBB	SO	WP	Bk	W	L	Pct	ShO	Sv-Op	Hld	ERC	ERA
2007	Nashv*	AAA	10	0	0	1	16.0	68	19	4	4	1	1	0	0	2	0	9	3	0	2	0	1.000	0	0--	-	3.75	2.25
2003	Det	AL	66	0	0	18	77.0	326	78	42	40	9	3	5	3	22	1	38	2	0	1	3	.250	0	3-6	5	3.97	4.68
2005	Det	AL	56	0	0	7	70.2	284	58	30	27	8	5	2	2	22	6	26	4	0	3	4	.429	0	0-1	11	2.91	3.44
2006	2 Tms		16	0	0	3	21.1	95	25	12	12	5	0	0	0	8	3	7	0	0	0	0	-	0	0-1	0	5.73	5.06

Year	Team	Lg	HOW MUCH HE PITCHED						WHAT HE GAVE UP												THE RESULTS							
			G	GS	CG	GF	IP	BFP	H	R	ER	HR	SH	SF	HB	TBB	IBB	SO	WP	Bk	W	L	Pct	ShO	Sv-Op	Hld	ERC	ERA
2007	Mil	NL	49	0	0	21	50.0	225	63	31	26	6	0	1	2	14	3	28	4	0	2	1	.667	0	0-0	2	5.27	4.68
06	Det	AL	9	0	0	3	11.1	49	13	4	4	2	0	0	0	1	0	4	0	0	0	0	-	0	0-0	0	5.10	3.18
06	Mil	NL	7	0	0	0	10.0	46	12	8	8	3	0	0	0	4	1	3	0	0	0	0	-	0	0-1	0	6.46	7.20
4 ML YEARS			187	0	0	50	219.0	930	224	115	105	28	6	11	7	66	13	99	10	0	6	8	.429	0	3-8	18	4.06	4.32

Matt Stairs

Bats: L **Throws:** R **Pos:** 1B-45; LF-43; PH-33; RF-17; DH-4; PR-1   **Ht:** 5'9" **Wt:** 215 **Born:** 2/27/1968 **Age:** 40

Year	Team	Lg	BATTING																			BASERUNNING				AVERAGES		
			G	AB	H	2B	3B	HR	(Hm	Rd)	TB	R	RBI	RC	TBB	IBB	SO	HBP	SH	SF	SB	CS	SB%	GDP	Avg	OBP	Slg
1992	Mon	NL	13	30	5	2	0	0	(0	0)	7	2	5	3	7	0	7	0	0	1	0	0	-	0	.167	.316	.233
1993	Mon	NL	6	8	3	1	0	0	(0	0)	4	1	2	1	0	0	1	0	0	0	0	0	-	1	.375	.375	.500
1995	Bos	AL	39	88	23	7	1	1	(0	1)	35	8	17	9	4	0	14	1	1	1	0	1	.00	4	.261	.298	.398
1996	Oak	AL	61	137	38	5	1	10	(5	5)	75	21	23	27	19	2	23	1	0	1	1	1	.50	2	.277	.367	.547
1997	Oak	AL	133	352	105	19	0	27	(20	7)	205	62	73	77	50	1	60	3	1	4	3	2	.60	6	.298	.386	.582
1998	Oak	AL	149	523	154	33	1	26	(16	10)	267	88	106	96	59	4	93	6	1	4	8	3	.73	13	.294	.370	.511
1999	Oak	AL	146	531	137	26	3	38	(15	23)	283	94	102	101	89	6	124	2	0	1	2	7	.22	8	.258	.366	.533
2000	Oak	AL	143	476	108	26	0	21	(9	12)	197	74	81	69	78	4	122	1	1	6	5	2	.71	7	.227	.333	.414
2001	ChC	NL	128	340	85	21	0	17	(5	12)	157	48	61	57	52	7	76	7	1	3	2	3	.40	4	.250	.358	.462
2002	Mil	NL	107	270	66	15	0	16	(6	10)	129	41	41	38	36	4	50	8	0	1	2	0	1.00	7	.244	.349	.478
2003	Pit	NL	121	305	89	20	1	20	(13	7)	171	49	57	58	45	3	64	5	0	2	0	1	.00	7	.292	.389	.561
2004	KC	AL	126	439	117	21	3	18	(6	12)	198	48	66	65	49	2	92	5	0	3	1	0	1.00	15	.267	.345	.451
2005	KC	AL	127	396	109	26	1	13	(5	8)	176	55	66	70	60	4	69	5	0	5	1	2	.33	9	.275	.373	.444
2006	3 Tms	AL	117	348	86	21	0	13	(6	7)	146	42	51	51	40	3	86	3	0	2	0	0	-	7	.247	.328	.420
2007	Tor	AL	125	357	103	28	1	21	(7	14)	196	58	64	65	44	5	66	2	0	2	2	1	.67	1	.289	.368	.549
06	KC	AL	77	226	59	14	0	8	(3	5)	97	31	32	35	31	2	52	2	0	2	0	0	-	5	.261	.352	.429
06	Tex	AL	26	81	17	4	0	3	(2	1)	30	6	11	10	6	1	22	1	0	0	0	0	-	1	.210	.273	.370
06	Det	AL	14	41	10	3	0	2	(1	1)	19	5	8	6	3	0	12	0	0	0	0	0	-	1	.244	.295	.463
15 ML YEARS			1541	4600	1228	271	12	241	(113	128)	2246	691	815	787	632	45	947	49	5	36	27	23	.54	97	.267	.359	.488

Jason Standridge

Pitches: R **Bats:** R **Pos:** RP-4   **Ht:** 6'4" **Wt:** 230 **Born:** 11/9/1978 **Age:** 29

Year	Team	Lg	HOW MUCH HE PITCHED						WHAT HE GAVE UP													THE RESULTS							
			G	GS	CG	GF	IP	BFP	H	R	ER	HR	SH	SF	HB	TBB	IBB	SO	WP	Bk	W	L	Pct	ShO	Sv-Op	Hld	ERC	ERA
2007	Omha*	AAA	5	0	0	4	4.2	24	6	2	2	0	0	0	0	5	1	3	1	0	2	1	.667	0	0- -	-	7.34	3.86
2001	TB	AL	9	1	0	6	19.1	87	19	10	10	5	0	0	0	14	1	9	0	0	0	0	-	0	0-0	0	6.63	4.66
2002	TB	AL	1	0	0	0	3.0	18	7	3	3	1	0	0	0	4	0	1	0	0	0	0	-	0	0-0	0	22.36	9.00
2003	TB	AL	8	7	1	1	35.1	157	38	25	25	7	1	1	1	16	0	20	1	0	0	5	.000	0	0-0	0	5.60	6.37
2004	TB	AL	3	1	0	1	10.0	48	14	10	10	5	0	1	0	4	0	7	1	0	0	0	-	0	0-0	0	9.60	9.00
2005	2 Tms		34	0	0	6	33.1	156	45	17	17	3	2	0	1	17	8	19	2	0	2	2	.500	0	0-0	5	6.33	4.59
2006	Cin	NL	21	0	0	2	18.2	86	17	14	10	2	1	0	1	14	0	18	0	0	1	1	.500	0	0-0	1	5.23	4.82
2007	KC	AL	4	0	0	2	7.2	41	11	10	7	2	1	0	0	5	2	6	0	0	0	1	.000	0	0-0	0	8.08	8.22
05	Tex	AL	2	0	0	0	2.1	16	7	3	3	0	0	0	0	1	1	2	1	0	0	0	-	0	0-0	0	14.52	11.57
05	Cin	NL	32	0	0	6	31.0	140	38	14	14	3	2	0	1	16	7	17	1	0	2	2	.500	0	0-0	5	5.76	4.06
7 ML YEARS			80	9	1	18	127.1	593	151	89	82	25	5	2	3	74	11	80	7	0	3	9	.250	0	0-0	6	6.69	5.80

Jason Stanford

Pitches: L **Bats:** L **Pos:** RP-6; SP-2   **Ht:** 6'2" **Wt:** 200 **Born:** 1/23/1977 **Age:** 31

Year	Team	Lg	HOW MUCH HE PITCHED						WHAT HE GAVE UP													THE RESULTS							
			G	GS	CG	GF	IP	BFP	H	R	ER	HR	SH	SF	HB	TBB	IBB	SO	WP	Bk	W	L	Pct	ShO	Sv-Op	Hld	ERC	ERA
2007	Buffalo*	AAA	18	14	0	1	87.2	380	84	45	40	8	4	5	9	34	0	60	5	0	5	1	.833	0	0- -	-	4.16	4.11
2003	Cle	AL	13	8	0	1	50.0	213	48	20	20	5	0	1	1	16	1	30	0	0	1	3	.250	0	0-0	0	3.55	3.60
2004	Cle	AL	2	2	0	0	11.0	50	12	1	1	0	1	0	1	5	0	5	1	0	1	0	1.000	0	0-0	0	4.38	0.82
2007	Cle	AL	8	2	0	2	26.1	118	32	15	14	1	0	1	2	7	0	16	0	0	1	1	.500	0	0-0	0	4.57	4.78
3 ML YEARS			23	12	0	3	87.1	381	92	36	35	6	1	2	4	28	1	51	1	0	2	5	.286	0	0-0	0	3.96	3.61

Craig Stansberry

Bats: R **Throws:** R **Pos:** PH-7; 2B-4; PR-2   **Ht:** 6'0" **Wt:** 185 **Born:** 3/8/1982 **Age:** 26

Year	Team	Lg	BATTING																			BASERUNNING				AVERAGES		
			G	AB	H	2B	3B	HR	(Hm	Rd)	TB	R	RBI	RC	TBB	IBB	SO	HBP	SH	SF	SB	CS	SB%	GDP	Avg	OBP	Slg
2003	Wmspt	A-	45	166	51	9	3	2	(-	-)	72	19	21	27	13	1	25	4	3	1	5	3	.63	2	.307	.370	.434
2004	Hickory	A	106	391	112	14	5	9	(-	-)	163	57	67	66	52	0	88	5	2	2	20	8	.71	6	.286	.376	.417
2005	Lynbrg	A+	24	94	33	7	2	3	(-	-)	53	17	19	23	11	1	13	2	0	0	7	1	.88	1	.351	.430	.564
2005	Altna	AA	116	421	100	22	11	18	(-	-)	198	62	66	66	44	0	116	6	5	7	15	5	.75	8	.238	.314	.470
2006	Altna	AA	72	260	67	18	3	10	(-	-)	121	46	30	43	31	0	62	4	1	1	8	3	.73	6	.258	.345	.465
2006	Indy	AAA	61	201	44	10	2	3	(-	-)	67	30	25	27	35	0	36	2	3	1	11	3	.79	5	.219	.339	.333
2007	Portlnd	AAA	124	466	127	33	3	14	(-	-)	208	83	75	80	70	3	95	6	0	6	10	10	.50	6	.273	.370	.446
2007	SD	NL	11	7	2	0	0	0	(0	0)	2	1	1	1	0	0	3	1	2	0	0	0	-	0	.286	.375	.286

Mike Stanton

Pitches: L **Bats:** L **Pos:** RP-69   **Ht:** 6'1" **Wt:** 215 **Born:** 6/2/1967 **Age:** 41

Year	Team	Lg	G	GS	CG	GF	IP	BFP	H	R	ER	HR	SH	SF	HB	TBB	IBB	SO	WP	Bk	W	L	Pct	ShO	Sv-Op	Hld	ERC	ERA
2007	Daytn*	A-	1	1	0	0	1.0	4	1	1	1	0	0	0	0	0	0	2	0	0	0	1	.000	0	0--	-	7.45	9.00
1989	Atl	NL	20	0	0	10	24.0	94	17	4	4	0	4	0	0	8	1	27	1	0	0	1	.000	0	7-8	2	1.72	1.50
1990	Atl	NL	7	0	0	4	7.0	42	16	16	14	1	1	0	1	4	2	7	1	0	0	3	.000	0	2-3	0	13.58	18.00
1991	Atl	NL	74	0	0	20	78.0	314	62	27	25	6	6	0	1	21	6	54	0	0	5	5	.500	0	7 10	15	2.31	2.88
1992	Atl	NL	65	0	0	23	63.2	264	59	32	29	6	1	2	2	20	2	44	3	0	5	4	.556	0	8-11	15	3.42	4.10
1993	Atl	NL	63	0	0	41	52.0	236	51	35	27	4	5	2	0	29	7	43	1	0	4	6	.400	0	27-33	5	4.08	4.67
1994	Atl	NL	49	0	0	15	45.2	197	41	18	18	2	2	1	3	26	3	35	1	0	3	1	.750	0	3-4	10	4.01	3.55
1995	2 Tms		48	0	0	22	40.1	178	48	23	19	6	2	1	1	14	2	23	2	1	2	1	.667	0	1-3	8	5.41	4.24
1996	2 Tms	AL	81	0	0	28	78.2	327	78	32	32	11	4	2	0	27	5	60	3	2	4	4	.500	0	1-6	22	4.08	3.66
1997	NYY	AL	64	0	0	15	66.2	283	50	19	19	3	2	0	3	34	2	70	3	2	6	1	.857	0	3-5	26	2.88	2.57
1998	NYY	AL	67	0	0	26	79.0	330	71	51	48	13	1	2	4	26	1	69	0	0	4	1	.800	0	6-10	18	3.88	5.47
1999	NYY	AL	73	1	0	10	62.1	271	71	30	30	5	4	2	1	18	4	59	2	0	2	2	.500	0	0-5	21	4.23	4.33
2000	NYY	AL	69	0	0	20	68.0	291	68	32	31	5	2	4	2	24	2	75	1	0	2	3	.400	0	0-4	15	3.78	4.10
2001	NYY	AL	76	0	0	16	80.1	342	80	25	23	4	2	3	4	29	9	78	3	1	9	4	.692	0	0-1	23	3.61	2.58
2002	NYY	AL	79	0	0	25	78.0	324	73	29	26	4	4	7	0	28	3	44	4	0	7	1	.875	0	6-9	17	3.23	3.00
2003	NYM	NL	50	0	0	24	45.1	194	37	25	23	6	1	3	2	19	4	34	2	1	2	7	.222	0	5-7	10	3.33	4.57
2004	NYM	NL	83	0	0	19	77.0	337	70	32	27	6	6	1	2	33	6	58	1	0	2	6	.250	0	0-6	25	3.41	3.16
2005	3 Tms		59	0	0	12	42.2	185	49	24	22	3	3	1	0	15	4	27	1	1	3	3	.500	0	0-1	9	4.42	4.64
2006	2 Tms	NL	82	0	0	22	67.2	290	70	30	30	2	2	4	2	27	11	48	5	1	7	7	.500	0	8-14	15	3.67	3.99
2007	Cin	NL	69	0	0	11	57.2	263	75	39	38	6	1	1	5	18	2	40	1	0	1	3	.250	0	0-3	10	5.85	5.93
95	Atl	NL	26	0	0	10	19.1	94	31	14	12	3	2	1	1	6	2	13	1	1	1	1	.500	0	1-2	4	7.86	5.59
95	Bos	AL	22	0	0	12	21.0	84	17	9	7	3	0	0	0	8	0	10	1	0	1	0	1.000	0	0-1	4	3.37	3.00
96	Bos	AL	59	0	0	19	56.1	239	58	24	24	9	3	2	0	23	4	46	3	2	4	3	.571	0	1-5	15	4.71	3.83
96	Tex	AL	22	0	0	9	22.1	88	20	8	8	2	1	0	0	4	1	14	0	0	0	1	.000	0	0-1	7	2.62	3.22
05	NYY	AL	28	0	0	6	14.0	64	17	11	11	1	0	1	0	6	0	12	1	0	1	2	.333	0	0-0	4	5.17	7.07
05	Was	NL	30	0	0	6	27.2	118	31	13	11	2	3	0	0	9	4	14	0	1	2	1	.667	0	0-1	5	4.11	3.58
05	Bos	AL	1	0	0	0	1.0	3	1	0	0	0	0	0	0	0	0	1	0	0	0	0	-	0	0-0	0	2.79	0.00
06	Was	NL	56	0	0	7	44.1	196	47	22	22	1	2	3	1	21	11	30	2	1	3	5	.375	0	0-3	10	3.81	4.47
06	SF	NL	26	0	0	15	23.1	94	23	8	8	1	0	1	1	6	0	18	3	0	4	2	.667	0	8-11	5	3.39	3.09
	19 ML YEARS		1178	1	0	363	1114.0	4762	1086	523	485	93	53	36	33	420	76	895	35	9	68	63	.519	0	84-143	266	3.75	3.92

Tim Stauffer

Pitches: R **Bats:** R **Pos:** SP-2   **Ht:** 6'1" **Wt:** 205 **Born:** 6/2/1982 **Age:** 26

Year	Team	Lg	G	GS	CG	GF	IP	BFP	H	R	ER	HR	SH	SF	HB	TBB	IBB	SO	WP	Bk	W	L	Pct	ShO	Sv-Op	Hld	ERC	ERA
2007	Portlnd*	AAA	25	20	0	0	130.2	572	147	73	63	12	8	4	4	36	0	96	7	0	8	5	.615	0	0--	-	4.30	4.34
2005	SD	NL	15	14	0	0	81.0	355	92	50	48	10	2	0	2	29	0	49	0	0	3	6	.333	0	0-0	0	5.00	5.33
2006	SD	NL	1	1	0	0	6.0	21	3	2	1	0	0	0	0	1	0	2	0	0	1	0	1.000	0	0-0	0	0.84	1.50
2007	SD	NL	2	2	0	0	7.2	45	15	18	10	5	0	0	1	6	0	6	0	0	0	1	.000	0	0-0	0	18.32	21.13
	3 ML YEARS		18	17	0	0	94.2	421	110	70	67	15	2	0	3	36	0	57	0	0	4	7	.364	0	0-0	0	5.54	6.37

Adam Stern

Bats: L **Throws:** R **Pos:** CF-2   **Ht:** 5'11" **Wt:** 180 **Born:** 2/12/1980 **Age:** 28

Year	Team	Lg	G	AB	H	2B	3B	HR	(Hm	Rd)	TB	R	RBI	RC	TBB	IBB	SO	HBP	SH	SF	SB	CS	SB%	GDP	Avg	OBP	Slg
2007	Norfolk*		78	289	78	11	6	1	(-	-)	104	40	23	36	24	1	65	1	6	2	17	6	.74	1	.270	.326	.360
2005	Bos	AL	36	15	2	0	0	1	(0	1)	5	4	2	1	0	0	4	1	0	0	1	1	.50	0	.133	.188	.333
2006	Bos	AL	10	20	3	1	0	0	(0	0)	4	3	4	2	0	0	4	1	0	0	1	0	1.00	0	.150	.190	.200
2007	Bal	AL	2	0	0	0	0	0	(0	0)	0	0	0	0	0	0	0	0	0	0	0	0	-	0	-	-	-
	3 ML YEARS		48	35	5	1	0	1	(0	1)	9	7	6	3	0	0	8	2	0	0	2	1	.67	0	.143	.189	.257

Mitch Stetter

Pitches: L **Bats:** L **Pos:** RP-6   **Ht:** 6'5" **Wt:** 208 **Born:** 1/16/1981 **Age:** 27

Year	Team	Lg	G	GS	CG	GF	IP	BFP	H	R	ER	HR	SH	SF	HB	TBB	IBB	SO	WP	Bk	W	L	Pct	ShO	Sv-Op	Hld	ERC	ERA
2003	Helena	R+	15	8	0	0	54.2	239	55	34	24	4	4	2	1	12	0	63	7	0	6	2	.750	0	0--	-	3.40	3.95
2004	Beloit	A	24	3	0	14	53.0	198	31	12	10	4	2	0	0	12	0	57	1	0	4	0	1.000	0	6--	-	1.41	1.70
2004	Hi Dsrt	A+	8	7	0	0	38.2	185	54	39	35	6	2	3	2	14	0	29	4	0	1	4	.200	0	0--	-	6.83	8.15
2005	Hntsvl	AA	32	0	0	22	51.2	205	45	15	14	3	1	0	2	11	1	47	0	0	2	3	.400	0	8--	-	2.61	2.44
2005	Nashv	AAA	27	0	0	4	25.1	111	23	17	13	5	2	1	0	11	1	23	2	0	1	1	.500	0	0--	-	4.17	4.62
2006	Nashv	AAA	51	0	0	6	38.1	169	38	20	19	3	6	3	3	16	3	36	3	0	2	5	.286	0	0--	-	4.09	4.46
2007	Brewrs	R	7	5	0	0	6.0	22	4	1	1	0	0	0	1	0	0	9	0	0	0	0	-	0	0--	-	1.29	1.50
2007	Nashv	AAA	24	0	0	4	14.2	55	8	7	7	1	0	2	0	5	0	19	1	0	1	0	1.000	0	1--	-	1.54	4.30
2007	Hntsvl	AA	2	0	0	0	1.0	3	0	0	0	0	0	0	0	0	0	2	0	0	0	0	-	0	0--	-	0.00	0.00
2007	Mil	NL	6	0	0	2	5.0	20	2	2	2	0	0	1	2	2	0	4	3	0	1	0	1.000	0	0-0	0	1.86	3.60

Chris Stewart

Bats: R **Throws:** R **Pos:** C-17; PR-2; PH-1   **Ht:** 6'4" **Wt:** 210 **Born:** 2/19/1982 **Age:** 26

Year	Team	Lg	G	AB	H	2B	3B	HR	(Hm	Rd)	TB	R	RBI	RC	TBB	IBB	SO	HBP	SH	SF	SB	CS	SB%	GDP	Avg	OBP	Slg
2002	Bristol	R+	42	158	44	9	0	1	(-	-)	56	25	12	19	12	0	17	2	0	0	2	3	.40	0	.278	.337	.354
2003	WinSa	A+	76	217	45	8	2	2	(-	-)	63	18	27	20	27	1	29	0	7	1	1	0	1.00	6	.207	.294	.290
2004	Brham	AA	83	260	60	11	2	1	(-	-)	78	26	17	24	22	0	59	4	13	2	2	4	.33	3	.231	.299	.300
2004	Charltt	AAA	5	14	1	1	0	0	(-	-)	2	1	1	0	1	0	3	1	0	0	0	0	-	0	.071	.188	.143

Year	Team	Lg	G	AB	H	2B	3B	HR	(Hm	Rd)	TB	R	RBI	RC	TBB	IBB	SO	HBP	SH	SF	SB	CS	SB%	GDP	Avg	OBP	Slg
2005	Brham	AA	95	311	89	21	0	11	(-	-)	143	39	51	49	24	2	37	3	10	2	3	3	.50	7	.286	.341	.460
2006	Charltt	AAA	89	272	72	17	3	4	(-	-)	107	40	28	35	15	0	35	5	8	1	3	0	1.00	5	.265	.314	.393
2007	Okla	AA	46	153	37	8	0	2	(-	-)	51	18	21	15	12	0	19	1	2	4	0	2	.00	4	.242	.294	.333
2006	CWS	AL	6	8	0	0	0	0	(0	0)	0	0	0	0	0	0	2	0	0	0	0	0	-	0	.000	.000	.000
2007	Tex	AL	17	37	9	2	0	0	(0	0)	11	4	3	3	3	0	6	0	3	0	0	0	-	2	.243	.300	.297
2 ML YEARS			23	45	9	2	0	0	(0	0)	11	4	3	3	3	0	8	0	3	0	0	0	-	2	.200	.250	.244

Ian Stewart

Bats: L **Throws:** R **Pos:** PH-29; 3B-11   **Ht:** 6'3" **Wt:** 205 **Born:** 4/5/1985 **Age:** 23

Year	Team	Lg	G	AB	H	2B	3B	HR	(Hm	Rd)	TB	R	RBI	RC	TBB	IBB	SO	HBP	SH	SF	SB	CS	SB%	GDP	Avg	OBP	Slg
2003	Casper	R+	57	224	71	14	5	10	(-	-)	125	40	43	49	29	3	54	3	0	1	4	1	.80	5	.317	.401	.558
2004	Ashvll	A	131	505	161	31	9	30	(-	-)	300	92	101	117	66	6	112	4	1	5	19	9	.68	7	.319	.398	.594
2005	Mdest	A+	112	435	119	32	7	17	(-	-)	216	83	86	78	52	0	113	5	0	7	2	2	.50	13	.274	.353	.497
2006	Tulsa	AA	120	462	124	41	7	10	(-	-)	209	75	71	74	50	2	103	11	1	4	3	8	.27	13	.268	.351	.452
2007	ColSpr	AAA	112	414	126	23	2	15	(-	-)	198	72	65	78	49	6	92	3	4	4	11	2	.85	10	.304	.379	.478
2007	Col	NL	35	43	9	4	0	1	(1	0)	16	3	9	5	1	0	17	2	0	0	0	0	-	0	.209	.261	.372

Shannon Stewart

Bats: R **Throws:** R **Pos:** LF-139; CF-6; PH-6; PR-3   **Ht:** 5'11" **Wt:** 210 **Born:** 2/25/1974 **Age:** 34

Year	Team	Lg	G	AB	H	2B	3B	HR	(Hm	Rd)	TB	R	RBI	RC	TBB	IBB	SO	HBP	SH	SF	SB	CS	SB%	GDP	Avg	OBP	Slg
1995	Tor	AL	12	38	8	0	0	0	(0	0)	8	2	1	3	5	0	5	1	0	0	2	0	1.00	0	.211	.318	.211
1996	Tor	AL	7	17	3	1	0	0	(0	0)	4	2	2	1	1	0	4	0	0	0	1	0	1.00	1	.176	.222	.235
1997	Tor	AL	44	168	48	13	7	0	(0	0)	75	25	22	29	19	1	24	4	0	2	10	3	.77	3	.286	.368	.446
1998	Tor	AL	144	516	144	29	3	12	(6	6)	215	90	55	88	67	1	77	15	6	1	51	18	.74	5	.279	.377	.417
1999	Tor	AL	145	608	185	28	2	11	(4	7)	250	102	67	95	59	0	83	8	3	4	37	14	.73	12	.304	.371	.411
2000	Tor	AL	136	583	186	43	5	21	(12	9)	302	107	69	106	37	1	79	6	1	4	20	5	.80	12	.319	.363	.518
2001	Tor	AL	155	640	202	44	7	12	(6	6)	296	103	60	109	46	1	72	11	0	1	27	10	.73	9	.316	.371	.463
2002	Tor	AL	141	577	175	38	6	10	(4	6)	255	103	45	92	54	2	60	9	0	1	14	2	.88	17	.303	.371	.442
2003	2 Tms	AL	136	573	176	44	2	13	(7	6)	263	90	73	93	52	3	66	6	2	11	4	6	.40	10	.307	.364	.459
2004	Min	AL	92	378	115	17	2	11	(5	6)	169	46	47	68	47	4	44	1	1	3	6	3	.67	5	.304	.380	.447
2005	Min	AL	132	551	151	27	3	10	(4	6)	214	69	56	68	34	2	73	8	1	5	7	5	.58	11	.274	.323	.388
2006	Min	AL	44	174	51	5	1	2	(0	2)	64	21	21	26	14	0	19	1	0	1	3	1	.75	7	.293	.347	.368
2007	Oak	AL	146	576	167	22	1	12	(2	10)	227	79	48	75	47	0	60	3	1	3	11	3	.79	15	.290	.345	.394
03	Tor	AL	71	303	89	22	2	7	(3	4)	136	47	35	51	27	2	30	2	0	8	1	2	.33	6	.294	.347	.449
03	Min	AL	65	270	87	22	0	6	(4	2)	127	43	38	42	25	1	36	4	2	3	3	4	.43	4	.322	.384	.470
13 ML YEARS			1334	5399	1611	311	39	114	(50	64)	2342	839	566	853	482	15	666	73	15	36	193	70	.73	107	.298	.362	.434

Kelly Stinnett

Bats: R **Throws:** R **Pos:** C-26; PR-1   **Ht:** 5'11" **Wt:** 235 **Born:** 2/4/1970 **Age:** 38

Year	Team	Lg	G	AB	H	2B	3B	HR	(Hm	Rd)	TB	R	RBI	RC	TBB	IBB	SO	HBP	SH	SF	SB	CS	SB%	GDP	Avg	OBP	Slg
2007	LsVgs*	AAA	31	102	20	2	0	3	(-	-)	31	10	10	8	9	0	22	1	1	0	0	0	-	5	.196	.268	.304
2007	Memp*	AAA	1	1	1	0	0	0	(-	-)	1	0	1	0	0	0	0	0	0	0	0	0	-	0	1.000	1.000	1.000
1994	NYM	NL	47	150	38	6	2	2	(0	2)	54	20	14	18	11	1	28	5	0	1	2	0	1.00	3	.253	.323	.360
1995	NYM	NL	77	196	43	8	1	4	(1	3)	65	23	18	24	29	3	65	6	0	0	2	0	1.00	3	.219	.338	.332
1996	Mil	AL	14	26	2	0	0	0	(0	0)	2	1	0	2	0	1	11	1	0	0	0	0	-	0	.077	.172	.077
1997	Mil	AL	30	36	9	4	0	0	(0	0)	13	2	3	4	3	0	9	0	0	0	0	0	-	0	.250	.308	.361
1998	Ari	NL	92	274	71	14	1	11	(5	6)	120	35	34	41	35	3	74	6	1	2	0	1	.00	9	.259	.353	.438
1999	Ari	NL	88	284	66	13	0	14	(3	11)	121	36	38	37	24	2	83	5	2	2	2	1	.67	4	.232	.302	.426
2000	Ari	NL	76	240	52	7	0	8	(2	6)	83	22	33	23	19	4	56	6	0	0	0	1	.00	5	.217	.291	.346
2001	Cin	NL	63	187	48	11	0	9	(6	3)	86	27	25	27	17	3	61	5	1	1	2	2	.50	5	.257	.333	.460
2002	Cin	NL	34	93	21	5	0	3	(1	2)	35	10	13	13	15	1	25	0	0	0	2	0	1.00	1	.226	.333	.376
2003	2 Tms	NL	67	186	44	13	0	3	(2	1)	66	14	19	20	14	3	52	4	2	1	0	0	-	3	.237	.302	.355
2004	KC	AL	20	59	18	0	0	3	(0	3)	27	10	7	9	5	0	16	2	3	0	0	0	-	0	.305	.379	.458
2005	Ari	NL	59	129	32	4	0	6	(2	4)	54	15	12	9	12	3	32	1	1	0	0	0	-	4	.248	.317	.419
2006	2 Tms	NL	41	91	19	3	0	1	(1	0)	25	6	9	7	5	1	33	1	2	0	0	0	-	0	.209	.258	.275
2007	StL	NL	26	82	13	3	0	1	(1	0)	19	7	5	3	5	2	22	0	0	0	0	0	-	0	.159	.207	.232
03	Cin	NL	60	179	41	13	0	3	(2	1)	63	14	19	18	13	3	51	4	2	1	0	0	-	3	.229	.294	.352
03	Phi	NL	7	7	3	0	0	0	(0	0)	3	0	0	2	1	0	1	0	0	0	0	0	-	0	.429	.500	.429
06	NYY	AL	34	79	18	3	0	1	(1	0)	24	6	9	7	5	1	29	1	2	0	0	0	-	0	.228	.282	.304
06	NYM	NL	7	12	1	0	0	0	(0	0)	1	0	0	0	0	0	4	0	0	0	0	0	-	0	.083	.083	.083
14 ML YEARS			734	2033	476	91	4	65	(24	41)	770	228	230	235	196	26	567	42	12	7	10	5	.67	39	.234	.313	.379

Mel Stocker

Bats: L **Throws:** R **Pos:** LF-4; PR-4; RF-2; PH-1   **Ht:** 5'10" **Wt:** 160 **Born:** 8/15/1980 **Age:** 27

Year	Team	Lg	G	AB	H	2B	3B	HR	(Hm	Rd)	TB	R	RBI	RC	TBB	IBB	SO	HBP	SH	SF	SB	CS	SB%	GDP	Avg	OBP	Slg
2001	Spkane	A-	28	73	17	2	2	0	(-	-)	23	10	7	9	14	0	20	0	1	0	4	2	.67	1	.233	.356	.315
2002	Spkane	A-	61	210	47	7	2	2	(-	-)	64	48	14	26	27	0	35	11	2	2	26	12	.68	6	.224	.340	.305
2003	Burlgtn	A	103	403	110	16	9	3	(-	-)	153	85	33	67	46	0	48	15	8	2	36	5	.88	0	.273	.367	.380
2003	Wilmg	A+	20	56	13	0	1	0	(-	-)	15	6	8	4	3	0	12	0	1	1	5	0	1.00	0	.232	.267	.268
2004	Wichta	AA	14	40	6	1	0	0	(-	-)	7	7	1	2	4	0	5	3	1	0	3	1	.75	3	.150	.277	.175
2004	Wilmg	A+	118	453	96	20	8	2	(-	-)	138	82	29	50	53	0	71	13	9	3	44	15	.75	5	.212	.310	.305

Year	Team	Lg	G	AB	H	2B	3B	HR	(Hm	Rd)	TB	R	RBI	RC	TBB	IBB	SO	HBP	SH	SF	SB	CS	SB%	GDP	Avg	OBP	Slg
2005	Wichta	AA	80	277	68	7	10	2	(-	-)	101	35	27	35	27	0	42	3	7	3	16	6	.73	7	.245	.316	.365
2005	Hi Dsrt	A+	7	26	6	0	1	0	(-	-)	8	3	4	2	1	0	3	0	0	0	2	1	.67	0	.231	.259	.308
2007	Hntsvl	AA	113	267	68	8	10	0	(-	-)	96	56	23	39	27	2	50	6	6	2	34	6	.85	4	.255	.334	.360
2007	Mil	NL	9	3	0	0	0	0	(0	0)	0	0	0	0	0	0	0	0	0	0	4	0	1.00	0	.000	.000	.000

Brian Stokes

Pitches: R Bats: R Pos: RP-59 **Ht: 6'1" Wt: 210 Born: 9/7/1979 Age: 28**

			HOW MUCH HE PITCHED					WHAT HE GAVE UP								THE RESULTS						
Year	Team	Lg	G	GS	CG	GF	IP	BFP	H	R	ER	HR	SH	SF	HB	TBB	IBB	SO	WP	Bk	W	L	Pct	ShO	Sv-Op	Hld	ERC	ERA
1999	Princtn	R+	33	0	0	27	37.0	163	33	20	16	2	2	1	6	21	0	39	8	1	2	3	.400	0	9--	-	3.88	3.89
2000	CtnSC	A	46	0	0	16	70.1	293	45	24	20	1	2	1	4	34	2	66	10	0	5	6	.455	0	5--	-	2.08	2.56
2001	Dkrsfld	A+	32	20	1	5	128.2	565	118	65	56	11	4	5	8	64	0	92	9	0	8	6	.571	0	1--	-	4.12	3.92
2002	Bkrsfld	A+	28	28	1	0	165.2	704	156	79	60	13	4	6	8	57	1	152	10	0	10	7	.588	1	0--	-	3.56	3.20
2003	Orlndo	AA	10	10	0	0	50.2	220	55	26	18	2	0	2	4	13	0	33	1	1	2	5	.286	0	0--	-	3.85	3.20
2005	Visalia	A+	4	4	0	0	17.0	71	15	8	8	3	0	1	0	5	0	21	0	0	1	2	.333	0	0--	-	3.45	4.24
2005	Mont	AA	16	16	1	0	93.1	379	82	36	36	8	3	1	2	28	2	70	4	0	4	6	.400	0	0--	-	3.05	3.47
2006	Drham	AAA	29	23	0	1	133.2	579	134	75	61	8	3	4	8	49	0	103	7	0	7	7	.500	0	0--	-	3.91	4.11
2006	TB	AL	5	4	0	0	24.0	110	31	13	13	2	0	3	1	9	0	15	0	0	1	0	1.000	0	0-0	-	5.75	4.88
2007	TB	AL	59	0	0	22	62.1	294	90	49	49	11	1	3	3	25	1	35	1	0	2	7	.222	0	0-2	8	7.70	7.07
	2 ML YEARS		64	4	0	22	86.1	404	121	62	62	13	1	6	4	34	1	50	1	0	3	7	.300	0	0-2	8	7.14	6.46

Ricky Stone

Pitches: R Bats: R Pos: RP-5 **Ht: 6'1" Wt: 195 Born: 2/28/1975 Age: 33**

			HOW MUCH HE PITCHED					WHAT HE GAVE UP								THE RESULTS						
Year	Team	Lg	G	GS	CG	GF	IP	BFP	H	R	ER	HR	SH	SF	HB	TBB	IBB	SO	WP	Bk	W	L	Pct	ShO	Sv-Op	Hld	ERC	ERA
2007	Lsvlle*	AAA	59	0	0	37	62.2	247	50	15	13	4	4	3	1	11	3	39	2	1	5	6	.455	0	16--	-	1.99	1.87
2001	Hou	NL	6	0	0	3	7.2	33	8	3	2	1	0	0	0	2	1	4	0	0	0	0	-	0	0-0	0	3.69	2.35
2002	Hou	NL	78	0	0	16	77.1	335	78	36	31	9	5	2	1	34	3	63	1	0	3	3	.500	0	1-2	12	4.43	3.61
2003	Hou	NL	65	0	0	20	83.0	350	76	36	34	11	4	1	6	31	4	47	1	0	6	4	.600	0	1-1	7	4.00	3.69
2004	2 Tms	NL	43	0	0	17	51.2	238	66	39	37	11	0	1	6	16	3	38	2	0	2	2	.500	0	0-0	1	6.60	6.45
2005	Cin	NL	23	0	0	4	30.2	143	48	24	23	8	0	2	2	7	2	15	2	0	0	0	-	0	0-0	2	8.46	6.75
2007	Cin	NL	5	0	0	3	5.1	23	7	6	6	4	0	0	1	0	0	3	0	0	0	0	-	0	0-0	0	10.09	10.13
04	Hou	NL	16	0	0	7	19.0	92	26	12	12	5	0	0	3	7	3	16	1	0	1	1	.500	0	0-0	1	7.81	5.68
04	SD	NL	27	0	0	10	32.2	146	40	27	25	6	0	1	3	9	0	22	1	0	1	1	.500	0	0-0	0	5.92	6.89
	6 ML YEARS		220	0	0	63	255.2	1122	283	144	133	44	9	6	16	90	13	170	6	0	11	9	.550	0	2-3	22	5.25	4.68

Huston Street

Pitches: R Bats: R Pos: RP-48 **Ht: 6'0" Wt: 195 Born: 8/2/1983 Age: 24**

			HOW MUCH HE PITCHED					WHAT HE GAVE UP								THE RESULTS						
Year	Team	Lg	G	GS	CG	GF	IP	BFP	H	R	ER	HR	SH	SF	HB	TBB	IBB	SO	WP	Bk	W	L	Pct	ShO	Sv-Op	Hld	ERC	ERA
2007	Scrmto*	AAA	1	1	0	0	1.0	4	1	0	0	0	0	0	0	0	0	2	0	0	0	0	-	0	0-0	-	1.95	0.00
2005	Oak	AL	67	0	0	47	78.1	306	53	17	15	3	3	2	2	26	4	72	1	0	5	1	.833	0	23-27	0	1.87	1.72
2006	Oak	AL	69	0	0	55	70.2	290	64	28	26	4	3	3	2	13	3	67	4	0	4	4	.500	0	37-48	1	2.49	3.31
2007	Oak	AL	48	0	0	35	50.0	199	35	20	16	5	2	1	0	12	3	63	0	0	5	2	.714	0	16-21	5	1.84	2.88
	3 ML YEARS		184	0	0	137	199.0	795	152	65	57	12	8	6	4	51	10	202	5	0	14	7	.667	0	76-96	6	2.08	2.58

Eric Stults

Pitches: L Bats: L Pos: RP-7; SP-5 **Ht: 6'0" Wt: 215 Born: 12/9/1979 Age: 28**

			HOW MUCH HE PITCHED					WHAT HE GAVE UP								THE RESULTS						
Year	Team	Lg	G	GS	CG	GF	IP	BFP	H	R	ER	HR	SH	SF	HB	TBB	IBB	SO	WP	Bk	W	L	Pct	ShO	Sv-Op	Hld	ERC	ERA
2002	Gr Falls	R+	5	0	0	1	8.0	34	6	4	2	0	0	0	0	3	0	9	0	0	1	0	1.000	0	1--	-	1.94	2.25
2002	VeroB	A+	13	6	0	1	42.0	185	39	19	14	3	2	2	1	20	0	40	2	0	3	1	.750	0	0--	-	3.79	3.00
2002	Jaxnvl	AA	1	0	0	0	1.0	3	0	0	0	0	0	0	0	0	0	0	0	0	0	0	-	0	0--	-	0.00	0.00
2003	Jaxnvl	AA	9	7	0	1	38.0	169	46	23	21	5	2	3	0	13	0	14	0	0	3	4	.429	0	1--	-	5.30	4.97
2003	VeroB	A+	1	1	0	0	3.0	13	6	2	2	0	0	0	0	1	0	1	0	0	0	1	.000	0	0--	-	11.17	6.00
2004	Clmbs	AAA	12	0	0	8	21.2	89	18	8	6	0	0	0	0	6	0	16	1	0	1	2	.333	0	3--	-	2.07	2.49
2004	VeroB	A+	7	0	0	1	10.0	46	11	4	3	0	0	0	1	4	0	6	0	0	2	1	.667	0	1--	-	4.16	2.70
2005	Jaxnvl	AA	12	12	0	0	68.0	291	73	33	25	6	2	1	0	14	0	58	0	0	4	3	.571	0	0--	-	3.56	3.31
2005	LsVgs	AAA	15	14	0	0	78.0	360	107	60	57	15	1	2	1	24	0	60	1	0	3	7	.300	0	0--	-	6.64	6.58
2006	LsVgs	AAA	26	26	1	0	153.1	658	153	85	72	10	5	9	5	68	5	128	7	0	10	11	.476	0	0--	-	4.15	4.23
2007	LsVgs	AAA	21	17	0	1	89.1	428	134	76	75	12	4	4	2	36	3	81	7	0	5	7	.417	0	0--	-	7.48	7.56
2006	LAD	NL	6	2	0	2	17.2	73	17	12	11	4	2	0	0	7	0	5	0	0	1	0	1.000	0	0-0	-	4.91	5.60
2007	LAD	NL	12	5	0	0	38.2	179	50	26	25	5	1	1	1	17	2	30	2	0	1	4	.200	0	0-0	1	6.25	5.82
	2 ML YEARS		18	7	0	2	56.1	252	67	38	36	9	3	1	1	24	2	35	2	0	2	4	.333	0	0-0	1	5.84	5.75

Cory Sullivan

Bats: L Throws: L Pos: CF-51; PH-32; PR-2; LF-1; RF-1 **Ht: 6'0" Wt: 180 Born: 8/20/1979 Age: 28**

			BATTING																	BASERUNNING				AVERAGES		
Year	Team	Lg	G	AB	H	2B	3B	HR	(Hm	Rd)	TB	R	RBI	RC	TBB	IBB	SO	HBP	SH	SF	SB	CS	SB%	GDP	Avg	OBP	Slg
2007	ColSpr*		53	206	54	9	3	1	(-	-)	72	29	21	24	18	0	44	1	3	0	4	3	.57	5	.262	.324	.350
2005	Col	NL	139	378	111	15	4	4	(1	3)	146	64	30	54	28	0	83	3	10	5	12	3	.80	6	.294	.343	.386
2006	Col	NL	126	386	103	26	10	2	(0	2)	155	47	30	47	32	3	100	1	19	5	10	6	.63	5	.267	.321	.402
2007	Col	NL	72	140	40	6	1	2	(0	2)	54	19	14	20	9	1	25	2	1	1	2	0	1.00	5	.286	.336	.386
	3 ML YEARS		337	904	254	47	15	8	(1	7)	355	130	74	121	69	4	208	6	30	11	24	9	.73	16	.281	.332	.393

Jeff Suppan

Pitches: R **Bats:** R **Pos:** SP-34 **Ht:** 6'2" **Wt:** 220 **Born:** 1/2/1975 **Age:** 33

Year	Team	Lg	G	GS	CG	GF	IP	BFP	H	R	ER	HR	SH	SF	HB	TBB	IBB	SO	WP	Bk	W	L	Pct	ShO	Sv-Op	Hld	ERC	ERA
1995	Bos	AL	8	3	0	1	22.2	100	29	15	15	4	1	0	1	5	1	19	0	0	1	2	.333	0	0-0	0	5.43	5.96
1996	Bos	AL	8	4	0	2	22.2	107	29	19	19	3	1	4	1	13	0	13	3	0	1	1	.500	0	0-0	0	7.03	7.54
1997	Bos	AL	23	22	0	1	112.1	503	140	75	71	12	0	4	4	36	1	67	5	0	7	3	.700	0	0-0	0	5.39	5.69
1998	2 Tms		17	14	1	2	78.2	345	91	56	50	13	3	2	1	22	1	51	2	0	1	7	.125	0	0-0	0	4.95	5.72
1999	KC	AL	32	32	4	0	208.2	887	222	113	105	28	7	5	3	62	4	103	5	1	10	12	.455	1	0-0	0	4.33	4.53
2000	KC	AL	35	33	3	0	217.0	948	240	121	119	36	5	6	7	84	3	128	7	1	10	9	.526	1	0-0	0	5.31	4.94
2001	KC	AL	34	34	1	0	218.1	946	227	120	106	26	5	6	12	74	3	120	6	0	10	14	.417	0	0-0	0	4.40	4.37
2002	KC	AL	33	33	3	0	208.0	912	229	134	123	32	4	11	7	68	3	109	10	1	9	16	.360	1	0-0	0	4.84	5.32
2003	2 Tms		32	31	3	0	204.0	873	217	98	95	23	11	6	8	51	5	110	7	0	13	11	.542	2	0-0	0	4.03	4.19
2004	StL	NL	31	31	0	0	188.0	811	192	98	87	25	8	8	5	65	1	110	4	1	16	9	.640	0	0-0	0	4.38	4.16
2005	StL	NL	32	32	0	0	194.1	834	206	93	77	24	11	5	7	63	1	114	6	1	16	10	.615	0	0-0	0	4.46	3.57
2006	StL	NL	32	32	0	0	190.0	837	207	100	87	21	9	3	8	69	6	104	8	0	12	7	.632	0	0-0	0	4.62	4.12
2007	Mil	NL	34	34	1	0	206.2	919	243	113	106	18	14	11	11	68	10	114	7	0	12	12	.500	0	0-0	0	4.84	4.62
98	Ari	NL	13	13	1	0	66.0	299	82	55	49	12	3	2	1	21	1	39	2	0	1	7	.125	0	0-0	0	5.73	6.68
98	KC	AL	4	1	0	2	12.2	46	9	1	1	1	0	0	0	1	0	12	0	0	0	0	-	0	0-0	0	1.51	0.71
03	Pit	NL	21	21	3	0	141.0	597	147	57	56	11	10	2	6	31	5	78	3	0	10	7	.588	2	0-0	0	3.55	3.57
03	Bos	AL	11	10	0	0	63.0	276	70	41	39	12	1	4	2	20	0	32	4	0	3	4	.429	0	0-0	0	5.15	5.57
13 ML YEARS			351	335	16	6	2071.1	9022	2272	1155	1060	265	79	69	77	680	39	1162	70	5	118	113	.511	5	0-0	1	4.67	4.61

Ichiro Suzuki

Bats: L **Throws:** R **Pos:** CF-155; DH-6 **Ht:** 5'9" **Wt:** 172 **Born:** 10/22/1973 **Age:** 34

Year	Team	Lg	G	AB	H	2B	3B	HR	(Hm	Rd)	TB	R	RBI	RC	TBB	IBB	SO	HBP	SH	SF	SB	CS	SB%	GDP	Avg	OBP	Slg
2001	Sea	AL	157	692	242	34	8	8	(5	3)	316	127	69	124	30	10	53	8	4	4	56	14	.80	3	.350	.381	.457
2002	Sea	AL	157	647	208	27	8	8	(4	4)	275	111	51	110	68	27	62	5	3	5	31	15	.67	8	.321	.388	.425
2003	Sea	AL	159	679	212	29	8	13	(8	5)	296	111	62	107	36	7	69	6	3	1	34	8	.81	3	.312	.352	.436
2004	Sea	AL	161	704	262	24	5	8	(4	4)	320	101	60	125	49	19	63	4	2	3	36	11	.77	6	.372	.414	.455
2005	Sea	AL	162	679	206	21	12	15	(8	7)	296	111	68	109	48	23	66	4	2	6	33	8	.80	5	.303	.350	.436
2006	Sea	AL	161	695	224	20	9	9	(6	3)	289	110	49	107	49	16	71	5	1	2	45	2	.96	3	.322	.370	.416
2007	Sea	AL	161	678	238	22	7	6	(3	3)	292	111	68	128	49	13	77	3	4	2	37	8	.82	7	.351	.396	.431
7 ML YEARS			1118	4774	1592	177	57	67	(38	29)	2084	782	427	810	329	115	461	35	19	23	272	66	.80	34	.333	.379	.437

Kurt Suzuki

Bats: R **Throws:** R **Pos:** C-66; DH-2; PH-2; PR-1 **Ht:** 6'0" **Wt:** 205 **Born:** 10/4/1983 **Age:** 24

Year	Team	Lg	G	AB	H	2B	3B	HR	(Hm	Rd)	TB	R	RBI	RC	TBB	IBB	SO	HBP	SH	SF	SB	CS	SB%	GDP	Avg	OBP	Slg
2004	Vancvr	A	46	175	52	10	3	3	(-	-)	77	27	31	32	18	0	26	12	3	3	0	1	.00	3	.297	.394	.440
2005	Stcktn	A+	114	441	122	26	5	12	(-	-)	194	85	65	79	63	0	61	12	2	5	5	3	.63	16	.277	.378	.440
2006	Mdland	AA	99	376	107	26	1	7	(-	-)	156	64	55	66	58	1	50	9	0	1	5	3	.63	15	.285	.392	.415
2007	Scrmto	AAA	55	211	59	9	0	3	(-	-)	77	32	27	29	21	1	41	4	1	3	0	0	-	10	.280	.351	.365
2007	Oak	AL	68	213	53	13	0	7	(4	3)	87	27	39	33	24	0	39	3	3	5	0	0	-	4	.249	.327	.408

Mark Sweeney

Bats: L **Throws:** L **Pos:** PH-90; 1B-13; LF-7; RF-3 **Ht:** 6'1" **Wt:** 215 **Born:** 10/26/1969 **Age:** 38

Year	Team	Lg	G	AB	H	2B	3B	HR	(Hm	Rd)	TB	R	RBI	RC	TBB	IBB	SO	HBP	SH	SF	SB	CS	SB%	GDP	Avg	OBP	Slg
1995	StL	NL	37	77	21	2	0	2	(0	2)	29	5	13	10	10	0	15	0	1	2	1	1	.50	3	.273	.348	.377
1996	StL	NL	98	170	45	9	0	3	(0	3)	63	32	22	27	33	2	29	1	5	0	3	0	1.00	4	.265	.387	.371
1997	2 Tms	NL	115	164	46	7	0	2	(2	0)	59	16	23	22	20	1	32	1	1	2	2	3	.40	3	.280	.358	.360
1998	SD	NL	122	192	45	8	3	2	(1	1)	65	17	15	21	26	0	37	1	0	3	1	2	.33	5	.234	.324	.339
1999	Cin	NL	37	31	11	3	0	2	(1	1)	20	6	7	7	4	1	9	0	0	0	0	0	-	2	.355	.429	.645
2000	Mil	NL	71	73	16	6	0	1	(0	1)	25	9	6	9	12	1	18	1	1	0	0	0	-	1	.219	.337	.342
2001	Mil	NL	48	89	23	3	1	3	(1	2)	37	9	11	14	12	0	23	0	2	0	2	1	.67	0	.258	.347	.416
2002	Mil	NL	48	65	11	3	0	1	(0	1)	17	3	4	1	4	0	19	0	0	1	0	0	-	1	.169	.217	.262
2003	Col	NL	67	97	25	9	0	2	(1	1)	40	13	14	15	9	1	27	0	0	1	0	1	.00	2	.258	.321	.412
2004	Col	NL	122	177	47	12	2	9	(6	3)	90	25	40	36	32	2	51	2	0	4	1	0	1.00	2	.266	.377	.508
2005	SD	NL	135	221	65	12	1	8	(3	5)	103	31	40	37	40	3	58	0	1	5	4	0	1.00	6	.294	.395	.466
2006	SF	NL	114	259	65	15	2	5	(0	5)	99	32	37	34	28	3	50	3	0	1	2	1	.67	1	.251	.330	.382
2007	2 Tms	NL	106	123	32	9	0	2	(0	2)	47	20	13	15	14	0	29	3	1	0	2	0	1.00	3	.260	.350	.382
97	StL	NL	44	61	13	3	0	0	(0	0)	16	5	4	5	9	1	14	1	1	1	0	1	.00	2	.213	.319	.262
97	SD	NL	71	103	33	4	0	2	(2	0)	43	11	19	17	11	0	18	0	0	1	2	2	.50	1	.320	.383	.417
07	SF	NL	76	90	23	8	0	2	(0	2)	37	18	10	13	13	0	18	1	1	0	2	0	1.00	1	.256	.368	.411
07	LAD	NL	30	33	9	1	0	0	(0	0)	10	2	3	2	1	0	11	0	0	0	0	0	-	2	.273	.294	.303
13 ML YEARS			1120	1738	452	98	9	42	(15	27)	694	218	245	248	244	14	397	12	12	17	16	9	.64	35	.260	.352	.399

Mike Sweeney

Bats: R **Throws:** R **Pos:** DH-65; 1B-6; PH-4 **Ht:** 6'3" **Wt:** 225 **Born:** 7/22/1973 **Age:** 34

Year	Team	Lg	G	AB	H	2B	3B	HR	(Hm	Rd)	TB	R	RBI	RC	TBB	IBB	SO	HBP	SH	SF	SB	CS	SB%	GDP	Avg	OBP	Slg
2007	Omha*	AAA	6	21	4	1	0	0	(-	-)	5	1	1	1	0	0	4	1	0	1	0	0	-	0	.190	.217	.238
1995	KC	AL	4	4	1	0	0	0	(0	0)	1	1	0	0	0	0	0	0	0	0	0	0	-	0	.250	.250	.250
1996	KC	AL	50	165	46	10	4	4	(1	3)	68	23	24	23	18	0	21	4	0	3	1	2	.33	7	.279	.358	.412
1997	KC	AL	84	240	58	8	0	7	(5	2)	87	30	31	25	17	0	33	6	1	2	3	2	.60	1	.242	.306	.363
1998	KC	AL	92	282	73	18	0	8	(6	2)	115	32	35	35	24	1	38	2	2	1	2	3	.40	7	.259	.320	.408

254

Year Team	Lg	G	AB	H	2B	3B	HR	(Hm	Rd)	TB	R	RBI	RC	TBB	IBB	SO	HBP	SH	SF	SB	CS	SB%	GDP	Avg	OBP	Slg
1999 KC	AL	150	575	185	44	2	22	(10	12)	299	101	102	109	54	0	48	10	0	4	6	1	.86	21	.322	.387	.520
2000 KC	AL	159	618	206	30	0	29	(17	12)	323	105	144	128	71	5	67	15	0	13	8	3	.73	15	.333	.407	.523
2001 KC	AL	147	559	170	46	0	29	(14	15)	303	97	99	109	64	13	64	2	1	6	10	3	.77	13	.304	.374	.542
2002 KC	AL	126	471	160	31	1	24	(14	10)	265	81	86	112	61	10	46	6	0	7	9	7	.56	9	.340	.417	.563
2003 KC	AL	108	392	115	18	1	16	(7	9)	183	62	83	83	64	5	56	2	0	5	3	2	.60	13	.293	.391	.467
2004 KC	AL	106	411	118	23	0	22	(8	14)	207	56	79	76	33	9	44	6	0	2	3	2	.60	7	.287	.347	.504
2005 KC	AL	122	470	141	39	0	21	(7	14)	243	63	83	80	33	7	61	4	1	6	3	0	1.00	16	.300	.347	.517
2006 KC	AL	60	217	56	15	0	8	(4	4)	95	23	33	33	28	5	48	4	0	3	2	0	1.00	5	.258	.349	.438
2007 KC	AL	74	265	69	15	1	7	(6	1)	107	26	38	39	17	4	29	5	0	2	0	0	-	9	.260	.315	.404
13 ML YEARS		1282	4669	1398	297	5	197	(99	98)	2296	700	837	851	484	59	555	66	5	54	50	25	.67	130	.299	.369	.492

Ryan Sweeney

Bats: L Throws: L Pos: LF-11; CF-3; PH-2   Ht: 6'4" Wt: 215 Born: 2/20/1985 Age: 23

Year Team	Lg	G	AB	H	2B	3B	HR	(Hm	Rd)	TB	R	RBI	RC	TBB	IBB	SO	HBP	SH	SF	SB	CS	SB%	GDP	Avg	OBP	Slg
2003 Bristol	R+	19	67	21	3	0	2	(-	-)	30	11	5	12	7	0	10	1	1	0	3	0	1.00	1	.313	.387	.448
2003 Gr Falls	R+	10	34	12	2	0	0	(-	-)	14	0	4	4	2	0	3	0	0	0	0	2	.00	1	.353	.389	.412
2004 WinSa	A+	134	515	146	22	3	7	(-	-)	195	71	66	69	40	1	65	7	3	2	8	6	.57	3	.283	.342	.379
2005 Brham	AA	113	429	128	22	3	1	(-	-)	159	64	47	60	35	4	53	7	7	5	6	6	.50	5	.298	.357	.371
2006 Charltt	AAA	118	449	133	25	3	13	(-	-)	203	64	70	71	35	5	73	3	3	2	7	7	.50	9	.296	.350	.452
2007 Charltt	AAA	105	397	107	17	2	10	(-	-)	158	50	47	58	48	2	71	1	2	2	8	5	.62	14	.270	.348	.398
2006 CWS	AL	18	35	8	0	0	0	(0	0)	8	1	5	1	0	0	7	0	0	0	0	0	-	1	.229	.229	.229
2007 CWS	AL	15	45	9	3	0	1	(1	0)	15	5	5	2	4	0	5	0	0	0	0	1	.00	2	.200	.265	.333
2 ML YEARS		33	80	17	3	0	1	(1	0)	23	6	10	3	4	0	12	0	0	0	0	1	.00	3	.213	.250	.288

Nick Swisher

Bats: B Throws: L Pos: CF-60; RF-57; 1B-44; DH-6; PH-1   Ht: 6'0" Wt: 216 Born: 11/25/1980 Age: 27

Year Team	Lg	G	AB	H	2B	3B	HR	(Hm	Rd)	TB	R	RBI	RC	TBB	IBB	SO	HBP	SH	SF	SB	CS	SB%	GDP	Avg	OBP	Slg
2004 Oak	AL	20	60	15	4	0	2	(1	1)	25	11	8	8	8	0	11	2	0	1	0	0	-	2	.250	.352	.417
2005 Oak	AL	131	462	109	32	1	21	(11	10)	206	66	74	62	55	3	110	4	0	1	0	1	.00	9	.236	.322	.446
2006 Oak	AL	157	556	141	24	2	35	(17	18)	274	106	95	95	97	7	152	11	2	6	1	2	.33	13	.254	.372	.493
2007 Oak	AL	150	539	141	36	1	22	(8	14)	245	84	78	89	100	12	131	10	1	9	3	2	.60	13	.262	.381	.455
4 ML YEARS		458	1617	406	96	4	80	(37	43)	750	267	255	254	260	22	404	27	3	17	4	5	.44	37	.251	.361	.464

Jon Switzer

Pitches: L Bats: L Pos: RP-21   Ht: 6'3" Wt: 190 Born: 8/13/1979 Age: 28

Year Team	Lg	G	GS	CG	GF	IP	BFP	H	R	ER	HR	SH	SF	HB	TBB	IBB	SO	WP	Bk	W	L	Pct	ShO	Sv-Op	Hld	ERC	ERA
2007 Drham*	AAA	23	0	0	6	33.0	126	26	4	3	0	1	1	1	8	1	23	0	0	0	0	-	0	1--	-	1.98	0.82
2003 TB	AL	5	0	0	1	9.2	46	13	8	8	2	0	1	4	3	0	7	1	0	0	0	-	0	0-0	0	8.88	7.45
2005 TB	AL	2	0	0	0	4.0	25	5	4	3	0	0	0	0	7	0	5	0	0	0	0	-	0	0-0	0	9.71	6.75
2006 TB	AL	40	0	0	6	33.2	157	38	19	17	5	2	1	1	19	3	18	3	0	2	2	.500	0	0-3	5	5.78	4.54
2007 TB	AL	21	0	0	2	19.0	88	27	17	17	2	0	1	0	7	1	13	1	0	0	2	.000	0	0-0	3	6.47	8.05
4 ML YEARS		68	0	0	9	66.1	316	83	48	45	9	2	3	5	36	4	43	5	0	2	4	.333	0	0-3	8	6.65	6.11

So Taguchi

Bats: R Throws: R Pos: CF-63; LF-41; PH-38; RF-8; PR-6; 2B-1   Ht: 5'10" Wt: 170 Born: 7/2/1969 Age: 38

Year Team	Lg	G	AB	H	2B	3B	HR	(Hm	Rd)	TB	R	RBI	RC	TBB	IBB	SO	HBP	SH	SF	SB	CS	SB%	GDP	Avg	OBP	Slg
2002 StL	NL	19	15	6	0	0	0	(0	0)	6	4	2	4	2	0	1	0	2	0	1	0	1.00	0	.400	.471	.400
2003 StL	NL	43	54	14	3	1	3	(1	2)	28	9	13	11	4	1	11	0	1	0	0	0	-	2	.259	.310	.519
2004 StL	NL	109	179	52	10	2	3	(1	2)	75	26	25	27	12	1	23	2	10	3	6	3	.67	6	.291	.337	.419
2005 StL	NL	143	396	114	21	2	8	(5	3)	163	45	53	59	20	2	62	2	2	4	11	2	.85	11	.288	.322	.412
2006 StL	NL	134	316	84	19	1	2	(0	2)	111	46	31	35	32	1	48	2	9	2	11	3	.79	9	.266	.335	.351
2007 StL	NL	130	307	89	15	0	3	(0	3)	113	48	30	41	23	0	32	6	3	1	7	4	.64	10	.290	.350	.368
6 ML YEARS		578	1267	359	68	6	19	(7	12)	496	178	154	177	93	5	177	12	27	10	36	12	.75	38	.283	.336	.391

Brian Tallet

Pitches: L Bats: L Pos: RP-48   Ht: 6'7" Wt: 220 Born: 9/21/1977 Age: 30

Year Team	Lg	G	GS	CG	GF	IP	BFP	H	R	ER	HR	SH	SF	HB	TBB	IBB	SO	WP	Bk	W	L	Pct	ShO	Sv-Op	Hld	ERC	ERA
2007 Syrcse*	AAA	7	0	0	3	6.2	27	4	2	1	1	0	1	0	3	0	11	0	0	0	0	-	0	0--	-	2.45	1.35
2002 Cle	AL	2	2	0	0	12.0	47	9	3	2	0	0	0	1	4	0	5	0	0	1	0	1.000	0	0-0	0	2.31	1.50
2003 Cle	AL	5	3	0	1	19.0	87	23	14	10	2	2	0	1	8	0	9	0	0	0	2	.000	0	0-0	0	5.65	4.74
2005 Cle	AL	2	0	0	0	4.2	24	6	4	4	2	0	0	1	3	0	2	0	0	0	0	-	0	0-0	0	10.55	7.71
2006 Tor	AL	44	1	0	8	54.1	229	45	24	23	5	1	5	3	31	4	37	2	1	3	0	1.000	0	0-0	5	3.97	3.81
2007 Tor	AL	48	0	0	11	62.1	267	49	26	24	1	2	3	6	28	7	54	1	0	2	4	.333	0	0-3	1	2.68	3.47
5 ML YEARS		101	6	0	20	152.1	654	132	71	63	10	5	8	12	74	11	107	3	1	6	6	.500	0	0-3	6	3.65	3.72

Taylor Tankersley

Pitches: L Bats: L Pos: RP-67   Ht: 6'1" Wt: 220 Born: 3/7/1983 Age: 25

Year	Team	Lg	G	GS	CG	GF	IP	BFP	H	R	ER	HR	SH	SF	HB	TBB	IBB	SO	WP	Bk	W	L	Pct	ShO	Sv-Op	Hld	ERC	ERA
2004	Jmstwn	A-	6	6	0	0	26.2	116	21	14	10	2	4	4	0	8	0	32	1	2	1	1	.500	0	0- -	-	2.21	3.38
2005	Grnsbr	A	12	12	0	0	66.0	297	74	45	38	12	0	1	2	25	0	63	3	1	2	7	.222	0	0- -	-	5.33	5.18
2005	Jupiter	A+	4	4	1	0	24.0	102	21	10	9	1	0	1	0	9	0	19	0	0	1	0	1.000	0	0- -	-	2.85	3.38
2006	Carlina	AA	22	0	0	14	28.1	110	11	4	3	0	6	1	1	14	1	40	1	0	4	1	.800	0	6- -	-	1.13	0.95
2007	Jupiter	A+	4	0	0	0	4.0	16	4	3	3	1	0	0	0	0	0	5	0	0	1	0	1.000	0	0- -	-	3.33	6.75
2007	Albq	AAA	7	0	0	1	5.2	22	3	3	3	1	2	0	0	2	0	5	0	0	0	1	1.000	0	0- -	-	1.94	4.76
2006	Fla	NL	49	0	0	10	41.0	178	33	14	13	4	3	3	1	26	5	46	3	0	2	1	.667	0	3-7	22	3.80	2.85
2007	Fla	NL	67	0	0	12	47.1	205	42	22	21	4	0	2	3	29	3	49	2	0	6	1	.857	0	1-3	16	4.45	3.99
	2 ML YEARS		116	0	0	22	88.1	383	75	36	34	8	3	5	4	55	8	95	5	0	8	2	.800	0	4-10	38	4.14	3.46

Jack Taschner

Pitches: L Bats: L Pos: RP-63   Ht: 6'3" Wt: 210 Born: 4/21/1978 Age: 30

Year	Team	Lg	G	GS	CG	GF	IP	BFP	H	R	ER	HR	SH	SF	HB	TBB	IBB	SO	WP	Bk	W	L	Pct	ShO	Sv-Op	Hld	ERC	ERA
2005	SF	NL	24	0	0	7	22.2	95	15	5	4	0	0	1	0	13	0	19	0	0	2	0	1.000	0	0-1	3	2.25	1.59
2006	SF	NL	24	0	0	6	19.1	101	31	23	18	4	0	2	0	7	0	15	3	0	0	1	.000	0	0-1	3	8.55	8.38
2007	SF	NL	63	0	0	16	50.0	222	44	31	30	4	2	3	1	29	2	51	2	0	3	1	.750	0	0-2	13	3.92	5.40
	3 ML YEARS		111	0	0	29	92.0	418	90	59	52	8	2	6	3	49	2	85	5	0	5	2	.714	0	0-4	19	4.36	5.09

Jordan Tata

Pitches: R Bats: R Pos: SP-3   Ht: 6'6" Wt: 220 Born: 9/20/1981 Age: 26

Year	Team	Lg	G	GS	CG	GF	IP	BFP	H	R	ER	HR	SH	SF	HB	TBB	IBB	SO	WP	Bk	W	L	Pct	ShO	Sv-Op	Hld	ERC	ERA
2003	Oneont	A-	16	12	0	2	73.1	306	64	32	21	7	5	4	6	20	0	60	4	1	4	3	.571	0	1- -	-	2.63	2.58
2004	WMich	A	28	28	1	0	166.1	705	167	77	62	7	12	3	9	68	2	116	15	0	8	11	.421	0	0- -	-	4.04	3.35
2005	Lkland	A+	25	25	2	0	155.0	628	138	55	48	12	2	1	8	41	1	134	11	1	13	2	.867	2	0- -	-	3.08	2.79
2006	Toledo	AAA	21	21	1	0	122.0	530	117	58	52	11	5	4	7	49	2	86	10	0	10	6	.625	1	0- -	-	3.96	3.84
2007	Toledo	AAA	14	14	0	0	82.2	338	67	31	28	8	3	2	1	28	0	50	2	0	4	5	.444	0	0- -	-	2.86	3.05
2006	Det	AL	8	0	0	2	14.2	65	14	11	10	1	0	2	0	7	1	6	0	0	0	0	-	0	0-0	0	3.69	6.14
2007	Det	AL	3	3	0	0	14.0	64	16	12	12	1	0	1	2	8	1	8	0	0	1	1	.500	0	0-0	0	6.06	7.71
	2 ML YEARS		11	3	0	2	28.2	129	30	23	22	2	0	3	2	15	2	14	0	0	1	1	.500	0	0-0	0	4.79	6.91

Ty Taubenheim

Pitches: R Bats: R Pos: SP-1   Ht: 6'5" Wt: 200 Born: 11/17/1982 Age: 25

Year	Team	Lg	G	GS	CG	GF	IP	BFP	H	R	ER	HR	SH	SF	HB	TBB	IBB	SO	WP	Bk	W	L	Pct	ShO	Sv-Op	Hld	ERC	ERA
2003	Helena	R+	14	0	0	2	50.1	196	47	13	12	3	4	0	2	3	0	44	2	1	6	1	.857	0	1- -	-	2.41	2.15
2004	Beloit	A	47	0	0	36	92.1	378	81	41	37	10	1	0	3	17	0	106	2	0	5	3	.625	0	12- -	-	2.72	3.61
2005	BrvdCt	A+	16	16	2	0	106.0	420	86	34	31	7	3	1	9	26	0	75	8	0	10	2	.833	1	0- -	-	2.69	2.63
2005	Hntsvl	AA	11	11	0	0	64.0	281	64	36	31	7	8	4	1	24	1	44	3	0	2	6	.250	0	0- -	-	3.98	4.36
2006	Syrcse	AAA	18	14	0	0	75.2	310	75	25	24	9	2	0	3	18	0	48	4	0	2	4	.333	0	0- -	-	3.77	2.85
2007	Syrcse	AAA	19	16	1	0	89.0	402	107	64	63	12	1	1	6	33	0	73	4	1	4	7	.364	1	0- -	-	5.71	6.37
2007	NHam	AA	5	5	0	0	31.1	123	21	7	7	2	1	0	2	11	0	29	3	0	2	1	.667	0	0- -	-	2.27	2.01
2006	Tor	AL	12	7	0	1	35.0	167	40	22	19	5	1	2	4	18	0	26	1	0	1	5	.167	0	0-0	0	6.05	4.89
2007	Tor	AL	1	1	0	0	5.0	24	5	5	5	1	0	1	1	4	0	4	1	0	0	0	-	0	0-0	0	7.56	9.00
	2 ML YEARS		13	8	0	1	40.0	191	45	27	24	6	1	3	5	22	0	30	2	0	1	5	.167	0	0-0	0	6.23	5.40

Julian Tavarez

Pitches: R Bats: L Pos: SP-23; RP-11   Ht: 6'2" Wt: 195 Born: 5/22/1973 Age: 35

Year	Team	Lg	G	GS	CG	GF	IP	BFP	H	R	ER	HR	SH	SF	HB	TBB	IBB	SO	WP	Bk	W	L	Pct	ShO	Sv-Op	Hld	ERC	ERA
1993	Cle	AL	8	7	0	0	37.0	172	53	29	27	7	0	1	2	13	2	19	3	1	2	2	.500	0	0-0	0	7.48	6.57
1994	Cle	AL	1	1	0	0	1.2	14	6	8	4	1	0	1	0	1	1	0	0	0	0	1	.000	0	0-0	0	24.13	21.60
1995	Cle	AL	57	0	0	15	85.0	350	76	36	23	7	0	2	3	21	0	68	3	2	10	2	.833	0	0-4	19	2.93	2.44
1996	Cle	AL	51	4	0	13	80.2	353	101	49	48	9	5	4	1	22	5	46	1	0	4	7	.364	0	0-0	13	5.12	5.36
1997	SF	NL	89	0	0	13	88.1	378	91	43	38	6	3	8	4	34	5	38	4	0	6	4	.600	0	0-3	26	4.13	3.87
1998	SF	NL	60	0	0	12	85.1	374	96	41	36	5	5	3	8	36	11	52	1	1	5	3	.625	0	1-6	10	4.89	3.80
1999	SF	NL	47	0	0	12	54.2	258	65	38	36	7	3	2	8	25	3	33	4	1	2	0	1.000	0	0-2	5	6.10	5.93
2000	Col	NL	51	12	0	8	120.0	530	124	68	59	11	3	4	7	53	9	62	2	1	11	5	.688	0	1-1	6	4.49	4.43
2001	ChC	NL	34	28	1	1	161.1	712	172	98	81	13	8	4	11	69	4	107	2	1	10	9	.526	0	0-0	2	4.70	4.52
2002	Fla	NL	29	27	0	1	153.2	714	188	100	92	9	13	2	15	74	7	67	7	2	10	12	.455	0	0-1	0	5.75	5.39
2003	Pit	NL	64	0	0	29	83.2	350	75	37	34	1	9	1	5	27	8	39	3	0	3	3	.500	0	11-14	9	2.72	3.66
2004	StL	NL	77	0	0	27	64.1	268	57	21	17	1	3	1	6	19	0	48	2	1	7	4	.636	0	4-6	19	2.87	2.38
2005	StL	NL	74	0	0	16	65.2	278	68	28	25	6	3	3	8	19	4	47	1	0	2	3	.400	0	4-6	32	4.29	3.43
2006	Bos	AL	58	6	1	11	98.2	431	110	54	49	10	3	6	4	44	3	56	2	0	5	4	.556	0	1-3	2	5.32	4.47
2007	Bos	AL	34	23	0	2	134.2	604	151	89	77	14	3	5	7	51	4	77	4	0	7	11	.389	0	0-0	1	4.83	5.15
	15 ML YEARS		734	108	2	160	1314.2	5786	1433	739	646	107	61	44	91	508	66	759	39	10	84	70	.545	0	22-46	144	4.63	4.42

Willy Taveras

Bats: R **Throws:** R **Pos:** CF-86; PH-8; DH-3; PR-1   **Ht:** 6'0" **Wt:** 160 **Born:** 12/25/1981 **Age:** 26

Year	Team	Lg	G	AB	H	2B	3B	HR	(Hm	Rd)	TB	R	RBI	RC	TBB	IBB	SO	HBP	SH	SF	SB	CS	SB%	GDP	Avg	OBP	Slg
2007	ColSpr*	AAA	4	14	5	0	0	0	(-	-)	5	0	0	1	0	0	2	1	0	0	1	2	.33	1	.357	.400	.357
2004	Hou	NL	10	1	0	0	0	0	(0	0)	0	2	0	0	0	0	1	0	1	0	1	0	1.00	0	.000	.000	.000
2005	Hou	NL	152	592	172	13	4	3	(2	1)	202	82	29	61	25	1	103	7	7	4	34	11	.76	4	.291	.325	.341
2006	Hou	NL	149	529	147	19	5	1	(0	1)	179	83	30	64	34	0	88	11	11	2	33	9	.79	6	.278	.333	.338
2007	Col	NL	97	372	119	13	2	2	(2	0)	142	64	24	56	21	0	55	7	7	1	33	9	.79	1	.320	.367	.382
	4 ML YEARS		408	1494	438	45	11	6	(4	2)	523	231	83	181	80	1	247	25	26	7	101	29	.78	11	.293	.338	.350

Mark Teahen

Bats: L **Throws:** R **Pos:** RF-137; 1B-9; CF-5; PH-4   **Ht:** 6'3" **Wt:** 210 **Born:** 9/6/1981 **Age:** 26

Year	Team	Lg	G	AB	H	2B	3B	HR	(Hm	Rd)	TB	R	RBI	RC	TBB	IBB	SO	HBP	SH	SF	SB	CS	SB%	GDP	Avg	OBP	Slg
2005	KC	AL	130	447	110	29	4	7	(3	4)	168	60	55	52	40	2	107	1	2	1	7	2	.78	13	.246	.309	.376
2006	KC	AL	109	393	114	21	7	18	(9	9)	203	70	69	79	40	2	85	2	2	2	10	0	1.00	5	.290	.357	.517
2007	KC	AL	144	544	155	31	8	7	(6	1)	223	78	60	82	55	8	127	3	4	2	13	5	.72	23	.285	.353	.410
	3 ML YEARS		383	1384	379	81	19	32	(18	14)	594	208	184	213	135	12	319	6	8	5	30	7	.81	41	.274	.340	.429

Mark Teixeira

Bats: B **Throws:** R **Pos:** 1B-128; DH-4   **Ht:** 6'3" **Wt:** 220 **Born:** 4/11/1980 **Age:** 28

Year	Team	Lg	G	AB	H	2B	3B	HR	(Hm	Rd)	TB	R	RBI	RC	TBB	IBB	SO	HBP	SH	SF	SB	CS	SB%	GDP	Avg	OBP	Slg
2007	Frisco*	AA	1	2	0	0	0	0	(-	-)	0	0	0	0	2	0	0	0	0	0	0	0	-	0	.000	.500	.000
2003	Tex	AL	146	529	137	29	5	26	(19	7)	254	66	84	78	44	5	120	14	0	2	1	2	.33	14	.259	.331	.480
2004	Tex	AL	145	545	153	34	2	38	(18	20)	305	101	112	120	68	12	117	10	0	2	4	1	.80	6	.281	.370	.560
2005	Tex	AL	162	644	194	41	3	43	(30	13)	370	112	144	148	72	5	124	11	0	3	4	0	1.00	18	.301	.379	.575
2006	Tex	AL	162	628	177	45	1	33	(12	21)	323	99	110	114	89	12	128	4	0	6	2	0	1.00	17	.282	.371	.514
2007	2 Tms		132	494	151	33	2	30	(14	16)	278	86	105	116	72	13	112	7	0	2	0	0	-	7	.306	.400	.563
07	Tex	AL	78	286	85	24	1	13	(5	8)	150	48	49	58	45	10	66	3	0	1	0	0	-	5	.297	.397	.524
07	Atl	NL	54	208	66	9	1	17	(9	8)	128	38	56	58	27	3	46	4	0	1	0	0	-	2	.317	.404	.615
	5 ML YEARS		747	2840	812	182	13	170	(93	77)	1530	464	555	576	345	47	601	46	0	15	11	3	.79	62	.286	.371	.539

Miguel Tejada

Bats: R **Throws:** R **Pos:** SS-125; DH-8; PH-1   **Ht:** 5'9" **Wt:** 215 **Born:** 5/25/1976 **Age:** 32

Year	Team	Lg	G	AB	H	2B	3B	HR	(Hm	Rd)	TB	R	RBI	RC	TBB	IBB	SO	HBP	SH	SF	SB	CS	SB%	GDP	Avg	OBP	Slg
2007	Frdrck*	A+	1	2	2	0	0	1	(-	-)	5	1	1	2	1	0	0	0	0	0	0	0	-	0	1.000	1.000	2.500
2007	Bowie*	AA	1	3	0	0	0	0	(-	-)	0	0	1	0	0	0	0	0	0	0	0	0	-	0	.000	.000	.000
1997	Oak	AL	26	99	20	3	2	2	(1	1)	33	10	10	7	2	0	22	3	0	0	2	0	1.00	3	.202	.240	.333
1998	Oak	AL	105	365	85	20	1	11	(5	6)	140	53	45	40	28	0	86	7	4	3	5	6	.45	8	.233	.298	.384
1999	Oak	AL	159	593	149	33	4	21	(12	9)	253	93	84	82	57	3	94	10	9	5	8	7	.53	11	.251	.325	.427
2000	Oak	AL	160	607	167	32	1	30	(16	14)	291	105	115	99	66	6	102	4	2	2	6	0	1.00	15	.275	.349	.479
2001	Oak	AL	162	622	166	31	3	31	(17	14)	296	107	113	94	43	5	89	13	1	4	11	5	.69	14	.267	.326	.476
2002	Oak	AL	162	662	204	30	0	34	(17	17)	336	108	131	123	38	3	84	11	0	4	7	2	.78	21	.308	.354	.508
2003	Oak	AL	162	636	177	42	0	27	(15	12)	300	98	106	103	53	7	65	6	0	8	10	0	1.00	12	.278	.336	.472
2004	Bal	AL	162	653	203	40	2	34	(17	17)	349	107	150	124	48	6	73	10	0	14	4	1	.80	24	.311	.360	.534
2005	Bal	AL	162	654	199	50	5	26	(16	10)	337	89	98	102	40	9	83	7	0	3	5	1	.83	26	.304	.349	.515
2006	Bal	AL	162	648	214	37	0	24	(17	7)	323	99	100	99	46	10	79	9	0	6	6	2	.75	28	.330	.379	.498
2007	Bal	AL	133	514	152	19	1	18	(12	6)	227	72	81	76	41	9	55	10	0	3	2	1	.67	22	.296	.357	.442
	11 ML YEARS		1555	6053	1736	337	19	258	(145	113)	2885	941	1033	949	462	58	832	90	16	52	66	25	.73	184	.287	.344	.477

Robinson Tejeda

Pitches: R **Bats:** R **Pos:** SP-19   **Ht:** 6'3" **Wt:** 229 **Born:** 3/24/1982 **Age:** 26

			HOW MUCH HE PITCHED					WHAT HE GAVE UP											THE RESULTS							
Year	Team	Lg	G	GS	CG	GF	IP	BFP	H	R	ER	HR	SH	SF	HB	TBB	IBB	SO	WP	Bk	W	L	Pct	ShO	Sv-Op	Hld	ERC	ERA
2007	Okla*	AAA	5	4	0	1	18.2	94	27	18	17	0	0	1	0	15	0	20	4	0	1	3	.250	0	0--	-	7.75	8.20
2005	Phi	NL	26	13	0	5	85.2	371	67	36	34	5	3	2	8	51	4	72	3	1	4	3	.571	0	0-0	1	3.64	3.57
2006	Tex	NL	14	14	0	0	73.2	329	83	40	35	10	1	5	3	32	1	40	1	1	5	5	.500	0	0-0	0	5.41	4.28
2007	Tex	AL	19	19	0	0	95.1	454	110	78	70	17	3	6	6	60	2	69	10	0	5	9	.357	0	0-0	0	6.77	6.61
	3 ML YEARS		59	46	0	5	254.2	1154	260	154	139	32	7	13	17	143	7	181	14	2	14	17	.452	0	0-0	1	5.28	4.91

Luis Terrero

Bats: R **Throws:** R **Pos:** CF-38; RF-15; PH-13; LF-5; PR-4; DH-1   **Ht:** 6'3" **Wt:** 205 **Born:** 5/18/1980 **Age:** 28

Year	Team	Lg	G	AB	H	2B	3B	HR	(Hm	Rd)	TB	R	RBI	RC	TBB	IBB	SO	HBP	SH	SF	SB	CS	SB%	GDP	Avg	OBP	Slg
2007	Charltt*	AAA	20	65	15	4	0	4	(-	-)	31	7	9	8	1	0	15	1	0	0	3	1	.75	4	.231	.254	.477
2003	Ari	NL	5	4	1	0	0	0	(0	0)	1	0	0	1	0	0	1	1	0	0	0	0	-	0	.250	.400	.250
2004	Ari	NL	62	229	56	14	0	4	(2	2)	82	21	14	25	20	2	78	5	1	0	10	2	.83	5	.245	.319	.358
2005	Ari	NL	88	161	37	6	1	4	(2	2)	57	23	20	17	14	0	40	6	2	1	3	2	.60	5	.230	.313	.354
2006	Bal	AL	27	40	8	1	0	1	(0	1)	12	4	6	3	1	0	7	1	0	0	0	3	.00	0	.200	.238	.300
2007	CWS	AL	61	117	27	2	0	5	(2	3)	44	18	12	18	12	0	35	9	1	0	4	3	.57	1	.231	.348	.376
	5 ML YEARS		243	551	129	23	1	14	(6	8)	196	66	52	64	47	2	161	22	4	1	17	10	.63	11	.234	.319	.356

Marcus Thames

Bats: R **Throws:** R **Pos:** LF-37; 1B-33; RF-9; PH-9; DH-6 **Ht:** 6'2" **Wt:** 220 **Born:** 3/6/1977 **Age:** 31

Year	Team	Lg	G	AB	H	2B	3B	HR	(Hm	Rd)	TB	R	RBI	RC	TBB	IBB	SO	HBP	SH	SF	SB	CS	SB%	GDP	Avg	OBP	Slg
2007	Toledo*	AAA	2	8	3	0	0	1	(-	-)	6	2	2	2	0	0	1	0	0	0	0	0	-	1	.375	.375	.750
2002	NYY	AL	7	13	3	1	0	1	(1	0)	7	2	2	2	0	0	4	0	0	0	0	0	-	0	.231	.231	.538
2003	Tex	AL	30	73	15	2	0	1	(0	1)	20	12	4	5	8	0	18	2	0	1	0	1	.00	2	.205	.298	.274
2004	Det	AL	61	165	42	12	0	10	(5	5)	84	24	33	30	16	0	42	2	0	1	0	1	.00	3	.255	.326	.509
2005	Det	AL	38	107	21	2	0	7	(3	4)	44	11	16	10	9	1	38	1	0	1	0	0	-	1	.196	.263	.411
2006	Det	AL	110	348	89	20	2	26	(11	15)	191	61	60	60	37	0	92	4	0	1	1	1	.50	0	.256	.333	.549
2007	Det	AL	86	269	65	15	0	18	(14	4)	134	37	54	39	13	1	72	1	0	1	2	1	.67	6	.242	.278	.498
	6 ML YEARS		332	975	235	52	2	63	(34	29)	480	147	169	146	83	2	266	10	0	5	3	4	.43	12	.241	.306	.492

Joe Thatcher

Pitches: L **Bats:** L **Pos:** RP-22 **Ht:** 6'2" **Wt:** 228 **Born:** 10/4/1981 **Age:** 26

			HOW MUCH HE PITCHED					WHAT HE GAVE UP										THE RESULTS							
Year	Team	Lg	G	GS	CG	GF	IP	BFP	H	R	ER	HR	SH	SF	HB	TBB	IBB	SO	WP	Bk	W	L	Pct	ShO	Sv-Op	Hld	ERC	ERA
2005	Helena	R+	6	0	0	6	7.2	32	8	3	3	1	0	0	1	1	0	10	0	0	2	0	1.000	0	2--	-	3.89	3.52
2005	BrvdCt	A+	7	0	0	4	9.0	32	6	0	0	0	0	0	0	0	0	14	3	0	0	0	-	0	2--	-	0.94	0.00
2006	WV	A	26	0	0	25	29.2	126	28	13	8	2	0	1	4	6	0	42	1	0	1	3	.250	0	10--	-	3.26	2.43
2006	BrvdCt	A+	16	0	0	12	30.2	114	12	6	1	1	2	0	2	9	0	32	0	0	3	1	.750	0	2--	-	0.98	0.29
2006	Hntsvl	AA	4	0	0	1	5.1	21	2	2	1	0	0	1	1	2	0	6	0	0	1	0	1.000	0	2--	-	1.18	1.69
2007	Hntsvl	AA	11	0	0	3	16.1	61	11	1	1	0	1	0	1	2	0	20	0	0	1	0	1.000	0	0--	-	1.32	0.55
2007	Nashv	AAA	24	0	0	5	21.2	94	19	5	5	0	2	0	1	7	1	33	4	1	2	1	.667	0	1--	-	2.44	2.08
2007	Portlnd	AAA	8	0	0	1	8.2	38	10	4	1	0	0	0	1	1	0	11	1	0	1	0	1.000	0	0--	-	3.47	1.04
2007	SD	NL	22	0	0	5	21.0	85	13	6	3	1	0	1	1	6	2	16	0	0	2	2	.500	0	0-0	2	1.49	1.29

Ryan Theriot

Bats: R **Throws:** R **Pos:** SS-108; 2B-37; PH-10; 3B-8; LF-4; PR-3; RF-2 **Ht:** 5'11" **Wt:** 175 **Born:** 12/7/1979 **Age:** 28

Year	Team	Lg	G	AB	H	2B	3B	HR	(Hm	Rd)	TB	R	RBI	RC	TBB	IBB	SO	HBP	SH	SF	SB	CS	SB%	GDP	Avg	OBP	Slg
2005	ChC	NL	9	13	2	1	0	0	(0	0)	3	3	0	0	1	0	2	0	0	0	0	0	-	0	.154	.214	.231
2006	ChC	NL	53	134	44	11	3	3	(3	0)	70	34	16	31	17	0	18	2	6	0	13	2	.87	5	.328	.412	.522
2007	ChC	NL	148	537	143	30	2	3	(3	0)	186	80	45	64	49	1	50	0	8	3	28	4	.88	12	.266	.326	.346
	3 ML YEARS		210	684	189	42	5	6	(6	0)	259	117	61	95	67	1	70	2	14	3	41	6	.87	17	.276	.341	.379

Curtis Thigpen

Bats: R **Throws:** R **Pos:** C-22; 1B-14; PR-10; DH-9; PH-5 **Ht:** 5'11" **Wt:** 190 **Born:** 4/19/1983 **Age:** 25

Year	Team	Lg	G	AB	H	2B	3B	HR	(Hm	Rd)	TB	R	RBI	RC	TBB	IBB	SO	HBP	SH	SF	SB	CS	SB%	GDP	Avg	OBP	Slg
2004	Auburn	A-	45	166	50	11	2	7	(-	-)	86	34	29	34	23	0	32	3	1	3	1	1	.50	2	.301	.390	.518
2005	Lansng	A	79	293	84	18	2	5	(-	-)	121	41	35	54	54	0	34	1	2	2	5	0	1.00	10	.287	.397	.413
2005	NHam	AA	39	141	40	8	0	4	(-	-)	60	18	15	21	9	0	19	3	4	0	0	0	-	1	.284	.340	.426
2006	NHam	AA	87	309	80	25	5	5	(-	-)	130	49	36	53	52	0	61	4	5	3	5	1	.83	7	.259	.370	.421
2006	Syrcse	AAA	13	53	14	3	0	1	(-	-)	20	3	9	5	2	0	9	1	0	0	1	0	1.00	5	.264	.304	.377
2007	Syrcse	AAA	50	179	51	10	0	3	(-	-)	70	20	20	26	17	2	23	2	1	3	1	0	1.00	5	.285	.348	.391
2007	Tor	AL	47	101	24	5	0	0	(0	0)	29	13	11	13	8	0	17	0	1	0	2	0	1.00	4	.238	.294	.287

Frank Thomas

Bats: R **Throws:** R **Pos:** DH-147; PH-8 **Ht:** 6'5" **Wt:** 275 **Born:** 5/27/1968 **Age:** 40

Year	Team	Lg	G	AB	H	2B	3B	HR	(Hm	Rd)	TB	R	RBI	RC	TBB	IBB	SO	HBP	SH	SF	SB	CS	SB%	GDP	Avg	OBP	Slg
1990	CWS	AL	60	191	63	11	3	7	(2	5)	101	39	31	46	44	0	54	2	0	3	0	1	.00	5	.330	.454	.529
1991	CWS	AL	158	559	178	31	2	32	(24	8)	309	104	109	134	138	13	112	1	0	2	1	2	.33	20	.318	.453	.553
1992	CWS	AL	160	573	185	46	2	24	(10	14)	307	108	115	132	122	6	88	5	0	11	6	3	.67	19	.323	.439	.536
1993	CWS	AL	153	549	174	36	0	41	(26	15)	333	106	128	137	112	23	54	2	0	13	4	2	.67	10	.317	.426	.607
1994	CWS	AL	113	399	141	34	1	38	(22	16)	291	106	101	127	109	12	61	2	0	7	2	3	.40	15	.353	.487	.729
1995	CWS	AL	145	493	152	27	0	40	(15	25)	299	102	111	132	136	29	74	6	0	12	3	2	.60	14	.308	.454	.606
1996	CWS	AL	141	527	184	26	0	40	(16	24)	330	110	134	137	109	26	70	5	0	8	1	1	.50	25	.349	.459	.626
1997	CWS	AL	146	530	184	35	0	35	(16	19)	324	110	125	139	109	9	69	3	0	7	1	1	.50	15	.347	.456	.611
1998	CWS	AL	160	585	155	35	2	29	(15	14)	281	109	109	111	110	2	93	6	0	11	7	0	1.00	14	.265	.381	.480
1999	CWS	AL	135	486	148	36	0	15	(9	6)	229	74	77	95	87	13	66	9	0	8	3	3	.50	15	.305	.414	.471
2000	CWS	AL	159	582	191	44	0	43	(30	13)	364	115	143	148	112	18	94	5	0	8	1	3	.25	13	.328	.436	.625
2001	CWS	AL	20	68	15	3	0	4	(2	2)	30	8	10	10	10	2	12	0	0	1	0	0	-	0	.221	.316	.441
2002	CWS	AL	148	523	132	29	1	28	(24	4)	247	77	92	96	88	2	115	7	0	10	3	0	1.00	10	.252	.361	.472
2003	CWS	AL	153	546	146	35	0	42	(29	13)	307	87	105	115	100	4	115	12	0	4	0	0	-	11	.267	.390	.562
2004	CWS	AL	74	240	65	16	0	18	(14	4)	135	53	49	59	64	3	57	6	0	1	0	2	.00	2	.271	.434	.563
2005	CWS	AL	34	105	23	3	0	12	(9	3)	62	19	26	18	16	0	31	0	0	3	0	0	-	2	.219	.315	.590
2006	Oak	AL	137	466	126	11	0	39	(23	16)	254	77	114	99	81	3	81	6	0	6	0	0	-	13	.270	.381	.545
2007	Tor	AL	155	531	147	30	0	26	(19	7)	255	63	95	97	81	3	94	7	0	5	0	0	-	14	.277	.377	.480
	18 ML YEARS		2251	7953	2409	488	11	513	(305	208)	4458	1467	1674	1832	1628	168	1340	84	0	120	32	23	.58	217	.303	.421	.561

Jim Thome

Bats: L **Throws:** R **Pos:** DH-123; PH-6; 1B-1   **Ht:** 6'3" **Wt:** 250 **Born:** 8/27/1970 **Age:** 37

								BATTING												BASERUNNING				AVERAGES		
Year	Team	Lg	G	AB	H	2B	3B	HR	(Hm | Rd)	TB	R	RBI	RC	TBB	IBB	SO	HBP	SH	SF	SB	CS	SB%	GDP	Avg	OBP	Slg
2007	Charltt*	AAA	5	14	3	1	0	0	(- | -)	4	2	5	2	6	2	3	0	0	0	0	0	-	1	.214	.450	.286
1991	Cle	AL	27	98	25	4	2	1	(0 | 1)	36	7	9	9	5	1	16	1	0	0	1	1	.50	4	.255	.298	.367
1992	Cle	AL	40	117	24	3	1	2	(1 | 1)	35	8	12	9	10	2	34	2	0	2	2	0	1.00	3	.205	.275	.299
1993	Cle	AL	47	154	41	11	0	7	(5 | 2)	73	28	22	30	29	1	36	4	0	5	2	1	.67	3	.266	.385	.474
1994	Cle	AL	98	321	86	20	1	20	(10 | 10)	168	58	52	56	46	5	84	0	1	1	3	3	.50	11	.268	.359	.523
1995	Cle	AL	137	452	142	29	3	25	(13 | 12)	252	92	73	109	97	3	113	5	0	3	4	3	.57	8	.314	.438	.558
1996	Cle	AL	151	505	157	28	5	38	(18 | 20)	309	122	116	132	123	8	141	6	0	2	2	2	.50	13	.311	.450	.612
1997	Cle	AL	147	496	142	25	0	40	(17 | 23)	287	104	102	120	120	9	146	3	0	8	1	1	.50	9	.286	.423	.579
1998	Cle	AL	123	440	129	34	2	30	(18 | 12)	257	89	85	104	89	8	141	4	0	7	1	0	1.00	7	.293	.413	.584
1999	Cle	AL	146	494	137	27	2	33	(19 | 14)	267	101	108	116	127	13	171	4	0	4	0	0	-	6	.277	.426	.540
2000	Cle	AL	158	557	150	33	1	37	(21 | 16)	296	106	106	119	118	4	171	4	0	5	1	0	1.00	8	.269	.398	.531
2001	Cle	AL	156	526	153	26	1	49	(30 | 19)	328	101	124	130	111	14	185	4	0	3	0	1	.00	5	.291	.416	.624
2002	Cle	AL	147	480	146	19	2	52	(30 | 22)	325	101	118	139	122	18	139	5	0	6	1	2	.33	5	.304	.445	.677
2003	Phi	NL	159	578	154	30	3	47	(28 | 19)	331	111	131	125	111	11	182	4	0	5	0	3	.00	5	.266	.385	.573
2004	Phi	NL	143	508	139	28	1	42	(19 | 23)	295	97	105	97	104	26	144	2	0	4	0	2	.00	10	.274	.396	.581
2005	Phi	NL	59	193	40	7	0	7	(6 | 1)	68	26	30	25	45	4	59	2	0	2	0	0	-	5	.207	.360	.352
2006	CWS	AL	143	490	141	26	0	42	(25 | 17)	293	108	109	120	107	12	147	6	0	7	0	0	-	4	.288	.416	.598
2007	CWS	AL	130	432	119	19	0	35	(21 | 14)	243	79	96	104	95	11	134	6	0	3	0	1	.00	10	.275	.410	.563
17 ML YEARS			2011	6841	1925	369	24	507	(281 | 226)	3863	1338	1398	1544	1459	150	2043	62	1	64	18	20	.47	120	.281	.409	.565

Brad Thompson

Pitches: R **Bats:** R **Pos:** RP-27; SP-17   **Ht:** 6'1" **Wt:** 190 **Born:** 1/31/1982 **Age:** 26

			HOW MUCH HE PITCHED						WHAT HE GAVE UP											THE RESULTS						
Year	Team	Lg	G	GS	CG	GF	IP	BFP	H	R	ER	HR	SH	SF	HB	TBB	IBB	SO	WP	Bk	W	L	Pct	ShO	Sv-Op	Hld	ERC	ERA
2007	Memp*	AAA	2	1	0	0	8.1	34	8	4	4	2	0	0	0	1	0	2	0	0	0	0	-	0	0--	-	3.55	4.32
2005	StL	NL	40	0	0	8	55.0	225	46	22	18	5	3	0	4	15	2	29	0	0	4	0	1.000	0	1-1	7	2.90	2.95
2006	StL	NL	43	1	0	16	56.2	245	58	23	21	4	3	0	5	20	3	32	1	0	1	2	.333	0	0-0	3	4.11	3.34
2007	StL	NL	44	17	0	10	129.1	580	157	76	68	23	4	2	13	40	2	53	4	0	8	6	.571	0	0-0	0	5.99	4.73
3 ML YEARS			127	18	0	34	241.0	1050	261	121	107	32	10	2	22	75	7	114	5	0	13	8	.619	0	1-1	10	4.79	4.00

Kevin Thompson

Bats: R **Throws:** R **Pos:** PR-8; LF-7; CF-6; RF-6; DH-3; PH-3   **Ht:** 5'10" **Wt:** 190 **Born:** 9/18/1979 **Age:** 28

								BATTING												BASERUNNING				AVERAGES		
Year	Team	Lg	G	AB	H	2B	3B	HR	(Hm	Rd)	TB	R	RBI	RC	TBB	IBB	SO	HBP	SH	SF	SB	CS	SB%	GDP	Avg	OBP	Slg
2000	Yanks	R	20	75	20	7	1	2	(-	-)	35	13	9	12	10	0	14	1	0	1	2	3	.40	1	.267	.356	.467
2001	StsInd	A-	68	260	68	11	4	6	(-	-)	105	46	33	41	36	0	48	5	1	2	11	5	.69	5	.262	.360	.404
2002	Grnsbr	A	62	226	64	24	3	3	(-	-)	103	44	31	45	37	1	42	6	0	1	14	3	.82	4	.283	.396	.456
2002	Tampa	A+	25	87	16	5	0	0	(-	-)	21	10	7	9	10	0	16	2	2	2	11	1	.92	3	.184	.258	.241
2002	StsInd	A-	36	139	42	5	2	4	(-	-)	63	25	14	24	17	1	24	0	1	1	6	3	.67	1	.302	.376	.453
2003	Tampa	A+	44	163	54	13	4	5	(-	-)	90	42	25	41	32	2	27	2	0	6	16	5	.76	3	.331	.433	.552
2003	Trntn	AA	86	328	74	16	2	5	(-	-)	109	48	20	42	37	1	57	4	3	2	47	8	.85	5	.226	.310	.332
2004	Tampa	A+	11	45	16	4	0	2	(-	-)	26	12	6	11	4	0	7	1	0	0	9	2	.82	0	.356	.420	.578
2004	Trntn	AA	69	270	76	17	0	9	(-	-)	120	43	17	46	30	1	40	4	2	0	29	10	.74	8	.281	.362	.444
2005	Trntn	AA	81	313	103	28	5	12	(-	-)	177	59	43	79	53	1	68	6	2	3	25	6	.81	5	.329	.432	.565
2005	Clmbs	AAA	58	209	52	17	0	2	(-	-)	75	28	28	29	23	0	45	6	4	4	18	5	.70	4	.249	.335	.359
2006	Clmbs	AAA	91	362	96	22	5	9	(-	-)	155	69	44	57	44	1	63	2	4	4	17	7	.71	3	.265	.345	.428
2007	S-WB	AAA	77	267	75	18	3	5	(-	-)	114	39	37	48	42	1	56	3	5	2	24	8	.75	8	.281	.382	.427
2006	NYY	AL	19	30	9	3	0	1	(1	0)	15	5	6	6	6	0	9	0	1	0	2	0	1.00	0	.300	.417	.500
2007	2 Tms	AL	22	35	5	3	0	0	(0	0)	8	4	3	2	3	0	13	0	0	0	0	0	-	0	.143	.211	.229
07	NYY	AL	13	21	4	3	0	0	(0	0)	7	2	2	2	2	0	10	0	0	0	0	0	-	0	.190	.261	.333
07	Oak	AL	9	14	1	0	0	0	(0	0)	1	2	1	0	1	0	3	0	0	0	0	0	-	0	.071	.133	.071
2 ML YEARS			41	65	14	6	0	1	(1	0)	23	9	9	8	9	0	22	0	1	0	2	0	1.00	0	.215	.311	.354

Mike Thompson

Pitches: R **Bats:** R **Pos:** RP-7   **Ht:** 6'4" **Wt:** 200 **Born:** 11/6/1980 **Age:** 27

			HOW MUCH HE PITCHED						WHAT HE GAVE UP											THE RESULTS						
Year	Team	Lg	G	GS	CG	GF	IP	BFP	H	R	ER	HR	SH	SF	HB	TBB	IBB	SO	WP	Bk	W	L	Pct	ShO	Sv-Op	Hld	ERC	ERA
1999	Padres	R	13	13	0	0	65.0	300	78	52	44	8	2	3	4	27	0	62	3	4	1	7	.125	0	0--	-	5.68	6.09
2000	FtWyn	A	6	6	0	0	26.1	122	28	19	15	1	2	3	6	15	0	17	3	0	1	3	.250	0	0--	-	5.48	5.13
2000	Idaho	R+	14	14	0	0	72.2	339	99	56	48	8	1	1	8	30	0	52	8	0	6	4	.600	0	0--	-	7.02	5.94
2001	Lk Els	A+	19	12	0	1	74.0	318	82	46	44	7	5	2	3	25	0	39	5	2	5	4	.556	0	0--	-	4.67	5.35
2001	FtWyn	A	1	1	0	0	6.0	28	8	4	4	0	0	0	0	2	0	1	0	0	0	1	.000	0	0--	-	4.83	6.00
2002	Lk Els	A+	25	22	0	1	123.0	573	144	93	76	14	3	6	7	53	0	79	3	1	5	7	.417	0	0--	-	5.40	5.56
2002	Mobile	AA	1	1	0	0	5.0	19	5	2	2	0	0	0	0	0	0	1	0	0	1	0	1.000	0	0--	-	3.24	3.60
2003	Lk Els	A+	28	22	0	1	136.1	590	163	78	67	8	4	6	2	31	0	75	7	0	10	11	.476	0	0--	-	4.27	4.42
2004	Mobile	AA	35	18	0	4	121.1	498	128	50	46	13	14	3	8	31	2	69	2	0	10	2	.833	0	0--	-	4.30	3.41
2005	Mobile	AA	18	18	2	0	114.2	487	116	50	41	6	6	2	5	27	0	68	5	0	6	6	.500	1	0--	-	3.31	3.22
2005	Portlnd	AAA	9	9	0	0	60.0	240	58	22	21	6	2	0	0	13	0	25	1	0	4	2	.667	0	0--	-	3.29	3.15
2006	Portlnd	AAA	13	13	0	0	69.1	288	69	30	29	4	0	2	4	20	1	41	1	0	6	1	.857	0	0--	-	3.62	3.76
2007	Portlnd	AAA	23	22	1	1	132.2	604	171	99	92	19	2	6	7	40	1	71	8	1	4	11	.267	0	0--	-	5.88	6.24
2006	SD	NL	19	16	0	2	92.0	405	103	56	51	13	5	2	7	30	4	35	1	0	4	5	.444	0	0-0	0	5.03	4.99
2007	SD	NL	7	0	0	4	15.2	75	19	15	12	2	2	3	3	7	2	5	0	0	0	1	.000	0	0-0	0	6.23	6.89
2 ML YEARS			26	16	0	6	107.2	480	122	71	63	15	7	5	10	37	6	40	1	0	4	6	.400	0	0-0	0	5.20	5.27

Rich Thompson

Pitches: R **Bats:** R **Pos:** RP-7   **Ht:** 6'1" **Wt:** 180 **Born:** 7/1/1984 **Age:** 23

			HOW MUCH HE PITCHED						WHAT HE GAVE UP												THE RESULTS						
Year	Team	Lg	G	GS	CG	GF	IP	BFP	H	R	ER	HR	SH	SF	HB	TBB	IBB	SO	WP	Bk	W	L	Pct	ShO	Sv-Op	Hld	ERC	ERA
2002	Angels	R	15	0	0	2	23.1	96	14	12	7	0	1	1	9	9	0	29	1	1	2	0	1.000	0	1--	-	1.54	2.70
2003	CRpds	A	31	0	0	23	37.2	145	18	5	1	1	2	1	0	13	0	54	6	0	1	2	.333	0	9--	-	1.14	0.24
2003	RCuca	A+	24	0	0	18	29.1	135	28	19	16	4	0	1	2	18	1	33	5	0	2	2	.500	0	8--	-	5.08	4.91
2004	RCuca	A+	41	5	0	17	77.2	339	76	36	34	9	1	0	3	33	2	71	4	1	3	2	.600	0	4--	-	4.26	3.94
2005	RCuca	A+	42	15	0	14	121.1	539	132	76	71	20	2	5	2	53	0	92	12	2	6	8	.429	0	3--	-	5.28	5.27
2006	Ark	AA	42	0	0	30	66.2	276	52	39	38	13	2	4	4	27	0	60	6	1	3	4	.429	0	10--	-	3.79	5.13
2006	Salt Lk	AAA	4	0	0	2	4.1	25	9	6	6	1	0	3	0	4	0	3	0	0	0	1	.000	0	1--	-	15.35	12.46
2007	RCuca	A+	1	0	0	0	2.0	7	1	0	0	0	1	0	0	0	0	3	1	0	0	0	-	0	0--	-	0.54	0.00
2007	Ark	AA	21	3	0	7	49.1	196	34	15	11	5	2	1	3	14	1	50	3	1	2	3	.400	0	1--	-	2.25	2.01
2007	Salt Lk	AAA	16	0	0	10	24.2	100	17	7	6	2	2	1	3	6	0	32	3	0	3	0	1.000	0	1--	-	2.18	2.19
2007	LAA	AL	7	0	0	2	6.2	32	10	8	8	4	0	0	0	3	0	9	2	0	0	0	-	0	0-0	0	11.85	10.80

John Thomson

Pitches: R **Bats:** R **Pos:** SP-2   **Ht:** 6'3" **Wt:** 220 **Born:** 10/1/1973 **Age:** 34

			HOW MUCH HE PITCHED						WHAT HE GAVE UP												THE RESULTS						
Year	Team	Lg	G	GS	CG	GF	IP	BFP	H	R	ER	HR	SH	SF	HB	TBB	IBB	SO	WP	Bk	W	L	Pct	ShO	Sv-Op	Hld	ERC	ERA
2007	Dnedin*	A+	2	2	0	0	11.0	46	13	8	5	2	0	0	1	1	0	11	0	0	1	0	1.000	0	0--	-	4.41	4.09
2007	Syrcse*	AAA	7	7	0	0	39.1	171	43	24	20	3	3	0	2	15	0	30	3	1	2	4	.333	0	0--	-	4.65	4.58
2007	Royals*	R	1	1	0	0	1.1	7	3	1	1	0	0	0	0	0	0	2	0	0	0	0	-	0	0--	-	9.13	6.75
2007	Wichta*	AA	2	2	0	0	5.0	25	7	8	8	4	0	1	0	2	0	4	0	0	0	2	.000	0	0--	-	11.56	14.40
2007	Omha*	AAA	1	1	0	0	3.1	20	9	8	8	1	0	0	2	0	0	2	0	0	0	1	.000	0	0--	-	19.66	21.60
1997	Col	NL	27	27	2	0	166.1	721	193	94	87	15	10	3	5	51	0	106	2	0	7	9	.438	1	0-0	0	4.74	4.71
1998	Col	NL	26	26	2	0	161.0	680	174	86	86	21	8	5	2	49	0	106	4	2	8	11	.421	0	0-0	0	4.51	4.81
1999	Col	NL	14	13	1	1	62.2	305	85	62	56	11	4	2	1	36	1	34	2	0	1	10	.091	0	0-0	0	7.60	8.04
2001	Col	NL	14	14	1	0	93.2	386	84	46	42	15	3	3	4	25	3	68	1	0	4	5	.444	1	0-0	0	3.52	4.04
2002	2 Tms	NL	30	30	0	0	181.2	800	201	116	95	28	13	10	2	44	9	107	2	0	9	14	.391	0	0-0	0	4.24	4.71
2003	Tex	AL	35	35	3	0	217.0	910	234	125	117	27	2	7	4	49	2	136	5	0	13	14	.481	1	0-0	0	4.10	4.85
2004	Atl	NL	33	33	0	0	198.1	834	210	93	82	20	11	4	6	52	5	133	3	0	14	8	.636	0	0-0	0	4.01	3.72
2005	Atl	NL	17	17	1	0	98.2	427	111	52	49	6	2	4	2	28	2	61	3	0	4	6	.400	0	0-0	0	4.09	4.47
2006	Atl	NL	18	15	0	1	80.1	361	93	55	43	11	5	7	2	32	4	46	1	0	2	7	.222	0	0-0	1	5.26	4.82
2007	KC	AL	2	2	0	0	10.2	46	13	5	4	0	0	2	0	3	0	3	0	1	1	1	.500	0	0-0	0	4.19	3.38
02	Col	NL	21	21	0	0	127.1	550	136	77	69	21	7	7	2	27	6	76	2	0	7	8	.467	0	0-0	0	4.02	4.88
02	NYM	NL	9	9	0	0	54.1	250	65	39	26	7	6	3	0	17	3	31	0	0	2	6	.250	0	0-0	0	4.74	4.31
10 ML YEARS			216	212	10	2	1270.1	5470	1398	734	661	154	58	47	28	369	26	800	23	3	63	85	.426	3	0-0	1	4.43	4.68

Scott Thorman

Bats: L **Throws:** R **Pos:** 1B-84; PH-46; PR-2   **Ht:** 6'3" **Wt:** 235 **Born:** 1/6/1982 **Age:** 26

			BATTING																		BASERUNNING				AVERAGES		
Year	Team	Lg	G	AB	H	2B	3B	HR	(Hm	Rd)	TB	R	RBI	RC	TBB	IBB	SO	HBP	SH	SF	SB	CS	SB%	GDP	Avg	OBP	Slg
2000	Braves	R	29	97	22	7	1	1	(-	-)	34	15	19	12	12	0	23	4	0	2	0	1	.00	1	.227	.330	.351
2002	Macon	A	127	470	138	38	3	16	(-	-)	230	57	82	86	51	5	83	7	0	6	2	2	.50	16	.294	.367	.489
2003	MrtlBh	A+	124	445	108	26	2	12	(-	-)	174	44	56	57	42	6	79	4	0	4	0	0	-	13	.243	.311	.391
2004	MrtlBh	A+	43	154	46	11	1	4	(-	-)	71	20	29	27	12	2	19	5	0	5	1	0	1.00	1	.299	.358	.461
2004	Grnville	AA	94	345	87	14	3	11	(-	-)	140	31	51	48	39	1	73	0	0	3	5	3	.63	5	.252	.326	.406
2005	Missi	AA	90	348	106	21	2	15	(-	-)	176	49	65	63	28	5	76	4	0	3	2	2	.50	3	.305	.360	.506
2005	Rchmd	AAA	52	210	58	10	3	6	(-	-)	92	23	27	29	9	0	42	3	0	2	0	0	-	3	.276	.313	.438
2006	Rchmd	AAA	81	309	92	16	2	15	(-	-)	157	38	48	57	31	6	48	1	0	3	4	2	.67	6	.298	.360	.508
2006	Atl	NL	55	128	30	11	0	5	(3	2)	56	13	14	14	5	0	21	0	0	0	1	0	1.00	0	.234	.263	.438
2007	Atl	NL	120	287	62	18	0	11	(4	7)	113	37	36	25	14	3	70	3	1	2	1	1	.50	6	.216	.258	.394
2 ML YEARS			175	415	92	29	0	16	(7	9)	169	50	50	39	19	3	91	3	1	2	2	1	.67	6	.222	.260	.407

Matt Thornton

Pitches: L **Bats:** L **Pos:** RP-68   **Ht:** 6'6" **Wt:** 230 **Born:** 9/15/1976 **Age:** 31

			HOW MUCH HE PITCHED						WHAT HE GAVE UP												THE RESULTS						
Year	Team	Lg	G	GS	CG	GF	IP	BFP	H	R	ER	HR	SH	SF	HB	TBB	IBB	SO	WP	Bk	W	L	Pct	ShO	Sv-Op	Hld	ERC	ERA
2004	Sea	AL	19	1	0	8	32.2	148	30	15	15	2	2	1	0	25	1	30	2	0	1	2	.333	0	0-0	4	4.75	4.13
2005	Sea	AL	55	0	0	15	57.0	262	54	33	33	13	1	1	0	42	2	57	7	0	0	4	.000	0	0-1	5	6.06	5.21
2006	CWS	AL	63	0	0	20	54.0	227	46	20	20	5	1	3	1	21	4	49	1	0	5	3	.625	0	2-5	18	3.12	3.33
2007	CWS	AL	68	0	0	13	56.1	249	59	31	30	4	0	2	2	26	6	55	3	0	4	4	.500	0	2-7	17	4.35	4.79
4 ML YEARS			205	1	0	56	200.0	886	189	99	98	24	4	7	3	114	13	191	13	0	10	13	.435	0	4-13	40	4.54	4.41

Erick Threets

Pitches: L **Bats:** L **Pos:** RP-3   **Ht:** 6'5" **Wt:** 240 **Born:** 11/4/1981 **Age:** 26

			HOW MUCH HE PITCHED						WHAT HE GAVE UP												THE RESULTS						
Year	Team	Lg	G	GS	CG	GF	IP	BFP	H	R	ER	HR	SH	SF	HB	TBB	IBB	SO	WP	Bk	W	L	Pct	ShO	Sv-Op	Hld	ERC	ERA
2001	SnJos	A+	14	14	0	0	59.1	270	49	34	28	2	1	3	7	40	0	60	14	3	0	10	.000	0	0--	-	4.07	4.25
2001	Hgrstn	A-	12	0	0	3	24.0	94	13	3	2	1	0	0	1	9	0	32	2	1	2	0	1.000	0	1--	-	1.55	0.75
2002	SnJos	A+	26	0	0	4	28.1	136	23	24	21	2	2	1	3	28	1	43	6	1	0	1	.000	0	1--	-	5.42	6.67
2003	Nrwich	AA	11	0	0	4	11.1	72	15	20	20	1	0	0	2	16	0	16	6	0	0	0	-	0	0--	-	12.88	15.88
2003	Hgrstn	A-	22	0	0	0	49.2	215	26	20	18	2	0	2	7	42	0	47	9	1	2	3	.400	0	0--	-	3.32	3.26
2005	Nrwich	AA	30	0	0	7	42.2	201	43	28	24	2	1	0	2	31	0	35	6	0	1	2	.333	0	2--	-	5.13	5.06
2006	Fresno	AAA	49	0	0	11	62.2	284	51	26	20	4	4	2	5	44	0	51	7	0	1	2	.667	0	0--	-	4.20	2.87
2007	Fresno	AAA	40	3	0	12	54.2	238	46	26	21	4	3	2	2	35	0	40	2	1	3	1	.750	0	1--	-	4.14	3.46
2007	SF	NL	3	0	0	1	2.1	15	5	5	5	0	0	0	0	3	0	1	1	0	0	0	-	0	0-0	0	14.38	19.29

Mike Timlin

Pitches: R **Bats:** R **Pos:** RP-50   **Ht:** 6'4" **Wt:** 210 **Born:** 3/10/1966 **Age:** 42

Year	Team	Lg	G	GS	CG	GF	IP	BFP	H	R	ER	HR	SH	SF	HB	TBB	IBB	SO	WP	Bk	W	L	Pct	ShO	Sv-Op	Hld	ERC	ERA
2007	Pawt*	AAA	8	2	0	1	8.2	37	9	4	4	0	1	1	0	3	0	3	1	0	0	0	-	0	0- -	-	3.39	4.15
1991	Tor	AL	63	3	0	17	108.1	463	94	43	38	6	6	2	1	50	11	85	5	0	11	6	.647	0	3-8	9	3.14	3.16
1992	Tor	AL	26	0	0	14	43.2	190	45	23	20	0	2	1	1	20	5	35	0	0	0	2	.000	0	1-1	1	3.68	4.12
1993	Tor	AL	54	0	0	27	55.2	254	63	32	29	7	1	3	1	27	3	49	1	0	4	2	.667	0	1-4	9	5.32	4.69
1994	Tor	AL	34	0	0	16	40.0	179	41	25	23	5	0	0	2	20	0	38	3	0	1	0	1.000	0	2-4	5	5.01	5.18
1995	Tor	AL	31	0	0	19	42.0	179	38	13	10	1	3	0	2	17	5	36	3	1	4	3	.571	0	5-9	4	3.04	2.14
1996	Tor	AL	59	0	0	56	56.2	230	47	25	23	4	2	3	2	18	4	52	3	0	1	6	.143	0	31-38	2	2.74	3.65
1997	2 Tms	AL	64	0	0	31	72.2	297	69	30	26	8	6	1	1	20	5	45	1	1	6	4	.600	0	10-18	9	3.40	3.22
1998	Sea	AL	70	0	0	40	79.1	321	78	26	26	5	4	2	3	16	2	60	0	0	3	3	.500	0	19-24	6	3.17	2.95
1999	Bal	AL	62	0	0	52	63.0	261	51	30	25	9	1	1	5	23	3	50	1	0	3	9	.250	0	27-36	0	3.46	3.57
2000	2 Tms	AL	62	0	0	40	64.2	295	67	33	30	8	7	2	4	35	6	52	0	0	5	4	.556	0	12-18	6	5.08	4.18
2001	StL	NL	67	0	0	19	72.2	307	78	35	33	6	1	2	3	19	4	47	3	1	4	5	.444	0	3-7	12	3.95	4.09
2002	2 Tms	NL	72	1	0	17	96.2	376	75	35	32	15	2	1	5	14	2	50	3	0	4	6	.400	0	0-4	20	2.46	2.98
2003	Bos	AL	72	0	0	13	83.2	340	77	37	33	11	4	1	4	9	3	65	0	0	6	4	.600	0	2-6	17	2.81	3.55
2004	Bos	AL	76	0	0	12	76.1	320	75	35	35	8	3	1	5	19	3	56	1	0	5	4	.556	0	1-4	20	3.64	4.13
2005	Bos	AL	81	0	0	27	80.1	342	86	23	20	2	3	6	2	20	5	59	3	0	7	3	.700	0	13-20	24	3.35	2.24
2006	Bos	AL	68	0	0	22	64.0	279	78	33	31	7	4	1	2	16	4	30	3	0	6	6	.500	0	9-17	21	4.86	4.36
2007	Bos	AL	50	0	0	19	55.1	222	46	23	21	7	5	2	3	14	3	31	0	0	2	1	.667	0	1-1	8	2.96	3.42
97	Tor	AL	38	0	0	26	47.0	190	41	17	15	6	4	1	1	15	4	36	1	1	3	2	.600	0	9-13	2	3.30	2.87
97	Sea	AL	26	0	0	5	25.2	107	28	13	11	2	2	0	0	5	1	9	0	0	3	2	.600	0	1-5	7	3.59	3.86
00	Bal	AL	37	0	0	31	35.0	157	37	22	19	6	5	1	2	15	3	26	0	0	2	3	.400	0	11-15	1	5.08	4.89
00	StL	NL	25	0	0	9	29.2	138	30	11	11	2	2	1	2	20	3	26	0	0	3	1	.750	0	1-3	5	5.05	3.34
02	StL	NL	42	1	0	10	61.0	236	48	19	17	9	2	0	4	7	2	35	1	0	1	3	.250	0	0-2	12	2.41	2.51
02	Phi	NL	30	0	0	7	35.2	140	27	16	15	6	0	1	1	7	0	15	2	0	3	3	.500	0	0-2	8	2.55	3.79
17 ML YEARS			1011	4	0	441	1155.0	4855	1108	501	455	109	54	29	46	357	68	840	30	3	71	69	.507	0	140-219	173	3.54	3.55

Brett Tomko

Pitches: R **Bats:** R **Pos:** RP-21; SP-19   **Ht:** 6'1" **Wt:** 220 **Born:** 4/7/1973 **Age:** 35

Year	Team	Lg	G	GS	CG	GF	IP	BFP	H	R	ER	HR	SH	SF	HB	TBB	IBB	SO	WP	Bk	W	L	Pct	ShO	Sv-Op	Hld	ERC	ERA
1997	Cin	NL	22	19	0	1	126.0	519	106	50	48	14	5	9	4	47	4	95	5	0	11	7	.611	0	0-0	0	3.31	3.43
1998	Cin	NL	34	34	1	0	210.2	887	198	111	104	22	12	2	7	64	3	162	9	1	13	12	.520	0	0-0	0	3.50	4.44
1999	Cin	NL	33	26	1	1	172.0	744	175	103	94	31	9	5	4	60	10	132	8	0	5	7	.417	0	0-0	1	4.51	4.92
2000	Sea	AL	32	8	0	10	92.1	401	92	53	48	12	5	5	3	40	4	59	1	1	7	5	.583	0	1-2	3	4.49	4.68
2001	Sea	AL	11	4	0	1	34.2	164	42	24	20	9	1	2	0	15	2	22	1	0	3	1	.750	0	0-1	0	6.31	5.19
2002	SD	NL	32	32	3	0	204.1	871	212	107	102	31	6	8	2	60	9	126	3	0	10	10	.500	0	0-0	0	4.18	4.49
2003	StL	NL	33	32	2	0	202.2	903	252	126	119	35	12	3	5	57	2	114	6	0	13	9	.591	0	0-0	0	5.63	5.28
2004	SF	NL	32	31	2	1	194.0	825	196	98	87	19	7	1	0	64	3	108	10	0	11	7	.611	1	0-0	0	3.82	4.04
2005	SF	NL	33	30	3	1	190.2	823	205	99	95	20	6	5	7	57	11	114	5	0	8	15	.348	0	1-1	1	4.18	4.48
2006	LAD	NL	44	15	0	2	112.1	491	123	67	59	17	7	7	2	29	0	76	3	1	8	7	.533	0	0-3	5	4.37	4.73
2007	2 Tms	NL	40	19	0	9	131.1	588	149	89	81	18	8	6	2	48	1	105	5	0	4	12	.250	0	0-0	0	4.90	5.55
07	LAD	NL	33	15	0	8	104.0	475	124	75	67	13	5	6	2	42	1	79	3	0	2	11	.154	0	0-0	0	5.39	5.80
07	SD	NL	7	4	0	1	27.1	113	25	14	14	5	3	0	0	6	0	26	2	0	2	1	.667	0	0-0	0	3.37	4.61
11 ML YEARS			346	250	12	26	1671.0	7216	1750	927	857	228	78	53	36	541	49	1113	56	3	93	92	.503	1	2-7	10	4.32	4.62

Yorvit Torrealba

Bats: R **Throws:** R **Pos:** C-112; PH-5   **Ht:** 5'11" **Wt:** 200 **Born:** 7/19/1978 **Age:** 29

Year	Team	Lg	G	AB	H	2B	3B	HR	(Hm	Rd)	TB	R	RBI	RC	TBB	IBB	SO	HBP	SH	SF	SB	CS	SB%	GDP	Avg	OBP	Slg
2001	SF	NL	3	4	2	0	1	0	(0	0)	4	0	2	2	0	0	0	0	0	0	0	0	-	0	.500	.500	1.000
2002	SF	NL	53	136	38	10	0	2	(0	2)	54	17	14	16	14	2	20	2	3	0	0	0	-	11	.279	.355	.397
2003	SF	NL	66	200	52	10	2	4	(3	1)	78	22	29	25	14	1	39	2	4	3	1	0	1.00	3	.260	.312	.390
2004	SF	NL	64	172	39	7	3	6	(3	3)	70	19	23	18	17	3	31	2	4	1	2	0	1.00	5	.227	.302	.407
2005	2 Tms		76	201	47	12	0	3	(2	1)	68	32	15	14	16	1	50	2	5	0	1	0	1.00	8	.234	.297	.338
2006	Col	NL	65	223	55	16	3	7	(3	4)	98	23	43	30	11	1	49	4	2	1	4	3	.57	7	.247	.293	.439
2007	Col	NL	113	396	101	22	1	8	(6	2)	149	47	47	34	34	1	73	6	6	1	2	1	.67	19	.255	.323	.376
05	SF	NL	34	93	21	8	0	1	(1	0)	32	18	7	7	9	1	25	1	2	0	1	0	1.00	3	.226	.301	.344
05	Sea	AL	42	108	26	4	0	2	(1	1)	36	14	8	7	7	0	25	1	3	0	0	0	-	5	.241	.293	.333
7 ML YEARS			440	1332	334	77	10	30	(17	13)	521	160	173	139	106	9	262	18	23	5	10	4	.71	55	.251	.313	.391

Salomon Torres

Pitches: R **Bats:** R **Pos:** RP-56   **Ht:** 5'11" **Wt:** 210 **Born:** 3/11/1972 **Age:** 36

Year	Team	Lg	G	GS	CG	GF	IP	BFP	H	R	ER	HR	SH	SF	HB	TBB	IBB	SO	WP	Bk	W	L	Pct	ShO	Sv-Op	Hld	ERC	ERA
2007	Pirates*	R	2	2	0	0	3.0	10	2	0	0	1	0	0	0	0	0	4	0	0	0	0	-	0	0- -	-	1.01	0.00
2007	Indy*	AAA	1	0	0	0	1.1	5	1	0	0	0	0	0	0	0	0	3	0	0	0	0	-	0	0- -	-	1.13	0.00
1993	SF	NL	8	8	0	0	44.2	196	37	21	20	5	7	1	1	27	3	23	3	1	3	5	.375	0	0-0	0	3.95	4.03
1994	SF	NL	16	14	1	2	84.1	378	95	55	51	10	4	8	7	34	2	42	4	1	2	8	.200	0	0-0	0	5.29	5.44
1995	2 Tms		20	14	1	4	80.0	384	100	61	56	16	1	0	2	49	3	47	1	2	3	9	.250	0	0-0	0	7.30	6.30
1996	Sea	AL	10	7	1	1	49.0	212	44	27	25	5	3	1	3	23	2	36	1	0	3	3	.500	1	0-0	0	3.98	4.59
1997	2 Tms		14	0	0	4	25.2	127	32	29	28	2	3	1	3	15	0	11	3	0	0	0	-	0	0-0	0	6.44	9.82
2002	Pit	NL	5	5	0	0	30.0	127	18	9	9	2	2	0	3	13	1	12	0	0	2	1	.667	0	0-0	0	4.07	2.70
2003	Pit	NL	41	16	0	7	121.0	518	128	65	64	19	4	1	7	42	5	84	3	0	7	5	.583	0	2-3	6	4.88	4.76
2004	Pit	NL	84	0	0	20	92.0	380	87	33	27	6	9	3	6	22	6	62	5	0	7	7	.500	0	0-4	30	3.12	2.64
2005	Pit	NL	78	0	0	32	94.2	388	76	34	29	7	3	2	6	36	7	55	5	0	5	5	.500	0	3-3	8	2.91	2.76
2006	Pit	NL	94	0	0	24	93.1	411	98	42	34	6	7	2	6	38	9	72	3	0	3	6	.333	0	12-15	20	4.23	3.28

261

Year Team	Lg	G	GS	CG	GF	IP	BFP	H	R	ER	HR	SH	SF	HB	TBB	IBB	SO	WP	Bk	W	L	Pct	ShO	Sv-Op	Hld	ERC	ERA
2007 Pit	NL	56	0	0	28	52.2	231	57	34	32	7	1	3	4	17	0	45	3	0	2	4	.333	0	12-18	5	4.78	5.47
95 SF	NL	4	1	0	2	8.0	40	13	8	8	4	0	0	0	7	0	2	0	0	0	1	.000	0	0-0	0	15.31	9.00
95 Sea	AL	16	13	1	2	72.0	344	87	53	48	12	1	0	2	42	3	45	1	2	3	8	.273	0	0-0	0	6.55	6.00
97 Sea	AL	2	0	0	1	3.1	21	7	10	10	0	0	0	1	3	0	0	0	0	0	0	-	0	0-0	0	13.67	27.00
97 Mon	NL	12	0	0	3	22.1	106	25	19	18	2	3	1	2	12	0	11	3	0	0	0	-	0	0-0	0	5.47	7.25
11 ML YEARS		426	64	3	122	767.1	3352	782	411	375	85	44	22	47	316	38	489	31	4	37	53	.411	1	29-43	69	4.50	4.40

Josh Towers

Pitches: R Bats: R Pos: SP-15; RP-10

Ht: 6'1" Wt: 188 Born: 2/26/1977 Age: 31

Year Team	Lg	G	GS	CG	GF	IP	BFP	H	R	ER	HR	SH	SF	HB	TBB	IBB	SO	WP	Bk	W	L	Pct	ShO	Sv-Op	Hld	ERC	ERA
2001 Bal	AL	24	20	1	2	140.1	586	165	74	70	21	3	4	6	16	0	58	1	0	8	10	.444	1	0-0	0	4.51	4.49
2002 Bal	AL	5	3	0	1	27.1	124	42	24	24	11	1	2	0	5	0	13	1	0	0	3	.000	0	0-0	0	9.00	7.90
2003 Tor	AL	14	8	1	2	64.1	265	67	34	32	15	0	2	4	7	1	42	1	0	8	1	.889	0	1-1	0	4.26	4.48
2004 Tor	AL	21	21	0	0	116.1	518	148	70	66	16	2	4	4	26	4	51	0	1	9	9	.500	0	0-0	0	5.50	5.11
2005 Tor	AL	33	33	2	0	208.2	876	237	101	86	24	3	7	6	29	2	112	1	1	13	12	.520	1	0-0	0	4.02	3.71
2006 Tor	AL	15	12	0	1	62.0	295	93	62	58	17	1	3	3	17	3	35	1	1	2	10	.167	0	0-0	0	8.05	8.42
2007 Tor	AL	25	15	0	6	107.0	469	129	73	64	18	3	4	6	22	2	76	1	0	5	10	.333	0	0-0	0	5.15	5.38
7 ML YEARS		137	112	4	12	726.0	3133	881	438	400	122	13	26	34	122	12	387	6	3	45	55	.450	2	1-1	0	5.03	4.96

J.R. Towles

Bats: R Throws: R Pos: C-14

Ht: 6'2" Wt: 195 Born: 2/11/1984 Age: 24

Year Team	Lg	G	AB	H	2B	3B	HR	(Hm	Rd)	TB	R	RBI	RC	TBB	IBB	SO	HBP	SH	SF	SB	CS	SB%	GDP	Avg	OBP	Slg
2004 Grnsvle	R	39	111	27	6	0	0	(-	-)	33	17	8	14	12	0	23	11	1	1	4	3	.57	1	.243	.370	.297
2005 Lxngtn	A	45	162	56	14	2	5	(-	-)	89	35	23	37	16	0	29	10	5	5	11	7	.61	3	.346	.436	.549
2006 Lxngtn	A	81	284	90	19	2	12	(-	-)	149	39	55	57	21	0	46	10	4	2	13	5	.72	3	.317	.382	.525
2007 Salem	A+	26	90	18	3	2	0	(-	-)	25	14	11	9	12	0	15	9	0	4	3	5	.38	2	.200	.339	.278
2007 CpChr	AA	61	216	70	12	2	11	(-	-)	119	47	49	50	23	1	35	15	3	0	9	4	.69	2	.324	.425	.551
2007 RdRck	AAA	13	43	12	0	0	0	(-	-)	12	5	2	3	4	0	7	1	2	0	2	4	.33	0	.279	.354	.279
2007 Hou	NL	14	40	15	5	0	1	(0	1)	23	9	12	11	3	1	1	1	0	0	0	1	.00	1	.375	.432	.575

Billy Traber

Pitches: L Bats: L Pos: RP-26; SP-2

Ht: 6'5" Wt: 200 Born: 9/18/1979 Age: 28

Year Team	Lg	G	GS	CG	GF	IP	BFP	H	R	ER	HR	SH	SF	HB	TBB	IBB	SO	WP	Bk	W	L	Pct	ShO	Sv-Op	Hld	ERC	ERA
2007 Clmbs*	AAA	14	4	0	0	40.1	168	40	21	13	2	3	3	1	7	1	29	1	0	2	3	.400	0	0- -	-	2.85	2.90
2003 Cle	AL	33	18	1	0	111.2	503	132	67	65	15	4	3	5	40	4	88	6	0	6	9	.400	1	0-0	1	5.31	5.24
2006 Was	NL	15	8	0	0	43.1	202	53	33	31	5	3	1	8	14	2	25	0	0	4	3	.571	0	0-0	2	5.81	6.44
2007 Was	NL	28	2	0	5	39.2	182	50	22	21	4	3	5	2	13	3	27	0	0	2	2	.500	0	0-1	2	5.30	4.76
3 ML YEARS		76	28	1	5	194.2	887	235	122	117	24	10	9	15	67	9	140	6	0	12	14	.462	1	0-1	5	5.42	5.41

Steve Trachsel

Pitches: R Bats: R Pos: SP-29

Ht: 6'4" Wt: 205 Born: 10/31/1970 Age: 37

Year Team	Lg	G	GS	CG	GF	IP	BFP	H	R	ER	HR	SH	SF	HB	TBB	IBB	SO	WP	Bk	W	L	Pct	ShO	Sv-Op	Hld	ERC	ERA
2007 Frdrck*	A+	1	1	0	0	7.0	28	7	3	2	0	0	0	0	1	0	4	1	0	0	1	.000	0	0- -	-	2.52	2.57
1993 ChC	NL	3	3	0	0	19.2	78	16	10	10	4	1	1	0	3	0	14	1	0	0	2	.000	0	0-0	0	2.71	4.58
1994 ChC	NL	22	22	1	0	146.0	612	133	57	52	19	3	3	3	54	4	108	6	0	9	7	.563	0	0-0	0	3.74	3.21
1995 ChC	NL	30	29	2	0	160.2	722	174	104	92	25	12	5	0	76	8	117	2	1	7	13	.350	0	0-0	0	5.13	5.15
1996 ChC	NL	31	31	3	0	205.0	845	181	82	69	30	3	3	8	62	3	132	5	2	13	9	.591	2	0-0	0	3.52	3.03
1997 ChC	NL	34	34	0	0	201.1	878	225	110	101	32	8	11	5	69	6	160	4	1	8	12	.400	0	0-0	0	5.04	4.51
1998 ChC	NL	33	33	1	0	208.0	894	204	107	103	27	9	7	8	84	5	149	3	2	15	8	.652	0	0-0	0	4.35	4.46
1999 ChC	NL	34	34	4	0	205.2	894	226	133	127	32	6	14	3	64	4	149	8	3	8	18	.308	0	0-0	0	4.69	5.56
2000 2 Tms	NL	34	34	3	0	200.2	882	232	116	107	26	6	6	6	74	2	110	4	0	8	15	.348	1	0-0	0	5.25	4.80
2001 NYM	NL	28	28	1	0	173.2	726	168	90	86	28	8	7	3	47	7	144	4	0	11	13	.458	1	0-0	0	3.80	4.46
2002 NYM	NL	30	30	1	0	173.2	741	170	80	65	16	9	3	0	69	4	105	4	0	11	11	.500	1	0-0	0	3.88	3.37
2003 NYM	NL	33	33	2	0	204.2	857	204	90	86	26	8	8	3	65	9	111	5	2	16	10	.615	2	0-0	0	3.97	3.78
2004 NYM	NL	33	33	0	0	202.2	881	203	104	90	25	11	8	5	83	9	117	4	2	12	13	.480	0	0-0	0	4.31	4.00
2005 NYM	NL	6	6	0	0	37.0	157	37	20	17	6	2	2	1	12	0	24	1	0	1	4	.200	0	0-0	0	4.34	4.14
2006 NYM	NL	30	30	1	0	164.2	736	185	94	91	23	4	7	4	78	1	79	4	0	15	8	.652	0	0-0	0	5.55	4.97
2007 2 Tms	NL	29	29	1	0	158.0	702	176	89	86	19	5	9	2	76	1	56	7	3	7	11	.389	0	0-0	0	5.34	4.90
00 TB	AL	23	23	3	0	137.2	606	160	76	70	16	2	5	6	49	1	78	3	0	6	10	.375	1	0-0	0	5.19	4.58
00 Tor	AL	11	11	0	0	63.0	276	72	40	37	10	4	1	0	25	1	32	1	0	2	5	.286	0	0-0	0	5.38	5.29
07 Bal	AL	25	25	1	0	140.2	623	151	73	70	16	3	7	2	69	0	45	6	3	6	8	.429	0	0-0	0	5.08	4.48
07 ChC	NL	4	4	0	0	17.1	79	25	16	16	3	2	2	0	7	1	11	1	0	1	3	.250	0	0-0	0	7.56	8.31
15 ML YEARS		410	409	20	0	2461.1	10605	2534	1286	1182	338	95	94	51	916	63	1575	62	16	141	154	.478	7	0-0	0	4.46	4.32

Chad Tracy

Bats: L Throws: R Pos: 3B-48; 1B-18; PH-15; DH-2   Ht: 6'2" Wt: 200 Born: 5/22/1980 Age: 28

							BATTING											BASERUNNING				AVERAGES		
Year Team	Lg	G	AB	H	2B	3B	HR	(Hm | Rd)	TB	R	RBI	RC	TBB	IBB	SO	HBP	SH	SF	SB	CS	SB%	GDP	Avg	OBP	Slg
2007 Tucsn*	AAA	3	15	7	2	0	1	(- | -)	12	3	4	4	0	0	1	0	0	0	0	0	-	1	.467	.467	.800
2004 Ari	NL	143	481	137	29	3	8	(6 | 2)	196	45	53	63	45	3	60	0	1	5	2	3	.40	11	.285	.343	.407
2005 Ari	NL	145	503	155	34	4	27	(9 | 18)	278	73	72	82	35	4	78	8	1	6	3	1	.75	10	.308	.359	.553
2006 Ari	NL	154	597	168	41	0	20	(14 | 6)	269	91	80	85	54	5	129	1	1	5	5	1	.83	11	.281	.343	.451
2007 Ari	NL	76	227	60	18	2	7	(3 | 4)	103	30	35	33	29	4	43	1	0	3	0	0	-	8	.264	.346	.454
4 ML YEARS		518	1808	520	122	9	62	(32 | 30)	846	239	240	263	163	16	310	14	3	19	10	5	.67	40	.288	.348	.468

Matt Treanor

Bats: R Throws: R Pos: C-53; PH-2   Ht: 6'0" Wt: 210 Born: 3/3/1976 Age: 32

							BATTING											BASERUNNING				AVERAGES		
Year Team	Lg	G	AB	H	2B	3B	HR	(Hm | Rd)	TB	R	RBI	RC	TBB	IBB	SO	HBP	SH	SF	SB	CS	SB%	GDP	Avg	OBP	Slg
2004 Fla	NL	29	55	13	2	0	0	(0 | 0)	15	7	1	4	4	0	13	2	0	0	0	0	-	3	.236	.311	.273
2005 Fla	NL	58	134	27	8	0	0	(0 | 0)	35	10	13	13	16	1	28	3	1	0	0	0	-	5	.201	.301	.261
2006 Fla	NL	67	157	36	6	1	2	(0 | 2)	50	12	14	16	19	4	34	5	2	2	0	1	.00	4	.229	.328	.318
2007 Fla	NL	55	171	46	7	1	4	(2 | 2)	67	16	19	26	19	1	29	5	2	1	0	0	-	2	.269	.357	.392
4 ML YEARS		209	517	122	23	2	6	(2 | 4)	167	45	47	59	58	6	104	15	5	3	0	1	.00	14	.236	.329	.323

Chin-hui Tsao

Pitches: R Bats: R Pos: RP-21   Ht: 6'1" Wt: 210 Born: 6/2/1981 Age: 27

		HOW MUCH HE PITCHED						WHAT HE GAVE UP												THE RESULTS						
Year Team	Lg	G	GS	CG	GF	IP	BFP	H	R	ER	HR	SH	SF	HB	TBB	IBB	SO	WP	Bk	W	L	Pct	ShO	Sv-Op	Hld	ERC	ERA
2007 LsVgs*	AAA	5	0	0	4	5.0	20	4	2	2	0	0	0	0	1	0	9	0	0	0	1	.000	0	2- -	-	1.70	3.60
2003 Col	NL	9	8	0	1	43.1	196	48	30	29	11	3	0	4	20	1	29	0	0	3	3	.500	0	0-0	0	6.56	6.02
2004 Col	NL	10	0	0	5	9.1	37	7	4	4	2	1	0	0	1	0	11	0	0	0	0	-	0	1-2	1	2.21	3.86
2005 Col	NL	10	0	0	9	11.0	56	16	8	8	3	1	1	1	5	1	4	1	0	1	0	1.000	0	3-4	0	8.44	6.55
2007 LAD	NL	21	0	0	6	24.2	97	18	12	12	3	0	0	1	8	0	16	0	0	0	1	.000	0	0-1	3	2.74	4.38
4 ML YEARS		50	8	0	21	88.1	386	89	54	53	19	5	1	6	34	2	60	1	0	4	4	.500	0	4-7	4	5.13	5.40

Troy Tulowitzki

Bats: R Throws: R Pos: SS-155   Ht: 6'3" Wt: 205 Born: 10/10/1984 Age: 23

							BATTING											BASERUNNING				AVERAGES		
Year Team	Lg	G	AB	H	2B	3B	HR	(Hm | Rd)	TB	R	RBI	RC	TBB	IBB	SO	HBP	SH	SF	SB	CS	SB%	GDP	Avg	OBP	Slg
2005 Mdest	A+	22	94	25	6	0	4	(- | -)	43	17	14	15	9	0	18	2	0	0	1	0	1.00	2	.266	.343	.457
2006 Tulsa	AA	104	423	123	34	2	13	(- | -)	200	75	61	76	46	3	71	10	1	5	6	5	.55	8	.291	.370	.473
2006 Col	NL	25	96	23	2	0	1	(- | -)	28	14	6	6	10	3	25	0	1	0	3	0	1.00	1	.240	.318	.292
2007 Col	NL	155	609	177	33	5	24	(15 | 9)	292	104	99	95	57	3	130	9	5	2	7	6	.54	14	.291	.359	.479
2 ML YEARS		180	705	200	35	5	25	(15 | 10)	320	119	105	105	67	6	155	10	6	2	10	6	.63	15	.284	.353	.454

Derrick Turnbow

Pitches: R Bats: R Pos: RP-77   Ht: 6'3" Wt: 210 Born: 1/25/1978 Age: 30

		HOW MUCH HE PITCHED						WHAT HE GAVE UP												THE RESULTS						
Year Team	Lg	G	GS	CG	GF	IP	BFP	H	R	ER	HR	SH	SF	HB	TBB	IBB	SO	WP	Bk	W	L	Pct	ShO	Sv-Op	Hld	ERC	ERA
2000 LAA	AL	24	1	0	16	38.0	181	36	21	20	7	0	0	2	36	0	25	3	1	0	0	-	0	0-0	1	7.05	4.74
2003 LAA	AL	11	0	0	7	15.1	53	7	1	1	0	0	0	0	3	0	15	0	0	2	0	1.000	0	0-0	0	0.79	0.59
2004 LAA	AL	4	0	0	4	6.1	26	2	0	0	0	0	0	0	7	0	3	0	0	0	0	-	0	0-0	0	2.47	0.00
2005 Mil	NL	69	0	0	62	67.1	271	49	15	13	5	0	1	2	24	2	64	9	0	7	1	.875	0	39-43	2	2.35	1.74
2006 Mil	NL	64	0	0	49	56.1	266	56	51	43	8	2	1	4	39	2	69	6	1	4	9	.308	0	24-32	4	5.69	6.87
2007 Mil	NL	77	0	0	13	68.0	292	44	36	35	4	1	2	2	46	0	84	7	0	4	5	.444	0	1-4	33	3.02	4.63
6 ML YEARS		249	1	0	151	251.1	1089	194	124	112	24	3	3	9	155	4	260	25	2	17	15	.531	0	64-79	40	3.74	4.01

Jason Tyner

Bats: L Throws: L Pos: LF-47; DH-22; RF-18; CF-17; PR-16; PH-15   Ht: 6'1" Wt: 180 Born: 4/23/1977 Age: 31

							BATTING											BASERUNNING				AVERAGES		
Year Team	Lg	G	AB	H	2B	3B	HR	(Hm | Rd)	TB	R	RBI	RC	TBB	IBB	SO	HBP	SH	SF	SB	CS	SB%	GDP	Avg	OBP	Slg
2000 2 Tms		50	124	28	4	0	0	(0 | 0)	32	9	13	9	5	0	16	2	8	3	7	2	.78	2	.226	.261	.258
2001 TB	AL	105	396	111	8	5	0	(0 | 0)	129	51	21	43	15	0	42	3	5	1	31	6	.84	6	.280	.311	.326
2002 TB	AL	44	168	36	2	1	0	(0 | 0)	40	17	9	8	7	0	19	1	3	1	7	1	.88	1	.214	.249	.238
2003 TB	AL	46	90	25	7	0	0	(0 | 0)	32	12	6	12	10	0	12	0	2	0	2	1	.67	1	.278	.350	.356
2005 Min	AL	18	56	18	1	1	0	(0 | 0)	21	8	5	8	4	0	4	0	0	0	2	0	1.00	2	.321	.367	.375
2006 Min	AL	62	218	68	5	2	0	(0 | 0)	77	29	18	30	11	2	18	1	0	2	4	2	.67	5	.312	.345	.353
2007 Min	AL	114	304	87	14	2	1	(0 | 1)	108	42	22	31	16	0	26	5	2	1	8	3	.73	12	.286	.331	.355
00 NYM	NL	13	41	8	2	0	0	(0 | 0)	10	3	5	2	1	0	4	1	3	2	1	1	.50	1	.195	.222	.244
00 TB	AL	37	83	20	2	0	0	(0 | 0)	22	6	8	7	4	0	12	1	5	1	6	1	.86	1	.241	.281	.265
7 ML YEARS		439	1356	373	41	11	1	(0 | 1)	439	168	94	141	68	2	137	12	20	8	61	15	.80	29	.275	.314	.324

Dan Uggla

Bats: R Throws: R Pos: 2B-158; DH-1; PR-1 · Ht: 5'11" Wt: 200 Born: 3/11/1980 Age: 28

Year	Team	Lg	G	AB	H	2B	3B	HR	(Hm	Rd)	TB	R	RBI	RC	TBB	IBB	SO	HBP	SH	SF	SB	CS	SB%	GDP	Avg	OBP	Slg
2001	Yakima	A-	72	278	77	21	0	5	(-	-)	113	39	40	40	20	0	52	9	1	4	8	4	.67	9	.277	.341	.406
2002	Lancst	A+	54	184	42	7	2	3	(-	-)	62	21	16	20	21	0	51	2	2	2	3	2	.60	2	.228	.311	.337
2002	Sbend	A	53	171	34	5	1	2	(-	-)	47	16	10	14	23	0	34	0	3	2	0	2	.00	2	.199	.291	.275
2003	Lancst	A+	134	534	155	31	7	23	(-	-)	269	104	90	98	46	0	105	11	11	6	24	9	.73	7	.290	.355	.504
2004	ElPaso	AA	83	294	76	12	2	4	(-	-)	104	29	30	31	15	0	55	4	2	2	10	7	.59	6	.259	.302	.354
2004	Lancst	A+	37	140	47	13	3	6	(-	-)	84	29	38	33	17	1	21	4	1	0	2	4	.33	0	.336	.422	.600
2005	Tenn	AA	135	498	148	33	3	21	(-	-)	250	88	87	96	52	5	103	14	3	2	15	8	.65	10	.297	.378	.502
2006	Fla	NL	154	611	172	26	7	27	(10	17)	293	105	90	97	48	1	123	9	7	8	6	6	.50	5	.282	.339	.480
2007	Fla	NL	159	632	155	49	3	31	(18	13)	303	113	88	81	68	0	167	13	4	11	2	1	.67	10	.245	.326	.479
2 ML YEARS			313	1243	327	75	10	58	(28	30)	596	218	178	178	116	1	290	22	11	19	8	7	.53	15	.263	.332	.479

B.J. Upton

Bats: R Throws: R Pos: CF-79; 2B-48; DH-3; PH-2; PR-1 · Ht: 6'3" Wt: 185 Born: 8/21/1984 Age: 23

Year	Team	Lg	G	AB	H	2B	3B	HR	(Hm	Rd)	TB	R	RBI	RC	TBB	IBB	SO	HBP	SH	SF	SB	CS	SB%	GDP	Avg	OBP	Slg
2007	Drham*	AAA	2	7	3	0	0	1	(-	-)	6	1	1	2	0	0	1	0	0	0	0	0	-	0	.429	.429	.857
2007	VeroB*	A+	7	17	4	0	0	1	(-	-)	7	4	3	5	0	2	0	2	0	2	0	0	-	0	.235	.375	.412
2004	TB	AL	45	159	41	8	2	4	(2	2)	65	19	12	22	15	0	46	1	1	1	4	1	.80	1	.258	.324	.409
2006	TB	AL	50	175	43	5	0	1	(1	0)	51	20	10	17	13	0	40	1	0	0	11	3	.79	1	.246	.302	.291
2007	TB	AL	129	474	142	25	1	24	(13	11)	241	86	82	93	65	4	154	4	1	4	22	8	.73	14	.300	.386	.508
3 ML YEARS			224	808	226	38	3	29	(16	13)	357	125	104	132	93	4	240	6	2	5	37	12	.76	16	.280	.356	.442

Justin Upton

Bats: R Throws: R Pos: RF-42; PH-2 · Ht: 6'3" Wt: 205 Born: 8/25/1987 Age: 20

Year	Team	Lg	G	AB	H	2B	3B	HR	(Hm	Rd)	TB	R	RBI	RC	TBB	IBB	SO	HBP	SH	SF	SB	CS	SB%	GDP	Avg	OBP	Slg
2006	Sbend	A	113	438	115	28	1	12	(-	-)	181	71	66	66	52	3	96	5	0	6	15	7	.68	6	.263	.343	.413
2007	Visalia	A+	32	126	43	6	2	5	(-	-)	68	27	17	29	19	1	28	3	0	2	9	4	.69	2	.341	.433	.540
2007	Mobile	AA	71	259	80	17	4	13	(-	-)	144	48	53	57	37	4	51	5	0	5	10	7	.59	6	.309	.399	.556
2007	Ari	NL	43	140	31	8	3	2	(2	0)	51	17	11	13	11	4	37	1	0	0	2	0	1.00	3	.221	.283	.364

Lino Urdaneta

Pitches: R Bats: R Pos: RP-2 · Ht: 6'1" Wt: 219 Born: 11/20/1979 Age: 28

Year	Team	Lg	G	GS	CG	GF	IP	BFP	H	R	ER	HR	SH	SF	HB	TBB	IBB	SO	WP	Bk	W	L	Pct	ShO	Sv-Op	Hld	ERC	ERA
1999	VeroB	A+	27	5	0	6	67.0	292	74	42	36	10	4	3	6	20	1	43	3	3	5	4	.556	0	0--	-	5.01	4.84
2000	VeroB	A+	27	5	0	7	78.0	351	103	60	47	7	2	5	3	24	1	40	6	0	5	4	.556	0	1--	-	5.71	5.42
2001	Wilmg	A+	10	4	0	3	23.2	110	31	23	20	7	0	2	3	11	0	16	2	0	1	2	.333	0	0--	-	8.71	7.61
2002	VeroB	A+	52	0	0	50	52.1	210	39	15	14	3	2	1	2	17	3	30	3	0	2	2	.500	0	32--	-	2.28	2.41
2002	Jaxnvl	AA	1	0	0	0	1.0	6	3	0	0	0	0	0	0	1	0	1	0	0	0	0	-	0	0--	-	22.91	0.00
2003	Jaxnvl	AA	44	0	0	25	65.0	279	68	37	31	4	5	4	3	24	5	42	0	0	0	8	.000	0	6--	-	4.06	4.29
2004	Toledo	AAA	9	1	0	0	13.0	65	22	14	14	4	0	0	1	3	0	4	0	0	0	2	.000	0	0--	-	9.57	9.69
2004	Lkland	A+	2	2	0	0	2.1	12	5	3	3	0	0	0	0	0	0	0	0	0	0	2	.000	0	0--	-	8.42	11.57
2005	StLuci	A+	3	0	0	1	4.2	17	2	1	1	0	0	0	0	1	0	4	0	0	0	0	-	0	0--	-	0.71	1.93
2005	Bnghtn	AA	1	0	0	0	1.2	8	2	1	1	0	0	0	0	1	1	0	0	0	0	0	-	0	0--	-	3.96	5.40
2006	Mets	R	6	0	0	0	7.0	29	8	3	1	0	1	0	0	6	0	6	0	0	0	0	-	0	0--	-	2.61	1.29
2006	Bnghtn	AA	5	0	0	1	4.0	15	3	1	1	0	0	0	0	1	0	2	1	0	0	1	.000	0	0--	-	1.79	2.25
2007	NewOr	AAA	10	0	0	9	12.1	51	12	8	8	3	1	1	0	2	0	2	1	0	1	0	1.000	0	6--	-	3.82	5.84
2007	Mets	R	2	0	0	1	4.0	14	2	0	0	0	0	0	0	2	0	0	0	0	0	0	-	0	1--	-	0.54	0.00
2007	StLuci	A+	2	0	0	0	2.0	11	0	0	0	0	0	0	1	1	0	0	0	0	0	0	-	0	0--	-	0.69	0.00
2007	Bnghtn	AA	16	0	0	10	22.2	100	26	13	12	1	0	1	1	8	2	12	0	0	1	1	.500	0	3--	-	4.36	4.76
2004	Det	AL	1	0	0	0	0.0	5	5	6	6	0	0	0	1	1	0	0	0	0	0	0	-	0	0-0	-	70.27	63.00
2007	NYM	NL	2	0	0	0	1.0	5	2	1	1	1	0	0	0	0	0	0	0	0	0	0	-	0	0-0	0	16.28	9.00
2 ML YEARS			3	0	0	0	1.0	11	7	7	7	1	0	0	1	1	0	0	0	0	0	0	-	0	0-0	0	70.27	63.00

Juan Uribe

Bats: R Throws: R Pos: SS-150 · Ht: 6'0" Wt: 225 Born: 3/22/1979 Age: 29

Year	Team	Lg	G	AB	H	2B	3B	HR	(Hm	Rd)	TB	R	RBI	RC	TBB	IBB	SO	HBP	SH	SF	SB	CS	SB%	GDP	Avg	OBP	Slg
2001	Col	NL	72	273	82	15	11	8	(3	5)	143	32	53	44	8	1	55	2	0	0	3	0	1.00	6	.300	.325	.524
2002	Col	NL	155	566	136	25	7	6	(4	2)	193	69	49	53	34	1	120	5	7	6	9	2	.82	17	.240	.286	.341
2003	Col	NL	87	316	80	19	3	10	(6	4)	135	45	33	45	17	0	60	3	6	1	7	2	.78	3	.253	.297	.427
2004	CWS	AL	134	502	142	31	6	23	(16	7)	254	82	74	81	32	1	96	3	11	5	9	11	.45	10	.283	.327	.506
2005	CWS	AL	146	481	121	23	4	16	(10	6)	198	58	71	59	34	0	77	4	11	10	4	6	.40	7	.252	.301	.412
2006	CWS	AL	132	463	109	28	2	21	(13	8)	204	53	71	52	13	1	82	3	9	7	1	1	.50	10	.235	.257	.441
2007	CWS	AL	150	513	120	18	2	20	(15	5)	202	55	68	52	34	2	112	4	7	5	1	9	.10	6	.234	.284	.394
7 ML YEARS			876	3114	790	159	34	104	(67	37)	1329	394	419	386	172	6	602	24	51	34	34	31	.52	59	.254	.295	.427

Chase Utley

Bats: L Throws: R Pos: 2B-132; 1B-1; PH-1   Ht: 6'1" Wt: 184 Born: 12/17/1978 Age: 29

Year Team	Lg	G	AB	H	2B	3B	HR	(Hm	Rd)	TB	R	RBI	RC	TBB	IBB	SO	HBP	SH	SF	SB	CS	SB%	GDP	Avg	OBP	Slg
2007 Rdng*	AA	3	10	1	0	0	0	(-	-)	1	0	0	0	1	0	2	0	0	0	0	0	-	0	.100	.182	.100
2003 Phi	NL	43	134	32	10	1	2	(1	1)	50	13	21	19	11	0	22	6	0	1	2	0	1.00	3	.239	.322	.373
2004 Phi	NL	94	267	71	11	2	13	(8	5)	125	36	57	37	15	1	40	2	1	2	4	1	.80	6	.266	.308	.468
2005 Phi	NL	147	543	158	39	6	28	(12	16)	293	93	105	102	69	5	109	9	0	7	16	3	.84	10	.291	.376	.540
2006 Phi	NL	160	658	203	40	4	32	(16	16)	347	131	102	122	63	1	132	14	0	4	15	4	.79	9	.309	.379	.527
2007 Phi	NL	132	530	176	48	5	22	(14	8)	300	104	103	111	50	1	89	25	1	7	9	1	.90	7	.332	.410	.566
5 ML YEARS		576	2132	640	148	18	97	(51	46)	1115	377	388	391	208	8	392	56	2	21	46	9	.84	35	.300	.374	.523

Wilson Valdez

Bats: R Throws: R Pos: 2B-12; SS-12; 3B-9; PR-7; PH-6; LF-2; CF-1   Ht: 5'11" Wt: 160 Born: 5/20/1978 Age: 30

Year Team	Lg	G	AB	H	2B	3B	HR	(Hm	Rd)	TB	R	RBI	RC	TBB	IBB	SO	HBP	SH	SF	SB	CS	SB%	GDP	Avg	OBP	Slg
2007 LsVgs*	AAA	90	361	124	19	1	4	(-	-)	157	81	29	68	43	1	34	1	4	2	14	6	.70	3	.343	.413	.435
2004 CWS	AL	19	43	10	1	0	1	(1	0)	14	8	4	2	2	0	5	0	1	0	1	2	.33	1	.233	.267	.326
2005 2 Tms		51	139	28	7	1	0	(0	0)	37	9	9	8	8	0	26	0	1	0	2	2	.50	2	.201	.245	.266
2007 LAD	NL	41	74	16	2	1	0	(0	0)	20	12	7	7	4	0	12	1	0	1	1	0	1.00	0	.216	.263	.270
05 Sea	AL	42	126	25	5	1	0	(0	0)	32	9	8	6	6	0	25	0	1	0	2	2	.50	1	.198	.235	.254
05 SD	NL	9	13	3	2	0	0	(0	0)	5	0	1	2	2	0	1	0	0	0	0	0	-	1	.231	.333	.385
3 ML YEARS		111	256	54	10	2	1	(1	0)	71	29	20	17	14	0	43	1	2	1	4	4	.50	3	.211	.254	.277

Javier Valentin

Bats: B Throws: R Pos: C-73; PH-43; PR-2; 1B-1; DH-1   Ht: 5'10" Wt: 215 Born: 9/19/1975 Age: 32

Year Team	Lg	G	AB	H	2B	3B	HR	(Hm	Rd)	TB	R	RBI	RC	TBB	IBB	SO	HBP	SH	SF	SB	CS	SB%	GDP	Avg	OBP	Slg
1997 Min	AL	4	7	2	0	0	0	(0	0)	2	1	0	1	0	0	3	0	0	0	0	0	-	0	.286	.286	.286
1998 Min	AL	55	162	32	7	1	3	(1	2)	50	11	18	10	11	1	30	0	3	1	0	0	-	7	.198	.247	.309
1999 Min	AL	78	218	54	12	1	5	(2	3)	83	22	28	27	22	0	39	1	1	5	0	0	-	4	.248	.313	.381
2002 Min	AL	4	4	2	0	0	0	(0	0)	2	0	0	0	0	0	0	0	0	0	0	0	-	0	.500	.500	.500
2003 TB	AL	49	135	30	7	1	3	(2	1)	48	13	15	11	5	0	31	1	0	1	0	0	-	7	.222	.254	.356
2004 Cin	NL	82	202	47	10	1	6	(2	4)	77	18	20	20	17	3	36	1	0	2	0	0	-	4	.233	.293	.381
2005 Cin	NL	76	221	62	11	0	14	(7	7)	115	36	50	41	30	3	37	0	0	3	0	0	-	5	.281	.362	.520
2006 Cin	NL	92	186	50	6	1	8	(6	2)	82	24	27	17	13	3	29	0	0	2	0	0	-	5	.269	.313	.441
2007 Cin	NL	97	243	67	21	0	2	(2	0)	94	19	34	31	19	2	25	1	0	2	0	0	-	5	.276	.328	.387
9 ML YEARS		537	1378	346	74	5	41	(22	19)	553	144	192	158	117	12	230	4	4	16	0	0	-	37	.251	.308	.401

Jose Valentin

Bats: B Throws: R Pos: 2B-45; PH-5; DH-1   Ht: 5'10" Wt: 190 Born: 10/12/1969 Age: 38

Year Team	Lg	G	AB	H	2B	3B	HR	(Hm	Rd)	TB	R	RBI	RC	TBB	IBB	SO	HBP	SH	SF	SB	CS	SB%	GDP	Avg	OBP	Slg
2007 StLuci*	A+	3	8	1	0	0	1	(-	-)	4	4	4	1	2	0	2	0	0	1	0	0	-	1	.125	.273	.500
1992 Mil	AL	4	3	0	0	0	0	(0	0)	0	1	1	0	0	0	0	0	0	0	0	0	-	0	.000	.000	.000
1993 Mil	AL	19	53	13	1	2	1	(1	0)	21	10	7	8	7	1	16	1	2	0	1	0	1.00	1	.245	.344	.396
1994 Mil	AL	97	285	68	10	0	11	(8	3)	120	47	46	43	38	1	75	2	4	2	12	3	.80	1	.239	.330	.421
1995 Mil	AL	112	338	74	23	3	11	(3	8)	136	62	49	42	37	0	83	0	7	4	16	8	.67	0	.219	.293	.402
1996 Mil	AL	154	552	143	33	7	24	(10	14)	262	90	95	91	66	9	145	0	6	4	17	4	.81	4	.259	.336	.475
1997 Mil	AL	136	494	125	23	1	17	(4	13)	201	58	58	64	39	4	109	4	4	5	19	8	.70	5	.253	.310	.407
1998 Mil	NL	151	428	96	24	0	16	(7	9)	168	65	49	57	63	8	105	1	2	3	10	7	.59	2	.224	.323	.393
1999 Mil	NL	89	256	58	9	5	10	(3	7)	107	45	38	40	48	7	52	2	2	5	3	2	.60	3	.227	.347	.418
2000 CWS	AL	144	568	155	37	6	25	(16	9)	279	107	92	97	59	1	106	4	13	4	19	2	.90	11	.273	.345	.491
2001 CWS	AL	124	438	113	22	2	28	(14	14)	223	74	68	74	50	2	114	3	8	3	9	6	.60	7	.258	.336	.509
2002 CWS	AL	135	474	118	26	4	25	(15	10)	227	70	75	75	43	2	99	2	3	5	3	3	.50	9	.249	.311	.479
2003 CWS	AL	144	503	119	26	2	28	(14	14)	233	79	74	72	54	4	114	3	7	2	8	3	.73	6	.237	.313	.463
2004 CWS	AL	125	450	97	20	3	30	(14	14)	213	74	70	64	43	4	139	3	6	2	8	6	.57	5	.216	.287	.473
2005 LAD	NL	56	147	25	4	2	2	(0	2)	39	17	14	14	31	2	38	4	0	2	3	1	.75	2	.170	.326	.265
2006 NYM	NL	137	384	104	24	3	18	(11	7)	188	56	62	57	37	5	71	0	5	6	6	2	.75	5	.271	.330	.490
2007 NYM	NL	51	166	40	11	1	3	(2	1)	62	18	18	17	15	4	28	0	1	1	2	1	.67	5	.241	.302	.373
16 ML YEARS		1678	5539	1348	302	41	249	(124	125)	2479	872	816	816	630	54	1294	29	70	49	136	56	.71	66	.243	.321	.448

Jose Valverde

Pitches: R Bats: R Pos: RP-65   Ht: 6'4" Wt: 255 Born: 7/24/1979 Age: 28

		HOW MUCH HE PITCHED						WHAT HE GAVE UP										THE RESULTS						
Year Team	Lg	G	GS	CG	GF	IP	BFP	H	R	ER	HR	SH	SF	HB	TBB	IBB	SO	WP	Bk	W	L	Pct	ShO	Sv-Op	Hld	ERC	ERA
2003 Ari	NL	54	0	0	33	50.1	204	24	16	12	4	0	1	2	26	2	71	2	0	2	1	.667	0	10-11	8	1.77	2.15
2004 Ari	NL	29	0	0	20	29.2	131	23	14	14	7	3	2	1	17	4	38	4	0	1	2	.333	0	8-10	5	4.25	4.25
2005 Ari	NL	61	0	0	34	66.1	268	51	19	18	5	3	1	2	20	1	75	3	0	3	4	.429	0	15-17	7	2.43	2.44
2006 Ari	NL	44	0	0	35	49.1	223	50	32	32	6	1	3	2	22	3	69	2	0	2	3	.400	0	18-22	1	4.42	5.84
2007 Ari	NL	65	0	0	59	64.1	265	46	21	19	7	0	1	3	26	1	78	1	0	1	4	.200	0	47-54	6	2.77	2.66
5 ML YEARS		253	0	0	181	260.0	1091	194	105	95	29	7	8	10	111	11	331	12	0	9	14	.391	0	98-114	21	2.93	3.29

John Van Benschoten

Pitches: R Bats: R Pos: SP-9; RP-2   **Ht: 6'4" Wt: 225 Born: 4/14/1980 Age: 28**

		HOW MUCH HE PITCHED						WHAT HE GAVE UP										THE RESULTS						
Year	Team	Lg	G	GS	CG	GF	IP	BFP	H	R	ER	HR	SH	SF	HB	TBB	IBB	SO	WP	Bk	W	L	Pct	ShO	Sv-Op Hld	ERC	ERA
2001	Wmspt	A-	9	9	0	0	25.2	104	23	11	10	0	0	0	1	10	0	19	5	0	0	2	.000	0	0- -	3.09	3.51
2002	Hickory	A	27	27	0	0	148.0	620	119	57	46	6	4	2	7	62	1	145	7	0	11	4	.733	0	0- -	2.86	2.80
2003	Lynbrg	A+	9	9	0	0	48.2	192	33	14	12	1	1	0	1	18	0	49	1	0	6	0	1.000	0	0- -	1.94	2.22
2003	Altna	AA	17	17	1	0	90.1	399	95	46	37	5	4	1	6	34	1	78	2	2	7	6	.538	0	0- -	4.16	3.69
2004	Nashv	AAA	23	23	0	0	131.2	574	135	75	69	16	2	3	9	49	1	101	4	1	4	11	.267	0	0- -	4.54	4.72
2006	Pirates	R	1	1	0	0	6.0	25	1	3	3	1	1	0	0	2	0	4	1	0	0	1	.000	0	0- -	0.75	4.50
2006	Altna	AA	1	1	0	0	5.0	21	3	2	2	0	0	1	0	3	0	3	1	0	1	0	1.000	0	0- -	2.03	3.60
2006	Indy	AAA	3	3	0	0	11.2	51	10	7	7	2	0	1	0	7	0	13	0	0	1	1	.500	0	0- -	4.58	5.40
2007	Indy	AAA	19	19	1	0	109.0	460	98	35	31	8	0	1	6	51	2	79	2	2	10	7	.588	1	0- -	3.89	2.56
2004	Pit	NL	6	5	0	0	28.2	135	33	27	22	3	2	2	2	19	0	18	1	0	1	3	.250	0	0-0 0	6.47	6.91
2007	Pit	NL	11	9	0	1	39.0	203	55	45	44	4	3	2	5	29	1	26	1	0	0	7	.000	0	0-0 0	8.51	10.15
	2 ML YEARS		17	14	0	1	67.2	338	88	72	66	7	5	4	7	48	1	44	2	0	1	10	.091	0	0-0 0	7.63	8.78

Rick Vanden Hurk

Pitches: R Bats: R Pos: SP-17; RP-1   **Ht: 6'5" Wt: 195 Born: 5/22/1985 Age: 23**

		HOW MUCH HE PITCHED						WHAT HE GAVE UP										THE RESULTS						
Year	Team	Lg	G	GS	CG	GF	IP	BFP	H	R	ER	HR	SH	SF	HB	TBB	IBB	SO	WP	Bk	W	L	Pct	ShO	Sv-Op Hld	ERC	ERA
2003	Mrlns	R	11	10	0	0	38.2	190	49	30	23	2	3	1	7	20	0	30	4	3	2	6	.250	0	0- -	6.40	5.35
2004	Jupiter	A+	14	14	0	0	58.0	252	54	22	21	2	2	7	4	31	0	43	6	0	2	3	.400	0	0- -	4.09	3.26
2005	Grnsbr	A	4	4	1	0	22.0	91	17	7	6	1	0	0	1	11	0	26	1	0	1	2	.333	0	0- -	3.11	2.45
2005	Jupiter	A+	2	2	0	0	6.2	28	7	4	3	0	0	0	1	0	0	6	0	0	0	1	.000	0	0- -	2.67	4.05
2006	Mrlns	R	5	5	0	0	15.0	56	4	2	2	0	1	0	0	8	0	26	1	0	0	0	-	0	0- -	0.86	1.20
2006	Jupiter	A+	3	3	0	0	10.0	40	5	4	3	1	0	0	0	6	0	15	0	0	0	0	-	0	0- -	2.26	2.70
2007	Carlna	AA	9	9	0	0	53.2	220	42	23	21	5	5	1	2	20	0	61	4	1	2	2	.500	0	0- -	2.93	3.52
2007	Albq	AAA	2	2	0	0	12.0	44	6	3	3	3	0	0	0	4	0	14	1	0	2	0	1.000	0	0- -	2.21	2.25
2007	Fla	NL	18	17	0	0	81.2	379	94	63	62	15	5	3	3	48	5	82	4	4	4	6	.400	0	0-0 0	6.50	6.83

Claudio Vargas

Pitches: R Bats: R Pos: SP-23; RP-6   **Ht: 6'3" Wt: 220 Born: 6/19/1978 Age: 30**

		HOW MUCH HE PITCHED						WHAT HE GAVE UP										THE RESULTS						
Year	Team	Lg	G	GS	CG	GF	IP	BFP	H	R	ER	HR	SH	SF	HB	TBB	IBB	SO	WP	Bk	W	L	Pct	ShO	Sv-Op Hld	ERC	ERA
2003	Mon	NL	23	20	0	0	114.0	492	111	59	55	16	5	4	7	41	5	62	2	0	6	8	.429	0	0-0 0	4.21	4.34
2004	Mon	NL	45	14	0	6	118.1	530	120	75	69	26	4	4	7	64	7	89	8	0	5	5	.500	0	0-0 3	5.84	5.25
2005	2 Tms	NL	25	23	0	0	132.1	586	146	81	77	25	6	1	7	47	5	95	6	0	9	9	.500	0	0-0 0	5.28	5.24
2006	Ari	NL	31	30	0	0	167.2	747	185	101	90	27	8	3	8	52	2	123	9	1	12	10	.545	0	0-0 0	4.81	4.83
2007	Mil	NL	29	23	0	1	134.1	605	153	80	76	23	5	7	2	54	3	107	4	0	11	6	.647	0	1-2 0	5.38	5.09
05	Was	NL	4	4	0	0	12.2	66	22	15	13	4	0	0	0	7	2	5	0	0	0	3	.000	0	0-0 0	11.04	9.24
05	Ari	NL	21	19	0	0	119.2	520	124	66	64	21	6	1	7	40	3	90	6	0	9	6	.600	0	0-0 0	4.74	4.81
	5 ML YEARS		153	110	0	8	666.2	2960	715	396	367	117	28	19	31	258	22	476	29	1	43	38	.531	0	1-2 3	5.09	4.95

Jason Vargas

Pitches: L Bats: L Pos: SP-2   **Ht: 6'0" Wt: 215 Born: 2/2/1983 Age: 25**

		HOW MUCH HE PITCHED						WHAT HE GAVE UP										THE RESULTS						
Year	Team	Lg	G	GS	CG	GF	IP	BFP	H	R	ER	HR	SH	SF	HB	TBB	IBB	SO	WP	Bk	W	L	Pct	ShO	Sv-Op Hld	ERC	ERA
2007	NewOr*	AAA	24	24	0	0	125.0	556	141	77	71	14	6	6	3	44	0	108	1	1	9	7	.563	0	0- -	4.75	5.11
2005	Fla	NL	17	13	1	0	73.2	325	71	34	33	4	4	1	4	31	4	59	0	0	5	5	.500	0	0-0 0	3.68	4.03
2006	Fla	NL	12	5	0	3	43.0	213	50	39	35	9	4	4	4	30	3	25	2	0	1	2	.333	0	0-0 0	7.30	7.33
2007	NYM	NL	2	2	0	0	10.1	51	17	14	14	4	0	0	0	2	1	4	1	1	0	1	.000	0	0-0 0	8.95	12.19
	3 ML YEARS		31	20	1	3	127.0	589	138	87	82	17	8	5	8	63	8	88	3	1	6	8	.429	0	0-0 0	5.25	5.81

Jason Varitek

Bats: B Throws: R Pos: C-125; PH-9   **Ht: 6'2" Wt: 230 Born: 4/11/1972 Age: 36**

			BATTING																		BASERUNNING				AVERAGES		
Year	Team	Lg	G	AB	H	2B	3B	HR	(Hm	Rd)	TB	R	RBI	RC	TBB	IBB	SO	HBP	SH	SF	SB	CS	SB%	GDP	Avg	OBP	Slg
1997	Bos	AL	1	1	1	0	0	0	(0	0)	1	0	0	1	0	0	0	0	0	0	0	0	-	0	1.000	1.000	1.000
1998	Bos	AL	86	221	56	13	0	7	(1	6)	90	31	33	26	17	1	45	2	4	3	2	2	.50	8	.253	.309	.407
1999	Bos	AL	144	483	130	39	2	20	(12	8)	233	70	76	75	46	2	85	2	5	8	1	2	.33	13	.269	.330	.482
2000	Bos	AL	139	448	111	31	1	10	(2	8)	174	55	65	59	60	3	84	6	1	4	1	1	.50	16	.248	.342	.388
2001	Bos	AL	51	174	51	11	1	7	(2	5)	85	19	25	30	21	3	35	1	1	1	0	0	-	6	.293	.371	.489
2002	Bos	AL	132	467	124	27	1	10	(6	4)	183	58	61	52	41	3	95	7	1	3	4	3	.57	13	.266	.332	.392
2003	Bos	AL	142	451	123	31	1	25	(13	12)	231	63	85	79	51	8	106	7	5	7	3	2	.60	10	.273	.351	.512
2004	Bos	AL	137	463	137	30	1	18	(8	10)	223	67	73	79	62	9	126	10	0	1	10	3	.77	11	.296	.390	.482
2005	Bos	AL	133	470	132	30	1	22	(7	15)	230	70	70	78	62	3	117	3	1	3	2	0	1.00	10	.281	.366	.489
2006	Bos	AL	103	365	87	19	2	12	(2	10)	146	46	55	45	46	7	87	2	1	2	1	2	.33	10	.238	.325	.400
2007	Bos	AL	131	435	111	15	3	17	(9	8)	183	57	68	61	71	9	122	8	0	4	1	2	.33	9	.255	.367	.421
	11 ML YEARS		1199	3978	1063	246	13	148	(62	86)	1779	536	611	585	477	48	902	48	19	36	25	17	.60	106	.267	.350	.447

Virgil Vasquez

Pitches: R **Bats:** R **Pos:** SP-3; RP-2   **Ht:** 6'3" **Wt:** 205 **Born:** 6/7/1982 **Age:** 26

Year	Team	Lg	G	GS	CG	GF	IP	BFP	H	R	ER	HR	SH	SF	HB	TBB	IBB	SO	WP	Bk	W	L	Pct	ShO	Sv-Op	Hld	ERC	ERA
2003	Oneont	A-	11	11	0	0	53.1	245	76	43	41	5	0	1	2	10	0	35	1	0	3	4	.429	0	0--	-	5.73	6.92
2004	WMich	A	27	27	0	0	168.1	681	156	73	68	14	8	5	15	34	1	120	6	1	14	6	.700	0	0--	-	3.23	3.64
2005	Lkland	A+	8	8	1	0	47.0	191	52	23	22	6	1	0	3	7	0	31	2	0	4	1	.800	1	0--	-	4.31	4.21
2005	Erie	AA	15	15	0	0	83.2	361	93	57	47	10	5	5	7	13	0	53	1	0	2	8	.200	0	0--	-	4.14	5.06
2006	Erie	AA	27	27	3	0	173.2	734	174	79	72	21	4	3	20	50	2	129	2	0	7	12	.368	0	0--	-	4.33	3.73
2007	Toledo	AAA	25	25	0	0	155.0	626	139	64	60	18	3	5	8	33	1	127	1	1	12	5	.706	2	0--	-	3.14	3.48
2007	Det	AL	5	3	0	0	16.2	81	27	16	16	7	0	0	1	5	0	7	0	0	0	1	.000	0	0-0	0	10.58	8.64

Javier Vazquez

Pitches: R **Bats:** R **Pos:** SP-32   **Ht:** 6'1" **Wt:** 210 **Born:** 7/25/1976 **Age:** 31

Year	Team	Lg	G	GS	CG	GF	IP	BFP	H	R	ER	HR	SH	SF	HB	TBB	IBB	SO	WP	Bk	W	L	Pct	ShO	Sv-Op	Hld	ERC	ERA
1998	Mon	NL	33	32	0	1	172.1	764	196	121	116	31	9	4	11	68	2	139	2	0	5	15	.250	0	0-0	0	5.79	6.06
1999	Mon	NL	26	26	3	0	154.2	667	154	98	86	20	3	3	4	52	4	113	2	0	9	8	.529	1	0-0	0	4.02	5.00
2000	Mon	NL	33	33	2	0	217.2	945	247	104	99	24	11	3	5	61	10	196	3	0	11	9	.550	1	0-0	0	4.45	4.05
2001	Mon	NL	32	32	5	0	223.2	898	197	92	85	24	9	2	3	44	4	208	3	1	16	11	.593	3	0-0	0	2.75	3.42
2002	Mon	NL	34	34	2	0	230.1	971	243	111	100	28	15	7	4	49	6	179	3	0	10	13	.435	0	0-0	0	3.80	3.91
2003	Mon	NL	34	34	4	0	230.2	938	198	93	83	28	6	6	4	57	5	241	11	1	13	12	.520	1	0-0	0	2.90	3.24
2004	NYY	AL	32	32	0	0	198.0	849	195	114	108	33	4	8	11	60	3	150	12	2	14	10	.583	0	0-0	0	4.23	4.91
2005	Ari	NL	33	33	3	0	215.2	904	223	114	106	35	13	5	5	46	4	192	7	0	11	15	.423	1	0-0	0	4.00	4.42
2006	CWS	AL	33	32	1	0	202.2	872	206	116	109	23	2	4	15	56	2	184	7	0	11	12	.478	0	0-0	0	4.02	4.84
2007	CWS	AL	32	32	2	0	216.2	882	197	95	90	29	5	7	7	50	2	213	5	0	15	8	.652	0	0-0	0	3.29	3.74
10 ML YEARS			322	320	22	1	2062.1	8690	2056	1056	981	275	77	47	69	543	42	1815	55	4	115	113	.504	7	0-0	0	3.84	4.28

Ramon Vazquez

Bats: L **Throws:** R **Pos:** 3B-71; SS-19; 2B-13; 1B-7; PH-4; PR-2   **Ht:** 5'11" **Wt:** 170 **Born:** 8/21/1976 **Age:** 31

Year	Team	Lg	G	AB	H	2B	3B	HR	(Hm	Rd)	TB	R	RBI	RC	TBB	IBB	SO	HBP	SH	SF	SB	CS	SB%	GDP	Avg	OBP	Slg
2007	Okla*	AAA	35	132	34	10	2	2	(-	-)	54	27	13	22	24	0	27	2	1	2	3	1	.75	1	.258	.375	.409
2001	Sea	AL	17	35	8	0	0	0	(0	0)	8	5	4	2	0	0	3	0	1	1	0	0	-	0	.229	.222	.229
2002	SD	NL	128	423	116	21	5	2	(0	2)	153	50	32	55	45	3	79	1	3	2	7	2	.78	6	.274	.344	.362
2003	SD	NL	116	422	110	17	4	3	(1	2)	144	56	30	49	52	2	88	2	5	3	10	3	.77	4	.261	.342	.341
2004	SD	NL	52	115	27	3	2	1	(1	0)	37	12	13	9	11	2	24	0	4	2	1	1	.50	2	.235	.297	.322
2005	2 Tms	AL	39	85	18	5	0	0	(0	0)	23	7	5	5	5	0	17	0	2	0	0	0	-	0	.212	.256	.271
2006	Cle	AL	34	67	14	2	0	1	(0	0)	19	11	8	7	6	0	18	0	2	2	0	0	-	3	.209	.267	.284
2007	Tex	AL	104	300	69	13	3	8	(2	6)	112	42	28	36	29	0	72	2	12	2	1	0	1.00	4	.230	.300	.373
05	Bos	AL	27	61	12	2	0	0	(0	0)	14	6	4	3	3	0	14	0	2	0	0	0	-	0	.197	.234	.230
05	Cle	AL	12	24	6	3	0	0	(0	0)	9	1	1	2	2	0	3	0	0	0	0	0	-	0	.250	.308	.375
7 ML YEARS			490	1447	362	61	14	15	(5	10)	496	183	120	163	148	7	301	5	29	12	19	6	.76	19	.250	.319	.343

Jorge Velandia

Bats: R **Throws:** R **Pos:** 2B-11; SS-4   **Ht:** 5'9" **Wt:** 180 **Born:** 1/12/1975 **Age:** 33

Year	Team	Lg	G	AB	H	2B	3B	HR	(Hm	Rd)	TB	R	RBI	RC	TBB	IBB	SO	HBP	SH	SF	SB	CS	SB%	GDP	Avg	OBP	Slg
2007	Drham*	AAA	120	433	108	24	4	5	(-	-)	155	44	32	47	28	0	95	3	7	6	6	6	.50	11	.249	.296	.358
1997	SD	NL	14	29	3	2	0	0	(0	0)	5	0	0	1	1	0	7	0	0	0	0	0	-	0	.103	.133	.172
1998	Oak	AL	8	4	1	0	0	0	(0	0)	1	0	0	0	0	0	1	0	0	0	0	0	-	0	.250	.250	.250
1999	Oak	AL	63	48	9	1	0	0	(0	0)	10	4	2	3	2	0	13	1	0	0	2	0	1.00	0	.188	.235	.208
2000	2 Tms	AL	33	31	3	1	0	0	(0	0)	4	2	2	1	2	0	8	1	0	0	0	0	-	0	.097	.176	.129
2001	NYM	NL	9	9	0	0	0	0	(0	0)	0	1	0	0	2	0	1	0	0	0	0	0	-	0	.000	.182	.000
2003	NYM	NL	23	58	11	3	1	0	(0	0)	16	6	8	6	10	1	15	0	3	1	0	0	-	1	.190	.304	.276
2007	TB	AL	14	50	16	4	0	2	(1	1)	26	7	11	12	8	0	17	1	1	0	0	0	-	0	.320	.424	.520
00	Oak	AL	18	24	3	1	0	0	(0	0)	4	1	2	1	0	0	6	1	0	0	0	0	-	0	.125	.160	.167
00	NYM	NL	15	7	0	0	0	0	(0	0)	0	1	0	0	2	0	2	0	0	0	0	0	-	0	.000	.222	.000
7 ML YEARS			164	229	43	11	1	2	(1	1)	62	20	23	23	25	1	62	3	4	1	2	0	1.00	1	.188	.275	.271

Eugenio Velez

Bats: B **Throws:** R **Pos:** PH-8; PR-5; 2B-4; LF-2   **Ht:** 6'1" **Wt:** 165 **Born:** 5/16/1982 **Age:** 26

Year	Team	Lg	G	AB	H	2B	3D	HR	(Hm	Rd)	TB	R	RBI	RC	TBB	IBB	SO	HBP	SH	SF	SB	CS	SB%	GDP	Avg	OBP	Slg
2003	Pulaski	R+	50	186	48	2	2	2	(-	-)	65	20	24	18	8	0	49	1	0	1	3	4	.43	7	.258	.291	.349
2003	Auburn	A-	7	26	5	2	0	1	(-	-)	10	2	7	2	1	0	10	0	0	0	0	0	-	0	.192	.222	.385
2004	Pulaski	R+	44	168	49	14	4	1	(-	-)	74	27	27	24	12	1	32	1	1	2	1	4	.20	4	.292	.339	.440
2004	Auburn	A-	10	19	5	0	0	0	(-	-)	5	5	2	2	3	0	5	1	0	0	0	0	-	2	.263	.391	.263
2005	Lansng	A	67	239	68	11	3	4	(-	-)	97	25	34	30	9	0	40	2	0	4	7	5	.58	2	.285	.311	.406
2006	Augsta	A	126	460	145	29	20	14	(-	-)	256	90	90	99	34	2	81	8	1	5	64	15	.81	9	.315	.369	.557
2007	Conn	AA	96	376	112	17	9	1	(-	-)	150	55	25	56	26	0	66	2	4	3	49	17	.74	6	.298	.344	.399
2007	Fresno	AAA	4	18	5	0	0	0	(-	-)	5	5	0	3	2	0	3	1	0	0	5	0	1.00	0	.278	.381	.278
2007	SF	NL	14	11	3	0	2	0	(0	0)	7	5	2	4	2	0	3	0	0	0	4	0	1.00	0	.273	.385	.636

.Jose Veras

Pitches: R **Bats:** R **Pos:** RP-9   **Ht:** 6'5" **Wt:** 236 **Born:** 10/20/1980 **Age:** 27

Year	Team	Lg	G	GS	CG	GF	IP	BFP	H	R	ER	HR	SH	SF	HB	TBB	IBB	SO	WP	Bk	W	L	Pct	ShO	Sv-Op	Hld	ERC	ERA
1998	DRays	R	5	4	0	0	16.0	79	19	14	12	1	0	0	1	12	0	19	1	0	1	1	.500	0	0--	-	6.49	6.75
1999	Princtn	R+	14	14	0	0	60.2	299	74	57	48	5	1	4	7	50	1	48	10	1	3	5	.375	0	0--	-	7.64	7.12
2000	CtnSC	A	20	20	1	0	106.2	493	125	74	57	7	2	1	11	41	0	102	11	1	8	8	.500	0	0--	-	5.07	4.81
2001	Bkrsfld	A+	27	27	0	0	153.0	678	163	104	77	13	5	4	20	55	0	138	14	2	9	8	.529	0	0--	-	4.72	4.53
2002	HudVal	A-	2	2	0	0	7.0	28	2	0	0	0	0	0	0	5	0	7	0	0	0	0	-	0	0--	-	1.21	0.00
2002	Bkrsfld	A+	11	11	0	0	59.0	283	77	44	35	10	1	5	3	30	0	57	2	2	3	4	.429	0	0--	-	7.08	5.34
2003	Orlndo	AA	27	22	1	1	130.1	551	108	59	50	11	3	3	6	53	0	118	8	1	6	9	.400	1	0--	-	3.22	3.45
2003	Drham	AAA	3	0	0	0	5.1	27	9	5	5	2	0	0	1	1	0	3	1	0	0	0	-	0	0--	-	10.48	8.44
2004	Drham	AAA	30	10	0	4	84.1	392	101	55	49	9	5	4	7	33	3	63	5	1	6	5	.545	0	0--	-	5.41	5.23
2004	Mont	AA	3	3	0	0	10.0	43	10	7	7	2	0	1	0	7	0	6	1	0	1	0	1.000	0	0--	-	6.55	6.30
2005	Okla	AAA	57	0	0	47	61.2	284	63	27	26	4	2	2	2	33	3	72	5	2	3	5	.375	0	24--	-	4.38	3.79
2006	Clmbs	AAA	50	0	0	35	59.2	220	49	17	16	3	4	2	1	19	2	68	1	0	5	3	.625	0	21--	-	2.85	2.41
2007	Yanks	R	2	2	0	0	2.0	8	2	0	0	0	0	0	0	0	0	1	0	0	0	0	-	0	0--	-	1.95	0.00
2007	Tampa	A+	2	1	0	0	3.0	11	0	0	0	0	0	0	0	2	0	5	0	0	0	0	-	0	0--	-	0.46	0.00
2007	S-WB	AAA	12	0	0	8	16.0	74	17	8	8	1	0	0	3	7	0	17	2	0	2	0	1.000	0	4--	-	4.99	4.50
2006	NYY	AL	12	0	0	4	11.0	42	8	5	5	2	0	0	0	4	0	6	1	1	0	0	-	0	1-1	1	3.19	4.09
2007	NYY	AL	9	0	0	3	9.1	41	6	6	6	0	0	0	0	7	1	7	1	0	0	0	-	0	2-2	1	2.52	5.79
	2 ML YEARS		21	0	0	7	20.1	83	14	11	11	2	0	0	0	11	1	13	2	1	0	0	-	0	3-3	2	2.92	4.87

Justin Verlander

Pitches: R **Bats:** R **Pos:** SP-32   **Ht:** 6'5" **Wt:** 200 **Born:** 2/20/1983 **Age:** 25

Year	Team	Lg	G	GS	CG	GF	IP	BFP	H	R	ER	HR	SH	SF	HB	TBB	IBB	SO	WP	Bk	W	L	Pct	ShO	Sv-Op	Hld	ERC	ERA
2005	Det	AL	2	2	0	0	11.1	54	15	9	9	1	0	0	1	5	0	7	1	0	0	2	.000	0	0-0	0	6.41	7.15
2006	Det	AL	30	30	1	0	186.0	776	187	78	75	21	2	4	6	60	1	124	5	1	17	9	.654	1	0-0	0	4.12	3.63
2007	Det	AL	32	32	1	0	201.2	866	181	88	82	20	3	1	19	67	3	183	17	2	18	6	.750	1	0-0	0	3.53	3.66
	3 ML YEARS		64	64	2	0	399.0	1696	383	175	166	42	5	5	26	132	4	314	23	3	35	17	.673	2	0-0	0	3.88	3.74

Jamie Vermilyea

Pitches: R **Bats:** R **Pos:** RP-2   **Ht:** 6'4" **Wt:** 195 **Born:** 2/10/1982 **Age:** 26

Year	Team	Lg	G	GS	CG	GF	IP	BFP	H	R	ER	HR	SH	SF	HB	TBB	IBB	SO	WP	Bk	W	L	Pct	ShO	Sv-Op	Hld	ERC	ERA
2003	Auburn	A-	9	2	0	1	30.1	119	22	10	8	0	2	1	3	5	0	53	0	0	5	1	.833	0	0--	-	1.63	2.37
2003	Dnedin	A+	9	0	0	3	21.2	86	21	6	6	1	0	0	1	2	1	25	1	0	0	2	.000	0	2--	-	2.57	2.49
2004	Dnedin	A+	18	6	0	2	55.1	226	54	22	19	4	1	0	1	13	1	37	2	0	5	1	.833	0	0--	-	3.23	3.09
2004	NHam	AA	20	6	1	10	57.1	223	43	20	16	2	1	0	3	12	0	39	1	0	3	2	.600	1	5--	-	1.94	2.51
2005	NHam	AA	27	4	0	6	65.2	273	67	21	17	5	1	1	3	16	2	52	0	0	3	3	.500	0	1--	-	3.61	2.33
2005	Syrcse	AAA	16	4	0	4	35.1	165	49	27	22	6	1	2	3	11	0	24	0	1	3	0	1.000	0	1--	-	6.95	5.60
2006	NHam	AA	5	1	0	2	16.1	63	15	4	3	0	1	0	0	0	0	7	0	0	0	0	-	0	1--	-	1.65	1.65
2006	Syrcse	AAA	25	17	0	5	114.2	486	129	57	49	9	8	5	2	28	0	64	1	0	6	7	.462	0	1--	-	4.14	3.85
2007	Syrcse	AAA	25	1	0	5	43.1	190	40	22	20	4	2	1	5	20	2	32	1	0	2	2	.500	0	1--	-	4.22	4.15
2007	Tor	AL	2	0	0	1	6.0	22	5	0	0	0	0	0	0	0	0	2	0	0	0	0	-	0	0-0	0	1.43	0.00

Shane Victorino

Bats: B **Throws:** R **Pos:** RF-114; PH-19; CF-4; PR-2   **Ht:** 5'9" **Wt:** 180 **Born:** 11/30/1980 **Age:** 27

Year	Team	Lg	G	AB	H	2B	3B	HR	(Hm	Rd)	TB	R	RBI	RC	TBB	IBB	SO	HBP	SH	SF	SB	CS	SB%	GDP	Avg	OBP	Slg
2007	Lakwd*	A-	1	5	1	0	0	0	(-	-)	1	1	0	0	0	0	1	0	0	0	0	0	-	0	.200	.200	.200
2007	Rdng*	AA	2	6	2	0	0	0	(-	-)	2	0	1	0	0	0	0	0	0	0	1	0	1.00	0	.333	.333	.333
2003	SD	NL	36	73	11	2	0	0	(0	0)	13	8	4	1	7	0	17	1	1	1	7	2	.78	5	.151	.232	.178
2005	Phi	NL	21	17	5	0	0	2	(1	1)	11	5	8	4	0	0	3	0	0	2	0	0	-	5	.294	.263	.647
2006	Phi	NL	153	415	119	19	8	6	(3	3)	172	70	46	58	24	0	54	14	8	1	4	3	.57	5	.287	.346	.414
2007	Phi	NL	131	456	128	23	3	12	(6	6)	193	78	46	65	37	1	62	10	5	2	37	4	.90	10	.281	.347	.423
	4 ML YEARS		341	961	263	44	11	20	(10	10)	389	161	104	128	68	1	136	25	14	6	48	9	.84	20	.274	.336	.405

Jose Vidro

Bats: B **Throws:** R **Pos:** DH-122; 1B-11; 2B-10; PH-10   **Ht:** 6'0" **Wt:** 193 **Born:** 8/27/1974 **Age:** 33

Year	Team	Lg	G	AB	H	2B	3B	HR	(Hm	Rd)	TB	R	RBI	RC	TBB	IBB	SO	HBP	SH	SF	SB	CS	SB%	GDP	Avg	OBP	Slg
1997	Mon	NL	67	169	42	12	1	2	(0	2)	62	19	17	19	11	0	20	2	0	3	1	0	1.00	1	.249	.297	.367
1998	Mon	NL	83	205	45	12	0	0	(0	0)	57	24	18	19	27	0	33	4	6	3	2	2	.50	5	.220	.318	.278
1999	Mon	NL	140	494	150	45	2	12	(5	7)	235	67	59	76	29	2	51	4	2	2	0	4	.00	12	.304	.346	.476
2000	Mon	NL	153	606	200	51	2	24	(11	13)	327	101	97	115	49	4	69	2	0	6	5	4	.56	17	.330	.379	.540
2001	Mon	NL	124	486	155	34	1	15	(6	9)	236	82	59	81	31	2	49	10	2	2	1	1	.80	18	.319	.371	.486
2002	Mon	NL	152	604	190	43	3	19	(11	8)	296	103	96	112	60	1	70	3	11	3	2	1	.67	12	.315	.378	.490
2003	Mon	NL	144	509	158	36	0	15	(7	8)	239	77	65	89	69	6	50	7	2	5	3	2	.60	16	.310	.397	.470
2004	Mon	NL	110	412	121	24	0	14	(6	8)	187	51	60	59	49	7	43	0	4	2	3	1	.75	14	.294	.367	.454
2005	Was	NL	87	309	85	21	2	7	(2	5)	131	38	32	41	31	3	30	1	2	4	0	0	-	8	.275	.339	.424
2006	Was	NL	126	463	134	26	1	7	(3	4)	183	52	47	60	41	3	48	3	0	4	1	0	1.00	16	.289	.348	.395
2007	Sea	AL	147	548	172	26	0	6	(2	4)	216	78	59	82	63	5	57	1	5	8	0	0	-	21	.314	.381	.394
	11 ML YEARS		1333	4805	1452	330	12	121	(53	68)	2169	692	609	753	460	33	520	37	34	42	21	15	.58	140	.302	.365	.451

Carlos Villanueva

Pitches: R **Bats:** R **Pos:** RP-53; SP-6   **Ht:** 6'3" **Wt:** 217 **Born:** 11/28/1983 **Age:** 24

			HOW MUCH HE PITCHED						WHAT HE GAVE UP												THE RESULTS							
Year	Team	Lg	G	GS	CG	GF	IP	BFP	H	R	ER	HR	SH	SF	HB	TBB	IBB	SO	WP	Bk	W	L	Pct	ShO	Sv-Op	Hld	ERC	ERA
2002	Giants	R	19	0	0	9	30.1	113	24	3	2	1	0	0	1	2	0	23	0	0	4	0	1.000	0	3--	-	1.64	0.59
2003	Giants	R	12	10	0	0	59.0	247	64	31	26	1	0	1	2	13	0	67	5	0	3	6	.333	0	0--	-	3.46	3.97
2004	Beloit	A	25	21	1	2	114.2	482	102	67	48	20	4	6	9	30	1	113	5	2	8	8	.500	1	1--	-	3.67	3.77
2005	BrvdCt	A+	21	21	0	0	112.1	447	78	31	29	11	0	2	3	32	0	124	8	4	8	1	.889	0	0--	-	2.15	2.32
2005	Hntsvl	AA	4	4	0	0	20.2	94	21	18	17	3	1	1	1	9	0	14	1	0	1	3	.250	0	0--	-	4.67	7.40
2006	Hntsvl	AA	11	10	1	0	62.1	259	60	31	26	6	1	0	1	14	0	59	6	0	4	5	.444	1	0--	-	3.21	3.75
2006	Nashv	AAA	11	9	1	1	66.1	263	42	20	20	6	3	1	2	26	0	61	2	0	7	1	.875	0	0--	-	2.23	2.71
2007	Nashv	AAA	2	2	0	0	8.1	30	3	3	3	1	0	0	1	1	0	9	1	0	0	0	-	0	0--	-	0.93	3.24
2006	Mil	NL	10	6	0	2	53.2	215	43	22	22	8	1	0	4	11	1	39	0	0	2	2	.500	0	0 0	0	2.85	3.69
2007	Mil	NL	59	6	0	8	114.1	489	101	52	50	16	4	1	3	53	3	99	3	0	8	5	.615	0	1-3	16	4.03	3.94
	2 ML YEARS		69	12	0	10	168.0	704	144	74	72	24	5	1	7	64	4	138	3	0	10	7	.588	0	1-3	16	3.64	3.86

Oscar Villarreal

Pitches: R **Bats:** L **Pos:** RP-51   **Ht:** 6'0" **Wt:** 215 **Born:** 11/22/1981 **Age:** 26

			HOW MUCH HE PITCHED						WHAT HE GAVE UP												THE RESULTS							
Year	Team	Lg	G	GS	CG	GF	IP	BFP	H	R	ER	HR	SH	SF	HB	TBB	IBB	SO	WP	Bk	W	L	Pct	ShO	Sv-Op	Hld	ERC	ERA
2003	Ari	NL	86	1	0	14	98.0	422	80	40	28	6	9	3	3	46	10	80	3	2	10	7	.588	0	0-4	10	2.97	2.57
2004	Ari	NL	17	0	0	4	18.0	84	25	14	14	3	3	0	1	7	1	17	5	0	2	0	.000	0	0-0	2	7.13	7.00
2005	Ari	NL	11	0	0	0	13.2	57	11	8	8	2	2	1	1	6	2	5	0	0	2	0	1.000	0	0-2	3	3.59	5.27
2006	Atl	NL	58	4	0	11	92.1	397	93	41	37	13	5	4	5	27	3	55	4	0	9	1	.900	0	0-4	2	4.10	3.61
2007	Atl	NL	51	0	0	11	76.1	336	75	40	36	6	3	9	4	32	8	58	6	0	2	2	.500	0	1-2	5	3.88	4.24
	5 ML YEARS		223	5	0	40	298.1	1296	284	143	123	30	22	17	14	118	24	215	18	2	23	12	.657	0	1-12	18	3.81	3.71

Ron Villone

Pitches: L **Bats:** L **Pos:** RP-37   **Ht:** 6'3" **Wt:** 245 **Born:** 1/16/1970 **Age:** 38

			HOW MUCH HE PITCHED						WHAT HE GAVE UP												THE RESULTS							
Year	Team	Lg	G	GS	CG	GF	IP	BFP	H	R	ER	HR	SH	SF	HB	TBB	IBB	SO	WP	Bk	W	L	Pct	ShO	Sv-Op	Hld	ERC	ERA
2007	S-WB*	AAA	17	0	0	4	23.2	102	21	6	5	0	2	2	1	10	0	27	1	0	0	1	.000	0	1--	-	2.97	1.90
1995	2 Tms		38	0	0	15	45.0	212	44	31	29	11	3	1	1	34	0	63	3	0	2	3	.400	0	1-5	6	6.57	5.80
1996	2 Tms		44	0	0	19	43.0	182	31	15	15	6	0	2	5	25	0	38	2	0	1	1	.500	0	2-3	9	4.08	3.14
1997	Mil	AL	50	0	0	15	52.2	238	54	23	20	4	2	0	1	36	2	40	3	0	1	0	1.000	0	0-2	8	5.30	3.42
1998	Cle	AL	25	0	0	6	27.0	129	30	18	18	3	2	2	2	22	0	15	0	0	0	0	-	0	0-0	1	7.01	6.00
1999	Cin	NL	29	22	0	2	142.2	610	114	70	67	8	9	3	5	73	2	97	6	0	9	7	.563	0	2-2	0	3.20	4.23
2000	Cin	NL	35	23	2	5	141.0	643	154	95	85	22	10	8	9	78	3	77	7	0	10	10	.500	0	0-0	1	5.97	5.43
2001	2 Tms		53	12	0	12	114.2	523	133	81	75	18	1	1	5	53	5	113	4	1	6	10	.375	0	0-0	6	6.81	5.89
2002	Pit	NL	45	7	0	6	93.0	399	95	63	60	8	5	3	5	34	3	55	1	0	4	6	.400	0	0-1	0	4.18	5.81
2003	Hou	NL	19	19	0	0	106.2	449	91	51	49	16	3	3	5	48	1	91	1	0	6	6	.500	0	0-0	0	4.04	4.13
2004	Sea	AL	56	10	0	14	117.0	523	102	64	53	12	4	4	12	64	3	86	6	0	8	6	.571	0	0-1	7	4.26	4.08
2005	2 Tms		79	0	0	24	64.0	287	57	34	29	4	3	5	7	35	2	70	3	1	5	5	.500	0	1-9	21	4.09	4.08
2006	NYY	AL	70	0	0	19	80.1	365	75	48	45	9	6	4	4	51	9	72	5	0	3	3	.500	0	0-1	6	4.69	5.04
2007	NYY	AL	37	0	0	13	42.1	176	36	20	20	5	0	1	3	18	3	25	4	0	0	0	-	0	0-1	4	3.74	4.25
95	Sea	AL	19	0	0	7	19.1	101	20	19	17	6	3	0	1	23	0	26	1	0	0	2	.000	0	0 3	3	9.67	7.91
95	SD	NL	19	0	0	8	25.2	111	24	12	12	5	0	1	0	11	0	37	2	0	2	1	.667	0	1-2	3	4.44	4.21
96	SD	NL	21	0	0	9	18.1	78	17	6	6	2	0	0	1	7	0	19	0	0	1	1	.500	0	0-1	4	3.90	2.95
96	Mil	AL	23	0	0	10	24.2	104	14	9	9	4	0	2	4	18	0	19	2	0	0	0	-	0	2-2	5	4.21	3.28
01	Col	NL	22	6	0	6	46.2	222	56	35	33	6	1	1	1	29	4	48	2	0	1	3	.250	0	0-0	2	6.30	6.36
01	Hou	NL	31	6	0	6	68.0	301	77	46	42	12	0	0	4	24	1	65	2	1	5	7	.417	0	0-0	4	5.46	5.56
05	Sea	AL	52	0	0	14	40.1	178	33	14	11	2	1	3	5	23	1	41	2	1	2	3	.400	0	1-6	17	3.79	2.45
05	Fla	NL	27	0	0	10	23.2	109	24	20	18	2	2	2	2	12	1	29	1	0	3	2	.600	0	0-3	4	4.61	6.85
	13 ML YEARS		580	93	2	150	1069.1	4736	1016	613	565	126	48	37	64	571	33	842	45	2	55	57	.491	0	6-25	69	4.66	4.76

Luis Vizcaino

Pitches: R **Bats:** R **Pos:** RP-77   **Ht:** 5'11" **Wt:** 210 **Born:** 8/6/1974 **Age:** 33

			HOW MUCH HE PITCHED						WHAT HE GAVE UP												THE RESULTS							
Year	Team	Lg	G	GS	CG	GF	IP	BFP	H	R	ER	HR	SH	SF	HB	TBB	IBB	SO	WP	Bk	W	L	Pct	ShO	Sv-Op	Hld	ERC	ERA
1999	Oak	AL	1	0	0	1	3.1	16	3	2	2	1	0	0	0	3	0	2	1	0	0	0	-	0	0-0	0	7.01	5.40
2000	Oak	AL	12	0	0	1	19.1	96	25	17	16	2	0	1	2	11	0	18	1	0	0	1	.000	0	0-0	0	6.83	7.45
2001	Oak	AL	36	0	0	15	36.2	156	38	19	19	8	0	1	0	12	1	31	3	0	2	1	.667	0	1-1	3	4.80	4.66
2002	Mil	NL	76	0	0	30	81.1	326	55	27	27	6	3	3	3	30	4	79	3	2	5	3	.625	0	5-6	19	2.20	2.99
2003	Mil	NL	75	0	0	21	62.0	272	64	45	44	16	2	1	1	25	3	61	3	0	4	3	.571	0	0-6	9	5.37	6.39
2004	Mil	NL	73	0	0	21	72.0	298	61	35	30	12	1	5	1	24	3	63	9	0	4	4	.500	0	1-5	21	3.40	3.75
2005	CWS	AL	65	0	0	20	70.0	305	74	30	29	8	4	1	2	29	6	43	3	0	6	5	.545	0	0-3	9	4.58	3.73
2006	Ari	NL	70	0	0	15	65.1	272	51	26	26	8	2	0	4	29	6	72	1	0	4	6	.400	0	0-2	25	3.34	3.58
2007	NYY	AL	77	0	0	13	75.1	334	66	37	36	6	2	6	2	43	11	62	1	0	8	2	.800	0	0-3	14	3.70	4.30
	9 ML YEARS		485	0	0	137	485.1	2075	437	238	229	67	14	18	15	206	34	431	25	2	33	25	.569	0	7-26	100	3.89	4.25

Omar Vizquel

Bats: B **Throws:** R **Pos:** SS-143; PH-3; PR-1   **Ht:** 5'9" **Wt:** 175 **Born:** 4/24/1967 **Age:** 41

			BATTING																		BASERUNNING				AVERAGES		
Year	Team	Lg	G	AB	H	2B	3B	HR	(Hm	Rd)	TB	R	RBI	RC	TBB	IBB	SO	HBP	SH	SF	SB	CS	SB%	GDP	Avg	OBP	Slg
1989	Sea	AL	143	387	85	7	3	1	(1	0)	101	45	20	25	28	0	40	1	13	2	1	4	.20	6	.220	.273	.261
1990	Sea	AL	81	255	63	3	2	2	(0	2)	76	19	18	22	18	0	22	0	10	2	4	1	.80	7	.247	.295	.298
1991	Sea	AL	142	426	98	16	4	1	(1	0)	125	42	41	39	45	0	37	0	8	3	7	2	.78	8	.230	.302	.293
1992	Sea	AL	136	483	142	20	4	0	(0	0)	170	49	21	54	32	0	38	2	9	1	15	13	.54	14	.294	.340	.352

Batting

Year Team	Lg	G	AB	H	2B	3B	HR	(Hm	Rd)	TB	R	RBI	RC	TBB	IBB	SO	HBP	SH	SF	SB	CS	SB%	GDP	Avg	OBP	Slg
1993 Sea	AL	158	560	143	14	2	2	(1	1)	167	68	31	53	50	2	71	4	13	3	12	14	.46	7	.255	.319	.298
1994 Cle	AL	69	286	78	10	1	1	(0	1)	93	39	33	32	23	0	23	0	11	2	13	4	.76	4	.273	.325	.325
1995 Cle	AL	136	542	144	28	0	6	(3	3)	190	87	56	70	59	0	59	1	10	10	29	11	.73	4	.266	.333	.351
1996 Cle	AL	151	542	161	36	1	9	(2	7)	226	98	64	87	56	0	42	4	12	9	35	9	.80	10	.297	.362	.417
1997 Cle	AL	153	565	158	23	6	5	(3	2)	208	89	49	75	57	1	58	2	16	2	43	12	.78	16	.280	.347	.368
1998 Cle	AL	151	576	166	30	6	2	(0	2)	214	86	50	82	62	1	64	4	12	6	37	12	.76	10	.288	.358	.372
1999 Cle	AL	144	574	191	36	4	5	(3	2)	250	112	66	106	65	0	50	1	17	7	42	9	.82	8	.333	.397	.436
2000 Cle	AL	156	613	176	27	3	7	(1	6)	230	101	66	92	87	0	72	5	7	5	22	10	.69	13	.287	.377	.375
2001 Cle	AL	155	611	156	26	8	2	(2	0)	204	84	50	66	61	0	72	2	15	4	13	9	.59	14	.255	.323	.334
2002 Cle	AL	151	582	160	31	5	14	(9	5)	243	85	72	91	56	3	64	8	7	10	18	10	.64	7	.275	.341	.418
2003 Cle	AL	64	250	61	13	2	2	(2	0)	84	43	19	25	29	0	20	0	5	1	8	3	.73	11	.244	.321	.336
2004 Cle	AL	148	567	165	28	3	7	(2	5)	220	82	59	86	57	0	62	1	20	6	19	6	.76	12	.291	.353	.388
2005 SF	NL	152	568	154	28	4	3	(0	3)	199	66	45	76	56	0	58	6	20	2	24	10	.71	10	.271	.341	.350
2006 SF	NL	153	579	171	22	10	4	(2	2)	225	88	58	90	56	3	51	6	13	5	24	7	.77	13	.295	.361	.389
2007 SF	NL	145	513	126	18	3	4	(2	2)	162	54	51	53	44	6	48	1	14	3	14	6	.70	14	.246	.305	.316
19 ML YEARS		2588	9479	2598	416	71	77	(34	43)	3387	1337	869	1224	941	16	951	47	232	83	380	152	.71	188	.274	.340	.357

Edinson Volquez

Pitches: R Bats: R Pos: SP-6 **Ht: 6'0" Wt: 200 Born: 7/3/1983 Age: 24**

Year Team	Lg	G	GS	CG	GF	IP	BFP	H	R	ER	HR	SH	SF	HB	TBB	IBB	SO	WP	Bk	W	L	Pct	ShO	Sv-Op	Hld	ERC	ERA
2007 Bkrsfld*	A+	7	7	0	0	35.1	153	27	28	28	4	1	2	2	20	0	38	5	0	0	4	.000	0	0--	-	3.70	7.13
2007 Frisco*	AA	11	11	0	0	58.1	238	46	23	23	9	0	0	2	19	0	62	1	0	8	1	.889	0	0--	-	3.14	3.55
2007 Okla*	AAA	8	8	0	0	51.0	197	25	8	8	0	3	1	1	21	0	66	3	0	6	1	.857	0	0--	-	1.27	1.41
2005 Tex	AL	6	3	0	0	12.2	75	25	22	20	3	0	1	2	10	0	11	0	0	0	4	.000	0	0-0	0	14.15	14.21
2006 Tex	AL	8	8	0	0	33.1	164	52	28	27	7	0	1	1	17	0	15	0	0	1	6	.143	0	0-0	0	9.27	7.29
2007 Tex	AL	6	6	0	0	34.0	149	34	18	17	4	0	2	2	15	0	29	0	0	2	1	.667	0	0-0	0	4.63	4.50
3 ML YEARS		20	17	0	0	80.0	388	111	68	64	14	0	4	5	42	0	55	0	0	3	11	.214	0	0-0	0	7.89	7.20

Joey Votto

Bats: L Throws: R Pos: 1B-17; LF-6; PH-3 **Ht: 6'3" Wt: 220 Born: 9/10/1983 Age: 24**

Year Team	Lg	G	AB	H	2B	3B	HR	(Hm	Rd)	TB	R	RBI	RC	TBB	IBB	SO	HBP	SH	SF	SB	CS	SB%	GDP	Avg	OBP	Slg
2002 Reds	R	50	175	47	13	3	9	(-	-)	93	29	33	33	21	1	45	1	0	5	7	2	.78	3	.269	.342	.531
2003 Billings	R+	70	240	76	17	3	6	(-	-)	117	47	38	57	56	3	80	4	0	1	4	0	1.00	4	.317	.452	.488
2003 Dayton	A	60	195	45	8	0	1	(-	-)	56	19	20	21	34	0	64	2	0	2	5	5	.29	3	.231	.348	.287
2004 Dayton	A	111	391	118	26	2	14	(-	-)	190	60	72	84	79	1	110	1	0	2	9	2	.82	6	.302	.419	.486
2004 Ptomc	A+	24	84	25	7	0	5	(-	-)	47	11	20	17	11	1	21	1	0	0	1	1	.50	1	.298	.385	.560
2005 Srsota	A+	124	464	119	23	2	17	(-	-)	197	64	83	68	52	2	122	3	1	9	4	5	.44	9	.256	.330	.425
2006 Chatt	AA	136	508	162	46	2	22	(-	-)	278	85	77	115	78	5	109	1	0	3	24	7	.77	13	.319	.408	.547
2007 Lsvlle	AAA	133	496	146	21	2	22	(-	-)	237	74	92	94	70	5	110	5	0	9	17	10	.63	7	.294	.381	.478
2007 Cin	NL	24	84	27	7	0	4	(4	0)	46	11	17	17	5	1	15	0	0	0	1	0	1.00	0	.321	.360	.548

Billy Wagner

Pitches: L Bats: L Pos: RP-66 **Ht: 5'11" Wt: 203 Born: 7/25/1971 Age: 36**

Year Team	Lg	G	GS	CG	GF	IP	BFP	H	R	ER	HR	SH	SF	HB	TBB	IBB	SO	WP	Bk	W	L	Pct	ShO	Sv-Op	Hld	ERC	ERA
1995 Hou	NL	1	0	0	0	0.1	1	0	0	0	0	0	0	0	0	0	0	0	0	0	0	-	0	-	0	0.00	0.00
1996 Hou	NL	37	0	0	20	51.2	212	28	16	14	6	7	2	3	30	2	67	1	0	2	2	.500	0	9-13	3	2.61	2.44
1997 Hou	NL	62	0	0	49	66.1	277	49	23	21	5	3	1	3	30	1	106	3	0	7	8	.467	0	23-29	1	2.85	2.85
1998 Hou	NL	58	0	0	50	60.0	247	46	19	18	6	4	0	0	25	1	97	2	0	4	3	.571	0	30-35	1	2.87	2.70
1999 Hou	NL	66	0	0	55	74.2	286	35	14	14	5	2	1	1	23	1	124	2	0	4	1	.800	0	39-42	1	1.20	1.57
2000 Hou	NL	28	0	0	19	27.2	129	28	19	19	6	0	0	1	18	0	28	7	0	2	4	.333	0	6-15	0	6.15	6.18
2001 Hou	NL	64	0	0	58	62.2	251	44	19	19	5	3	1	5	20	0	79	3	0	2	5	.286	0	39-41	0	2.42	2.73
2002 Hou	NL	70	0	0	61	75.0	289	51	21	21	7	2	3	2	22	5	88	6	0	4	2	.667	0	35-41	0	2.08	2.52
2003 Hou	NL	78	0	0	67	86.0	335	52	18	17	8	1	0	3	23	5	105	4	0	1	4	.200	0	44-47	0	1.63	1.78
2004 Phi	NL	45	0	0	38	48.1	182	31	16	13	5	3	0	2	6	1	59	1	0	4	0	1.000	0	21-25	1	1.52	2.42
2005 Phi	NL	75	0	0	70	77.2	297	45	17	13	6	0	2	3	20	2	87	3	1	4	3	.571	0	38-41	0	1.53	1.51
2006 NYM	NL	70	0	0	59	72.1	297	59	22	18	7	2	0	4	21	1	94	2	0	3	2	.600	0	40-45	0	2.83	2.24
2007 NYM	NL	66	0	0	57	68.1	282	55	22	20	6	1	2	2	22	4	80	4	0	2	2	.500	0	34-39	0	2.66	2.63
13 ML YEARS		720	0	0	603	771.0	3085	523	226	206	72	28	12	29	260	23	1014	38	1	39	36	.520	0	358-413	7	2.23	2.40

Ryan Wagner

Pitches: R Bats: R Pos: RP-14 **Ht: 6'4" Wt: 210 Born: 7/15/1982 Age: 25**

Year Team	Lg	G	GS	CG	GF	IP	BFP	H	R	ER	HR	SH	SF	HB	TBB	IBB	SO	WP	Bk	W	L	Pct	ShO	Sv-Op	Hld	ERC	ERA
2003 Cin	NL	17	0	0	3	21.2	88	13	4	4	2	0	1	0	12	1	25	4	0	2	0	1.000	0	0-1	6	2.46	1.66
2004 Cin	NL	49	0	0	5	51.2	242	59	31	27	7	2	3	2	27	2	37	6	0	3	2	.600	0	0-3	8	5.66	4.70
2005 Cin	NL	42	0	0	6	45.2	210	56	33	31	4	1	3	4	17	1	39	2	0	3	2	.600	0	0-1	12	5.48	6.11
2006 Was	NL	26	0	0	5	30.2	141	36	21	16	3	1	0	2	15	3	20	3	1	3	3	.500	0	0-2	3	5.55	4.70
2007 Was	NL	14	0	0	0	15.2	73	20	11	10	2	1	0	0	8	2	9	1	0	0	2	.000	0	0-0	1	6.18	5.74
5 ML YEARS		148	0	0	23	165.1	754	184	100	88	18	5	7	8	79	9	130	16	1	11	9	.550	0	0-7	30	5.18	4.79

Adam Wainwright

Pitches: R **Bats:** R **Pos:** SP-32   **Ht:** 6'7" **Wt:** 230 **Born:** 8/30/1981 **Age:** 26

			HOW MUCH HE PITCHED				WHAT HE GAVE UP											THE RESULTS					
Year	Team	Lg	G	GS	CG	GF	IP	BFP	H	R	ER	HR	SH	SF	HB	TBB	IBB	SO	WP	Bk	W	L	Pct	ShO	Sv-Op Hld	ERC	ERA
2005	StL	NL	2	0	0	1	2.0	9	2	3	3	1	0	0	0	1	0	0	0	0	0	0	-	0	0-0 0	7.30	13.50
2006	StL	NL	61	0	0	10	75.0	309	64	26	26	6	4	1	4	22	2	72	3	0	2	1	.667	0	3-5 17	2.92	3.12
2007	StL	NL	32	32	1	0	202.0	882	212	93	83	13	9	5	9	70	4	136	6	0	14	12	.538	0	0-0 0	4.01	3.70
3 ML YEARS			95	32	1	11	279.0	1200	278	122	112	20	13	6	13	93	6	208	9	0	16	13	.552	0	3-5 17	3.73	3.61

Tim Wakefield

Pitches: R **Bats:** R **Pos:** SP-31   **Ht:** 6'2" **Wt:** 210 **Born:** 8/2/1966 **Age:** 41

			HOW MUCH HE PITCHED						WHAT HE GAVE UP											THE RESULTS					
Year	Team	Lg	G	GS	CG	GF	IP	BFP	H	R	ER	HR	SH	SF	HB	TBB	IBB	SO	WP	Bk	W	L	Pct	ShO	Sv-Op Hld	ERC	ERA
1992	Pit	NL	13	13	4	0	92.0	373	76	26	22	3	6	4	1	35	1	51	3	1	8	1	.889	1	0-0 0	2.72	2.15
1993	Pit	NL	24	20	3	1	128.1	595	145	83	80	14	7	5	9	75	2	59	6	0	6	11	.353	2	0-0 0	5.97	5.61
1995	Bos	AL	27	27	6	0	195.1	804	163	76	64	22	3	7	9	68	0	119	11	0	16	8	.667	1	0-0 0	3.28	2.95
1996	Bos	AL	32	32	6	0	211.2	963	238	151	121	38	1	9	12	90	0	140	4	1	14	13	.519	0	0-0 0	5.68	5.14
1997	Bos	AL	35	29	4	2	201.1	866	193	109	95	24	3	7	16	87	5	151	6	0	12	15	.444	2	0-0 1	4.47	4.25
1998	Bos	AL	36	33	2	1	216.0	939	211	123	110	30	1	8	14	79	1	146	6	1	17	8	.680	0	0-0 0	4.30	4.58
1999	Bos	AL	49	17	0	28	140.0	635	146	93	79	19	1	8	5	72	2	104	1	0	6	11	.353	0	15-18 0	5.12	5.08
2000	Bos	AL	51	17	0	13	159.1	706	170	107	97	31	4	8	4	65	3	102	4	0	6	10	.375	0	0-1 3	5.23	5.48
2001	Bos	AL	45	17	0	5	168.2	732	156	84	73	13	3	9	18	73	5	148	5	1	9	12	.429	0	3-5 3	4.02	3.90
2002	Bos	AL	45	15	0	10	163.1	657	121	57	51	15	1	4	9	51	2	134	5	2	11	5	.688	0	3-5 5	2.54	2.81
2003	Bos	AL	35	33	0	2	202.1	872	193	106	92	23	2	4	12	71	0	169	8	0	11	7	.611	0	1-1 0	3.92	4.09
2004	Bos	AL	32	30	0	0	188.1	831	197	121	102	29	2	4	16	63	3	116	9	0	12	10	.545	0	0-0 1	4.73	4.87
2005	Bos	AL	33	33	3	0	225.1	943	210	113	104	35	1	6	11	68	4	151	8	0	16	12	.571	0	0-0 0	3.87	4.15
2006	Bos	AL	23	23	1	0	140.0	610	135	80	72	19	1	3	10	51	0	90	6	0	7	11	.389	0	0-0 0	4.22	4.63
2007	Bos	AL	31	31	0	0	189.0	800	191	104	100	22	2	6	4	64	1	110	10	0	17	12	.586	0	0-0 0	4.14	4.76
15 ML YEARS			511	370	29	62	2621.0	11326	2545	1433	1262	337	38	92	150	1012	29	1790	92	6	168	146	.535	6	22-30 13	4.27	4.33

Jamie Walker

Pitches: L **Bats:** L **Pos:** RP-81   **Ht:** 6'2" **Wt:** 194 **Born:** 7/1/1971 **Age:** 36

			HOW MUCH HE PITCHED						WHAT HE GAVE UP											THE RESULTS					
Year	Team	Lg	G	GS	CG	GF	IP	BFP	H	R	ER	HR	SH	SF	HB	TBB	IBB	SO	WP	Bk	W	L	Pct	ShO	Sv-Op Hld	ERC	ERA
1997	KC	AL	50	0	0	15	43.0	197	46	28	26	6	2	2	3	20	3	24	2	0	3	3	.500	0	0-1 3	5.10	5.44
1998	KC	AL	6	2	0	2	17.1	86	30	20	19	5	1	1	2	3	0	15	0	0	0	1	.000	0	0-0 1	9.69	9.87
2002	Det	AL	57	0	0	16	43.2	175	32	19	18	9	0	1	4	9	1	40	1	1	1	1	.500	0	1-4 5	2.86	3.71
2003	Det	AL	78	0	0	19	65.0	273	61	30	24	9	5	2	2	17	1	45	1	0	4	3	.571	0	3-7 12	3.51	3.32
2004	Det	AL	70	0	0	18	64.2	277	69	28	23	8	1	1	1	12	3	53	4	0	3	4	.429	0	1-7 18	3.65	3.20
2005	Det	AL	66	0	0	11	48.2	208	49	22	20	5	1	1	2	13	3	30	0	0	4	3	.571	0	0-2 14	3.63	3.70
2006	Det	AL	56	0	0	14	48.0	196	47	15	15	8	1	0	0	8	3	37	1	0	1	0	1.000	0	0-0 11	3.38	2.81
2007	Bal	AL	81	0	0	19	61.1	258	57	25	22	6	0	5	2	17	4	41	3	0	3	2	.600	0	7-13 21	3.19	3.23
8 ML YEARS			464	2	0	114	391.2	1670	391	187	167	56	11	13	16	99	18	285	12	1	18	18	.500	0	12-34 85	3.81	3.84

Todd Walker

Bats: L **Throws:** R **Pos:** 1B-10; PH-7; DH-2; LF-1   **Ht:** 6'0" **Wt:** 180 **Born:** 5/25/1973 **Age:** 35

			BATTING																			BASERUNNING				AVERAGES		
Year	Team	Lg	G	AB	H	2B	3B	HR	(Hm	Rd)	TB	R	RBI	RC	TBB	IBB	SO	HBP	SH	SF	SB	CS	SB%	GDP	Avg	OBP	Slg
1996	Min	AL	25	82	21	6	0	0	(0	0)	27	8	6	7	4	0	13	0	0	3	2	0	1.00	4	.256	.281	.329
1997	Min	AL	52	156	37	7	1	3	(2	1)	55	15	16	16	11	1	30	1	1	2	7	0	1.00	5	.237	.288	.353
1998	Min	AL	143	528	167	41	3	12	(7	5)	250	85	62	90	47	9	65	2	0	4	19	7	.73	13	.316	.372	.473
1999	Min	AL	143	531	148	37	4	6	(4	2)	211	62	46	70	52	5	83	1	0	2	18	10	.64	15	.279	.343	.397
2000	2 Tms		80	248	72	11	4	9	(5	4)	118	42	44	43	27	0	29	1	1	6	7	1	.88	5	.290	.355	.476
2001	2 Tms	NL	151	551	163	35	2	17	(13	4)	253	93	75	84	51	1	82	1	4	3	1	8	.11	4	.296	.355	.459
2002	Cin	NL	155	612	183	42	3	11	(7	4)	264	79	64	90	50	7	81	3	7	3	8	5	.62	9	.299	.353	.431
2003	Bos	AL	144	587	166	38	4	13	(6	7)	251	92	85	84	48	0	54	1	1	1	1	1	.50	17	.283	.333	.428
2004	ChC	NL	129	372	102	19	4	15	(6	9)	174	60	50	61	43	8	52	4	1	4	0	3	.00	2	.274	.352	.468
2005	ChC	NL	110	397	121	25	3	12	(5	7)	188	50	40	56	31	1	40	1	2	2	1	1	.50	8	.305	.355	.474
2006	2 Tms	NL	138	442	123	22	2	9	(4	5)	176	56	53	60	55	2	38	1	1	5	2	1	.67	8	.278	.356	.398
2007	Oak	AL	18	48	13	1	0	0	(0	0)	14	5	4	4	2	0	4	0	0	2	0	0	-	2	.271	.288	.292
00 Min		AL	23	77	18	1	0	2	(0	2)	25	14	8	7	7	0	10	0	0	3	3	0	1.00	3	.234	.287	.325
00 Col		NL	57	171	54	10	4	7	(5	2)	93	28	36	36	20	0	19	1	1	3	4	1	.80	2	.316	.385	.544
01 Col		NL	85	290	86	18	2	12	(10	2)	144	52	43	47	25	1	40	0	3	3	1	3	.25	8	.297	.349	.497
01 Cin		NL	66	261	77	17	0	5	(3	2)	109	41	32	37	26	0	42	1	1	0	0	5	.00	6	.295	.361	.418
06 ChC		NL	94	318	88	16	1	6	(3	3)	124	38	40	40	38	1	27	1	1	4	0	1	.00	7	.277	.352	.390
06 SD		NL	44	124	35	6	1	3	(1	2)	52	18	13	20	17	1	11	0	0	1	2	0	1.00	1	.282	.366	.419
12 ML YEARS			1288	4554	1316	284	30	107	(58	49)	1981	647	545	665	421	34	571	16	18	46	66	37	.64	102	.289	.348	.435

Tyler Walker

Pitches: R **Bats:** R **Pos:** RP-15   **Ht:** 6'3" **Wt:** 275 **Born:** 5/15/1976 **Age:** 32

			HOW MUCH HE PITCHED						WHAT HE GAVE UP											THE RESULTS					
Year	Team	Lg	G	GS	CG	GF	IP	BFP	H	R	ER	HR	SH	SF	HB	TBB	IBB	SO	WP	Bk	W	L	Pct	ShO	Sv-Op Hld	ERC	ERA
2007	SnJos*	A+	10	0	0	6	10.1	41	9	2	2	0	0	0	2	0	0	15	0	0	0	0	-	0	3-- -	2.05	1.74
2007	Fresno*	AAA	20	0	0	13	23.0	104	25	12	12	5	1	0	0	10	0	23	1	0	1	2	.333	0	7-- -	5.46	4.70
2002	NYM	NL	5	1	0	3	10.2	49	11	7	7	3	0	0	0	5	1	7	0	0	1	0	1.000	0	0-0 0	5.46	5.91
2004	SF	NL	52	0	0	13	63.2	275	69	31	30	8	3	7	1	24	1	48	1	0	5	1	.833	0	1-1 5	4.76	4.24
2005	SF	NL	67	0	0	39	61.2	279	68	31	29	9	5	1	3	27	6	54	4	0	6	4	.600	0	23-28 5	5.15	4.23
2006	2 Tms		26	0	0	17	25.1	111	27	20	20	1	1	0	0	12	0	19	1	0	1	4	.200	0	10-14 1	4.35	7.11

Year Team	Lg	G	GS	CG	GF	IP	BFP	H	R	ER	HR	SH	SF	HB	TBB	IBB	SO	WP	Bk	W	L	Pct	ShO	Sv-Op	Hld	ERC	ERA
2007 SF	NL	15	0	0	1	14.1	53	12	2	2	0	0	1	0	4	1	9	0	0	2	0	1.000	0	0-1	7	2.30	1.26
06 SF	NL	6	0	0	1	5.1	28	9	9	9	1	0	0	0	5	0	3	1	0	0	1	.000	0	0-2	1	12.35	15.19
06 TB	AL	20	0	0	16	20.0	83	18	11	11	0	1	0	0	7	0	16	0	0	1	3	.250	0	10-12	0	2.70	4.95
5 ML YEARS		165	1	0	73	175.2	767	187	91	88	21	9	9	4	72	9	137	6	0	15	9	.625	0	34-44	15	4.67	4.51

Chien-Ming Wang

Pitches: R **Bats:** R **Pos:** SP-30   **Ht:** 6'3" **Wt:** 225 **Born:** 3/31/1980 **Age:** 28

Year Team	Lg	G	GS	CG	GF	IP	BFP	H	R	ER	HR	SH	SF	HB	TBB	IBB	SO	WP	Bk	W	L	Pct	ShO	Sv-Op	Hld	ERC	ERA
2007 Tampa*	A+	1	1	0	0	5.0	22	5	3	3	0	0	0	1	1	0	4	0	0	0	0	-	0	0--	-	3.28	5.40
2005 NYY	AL	18	17	0	0	116.1	486	113	58	52	9	3	4	6	32	3	47	3	0	8	5	.615	0	0-0	0	3.47	4.02
2006 NYY	AL	34	33	2	1	218.0	900	233	92	88	12	3	2	2	52	4	76	6	1	19	6	.760	1	1-1	0	3.62	3.63
2007 NYY	AL	30	30	1	0	199.1	823	199	84	82	9	2	3	8	59	1	104	9	1	19	7	.731	0	0-0	0	3.54	3.70
3 ML YEARS		82	80	3	1	533.2	2209	545	234	222	30	8	9	16	143	8	227	18	2	46	18	.719	1	1-1	0	3.56	3.74

Daryle Ward

Bats: L **Throws:** L **Pos:** PH-54; 1B-16; RF-10; LF-1   **Ht:** 6'2" **Wt:** 240 **Born:** 6/27/1975 **Age:** 33

Year Team	Lg	G	AB	H	2B	3B	HR	(Hm	Rd)	TB	R	RBI	RC	TBB	IBB	SO	HBP	SH	SF	SB	CS	SB%	GDP	Avg	OBP	Slg
2007 Iowa*	AAA	4	13	1	1	0	0	(-	-)	2	0	1	0	0	0	2	0	0	0	0	0	-	0	.077	.077	.154
1998 Hou	NL	4	3	1	0	0	0	(0	0)	1	1	0	1	1	0	2	0	0	0	0	0	-		.333	.500	.333
1999 Hou	NL	64	150	41	6	0	8	(2	6)	71	11	30	21	9	0	31	0	0	2	0	0	-	4	.273	.311	.473
2000 Hou	NL	119	264	68	10	2	20	(13	7)	142	36	47	40	15	2	61	0	0	2	0	0	-	6	.258	.295	.538
2001 Hou	NL	95	213	56	15	0	9	(5	4)	98	21	39	31	19	4	48	1	0	2	0	0	-	3	.263	.323	.460
2002 Hou	NL	136	453	125	31	0	12	(9	3)	192	41	72	61	33	5	82	1	0	4	1	3	.25	9	.276	.324	.424
2003 LAD	NL	52	109	20	1	0	0	(0	0)	21	6	9	1	3	0	19	1	0	1	0	0	-	4	.183	.211	.193
2004 Pit	NL	79	293	73	17	2	15	(8	7)	139	39	57	40	22	3	45	3	0	3	0	0	-	8	.249	.305	.474
2005 Pit	NL	133	407	106	21	1	12	(7	5)	165	46	63	49	37	10	60	1	0	8	0	2	.00	18	.260	.318	.405
2006 2 Tms	NL	98	130	40	10	0	7	(3	4)	71	17	26	26	15	1	27	2	0	3	0	1	.00	5	.308	.380	.546
2007 ChC	NL	79	110	36	13	0	3	(2	1)	58	16	19	19	22	8	23	0	0	1	0	0	-	6	.327	.436	.527
06 Was	NL	78	104	32	9	0	6	(3	3)	59	15	19	19	14	1	21	2	0	3	0	1	.00	5	.308	.390	.567
06 Atl	NL	20	26	8	1	0	1	(0	1)	12	2	7	7	1	0	6	0	0	0	0	0	-		.308	.333	.462
10 ML YEARS		859	2132	566	124	5	86	(49	37)	958	234	362	289	176	33	398	9	0	26	1	6	.14	63	.265	.321	.449

John Wasdin

Pitches: R **Bats:** R **Pos:** RP-12   **Ht:** 6'2" **Wt:** 190 **Born:** 8/5/1972 **Age:** 35

Year Team	Lg	G	GS	CG	GF	IP	BFP	H	R	ER	HR	SH	SF	HB	TBB	IBB	SO	WP	Bk	W	L	Pct	ShO	Sv-Op	Hld	ERC	ERA
2007 Indy*	AAA	7	7	0	0	35.1	149	43	25	25	10	0	0	3	3	0	40	4	0	1	1	.500	0	0--	-	5.44	6.37
1995 Oak	AL	5	2	0	3	17.1	69	14	9	9	4	0	0	1	3	0	6	0	0	1	1	.500	0	0-0	0	3.19	4.67
1996 Oak	AL	25	21	1	2	131.1	575	145	96	87	24	3	6	4	50	5	75	2	2	8	7	.533	0	0-1	0	5.32	5.96
1997 Bos	AL	53	7	0	10	124.2	534	121	68	61	18	4	7	3	38	4	84	4	0	4	6	.400	0	0-2	0	3.82	4.40
1998 Bos	AL	47	8	0	13	96.0	424	111	57	56	14	3	6	2	27	8	59	1	0	6	4	.600	0	0-1	0	4.70	5.25
1999 Bos	AL	45	0	0	17	74.1	302	66	38	34	14	2	2	0	18	0	57	2	0	8	3	.727	0	2-5	0	3.41	4.12
2000 2 Tms		39	4	1	12	80.1	352	90	48	48	14	1	7	5	24	3	71	3	0	1	6	.143	0	1-2	0	5.09	5.38
2001 2 Tms		44	0	0	7	74.0	330	86	44	42	11	0	5	6	24	6	64	3	0	3	2	.600	0	0-5	0	5.27	5.11
2003 Tor	AL	3	2	0	0	5.0	35	16	13	13	2	0	1	0	4	0	5	0	0	1	0	1.000	0	0-0	0	25.15	23.40
2004 Tex	AL	15	10	0	0	65.0	301	83	52	49	18	1	2	3	23	2	36	0	0	2	4	.333	0	0-0	0	6.97	6.78
2005 Tex	AL	31	6	0	7	75.2	319	77	37	36	9	1	2	1	20	2	44	2	0	3	2	.600	0	4-6	4	3.77	4.28
2006 Tex	AL	9	5	0	3	30.0	141	33	19	17	6	0	0	4	13	0	16	0	0	2	2	.500	0	0-0	0	5.93	5.10
2007 Pit	NL	12	0	0	4	19.2	93	32	13	13	0	1	0	1	8	4	10	1	0	1	1	.500	0	0-0	0	7.40	5.95
00 Bos	AL	25	1	0	10	44.2	198	48	25	25	8	0	5	2	15	2	36	1	0	1	3	.250	0	1-2	0	4.83	5.04
00 Col	NL	14	3	1	2	35.2	154	42	23	23	6	1	2	3	9	1	35	2	0	0	3	.000	0	0-0	0	5.43	5.80
01 Col	NL	18	0	0	2	24.1	110	32	19	19	7	0	1	1	8	2	17	1	0	2	1	.667	0	0-3	0	7.27	7.03
01 Bal	AL	26	0	0	5	49.2	220	54	25	23	4	0	4	5	16	4	47	2	0	1	1	.500	0	0-0	0	4.36	4.17
12 ML YEARS		328	65	2	78	793.1	3475	874	494	465	135	15	39	29	252	34	527	18	2	39	39	.500	0	7-22	4	4.89	5.28

Jarrod Washburn

Pitches: L **Bats:** L **Pos:** SP-32   **Ht:** 6'1" **Wt:** 190 **Born:** 8/13/1974 **Age:** 33

Year Team	Lg	G	GS	CG	GF	IP	BFP	H	R	ER	HR	SH	SF	HB	TBB	IBB	SO	WP	Bk	W	L	Pct	ShO	Sv-Op	Hld	ERC	ERA
1998 LAA	AL	15	11	0	0	74.0	317	70	40	38	11	3	4	1	27	1	48	0	0	6	3	.667	0	0-0	1	4.09	4.62
1999 LAA	AL	16	10	0	3	61.2	264	61	36	36	6	1	2	1	26	0	39	2	0	4	5	.444	0	0-0	1	4.20	5.25
2000 LAA	AL	14	14	0	0	84.1	340	64	38	35	16	1	3	1	37	0	49	1	0	7	2	.778	0	0-0	3	3.66	3.74
2001 LAA	AL	30	30	1	0	193.1	813	196	89	81	25	4	4	7	54	4	126	3	1	11	10	.524	0	0-0	4	4.03	3.77
2002 LAA	AL	32	32	1	0	206.0	852	183	75	72	19	4	7	3	59	1	139	5	1	18	6	.750	0	0-0	3	3.02	3.15
2003 LAA	AL	32	32	2	0	207.1	876	205	106	102	34	5	6	11	54	4	118	4	1	10	15	.400	0	0-0	4	4.07	4.43
2004 LAA	AL	25	25	1	0	149.1	640	159	81	77	20	2	4	4	40	1	86	5	0	11	8	.579	1	0-0	4	4.23	4.64
2005 LAA	AL	29	29	1	0	177.1	740	184	66	63	19	4	6	8	51	0	94	2	0	8	8	.500	1	0-0	4	4.19	3.20
2006 Sea	AL	31	31	0	0	187.0	809	198	103	97	25	3	6	7	55	2	103	3	0	8	14	.364	0	0-0	4	4.33	4.67
2007 Sea	AL	32	32	1	0	193.2	839	201	102	93	23	9	6	8	67	5	114	2	1	10	15	.400	1	0-0	2	4.33	4.32
10 ML YEARS		256	246	7	3	1534.0	6490	1521	736	694	198	35	47	53	470	18	916	27	3	93	86	.520	3	0-0	2	4.00	4.07

Ehren Wassermann

Pitches: R **Bats:** B **Pos:** RP-33   **Ht:** 6'0" **Wt:** 185 **Born:** 12/6/1980 **Age:** 27

			HOW MUCH HE PITCHED						WHAT HE GAVE UP												THE RESULTS						
Year	Team	Lg	G	GS	CG	GF	IP	BFP	H	R	ER	HR	SH	SF	HB	TBB	IBB	SO	WP	Bk	W	L	Pct	ShO	Sv-Op	Hld	ERC	ERA
2003	Bristol	R+	4	0	0	2	3.2	22	9	6	6	0	0	0	0	3	1	4	3	0	0	1	.000	0	0--	-	14.40	14.73
2003	Knapol	A-	6	0	0	5	9.0	36	8	1	1	0	2	0	1	3	1	10	1	0	1	1	.500	0	0--	-	2.98	1.00
2004	Knapol	A-	50	0	0	47	55.2	230	44	20	17	1	1	0	4	16	3	42	4	0	2	3	.400	0	30--	-	2.19	2.75
2004	WinSa	A+	10	0	0	4	10.0	47	11	4	3	1	0	0	1	5	3	5	1	0	1	0	1.000	0	1--	-	4.78	2.70
2005	WinSa	A+	42	0	0	38	46.0	183	41	10	7	0	3	3	2	9	0	37	3	0	4	2	.667	0	20--	-	2.33	1.37
2005	Brham	AA	15	0	0	5	22.0	95	24	6	5	0	0	1	2	8	1	21	2	0	2	0	1.000	0	0--	-	4.10	2.05
2006	Brham	AA	61	0	0	54	63.1	274	60	26	18	3	5	1	6	25	2	47	7	1	4	8	.333	0	22--	-	3.72	2.56
2007	Charltt	AAA	38	0	0	14	42.2	178	34	13	10	0	6	1	5	18	2	33	1	0	4	3	.333	0	5--	-	2.80	2.11
2007	CWS	AL	33	0	0	6	23.0	94	20	9	7	0	0	1	2	7	4	14	1	0	1	1	.500	0	0-1	9	2.47	2.74

Tommy Watkins

Bats: R **Throws:** R **Pos:** 3B-8; SS-1; DH-1; PH-1   **Ht:** 5'10" **Wt:** 200 **Born:** 6/18/1980 **Age:** 28

			BATTING																		BASERUNNING				AVERAGES		
Year	Team	Lg	G	AB	H	2B	3B	HR	(Hm	Rd)	TB	R	RBI	RC	TBB	IBB	SO	HBP	SH	SF	SB	CS	SB%	GDP	Avg	OBP	Slg
1998	Twins	R	33	73	16	5	0	0	(-	-)	21	8	8	8	9	0	11	0	1	1	5	0	1.00	1	.219	.301	.288
1999	Twins	R	49	152	40	10	0	1	(-	-)	53	30	12	23	28	1	21	2	7	1	4	4	.50	5	.263	.383	.349
2000	Elizab	R+	37	113	25	2	1	0	(-	-)	29	15	15	11	14	0	23	2	2	2	4	1	.80	5	.221	.313	.257
2001	QuadC	A	73	191	44	9	0	2	(-	-)	59	31	16	22	28	0	36	2	6	1	4	2	.67	4	.230	.333	.309
2002	FtMyrs	A+	94	269	63	10	0	2	(-	-)	79	38	24	27	29	0	46	3	7	2	10	5	.67	5	.234	.314	.294
2003	FtMyrs	A+	104	347	90	9	2	1	(-	-)	106	53	35	39	34	0	44	5	8	3	11	5	.69	5	.259	.332	.305
2004	NwBrit	AA	116	397	106	21	1	8	(-	-)	153	64	47	57	45	0	77	5	12	4	20	9	.69	5	.267	.346	.385
2005	NwBrit	AA	115	319	73	19	0	4	(-	-)	104	50	23	34	31	0	65	5	13	0	12	7	.63	7	.229	.307	.326
2006	NwBrit	AA	32	101	22	2	1	0	(-	-)	26	9	8	8	10	0	26	1	2	0	3	1	.75	5	.218	.295	.257
2006	Roch	AAA	60	174	48	9	0	4	(-	-)	69	25	23	26	18	0	25	1	5	1	7	2	.78	2	.276	.345	.397
2007	Roch	AAA	110	349	95	22	0	8	(-	-)	141	53	49	52	39	1	63	4	7	3	12	7	.63	10	.272	.349	.404
2007	Min	AL	9	28	10	0	0	0	(0	0)	10	2	0	4	4	0	4	0	0	0	1	0	1.00	1	.357	.438	.357

Brandon Watson

Bats: L **Throws:** R **Pos:** CF-5; LF-1   **Ht:** 6'1" **Wt:** 170 **Born:** 9/30/1981 **Age:** 26

			BATTING																		BASERUNNING				AVERAGES		
Year	Team	Lg	G	AB	H	2B	3B	HR	(Hm	Rd)	TB	R	RBI	RC	TBB	IBB	SO	HBP	SH	SF	SB	CS	SB%	GDP	Avg	OBP	Slg
2007	Clmbs*	AAA	103	399	125	11	6	2	(-	-)	154	47	29	56	21	1	51	2	14	4	17	8	.68	3	.313	.347	.386
2005	Was	NL	26	40	7	1	1	1	(0	1)	13	8	5	3	4	0	8	0	4	0	0	2	.00	0	.175	.250	.325
2006	2 Tms	NL	10	28	5	0	0	0	(0	0)	5	0	0	1	1	0	3	0	0	0	1	2	.33	0	.179	.207	.179
2007	Was	NL	5	18	5	1	0	0	(0	0)	6	2	2	2	1	1	1	0	0	0	1	0	1.00	0	.278	.316	.333
06	Was	NL	9	28	5	0	0	0	(0	0)	5	0	0	1	1	0	3	0	0	0	0	2	.00	0	.179	.207	.179
06	Cin	NL	1	0	0	0	0	0	(0	0)	0	0	0	0	0	0	0	0	0	0	0	1	1.00	0	-	-	-
3 ML YEARS			40	86	17	2	1	1	(0	1)	24	10	7	6	6	1	12	0	4	0	2	4	.33	0	.198	.250	.279

David Weathers

Pitches: R **Bats:** R **Pos:** RP-70   **Ht:** 6'3" **Wt:** 230 **Born:** 9/25/1969 **Age:** 38

			HOW MUCH HE PITCHED						WHAT HE GAVE UP												THE RESULTS						
Year	Team	Lg	G	GS	CG	GF	IP	BFP	H	R	ER	HR	SH	SF	HB	TBB	IBB	SO	WP	Bk	W	L	Pct	ShO	Sv-Op	Hld	ERC	ERA
1991	Tor	AL	15	0	0	4	14.2	79	15	9	8	1	2	1	2	17	3	13	0	0	1	0	1.000	0	0-0	1	6.88	4.91
1992	Tor	AL	2	0	0	0	3.1	15	5	3	3	1	0	0	0	2	0	3	0	0	0	0	-	0	0-0	0	10.97	8.10
1993	Fla	NL	14	6	0	2	45.2	202	57	26	26	3	2	0	1	13	1	34	6	0	2	3	.400	0	0-0	0	4.86	5.12
1994	Fla	NL	24	24	0	0	135.0	622	166	87	79	13	12	4	4	59	9	72	7	1	8	12	.400	0	0-0	0	5.52	5.27
1995	Fla	NL	28	15	0	0	90.1	419	104	68	60	8	7	3	5	52	3	60	3	0	4	5	.444	0	0-0	1	5.79	5.98
1996	2 Tms	NL	42	12	0	9	88.2	409	108	60	54	8	5	2	6	42	5	53	3	0	2	4	.333	0	0-0	3	5.80	5.48
1997	2 Tms	NL	19	1	0	5	25.2	126	38	24	24	3	2	1	1	15	0	18	3	0	1	3	.250	0	0-1	0	8.27	8.42
1998	2 Tms	NL	44	9	0	9	110.0	492	130	69	60	6	6	2	3	41	3	94	7	2	6	5	.545	0	0-1	3	4.73	4.91
1999	Mil	NL	63	0	0	14	93.0	414	102	49	48	14	4	4	2	38	3	74	1	1	7	4	.636	0	2-6	9	5.04	4.65
2000	Mil	NL	69	0	0	23	76.1	320	73	29	26	7	4	1	2	32	8	50	0	0	3	5	.375	0	1-7	14	3.90	3.07
2001	2 Tms	NL	80	0	0	25	86.0	351	65	24	23	6	10	3	3	34	8	66	0	0	4	5	.444	0	4-10	16	2.59	2.41
2002	NYM	NL	71	0	0	12	77.1	331	69	30	25	6	4	3	2	36	7	61	2	0	6	3	.667	0	0-5	18	3.60	2.91
2003	NYM	NL	77	0	0	20	87.2	384	87	33	30	6	8	0	6	40	6	75	1	0	1	6	.143	0	7-9	26	4.21	3.08
2004	3 Tms	NL	66	2	0	20	82.1	357	85	44	38	12	5	2	5	35	2	61	1	1	7	7	.500	0	0-4	12	5.01	4.15
2005	Cin	NL	73	0	0	41	77.2	331	71	36	34	7	4	2	2	29	2	61	4	0	7	4	.636	0	15-19	8	3.46	3.94
2006	Cin	NL	67	0	0	32	73.2	314	61	31	29	12	5	3	2	34	4	50	0	0	4	4	.500	0	12-19	9	3.79	3.54
2007	Cin	NL	70	0	0	60	77.2	328	67	33	31	4	5	4	5	27	4	48	1	0	2	6	.250	0	33-39	15	2.95	3.59
96	Fla	NL	31	8	0	8	71.1	319	85	41	36	7	5	1	4	28	4	40	2	0	2	2	.500	0	0-0	3	5.35	4.54
96	NYY	AL	11	4	0	1	17.1	90	23	19	18	1	0	1	2	14	1	13	1	0	0	2	.000	0	0-0	0	7.66	9.35
97	NYY	AL	10	0	0	3	9.0	47	15	10	10	1	0	0	0	7	0	4	2	0	0	1	.000	0	0-1	0	10.26	10.00
97	Cle	AL	9	1	0	2	16.2	79	23	14	14	2	2	1	1	8	0	14	1	0	1	2	.333	0	0-0	0	7.23	7.56
98	Cin	NL	16	9	0	0	62.1	294	86	47	43	3	4	1	1	27	2	51	5	1	2	4	.333	0	0-0	0	6.04	6.21
98	Mil	NL	28	0	0	9	47.2	198	44	22	17	3	2	1	2	14	1	43	2	1	4	1	.800	0	0-1	3	3.15	3.21
01	Mil	NL	52	0	0	21	57.2	233	37	14	13	3	8	1	2	25	7	46	0	0	3	4	.429	0	4-7	10	2.01	2.03
01	ChC	NL	28	0	0	4	28.1	118	28	10	10	3	2	2	1	9	1	20	0	0	1	1	.500	0	0-3	6	3.90	3.18
04	NYM	NL	32	0	0	10	33.2	156	41	19	16	5	2	2	2	15	0	25	1	1	5	3	.625	0	0-1	6	6.15	4.28
04	Hou	NL	26	0	0	9	32.0	137	31	20	17	5	3	0	3	13	1	26	0	0	1	3	.400	0	0-3	5	4.77	4.78
04	Fla	NL	8	2	0	1	16.2	64	13	5	5	2	1	0	0	7	1	10	0	0	1	0	1.000	0	0-0	1	3.28	2.70
17 ML YEARS			824	69	0	276	1245.0	5493	1303	655	598	117	87	36	52	546	68	893	39	5	65	76	.461	0	74-120	120	4.54	4.32

Jeff Weaver

Pitches: R **Bats:** R **Pos:** SP-27   **Ht:** 6'5" **Wt:** 200 **Born:** 8/22/1976 **Age:** 31

Year	Team	Lg	G	GS	CG	GF	IP	BFP	H	R	ER	HR	SH	SF	HB	TBB	IBB	SO	WP	Bk	W	L	Pct	ShO	Sv-Op	Hld	ERC	ERA
1999	Det	AL	30	29	0	1	163.2	717	176	104	101	27	5	5	17	56	2	114	0	0	9	12	.429	0	0-0	0	5.21	5.55
2000	Det	AL	31	30	2	0	200.0	849	205	102	96	26	3	9	15	52	2	136	3	2	11	15	.423	0	0-0	0	4.18	4.32
2001	Det	AL	33	33	5	0	229.1	985	235	116	104	19	12	7	14	68	4	152	3	0	13	16	.448	0	0-0	0	3.89	4.08
2002	2 Tms	AL	32	25	3	3	199.2	840	193	88	78	16	6	3	11	48	4	132	6	0	11	11	.500	3	2-2	0	3.30	3.52
2003	NYY	AL	32	24	0	3	159.1	735	211	113	106	16	9	9	11	47	2	93	2	0	7	9	.438	0	0-0	1	5.77	5.99
2004	LAD	NL	34	34	0	0	220.0	935	219	103	98	19	5	7	14	67	9	153	9	0	13	13	.500	0	0-0	0	3.79	4.01
2005	LAD	NL	34	34	3	0	224.0	930	220	111	105	35	8	3	18	43	1	157	2	0	14	11	.560	2	0-0	0	3.87	4.22
2006	2 Tms		31	31	0	0	172.0	770	213	117	110	34	7	4	10	47	1	107	5	0	8	14	.364	0	0-0	0	5.90	5.76
2007	Sea	AL	27	27	3	0	146.2	657	190	105	101	23	4	7	8	35	5	80	3	1	7	13	.350	2	0-0	0	5.74	6.20
02	Det	AL	17	17	3	0	121.2	509	112	50	43	4	5	2	8	33	1	75	4	0	6	8	.429	3	0-0	0	2.94	3.18
02	NYY	AL	15	8	0	3	78.0	331	81	38	35	12	1	1	3	15	3	57	2	0	5	3	.625	0	2-2	0	3.86	4.04
06	LAA	AL	16	16	0	0	88.2	397	114	68	62	18	2	1	4	21	0	62	4	0	3	10	.231	0	0-0	0	6.03	6.29
06	StL	NL	15	15	0	0	83.1	373	99	49	48	16	5	3	6	26	1	45	1	0	5	4	.556	0	0-0	0	5.78	5.18
9 ML YEARS			284	267	16	7	1714.2	7418	1862	959	899	215	59	54	118	463	30	1124	33	3	93	114	.449	7	2-2	1	4.48	4.72

Jered Weaver

Pitches: R **Bats:** R **Pos:** SP-28   **Ht:** 6'7" **Wt:** 205 **Born:** 10/4/1982 **Age:** 25

Year	Team	Lg	G	GS	CG	GF	IP	BFP	H	R	ER	HR	SH	SF	HB	TBB	IBB	SO	WP	Bk	W	L	Pct	ShO	Sv-Op	Hld	ERC	ERA
2005	RCuca	A+	7	7	0	0	33.0	131	25	18	14	3	0	1	1	7	0	49	1	0	4	1	.800	0	0- -	-	2.17	3.82
2005	Ark	AA	8	8	0	0	43.0	192	43	22	19	5	0	1	0	19	0	46	1	0	3	3	.500	0	0- -	-	4.23	3.98
2006	Salt Lk	AAA	12	11	2	0	77.0	295	63	19	18	7	0	1	2	10	0	93	0	0	6	1	.857	2	0- -	-	2.24	2.10
2007	RCuca	A+	2	2	0	0	11.0	41	5	1	1	1	0	0	0	3	0	12	0	0	1	0	1.000	0	0- -	-	1.16	0.82
2006	LAA	AL	19	19	0	0	123.0	490	94	36	35	15	2	2	3	33	1	105	2	0	11	2	.846	0	0-0	0	2.57	2.56
2007	LAA	AL	28	28	0	0	161.0	695	178	77	70	17	5	5	2	45	3	115	4	0	13	7	.650	0	0-0	0	4.24	3.91
2 ML YEARS			47	47	0	0	284.0	1185	272	113	105	32	7	7	5	78	4	220	6	0	24	9	.727	0	0-0	0	3.49	3.33

Brandon Webb

Pitches: R **Bats:** R **Pos:** SP-34   **Ht:** 6'2" **Wt:** 230 **Born:** 5/9/1979 **Age:** 29

Year	Team	Lg	G	GS	CG	GF	IP	BFP	H	R	ER	HR	SH	SF	HB	TBB	IBB	SO	WP	Bk	W	L	Pct	ShO	Sv-Op	Hld	ERC	ERA
2003	Ari	NL	29	28	1	1	180.2	750	140	65	57	12	9	1	13	68	4	172	9	1	10	9	.526	1	0-0	0	2.80	2.84
2004	Ari	NL	35	35	1	0	208.0	933	194	111	83	17	14	6	11	119	11	164	17	1	7	16	.304	0	0-0	0	4.32	3.59
2005	Ari	NL	33	33	1	0	229.0	943	229	98	90	21	10	7	2	59	4	172	14	1	14	12	.538	0	0-0	0	3.54	3.54
2006	Ari	NL	33	33	5	0	235.0	950	216	91	81	15	10	6	6	50	4	178	5	2	16	8	.667	3	0-0	0	2.81	3.10
2007	Ari	NL	34	34	4	0	236.1	975	209	91	79	12	9	6	5	72	6	194	3	0	18	10	.643	3	0-0	0	2.82	3.01
5 ML YEARS			164	163	12	1	1089.0	4551	988	456	390	77	52	26	37	368	29	880	48	5	65	55	.542	7	0-0	0	3.24	3.22

Rickie Weeks

Bats: R **Throws:** R **Pos:** 2B-115; PH-4   **Ht:** 6'0" **Wt:** 205 **Born:** 9/13/1982 **Age:** 25

Year	Team	Lg	G	AB	H	2B	3B	HR	(Hm	Rd)	TB	R	RBI	RC	TBB	IBB	SO	HBP	SH	SF	SB	CS	SB%	GDP	Avg	OBP	Slg
2007	Nashv*	AAA	6	22	10	3	1	0	(-	-)	15	5	3	7	5	0	6	1	0	0	1	2	.33	1	.455	.571	.682
2003	Mil	NL	7	12	2	1	0	0	(0	0)	3	1	0	0	1	0	6	1	0	0	0	0	-	0	.167	.286	.250
2005	Mil	NL	96	360	86	13	2	13	(8	5)	142	56	42	49	40	2	96	11	2	1	15	2	.88	11	.239	.333	.394
2006	Mil	NL	95	359	100	15	3	8	(6	2)	145	73	34	53	30	1	92	19	2	3	19	5	.79	6	.279	.363	.404
2007	Mil	NL	118	409	96	21	6	16	(5	11)	177	87	36	65	78	5	116	14	3	2	25	2	.93	3	.235	.374	.433
4 ML YEARS			316	1140	284	50	11	37	(19	18)	467	217	112	167	149	8	310	45	7	6	59	9	.87	20	.249	.357	.410

Todd Wellemeyer

Pitches: R **Bats:** R **Pos:** RP-21; SP-11   **Ht:** 6'3" **Wt:** 205 **Born:** 8/30/1978 **Age:** 29

Year	Team	Lg	G	GS	CG	GF	IP	BFP	H	R	ER	HR	SH	SF	HB	TBB	IBB	SO	WP	Bk	W	L	Pct	ShO	Sv-Op	Hld	ERC	ERA
2007	Sprgfld*	AA	1	1	0	0	1.0	7	3	2	0	0	0	0	0	1	0	2	0	0	0	0	-	0	0- -	-	19.55	0.00
2003	ChC	NL	15	0	0	8	27.2	122	25	22	20	5	1	0	0	19	1	30	0	0	1	1	.500	0	1-1	1	5.33	6.51
2004	ChC	NL	20	0	0	7	24.1	119	27	16	16	1	3	2	0	20	2	30	0	1	2	1	.667	0	0-0	0	5.67	5.92
2005	ChC	NL	22	0	0	6	32.1	146	32	23	22	7	2	1	0	22	1	32	3	0	2	1	.667	0	1-1	3	6.09	6.12
2006	2 Tms		46	0	0	10	78.1	345	68	38	36	6	3	6	4	50	3	54	9	0	1	4	.200	0	1-1	3	4.28	4.14
2007	2 Tms		32	11	0	7	79.1	353	77	50	40	11	3	4	3	40	2	60	4	0	3	3	.500	0	0-0	2	4.68	4.54
06	Fla	NL	18	0	0	6	21.1	97	20	13	13	1	1	3	2	13	1	17	2	0	0	2	.000	0	0-0	0	4.41	5.48
06	KC	AL	28	0	0	4	57.0	248	48	25	23	5	2	3	2	37	2	37	7	0	1	2	.333	0	1-1	3	4.23	3.63
07	KC	AL	12	0	0	5	15.2	84	25	19	18	4	1	0	1	11	2	9	2	0	0	1	.000	0	0-0	1	10.40	10.34
07	StL	NL	20	11	0	2	63.2	269	52	31	22	7	2	4	2	29	0	51	2	0	3	2	.600	0	0-0	1	3.48	3.11
5 ML YEARS			135	11	0	38	242.0	1085	229	149	134	30	12	13	7	151	9	206	16	1	9	10	.474	0	3-3	9	4.91	4.98

David Wells

Pitches: L **Bats:** L **Pos:** SP-29   **Ht:** 6'3" **Wt:** 248 **Born:** 5/20/1963 **Age:** 45

Year	Team	Lg	G	GS	CG	GF	IP	BFP	H	R	ER	HR	SH	SF	HB	TBB	IBB	SO	WP	Bk	W	L	Pct	ShO	Sv-Op	Hld	ERC	ERA
1987	Tor	AL	18	2	0	6	29.1	132	37	14	13	0	1	0	0	12	0	32	4	0	4	3	.571	0	1-2	2	4.91	3.99
1988	Tor	AL	41	0	0	15	64.1	279	65	36	33	12	2	2	2	31	9	56	6	2	3	5	.375	0	4-6	8	5.11	4.62
1989	Tor	AL	54	0	0	19	86.1	352	66	25	23	5	3	2	0	28	7	78	6	3	7	4	.636	0	2-9	8	2.16	2.40
1990	Tor	AL	43	25	0	8	189.0	759	165	72	66	14	9	2	2	45	3	115	7	1	11	6	.647	0	3-3	3	2.67	3.14
1991	Tor	AL	40	28	2	3	198.1	811	188	88	82	24	6	6	2	49	1	106	10	3	15	10	.600	0	1-2	3	3.41	3.72
1992	Tor	AL	41	14	0	14	120.0	529	138	84	72	16	3	4	8	36	6	62	3	1	7	9	.438	0	2-4	3	4.98	5.40
1993	Det	AL	32	30	0	0	187.0	776	183	93	87	26	3	3	7	42	6	139	13	0	11	9	.550	0	0-0	1	3.64	4.19
1994	Det	AL	16	16	5	0	111.1	464	113	54	49	13	3	1	2	24	6	71	5	0	5	7	.417	1	0-0	0	3.54	3.96
1995	2 Tms		29	29	6	0	203.0	839	194	88	73	23	7	3	2	53	9	133	7	2	16	8	.667	0	0-0	0	3.37	3.24
1996	Bal	AL	34	34	3	0	224.1	946	247	132	128	32	8	14	7	51	7	130	4	2	11	14	.440	0	0-0	0	4.39	5.14
1997	NYY	AL	32	32	5	0	218.0	922	239	109	102	24	7	3	6	45	0	156	6	0	16	10	.615	2	0-0	0	4.04	4.21
1998	NYY	AL	30	30	8	0	214.1	851	195	86	83	29	2	2	1	29	0	163	2	0	18	4	.818	5	0-0	0	2.83	3.49
1999	Tor	AL	34	34	7	0	231.2	987	246	132	124	32	6	6	6	62	2	169	1	0	17	10	.630	0	0-0	0	4.26	4.82
2000	Tor	AL	35	35	9	0	229.2	972	266	115	105	23	6	7	8	31	0	166	9	1	20	8	.714	1	0-0	0	4.05	4.11
2001	CWS	AL	16	16	1	0	100.2	432	120	55	50	12	2	2	3	21	1	59	2	0	5	7	.417	0	0-0	0	4.69	4.47
2002	NYY	AL	31	31	2	0	206.1	873	210	100	86	21	6	5	5	45	2	137	4	0	19	7	.731	1	0-0	0	3.50	3.75
2003	NYY	AL	31	30	4	0	213.0	887	242	101	98	24	6	7	8	20	0	101	3	0	15	7	.682	1	0-0	0	3.87	4.14
2004	SD	NL	31	31	0	0	195.2	804	203	85	81	23	14	4	2	20	1	101	2	1	12	8	.600	0	0-0	0	3.23	3.73
2005	Bos	AL	30	30	2	0	184.0	780	220	95	91	21	1	6	9	21	0	107	4	1	15	7	.682	0	0-0	0	4.36	4.45
2006	2 Tms		13	13	0	0	75.1	324	97	41	37	11	2	1	0	12	0	38	0	0	3	5	.375	0	0-0	0	5.14	4.42
2007	2 Tms	NL	29	29	0	0	157.1	694	201	97	95	22	9	4	3	42	5	82	1	0	9	9	.500	0	0-0	0	5.54	5.43
95	Det	AL	18	18	3	0	130.1	539	120	54	44	17	3	2	2	37	5	83	6	1	10	3	.769	0	0-0	0	3.40	3.04
95	Cin	NL	11	11	3	0	72.2	300	74	34	29	6	4	1	0	16	4	50	1	1	6	5	.545	0	0-0	0	3.31	3.59
06	Bos	AL	8	8	0	0	47.0	206	64	30	26	10	1	1	0	8	0	24	0	0	2	3	.400	0	0-0	0	6.16	4.98
06	SD	NL	5	5	0	0	28.1	118	33	11	11	1	1	0	0	4	0	14	0	0	1	2	.333	0	0-0	0	3.58	3.49
07	SD	NL	22	22	0	0	118.2	532	156	74	73	17	9	3	3	33	4	63	1	0	5	8	.385	0	0-0	0	5.84	5.54
07	LAD	NL	7	7	0	0	38.2	162	45	23	22	5	0	1	0	9	1	19	0	0	4	1	.800	0	0-0	0	4.64	5.12
21 ML YEARS			660	489	54	65	3439.0	14413	3635	1702	1578	407	106	84	83	719	65	2201	101	17	239	157	.604	12	13-26	28	3.84	4.13

Kip Wells

Pitches: R **Bats:** R **Pos:** SP-26; RP-8   **Ht:** 6'3" **Wt:** 205 **Born:** 4/21/1977 **Age:** 31

Year	Team	Lg	G	GS	CG	GF	IP	BFP	H	R	ER	HR	SH	SF	HB	TBB	IBB	SO	WP	Bk	W	L	Pct	ShO	Sv-Op	Hld	ERC	ERA
1999	CWS	AL	7	7	0	0	35.2	153	33	17	16	2	0	2	3	15	0	29	1	2	4	1	.800	0	0-0	0	3.80	4.04
2000	CWS	AL	20	20	0	0	98.2	468	126	78	66	15	1	3	2	58	4	71	7	0	6	9	.400	0	0-0	0	7.01	6.02
2001	CWS	AL	40	20	0	0	133.1	603	145	80	71	14	8	6	12	61	5	88	11	0	10	11	.476	0	0-2	0	5.16	4.79
2002	Pit	NL	33	33	1	0	198.1	845	197	92	79	21	7	5	7	71	11	134	7	0	12	14	.462	1	0-0	0	4.00	3.58
2003	Pit	NL	31	31	1	0	197.1	835	171	77	72	24	15	2	7	76	7	147	7	0	10	9	.526	0	0-0	0	3.49	3.28
2004	Pit	NL	24	24	0	0	138.1	621	145	71	70	14	5	6	6	66	4	116	3	0	5	7	.417	0	0-0	0	4.77	4.55
2005	Pit	NL	33	33	1	0	182.0	828	186	116	103	23	9	10	12	99	8	132	8	0	8	18	.308	1	0-0	0	5.14	5.09
2006	2 Tms		9	9	0	0	44.1	208	61	33	32	3	1	1	4	21	1	20	5	0	2	5	.286	0	0-0	0	6.90	6.50
2007	StL	NL	34	26	0	4	162.2	750	186	116	103	19	8	7	9	78	9	122	8	1	7	17	.292	0	0-0	0	5.44	5.70
06	Pit	NL	7	7	0	0	36.1	168	46	27	27	3	1	1	4	10	1	16	5	0	1	5	.167	0	0-0	0	6.51	6.69
06	Tex	AL	2	2	0	0	8.0	40	15	6	5	0	0	0	0	3	0	4	0	0	1	0	1.000	0	0-0	0	8.77	5.63
9 ML YEARS			231	203	3	7	1190.2	5311	1250	678	612	135	54	42	62	545	49	870	60	3	64	91	.413	2	0-2	6	4.83	4.63

Vernon Wells

Bats: R **Throws:** R **Pos:** CF-148; PH-5   **Ht:** 6'1" **Wt:** 225 **Born:** 12/8/1978 **Age:** 29

Year	Team	Lg	G	AB	H	2B	3B	HR	(Hm	Rd)	TB	R	RBI	RC	TBB	IBB	SO	HBP	SH	SF	SB	CS	SB%	GDP	Avg	OBP	Slg
1999	Tor	AL	24	88	23	5	0	1	(1	0)	31	8	8	7	4	0	18	0	0	0	1	1	.50	6	.261	.293	.352
2000	Tor	AL	3	2	0	0	0	0	(0	0)	0	0	0	0	0	0	0	0	0	0	0	0	-	0	.000	.000	.000
2001	Tor	AL	30	96	30	8	0	1	(1	0)	41	14	6	16	5	0	15	1	0	1	5	0	1.00	0	.313	.350	.427
2002	Tor	AL	159	608	167	34	4	23	(10	13)	278	87	100	88	27	0	85	3	2	8	9	4	.69	15	.275	.305	.457
2003	Tor	AL	161	678	215	49	5	33	(13	20)	373	118	117	124	42	2	80	7	0	8	4	1	.80	21	.317	.359	.550
2004	Tor	AL	134	536	146	34	2	23	(14	9)	253	82	67	72	51	2	83	2	0	1	9	2	.82	17	.272	.337	.472
2005	Tor	AL	156	620	167	30	3	28	(14	14)	287	78	97	96	47	3	86	3	0	8	8	3	.73	13	.269	.320	.463
2006	Tor	AL	154	611	185	40	5	32	(24	8)	331	91	106	107	54	0	90	3	0	9	17	4	.81	13	.303	.357	.542
2007	Tor	AL	149	584	143	36	4	16	(8	8)	235	85	80	74	49	4	89	3	0	6	10	4	.71	9	.245	.304	.402
9 ML YEARS			970	3823	1076	236	23	157	(85	72)	1829	563	581	584	279	11	546	22	2	41	63	19	.77	94	.281	.331	.478

Jayson Werth

Bats: R **Throws:** R **Pos:** RF-58; LF-37; PH-21; CF-2; PR-2; 1B-1   **Ht:** 6'4" **Wt:** 210 **Born:** 5/20/1979 **Age:** 29

Year	Team	Lg	G	AB	H	2B	3B	HR	(Hm	Rd)	TB	R	RBI	RC	TBB	IBB	SO	HBP	SH	SF	SB	CS	SB%	GDP	Avg	OBP	Slg
2007	Clrwtr*	A+	4	13	1	0	0	0	(-	-)	1	3	0	0	2	0	4	0	0	0	0	0	-	1	.077	.200	.077
2002	Tor	AL	15	46	12	2	1	0	(0	0)	16	4	6	5	6	0	11	0	0	1	1	0	1.00	4	.261	.340	.348
2003	Tor	AL	26	48	10	4	0	2	(0	2)	20	7	10	6	3	0	22	0	0	0	1	0	1.00	0	.208	.255	.417
2004	LAD	NL	89	290	76	11	3	16	(11	5)	141	56	47	47	30	0	85	4	1	1	4	1	.80	1	.262	.338	.486
2005	LAD	NL	102	337	79	22	2	7	(1	6)	126	46	43	44	48	2	114	6	1	3	11	2	.85	10	.234	.338	.374
2007	Phi	NL	94	255	76	11	3	8	(1	7)	117	43	49	57	44	1	73	2	2	1	7	1	.88	6	.298	.404	.459
5 ML YEARS			326	976	253	50	9	33	(13	20)	420	156	155	159	131	3	305	12	4	6	24	4	.86	15	.259	.352	.430

Jake Westbrook

Pitches: R Bats: R Pos: SP-25 Ht: 6'3" Wt: 200 Born: 9/29/1977 Age: 30

Year Team	Lg	G	GS	CG	GF	IP	BFP	H	R	ER	HR	SH	SF	HB	TBB	IBB	SO	WP	Bk	W	L	Pct	ShO	Sv-Op	Hld	ERC	ERA
2007 Lk Cty*	A-	1	1	0	0	5.0	21	6	5	4	0	0	0	0	4	1	5	2	0	0	1	.000	0	0--	-	2.89	7.20
2007 Buffalo*	AAA	2	2	0	0	5.1	30	9	7	5	0	0	1	0	5	0	5	0	0	0	1	.000	0	0--	-	9.56	8.44
2007 Akron*	AA	1	1	0	0	2.1	13	5	4	4	0	0	0	0	3	0	1	0	0	0	1	.000	0	0--	-	16.68	15.43
2000 NYY	AL	3	2	0	1	6.2	38	15	10	10	1	0	2	0	4	1	1	0	0	0	2	.000	0	0-0	0	13.53	13.50
2001 Cle	AL	23	6	0	3	64.2	290	79	43	42	6	1	5	4	22	4	48	4	0	4	4	.500	0	0-0	5	5.25	5.85
2002 Cle	AL	11	4	0	1	41.2	185	50	30	27	6	2	1	1	12	1	20	1	0	1	3	.250	0	0-2	1	5.12	5.83
2003 Cle	AL	34	22	1	4	133.0	580	142	70	64	9	4	3	12	56	1	58	3	0	7	10	.412	0	0-0	1	4.78	4.33
2004 Cle	AL	33	30	5	2	215.2	895	208	95	81	19	6	6	5	61	3	116	4	1	14	9	.609	1	0-0	0	3.45	3.38
2005 Cle	AL	34	34	2	0	210.2	895	218	121	105	19	5	4	7	56	3	119	3	0	15	15	.500	0	0-0	0	3.78	4.49
2006 Cle	AL	32	32	3	0	211.1	904	247	106	98	15	5	4	4	55	4	109	5	0	15	10	.600	2	0-0	0	4.39	4.17
2007 Cle	AL	25	25	0	0	152.0	648	159	78	73	13	6	4	6	55	5	93	3	0	6	9	.400	0	0-0	0	4.28	4.32
8 ML YEARS		195	155	11	11	1035.2	4435	1118	553	500	88	29	29	39	321	22	564	23	1	62	62	.500	3	0-2	7	4.23	4.35

Dan Wheeler

Pitches: R Bats: R Pos: RP-70 Ht: 6'3" Wt: 222 Born: 12/10/1977 Age: 30

Year Team	Lg	G	GS	CG	GF	IP	BFP	H	R	ER	HR	SH	SF	HB	TBB	IBB	SO	WP	Bk	W	L	Pct	ShO	Sv-Op	Hld	ERC	ERA
1999 TB	AL	6	6	0	0	30.2	136	35	20	20	7	1	0	0	13	1	32	1	0	0	4	.000	0	0-0	0	5.96	5.87
2000 TB	AL	11	2	0	6	23.0	111	29	14	14	2	1	1	2	11	2	17	2	0	1	1	.500	0	0-1	1	5.87	5.48
2001 TB	AL	13	0	0	3	17.2	87	30	17	17	3	0	2	0	5	0	12	1	1	1	0	1.000	0	0-0	0	8.38	8.66
2003 NYM	NL	35	0	0	10	51.0	215	49	23	21	6	0	3	1	17	4	35	1	0	1	3	.250	0	2-3	5	3.69	3.71
2004 2 Tms	NL	46	1	0	11	65.0	287	76	33	31	10	2	1	1	20	2	55	4	1	3	1	.750	0	0-0	5	5.05	4.29
2005 Hou	NL	71	0	0	20	73.1	288	53	18	18	7	5	1	3	19	3	69	0	0	2	3	.400	0	3-5	17	2.22	2.21
2006 Hou	NL	75	0	0	25	71.1	295	58	22	20	5	3	3	2	24	8	68	0	0	3	5	.375	0	9-12	24	2.57	2.52
2007 2 Tms		70	0	0	29	74.2	321	74	48	44	11	3	3	3	23	3	82	2	0	1	9	.100	0	11-18	18	4.04	5.30
04 NYM	NL	32	1	0	7	50.2	232	65	29	27	9	2	1	0	17	2	46	4	1	3	1	.750	0	0-0	3	5.91	4.80
04 Hou	NL	14	0	0	4	14.1	55	11	4	4	1	0	0	1	3	0	9	0	0	0	0	-	0	0-0	2	2.35	2.51
07 Hou	NL	45	0	0	25	49.2	205	46	28	28	8	1	1	2	13	1	56	1	0	1	4	.200	0	11-15	6	3.69	5.07
07 TB	AL	25	0	0	4	25.0	116	28	20	16	3	2	2	1	10	2	26	1	0	0	5	.000	0	0-3	12	4.72	5.76
8 ML YEARS		327	9	0	104	406.2	1740	404	195	185	51	15	14	12	132	23	370	11	2	12	26	.316	0	25-39	65	3.93	4.09

Bill White

Pitches: L Bats: L Pos: RP-9 Ht: 6'3" Wt: 215 Born: 11/20/1978 Age: 29

Year Team	Lg	G	GS	CG	GF	IP	BFP	H	R	ER	HR	SH	SF	HB	TBB	IBB	SO	WP	Bk	W	L	Pct	ShO	Sv-Op	Hld	ERC	ERA
2000 DBcks	R	4	1	0	0	6.0	25	3	4	4	0	0	1	0	5	0	9	3	0	0	1	.000	0	0--	-	2.39	6.00
2000 Sbend	A	1	1	0	0	2.2	14	3	1	1	0	0	0	0	3	0	5	1	0	0	0	-	0	0--	-	6.72	3.38
2001 Sbend	A	19	19	0	0	111.1	465	90	53	47	9	4	2	4	53	0	103	5	1	9	3	.750	0	0--	-	3.39	3.80
2001 ElPaso	AA	7	7	0	0	37.2	165	38	23	19	2	2	2	3	20	0	26	6	1	0	4	.000	0	0--	-	4.76	4.54
2002 Yakima	A-	3	3	0	0	8.2	46	10	9	9	2	0	0	0	10	0	11	1	1	0	1	.000	0	0--	-	9.22	9.35
2002 Lancst	A+	6	6	0	0	19.1	102	31	23	22	4	0	2	0	16	0	15	2	0	0	3	.000	0	0--	-	10.89	10.24
2003 ElPaso	AA	15	6	0	2	39.0	179	42	27	27	4	1	2	8	22	0	25	5	1	1	3	.250	0	0--	-	6.26	6.23
2004 Lancst	A+	14	0	0	6	18.1	81	16	8	4	2	0	0	3	7	0	23	2	0	1	1	.500	0	1--	-	3.91	1.96
2004 ElPaso	AA	31	0	0	10	35.1	198	42	37	29	2	0	1	1	34	3	40	8	0	2	3	.400	0	0--	-	6.35	7.39
2005 Tenn	AA	60	0	0	7	42.1	192	40	28	20	1	3	1	4	26	0	33	4	0	0	2	.000	0	0--	-	4.39	4.25
2006 Tenn	AA	54	0	0	20	63.2	280	59	27	25	6	6	2	5	33	2	76	3	1	0	1	.000	0	12--	-	4.37	3.53
2007 Okla	AAA	1	0	0	0	1.2	10	2	0	0	0	0	0	0	2	0	2	0	0	0	0	-	0	0--	-	6.68	0.00
2007 Frisco	AA	43	0	0	7	48.2	227	48	26	24	4	3	1	7	26	0	64	7	1	2	0	1.000	0	2--	-	4.84	4.44
2007 Tex	AL	9	0	0	1	9.1	42	8	5	5	1	0	0	2	7	1	9	0	0	2	0	1.000	0	0-0	3	5.63	4.82

Rick White

Pitches: R Bats: R Pos: RP-29 Ht: 6'4" Wt: 245 Born: 12/23/1968 Age: 39

Year Team	Lg	G	GS	CG	GF	IP	BFP	H	R	ER	HR	SH	SF	HB	TBB	IBB	SO	WP	Bk	W	L	Pct	ShO	Sv-Op	Hld	ERC	ERA
2007 CpChr*	AA	2	2	0	0	3.0	12	3	1	1	0	0	0	0	0	0	3	0	0	0	0	-	0	0--	-	1.95	3.00
2007 Tacom*	AAA	7	0	0	6	9.0	35	4	1	1	1	0	0	0	5	1	6	0	0	1	1	.500	0	2--	-	1.79	1.00
1994 Pit	NL	43	5	0	23	75.1	317	79	35	32	9	7	5	6	17	3	38	2	2	4	5	.444	0	6-9	3	4.11	3.82
1995 Pit	NL	15	9	0	2	55.0	247	66	33	29	3	3	3	2	18	0	29	2	0	2	3	.400	0	0-0	0	4.70	4.75
1998 TB	AL	38	3	0	12	68.2	289	66	32	29	8	0	3	2	23	2	39	3	0	2	6	.250	0	0-0	2	3.82	3.80
1999 TB	AL	63	1	0	11	108.0	480	132	56	49	8	2	5	1	38	5	81	3	0	5	3	.625	0	0-2	4	4.96	4.08
2000 2 Tms		66	0	0	14	99.2	420	83	44	39	9	1	3	7	38	5	67	3	0	5	9	.357	0	3-7	4	3.21	3.52
2001 NYM	NL	55	0	0	15	69.2	299	71	38	30	7	2	2	2	17	4	51	1	0	4	5	.444	0	2-4	10	3.52	3.88
2002 2 Tms	NL	61	0	0	10	62.2	264	62	33	30	4	3	4	1	21	5	41	3	0	5	7	.417	0	0-1	16	3.49	4.31
2003 2 Tms		49	0	0	15	67.0	293	74	48	43	13	2	2	4	21	2	54	2	0	1	2	.333	0	1-1	4	5.22	5.78
2004 Cle	AL	59	0	0	20	78.1	340	88	52	46	15	6	3	2	29	7	44	2	0	5	5	.500	0	1-3	2	5.41	5.29
2005 Pit	NL	71	0	0	23	75.0	338	90	39	31	3	9	4	4	29	10	40	4	0	4	7	.364	0	2-3	12	4.71	3.72
2006 2 Tms	NL	64	0	0	20	64.2	276	72	44	37	8	5	2	3	20	1	40	4	2	4	1	.800	0	1-2	7	4.82	5.15
2007 2 Tms		29	0	0	7	34.2	162	47	31	30	4	2	0	0	18	5	18	1	0	1	1	.500	0	0-1	4	6.68	7.79
00 TB	AL	44	0	0	8	71.1	293	57	30	27	7	1	2	5	26	3	47	3	0	3	6	.333	0	2-5	2	3.09	3.41
00 NYM	NL	22	0	0	6	28.1	127	26	14	12	2	0	1	2	12	2	20	0	0	2	3	.400	0	1-2	2	3.51	3.81
02 Col	NL	41	0	0	8	40.2	182	49	30	28	4	1	4	1	18	4	27	3	0	2	6	.250	0	0-1	9	5.47	6.20
02 StL	NL	20	0	0	2	22.0	82	13	3	2	0	2	0	0	3	1	14	0	0	3	1	.750	0	0-0	7	0.94	0.82
03 CWS	AL	34	0	0	12	47.2	207	56	39	35	11	1	2	1	13	2	37	0	0	1	2	.333	0	1-1	3	5.58	6.61
03 Hou	NL	15	0	0	3	19.1	86	18	9	8	2	1	0	3	8	0	17	2	0	0	0	-	0	0-0	1	4.33	3.72
06 Cin	NL	26	0	0	10	27.1	118	34	23	19	5	3	2	1	5	1	17	2	2	1	0	1.000	0	1-2	2	5.35	6.26

Year	Team	Lg	G	GS	CG	GF	IP	BFP	H	R	ER	HR	SH	SF	HB	TBB	IBB	SO	WP	Bk	W	L	Pct	ShO	Sv-Op	Hld	ERC	ERA
06	Phi	NL	38	0	0	10	37.1	158	38	21	18	3	2	0	2	15	0	23	2	0	3	1	.750	0	0-0	5	4.42	4.34
07	Hou	NL	23	0	0	5	29.1	133	36	25	25	4	1	0	0	14	0	15	0	0	0	1	1.000	0	0-1	4	5.85	7.67
07	Sea	AL	6	0	0	2	5.1	29	11	6	5	0	1	0	0	4	1	3	1	0	0	1	.000	0	0-0	0	11.63	8.44
12 ML YEARS			613	18	0	172	858.2	3725	930	485	425	91	42	36	34	289	49	542	30	4	42	54	.438	0	16-33	68	4.43	4.45

Rondell White

Bats: R **Throws:** R **Pos:** LF-16; DH 16; PH-8

Ht: 6'1" **Wt:** 225 **Born:** 2/23/1972 **Age:** 36

Year	Team	Lg	G	AB	H	2B	3B	HR	(Hm	Rd)	TB	R	RBI	RC	TBB	IBB	SO	HBP	SH	SF	SB	CS	SB%	GDP	Avg	OBP	Slg
2007 Twins*	R		7	23	10	4	0	0	(-	-)	14	1	3	6	3	0	2	0	0	0	0	0	-	0	.435	.500	.609
2007 FtMyrs*	A+		5	15	4	1	0	0	(-	-)	5	3	1	1	1	0	1	1	0	0	0	0	-	0	.267	.353	.333
1993	Mon	NL	23	73	19	3	1	2	(1	1)	30	9	15	9	7	0	16	0	2	1	1	2	.33	2	.260	.321	.411
1994	Mon	NL	40	97	27	10	1	2	(1	1)	45	16	13	16	9	0	18	3	0	0	1	1	.50	1	.278	.358	.464
1995	Mon	NL	130	474	140	33	4	13	(6	7)	220	87	57	79	41	1	87	6	0	4	25	5	.83	11	.295	.356	.464
1996	Mon	NL	88	334	98	19	4	6	(2	4)	143	35	41	46	22	0	53	2	0	1	14	6	.70	11	.293	.340	.428
1997	Mon	NL	151	592	160	29	5	28	(9	19)	283	84	82	84	31	3	111	10	1	4	16	8	.67	18	.270	.316	.478
1998	Mon	NL	97	357	107	21	2	17	(9	8)	183	54	58	65	30	2	57	7	0	3	16	7	.70	7	.300	.363	.513
1999	Mon	NL	138	539	168	26	6	22	(10	12)	272	83	64	91	32	2	85	11	0	6	10	6	.63	17	.312	.359	.505
2000	2 Tms	NL	94	357	111	26	0	13	(3	10)	176	59	61	64	33	0	79	4	0	2	5	3	.63	4	.311	.374	.493
2001	ChC	NL	95	323	99	19	1	17	(7	10)	171	43	50	57	26	4	56	7	1	0	1	0	1.00	14	.307	.371	.529
2002	NYY	AL	126	455	109	21	0	14	(5	9)	172	59	62	43	25	1	86	8	1	5	1	2	.33	11	.240	.288	.378
2003	2 Tms	NL	137	488	141	23	4	22	(5	17)	238	62	87	72	31	2	79	10	0	5	1	4	.20	11	.289	.341	.488
2004	Det	AL	121	448	121	21	2	19	(5	14)	203	76	67	69	39	4	77	8	0	3	1	2	.33	13	.270	.337	.453
2005	Det	AL	97	374	117	24	3	12	(7	5)	183	49	53	61	17	0	48	5	0	4	1	0	1.00	6	.313	.348	.489
2006	Min	AL	99	337	83	17	1	7	(4	3)	123	32	38	27	11	2	54	4	0	3	1	1	.50	11	.246	.276	.365
2007	Min	AL	38	109	19	4	0	4	(0	4)	35	8	20	12	6	0	19	3	0	1	0	0	-	2	.174	.235	.321
00	Mon	NL	75	290	89	24	0	11	(3	8)	146	52	54	53	28	0	67	2	0	2	5	1	.83	4	.307	.370	.503
00	ChC	NL	19	67	22	2	0	2	(0	2)	30	7	7	11	5	0	12	2	0	0	0	2	.00	0	.328	.392	.448
03	SD	NI	115	413	115	17	3	18	(4	14)	192	49	66	54	25	2	71	8	0	3	1	4	.20	11	.278	.330	.465
03	KC	AL	22	75	26	6	1	4	(1	3)	46	13	21	18	6	0	8	2	0	2	0	0	-	2	.347	.400	.613
15 ML YEARS			1474	5357	1519	296	34	198	(74	124)	2477	756	768	795	360	21	925	88	5	42	94	47	.67	143	.284	.336	.462

Sean White

Pitches: R **Bats:** R **Pos:** RP-15

Ht: 6'4" **Wt:** 215 **Born:** 4/25/1981 **Age:** 27

Year	Team	Lg	G	GS	CG	GF	IP	BFP	H	R	FR	HR	SH	SF	HB	TBB	IDD	SO	WP	Bk	W	L	Pct	ShO	Sv-Op	Hld	ERC	ERA
2003	Danvle	R	14	10	0	2	51.1	219	53	22	17	1	1	0	5	16	0	32	4	0	3	3	.500	0	1--	-	3.79	2.98
2004	Rome	A	13	1	0	4	36.1	160	42	30	26	4	1	2	0	12	0	20	1	0	3	2	.600	0	1--	-	4.74	0.44
2004	MrtlBh	A+	18	10	0	0	70.0	291	62	34	28	2	3	4	0	24	0	41	4	0	6	6	.500	0	0--	-	2.77	3.60
2005	MrtlBh	A+	18	18	0	0	97.0	417	112	46	40	5	3	1	5	29	0	65	11	0	9	3	.750	0	0--	-	4.52	3.71
2005	Missi	AA	8	8	0	0	50.1	211	43	25	23	2	2	0	4	18	2	33	6	0	2	5	.286	0	0--	-	2.97	4.11
2006	Missi	AA	21	16	0	2	102.1	469	124	58	50	5	5	3	3	43	3	73	6	0	5	6	.455	0	1--	-	4.86	4.40
2006	Braves	R	3	0	0	0	7.0	24	3	0	0	0	0	0	0	0	0	6	1	0	0	0	-	0	0--	-	0.40	0.00
2007	Ms	R	3	3	0	0	10.1	54	19	10	9	0	0	0	1	4	0	11	4	0	0	2	.000	0	0--	-	8.74	7.84
2007	Tacom	AAA	2	2	0	0	10.2	45	11	4	3	0	0	0	0	2	0	7	0	0	1	1	.500	0	0--	-	3.11	2.53
2007	Wisc	A-	1	1	0	0	5.0	18	2	0	0	0	0	0	0	1	0	4	0	0	1	0	1.000	0	0--	-	0.63	0.00
2007	Sea	AL	15	0	0	4	35.1	165	35	24	22	2	0	3	8	20	0	16	5	1	1	1	.500	0	0-0	0	5.24	5.60

Bob Wickman

Pitches: R **Bats:** R **Pos:** RP-57

Ht: 6'1" **Wt:** 240 **Born:** 2/6/1969 **Age:** 39

Year	Team	Lg	G	GS	CG	GF	IP	BFP	H	R	ER	HR	SH	SF	HB	TBB	IBB	SO	WP	Bk	W	L	Pct	ShO	Sv-Op	Hld	ERC	ERA
1992	NYY	AL	8	8	0	0	50.1	213	51	25	23	2	1	3	2	20	0	21	3	0	6	1	.857	0	0-0	0	3.99	4.11
1993	NYY	AL	41	19	1	9	140.0	629	156	82	72	13	4	1	5	69	7	70	2	0	14	4	.778	1	4-8	2	5.16	4.63
1994	NYY	AL	53	0	0	19	70.0	286	54	26	24	3	0	5	1	27	3	56	2	0	5	4	.556	0	6-10	11	2.45	3.09
1995	NYY	AL	63	1	0	14	80.0	347	77	38	36	6	4	1	5	33	3	51	2	0	2	4	.333	0	1-10	21	3.92	4.05
1996	2 Tms	AL	70	0	0	18	95.2	429	106	50	47	10	2	4	5	44	3	75	4	0	7	1	.875	0	0-4	10	5.17	4.42
1997	Mil	AL	74	0	0	20	95.2	405	89	32	29	8	6	2	3	41	7	78	8	0	7	6	.538	0	1-5	28	3.76	2.73
1998	Mil	NL	72	0	0	51	82.1	358	79	38	34	5	10	3	4	39	2	71	1	0	6	9	.400	0	25-32	9	4.05	3.72
1999	Mil	NL	71	0	0	63	74.1	331	75	31	28	6	3	2	2	38	6	60	2	0	3	8	.273	0	37-45	0	4.38	3.39
2000	2 Tms		69	0	0	60	72.2	309	64	30	25	1	3	1	1	32	5	55	2	0	3	5	.375	0	30-37	0	2.92	3.10
2001	Cle	AL	70	0	0	56	67.2	270	61	18	18	4	0	0	2	14	2	66	2	0	5	0	1.000	0	32-35	4	2.69	2.39
2002	Cle	AL	36	0	0	34	34.1	159	42	22	17	3	0	0	1	10	0	36	0	0	1	3	.250	0	20-22	0	4.72	4.46
2004	Cle	AL	30	0	0	21	29.2	129	33	14	14	4	0	0	0	11	0	26	0	0	0	2	.000	0	13-14	4	5.09	4.25
2005	Cle	AL	64	0	0	55	62.0	257	57	17	17	9	2	2	1	21	3	41	0	1	0	4	.000	0	45-50	0	3.74	2.47
2006	2 Tms		57	0	0	55	54.0	233	53	22	16	2	5	3	1	13	0	42	1	0	1	6	.143	0	33-37	0	2.89	2.67
2007	2 Tms		57	0	0	40	50.1	232	54	24	20	4	2	1	3	21	4	37	3	1	3	4	.429	0	20-26	0	4.33	3.58
96	NYY	AL	58	0	0	14	79.0	358	94	41	41	7	1	4	5	34	1	61	3	0	4	1	.800	0	0-3	6	5.51	4.67
96	Mil	AL	12	0	0	4	16.2	71	12	9	6	3	1	0	0	10	2	14	1	0	3	0	1.000	0	0-1	4	3.66	3.24
00	Mil	NL	43	0	0	36	46.0	194	37	18	15	1	0	1	1	20	2	44	2	0	2	5	.500	0	16-20	0	2.62	2.93
00	Cle	AL	26	0	0	24	26.2	115	27	12	10	0	3	0	0	12	3	11	0	0	1	0	.250	0	14-17	0	3.47	3.38
06	Cle	AL	29	0	0	29	28.0	126	29	15	13	1	4	3	1	11	0	17	1	0	1	4	.200	0	15-18	0	3.79	4.18
06	Atl	NL	28	0	0	26	26.0	107	24	7	3	1	1	0	0	2	0	25	0	0	0	2	.000	0	18-19	0	1.99	1.04
07	Atl	NL	49	0	0	39	43.2	204	48	22	19	4	2	0	2	20	4	35	2	1	3	3	.500	0	20-26	0	4.64	3.92
07	Ari	NL	8	0	0	1	6.2	28	6	2	1	0	0	1	1	1	0	2	1	0	0	1	.000	0	0-0	1	2.46	1.35
15 ML YEARS			835	28	1	511	1059.0	4586	1051	469	420	80	42	28	38	432	45	785	32	2	63	61	.508	1	267-335	90	3.97	3.57

277

Ty Wigginton

Bats: R **Throws:** R **Pos:** 3B-80; 2B-39; 1B-18; DH-15; PH-3; LF-1; RF-1   **Ht:** 6'0" **Wt:** 225 **Born:** 10/11/1977 **Age:** 30

								BATTING												BASERUNNING				AVERAGES		
Year	Team	Lg	G	AB	H	2B	3B	HR	(Hm | Rd)	TB	R	RBI	RC	TBB	IBB	SO	HBP	SH	SF	SB	CS	SB%	GDP	Avg	OBP	Slg
2002	NYM	NL	46	116	35	8	0	6	(4 | 2)	61	18	18	15	8	0	19	2	0	1	2	1	.67	4	.302	.354	.526
2003	NYM	NL	156	573	146	36	6	11	(4 | 7)	227	73	71	76	46	2	124	9	1	4	12	2	.86	15	.255	.318	.396
2004	2 Tms		144	494	129	30	2	17	(6 | 11)	214	63	66	59	45	6	82	2	1	3	7	1	.88	15	.261	.324	.433
2005	Pit	NL	57	155	40	9	1	7	(1 | 6)	72	20	25	22	14	0	30	1	1	0	0	1	.00	3	.258	.324	.465
2006	TB	AL	122	444	122	25	1	24	(18 | 6)	221	55	79	69	32	3	97	6	1	3	4	3	.57	11	.275	.330	.498
2007	2 Tms		148	547	152	33	0	22	(15 | 7)	251	71	67	64	41	0	113	8	0	8	3	4	.43	16	.278	.333	.459
04	NYM	NL	86	312	89	23	2	12	(5 | 7)	152	46	42	38	23	4	48	1	1	2	6	1	.86	11	.285	.334	.487
04	Pit	NL	58	182	40	7	0	5	(1 | 4)	62	17	24	21	22	2	34	1	0	1	1	0	1.00	4	.220	.306	.341
07	TB	AL	98	378	104	21	0	16	(9 | 7)	173	47	49	42	28	0	73	5	0	6	1	4	.20	8	.275	.329	.458
07	Hou	NL	50	169	48	12	0	6	(6 | 0)	78	24	18	22	13	0	40	3	0	2	2	0	1.00	8	.284	.342	.462
	6 ML YEARS		673	2329	624	141	10	87	(48 | 39)	1046	300	326	305	186	11	465	28	4	19	28	12	.70	64	.268	.327	.449

Brad Wilkerson

Bats: L **Throws:** L **Pos:** 1B-68; LF-36; RF-19; PH-7; PR-2; CF-1; DH-1   **Ht:** 6'0" **Wt:** 205 **Born:** 6/1/1977 **Age:** 31

								BATTING												BASERUNNING				AVERAGES		
Year	Team	Lg	G	AB	H	2B	3B	HR	(Hm | Rd)	TB	R	RBI	RC	TBB	IBB	SO	HBP	SH	SF	SB	CS	SB%	GDP	Avg	OBP	Slg
2007	Frisco*	AA	3	10	2	1	0	0	(- | -)	3	3	0	1	4	0	1	0	0	0	0	0	-	1	.200	.429	.300
2001	Mon	NL	47	117	24	7	2	1	(1 | 0)	38	11	5	12	17	1	41	0	1	1	2	1	.67	2	.205	.304	.325
2002	Mon	NL	153	507	135	27	8	20	(12 | 8)	238	92	59	83	81	7	161	5	6	4	7	8	.47	5	.266	.370	.469
2003	Mon	NL	146	504	135	34	4	19	(9 | 10)	234	78	77	90	89	0	155	4	2	3	13	10	.57	5	.268	.380	.464
2004	Mon	NL	160	572	146	39	4	32	(15 | 17)	285	112	67	95	106	8	152	4	3	3	13	6	.68	6	.255	.374	.498
2005	Was	NL	148	565	140	42	7	11	(6 | 5)	229	76	57	83	84	9	147	7	3	2	8	10	.44	6	.248	.351	.405
2006	Tex	AL	95	320	71	15	2	15	(5 | 10)	135	56	44	39	37	1	116	3	2	3	3	2	.60	6	.222	.306	.422
2007	Tex	AL	119	338	79	17	1	20	(12 | 8)	158	54	62	58	43	0	107	1	3	4	4	1	.80	2	.234	.319	.467
	7 ML YEARS		868	2923	730	181	26	118	(60 | 58)	1317	479	371	460	457	26	879	24	20	20	50	38	.57	32	.250	.354	.451

Dave Williams

Pitches: L **Bats:** L **Pos:** SP-1; RP-1   **Ht:** 6'3" **Wt:** 214 **Born:** 3/12/1979 **Age:** 29

			HOW MUCH HE PITCHED						WHAT HE GAVE UP											THE RESULTS						
Year	Team	Lg	G	GS	CG	GF	IP	BFP	H	R	ER	HR	SH	SF	HB	TBB	IBB	SO	WP	Bk	W	L	Pct	ShO	Sv-Op	Hld	ERC	ERA
2007	StLuci*	A+	1	1	0	0	5.0	20	4	3	3	1	0	0	0	2	0	3	0	0	0	0	-	0	0--	-	3.78	5.40
2007	NewOr*	AAA	10	10	0	0	61.1	255	58	31	27	11	2	2	6	13	0	38	0	0	3	4	.429	0	0--	-	3.97	3.96
2001	Pit	NL	22	18	0	1	114.0	472	100	53	47	15	3	8	7	45	4	57	0	0	3	7	.300	0	0-0	1	3.89	3.71
2002	Pit	NL	9	9	0	0	43.1	195	38	26	24	9	2	1	4	24	2	33	2	2	2	5	.286	0	0-0	0	4.99	4.98
2004	Pit	NL	10	6	0	0	38.2	162	31	21	19	4	1	1	3	13	2	33	0	0	2	3	.400	0	0-0	0	2.97	4.42
2005	Pit	NL	25	25	1	0	138.2	600	137	74	68	20	7	2	8	58	5	88	3	0	10	11	.476	1	0-0	0	4.62	4.41
2006	2 Tms	NL	14	13	0	1	69.0	320	93	52	50	14	6	3	6	20	1	32	2	1	5	4	.556	0	0-0	0	6.82	6.52
2007	NYM	NL	2	1	0	1	4.1	29	12	11	11	2	0	1	0	5	1	2	1	0	0	1	.000	0	0-0	0	24.43	22.85
06	Cin	NL	8	8	0	0	40.0	194	54	34	32	9	3	3	4	16	0	16	1	1	2	3	.400	0	0-0	0	7.46	7.20
06	NYM	NL	6	5	0	1	29.0	126	39	18	18	5	3	0	2	4	1	16	1	0	3	1	.750	0	0-0	0	5.93	5.59
	6 ML YEARS		82	72	1	3	408.0	1778	411	237	219	64	19	16	28	165	15	245	8	3	22	31	.415	1	0-0	1	4.80	4.83

Jerome Williams

Pitches: R **Bats:** R **Pos:** SP-6   **Ht:** 6'3" **Wt:** 240 **Born:** 12/4/1981 **Age:** 26

			HOW MUCH HE PITCHED						WHAT HE GAVE UP											THE RESULTS						
Year	Team	Lg	G	GS	CG	GF	IP	BFP	H	R	ER	HR	SH	SF	HB	TBB	IBB	SO	WP	Bk	W	L	Pct	ShO	Sv-Op	Hld	ERC	ERA
2007	Clmbs*	AAA	1	1	0	0	6.0	24	4	1	1	1	0	0	1	0	0	5	0	0	0	0	-	0	0--	-	3.20	1.50
2007	Hrsbrg*	AA	14	4	0	0	35.2	177	53	47	36	8	3	2	4	16	2	26	2	0	0	3	.000	0	0--	-	8.68	9.08
2007	Roch*	AAA	8	1	0	4	11.0	57	18	11	11	0	0	1	1	7	0	6	0	0	0	1	.000	0	1---	-	8.62	9.00
2003	SF	NL	21	21	2	0	131.0	545	116	54	48	10	6	3	7	49	3	88	2	1	7	5	.583	1	0-0	0	3.42	3.30
2004	SF	NL	22	22	0	0	129.1	559	123	69	61	14	4	9	17	44	1	80	2	1	10	7	.588	0	0-0	0	4.14	4.24
2005	2 Tms	NL	22	20	0	0	122.2	532	119	62	58	14	11	8	10	49	1	70	2	0	6	10	.375	0	0-0	1	4.34	4.26
2006	ChC	NL	5	2	0	1	12.1	61	15	12	10	2	0	3	1	11	1	5	0	0	2	0	.000	0	0-0	0	8.42	7.30
2007	Was	NL	6	6	0	0	30.0	140	34	26	24	6	1	1	3	18	0	15	2	1	0	5	.000	0	0-0	0	6.43	7.20
05	SF	NL	4	3	0	0	16.2	73	21	12	12	2	1	0	1	4	1	11	0	0	0	2	.000	0	0-0	0	5.32	6.48
05	ChC	NL	18	17	0	0	106.0	459	98	50	46	12	10	8	9	45	0	59	2	0	6	8	.429	0	0-0	1	4.19	3.91
	5 ML YEARS		76	71	2	1	425.1	1837	407	223	201	46	22	24	35	171	6	258	8	3	23	29	.442	1	0-0	1	4.23	4.25

Todd Williams

Pitches: R **Bats:** R **Pos:** RP-14   **Ht:** 6'3" **Wt:** 210 **Born:** 2/13/1971 **Age:** 37

			HOW MUCH HE PITCHED						WHAT HE GAVE UP											THE RESULTS						
Year	Team	Lg	G	GS	CG	GF	IP	BFP	H	R	ER	HR	SH	SF	HB	TBB	IBB	SO	WP	Bk	W	L	Pct	ShO	Sv-Op	Hld	ERC	ERA
2007	Norfolk*	AAA	9	0	0	3	11.2	42	7	1	0	0	0	0	1	0	7	0	0	1	0	1.000	0	1--	-	0.92	0.00
2007	Tulsa*	AA	2	0	0	2	2.0	7	2	1	0	0	0	0	0	0	0	0	0	0	0	-	0	0--	-	2.31	0.00
2007	ColSpr*	AAA	6	0	0	1	6.1	29	10	5	5	2	0	1	1	2	1	4	1	0	1	1	.500	0	0--	-	10.38	7.11
1995	LAD	NL	16	0	0	5	19.1	83	19	11	11	3	3	1	0	7	2	8	0	0	2	2	.500	0	0-1	0	4.01	5.12
1998	Cin	NL	6	0	0	2	9.1	50	15	8	8	1	0	0	0	6	4	0	0	0	0	1	.000	0	0-0	0	8.58	7.71
1999	Sea	AL	13	0	0	7	9.2	47	11	5	5	1	1	0	1	7	0	7	0	0	0	0	-	0	0-0	0	6.67	4.66
2001	NYY	AL	15	0	0	6	15.1	82	22	9	8	2	2	1	0	9	2	13	0	0	1	0	1.000	0	0-0	0	7.01	4.70
2004	Bal	AL	29	0	0	7	31.1	126	26	10	10	2	0	0	5	9	0	13	1	0	2	0	1.000	0	0-0	3	3.25	2.87
2005	Bal	AL	72	0	0	12	76.1	321	72	34	28	5	2	4	3	26	4	38	4	1	5	5	.500	0	1-3	18	3.40	3.30
2006	Bal	AL	62	0	0	5	57.0	260	76	36	30	8	3	1	2	19	3	24	6	0	2	4	.333	0	1-5	13	6.19	4.74
2007	Bal	AL	14	0	0	5	14.1	64	19	12	12	2	1	0	1	4	0	9	0	0	0	2	.000	0	0-1	5	6.25	7.53
	8 ML YEARS		227	0	0	49	232.2	1033	260	125	112	23	10	9	14	87	11	116	11	1	12	14	.462	0	2-10	38	4.81	4.33

278

Woody Williams

Pitches: R **Bats:** R **Pos:** SP-31; RP-2   **Ht:** 6'0" **Wt:** 200 **Born:** 8/19/1966 **Age:** 41

		HOW MUCH HE PITCHED						WHAT HE GAVE UP												THE RESULTS						
Year	Team	Lg	G	GS	CG	GF	IP	BFP	H	R	ER	HR	SH	SF	HB	TBB	IBB	SO	WP	Bk	W	L	Pct	ShO	Sv-Op	Hld	ERC	ERA
1993	Tor	AL	30	0	0	9	37.0	172	40	18	18	2	1	1	1	22	3	24	2	1	3	1	.750	0	0-2	4	4.85	4.38
1994	Tor	AL	38	0	0	14	59.1	253	44	24	24	5	1	2	2	33	1	56	4	0	1	3	.250	0	0-0	5	3.25	3.64
1995	Tor	AL	23	3	0	10	53.2	232	44	23	22	6	2	0	2	28	1	41	0	0	1	2	.333	0	0-1	1	3.72	3.69
1996	Tor	AL	12	10	1	0	59.0	255	64	33	31	8	2	1	1	21	1	43	2	0	4	5	.444	0	0-0	0	4.73	4.73
1997	Tor	AL	31	31	0	0	194.2	833	201	98	94	31	6	8	5	66	3	124	7	0	9	14	.391	0	0-0	0	4.55	4.35
1998	Tor	AL	32	32	1	0	209.2	894	196	112	104	36	5	6	2	81	3	151	2	1	10	9	.526	1	0-0	0	4.15	4.46
1999	SD	NL	33	33	0	0	208.1	887	213	106	102	33	9	9	2	73	5	137	9	0	12	12	.500	0	0-0	0	4.46	4.41
2000	SD	NL	23	23	4	0	168.0	700	152	74	70	23	4	3	3	54	2	111	4	0	10	8	.556	0	0-0	0	3.55	3.75
2001	2 Tms	NL	34	34	3	0	220.0	922	224	110	99	35	13	8	8	56	5	154	5	0	15	9	.625	1	0-0	0	4.15	4.05
2002	StL	NL	17	17	1	0	103.1	412	84	30	29	10	3	1	4	25	2	76	2	0	9	4	.692	0	0-0	0	2.63	2.53
2003	StL	NL	34	33	0	1	220.2	944	220	101	95	20	11	6	11	55	2	153	3	0	18	9	.667	0	0-1	0	3.52	3.87
2004	StL	NL	31	31	0	0	189.2	817	193	93	88	20	9	5	9	58	3	131	12	1	11	8	.579	0	0-0	0	3.97	4.18
2005	SD	NL	28	28	0	0	159.2	697	174	92	86	24	6	5	3	51	1	106	1	0	9	12	.429	0	0-0	0	4.65	4.85
2006	SD	NL	25	24	0	0	145.1	624	152	68	59	21	7	5	7	35	3	72	4	1	12	5	.706	0	0-0	0	4.12	3.65
2007	Hou	NL	33	31	0	0	188.0	833	216	114	110	35	9	4	12	53	5	101	1	2	8	15	.348	0	0-0	0	5.26	5.27
01	SD	NL	23	23	0	0	145.0	632	170	88	80	28	8	8	5	37	4	102	4	0	8	8	.500	0	0-0	0	5.26	4.97
01	StL	NL	11	11	3	0	75.0	290	54	22	19	7	5	0	3	19	1	52	1	0	7	1	.875	1	0-0	0	2.24	2.28
15 ML YEARS			424	330	10	34	2216.1	9475	2217	1096	1031	309	89	64	72	711	40	1480	58	6	132	116	.532	2	0-4	10	4.13	4.19

Scott Williamson

Pitches: R **Bats:** R **Pos:** RP-16   **Ht:** 6'0" **Wt:** 197 **Born:** 2/17/1976 **Age:** 32

		HOW MUCH HE PITCHED						WHAT HE GAVE UP												THE RESULTS						
Year	Team	Lg	G	GS	CG	GF	IP	BFP	H	R	ER	HR	SH	SF	HB	TBB	IBB	SO	WP	Bk	W	L	Pct	ShO	Sv-Op	Hld	ERC	ERA
2007	Dlmrva*	A-	1	0	0	0	2.0	9	2	1	1	0	0	0	0	1	0	2	0	0	1	0	1.000	0	0--	-	3.63	4.50
2007	Frdrck*	A+	2	1	0	0	2.0	12	4	3	3	0	0	1	2	0	0	2	0	0	0	1	.000	0	0--	-	12.01	13.50
2007	Bowie*	AA	1	1	0	0	2.0	12	5	6	6	0	0	0	0	1	0	4	1	0	0	1	.000	0	0--	-	13.27	27.00
2007	S-WB*	AAA	4	0	0	1	3.2	19	5	4	4	1	0	0	0	3	0	7	0	0	0	1	.000	0	0--	-	9.47	9.82
1999	Cin	NL	62	0	0	40	93.1	366	54	29	25	8	5	2	1	43	6	107	13	0	12	7	.632	0	19-26	5	2.05	2.41
2000	Cin	NL	48	10	0	13	112.0	495	92	45	41	7	4	2	3	75	7	136	21	1	5	8	.385	0	6-8	6	3.85	3.29
2001	Cin	NL	2	0	0	0	0.2	6	1	0	0	0	0	0	0	2	0	1	0	0	0	0	-	0	0-0	1	24.61	0.00
2002	Cin	NL	63	0	0	23	74.0	299	46	27	24	5	5	2	2	36	5	84	8	1	3	4	.429	0	8-12	3	2.24	2.92
2003	2 Tms		66	0	0	40	62.2	276	54	30	29	7	2	1	1	34	6	74	11	0	5	4	.556	0	21-28	5	3.78	4.16
2004	Bos	AL	28	0	0	5	28.2	120	11	6	4	0	0	3	3	18	1	28	4	0	0	1	.000	0	1-2	3	1.47	1.26
2005	ChC	NL	17	0	0	4	14.1	65	15	9	9	3	2	0	2	6	0	23	4	1	0	0	-	0	0-0	3	5.79	5.65
2006	2 Tms	NL	42	0	0	10	39.1	176	41	26	25	4	0	2	1	22	1	42	8	1	2	4	.333	0	0-0	3	5.09	5.72
2007	Bal	AL	16	0	0	2	14.1	61	12	8	7	1	0	2	0	8	0	16	1	0	1	0	1.000	0	0-1	1	3.62	4.40
03	Cin	NL	42	0	0	34	42.1	187	34	15	15	6	2	0	1	25	4	53	7	0	5	3	.625	0	21-26	0	3.07	3.10
03	Bos	AL	24	0	0	6	20.1	89	20	15	14	1	0	1	0	9	2	21	4	0	0	1	.000	0	0-2	5	3.58	6.20
06	ChC	NL	31	0	0	5	28.1	127	27	17	16	2	0	1	1	16	1	32	7	1	2	3	.400	0	0-0	3	4.28	5.08
06	SD	NL	11	0	0	5	11.0	49	14	9	9	2	0	1	0	6	0	10	1	0	0	1	.000	0	0-0	0	7.42	7.36
9 ML YEARS			344	10	0	137	439.1	1864	326	180	164	35	18	14	14	244	26	510	71	4	28	28	.500	0	55-77	35	3.16	3.36

Josh Willingham

Bats: R **Throws:** R **Pos:** LF-137; PH-4; DH-3   **Ht:** 6'2" **Wt:** 215 **Born:** 2/17/1979 **Age:** 29

							BATTING												BASERUNNING				AVERAGES		
Year	Team	Lg	G	AB	H	2B	3B	HR	(Hm | Rd)	TB	R	RBI	RC	TBB	IBB	SO	HBP	SH	SF	SB	CS	SB%	GDP	Avg	OBP	Slg
2004	Fla	NL	12	25	5	0	0	1	(0 | 1)	8	2	1	1	4	0	8	0	0	0	0	0	-	1	.200	.310	.320
2005	Fla	NL	16	23	7	1	0	0	(0 | 0)	8	3	4	3	2	0	5	2	1	0	0	0	-	1	.304	.407	.348
2006	Fla	NL	142	502	139	28	2	26	(11 | 15)	249	62	74	74	54	2	109	11	0	6	2	0	1.00	13	.277	.356	.496
2007	Fla	NL	144	521	138	32	4	21	(10 | 11)	241	75	89	94	66	1	122	16	0	1	8	1	.89	11	.265	.364	.463
4 ML YEARS			314	1071	289	61	6	48	(21 | 27)	506	142	168	172	126	3	244	29	1	7	10	1	.91	26	.270	.360	.472

Dontrelle Willis

Pitches: L **Bats:** L **Pos:** SP-35   **Ht:** 6'4" **Wt:** 225 **Born:** 1/12/1982 **Age:** 26

		HOW MUCH HE PITCHED						WHAT HE GAVE UP												THE RESULTS						
Year	Team	Lg	G	GS	CG	GF	IP	BFP	H	R	ER	HR	SH	SF	HB	TBB	IBB	SO	WP	Bk	W	L	Pct	ShO	Sv-Op	Hld	ERC	ERA
2003	Fla	NL	27	27	2	0	160.2	668	148	61	59	13	3	1	3	58	0	142	7	1	14	6	.700	2	0-0	0	3.49	3.30
2004	Fla	NL	32	32	2	0	197.0	848	210	99	88	20	8	2	8	61	8	139	2	0	10	11	.476	0	0-0	0	4.21	4.02
2005	Fla	NL	34	34	7	0	236.1	960	213	79	69	11	14	5	8	55	3	170	2	1	22	10	.688	5	0-0	0	2.71	2.63
2006	Fla	NL	34	34	4	0	223.1	975	234	106	96	21	11	6	19	83	6	160	6	1	12	12	.500	1	0-0	0	4.53	3.87
2007	Fla	NL	35	35	0	0	205.1	942	241	131	118	29	15	7	14	87	4	146	9	1	10	15	.400	0	0-0	0	5.72	5.17
5 ML YEARS			162	162	15	0	1022.2	4393	1046	476	430	94	51	21	52	344	21	757	26	4	68	54	.557	8	0-0	0	4.09	3.78

Reggie Willits

Bats: B **Throws:** R **Pos:** LF-64; RF-31; CF-30; DH-14; PH-8; PR-4   **Ht:** 5'11" **Wt:** 185 **Born:** 5/30/1981 **Age:** 27

							BATTING												BASERUNNING				AVERAGES		
Year	Team	Lg	G	AB	H	2B	3B	HR	(Hm | Rd)	TB	R	RBI	RC	TBB	IBB	SO	HBP	SH	SF	SB	CS	SB%	GDP	Avg	OBP	Slg
2003	Provo	R+	59	230	69	14	4	4	(- | -)	103	53	27	46	37	0	52	6	3	0	14	4	.78	2	.300	.410	.448
2004	RCuca	A+	135	526	150	17	5	5	(- | -)	192	99	52	84	73	2	112	8	8	10	44	15	.75	4	.285	.374	.365
2005	Ark	AA	123	487	148	23	6	2	(- | -)	189	75	46	80	54	0	78	8	4	8	40	14	.74	5	.304	.377	.388
2006	Salt Lk	AAA	97	352	115	18	4	3	(- | -)	150	85	39	75	77	2	50	2	4	2	31	15	.67	5	.327	.448	.426
2006	LAA	AL	28	45	12	1	0	0	(0 | 0)	13	12	2	6	11	0	10	0	2	0	4	3	.57	0	.267	.411	.289
2007	LAA	AL	136	430	126	20	1	0	(0 | 0)	148	74	34	68	69	2	83	3	11	5	27	8	.77	7	.293	.391	.344
2 ML YEARS			164	475	138	21	1	0	(0 | 0)	161	86	36	74	80	2	93	3	13	5	31	11	.74	7	.291	.393	.339

Brian Wilson

Pitches: R Bats: R Pos: RP-24 Ht: 6'1" Wt: 205 Born: 3/16/1982 Age: 26

			HOW MUCH HE PITCHED						WHAT HE GAVE UP										THE RESULTS						
Year	Team	Lg	G	GS	CG	GF	IP	BFP	H	R	ER	HR	SH	SF	HB	TBB	IBB	SO	WP	Bk	W	L	Pct	ShO	Sv-Op	Hld	ERC	ERA
2004	Hgrstn	A	23	3	0	12	57.1	259	63	37	34	7	0	0	3	22	1	41	1	0	2	5	.286	0	3- -	-	4.82	5.34
2005	Augsta	A	26	0	0	24	33.0	129	23	7	3	0	1	0	3	7	0	30	0	0	5	1	.833	0	13- -	-	1.64	0.82
2005	Nrwich	AA	15	0	0	15	15.2	58	6	1	1	0	0	0	1	5	0	22	0	0	0	0	-	0	8- -	-	0.90	0.57
2005	Fresno	AAA	9	0	0	2	11.1	52	8	7	5	0	1	1	0	8	0	13	1	0	1	1	.500	0	0- -	-	2.72	3.97
2006	Fresno	AAA	24	0	0	14	28.0	115	20	9	9	2	0	1	1	14	0	30	0	0	1	3	.250	0	7- -	-	2.93	2.89
2006	SnJos	A+	1	0	0	0	1.0	5	1	1	1	0	0	0	0	1	0	1	0	0	0	0	-	0	0- -	-	5.48	9.00
2007	SnJos	A+	3	0	0	3	3.0	11	1	0	0	0	0	0	0	0	0	6	0	0	0	0	-	0	2- -	-	0.23	0.00
2007	Fresno	AAA	31	0	0	25	34.1	155	24	13	8	0	1	1	5	24	1	37	2	0	1	2	.333	0	11- -	-	3.25	2.10
2006	SF	NL	31	0	0	9	30.0	141	32	19	18	1	1	4	1	21	2	23	0	0	2	3	.400	0	1-2	4	5.11	5.40
2007	SF	NL	24	0	0	9	23.2	93	16	6	6	1	0	0	1	7	0	18	0	0	1	2	.333	0	6-7	9	1.87	2.28
	2 ML YEARS		55	0	0	18	53.2	234	48	25	24	2	1	4	2	28	2	41	0	0	3	5	.375	0	7-9	13	3.59	4.02

C.J. Wilson

Pitches: L Bats: L Pos: RP-66 Ht: 6'1" Wt: 215 Born: 11/18/1980 Age: 27

			HOW MUCH HE PITCHED						WHAT HE GAVE UP										THE RESULTS						
Year	Team	Lg	G	GS	CG	GF	IP	BFP	H	R	ER	HR	SH	SF	HB	TBB	IBB	SO	WP	Bk	W	L	Pct	ShO	Sv-Op	Hld	ERC	ERA
2005	Tex	AL	24	6	0	5	48.0	220	63	39	37	7	5	1	2	18	1	30	4	1	1	7	.125	0	1-1	4	6.03	6.94
2006	Tex	AL	44	0	0	12	44.1	191	39	23	20	7	1	0	5	18	1	43	0	0	2	4	.333	0	1-2	7	4.25	4.06
2007	Tex	AL	66	0	0	22	68.1	285	50	25	23	4	2	4	6	33	1	63	5	0	2	1	.667	0	12-14	15	3.01	3.03
	3 ML YEARS		134	6	0	39	160.2	696	152	87	80	16	4	6	13	69	3	136	9	1	5	12	.294	0	14-17	26	4.21	4.48

Craig Wilson

Bats: R Throws: R Pos: 1B-20; PH-6 Ht: 6'2" Wt: 225 Born: 11/30/1976 Age: 31

			BATTING																		BASERUNNING				AVERAGES		
Year	Team	Lg	G	AB	H	2B	3B	HR	(Hm	Rd)	TB	R	RBI	RC	TBB	IBB	SO	HBP	SH	SF	SB	CS	SB%	GDP	Avg	OBP	Slg
2007	Charltt*	AAA	15	61	11	2	0	1	(-	-)	16	8	5	4	7	0	28	1	0	0	0	0	-	3	.180	.275	.262
2001	Pit	NL	88	158	49	3	1	13	(8	5)	93	27	32	34	15	1	53	7	1	2	3	1	.75	4	.310	.390	.589
2002	Pit	NL	131	368	97	16	1	16	(3	13)	163	48	57	55	32	0	116	21	1	2	2	3	.40	10	.264	.355	.443
2003	Pit	NL	116	309	81	15	4	18	(9	9)	158	49	48	49	35	4	89	13	0	1	3	1	.75	6	.262	.360	.511
2004	Pit	NL	155	561	148	35	5	29	(16	13)	280	97	82	84	50	3	169	30	0	3	2	2	.50	11	.264	.354	.499
2005	Pit	NL	59	197	52	14	1	5	(3	2)	83	23	22	28	30	2	69	10	0	1	3	0	1.00	6	.264	.387	.421
2006	2 Tms	NL	125	359	90	15	2	17	(10	7)	160	53	49	48	28	2	122	6	0	2	1	0	1.00	10	.251	.314	.446
2007	Atl	NL	24	58	10	2	0	1	(0	1)	15	6	2	3	6	0	25	3	0	0	0	0	-	4	.172	.304	.259
06	Pit	NL	85	255	68	11	2	13	(8	5)	122	38	41	43	24	2	88	5	0	2	1	0	1.00	6	.267	.339	.478
06	NYY	AL	40	104	22	4	0	4	(2	2)	38	15	8	5	4	0	34	1	0	0	0	0	-	4	.212	.248	.365
	7 ML YEARS		698	2010	527	100	14	99	(49	50)	952	303	292	301	198	12	643	90	2	11	14	7	.67	47	.262	.353	.474

Jack Wilson

Bats: R Throws: R Pos: SS-131; PH-4 Ht: 6'0" Wt: 195 Born: 12/29/1977 Age: 30

			BATTING																		BASERUNNING				AVERAGES		
Year	Team	Lg	G	AB	H	2B	3B	HR	(Hm	Rd)	TB	R	RBI	RC	TBB	IBB	SO	HBP	SH	SF	SB	CS	SB%	GDP	Avg	OBP	Slg
2001	Pit	NL	108	390	87	17	1	3	(0	3)	115	44	25	27	16	2	70	1	17	1	1	3	.25	4	.223	.255	.295
2002	Pit	NL	147	527	133	22	4	4	(2	2)	175	77	47	60	37	2	74	4	17	1	5	2	.71	7	.252	.306	.332
2003	Pit	NL	150	558	143	21	3	9	(2	7)	197	58	62	62	36	3	74	4	11	6	5	5	.50	11	.256	.303	.353
2004	Pit	NL	157	652	201	41	12	11	(7	4)	299	82	59	84	26	0	71	3	7	5	8	4	.67	15	.308	.335	.459
2005	Pit	NL	158	587	151	24	7	8	(5	3)	213	60	52	60	31	6	58	6	11	4	7	3	.70	11	.257	.299	.363
2006	Pit	NL	142	543	148	27	1	8	(5	3)	201	70	35	58	33	0	65	4	9	5	4	3	.57	15	.273	.316	.370
2007	Pit	NL	135	477	141	29	2	12	(3	9)	210	67	56	70	38	9	46	6	7	7	2	5	.29	8	.296	.350	.440
	7 ML YEARS		997	3734	1004	181	30	55	(22	33)	1410	458	336	421	217	22	458	28	79	29	32	25	.56	71	.269	.312	.378

Josh Wilson

Bats: R Throws: R Pos: SS-57; 2B-27; PH-16; 3B-8; PR-2 Ht: 6'1" Wt: 160 Born: 3/26/1981 Age: 27

			BATTING																		BASERUNNING				AVERAGES		
Year	Team	Lg	G	AB	H	2B	3B	HR	(Hm	Rd)	TB	R	RBI	RC	TBB	IBB	SO	HBP	SH	SF	SB	CS	SB%	GDP	Avg	OBP	Slg
1999	Mrlns	R	53	203	54	9	4	0	(-	-)	71	29	27	30	24	0	36	5	1	4	14	2	.88	4	.266	.352	.350
2000	Kane	A	13	52	14	3	1	1	(-	-)	22	2	6	7	3	0	14	1	0	1	0	0	-	2	.269	.316	.423
2000	Utica	A-	66	259	89	13	6	3	(-	-)	123	43	43	51	29	3	47	5	1	1	9	8	.53	6	.344	.418	.475
2001	Kane	A	123	506	144	28	5	4	(-	-)	194	65	61	58	28	0	60	4	4	4	17	11	.61	10	.285	.325	.383
2002	Jupiter	A+	111	398	102	17	1	11	(-	-)	154	51	50	49	28	0	67	10	3	4	7	10	.41	6	.256	.318	.387
2002	Portlnd	AA	12	41	14	3	0	2	(-	-)	23	5	5	7	2	0	6	1	0	1	0	1	.00	0	.341	.372	.561
2003	Carlina	AA	118	434	110	30	6	3	(-	-)	161	53	58	49	27	0	70	2	2	10	6	5	.55	9	.253	.294	.371
2004	Carlina	AA	81	311	98	21	1	10	(-	-)	151	63	41	61	42	1	50	1	2	2	8	4	.67	4	.315	.396	.486
2004	Albq	AAA	56	240	67	12	2	5	(-	-)	98	32	23	34	19	0	51	2	2	0	6	1	.86	5	.279	.337	.408
2005	Albq	AAA	143	526	135	31	6	17	(-	-)	229	88	82	79	48	2	114	9	2	12	17	7	.71	8	.257	.323	.435
2006	ColSpr	AAA	89	335	103	18	4	10	(-	-)	159	61	45	63	37	2	41	4	1	7	15	4	.79	5	.307	.376	.475
2005	Fla	NL	11	10	1	1	0	0	(0	0)	2	0	0	4	1	0	0	0	1	0	0	0	-	0	.100	.182	.200
2007	2 Tms		105	282	67	15	3	2	(0	2)	94	28	24	24	17	0	57	5	3	3	6	2	.75	5	.238	.290	.333
07	Was	NL	15	19	1	0	0	0	(0	0)	1	3	0	0	5	0	6	1	0	0	0	0	-	0	.053	.280	.053
07	TB	AL	90	263	66	15	3	2	(0	2)	93	25	24	24	12	0	51	4	3	3	6	2	.75	5	.251	.291	.354
	2 ML YEARS		116	292	68	16	3	2	(0	2)	96	30	24	24	17	0	61	6	3	3	6	2	.75	5	.233	.286	.329

Preston Wilson

Bats: R **Throws:** R **Pos:** RF-16; PH-11   **Ht:** 6'2" **Wt:** 220 **Born:** 7/19/1974 **Age:** 33

Year Team	Lg	G	AB	H	2B	3B	HR	(Hm	Rd)	TB	R	RBI	RC	TBB	IBB	SO	HBP	SH	SF	SB	CS	SB%	GDP	Avg	OBP	Slg
1998 2 Tms	NL	22	51	8	2	0	1	(1	0)	13	7	3	3	6	0	21	1	2	0	1	1	.50	0	.157	.259	.255
1999 Fla	NL	149	482	135	21	4	26	(8	18)	242	67	71	81	46	3	156	9	0	6	11	4	.73	15	.280	.350	.502
2000 Fla	NL	161	605	160	35	3	31	(12	19)	294	94	121	97	55	1	187	8	0	6	36	14	.72	11	.264	.331	.486
2001 Fla	NL	123	468	128	30	2	23	(9	14)	231	70	71	73	36	2	107	6	0	3	20	8	.71	14	.274	.331	.494
2002 Fla	NL	141	510	124	22	2	23	(8	15)	219	80	65	58	58	3	140	9	2	3	20	11	.65	17	.243	.329	.429
2003 Col	NL	155	600	169	43	1	36	(21	15)	322	94	141	111	54	1	139	4	0	3	14	7	.67	23	.282	.343	.537
2004 Col	NL	58	202	50	11	0	6	(3	3)	79	24	29	19	17	2	49	3	0	0	2	1	.67	9	.248	.315	.391
2005 2 Tms	NL	139	520	135	29	2	25	(13	12)	243	73	90	72	45	0	148	7	1	3	6	6	.50	18	.260	.325	.467
2006 2 Tms	NL	135	501	132	25	2	17	(12	5)	212	58	72	60	29	3	121	4	0	3	12	2	.86	20	.263	.307	.423
2007 StL	NL	25	64	14	3	0	1	(0	1)	20	6	5	5	4	0	17	0	0	0	2	1	.67	2	.219	.265	.313
98 NYM	NL	8	20	6	2	0	0	(0	0)	8	3	2	3	2	0	8	0	0	0	1	1	.50	0	.300	.364	.400
98 Fla	NL	14	31	2	0	0	1	(1	0)	5	4	1	0	4	0	13	1	2	0	0	0	-	0	.065	.194	.161
05 Col	NL	71	267	69	15	1	15	(10	5)	131	39	47	33	25	0	77	1	1	2	3	2	.60	8	.258	.322	.491
05 Was	NL	68	253	66	14	1	10	(3	7)	112	34	43	39	20	0	71	6	0	1	3	4	.43	10	.261	.329	.443
06 Hou	NL	102	390	105	22	2	9	(7	2)	158	40	55	44	22	2	94	2	0	3	6	2	.75	18	.269	.309	.405
06 StL	NL	33	111	27	3	0	8	(5	3)	54	18	17	16	7	1	27	2	0	0	6	0	1.00	2	.243	.300	.486
10 ML YEARS		1108	4003	1055	221	16	189	(87	102)	1875	573	668	579	350	15	1085	51	5	27	124	55	.69	129	.264	.329	.468

Vance Wilson

Bats: R **Throws:** R **Pos:** C   **Ht:** 5'11" **Wt:** 215 **Born:** 3/17/1973 **Age:** 35

Year Team	Lg	G	AB	H	2B	3B	HR	(Hm	Rd)	TB	R	RBI	RC	TBB	IBB	SO	HBP	SH	SF	SB	CS	SB%	GDP	Avg	OBP	Slg
2007 Toledo*	AAA	3	11	3	0	0	0	(-	-)	3	2	0	1	0	0	2	1	0	0	0	0	-	2	.273	.333	.273
1999 NYM	NL	1	0	0	0	0	0	(0	0)	0	0	0	0	0	0	0	0	0	0	0	0	-	0	-	-	-
2000 NYM	NL	4	4	0	0	0	0	(0	0)	0	0	0	0	0	0	2	0	0	0	0	0	-	0	.000	.000	.000
2001 NYM	NL	32	57	17	3	0	0	(0	0)	20	3	6	6	2	0	16	2	0	1	0	1	.00	1	.298	.339	.351
2002 NYM	NL	74	163	40	7	0	5	(3	2)	62	19	26	21	5	0	32	8	2	0	0	1	.00	6	.245	.301	.380
2003 NYM	NL	96	268	65	9	1	8	(3	5)	100	28	39	31	15	1	56	5	2	2	1	2	.33	6	.243	.293	.373
2004 NYM	NL	79	157	43	10	1	4	(1	3)	67	18	21	23	11	2	24	5	1	3	1	0	1.00	4	.274	.335	.427
2005 Det	AL	61	152	30	4	0	3	(1	2)	43	18	19	13	11	0	26	6	2	2	0	0	-	6	.197	.275	.283
2006 Det	AL	56	152	43	9	0	5	(3	2)	67	18	18	17	2	0	33	3	10	1	0	4	.00	1	.283	.304	.441
8 ML YEARS		403	953	238	42	2	25	(11	14)	359	104	129	111	46	3	189	29	17	9	2	8	.20	23	.250	.302	.377

Randy Winn

Bats: B **Throws:** R **Pos:** RF-104; CF-36; LF-24; PH-7; 3B-1; PR-1   **Ht:** 0'2" **Wt:** 195 **Born:** 6/9/1974 **Age:** 34

Year Team	Lg	G	AB	H	2B	3B	HR	(Hm	Rd)	TB	R	RBI	RC	TBB	IBB	SO	HBP	SH	SF	SB	CS	SB%	GDP	Avg	OBP	Slg
1998 TB	AL	109	338	94	9	9	1	(0	1)	124	51	17	44	29	0	69	1	11	0	26	12	.68	2	.278	.337	.367
1999 TB	AL	70	303	81	16	4	2	(2	0)	111	44	24	32	17	0	63	1	1	2	9	9	.50	3	.267	.307	.366
2000 TB	AL	51	159	40	5	0	1	(1	0)	48	28	16	18	26	0	25	2	2	1	6	7	.46	2	.252	.362	.302
2001 TB	AL	128	429	117	25	6	6	(3	3)	172	54	50	56	38	0	81	6	5	2	12	10	.55	10	.273	.339	.401
2002 TB	AL	152	607	181	39	9	14	(9	5)	280	87	75	104	55	3	109	6	1	5	27	8	.77	9	.298	.360	.461
2003 Sea	AL	157	600	177	37	4	11	(6	5)	255	103	75	96	41	0	108	8	6	5	23	5	.82	9	.295	.346	.425
2004 Sea	AL	157	626	179	34	6	14	(6	8)	267	84	81	91	53	1	98	8	9	7	21	7	.75	16	.286	.346	.427
2005 2 Tms		160	617	189	47	6	20	(9	11)	308	85	63	95	48	4	91	5	10	3	19	11	.63	11	.306	.360	.499
2006 SF	NL	149	573	150	34	5	11	(5	6)	227	82	56	69	48	3	63	7	3	4	10	8	.56	7	.262	.324	.396
2007 SF	NL	155	593	178	42	1	14	(4	10)	264	73	65	86	44	3	85	7	4	5	15	3	.83	12	.300	.353	.445
05 Sea	AL	102	386	106	25	1	6	(2	4)	151	46	37	52	37	3	53	4	6	3	12	6	.67	7	.275	.342	.391
05 SF	NL	58	231	83	22	5	14	(7	7)	157	39	26	43	11	1	38	1	4	0	7	5	.58	4	.359	.391	.680
10 ML YEARS		1297	4845	1386	288	50	94	(45	49)	2056	691	522	691	399	14	792	51	52	34	168	80	.68	81	.286	.345	.424

Dewayne Wise

Bats: L **Throws:** L **Pos:** CF-4; PH-1   **Ht:** 6'1" **Wt:** 180 **Born:** 2/24/1978 **Age:** 30

Year Team	Lg	G	AB	H	2B	3B	HR	(Hm	Rd)	TB	R	RBI	RC	TBB	IBB	SO	HBP	SH	SF	SB	CS	SB%	GDP	Avg	OBP	Slg
2007 Reds*	R	2	6	3	1	0	0	(-	-)	4	2	0	1	0	0	2	0	0	0	1	0	1.00	0	.500	.500	.667
2007 Lsvlle*	AAA	54	207	52	11	7	7	(-	-)	98	34	20	29	8	1	56	2	4	1	8	2	.80	5	.251	.284	.473
2000 Tor	AL	28	22	3	0	0	0	(0	0)	3	3	0	0	1	0	5	0	0	0	1	0	1.00	0	.136	.208	.136
2002 Tor	AL	42	112	20	4	1	3	(2	1)	35	14	13	8	4	0	15	0	0	0	5	0	1.00	0	.179	.207	.313
2004 Atl	NL	77	162	37	9	4	6	(3	3)	72	24	17	20	9	1	28	1	2	1	6	1	.86	1	.228	.272	.444
2006 Cin	NL	31	38	7	2	0	0	(0	0)	9	3	1	0	0	0	6	0	2	0	0	0	-	2	.184	.184	.237
2007 Cin	NL	5	5	1	0	1	0	(0	0)	3	1	1	1	1	1	1	0	0	0	0	0	-	0	.200	.333	.600
5 ML YEARS		183	339	68	15	6	9	(5	4)	122	45	32	29	15	2	55	2	4	1	12	1	.92	3	.201	.238	.360

Matt Wise

Pitches: R **Bats:** R **Pos:** RP-56   **Ht:** 6'4" **Wt:** 195 **Born:** 11/18/1975 **Age:** 32

Year Team	Lg	G	GS	CG	GF	IP	BFP	H	R	ER	HR	SH	SF	HB	TBB	IBB	SO	WP	Bk	W	L	Pct	ShO	Sv-Op	Hld	ERC	ERA
2000 LAA	AL	8	6	0	0	37.1	163	40	23	23	7	0	2	1	13	1	20	1	0	3	3	.500	0	0-0	0	4.96	5.54
2001 LAA	AL	11	9	0	2	49.1	211	47	27	24	11	2	1	2	18	1	50	1	0	1	4	.200	0	0-0	0	4.65	4.38
2002 LAA	AL	7	0	0	6	8.1	33	7	3	3	0	1	0	1	1	0	6	0	0	0	0	-	0	0-0	0	2.07	3.24
2004 Mil	NL	30	3	0	5	52.2	222	51	27	26	3	1	2	2	15	1	30	2	0	1	2	.333	0	0-0	3	3.27	4.44

Year Team	Lg	G	GS	CG	GF	IP	BFP	H	R	ER	HR	SH	SF	HB	TBB	IBB	SO	WP	Bk	W	L	Pct	ShO	Sv-Op	Hld	ERC	ERA
2005 Mil	NL	49	0	0	11	64.1	262	37	25	24	6	1	2	3	25	5	62	1	1	4	4	.500	0	1-3	10	1.83	3.36
2006 Mil	NL	40	0	0	9	44.1	188	45	24	19	6	3	1	2	14	2	27	0	1	5	6	.455	0	0-4	14	4.23	3.86
2007 Mil	NL	56	0	0	9	53.2	236	61	30	25	5	1	3	1	17	1	43	0	1	3	2	.600	0	1-2	13	4.49	4.19
7 ML YEARS		201	18	0	42	310.0	1315	288	159	144	38	9	11	12	103	11	238	4	3	17	21	.447	0	2-9	40	3.65	4.18

Jay Witasick

Pitches: R Bats: R Pos: RP-36   Ht: 6'4" Wt: 249 Born: 8/28/1972 Age: 35

		HOW MUCH HE PITCHED						WHAT HE GAVE UP												THE RESULTS						
Year Team	Lg	G	GS	CG	GF	IP	BFP	H	R	ER	HR	SH	SF	HB	TBB	IBB	SO	WP	Bk	W	L	Pct	ShO	Sv-Op	Hld	ERC	ERA
2007 VeroB*	A+	2	2	0	0	2.0	7	1	0	0	0	0	0	0	1	0	1	0	0	0	0	-	0	0--	-	1.62	0.00
2007 Drham*	AAA	6	0	0	3	7.1	28	2	0	0	0	0	0	0	2	0	8	3	0	1	0	1.000	0	1--	-	0.44	0.00
1996 Oak	AL	12	0	0	6	13.0	55	12	9	9	5	0	1	0	5	0	12	2	0	1	1	.500	0	0-1	0	5.52	6.23
1997 Oak	AL	8	0	0	1	11.0	53	14	7	7	2	1	0	0	6	0	8	0	0	0	0	-	0	0-0	1	6.81	5.73
1998 Oak	AL	7	3	0	1	27.0	131	36	24	19	9	0	0	0	15	1	29	2	0	1	3	.250	0	0-0	0	8.53	6.33
1999 KC	AL	32	28	1	2	158.1	732	191	108	98	23	4	8	8	83	1	102	5	2	9	12	.429	1	0-0	0	6.45	5.57
2000 2 Tms		33	25	2	2	150.0	697	178	107	97	24	8	4	7	73	5	121	5	1	6	10	.375	0	0-0	0	6.09	5.82
2001 2 Tms		63	0	0	17	79.0	352	78	41	29	8	3	2	6	33	4	106	4	0	8	2	.800	0	1-4	10	4.22	3.30
2002 SF	NL	44	0	0	9	68.1	276	58	19	18	3	2	1	4	21	3	54	3	0	1	0	1.000	0	0-0	4	2.78	2.37
2003 SD	NL	46	0	0	14	45.2	202	42	24	23	6	3	1	1	25	4	42	5	0	3	7	.300	0	2-7	12	4.34	4.53
2004 SD	NL	44	0	0	20	61.2	266	57	28	22	8	3	2	1	26	2	57	4	0	0	1	.000	0	1-3	2	3.92	3.21
2005 2 Tms		60	0	0	11	63.1	277	53	26	20	4	4	0	6	29	5	73	5	0	1	5	.167	0	1-4	17	3.31	2.84
2006 Oak	AL	20	0	0	8	22.2	111	25	17	17	3	0	0	1	21	2	23	1	0	1	0	1.000	0	0-0	2	7.25	6.75
2007 2 Tms		36	0	0	10	31.1	146	31	19	18	2	1	1	1	27	2	18	4	0	1	0	1.000	0	0-1	4	5.72	5.17
00 KC	AL	22	14	2	2	89.1	410	109	65	59	15	3	3	4	38	0	67	3	0	3	8	.273	0	0-0	0	6.19	5.94
00 SD	NL	11	11	0	0	60.2	287	69	42	38	9	5	1	3	35	5	54	2	1	3	2	.600	0	0-0	0	5.94	5.64
01 SD	NL	31	0	0	9	38.2	164	31	14	8	3	3	0	4	15	3	53	3	0	5	2	.714	0	1-3	5	3.05	1.86
01 NYY	AL	32	0	0	8	40.1	188	47	27	21	5	0	2	2	18	1	53	1	0	3	0	1.000	0	0-1	5	5.43	4.69
05 Col	NL	32	0	0	7	35.2	148	27	11	10	2	4	0	3	12	3	40	2	0	0	4	.000	0	0-1	11	2.43	2.52
05 Oak	AL	28	0	0	4	27.2	129	26	15	10	2	0	0	3	17	2	33	3	0	1	1	.500	0	1-3	6	4.54	3.25
07 Oak	AL	16	0	0	5	15.0	65	14	6	6	1	0	0	1	9	1	10	2	0	1	0	1.000	0	0-1	1	4.56	3.60
07 TB	AL	20	0	0	5	16.1	81	17	13	12	1	1	1	0	18	1	8	2	0	0	0	-	0	0-0	3	6.81	6.61
12 ML YEARS		405	56	3	101	731.1	3298	775	429	377	97	29	20	35	364	29	645	40	3	32	41	.438	1	5-20	52	5.18	4.64

Randy Wolf

Pitches: L Bats: L Pos: SP-18   Ht: 5'10" Wt: 200 Born: 8/22/1976 Age: 31

		HOW MUCH HE PITCHED						WHAT HE GAVE UP												THE RESULTS						
Year Team	Lg	G	GS	CG	GF	IP	BFP	H	R	ER	HR	SH	SF	HB	TBB	IBB	SO	WP	Bk	W	L	Pct	ShO	Sv-Op	Hld	ERC	ERA
2007 InldEm*	A+	1	1	0	0	4.0	18	6	3	3	2	0	0	0	1	0	4	0	0	0	0	-	0	0--	-	10.07	6.75
1999 Phi	NL	22	21	0	0	121.2	552	126	78	75	20	5	1	5	67	0	116	4	0	6	9	.400	0	0-0	0	5.54	5.55
2000 Phi	NL	32	32	1	0	206.1	889	210	107	100	25	10	8	8	83	2	160	1	0	11	9	.550	0	0-0	0	4.54	4.36
2001 Phi	NL	28	25	4	1	163.0	684	150	74	67	15	11	7	10	51	4	152	1	0	10	11	.476	2	0-0	0	3.46	3.70
2002 Phi	NL	31	31	3	0	210.2	855	172	77	75	23	7	6	7	63	5	172	4	0	11	9	.550	2	0-0	0	2.88	3.20
2003 Phi	NL	33	33	2	0	200.0	850	176	101	94	27	8	4	6	78	4	177	6	0	16	10	.615	2	0-0	0	3.67	4.23
2004 Phi	NL	23	23	1	0	136.2	585	145	73	65	20	6	3	5	36	4	89	2	0	5	8	.385	1	0-0	0	4.29	4.28
2005 Phi	NL	13	13	0	0	80.0	346	87	40	39	14	4	1	6	26	2	61	1	0	6	4	.600	0	0-0	0	5.17	4.39
2006 Phi	NL	12	12	0	0	56.2	261	63	37	35	13	2	3	2	33	2	44	2	0	4	0	1.000	0	0-0	0	6.63	5.56
2007 LAD	NL	18	18	0	0	102.2	458	110	55	54	10	5	5	6	39	2	94	4	0	9	6	.600	0	0-0	0	4.52	4.73
9 ML YEARS		212	208	11	1	1277.2	5480	1239	642	604	167	58	38	55	476	25	1065	25	0	78	66	.542	7	0-0	0	4.16	4.25

Ross Wolf

Pitches: R Bats: R Pos: RP-14   Ht: 6'0" Wt: 180 Born: 10/18/1982 Age: 25

		HOW MUCH HE PITCHED						WHAT HE GAVE UP												THE RESULTS						
Year Team	Lg	G	GS	CG	GF	IP	BFP	H	R	ER	HR	SH	SF	HB	TBB	IBB	SO	WP	Bk	W	L	Pct	ShO	Sv-Op	Hld	ERC	ERA
2002 Jmstwn	A-	11	11	0	0	46.1	209	56	30	24	4	1	3	3	12	0	18	2	1	2	4	.333	0	0--	-	4.77	4.66
2003 Grnsbr	A	27	0	0	6	50.1	192	32	10	9	2	4	1	2	10	2	26	0	0	6	1	.857	0	2--	-	1.42	1.61
2004 Jupiter	A+	43	0	0	22	90.0	386	87	33	26	2	1	1	4	28	6	58	3	0	11	7	.611	0	5--	-	3.04	2.60
2005 Carlina	AA	54	1	0	15	78.0	373	106	54	44	6	4	5	1	31	4	59	3	0	4	5	.556	0	1--	-	5.79	5.08
2006 Carlina	AA	12	0	0	3	18.0	66	12	3	2	0	1	0	0	2	1	12	1	0	1	2	.333	0	0--	-	1.11	1.00
2006 Albq	AAA	48	0	0	9	48.2	217	65	28	28	1	4	1	3	15	1	29	2	0	4	1	.800	0	0--	-	5.42	5.18
2007 Albq	AAA	46	0	0	10	47.1	206	54	24	18	5	2	3	0	17	1	23	0	1	3	4	.571	0	2--	-	4.78	3.42
2007 Fla	NL	14	0	0	2	12.1	66	24	16	16	4	1	0	1	3	0	6	1	0	0	1	.000	0	0-0	0	11.46	11.68

Brian Wolfe

Pitches: R Bats: R Pos: RP-38   Ht: 6'2" Wt: 200 Born: 11/29/1980 Age: 27

		HOW MUCH HE PITCHED						WHAT HE GAVE UP												THE RESULTS						
Year Team	Lg	G	GS	CG	GF	IP	BFP	H	R	ER	HR	SH	SF	HB	TBB	IBB	SO	WP	Bk	W	L	Pct	ShO	Sv-Op	Hld	ERC	ERA
1999 Twins	R	9	5	2	0	38.0	153	33	14	12	2	1	1	1	9	0	40	2	0	4	0	1.000	0	0--	-	2.59	2.84
2000 QuadC	A	31	18	0	2	123.1	541	148	73	65	13	2	6	4	34	1	91	7	1	5	9	.357	0	0--	-	4.90	4.74
2001 QuadC	A	28	23	2	2	160.0	641	128	64	50	11	2	4	5	32	2	128	8	0	13	8	.619	2	0--	-	2.18	2.81
2002 FtMyrs	A+	25	23	0	0	132.0	584	160	84	68	17	5	4	7	34	0	85	5	3	6	9	.400	0	0--	-	5.15	4.64
2003 FtMyrs	A+	7	7	0	0	46.1	185	41	15	13	0	5	0	1	6	0	22	2	0	4	2	.667	0	0--	-	2.31	2.53
2003 NwBrit	AA	30	10	1	11	82.2	375	111	65	59	10	2	5	3	24	2	42	0	1	5	7	.417	0	3--	-	5.95	6.42
2004 NwBrit	AA	7	0	0	1	11.0	50	16	10	10	3	1	0	0	3	0	6	0	0	1	1	.500	0	0--	-	7.80	8.18
2005 Roch	AAA	3	0	0	0	6.1	31	10	8	6	1	0	0	0	2	0	5	0	0	0	2	.000	0	0--	-	7.54	8.53
2005 NwBrit	AA	5	0	0	2	7.2	37	10	6	6	0	0	0	0	7	1	4	0	0	1	0	1.000	0	0--	-	7.28	7.04
2005 BrvdCt	A+	18	0	0	13	22.2	91	19	3	2	0	0	0	0	8	0	22	1	0	1	1	.500	0	8--	-	2.47	0.79
2005 Hntsvl	AA	16	0	0	7	24.0	115	32	12	9	1	2	1	1	8	2	19	3	0	3	2	.600	0	0--	-	5.07	3.38

Year	Team	Lg	G	GS	CG	GF	IP	BFP	H	R	ER	HR	SH	SF	HB	TBB	IBB	SO	WP	Bk	W	L	Pct	ShO	Sv-Op	Hld	ERC	ERA
2006	Dnedin	A+	5	5	0	0	24.0	110	33	20	16	3	0	1	2	3	0	17	1	0	1	4	.200	0	0- -	-	5.53	6.00
2006	NHam	AA	24	2	0	6	42.1	198	54	30	27	5	2	1	1	15	1	34	2	1	1	3	.250	0	0- -	-	5.52	5.74
2007	Syrcse	AAA	17	0	0	6	26.0	100	18	4	3	1	0	0	0	6	1	23	1	0	2	0	1.000	0	0- -	-	1.58	1.04
2007	Tor	AL	38	0	0	12	45.1	174	36	17	15	5	0	2	2	9	2	22	0	0	3	1	.750	0	0-2	6	2.52	2.98

Brandon Wood

Bats: R Throws: R Pos: 3B-10; SS-3; PH-2; PR-1   Ht: 6'3" Wt: 185 Born: 3/2/1985 Age: 23

Year	Team	Lg	G	AB	H	2B	3B	HR	(Hm	Rd)	TB	R	RBI	RC	TBB	IBB	SO	HBP	SH	SF	SB	CS	SB%	GDP	Avg	OBP	Slg
2003	Angels	R	19	78	24	8	2	0	(-	-)	36	14	13	13	4	0	15	2	0	2	3	0	1.00	2	.308	.349	.462
2003	Provo	R+	42	162	45	13	2	5	(-	-)	77	25	31	27	16	0	48	2	0	1	1	1	.50	2	.278	.348	.475
2004	CRpds	A	125	478	120	30	5	11	(-	-)	193	65	64	67	46	3	117	5	4	2	21	5	.81	8	.251	.322	.404
2005	RCuca	A+	130	536	172	51	4	43	(-	-)	360	109	115	131	48	5	128	7	2	2	7	3	.70	12	.321	.383	.672
2005	Salt Lk	AAA	4	19	6	2	1	0	(-	-)	10	1	1	3	0	0	6	0	0	0	0	0	-	0	.316	.316	.526
2006	Ark	AA	118	453	125	42	4	25	(-	-)	250	74	83	92	54	1	149	6	2	7	19	3	.86	10	.276	.356	.552
2007	Salt Lk	AAA	111	437	119	27	1	23	(-	-)	217	73	77	76	45	0	120	1	0	5	10	1	.91	10	.272	.338	.497
2007	LAA	AL	13	33	5	1	0	1	(0	1)	9	2	3	1	0	0	12	0	0	0	0	0	-	0	.152	.152	.273

Jason Wood

Bats: R Throws: R Pos: PH-54; 1B-46; 3B-7; 2B-2; LF-1; DH-1; PR-1   Ht: 6'1" Wt: 200 Born: 12/16/1969 Age: 38

Year	Team	Lg	G	AB	H	2B	3B	HR	(Hm	Rd)	TB	R	RBI	RC	TBB	IBB	SO	HBP	SH	SF	SB	CS	SB%	GDP	Avg	OBP	Slg
1998	2 Tms	AL	13	24	8	2	0	1	(0	1)	13	6	1	4	3	0	5	0	0	0	0	1	.00	0	.333	.407	.542
1999	Det	AL	27	44	7	1	0	1	(1	0)	11	5	8	1	2	0	13	0	1	0	0	0	-	0	.159	.196	.250
2006	Fla	NL	12	13	6	2	0	0	(0	0)	8	3	1	4	1	0	2	0	0	0	1	0	1.00	0	.462	.500	.615
2007	Fla	NL	98	117	28	6	0	3	(2	1)	43	11	26	16	8	0	38	0	1	1	0	0	-	1	.239	.286	.368
98	Oak	AL	3	1	0	0	0	0	(0	0)	0	1	0	0	0	0	1	0	0	0	0	0	-	0	.000	.000	.000
98	Det	AL	10	23	8	2	0	1	(0	1)	13	5	1	4	3	0	4	0	0	0	0	1	.00	0	.348	.423	.565
4 ML YEARS			150	198	49	11	0	5	(3	2)	75	25	36	25	14	0	58	0	2	1	1	1	.50	1	.247	.296	.379

Kerry Wood

Pitches: R Bats: R Pos: RP-22   Ht: 6'5" Wt: 225 Born: 6/16/1977 Age: 31

Year	Team	Lg	G	GS	CG	GF	IP	BFP	H	R	ER	HR	SH	SF	HB	TBB	IBB	SO	WP	Bk	W	L	Pct	ShO	Sv-Op	Hld	ERC	ERA
2007	Cubs*	R	4	4	0	0	4.0	17	4	2	1	0	0	0	0	1	0	5	1	0	0	1	.000	0	0- -	-	2.77	2.25
2007	Peoria*	A-	3	1	0	0	3.0	11	1	0	0	0	0	0	0	1	0	3	1	0	1	0	1.000	0	0- -	-	0.09	0.00
2007	Tenn*	AA	1	0	0	0	1.2	6	0	0	0	0	0	0	0	1	0	1	0	0	0	0	-	0	0- -	-	0.38	0.00
1998	ChC	NL	26	26	1	0	166.2	699	117	69	63	14	2	4	11	85	1	233	6	3	13	6	.684	1	0-0	0	3.03	3.40
2000	ChC	NL	23	23	1	0	137.0	603	112	77	73	17	7	5	9	87	0	132	5	1	8	7	.533	0	0-0	0	4.43	4.80
2001	ChC	NL	28	28	1	0	174.1	740	127	70	65	16	4	5	10	92	3	217	9	0	12	6	.667	1	0-0	0	3.22	3.36
2002	ChC	NL	33	33	4	0	213.2	895	169	92	87	22	13	5	16	97	5	217	8	1	12	11	.522	1	0-0	0	3.46	3.66
2003	ChC	NL	32	32	4	0	211.0	887	152	77	75	24	11	6	21	100	2	266	11	0	14	11	.560	2	0-0	0	3.31	3.20
2004	ChC	NL	22	22	0	0	140.1	595	127	62	58	16	6	6	11	51	0	144	7	0	8	9	.471	0	0-0	0	3.83	3.72
2005	ChC	NL	21	10	0	4	66.0	273	52	32	31	14	2	1	2	26	0	77	0	0	3	4	.429	0	0-0	4	3.75	4.23
2006	ChC	NL	4	4	0	0	19.2	86	19	13	9	5	0	2	1	8	0	13	1	0	1	2	.333	0	0-0	0	5.17	4.12
2007	ChC	NL	22	0	0	2	24.1	101	18	9	9	0	1	0	0	13	1	24	1	0	1	1	.500	0	0-0	0	2.49	3.33
9 ML YEARS			211	178	11	6	1153.0	4879	893	501	470	128	46	34	81	559	12	1323	47	5	72	57	.558	5	0-0	4	3.52	3.67

Mike Wood

Pitches: R Bats: R Pos: RP-17; SP-4   Ht: 6'3" Wt: 220 Born: 4/26/1980 Age: 28

Year	Team	Lg	G	GS	CG	GF	IP	BFP	H	R	ER	HR	SH	SF	HB	TBB	IBB	SO	WP	Bk	W	L	Pct	ShO	Sv-Op	Hld	ERC	ERA
2007	Okla*	AAA	16	15	1	0	97.2	389	83	40	35	7	3	3	4	21	0	73	3	1	9	3	.750	0	0- -	-	2.61	3.23
2003	Oak	AL	7	1	0	2	13.2	72	24	17	16	1	1	0	2	7	2	15	2	0	2	1	.667	0	0-0	0	9.45	10.54
2004	KC	AL	17	17	0	0	100.0	432	112	67	66	16	5	2	6	28	3	54	6	1	3	8	.273	0	0-0	0	4.96	5.94
2005	KC	AL	47	10	0	10	115.0	520	129	66	57	18	5	5	8	52	5	60	7	0	5	8	.385	0	2-2	7	5.67	4.46
2006	KC	AL	23	7	0	2	64.2	307	86	51	41	10	1	2	7	23	3	29	3	0	3	3	.500	0	0-0	1	6.57	5.71
2007	Tex	AL	21	4	0	3	50.2	234	68	36	30	9	1	2	4	15	1	25	3	0	3	2	.600	0	0-0	3	6.57	5.33
5 ML YEARS			115	39	0	17	344.0	1565	419	237	210	54	13	11	27	125	14	183	21	1	16	22	.421	0	2-2	11	5.90	5.49

Jake Woods

Pitches: L Bats: L Pos: RP-4   Ht: 6'1" Wt: 190 Born: 9/3/1981 Age: 26

Year	Team	Lg	G	GS	CG	GF	IP	BFP	H	R	ER	HR	SH	SF	HB	TBB	IBB	SO	WP	Bk	W	L	Pct	ShO	Sv-Op	Hld	ERC	ERA
2007	Tacom*	AAA	25	18	0	3	114.2	519	151	88	88	17	5	1	7	42	0	79	3	1	5	7	.417	0	1- -	-	6.63	6.91
2005	LAA	AL	28	0	0	10	27.2	122	30	18	14	7	1	0	2	8	0	20	2	0	1	1	.500	0	0-0	2	5.44	4.55
2006	Sea	AL	37	8	0	10	105.0	473	115	51	49	12	2	2	2	53	5	66	4	0	7	4	.636	0	1-1	2	5.16	4.20
2007	Sea	AL	4	0	0	2	10.2	49	9	8	7	1	0	0	1	7	0	4	0	0	0	0	-	0	0-0	0	4.41	5.91
3 ML YEARS			69	8	0	22	143.1	644	154	77	70	20	3	2	5	68	5	90	6	0	8	5	.615	0	1-1	4	5.17	4.40

Chris Woodward

Bats: R Throws: R Pos: PH-46; 3B-24; SS-13; 2B-11; PR-10; 1B-6   Ht: 6'0" Wt: 190 Born: 6/27/1976 Age: 32

									BATTING													BASERUNNING				AVERAGES		
Year	Team	Lg	G	AB	H	2B	3B	HR	(Hm	Rd)	TB	R	RBI	RC	TBB	IBB	SO	HBP	SH	SF	SB	CS	SB%	GDP	Avg	OBP	Slg
1999	Tor	AL	14	26	6	1	0	0	(0	0)	7	1	2	2	2	0	6	0	0	1	0	0	-	1	.231	.276	.269
2000	Tor	AL	37	104	19	7	0	3	(1	2)	35	16	14	9	10	3	28	0	1	0	1	0	1.00	1	.183	.254	.337
2001	Tor	AL	37	63	12	3	2	2	(2	0)	25	9	5	4	1	0	14	0	2	0	0	1	.00	1	.190	.203	.397
2002	Tor	AL	90	312	86	13	4	13	(9	4)	146	48	45	45	26	0	72	3	1	8	3	0	1.00	8	.276	.330	.468
2003	Tor	AL	104	349	91	22	2	7	(4	3)	138	49	44	42	28	0	72	3	0	6	1	2	.33	6	.261	.316	.395
2004	Tor	AL	69	213	50	13	4	1	(0	1)	74	21	24	24	14	0	46	1	2	2	1	2	.33	3	.235	.283	.347
2005	NYM	NL	81	173	49	10	0	3	(2	1)	68	16	18	20	13	0	46	2	2	2	0	0	-	2	.283	.337	.393
2006	NYM	NL	83	222	48	10	1	3	(2	1)	69	25	25	18	23	2	55	1	4	3	1	1	.50	2	.216	.289	.311
2007	Atl	NL	92	136	27	6	1	1	(1	0)	38	16	8	9	10	1	29	0	4	1	1	0	1.00	3	.199	.252	.279
	9 ML YEARS		607	1598	388	85	14	33	(21	12)	600	201	186	173	127	6	368	10	16	23	8	6	.57	27	.243	.299	.375

Chase Wright

Pitches: L Bats: L Pos: SP-2; RP-1   Ht: 6'2" Wt: 205 Born: 2/8/1983 Age: 25

				HOW MUCH HE PITCHED						WHAT HE GAVE UP											THE RESULTS						ERC	ERA
Year	Team	Lg	G	GS	CG	GF	IP	BFP	H	R	ER	HR	SH	SF	HB	TBB	IBB	SO	WP	Bk	W	L	Pct	ShO	Sv-Op	Hld		
2001	Yanks	R	10	7	0	1	25.0	131	33	28	22	0	2	3	1	21	1	33	7	1	2	3	.400	0	0--	-	6.79	7.92
2002	Yanks	R	10	7	0	0	42.0	194	32	19	16	0	6	1	1	39	0	23	10	1	2	3	.400	0	0--	-	4.06	3.43
2003	Btl Crk	A	7	2	0	2	14.0	71	12	11	10	1	0	0	2	16	0	10	3	1	1	1	.500	0	0--	-	6.48	6.43
2003	StlsInd	A-	14	14	1	0	81.0	342	82	42	32	2	4	1	2	30	0	68	11	1	3	5	.375	0	0--	-	3.68	3.56
2004	Btl Crk	A	18	18	0	0	86.0	405	100	60	52	4	2	4	2	57	0	51	12	0	5	8	.385	0	0--	-	5.79	5.44
2004	StlsInd	A-	1	1	0	0	3.0	20	5	5	3	0	0	0	2	3	0	3	0	0	0	1	.000	0	0--	-	12.02	9.00
2005	CtnSC	A	25	24	0	0	144.0	613	128	71	60	10	5	4	7	69	0	110	12	1	10	4	.714	0	0--	-	3.81	3.75
2006	Tampa	A+	37	14	1	6	119.2	489	95	32	25	1	5	2	4	43	0	100	3	1	12	3	.800	1	0--	-	2.39	1.88
2007	S-WB	AAA	15	14	0	0	85.1	371	79	44	38	7	3	1	6	42	0	40	7	1	8	3	.727	0	1--	-	4.21	4.01
2007	Trntn	AA	10	10	1	0	59.2	247	55	25	24	8	1	1	3	21	0	41	2	1	5	2	.714	1	0--	-	4.00	3.62
2007	NYY	AL	3	2	0	0	10.0	49	12	8	8	5	0	0	2	6	0	8	0	0	2	0	1.000	0	0-0	0	10.50	7.20

David Wright

Bats: R Throws: R Pos: 3B-159; PH-1   Ht: 6'0" Wt: 217 Born: 12/20/1982 Age: 25

									BATTING													BASERUNNING				AVERAGES		
Year	Team	Lg	G	AB	H	2B	3B	HR	(Hm	Rd)	TB	R	RBI	RC	TBB	IBB	SO	HBP	SH	SF	SB	CS	SB%	GDP	Avg	OBP	Slg
2004	NYM	NL	69	263	77	17	1	14	(8	6)	138	41	40	42	14	0	40	3	0	3	6	0	1.00	7	.293	.332	.525
2005	NYM	NL	160	575	176	42	1	27	(12	15)	301	99	102	105	72	2	113	7	0	3	17	7	.71	16	.306	.388	.523
2006	NYM	NL	154	582	181	40	5	26	(13	13)	309	96	116	119	66	13	113	5	0	8	20	5	.80	15	.311	.381	.531
2007	NYM	NL	160	604	196	42	1	30	(16	14)	330	113	107	127	94	6	115	6	0	7	34	5	.87	14	.325	.416	.546
	4 ML YEARS		543	2024	630	141	8	97	(49	48)	1078	349	365	393	246	21	381	21	0	21	77	17	.82	52	.311	.388	.533

Jamey Wright

Pitches: R Bats: R Pos: RP-11; SP-9   Ht: 6'5" Wt: 205 Born: 12/24/1974 Age: 33

				HOW MUCH HE PITCHED						WHAT HE GAVE UP											THE RESULTS						ERC	ERA
Year	Team	Lg	G	GS	CG	GF	IP	BFP	H	R	ER	HR	SH	SF	HB	TBB	IBB	SO	WP	Bk	W	L	Pct	ShO	Sv-Op	Hld		
2007	Frisco*	AA	1	1	0	0	4.0	17	6	2	2	0	0	0	0	0	0	2	0	0	0	0	-	0	0--	-	4.76	4.50
2007	Okla*	AAA	3	3	0	0	16.1	72	21	11	8	2	0	0	0	3	0	11	0	0	2	1	.667	0	0--	-	4.95	4.41
1996	Col	NL	16	15	0	0	91.1	406	105	60	50	8	4	2	7	41	1	45	1	2	4	4	.500	0	0-0	1	5.50	4.93
1997	Col	NL	26	26	1	0	149.2	698	198	113	104	19	8	3	11	71	3	59	6	2	8	12	.400	0	0-0	0	6.96	6.25
1998	Col	NL	34	34	1	0	206.1	919	235	143	130	24	8	6	11	95	3	86	6	3	9	14	.391	0	0-0	0	5.57	5.67
1999	Col	NL	16	16	0	0	94.1	423	110	52	51	10	3	4	4	54	3	49	3	0	4	3	.571	0	0-0	0	6.19	4.87
2000	Mil	NL	26	25	0	1	164.2	718	157	81	75	12	4	6	18	88	5	96	9	2	7	9	.438	0	0-0	0	4.67	4.10
2001	Mil	NL	33	33	1	0	194.2	868	201	115	106	26	7	5	20	98	10	129	6	1	11	12	.478	1	0-0	0	5.36	4.90
2002	2 Tms	NL	23	22	1	0	129.1	585	130	80	76	17	9	6	11	75	9	77	9	0	7	13	.350	1	0-0	0	5.35	5.29
2003	KC	AL	4	4	2	0	25.1	106	23	14	12	1	0	0	1	11	0	19	0	1	1	2	.333	1	0-0	0	3.53	4.26
2004	Col	NL	14	14	0	0	78.2	361	82	39	36	8	1	1	6	45	3	41	3	0	2	3	.400	0	0-0	0	5.26	4.12
2005	Col	NL	34	27	0	1	171.1	782	201	119	104	22	4	3	15	81	4	101	2	2	8	16	.333	0	0-0	1	6.02	5.46
2006	SF	NL	34	21	0	2	156.0	676	167	95	90	16	5	4	10	64	4	79	6	0	6	10	.375	0	0-0	0	4.89	5.19
2007	Tex	AL	20	9	0	3	77.0	330	72	35	31	6	3	2	5	41	2	39	4	0	4	5	.444	0	0-0	1	4.44	3.62
02	Mil	NL	19	19	1	0	114.1	515	115	72	68	15	9	6	11	63	8	69	8	0	5	13	.278	1	0-0	0	5.28	5.35
02	StL	NL	4	3	0	0	15.0	70	15	8	8	2	0	0	0	12	1	8	1	0	2	0	1.000	0	0-0	0	5.87	4.80
	12 ML YEARS		280	246	6	7	1538.2	6872	1681	946	865	169	56	42	119	764	47	820	55	12	71	103	.408	3	0-0	3	5.46	5.06

Jaret Wright

Pitches: R Bats: R Pos: SP-3   Ht: 6'2" Wt: 245 Born: 12/29/1975 Age: 32

				HOW MUCH HE PITCHED						WHAT HE GAVE UP											THE RESULTS						ERC	ERA
Year	Team	Lg	G	GS	CG	GF	IP	BFP	H	R	ER	HR	SH	SF	HB	TBB	IBB	SO	WP	Bk	W	L	Pct	ShO	Sv-Op	Hld		
2007	Frdrck*	A+	1	1	0	0	4.2	18	3	1	1	0	0	0	0	2	0	6	0	0	0	0	-	0	0--	-	1.84	1.93
2007	Bowie*	AA	3	2	0	0	3.0	11	3	1	1	0	0	0	0	0	0	4	0	0	0	0	-	0	0--	-	2.18	3.00
1997	Cle	AL	16	16	0	0	90.1	388	81	45	44	9	3	4	5	35	0	63	1	0	8	3	.727	0	0-0	0	3.63	4.38
1998	Cle	AL	32	32	1	0	192.2	855	207	109	101	22	4	6	11	87	4	140	6	0	12	10	.545	1	0-0	0	5.07	4.72
1999	Cle	AL	26	26	0	0	133.2	609	144	99	90	18	3	3	7	77	1	91	4	0	8	10	.444	0	0-0	0	5.77	6.06
2000	Cle	AL	9	9	1	0	51.2	217	44	27	27	6	0	1	1	28	0	36	2	0	3	4	.429	0	0-0	0	4.13	4.70
2001	Cle	AL	7	7	0	0	29.0	140	36	23	21	2	2	1	0	22	0	18	1	1	2	2	.500	0	0-0	0	6.82	6.52
2002	Cle	AL	8	6	0	1	18.1	116	40	34	32	3	0	3	2	19	0	12	1	0	2	3	.400	0	0-0	0	15.90	15.71
2003	2 Tms	NL	50	0	0	17	56.1	269	76	46	46	9	2	4	3	31	2	50	12	0	2	5	.286	0	2-5	4	7.59	7.35
2004	Atl	NL	32	32	0	0	186.1	781	168	79	68	11	8	6	3	70	5	159	3	0	15	8	.652	0	0-0	0	3.20	3.28
2005	NYY	AL	13	13	0	0	63.2	302	81	51	43	8	0	5	6	32	1	34	4	0	5	5	.500	0	0-0	0	6.72	6.08

	HOW MUCH HE PITCHED						WHAT HE GAVE UP													THE RESULTS							
Year Team	Lg	G	GS	CG	GF	IP	BFP	H	R	ER	HR	SH	SF	HB	TBB	IBB	SO	WP	Bk	W	L	Pct	ShO	Sv-Op	Hld	ERC	ERA
2006 NYY	AL	30	27	0	0	140.1	625	157	76	70	10	3	3	7	57	0	84	6	0	11	7	.611	0	0-0	1	4.78	4.49
2007 Bal	AL	3	3	0	0	10.1	48	12	11	8	1	0	0	0	9	0	7	0	0	0	3	.000	0	0-0	0	7.40	6.97
03 SD	NL	39	0	0	14	47.1	233	69	44	44	9	1	4	2	28	2	41	10	0	1	5	.167	0	2-4	1	8.71	8.37
03 Atl	NL	11	0	0	3	9.0	36	7	2	2	0	1	0	1	3	0	9	2	0	1	0	1.000	0	0-1	3	2.51	2.00
11 ML YEARS		226	171	2	18	972.2	4350	1046	600	550	99	25	36	45	467	13	694	40	1	68	60	.531	2	2-5	5	5.04	5.09

Mike Wuertz

Pitches: R **Bats:** R **Pos:** RP-73   **Ht:** 6'3" **Wt:** 205 **Born:** 12/15/1978 **Age:** 29

	HOW MUCH HE PITCHED						WHAT HE GAVE UP													THE RESULTS							
Year Team	Lg	G	GS	CG	GF	IP	BFP	H	R	ER	HR	SH	SF	HB	TBB	IBB	SO	WP	Bk	W	L	Pct	ShO	Sv-Op	Hld	ERC	ERA
2004 ChC	NL	31	0	0	11	29.0	124	22	14	14	4	4	2	0	17	1	30	2	1	1	0	1.000	0	1-1	1	3.67	4.34
2005 ChC	NL	75	0	0	12	75.2	319	60	36	32	6	3	2	0	40	7	89	7	0	6	2	.750	0	0-3	18	3.17	3.81
2006 ChC	NL	41	0	0	4	40.2	175	35	14	12	5	3	0	1	16	2	42	1	0	3	1	.750	0	0-1	6	3.37	2.66
2007 ChC	NL	73	0	0	19	72.1	312	64	30	28	8	3	1	0	35	6	79	6	0	2	3	.400	0	0-0	8	3.68	3.48
4 ML YEARS		220	0	0	46	217.2	930	181	94	86	23	13	5	1	108	16	240	16	1	12	6	.667	0	1-5	33	3.44	3.56

Tyler Yates

Pitches: R **Bats:** R **Pos:** RP-75   **Ht:** 6'4" **Wt:** 240 **Born:** 8/7/1977 **Age:** 30

	HOW MUCH HE PITCHED						WHAT HE GAVE UP													THE RESULTS							
Year Team	Lg	G	GS	CG	GF	IP	BFP	H	R	ER	HR	SH	SF	HB	TBB	IBB	SO	WP	Bk	W	L	Pct	ShO	Sv-Op	Hld	ERC	ERA
2004 NYM	NL	21	7	0	2	46.2	228	61	36	33	6	2	2	3	25	3	35	1	1	2	4	.333	0	0-0	2	6.73	6.36
2006 Atl	NL	56	0	0	11	50.0	217	42	23	22	6	2	0	0	31	8	46	1	0	2	5	.286	0	1-6	12	3.95	3.96
2007 Atl	NL	75	0	0	14	66.0	294	64	44	38	6	4	1	3	31	8	69	2	0	2	3	.400	0	2-3	13	4.02	5.18
3 ML YEARS		152	7	0	27	162.2	739	167	103	93	18	8	3	6	87	19	150	4	1	6	12	.333	0	3-9	27	4.73	5.15

Kevin Youkilis

Bats: R **Throws:** R **Pos:** 1B-135, 3D-13; PH-4   **Ht:** 6'1" **Wt:** 220 **Born:** 3/15/1979 **Age:** 29

	BATTING																			BASERUNNING				AVERAGES		
Year Team	Lg	G	AB	H	2B	3B	HR	(Hm	Rd)	TB	R	RBI	RC	TBB	IBB	SO	HBP	SH	SF	SB	CS	SB%	GDP	Avg	OBP	Slg
2004 Bos	AL	72	208	54	11	0	7	(2	5)	86	38	35	36	33	0	45	4	0	3	0	1	.00	1	.260	367	.413
2005 Bos	AL	44	79	22	7	1	1	(0	1)	32	11	9	13	14	0	19	2	0	0	0	1	.00	0	.278	.400	.405
2006 Bos	AL	147	569	159	42	2	13	(6	7)	244	100	72	104	91	0	120	9	0	11	5	2	.71	12	.279	.381	.429
2007 Bos	AL	145	528	152	35	2	16	(8	0)	239	85	83	101	77	0	105	15	0	5	4	2	.67	9	.288	.390	.453
4 ML YEARS		408	1384	387	95	4	37	(16	21)	601	234	199	254	215	0	289	30	0	19	9	6	.60	22	.280	.383	.434

Shane Youman

Pitches: L **Bats:** L **Pos:** SP-8; RP-8   **Ht:** 6'4" **Wt:** 220 **Born:** 10/11/1979 **Age:** 28

	HOW MUCH HE PITCHED						WHAT HE GAVE UP													THE RESULTS							
Year Team	Lg	G	GS	CG	GF	IP	BFP	H	R	ER	HR	SH	SF	HB	TBB	IBB	SO	WP	Bk	W	L	Pct	ShO	Sv-Op	Hld	ERC	ERA
2002 Wmspt	A-	20	0	0	12	37.1	143	25	7	6	1	1	0	2	8	0	40	1	0	4	0	1.000	0	5--	-	1.59	1.45
2003 Hickory	A	40	1	0	28	50.1	236	51	31	26	2	4	1	2	35	2	58	5	0	6	3	.667	0	12--	-	4.87	4.65
2004 Lynbrg	A+	47	0	0	11	74.0	325	67	28	26	5	1	1	1	35	5	62	2	0	4	2	.667	0	2--	-	3.46	3.16
2005 Altna	AA	44	5	0	15	101.0	457	102	54	44	10	10	0	2	48	4	77	5	0	8	6	.571	0	2--	-	4.30	3.92
2006 Altna	AA	23	11	0	3	95.1	375	70	27	16	4	3	2	1	20	1	64	1	0	7	2	.778	0	1--	-	1.71	1.51
2006 Indy	AAA	8	7	0	0	42.1	175	42	20	19	2	2	1	0	10	0	19	2	0	4	0	1.000	0	0--	-	3.07	4.04
2007 Indy	AAA	15	15	0	0	82.1	367	94	45	43	4	3	4	0	36	1	61	2	0	4	6	.400	0	0--	-	4.55	4.70
2006 Pit	NL	5	3	0	0	21.2	88	15	7	7	1	2	1	0	10	0	5	0	0	0	2	.000	0	0-0	0	2.37	2.91
2007 Pit	NL	16	8	0	3	57.1	257	65	40	38	5	10	2	4	23	1	29	2	0	3	5	.375	0	0-0	0	5.02	5.97
2 ML YEARS		21	11	0	3	79.0	345	80	47	45	6	12	3	4	33	1	34	2	0	3	7	.300	0	0-0	0	4.24	5.13

Chris Young

Pitches: R **Bats:** R **Pos:** SP-30   **Ht:** 6'10" **Wt:** 260 **Born:** 5/25/1979 **Age:** 29

	HOW MUCH HE PITCHED						WHAT HE GAVE UP													THE RESULTS							
Year Team	Lg	G	GS	CG	GF	IP	BFP	H	R	ER	HR	SH	SF	HB	TBB	IBB	SO	WP	Bk	W	L	Pct	ShO	Sv-Op	Hld	ERC	ERA
2004 Tex	AL	7	7	0	0	36.1	158	36	21	19	7	1	0	2	10	0	27	1	0	3	2	.600	0	0-0	0	4.26	4.71
2005 Tex	AL	31	31	0	0	164.2	700	162	84	78	19	2	4	7	45	2	137	3	0	12	7	.632	0	0-0	0	3.71	4.26
2006 SD	NL	31	31	0	0	179.1	735	134	72	69	28	8	3	6	69	4	164	6	1	11	5	.688	0	0-0	0	3.12	3.46
2007 SD	NL	30	30	0	0	173.0	705	118	66	60	10	3	6	7	72	0	167	7	4	9	8	.529	0	0-0	0	2.35	3.12
4 ML YEARS		99	99	0	0	553.1	2298	450	243	226	64	14	13	22	196	6	495	17	5	35	22	.614	0	0-0	0	3.12	3.68

Chris Young

Bats: R **Throws:** R **Pos:** CF-146; PH-1; PR-1   **Ht:** 6'2" **Wt:** 180 **Born:** 9/5/1983 **Age:** 24

	BATTING																			BASERUNNING				AVERAGES		
Year Team	Lg	G	AB	H	2B	3B	HR	(Hm	Rd)	TB	R	RBI	RC	TBB	IBB	SO	HBP	SH	SF	SB	CS	SB%	GDP	Avg	OBP	Slg
2002 WhSox	R	55	184	40	13	1	5	(-	-)	70	26	17	21	19	0	54	5	2	0	7	8	.47	1	.217	.308	.380
2003 Bristol	R+	64	238	69	18	3	7	(-	-)	114	47	28	43	23	0	40	4	3	4	21	7	.75	0	.290	.357	.479
2003 Gr Falls	R+	10	34	6	3	0	0	(-	-)	9	5	0	1	1	0	10	0	0	0	0	0	-	0	.176	.200	.265
2004 Knapol	A-	135	465	122	31	5	24	(-	-)	235	83	56	91	66	1	145	11	6	3	31	9	.78	2	.262	.365	.505
2005 Brham	AA	126	466	129	41	3	26	(-	-)	254	100	77	101	70	1	129	7	7	3	32	6	.84	4	.277	.377	.545
2006 Tucsn	AAA	100	402	111	32	4	21	(-	-)	214	78	77	81	52	2	71	6	1	5	17	5	.77	6	.276	.363	.532
2006 Ari	NL	30	70	17	4	0	2	(1	1)	27	10	10	11	6	0	12	1	0	1	2	1	.67	0	.243	.308	.386
2007 Ari	NL	148	569	135	29	3	32	(14	18)	266	85	68	68	43	1	141	6	1	5	27	6	.82	5	.237	.295	.467
2 ML YEARS		178	639	152	33	3	34	(15	19)	293	95	78	79	49	1	153	7	1	6	29	7	.81	5	.238	.297	.459

Delmon Young

Throws: R **Pos:** RF-133; CF-29; DH-4   **Ht:** 6'3" **Wt:** 215 **Born:** 9/14/1985 **Age:** 22

Year Team	Lg	G	AB	H	2B	3B	HR	(Hm	Rd)	TB	R	RBI	RC	TBB	IBB	SO	HBP	SH	SF	SB	CS	SB%	GDP	Avg	OBP	Slg
nSC	A	131	513	165	26	5	25	(-	-)	276	95	116	108	53	6	120	6	0	6	21	6	.78	11	.322	.388	.538
lont	AA	84	330	111	13	4	20	(-	-)	192	59	71	74	25	5	66	7	0	8	25	8	.76	10	.336	.386	.582
Drham	AAA	52	228	65	13	3	6	(-	-)	102	33	28	30	4	0	33	2	0	0	7	4	.64	6	.285	.303	.447
Drham	AAA	86	342	108	22	4	8	(-	-)	162	50	59	59	15	1	65	3	0	10	22	4	.85	12	.316	.341	.474
6 TB	AL	30	126	40	9	1	3	(1	2)	60	16	10	15	1	0	24	3	0	1	2	2	.50	0	.317	.336	.476
07 TB	AL	162	645	186	38	0	13	(9	4)	263	65	93	90	26	2	127	3	0	7	10	3	.77	23	.288	.316	.408
2 ML YEARS		192	771	226	47	1	16	(10	6)	323	81	103	105	27	2	151	6	0	8	12	5	.71	23	.293	.319	.419

Delwyn Young

Bats: B **Throws:** R **Pos:** PH-12; LF-6; 2B-2; PR-1   **Ht:** 5'10" **Wt:** 210 **Born:** 6/30/1982 **Age:** 26

Year Team	Lg	G	AB	H	2B	3B	HR	(Hm	Rd)	TB	R	RBI	RC	TBB	IBB	SO	HBP	SH	SF	SB	CS	SB%	GDP	Avg	OBP	Slg
2002 Gr Falls	R+	59	240	72	18	1	10	(-	-)	122	42	41	46	27	2	60	4	0	0	4	2	.67	2	.300	.380	.508
2003 SoGA	A	119	443	143	38	7	15	(-	-)	240	67	73	90	36	1	87	8	2	4	5	2	.71	2	.323	.381	.542
2004 VeroB	A+	129	470	132	36	3	22	(-	-)	240	76	85	89	57	8	134	7	2	4	11	4	.73	11	.281	.364	.511
2005 Jaxnvl	AA	95	371	110	25	1	16	(-	-)	185	52	62	63	27	4	86	3	1	4	1	3	.25	9	.296	.346	.499
2005 LsVgs	AAA	36	160	52	12	0	4	(-	-)	76	23	14	27	8	0	35	1	1	0	0	0	-	3	.325	.361	.475
2006 LsVgs	AAA	140	532	145	42	1	18	(-	-)	243	76	98	80	42	5	104	3	1	5	3	4	.43	11	.273	.326	.457
2007 LsVgs	AAA	121	490	165	54	5	17	(-	-)	280	107	98	104	38	3	105	3	0	6	4	3	.57	13	.337	.384	.571
2006 LAD	NL	8	5	0	0	0	0	(0	0)	0	0	0	0	0	0	1	0	0	0	0	0	-	0	.000	.000	.000
2007 LAD	NL	19	34	13	1	1	2	(2	0)	22	4	3	8	2	0	5	0	0	0	1	0	1.00	0	.382	.417	.647
2 ML YEARS		27	39	13	1	1	2	(2	0)	22	4	3	8	2	0	6	0	0	0	1	0	1.00	0	.333	.366	.564

Dmitri Young

Bats: B **Throws:** R **Pos:** 1B-116; PH-13; DH-7   **Ht:** 6'2" **Wt:** 240 **Born:** 10/11/1973 **Age:** 34

Year Team	Lg	G	AB	H	2B	3B	HR	(Hm	Rd)	TB	R	RBI	RC	TBB	IBB	SO	HBP	SH	SF	SB	CS	SB%	GDP	Avg	OBP	Slg
1996 StL	NL	16	29	7	0	0	0	(0	0)	7	3	2	2	4	0	5	1	0	0	0	1	.00	1	.241	.353	.241
1997 StL	NL	110	333	86	14	3	5	(2	3)	121	38	34	40	38	3	63	2	1	3	6	5	.55	8	.258	.335	.363
1998 Cin	NL	144	536	166	48	1	14	(3	11)	258	81	83	88	47	4	94	2	0	5	2	4	.33	16	.310	.364	.481
1999 Cin	NL	127	373	112	30	2	14	(9	5)	188	63	56	63	30	1	71	2	0	4	3	1	.75	11	.300	.352	.504
2000 Cin	NL	152	548	166	37	6	18	(6	12)	269	68	88	86	36	6	80	3	1	5	0	3	.00	16	.303	.346	.491
2001 Cin	NL	142	540	163	28	3	21	(8	13)	260	68	69	83	37	10	77	5	1	3	8	5	.62	12	.302	.350	.481
2002 Det	AL	54	201	57	14	0	7	(5	2)	92	25	27	27	12	5	39	2	0	1	2	0	1.00	12	.284	.329	.458
2003 Det	AL	155	562	167	34	7	29	(10	19)	302	78	85	101	58	16	130	11	0	4	2	1	.67	16	.297	.372	.537
2004 Det	AL	104	389	106	23	2	18	(8	10)	187	72	60	57	33	4	71	6	0	4	0	1	.00	8	.272	.336	.481
2005 Det	AL	126	469	127	25	3	21	(10	11)	221	61	72	60	29	7	100	9	0	1	1	0	1.00	16	.271	.325	.471
2006 Det	AL	48	172	43	4	1	7	(2	5)	70	19	23	20	11	0	39	0	0	1	1	1	.50	3	.250	.293	.407
2007 Was	NL	136	460	147	38	1	13	(7	6)	226	57	74	74	44	6	74	1	0	3	0	0	-	13	.320	.378	.491
12 ML YEARS		1314	4612	1347	295	29	167	(70	97)	2201	633	673	701	379	62	843	44	3	34	25	22	.53	142	.292	.349	.477

Michael Young

Bats: R **Throws:** R **Pos:** SS-150; DH-6   **Ht:** 6'1" **Wt:** 200 **Born:** 10/19/1976 **Age:** 31

Year Team	Lg	G	AB	H	2B	3B	HR	(Hm	Rd)	TB	R	RBI	RC	TBB	IBB	SO	HBP	SH	SF	SB	CS	SB%	GDP	Avg	OBP	Slg
2000 Tex	AL	2	2	0	0	0	0	(0	0)	0	0	0	0	0	0	1	0	0	0	0	0	-	0	.000	.000	.000
2001 Tex	AL	106	386	96	18	4	11	(7	4)	155	57	49	45	26	0	91	3	9	5	3	1	.75	9	.249	.298	.402
2002 Tex	AL	156	573	150	26	8	9	(3	6)	219	77	62	64	41	1	112	0	13	6	6	7	.46	14	.262	.308	.382
2003 Tex	AL	160	666	204	33	9	14	(9	5)	297	106	72	106	36	1	103	1	3	7	13	2	.87	14	.306	.339	.446
2004 Tex	AL	160	690	216	33	9	22	(9	13)	333	114	99	124	44	1	89	1	0	4	12	3	.80	11	.313	.353	.483
2005 Tex	AL	159	668	221	40	5	24	(12	12)	343	114	91	131	58	0	91	3	0	3	5	2	.71	20	.331	.385	.513
2006 Tex	AL	162	691	217	52	3	14	(8	6)	317	93	103	120	48	0	96	1	0	8	7	3	.70	27	.314	.356	.459
2007 Tex	AL	156	639	201	37	1	9	(8	1)	267	80	94	107	47	5	107	5	0	1	13	3	.81	21	.315	.366	.418
8 ML YEARS		1061	4315	1305	239	39	103	(56	47)	1931	641	570	697	300	8	690	14	25	34	59	21	.74	116	.302	.347	.448

Mike Zagurski

Pitches: L **Bats:** L **Pos:** RP-25   **Ht:** 6'0" **Wt:** 225 **Born:** 1/27/1983 **Age:** 25

		HOW MUCH HE PITCHED						WHAT HE GAVE UP											THE RESULTS						
Year Team	Lg	G	GS	CG	GF	IP	BFP	H	R	ER	HR	SH	SF	HB	TBB	IBB	SO	WP	Bk	W	L	Pct	ShO	Sv-Op Hld	ERC	ERA
2005 Batvia	A-	15	8	0	3	45.0	197	47	29	23	2	1	1	3	15	0	43	1	1	3	4	.429	0	0- -	3.89	4.60
2006 Lakwd	A	42	0	0	13	56.1	231	46	22	22	0	3	0	0	22	0	75	4	0	4	4	.500	0	1- -	2.44	3.51
2007 Clrwtr	A+	12	0	0	8	16.1	59	6	2	2	0	2	0	1	4	0	30	0	0	0	0	-	0	5- -	0.73	1.10
2007 Rdng	AA	6	0	0	3	7.0	26	2	1	1	0	0	0	0	2	0	8	0	0	0	0	-	0	0- -	0.50	1.29
2007 Ottawa	AAA	7	0	0	1	9.0	39	7	2	2	0	0	0	0	6	0	11	1	0	0	0	-	0	0- -	3.17	2.00
2007 Phi	NL	25	0	0	4	21.1	101	25	14	14	3	1	1	1	11	2	21	2	0	1	0	1.000	0	0-2 5	5.75	5.91

Carlos Zambrano

Pitches: R **Bats:** B **Pos:** SP-34   **Ht:** 6'5" **Wt:** 255 **Born:** 6/1/1981 **Age:** 27

			HOW MUCH HE PITCHED						WHAT HE GAVE UP												THE RESULTS						
Year	Team	Lg	G	GS	CG	GF	IP	BFP	H	R	ER	HR	SH	SF	HB	TBB	IBB	SO	WP	Bk	W	L	Pct	ShO	Sv-Op	Hld	ERC	ERA
2001	ChC	NL	6	1	0	1	7.2	42	11	13	13	2	1	1	1	8	0	4	1	0	1	2	.333	0	0-1	0	11.86	15.26
2002	ChC	NL	32	16	0	3	108.1	477	94	53	44	9	9	1	4	63	2	93	6	0	4	8	.333	0	0-0	0	4.02	3.66
2003	ChC	NL	32	32	3	0	214.0	907	188	88	74	9	11	6	10	94	12	168	6	1	13	11	.542	1	0-0	0	3.28	3.11
2004	ChC	NL	31	31	1	0	209.2	887	174	73	64	14	10	3	20	81	4	188	6	2	16	8	.667	1	0-0	0	3.20	2.75
2005	ChC	NL	33	33	2	0	223.1	909	170	88	81	21	9	5	8	86	3	202	7	0	14	6	.700	0	0-0	0	2.86	3.26
2006	ChC	NL	33	33	0	0	214.0	917	162	91	81	20	11	4	9	115	4	210	9	1	16	7	.696	0	0-0	0	3.34	3.41
2007	ChC	NL	34	34	1	0	216.1	925	187	100	95	23	6	3	14	101	4	177	3	0	18	13	.581	0	0-0	0	3.88	3.95
	7 ML YEARS		201	180	7	4	1193.1	5064	986	506	452	98	57	23	66	548	29	1042	38	4	82	55	.599	2	0-1	0	3.42	3.41

Victor Zambrano

Pitches: R **Bats:** B **Pos:** RP-9; SP-4   **Ht:** 6'0" **Wt:** 205 **Born:** 8/6/1975 **Age:** 32

			HOW MUCH HE PITCHED						WHAT HE GAVE UP												THE RESULTS						
Year	Team	Lg	G	GS	CG	GF	IP	BFP	H	R	ER	HR	SH	SF	HB	TBB	IBB	SO	WP	Bk	W	L	Pct	ShO	Sv-Op	Hld	ERC	ERA
2007	Dnedin*	A+	1	1	0	0	4.0	21	1	2	2	0	0	0	1	7	0	3	0	0	0	0	-	0	0--	-	4.84	4.50
2007	NHam*	AA	1	1	0	0	6.1	29	10	5	4	1	0	0	1	0	0	4	0	0	0	0	-	0	0--	-	7.08	5.68
2007	Syrcse*	AAA	8	8	0	0	41.1	195	50	34	34	4	0	0	7	22	1	37	8	0	3	2	.600	0	0--	-	6.61	7.40
2007	Indy*	AAA	5	5	0	0	26.2	103	17	9	8	1	0	1	1	9	0	25	1	0	2	0	1.000	0	0--	-	1.83	2.70
2001	TB	AL	36	0	0	19	51.1	212	38	21	18	6	2	0	3	18	0	58	4	0	6	2	.750	0	2-6	5	2.80	3.16
2002	TB	AL	42	11	0	11	114.0	519	120	77	70	15	7	8	4	68	5	73	10	0	8	8	.500	0	1-3	6	5.52	5.53
2003	TB	AL	34	28	1	2	188.1	836	165	97	88	21	3	10	20	106	2	132	15	3	12	10	.545	0	0-0	2	4.51	4.21
2004	2 Tms		26	25	0	0	142.0	650	119	77	69	13	1	10	16	102	2	123	6	0	11	7	.611	0	0-0	1	4.75	4.37
2005	NYM	NL	31	27	0	2	166.1	748	170	85	77	12	6	6	15	77	2	112	8	2	7	12	.368	0	0-0	0	4.55	4.17
2006	NYM	NL	5	5	0	0	21.1	97	25	16	16	5	0	0	0	11	0	15	1	0	1	2	.333	0	0-0	0	6.69	6.75
2007	2 Tms		13	4	0	2	23.0	125	32	26	26	6	2	2	5	22	2	16	2	0	0	3	.000	0	0-0	0	11.33	10.17
04	TB	AL	23	22	0	0	128.0	588	107	68	63	13	0	10	16	96	2	109	5	0	9	7	.563	0	0-0	1	5.01	4.43
04	NYM	NL	3	3	0	0	14.0	62	12	9	6	0	1	0	0	6	0	14	1	0	2	0	1.000	0	0-0	0	2.57	3.86
07	Tor	AL	8	2	0	2	10.2	62	20	13	13	5	1	1	1	11	2	5	1	0	0	2	.000	0	0-0	0	16.93	10.97
07	Bal	AL	5	2	0	0	12.1	63	12	13	13	1	1	1	4	11	0	11	1	0	0	1	.000	0	0-0	0	7.02	9.49
	7 ML YEARS		187	100	1	36	706.1	3187	669	399	364	78	21	36	63	404	13	529	46	5	45	44	.506	0	3-9	14	4.85	4.64

Mauro Zarate

Pitches: R **Bats:** R **Pos:** RP-4   **Ht:** 6'1" **Wt:** 180 **Born:** 2/8/1983 **Age:** 25

			HOW MUCH HE PITCHED						WHAT HE GAVE UP												THE RESULTS						
Year	Team	Lg	G	GS	CG	GF	IP	BFP	H	R	ER	HR	SH	SF	HB	TBB	IBB	SO	WP	Bk	W	L	Pct	ShO	Sv-Op	Hld	ERC	ERA
2004	Grnsbr	A	10	10	0	0	43.2	205	69	46	41	13	3	1	5	12	0	29	0	0	1	4	.200	0	0--	-	9.67	8.45
2004	Mrlns	R	17	0	0	7	42.0	175	35	18	11	3	0	1	5	7	0	28	2	0	2	2	.500	0	3--	-	2.50	2.36
2005	Jmstwn	A-	24	0	0	19	27.1	116	24	13	13	3	2	1	2	8	0	35	0	0	1	3	.250	0	7--	-	3.27	4.28
2006	Grnsbr	A	53	0	0	27	79.0	346	75	33	28	7	3	3	3	30	0	80	2	1	3	5	.375	0	7--	-	3.68	3.19
2007	Jupiter	A+	14	0	0	4	26.0	108	19	7	7	1	2	1	0	11	2	20	2	0	2	2	.500	0	1--	-	2.20	2.42
2007	Carlina	AA	17	0	0	3	25.2	102	14	7	4	2	1	0	0	9	0	32	0	0	0	1	.000	0	1--	-	1.52	1.40
2007	Albq	AAA	25	0	0	2	34.0	143	29	9	9	2	3	4	2	12	0	23	1	0	2	0	1.000	0	0--	-	3.03	2.38
2007	Fla	NL	4	0	0	0	5.0	30	11	7	6	3	0	0	1	1	0	3	1	0	0	0	-	0	0-0	0	15.01	10.00

Gregg Zaun

Bats: B **Throws:** R **Pos:** C-103; PH-16; DH-1   **Ht:** 5'10" **Wt:** 190 **Born:** 4/14/1971 **Age:** 37

			BATTING																		BASERUNNING				AVERAGES		
Year	Team	Lg	G	AB	H	2B	3B	HR	(Hm	Rd)	TB	R	RBI	RC	TBB	IBB	SO	HBP	SH	SF	SB	CS	SB%	GDP	Avg	OBP	Slg
2007	Syrcse*	AAA	3	11	1	0	0	0	(-	-)	1	1	0	0	1	0	2	0	0	0	0	0	-	2	.091	.167	.091
1995	Bal	AL	40	104	27	5	0	3	(1	2)	41	18	14	15	16	0	14	0	2	0	1	1	.50	2	.260	.358	.394
1996	2 Tms		60	139	34	9	1	2	(1	1)	51	20	15	16	14	3	20	2	1	2	1	0	1.00	5	.245	.318	.367
1997	Fla	NL	58	143	43	10	2	2	(0	2)	63	21	20	27	26	4	18	2	1	0	1	0	1.00	3	.301	.415	.441
1998	Fla	NL	106	298	56	12	2	5	(2	3)	87	19	29	23	35	2	52	1	2	2	5	2	.71	7	.188	.274	.292
1999	Tex	AL	43	93	23	2	1	1	(0	1)	30	12	12	10	10	0	7	0	1	2	1	0	1.00	2	.247	.314	.323
2000	KC	AL	83	234	64	11	0	7	(2	5)	96	36	33	40	43	3	34	3	0	2	7	3	.70	4	.274	.390	.410
2001	KC	AL	39	125	40	9	0	6	(1	5)	67	15	18	24	12	0	16	0	0	1	1	2	.33	2	.320	.377	.536
2002	Hou	NL	76	185	41	7	1	3	(3	0)	59	18	24	17	12	1	36	2	2	1	1	0	1.00	4	.222	.275	.319
2003	2 Tms		74	166	38	8	0	4	(1	3)	58	15	21	20	19	0	21	1	1	2	1	1	.50	5	.229	.309	.349
2004	Tor	AL	107	338	91	24	0	6	(2	4)	133	46	36	50	47	3	61	6	0	1	0	2	.00	7	.269	.367	.393
2005	Tor	AL	133	434	109	18	1	11	(4	7)	162	61	61	65	73	2	70	0	0	5	2	3	.40	11	.251	.355	.373
2006	Tor	AL	99	290	79	19	0	12	(7	5)	134	39	40	41	41	3	42	3	0	5	0	0	.00	10	.272	.363	.462
2007	Tor	AL	110	331	80	24	1	10	(6	4)	136	43	52	48	51	8	55	2	1	6	0	0	-	9	.242	.341	.411
96	Bal	AL	50	108	25	8	1	1	(1	0)	38	16	13	12	11	2	15	2	0	2	0	0	-	3	.231	.309	.352
96	Fla	NL	10	31	9	1	0	1	(0	1)	13	4	2	4	3	1	5	0	1	0	1	0	1.00	2	.290	.353	.419
03	Hou	NL	59	120	26	7	0	1	(1	0)	36	9	13	12	14	0	14	1	1	2	1	0	1.00	5	.217	.299	.300
03	Col	NL	15	46	12	1	0	3	(0	3)	22	6	8	8	5	0	7	0	0	0	0	1	.00	0	.261	.333	.478
	13 ML YEARS		1028	2880	725	158	9	72	(33	39)	1117	363	375	396	399	29	446	22	11	29	21	16	.57	71	.252	.344	.388

Ryan Zimmerman

Throws: R **Pos:** 3B-161; DH-1 **Ht:** 6'2" **Wt:** 210 **Born:** 9/28/1984 **Age:** 23

	Lg	G	AB	H	2B	3B	HR	(Hm	Rd)	TB	R	RBI	RC	TBB	IBB	SO	HBP	SH	SF	SB	CS	SB%	GDP	Avg	OBP	Slg
	NL	20	58	23	10	0	0	(0	0)	33	6	6	9	3	0	12	0	0	1	0	0	-	1	.397	.419	.569
	NL	157	614	176	47	3	20	(10	10)	289	84	110	101	61	7	120	2	1	4	11	8	.58	15	.287	.351	.471
	NL	**162**	653	174	43	5	24	(11	13)	299	99	91	83	61	3	125	3	0	5	4	1	.80	26	.266	.330	.458
ML YEARS		339	1325	373	100	8	44	(21	23)	621	189	207	193	125	10	257	5	1	10	15	9	.63	42	.282	.343	.469

Barry Zito

Pitches: L **Bats:** L **Pos:** SP-33; RP-1 **Ht:** 6'4" **Wt:** 210 **Born:** 5/13/1978 **Age:** 30

			HOW MUCH HE PITCHED						WHAT HE GAVE UP											THE RESULTS						
Year	Team	Lg	G	GS	CG	GF	IP	BFP	H	R	ER	HR	SH	SF	HB	TBB	IBB	SO	WP	Bk	W	L	Pct	ShO	Sv-Op	Hld	ERC	ERA
2000	Oak	AL	14	14	1	0	92.2	376	64	30	28	6	1	0	2	45	2	78	2	0	7	4	.636	1	0-0	0	2.63	2.72
2001	Oak	AL	35	**35**	3	0	214.1	902	184	92	83	18	5	4	13	80	0	205	6	1	17	8	.680	2	0-0	0	3.33	3.49
2002	Oak	AL	35	**35**	1	0	229.1	939	182	79	70	24	9	7	9	78	2	182	2	1	**23**	5	.821	0	0-0	0	2.92	2.75
2003	Oak	AL	35	35	4	0	231.2	957	186	98	85	19	7	7	6	88	3	146	4	0	14	12	.538	1	0-0	0	2.91	3.30
2004	Oak	AL	34	34	0	0	213.0	926	216	116	106	28	7	9	9	81	2	163	4	1	11	11	.500	0	0-0	0	4.45	4.48
2005	Oak	AL	35	**35**	0	0	228.1	953	185	106	98	26	8	7	13	89	0	171	4	0	14	13	.519	0	0-0	0	3.32	3.86
2006	Oak	AL	34	**34**	0	0	221.0	**945**	211	99	94	27	7	6	13	99	5	151	4	2	16	10	.615	0	0-0	0	4.47	3.83
2007	SF	NL	34	33	0	0	196.2	850	182	105	99	24	12	4	4	83	4	131	5	0	11	13	.458	0	0-0	0	3.91	4.53
	8 ML YEARS		256	255	9	0	1627.0	6848	1410	725	663	172	56	44	69	643	18	1227	31	5	113	76	.598	4	0-0	0	3.53	3.67

Ben Zobrist

Bats: B **Throws:** R **Pos:** SS-30; PR-2; PH-1 **Ht:** 6'3" **Wt:** 200 **Born:** 5/26/1981 **Age:** 27

								BATTING														BASERUNNING			AVERAGES		
Year	Team	Lg	G	AB	H	2B	3B	HR	(Hm	Rd)	TB	R	RBI	RC	TBB	IBB	SO	HBP	SH	SF	SB	CS	SB%	GDP	Avg	OBP	Slg
2004	TriCity	A-	68	257	87	14	3	4	(-	-)	119	50	45	56	43	0	31	4	4	2	15	4	.79	5	.339	.438	.463
2005	Lxngtn	A	68	247	75	17	2	2	(-	-)	102	45	32	49	47	2	35	5	4	7	16	5	.76	2	.304	.415	.413
2005	Salem	A+	42	141	47	12	1	3	(-	-)	70	25	13	35	37	1	17	1	1	0	2	1	.67	3	.333	.475	.496
2006	CpChr	AA	83	315	103	26	6	3	(-	-)	149	57	30	67	55	1	46	5	5	1	9	5	.64	7	.327	.434	.473
2006	Drham	AAA	18	69	21	3	1	0	(-	-)	26	12	6	11	10	0	9	1	2	0	4	1	.80	0	.304	.400	.377
2007	Drham	AAA	61	222	62	14	2	7	(-	-)	101	42	22	45	43	0	38	5	3	3	8	3	.73	4	.279	.403	.455
2006	TB	AL	52	183	41	6	2	2	(2	0)	57	10	18	13	10	1	26	0	2	3	2	3	.40	2	.224	.260	.311
2007	TB	AL	31	97	15	2	0	1	(0	1)	20	8	9	0	3	0	21	1	2	2	2	0	1.00	1	.155	.184	.206
	2 ML YEARS		83	280	56	8	2	3	(2	1)	77	18	27	13	13	1	47	1	4	5	4	3	.57	3	.200	.234	.275

Joel Zumaya

Pitches: R **Bats:** R **Pos:** RP-28 **Ht:** 6'3" **Wt:** 210 **Born:** 11/9/1984 **Age:** 23

			HOW MUCH HE PITCHED						WHAT HE GAVE UP											THE RESULTS						
Year	Team	Lg	G	GS	CG	GF	IP	BFP	H	R	ER	HR	SH	SF	HB	TBB	IBB	SO	WP	Bk	W	L	Pct	ShO	Sv-Op	Hld	ERC	ERA
2002	Tigers	R	9	8	0	0	37.1	143	21	9	8	2	0	2	1	11	0	46	3	0	2	1	.667	0	0--	-	1.46	1.93
2003	WMich	A	19	19	0	0	90.1	376	69	35	28	3	3	2	3	38	0	126	4	0	7	5	.583	0	0--	-	2.57	2.79
2004	Lkland	A+	20	20	1	0	115.2	479	90	60	56	10	7	4	9	58	0	108	7	1	7	7	.500	1	0--	-	3.58	4.36
2004	Erie	AA	4	4	0	0	20.0	90	19	20	14	6	1	1	2	10	0	29	0	0	2	2	.500	0	0--	-	6.04	6.30
2005	Erie	AA	18	18	0	0	107.1	438	71	40	33	8	1	4	2	52	0	143	4	4	8	3	.727	0	0--	-	2.53	2.77
2005	Toledo	AAA	8	8	1	0	44.0	186	30	13	13	2	1	1	5	24	1	56	2	0	1	2	.333	0	0--	-	2.95	2.66
2007	Toledo	AAA	3	0	0	0	2.2	13	3	2	2	0	0	0	0	2	0	2	0	0	0	0	-	0	0--	-	5.24	6.75
2006	Det	AL	62	0	0	12	83.1	350	56	20	18	6	2	4	2	42	2	97	4	0	6	3	.667	0	1-6	30	2.55	1.94
2007	Det	AL	28	0	0	7	33.2	142	23	16	16	3	1	1	1	17	2	27	3	0	2	3	.400	0	1-5	8	2.68	4.28
	2 ML YEARS		90	0	0	19	117.0	492	79	36	34	9	3	5	3	59	4	124	7	0	8	6	.571	0	2-11	38	2.59	2.62

2007 Fielding Statistics

The following pages offer all of the traditional fielding statistics for the 2007 season. But keep in mind, these fielding stats are not official; there will most likely be a few discrepancies when the official, Major League Baseball-sanctioned results arrive later this year. But we had a choice: publish the book in November or wait for the official totals. Well, we hope you'll agree it's worth putting the book out early. Our totals may not be official, but they're no less accurate.

Each position is broken down into "The Regulars" and "The Rest." This way, we get a clearer sense of how the starters at each position compare to one another, and we don't have to sift through the handful of games played by players away from their regular positions. September call-ups and players playing out of position have their own lists, so if you want to know how many double plays Scott Spiezo turned at second base in 2007, we have that too.

The last column for the non-catchers is Range Factor, labeled "Rng." Range Factor is the number of successful chances (putouts plus assists) times nine, divided by the number of defensive innings played.

Don't miss our "Catchers Special" section where we offer catcher statistics like catcher ERA and caught stealing percentages. These are the stats that keep guys like Yadier Molina in the big leagues, because we all know he ain't here for his bat.

A few clarifications before you start reading: One, **PCS** is the number of Total Caught Stealing attributed to the pitcher, not to the catcher in question. So **CS%** is the percentage of runners caught stealing not including **PCS**. Two, if you are looking for a pitcher's fielding statistics, you will find them in the "Pitchers Hitting, Fielding & Holding Runners" section. And third, if you are interested in seeing fielding leader boards you can find them for position players in the Leader Board section and in The 2007 Fielding Bible Awards section.

First Basemen - Regulars

Player	Tm	G	GS	Inn	PO	A	E	DP	Pct.	Rng
Youkilis,Kevin	Bos	135	124	1094.0	990	90	0	101	1.000	-
Millar,Kevin	Bal	101	101	873.0	852	66	1	94	.999	-
Helton,Todd	Col	153	152	1337.0	1448	95	2	153	.999	-
Sexson,Richie	Sea	116	115	991.2	1000	72	2	102	.998	-
Casey,Sean	Det	131	105	989.0	992	42	2	87	.998	-
Kotchman,Casey	LAA	130	116	1033.0	978	68	3	103	.997	-
Klesko,Ryan	SF	100	89	804.2	755	66	3	73	.996	-
Morneau,Justin	Min	143	143	1259.1	1189	102	5	122	.996	-
Konerko,Paul	CWS	141	140	1227.2	1180	71	5	131	.996	-
Teixeira,Mark	TOT	128	128	1098.0	1108	77	5	120	.996	-
Hatteberg,Scott	Cin	96	85	772.2	657	50	3	66	.996	-
Overbay,Lyle	Tor	119	107	972.1	1060	101	5	107	.996	-
LaRoche,Adam	Pit	151	148	1301.1	1296	81	6	154	.996	-
Johnson,Dan	Oak	97	96	854.2	869	40	4	80	.996	-
Gload,Ross	KC	89	74	675.2	623	45	3	78	.996	-
Pujols,Albert	StL	154	153	1324.2	1325	124	8	132	.995	-
Lee,Derrek	ChC	147	146	1274.1	1165	87	7	99	.994	-
Gonzalez,Adrian	SD	161	161	1462.2	1470	140	10	134	.994	-
Delgado,Carlos	NYM	138	138	1219.1	1133	74	8	101	.993	-
Pena,Carlos	TB	144	137	1221.0	1054	130	8	116	.993	-
Garko,Ryan	Cle	125	121	1066.1	1073	71	8	115	.993	-
Jacobs,Mike	Fla	108	104	903.0	793	45	7	91	.992	-
Berkman,Lance	Hou	126	122	1066.1	1015	103	10	86	.991	-
Howard,Ryan	Phi	140	138	1241.0	1191	103	12	124	.991	-
Thorman,Scott	Atl	84	66	608.1	571	56	6	46	.991	-
Young,Dmitri	Was	116	116	884.2	788	61	9	90	.990	-
Fielder,Prince	Mil	153	151	1338.0	1163	99	14	115	.989	-
Loney,James	LAD	93	85	774.2	725	61	9	87	.989	-
Jackson,Conor	Ari	108	107	867.2	859	48	11	86	.988	-

First Basemen - The Rest

Player	Tm	G	GS	Inn	PO	A	E	DP	Pct.	Rng
Amezaga,Alfredo	Fla	4	0	4.2	4	1	0	0	1.000	-
Anderson,Marlon	LAD	2	1	8.0	9	1	1	0	.909	-
Anderson,Marlon	NYM	1	1	7.0	7	0	0	0	1.000	-
Atkins,Garrett	Col	10	2	32.1	31	3	1	3	.971	-
Aurilia,Rich	SF	55	42	371.0	375	18	2	42	.995	-
Ausmus,Brad	Hou	5	0	7.0	6	1	0	1	1.000	-
Bailey,Jeff	Bos	3	2	17.2	16	2	0	1	1.000	-
Baker,Jeff	Col	20	9	96.2	120	2	3	12	.976	-
Barajas,Rod	Phi	1	0	1.0	1	1	0	0	1.000	-
Barton,Daric	Oak	18	18	157.2	153	7	0	19	1.000	-
Batista,Tony	Was	27	12	127.0	121	3	1	16	.992	-
Belliard,Ronnie	Was	9	4	42.0	39	0	1	5	.975	-
Bennett,Gary	StL	1	0	1.0	1	0	0	1	1.000	-
Betemit,Wilson	NYY	14	9	74.1	67	4	0	9	1.000	-
Blake,Casey	Cle	12	5	49.2	39	5	0	4	1.000	-
Blanco,Henry	ChC	2	1	15.0	8	1	0	0	1.000	-
Bloomquist,Willie	Sea	4	0	5.2	5	1	0	0	1.000	-
Blum,Geoff	SD	1	1	9.0	13	1	0	2	1.000	-
Boone,Aaron	Fla	48	46	388.0	352	26	5	34	.987	-
Branyan,Russell	StL	4	0	6.1	6	0	0	1	1.000	-
Brazell,Craig	KC	1	0	3.0	7	0	0	2	1.000	-
Broussard,Ben	Sea	52	36	337.0	281	21	2	39	.993	-
Butler,Billy	KC	13	11	83.0	79	8	2	6	.978	-
Cairo,Miguel	NYY	22	17	156.1	162	9	4	16	.977	-
Cairo,Miguel	StL	2	1	9.2	11	1	0	2	1.000	-
Cantu,Jorge	TB	7	7	51.0	49	3	0	5	1.000	-
Cantu,Jorge	Cin	14	13	104.1	86	4	0	7	1.000	-
Casto,Kory	Was	2	1	9.0	13	0	0	1	1.000	-
Catalanotto,Frank	Tex	14	13	96.0	94	6	0	8	1.000	-
Cirillo,Jeff	Min	8	8	70.0	65	4	3	4	.958	-
Cirillo,Jeff	Ari	2	0	3.0	1	1	0	0	1.000	-
Clark,Howie	Tor	3	2	13.0	17	1	0	3	1.000	-
Clark,Tony	Ari	83	43	452.2	432	32	2	50	.996	-
Conine,Jeff	Cin	56	49	431.2	390	21	3	50	.993	-
Conine,Jeff	NYM	11	7	77.0	79	2	2	6	.976	-
Cora,Alex	Bos	1	0	3.0	1	0	1	0	.500	-
Coste,Chris	Phi	1	1	7.0	6	0	0	1	1.000	-
Cuddyer,Michael	Min	4	4	39.0	30	4	0	4	1.000	-
Damon,Johnny	NYY	5	0	8.1	9	0	1	1	.900	-

Player	Tm	G	GS	Inn	PO	A	E	DP	Pct.	Rng
DeRosa,Mark	ChC	9	5	55.2	49	0	1	9	.980	-
Diaz,Matt	Atl	2	0	2.2	3	1	0	1	1.000	-
Dillon,Joe	Mil	5	3	28.0	25	2	0	5	1.000	-
Dobbs,Greg	Phi	14	10	97.2	102	6	0	8	1.000	-
Doumit,Ryan	Pit	3	2	18.2	12	0	0	1	1.000	-
Duncan,Chris	StL	11	1	32.0	25	1	0	3	1.000	-
Duncan,Shelley	NYY	9	2	32.0	24	3	0	6	1.000	-
Easley,Damion	NYM	2	2	14.0	20	0	0	2	1.000	-
Edmonds,Jim	StL	1	0	0.0	0	0	0	0	-	-
Eldred,Brad	Pit	4	2	22.0	23	1	0	3	1.000	-
Ensberg,Morgan	SD	1	1	9.0	7	1	1	1	.889	-
Erstad,Darin	CWS	22	19	173.2	174	14	1	18	.995	-
Feliz,Pedro	SF	4	3	31.0	27	2	0	5	1.000	-
Fick,Robert	Was	84	29	383.1	344	22	4	32	.989	-
Fox,Jake	ChC	1	0	2.0	3	0	0	2	1.000	-
Franco,Julio	NYM	6	4	40.0	22	3	0	3	1.000	-
Franco,Julio	Atl	10	10	91.1	101	10	0	11	1.000	-
Garciaparra,Nomar	LAD	68	66	571.0	556	27	4	52	.993	-
Giambi,Jason	NYY	18	16	121.0	108	6	1	10	.991	-
Gomez,Chris	Bal	36	9	116.2	131	9	0	7	1.000	-
Gomez,Chris	Cle	8	2	34.2	25	2	0	2	1.000	-
Gonzalez,Andy	CWS	5	0	8.1	7	0	0	1	1.000	-
Gordon,Alex	KC	32	16	154.0	132	8	1	16	.993	-
Graffanino,Tony	Mil	9	7	68.1	64	6	0	7	1.000	-
Green,Shawn	NYM	17	10	95.0	81	5	1	3	.989	-
Guillen,Carlos	Det	36	15	178.2	185	17	1	15	.995	-
Guzman,Joel	TB	2	2	17.0	11	1	1	2	.923	-
Hafner,Travis	Cle	11	10	91.0	97	4	0	8	1.000	-
Hammock,Robby	Ari	1	0	1.0	1	0	0	1	1.000	-
Helms,Wes	Phi	18	12	102.2	93	4	1	12	.990	-
Hernandez,Ramon	Bal	1	0	1.0	0	0	0	0	-	-
Hessman,Mike	Det	12	11	84.1	74	2	0	15	1.000	-
Hillenbrand,Shea	LAA	6	6	47.0	38	2	1	5	.976	-
Hillenbrand,Shea	LAD	2	1	6.0	6	0	0	1	1.000	-
Hinske,Eric	Bos	43	29	276.0	256	22	3	25	.989	-
Hoover,Paul	Fla	1	0	3.0	1	0	0	0	1.000	-
House,J.R.	Bal	1	0	2.0	2	0	0	0	1.000	-
Huff,Aubrey	Bal	51	49	421.0	424	24	3	41	.993	-
Jones,Garrett	Min	8	7	63.0	57	4	0	5	1.000	-
Kata,Matt	Tex	4	1	20.0	25	0	0	2	1.000	-
Keppinger,Jeff	Cin	1	0	2.0	2	0	0	0	1.000	-
Koshansky,Joe	Col	3	0	6.0	9	0	0	0	1.000	-
LaForest,Pete	SD	1	0	4.0	2	2	1	1	.800	-
Lamb,Mike	Hou	43	22	225.2	198	29	3	25	.987	-
LeCroy,Matthew	Min	1	0	2.0	3	0	0	0	1.000	-
Loretta,Mark	Hou	24	18	153.0	148	15	1	8	.994	-
Luna,Hector	Tor	2	1	10.0	7	1	0	0	1.000	-
Mackowiak,Rob	CWS	5	2	23.0	23	1	0	2	1.000	-
Martinez,Ramon	LAD	1	0	3.0	2	0	0	0	1.000	-
Martinez,Victor	Cle	30	24	221.0	187	13	1	18	.995	-
McClain,Scott	SF	3	1	9.2	8	0	0	0	1.000	-
Mientkiewicz,Doug	NYY	70	48	458.0	482	23	2	59	.996	-
Miller,Damian	Mil	1	1	6.0	4	0	1	0	.800	-
Molina,Yadier	StL	1	0	1.0	1	0	0	0	1.000	-
Moore,Scott	ChC	1	1	9.0	10	1	0	1	1.000	-
Moore,Scott	Bal	3	3	26.0	19	2	0	1	1.000	-
Morales,Kendry	LAA	19	12	121.0	119	9	0	11	1.000	-
Morse,Mike	Sea	5	3	28.0	35	1	0	1	1.000	-
Munson,Eric	Hou	5	0	10.2	11	0	0	0	1.000	-
Niekro,Lance	SF	3	3	22.0	24	2	0	4	1.000	-
Nieves,Wil	NYY	1	0	1.0	1	0	0	0	1.000	-
Norton,Greg	TB	3	1	8.2	5	1	0	0	1.000	-
Ortiz,David	Bos	7	7	48.0	37	3	0	3	1.000	-
Ortmeier,Dan	SF	22	20	171.1	171	11	0	10	1.000	-
Pearce,Steve	Pit	2	2	9.0	12	0	0	5	1.000	-
Phelps,Josh	NYY	29	20	162.2	167	9	3	16	.983	-
Phelps,Josh	Pit	22	8	96.2	107	5	0	12	1.000	-
Phillips,Andy	NYY	57	49	431.0	380	28	0	44	1.000	-
Phillips,Jason	Tor	4	3	23.0	22	2	0	2	1.000	-
Phillips,Paul	KC	1	1	1.0	2	0	0	0	1.000	-
Posada,Jorge	NYY	1	1	6.0	6	0	0	1	1.000	-
Quinlan,Robb	LAA	34	28	234.0	214	16	1	25	.996	-
Rodriguez,Luis	Min	3	0	3.1	3	1	0	1	1.000	-
Rottino,Vinny	Mil	1	0	4.0	4	0	0	1	1.000	-

Player	Tm	G	GS	Inn	PO	A	E	DP	Pct.	Rng
Saenz,Olmedo	LAD	13	8	75.0	60	4	0	6	1.000	-
Saltalamacchia,J	Atl	14	11	103.1	96	9	2	7	.981	-
Saltalamacchia,J	Tex	24	24	199.0	204	12	9	21	.960	-
Schneider,Brian	Was	1	0	0.2	0	0	0	0	-	-
Shealy,Ryan	KC	52	49	421.0	402	29	0	37	1.000	-
Smith,Jason	KC	3	1	11.1	12	0	0	1	1.000	-
Snyder,Chris	Ari	2	0	2.0	1	0	0	0	1.000	-
Spiezio,Scott	StL	9	7	61.0	72	2	0	6	1.000	-
Stairs,Matt	Tor	45	37	334.1	377	31	6	32	.986	-
Sweeney,Mark	SF	9	4	44.0	51	2	0	4	1.000	-
Sweeney,Mark	LAD	4	1	12.1	10	0	0	0	1.000	-
Sweeney,Mike	KC	6	6	39.1	40	2	1	5	.977	-
Swisher,Nick	Oak	44	39	346.2	391	25	3	31	.993	-
Teahen,Mark	KC	9	5	49.0	45	0	0	4	1.000	-
Teixeira,Mark	Tex	74	74	624.0	614	47	1	74	.998	-
Teixeira,Mark	Atl	54	54	474.0	494	30	4	46	.992	-
Thames,Marcus	Det	33	31	195.1	180	15	2	17	.990	-
Thigpen,Curtis	Tor	14	12	96.0	99	10	1	11	.991	-
Thome,Jim	CWS	1	1	8.0	6	0	0	0	1.000	-
Tracy,Chad	Ari	18	12	114.2	122	5	1	9	.992	-
Utley,Chase	Phi	1	1	8.0	6	0	0	2	1.000	-
Valentin,Javier	Cin	1	0	2.0	3	0	0	1	1.000	-
Vazquez,Ramon	Tex	7	3	35.0	31	0	0	3	1.000	-
Vidro,Jose	Sea	11	8	72.0	78	5	0	5	1.000	-
Votto,Joey	Cin	17	15	137.0	107	11	0	15	1.000	-
Walker,Todd	Oak	10	9	89.0	87	8	0	10	1.000	-
Ward,Daryle	ChC	16	9	90.2	90	5	1	12	.990	-
Werth,Jayson	Phi	1	0	1.0	1	0	0	0	1.000	-
Wigginton,Ty	TB	17	15	132.0	116	15	0	14	1.000	-
Wigginton,Ty	Hou	1	0	2.0	3	0	0	0	1.000	-
Wilkerson,Brad	Tex	68	47	456.0	497	19	3	51	.994	-
Wilson,Craig	Atl	20	17	141.2	133	10	1	15	.993	-
Wood,Jason	Fla	46	12	145.0	112	10	3	16	.976	-
Woodward,Chris	Atl	6	4	35.0	28	1	1	3	.967	-

Second Basemen - Regulars

Player	Tm	G	GS	Inn	PO	A	E	DP	Pct.	Rng
Kinsler,Ian	Tex	130	129	1136.2	283	436	17	98	.977	5.69
Ellis,Mark	Oak	150	149	1322.0	302	499	5	104	.994	5.45
Matsui,Kaz	Col	102	96	863.1	200	311	4	84	.992	5.33
Kennedy,Adam	StL	79	74	630.1	156	211	7	46	.981	5.24
Cano,Robinson	NYY	159	157	1408.2	320	497	13	136	.984	5.22
Iguchi,Tadahito	TOT	121	118	1043.1	260	337	6	96	.990	5.15
Lopez,Jose	Sea	146	139	1231.1	280	423	8	105	.989	5.14
Hill,Aaron	Tor	160	158	1410.0	244	560	14	114	.983	5.13
Utley,Chase	Phi	132	130	1167.0	289	372	10	85	.985	5.10
Polanco,Placido	Det	141	138	1209.0	294	389	0	101	1.000	5.08
Phillips,Brandon	Cin	156	154	1371.0	341	433	8	113	.990	5.08
Giles,Marcus	SD	112	106	947.2	203	332	7	75	.987	5.08
Barfield,Josh	Cle	120	115	1032.0	242	338	15	73	.975	5.06
Belliard,Ronnie	Was	113	113	1004.2	277	286	6	73	.989	5.04
Roberts,Brian	Bal	154	151	1329.2	278	457	7	110	.991	4.97
Hudson,Orlando	Ari	137	137	1183.1	258	387	10	96	.985	4.91
Sanchez,Freddy	Pit	146	146	1272.2	313	379	9	121	.987	4.89
Pedroia,Dustin	Bos	137	132	1141.1	259	360	6	78	.990	4.88
Kendrick,Howie	LAA	86	85	751.1	146	254	9	54	.978	4.79
Durham,Ray	SF	124	117	1028.0	244	300	12	86	.978	4.76
Johnson,Kelly	Atl	133	127	1153.1	227	383	14	83	.978	4.76
Weeks,Rickie	Mil	116	111	984.0	232	286	13	73	.975	4.74
Uggla,Dan	Fla	158	156	1383.2	323	402	11	111	.985	4.72
Kent,Jeff	LAD	133	132	1084.1	235	328	14	76	.976	4.67
Grudzielanek,Mark	KC	116	110	947.1	184	300	6	68	.988	4.60
DeRosa,Mark	ChC	93	88	708.2	168	193	6	45	.984	4.58
Castillo,Luis	TOT	135	133	1158.1	253	315	5	75	.991	4.41
Biggio,Craig	Hou	114	111	936.2	191	267	10	54	.979	4.40

Second Basemen - The Rest

Player	Tm	G	GS	Inn	PO	A	E	DP	Pct.	Rng
Abreu,Tony	LAD	25	10	115.2	19	48	0	10	1.000	5.21
Adams,Russ	Tor	2	2	17.0	4	3	0	0	1.000	3.71
Amezaga,Alfredo	Fla	11	6	56.0	21	21	2	7	.955	6.75
Anderson,Marlon	LAD	1	0	2.0	0	0	0	0	-	.00

Player	Tm	G	GS	Inn	PO	A	E	DP	Pct.	Rng
Aurilia,Rich	SF	9	7	70.1	18	19	1	7	.974	4.73
Ausmus,Brad	Hou	1	1	2.0	0	1	0	0	1.000	4.50
Aybar,Erick	LAA	43	35	320.1	60	106	4	25	.976	4.66
Barden,Brian	StL	2	2	9.0	2	4	0	0	1.000	6.00
Barmes,Clint	Col	5	1	16.0	1	5	0	0	1.000	3.38
Bellhorn,Mark	Cin	1	0	1.2	0	1	0	1	1.000	5.40
Berroa,Angel	KC	1	0	4.0	0	0	0	0	-	.00
Betemit,Wilson	LAD	1	1	6.0	1	0	0	1	1.000	1.50
Betemit,Wilson	NYY	2	2	17.0	3	7	0	1	1.000	5.29
Bloomquist,Willie	Sea	20	15	138.0	23	38	4	9	.938	3.98
Blum,Geoff	SD	61	55	494.0	86	165	2	26	.992	4.57
Bonifacio,Emilio	Ari	6	6	46.0	9	15	1	6	.960	4.70
Burke,Chris	Hou	58	31	311.0	56	103	3	17	.981	4.60
Bynum,Freddie	Bal	4	2	18.0	2	7	0	0	1.000	4.50
Cabrera,Asdrubal	Cle	40	34	321.0	70	119	1	28	.995	5.30
Cairo,Miguel	NYY	3	3	23.0	6	7	0	0	1.000	5.09
Cairo,Miguel	StL	9	4	42.2	9	13	0	1	1.000	4.64
Callaspo,Alberto	Ari	10	3	41.0	4	12	0	4	1.000	3.51
Cantu,Jorge	TB	1	0	3.0	2	2	0	2	1.000	12.00
Cantu,Jorge	Cin	1	1	8.0	1	3	0	0	1.000	4.50
Carroll,Jamey	Col	60	49	431.1	81	164	2	37	.992	5.11
Casilla,Alexi	Min	52	47	421.0	80	147	10	38	.958	4.85
Castillo,Jose	Pit	20	13	129.0	45	25	4	11	.946	4.88
Castillo,Luis	Min	85	85	726.1	154	220	3	48	.992	4.63
Castillo,Luis	NYM	50	48	432.0	99	95	2	27	.990	4.04
Castro,Juan	Cin	8	2	25.0	6	5	2	0	.846	3.96
Cedeno,Ronny	ChC	8	3	33.0	10	14	0	3	1.000	6.55
Cintron,Alex	CWS	14	14	117.2	22	24	3	6	.939	3.52
Cirillo,Jeff	Ari	2	0	3.0	0	0	0	0	-	.00
Clark,Howie	Tor	3	2	19.0	2	4	0	0	1.000	2.84
Cora,Alex	Bos	47	30	297.1	67	95	1	20	.994	4.90
Cortez,Fernando	KC	6	3	33.0	12	11	1	4	.958	6.27
Counsell,Craig	Mil	62	50	468.0	112	128	6	33	.976	4.62
Dillon,Joe	Mil	3	2	25.0	10	6	0	2	1.000	5.76
Dobbs,Greg	Phi	4	0	7.0	0	7	0	0	1.000	9.00
Easley,Damion	NYM	39	36	334.2	79	114	4	24	.980	5.19
Escobar,Yunel	Atl	21	20	164.1	28	49	3	10	.963	4.22
Fahey,Brandon	Bal	9	2	31.0	10	15	0	4	1.000	7.26
Figgins,Chone	LAA	9	6	58.0	9	15	1	1	.960	3.72
Fontenot,Mike	ChC	62	50	468.0	112	128	6	33	.976	4.62
Frandsen,Kevin	SF	49	37	343.1	81	108	4	24	.979	4.95
Freel,Ryan	Cin	2	1	9.0	3	3	0	1	1.000	6.00
Furmaniak,J.J.	Oak	4	1	13.0	3	4	0	2	1.000	4.85
German,Esteban	KC	56	45	406.0	83	105	3	27	.984	4.17
Gomez,Chris	Bal	6	5	43.0	8	20	0	6	1.000	5.86
Gomez,Chris	Cle	4	4	25.0	12	9	0	3	1.000	7.56
Gonzalez,Andy	CWS	4	2	24.0	4	4	0	1	1.000	3.00
Gotay,Ruben	NYM	37	33	296.1	72	71	3	14	.979	4.34
Graffanino,Tony	Mil	30	27	240.1	65	69	1	23	.993	5.02
Green,Nick	Sea	2	1	8.0	2	2	0	1	1.000	4.50
Hairston,Jerry	Tex	16	15	107.0	25	41	0	12	1.000	5.55
Harris,Brendan	TB	47	45	404.0	75	96	1	26	.994	3.81
Hernandez,Luis	Bal	2	2	17.0	4	3	0	1	1.000	3.71
Iguchi,Tadahito	CWS	90	88	778.0	188	247	6	66	.986	5.03
Iguchi,Tadahito	Phi	31	30	265.1	72	90	0	30	1.000	5.49
Infante,Omar	Det	20	12	124.1	30	38	1	8	.986	4.92
Iwamura,Akinori	TB	1	1	9.0	2	2	0	1	1.000	4.00
Izturis,Maicer	LAA	40	36	305.1	50	91	0	24	1.000	4.16
Jimenez,D'Angelo	Was	10	7	68.2	13	22	0	3	1.000	4.59
Kata,Matt	Tex	2	1	13.0	3	1	1	2	.800	2.77
Kata,Matt	Pit	10	2	34.0	14	14	0	6	1.000	7.41
Kelly,Don	Pit	3	1	12.0	1	2	0	1	1.000	2.25
Keppinger,Jeff	Cin	3	3	26.0	10	7	0	2	1.000	5.88
Lopez,Felipe	Was	43	42	373.1	90	113	1	34	.995	4.89
Lopez,Pedro	Cin	1	1	9.0	1	1	0	1	1.000	2.00
Loretta,Mark	Hou	49	18	201.0	47	50	0	14	1.000	4.34
Martinez,Ramon	LAD	36	14	178.0	36	38	1	8	.987	3.74
Miles,Aaron	StL	65	63	590.2	152	160	5	39	.984	4.75
Murphy,Donnie	Oak	2	0	3.0	1	1	0	1	1.000	6.00
Newhan,David	NYM	1	1	9.0	1	1	1	0	.667	2.00
Nunez,Abraham	Phi	4	2	19.0	11	4	0	2	1.000	7.11
Ojeda,Augie	Ari	26	16	164.2	29	70	0	18	1.000	5.41
Orr,Pete	Atl	4	2	20.0	9	3	0	2	1.000	5.40
Ozuna,Pablo	CWS	3	3	29.1	12	10	0	3	1.000	6.75

Player	Tm	G	GS	Inn	PO	A	E	DP	Pct.	Rng
Pena,Tony F	KC	1	0	6.0	2	3	0	1	1.000	7.50
Perez,Neifi	Det	7	4	40.0	7	14	0	5	1.000	4.73
Phillips,Andy	NYY	1	0	2.0	0	1	0	0	1.000	4.50
Prado,Martin	Atl	10	7	64.1	14	34	3	3	.941	6.72
Punto,Nick	Min	25	18	172.1	46	63	3	11	.973	5.69
Quintanilla,Omar	Col	25	17	161.1	39	49	0	15	1.000	4.91
Raburn,Ryan	Det	10	8	74.0	10	26	1	5	.973	4.38
Ransom,Cody	Hou	3	1	14.0	3	3	0	0	1.000	3.86
Relaford,Desi	Tex	12	6	70.1	11	27	0	6	1.000	4.86
Reynolds,Mark	Ari	2	0	2.0	1	0	0	0	1.000	4.50
Richar,Danny	CWS	56	55	491.2	103	139	3	37	.988	4.43
Rivas,Luis	Cle	2	2	15.0	3	4	0	1	1.000	4.20
Roberts,Ryan	Tor	1	0	2.2	0	1	0	0	1.000	3.38
Robles,Oscar	SD	8	2	35.2	4	15	0	1	1.000	4.79
Rodriguez,Luis	Min	21	12	117.0	24	38	1	10	.984	4.77
Rouse,Mike	Cle	14	7	69.2	21	24	1	4	.978	5.81
Ryan,Brendan	StL	17	15	125.0	20	45	3	9	.956	4.68
Sadler,Donnie	Ari	1	0	1.0	1	0	0	0	1.000	9.00
Scutaro,Marco	Oak	13	12	110.0	19	44	0	10	1.000	5.15
Smith,Jason	KC	7	4	41.0	9	9	1	5	.947	3.95
Soriano,Alfonso	ChC	1	0	1.0	0	0	0	0	-	.00
Spiezio,Scott	StL	5	4	36.0	8	8	1	3	.941	4.00
Stansberry,Craig	SD	4	0	7.1	2	2	0	1	1.000	4.91
Taguchi,So	StL	1	0	2.0	1	0	1	0	.500	4.50
Theriot,Ryan	ChC	37	21	236.0	47	70	1	17	.992	4.46
Upton,B.J.	TB	48	48	416.1	106	133	12	26	.952	5.17
Valdez,Wilson	LAD	12	5	59.0	16	25	0	5	1.000	6.25
Valentin,Jose	NYM	45	44	380.1	102	116	5	22	.978	5.16
Vazquez,Ramon	Tex	13	11	103.0	18	32	0	9	1.000	4.37
Velandia,Jorge	TB	11	11	94.1	17	29	0	7	1.000	4.39
Velez,Eugenio	SF	4	1	12.0	5	4	1	2	.900	6.75
Vidro,Jose	Sea	10	7	57.0	19	12	1	2	.969	4.89
Wigginton,Ty	TB	39	37	321.0	74	89	3	24	.982	4.57
Wilson,Josh	TB	27	20	182.0	44	68	6	19	.949	5.54
Wood,Jason	Fla	2	0	4.0	2	0	0	1	1.000	4.50
Woodward,Chris	Atl	11	6	54.1	12	16	0	4	1.000	4.64
Young,Delwyn	LAD	2	0	5.0	3	0	0	0	1.000	5.40

Third Basemen - Regulars

Player	Tm	G	GS	Inn	PO	A	E	DP	Pct.	Rng
Zimmerman,Ryan	Was	161	161	1431.2	140	348	23	39	.955	3.07
Rolen,Scott	StL	112	108	935.0	85	226	10	22	.969	2.99
Bautista,Jose	Pit	126	122	1064.2	95	251	15	16	.958	2.92
Feliz,Pedro	SF	143	137	1220.0	93	302	11	28	.973	2.91
Mora,Melvin	Bal	120	120	1051.1	79	260	10	18	.971	2.90
Beltre,Adrian	Sea	147	146	1279.1	121	287	18	24	.958	2.87
Ramirez,Aramis	ChC	126	126	1091.1	88	260	10	19	.972	2.87
Inge,Brandon	Det	150	146	1309.2	91	325	18	25	.959	2.86
Punto,Nick	Min	108	93	828.1	83	171	7	11	.973	2.76
Gordon,Alex	KC	137	129	1135.0	99	247	14	22	.961	2.74
Wigginton,Ty	TOT	80	74	647.1	57	140	8	6	.961	2.74
Wright,David	NYM	159	159	1418.1	107	324	21	24	.954	2.73
Chavez,Eric	Oak	88	87	774.2	66	169	6	16	.975	2.73
Fields,Josh	CWS	79	78	689.2	47	159	9	13	.958	2.69
Blake,Casey	Cle	145	134	1209.0	99	258	14	24	.962	2.66
Glaus,Troy	Tor	114	110	928.0	63	197	9	24	.967	2.52
Cabrera,Miguel	Fla	154	153	1310.2	100	266	23	33	.941	2.51
Lowell,Mike	Bos	154	150	1324.1	105	264	15	34	.961	2.51
Jones,Chipper	Atl	126	126	1080.2	75	226	9	17	.971	2.51
Encarnacion,Edwin	Cin	137	134	1168.0	112	212	16	21	.953	2.50
Rodriguez,Alex	NYY	154	154	1330.0	106	251	13	30	.965	2.42
Iwamura,Akinori	TB	120	120	1042.1	79	197	7	17	.975	2.38
Kouzmanoff,Kevin	SD	136	128	1135.1	91	209	22	12	.932	2.38
Figgins,Chone	LAA	99	96	836.2	52	165	13	14	.943	2.33
Atkins,Garrett	Col	154	153	1319.0	84	252	13	34	.963	2.29
Reynolds,Mark	Ari	104	97	842.1	55	157	11	21	.951	2.27
Braun,Ryan	Mil	112	112	945.1	61	161	26	12	.895	2.11

Third Basemen - The Rest

Player	Tm	G	GS	Inn	PO	A	E	DP	Pct.	Rng
Abreu,Tony	LAD	28	23	198.1	14	57	4	6	.947	3.22
Adams,Russ	Tor	16	14	123.0	6	11	3	0	.850	1.24

Player	Tm	G	GS	Inn	PO	A	E	DP	Pct.	Rng
Amezaga,Alfredo	Fla	12	4	46.2	11	6	0	0	1.000	3.28
Aurilia,Rich	SF	22	21	177.2	15	39	4	6	.931	2.74
Ausmus,Brad	Hou	2	0	5.0	0	0	0	0	-	.00
Aybar,Erick	LAA	1	1	9.0	0	2	0	0	1.000	2.00
Baker,Jeff	Col	2	2	18.0	0	3	0	0	1.000	1.50
Barden,Brian	Ari	3	2	17.0	0	2	0	1	1.000	1.06
Barden,Brian	StL	1	0	5.0	2	0	0	0	1.000	3.60
Barmes,Clint	Col	1	0	2.0	0	0	0	0	-	.00
Basak,Chris	NYY	3	0	5.0	0	1	0	0	1.000	1.80
Batista,Tony	Was	2	0	3.0	0	1	0	0	1.000	3.00
Bellhorn,Mark	Cin	2	1	13.0	0	4	0	0	1.000	2.77
Belliard,Ronnie	Was	2	1	11.0	1	3	0	0	1.000	3.27
Berroa,Angel	KC	1	0	0.1	0	0	0	0	-	.00
Betemit,Wilson	LAD	53	39	353.0	20	60	4	6	.952	2.04
Betemit,Wilson	NYY	14	5	55.2	1	14	2	3	.882	2.43
Blalock,Hank	Tex	39	39	339.1	18	69	6	9	.935	2.31
Bloomquist,Willie	Sea	20	13	128.0	11	29	0	2	1.000	2.81
Blum,Geoff	SD	13	2	54.1	2	8	0	0	1.000	1.66
Boone,Aaron	Fla	12	5	68.1	6	9	0	0	1.000	1.98
Branyan,Russell	SD	24	18	155.2	10	40	0	9	1.000	2.89
Branyan,Russell	Phi	1	1	5.0	1	0	0	0	1.000	1.80
Branyan,Russell	StL	9	5	50.0	6	20	1	5	.963	4.68
Brown,Matt	LAA	4	1	14.0	1	3	0	1	1.000	2.57
Bruntlett,Eric	Hou	3	0	9.0	1	2	0	1	1.000	3.00
Buscher,Brian	Min	27	24	201.1	17	31	4	6	.923	2.15
Cabrera,Asdrubal	Cle	1	0	1.1	0	1	0	0	1.000	6.75
Cairo,Miguel	NYY	7	3	35.0	1	9	1	2	.909	2.57
Cairo,Miguel	StL	15	9	89.0	4	23	1	4	.964	2.73
Callaspo,Alberto	Ari	18	11	119.1	11	23	1	5	.971	2.56
Cantu,Jorge	Cin	1	0	4.0	0	0	0	0	-	.00
Carroll,Jamey	Col	35	1	64.2	5	13	2	5	.900	2.51
Castillo,Jose	Pit	34	27	253.1	23	83	4	6	.964	3.77
Castro,Juan	Cin	17	5	64.0	8	9	1	0	.944	2.39
Cedeno,Ronny	ChC	4	1	14.0	3	3	0	1	1.000	3.86
Cintron,Alex	CWS	19	12	112.2	9	27	5	3	.878	2.88
Cirillo,Jeff	Min	15	12	106.0	6	29	0	3	1.000	2.97
Cirillo,Jeff	Ari	11	5	58.0	5	13	0	2	1.000	2.79
Clark,Howie	Tor	10	7	65.0	4	17	0	2	1.000	2.91
Clayton,Royce	Bos	3	0	6.1	0	2	0	0	1.000	2.84
Conine,Jeff	Cin	1	0	1.0	0	0	0	0	-	.00
Counsell,Craig	Mil	50	27	297.2	21	73	0	10	1.000	2.84
Crede,Joe	CWS	46	45	388.1	36	97	4	18	.971	3.08
DeRosa,Mark	ChC	37	31	287.1	24	68	4	3	.958	2.88
Dillon,Joe	Mil	3	0	7.0	1	2	0	1	1.000	3.86
Dobbs,Greg	Phi	68	57	418.0	44	77	7	7	.945	2.61
Easley,Damion	NYM	2	0	4.0	0	2	1	0	.667	4.50
Ensberg,Morgan	Hou	68	52	492.1	36	107	11	12	.929	2.61
Ensberg,Morgan	SD	12	10	92.2	3	29	1	3	.970	3.11
Escobar,Yunel	Atl	22	19	159.1	20	28	4	4	.923	2.71
Fahey,Brandon	Bal	2	0	3.1	0	1	1	0	.500	2.70
Franco,Julio	NYM	2	2	18.0	1	4	0	0	1.000	2.50
Frandsen,Kevin	SF	9	4	55.2	2	11	0	2	1.000	2.10
Freel,Ryan	Cin	19	15	124.0	17	29	2	3	.958	3.34
Furmaniak,J.J.	Oak	2	2	12.0	0	2	0	0	1.000	1.50
Garciaparra,Nomar	LAD	43	41	354.2	32	64	6	3	.941	2.44
German,Esteban	KC	46	32	281.2	16	49	5	5	.929	2.08
Gomez,Chris	Bal	25	18	177.0	13	42	3	9	.948	2.80
Gomez,Chris	Cle	6	6	58.0	6	16	0	3	1.000	3.41
Gonzalez,Alberto	NYY	1	0	2.0	0	0	0	0	-	.00
Gonzalez,Andy	CWS	25	21	188.0	15	42	9	6	.864	2.73
Gotay,Ruben	NYM	2	1	11.0	0	5	0	0	1.000	4.09
Graffanino,Tony	Mil	23	23	194.1	28	43	2	3	.973	3.29
Guzman,Joel	TB	8	4	44.0	3	7	0	1	1.000	2.05
Hairston,Jerry	Tex	10	4	44.2	3	13	1	1	.941	3.22
Hammock,Robby	Ari	1	0	13.2	0	2	1	0	.667	1.32
Hannahan,Jack	Oak	41	40	361.2	19	78	3	10	.970	2.41
Harris,Brendan	TB	4	2	24.2	2	1	1	0	.750	1.09
Harris,Willie	Atl	2	0	9.0	0	4	1	0	.800	4.00
Headley,Chase	SD	5	5	38.1	2	3	1	0	.833	1.17
Helms,Wes	Phi	68	53	441.2	27	97	9	3	.932	2.53
Hessman,Mike	Det	4	3	28.0	1	5	0	0	1.000	1.93
Hillenbrand,Shea	LAD	18	17	154.0	14	35	4	5	.925	2.86
House,J.R.	Bal	2	0	2.0	0	0	0	0	-	.00
Huff,Aubrey	Bal	15	15	122.0	9	24	1	1	.971	2.43

Player	Tm	G	GS	Inn	PO	A	E	DP	Pct.	Rng
Infante,Omar	Det	9	8	72.2	6	22	1	1	.966	3.47
Inglett,Joe	Tor	1	1	9.0	0	0	0	0	-	.00
Izturis,Cesar	Pit	11	5	49.0	3	11	0	0	1.000	2.57
Izturis,Maicer	LAA	53	50	447.0	21	91	3	10	.974	2.26
Jackson,Conor	Ari	2	0	2.0	1	0	0	0	1.000	4.50
Jimenez,D'Angelo	Was	1	0	1.0	0	0	0	0	-	.00
Kata,Matt	Tex	7	6	44.1	3	7	2	0	.833	2.03
Kata,Matt	Pit	10	8	80.2	2	16	1	1	.947	2.01
Keppinger,Jeff	Cin	13	7	75.2	7	23	1	3	.968	3.57
Lamb,Mike	Hou	58	46	416.1	29	88	8	8	.936	2.53
LaRoche,Andy	LAD	30	28	237.0	22	48	3	8	.959	2.66
LaRue,Jason	KC	1	0	6.0	0	1	0	0	1.000	1.50
Lopez,Jose	Sea	3	2	15.0	2	5	1	1	.875	4.20
Loretta,Mark	Hou	23	17	141.1	11	28	0	1	1.000	2.48
Luna,Hector	Tor	15	10	100.1	6	23	2	3	.935	2.60
Mabry,John	Col	4	4	27.0	3	4	1	0	.875	2.33
Mackowiak,Rob	CWS	1	0	1.0	0	0	0	0	-	.00
Marte,Andy	Cle	19	16	135.2	16	27	4	2	.915	2.85
Martinez,Ramon	LAD	17	10	104.0	2	33	1	2	.972	3.03
McDonald,John	Tor	15	8	93.0	10	29	1	5	.975	3.77
Melhuse,Adam	Oak	1	0	2.0	0	1	0	0	1.000	4.50
Melhuse,Adam	Tex	5	3	31.0	0	12	0	1	1.000	3.48
Metcalf,Travis	Tex	55	49	430.1	35	89	7	14	.947	2.59
Miles,Aaron	StL	3	2	19.0	0	8	0	1	1.000	3.79
Moore,Scott	Bal	12	9	83.0	6	12	0	2	1.000	1.95
Morse,Mike	Sea	3	1	12.0	0	5	0	2	1.000	3.75
Murphy,Donnie	Oak	1	0	2.0	0	1	0	0	1.000	4.50
Newhan,David	NYM	1	0	1.0	0	0	0	0	-	.00
Nunez,Abraham	Phi	113	51	593.2	41	175	9	12	.960	3.27
Ojeda,Augie	Ari	7	0	14.2	0	3	0	0	1.000	1.84
Olmedo,Ray	Tor	2	0	7.0	2	2	0	0	1.000	5.14
Orr,Pete	Atl	14	7	63.0	4	13	1	1	.944	2.43
Ozuna,Pablo	CWS	9	6	61.0	5	9	3	0	.824	2.07
Perez,Neifi	Det	3	3	24.0	2	10	1	0	.923	4.50
Phillips,Andy	NYY	9	0	17.0	1	2	0	0	1.000	1.59
Prado,Martin	Atl	9	4	44.0	4	7	0	0	1.000	2.25
Quinlan,Robb	LAA	10	5	53.1	4	7	1	0	.917	1.86
Raburn,Ryan	Det	3	2	13.0	1	1	0	1	1.000	1.38
Ransom,Cody	Hou	2	1	8.0	1	1	0	0	1.000	2.25
Roberts,Ryan	Tor	3	3	22.0	0	2	1	0	.667	.82
Robles,Oscar	SD	4	0	8.1	2	3	0	0	1.000	5.40
Rodriguez,Luis	Min	38	25	232.0	25	43	3	7	.958	2.64
Rouse,Mike	Cle	14	6	58.2	4	11	1	3	.938	2.30
Ryan,Brendan	StL	24	18	150.0	19	41	4	7	.938	3.60
Saenz,Olmedo	LAD	3	0	6.0	0	1	0	0	1.000	1.50
Sardinha,Bronson	NYY	1	0	6.0	0	0	0	0	-	.00
Scutaro,Marco	Oak	36	33	295.2	23	64	9	2	.906	2.65
Smith,Jason	Tor	15	9	101.1	12	28	0	5	1.000	3.55
Smith,Jason	KC	4	1	14.1	1	2	1	0	.750	1.88
Spiezio,Scott	StL	27	20	187.2	22	42	3	5	.955	3.07
Stewart,Ian	Col	11	3	41.1	5	16	0	1	1.000	4.57
Theriot,Ryan	ChC	8	4	54.0	5	7	2	0	.857	2.00
Tracy,Chad	Ari	48	46	374.0	29	73	4	6	.962	2.45
Valdez,Wilson	LAD	9	4	43.0	2	9	0	2	1.000	2.30
Vazquez,Ramon	Tex	71	61	540.1	46	123	7	17	.960	2.81
Watkins,Thomas	Min	8	8	69.0	4	15	0	1	1.000	2.48
Wigginton,Ty	TB	32	30	254.2	23	52	5	3	.938	2.65
Wigginton,Ty	Hou	48	46	392.2	34	88	3	3	.976	2.80
Wilson,Josh	TB	8	6	64.0	3	19	3	4	.880	3.09
Winn,Randy	SF	1	0	0.1	1	0	0	0	1.000	27.00
Wood,Brandon	LAA	10	9	75.0	12	14	1	2	.963	3.12
Wood,Jason	Fla	7	0	18.0	1	1	0	0	1.000	1.00
Woodward,Chris	Atl	24	6	100.1	5	16	3	2	.875	1.88
Youkilis,Kevin	Bos	13	12	108.0	5	30	3	4	.921	2.92

Shortstops - Regulars

Player	Tm	G	GS	Inn	PO	A	E	DP	Pct.	Rng
Tulowitzki,Troy	Col	155	155	1375.0	262	561	11	114	.987	5.39
McDonald,John	Tor	102	93	799.1	148	294	8	66	.982	4.98
Furcal,Rafael	LAD	138	138	1210.0	241	426	19	99	.972	4.96
Wilson,Jack	Pit	131	131	1142.0	177	452	11	112	.983	4.96
Uribe,Juan	CWS	150	147	1305.1	245	443	17	102	.976	4.74
Vizquel,Omar	SF	143	136	1219.1	198	444	9	90	.986	4.74

Player	Tm	G	GS	Inn	PO	A	E	DP	Pct.	Rng
Peralta,Jhonny	Cle	152	149	1348.0	249	452	19	106	.974	4.68
Bartlett,Jason	Min	138	135	1194.0	205	415	26	97	.960	4.67
Betancourt,Yuniesky	Sea	152	147	1302.1	239	435	23	110	.967	4.66
Young,Michael	Tex	150	150	1291.1	211	446	19	107	.972	4.58
Crosby,Bobby	Oak	92	92	813.2	131	282	14	61	.967	4.57
Pena,Tony F	KC	150	145	1273.2	208	438	23	98	.966	4.56
Eckstein,David	StL	114	112	943.2	164	310	20	59	.960	4.52
Cabrera,Orlando	LAA	153	153	1330.2	239	415	11	104	.983	4.42
Rollins,Jimmy	Phi	162	162	1441.1	227	479	11	110	.985	4.41
Greene,Khalil	SD	153	153	1396.1	218	461	11	98	.984	4.38
Drew,Stephen	Ari	147	143	1283.1	212	409	17	98	.973	4.36
Lopez,Felipe	Was	111	104	927.0	154	289	20	56	.957	4.30
Guillen,Carlos	Det	132	129	1074.0	160	352	24	79	.955	4.29
Tejada,Miguel	Bal	124	122	1068.2	149	358	15	77	.971	4.27
Ramirez,Hanley	Fla	151	150	1301.2	225	392	24	98	.963	4.24
Gonzalez,Alex	Cin	103	98	872.2	147	264	16	73	.963	4.24
Lugo,Julio	Bos	145	139	1228.1	214	360	19	70	.968	4.21
Renteria,Edgar	Atl	121	121	1019.1	147	322	11	71	.977	4.14
Reyes,Jose	NYM	160	160	1431.1	203	445	12	88	.982	4.07
Theriot,Ryan	ChC	108	101	859.0	126	260	8	56	.980	4.04
Jeter,Derek	NYY	155	153	1318.1	199	390	18	104	.970	4.02
Izturis,Cesar	TOT	90	69	655.2	96	196	8	53	.973	4.01
Hardy,J.J.	Mil	149	145	1271.2	168	397	13	83	.978	4.00
Harris,Brendan	TB	87	86	751.2	111	221	11	54	.968	3.98

Shortstops - The Rest

Player	Tm	G	GS	Inn	PO	A	E	DP	Pct.	Rng
Abreu,Tony	LAD	7	5	44.0	7	18	1	3	.962	5.11
Amezaga,Alfredo	Fla	18	11	122.0	16	35	1	4	.981	3.76
Andino,Robert	Fla	3	1	20.0	3	4	0	1	1.000	3.15
Aurilia,Rich	SF	12	11	94.0	14	35	2	6	.961	4.69
Aybar,Erick	LAA	20	7	79.0	14	24	3	2	.927	4.33
Barden,Brian	StL	6	0	25.1	3	11	0	2	1.000	4.97
Barmes,Clint	Col	8	3	35.0	8	12	1	3	.952	5.14
Basak,Chris	NYY	1	0	1.0	0	0	0	0	-	.00
Belliard,Ronnie	Was	4	4	30.0	0	9	0	1	1.000	4.50
Berroa,Angel	KC	4	2	21.2	4	11	0	6	1.000	6.23
Betemit,Wilson	LAD	2	0	7.0	0	1	0	0	1.000	1.29
Betemit,Wilson	NYY	8	4	39.0	9	9	1	2	.947	4.15
Bloomquist,Willie	Sea	20	15	124.0	23	39	1	5	.984	4.50
Blum,Geoff	SD	12	10	88.1	14	26	3	4	.930	4.08
Bruntlett,Eric	Hou	63	34	348.2	62	109	7	23	.961	4.41
Burke,Chris	Hou	7	1	24.0	3	9	0	0	1.000	4.50
Bynum,Freddie	Bal	15	7	66.0	13	16	1	2	.967	3.95
Cabrera,Asdrubal	Cle	7	6	42.0	8	21	0	5	1.000	6.21
Cairo,Miguel	NYY	16	3	52.2	7	22	0	4	1.000	4.96
Callaspo,Alberto	Ari	9	9	75.0	11	25	2	3	.947	4.32
Carroll,Jamey	Col	11	5	57.0	10	22	0	5	1.000	5.05
Casilla,Alexi	Min	5	3	30.0	4	8	0	2	1.000	3.60
Castillo,Jose	Pit	8	7	63.0	15	20	1	7	.972	5.00
Castro,Juan	Cin	16	11	89.1	10	27	0	5	1.000	3.73
Cedeno,Ronny	ChC	15	10	110.0	14	33	2	5	.959	3.85
Cintron,Alex	CWS	17	15	132.1	34	45	2	14	.975	5.37
Clark,Howie	Tor	2	0	3.0	0	0	0	0	-	.00
Clayton,Royce	Tor	68	56	500.0	73	176	7	30	.973	4.48
Clayton,Royce	Bos	1	1	8.0	0	3	1	0	.750	3.38
Cora,Alex	Bos	33	22	202.1	25	69	3	18	.969	4.18
Counsell,Craig	Mil	27	17	170.2	20	55	1	14	.987	3.96
Cruz,Enrique	Cin	1	0	2.2	0	0	1	0	.000	.00
DeRosa,Mark	ChC	1	0	8.0	1	1	0	0	1.000	2.25
Escobar,Yunel	Atl	53	36	363.0	59	113	4	22	.977	4.26
Everett,Adam	Hou	66	62	535.1	96	197	8	37	.973	4.93
Fahey,Brandon	Bal	18	9	94.0	11	24	0	5	1.000	3.35
Figueroa,Luis	SF	1	0	2.0	1	3	0	1	1.000	18.00
Fontenot,Mike	ChC	3	3	19.0	2	0	2	0	.500	.95
Frandsen,Kevin	SF	22	15	138.1	28	38	1	7	.985	4.29
Furmaniak,J.J.	Oak	3	2	21.0	5	5	1	3	.909	4.29
German,Esteban	KC	4	1	12.0	0	1	1	1	.500	.75
Gomez,Chris	Bal	10	10	71.0	13	31	0	9	1.000	5.58
Gonzalez,Alberto	NYY	11	2	39.2	11	12	1	3	.958	5.22
Gonzalez,Andy	CWS	1	0	2.0	0	0	0	0	-	.00
Gordon,Alex	KC	1	0	6.0	2	1	0	0	1.000	4.50
Gotay,Ruben	NYM	5	2	20.0	4	5	0	1	1.000	4.05

Player	Tm	G	GS	Inn	PO	A	E	DP	Pct.	Rng
Graffanino,Tony	Mil	1	0	2.0	0	0	0	0	-	.00
Green,Nick	Sea	3	0	6.0	0	2	0	0	1.000	3.00
Grudzielanek,Mark	KC	3	0	4.0	1	2	0	0	1.000	6.75
Guzman,Cristian	Was	44	42	376.0	67	105	8	33	.956	4.12
Guzman,Joel	TB	3	0	9.0	0	0	0	0	-	.00
Hairston,Jerry	Tex	2	0	3.0	1	0	0	0	1.000	3.00
Hernandez,Anderson	NYM	1	0	1.0	0	0	0	0	-	.00
Hernandez,Luis	Bal	23	14	139.0	31	52	3	17	.965	5.37
Hu,Chin-Lung	LAD	10	7	70.0	11	22	1	8	.971	4.24
Infante,Omar	Det	14	7	79.2	15	17	2	5	.941	3.62
Izturis,Cesar	ChC	60	48	450.2	57	130	7	28	.964	3.73
Izturis,Cesar	Pit	30	21	205.0	39	66	1	25	.991	4.61
Izturis,Maicer	LAA	3	2	19.0	8	3	1	1	.917	5.21
Jimenez,D'Angelo	Was	11	9	77.1	17	19	3	4	.923	4.19
Jones,Chipper	Atl	1	0	7.0	1	1	0	0	1.000	2.57
Kata,Matt	Tex	6	2	25.0	7	6	0	2	1.000	4.68
Kata,Matt	Pit	3	1	16.2	2	5	0	1	1.000	3.78
Kelly,Don	Pit	5	2	20.0	5	6	0	1	1.000	4.95
Kennedy,Adam	StL	1	0	2.0	0	3	0	0	1.000	13.50
Keppinger,Jeff	Cin	47	43	390.2	62	124	2	27	.989	4.28
Lopez,Pedro	Cin	12	10	93.1	23	24	1	10	.979	4.53
Loretta,Mark	Hou	72	58	486.2	80	157	6	29	.975	4.38
Martinez,Ramon	LAD	8	6	54.2	8	15	0	4	1.000	3.79
Miles,Aaron	StL	40	33	301.0	73	91	9	24	.948	4.90
Morse,Mike	Sea	1	0	2.0	0	0	0	0	-	.00
Murphy,Donnie	Oak	31	30	265.1	35	91	5	22	.962	4.27
Nunez,Abraham	Phi	8	0	17.0	0	3	0	1	1.000	1.59
Ojeda,Augie	Ari	12	9	75.2	18	23	0	3	1.000	4.88
Olmedo,Ray	Tor	24	12	134.1	24	60	1	15	.988	5.63
Ozuna,Pablo	CWS	1	0	1.0	0	0	0	0	-	.00
Perez,Neifi	Det	24	9	107.2	13	27	2	7	.952	3.34
Phillips,Brandon	Cin	1	0	1.0	0	1	0	0	1.000	9.00
Punto,Nick	Min	27	24	210.2	44	70	3	17	.974	4.87
Quintanilla,Omar	Col	2	0	5.0	1	2	0	0	1.000	5.40
Ransom,Cody	Hou	12	7	70.0	16	21	2	4	.949	4.76
Rivas,Luis	Cle	1	0	7.0	0	4	1	0	.800	5.14
Rouse,Mike	Cle	11	7	65.2	10	32	1	5	.977	5.76
Ryan,Brendan	StL	28	17	163.2	31	65	3	15	.970	5.28
Sanchez,Freddy	Pit	1	0	1.0	0	0	0	0	-	.00
Santiago,Ramon	Det	31	17	186.0	29	62	2	12	.978	4.40
Scutaro,Marco	Oak	43	38	348.0	52	111	5	22	.970	4.22
Smith,Jason	Tor	3	1	12.0	1	6	1	2	.875	5.25
Smith,Jason	Ari	1	1	7.0	0	2	0	0	1.000	2.57
Smith,Jason	KC	20	14	120.0	22	39	3	6	.953	4.58
Valdez,Wilson	LAD	12	6	64.1	7	26	0	4	1.000	4.62
Vazquez,Ramon	Tex	19	10	110.2	16	42	0	8	1.000	4.72
Velandia,Jorge	TB	4	3	27.0	7	12	0	4	1.000	6.33
Watkins,Thomas	Min	1	0	2.0	1	0	0	0	1.000	4.50
Wilson,Josh	Was	7	3	36.1	5	15	5	2	.800	4.95
Wilson,Josh	TB	50	47	417.1	67	118	8	30	.959	3.99
Wood,Brandon	LAA	3	0	6.1	0	2	0	0	1.000	2.84
Woodward,Chris	Atl	13	5	67.0	7	20	2	5	.931	3.63
Zobrist,Ben	TB	30	26	224.2	37	63	6	17	.943	4.01

Player	Tm	G	GS	Inn	PO	A	E	DP	Pct.	Rng
Ibanez,Raul	Sea	131	131	1114.1	224	10	6	2	.975	1.89
Dunn,Adam	Cin	144	142	1189.2	244	4	6	0	.976	1.88
Anderson,Garret	LAA	85	85	724.1	143	7	2	0	.987	1.86
Alou,Moises	NYM	84	84	703.0	138	7	4	0	.973	1.86
Gonzalez,Luis	LAD	127	126	996.0	192	4	1	0	.995	1.77
Lee,Carlos	Hou	157	157	1369.1	261	8	4	2	.985	1.77
Bonds,Barry	SF	110	110	842.0	162	2	4	0	.976	1.75
Ramirez,Manny	Bos	120	120	994.2	182	8	2	0	.990	1.72
Willingham,Josh	Fla	137	137	1176.1	211	9	3	0	.987	1.68
Burrell,Pat	Phi	138	138	1028.1	176	8	10	0	.948	1.61

Left Fielders - The Rest

Player	Tm	G	GS	Inn	PO	A	E	DP	Pct.	Rng
Abercrombie,Reggie	Fla	3	1	11.0	3	0	0	0	1.000	2.45
Amezaga,Alfredo	Fla	2	0	2.0	1	0	0	0	1.000	4.50
Anderson,Brian	CWS	5	0	11.1	1	0	0	0	1.000	.79
Anderson,Josh	Hou	3	0	6.0	1	0	0	0	1.000	1.50
Anderson,Marlon	NYM	12	6	60.1	16	0	0	0	1.000	2.39
Ankiel,Rick	StL	2	2	16.0	6	1	0	0	1.000	3.94
Aybar,Erick	LAA	6	4	29.0	5	0	0	0	1.000	1.55
Baker,Jeff	Col	6	1	18.0	5	0	0	0	1.000	2.50
Balentien,Wladimir	Sea	1	0	1.0	0	0	0	0	-	.00
Barker,Sean	Col	1	0	1.0	0	0	0	0	-	.00
Bautista,Jose	Pit	2	1	12.2	1	0	0	0	1.000	.71
Betemit,Wilson	NYY	1	0	1.0	1	0	0	0	1.000	9.00
Bloomquist,Willie	Sea	13	6	60.0	12	0	0	0	1.000	1.80
Blum,Geoff	SD	9	3	45.0	14	0	0	0	1.000	2.80
Bocachica,Hiram	SD	2	1	11.0	3	0	0	0	1.000	2.45
Borchard,Joe	Fla	14	6	67.2	15	0	1	0	.938	2.00
Botts,Jason	Tex	28	28	212.0	62	1	0	0	1.000	2.67
Bourn,Michael	Phi	79	6	217.2	52	0	0	0	1.000	2.15
Bradley,Milton	SD	40	40	326.1	72	3	2	1	.974	2.07
Branyan,Russell	SD	12	9	78.1	14	0	1	0	.933	1.61
Branyan,Russell	Phi	1	0	1.0	0	0	0	0	-	.00
Broussard,Ben	Sea	10	8	67.0	14	0	0	0	1.000	1.88
Brown,Dee	Oak	4	0	5.2	2	0	0	0	1.000	3.18
Bruntlett,Eric	Hou	4	0	8.1	1	0	0	0	1.000	1.08
Buck,Travis	Oak	18	16	128.0	26	1	0	0	1.000	1.90
Burke,Chris	Hou	3	1	16.0	5	1	0	0	1.000	3.38
Butler,Billy	KC	6	5	43.0	4	0	1	0	.800	.84
Bynum,Freddie	Bal	23	9	100.0	27	2	0	0	1.000	2.61
Byrd,Marlon	Tex	18	13	116.2	31	0	0	0	1.000	2.39
Cabrera,Melky	NYY	16	14	142.0	34	2	0	0	1.000	2.28
Cairo,Miguel	NYY	3	1	13.0	2	0	0	0	1.000	1.38
Cairo,Miguel	StL	1	0	1.0	0	0	0	0	-	.00
Callaspo,Alberto	Ari	3	1	19.0	3	0	0	0	1.000	1.42
Carroll,Brett	Fla	7	1	18.2	3	1	0	1	1.000	1.93
Casto,Kory	Was	12	11	91.2	18	0	0	0	1.000	1.77
Catalanotto,Frank	Tex	64	60	483.1	98	2	0	0	1.000	1.86
Chavez,Endy	NYM	37	19	195.0	46	1	0	0	1.000	2.17
Choo,Shin-Soo	Cle	3	3	32.0	10	1	0	1	1.000	3.09
Clark,Brady	LAD	32	4	92.2	14	0	0	0	1.000	1.36
Clark,Brady	SD	6	1	21.1	4	0	0	0	1.000	1.69
Clevlen,Brent	Det	8	0	13.0	2	0	0	0	1.000	1.38
Coats,Buck	Cin	5	2	24.0	10	1	0	0	1.000	4.13
Conine,Jeff	NYM	2	1	10.0	0	0	0	0	-	.00
Costa,Shane	KC	15	11	98.0	31	0	1	0	.969	2.85
Cruz,Jose	SD	49	38	365.1	89	4	1	1	.989	2.29
Cruz,Nelson	Tex	16	14	118.0	19	1	0	0	1.000	1.53
Cust,Jack	Oak	14	12	81.2	14	0	1	0	.933	1.54
Damon,Johnny	NYY	32	31	271.0	71	2	2	0	.973	2.42
DaVanon,Jeff	Ari	2	0	5.0	1	0	0	0	1.000	1.80
DaVanon,Jeff	Oak	1	1	8.0	4	0	0	0	1.000	4.50
Davis,Rajai	SF	7	1	20.2	7	0	0	0	1.000	3.05
Dellucci,David	Cle	51	44	382.1	97	3	0	0	1.000	2.35
DeRosa,Mark	ChC	4	1	8.0	2	0	0	0	1.000	2.25
Diaz,Victor	Tex	3	1	10.1	2	0	0	0	1.000	1.74
Dillon,Joe	Mil	8	5	43.1	13	0	0	0	1.000	2.70
Dobbs,Greg	Phi	14	10	82.2	18	0	1	0	.947	1.96
Dukes,Elijah	TB	3	1	12.0	5	0	0	0	1.000	3.75
Duncan,Shelley	NYY	4	0	12.0	3	0	0	0	1.000	2.25
Easley,Damion	NYM	3	3	26.0	4	0	0	0	1.000	1.38
Ellison,Jason	Sea	18	5	63.0	11	0	1	0	.917	1.57

Left Fielders - Regulars

Player	Tm	G	GS	Inn	PO	A	E	DP	Pct.	Rng
Church,Ryan	Was	91	87	719.1	196	3	3	1	.985	2.49
Brown,Emil	KC	78	66	606.1	155	7	6	2	.964	2.40
Payton,Jay	Bal	123	100	904.0	232	2	5	1	.979	2.33
Jenkins,Geoff	Mil	121	109	973.2	242	7	3	2	.988	2.30
Byrnes,Eric	Ari	123	113	970.2	239	9	4	0	.984	2.30
Soriano,Alfonso	ChC	122	122	1064.0	244	19	6	4	.978	2.22
Crawford,Carl	TB	139	136	1186.1	286	3	4	1	.986	2.19
Stewart,Shannon	Oak	139	128	1154.0	277	4	3	2	.989	2.19
Diaz,Matt	Atl	95	77	678.1	155	4	2	1	.988	2.11
Kubel,Jason	Min	84	81	700.1	159	2	2	2	.988	2.07
Harris,Willie	Atl	85	69	620.1	138	4	3	1	.979	2.06
Bay,Jason	Pit	142	142	1237.0	265	13	8	3	.972	2.02
Matsui,Hideki	NYY	112	111	980.0	213	6	3	0	.986	2.01
Holliday,Matt	Col	157	157	1383.2	296	7	3	0	.990	1.97
Lind,Adam	Tor	80	72	651.2	137	5	0	0	1.000	1.96
Monroe,Craig	TOT	102	88	805.2	166	6	3	1	.983	1.92

Player	Tm	G	GS	Inn	PO	A	E	DP	Pct.	Rng
Ellison,Jason	Cin	14	2	30.0	10	0	0	0	1.000	3.00
Ellsbury,Jacoby	Bos	22	15	144.0	37	0	0	0	1.000	2.31
Erstad,Darin	CWS	12	4	43.2	15	0	0	0	1.000	3.09
Ethier,Andre	LAD	60	26	306.0	73	2	1	0	.987	2.21
Evans,Terry	LAA	2	1	8.1	2	0	0	0	1.000	2.16
Fahey,Brandon	Bal	7	1	20.0	7	0	0	0	1.000	3.15
Feliz,Pedro	SF	2	2	17.0	5	0	0	0	1.000	2.65
Fick,Robert	Was	14	10	67.0	14	1	1	0	.938	2.01
Fields,Josh	CWS	21	21	179.1	34	2	2	0	.947	1.81
Figueroa,Luis	SF	1	0	1.0	0	0	0	0	-	.00
Floyd,Cliff	ChC	17	15	132.2	32	0	0	0	1.000	2.17
Ford,Lew	Min	35	25	233.1	46	1	1	1	.979	1.81
Francisco,Ben	Cle	14	11	102.1	26	0	0	0	1.000	2.29
Frandsen,Kevin	SF	10	3	40.1	8	1	0	0	1.000	2.01
Freel,Ryan	Cin	1	0	2.0	0	0	0	0	-	.00
Fuld,Sam	ChC	1	0	1.0	0	0	0	0	-	.00
Furmaniak,J.J.	Oak	1	0	3.0	0	0	0	0	-	.00
Gathright,Joey	KC	64	59	519.1	154	3	3	0	.981	2.72
German,Esteban	KC	8	5	42.0	6	2	0	0	1.000	1.71
Gibbons,Jay	Bal	43	41	326.1	75	1	2	1	.974	2.10
Gload,Ross	KC	8	7	53.2	10	1	0	0	1.000	1.84
Gomes,Jonny	TB	26	20	186.1	42	2	0	1	1.000	2.13
Gomez,Carlos	NYM	27	20	179.1	46	2	1	1	.980	2.41
Gonzalez,Andy	CWS	18	15	121.0	31	1	0	0	1.000	2.38
Gorneault,Nick	LAA	2	1	15.0	5	1	1	0	.857	3.60
Graffanino,Tony	Mil	3	3	22.0	7	0	0	0	1.000	2.86
Granderson,Curtis	Det	2	0	5.0	4	0	0	0	1.000	7.20
Gross,Gabe	Mil	3	1	12.1	0	0	0	0	-	.00
Gutierrez,Franklin	Cle	9	7	58.2	7	0	0	0	1.000	1.07
Guzman,Freddy	Tex	1	0	1.0	0	0	0	0	-	.00
Gwynn,Tony	Mil	4	0	6.0	1	0	0	0	1.000	1.50
Hairston,Jerry	Tex	21	4	62.0	15	1	1	0	.941	2.32
Hairston,Scott	Ari	52	42	380.0	90	3	3	1	.969	2.20
Hairston,Scott	SD	25	18	180.1	24	1	0	0	1.000	1.25
Hamilton,Josh	Cin	9	2	27.0	5	0	0	0	1.000	1.67
Hammock,Robby	Ari	5	3	32.0	6	0	0	0	1.000	1.69
Haynes,Nathan	LAA	8	1	25.0	5	1	0	0	1.000	2.16
Hernandez,Luis	Bal	1	0	1.0	0	0	0	0	-	.00
Hessman,Mike	Det	1	0	4.0	1	0	0	0	1.000	2.25
Hinske,Eric	Bos	24	10	101.0	26	1	0	0	1.000	2.41
Hopper,Norris	Cin	34	7	115.0	37	1	0	0	1.000	2.97
Huber,Justin	KC	3	2	18.0	2	0	0	0	1.000	1.00
Infante,Omar	Det	1	0	1.0	0	0	0	0	-	.00
Jackson,Conor	Ari	2	1	9.0	3	0	0	0	1.000	3.00
Johnson,Ben	NYM	5	5	45.0	12	0	0	0	1.000	2.40
Johnson,Reed	Tor	70	54	503.0	108	2	0	0	1.000	1.97
Jones,Adam	Sea	26	11	119.0	24	2	1	1	.963	1.97
Jones,Brandon	Atl	5	5	43.0	5	0	0	0	1.000	1.05
Jones,Garrett	Min	5	2	19.0	4	0	1	0	.800	1.89
Jones,Jacque	ChC	2	2	18.1	2	0	0	0	1.000	.98
Kata,Matt	Tex	10	4	54.0	12	2	0	1	1.000	2.33
Kata,Matt	Pit	2	1	10.0	2	0	0	0	1.000	1.80
Kelly,Don	Pit	1	0	1.0	1	0	0	0	1.000	9.00
Kendall,Jason	Oak	2	0	2.1	1	0	0	0	1.000	3.86
Keppinger,Jeff	Cin	1	1	11.0	5	0	0	0	1.000	4.09
Kielty,Bobby	Oak	2	2	13.0	4	1	0	1	1.000	3.46
Kielty,Bobby	Bos	10	5	57.0	14	1	0	0	1.000	2.37
Klesko,Ryan	SF	2	1	8.0	2	0	0	0	1.000	2.25
Knott,Jon	Bal	2	2	12.0	4	0	0	0	1.000	3.00
Laird,Gerald	Tex	1	0	1.0	0	0	0	0	-	.00
Lane,Jason	Hou	4	0	6.0	0	0	0	0	-	.00
Langerhans,Ryan	Atl	19	11	114.0	18	0	0	0	1.000	1.42
Langerhans,Ryan	Was	47	4	119.1	29	0	0	0	1.000	2.19
LaRoche,Andy	LAD	1	0	1.0	0	0	0	0	-	.00
Ledee,Ricky	NYM	11	9	89.0	22	0	0	0	1.000	2.22
Lewis,Fred	SF	24	10	115.0	32	0	1	0	.970	2.50
Linden,Todd	SF	18	1	49.0	12	0	0	0	1.000	2.20
Linden,Todd	Fla	13	13	119.0	25	0	0	0	1.000	1.89
Lofton,Kenny	Cle	50	42	387.2	82	3	0	1	1.000	1.97
Ludwick,Ryan	StL	49	37	324.0	86	1	0	0	1.000	2.42
Mabry,John	Col	1	0	2.0	1	0	0	0	1.000	4.50
Mackowiak,Rob	CWS	58	49	424.2	90	3	2	1	.979	1.97
Mackowiak,Rob	SD	7	5	35.0	8	0	1	0	.889	2.06
Maxwell,Justin	Was	1	1	6.0	1	0	0	0	1.000	1.50

Player	Tm	G	GS	Inn	PO	A	E	DP	Pct.	Rng
Maybin,Cameron	Det	10	9	80.0	22	0	0	0	1.000	2.48
McAnulty,Paul	SD	4	2	22.2	5	0	0	0	1.000	1.99
McLouth,Nate	Pit	24	9	110.1	19	0	0	0	1.000	1.55
Mench,Kevin	Mil	51	44	377.2	55	3	0	1	1.000	1.38
Michaels,Jason	Cle	74	55	499.2	117	4	0	0	1.000	2.18
Miles,Aaron	StL	1	0	0.2	0	0	0	0	-	.00
Millar,Kevin	Bal	3	2	15.0	1	0	0	0	1.000	.60
Milledge,Lastings	NYM	11	8	77.0	20	0	0	0	1.000	2.34
Mohr,Dustan	TB	3	2	18.0	3	0	0	0	1.000	1.50
Monroe,Craig	Det	97	88	795.2	162	6	3	1	.982	1.90
Monroe,Craig	ChC	5	0	10.0	4	0	0	0	1.000	3.60
Moore,Scott	Bal	1	0	2.0	0	0	0	0	-	.00
Moss,Brandon	Bos	13	4	52.0	11	1	0	0	1.000	2.08
Murphy,David	Bos	1	0	1.0	1	0	0	0	1.000	9.00
Murphy,David	Tex	31	5	94.1	25	0	1	0	.962	2.39
Murphy,Tommy	LAA	5	3	28.0	12	1	0	0	1.000	4.18
Murton,Matt	ChC	28	21	185.2	50	1	0	0	1.000	2.47
Nady,Xavier	Pit	10	9	76.2	14	0	0	0	1.000	1.64
Newhan,David	NYM	8	7	67.2	20	0	0	0	1.000	2.66
Nix,Laynce	Mil	1	0	1.1	0	0	0	0	-	.00
Norton,Greg	TB	3	2	20.0	1	0	0	0	1.000	.45
Orr,Pete	Atl	1	0	0.2	0	0	0	0	-	.00
Ortmeier,Dan	SF	22	8	93.1	29	0	0	0	1.000	2.80
Owens,Jerry	CWS	11	2	35.2	5	0	0	0	1.000	1.26
Ozuna,Pablo	CWS	7	6	43.0	13	0	1	0	.929	2.72
Pagan,Angel	ChC	2	0	3.0	0	0	0	0	-	.00
Palmeiro,Orlando	Hou	11	3	40.0	13	1	0	0	1.000	3.15
Patterson,Eric	ChC	2	1	7.0	1	0	0	0	1.000	1.29
Pena,Wily Mo	Bos	22	8	89.0	13	1	0	0	1.000	1.42
Pena,Wily Mo	Was	33	33	274.1	55	0	0	0	1.000	1.80
Perez,Timo	Det	21	19	158.0	41	2	2	0	.956	2.45
Pie,Felix	ChC	2	0	5.0	1	0	0	0	1.000	1.80
Podsednik,Scott	CWS	54	52	460.1	108	4	4	1	.966	2.19
Putnam,Danny	Oak	1	0	7.0	4	0	0	0	1.000	5.14
Quentin,Carlos	Ari	3	1	7.1	3	0	0	0	1.000	3.68
Quinlan,Robb	LAA	16	8	77.0	17	0	0	0	1.000	1.99
Rabe,Josh	Min	7	5	48.0	12	1	0	0	1.000	2.44
Raburn,Ryan	Det	10	7	58.0	16	1	0	1	1.000	2.64
Redman,Tike	Bal	9	7	58.1	16	0	0	0	1.000	2.47
Reed,Jeremy	Sea	3	1	10.0	3	0	0	0	1.000	2.70
Relaford,Desi	Tex	2	0	2.0	0	0	0	0	-	.00
Restovich,Mike	Was	6	6	39.0	10	0	0	0	1.000	2.31
Rivera,Juan	LAA	2	2	15.0	0	0	0	0	-	.00
Roberson,Chris	Phi	1	0	1.0	0	0	0	0	-	.00
Roberts,Dave	SF	20	7	83.1	24	0	0	0	1.000	2.59
Roberts,Ryan	Tor	1	1	6.0	3	0	0	0	1.000	4.50
Ross,Cody	Fla	8	4	47.0	16	1	1	1	.944	3.26
Rottino,Vinny	Mil	1	0	2.0	0	0	0	0	-	.00
Ruggiano,Justin	TB	1	1	7.0	2	0	0	0	1.000	2.57
Salazar,Jeff	Ari	6	1	17.0	3	0	0	0	1.000	1.59
Sanders,Reggie	KC	9	7	57.0	11	0	0	0	1.000	1.74
Sardinha,Bronson	NYY	1	1	9.0	3	0	1	0	.750	3.00
Schumaker,Skip	StL	23	10	122.2	20	0	1	0	.952	1.47
Scott,Luke	Hou	5	1	18.0	4	0	0	0	1.000	2.00
Scutaro,Marco	Oak	6	1	19.1	2	0	0	0	1.000	.93
Sheffield,Gary	Det	7	7	56.0	12	1	0	0	1.000	2.09
Sledge,Terrmel	SD	54	46	399.1	77	2	1	0	.988	1.78
Snelling,Chris	Was	20	10	129.0	28	1	0	0	1.000	2.02
Snelling,Chris	Oak	1	1	9.0	1	0	0	0	1.000	1.00
Snyder,Chris	Ari	1	0	1.0	0	0	0	0	-	.00
Spiezio,Scott	StL	3	2	12.0	1	0	0	0	1.000	.75
Spilborghs,Ryan	Col	15	5	66.1	15	0	0	0	1.000	2.04
Stairs,Matt	Tor	43	35	288.0	46	3	0	0	1.000	1.53
Stocker,Mel	Mil	4	0	6.0	3	0	0	0	1.000	4.50
Sullivan,Cory	Col	1	0	1.0	0	0	0	0	-	.00
Sweeney,Mark	SF	7	5	42.1	6	0	0	0	1.000	1.28
Sweeney,Ryan	CWS	11	10	92.2	19	1	0	1	1.000	1.94
Taguchi,So	StL	41	21	212.1	49	2	2	1	.962	2.16
Terrero,Luis	CWS	5	3	29.0	2	0	0	0	1.000	.62
Thames,Marcus	Det	37	32	276.2	67	1	2	1	.971	2.21
Theriot,Ryan	ChC	4	0	11.0	4	0	0	0	1.000	3.27
Thompson,Kevin	NYY	5	2	22.2	6	0	0	0	1.000	2.38
Thompson,Kevin	Oak	2	1	16.0	2	0	0	0	1.000	1.13
Tyner,Jason	Min	47	33	311.0	89	3	0	0	1.000	2.66

Player	Tm	G	GS	Inn	PO	A	E	DP	Pct.	Rng
Valdez,Wilson	LAD	2	1	8.1	1	0	0	0	1.000	1.08
Velez,Eugenio	SF	2	0	4.0	0	0	0	0	-	.00
Votto,Joey	Cin	6	6	51.0	14	0	1	0	.933	2.47
Walker,Todd	Oak	1	0	1.0	0	0	0	0	-	.00
Ward,Daryle	ChC	1	0	1.0	0	0	0	0	-	.00
Watson,Brandon	Was	1	0	1.0	0	0	0	0	-	.00
Werth,Jayson	Phi	37	8	127.2	35	2	0	1	1.000	2.61
White,Rondell	Min	16	16	125.0	24	0	0	0	1.000	1.73
Wigginton,Ty	Hou	1	0	1.0	0	0	0	0	-	.00
Wilkerson,Brad	Tex	36	33	275.1	73	2	2	0	.974	2.45
Willits,Reggie	LAA	64	57	513.1	151	3	1	1	.994	2.70
Winn,Randy	SF	23	14	137.2	27	2	0	0	1.000	1.90
Wood,Jason	Fla	1	0	2.0	0	0	0	0	-	.00
Young,Delwyn	LAD	6	5	46.0	8	0	0	0	1.000	1.57

Center Fielders - Regulars

Player	Tm	G	GS	Inn	PO	A	E	DP	Pct.	Rng
Crisp,Coco	Bos	144	137	1216.1	408	7	1	4	.998	3.07
Granderson,Curtis	Det	157	140	1285.0	424	10	5	4	.989	3.04
Cabrera,Melky	NYY	131	117	1072.2	346	14	4	1	.989	3.02
Amezaga,Alfredo	Fla	87	71	643.2	208	8	5	1	.977	3.02
Logan,Nook	Was	111	79	755.1	248	2	2	0	.992	2.98
Upton,B.J.	TB	78	74	664.2	204	11	2	2	.991	2.91
Suzuki,Ichiro	Sea	155	155	1339.1	424	8	1	3	.998	2.90
Matthews Jr.,Gary	LAA	135	133	1144.2	362	7	5	3	.987	2.90
Beltran,Carlos	NYM	141	141	1240.1	389	6	5	2	.988	2.87
Pence,Hunter	Hou	95	95	844.2	260	6	4	0	.985	2.83
Jones,Jacque	ChC	84	79	645.0	195	8	4	0	.981	2.83
Taveras,Willy	Col	86	85	714.0	212	7	4	0	.982	2.76
Edmonds,Jim	StL	103	99	828.1	244	8	5	4	.981	2.74
Roberts,Dave	SF	92	87	756.2	223	6	3	0	.987	2.72
DeJesus,David	KC	156	153	1351.1	401	5	4	0	.990	2.70
Hunter,Torii	Min	155	155	1314.2	387	5	2	0	.995	2.68
Jones,Andruw	Atl	154	153	1346.0	396	3	2	1	.995	2.67
Owens,Jerry	CWS	84	81	708.2	208	1	2	1	.991	2.65
Hall,Bill	Mil	130	116	1022.1	295	5	9	0	.971	2.64
Rowand,Aaron	Phi	161	155	1373.2	392	11	2	2	.995	2.64
Sizemore,Grady	Cle	160	157	1408.2	399	4	2	2	.995	2.57
Young,Chris	Ari	146	144	1263.0	354	6	6	2	.984	2.57
Cameron,Mike	SD	150	148	1329.0	365	7	5	2	.987	2.52
Lofton,Kenny	TOT	83	82	690.1	188	5	3	3	.985	2.52
Patterson,Corey	Bal	132	118	1057.1	281	8	3	1	.990	2.46
Pierre,Juan	LAD	162	160	1416.2	366	4	5	0	.987	2.35
Wells,Vernon	Tor	148	143	1279.0	321	5	3	0	.991	2.29

Center Fielders - The Rest

Player	Tm	G	GS	Inn	PO	A	E	DP	Pct.	Rng
Abercrombie,Reggie	Fla	17	15	124.1	54	2	1	0	.982	4.05
Anderson,Brian	CWS	3	3	24.0	8	0	1	0	.889	3.00
Anderson,Josh	Hou	15	15	134.0	30	0	1	0	.968	2.01
Anderson,Marlon	NYM	3	3	22.0	6	0	0	0	1.000	2.45
Ankiel,Rick	StL	22	14	137.0	27	0	0	0	1.000	1.77
Baldelli,Rocco	TB	20	20	162.0	62	3	0	1	1.000	3.61
Barker,Sean	Col	1	0	2.0	1	0	0	0	1.000	4.50
Barmes,Clint	Col	5	2	17.0	3	0	1	0	.750	1.59
Bautista,Jose	Pit	5	4	30.0	6	0	0	0	1.000	1.80
Berkman,Lance	Hou	1	0	1.0	0	0	0	0	-	.00
Bloomquist,Willie	Sea	7	1	20.0	8	0	0	0	1.000	3.60
Bocachica,Hiram	Oak	6	5	46.0	10	0	1	0	.909	1.96
Bocachica,Hiram	SD	6	3	35.0	11	1	0	1	1.000	3.09
Bourn,Michael	Phi	12	6	56.2	16	0	0	0	1.000	2.54
Bradley,Milton	Oak	15	15	125.0	29	0	0	0	1.000	2.09
Bruntlett,Eric	Hou	2	1	12.2	9	0	0	0	1.000	6.39
Buck,Travis	Oak	5	3	28.0	9	0	0	0	1.000	2.89
Burke,Chris	Hou	26	23	201.0	50	1	1	0	.981	2.28
Bynum,Freddie	Bal	5	4	41.0	9	0	0	0	1.000	1.98
Byrd,Marlon	Tex	63	54	496.1	114	4	2	1	.983	2.14
Byrnes,Eric	Ari	23	17	169.0	50	0	0	0	1.000	2.66
Carroll,Brett	Fla	12	9	81.0	29	0	2	0	.935	3.22
Carroll,Jamey	Col	1	0	1.0	1	0	0	0	1.000	9.00
Chavez,Endy	NYM	10	5	58.0	24	0	0	0	1.000	3.72
Church,Ryan	Was	41	39	326.0	118	1	0	0	1.000	3.29

Player	Tm	G	GS	Inn	PO	A	E	DP	Pct.	Rng
Clark,Brady	LAD	2	2	14.0	4	0	0	0	1.000	2.57
Clark,Brady	SD	12	9	87.1	26	0	0	0	1.000	2.68
Clevlen,Brent	Det	1	1	6.0	0	0	0	0	-	.00
Coats,Buck	Cin	2	1	17.0	4	0	0	0	1.000	2.12
Cruz,Jose	SD	3	2	17.0	4	0	0	0	1.000	2.12
Damon,Johnny	NYY	48	45	377.0	121	1	0	0	1.000	2.91
DaVanon,Jeff	Oak	23	14	144.2	36	1	0	0	1.000	2.30
Davis,Rajai	Pit	12	12	83.0	27	0	0	0	1.000	2.93
Davis,Rajai	SF	46	31	296.1	97	3	0	0	1.000	3.04
De Aza,Alejandro	Fla	35	34	303.2	85	3	1	0	.989	2.61
Drew,J.D.	Bos	4	3	29.1	12	0	1	0	.923	3.68
Duffy,Chris	Pit	68	58	534.2	172	3	1	0	.994	2.95
Dukes,Elijah	TB	38	37	332.1	82	3	0	1	1.000	2.30
Ellison,Jason	Sea	7	3	40.0	10	0	0	0	1.000	2.25
Ellison,Jason	Cin	1	1	11.0	8	0	0	0	1.000	6.55
Ellsbury,Jacoby	Bos	16	12	107.0	38	0	0	0	1.000	3.20
Encarnacion,Juan	StL	2	0	3.2	1	0	0	0	1.000	2.45
Erstad,Darin	CWS	45	43	371.1	105	1	1	0	.991	2.57
Finley,Steve	Col	26	15	155.1	45	1	0	1	1.000	2.67
Ford,Lew	Min	14	0	37.0	7	0	0	0	1.000	1.70
Freel,Ryan	Cin	59	49	444.1	136	3	2	0	.986	2.82
Fuld,Sam	ChC	1	0	1.0	0	0	0	0	-	.00
Gathright,Joey	KC	10	5	56.0	16	0	1	0	.941	2.57
Giles,Brian	SD	1	1	6.0	1	0	0	0	1.000	1.50
Gomez,Carlos	NYM	4	0	12.0	4	0	0	0	1.000	3.00
Gonzalez,Andy	CWS	9	6	53.0	16	1	0	1	1.000	2.89
Gross,Gabe	Mil	5	3	26.0	9	1	0	1	1.000	3.46
Gutierrez,Franklin	Cle	8	2	32.0	11	0	0	0	1.000	3.09
Guzman,Freddy	Tex	3	1	12.0	5	0	0	0	1.000	3.75
Gwynn,Tony	Mil	27	15	153.1	34	0	1	0	.971	2.00
Hairston,Jerry	Tex	22	14	134.1	50	2	1	0	.981	3.48
Hairston,Scott	Ari	1	0	1.0	0	0	0	0	-	.00
Hairston,Scott	SD	2	0	5.0	1	0	0	0	1.000	1.80
Hamilton,Josh	Cin	71	64	555.2	168	6	4	2	.978	2.82
Harris,Willie	Atl	20	9	110.1	35	0	0	0	1.000	2.85
Hart,Corey	Mil	34	28	232.1	71	1	2	0	.973	2.79
Haynes,Nathan	LAA	12	5	59.1	10	0	0	0	1.000	1.52
Hopper,Norris	Cin	55	46	408.1	133	2	1	1	.993	2.98
Infante,Omar	Det	12	10	68.0	19	0	0	0	1.000	2.51
Jimerson,Charlton	Sea	1	0	1.0	0	0	0	0	-	.00
Johnson,Reed	Tor	1	1	8.0	1	0	0	0	1.000	1.13
Jones,Adam	Sea	7	3	34.0	10	0	1	0	.909	2.65
Kearns,Austin	Was	6	1	21.2	6	0	0	0	1.000	2.49
Kemp,Matt	LAD	6	0	17.1	8	0	0	0	1.000	4.15
Kielty,Bobby	Oak	1	0	2.0	0	0	0	0	-	.00
Kotsay,Mark	Oak	56	53	472.2	141	5	2	3	.986	2.78
Lane,Jason	Hou	36	27	260.2	80	2	0	1	1.000	2.83
Lane,Jason	SD	1	0	1.1	1	0	0	0	1.000	6.75
Langerhans,Ryan	Oak	2	2	14.0	5	1	1	0	.857	3.86
Langerhans,Ryan	Was	38	33	260.2	89	0	1	0	.989	3.07
Lewis,Fred	SF	5	4	41.0	12	0	0	0	1.000	2.63
Linden,Todd	SF	9	9	75.0	23	2	2	0	.926	3.00
Linden,Todd	Fla	4	3	31.2	10	0	0	0	1.000	2.84
Lofton,Kenny	Tex	80	79	669.1	186	5	3	3	.985	2.57
Lofton,Kenny	Cle	3	3	21.0	2	0	0	0	1.000	.86
Ludwick,Ryan	StL	6	3	22.0	7	0	0	0	1.000	2.86
Mackowiak,Rob	SD	1	0	4.0	0	0	0	0	-	.00
Mahar,Kevin	Tex	5	4	37.1	9	0	0	0	1.000	2.17
Maxwell,Justin	Was	5	5	41.0	16	0	0	0	1.000	3.51
Maybin,Cameron	Det	5	2	25.0	10	0	0	0	1.000	3.60
McLouth,Nate	Pit	66	53	495.1	142	2	2	1	.986	2.62
Michaels,Jason	Cle	1	0	1.0	1	0	0	0	1.000	9.00
Milledge,Lastings	NYM	14	13	120.0	41	2	1	0	.977	3.23
Mohr,Dustan	TB	1	1	8.0	6	0	0	0	1.000	6.75
Monroe,Craig	ChC	7	7	39.0	10	0	0	0	1.000	2.31
Morgan,Nyjer	Pit	28	25	221.2	84	2	1	2	.989	3.49
Murphy,David	Tex	10	10	78.2	23	0	0	0	1.000	2.63
Murphy,Tommy	LAA	2	0	4.0	1	0	0	0	1.000	2.25
Murton,Matt	ChC	1	0	1.0	0	0	0	0	-	.00
Nady,Xavier	Pit	11	10	83.0	17	0	1	0	.944	1.84
Nix,Laynce	Mil	4	0	10.1	1	0	0	0	1.000	.87
Ortmeier,Dan	SF	1	0	0.1	0	0	0	0	-	.00
Pagan,Angel	ChC	34	28	236.0	60	0	0	0	1.000	2.29
Payton,Jay	Bal	17	14	107.1	41	1	2	1	.955	3.52

Player	Tm	G	GS	Inn	PO	A	E	DP	Pct.	Rng
Pena,Wily Mo	Bos	12	10	86.0	23	2	2	1	.926	2.62
Pie,Felix	ChC	80	36	424.1	120	1	0	0	1.000	2.57
Podsednik,Scott	CWS	3	2	20.0	2	0	0	0	1.000	.90
Putnam,Danny	Oak	6	4	46.0	7	0	0	0	1.000	1.37
Raburn,Ryan	Det	13	9	63.1	15	0	0	0	1.000	2.13
Redman,Tike	Bal	28	25	231.0	78	1	1	1	.988	3.08
Reed,Eric	Fla	4	2	20.0	4	0	0	0	1.000	1.80
Rios,Alex	Tor	22	18	161.2	44	1	2	0	.957	2.51
Roberson,Chris	Phi	2	0	10.0	4	0	0	0	1.000	3.60
Ross,Cody	Fla	36	28	239.1	63	2	1	1	.985	2.44
Ruggiano,Justin	TB	3	2	20.0	3	0	0	0	1.000	1.35
Salazar,Jeff	Ari	1	1	8.0	2	0	0	0	1.000	2.25
Schumaker,Skip	StL	15	5	64.1	20	1	0	0	1.000	2.94
Scott,Luke	Hou	3	1	10.2	4	0	0	0	1.000	3.38
Snelling,Chris	Oak	5	5	38.2	8	1	0	0	1.000	2.09
Soriano,Alfonso	ChC	12	12	100.1	29	0	0	0	1.000	2.60
Spilborghs,Ryan	Col	46	37	325.2	75	2	1	1	.987	2.13
Stern,Adam	Bal	2	0	2.0	0	0	0	0	-	.00
Stewart,Shannon	Oak	6	3	32.0	12	0	1	0	.923	3.38
Sullivan,Cory	Col	51	24	257.0	77	1	0	1	1.000	2.73
Sweeney,Ryan	CWS	3	3	26.0	6	0	0	0	1.000	2.08
Swisher,Nick	Oak	59	56	481.0	139	1	2	0	.986	2.62
Taguchi,So	StL	63	41	380.1	118	1	1	1	.992	2.82
Teahen,Mark	KC	5	4	30.0	8	0	0	0	1.000	2.40
Terrero,Luis	CWS	38	24	237.2	70	2	1	1	.986	2.73
Thompson,Kevin	NYY	1	0	1.0	0	0	0	0	-	.00
Thompson,Kevin	Oak	5	2	18.0	2	0	1	0	.667	1.00
Tyner,Jason	Min	17	7	85.0	19	0	0	0	1.000	2.01
Valdez,Wilson	LAD	1	0	2.0	1	0	0	0	1.000	4.50
Victorino,Shane	Phi	4	1	16.0	3	0	0	0	1.000	1.69
Watson,Brandon	Was	5	5	42.0	9	0	0	0	1.000	1.93
Werth,Jayson	Phi	2	0	2.0	3	0	0	0	1.000	13.50
Wilkerson,Brad	Tex	1	0	2.0	1	0	0	0	1.000	4.50
Willits,Reggie	LAA	30	24	227.0	68	0	1	0	.986	2.70
Winn,Randy	SF	36	31	284.1	82	0	0	0	1.000	2.60
Wise,Dewayne	Cin	4	1	13.1	6	0	0	0	1.000	4.05
Young,Delmon	TB	29	28	242.2	62	0	3	0	.954	2.30

Right Fielders - Regulars

Player	Tm	G	GS	Inn	PO	A	E	DP	Pct.	Rng
Hart,Corey	Mil	113	94	864.1	253	3	1	0	.996	2.67
Teahen,Mark	KC	137	130	1150.2	318	17	6	7	.982	2.62
Kearns,Austin	Was	158	156	1376.1	374	9	2	4	.995	2.50
Victorino,Shane	Phi	114	100	918.2	229	10	3	4	.988	2.34
Hermida,Jeremy	Fla	116	114	985.2	247	7	9	1	.966	2.32
Griffey Jr.,Ken	Cin	133	131	1163.0	291	5	8	2	.974	2.29
Dye,Jermaine	CWS	135	135	1156.0	284	9	3	3	.990	2.28
Cruz,Nelson	Tex	82	65	604.1	148	5	5	1	.968	2.28
Scott,Luke	Hou	101	90	817.0	196	8	3	2	.986	2.25
Winn,Randy	SF	104	98	869.0	209	3	2	0	.991	2.20
Francoeur,Jeff	Atl	162	162	1440.2	327	19	5	2	.986	2.16
Abreu,Bobby	NYY	157	150	1333.0	313	6	4	1	.988	2.15
Young,Delmon	TB	133	127	1134.0	252	16	4	7	.985	2.13
Ethier,Andre	LAD	102	91	779.2	176	8	4	1	.979	2.12
Guerrero,Vladimir	LAA	108	108	930.2	208	5	9	3	.959	2.06
Markakis,Nick	Bal	161	158	1399.2	303	13	2	4	.994	2.03
Cuddyer,Michael	Min	140	140	1224.1	256	19	4	2	.986	2.02
Green,Shawn	NYM	110	107	919.2	203	2	3	0	.986	2.01
Nady,Xavier	Pit	94	89	748.0	161	4	0	0	1.000	1.99
Guillen,Jose	Sea	150	150	1273.2	268	9	8	3	.972	1.96
Ordonez,Magglio	Det	143	142	1221.0	261	4	1	2	.996	1.95
Kemp,Matt	LAD	88	66	619.2	129	2	4	1	.970	1.90
Giles,Brian	SD	120	119	1062.2	216	2	5	1	.978	1.85
Encarnacion,Juan	StL	74	72	615.1	124	2	8	0	.940	1.84
Hawpe,Brad	Col	142	137	1236.2	246	6	6	1	.977	1.83
Drew,J.D.	Bos	133	123	1062.0	212	3	5	1	.977	1.82
Rios,Alex	Tor	147	139	1250.0	243	10	5	1	.981	1.82
Nixon,Trot	Cle	87	82	675.0	129	4	4	2	.971	1.77

Right Fielders - The Rest

Player	Tm	G	GS	Inn	PO	A	E	DP	Pct.	Rng
Abercrombie,Reggie	Fla	2	1	9.1	3	0	0	0	1.000	2.89

Player	Tm	G	GS	Inn	PO	A	E	DP	Pct.	Rng
Ambres,Chip	NYM	1	0	2.0	0	0	0	0	-	.00
Amezaga,Alfredo	Fla	3	0	3.0	2	0	0	0	1.000	6.00
Anderson,Josh	Hou	1	0	2.0	1	0	0	0	1.000	4.50
Anderson,Marlon	NYM	1	1	8.0	2	2	0	0	1.000	4.50
Ankiel,Rick	StL	27	24	197.2	58	2	2	0	.968	2.73
Aybar,Erick	LAA	2	0	3.0	0	0	0	0	-	.00
Baker,Jeff	Col	13	12	92.0	22	1	0	0	1.000	2.25
Balentien,Wladimir	Sea	2	0	4.0	0	0	0	0	-	.00
Bautista,Jose	Pit	16	13	130.0	23	1	2	0	.923	1.66
Berkman,Lance	Hou	31	27	229.2	49	1	2	1	.962	1.96
Betemit,Wilson	LAD	1	0	1.2	0	0	0	0	-	.00
Blake,Casey	Cle	7	7	54.0	13	2	0	2	1.000	2.50
Bloomquist,Willie	Sea	4	0	4.0	2	0	0	0	1.000	4.50
Bocachica,Hiram	SD	15	11	101.0	21	1	0	0	1.000	1.96
Borchard,Joe	Fla	34	31	277.1	78	1	1	1	.988	2.56
Bourn,Michael	Phi	6	3	29.2	8	0	0	0	1.000	2.43
Bradley,Milton	Oak	3	3	23.0	5	0	0	0	1.000	1.96
Bradley,Milton	SD	1	0	6.0	1	0	0	0	1.000	1.50
Broussard,Ben	Sea	12	10	82.0	21	0	0	0	1.000	2.30
Brown,Dee	Oak	4	0	8.0	1	0	0	0	1.000	1.13
Brown,Emil	KC	21	17	150.2	42	1	0	0	1.000	2.57
Bruntlett,Eric	Hou	1	0	2.0	0	0	1	0	.000	.00
Buck,Travis	Oak	65	56	509.1	110	2	0	0	1.000	1.98
Burke,Chris	Hou	20	15	132.0	26	1	1	1	.964	1.84
Byrd,Marlon	Tex	40	36	304.1	78	5	1	4	.988	2.45
Byrnes,Eric	Ari	35	29	250.1	62	3	1	1	.985	2.34
Cabrera,Melky	NYY	5	4	35.0	5	0	0	0	1.000	1.29
Callaspo,Alberto	Ari	7	7	61.0	12	1	0	0	1.000	1.92
Carroll,Brett	Fla	5	2	22.0	13	0	0	0	1.000	5.32
Carroll,Jamey	Col	2	1	10.0	1	0	0	0	1.000	.90
Castillo,Jose	Pit	1	0	3.0	3	0	0	0	1.000	9.00
Chavez,Endy	NYM	24	8	100.0	31	0	0	0	1.000	2.79
Choo,Shin-Soo	Cle	1	0	11.0	0	0	0	0	-	.00
Clark,Brady	LAD	13	5	48.0	11	0	1	0	.917	2.06
Clark,Brady	SD	2	1	11.0	1	0	0	0	1.000	.82
Cleven,Brent	Det	4	0	5.1	2	0	0	0	1.000	3.38
Coats,Buck	Cin	5	2	27.2	4	1	1	0	.833	1.63
Conine,Jeff	Cin	1	0	4.0	1	0	0	0	1.000	2.25
Conine,Jeff	NYM	1	0	2.0	1	0	0	0	1.000	4.50
Costa,Shane	KC	13	7	73.0	23	0	0	0	1.000	2.84
Cruz,Jose	SD	23	20	178.1	54	1	0	1	1.000	2.78
Cust,Jack	Oak	48	46	382.0	79	1	3	0	.964	1.88
Damon,Johnny	NYY	1	0	3.0	1	0	0	0	1.000	3.00
DaVanon,Jeff	Ari	7	5	52.0	10	0	1	0	.909	1.73
DaVanon,Jeff	Oak	1	0	1.0	0	0	0	0	-	.00
Davis,Rajai	SF	1	1	8.0	0	0	0	0	-	.00
DeRosa,Mark	ChC	22	13	138.2	28	1	0	0	1.000	1.88
Diaz,Matt	Atl	5	0	15.2	3	0	0	0	1.000	1.72
Diaz,Victor	Tex	24	19	161.1	33	0	1	0	.971	1.84
Dillon,Joe	Mil	1	1	6.0	1	0	0	0	1.000	1.50
Dobbs,Greg	Phi	3	1	10.0	3	0	0	0	1.000	2.70
Doumit,Ryan	Pit	38	33	311.0	62	5	1	2	.985	1.94
Dukes,Elijah	TB	1	0	1.1	0	0	0	0	-	.00
Duncan,Shelley	NYY	8	4	43.0	11	2	0	1	1.000	2.72
Easley,Damion	NYM	6	5	43.0	9	0	0	0	1.000	1.88
Eldred,Brad	Pit	8	7	51.2	8	0	0	0	1.000	1.39
Ellison,Jason	Sea	29	0	41.0	8	0	0	0	1.000	1.76
Ellison,Jason	Cin	11	9	82.0	26	1	0	0	1.000	2.96
Ellsbury,Jacoby	Bos	1	1	6.0	0	0	0	0	-	.00
Erstad,Darin	CWS	9	8	76.1	12	1	0	0	1.000	1.53
Evans,Terry	LAA	6	2	23.0	2	0	0	0	1.000	.78
Feliz,Pedro	SF	1	0	2.0	0	0	0	0	-	.00
Fick,Robert	Was	7	3	30.2	4	0	0	0	1.000	1.17
Figgins,Chone	LAA	11	11	86.0	17	1	0	0	1.000	1.88
Finley,Steve	Col	3	0	6.0	1	0	0	0	1.000	1.50
Floyd,Cliff	ChC	63	60	412.1	69	1	0	0	1.000	1.53
Ford,Lew	Min	3	2	23.0	6	0	0	0	1.000	2.35
Fox,Jake	ChC	3	3	22.0	2	0	0	0	1.000	.82
Francisco,Ben	Cle	5	3	28.0	6	0	0	0	1.000	1.93
Frandsen,Kevin	SF	3	2	18.0	5	0	1	0	.833	2.50
Fuld,Sam	ChC	6	1	22.0	9	1	0	1	1.000	4.09
Furmaniak,J.J.	Oak	2	0	3.0	1	0	0	0	1.000	3.00
Gall,John	Fla	1	1	6.0	1	0	0	0	1.000	1.50
Gibbons,Jay	Bal	2	2	14.0	3	0	0	0	1.000	1.93

Player	Tm	G	GS	Inn	PO	A	E	DP	Pct.	Rng
Gomes,Jonny	TB	32	30	252.2	53	3	0	1	1.000	1.99
Gomez,Carlos	NYM	22	14	133.2	35	1	2	0	.947	2.42
Gonzalez,Andy	CWS	10	6	63.0	15	0	0	0	1.000	2.14
Griffin,John-Ford	Tor	3	3	24.0	5	0	0	0	1.000	1.88
Gross,Gabe	Mil	45	39	288.2	70	2	2	0	.973	2.24
Gutierrez,Franklin	Cle	88	59	578.2	136	3	1	1	.993	2.16
Gwynn,Tony	Mil	10	7	62.2	14	1	0	0	1.000	2.15
Hairston,Jerry	Tex	6	4	39.0	8	0	0	0	1.000	1.85
Hamilton,Josh	Cin	10	9	81.0	27	1	0	0	1.000	3.11
Hammock,Robby	Ari	2	0	4.1	1	0	0	0	1.000	2.08
Haynes,Nathan	LAA	13	2	37.0	11	0	0	0	1.000	2.68
Hill,Koyie	ChC	1	0	1.0	0	0	0	0	-	.00
Hinske,Eric	Bos	12	9	82.1	16	0	0	0	1.000	1.75
Hopper,Norris	Cin	13	10	84.2	27	2	0	0	1.000	3.08
Infante,Omar	Det	6	0	13.0	4	0	0	0	1.000	2.77
Jimerson,Charlton	Sea	2	0	2.0	1	0	0	0	1.000	4.50
Johnson,Ben	NYM	4	2	23.0	7	0	0	0	1.000	2.74
Johnson,Reed	Tor	8	7	71.2	13	1	0	0	1.000	1.76
Jones,Adam	Sea	6	2	23.2	5	0	0	0	1.000	1.90
Jones,Garrett	Min	1	1	8.0	3	0	0	0	1.000	3.38
Jones,Jacque	ChC	67	32	349.0	75	0	0	0	1.000	1.93
Kata,Matt	Pit	1	0	1.0	0	0	0	0	-	.00
Kelly,Don	Pit	1	0	0.0	0	0	0	0	-	
Kennedy,Adam	StL	1	0	1.2	0	0	0	0	-	.00
Keppinger,Jeff	Cin	1	1	7.1	1	1	0	0	1.000	2.45
Kielty,Bobby	Oak	7	6	53.0	9	0	0	0	1.000	1.53
Kielty,Bobby	Bos	10	6	67.0	14	0	0	0	1.000	1.88
Klesko,Ryan	SF	1	1	9.0	2	0	0	0	1.000	2.00
Lamb,Mike	Hou	1	0	0.2	0	0	0	0	-	.00
Lane,Jason	Hou	18	15	127.2	43	0	0	0	1.000	3.03
Lane,Jason	SD	1	0	2.0	0	0	0	0	-	.00
Langerhans,Ryan	Was	7	2	27.0	10	0	0	0	1.000	3.33
Lewis,Fred	SF	27	24	205.2	53	0	0	0	1.000	2.32
Linden,Todd	SF	3	2	16.0	3	0	1	0	.750	1.69
Linden,Todd	Fla	8	3	34.0	5	0	0	0	1.000	1.32
Loney,James	LAD	1	0	1.0	0	0	0	0	-	.00
Lowry,Noah	SF	1	0	0.1	0	0	0	0	-	.00
Ludwick,Ryan	StL	41	25	252.1	60	0	1	0	.984	2.14
Luna,Hector	Tor	1	0	1.0	0	0	0	0	-	.00
Mackowiak,Rob	CWS	14	9	88.2	22	1	1	0	.958	2.33
Mackowiak,Rob	SD	9	6	62.0	16	1	0	0	1.000	2.47
Mahar,Kevin	Tex	2	0	3.0	1	0	0	0	1.000	3.00
McAnulty,Paul	SD	5	4	40.1	11	0	0	0	1.000	2.45
McDonald,Darnell	Min	3	3	25.0	2	1	0	1	1.000	1.08
McLouth,Nate	Pit	18	4	68.0	22	0	1	0	.957	2.91
Mench,Kevin	Mil	33	21	219.2	56	3	2	1	.967	2.42
Michaels,Jason	Cle	27	10	116.0	29	0	1	0	.967	2.25
Milledge,Lastings	NYM	28	25	221.0	51	0	1	0	.981	2.08
Mohr,Dustan	TB	1	1	9.0	0	0	0	0	-	.00
Monroe,Craig	Det	1	0	4.0	1	0	0	0	1.000	2.25
Monroe,Craig	ChC	8	6	46.0	8	0	0	0	1.000	1.57
Morales,Kendry	LAA	6	1	16.0	4	0	0	0	1.000	2.25
Morse,Mike	Sea	1	0	3.0	0	0	0	0	-	.00
Moss,Brandon	Bos	4	1	12.0	1	0	0	0	1.000	.75
Murphy,David	Bos	1	0	4.0	1	0	0	0	1.000	2.25
Murphy,David	Tex	14	10	76.0	13	4	0	1	1.000	2.01
Murphy,Tommy	LAA	9	5	55.1	16	0	0	0	1.000	2.60
Murton,Matt	ChC	41	32	282.2	65	2	4	1	.944	2.13
Norton,Greg	TB	6	4	31.2	3	1	0	0	1.000	1.14
Ortmeier,Dan	SF	13	9	89.0	17	0	0	0	1.000	1.72
Pagan,Angel	ChC	29	4	92.0	20	0	0	0	1.000	1.96
Palmeiro,Orlando	Hou	16	2	37.0	7	1	0	0	1.000	1.95
Payton,Jay	Bal	6	2	25.0	8	0	0	0	1.000	2.88
Pearce,Steve	Pit	18	16	135.0	31	1	0	0	1.000	2.13
Pena,Wily Mo	Bos	36	22	205.1	43	0	1	0	.977	1.88
Pena,Wily Mo	Was	1	1	9.0	2	0	0	0	1.000	2.00
Pence,Hunter	Hou	14	13	115.2	36	0	2	0	.947	2.80
Perez,Timo	Det	4	3	27.0	3	0	0	0	1.000	1.00
Putnam,Danny	Oak	4	3	28.0	8	0	1	0	.889	2.57
Quentin,Carlos	Ari	75	63	577.0	138	2	1	0	.993	2.18
Quinlan,Robb	LAA	2	0	19.0	3	0	0	0	1.000	1.42
Rabe,Josh	Min	2	1	12.0	2	0	0	0	1.000	1.50
Raburn,Ryan	Det	16	9	90.0	24	0	0	0	1.000	2.40
Reed,Jeremy	Sea	1	0	1.0	0	0	0	0	-	.00

Player	Tm	G	GS	Inn	PO	A	E	DP	Pct.	Rng
Restovich,Mike	Was	2	0	3.2	1	0	0	0	1.000	2.45
Reynolds,Mark	Ari	2	0	3.0	1	0	0	0	1.000	3.00
Rivera,Juan	LAA	7	7	53.0	9	1	0	0	1.000	1.70
Roberson,Chris	Phi	16	3	54.0	14	1	1	1	.938	2.50
Ross,Cody	Fla	19	10	106.1	30	2	1	2	.970	2.71
Ruggiano,Justin	TB	1	0	1.0	1	0	0	0	1.000	9.00
Salazar,Jeff	Ari	27	20	178.0	47	3	0	1	1.000	2.53
Sanders,Reggie	KC	9	8	63.0	27	0	0	0	1.000	3.86
Sardinha,Bronson	NYY	4	1	12.2	3	0	0	0	1.000	2.13
Schierholtz,Nate	SF	30	24	229.1	48	0	1	0	.980	1.88
Schumaker,Skip	StL	26	12	115.1	24	0	1	0	.960	1.87
Scutaro,Marco	Oak	4	2	26.0	8	0	0	0	1.000	2.77
Sheffield,Gary	Det	7	5	50.0	13	0	0	0	1.000	2.34
Sledge,Terrmel	SD	6	2	21.1	11	0	0	0	1.000	4.64
Smith,Seth	Col	1	0	2.0	0	0	0	0	-	.00
Sosa,Sammy	Tex	16	16	131.0	32	1	0	0	1.000	2.27
Spiezio,Scott	StL	15	13	106.1	17	0	1	0	.944	1.44
Spilborghs,Ryan	Col	20	13	124.1	25	0	0	0	1.000	1.81
Stairs,Matt	Tor	17	13	102.0	20	0	0	0	1.000	1.76
Stocker,Mel	Mil	2	0	3.0	0	0	0	0	-	.00
Sullivan,Cory	Col	1	0	1.0	0	0	0	0	-	.00
Sweeney,Mark	SF	3	1	7.1	1	0	0	0	1.000	1.23
Swisher,Nick	Oak	57	46	413.2	107	2	0	0	1.000	2.37
Taguchi,So	StL	8	2	23.1	5	0	0	0	1.000	1.93
Terrero,Luis	CWS	15	4	56.2	12	0	0	0	1.000	1.91
Thames,Marcus	Det	9	3	37.0	10	0	0	0	1.000	2.43
Theriot,Ryan	ChC	2	1	7.0	1	0	0	0	1.000	1.29
Thompson,Kevin	NYY	5	3	24.0	8	0	0	0	1.000	3.00
Thompson,Kevin	Oak	1	0	1.0	0	0	0	0	-	.00
Tyner,Jason	Min	18	15	144.1	37	0	1	0	.974	2.31
Upton,Justin	Ari	42	38	315.1	65	1	5	0	.930	1.88
Ward,Daryle	ChC	10	10	74.0	25	1	0	0	1.000	3.16
Werth,Jayson	Phi	58	55	446.0	109	7	2	1	.983	2.34
Wigginton,Ty	Hou	1	0	1.0	0	0	0	0	-	.00
Wilkerson,Brad	Tex	19	12	111.0	27	0	0	0	1.000	2.19
Willits,Reggie	LAA	31	24	212.0	41	3	1	0	.978	1.87
Wilson,Preston	StL	16	14	123.2	27	0	2	0	.931	1.96

Catchers - Regulars

Player	Tm	G	GS	Inn	PO	A	E	DP	PB	Pct.
Snyder,Chris	Ari	106	103	891.1	722	58	1	9	9	.999
Mauer,Joe	Min	91	88	777.2	598	35	1	5	4	.998
Johjima,Kenji	Sea	133	128	1106.2	805	56	2	15	5	.998
Pierzynski,A.J.	CWS	130	116	1058.0	796	46	2	6	14	.998
Ruiz,Carlos	Phi	111	100	912.2	688	54	2	4	5	.997
Bard,Josh	SD	108	103	927.1	751	39	3	4	3	.996
Martinez,Victor	Cle	121	118	1042.2	779	53	4	8	6	.995
Ausmus,Brad	Hou	114	101	906.2	763	47	4	5	2	.995
Posada,Jorge	NYY	138	125	1111.1	799	54	5	6	13	.994
Varitek,Jason	Bos	125	121	1064.0	937	39	6	8	4	.994
Rodriguez,Ivan	Det	127	119	1052.2	834	50	6	7	7	.993
Ross,Dave	Cin	108	98	837.1	662	50	5	7	6	.993
Estrada,Johnny	Mil	113	111	961.0	803	37	6	6	5	.993
Schneider,Brian	Was	122	120	1051.1	702	53	6	4	5	.992
Paulino,Ronny	Pit	129	119	1088.0	784	58	7	9	8	.992
Molina,Bengie	SF	129	125	1104.0	808	61	8	4	16	.991
Barrett,Michael	TOT	95	83	768.0	613	34	6	2	12	.991
Molina,Yadier	StL	107	101	861.1	582	63	6	8	7	.991
Torrealba,Yorvit	Col	112	105	935.1	679	56	7	7	4	.991
Kendall,Jason	TOT	132	130	1146.0	847	58	9	6	12	.990
Hernandez,Ramon	Bal	104	97	855.0	636	44	7	4	9	.990
Buck,John	KC	112	104	924.1	697	29	8	6	3	.989
Lo Duca,Paul	NYM	113	112	974.0	754	34	9	5	2	.989
Martin,Russell	LAD	145	143	1254.0	1065	85	14	11	5	.988
Zaun,Gregg	Tor	103	93	838.1	590	41	8	4	2	.987
McCann,Brian	Atl	132	130	1139.0	907	53	13	9	6	.987
Olivo,Miguel	Fla	119	111	990.1	787	64	12	9	16	.986
Navarro,Dioner	TB	112	110	956.1	814	67	14	11	6	.984
Laird,Gerald	Tex	119	114	987.1	675	75	12	13	9	.984

Catchers - The Rest

Player	Tm	G	GS	Inn	PO	A	E	DP	PB	Pct.
Alfonzo,Eliezer	SF	17	12	122.0	97	7	3	0	1	.972
Alomar Jr.,Sandy	NYM	6	4	41.0	29	5	0	0	0	1.000
Bako,Paul	Bal	57	47	421.0	324	24	4	5	8	.989
Barajas,Rod	Phi	38	37	303.0	252	14	0	3	1	1.000
Barrett,Michael	ChC	55	52	475.1	389	18	5	2	8	.988
Barrett,Michael	SD	40	31	292.2	224	16	1	0	4	.996
Bellorin,Edwin	Col	2	1	5.0	3	0	0	0	0	1.000
Bennett,Gary	StL	52	41	370.1	244	9	1	1	2	.996
Biggio,Craig	Hou	1	1	2.0	1	0	0	0	0	1.000
Blanco,Henry	ChC	14	13	109.0	102	4	0	1	2	1.000
Bowen,Rob	SD	26	22	208.0	136	13	3	2	2	.980
Bowen,Rob	ChC	9	9	76.1	78	3	1	1	0	.988
Bowen,Rob	Oak	21	14	130.2	92	4	1	0	1	.990
Budde,Ryan	LAA	10	5	46.1	36	1	1	0	0	.974
Burke,Jamie	Sea	48	34	321.2	259	9	1	0	3	.996
Casanova,Raul	TB	23	19	168.2	138	9	3	3	4	.980
Cash,Kevin	Bos	12	8	82.0	56	8	1	2	0	.985
Castillo,Alberto	Bal	11	11	91.2	92	7	0	1	1	1.000
Castro,Ramon	NYM	50	35	330.2	303	12	4	1	1	.987
Coste,Chris	Phi	31	25	242.2	157	12	0	3	2	1.000
Cota,Humberto	Pit	5	5	41.0	30	2	0	0	0	1.000
DiFelice,Mike	NYM	16	11	106.2	83	7	2	0	2	.978
Doumit,Ryan	Pit	28	28	223.2	149	7	2	2	5	.987
Esposito,Brian	StL	1	0	1.0	1	0	0	0	0	1.000
Fasano,Sal	Tor	16	14	120.1	93	5	3	0	1	.970
Feliz,Pedro	SF	1	0	0.1	0	0	0	0	0	-
Flores,Jesus	Was	55	42	395.1	262	30	4	1	4	.986
Gil,Geronimo	Col	4	3	35.0	21	3	0	0	1	1.000
Hall,Toby	CWS	37	35	292.2	187	10	3	1	5	.985
Hammock,Robby	Ari	12	2	39.0	41	6	0	0	1	1.000
Hanigan,Ryan	Cin	3	2	20.0	16	0	0	0	0	1.000
Heintz,Chris	Min	21	14	137.1	106	9	0	0	1	1.000
Hill,Koyie	ChC	31	25	232.1	190	11	1	3	1	.995
Hoover,Paul	Fla	1	1	12.2	12	0	0	0	0	1.000
House,J.R.	Bal	9	5	40.0	31	2	0	0	1	1.000
Iannetta,Chris	Col	60	54	496.2	301	27	1	1	4	.997
Johnson,Rob	Sea	4	0	6.0	2	0	0	0	0	1.000
Jorgensen,Ryan	Cin	4	4	34.0	29	1	1	0	0	.968
Kendall,Jason	Oak	80	80	714.1	485	34	4	4	7	.992
Kendall,Jason	ChC	52	50	431.2	362	24	5	2	5	.987
LaForest,Pete	SD	7	7	56.2	49	1	1	0	0	.980
LaRue,Jason	KC	65	54	474.1	311	24	5	3	2	.985
LeCroy,Matthew	Min	4	4	35.0	22	0	1	0	1	.957
Lieberthal,Mike	LAD	31	17	167.0	136	11	3	3	0	.980
Lucy,Donny	CWS	5	4	33.0	27	1	0	0	0	1.000
Maldonado,Carlos	Pit	13	8	79.0	64	2	0	0	0	1.000
Mathis,Jeff	LAA	57	52	467.0	383	42	4	2	5	.991
Melhuse,Adam	Oak	10	7	64.0	42	5	0	1	1	1.000
Melhuse,Adam	Tex	15	13	123.0	80	5	0	0	2	1.000
Miller,Corky	Atl	11	6	62.0	49	3	0	1	1	1.000
Miller,Damian	Mil	56	50	446.1	359	28	1	2	1	.997
Mirabelli,Doug	Bos	46	33	292.2	194	19	1	4	6	.995
Moeller,Chad	Cin	17	9	86.2	72	5	0	0	0	1.000
Moeller,Chad	LAD	7	2	29.0	25	1	0	0	0	1.000
Molina,Gustavo	CWS	9	7	57.0	41	1	0	0	1	1.000
Molina,Gustavo	Bal	7	2	25.0	12	2	0	0	0	1.000
Molina,Jose	LAA	40	37	323.0	283	17	4	2	2	.987
Molina,Jose	NYY	29	16	169.1	153	13	0	1	2	1.000
Montero,Miguel	Ari	73	57	510.2	340	30	6	5	5	.984
Morales,Jose	Min	1	1	4.0	5	1	0	0	0	1.000
Munson,Eric	Hou	43	36	309.1	215	14	2	2	2	.991
Napoli,Mike	LAA	75	68	598.2	460	32	7	2	1	.986
Nieves,Wil	NYY	25	21	169.0	111	6	2	1	1	.983
Paul,Josh	TB	35	30	277.2	228	21	2	3	4	.992
Pena,Brayan	Atl	10	5	59.1	52	2	0	1	1	1.000
Phelps,Josh	NYY	1	0	1.0	0	0	0	0	0	-
Phelps,Josh	Pit	3	2	16.0	9	1	0	0	0	1.000
Phillips,Jason	Tor	49	41	363.2	308	14	3	2	2	.991
Phillips,Paul	KC	7	3	38.2	29	1	0	0	0	1.000
Quintero,Humberto	Hou	26	15	151.2	97	13	2	0	1	.982
Quiroz,Guillermo	Tex	8	2	28.2	25	0	2	0	0	.926
Rabelo,Mike	Det	49	43	394.2	246	21	5	5	3	.982
Redmond,Mike	Min	56	55	482.2	385	24	0	4	0	1.000
Riggans,Shawn	TB	3	3	27.0	31	1	2	0	0	.941
Rivera,Mike	Mil	11	1	37.0	33	2	0	0	0	1.000
Rodriguez,Guillermo	SF	33	25	227.1	179	17	4	1	4	.980
Saltalamacchia,J	Atl	25	20	187.0	138	12	1	3	2	.993
Saltalamacchia,J	Tex	22	22	185.2	127	5	2	1	0	.985
Sammons,Clint	Atl	2	1	9.0	5	1	0	0	0	1.000
Shoppach,Kelly	Cle	58	44	420.0	287	28	4	6	2	.987
Soto,Geovany	ChC	16	13	122.0	109	10	0	0	0	1.000
Stewart,Chris	Tex	17	11	105.1	99	5	2	3	3	.981
Stinnett,Kelly	StL	26	20	203.0	153	9	4	0	1	.976
Suzuki,Kurt	Oak	66	61	539.0	431	32	2	0	7	.996
Thigpen,Curtis	Tor	22	14	126.1	103	11	0	1	1	1.000
Towles,J.R.	Hou	14	9	95.0	65	6	0	1	1	1.000
Treanor,Matt	Fla	53	50	440.2	385	16	3	2	3	.993
Valentin,Javier	Cin	73	49	471.2	341	19	1	4	8	.997

Catchers Special - Regulars

Player	Tm	G	GS	Inn	SBA	CS	PCS	CS%	ER	CERA
Molina,Yadier	StL	107	101	861.1	50	27	4	.50	414	4.33
Mauer,Joe	Min	91	88	777.2	45	24	5	.48	327	3.78
Laird,Gerald	Tex	119	114	987.1	98	39	0	.40	524	4.78
Johjima,Kenji	Sea	133	128	1106.2	86	40	10	.39	624	5.07
Ross,Dave	Cin	108	98	837.1	61	25	2	.39	425	4.57
Martinez,Victor	Cle	121	118	1042.2	103	33	3	.30	465	4.01
Schneider,Brian	Was	122	120	1051.1	77	24	2	.29	560	4.79
Rodriguez,Ivan	Det	127	119	1052.2	68	21	2	.29	515	4.40
Martin,Russell	LAD	145	143	1254.0	123	41	8	.29	550	3.95
Olivo,Miguel	Fla	119	111	990.1	76	25	5	.28	555	5.04
Snyder,Chris	Ari	106	103	891.1	81	29	11	.26	369	3.73
Navarro,Dioner	TB	112	110	956.1	101	30	6	.25	584	6.50
Ruiz,Carlos	Phi	111	100	912.2	83	26	7	.25	465	4.59
Molina,Bengie	SF	129	125	1104.0	76	23	6	.24	504	4.11
Varitek,Jason	Bos	125	121	1064.0	83	20	1	.23	449	3.80
Posada,Jorge	NYY	132	124	1111.1	134	32	4	.22	556	4.50
Paulino,Ronny	Pit	129	119	1000.0	101	27	8	.20	557	4.61
Hernandez,Ramon	Bal	104	97	855.0	88	20	3	.20	494	5.20
McCann,Brian	Atl	132	130	1139.0	89	19	2	.20	492	3.89
Lo Duca,Paul	NYM	113	112	974.0	94	22	5	.19	447	4.13
Torrealba,Yorvit	Col	112	105	935.1	76	15	2	.18	428	4.12
Buck,John	KC	112	104	924.1	56	12	3	.17	455	4.43
Pierzynski,A.J.	CWS	130	116	1058.0	82	20	8	.16	519	4.41
Ausmus,Brad	Hou	114	101	906.2	64	17	8	.16	432	4.29
Zaun,Gregg	Tor	103	93	838.1	86	13	1	.14	331	3.55
Kendall,Jason	TOT	132	130	1146.0	131	20	7	.10	476	3.74
Barrett,Michael	TOT	95	83	768.0	86	14	6	.10	355	4.16
Estrada,Johnny	Mil	113	111	961.0	84	11	5	.08	474	4.44
Bard,Josh	SD	108	103	927.1	131	10	2	.06	354	3.44

Catchers Special - The Rest

Player	Tm	G	GS	Inn	SBA	CS	PCS	CS%	ER	CERA
Alfonzo,Eliezer	SF	17	12	122.0	16	5	0	.31	50	3.69
Alomar Jr.,Sandy	NYM	6	4	41.0	3	3	0	1.00	26	5.71
Bako,Paul	Bal	57	47	421.0	35	7	1	.18	232	4.96
Barajas,Rod	Phi	38	37	303.0	21	7	1	.33	174	5.17
Barrett,Michael	ChC	55	52	475.1	39	7	5	.06	220	4.17
Barrett,Michael	SD	40	31	292.2	47	7	1	.13	135	4.15
Bellorin,Edwin	Col	2	1	5.0	0	0	0	-	2	3.60
Bennett,Gary	StL	52	41	370.1	28	4	2	.08	215	5.23
Biggio,Craig	Hou	1	1	2.0	0	0	0	-	1	4.50
Blanco,Henry	ChC	14	13	109.0	11	3	1	.20	58	4.79
Bowen,Rob	SD	26	22	208.0	26	3	1	.08	80	3.46
Bowen,Rob	ChC	9	9	76.1	5	1	0	.20	40	4.72
Bowen,Rob	Oak	21	14	130.2	8	1	0	.13	73	5.03
Budde,Ryan	LAA	10	5	46.1	1	1	1	-	22	4.27
Burke,Jamie	Sea	48	34	321.2	28	5	2	.12	134	3.75
Casanova,Raul	TB	23	19	168.2	14	5	1	.31	131	6.99
Cash,Kevin	Bos	12	8	82.0	11	2	0	.18	36	3.95
Castillo,Alberto	Bal	11	11	91.2	13	4	0	.31	48	4.71
Castro,Ramon	NYM	50	35	330.2	30	3	1	.07	157	4.27
Coste,Chris	Phi	31	25	242.2	21	6	0	.29	133	4.93
Cota,Humberto	Pit	5	5	41.0	8	1	0	.13	26	5.71

Player	Tm	G	GS	Inn	SBA	CS	PCS	CS%	ER	CERA
DiFelice,Mike	NYM	16	11	106.2	7	1	0	.14	59	4.98
Doumit,Ryan	Pit	28	28	223.2	27	6	2	.16	137	5.51
Esposito,Brian	StL	1	0	1.0	0	0	0	-	0	0.00
Fasano,Sal	Tor	16	14	120.1	14	3	0	.21	79	5.91
Feliz,Pedro	SF	1	0	0.1	1	0	0	.00	1	27.00
Flores,Jesus	Was	55	42	395.1	40	13	2	.29	176	4.01
Gil,Geronimo	Col	4	3	35.0	2	0	0	.00	16	4.11
Hall,Toby	CWS	37	35	292.2	29	3	0	.10	199	6.12
Hammock,Robby	Ari	12	2	39.0	4	3	0	.75	20	4.62
Hanigan,Ryan	Cin	3	2	20.0	1	0	0	.00	9	4.05
Heintz,Chris	Min	21	14	137.1	14	1	0	.07	92	6.03
Hill,Koyie	ChC	31	25	232.1	14	4	0	.29	77	2.98
Hoover,Paul	Fla	2	1	12.2	2	1	1	.00	10	7.11
House,J.R.	Bal	9	5	46.0	4	1	0	.25	40	7.83
Iannetta,Chris	Col	60	54	496.2	43	10	2	.20	260	4.71
Johnson,Rob	Sea	4	0	6.0	0	0	0	-	2	3.00
Jorgensen,Ryan	Cin	4	4	34.0	0	0	0	-	24	6.35
Kendall,Jason	Oak	80	80	714.1	74	15	4	.16	270	3.40
Kendall,Jason	ChC	52	50	431.2	57	5	3	.04	206	4.29
LaForest,Pete	SD	7	7	56.2	5	0	0	.00	45	7.15
LaRue,Jason	KC	65	55	474.1	40	14	1	.33	251	4.76
LeCroy,Matthew	Min	4	4	35.0	8	0	0	.00	10	2.57
Lieberthal,Mike	LAD	31	17	167.0	19	5	1	.22	114	6.14
Lucy,Donny	CWS	5	4	33.0	8	0	0	.00	19	5.18
Maldonado,Carlos	Pit	13	8	79.0	5	1	0	.20	62	7.06
Mathis,Jeff	LAA	57	52	467.0	48	8	0	.17	202	3.89
Melhuse,Adam	Oak	10	7	64.0	9	3	1	.25	31	4.36
Melhuse,Adam	Tex	15	13	123.0	11	1	0	.09	55	4.02
Miller,Corky	Atl	11	6	62.0	3	1	0	.33	31	4.50
Miller,Damian	Mil	56	50	446.1	36	12	1	.31	221	4.46
Mirabelli,Doug	Bos	46	33	292.2	45	10	0	.22	133	4.09
Moeller,Chad	Cin	17	9	86.2	12	1	0	.08	69	7.17
Moeller,Chad	LAD	7	2	29.0	0	0	0	-	13	4.03
Molina,Gustavo	CWS	9	7	57.0	2	0	0	.00	27	4.26
Molina,Gustavo	Bal	7	2	25.0	1	0	0	.00	15	5.40
Molina,Jose	LAA	40	37	323.0	25	7	0	.28	165	4.60
Molina,Jose	NYY	29	16	169.1	19	6	1	.28	87	4.62
Montero,Miguel	Ari	73	57	510.2	45	10	1	.20	273	4.81
Morales,Jose	Min	1	1	4.0	0	0	0	-	3	6.75
Munson,Eric	Hou	43	36	309.1	29	3	0	.10	201	5.85
Napoli,Mike	LAA	75	68	598.2	64	15	2	.21	285	4.28
Nieves,Wil	NYY	25	21	169.0	27	6	0	.22	82	4.37
Paul,Josh	TB	35	30	277.2	22	9	0	.41	151	4.89
Pena,Brayan	Atl	10	5	59.1	8	4	2	.33	40	6.07
Phelps,Josh	NYY	1	0	1.0	0	0	0	-	0	0.00
Phelps,Josh	Pit	3	2	16.0	4	0	0	.00	13	7.31
Phillips,Jason	Tor	49	41	363.2	47	4	2	.04	162	4.01
Phillips,Paul	KC	7	3	38.2	0	0	0	-	13	3.03
Quintero,Humberto	Hou	26	15	151.2	13	5	0	.38	86	5.10
Quiroz,Guillermo	Tex	8	2	28.2	5	0	0	.00	20	6.28
Rabelo,Mike	Det	49	43	394.2	36	10	2	.24	222	5.06
Redmond,Mike	Min	56	55	482.2	39	16	3	.36	235	4.38
Riggans,Shawn	TB	3	3	27.0	3	0	0	.00	13	4.33
Rivera,Mike	Mil	11	1	37.0	3	1	0	.33	18	4.38
Rodriguez,Guillermo	SF	33	25	227.1	17	5	1	.25	123	4.87
Saltalamacchia,J	Atl	25	20	187.0	26	5	0	.19	98	4.72
Saltalamacchia,J	Tex	22	22	185.2	19	3	2	.06	99	4.80
Sammons,Clint	Atl	2	1	9.0	2	1	0	.50	4	4.00
Shoppach,Kelly	Cle	58	44	420.0	36	13	0	.36	194	4.16
Soto,Geovany	ChC	16	13	122.0	14	4	0	.29	49	3.61
Stewart,Chris	Tex	17	11	105.1	12	4	0	.33	58	4.96
Stinnett,Kelly	StL	26	20	203.0	14	3	0	.21	116	5.14
Suzuki,Kurt	Oak	66	61	539.0	36	7	0	.19	318	5.31
Thigpen,Curtis	Tor	22	14	126.1	11	4	0	.36	72	5.13
Towles,J.R.	Hou	14	9	95.0	6	3	0	.50	45	4.26
Treanor,Matt	Fla	53	50	440.2	49	7	1	.13	230	4.70
Valentin,Javier	Cin	73	49	471.2	45	5	0	.11	271	5.17

Player Baserunning

Bill James

It is universally recognized that there is a difference between being a good base stealer and being a good baserunner. One can be a good base*runner* by reading the ball well off the bat, figuring out quickly whether the ball will be caught or will drop, making good decisions and, to an extent, running good routes. It is difficult to be a good base stealer by making good decisions. That requires speed. One can be a good baserunner without being a good base stealer; one can be a good base stealer without being a good baserunner, and somebody should have zapped me with a stun gun two or three sentences ago for belaboring the obvious.

For a time in the 19th century, the official statistics of the game attempted to acknowledge this "other" baserunning ability by crediting players with stolen bases (sometimes) for going first to third on a single, or scoring from first on a double. This was a poorly conceived idea. It amounted to polluting the Stolen Base counts with things that were not actually Stolen Bases.

After a few years they stopped doing that, and, like Mark Twain's cat who would not sit on a cold stove lid either, they stopped doing *anything* to document base*running*, other than base *stealing*. And I understand, you know. . .they didn't have computers, they couldn't keep track of everything.

So we're trying to document base*running*, as opposed to base stealing. This is how we do it. When a runner is on first base and a single is hit the runner from first goes to third 27% of the time. Suppose that a given runner is on first 100 times when a single is hit, and he goes to third 50 times. That would be +23—23 bases better than average.

But I kind of tricked you there. No runner is on first base when a single is hit 100 times in a season, nor anything remotely like 100 times in a season. When people have no data on x, they sometimes will tend to exaggerate the importance of x. What *actual* studies of baserunning will show is that the number of bases gained and lost is not all that large. If you're on first base when a single is hit 30 times in a season, that's a huge number. If you're five bases above average there (+5) that's a big number for that category.

We check several things like this. . . .runners going from first to third on a single, runners scoring from second on a single (59% do), runners scoring from first on a double (44%). If a player does better than the average bloke in these categories, we credit him with plus bases. If he does worse, he comes out with minus bases.

We also look at Bases Taken, which is baserunners moving up on a Wild Pitch, a Passed Ball, a Balk, a Sac Fly or Defensive Indifference, and we look at baserunning outs. When a player is doubled off or runs into an out, we charge him three bases for that, or, if he prefers, we zap him with a stun gun. That, again, is pro-rated to the average, so that if a player *doesn't* run into outs, he gets credit for that.

We look at runs scored as a percentage of times on base, and we make an adjustment for that. But there are still a good many elements of baserunning that we *don't* consider. We don't make an adjustment for reaching base on errors, or for grounding into double plays. We don't give credit for reaching base after a strikeout. We don't give credit for moving from second to third on a fly ball, or for moving from first to second on a ground out. For that matter, if a runner moved from first to third on a ground out—and I actually saw that happen in 2006—we wouldn't give credit for that either. We don't include all baserunning outs, only baserunning outs which occur in certain situations.

"Baserunning" is a very complicated concept, and we're working on measuring it all, but we're not there yet. Vacuuming up all the data we can find and putting it ALL into one of these categories might not turn out to be a smart line of analysis in the long run, because we might not have a clear understanding of what we're seeing.

We did add one thing this year, which is credit for stolen bases. SBG is Stolen Base Gain, figured as Stolen Bases minus two times caught stealing. Base Stealing is part of Base Running, broadly defined. The title at the head of the page doesn't say "Baserunning other than Base Stealing"; it just says "Baserunning." Base stealing isn't *all* of baserunning, but it is part of baserunning.

In 2007, interestingly enough, the top base stealer in the majors was also the best baserunner in the majors, independent of stolen bases. Jose Reyes led the majors in bags stolen, with 78, and also in bases stolen base gain, with 36. But setting that aside, Reyes was also the best base runner in the majors, based on the other things we have introduced here. Reyes was 19-for-25 scoring from second on a single (+4), 5-for-5 scoring from first on a double (+3), picked up 32 bases from things like Wild Pitches and Sac Flies, and, most impressively, ran into an out only once all year. Altogether he was +34 not counting the stolen bases—the best in the majors.

And the worst was: Colorado's Todd Helton. I don't know what happened to Helton, honestly; in 2006 he scored as an above-average baserunner. Last year he was 5-for-42 moving first to third on a single. He moved up only 9 bases on baserunning opportunities (in 2006 his total was 22), and he ran into six outs. It's an ugly combination—minus 33 if you don't count base stealing, minus 35 if you do.

There is season-to-season fluctuation in this data, as there is in every category. Last year Adrian Gonzalez ranked as the second-worst baserunner in the major leagues, in large part because he was doubled off six times. Last year he wasn't doubled off at all, and ranked at +5 as a baserunner.

But that's the exception. Most guys who are good one year are going to be good the next; most guys who are + base stealers are also going to be + baserunners otherwise. David DeJesus scored at +24 in 2006 (not counting base stealing) and at +24 in 2007. Frank Thomas scored at –23 in 2006, -29 in 2007. Chone Figgins was +28 in 2006, +14 in 2007. Pat Burrell was –20 in 2006, -16 in 2007. Mark Ellis was +24 in 2006, +8 in 2007. David Ortiz—an extremely smart baserunner although very slow—was +0 in 2006, +4 in 2007. Bengie Molina was –15 in 2006, -20 in 2007.

In 2006 the best major league player at going from first to third on a single was Mike Cameron, who went 1-to-3 15 times in 22 opportunties. In 2007 the best major leaguer at this was, once again, Mike Cameron, this time 15 for 23. On the other end of that scale was Jason Varitek, who was 0 for 18.

Rob Mackowiak was on second base when a single was hit 11 times in 2007, and scored all 11 times, making him the major league leader in that area. Bengie Molina was 0 for 9.

Ronnie Belliard was on first when a double was hit 7 times in 2007, and scored all 7 times. Todd Helton was 0 for 10.

2007 Baserunning

Player	On Base	Scored	1st to 3rd Moved	1st to 3rd Chances	2nd to Home Moved	2nd to Home Chances	1st to Home Moved	1st to Home Chances	Bases Taken	Out Adv.	Doubled Off	BR Outs	BR Gain	SB Gain	Rating
Abreu, Bobby	271	39%	6	24	14	27	3	5	17	1	1	2	+9	+9	+18
Abreu, Tony	60	28%	3	7	1	2	1	1	3	0	0	0	+2	0	+2
Alou, Moises	143	27%	4	14	7	11	1	3	10	0	3	3	-5	+3	-2
Amezaga, Alfredo	176	25%	4	11	4	11	2	7	11	0	0	0	0	-1	-1
Anderson, Garret	153	33%	5	20	17	21	1	6	8	0	2	2	+1	+1	+2
Ankiel, Rick	55	36%	2	7	5	6	1	1	3	0	0	0	+4	+1	+5
Atkins, Garrett	245	24%	5	23	14	25	2	3	10	2	2	4	-17	+1	-16
Aurilia, Rich	119	29%	2	14	7	11	4	5	12	0	1	1	+5	0	+5
Ausmus, Brad	135	26%	2	9	7	14	0	1	2	0	1	1	-10	+4	-6
Aybar, Erick	68	25%	3	6	4	4	2	2	5	0	2	3	-3	-4	-7
Bako, Paul	53	23%	3	15	2	3	0	3	2	0	0	0	-3	-2	-5
Barajas, Rod	53	23%	1	5	4	4	1	2	1	0	0	0	-1	-2	-3
Bard, Josh	170	22%	4	19	4	12	0	1	5	1	1	2	-16	-2	-18
Barfield, Josh	154	32%	3	13	9	12	5	6	19	1	0	1	+16	+4	+20
Barrett, Michael	109	18%	5	13	3	12	1	3	7	1	1	2	-10	-2	-12
Bartlett, Jason	220	32%	14	27	15	22	5	6	13	0	2	2	+12	+17	+29
Bautista, Jose	207	29%	3	18	16	23	5	11	13	1	2	3	-3	0	-3
Bay, Jason	211	27%	3	22	12	29	6	12	13	1	0	1	-7	+2	-5
Belliard, Ronnie	190	24%	7	21	12	16	7	7	8	1	0	1	+3	+3	+6
Beltran, Carlos	207	29%	9	29	11	18	4	5	18	1	2	3	+5	+19	+24
Beltre, Adrian	202	30%	7	15	12	26	1	6	19	2	3	5	-5	+10	+5
Bennett, Gary	50	20%	1	9	2	7	0	1	4	0	2	2	-9	-1	-10
Berkman, Lance	245	25%	8	34	6	16	3	5	16	3	0	3	-9	+1	-8
Betancourt, Yuniesky	193	33%	11	26	16	26	1	3	19	0	1	1	+15	-3	+12
Betemit, Wilson	89	21%	1	8	1	8	2	3	7	0	2	2	-9	0	-9
Biggio, Craig	172	34%	6	25	9	15	2	5	12	1	0	1	+4	-2	+2
Blake, Casey	236	27%	10	27	19	22	4	6	19	0	0	0	+18	-6	+12
Blalock, Hank	80	28%	0	6	6	10	0	1	9	0	2	2	-2	+2	0
Bloomquist, Willie	86	30%	6	15	9	12	1	3	15	0	0	0	+6	-3	+3
Blum, Geoff	122	24%	4	15	5	7	0	2	9	0	0	0	+2	0	+2
Bonds, Barry	214	22%	2	18	9	20	0	6	16	1	0	1	-8	+5	-3
Boone, Aaron	90	24%	1	9	3	6	2	2	5	1	1	2	-7	+2	-5
Borchard, Joe	62	26%	2	6	2	7	1	1	3	0	1	1	-4	+4	0
Botts, Jason	62	27%	2	10	2	3	0	1	6	0	0	0	+2	+1	+3
Bourn, Michael	82	34%	3	9	3	5	1	2	6	1	1	2	-1	+16	+15
Bowen, Rob	69	25%	0	5	8	9	0	3	6	0	0	0	+2	-3	-1
Bradley, Milton	87	28%	0	7	6	9	0	5	7	1	0	2	-6	+1	-5
Branyan, Russell	53	23%	1	2	2	7	0	2	5	1	0	1	-4	+1	-3
Braun, Ryan	166	34%	3	13	9	15	2	2	19	1	0	1	+13	+5	+18
Broussard, Ben	88	23%	2	18	4	9	0	1	6	2	1	3	-13	+2	-11
Brown, Emil	140	27%	5	9	6	10	2	3	10	0	2	2	+1	+8	+9
Bruntlett, Eric	73	22%	0	5	4	6	0	0	1	0	0	0	-4	0	-4
Buck, John	121	19%	2	14	6	9	3	4	11	0	1	1	0	-2	-2
Buck, Travis	129	26%	4	14	7	16	1	3	12	0	1	1	+0	+2	+2
Burke, Chris	117	28%	4	9	5	10	0	1	8	0	0	0	+4	+3	+7
Burke, Jamie	50	36%	1	8	4	7	1	3	2	0	0	0	0	-2	-2
Burrell, Pat	219	21%	2	18	10	22	4	8	6	1	0	1	-16	0	-16
Butler, Billy	133	23%	3	10	2	9	0	3	7	1	0	1	-8	0	-8
Bynum, Freddie	58	33%	4	10	4	6	0	0	3	0	1	1	+0	+6	+6
Byrd, Marlon	181	28%	5	15	12	16	4	6	13	0	0	0	+10	-1	+9
Byrnes, Eric	249	33%	4	16	12	17	5	8	17	0	0	0	+14	+36	+50
Cabrera, Asdrubal	68	40%	5	9	5	6	2	2	6	0	0	0	+11	0	+11
Cabrera, Melky	211	27%	8	23	12	19	2	6	11	0	3	4	-8	+3	-5
Cabrera, Miguel	246	23%	4	21	9	23	2	7	7	0	2	3	-23	0	-23
Cabrera, Orlando	262	35%	11	36	15	23	9	13	24	0	0	0	+26	+12	+38
Cairo, Miguel	79	25%	1	4	8	12	0	0	5	1	0	1	-1	+6	+5
Callaspo, Alberto	50	20%	2	7	5	6	0	0	7	1	0	1	+2	-1	+1
Cameron, Mike	209	32%	15	23	17	23	4	9	11	0	0	0	+18	+8	+26
Cano, Robinson	242	31%	4	25	25	33	4	4	14	2	3	5	-4	-6	-10
Carroll, Jamey	116	37%	1	11	12	17	6	6	8	0	1	2	+4	+2	+6
Casey, Sean	180	20%	2	10	6	13	2	6	12	0	1	1	-6	-2	-8
Casilla, Alexi	65	23%	3	8	1	2	1	1	4	0	0	0	+1	+9	+10

2007 Baserunning

Player	On Base	Scored	1st to 3rd		2nd to Home		1st to Home		Bases Taken	Out Adv.	Doubled Off	BR Outs	BR Gain	SB Gain	Rating
			Moved	Chances	Moved	Chances	Moved	Chances							
Castillo, Jose	68	26%	1	4	4	9	1	1	8	0	0	0	+4	0	+4
Castillo, Luis	248	36%	7	31	20	25	2	7	27	0	5	5	+12	+7	+19
Catalanotto, Frank	132	31%	5	22	7	11	4	7	9	2	1	3	-4	0	-4
Chavez, Endy	65	29%	2	6	3	5	0	0	4	0	0	0	+2	+1	+3
Chavez, Eric	108	20%	3	9	3	6	1	3	11	0	0	0	+6	0	+6
Church, Ryan	188	22%	5	17	10	18	1	2	9	0	0	0	-2	-1	-3
Cintron, Alex	61	34%	4	6	1	3	0	5	4	0	0	0	+2	0	+2
Cirillo, Jeff	78	28%	0	4	6	6	1	2	3	0	1	1	-2	+2	+0
Clark, Brady	59	22%	0	5	2	7	0	0	4	0	0	0	-3	-5	-8
Clark, Tony	62	23%	0	6	2	3	1	4	3	0	0	0	-3	0	-3
Clayton, Royce	78	29%	0	5	6	11	0	1	11	0	1	1	+3	0	+3
Conine, Jeff	99	19%	0	2	5	5	2	3	7	0	0	0	+2	+4	+6
Cora, Alex	82	33%	2	3	2	6	0	2	7	0	0	0	+4	-1	+3
Counsell, Craig	109	26%	1	5	4	11	3	5	10	1	1	3	-6	0	-6
Crawford, Carl	237	35%	5	20	14	23	4	8	26	0	4	4	+10	+30	+40
Crisp, Coco	226	35%	9	23	14	23	5	6	25	2	0	2	+21	+16	+37
Crosby, Bobby	113	28%	4	8	5	9	0	3	11	1	0	1	+4	+6	+10
Cruz, Jose	91	34%	2	9	5	8	1	2	8	1	1	2	+0	+4	+4
Cruz, Nelson	102	25%	0	9	6	7	2	3	5	0	2	2	-6	-6	-12
Cuddyer, Michael	237	30%	16	28	11	19	2	9	19	2	2	4	+5	+5	+10
Cust, Jack	187	19%	3	21	8	12	0	5	8	0	1	1	-12	-4	-16
Damon, Johnny	228	36%	18	34	17	29	1	7	21	2	0	2	+18	+21	+39
Davis, Rajai	93	33%	6	13	2	3	2	3	12	0	0	0	+13	+10	+23
DeJesus, David	253	37%	15	36	14	24	3	4	29	1	2	3	+24	+2	+26
Delgado, Carlos	186	25%	3	22	9	16	0	3	8	2	2	4	-18	+4	-14
Dellucci, David	63	33%	2	7	5	7	1	2	3	1	0	1	0	0	0
DeRosa, Mark	225	24%	5	19	13	17	2	6	21	0	2	2	+5	-3	+2
Diaz, Matt	146	22%	4	20	11	18	0	3	10	2	0	2	-7	+4	-3
Dobbs, Greg	114	31%	0	8	4	0	5	7	7	0	0	0	+4	+3	+7
Doumit, Ryan	92	26%	2	10	7	8	0	1	9	0	1	1	+3	-3	0
Drew, J.D.	221	33%	7	27	8	13	2	4	14	0	1	1	+6	0	+6
Drew, Stephen	193	25%	5	15	9	17	1	4	14	0	2	2	-3	+9	+6
Duffy, Chris	92	30%	3	10	4	7	0	0	9	0	2	2	+0	+5	+5
Dukes, Elijah	64	27%	3	8	2	3	2	2	3	0	0	0	+2	-6	-4
Duncan, Chris	142	21%	9	17	10	13	1	2	13	0	0	0	+11	0	+11
Dunn, Adam	215	28%	6	20	5	17	6	10	12	0	1	1	-2	+5	+3
Durham, Ray	169	27%	7	12	12	17	3	5	7	1	0	1	+3	+6	+9
Dye, Jermaine	166	24%	2	12	9	19	2	5	5	1	1	2	-14	0	-14
Easley, Damion	73	19%	1	6	3	5	0	0	9	0	0	0	+3	-2	+1
Eckstein, David	181	30%	5	18	7	11	3	7	14	3	0	3	0	+8	+8
Edmonds, Jim	126	21%	6	18	3	5	1	3	13	1	1	2	0	-4	-4
Ellis, Mark	225	29%	8	22	11	22	5	10	16	0	0	0	+8	+1	+9
Ellison, Jason	53	28%	0	6	3	6	1	1	3	0	0	0	-1	-2	-3
Ellsbury, Jacoby	54	31%	3	4	4	7	1	1	6	0	1	1	+4	+9	+13
Encarnacion, Edwin	215	23%	5	23	7	12	3	6	6	0	0	0	-7	+6	-1
Encarnacion, Juan	105	32%	5	11	9	12	2	6	8	1	1	2	+3	-2	+1
Ensberg, Morgan	104	34%	4	14	2	7	3	4	12	2	2	4	-3	-2	-5
Erstad, Darin	120	24%	2	11	7	8	3	4	8	0	0	0	+4	+3	+7
Escobar, Yunel	151	32%	8	27	12	16	1	4	8	0	0	0	+7	-1	+6
Estrada, Johnny	134	22%	3	16	3	11	0	1	6	0	0	0	-7	0	-7
Ethier, Andre	178	21%	3	24	14	17	0	3	10	0	1	1	-5	-8	-13
Everett, Adam	79	20%	4	8	4	7	1	2	3	1	1	2	-6	0	-6
Feliz, Pedro	176	23%	6	23	13	18	1	5	11	3	1	4	-10	-2	-12
Fick, Robert	76	29%	1	6	4	4	2	2	5	0	0	0	+4	-2	+2
Fielder, Prince	227	26%	2	23	6	11	3	8	15	0	0	0	-1	-2	-3
Fields, Josh	118	26%	3	15	5	7	0	2	4	0	1	1	-6	-1	-7
Figgins, Chone	206	38%	17	30	16	22	3	6	18	0	5	5	+14	+17	+31
Flores, Jesus	68	25%	1	2	4	7	0	2	2	0	0	0	-2	-2	-4
Floyd, Cliff	120	26%	3	15	4	7	0	2	9	0	0	0	+1	0	+1
Fontenot, Mike	88	33%	1	7	6	8	2	2	13	0	0	1	+9	-3	+6
Ford, Lew	53	19%	1	3	1	3	0	1	3	0	1	1	-5	+1	-4
Francoeur, Jeff	245	27%	10	28	12	20	2	5	19	1	2	4	-2	+1	-1
Frandsen, Kevin	107	20%	1	9	3	8	1	2	4	0	1	1	-9	-2	-11
Freel, Ryan	102	40%	5	12	5	9	3	3	12	0	3	3	+6	-1	+5

305

2007 Baserunning

Player	On Base	Scored	1st to 3rd Moved	1st to 3rd Chances	2nd to Home Moved	2nd to Home Chances	1st to Home Moved	1st to Home Chances	Bases Taken	Out Adv.	Doubled Off	BR Outs	BR Gain	SB Gain	Rating
Furcal, Rafael	230	35%	11	36	19	30	0	0	13	1	2	3	+3	+13	+16
Garciaparra, Nomar	164	20%	3	23	11	18	1	4	5	1	0	2	-16	+1	-15
Garko, Ryan	191	21%	3	29	7	21	0	5	7	5	0	5	-32	-2	-34
Gathright, Joey	103	27%	4	11	5	7	1	1	14	1	1	2	+6	-7	-1
German, Esteban	164	27%	4	12	7	13	2	3	10	0	1	1	+1	-3	-2
Giambi, Jason	97	18%	1	7	2	7	1	6	3	2	0	2	-15	+1	-14
Gibbons, Jay	75	29%	1	7	2	6	1	4	5	2	0	2	-7	0	-7
Giles, Brian	197	30%	11	21	11	13	7	8	15	0	2	2	+14	-8	+6
Giles, Marcus	158	30%	11	19	10	15	4	7	16	0	0	0	+19	+4	+23
Glaus, Troy	157	25%	3	16	6	12	0	3	10	0	2	2	-7	-2	-9
Gload, Ross	122	25%	2	13	8	13	1	4	14	0	0	0	+6	-2	+4
Gomes, Jonny	122	25%	1	5	7	11	0	1	15	0	3	3	0	+4	+4
Gomez, Carlos	52	23%	1	1	5	7	0	0	3	0	0	0	+2	+6	+8
Gomez, Chris	94	21%	4	12	4	6	0	1	8	0	0	0	+3	-3	0
Gonzalez, Adrian	231	31%	3	17	10	21	4	8	19	1	0	1	+5	0	+5
Gonzalez, Alex	140	28%	4	12	3	6	3	5	12	0	0	0	+7	-2	+5
Gonzalez, Andy	70	21%	1	10	2	3	0	1	8	0	1	1	-1	-9	-10
Gonzalez, Luis	189	29%	3	24	9	23	1	2	15	1	0	1	-3	+2	-1
Gordon, Alex	185	24%	5	15	9	17	1	2	16	0	0	0	+6	+6	+12
Gotay, Ruben	76	28%	4	9	5	10	1	5	6	0	0	0	+2	-3	-1
Graffanino, Tony	87	29%	3	11	2	7	2	2	7	0	0	0	+3	-2	+1
Granderson, Curtis	236	42%	14	39	15	34	3	7	23	0	4	4	+11	+24	+35
Green, Shawn	185	28%	3	19	10	17	2	2	13	2	1	3	-5	+9	+4
Greene, Khalil	192	32%	0	16	12	18	3	5	14	0	0	0	+7	+4	+11
Griffey Jr., Ken	212	22%	4	25	8	17	0	6	17	2	0	2	-9	+4	-5
Gross, Gabe	70	30%	3	6	4	4	1	1	9	0	0	0	+10	+1	+11
Grudzielanek, Mark	178	36%	10	24	12	23	3	6	14	0	2	2	+8	-3	+5
Guerrero, Vladimir	262	24%	15	32	9	16	2	2	20	4	1	5	-5	-4	-9
Guillen, Carlos	216	30%	10	24	10	22	2	4	16	0	0	0	+9	-3	+6
Guillen, Jose	243	25%	10	22	12	19	1	8	17	3	1	4	-5	+3	-2
Gutierrez, Franklin	103	27%	4	10	5	8	1	4	9	0	0	0	+5	+2	+7
Guzman, Cristian	79	37%	7	12	5	6	2	2	5	0	0	0	+10	+2	+12
Gwynn, Tony	51	25%	0	2	3	6	1	2	9	1	0	1	+3	+6	+9
Hafner, Travis	248	23%	10	30	5	10	4	8	16	0	0	1	0	-1	-1
Hairston, Scott	88	30%	3	12	3	5	0	2	7	0	2	2	-3	+2	-1
Hall, Bill	159	28%	5	20	7	15	5	6	14	1	1	2	+2	-6	-4
Hamilton, Josh	112	29%	6	13	3	8	1	3	8	0	1	1	+1	-3	-2
Hannahan, Jack	63	21%	1	9	2	5	2	3	3	1	1	2	-9	+1	-8
Hardy, J.J.	206	31%	4	21	8	14	2	6	14	1	2	4	-7	-4	-11
Harris, Brendan	207	29%	4	13	13	20	1	1	17	1	2	3	+2	+2	+4
Harris, Willie	152	36%	5	14	7	12	2	4	19	0	1	1	+15	-5	+10
Hart, Corey	199	31%	3	10	12	14	2	2	18	1	0	1	+14	+9	+23
Hatteberg, Scott	163	25%	3	20	9	13	1	6	10	1	0	1	-4	0	-4
Hawpe, Brad	218	23%	6	22	12	16	2	6	10	2	0	2	-6	-4	-10
Helms, Wes	101	16%	1	7	4	12	1	3	6	1	1	2	-12	0	-12
Helton, Todd	295	23%	5	42	19	26	0	10	9	3	3	6	-33	-2	-35
Hermida, Jeremy	171	21%	2	18	6	20	2	6	8	0	1	1	-15	-5	-20
Hernandez, Ramon	145	21%	2	17	6	16	1	4	5	0	0	0	-11	-5	-16
Hill, Aaron	231	30%	4	24	16	25	2	5	14	1	3	4	-7	-2	-9
Hillenbrand, Shea	81	26%	2	7	7	8	0	4	6	0	1	1	0	-6	-6
Hinske, Eric	73	26%	2	5	2	9	1	2	3	0	0	0	-3	+3	+0
Holliday, Matt	278	30%	14	33	17	23	5	9	21	0	0	0	+21	+3	+24
Hopper, Norris	137	37%	5	21	14	17	3	5	11	1	1	2	+8	+2	+10
Howard, Ryan	215	22%	2	19	11	19	2	8	18	3	1	4	-12	+1	-11
Hudson, Orlando	224	26%	10	25	7	10	4	7	18	1	1	2	+7	+6	+13
Huff, Aubrey	206	26%	6	26	11	20	0	3	19	0	0	0	+6	-1	+5
Hunter, Torii	219	30%	13	21	13	19	3	5	14	1	2	3	+8	0	+8
Iannetta, Chris	81	22%	0	6	5	9	0	0	1	1	1	2	-12	0	-12
Ibanez, Raul	226	26%	4	25	8	18	7	9	13	0	2	2	-6	0	-6
Iguchi, Tadahito	190	31%	6	17	7	12	2	6	13	0	1	1	+5	+10	+15
Infante, Omar	66	33%	1	7	8	8	0	2	6	0	1	2	0	+2	+2
Inge, Brandon	181	28%	5	17	10	18	1	5	17	0	3	4	-4	+5	+1
Iwamura, Akinori	208	36%	8	31	20	27	4	10	22	0	1	1	+19	-4	+15
Izturis, Cesar	120	26%	4	17	12	15	2	4	7	0	0	0	+4	-3	+1

306

2007 Baserunning

Player	On Base	Scored	1st to 3rd		2nd to Home		1st to Home		Bases Taken	Out Adv.	Doubled Off	BR Outs	BR Gain	SB Gain	Rating
			Moved	Chances	Moved	Chances	Moved	Chances							
Izturis, Maicer	135	30%	6	15	8	15	3	9	14	0	1	1	+7	+5	+12
Jackson, Conor	174	24%	4	14	8	14	4	6	12	1	1	2	-2	-2	-4
Jacobs, Mike	137	29%	1	10	6	13	3	4	6	0	0	0	-1	-3	-4
Jenkins, Geoff	138	17%	1	17	0	5	0	2	13	1	0	1	-8	-2	-10
Jeter, Derek	307	29%	6	20	17	21	7	9	19	0	0	0	+14	-1	+13
Johjima, Kenji	171	22%	2	21	12	23	0	5	8	1	2	3	-19	-4	-23
Johnson, Dan	168	21%	6	17	6	11	2	6	10	0	1	1	-4	0	-4
Johnson, Kelly	228	33%	12	27	8	21	4	8	18	0	0	0	+13	-1	+12
Johnson, Reed	101	29%	1	11	2	6	1	4	11	1	0	1	0	0	0
Jones, Andruw	208	27%	2	21	11	17	0	4	17	1	0	1	+1	+1	+2
Jones, Chipper	253	31%	5	27	18	28	3	6	16	0	1	2	+2	+3	+5
Jones, Jacque	186	25%	2	19	9	15	2	4	13	3	1	4	-11	0	-11
Kata, Matt	51	35%	0	2	7	9	0	0	2	0	0	0	+2	+1	+3
Kearns, Austin	253	27%	6	22	14	22	4	9	23	0	3	3	+4	-2	+2
Kemp, Matt	120	31%	6	10	5	9	4	7	3	0	3	3	-6	0	-6
Kendall, Jason	171	25%	5	18	8	14	1	4	16	0	2	2	+0	-5	-5
Kendrick, Howie	138	36%	6	13	13	18	5	9	11	0	1	2	+9	-3	+6
Kennedy, Adam	95	25%	4	12	5	9	0	5	10	0	2	2	-2	+2	0
Kent, Jeff	209	28%	9	19	6	13	3	7	14	0	2	2	+1	-5	-4
Keppinger, Jeff	114	30%	5	9	5	11	1	2	7	1	0	1	+1	0	+1
Kinsler, Ian	193	39%	6	20	19	27	2	5	16	0	1	1	+16	+19	+35
Klesko, Ryan	145	31%	3	15	8	15	1	4	8	0	1	1	-2	+3	+1
Konerko, Paul	211	19%	3	25	9	19	0	3	8	0	0	0	-14	-2	-16
Kotchman, Casey	190	28%	0	17	8	20	1	7	13	4	0	4	-17	-6	-23
Kotsay, Mark	74	26%	5	9	2	5	1	3	8	1	0	1	+3	-1	+2
Kouzmanoff, Kevin	173	23%	2	14	4	10	0	4	8	0	0	0	-8	+1	-7
Kubel, Jason	153	23%	3	15	7	15	1	5	8	2	1	3	-14	+5	-9
Laird, Gerald	126	31%	4	10	4	7	0	0	7	0	1	1	+1	+2	+3
Lamb, Mike	129	26%	5	16	3	5	2	4	11	0	0	0	+6	0	+6
Lane, Jason	52	19%	1	4	2	5	0	0	1	0	0	0	-4	-1	-5
Langerhans, Ryan	72	29%	3	10	1	5	0	0	2	0	0	0	-2	+1	-1
LaRoche, Adam	206	24%	4	23	9	17	3	7	11	0	0	0	-3	-1	-4
Lee, Carlos	239	25%	4	21	13	28	4	11	10	0	3	3	-17	0	-17
Lee, Derrek	261	26%	6	37	21	27	2	8	11	2	3	5	-16	-4	-20
Lewis, Fred	80	39%	4	13	9	13	0	1	7	0	1	1	+5	+3	+8
Lind, Adam	84	27%	5	9	6	8	1	1	5	0	1	2	0	-3	-3
Linden, Todd	78	26%	4	11	1	7	0	2	5	1	1	2	-8	+4	-4
Lo Duca, Paul	166	22%	2	16	6	11	0	3	10	2	1	4	-16	+2	-14
Lofton, Kenny	219	36%	8	26	17	24	6	8	15	1	2	3	+9	+9	+18
Logan, Nook	128	30%	2	9	6	12	1	2	9	0	1	1	+0	+13	+13
Loney, James	135	19%	5	19	3	8	3	4	6	1	1	2	-10	-2	-12
Lopez, Felipe	226	27%	8	28	9	16	6	7	10	4	2	6	-15	+6	-9
Lopez, Jose	173	27%	4	26	8	17	5	7	9	1	2	3	-11	-4	-15
Loretta, Mark	189	25%	4	28	7	16	2	7	8	0	1	1	-11	-3	-14
Lowell, Mike	250	23%	4	25	12	23	3	6	14	2	0	2	-10	-1	-11
Ludwick, Ryan	114	25%	5	16	3	11	2	2	9	1	0	1	-2	-4	-6
Lugo, Julio	215	29%	1	20	15	23	4	9	16	1	1	2	-1	+21	+20
Mackowiak, Rob	114	30%	4	12	11	11	4	7	4	0	0	0	+6	+2	+8
Markakis, Nick	256	29%	6	25	13	23	5	9	16	0	0	0	+6	+6	+12
Martin, Russell	232	29%	6	30	14	23	2	5	20	2	3	5	-5	+3	-2
Martinez, Victor	235	23%	3	21	11	20	0	6	24	0	1	1	+1	0	+1
Mathis, Jeff	54	37%	0	5	3	5	0	0	3	0	0	0	+1	-2	-1
Matsui, Hideki	243	31%	7	30	17	25	4	10	15	0	1	1	+5	0	+5
Matsui, Kaz	169	47%	2	11	21	28	3	6	15	0	1	1	+20	+24	+44
Matthews Jr., Gary	194	31%	10	21	16	22	4	4	13	0	1	1	+14	+10	+24
Mauer, Joe	185	30%	8	18	9	17	2	6	15	0	1	1	+7	+5	+12
McCann, Brian	168	20%	4	11	2	11	1	6	8	0	0	0	-9	-2	-11
McDonald, John	121	26%	1	6	5	8	1	1	5	1	0	1	-4	+3	-1
McLouth, Nate	129	38%	3	7	8	14	1	7	11	0	2	2	+3	+20	+23
Mench, Kevin	108	29%	2	8	8	10	0	1	11	0	0	0	+8	+1	+9
Metcalf, Travis	56	36%	1	3	7	8	0	1	3	0	1	1	+1	-2	-1
Michaels, Jason	109	33%	3	14	9	13	3	7	13	1	3	4	-1	-5	-6
Mientkiewicz, Doug	68	31%	1	8	2	6	0	3	6	0	0	0	0	0	0
Miles, Aaron	163	33%	13	29	8	13	2	5	16	0	3	3	+8	0	+8

307

2007 Baserunning

Player	On Base	Scored	1st to 3rd Moved	1st to 3rd Chances	2nd to Home Moved	2nd to Home Chances	1st to Home Moved	1st to Home Chances	Bases Taken	Out Adv.	Doubled Off	BR Outs	BR Gain	SB Gain	Rating
Millar, Kevin	201	23%	4	23	6	12	0	5	12	0	1	1	-8	-1	-9
Milledge, Lastings	72	28%	2	5	6	8	0	1	2	1	0	1	-3	-1	-4
Miller, Damian	64	23%	1	5	4	5	0	2	2	0	1	1	-5	+1	-4
Molina, Bengie	151	13%	0	12	0	9	0	4	4	0	0	0	-20	0	-20
Molina, Jose	61	28%	1	7	1	7	0	2	3	0	0	0	-4	0	-4
Molina, Yadier	141	17%	2	19	5	13	1	1	7	1	0	1	-12	-1	-13
Monroe, Craig	113	36%	2	15	14	25	1	2	1	0	1	1	-6	-8	-14
Montero, Miguel	67	30%	2	7	3	7	0	1	7	1	0	1	+0	0	+0
Mora, Melvin	177	30%	4	16	11	15	4	6	11	2	1	3	-1	+3	+2
Morneau, Justin	217	24%	4	26	12	21	3	7	13	2	0	2	-8	-1	-9
Murton, Matt	96	28%	2	10	5	12	2	2	7	1	1	2	-5	+1	-4
Nady, Xavier	150	23%	3	15	8	13	6	10	4	0	0	0	-4	+1	-3
Napoli, Mike	92	33%	5	12	8	9	1	1	8	0	2	2	+5	+1	+6
Navarro, Dioner	122	30%	4	14	9	14	1	4	13	0	0	0	+9	+1	+10
Nixon, Trot	123	22%	4	14	3	10	0	2	13	1	0	2	-4	0	-4
Norton, Greg	82	26%	1	8	4	8	0	5	6	0	0	0	-2	-1	-3
Nunez, Abraham	107	22%	1	8	5	8	2	4	9	1	2	3	-7	+2	-5
Ojeda, Augie	51	29%	2	8	1	2	2	3	3	0	0	0	+1	+1	+2
Olivo, Miguel	124	22%	2	12	3	9	1	1	10	0	1	1	-4	-1	-5
Ordonez, Magglio	282	32%	8	32	13	22	4	11	17	1	2	3	-2	+2	+0
Ortiz, David	271	30%	8	36	18	31	1	9	27	3	0	3	+4	+1	+5
Ortmeier, Dan	60	23%	1	2	4	4	1	1	4	0	1	1	+0	0	+0
Overbay, Lyle	148	26%	7	20	6	9	3	5	9	1	1	2	-1	+2	+1
Owens, Jerry	136	32%	5	8	13	16	1	4	13	1	0	1	+12	+16	+28
Pagan, Angel	59	29%	4	7	6	9	0	0	3	0	1	2	-2	+2	0
Patterson, Corey	172	33%	9	16	15	21	1	3	9	1	0	1	+9	+19	+28
Paulino, Ronny	160	28%	4	18	5	5	1	2	5	1	2	3	-9	-2	-11
Payton, Jay	169	24%	7	26	3	6	1	6	9	1	0	2	-8	+1	-7
Pedroia, Dustin	228	34%	2	26	14	22	4	8	21	1	4	5	-2	+5	+3
Pena, Carlos	212	25%	12	37	10	23	0	2	17	1	1	2	-2	+1	-1
Pena, Tony F	175	32%	6	25	11	14	1	3	18	0	1	1	+12	-7	+5
Pena, Wily Mo	111	26%	2	10	5	11	3	6	9	0	1	1	-1	0	-1
Pence, Hunter	181	22%	4	20	5	9	4	4	12	1	2	3	-7	+1	-6
Peralta, Jhonny	232	28%	2	21	8	17	2	5	17	1	2	3	-7	-4	-11
Phelps, Josh	74	19%	0	6	4	7	1	3	6	1	0	1	-4	0	-4
Phillips, Andy	76	33%	1	8	3	5	1	2	2	0	0	0	-1	-6	-7
Phillips, Brandon	234	33%	8	13	17	23	4	6	17	3	1	4	+9	+16	+25
Piazza, Mike	108	23%	1	12	1	6	0	4	2	1	2	3	-20	0	-20
Pie, Felix	74	32%	3	8	4	9	2	2	9	0	0	0	+8	+6	+14
Pierre, Juan	269	35%	11	37	27	37	9	11	24	1	3	4	+18	+34	+52
Pierzynski, A.J.	155	26%	1	16	5	9	2	8	9	1	0	1	-7	-1	-8
Podsednik, Scott	81	35%	0	2	7	10	1	1	7	2	1	3	-2	+2	0
Polanco, Placido	266	36%	9	30	17	32	6	12	21	0	1	1	+14	+1	+15
Posada, Jorge	248	29%	6	30	16	28	0	7	21	2	2	5	-9	+2	-7
Pujols, Albert	280	24%	12	37	14	21	2	4	18	2	0	2	+1	-10	-9
Punto, Nick	172	30%	6	16	11	19	2	4	16	1	2	3	+3	+4	+7
Quentin, Carlos	86	28%	0	8	6	10	2	2	7	1	1	2	-3	-2	-5
Quinlan, Robb	74	24%	3	9	3	6	1	4	4	0	0	0	-1	-1	-2
Rabelo, Mike	61	21%	1	6	2	3	0	1	1	1	0	1	-7	0	-7
Raburn, Ryan	50	48%	2	8	4	6	2	5	10	0	0	0	+11	+3	+14
Ramirez, Aramis	204	23%	3	24	11	19	4	8	13	0	1	1	-5	0	-5
Ramirez, Hanley	268	35%	5	16	15	28	5	8	20	1	1	2	+11	+23	+34
Ramirez, Manny	224	29%	4	21	7	17	3	9	16	1	0	1	-1	0	-1
Redman, Tike	52	40%	1	3	5	9	1	1	5	0	0	0	+5	+5	+10
Redmond, Mike	112	20%	3	11	1	4	2	3	6	0	0	0	-2	0	-2
Renteria, Edgar	221	34%	7	28	14	18	4	5	19	0	0	0	+19	+7	+26
Reyes, Jose	285	37%	6	21	19	25	5	5	32	0	1	1	+34	+36	+70
Reynolds, Mark	136	33%	3	10	6	9	0	4	18	0	0	0	+14	-2	+12
Richar, Danny	60	40%	7	9	5	8	1	2	6	1	0	1	+8	-5	+3
Rios, Alex	247	36%	7	24	18	28	5	6	20	0	2	2	+15	+9	+24
Roberts, Brian	270	34%	7	24	17	27	5	11	14	0	5	5	-5	+36	+31
Roberts, Dave	159	37%	6	14	12	21	3	6	13	1	1	2	+8	+21	+29
Rodriguez, Alex	276	32%	11	29	20	28	4	8	18	0	1	1	+15	+16	+31
Rodriguez, Ivan	167	23%	7	19	10	18	3	5	7	2	0	2	-6	-2	-8

308

2007 Baserunning

Player	On Base	Scored	1st to 3rd Moved	1st to 3rd Chances	2nd to Home Moved	2nd to Home Chances	1st to Home Moved	1st to Home Chances	Bases Taken	Out Adv.	Doubled Off	BR Outs	BR Gain	SB Gain	Rating
Rodriguez, Luis	52	31%	3	8	2	3	0	2	5	0	2	2	-2	+1	-1
Rolen, Scott	152	31%	5	13	12	13	3	5	10	0	2	2	+6	-1	+5
Rollins, Jimmy	262	41%	13	24	17	22	5	11	20	0	0	0	+32	+29	+61
Ross, Cody	79	28%	2	5	5	7	1	3	7	0	1	1	+2	+2	+4
Ross, Dave	86	17%	0	6	5	11	0	0	5	1	1	2	-11	0	-11
Rowand, Aaron	255	31%	4	26	18	25	4	9	14	0	1	1	+3	0	+3
Ruiz, Carlos	161	22%	2	5	3	7	0	0	14	1	2	3	-5	+4	-1
Ryan, Brendan	74	35%	3	10	4	7	2	5	7	0	0	0	+6	+7	+13
Saltalamacchia, J.	98	29%	3	10	4	9	0	0	4	0	1	1	-4	0	-4
Sanchez, Freddy	240	28%	5	27	17	21	5	8	14	0	2	2	+2	-2	0
Schneider, Brian	165	16%	3	12	5	8	0	4	6	0	2	2	-15	0	-15
Schumaker, Skip	72	24%	2	5	3	9	1	1	6	2	0	2	-5	-1	-6
Scott, Luke	144	22%	1	16	10	12	1	1	10	0	0	0	+1	+1	+2
Scutaro, Marco	131	32%	4	11	10	14	3	7	9	0	1	1	+5	0	+5
Sexson, Richie	145	26%	1	19	4	9	0	4	4	0	0	0	-10	+1	-9
Shealy, Ryan	58	26%	1	8	1	5	0	3	8	2	1	3	-8	0	-8
Sheffield, Gary	222	37%	2	19	19	27	8	10	20	1	0	1	+18	+12	+30
Shoppach, Kelly	52	37%	1	11	3	9	2	3	4	0	0	0	0	0	0
Sizemore, Grady	278	34%	10	23	21	26	5	7	34	0	4	4	+27	+13	+40
Sledge, Terrmel	71	21%	2	8	2	5	2	3	1	0	1	1	-7	-3	-10
Snyder, Chris	130	18%	1	11	8	16	2	4	6	1	0	1	-10	-2	-12
Soriano, Alfonso	188	34%	9	15	12	19	4	4	14	2	2	4	+6	+7	+13
Sosa, Sammy	138	23%	3	13	5	8	1	4	5	1	1	2	-10	0	-10
Spiezio, Scott	90	30%	1	11	4	9	1	3	7	0	2	2	-6	-2	-8
Spilborghs, Ryan	112	26%	1	12	5	9	2	2	2	1	0	1	-8	+2	-6
Stairs, Matt	137	27%	3	8	10	19	1	8	7	1	0	1	-5	0	-5
Stewart, Shannon	228	29%	9	27	11	17	5	11	22	0	1	1	+14	+5	+19
Sullivan, Cory	56	30%	3	9	4	7	0	0	4	0	0	0	+3	+2	+5
Suzuki, Ichiro	312	34%	16	39	21	32	5	11	31	1	1	2	+26	+21	+47
Suzuki, Kurt	86	23%	1	9	3	6	0	1	6	0	0	0	-1	0	-1
Sweeney, Mark	53	34%	1	6	3	5	1	2	7	1	1	2	-1	+2	+1
Sweeney, Mike	97	20%	0	5	3	5	1	2	9	0	1	1	-2	0	-2
Swisher, Nick	239	26%	15	32	11	17	3	4	24	1	2	3	+12	-1	+11
Taguchi, So	135	33%	3	14	9	18	2	4	11	0	3	3	-3	-1	-4
Taveras, Willy	162	38%	12	19	10	15	1	3	22	1	1	2	+23	+15	+38
Teahen, Mark	223	32%	9	18	11	17	6	8	22	0	1	1	+20	+3	+23
Teixeira, Mark	210	27%	2	13	9	14	1	4	18	1	1	2	+1	0	+1
Tejada, Miguel	210	26%	7	26	7	19	5	9	15	1	1	3	-7	0	-7
Terrero, Luis	52	25%	3	6	4	4	1	1	5	0	0	0	+6	-2	+4
Thames, Marcus	72	26%	3	6	7	8	1	2	1	0	0	0	+1	0	+1
Theriot, Ryan	228	34%	7	21	15	23	3	6	13	2	3	5	-4	+20	+16
Thomas, Frank	220	17%	2	27	3	14	1	9	11	2	1	3	-29	0	-29
Thome, Jim	192	23%	3	18	7	15	0	4	12	2	0	2	-11	-2	-13
Thorman, Scott	74	35%	4	7	3	10	0	0	9	0	1	1	+4	-1	+3
Torrealba, Yorvit	148	26%	2	13	10	18	3	4	10	0	0	0	+2	0	+2
Tracy, Chad	87	26%	2	3	8	13	0	1	9	2	0	2	+0	0	+0
Treanor, Matt	72	17%	0	3	2	5	0	4	4	2	1	3	-14	0	-14
Tulowitzki, Troy	243	33%	8	23	22	27	1	2	14	1	2	3	+7	-5	+2
Tyner, Jason	133	31%	6	20	11	17	1	3	13	0	1	1	+7	+2	+9
Uggla, Dan	233	35%	8	24	20	27	9	12	17	0	1	1	+19	0	+19
Upton, B.J.	211	29%	10	23	12	16	4	5	23	1	0	1	+20	+6	+26
Uribe, Juan	153	23%	6	13	3	7	1	6	7	0	1	1	-5	-17	-22
Utley, Chase	243	34%	10	21	15	20	3	6	16	1	0	1	+16	+7	+23
Valentin, Javier	92	18%	0	9	3	12	1	3	1	0	2	2	-18	0	-18
Valentin, Jose	60	25%	0	2	5	6	1	3	8	0	0	0	+6	0	+6
Varitek, Jason	183	22%	0	18	5	15	0	2	7	0	2	2	-20	-3	-23
Vazquez, Ramon	105	32%	4	18	10	13	1	2	5	1	1	2	-2	+1	-1
Victorino, Shane	189	35%	7	18	12	16	3	10	19	2	1	4	+7	+29	+36
Vidro, Jose	253	28%	7	29	14	23	4	9	12	0	0	0	+2	0	+2
Vizquel, Omar	186	27%	5	17	13	17	4	8	10	1	2	3	-3	+2	-1
Ward, Daryle	57	23%	1	5	5	6	2	3	4	0	0	0	+2	0	+2
Weeks, Rickie	191	37%	9	20	12	16	4	7	17	0	4	4	+10	+21	+31
Wells, Vernon	202	34%	6	19	11	16	8	9	14	2	2	4	+4	+2	+6
Werth, Jayson	124	28%	2	8	4	7	2	4	12	1	0	1	+4	+5	+9

2007 Baserunning

Player	On Base	Scored	1st to 3rd Moved	1st to 3rd Chances	2nd to Home Moved	2nd to Home Chances	1st to Home Moved	1st to Home Chances	Bases Taken	Out Adv.	Doubled Off	BR Outs	BR Gain	SB Gain	Rating
Wigginton, Ty	204	24%	4	21	9	17	2	5	21	1	0	1	+4	-5	-1
Wilkerson, Brad	117	29%	3	11	10	16	1	3	9	0	0	0	+5	+2	+7
Willingham, Josh	222	24%	9	20	8	16	1	4	8	0	1	1	-5	+6	+1
Willits, Reggie	210	35%	14	43	10	20	4	8	20	1	3	4	+6	+11	+17
Wilson, Jack	193	28%	6	16	10	19	5	7	15	0	2	2	+4	-8	-4
Wilson, Josh	101	26%	0	3	7	12	2	4	9	1	2	3	-6	+2	-4
Winn, Randy	239	25%	5	26	13	23	2	3	11	1	1	2	-9	+9	0
Woodward, Chris	52	29%	1	3	3	6	0	1	6	0	0	0	+3	+1	+4
Wright, David	288	29%	9	26	15	19	4	8	17	0	3	3	+3	+24	+27
Youkilis, Kevin	244	28%	9	21	10	18	6	10	21	0	2	2	+10	0	+10
Young, Chris	175	30%	8	24	9	13	0	1	14	0	0	0	+11	+15	+26
Young, Delmon	226	23%	8	19	12	19	4	6	13	1	1	2	-1	+4	+3
Young, Dmitri	187	24%	4	16	4	15	1	7	12	1	0	1	-9	0	-9
Young, Michael	270	26%	6	27	17	24	1	4	16	2	1	3	-5	+7	+2
Zaun, Gregg	131	25%	0	14	8	19	0	1	9	1	3	4	-17	0	-17
Zimmerman, Ryan	237	32%	8	29	14	20	2	8	16	0	2	2	+4	+2	+6

Team Baserunning

Bill James

Last year, when we introduced the new baserunning data, we neglected to include team totals. There will be a time in the future, probably not too long from now, when this baserunning data will be published for all teams and all players over the last 50 years. When that happens, we'll be in a better position to understand the role of baserunning (other than base stealing) in creating runs. This data is the first step along that road.

2007 Team Baserunning

Team	On Base	Scored	1st to 3rd Moved	1st to 3rd Chances	2nd to Home Moved	2nd to Home Chances	1st to Home Moved	1st to Home Chances	Bases Taken	Out Adv.	Doubled Off	BR Outs	BR Gain	SB Gain	Rating
New York Mets	2221	28%	55	217	125	193	19	47	170	11	16	28	+3	+108	+111
Philadelphia Phillies	2347	29%	53	214	117	193	34	81	168	12	11	24	+4	+100	+104
Tampa Bay Devil Rays	2134	28%	64	223	127	208	26	60	193	7	15	22	+47	+35	+82
Arizona D-Backs	1960	28%	51	185	93	160	26	56	160	10	9	19	+21	+61	+82
Los Angeles Angels	2251	31%	100	277	139	219	37	86	175	10	19	31	+47	+29	+76
Detroit Tigers	2236	32%	70	247	138	242	35	78	159	5	14	21	+32	+43	+75
New York Yankees	2472	31%	73	263	154	246	31	72	159	10	12	24	+21	+43	+64
Texas Rangers	2078	31%	50	204	138	201	23	50	142	7	15	22	+25	+38	+63
Milwaukee Brewers	2018	28%	43	189	86	150	25	50	171	7	9	18	+29	+32	+61
Kansas City Royals	2126	28%	72	216	107	192	24	49	197	5	13	18	+69	-10	+59
Boston Red Sox	2418	29%	54	244	113	214	32	75	187	10	12	22	+4	+48	+52
Minnesota Twins	2177	28%	89	240	119	198	26	64	154	10	19	29	-1	+52	+51
Atlanta Braves	2228	28%	68	246	113	199	19	53	174	6	5	13	+40	+4	+44
Colorado Rockies	2350	29%	65	248	162	241	25	55	145	12	13	26	+0	+38	+38
Cleveland Indians	2270	28%	66	246	123	199	31	66	199	10	11	24	+41	-10	+31
Baltimore Orioles	2222	28%	64	249	108	193	26	72	138	8	10	20	-30	+60	+30
San Diego Padres	2031	28%	65	200	106	179	27	59	137	8	8	16	+19	+7	+26
San Francisco Giants	2121	26%	56	213	113	194	26	60	129	9	11	20	-35	+53	+18
Oakland Athletics	2197	26%	74	239	97	176	25	70	173	7	13	21	+2	+12	+14
Seattle Mariners	2243	29%	71	271	133	233	28	71	150	10	14	24	-19	+21	+2
Cincinnati Reds	2122	27%	55	204	100	187	31	66	142	13	12	25	-33	+35	+2
Los Angeles Dodgers	2211	27%	69	269	133	225	32	62	134	7	19	27	-40	+37	-3
Chicago Cubs	2213	27%	55	234	135	216	30	61	159	12	17	31	-28	+20	-8
Florida Marlins	2158	27%	44	180	94	201	31	66	134	6	13	20	-46	+37	-9
Washington Nationals	2114	26%	58	204	97	171	28	58	129	8	13	21	-33	+23	-10
Pittsburgh Pirates	2060	28%	44	207	120	196	39	79	133	7	15	22	-21	+8	-13
St Louis Cardinals	2153	27%	83	274	111	195	24	62	172	11	17	29	-8	-10	-18
Toronto Blue Jays	2086	28%	44	209	107	194	24	55	150	10	17	28	-38	+13	-25
Chicago White Sox	1943	26%	50	184	101	157	16	58	116	8	7	15	-23	-12	-35
Houston Astros	2153	26%	53	237	97	182	24	51	128	7	11	18	-49	-1	-50
MLB Totals	65313	28%	1858	6833	3506	5954	824	1892	4677	263	390	678			

Pitchers Hitting, Fielding & Holding Runners, and Hitters Pitching

Have you ever wondered how a pitcher performed at the plate? What about how position players do in the rare occasions when they are called on to pitch? All of this information can be found in the forthcoming pages. Pitchers have their 2007 and career hitting statistics present, as well as their 2007 fielding statistics and data on how well they held runners in 2007. All active position players who have pitched have their career pitching statistics listed, as well as any 2007 pitching statistics that they may have accrued.

Pitchers Hitting, Fielding and Holding Runners

Pitcher	T	2007 Hitting						Career Hitting										2007 Fielding and Holding Runners											
		Avg	AB	H	HR	RBI	SH	Avg	AB	H	2B	3B	HR	RBI	BB	SO	SH	G	Inn	PO	A	E	DP	Pct	SBA	CS	PCS	PPO	CS%
Aardsma,David, CWS	R	-	0	0	0	0	0	.000	2	0	0	0	0	0	0	0	1	25	32.1	2	4	1	0	.857	0	0	0	0	-
Abreu,Winston, Was	R	.000	2	0	0	0	0	.000	2	0	0	0	0	0	0	1	0	26	30.1	2	1	0	0	1.000	4	0	0	0	.00
Accardo,Jeremy, Tor	R	-	0	0	0	0	0	.143	7	1	0	0	0	0	0	1	0	64	67.1	6	3	0	0	1.000	11	1	0	0	.09
Acosta,Manny, Atl	R	-	0	0	0	0	0	-	0	0	0	0	0	0	0	0	0	21	23.2	2	7	0	1	1.000	4	0	0	1	.00
Adkins,Jon, NYM	R	-	0	0	0	0	0	.000	1	0	0	0	0	0	0	1	0	1	1.0	0	0	0	0	-	0	0	0	0	-
Affeldt,Jeremy, Col	L	-	0	0	0	0	0	.222	9	2	0	0	0	2	1	2	0	75	59.0	2	12	0	0	1.000	8	1	0	0	.13
Albaladejo,Jonathan, Was	R	-	0	0	0	0	0	-	0	0	0	0	0	0	0	0	0	14	14.1	0	1	0	0	1.000	1	0	0	0	.00
Albers,Matt, Hou	R	.069	29	2	0	0	3	.061	33	2	0	0	0	0	0	20	3	31	110.2	7	13	1	2	.952	14	3	0	0	.21
Alfonseca,Antonio, Phi	R	.000	1	0	0	0	0	.143	14	2	0	0	0	2	0	8	1	61	49.2	1	4	0	0	1.000	7	0	0	0	.00
Aquino,Greg, Mil	R	-	0	0	0	0	0	.000	2	0	0	0	0	0	0	0	0	15	14.0	0	1	0	0	1.000	0	0	0	0	-
Arias,Alberto, Col	R	.000	2	0	0	0	0	.000	2	0	0	0	0	0	0	2	0	6	7.1	0	1	0	0	1.000	0	0	0	0	-
Armas Jr.,Tony, Pit	R	.115	26	3	0	2	2	.098	265	26	2	1	0	10	4	99	27	31	97.0	5	8	0	0	1.000	13	2	0	0	.15
Arroyo,Bronson, Cin	R	.143	70	10	1	3	6	.112	206	23	7	0	3	10	6	94	19	34	210.2	11	27	1	0	.974	9	6	0	2	.67
Ascanio,Jose, Atl	R	-	0	0	0	0	0	-	0	0	0	0	0	0	0	0	0	13	16.0	1	3	0	0	1.000	0	0	0	0	-
Atchison,Scott, SF	R	.000	2	0	0	0	0	.000	2	0	0	0	0	0	0	1	0	22	30.2	2	6	0	1	1.000	4	0	0	0	.00
Ayala,Luis, Was	R	-	0	0	0	0	0	.308	13	4	1	0	0	0	0	3	2	44	42.1	3	8	0	0	1.000	2	1	0	0	.50
Backe,Brandon, Hou	R	.400	10	4	1	1	0	.247	85	21	3	2	2	13	6	29	8	5	28.2	2	6	0	1	1.000	1	1	0	0	1.00
Bacsik,Mike, Was	L	.103	29	3	0	1	4	.100	50	5	2	0	0	3	1	10	7	29	118.0	12	13	1	2	.962	4	2	0	0	.50
Baek,Cha Seung, Sea	R	.000	1	0	0	0	0	.000	1	0	0	0	0	0	0	1	0	14	73.1	4	8	0	0	1.000	3	2	0	0	.67
Baez,Danys, Bal	R	-	0	0	0	0	0	.000	3	0	0	0	0	0	0	1	0	53	50.1	6	9	0	0	1.000	6	0	0	0	.00
Bailey,Homer, Cin	R	.273	11	3	0	2	1	.273	11	3	1	0	0	2	0	5	1	9	45.1	3	3	1	0	.857	9	0	0	1	.00
Baker,Scott, Min	R	.000	6	0	0	0	0	.000	9	0	0	0	0	0	0	4	0	24	143.2	9	10	2	1	.905	15	4	0	0	.27
Bale,John, KC	L	-	0	0	0	0	0	.118	17	2	0	0	0	0	0	8	0	26	40.0	1	8	0	1	1.000	0	0	0	0	-
Balfour,Grant, Mil-TB	R	-	0	0	0	0	0	-	0	0	0	0	0	0	0	0	0	25	24.2	1	5	0	0	1.000	4	1	1	1	.25
Banks,Josh, Tor	R	-	0	0	0	0	0	-	0	0	0	0	0	0	0	0	0	3	7.1	1	2	0	0	1.000	0	0	0	0	-
Bannister,Brian, KC	R	.333	3	1	0	0	0	.333	15	5	3	0	0	2	0	4	1	27	165.0	12	21	0	1	1.000	12	5	0	2	.42
Barone,Daniel, Fla	R	.111	9	1	0	0	2	.111	9	1	0	0	0	0	0	7	2	16	41.0	0	5	0	0	1.000	2	1	1	0	.50
Barry,Kevin, Atl	R	-	0	0	0	0	0	.000	2	0	0	0	0	0	0	1	0	1	2.0	0	0	0	0	-	0	0	0	0	-
Batista,Miguel, Sea	R	.000	6	0	0	0	0	.093	290	27	5	0	2	9	11	161	23	33	193.0	14	27	2	2	.953	23	9	1	0	.39
Bautista,Denny, Col	R	.000	1	0	0	0	0	.000	2	0	0	0	0	0	0	1	0	9	8.2	0	0	0	0	-	1	0	0	0	.00
Bayliss,Jonah, Pit	R	-	0	0	0	0	0	-	0	0	0	0	0	0	0	0	0	39	37.2	3	4	0	0	1.000	5	1	0	0	.20
Bazardo,Yorman, Det	R	-	0	0	0	0	0	.000	1	0	0	0	0	0	0	1	0	11	23.2	2	3	0	1	1.000	1	0	0	0	.00
Bean,Colter, NYY	R	-	0	0	0	0	0	-	0	0	0	0	0	0	0	0	0	3	3.0	0	1	0	0	1.000	1	0	0	0	.00
Beckett,Josh, Bos	R	.182	11	2	0	1	0	.151	205	31	9	0	2	15	10	74	25	30	200.2	18	12	2	1	.938	20	6	0	1	.30
Bedard,Erik, Bal	L	.400	5	2	0	1	1	.182	11	2	0	0	0	1	1	4	1	28	182.0	6	17	0	2	1.000	7	2	0	0	.29
Beimel,Joe, LAD	L	.000	1	0	0	0	0	.233	43	10	1	0	0	1	2	17	6	83	67.1	11	22	1	6	.971	5	3	3	2	.60
Belisle,Matt, Cin	R	.060	50	3	0	1	8	.063	63	4	1	0	1	3	3	38	11	30	177.2	18	12	0	0	1.000	17	6	0	0	.35
Bell,Heath, SD	R	-	0	0	0	0	0	.000	5	0	0	0	0	0	0	2	0	81	93.2	7	17	0	1	1.000	11	3	1	0	.27
Bell,Rob, Bal	R	-	0	0	0	0	0	.083	60	5	2	0	0	0	3	34	5	30	53.0	4	4	0	0	1.000	10	1	0	0	.10
Benitez,Armando, SF-Fla	R	-	0	0	0	0	0	.000	8	0	0	0	0	2	0	4	0	55	50.1	2	2	1	0	.800	6	0	0	0	.00
Bennett,Jeff, Atl	R	.000	4	0	0	0	0	.000	6	0	0	0	0	0	0	4	0	3	13.0	0	4	0	0	1.000	0	0	0	0	-
Benoit,Joaquin, Tex	R	-	0	0	0	0	0	.000	9	0	0	0	0	0	0	4	0	70	82.0	5	7	0	2	1.000	4	2	0	0	.50
Bergmann,Jason, Was	R	.135	37	5	0	0	6	.125	48	6	0	0	0	0	3	19	8	21	115.1	6	10	1	2	.941	11	3	0	2	.27
Betancourt,Rafael, Cle	R	.000	1	0	0	0	0	.000	1	0	0	0	0	0	0	1	0	68	79.1	2	4	0	1	1.000	8	4	0	0	.50
Billingsley,Chad, LAD	R	.111	36	4	0	2	4	.100	60	6	1	0	0	4	3	34	5	43	147.0	8	17	0	0	1.000	11	6	2	0	.55
Birkins,Kurt, Bal	L	-	0	0	0	0	0	-	0	0	0	0	0	0	0	0	0	19	34.1	0	4	0	0	1.000	1	0	0	0	.00
Bisenius,Joe, Phi	R	-	0	0	0	0	0	-	0	0	0	0	0	0	0	0	0	2	2.0	0	0	0	0	-	0	0	0	0	-
Blackburn,Nick, Min	R	-	0	0	0	0	0	-	0	0	0	0	0	0	0	0	0	6	11.2	0	0	0	0	-	1	1	0	0	1.00
Blackley,Travis, SF	L	.333	3	1	0	0	0	.333	3	1	0	0	0	0	0	1	0	2	8.2	0	0	0	0	-	0	0	0	0	-
Blanton,Joe, Oak	R	.000	4	0	0	0	1	.111	9	1	0	0	0	0	0	4	3	34	230.0	15	27	0	2	1.000	23	4	1	1	.17
Blevins,Jerry, Oak	L	-	0	0	0	0	0	-	0	0	0	0	0	0	0	0	0	6	4.2	0	0	0	0	-	0	0	0	0	-
Bonderman,Jeremy, Det	R	.167	6	1	0	0	0	.040	25	1	0	0	0	0	0	15	0	28	174.1	17	15	3	2	.914	23	4	0	1	.17
Bonser,Boof, Min	R	.000	3	0	0	0	2	.000	6	0	0	0	0	0	0	1	3	31	173.0	16	13	3	0	.906	18	7	1	0	.39
Booker,Chris, Was	R	-	0	0	0	0	0	-	0	0	0	0	0	0	0	0	0	3	1.0	0	0	0	0	-	0	0	0	0	-
Bootcheck,Chris, LAA	R	-	0	0	0	0	0	-	0	0	0	0	0	0	0	0	0	51	77.1	4	11	0	2	1.000	8	2	0	0	.25
Borkowski,Dave, Hou	R	.000	2	0	0	0	0	.000	7	0	0	0	0	0	0	2	0	64	71.2	6	18	1	3	.960	2	0	0	0	.00
Borowski,Joe, Cle	R	-	0	0	0	0	0	.222	9	2	0	0	0	0	0	7	1	69	65.2	4	6	0	1	1.000	11	2	0	1	.18
Bowie,Micah, Was	L	.091	11	1	0	1	2	.154	26	4	0	0	0	4	1	7	2	30	57.1	4	4	0	0	1.000	5	2	0	0	.40
Boyer,Blaine, Atl	R	-	0	0	0	0	0	-	0	0	0	0	0	0	0	0	0	5	5.1	1	1	0	0	1.000	1	0	0	0	.00
Braden,Dallas, Oak	L	-	0	0	0	0	0	-	0	0	0	0	0	0	0	0	0	20	72.1	4	9	1	0	.929	3	1	1	1	.33
Bradford,Chad, Bal	R	-	0	0	0	0	0	-	0	0	0	0	0	0	0	0	0	78	64.2	4	15	1	1	.950	5	1	0	0	.20
Braun,Ryan, KC	R	-	0	0	0	0	0	-	0	0	0	0	0	0	0	0	0	26	39.1	1	7	0	0	1.000	4	1	0	0	.25
Bray,Bill, Cin	L	-	0	0	0	0	0	.000	1	0	0	0	0	0	0	1	0	19	14.1	1	1	0	0	1.000	1	0	0	0	.00
Brazoban,Yhency, LAD	R	-	0	0	0	0	0	.000	3	0	0	0	0	0	0	2	0	4	1.2	0	1	0	0	1.000	1	0	0	0	.00
Britton,Chris, NYY	R	-	0	0	0	0	0	-	0	0	0	0	0	0	0	0	0	11	12.2	0	1	0	0	1.000	1	0	0	0	.00
Broadway,Lance, CWS	R	-	0	0	0	0	0	-	0	0	0	0	0	0	0	0	0	4	10.1	1	1	0	0	1.000	0	0	0	0	-
Brocail,Doug, SD	R	.500	2	1	0	0	0	.500	2	1	0	0	0	0	0	1	0	67	76.2	10	16	0	0	1.000	3	0	0	0	.00
Brower,Jim, NYY	R	-	0	0	0	0	0	.203	59	12	1	0	0	4	1	20	4	3	3.1	0	0	0	0	-	2	0	0	0	.00

Pitchers Hitting, Fielding and Holding Runners

Pitcher	T	2007 Hitting						Career Hitting										2007 Fielding and Holding Runners											
		Avg	AB	H	HR	RBI	SH	Avg	AB	H	2B	3B	HR	RBI	BB	SO	SH	G	Inn	PO	A	E	DP	Pct	SBA	CS	PCS	PPO	CS%
Brown,Andrew, Oak	R	-	0	0	0	0	0	-	0	0	0	0	0	0	0	0	0	33	41.2	2	4	0	0	1.000	3	0	0	0	.00
Broxton,Jonathan, LAD	R	-	0	0	0	0	0	.000	2	0	0	0	0	0	1	2	1	83	82.0	9	7	0	1	1.000	9	3	1	0	.33
Bruney,Brian, NYY	R	-	0	0	0	0	0	.000	1	0	0	0	0	0	0	0	0	58	50.0	1	2	1	0	.750	9	5	0	0	.56
Buchholz,Clay, Bos	R	-	0	0	0	0	0	-	0	0	0	0	0	0	0	0	0	4	22.2	1	3	1	0	.800	0	0	0	1	-
Buchholz,Taylor, Col	R	.130	23	3	0	1	1	.075	53	4	0	0	0	1	3	22	5	41	93.2	3	9	1	0	.923	7	0	0	0	.00
Buckner,Billy, KC	R	-	0	0	0	0	0	-	0	0	0	0	0	0	0	0	0	7	34.0	1	3	0	2	1.000	1	0	0	0	.00
Buehrle,Mark, CWS	L	.000	5	0	0	0	1	.067	30	2	0	0	0	1	1	17	4	30	201.0	13	34	1	3	.979	5	3	3	2	.60
Bukvich,Ryan, CWS	R	-	0	0	0	0	0	-	0	0	0	0	0	0	0	0	0	45	35.2	2	6	1	1	.889	1	0	0	0	.00
Bulger,Jason, LAA	R	-	0	0	0	0	0	-	0	0	0	0	0	0	0	0	0	6	6.1	0	0	0	0	-	0	0	0	0	-
Bullington,Bryan, Pit	R	.333	3	1	0	0	1	.333	3	1	0	0	0	0	0	0	1	5	17.0	1	1	0	0	1.000	2	0	0	0	.00
Burgos,Ambiorix, NYM	R	-	0	0	0	0	0	-	0	0	0	0	0	0	0	0	0	17	23.2	1	2	0	0	1.000	1	0	0	0	.00
Burnett,A.J., Tor	R	.000	2	0	0	0	0	.132	258	34	6	3	3	9	12	124	33	25	165.2	17	15	2	2	.941	31	0	0	0	.00
Burres,Brian, Bal	L	.500	2	1	0	1	1	.500	2	1	0	0	0	1	0	1	1	37	121.0	3	9	1	0	.923	16	5	1	0	.31
Burton,Jared, Cin	R	-	0	0	0	0	0	-	0	0	0	0	0	0	0	0	0	47	43.0	3	3	1	0	.857	5	1	0	1	.20
Bush,David, Mil	R	.127	55	7	0	2	6	.151	119	18	5	0	0	11	0	36	15	33	186.1	23	18	1	4	.976	22	7	0	0	.32
Byrd,Paul, Cle	R	.000	2	0	0	0	0	.159	151	24	0	0	0	10	12	37	27	31	192.1	15	20	0	3	1.000	13	2	0	2	.15
Byrdak,Tim, Det	L	-	0	0	0	0	0	-	0	0	0	0	0	0	0	0	0	39	45.0	0	2	2	0	.500	3	1	0	0	.33
Cabrera,Daniel, Bal	R	.000	3	0	0	0	0	.000	9	0	0	0	0	0	0	9	1	34	204.1	5	12	1	0	.944	28	4	0	0	.14
Cabrera,Fern, Cle-Bal	R	-	0	0	0	0	0	-	0	0	0	0	0	0	0	0	0	33	43.2	2	2	0	0	1.000	8	4	1	0	.50
Cain,Matt, SF	R	.070	57	4	2	4	7	.101	129	13	3	0	2	5	3	66	16	32	200.0	6	25	0	2	1.000	13	5	0	0	.38
Calero,Kiko, Oak	R	-	0	0	0	0	0	.167	6	1	0	0	0	1	0	2	0	46	40.2	1	4	0	2	1.000	8	0	0	0	.00
Cali,Carmen, Min	L	-	0	0	0	0	0	-	0	0	0	0	0	0	0	0	0	24	21.0	2	5	0	0	1.000	0	0	0	0	-
Cameron,Kevin, SD	R	.000	4	0	0	0	0	.000	4	0	0	0	0	0	0	3	0	48	58.0	5	9	2	1	.875	9	0	0	0	.00
Camp,Shawn, TB	R	-	0	0	0	0	0	-	0	0	0	0	0	0	0	0	0	50	40.0	3	5	0	1	1.000	2	0	0	0	.00
Campillo,Jorge, Sea	R	-	0	0	0	0	0	-	0	0	0	0	0	0	0	0	0	5	13.1	0	2	0	1	1.000	3	1	0	0	.33
Capellan,Jose, Mil-Det	R	-	0	0	0	0	0	.000	4	0	0	0	0	0	0	3	0	17	26.0	1	2	1	0	.750	4	1	0	0	.25
Capps,Matt, Pit	R	1.000	1	1	0	0	0	.333	3	1	0	0	0	0	1	1	0	76	79.0	1	8	0	0	1.000	1	0	0	0	.00
Capuano,Chris, Mil	L	.220	41	9	1	3	5	.161	218	35	6	0	1	17	7	99	15	29	150.0	8	29	1	2	.974	6	0	0	2	.00
Carlyle,Buddy, Atl	R	.139	36	5	0	3	7	.139	36	5	0	0	0	3	0	12	7	22	107.0	7	16	1	3	.958	6	2	0	0	.33
Carmona,Fausto, Cle	R	.000	4	0	0	0	1	.000	4	0	0	0	0	0	0	3	1	32	215.0	23	39	2	5	.969	18	5	0	2	.28
Carpenter,Chris, StL	R	.000	1	0	0	0	0	.095	222	21	2	0	0	5	7	76	25	1	6.0	1	1	0	0	1.000	0	0	0	0	-
Carrasco,Hector, LAA	R	-	0	0	0	0	0	.038	26	1	0	0	0	0	0	19	2	29	38.1	4	5	1	2	.900	0	0	0	0	-
Carvajal,Marcos, Fla	R	-	0	0	0	0	0	.250	4	1	0	0	0	2	0	3	0	3	4.0	1	0	1	0	.500	1	0	0	0	.00
Casilla,Santiago, Oak	R	-	0	0	0	0	0	-	0	0	0	0	0	0	0	0	0	46	50.2	1	1	0	0	1.000	9	0	0	0	.00
Cassel,Jack, SD	R	.125	8	1	0	0	0	.125	8	1	0	0	0	0	0	3	0	6	22.2	0	5	0	0	1.000	0	0	0	0	-
Castro,Fabio, Phi	L	-	0	0	0	0	1	.000	2	0	0	0	0	0	1	1	1	10	12.0	1	0	0	0	1.000	0	0	0	0	-
Cate,Troy, StL	L	.000	1	0	0	0	0	.000	1	0	0	0	0	0	0	0	0	14	16.0	2	0	0	0	1.000	0	0	0	0	-
Cavazos,Andy, StL	R	-	0	0	0	0	0	-	0	0	0	0	0	0	0	0	0	17	20.0	0	1	0	1	1.000	0	0	0	0	-
Chacin,Gustavo, Tor	L	-	0	0	0	0	0	.000	7	0	0	0	0	0	0	2	1	5	27.1	0	1	0	0	1.000	0	0	0	0	-
Chacon,Shawn, Pit	R	.273	11	3	0	0	2	.155	174	27	4	0	1	10	3	68	18	64	96.0	3	20	1	4	.958	11	4	2	0	.36
Chamberlain,Joba, NYY	R	-	0	0	0	0	0	-	0	0	0	0	0	0	0	0	0	19	24.0	0	1	0	0	1.000	1	0	0	0	.00
Chen,Bruce, Tex	L	-	0	0	0	0	0	.130	115	15	1	0	0	3	2	53	17	5	10.0	0	0	0	0	-	0	0	0	0	-
Cherry,Rocky, ChC-Bal	R	.000	1	0	0	0	0	.000	1	0	0	0	0	0	0	0	0	22	31.1	1	2	1	0	.750	1	0	0	0	.00
Chico,Matt, Was	L	.167	48	8	0	3	9	.167	48	8	0	0	0	3	0	11	9	31	167.0	2	18	0	1	1.000	15	6	1	1	.40
Choate,Randy, Ari	L	-	0	0	0	0	0	.000	5	0	0	0	0	0	0	3	0	2	2.0	0	0	0	0	-	0	0	0	0	-
Chulk,Vinnie, SF	R	.333	3	1	0	0	0	.250	4	1	0	0	0	0	0	0	0	57	53.0	2	4	1	1	.857	3	1	1	0	.33
Clarke,Darren, Col	R	-	0	0	0	0	0	-	0	0	0	0	0	0	0	0	0	2	1.1	0	1	0	0	1.000	0	0	0	0	-
Clemens,Roger, NYY	R	.500	2	1	0	0	0	.173	179	31	6	0	0	12	13	61	18	18	99.0	4	15	0	2	1.000	19	4	0	0	.21
Clippard,Tyler, NYY	R	.500	2	1	0	0	1	.500	2	1	0	0	0	0	0	1	1	6	27.0	2	2	0	1	1.000	5	0	0	0	.00
Coffey,Todd, Cin	R	-	0	0	0	0	0	.000	3	0	0	0	0	0	0	3	0	58	51.0	1	8	0	0	1.000	6	0	0	0	.00
Collazo,Willie, NYM	L	-	0	0	0	0	0	-	0	0	0	0	0	0	0	0	0	6	5.2	0	1	0	0	1.000	0	0	0	0	-
Colome,Jesus, Was	R	.000	1	0	0	0	0	.000	2	0	0	0	0	0	0	2	1	61	66.0	5	6	0	0	1.000	3	0	0	0	.00
Colon,Bartolo, LAA	R	.000	3	0	0	0	0	.120	83	10	0	0	0	5	0	47	5	19	99.1	3	8	1	1	.917	4	2	0	0	.50
Colyer,Steve, Atl	L	-	0	0	0	0	0	-	0	0	0	0	0	0	1	0	0	7	3.2	0	2	0	0	1.000	2	2	2	0	1.00
Condrey,Clay, Phi	R	.000	4	0	0	0	0	.091	22	2	0	0	0	0	0	13	0	39	50.0	7	7	0	1	1.000	2	1	0	0	.50
Contreras,Jose, CWS	R	.000	1	0	0	0	0	.000	19	0	0	0	0	0	3	12	0	32	189.0	5	22	6	2	.818	31	6	1	0	.19
Cook,Aaron, Col	R	.238	42	10	0	1	13	.137	204	28	3	1	0	6	12	67	40	25	166.0	13	34	0	1	1.000	10	2	0	0	.20
Corcoran,Tim, TB	R	-	0	0	0	0	0	.000	4	0	0	0	0	0	0	3	1	9	17.1	1	2	0	0	1.000	1	1	0	0	1.00
Cordero,Chad, Was	R	.000	1	0	0	0	0	.000	5	0	0	0	0	0	0	4	2	76	75.0	0	3	0	0	1.000	4	2	0	0	.50
Cordero,Francisco, Mil	R	-	0	0	0	0	0	.000	1	0	0	0	0	0	0	1	0	66	63.1	2	6	0	1	1.000	3	0	0	0	.00
Corey,Bryan, Bos	R	-	0	0	0	0	0	-	0	0	0	0	0	0	0	0	0	9	9.1	0	4	0	1	1.000	1	0	0	0	.00
Cormier,Lance, Atl	R	.000	16	0	0	0	5	.119	42	5	1	0	0	2	2	14	4	10	45.2	3	6	0	1	1.000	4	0	0	0	.00
Cormier,Rheal, Cin	L	-	0	0	0	0	0	.188	192	36	4	1	0	12	5	45	30	6	3.0	0	2	0	0	1.000	0	0	0	0	-
Corpas,Manny, Col	R	-	0	0	0	0	0	-	0	0	0	0	0	0	0	0	0	78	78.0	7	9	0	0	1.000	3	3	0	0	1.00
Correia,Kevin, SF	R	.067	15	1	0	0	3	.105	57	6	1	0	0	2	5	23	5	59	101.2	9	8	0	0	1.000	13	3	0	0	.23
Cotts,Neal, ChC	L	-	0	0	0	0	0	1.000	1	1	0	0	0	0	0	0	0	16	16.2	0	2	0	0	1.000	2	1	1	0	.50
Coutlangus,Jon, Cin	L	-	0	0	0	0	0	-	0	0	0	0	0	0	0	0	0	64	41.0	0	9	1	1	1.000	4	1	1	0	.25
Crain,Jesse, Min	R	-	0	0	0	0	0	-	0	0	0	0	0	0	0	0	0	18	16.1	5	2	0	1	1.000	1	1	0	0	1.00
Cruz,Juan, Ari	R	.000	2	0	0	0	0	.114	70	8	1	1	0	2	4	28	7	53	61.0	1	6	0	0	1.000	4	2	0	0	.50
Danks,John, CWS	L	.000	2	0	0	0	0	.000	2	0	0	0	0	0	0	2	0	26	139.0	5	17	1	1	.957	11	1	1	1	.09

Pitchers Hitting, Fielding and Holding Runners

Pitcher	T	2007 Hitting Avg	AB	H	HR	RBI	SH	Career Hitting Avg	AB	H	2B	3B	HR	RBI	BB	SO	SH	2007 Fielding and Holding Runners G	Inn	PO	A	E	DP	Pct	SBA	CS	PCS	PPO	CS%
Davidson,Dave, Pit	L	-	0	0	0	0	0	-	0	0	0	0	0	0	0	0	0	2	2.0	0	0	0	0	-	0	0	0	0	-
Davies,Kyle, Atl-KC	R	.192	26	5	1	4	2	.141	64	9	1	0	2	9	4	23	13	28	136.0	8	16	2	1	.923	17	3	0	0	.18
Davis,Doug, Ari	L	.069	58	4	0	1	9	.070	284	20	3	1	0	6	4	132	30	33	192.2	5	38	2	2	.956	12	6	6	2	.50
Davis,Jason, Cle-Sea	R	-	0	0	0	0	0	.111	9	1	0	0	1	1	0	5	2	24	37.0	4	3	1	3	.875	2	0	0	0	.00
Davis,Kane, Phi	R	-	0	0	0	0	0	.000	6	0	0	0	0	0	0	6	0	11	11.1	0	0	0	0	-	3	2	0	0	.67
Day,Dewon, CWS	R	-	0	0	0	0	0	-	0	0	0	0	0	0	0	0	0	13	12.0	1	0	1	0	.500	1	0	0	0	.00
De Jong,Jordan, Tor	R	-	0	0	0	0	0	-	0	0	0	0	0	0	0	0	0	6	9.0	0	1	0	0	1.000	3	0	0	0	.00
de la Cruz,Eulogio, Det	R	-	0	0	0	0	0	-	0	0	0	0	0	0	0	0	0	6	6.2	0	0	0	0	-	0	0	0	0	-
de la Rosa,Jorge, KC	L	.000	5	0	0	0	0	.000	16	0	0	0	0	0	0	11	1	26	130.0	3	13	1	1	.941	10	4	2	0	.40
Delcarmen,Manny, Bos	R	-	0	0	0	0	0	-	0	0	0	0	0	0	0	0	0	44	44.0	2	6	0	0	1.000	4	2	0	0	.50
Dempster,Ryan, ChC	R	.000	1	0	0	0	0	.076	314	24	5	1	0	7	6	135	32	66	66.2	4	7	0	1	1.000	9	0	0	0	.00
DePaula,Julio, Min	R	-	0	0	0	0	0	-	0	0	0	0	0	0	0	0	0	16	20.0	2	2	1	0	.800	0	0	0	0	-
DeSalvo,Matt, NYY	R	-	0	0	0	0	0	-	0	0	0	0	0	0	0	0	0	7	27.2	1	4	0	1	1.000	4	0	0	0	.00
Dessens,Elmer, Mil-Col	R	.000	6	0	0	0	1	.163	240	39	4	1	0	16	22	65	38	17	34.0	2	8	0	1	1.000	1	0	0	0	.00
Detwiler,Ross, Was	L	-	0	0	0	0	0	-	0	0	0	0	0	0	0	0	0	1	1.0	0	0	0	0	-	0	0	0	0	-
Devine,Joey, Atl	R	-	0	0	0	0	0	.000	1	0	0	0	0	0	0	1	0	10	8.1	0	0	0	0	-	0	0	0	0	-
DiNardo,Lenny, Oak	L	.250	4	1	0	0	0	.200	5	1	0	0	0	0	0	3	0	35	131.1	1	15	2	0	.889	6	3	0	0	.50
Dohmann,Scott, TB	R	-	0	0	0	0	0	.000	3	0	0	0	0	0	0	2	1	31	32.2	4	2	0	0	1.000	5	2	1	0	.40
Donnelly,Brendan, Bos	R	-	0	0	0	0	0	.000	1	0	0	0	0	0	0	0	0	27	20.2	1	1	0	0	1.000	2	0	0	0	.00
Dotel,Octavio, KC-Atl	R	-	0	0	0	0	0	.068	74	5	0	0	0	1	5	42	9	33	30.2	1	1	0	0	1.000	2	0	0	0	.00
Dove,Dennis, StL	R	-	0	0	0	0	0	-	0	0	0	0	0	0	0	0	0	3	3.0	0	0	0	0	-	0	0	0	0	-
Downs,Scott, Tor	L	-	0	0	0	0	0	.068	44	3	0	0	0	1	3	17	10	81	58.0	3	13	1	1	.941	1	1	1	0	1.00
Doyne,Cory, Bal	R	-	0	0	0	0	0	-	0	0	0	0	0	0	0	0	0	5	3.2	0	0	0	0	-	0	0	0	0	-
Driskill,Travis, Hou	R	-	0	0	0	0	1	.000	5	0	0	0	0	0	1	4	1	2	6.0	1	0	0	0	1.000	1	0	0	0	.00
Duchscherer,Justin, Oak	R	-	0	0	0	0	0	-	0	0	0	0	0	0	0	0	0	17	16.1	2	4	0	0	1.000	3	0	0	0	.00
Duckworth,Brandon, KC	R	1.000	1	1	0	0	0	.221	113	25	4	0	0	8	10	22	10	26	46.2	7	6	0	1	1.000	1	0	0	0	.00
Duke,Zach, Pit	L	.250	32	8	0	3	3	.195	128	25	3	0	0	11	3	54	12	20	107.1	2	22	0	3	1.000	10	5	2	0	.50
Dumatrait,Phil, Cin	L	.000	6	0	0	0	0	.000	6	0	0	0	0	0	0	4	0	6	18.0	2	1	0	0	1.000	0	0	0	0	-
Durbin,Chad, Det	R	.000	4	0	0	1	0	.000	6	0	0	0	0	1	0	1	0	36	127.2	4	15	0	0	1.000	7	2	0	0	.29
Durbin,J.D., Ari-Phi	R	.263	19	5	0	0	3	.263	19	5	1	0	0	0	0	5	3	19	65.1	8	7	0	0	1.000	4	1	0	0	.25
Eaton,Adam, Phi	R	.210	62	13	1	5	6	.195	313	61	14	1	3	24	27	107	23	30	161.2	18	18	2	1	.947	15	9	1	0	.60
Elarton,Scott, KC	R	.000	1	0	0	0	0	.139	165	23	3	0	0	3	5	53	28	9	37.0	1	2	0	1	1.000	2	0	0	0	.00
Embree,Alan, Oak	L	-	0	0	0	0	0	.000	3	0	0	0	0	0	1	2	0	68	68.0	3	5	0	0	1.000	5	1	1	0	.20
Ennis,John, Phi	R	.333	3	1	0	0	0	.250	4	1	0	0	0	0	0	1	0	3	7.2	1	0	0	0	1.000	1	0	0	0	.00
Escobar,Kelvim, LAA	R	.333	6	2	0	0	1	.111	27	3	0	0	0	1	0	13	2	30	195.2	13	18	2	4	.939	20	3	0	0	.15
Eveland,Dana, Ari	L	-	0	0	0	0	0	.000	8	0	0	0	0	0	4	3	1	5	5.0	0	2	0	0	1.000	1	0	0	0	.00
Eyre,Scott, ChC	L	.000	1	0	0	0	0	.154	13	2	0	0	0	0	1	6	0	55	52.1	0	2	0	1	1.000	9	1	0	0	.11
Eyre,Willie, Tex	R	-	0	0	0	0	0	.000	1	0	0	0	0	0	0	0	0	33	68.0	6	11	0	1	1.000	4	2	0	0	.50
Falkenborg,Brian, StL	R	.000	1	0	0	0	0	.000	4	0	0	0	0	0	1	4	0	16	18.2	2	2	0	1	1.000	1	0	0	0	.00
Farnsworth,Kyle, NYY	R	-	0	0	0	0	0	.074	54	4	1	0	0	3	2	18	8	64	60.0	3	7	3	0	.769	11	2	0	0	.18
Feierabend,Ryan, Sea	L	-	0	0	0	0	0	-	0	0	0	0	0	0	0	0	0	13	49.1	1	8	0	0	1.000	3	3	2	3	1.00
Feldman,Scott, Tex	R	-	0	0	0	0	0	-	0	0	0	0	0	0	0	0	0	29	39.0	1	7	0	1	1.000	8	2	0	0	.25
Feliciano,Pedro, NYM	L	-	0	0	0	0	0	.000	6	0	0	0	0	0	1	2	1	78	64.0	2	15	2	1	.895	3	0	0	0	.00
Field,Nate, Fla	R	-	0	0	0	0	0	-	0	0	0	0	0	0	0	0	0	1	1.0	0	0	0	0	-	0	0	0	0	-
Flores,Randy, StL	L	.000	1	0	0	0	0	.000	8	0	0	0	0	0	0	5	0	70	55.0	1	9	0	0	1.000	2	0	0	0	.00
Flores,Ron, Oak	L	-	0	0	0	0	0	.000	1	0	0	0	0	0	0	0	0	17	17.2	0	0	1	0	.000	0	0	0	0	-
Floyd,Gavin, CWS	R	-	0	0	0	0	0	.048	42	2	0	0	0	0	0	22	0	16	70.0	7	4	1	0	.917	12	0	0	0	.00
Fogg,Josh, Col	R	.132	53	7	0	1	9	.118	304	36	3	0	0	11	11	103	50	30	165.2	12	19	0	4	1.000	14	2	0	0	.14
Fossum,Casey, TB	L	-	0	0	0	0	0	.087	46	4	0	0	0	0	1	16	4	40	76.0	4	15	0	0	1.000	10	0	0	0	.00
Francis,Jeff, Col	L	.188	64	12	0	3	13	.130	193	25	5	0	0	13	17	71	32	34	215.1	12	33	0	2	1.000	13	4	3	1	.31
Francisco,Frank, Tex	R	-	0	0	0	0	0	-	0	0	0	0	0	0	0	0	0	59	59.1	2	3	2	0	.714	8	4	0	0	.50
Franklin,Ryan, StL	R	.500	2	1	0	1	0	.118	17	2	0	0	0	1	2	8	2	69	80.0	4	8	0	1	1.000	4	2	0	1	.50
Frasor,Jason, Tor	R	-	0	0	0	0	0	-	0	0	0	0	0	0	0	0	0	51	57.0	2	7	0	0	1.000	7	2	0	0	.29
Fuentes,Brian, Col	L	-	0	0	0	0	0	.000	1	0	0	0	0	0	0	0	0	64	61.1	0	6	1	0	.857	2	1	1	0	.50
Fultz,Aaron, Cle	L	-	0	0	0	0	0	.263	19	5	0	0	0	0	3	1	1	49	37.0	7	2	0	0	1.000	3	2	0	0	.67
Gabbard,Kason, Bos-Tex	L	-	0	0	0	0	0	-	0	0	0	0	0	0	0	0	0	15	81.1	5	20	0	3	1.000	7	2	1	0	.29
Gagne,Eric, Tex-Bos	R	-	0	0	0	0	0	.140	86	12	2	1	1	3	1	25	12	54	52.0	2	8	0	0	1.000	1	0	0	0	.00
Galarraga,Armando, Tex	R	-	0	0	0	0	0	-	0	0	0	0	0	0	0	0	0	3	8.2	1	0	0	0	1.000	3	1	0	0	.33
Gallagher,Sean, ChC	R	.000	1	0	0	0	0	.000	1	0	0	0	0	0	0	0	0	8	14.2	0	1	0	1	1.000	0	0	0	0	-
Gallardo,Yovani, Mil	R	.250	40	10	2	6	1	.250	40	10	3	0	2	6	1	10	1	20	110.1	12	13	1	0	.962	5	1	1	1	.20
Garcia,Anderson, Phi	R	-	0	0	0	0	0	-	0	0	0	0	0	0	0	0	0	1	0.2	0	0	0	0	-	0	0	0	0	-
Garcia,Freddy, Phi	R	.235	17	4	0	2	2	.207	58	12	2	0	0	4	2	19	13	11	58.0	4	6	0	0	1.000	5	0	0	1	.00
Garcia,Harvey, Fla	R	-	0	0	0	0	0	-	0	0	0	0	0	0	0	0	0	8	12.1	1	1	1	0	.667	0	0	0	0	-
Gardner,Lee, Fla	R	.000	4	0	0	0	0	.000	4	0	0	0	0	0	0	3	0	62	74.1	5	8	1	1	.929	3	0	0	0	.00
Garland,Jon, CWS	R	-	0	0	0	0	2	.176	17	3	0	0	1	3	1	5	7	32	208.1	20	28	1	4	.980	8	6	1	1	.75
Garza,Matt, Min	R	.000	2	0	0	0	1	.000	2	0	0	0	0	0	0	1	1	16	83.0	1	10	2	0	.846	4	3	1	0	.75
Gaudin,Chad, Oak	R	.000	3	0	0	0	0	.000	4	0	0	0	0	0	1	2	2	34	199.1	22	20	1	1	.977	13	1	0	0	.08
Geary,Geoff, Phi	R	.000	4	0	0	0	0	.125	16	2	1	0	0	1	1	10	0	57	67.1	4	9	2	1	.867	4	2	0	0	.50
Germano,Justin, SD	R	.156	32	5	0	2	6	.122	41	5	1	0	0	2	3	18	8	26	133.1	11	21	0	1	1.000	20	2	0	0	.10
Giese,Dan, SF	R	-	0	0	0	0	0	-	0	0	0	0	0	0	0	0	0	8	9.1	2	2	0	0	1.000	1	1	1	0	1.00

Pitchers Hitting, Fielding and Holding Runners

Pitcher	T	2007 Hitting						Career Hitting										2007 Fielding and Holding Runners											
		Avg	AB	H	HR	RBI	SH	Avg	AB	H	2B	3B	HR	RBI	BB	SO	SH	G	Inn	PO	A	E	DP	Pct	SBA	CS	PCS	PPO	CS%
Glavine,Tom, NYM	L	.214	56	12	0	4	12	.187	1304	244	25	2	1	89	98	324	213	34	200.1	6	26	1	2	.970	13	8	2	0	.62
Glover,Gary, TB		-	0	0	0	0	0	.071	28	2	0	0	0	1	2	14	3	67	77.1	7	8	0	0	1.000	8	2	0	0	.25
Gobble,Jimmy, KC	L	-	0	0	0	0	0	.000	2	0	0	0	0	0	0	1	1	74	53.2	2	9	1	2	.917	3	1	0	0	.33
Gonzalez,Edgar, Ari	R	.190	21	4	0	0	3	.157	51	8	0	0	0	0	0	10	5	32	102.0	5	12	0	1	1.000	5	3	1	0	.60
Gonzalez,Enrique, Ari	R	-	0	0	0	0	0	.281	32	9	1	0	0	3	0	8	3	1	2.0	1	1	0	0	1.000	1	0	0	0	.00
Gonzalez,Mike, Atl	L	-	0	0	0	0	0	.500	2	1	1	0	0	2	0	0	0	18	17.0	0	2	0	0	1.000	2	1	0	0	.50
Gordon,Tom, Phi	R	-	0	0	0	0	0	.000	2	0	0	0	0	0	0	0	0	44	40.0	6	7	0	0	1.000	2	1	0	0	.50
Gorzelanny,Tom, Pit	L	.063	63	4	0	3	6	.048	83	4	0	0	0	4	3	43	8	32	201.2	12	22	1	1	.971	22	5	2	1	.23
Gosling,Mike, Cin	L	.000	5	0	0	0	0	.000	17	0	0	0	0	0	1	11	2	23	33.0	2	2	0	0	1.000	3	1	1	0	.33
Grabow,John, Pit	L	.000	1	0	0	0	0	.000	3	0	0	0	0	0	0	1	0	63	51.2	2	4	0	0	1.000	10	0	0	0	.00
Green,Sean, Sea	R	-	0	0	0	0	0	-	0	0	0	0	0	0	0	0	0	64	68.0	7	15	1	1	.957	4	4	0	1	1.00
Gregg,Kevin, Fla	R	.000	2	0	0	0	0	.000	5	0	0	0	0	0	0	4	0	74	84.0	3	9	0	0	1.000	3	0	0	1	.00
Greinke,Zack, KC	R	.000	1	0	0	0	0	.200	5	1	0	0	1	1	0	2	0	52	122.1	11	7	0	0	1.000	10	3	0	1	.30
Grilli,Jason, Det	R	-	0	0	0	0	0	-	0	0	0	0	0	0	0	0	0	57	79.2	0	13	2	0	.867	3	2	0	0	.67
Gronkiewicz,Lee, Tor	R	-	0	0	0	0	0	-	0	0	0	0	0	0	0	0	0	1	4.0	1	0	0	0	1.000	0	0	0	0	-
Guardado,Eddie, Cin	L	-	0	0	0	0	0	.000	1	0	0	0	0	0	0	0	0	15	13.2	0	2	0	0	1.000	0	0	0	0	-
Guerrier,Matt, Min	R	-	0	0	0	0	0	.000	2	0	0	0	0	0	0	0	1	73	88.0	13	9	0	1	1.000	8	2	0	1	.25
Guthrie,Jeremy, Bal	R	.000	7	0	0	0	0	.000	7	0	0	0	0	0	0	4	0	32	175.1	16	21	1	2	.974	9	5	0	1	.56
Gutierrez,Juan, Hou	R	.000	6	0	0	0	1	.000	6	0	0	0	0	0	0	4	1	7	21.1	1	1	0	0	1.000	2	1	0	0	.50
Guzman,Angel, ChC	R	.000	7	0	0	0	0	.105	19	2	1	0	0	2	0	6	4	12	30.1	1	7	0	1	1.000	4	0	0	0	.00
Gwyn,Marc, LAA	R	-	0	0	0	0	0	-	0	0	0	0	0	0	0	0	0	3	5.1	1	0	0	0	1.000	0	0	0	0	-
Haeger,Charlie, CWS	R	-	0	0	0	0	0	-	0	0	0	0	0	0	0	0	0	8	11.1	1	2	0	0	1.000	2	0	0	0	.00
Halladay,Roy, Tor	R	.500	4	2	0	1	0	.091	33	3	0	0	0	1	0	14	2	31	225.1	20	35	2	3	.965	27	7	1	0	.26
Hamels,Cole, Phi	L	.141	64	9	0	2	5	.130	108	14	2	0	0	5	8	50	7	28	183.1	6	22	1	0	.966	16	2	2	0	.13
Hammel,Jason, TB	R	1.000	1	1	0	1	0	1.000	1	1	1	0	0	1	0	0	0	24	85.0	8	4	1	0	.923	19	3	0	0	.16
Hampson,Justin, SD	L	.000	4	0	0	0	0	.000	7	0	0	0	0	0	1	2	1	39	53.1	3	14	0	1	1.000	7	2	1	0	.29
Hancock,Josh, StL	R	.000	1	0	0	0	0	.083	24	2	0	0	0	1	4	18	2	8	12.2	1	2	0	0	1.000	0	0	0	0	-
Hanrahan,Joel, Was	R	.286	14	4	0	3	3	.286	14	4	2	1	0	3	0	5	3	12	51.0	2	3	0	0	1.000	6	2	0	0	.33
Hansack,Devern, Bos	R	-	0	0	0	0	0	-	0	0	0	0	0	0	0	0	0	3	7.2	0	2	0	0	1.000	0	0	0	0	-
Happ,J.A., Phi	L	.000	1	0	0	0	0	.000	1	0	0	0	0	0	0	1	0	1	4.0	0	0	0	0	-	0	0	0	0	-
Harang,Aaron, Cin	R	.095	74	7	0	2	11	.073	300	22	2	0	0	7	2	150	24	34	231.2	10	21	0	1	1.000	21	8	0	0	.38
Harden,Rich, Oak	R	-	0	0	0	0	0	.000	5	0	0	0	0	0	0	3	0	7	25.2	3	0	0	0	1.000	2	1	0	0	.50
Haren,Dan, Oak	R	.000	4	0	0	0	0	.075	53	4	3	0	0	3	1	19	3	34	222.2	14	15	1	1	.967	26	6	0	0	.23
Harikkala,Tim, Col	R	1.000	1	1	0	1	0	.250	4	1	0	0	0	1	0	3	1	1	3.1	0	1	0	0	1.000	1	0	0	0	.00
Hart,Kevin, ChC	R	-	0	0	0	0	0	-	0	0	0	0	0	0	0	0	0	8	11.0	0	1	0	0	1.000	1	0	0	0	.00
Hawkins,LaTroy, Col	R	.000	1	0	0	0	0	.000	6	0	0	0	0	0	0	5	1	62	55.1	9	12	0	2	1.000	3	1	0	0	.33
Heilman,Aaron, NYM	R	-	0	0	0	0	0	.023	43	1	0	0	0	1	2	23	1	81	86.0	4	13	0	1	1.000	10	2	0	0	.20
Hendrickson,Mark, LAD	L	.037	27	1	0	1	1	.065	62	4	1	0	1	2	5	32	3	39	122.2	3	22	0	0	1.000	13	2	2	0	.15
Henn,Sean, NYY	L	.000	1	0	0	0	0	.000	1	0	0	0	0	0	0	1	0	20	36.2	3	3	0	1	1.000	1	1	0	1	1.00
Hennessey,Brad, SF	R	.000	1	0	0	0	0	.225	80	18	2	0	2	7	1	25	5	69	68.1	4	10	0	0	1.000	5	1	1	0	.20
Hensley,Clay, SD	R	.214	14	3	0	2	2	.118	68	8	2	0	0	4	3	39	7	13	50.0	6	11	0	0	1.000	11	1	0	0	.09
Herges,Matt, Col	R	.000	6	0	0	0	0	.182	33	6	0	0	0	1	1	19	2	35	48.2	2	7	0	0	1.000	1	1	0	1	1.00
Hernandez,Felix, Sea	R	.250	4	1	0	1	0	.125	8	1	0	0	0	1	0	6	1	30	190.1	13	24	1	2	.974	15	5	0	1	.33
Hernandez,Livan, Ari	R	.213	75	16	1	5	3	.232	789	183	34	2	9	73	6	107	85	33	204.1	13	39	0	2	1.000	25	5	0	2	.20
Hernandez,Orlando, NYM	R	.167	48	8	0	3	6	.155	116	18	3	1	0	5	1	41	15	27	147.2	14	20	0	2	1.000	20	6	1	0	.30
Hernandez,Rob, Cle-LAD	R	-	0	0	0	0	0	.500	2	1	0	0	0	0	0	1	0	50	46.1	1	4	3	0	.625	3	1	0	0	.33
Hernandez,Yoel, Phi	R	-	0	0	0	0	0	-	0	0	0	0	0	0	0	0	0	14	15.1	2	1	0	0	1.000	2	0	0	0	.00
Hill,Rich, ChC	L	.127	63	8	0	5	3	.131	99	13	3	0	0	5	2	46	6	32	195.0	4	22	4	0	.867	28	5	4	0	.18
Hill,Shawn, Was	R	.077	26	2	0	0	7	.088	34	3	0	0	0	0	3	16	10	16	97.1	2	16	1	1	.947	9	3	0	0	.33
Hirsh,Jason, Col	R	.097	31	3	0	2	2	.065	46	3	0	0	0	2	1	26	4	19	112.1	0	12	0	1	1.000	4	0	0	1	.00
Hochevar,Luke, KC	R	-	0	0	0	0	0	-	0	0	0	0	0	0	0	0	0	4	12.2	1	4	0	1	1.000	0	0	0	0	-
Hoey,Jim, Bal	R	-	0	0	0	0	0	-	0	0	0	0	0	0	0	0	0	23	24.2	1	1	1	0	.667	3	0	0	0	.00
Hoffman,Trevor, SD	R	-	0	0	0	0	0	.121	33	4	2	0	0	5	0	10	2	61	57.1	3	4	0	0	1.000	4	1	0	0	.25
Houlton,D.J., LAD	R	-	0	0	0	0	0	.100	30	3	1	0	0	1	3	18	2	18	28.0	3	2	1	1	.833	3	2	0	0	.67
Howell,J.P., TB	L	.333	6	2	0	1	0	.222	9	2	0	0	0	1	0	3	0	10	51.0	7	10	0	1	1.000	3	1	1	0	.33
Howry,Bob, ChC	R	-	0	0	0	0	0	.500	2	1	0	0	0	0	0	0	0	78	81.1	1	8	0	0	1.000	2	0	0	0	.00
Huber,Jon, Sea	R	-	0	0	0	0	0	-	0	0	0	0	0	0	0	0	0	9	11.1	1	0	0	0	1.000	0	0	0	0	-
Hudson,Luke, KC	R	-	0	0	0	0	0	.244	41	10	2	0	0	5	3	12	3	1	2.0	0	0	0	0	-	0	0	0	0	-
Hudson,Tim, Atl	R	.263	76	20	0	9	4	.165	230	38	7	1	0	19	10	71	22	34	224.1	27	43	0	2	1.000	13	4	0	2	.31
Hughes,Phil, NYY	R	-	0	0	0	0	0	-	0	0	0	0	0	0	0	0	0	13	72.2	4	9	1	1	.929	12	3	0	0	.25
Hull,Eric, LAD	R	-	0	0	0	0	0	-	0	0	0	0	0	0	0	0	0	5	6.2	0	0	0	0	-	0	0	0	0	-
Humber,Philip, NYM	R	.000	1	0	0	0	0	.000	1	0	0	0	0	0	0	0	1	3	7.0	0	0	0	0	-	0	0	0	0	-
Igawa,Kei, NYY	L	-	0	0	0	0	1	-	0	0	0	0	0	0	1	0	1	14	67.2	1	3	1	1	.800	2	1	0	0	.50
Isringhausen,Jason, StL	R	-	0	0	0	0	0	.206	102	21	4	1	2	16	5	35	8	63	65.1	5	5	0	1	1.000	1	0	0	0	.00
Jackson,Edwin, TB	R	.500	2	1	0	0	0	.182	22	4	0	0	0	2	2	6	3	32	161.0	11	14	2	0	.926	22	5	1	0	.23
James,Chuck, Atl	L	.113	53	6	0	2	8	.090	89	8	1	0	0	3	3	30	12	30	161.1	7	13	1	0	.952	14	5	1	0	.36
Janssen,Casey, Tor	R	-	0	0	0	0	0	.000	1	0	0	0	0	0	0	0	1	70	72.2	6	5	2	0	.846	2	1	0	0	.50
Jenks,Bobby, CWS	R	-	0	0	0	0	0	-	0	0	0	0	0	0	0	0	0	66	65.0	3	12	0	1	1.000	5	0	0	0	.00
Jennings,Jason, Hou	R	.077	26	2	0	1	1	.207	328	68	14	0	2	26	19	80	28	19	99.0	6	5	0	0	1.000	18	3	1	0	.17
Jimenez,Kelvin, StL	R	.000	2	0	0	0	0	.000	2	0	0	0	0	0	0	1	2	34	42.0	2	6	0	0	1.000	4	0	0	0	.00

Pitcher	T	2007 Hitting						Career Hitting										2007 Fielding and Holding Runners											
		Avg	AB	H	HR	RBI	SH	Avg	AB	H	2B	3B	HR	RBI	BB	SO	SH	G	Inn	PO	A	E	DP	Pct	SBA	CS	PCS	PPO	CS%
Jimenez,Ubaldo, Col	R	.083	24	2	0	0	4	.111	27	3	0	0	0	0	3	7	4	15	82.0	8	14	3	1	.880	16	0	0	0	.00
Johnson,Jim, Bal	R	-	0	0	0	0	0	-	0	0	0	0	0	0	0	0	0	1	2.0	0	0	0	0	-	0	0	0	0	-
Johnson,Josh, Fla	R	.000	2	0	0	0	1	.104	48	5	2	0	0	3	1	26	7	4	15.2	2	1	1	0	.750	2	1	0	0	.50
Johnson,Randy, Ari	L	.067	15	1	0	0	2	.126	549	69	13	0	1	35	14	254	37	10	56.2	0	8	0	0	1.000	8	4	2	0	.50
Johnson,Tyler, StL	L	-	0	0	0	0	1	.000	1	0	0	0	0	0	0	1	1	55	38.0	0	3	0	0	1.000	0	0	0	0	-
Jones,Greg, LAA	R	-	0	0	0	0	0	-	0	0	0	0	0	0	0	0	0	9	8.2	0	1	0	0	1.000	0	0	0	0	-
Jones,Todd, Det	R	-	0	0	0	0	0	.211	19	4	1	0	0	0	1	6	0	63	61.1	2	7	1	0	.900	1	0	0	0	.00
Julio,Jorge, Fla-Col	R	-	0	0	0	0	0	.000	1	0	0	0	0	0	2	1	0	68	62.0	1	3	0	0	1.000	14	2	0	0	.14
Jurrjens,Jair, Det	R	-	0	0	0	0	0	-	0	0	0	0	0	0	0	0	0	7	30.2	0	4	0	0	1.000	2	0	0	0	.00
Karstens,Jeff, NYY	R	-	0	0	0	0	0	-	0	0	0	0	0	0	0	0	0	7	14.2	0	1	0	0	1.000	1	0	0	0	.00
Kazmir,Scott, TB	L	.500	2	1	0	1	0	.167	6	1	0	0	0	1	0	2	0	34	206.2	7	18	3	2	.893	20	8	2	1	.40
Keisler,Randy, StL	L	.167	6	1	0	0	0	.200	25	5	2	0	1	2	0	7	0	4	17.1	0	4	0	0	1.000	0	0	0	0	-
Kendrick,Kyle, Phi	R	.154	39	6	0	2	5	.154	39	6	0	0	0	2	3	17	5	20	121.0	8	19	0	1	1.000	10	2	0	0	.20
Kennedy,Ian, NYY	R	-	0	0	0	0	0	-	0	0	0	0	0	0	0	0	0	3	19.0	0	2	0	0	1.000	2	1	0	0	.50
Kennedy,Joe, Oak-Ari-Tor	L	.333	3	1	0	2	0	.176	91	16	2	1	0	8	3	25	9	39	110.2	2	20	5	1	.815	13	5	2	0	.38
Kensing,Logan, Fla	R	.000	1	0	0	0	0	.000	4	0	0	0	0	0	0	2	1	9	13.1	1	1	0	0	1.000	2	0	0	0	.00
Keppel,Bobby, Col	R	-	0	0	0	0	0	.000	2	0	0	0	0	0	0	0	0	4	4.0	0	0	0	0	-	0	0	0	0	-
Kim,B-H, Col-Fla-Ari	R	.061	33	2	0	1	7	.124	153	19	3	0	0	10	6	39	19	28	118.1	5	10	3	0	.833	29	6	0	0	.21
King,Ray, Was-Mil	L	-	0	0	0	0	0	.000	6	0	0	0	0	0	0	3	0	67	39.2	2	6	1	1	.889	5	1	0	0	.20
Kline,Steve, SF	L	.000	1	0	0	0	0	.143	14	2	1	0	0	2	0	6	4	68	46.0	3	3	1	0	.857	4	2	0	0	.50
Kolb,Dan, Pit	R	-	0	0	0	0	0	.000	1	0	0	0	0	0	0	1	0	3	3.0	0	1	0	0	1.000	0	0	0	0	.00
Komine,Shane, Oak	R	-	0	0	0	0	0	-	0	0	0	0	0	0	0	0	0	2	7.2	0	0	0	0	-	0	0	0	0	-
Koplove,Mike, Cle	R	-	0	0	0	0	0	.000	5	0	0	0	0	0	0	2	0	5	6.0	0	1	0	0	1.000	2	0	0	0	.00
Koronka,John, Tex	L	.000	2	0	0	0	0	.000	12	0	0	0	0	0	1	7	0	2	10.1	0	0	0	0	-	0	0	0	0	-
Kuo,Hong-Chih, LAD	L	.167	6	1	1	1	2	.143	14	2	1	0	1	1	0	9	5	8	30.1	0	4	1	0	.800	3	0	0	0	.00
Kuwata,Masumi, Pit	R	-	0	0	0	0	0	-	0	0	0	0	0	0	0	0	0	19	21.0	1	4	0	0	1.000	4	0	0	0	.00
Lackey,John, LAA	R	.000	2	0	0	0	0	.000	16	0	0	0	0	0	0	4	0	33	224.0	22	25	2	5	.959	25	6	1	1	.24
Laffey,Aaron, Cle	L	-	0	0	0	0	0	-	0	0	0	0	0	0	0	0	0	9	49.1	3	13	0	1	1.000	4	3	0	0	.75
Lannan,John, Was	L	.154	13	2	0	1	0	.154	13	2	1	0	0	1	0	5	0	6	34.2	2	6	0	1	1.000	6	2	1	0	.33
Lara,Juan, Cle	L	-	0	0	0	0	0	-	0	0	0	0	0	0	0	0	0	1	1.1	0	0	0	0	-	0	0	0	0	-
Lawrence,Brian, NYM	R	.250	12	3	0	3	0	.131	289	38	7	0	1	20	13	97	22	6	29.0	2	3	0	1	1.000	6	1	0	0	.17
League,Brandon, Tor	R	-	0	0	0	0	0	-	0	0	0	0	0	0	0	0	0	14	11.2	0	4	1	0	.800	1	1	0	0	1.00
Ledezma,Wil, Det-Atl-SD	L	.000	2	0	0	0	0	.000	2	0	0	0	0	0	0	0	0	44	59.1	4	6	1	0	.909	10	3	1	0	.30
Lee,Cliff, Cle	L	.000	5	0	0	0	0	.091	22	2	0	0	0	0	0	7	0	20	97.1	7	5	1	2	.923	5	1	0	0	.20
Leicester,Jon, Bal	R	-	0	0	0	0	0	.000	1	0	0	0	0	0	0	0	1	10	32.0	3	2	0	0	1.000	2	0	0	0	.00
Lerew,Anthony, Atl	R	.000	3	0	0	0	0	.000	3	0	0	0	0	0	0	0	0	9	11.2	1	4	0	0	1.000	1	0	0	0	.00
Lester,Jon, Bos	L	-	0	0	0	0	0	.000	4	0	0	0	0	0	0	3	0	12	63.0	6	4	1	0	.909	6	2	1	0	.33
Lewis,Colby, Oak	R	-	0	0	0	0	0	.000	1	0	0	0	0	0	0	1	0	26	37.2	1	3	0	1	1.000	1	0	0	0	.00
Lewis,Jensen, Cle	R	-	0	0	0	0	0	-	0	0	0	0	0	0	0	0	0	26	29.1	2	1	1	0	.750	1	1	1	0	1.00
Lidge,Brad, Hou	R	-	0	0	0	0	0	.286	7	2	1	0	0	2	0	4	0	66	67.0	3	4	0	1	1.000	3	0	0	0	.00
Lieber,Jon, Phi	R	.059	17	1	0	1	1	.140	607	85	17	0	0	25	30	230	54	14	78.0	5	5	2	1	.833	2	0	0	0	.00
Lilly,Ted, ChC	L	.137	73	10	0	5	3	.115	96	11	1	0	0	5	1	42	7	34	207.0	5	25	2	1	.938	18	4	2	0	.22
Lincecum,Tim, SF	R	.093	43	4	0	0	6	.093	43	4	1	0	0	0	2	21	6	24	146.1	11	13	0	1	1.000	12	2	0	0	.17
Lindstrom,Matt, Fla	R	.000	1	0	0	0	0	.000	1	0	0	0	0	0	0	1	0	71	67.0	7	6	1	2	.929	2	1	0	0	.50
Linebrink,Scott, SD-Mil	R	.000	1	0	0	0	0	.222	18	4	1	0	0	0	0	10	2	71	70.1	6	8	2	2	.875	9	3	0	0	.33
Litsch,Jesse, Tor	R	.000	1	0	0	0	0	.000	1	0	0	0	0	0	0	0	0	20	111.0	10	21	0	2	1.000	9	3	0	0	.33
Littleton,Wes, Tex	R	.000	1	0	0	0	0	.000	1	0	0	0	0	0	0	1	0	35	48.0	2	9	0	0	1.000	4	1	0	0	.25
Livingston,Bobby, Cin	L	.280	25	7	0	2	4	.280	25	7	0	0	0	2	2	7	4	10	56.1	3	14	0	0	1.000	2	0	0	0	.00
Liz,Radhames, Bal	R	-	0	0	0	0	0	-	0	0	0	0	0	0	0	0	0	9	24.2	0	0	0	0	-	4	1	0	0	.25
Loaiza,Esteban, Oak-LAD	R	.143	7	1	0	2	2	.166	265	44	4	1	0	17	3	68	33	7	37.1	1	2	0	0	1.000	1	0	0	0	.00
Loe,Kameron, Tex	R	.500	2	1	0	0	0	.500	2	1	0	0	0	0	1	0	0	28	136.0	8	29	3	3	.925	16	5	0	1	.31
Loewen,Adam, Bal	L	-	0	0	0	0	0	.000	2	0	0	0	0	0	0	0	0	6	30.1	3	5	0	0	1.000	0	0	0	0	-
Logan,Boone, CWS	L	-	0	0	0	0	0	-	0	0	0	0	0	0	0	0	0	68	50.2	2	3	2	0	.714	8	1	1	0	.13
Lohse,Kyle, Cin-Phi	R	.163	49	8	0	2	12	.174	92	16	2	0	0	6	2	30	17	34	192.2	12	21	1	0	.971	20	8	0	1	.40
Looper,Braden, StL	R	.189	53	10	0	6	5	.190	63	12	3	0	0	6	4	24	6	31	175.0	11	18	0	1	1.000	6	1	0	0	.17
Lopez,Aquilino, Det	R	.000	1	0	0	0	0	.000	1	0	0	0	0	0	0	0	0	10	17.1	1	0	0	0	1.000	0	0	0	0	-
Lopez,Javier, Bos	L	-	0	0	0	0	0	.143	7	1	0	0	0	1	0	3	1	61	40.2	5	6	0	1	1.000	1	1	0	0	1.00
Lopez,Rodrigo, Col	R	.045	22	1	0	0	1	.048	42	2	0	0	0	0	1	25	2	14	79.1	6	15	0	0	1.000	12	4	0	1	.33
Lowe,Derek, LAD	R	.119	59	7	0	1	6	.120	208	25	5	0	0	9	13	61	28	33	199.1	15	24	0	3	1.000	26	12	0	0	.46
Lowe,Mark, Sea	R	-	0	0	0	0	0	-	0	0	0	0	0	0	0	0	0	4	2.2	0	0	0	0	-	1	0	0	0	.00
Lowry,Noah, SF	L	.088	57	5	1	5	4	.178	197	35	10	0	2	14	7	48	27	26	156.0	10	22	4	1	.889	11	4	0	0	.36
Lugo,Ruddy, TB-Oak	R	-	0	0	0	0	0	-	0	0	0	0	0	0	0	0	0	38	48.1	3	8	0	0	1.000	4	2	0	0	.50
Lyon,Brandon, Ari	R	-	0	0	0	0	0	-	0	0	0	0	0	0	0	1	0	73	74.0	3	9	1	0	.923	6	1	0	0	.17
MacDougal,Mike, CWS	R	-	0	0	0	0	0	-	0	0	0	0	0	0	0	0	0	54	42.1	3	4	0	0	1.000	9	0	0	0	.00
Maddux,Greg, SD	R	.145	62	9	0	0	9	.173	1536	266	35	2	5	81	33	404	174	34	198.0	19	51	1	5	.986	39	2	0	1	.05
Madson,Ryan, Phi	R	.000	3	0	0	0	1	.133	45	6	1	0	0	2	2	17	7	38	56.0	2	10	0	0	1.000	4	3	0	0	.75
Mahay,Ron, Tex-Atl	L	.000	1	0	0	0	0	.250	8	2	1	0	0	0	0	2	0	58	67.0	3	8	0	0	1.000	4	3	0	0	.75
Maholm,Paul, Pit	L	.186	59	11	0	5	2	.147	129	19	1	0	0	7	5	66	4	29	177.2	4	32	1	1	.973	17	6	1	0	.35
Maine,John, NYM	R	.109	55	6	1	3	14	.084	83	7	1	0	1	3	5	44	17	32	191.0	5	16	0	1	1.000	17	5	0	1	.29
Majewski,Gary, Cin	R	.000	2	0	0	0	0	.000	13	0	0	0	0	0	0	8	2	32	23.0	2	0	1	0	.667	1	0	0	0	.00

Pitchers Hitting, Fielding and Holding Runners

Pitcher	T	2007 Hitting Avg	AB	H	HR	RBI	SH	Career Hitting Avg	AB	H	2B	3B	HR	RBI	BB	SO	SH	2007 Fielding and Holding Runners G	Inn	PO	A	E	DP	Pct	SBA	CS	PCS	PPO	CS%
Marcum,Shaun, Tor	R	.000	4	0	0	0	0	.000	4	0	0	0	0	0	1	2	0	38	159.0	19	27	0	6	1.000	8	2	0	1	.25
Marmol,Carlos, ChC	R	.000	6	0	0	0	1	.207	29	6	1	0	1	1	0	10	2	59	69.1	4	7	0	1	1.000	9	0	0	1	.00
Maroth,Mike, Det-StL	L	.214	14	3	0	1	1	.233	30	7	1	0	0	3	2	12	4	27	116.1	2	22	0	4	1.000	7	6	4	2	.86
Marquis,Jason, ChC	R	.139	72	10	1	4	4	.207	382	79	22	2	3	30	8	92	19	34	191.2	15	27	2	2	.955	22	2	0	0	.09
Marshall,Jay, Oak	L	-	0	0	0	0	0	-	0	0	0	0	0	0	0	0	0	42	42.0	1	16	1	1	.944	1	0	0	0	.00
Marshall,Sean, ChC	L	.103	29	3	0	0	4	.116	69	8	1	0	1	2	1	32	7	21	103.1	12	12	1	3	.960	7	2	1	0	.29
Marte,Damaso, Pit	L	.000	2	0	0	0	0	.000	8	0	0	0	0	0	0	2	0	65	45.1	1	7	0	0	1.000	1	1	1	0	1.00
Martin,Tom, Col	L	.000	1	0	0	0	1	.000	12	0	0	0	0	0	4	1	26	25.2	0	1	0	0	1.000	1	0	0	0	.00
Martinez,Carlos, Fla	R	.000	1	0	0	0	0	.000	1	0	0	0	0	0	0	1	0	2	2.2	0	0	0	-		0	0	0	0	-
Martinez,Pedro, NYM	R	.111	9	1	0	0	2	.094	381	36	5	2	0	13	14	169	55	5	28.0	1	0	0	1.000	3	0	0	0	.00
Masset,Nick, CWS	R	.000	1	0	0	0	1	.000	1	0	0	0	0	0	0	1	1	27	39.1	0	3	0	0	1.000	9	1	0	0	.11
Mastny,Tom, Cle	R	-	0	0	0	0	0	-	0	0	0	0	0	0	0	0	0	51	57.2	2	11	1	1	.929	6	2	0	0	.33
Mateo,Julio, Sea	R	-	0	0	0	0	0	-	0	0	0	0	0	0	0	0	0	9	12.0	1	1	0	0	1.000	1	1	0	0	1.00
Matsuzaka,Daisuke, Bos	R	.000	4	0	0	0	0	.000	4	0	0	0	0	0	0	2	0	32	204.2	11	23	0	3	1.000	25	1	0	0	.28
McBeth,Marcus, Cin	R	-	0	0	0	0	0	-	0	0	0	0	0	0	0	0	0	23	19.2	1	5	0	1	1.000	7	0	0	0	.00
McBride,Macay, Atl-Det	L	-	0	0	0	0	0	-	0	0	0	0	0	0	0	0	0	38	30.2	2	3	0	0	1.000	1	0	0	0	.00
McCarthy,Brandon, Tex	R	.000	2	0	0	0	1	.000	5	0	0	0	0	0	0	4	1	23	101.2	10	6	2	1	.889	22	5	0	0	.23
McClellan,Zach, Col	R	.000	1	0	0	0	0	.000	1	0	0	0	0	0	0	1	0	12	14.0	0	4	0	0	1.000	1	1	0	0	1.00
McClung,Seth, Mil	R	-	0	0	0	0	0	.000	1	0	0	0	0	0	0	0	1	14	12.0	1	0	0	0	1.000	0	0	0	0	-
McGowan,Dustin, Tor	R	.286	7	2	0	0	0	.286	7	2	0	0	0	0	0	3	0	27	169.2	17	29	4	2	.920	30	1	0	0	.03
McLeary,Marty, Pit	R	.000	2	0	0	0	0	.000	7	0	0	0	0	0	0	3	0	4	7.2	0	0	0	-		1	0	0	0	.00
McLemore,Mark, Hou	L	-	0	0	0	0	0	-	0	0	0	0	0	0	0	0	0	29	35.0	1	0	0	0	1.000	1	0	0	0	.00
Meche,Gil, KC	R	.000	4	0	0	0	0	.118	17	2	0	0	1	0	7	0	34	216.0	15	22	3	5	.925	9	5	1	1	.56				
Medders,Brandon, Ari	R	-	0	0	0	0	0	.000	3	0	0	0	0	0	0	1	0	30	29.1	4	1	1	0	.833	5	5	0	0	1.00
Meloan,Jonathan, LAD	R	-	0	0	0	0	0	-	0	0	0	0	0	0	0	0	0	5	7.1	1	0	0	0	1.000	1	1	0	0	.00
Mendoza,Luis, Tex	R	-	0	0	0	0	0	-	0	0	0	0	0	0	0	0	0	6	16.0	2	4	0	0	1.000	1	1	0	1	1.00
Meredith,Cla, SD	R	.000	1	0	0	0	0	.000	1	0	0	0	0	0	0	1	0	80	79.2	6	15	0	1	1.000	9	2	0	0	.22
Mesa,Jose, Det-Phi	R	-	0	0	0	0	0	.000	2	0	0	0	0	0	1	1	0	56	50.2	2	5	0	0	1.000	1	0	0	0	.00
Messenger,Randy, Fla-SF	R	.000	1	0	0	0	1	.167	6	1	0	0	0	1	3	1	60	64.1	2	9	1	0	.917	6	1	1	0	.17			
Meyer,Dan, Oak	L	-	0	0	0	0	0	-	0	0	0	0	0	0	0	0	0	6	16.1	0	0	0	-		1	0	0	0	.00
Miller,Andrew, Det	L	.000	5	0	0	0	0	.000	5	0	0	0	0	0	0	5	0	13	64.0	2	8	2	1	.833	11	1	0	0	.09
Miller,Jason, Min	L	-	0	0	0	0	0	-	0	0	0	0	0	0	0	0	0	4	4.0	0	0	0	-		1	0	0	0	.00
Miller,Justin, Fla	R	.000	2	0	0	0	0	.000	4	0	0	0	0	0	0	1	0	62	61.2	2	5	0	0	1.000	3	2	1	0	.67
Miller,Matt, Cle	R	-	0	0	0	0	0	-	0	0	0	0	0	0	0	0	0	2	1.0	0	1	0	0	1.000	0	0	0	0	-
Miller,Trever, Hou	L	-	0	0	0	0	0	.167	6	1	1	0	0	0	0	1	2	76	46.1	1	3	0	0	1.000	3	0	0	0	.00
Miller,Wade, ChC	R	.250	4	1	0	0	0	.172	273	47	9	0	0	17	4	86	30	3	13.2	0	1	0	0	1.000	2	1	0	0	.50
Millwood,Kevin, Tex	R	.000	4	0	0	0	0	.121	437	53	14	0	2	24	19	200	51	31	172.2	4	13	3	0	.850	19	5	0	0	.26
Milton,Eric, Cin	L	.143	7	1	0	2	2	.183	197	36	5	1	2	16	10	87	18	6	31.1	0	6	0	0	1.000	2	0	0	0	.00
Miner,Zach, Det	R	-	0	0	0	0	0	.167	6	1	1	0	0	0	0	3	0	34	53.2	1	8	2	0	.818	10	6	0	0	.60
Misch,Pat, SF	L	.111	9	1	0	0	1	.111	9	1	0	0	0	0	0	3	1	18	40.1	2	4	1	0	.857	4	1	1	0	.25
Mitre,Sergio, Fla	R	.079	38	3	0	0	7	.141	78	11	4	0	0	2	3	33	13	27	149.0	18	29	1	0	.979	15	3	1	0	.20
Moehler,Brian, Hou	R	.200	5	1	0	0	0	.057	106	6	1	0	0	5	4	45	13	42	59.2	8	7	0	3	1.000	3	0	0	0	.00
Morales,Franklin, Col	L	.308	13	4	0	1	1	.308	13	4	0	0	0	1	1	5	1	8	39.1	0	11	0	1	1.000	5	1	0	1	.20
Morillo,Juan, Col	R	.000	1	0	0	0	0	.000	1	0	0	0	0	0	0	0	0	4	3.2	0	0	0	-		1	0	0	0	.00
Morris,Matt, SF-Pit	R	.228	57	13	1	3	11	.168	536	90	17	0	2	37	27	212	81	32	198.2	16	28	1	3	.978	17	2	0	0	.12
Morrow,Brandon, Sea	R	-	0	0	0	0	0	-	0	0	0	0	0	0	0	0	0	60	63.1	1	2	0	0	1.000	5	2	0	0	.40
Moseley,Dustin, LAA	R	-	0	0	0	0	0	-	0	0	0	0	0	0	0	0	0	46	92.0	4	4	1	1	.889	9	3	0	0	.33
Mota,Guillermo, NYM	R	.000	1	0	0	0	0	.206	34	7	1	0	2	6	0	17	0	52	59.1	1	14	1	0	.938	7	0	0	0	.00
Moyer,Jamie, Phi	L	.123	73	9	0	2	8	.142	268	38	4	0	9	18	89	34	33	199.1	14	32	1	0	.979	15	6	4	0	.40			
Moylan,Peter, Atl	R	.000	4	0	0	0	0	.000	4	0	0	0	0	0	1	3	0	80	90.0	7	20	0	1	1.000	11	2	0	1	.18
Mujica,Edward, Cle	R	-	0	0	0	0	0	-	0	0	0	0	0	0	0	0	0	10	13.0	0	0	0	-		1	0	0	0	.00
Mulder,Mark, StL	L	.500	2	1	0	0	0	.162	111	18	2	0	1	9	9	45	8	3	11.0	0	3	0	0	1.000	1	1	1	0	1.00
Muniz,Carlos, NYM	R	-	0	0	0	0	0	-	0	0	0	0	0	0	0	0	0	2	2.1	0	0	0	-		1	0	0	0	.00
Munoz,Arnie, Was	L	-	0	0	0	0	0	.000	1	0	0	0	0	0	0	0	0	13	5.1	0	0	0	-		0	0	0	0	-
Munter,Scott, SF	R	-	0	0	0	0	0	1.000	1	1	0	0	0	0	0	1	0	12	10.2	1	1	0	0	1.000	0	0	0	0	.00
Murphy,Bill, Ari	L	-	0	0	0	0	0	-	0	0	0	0	0	0	0	0	0	10	6.1	0	1	0	0	1.000	0	0	0	0	-
Murray,A.J., Tex	L	-	0	0	0	0	0	-	0	0	0	0	0	0	0	0	0	14	28.0	1	4	0	0	1.000	4	0	0	0	.00
Musser,Neal, KC	L	.000	1	0	0	0	0	.000	1	0	0	0	0	0	0	0	0	17	24.2	0	0	0	-		4	1	0	0	.25
Mussina,Mike, NYY	R	.000	2	0	0	0	0	.170	47	8	1	0	0	5	1	9	1	28	152.0	12	24	0	4	1.000	27	3	0	0	.11
Myers,Brett, Phi	R	.000	6	0	0	0	1	.126	270	34	7	0	9	14	91	35	51	68.2	6	10	0	1	1.000	7	1	0	0	.14			
Myers,Mike, NYY-CWS	L	.000	1	0	0	0	0	.000	2	0	0	0	0	0	0	1	0	72	54.1	3	13	0	1	1.000	8	2	1	0	.25
Nathan,Joe, Min	R	-	0	0	0	0	0	.159	63	10	3	0	2	4	3	17	10	68	71.2	1	3	1	0	.800	7	0	0	0	.00
Neshek,Pat, Min	R	-	0	0	0	0	0	-	0	0	0	0	0	0	0	0	0	74	70.1	3	8	0	0	1.000	3	2	0	0	.67
Newman,Josh, Col	L	-	0	0	0	0	0	-	0	0	0	0	0	0	0	0	0	2	3.0	0	0	0	-		0	0	0	0	-
Nippert,Dustin, Ari	R	.000	2	0	0	0	0	.125	8	1	0	0	0	0	1	6	0	36	45.1	1	3	1	1	.800	1	0	0	0	.00
Nolasco,Ricky, Fla	R	.000	6	0	0	0	1	.149	47	7	0	0	1	5	2	22	7	5	21.1	1	1	0	0	1.000	3	1	0	0	.33
Nunez,Leo, KC	R	-	0	0	0	0	0	-	0	0	0	0	0	0	0	0	0	13	43.2	2	0	0	0	1.000	5	0	0	0	.00
Obermueller,Wes, Fla	R	.063	16	1	0	0	3	.237	93	22	5	1	0	6	1	26	8	18	59.0	8	7	0	2	1.000	8	2	0	0	.25
O'Flaherty,Eric, Sea	L	.000	1	0	0	0	0	.000	1	0	0	0	0	0	0	1	0	56	52.1	0	10	0	2	1.000	4	2	1	0	.50
Ohka,Tomo, Tor	R	-	0	0	0	0	0	.139	238	33	2	0	0	15	10	94	24	10	56.0	4	3	2	0	.778	1	1	0	0	1.00

Pitchers Hitting, Fielding and Holding Runners

Pitcher	T	2007 Hitting						Career Hitting										2007 Fielding and Holding Runners											
		Avg	AB	H	HR	RBI	SH	Avg	AB	H	2B	3B	HR	RBI	BB	SO	SH	G	Inn	PO	A	E	DP	Pct	SBA	CS	PCS	PPO	CS%
Ohlendorf,Ross, NYY	R	-	0	0	0	0	0	-	0	0	0	0	0	0	0	0	0	6	6.1	0	0	0	0	-	0	0	0	0	-
Ohman,Will, ChC	L	-	0	0	0	0	0	1.000	1	1	0	0	0	0	0	0	0	56	36.1	3	4	0	1	1.000	4	0	0	0	.00
Okajima,Hideki, Bos	L	-	0	0	0	0	0	-	0	0	0	0	0	0	0	0	0	66	69.0	1	11	0	1	1.000	5	0	0	0	.00
Oliver,Darren, LAA	L	-	0	0	0	0	0	.221	217	48	11	0	1	20	8	74	15	61	64.1	2	11	1	1	.929	3	0	0	0	.00
Olsen,Scott, Fla	L	.176	51	9	0	3	9	.179	112	20	5	0	0	11	1	42	16	33	176.2	3	21	0	0	1.000	16	6	2	0	.38
Olson,Garrett, Bal	L	-	0	0	0	0	0	-	0	0	0	0	0	0	0	0	0	7	32.1	0	5	2	0	.714	4	1	1	0	.25
Ortiz,Ramon, Min-Col	R	.250	4	1	0	1	0	.081	136	11	2	0	1	4	5	57	14	38	104.0	10	12	2	3	.917	11	3	0	0	.27
Ortiz,Russ, SF	R	.176	17	3	0	3	2	.207	479	99	23	0	6	47	34	126	58	12	49.0	6	9	0	1	1.000	6	2	0	0	.33
Orvella,Chad, TB	R	-	0	0	0	0	0	-	0	0	0	0	0	0	0	0	0	10	8.0	0	3	1	0	.750	3	0	0	0	.00
Osoria,Franquelis, Pit	R	.000	4	0	0	0	1	.000	9	0	0	0	0	0	0	6	1	25	28.1	1	8	0	0	1.000	1	0	0	0	.00
Oswalt,Roy, Hou	R	.125	64	8	0	3	11	.153	437	67	7	0	1	26	19	124	68	33	212.0	20	36	0	3	1.000	6	1	0	0	.17
Otsuka,Akinori, Tex	R	-	0	0	0	0	0	.000	2	0	0	0	0	0	0	1	0	34	32.1	2	2	1	0	.800	5	2	0	0	.40
Owens,Henry, Fla	R	-	0	0	0	0	0	-	0	0	0	0	0	0	0	0	0	22	23.0	1	2	0	0	1.000	1	0	0	0	.00
Owings,Micah , Ari	R	.333	60	20	4	15	1	.333	60	20	7	1	4	15	2	16	1	29	152.2	6	20	2	1	.929	7	3	0	0	.43
Padilla,Vicente, Tex	R	.500	2	1	0	0	0	.096	208	20	3	1	0	13	14	110	20	23	120.1	6	12	1	2	.947	6	3	1	0	.50
Papelbon,Jonathan, Bos	R	-	0	0	0	0	0	-	0	0	0	0	0	0	0	0	0	59	58.1	4	0	0	0	1.000	4	0	0	0	.00
Park,Chan Ho, NYM	R	.000	1	0	0	0	0	.182	406	74	15	1	2	30	17	145	50	1	4.0	1	0	0	0	1.000	0	0	0	0	-
Paronto,Chad, Atl	R	-	0	0	0	0	0	.000	1	0	0	0	0	0	0	1	0	41	40.1	1	7	0	1	1.000	8	2	0	0	.25
Parra,Manny, Mil	L	.222	9	2	0	2	1	.222	9	2	2	0	0	2	0	3	1	9	26.1	0	3	0	1	1.000	0	0	0	0	-
Parrish,John, Bal-Sea	L	-	0	0	0	0	0	.000	1	0	0	0	0	0	0	0	0	53	52.0	2	8	0	1	1.000	0	0	0	1	-
Patterson,John, Was	R	.000	10	0	0	0	0	.106	132	14	3	0	0	2	2	56	17	7	31.1	1	2	0	0	1.000	8	1	0	0	.13
Patton,Troy, Hou	L	.333	3	1	0	0	0	.333	3	1	0	0	0	0	0	1	0	3	12.2	0	0	0	0	-	0	0	0	0	-
Paulino,Felipe, Hou	R	.000	6	0	0	0	0	.000	6	0	0	0	0	0	0	4	0	5	19.0	4	1	0	0	1.000	0	0	0	0	-
Pavano,Carl, NYY	R	-	0	0	0	0	0	.139	295	41	8	2	2	14	4	116	34	2	11.1	1	2	0	0	1.000	3	0	0	0	.00
Peavy,Jake, SD	R	.233	73	17	0	7	8	.174	333	58	12	1	2	24	14	100	36	34	223.1	21	27	0	1	1.000	23	2	0	1	.09
Peguero,Jailen, Ari	R	-	0	0	0	0	0	-	0	0	0	0	0	0	0	0	0	18	14.2	0	3	0	0	1.000	1	1	0	0	1.00
Pelfrey,Mike, NYM	R	.095	21	2	0	0	0	.067	30	2	1	0	0	0	1	13	0	15	72.2	1	7	0	0	1.000	8	0	0	1	.00
Pena,Tony, Ari	R	.250	4	1	0	1	0	.167	6	1	0	0	0	1	0	2	0	75	85.1	4	8	1	1	.923	1	0	0	2	.00
Penny,Brad, LAD	R	.246	65	16	0	7	7	.156	454	71	16	2	2	28	3	148	32	33	208.0	13	23	0	2	1.000	19	5	0	0	.26
Peralta,Joel, KC	R	1.000	1	1	0	2	0	1.000	1	1	1	0	0	2	0	0	0	62	87.2	4	7	0	1	1.000	8	0	0	1	.00
Percival,Troy, StL	R	.000	4	0	0	0	0	.000	5	0	0	0	0	0	0	5	0	34	40.0	2	0	0	0	1.000	5	3	0	0	.60
Perez,Juan, Pit	L	-	0	0	0	0	0	-	0	0	0	0	0	0	0	0	0	17	12.1	0	3	0	0	1.000	1	0	0	0	.00
Perez,Odalis, KC	L	.200	5	1	0	0	0	.129	287	37	8	0	1	10	6	73	41	26	137.1	7	17	0	0	1.000	12	3	1	0	.25
Perez,Oliver, NYM	L	.161	56	9	0	1	6	.161	254	41	2	0	0	11	8	82	30	29	177.0	1	14	3	0	.833	16	3	2	1	.19
Perez,Rafael, Cle	L	-	0	0	0	0	0	-	0	0	0	0	0	0	0	0	0	44	60.2	4	5	2	0	.818	3	1	0	0	.33
Perkins,Glen, Min	L	-	0	0	0	0	0	-	0	0	0	0	0	0	0	0	0	19	28.2	0	3	0	2	1.000	2	1	0	0	.50
Petit,Yusmeiro, Ari	R	.063	16	1	0	0	2	.095	21	2	0	0	0	1	0	10	2	14	57.0	0	5	0	0	1.000	4	0	0	0	.00
Petrick,Billy, ChC	R	-	0	0	0	0	0	-	0	0	0	0	0	0	0	0	0	8	9.2	0	0	0	0	-	2	1	0	0	.50
Pettitte,Andy, NYY	L	.000	4	0	0	0	0	.134	179	24	5	0	1	12	6	57	31	36	215.1	13	28	1	2	.976	26	8	4	1	.31
Phillips,Heath, CWS	L	-	0	0	0	0	0	-	0	0	0	0	0	0	0	0	0	6	7.1	1	4	0	1	1.000	0	0	0	1	-
Pignatiello,Carmen, ChC	L	-	0	0	0	0	0	-	0	0	0	0	0	0	0	0	0	4	2.0	0	0	0	0	-	1	1	0	0	1.00
Pineiro,Joel, Bos-StL	R	.056	18	1	0	0	4	.071	42	3	1	0	0	2	2	23	8	42	97.2	8	18	2	0	.929	6	2	0	0	.33
Pinto,Renyel, Fla	L	.000	3	0	0	0	0	.000	4	0	0	0	0	0	0	2	0	57	58.2	2	4	0	1	1.000	5	3	0	0	.60
Ponson,Sidney, Min	R	-	0	0	0	0	0	.143	63	9	3	0	0	1	3	20	11	7	37.2	4	3	1	0	.875	3	2	0	0	.67
Prinz,Bret, CWS	R	-	0	0	0	0	0	-	0	0	0	0	0	0	0	0	0	3	3.1	0	0	0	0	-	0	0	0	0	-
Proctor,Scott, NYY-LAD	R	.000	3	0	0	0	0	.000	3	0	0	0	0	0	0	3	0	83	86.1	3	7	0	1	1.000	13	4	0	0	.31
Putz,J.J., Sea	R	-	0	0	0	0	0	-	0	0	0	0	0	0	0	0	0	68	71.2	6	5	0	0	1.000	3	0	0	0	.00
Qualls,Chad, Hou	R	-	0	0	0	0	0	.000	2	0	0	0	0	0	0	2	0	79	82.2	5	14	0	2	1.000	12	5	1	0	.42
Rakers,Aaron, SD	R	-	0	0	0	0	0	-	0	0	0	0	0	0	0	0	0	1	1.0	0	0	0	0	-	0	0	0	0	-
Ramirez,Edwar, NYY	R	-	0	0	0	0	0	-	0	0	0	0	0	0	0	0	0	21	21.0	2	2	0	0	1.000	2	0	0	0	.00
Ramirez,Elizardo, Cin	R	.200	5	1	0	0	0	.154	39	6	1	0	0	3	2	12	2	4	16.1	2	0	0	0	1.000	1	0	0	0	.00
Ramirez,Erasmo, Oak-Fla	L	-	0	0	0	0	0	-	0	0	0	0	0	0	0	0	0	7	6.1	0	2	0	1	1.000	0	0	0	0	-
Ramirez,Horacio, Sea	L	-	0	0	0	0	0	.151	179	27	3	1	0	5	2	36	13	20	98.0	4	26	0	3	1.000	14	5	3	0	.36
Ramirez,Ramon, Col	R	-	0	0	0	0	0	.500	4	2	0	0	0	0	0	2	1	22	17.1	1	2	0	0	1.000	3	0	0	0	.00
Randolph,Stephen, Hou	L	-	0	0	0	0	0	.333	15	5	3	0	0	3	0	5	1	14	13.1	0	1	0	0	1.000	2	0	0	0	.00
Rapada,Clay, ChC-Det	L	-	0	0	0	0	0	-	0	0	0	0	0	0	0	0	0	5	5.2	0	0	0	0	-	0	0	0	0	-
Rasner,Darrell, NYY	R	-	0	0	0	0	0	-	0	0	0	0	0	0	0	0	0	6	24.2	1	2	0	0	1.000	4	1	0	0	.25
Rauch,Jon, Was	R	.000	3	0	0	0	0	.100	20	2	0	0	1	3	0	14	1	88	87.1	5	5	0	0	1.000	6	1	1	0	.17
Ray,Chris, Bal	R	-	0	0	0	0	0	-	0	0	0	0	0	0	0	0	0	43	42.2	5	5	1	0	.909	3	1	0	0	.33
Redding,Tim, Was	R	.071	28	2	0	2	1	.141	149	21	4	0	0	7	2	71	14	15	84.0	2	14	1	1	.941	8	3	0	0	.38
Redman,Mark, Atl-Col	L	.000	13	0	0	0	0	.056	143	8	0	0	0	3	6	64	10	11	41.1	0	3	0	0	1.000	2	1	0	0	.50
Reitsma,Chris, Sea	R	-	0	0	0	0	0	.103	87	9	1	0	0	5	3	42	14	26	23.2	1	4	0	0	1.000	4	0	0	0	.00
Resop,Chris, LAA	R	-	0	0	0	0	0	.000	1	0	0	0	0	0	0	1	0	4	4.1	0	0	0	0	-	0	0	0	0	-
Reyes,Al, TB	R	-	0	0	0	0	0	.250	12	3	0	0	0	1	0	6	2	61	60.2	2	3	0	0	1.000	2	0	0	0	.00
Reyes,Anthony, StL	R	.077	26	2	0	1	6	.091	55	5	0	0	0	1	0	21	8	22	107.1	7	9	0	1	1.000	6	2	0	2	.33
Reyes,Dennys, Min	L	-	0	0	0	0	0	.074	54	4	1	0	0	0	2	25	2	50	29.1	1	5	1	0	.857	4	3	3	0	.75
Reyes,Jo-Jo, Atl	L	.158	19	3	0	0	4	.158	19	3	0	0	0	0	0	7	4	11	50.2	1	7	0	1	1.000	3	1	1	0	.33
Rheinecker,John, Tex	L	-	0	0	0	0	0	-	0	0	0	0	0	0	0	0	0	23	50.1	3	10	0	0	1.000	0	0	0	0	-
Ridgway,Jeff, TB	L	-	0	0	0	0	0	-	0	0	0	0	0	0	0	0	0	3	0.1	0	0	0	0	-	0	0	0	0	-
Rincon,Juan, Min	R	-	0	0	0	0	0	.500	2	1	0	0	0	0	0	1	0	63	59.2	3	11	1	1	.933	4	1	0	0	.25

Pitchers Hitting, Fielding and Holding Runners

Pitcher	T	Avg	AB	H	HR	RBI	SH	Avg	AB	H	2B	3B	HR	RBI	BB	SO	SH	G	Inn	PO	A	E	DP	Pct	SBA	CS	PCS	PPO	CS%
Ring,Royce, SD-Atl	L	-	0	0	0	0	0		0	0	0	0	0	0	0	0	0	26	20.0	1	5	0	0	1.000	2	1	0	0	.50
Riske,David, KC	R	-	0	0	0	0	0	.000	0	0	0	0	0	0	0	0	0	65	69.2	5	11	0	2	1.000	5	1	0	0	.20
Rivera,Mariano, NYY	R	-	0	0	0	0	0	.000	1	0	0	0	0	0	0	1	0	67	71.1	6	10	0	1	1.000	3	1	0	0	.33
Rivera,Saul, Was	R	.000	1	0	0	0	0	.000	5	0	0	0	0	0	1	2	0	85	93.0	4	26	0	2	1.000	4	2	0	0	.50
Robertson,Connor, Oak	R	-	0	0	0	0	0	-	0	0	0	0	0	0	0	0	0	3	2.0	0	1	0	0	1.000	0	0	0	0	-
Robertson,Nate, Det	L	-	0	0	0	0	0	.071	14	1	0	0	0	1	0	6	1	30	177.2	4	28	2	2	.941	11	4	1	0	.36
Rodney,Fernando, Det	R	-	0	0	0	0	0	.000	1	0	0	0	0	0	0	0	0	48	50.2	2	12	1	0	.933	8	2	0	0	.25
Rodriguez,Francisco, LAA	R	-	0	0	0	0	0	-	0	0	0	0	0	0	0	0	0	64	67.1	4	2	0	0	1.000	13	1	0	0	.08
Rodriguez,Wandy, Hou	L	.122	49	6	0	2	12	.119	126	15	1	0	0	4	5	41	18	31	182.2	11	25	1	1	.973	22	9	6	0	.41
Rogers,Brian, Pit	R	-	0	0	0	0	0	-	0	0	0	0	0	0	0	0	0	3	2.0	0	1	0	0	1.000	1	0	0	0	.00
Rogers,Kenny, Det	L	.000	2	0	0	0	0	.138	65	9	1	1	0	4	4	24	4	11	63.0	7	10	1	0	.944	9	0	0	2	
Romero,J.C., Bos-Phi	L	.000	1	0	0	0	0	.250	4	1	1	0	0	0	0	1	0	74	56.1	6	10	1	0	.941	6	2	1	0	.33
Rosario,Francisco, Phi	R	-	0	0	0	0	1	.000	1	0	0	0	0	0	0	0	1	23	26.1	1	4	0	0	1.000	4	1	0	0	.25
Rowland-Smith,R, Sea	L	-	0	0	0	0	0	-	0	0	0	0	0	0	0	0	0	26	38.2	1	5	1	1	.857	2	2	1	1	1.00
Ryan,B.J., Tor	L	-	0	0	0	0	0	.000	2	0	0	0	0	0	0	0	0	5	4.1	0	0	0	0	-	0	0	0	0	-
Ryu,Jae Kuk, TB	R	-	0	0	0	0	0	.000	1	0	0	0	0	0	0	1	0	17	23.1	1	1	0	0	1.000	4	2	0	0	.50
Saarloos,Kirk, Cin	R	.200	5	1	0	2	1	.073	41	3	2	0	0	5	1	12	9	34	42.2	2	11	1	1	.929	2	0	0	0	.00
Sabathia,C.C., Cle	L	.667	3	2	0	0	0	.297	37	11	1	0	1	6	1	10	1	34	241.0	1	24	1	0	.962	20	10	1	0	.50
Saito,Takashi, LAD	R	-	0	0	0	0	0	-	0	0	0	0	0	0	0	0	0	63	64.1	3	10	0	5	1.000	2	0	0	0	.00
Salas,Juan, TB	R	-	0	0	0	0	0	-	0	0	0	0	0	0	0	0	0	34	36.1	4	4	0	0	1.000	3	1	1	0	.33
Salmon,Brad, Cin	R	-	0	0	0	0	0	-	0	0	0	0	0	0	0	0	0	26	24.0	0	2	0	0	1.000	2	0	0	0	.00
Sampson,Chris, Hou	R	.154	26	4	0	0	8	.129	31	4	0	0	0	0	0	12	10	24	121.2	27	23	0	2	1.000	4	1	0	1	.25
Sanches,Brian, Phi	R	-	0	0	0	0	0	-	0	0	0	0	0	0	0	0	0	12	14.2	0	1	0	0	1.000	3	2	0	0	.67
Sanchez,Anibal, Fla	R	.091	11	1	0	0	1	.109	46	5	0	0	0	2	2	21	4	6	30.0	2	8	2	0	.833	1	0	0	0	.00
Sanchez,Jonathan, SF	L	.167	6	1	0	1	1	.077	13	1	1	0	0	1	1	7	1	33	52.0	0	6	0	1	1.000	5	4	1	0	.80
Sanchez,Romulo, Pit	R	.000	1	0	0	0	0	.000	1	0	0	0	0	0	0	1	0	16	18.0	4	1	0	0	1.000	0	0	0	0	-
Santana,Ervin, LAA	R	.200	5	1	0	2	0	.222	9	2	1	0	0	2	0	6	0	28	150.0	6	13	0	2	1.000	14	3	0	0	.21
Santana,Johan, Min	L	.286	7	2	0	1	0	.258	31	8	1	1	0	3	1	4	0	33	219.0	14	26	0	1	1.000	11	5	3	1	.45
Santos,Victor, Cin-Bal	R	.000	3	0	0	0	1	.097	124	12	2	0	0	2	2	48	17	36	63.1	4	5	1	0	.900	6	2	0	1	.33
Sarfate,Dennis, Hou	R	-	0	0	0	0	0	-	0	0	0	0	0	0	0	0	0	7	8.1	1	0	0	0	1.000	0	0	0	0	-
Saunders,Joe, LAA	L	-	0	0	0	0	0	-	0	0	0	0	0	0	0	0	0	18	107.1	3	14	0	0	1.000	11	4	2	0	.36
Schilling,Curt, Bos	R	.500	2	1	0	0	0	.151	773	117	13	1	0	29	25	270	102	24	151.0	12	9	0	0	1.000	6	1	0	1	.17
Schmidt,Jason, LAD	R	.143	7	1	1	1	1	.105	591	62	9	0	7	21	22	282	89	6	25.2	1	2	0	0	1.000	1	0	0	0	.00
Schoeneweis,Scott, NYM	L	-	0	0	0	0	0	.286	7	2	1	0	0	1	2	2	0	70	59.0	5	4	1	1	.900	7	1	1	0	.14
Schroder,Chris, Was	R	.000	2	0	0	0	0	.000	4	0	0	0	0	0	0	2	0	37	45.1	3	3	0	0	1.000	4	1	0	0	.25
Schultz,Mike, Ari	R	-	0	0	0	0	0	-	0	0	0	0	0	0	0	0	0	1	1.0	0	0	0	0	-	0	0	0	0	-
Seanez,Rudy, LAD	R	.000	1	0	0	0	0	.000	5	0	0	0	0	0	1	5	0	73	76.0	2	6	0	0	1.000	11	1	0	0	.09
Seay,Bobby, Det	L	.000	1	0	0	0	0	.000	1	0	0	0	0	0	0	1	0	58	46.1	2	5	0	0	1.000	2	1	0	0	.50
Soddon,Chris, Fla	I	.000	3	0	0	0	2	.000	3	0	0	0	0	0	0	2	2	7	17.1	0	5	0	0	1.000	3	0	0	0	.00
Segovia,Zack, Phi	R	.000	2	0	0	0	0	.000	2	0	0	0	0	0	0	0	0	1	5.0	0	1	0	0	1.000	0	0	0	0	-
Sele,Aaron, NYM	R	.000	4	0	0	0	1	.155	58	9	2	0	0	1	3	13	12	34	53.2	2	9	0	1	1.000	0	0	0	0	
Seo,Jae, TB	R	-	0	0	0	0	0	.115	131	15	3	0	0	5	9	45	11	11	52.0	3	2	0	1	1.000	5	2	0	0	.40
Serafini,Dan, Col	L	-	0	0	0	0	0	.070	43	3	0	0	0	2	3	19	5	3	0.1	0	0	0	0	-	0	0	0	0	-
Sharpless,Josh, Pit	R	-	0	0	0	0	0	-	0	0	0	0	0	0	0	0	0	6	4.1	1	0	0	0	1.000	0	0	0	0	-
Shearn,Tom, Cin	R	.000	11	0	0	0	1	.000	11	0	0	0	0	0	1	4	1	7	32.2	3	2	0	0	1.000	0	0	0	0	
Sheets,Ben, Mil	R	.067	45	3	0	0	6	.077	366	28	1	0	0	7	16	180	36	24	141.1	9	10	0	0	1.000	21	0	0	1	.00
Sherrill,George, Sea	L	-	0	0	0	0	0	-	0	0	0	0	0	0	0	0	0	73	45.2	0	6	1	0	.857	0	0	0	0	-
Shields,James, TB	R	.167	6	1	0	0	1	.286	14	4	0	0	0	0	0	3	1	31	215.0	30	24	1	3	.982	15	6	0	0	.40
Shields,Scot, LAA	R	-	0	0	0	0	0	.000	3	0	0	0	0	0	0	2	0	71	77.0	5	9	2	1	.875	4	1	0	1	.25
Shouse,Brian, Mil	L	-	0	0	0	0	0	-	0	0	0	0	0	0	0	0	0	73	47.2	2	10	0	0	1.000	8	2	1	0	.25
Shuey,Paul, Bal	R	-	0	0	0	0	0	.143	7	1	0	0	0	0	0	3	0	25	25.2	1	1	0	0	1.000	3	1	0	0	.33
Silva,Carlos, Min	R	.000	4	0	0	0	2	.130	23	3	1	0	0	1	1	7	3	33	202.0	14	26	0	2	1.000	15	7	0	0	.47
Simontacchi,Jason, Was	R	.053	19	1	0	0	1	.174	109	19	1	0	0	2	2	34	5	13	70.2	3	12	0	3	1.000	3	3	0	4	1.00
Sisco,Andy, CWS	L	-	0	0	0	0	0	.000	1	0	0	0	0	0	0	1	0	19	14.0	1	0	0	0	1.000	3	0	0	0	.00
Slaten,Doug, Ari	L	-	0	0	0	0	0	-	0	0	0	0	0	0	0	0	0	61	36.1	0	1	1	0	.500	3	0	0	0	.00
Slowey,Kevin, Min	R	-	0	0	0	0	0	-	0	0	0	0	0	0	0	0	0	13	66.2	4	2	0	0	1.000	0	0	0	0	-
Smith,Joe, NYM	R	.000	1	0	0	0	0	.000	1	0	0	0	0	0	0	1	0	54	44.1	2	9	0	0	1.000	6	1	0	0	.17
Smith,Matt, Phi	L	-	0	0	0	0	0	-	0	0	0	0	0	0	0	0	0	9	4.0	0	1	1	0	.500	1	0	0	0	.00
Smoltz,John, Atl	R	.093	54	5	0	2	13	.162	925	150	26	2	5	60	78	356	135	32	205.2	19	29	3	1	.941	15	4	0	1	.27
Snell,Ian, Pit	R	.088	57	5	0	2	12	.066	121	8	1	0	0	4	5	56	22	32	208.0	11	15	0	1	1.000	20	6	0	0	.30
Snyder,Kyle, Bos	R	-	0	0	0	0	0	.000	2	0	0	0	0	0	0	1	0	46	54.1	4	7	1	0	.917	7	2	0	1	.29
Sonnanstine,Andy, TB	R	.400	5	2	0	1	0	.400	5	2	0	0	0	1	0	2	0	22	130.2	16	13	2	3	.935	9	8	0	0	.89
Soria,Joakim, KC	R	-	0	0	0	0	0	-	0	0	0	0	0	0	0	0	0	62	69.0	4	9	1	0	.929	0	0	0	1	
Soriano,Rafael, Atl	R	-	0	0	0	0	0	.000	4	0	0	0	0	0	0	1	0	71	72.0	2	2	1	0	.800	9	2	0	0	.22
Sosa,Jorge, NYM	R	.200	25	5	0	1	2	.138	80	11	2	0	3	4	6	35	11	42	112.2	2	8	0	0	1.000	6	2	0	0	.33
Sowers,Jeremy, Cle	L	1.000	1	1	0	0	0	1.000	1	1	0	0	0	0	1	0	0	13	67.1	5	7	0	2	1.000	12	2	0	0	.17
Speier,Justin, LAA	R	-	0	0	0	0	0	.176	17	3	0	0	0	0	0	8	0	51	50.0	4	3	1	0	.875	5	3	0	0	.60
Speier,Ryan, Col	R	-	0	0	0	0	0	.000	2	0	0	0	0	0	0	0	0	20	18.0	0	2	0	0	1.000	2	1	0	0	.50
Speigner,Levale, Was	R	.000	4	0	0	0	3	.000	4	0	0	0	0	0	1	2	3	19	40.0	7	8	1	1	.938	1	1	0	0	1.00
Springer,Russ, StL	R	.000	1	0	0	0	0	.074	27	2	0	0	0	0	0	17	4	76	66.0	1	5	0	1	1.000	6	3	0	0	.50

Pitchers Hitting, Fielding and Holding Runners

Pitcher	T	2007 Hitting						Career Hitting										2007 Fielding and Holding Runners											
		Avg	AB	H	HR	RBI	SH	Avg	AB	H	2B	3B	HR	RBI	BB	SO	SH	G	Inn	PO	A	E	DP	Pct	SBA	CS	PCS	PPO	CS%
Spurling,Chris, Mil	R	-	0	0	0	0	0		0	0	0	0	0	0	0	0	0	49	50.0	7	4	1	0	.917	2	0	0	0	.00
Standridge,Jason, KC	R	-	0	0	0	0	0	-	0	0	0	0	0	0	1	0	0	4	7.2	0	1	0	0	1.000	0	0	0	0	-
Stanford,Jason, Cle	L	.000	2	0	0	0	1	.000	2	0	0	0	0	0	0	2	1	8	26.1	1	6	0	0	1.000	1	0	0	0	.00
Stanton,Mike, Cin	L	.000	2	0	0	0	0	.333	24	8	1	0	0	3	1	3	1	69	57.2	2	4	2	1	.750	5	1	0	1	.20
Stauffer,Tim, SD	R	.250	4	1	0	2	1	.167	30	5	1	0	0	3	0	13	4	2	7.2	0	0	0	0	-	0	0	0	0	-
Stetter,Mitch, Mil	L	-	0	0	0	0	0	-	0	0	0	0	0	0	0	0	0	6	5.0	0	0	0	0	-	0	0	0	0	-
Stokes,Brian, TB	R	-	0	0	0	0	0	-	0	0	0	0	0	0	0	0	0	59	62.1	9	6	0	1	1.000	4	1	0	0	.25
Stone,Ricky, Cin	R	-	0	0	0	0	0	.000	10	0	0	0	0	0	0	4	1	5	5.1	0	0	0	0	-	0	0	0	0	-
Street,Huston, Oak	R	-	0	0	0	0	0	-	0	0	0	0	0	0	0	0	0	48	50.0	2	7	1	0	.900	7	2	0	0	.29
Stults,Eric, LAD	L	.333	12	4	0	0	0	.412	17	7	2	0	0	0	0	6	1	12	38.2	0	7	0	0	1.000	3	0	0	0	.00
Suppan,Jeff, Mil	R	.131	61	8	0	2	11	.183	311	57	4	0	1	17	15	69	47	34	206.2	17	32	1	7	.980	7	0	0	0	.00
Switzer,Jon, TB	L	-	0	0	0	0	0	-	0	0	0	0	0	0	0	0	0	21	19.0	0	4	0	1	1.000	1	1	0	1	1.00
Tallet,Brian, Tor	L	-	0	0	0	0	0	.000	2	0	0	0	0	0	0	1	0	48	62.1	3	6	1	0	.900	10	1	1	0	.10
Tankersley,Taylor, Fla	L	-	0	0	0	0	0	.000	2	0	0	0	0	0	0	2	0	67	47.1	0	8	0	1	1.000	5	4	2	0	.80
Taschner,Jack, SF	L	.000	1	0	0	0	1	.000	1	0	0	0	0	0	0	0	1	63	50.0	1	4	0	0	1.000	3	0	0	0	.00
Tata,Jordan, Det	R	-	0	0	0	0	0	-	0	0	0	0	0	0	0	0	0	3	14.0	0	1	0	0	1.000	0	0	0	0	-
Taubenheim,Ty, Tor	R	-	0	0	0	0	0	.333	3	1	0	0	0	0	0	2	0	1	5.0	0	0	0	0	-	0	0	0	0	-
Tavarez,Julian, Bos	R	.250	4	1	0	0	0	.115	139	16	0	0	0	8	7	60	21	34	134.2	11	9	1	2	.952	0	0	0	0	-
Tejeda,Robinson, Tex	R	.000	3	0	0	0	1	.080	25	2	0	1	0	0	0	13	7	19	95.1	4	15	1	2	.950	17	5	0	0	.29
Thatcher,Joe, SD	L	-	0	0	0	0	0	-	0	0	0	0	0	0	0	0	0	22	21.0	1	1	2	0	.500	3	0	0	0	.00
Thompson,Brad, StL	R	.167	24	4	0	0	7	.188	32	6	0	0	0	0	0	14	8	44	129.1	8	10	0	1	1.000	8	4	1	1	.50
Thompson,Mike, SD	R	.000	2	0	0	0	0	.148	27	4	0	0	0	0	1	13	3	7	15.2	2	1	2	0	.600	1	0	0	0	.00
Thompson,Rich, LAA	R	-	0	0	0	0	0	-	0	0	0	0	0	0	0	0	0	7	6.2	1	0	0	0	1.000	1	1	0	0	1.00
Thomson,John, KC	R	-	0	0	0	0	0	.198	318	63	6	1	0	22	12	133	48	2	10.2	1	1	0	0	1.000	1	0	0	0	.00
Thornton,Matt, CWS	L	.000	1	0	0	0	0	.000	1	0	0	0	0	0	0	1	0	68	56.1	5	8	0	2	1.000	2	1	1	0	.50
Threets,Erick, SF	L	-	0	0	0	0	0	-	0	0	0	0	0	0	0	0	0	3	2.1	0	0	0	0	-	0	0	0	0	-
Timlin,Mike, Bos	R	-	0	0	0	0	0	.000	7	0	0	0	0	0	0	4	0	50	55.1	4	9	2	1	.867	5	2	0	0	.40
Tomko,Brett, LAD-SD	R	.000	31	0	0	1	5	.158	450	71	9	0	29	19	177	71		40	131.1	7	15	2	2	.917	13	5	0	0	.38
Torres,Salomon, Pit	R	-	0	0	0	0	0	.147	102	15	1	1	0	1	2	46	12	56	52.2	2	5	2	0	.778	3	1	0	0	.33
Towers,Josh, Tor	R	.000	1	0	0	0	0	.063	16	1	0	0	0	0	0	3	2	25	107.0	16	19	3	2	.921	15	2	0	0	.13
Traber,Billy, Was	L	.000	4	0	0	0	0	.048	21	1	0	0	0	0	1	13	2	28	39.2	1	5	1	0	.857	6	1	0	0	.17
Trachsel,Steve, Bal-ChC	R	.083	12	1	0	0	0	.163	651	106	17	1	3	40	26	200	87	29	158.0	17	35	0	2	1.000	26	7	3	1	.27
Tsao,Chin-hui, LAD	R	-	0	0	0	0	0	.154	13	2	1	0	0	0	0	1	2	21	24.2	1	6	0	1	1.000	2	0	0	0	.00
Turnbow,Derrick, Mil	R	-	0	0	0	0	0	.000	2	0	0	0	0	0	0	1	0	77	68.0	7	14	0	1	1.000	6	3	1	0	.50
Urdaneta,Lino, NYM	R	-	0	0	0	0	0	-	0	0	0	0	0	0	0	0	0	2	1.0	0	0	0	0	-	0	0	0	0	-
Valverde,Jose, Ari	R	-	0	0	0	0	0	1.000	1	1	1	0	0	0	0	0	0	65	64.1	5	2	0	0	1.000	6	2	1	0	.33
Van Benschoten,John, Pit	R	.143	7	1	0	0	2	.133	15	2	1	0	1	2	2	6	4	11	39.0	0	5	0	0	1.000	7	1	0	1	.14
Vanden Hurk,Rick, Fla	R	.043	23	1	0	0	3	.043	23	1	0	0	0	0	1	12	3	18	81.2	2	4	1	1	.857	11	3	0	1	.27
Vargas,Claudio, Mil	R	.132	38	5	0	0	5	.085	177	15	4	0	0	7	3	51	32	29	134.1	6	15	2	0	.913	16	5	2	0	.31
Vargas,Jason, NYM	L	.000	2	0	0	0	1	.295	44	13	3	0	3	2	9	1		2	10.1	0	0	0	0	-	2	0	0	0	.00
Vasquez,Virgil, Det	R	-	0	0	0	0	0	-	0	0	0	0	0	0	0	0	0	5	16.2	1	4	0	0	1.000	1	0	0	0	.00
Vazquez,Javier, CWS	R	.000	6	0	0	0	1	.212	433	92	10	2	1	24	17	70	74	32	216.2	10	28	2	4	.950	10	4	0	0	.40
Veras,Jose, NYY	R	-	0	0	0	0	0	-	0	0	0	0	0	0	0	0	0	9	9.1	0	0	0	0	-	2	0	0	0	.00
Verlander,Justin, Det	R	.000	4	0	0	0	1	.000	5	0	0	0	0	0	0	3	2	32	201.2	7	17	0	0	1.000	5	1	0	2	.20
Vermilyea,Jamie, Tor	R	-	0	0	0	0	0	-	0	0	0	0	0	0	0	0	0	2	6.0	0	1	0	0	1.000	0	0	0	0	-
Villanueva,Carlos, Mil	R	.077	13	1	0	0	4	.071	28	2	0	0	0	1	0	12	6	59	114.1	2	9	0	0	1.000	9	3	1	0	.33
Villarreal,Oscar, Atl	R	.250	4	1	0	0	1	.071	14	1	0	0	0	0	0	6	3	51	76.1	4	9	0	0	1.000	3	0	0	0	.00
Villone,Ron, NYY	L	-	0	0	0	0	0	.130	169	22	3	1	1	7	1	50	12	37	42.1	1	4	0	1	1.000	0	0	0	0	-
Vizcaino,Luis, NYY	R	.000	2	0	0	0	0	.000	4	0	0	0	0	0	0	4	0	77	75.1	7	7	0	0	1.000	7	2	0	0	.29
Volquez,Edinson, Tex	R	-	0	0	0	0	0	-	0	0	0	0	0	0	0	0	0	6	34.0	0	2	0	0	1.000	2	0	0	0	.00
Wagner,Billy, NYM	L	-	0	0	0	0	0	.100	20	2	0	0	0	1	1	12	0	66	68.1	1	7	1	0	.889	0	0	0	0	-
Wagner,Ryan, Was	R	-	0	0	0	0	0	.250	4	1	0	0	0	0	0	2	1	14	15.2	3	1	1	0	.800	1	0	0	0	.00
Wainwright,Adam, StL	R	.290	62	18	1	6	9	.309	68	21	4	0	2	7	3	18	9	32	202.0	13	28	2	4	.953	14	8	1	0	.57
Wakefield,Tim, Bos	R	.000	2	0	0	0	0	.122	98	12	2	0	1	4	2	37	13	31	189.0	14	22	0	3	1.000	49	8	0	0	.16
Walker,Jamie, Bal	L	-	0	0	0	0	0	-	0	0	0	0	0	0	0	0	0	81	61.1	0	5	0	0	1.000	3	1	0	0	.33
Walker,Tyler, SF	R	-	0	0	0	0	0	.000	10	0	0	0	0	0	1	6	0	15	14.1	1	0	0	1	1.000	1	1	0	0	1.00
Wang,Chien-Ming, NYY	R	.000	3	0	0	0	0	.000	8	0	0	0	0	0	0	6	0	30	199.1	11	34	0	3	1.000	21	7	0	0	.33
Wasdin,John, Pit	R	.000	4	0	0	0	0	.158	19	3	1	0	0	1	1	6	1	12	19.2	0	3	0	0	1.000	2	2	1	0	1.00
Washburn,Jarrod, Sea	L	.500	2	1	0	1	0	.281	32	9	0	0	4	5	9	7		32	193.2	8	23	1	0	.969	11	5	4	0	.45
Wassermann,E., CWS	R	-	0	0	0	0	0	-	0	0	0	0	0	0	0	0	0	33	23.0	1	4	1	0	.833	2	0	0	0	.00
Weathers,David, Cin	R	-	0	0	0	0	0	.101	139	14	0	0	2	4	7	85	16	70	77.2	3	8	0	0	1.000	6	1	0	0	.17
Weaver,Jeff, Sea	R	.000	1	0	0	0	1	.205	190	39	6	1	0	13	6	64	22	27	146.2	5	11	1	0	.941	12	3	0	1	.25
Weaver,Jered, LAA	R	.250	4	1	0	0	0	.250	4	1	0	0	0	0	0	1	0	28	161.0	10	17	2	1	.931	21	2	0	1	.10
Webb,Brandon, Ari	R	.082	73	6	0	3	8	.106	322	34	5	0	0	18	9	151	42	34	236.1	20	50	5	0	.933	35	9	2	0	.26
Wellemeyer,Todd, KC-StL	R	.125	16	2	0	1	3	.130	23	3	0	0	0	1	1	12	4	32	79.1	3	5	0	0	1.000	5	1	0	0	.20
Wells,David, SD-LAD	L	.151	53	8	0	1	6	.129	178	23	2	0	0	5	3	59	18	29	157.1	7	22	3	0	.906	18	7	3	0	.39
Wells,Kip, StL	R	.321	53	17	1	5	1	.201	303	61	10	1	4	17	4	131	26	34	162.2	10	21	4	0	.886	22	5	1	1	.23
Westbrook,Jake, Cle	R	.000	2	0	0	0	0	.167	12	2	1	0	0	1	1	8	3	25	152.0	19	29	0	5	1.000	21	7	0	2	.33
Wheeler,Dan, Hou-TB	R	-	0	0	0	0	0	.143	7	1	0	0	0	0	0	1	1	70	74.2	10	5	0	0	1.000	4	0	0	0	.00
White,Bill, Tex	L	-	0	0	0	0	0	-	0	0	0	0	0	0	0	0	0	9	9.1	0	0	0	0	-	1	0	0	0	.00

Pitchers Hitting, Fielding and Holding Runners

Pitcher	T	2007 Hitting						Career Hitting										2007 Fielding and Holding Runners											
		Avg	AB	H	HR	RBI	SH	Avg	AB	H	2B	3B	HR	RBI	BB	SO	SH	G	Inn	PO	A	E	DP	Pct	SBA	CS	PCS	PPO	CS%
White, Rick, Hou-Sea	R	.000	1	0	0	0	0	.093	43	4	1	0	0	1	0	13	2	29	34.2	1	9	0	0	1.000	0	0	0	1	-
White, Sean, Sea	R	-	0	0	0	0	0	-	0	0	0	0	0	0	0	0	0	15	35.1	1	6	0	0	1.000	3	1	0	1	.33
Wickman, Bob, Atl-Ari	R	-	0	0	0	0	0	.000	2	0	0	0	0	0	0	0	0	57	50.1	4	5	3	0	.750	8	0	0	0	.00
Williams, Dave, NYM	L	.000	1	0	0	0	0	.122	123	15	3	0	1	9	4	65	9	2	4.1	0	3	0	0	1.000	0	0	0	0	-
Williams, Jerome, Was	R	.143	7	1	0	0	1	.112	116	13	2	0	0	1	1	54	19	6	30.0	2	2	1	0	.800	2	0	0	0	.00
Williams, Todd, Bal	R	-	0	0	0	0	0	-	0	0	0	0	0	0	0	0	0	14	14.1	2	2	0	0	1.000	0	0	0	0	-
Williams, Woody, Hou	R	.102	59	6	1	2	5	.194	540	105	25	1	4	43	17	183	45	33	188.0	17	33	1	3	.980	15	4	0	0	.27
Williamson, Scott, Bal	R	-	0	0	0	0	0	.043	23	1	0	0	0	0	3	14	7	16	14.1	1	1	0	0	1.000	7	0	0	0	.00
Willis, Dontrelle, Fla	L	.286	63	18	2	7	11	.234	351	82	10	5	8	35	21	64	29	35	205.1	7	36	5	3	.896	7	1	0	1	.14
Wilson, Brian, SF	R	-	0	0	0	0	1	.000	2	0	0	0	0	0	0	1	1	24	23.2	1	0	0	0	1.000	2	2	0	0	1.00
Wilson, C.J., Tex	L	-	0	0	0	0	0	-	0	0	0	0	0	0	0	0	0	66	68.1	4	12	1	1	.941	2	0	0	0	.00
Wise, Matt, Mil	R	1.000	1	1	0	0	0	.286	7	2	0	0	0	1	0	2	1	56	53.2	4	1	1	0	.833	9	0	0	0	.00
Witasick, Jay, Oak-TB	R	-	0	0	0	0	0	.071	42	3	0	0	0	3	1	22	2	36	31.1	2	2	1	0	.800	2	1	0	0	.50
Wolf, Randy, LAD	L	.167	30	5	0	2	3	.191	383	73	21	0	4	36	25	125	52	18	102.2	4	13	0	0	1.000	7	3	0	0	.43
Wolf, Ross, Fla	R	.000	1	0	0	0	0	.000	1	0	0	0	0	0	0	1	0	14	12.1	0	1	0	0	1.000	0	0	0	0	-
Wolfe, Brian, Tor	R	-	0	0	0	0	0	-	0	0	0	0	0	0	0	0	0	38	45.1	5	2	1	0	.875	0	0	0	0	-
Wood, Kerry, ChC	R	.000	1	0	0	0	0	.171	345	59	6	0	7	32	11	113	46	22	24.1	0	0	0	0	-	1	1	0	0	1.00
Wood, Mike, Tex	R	-	0	0	0	0	0	.000	5	0	0	0	0	0	0	2	0	21	50.2	4	8	1	0	.923	2	1	0	0	.50
Woods, Jake, Sea	L	-	0	0	0	0	0	-	0	0	0	0	0	0	0	0	0	4	10.2	0	0	0	0	-	2	0	0	0	.00
Wright, Chase, NYY	L	-	0	0	0	0	0	-	0	0	0	0	0	0	0	0	0	3	10.0	0	0	0	0	-	1	0	0	0	.00
Wright, Jamey, Tex	R	.000	1	0	0	0	1	.147	436	64	15	1	1	17	12	175	51	20	77.0	5	14	1	2	.950	8	4	0	1	.50
Wright, Jaret, Bal	R	-	0	0	0	0	0	.141	78	11	2	0	1	6	3	42	10	3	10.1	2	1	0	0	1.000	3	1	0	1	.33
Wuertz, Mike, ChC	R	.000	2	0	0	0	0	.000	5	0	0	0	0	0	0	4	1	73	72.1	2	9	0	0	1.000	8	1	0	0	.13
Yates, Tyler, Atl	R	.000	1	0	0	0	0	.083	12	1	0	0	0	0	0	6	1	75	66.0	4	6	2	0	.833	8	1	0	0	.13
Youman, Shane, Pit	L	.083	12	1	0	0	2	.211	19	4	0	0	0	1	1	8	2	16	57.1	3	13	0	0	1.000	5	1	1	0	.20
Young, Chris, SD	R	.130	46	6	0	2	6	.124	105	13	3	1	0	6	5	44	14	30	173.0	7	13	1	1	.952	44	0	0	2	.00
Zagurski, Mike, Phi	L	-	0	0	0	0	0	-	0	0	0	0	0	0	0	0	0	25	21.1	0	1	0	0	1.000	0	0	0	0	-
Zambrano, Carlos, ChC	R	.247	81	20	2	5	5	.219	411	90	15	2	12	33	5	151	28	34	216.1	20	28	1	1	.980	7	3	0	1	.43
Zambrano, Victor, Tor-Bal	R	-	0	0	0	0	0	.123	73	9	1	1	0	3	0	28	8	13	23.0	0	3	0	0	1.000	3	1	0	0	.33
Zarate, Mauro, Fla	R	-	0	0	0	0	0	-	0	0	0	0	0	0	0	0	0	4	5.0	0	0	2	0	.000	0	0	0	0	-
Zito, Barry, SF	L	.113	62	7	0	3	4	.088	91	8	0	0	0	3	2	31	7	34	196.2	3	21	0	1	1.000	6	1	1	0	.17
Zumaya, Joel, Det	R	-	0	0	0	0	0	-	0	0	0	0	0	0	0	0	0	28	33.2	3	1	0	0	1.000	3	0	0	0	.00

Hitters Pitching

Player	2007 Pitching											Career Pitching										
	G	W	L	Sv	IP	H	R	ER	BB	SO	ERA	G	W	L	Sv	IP	H	R	ER	BB	SO	ERA
Ankiel,Rick, StL	0	0	0	0	0.0	0	0	0	0	0	-	51	13	10	1	242.0	198	119	105	130	269	3.90
Cirillo,Jeff, Ari	1	0	0	0	1.0	0	0	0	2	1	0.00	1	0	0	0	1.0	0	0	0	2	1	0.00
Finley,Steve, Col	0	0	0	0	0.0	0	0	0	0	0	-	1	0	0	0	1.0	0	0	0	1	0	0.00
Jimenez,D'Angelo, Was	0	0	0	0	0.0	0	0	0	0	0	-	1	0	0	0	1.1	0	0	0	0	0	0.00
Loretta,Mark, Hou	0	0	0	0	0.0	0	0	0	0	0	-	1	0	0	0	1.0	1	0	0	1	2	0.00
Mabry,John, Col	0	0	0	0	0.0	0	0	0	0	0	-	2	0	0	0	1.0	6	7	7	4	0	63.00
Miles,Aaron, StL	2	0	0	0	2.0	3	2	2	0	0	9.00	2	0	0	0	2.0	3	2	2	0	0	9.00
Nunez,Abraham, Phi	0	0	0	0	0.0	0	0	0	0	0	-	1	0	0	0	0.1	0	0	0	0	0	0.00
Ojeda,Augie, Ari	1	0	0	0	1.0	0	0	0	0	0	0.00	1	0	0	0	1.0	0	0	0	0	0	0.00
Relaford,Desi, Tex	0	0	0	0	0.0	0	0	0	0	0	-	1	0	0	0	1.0	0	0	0	0	1	0.00
Spiezio,Scott, StL	1	0	0	0	1.0	0	0	0	1	0	0.00	1	0	0	0	1.0	0	0	0	1	0	0.00
Wilson,Josh, TB	1	0	0	0	1.0	1	0	0	1	0	0.00	1	0	0	0	1.0	1	0	0	1	0	0.00
Wood,Jason, Fla	1	0	0	0	1.0	0	0	0	0	0	0.00	1	0	0	0	1.0	0	0	0	0	0	0.00

Manufactured Runs

Bill James

We began here last year an effort to document Manufactured Runs. The term "manufactured run", which came into use in the 1970s, describes a run which is put together out of small parts—infield hits, bunts, moving up on ground outs, stealing bases, hitting and running, scoring on fly balls, etc. Drawing a walk and swatting a two-run homer is not manufacturing runs as the term is used by Tim McCarver and lesser broadcasters. A walk, a bunt, a stolen base, a fly ball. . .that's a manufactured run.

In order to study Manufactured Runs we had to come up with a technical definition of them, which is: a run is considered a manufactured run if at least two of the four bases result from doing something other than playing station-to-station baseball. We divide Manufactured Runs into two classes:

MR-1 are Manufactured Runs which result at least in part from deliberate acts such as stolen bases and bunts.

MR-2 are Manufactured Runs which result from things like wild pitches, runners moving up on ground outs or fly outs, taking advantage of errors and taking extra bases on singles.

If you have a walk, a single (runner goes to third) and a sac fly (runner scores) that's a manufactured run, because a walk and a single don't make up a run, but you've turned them into a run. But it's not an MR-1 because you haven't used a bunt or a stolen base or a pinch runner to make it happen.

Last year we presented the first data on Manufactured Runs, which was a count of the Manufactured Runs by each major league team. This year we have expanded this to include two new categories: Manufactured Runs *allowed* by each team, and Manufactured Run Contributions of individual players. These are among the things we have learned by studying the issue:

1. The average major league team manufactures just about one run per game played, or 165 per season.

2. The number of Manufactured Runs in the major leagues was slightly up last year, about 2%.

3. The best major league team at manufacturing runs was the team that most knowledgeable people would have guessed: the Los Angeles Angels. The Angels are famous for being aggressive about moving runners. To be successful doing that, they *have* to manufacture runs—and the Angels were certainly successful in 2007.

4. The best team at manufacturing runs in 2006, the Minnesota Twins, was second in 2007.

5. There is no large difference in the number of runs manufactured by American League and National League teams.

6. The most difficult teams against which to manufacture a run were the Chicago Cubs in the National League (125 MR allowed) and the Red Sox in the American.

7. The easiest teams to manufacture a run against were the White Sox in the American League and the Marlins in the National, 200 runs each.

8. The eight teams that made the playoffs manufactured an average of 185 runs—20 above average—but allowed the opposition to manufacture only 151, 14 below average.   Thus, in 2007 at least, manufacturing runs was slightly more characteristic of successful teams than was preventing the opposition from scoring them.

9. The best major leaguer at manufacturing a run was also the best baserunner and the best base stealer—Jose Reyes of the Mets. Reyes contributed to 52 manufactured runs, nine more than second-place Ichiro Suzuki.

10. All of the players who contributed to the most manufactured runs in 2006 were the players you would expect to find on the list—Juan Pierre, Grady Sizemore, Rafael Furcal, Brian Roberts. It is difficult to say that there are any surprises on the list of the players who contributed to the most manufactured runs, except perhaps at the bottom of the NL list—Chris Young, Troy Tulowitzki and Shane Victorino.

American League

Team	MR	MR1	MR2
Los Angeles Angels	223	71	152
Minnesota Twins	218	76	142
New York Yankees	206	74	132
Texas Rangers	192	68	124
Seattle Mariners	183	63	120
Cleveland Indians	181	59	122
Tampa Bay Devil Rays	178	68	110
Boston Red Sox	176	61	115
Kansas City Royals	174	50	124
Detroit Tigers	174	68	106
Baltimore Orioles	169	78	91
Oakland Athletics	137	34	103
Toronto Blue Jays	135	40	95
Chicago White Sox	132	43	89

American League Opponents

Team	MR	MR1	MR2
Chicago White Sox	200	69	131
Texas Rangers	195	58	137
Tampa Bay Devil Rays	194	64	130
Baltimore Orioles	192	70	122
New York Yankees	184	76	108
Oakland Athletics	181	68	113
Toronto Blue Jays	176	60	116
Detroit Tigers	174	51	123
Seattle Mariners	173	52	121
Los Angeles Angels	162	62	100
Kansas City Royals	157	42	115
Cleveland Indians	156	53	103
Minnesota Twins	136	49	87
Boston Red Sox	134	47	87

National League

Team	MR	MR1	MR2
Colorado Rockies	211	98	113
Los Angeles Dodgers	199	94	105
New York Mets	181	101	80
Philadelphia Phillies	160	63	106
Chicago Cubs	159	45	114
St Louis Cardinals	157	44	113
Arizona Diamondbacks	155	49	106
Pittsburgh Pirates	153	51	102
San Francisco Giants	152	69	83
San Diego Padres	143	43	100
Cincinnati Reds	141	64	77
Florida Marlins	136	56	80
Atlanta Braves	135	36	99
Houston Astros	134	43	91
Milwaukee Brewers	122	42	80
Washington Nationals	121	39	82

National League Opponents

Team	MR	MR1	MR2
Florida Marlins	200	57	143
Los Angeles Dodgers	182	71	111
Pittsburgh Pirates	177	67	110
San Diego Padres	174	85	89
Milwaukee Brewers	166	59	107
Arizona Diamondbacks	158	57	101
San Francisco Giants	156	62	94
Atlanta Braves	156	68	88
New York Mets	155	62	93
Washington Nationals	154	59	95
St Louis Cardinals	153	47	106
Colorado Rockies	151	55	96
Cincinnati Reds	149	60	89
Philadelphia Phillies	140	48	92
Houston Astros	136	51	85
Chicago Cubs	125	61	64

Top Three From Each Team

American League Top Ten

Player	Tm	MRC	MRC1	MRC2
Suzuki, Ichiro	Sea	43	20	23
Sizemore, Grady	Cle	39	20	19
Roberts, Brian	Bal	35	26	9
Granderson, Curtis	Det	34	17	17
Crawford, Carl	TB	34	18	16
Crisp, Coco	Bos	32	13	19
Bartlett, Jason	Min	32	11	21
Damon, Johnny	NYY	30	11	19
DeJesus, David	KC	29	8	21
Cabrera, Orlando	LAA	29	7	22

National League Top Ten

Player	Tm	MRC	MRC1	MRC2
Reyes, Jose	NYM	52	35	17
Pierre, Juan	LAD	40	28	12
Furcal, Rafael	LAD	39	26	13
Taveras, Willy	Col	33	24	9
Rollins, Jimmy	Phi	32	15	17
Ramirez, Hanley	Fla	31	20	11
Matsui, Kaz	Col	29	17	12
Young, Chris	Ari	27	14	13
Tulowitzki, Troy	Col	26	13	13
Victorino, Shane	Phi	26	13	13

MRC = Manufactured Run Contributions

Arizona Diamondbacks

Player	MRC	MRC1	MRC2
Young, Chris	27	14	13
Byrnes, Eric	20	10	10
Hudson, Orlando	17	4	13

Atlanta Braves

Player	MRC	MRC1	MRC2
Escobar, Yunel	16	4	12
Francoeur, Jeff	14	3	11
Jones, Andruw	14	1	13
Johnson, Kelly	14	4	10
Harris, Willie	14	6	8

Baltimore Orioles

Player	MRC	MRC1	MRC2
Roberts, Brian	35	26	9
Mora, Melvin	22	7	15
Patterson, Corey	21	17	4

Boston Red Sox

Player	MRC	MRC1	MRC2
Crisp, Coco	32	13	19
Lugo, Julio	23	15	8
Ortiz, David	18	1	17

Chicago Cubs

Player	MRC	MRC1	MRC2
Theriot, Ryan	22	6	16
Ramirez, Aramis	14	2	12
Soriano, Alfonso	14	7	7

Chicago White Sox

Player	MRC	MRC1	MRC2
Owens, Jerry	15	7	8
Podsednik, Scott	13	7	6
Uribe, Juan	12	2	10

Cincinnati Reds

Player	MRC	MRC1	MRC2
Hopper, Norris	23	15	8
Phillips, Brandon	21	11	10
Encarnacion, Edwin	14	4	10

Cleveland Indians

Player	MRC	MRC1	MRC2
Sizemore, Grady	39	20	19
Peralta, Jhonny	18	5	13
Blake, Casey	17	1	16
Barfield, Josh	17	7	10

Colorado Rockies

Player	MRC	MRC1	MRC2
Taveras, Willy	33	24	9
Matsui, Kaz	29	17	12
Tulowitzki, Troy	26	13	13

Detroit Tigers

Player	MRC	MRC1	MRC2
Granderson, Curtis	34	17	17
Sheffield, Gary	21	10	11
Ordonez, Magglio	18	4	14

Florida Marlins

Player	MRC	MRC1	MRC2
Ramirez, Hanley	31	20	11
Uggla, Dan	18	3	15
Willingham, Josh	9	5	4
Olivo, Miguel	9	4	5
Ross, Cody	9	0	9

Houston Astros

Player	MRC	MRC1	MRC2
Biggio, Craig	17	5	12
Lamb, Mike	12	1	11
Lee, Carlos	11	1	10

Kansas City Royals

Player	MRC	MRC1	MRC2
DeJesus, David	29	8	21
Pena, Tony	25	6	19
Grudzielanek, Mark	22	3	19

Los Angeles Angels

Player	MRC	MRC1	MRC2
Cabrera, Orlando	29	7	22
Figgins, Chone	28	18	10
Willits, Reggie	26	16	10

Los Angeles Dodgers

Player	MRC	MRC1	MRC2
Pierre, Juan	40	28	12
Furcal, Rafael	39	26	13
Martin, Russell	20	7	13
Kent, Jeff	20	2	18

Milwaukee Brewers

Player	MRC	MRC1	MRC2
Weeks, Rickie	15	8	7
Hart, Corey	15	6	9
Braun, Ryan	12	6	6

Minnesota Twins

Player	MRC	MRC1	MRC2
Bartlett, Jason	32	11	21
Cuddyer, Michael	24	4	20
Hunter, Torii	24	12	12
Punto, Nick	24	12	12

New York Mets

Player	MRC	MRC1	MRC2
Reyes, Jose	52	35	17
Wright, David	16	9	7
Beltran, Carlos	13	5	8

New York Yankees

Player	MRC	MRC1	MRC2
Damon, Johnny	30	11	19
Abreu, Bobby	27	13	14
Rodriguez, Alex	24	9	15

Seattle Mariners

Player	MRC	MRC1	MRC2
Suzuki, Ichiro	43	20	23
Betancourt, Yuniesky	25	10	15
Vidro, Jose	19	2	17

Oakland Athletics

Player	MRC	MRC1	MRC2
Stewart, Shannon	17	6	11
Ellis, Mark	15	2	13
Swisher, Nick	14	3	11

St Louis Cardinals

Player	MRC	MRC1	MRC2
Miles, Aaron	23	9	14
Taguchi, So	16	1	15
Eckstein, David	12	4	8

Philadelphia Phillies

Player	MRC	MRC1	MRC2
Rollins, Jimmy	32	15	17
Victorino, Shane	26	13	13
Burrell, Pat	14	7	7
Rowand, Aaron	14	0	14

Tampa Bay Devil Rays

Player	MRC	MRC1	MRC2
Crawford, Carl	34	18	16
Iwamura, Akinori	24	10	14
Young, Delmon	17	5	12
Upton, B.J.	17	9	8

Pittsburgh Pirates

Player	MRC	MRC1	MRC2
Wilson, Jack	21	12	9
McLouth, Nate	15	6	9
Bautista, Jose	15	1	14

Texas Rangers

Player	MRC	MRC1	MRC2
Kinsler, Ian	27	13	14
Young, Michael	19	6	13
Lofton, Kenny	17	7	10
Byrd, Marlon	17	5	12

San Diego Padres

Player	MRC	MRC1	MRC2
Giles, Brian	19	4	15
Cameron, Mike	19	8	11
Giles, Marcus	17	6	11

Toronto Blue Jays

Player	MRC	MRC1	MRC2
Hill, Aaron	17	5	12
Rios, Alex	17	6	11
Wells, Vernon	14	3	11

San Francisco Giants

Player	MRC	MRC1	MRC2
Roberts, Dave	21	14	7
Winn, Randy	19	10	9
Feliz, Pedro	14	3	11

Washington Nationals

Player	MRC	MRC1	MRC2
Kearns, Austin	18	3	15
Lopez, Felipe	14	7	7
Zimmerman, Ryan	14	1	13

Manager's Record

Bill James

Since the mid-1990s we have been engaged in an effort to build a Manager's Record. The basic goal of this effort is to help the reader understand better how one manager is functionally different from another. Last year we added "RCD"...Relievers used on Consecutive Days. Manny Acta of Washington in 2007 used a reliever who had also pitched the previous day 183 times. Jim Leyland used relievers on consecutive days only 70 times. That's a very real difference between those two managers. Acta is willing to use his relievers on back-to-back days. Leyland would prefer not to. The data makes this crystal clear.

There are a couple of new things in this chart this year, and I'll explain the less significant one first. One problem we have had with developing a manager's record is that the differences we are trying to measure keep disappearing on us. We used to measure "Long Outings" as outings in which a manager allowed his starting pitcher to throw more than 130 pitches. This gradually became a useless chart, inasmuch as, after a time, nobody was throwing 130 pitches in a game.

Last year we were measuring "Long Outings" as more than 120 pitches, but this, too, was rapidly heading in the direction of zero, so we changed the definition of a Long Outing to more than 110 pitches. We made this change retroactive to 2002. In many of the charts below there is a little line in the "LO" column between 2001 and 2002. This marks where the new definition takes effect.

Bruce Bochy of San Francisco left his starter in the game to throw more than 110 pitches 36 times in 2007. Ron Washington of Texas did this only 4 times. Again, that seems like a substantial difference between the two managers.

We are trying to create a situation in which the people who call in to talk shows at least have the opportunity to know what they are talking about. We're trying to create a factual reference to distinguish one manager from another, in the same way that we can distinguish Alfonso Soriano from Johnny Estrada without relying on "one time I saw Johnny Estrada steal second base standing up." We KNOW how many bases Johnny Estrada steals; we KNOW how many Alfonso Soriano steals. We are trying to create a situation in which we have a similar factual reference set about managers.

The other new thing this year is a breakdown of Intentional Walks into the categories we are calling "Good", "Not Good" and "Bomb". We try to avoid, in compiling the manager's record, making judgments about the manager's decisions. We are not trying to say whether someone is a good manager or a bad manager. We are trying to describe how one manager is *different* from the next.

But whether or not an intentional walk has blown up in a manager's face is, I think, a reasonably objective thing. Mike Scioscia walks David Ortiz in the ninth inning of the second game of the American League Division Series, and

Manny Ramirez hits a walk-off three-run homer.   Nobody is going to argue that that's a successful outcome.   Our desire to avoid judgments doesn't mean that we don't count Wins and Losses.   The desire to avoid making subjective judgments doesn't preclude us from noting successes and failures, if those successes and failures are clearly defined.

We sorted Intentional Walks into three categories of outcomes:

Good.

Not Good.

Bomb.

If no runs scored in the inning after the intentional walk, that was a good outcome.

If the next batter after the intentional walk grounded into a double play, that was always counted as a good outcome, even if a run scored on the play.

If one run scored in the inning after the intentional walk (and there was no double play), that was not a good outcome, but it's not necessarily a bad outcome, either, so we called it NG (Not Good).   Runners on first and third, nobody out, you issue an intentional walk and the next guy hits a sac fly, that's not a good outcome, but it's not really a bad outcome, either.   It's just not exactly what you were hoping for.

If more than one run scored in the inning after the intentional walk, that was counted as the IBB exploding on the manager, or "Bomb".

We talked about using some more parameters to categorize these things. . .for example, if you get out of the inning with a lead, it's always a good outcome, or if the runner who is intentionally walked comes around to score, it's always a bad outcome/bomb.   Ultimately, we decided that it wasn't necessary or helpful to introduce those complications.   If multiple runs score after an intentional walk, that's a clear failure, isn't it?   You're not TRYING to set up a situation in which multiple runs will score.   You're trying to avoid that.   If it happens, the IBB has exploded on you—period.

Again, I would caution against using these numbers to rush to judgment on the manager.   Ned Yost of the Brewers issued 34 intentional walks in 2006, 37 in 2007.   In 2006 14 of these intentional walks got a good outcome, 20 of them did not, and 12 of them exploded on him.   That's a very poor record.

In 2007, issuing essentially the same number of intentional walks, Yost got a good outcome 28 times (although the other 9 were all bombs.) That's a very good ratio, 28 to 9.

It is unlikely that this data "proves" or "indicates" that Yost was stupid in 2006 or that he was brilliant in 2007.   It simply indicates that these decisions did not work out for him in 2006, whereas they worked out much better in 2007.

Clint Hurdle in 2006 ordered 23 intentional walks that exploded in his face. This appears to be the record for the new category.   Mike Scioscia, victimized by the IBB in the 2007 playoffs, has had only 3 to 6 per season explode on him—exceptionally low totals, consistently since 2002.   We hope that this proves to be a useful distinction among managers, rather than simply something that the press and the talk show guys use to beat up on managers they don't like.

While I'm here, let me discuss a few other differences between managers:

Bob Melvin of Arizona used 146 different lineups in 2007, whereas Charlie Manuel of Philadelphia used only 87 (ignoring the pitchers). These things are in keeping with the career tendencies of these managers. Melvin in the past has used as many as 151 lineups in a season, whereas the 87 used by Manuel was actually his highest total in several years. Manuel clearly likes a set lineup.

73% of the hitters in the lineup for Bruce Bochy in 2007 had the platoon advantage at the start of the game, whereas only 49% of Jim Tracy's guys started the game with the platoon edge. This may indicate something about the manager; it may just be the talent they had. Bochy has led the league before, with 65% in 1998, whereas Tracy's figure in 2006 was 43%. But their career data is not dramatically different.

Tony LaRussa in 2007 used 317 pinch hitters, the most in the majors; in the past he has used as many as 352 (twice). Bob Geren of Oakland used only 64 pinch hitters—a difference which is certainly exaggerated by the Designated Hitter rule, but would probably be there anyway.

Charlie Manuel led the majors in pinch runners used, 56, which probably only indicates that he had a couple of really slow guys in his lineup.

Manny Acta led the majors in the number of Defensive Substitutes ordered into the game, 78. Acta had very "aggressive" numbers across the board, leading the majors in Defensive Substitutes (DS), Relievers Used (Rel) and Relievers Used on Consecutive Days (RCD). Since he was a first-year manager, it is difficult to reach any firm conclusions as to what extent this reflects his preferences, and to what extent it simply reflects the talent he had to work with.

Categories of this record are Games Managed (G), Number of Different Lineups Used (LUp), the percentage of players who had the platoon advatange at the start of the game (PL%), Pinch Hitters Used (PH), Pinch Runners Used (PR), Defensive Substitutes Used (DS), Quick Hooks (Quick), Slow Hooks (Slow), Long Outings by Starting Pitchers (LO), Relievers Used on Consecutive Days (RCD), Long Saves (LS), Relivers Used (Rel), Stolen Base Attempts (SBA), Sacrifice Bunts Attempts (SacA), Runners Moving with the Pitch (RM), Pitchouts ordered (PO), Intentional Walks issued (#), Intentional Walks resulting in a Good Outcome (Good), Intentional Walks resulting Not in a Good Outcome (NG), Intentional Walks Blowing up on the Manager (Bomb), Wins (W), Losses (L) and Winning Percentage (Pct.).

Manny Acta

Year	Team	Lg	G	LUp	PL%	PH	PR	DS	Quick	Slow	LO	RCD	LS	Rel	SBA	SacA	RM	PO	#	Good	NG	Bomb	W	L	Pct
2007	Nationals	NL	162	101	.65	295	32	78	53	28	5	183	1	588	92	86	70	28	44	28	16	8	73	89	.451
	162-Game Average			101	.65	295	32	78	53	28	5	183	1	588	92	86	70	28	44	28	16	8	73	89	.451

Buddy Bell

Year	Team	Lg	G	LUp	PL%	PH	PR	DS	Quick	Slow	LO	RCD	LS	Rel	SBA	SacA	RM	PO	#	Good	NG	Bomb	W	L	Pct
1996	Tigers	AL	162	128	.50	123	29	17	17	27	26	82	8	426	137	63		13	40	6	34	19	53	109	.327
1997	Tigers	AL	162	116	.61	163	19	22	24	7	12	113	11	417	233	44		32	24	8	16	10	79	83	.488
1998	Tigers	AL	137	88	.58	102	25	7	15	15	10	89	4	362	143	24		38	29	8	21	15	52	85	.380
2000	Rockies	NL	162	106	.64	285	21	8	12	18	10	106	8	480	192	100		40	53	20	33	16	82	80	.506
2001	Rockies	NL	162	116	.61	314	27	14	18	30	8	117	6	476	186	108		43	43	12	31	13	73	89	.451
2002	Rockies	NL	22	15	.55	48	1	5	5	11	3	21	0	69	17	9	5	5	11	5	6	4	6	16	.273
2005	Royals	AL	112	93	.61	97	18	8	32	23	3	50	4	310	48	38	80	25	17	9	8	6	43	69	.384
2006	Royals	AL	152	132	.57	87	27	25	40	37	13	86	6	439	95	63	81	13	40	20	20	10	58	94	.382
2007	Royals	AL	162	141	.55	119	30	28	49	28	16	74	10	448	122	59	125	25	54	33	21	9	69	93	.426
	162-Game Average			123	.58	176	26	18	28	26	13	267	21	450	154	67	105	31	41	16	25	13	68	94	.420

Bud Black

Year	Team	Lg	G	LUp	PL%	PH	PR	DS	Quick	Slow	LO	RCD	LS	Rel	SBA	SacA	RM	PO	#	Good	NG	Bomb	W	L	Pct
2007	Padres	NL	163	115	.62	279	18	13	63	28	13	122	0	485	79	85	73	56	48	28	20	11	89	74	.546
	162-Game Average			114	.62	277	18	13	63	28	13	121	0	482	79	84	73	56	48	28	20	11	88	74	.543

Bruce Bochy

Year	Team	Lg	G	LUp	PL%	PH	PR	DS	Quick	Slow	LO	RCD	LS	Rel	SBA	SacA	RM	PO	#	Good	NG	Bomb	W	L	Pct
1995	Padres	NL	144	96	.59	262	30	23	44	41	17	38	3	337	170	68		38	26	8	18	11	70	74	.486
1996	Padres	NL	162	114	.52	289	29	15	51	33	10	67	12	411	164	73		65	42	24	18	12	91	71	.562
1997	Padres	NL	162	111	.60	291	26	9	45	45	3	81	11	426	200	84		58	24	7	17	11	76	86	.469
1998	Padres	NL	162	110	.65	280	62	44	44	45	9	81	12	369	116	84		27	30	16	14	10	98	64	.605
1999	Padres	NL	162	137	.60	298	51	21	44	36	4	68	5	403	241	60		29	39	20	19	13	74	88	.457
2000	Padres	NL	162	134	.52	285	44	14	41	47	14	105	5	443	184	52		27	40	11	29	11	76	86	.469
2001	Padres	NL	162	116	.60	255	54	27	32	47	6	85	10	422	173	43		23	40	17	23	13	79	83	.488
2002	Padres	NL	162	123	.66	273	46	56	40	40	17	106	4	459	115	63	59	12	61	38	23	14	66	96	.407
2003	Padres	NL	162	134	.58	339	20	29	34	43	16	100	3	473	115	63	41	6	52	33	19	12	64	98	.395
2004	Padres	NL	162	96	.54	284	38	47	46	32	15	76	3	437	77	75	90	14	39	24	15	10	87	75	.537
2005	Padres	NL	162	128	.58	285	31	49	46	36	23	87	1	456	143	89	111	16	45	33	12	8	82	80	.506
2006	Padres	NL	162	111	.60	264	64	48	42	42	24	111	2	475	154	77	106	21	63	43	20	10	88	74	.543
2007	Giants	NL	162	128	.73	264	50	45	26	50	36	132	2	496	152	86	119	10	41	29	12	3	71	91	.438
	162-Game Average			119	.60	285	42	33	42	42	15	190	12	435	155	71	88	27	42	24	19	11	79	83	.488

Cecil Cooper

Year	Team	Lg	G	LUp	PL%	PH	PR	DS	Quick	Slow	LO	RCD	LS	Rel	SBA	SacA	RM	PO	#	Good	NG	Bomb	W	L	Pct
2007	Astros	NL	31	26	.42	63	8	23	10	5	2	11	0	88	19	16	20	4	14	8	6	4	15	16	.484
	162-Game Average			136	.42	329	42	120	52	26	10	57	0	460	99	84	105	21	73	42	31	21	78	84	.481

Bobby Cox

Year	Team	Lg	G	LUp	PL%	PH	PR	DS	Quick	Slow	LO	RCD	LS	Rel	SBA	SacA	RM	PO	#	Good	NG	Bomb	W	L	Pct
1994	Braves	NL	114	64	.60	163	30	25	22	31	5	60	5	244	79	83		44	39	20	19	9	68	46	.596
1995	Braves	NL	144	59	.56	224	48	40	41	34	13	80	6	339	116	77		41	38	23	15	4	90	54	.625
1996	Braves	NL	162	89	.62	254	32	27	48	43	19	110	9	408	126	90		34	48	22	26	14	96	66	.593
1997	Braves	NL	162	87	.64	276	58	29	40	37	23	90	4	374	166	112		13	46	32	14	10	101	62	.620
1998	Braves	NL	162	80	.64	245	28	25	44	33	14	70	1	354	141	97		40	26	11	15	8	106	56	.654
1999	Braves	NL	162	76	.58	272	51	34	44	39	13	99	6	394	214	89		54	37	17	20	11	103	59	.636
2000	Braves	NL	162	103	.59	252	72	11	52	41	6	81	13	376	204	109		59	34	17	17	5	95	67	.586
2001	Braves	NL	162	113	.57	278	50	23	49	40	4	93	8	412	131	84		90	55	27	28	13	88	74	.543
2002	Braves	NL	161	105	.48	289	38	44	58	30	20	113	9	469	115	84	37	46	63	41	22	12	101	59	.631
2003	Braves	NL	162	69	.52	262	49	45	40	45	23	113	10	489	90	85	23	49	69	51	18	11	101	61	.623
2004	Braves	NL	162	105	.70	263	80	28	49	33	25	128	16	483	118	104	75	22	50	30	20	14	96	66	.593
2005	Braves	NL	162	110	.69	247	54	35	46	27	20	125	7	484	124	104	93	11	52	34	18	11	90	72	.556
2006	Braves	NL	162	85	.58	299	24	35	44	38	24	144	3	522	87	99	56	24	69	48	21	12	79	83	.488
2007	Braves	NL	162	86	.68	290	33	21	60	24	10	143	1	528	94	77	68	28	89	58	31	16	84	78	.519
	162-Game Average			91	.60	266	48	31	47	36	16	242	16	432	133	95	59	41	53	32	21	11	96	66	.593

Terry Francona

Year	Team	Lg	G	LINEUPS		SUBSTITUTION			PITCHER USAGE						TACTICS				INTENTIONAL BB				RESULTS		
				LUp	PL%	PH	PR	DS	Quick	Slow	LO	RCD	LS	Rel	SBA	SacA	RM	PO	#	Good	NG	Bomb	W	L	Pct
1997	Phillies	NL	162	98	.66	288	19	28	28	54	22	102	9	409	148	91		30	31	12	19	9	68	94	.420
1998	Phillies	NL	162	84	.53	256	20	19	34	57	20	88	7	385	142	85		16	23	6	17	8	75	87	.463
1999	Phillies	NL	162	85	.51	239	13	31	29	41	16	111	7	441	160	81		27	17	7	10	6	77	85	.475
2000	Phillies	NL	162	108	.53	278	17	14	38	43	25	102	5	414	132	89		16	17	7	10	7	65	97	.401
2004	Red Sox	AL	162	141	.65	139	87	60	39	48	32	105	8	437	98	18	84	27	28	22	6	4	98	64	.605
2005	Red Sox	AL	162	104	.67	110	46	37	25	55	30	99	3	442	57	21	79	11	28	18	10	5	95	67	.586
2006	Red Sox	AL	162	116	.59	93	54	49	36	42	13	94	9	454	74	33	95	16	25	11	14	7	86	76	.531
2007	Red Sox	AL	162	109	.60	84	34	23	41	35	32	89	4	451	120	45	90	14	20	14	6	4	96	66	.593
	162-Game Average			106	.59	186	36	33	34	47	24	198	13	429	116	58	87	20	24	12	12	6	82	80	.506

Ron Gardenhire

Year	Team	Lg	G	LINEUPS		SUBSTITUTION			PITCHER USAGE						TACTICS				INTENTIONAL BB				RESULTS		
				LUp	PL%	PH	PR	DS	Quick	Slow	LO	RCD	LS	Rel	SBA	SacA	RM	PO	#	Good	NG	Bomb	W	L	Pct
2002	Twins	AL	161	111	.69	157	42	42	51	22	10	84	1	435	141	45	30	11	24	16	8	4	94	67	.584
2003	Twins	AL	162	126	.63	144	50	26	49	33	13	85	2	399	138	59	37	14	35	16	19	6	90	72	.556
2004	Twins	AL	163	131	.59	148	55	29	54	21	20	106	4	435	162	66	105	19	27	15	12	7	92	70	.568
2005	Twins	AL	162	135	.58	104	45	26	50	21	5	87	1	396	146	59	138	16	38	28	10	3	83	79	.512
2006	Twins	AL	162	97	.62	93	36	21	60	29	3	82	5	421	143	48	127	11	25	14	11	4	96	66	.593
2007	Twins	AL	162	139	.63	104	42	25	45	30	8	99	4	438	142	45	148	11	33	14	19	9	79	83	.488
	162-Game Average			123	.62	125	45	28	52	26	10	91	3	421	145	54	98	14	30	17	13	6	89	73	.549

Phil Garner

Year	Team	Lg	G	LINEUPS		SUBSTITUTION			PITCHER USAGE						TACTICS				INTENTIONAL BB				RESULTS		
				LUp	PL%	PH	PR	DS	Quick	Slow	LO	RCD	LS	Rel	SBA	SacA	RM	PO	#	Good	NG	Bomb	W	L	Pct
1994	Brewers	AL	115	94	.53	53	33	24	31	35	0	44	5	252	96	46		23	16	6	10	9	53	62	.461
1995	Brewers	AL	144	120	.58	83	67	52	42	42	10	52	4	321	145	64		52	23	2	21	12	65	79	.451
1996	Brewers	AL	162	114	.58	115	48	46	50	36	13	61	12	385	149	72		82	20	1	19	11	80	82	.494
1997	Brewers	AL	161	128	.59	190	42	36	51	34	6	93	6	367	158	65		55	21	11	10	6	78	83	.484
1998	Brewers	NL	162	125	.58	265	54	46	52	43	6	90	9	416	140	85		59	21	12	9	4	74	88	.457
1999	Brewers	NL	112	69	.57	182	15	5	28	26	4	45	5	294	75	85		57	19	10	9	8	52	60	.464
2000	Tigers	Al	162	128	.53	126	30	25	35	30	8	109	3	429	121	58		26	13	5	8	6	79	83	.488
2001	Tigers	AL	162	116	.64	93	40	14	25	51	9	81	3	391	194	58		36	29	10	19	11	00	90	.407
2002	Tigers	AL	6	3	.63	1	1	0	1	3	3	2	0	15	4	0	3	0	2	0	2	2	0	6	.000
2004	Astros	NL	74	31	.54	163	28	35	27	14	14	71	4	241	78	40	36	7	24	20	4	1	48	26	.649
2005	Astros	NL	163	101	.48	251	40	63	55	34	21	118	3	434	159	99	148	10	29	17	12	7	89	73	.549
2006	Astros	NL	162	111	.47	287	17	47	55	36	18	157	2	497	115	123	114	26	65	31	34	17	82	80	.506
2007	Astros	NL	131	99	.52	230	14	36	31	44	17	120	0	388	79	88	84	23	48	27	21	11	58	73	.443
	162-Game Average			117	.55	193	41	41	46	41	12	316	17	418	143	83	117	43	31	14	17	10	78	84	.481

Bob Geren

Year	Team	Lg	G	LINEUPS		SUBSTITUTION			PITCHER USAGE						TACTICS				INTENTIONAL BB				RESULTS		
				LUp	PL%	PH	PR	DS	Quick	Slow	LO	RCD	LS	Rel	SBA	SacA	RM	PO	#	Good	NG	Bomb	W	L	Pct
2007	Athletics	AL	162	140	.57	64	31	24	39	43	14	112	9	446	72	31	91	22	60	38	22	10	76	86	.469
	162-Game Average			140	.57	64	31	24	39	43	14	112	9	446	72	31	91	22	60	38	22	10	76	86	.469

John Gibbons

Year	Team	Lg	G	LINEUPS		SUBSTITUTION			PITCHER USAGE						TACTICS				INTENTIONAL BB				RESULTS		
				LUp	PL%	PH	PR	DS	Quick	Slow	LO	RCD	LS	Rel	SBA	SacA	RM	PO	#	Good	NG	Bomb	W	L	Pct
2004	Blue Jays	AL	51	36	.68	55	3	2	15	8	7	22	1	130	34	2	39	21	11	5	6	3	20	30	.400
2005	Blue Jays	AL	162	124	.66	148	11	37	55	18	9	77	12	432	107	28	128	45	29	13	16	9	80	82	.494
2006	Blue Jays	AL	162	120	.53	112	32	40	59	32	17	94	16	482	98	20	126	40	56	32	24	12	87	75	.537
2007	Blue Jays	AL	162	131	.46	139	48	33	45	37	31	75	9	420	79	35	99	37	34	17	17	6	83	79	.512
	162-Game Average			124	.56	137	28	34	53	29	19	81	11	442	96	26	118	43	39	20	19	9	82	80	.506

Fredi Gonzalez

Year	Team	Lg	G	LINEUPS		SUBSTITUTION			PITCHER USAGE						TACTICS				INTENTIONAL BB				RESULTS		
				LUp	PL%	PH	PR	DS	Quick	Slow	LO	RCD	LS	Rel	SBA	SacA	RM	PO	#	Good	NG	Bomb	W	L	Pct
2007	Marlins	NL	162	96	.50	284	29	34	33	56	20	138	5	560	139	91	79	22	60	36	24	16	71	91	.438
	162-Game Average			96	.50	284	29	34	33	56	20	138	5	560	139	91	79	22	60	36	24	16	71	91	.438

Ozzie Guillen

Year	Team	Lg	G	LINEUPS		SUBSTITUTION			PITCHER USAGE						TACTICS				INTENTIONAL BB				RESULTS		
				LUp	PL%	PH	PR	DS	Quick	Slow	LO	RCD	LS	Rel	SBA	SacA	RM	PO	#	Good	NG	Bomb	W	L	Pct
2004	White Sox	AL	162	134	.55	160	46	15	27	65	48	86	8	399	129	79	77	17	36	15	21	8	83	79	.512
2005	White Sox	AL	162	112	.51	100	32	21	31	56	35	114	5	412	204	68	148	15	42	27	15	6	99	63	.611
2006	White Sox	AL	162	87	.60	135	42	38	27	66	35	83	7	398	141	61	83	27	59	39	20	9	90	72	.556
2007	White Sox	AL	162	124	.56	100	26	23	26	53	33	131	2	463	123	54	92	13	50	24	26	15	72	90	.444
	162-Game Average			114	.55	124	37	24	28	60	38	104	6	418	149	66	100	18	47	26	21	10	86	76	.531

Mike Hargrove

Year	Team	Lg	G	LINEUPS		SUBSTITUTION			PITCHER USAGE						TACTICS				INTENTIONAL BB				RESULTS		
				LUp	PL%	PH	PR	DS	Quick	Slow	LO	RCD	LS	Rel	SBA	SacA	RM	PO	#	Good	NG	Bomb	W	L	Pct
1994	Indians	AL	113	53	.67	79	18	31	23	31	3	41	4	222	179	43		40	22	8	14	7	66	47	.584
1995	Indians	AL	144	64	.66	101	34	21	36	23	12	61	3	335	185	40		22	12	5	7	3	100	44	.694
1996	Indians	AL	161	96	.56	115	20	25	39	31	14	70	5	382	210	58		41	31	11	20	11	99	62	.615
1997	Indians	AL	162	109	.58	86	17	14	34	46	14	101	9	429	177	60		37	30	7	23	10	86	75	.534
1998	Indians	AL	162	108	.62	88	21	32	29	39	19	104	9	423	203	53		47	39	17	22	13	89	73	.549
1999	Indians	AL	162	123	.66	99	25	22	41	44	15	99	3	466	197	82		28	36	14	22	13	97	65	.599
2000	Orioles	AL	162	107	.54	77	42	19	25	55	24	84	2	396	191	36		31	21	10	11	2	74	88	.457
2001	Orioles	AL	162	139	.53	82	27	20	39	42	3	74	10	392	186	57		71	17	7	10	7	63	98	.391
2002	Orioles	AL	162	125	.52	129	24	22	32	44	32	74	6	407	158	54	13	39	34	22	12	6	67	95	.414
2003	Orioles	AL	163	120	.52	78	37	22	29	52	48	89	5	425	125	67	45	16	43	20	23	11	71	91	.438
2005	Mariners	AL	162	97	.52	125	24	18	30	45	31	73	1	433	149	61	120	36	32	21	11	7	69	93	.426
2006	Mariners	AL	162	84	.51	121	21	20	24	49	24	81	14	429	143	39	119	17	50	26	24	16	78	84	.481
2007	Mariners	AL	78	48	.47	41	18	21	20	26	9	44	7	209	55	22	58	13	20	12	8	4	45	33	.577
	162-Game Average			106	.57	101	27	24	33	44	21	222	17	411	179	56	79	36	32	15	17	9	83	79	.512

Clint Hurdle

Year	Team	Lg	G	LINEUPS		SUBSTITUTION			PITCHER USAGE						TACTICS				INTENTIONAL BB				RESULTS		
				LUp	PL%	PH	PR	DS	Quick	Slow	LO	RCD	LS	Rel	SBA	SacA	RM	PO	#	Good	NG	Bomb	W	L	Pct
2002	Rockies	NL	140	100	.52	283	30	41	30	44	17	104	3	437	139	44	41	13	38	22	16	11	67	73	.479
2003	Rockies	NL	162	108	.47	317	17	32	35	40	5	87	4	500	100	82	26	16	51	31	20	13	74	88	.457
2004	Rockies	NL	162	131	.57	330	24	36	33	60	20	74	1	473	77	126	52	11	84	54	30	12	68	94	.420
2005	Rockies	NL	162	135	.60	273	21	40	42	60	17	89	2	459	97	114	119	22	54	28	26	15	67	95	.414
2006	Rockies	NL	162	111	.49	259	17	22	34	52	17	107	2	499	135	155	109	28	81	45	36	23	76	86	.469
2007	Rockies	NL	163	96	.51	283	32	29	45	37	13	112	1	529	131	112	109	26	61	30	31	14	90	73	.552
	162-Game Average			116	.53	297	24	34	37	50	15	98	2	493	116	108	78	20	63	36	27	15	75	87	.463

Tony LaRussa

Year	Team	Lg	G	LINEUPS		SUBSTITUTION			PITCHER USAGE						TACTICS				INTENTIONAL BB				RESULTS		
				LUp	PL%	PH	PR	DS	Quick	Slow	LO	RCD	LS	Rel	SBA	SacA	RM	PO	#	Good	NG	Bomb	W	L	Pct
1994	Athletics	AL	114	97	.62	89	28	14	43	21	5	60	4	308	130	31		32	23	13	10	4	51	63	.447
1995	Athletics	AL	144	120	.54	113	38	24	33	38	19	46	7	358	158	42		42	17	9	8	4	67	77	.465
1996	Cardinals	NL	162	120	.52	246	25	13	32	48	24			413	207	117		41	38				88	74	.543
1997	Cardinals	NL	162	146	.54	307	17	18	34	42	16	81	2	399	224	77		79	26	18	8	2	73	89	.451
1998	Cardinals	NL	162	146	.52	259	7	18	62	31	13	82	14	429	174	85		34	32	19	13	8	83	79	.512
1999	Cardinals	NL	161	138	.47	264	32	28	50	41	13	96	14	454	182	103		30	31	13	18	11	75	86	.466
2000	Cardinals	NL	162	137	.53	240	35	25	40	31	11	63	18	386	138	107		34	21	14	7	6	95	67	.586
2001	Cardinals	NL	162	117	.47	256	26	13	46	36	7	140	7	485	126	102		25	31	16	15	4	93	69	.574
2002	Cardinals	NL	162	117	.52	352	35	41	55	33	23	110	6	472	128	105	57	13	39	25	14	8	97	65	.599
2003	Cardinals	NL	162	126	.50	352	28	51	38	49	36	113	9	460	114	108	56	9	36	28	8	2	85	77	.525
2004	Cardinals	NL	162	119	.53	321	33	75	30	43	31	120	16	469	158	87	128	7	24	17	7	4	105	57	.648
2005	Cardinals	NL	162	138	.55	270	25	48	40	38	22	88	4	436	119	92	153	9	27	16	11	7	100	62	.617
2006	Cardinals	NL	162	131	.56	272	11	52	49	34	21	95	6	469	91	85	117	13	35	21	14	3	83	78	.516
2007	Cardinals	NL	162	150	.60	317	19	37	46	44	8	102	5	516	89	85	120	23	25	10	15	11	78	84	.481
	162-Game Average			133	.53	269	26	34	44	39	18	200	19	446	150	90	105	29	30	19	11	5	86	76	.531

Jim Leyland

Year	Team	Lg	G	LINEUPS		SUBSTITUTION			PITCHER USAGE						TACTICS				INTENTIONAL BB				RESULTS		
				LUp	PL%	PH	PR	DS	Quick	Slow	LO	RCD	LS	Rel	SBA	SacA	RM	PO	#	Good	NG	Bomb	W	L	Pct
1995	Pirates	NL	144	124	.56	282	8	4	13	12	11	71	4	391	139	69		51	36	16	20	10	58	86	.403
1996	Pirates	NL	162	117	.53	299	18	14	27	8	11	60	11	422	175	101		46	31	4	27	13	73	89	.451
1997	Marlins	NL	162	105	.59	258	36	31	21	12	18	65	2	404	173	91		38	31	15	16	9	92	70	.568
1998	Marlins	NL	162	96	.59	277	13	15	18	24	31	73	8	420	172	91		31	45	20	25	11	54	108	.333
1999	Rockies	NL	162	124	.56	294	11	12	11	29	21	72	5	421	113	88		11	29	7	22	14	72	90	.444
2006	Tigers	AL	162	120	.53	81	34	37	51	30	16	52	3	390	100	57	124	9	35	23	12	9	95	67	.586
2007	Tigers	AL	162	108	.53	77	31	49	46	43	14	70	5	443	133	35	123	20	41	24	17	13	88	74	.543
	162-Game Average			115	.56	228	22	24	27	23	18	232	19	420	146	77	124	30	36	16	20	11	77	85	.475

336

Grady Little

Year	Team	Lg	G	LINEUPS		SUBSTITUTION			PITCHER USAGE						TACTICS				INTENTIONAL BB				RESULTS		
				LUp	PL%	PH	PR	DS	Quick	Slow	LO	RCD	LS	Rel	SBA	SacA	RM	PO	#	Good	NG	Bomb	W	L	Pct
2002	Red Sox	AL	162	120	.59	138	54	23	59	27	18	53	11	338	108	32	25	46	29	18	11	3	93	69	.574
2003	Red Sox	AL	162	118	.64	130	80	32	43	36	19	78	8	437	123	32	42	28	41	22	19	13	95	67	.586
2006	Dodgers	NL	162	118	.67	291	34	37	56	27	11	106	9	454	177	82	137	63	40	22	18	7	88	74	.543
2007	Dodgers	NL	162	112	.61	273	35	61	44	31	11	125	4	483	187	77	133	45	34	21	13	7	82	80	.506
	162-Game Average			117	.63	208	51	38	51	30	15	91	8	428	149	56	84	46	36	21	15	8	90	72	.556

Pete Mackanin

Year	Team	Lg	G	LINEUPS		SUBSTITUTION			PITCHER USAGE						TACTICS				INTENTIONAL BB				RESULTS		
				LUp	PL%	PH	PR	DS	Quick	Slow	LO	RCD	LS	Rel	SBA	SacA	RM	PO	#	Good	NG	Bomb	W	L	Pct
2005	Pirates	NL	26	24	.52	54	1	5	11	4	1	22	0	94	19	19	20	2	5	2	3	1	12	14	.462
2007	Reds	NL	80	57	.59	130	10	26	20	22	9	58	3	266	62	44	36	12	18	10	8	3	41	39	.513
	162-Game Average			124	.57	281	17	47	47	40	15	122	5	550	124	96	86	21	35	18	17	6	81	81	.500

Joe Maddon

Year	Team	Lg	G	LINEUPS		SUBSTITUTION			PITCHER USAGE						TACTICS				INTENTIONAL BB				RESULTS		
				LUp	PL%	PH	PR	DS	Quick	Slow	LO	RCD	LS	Rel	SBA	SacA	RM	PO	#	Good	NG	Bomb	W	L	Pct
2006	Devil Rays	AL	162	145	.57	81	26	51	41	37	16	79	10	444	186	51	126	48	39	19	20	13	61	101	.377
2007	Devil Rays	AL	162	122	.53	80	19	16	31	56	19	113	1	483	179	40	118	50	31	18	13	4	66	96	.407
	162-Game Average			134	.55	81	23	34	36	47	18	96	6	464	183	46	122	49	35	19	17	9	64	98	.395

Charlie Manuel

Year	Team	Lg	G	LINEUPS		SUBSTITUTION			PITCHER USAGE						TACTICS				INTENTIONAL BB				RESULTS		
				LUp	PL%	PH	PR	DS	Quick	Slow	LO	RCD	LS	Rel	SBA	SacA	RM	PO	#	Good	NG	Bomb	W	L	Pct
2000	Indians	AL	162	102	.64	73	40	26	21	12	20	104	7	462	147	59		30	38	21	17	9	90	72	.556
2001	Indians	AL	162	114	.61	105	30	49	28	17	10	120	3	484	120	67		43	34	20	14	11	91	71	.562
2002	Indians	AL	87	68	.61	60	10	19	13	17	25	47	0	225	57	19	12	3	21	12	9	4	39	48	.448
2005	Phillies	NL	162	80	.64	265	36	19	42	28	13	119	6	442	143	86	76	11	51	35	16	9	88	74	.543
2006	Phillies	NL	162	81	.65	301	42	49	28	42	22	126	2	500	117	79	69	16	63	35	28	12	85	77	.525
2007	Phillies	NL	162	87	.64	264	56	75	40	40	19	128	6	498	157	84	90	30	62	41	21	16	89	73	.549
	162-Game Average			96	.63	193	39	43	31	28	20	182	7	472	134	71	70	24	40	30	10	11	87	75	.537

John McLaren

Year	Team	Lg	G	LINEUPS		SUBSTITUTION			PITCHER USAGE						TACTICS				INTENTIONAL BB				RESULTS		
				LUp	PL%	PH	PR	DS	Quick	Slow	LO	RCD	LS	Rel	SBA	SacA	RM	PO	#	Good	NG	Bomb	W	L	Pct
2007	Mariners	AL	84	52	.48	55	40	18	17	23	19	49	6	247	56	20	76	18	19	10	9	5	43	41	.512
	162-Game Average			100	.48	106	77	35	33	44	37	95	12	476	108	39	147	35	37	19	17	10	83	79	.512

Bob Melvin

Year	Team	Lg	G	LINEUPS		SUBSTITUTION			PITCHER USAGE						TACTICS				INTENTIONAL BB				RESULTS		
				LUp	PL%	PH	PR	DS	Quick	Slow	LO	RCD	LS	Rel	SBA	SacA	RM	PO	#	Good	NG	Bomb	W	L	Pct
2003	Mariners	AL	162	111	.62	81	62	33	27	46	43	56	6	366	145	44	37	5	24	14	10	4	93	69	.574
2004	Mariners	AL	162	151	.59	127	86	26	21	62	43	82	5	414	152	56	111	24	32	18	14	8	63	99	.389
2005	Diamondbacks	NL	162	120	.68	310	26	38	26	56	36	123	11	458	93	93	101	30	43	27	16	9	77	85	.475
2006	Diamondbacks	NL	162	114	.72	278	11	35	37	42	15	86	0	461	106	81	60	30	44	28	16	8	76	86	.469
2007	Diamondbacks	NL	162	146	.57	243	11	61	35	42	31	96	2	469	133	74	70	25	38	30	8	4	90	72	.556
	162-Game Average			128	.64	208	39	39	29	50	34	89	5	434	126	70	76	23	36	23	13	7	80	82	.494

Jerry Narron

Year	Team	Lg	G	LINEUPS		SUBSTITUTION			PITCHER USAGE						TACTICS				INTENTIONAL BB				RESULTS		
				LUp	PL%	PH	PR	DS	Quick	Slow	LO	RCD	LS	Rel	SBA	SacA	RM	PO	#	Good	NG	Bomb	W	L	Pct
2001	Rangers	AL	134	94	.66	92	14	19	9	18	6	60	5	340	106	29		5	16	2	14	8	62	72	.463
2002	Rangers	AL	162	128	.52	159	63	38	30	50	26	121	5	487	96	58	48	6	32	19	13	3	72	90	.444
2005	Reds	NL	93	73	.61	156	9	14	13	22	12	71	5	287	50	45	53	7	25	21	4	2	46	46	.500
2006	Reds	NL	162	140	.56	273	23	46	33	47	41	121	2	476	157	86	89	11	55	38	17	9	80	82	.494
2007	Reds	NL	82	63	.58	135	6	26	11	33	21	74	8	256	66	56	45	8	29	16	13	7	31	51	.378
	162-Game Average			128	.58	209	29	37	25	44	27	145	8	473	122	70	76	9	40	25	16	7	75	87	.463

Sam Perlozzo

Year	Team	Lg	G	LINEUPS		SUBSTITUTION			PITCHER USAGE						TACTICS				INTENTIONAL BB				RESULTS		
				LUp	PL%	PH	PR	DS	Quick	Slow	LO	RCD	LS	Rel	SBA	SacA	RM	PO	#	Good	NG	Bomb	W	L	Pct
2005	Orioles	AL	55	47	.61	28	23	26	15	11	5	46	2	180	41	24	25	8	3	1	2	1	23	32	.418
2006	Orioles	AL	162	124	.56	72	46	49	29	46	14	102	10	472	153	56	76	30	26	15	11	7	70	92	.432
2007	Orioles	AL	69	48	.60	29	26	25	16	15	13	64	1	211	62	30	29	13	8	3	5	5	29	40	.420
	162-Game Average			124	.58	73	54	57	34	41	18	120	7	489	145	62	74	29	21	11	10	7	69	93	.426

Lou Piniella

Year	Team	Lg	G	LINEUPS		SUBSTITUTION			PITCHER USAGE						TACTICS				INTENTIONAL BB				RESULTS		
				LUp	PL%	PH	PR	DS	Quick	Slow	LO	RCD	LS	Rel	SBA	SacA	RM	PO	#	Good	NG	Bomb	W	L	Pct
1994	Mariners	AL	112	98	.49	113	24	6	30	35	4	54	9	252	69	54		37	28	10	18	9	49	63	.438
1995	Mariners	AL	145	98	.56	137	41	22	37	39	30	58	20	324	151	66		40	32	13	19	12	79	66	.545
1996	Mariners	AL	161	99	.55	190	28	14	56	21	15	91	14	403	129	65		40	40	19	21	13	85	76	.528
1997	Mariners	AL	162	84	.57	147	35	27	38	47	25	79	11	392	129	61		32	30	12	18	10	90	72	.556
1998	Mariners	AL	161	111	.53	99	38	43	38	54	32	81	4	368	154	58		20	18	3	15	7	76	85	.472
1999	Mariners	AL	162	130	.46	122	38	30	31	40	21	51	10	346	175	49		31	27	3	24	8	79	83	.488
2000	Mariners	AL	162	130	.50	109	43	52	51	37	1	64	11	383	178	73		22	32	15	17	8	91	71	.562
2001	Mariners	AL	162	115	.64	121	44	64	55	33	5	62	9	392	216	62		33	23	14	9	3	116	46	.716
2002	Mariners	AL	162	129	.64	98	135	50	47	38	33	52	7	343	195	59	31	25	34	15	19	11	93	69	.574
2003	Devil Rays	AL	162	124	.60	188	43	26	38	41	29	59	5	372	184	53	52	23	37	21	16	10	63	99	.389
2004	Devil Rays	AL	162	137	.63	121	30	37	50	34	23	57	15	401	174	44	87	16	35	16	19	9	70	91	.435
2005	Devil Rays	AL	162	135	.54	127	18	52	38	54	32	67	10	401	200	53	128	16	41	19	22	13	67	95	.414
2007	Cubs	NL	162	125	.51	263	52	51	35	38	33	98	3	478	119	60	89	17	46	28	18	4	85	77	.525
	162-Game Average			121	.56	146	45	38	43	41	23	175	26	386	165	60	77	28	34	15	19	9	83	79	.512

Willie Randolph

Year	Team	Lg	G	LINEUPS		SUBSTITUTION			PITCHER USAGE						TACTICS				INTENTIONAL BB				RESULTS		
				LUp	PL%	PH	PR	DS	Quick	Slow	LO	RCD	LS	Rel	SBA	SacA	RM	PO	#	Good	NG	Bomb	W	L	Pct
2005	Mets	NL	162	105	.64	222	10	51	47	34	20	74	5	392	193	89	118	18	43	28	15	9	83	79	.512
2006	Mets	NL	162	101	.68	247	9	24	40	40	15	119	4	474	181	100	103	16	39	25	14	9	97	65	.599
2007	Mets	NL	162	102	.68	269	21	28	26	44	27	122	3	499	246	97	100	10	40	26	14	7	88	74	.543
	162-Game Average			103	.67	246	13	34	38	39	21	105	4	455	207	95	107	15	41	26	14	8	89	73	.549

Mike Scioscia

Year	Team	Lg	G	LINEUPS		SUBSTITUTION			PITCHER USAGE						TACTICS				INTENTIONAL BB				RESULTS		
				LUp	PL%	PH	PR	DS	Quick	Slow	LO	RCD	LS	Rel	SBA	SacA	RM	PO	#	Good	NG	Bomb	W	L	Pct
2000	Angels	AL	162	75	.62	110	41	4	56	42	6	95	9	441	145	63		40	32	16	16	7	82	80	.506
2001	Angels	AL	162	130	.62	118	30	8	29	41	5	81	9	384	168	66		50	33	8	25	12	75	87	.463
2002	Angels	AL	162	102	.64	170	60	24	34	32	34	88	8	400	168	61	41	29	24	15	9	5	99	63	.611
2003	Angels	AL	162	130	.64	134	54	40	50	48	11	60	4	375	190	64	79	25	38	26	12	3	77	85	.475
2004	Angels	AL	162	126	.57	115	43	46	35	40	22	61	11	343	189	69	196	32	27	18	9	3	92	70	.568
2005	Angels	AL	162	124	.65	92	37	37	47	37	24	88	9	379	218	58	160	43	24	15	9	4	95	67	.586
2006	Angels	AL	162	114	.63	103	45	38	38	47	21	99	9	380	205	37	163	22	27	18	9	6	89	73	.549
2007	Angels	AL	162	127	.66	103	26	19	39	40	14	94	4	396	194	41	166	44	22	12	10	5	94	68	.580
	162-Game Average			116	.63	118	42	27	41	41	17	111	11	387	185	57	134	36	28	16	12	6	88	74	.543

Joe Torre

Year	Team	Lg	G	LINEUPS		SUBSTITUTION			PITCHER USAGE						TACTICS				INTENTIONAL BB				RESULTS		
				LUp	PL%	PH	PR	DS	Quick	Slow	LO	RCD	LS	Rel	SBA	SacA	RM	PO	#	Good	NG	Bomb	W	L	Pct
1994	Cardinals	NL	115	79	.68	192	9	0	36	29	6	106	4	330	122	57		33	13	3	10	6	53	61	.465
1995	Cardinals	NL	47	36	.51	99	6	4	17	11	1	41	2	146	42	26		14	11	5	6	2	20	27	.426
1996	Yankees	AL	162	131	.57	92	62	55	59	23	22	97	10	411	142	53		19	27	9	18	14	92	70	.568
1997	Yankees	AL	162	118	.61	75	70	23	35	41	19	84	14	368	157	54		14	29	11	18	10	96	66	.593
1998	Yankees	AL	162	96	.62	94	36	28	43	38	27	71	17	334	216	44		9	18	10	8	4	114	48	.704
1999	Yankees	AL	162	76	.63	103	57	10	29	51	26	80	12	276	129	31		12	15	5	10	8	98	64	.605
2000	Yankees	AL	161	112	.63	86	49	27	43	53	27	92	16	382	147	22		8	16	2	14	7	87	74	.540
2001	Yankees	AL	161	94	.56	76	33	14	37	45	10	77	17	362	214	41		21	22	13	9	6	95	65	.594
2002	Yankees	AL	161	108	.62	92	60	31	37	48	45	86	13	334	138	34	38	17	44	33	11	4	103	58	.640
2003	Yankees	AL	163	104	.65	118	48	18	26	51	52	75	10	367	131	39	69	33	36	21	15	8	101	61	.623
2004	Yankees	AL	163	116	.65	99	42	47	47	35	29	129	0	436	117	48	126	33	32	16	16	9	101	61	.623
2005	Yankees	AL	162	117	.64	94	65	47	44	45	28	92	7	418	111	40	123	50	25	11	14	9	95	67	.586
2006	Yankees	AL	162	120	.66	108	50	59	50	28	9	109	7	490	174	48	115	50	41	22	19	4	97	65	.599
2007	Yankees	AL	162	102	.68	99	34	22	51	29	10	113	13	522	163	51	152	41	33	17	16	7	94	68	.580
	162-Game Average			109	.63	110	48	30	43	41	24	209	25	399	154	45	104	27	28	14	14	8	96	66	.593

Jim Tracy

Year	Team	Lg	G	LUp	PL%	PH	PR	DS	Quick	Slow	LO	RCD	LS	Rel	SBA	SacA	RM	PO	#	Good	NG	Bomb	W	L	Pct
2001	Dodgers	NL	162	111	.50	264	34	20	46	42	8	84	4	409	131	81		10	25	7	18	9	86	76	.531
2002	Dodgers	NL	162	102	.52	331	44	37	48	35	21	118	9	423	133	80	35	18	45	31	14	5	92	70	.568
2003	Dodgers	NL	162	103	.64	269	22	64	52	29	22	**148**	**11**	438	116	97	32	10	35	23	12	8	85	77	.525
2004	Dodgers	NL	162	94	**.70**	**336**	34	19	48	31	16	128	**16**	459	143	79	90	7	47	32	15	8	93	69	.574
2005	Dodgers	NL	162	129	.64	303	31	37	44	40	20	126	2	459	93	76	97	17	34	21	13	6	71	91	.438
2006	Pirates	NL	162	121	.43	264	22	23	37	43	12	156	3	505	91	80	74	12	62	39	23	15	67	95	.414
2007	Pirates	NL	162	124	.49	240	12	26	33	40	13	113	0	495	98	80	90	12	55	30	25	11	68	**94**	.420
	162-Game Average			112	.56	287	28	32	44	37	16	146	8	455	115	82	70	12	43	26	17	9	80	82	.494

Dave Trembley

Year	Team	Lg	G	LUp	PL%	PH	PR	DS	Quick	Slow	LO	RCD	LS	Rel	SBA	SacA	RM	PO	#	Good	NG	Bomb	W	L	Pct
2007	Orioles	AL	93	71	.60	63	29	16	21	25	16	47	3	279	124	32	83	32	29	15	14	8	40	53	.430
	162-Game Average			124	.60	110	51	28	37	44	28	82	5	486	216	56	145	56	51	26	24	14	70	92	.432

Ron Washington

Year	Team	Lg	G	LUp	PL%	PH	PR	DS	Quick	Slow	LO	RCD	LS	Rel	SBA	SacA	RM	PO	#	Good	NG	Bomb	W	L	Pct
2007	Rangers	AL	162	139	.60	89	30	**53**	47	46	4	78	9	467	113	**76**	67	13	38	19	19	11	75	87	.463
	162-Game Average			139	.60	89	30	53	47	46	4	78	9	467	113	76	67	13	38	19	19	11	75	87	.463

Eric Wedge

Year	Team	Lg	G	LUp	PL%	PH	PR	DS	Quick	Slow	LO	RCD	LS	Rel	SBA	SacA	RM	PO	#	Good	NG	Bomb	W	L	Pct
2003	Indians	AL	162	**145**	.67	117	43	27	47	34	18	89	5	428	147	67	54	12	37	22	15	8	68	94	.420
2004	Indians	AL	162	114	**.72**	110	41	20	42	38	22	121	0	479	149	56	96	25	47	26	**18**	8	80	82	.494
2005	Indians	AL	162	111	.66	88	18	16	45	45	15	90	3	409	98	53	79	9	20	11	9	7	93	69	.574
2006	Indians	AL	162	111	.59	98	13	13	28	52	27	48	1	377	78	40	81	15	35	21	14	11	78	84	.481
2007	Indians	AL	162	117	.60	116	41	25	34	38	20	79	2	395	113	40	108	16	42	24	18	9	**96**	66	.593
	162-Game Average			120	.65	106	31	20	39	41	20	85	2	418	117	51	84	15	36	21	15	11	83	79	.512

Ned Yost

Year	Team	Lg	G	LUp	PL%	PH	PR	DS	Quick	Slow	LO	RCD	LS	Rel	SBA	SacA	RM	PO	#	Good	NG	Bomb	W	L	Pct
2003	Brewers	NL	162	97	.44	304	22	39	23	**59**	18	90	6	460	138	85	40	23	43	28	15	9	68	94	.420
2004	Brewers	NL	162	131	.60	317	28	20	39	40	27	63	2	423	**178**	79	78	7	27	16	11	8	67	94	.416
2005	Brewers	NL	162	99	.46	259	18	35	26	41	**42**	71	2	395	113	89	97	50	52	23	**29**	10	81	81	.500
2006	Brewers	NL	162	106	.48	238	12	14	33	44	18	77	4	427	108	80	77	16	34	14	20	12	75	87	.463
2007	Brewers	NL	162	109	.60	259	11	41	37	42	18	117	**7**	492	128	74	94	19	37	28	9	9	83	79	.512
	162-Game Average			109	.52	276	18	30	32	45	25	84	4	440	133	82	77	23	39	22	17	10	75	87	.463

Categories of this record are Games Managed (G), Number of Different Lineups Used (LUp), the percentage of players who had the platoon advatange at the start of the game (PL%), Pinch Hitters Used (PH), Pinch Runners Used (PR), Defensive Substitutes Used (DS), Quick Hooks (Quick), Slow Hooks (Slow), Long Outings by Starting Pitchers (LO), Relievers Used on Consecutive Days (RCD), Long Saves (LS), Relivers Used (Rel), Stolen Base Attempts (SBA), Sacrifice Bunts Attempts (SacA), Runners Moving with the Pitch (RM), Pitchouts ordered (PO), Intentional Walks issued (#), Intentional Walks resulting in a Good Outcome (Good), Intentional Walks resulting Not in a Good Outcome (NG), Intentional Walks Blowing up on the Manager (Bomb), Wins (W), Losses (L) and Winning Percentage (Pct.).

2007 American League Managers

Manager	G	LINEUPS		SUBSTITUTION			PITCHER USAGE						TACTICS				INTENTIONAL BB				RESULTS		
		LUp	PL%	PH	PR	DS	Quick	Slow	LO	RCD	LS	Rel	SBA	SacA	RM	PO	#	Good	NG	Bomb	W	L	Pct
Buddy Bell, KC	162	141	.55	119	30	28	49	28	16	74	10	448	122	59	125	25	54	33	21	9	69	93	.426
Terry Francona, Bos	162	109	.60	84	34	23	41	35	32	89	4	451	120	45	90	14	20	14	6	4	96	66	.593
Ron Gardenhire, Min	162	139	.63	104	42	25	45	30	8	99	4	438	142	45	148	11	33	14	19	9	79	83	.488
Bob Geren, Oak	162	140	.57	64	31	24	39	43	14	112	9	446	72	31	91	22	60	38	22	10	76	86	.469
John Gibbons, Tor	162	131	.46	139	48	33	45	37	31	75	9	420	79	35	99	37	34	17	17	6	83	79	.512
Ozzie Guillen, CWS	162	124	.56	100	26	23	26	53	33	131	2	463	123	54	92	13	50	24	26	15	72	90	.444
Jim Leyland, Det	162	108	.53	77	31	49	46	43	14	70	5	443	133	35	123	20	41	24	17	13	88	74	.543
Joe Maddon, TB	162	122	.53	80	19	16	31	56	19	113	1	483	179	40	118	50	31	18	13	4	66	96	.407
Mike Scioscia, LAA	162	127	.66	103	26	19	39	40	14	94	4	396	194	41	166	44	22	12	10	5	94	68	.580
Joe Torre, NYY	162	102	.68	99	34	22	51	29	10	113	13	522	163	51	152	41	33	17	16	7	94	68	.580
Ron Washington, Tex	162	139	.60	89	30	53	47	46	4	78	9	467	113	76	67	13	38	19	19	11	75	87	.463
Eric Wedge, Cle	162	117	.60	116	41	25	34	38	20	79	2	395	113	40	108	16	42	24	18	9	96	66	.593
162-Game Average		121	.57	96	39	32	40	41	21	97	7	454	134	48	116	28	38	21	17	9	81	81	.500

Manager	G	LINEUPS		SUBSTITUTION			PITCHER USAGE						TACTICS				INTENTIONAL BB				RESULTS		
		LUp	PL%	PH	PR	DS	Quick	Slow	LO	RCD	LS	Rel	SBA	SacA	RM	PO	#	Good	NG	Bomb	W	L	Pct
Mike Hargrove, Sea	78	48	.47	41	18	21	20	26	9	44	7	209	55	22	58	13	20	12	8	4	45	33	.577
John McLaren, Sea	84	52	.48	55	40	18	17	23	19	49	6	247	56	20	76	18	19	10	9	5	43	41	.512
Sam Perlozzo, Bal	69	48	.60	29	26	25	16	15	13	64	1	211	62	30	29	13	8	3	5	5	29	40	.420
Dave Trembley, Bal	93	71	.60	63	29	16	21	25	16	47	3	279	124	32	83	32	29	15	14	8	40	53	.430

2007 National League Managers

Manager	G	LINEUPS		SUBSTITUTION			PITCHER USAGE						TACTICS				INTENTIONAL BB				RESULTS		
		LUp	PL%	PH	PR	DS	Quick	Slow	LO	RCD	LS	Rel	SBA	SacA	RM	PO	#	Good	NG	Bomb	W	L	Pct
Manny Acta, Was	162	101	.65	295	32	78	53	28	5	183	1	588	92	86	70	28	44	28	16	8	73	89	.451
Bud Black, SD	163	115	.62	279	18	13	63	28	13	122	0	485	79	85	73	56	48	28	20	11	89	74	.546
Bruce Bochy, SF	162	128	.73	264	50	45	26	50	36	132	2	496	152	86	119	10	41	29	12	3	71	91	.438
Bobby Cox, Atl	162	86	.68	290	33	21	60	24	10	143	1	528	94	77	68	28	89	58	31	16	84	78	.519
Fredi Gonzalez, Fla	162	96	.50	284	29	34	33	56	20	138	5	560	139	91	79	22	60	36	24	16	71	91	.438
Clint Hurdle, Col	163	96	.51	283	32	29	45	37	13	112	1	529	131	112	109	26	61	30	31	14	90	73	.552
Tony LaRussa, StL	162	150	.60	317	19	37	46	44	8	102	5	516	89	85	120	23	25	10	15	11	78	84	.481
Grady Little, LAD	162	112	.61	273	35	61	44	31	11	125	4	483	187	77	133	45	34	21	13	7	82	80	.506
Charlie Manuel, Phi	162	87	.64	264	56	75	40	40	19	128	6	498	157	84	90	30	62	41	21	16	89	73	.549
Bob Melvin, Ari	162	146	.57	243	11	61	35	42	31	96	2	469	133	74	70	25	38	30	8	4	90	72	.556
Lou Piniella, ChC	162	125	.51	263	52	51	35	38	33	98	3	478	119	60	89	17	46	28	18	4	85	77	.525
Willie Randolph, NYM	162	102	.68	269	21	28	26	44	27	122	3	499	246	97	100	10	40	26	14	7	88	74	.543
Jim Tracy, Pit	162	124	.49	240	12	26	33	40	13	113	0	495	98	80	90	12	55	30	25	11	68	94	.420
Ned Yost, Mil	162	109	.60	259	11	41	37	42	18	117	7	492	128	74	94	19	37	28	9	9	83	79	.512
162-Game Average		115	.58	276	28	48	40	41	19	122	3	505	128	87	93	24	50	31	20	11	80	82	.494

Manager	G	LINEUPS		SUBSTITUTION			PITCHER USAGE						TACTICS				INTENTIONAL BB				RESULTS		
		LUp	PL%	PH	PR	DS	Quick	Slow	LO	RCD	LS	Rel	SBA	SacA	RM	PO	#	Good	NG	Bomb	W	L	Pct
Cecil Cooper, Hou	31	26	.42	63	8	23	10	5	2	11	0	88	19	16	20	4	14	8	6	4	15	16	.484
Phil Garner, Hou	131	99	.52	230	14	36	31	44	17	120	0	388	79	88	84	23	48	27	21	11	58	73	.443
Pete Mackanin, Cin	80	57	.59	130	10	26	20	22	9	58	3	266	62	44	36	12	18	10	8	3	41	39	.513
Jerry Narron, Cin	82	63	.58	135	6	26	11	33	21	74	8	256	66	56	45	8	29	16	13	7	31	51	.378

Categories of this record are Games Managed (G), Number of Different Lineups Used (LUp), the percentage of players who had the platoon advatange at the start of the game (PL%), Pinch Hitters Used (PH), Pinch Runners Used (PR), Defensive Substitutes Used (DS), Quick Hooks (Quick), Slow Hooks (Slow), Long Outings by Starting Pitchers (LO), Relievers Used on Consecutive Days (RCD), Long Saves (LS), Relivers Used (Rel), Stolen Base Attempts (SBA), Sacrifice Bunts Attempts (SacA), Runners Moving with the Pitch (RM), Pitchouts ordered (PO), Intentional Walks issued (#), Intentional Walks resulting in a Good Outcome (Good), Intentional Walks resulting Not in a Good Outcome (NG), Intentional Walks Blowing up on the Manager (Bomb), Wins (W), Losses (L) and Winning Percentage (Pct.).

2007 Park Indices

Park indices are calculated in a way that neutralizes the effect of a team's makeup and isolates the effects of the park. The isolation is figured by comparing what both the team and its opponents accomplished at home, and comparing that to what the same team and its opponents accomplished on the road.

To calculate the park index for home runs in a given ballpark, we take the total home runs of both the home team and its opponents at the ballpark and compare it to the total home runs of the home team and its opponents in other games. We then divide each of those totals by the at-bats in the equivalent situations, so that if there are more at-bats in either situation the index is not skewed. The result is then multiplied by 100 to yield the familiar form.

The park indices for doubles, triples, walks, strikeouts and home runs by lefties and righties are determined like home runs above—relative to at-bats. Indices of at-bats, runs, hits, errors and infield fielding errors (E-Infield) are calculated relative to games. The three batting average indices are calculated as is, since these are already relative to at-bats.

A park with an index of exactly 100 is neutral and can be said to have had no effect on that particular stat. An index above 100 means the ballpark favors that statistic. For example, if a park has a home run index of 120, it was 20% easier to hit home runs in that park then the rest of the parks in that team's league.

Something new in last year's *Handbook* and kept the same for this season: We are no longer ignoring interleague games in the data. In the past we did not include interleague games due to the designated hitter rule only being used in American League parks, as well as because the schedules are very unbalanced. However, we felt that having the complete data was more important than trying to remove some statistical "noise," so now if you are interested in a team's home/road splits you will (except as noted below) be able to find them here as well.

There are lots of twists and turns included in the 2007 data. The simple ones are that the historical data for Citizens Bank Park, PETCO Park and Busch Stadium show only two-year data instead of three. For Citizens Bank and PETCO, that's because major renovations took place before the 2006 season. For Busch, it's because it opened in 2006. As for the complexities, a snow-out three-game makeup series between the Angels and Indians played in Milwaukee was considered all away games because none of the games were played in either team's home park. A scheduled three-game series between the Rangers and Devil Rays in Orlando was handled the same way. Finally, there was another snow-out makeup single game played between the Indians and Mariners in Seattle, in which the Indians batted last as the home team. For the purposes of Park Indices, we considered the Mariners the home team anyway, since the game was played at Safeco Field.

Arizona Diamondbacks - Chase Field

| | 2007 Season | | | | | | | 2005-2007 | | | | | | |
| | Home Games | | | Away Games | | | | Home Games | | | Away Games | | | |
	D'Backs	Opp	Total	D'Backs	Opp	Total	Index	D'Backs	Opp	Total	D'Backs	Opp	Total	Index
G	81	81	162	81	81	162		243	243	486	243	243	486	
Avg	.260	.265	.263	.241	.259	.250	105	.267	.275	.271	.249	.263	.256	106
AB	2626	2825	5451	2772	2688	5460	100	8125	8647	16772	8468	8179	16647	101
R	386	374	760	326	358	684	111	1124	1276	2400	1057	1100	2157	111
H	683	750	1433	667	696	1363	105	2170	2374	4544	2105	2155	4260	107
2B	151	149	300	135	144	279	108	465	506	971	443	453	896	108
3B	31	22	53	9	12	21	253	77	72	149	28	52	80	185
HR	91	88	179	80	81	161	111	274	290	564	248	240	488	115
BB	277	279	556	255	267	522	107	822	861	1683	820	758	1578	106
SO	495	538	1033	616	550	1166	89	1456	1634	3090	1714	1607	3321	92
E	54	41	95	52	43	95	100	146	136	282	158	143	301	94
E-Infield	23	16	39	20	15	35	111	70	61	131	56	57	113	116
LHB-Avg	.261	.275	.269	.249	.267	.259	104	.277	.287	.282	.262	.266	.264	107
LHB-HR	32	45	77	21	42	63	127	144	141	285	119	110	229	123
RHB-Avg	.260	.258	.259	.236	.252	.243	106	.257	.265	.261	.236	.262	.249	105
RHB-HR	59	43	102	59	39	98	102	130	149	279	129	130	259	107

Atlanta Braves - Turner Field

| | 2007 Season | | | | | | | 2005-2007 | | | | | | |
| | Home Games | | | Away Games | | | | Home Games | | | Away Games | | | |
	Braves	Opp	Total	Braves	Opp	Total	Index	Braves	Opp	Total	Braves	Opp	Total	Index
G	81	81	162	81	81	162		243	243	486	243	243	486	
Avg	.266	.254	.260	.282	.265	.274	95	.277	.263	.270	.264	.271	.267	101
AB	2715	2794	5509	2974	2763	5737	96	8144	8479	16623	8614	8223	16837	99
R	377	359	736	433	374	807	91	1213	1079	2292	1215	1133	2348	98
H	723	711	1434	839	731	1570	91	2254	2227	4481	2271	2231	4502	100
2B	134	126	260	194	146	340	80	459	421	880	489	440	929	96
3B	13	18	31	14	21	35	92	49	42	91	41	55	96	96
HR	82	88	170	94	84	178	99	271	248	519	311	252	563	93
BB	279	284	563	255	253	508	115	821	794	1615	773	835	1608	102
SO	557	579	1136	592	527	1119	106	1633	1630	3263	1769	1454	3223	103
E	55	41	96	52	52	104	92	142	154	296	150	141	291	102
E-Infield	25	19	44	24	26	50	88	65	67	132	69	62	131	101
LHB-Avg	.263	.266	.264	.270	.262	.266	99	.283	.266	.274	.266	.276	.271	101
LHB-HR	34	36	70	48	29	77	94	109	104	213	147	113	260	83
RHB-Avg	.269	.247	.257	.291	.267	.279	92	.272	.260	.266	.262	.267	.264	101
RHB-HR	48	52	100	46	55	101	103	162	144	306	164	139	303	102

Baltimore Orioles - Oriole Park at Camden Yards

| | 2007 Season | | | | | | | 2005-2007 | | | | | | |
| | Home Games | | | Away Games | | | | Home Games | | | Away Games | | | |
	Orioles	Opp	Total	Orioles	Opp	Total	Index	Orioles	Opp	Total	Orioles	Opp	Total	Index
G	81	81	162	81	81	162		243	243	486	243	243	486	
Avg	.280	.276	.278	.264	.260	.262	106	.278	.270	.274	.267	.274	.271	101
AB	2786	2900	5686	2845	2659	5504	103	8257	8548	16805	8535	8110	16645	101
R	386	468	854	370	400	770	111	1132	1264	2396	1121	1303	2424	99
H	779	800	1579	750	691	1441	110	2295	2307	4602	2282	2221	4503	102
2B	135	154	289	171	129	300	93	403	406	809	487	423	910	88
3B	17	10	27	13	7	20	131	41	24	65	36	43	79	81
HR	83	84	167	59	77	136	119	276	277	553	219	280	499	110
BB	246	350	596	254	346	600	96	735	943	1678	686	946	1632	102
SO	433	535	968	506	552	1058	89	1240	1580	2820	1479	1575	3054	91
E	36	44	80	43	49	92	87	131	145	276	157	154	311	89
E-Infield	12	15	27	18	21	39	69	48	56	104	63	64	127	82
LHB-Avg	.290	.295	.292	.262	.266	.264	111	.276	.280	.278	.275	.289	.281	99
LHB-HR	38	35	73	31	36	67	101	110	109	219	93	127	220	97
RHB-Avg	.269	.263	.265	.265	.256	.260	102	.279	.263	.271	.262	.264	.263	103
RHB-HR	45	49	94	28	41	69	137	166	168	334	126	153	279	120

Boston Red Sox - Fenway Park

	2007 Season							2005-2007						
	Home Games			Away Games				Home Games			Away Games			
	Red Sox	Opp	Total	Red Sox	Opp	Total	Index	Red Sox	Opp	Total	Red Sox	Opp	Total	Index
G	81	81	162	81	81	162		243	243	486	243	243	486	
Avg	.297	.261	.279	.262	.233	.248	113	.287	.268	.278	.265	.267	.266	104
AB	2759	2799	5558	2830	2661	5491	101	8234	8546	16780	8600	8172	16772	100
R	472	352	824	395	305	700	118	1377	1151	2528	1220	1136	2356	107
H	820	730	1550	741	620	1361	114	2367	2291	4658	2283	2179	4462	104
2B	191	181	372	161	114	275	134	568	588	1156	450	409	859	135
3B	17	10	27	18	10	28	95	35	43	78	37	46	83	94
HR	79	69	148	87	82	169	87	254	222	476	303	274	577	82
BB	350	221	571	339	261	600	94	1010	700	1710	1004	731	1735	99
SO	492	568	1060	550	581	1131	93	1493	1625	3118	1649	1553	3202	97
E	36	43	79	45	48	93	85	113	156	269	143	137	280	96
E-Infield	12	21	33	20	17	37	89	52	70	122	52	57	109	112
LHB-Avg	.293	.249	.270	.262	.234	.248	109	.285	.272	.278	.267	.261	.264	105
LHB-HR	33	30	63	40	37	77	79	109	101	210	152	126	278	74
RHB-Avg	.300	.271	.286	.261	.233	.248	115	.289	.265	.277	.264	.271	.268	104
RHB-HR	46	39	85	47	45	92	93	145	121	266	151	148	299	90

Chicago Cubs - Wrigley Field

	2007 Season							2005-2007						
	Home Games			Away Games				Home Games			Away Games			
	Cubs	Opp	Total	Cubs	Opp	Total	Index	Cubs	Opp	Total	Cubs	Opp	Total	Index
G	81	81	162	81	81	162		243	243	486	243	243	486	
Avg	.278	.251	.264	.265	.240	.253	104	.276	.247	.261	.263	.253	.258	101
AB	2796	2844	5640	2847	2608	5455	103	8292	8455	16747	8522	7916	16438	102
R	408	370	778	344	320	664	117	1136	1158	2294	1035	1080	2115	108
H	776	713	1489	754	627	1381	108	2289	2090	4379	2243	2003	4246	103
2B	174	164	338	166	116	282	116	483	438	921	451	376	827	109
3B	13	14	27	15	15	30	87	50	44	94	47	36	83	111
HR	84	85	169	67	80	147	111	264	306	570	247	255	502	111
BB	265	300	565	235	273	508	108	662	903	1565	652	933	1585	97
SO	542	640	1182	512	571	1083	106	1435	1990	3425	1467	1727	3194	105
E	50	72	122	44	58	102	120	165	176	341	136	185	321	106
E-Infield	25	29	54	15	27	42	129	75	72	147	52	86	138	107
LHB-Avg	.245	.254	.250	.252	.242	.247	101	.260	.249	.255	.255	.256	.255	100
LHB-HR	14	25	39	13	23	36	109	77	113	190	67	96	163	119
RHB-Avg	.294	.249	.271	.272	.240	.256	106	.287	.246	.266	.269	.251	.260	102
RHB-HR	70	60	130	54	57	111	111	187	193	380	180	159	339	107

Chicago White Sox - U.S. Cellular Field

	2007 Season							2005-2007						
	Home Games			Away Games				Home Games			Away Games			
	White Sox	Opp	Total	White Sox	Opp	Total	Index	White Sox	Opp	Total	White Sox	Opp	Total	Index
G	81	81	162	81	81	162		243	243	486	243	243	486	
Avg	.247	.282	.265	.246	.270	.258	103	.262	.268	.265	.265	.263	.264	101
AB	2650	2903	5553	2791	2728	5519	101	8092	8666	16758	8535	8213	16748	100
R	351	446	797	342	393	735	108	1179	1181	2360	1123	1097	2220	106
H	654	819	1473	687	737	1424	103	2118	2325	4443	2259	2157	4416	101
2B	113	158	271	136	139	275	98	373	433	806	420	438	858	94
3B	7	11	18	13	25	38	47	24	35	59	39	55	94	63
HR	110	90	200	80	84	164	121	361	299	660	265	242	507	130
BB	269	238	507	263	261	524	96	751	715	1466	718	676	1394	105
SO	526	528	1054	623	487	1110	94	1519	1584	3103	1688	1483	3171	98
E	60	45	105	48	45	93	113	137	146	283	155	139	294	96
E-Infield	22	15	37	17	25	42	88	51	61	112	61	63	124	90
LHB-Avg	.249	.284	.266	.266	.278	.271	98	.258	.269	.264	.276	.261	.268	98
LHB-HR	42	34	76	29	30	59	125	111	127	238	74	91	165	140
RHB-Avg	.245	.281	.265	.231	.265	.249	106	.264	.268	.266	.258	.264	.261	102
RHB-HR	68	56	124	51	54	105	119	250	172	422	191	151	342	126

Cincinnati Reds - Great American Ballpark

| | 2007 Season | | | | | | | 2005-2007 | | | | | | |
| | Home Games | | | Away Games | | | | Home Games | | | Away Games | | | |
	Reds	Opp	Total	Reds	Opp	Total	Index	Reds	Opp	Total	Reds	Opp	Total	Index
G	81	81	162	81	81	162		244	244	488	243	243	486	
Avg	.265	.272	.268	.269	.293	.281	96	.268	.280	.274	.256	.287	.271	101
AB	2766	2926	5692	2841	2763	5604	102	8205	8786	16991	8482	8285	16767	101
R	416	439	855	367	414	781	109	1267	1328	2595	1085	1215	2300	112
H	732	796	1528	764	809	1573	97	2198	2460	4658	2170	2378	4548	102
2B	153	174	327	140	171	311	104	454	555	1009	465	488	953	104
3B	12	10	22	11	16	27	80	19	32	51	31	56	87	58
HR	117	114	231	87	84	171	133	367	351	718	276	279	555	128
BB	284	234	518	252	248	500	102	909	708	1617	852	730	1582	101
SO	558	556	1114	555	512	1067	103	1746	1634	3380	1862	1442	3304	101
E	58	44	102	37	53	90	113	167	126	293	160	143	303	96
E-Infield	23	22	45	18	26	44	102	66	56	122	59	56	115	106
LHB-Avg	.287	.271	.278	.270	.273	.271	103	.280	.282	.281	.263	.272	.267	105
LHB-HR	59	46	105	46	32	78	134	182	140	322	143	102	245	128
RHB-Avg	.251	.273	.262	.268	.307	.287	91	.259	.279	.270	.251	.296	.274	98
RHB-HR	58	68	126	41	52	93	132	185	211	396	133	177	310	127

Cleveland Indians - Jacobs Field

| | 2007 Season | | | | | | | 2005-2007 | | | | | | |
| | Home Games | | | Away Games | | | | Home Games | | | Away Games | | | |
	Indians	Opp	Total	Indians	Opp	Total	Index	Indians	Opp	Total	Indians	Opp	Total	Index
G	77	77	154	85	85	170		239	239	478	247	247	494	
Avg	.277	.274	.275	.261	.263	.262	105	.274	.262	.268	.272	.269	.271	99
AB	2580	2748	5328	3024	2915	5939	99	7991	8345	16336	8841	8452	17293	98
R	413	354	767	398	350	748	113	1215	1023	2238	1256	1105	2361	98
H	714	752	1466	790	767	1557	104	2193	2188	4381	2409	2277	4686	97
2B	130	147	277	175	159	334	92	481	424	905	512	444	956	100
3B	8	10	18	19	12	31	65	27	25	52	57	35	92	60
HR	95	68	163	83	78	161	113	280	220	500	301	249	550	96
BB	284	199	483	306	211	517	104	840	610	1450	809	642	1451	106
SO	540	567	1107	662	480	1142	108	1646	1598	3244	1853	1447	3300	104
E	42	48	90	50	45	95	105	155	151	306	161	131	292	108
E-Infield	22	23	45	23	18	41	121	76	62	138	73	58	131	109
LHB-Avg	.266	.272	.269	.269	.275	.272	99	.284	.274	.279	.283	.280	.282	99
LHB-HR	31	24	55	43	27	70	89	137	80	217	148	89	237	98
RHB-Avg	.284	.275	.280	.255	.255	.255	110	.267	.255	.261	.264	.263	.263	99
RHB-HR	64	44	108	40	51	91	130	143	140	283	153	160	313	95

Colorado Rockies - Coors Field

| | 2007 Season | | | | | | | 2005-2007 | | | | | | |
| | Home Games | | | Away Games | | | | Home Games | | | Away Games | | | |
	Rockies	Opp	Total	Rockies	Opp	Total	Index	Rockies	Opp	Total	Rockies	Opp	Total	Index
G	82	82	164	81	81	162		244	244	488	243	243	486	
Avg	.298	.274	.286	.261	.259	.260	110	.297	.283	.290	.247	.269	.258	113
AB	2836	2910	5746	2855	2710	5565	102	8412	8729	17141	8383	8066	16449	104
R	478	396	874	382	362	744	116	1385	1256	2641	1028	1176	2204	119
H	845	796	1641	746	701	1447	112	2501	2474	4975	2071	2172	4243	117
2B	164	178	342	149	120	269	123	481	529	1010	437	457	894	108
3B	22	27	49	14	18	32	148	75	73	148	49	59	108	132
HR	103	82	185	68	82	150	119	264	259	523	214	235	449	112
BB	319	231	550	303	273	576	92	888	804	1692	804	857	1661	98
SO	522	472	994	630	495	1125	86	1508	1468	2976	1855	1432	3287	87
E	40	60	100	28	48	76	130	138	190	328	139	162	301	109
E-Infield	11	19	30	7	15	22	135	54	60	114	48	67	115	99
LHB-Avg	.289	.256	.270	.273	.263	.268	101	.292	.283	.287	.257	.280	.269	107
LHB-HR	33	29	62	21	39	60	104	74	108	182	79	108	187	96
RHB-Avg	.302	.285	.294	.255	.256	.255	115	.300	.284	.292	.241	.261	.251	117
RHB-HR	70	53	123	47	43	90	129	190	151	341	135	127	262	123

Detroit Tigers - Comerica Park

| | 2007 Season | | | | | | | 2005-2007 | | | | | | |
| | Home Games | | | Away Games | | | | Home Games | | | Away Games | | | |
	Tigers	Opp	Total	Tigers	Opp	Total	Index	Tigers	Opp	Total	Tigers	Opp	Total	Index
G	81	81	162	81	81	162		243	243	486	243	243	486	
Avg	.287	.268	.278	.286	.265	.276	101	.279	.266	.272	.276	.264	.271	101
AB	2807	2879	5686	2950	2745	5695	100	8334	8618	16952	8667	8069	16736	101
R	446	417	863	441	380	821	105	1201	1142	2343	1231	1117	2348	100
H	807	771	1578	845	727	1572	100	2326	2289	4615	2395	2133	4528	102
2B	164	151	315	188	137	325	97	423	414	837	506	395	901	92
3B	32	27	59	18	19	37	160	85	07	152	50	52	102	147
HR	99	88	187	78	86	164	114	269	255	524	279	272	551	94
BB	246	288	534	228	278	506	106	651	779	1430	637	737	1374	103
SO	493	530	1023	561	517	1078	95	1499	1516	3015	1726	1441	3167	94
E	57	41	98	42	47	89	110	163	155	318	152	138	290	110
E-Infield	24	13	37	20	21	41	90	72	67	139	61	60	121	115
LHB-Avg	.290	.255	.270	.298	.266	.280	96	.273	.266	.269	.279	.264	.270	99
LHB-HR	21	30	51	22	36	58	88	74	88	162	65	103	168	95
RHB-Avg	.286	.277	.282	.281	.264	.274	103	.282	.266	.274	.275	.265	.271	101
RHB-HR	78	58	136	56	50	106	128	195	167	362	214	169	383	93

Florida Marlins - Dolphins Stadium

| | 2007 Season | | | | | | | 2005-2007 | | | | | | |
| | Home Games | | | Away Games | | | | Home Games | | | Away Games | | | |
	Marlins	Opp	Total	Marlins	Opp	Total	Index	Marlins	Opp	Total	Marlins	Opp	Total	Index
G	81	81	162	81	81	162		243	243	486	243	243	486	
Avg	.271	.280	.276	.263	.290	.277	100	.266	.267	.266	.270	.279	.274	97
AB	2803	2949	5752	2824	2724	5548	104	8112	8526	16638	8519	8123	16642	100
R	409	459	868	381	432	813	107	1106	1168	2274	1159	1227	2386	95
H	760	826	1586	744	791	1535	103	2158	2273	4431	2299	2268	4567	97
2B	171	173	344	169	129	298	111	452	459	911	503	417	920	99
3B	23	18	41	15	13	28	141	67	67	134	45	57	102	131
HR	110	79	189	91	97	188	97	251	210	461	260	248	508	91
BB	261	371	632	260	290	550	111	815	972	1787	715	874	1589	112
SO	660	662	1322	672	480	1152	111	1750	1882	3632	1749	1473	3222	113
E	67	48	115	70	54	124	93	168	156	324	198	167	365	89
E-Infield	26	15	41	24	15	39	105	54	53	107	76	55	131	82
LHB-Avg	.242	.267	.256	.281	.276	.278	92	.251	.267	.260	.275	.272	.273	95
LHB-HR	24	28	52	20	24	44	108	65	86	151	60	81	141	105
RHB-Avg	.285	.288	.286	.257	.299	.276	104	.273	.266	.270	.268	.284	.275	98
RHB-HR	86	51	137	71	73	144	94	186	124	310	200	167	367	85

Houston Astros - Minute Maid Park

| | 2007 Season | | | | | | | 2005-2007 | | | | | | |
| | Home Games | | | Away Games | | | | Home Games | | | Away Games | | | |
	Astros	Opp	Total	Astros	Opp	Total	Index	Astros	Opp	Total	Astros	Opp	Total	Index
G	81	81	162	81	81	162		243	243	486	244	244	488	
Avg	.266	.262	.264	.254	.286	.270	98	.264	.250	.257	.251	.267	.259	99
AB	2770	2950	5720	2835	2779	5614	102	8086	8544	16630	8502	8187	16689	100
R	361	367	728	362	446	808	90	1093	1005	2098	1058	1136	2194	96
H	737	772	1509	720	794	1514	100	2132	2140	4272	2132	2187	4319	99
2B	139	169	308	154	176	330	92	405	441	846	444	484	928	91
3B	22	15	37	8	22	30	121	56	40	96	33	52	85	113
HR	83	108	191	84	98	182	103	274	280	554	228	263	491	113
BB	276	249	525	271	261	532	97	822	675	1497	791	755	1546	97
SO	492	651	1143	551	458	1009	111	1491	1852	3343	1665	1581	3246	103
E	46	34	80	57	51	108	74	140	119	259	132	159	291	89
E-Infield	27	21	48	23	22	45	107	77	50	127	54	74	128	100
LHB-Avg	.247	.266	.259	.276	.278	.278	93	.254	.256	.255	.277	.263	.269	95
LHB-HR	27	43	70	35	33	68	102	85	106	191	95	91	186	104
RHB-Avg	.273	.258	.266	.246	.291	.266	100	.267	.247	.258	.241	.270	.254	102
RHB-HR	56	65	121	49	65	114	104	189	174	363	133	172	305	119

Kansas City Royals - Ewing M. Kauffman Stadium

| | 2007 Season | | | | | | | 2005-2007 | | | | | | |
| | Home Games | | | Away Games | | | | Home Games | | | Away Games | | | |
	Royals	Opp	Total	Royals	Opp	Total	Index	Royals	Opp	Total	Royals	Opp	Total	Index
G	81	81	162	81	81	162		243	243	486	243	243	486	
Avg	.267	.283	.275	.256	.270	.263	105	.275	.287	.281	.255	.286	.271	104
AB	2678	2874	5552	2856	2718	5574	100	8154	8670	16824	8472	8190	16662	101
R	355	399	754	351	379	730	103	1136	1348	2484	1028	1336	2364	105
H	715	812	1527	732	735	1467	104	2244	2489	4733	2163	2346	4509	105
2B	162	219	381	138	161	299	128	495	595	1090	429	473	902	120
3B	28	13	41	18	17	35	118	63	49	112	54	50	104	107
HR	49	79	128	53	89	142	90	165	261	426	187	298	485	87
BB	211	266	477	217	254	471	102	683	882	1565	643	855	1498	103
SO	483	501	984	586	492	1078	92	1442	1420	2862	1675	1401	3076	92
E	43	43	86	63	64	127	68	156	157	313	173	168	341	92
E-Infield	16	20	36	21	20	41	88	65	62	127	68	58	126	101
LHB-Avg	.270	.276	.273	.262	.259	.260	105	.274	.281	.278	.261	.280	.270	103
LHB-HR	19	33	52	23	35	58	89	63	105	168	71	120	191	86
RHB-Avg	.264	.287	.277	.252	.279	.265	104	.276	.291	.284	.251	.290	.271	105
RHB-HR	30	46	76	30	54	84	91	102	156	258	116	178	294	88

Los Angeles Angels - Angel Stadium of Anaheim

| | 2007 Season | | | | | | | 2005-2007 | | | | | | |
| | Home Games | | | Away Games | | | | Home Games | | | Away Games | | | |
	Angels	Opp	Total	Angels	Opp	Total	Index	Angels	Opp	Total	Angels	Opp	Total	Index
G	81	81	162	81	81	162		243	243	486	243	243	486	
Avg	.305	.260	.282	.263	.273	.268	105	.284	.254	.269	.269	.262	.265	101
AB	2762	2849	5611	2792	2714	5506	102	8230	8532	16762	8557	8165	16722	100
R	460	348	808	362	383	745	108	1187	1005	2192	1162	1101	2263	97
H	843	740	1583	735	740	1475	107	2338	2171	4509	2299	2138	4437	102
2B	176	165	341	148	124	272	123	455	461	916	456	413	869	105
3B	13	11	24	10	23	33	71	42	35	77	40	53	93	83
HR	61	68	129	62	83	145	87	201	214	415	228	253	481	86
BB	274	236	510	233	241	474	106	748	670	1418	692	721	1413	100
SO	414	581	995	469	575	1044	94	1274	1749	3023	1371	1697	3068	98
E	55	68	123	46	54	100	123	163	172	335	149	156	305	110
E-Infield	23	32	55	18	20	38	145	65	71	136	62	60	122	111
LHB-Avg	.326	.254	.290	.255	.278	.266	109	.285	.260	.272	.267	.270	.268	102
LHB-HR	28	19	47	26	40	66	76	71	92	163	88	129	217	79
RHB-Avg	.290	.264	.277	.270	.268	.269	103	.284	.250	.266	.270	.255	.263	101
RHB-HR	33	49	82	36	43	79	95	130	122	252	140	124	264	91

Los Angeles Dodgers - Dodger Stadium

| | 2007 Season | | | | | | | 2005-2007 | | | | | | |
| | Home Games | | | Away Games | | | | Home Games | | | Away Games | | | |
	Dodgers	Opp	Total	Dodgers	Opp	Total	Index	Dodgers	Opp	Total	Dodgers	Opp	Total	Index
G	81	81	162	81	81	162		243	243	486	243	243	486	
Avg	.277	.263	.270	.273	.259	.266	101	.273	.259	.266	.263	.270	.267	100
AB	2757	2846	5603	2856	2682	5538	101	8102	8464	16566	8572	8168	16740	99
R	376	374	750	359	353	712	105	1157	1081	2238	1083	1152	2235	100
H	765	748	1513	779	695	1474	103	2212	2193	4405	2258	2208	4466	99
2B	123	141	264	153	138	291	90	421	445	866	446	448	894	98
3B	13	8	21	22	14	36	58	42	25	67	72	60	132	51
HR	69	72	141	60	74	134	104	237	240	477	194	240	434	111
BB	278	253	531	233	265	498	105	904	731	1635	749	750	1499	110
SO	429	645	1074	435	539	974	109	1389	1782	3171	1528	1474	3002	107
E	55	55	110	59	46	105	105	164	160	324	171	141	312	104
E-Infield	16	16	32	28	25	53	60	66	61	127	75	69	144	88
LHB-Avg	.282	.249	.267	.279	.246	.265	101	.280	.264	.272	.264	.279	.271	100
LHB-HR	30	30	60	31	19	50	118	111	107	218	91	96	187	118
RHB-Avg	.273	.272	.272	.266	.268	.267	102	.266	.256	.261	.263	.263	.263	99
RHB-HR	39	42	81	29	55	84	96	126	133	259	103	144	247	106

Milwaukee Brewers - Miller Park

	2007 Season							2005-2007						
	Home Games			Away Games				Home Games			Away Games			
	Brewers	Opp	Total	Brewers	Opp	Total	Index	Brewers	Opp	Total	Brewers	Opp	Total	Index
G	81	81	162	81	81	162		243	243	486	243	243	486	
Avg	.268	.252	.260	.256	.287	.271	96	.262	.246	.254	.257	.278	.267	95
AB	2702	2845	5547	2852	2775	5627	99	7950	8391	16341	8485	8230	16715	98
R	430	363	793	371	413	784	101	1191	1096	2287	1066	1210	2276	100
H	724	717	1441	731	796	1527	94	2085	2064	4149	2183	2285	4468	93
2B	170	153	323	140	168	308	106	477	464	941	461	512	973	99
3B	15	6	21	22	20	42	51	43	32	75	33	50	80	86
HR	121	86	207	110	75	185	114	308	257	565	278	250	528	109
BB	263	266	529	238	241	479	112	808	812	1620	726	778	1504	110
SO	550	625	1175	587	549	1136	105	1706	1885	3591	1826	1607	3433	107
E	60	46	106	49	47	96	110	183	148	331	162	131	293	113
E-Infield	20	21	41	19	20	39	105	66	70	136	69	56	125	109
LHB-Avg	.261	.247	.253	.252	.282	.267	95	.253	.251	.252	.266	.272	.269	94
LHB-HR	45	32	77	44	35	79	101	105	94	199	111	97	208	99
RHB-Avg	.271	.255	.264	.259	.290	.274	96	.266	.243	.255	.253	.281	.266	96
RHB-HR	76	54	130	66	40	106	123	203	163	366	167	153	320	116

Minnesota Twins - Hubert H. Humphrey Metrodome Surface: AstroTurf

	2007 Season							2005-2007						
	Home Games			Away Games				Home Games			Away Games			
	Twins	Opp	Total	Twins	Opp	Total	Index	Twins	Opp	Total	Twins	Opp	Total	Index
G	81	81	162	81	81	162		243	243	486	243	243	486	
Avg	.263	.255	.259	.266	.284	.275	94	.275	.253	.264	.266	.279	.272	97
AB	2708	2863	5571	2914	2725	5639	101	8160	8525	16685	8528	8239	16767	100
R	327	343	670	391	382	773	87	1096	984	2080	1111	1086	2197	95
H	711	731	1442	749	774	1523	95	2244	2157	4401	2265	2296	4561	96
2B	126	150	276	147	147	294	93	389	415	804	428	419	847	95
3B	19	14	33	17	13	30	109	59	36	95	43	42	85	112
HR	48	82	130	70	103	173	75	184	242	426	211	294	505	85
BB	255	214	469	257	206	463	101	718	518	1236	769	606	1375	90
SO	397	593	990	442	501	943	104	1323	1721	3044	1366	1502	2868	107
E	48	57	105	47	62	109	96	139	170	309	142	171	313	99
E-Infield	19	19	38	21	25	46	83	63	55	118	56	70	126	94
LHB-Avg	.253	.273	.263	.283	.306	.293	90	.274	.268	.271	.279	.288	.283	96
LHB-HR	25	43	68	34	49	83	81	79	110	189	103	136	239	80
RHB-Avg	.271	.241	.255	.251	.267	.259	99	.276	.242	.258	.254	.272	.263	98
RHB-HR	23	39	62	36	54	90	69	105	132	237	108	158	266	89

New York Mets - Shea Stadium

	2007 Season							2005-2007						
	Home Games			Away Games				Home Games			Away Games			
	Mets	Opp	Total	Mets	Opp	Total	Index	Mets	Opp	Total	Mets	Opp	Total	Index
G	81	81	162	81	81	162		243	243	486	243	243	486	
Avg	.270	.247	.258	.280	.263	.272	95	.262	.248	.255	.269	.260	.265	96
AB	2690	2811	5501	2915	2747	5662	97	8100	8442	16542	8568	8104	16672	99
R	367	376	743	437	374	811	92	1125	1035	2160	1235	1094	2329	93
H	727	693	1420	816	722	1538	92	2124	2096	4220	2309	2111	4420	95
2B	139	142	281	155	154	309	94	427	424	851	469	423	892	96
3B	14	17	31	13	16	29	110	46	34	80	54	38	92	88
HR	83	79	162	94	86	180	93	262	224	486	290	256	546	90
BB	264	284	548	285	286	571	99	796	785	1581	786	803	1589	100
SO	459	582	1041	522	552	1074	100	1484	1708	3192	1643	1599	3242	99
E	51	48	99	50	57	107	93	165	161	326	146	172	318	103
E-Infield	22	22	44	14	20	34	129	67	64	131	53	66	119	110
LHB-Avg	.268	.270	.269	.267	.268	.268	100	.259	.260	.259	.266	.257	.262	99
LHB-HR	34	35	69	45	30	75	95	132	92	224	157	98	255	89
RHB-Avg	.272	.232	.250	.293	.260	.275	91	.265	.240	.252	.273	.263	.268	94
RHB-HR	49	44	93	49	56	105	91	130	132	262	133	158	291	91

New York Yankees - Yankee Stadium

| | 2007 Season | | | | | | | 2005-2007 | | | | | | |
| | Home Games | | | Away Games | | | | Home Games | | | Away Games | | | |
	Yankees	Opp	Total	Yankees	Opp	Total	Index	Yankees	Opp	Total	Yankees	Opp	Total	Index
G	81	81	162	81	81	162		243	243	486	243	243	486	
Avg	.300	.263	.281	.280	.274	.277	101	.291	.262	.277	.276	.270	.273	101
AB	2820	2852	5672	2897	2734	5631	101	8294	8538	16832	8698	8196	16894	100
R	520	382	902	448	395	843	107	1447	1117	2564	1337	1216	2553	100
H	845	749	1594	811	749	1560	102	2416	2240	4656	2400	2216	4616	101
2B	150	162	312	176	165	341	91	430	444	874	482	472	954	92
3B	11	11	22	21	16	37	59	27	34	61	42	46	88	70
HR	107	81	188	94	69	163	115	344	246	590	296	238	534	111
BB	334	268	602	303	310	613	97	960	712	1672	963	825	1788	94
SO	465	552	1017	526	457	983	103	1430	1581	3011	1603	1432	3035	100
E	45	58	103	43	56	99	104	148	171	319	139	163	302	106
E-Infield	22	27	49	21	23	44	111	70	86	156	58	75	133	117
LHB-Avg	.299	.270	.287	.273	.291	.280	102	.285	.259	.274	.277	.273	.275	99
LHB-HR	64	40	104	51	29	80	132	185	113	298	171	80	251	119
RHB-Avg	.301	.258	.274	.292	.261	.274	100	.300	.265	.280	.275	.269	.271	103
RHB-HR	43	41	84	43	40	83	98	159	133	292	125	158	283	104

Oakland Athletics - McAfee Coliseum

| | 2007 Season | | | | | | | 2005-2007 | | | | | | |
| | Home Games | | | Away Games | | | | Home Games | | | Away Games | | | |
	Athletics	Opp	Total	Athletics	Opp	Total	Index	Athletics	Opp	Total	Athletics	Opp	Total	Index
G	81	81	162	81	81	162		243	243	486	243	243	486	
Avg	.240	.249	.245	.271	.278	.274	89	.256	.252	.254	.263	.266	.264	96
AB	2669	2818	5487	2908	2756	5664	97	8102	8459	16561	8602	8175	16777	99
R	331	350	681	410	408	818	83	1094	1041	2135	1190	1102	2292	93
H	641	703	1344	789	765	1554	86	2073	2135	4208	2262	2173	4435	95
2B	127	127	254	168	155	323	81	425	416	841	446	412	858	99
3B	14	20	34	2	25	27	130	36	44	80	22	58	80	101
HR	77	59	136	94	79	173	81	232	205	437	269	249	518	85
BB	334	279	613	330	251	581	109	894	795	1689	957	768	1725	99
SO	473	514	987	646	522	1168	87	1292	1531	2823	1622	1583	3205	89
E	51	45	96	39	48	87	110	129	137	266	133	149	282	94
E-Infield	16	15	31	12	24	36	86	48	51	99	52	76	128	77
LHB-Avg	.245	.242	.244	.258	.282	.269	91	.257	.255	.256	.249	.274	.260	98
LHB-HR	47	21	68	46	22	68	103	126	77	203	138	90	228	90
RHB-Avg	.236	.254	.246	.282	.275	.278	88	.255	.250	.252	.275	.260	.267	94
RHB-HR	30	38	68	48	57	105	67	106	128	234	131	159	290	82

Philadelphia Phillies - Citizens Bank Park

| | 2007 Season | | | | | | | 2006-2007 | | | | | | |
| | Home Games | | | Away Games | | | | Home Games | | | Away Games | | | |
	Phillies	Opp	Total	Phillies	Opp	Total	Index	Phillies	Opp	Total	Phillies	Opp	Total	Index
G	81	81	162	81	81	162		162	162	324	162	162	324	
Avg	.280	.273	.277	.268	.278	.273	101	.277	.274	.276	.264	.277	.270	102
AB	2754	2840	5594	2934	2802	5736	98	5504	5717	11221	5871	5602	11473	98
R	450	421	871	442	400	842	103	894	841	1735	863	792	1655	105
H	771	776	1547	787	779	1566	99	1525	1567	3092	1551	1549	3100	100
2B	146	174	320	180	171	351	93	297	342	639	323	338	661	99
3B	21	10	31	20	16	36	88	36	27	63	46	39	85	76
HR	116	125	241	97	73	170	145	228	246	474	201	163	364	133
BB	298	276	574	343	282	625	94	599	531	1130	668	539	1207	96
SO	568	560	1128	637	490	1127	103	1128	1174	2302	1280	1014	2294	103
E	43	66	109	46	52	98	111	96	123	219	97	103	200	110
E-Infield	17	31	48	21	26	47	102	39	57	96	42	51	93	103
LHB-Avg	.280	.286	.283	.267	.281	.273	104	.280	.283	.281	.272	.277	.274	103
LHB-HR	58	48	106	52	22	74	145	126	92	218	115	58	173	130
RHB-Avg	.280	.266	.272	.270	.276	.273	100	.274	.269	.271	.256	.276	.267	102
RHB-HR	58	77	135	45	51	96	145	102	154	256	86	105	191	136

Pittsburgh Pirates - PNC Park

| | 2007 Season | | | | | | | 2005-2007 | | | | | | |
| | Home Games | | | Away Games | | | Index | Home Games | | | Away Games | | | Index |
	Pirates	Opp	Total	Pirates	Opp	Total		Pirates	Opp	Total	Pirates	Opp	Total	
G	81	81	162	81	81	162		243	243	486	243	243	486	
Avg	.272	.280	.276	.254	.296	.274	101	.274	.275	.274	.250	.283	.266	103
AB	2721	2857	5578	2848	2796	5644	99	8262	8592	16854	8438	8030	16468	102
R	373	390	763	351	456	807	95	1097	1147	2244	998	1265	2263	99
H	741	800	1541	722	827	1549	99	2260	2359	4619	2110	2269	4379	105
2B	170	172	342	152	165	317	109	493	501	994	407	458	865	112
3B	12	7	19	19	14	33	58	47	33	80	39	46	85	92
HR	65	76	141	83	98	181	79	194	221	415	234	271	505	80
BB	221	237	458	242	281	523	89	711	826	1537	682	924	1606	94
SO	539	496	1035	596	501	1097	95	1636	1556	3192	1791	1459	3250	96
E	32	47	79	51	52	103	77	141	151	292	163	167	330	88
E-Infield	16	14	30	26	16	42	71	66	62	128	76	67	143	90
LHB-Avg	.276	.273	.275	.236	.282	.260	106	.267	.280	.273	.234	.274	.254	108
LHB-HR	25	34	59	23	30	53	107	69	86	155	57	94	151	100
RHB-Avg	.270	.283	.277	.261	.302	.281	99	.277	.272	.274	.258	.286	.272	101
RHB-HR	40	42	82	60	68	128	66	125	135	260	177	177	354	72

San Diego Padres - PETCO Park

| | 2007 Season | | | | | | | 2006-2007 | | | | | | |
| | Home Games | | | Away Games | | | Index | Home Games | | | Away Games | | | Index |
	Padres	Opp	Total	Padres	Opp	Total		Padres	Opp	Total	Padres	Opp	Total	
G	81	81	162	82	82	164		162	162	324	163	163	326	
Avg	.235	.235	.235	.265	.264	.265	89	.240	.239	.240	.272	.260	.266	90
AB	2659	2822	5481	2953	2811	5764	96	5357	5666	11023	5831	5524	11355	98
R	323	278	601	418	388	806	75	638	615	1253	834	730	1564	81
H	626	663	1289	782	743	1525	86	1287	1356	2643	1586	1435	3021	88
2B	126	118	244	196	152	348	74	244	244	488	376	290	666	75
3B	19	16	35	12	22	34	108	41	32	73	28	41	69	109
HR	72	45	117	99	74	173	71	147	137	284	185	158	343	85
BB	268	219	487	289	255	544	94	550	450	1000	571	486	1057	98
SO	637	599	1236	592	537	1129	115	1185	1195	2380	1148	1038	2186	112
E	38	27	65	54	49	103	64	78	73	151	106	99	205	74
E-Infield	16	9	25	23	25	48	53	30	23	53	43	45	88	61
LHB-Avg	.245	.244	.245	.264	.263	.263	93	.262	.237	.250	.270	.263	.267	94
LHB-HR	31	23	54	49	34	83	67	60	63	123	90	75	165	78
RHB-Avg	.227	.228	.228	.266	.265	.265	86	.222	.241	.232	.274	.257	.265	87
RHB-HR	41	22	63	50	40	90	75	87	74	161	95	83	178	92

San Francisco Giants - Pacific Bell Park

| | 2007 Season | | | | | | | 2005-2007 | | | | | | |
| | Home Games | | | Away Games | | | Index | Home Games | | | Away Games | | | Index |
	Giants	Opp	Total	Giants	Opp	Total		Giants	Opp	Total	Giants	Opp	Total	
G	81	81	162	81	81	162		243	243	486	242	242	484	
Avg	.259	.270	.265	.249	.250	.249	106	.261	.261	.261	.255	.263	.259	101
AB	2737	2908	5645	2801	2626	5427	104	8048	8498	16546	8424	8013	16437	100
R	336	361	697	347	359	706	99	1031	1120	2151	1047	1135	2182	98
H	710	786	1496	697	656	1353	111	2102	2216	4318	2150	2104	4254	101
2B	133	169	302	134	151	285	102	438	447	885	425	448	873	101
3B	20	25	45	17	16	33	131	61	69	130	54	59	113	114
HR	54	64	118	77	69	146	78	179	201	380	243	236	479	79
BB	264	274	538	268	319	587	88	738	842	1580	719	927	1646	95
SO	425	537	962	482	520	1002	92	1232	1555	2787	1467	1466	2933	94
E	46	50	96	42	46	88	109	136	150	286	133	130	263	108
E-Infield	23	20	43	19	16	35	123	63	54	117	58	59	117	100
LHB-Avg	.268	.265	.266	.243	.256	.248	107	.265	.262	.263	.262	.263	.263	100
LHB-HR	27	21	48	30	23	53	84	69	62	131	96	83	179	71
RHB-Avg	.250	.274	.264	.254	.246	.250	106	.258	.260	.259	.250	.262	.256	101
RHB-HR	27	43	70	47	46	93	74	110	139	249	147	153	300	84

Seattle Mariners - Safeco Field

| | 2007 Season | | | | | | | 2005-2007 | | | | | | |
| | Home Games | | | Away Games | | | | Home Games | | | Away Games | | | |
	Mariners	Opp	Total	Mariners	Opp	Total	Index	Mariners	Opp	Total	Mariners	Opp	Total	Index
G	82	82	164	80	80	160		244	244	488	242	242	484	
Avg	.283	.275	.279	.290	.289	.290	96	.269	.264	.266	.273	.282	.277	96
AB	2766	2907	5673	2918	2699	5617	99	8202	8599	16801	8659	8147	16806	99
R	386	406	792	408	407	815	95	1093	1139	2232	1156	1217	2373	93
H	782	798	1580	847	780	1627	95	2209	2267	4476	2368	2294	4662	95
2B	124	177	301	160	154	314	95	388	469	857	451	456	907	95
3B	9	9	18	13	25	38	47	43	27	70	55	52	107	65
HR	77	75	152	76	72	148	102	221	239	460	234	270	504	91
BB	210	277	487	179	269	448	108	636	840	1476	623	762	1385	107
SO	449	560	1009	412	460	872	115	1452	1615	3067	1369	1364	2733	112
E	49	65	114	41	55	96	116	131	171	302	133	193	326	92
E-Infield	18	26	44	15	24	39	110	50	58	108	63	80	143	75
LHB-Avg	.322	.270	.293	.306	.281	.293	100	.293	.267	.279	.281	.270	.275	101
LHB-HR	18	32	50	24	32	56	88	73	102	175	86	101	187	92
RHB-Avg	.262	.278	.270	.282	.294	.288	94	.254	.261	.258	.269	.290	.279	93
RHB-HR	59	43	102	52	40	92	110	148	137	285	148	169	317	91

St Louis Cardinals - Busch Stadium

| | 2007 Season | | | | | | | 2006-2007 | | | | | | |
| | Home Games | | | Away Games | | | | Home Games | | | Away Games | | | |
	Cardinals	Opp	Total	Cardinals	Opp	Total	Index	Cardinals	Opp	Total	Cardinals	Opp	Total	Index
G	81	81	162	81	81	162		161	161	322	162	162	324	
Avg	.283	.269	.275	.265	.273	.269	102	.278	.261	.269	.265	.278	.272	99
AB	2704	2866	5570	2825	2729	5554	100	5412	5659	11071	5639	5432	11071	101
R	365	385	750	360	444	804	93	764	733	1497	742	858	1600	94
H	764	770	1534	749	744	1493	103	1502	1478	2980	1495	1511	3006	100
2B	132	162	294	147	157	304	96	272	303	575	299	326	625	92
3B	7	19	26	6	19	25	104	21	31	52	19	41	60	87
HR	62	67	129	79	101	180	71	147	158	305	178	203	381	80
BB	251	246	497	255	263	518	96	524	497	1021	513	516	1029	99
SO	405	462	867	504	483	987	88	844	957	1801	987	958	1945	93
E	67	51	118	54	47	101	117	123	101	224	96	102	198	114
E-Infield	29	24	53	25	20	45	118	55	44	99	43	47	90	111
LHB-Avg	.282	.267	.274	.245	.283	.266	103	.274	.266	.270	.252	.289	.273	99
LHB-HR	26	28	54	29	46	75	68	53	73	126	64	90	154	79
RHB-Avg	.283	.270	.277	.275	.266	.271	102	.279	.257	.269	.271	.271	.271	99
RHB-HR	36	39	75	50	55	105	74	94	85	179	114	113	227	81

Tampa Bay Devil Rays - Tropicana Field Surface: NexTurf

| | 2007 Season | | | | | | | 2005-2007 | | | | | | |
| | Home Games | | | Away Games | | | | Home Games | | | Away Games | | | |
	Devil Rays	Opp	Total	Devil Rays	Opp	Total	Index	Devil Rays	Opp	Total	Devil Rays	Opp	Total	Index
G	78	78	156	84	84	168		240	240	480	246	246	492	
Avg	.256	.284	.271	.279	.296	.287	94	.265	.277	.271	.266	.294	.280	97
AB	2598	2802	5400	2995	2882	5877	99	7980	8544	16524	8639	8335	16974	100
R	351	423	774	431	521	952	88	1117	1281	2398	1104	1455	2559	96
H	665	797	1462	835	852	1687	93	2115	2368	4483	2299	2451	4750	97
2B	116	170	286	175	164	339	92	387	475	862	460	508	968	91
3B	17	18	35	19	20	39	98	65	52	117	44	54	98	123
HR	93	88	181	94	111	205	96	264	281	545	270	292	562	100
BB	245	268	513	300	300	600	93	705	866	1571	693	923	1616	100
SO	585	610	1195	739	584	1323	98	1603	1652	3255	1817	1470	3287	102
E	51	51	102	66	51	117	94	172	151	323	185	122	307	108
E-Infield	23	22	45	32	19	51	95	76	59	135	79	39	118	117
LHB-Avg	.270	.287	.279	.282	.307	.295	95	.268	.282	.276	.269	.293	.281	98
LHB-HR	38	38	76	39	49	88	92	97	119	216	103	114	217	104
RHB-Avg	.247	.283	.265	.277	.287	.282	94	.263	.274	.269	.264	.295	.279	96
RHB-HR	55	50	105	55	62	117	99	167	162	329	167	178	345	97

Texas Rangers - Rangers Ballpark in Arlington

| | 2007 Season | | | | | | | 2005-2007 | | | | | | |
| | Home Games | | | Away Games | | | | Home Games | | | Away Games | | | |
	Rangers	Opp	Total	Rangers	Opp	Total	Index	Rangers	Opp	Total	Rangers	Opp	Total	Index
G	81	81	162	81	81	162		243	243	486	243	243	486	
Avg	.277	.263	.270	.249	.286	.267	101	.279	.271	.275	.260	.283	.271	101
AB	2728	2870	5598	2827	2690	5517	101	8318	8688	17006	8612	8172	16784	101
R	421	400	821	395	444	839	98	1318	1237	2555	1198	1249	2447	104
H	755	755	1510	705	770	1475	102	2323	2356	4679	2236	2316	4552	103
2B	141	156	297	157	158	315	93	484	475	959	482	447	929	102
3B	25	13	38	11	12	23	163	52	42	94	36	33	69	134
HR	95	72	167	84	83	167	99	341	237	578	281	239	520	110
BB	252	317	569	251	351	602	93	759	824	1583	744	862	1606	97
SO	603	528	1131	621	448	1069	104	1656	1481	3137	1741	1399	3140	99
E	63	48	111	61	56	117	95	169	139	308	161	149	310	99
E-Infield	30	15	45	24	25	49	92	80	70	150	61	79	140	107
LHB-Avg	.278	.252	.264	.246	.295	.271	97	.269	.269	.269	.257	.280	.269	100
LHB-HR	45	39	84	34	40	74	108	144	136	280	115	101	216	124
RHB-Avg	.276	.272	.274	.252	.280	.265	104	.286	.273	.280	.261	.286	.273	103
RHB-HR	50	33	83	50	43	93	90	197	101	298	166	138	304	99

Toronto Blue Jays - Rogers Centre Surface: AstroTurf

| | 2007 Season | | | | | | | 2005-2007 | | | | | | |
| | Home Games | | | Away Games | | | | Home Games | | | Away Games | | | |
	Blue Jays	Opp	Total	Blue Jays	Opp	Total	Index	Blue Jays	Opp	Total	Blue Jays	Opp	Total	Index
G	81	81	162	81	81	162		243	243	486	243	243	486	
Avg	.260	.235	.247	.258	.267	.263	94	.277	.250	.263	.263	.268	.265	99
AB	2665	2760	5425	2871	2752	5623	96	8202	8477	16679	8511	8146	16657	100
R	380	325	705	373	374	747	94	1230	1036	2266	1107	1122	2229	102
H	692	648	1340	742	735	1477	91	2270	2123	4393	2235	2182	4417	99
2B	169	137	306	175	115	290	109	522	401	923	477	405	882	105
3B	12	14	26	12	10	22	122	52	37	89	38	28	66	135
HR	90	83	173	75	74	149	120	287	280	567	213	247	460	123
BB	269	222	491	264	257	521	98	749	674	1423	784	753	1537	92
SO	539	582	1121	505	495	1000	117	1433	1670	3111	1472	1423	2895	107
E	47	44	91	55	38	93	98	144	137	281	152	121	273	103
E-Infield	22	21	43	19	17	36	119	59	53	112	64	52	116	97
LHB-Avg	.261	.249	.253	.237	.270	.258	98	.276	.250	.262	.256	.267	.262	100
LHB-HR	32	47	79	23	35	58	144	96	119	215	77	95	172	126
RHB-Avg	.259	.222	.243	.267	.264	.266	92	.277	.251	.264	.266	.269	.267	99
RHB-HR	58	36	94	52	39	91	106	191	161	352	136	162	288	121

Washington Nationals - RFK Stadium

| | 2007 Season | | | | | | | 2005-2007 | | | | | | |
| | Home Games | | | Away Games | | | | Home Games | | | Away Games | | | |
	Nationals	Opp	Total	Nationals	Opp	Total	Index	Nationals	Opp	Total	Nationals	Opp	Total	Index
G	81	81	162	81	81	162		243	243	486	243	243	486	
Avg	.259	.259	.259	.254	.280	.267	97	.252	.256	.254	.261	.281	.271	94
AB	2695	2833	5528	2825	2751	5576	99	7951	8505	16456	8490	8231	16721	98
R	324	355	679	349	428	777	87	986	1087	2073	1072	1241	2313	90
H	697	733	1430	718	769	1487	96	2006	2178	4184	2213	2315	4528	92
2B	162	152	314	147	148	295	107	450	434	884	492	450	942	95
3B	15	11	26	16	16	32	82	51	39	90	34	51	85	108
HR	48	77	125	75	110	185	68	168	234	402	236	286	522	78
BB	255	277	532	269	303	572	94	795	788	1583	814	915	1729	93
SO	521	495	1016	607	436	1043	98	1574	1548	3122	1800	1340	3140	101
E	48	52	100	61	33	94	106	151	152	303	181	118	299	101
E-Infield	17	21	38	24	12	36	106	63	59	122	65	51	116	105
LHB-Avg	.255	.255	.255	.245	.268	.255	100	.258	.260	.259	.262	.276	.269	96
LHB-HR	18	32	50	31	43	74	69	66	104	170	92	120	212	81
RHB-Avg	.262	.261	.261	.262	.287	.275	95	.248	.253	.250	.259	.285	.272	92
RHB-HR	30	45	75	44	67	111	67	102	130	232	144	166	310	76

2007 American League Ballpark Index Rankings - Runs

Home Park	Avg	AB	R	H	2B	3B	HR	BB	SO	E	E-Inf	LHB Avg	LHB HR	RHB Avg	RHB HR
Red Sox (Fenway Park)	113	101	118	114	134	95	87	94	93	85	89	109	79	115	93
Indians (Jacobs Field)	105	99	113	104	92	65	113	104	108	105	121	99	89	110	130
Orioles (Oriole Park at Camden Yards)	106	103	111	110	93	131	119	96	89	87	69	111	101	102	137
Angels (Angel Stadium of Anaheim)	105	102	108	107	123	71	87	106	94	123	145	109	76	103	95
White Sox (U.S. Cellular Field)	103	101	108	103	98	47	121	96	94	113	88	98	125	106	119
Yankees (Yankee Stadium)	101	101	107	102	91	59	115	97	103	104	111	102	132	100	98
Tigers (Comerica Park)	101	100	105	100	97	160	114	106	95	110	90	96	88	103	128
Royals (Ewing M. Kauffman Stadium)	105	100	103	104	128	118	90	102	92	68	88	105	89	104	91
Rangers (Rangers Ballpark in Arlington)	101	101	98	102	93	163	99	93	104	95	92	97	108	104	90
Mariners (Safeco Field)	96	99	95	95	95	47	102	108	115	116	110	100	88	94	110
Blue Jays (Rogers Centre)	94	96	94	91	109	122	120	98	117	98	119	98	144	92	106
Devil Rays (Tropicana Field)	94	99	88	93	92	98	96	93	98	94	95	95	92	94	99
Twins (Hubert H. Humphrey Metrodome)	94	101	87	95	93	109	75	101	104	96	83	90	81	99	69
Athletics (McAfee Coliseum)	89	97	83	86	81	130	81	109	87	110	86	91	103	88	67

2007 National League Ballpark Index Rankings - Runs

Home Park	Avg	AB	R	H	2B	3B	HR	BB	SO	E	E-Inf	LHB Avg	LHB HR	RHB Avg	RHB HR
Cubs (Wrigley Field)	104	103	117	108	116	87	111	108	106	120	129	101	109	106	111
Rockies (Coors Field)	110	102	116	112	123	148	119	92	86	130	135	101	104	115	129
Diamondbacks (Chase Field)	105	100	111	105	108	253	111	107	89	100	111	104	127	106	102
Reds (Great American Ballpark)	96	102	109	97	104	80	133	102	103	113	102	103	134	91	132
Marlins (Dolphins Stadium)	100	104	107	103	111	141	97	111	111	93	105	92	108	104	94
Dodgers (Dodger Stadium)	101	101	105	103	90	58	104	105	109	105	60	101	118	102	96
Phillies (Citizens Bank Park)	101	98	103	99	93	88	145	94	103	111	102	104	145	100	145
Brewers (Miller Park)	96	99	101	94	106	51	114	112	105	110	105	95	101	96	123
Giants (Pacific Bell Park)	106	104	99	111	102	131	78	88	92	109	123	107	84	106	74
Pirates (PNC Park)	101	99	95	99	109	58	79	89	95	77	71	106	107	99	66
Cardinals (Busch Stadium)	102	100	93	103	96	104	71	96	88	117	118	103	68	102	74
Mets (Shea Stadium)	95	97	92	92	94	110	93	99	100	93	129	100	95	91	91
Braves (Turner Field)	95	96	91	91	80	92	99	115	106	92	88	99	94	92	103
Astros (Minute Maid Park)	98	102	90	100	92	121	103	97	111	74	107	93	102	100	104
Nationals (RFK Stadium)	97	99	87	96	107	82	68	94	98	106	106	100	69	95	67
Padres (PETCO Park)	89	96	75	86	74	108	71	94	115	64	53	93	67	86	75

2007 AL Home Runs

Home Park	Index
White Sox	121
Blue Jays	120
Orioles	119
Yankees	115
Tigers	114
Indians	113
Mariners	102
Rangers	99
Devil Rays	96
Royals	90
Angels	87
Red Sox	87
Athletics	81
Twins	75

2007 AL LHB Home Runs

Home Park	Index
Blue Jays	144
Yankees	132
White Sox	125
Rangers	108
Athletics	103
Orioles	101
Devil Rays	92
Indians	89
Royals	89
Tigers	88
Mariners	88
Twins	81
Red Sox	79
Angels	76

2007 AL RHB Home Runs

Home Park	Index
Orioles	137
Indians	130
Tigers	128
White Sox	119
Mariners	110
Blue Jays	106
Devil Rays	99
Yankees	98
Angels	95
Red Sox	93
Royals	91
Rangers	90
Twins	69
Athletics	67

2007 NL Home Runs

Home Park	Index
Phillies	145
Reds	133
Rockies	119
Brewers	114
Diamondbacks	111
Cubs	111
Dodgers	104
Astros	103
Braves	99
Marlins	97
Mets	93
Pirates	79
Giants	78
Cardinals	71
Padres	71
Nationals	68

2007 NL LHB Home Runs

Home Park	Index
Phillies	145
Reds	134
Diamondbacks	127
Dodgers	118
Cubs	109
Marlins	108
Pirates	107
Rockies	104
Astros	102
Brewers	101
Mets	95
Braves	94
Giants	84
Nationals	69
Cardinals	68
Padres	67

2007 NL RHB Home Runs

Home Park	Index
Phillies	145
Reds	132
Rockies	129
Brewers	123
Cubs	111
Astros	104
Braves	103
Diamondbacks	102
Dodgers	96
Marlins	94
Mets	91
Padres	75
Giants	74
Cardinals	74
Nationals	67
Pirates	66

2007 AL Avg	
Home Park	Index
Red Sox	113
Orioles	106
Angels	105
Indians	105
Royals	105
White Sox	103
Yankees	101
Rangers	101
Tigers	101
Mariners	96
Devil Rays	94
Twins	94
Blue Jays	94
Athletics	89

2007 AL LHB Avg	
Home Park	Index
Orioles	111
Red Sox	109
Angels	109
Royals	105
Yankees	102
Mariners	100
Indians	99
White Sox	98
Blue Jays	98
Rangers	97
Tigers	96
Devil Rays	95
Athletics	91
Twins	90

2007 AL RHB Avg	
Home Park	Index
Red Sox	115
Indians	110
White Sox	106
Royals	104
Rangers	104
Tigers	103
Angels	103
Orioles	102
Yankees	100
Twins	99
Devil Rays	94
Mariners	94
Blue Jays	92
Athletics	88

2007 NL Avg	
Home Park	Index
Rockies	110
Giants	106
Diamondbacks	105
Cubs	104
Cardinals	102
Dodgers	101
Phillies	101
Pirates	101
Marlins	100
Astros	98
Nationals	97
Brewers	96
Reds	96
Braves	95
Mets	95
Padres	89

2007 NL LHB Avg	
Home Park	Index
Giants	107
Pirates	106
Diamondbacks	104
Phillies	104
Cardinals	103
Reds	103
Rockies	101
Cubs	101
Dodgers	101
Mets	100
Nationals	100
Braves	99
Brewers	95
Astros	93
Padres	93
Marlins	92

2007 NL RHB Avg	
Home Park	Index
Rockies	115
Diamondbacks	106
Cubs	106
Giants	106
Marlins	104
Cardinals	102
Dodgers	102
Astros	100
Phillies	100
Pirates	99
Brewers	96
Nationals	95
Braves	92
Reds	91
Mets	91
Padres	86

2007 AL Doubles	
Home Park	Index
Red Sox	134
Royals	128
Angels	123
Blue Jays	109
White Sox	98
Tigers	97
Mariners	95
Twins	93
Orioles	93
Rangers	93
Indians	92
Devil Rays	92
Yankees	91
Athletics	81

2007 AL Triples	
Home Park	Index
Rangers	163
Tigers	160
Orioles	131
Athletics	130
Blue Jays	122
Royals	118
Twins	109
Devil Rays	98
Red Sox	95
Angels	71
Indians	65
Yankees	59
White Sox	47
Mariners	47

2007 AL Errors	
Home Park	Index
Angels	123
Mariners	116
White Sox	113
Athletics	110
Tigers	110
Indians	105
Yankees	104
Blue Jays	98
Twins	96
Rangers	95
Devil Rays	94
Orioles	87
Red Sox	85
Royals	68

2007 NL Doubles	
Home Park	Index
Rockies	123
Cubs	116
Marlins	111
Pirates	109
Diamondbacks	108
Nationals	107
Brewers	106
Reds	104
Giants	102
Cardinals	96
Mets	94
Phillies	93
Astros	92
Dodgers	90
Braves	80
Padres	74

2007 NL Triples	
Home Park	Index
Diamondbacks	253
Rockies	148
Marlins	141
Giants	131
Astros	121
Mets	110
Padres	108
Cardinals	104
Braves	92
Phillies	88
Cubs	87
Nationals	82
Reds	80
Pirates	58
Dodgers	58
Brewers	51

2007 NL Errors	
Home Park	Index
Rockies	130
Cubs	120
Cardinals	117
Reds	113
Phillies	111
Brewers	110
Giants	109
Nationals	106
Dodgers	105
Diamondbacks	100
Marlins	93
Mets	93
Braves	92
Pirates	77
Astros	74
Padres	64

2005-2007 American League Ballpark Index Rankings - Runs

Home Park	TOTALS											LHB		RHB	
	Avg	AB	R	H	2B	3B	HR	BB	SO	E	E-Inf	Avg	HR	Avg	HR
Red Sox (Fenway Park)	104	100	107	104	135	94	82	99	97	96	112	105	74	104	90
White Sox (U.S. Cellular Field)	101	100	106	101	94	63	130	105	98	96	90	98	140	102	126
Royals (Ewing M. Kauffman Stadium)	104	101	105	105	120	107	87	103	92	92	101	103	86	105	88
Rangers (Rangers Ballpark in Arlington)	101	101	104	103	102	134	110	97	99	99	107	100	124	103	99
Blue Jays (Rogers Centre)	99	100	102	99	105	135	123	92	107	103	97	100	126	99	121
Yankees (Yankee Stadium)	101	100	100	101	92	70	111	94	100	106	117	99	119	103	104
Tigers (Comerica Park)	101	101	100	102	92	147	94	103	94	110	115	99	95	101	93
Orioles (Oriole Park at Camden Yards)	101	101	99	102	88	81	110	102	91	89	82	99	97	103	120
Indians (Jacobs Field)	99	98	98	97	100	60	96	106	104	108	109	99	98	99	95
Angels (Angel Stadium of Anaheim)	101	100	97	102	105	83	86	100	98	110	111	102	79	101	91
Devil Rays (Tropicana Field)	97	100	96	97	91	123	100	100	102	108	117	98	104	96	97
Twins (Hubert H. Humphrey Metrodome)	97	100	95	96	95	112	85	90	107	99	94	96	80	98	89
Mariners (Safeco Field)	96	99	93	95	95	65	91	107	112	92	75	101	92	93	91
Athletics (McAfee Coliseum)	96	99	93	95	99	101	85	99	89	94	77	98	90	94	82

2005-2007 National League Ballpark Index Rankings - Runs

Home Park	TOTALS											LHB		RHB	
	Avg	AB	R	H	2B	3B	HR	BB	SO	E	E-Inf	Avg	HR	Avg	HR
Rockies (Coors Field)	113	104	119	117	108	132	112	98	87	109	99	107	96	117	123
Reds (Great American Ballpark)	101	101	112	102	104	58	128	101	101	96	106	105	128	98	127
Diamondbacks (Chase Field)	106	101	111	107	108	185	115	106	92	94	116	107	123	105	107
Cubs (Wrigley Field)	101	102	108	103	109	111	111	97	105	106	107	100	119	102	107
Phillies (Citizens Bank Park) *	102	98	105	100	99	76	133	96	103	110	103	103	130	102	136
Brewers (Miller Park)	95	98	100	93	99	86	109	110	107	113	109	94	99	96	116
Dodgers (Dodger Stadium)	100	100	100	99	98	51	111	110	107	104	88	100	118	99	106
Pirates (PNC Park)	103	102	99	105	112	92	80	94	96	88	90	108	100	101	72
Giants (Pacific Bell Park)	101	100	98	101	101	114	79	95	94	108	100	100	71	101	84
Braves (Turner Field)	101	99	98	100	96	96	93	102	103	102	101	101	83	101	102
Astros (Minute Maid Park)	99	100	96	99	91	113	113	97	103	89	100	95	104	102	119
Marlins (Dolphins Stadium)	97	100	95	97	99	131	91	112	113	89	82	95	105	98	85
Cardinals (Busch Stadium) *	99	101	94	100	92	87	80	99	93	114	111	99	79	99	81
Mets (Shea Stadium)	96	99	93	95	96	88	90	100	99	103	110	99	89	94	91
Nationals (RFK Stadium)	94	98	90	92	95	108	78	93	101	101	105	96	81	92	76
Padres (PETCO Park) *	90	98	81	88	75	109	85	98	112	74	61	94	78	87	92

2005-2007 AL Home Runs

Home Park	Index
White Sox	130
Blue Jays	123
Yankees	111
Orioles	110
Rangers	110
Devil Rays	100
Indians	96
Tigers	94
Mariners	91
Royals	87
Angels	86
Athletics	85
Twins	85
Red Sox	82

2005-2007 AL LHB Home Runs

Home Park	Index
White Sox	140
Blue Jays	126
Rangers	124
Yankees	119
Devil Rays	104
Indians	98
Orioles	97
Tigers	95
Mariners	92
Athletics	90
Royals	86
Twins	80
Angels	79
Red Sox	74

2005-2007 AL RHB Home Runs

Home Park	Index
White Sox	126
Blue Jays	121
Orioles	120
Yankees	104
Rangers	99
Devil Rays	97
Indians	95
Tigers	93
Angels	91
Mariners	91
Red Sox	90
Twins	89
Royals	88
Athletics	82

2005-2007 NL Home Runs

Home Park	Index
Phillies *	133
Reds	128
Diamondbacks	115
Astros	113
Rockies	112
Cubs	111
Dodgers	111
Brewers	109
Braves	93
Marlins	91
Mets	90
Padres *	85
Pirates	80
Cardinals *	80
Giants	79
Nationals	78

2005-2007 NL LHB Home Runs

Home Park	Index
Phillies *	130
Reds	128
Diamondbacks	123
Cubs	119
Dodgers	118
Marlins	105
Astros	104
Pirates	100
Brewers	99
Rockies	96
Mets	89
Braves	83
Nationals	81
Cardinals *	79
Padres *	78
Giants	71

2005-2007 NL RHB Home Runs

Home Park	Index
Phillies *	136
Reds	127
Rockies	123
Astros	119
Brewers	116
Cubs	107
Diamondbacks	107
Dodgers	106
Braves	102
Padres *	92
Mets	91
Marlins	85
Giants	84
Cardinals *	81
Nationals	76
Pirates	72

* Data since 2006

2005-2007 AL Avg	
Home Park	Index
Red Sox	104
Royals	104
Rangers	101
Angels	101
Yankees	101
Orioles	101
Tigers	101
White Sox	101
Blue Jays	99
Indians	99
Twins	97
Devil Rays	97
Athletics	96
Mariners	96

2005-2007 AL LHB Avg	
Home Park	Index
Red Sox	105
Royals	103
Angels	102
Mariners	101
Blue Jays	100
Rangers	100
Yankees	99
Tigers	99
Indians	99
Orioles	99
Athletics	98
White Sox	98
Devil Rays	98
Twins	96

2005-2007 AL RHB Avg	
Home Park	Index
Royals	105
Red Sox	104
Yankees	103
Orioles	103
Rangers	103
White Sox	102
Angels	101
Tigers	101
Indians	99
Blue Jays	99
Twins	98
Devil Rays	96
Athletics	94
Mariners	93

2005-2007 NL Avg	
Home Park	Index
Rockies	113
Diamondbacks	106
Pirates	103
Phillies *	102
Cubs	101
Reds	101
Giants	101
Braves	101
Dodgers	100
Astros	99
Cardinals *	99
Marlins	97
Mets	96
Brewers	95
Nationals	94
Padres *	90

2005-2007 NL LHB Avg	
Home Park	Index
Pirates	108
Diamondbacks	107
Rockies	107
Reds	105
Phillies *	103
Braves	101
Dodgers	100
Giants	100
Cubs	100
Mets	99
Cardinals *	99
Nationals	96
Marlins	95
Astros	95
Brewers	94
Padres *	94

2005-2007 NL RHB Avg	
Home Park	Index
Rockies	117
Diamondbacks	105
Cubs	102
Phillies *	102
Astros	102
Giants	101
Pirates	101
Braves	101
Cardinals *	99
Dodgers	99
Reds	98
Marlins	98
Brewers	96
Mets	94
Nationals	92
Padres *	87

2005-2007 AL Doubles	
Home Park	Index
Red Sox	135
Royals	120
Angels	105
Blue Jays	105
Rangers	102
Indians	100
Athletics	99
Twins	95
Mariners	95
White Sox	94
Yankees	92
Tigers	92
Devil Rays	91
Orioles	88

2005-2007 AL Triples	
Home Park	Index
Tigers	147
Blue Jays	135
Rangers	134
Devil Rays	123
Twins	112
Royals	107
Athletics	101
Red Sox	94
Angels	83
Orioles	81
Yankees	70
Mariners	65
White Sox	63
Indians	60

2005-2007 AL Errors	
Home Park	Index
Angels	110
Tigers	110
Indians	108
Devil Rays	108
Yankees	106
Blue Jays	103
Rangers	99
Twins	99
White Sox	96
Red Sox	96
Athletics	94
Mariners	92
Royals	92
Orioles	89

2005-2007 NL Doubles	
Home Park	Index
Pirates	112
Cubs	109
Rockies	108
Diamondbacks	108
Reds	104
Giants	101
Marlins	99
Brewers	99
Phillies *	99
Dodgers	98
Mets	96
Braves	96
Nationals	95
Cardinals *	92
Astros	91
Padres *	75

2005-2007 NL Triples	
Home Park	Index
Diamondbacks	185
Rockies	132
Marlins	131
Giants	114
Astros	113
Cubs	111
Padres *	109
Nationals	108
Braves	96
Pirates	92
Mets	88
Cardinals *	87
Brewers *	86
Phillies	76
Reds	58
Dodgers	51

2005-2007 NL Errors	
Home Park	Index
Cardinals *	114
Brewers	113
Phillies *	110
Rockies	109
Giants	108
Cubs	106
Dodgers	104
Mets	103
Braves	102
Nationals	101
Reds	96
Diamondbacks	94
Astros	89
Marlins	89
Pirates	88
Padres *	74

* Data since 2006

2007 Lefty/Righty Statistics

In the following section are lefty/righty splits for all batters and pitchers who appeared during the 2007 season. The batting side of each hitter is shown below his name; for pitchers, the hand that he throws with is indicated.

Which players benefited the most from a platoon advantage? Which players should have been part of a platoon but weren't? Which pitchers were equally tough on lefties and righties? It's all in the pages that follow.

Batter	vs	Avg	AB	H	2B	3B	HR	RBI	BB	SO	OBP	Slg
Abercrombie,Reggie	L	.162	37	6	1	0	2	2	2	12	.205	.351
Bats Right	R	.231	39	9	2	0	0	3	0	10	.268	.282
Abreu,Bobby	L	.262	149	39	8	1	1	21	16	29	.329	.349
Bats Left	R	.289	456	132	32	4	15	80	68	86	.382	.476
Abreu,Tony	L	.214	42	9	4	1	1	7	2	6	.283	.429
Bats Both	R	.290	124	36	10	0	1	10	5	15	.318	.395
Adams,Russ	L	.000	6	0	0	0	0	0	1	0	.143	.000
Bats Left	R	.259	54	14	3	0	2	12	6	14	.333	.426
Alfonzo,Eliezer	L	.150	20	3	1	0	0	3	0	10	.150	.200
Bats Right	R	.295	44	13	1	1	1	3	2	13	.340	.432
Alomar Jr.,Sandy	L	.200	5	1	0	0	0	0	0	0	.200	.200
Bats Right	R	.118	17	2	1	0	0	0	0	3	.118	.176
Alou,Moises	L	.360	86	31	9	0	4	13	14	9	.451	.605
Bats Right	R	.335	242	81	10	1	9	36	13	21	.368	.496
Ambres,Chip	L	-	0	0	0	0	0	0	0	0	-	-
Bats Right	R	.333	3	1	0	0	0	1	0	1	.333	.333
Amezaga,Alfredo	L	.224	58	13	5	0	0	2	1	11	.233	.310
Bats Both	R	.269	342	92	9	9	2	28	34	41	.339	.365
Anderson,Brian	L	.000	8	0	0	0	0	0	1	3	.111	.000
Bats Right	R	.222	9	2	1	0	0	0	1	4	.300	.333
Anderson,Garret	L	.288	104	30	3	0	6	25	5	20	.315	.490
Bats Left	R	.300	313	94	28	1	10	55	22	34	.342	.492
Anderson,Josh	L	.389	18	7	1	0	0	4	1	0	.450	.444
Bats Left	R	.347	49	17	2	0	0	7	4	6	.400	.388
Anderson,Marlon	L	.143	7	1	0	0	0	1	0	1	.125	.143
Bats Left	R	.307	88	27	7	0	3	26	8	16	.361	.489
Andino,Robert	L	.333	3	1	1	0	0	0	0	1	.333	.667
Bats Right	R	.400	10	4	0	0	0	0	0	1	.400	.400
Ankiel,Rick	L	.391	46	18	6	0	4	16	2	13	.400	.783
Bats Left	R	.246	126	31	2	1	7	23	11	28	.302	.444
Atkins,Garrett	L	.286	175	50	7	0	6	26	20	22	.354	.429
Bats Right	R	.307	430	132	28	1	19	85	47	74	.372	.509
Aurilia,Rich	L	.240	129	31	8	1	4	13	4	15	.265	.411
Bats Right	R	.260	200	52	11	1	1	20	18	30	.329	.340
Ausmus,Brad	L	.239	88	21	5	0	1	7	12	8	.337	.330
Bats Right	R	.234	261	61	11	3	2	18	25	66	.312	.322
Aybar,Erick	L	.304	46	14	2	0	1	5	3	7	.340	.413
Bats Both	R	.216	148	32	3	1	0	14	7	25	.259	.250
Bailey,Jeff	L	.167	6	1	0	0	1	1	0	0	.167	.667
Bats Right	R	.000	3	0	0	0	0	0	0	1	.000	.000
Baker,Jeff	L	.246	61	15	0	1	3	7	8	16	.333	.426
Bats Right	R	.205	83	17	2	1	1	5	5	24	.267	.289
Bako,Paul	L	.192	26	5	1	0	0	1	2	7	.250	.231
Bats Left	R	.208	130	27	2	1	1	7	13	43	.283	.262
Baldelli,Rocco	L	.156	32	5	1	0	3	6	3	6	.250	.469
Bats Right	R	.219	105	23	5	0	2	6	6	29	.274	.324
Balentien,Wladimir	L	.000	1	0	0	0	0	0	0	0	.000	.000
Bats Right	R	1.000	2	2	1	0	1	4	0	0	.667	3.000
Barajas,Rod	L	.226	31	7	3	0	2	5	7	8	.400	.516
Bats Right	R	.231	91	21	5	0	2	5	14	16	.333	.352
Bard,Josh	L	.376	109	41	12	0	1	16	16	12	.452	.514
Bats Both	R	.250	280	70	15	2	4	35	34	46	.329	.361
Barden,Brian	L	.125	8	1	1	0	0	0	1	2	.222	.250
Bats Right	R	.185	27	5	0	0	0	0	1	5	.214	.185
Barfield,Josh	L	.211	114	24	3	1	2	11	5	28	.242	.307
Bats Right	R	.255	306	78	16	2	1	39	9	62	.280	.330
Barker,Sean	L	-	0	0	0	0	0	0	0	0	-	-
Bats Right	R	.000	2	0	0	0	0	0	0	1	.333	.000
Barmes,Clint	L	.444	9	4	2	0	0	1	0	1	.444	.667
Bats Right	R	.143	28	4	1	0	0	0	1	12	.172	.179
Barrett,Michael	L	.222	63	14	3	0	3	6	6	10	.286	.413
Bats Right	R	.249	281	70	14	0	6	35	13	47	.279	.363
Bartlett,Jason	L	.319	138	44	13	2	1	9	15	16	.394	.464
Bats Right	R	.245	372	91	7	5	4	34	35	57	.318	.323
Barton,Daric	L	.296	27	8	5	0	1	2	6	7	.441	.593
Bats Left	R	.378	45	17	4	0	3	6	4	4	.420	.667
Basak,Chris	L	.000	1	0	0	0	0	0	0	0	.000	.000
Bats Right	R	-	0	0	0	0	0	0	0	0	-	-
Batista,Tony	L	.234	47	11	0	0	1	7	6	6	.327	.298
Bats Right	R	.278	54	15	3	0	1	9	6	8	.365	.389
Bautista,Jose	L	.256	121	31	8	0	4	14	21	21	.366	.421
Bats Right	R	.253	411	104	28	2	11	49	47	80	.331	.411
Bay,Jason	L	.227	128	29	8	0	5	21	20	32	.336	.406
Bats Right	R	.254	410	104	17	2	16	63	39	109	.325	.422
Bellhorn,Mark	L	.250	4	1	0	0	0	0	0	2	.250	.250
Bats Both	R	.000	10	0	0	0	0	1	4	3	.286	.000
Belliard,Ronnie	L	.329	140	46	12	0	5	19	11	17	.370	.521
Bats Right	R	.275	371	102	23	1	6	39	23	55	.317	.391
Bellorin,Edwin	L	.000	1	0	0	0	0	0	0	0	.000	.000
Bats Right	R	.000	1	0	0	0	0	0	0	0	.000	.000
Beltran,Carlos	L	.304	158	48	7	0	11	30	21	21	.383	.557
Bats Both	R	.265	396	105	26	3	22	82	48	90	.341	.513
Beltre,Adrian	L	.280	125	35	9	0	8	32	11	27	.338	.544
Bats Right	R	.274	470	129	32	2	18	67	27	77	.314	.466
Bennett,Gary	L	.227	44	10	1	0	0	4	1	2	.234	.250
Bats Right	R	.261	111	29	6	0	2	13	7	14	.306	.369
Berkman,Lance	L	.265	132	35	6	1	5	24	19	24	.361	.439
Bats Both	R	.282	429	121	18	1	29	78	75	101	.394	.531
Berroa,Angel	L	.200	5	1	0	0	0	0	0	2	.333	.200
Bats Right	R	.000	6	0	0	0	0	0	1	2	.000	.000
Betancourt,Yuniesky	L	.333	114	38	11	1	4	17	6	10	.364	.553
Bats Right	R	.277	422	117	27	1	5	50	9	38	.292	.382
Betemit,Wilson	L	.239	46	11	3	0	1	4	4	20	.300	.370
Bats Both	R	.227	194	44	9	0	13	46	34	62	.341	.474
Biggio,Craig	L	.323	130	42	9	2	2	9	8	22	.357	.469
Bats Right	R	.227	387	88	22	1	8	41	15	90	.260	.351
Blake,Casey	L	.256	160	41	12	1	6	20	28	30	.370	.456
Bats Right	R	.276	428	118	24	3	12	58	26	93	.327	.430
Blalock,Hank	L	.298	47	14	4	1	0	6	5	9	.370	.426
Bats Left	R	.292	161	47	12	2	10	27	16	29	.354	.578
Blanco,Henry	L	.050	20	1	0	0	0	2	1	3	.095	.050
Bats Right	R	.235	34	8	3	0	0	2	1	9	.250	.324
Bloomquist,Willie	L	.238	42	10	0	0	2	5	5	8	.319	.381
Bats Right	R	.290	131	38	3	0	0	8	5	27	.321	.313
Blum,Geoff	L	.238	80	19	6	0	0	11	8	13	.303	.313
Bats Both	R	.256	250	64	15	1	5	22	24	39	.324	.384
Bocachica,Hiram	L	.184	38	7	4	0	0	2	4	9	.256	.289
Bats Right	R	.214	42	9	0	0	2	3	3	9	.267	.357
Bonds,Barry	L	.265	117	31	6	0	8	25	44	20	.470	.521
Bats Left	R	.283	223	63	8	0	20	41	88	34	.486	.587
Bonifacio,Emilio	L	.200	5	1	0	0	0	0	0	0	.200	.200
Bats Both	R	.222	18	4	1	0	0	2	4	3	.364	.278
Boone,Aaron	L	.213	47	10	2	0	0	4	9	8	.350	.255
Bats Right	R	.310	142	44	9	0	5	24	12	33	.401	.479
Borchard,Joe	L	.188	32	6	1	0	0	2	3	10	.257	.219
Bats Both	R	.197	147	29	8	0	4	17	18	50	.293	.333
Botts,Jason	L	.333	42	14	4	0	0	4	5	16	.404	.429
Bats Both	R	.208	125	26	4	1	2	10	14	43	.301	.304
Bourn,Michael	L	.154	26	4	1	0	0	1	3	4	.241	.192
Bats Left	R	.312	93	29	2	3	1	5	10	17	.379	.430
Bowen,Rob	L	.250	48	12	5	0	1	2	8	10	.357	.417
Bats Both	R	.222	108	24	5	0	3	16	19	51	.338	.352
Bradley,Milton	L	.304	69	21	3	1	5	16	8	12	.372	.594
Bats Both	R	.307	140	43	6	0	8	21	23	29	.416	.521
Branyan,Russell	L	.158	19	3	1	0	0	2	6	7	.385	.211
Bats Left	R	.201	144	29	4	1	10	24	22	62	.310	.451
Braun,Ryan	L	.450	111	50	8	2	15	35	16	19	.516	.964
Bats Right	R	.282	340	96	18	4	19	62	13	93	.319	.526
Brazell,Craig	L	1.000	1	1	0	0	0	0	0	0	1.000	1.000
Bats Left	R	.000	3	0	0	0	0	0	1	1	.250	.000
Broussard,Ben	L	.250	16	4	0	0	0	3	2	0	.368	.250
Bats Right	R	.277	224	62	10	0	7	26	15	50	.327	.415
Brown,Dee	L	.000	1	0	0	0	0	0	0	0	.000	.000
Bats Left	R	.000	2	0	0	0	0	0	0	1	.000	.000
Brown,Emil	L	.317	145	46	5	1	4	31	14	23	.375	.448
Bats Right	R	.217	221	48	8	0	2	31	10	48	.249	.281
Brown,Matt	L	.000	3	0	0	0	0	0	2	1	.400	.000
Bats Right	R	.000	2	0	0	0	0	0	0	0	.000	.000
Bruntlett,Eric	L	.237	59	14	2	0	0	5	9	11	.348	.271
Bats Right	R	.253	79	20	3	0	0	9	11	16	.344	.291
Buck,John	L	.189	74	14	3	0	5	11	12	21	.307	.432
Bats Right	R	.231	273	63	15	0	13	37	24	71	.309	.429
Buck,Travis	L	.323	65	21	6	0	4	11	6	11	.405	.600
Bats Left	R	.277	220	61	16	5	3	23	33	55	.368	.436
Budde,Ryan	L	.333	3	1	1	0	0	1	0	0	.333	.667
Bats Right	R	.133	15	2	0	0	0	0	0	6	.133	.133
Burke,Chris	L	.292	106	31	5	2	2	11	10	10	.370	.434
Bats Right	R	.197	213	42	14	0	4	17	17	42	.271	.319
Burke,Jamie	L	.280	25	7	1	0	1	7	3	2	.357	.440
Bats Right	R	.307	88	27	7	0	0	5	4	15	.365	.386
Burrell,Pat	L	.255	141	36	9	0	10	33	40	36	.418	.532
Bats Right	R	.257	331	85	17	0	20	64	74	84	.391	.489

Batters vs. Left-Handed and Right-Handed Pitchers

Batter	vs	Avg	AB	H	2B	3B	HR	RBI	BB	SO	OBP	Slg
Buscher,Brian	L	.200	10	2	0	0	0	1	1	5	.250	.200
Bats Left	R	.250	72	18	1	0	2	9	9	11	.333	.347
Butler,Billy	L	.340	97	33	9	1	4	21	10	15	.404	.577
Bats Right	R	.272	232	63	14	1	4	31	17	40	.323	.392
Bynum,Freddie	L	.263	19	5	2	0	0	2	1	5	.333	.368
Bats Left	R	.260	77	20	6	2	2	9	1	25	.278	.468
Byrd,Marlon	L	.327	104	34	6	2	1	16	7	24	.374	.452
Bats Right	R	.300	310	93	11	6	9	54	22	64	.348	.461
Byrnes,Eric	L	.248	145	36	5	2	7	16	17	24	.331	.455
Bats Right	R	.297	481	143	25	6	14	67	40	74	.360	.462
Cabrera,Asdrubal	L	.340	47	16	4	1	2	7	1	10	.354	.596
Bats Both	R	.259	112	29	5	1	1	15	16	19	.353	.348
Cabrera,Melky	L	.250	148	37	8	0	1	10	14	16	.317	.324
Bats Both	R	.282	397	112	16	8	7	63	29	52	.331	.416
Cabrera,Miguel	L	.364	118	43	9	1	9	30	29	25	.487	.686
Bats Right	R	.309	470	145	29	1	25	89	50	102	.376	.534
Cabrera,Orlando	L	.308	133	41	10	0	4	21	13	15	.369	.474
Bats Right	R	.299	505	151	25	1	4	65	31	49	.339	.376
Cairo,Miguel	L	.254	59	15	2	1	0	10	2	10	.302	.322
Bats Right	R	.252	115	29	7	1	0	5	9	14	.304	.330
Callaspo,Alberto	L	.219	32	7	4	0	0	2	3	2	.286	.344
Bats Both	R	.214	112	24	4	0	0	5	6	12	.258	.250
Cameron,Mike	L	.294	153	45	6	3	7	24	26	32	.404	.510
Bats Right	R	.222	418	93	27	3	14	54	41	128	.298	.402
Cano,Robinson	L	.328	192	63	11	1	6	39	12	28	.374	.490
Bats Left	R	.296	425	126	30	6	13	58	27	57	.344	.487
Cantu,Jorge	L	.232	69	16	3	0	1	5	8	16	.316	.319
Bats Right	R	.283	46	13	6	0	0	8	4	10	.352	.413
Carroll,Brett	L	.240	25	6	1	0	0	2	1	7	.269	.280
Bats Right	R	.125	24	3	0	0	0	0	2	8	.192	.125
Carroll,Jamey	L	.262	103	27	5	0	2	14	11	11	.336	.369
Bats Right	R	.194	124	24	4	1	0	8	17	23	.301	.242
Casanova,Raul	L	.250	20	5	0	0	2	5	1	9	.261	.550
Bats Both	R	.254	59	15	1	1	4	6	6	8	.333	.508
Casey,Sean	L	.365	63	23	6	1	0	14	0	8	.437	.492
Bats Left	R	.285	390	111	24	0	4	40	31	34	.339	.377
Cash,Kevin	L	.077	13	1	1	0	0	0	2	7	.200	.154
Bats Right	R	.143	14	2	0	0	0	4	2	6	.278	.143
Casilla,Alexi	L	.274	84	23	4	0	0	7	3	7	.295	.321
Bats Right	R	.181	105	19	1	1	0	2	6	22	.225	.210
Castillo,Alberto	L	.263	19	5	2	0	1	3	1	6	.286	.526
Bats Right	R	.000	12	0	0	0	0	0	2	4	.143	.000
Castillo,Jose	L	.246	65	16	4	0	0	6	3	13	.290	.308
Bats Right	R	.244	156	38	14	1	0	18	3	35	.261	.346
Castillo,Luis	L	.296	142	42	12	2	1	15	12	11	.348	.430
Bats Both	R	.303	406	123	7	3	0	23	41	34	.366	.335
Casto,Kory	L	.071	14	1	0	0	0	0	1	6	.133	.071
Bats Left	R	.150	40	6	2	0	0	3	1	11	.167	.200
Castro,Juan	L	.226	31	7	3	0	0	2	3	4	.294	.323
Bats Right	R	.155	58	9	2	0	0	3	1	17	.164	.190
Castro,Ramon	L	.276	29	8	1	0	2	5	4	8	.364	.517
Bats Right	R	.287	115	33	5	0	9	26	6	31	.323	.565
Catalanotto,Frank	L	.231	13	3	0	0	0	1	3	3	.375	.231
Bats Left	R	.261	318	83	20	4	11	43	25	34	.335	.453
Cedeno,Ronny	L	.176	34	6	1	0	0	5	0	5	.176	.206
Bats Right	R	.225	40	9	1	0	4	8	3	13	.273	.550
Chavez,Endy	L	.276	29	8	2	0	1	4	0	1	.276	.448
Bats Left	R	.289	121	35	5	2	0	13	9	15	.336	.364
Chavez,Eric	L	.234	124	29	9	2	3	16	11	30	.292	.411
Bats Left	R	.244	217	53	12	0	12	30	23	46	.314	.465
Choo,Shin-Soo	L	.000	3	0	0	0	0	0	1	1	.250	.000
Bats Left	R	.357	14	5	0	0	0	5	1	4	.375	.357
Church,Ryan	L	.229	118	27	10	0	1	19	15	31	.316	.319
Bats Left	R	.287	352	101	33	1	14	51	34	76	.360	.506
Cintron,Alex	L	.238	21	5	1	0	0	5	2	4	.304	.286
Bats Both	R	.244	164	40	6	1	2	14	7	31	.277	.329
Cirillo,Jeff	L	.271	70	19	6	1	1	11	6	7	.321	.429
Bats Right	R	.236	123	29	7	1	1	16	13	12	.314	.333
Clark,Brady	L	.308	39	12	3	1	0	4	5	2	.386	.436
Bats Right	R	.235	68	16	2	1	0	7	9	16	.333	.294
Clark,Howie	L	.000	2	0	0	0	0	0	0	1	.000	.000
Bats Left	R	.213	47	10	2	0	0	2	7	4	.309	.255
Clark,Tony	L	.219	32	7	1	0	2	3	3	9	.286	.438
Bats Both	R	.254	189	48	4	1	15	48	18	50	.314	.524
Clayton,Royce	L	.246	57	14	4	0	0	1	6	15	.317	.316
Bats Right	R	.246	138	34	10	0	1	11	8	38	.287	.341
Clement,Jeff	L	.000	1	0	0	0	0	0	0	1	.000	.000
Bats Left	R	.400	15	6	1	0	2	3	3	2	.500	.867
Clevlen,Brent	L	.167	6	1	0	0	0	0	0	4	.167	.167
Bats Right	R	.000	4	0	0	0	0	0	0	0	.000	.000
Coats,Buck	L	.500	10	5	3	0	0	1	1	4	.545	.800
Bats Left	R	.083	24	2	1	0	0	1	2	11	.148	.125
Conine,Jeff	L	.252	147	37	10	0	6	25	20	23	.331	.442
Bats Right	R	.257	109	28	3	1	0	12	7	13	.297	.303
Cora,Alex	L	.179	28	5	0	0	0	3	0	2	.207	.179
Bats Left	R	.257	179	46	10	5	3	15	7	21	.311	.410
Cortez,Fernando	L	.500	2	1	0	0	0	1	0	0	.500	.500
Bats Left	R	.250	12	3	1	0	0	0	1	0	.308	.333
Costa,Shane	L	.125	8	1	0	0	0	0	1	2	.222	.125
Bats Right	R	.232	95	22	6	1	0	12	4	21	.260	.316
Coste,Chris	L	.405	37	15	2	0	0	3	0	2	.405	.459
Bats Right	R	.228	92	21	1	0	5	19	4	18	.276	.402
Cota,Humberto	L	-	0	0	0	0	0	0	0	0	-	-
Bats Left	R	.286	14	4	1	0	0	3	2	2	.389	.357
Counsell,Craig	L	.157	51	8	1	1	1	5	6	16	.259	.275
Bats Right	R	.234	231	54	11	1	2	19	35	31	.337	.316
Crawford,Carl	L	.318	195	62	14	5	3	38	8	38	.350	.487
Bats Left	R	.314	389	122	23	4	8	42	24	74	.357	.455
Crede,Joe	L	.206	34	7	0	0	0	5	5	5	.308	.206
Bats Right	R	.218	133	29	5	0	4	17	5	19	.245	.346
Crisp,Coco	L	.270	148	40	8	0	4	19	17	26	.345	.405
Bats Both	R	.267	378	101	20	7	2	41	33	58	.324	.373
Crosby,Bobby	L	.222	99	22	6	0	3	8	7	17	.274	.374
Bats Right	R	.228	250	57	10	0	5	23	16	45	.280	.328
Cruz,Enrique	L	-	0	0	0	0	0	0	0	0	-	-
Bats Right	R	.000	1	0	0	0	0	0	0	0	.000	.000
Cruz,Jose	L	.221	86	19	5	1	2	6	13	24	.323	.372
Bats Both	R	.241	170	41	7	2	4	15	18	41	.312	.376
Cruz,Nelson	L	.212	99	21	4	0	2	14	8	27	.269	.313
Bats Right	R	.245	208	51	11	2	7	20	13	60	.296	.418
Cuddyer,Michael	L	.308	159	49	14	2	3	19	20	29	.387	.478
Bats Right	R	.263	388	102	14	3	13	62	44	78	.344	.415
Cust,Jack	L	.218	124	27	3	0	7	26	30	60	.374	.411
Bats Left	R	.273	271	74	15	1	19	56	72	105	.424	.546
Damon,Johnny	L	.281	139	39	5	1	1	14	14	26	.353	.353
Bats Left	R	.266	394	105	22	1	11	49	52	53	.350	.411
DaVanon,Jeff	L	.429	14	6	0	0	0	0	1	4	.467	.429
Bats Both	R	.173	75	13	3	1	0	6	11	23	.281	.240
Davis,Rajai	L	.299	97	20	5	1	1	6	13	13	.384	.402
Bats Right	R	.258	93	24	6	1	0	3	8	15	.337	.344
De Aza,Alejandro	L	.313	32	10	1	1	0	1	0	4	.333	.406
Bats Left	R	.205	112	23	7	1	0	7	6	33	.242	.286
DeJesus,David	L	.240	175	42	9	0	2	16	19	30	.332	.326
Bats Left	R	.267	430	115	20	9	5	42	45	53	.358	.391
Delgado,Carlos	L	.267	176	47	9	0	4	30	13	44	.318	.386
Bats Left	R	.254	362	92	21	0	20	57	39	74	.340	.478
Dellucci,David	L	.167	24	4	2	0	0		2	8	.231	.250
Bats Left	R	.240	154	37	9	2	4	20	15	32	.306	.403
DeRosa,Mark	L	.283	145	41	11	0	1	18	17	24	.366	.379
Bats Right	R	.297	357	106	17	3	9	54	41	69	.373	.437
Diaz,Matt	L	.356	188	67	15	0	9	27	10	27	.384	.580
Bats Right	R	.318	170	54	6	0	3	18	6	36	.350	.406
Diaz,Victor	L	.212	52	11	2	0	5	16	1	18	.222	.538
Bats Right	R	.269	52	14	2	0	4	9	0	15	.296	.538
DiFelice,Mike	L	.200	10	2	1	1	0	4	0	1	.182	.500
Bats Right	R	.267	30	8	1	0	0	1	2	11	.353	.300
Dillon,Joe	L	.556	18	10	2	1	0	4	3	4	.636	.778
Bats Right	R	.276	58	16	6	1	0	6	2	10	.300	.414
Dobbs,Greg	L	.214	28	6	0	0	0		1	5	.267	.214
Bats Left	R	.277	296	82	20	4	10	54	27	52	.335	.473
Doumit,Ryan	L	.246	57	14	4	0	0	5	3	16	.317	.316
Bats Both	R	.282	195	55	15	2	9	27	19	43	.347	.518
Drew,J.D.	L	.224	116	26	7	1	2	18	10	35	.285	.353
Bats Left	R	.286	350	100	23	3	9	46	69	65	.400	.446
Drew,Stephen	L	.246	138	34	8	2	1	18	15	32	.318	.355
Bats Left	R	.235	405	95	20	2	11	42	45	68	.311	.375
Duffy,Chris	L	.211	57	12	1	2	1	5	3	13	.262	.351
Bats Left	R	.261	184	48	10	1	2	17	18	30	.329	.359
Dukes,Elijah	L	.260	50	13	1	1	4	7	6	7	.339	.560
Bats Right	R	.164	134	22	2	1	6	14	27	37	.311	.328
Duncan,Chris	L	.213	80	17	5	0	1	13	8	31	.289	.313
Bats Left	R	.271	295	80	15	0	20	57	47	92	.371	.525

Batters vs. Left-Handed and Right-Handed Pitchers

Batter	vs	Avg	AB	H	2B	3B	HR	RBI	BB	SO	OBP	Slg
Duncan,Shelley	L	.303	33	10	1	0	3	10	4	10	.378	.606
Bats Right	R	.220	41	9	0	0	4	7	4	10	.289	.512
Dunn,Adam	L	.239	188	45	8	1	9	29	30	68	.353	.436
Bats Left	R	.278	334	93	19	1	31	77	71	97	.404	.620
Durham,Ray	L	.200	125	25	4	1	6	19	17	24	.294	.392
Bats Both	R	.224	339	76	17	1	5	52	36	51	.296	.324
Dye,Jermaine	L	.292	130	38	9	0	8	22	17	21	.378	.546
Bats Right	R	.241	378	91	25	0	20	56	28	86	.295	.466
Easley,Damion	L	.371	89	33	2	0	6	16	12	17	.446	.596
Bats Right	R	.202	104	21	4	0	4	10	7	18	.282	.356
Eckstein,David	L	.298	131	39	9	0	0	8	7	6	.343	.366
Bats Right	R	.314	303	95	14	0	3	23	17	16	.362	.389
Edmonds,Jim	L	.198	81	16	3	0	3	17	10	23	.286	.346
Bats Left	R	.268	284	76	12	2	9	36	31	52	.336	.419
Eldred,Brad	L	.105	19	2	1	0	0	1	1	8	.150	.158
Bats Right	R	.111	27	3	0	0	2	2	0	8	.111	.333
Ellis,Mark	L	.313	150	47	8	1	11	28	16	20	.384	.600
Bats Right	R	.263	433	114	25	2	8	48	28	74	.318	.386
Ellison,Jason	L	.139	36	5	0	0	0	0	3	11	.225	.139
Bats Right	R	.293	58	17	1	0	1	2	3	16	.328	.362
Ellsbury,Jacoby	L	.346	26	9	2	0	0	7	2	3	.379	.423
Bats Left	R	.356	90	32	5	1	3	11	6	12	.398	.533
Encarnacion,Edwin	L	.284	155	44	8	1	4	21	20	30	.378	.426
Bats Right	R	.291	347	101	17	0	12	55	19	56	.346	.444
Encarnacion,Juan	L	.290	107	31	6	0	3	21	5	15	.325	.430
Bats Right	R	.278	176	49	11	1	6	26	13	28	.323	.455
Ensberg,Morgan	L	.257	105	27	3	0	7	16	14	28	.345	.486
Bats Right	R	.215	177	38	10	0	5	23	24	39	.305	.356
Erstad,Darin	L	.157	83	13	1	1	1	8	5	14	.205	.229
Bats Left	R	.282	227	64	12	0	3	24	23	30	.347	.374
Escobar,Yunel	L	.355	141	50	12	0	1	14	9	16	.409	.461
Bats Right	R	.303	178	54	13	0	4	14	18	28	.367	.444
Esposito,Brian	L	-	0	0	0	0	0	0	0	0	-	-
Bats Right	R	-	0	0	0	0	0	0	0	0	-	-
Estrada,Johnny	L	.313	134	42	7	0	3	17	1	16	.321	.433
Bats Both	R	.263	308	81	18	0	7	37	11	27	.285	.390
Ethier,Andre	L	.279	111	31	10	0	1	16	7	22	.319	.396
Bats Left	R	.286	336	96	22	2	12	48	39	46	.360	.470
Evans,Terry	L	.167	6	1	0	0	1	2	0	0	.167	.667
Bats Right	R	.000	5	0	0	0	0	0	2	4	.286	.000
Everett,Adam	L	.214	56	12	3	0	0	5	6	4	.290	.268
Bats Right	R	.238	164	39	8	1	2	10	8	27	.277	.335
Fahey,Brandon	L	.000	9	0	0	0	0	0	0	2	.000	.000
Bats Left	R	.200	45	9	1	1	0	1	2	7	.234	.267
Fasano,Sal	L	.125	8	1	0	0	0	1	1	3	.222	.125
Bats Right	R	.189	37	7	3	0	1	3	1	16	.231	.351
Feliz,Pedro	L	.257	152	39	9	1	2	14	9	18	.298	.368
Bats Right	R	.252	405	102	19	1	18	58	20	52	.287	.437
Fick,Robert	L	.143	42	6	0	0	1	2	4	15	.217	.214
Bats Left	R	.258	155	40	6	1	1	14	15	27	.333	.329
Fielder,Prince	L	.261	188	49	11	0	10	32	19	37	.355	.479
Bats Left	R	.301	385	116	24	2	40	87	71	84	.414	.686
Fields,Josh	L	.321	106	34	7	0	11	25	9	35	.371	.698
Bats Right	R	.213	267	57	10	1	12	42	26	90	.284	.393
Figgins,Chone	L	.326	92	30	8	2	0	12	10	18	.388	.457
Bats Both	R	.331	350	116	16	4	3	46	41	63	.394	.426
Figueroa,Luis	L	.000	1	0	0	0	0	0	0	0	.000	.000
Bats Both	R	.250	4	1	0	0	0	0	0	0	.250	.250
Finley,Steve	L	.267	15	4	0	0	0	0	0	0	.267	.267
Bats Left	R	.165	79	13	3	0	1	2	8	4	.241	.241
Flores,Jesus	L	.270	89	24	5	0	3	11	10	24	.343	.427
Bats Right	R	.220	91	20	4	0	1	14	4	24	.276	.297
Floyd,Cliff	L	.303	33	10	4	0	0	5	5	6	.395	.424
Bats Left	R	.281	249	70	6	1	9	40	30	41	.370	.422
Fontenot,Mike	L	.212	52	11	3	0	1	6	4	15	.259	.327
Bats Left	R	.297	182	54	9	4	2	23	18	28	.358	.423
Ford,Lew	L	.256	43	11	4	0	1	4	6	9	.347	.419
Bats Right	R	.219	73	16	2	0	2	10	5	15	.296	.329
Fox,Jake	L	.200	10	2	2	0	0	1	1	1	.273	.400
Bats Right	R	.000	4	0	0	0	0	0	0	1	.000	.000
Francisco,Ben	L	.286	7	2	1	0	0	1	0	1	.286	.429
Bats Right	R	.273	55	15	4	0	3	11	3	18	.305	.509
Franco,Julio	L	.250	28	7	1	0	1	5	7	9	.400	.393
Bats Right	R	.210	62	13	2	0	0	11	7	14	.282	.242
Francoeur,Jeff	L	.317	208	66	11	0	8	46	16	33	.367	.486
Bats Right	R	.281	434	122	29	0	11	59	26	96	.323	.424

Batter	vs	Avg	AB	H	2B	3B	HR	RBI	BB	SO	OBP	Slg
Frandsen,Kevin	L	.262	107	28	6	0	4	9	6	5	.301	.430
Bats Right	R	.274	157	43	6	1	1	22	15	19	.350	.344
Freel,Ryan	L	.143	112	16	5	2	1	8	3	19	.172	.250
Bats Right	R	.315	165	52	8	1	2	8	15	28	.392	.412
Fuld,Sam	L	.000	1	0	0	0	0	0	0	0	.000	.000
Bats Left	R	.000	5	0	0	0	0	0	3	3	.375	.000
Furcal,Rafael	L	.313	160	50	8	2	0	16	12	20	.356	.388
Bats Both	R	.254	421	107	15	2	6	31	43	48	.324	.342
Furmaniak,J.J.	L	.250	4	1	1	0	0	1	1	2	.400	.500
Bats Right	R	.154	13	2	0	0	0	0	2	6	.353	.154
Gall,John	L	.000	1	0	0	0	0	0	0	0	.500	.000
Bats Right	R	.000	3	0	0	0	0	0	0	1	.000	.000
Garciaparra,Nomar	L	.213	94	20	5	0	2	9	9	7	.282	.330
Bats Right	R	.303	337	102	12	0	5	50	22	34	.342	.383
Garko,Ryan	L	.310	142	44	9	0	7	17	16	31	.393	.521
Bats Right	R	.281	342	96	20	1	14	44	18	63	.344	.468
Gathright,Joey	L	.282	39	11	1	0	0	5	2	10	.317	.308
Bats Left	R	.312	189	59	7	0	0	14	18	26	.381	.349
German,Esteban	L	.277	148	41	8	3	3	13	19	22	.361	.432
Bats Right	R	.255	200	51	7	3	1	24	24	38	.343	.335
Giambi,Jason	L	.239	71	17	3	0	5	12	4	21	.289	.493
Bats Left	R	.235	183	43	5	0	9	27	36	45	.379	.410
Gibbons,Jay	L	.283	46	13	5	0	0	6	2	10	.320	.391
Bats Left	R	.219	224	49	9	0	6	22	13	42	.263	.339
Gil,Geronimo	L	.000	6	0	0	0	0	0	0	1	.000	.000
Bats Right	R	.125	8	1	0	0	0	0	1	4	.222	.125
Gil,Jerry	L	-	0	0	0	0	0	0	0	0	-	-
Bats Right	R	-	0	0	0	0	0	0	0	0	-	-
Giles,Brian	L	.241	158	38	8	0	2	16	25	22	.346	.329
Bats Left	R	.286	325	93	19	2	11	35	39	39	.368	.458
Giles,Marcus	L	.237	135	32	9	1	1	16	15	21	.311	.341
Bats Right	R	.225	285	64	10	2	3	23	29	61	.301	.305
Glaus,Troy	L	.361	83	30	6	0	9	22	18	24	.476	.759
Bats Right	R	.235	302	71	13	1	11	40	43	78	.334	.394
Gload,Ross	L	.388	49	19	2	1	0	11	1	5	.385	.469
Bats Left	R	.269	271	73	20	2	7	40	15	34	.306	.435
Gomes,Jonny	L	.313	96	30	5	1	5	12	10	32	.376	.542
Bats Right	R	.218	252	55	15	1	12	37	25	94	.302	.429
Gomez,Carlos	L	.254	59	15	3	0	1	6	0	7	.258	.356
Bats Right	R	.212	66	14	0	0	1	6	8	20	.312	.258
Gomez,Chris	L	.292	89	26	3	1	0	6	5	6	.330	.348
Bats Right	R	.301	133	40	9	0	1	15	5	20	.321	.391
Gonzalez,Adrian	L	.263	205	54	13	1	9	32	19	41	.328	.468
Bats Left	R	.290	441	128	33	2	21	68	46	99	.356	.517
Gonzalez,Alberto	L	.333	3	1	0	0	0	0	0	0	.333	.333
Bats Right	R	.000	11	0	0	0	0	1	1	1	.083	.000
Gonzalez,Alex	L	.234	111	26	6	1	2	12	12	26	.315	.360
Bats Right	R	.287	282	81	21	0	14	43	12	49	.329	.511
Gonzalez,Andy	L	.185	81	15	2	0	1	5	13	25	.298	.247
Bats Right	R	.185	108	20	4	0	1	6	12	36	.267	.250
Gonzalez,Luis	L	.317	101	32	4	0	5	17	8	12	.384	.505
Bats Left	R	.267	363	97	19	2	10	51	48	44	.353	.413
Gordon,Alex	L	.217	143	31	12	1	5	21	7	35	.266	.420
Bats Left	R	.258	400	103	24	3	10	39	34	102	.330	.408
Gorneault,Nick	L	.000	2	0	0	0	0	0	1	0	.333	.000
Bats Right	R	.000	2	0	0	0	0	0	0	1	.000	.000
Gotay,Ruben	L	.194	36	7	1	0	0	2	5	13	.286	.222
Bats Both	R	.318	154	49	11	0	4	22	11	29	.367	.468
Graffanino,Tony	L	.231	91	21	2	0	3	11	11	14	.311	.352
Bats Right	R	.243	140	34	6	0	6	19	13	30	.318	.414
Granderson,Curtis	L	.160	119	19	4	0	3	10	8	40	.225	.269
Bats Left	R	.337	493	166	34	23	20	64	44	101	.393	.621
Green,Nick	L	.000	4	0	0	0	0	0	0	2	.000	.000
Bats Right	R	.000	3	0	0	0	0	0	0	1	.000	.000
Green,Shawn	L	.195	118	23	5	0	2	12	9	27	.264	.288
Bats Left	R	.326	328	107	25	1	8	34	28	35	.383	.482
Greene,Khalil	L	.268	157	42	12	1	6	27	16	28	.343	.471
Bats Right	R	.249	454	113	32	2	21	70	16	100	.272	.467
Griffey Jr.,Ken	L	.236	191	45	6	1	9	28	24	37	.317	.419
Bats Left	R	.300	337	101	18	0	21	65	61	62	.402	.540
Griffin,John-Ford	L	-	0	0	0	0	0	0	0	0	-	-
Bats Left	R	.300	10	3	1	0	1	3	3	5	.429	.700
Gross,Gabe	L	.091	11	1	0	0	0	0	4	5	.333	.091
Bats Left	R	.244	172	42	12	2	7	24	21	32	.328	.459
Grudzielanek,Mark	L	.321	140	45	11	2	2	20	10	18	.373	.471
Bats Right	R	.294	313	92	21	1	4	31	13	42	.333	.406

Batters vs. Left-Handed and Right-Handed Pitchers

Batter	vs	Avg	AB	H	2B	3B	HR	RBI	BB	SO	OBP	Slg
Guerrero,Vladimir	L	.321	109	35	10	0	5	19	21	9	.432	.550
Bats Right	R	.325	465	151	35	1	22	106	50	53	.396	.546
Guillen,Carlos	L	.302	116	35	9	1	6	26	13	19	.369	.552
Bats Both	R	.295	448	132	26	8	15	76	42	74	.354	.489
Guillen,Jose	L	.362	138	50	12	1	7	23	15	20	.433	.616
Bats Right	R	.268	455	122	16	1	16	76	26	98	.327	.413
Gutierrez,Franklin	L	.330	94	31	7	1	4	11	6	28	.366	.553
Bats Right	R	.232	177	41	6	1	9	25	15	49	.292	.429
Guzman,Cristian	L	.357	42	15	2	1	0	3	0	6	.357	.452
Bats Both	R	.318	132	42	4	5	2	11	15	15	.387	.470
Guzman,Freddy	L	1.000	1	1	0	0	1	1	0	0	1.000	4.000
Bats Both	R	.000	5	0	0	0	0	0	0	2	.000	.000
Guzman,Joel	L	.125	8	1	0	0	0	1	0	4	.125	.125
Bats Right	R	.276	29	8	1	2	0	3	2	6	.323	.448
Gwynn,Tony	L	.316	19	6	0	0	0	3	1	6	.350	.316
Bats Left	R	.250	104	26	3	2	0	7	11	18	.322	.317
Hafner,Travis	L	.274	197	54	7	1	8	36	36	44	.396	.442
Bats Left	R	.261	348	91	18	1	16	64	66	71	.379	.457
Hairston,Jerry	L	.228	79	18	3	0	1	8	4	9	.262	.304
Bats Right	R	.150	80	12	4	0	2	8	7	15	.237	.275
Hairston,Scott	L	.235	85	20	4	0	3	7	8	13	.301	.388
Bats Right	R	.247	178	44	14	2	8	29	18	42	.318	.483
Hall,Bill	L	.270	148	40	13	0	5	21	15	41	.335	.459
Bats Right	R	.247	304	75	22	0	9	42	25	87	.305	.408
Hall,Toby	L	.288	52	15	3	0	0	2	3	4	.321	.346
Bats Right	R	.141	64	9	1	0	0	1	0	8	.141	.156
Hamilton,Josh	L	.222	72	16	2	0	1	4	8	29	.296	.292
Bats Left	R	.314	226	71	15	2	18	43	25	36	.391	.637
Hammock,Robby	L	.286	21	6	1	0	0	0	1	2	.318	.333
Bats Right	R	.208	24	5	1	0	0	0	2	5	.296	.250
Hanigan,Ryan	L	.000	3	0	0	0	0	0	0	1	.000	.000
Bats Right	R	.429	7	3	1	0	0	2	1	1	.500	.571
Hannahan,Jack	L	.400	35	14	5	0	1	9	2	0	.421	.629
Bats Left	R	.239	109	26	7	0	2	15	19	30	.354	.358
Hardy,J.J.	L	.316	152	48	11	1	9	32	14	14	.371	.579
Bats Right	R	.264	440	116	19	0	17	48	26	59	.306	.423
Harris,Brendan	L	.345	142	49	11	0	3	12	15	27	.411	.486
Bats Right	R	.264	379	100	24	3	9	47	27	69	.317	.414
Harris,Willie	L	.191	47	9	2	0	0	3	6	17	.291	.234
Bats Left	R	.283	297	84	18	8	2	29	34	54	.350	.418
Hart,Corey	L	.331	160	53	10	4	9	25	17	29	.419	.613
Bats Right	R	.278	345	96	23	5	15	56	19	70	.320	.504
Hatteberg,Scott	L	.205	39	8	2	0	1	4	2	6	.244	.333
Bats Left	R	.323	322	104	25	1	9	43	47	29	.411	.491
Hawpe,Brad	L	.214	126	27	4	2	5	22	11	44	.283	.397
Bats Left	R	.315	390	123	29	2	24	94	70	93	.418	.585
Haynes,Nathan	L	.000	2	0	0	0	0	0	0	0	.000	.000
Bats Left	R	.279	43	12	0	1	0	1	3	11	.326	.326
Headley,Chase	L	.167	6	1	0	0	0	0	0	0	.167	.167
Bats Both	R	.250	12	3	1	0	0	0	2	4	.400	.333
Heintz,Chris	L	.313	16	5	0	0	0	1	0	1	.313	.313
Bats Right	R	.225	40	9	0	0	0	6	3	11	.279	.225
Helms,Wes	L	.282	117	33	10	0	3	19	10	26	.346	.444
Bats Right	R	.221	163	36	9	0	2	20	9	36	.261	.313
Helton,Todd	L	.285	165	47	9	0	1	22	28	26	.386	.358
Bats Left	R	.334	392	131	33	2	16	69	88	48	.454	.551
Hermida,Jeremy	L	.292	113	33	5	0	5	16	7	30	.344	.469
Bats Left	R	.297	316	94	27	1	13	47	40	75	.377	.513
Hernandez,Anderson	L	.000	1	0	0	0	0	0	0	1	.000	.000
Bats Both	R	.500	2	1	0	0	0	0	0	0	.500	.500
Hernandez,Luis	L	.300	20	6	1	0	1	3	1	3	.333	.500
Bats Both	R	.286	49	14	1	0	0	4	0	7	.286	.306
Hernandez,Ramon	L	.250	96	24	5	0	4	21	10	13	.327	.427
Bats Right	R	.261	268	70	13	0	5	41	26	46	.334	.366
Hessman,Mike	L	.208	24	5	0	0	0	2	2	11	.269	.208
Bats Right	R	.259	27	7	0	0	4	10	3	6	.323	.704
Hill,Aaron	L	.317	145	46	13	1	7	26	8	29	.351	.566
Bats Right	R	.283	463	131	34	1	10	52	33	73	.328	.425
Hill,Koyie	L	.182	22	4	1	0	0	4	1	4	.208	.227
Bats Both	R	.155	71	11	3	0	2	8	7	14	.238	.282
Hillenbrand,Shea	L	.260	73	19	1	1	1	7	3	4	.286	.342
Bats Right	R	.247	194	48	4	1	3	24	4	26	.264	.325
Hinske,Eric	L	.200	20	4	1	0	1	4	4	7	.360	.400
Bats Left	R	.205	166	34	11	3	5	17	24	47	.311	.398
Holliday,Matt	L	.301	143	43	8	2	9	30	17	27	.384	.573
Bats Right	R	.351	493	173	42	4	27	107	46	99	.412	.617

Batter	vs	Avg	AB	H	2B	3B	HR	RBI	BB	SO	OBP	Slg
Hoover,Paul	L	.667	3	2	0	0	0	0	0	0	.667	.667
Bats Right	R	.200	5	1	0	0	0	0	0	2	.200	.200
Hopper,Norris	L	.351	111	39	6	2	0	4	6	8	.385	.441
Bats Right	R	.316	196	62	8	0	0	10	14	25	.363	.357
House,J.R.	L	.077	13	1	0	0	0	0	0	3	.143	.077
Bats Right	R	.280	25	7	2	0	3	3	1	8	.333	.720
Howard,Ryan	L	.225	209	47	8	0	16	46	32	85	.333	.493
Bats Left	R	.297	320	95	18	0	31	90	75	114	.428	.644
Hu,Chin-Lung	L	.200	10	2	0	1	0	0	0	1	.200	.400
Bats Right	R	.263	19	5	0	0	2	5	0	7	.263	.579
Huber,Justin	L	.100	10	1	0	0	0	0	0	2	.100	.100
Bats Right	R	-	0	0	0	0	0	0	0	0	-	-
Hudson,Orlando	L	.281	135	38	5	3	3	16	12	18	.338	.430
Bats Both	R	.298	382	114	23	6	7	47	58	69	.388	.445
Huff,Aubrey	L	.305	131	40	4	1	3	17	11	24	.359	.420
Bats Left	R	.272	419	114	30	4	12	55	37	63	.330	.449
Hunter,Torii	L	.314	169	53	10	0	10	26	11	25	.356	.550
Bats Right	R	.276	431	119	35	1	18	81	29	76	.326	.487
Iannetta,Chris	L	.204	49	10	1	2	2	10	11	14	.350	.429
Bats Right	R	.223	148	33	7	1	2	17	18	44	.324	.324
Ibanez,Raul	L	.256	160	41	8	1	2	23	8	28	.294	.356
Bats Left	R	.305	413	126	27	4	19	82	45	69	.371	.528
Iguchi,Tadahito	L	.266	143	38	8	2	4	13	22	25	.363	.434
Bats Right	R	.267	322	86	19	2	5	30	35	63	.339	.385
Infante,Omar	L	.281	64	18	3	1	2	10	6	9	.343	.453
Bats Right	R	.265	102	27	3	0	0	7	3	20	.283	.294
Inge,Brandon	L	.333	111	37	10	0	3	20	14	25	.419	.505
Bats Right	R	.209	397	83	15	2	11	51	33	125	.281	.340
Inglett,Joe	L	.000	1	0	0	0	0	0	0	0	.000	.000
Bats Left	R	.750	4	3	0	1	0	2	0	0	.750	1.250
Iwamura,Akinori	L	.323	155	50	8	0	5	12	18	40	.391	.471
Bats Left	R	.268	336	90	13	10	2	22	40	74	.344	.384
Izturis,Cesar	L	.186	86	16	1	0	0	5	5	5	.231	.198
Bats Both	R	.285	228	65	13	2	0	11	14	14	.329	.360
Izturis,Maicer	L	.280	75	21	2	1	1	11	10	11	.365	.373
Bats Both	R	.291	261	76	15	1	5	40	23	28	.344	.414
Jackson,Conor	L	.320	122	39	8	1	6	21	18	10	.408	.549
Bats Right	R	.270	293	79	21	0	9	39	35	37	.351	.433
Jacobs,Mike	L	.290	107	31	4	1	5	13	5	29	.333	.486
Bats Left	R	.257	319	82	23	1	12	41	26	72	.312	.448
Jenkins,Geoff	L	.215	65	14	4	0	3	14	3	19	.282	.415
Bats Left	R	.262	355	93	20	2	18	50	29	97	.326	.482
Jeter,Derek	L	.317	139	44	13	1	2	15	19	24	.409	.468
Bats Right	R	.324	500	162	26	3	10	58	37	76	.382	.448
Jimenez,D'Angelo	L	.200	30	6	1	0	1	3	9	7	.385	.333
Bats Both	R	.264	72	19	6	0	1	7	12	15	.376	.389
Jimerson,Charlton	L	-	0	0	0	0	0	0	0	0	-	-
Bats Right	R	1.000	2	2	0	0	1	1	0	0	1.000	2.500
Johjima,Kenji	L	.327	104	34	11	0	3	14	3	11	.358	.519
Bats Right	R	.276	381	105	18	0	11	47	12	30	.312	.409
Johnson,Ben	L	.214	14	3	0	0	0	0	0	5	.214	.214
Bats Right	R	.154	13	2	1	0	0	1	2	6	.250	.231
Johnson,Dan	L	.234	154	36	7	1	8	23	22	30	.335	.448
Bats Left	R	.237	262	62	13	0	10	39	50	47	.358	.401
Johnson,Kelly	L	.272	158	43	7	4	2	17	22	39	.366	.405
Bats Left	R	.278	363	101	19	6	14	51	57	78	.378	.479
Johnson,Reed	L	.325	77	25	6	2	2	6	5	9	.381	.532
Bats Right	R	.202	198	40	7	0	0	8	11	47	.275	.237
Johnson,Rob	L	-	0	0	0	0	0	0	0	0	-	-
Bats Right	R	.333	3	1	0	0	0	0	0	0	.333	.333
Jones,Adam	L	.310	29	9	0	1	2	4	2	8	.355	.586
Bats Right	R	.194	36	7	2	0	0	0	2	13	.256	.250
Jones,Andruw	L	.225	182	41	8	1	10	33	28	48	.339	.445
Bats Right	R	.221	390	86	19	1	16	61	42	90	.297	.397
Jones,Brandon	L	.500	4	2	1	0	0	2	0	0	.500	.750
Bats Left	R	.067	15	1	0	0	0	2	0	8	.118	.067
Jones,Chipper	L	.274	201	55	12	2	7	28	22	30	.345	.458
Bats Both	R	.378	312	118	30	2	22	74	60	45	.472	.699
Jones,Garrett	L	.077	13	1	1	0	0	0	0	7	.077	.154
Bats Left	R	.234	64	15	1	1	2	5	6	13	.296	.375
Jones,Jacque	L	.295	78	23	5	2	0	12	7	12	.353	.410
Bats Left	R	.283	375	106	28	0	5	54	27	58	.332	.397
Jorgensen,Ryan	L	.143	7	1	0	0	1	2	0	4	.143	.571
Bats Right	R	.250	8	2	0	0	1	4	0	1	.250	.625
Kata,Matt	L	.113	53	6	2	0	1	6	2	13	.161	.208
Bats Both	R	.276	105	29	7	1	2	10	3	20	.303	.419

Batters vs. Left-Handed and Right-Handed Pitchers

Batter	vs	Avg	AB	H	2B	3B	HR	RBI	BB	SO	OBP	Slg
Kearns,Austin	L	.292	137	40	12	1	4	18	25	19	.401	.482
Bats Right	R	.258	450	116	23	0	12	56	46	87	.339	.389
Kelly,Don	L	.000	2	0	0	0	0	0	0	1	.000	.000
Bats Left	R	.160	25	4	0	0	0	0	3	2	.300	.160
Kemp,Matt	L	.390	100	39	5	2	3	17	9	21	.432	.570
Bats Right	R	.318	192	61	7	3	7	25	7	45	.340	.495
Kendall,Jason	L	.198	126	25	5	0	1	10	10	11	.261	.262
Bats Right	R	.259	340	88	15	1	2	31	21	31	.315	.326
Kendrick,Howie	L	.325	80	26	5	1	2	10	3	8	.349	.488
Bats Right	R	.322	258	83	19	1	3	29	6	53	.346	.438
Kennedy,Adam	L	.122	41	5	1	1	0	1	3	9	.200	.195
Bats Left	R	.235	238	56	8	0	3	17	19	24	.296	.307
Kent,Jeff	L	.299	97	29	7	0	5	20	23	16	.424	.526
Bats Right	R	.302	397	120	29	1	15	59	34	45	.362	.494
Keppinger,Jeff	L	.362	69	25	6	1	2	11	5	1	.421	.565
Bats Right	R	.320	172	55	10	1	3	21	19	11	.392	.442
Kielty,Bobby	L	.260	50	13	2	0	0	7	6	14	.333	.300
Bats Both	R	.162	37	6	1	0	1	5	2	12	.220	.270
Kinsler,Ian	L	.339	115	39	7	1	6	18	18	19	.425	.574
Bats Right	R	.239	368	88	15	1	14	43	44	64	.333	.399
Klesko,Ryan	L	.262	65	17	5	1	2	6	5	22	.324	.462
Bats Left	R	.259	297	77	22	2	4	38	41	46	.348	.387
Knott,Jon	L	.000	9	0	0	0	0	1	3	3	.231	.000
Bats Right	R	.600	5	3	0	0	1	3	1	0	.667	1.200
Konerko,Paul	L	.296	152	45	11	0	12	25	22	23	.383	.605
Bats Right	R	.244	397	97	23	0	19	65	56	79	.338	.446
Koshansky,Joe	L	.000	1	0	0	0	0	0	0	0	.000	.000
Bats Left	R	.091	11	1	1	0	0	2	2	4	.214	.182
Kotchman,Casey	L	.315	73	23	6	0	0	12	7	5	.378	.397
Bats Left	R	.292	370	108	31	3	11	56	46	38	.371	.481
Kotsay,Mark	L	.130	46	6	1	0	0	4	3	4	.180	.152
Bats Left	R	.238	160	38	13	0	1	16	16	16	.307	.338
Kouzmanoff,Kevin	L	.356	146	52	12	1	7	30	6	25	.376	.596
Bats Right	R	.240	338	81	18	1	11	44	26	69	.309	.396
Kubel,Jason	L	.236	72	17	4	0	1	8	11	23	.333	.333
Bats Left	R	.280	346	97	27	2	12	57	30	56	.336	.474
LaForest,Pete	L	.667	6	4	0	0	1	3	0	2	.667	1.167
Bats Left	R	.200	30	6	1	0	0	1	7	10	.351	.233
Laird,Gerald	L	.239	109	26	5	0	4	13	9	31	.297	.394
Bats Right	R	.218	298	65	13	3	5	34	21	72	.271	.332
Lamb,Mike	L	.362	47	17	3	0	3	12	6	4	.439	.617
Bats Left	R	.277	264	73	11	2	8	28	30	41	.353	.424
Lane,Jason	L	.151	73	11	2	0	5	18	3	9	.179	.384
Bats Right	R	.194	98	19	3	0	3	9	13	22	.304	.316
Langerhans,Ryan	L	.219	32	7	2	0	2	9	1	11	.242	.469
Bats Left	R	.157	178	28	5	2	4	14	28	70	.276	.275
LaRoche,Adam	L	.299	147	44	14	0	3	30	11	41	.352	.456
Bats Left	R	.262	416	109	28	0	18	58	51	90	.342	.459
LaRoche,Andy	L	.200	25	5	0	0	0	2	4	7	.310	.200
Bats Right	R	.235	68	16	5	0	1	8	16	17	.384	.353
LaRue,Jason	L	.160	50	8	1	0	3	5	3	21	.250	.360
Bats Right	R	.143	119	17	8	0	1	8	14	45	.235	.235
LeCroy,Matthew	L	.125	8	1	0	0	0	0	0	2	.125	.125
Bats Right	R	.167	12	2	1	0	0	0	0	2	.167	.250
Ledee,Ricky	L	-	0	0	0	0	0	0	0	0	-	-
Bats Right	R	.222	36	8	3	0	1	6	5	10	.310	.389
Lee,Carlos	L	.338	148	50	10	0	7	29	16	11	.408	.547
Bats Right	R	.292	479	140	33	1	25	90	37	52	.337	.522
Lee,Derrek	L	.339	124	42	14	0	6	19	17	22	.418	.597
Bats Right	R	.312	443	138	29	1	16	63	54	92	.395	.490
Lewis,Fred	L	.276	29	8	0	1	0	1	1	5	.323	.345
Bats Left	R	.289	128	37	6	1	3	18	18	27	.385	.422
Lieberthal,Mike	L	.167	18	3	1	0	0	0	1	3	.211	.222
Bats Right	R	.254	59	15	1	0	0	1	3	8	.302	.271
Lind,Adam	L	.194	67	13	1	0	2	10	4	12	.243	.299
Bats Left	R	.251	223	56	13	0	9	36	12	53	.289	.430
Linden,Todd	L	.262	65	17	1	0	0	5	7	24	.333	.277
Bats Both	R	.235	119	28	7	1	1	6	12	35	.311	.336
Lo Duca,Paul	L	.341	126	43	8	0	4	21	8	8	.376	.500
Bats Right	R	.245	319	78	10	1	5	33	16	25	.285	.329
Lofton,Kenny	L	.223	94	21	3	0	0	6	10	11	.290	.255
Bats Left	R	.313	396	124	22	6	7	32	46	40	.386	.452
Logan,Nook	L	.305	131	40	10	3	0	7	10	32	.352	.427
Bats Right	R	.237	194	46	8	1	0	14	9	54	.271	.289
Loney,James	L	.319	94	30	5	2	2	13	11	15	.387	.479
Bats Left	R	.336	250	84	13	2	13	54	17	33	.379	.560

Batter	vs	Avg	AB	H	2B	3B	HR	RBI	BB	SO	OBP	Slg
Lopez,Felipe	L	.269	182	49	7	1	4	19	15	33	.335	.385
Bats Both	R	.235	421	99	18	5	5	31	38	76	.296	.337
Lopez,Jose	L	.244	119	29	3	0	3	13	7	13	.285	.345
Bats Right	R	.254	405	103	14	2	8	49	13	51	.284	.358
Lopez,Pedro	L	.125	16	2	0	0	0	0	0	4	.125	.125
Bats Right	R	.207	29	6	2	0	0	0	1	6	.258	.276
Loretta,Mark	L	.317	104	33	5	0	2	12	14	11	.395	.423
Bats Right	R	.278	356	99	18	2	2	29	30	30	.339	.357
Lowell,Mike	L	.323	161	52	14	0	3	33	17	22	.383	.466
Bats Right	R	.325	428	139	23	2	18	87	36	49	.376	.514
Lucy,Donny	L	.500	2	1	0	0	0	0	0	1	.500	.500
Bats Right	R	.154	13	2	0	0	0	0	0	5	.154	.154
Ludwick,Ryan	L	.221	122	27	10	0	3	15	10	32	.307	.377
Bats Right	R	.298	181	54	12	0	11	37	16	40	.362	.547
Lugo,Julio	L	.226	155	35	5	2	3	23	19	24	.309	.342
Bats Right	R	.241	415	100	31	0	5	50	29	58	.289	.352
Luna,Hector	L	.278	18	5	0	0	1	4	1	3	.300	.444
Bats Right	R	.083	24	2	0	0	0	0	1	7	.154	.083
Mabry,John	L	.000	1	0	0	0	0	0	0	1	.000	.000
Bats Left	R	.121	33	4	1	0	1	5	5	9	.237	.242
Macias,Drew	L	-	0	0	0	0	0	0	0	0	-	-
Bats Left	R	-	0	0	0	0	0	0	0	0	-	-
Mackowiak,Rob	L	.283	46	13	2	0	0	4	2	11	.340	.326
Bats Left	R	.259	247	64	12	2	6	34	24	60	.337	.397
Mahar,Kevin	L	.222	9	2	1	0	0	1	0	4	.222	.333
Bats Right	R	.111	9	1	0	0	0	0	0	3	.111	.111
Maldonado,Carlos	L	.250	4	1	0	0	1	1	2	0	.500	1.000
Bats Right	R	.200	20	4	1	0	1	3	3	8	.292	.400
Markakis,Nick	L	.274	197	54	11	2	7	38	12	35	.318	.457
Bats Left	R	.311	440	137	32	1	16	74	49	77	.382	.498
Marte,Andy	L	.278	18	5	0	0	0	1	1	2	.316	.278
Bats Right	R	.154	39	6	4	0	1	7	1	7	.195	.333
Martin,Russell	L	.357	129	46	8	0	8	26	22	18	.458	.605
Bats Right	R	.273	411	112	24	3	11	61	45	71	.347	.426
Martinez,Ramon	L	.200	55	11	2	0	0	13	6	6	.270	.236
Bats Right	R	.189	74	14	2	0	0	14	5	9	.232	.216
Martinez,Victor	L	.289	197	57	12	0	7	34	23	23	.368	.457
Bats Both	R	.307	365	112	28	0	18	80	39	53	.377	.532
Mathis,Jeff	L	.242	33	8	2	0	1	4	3	17	.297	.394
Bats Right	R	.203	138	28	10	0	3	19	12	32	.271	.341
Matsui,Hideki	L	.274	164	45	3	1	8	28	23	27	.363	.451
Bats Left	R	.290	383	111	25	3	17	75	50	46	.368	.504
Matsui,Kaz	L	.271	70	19	3	1	1	6	4	12	.311	.386
Bats Both	R	.291	340	99	21	5	3	31	30	57	.348	.409
Matthews Jr.,Gary	L	.175	120	21	6	0	3	16	15	32	.263	.300
Bats Both	R	.275	396	109	20	3	15	56	40	70	.342	.455
Mauer,Joe	L	.283	138	39	5	0	0	16	15	25	.354	.319
Bats Left	R	.299	268	80	22	3	7	44	42	26	.395	.481
Maxwell,Justin	L	.375	16	6	0	0	2	5	0	5	.375	.750
Bats Right	R	.100	10	1	0	0	0	0	1	3	.182	.100
Maybin,Cameron	L	.000	14	0	0	0	0	0	0	6	.000	.000
Bats Right	R	.200	35	7	3	0	1	2	3	15	.282	.371
McAnulty,Paul	L	.286	14	4	1	0	1	2	1	4	.333	.571
Bats Left	R	.154	26	4	0	0	0	3	2	6	.214	.154
McCann,Brian	L	.264	174	46	10	0	8	37	8	30	.296	.460
Bats Left	R	.273	330	90	28	0	10	55	27	44	.332	.448
McClain,Scott	L	.143	7	1	0	0	0	0	0	2	.143	.143
Bats Right	R	.250	4	1	0	0	0	0	0	0	.250	.250
McDonald,Darnell	L	.000	3	0	0	0	0	0	0	0	.000	.000
Bats Right	R	.143	7	1	0	0	0	0	0	3	.250	.143
McDonald,John	L	.329	85	28	9	1	0	13	3	14	.360	.459
Bats Right	R	.223	242	54	11	1	1	18	8	34	.250	.289
McLouth,Nate	L	.269	67	18	5	0	1	6	10	20	.351	.388
Bats Left	R	.256	262	67	16	3	12	27	34	57	.351	.477
Melhuse,Adam	L	.222	27	6	2	0	1	3	0	6	.222	.407
Bats Both	R	.209	67	14	2	0	0	6	7	20	.293	.239
Melillo,Kevin	L	-	0	0	0	0	0	0	0	0	-	-
Bats Left	R	-	0	0	0	0	0	0	1	0	1.000	-
Mench,Kevin	L	.314	156	49	10	2	8	26	8	10	.343	.558
Bats Right	R	.212	132	28	10	1	0	11	8	11	.261	.303
Metcalf,Travis	L	.237	59	14	5	1	1	5	5	11	.288	.407
Bats Right	R	.265	102	27	7	0	4	16	8	30	.318	.451
Michaels,Jason	L	.287	136	39	6	0	5	28	15	21	.359	.441
Bats Right	R	.252	131	33	5	1	2	11	5	29	.285	.351
Mientkiewicz,Doug	L	.231	26	6	1	0	0	4	3	5	.344	.269
Bats Left	R	.286	140	40	11	0	5	20	13	18	.351	.471

Batters vs. Left-Handed and Right-Handed Pitchers

Batter	vs	Avg	AB	H	2B	3B	HR	RBI	BB	SO	OBP	Slg
Miles,Aaron	L	.286	119	34	4	1	0	10	16	11	.368	.336
Bats Both	R	.292	295	86	12	0	2	22	9	29	.311	.353
Millar,Kevin	L	.250	140	35	3	0	8	18	21	24	.364	.443
Bats Right	R	.256	336	86	23	1	9	45	55	70	.365	.411
Milledge,Lastings	L	.317	60	19	3	1	3	6	7	12	.406	.550
Bats Right	R	.250	124	31	6	0	4	23	6	30	.309	.395
Miller,Corky	L	.250	8	2	0	0	0	2	0	1	.250	.250
Bats Right	R	.263	19	5	2	0	1	2	1	4	.333	.526
Miller,Damian	L	.235	51	12	2	0	1	6	7	11	.322	.333
Bats Both	R	.237	135	32	7	0	3	18	7	28	.286	.356
Mirabelli,Doug	L	.250	16	4	0	0	1	2	2	6	.333	.438
Bats Right	R	.194	98	19	3	0	4	14	9	35	.269	.347
Moeller,Chad	L	.238	21	5	1	0	1	1	0	4	.238	.429
Bats Right	R	.114	35	4	0	0	0	1	0	14	.139	.114
Mohr,Dustan	L	.250	8	2	0	0	1	2	0	3	.250	.625
Bats Right	R	.000	8	0	0	0	0	0	0	0	.000	.000
Molina,Bengie	L	.271	133	36	4	0	6	21	5	16	.295	.436
Bats Right	R	.277	364	101	15	1	13	60	10	37	.300	.431
Molina,Gustavo	L	.000	10	0	0	0	0	0	1	2	.091	.000
Bats Right	R	.176	17	3	1	0	0	1	0	5	.167	.235
Molina,Jose	L	.360	50	18	4	0	1	7	0	10	.353	.500
Bats Right	R	.220	141	31	9	0	0	12	5	33	.247	.284
Molina,Yadier	L	.288	104	30	8	0	2	14	17	13	.388	.423
Bats Right	R	.269	249	67	7	0	4	26	17	30	.319	.345
Monroe,Craig	L	.271	129	35	11	0	6	26	8	28	.309	.496
Bats Right	R	.194	263	51	12	0	6	33	18	79	.247	.308
Montero,Miguel	L	.286	21	6	0	0	0	7	0	3	.304	.286
Bats Left	R	.218	193	42	7	0	10	30	20	32	.291	.409
Moore,Scott	L	.000	4	0	0	0	0	0	0	1	.000	.000
Bats Left	R	.250	48	12	2	0	1	11	1	16	.255	.354
Mora,Melvin	L	.254	114	29	6	1	3	17	18	19	.358	.404
Bats Right	R	.280	353	99	17	0	11	41	29	64	.335	.422
Morales,Jose	L	-	0	0	0	0	0	0	0	0	-	-
Bats Both	R	1.000	3	3	1	0	0	0	0	0	1.000	1.333
Morales,Kendry	L	.241	29	7	2	0	0	1	0	7	.267	.310
Bats Both	R	.311	90	28	8	0	4	14	6	14	.354	.533
Morgan,Nyjer	L	.259	27	7	1	1	1	2	4	6	.355	.481
Bats Left	R	.313	80	25	2	3	0	5	5	13	.360	.413
Morneau,Justin	L	.228	202	46	9	2	8	40	14	36	.283	.411
Bats Left	R	.294	388	114	22	1	23	71	50	55	.373	.534
Morse,Mike	L	.571	7	4	2	0	0	1	0	0	.571	.857
Bats Right	R	.364	11	4	0	0	0	2	1	4	.462	.364
Morton,Colt	L	-	0	0	0	0	0	0	0	0	-	-
Bats Right	R	.000	1	0	0	0	0	0	0	0	.000	.000
Moss,Brandon	L	.250	4	1	0	0	0	0	1	1	.400	.250
Bats Left	R	.286	21	6	2	1	0	1	3	5	.375	.476
Munson,Eric	L	.216	37	8	1	0	1	4	3	6	.275	.324
Bats Left	R	.242	95	23	3	0	3	11	13	9	.327	.368
Murphy,David	L	.409	22	9	3	1	0	2	1	4	.435	.636
Bats Left	R	.325	83	27	9	1	2	12	6	16	.371	.530
Murphy,Donnie	L	.279	43	12	3	0	4	12	3	12	.340	.628
Bats Right	R	.187	75	14	5	0	2	9	7	23	.262	.333
Murphy,Tommy	L	.111	9	1	0	0	0	0	0	1	.111	.111
Bats Both	R	.207	29	6	1	0	0	2	0	8	.233	.241
Murton,Matt	L	.319	91	29	8	0	3	9	10	14	.386	.505
Bats Right	R	.257	144	37	5	0	5	13	16	25	.331	.396
Myrow,Brian	L	-	0	0	0	0	0	0	0	0	-	-
Bats Left	R	.100	10	1	1	0	0	1	1	4	.250	.200
Nady,Xavier	L	.295	95	28	5	1	3	16	6	21	.356	.463
Bats Right	R	.274	336	92	18	0	17	56	17	80	.322	.479
Napoli,Mike	L	.291	55	16	3	0	2	6	7	11	.373	.455
Bats Right	R	.232	164	38	8	1	8	28	26	52	.344	.439
Navarro,Dioner	L	.226	93	21	5	0	5	10	7	15	.277	.441
Bats Both	R	.227	295	67	14	2	4	34	26	52	.288	.329
Newhan,David	L	.000	2	0	0	0	0	0	0	0	.000	.000
Bats Left	R	.208	72	15	1	1	1	6	8	19	.296	.292
Niekro,Lance	L	.167	12	2	0	0	0	0	1	3	.231	.167
Bats Right	R	.200	5	1	0	0	0	0	0	2	.200	.200
Nieves,Wil	L	.200	15	3	1	0	0	2	0	1	.200	.267
Bats Right	R	.152	46	7	3	0	0	6	2	8	.188	.217
Nix,Laynce	L	.000	3	0	0	0	0	0	0	2	.000	.000
Bats Left	R	.000	9	0	0	0	0	0	0	2	.000	.000
Nixon,Trot	L	.224	49	11	3	0	0	8	5	15	.286	.286
Bats Left	R	.256	258	66	14	0	3	23	39	44	.352	.345
Norton,Greg	L	.174	23	4	2	0	0	2	3	9	.269	.261
Bats Both	R	.251	179	45	7	0	4	21	34	46	.369	.358
Nunez,Abraham	L	.284	74	21	3	1	0	4	7	13	.354	.351
Bats Both	R	.213	178	38	7	0	0	12	23	35	.303	.253
Ojeda,Augie	L	.250	48	12	2	1	0	5	5	6	.315	.333
Bats Both	R	.292	65	19	0	1	1	7	10	7	.382	.369
Olivo,Miguel	L	.295	95	28	8	1	2	13	7	23	.343	.463
Bats Right	R	.221	357	79	12	3	14	47	7	100	.240	.389
Olmedo,Ray	L	.000	6	0	0	0	0	0	0	0	.000	.000
Bats Both	R	.244	45	11	4	0	0	1	2	9	.277	.333
Ordonez,Magglio	L	.410	122	50	13	0	8	30	24	15	.500	.713
Bats Right	R	.351	473	166	41	0	20	109	52	64	.415	.564
Orr,Pete	L	.000	8	0	0	0	0	0	1	2	.111	.000
Bats Left	R	.228	57	13	1	0	0	2	2	12	.254	.246
Ortiz,David	L	.308	182	56	13	0	5	33	23	34	.390	.462
Bats Left	R	.343	367	126	39	1	30	84	88	69	.470	.700
Ortmeier,Dan	L	.257	70	18	3	2	4	7	3	16	.297	.529
Bats Both	R	.310	87	27	4	2	2	9	4	25	.333	.471
Overbay,Lyle	L	.287	108	31	6	1	4	14	5	24	.322	.472
Bats Left	R	.224	317	71	24	1	6	30	42	54	.313	.363
Owens,Jerry	L	.235	68	16	1	1	0	4	7	13	.316	.279
Bats Left	R	.274	288	79	8	1	1	13	20	50	.326	.319
Ozuna,Pablo	L	.256	39	10	3	0	0	0	0	4	.256	.333
Bats Right	R	.231	39	9	0	0	0	3	3	5	.302	.231
Pagan,Angel	L	.236	72	17	6	0	4	12	4	15	.269	.486
Bats Both	R	.289	76	22	4	2	0	9	6	17	.341	.395
Palmeiro,Orlando	L	.200	5	1	0	0	0	0	2	0	.429	.200
Bats Left	R	.235	98	23	3	0	0	6	14	8	.336	.265
Patterson,Corey	L	.310	142	44	8	0	4	20	6	11	.344	.451
Bats Left	R	.251	319	80	18	2	4	25	15	54	.286	.357
Patterson,Eric	L	-	0	0	0	0	0	0	0	0	-	-
Bats Right	R	.250	8	2	1	0	0	0	0	3	.250	.375
Paul,Josh	L	.242	33	8	1	0	1	5	1	10	.265	.364
Bats Right	R	.167	72	12	2	0	0	4	5	20	.221	.194
Paulino,Ronny	L	.407	108	44	5	0	5	17	10	10	.462	.593
Bats Right	R	.218	349	76	20	0	6	38	23	69	.267	.327
Payton,Jay	L	.285	123	35	8	0	3	11	11	9	.353	.423
Bats Right	R	.244	311	76	13	5	4	47	11	33	.267	.357
Pearce,Steve	L	.429	14	6	2	0	0	0	1	4	.429	.571
Bats Right	R	.259	54	14	3	1	0	6	5	11	.322	.352
Pedroia,Dustin	L	.348	164	57	8	0	3	21	18	10	.418	.451
Bats Right	R	.303	356	108	31	1	5	29	29	32	.362	.438
Pena,Brayan	L	.222	18	4	0	0	1	2	0	2	.222	.389
Bats Both	R	.200	15	3	0	0	0	1	0	1	.200	.200
Pena,Carlos	L	.271	133	36	5	1	11	39	22	39	.381	.571
Bats Left	R	.286	357	102	24	0	35	82	81	103	.421	.647
Pena,Tony F	L	.271	133	36	6	1	1	10	2	19	.285	.353
Bats Right	R	.266	376	100	19	6	1	37	8	59	.284	.356
Pena,Wily Mo	L	.330	112	37	7	1	4	16	10	36	.395	.518
Bats Right	R	.203	177	36	6	0	9	23	12	58	.269	.390
Pence,Hunter	L	.354	99	35	5	3	4	16	9	12	.407	.586
Bats Right	R	.314	357	112	25	6	13	53	17	83	.346	.527
Peralta,Jhonny	L	.275	142	39	7	0	6	15	20	38	.370	.451
Bats Right	R	.269	432	116	20	1	15	57	41	108	.331	.424
Perez,Neifi	L	.217	23	5	1	0	1	4	1	4	.250	.391
Bats Both	R	.146	41	6	2	0	0	2	3	4	.205	.195
Perez,Timo	L	.429	7	3	0	1	0	1	0	2	.429	.714
Bats Left	R	.386	83	32	9	1	0	12	6	4	.427	.518
Phelps,Josh	L	.314	86	27	4	0	4	13	9	17	.392	.500
Bats Right	R	.296	71	21	2	2	3	18	11	25	.407	.507
Phillips,Andy	L	.280	50	14	3	0	0	9	3	13	.315	.340
Bats Right	R	.296	135	40	4	1	2	16	9	13	.347	.385
Phillips,Brandon	L	.341	208	71	8	1	15	32	12	27	.378	.606
Bats Right	R	.262	442	116	18	5	15	62	21	82	.310	.428
Phillips,Jason	L	.191	47	9	4	0	0	5	2	7	.240	.277
Bats Right	R	.216	97	21	3	0	1	7	8	14	.283	.278
Phillips,Paul	L	.000	5	0	0	0	0	1	1	0	.167	.000
Bats Right	R	.222	9	2	1	0	0	0	1	1	.222	.333
Piazza,Mike	L	.292	89	26	7	0	1	13	7	20	.344	.404
Bats Right	R	.268	220	59	10	1	7	31	11	41	.300	.418
Pie,Felix	L	.111	36	4	0	0	0	4	2	9	.158	.111
Bats Left	R	.241	141	34	9	3	2	16	12	34	.299	.390
Pierre,Juan	L	.274	190	52	6	0	0	12	11	10	.315	.305
Bats Left	R	.301	478	144	18	8	0	29	22	27	.338	.372
Pierzynski,A.J.	L	.252	107	27	3	0	5	13	6	17	.296	.421
Bats Left	R	.266	365	97	21	0	9	37	19	49	.313	.397
Podsednik,Scott	L	.279	61	17	3	2	0	1	8	11	.380	.393
Bats Left	R	.229	153	35	10	2	2	10	5	25	.263	.359

Batters vs. Left-Handed and Right-Handed Pitchers

Batter	vs	Avg	AB	H	2B	3B	HR	RBI	BB	SO	OBP	Slg
Polanco,Placido	L	.326	144	47	7	1	3	10	6	7	.362	.451
Bats Right	R	.345	443	153	29	2	6	57	31	23	.396	.460
Posada,Jorge	L	.331	145	48	9	1	6	28	21	40	.411	.531
Bats Both	R	.341	361	123	33	0	14	62	53	58	.432	.548
Prado,Martin	L	.211	38	8	2	0	0	2	1	3	.231	.263
Bats Right	R	.429	21	9	1	0	0	0	2	3	.478	.476
Pujols,Albert	L	.367	150	55	14	0	9	21	39	16	.500	.640
Bats Right	R	.313	415	130	24	1	23	82	60	42	.400	.542
Punto,Nick	L	.175	154	27	6	2	0	7	14	22	.243	.240
Bats Both	R	.226	318	72	12	2	1	18	41	68	.313	.286
Putnam,Danny	L	.222	9	2	0	0	1	2	1	4	.300	.556
Bats Left	R	.211	19	4	0	0	0	0	2	7	.286	.211
Quentin,Carlos	L	.172	64	11	3	0	2	8	7	16	.276	.313
Bats Right	R	.230	165	38	13	0	3	23	11	38	.306	.364
Quinlan,Robb	L	.269	119	32	7	0	2	14	8	17	.313	.378
Bats Right	R	.203	59	12	2	0	1	7	6	10	.288	.288
Quintanilla,Omar	L	.100	10	1	0	0	0	0	1	3	.182	.100
Bats Left	R	.250	60	15	4	0	0	5	4	12	.297	.317
Quintero,Humberto	L	.211	19	4	1	0	0	0	0	4	.250	.263
Bats Right	R	.235	34	8	1	0	0	1	2	9	.297	.265
Quiroz,Guillermo	L	.500	2	1	1	0	0	1	1	0	.667	1.000
Bats Right	R	.375	8	3	0	0	0	1	0	2	.375	.375
Rabe,Josh	L	.200	20	4	0	0	0	0	0	4	.200	.200
Bats Right	R	.182	11	2	0	0	0	2	0	3	.182	.182
Rabelo,Mike	L	.276	29	8	3	0	0	6	1	1	.323	.379
Bats Both	R	.252	139	35	7	2	1	12	5	40	.295	.353
Raburn,Ryan	L	.259	58	15	7	0	1	9	6	14	.328	.431
Bats Right	R	.338	80	27	5	2	3	18	2	19	.349	.563
Ramirez,Aramis	L	.395	114	45	6	0	12	31	11	12	.457	.763
Bats Right	R	.286	392	112	29	4	14	70	32	54	.339	.487
Ramirez,Hanley	L	.399	148	59	13	4	8	27	14	11	.451	.703
Bats Right	R	.312	491	153	35	2	21	54	38	84	.366	.519
Ramirez,Manny	L	.344	128	44	8	0	9	22	33	26	.478	.617
Bats Right	R	.279	355	99	25	1	11	66	38	66	.353	.448
Ransom,Cody	L	.333	9	3	0	0	1	3	0	1	.333	.667
Bats Right	R	.192	26	5	2	0	0	0	9	8	.432	.269
Redman,Tike	L	.133	30	4	0	1	0	1	1	5	.156	.200
Bats Left	R	.373	102	38	9	1	2	15	4	13	.396	.539
Redmond,Mike	L	.330	88	29	7	0	1	12	11	3	.410	.443
Bats Right	R	.277	184	51	6	0	0	26	7	20	.313	.310
Reed,Eric	L	.000	3	0	0	0	0	0	0	2	.000	.000
Bats Left	R	.118	17	2	0	0	0	0	1	4	.167	.118
Reed,Jeremy	L	-	0	0	0	0	0	0	0	0	-	-
Bats Left	R	.176	17	3	0	1	0	0	0	3	.176	.294
Relaford,Desi	L	.100	10	1	0	0	0	0	1	2	.182	.100
Bats Both	R	.125	16	2	0	0	0	1	1	4	.176	.125
Renteria,Edgar	L	.349	175	61	12	0	5	23	19	31	.415	.503
Bats Right	R	.323	319	103	18	1	7	34	27	46	.376	.451
Restovich,Mike	L	.045	22	1	0	0	0	1	1	7	.087	.045
Bats Right	R	.500	6	3	1	0	0	0	1	1	.500	.667
Reyes,Jose	L	.318	192	61	13	2	1	12	17	15	.373	.422
Bats Both	R	.266	489	130	23	10	11	45	60	63	.347	.421
Reynolds,Mark	L	.278	108	30	4	1	5	17	12	33	.347	.472
Bats Right	R	.279	258	72	16	3	12	45	25	96	.349	.504
Richar,Danny	L	.205	39	8	1	0	2	6	6	10	.311	.385
Bats Left	R	.236	148	35	8	3	4	9	10	23	.283	.412
Riggans,Shawn	L	1.000	1	1	0	0	0	2	0	0	1.000	1.000
Bats Right	R	.000	9	0	0	0	0	0	0	1	.000	.000
Rios,Alex	L	.345	145	50	17	1	6	26	20	18	.422	.600
Bats Right	R	.283	498	141	26	6	18	59	35	85	.334	.468
Rivas,Luis	L	.667	3	2	0	0	1	3	0	0	.667	1.667
Bats Right	R	.125	8	1	0	1	0	1	0	0	.125	.375
Rivera,Juan	L	.276	29	8	0	0	2	6	0	3	.276	.483
Bats Right	R	.286	14	4	1	0	0	2	1	1	.333	.357
Rivera,Mike	L	.500	2	1	0	0	1	2	0	0	.500	2.000
Bats Right	R	.182	11	2	0	0	1	1	1	3	.250	.455
Roberson,Chris	L	.111	9	1	0	0	0	0	0	1	.111	.111
Bats Both	R	.368	19	7	0	0	0	1	1	3	.400	.368
Roberts,Brian	L	.268	179	48	10	0	1	9	35	35	.386	.341
Bats Both	R	.299	442	132	32	5	11	48	54	64	.373	.468
Roberts,Dave	L	.156	77	12	0	1	0	1	7	22	.226	.182
Bats Left	R	.285	319	91	17	8	2	22	35	44	.356	.408
Roberts,Ryan	L	.000	3	0	0	0	0	0	2	3	.400	.000
Bats Right	R	.100	10	1	0	0	0	0	0	4	.182	.100
Robles,Oscar	L	.333	3	1	0	0	0	1	0	0	.333	.333
Bats Left	R	.217	23	5	0	0	0	1	2	4	.280	.217

Batter	vs	Avg	AB	H	2B	3B	HR	RBI	BB	SO	OBP	Slg
Rodriguez,Alex	L	.272	136	37	14	0	7	25	36	22	.432	.529
Bats Right	R	.327	447	146	17	0	47	131	59	98	.419	.680
Rodriguez,Guillermo	L	.269	26	7	1	0	0	2	4	5	.367	.308
Bats Right	R	.246	61	15	5	0	1	12	6	12	.309	.377
Rodriguez,Ivan	L	.302	126	38	13	1	1	11	0	20	.302	.444
Bats Right	R	.274	376	103	18	2	10	52	9	76	.291	.412
Rodriguez,Luis	L	.226	31	7	0	0	0	3	4	4	.314	.226
Bats Both	R	.218	124	27	5	1	2	9	8	10	.272	.323
Rolen,Scott	L	.204	103	21	5	0	2	15	13	17	.306	.311
Bats Right	R	.287	289	83	19	2	6	43	24	39	.341	.429
Rollins,Jimmy	L	.321	212	68	16	2	9	25	16	16	.374	.542
Bats Both	R	.286	504	144	22	18	21	69	33	69	.331	.526
Ross,Cody	L	.385	65	25	5	0	6	23	10	7	.474	.738
Bats Right	R	.306	108	33	14	0	6	16	10	31	.372	.602
Ross,Dave	L	.248	117	29	5	0	7	14	8	32	.291	.470
Bats Right	R	.175	194	34	5	0	10	25	22	60	.259	.356
Rottino,Vinny	L	.500	4	2	1	0	0	3	0	1	.500	.750
Bats Right	R	.000	5	0	0	0	0	0	0	0	.000	.000
Rouse,Mike	L	.000	11	0	0	0	0	0	0	6	.000	.000
Bats Left	R	.143	56	8	1	0	0	4	7	14	.234	.161
Rowand,Aaron	L	.315	184	58	18	0	8	30	15	43	.374	.543
Bats Right	R	.306	428	131	27	0	19	59	32	76	.374	.502
Ruggiano,Justin	L	-	0	0	0	0	0	0	0	0	-	-
Bats Right	R	.214	14	3	0	0	0	3	1	5	.267	.214
Ruiz,Carlos	L	.189	90	17	6	1	1	12	9	7	.265	.311
Bats Right	R	.282	284	80	23	1	5	42	33	42	.363	.423
Ryan,Brendan	L	.354	79	28	2	0	2	5	7	6	.407	.456
Bats Right	R	.238	101	24	7	0	2	7	8	13	.300	.366
Sadler,Donnie	L	-	0	0	0	0	0	0	0	0	-	-
Bats Right	R	.000	1	0	0	0	0	0	0	0	.000	.000
Saenz,Olmedo	L	.170	47	8	1	0	3	5	10	6	.310	.383
Bats Right	R	.206	63	13	4	0	1	13	6	19	.284	.317
Salazar,Jeff	L	.300	10	3	1	0	0	2	0	2	.300	.400
Bats Left	R	.274	84	23	5	1	1	8	9	17	.344	.393
Saltalamacchia,J.	L	.226	115	26	3	0	4	9	7	28	.268	.357
Bats Both	R	.290	193	56	10	1	7	24	12	47	.335	.461
Sammons,Clint	L	1.000	1	1	0	0	0	0	0	0	1.000	2.000
Bats Right	R	.500	2	1	0	0	0	0	0	0	.500	.500
Sanchez,Freddy	L	.364	162	59	16	1	4	20	12	12	.407	.549
Bats Right	R	.282	440	124	26	3	7	61	20	64	.319	.402
Sanders,Reggie	L	.346	26	9	3	0	1	6	3	5	.414	.577
Bats Right	R	.298	47	14	4	0	1	5	8	10	.411	.447
Santiago,Ramon	L	.300	10	3	2	1	0	0	1	2	.417	.700
Bats Both	R	.281	57	16	3	0	0	7	0	8	.305	.333
Sardinha,Bronson	L	.500	2	1	0	0	0	0	0	0	.500	.500
Bats Left	R	.286	7	2	0	0	0	2	2	1	.400	.286
Schierholtz,Nate	L	.500	18	9	1	1	0	1	0	3	.500	.667
Bats Left	R	.266	94	25	4	2	0	9	2	16	.283	.351
Schneider,Brian	L	.212	113	24	6	1	1	17	21	21	.326	.310
Bats Left	R	.244	295	72	15	0	5	37	35	35	.325	.346
Schumaker,Skip	L	.375	24	9	0	0	0	5	4	4	.464	.375
Bats Left	R	.327	153	50	12	2	2	14	4	16	.340	.471
Scott,Luke	L	.271	59	16	4	0	5	15	7	18	.358	.492
Bats Left	R	.252	310	78	24	5	15	49	46	77	.349	.506
Scutaro,Marco	L	.309	81	25	2	0	3	12	15	13	.417	.444
Bats Right	R	.245	257	63	11	0	4	29	20	27	.302	.335
Sexson,Richie	L	.238	105	25	7	0	4	15	15	25	.333	.419
Bats Right	R	.195	329	64	14	0	17	48	36	75	.283	.392
Shealy,Ryan	L	.125	48	6	0	0	0	2	4	17	.208	.125
Bats Right	R	.258	124	32	6	0	3	19	9	36	.316	.379
Sheffield,Gary	L	.245	110	27	4	1	6	22	21	15	.368	.464
Bats Right	R	.271	384	104	16	0	19	53	63	56	.380	.461
Shoppach,Kelly	L	.265	34	9	1	0	5	11	6	11	.390	.735
Bats Right	R	.260	127	33	12	0	2	19	5	45	.286	.402
Sizemore,Grady	L	.284	208	59	8	2	6	30	28	56	.384	.428
Bats Left	R	.274	420	115	26	3	18	48	73	99	.394	.479
Sledge,Terrmel	L	.111	27	3	3	0	0	5	4	11	.242	.222
Bats Left	R	.225	173	39	6	0	7	18	23	49	.322	.382
Smith,Jason	L	.067	15	1	0	0	0	0	1	8	.125	.067
Bats Left	R	.214	126	27	3	2	6	18	5	45	.248	.413
Smith,Seth	L	-	0	0	0	0	0	0	0	0	-	-
Bats Left	R	.625	8	5	0	0	0	0	0	1	.625	.875
Snelling,Chris	L	.235	17	4	0	0	0	0	2	4	.381	.235
Bats Left	R	.250	52	13	1	1	1	6	10	13	.400	.365
Snyder,Chris	L	.316	117	37	10	0	4	23	16	19	.407	.504
Bats Right	R	.215	209	45	10	0	9	24	24	48	.306	.392

Batters vs. Left-Handed and Right-Handed Pitchers

Batter	vs	Avg	AB	H	2B	3B	HR	RBI	BB	SO	OBP	Slg
Soriano,Alfonso	L	.254	126	32	5	1	9	16	9	30	.301	.524
Bats Right	R	.311	453	141	37	4	24	54	22	100	.347	.570
Sosa,Sammy	L	.328	119	39	13	0	7	37	17	29	.410	.613
Bats Right	R	.222	293	65	11	1	14	55	17	83	.267	.410
Soto,Geovany	L	.444	27	12	2	0	1	5	2	5	.467	.630
Bats Right	R	.333	27	9	4	0	2	3	3	9	.400	.704
Spiezio,Scott	L	.310	71	22	6	0	1	7	9	6	.395	.437
Bats Both	R	.250	152	38	8	0	3	24	18	34	.335	.362
Spilborghs,Ryan	L	.356	87	31	5	0	5	22	12	7	.426	.586
Bats Right	R	.271	177	48	9	1	6	29	16	38	.332	.435
Stairs,Matt	L	.289	45	13	6	0	0	11	8	12	.396	.422
Bats Left	R	.288	312	90	22	1	21	53	36	54	.364	.567
Stansberry,Craig	L	.333	3	1	0	0	0	0	0	2	.333	.333
Bats Right	R	.250	4	1	0	0	0	1	0	1	.400	.250
Stern,Adam	L	-	0	0	0	0	0	0	0	0	-	-
Bats Left	R	-	0	0	0	0	0	0	0	0	-	-
Stewart,Chris	L	.400	5	2	2	0	0	2	1	0	.500	.800
Bats Right	R	.219	32	7	0	0	0	1	2	6	.265	.219
Stewart,Ian	L	.100	10	1	1	0	0	0	0	4	.182	.200
Bats Left	R	.242	33	8	3	0	1	9	1	13	.286	.424
Stewart,Shannon	L	.269	167	45	4	0	4	15	17	16	.333	.365
Bats Right	R	.298	409	122	18	1	8	33	30	44	.350	.406
Stinnett,Kelly	L	.105	19	2	0	0	0	0	1	6	.150	.105
Bats Right	R	.175	63	11	3	0	1	5	4	16	.224	.270
Stocker,Mel	L	.000	2	0	0	0	0	0	0	0	.000	.000
Bats Left	R	.000	1	0	0	0	0	0	0	0	.000	.000
Sullivan,Cory	L	.353	17	6	0	0	0	1	1	3	.389	.353
Bats Left	R	.276	123	34	6	1	2	13	8	22	.328	.390
Suzuki,Ichiro	L	.331	172	57	6	2	1	10	13	17	.380	.407
Bats Left	R	.358	506	181	16	5	5	58	36	60	.402	.439
Suzuki,Kurt	L	.151	53	8	3	0	3	12	7	10	.246	.377
Bats Right	R	.281	160	45	10	0	4	27	17	29	.353	.419
Sweeney,Mark	L	.250	12	3	0	0	0	3	0	2	.250	.250
Bats Left	R	.261	111	29	9	0	2	10	14	27	.359	.396
Sweeney,Mike	L	.301	83	25	6	1	2	13	6	6	.352	.470
Bats Right	R	.242	182	44	9	0	5	25	11	23	.298	.374
Sweeney,Ryan	L	.167	6	1	1	0	0	0	0	1	.167	.333
Bats Left	R	.205	39	8	2	0	1	5	4	4	.279	.333
Swisher,Nick	L	.291	151	44	8	0	6	22	42	30	.458	.464
Bats Both	R	.250	388	97	28	1	16	56	58	101	.348	.451
Taguchi,So	L	.314	159	50	6	0	2	19	11	15	.370	.390
Bats Right	R	.264	148	39	9	0	1	11	12	17	.329	.345
Taveras,Willy	L	.371	89	33	4	2	0	7	7	10	.417	.461
Bats Right	R	.304	283	86	9	0	2	17	14	45	.351	.357
Teahen,Mark	L	.255	157	40	6	4	0	12	14	41	.328	.344
Bats Left	R	.297	387	115	25	4	7	48	41	86	.363	.437
Teixeira,Mark	L	.357	154	55	14	0	6	36	21	33	.435	.565
Bats Both	R	.282	340	96	19	2	24	69	51	79	.384	.562
Tejada,Miguel	L	.323	124	40	8	0	5	18	15	13	.404	.508
Bats Right	R	.287	390	112	11	1	13	63	26	42	.342	.421
Terrero,Luis	L	.196	51	10	0	0	3	4	8	18	.349	.373
Bats Right	R	.258	66	17	2	0	2	8	4	17	.347	.379
Thames,Marcus	L	.310	87	27	9	0	5	17	4	20	.341	.586
Bats Right	R	.209	182	38	6	0	13	37	9	52	.249	.456
Theriot,Ryan	L	.286	126	36	11	0	3	10	13	9	.353	.444
Bats Right	R	.260	411	107	19	2	0	35	36	41	.318	.316
Thigpen,Curtis	L	.256	43	11	1	0	0	6	4	6	.319	.279
Bats Right	R	.224	58	13	4	0	0	5	4	11	.274	.293
Thomas,Frank	L	.336	122	41	9	0	9	32	21	24	.431	.631
Bats Right	R	.259	409	106	21	0	17	63	60	70	.360	.435
Thome,Jim	L	.196	143	28	4	0	6	23	23	47	.314	.350
Bats Left	R	.315	289	91	15	0	29	73	72	87	.455	.668
Thompson,Kevin	L	.176	17	3	1	0	0	3	2	5	.263	.235
Bats Right	R	.111	18	2	2	0	0	0	1	8	.158	.222
Thorman,Scott	L	.176	68	12	3	0	0	4	4	19	.227	.221
Bats Left	R	.228	219	50	15	0	11	32	10	51	.268	.447
Torrealba,Yorvit	L	.264	87	23	5	0	1	4	11	16	.354	.356
Bats Right	R	.252	309	78	17	1	7	43	23	57	.314	.382
Towles,J.R.	L	.333	9	3	0	0	0	1	1	0	.400	.333
Bats Right	R	.387	31	12	5	0	1	11	2	1	.441	.645
Tracy,Chad	L	.174	46	8	1	1	0	2	0	13	.174	.239
Bats Left	R	.287	181	52	17	1	7	33	29	30	.383	.508
Treanor,Matt	L	.245	53	13	1	0	1	1	8	13	.365	.321
Bats Right	R	.280	118	33	6	1	3	18	11	16	.353	.424
Tulowitzki,Troy	L	.333	138	46	8	1	6	21	15	21	.396	.536
Bats Right	R	.278	471	131	25	4	18	78	42	109	.348	.463

Batter	vs	Avg	AB	H	2B	3B	HR	RBI	BB	SO	OBP	Slg
Tyner,Jason	L	.233	60	14	3	0	0	3	5	6	.324	.283
Bats Left	R	.299	244	73	11	2	1	19	11	20	.333	.373
Uggla,Dan	L	.245	139	34	12	0	8	22	16	35	.325	.504
Bats Right	R	.245	493	121	37	3	23	66	52	132	.326	.473
Upton,B.J.	L	.281	121	34	4	0	8	24	22	36	.389	.512
Bats Right	R	.306	353	108	21	1	16	58	43	118	.385	.507
Upton,Justin	L	.200	40	8	2	2	1	3	4	11	.273	.425
Bats Right	R	.230	100	23	6	1	1	8	7	26	.287	.340
Uribe,Juan	L	.257	140	36	5	1	7	22	8	28	.300	.457
Bats Right	R	.225	373	84	13	1	13	46	26	84	.278	.370
Utley,Chase	L	.318	192	61	20	0	5	39	22	46	.427	.500
Bats Left	R	.340	338	115	28	5	17	64	28	43	.400	.604
Valdez,Wilson	L	.174	23	4	1	1	0	2	2	2	.240	.304
Bats Right	R	.235	51	12	1	0	0	5	2	10	.273	.255
Valentin,Javier	L	.290	31	9	6	0	0	7	4	3	.371	.484
Bats Both	R	.274	212	58	15	0	2	27	15	22	.322	.373
Valentin,Jose	L	.275	51	14	3	0	1	8	3	4	.315	.392
Bats Both	R	.226	115	26	8	1	2	10	12	24	.297	.365
Varitek,Jason	L	.264	121	32	3	0	5	20	22	29	.388	.413
Bats Both	R	.252	314	79	12	3	12	48	49	93	.358	.424
Vazquez,Ramon	L	.184	76	14	3	0	0	2	7	22	.259	.224
Bats Left	R	.246	224	55	10	3	8	26	22	50	.315	.424
Velandia,Jorge	L	.000	7	0	0	0	0	1	3	3	.300	.000
Bats Right	R	.372	43	16	4	0	2	10	5	14	.449	.605
Velez,Eugenio	L	.000	1	0	0	0	0	0	0	1	.000	.000
Bats Both	R	.300	10	3	0	2	0	2	2	2	.417	.700
Victorino,Shane	L	.291	134	39	10	1	5	15	11	21	.364	.493
Bats Both	R	.276	322	89	13	2	7	31	26	41	.339	.394
Vidro,Jose	L	.328	137	45	7	0	0	14	13	12	.382	.380
Bats Both	R	.309	411	127	19	0	6	45	50	45	.380	.399
Vizquel,Omar	L	.243	136	33	4	0	2	16	9	14	.290	.316
Bats Both	R	.247	377	93	14	3	2	35	35	34	.310	.316
Votto,Joey	L	.269	26	7	2	0	0	1	1	2	.296	.346
Bats Left	R	.345	58	20	5	0	4	16	4	13	.387	.638
Walker,Todd	L	.188	16	3	0	0	0	0	2	2	.278	.188
Bats Left	R	.313	32	10	1	0	0	4	0	2	.294	.344
Ward,Daryle	L	.250	8	2	1	0	0	0	2	1	.400	.375
Bats Left	R	.333	102	34	12	0	3	19	20	22	.439	.539
Watkins,Tommy	L	.357	14	5	0	0	0	0	2	1	.438	.357
Bats Right	R	.357	14	5	0	0	0	0	2	3	.438	.357
Watson,Brandon	L	.000	2	0	0	0	0	0	0	0	.000	.000
Bats Left	R	.313	16	5	1	0	0	2	1	1	.353	.375
Weeks,Rickie	L	.258	124	32	9	0	4	9	30	28	.421	.427
Bats Right	R	.225	285	64	12	6	12	27	48	88	.352	.435
Wells,Vernon	L	.311	132	41	7	0	4	18	15	16	.380	.455
Bats Right	R	.226	452	102	29	4	12	62	34	73	.280	.387
Werth,Jayson	L	.375	88	33	4	0	5	22	15	15	.467	.591
Bats Right	R	.257	167	43	7	3	3	27	29	58	.371	.389
White,Rondell	L	.143	42	6	2	0	2	7	3	8	.217	.333
Bats Right	R	.194	67	13	2	0	2	13	3	11	.247	.313
Wigginton,Ty	L	.284	141	40	10	0	10	19	19	31	.367	.567
Bats Right	R	.276	406	112	23	0	12	48	22	82	.320	.421
Wilkerson,Brad	L	.258	97	25	5	0	7	20	10	27	.333	.526
Bats Left	R	.224	241	54	12	1	13	42	33	80	.313	.444
Willingham,Josh	L	.218	133	29	5	0	2	10	20	39	.320	.301
Bats Right	R	.281	388	109	27	4	19	79	46	83	.379	.518
Willits,Reggie	L	.333	126	42	6	0	0	8	15	17	.406	.381
Bats Both	R	.276	304	84	14	1	0	26	54	66	.385	.329
Wilson,Craig	L	.209	43	9	2	0	1	1	5	16	.320	.326
Bats Right	R	.067	15	1	0	0	0	1	3	9	.263	.067
Wilson,Jack	L	.320	100	32	8	0	6	18	13	7	.397	.580
Bats Right	R	.289	377	109	21	2	6	38	25	39	.337	.403
Wilson,Josh	L	.256	82	21	7	0	0	7	5	20	.303	.341
Bats Right	R	.230	200	46	8	3	2	17	12	37	.284	.330
Wilson,Preston	L	.208	24	5	2	0	1	5	2	4	.269	.417
Bats Right	R	.225	40	9	1	0	0	0	2	13	.262	.250
Winn,Randy	L	.351	185	65	13	0	7	20	16	23	.399	.535
Bats Both	R	.277	408	113	29	1	7	45	28	62	.332	.404
Wise,Dewayne	L	-	0	0	0	0	0	0	0	0	-	-
Bats Left	R	.200	5	1	0	1	0	1	1	1	.333	.600
Wood,Brandon	L	.200	15	3	1	0	0	1	0	7	.200	.267
Bats Right	R	.111	18	2	0	0	1	2	0	5	.111	.278
Wood,Jason	L	.244	45	11	2	0	1	9	3	15	.286	.356
Bats Right	R	.236	72	17	4	0	2	17	5	23	.286	.375
Woodward,Chris	L	.229	70	16	2	0	1	5	9	12	.313	.300
Bats Right	R	.167	66	11	4	1	0	3	1	17	.179	.258
Wright,David	L	.361	166	60	16	0	11	35	27	21	.449	.657

Batters vs. Left-Handed and Right-Handed Pitchers

Batter	vs	Avg	AB	H	2B	3B	HR	RBI	BB	SO	OBP	Slg
	R	.311	438	136	26	1	19	72	67	94	.404	.505
Youkilis,Kevin	L	.290	145	42	9	1	2	13	25	34	.408	.407
Bats Right	R	.287	383	110	26	1	14	70	52	71	.384	.470
Young,Chris	L	.246	134	33	6	0	6	10	16	32	.331	.425
Bats Right	R	.234	435	102	23	3	26	58	27	109	.284	.480
Young,Delmon	L	.299	164	49	15	0	2	25	7	35	.326	.427
Bats Right	R	.285	481	137	23	0	11	68	19	92	.312	.401
Young,Delwyn	L	.333	15	5	0	0	1	2	1	4	.375	.533
Bats Both	R	.421	19	8	1	1	1	1	1	1	.450	.737
Young,Dmitri	L	.301	133	40	12	1	2	22	7	25	.333	.451
Bats Both	R	.327	327	107	26	0	11	52	37	49	.395	.508
Young,Michael	L	.309	152	47	13	1	1	17	13	27	.369	.428
Bats Right	R	.316	487	154	24	0	8	77	34	80	.365	.415
Zaun,Gregg	L	.290	69	20	8	0	0	9	13	12	.391	.406
Bats Both	R	.229	262	60	16	1	10	43	38	43	.327	.412
Zimmerman,Ryan	L	.374	147	55	12	3	8	27	19	21	.443	.660
Bats Right	R	.235	506	119	31	2	16	64	42	104	.295	.399
Zobrist,Ben	L	.182	22	4	0	0	0	3	0	4	.167	.182
Bats Both	R	.147	75	11	2	0	1	6	3	17	.190	.213
AL	L	.275	-	-	-	-	-	-	-	-	.346	.431
	R	.269	-	-	-	-	-	-	-	-	.335	.420
NL	L	.272	-	-	-	-	-	-	-	-	.342	.430
	R	.264	-	-	-	-	-	-	-	-	.331	.420
MLB	L	.273	-	-	-	-	-	-	-	-	.344	.431
	R	.266	-	-	-	-	-	-	-	-	.333	.420

Pitchers vs. Left-Handed and Right-Handed Batters

Pitcher	vs	Avg	AB	H	2B	3B	HR	RBI	BB	SO	OBP	Slg
Aardsma,David	L	.283	46	13	1	1	0	2	13	15	.441	.348
Throws Right	R	.310	84	26	5	2	4	24	4	21	.344	.560
Abreu,Winston	L	.222	45	10	4	0	1	12	3	7	.271	.378
Throws Right	R	.351	77	27	4	0	6	17	6	19	.393	.636
Accardo,Jeremy	L	.161	124	20	3	0	0	4	12	23	.234	.185
Throws Right	R	.250	124	31	3	0	4	17	12	34	.326	.371
Acosta,Manny	L	.250	36	9	1	0	2	4	4	11	.325	.444
Throws Right	R	.093	43	4	0	0	0	4	10	11	.264	.093
Adkins,Jon	L	.000	1	0	0	0	0	0	0	0	.000	.000
Throws Right	R	.000	2	0	0	0	0	0	0	0	.000	.000
Affeldt,Jeremy	L	.250	80	20	7	1	1	12	13	17	.347	.400
Throws Left	R	.211	128	27	5	4	2	21	20	29	.323	.359
Albaladejo,Jonathan	L	.182	22	4	2	0	1	5	1	5	.217	.409
Throws Right	R	.120	25	3	0	0	0	4	1	7	.179	.120
Albers,Matt	L	.280	189	53	7	3	9	34	28	28	.367	.492
Throws Right	R	.298	248	74	19	1	9	36	22	43	.366	.492
Alfonseca,Antonio	L	.370	81	30	7	1	1	14	12	6	.453	.519
Throws Right	R	.278	126	35	10	0	2	18	15	18	.355	.405
Aquino,Greg	L	.304	23	7	2	0	1	5	2	5	.360	.522
Throws Right	R	.200	30	6	0	1	1	10	3	7	.273	.367
Arias,Alberto	L	.385	13	5	1	0	1	7	3	1	.500	.692
Throws Right	R	.231	13	3	2	0	0	2	2	2	.333	.385
Armas Jr.,Tony	L	.280	186	52	10	1	11	38	27	45	.366	.522
Throws Right	R	.294	201	59	12	0	7	30	11	28	.348	.458
Arroyo,Bronson	L	.274	358	98	17	1	14	44	29	55	.339	.444
Throws Right	R	.285	470	134	36	1	14	56	34	101	.337	.455
Ascanio,Jose	L	.280	25	7	3	0	1	5	3	4	.357	.520
Throws Right	R	.238	42	10	2	1	2	6	3	9	.289	.476
Atchison,Scott	L	.278	36	10	2	0	2	3	5	11	.357	.500
Throws Right	R	.272	81	22	5	0	3	12	5	14	.318	.444
Ayala,Luis	L	.243	70	17	2	1	0	6	7	11	.313	.300
Throws Right	R	.286	91	26	2	0	5	16	5	17	.316	.473
Backe,Brandon	L	.245	49	12	2	0	0	4	3	5	.296	.286
Throws Right	R	.250	60	15	5	0	4	8	8	6	.348	.533
Bacsik,Mike	L	.287	94	27	6	0	6	13	4	15	.340	.543
Throws Left	R	.297	384	114	14	3	20	54	25	30	.341	.505
Baek,Cha Seung	L	.267	135	36	9	3	3	18	8	25	.320	.444
Throws Right	R	.305	167	51	12	1	3	22	6	24	.329	.443
Baez,Danys	L	.346	78	27	7	0	3	20	15	11	.453	.551
Throws Right	R	.200	115	23	3	1	5	16	14	18	.319	.374
Bailey,Homer	L	.284	81	23	8	0	1	13	17	15	.408	.420
Throws Right	R	.233	86	20	6	0	2	11	11	13	.317	.372
Baker,Scott	L	.323	260	84	12	3	7	30	18	46	.375	.473
Throws Right	R	.257	304	78	21	0	8	33	11	56	.284	.405
Bale,John	L	.281	64	18	3	0	1	9	8	19	.360	.375
Throws Left	R	.297	91	27	3	1	0	10	9	23	.356	.352
Balfour,Grant	L	.370	46	17	2	2	0	8	12	14	.492	.500
Throws Right	R	.265	49	13	2	1	2	13	8	16	.367	.469
Banks,Josh	L	.273	22	6	2	0	0	0	2	2	.333	.364
Throws Right	R	.500	10	5	1	0	1	5	0	0	.455	.900
Bannister,Brian	L	.281	302	85	30	3	7	30	26	37	.343	.470
Throws Right	R	.219	324	71	17	1	8	42	18	40	.264	.352
Barone,Daniel	L	.258	66	17	2	0	2	12	12	8	.363	.379
Throws Right	R	.347	95	33	5	1	9	17	7	10	.398	.705
Barry,Kevin	L	.500	6	3	2	0	0	2	0	2	.500	.833
Throws Right	R	.500	6	3	0	0	0	3	2	2	.625	.500
Batista,Miguel	L	.295	369	109	27	3	9	47	48	57	.375	.458
Throws Right	R	.258	388	100	22	0	9	40	37	76	.332	.384
Bautista,Denny	L	.480	25	12	2	0	0	8	3	4	.536	.560
Throws Right	R	.353	17	6	1	0	0	3	1	4	.421	.412
Bayliss,Jonah	L	.333	42	14	2	1	5	14	10	8	.462	.786
Throws Right	R	.319	116	37	10	0	3	22	8	21	.370	.483
Bazardo,Yorman	L	.289	45	13	4	0	2	4	3	6	.333	.511
Throws Right	R	.143	42	6	2	0	0	4	2	9	.229	.190
Bean,Colter	L	1.000	1	1	1	0	0	0	2	0	1.000	2.000
Throws Right	R	.308	13	4	1	0	0	5	3	2	.438	.385
Beckett,Josh	L	.255	380	97	22	3	6	32	27	101	.308	.376
Throws Right	R	.235	392	92	23	0	11	40	13	93	.263	.378
Bedard,Erik	L	.229	131	30	2	1	5	12	17	39	.322	.374
Throws Left	R	.208	534	111	20	1	14	48	40	182	.266	.328
Beimel,Joe	L	.188	96	18	6	0	0	6	7	25	.240	.250
Throws Left	R	.294	153	45	10	0	1	22	17	14	.366	.379
Belisle,Matt	L	.298	325	97	18	1	15	54	27	48	.349	.498
Throws Right	R	.303	380	115	26	2	11	47	16	77	.337	.468
Bell,Heath	L	.216	153	33	3	0	3	13	18	47	.301	.294
Throws Right	R	.157	172	27	4	2	0	14	12	55	.216	.203
Bell,Rob	L	.391	92	36	7	0	2	18	17	9	.477	.533
Throws Right	R	.282	131	37	9	1	5	26	7	19	.317	.481
Benitez,Armando	L	.273	88	24	5	0	3	11	19	23	.402	.432
Throws Right	R	.243	103	25	7	1	5	23	10	34	.313	.476
Bennett,Jeff	L	.357	14	5	1	0	1	2	3	3	.471	.643
Throws Right	R	.237	38	9	1	0	2	3	0	11	.231	.421
Benoit,Joaquin	L	.172	134	23	4	0	3	11	7	46	.221	.269
Throws Right	R	.268	168	45	13	1	3	19	21	41	.349	.411
Bergmann,Jason	L	.263	209	55	15	1	14	32	25	43	.343	.545
Throws Right	R	.200	220	44	13	0	4	22	17	43	.261	.314
Betancourt,Rafael	L	.241	108	26	9	0	1	7	4	25	.265	.352
Throws Right	R	.147	170	25	3	1	3	9	5	55	.170	.229
Billingsley,Chad	L	.277	253	70	17	2	3	23	30	50	.353	.395
Throws Right	R	.210	291	61	7	1	12	33	34	91	.296	.364
Birkins,Kurt	L	.345	58	20	5	0	0	11	5	11	.415	.431
Throws Left	R	.337	95	32	8	1	3	25	9	19	.400	.537
Bisenius,Joe	L	.200	5	1	1	0	0	2	2	3	.429	.400
Throws Right	R	.500	2	1	0	0	0	0	0	0	.500	.500
Blackburn,Nick	L	.478	23	11	0	0	1	3	2	1	.520	.609
Throws Right	R	.276	29	8	0	1	1	6	0	7	.276	.448
Blackley,Travis	L	.111	9	1	0	0	0	3	1	3	.200	.111
Throws Left	R	.360	25	9	2	1	2	4	4	2	.448	.760
Blanton,Joe	L	.291	422	123	26	4	2	40	24	57	.328	.386
Throws Right	R	.248	471	117	16	0	14	50	16	83	.275	.372
Blevins,Jerry	L	.333	9	3	1	0	0	1	0	1	.333	.444
Throws Left	R	.357	14	5	1	0	1	4	2	2	.438	.643
Bonderman,Jeremy	L	.268	396	106	24	4	16	55	29	83	.318	.470
Throws Right	R	.291	299	87	17	2	7	33	19	62	.338	.431
Bonser,Boof	L	.349	373	130	26	3	16	49	34	73	.407	.563
Throws Right	R	.214	322	69	14	0	11	45	31	63	.285	.360
Booker,Chris	L	.500	2	1	0	0	1	2	1	0	.667	2.000
Throws Right	R	.000	1	0	0	0	0	1	0	1	.000	.000
Bootcheck,Chris	L	.302	126	38	7	2	2	16	12	19	.359	.437
Throws Right	R	.253	170	43	8	2	5	26	12	37	.316	.412
Borkowski,Dave	L	.300	110	33	8	2	2	17	23	25	.421	.464
Throws Right	R	.256	168	43	11	0	6	36	11	38	.307	.429
Borowski,Joe	L	.293	140	41	2	0	4	16	12	34	.349	.393
Throws Right	R	.286	126	36	10	0	5	21	6	24	.314	.484
Bowie,Micah	L	.250	68	17	0	1	1	9	1	14	.278	.324
Throws Left	R	.266	143	38	5	0	6	18	26	28	.372	.427
Boyer,Blaine	L	.500	10	5	0	0	0	2	0	1	.500	.500
Throws Right	R	.357	14	5	1	0	0	0	1	2	.400	.429
Braden,Dallas	L	.214	56	12	0	2	1	5	4	9	.267	.339
Throws Left	R	.324	244	79	15	3	8	49	22	40	.384	.508
Bradford,Chad	L	.321	81	26	3	0	1	13	7	9	.402	.395
Throws Right	R	.282	181	51	6	0	0	22	9	20	.321	.315
Braun,Ryan	L	.315	73	23	10	0	2	12	12	14	.402	.534
Throws Right	R	.284	81	23	4	0	2	17	10	10	.351	.407
Bray,Bill	L	.158	19	3	1	0	0	4	2	6	.227	.211
Throws Left	R	.342	38	13	2	2	1	5	3	8	.390	.579
Brazoban,Yhency	L	.167	6	1	0	0	0	2	1	5	.286	.167
Throws Right	R	.667	3	2	2	0	0	3	2	0	.800	1.333
Britton,Chris	L	.118	17	2	0	0	1	3	1	2	.167	.294
Throws Right	R	.241	29	7	2	0	1	2	3	3	.313	.414
Broadway,Lance	L	.188	16	3	1	0	0	1	5	4	.364	.250
Throws Right	R	.105	19	2	1	0	0	0	0	10	.105	.158
Brocail,Doug	L	.182	137	25	3	2	3	18	15	24	.261	.299
Throws Right	R	.268	153	41	6	1	5	20	9	19	.317	.418
Brower,Jim	L	.286	7	2	1	0	0	2	0	0	.250	.429
Throws Right	R	.667	9	6	2	0	0	3	2	1	.692	.889
Brown,Andrew	L	.242	66	16	6	0	0	7	9	21	.333	.333
Throws Right	R	.247	89	22	7	1	1	13	8	22	.327	.382
Broxton,Jonathan	L	.200	145	29	4	0	3	18	20	47	.299	.290
Throws Right	R	.247	162	40	7	2	3	15	5	52	.269	.370
Bruney,Brian	L	.303	66	20	3	1	4	15	22	11	.467	.561
Throws Right	R	.209	115	24	6	0	1	12	15	28	.304	.287
Buchholz,Clay	L	.217	46	10	3	0	0	3	6	15	.321	.283
Throws Right	R	.133	30	4	0	0	0	2	4	7	.229	.133
Buchholz,Taylor	L	.268	168	45	11	1	4	21	9	37	.306	.417
Throws Right	R	.306	196	60	8	2	4	27	11	24	.341	.429
Buckner,Billy	L	.314	70	22	6	1	4	11	11	11	.402	.600
Throws Right	R	.268	56	15	5	0	1	7	5	6	.328	.411
Buehrle,Mark	L	.314	153	48	14	0	5	17	9	20	.358	.503
Throws Left	R	.258	620	160	30	2	17	57	36	95	.300	.395
Bukvich,Ryan	L	.209	43	9	1	1	1	5	10	5	.370	.349
Throws Right	R	.278	97	27	4	1	4	21	14	13	.374	.464
Bulger,Jason	L	.222	9	2	0	0	0	0	3	5	.417	.222

Pitchers vs. Left-Handed and Right-Handed Batters

Pitcher	vs	Avg	AB	H	2B	3B	HR	RBI	BB	SO	OBP	Slg
Throws Right	R	.231	13	3	0	0	0	2	0	3	.231	.231
Bullington,Bryan	L	.481	27	13	2	0	3	8	1	1	.500	.889
Throws Right	R	.256	43	11	1	0	0	3	4	6	.319	.279
Burgos,Ambiorix	L	.273	44	12	4	0	2	6	3	7	.333	.500
Throws Right	R	.122	41	5	1	0	1	3	6	12	.245	.220
Burnett,A.J.	L	.200	330	66	11	0	12	30	36	106	.294	.342
Throws Right	R	.231	281	65	8	1	11	34	30	70	.312	.384
Burres,Brian	L	.306	134	41	6	0	5	27	19	26	.392	.463
Throws Left	R	.281	352	99	19	2	9	43	47	70	.374	.423
Burton,Jared	L	.130	54	7	1	0	1	4	15	12	.314	.204
Throws Right	R	.219	96	21	3	0	1	8	7	24	.286	.281
Bush,David	L	.246	321	79	19	2	9	34	26	66	.310	.402
Throws Right	R	.324	426	138	35	0	18	66	18	68	.361	.533
Byrd,Paul	L	.322	407	131	29	3	7	55	14	27	.345	.459
Throws Right	R	.280	386	108	18	1	20	41	14	61	.311	.487
Byrdak,Tim	L	.176	68	12	7	1	2	13	10	24	.280	.397
Throws Left	R	.268	97	26	5	0	1	12	16	25	.365	.351
Cabrera,Daniel	L	.294	391	115	21	2	15	69	62	83	.399	.473
Throws Right	R	.236	390	92	16	0	10	45	46	83	.326	.354
Cabrera,Fernando	L	.319	69	22	4	2	6	19	21	16	.473	.696
Throws Right	R	.267	105	28	6	0	3	15	10	32	.328	.410
Cain,Matt	L	.248	343	85	20	5	3	41	45	72	.335	.362
Throws Right	R	.224	392	88	20	2	11	31	34	91	.291	.370
Calero,Kiko	L	.245	49	12	2	0	1	8	9	8	.361	.347
Throws Right	R	.315	108	34	5	4	2	19	12	23	.379	.491
Cali,Carmen	L	.255	47	12	1	0	2	6	6	9	.340	.404
Throws Left	R	.278	36	10	4	0	0	3	10	5	.458	.389
Cameron,Kevin	L	.255	110	28	3	0	0	5	14	21	.339	.282
Throws Right	R	.243	111	27	2	0	0	11	22	29	.363	.261
Camp,Shawn	L	.370	54	20	7	0	1	15	10	12	.470	.556
Throws Right	R	.368	117	43	4	0	6	33	8	24	.417	.556
Campillo,Jorge	L	.238	21	5	0	1	0	1	4	4	.360	.333
Throws Right	R	.394	33	13	3	2	2	13	2	5	.432	.788
Capellan,Jose	L	.313	32	10	0	2	3	8	5	3	.405	.719
Throws Right	R	.250	72	18	2	0	4	11	4	17	.295	.444
Capps,Matt	L	.281	114	32	6	0	2	11	12	18	.357	.386
Throws Right	R	.181	177	32	7	0	3	15	4	46	.202	.271
Capuano,Chris	L	.259	116	30	5	0	2	14	12	31	.331	.353
Throws Left	R	.293	478	140	29	2	18	62	42	101	.357	.475
Carlyle,Buddy	L	.343	198	68	17	3	11	35	16	36	.391	.626
Throws Right	R	.229	214	49	14	2	8	28	16	38	.284	.425
Carmona,Fausto	L	.275	440	121	19	4	6	26	39	57	.333	.377
Throws Right	R	.216	361	78	8	0	10	46	22	80	.280	.321
Carpenter,Chris	L	.375	16	6	1	0	0	3	1	2	.444	.438
Throws Right	R	.300	10	3	0	0	0	2	0	1	.300	.300
Carrasco,Hector	L	.188	69	13	1	1	1	7	11	16	.300	.275
Throws Right	R	.333	93	31	7	2	7	24	12	17	.411	.677
Carvajal,Marcos	L	.364	11	4	1	0	0	3	2	1	.462	.455
Throws Right	R	.400	10	4	0	0	0	1	0	1	.364	.400
Casilla,Santiago	L	.212	66	14	2	0	3	10	11	11	.316	.379
Throws Right	R	.230	126	29	6	1	3	18	12	41	.300	.365
Cassel,Jack	L	.375	32	12	2	0	0	1	3	2	.429	.438
Throws Right	R	.300	60	18	3	0	1	6	2	9	.333	.400
Castro,Fabio	L	.063	16	1	0	0	0	0	4	8	.250	.063
Throws Left	R	.296	27	8	2	0	2	7	9	6	.472	.593
Cate,Troy	L	.259	27	7	1	0	0	1	3	6	.333	.296
Throws Left	R	.314	35	11	1	0	1	4	6	6	.395	.429
Cavazos,Andy	L	.357	42	15	2	0	3	12	7	7	.440	.619
Throws Right	R	.308	39	12	5	1	2	10	9	8	.442	.641
Chacin,Gustavo	L	.269	26	7	1	1	2	6	2	0	.345	.615
Throws Left	R	.265	83	22	5	0	4	8	5	11	.315	.470
Chacon,Shawn	L	.317	126	40	6	2	4	20	25	21	.438	.492
Throws Right	R	.236	233	55	14	1	5	26	23	58	.313	.369
Chamberlain,Joba	L	.132	38	5	3	0	0	0	2	15	.195	.211
Throws Right	R	.156	45	7	1	0	1	1	4	19	.224	.244
Chen,Bruce	L	.400	10	4	1	0	1	7	0	0	.400	.800
Throws Left	R	.233	30	7	3	0	2	6	6	7	.361	.533
Cherry,Rocky	L	.167	42	7	1	0	2	5	10	12	.333	.333
Throws Right	R	.299	77	23	9	0	2	14	9	11	.382	.494
Chico,Matt	L	.273	132	36	9	0	5	10	11	27	.333	.455
Throws Left	R	.283	520	147	29	4	21	76	63	67	.358	.475
Choate,Randy	L	1.000	3	3	0	0	0	0	0	0	1.000	1.000
Throws Left	R	-	0	0	0	0	0	0	0	0	-	-
Chulk,Vinnie	L	.290	69	20	6	1	1	10	7	11	.364	.449
Throws Right	R	.250	132	33	6	2	2	20	7	30	.285	.371
Clarke,Darren	L	1.000	1	1	0	0	0	0	0	0	1.000	1.000

Pitcher	vs	Avg	AB	H	2B	3B	HR	RBI	BB	SO	OBP	Slg
Throws Right	R	.200	5	1	0	0	0	0	1	1	.333	.200
Clemens,Roger	L	.233	163	38	6	2	5	22	19	27	.311	.387
Throws Right	R	.282	216	61	9	2	4	25	12	41	.332	.398
Clippard,Tyler	L	.208	53	11	3	0	2	5	8	9	.311	.377
Throws Right	R	.333	54	18	4	0	4	13	9	9	.429	.630
Coffey,Todd	L	.343	70	24	0	0	2	8	9	11	.432	.429
Throws Right	R	.313	147	46	4	0	10	37	10	32	.369	.544
Collazo,Willie	L	.111	9	1	0	0	0	1	3	0	.333	.111
Throws Left	R	.462	13	6	2	0	0	2	2	0	.533	.615
Colome,Jesus	L	.311	106	33	3	2	4	18	12	11	.369	.491
Throws Right	R	.218	142	31	6	0	2	15	15	32	.294	.303
Colon,Bartolo	L	.313	163	51	9	0	7	25	15	35	.383	.497
Throws Right	R	.325	249	81	16	0	8	40	14	41	.361	.486
Colyer,Steve	L	.429	7	3	0	0	0	1	3	2	.600	.429
Throws Left	R	.545	11	6	1	0	1	3	1	2	.583	.909
Condrey,Clay	L	.299	87	26	5	0	1	18	9	13	.367	.391
Throws Right	R	.302	116	35	3	3	3	20	7	14	.357	.457
Contreras,Jose	L	.333	411	137	22	3	13	75	40	58	.390	.496
Throws Right	R	.270	352	95	17	2	8	41	22	55	.332	.398
Cook,Aaron	L	.263	320	84	16	2	7	33	21	18	.310	.391
Throws Right	R	.295	319	94	22	0	8	44	23	43	.349	.439
Corcoran,Tim	L	.316	19	6	4	0	0	4	6	3	.480	.526
Throws Right	R	.234	47	11	1	0	2	11	6	3	.333	.383
Cordero,Chad	L	.221	140	31	7	1	2	5	12	29	.283	.329
Throws Right	R	.295	149	44	9	0	6	24	17	33	.365	.477
Cordero,Francisco	L	.225	102	23	4	0	2	8	13	40	.319	.324
Throws Right	R	.212	137	29	7	0	2	15	5	46	.238	.307
Corey,Bryan	L	.167	12	2	1	0	0	1	3	3	.333	.250
Throws Right	R	.286	14	4	1	0	0	1	1	3	.313	.357
Cormier,Lance	L	.257	74	19	4	0	5	12	9	15	.337	.514
Throws Right	R	.333	111	37	7	1	11	23	13	12	.403	.712
Cormier,Rheal	L	.200	5	1	0	0	0	0	1	1	.333	.200
Throws Left	R	.500	6	3	1	0	1	4	0	0	.571	1.167
Corpas,Manny	L	.234	141	33	4	0	4	16	9	22	.283	.348
Throws Right	R	.214	140	30	4	0	2	9	11	36	.276	.286
Correia,Kevin	L	.217	143	31	7	1	3	10	18	36	.304	.343
Throws Right	R	.257	245	63	13	1	6	29	22	44	.320	.392
Cotts,Neal	L	.240	25	6	0	0	1	9	4	6	.345	.360
Throws Left	R	.250	36	9	5	0	0	5	5	8	.370	.389
Coutlangus,Jon	L	.231	65	15	3	0	0	8	16	19	.393	.277
Throws Left	R	.264	87	23	3	1	3	15	11	19	.356	.425
Crain,Jesse	L	.269	26	7	1	0	2	7	2	3	.333	.538
Throws Right	R	.308	39	12	3	0	2	8	2	7	.341	.538
Cruz,Juan	L	.269	108	29	6	1	4	13	24	34	.412	.454
Throws Right	R	.143	112	16	6	0	3	13	8	53	.211	.277
Danks,John	L	.281	121	34	8	0	7	25	16	23	.370	.521
Throws Left	R	.292	432	126	30	1	21	60	38	86	.350	.512
Davidson,Dave	L	.500	2	1	1	0	0	2	1	0	.750	1.000
Throws Left	R	.455	11	5	1	0	1	4	1	0	.538	.818
Davies,Kyle	L	.275	265	73	16	5	11	41	41	55	.373	.498
Throws Right	R	.293	280	82	18	2	11	47	29	44	.365	.489
Davis,Doug	L	.252	163	41	8	0	7	23	15	34	.330	.429
Throws Left	R	.290	587	170	32	4	14	69	80	110	.375	.429
Davis,Jason	L	.267	60	16	3	1	1	13	8	12	.352	.400
Throws Right	R	.302	86	26	2	0	3	11	17	7	.419	.430
Davis,Kane	L	.316	19	6	1	1	0	3	6	3	.462	.474
Throws Right	R	.355	31	11	1	0	2	4	2	7	.394	.581
Day,Dewon	L	.375	24	9	3	1	0	9	3	1	.444	.583
Throws Right	R	.333	30	10	1	0	1	4	6	6	.474	.467
De Jong,Jordan	L	.391	23	9	5	0	0	9	2	3	.440	.609
Throws Right	R	.143	14	2	0	0	0	0	3	4	.294	.143
de la Cruz,Eulogio	L	.250	12	3	1	0	0	2	3	3	.400	.333
Throws Right	R	.438	16	7	1	0	1	5	1	2	.471	.688
de la Rosa,Jorge	L	.234	107	25	4	0	1	5	10	19	.305	.299
Throws Left	R	.321	420	135	40	1	19	68	43	63	.384	.557
Delcarmen,Manny	L	.167	60	10	0	1	2	7	10	11	.278	.300
Throws Right	R	.194	93	18	1	1	2	7	7	30	.265	.290
Dempster,Ryan	L	.259	112	29	5	3	4	19	16	33	.349	.464
Throws Right	R	.224	134	30	3	0	4	10	14	22	.300	.336
DePaula,Julio	L	.341	41	14	3	1	2	9	5	3	.417	.610
Throws Right	R	.372	43	16	1	0	3	10	5	5	.460	.605
DeSalvo,Matt	L	.359	39	14	5	1	1	6	8	1	.479	.615
Throws Right	R	.274	73	20	6	0	1	11	10	9	.376	.397
Dessens,Elmer	L	.391	64	25	7	1	3	14	5	9	.435	.672
Throws Right	R	.260	77	20	4	1	3	18	7	13	.318	.455
Detwiler,Ross	L	.000	1	0	0	0	0	0	0	1	.000	.000

Pitchers vs. Left-Handed and Right-Handed Batters

Pitcher	vs	Avg	AB	H	2B	3B	HR	RBI	BB	SO	OBP	Slg
Throws Left	R	.000	3	0	0	0	0	0	0	0	.000	.000
Devine,Joey	L	.300	10	3	0	0	0	0	3	1	.462	.300
Throws Right	R	.211	19	4	0	0	0	2	5	6	.360	.211
DiNardo,Lenny	L	.304	102	31	4	0	4	15	10	8	.374	.461
Throws Left	R	.271	387	105	19	0	9	48	40	51	.337	.390
Dohmann,Scott	L	.241	54	13	2	0	1	7	9	13	.344	.333
Throws Right	R	.271	59	16	3	1	2	8	9	13	.357	.458
Donnelly,Brendan	L	.212	33	7	2	0	0	7	4	5	.297	.273
Throws Right	R	.250	48	12	2	1	0	3	1	10	.321	.333
Dotel,Octavio	L	.265	49	13	3	0	1	3	7	11	.368	.388
Throws Right	R	.225	71	16	4	1	3	13	5	30	.304	.437
Dove,Dennis	L	.200	5	1	0	0	1	1	1	1	.333	.800
Throws Right	R	.444	9	4	1	0	1	4	0	0	.444	.889
Downs,Scott	L	.209	110	23	2	0	1	15	13	32	.294	.255
Throws Left	R	.238	101	24	3	0	2	8	11	25	.313	.327
Doyne,Cory	L	.462	13	6	1	0	1	5	1	1	.467	.769
Throws Right	R	.250	4	1	0	0	0	0	2	1	.571	.250
Driskill,Travis	L	.250	12	3	2	0	1	4	1	3	.308	.667
Throws Right	R	.467	15	7	1	0	0	2	0	1	.438	.533
Duchscherer,Justin	L	.400	30	12	5	2	0	2	5	4	.472	.700
Throws Right	R	.176	34	6	0	0	3	7	3	9	.237	.441
Duckworth,Brandon	L	.266	79	21	6	1	1	11	11	8	.352	.405
Throws Right	R	.283	106	30	6	0	2	12	12	13	.361	.396
Duke,Zach	L	.341	82	28	5	0	3	15	3	13	.372	.512
Throws Left	R	.363	366	133	33	2	11	52	22	28	.398	.555
Dumatrait,Phil	L	.471	17	8	4	0	1	7	0	2	.471	.882
Throws Left	R	.443	70	31	7	0	5	17	12	7	.518	.757
Durbin,Chad	L	.281	249	70	15	0	7	27	26	31	.350	.426
Throws Right	R	.255	247	63	8	0	14	37	23	35	.329	.457
Durbin,J.D.	L	.301	123	37	8	0	4	18	22	19	.411	.463
Throws Right	R	.297	138	41	11	0	2	24	15	21	.368	.420
Eaton,Adam	L	.322	295	95	20	4	16	58	41	40	.409	.580
Throws Right	R	.284	342	97	21	0	14	44	30	57	.351	.468
Elarton,Scott	L	.325	80	26	10	1	6	21	14	10	.421	.700
Throws Right	R	.351	77	27	4	0	6	13	7	3	.416	.636
Embree,Alan	L	.206	73	15	3	1	1	9	6	13	.266	.315
Throws Left	R	.278	187	52	9	1	4	24	13	38	.319	.401
Ennis,John	L	.400	15	6	2	0	0	2	2	3	.471	.533
Throws Right	R	.300	20	6	0	0	1	3	1	5	.333	.450
Escobar,Kelvim	L	.264	356	94	23	3	6	35	33	81	.332	.396
Throws Right	R	.233	378	88	17	1	5	34	33	79	.292	.323
Eveland,Dana	L	.500	6	3	1	0	0	2	4	0	.700	.667
Throws Left	R	.313	16	5	2	0	0	5	1	3	.333	.438
Eyre,Scott	L	.253	75	19	2	2	3	19	9	18	.333	.453
Throws Left	R	.317	126	40	9	2	0	12	26	27	.435	.421
Eyre,Willie	L	.248	113	28	6	1	3	17	16	13	.344	.398
Throws Right	R	.323	155	50	11	0	5	22	16	29	.386	.490
Falkenborg,Brian	L	.321	28	9	2	0	2	9	2	6	.367	.607
Throws Right	R	.277	47	13	3	0	0	3	6	10	.370	.340
Farnsworth,Kyle	L	.273	110	30	4	0	5	16	20	22	.379	.445
Throws Right	R	.242	124	30	6	0	4	15	7	26	.293	.387
Feierabend,Ryan	L	.304	46	14	3	0	1	4	9	8	.431	.435
Throws Left	R	.366	161	59	15	1	9	34	14	19	.421	.640
Feldman,Scott	L	.316	57	18	5	0	1	10	17	5	.474	.456
Throws Right	R	.265	98	26	7	0	2	16	15	14	.371	.398
Feliciano,Pedro	L	.168	95	16	1	0	1	10	11	30	.273	.211
Throws Left	R	.221	140	31	9	3	2	16	20	31	.325	.371
Field,Nate	L	.750	4	3	1	0	0	3	0	1	.750	1.000
Throws Right	R	.000	2	0	0	0	0	0	1	1	.333	.000
Flores,Randy	L	.326	95	31	3	2	1	12	7	15	.385	.432
Throws Left	R	.299	134	40	7	2	1	27	8	32	.338	.403
Flores,Ron	L	.095	21	2	1	0	0	0	4	6	.240	.143
Throws Left	R	.298	47	14	4	1	2	10	8	9	.393	.553
Floyd,Gavin	L	.314	137	43	5	1	8	16	12	22	.377	.540
Throws Right	R	.286	147	42	4	0	9	27	7	27	.331	.497
Fogg,Josh	L	.279	315	88	22	8	11	46	32	37	.348	.505
Throws Right	R	.305	348	106	23	2	12	44	27	57	.370	.486
Fossum,Casey	L	.369	111	41	8	0	4	27	8	17	.403	.550
Throws Left	R	.322	211	68	12	1	11	46	19	36	.387	.545
Francis,Jeff	L	.242	194	47	5	1	6	21	12	44	.292	.371
Throws Left	R	.289	647	187	40	1	19	70	51	121	.344	.442
Francisco,Frank	L	.221	95	21	6	1	1	10	20	21	.364	.337
Throws Right	R	.286	126	36	9	1	2	17	18	28	.375	.421
Franklin,Ryan	L	.238	130	31	5	1	4	12	4	14	.261	.385
Throws Right	R	.231	169	39	9	0	4	19	7	30	.271	.355
Frasor,Jason	L	.245	94	23	4	1	2	21	15	26	.348	.372

Pitcher	vs	Avg	AB	H	2B	3B	HR	RBI	BB	SO	OBP	Slg
Throws Right	R	.200	120	24	9	0	1	7	8	33	.256	.300
Fuentes,Brian	L	.204	54	11	3	1	0	5	7	20	.302	.296
Throws Left	R	.207	169	35	3	0	6	19	16	36	.298	.331
Fultz,Aaron	L	.191	68	13	5	1	1	12	10	12	.291	.338
Throws Left	R	.265	68	18	3	0	1	10	8	16	.342	.353
Gabbard,Kason	L	.236	72	17	2	0	3	14	6	17	.309	.389
Throws Left	R	.230	222	51	14	0	5	22	35	38	.347	.360
Gagne,Eric	L	.224	98	22	6	0	0	8	8	25	.290	.286
Throws Right	R	.265	102	27	6	0	3	15	13	26	.348	.412
Galarraga,Armando	L	.263	19	5	0	0	2	4	4	3	.375	.579
Throws Right	R	.231	13	3	1	0	0	2	3	3	.375	.308
Gallagher,Sean	L	.294	34	10	4	0	1	5	3	4	.368	.500
Throws Right	R	.346	26	9	2	0	2	10	9	1	.500	.654
Gallardo,Yovani	L	.247	170	42	11	0	3	13	21	46	.328	.365
Throws Right	R	.244	250	61	13	2	5	30	16	55	.293	.372
Garcia,Anderson	L	1.000	1	1	0	0	0	0	0	0	1.000	1.000
Throws Right	R	.333	3	1	0	0	0	0	0	0	.333	.333
Garcia,Freddy	L	.292	106	31	9	1	4	14	10	24	.353	.509
Throws Right	R	.339	127	43	10	1	8	16	9	26	.397	.622
Garcia,Harvey	L	.409	22	9	1	0	2	2	4	3	.500	.727
Throws Right	R	.200	25	5	0	0	1	3	3	12	.286	.320
Gardner,Lee	L	.308	130	40	6	1	1	13	13	17	.368	.392
Throws Right	R	.208	154	32	5	0	1	12	5	35	.244	.260
Garland,Jon	L	.259	406	105	21	5	9	50	36	50	.321	.401
Throws Right	R	.281	406	114	25	2	10	56	21	48	.315	.426
Garza,Matt	L	.314	156	49	8	0	5	17	22	39	.403	.462
Throws Right	R	.276	170	47	8	1	3	17	10	28	.319	.388
Gaudin,Chad	L	.282	393	111	21	5	11	46	68	49	.389	.445
Throws Right	R	.250	376	94	19	3	10	48	32	105	.316	.396
Geary,Geoff	L	.248	105	26	5	1	1	13	14	12	.341	.343
Throws Right	R	.309	149	46	7	0	7	33	11	26	.381	.497
Germano,Justin	L	.244	246	60	13	1	7	24	22	34	.311	.390
Throws Right	R	.272	268	73	19	1	7	37	18	44	.332	.429
Giese,Dan	L	.143	14	2	1	0	1	1	1	3	.200	.429
Throws Right	R	.300	20	6	1	0	3	3	1	4	.333	.800
Glavine,Tom	L	.326	187	61	4	2	4	20	18	26	.391	.433
Throws Left	R	.266	593	158	34	6	19	70	46	63	.320	.440
Glover,Gary	L	.286	133	38	3	4	5	18	16	24	.364	.481
Throws Right	R	.290	169	49	11	1	7	24	11	27	.330	.491
Gobble,Jimmy	L	.241	108	26	9	1	2	14	13	40	.325	.398
Throws Left	R	.319	94	30	6	1	4	20	10	10	.377	.532
Gonzalez,Edgar	L	.313	201	63	17	1	12	34	17	35	.365	.587
Throws Right	R	.237	198	47	9	0	6	28	11	27	.288	.374
Gonzalez,Enrique	L	.500	4	2	0	0	0	3	1	0	.600	.500
Throws Right	R	.333	6	2	1	0	0	0	0	0	.333	.500
Gonzalez,Mike	L	.333	24	8	2	0	0	3	3	4	.407	.417
Throws Left	R	.189	37	7	2	1	0	2	5	9	.279	.297
Gordon,Tom	L	.310	71	22	4	0	6	10	5	14	.351	.620
Throws Right	R	.222	81	18	3	0	1	7	8	18	.304	.296
Gorzelanny,Tom	L	.217	129	28	4	0	3	14	6	30	.254	.318
Throws Left	R	.284	654	186	46	2	15	68	62	105	.352	.430
Gosling,Mike	L	.260	50	13	5	0	1	9	6	20	.345	.420
Throws Left	R	.354	82	29	6	0	4	13	22	12	.490	.573
Grabow,John	L	.238	80	19	2	1	1	12	5	21	.279	.325
Throws Left	R	.303	122	37	3	0	5	20	14	21	.377	.451
Green,Sean	L	.329	73	24	4	3	0	9	17	5	.453	.466
Throws Right	R	.286	185	53	10	1	2	35	17	48	.346	.384
Gregg,Kevin	L	.162	148	24	7	1	1	12	22	49	.271	.243
Throws Right	R	.247	158	39	4	0	6	25	18	38	.346	.386
Greinke,Zack	L	.266	237	63	21	2	5	21	19	47	.318	.435
Throws Right	R	.263	224	59	14	0	7	32	17	59	.321	.420
Grilli,Jason	L	.237	97	23	5	1	1	16	19	26	.361	.340
Throws Right	R	.275	211	58	13	0	4	35	13	36	.325	.393
Gronkiewicz,Lee	L	.143	7	1	0	0	0	0	2	0	.333	.143
Throws Right	R	.167	6	1	0	0	1	1	0	2	.167	.667
Guardado,Eddie	L	.333	12	4	2	0	1	5	1	1	.429	.750
Throws Left	R	.273	44	12	5	0	1	8	3	7	.313	.455
Guerrier,Matt	L	.264	140	37	2	1	6	20	11	22	.320	.421
Throws Right	R	.187	182	34	8	0	3	12	10	46	.242	.280
Guthrie,Jeremy	L	.255	341	87	24	1	14	47	22	68	.302	.455
Throws Right	R	.243	321	78	13	0	9	35	25	55	.299	.368
Gutierrez,Juan	L	.216	37	8	4	0	1	4	1	7	.225	.405
Throws Right	R	.362	47	17	5	0	2	9	5	9	.415	.596
Guzman,Angel	L	.333	60	20	3	0	1	7	5	14	.379	.433
Throws Right	R	.218	55	12	6	0	1	5	4	12	.295	.382
Gwyn,Marc	L	.300	10	3	0	0	2	6	4	2	.500	.900

Pitchers vs. Left-Handed and Right-Handed Batters

Pitcher	vs	Avg	AB	H	2B	3B	HR	RBI	BB	SO	OBP	Slg
Throws Right	R	.400	15	6	1	0	1	3	1	1	.412	.667
Haeger,Charlie	L	.286	21	6	0	0	2	4	5	0	.444	.571
Throws Right	R	.407	27	11	0	0	1	7	3	1	.452	.519
Halladay,Roy	L	.265	464	123	20	1	8	37	29	76	.311	.364
Throws Right	R	.270	403	109	22	1	7	49	19	63	.300	.382
Hamels,Cole	L	.247	97	24	10	0	2	14	9	31	.308	.412
Throws Left	R	.236	590	139	27	1	23	54	34	146	.279	.402
Hammel,Jason	L	.310	174	54	8	3	7	25	25	37	.397	.511
Throws Right	R	.277	166	46	16	1	5	33	15	27	.344	.476
Hampson,Justin	L	.213	61	13	3	1	1	6	2	7	.246	.344
Throws Left	R	.255	137	35	9	0	0	12	14	27	.333	.321
Hancock,Josh	L	.389	18	7	1	0	2	4	1	2	.421	.778
Throws Right	R	.226	31	7	1	0	0	1	4	7	.314	.258
Hanrahan,Joel	L	.267	101	27	5	0	4	11	21	24	.393	.436
Throws Right	R	.305	105	32	5	0	5	21	17	19	.398	.495
Hansack,Devern	L	.333	21	7	2	0	1	3	2	2	.391	.571
Throws Right	R	.167	12	2	1	0	1	2	3	3	.333	.500
Happ,J.A.	L	.333	3	1	1	0	0	0	1	1	.500	.667
Throws Left	R	.375	16	6	0	0	3	5	1	4	.412	.938
Harang,Aaron	L	.237	388	92	18	1	9	36	32	94	.299	.358
Throws Right	R	.246	491	121	31	2	19	57	20	124	.282	.434
Harden,Rich	L	.292	48	14	2	0	2	2	4	11	.346	.458
Throws Right	R	.098	41	4	1	0	1	4	7	16	.229	.195
Haren,Dan	L	.230	431	99	25	5	9	36	37	100	.290	.374
Throws Right	R	.264	436	115	18	2	15	47	18	92	.293	.417
Harikkala,Tim	L	.500	8	4	0	0	0	1	0	2	.500	.500
Throws Right	R	.500	10	5	0	0	0	2	1	0	.545	.500
Hart,Kevin	L	.000	13	0	0	0	0	0	1	7	.071	.000
Throws Right	R	.292	24	7	2	1	0	2	3	6	.370	.458
Hawkins,LaTroy	L	.237	97	23	3	1	5	10	9	16	.299	.443
Throws Right	R	.266	109	29	2	2	1	10	7	13	.310	.349
Heilman,Aaron	L	.234	124	29	8	1	5	16	11	32	.302	.435
Throws Right	R	.218	197	43	6	1	3	23	9	31	.263	.305
Hendrickson,Mark	L	.258	93	24	3	0	2	12	8	22	.317	.355
Throws Left	R	.300	393	118	18	2	13	56	21	70	.334	.455
Henn,Sean	L	.288	59	17	0	1	2	10	5	10	.364	.424
Throws Left	R	.297	91	27	9	0	4	21	22	18	.439	.527
Hennessey,Brad	L	.245	102	25	7	0	5	16	16	19	.353	.461
Throws Right	R	.265	155	41	9	1	2	15	7	21	.305	.374
Hensley,Clay	L	.287	94	27	7	0	1	15	18	13	.398	.394
Throws Right	R	.324	108	35	8	0	4	23	14	17	.407	.509
Herges,Matt	L	.216	74	16	2	1	3	11	5	13	.263	.392
Throws Right	R	.184	98	18	6	1	1	7	10	17	.259	.296
Hernandez,Felix	L	.300	373	112	25	3	14	48	39	88	.368	.496
Throws Right	R	.261	372	97	11	1	6	34	14	77	.290	.344
Hernandez,Livan	L	.295	400	118	16	1	18	64	51	36	.379	.475
Throws Right	R	.320	403	129	26	4	16	46	28	54	.362	.524
Hernandez,Orlando	L	.245	265	65	11	3	11	36	38	47	.341	.434
Throws Right	R	.167	263	44	10	0	12	24	26	81	.251	.342
Hernandez,Roberto	L	.259	85	22	6	0	2	17	9	18	.333	.400
Throws Right	R	.356	104	37	13	0	3	19	16	13	.451	.567
Hernandez,Yoel	L	.296	27	8	1	0	1	5	0	2	.296	.444
Throws Right	R	.308	39	12	3	0	1	11	1	11	.325	.462
Hill,Rich	L	.191	152	29	9	0	3	15	12	49	.263	.309
Throws Left	R	.247	572	141	23	1	24	70	51	134	.316	.416
Hill,Shawn	L	.288	170	49	13	2	4	20	11	26	.341	.459
Throws Right	R	.189	196	37	3	1	5	17	14	39	.250	.291
Hirsh,Jason	L	.236	199	47	7	6	6	20	29	35	.332	.422
Throws Right	R	.250	224	56	15	1	12	38	19	40	.310	.487
Hochevar,Luke	L	.273	22	6	3	0	0	2	3	1	.385	.409
Throws Right	R	.208	24	5	0	0	1	1	1	4	.296	.333
Hoey,Jim	L	.351	37	13	2	0	2	11	8	5	.447	.568
Throws Right	R	.218	55	12	4	0	0	6	10	13	.338	.291
Hoffman,Trevor	L	.299	97	29	7	1	1	11	12	23	.376	.423
Throws Right	R	.169	118	20	9	2	1	13	3	21	.187	.305
Houlton,D.J.	L	.255	51	13	1	0	2	7	3	8	.296	.392
Throws Right	R	.278	54	15	1	0	3	8	4	13	.322	.463
Howell,J.P.	L	.296	54	16	3	0	3	17	5	11	.356	.519
Throws Left	R	.325	163	53	12	0	5	24	16	38	.393	.491
Howry,Bob	L	.192	130	25	4	2	2	12	12	31	.266	.300
Throws Right	R	.283	180	51	5	2	6	21	7	41	.312	.433
Huber,Jon	L	.400	15	6	0	0	0	1	1	1	.438	.400
Throws Right	R	.250	28	7	2	0	1	3	3	7	.323	.429
Hudson,Luke	L	.143	7	1	0	0	1	2	2	0	.333	.571
Throws Right	R	.500	2	1	1	0	0	2	2	0	.750	1.000
Hudson,Tim	L	.261	445	116	11	6	6	38	35	48	.320	.353

Pitcher	vs	Avg	AB	H	2B	3B	HR	RBI	BB	SO	OBP	Slg
Throws Right	R	.261	402	105	18	3	4	35	18	84	.295	.351
Hughes,Phil	L	.264	129	34	11	0	6	18	19	27	.358	.488
Throws Right	R	.210	143	30	6	0	2	13	10	31	.269	.294
Hull,Eric	L	.000	8	0	0	0	0	0	1	3	.111	.000
Throws Right	R	.267	15	4	1	0	0	3	2	2	.353	.333
Humber,Philip	L	.375	16	6	1	1	1	2	1	1	.412	.750
Throws Right	R	.214	14	3	2	0	0	2	1	1	.267	.357
Igawa,Kei	L	.320	75	24	3	1	3	13	7	12	.407	.507
Throws Left	R	.264	197	52	15	2	12	33	30	41	.361	.543
Isringhausen,Jason	L	.196	97	19	6	0	0	7	12	25	.297	.258
Throws Right	R	.167	138	23	2	1	4	13	16	29	.252	.283
Jackson,Edwin	L	.313	336	105	24	3	9	52	56	70	.409	.482
Throws Right	R	.285	316	90	10	2	10	46	32	58	.354	.424
James,Chuck	L	.252	131	33	8	0	7	18	11	28	.308	.473
Throws Left	R	.268	488	131	25	1	25	50	47	88	.332	.477
Janssen,Casey	L	.257	101	26	7	0	0	8	9	14	.315	.327
Throws Right	R	.241	170	41	9	0	4	23	11	25	.296	.365
Jenks,Bobby	L	.237	97	23	2	0	0	11	6	29	.283	.258
Throws Right	R	.169	130	22	3	0	2	12	7	27	.210	.238
Jennings,Jason	L	.309	162	50	11	1	5	30	19	29	.371	.481
Throws Right	R	.295	234	69	17	0	14	37	15	42	.340	.547
Jimenez,Kelvin	L	.271	59	16	4	0	1	16	10	12	.377	.390
Throws Right	R	.345	116	40	11	1	1	18	7	12	.398	.483
Jimenez,Ubaldo	L	.244	156	38	7	4	5	20	25	29	.355	.436
Throws Right	R	.212	151	32	9	0	5	20	12	39	.286	.371
Johnson,Jim	L	.333	3	1	0	0	0	0	2	0	.600	.333
Throws Right	R	.400	5	2	0	0	0	2	0	1	.333	.400
Johnson,Josh	L	.419	31	13	1	0	1	8	10	7	.561	.548
Throws Right	R	.361	36	13	2	1	0	7	2	7	.385	.472
Johnson,Randy	L	.182	33	6	0	0	1	3	1	11	.270	.273
Throws Left	R	.257	179	46	5	0	6	19	12	61	.307	.385
Johnson,Tyler	L	.224	67	15	3	2	2	18	6	14	.307	.418
Throws Left	R	.211	76	16	3	0	2	8	10	10	.307	.329
Jones,Greg	L	.250	20	5	1	0	1	8	2	3	.318	.450
Throws Right	R	.313	16	5	2	0	1	4	3	2	.450	.625
Jones,Todd	L	.265	136	36	7	2	1	18	15	25	.338	.368
Throws Right	R	.269	104	28	3	1	2	10	8	8	.321	.375
Julio,Jorge	L	.227	97	22	7	0	0	10	15	18	.325	.299
Throws Right	R	.322	143	46	8	0	8	34	16	38	.396	.545
Jurrjens,Jair	L	.262	61	16	3	3	2	6	10	6	.366	.508
Throws Right	R	.167	48	8	1	0	2	9	1	7	.196	.313
Karstens,Jeff	L	.424	33	14	5	0	3	10	4	3	.486	.848
Throws Right	R	.371	35	13	4	0	1	8	5	2	.439	.571
Kazmir,Scott	L	.217	212	46	7	1	7	21	11	56	.262	.358
Throws Left	R	.263	570	150	32	3	11	56	78	183	.355	.388
Keisler,Randy	L	.154	13	2	2	0	0	2	2	2	.250	.308
Throws Left	R	.345	55	19	2	3	3	10	3	3	.373	.655
Kendrick,Kyle	L	.321	224	72	16	1	11	26	19	18	.374	.549
Throws Right	R	.241	237	57	12	0	5	22	6	31	.277	.354
Kennedy,Ian	L	.161	31	5	1	0	0	1	6	7	.297	.194
Throws Right	R	.216	37	8	2	0	1	5	3	8	.275	.351
Kennedy,Joe	L	.204	98	20	2	0	0	12	16	15	.341	.224
Throws Left	R	.306	324	99	17	3	9	47	39	36	.379	.460
Kensing,Logan	L	.250	28	7	1	0	0	1	5	9	.364	.286
Throws Right	R	.190	21	4	0	0	0	0	2	4	.320	.190
Keppel,Bobby	L	.222	9	2	1	0	1	2	1	0	.300	.667
Throws Right	R	.500	8	4	0	0	0	1	2	1	.600	.500
Kim,Byung-Hyun	L	.316	237	75	15	3	14	35	43	54	.443	.582
Throws Right	R	.242	231	56	10	1	6	40	25	53	.321	.372
King,Ray	L	.187	75	14	3	0	3	14	10	13	.284	.347
Throws Left	R	.311	74	23	8	1	3	11	11	12	.407	.568
Kline,Steve	L	.318	85	27	4	0	0	4	8	9	.383	.365
Throws Left	R	.287	108	31	7	0	2	13	10	8	.353	.407
Kolb,Dan	L	1.000	2	2	0	0	1	2	1	0	.750	2.500
Throws Right	R	.364	11	4	1	0	0	1	1	2	.417	.455
Komine,Shane	L	.333	9	3	0	0	1	2	0	1	.333	.667
Throws Right	R	.158	19	3	1	0	1	2	1	0	.227	.368
Koplove,Mike	L	.125	8	1	0	0	0	1	2	1	.300	.125
Throws Right	R	.333	15	5	4	0	0	2	0	3	.375	.600
Koronka,John	L	.250	8	2	0	1	0	3	0	0	.222	.500
Throws Left	R	.400	35	14	3	0	0	3	5	2	.488	.486
Kuo,Hong-Chih	L	.240	25	6	1	0	0	2	3	11	.321	.280
Throws Left	R	.296	98	29	6	1	3	21	11	16	.369	.469
Kuwata,Masumi	L	.200	25	5	0	1	1	5	10	3	.417	.400
Throws Right	R	.345	58	20	6	0	5	20	5	9	.394	.707
Lackey,John	L	.280	421	118	21	2	9	41	23	88	.330	.404

Pitchers vs. Left-Handed and Right-Handed Batters

Pitcher	vs	Avg	AB	H	2B	3B	HR	RBI	BB	SO	OBP	Slg
Throws Right	R	.229	442	101	20	3	9	36	29	91	.281	.348
Laffey,Aaron	L	.322	59	19	5	0	1	8	6	10	.412	.458
Throws Left	R	.271	129	35	8	0	1	12	6	15	.304	.357
Lannan,John	L	.273	22	6	0	0	1	5	4	6	.429	.409
Throws Left	R	.273	110	30	4	1	2	10	13	5	.350	.382
Lara,Juan	L	.500	2	1	0	0	1	2	0	0	.500	2.000
Throws Left	R	.250	4	1	0	0	0	0	1	2	.400	.250
Lawrence,Brian	L	.407	54	22	3	0	2	9	6	5	.467	.574
Throws Right	R	.300	70	21	5	0	2	13	7	13	.372	.457
League,Brandon	L	.458	24	11	3	0	1	6	2	1	.481	.708
Throws Right	R	.308	26	8	1	0	0	4	5	6	.419	.346
Ledezma,Wil	L	.312	77	24	3	0	3	17	9	19	.384	.468
Throws Left	R	.288	160	46	13	1	4	22	29	28	.391	.456
Lee,Cliff	L	.327	107	35	7	0	5	17	9	18	.385	.533
Throws Left	R	.267	288	77	21	1	12	49	27	48	.341	.472
Leicester,Jon	L	.242	66	16	10	0	2	11	10	8	.354	.485
Throws Right	R	.328	61	20	3	1	1	11	3	8	.369	.459
Lerew,Anthony	L	.222	18	4	1	0	1	2	6	5	.417	.444
Throws Right	R	.345	29	10	1	0	3	6	1	4	.367	.690
Lester,Jon	L	.231	65	15	2	0	3	10	10	12	.325	.400
Throws Left	R	.267	172	46	5	0	7	23	21	38	.345	.419
Lewis,Colby	L	.386	44	17	7	0	2	14	8	9	.481	.682
Throws Right	R	.255	106	27	2	1	5	22	6	14	.308	.434
Lewis,Jensen	L	.244	41	10	0	0	0	4	4	9	.304	.244
Throws Right	R	.229	70	16	4	1	1	6	6	25	.299	.357
Lidge,Brad	L	.184	103	19	5	3	3	11	11	34	.280	.379
Throws Right	R	.243	144	35	9	0	6	19	19	54	.335	.431
Lieber,Jon	L	.310	142	44	8	1	4	21	13	18	.371	.465
Throws Right	R	.278	169	47	12	2	3	24	9	36	.315	.426
Lilly,Ted	L	.258	151	39	11	1	3	16	8	38	.294	.404
Throws Left	R	.230	617	142	32	1	25	70	47	136	.284	.407
Lincecum,Tim	L	.214	266	57	15	4	8	31	34	71	.300	.391
Throws Right	R	.238	273	65	11	2	4	30	31	79	.316	.337
Lindstrom,Matt	L	.263	99	26	2	0	0	11	7	21	.315	.283
Throws Right	R	.255	157	40	8	0	2	18	14	41	.324	.344
Linebrink,Scott	L	.215	121	26	5	0	6	15	14	23	.301	.405
Throws Right	R	.284	148	42	5	0	6	18	11	27	.333	.439
Litsch,Jesse	L	.308	224	69	14	3	6	27	26	28	.385	.478
Throws Right	R	.229	205	47	5	0	8	20	10	22	.275	.371
Littleton,Wes	L	.236	72	17	1	0	4	13	4	8	.278	.417
Throws Right	R	.279	111	31	8	0	2	16	12	16	.357	.405
Livingston,Bobby	L	.341	44	15	3	0	3	6	3	9	.396	.614
Throws Left	R	.321	193	62	16	1	5	26	5	18	.338	.492
Liz,Radhames	L	.244	45	11	1	0	1	6	14	10	.417	.333
Throws Right	R	.275	51	14	3	0	2	13	9	14	.393	.451
Loaiza,Esteban	L	.294	51	15	3	1	3	7	12	7	.429	.569
Throws Right	R	.239	88	21	1	0	7	17	8	13	.306	.489
Loe,Kameron	L	.328	274	90	20	4	7	52	27	30	.388	.507
Throws Right	R	.262	275	72	15	1	6	31	29	48	.335	.389
Loewen,Adam	L	.227	22	5	1	0	0	4	5	3	.370	.273
Throws Left	R	.242	91	22	4	0	1	6	21	19	.400	.319
Logan,Boone	L	.221	86	19	3	0	1	12	10	22	.296	.291
Throws Left	R	.357	112	40	4	1	6	33	10	13	.397	.571
Lohse,Kyle	L	.276	348	96	21	1	12	49	28	61	.333	.445
Throws Right	R	.282	394	111	32	2	10	46	29	61	.343	.449
Looper,Braden	L	.279	298	83	20	2	10	38	22	50	.328	.460
Throws Right	R	.261	383	100	21	0	12	49	29	37	.315	.410
Lopez,Aquilino	L	.258	31	8	1	1	1	5	4	3	.351	.452
Throws Right	R	.286	35	10	0	0	1	4	2	4	.333	.371
Lopez,Javier	L	.293	82	24	5	2	1	20	8	18	.366	.439
Throws Left	R	.176	68	12	3	0	1	5	10	8	.300	.265
Lopez,Rodrigo	L	.270	159	43	9	3	7	22	11	23	.316	.497
Throws Right	R	.276	145	40	8	0	4	18	10	20	.314	.414
Lowe,Derek	L	.271	365	99	14	3	7	36	38	63	.338	.384
Throws Right	R	.239	398	95	19	0	13	52	21	84	.279	.384
Lowe,Mark	L	.667	3	2	1	0	1	1	2	0	.800	2.000
Throws Right	R	.000	7	0	0	0	0	0	1	3	.125	.000
Lowry,Noah	L	.216	111	24	2	0	1	8	12	18	.296	.261
Throws Left	R	.278	472	131	21	8	11	60	75	69	.379	.426
Lugo,Ruddy	L	.244	78	19	6	1	3	22	17	11	.388	.462
Throws Right	R	.274	106	29	9	1	0	22	20	23	.386	.377
Lyon,Brandon	L	.233	129	30	6	1	0	7	8	19	.277	.295
Throws Right	R	.267	150	40	13	1	2	20	14	21	.329	.407
MacDougal,Mike	L	.298	47	14	4	1	1	7	10	12	.421	.489
Throws Right	R	.288	125	36	9	0	2	25	23	27	.404	.408
Maddux,Greg	L	.280	347	97	26	2	4	31	13	49	.305	.401

Pitcher	vs	Avg	AB	H	2B	3B	HR	RBI	BB	SO	OBP	Slg
Throws Right	R	.289	429	124	21	6	10	52	12	55	.313	.436
Madson,Ryan	L	.170	88	15	4	0	2	6	16	24	.300	.284
Throws Right	R	.275	120	33	5	1	3	16	7	19	.313	.408
Mahay,Ron	L	.189	106	20	5	0	2	12	8	27	.250	.292
Throws Left	R	.242	132	32	8	2	2	15	29	28	.377	.379
Maholm,Paul	L	.238	105	25	2	0	3	11	7	25	.287	.343
Throws Left	R	.305	586	179	34	3	19	86	42	80	.355	.471
Maine,John	L	.237	334	79	17	3	13	40	50	82	.337	.422
Throws Right	R	.234	381	89	17	2	10	41	25	98	.285	.367
Majewski,Gary	L	.333	27	9	2	0	1	6	2	1	.379	.519
Throws Right	R	.420	81	34	4	0	2	11	1	9	.440	.543
Marcum,Shaun	L	.259	321	83	20	2	17	38	31	59	.329	.492
Throws Right	R	.237	278	66	10	1	10	36	18	63	.287	.388
Marmol,Carlos	L	.209	86	18	2	0	1	6	17	30	.349	.267
Throws Right	R	.146	157	23	3	0	2	7	18	66	.242	.204
Maroth,Mike	L	.299	97	29	7	1	3	12	13	23	.389	.485
Throws Left	R	.359	387	139	30	2	23	80	37	28	.414	.625
Marquis,Jason	L	.274	314	86	20	3	9	49	51	48	.382	.443
Throws Right	R	.242	429	104	20	1	13	51	25	61	.297	.385
Marshall,Jay	L	.296	71	21	3	1	0	11	6	9	.351	.366
Throws Left	R	.299	97	29	6	0	3	23	16	9	.415	.454
Marshall,Sean	L	.203	69	14	2	2	1	5	6	9	.267	.333
Throws Left	R	.280	332	93	16	1	12	42	29	58	.338	.443
Marte,Damaso	L	.094	64	6	2	0	0	3	10	25	.227	.125
Throws Left	R	.271	96	26	8	1	2	14	8	26	.327	.438
Martin,Tom	L	.289	38	11	1	2	1	6	4	5	.372	.500
Throws Left	R	.309	68	21	2	0	3	7	5	5	.356	.471
Martinez,Carlos	L	.333	6	2	1	0	1	1	0	1	.333	1.000
Throws Right	R	.333	6	2	0	0	2	3	1	1	.429	1.333
Martinez,Pedro	L	.319	47	15	4	0	0	2	3	11	.353	.404
Throws Right	R	.261	69	18	8	0	0	8	4	21	.316	.377
Masset,Nick	L	.338	68	23	3	0	1	17	9	10	.418	.426
Throws Right	R	.312	93	29	5	2	1	13	17	11	.416	.441
Mastny,Tom	L	.282	85	24	6	0	3	13	16	13	.402	.459
Throws Right	R	.283	138	39	8	1	3	21	16	39	.357	.420
Mateo,Julio	L	.200	15	3	0	0	0	1	4	1	.368	.200
Throws Right	R	.281	32	9	3	0	0	9	1	3	.303	.375
Matsuzaka,Daisuke	L	.238	369	88	18	2	14	53	50	105	.332	.412
Throws Right	R	.253	407	103	24	1	11	39	30	96	.321	.398
McBeth,Marcus	L	.273	33	9	3	1	2	4	3	6	.333	.606
Throws Right	R	.295	44	13	2	0	0	5	4	11	.360	.341
McBride,Macay	L	.263	57	15	1	0	2	14	5	17	.344	.386
Throws Left	R	.254	71	18	1	0	2	7	20	13	.418	.352
McCarthy,Brandon	L	.292	195	57	14	0	7	26	23	29	.364	.472
Throws Right	R	.263	205	54	17	1	2	31	25	30	.347	.385
McClellan,Zach	L	.394	33	13	5	0	0	6	4	5	.447	.545
Throws Right	R	.292	24	7	1	0	0	1	1	8	.320	.333
McClung,Seth	L	.313	16	5	1	1	0	0	1	4	.353	.500
Throws Right	R	.214	28	6	2	0	0	5	4	7	.324	.286
McGowan,Dustin	L	.257	338	87	19	2	12	47	35	78	.326	.432
Throws Right	R	.198	298	59	8	1	2	21	26	66	.262	.252
McLeary,Marty	L	.294	17	5	1	0	3	9	1	1	.333	.882
Throws Right	R	.267	15	4	1	0	1	2	1	4	.313	.533
McLemore,Mark	L	.419	43	18	6	0	1	7	6	10	.480	.628
Throws Left	R	.204	98	20	6	0	4	11	12	25	.297	.388
Meche,Gil	L	.242	414	100	15	4	11	43	38	91	.306	.377
Throws Right	R	.284	415	118	22	0	11	50	24	65	.322	.417
Medders,Brandon	L	.186	43	8	1	0	3	7	11	12	.352	.419
Throws Right	R	.328	67	22	2	0	6	8	5	11	.384	.627
Meloan,Jonathan	L	.231	13	3	1	1	0	5	4	2	.412	.462
Throws Right	R	.333	15	5	2	0	1	3	4	5	.500	.667
Mendoza,Luis	L	.281	32	9	1	0	0	4	3	2	.324	.313
Throws Right	R	.167	24	4	2	0	1	2	1	5	.259	.375
Meredith,Cla	L	.286	133	38	6	0	4	31	9	17	.336	.421
Throws Right	R	.303	185	56	5	0	2	24	8	42	.333	.362
Mesa,Jose	L	.263	76	20	3	1	2	15	13	13	.363	.408
Throws Right	R	.280	118	33	6	2	7	29	12	16	.346	.542
Messenger,Randy	L	.342	111	38	6	1	0	14	12	19	.403	.414
Throws Right	R	.320	147	47	9	0	4	32	9	15	.354	.463
Meyer,Dan	L	.400	20	8	0	2	1	6	2	1	.435	.750
Throws Left	R	.250	48	12	2	1	1	10	7	10	.345	.396
Miller,Andrew	L	.175	57	10	2	0	0	5	8	23	.304	.211
Throws Left	R	.312	202	63	7	3	8	34	31	33	.414	.495
Miller,Jason	L	.200	5	1	0	0	1	1	0	2	.200	.800
Throws Left	R	.429	14	6	3	0	1	7	3	0	.529	.857
Miller,Justin	L	.324	74	24	4	2	3	13	8	18	.390	.554

Pitchers vs. Left-Handed and Right-Handed Batters

Pitcher	vs	Avg	AB	H	2B	3B	HR	RBI	BB	SO	OBP	Slg
Throws Right	R	.184	158	29	7	2	2	15	16	56	.259	.291
Miller,Matt	L	.000	1	0	0	0	0	0	0	0	.000	.000
Throws Right	R	.500	4	2	0	0	0	1	0	0	.500	.500
Miller,Trever	L	.209	91	19	5	1	2	14	9	30	.301	.352
Throws Left	R	.289	90	26	6	1	4	14	14	16	.390	.511
Miller,Wade	L	.412	34	14	4	0	4	13	4	5	.474	.882
Throws Right	R	.345	29	10	2	0	1	2	2	1	.387	.517
Millwood,Kevin	L	.288	313	90	18	3	11	46	43	60	.373	.470
Throws Right	R	.311	395	123	22	0	8	54	24	63	.360	.428
Milton,Eric	L	.300	20	6	2	0	1	4	1	7	.333	.550
Throws Left	R	.297	111	33	10	1	3	15	8	11	.345	.486
Miner,Zach	L	.207	82	17	1	3	0	9	8	16	.275	.293
Throws Right	R	.317	123	39	7	0	3	15	14	18	.387	.447
Misch,Pat	L	.238	42	10	6	0	0	1	5	9	.319	.381
Throws Left	R	.316	117	37	7	2	3	24	7	17	.359	.487
Mitre,Sergio	L	.271	291	79	14	0	4	38	25	30	.328	.361
Throws Right	R	.332	304	101	13	3	5	42	16	50	.375	.444
Moehler,Brian	L	.303	89	27	5	0	4	16	11	18	.376	.494
Throws Right	R	.268	149	40	4	1	4	13	6	18	.297	.389
Morales,Franklin	L	.129	31	4	1	1	0	1	2	7	.206	.226
Throws Left	R	.273	110	30	5	0	2	13	12	19	.344	.373
Morillo,Juan	L	.111	9	1	0	0	0	0	1	3	.200	.111
Throws Right	R	.400	5	2	0	0	1	4	0	0	.500	1.000
Morris,Matt	L	.293	352	103	28	2	6	47	33	45	.350	.435
Throws Right	R	.309	443	137	33	2	12	59	28	57	.359	.474
Morrow,Brandon	L	.278	90	25	6	0	2	11	27	22	.437	.411
Throws Right	R	.221	140	31	9	0	1	15	23	44	.331	.307
Moseley,Dustin	L	.224	161	36	11	3	2	15	12	31	.277	.366
Throws Right	R	.323	189	61	8	1	5	23	15	19	.378	.455
Mota,Guillermo	L	.235	98	23	6	0	3	16	5	17	.279	.388
Throws Right	R	.284	141	40	9	0	5	23	13	30	.348	.454
Moyer,Jamie	L	.309	152	47	13	1	6	28	12	24	.361	.526
Throws Left	R	.279	628	175	44	3	24	77	54	109	.338	.473
Moylan,Peter	L	.242	128	31	7	2	0	11	20	28	.351	.328
Throws Right	R	.184	185	34	2	0	6	25	11	35	.245	.292
Mujica,Edward	L	.320	25	8	2	1	1	2	1	4	.333	.600
Throws Right	R	.344	32	11	2	1	2	9	1	3	.364	.656
Mulder,Mark	L	.455	11	5	1	0	2	5	0	1	.455	1.091
Throws Left	R	.436	39	17	7	0	2	10	7	2	.532	.769
Muniz,Carlos	L	.000	2	0	0	0	0	0	0	1	.000	.000
Throws Right	R	.167	6	1	0	0	0	0	2	1	.375	.167
Munoz,Arnie	L	.286	7	2	0	0	1	4	3	0	.583	.714
Throws Left	R	.267	15	4	1	0	1	3	4	3	.421	.533
Munter,Scott	L	.273	11	3	0	0	0	2	3	1	.429	.273
Throws Right	R	.407	27	11	2	1	0	11	1	3	.400	.556
Murphy,Bill	L	.462	13	6	1	0	0	6	4	1	.588	.538
Throws Left	R	.231	13	3	0	0	0	1	3	1	.412	.231
Murray,A.J.	L	.308	26	8	0	2	2	6	4	5	.400	.692
Throws Left	R	.215	79	17	4	1	4	8	11	13	.308	.443
Musser,Neal	L	.395	38	15	3	0	3	7	3	7	.439	.711
Throws Left	R	.266	64	17	5	0	2	10	11	12	.373	.438
Mussina,Mike	L	.315	305	96	25	0	6	36	16	46	.348	.456
Throws Right	R	.307	300	92	24	1	8	47	19	45	.351	.473
Myers,Brett	L	.183	115	21	5	0	3	9	14	38	.269	.304
Throws Right	R	.274	146	40	5	2	6	23	13	45	.338	.459
Myers,Mike	L	.295	105	31	7	0	1	19	13	22	.372	.390
Throws Left	R	.259	108	28	6	0	5	25	10	5	.328	.454
Nathan,Joe	L	.221	122	27	7	0	2	11	12	34	.292	.328
Throws Right	R	.199	136	27	7	0	2	7	7	43	.238	.294
Neshek,Pat	L	.181	94	17	5	0	3	16	13	21	.288	.330
Throws Right	R	.185	146	27	6	1	4	19	14	53	.252	.322
Newman,Josh	L	.000	5	0	0	0	0	0	0	2	.000	.000
Throws Left	R	.667	3	2	1	0	0	1	0	1	.667	1.000
Nippert,Dustin	L	.238	80	19	4	0	1	9	12	17	.337	.325
Throws Right	R	.290	100	29	8	0	4	20	4	21	.317	.490
Nolasco,Ricky	L	.293	41	12	1	0	0	1	7	7	.400	.317
Throws Right	R	.350	40	14	1	1	3	15	2	4	.348	.650
Nunez,Leo	L	.275	69	19	4	0	6	12	6	15	.325	.594
Throws Right	R	.248	101	25	6	0	2	5	4	22	.276	.366
Obermueller,Wes	L	.309	123	38	7	2	6	28	16	19	.390	.545
Throws Right	R	.304	112	34	8	0	1	19	20	16	.416	.402
O'Flaherty,Eric	L	.183	93	17	0	1	0	6	11	18	.278	.204
Throws Left	R	.277	101	28	7	0	1	12	9	18	.354	.376
Ohka,Tomo	L	.299	97	29	6	0	6	14	12	9	.376	.546
Throws Right	R	.300	130	39	6	0	4	17	10	12	.348	.438
Ohlendorf,Ross	L	.267	15	4	0	0	1	2	0	8	.267	.467
Throws Right	R	.111	9	1	0	0	0	1	2	1	.273	.111
Ohman,Will	L	.236	72	17	5	0	2	10	10	20	.329	.389
Throws Left	R	.325	77	25	9	0	1	14	6	13	.381	.481
Okajima,Hideki	L	.236	89	21	3	1	2	5	7	23	.289	.360
Throws Left	R	.182	159	29	3	0	4	10	10	40	.235	.277
Oliver,Darren	L	.289	90	26	7	0	3	17	9	22	.343	.467
Throws Left	R	.209	153	32	4	0	2	13	14	29	.278	.275
Olsen,Scott	L	.331	142	47	7	0	5	28	11	28	.383	.486
Throws Left	R	.311	576	179	38	2	24	92	74	105	.384	.509
Olson,Garrett	L	.261	23	6	2	0	0	6	5	9	.393	.348
Throws Left	R	.340	106	36	5	0	4	21	23	19	.455	.500
Ortiz,Ramon	L	.313	195	61	8	1	8	38	14	15	.358	.487
Throws Right	R	.287	230	66	21	0	8	36	8	36	.321	.483
Ortiz,Russ	L	.346	81	28	7	1	3	15	14	9	.465	.568
Throws Right	R	.259	112	29	9	0	1	14	6	18	.306	.366
Orvella,Chad	L	.500	16	8	3	0	0	6	3	2	.579	.688
Throws Right	R	.345	29	10	2	1	3	10	7	4	.486	.793
Osoria,Franquelis	L	.353	34	12	1	0	2	8	5	2	.436	.559
Throws Right	R	.263	80	21	1	0	1	9	3	11	.322	.313
Oswalt,Roy	L	.272	427	116	27	4	5	31	37	88	.328	.389
Throws Right	R	.259	406	105	24	1	9	42	23	66	.309	.389
Otsuka,Akinori	L	.172	58	10	1	0	0	5	6	14	.246	.190
Throws Right	R	.262	61	16	6	0	0	4	3	9	.292	.361
Owens,Henry	L	.262	42	11	2	0	2	4	6	5	.354	.452
Throws Right	R	.174	46	8	4	0	1	2	4	11	.240	.326
Owings,Micah	L	.265	298	79	16	4	15	47	30	51	.339	.497
Throws Right	R	.240	279	67	17	3	5	28	20	55	.312	.376
Padilla,Vicente	L	.329	231	76	8	0	8	34	30	34	.410	.468
Throws Right	R	.271	258	70	10	1	8	39	20	37	.338	.411
Papelbon,Jonathan	L	.104	115	12	4	0	3	9	11	56	.183	.217
Throws Right	R	.200	90	18	1	0	2	8	4	28	.265	.278
Park,Chan Ho	L	.375	8	3	1	0	1	2	0	1	.375	.875
Throws Right	R	.300	10	3	0	0	1	5	2	3	.417	.600
Paronto,Chad	L	.333	66	22	2	1	1	14	9	4	.410	.439
Throws Right	R	.287	87	25	5	0	0	13	10	10	.370	.345
Parra,Manny	L	.174	23	4	0	0	1	3	1	10	.208	.304
Throws Left	R	.280	75	21	3	1	0	13	11	16	.374	.347
Parrish,John	L	.293	92	27	7	0	1	12	8	13	.353	.402
Throws Left	R	.298	121	36	6	0	1	26	29	28	.437	.372
Patterson,John	L	.328	58	19	6	0	2	11	13	7	.444	.534
Throws Right	R	.294	68	20	4	1	3	8	9	8	.377	.515
Patton,Troy	L	.100	10	1	1	0	0	0	0	1	.100	.200
Throws Left	R	.243	37	9	2	0	3	5	4	7	.349	.541
Paulino,Felipe	L	.310	29	9	1	0	3	7	5	3	.412	.655
Throws Right	R	.277	47	13	5	1	2	8	2	8	.306	.553
Pavano,Carl	L	.208	24	5	1	0	0	2	1	1	.240	.250
Throws Right	R	.350	20	7	2	0	1	4	1	3	.381	.600
Peavy,Jake	L	.242	409	99	21	4	8	39	41	101	.314	.372
Throws Right	R	.174	403	70	10	3	5	23	27	139	.228	.251
Peguero,Jailen	L	.240	25	6	2	1	0	5	7	5	.394	.400
Throws Right	R	.367	30	11	1	0	2	6	6	4	.486	.600
Pelfrey,Mike	L	.323	130	42	6	0	5	24	24	19	.428	.485
Throws Right	R	.277	155	43	8	2	1	16	15	26	.367	.374
Pena,Tony	L	.245	139	34	6	2	6	22	14	23	.316	.446
Throws Right	R	.176	165	29	5	1	2	15	17	40	.266	.255
Penny,Brad	L	.229	353	81	20	1	1	29	39	70	.305	.300
Throws Right	R	.286	412	118	27	0	8	40	34	65	.343	.410
Peralta,Joel	L	.248	125	31	6	4	4	15	9	21	.299	.456
Throws Right	R	.290	214	62	15	2	5	34	10	45	.322	.449
Percival,Troy	L	.220	59	13	3	1	1	6	4	12	.270	.356
Throws Right	R	.136	81	11	1	0	2	4	6	24	.195	.222
Perez,Juan	L	.313	16	5	1	0	0	0	3	6	.421	.375
Throws Left	R	.273	33	9	2	0	2	6	5	4	.368	.515
Perez,Odalis	L	.301	123	37	11	0	2	22	13	14	.364	.439
Throws Left	R	.323	436	141	36	1	12	58	37	50	.377	.493
Perez,Oliver	L	.206	141	29	2	1	5	18	15	47	.285	.340
Throws Left	R	.235	527	124	32	0	17	60	64	127	.322	.393
Perez,Rafael	L	.145	83	12	2	0	2	6	7	22	.209	.241
Throws Left	R	.213	136	29	4	1	3	11	8	40	.257	.324
Perkins,Glen	L	.250	36	9	2	0	1	5	3	9	.300	.389
Throws Left	R	.222	63	14	2	0	1	6	9	11	.338	.302
Petit,Yusmeiro	L	.274	95	26	7	3	6	14	15	14	.373	.600
Throws Right	R	.250	128	32	8	0	6	11	3	26	[illegible]	.453
Petrick,Billy	L	.154	13	2	1	0	0	0	3	3	.313	.231
Throws Right	R	[illegible]	22	6	0	0	3	8	4	3	.385	.682
Pettitte,Andy	L	.298	198	59	9	3	7	26	19	34	.356	.480

Pitchers vs. Left-Handed and Right-Handed Batters

Pitcher	vs	Avg	AB	H	2B	3B	HR	RBI	BB	SO	OBP	Slg
Throws Left	R	.282	634	179	40	2	9	67	50	107	.332	.394
Phillips,Heath	L	.375	8	3	0	0	0	2	2	0	.500	.375
Throws Left	R	.318	22	7	2	0	1	2	2	2	.375	.545
Pignatiello,Carmen	L	.500	6	3	0	0	1	2	0	3	.500	1.000
Throws Left	R	.000	2	0	0	0	0	0	0	0	.000	.000
Pineiro,Joel	L	.250	160	40	9	0	7	19	16	28	.318	.438
Throws Right	R	.308	227	70	21	1	7	26	10	32	.342	.502
Pinto,Renyel	L	.210	62	13	1	0	0	3	10	23	.333	.226
Throws Left	R	.227	141	32	7	0	7	19	22	33	.331	.426
Ponson,Sidney	L	.265	83	22	5	1	2	16	11	12	.358	.422
Throws Right	R	.410	78	32	5	0	5	14	6	11	.465	.667
Prinz,Bret	L	.333	6	2	1	0	1	1	0	0	.333	1.000
Throws Right	R	.250	8	2	0	0	0	0	2	1	.400	.250
Proctor,Scott	L	.250	136	34	7	1	4	18	23	23	.362	.404
Throws Right	R	.237	186	44	4	1	8	24	21	41	.319	.398
Putz,J.J.	L	.148	128	19	3	0	4	6	5	44	.187	.266
Throws Right	R	.158	114	18	3	0	2	10	8	38	.218	.237
Qualls,Chad	L	.248	129	32	3	0	1	7	9	35	.295	.295
Throws Right	R	.289	180	52	3	2	9	29	16	43	.355	.478
Rakers,Aaron	L	.500	2	1	0	0	0	0	0	0	.500	.500
Throws Right	R	.000	2	0	0	0	0	0	0	0	.000	.000
Ramirez,Edwar	L	.342	38	13	3	0	3	17	8	10	.457	.658
Throws Right	R	.239	46	11	2	0	3	8	6	21	.357	.478
Ramirez,Elizardo	L	.258	31	8	1	0	3	8	6	4	.378	.581
Throws Right	R	.364	33	12	0	0	2	6	2	4	.400	.545
Ramirez,Erasmo	L	.182	11	2	1	0	0	0	2	0	.308	.273
Throws Left	R	.357	14	5	0	0	0	1	1	1	.400	.357
Ramirez,Horacio	L	.330	100	33	8	1	2	14	10	13	.391	.490
Throws Left	R	.340	312	106	19	2	11	61	32	27	.403	.519
Ramirez,Ramon	L	.240	25	6	1	0	0	3	4	7	.344	.280
Throws Right	R	.357	42	15	7	0	2	15	2	8	.306	.667
Randolph,Stephen	L	.364	22	8	3	1	2	5	5	10	.481	.804
Throws Left	R	.361	36	13	4	0	2	9	12	12	.520	.639
Rapada,Clay	L	.143	7	1	0	0	1	3	2	3	.333	.571
Throws Left	R	.500	4	2	1	0	1	2	0	1	.500	1.500
Rasner,Darrell	L	.375	48	18	3	0	2	7	5	3	.426	.563
Throws Right	R	.212	52	11	3	0	2	5	3	8	.281	.385
Rauch,Jon	L	.208	149	31	5	0	6	20	11	25	.259	.362
Throws Right	R	.249	177	44	8	2	1	18	10	46	.284	.333
Ray,Chris	L	.233	73	17	1	1	1	6	13	17	.356	.315
Throws Right	R	.212	85	18	5	0	4	20	5	27	.261	.412
Redding,Tim	L	.245	147	36	6	0	5	19	19	22	.329	.388
Throws Right	R	.282	170	48	9	0	5	13	19	25	.368	.424
Redman,Mark	L	.250	44	11	0	0	1	6	3	8	.298	.318
Throws Left	R	.358	134	48	12	1	5	29	14	19	.421	.575
Reitsma,Chris	L	.357	42	15	4	0	2	15	3	7	.400	.595
Throws Right	R	.361	61	22	5	0	1	10	6	4	.412	.492
Resop,Chris	L	.286	7	2	0	0	0	0	1	1	.375	.286
Throws Right	R	.333	6	2	0	0	1	4	0	1	.286	.833
Reyes,Al	L	.240	121	29	8	0	7	20	13	36	.316	.479
Throws Right	R	.187	107	20	2	0	6	15	8	34	.248	.374
Reyes,Anthony	L	.290	200	58	12	1	7	36	7	36	.310	.465
Throws Right	R	.234	214	50	16	3	9	37	36	38	.361	.463
Reyes,Dennys	L	.273	66	18	3	0	0	9	8	12	.354	.318
Throws Left	R	.364	44	16	3	0	1	4	13	9	.509	.500
Reyes,Jo-Jo	L	.129	31	4	0	0	1	3	8	9	.308	.226
Throws Left	R	.317	161	51	13	0	8	29	22	18	.398	.547
Rheinecker,John	L	.229	70	16	4	0	2	10	5	21	.289	.371
Throws Left	R	.328	137	45	6	0	7	23	23	19	.426	.526
Ridgway,Jeff	L	1.000	4	4	0	0	1	5	1	0	1.000	1.750
Throws Left	R	.750	4	3	0	1	0	2	0	0	.800	1.250
Rincon,Juan	L	.313	115	36	6	1	5	22	15	24	.402	.513
Throws Right	R	.236	123	29	4	0	4	15	13	25	.312	.366
Ring,Royce	L	.206	34	7	1	0	1	6	10	13	.378	.324
Throws Left	R	.167	36	6	0	0	0	5	7	8	.302	.167
Riske,David	L	.202	99	20	5	1	2	8	11	26	.279	.333
Throws Right	R	.265	155	41	8	0	6	22	16	26	.333	.432
Rivera,Mariano	L	.255	137	35	4	1	1	11	4	32	.287	.321
Throws Right	R	.241	137	33	6	2	3	18	8	42	.300	.380
Rivera,Saul	L	.271	144	39	7	1	0	14	19	28	.356	.333
Throws Right	R	.244	201	49	18	0	1	18	23	36	.322	.348
Robertson,Connor	L	1.000	2	2	2	0	0	2	0	0	.667	2.000
Throws Right	R	.444	9	4	1	0	0	1	2	2	.583	.556
Robertson,Nate	L	.296	189	56	9	1	3	19	8	34	.330	.402
Throws Left	R	.278	514	143	31	3	19	72	55	85	.346	.461
Rodney,Fernando	L	.247	85	21	2	1	2	8	11	22	.347	.365

Pitcher	vs	Avg	AB	H	2B	3B	HR	RBI	BB	SO	OBP	Slg
Throws Right	R	.231	108	25	8	0	3	21	10	32	.298	.389
Rodriguez,Francisco	L	.187	107	20	7	0	0	12	18	44	.297	.252
Throws Right	R	.217	138	30	5	2	3	16	16	46	.301	.348
Rodriguez,Wandy	L	.252	127	32	6	0	3	17	9	34	.301	.370
Throws Left	R	.254	578	147	39	5	19	73	53	124	.320	.438
Rogers,Brian	L	.500	2	1	0	0	0	1	0	0	.500	.500
Throws Right	R	.500	4	2	0	0	2	3	1	1	.500	2.000
Rogers,Kenny	L	.197	66	13	2	1	1	2	9	11	.303	.303
Throws Left	R	.289	180	52	11	2	7	31	16	25	.342	.489
Romero,J.C.	L	.208	77	16	6	1	0	6	14	20	.333	.312
Throws Left	R	.198	116	23	6	0	3	9	26	22	.350	.328
Rosario,Francisco	L	.340	50	17	5	0	1	8	6	13	.414	.500
Throws Right	R	.304	56	17	5	0	2	10	7	12	.403	.500
Rowland-Smith,Ryan	L	.275	51	14	2	1	1	15	5	19	.322	.412
Throws Left	R	.266	94	25	8	0	3	11	10	23	.346	.447
Ryan,B.J.	L	.333	3	1	0	0	0	0	0	2	.333	.333
Throws Left	R	.333	18	6	1	0	1	6	4	1	.455	.556
Ryu,Jae Kuk	L	.354	48	17	4	1	1	5	8	5	.456	.542
Throws Right	R	.298	47	14	4	0	1	12	3	9	.377	.447
Saarloos,Kirk	L	.338	68	23	5	1	3	12	6	11	.400	.574
Throws Right	R	.284	109	31	8	0	5	20	13	16	.371	.495
Sabathia,C.C.	L	.203	202	41	14	0	3	12	4	75	.229	.317
Throws Left	R	.275	716	197	46	1	17	77	33	134	.310	.413
Saito,Takashi	L	.186	113	21	3	0	4	9	5	25	.240	.319
Throws Right	R	.114	105	12	1	0	1	5	8	53	.177	.152
Salas,Juan	L	.260	77	20	2	0	4	13	8	15	.337	.442
Throws Right	R	.235	68	16	6	0	3	8	9	11	.358	.456
Salmon,Brad	L	.310	29	9	2	0	2	7	4	4	.394	.586
Throws Right	R	.213	61	13	1	0	1	8	6	18	.294	.279
Sampson,Chris	L	.291	223	65	12	4	9	25	13	23	.333	.502
Throws Right	R	.292	250	73	9	0	11	35	17	28	.344	.460
Sanches,Brian	L	.300	20	6	2	0	1	4	5	3	.440	.550
Throws Right	R	.206	34	7	1	0	5	7	7	6	.357	.676
Sanchez,Anibal	L	.329	70	23	5	0	2	12	11	7	.420	.486
Throws Right	R	.357	56	20	4	1	1	5	8	7	.441	.518
Sanchez,Jonathan	L	.197	61	12	1	0	2	2	9	24	.310	.311
Throws Left	R	.321	140	45	7	0	6	21	19	38	.412	.500
Sanchez,Romulo	L	.353	17	6	0	0	0	1	2	1	.421	.353
Throws Right	R	.217	46	10	4	0	2	8	6	10	.315	.435
Santana,Ervin	L	.284	275	78	19	3	11	37	36	61	.373	.495
Throws Right	R	.292	329	96	19	2	15	54	22	65	.343	.498
Santana,Johan	L	.197	198	39	8	0	9	21	20	62	.276	.374
Throws Left	R	.234	616	144	32	4	24	63	32	173	.273	.416
Santos,Victor	L	.280	100	28	6	1	5	19	14	20	.365	.510
Throws Right	R	.307	140	43	9	0	10	32	19	28	.394	.586
Sarfate,Dennis	L	.182	11	2	1	0	0	1	0	4	.167	.273
Throws Right	R	.167	18	3	1	0	0	0	1	10	.211	.222
Saunders,Joe	L	.274	84	23	2	1	0	5	3	12	.299	.321
Throws Left	R	.304	349	106	25	1	11	46	31	57	.358	.476
Schilling,Curt	L	.274	336	92	20	1	14	41	13	62	.301	.464
Throws Right	R	.277	264	73	15	1	7	23	10	39	.304	.420
Schmidt,Jason	L	.250	48	12	3	0	1	7	3	10	.294	.375
Throws Right	R	.333	60	20	4	1	3	9	11	12	.444	.583
Schoeneweis,Scott	L	.204	93	19	4	0	0	6	11	21	.308	.247
Throws Left	R	.316	136	43	9	1	8	23	17	20	.390	.574
Schroder,Chris	L	.250	64	16	3	0	2	5	8	14	.333	.391
Throws Right	R	.183	109	20	5	0	0	7	7	29	.246	.229
Schultz,Mike	L	1.000	1	1	0	0	0	0	0	0	1.000	1.000
Throws Right	R	.000	2	0	0	0	0	0	0	1	.000	.000
Seanez,Rudy	L	.269	119	32	4	1	3	9	7	33	.320	.395
Throws Right	R	.264	174	46	3	0	7	26	20	40	.342	.402
Seay,Bobby	L	.209	91	19	4	1	0	5	7	24	.270	.275
Throws Left	R	.250	76	19	5	1	1	9	8	14	.326	.382
Seddon,Chris	L	.214	14	3	0	0	0	2	1	3	.313	.214
Throws Left	R	.377	69	26	5	0	2	16	4	7	.405	.536
Segovia,Zack	L	.250	8	2	0	0	1	3	1	0	.300	.625
Throws Right	R	.500	12	6	2	1	0	2	0	2	.500	.833
Sele,Aaron	L	.420	81	34	9	3	2	15	10	8	.473	.679
Throws Right	R	.321	137	44	14	0	3	22	11	21	.373	.489
Seo,Jae	L	.375	112	42	7	1	5	21	6	18	.418	.589
Throws Right	R	.368	114	42	7	2	6	26	10	10	.424	.623
Serafini,Dan	L	.000	1	0	0	0	0	0	2	0	.750	.000
Throws Left	R	-	0	0	0	0	0	0	0	0	-	-
Sharpless,Josh	L	.250	8	2	1	0	0	0	1	1	.333	.375
Throws Right	R	.455	11	5	2	0	3	8	0	0	.455	1.455
Shearn,Tom	L	.200	50	10	3	0	2	8	5	9	.268	.380

Pitchers vs. Left-Handed and Right-Handed Batters

Pitcher	vs	Avg	AB	H	2B	3B	HR	RBI	BB	SO	OBP	Slg
Throws Right	R	.306	72	22	4	0	6	11	8	7	.375	.611
Sheets,Ben	L	.200	255	51	5	2	9	23	13	53	.241	.341
Throws Right	R	.300	290	87	18	3	8	35	24	53	.349	.466
Sherrill,George	L	.156	90	14	3	0	3	14	10	40	.240	.289
Throws Left	R	.212	66	14	3	0	1	9	7	16	.284	.303
Shields,James	L	.243	387	94	20	4	10	39	19	81	.280	.393
Throws Right	R	.250	432	108	21	1	18	47	17	103	.290	.428
Shields,Scot	L	.214	145	31	8	0	6	29	17	47	.301	.393
Throws Right	R	.226	137	31	3	0	1	7	16	30	.318	.270
Shouse,Brian	L	.214	84	18	4	0	0	11	6	21	.264	.262
Throws Left	R	.295	95	28	4	0	0	11	8	11	.358	.337
Shuey,Paul	L	.355	31	11	3	0	3	15	11	7	.524	.742
Throws Right	R	.301	73	22	4	2	0	6	10	15	.386	.411
Silva,Carlos	L	.294	394	116	20	4	14	49	28	45	.340	.472
Throws Right	R	.280	403	113	21	3	6	38	8	44	.299	.392
Simontacchi,Jason	L	.311	135	42	10	3	6	26	7	20	.347	.563
Throws Right	R	.346	153	53	11	0	7	20	16	22	.409	.556
Sisco,Andy	L	.250	32	8	3	0	0	4	3	7	.314	.344
Throws Left	R	.367	30	11	3	0	2	7	8	6	.513	.667
Slaten,Doug	L	.268	82	22	6	0	1	15	8	19	.333	.378
Throws Left	R	.284	67	19	4	0	3	3	6	9	.342	.478
Slowey,Kevin	L	.267	146	39	10	1	8	16	9	21	.310	.514
Throws Right	R	.309	139	43	9	1	8	21	2	26	.317	.561
Smith,Joe	L	.298	47	14	4	0	1	10	7	13	.411	.447
Throws Right	R	.266	128	34	6	0	2	26	14	32	.361	.359
Smith,Matt	L	.400	5	2	0	0	0	2	6	1	.727	.400
Throws Left	R	.182	11	2	1	0	0	1	5	0	.438	.273
Smoltz,John	L	.262	385	101	16	3	8	28	35	76	.327	.382
Throws Right	R	.237	401	95	23	0	10	36	12	121	.259	.369
Snell,Ian	L	.284	380	108	21	1	13	46	42	76	.353	.447
Throws Right	R	.245	412	101	23	3	9	41	26	101	.300	.381
Snyder,Kyle	L	.195	82	16	3	0	3	10	11	15	.313	.341
Throws Right	R	.242	120	29	6	0	4	18	21	26	.366	.392
Sonnanstine,Andy	L	.318	267	85	18	1	11	44	15	42	.352	.517
Throws Right	R	.266	248	66	19	2	7	33	11	55	.307	.444
Soria,Joakim	L	.167	96	16	4	1	0	5	7	25	.217	.229
Throws Right	R	.200	150	30	4	0	3	13	12	50	.264	.287
Soriano,Rafael	L	.164	122	20	3	1	6	16	10	28	.233	.352
Throws Right	R	.197	137	27	4	0	6	12	5	42	.231	.358
Sosa,Jorge	L	.326	184	60	14	2	7	32	24	30	.400	.538
Throws Right	R	.202	243	49	14	0	3	27	17	39	.253	.296
Sowers,Jeremy	L	.206	63	13	3	0	1	7	7	6	.292	.302
Throws Left	R	.338	210	71	17	1	9	40	14	18	.381	.557
Speier,Justin	L	.222	81	18	3	0	3	8	8	26	.289	.370
Throws Right	R	.186	97	18	3	1	3	10	4	21	.245	.330
Speier,Ryan	L	.333	24	8	4	0	0	3	4	6	.429	.500
Throws Right	R	.279	43	12	2	0	1	4	4	7	.354	.395
Speigner,Levale	L	.329	70	23	3	0	3	16	10	6	.407	.500
Throws Right	R	.350	100	35	11	1	1	26	13	13	.417	.510
Springer,Russ	L	.235	68	16	4	1	1	5	7	17	.316	.368
Throws Right	R	.158	158	25	2	1	2	16	12	49	.219	.222
Spurling,Chris	L	.315	89	28	5	0	4	18	10	11	.386	.506
Throws Right	R	.294	119	35	7	1	2	19	4	17	.323	.420
Standridge,Jason	L	.308	13	4	1	0	1	2	1	2	.357	.615
Throws Right	R	.318	22	7	2	0	1	5	4	4	.423	.545
Stanford,Jason	L	.407	27	11	2	0	1	8	3	4	.469	.593
Throws Left	R	.259	81	21	3	0	0	7	4	12	.302	.296
Stanton,Mike	L	.306	98	30	4	1	2	22	1	21	.333	.429
Throws Left	R	.321	140	45	11	0	4	24	17	19	.400	.486
Stauffer,Tim	L	.467	15	7	0	0	4	8	2	3	.529	1.267
Throws Right	R	.348	23	8	1	0	1	8	4	3	.464	.522
Stetter,Mitch	L	.222	9	2	2	0	0	0	1	4	.364	.444
Throws Left	R	.000	6	0	0	0	0	2	1	0	.222	.000
Stokes,Brian	L	.346	127	44	6	0	6	18	14	19	.415	.535
Throws Right	R	.341	135	46	10	0	5	33	11	16	.391	.526
Stone,Ricky	L	.143	14	2	0	1	1	1	0	2	.143	.500
Throws Right	R	.625	8	5	1	0	3	7	0	1	.667	1.875
Street,Huston	L	.224	85	19	3	0	4	13	10	32	.302	.400
Throws Right	R	.162	99	16	3	0	1	7	2	31	.178	.222
Stults,Eric	L	.353	34	12	2	0	2	8	1	5	.371	.588
Throws Left	R	.304	125	38	8	1	3	15	16	25	.385	.456
Suppan,Jeff	L	.334	347	116	26	2	8	42	32	47	.397	.490
Throws Right	R	.271	468	127	34	1	10	65	36	67	.325	.412
Switzer,Jon	L	.242	33	8	2	0	1	5	2	5	.278	.394
Throws Left	R	.404	47	19	7	0	1	10	5	8	.462	.617
Tallet,Brian	L	.247	89	22	5	2	0	17	11	25	.349	.348

Pitcher	vs	Avg	AB	H	2B	3B	HR	RBI	BB	SO	OBP	Slg
Throws Left	R	.194	139	27	5	1	1	15	17	29	.289	.266
Tankersley,Taylor	L	.179	78	14	3	0	2	11	10	25	.286	.295
Throws Left	R	.301	93	28	2	1	2	11	19	24	.421	.409
Taschner,Jack	L	.316	79	25	8	0	2	21	10	18	.391	.494
Throws Left	R	.176	108	19	6	0	2	11	19	33	.297	.287
Tata,Jordan	L	.375	24	9	5	2	0	7	7	5	.500	.750
Throws Right	R	.241	29	7	2	0	1	4	1	3	.313	.414
Taubenheim,Ty	L	.286	7	2	1	0	0	1	2	1	.444	.429
Throws Right	R	.273	11	3	1	0	1	2	2	3	.400	.636
Tavarez,Julian	L	.260	265	69	15	0	6	32	31	43	.338	.385
Throws Right	R	.300	273	82	22	1	8	47	20	34	.358	.476
Tejeda,Robinson	L	.317	186	59	13	2	12	32	32	26	.421	.602
Throws Right	R	.264	193	51	11	0	5	38	28	43	.361	.399
Thatcher,Joe	L	.200	25	5	2	0	1	5	4	8	.310	.400
Throws Left	R	.151	53	8	2	0	0	2	2	8	.196	.189
Thompson,Brad	L	.343	233	80	18	2	10	31	19	18	.403	.567
Throws Right	R	.267	288	77	13	1	13	44	21	35	.333	.455
Thompson,Mike	L	.308	26	8	3	0	1	11	3	3	.367	.538
Throws Right	R	.324	34	11	4	0	1	9	4	2	.419	.529
Thompson,Rich	L	.200	10	2	0	0	0	1	1	3	.273	.200
Throws Right	R	.421	19	8	1	1	4	8	2	6	.476	1.211
Thomson,John	L	.261	23	6	1	1	0	1	0	1	.261	.391
Throws Right	R	.389	18	7	3	0	0	4	3	2	.435	.556
Thornton,Matt	L	.283	92	26	7	2	1	13	10	24	.365	.435
Throws Left	R	.260	127	33	9	2	3	27	16	31	.338	.433
Threets,Erick	L	.750	4	3	1	0	0	2	1	0	.800	1.000
Throws Left	R	.250	8	2	2	0	0	2	2	1	.400	.500
Timlin,Mike	L	.173	81	14	0	0	2	9	7	16	.253	.247
Throws Right	R	.274	117	32	5	1	5	15	7	15	.317	.462
Tomko,Brett	L	.276	246	68	14	2	10	36	26	43	.345	.472
Throws Right	R	.291	278	81	21	1	8	46	22	62	.341	.460
Torres,Salomon	L	.275	80	22	3	0	4	11	10	21	.352	.463
Throws Right	R	.278	126	35	6	0	3	22	7	24	.331	.397
Towers,Josh	L	.305	213	65	10	5	10	36	16	37	.361	.540
Throws Right	R	.290	221	64	10	1	8	28	6	39	.313	.452
Traber,Billy	L	.176	51	9	0	0	3	12	3	15	.214	.353
Throws Left	R	.380	108	41	13	0	1	18	10	12	.431	.528
Trachsel,Steve	L	.250	268	67	12	1	7	24	49	30	.364	.381
Throws Right	R	.319	342	109	21	3	12	57	27	26	.364	.503
Tsao,Chin-hui	L	.195	41	8	2	0	2	7	4	5	.283	.390
Throws Right	R	.213	47	10	3	0	1	3	4	11	.275	.340
Turnbow,Derrick	L	.172	93	16	2	0	3	12	18	34	.306	.290
Throws Right	R	.189	148	28	2	2	1	21	28	50	.322	.250
Urdaneta,Lino	L	.000	1	0	0	0	0	0	0	0	.000	.000
Throws Right	R	.500	4	2	0	0	1	3	0	0	.500	1.250
Valverde,Jose	L	.202	124	25	3	1	4	10	13	32	.286	.339
Throws Right	R	.189	111	21	5	0	3	10	13	46	.280	.315
Van Benschoten,John	L	.311	61	19	1	0	1	11	19	12	.476	.377
Throws Right	R	.350	103	36	10	0	3	28	10	14	.424	.534
Vanden Hurk,Rick	L	.289	152	44	13	3	5	21	28	39	.396	.513
Throws Right	R	.298	168	50	11	0	10	37	20	43	.380	.542
Vargas,Claudio	L	.320	247	79	15	1	11	35	29	42	.391	.522
Throws Right	R	.255	290	74	14	0	12	42	25	65	.312	.428
Vargas,Jason	L	.000	3	0	0	0	0	1	1	0	.250	.000
Throws Left	R	.370	46	17	0	0	4	10	1	4	.383	.630
Vasquez,Virgil	L	.400	35	14	1	1	5	7	1	4	.417	.914
Throws Right	R	.325	40	13	3	1	2	9	4	3	.400	.600
Vazquez,Javier	L	.230	370	85	23	3	14	45	27	99	.286	.422
Throws Right	R	.253	443	112	17	2	15	44	23	114	.293	.402
Veras,Jose	L	.154	13	2	1	0	0	0	4	4	.353	.231
Throws Right	R	.190	21	4	1	0	0	2	3	3	.292	.238
Verlander,Justin	L	.232	413	96	17	2	13	49	40	102	.312	.378
Throws Right	R	.234	363	85	16	0	7	26	27	81	.307	.336
Vermilyea,Jamie	L	.125	8	1	1	0	0	0	0	1	.125	.250
Throws Right	R	.286	14	4	0	0	0	0	0	1	.286	.286
Villanueva,Carlos	L	.250	172	43	11	1	7	17	23	42	.345	.448
Throws Right	R	.227	256	58	16	0	9	34	30	57	.309	.395
Villarreal,Oscar	L	.315	124	39	8	2	4	26	18	23	.388	.508
Throws Right	R	.220	164	36	7	0	2	21	14	35	.290	.299
Villone,Ron	L	.239	67	16	1	0	2	8	5	4	.311	.343
Throws Left	R	.230	87	20	1	0	3	16	13	21	.333	.345
Vizcaino,Luis	L	.265	117	31	10	0	3	20	18	16	.362	.427
Throws Right	R	.213	164	35	14	0	3	25	25	46	.314	.354
Volquez,Edinson	L	.222	63	14	0	1	2	7	6	21	.282	.349
Throws Right	R	.299	67	20	5	0	2	10	9	8	.397	.463
Wagner,Billy	L	.241	54	13	4	0	1	9	6	22	.328	.370

Pitchers vs. Left-Handed and Right-Handed Batters

Pitcher	vs	Avg	AB	H	2B	3B	HR	RBI	BB	SO	OBP	Slg
Throws Left	R	.209	201	42	5	1	5	15	16	58	.268	.318
Wagner,Ryan	L	.269	26	7	1	0	0	5	3	2	.345	.308
Throws Right	R	.342	38	13	4	0	2	9	5	7	.419	.605
Wainwright,Adam	L	.249	341	85	17	3	6	36	31	74	.317	.370
Throws Right	R	.283	448	127	30	1	7	46	39	62	.345	.402
Wakefield,Tim	L	.247	304	75	17	3	7	27	35	38	.327	.391
Throws Right	R	.276	420	116	30	0	15	62	29	72	.323	.455
Walker,Jamie	L	.216	111	24	3	1	2	18	8	23	.279	.315
Throws Left	R	.268	123	33	5	0	4	18	9	18	.309	.407
Walker,Tyler	L	.182	22	4	1	0	0	2	3	2	.269	.227
Throws Right	R	.308	26	8	3	0	0	3	1	7	.333	.423
Wang,Chien-Ming	L	.286	391	112	25	3	7	50	34	34	.344	.419
Throws Right	R	.242	360	87	13	3	2	22	25	70	.302	.311
Wasdin,John	L	.296	27	8	4	0	1	4	3	3	.355	.556
Throws Right	R	.421	57	24	3	1	0	5	5	7	.468	.509
Washburn,Jarrod	L	.213	197	42	6	1	4	19	17	48	.278	.315
Throws Left	R	.288	552	159	35	3	19	68	50	66	.352	.466
Wassermann,Ehren	L	.533	15	8	1	1	0	2	3	1	.632	.733
Throws Right	R	.174	69	12	2	0	0	9	4	13	.227	.203
Weathers,David	L	.254	122	31	7	2	1	17	15	19	.336	.369
Throws Right	R	.218	165	36	8	3	3	20	12	29	.284	.358
Weaver,Jeff	L	.324	315	102	29	4	15	51	22	41	.374	.584
Throws Right	R	.306	288	88	15	1	8	45	13	39	.338	.448
Weaver,Jered	L	.291	320	93	15	2	6	28	27	45	.348	.406
Throws Right	R	.269	316	85	16	1	11	44	18	70	.306	.430
Webb,Brandon	L	.272	456	124	29	4	8	57	48	77	.342	.406
Throws Right	R	.199	427	85	13	0	4	28	24	117	.244	.258
Wellemeyer,Todd	L	.311	148	46	8	0	6	23	22	22	.395	.486
Throws Right	R	.200	155	31	6	0	5	21	18	38	.292	.335
Wells,David	L	.288	132	38	3	4	5	19	6	24	.321	.485
Throws Left	R	.323	504	163	39	1	17	70	36	58	.369	.506
Wells,Kip	L	.287	279	80	17	4	11	48	36	50	.371	.495
Throws Right	R	.287	369	106	20	5	8	54	42	72	.366	.434
Westbrook,Jake	L	.288	299	86	11	0	9	38	36	52	.388	.415
Throws Right	R	.263	278	73	10	2	4	29	19	41	.313	.356
Wheeler,Dan	L	.260	127	33	12	0	4	15	13	31	.324	.449
Throws Right	R	.253	162	41	9	0	7	38	10	51	.307	.438
White,Bill	L	.286	14	4	1	0	0	2	1	6	.333	.357
Throws Left	R	.211	19	4	0	0	1	1	0	3	.444	.368
White,Rick	L	.298	47	14	1	0	1	11	9	5	.411	.383
Throws Right	R	.347	95	33	6	3	3	18	9	13	.404	.568
White,Sean	L	.250	60	15	3	0	2	11	12	6	.378	.400
Throws Right	R	.270	74	20	9	0	0	16	8	10	.385	.392
Wickman,Bob	L	.277	94	26	5	2	2	7	14	15	.370	.436
Throws Right	R	.252	111	28	6	1	2	21	7	22	.311	.378
Williams,Dave	L	.333	3	1	0	0	1	3	0	0	.333	1.333
Throws Left	R	.550	20	11	2	1	1	8	5	2	.615	.900
Williams,Jerome	L	.281	57	16	2	1	1	3	10	5	.388	.404
Throws Right	R	.286	63	18	3	0	5	19	8	10	.361	.571
Williams,Todd	L	.429	21	9	1	0	1	10	2	3	.478	.619
Throws Right	R	.270	37	10	0	0	1	4	2	6	.325	.351
Williams,Woody	L	.279	344	96	20	1	22	53	30	50	.340	.535
Throws Right	R	.292	411	120	26	2	13	55	23	51	.342	.460
Williamson,Scott	L	.353	17	6	1	0	0	2	3	2	.450	.412
Throws Right	R	.176	34	6	1	0	1	4	5	14	.268	.294
Willis,Dontrelle	L	.123	106	13	2	0	0	8	11	33	.215	.142
Throws Left	R	.320	713	228	51	5	29	111	76	113	.392	.527
Wilson,Brian	L	.304	23	7	2	0	1	3	7	6	.467	.522
Throws Right	R	.145	62	9	2	0	0	2	0	12	.159	.177
Wilson,C.J.	L	.112	98	11	2	0	1	12	11	39	.217	.163
Throws Left	R	.275	142	39	5	0	3	22	22	24	.381	.373
Wise,Matt	L	.264	72	19	5	2	1	7	9	15	.346	.431
Throws Right	R	.296	142	42	8	0	4	23	8	28	.331	.437
Witasick,Jay	L	.310	42	13	4	0	0	6	18	3	.517	.405
Throws Right	R	.243	74	18	4	1	2	12	9	15	.329	.405
Wolf,Randy	L	.250	72	18	3	1	4	15	3	26	.276	.486
Throws Left	R	.278	331	92	24	0	6	35	36	68	.355	.405
Wolf,Ross	L	.269	26	7	2	1	1	8	2	2	.345	.538
Throws Right	R	.486	35	17	1	0	3	11	1	4	.500	.771
Wolfe,Brian	L	.348	69	24	7	0	4	16	5	12	.400	.623
Throws Right	R	.130	92	12	2	0	1	10	4	10	.172	.185
Wood,Kerry	L	.148	27	4	1	0	0	2	4	8	.258	.185
Throws Right	R	.233	60	14	7	0	0	9	9	16	.333	.350
Wood,Mike	L	.342	114	39	9	1	5	17	13	12	.408	.570
Throws Right	R	.296	98	29	7	0	4	18	2	13	.330	.490
Woods,Jake	L	.091	11	1	0	0	0	2	1	2	.231	.091

Pitcher	vs	Avg	AB	H	2B	3B	HR	RBI	BB	SO	OBP	Slg
Throws Left	R	.267	30	8	2	0	1	7	6	2	.389	.433
Wright,Chase	L	.250	12	3	0	0	2	2	1	4	.308	.750
Throws Left	R	.310	29	9	2	0	3	5	5	4	.444	.690
Wright,Jamey	L	.268	112	30	7	1	3	11	29	17	.420	.429
Throws Right	R	.253	166	42	5	1	3	20	12	22	.317	.349
Wright,Jaret	L	.300	20	6	3	0	0	2	8	4	.500	.450
Throws Right	R	.316	19	6	0	0	1	5	1	3	.350	.474
Wuertz,Mike	L	.238	80	19	4	0	2	6	13	23	.344	.363
Throws Right	R	.233	193	45	13	1	6	23	22	56	.310	.404
Yates,Tyler	L	.310	100	31	10	3	3	13	13	25	.400	.560
Throws Right	R	.213	155	33	4	0	3	17	18	44	.297	.297
Youman,Shane	L	.306	36	11	2	0	2	7	4	6	.381	.528
Throws Left	R	.297	182	54	14	0	3	30	19	23	.371	.423
Young,Chris	L	.231	294	68	10	6	6	34	33	67	.311	.367
Throws Right	R	.155	322	50	9	2	4	23	39	100	.254	.233
Zagurski,Mike	L	.216	37	8	0	0	0	7	3	9	.286	.216
Throws Left	R	.340	50	17	5	0	3	12	8	12	.431	.620
Zambrano,Carlos	L	.268	400	107	23	3	9	39	64	84	.373	.408
Throws Right	R	.200	401	80	11	1	14	46	37	93	.283	.337
Zambrano,Victor	L	.351	37	13	1	1	2	13	13	5	.519	.595
Throws Right	R	.333	57	19	0	0	4	14	9	11	.451	.544
Zarate,Mauro	L	.333	12	4	0	0	2	5	0	1	.333	.833
Throws Right	R	.438	16	7	1	0	1	2	1	2	.500	.688
Zito,Barry	L	.242	186	45	14	1	5	22	18	43	.316	.409
Throws Left	R	.244	561	137	24	4	19	70	65	88	.323	.403
Zumaya,Joel	L	.271	48	13	2	0	2	10	6	11	.357	.438
Throws Right	R	.135	74	10	2	0	1	10	11	16	.247	.203
AL	L	.272	-	-	-	-	-	-	-	-	.345	.429
	R	.267	-	-	-	-	-	-	-	-	.329	.415
NL	L	.266	-	-	-	-	-	-	-	-	.341	.423
	R	.268	-	-	-	-	-	-	-	-	.332	.424
MLB	L	.269	-	-	-	-	-	-	-	-	.343	.426
	R	.268	-	-	-	-	-	-	-	-	.331	.420

2007 Leader Boards

Many of our leader boards are derived from the complex pitch data collected by Baseball Info Solutions. Their pitch charting data is the most complete and thorough in baseball, and the information found in these leader boards cannot be found anywhere else. We have everything from the pitchers who hurl knee-buckling curves to the sliders that hang just a little too long—and wind up getting blasted.

Speaking of blasting, we also have a leader board for the longest home runs hit in 2007. Last year, the National League Most Valuable Player (and home run leader) also hit the longest home run in baseball. On April 23, 2006, the Philadelphia Phillies' Ryan Howard deposited a Sergio Mitre pitch over the batter's eye and onto the walkway at Citizens Bank Park—496 feet from home plate. So,…did anybody beat that in 2007?

Here are some definitions to help clarify parts of the leader boards that may not be familiar to all readers:

OPS stands for "On Base Percentage Plus Slugging Percentage." OPS versus different types of pitches is new on our leader boards this year. It corrects certain flaws in BPS (Batting average Plus Slugging) versus pitch that we used in previous years and is based on a new method developed by Bill James.

OutZ is "Pitches Outside the Strike Zone."

Holds Adjusted Saves Percentage is calculated by dividing holds plus saves by holds plus save opportunities.

2007 American League Batting Leaders

Batting Average (minimum 502 PA)		On Base Percentage (minimum 502 PA)		Slugging Average (minimum 502 PA)		Home Runs	
Ordonez,Magglio, Det	.363	Ortiz,David, Bos	.445	Rodriguez,Alex, NYY	.645	Rodriguez,Alex, NYY	54
Suzuki,Ichiro, Sea	.351	Ordonez,Magglio, Det	.434	Pena,Carlos, TB	.627	Pena,Carlos, TB	46
Polanco,Placido, Det	.341	Posada,Jorge, NYY	.426	Ortiz,David, Bos	.621	Ortiz,David, Bos	35
Posada,Jorge, NYY	.338	Rodriguez,Alex, NYY	.422	Ordonez,Magglio, Det	.595	Thome,Jim, CWS	35
Ortiz,David, Bos	.332	Pena,Carlos, TB	.411	Thome,Jim, CWS	.563	Konerko,Paul, CWS	31
Figgins,Chone, LAA	.330	Thome,Jim, CWS	.410	Granderson,Curtis, Det	.552	Morneau,Justin, Min	31
Lowell,Mike, Bos	.324	Cust,Jack, Oak	.408	Guerrero,Vladimir, LAA	.547	Dye,Jermaine, CWS	28
Guerrero,Vladimir, LAA	.324	Guerrero,Vladimir, LAA	.403	Posada,Jorge, NYY	.543	Hunter,Torii, Min	28
Jeter,Derek, NYY	.322	Suzuki,Ichiro, Sea	.396	Upton,B.J., TB	.508	Ordonez,Magglio, Det	28
Pedroia,Dustin, Bos	.317	Figgins,Chone, LAA	.393	Martinez,Victor, Cle	.505	Guerrero,Vladimir, LAA	27

Games		Plate Appearances		At Bats		Hits	
Sizemore,Grady, Cle	162	Sizemore,Grady, Cle	748	Suzuki,Ichiro, Sea	678	Suzuki,Ichiro, Sea	238
Young,Delmon, TB	162	Suzuki,Ichiro, Sea	736	Young,Delmon, TB	645	Ordonez,Magglio, Det	216
Markakis,Nick, Bal	161	Roberts,Brian, Bal	716	Rios,Alex, Tor	643	Jeter,Derek, NYY	206
Rios,Alex, Tor	161	Jeter,Derek, NYY	714	Jeter,Derek, NYY	639	Young,Michael, Tex	201
Suzuki,Ichiro, Sea	161	Rios,Alex, Tor	711	Young,Michael, Tex	639	Polanco,Placido, Det	200
Cano,Robinson, NYY	160	Markakis,Nick, Bal	710	Cabrera,Orlando, LAA	638	Cabrera,Orlando, LAA	192
Hill,Aaron, Tor	160	Rodriguez,Alex, NYY	708	Markakis,Nick, Bal	637	Lowell,Mike, Bos	191
Hunter,Torii, Min	160	DeJesus,David, KC	703	Sizemore,Grady, Cle	628	Markakis,Nick, Bal	191
3 tied with	158	Cabrera,Orlando, LAA	701	Roberts,Brian, Bal	621	Rios,Alex, Tor	191
		Abreu,Bobby, NYY	699	Cano,Robinson, NYY	617	Cano,Robinson, NYY	189

Singles		Doubles		Triples		Total Bases	
Suzuki,Ichiro, Sea	203	Ordonez,Magglio, Det	54	Granderson,Curtis, Det	23	Rodriguez,Alex, NYY	376
Young,Michael, Tex	154	Ortiz,David, Bos	52	Iwamura,Akinori, TB	10	Ordonez,Magglio, Det	354
Polanco,Placido, Det	152	Hill,Aaron, Tor	47	Crawford,Carl, TB	9	Ortiz,David, Bos	341
Jeter,Derek, NYY	151	Guerrero,Vladimir, LAA	45	DeJesus,David, KC	9	Granderson,Curtis, Det	338
Cabrera,Orlando, LAA	148	Hunter,Torii, Min	45	Guillen,Carlos, Det	9	Rios,Alex, Tor	320
Vidro,Jose, Sea	140	Markakis,Nick, Bal	43	Byrd,Marlon, Tex	8	Guerrero,Vladimir, LAA	314
Young,Delmon, TB	135	Rios,Alex, Tor	43	Cabrera,Melky, NYY	8	Markakis,Nick, Bal	309
Ordonez,Magglio, Det	134	Posada,Jorge, NYY	42	Teahen,Mark, KC	8	Pena,Carlos, TB	307
Stewart,Shannon, Oak	132	Roberts,Brian, Bal	42	6 tied with	7	Hunter,Torii, Min	303
Lowell,Mike, Bos	131	2 tied with	41			Cano,Robinson, NYY	301

Runs Scored		RBI		Walks		Strikeouts	
Rodriguez,Alex, NYY	143	Rodriguez,Alex, NYY	156	Ortiz,David, Bos	111	Cust,Jack, Oak	164
Abreu,Bobby, NYY	123	Ordonez,Magglio, Det	139	Cust,Jack, Oak	105	Sizemore,Grady, Cle	155
Granderson,Curtis, Det	122	Guerrero,Vladimir, LAA	125	Pena,Carlos, TB	103	Upton,B.J., TB	154
Sizemore,Grady, Cle	118	Pena,Carlos, TB	121	Hafner,Travis, Cle	102	Inge,Brandon, Det	150
Ordonez,Magglio, Det	117	Lowell,Mike, Bos	120	Sizemore,Grady, Cle	101	Peralta,Jhonny, Cle	146
Ortiz,David, Bos	116	Ortiz,David, Bos	117	Swisher,Nick, Oak	100	Pena,Carlos, TB	142
Rios,Alex, Tor	114	Martinez,Victor, Cle	114	Rodriguez,Alex, NYY	95	Granderson,Curtis, Det	141
Suzuki,Ichiro, Sea	111	Markakis,Nick, Bal	112	Thome,Jim, CWS	95	Gordon,Alex, KC	137
Sheffield,Gary, Det	107	Morneau,Justin, Min	111	Roberts,Brian, Bal	89	Thome,Jim, CWS	134
Polanco,Placido, Det	105	Hunter,Torii, Min	107	2 tied with	84	Swisher,Nick, Oak	131

2007 American League Batting Leaders

Intentional Walks

Guerrero,Vladimir, LAA	28
Hafner,Travis, Cle	17
Ramirez,Manny, Bos	13
Suzuki,Ichiro, Sea	13
Martinez,Victor, Cle	12
Ortiz,David, Bos	12
Swisher,Nick, Oak	12
4 tied with	11

BA Bases Loaded
(minimum 10 PA)

Lopez,Jose, Sea	.667
Suzuki,Ichiro, Sea	.615
McDonald,John, Tor	.600
Crawford,Carl, TB	.571
Piazza,Mike, Oak	.556
Hill,Aaron, Tor	.545
Posada,Jorge, NYY	.545
Ibanez,Raul, Sea	.526
5 tied with	.500

Sacrifice Hits

Patterson,Corey, Bal	13
McDonald,John, Tor	12
Vazquez,Ramon, Tex	12
Willits,Reggie, LAA	11
Cabrera,Melky, NYY	10
Gathright,Joey, KC	10
Crisp,Coco, Bos	9
Lopez,Jose, Sea	9
4 tied with	8

Sacrifice Flies

Cabrera,Orlando, LAA	11
Martinez,Victor, Cle	11
Matsui,Hideki, NYY	10
Cabrera,Melky, NYY	9
Morneau,Justin, Min	9
Rodriguez,Alex, NYY	9
Swisher,Nick, Oak	9
7 tied with	8

BA Close & Late
(minimum 50 PA)

Johjima,Kenji, Sea	.457
Suzuki,Ichiro, Sea	.402
Markakis,Nick, Bal	.389
Rodriguez,Alex, NYY	.357
Varitek,Jason, Bos	.351
Martinez,Victor, Cle	.347
Guerrero,Vladimir, LAA	.342
Wigginton,Ty, TB	.340
Roberts,Brian, Bal	.330
Jeter,Derek, NYY	.325

Batting Average w/ RISP
(minimum 100 PA)

Ordonez,Magglio, Det	.429
Izturis,Maicer, LAA	.406
Suzuki,Ichiro, Sea	.397
Young,Michael, Tex	.376
Polanco,Placido, Det	.364
Ortiz,David, Bos	.362
Lowell,Mike, Bos	.356
Martinez,Victor, Cle	.356
Jeter,Derek, NYY	.354
Guerrero,Vladimir, LAA	.354

SLG vs. LHP
(minimum 125 PA)

Ordonez,Magglio, Det	.713
Thomas,Frank, Tor	.631
Ramirez,Manny, Bos	.617
Guillen,Jose, Sea	.616
Sosa,Sammy, Tex	.613
Konerko,Paul, CWS	.605
Ellis,Mark, Oak	.600
Rios,Alex, Tor	.600
Kinsler,Ian, Tex	.574
Pena,Carlos, TB	.571

SLG vs. RHP
(minimum 377 PA)

Ortiz,David, Bos	.700
Rodriguez,Alex, NYY	.680
Pena,Carlos, TB	.647
Granderson,Curtis, Det	.621
Ordonez,Magglio, Det	.564
Posada,Jorge, NYY	.548
Guerrero,Vladimir, LAA	.546
Morneau,Justin, Min	.534
Martinez,Victor, Cle	.532
Ibanez,Raul, Sea	.528

Leadoff Hitters OBP
(minimum 150 PA)

Figgins,Chone, LAA	.415
Suzuki,Ichiro, Sea	.396
Sizemore,Grady, Cle	.389
Buck,Travis , Oak	.383
Roberts,Brian, Bal	.376
Lofton,Kenny, Tex-Cle	.376
Catalanotto,Frank, Tex	.368
Granderson,Curtis, Det	.362
Willits,Reggie, LAA	.359
DeJesus,David, KC	.358

Cleanup Hitters SLG
(minimum 150 PA)

Rodriguez,Alex, NYY	.654
Ordonez,Magglio, Det	.593
Guillen,Jose, Sea	.542
Dye,Jermaine, CWS	.541
Guerrero,Vladimir, LAA	.538
Martinez,Victor, Cle	.533
Pena,Carlos, TB	.516
Konerko,Paul, CWS	.501
Ramirez,Manny, Bos	.501
Byrd,Marlon, Tex	.500

BA vs. LHP
(minimum 125 PA)

Ordonez,Magglio, Det	.410
Guillen,Jose, Sea	.362
Pedroia,Dustin, Bos	.348
Harris,Brendan, TB	.345
Rios,Alex, Tor	.345
Ramirez,Manny, Bos	.344
Kinsler,Ian, Tex	.339
Thomas,Frank, Tor	.336
Inge,Brandon, Det	.333
Willits,Reggie, LAA	.333

BA vs. RHP
(minimum 377 PA)

Suzuki,Ichiro, Sea	.358
Ordonez,Magglio, Det	.351
Polanco,Placido, Det	.345
Ortiz,David, Bos	.343
Posada,Jorge, NYY	.341
Granderson,Curtis, Det	.337
Figgins,Chone, LAA	.331
Rodriguez,Alex, NYY	.327
Lowell,Mike, Bos	.325
Guerrero,Vladimir, LAA	.325

Home BA
(minimum 251 PA)

Ordonez,Magglio, Det	.389
Lowell,Mike, Bos	.373
Suzuki,Ichiro, Sea	.365
Ortiz,David, Bos	.365
Pedroia,Dustin, Bos	.351
Polanco,Placido, Det	.341
Jeter,Derek, NYY	.334
Guerrero,Vladimir, LAA	.332
Posada,Jorge, NYY	.332
Vidro,Jose, Sea	.330

Away BA
(minimum 251 PA)

Posada,Jorge, NYY	.344
Crawford,Carl, TB	.342
Polanco,Placido, Det	.341
Ordonez,Magglio, Det	.340
Suzuki,Ichiro, Sea	.337
Upton,B.J., TB	.335
Rodriguez,Alex, NYY	.326
Stewart,Shannon, Oak	.324
Cabrera,Orlando, LAA	.318
Granderson,Curtis, Det	.318

OBP vs. LHP
(minimum 125 PA)

Ordonez,Magglio, Det	.500
Ramirez,Manny, Bos	.478
Swisher,Nick, Oak	.458
Guillen,Jose, Sea	.433
Guerrero,Vladimir, LAA	.432
Rodriguez,Alex, NYY	.432
Thomas,Frank, Tor	.431
Kinsler,Ian, Tex	.425
Rios,Alex, Tor	.422
Inge,Brandon, Det	.419

OBP vs. RHP
(minimum 377 PA)

Ortiz,David, Bos	.470
Posada,Jorge, NYY	.432
Pena,Carlos, TB	.421
Rodriguez,Alex, NYY	.419
Ordonez,Magglio, Det	.415
Suzuki,Ichiro, Sea	.402
Drew,J.D., Bos	.400
Polanco,Placido, Det	.396
Guerrero,Vladimir, LAA	.396
Figgins,Chone, LAA	.394

2007 American League Batting Leaders

Stolen Bases	
Crawford,Carl, TB	50
Roberts,Brian, Bal	50
Figgins,Chone, LAA	41
Patterson,Corey, Bal	37
Suzuki,Ichiro, Sea	37
Lugo,Julio, Bos	33
Sizemore,Grady, Cle	33
Owens,Jerry, CWS	32
Crisp,Coco, Bos	28
2 tied with	27

Caught Stealing	
Figgins,Chone, LAA	12
Crawford,Carl, TB	10
Sizemore,Grady, Cle	10
Hunter,Torii, Min	9
Patterson,Corey, Bal	9
Uribe,Juan, CWS	9
9 tied with	8

Highest SB Success Pct	
(minimum 20 SBA)	
Granderson,Curtis, Det	96.3
Kinsler,Ian, Tex	92.0
Damon,Johnny, NYY	90.0
Bartlett,Jason, Min	88.5
Roberts,Brian, Bal	87.7
Rodriguez,Alex, NYY	85.7
Lugo,Julio, Bos	84.6
Cabrera,Orlando, LAA	83.3
Crawford,Carl, TB	83.3
Crisp,Coco, Bos	82.4

Lowest SB Success Pct	
(minimum 20 SBA)	
Iwamura,Akinori, TB	60.0
Guillen,Carlos, Det	61.9
Jeter,Derek, NYY	65.2
Hunter,Torii, Min	66.7
Punto,Nick, Min	72.7
Upton,B.J., TB	73.3
Markakis,Nick, Bal	75.0
Abreu,Bobby, NYY	75.8
Lofton,Kenny, Tex-Cle	76.7
Sizemore,Grady, Cle	76.7

Steals of Third	
Roberts,Brian, Bal	19
Crawford,Carl, TB	9
Lugo,Julio, Bos	8
Bartlett,Jason, Min	6
Patterson,Corey, Bal	6
Suzuki,Ichiro, Sea	6
Cabrera,Orlando, LAA	5
Guillen,Carlos, Det	5
5 tied with	4

Grounded Into DP	
Teahen,Mark, KC	23
Young,Delmon, TB	23
Johjima,Kenji, Sea	22
Markakis,Nick, Bal	22
Mora,Melvin, Bal	22
Tejada,Miguel, Bal	22
7 tied with	21

Grounded Into DP Pct	
(minimum 50 GIDP Ops)	
Giambi,Jason, NYY	1.52
Gomes,Jonny, TB	1.56
Iwamura,Akinori, TB	2.67
Wilkerson,Brad, Tex	2.94
Patterson,Corey, Bal	3.13
Sizemore,Grady, Cle	3.16
Barfield,Josh, Cle	3.23
Laird,Gerald, Tex	3.57
Granderson,Curtis, Det	3.66
Damon,Johnny, NYY	4.71

Hit By Pitch	
DeJesus,David, KC	23
Rodriguez,Alex, NYY	21
Garko,Ryan, Cle	20
Guillen,Jose, Sea	19
Sizemore,Grady, Cle	17
Youkilis,Kevin, Bos	15
Jeter,Derek, NYY	14
Gordon,Alex, KC	13
5 tied with	11

Pitches Seen	
Sizemore,Grady, Cle	3112
Abreu,Bobby, NYY	3063
Roberts,Brian, Bal	3013
Swisher,Nick, Oak	2803
Suzuki,Ichiro, Sea	2772
Blake,Casey, Cle	2764
Ortiz,David, Bos	2742
Rodriguez,Alex, NYY	2698
Hafner,Travis, Cle	2697
Granderson,Curtis, Det	2692

At Bats Per Home Run	
(minimum 502 PA)	
Pena,Carlos, TB	10.7
Rodriguez,Alex, NYY	10.8
Thome,Jim, CWS	12.3
Cust,Jack, Oak	15.2
Ortiz,David, Bos	15.7
Konerko,Paul, CWS	17.7
Dye,Jermaine, CWS	18.1
Morneau,Justin, Min	19.0
Upton,B.J., TB	19.8
Sheffield,Gary, Det	19.8

Highest GB/FB Ratio	
(minimum 502 PA)	
Suzuki,Ichiro, Sea	2.90
Jeter,Derek, NYY	2.84
Pena,Tony F, KC	2.64
Figgins,Chone, LAA	2.49
Young,Michael, Tex	2.39
Rodriguez,Ivan, Det	2.30
Willits,Reggie, LAA	2.13
Cabrera,Melky, NYY	2.03
Cano,Robinson, NYY	1.99
Vidro,Jose, Sea	1.99

Lowest GB/FB Ratio	
(minimum 502 PA)	
Thomas,Frank, Tor	0.62
Millar,Kevin, Bal	0.65
Ellis,Mark, Oak	0.71
Uribe,Juan, CWS	0.81
Sizemore,Grady, Cle	0.82
Kinsler,Ian, Tex	0.86
Dye,Jermaine, CWS	0.88
Granderson,Curtis, Det	0.88
Lowell,Mike, Bos	0.90
Swisher,Nick, Oak	0.92

Pitches Per Plate App	
(minimum 502 PA)	
Willits,Reggie, LAA	4.45
Cust,Jack, Oak	4.40
Abreu,Bobby, NYY	4.38
Millar,Kevin, Bal	4.34
Damon,Johnny, NYY	4.31
Youkilis,Kevin, Bos	4.27
Swisher,Nick, Oak	4.25
Inge,Brandon, Det	4.24
Roberts,Brian, Bal	4.21
Thome,Jim, CWS	4.20

Pct Pitches Taken	
(minimum 1500 Pitches)	
Willits,Reggie, LAA	65.1
Johnson,Dan, Oak	64.6
Mauer,Joe, Min	64.3
Abreu,Bobby, NYY	64.1
Cust,Jack, Oak	64.1
Castillo,Luis, Min	62.9
Swisher,Nick, Oak	62.8
Hafner,Travis, Cle	62.7
Glaus,Troy, Tor	62.6
Matsui,Hideki, NYY	62.2

Best BPS on OutZ	
(minimum 502 PA)	
Pedroia,Dustin, Bos	.664
Guerrero,Vladimir, LAA	.662
Sheffield,Gary, Det	.654
Lofton,Kenny, Tex-Cle	.649
Polanco,Placido, Det	.631
Lowell,Mike, Bos	.623
Suzuki,Ichiro, Sea	.616
Cabrera,Melky, NYY	.612
Martinez,Victor, Cle	.586
Stewart,Shannon, Oak	.577

Worst BPS on OutZ	
(minimum 502 PA)	
Cust,Jack, Oak	.083
Ramirez,Manny, Bos	.189
Thome,Jim, CWS	.229
Peralta,Jhonny, Cle	.234
Inge,Brandon, Det	.246
Upton,B.J., TB	.278
Hill,Aaron, Tor	.280
Gordon,Alex, KC	.294
Crisp,Coco, Bos	.300
Millar,Kevin, Bal	.300

2007 American League Batting Leaders

Best OPS vs Fastballs
(minimum 251 PA)

Rodriguez,Alex, NYY	1.130
Pena,Carlos, TB	1.129
Ortiz,David, Bos	1.113
Cust,Jack, Oak	1.062
Thome,Jim, CWS	1.059
Posada,Jorge, NYY	1.039
Ordonez,Magglio, Det	1.028
Granderson,Curtis, Det	1.017
Upton,B.J., TB	1.012
Kotchman,Casey, LAA	.989

Best OPS vs Curveballs
(minimum 50 PA)

Hill,Aaron, Tor	1.298
Ortiz,David, Bos	1.087
Guerrero,Vladimir, LAA	1.019
Morneau,Justin, Min	1.015
Suzuki,Ichiro, Sea	1.002
Cano,Robinson, NYY	.982
Pena,Carlos, TB	.938
Sizemore,Grady, Cle	.903
Ellis,Mark, Oak	.856
Hunter,Torii, Min	.850

Best OPS vs Changeups
(minimum 50 PA)

Ordonez,Magglio, Det	1.146
Lowell,Mike, Bos	1.094
Cuddyer,Michael, Min	1.065
Mackowiak,Rob, CWS	1.058
Guillen,Jose, Sea	1.012
Ortiz,David, Bos	.974
Wells,Vernon, Tor	.974
Mora,Melvin, Bal	.934
Cano,Robinson, NYY	.932
2 tied with	.925

Best OPS vs Sliders
(minimum 32 PA)

Roberts,Brian, Bal	1.146
Rodriguez,Alex, NYY	1.075
Hunter,Torii, Min	1.052
Pena,Carlos, TB	1.030
Tyner,Jason, Min	1.030
Guerrero,Vladimir, LAA	1.018
Abreu,Bobby, NYY	1.011
Kubel,Jason, Min	1.004
Lowell,Mike, Bos	.999
Posada,Jorge, NYY	.994

OPS
(minimum 502 PA)

Rodriguez,Alex, NYY	1.067
Ortiz,David, Bos	1.066
Pena,Carlos, TB	1.037
Ordonez,Magglio, Det	1.029
Thome,Jim, CWS	.973
Posada,Jorge, NYY	.970
Guerrero,Vladimir, LAA	.950
Granderson,Curtis, Det	.913
Cust,Jack, Oak	.912
Upton,B.J., TB	.894

OPS First Half
(minimum 251 PA)

Rodriguez,Alex, NYY	1.075
Ordonez,Magglio, Det	1.050
Pena,Carlos, TB	1.004
Ortiz,David, Bos	.990
Sheffield,Gary, Det	.970
Guillen,Carlos, Det	.968
Guerrero,Vladimir, LAA	.962
Teixeira,Mark, Tex	.959
Morneau,Justin, Min	.944
Martinez,Victor, Cle	.936

OPS Second Half
(minimum 251 PA)

Ortiz,David, Bos	1.153
Pena,Carlos, TB	1.066
Posada,Jorge, NYY	1.061
Rodriguez,Alex, NYY	1.058
Ordonez,Magglio, Det	1.004
Thome,Jim, CWS	.967
Cano,Robinson, NYY	.953
Granderson,Curtis, Det	.948
Dye,Jermaine, CWS	.947
Markakis,Nick, Bal	.939

OPS by Catchers
(minimum 251 PA)

Posada,Jorge, NYY	.969
Martinez,Victor, Cle	.902
Mauer,Joe, Min	.822
Napoli,Mike, LAA	.792
Varitek,Jason, Bos	.784
Johjima,Kenji, Sea	.761
Zaun,Gregg, Tor	.747
Buck,John, KC	.744
Rodriguez,Ivan, Det	.723
Hernandez,Ramon, Bal	.712

OPS by First Basemen
(minimum 251 PA)

Pena,Carlos, TB	1.042
Teixeira,Mark, Tex	.878
Youkilis,Kevin, Bos	.845
Garko,Ryan, Cle	.842
Konerko,Paul, CWS	.826
Morneau,Justin, Min	.821
Kotchman,Casey, LAA	.813
Millar,Kevin, Bal	.799
Gload,Ross, KC	.766
2 tied with	.748

OPS by Second Basemen
(minimum 251 PA)

Polanco,Placido, Det	.840
Cano,Robinson, NYY	.839
Pedroia,Dustin, Bos	.821
Roberts,Brian, Bal	.806
Kinsler,Ian, Tex	.797
Kendrick,Howie, LAA	.794
Hill,Aaron, Tor	.793
Ellis,Mark, Oak	.778
Grudzielanek,Mark, KC	.767
Iguchi,Tadahito, CWS	.723

OPS by Third Basemen
(minimum 251 PA)

Rodriguez,Alex, NYY	1.064
Lowell,Mike, Bos	.879
Figgins,Chone, LAA	.841
Glaus,Troy, Tor	.837
Beltre,Adrian, Sea	.810
Mora,Melvin, Bal	.769
Iwamura,Akinori, TB	.768
Blake,Casey, Cle	.761
Chavez,Eric, Oak	.754
Fields,Josh, CWS	.751

OPS by Shortstops
(minimum 251 PA)

Jeter,Derek, NYY	.841
Guillen,Carlos, Det	.831
Tejada,Miguel, Bal	.817
Harris,Brendan, TB	.811
Young,Michael, Tex	.788
Peralta,Jhonny, Cle	.773
Cabrera,Orlando, LAA	.745
Betancourt,Yuniesky, Sea	.729
Bartlett,Jason, Min	.702
Uribe,Juan, CWS	.678

OPS by Left Fielders
(minimum 251 PA)

Anderson,Garret, LAA	.887
Ramirez,Manny, Bos	.881
Matsui,Hideki, NYY	.880
Ibanez,Raul, Sea	.859
Crawford,Carl, TB	.824
Kubel,Jason, Min	.745
Stewart,Shannon, Oak	.731
Lind,Adam, Tor	.674
Payton,Jay, Bal	.671
2 tied with	.641

OPS by Center Fielders
(minimum 251 PA)

Granderson,Curtis, Det	.913
Sizemore,Grady, Cle	.853
Swisher,Nick, Oak	.849
Upton,B.J., TB	.847
Hunter,Torii, Min	.840
Suzuki,Ichiro, Sea	.820
Lofton,Kenny, Tex-Cle	.817
Matthews Jr.,Gary, LAA	.754
DeJesus,David, KC	.724
Cabrera,Melky, NYY	.721

OPS by Right Fielders
(minimum 251 PA)

Ordonez,Magglio, Det	1.046
Guerrero,Vladimir, LAA	.987
Rios,Alex, Tor	.878
Markakis,Nick, Bal	.848
Gutierrez,Franklin, Cle	.845
Guillen,Jose, Sea	.820
Abreu,Bobby, NYY	.811
Dye,Jermaine, CWS	.811
Drew,J.D., Bos	.799
Cuddyer,Michael, Min	.795

OPS by Designated Hitters
(minimum 125 PA)

Ortiz,David, Bos	1.080
Thome,Jim, CWS	.969
Kubel,Jason, Min	.875
Cust,Jack, Oak	.874
Hafner,Travis, Cle	.869
Thomas,Frank, Tor	.860
Guerrero,Vladimir, LAA	.852
Sheffield,Gary, Det	.829
Sosa,Sammy, Tex	.819
Butler,Billy, KC	.792

2007 American League Batting Leaders

OPS Batting Left vs. LHP	
(minimum 125 PA)	
Pena,Carlos, TB	.953
Cano,Robinson, NYY	.864
Iwamura,Akinori, TB	.862
Ortiz,David, Bos	.852
Crawford,Carl, TB	.837
Hafner,Travis, Cle	.837
Matsui,Hideki, NYY	.814
Sizemore,Grady, Cle	.812
Patterson,Corey, Bal	.795
Suzuki,Ichiro, Sea	.787

OPS Batting Left vs. RHP	
(minimum 377 PA)	
Ortiz,David, Bos	1.171
Pena,Carlos, TB	1.068
Granderson,Curtis, Det	1.014
Posada,Jorge, NYY	.981
Martinez,Victor, Cle	.908
Morneau,Justin, Min	.905
Ibanez,Raul, Sea	.899
Markakis,Nick, Bal	.880
Matsui,Hideki, NYY	.872
Sizemore,Grady, Cle	.872

OPS Batting Right vs. LHP	
(minimum 125 PA)	
Ordonez,Magglio, Det	1.213
Ramirez,Manny, Bos	1.095
Thomas,Frank, Tor	1.062
Guillen,Jose, Sea	1.049
Sosa,Sammy, Tex	1.024
Rios,Alex, Tor	1.022
Kinsler,Ian, Tex	.999
Konerko,Paul, CWS	.988
Ellis,Mark, Oak	.984
Guerrero,Vladimir, LAA	.982

OPS Batting Right vs. RHP	
(minimum 377 PA)	
Rodriguez,Alex, NYY	1.099
Ordonez,Magglio, Det	.980
Guerrero,Vladimir, LAA	.942
Upton,B.J., TB	.892
Lowell,Mike, Bos	.890
Polanco,Placido, Det	.857
Youkilis,Kevin, Bos	.854
Sheffield,Gary, Det	.841
Jeter,Derek, NYY	.830
Hunter,Torii, Min	.813

OPS vs. LHP	
(minimum 125 PA)	
Ordonez,Magglio, Det	1.213
Ramirez,Manny, Bos	1.095
Thomas,Frank, Tor	1.062
Guillen,Jose, Sea	1.049
Sosa,Sammy, Tex	1.024
Rios,Alex, Tor	1.022
Kinsler,Ian, Tex	.999
Konerko,Paul, CWS	.988
Ellis,Mark, Oak	.984
Guerrero,Vladimir, LAA	.982

OPS vs. RHP	
(minimum 377 PA)	
Ortiz,David, Bos	1.171
Rodriguez,Alex, NYY	1.099
Pena,Carlos, TB	1.068
Granderson,Curtis, Det	1.014
Posada,Jorge, NYY	.981
Ordonez,Magglio, Det	.980
Guerrero,Vladimir, LAA	.942
Martinez,Victor, Cle	.908
Morneau,Justin, Min	.907
Ibanez,Raul, Sea	.899

RC Per 27 Outs vs. LHP	
(minimum 125 PA)	
Ordonez,Magglio, Det	12.7
Sosa,Sammy, Tex	10.6
Kinsler,Ian, Tex	10.4
Thomas,Frank, Tor	9.7
Ramirez,Manny, Bos	8.8
Swisher,Nick, Oak	8.7
Guillen,Jose, Sea	8.5
Pena,Carlos, TB	8.4
Inge,Brandon, Det	8.1
Ellis,Mark, Oak	7.8

RC Per 27 Outs vs. RHP	
(minimum 377 PA)	
Ortiz,David, Bos	11.2
Rodriguez,Alex, NYY	10.5
Ordonez,Magglio, Det	8.9
Pena,Carlos, TB	8.2
Guerrero,Vladimir, LAA	8.2
Granderson,Curtis, Det	8.1
Suzuki,Ichiro, Sea	8.0
Posada,Jorge, NYY	7.8
Figgins,Chone, LAA	7.7
Martinez,Victor, Cle	7.5

Highest RBI %	
(minimum 502 PA)	
Rodriguez,Alex, NYY	13.65
Pena,Carlos, TB	13.24
Thome,Jim, CWS	12.55
Ordonez,Magglio, Det	12.31
Guerrero,Vladimir, LAA	11.59
Ortiz,David, Bos	11.33
Martinez,Victor, Cle	11.04
Cust,Jack, Oak	10.88
Lowell,Mike, Bos	10.53
Thomas,Frank, Tor	10.42

Lowest RBI %	
(minimum 502 PA)	
Punto,Nick, Min	3.08
Iwamura,Akinori, TB	4.55
Willits,Reggie, LAA	4.69
Lofton,Kenny, Tex-Cle	4.88
Bartlett,Jason, Min	5.11
Stewart,Shannon, Oak	5.25
Pena,Tony F, KC	5.50
Patterson,Corey, Bal	5.53
Roberts,Brian, Bal	5.68
Pedroia,Dustin, Bos	5.82

Highest Strikeout per PA	
(minimum 502 PA)	
Cust,Jack, Oak	.323
Upton,B.J., TB	.281
Inge,Brandon, Det	.260
Thome,Jim, CWS	.250
Varitek,Jason, Bos	.236
Pena,Carlos, TB	.232
Gordon,Alex, KC	.228
Peralta,Jhonny, Cle	.226
Granderson,Curtis, Det	.209
Teahen,Mark, KC	.209

Lowest Strikeout per PA	
(minimum 502 PA)	
Polanco,Placido, Det	.047
Pedroia,Dustin, Bos	.072
Johjima,Kenji, Sea	.080
Kotchman,Casey, LAA	.085
Betancourt,Yuniesky, Sea	.086
Cabrera,Orlando, LAA	.091
Lofton,Kenny, Tex-Cle	.091
Vidro,Jose, Sea	.091
Guerrero,Vladimir, LAA	.094
Stewart,Shannon, Oak	.095

Home Runs At Home	
Rodriguez,Alex, NYY	26
Pena,Carlos, TB	23
Thome,Jim, CWS	21
Thomas,Frank, Tor	19
Konerko,Paul, CWS	17
Ordonez,Magglio, Det	17
Matsui,Hideki, NYY	16
Ortiz,David, Bos	16
Peralta,Jhonny, Cle	16
4 tied with	15

Home Runs Away	
Rodriguez,Alex, NYY	28
Pena,Carlos, TB	23
Ortiz,David, Bos	19
Hunter,Torii, Min	17
Morneau,Justin, Min	16
Beltre,Adrian, Sea	15
7 tied with	14

Longest Avg Home Run	
(min 10 over the wall)	
Hafner,Travis, Cle	410
Gomes,Jonny, TB	408
Beltre,Adrian, Sea	406
Teixeira,Mark, Tex	404
Cust,Jack, Oak	404
Drew,J.D., Bos	403
Morneau,Justin, Min	403
Pena,Carlos, TB	402
Guerrero,Vladimir, LAA	401
Thome,Jim, CWS	401

Shortest Avg Home Run	
(min 10 over the wall)	
Millar,Kevin, Bal	363
Hill,Aaron, Tor	364
Roberts,Brian, Bal	367
Mora,Melvin, Bal	369
Zaun,Gregg, Tor	371
Crawford,Carl, TB	372
Polanco,Placido, Det	373
Tejada,Miguel, Bal	373
Inge,Brandon, Det	373
Markakis,Nick, Bal	377

2007 American League Batting Leaders

Under Age 26: AB Per HR
(minimum 502 PA)

Upton,B.J., TB	19.8
Kinsler,Ian, Tex	24.2
Sizemore,Grady, Cle	26.2
Peralta,Jhonny, Cle	27.3
Markakis,Nick, Bal	27.7
Cano,Robinson, NYY	32.5
Hill,Aaron, Tor	35.8
Gordon,Alex, KC	36.2
Kotchman,Casey, LAA	40.3
Lopez,Jose, Sea	47.6

Under Age 26: OPS
(minimum 502 PA)

Upton,B.J., TB	.894
Sizemore,Grady, Cle	.852
Markakis,Nick, Bal	.848
Cano,Robinson, NYY	.841
Kotchman,Casey, LAA	.840
Pedroia,Dustin, Bos	.823
Kinsler,Ian, Tex	.796
Hill,Aaron, Tor	.792
Peralta,Jhonny, Cle	.771
2 tied with	.725

Under Age 26: RC/27 Outs
(minimum 502 PA)

Sizemore,Grady, Cle	7.0
Upton,B.J., TB	6.9
Kotchman,Casey, LAA	5.8
Markakis,Nick, Bal	5.7
Pedroia,Dustin, Bos	5.7
Kinsler,Ian, Tex	5.5
Cano,Robinson, NYY	5.5
Peralta,Jhonny, Cle	5.1
Hill,Aaron, Tor	5.1
Young,Delmon, TB	4.9

Longest Home Run

Ramirez,Manny, Bos, 7/26	481
Gomes,Jonny, TB, 7/30	465
Gomes,Jonny, TB, 9/5	460
Ibanez,Raul, Sea, 6/20	460
Teixeira,Mark, Tex, 5/27	453
Pena,Carlos, TB, 6/17	450
Sosa,Sammy, Tex, 9/9	450
Byrd,Marlon, Tex, 6/22	449
Pena,Carlos, TB, 6/9	447
Cruz,Nelson, Tex, 7/31	446

Swing and Miss %
(minimum 1500 Pitches Seen)

Cust,Jack, Oak	25.4
Sosa,Sammy, Tex	24.5
Pena,Carlos, TB	22.7
Gomes,Jonny, TB	21.4
Buck,John, KC	20.2
Young,Delmon, TB	19.8
Thome,Jim, CWS	19.6
Sexson,Richie, Sea	19.4
Upton,B.J., TB	18.2
Glaus,Troy, Tor	18.0

Highest First Swing %
(minimum 502 PA)

Young,Delmon, TB	51.4
Guerrero,Vladimir, LAA	48.0
Crawford,Carl, TB	43.1
Pena,Tony F, KC	41.6
Ordonez,Magglio, Det	39.2
Pierzynski,A.J., CWS	38.0
Gordon,Alex, KC	37.8
Patterson,Corey, Bal	37.5
Guillen,Carlos, Det	34.7
Cano,Robinson, NYY	34.5

Lowest First Swing %
(minimum 502 PA)

Willits,Reggie, LAA	4.6
Abreu,Bobby, NYY	8.8
Damon,Johnny, NYY	9.3
Youkilis,Kevin, Bos	10.6
Granderson,Curtis, Det	13.6
Pedroia,Dustin, Bos	14.5
Stewart,Shannon, Oak	14.9
Lowell,Mike, Bos	15.8
Mora,Melvin, Bal	15.8
Sheffield,Gary, Det	16.0

Home RC Per 27 Outs
(minimum 251 PA)

Ordonez,Magglio, Det	11.0
Ortiz,David, Bos	10.8
Pena,Carlos, TB	9.8
Cust,Jack, Oak	9.5
Rodriguez,Alex, NYY	9.3
Lowell,Mike, Bos	8.9
Sizemore,Grady, Cle	8.9
Thome,Jim, CWS	8.8
Suzuki,Ichiro, Sea	8.2
Thomas,Frank, Tor	7.7

Road RC Per 27 Outs
(minimum 251 PA)

Rodriguez,Alex, NYY	10.6
Guerrero,Vladimir, LAA	8.7
Posada,Jorge, NYY	8.6
Upton,B.J., TB	8.5
Ordonez,Magglio, Det	8.5
Ortiz,David, Bos	8.2
Thome,Jim, CWS	7.9
Youkilis,Kevin, Bos	7.8
Martinez,Victor, Cle	7.3
Pena,Carlos, TB	7.2

2007 National League Batting Leaders

Batting Average (minimum 502 PA)		On Base Percentage (minimum 502 PA)		Slugging Average (minimum 502 PA)		Home Runs	
Holliday,Matt, Col	.340	Helton,Todd, Col	.434	Braun,Ryan, Mil	.634	Fielder,Prince, Mil	50
Jones,Chipper, Atl	.337	Pujols,Albert, StL	.429	Fielder,Prince, Mil	.618	Howard,Ryan, Phi	47
Utley,Chase, Phi	.332	Jones,Chipper, Atl	.425	Holliday,Matt, Col	.607	Dunn,Adam, Cin	40
Renteria,Edgar, Atl	.332	Wright,David, NYM	.416	Jones,Chipper, Atl	.604	Holliday,Matt, Col	36
Ramirez,Hanley, Fla	.332	Utley,Chase, Phi	.410	Howard,Ryan, Phi	.584	Berkman,Lance, Hou	34
Pujols,Albert, StL	.327	Holliday,Matt, Col	.405	Pujols,Albert, StL	.568	Braun,Ryan, Mil	34
Wright,David, NYM	.325	Cabrera,Miguel, Fla	.401	Utley,Chase, Phi	.566	Cabrera,Miguel, Fla	34
Cabrera,Miguel, Fla	.320	Lee,Derrek, ChC	.400	Cabrera,Miguel, Fla	.565	Beltran,Carlos, NYM	33
Helton,Todd, Col	.320	Burrell,Pat, Phi	.400	Ramirez,Hanley, Fla	.562	Soriano,Alfonso, ChC	33
Young,Dmitri, Was	.320	Fielder,Prince, Mil	.395	Soriano,Alfonso, ChC	.560	3 tied with	32

Games		Plate Appearances		At Bats		Hits	
Francoeur,Jeff, Atl	162	Rollins,Jimmy, Phi	778	Rollins,Jimmy, Phi	716	Holliday,Matt, Col	216
Lee,Carlos, Hou	162	Reyes,Jose, NYM	765	Reyes,Jose, NYM	681	Ramirez,Hanley, Fla	212
Pierre,Juan, LAD	162	Pierre,Juan, LAD	729	Pierre,Juan, LAD	668	Rollins,Jimmy, Phi	212
Rollins,Jimmy, Phi	162	Uggla,Dan, Fla	728	Zimmerman,Ryan, Was	653	Pierre,Juan, LAD	196
Zimmerman,Ryan, Was	162	Zimmerman,Ryan, Was	722	Phillips,Brandon, Cin	650	Wright,David, NYM	196
Gonzalez,Adrian, SD	161	Gonzalez,Adrian, SD	720	Gonzalez,Adrian, SD	646	Reyes,Jose, NYM	191
Kearns,Austin, Was	161	Holliday,Matt, Col	713	Francoeur,Jeff, Atl	642	Lee,Carlos, Hou	190
Rowand,Aaron, Phi	161	Wright,David, NYM	711	Ramirez,Hanley, Fla	639	Rowand,Aaron, Phi	189
3 tied with	160	Ramirez,Hanley, Fla	706	Holliday,Matt, Col	636	Cabrera,Miguel, Fla	188
		Phillips,Brandon, Cin	702	Uggla,Dan, Fla	632	Francoeur,Jeff, Atl	188

Singles		Doubles		Triples		Total Bases	
Pierre,Juan, LAD	164	Holliday,Matt, Col	50	Rollins,Jimmy, Phi	20	Holliday,Matt, Col	386
Reyes,Jose, NYM	131	Uggla,Dan, Fla	49	Reyes,Jose, NYM	12	Rollins,Jimmy, Phi	380
Francoeur,Jeff, Atl	129	Ramirez,Hanley, Fla	48	Johnson,Kelly, Atl	10	Ramirez,Hanley, Fla	359
Ramirez,Hanley, Fla	129	Utley,Chase, Phi	48	Amezaga,Alfredo, Fla	9	Fielder,Prince, Mil	354
Sanchez,Freddy, Pit	126	Gonzalez,Adrian, SD	46	Hart,Corey, Mil	9	Cabrera,Miguel, Fla	332
Phillips,Brandon, Cin	125	Rowand,Aaron, Phi	45	Hudson,Orlando, Ari	9	Lee,Carlos, Hou	331
Furcal,Rafael, LAD	124	Greene,Khalil, SD	44	Pence,Hunter, Hou	9	Wright,David, NYM	330
Holliday,Matt, Col	124	4 tied with	43	Roberts,Dave, SF	9	Gonzalez,Adrian, SD	324
Rollins,Jimmy, Phi	124			3 tied with	8	Soriano,Alfonso, ChC	324
Wright,David, NYM	123					Pujols,Albert, StL	321

Runs Scored		RBI		Walks		Strikeouts	
Rollins,Jimmy, Phi	139	Holliday,Matt, Col	137	Bonds,Barry, SF	132	Howard,Ryan, Phi	199
Ramirez,Hanley, Fla	125	Howard,Ryan, Phi	136	Helton,Todd, Col	116	Uggla,Dan, Fla	167
Holliday,Matt, Col	120	Cabrera,Miguel, Fla	119	Burrell,Pat, Phi	114	Dunn,Adam, Cin	165
Reyes,Jose, NYM	119	Fielder,Prince, Mil	119	Howard,Ryan, Phi	107	Cameron,Mike, SD	160
Uggla,Dan, Fla	113	Lee,Carlos, Hou	119	Dunn,Adam, Cin	101	Bay,Jason, Pit	141
Wright,David, NYM	113	Hawpe,Brad, Col	116	Pujols,Albert, StL	99	Young,Chris, Ari	141
Fielder,Prince, Mil	109	Beltran,Carlos, NYM	112	Berkman,Lance, Hou	94	Gonzalez,Adrian, SD	140
Jones,Chipper, Atl	108	Atkins,Garrett, Col	111	Wright,David, NYM	94	Jones,Andruw, Atl	138
Phillips,Brandon, Cin	107	Wright,David, NYM	107	Fielder,Prince, Mil	90	Hawpe,Brad, Col	137
Rowand,Aaron, Phi	105	Dunn,Adam, Cin	106	Griffey Jr.,Ken, Cin	85	LaRoche,Adam, Pit	131

2007 National League Batting Leaders

Intentional Walks

Bonds,Barry, SF	43
Howard,Ryan, Phi	35
Cabrera,Miguel, Fla	23
Pujols,Albert, StL	22
Fielder,Prince, Mil	21
Helton,Todd, Col	16
Griffey Jr.,Ken, Cin	14
Reyes,Jose, NYM	13
Ethier,Andre, LAD	12
2 tied with	11

BA Bases Loaded
(minimum 10 PA)

Keppinger,Jeff, Cin	.667
Zimmerman,Ryan, Was	.625
Estrada,Johnny, Mil	.600
Diaz,Matt, Atl	.500
Frandsen,Kevin, SF	.500
Lamb,Mike, Hou	.500
Tulowitzki,Troy, Col	.478
Cabrera,Miguel, Fla	.471
Encarnacion,Edwin, Cin	.471
4 tied with	.455

Sacrifice Hits

Pierre,Juan, LAD	20
Maine,John, NYM	14
Vizquel,Omar, SF	14
Cook,Aaron, Col	13
Francis,Jeff, Col	13
Smoltz,John, Atl	13
Glavine,Tom, NYM	12
Lohse,Kyle, Cin-Phi	12
Rodriguez,Wandy, Hou	12
Snell,Ian, Pit	12

Sacrifice Flies

Lee,Carlos, Hou	13
Greene,Khalil, SD	11
Uggla,Dan, Fla	11
Atkins,Garrett, Col	10
Beltran,Carlos, NYM	10
Lo Duca,Paul, NYM	10
Durham,Ray, SF	9
Griffey Jr.,Ken, Cin	9
Jones,Andruw, Atl	9
Sanchez,Freddy, Pit	9

BA Close & Late
(minimum 50 PA)

Eckstein,David, StL	.442
Pujols,Albert, StL	.403
Rowand,Aaron, Phi	.382
Hudson,Orlando, Ari	.380
Loney,James, LAD	.378
Molina,Yadier, StL	.353
Lee,Derrek, ChC	.346
Wright,David, NYM	.346
Hatteberg,Scott, Cin	.344
Valentin,Javier, Cin	.344

Batting Average w/ RISP
(minimum 100 PA)

Loney,James, LAD	.419
Bard,Josh, SD	.406
Cabrera,Miguel, Fla	.378
Garciaparra,Nomar, LAD	.373
Lee,Derrek, ChC	.364
Encarnacion,Edwin, Cin	.360
Jones,Jacque, ChC	.358
Willingham,Josh, Fla	.345
Sanchez,Freddy, Pit	.344
Francoeur,Jeff, Atl	.341

SLG vs. LHP
(minimum 125 PA)

Braun,Ryan, Mil	.964
Ramirez,Aramis, ChC	.763
Ramirez,Hanley, Fla	.703
Cabrera,Miguel, Fla	.686
Zimmerman,Ryan, Was	.660
Wright,David, NYM	.657
Pujols,Albert, StL	.640
Hart,Corey, Mil	.613
Phillips,Brandon, Cin	.606
Martin,Russell, LAD	.605

SLG vs. RHP
(minimum 377 PA)

Jones,Chipper, Atl	.699
Fielder,Prince, Mil	.686
Howard,Ryan, Phi	.644
Dunn,Adam, Cin	.620
Holliday,Matt, Col	.617
Utley,Chase, Phi	.604
Hawpe,Brad, Col	.585
Soriano,Alfonso, ChC	.570
Helton,Todd, Col	.551
Pujols,Albert, StL	.542

Leadoff Hitters OBP
(minimum 150 PA)

Ramirez,Hanley, Fla	.405
Escobar,Yunel, Atl	.400
Hopper,Norris, Cin	.392
Weeks,Rickie, Mil	.385
Johnson,Kelly, Atl	.372
Taveras,Willy, Col	.372
Giles,Brian, SD	.368
Davis,Rajai, Pit-SF	.367
Byrnes,Eric, Ari	.360
McLouth,Nate, Pit	.360

Cleanup Hitters SLG
(minimum 150 PA)

Fielder,Prince, Mil	.677
Beltran,Carlos, NYM	.619
Teixeira,Mark, Atl	.615
Howard,Ryan, Phi	.586
Bonds,Barry, SF	.586
Cabrera,Miguel, Fla	.578
Gonzalez,Adrian, SD	.553
Ramirez,Aramis, ChC	.553
Jackson,Conor, Ari	.538
Lee,Carlos, Hou	.526

BA vs. LHP
(minimum 125 PA)

Braun,Ryan, Mil	.450
Ramirez,Hanley, Fla	.399
Ramirez,Aramis, ChC	.395
Bard,Josh, SD	.376
Zimmerman,Ryan, Was	.374
Pujols,Albert, StL	.367
Cabrera,Miguel, Fla	.364
Sanchez,Freddy, Pit	.364
Wright,David, NYM	.361
Martin,Russell, LAD	.357

BA vs. RHP
(minimum 377 PA)

Jones,Chipper, Atl	.378
Holliday,Matt, Col	.351
Utley,Chase, Phi	.340
Helton,Todd, Col	.334
Hawpe,Brad, Col	.315
Pujols,Albert, StL	.313
Ramirez,Hanley, Fla	.312
Lee,Derrek, ChC	.312
Soriano,Alfonso, ChC	.311
Wright,David, NYM	.311

Home BA
(minimum 251 PA)

Holliday,Matt, Col	.376
Utley,Chase, Phi	.372
Lee,Derrek, ChC	.371
Atkins,Garrett, Col	.349
Lee,Carlos, Hou	.345
Ramirez,Hanley, Fla	.345
Ramirez,Aramis, ChC	.337
Pence,Hunter, Hou	.336
Cabrera,Miguel, Fla	.336
Wright,David, NYM	.335

Away BA
(minimum 251 PA)

Pujols,Albert, StL	.358
Jones,Chipper, Atl	.353
Renteria,Edgar, Atl	.336
Martin,Russell, LAD	.329
Soriano,Alfonso, ChC	.325
Hermida,Jeremy, Fla	.324
Braun,Ryan, Mil	.322
Ramirez,Hanley, Fla	.319
Wright,David, NYM	.316
Francoeur,Jeff, Atl	.316

OBP vs. LHP
(minimum 125 PA)

Braun,Ryan, Mil	.516
Pujols,Albert, StL	.500
Cabrera,Miguel, Fla	.487
Bonds,Barry, SF	.470
Martin,Russell, LAD	.458
Ramirez,Aramis, ChC	.457
Bard,Josh, SD	.452
Ramirez,Hanley, Fla	.451
Wright,David, NYM	.449
Zimmerman,Ryan, Was	.443

OBP vs. RHP
(minimum 377 PA)

Jones,Chipper, Atl	.472
Helton,Todd, Col	.454
Howard,Ryan, Phi	.428
Hawpe,Brad, Col	.418
Fielder,Prince, Mil	.414
Holliday,Matt, Col	.412
Dunn,Adam, Cin	.404
Wright,David, NYM	.404
Griffey Jr.,Ken, Cin	.402
2 tied with	.400

2007 National League Batting Leaders

Stolen Bases

Reyes,Jose, NYM	78
Pierre,Juan, LAD	64
Ramirez,Hanley, Fla	51
Byrnes,Eric, Ari	50
Rollins,Jimmy, Phi	41
Victorino,Shane, Phi	37
Wright,David, NYM	34
Taveras,Willy, Col	33
Matsui,Kaz, Col	32
Phillips,Brandon, Cin	32

Caught Stealing

Reyes,Jose, NYM	21
Pierre,Juan, LAD	15
Ramirez,Hanley, Fla	14
Harris,Willie, Atl	11
Lopez,Felipe, Was	9
Martin,Russell, LAD	9
Taveras,Willy, Col	9
Freel,Ryan, Cin	8
Phillips,Brandon, Cin	8
3 tied with	7

Highest SB Success Pct
(minimum 20 SBA)

McLouth,Nate, Pit	95.7
Weeks,Rickie, Mil	92.6
Beltran,Carlos, NYM	92.0
Victorino,Shane, Phi	90.2
Matsui,Kaz, Col	88.9
Byrnes,Eric, Ari	87.7
Theriot,Ryan, ChC	87.5
Rollins,Jimmy, Phi	87.2
Wright,David, NYM	87.2
Roberts,Dave, SF	86.1

Lowest SB Success Pct
(minimum 20 SBA)

Harris,Willie, Atl	60.7
Amezaga,Alfredo, Fla	65.0
Freel,Ryan, Cin	65.2
Hopper,Norris, Cin	70.0
Martin,Russell, LAD	70.0
Vizquel,Omar, SF	70.0
Lopez,Felipe, Was	72.7
Braun,Ryan, Mil	75.0
Soriano,Alfonso, ChC	76.0
Hart,Corey, Mil	76.7

Steals of Third

Pierre,Juan, LAD	18
Reyes,Jose, NYM	16
Ramirez,Hanley, Fla	13
Beltran,Carlos, NYM	8
Phillips,Brandon, Cin	8
Young,Chris, Ari	8
Byrnes,Eric, Ari	7
Freel,Ryan, Cin	7
Davis,Rajai, Pit-SF	6
Theriot,Ryan, ChC	6

Grounded Into DP

Lee,Carlos, Hou	27
Pujols,Albert, StL	27
Phillips,Brandon, Cin	26
Zimmerman,Ryan, Was	26
Holliday,Matt, Col	23
Hudson,Orlando, Ari	21
Jones,Chipper, Atl	21
McCann,Brian, Atl	19
Torrealba,Yorvit, Col	19
5 tied with	18

Grounded Into DP Pct
(minimum 50 GIDP Ops)

Werth,Jayson, Phi	0.00
Ludwick,Ryan, StL	1.33
Matsui,Kaz, Col	1.47
Teixeira,Mark, Atl	3.39
Gonzalez,Adrian, SD	4.35
Cruz,Jose, SD	4.55
Drew,Stephen, Ari	4.55
Weeks,Rickie, Mil	4.62
Duncan,Chris, StL	4.88
Encarnacion,Edwin, Cin	5.00

Hit By Pitch

Utley,Chase, Phi	25
Rowand,Aaron, Phi	19
Willingham,Josh, Fla	16
Encarnacion,Edwin, Cin	14
Fielder,Prince, Mil	14
Weeks,Rickie, Mil	14
Boone,Aaron, Fla	13
Hart,Corey, Mil	13
Uggla,Dan, Fla	13
4 tied with	12

Pitches Seen

Rollins,Jimmy, Phi	3001
Helton,Todd, Col	2974
Zimmerman,Ryan, Was	2884
Uggla,Dan, Fla	2860
Wright,David, NYM	2833
Reyes,Jose, NYM	2814
Gonzalez,Adrian, SD	2766
Pujols,Albert, StL	2752
Howard,Ryan, Phi	2723
Lopez,Felipe, Was	2701

At Bats Per Home Run
(minimum 502 PA)

Howard,Ryan, Phi	11.3
Fielder,Prince, Mil	11.5
Dunn,Adam, Cin	13.1
Burrell,Pat, Phi	15.7
Berkman,Lance, Hou	16.5
Beltran,Carlos, NYM	16.8
Cabrera,Miguel, Fla	17.3
Soriano,Alfonso, ChC	17.5
Griffey Jr.,Ken, Cin	17.6
Pujols,Albert, StL	17.7

Highest GB/FB Ratio
(minimum 502 PA)

Pierre,Juan, LAD	2.62
Winn,Randy, SF	2.28
Hudson,Orlando, Ari	2.25
Theriot,Ryan, ChC	2.13
Lopez,Felipe, Was	1.92
Furcal,Rafael, LAD	1.86
Renteria,Edgar, Atl	1.80
Martin,Russell, LAD	1.69
Ethier,Andre, LAD	1.61
Kearns,Austin, Was	1.59

Lowest GB/FB Ratio
(minimum 502 PA)

Burrell,Pat, Phi	0.65
Uggla,Dan, Fla	0.75
Soriano,Alfonso, ChC	0.79
Griffey Jr.,Ken, Cin	0.81
Young,Chris, Ari	0.82
Greene,Khalil, SD	0.84
Howard,Ryan, Phi	0.84
Dunn,Adam, Cin	0.84
Byrnes,Eric, Ari	0.85
Atkins,Garrett, Col	0.85

Pitches Per Plate App
(minimum 502 PA)

Helton,Todd, Col	4.36
Burrell,Pat, Phi	4.22
Howard,Ryan, Phi	4.20
Weeks,Rickie, Mil	4.18
Dunn,Adam, Cin	4.18
Bautista,Jose, Pit	4.14
Johnson,Kelly, Atl	4.12
Pujols,Albert, StL	4.05
Cameron,Mike, SD	4.03
Lopez,Felipe, Was	4.03

Pct Pitches Taken
(minimum 1500 Pitches)

Bonds,Barry, SF	67.2
Hatteberg,Scott, Cin	65.4
Giles,Brian, SD	64.5
Burrell,Pat, Phi	63.8
Pujols,Albert, StL	62.9
Weeks,Rickie, Mil	62.4
Jackson,Conor, Ari	61.8
McLouth,Nate, Pit	61.6
Snyder,Chris, Ari	61.5
Lopez,Felipe, Was	61.2

Best BPS on OutZ
(minimum 502 PA)

Hart,Corey, Mil	.699
Giles,Brian, SD	.676
Holliday,Matt, Col	.630
Wright,David, NYM	.623
Pujols,Albert, StL	.611
Gonzalez,Luis, LAD	.608
Renteria,Edgar, Atl	.607
Pierre,Juan, LAD	.602
Ramirez,Hanley, Fla	.595
Lee,Carlos, Hou	.572

Worst BPS on OutZ
(minimum 502 PA)

Cameron,Mike, SD	.138
Willingham,Josh, Fla	.189
Church,Ryan, Was	.242
Berkman,Lance, Hou	.246
Bautista,Jose, Pit	.256
Kouzmanoff,Kevin, SD	.277
Drew,Stephen, Ari	.292
Durham,Ray, SF	.299
Burrell,Pat, Phi	.304
Young,Chris, Ari	.312

2007 National League Batting Leaders

Best OPS vs Fastballs
(minimum 251 PA)

Jones,Chipper, Atl	1.117
Howard,Ryan, Phi	1.055
Pujols,Albert, StL	1.016
Dunn,Adam, Cin	1.012
Wright,David, NYM	1.003
Bonds,Barry, SF	.998
Cabrera,Miguel, Fla	.996
Utley,Chase, Phi	.977
Lee,Derrek, ChC	.976
Rowand,Aaron, Phi	.960

Best OPS vs Curveballs
(minimum 50 PA)

Fielder,Prince, Mil	1.306
Gonzalez,Luis, LAD	1.084
Hawpe,Brad, Col	1.043
Rollins,Jimmy, Phi	.945
Ramirez,Hanley, Fla	.929
Phillips,Brandon, Cin	.923
DeRosa,Mark, ChC	.909
Francoeur,Jeff, Atl	.907
Gonzalez,Adrian, SD	.893
Bay,Jason, Pit	.844

Best OPS vs Changeups
(minimum 50 PA)

Braun,Ryan, Mil	1.249
Holliday,Matt, Col	1.238
Kearns,Austin, Was	1.171
Diaz,Matt, Atl	1.153
Hawpe,Brad, Col	1.143
Helton,Todd, Col	1.119
Ramirez,Aramis, ChC	1.076
Utley,Chase, Phi	1.067
Fielder,Prince, Mil	1.058
Soriano,Alfonso, ChC	1.053

Best OPS vs Sliders
(minimum 32 PA)

McLouth,Nate, Pit	1.242
Jones,Chipper, Atl	1.176
Holliday,Matt, Col	1.153
Hamilton,Josh, Cin	1.148
Victorino,Shane, Phi	1.121
Hatteberg,Scott, Cin	1.103
Lee,Carlos, Hou	1.087
Utley,Chase, Phi	1.086
Hairston,Scott, Ari-SD	1.076
Hermida,Jeremy, Fla	1.074

OPS
(minimum 502 PA)

Jones,Chipper, Atl	1.029
Fielder,Prince, Mil	1.013
Holliday,Matt, Col	1.012
Pujols,Albert, StL	.997
Utley,Chase, Phi	.976
Howard,Ryan, Phi	.976
Cabrera,Miguel, Fla	.965
Wright,David, NYM	.963
Ramirez,Hanley, Fla	.948
Dunn,Adam, Cin	.940

OPS First Half
(minimum 251 PA)

Bonds,Barry, SF	1.101
Jones,Chipper, Atl	1.011
Fielder,Prince, Mil	.996
Utley,Chase, Phi	.972
Cabrera,Miguel, Fla	.969
Holliday,Matt, Col	.964
Griffey Jr.,Ken, Cin	.958
Pence,Hunter, Hou	.956
Hawpe,Brad, Col	.949
Howard,Ryan, Phi	.933

OPS Second Half
(minimum 251 PA)

Pujols,Albert, StL	1.081
Holliday,Matt, Col	1.073
Wright,David, NYM	1.061
Jones,Chipper, Atl	1.046
Fielder,Prince, Mil	1.034
Howard,Ryan, Phi	1.016
Burrell,Pat, Phi	1.010
Dunn,Adam, Cin	.986
Braun,Ryan, Mil	.976
Ramirez,Hanley, Fla	.975

OPS by Catchers
(minimum 251 PA)

Martin,Russell, LAD	.857
Snyder,Chris, Ari	.779
McCann,Brian, Atl	.775
Bard,Josh, SD	.772
Ruiz,Carlos, Phi	.734
Molina,Bengie, SF	.726
Molina,Yadier, StL	.714
Paulino,Ronny, Pit	.708
Torrealba,Yorvit, Col	.704
Estrada,Johnny, Mil	.691

OPS by First Basemen
(minimum 251 PA)

Fielder,Prince, Mil	1.013
Pujols,Albert, StL	.992
Howard,Ryan, Phi	.968
Helton,Todd, Col	.935
Loney,James, LAD	.920
Berkman,Lance, Hou	.909
Lee,Derrek, ChC	.900
Hatteberg,Scott, Cin	.891
Young,Dmitri, Was	.872
Jackson,Conor, Ari	.855

OPS by Second Basemen
(minimum 251 PA)

Utley,Chase, Phi	.983
Kent,Jeff, LAD	.877
DeRosa,Mark, ChC	.848
Johnson,Kelly, Atl	.839
Phillips,Brandon, Cin	.818
Hudson,Orlando, Ari	.807
Uggla,Dan, Fla	.806
Weeks,Rickie, Mil	.801
Sanchez,Freddy, Pit	.788
Belliard,Ronnie, Was	.754

OPS by Third Basemen
(minimum 251 PA)

Jones,Chipper, Atl	1.040
Braun,Ryan, Mil	1.006
Cabrera,Miguel, Fla	.966
Wright,David, NYM	.961
Ramirez,Aramis, ChC	.914
Atkins,Garrett, Col	.864
Reynolds,Mark, Ari	.850
Zimmerman,Ryan, Was	.793
Encarnacion,Edwin, Cin	.789
Kouzmanoff,Kevin, SD	.784

OPS by Shortstops
(minimum 251 PA)

Ramirez,Hanley, Fla	.943
Rollins,Jimmy, Phi	.875
Renteria,Edgar, Atl	.863
Tulowitzki,Troy, Col	.838
Gonzalez,Alex, Cin	.804
Hardy,J.J., Mil	.786
Wilson,Jack, Pit	.781
Reyes,Jose, NYM	.775
Greene,Khalil, SD	.759
Eckstein,David, StL	.742

OPS by Left Fielders
(minimum 251 PA)

Bonds,Barry, SF	1.067
Holliday,Matt, Col	1.020
Dunn,Adam, Cin	.945
Burrell,Pat, Phi	.931
Diaz,Matt, Atl	.921
Soriano,Alfonso, ChC	.915
Alou,Moises, NYM	.914
Lee,Carlos, Hou	.888
Duncan,Chris, StL	.826
Willingham,Josh, Fla	.825

OPS by Center Fielders
(minimum 251 PA)

Hamilton,Josh, Cin	.950
Pence,Hunter, Hou	.922
Rowand,Aaron, Phi	.891
Beltran,Carlos, NYM	.880
Jones,Jacque, ChC	.765
Young,Chris, Ari	.764
Cameron,Mike, SD	.759
Taveras,Willy, Col	.756
Hall,Bill, Mil	.739
Edmonds,Jim, StL	.727

OPS by Right Fielders
(minimum 251 PA)

Hawpe,Brad, Col	.936
Kemp,Matt, LAD	.913
Scott,Luke, Hou	.885
Griffey Jr.,Ken, Cin	.884
Hermida,Jeremy, Fla	.867
Winn,Randy, SF	.830
Nady,Xavier, Pit	.810
Ethier,Andre, LAD	.796
Hart,Corey, Mil	.796
Francoeur,Jeff, Atl	.782

OPS by Pitchers
(minimum 66 PA)

Willis,Dontrelle, Fla	.848
Wainwright,Adam, StL	.668
Penny,Brad, LAD	.618
Zambrano,Carlos, ChC	.615
Hudson,Tim, Atl	.594
Peavy,Jake, SD	.581
Morris,Matt, SF-Pit	.557
Glavine,Tom, NYM	.527
Eaton,Adam, Phi	.517
Hernandez,Livan, Ari	.484

2007 National League Batting Leaders

OPS Batting Left vs. LHP
(minimum 125 PA)

Bonds,Barry, SF	.991
Utley,Chase, Phi	.927
Fielder,Prince, Mil	.834
Howard,Ryan, Phi	.826
LaRoche,Adam, Pit	.808
Gonzalez,Adrian, SD	.796
Dunn,Adam, Cin	.789
Johnson,Kelly, Atl	.771
McCann,Brian, Atl	.752
Helton,Todd, Col	.743

OPS Batting Left vs. RHP
(minimum 377 PA)

Jones,Chipper, Atl	1.171
Fielder,Prince, Mil	1.100
Howard,Ryan, Phi	1.072
Dunn,Adam, Cin	1.024
Helton,Todd, Col	1.005
Utley,Chase, Phi	1.004
Hawpe,Brad, Col	1.002
Griffey Jr.,Ken, Cin	.943
Berkman,Lance, Hou	.926
Gonzalez,Adrian, SD	.873

OPS Batting Right vs. LHP
(minimum 125 PA)

Braun,Ryan, Mil	1.480
Ramirez,Aramis, ChC	1.220
Cabrera,Miguel, Fla	1.173
Ramirez,Hanley, Fla	1.157
Pujols,Albert, StL	1.140
Wright,David, NYM	1.106
Zimmerman,Ryan, Was	1.103
Martin,Russell, LAD	1.062
Hart,Corey, Mil	1.032
Lee,Derrek, ChC	1.015

OPS Batting Right vs. RHP
(minimum 377 PA)

Holliday,Matt, Col	1.028
Pujols,Albert, StL	.942
Soriano,Alfonso, ChC	.917
Cabrera,Miguel, Fla	.910
Wright,David, NYM	.908
Willingham,Josh, Fla	.897
Lee,Derrek, ChC	.885
Ramirez,Hanley, Fla	.884
Atkins,Garrett, Col	.882
Burrell,Pat, Phi	.881

OPS vs. LHP
(minimum 125 PA)

Braun,Ryan, Mil	1.480
Ramirez,Aramis, ChC	1.220
Cabrera,Miguel, Fla	1.173
Ramirez,Hanley, Fla	1.154
Pujols,Albert, StL	1.140
Wright,David, NYM	1.106
Zimmerman,Ryan, Was	1.103
Martin,Russell, LAD	1.062
Hart,Corey, Mil	1.032
Lee,Derrek, ChC	1.015

OPS vs. RHP
(minimum 377 PA)

Jones,Chipper, Atl	1.171
Fielder,Prince, Mil	1.100
Howard,Ryan, Phi	1.072
Holliday,Matt, Col	1.028
Dunn,Adam, Cin	1.024
Helton,Todd, Col	1.005
Utley,Chase, Phi	1.004
Hawpe,Brad, Col	1.002
Griffey Jr.,Ken, Cin	.943
Pujols,Albert, StL	.942

RC Per 27 Outs vs. LHP
(minimum 125 PA)

Braun,Ryan, Mil	16.9
Ramirez,Aramis, ChC	13.3
Cabrera,Miguel, Fla	12.1
Ramirez,Hanley, Fla	11.6
Zimmerman,Ryan, Was	9.7
Utley,Chase, Phi	9.1
Hart,Corey, Mil	9.0
Snyder,Chris, Ari	9.0
Burrell,Pat, Phi	8.9
Lee,Derrek, ChC	8.9

RC Per 27 Outs vs. RHP
(minimum 377 PA)

Jones,Chipper, Atl	11.2
Howard,Ryan, Phi	10.0
Fielder,Prince, Mil	9.3
Helton,Todd, Col	8.8
Hawpe,Brad, Col	8.4
Holliday,Matt, Col	8.2
Dunn,Adam, Cin	7.9
Wright,David, NYM	7.5
Utley,Chase, Phi	7.5
Berkman,Lance, Hou	7.4

Highest RBI %
(minimum 502 PA)

Howard,Ryan, Phi	13.03
Fielder,Prince, Mil	12.05
Holliday,Matt, Col	12.04
Hawpe,Brad, Col	11.57
Cabrera,Miguel, Fla	11.53
Beltran,Carlos, NYM	11.19
Utley,Chase, Phi	10.99
Ramirez,Aramis, ChC	10.99
Dunn,Adam, Cin	10.98
Burrell,Pat, Phi	10.86

Lowest RBI %
(minimum 502 PA)

Pierre,Juan, LAD	3.72
Furcal,Rafael, LAD	5.06
Theriot,Ryan, ChC	5.14
Reyes,Jose, NYM	5.30
Weeks,Rickie, Mil	5.32
Lopez,Felipe, Was	5.33
Loretta,Mark, Hou	5.40
Vizquel,Omar, SF	5.59
Victorino,Shane, Phi	6.05
Biggio,Craig, Hou	6.06

Highest Strikeout per PA
(minimum 502 PA)

Howard,Ryan, Phi	.307
Dunn,Adam, Cin	.261
Hall,Bill, Mil	.254
Cameron,Mike, SD	.246
Bay,Jason, Pit	.230
Uggla,Dan, Fla	.229
Weeks,Rickie, Mil	.229
Hawpe,Brad, Col	.226
Young,Chris, Ari	.226
Soriano,Alfonso, ChC	.211

Lowest Strikeout per PA
(minimum 502 PA)

Pierre,Juan, LAD	.051
Loretta,Mark, Hou	.080
Vizquel,Omar, SF	.083
Theriot,Ryan, ChC	.084
Pujols,Albert, StL	.085
Wilson,Jack, Pit	.086
Lee,Carlos, Hou	.090
Reyes,Jose, NYM	.102
Molina,Bengie, SF	.103
2 tied with	.106

Home Runs At Home

Fielder,Prince, Mil	27
Holliday,Matt, Col	25
Howard,Ryan, Phi	23
Cabrera,Miguel, Fla	19
Dunn,Adam, Cin	19
Hawpe,Brad, Col	19
Rollins,Jimmy, Phi	18
Uggla,Dan, Fla	18
6 tied with	17

Home Runs Away

Howard,Ryan, Phi	24
Fielder,Prince, Mil	23
Beltran,Carlos, NYM	22
Berkman,Lance, Hou	21
Dunn,Adam, Cin	21
Gonzalez,Adrian, SD	20
Pujols,Albert, StL	20
Soriano,Alfonso, ChC	20
Young,Chris, Ari	18
Braun,Ryan, Mil	17

Longest Avg Home Run
(min 10 over the wall)

Thorman,Scott, Atl	409
Holliday,Matt, Col	409
Spilborghs,Ryan, Col	408
Delgado,Carlos, NYM	407
Cabrera,Miguel, Fla	406
Ludwick,Ryan, StL	405
Edmonds,Jim, StL	405
Hermida,Jeremy, Fla	405
Fielder,Prince, Mil	404
Kent,Jeff, LAD	403

Shortest Avg Home Run
(min 10 over the wall)

Biggio,Craig, Hou	360
Wilson,Jack, Pit	361
Rollins,Jimmy, Phi	370
Lee,Carlos, Hou	377
Branyan,Russ, SD-Phi-StL	378
Diaz,Matt, Atl	378
Sanchez,Freddy, Pit	379
McLouth,Nate, Pit	379
Bradley,Milton, SD	379
Estrada,Johnny, Mil	380

2007 National League Batting Leaders

Under Age 26: AB Per HR
(minimum 502 PA)

Fielder,Prince, Mil	11.5
Cabrera,Miguel, Fla	17.3
Young,Chris, Ari	17.8
Wright,David, NYM	20.1
Hart,Corey, Mil	21.0
Gonzalez,Adrian, SD	21.5
Ramirez,Hanley, Fla	22.0
Hardy,J.J., Mil	22.8
Tulowitzki,Troy, Col	25.4
Weeks,Rickie, Mil	25.6

Under Age 26: OPS
(minimum 502 PA)

Fielder,Prince, Mil	1.013
Cabrera,Miguel, Fla	.965
Wright,David, NYM	.963
Ramirez,Hanley, Fla	.948
Hart,Corey, Mil	.892
Gonzalez,Adrian, SD	.849
Martin,Russell, LAD	.843
Tulowitzki,Troy, Col	.838
Johnson,Kelly, Atl	.831
Weeks,Rickie, Mil	.807

Under Age 26: RC/27 Outs
(minimum 502 PA)

Fielder,Prince, Mil	7.9
Wright,David, NYM	7.9
Cabrera,Miguel, Fla	7.7
Ramirez,Hanley, Fla	6.7
Hart,Corey, Mil	6.6
Encarnacion,Edwin, Cin	6.4
Gonzalez,Adrian, SD	6.1
Johnson,Kelly, Atl	5.9
Tulowitzki,Troy, Col	5.6
Martin,Russell, LAD	5.5

Longest Home Run

Howard,Ryan, Phi, 6/27	505
Fielder,Prince, Mil, 9/24	480
Byrnes,Eric, Ari, 5/8	473
Ludwick,Ryan, StL, 7/1	473
Cabrera,Miguel, Fla, 7/15	471
Dunn,Adam, Cin, 9/11	471
Jones,Chipper, Atl, 8/9	470
Cabrera,Miguel, Fla, 4/22	467
Uggla,Dan, Fla, 4/22	466
Fielder,Prince, Mil, 5/21	462

Swing and Miss %
(minimum 1500 Pitches Seen)

Howard,Ryan, Phi	25.0
Reynolds,Mark, Ari	24.4
Olivo,Miguel, Fla	24.2
Hawpe,Brad, Col	22.3
Jones,Andruw, Atl	20.4
Uggla,Dan, Fla	20.3
Jenkins,Geoff, Mil	20.0
Francoeur,Jeff, Atl	19.7
Dunn,Adam, Cin	19.5
Soriano,Alfonso, ChC	10.1

Highest First Swing %
(minimum 502 PA)

Francoeur,Jeff, Atl	44.1
Holliday,Matt, Col	42.9
Hawpe,Brad, Col	40.2
Cabrera,Miguel, Fla	39.5
Young,Dmitri, Was	38.6
Phillips,Brandon, Cin	37.2
Kent,Jeff, LAD	35.8
Soriano,Alfonso, ChC	35.7
Berkman,Lance, Hou	35.6
Tulowitzki,Troy, Col	35.3

Lowest First Swing %
(minimum 502 PA)

Hardy,J.J., Mil	7.9
Pujols,Albert, StL	11.7
Pierre,Juan, LAD	13.5
Weeks,Rickie, Mil	14.4
Lopez,Felipe, Was	15.0
Utley,Chase, Phi	15.0
Rollins,Jimmy, Phi	16.3
Loretta,Mark, Hou	16.9
Gonzalez,Luis, LAD	18.3
Zimmerman,Ryan, Was	18.5

Home RC Per 27 Outs
(minimum 251 PA)

Fielder,Prince, Mil	10.0
Holliday,Matt, Col	10.0
Utley,Chase, Phi	10.0
Burrell,Pat, Phi	9.7
Lee,Derrek, ChC	9.6
Helton,Todd, Col	9.0
Bonds,Barry, SF	8.7
Ramirez,Aramis, ChC	8.5
Cabrera,Miguel, Fla	8.4
Atkins,Garrett, Col	7.8

Road RC Per 27 Outs
(minimum 251 PA)

Jones,Chipper, Atl	9.1
Pujols,Albert, StL	8.9
Howard,Ryan, Phi	8.6
Berkman,Lance, Hou	8.3
Wright,David, NYM	8.2
Braun,Ryan, Mil	7.4
Gonzalez,Adrian, SD	7.4
Hermida,Jeremy, Fla	7.2
Johnson,Kelly, Atl	7.1
Cabrera,Miguel, Fla	7.1

2007 American League Pitching Leaders

Earned Run Average
(minimum 162 IP)

Lackey,John, LAA	3.01
Carmona,Fausto, Cle	3.06
Haren,Dan, Oak	3.07
Bedard,Erik, Bal	3.16
Sabathia,C.C., Cle	3.21
Beckett,Josh, Bos	3.27
Santana,Johan, Min	3.33
Escobar,Kelvim, LAA	3.40
Kazmir,Scott, TB	3.48
Buehrle,Mark, CWS	3.63

Winning Percentage
(minimum 15 Decisions)

Verlander,Justin, Det	.750
Beckett,Josh, Bos	.741
Sabathia,C.C., Cle	.731
Wang,Chien-Ming, NYY	.731
Bedard,Erik, Bal	.722
Escobar,Kelvim, LAA	.720
Carmona,Fausto, Cle	.704
Halladay,Roy, Tor	.696
Lackey,John, LAA	.679
2 tied with	.667

Opponent Batting Average
(minimum 162 IP)

Bedard,Erik, Bal	.212
Burnett,A.J., Tor	.214
Santana,Johan, Min	.225
McGowan,Dustin, Tor	.230
Verlander,Justin, Det	.233
Vazquez,Javier, CWS	.242
Beckett,Josh, Bos	.245
Matsuzaka,Daisuke, Bos	.246
Shields,James, TB	.247
Haren,Dan, Oak	.247

Baserunners Per 9 IP
(minimum 162 IP)

Santana,Johan, Min	9.82
Bedard,Erik, Bal	10.04
Shields,James, TB	10.38
Beckett,Josh, Bos	10.50
Vazquez,Javier, CWS	10.55
Sabathia,C.C., Cle	10.57
Haren,Dan, Oak	10.99
McGowan,Dustin, Tor	11.09
Guthrie,Jeremy, Bal	11.09
Blanton,Joe, Oak	11.11

Games

Downs,Scott, Tor	81
Walker,Jamie, Bal	81
Bradford,Chad, Bal	78
Vizcaino,Luis, NYY	77
Gobble,Jimmy, KC	74
Neshek,Pat, Min	74
Guerrier,Matt, Min	73
Sherrill,George, Sea	73
Myers,Mike, NYY-CWS	72
Shields,Scot, LAA	71

Games Started

Blanton,Joe, Oak	34
Cabrera,Daniel, Bal	34
Gaudin,Chad, Oak	34
Haren,Dan, Oak	34
Kazmir,Scott, TB	34
Meche,Gil, KC	34
Pettitte,Andy, NYY	34
Sabathia,C.C., Cle	34
3 tied with	33

Complete Games

Halladay,Roy, Tor	7
Sabathia,C.C., Cle	4
Blanton,Joe, Oak	3
Buehrle,Mark, CWS	3
Escobar,Kelvim, LAA	3
Weaver,Jeff, Sea	3
10 tied with	2

Shutouts

Byrd,Paul, Cle	2
Contreras,Jose, CWS	2
Lackey,John, LAA	2
Weaver,Jeff, Sea	2
19 tied with	1

Wins

Beckett,Josh, Bos	20
Carmona,Fausto, Cle	19
Lackey,John, LAA	19
Sabathia,C.C., Cle	19
Wang,Chien-Ming, NYY	19
Escobar,Kelvim, LAA	18
Verlander,Justin, Det	18
Wakefield,Tim, Bos	17
Batista,Miguel, Sea	16
Halladay,Roy, Tor	16

Losses

Cabrera,Daniel, Bal	18
Contreras,Jose, CWS	17
Jackson,Edwin, TB	15
Washburn,Jarrod, Sea	15
Millwood,Kevin, Tex	14
Santana,Ervin, LAA	14
Silva,Carlos, Min	14
7 tied with	13

No Decisions

Guthrie,Jeremy, Bal	15
Kazmir,Scott, TB	12
Meche,Gil, KC	12
Buehrle,Mark, CWS	11
Jackson,Edwin, TB	11
Shields,James, TB	11
Trachsel,Steve, Bal	11
8 tied with	10

Wild Pitches

Verlander,Justin, Det	17
Batista,Miguel, Sea	15
McGowan,Dustin, Tor	13
Bonderman,Jeremy, Det	12
Haren,Dan, Oak	10
Kazmir,Scott, TB	10
Tejeda,Robinson, Tex	10
Wakefield,Tim, Bos	10
4 tied with	9

Strikeouts

Kazmir,Scott, TB	239
Santana,Johan, Min	235
Bedard,Erik, Bal	221
Vazquez,Javier, CWS	213
Sabathia,C.C., Cle	209
Matsuzaka,Daisuke, Bos	201
Beckett,Josh, Bos	194
Haren,Dan, Oak	192
Shields,James, TB	184
Verlander,Justin, Det	183

Walks Allowed

Cabrera,Daniel, Bal	108
Gaudin,Chad, Oak	100
Kazmir,Scott, TB	89
Jackson,Edwin, TB	88
Batista,Miguel, Sea	85
Matsuzaka,Daisuke, Bos	80
Pettitte,Andy, NYY	69
Trachsel,Steve, Bal	69
3 tied with	67

Intentional Walks Allowed

Vizcaino,Luis, NYY	11
Mastny,Tom, Cle	9
Gaudin,Chad, Oak	8
Tallet,Brian, Tor	7
12 tied with	6

Hit Batters

Verlander,Justin, Det	19
Cabrera,Daniel, Bal	15
Contreras,Jose, CWS	15
Matsuzaka,Daisuke, Bos	13
Burnett,A.J., Tor	12
Lackey,John, LAA	12
Carmona,Fausto, Cle	11
Shields,James, TB	10
Padilla,Vicente, Tex	9
10 tied with	8

2007 American League Pitching Leaders

Runs Allowed

Contreras,Jose, CWS	134
Cabrera,Daniel, Bal	133
Jackson,Edwin, TB	116
Garland,Jon, CWS	114
Millwood,Kevin, Tex	111
Bonser,Boof, Min	108
Gaudin,Chad, Oak	108
Byrd,Paul, Cle	107
Blanton,Joe, Oak	106
Pettitte,Andy, NYY	106

Hits Allowed

Blanton,Joe, Oak	240
Byrd,Paul, Cle	239
Pettitte,Andy, NYY	238
Sabathia,C.C., Cle	238
Contreras,Jose, CWS	232
Halladay,Roy, Tor	232
Silva,Carlos, Min	229
Garland,Jon, CWS	219
Lackey,John, LAA	219
Meche,Gil, KC	218

Doubles Allowed

Sabathia,C.C., Cle	60
Batista,Miguel, Sea	49
Mussina,Mike, NYY	49
Pettitte,Andy, NYY	49
Bannister,Brian, KC	47
Byrd,Paul, Cle	47
Perez,Odalis, KC	47
Wakefield,Tim, Bos	47
Garland,Jon, CWS	46
Beckett,Josh, Bos	45

Home Runs Allowed

Santana,Johan, Min	33
Vazquez,Javier, CWS	29
Danks,John, CWS	28
Shields,James, TB	28
Bonser,Boof, Min	27
Byrd,Paul, Cle	27
Marcum,Shaun, Tor	27
Santana,Ervin, LAA	26
Cabrera,Daniel, Bal	25
Matsuzaka,Daisuke, Bos	25

Run Support Per Nine IP
(minimum 162 IP)

Verlander,Justin, Det	7.32
Wang,Chien-Ming, NYY	7.04
Pettitte,Andy, NYY	6.77
Beckett,Josh, Bos	6.59
Escobar,Kelvim, LAA	6.44
Hernandez,Felix, Sea	6.29
Bonderman,Jeremy, Det	6.25
Byrd,Paul, Cle	6.08
Halladay,Roy, Tor	6.03
Wakefield,Tim, Bos	5.76

% Pitches In Strike Zone
(minimum 162 IP)

Byrd,Paul, Cle	58.7
Silva,Carlos, Min	55.8
Santana,Johan, Min	54.7
Bannister,Brian, KC	54.2
Bedard,Erik, Bal	53.6
Wakefield,Tim, Bos	53.3
Halladay,Roy, Tor	53.3
Blanton,Joe, Oak	53.0
Beckett,Josh, Bos	53.0
Verlander,Justin, Det	53.0

Pitches Per Start
(minimum 30 GS)

Matsuzaka,Daisuke, Bos	108.8
Vazquez,Javier, CWS	108.3
Halladay,Roy, Tor	107.4
Haren,Dan, Oak	106.9
Kazmir,Scott, TB	106.1
Sabathia,C.C., Cle	105.3
Meche,Gil, KC	105.3
Cabrera,Daniel, Bal	104.9
Verlander,Justin, Det	104.8
Buehrle,Mark, CWS	103.4

Pitches Per Batter
(minimum 162 IP)

Byrd,Paul, Cle	3.40
Wang,Chien-Ming, NYY	3.48
Contreras,Jose, CWS	3.50
Carmona,Fausto, Cle	3.57
Halladay,Roy, Tor	3.59
Wakefield,Tim, Bos	3.60
Silva,Carlos, Min	3.60
Bonderman,Jeremy, Det	3.62
Shields,James, TB	3.64
Lackey,John, LAA	3.66

Quality Starts

Haren,Dan, Oak	28
Carmona,Fausto, Cle	26
Sabathia,C.C., Cle	25
Lackey,John, LAA	24
Meche,Gil, KC	23
Pettitte,Andy, NYY	22
5 tied with	21

Batters Faced

Sabathia,C.C., Cle	975
Blanton,Joe, Oak	950
Haren,Dan, Oak	935
Lackey,John, LAA	929
Halladay,Roy, Tor	927
Cabrera,Daniel, Bal	922
Pettitte,Andy, NYY	916
Meche,Gil, KC	906
Kazmir,Scott, TB	887
Gaudin,Chad, Oak	886

Innings Pitched

Sabathia,C.C., Cle	241.0
Blanton,Joe, Oak	230.0
Halladay,Roy, Tor	225.1
Lackey,John, LAA	224.0
Haren,Dan, Oak	222.2
Santana,Johan, Min	219.0
Vazquez,Javier, CWS	216.2
Meche,Gil, KC	216.0
Pettitte,Andy, NYY	215.1
2 tied with	215.0

Most Pitches in a Game

Burnett,A.J., Tor, 6/7	130
Matsuzaka,D, Bos, 6/5	130
Verlander,Justin, Det, 9/1	129
Halladay,Roy, Tor, 9/4	126
Halladay,Roy, Tor, 7/28	126
Matsuzaka,D, Bos, 6/22	126
Burnett,A.J., Tor, 5/27	125
Halladay,Roy, Tor, 8/19	125
4 tied with	124

Stolen Bases Allowed

Wakefield,Tim, Bos	41
Burnett,A.J., Tor	31
McGowan,Dustin, Tor	29
Contreras,Jose, CWS	25
Cabrera,Daniel, Bal	24
Mussina,Mike, NYY	24
Halladay,Roy, Tor	20
Haren,Dan, Oak	20
4 tied with	19

Caught Stealing Off

Sabathia,C.C., Cle	10
Batista,Miguel, Sea	9
Kazmir,Scott, TB	8
Pettitte,Andy, NYY	8
Sonnanstine,Andy, TB	8
Wakefield,Tim, Bos	8
6 tied with	7

Stolen Base Pct Allowed
(minimum 162 IP)

Garland,Jon, CWS	25.0
Buehrle,Mark, CWS	40.0
Guthrie,Jeremy, Bal	44.4
Meche,Gil, KC	44.4
Sabathia,C.C., Cle	50.0
Silva,Carlos, Min	53.3
Santana,Johan, Min	54.5
Washburn,Jarrod, Sea	54.5
Bannister,Brian, KC	58.3
3 tied with	60.0

Pickoffs

Buehrle,Mark, CWS	5
Feierabend,Ryan, Sea	5
Pettitte,Andy, NYY	5
Maroth,Mike, Det	4
Santana,Johan, Min	4
Washburn,Jarrod, Sea	4
Kazmir,Scott, TB	3
Ramirez,Horacio, Sea	3
Reyes,Dennys, Min	3
Trachsel,Steve, Bal	3

2007 American League Pitching Leaders

Strikeouts Per 9 IP
(minimum 162 IP)

Bedard,Erik, Bal	10.93
Kazmir,Scott, TB	10.41
Santana,Johan, Min	9.66
Burnett,A.J., Tor	9.56
Vazquez,Javier, CWS	8.85
Matsuzaka,Daisuke, Bos	8.84
Beckett,Josh, Bos	8.70
Verlander,Justin, Det	8.17
Sabathia,C.C., Cle	7.80
Hernandez,Felix, Sea	7.80

Opp On-Base Percentage
(minimum 162 IP)

Santana,Johan, Min	.273
Bedard,Erik, Bal	.278
Shields,James, TB	.285
Beckett,Josh, Bos	.286
Vazquez,Javier, CWS	.290
Haren,Dan, Oak	.292
Sabathia,C.C., Cle	.292
McGowan,Dustin, Tor	.296
Guthrie,Jeremy, Bal	.300
Blanton,Joe, Oak	.301

Opp Slugging Average
(minimum 162 IP)

Bedard,Erik, Bal	.337
McGowan,Dustin, Tor	.347
Carmona,Fausto, Cle	.352
Verlander,Justin, Det	.358
Escobar,Kelvim, LAA	.358
Burnett,A.J., Tor	.362
Wang,Chien-Ming, NYY	.368
Halladay,Roy, Tor	.373
Lackey,John, LAA	.375
Beckett,Josh, Bos	.377

Opponent OPS

Bedard,Erik, Bal	.615
McGowan,Dustin, Tor	.644
Carmona,Fausto, Cle	.661
Beckett,Josh, Bos	.663
Burnett,A.J., Tor	.664
Verlander,Justin, Det	.668
Escobar,Kelvim, LAA	.669
Halladay,Roy, Tor	.678
Blanton,Joe, Oak	.679
Santana,Johan, Min	.679

Home Runs Per Nine IP
(minimum 162 IP)

Wang,Chien-Ming, NYY	0.41
Escobar,Kelvim, LAA	0.51
Halladay,Roy, Tor	0.60
Blanton,Joe, Oak	0.63
Pettitte,Andy, NYY	0.67
Carmona,Fausto, Cle	0.67
Lackey,John, LAA	0.72
McGowan,Dustin, Tor	0.74
Sabathia,C.C., Cle	0.75
Beckett,Josh, Bos	0.76

Batting Average vs. LHB
(minimum 125 BF)

Papelbon,Jonathan, Bos	.104
Putz,J.J., Sea	.148
Accardo,Jeremy, Tor	.161
Benoit,Joaquin, Tex	.172
Rodriguez,Francisco, LAA	.187
Santana,Johan, Min	.197
Burnett,A.J., Tor	.200
Sabathia,C.C., Cle	.203
Downs,Scott, Tor	.209
Washburn,Jarrod, Sea	.213

Batting Average vs. RHB
(minimum 225 BF)

McGowan,Dustin, Tor	.198
Bedard,Erik, Bal	.208
Bonser,Boof, Min	.214
Carmona,Fausto, Cle	.216
Bannister,Brian, KC	.219
Lackey,John, LAA	.229
Gabbard,Kason, Bos-Tex	.230
Burnett,A.J., Tor	.231
Escobar,Kelvim, LAA	.233
Santana,Johan, Min	.234

Opp BA w/ RISP
(minimum 125 BF)

Haren,Dan, Oak	.181
Bedard,Erik, Bal	.197
Beckett,Josh, Bos	.207
Santana,Johan, Min	.219
Vazquez,Javier, CWS	.221
Greinke,Zack, KC	.224
Durbin,Chad, Det	.227
Matsuzaka,Daisuke, Bos	.229
Baker,Scott, Min	.230
Burnett,A.J., Tor	.232

OBP vs. Leadoff Hitter
(minimum 150 BF)

Beckett,Josh, Bos	.251
Shields,James, TB	.259
Burnett,A.J., Tor	.260
Santana,Johan, Min	.264
Bonderman,Jeremy, Det	.275
Wakefield,Tim, Bos	.278
Verlander,Justin, Det	.281
Lackey,John, LAA	.283
Schilling,Curt, Bos	.284
Garland,Jon, CWS	.284

Strikeouts / Walks Ratio
(minimum 162 IP)

Sabathia,C.C., Cle	5.65
Shields,James, TB	5.11
Beckett,Josh, Bos	4.85
Santana,Johan, Min	4.52
Vazquez,Javier, CWS	4.26
Bedard,Erik, Bal	3.88
Blanton,Joe, Oak	3.50
Haren,Dan, Oak	3.49
Lackey,John, LAA	3.44
Byrd,Paul, Cle	3.14

Highest GB/FB Ratio
(minimum 162 IP)

Carmona,Fausto, Cle	3.47
Hernandez,Felix, Sea	3.28
Wang,Chien-Ming, NYY	3.14
Halladay,Roy, Tor	2.28
Burnett,A.J., Tor	2.15
McGowan,Dustin, Tor	2.05
Gaudin,Chad, Oak	2.01
Pettitte,Andy, NYY	1.79
Millwood,Kevin, Tex	1.78
Blanton,Joe, Oak	1.74

Lowest GB/FB Ratio
(minimum 162 IP)

Washburn,Jarrod, Sea	0.97
Santana,Johan, Min	0.98
Wakefield,Tim, Bos	1.04
Matsuzaka,Daisuke, Bos	1.06
Byrd,Paul, Cle	1.06
Vazquez,Javier, CWS	1.07
Kazmir,Scott, TB	1.18
Verlander,Justin, Det	1.19
Bannister,Brian, KC	1.22
Shields,James, TB	1.26

Sacrifice Flies Allowed

Contreras,Jose, CWS	10
Pettitte,Andy, NYY	9
Blanton,Joe, Oak	8
Haren,Dan, Oak	8
Kennedy,Joe, Oak-Tor	8
9 tied with	7

Sacrifice Hits Allowed

Cabrera,Daniel, Bal	13
Washburn,Jarrod, Sea	9
Contreras,Jose, CWS	8
Buehrle,Mark, CWS	7
Danks,John, CWS	7
DiNardo,Lenny, Oak	7
10 tied with	6

GIDP Induced

Carmona,Fausto, Cle	32
Wang,Chien-Ming, NYY	32
Pettitte,Andy, NYY	29
Escobar,Kelvim, LAA	28
Halladay,Roy, Tor	28
DiNardo,Lenny, Oak	27
Gaudin,Chad, Oak	26
Silva,Carlos, Min	24
Lackey,John, LAA	23
Sabathia,C.C., Cle	23

GIDP Per Nine IP
(minimum 162 IP)

Wang,Chien-Ming, NYY	1.44
Carmona,Fausto, Cle	1.34
Escobar,Kelvim, LAA	1.29
Pettitte,Andy, NYY	1.21
Gaudin,Chad, Oak	1.17
Halladay,Roy, Tor	1.12
Silva,Carlos, Min	1.07
Burnett,A.J., Tor	1.03
Hernandez,Felix, Sea	0.95
Millwood,Kevin, Tex	0.94

2007 American League Pitching Leaders

Saves			Blown Saves			Save Pct (minimum 20 Save Ops)			Save Opportunities	
Borowski,Joe, Cle	45		Borowski,Joe, Cle	8		Putz,J.J., Sea	95.2		Borowski,Joe, Cle	53
Jenks,Bobby, CWS	40		Benoit,Joaquin, Tex	7		Papelbon,Jonathan, Bos	92.5		Jenks,Bobby, CWS	46
Putz,J.J., Sea	40		Jenks,Bobby, CWS	6		Nathan,Joe, Min	90.2		Rodriguez,Francisco, LAA	46
Rodriguez,Francisco, LAA	40		Jones,Todd, Det	6		Rivera,Mariano, NYY	88.2		Jones,Todd, Det	44
Jones,Todd, Det	38		Rodriguez,Francisco, LAA	6		Jenks,Bobby, CWS	87.0		Putz,J.J., Sea	42
Nathan,Joe, Min	37		Shields,Scot, LAA	6		Rodriguez,Francisco, LAA	87.0		Nathan,Joe, Min	41
Papelbon,Jonathan, Bos	37		Walker,Jamie, Bal	6		Reyes,Al, TB	86.7		Papelbon,Jonathan, Bos	40
Accardo,Jeremy, Tor	30		5 tied with	5		Jones,Todd, Det	86.4		Accardo,Jeremy, Tor	35
Rivera,Mariano, NYY	30					Accardo,Jeremy, Tor	85.7		Rivera,Mariano, NYY	34
Reyes,Al, TB	26					Borowski,Joe, Cle	84.9		Reyes,Al, TB	30

Easy Saves			Regular Saves			Tough Saves			Holds Adjusted Saves % (minimum 20 Save Ops)	
Borowski,Joe, Cle	30		Jones,Todd, Det	17		Putz,J.J., Sea	8		Putz,J.J., Sea	95.2
Jenks,Bobby, CWS	30		Papelbon,Jonathan, Bos	16		Accardo,Jeremy, Tor	4		Papelbon,Jonathan, Bos	92.9
Rodriguez,Francisco, LAA	30		Borowski,Joe, Cle	15		Rivera,Mariano, NYY	4		Nathan,Joe, Min	90.2
Nathan,Joe, Min	25		Putz,J.J., Sea	14		Embree,Alan, Oak	3		Embree,Alan, Oak	89.2
Jones,Todd, Det	21		Rivera,Mariano, NYY	14		Jenks,Bobby, CWS	2		Rivera,Mariano, NYY	88.2
Papelbon,Jonathan, Bos	20		Accardo,Jeremy, Tor	11		Nathan,Joe, Min	2		Jenks,Bobby, CWS	87.0
Putz,J.J., Sea	18		Nathan,Joe, Min	10		Rodriguez,Francisco, LAA	2		Rodriguez,Francisco, LAA	87.0
Reyes,Al, TB	17		Reyes,Al, TB	9		Soria,Joakim, KC	2		Reyes,Al, TB	86.7
Accardo,Jeremy, Tor	15		Jenks,Bobby, CWS	8		10 tied with	1		Soria,Joakim, KC	86.7
Ray,Chris, Bal	13		Rodriguez,Francisco, LAA	8					Accardo,Jeremy, Tor	86.5

Relief Wins			Relief Losses			Relief Games			Holds	
Vizcaino,Luis, NYY	8		Bradford,Chad, Bal	7		Downs,Scott, Tor	81		Betancourt,Rafael, Cle	31
Benoit,Joaquin, Tex	7		Stokes,Brian, TB	7		Walker,Jamie, Bal	81		Shields,Scot, LAA	31
Mastny,Tom, Cle	7		Baez,Danys, Bal	6		Bradford,Chad, Bal	78		Okajima,Hideki, Bos	27
Neshek,Pat, Min	7		Ray,Chris, Bal	6		Vizcaino,Luis, NYY	77		Downs,Scott, Tor	24
O'Flaherty,Eric, Sea	7		Rodney,Fernando, Det	6		Gobble,Jimmy, KC	74		Janssen,Casey, Tor	24
Glover,Gary, TB	6		10 tied with	5		Neshek,Pat, Min	74		Speier,Justin, LAA	24
Lugo,Ruddy, TB-Oak	6					Guerrier,Matt, Min	73		Sherrill,George, Sea	22
Putz,J.J., Sea	6					Sherrill,George, Sea	73		Francisco,Frank, Tex	21
6 tied with	5					Myers,Mike, NYY-CWS	72		Walker,Jamie, Bal	21
						Shields,Scot, LAA	71		3 tied with	19

Relief Innings			Inherited Runners Scrd % (minimum 30 IR)			Relief Opp On Base Pct (minimum 50 IP)			Relief Opp Slugging Avg (minimum 50 IP)	
Guerrier,Matt, Min	88.0		Francisco,Frank, Tex	6.8		Putz,J.J., Sea	.202		Papelbon,Jonathan, Bos	.244
Peralta,Joel, KC	87.2		Betancourt,Rafael, Cle	9.1		Betancourt,Rafael, Cle	.208		Jenks,Bobby, CWS	.247
Benoit,Joaquin, Tex	82.0		Seay,Bobby, Det	14.3		Papelbon,Jonathan, Bos	.219		Putz,J.J., Sea	.252
Grilli,Jason, Det	79.2		Casilla,Santiago, Oak	16.1		Perez,Rafael, Cle	.238		Soria,Joakim, KC	.264
Betancourt,Rafael, Cle	79.1		Perez,Rafael, Cle	16.2		Street,Huston, Oak	.239		Betancourt,Rafael, Cle	.277
Bootcheck,Chris, LAA	77.1		Marshall,Jay, Oak	16.7		Jenks,Bobby, CWS	.242		Accardo,Jeremy, Tor	.278
Glover,Gary, TB	77.1		Speier,Justin, LAA	16.7		Soria,Joakim, KC	.245		Wilson,C.J., Tex	.288
Shields,Scot, LAA	77.0		Greinke,Zack, KC	20.6		Okajima,Hideki, Bos	.255		Downs,Scott, Tor	.289
Vizcaino,Luis, NYY	75.1		Putz,J.J., Sea	21.9		Nathan,Joe, Min	.264		Perez,Rafael, Cle	.292
Janssen,Casey, Tor	72.2		Sherrill,George, Sea	22.5		Speier,Justin, LAA	.265		O'Flaherty,Eric, Sea	.294

2007 American League Pitching Leaders

Relief Opp BA Vs LHB
(minimum 50 AB)

Papelbon,Jonathan, Bos	.104
Wilson,C.J., Tex	.112
Perez,Rafael, Cle	.145
Putz,J.J., Sea	.148
Sherrill,George, Sea	.156
Accardo,Jeremy, Tor	.161
Delcarmen,Manny, Bos	.164
Soria,Joakim, KC	.167
Benoit,Joaquin, Tex	.172
Otsuka,Akinori, Tex	.172

Relief Opp BA Vs RHB
(minimum 50 AB)

Wolfe,Brian, Tor	.130
Zumaya,Joel, Det	.135
Betancourt,Rafael, Cle	.148
Putz,J.J., Sea	.158
Street,Huston, Oak	.162
Jenks,Bobby, CWS	.169
Durbin,Chad, Det	.172
Wassermann,Ehren, CWS	.174
Lopez,Javier, Bos	.176
Okajima,Hideki, Bos	.182

Relief Opp Batting Average
(minimum 50 IP)

Papelbon,Jonathan, Bos	.146
Putz,J.J., Sea	.153
Neshek,Pat, Min	.183
Betancourt,Rafael, Cle	.183
Soria,Joakim, KC	.187
Perez,Rafael, Cle	.187
Street,Huston, Oak	.190
Jenks,Bobby, CWS	.198
Okajima,Hideki, Bos	.202
Speier,Justin, LAA	.202

Relief Earned Run Average
(minimum 50 IP)

Putz,J.J., Sea	1.38
Betancourt,Rafael, Cle	1.47
Perez,Rafael, Cle	1.78
Papelbon,Jonathan, Bos	1.85
Nathan,Joe, Min	1.88
Accardo,Jeremy, Tor	2.14
Downs,Scott, Tor	2.17
Okajima,Hideki, Bos	2.22
Guerrier,Matt, Min	2.35
Janssen,Casey, Tor	2.35

Rel OBP 1st Batter Faced
(minimum 40 BF)

Perez,Rafael, Cle	.091
Betancourt,Rafael, Cle	.147
Papelbon,Jonathan, Bos	.169
Soria,Joakim, KC	.177
Speier,Justin, LAA	.180
Putz,J.J., Sea	.191
Delcarmen,Manny, Bos	.205
Reyes,Al, TB	.213
Neshek,Pat, Min	.233
Snyder,Kyle, Bos	.239

Rel Opp BA w/ Runners On
(minimum 50 IP)

Putz,J.J., Sea	.109
Okajima,Hideki, Bos	.168
Betancourt,Rafael, Cle	.173
Proctor,Scott, NYY	.173
Speier,Justin, LAA	.179
Papelbon,Jonathan, Bos	.187
Perez,Rafael, Cle	.191
Benoit,Joaquin, Tex	.192
Riske,David, KC	.193
Neshek,Pat, Min	.197

Relief Opp BA w/ RISP
(minimum 50 IP)

Putz,J.J., Sea	.097
Okajima,Hideki, Bos	.130
Papelbon,Jonathan, Bos	.132
Proctor,Scott, NYY	.148
Perez,Rafael, Cle	.164
Guerrier,Matt, Min	.169
Accardo,Jeremy, Tor	.169
Neshek,Pat, Min	.181
Mastny,Tom, Cle	.188
Riske,David, KC	.194

Fastest Avg Fastball-Relief
(minimum 50 IP)

Greinke,Zack, KC	95.4
Nathan,Joe, Min	94.8
Morrow,Brandon, Sea	94.8
Putz,J.J., Sea	94.7
Farnsworth,Kyle, NYY	94.7
Stokes,Brian, TB	94.4
Thornton,Matt, CWS	94.3
Papelbon,Jonathan, Bos	94.3
Accardo,Jeremy, Tor	94.1
Jenks,Bobby, CWS	93.9

Fastest Average Fastball
(minimum 162 IP)

Hernandez,Felix, Sea	95.6
Burnett,A.J., Tor	95.1
Verlander,Justin, Det	94.8
McGowan,Dustin, Tor	94.7
Beckett,Josh, Bos	94.6
Cabrera,Daniel, Bal	94.3
Escobar,Kelvim, LAA	93.7
Carmona,Fausto, Cle	93.5
Guthrie,Jeremy, Bal	93.4
Sabathia,C.C., Cle	92.9

Slowest Average Fastball
(minimum 162 IP)

Wakefield,Tim, Bos	74.2
Byrd,Paul, Cle	85.6
Buehrle,Mark, CWS	85.9
Washburn,Jarrod, Sea	87.7
Robertson,Nate, Det	88.5
Pettitte,Andy, NYY	89.1
Bannister,Brian, KC	89.2
Garland,Jon, CWS	89.3
Blanton,Joe, Oak	89.3
Contreras,Jose, CWS	90.1

Pitches 100+ Velocity

Zumaya,Joel, Det	30
Verlander,Justin, Det	17
Chamberlain,Joba, NYY	11
Burnett,A.J., Tor	3
Hoey,Jim, Bal	2
Morrow,Brandon, Sea	2
9 tied with	1

Pitches 95+ Velocity

Hernandez,Felix, Sea	1058
Verlander,Justin, Det	1016
Cabrera,Daniel, Bal	910
Burnett,A.J., Tor	886
Beckett,Josh, Bos	809
Jackson,Edwin, TB	696
McGowan,Dustin, Tor	693
Greinke,Zack, KC	522
Carmona,Fausto, Cle	481
Morrow,Brandon, Sea	470

Pitches Less Than 80 MPH

Wakefield,Tim, Bos	2194
Gabbard,Kason, Bos-Tex	908
Myers,Mike, NYY-CWS	884
Bedard,Erik, Bal	798
Buehrle,Mark, CWS	792
Maroth,Mike, Det	698
Weaver,Jeff, Sea	660
Byrd,Paul, Cle	632
Washburn,Jarrod, Sea	623
Meche,Gil, KC	622

Lowest % Fastballs
(minimum 162 IP)

Wakefield,Tim, Bos	13.4
Batista,Miguel, Sea	40.3
Buehrle,Mark, CWS	43.3
Shields,James, TB	45.9
Halladay,Roy, Tor	46.0
Meche,Gil, KC	47.1
Haren,Dan, Oak	50.5
Blanton,Joe, Oak	50.9
Escobar,Kelvim, LAA	51.2
Vazquez,Javier, CWS	52.0

Highest % Fastballs
(minimum 162 IP)

Wang,Chien-Ming, NYY	75.4
Cabrera,Daniel, Bal	72.4
Carmona,Fausto, Cle	70.7
Kazmir,Scott, TB	68.9
Gaudin,Chad, Oak	68.6
Silva,Carlos, Min	66.7
Guthrie,Jeremy, Bal	66.3
Burnett,A.J., Tor	65.4
Garland,Jon, CWS	64.0
Millwood,Kevin, Tex	62.7

Highest % Curveballs
(minimum 162 IP)

Bedard,Erik, Bal	33.9
Burnett,A.J., Tor	25.8
Beckett,Josh, Bos	24.9
Meche,Gil, KC	21.7
Halladay,Roy, Tor	21.4
Lackey,John, LAA	19.8
Bonser,Boof, Min	18.7
Verlander,Justin, Det	18.6
Blanton,Joe, Oak	13.5
Bannister,Brian, KC	12.4

2007 American League Pitching Leaders

Highest % Changeups
(minimum 162 IP)

Shields,James, TB	29.7
Santana,Johan, Min	28.8
Silva,Carlos, Min	22.5
Buehrle,Mark, CWS	18.7
Verlander,Justin, Det	18.5
Sabathia,C.C., Cle	18.2
Byrd,Paul, Cle	16.6
Robertson,Nate, Det	16.5
Blanton,Joe, Oak	14.2
Vazquez,Javier, CWS	13.9

Highest % Sliders
(minimum 162 IP)

Bonderman,Jeremy, Det	34.5
Robertson,Nate, Det	22.6
Cabrera,Daniel, Bal	22.5
Guthrie,Jeremy, Bal	21.9
Haren,Dan, Oak	21.7
Gaudin,Chad, Oak	21.2
Sabathia,C.C., Cle	20.7
Hernandez,Felix, Sea	20.1
Bonser,Boof, Min	19.6
McGowan,Dustin, Tor	18.7

Balks

Trachsel,Steve, Bal	3
Batista,Miguel, Sea	2
Cabrera,Daniel, Bal	2
Davis,Jason, Cle-Sea	2
Farnsworth,Kyle, NYY	2
Feldman,Scott, Tex	2
Ledezma,Wil, Det	2
Verlander,Justin, Det	2
44 tied with	1

Strikeout/Hit Ratio
(minimum 50 IP)

Papelbon,Jonathan, Bos	2.80
Putz,J.J., Sea	2.22
Rodriguez,Francisco, LAA	1.80
Street,Huston, Oak	1.80
Neshek,Pat, Min	1.68
Soria,Joakim, KC	1.63
Betancourt,Rafael, Cle	1.57
Bedard,Erik, Bal	1.57
Perez,Rafael, Cle	1.51
Reyes,Al, TB	1.43

Opp OPS vs Fastballs
(minimum 251 BF)

Beckett,Josh, Bos	.645
Shields,Scot, LAA	.650
Kazmir,Scott, TB	.673
Bedard,Erik, Bal	.677
Burnett,A.J., Tor	.685
Carmona,Fausto, Cle	.686
Verlander,Justin, Det	.686
Wang,Chien-Ming, NYY	.692
Santana,Johan, Min	.707
Greinke,Zack, KC	.709

Opp OPS vs Curveballs
(minimum 100 BF)

Bedard,Erik, Bal	.429
Burnett,A.J., Tor	.514
Beckett,Josh, Bos	.554
Meche,Gil, KC	.585
Lackey,John, LAA	.624
Trachsel,Steve, Bal	.639
Verlander,Justin, Det	.642
Bonser,Boof, Min	.701
Blanton,Joe, Oak	.710
Mussina,Mike, NYY	.730

Opp OPS vs Changeups
(minimum 100 BF)

Meche,Gil, KC	.481
Okajima,Hideki, Bos	.503
Shields,James, TB	.562
Kennedy,Joe, Oak-Tor	.578
Pettitte,Andy, NYY	.584
Blanton,Joe, Oak	.614
Vazquez,Javier, CWS	.614
Verlander,Justin, Det	.640
Santana,Johan, Min	.657
Sabathia,C.C., Cle	.660

Opp OPS vs Sliders
(minimum 64 BF)

Perez,Rafael, Cle	.479
Street,Huston, Oak	.482
Durbin,Chad, Det	.502
Speier,Justin, LAA	.502
McGowan,Dustin, Tor	.504
Rodriguez,Francisco, LAA	.504
Neshek,Pat, Min	.528
Sabathia,C.C., Cle	.529
Blanton,Joe, Oak	.533
Casilla,Santiago, Oak	.544

Earned Runs

Cabrera,Daniel, Bal	126
Contreras,Jose, CWS	117
Jackson,Edwin, TB	103
Blanton,Joe, Oak	101
Weaver,Jeff, Sea	101
Matsuzaka,Daisuke, Bos	100
Wakefield,Tim, Bos	100
Millwood,Kevin, Tex	99
4 tied with	98

Hits Per Nine Innings
(minimum 162 IP)

Bedard,Erik, Bal	6.97
Burnett,A.J., Tor	7.12
Santana,Johan, Min	7.52
McGowan,Dustin, Tor	7.74
Verlander,Justin, Det	8.08
Vazquez,Javier, CWS	8.18
Carmona,Fausto, Cle	8.33
Escobar,Kelvim, LAA	8.37
Matsuzaka,Daisuke, Bos	8.40
Shields,James, TB	8.46

2007 National League Pitching Leaders

Earned Run Average (minimum 162 IP)		Winning Percentage (minimum 15 Decisions)		Opponent Batting Average (minimum 162 IP)		Baserunners Per 9 IP (minimum 162 IP)	
Peavy,Jake, SD	2.54	Penny,Brad, LAD	.800	Young,Chris, SD	.192	Peavy,Jake, SD	9.79
Webb,Brandon, Ari	3.01	Peavy,Jake, SD	.760	Peavy,Jake, SD	.208	Young,Chris, SD	10.25
Penny,Brad, LAD	3.03	Hamels,Cole, Phi	.750	Perez,Oliver, NYM	.229	Hamels,Cole, Phi	10.26
Smoltz,John, Atl	3.11	Harang,Aaron, Cin	.727	Zambrano,Carlos, ChC	.233	Lilly,Ted, ChC	10.39
Young,Chris, SD	3.12	Billingsley,Chad, LAD	.706	Hill,Rich, ChC	.235	Harang,Aaron, Cin	10.61
Oswalt,Roy, Hou	3.18	Sheets,Ben, Mil	.706	Maine,John, NYM	.235	Smoltz,John, Atl	10.81
Hudson,Tim, Atl	3.33	Oswalt,Roy, Hou	.667	Cain,Matt, SF	.235	Webb,Brandon, Ari	10.89
Hamels,Cole, Phi	3.39	Francis,Jeff, Col	.654	Lilly,Ted, ChC	.236	Hill,Rich, ChC	11.31
Perez,Oliver, NYM	3.56	Lilly,Ted, ChC	.652	Webb,Brandon, Ari	.237	Hudson,Tim, Atl	11.31
Cain,Matt, SF	3.65	Vargas,Claudio, Mil	.647	Hamels,Cole, Phi	.237	Maddux,Greg, SD	11.45

Games		Games Started		Complete Games		Shutouts	
Rauch,Jon, Was	88	Willis,Dontrelle, Fla	35	Webb,Brandon, Ari	4	Webb,Brandon, Ari	3
Rivera,Saul, Was	85	11 tied with	34	Lowe,Derek, LAD	3	13 tied with	1
Beimel,Joe, LAD	83			Morris,Matt, SF-Pit	3		
Broxton,Jonathan, LAD	83			Cook,Aaron, Col	2		
Bell,Heath, SD	81			Hamels,Cole, Phi	2		
Heilman,Aaron, NYM	81			Harang,Aaron, Cin	2		
Meredith,Cla, SD	80			Lohse,Kyle, Cin-Phi	2		
Moylan,Peter, Atl	80			Maholm,Paul, Pit	2		
Qualls,Chad, Hou	79			Owings,Micah , Ari	2		
3 tied with	78			Sheets,Ben, Mil	2		

Wins		Losses		No Decisions		Wild Pitches	
Peavy,Jake, SD	19	Wells,Kip, StL	17	Chico,Matt, Was	15	Cain,Matt, SF	12
Webb,Brandon, Ari	18	Cain,Matt, SF	16	Mitre,Sergio, Fla	14	Harang,Aaron, Cin	12
Zambrano,Carlos, ChC	18	Arroyo,Bronson, Cin	15	Belisle,Matt, Cin	13	Snell,Ian, Pit	12
Francis,Jeff, Col	17	Maholm,Paul, Pit	15	Glavine,Tom, NYM	13	Capuano,Chris, Mil	10
Harang,Aaron, Cin	16	Olsen,Scott, Fla	15	Hill,Rich, ChC	13	Davis,Doug, Ari	10
Hudson,Tim, Atl	16	Williams,Woody, Hou	15	Penny,Brad, LAD	13	Lincecum,Tim, SF	10
Penny,Brad, LAD	16	Willis,Dontrelle, Fla	15	Young,Chris, SD	13	Willis,Dontrelle, Fla	9
4 tied with	15	Lowe,Derek, LAD	14	Harang,Aaron, Cin	12	Olsen,Scott, Fla	8
		Reyes,Anthony, StL	14	Lincecum,Tim, SF	12	Smoltz,John, Atl	8
		3 tied with	13	Marquis,Jason, ChC	12	Wells,Kip, StL	8

Strikeouts		Walks Allowed		Intentional Walks Allowed		Hit Batters	
Peavy,Jake, SD	240	Zambrano,Carlos, ChC	101	Moylan,Peter, Atl	12	Kim,B-H, Col-Fla-Ari	16
Harang,Aaron, Cin	218	Davis,Doug, Ari	95	Chacon,Shawn, Pit	11	Owings,Micah , Ari	14
Smoltz,John, Atl	197	Lowry,Noah, SF	87	Capps,Matt, Pit	10	Willis,Dontrelle, Fla	14
Webb,Brandon, Ari	194	Willis,Dontrelle, Fla	87	Suppan,Jeff, Mil	10	Zambrano,Carlos, ChC	14
Hill,Rich, ChC	183	Olsen,Scott, Fla	85	Affeldt,Jeremy, Col	9	Arroyo,Bronson, Cin	13
Maine,John, NYM	180	Zito,Barry, SF	83	Borkowski,Dave, Hou	9	Fogg,Josh, Col	13
Hamels,Cole, Phi	177	Cain,Matt, SF	79	Smoltz,John, Atl	9	Marquis,Jason, ChC	13
Snell,Ian, Pit	177	Hernandez,Livan, Ari	79	Wells,Kip, StL	9	Thompson,Brad, StL	13
Zambrano,Carlos, ChC	177	Perez,Oliver, NYM	79	5 tied with	8	3 tied with	12
2 tied with	174	Wells,Kip, StL	78				

2007 National League Pitching Leaders

Runs Allowed

Olsen,Scott, Fla	134
Willis,Dontrelle, Fla	131
Morris,Matt, SF-Pit	123
Moyer,Jamie, Phi	118
Eaton,Adam, Phi	117
Hernandez,Livan, Ari	116
Wells,Kip, StL	116
Williams,Woody, Hou	114
Suppan,Jeff, Mil	113
2 tied with	111

Hits Allowed

Hernandez,Livan, Ari	247
Suppan,Jeff, Mil	243
Willis,Dontrelle, Fla	241
Morris,Matt, SF-Pit	240
Francis,Jeff, Col	234
Arroyo,Bronson, Cin	232
Olsen,Scott, Fla	226
Moyer,Jamie, Phi	222
3 tied with	221

Doubles Allowed

Morris,Matt, SF-Pit	61
Suppan,Jeff, Mil	60
Moyer,Jamie, Phi	57
Bush,David, Mil	54
Arroyo,Bronson, Cin	53
Lohse,Kyle, Cin-Phi	53
Willis,Dontrelle, Fla	53
Oswalt,Roy, Hou	51
Gorzelanny,Tom, Pit	50
Harang,Aaron, Cin	49

Home Runs Allowed

Williams,Woody, Hou	35
Hernandez,Livan, Ari	34
James,Chuck, Atl	32
Eaton,Adam, Phi	30
Moyer,Jamie, Phi	30
Olsen,Scott, Fla	29
Willis,Dontrelle, Fla	29
Arroyo,Bronson, Cin	28
Harang,Aaron, Cin	28
Lilly,Ted, ChC	28

Run Support Per Nine IP
(minimum 162 IP)

Willis,Dontrelle, Fla	6.27
Hudson,Tim, Atl	6.18
Lilly,Ted, ChC	6.00
Hamels,Cole, Phi	5.99
Penny,Brad, LAD	5.93
Fogg,Josh, Col	5.92
Harang,Aaron, Cin	5.87
Peavy,Jake, SD	5.84
Maine,John, NYM	5.84
Belisle,Matt, Cin	5.83

% Pitches In Strike Zone
(minimum 162 IP)

Maddux,Greg, SD	57.6
Oswalt,Roy, Hou	56.1
Hill,Rich, ChC	55.6
Harang,Aaron, Cin	55.1
Hamels,Cole, Phi	54.4
Morris,Matt, SF-Pit	54.0
Maholm,Paul, Pit	53.7
Bush,David, Mil	53.7
Arroyo,Bronson, Cin	53.7
Belisle,Matt, Cin	53.7

Pitches Per Start
(minimum 30 GS)

Zambrano,Carlos, ChC	108.6
Peavy,Jake, SD	106.2
Harang,Aaron, Cin	105.6
Cain,Matt, SF	104.7
Gorzelanny,Tom, Pit	103.5
Oswalt,Roy, Hou	103.1
Zito,Barry, SF	102.8
Francis,Jeff, Col	102.5
Maine,John, NYM	102.2
Hernandez,Livan, Ari	101.8

Pitches Per Batter
(minimum 162 IP)

Maddux,Greg, SD	3.26
Hudson,Tim, Atl	3.42
Morris,Matt, SF-Pit	3.44
Cook,Aaron, Col	3.45
Maholm,Paul, Pit	3.46
Webb,Brandon, Ari	3.53
Snell,Ian, Pit	3.54
Marquis,Jason, ChC	3.58
Smoltz,John, Atl	3.59
Fogg,Josh, Col	3.59

Quality Starts

Peavy,Jake, SD	28
Penny,Brad, LAD	26
Smoltz,John, Atl	26
Hudson,Tim, Atl	25
Glavine,Tom, NYM	23
Arroyo,Bronson, Cin	22
Cain,Matt, SF	22
Snell,Ian, Pit	22
Webb,Brandon, Ari	22
2 tied with	21

Batters Faced

Webb,Brandon, Ari	975
Harang,Aaron, Cin	948
Willis,Dontrelle, Fla	942
Hudson,Tim, Atl	925
Zambrano,Carlos, ChC	925
Francis,Jeff, Col	922
Arroyo,Bronson, Cin	921
Suppan,Jeff, Mil	919
Hernandez,Livan, Ari	913
Oswalt,Roy, Hou	910

Innings Pitched

Webb,Brandon, Ari	236.1
Harang,Aaron, Cin	231.2
Hudson,Tim, Atl	224.1
Peavy,Jake, SD	223.1
Zambrano,Carlos, ChC	216.1
Francis,Jeff, Col	215.1
Oswalt,Roy, Hou	212.0
Arroyo,Bronson, Cin	210.2
Penny,Brad, LAD	208.0
Snell,Ian, Pit	208.0

Most Pitches in a Game

Hernandez,O, NYM, 8/14	130
Arroyo,Bronson, Cin, 5/16	129
Zambrano,C, ChC, 6/11	128
Bush,David, Mil, 8/16	127
Lilly,Ted, ChC, 8/9	127
Morris,Matt, SF-Pit, 5/20	127
Kim,B.H., Col-Fla-Ari, 8/1	126
Zito,Barry, SF, 4/21	126
6 tied with	125

Stolen Bases Allowed

Young,Chris, SD	44
Maddux,Greg, SD	37
Webb,Brandon, Ari	26
Hill,Rich, ChC	23
Kim,B-H, Col-Fla-Ari	23
Peavy,Jake, SD	21
Sheets,Ben, Mil	21
Hernandez,Livan, Ari	20
Marquis,Jason, ChC	20
Germano,Justin, SD	18

Caught Stealing Off

Lowe,Derek, LAD	12
Eaton,Adam, Phi	9
Rodriguez,Wandy, Hou	9
Webb,Brandon, Ari	9
Glavine,Tom, NYM	8
Harang,Aaron, Cin	8
Lohse,Kyle, Cin-Phi	8
Wainwright,Adam, StL	8
Bush,David, Mil	7
Wells,David, SD-LAD	7

Stolen Base Pct Allowed
(minimum 162 IP)

Arroyo,Bronson, Cin	33.3
Glavine,Tom, NYM	38.5
Wainwright,Adam, StL	42.9
Davis,Doug, Ari	50.0
Lowe,Derek, LAD	53.8
Zambrano,Carlos, ChC	57.1
Rodriguez,Wandy, Hou	59.1
Chico,Matt, Was	60.0
Lohse,Kyle, Cin-Phi	60.0
Moyer,Jamie, Phi	60.0

Pickoffs

Davis,Doug, Ari	8
Rodriguez,Wandy, Hou	6
Beimel,Joe, LAD	5
Simontacchi,Jason, Was	5
Francis,Jeff, Col	4
Hill,Rich, ChC	4
Moyer,Jamie, Phi	4
Gorzelanny,Tom, Pit	3
Perez,Oliver, NYM	3
Wells,David, SD-LAD	3

2007 National League Pitching Leaders

Strikeouts Per 9 IP
(minimum 162 IP)

Peavy,Jake, SD	9.67
Perez,Oliver, NYM	8.85
Hamels,Cole, Phi	8.69
Young,Chris, SD	8.69
Smoltz,John, Atl	8.62
Maine,John, NYM	8.48
Harang,Aaron, Cin	8.47
Hill,Rich, ChC	8.45
Rodriguez,Wandy, Hou	7.78
Snell,Ian, Pit	7.66

Opp On-Base Percentage
(minimum 162 IP)

Peavy,Jake, SD	.272
Young,Chris, SD	.281
Hamels,Cole, Phi	.283
Lilly,Ted, ChC	.286
Harang,Aaron, Cin	.289
Smoltz,John, Atl	.293
Webb,Brandon, Ari	.296
Hill,Rich, ChC	.305
Lowe,Derek, LAD	.308
Hudson,Tim, Atl	.309

Opp Slugging Average
(minimum 162 IP)

Young,Chris, SD	.297
Peavy,Jake, SD	.312
Webb,Brandon, Ari	.334
Hudson,Tim, Atl	.352
Penny,Brad, LAD	.359
Cain,Matt, SF	.366
Zambrano,Carlos, ChC	.372
Smoltz,John, Atl	.375
Perez,Oliver, NYM	.382
Lowe,Derek, LAD	.384

Opponent OPS

Young,Chris, SD	.578
Peavy,Jake, SD	.584
Webb,Brandon, Ari	.630
Hudson,Tim, Atl	.660
Smoltz,John, Atl	.669
Cain,Matt, SF	.678
Penny,Brad, LAD	.685
Hamels,Cole, Phi	.686
Harang,Aaron, Cin	.690
2 tied with	.692

Home Runs Per Nine IP
(minimum 162 IP)

Penny,Brad, LAD	0.39
Hudson,Tim, Atl	0.40
Webb,Brandon, Ari	0.46
Young,Chris, SD	0.52
Peavy,Jake, SD	0.52
Wainwright,Adam, StL	0.58
Oswalt,Roy, Hou	0.59
Cain,Matt, SF	0.63
Maddux,Greg, SD	0.64
Suppan,Jeff, Mil	0.78

Batting Average vs. LHB
(minimum 125 BF)

Gregg,Kevin, Fla	.162
Soriano,Rafael, Atl	.164
Brocail,Doug, SD	.182
Myers,Brett, Phi	.183
Hill,Rich, ChC	.191
Howry,Bob, ChC	.192
Broxton,Jonathan, LAD	.200
Sheets,Ben, Mil	.200
Valverde,Jose, Ari	.202
Perez,Oliver, NYM	.206

Batting Average vs. RHB
(minimum 225 BF)

Young,Chris, SD	.155
Hernandez,Orlando, NYM	.167
Peavy,Jake, SD	.174
Webb,Brandon, Ari	.199
Zambrano,Carlos, ChC	.200
Bergmann,Jason, Was	.200
Sosa,Jorge, NYM	.202
Billingsley,Chad, LAD	.210
Cain,Matt, SF	.224
Villanueva,Carlos, Mil	.227

Opp BA w/ RISP
(minimum 125 BF)

Smoltz,John, Atl	.178
Hamels,Cole, Phi	.200
Rivera,Saul, Was	.204
Kendrick,Kyle, Phi	.207
Harang,Aaron, Cin	.213
Chico,Matt, Was	.214
Hernandez,Orlando, NYM	.214
Perez,Oliver, NYM	.216
James,Chuck, Atl	.218
Lilly,Ted, ChC	.220

OBP vs. Leadoff Hitter
(minimum 150 BF)

Webb,Brandon, Ari	.251
Peavy,Jake, SD	.256
Lilly,Ted, ChC	.256
Hudson,Tim, Atl	.264
Oswalt,Roy, Hou	.271
Young,Chris, SD	.275
Maine,John, NYM	.276
Harang,Aaron, Cin	.286
Maddux,Greg, SD	.286
Marquis,Jason, ChC	.289

Strikeouts / Walks Ratio
(minimum 162 IP)

Harang,Aaron, Cin	4.19
Smoltz,John, Atl	4.19
Maddux,Greg, SD	4.16
Hamels,Cole, Phi	4.12
Peavy,Jake, SD	3.53
Lilly,Ted, ChC	3.16
Bush,David, Mil	3.05
Belisle,Matt, Cin	2.91
Hill,Rich, ChC	2.90
Webb,Brandon, Ari	2.69

Highest GB/FB Ratio
(minimum 162 IP)

Lowe,Derek, LAD	4.29
Webb,Brandon, Ari	3.82
Hudson,Tim, Atl	3.54
Cook,Aaron, Col	3.04
Maddux,Greg, SD	2.16
Oswalt,Roy, Hou	2.06
Maholm,Paul, Pit	2.06
Penny,Brad, LAD	1.96
Morris,Matt, SF-Pit	1.89
Wells,Kip, StL	1.83

Lowest GB/FB Ratio
(minimum 162 IP)

Young,Chris, SD	0.58
Perez,Oliver, NYM	0.76
Chico,Matt, Was	0.80
Lilly,Ted, ChC	0.80
Arroyo,Bronson, Cin	0.93
Hill,Rich, ChC	0.95
Maine,John, NYM	0.98
Cain,Matt, SF	0.99
Williams,Woody, Hou	1.00
Lohse,Kyle, Cin-Phi	1.04

Sacrifice Flies Allowed

Suppan,Jeff, Mil	11
Chico,Matt, Was	10
Mitre,Sergio, Fla	10
Belisle,Matt, Cin	9
Gorzelanny,Tom, Pit	9
Lilly,Ted, ChC	9
Penny,Brad, LAD	9
Villarreal,Oscar, Atl	9
5 tied with	8

Sacrifice Hits Allowed

Hernandez,Livan, Ari	17
Maddux,Greg, SD	15
Willis,Dontrelle, Fla	15
Lohse,Kyle, Cin-Phi	14
Lowry,Noah, SF	14
Olsen,Scott, Fla	14
Suppan,Jeff, Mil	14
Maholm,Paul, Pit	13
Marquis,Jason, ChC	13
Penny,Brad, LAD	13

GIDP Induced

Maholm,Paul, Pit	29
Penny,Brad, LAD	29
Cook,Aaron, Col	27
Hudson,Tim, Atl	26
Lowry,Noah, SF	25
Morris,Matt, SF-Pit	24
Davis,Doug, Ari	23
Duke,Zach, Pit	23
Suppan,Jeff, Mil	23
2 tied with	22

GIDP Per Nine IP
(minimum 162 IP)

Maholm,Paul, Pit	1.47
Cook,Aaron, Col	1.46
Penny,Brad, LAD	1.25
Morris,Matt, SF-Pit	1.09
Davis,Doug, Ari	1.07
Hudson,Tim, Atl	1.04
Suppan,Jeff, Mil	1.00
Hernandez,Livan, Ari	0.97
Lowe,Derek, LAD	0.95
Glavine,Tom, NYM	0.94

2007 National League Pitching Leaders

Saves

Valverde,Jose, Ari	47
Cordero,Francisco, Mil	44
Hoffman,Trevor, SD	42
Saito,Takashi, LAD	39
Cordero,Chad, Was	37
Wagner,Billy, NYM	34
Weathers,David, Cin	33
Gregg,Kevin, Fla	32
Isringhausen,Jason, StL	32
Dempster,Ryan, ChC	28

Blown Saves

Cordero,Chad, Was	9
Lidge,Brad, Hou	8
Benitez,Armando, SF-Fla	7
Chacon,Shawn, Pit	7
Cordero,Francisco, Mil	7
Fuentes,Brian, Col	7
Hoffman,Trevor, SD	7
Julio,Jorge, Fla-Col	7
Linebrink,Scott, SD-Mil	7
Valverde,Jose, Ari	7

Save Pct
(minimum 20 Save Ops)

Isringhausen,Jason, StL	94.1
Saito,Takashi, LAD	90.7
Dempster,Ryan, ChC	90.3
Gregg,Kevin, Fla	88.9
Myers,Brett, Phi	87.5
Wagner,Billy, NYM	87.2
Valverde,Jose, Ari	87.0
Corpas,Manny, Col	86.4
Cordero,Francisco, Mil	86.3
2 tied with	85.7

Save Opportunities

Valverde,Jose, Ari	54
Cordero,Francisco, Mil	51
Hoffman,Trevor, SD	49
Cordero,Chad, Was	46
Saito,Takashi, LAD	43
Wagner,Billy, NYM	39
Weathers,David, Cin	39
Gregg,Kevin, Fla	36
Isringhausen,Jason, StL	34
Dempster,Ryan, ChC	31

Easy Saves

Hoffman,Trevor, SD	31
Cordero,Chad, Was	25
Valverde,Jose, Ari	25
Cordero,Francisco, Mil	22
Saito,Takashi, LAD	22
Wagner,Billy, NYM	22
Isringhausen,Jason, StL	21
Gregg,Kevin, Fla	20
Dempster,Ryan, ChC	19
Fuentes,Brian, Col	16

Regular Saves

Valverde,Jose, Ari	21
Cordero,Francisco, Mil	19
Weathers,David, Cin	18
Saito,Takashi, LAD	16
Cordero,Chad, Was	12
Wagner,Billy, NYM	12
Hoffman,Trevor, SD	11
Gregg,Kevin, Fla	10
Lidge,Brad, Hou	10
Isringhausen,Jason, StL	9

Tough Saves

Cordero,Francisco, Mil	3
Weathers,David, Cin	3
Gregg,Kevin, Fla	2
Isringhausen,Jason, StL	2
15 tied with	1

Holds Adjusted Saves %
(minimum 20 Save Ops)

Isringhausen,Jason, StL	94.1
Corpas,Manny, Col	92.1
Capps,Matt, Pit	91.7
Saito,Takashi, LAD	90.9
Gregg,Kevin, Fla	90.5
Dempster,Ryan, ChC	90.3
Myers,Brett, Phi	88.9
Wagner,Billy, NYM	87.2
Valverde,Jose, Ari	87.0
Hennessey,Brad, SF	86.5

Relief Wins

Rauch,Jon, Was	8
Springer,Russ, StL	8
Heilman,Aaron, NYM	7
8 tied with	6

Relief Losses

Benitez,Armando, SF-Fla	8
Capps,Matt, Pit	7
Dempster,Ryan, ChC	7
Heilman,Aaron, NYM	7
Howry,Bob, ChC	7
Correia,Kevin, SF	6
Linebrink,Scott, SD-Mil	6
Meredith,Cla, SD	6
Rivera,Saul, Was	6
Weathers,David, Cin	6

Relief Games

Rauch,Jon, Was	88
Rivera,Saul, Was	85
Beimel,Joe, LAD	83
Broxton,Jonathan, LAD	83
Bell,Heath, SD	81
Heilman,Aaron, NYM	81
Meredith,Cla, SD	80
Moylan,Peter, Atl	80
Qualls,Chad, Hou	79
3 tied with	78

Holds

Lyon,Brandon, Ari	35
Bell,Heath, SD	34
Rauch,Jon, Was	33
Turnbow,Derrick, Mil	33
Broxton,Jonathan, LAD	32
Pena,Tony, Ari	30
Franklin,Ryan, StL	25
Heilman,Aaron, NYM	22
Howry,Bob, ChC	22
Romero,J.C., Phi	22

Relief Innings

Bell,Heath, SD	93.2
Rivera,Saul, Was	93.0
Moylan,Peter, Atl	90.0
Rauch,Jon, Was	87.1
Heilman,Aaron, NYM	86.0
Pena,Tony, Ari	85.1
Gregg,Kevin, Fla	84.0
Qualls,Chad, Hou	82.2
Broxton,Jonathan, LAD	82.0
Howry,Bob, ChC	81.1

Inherited Runners Scrd %
(minimum 30 IR)

Marmol,Carlos, ChC	12.2
Wuertz,Mike, ChC	13.2
Schoeneweis,Scott, NYM	16.3
Beimel,Joe, LAD	17.5
Kline,Steve, SF	18.8
Feliciano,Pedro, NYM	20.0
Tankersley,Taylor, Fla	20.0
Bell,Heath, SD	20.6
Miller,Trever, Hou	20.8
Pinto,Renyel, Fla	21.1

Relief Opp On Base Pct
(minimum 50 IP)

Saito,Takashi, LAD	.209
Soriano,Rafael, Atl	.232
Springer,Russ, StL	.248
Bell,Heath, SD	.257
Capps,Matt, Pit	.266
Franklin,Ryan, StL	.267
Isringhausen,Jason, StL	.271
Rauch,Jon, Was	.273
Cordero,Francisco, Mil	.274
Hoffman,Trevor, SD	.276

Relief Opp Slugging Avg
(minimum 50 IP)

Marmol,Carlos, ChC	.226
Saito,Takashi, LAD	.239
Bell,Heath, SD	.246
Springer,Russ, StL	.265
Turnbow,Derrick, Mil	.266
Cameron,Kevin, SD	.271
Isringhausen,Jason, StL	.272
Feliciano,Pedro, NYM	.306
Moylan,Peter, Atl	.307
Cordero,Francisco, Mil	.314

2007 National League Pitching Leaders

Relief Opp BA Vs LHB (minimum 50 AB)	
Marte,Damaso, Pit	.094
Burton,Jared, Cin	.130
Sanchez,Jonathan, SF	.160
Gregg,Kevin, Fla	.162
Soriano,Rafael, Atl	.164
Myers,Brett, Phi	.165
Feliciano,Pedro, NYM	.168
Madson,Ryan, Phi	.170
Turnbow,Derrick, Mil	.172
Tankersley,Taylor, Fla	.179

Relief Opp BA Vs RHB (minimum 50 AB)	
Saito,Takashi, LAD	.114
Romero,J.C., Phi	.133
Percival,Troy, StL	.138
Cruz,Juan, Ari	.143
Wilson,Brian, SF	.145
Marmol,Carlos, ChC	.146
Thatcher,Joe, SD	.151
Bell,Heath, SD	.157
Springer,Russ, StL	.158
Billingsley,Chad, LAD	.164

Relief Opp Batting Average (minimum 50 IP)	
Saito,Takashi, LAD	.151
Marmol,Carlos, ChC	.169
Isringhausen,Jason, StL	.179
Springer,Russ, StL	.181
Soriano,Rafael, Atl	.181
Turnbow,Derrick, Mil	.183
Bell,Heath, SD	.185
Valverde,Jose, Ari	.196
Feliciano,Pedro, NYM	.200
Cruz,Juan, Ari	.205

Relief Earned Run Average (minimum 50 IP)	
Saito,Takashi, LAD	1.40
Marmol,Carlos, ChC	1.43
Moylan,Peter, Atl	1.80
Gardner,Lee, Fla	1.94
Bell,Heath, SD	2.02
Corpas,Manny, Col	2.08
Springer,Russ, StL	2.18
Capps,Matt, Pit	2.28
Isringhausen,Jason, StL	2.48
Wagner,Billy, NYM	2.63

Rel OBP 1st Batter Faced (minimum 40 BF)	
Saito,Takashi, LAD	.175
Gardner,Lee, Fla	.177
Myers,Brett, Phi	.184
Bell,Heath, SD	.185
Soriano,Rafael, Atl	.197
Marmol,Carlos, ChC	.203
Cordero,Francisco, Mil	.212
Hoffman,Trevor, SD	.213
Howry,Bob, ChC	.218
Fuentes,Brian, Col	.219

Rel Opp BA w/ Runners On (minimum 50 IP)	
Marmol,Carlos, ChC	.154
Feliciano,Pedro, NYM	.165
Pinto,Renyel, Fla	.167
Springer,Russ, StL	.167
Saito,Takashi, LAD	.169
Isringhausen,Jason, StL	.170
Valverde,Jose, Ari	.194
Wagner,Billy, NYM	.198
Moylan,Peter, Atl	.199
Pena,Tony, Ari	.205

Relief Opp BA w/ RISP (minimum 50 IP)	
Marmol,Carlos, ChC	.110
Isringhausen,Jason, StL	.135
Feliciano,Pedro, NYM	.136
Pinto,Renyel, Fla	.138
Saito,Takashi, LAD	.152
Valverde,Jose, Ari	.170
Springer,Russ, StL	.170
Miller,Justin, Fla	.177
Myers,Brett, Phi	.178
Cruz,Juan, Ari	.179

Fastest Avg Fastball-Relief (minimum 50 IP)	
Lindstrom,Matt, Fla	96.6
Lidge,Brad, Hou	95.4
Broxton,Jonathan, LAD	95.2
Julio,Jorge, Fla-Col	95.1
Turnbow,Derrick, Mil	95.1
Yates,Tyler, Atl	95.0
Pena,Tony, Ari	95.0
Bell,Heath, SD	94.7
Wagner,Billy, NYM	94.6
Soriano,Rafael, Atl	94.6

Fastest Average Fastball (minimum 162 IP)	
Penny,Brad, LAD	93.4
Cain,Matt, SF	93.2
Oswalt,Roy, Hou	92.7
Smoltz,John, Atl	92.5
Peavy,Jake, SD	92.5
Snell,Ian, Pit	92.4
Zambrano,Carlos, ChC	91.6
Maine,John, NYM	91.2
Belisle,Matt, Cin	91.1
Hudson,Tim, Atl	90.9

Slowest Average Fastball (minimum 162 IP)	
Moyer,Jamie, Phi	81.1
Hernandez,Livan, Ari	83.6
Glavine,Tom, NYM	83.7
Davis,Doug, Ari	84.1
Zito,Barry, SF	84.5
Maddux,Greg, SD	84.7
Chico,Matt, Was	85.5
Williams,Woody, Hou	86.5
Francis,Jeff, Col	86.6
Morris,Matt, SF-Pit	87.4

Pitches 100+ Velocity	
Lindstrom,Matt, Fla	9
Jimenez,Ubaldo, Col	7
Broxton,Jonathan, LAD	3
Turnbow,Derrick, Mil	2
Yates,Tyler, Atl	2
9 tied with	1

Pitches 95+ Velocity	
Julio,Jorge, Fla-Col	750
Lincecum,Tim, SF	647
Lindstrom,Matt, Fla	606
Penny,Brad, LAD	579
Jimenez,Ubaldo, Col	574
Bell,Heath, SD	484
Lidge,Brad, Hou	475
Broxton,Jonathan, LAD	473
Soriano,Rafael, Atl	437
Yates,Tyler, Atl	432

Pitches Less Than 80 MPH	
Morris,Matt, SF-Pit	1550
Glavine,Tom, NYM	1419
Arroyo,Bronson, Cin	1376
Wells,David, SD-LAD	1354
Moyer,Jamie, Phi	1316
Zito,Barry, SF	1149
Kim,B-H, Col-Fla-Ari	1119
Hernandez,Livan, Ari	1077
Davis,Doug, Ari	915
Hernandez,Orlando, NYM	892

Lowest % Fastballs (minimum 162 IP)	
Moyer,Jamie, Phi	37.1
Davis,Doug, Ari	39.4
Fogg,Josh, Col	42.0
Arroyo,Bronson, Cin	42.7
Smoltz,John, Atl	43.7
Morris,Matt, SF-Pit	43.9
Glavine,Tom, NYM	49.4
Snell,Ian, Pit	50.0
Lohse,Kyle, Cin-Phi	51.6
Bush,David, Mil	52.6

Highest % Fastballs (minimum 162 IP)	
Cook,Aaron, Col	78.4
Willis,Dontrelle, Fla	74.1
Young,Chris, SD	73.8
Webb,Brandon, Ari	72.1
Penny,Brad, LAD	71.0
Maddux,Greg, SD	69.9
Olsen,Scott, Fla	68.7
Harang,Aaron, Cin	68.1
Zambrano,Carlos, ChC	66.4
Rodriguez,Wandy, Hou	66.0

Highest % Curveballs (minimum 162 IP)	
Morris,Matt, SF-Pit	28.1
Arroyo,Bronson, Cin	27.2
Hill,Rich, ChC	26.6
Rodriguez,Wandy, Hou	24.0
Maholm,Paul, Pit	19.7
Bush,David, Mil	19.6
Williams,Woody, Hou	19.4
Wainwright,Adam, StL	18.3
Zito,Barry, SF	18.3
Davis,Doug, Ari	16.8

2007 National League Pitching Leaders

Highest % Changeups
(minimum 162 IP)

Glavine,Tom, NYM	44.1
Hamels,Cole, Phi	34.5
Moyer,Jamie, Phi	28.2
Francis,Jeff, Col	24.1
Fogg,Josh, Col	20.4
Maddux,Greg, SD	20.1
Zito,Barry, SF	19.7
Lohse,Kyle, Cin-Phi	17.7
Chico,Matt, Was	17.5
Gorzelanny,Tom, Pit	16.6

Highest % Sliders
(minimum 162 IP)

Snell,Ian, Pit	35.5
Smoltz,John, Atl	32.7
Perez,Oliver, NYM	26.2
Lohse,Kyle, Cin-Phi	22.7
Peavy,Jake, SD	22.7
Hernandez,Livan, Ari	21.7
Maine,John, NYM	21.0
Morris,Matt, SF-Pit	20.8
Olsen,Scott, Fla	20.7
Harang,Aaron, Cin	19.2

Balks

Vanden Hurk,Rick, Fla	4
Young,Chris, SD	4
Benitez,Armando, SF-Fla	3
Looper,Braden, StL	3
7 tied with	2

Strikeout/Hit Ratio
(minimum 50 IP)

Saito,Takashi, LAD	2.36
Marmol,Carlos, ChC	2.34
Cruz,Juan, Ari	1.93
Turnbow,Derrick, Mil	1.91
Bell,Heath, SD	1.70
Valverde,Jose, Ari	1.70
Cordero,Francisco, Mil	1.65
Lidge,Brad, Hou	1.63
Springer,Russ, StL	1.61
Soriano,Rafael, Atl	1.49

Opp OPS vs Fastballs
(minimum 251 BF)

Peavy,Jake, SD	.550
Young,Chris, SD	.563
Moylan,Peter, Atl	.579
Bergmann,Jason, Was	.612
Webb,Brandon, Ari	.634
Smoltz,John, Atl	.638
Hernandez,Orlando, NYM	.644
Sheets,Ben, Mil	.648
Gallardo,Yovani, Mil	.652
Penny,Brad, LAD	.655

Opp OPS vs Curveballs
(minimum 100 BF)

Rodriguez,Wandy, Hou	.487
Webb,Brandon, Ari	.571
Lilly,Ted, ChC	.572
Davis,Doug, Ari	.600
Wainwright,Adam, StL	.612
Penny,Brad, LAD	.674
Hill,Rich, ChC	.680
Oswalt,Roy, Hou	.730
Maholm,Paul, Pit	.732
2 tied with	.735

Opp OPS vs Changeups
(minimum 100 BF)

Lowe,Derek, LAD	.569
Lohse,Kyle, Cin-Phi	.584
Chico,Matt, Was	.603
Webb,Brandon, Ari	.604
Heilman,Aaron, NYM	.634
Zito,Barry, SF	.636
Mota,Guillermo, NYM	.637
Francis,Jeff, Col	.645
Mitre,Sergio, Fla	.664
Villanueva,Carlos, Mil	.679

Opp OPS vs Sliders
(minimum 64 BF)

Corpas,Manny, Col	.422
Marmol,Carlos, ChC	.438
Johnson,Tyler, StL	.448
Johnson,Randy, Ari	.470
Hampson,Justin, SD	.496
Cruz,Juan, Ari	.506
Franklin,Ryan, StL	.509
Peavy,Jake, SD	.532
Rauch,Jon, Was	.542
Dempster,Ryan, ChC	.549

Earned Runs

Willis,Dontrelle, Fla	118
Olsen,Scott, Fla	114
Eaton,Adam, Phi	113
Hernandez,Livan, Ari	112
Moyer,Jamie, Phi	111
Williams,Woody, Hou	110
Morris,Matt, SF-Pit	108
Bush,David, Mil	106
Suppan,Jeff, Mil	106
Belisle,Matt, Cin	105

Hits Per Nine Innings
(minimum 162 IP)

Young,Chris, SD	6.14
Peavy,Jake, SD	6.81
Perez,Oliver, NYM	7.78
Zambrano,Carlos, ChC	7.78
Cain,Matt, SF	7.79
Hill,Rich, ChC	7.85
Lilly,Ted, ChC	7.87
Maine,John, NYM	7.92
Webb,Brandon, Ari	7.96
Hamels,Cole, Phi	8.00

2007 American League Fielding Leaders

2B Pivot %
(minimum 98 G)

Cano,Robinson, NYY	0.727
Kinsler,Ian, Tex	0.681
Pedroia,Dustin, Bos	0.677
Hill,Aaron, Tor	0.647
Lopez,Jose, Sea	0.647
Polanco,Placido, Det	0.630
Ellis,Mark, Oak	0.629
Grudzielanek,Mark, KC	0.613
Roberts,Brian, Bal	0.596
Barfield,Josh, Cle	0.551

SS Pivot %
(minimum 98 G)

Pena,Tony F, KC	0.776
Bartlett,Jason, Min	0.734
Jeter,Derek, NYY	0.720
Cabrera,Orlando, LAA	0.681
Betancourt,Yuniesky, Sea	0.663
McDonald,John, Tor	0.651
Uribe,Juan, CWS	0.624
Guillen,Carlos, Det	0.623
Peralta,Jhonny, Cle	0.622
Tejada,Miguel, Bal	0.551

Highest Pct CS by Catchers
(minimum 600 INN or 50 SBA)

Mauer,Joe, Min	47.5
Laird,Gerald, Tex	39.8
Johjima,Kenji, Sea	39.5
Martinez,Victor, Cle	30.0
Rodriguez,Ivan, Det	28.8
Navarro,Dioner, TB	25.3
Varitek,Jason, Bos	23.2
Posada,Jorge, NYY	21.5
Napoli,Mike, LAA	21.0
Hernandez,Ramon, Bal	20.0

Lowest Pct CS by Catchers
(minimum 600 INN or 50 SBA)

Zaun,Gregg, Tor	14.1
Kendall,Jason, Oak	15.7
Pierzynski,A.J., CWS	16.2
Buck,John, KC	17.0
Hernandez,Ramon, Bal	20.0
Napoli,Mike, LAA	21.0
Posada,Jorge, NYY	21.5
Varitek,Jason, Bos	23.2
Navarro,Dioner, TB	25.3
Rodriguez,Ivan, Det	28.8

2B Double Play %
(minimum 98 G)

Cano,Robinson, NYY	0.652
Hill,Aaron, Tor	0.570
Pedroia,Dustin, Bos	0.563
Lopez,Jose, Sea	0.555
Polanco,Placido, Det	0.550
Grudzielanek,Mark, KC	0.549
Ellis,Mark, Oak	0.537
Kinsler,Ian, Tex	0.537
Roberts,Brian, Bal	0.493
Barfield,Josh, Cle	0.459

3B Double Play %
(minimum 98 G)

Lowell,Mike, Bos	0.483
Glaus,Troy, Tor	0.471
Rodriguez,Alex, NYY	0.397
Blake,Casey, Cle	0.368
Inge,Brandon, Det	0.353
Gordon,Alex, KC	0.351
Iwamura,Akinori, TB	0.349
Figgins,Chone, LAA	0.324
Mora,Melvin, Bal	0.309
Beltre,Adrian, Sea	0.306

SS Double Play %
(minimum 98 G)

Cabrera,Orlando, LAA	0.647
Jeter,Derek, NYY	0.645
Pena,Tony F, KC	0.634
Bartlett,Jason, Min	0.610
Betancourt,Yuniesky, Sea	0.601
Uribe,Juan, CWS	0.596
Peralta,Jhonny, Cle	0.586
McDonald,John, Tor	0.578
Guillen,Carlos, Det	0.565
Young,Michael, Tex	0.563

Errors

Bartlett,Jason, Min	26
Guillen,Carlos, Det	25
Betancourt,Yuniesky, Sea	23
Pena,Tony F, KC	23
Lugo,Julio, Bos	19
Peralta,Jhonny, Cle	19
Young,Michael, Tex	19
Beltre,Adrian, Sea	18
Inge,Brandon, Det	18
Jeter,Derek, NYY	18

Fielding Errors

Guillen,Carlos, Det	17
Bartlett,Jason, Min	15
Kinsler,Ian, Tex	13
Pena,Tony F, KC	13
Peralta,Jhonny, Cle	13
Wilson,Josh, TB	13
Betancourt,Yuniesky, Sea	11
Jeter,Derek, NYY	11
Lugo,Julio, Bos	11
2 tied with	10

Throwing Errors

Beltre,Adrian, Sea	12
Betancourt,Yuniesky, Sea	12
Navarro,Dioner, TB	12
Bartlett,Jason, Min	11
Pena,Tony F, KC	10
Uribe,Juan, CWS	10
Crosby,Bobby, Oak	9
Gordon,Alex, KC	9
Laird,Gerald, Tex	9
Young,Michael, Tex	9

Range Factor for 2B
(minimum 98 games)

Kinsler,Ian, Tex	5.69
Ellis,Mark, Oak	5.45
Cano,Robinson, NYY	5.22
Lopez,Jose, Sea	5.14
Hill,Aaron, Tor	5.13
Polanco,Placido, Det	5.08
Barfield,Josh, Cle	5.06
Roberts,Brian, Bal	4.97
Pedroia,Dustin, Bos	4.88
Grudzielanek,Mark, KC	4.60

Range Factor for 3B
(minimum 98 games)

Mora,Melvin, Bal	2.90
Beltre,Adrian, Sea	2.87
Inge,Brandon, Det	2.86
Punto,Nick, Min	2.76
Gordon,Alex, KC	2.74
Blake,Casey, Cle	2.66
Glaus,Troy, Tor	2.52
Lowell,Mike, Bos	2.51
Rodriguez,Alex, NYY	2.42
Iwamura,Akinori, TB	2.38

Range Factor for SS
(minimum 98 games)

McDonald,John, Tor	4.98
Uribe,Juan, CWS	4.74
Peralta,Jhonny, Cle	4.68
Bartlett,Jason, Min	4.67
Betancourt,Yuniesky, Sea	4.66
Young,Michael, Tex	4.58
Pena,Tony F, KC	4.56
Cabrera,Orlando, LAA	4.42
Guillen,Carlos, Det	4.29
Tejada,Miguel, Bal	4.27

2007 National League Fielding Leaders

2B Pivot % (minimum 98 G)		SS Pivot % (minimum 98 G)		Highest Pct CS by Catchers (minimum 600 INN or 50 SBA)		Lowest Pct CS by Catchers (minimum 600 INN or 50 SBA)	
Hudson,Orlando, Ari	0.750	Theriot,Ryan, ChC	0.750	Molina,Yadier, StL	50.0	Kendall,Jason, ChC	3.7
Belliard,Ronnie, Was	0.743	Rollins,Jimmy, Phi	0.679	Ross,Dave, Cin	39.0	Bard,Josh, SD	6.2
Giles,Marcus, SD	0.726	Tulowitzki,Troy, Col	0.674	Schneider,Brian, Was	29.3	Estrada,Johnny, Mil	7.6
Uggla,Dan, Fla	0.723	Hardy,J.J., Mil	0.672	Martin,Russell, LAD	29.3	Barrett,Michael, ChC-SD	10.0
Phillips,Brandon, Cin	0.722	Furcal,Rafael, LAD	0.657	Olivo,Miguel, Fla	28.2	Ausmus,Brad, Hou	17.5
Sanchez,Freddy, Pit	0.693	Gonzalez,Alex, Cin	0.646	Snyder,Chris, Ari	25.7	Torrealba,Yorvit, Col	17.6
Durham,Ray, SF	0.663	Wilson,Jack, Pit	0.643	Ruiz,Carlos, Phi	25.0	Lo Duca,Paul, NYM	19.1
Johnson,Kelly, Atl	0.662	Reyes,Jose, NYM	0.639	Molina,Bengie, SF	24.3	McCann,Brian, Atl	19.5
Weeks,Rickie, Mil	0.662	Drew,Stephen, Ari	0.632	Paulino,Ronny, Pit	20.4	Paulino,Ronny, Pit	20.4
Matsui,Kaz, Col	0.662	Renteria,Edgar, Atl	0.614	McCann,Brian, Atl	19.5	Molina,Bengie, SF	24.3

2B Double Play % (minimum 98 G)		3B Double Play % (minimum 98 G)		SS Double Play % (minimum 98 G)	
Matsui,Kaz, Col	0.595	Reynolds,Mark, Ari	0.538	Wilson,Jack, Pit	0.673
Sanchez,Freddy, Pit	0.546	Zimmerman,Ryan, Was	0.432	Gonzalez,Alex, Cin	0.663
Hudson,Orlando, Ari	0.533	Rolen,Scott, StL	0.412	Theriot,Ryan, ChC	0.658
Uggla,Dan, Fla	0.520	Atkins,Garrett, Col	0.405	Tulowitzki,Troy, Col	0.647
Weeks,Rickie, Mil	0.519	Nunez,Abraham, Phi	0.393	Furcal,Rafael, LAD	0.627
Johnson,Kelly, Atl	0.513	Cabrera,Miguel, Fla	0.380	Renteria,Edgar, Atl	0.624
Phillips,Brandon, Cin	0.510	Encarnacion,Edwin, Cin	0.375	Hardy,J.J., Mil	0.623
Durham,Ray, SF	0.510	Feliz,Pedro, SF	0.357	Vizquel,Omar, SF	0.622
Belliard,Ronnie, Was	0.493	Braun,Ryan, Mil	0.316	Drew,Stephen, Ari	0.621
Giles,Marcus, SD	0.489	Kouzmanoff,Kevin, SD	0.293	Rollins,Jimmy, Phi	0.612

Errors		Fielding Errors		Throwing Errors	
Braun,Ryan, Mil	26	Gonzalez,Alex, Cin	14	Braun,Ryan, Mil	16
Ramirez,Hanley, Fla	24	Cabrera,Miguel, Fla	13	Lopez,Felipe, Was	15
Cabrera,Miguel, Fla	23	Eckstein,David, StL	13	Zimmerman,Ryan, Was	15
Zimmerman,Ryan, Was	23	Drew,Stephen, Ari	12	Martin,Russell, LAD	14
Kouzmanoff,Kevin, SD	22	Kouzmanoff,Kevin, SD	12	Ramirez,Hanley, Fla	13
Lopez,Felipe, Was	21	Bautista,Jose, Pit	11	Furcal,Rafael, LAD	11
Wright,David, NYM	21	Durham,Ray, SF	11	Wright,David, NYM	11
Eckstein,David, StL	20	Kent,Jeff, LAD	11	Cabrera,Miguel, Fla	10
Furcal,Rafael, LAD	19	Ramirez,Hanley, Fla	11	Kouzmanoff,Kevin, SD	10
2 tied with	17	Rollins,Jimmy, Phi	11	2 tied with	9

Range Factor for 2B (minimum 98 games)		Range Factor for 3B (minimum 98 games)		Range Factor for SS (minimum 98 games)	
Matsui,Kaz, Col	5.33	Nunez,Abraham, Phi	3.27	Tulowitzki,Troy, Col	5.39
Utley,Chase, Phi	5.10	Zimmerman,Ryan, Was	3.07	Furcal,Rafael, LAD	4.96
Giles,Marcus, SD	5.08	Rolen,Scott, StL	2.99	Wilson,Jack, Pit	4.96
Phillips,Brandon, Cin	5.08	Bautista,Jose, Pit	2.92	Vizquel,Omar, SF	4.74
Belliard,Ronnie, Was	5.04	Feliz,Pedro, SF	2.91	Eckstein,David, StL	4.52
Hudson,Orlando, Ari	4.91	Ramirez,Aramis, ChC	2.87	Rollins,Jimmy, Phi	4.41
Sanchez,Freddy, Pit	4.89	Wright,David, NYM	2.73	Greene,Khalil, SD	4.38
Durham,Ray, SF	4.76	Cabrera,Miguel, Fla	2.51	Drew,Stephen, Ari	4.36
Johnson,Kelly, Atl	4.76	Jones,Chipper, Atl	2.51	Lopez,Felipe, Was	4.30
Weeks,Rickie, Mil	4.74	Encarnacion,Edwin, Cin	2.50	Ramirez,Hanley, Fla	4.27

2007 Active Career Batting Leaders

Batting Average (minimum 1000 PA)		On Base Percentage (minimum 1000 PA)		Slugging Average (minimum 1000 PA)		Home Runs	
Suzuki,Ichiro	.333	Bonds,Barry	.444	Pujols,Albert	.620	Bonds,Barry	762
Helton,Todd	.332	Helton,Todd	.430	Howard,Ryan	.610	Sosa,Sammy	609
Pujols,Albert	.332	Thomas,Frank	.421	Bonds,Barry	.607	Griffey Jr.,Ken	593
Guerrero,Vladimir	.325	Pujols,Albert	.420	Ramirez,Manny	.593	Rodriguez,Alex	518
Holliday,Matt	.319	Berkman,Lance	.412	Helton,Todd	.583	Thomas,Frank	513
Jeter,Derek	.317	Giambi,Jason	.411	Guerrero,Vladimir	.579	Thome,Jim	507
Garciaparra,Nomar	.315	Ramirez,Manny	.409	Rodriguez,Alex	.578	Ramirez,Manny	490
Cano,Robinson	.314	Thome,Jim	.409	Thome,Jim	.565	Sheffield,Gary	480
Mauer,Joe	.313	Abreu,Bobby	.408	Thomas,Frank	.561	Delgado,Carlos	431
Ramirez,Manny	.313	Giles,Brian	.404	Berkman,Lance	.559	Piazza,Mike	427

Games		At Bats		Hits		Total Bases	
Bonds,Barry	2986	Biggio,Craig	10876	Biggio,Craig	3060	Bonds,Barry	5976
Biggio,Craig	2850	Bonds,Barry	9847	Bonds,Barry	2935	Griffey Jr.,Ken	4884
Vizquel,Omar	2588	Vizquel,Omar	9479	Vizquel,Omar	2598	Biggio,Craig	4711
Finley,Steve	2583	Finley,Steve	9397	Franco,Julio	2586	Sosa,Sammy	4704
Franco,Julio	2527	Griffey Jr.,Ken	8826	Griffey Jr.,Ken	2558	Thomas,Frank	4458
Gonzalez,Luis	2455	Gonzalez,Luis	8816	Finley,Steve	2548	Sheffield,Gary	4449
Griffey Jr.,Ken	2378	Sosa,Sammy	8813	Sheffield,Gary	2521	Rodriguez,Alex	4251
Sheffield,Gary	2362	Franco,Julio	8677	Gonzalez,Luis	2502	Gonzalez,Luis	4244
Sosa,Sammy	2354	Sheffield,Gary	8531	Rodriguez,Ivan	2495	Ramirez,Manny	4184
Thomas,Frank	2251	Rodriguez,Ivan	8247	Lofton,Kenny	2428	Finley,Steve	4157

Doubles		Triples		Runs Scored		RBI	
Biggio,Craig	668	Finley,Steve	124	Bonds,Barry	2227	Bonds,Barry	1996
Bonds,Barry	601	Lofton,Kenny	116	Biggio,Craig	1844	Griffey Jr.,Ken	1701
Gonzalez,Luis	570	Damon,Johnny	87	Griffey Jr.,Ken	1545	Thomas,Frank	1674
Kent,Jeff	537	Rollins,Jimmy	81	Sheffield,Gary	1540	Sosa,Sammy	1667
Rodriguez,Ivan	504	Durham,Ray	79	Lofton,Kenny	1528	Ramirez,Manny	1604
Thomas,Frank	488	Bonds,Barry	77	Rodriguez,Alex	1501	Sheffield,Gary	1576
Griffey Jr.,Ken	473	Crawford,Carl	74	Sosa,Sammy	1475	Rodriguez,Alex	1503
Ramirez,Manny	471	Guzman,Cristian	73	Thomas,Frank	1467	Kent,Jeff	1459
Anderson,Garret	462	Vizquel,Omar	71	Finley,Steve	1443	Thome,Jim	1398
Helton,Todd	455	Pierre,Juan	69	Gonzalez,Luis	1382	Gonzalez,Luis	1392

Walks		Intentional Walks		Hit By Pitch		Strikeouts	
Bonds,Barry	2558	Bonds,Barry	688	Biggio,Craig	285	Sosa,Sammy	2306
Thomas,Frank	1628	Griffey Jr.,Ken	230	Kendall,Jason	218	Thome,Jim	2043
Thome,Jim	1459	Guerrero,Vladimir	223	Delgado,Carlos	160	Biggio,Craig	1753
Sheffield,Gary	1377	Thomas,Frank	168	Giambi,Jason	135	Sanders,Reggie	1614
Griffey Jr.,Ken	1162	Delgado,Carlos	167	Jeter,Derek	129	Delgado,Carlos	1601
Biggio,Craig	1160	Ramirez,Manny	167	Sheffield,Gary	128	Griffey Jr.,Ken	1593
Jones,Chipper	1152	Helton,Todd	162	Rodriguez,Alex	127	Edmonds,Jim	1587
Giambi,Jason	1129	Sosa,Sammy	154	Easley,Damion	125	Ramirez,Manny	1543
Ramirez,Manny	1125	Thome,Jim	150	Kent,Jeff	118	Bonds,Barry	1539
Gonzalez,Luis	1114	Gonzalez,Luis	149	Eckstein,David	116	Rodriguez,Alex	1524

2007 Active Career Batting Leaders

Sacrifice Hits		Sacrifice Flies		Stolen Bases		Seasons Played	
Vizquel,Omar	232	Thomas,Frank	120	Lofton,Kenny	622	Clemens,Roger	24
Glavine,Tom	213	Sheffield,Gary	108	Bonds,Barry	514	Franco,Julio	23
Maddux,Greg	174	Conine,Jeff	103	Biggio,Craig	414	Bonds,Barry	22
Smoltz,John	135	Kent,Jeff	101	Pierre,Juan	389	Maddux,Greg	22
Clayton,Royce	113	Griffey Jr.,Ken	94	Vizquel,Omar	380	Glavine,Tom	21
Schilling,Curt	102	Gonzalez,Luis	93	Damon,Johnny	333	Moyer,Jamie	21
Biggio,Craig	101	Bonds,Barry	91	Castillo,Luis	325	Wells,David	21
Perez,Neifi	99	Delgado,Carlos	83	Finley,Steve	320	5 tied with	20
Pierre,Juan	96	Vizquel,Omar	83	Sanders,Reggie	304		
Finley,Steve	91	Ramirez,Manny	82	Abreu,Bobby	296		

At Bats Per Home Run (minimum 1000 AB)		Grounded Into DP		Highest SB Success Pct (minimum 100 SBA)		Lowest SB Success Pct (minimum 100 SBA)	
Howard,Ryan	11.3	Franco,Julio	312	Beltran,Carlos	88.0	Perez,Neifi	55.9
Bonds,Barry	12.9	Rodriguez,Ivan	271	Byrnes,Eric	87.8	Edmonds,Jim	56.8
Thome,Jim	13.5	Piazza,Mike	229	Crawford,Carl	82.9	Gonzalez,Luis	59.9
Dunn,Adam	14.1	Clayton,Royce	218	Roberts,Dave	81.2	Kent,Jeff	61.4
Rodriguez,Alex	14.2	Thomas,Frank	217	Rollins,Jimmy	81.0	Guillen,Carlos	62.0
Pujols,Albert	14.4	Ramirez,Manny	213	Cabrera,Orlando	80.9	Anderson,Garret	62.3
Ramirez,Manny	14.4	Kent,Jeff	211	Rodriguez,Alex	80.5	Cirillo,Jeff	63.0
Sosa,Sammy	14.5	Sheffield,Gary	206	Suzuki,Ichiro	80.5	Kotsay,Mark	63.6
Griffey Jr.,Ken	14.9	Gonzalez,Luis	203	Patterson,Corey	80.4	Walker,Todd	64.1
Fielder,Prince	15.0	Sosa,Sammy	202	Reyes,Jose	80.1	Jones,Jacque	65.1

Strikeouts / Walks Ratio (minimum 1000 AB)		At Bats Per GIDP (minimum 1000 AB)		OPS (minimum 1000 PA)		Secondary Average (minimum 1000 PA)	
Bonds,Barry	.602	Matsui,Kaz	197.1	Bonds,Barry	1.051	Bonds,Barry	.621
Giles,Brian	.703	Suzuki,Ichiro	140.4	Pujols,Albert	1.040	Thome,Jim	.499
Sheffield,Gary	.757	Granderson,Curtis	139.5	Helton,Todd	1.014	Howard,Ryan	.491
Pujols,Albert	.764	Taveras,Willy	135.8	Howard,Ryan	1.007	Dunn,Adam	.489
Helton,Todd	.776	Reyes,Jose	119.9	Ramirez,Manny	1.002	Thomas,Frank	.466
Thomas,Frank	.823	Roberts,Dave	113.0	Thomas,Frank	.982	Berkman,Lance	.456
Palmeiro,Orlando	.868	Branyan,Russell	109.9	Thome,Jim	.974	Ramirez,Manny	.444
Mauer,Joe	.880	Maddux,Greg	109.7	Berkman,Lance	.971	Pujols,Albert	.444
Hatteberg,Scott	.894	Patterson,Corey	106.9	Guerrero,Vladimir	.970	Giambi,Jason	.442
Kendall,Jason	.915	Damon,Johnny	104.3	Rodriguez,Alex	.967	Abreu,Bobby	.435

Highest Strikeout per PA (minimum 1000 PA)		Lowest Strikeout per PA (minimum 1000 PA)		Plate Appearances		At Bats Per RBI (minimum 1000 AB)	
Branyan,Russell	.348	Pierre,Juan	.055	Bonds,Barry	12606	Howard,Ryan	4.1
Smoltz,John	.312	Polanco,Placido	.064	Biggio,Craig	12503	Ramirez,Manny	4.4
Pena,Wily Mo	.311	Lo Duca,Paul	.069	Vizquel,Omar	10782	Pujols,Albert	4.7
Bellhorn,Mark	.290	Eckstein,David	.071	Finley,Steve	10460	Thomas,Frank	4.8
Gomes,Jonny	.284	Kendall,Jason	.076	Griffey Jr.,Ken	10167	Ortiz,David	4.8
Howard,Ryan	.283	Johjima,Kenji	.082	Sheffield,Gary	10153	Delgado,Carlos	4.8
Wilson,Craig	.278	Hall,Toby	.083	Gonzalez,Luis	10144	Hafner,Travis	4.8
Werth,Jayson	.270	Cabrera,Orlando	.085	Sosa,Sammy	9896	Rodriguez,Alex	4.9
Ross,Dave	.269	Palmeiro,Orlando	.085	Thomas,Frank	9785	Thome,Jim	4.9
Dunn,Adam	.266	Perez,Timo	.087	Franco,Julio	9731	Bonds,Barry	4.9

2007 Active Career Pitching Leaders

Earned Run Average (minimum 750 IP)		Winning Percentage (minimum 100 Decisions)		Opponent Batting Average (minimum 750 IP)		Baserunners Per 9 IP (minimum 750 IP)	
Rivera,Mariano	2.35	Martinez,Pedro	.692	Wagner,Billy	.190	Wagner,Billy	9.48
Wagner,Billy	2.40	Santana,Johan	.679	Benitez,Armando	.196	Hoffman,Trevor	9.52
Hoffman,Trevor	2.73	Oswalt,Roy	.675	Hoffman,Trevor	.209	Martinez,Pedro	9.71
Martinez,Pedro	2.80	Halladay,Roy	.669	Martinez,Pedro	.210	Rivera,Mariano	9.75
Oswalt,Roy	3.07	Hudson,Tim	.659	Wood,Kerry	.215	Santana,Johan	10.03
Benitez,Armando	3.11	Clemens,Roger	.658	Rivera,Mariano	.216	Schilling,Curt	10.38
Maddux,Greg	3.11	Johnson,Randy	.654	Johnson,Randy	.218	Maddux,Greg	10.51
Clemens,Roger	3.12	Pettitte,Andy	.640	Santana,Johan	.221	Smoltz,John	10.67
Santana,Johan	3.22	Mussina,Mike	.635	Zambrano,Carlos	.226	Clemens,Roger	10.84
Webb,Brandon	3.22	Mulder,Mark	.632	Clemens,Roger	.229	Mussina,Mike	10.85

Games		Games Started		Complete Games		Shutouts	
Stanton,Mike	1178	Clemens,Roger	707	Clemens,Roger	118	Clemens,Roger	46
Mesa,Jose	1022	Maddux,Greg	707	Maddux,Greg	109	Johnson,Randy	37
Timlin,Mike	1011	Glavine,Tom	669	Johnson,Randy	98	Maddux,Greg	35
Hernandez,Rob	1010	Johnson,Randy	556	Schilling,Curt	83	Glavine,Tom	25
Jones,Todd	937	Moyer,Jamie	551	Mussina,Mike	57	Mussina,Mike	23
Myers,Mike	883	Mussina,Mike	502	Glavine,Tom	56	Schilling,Curt	20
Hoffman,Trevor	882	Wells,David	489	Wells,David	54	Martinez,Pedro	17
Gordon,Tom	853	Smoltz,John	461	Smoltz,John	53	Smoltz,John	16
Wickman,Bob	835	Rogers,Kenny	444	Martinez,Pedro	46	Carpenter,Chris	12
Weathers,David	824	Schilling,Curt	436	Hernandez,Livan	43	Wells,David	12

Wins		Losses		Innings Pitched		Batters Faced	
Clemens,Roger	354	Maddux,Greg	214	Clemens,Roger	4916.2	Clemens,Roger	20240
Maddux,Greg	347	Glavine,Tom	199	Maddux,Greg	4814.1	Maddux,Greg	19617
Glavine,Tom	303	Clemens,Roger	184	Glavine,Tom	4350.0	Glavine,Tom	18323
Johnson,Randy	284	Moyer,Jamie	178	Johnson,Randy	3855.1	Johnson,Randy	15877
Mussina,Mike	250	Wells,David	157	Moyer,Jamie	3550.1	Moyer,Jamie	15102
Wells,David	239	Trachsel,Steve	154	Wells,David	3439.0	Wells,David	14413
Moyer,Jamie	230	Johnson,Randy	150	Smoltz,John	3367.0	Smoltz,John	13810
Schilling,Curt	216	Schilling,Curt	146	Mussina,Mike	3362.1	Mussina,Mike	13774
Rogers,Kenny	210	Wakefield,Tim	146	Schilling,Curt	3261.0	Rogers,Kenny	13498
Martinez,Pedro	209	Smoltz,John	145	Rogers,Kenny	3129.0	Schilling,Curt	13284

Strikeouts		Walks Allowed		Hit Batters		Wild Pitches	
Clemens,Roger	4672	Clemens,Roger	1580	Johnson,Randy	182	Clemens,Roger	143
Johnson,Randy	4616	Glavine,Tom	1463	Clemens,Roger	159	Smoltz,John	143
Maddux,Greg	3273	Johnson,Randy	1422	Wakefield,Tim	150	Gordon,Tom	106
Schilling,Curt	3116	Rogers,Kenny	1104	Maddux,Greg	131	Johnson,Randy	102
Martinez,Pedro	3030	Moyer,Jamie	1012	Martinez,Pedro	131	Clement,Matt	101
Smoltz,John	2975	Wakefield,Tim	1012	Park,Chan Ho	126	Wells,David	101
Mussina,Mike	2663	Smoltz,John	984	Wright,Jamey	119	Schmidt,Jason	93
Glavine,Tom	2570	Maddux,Greg	969	Rogers,Kenny	118	Wakefield,Tim	92
Wells,David	2201	Gordon,Tom	957	Weaver,Jeff	118	Batista,Miguel	85
Moyer,Jamie	2125	Trachsel,Steve	916	Moyer,Jamie	117	Carrasco,Hector	85

2007 Active Career Pitching Leaders

Saves		Save Pct (minimum 50 Save Ops)		Home Runs Allowed		Strikeouts Per 9 IP (minimum 750 IP)	
Hoffman,Trevor	524	Gagne,Eric	94.7	Moyer,Jamie	444	Wagner,Billy	11.84
Rivera,Mariano	443	Smoltz,John	91.7	Wells,David	407	Benitez,Armando	10.91
Wagner,Billy	358	Saito,Takashi	91.3	Johnson,Randy	368	Johnson,Randy	10.78
Hernandez,Rob	326	Nathan,Joe	89.9	Clemens,Roger	363	Wood,Kerry	10.33
Percival,Troy	324	Hoffman,Trevor	89.3	Mussina,Mike	359	Martinez,Pedro	10.20
Mesa,Jose	321	Rivera,Mariano	88.2	Schilling,Curt	347	Hoffman,Trevor	9.63
Jones,Todd	301	Jenks,Bobby	87.9	Glavine,Tom	345	Santana,Johan	9.50
Benitez,Armando	289	Papelbon,Jonathan	87.8	Trachsel,Steve	338	Perez,Oliver	9.47
Isringhausen,Jason	281	Wagner,Billy	86.7	Wakefield,Tim	337	Peavy,Jake	9.02
Wickman,Bob	267	Valverde,Jose	86.0	Maddux,Greg	332	Kim,B-H	8.63

Opp On-Base Percentage (minimum 750 IP)		Opp Slugging Average (minimum 750 IP)		Hits Per Nine Innings (minimum 750 IP)		Home Runs Per Nine IP (minimum 750 IP)	
Hoffman,Trevor	.265	Rivera,Mariano	.294	Wagner,Billy	6.11	Rivera,Mariano	0.46
Wagner,Billy	.266	Wagner,Billy	.300	Benitez,Armando	6.30	Maddux,Greg	0.62
Rivera,Mariano	.271	Martinez,Pedro	.328	Martinez,Pedro	6.89	Webb,Brandon	0.64
Martinez,Pedro	.271	Benitez,Armando	.336	Hoffman,Trevor	6.91	Clemens,Roger	0.66
Santana,Johan	.278	Hoffman,Trevor	.337	Wood,Kerry	6.97	Wickman,Bob	0.68
Schilling,Curt	.286	Clemens,Roger	.341	Johnson,Randy	7.16	Isringhausen,Jason	0.70
Maddux,Greg	.291	Isringhausen,Jason	.345	Rivera,Mariano	7.17	Oswalt,Roy	0.71
Smoltz,John	.292	Johnson,Randy	.346	Santana,Johan	7.34	Glavine,Tom	0.71
Clemens,Roger	.294	Zambrano,Carlos	.349	Zambrano,Carlos	7.44	Hudson,Tim	0.72
Mussina,Mike	.296	Webb,Brandon	.354	Clemens,Roger	7.66	Martinez,Pedro	0.72

Strikeouts / Walks Ratio (minimum 750 IP)		Stolen Base Pct Allowed (minimum 750 IP)		GIDP Induced		GIDP Per Nine IP (minimum 750 IP)	
Schilling,Curt	4.38	Maroth,Mike	37.5	Glavine,Tom	413	Tavarez,Julian	1.28
Martinez,Pedro	4.28	Carpenter,Chris	38.3	Maddux,Greg	406	Westbrook,Jake	1.28
Sheets,Ben	3.94	Buehrle,Mark	41.3	Clemens,Roger	330	Silva,Carlos	1.23
Wagner,Billy	3.90	Rogers,Kenny	41.7	Rogers,Kenny	323	Wright,Jamey	1.22
Hoffman,Trevor	3.81	Meche,Gil	45.3	Moyer,Jamie	292	Mulder,Mark	1.14
Santana,Johan	3.79	Zambrano,Carlos	46.3	Pettitte,Andy	291	Schoeneweis,Scott	1.12
Lieber,Jon	3.67	Santana,Johan	49.1	Mussina,Mike	269	Wickman,Bob	1.11
Oswalt,Roy	3.62	Redman,Mark	50.0	Wells,David	266	Robertson,Nate	1.07
Rivera,Mariano	3.60	Garland,Jon	50.6	Smoltz,John	240	White,Rick	1.05
Mussina,Mike	3.53	Ohka,Tomo	50.7	Johnson,Randy	236	Torres,Salomon	1.04

Complete Game % (minimum 100 GS)		Quality Start Pct (minimum 100 GS)		Walks Per 9 IP (minimum 750 IP)		Games Finished	
Schilling,Curt	0.19	Oswalt,Roy	69.9	Silva,Carlos	1.63	Hoffman,Trevor	732
Johnson,Randy	0.18	Martinez,Pedro	69.5	Lieber,Jon	1.74	Hernandez,Rob	667
Clemens,Roger	0.17	Johnson,Randy	68.2	Maddux,Greg	1.81	Rivera,Mariano	659
Maddux,Greg	0.15	Peavy,Jake	66.9	Wells,David	1.88	Mesa,Jose	633
Halladay,Roy	0.14	Webb,Brandon	66.3	Sheets,Ben	1.95	Wagner,Billy	603
Mulder,Mark	0.12	Schilling,Curt	66.1	Schilling,Curt	1.96	Jones,Todd	582
Hernandez,Livan	0.12	Clemens,Roger	65.8	Mussina,Mike	2.02	Benitez,Armando	525
Martinez,Pedro	0.12	Maddux,Greg	65.5	Oswalt,Roy	2.06	Wickman,Bob	511
Smoltz,John	0.11	Glavine,Tom	64.4	Buehrle,Mark	2.06	Percival,Troy	498
Ponson,Sidney	0.11	Santana,Johan	64.0	Byrd,Paul	2.16	Timlin,Mike	441

2007 American League Bill James Leaders

Top Game Scores

Pitcher	Date	Opp	IP	H	R	ER	BB	SO	GS
Bedard,Erik, Bal	7/7	Tex	9.0	2	0	0	0	15	98
Santana,Johan, Min	8/19	Tex	8.0	2	0	0	0	17	95
Verlander,Justin, Det	6/12	Mil	9.0	0	0	0	4	12	95
Buehrle,Mark, CWS	4/18	Tex	9.0	0	0	0	1	8	94
Baker,Scott, Min	8/31	KC	9.0	1	0	0	1	9	93
Buchholz,Clay, Bos	9/1	Bal	9.0	0	0	0	3	9	93
McGowan,Dustin, Tor	6/24	Col	9.0	1	0	0	1	7	91
Hernandez,Felix, Sea	4/11	Bos	9.0	1	0	0	2	6	89
Schilling,Curt, Bos	6/7	Oak	9.0	1	0	0	0	4	89
Gabbard,Kason, Bos	7/16	KC	9.0	3	0	0	1	8	88
Greinke,Zack, KC	9/20	CWS	8.0	2	0	0	0	10	88

Worst Game Scores

Pitcher	Date	Opp	IP	H	R	ER	BB	SO	GS
Garland,Jon, CWS	7/6	Min	3.1	11	12	11	3	0	-11
Lewis,Colby, Oak	5/22	CWS	3.1	12	10	10	2	0	-6
Feierabend,Ryan, Sea	7/3	KC	1.1	8	10	10	2	0	-4
Shields,James, TB	7/22	NYY	3.1	10	10	10	4	1	-3
Bonderman,Jeremy, Det	7/29	LAA	2.1	9	11	10	3	4	-2
Contreras,Jose, CWS	7/25	Det	4.2	12	9	9	3	3	4
Loe,Kameron, Tex	6/7	Det	2.2	9	9	9	1	1	4
Garland,Jon, CWS	8/2	NYY	1.1	9	8	8	0	1	5
Batista,Miguel, Sea	8/22	Min	2.0	9	8	8	1	1	6
Carmona,Fausto, Cle	6/27	Oak	1.0	7	8	8	2	1	6
Halladay,Roy, Tor	6/5	TB	3.1	12	8	7	1	1	6
Westbrook,Jake, Cle	4/17	NYY	1.2	8	8	8	2	1	6

Runs Created

Rodriguez,Alex, NYY	159
Ordonez,Magglio, Det	146
Ortiz,David, Bos	138
Suzuki,Ichiro, Sea	128
Guerrero,Vladimir, LAA	127
Sizemore,Grady, Cle	123
Pena,Carlos, TB	114
Jeter,Derek, NYY	112
Martinez,Victor, Cle	108
Young,Michael, Tex	107

Runs Created Per 27 Outs

Rodriguez,Alex, NYY	9.9
Ordonez,Magglio, Det	9.6
Ortiz,David, Bos	9.5
Thome,Jim, CWS	8.5
Pena,Carlos, TB	8.3
Guerrero,Vladimir, LAA	8.1
Cust,Jack, Oak	7.5
Posada,Jorge, NYY	7.4
Suzuki,Ichiro, Sea	7.4
Figgins,Chone, LAA	7.2

Offensive Winning %

Rodriguez,Alex, NYY	.801
Ordonez,Magglio, Det	.790
Ortiz,David, Bos	.771
Pena,Carlos, TB	.759
Cust,Jack, Oak	.748
Thome,Jim, CWS	.732
Guerrero,Vladimir, LAA	.725
Suzuki,Ichiro, Sea	.711
Posada,Jorge, NYY	.692
Upton,B.J., TB	.687

Secondary Average
(minimum 502 PA)

Pena,Carlos, TB	.557
Rodriguez,Alex, NYY	.535
Cust,Jack, Oak	.514
Thome,Jim, CWS	.507
Ortiz,David, Bos	.497
Sheffield,Gary, Det	.411
Sizemore,Grady, Cle	.398
Upton,B.J., TB	.392
Swisher,Nick, Oak	.384
Granderson,Curtis, Det	.377

Isolated Power
(minimum 502 PA)

Pena,Carlos, TB	.345
Rodriguez,Alex, NYY	.331
Ortiz,David, Bos	.290
Thome,Jim, CWS	.287
Granderson,Curtis, Det	.250
Cust,Jack, Oak	.248
Dye,Jermaine, CWS	.232
Ordonez,Magglio, Det	.232
Konerko,Paul, CWS	.231
Guerrero,Vladimir, LAA	.223

Power / Speed Number

Rodriguez,Alex, NYY	33.2
Sizemore,Grady, Cle	27.8
Granderson,Curtis, Det	24.4
Sheffield,Gary, Det	23.4
Upton,B.J., TB	23.0
Hunter,Torii, Min	21.9
Kinsler,Ian, Tex	21.4
Markakis,Nick, Bal	20.2
Rios,Alex, Tor	19.9
Abreu,Bobby, NYY	19.5

Speed Scores (2006-2007)

Patterson,Corey, Bal	8.67
Granderson,Curtis, Det	8.63
Crawford,Carl, TB	8.22
Suzuki,Ichiro, Sea	8.09
Sizemore,Grady, Cle	7.96
Figgins,Chone, LAA	7.73
Damon,Johnny, NYY	7.68
Crisp,Coco, Bos	7.47
Lugo,Julio, Bos	7.02
DeJesus,David, KC	6.94

Cheap Wins

Byrd,Paul, Cle	8
Hernandez,Felix, Sea	6
Bonderman,Jeremy, Det	5
Matsuzaka,Daisuke, Bos	5
Perez,Odalis, KC	5
Ramirez,Horacio, Sea	5
Robertson,Nate, Det	5
Sabathia,C.C., Cle	5
Silva,Carlos, Min	5
9 tied with	4

Tough Losses

Matsuzaka,Daisuke, Bos	7
Meche,Gil, KC	7
Santana,Johan, Min	7
Cabrera,Daniel, Bal	6
Contreras,Jose, CWS	5
Garland,Jon, CWS	5
Haren,Dan, Oak	5
7 tied with	4

2007 National League Bill James Leaders

Top Game Scores

Pitcher	Date	Opp	IP	H	R	ER	BB	SO	GS
Lieber,Jon, Phi	6/9	KC	9.0	3	0	0	0	11	92
Harang,Aaron, Cin	8/29	Pit	9.0	2	0	0	1	8	90
Maine,John, NYM	9/29	Fla	7.2	1	0	0	2	14	89
Webb,Brandon, Ari	8/17	Atl	9.0	2	0	0	1	6	88
Hamels,Cole, Phi	4/21	Cin	9.0	5	1	1	2	15	86
Marquis,Jason, ChC	5/9	Pit	9.0	3	0	0	0	5	86
Morris,Matt, SF	5/20	Oak	9.0	2	1	1	2	9	86
Owings,Micah , Ari	9/18	SF	9.0	2	0	0	1	4	86
Peavy,Jake, SD	4/25	Ari	7.0	2	0	0	3	16	86
Rodriguez,Wandy, Hou	7/6	NYM	9.0	4	0	0	1	8	86
Webb,Brandon, Ari	8/11	Was	9.0	5	0	0	1	10	86

Worst Game Scores

Pitcher	Date	Opp	IP	H	R	ER	BB	SO	GS
Gallardo,Yovani, Mil	8/8	Col	2.2	12	11	11	3	1	-12
Jennings,Jason, Hou	7/29	SD	0.2	8	11	11	3	0	-11
Stauffer,Tim, SD	8/26	Phi	4.0	11	11	11	3	3	-4
Maholm,Paul, Pit	9/16	Hou	2.2	11	10	10	0	1	-3
Simontacchi,J., Was	6/19	Det	3.0	10	10	10	2	1	-2
Hanrahan,Joel, Was	8/26	Col	2.2	8	9	9	5	1	2
Lowe,Derek, LAD	7/19	NYM	3.0	10	9	8	3	0	2
Maroth,Mike, StL	7/19	Atl	5.0	11	10	10	3	0	2
Vargas,Jason, NYM	7/3	Col	3.1	11	9	9	2	2	2
Hensley,Clay, SD	4/16	ChC	5.0	11	10	10	3	1	3

Runs Created

Holliday,Matt, Col	134
Wright,David, NYM	127
Fielder,Prince, Mil	125
Rollins,Jimmy, Phi	124
Cabrera,Miguel, Fla	122
Howard,Ryan, Phi	119
Pujols,Albert, StL	118
Helton,Todd, Col	115
Ramirez,Hanley, Fla	115
Utley,Chase, Phi	111

Runs Created Per 27 Outs

Utley,Chase, Phi	8.1
Jones,Chipper, Atl	8.1
Holliday,Matt, Col	8.0
Fielder,Prince, Mil	7.9
Wright,David, NYM	7.9
Howard,Ryan, Phi	7.9
Cabrera,Miguel, Fla	7.7
Helton,Todd, Col	7.7
Pujols,Albert, StL	7.5
Hawpe,Brad, Col	7.2

Offensive Winning %

Jones,Chipper, Atl	.753
Wright,David, NYM	.743
Fielder,Prince, Mil	.734
Utley,Chase, Phi	.731
Pujols,Albert, StL	.722
Howard,Ryan, Phi	.721
Cabrera,Miguel, Fla	.721
Holliday,Matt, Col	.717
Helton,Todd, Col	.701
Berkman,Lance, Hou	.690

Secondary Average
(minimum 502 PA)

Howard,Ryan, Phi	.520
Dunn,Adam, Cin	.500
Fielder,Prince, Mil	.490
Burrell,Pat, Phi	.487
Weeks,Rickie, Mil	.450
Jones,Chipper, Atl	.437
Wright,David, NYM	.434
Pujols,Albert, StL	.419
Beltran,Carlos, NYM	.415
Berkman,Lance, Hou	.412

Isolated Power
(minimum 502 PA)

Fielder,Prince, Mil	.330
Howard,Ryan, Phi	.316
Dunn,Adam, Cin	.289
Holliday,Matt, Col	.267
Jones,Chipper, Atl	.267
Soriano,Alfonso, ChC	.261
Beltran,Carlos, NYM	.249
Hawpe,Brad, Col	.248
Burrell,Pat, Phi	.246
Cabrera,Miguel, Fla	.245

Power / Speed Number

Ramirez,Hanley, Fla	37.0
Rollins,Jimmy, Phi	34.6
Wright,David, NYM	31.9
Phillips,Brandon, Cin	31.0
Byrnes,Eric, Ari	29.6
Young,Chris, Ari	29.3
Beltran,Carlos, NYM	27.1
Soriano,Alfonso, ChC	24.1
Hart,Corey, Mil	23.5
Reyes,Jose, NYM	20.8

Speed Scores (2006-2007)

Reyes,Jose, NYM	8.88
Roberts,Dave, SF	8.63
Rollins,Jimmy, Phi	8.41
Taveras,Willy, Col	8.09
Pierre,Juan, LAD	7.98
Ramirez,Hanley, Fla	7.90
Victorino,Shane, Phi	7.42
Beltran,Carlos, NYM	7.38
Cameron,Mike, SD	7.18
Byrnes,Eric, Ari	7.16

Cheap Wins

Suppan,Jeff, Mil	7
Eaton,Adam, Phi	5
Olsen,Scott, Fla	5
Chico,Matt, Was	4
Hernandez,Livan, Ari	4
Kendrick,Kyle, Phi	4
Lowry,Noah, SF	4
Maddux,Greg, SD	4
Willis,Dontrelle, Fla	4
13 tied with	3

Tough Losses

Cain,Matt, SF	8
Lowe,Derek, LAD	5
Reyes,Anthony, StL	5
Perez,Oliver, NYM	4
Smoltz,John, Atl	4
Snell,Ian, Pit	4
Willis,Dontrelle, Fla	4
13 tied with	3

Additional Bill James Leaders

AL Batters Win Shares
(2007)

Rodriguez,Alex, NYY	37
Ordonez,Magglio, Det	34
Suzuki,Ichiro, Sea	33
Guerrero,Vladimir, LAA	29
Martinez,Victor, Cle	29
Sizemore,Grady, Cle	29
Pena,Carlos, TB	28
Ortiz,David, Bos	27
Cabrera,Orlando, LAA	25
Granderson,Curtis, Det	25

NL Batters Win Shares
(2007)

Wright,David, NYM	34
Pujols,Albert, StL	32
Cabrera,Miguel, Fla	29
Utley,Chase, Phi	28
Fielder,Prince, Mil	27
Holliday,Matt, Col	27
Ramirez,Hanley, Fla	27
Rollins,Jimmy, Phi	27
Howard,Ryan, Phi	26
3 tied with	25

AL Pitchers Win Shares
(2007)

Sabathia,C.C., Cle	24
Carmona,Fausto, Cle	22
Lackey,John, LAA	21
Putz,J.J., Sea	20
Beckett,Josh, Bos	18
Escobar,Kelvim, LAA	18
Vazquez,Javier, CWS	18
4 tied with	17

NL Pitchers Win Shares
(2007)

Webb,Brandon, Ari	22
Peavy,Jake, SD	21
Penny,Brad, LAD	20
Harang,Aaron, Cin	17
Hudson,Tim, Atl	17
Oswalt,Roy, Hou	17
Saito,Takashi, LAD	17
Zambrano,Carlos, ChC	16
3 tied with	15

Batters Win Shares
(Career)

Bonds,Barry	705
Biggio,Craig	428
Sheffield,Gary	418
Thomas,Frank	400
Griffey Jr.,Ken	381
Rodriguez,Alex	377
Ramirez,Manny	348
Kent,Jeff	330
Jones,Chipper	326
2 tied with	325

Pitchers Win Shares
(Career)

Clemens,Roger	437
Maddux,Greg	392
Glavine,Tom	313
Johnson,Randy	309
Smoltz,John	286
Mussina,Mike	254
Schilling,Curt	252
Martinez,Pedro	251
Wells,David	210
2 tied with	202

2007 AL Component ERA
(minimum 162 IP)

Bedard,Erik, Bal	2.71
Santana,Johan, Min	2.98
Beckett,Josh, Bos	2.99
McGowan,Dustin, Tor	3.07
Sabathia,C.C., Cle	3.12
Shields,James, TB	3.24
Escobar,Kelvim, LAA	3.25
Vazquez,Javier, CWS	3.29
Blanton,Joe, Oak	3.30
Haren,Dan, Oak	3.32

2007 NL Component ERA
(minimum 162 IP)

Peavy,Jake, SD	2.27
Young,Chris, SD	2.35
Webb,Brandon, Ari	2.82
Smoltz,John, Atl	3.07
Hudson,Tim, Atl	3.12
Hamels,Cole, Phi	3.12
Lilly,Ted, ChC	3.14
Harang,Aaron, Cin	3.22
Cain,Matt, SF	3.23
Penny,Brad, LAD	3.41

Highest Avg Game Score
(AL - minimum 30 GS)

Santana,Johan, Min	59.45
Beckett,Josh, Bos	57.80
Sabathia,C.C., Cle	57.79
Vazquez,Javier, CWS	56.78
Lackey,John, LAA	56.45
Carmona,Fausto, Cle	56.16
Haren,Dan, Oak	56.09
Shields,James, TB	55.97
Escobar,Kelvim, LAA	55.37
Kazmir,Scott, TB	55.06

Lowest Avg Game Score
(AL - minimum 30 GS)

Contreras,Jose, CWS	42.13
Jackson,Edwin, TB	43.00
Millwood,Kevin, Tex	44.58
Cabrera,Daniel, Bal	46.09
Byrd,Paul, Cle	46.10
Bonser,Boof, Min	46.80
Robertson,Nate, Det	47.10
Batista,Miguel, Sea	48.09
Wakefield,Tim, Bos	48.35
Gaudin,Chad, Oak	48.41

Lowest Offensive Win %
(AL)

Punto,Nick, Min	.236
Uribe,Juan, CWS	.293
Pena,Tony F, KC	.300
Pierzynski,A.J., CWS	.317
Lopez,Jose, Sea	.325
Lugo,Julio, Bos	.344
Patterson,Corey, Bal	.352
Rodriguez,Ivan, Det	.375
Blake,Casey, Cle	.386
Johjima,Kenji, Sea	.411

Highest Avg Game Score
(NL - minimum 30 GS)

Peavy,Jake, SD	62.18
Webb,Brandon, Ari	57.97
Young,Chris, SD	57.87
Smoltz,John, Atl	57.16
Harang,Aaron, Cin	56.79
Lilly,Ted, ChC	54.94
Cain,Matt, SF	54.69
Hill,Rich, ChC	54.59
Penny,Brad, LAD	54.42
Hudson,Tim, Atl	54.29

Lowest Avg Game Score
(NL - minimum 30 GS)

Eaton,Adam, Phi	41.63
Olsen,Scott, Fla	41.64
Hernandez,Livan, Ari	44.48
Morris,Matt, SF-Pit	44.66
Willis,Dontrelle, Fla	45.17
Belisle,Matt, Cin	45.57
Chico,Matt, Was	45.71
Williams,Woody, Hou	46.06
Suppan,Jeff, Mil	46.29
Moyer,Jamie, Phi	46.58

Lowest Offensive Win %
(NL)

Durham,Ray, SF	.325
Vizquel,Omar, SF	.343
Biggio,Craig, Hou	.345
Lopez,Felipe, Was	.384
Pierre,Juan, LAD	.389
Furcal,Rafael, LAD	.393
Young,Chris, Ari	.402
Theriot,Ryan, ChC	.404
Jones,Andruw, Atl	.434
Feliz,Pedro, SF	.441

410

Win Shares

Bill James initially devised Win Shares as a way to relate a player's individual statistics to the number of wins he contributed to his team. As a single number, Win Shares allows us to easily compare the accomplishments of each player and to compare players across positions.

We credit a team with three Win Shares for each win. If a team wins 100 games, the players on the team will be credited with 300 Win Shares—or 300 thirds-of-a-win. If a team wins 70 games, the players on the team will be credited with 210 Win Shares, and so on.

The following pages contain the sum of a player's Win Shares prior to 1998, followed by his individual season totals from 1998 through 2007. Career totals are also included for each player.

The quality of the team does not affect an individual player's Win Shares. A great player on a bad team will rate just as well as a great player on a good team. In 2007 for example, Jim Thome's 21 Win Shares for the 90-loss Chicago White Sox were the absolute equivalent of Jake Peavy's 21 Win Shares for the San Diego Padres, a team that won 89 games.

Win Shares are also a great tool for evaluating award voting and Hall of Fame credentials. Do this year's Most Valuable Player or Cy Young Award winner match up with the leaders in Win Shares? Generally, 30 Win Shares indicates an MVP-caliber season; 20 Win Shares indicates a season worthy of the Cy Young Award.

Based on Win Shares, the 2007 American League MVP should be Alex Rodriguez (37) while the National League MVP should be his cross-town doppelganger, David Wright (34). The Cy Young race in the AL will most likely come down to Fausto Carmona (22), John Lackey (21), and C.C. Sabathia (24); while the NL race will feature a death-cage match between Jake Peavy (21) and defending-champion Brandon Webb (22). As for the rookies, Dustin Pedroia is the favorite in the AL with 18 win shares, while Troy Tulowitzki (24) should eek out Ryan Braun (22) in the National League.

Win Shares can also be used to assess the value of trades. Does your favorite team have a net gain or loss from their transaction? Win Shares also adjusts for offensive environment, so it is a great tool to use for looking at the greatest individual seasons in baseball history, as well as the greatest players of all time. For a complete description of how Win Shares are calculated as well as countless essays using Win Shares to analyze various facets of the game, check out Bill James' book, *Win Shares*.

WIN SHARES BY YEAR

Player	<98	98	99	00	01	02	03	04	05	06	07	Career
Aardsma,David								0		4	1	5
Abercrombie,Reggie										3	1	4
Abreu,Bobby	6	26	26	23	26	29	28	33	25	27	18	267
Abreu,Tony											4	4
Abreu,Winston										0	0	0
Accardo,Jeremy									2	4	14	20
Acosta,Manny											2	2
Adams,Russ								2	10	3	1	16
Adkins,Jon							0	3	0	3	0	6
Affeldt,Jeremy						5	12	4	1	3	5	30
Albaladejo,Jonathan											2	2
Albers,Matt										0	0	0
Alfonseca,Antonio	0	3	11	10	9	7	1	8	1	0	3	53
Alfonzo,Eliezer										9	1	10
Alomar Jr.,Sandy	78	6	4	8	4	5	4	1	2	3	0	115
Alou,Moises	112	29		17	21	9	20	23	18	14	12	275
Ambres,Chip							1		0			1
Amezaga,Alfredo						2	1	1	0	5	5	14
Anderson,Brian								0	5	0		5
Anderson,Garret	33	18	16	15	17	23	25	14	16	14	13	204
Anderson,Josh											3	3
Anderson,Marlon		2	8	2	16	10	12	3	4	8	4	69
Andino,Robert									0	0	0	0
Ankiel,Rick			3	14	0			0			8	25
Aquino,Greg								6	0	3	0	9
Arias,Alberto											0	0
Armas Jr.,Tony			0	5	12	7	4	2	2	4	1	37
Arroyo,Bronson				0	3	2	2	11	11	20	11	60
Ascanio,Jose											0	0
Atchison,Scott								2	0		2	4
Atkins,Garrett							0	2	13	23	18	56
Aurilia,Rich	12	13	18	20	33	15	13	7	16	15	5	167
Ausmus,Brad	42	14	17	16	10	10	12	7	15	7	7	157
Ayala,Luis							11	10	8		4	33
Aybar,Erick										1	2	3
Aybar,Willy										6	6	12
Backe,Brandon						0	1	5	7	3	3	19
Bacsik,Mike					0	2	0	1			2	5
Baek,Cha Seung								0		3	3	6
Baez,Danys					6	11	9	10	10	6	1	53
Bailey,Homer											2	2
Bailey,Jeff											0	0
Baker,Jeff									1	3	1	5
Baker,Scott									4	0	8	12
Bako,Paul		5	5	5	3	3	5	2	1	2	2	33
Baldelli,Rocco							14	14		12	2	42
Bale,John				0	0	2		2			3	7
Balentien,Wladimir											0	0
Balfour,Grant					0		2	3			0	5
Banks,Josh											0	0
Bannister,Brian										3	11	14
Barajas,Rod			1	0	1	3	5	9	11	7	3	40
Bard,Josh						1	7	2	2	10	16	38
Barden,Brian											0	0
Barfield,Josh										18	8	26
Barker,Sean											0	0
Barmes,Clint							1	3	9	6	0	19
Barone,Daniel											0	0
Barrett,Michael		1	11	1	2	12	7	14	18	13	3	82
Barry,Kevin										1	0	1
Bartlett,Jason								0	6	13	16	35
Barton,Daric											3	3
Basak,Chris											0	0
Batista,Miguel	0	6	6	0	11	9	14	11	8	10	12	87
Batista,Tony	11	10	21	18	12	14	11	12		4	2	115
Bautista,Denny								0	1	1	0	2
Bautista,Jose								0	0	9	12	21
Bay,Jason							5	15	30	21	12	83
Bayliss,Jonah									0	1	0	1
Bazardo,Yorman									0		3	3
Bean,Colter									0	0	0	0
Beckett,Josh					3	5	11	9	12	11	18	69
Bedard,Erik							0	6	8	13	17	44
Beimel,Joe					4	3	2	0	1	7	6	23
Belisle,Matt								0	4	3	5	12
Bell,Heath								2	0	1	13	16
Bell,Rob				5	1	2	3	6	0	1		18
Bellhorn,Mark	5	0		0	1	18	4	20	5	4	0	57
Belliard,Ronnie		0	15	17	13	1	11	18	18	11	15	119
Bellorin,Edwin										0		0
Beltran,Carlos		2	18	5	27	20	28	29	21	34	25	209
Beltre,Adrian			4	15	12	16	15	33	13	17	16	163
Benitez,Armando	16	10	19	17	14	12	10	18	4	6	2	128
Bennett,Gary	0	1	2	3	1	4	6	2	5	2	2	28
Bennett,Jeff								2			1	3
Benoit,Joaquin					0	3	5	4	6	4	10	32
Benson,Kris			12	14			5	2	10	10	8	61
Bergmann,Jason									2	0	5	7
Berkman,Lance			1	10	32	29	25	30	20	31	24	202
Berroa,Angel						1	1	16	12	12	4	46
Betancourt,Rafael							4	5	7	5	16	37
Betancourt,Yuniesky									3	13	19	35
Betemit,Wilson					0			1	7	9	8	25
Biggio,Craig	240	35	31	11	25	15	20	16	18	11	6	428
Billingsley,Chad										6	12	18
Birkins,Kurt										2	0	2
Bisenius,Joe											0	0
Blackburn,Nick											0	0
Blackley,Travis									0		0	0
Blake,Casey			1	0	1	0	11	17	9	11	11	61
Blalock,Hank						1	17	24	14	13	8	77
Blanco,Henry	0		6	9	6	4	2	5	5	6	0	43
Blanton,Joe								0	13	10	13	36
Blevins,Jerry											0	0
Bloomquist,Willie						3	3	2	4	5	2	19
Blum,Geoff			3	10	8	15	5	3	7	6	9	66
Bocachica,Hiram				0	3	1	0	1	0	0	1	6
Bonderman,Jeremy							2	8	9	13	7	39
Bonds,Barry	384	34	19	32	54	49	39	48	2	25	19	705
Bonifacio,Emilio											1	1
Bonser,Boof										6	4	10
Booker,Chris									0	1	0	1
Boone,Aaron	0	6	15	10	13	19	23		9	7	7	109
Bootcheck,Chris								0	1	0	4	5
Borchard,Joe						1	0	1	0	4	1	7
Borkowski,Dave			1	0	0		2			4	3	10
Borowski,Joe	4	0			0	8	14	0	3	9	8	46
Botts,Jason									0	1	2	3
Bourn,Michael										0	4	4
Bowen,Rob								0	1	2	5	8
Bowie,Micah			2	0						3	3	8
Boyer,Blaine									4	0	0	4
Braden,Dallas											0	0
Bradford,Chad		3	0	2	3	9	9	5	2	7	6	46
Bradley,Milton				3	3	6	18	16	10	13	11	80
Branyan,Russell		0	1	5	10	8	6	5	9	6	5	55
Braun,Ryan, Mil											22	22
Braun,Ryan, KC										0	0	0
Bray,Bill										3	1	4
Brazell,Craig								0				0
Brazoban,Yhency								4	4	0	0	8
Britton,Chris										4	1	5
Broadway,Lance											2	2
Brocail,Doug	15	8	12	5				4	3	1	6	54
Broussard,Ben						0	9	16	10	11	5	51
Brower,Jim			2	1	8	5	7	8	1	0	0	32
Brown,Andrew										1	2	3
Brown,Dee			0	0	0	4	0	2	3			9
Brown,Emil	1	0	0	1	2				18	13	8	43
Brown,Matt											0	0
Broxton,Jonathan									0	9	10	19
Bruney,Brian								2	0	3	2	7
Bruntlett,Eric							1	2	3	4	4	14
Buchholz,Clay											3	3
Buchholz,Taylor										1	5	6
Buck,John								4	10	8	7	29

Player	<98	98	99	00	01	02	03	04	05	06	07	Career
Buck,Travis											10	10
Buckner,Billy											1	1
Budde,Ryan											0	0
Buehrle,Mark				4	18	17	13	17	22	9	17	117
Bukvich,Ryan					1	0	1	0			2	4
Bulger,Jason								1	0	1		2
Bullington,Bryan								0		0		0
Burgos,Ambiorix								4	3	2		9
Burke,Chris						0	6	10	5			21
Burke,Jamie				0		1	5	0			6	12
Burnett,A.J.		3	5	9	14	0	7	11	9	11		69
Burrell,Pat			12	17	25	9	14	24	15	20		136
Burres,Brian										1	3	4
Burton,Jared											5	5
Buscher,Brian											1	1
Bush,David							7	6	12	6		31
Butler,Billy											7	7
Bynum,Freddie								0	3	2		5
Byrd,Marlon					0	16	5	6	2	13		42
Byrd,Paul	6	7	10	0	6	19		7	13	6	12	86
Byrdak,Tim		0	0	0				1	0	4		5
Byrnes,Eric			0	1	2	16	17	9	13	24		82
Cabrera,Asdrubal											7	7
Cabrera,Daniel							8	7	7	6		28
Cabrera,Fern							0	4	2	1		7
Cabrera,Melky								0	13	12		25
Cabrera,Miguel							12	19	27	33	29	120
Cabrera,Orlando	0	6	8	9	26	14	20	11	15	18	25	152
Cain,Matt									5	11	12	28
Cairo,Miguel	0	10	10	10	4	3	3	14	5	5	4	68
Calero,Kiko							3	6	5	7	1	22
Cali,Carmen							0	0			1	1
Callaspo,Alberto										1	1	2
Cameron,Kevin											4	4
Cameron,Mike	17	6	19	19	29	18	21	15	11	25	20	200
Camp,Shawn								4	0	5	0	9
Campillo,Jorge								0	0	0		0
Cano,Robinson									12	17	21	50
Cantu,Jorge								4	18	5	1	28
Capellan,Jose							0	1	5	0		6
Capps,Matt								0	7	14		21
Capuano,Chris							1	4	13	14	5	37
Carlyle,Buddy			0	0					0		3	3
Carmona,Fausto										1	22	23
Carpenter,Chris	2	11	9	5	13	3		12	20	19	0	94
Carrasco,Hector	21	5	3	6	4		2		10	8	0	59
Carroll,Brett											0	0
Carroll,Jamey							3	3	6	9	13	5	39
Carvajal,Marcos								2	0			2
Casanova,Raul	2	0		8	6	1		0			1	18
Casey,Sean	0	10	23	17	18	6	17	28	13	10	9	151
Cash,Kevin					0	0	3	0		0		3
Casilla,Alexi										0	1	1
Casilla,Santiago							0	0	0	4		4
Cassel,Jack											1	1
Castillo,Alberto	2	3	7	4	3	0	1	2	4		1	27
Castillo,Jose								9	9	7	2	27
Castillo,Luis	6	3	14	18	14	20	22	22	18	18	16	171
Casto,Kory											0	0
Castro,Fabio										3	0	3
Castro,Juan	3	3	0	3	1	2	8	5	7	6	1	39
Castro,Ramon			1	3	0	4	2	1	7	2	6	26
Catalanotto,Frank	1	4	5	8	17	7	15	5	16	14	9	101
Cate,Troy											1	1
Cavazos,Andy											0	0
Cedeno,Ronny								2	5	1		8
Chacin,Gustavo							1	14	5	1		21
Chacon,Shawn				7	4	9	2	11	1	6		40
Chamberlain,Joba											5	5
Chavez,Endy				0	3	10	10	1	13	4		41
Chavez,Eric		2	9	16	26	24	25	18	20	16	6	162
Chen,Bruce		1	1	11	4	1	0	4	13	0	0	35
Cherry,Rocky											1	1

Player	<98	98	99	00	01	02	03	04	05	06	07	Career
Chico,Matt											5	5
Choate,Randy			1	4	0	0	3	0	1	0		9
Choo,Shin-Soo								0	4	1		5
Chulk,Vinnie					0	4	5	2	5			16
Church,Ryan						1	8	9	16			34
Cintron,Alex				0	1	14	8	7	6	4		40
Cirillo,Jeff	56	26	22	19	14	9	3	1	6	8	5	169
Clark,Brady				0	4	1	7	12	22	8	2	56
Clark,Howie					0	3	1		0	0	4	4
Clark,Tony	34	15	19	6	16	1	4	7	18	0	4	124
Clarke,Darren											0	0
Claussen,Brandon						1	0	7	1			9
Clayton,Royce	66	12	15	8	10	8	7	11	11	7	4	159
Clemens,Roger	282	25	10	16	19	11	15	19	24	11	5	437
Clement,Jeff											2	2
Clement,Matt		1	6	5	4	11	10	12	11	1		61
Clevlen,Brent									2	0		2
Clippard,Tyler											1	1
Coats,Buck										0	0	0
Coffey,Todd									3	9	1	13
Collazo,Willie											0	0
Colome,Jesus					4	0	4	5	2	0	5	20
Colon,Bartolo	2	16	16	15	14	22	17	10	18	1	1	132
Colyer,Steve						2	0			0		2
Condrey,Clay					2	0			2	3		7
Conine,Jeff	79	6	10	9	24	9	16	17	10	8	5	193
Contreras,Jose						7	6	17	13	5		48
Cook,Aaron					2	3	6	6	12	9		38
Cora,Alex		1	0	6	6	13	13	17	5	6	4	71
Corcoran,Tim								0	5	0		5
Cordero,Chad						2	12	15	12	10		51
Cordero,Francisco		2	3	0	8	12	17	11	12	12		77
Corey,Bryan		0			0			3	1			4
Cormier,Lance							0	4	2	0		6
Cormier,Rheal	33		5	4	4	1	14	7	1	6	0	75
Corpas,Manny									3	15		18
Correia,Kevin							3	0	2	6	8	19
Cortez,Fernando								0	0			0
Costa,Shane									0	3	1	4
Coste,Chris										8	4	12
Cota,Humberto			0	0	0	2	6	1	1			10
Cotts,Neal					0	2	9	2	1			14
Counsell,Craig	8	13	2	5	14	15	5	10	22	9	6	109
Coutlangus,Jon										3		3
Crain,Jesse							4	10	7	0		21
Crawford,Carl					6	13	20	22	21	20		102
Crede,Joe			0	1	6	13	8	15	19	4		66
Crisp,Coco				3	7	14	20	9	16			69
Crosby,Bobby					0	14	12	8	4			38
Cruz,Enrique					0			0		0		0
Cruz,Jose	11	12	11	15	16	13	17	14	11	4	5	129
Cruz,Juan				4	3	0	7	0	6	6		26
Cruz,Nelson								0	3	4		7
Cuddyer,Michael				0	3	1	10	7	22	16		59
Cust,Jack				0	0	4	0		0	19		23
Damon,Johnny	26	17	18	26	17	22	18	26	25	21	15	231
Danks,John										4		4
DaVanon,Jeff		0		1	1	12	9	4	7	1		35
Davidson,Dave										0	0	0
Davies,Kyle									4	0	1	5
Davis,Doug		0	5	8	3	7	16	12	8	11		70
Davis,Jason					2	5	2	2	4	1		16
Davis,Kane		0	5	0		2			0			7
Davis,Rajai									0	5		5
Day,Dewon											0	0
De Aza,Alejandro											1	1
De Jong,Jordan										0		0
de la Cruz,Eulogio											0	0
de la Rosa,Jorge								0	2	2	3	7
DeJesus,David						0	9	16	14	15		54
Delcarmen,Manny									1	3	6	10
Delgado,Carlos	33	24	21	36	23	26	32	16	29	22	13	275
Dellucci,David	1	10	5	1	7	4	4	10	15	8	2	67

413

WIN SHARES BY YEAR

Player	<98	98	99	00	01	02	03	04	05	06	07	Career
Dempster,Ryan		0	6	17	7	4	0	2	14	6	8	64
Denorfia,Chris									0	2		2
DePaula,Julio											0	0
DeRosa,Mark		0	0	1	6	7	5	2	4	14	16	55
DeSalvo,Matt											0	0
Dessens,Elmer	2	1		10	10	15	7	5	4	5	0	59
Detwiler,Ross											0	0
Devine,Joey									0	0	1	1
Diaz,Matt						0	0	2	7	11		20
Diaz,Victor								1	7	0	2	10
DiFelice,Mike	6	5	8	2	1	4	6	0	0	0	1	33
Dillon,Joe										0	3	3
DiNardo,Lenny								1	1	0	6	8
Dobbs,Greg								1	2	1	7	11
Dohmann,Scott								3	1	1	3	8
Donnelly,Brendan						6	12	5	6	5	2	36
Dotel,Octavio			3	7	12	17	12	14	2	0	3	70
Doumit,Ryan									6	2	6	14
Dove,Dennis											0	0
Downs,Scott			3				0	0	5	6	8	22
Doyne,Cory											0	0
Drew,J.D.		3	10	18	22	15	13	31	12	19	12	155
Drew,Stephen										6	16	22
Driskill,Travis					5	1	0	0			0	6
Duchscherer,Justin					0		1	9	11	10	1	32
Duckworth,Brandon					5	2	2	0	0	0	2	11
Duffy,Chris									5	6	5	16
Duke,Zach									10	10	2	22
Dukes,Elijah											2	2
Dumatrait,Phil											0	0
Duncan,Chris									0	10	17	27
Duncan,Shelley											3	3
Dunn,Adam					10	20	13	29	25	18	18	133
Durbin,Chad			0	0	8	0	0	1		1	6	16
Durbin,J.D.								0			3	3
Durham,Ray	38	25	20	19	21	20	16	19	14	20	6	218
Dye,Jermaine	7	2	16	21	18	13	2	12	17	25	11	144
Easley,Damion	39	23	13	14	15	5	0	8	9	5	8	139
Eaton,Adam				9	5	0	7	6	5	4	2	38
Eckstein,David					12	21	11	10	27	13	12	106
Edmonds,Jim	66	24	5	29	30	29	22	33	25	11	9	283
Elarton,Scott			5	10	11	0		0	5	7	4	42
Eldred,Brad								1		0		1
Ellis,Mark					14	18		21	14	20		87
Ellison,Jason						0	1	6	0	0		7
Ellsbury,Jacoby											6	6
Embree,Alan	7	3	6	3	2	7	5	4	0	5	8	50
Encarnacion,Edwin								4	14	16		34
Encarnacion,Juan	1	4	8	14	5	14	15	12	18	15	5	111
Ennis,John						0		0				0
Ensberg,Morgan				0		2	15	11	27	16	6	77
Erstad,Darin	22	21	9	30	14	17	3	15	15	1	5	152
Escobar,Alex					1		1	3		4		9
Escobar,Kelvim	6	7	7	8	11	9	12	14	5	12	18	109
Escobar,Yunel											12	12
Esposito,Brian											0	0
Estes,Shawn	20	3	6	10	7	4	0	9	5	0		64
Estrada,Johnny					5	0	0	18	9	13	7	52
Ethier,Andre										11	13	24
Evans,Terry											0	0
Eveland,Dana								0	0	0	0	0
Everett,Adam					0	1	11	12	14	13	4	55
Eyre,Scott	2	2	0	0	2	4	5	4	9	5	3	36
Eyre,Willie										2	2	4
Fahey,Brandon										4	1	5
Falkenborg,Brian			0				0	0	0	0		0
Farnsworth,Kyle			5	0	9	0	7	3	14	5	3	46
Fasano,Sal	5	7	3	2	2	0			3	3	0	25
Feierabend,Ryan										1	0	1
Feldman,Scott									1	3	1	5
Feliciano,Pedro						0	3	1		8	6	18
Feliz,Pedro			0	0	2	8	9	9	13	12		53
Fick,Robert		2	2	4	10	12	14	2	6	1	1	54
Field,Nate					0	2	3	0	1	0		6
Fielder,Prince									2	16	27	45
Fields,Josh										0	12	12
Figgins,Chone					0	8	20	22	17	21		88
Figueroa,Luis				0						0	0	0
Finley,Steve	147	15	24	21	15	24	18	16	6	10	1	297
Flores,Jesus											6	6
Flores,Randy					1		2	3	1	3		10
Flores,Ron									1	3	1	5
Floyd,Cliff	22	18	9	19	26	22	15	13	24	9	8	185
Floyd,Gavin									2	0	2	4
Fogg,Josh					2	10	4	7	3	6	6	38
Fontenot,Mike									0		5	5
Ford,Lew							4	21	12	3	2	42
Fossum,Casey					2	6	3	0	5	4	0	20
Fox,Jake										0		0
Francis,Jeff								2	6	13	14	35
Francisco,Ben										1		1
Francisco,Frank								6		0	3	9
Franco,Julio	241	0		3	6	6	12	7	3	2		280
Francoeur,Jeff									12	15	20	47
Frandsen,Kevin										0	4	4
Franklin,Ryan		1			5	6	13	6	6	4	8	49
Frasor,Jason								9	6	4	3	22
Freel,Ryan					0		3	19	11	11	4	48
Fuentes,Brian					1	2	10	2	14	12	10	51
Fuld,Sam											0	0
Fultz,Aaron		3	3	1	3	3	7	4	5			29
Furcal,Rafael				17	9	20	25	20	26	27	15	159
Furmaniak,J.J.									0		0	0
Gabbard,Kason										2	5	7
Gagne,Eric			3	2	4	20	25	19	3	1	7	84
Galarraga,Armando											0	0
Gall,John									1	0	0	1
Gallagher,Sean											0	0
Gallardo,Yovani											9	9
Garcia,Anderson										0	0	0
Garcia,Freddy			16	8	18	11	8	15	17	14	1	108
Garcia,Harvey											0	0
Garciaparra,Nomar	28	27	32	29	3	26	25	11	5	17	11	214
Gardner,Lee							0			0	7	7
Garko,Ryan									0	6	12	18
Garland,Jon				1	8	8	10	11	20	15	13	86
Garza,Matt										1	4	5
Gathright,Joey							0	4	7	6		17
Gaudin,Chad							3	1	0	7	9	20
Geary,Geoff						0	1	3	10	3		17
German,Esteban						0	0	2	1	11	8	22
Germano,Justin									0		4	4
Giambi,Jason	38	23	30	38	38	34	28	8	24	22	6	289
Gibbons,Jay					4	12	18	4	15	9	1	63
Giese,Dan										0	0	0
Gil,Geronimo					2	7	3	1	1		0	14
Gil,Jerry								1			0	1
Giles,Brian	20	14	27	27	29	31	25	23	32	21	17	266
Giles,Marcus					9	5	28	17	23	17	12	111
Glaus,Troy		3	16	25	21	22	9	8	23	16	14	157
Glavine,Tom	162	23	14	21	16	19	7	14	14	13	10	313
Gload,Ross				0		0		7	0	4	7	18
Glover,Gary		0		4	5	3	1	1			4	18
Gobble,Jimmy							3	5	1	4	5	18
Gomes,Jonny							0	0	14	6	8	28
Gomez,Carlos											2	2
Gomez,Chris	34	15	6	1	8	11	2	8	4	5	4	98
Gonzalez,Adrian								1	1	16	25	43
Gonzalez,Alberto											0	0
Gonzalez,Alex	1	11	3	10	3	20	15	14	10	10		97
Gonzalez,Andy											1	1
Gonzalez,Edgar							1	0	0	3	5	9
Gonzalez,Enrique										3	0	3
Gonzalez,Luis	103	12	26	27	37	27	24	10	19	12	12	309
Gonzalez,Mike							0	8	6	11	3	28
Gordon,Alex											12	12

414

	WIN SHARES BY YEAR											
Player	<98	98	99	00	01	02	03	04	05	06	07	Career
Gordon,Tom	97	17	2		8	3	11	15	10	10	4	177
Gorneault,Nick											0	0
Gorzelanny,Tom									0	3	11	14
Gosling,Mike							1	1	0	1		3
Gotay,Ruben							3	5			6	14
Grabow,John						0	1	2	5	3		11
Graffanino,Tony	7	4	7	6	3	7	9	7	13	12	5	80
Granderson,Curtis							0	6	20	25		51
Green,Nick						8	6	2	0			16
Green,Sean									2	5		7
Green,Shawn	32	21	24	22	34	29	20	15	17	11	12	237
Greene,Khalil							1	20	16	13	19	69
Gregg,Kevin						2	6	2	4	10		24
Greinke,Zack								9	3	1	9	22
Griffey Jr.,Ken	215	29	31	24	14	5	6	15	19	9	14	381
Griffin,John-Ford								0		1		1
Grilli,Jason			0	1		0	1	4	4			10
Gronkiewicz,Lee										0		0
Gross,Gabe							2	2	10	4		18
Grudzielanek,Mark	34	13	13	15	17	12	18	8	18	13	12	173
Guardado,Eddie	14	5	4	8	12	14	15	8	10	3	0	93
Guerrero,Vladimir	10	29	28	29	23	28	18	27	27	24	29	272
Guerrier,Matt							0	5	5	9		19
Guillen,Carlos		2	0	8	14	12	12	22	8	25	19	122
Guillen,Jose	7	11	3	6	2	2	20	20	15	3	18	107
Guthrie,Jeremy							1	0	0	12		13
Gutierrez,Franklin							0	1	6			7
Gutierrez,Juan										0		0
Guzman,Angel								0	2			2
Guzman,Cristian			5	12	18	14	13	16	6		7	91
Guzman,Freddy							1	0	0	1		1
Guzman,Joel								0	0	0		0
Gwyn,Marc										0		0
Gwynn,Tony									1	3		4
Haeger,Charlie										2	0	2
Hafner,Travis					1	7	21	26	24	16		95
Hairston,Jerry		0	5	4	10	12	7	8	9	1	2	58
Hairston,Scott							3	0	0	7		10
Hall,Bill					1	4	7	17	20	10		59
Hall,Toby			0	6	7	10	8	11	3	0		45
Halladay,Roy		2	10	0	9	21	23	0	16	20	16	125
Hamels,Cole									8	15		23
Hamilton,Josh											11	11
Hammel,Jason								0	2			2
Hammock,Robby						6	3	0	1			10
Hampson,Justin								0	4			4
Hancock,Josh					0	0	2	1	5	1		9
Hanigan,Ryan										1		1
Hannahan,Jack							0	5				5
Hanrahan,Joel								2				2
Hansack,Devern							1	0				1
Happ,J.A.								0				0
Harang,Aaron				4	2	5	11	18	17			57
Harden,Rich				4	14	12	4	2				36
Hardy,J.J.					11	3	19					33
Haren,Dan				1	2	13	14	17				47
Harikkala,Tim	0	0			5	0	0					5
Harris,Brendan					0	1	0	13				14
Harris,Willie			0	2	2	10	4	1	9			28
Hart,Corey					0	0	5	21				26
Hart,Kevin								2				2
Hatteberg,Scott	6	11	4	5	5	16	14	17	8	15	10	111
Hawkins,LaTroy	2	6	3	12	3	11	13	16	5	4	5	80
Hawpe,Brad					1	8	15	20				44
Haynes,Nathan								1				1
Headley,Chase								0				0
Heilman,Aaron			0	0	10	8	8					26
Heintz,Chris					1	0	1					2
Helms,Wes		1		0	5	1	12	4	5	10	2	40
Helton,Todd	2	17	19	29	26	27	34	30	25	21	22	252
Hendrickson,Mark					4	4	7	4	8	3		30
Henn,Sean						0	0	0				0
Hennessey,Brad					1	6	6	10				23

	WIN SHARES BY YEAR											
Player	<98	98	99	00	01	02	03	04	05	06	07	Career
Hensley,Clay								5	11	0		16
Herges,Matt		1	10	9	4	7	3	1	3	5		43
Hermida,Jeremy							3	6	13			22
Hernandez,A.							0	1	0			1
Hernandez,Felix							8	8	14			30
Hernandez,Livan	9	6	9	14	5	7	22	19	13	10	10	124
Hernandez,Luis									1			1
Hernandez,Orlando		13	14	12	4	11		8	5	7	9	83
Hernandez,Ramon		6	10	13	12	19	13	10	21	11		115
Hernandez,Rob	72	10	14	12	9	7	3	1	10	5	1	144
Hernandez,Yoel									0			0
Hessman,Mike				1	0			1				2
Hill,Aaron							9	14	20			43
Hill,Koyie				0	1	1		1				3
Hill,Rich						0	5	13				18
Hill,Shawn				0			1	6				7
Hillenbrand,Shea				5	17	11	13	15	8	1		70
Hinske,Eric				22	12	6	11	7	3			61
Hirsh,Jason							0	5				5
Hochevar,Luke								1				1
Hoey,Jim							0	0				0
Hoffman,Trevor	58	20	14	13	9	8	1	11	10	14	11	169
Holliday,Matt							9	17	19	27		72
Hoover,Paul		0	0				0	0				0
Hopper,Norris							2	7				9
Houlton,D.J.						2		1				3
House,J.R.				0	0		0	0				0
Howard,Ryan					1	10	29	26				66
Howell,J.P.					1	2	0					3
Howry,Bob	7	10	9	5	3	0	4	11	9	11		69
Hu,Chin-Lung								1				1
Huber,Jon							3	1				4
Huber,Justin					0	0	0					0
Hudson,Luke			0		4	1	5	0				10
Hudson,Orlando				7	18	16	15	20	21			97
Hudson,Tim		12	15	17	23	23	16	14	7	17		144
Huff,Aubrey		3	5	12	21	20	14	9	12			96
Hughes,Phil							4					4
Hull,Eric							0					0
Humber,Philip							0	0				0
Hunter,Torii	0	0	5	8	19	20	15	13	11	17	22	130
Iannetta,Chris							1	5				6
Ibanez,Raul	0	1	4	1	9	12	15	12	17	25	23	119
Igawa,Kei							1					1
Iguchi,Tadahito						18	19	15				52
Infante,Omar			3	3	12	7	5	4				34
Inge,Brandon			3	4	5	13	17	17	12			71
Inglett,Joe							6	1				7
Isringhausen,Jason	14		4	10	14	13	7	15	12	8	12	109
Iwamura,Akinori							13					13
Izturis,Cesar			4	4	11	25	6	3	5			58
Izturis,Maicer				1	6	13	16					36
Jackson,Conor					0	12	13					25
Jackson,Edwin			2	0	0	1	2					5
Jacobs,Mike					5	12	7					24
James,Chuck					1	8	8					17
Janssen,Casey					4	10						14
Jenkins,Geoff	1	18	20	11	4	20	12	20	15	11		132
Jenks,Bobby					6	12	16					34
Jennings,Jason			3	14	9	9	5	14	0			54
Jeter,Derek	38	27	35	23	28	24	18	26	26	32	24	301
Jimenez,D'Angelo	1		8	13	17	23	1	1	3			67
Jimenez,Kelvin							0					0
Jimenez,Ubaldo							0	4				4
Jimerson,Charlton						0	0	1				1
Johjima,Kenji						20	17					37
Johnson,Ben						1	2	0				3
Johnson,Dan						9	5	10				24
Johnson,Jim						0	0					0
Johnson,Josh					1	12	0					13
Johnson,Kelly					9		19					28
Johnson,Nick			0	11	14	6	20	25				76
Johnson,Randy	129	19	26	26	26	29	6	21	15	8	4	309

WIN SHARES BY YEAR

Player	<98	98	99	00	01	02	03	04	05	06	07	Career
Johnson,Reed							11	9	10	16	3	49
Johnson,Rob											0	0
Johnson,Tyler									0	1	2	3
Jones,Adam										1	0	1
Jones,Andruw	16	26	28	30	22	27	23	17	21	22	15	247
Jones,Brandon											0	0
Jones,Chipper	69	29	32	27	29	31	26	18	18	22	25	326
Jones,Garrett											0	0
Jones,Greg						1			0	0	0	1
Jones,Jacque			9	11	10	25	14	13	13	15	14	124
Jones,Todd	39	7	10	10	5	6	1	6	15	9	8	116
Jorgensen,Ryan							0				1	1
Julio,Jorge					1	13	6	8	1	7	4	40
Jurrjens,Jair										2		2
Karstens,Jeff										3	0	3
Kata,Matt						8	3	0			1	12
Kazmir,Scott							1	10	13	13		37
Kearns,Austin					16	12	5	10	17	20		80
Keisler,Randy				0	0		0		0	1	0	1
Kelly,Don											0	0
Kemp,Matt										3	10	13
Kendall,Jason	34	26	13	24	9	14	20	25	14	23	7	209
Kendrick,Howie										6	9	15
Kendrick,Kyle											9	9
Kennedy,Adam			2	11	8	17	14	13	17	15	2	99
Kennedy,Ian											2	2
Kennedy,Joe				6	9	0	13	3	6	4		41
Kensing,Logan								0	0	2	2	4
Kent,Jeff	85	25	23	37	27	28	20	22	28	18	17	330
Keppel,Bobby										1	0	1
Keppinger,Jeff						2				1	9	12
Kielty,Bobby				1	15	12	4	10	8	1		51
Kim,B-H		2	8	16	20	14	0	6	5	3		74
King,Ray			0	4	5	5	5	8	3	2	2	34
Kinney,Josh										2		2
Kinsler,Ian										12	17	29
Klesko,Ryan	63	13	18	23	29	30	13	18	15	1	7	230
Kline,Steve	1	6	7	9	12	6	5	7	3	5	2	63
Knott,Jon							0			0	1	1
Kolb,Dan			2	0	1	2	9	11	0	3	0	28
Komine,Shane										0	0	0
Konerko,Paul	0	2	14	15	17	17	4	20	24	21	16	150
Koplove,Mike					0	7	5	6	2	0	0	20
Koronka,John								0	4	0		4
Koshansky,Joe											0	0
Kotchman,Casey								2	4	0	15	21
Kotsay,Mark	1	13	6	12	16	22	14	21	19	11	3	138
Kouzmanoff,Kevin										1	15	16
Kroon,Marc	0	0					0					0
Kubel,Jason								3		1	12	16
Kuo,Hong-Chih									0	3	0	3
Kuwata,Masumi											0	0
Lackey,John						7	8	10	16	16	21	78
Laffey,Aaron											3	3
LaForest,Pete							0		0		2	2
Laird,Gerald							1	3	1	5	10	20
Lamb,Mike				6	8	7	0	12	6	9	10	58
Lane,Jason						3	1	5	14	7	2	32
Langerhans,Ryan							0	0	12	8	5	25
Lannan,John											2	2
Lara,Juan										0	0	0
LaRoche,Adam								7	11	16	16	50
LaRoche,Andy											2	2
LaRue,Jason			2	3	9	11	10	15	17	5	2	74
Lawrence,Brian					6	8	8	8	4	0		34
League,Brandon								1	0	5	0	6
LeCroy,Matthew			2	3	4	12	4	8	2	0		35
Ledee,Ricky		2	9	10	4	4	7	5	7	0	1	49
Ledezma,Wil							2	3	0	4	2	11
Lee,Carlos			10	14	15	17	20	22	21	22	21	162
Lee,Cliff						1	3	6	13	10	1	34
Lee,Derrek	2	10	1	16	16	22	25	19	34	4	21	170
Leicester,Jon								3	0		0	3

WIN SHARES BY YEAR

Player	<98	98	99	00	01	02	03	04	05	06	07	Career
Lerew,Anthony									0	0	0	0
Lester,Jon										5	4	9
Lewis,Colby						0	1	1		0	0	2
Lewis,Fred										1	5	6
Lewis,Jensen											4	4
Lidge,Brad						1	8	22	15	7	10	63
Lieber,Jon	24	8	13	12	16	7		10	12	6	3	111
Lieberthal,Mike	19	8	20	14	3	15	16	9	11	6	1	122
Lilly,Ted			0	0	3	6	10	15	4	11	15	64
Lincecum,Tim											8	8
Lind,Adam										3	7	10
Linden,Todd							1	0	1	2	3	7
Lindstrom,Matt											5	5
Linebrink,Scott				1	1	0	5	10	11	8	5	41
Liriano,Francisco									0	16		16
Litsch,Jesse											7	7
Littleton,Wes										6	3	9
Livingston,Bobby										0	2	2
Liz,Radhames											0	0
Lo Duca,Paul		0	2	2	28	19	19	20	11	16	9	126
Loaiza,Esteban	18	6	8	12	8	4	23	7	12	7	2	107
Loe,Kameron								0	8	2	3	13
Loewen,Adam									4	2	0	6
Lofton,Kenny	135	21	16	17	13	19	18	7	15	12	15	288
Logan,Boone										0	3	3
Logan,Nook							3	5	2	6		16
Lohse,Kyle					3	11	11	6	10	4	9	54
Loney,James										3	16	19
Looper,Braden		0	5	5	7	11	12	13	6	8	6	73
Lopez,Aquilino							10	1	1		1	13
Lopez,Felipe					5	6	3	9	21	16	11	71
Lopez,Javier							7	0	0	2	4	13
Lopez,Jose								3	5	16	10	34
Lopez,Pedro									1		1	2
Lopez,Rodrigo			0		15	2	14	8	4	4		47
Loretta,Mark	15	16	14	12	9	10	24	32	15	17	12	176
Lowe,Derek	1	7	19	19	11	22	12	6	11	15	11	134
Lowe,Mark										3	0	3
Lowell,Mike		0	8	20	20	19	23	22	8	16	23	159
Lowry,Noah							1	6	15	7	10	39
Lucy,Donny											0	0
Ludwick,Ryan							0	6	0	0	10	16
Lugo,Julio				9	9	9	14	20	24	13	11	109
Lugo,Ruddy										7	3	10
Luna,Hector								4	5	9	0	18
Lyon,Brandon						4	0	5	0	6	11	26
Mabry,John	31	5	3	3	1	8	2	8	3	3	0	67
MacDougal,Mike					1	0	9	0	8	5	0	23
Macias,Drew										0	0	0
Mackowiak,Rob					4	12	6	14	12	6	7	61
Maddux,Greg	231	25	17	24	20	19	11	13	11	12	9	392
Madson,Ryan							0	9	6	4	5	24
Mahar,Kevin											0	0
Mahay,Ron	3	2	3	1	2	0	5	8	0	4	7	35
Maholm,Paul									4	7	5	16
Maine,John								0	0	6	11	17
Majewski,Gary								1	8	4	0	13
Maldonado,Carlos										0	0	0
Marcum,Shaun									1	3	10	14
Markakis,Nick										12	20	32
Marmol,Carlos										1	11	12
Maroth,Mike						6	4	11	8	4	3	36
Marquis,Jason				1	8	3	1	14	12	2	8	49
Marshall,Jay										0		0
Marshall,Sean										2	6	8
Marte,Andy									0	4	0	4
Marte,Damaso			0		1	9	15	9	4	4	5	47
Martin,Russell										14	22	36
Martin,Tom	7	0	0	2	0	0	5	2	0	3	1	20
Martinez,Carlos										1	0	1
Martinez,Pedro	78	21	27	29	12	21	20	16	19	6	2	251
Martinez,Ramon		0	5	7	9	9	7	6	2	5	2	52
Martinez,Victor						1	3	20	22	18	29	93

WIN SHARES BY YEAR

Player	<98	98	99	00	01	02	03	04	05	06	07	Career
Masset,Nick										1	0	1
Mastny,Tom										1	4	5
Mateo,Julio						1	7	3	7	4	1	23
Mathieson,Scott										U		U
Mathis,Jeff									0	0	2	2
Matsui,Hideki							19	28	23	6	16	92
Matsui,Kaz								13	5	7	14	39
Matsuzaka,Daisuke											12	12
Matthews Jr.,Gary			1	1	10	10	9	11	11	21	14	88
Mauer,Joe								6	22	30	21	79
Maxwell,Justin											1	1
Maybin,Cameron											0	0
McAnulty,Paul									0	1	0	1
McBeth,Marcus											1	1
McBride,Macay									0	4	1	5
McCann,Brian									6	22	15	43
McCarthy,Brandon									5	5	3	13
McClain,Scott	0								0			0
McClellan,Zach											0	0
McClung,Seth							2		1	2	0	5
McDonald,Darnell							0					0
McDonald,John			0	0	0	5	2	1	4	3	8	23
McGowan,Dustin									0	0	11	11
McLeary,Marty							0		2	0		2
McLemore,Mark											3	3
McLouth,Nate									1	2	10	13
McPherson,Dallas								1	6	3		10
Meche,Gil			6	6			8	5	5	8	13	51
Medders,Brandon									5	6	2	13
Melhuse,Adam			0	0			4	5	2	1	2	14
Melillo,Kevin											0	0
Meloan,Jonathan											0	0
Mench,Kevin					10		4	13	12	9	8	56
Mendoza,Luis											2	2
Meredith,Cla									0	9	5	14
Mesa,Jose	61	5	5	3	14	13	0	12	5	6	1	125
Messenger,Randy									1	1	3	5
Metcalf,Travis											3	3
Meyer,Dan						0				0		0
Michaels,Jason					0	3	5	10	12	9	7	46
Mientkiewicz,Doug		0	3	0	18	17	20	6	4	8	4	80
Miles,Aaron							1	12	8	10	10	41
Millar,Kevin		0	12	10	20	14	16	17	11	13	12	125
Milledge,Lastings										4	6	10
Miller,Andrew										0	2	2
Miller,Corky				2	5	1	0	0	0		1	9
Miller,Damian	2	6	10	11	10	10	10	14	8	9	3	93
Miller,Jason										0	0	0
Miller,Justin					3		2	0			5	10
Miller,Matt						1	5	4	1	0		11
Miller,Trever	0	4	2	0			4	4	2	6	2	24
Miller,Wade			0	4	17	13	9	7	4		1	55
Millwood,Kevin	3	10	22	10	5	19	11	5	14	13	5	117
Milton,Eric		6	12	11	15	9	2	9	0	7	1	72
Miner,Zach										4	5	9
Mirabelli,Doug	1	1	3	6	7	4	2	7	4	2	2	39
Misch,Pat										0	2	2
Mitre,Sergio							0	0	2	0	4	6
Moehler,Brian		9	17	10	10	1	2	0		5	3	57
Moeller,Chad				2	0	6	6	5	3	1	0	23
Mohr,Dustan					1	11	6	9	3	0	0	30
Molina,Bengie		0	3	13	7	10	16	11	15	11	13	99
Molina,Gustavo											0	0
Molina,Jose			0		1	2	2	6	7	5	4	27
Molina,Yadier								5	14	9	12	40
Monroe,Craig					1	0	10	11	13	13	3	51
Montero,Miguel										0	3	3
Moore,Scott										1	1	2
Mora,Melvin			0	12	11	16	16	24	20	18	10	127
Morales,Franklin											4	4
Morales,Jose											1	1
Morales,Kendry										2	2	4
Morgan,Nyjer											4	4

WIN SHARES BY YEAR

Player	<98	98	99	00	01	02	03	04	05	06	07	Career
Morillo,Juan										0	0	0
Morneau,Justin							1	9	7	26	18	61
Morris,Matt	16	10		6	17	14	10	7	9	8	7	104
Morrow,Brandon											5	5
Morse,Mike									5	2	2	9
Morton,Colt											0	0
Moseley,Dustin										0	6	6
Moss,Brandon											1	1
Mota,Guillermo			5	1	2	2	14	12	3	3	1	43
Moyer,Jamie	77	18	18	5	15	16	18	5	12	10	8	202
Moylan,Peter										1	9	10
Mujica,Edward										1	0	1
Mulder,Mark				5	18	19	17	15	13	1	0	88
Muniz,Carlos											0	0
Munoz,Arnie								0				0
Munson,Eric				0	0	0	7	9	0	1	1	18
Munter,Scott									4	0	1	5
Murphy,Bill										0		0
Murphy,David										0	5	5
Murphy,Donnie									0	0	3	3
Murphy,Tommy										2	0	2
Murray,A.J.											1	1
Murton,Matt									4	13	5	22
Musser,Neal											1	1
Mussina,Mike	111	15	17	18	20	15	19	9	10	14	6	254
Myers,Brett						3	9	4	14	12	9	51
Myers,Mike	4	6	2	7	4	3	1	3	4	3	4	41
Myrow,Brian										1	0	1
Nady,Xavier			0				7	1	8	12	10	38
Napoli,Mike										10	8	18
Nathan,Joe			5	2		1	11	19	17	20	16	91
Navarro,Dioner								0	4	5	6	15
Nelson,Joe			0						0	5		5
Neshek,Pat										6	8	14
Newhan,David			1	0	0			13	2	0	1	17
Newman,Josh											0	0
Niekro,Lance								0	6	3	0	9
Nieve,Fernando										6		6
Nieves,Wil					1				0	0	1	2
Nippert,Dustin									1	0	1	2
Nix,Laynce							4	7	4		0	15
Nixon,Trot	0	0	10	14	20	16	19	4	15	10	4	112
Nolasco,Ricky									5	0		5
Norton,Greg	1	4	11	3	3	3	4	0		9	5	43
Nunez,Abraham	1	1	4	1	6	5	4	2	12	4	3	43
Nunez,Leo									0	1	3	4
Obermueller,Wes						0	2	4	1		0	7
O'Flaherty,Eric										0	4	4
Ohka,Tomo			0	6	2	14	12	5	10	4	1	54
Ohlendorf,Ross											1	1
Ohman,Will			0	0					4	5	2	11
Ojeda,Augie				2	2	1	0		3		4	12
Okajima,Hideki											11	11
Oliver,Darren	33	4	13	0	3	3	10	1		6	5	78
Olivo,Miguel						1	8	7	7	13	7	43
Olmedo,Ray							2	0	1	0	1	4
Olsen,Scott									1	10	1	12
Olson,Garrett											0	0
Ordonez,Magglio	3	13	20	22	25	25	23	8	10	19	34	202
Orr,Pete									3	2	0	5
Ortiz,David	2	9	0	8	7	11	15	24	30	27	27	160
Ortiz,Ramon			1	6	12	14	5	7	3	3	3	54
Ortiz,Russ	3	12	7	15	13	16	12	0	1	1		80
Ortmeier,Dan									0	0	3	3
Orvella,Chad									3	0	0	3
Osoria,Franquelis									1	0	1	2
Oswalt,Roy					15	20	10	18	21	20	17	121
Otsuka,Akinori								11	4	13	5	33
Overbay,Lyle					0	0	6	17	17	17	6	63
Owens,Henry										0	3	3
Owens,Jerry										0	6	6
Owings,Micah											13	13
Ozuna,Pablo		1				1	1		4	6	0	13

WIN SHARES BY YEAR

Player	<98	98	99	00	01	02	03	04	05	06	07	Career
Padilla,Vicente			0	6	3	14	13	5	6	12	2	61
Pagan,Angel										3	5	8
Palmeiro,Orlando	4	5	6	7	4	8	6	3	6	1	2	52
Papelbon,Jonathan									4	19	15	38
Park,Chan Ho	20	13	6	18	16	5	0	4	5	4	0	91
Paronto,Chad					0	2	0			4	3	9
Parra,Manny											2	2
Parrish,John				0	0		2	6	2		2	12
Patterson,Corey				0	3	8	13	17	4	13	8	66
Patterson,Eric											0	0
Patterson,John						3	0	2	14	2	0	21
Patton,Troy											1	1
Paul,Josh			0	3	4	2	1	2	1	4	1	18
Paulino,Felipe											0	0
Paulino,Ronny									0	14	10	24
Pavano,Carl		6	3	8	0	3	9	19	3		1	52
Payton,Jay		0	0	14	3	15	15	15	12	15	7	96
Pearce,Steve											2	2
Peavy,Jake						3	7	15	16	12	21	74
Pedroia,Dustin										2	18	20
Peguero,Jailen											0	0
Pelfrey,Mike										0	1	1
Pena,Brayan									0	1	0	1
Pena,Carlos						3	11	9	11	7	28	69
Pena,Tony										1	11	12
Pena,Tony F										0	11	11
Pena,Wily Mo						0	1	14	6	8	5	34
Pence,Hunter											18	18
Penn,Hayden										0	0	0
Penny,Brad				5	12	4	10	10	9	11	20	81
Peralta,Jhonny							4	0	25	15	21	65
Peralta,Joel									2	5	6	13
Percival,Troy	38	12	11	8	14	13	8	9	2		4	119
Perez,Juan										0	0	0
Perez,Neifi	9	12	14	15	11	6	8	7	12	4	1	99
Perez,Odalis	1	1		3	17	6	13	4	2	3		50
Perez,Oliver						4	1	16	2	0	10	33
Perez,Rafael										1	9	10
Perez,Timo				2	4	14	5	6	1	0	4	36
Perkins,Glen										1	2	3
Petit,Yusmeiro										0	3	3
Petrick,Billy											0	0
Pettitte,Andy	49	13	10	14	13	11	15	5	21	12	13	176
Phelps,Josh				0	0	10	10	5	4		5	34
Phillips,Andy								0	0	1	3	4
Phillips,Brandon						1	4	0	0	14	17	36
Phillips,Heath											1	1
Phillips,Jason				0	1	13	5	7	0	1		27
Phillips,Paul							0	2	2	0		4
Piazza,Mike	152	33	21	28	21	19	11	12	12	11	5	325
Pie,Felix											5	5
Pierre,Juan				3	17	15	20	22	14	15	12	118
Pierzynski,A.J.		1	0	3	15	18	22	12	11	14	8	104
Pignatiello,Carmen											0	0
Pineiro,Joel				0	7	14	13	5	3	0	5	47
Pinto,Renyel										2	4	6
Podsednik,Scott					0	1	22	13	12	9	1	58
Polanco,Placido		2	3	11	14	16	18	17	22	14	24	141
Ponson,Sidney		5	10	11	4	10	15	8	0	3	0	66
Posada,Jorge	6	15	10	29	23	22	28	21	19	24	24	221
Prado,Martin										2	1	3
Prinz,Bret				7	0	0	1	0		0		8
Prior,Mark						8	22	7	12	0		49
Proctor,Scott								1	0	9	6	16
Pujols,Albert					29	32	41	37	34	37	32	242
Punto,Nick					0	0	1	4	6	12	5	28
Putnam,Danny											0	0
Putz,J.J.							0	3	5	17	20	45
Qualls,Chad								4	7	9	9	29
Quentin,Carlos										5	5	10
Quinlan,Robb							0	8	2	8	1	19
Quintanilla,Omar									1	0	1	2
Quintero,Humberto							0	1	1	0	1	3

WIN SHARES BY YEAR

Player	<98	98	99	00	01	02	03	04	05	06	07	Career
Quiroz,Guillermo								0	0	0	1	1
Rabe,Josh										1	0	1
Rabelo,Mike										0	2	2
Raburn,Ryan										0	4	4
Rakers,Aaron									0	1	0	1
Ramirez,Aramis		2	0	3	27	6	19	19	18	21	21	136
Ramirez,Edwar											0	0
Ramirez,Elizardo								1	0	3	0	4
Ramirez,Erasmo								4	3	1	0	8
Ramirez,Hanley									0	25	27	52
Ramirez,Horacio							9	5	8	3	0	25
Ramirez,Manny	80	25	35	27	25	29	28	25	33	27	14	348
Ramirez,Ramon										7	0	7
Randolph,Stephen							6	3			0	9
Ransom,Cody				0	0	0	2			2		4
Rapada,Clay											0	0
Rasner,Darrell									0	1	1	2
Rauch,Jon						0		4	2	8	10	24
Ray,Chris									4	12	6	22
Redding,Tim					2	1	10	1	0		5	19
Redman,Mark			0	10	3	10	11	10	4	6	2	56
Redman,Tike				1	1	9	10	5		5		31
Redmond,Mike		4	12	5	6	13	1	6	7	6	11	71
Reed,Eric										0	0	0
Reed,Jeremy								3	9	1	0	13
Reitsma,Chris					3	7	8	7	9	0	0	34
Relaford,Desi	1	5	4	12	13	9	11	5	2		0	62
Renteria,Edgar	30	11	13	15	13	26	25	16	15	19	19	202
Repko,Jason									5	4	0	9
Resop,Chris									0	1	0	1
Restovich,Mike						0	2	1	1	0	0	4
Reyes,Al	5	4	5	1	2	2	1	2	9		6	37
Reyes,Anthony									1	3	0	4
Reyes,Dennys	2	2	5	2	1	4	0	4	1	9	2	32
Reyes,Jo-Jo											0	0
Reyes,Jose							12	4	16	28	24	84
Reynolds,Mark											14	14
Rheinecker,John										2	1	3
Richar,Danny											3	3
Ridgway,Jeff											0	0
Riggans,Shawn										1	0	1
Rincon,Juan					0	0	7	12	10	8	2	39
Ring,Royce									0	1	2	3
Rios,Alex								7	9	18	22	56
Riske,David		0		3	2	10	7	5	4	8		39
Rivas,Luis		1		8	6	6	9	4		0		34
Rivera,Juan					0	1	4	12	9	18	1	45
Rivera,Mariano	35	14	17	16	19	9	18	18	19	16	12	193
Rivera,Mike				0	1	0				4	0	5
Rivera,Saul										5	7	12
Roberson,Chris										0	0	0
Roberts,Brian					3	2	13	16	28	13	22	97
Roberts,Dave		2	0	0	19	8	12	14	19	10		84
Roberts,Ryan										0	0	0
Robertson,Connor											0	0
Robertson,Nate						0	1	8	7	14	8	38
Robles,Oscar									9	0	1	10
Rodney,Fernando						0	1		6	8	3	18
Rodriguez,Alex	58	30	23	37	37	35	32	29	34	25	37	377
Rodriguez,Francisco						1	9	17	14	17	15	73
Rodriguez,Guillermo											3	3
Rodriguez,Ivan	114	27	28	19	18	11	23	22	10	24	12	308
Rodriguez,Luis									6	1	1	8
Rodriguez,Wandy									2	2	7	11
Rogers,Brian										0	0	0
Rogers,Kenny	82	19	12	15	2	15	11	14	15	14	3	202
Rolen,Scott	31	30	15	18	29	26	25	35	5	21	11	246
Rollins,Jimmy				1	20	17	19	24	21	25	28	155
Romero,J.C.			1	0	1	14	3	8	5	0	8	40
Rosario,Francisco										0	0	0
Ross,Cody						1			0	6	10	17
Ross,Dave						1	4	2	3	13	7	30
Rottino,Vinny										0	0	0

WIN SHARES BY YEAR

Player	<98	98	99	00	01	02	03	04	05	06	07	Career
Rouse,Mike										1	1	2
Rowand,Aaron				5	7	6	20	18	7	21		84
Rowland-Smith,R											2	2
Ruggiano,Justin											0	0
Ruiz,Carlos										2	13	15
Ryan,B.J.			2	2	3	3	6	11	14	19	0	60
Ryan,Brendan											5	5
Ryan,Jae Kuk										0	0	0
Saarloos,Kirk					1	2	2	9	6	0		20
Sabathia,C.C.				12	13	13	11	12	15	24		100
Sadler,Donnie		3	1	2	2	1	1	0			0	10
Saenz,Olmedo	0		7	8	1	5		4	11	7	0	43
Saito,Takashi										18	17	35
Salas,Juan										0	2	2
Salazar,Jeff										2	4	6
Salmon,Brad											1	1
Saltalamacchia,J											5	5
Sammons,Clint											0	0
Sampson,Chris										4	5	9
Sanches,Brian									0	0	0	
Sanchez,Anibal										10	1	11
Sanchez,Duaner						0	0	6	7	6		19
Sanchez,Freddy						0	0	0	12	23	21	56
Sanchez,Jonathan										2	0	2
Sanchez,Romulo											1	1
Sanders,Reggie	91	14	19	6	14	14	18	14	11	5	3	209
Santana,Ervin									6	12	3	21
Santana,Johan				2	2	10	16	26	23	24	17	120
Santiago,Ramon					4	5	0	0	1	2		12
Santos,Victor					5	0	0	5	3	1	2	16
Sardinha,Bronson									0			0
Sarfate,Dennis									0	2		2
Saunders,Joe									0	4	7	11
Schierholtz,Nate											2	2
Schilling,Curt	86	22	15	16	24	24	15	21	4	15	10	252
Schmidt,Jason	10	11	13	1	9	10	22	19	9	15	0	119
Schneider,Brian				1	2	7	13	17	16	9	11	76
Schoeneweis,Scott			1	6	9	5	3	4	6	6	2	42
Schroder,Chris									0	3		3
Schultz,Mike										0		0
Schumaker,Skip									0	0	7	7
Scott,Luke									0	11	11	22
Scutaro,Marco						0	2	11	11	11	8	43
Seanez,Rudy	3	5	7	2	3	1	0	4	7	2	6	40
Seay,Bobby				0		1	2	0	0	6		9
Seddon,Chris											0	0
Segovia,Zack										0		0
Sele,Aaron	38	14	13	12	14	5	2	5	2	5	1	111
Seo,Jae					0	9	3	9	4	0		25
Serafini,Dan	2	2	0	2		0			0			6
Sexson,Richie	0	5	10	16	19	21	26	3	24	19	7	150
Sharpless,Josh									2	0		2
Shealy,Ryan									2	6	1	9
Shearn,Tom											2	2
Sheets,Ben					6	8	9	21	11	7	10	72
Sheffield,Gary	161	30	24	31	30	26	35	30	31	4	16	418
Sherrill,George						1	2	3	8			14
Shields,James									6	12		18
Shields,Scot				2	6	12	11	13	11	8		63
Shoppach,Kelly								0	3	7		10
Shouse,Brian	0	0			0	6	6	2	3	5		22
Shuey,Paul	8	6	10	8	6	7	7			0		52
Silva,Carlos				7	5	14	14	2	11			53
Simontacchi,Jason				8	2	0						10
Sisco,Andy						5	0	0				5
Sizemore,Grady						5	24	24	29			82
Slaten,Doug									1	4		5
Sledge,Terrmel						13	1	1	3			18
Slowey,Kevin										3		3
Smith,Jason				0	0	0	2	1	3	2		8
Smith,Joe										3		3
Smith,Matt								4	0			4
Smith,Seth										1		1

Player	<98	98	99	00	01	02	03	04	05	06	07	Career
Smoltz,John	147	16	18		8	17	16	16	19	15	14	286
Snell,Ian								0	1	8	11	20
Snelling,Chris				0			1	2	2			5
Snyder,Chris						2	4	7	16			29
Snyder,Kyle				4		0	1	3				8
Sonnanstine,Andy										3		3
Soria,Joakim										13		13
Soriano,Alfonso			0	0	16	28	27	16	16	26	20	149
Soriano,Rafael						1	7	0	1	7	9	25
Sosa,Jorge						2	5	3	14	2	6	32
Sosa,Sammy	113	35	26	30	42	27	22	12	4		11	322
Soto,Geovany									0	0	3	3
Sowers,Jeremy									7	0		7
Speier,Justin		0	1	7	5	7	8	7	7	6	7	55
Speier,Ryan									2	2		4
Speigner,Levale										0		0
Spiezio,Scott	12	10	6	6	9	17	12	4	0	12	7	95
Spilborghs,Ryan									0	3	9	12
Springer,Russ	12	3	5	3	0		0	1	3	5	8	40
Spurling,Chris							4	5	1	2		12
Stairs,Matt	21	20	20	10	11	7	13	11	14	7	13	147
Standridge,Jason					1	0	0	0	2	1	0	4
Stanford,Jason					3	1		1				5
Stansberry,Craig										0		0
Stanton,Mike	50	4	4	6	10	10	3	7	2	8	1	105
Stauffer,Tim								0	1	0		1
Stern,Adam								0	0	0		0
Stetter,Mitch										1		1
Stewart,Chris									0	1		1
Stewart,Ian										1		1
Stewart,Shannon	7	18	17	17	18	17	19	13	11	5	13	155
Stinnett,Kelly	9	10	6	5	5	4	4	2	1	2	1	49
Stocker,Mel										0	0	0
Stokes,Brian									1	0		1
Stone,Ricky				1	5	6	0	0		0		12
Street,Huston								16	14	10		40
Stults,Eric									1	1		2
Sullivan,Cory								10	6	4		20
Suppan,Jeff	5	2	12	12	9	14	9	13	12	9		109
Suzuki,Ichiro				36	26	23	27	22	24	33		191
Suzuki,Kurt										7		7
Sweeney,Mark	13	3	2	1	1	0	2	6	9	5	2	44
Sweeney,Mike	9	8	16	26	18	18	15	14	16	5	5	150
Sweeney,Ryan									0	0		0
Swisher,Nick							1	12	20	18		51
Switzer,Jon					0		0	2	0			2
Taguchi,So					1	3	6	12	6	9		37
Tallet,Brian					2	0		0	4	4		10
Tankersley,Taylor									5	4		9
Taschner,Jack							3	0	2			5
Tata,Jordan								0	0	0		0
Taubenheim,Ty									1	0		1
Tavarez,Julian	20	5	1	10	6	2	10	9	6	5	4	78
Taveras,Willy							0	13	13	11		37
Teahen,Mark								9	18	15		42
Teixeira,Mark						13	24	33	21	25		116
Tejada,Miguel	1	7	20	23	25	32	25	28	26	23	14	224
Tejeda,Robinson								5	4	0		9
Terrero,Luis					0	3	3	0	3			9
Thames,Marcus				0	0	6	1	11	6			24
Thatcher,Joe										2		2
Theriot,Ryan							0	6	11			17
Thigpen,Curtis									2			2
Thomas,Frank	232	25	16	34	1	16	23	12	3	21	17	400
Thome,Jim	96	19	26	20	31	33	30	20	4	25	21	325
Thompson,Brad								5	5	4		14
Thompson,Kevin									1	0		1
Thompson,Mike									2	0		2
Thompson,Rich									0			0
Thomson,John	10	9	0		7	7	11	13	4	2	1	64
Thorman,Scott									2	2		4
Thornton,Matt						2	1	7	4			14
Threets,Erick									0			0

WIN SHARES BY YEAR

Player	<98	98	99	00	01	02	03	04	05	06	07	Career
Timlin,Mike	43	12	9	6	5	8	8	7	14	6	5	123
Tomko,Brett	10	9	6	5	1	6	6	10	8	5	1	67
Torrealba,Yorvit					1	4	7	4	4	6	6	32
Torres,Salomon	6					3	5	11	10	9	3	47
Towers,Josh					6	0	5	6	13	0	2	32
Towles,J.R.											3	3
Traber,Billy							3			0	1	4
Trachsel,Steve	39	13	6	11	8	10	13	10	1	6	8	125
Tracy,Chad								11	19	14	6	50
Treanor,Matt							1	2	5	6		14
Tsao,Chin-hui							1	1	0		1	3
Tulowitzki,Troy										1	24	25
Turnbow,Derrick				2			2	1	17	2	6	30
Tyner,Jason				1	6	1	2		2	7	4	23
Uggla,Dan										23	16	39
Upton,B.J.								4		2	22	28
Upton,Justin											1	1
Urdaneta,Lino							0			0		0
Uribe,Juan				7	10	9	18	17	11	13		85
Utley,Chase							5	8	25	27	28	93
Valdez,Wilson								1	2		2	5
Valentin,Javier	0	2	5			0	2	4	11	3	6	33
Valentin,Jose	55	15	8	24	15	16	18	14	2	15	3	185
Valverde,Jose							11	3	13	4	14	45
Van Benschoten,J.							0			0		0
Vanden Hurk,Rick										0		0
Vargas,Claudio							6	3	6	7	5	27
Vargas,Jason									4	1	0	5
Varitek,Jason	0	5	12	7	8	12	17	18	18	7	14	118
Vasquez,Virgil										0		0
Vazquez,Javier		0	8	14	21	13	21	9	12	11	18	127
Vazquez,Ramon				0	14	10	1	1	1	1	6	33
Velandia,Jorge	0	0	1	0	0		2				3	6
Velez,Eugenio											1	1
Veras,Jose										1	1	2
Verlander,Justin									0	15	16	31
Vermilyea,Jamie											1	1
Victorino,Shane							0		1	11	11	23
Vidro,Jose	3	2	11	25	18	29	19	11	10	12	16	156
Villanueva,Carlos										4	8	12
Villarreal,Oscar							11	0	1	7	3	22
Villone,Ron	11	1	8	5	3	2	5	6	5	3	2	51
Vizcaino,Luis				0	0	2	8	1	6	6	7	36
Vizquel,Omar	98	18	22	16	12	21	5	18	20	20	12	262
Volquez,Edinson									0	0	2	2
Votto,Joey											3	3
Wagner,Billy	19	11	20	1	13	16	19	10	18	14	12	153
Wagner,Ryan							3	2	1	1	0	7
Wainwright,Adam								0	9	13		22
Wakefield,Tim	51	11	8	5	11	15	12	8	15	7	10	153
Walker,Jamie	2	0			4	7	6	4	5	8		36
Walker,Todd	3	19	9	5	12	22	15	13	13	11	0	122
Walker,Tyler					0		4	7	3	3	3	17
Wang,Chien-Ming									7	16	15	38
Ward,Daryle		0	3	3	5	10	0	7	7	6	4	45
Wasdin,John	12	4	7	3	3		0	1	6	1	0	37
Washburn,Jarrod		4	3	7	15	18	10	8	14	7	10	96
Wassermann,Ehren											3	3
Watkins,Tommy											1	1
Watson,Brandon								0	0	0		0
Weathers,David	8	4	6	7	10	7	8	5	8	10	13	86
Weaver,Jeff		7	12	13	14	2	11	13	3	1		76
Weaver,Jered										14	12	26
Webb,Brandon						17	11	17	20	22		87
Weeks,Rickie						0		9	10	14		33
Wellemeyer,Todd						0	1	0	4	4		9
Wells,David	99	18	13	18	5	15	14	10	11	4	3	210
Wells,Kip		3	2	6	13	16	6	3	0	2		51
Wells,Vernon		1	0	3	18	26	13	20	24	15		120
Werth,Jayson					1	1	11	9			13	35
Westbrook,Jake			0	2	1	6	15	8	13	9		54
Wheeler,Dan		1	1	0		3	3	10	12	4		34
White,Bill										1		1

WIN SHARES BY YEAR

Player	<98	98	99	00	01	02	03	04	05	06	07	Career
White,Rick	9	5	7	9	5	5	1	3	5	2	0	51
White,Rondell	48	16	15	14	12	6	15	11	12	1	1	151
White,Sean											1	1
Wickman,Bob	43	11	11	12	14	4		3	10	8	5	121
Wigginton,Ty					3	15	10	4	13	11		56
Wilkerson,Brad			1	17	18	19	19	5	11			90
Williams,Dave			7	1		2	6	1	0			17
Williams,Jerome						9	7	6	0	0		22
Williams,Todd	1	0	1		1		3	7	2	0		15
Williams,Woody	25	12	10	12	11	10	13	8	3	10	4	118
Williamson,Scott		17	11	0	10	7	4	0	1	1		51
Willingham,Josh							0	0	14	19		33
Willis,Dontrelle						14	9	22	13	7		65
Willits,Reggie									1	14		15
Wilson,Brian										1	5	6
Wilson,C.J.								0	3	9		12
Wilson,Craig				8	11	10	16	5	8	0		58
Wilson,Jack				5	12	11	22	14	12	19		95
Wilson,Josh									0	3		3
Wilson,Preston		1	13	20	10	10	20	2	14	9	0	99
Wilson,Vance			0	0	1	5	7	5	3	5		26
Winn,Randy		5	4	2	10	23	21	17	22	13	16	133
Wise,Dewayne			0	1		3		0	0	0		4
Wise,Matt			2	2	1		3	7	4	4		23
Witasick,Jay	0	0	5	3	6	6	2	3	6	0	1	32
Wolf,Randy			4	13	11	15	12	6	4	2	5	72
Wolf,Ross										0		0
Wolfe,Brian										4		4
Wood,Brandon										0		0
Wood,Jason		0	0						1	3		4
Wood,Kerry		14		7	13	12	18	9	4	2	2	81
Wood,Mike						0	2	5	1	1		9
Woods,Jake									1	6	0	7
Woodward,Chris			0	2	1	10	9	4	4	3	1	34
Wright,Chase											0	0
Wright,David							9	26	30	34		99
Wright,Jamey	8	8	7	9	7	2	2	5	4	4	5	61
Wright,Jaret	6	11	3	3	0	0	1	14	1	7	0	46
Wuertz,Mike								2	6	4	6	18
Yates,Tyler							0		3	2		5
Youkilis,Kevin							8	3	22	20		53
Youman,Shane									2	1		3
Young,Chris, SD								2	10	12	12	36
Young,Chris, Ari										2	14	16
Young,Delmon										2	17	19
Young,Delwyn										0	2	2
Young,Dmitri	5	16	10	14	13	5	19	8	9	2	16	117
Young,Michael			0	7	11	21	25	29	26	23		142
Zagurski,Mike											1	1
Zambrano,Carlos				0	5	18	20	18	17	16		94
Zambrano,Victor				6	4	10	8	7	0	0		35
Zarate,Mauro										0		0
Zaun,Gregg	15	3	3	9	4	2	2	11	14	8	9	80
Zimmerman,Ryan									2	24	20	46
Zito,Barry			9	15	25	18	12	13	17	8		117
Zobrist,Ben										2	1	3
Zumaya,Joel										12	3	15

Young Talent Inventory

Bill James

We are sitting in a historic bubble of young talent. About a year ago a
reporter (John Tomase) asked me an extremely interesting question: Why do you
think that there are so many great young players around right now? I replied in
my usual annoyingly cautious fashion that I didn't know whether there was or was
not an unusual amount of young talent around at the moment, but then later I
decided to study the issue.

Conclusion: there is no doubt that there is an unusual amount of great
young talent around right now. Arguably, there is more outstanding young talent
around right now than at any other moment in baseball history—not more per
team, but there are more teams. The moment at which there had been the most
young talent in baseball, before 2007, was 1964. Among the players in 1964 who
were 25 years old or younger and already doing some good work in The Show:
Dick Allen, Ken Berry, Jim Bouton, Lou Brock, Gates Brown, Wally Bunker,
Johnny Callison, Rico Carty, Dean Chance, Tony Conigliaro, Willie Davis, Larry
Dierker, Al Downing, Sammy Ellis, Dick Ellsworth, Ron Fairly, Bill Freehan, Jim
Fregosi, Dave Giusti, Dick Green, Jim Ray Hart, Alex Johnson, Deron Johnson,
Jim Kaat, Mickey Lolich, Jim Maloney, Dick McAuliffe, Tim McCarver, Sam
McDowell, Dave McNally, Tony Oliva, Claude Osteen, Milt Pappas, Gaylord
Perry, Vada Pinson, Boog Powell, Pete Rose, Ray Sadecki, Ron Santo, Willie
Stargell, Mel Stottlemyre, Luis Tiant, Joe Torre, Pete Ward, Don Wert, Zoilo
Versalles and Carl Yastrzemski. That was greatest explosion of young talent in
baseball history—until now. What we have now is even better than that.

Who is the best young player in baseball? A deceptively tricky question,
in that it requires us to combine two unlike factors—youth and talent—into one
measurement. C. C. Sabathia is certainly a better pitcher right now than Felix
Hernandez, but Sabathia was 26 in 2007; Hernandez was 21. Does Hernandez'
youth outweigh Sabathia's production? Alex Rios is probably a better player
right now than Jeff Francoeur, but Francoeur is three years younger. Both players
are 1) clearly still young, and 2) clearly very good. How do you balance
Francoeur's additional youth against Rios' additional accomplishments?

You just have to pick a method and roll with it. We're not talking here
about *prospects* or minor league players. We're discussing proven major league
players who are still young. This was my method, in short. First, I eliminated
from my study all players who were 29 years old in 2007 or older, since 29-year-
olds in 2007 are now 30, and 30-year-old baseball players are not young. A 28-
year-old player can be considered to have a little bit of youth left; a 30-year-old,
no way. Second, I figured the runs created by each player—for Rios, 105. Third,

I made a "speed adjustment", since speed correlates strongly with defensive value, and defensive value is more difficult to measure. Fourth, I divided that total by the runs scored/runs allowed per game by the player's team, thus building in context adjustments. Fifth, I multiplied that by the number of years the player had left before he was 33 years old. For Alex Rios, this creates an output of 216, which ranks. . .well, I'll get to that in a moment. For the pitchers, I developed a similar method based on runs allowed.

Why 33 years old, rather than 30? I tried it the other way and it doesn't work. Suppose that you have a 27-year-old player and a 24-year-old player of the same accomplishment. . .Jose Reyes and Albert Pujols, or Justin Verlander and Josh Beckett, or Edwin Encarnacion and Felipe Lopez. The 24-year-old *is* more valuable, and we want him to rank higher, but he's not *twice* as valuable. If we subtract his age from 30, that's 3 "years left" for the 27-year-olds, 6 years left for the 24-year-olds. It causes moderately good 22-year-olds to vault ahead of MVP-level 27-year-olds. Subtracting from 33 flattens the slope, creating better balance.

Combining youth *and* performance, Felix Hernandez ranks well ahead of Sabathia, Francoeur a little ahead of Rios, which is just my ranking. . .feel free to second guess, bitch and moan, or do your own ranking. Without further ado, here is my post-2007 Young Talent Inventory, starting with the 25 best young players in baseball today:

1. **Prince Fielder,** Milwaukee first baseman. I don't think Fielder should be the NL MVP, although he will get some votes, and, let's face it, he is not exactly a Prince of a Fielder. But 23-year-olds who hit 50 home runs don't come around every year.

Fielder has a "score" in our system of 323, but since the numbers are only relevant one to another, I'll skip those from now on. But I will list their ages, so that I don't have to comment on that. . .ages are as of June 30, 2007.

2. **Hanley Ramirez,** Florida shortstop (23). Ramirez followed up his Rookie-of-the-Year campaign with one of the greatest seasons ever by a young shortstop—.332 with 29 homers, 51 stolen bases, 48 doubles. Ramirez is lean, extremely strong and extremely fast, and, as a shortstop, he seems to be headed to third base.

3. **Fausto Carmona,** Cleveland starting pitcher (23). The third young ground-ball pitcher to have a breakthrough season in the last three years, following Brandon Webb and Chien-Ming Wang—and he was the best of the three in 2007.

4. **David Wright,** New York Mets third baseman (24). Wright vs. Reyes is too close to call. Can I keep them both for a couple of years and then decide?

5. **Felix Hernandez,** Seattle starting pitcher (21). The ace of the Seattle staff fired a one-hitter in his second start of the season, then struggled for two months. But he was 8-1 after July 27.

6. **Scott Kazmir,** Tampa Bay lefty (23). Sort of a shorter Steve Carlton, he battled the league's strictest pitch counts and missed leading the major leagues in strikeouts by one. He now has three straight winning seasons, which isn't that easy to do starting about five times a year against Toronto, Boston and the Yankees with the Tampa Bay Devil Rays behind you.

7. **Jose Reyes**, Mets shortstop (24). Probably baseball's best baserunner, he has three straight seasons of 60+ stolen bases, has hit 46 triples in the last three years—and has nearly tripled his walks over the last two years, from 27 to 77.

8. **Matt Cain,** San Francisco starting pitcher (22). His 7-16 record disguises one of the league's best pitchers, slider is probably his best pitch. He had the same number of quality starts last year as Brandon Webb (22), but whereas Webb was 17-2 with 3 no-decisions in those games, Cain was 6-8 with 8 no-decisions.

9. **Grady Sizemore,** Cleveland center fielder (24). Might have ranked first a year or two ago, although the competition was stiff. I've been trying to use comparable players to suggest an idea of where these guys might fit into history, but I keep coming up empty. Jose Reyes is sort of like Garry Templeton, but almost certainly better. Sizemore is along the lines of Vada Pinson or Enos Slaughter, but probably better than either one if he stays healthy. David Wright is kind of like Mike Schmidt, but not really. . .he out-hits Schmidt by 50 points, and probably won't quite match his power or defense. He's like Ron Santo, but faster. All of these guys are originals.

       The Indians had Hall of Fame center fielders for most of their first 55 years, in Tris Speaker, Earl Averill and Larry Doby. It's been awhile. Kenny Lofton has had a fantastic career, and I wouldn't dismiss the notion that he deserves Hall of Fame consideration, but he's bounced in and out of Cleveland like a bad penny, chopping up his career into little parts until he wound up as the premise of a moving company commercial. Let's hope that doesn't happen to Grady.

10. **Cole Hamels,** Philadelphia starting pitcher (23). Uses the changeup more often than a high school cheerleader. His health is the only thing that will keep him from being great—but remember, arm injuries don't strike down *some* great young pitchers, they strike down *most* great young pitchers.

11. **Ryan Zimmerman**, Washington third baseman (22). A Ken Boyer, Scott Rolen-type third baseman. You'll know if the Washington press corps ever starts going to baseball games, because if they do Zimmerman will be more famous than Britney Spears.

12. **Troy Tulowitzki**, Colorado shortstop (22). The complete package, apart from so-so speed. Coming out of college I thought he would be too muscular to play short, but he's a fantastic shortstop, also scored 100 runs as a rookie and drove in 99. You might compare him to Ripken, but he's much more athletic at short than Ripken was, although Ripken was an outstanding shortstop in his best years.

13. **Miguel Cabrera**, Florida third baseman (24). He's fat and he looks lazy, but he hits .320 and drives in 115 runs every year. As a hitter, he's in a class with Albert Pujols, Manny Ramirez and Albert Belle, just crushes the ball about 200 times a year. As a third baseman he's in a class with guys who really need to work on playing third base.

14. **Ryan Braun,** Milwaukee third baseman (23). Harmon Killebrew-type power, a little like a right-handed Jim Thome. He probably won't make it as a third baseman, either, which kind of sets up an interesting quandary for the Brewers, as to where they're going to hide his glove with Fielder over at first. But this guy may be a better hitter than Fielder, and it might be the smart thing for the Brewers to do to say screw the defense, we can give you seven runs and beat you with a football score. They could be the first team ever to have 50 home runs at each corner of the infield.

15. **Justin Verlander,** Detroit starting pitcher (24). As a rookie I was a little skeptical of him because, despite the 100-MPH fastball and the 17 wins, he struck out only 124 batters. But last year he was much more confident with his curve ball and his change, and his strikeouts were way up. There are Cy Young Awards in his future.

16. **Nick Markakis,** Baltimore right fielder (23). A beautiful left-handed stroke, sort of in the mold of Paul O'Neill, Mike Greenwell or Garret Anderson as a hitter, possibly even Billy Williams. Decent right fielder.

17. **Jake Peavy,** San Diego starting pitcher (26). Often cited as the best starting pitcher in baseball, which probably has quite a bit to do with park effects. Padre

fans at this moment are bellowing that Peavy was 10-1 with a 2.57 ERA on the road, as if this should preclude us from taking park effects into account.

18. **Adrian Gonzalez,** San Diego first baseman (25). Graceful but slow, he is somewhere between Rafael Palmeiro, Kent Hrbek and the Crime Dog. He hit .295 on the road with 33 doubles, 21 homers, 68 RBI—more than twice as many doubles, homers and RBI on the road as he had at home.

19. **Tom Gorzelanny,** Pittsburgh lefty (24). The heir to the mantle of Tom Glavine, Jamie Moyer, Kenny Rogers and Jimmy Key, which actually I think belongs to Ed Lopat and was stolen from Lopat by Johnny Podres or Claude Osteen or somebody, and lent to Randy Jones and then John Tudor.

20. **James Shields**, Tampa Bay (25). He plays Drysdale to Kazmir's Koufax, had an outstanding season despite allowing 28 home runs and working against hard pitch counts. Never wastes a pitch, with a strikeout/walk ratio of 184-36. He had 48 innings of ten pitches or less, only 32 innings of 20 pitches or more—a better ratio of quick innings to long innings than any of the big three Cy Young candidates (Beckett, Sabathia and Lackey. Beckett's ratio was 44-45, Sabathia's 58-55, Lackey's 57-40. Carmona actually was better than Shields, at 56-36.)

21. **C. C. Sabathia**, Cleveland lefty (26). I have to tell you, as a baseball fan, I absolutely adore C. C. Sabathia. I always have. I've compared all these players to somebody else. It is sacrilege to compare C. C. Sabathia to any other pitcher. He is totally unique. For one thing, although listed weights of baseball players are so bogus that it's hard to see the point of listing them, C. C. has to be the heaviest player in major league history. He's huge—6'7"and has an aircraft carrier frame supporting large piles of necessary and unnecessary flesh, all of this adorned with comic little ears that stick out from his face as if the Lord couldn't find a flat place to put them. He has a unique delivery, hanging his massive leg in the air in seeming defiance of both gravity and nature, yet he is balanced and graceful. He projects a sort of genial warrior calm on the mound. He was an outstanding pitcher when he reached the majors in 2001 and has gotten steadily better, cutting his walks from 95 in 180 innings to 37 in 241 innings. He's 26 now, like Peavy, and his age is pushing him downward on this list; he is less of a young talent, and more of a mature product. But I don't think I've ever missed a C. C. Sabathia start in Kansas City when I was near KC or in Boston since I've been in Boston, and I hope he pitches forever.

22. **Curtis Granderson,** Detroit center fielder (26). Came out of nowhere to be a sensational center fielder for Detroit these last two years, 26/27 as a base stealer

with an unheard-of 23 triples, brilliant defense. Engaging personality. Somewhere between Kenny Lofton and Andy Van Slyke, but could be better than either of them.

23. **Brandon Webb**, Arizona starting pitcher (26). Followed up a Cy Young season (2006) by increasing his innings pitched, strikeouts and wins, and cutting his ERA. I would bet that nobody has ever done that before.

24. **Chad Billingsley,** Dodger starter (22). A starter in 2006, he was in the bullpen until late June 2007, moved back to the rotation for 20 starts and was much better than he was as a rookie. Not that he was bad as a rookie. . .he was 7-4, 3.80 ERA. 2007 he was 12-5, 3.31. Uses a five-pitch mix with a cutter as the featured pitch. Fly ball pitcher, tough to run on. . .may not have the conditioning to endure as a front-line starter.

25. **Chris Young,** Arizona center fielder (23). Not your typical leadoff man, with 32 homers and a .237 average, but I guess it worked. Trim right-handed hitter with 40/40 potential, doesn't get cheated when he swings.

26-30 Jeff Francoeur, B. J. Upton, Russell Martin, Francisco Rodriguez, Alex Rios
31-35 Ian Snell, Dustin Pedroia, Chad Cordero, Matt Holliday, Dan Haren
36-40 Matt Capps, Hunter Pence, Adam Wainwright, Corey Hart, Robinson Cano
41-45 Delmon Young, Joe Blanton, Carl Crawford, Jeremy Accardo, Jeff Francis
46-50 Bobby Jenks, Chad Gaudin, Manny Corpas, Kelly Johnson, Kyle Kendrick

The number one team in terms of Young Talent is the Colorado Rockies, and here I'm going to have to revert to giving the values I assigned to each player, even though there is no real frame of reference for it. I credit the Rockies with 1,902 points worth of young talent—1,008 to the hitters, 895 for the pitchers, it rounds down. This is a team-by-team summary:

1. Rockies   **Hitters: 1008 Pitchers: 895 Total   1902**
Four Grade-A young players, in Tulowitzki, Holliday, Jeff Francis and Manny Corpas Delecti, with three more young and somewhat good or good and somewhat young talents in Brad Hawpe, Garrett Atkins and Willy Taveras.

2. Tampa Bay   **Hitters: 1072 Pitchers: 778 Total   1850**
Five Grade-A young players—Kazmir, Shields, B. J. Upton, Delmon Young and Carl Crawford. I know that a lot of people would list Delmon Young

in the top five young players in baseball, but I don't see that his performance justifies that, and this isn't about scouting reports or press clippings, it's about performance. Edwin Jackson just misses being A grade, and Sonnanstine ain't bad, either.

3. Arizona   Hitters: 930   Pitchers: 861 Total: 1791

Four young players among the top 75 in baseball, which is how I defined "Grade A"—Brandon Webb, Chris Young, Jose Valverde and Mark Reynolds, backed by Stephen Drew, Conor Jackson, Micah Owings and others.

4. Florida Marlins   Hitters: 1181 Pitchers: 605 Total: 1787

Hanley, Cabrera and Jeremy Hermida are Grade A, Dontrelle Willis has slipped to a B because of his off season and Dan Uggla is a B because he is 27, but he's good, too. Scott Olsen is in there.

5. Cleveland Indians Hitters: 970   Pitchers: 735 Total: 1705

Three players on the top 25 list (above), backed by Jhonny Peralta, Ryan Garko and Victor Martinez. Victor is 28, which is half-young.

6. Milwaukee   Hitters: 1237 Pitchers: 440 Total: 1677

They have the best young position players in baseball, and I believe they are the only team that has six Grade A young players (Fielder, Braun, Corey Hart, J. J. Hardy, Yovani Gallardo and Rickie Weeks.)   But the great young pitchers they had a couple of years ago all looked at the defense behind them and decided their best shot was to hide out on the disabled list for a couple of years.

7. Pittsburgh   Hitters: 752   Pitchers: 867 Total: 1619

The future is looking better with two good young starters (Gorzelanny and Snell), and a crack reliever (Capps). Maholm is a maybe (another starter) and Jose Bautista's a maybe at third. . .team needs Jason Bay to get back where he was.

8. Kansas City   Hitters: 837   Pitchers: 664 Total: 1501

More depth than flash, with reliever Joakim Soria and third baseman Alex Gordon scoring as low A's, but lots of depth with Greinke, Teahen, Butler, Bannister, DeJesus and Pena.

9. Oakland   Hitters: 617   Pitchers: 851 Total: 1468

Oakland has a different set of expectations than most of the young teams, like Pittsburgh and Kansas City, Tampa Bay. Oakland is accustomed to winning. Three starters are Grade A (Haren, Blanton and Gaudin), Huston Street, Travis

Buck and Nick Swisher are B's and could be A's, but the injuries to Chavez, the failure of Dan Johnson to develop, and the wipeout of Rich (Hardy Harr) Harden have pushed the team at least temporarily off course.

10. Toronto   **Hitters: 561**   **Pitchers: 841**   **Total: 1402**
       Grade A: Alex Rios, Jeremy Accardo, Aaron Hill
       Grade B: Dustin McGowan, Shaun Marcum, Jesse Litsch, Casey Janssen

11. Minnesota   **Hitters: 679**   **Pitchers: 717**   **Total: 1396**
       Grade A: Morneau
       Grade B: Mauer, Santana, Kubel, Baker, Bartlett, Bonser, Cuddyer
       Mauer being evaluated in an off year, Santana is great but no longer so young.

12. Philadelphia   **Hitters: 737**   **Pitchers: 640**   **Total: 1377**
       Grade A: Cole Hamels, Kyle Kendrick, Jimmy Rollins
       Grade B: Ryan Howard, Chase Utley, Brett Myers, Shane Victorino
       Most of the team has exited "young" and entered "prime", but is holding on to pieces of their youth.

13. Washington   **Hitters: 732**   **Pitchers: 538**   **Total: 1270**
       Grade A: Ryan Zimmerman, Chad Cordero
       Grade B: Matt Chico, Austin Kearns, Felipe Lopez

14. San Diego   **Hitters: 580**   **Pitchers: 645**   **Total: 1225**
       Grade A: Peavy and Adrian Gonzalez
       Grade B: Kouzmanoff, Khalil Greene, Justin Germano, Chris Young

15. LA Angels   **Hitters: 524**   **Pitchers: 674**   **Total: 1198**
       Grade A: K-Rod is still young enough to Grade A, although it seems like he has been around forever. Also Jered Weaver.
       Grade B: Kotchman and Howie Kendrick

16. Atlanta   **Hitters: 884**   **Pitchers: 301**   **Total: 1185**
       Grade A: Francoeur and Kelly Johnson
       Grade B: Brian McCann, Mark Teixeira, Chuck James, Yunel Escobar
       A year ago McCann rated very, very high after what may have been a fluke year.

17. New York Mets   **Hitters: 711**   **Pitchers: 455**   **Total: 1166**
       Grade A: Wright, Reyes, John Maine and Oliver Perez

Grade B: None

Competitive teams don't have as much room to let young players thrash around, and consequently most of the top teams don't show as having a lot of young talent. They may **have** the young talent; it just isn't in the lineup yet.

18. Boston Red Sox   Hitters: 500   Pitchers: 656 Total: 1156

Grade A: Dustin Pedroia, Jon Papelbon, Josh Beckett and Daisuke Matsuzaka.

Grade B: Youkilis and Coco Crisp.

The young players Boston is most excited about, Ellsbury and Buchholz, don't show up yet because they spent most of the 2007 season in the minors.

19. San Francisco   Hitters: 220   Pitchers: 877 Total: 1098

Grade A: Matt Cain

Grade B: Lincecum and Noah Lowry.

The young pitching is very good, but it would be the understatement of the Bay to say that the lineup needs a lot of work.

20. Dodgers   Hitters: 702   Pitchers: 347   Total: 1049

Grade A: Billingsley, Russell Martin, James Loney and Matt Kemp

Grade B: Andre Ethier, Jonathan Broxton.

21. Texas Rangers   Hitters: 450   Pitchers: 491   Total: 941

Grade A: None

Grade B: Kinsler

Players acquired in mid-season (Saltalamacchia, Gabbard, Murphy) may grade better next year.

22. Baltimore   Hitters: 336   Pitchers: 552   Total: 888

Grade A: Markakis

Grade B: Erik Bedard, Daniel Cabrera, Jeremy Guthrie.

Bedard is great, but not a Grade A *young* player because he is 28.

23. Cincinnati Reds   Hitters: 686   Pitchers: 201   Total 887

Grade A: Brandon Phillips

Grade B: Edwin Encarnacion, Adam Dunn

24. White Sox   Hitters: 252   Pitchers: 636   Total: 888

Grade A: Bobby Jenks

Grade B: Jon Garland, Mark Buerhle, John Danks

25. Seattle   Hitters: 339   Pitchers: 543   Total: 882
> Grade A: Felix Hernandez
> Grade B: Yuniesky Betancourt, Jose Lopez

26. Cardinals   Hitters: 557   Pitchers: 307   Total: 864
> Grade A: Adam Wainwright, Albert Pujols
> Grade B: None
> Let me note that there is almost no difference here between spots 22 and 26. . .they're all really about even.

27. Yankees   Hitters: 432   Pitchers: 390   Total: 822
> Grade A: Robinson Cano, Melky Cabrera, Chien-Ming Wang
> Grade B: None

28. Detroit   Hitters: 270   Pitchers: 545   Total: 814
> Grade A: Verlander, Granderson, Bonderman
> Grade B: None
> Grade C: None
> The Cardinals at least have three C's, in Chris Duncan, Brad Thompson and Yadier Molina. The Tigers are heavily dependant on the veteran stars that they brought in.

29. Cubs   Hitters: 228   Pitchers: 541   Total: 769
> Grade A: Carlos Zambrano
> Grade B: Rich Hill, Carlos Marmol
> Theriot, Marshall and Murton are C's.

30. Astros   Hitters: 255   Pitchers: 171   Total: 425
> Grade A: Hunter Pence
> Grade B: None

It will be interesting to see, looking backward ten years from now, to what extent the possession of young talent has predicted the pennant races of 2008-2012. I sort-of studied that a year ago, but only time and repetitions will really show us what that relationship is.

Bill James

(Editor's note: Bill James will explore the Young Talent Inventory in more depth in both *The Bill James Gold Mine 2008* and Bill James Online coming out in February 2008.)

Projected Batting Records

Bill James

Hi guys.   Well, it is time to 'fess up again.   We didn't nail them all.

This is the part of the book in which we attempt to tell you, in November of 2007, what Jason Bay's batting average will be in 2008. . . and not only Jason Bay, but also Carlos Quentin, Jerry Owens, Jhonny Peralta, Wily Mo Pena, Orlando Hudson and 400 other guys, and not only what his batting average will be but also how many games he will play, how many home runs he will hit, how many runs he will drive in, how many bases he will steal, and who he will vote for in the local elections.   We come pretty close sometimes —more on that later—and sometimes, we're just entirely wrong.   Let's start by looking at a few of the cases in which we were just entirely wrong last year:

Carlos Quentin

	G	AB	R	H	D	T	HR	RBI	BB	SO	SB	Avg	Slg
Actual	81	229	29	49	16	0	5	31	18	54	2	214	349
Projected	158	631	104	170	48	5	25	100	72	98	9	269	480

Quentin, a .309 hitter while slicing through the Arizona farm system, came to the big leagues for the last two months of 2006 and hit 9 homers, driving in 32 runs in a third of a season.   We figured he was over the hump.   Turned out he wasn't.   But we were closer on him than we were on Carlos Pena:

Carlos Pena

	G	AB	R	H	D	T	HR	RBI	BB	SO	SB	Avg	Slg
Actual	148	490	99	138	29	1	46	121	103	142	1	282	627
Projected	68	152	23	39	8	1	8	24	22	42	1	257	480

We hammered his stolen bases and his triples, though; you have to give us that.   We appear to have had Albert Pujols' projection confused with Prince Fielder's:

Albert Pujols

	G	AB	R	H	D	T	HR	RBI	BB	SO	SB	Avg	Slg
Actual	158	565	99	185	38	1	32	103	99	58	2	327	568
Projected	155	591	136	197	46	2	50	141	94	59	7	333	672

Prince Fielder

	G	AB	R	H	D	T	HR	RBI	BB	SO	SB	Avg	Slg
Actual	158	573	109	165	35	2	50	119	90	121	2	288	618
Projected	157	528	78	148	33	1	30	87	58	113	7	280	517

We got their batting averages about right, but we messed up their power and also, for some odd reason, we expected that Pujols would get to play in the 2007 All-Star game.   Jorge Posada, on the other hand, we got his power right but we were 72 points off on his batting average:

Jorge Posada

	G	AB	R	H	D	T	HR	RBI	BB	SO	SB	Avg	Slg
Actual	144	506	91	171	42	1	20	90	74	98	2	338	543
Projected	143	497	70	132	29	1	22	89	78	113	2	266	461

We appear to have confused Aaron Rowand with Vernon Wells:

Vernon Wells

	G	AB	R	H	D	T	HR	RBI	BB	SO	SB	Avg	Slg
Actual	149	584	85	143	36	4	16	80	49	89	10	245	402
Projected	156	618	91	178	40	3	30	100	50	89	12	288	508

Aaron Rowand

	G	AB	R	H	D	T	HR	RBI	BB	SO	SB	Avg	Slg
Actual	161	612	105	189	45	0	27	89	47	119	6	309	515
Projected	143	531	78	145	33	2	16	65	29	101	12	273	433

One year we did that with the two Alex Gonzalezes; our projection for one Alex Gonzalez was almost perfect for the other one, and vice versa.   In that case we probably really *did* have them confused.   We didn't see the power spikes coming for B. J. Upton, Brandon Phillips, Hanley Ramirez or J. J. Hardy:

B. J. Upton

	G	AB	R	H	D	T	HR	RBI	BB	SO	SB	Avg	Slg
Actual	129	474	86	142	25	1	24	82	65	154	22	300	508
Projected	144	480	74	127	24	3	11	47	60	112	43	265	396

Brandon Phillips

	G	AB	R	H	D	T	HR	RBI	BB	SO	SB	Avg	Slg
Actual	158	650	107	187	26	6	30	94	33	109	32	288	485
Projected	149	527	68	136	30	1	14	59	35	83	17	258	398

Hanley Ramirez

	G	AB	R	H	D	T	HR	RBI	BB	SO	SB	Avg	Slg
Actual	154	639	125	212	48	6	29	81	52	95	51	332	562
Projected	158	594	104	169	41	9	14	59	53	102	46	285	455

J.J. Hardy

	G	AB	R	H	D	T	HR	RBI	BB	SO	SB	Avg	Slg
Actual	151	592	89	164	30	1	26	80	40	73	2	277	463
Projected	115	417	53	105	24	0	13	55	45	57	1	252	403

Nor did we anticipate the power declines of Marcus Giles, Richie Sexson, Carlos Delgado or Pronk:

Marcus Giles

	G	AB	R	H	D	T	HR	RBI	BB	SO	SB	Avg	Slg
Actual	116	420	52	96	19	3	4	39	44	82	10	229	317
Projected	148	569	95	160	39	2	15	66	65	105	12	281	436

Richie Sexson

	G	AB	R	H	D	T	HR	RBI	BB	SO	SB	Avg	Slg
Actual	121	434	58	89	21	0	21	63	51	100	1	205	399
Projected	146	549	81	143	31	1	34	107	70	152	1	260	506

Carlos Delgado

	G	AB	R	H	D	T	HR	RBI	BB	SO	SB	Avg	Slg
Actual	139	538	71	139	30	0	24	87	52	118	4	258	448
Projected	150	555	93	153	36	1	37	118	88	136	0	276	544

Travis Hafner

	G	AB	R	H	D	T	HR	RBI	BB	SO	SB	Avg	Slg
Actual	152	545	80	145	25	2	24	100	102	115	1	266	451
Projected	145	526	102	157	39	1	37	115	94	129	0	298	587

We were blindsided by the poor seasons of Andruw Jones and Jason Bay:

Andruw Jones

	G	AB	R	H	D	T	HR	RBI	BB	SO	SB	Avg	Slg
Actual	154	572	83	127	27	2	26	94	70	138	5	222	413
Projected	159	594	102	157	32	2	40	115	74	131	5	264	527

Jason Bay

	G	AB	R	H	D	T	HR	RBI	BB	SO	SB	Avg	Slg
Actual	145	538	78	133	25	2	21	84	59	141	4	247	418
Projected	157	578	105	173	34	4	35	109	97	141	13	299	554

We didn't anticipate the injuries to Eric Chavez, Hank Blalock, Scott Rolen, or Joe Crede. . .was there like Freddie Kreuger or somebody attacking the major leagues' top third basemen?   We didn't even anticipate the injury to Rocco Baldelli, although in retrospect, we must have been the only people who didn't.

We dramatically over-projected playing time for many young players, among them Erick Aybar, Justin Huber, Ben Zobrist, Ryan Shealy, Matt Murton and Andy Marte.   I don't mind that.   I pitch a fit in the office about projections like this:

Troy Tulowitzki

	G	AB	R	H	D	T	HR	RBI	BB	SO	SB	Avg	Slg
Actual	155	609	104	177	33	5	24	99	57	130	7	291	479
Projected	129	447	68	123	31	2	12	50	43	76	8	275	434

I can't stand that, because to me, that's a gutless projection.   As I see it, nobody really expects us to know in October, 2007, which rookies will have how much playing time in 2008; we do the best we can to figure it out, but anybody who thinks we know that probably believes that Steve Moyer is secretly Batman. Our job, in my mind, is to answer this question: If this young player gets a chance to play, what will he do? What will his hitting stats be?

We miss *that* one sometimes, too—Alex Gordon—but I don't mind that. I hate the Tulowitzki-type projection because we gave a projection that was timid and compromised, rather than bold and plain spoken. I also foam at the mouth about projections like this one:

Franklin Gutierrez

	G	AB	R	H	D	T	HR	RBI	BB	SO	SB	Avg	Slg
Actual	100	271	41	72	13	2	13	36	21	77	8	266	472
Projected	49	105	18	27	8	0	2	10	10	23	3	257	390

What use is it to anybody to say that a young player is going to have 105 at bats and hit .257 with 2 homers?   In 105 at bats, *anybody* could hit .257 with 2 homers, Alex Rodriguez or Adam Everett, Albert Pujols or John Flaherty.   What use is it to show numbers that could be anybody's? If that's the only thing we have to offer about a young player, we should just keep quiet. Another one of those is Kevin Frandsen. If we'd just projected him into some reasonable amount of backup playing time, it would have been a great projection:

Kevin Frandsen

	G	AB	R	H	D	T	HR	RBI	BB	SO	SB	Avg	Slg
Actual	109	264	26	71	12	1	5	31	21	24	4	269	379
Projected	59	148	20	40	11	1	2	14	5	15	3	270	399

We were way off on Jim Edmonds, Magglio Ordonez, Marlon Byrd, Craig Monroe and Josh Barfield.   I mentioned Alex Gordon:

Alex Gordon

	G	AB	R	H	D	T	HR	RBI	BB	SO	SB	Avg	Slg
Actual	151	543	60	134	36	4	15	60	41	137	14	247	411
Projected	118	413	79	126	33	1	20	72	53	92	21	305	535

Which some people will take as evidence that we can't project what players will hit in the majors based on what they hit in the minors.   Nonsense; we project what players will hit all the time based on what they hit in the minors, and many times we're just about right. Look at our projections last year for Ryan Theriot, Ryan Garko, Josh Fields, Dustin Pedroia, Delmon Young and Chris Coste:

Ryan Theriot

	G	AB	R	H	D	T	HR	RBI	BB	SO	SB	Avg	Slg
Actual	148	537	80	143	30	2	3	45	49	50	28	266	346
Projected	149	536	77	154	29	6	3	49	57	59	31	287	381

Ryan Garko

	G	AB	R	H	D	T	HR	RBI	BB	SO	SB	Avg	Slg
Actual	138	484	62	140	29	1	21	61	34	94	0	289	483
Projected	149	527	72	141	30	1	20	95	54	100	3	268	442

Josh Fields

	G	AB	R	H	D	T	HR	RBI	BB	SO	SB	Avg	Slg
Actual	100	373	54	91	17	1	23	67	35	125	1	244	480
Projected	135	489	81	134	31	2	22	73	55	143	12	274	481

Dustin Pedroia

	G	AB	R	H	D	T	HR	RBI	BB	SO	SB	Avg	Slg
Actual	139	520	86	165	39	1	8	50	47	42	7	317	442
Projected	157	619	79	176	47	3	10	72	67	43	3	284	418

Delmon Young

	G	AB	R	H	D	T	HR	RBI	BB	SO	SB	Avg	Slg
Actual	162	645	65	186	38	0	13	93	26	127	10	288	408
Projected	157	594	83	179	34	6	18	89	23	110	33	301	470

Chris Coste

	G	AB	R	H	D	T	HR	RBI	BB	SO	SB	Avg	Slg
Actual	48	129	15	36	3	0	5	22	4	20	0	279	419
Projected	68	203	22	55	12	0	6	28	12	32	1	271	419

We just missed on Gordon because he had an off year, or we made a projection based on insufficient data. Sometimes a super-talented young player shoots through the minors before we have enough data to get a good read on his skills. Don't know what else we can do about that.

I made a transition there from bad projections to good ones. I had to; we were about to run out of bad projections. I had named just about every player in the majors whose performance was substantially different than we had projected. The reality is, most player's performance *wasn't* much different than we projected it to be—in 2007 or in any other year. We project, basically, that every player will continue to do in the future whatever he has done in the past. If a player has hit .250 in the past, we project that he will continue to hit .250. If he has hit .350 in the past, we project that he will continue to hit .350. If he hit .350 in 2006 and .250 in 2007, we project that he will hit .300 in 2008. We're pretty close to right most of the time, because most players in any season will continue to do about what they have done in the past.

Of course, we change the player's projections based on their age and some other things. We're often close to right, and sometimes, by dumb luck, we're close to spookily right. Like Brad Ausmus, Rob Mackowiak, Jeff Conine, Pedro Feliz, Carlos Beltran, Adrian Beltre and Mike Lamb:

Brad Ausmus

	G	AB	R	H	D	T	HR	RBI	BB	SO	SB	Avg	Slg
Actual	117	349	38	82	16	3	3	25	37	74	6	235	324
Projected	123	360	34	85	14	1	3	33	37	57	2	236	306

Rob Mackowiak

	G	AB	R	H	D	T	HR	RBI	BB	SO	SB	Avg	Slg
Actual	113	293	40	77	14	2	6	38	26	71	4	263	386
Projected	115	267	33	71	13	1	7	32	27	63	5	266	401

Jeff Conine

	G	AB	R	H	D	T	HR	RBI	BB	SO	SB	Avg	Slg
Actual	101	256	25	65	13	1	6	37	27	36	4	254	383
Projected	124	272	28	72	15	1	5	35	24	40	2	265	382

Pedro Feliz

	G	AB	R	H	D	T	HR	RBI	BB	SO	SB	Avg	Slg
Actual	150	557	61	141	28	2	20	72	29	70	2	253	418
Projected	144	491	60	122	27	2	19	75	27	92	1	248	428

Carlos Beltran

	G	AB	R	H	D	T	HR	RBI	BB	SO	SB	Avg	Slg
Actual	144	554	93	153	33	3	33	112	69	111	23	276	525
Projected	153	582	114	161	35	4	32	105	80	108	22	277	515

Adrian Beltre

	G	AB	R	H	D	T	HR	RBI	BB	SO	SB	Avg	Slg
Actual	149	595	87	164	41	2	26	99	38	104	14	276	482
Projected	154	582	78	158	34	2	26	89	46	104	8	271	471

Mike Lamb

	G	AB	R	H	D	T	HR	RBI	BB	SO	SB	Avg	Slg
Actual	124	311	45	90	14	2	11	40	36	45	0	289	453
Projected	124	338	51	94	18	2	11	46	31	56	1	278	441

We were on target about both of the Red Sox catchers:

Jason Varitek

	G	AB	R	H	D	T	HR	RBI	BB	SO	SB	Avg	Slg
Actual	131	435	57	111	15	3	17	68	71	122	1	255	421
Projected	129	468	60	121	29	1	17	69	56	118	2	259	434

Doug Mirabelli

	G	AB	R	H	D	T	HR	RBI	BB	SO	SB	Avg	Slg
Actual	48	114	9	23	3	0	5	16	11	41	0	202	360
Projected	56	150	15	32	8	0	5	20	15	49	0	213	367

I remember we had a long debate about whether 2007 would be Bengie Molina's year to steal a base or hit a triple, and it looks like we picked the wrong one:

Bengie Molina

	G	AB	R	H	D	T	HR	RBI	BB	SO	SB	Avg	Slg
Actual	134	497	38	137	19	1	19	81	15	53	0	276	433
Projected	127	465	47	128	21	0	16	68	23	49	1	275	424

Good prediction, anyway. Actually, we did pretty well on all three Molinas, although we were a little off on Yadier's batting average:

Jose Molina

	G	AB	R	H	D	T	HR	RBI	BB	SO	SB	Avg	Slg
Actual	69	191	18	49	13	0	1	19	5	43	2	257	340
Projected	90	243	22	60	13	0	4	27	11	50	1	247	350

Yadier Molina

	G	AB	R	H	D	T	HR	RBI	BB	SO	SB	Avg	Slg
Actual	111	353	30	97	15	0	6	40	34	43	1	275	368
Projected	118	360	30	88	19	0	6	46	24	32	1	244	347

Center fielders and catchers. . .we had real good projections last year for center fielders and catchers.   We had good projections for Mike Cameron, Juan Pierre, Dave Roberts and Kenny Lofton:

Mike Cameron

	G	AB	R	H	D	T	HR	RBI	BB	SO	SB	Avg	Slg
Actual	151	571	88	138	33	6	21	78	67	160	18	242	431
Projected	136	523	80	131	31	4	21	76	68	146	20	250	446

Juan Pierre

	G	AB	R	H	D	T	HR	RBI	BB	SO	SB	Avg	Slg
Actual	162	668	96	196	24	8	0	41	33	37	64	293	353
Projected	158	633	89	189	25	8	2	42	38	37	49	299	373

Dave Roberts

	G	AB	R	H	D	T	HR	RBI	BB	SO	SB	Avg	Slg
Actual	114	396	61	103	17	9	2	23	42	66	31	260	364
Projected	118	354	55	95	12	5	3	28	39	48	28	268	356

Kenny Lofton

	G	AB	R	H	D	T	HR	RBI	BB	SO	SB	Avg	Slg
Actual	136	490	86	145	25	6	7	38	56	51	23	296	414
Projected	134	484	83	139	20	5	6	43	50	52	23	287	386

Garrett Atkins' projection looks better than it is because we got his games played and at bats exactly right:

Garrett Atkins

	G	AB	R	H	D	T	HR	RBI	BB	SO	SB	Avg	Slg
Actual	157	605	83	182	35	1	25	111	67	96	3	301	486
Projected	157	605	97	188	45	1	22	104	67	71	2	311	498

Which actually isn't all that remarkable, because those are almost the same numbers he had in 2006. David Wright and Miguel Cabrera are easy, because they're great every year:

David Wright

	G	AB	R	H	D	T	HR	RBI	BB	SO	SB	Avg	Slg
Actual	160	604	113	196	42	1	30	107	94	115	34	325	546
Projected	150	567	100	179	42	3	29	112	66	99	18	316	554

Miguel Cabrera

	G	AB	R	H	D	T	HR	RBI	BB	SO	SB	Avg	Slg
Actual	157	588	91	188	38	2	34	119	79	127	2	320	565
Projected	160	609	113	200	48	3	32	125	80	119	7	328	575

Whereas it took some serious luck to come as close as we did on Ian Kinsler, Dioner Navarro and Brad Hawpe:

Ian Kinsler

	G	AB	R	H	D	T	HR	RBI	BB	SO	SB	Avg	Slg
Actual	130	483	96	127	22	2	20	61	62	83	23	263	441
Projected	155	539	84	145	33	1	20	74	47	78	15	269	445

Dioner Navarro

	G	AB	R	H	D	T	HR	RBI	BB	SO	SB	Avg	Slg
Actual	119	388	46	88	19	2	9	44	33	67	3	227	356
Projected	135	387	41	97	18	0	8	38	42	58	3	251	359

Brad Hawpe

	G	AB	R	H	D	T	HR	RBI	BB	SO	SB	Avg	Slg
Actual	152	516	80	150	33	4	29	116	81	137	0	291	539
Projected	152	586	80	170	37	5	26	101	83	132	5	290	503

We had other good projections. We had good projections on Luis Castillo, Pat Burrell, Geoff Blum, Willie Bloomquist, Derek Jeter, Miguel Cairo, Carlos Lee, Luis Gonzalez, Xavier Nady, Chris Gomez, Brian Roberts and Kenji Johjima. So Taguchi, Raul Ibanez, Kelly Shoppach, Jhonny Peralta and Kevin Youkilis. Most players do about what their history suggests they should do, and when they do, we have a good projection. There are other people who do these projections, and who claim to be better at it than we are, and you absolutely should feel free to believe them if you want to.

Addendum from Baseball Info Solutions:

Where did our annual Injury Projections disappear to? They went on the DL, of course. Seriously, Sig Mejdal, the St. Louis Cardinal employee who has done them for us, has not been able to share any of the improvements that he has made to the system and with others producing their own Injury Projections, he felt that he would step aside instead of sharing an "out of date" system. There is a good chance Injury Projections will return in the future.

2008 Hitter Projections

Hitter	Team	Age	G	AB	H	2B	3B	HR	R	RBI	RC	RC27	BB	SO	SB	CS	SB%	Avg	OBP	Slg	OPS
Abreu,Bobby	NYY	34	160	596	170	42	2	20	107	99	111	6.63	110	130	25	9	.74	.285	.399	.463	.862
Abreu,Tony	LAD	23	59	198	57	14	1	2	27	19	26	4.76	11	29	3	1	.75	.288	.332	.399	.731
Alou,Moises	NYM	41	123	455	133	25	1	19	60	71	78	6.28	46	48	3	1	.75	.292	.360	.477	.837
Amezaga,Alfredo	Fla	30	118	328	87	12	4	2	39	23	37	3.88	29	41	12	7	.63	.265	.331	.345	.675
Anderson,Garret	LAA	36	135	506	144	32	1	18	63	86	75	5.37	28	77	2	1	.67	.285	.322	.458	.781
Anderson,Marlon	NYM	34	51	122	32	6	1	3	16	15	16	4.57	10	21	3	1	.75	.262	.323	.402	.725
Ankiel,Rick	StL	28	131	456	117	19	2	29	67	94	68	5.18	29	97	4	2	.67	.257	.301	.498	.799
Antonelli,Matthew	LAD	23	62	229	63	12	1	7	41	29	37	5.63	35	47	13	5	.72	.275	.371	.428	.799
Atkins,Garrett	Col	28	157	605	188	43	1	24	92	113	116	7.22	69	81	2	1	.67	.311	.384	.504	.888
Aurilia,Rich	SF	36	106	333	89	18	1	10	42	41	45	4.80	26	49	1	0	1.00	.267	.324	.417	.742
Ausmus,Brad	Hou	39	68	210	48	8	1	2	20	18	19	3.03	22	39	2	1	.67	.229	.316	.305	.621
Aybar,Erick	LAA	24	60	175	45	8	1	2	23	16	17	3.25	8	22	10	6	.62	.257	.293	.349	.642
Baker,Jeff	Col	27	96	227	62	13	2	9	29	35	34	5.33	17	51	2	1	.67	.273	.327	.467	.793
Bako,Paul	Bal	36	55	140	28	5	0	1	11	10	10	2.32	14	43	0	0	.00	.200	.277	.257	.535
Baldelli,Rocco	TB	26	131	456	129	26	4	17	70	64	69	5.40	25	89	14	5	.74	.283	.329	.469	.798
Balentien,Wladimir	Sea	23	94	319	81	16	1	15	49	55	48	5.16	38	83	11	4	.73	.254	.333	.451	.785
Barajas,Rod	Phi	32	70	190	46	12	0	7	24	25	23	4.15	14	34	0	0	.00	.242	.304	.416	.720
Bard,Josh	SD	30	110	326	93	22	1	6	35	44	49	5.47	38	46	0	0	.00	.285	.360	.414	.774
Barfield,Josh	Cle	25	85	275	75	14	1	5	36	33	33	4.21	15	50	10	4	.71	.273	.315	.385	.701
Barrett,Michael	SD	31	116	382	100	24	1	12	42	48	51	4.69	29	57	1	1	.50	.262	.319	.424	.743
Bartlett,Jason	Min	28	134	482	138	25	4	5	74	44	65	4.83	43	63	17	6	.74	.286	.353	.386	.739
Barton,Daric	Oak	22	127	496	136	38	3	10	75	61	76	5.44	69	66	4	3	.57	.274	.364	.423	.787
Bautista,Jose	Pit	27	129	465	120	30	2	15	64	60	67	5.01	56	92	5	3	.62	.258	.345	.428	.773
Bay,Jason	Pit	29	148	518	143	31	3	26	84	91	94	6.47	73	138	7	3	.70	.276	.374	.498	.872
Belliard,Ronnie	Was	33	153	567	156	38	1	13	70	66	77	4.85	45	85	3	2	.60	.275	.331	.414	.745
Beltran,Carlos	NYM	31	151	579	159	35	4	32	107	106	110	6.73	78	112	23	5	.82	.275	.364	.515	.878
Beltre,Adrian	Sea	29	154	598	163	37	2	27	82	95	92	5.45	44	106	10	4	.71	.273	.327	.477	.803
Bennett,Gary	StL	36	71	176	41	8	0	2	13	19	16	3.08	13	27	1	0	1.00	.233	.289	.313	.602
Berkman,Lance	Hou	32	154	568	165	36	2	35	100	113	124	7.92	106	119	6	4	.60	.290	.408	.546	.954
Betancourt,Yuniesky	Sea	26	148	538	154	33	5	9	67	59	68	4.53	18	45	8	6	.57	.286	.311	.416	.727
Betemit,Wilson	NYY	26	132	331	87	18	1	17	48	55	54	5.73	42	91	1	1	.50	.263	.346	.477	.823
Blake,Casey	Cle	34	135	450	130	27	1	16	61	59	61	4.71	42	102	3	3	.50	.258	.331	.429	.760
Blalock,Hank	Tex	27	127	486	134	29	2	20	70	77	77	5.66	48	91	4	2	.67	.276	.343	.467	.810
Bloomquist,Willie	Sea	30	79	178	47	7	1	1	26	14	19	3.69	13	30	8	3	.73	.264	.318	.331	.649
Blum,Geoff	SD	35	121	335	81	18	1	6	34	35	36	3.69	28	57	1	0	1.00	.242	.304	.355	.659
Bonds,Barry	SF	43	122	320	91	17	1	26	69	63	92	10.40	125	50	4	1	.80	.284	.491	.588	1.079
Boone,Aaron	Fla	35	98	293	73	15	1	8	38	39	35	4.10	24	59	4	2	.67	.249	.325	.389	.714
Borchard,Joe	Fla	29	67	109	26	4	0	5	14	14	14	4.33	12	30	1	1	.50	.239	.320	.413	.733
Botts,Jason	Tex	27	81	279	78	21	2	9	42	42	48	6.18	41	81	1	1	.50	.280	.376	.466	.842
Bourn,Michael	Phi	25	74	123	34	3	2	1	23	9	17	4.80	14	24	14	3	.82	.276	.350	.358	.708
Bowen,Rob	Oak	27	57	152	35	8	0	4	22	16	18	4.00	23	48	1	0	1.00	.230	.335	.362	.697
Bradley,Milton	SD	30	71	252	70	14	1	10	39	36	42	5.90	34	52	3	3	.67	.278	.370	.460	.831
Branyan,Russell	StL	32	91	200	44	10	0	12	26	31	28	4.64	29	84	1	1	.50	.220	.325	.450	.775
Braun,Ryan	Mil	24	158	570	186	42	5	46	121	122	141	9.35	47	114	20	8	.71	.326	.383	.660	1.042
Brignac,Reid	TB	22	70	211	54	11	2	7	34	31	29	4.74	19	39	7	2	.78	.256	.317	.427	.744
Broussard,Ben	Sea	31	123	356	95	20	1	14	45	51	51	5.06	28	79	2	1	.67	.267	.329	.447	.776
Brown,Emil	KC	33	96	329	87	18	1	8	41	50	42	4.46	28	66	7	3	.70	.264	.328	.398	.726
Bruce,Jay	Cin	21	143	535	165	41	4	36	77	82	115	7.95	46	141	9	6	.60	.308	.363	.602	.965
Bruntlett,Eric	Hou	30	110	258	64	11	2	2	31	24	28	3.66	30	45	11	5	.69	.248	.329	.329	.658
Buck,John	KC	27	126	430	104	23	0	19	51	60	56	4.47	37	99	0	0	.00	.242	.312	.428	.740
Buck,Travis	Oak	24	112	408	118	35	6	10	59	49	73	6.48	54	83	7	3	.70	.289	.376	.478	.854
Burke,Chris	Hou	28	122	357	92	22	2	8	53	35	45	4.33	29	56	13	5	.72	.258	.327	.398	.725
Burke,Jamie	Sea	36	65	143	37	8	0	3	17	16	16	3.92	9	18	0	1	.50	.259	.312	.378	.689
Burrell,Pat	Phi	31	156	540	138	29	1	31	82	104	99	6.40	107	149	0	0	.00	.256	.382	.485	.867
Buscher,Brian	Min	27	102	336	90	18	1	9	39	43	46	4.82	34	45	3	2	.60	.268	.335	.408	.743
Butler,Billy	KC	22	145	512	152	35	2	17	73	90	88	6.36	54	75	1	0	1.00	.297	.365	.473	.838
Byrd,Marlon	Tex	30	116	376	105	20	3	9	50	48	52	4.93	29	78	5	3	.62	.279	.339	.420	.759
Byrnes,Eric	Ari	32	146	521	139	31	3	18	79	66	76	5.08	43	86	28	7	.80	.267	.331	.441	.772
Cabrera,Asdrubal	Cle	22	110	347	96	21	2	6	61	42	48	4.86	35	55	15	6	.71	.277	.345	.401	.745
Cabrera,Melky	NYY	23	150	541	153	26	5	10	75	73	75	4.96	48	65	14	5	.74	.283	.345	.405	.749
Cabrera,Miguel	Fla	25	159	606	198	44	2	35	100	128	142	9.00	81	123	3	2	.60	.327	.411	.579	.990
Cabrera,Orlando	LAA	33	156	619	169	39	1	9	83	73	78	4.46	46	62	17	5	.77	.273	.326	.383	.709
Cairo,Miguel	StL	34	74	164	41	8	1	1	20	16	17	3.54	11	23	7	2	.78	.250	.313	.329	.642
Callaspo,Alberto	Ari	25	74	201	57	11	2	3	27	21	27	4.81	16	14	2	2	.50	.284	.339	.403	.742
Cameron,Mike	SD	35	146	570	139	33	4	22	84	80	80	4.75	69	165	18	7	.72	.244	.333	.432	.764
Cano,Robinson	NYY	25	150	590	190	44	5	19	90	95	107	6.90	32	70	4	3	.57	.322	.362	.510	.872
Cantu,Jorge	Cin	25	75	180	49	13	1	6	21	29	26	5.16	11	33	0	0	.00	.272	.328	.456	.784
Carroll,Jamey	Col	34	82	195	51	9	1	1	33	15	22	3.89	24	31	4	3	.57	.262	.351	.333	.685
Casey,Sean	Det	33	129	422	123	26	1	8	50	56	61	5.29	38	42	1	1	.50	.291	.357	.415	.772
Casilla,Alexi	Min	23	98	312	80	12	1	2	44	30	36	3.56	28	46	24	9	.73	.256	.318	.321	.638
Castillo,Jose	Pit	27	98	275	72	15	1	6	30	34	32	4.08	15	50	1	1	.50	.262	.305	.389	.694
Castillo,Luis	NYM	32	146	575	172	18	4	3	89	40	77	4.85	64	56	20	10	.67	.299	.370	.360	.730
Casto,Kory	Was	26	71	131	31	6	1	4	18	16	16	4.12	17	32	1	1	.50	.237	.324	.389	.714
Castro,Ramon	NYM	32	92	290	73	15	0	16	37	50	43	5.15	29	74	0	0	.00	.252	.322	.469	.791
Catalanotto,Frank	Tex	34	132	452	128	31	3	10	66	56	67	5.34	43	52	2	2	.50	.283	.356	.431	.787
Chavez,Endy	NYM	30	99	209	57	10	2	2	28	19	25	4.19	14	23	7	3	.70	.273	.318	.368	.687
Chavez,Eric	Oak	30	133	495	128	30	1	24	74	80	80	5.64	63	104	5	2	.71	.259	.343	.469	.812
Church,Ryan	Was	29	130	417	114	30	1	15	55	66	67	5.71	46	93	4	2	.67	.273	.353	.463	.815
Cintron,Alex	CWS	29	54	126	34	7	1	2	15	14	15	4.19	6	17	1	1	.50	.270	.308	.389	.697
Cirillo,Jeff	Ari	38	65	140	38	8	0	2	17	17	17	4.29	12	17	1	1	.50	.271	.338	.371	.709

442

2008 Hitter Projections

Hitter	Team	Age	G	AB	H	2B	3B	HR	R	RBI	RC	RC27	BB	SO	SB	CS	SB%	Avg	OBP	Slg	OPS
Clark,Brady	SD	35	74	147	39	7	0	2	19	14	17	4.02	15	21	2	2	.50	.265	.361	.354	.715
Clark,Tony	Ari	36	85	190	46	9	0	12	24	36	28	5.06	19	54	0	0	.00	.242	.314	.479	.793
Clayton,Royce	Bos	38	45	110	26	6	0	1	13	9	10	3.06	8	25	2	1	.67	.236	.300	.318	.618
Clement,Jeff	Sea	24	50	114	29	8	0	4	15	16	16	4.89	12	23	0	0	.00	.254	.325	.430	.755
Cora,Alex	Bos	32	52	153	37	6	1	2	17	13	15	3.33	10	19	2	1	.67	.242	.326	.333	.659
Costa,Shane	KC	26	75	185	52	14	1	4	25	18	26	5.04	12	21	4	1	.80	.281	.332	.432	.764
Coste,Chris	Phi	35	60	156	41	7	0	5	16	23	19	4.30	8	23	0	0	.00	.263	.307	.404	.711
Counsell,Craig	Mil	37	106	302	72	13	1	3	40	22	31	3.46	37	46	6	3	.67	.238	.331	.318	.649
Crawford,Carl	TB	26	154	619	185	30	13	13	94	75	98	5.73	34	102	49	11	.82	.299	.339	.452	.792
Crede,Joe	CWS	30	138	438	113	23	0	19	54	67	58	4.64	26	60	0	0	.00	.258	.306	.441	.746
Crisp,Coco	Bos	28	125	450	124	26	3	8	67	48	61	4.76	39	69	19	7	.73	.276	.335	.400	.735
Crosby,Bobby	Oak	28	108	375	92	21	1	11	51	41	46	4.18	35	65	8	3	.73	.245	.313	.395	.708
Cruz,Jose	SD	34	97	257	61	14	1	9	35	30	35	4.60	38	65	5	2	.71	.237	.336	.405	.740
Cruz,Nelson	Tex	27	103	362	99	21	1	18	53	60	58	5.65	34	92	6	4	.60	.273	.338	.486	.824
Cuddyer,Michael	Min	29	149	549	151	33	4	19	87	82	87	5.66	64	115	5	2	.71	.275	.356	.454	.810
Cust,Jack	Oak	29	138	500	127	26	1	30	85	88	99	6.90	124	176	0	0	.00	.254	.402	.490	.892
Damon,Johnny	NYY	34	152	604	168	33	3	15	107	70	90	5.28	66	85	23	7	.77	.278	.352	.417	.769
Davis,Rajai	SF	27	125	407	115	22	3	3	58	29	54	4.57	36	54	46	15	.75	.283	.344	.373	.717
De Aza,Alejandro	Fla	24	93	315	83	19	3	4	50	23	38	4.15	24	67	15	6	.71	.263	.318	.381	.699
DeJesus,David	KC	28	148	580	163	34	6	9	95	62	82	5.05	59	83	8	5	.62	.281	.361	.407	.768
Delgado,Carlos	NYM	36	144	520	140	32	1	30	79	101	95	6.48	73	123	2	1	.67	.269	.373	.508	.881
Dellucci,David	Cle	34	43	160	40	8	1	6	25	22	23	4.94	20	41	2	1	.67	.250	.344	.425	.769
Denorfia,Chris	Cin	27	86	287	89	17	1	8	43	38	50	6.44	30	45	9	4	.69	.310	.375	.460	.835
DeRosa,Mark	ChC	33	143	506	141	29	1	11	68	64	70	4.97	49	97	1	1	.50	.279	.348	.405	.753
Diaz,Matt	Atl	30	134	406	134	28	2	13	53	57	73	6.93	18	67	5	2	.71	.330	.364	.505	.869
Diaz,Victor	Tex	26	67	185	49	10	1	9	23	32	27	5.12	12	52	2	1	.67	.265	.313	.476	.789
Dobbs,Greg	Phi	29	113	305	85	17	2	7	39	45	42	4.92	25	53	5	2	.71	.279	.335	.416	.752
Doumit,Ryan	Pit	27	104	322	90	23	2	13	48	54	53	5.89	29	69	3	2	.60	.280	.354	.484	.838
Drew,J.D.	Bos	32	143	510	142	29	3	20	90	78	92	6.45	92	112	5	3	.62	.278	.393	.465	.857
Drew,Stephen	Ari	25	150	545	143	30	5	15	68	65	76	4.88	55	93	8	3	.73	.262	.332	.418	.751
Duffy,Chris	Pit	27	97	319	90	15	3	4	48	28	42	4.63	23	55	20	7	.74	.282	.340	.386	.726
Dukes,Elijah	TB	24	72	233	59	9	3	11	40	36	37	5.44	34	46	6	3	.67	.253	.351	.459	.810
Duncan,Chris	StL	27	131	434	116	23	1	26	66	77	78	6.36	59	119	2	1	.67	.267	.356	.505	.861
Duncan,Shelley	NYY	28	71	149	39	7	0	10	23	28	26	6.15	16	36	1	0	1.00	.262	.333	.510	.843
Dunn,Adam	Cin	28	158	566	142	31	4	43	107	103	116	7.06	118	183	8	3	.73	.251	.386	.537	.923
Durham,Ray	SF	36	135	446	115	25	2	13	66	57	61	4.73	49	70	8	4	.67	.258	.337	.410	.747
Dye,Jermaine	CWS	34	136	513	136	29	1	29	77	88	84	5.76	50	112	3	2	.60	.265	.336	.495	.831
Easley,Damion	NYM	38	66	162	38	8	0	6	20	20	19	3.95	16	29	1	1	.50	.235	.326	.395	.721
Eckstein,David	StL	33	140	552	160	24	1	4	77	41	67	4.39	39	39	11	5	.69	.290	.352	.359	.711
Edmonds,Jim	StL	38	110	351	94	21	1	19	56	62	64	6.45	56	93	2	1	.67	.268	.372	.496	.867
Ellis,Mark	Oak	31	146	541	146	30	3	15	81	65	74	4.82	48	87	6	4	.60	.270	.338	.420	.758
Ellsbury,Jacoby	Bos	24	125	463	148	29	5	5	78	46	79	6.32	39	55	42	10	.81	.320	.374	.436	.810
Encarnacion,Edwin	Cin	25	137	494	146	34	1	20	73	82	85	6.30	43	82	8	3	.73	.296	.366	.490	.856
Ensberg,Morgan	SD	32	119	340	85	17	1	17	52	53	55	5.59	56	78	1	1	.50	.250	.361	.456	.817
Erstad,Darin	CWS	34	71	193	50	9	1	3	25	20	22	3.97	16	33	4	1	.80	.259	.322	.363	.685
Escobar,Alex	Was	29	98	363	98	20	2	11	50	53	52	5.03	39	81	6	4	.60	.270	.341	.427	.700
Escobar,Yunel	Atl	25	120	410	126	27	2	5	59	46	63	5.65	42	60	9	6	.60	.307	.376	.420	.795
Estrada,Johnny	Mil	32	127	468	133	30	0	10	45	65	60	4.68	20	48	0	0	.00	.284	.319	.413	.732
Ethier,Andre	LAD	26	153	514	156	33	4	16	72	75	89	6.43	51	80	2	2	.50	.304	.371	.477	.847
Everett,Adam	Hou	31	148	492	121	25	2	7	54	48	50	3.46	30	76	11	5	.69	.246	.295	.348	.642
Feliz,Pedro	SF	33	140	480	121	26	2	18	57	70	59	4.26	26	76	1	1	.50	.252	.292	.425	.717
Fick,Robert	Was	34	69	106	26	5	0	2	12	12	12	3.90	11	20	0	0	.00	.245	.328	.349	.677
Fielder,Prince	Mil	24	157	560	162	35	1	44	101	111	125	8.13	79	113	4	2	.67	.289	.388	.591	.979
Fields,Josh	CWS	25	148	530	144	31	1	30	86	92	93	6.17	64	156	12	6	.67	.272	.351	.504	.855
Figgins,Chone	LAA	30	143	548	161	25	7	5	90	58	80	5.16	58	94	41	16	.72	.294	.361	.392	.754
Flores,Jesus	Was	23	79	231	59	12	0	6	29	35	28	4.23	19	56	0	0	.00	.255	.320	.385	.705
Floyd,Cliff	ChC	35	95	305	82	17	1	13	46	48	48	5.57	35	58	3	1	.75	.269	.359	.459	.818
Fontenot,Mike	ChC	28	90	298	83	20	3	5	43	32	43	5.13	30	51	5	3	.62	.279	.345	.416	.761
Ford,Lew	Min	31	68	154	40	9	1	3	22	17	20	4.48	16	28	4	2	.67	.260	.352	.390	.742
Francoeur,Jeff	Atl	24	158	562	162	35	2	22	77	98	87	5.61	32	106	5	3	.62	.288	.333	.475	.808
Frandsen,Kevin	SF	26	119	408	115	26	2	7	53	44	53	4.61	25	37	9	6	.60	.282	.330	.407	.736
Freel,Ryan	Cin	32	114	381	101	20	2	5	59	23	48	4.29	41	68	25	11	.69	.265	.347	.367	.715
Furcal,Rafael	LAD	30	153	623	178	30	5	11	102	56	90	5.14	63	82	28	10	.74	.286	.352	.403	.755
Garciaparra,Nomar	LAD	34	113	370	108	22	2	11	51	56	57	5.63	27	34	3	1	.75	.292	.347	.451	.798
Garko,Ryan	Cle	27	142	520	144	31	1	22	70	81	81	5.59	45	95	1	1	.50	.277	.348	.467	.816
Gathright,Joey	KC	27	118	463	132	18	4	1	72	40	60	4.52	54	68	34	14	.71	.285	.365	.348	.712
German,Esteban	KC	30	123	396	114	19	4	4	59	43	56	5.04	46	62	14	7	.67	.288	.366	.386	.753
Giambi,Jason	NYY	37	123	389	95	18	0	25	63	74	72	6.52	84	97	1	1	.50	.249	.400	.493	.894
Gibbons,Jay	Bal	31	92	274	70	17	0	10	32	38	36	4.59	20	44	0	0	.00	.255	.311	.427	.738
Giles,Brian	SD	37	126	504	138	30	2	16	76	70	83	5.83	86	63	6	4	.60	.274	.384	.437	.820
Giles,Marcus	SD	30	107	368	98	24	2	7	56	40	50	4.74	40	70	8	4	.67	.266	.346	.399	.746
Glaus,Troy	Tor	31	145	526	132	28	1	32	88	93	91	5.97	86	139	2	2	.50	.251	.360	.490	.851
Gload,Ross	KC	32	109	316	97	21	1	9	40	49	50	5.88	18	37	2	2	.50	.307	.346	.465	.811
Gomes,Jonny	TB	27	110	335	85	19	2	18	50	53	55	5.61	45	104	11	5	.69	.254	.354	.484	.838
Gomez,Carlos	NYM	22	72	181	49	9	2	3	24	19	24	4.55	13	35	20	5	.80	.271	.327	.392	.719
Gomez,Chris	Cle	37	91	221	61	11	0	2	23	21	25	4.04	14	25	1	1	.50	.276	.322	.353	.675
Gonzalez,Adrian	SD	26	154	550	162	38	2	27	87	102	104	6.84	53	104	0	0	.00	.295	.359	.518	.877
Gonzalez,Alex	Cin	31	120	425	108	28	1	13	51	55	52	4.25	26	82	1	1	.50	.254	.308	.416	.724
Gonzalez,Luis	LAD	40	113	366	97	22	1	12	51	51	56	5.39	50	47	3	1	.75	.265	.363	.429	.792
Gordon,Alex	KC	24	152	546	151	40	3	20	80	76	88	5.72	52	125	18	5	.78	.277	.349	.471	.820
Gotay,Ruben	NYM	25	63	128	33	8	1	3	17	16	16	4.33	11	24	2	1	.67	.258	.321	.406	.728

443

2008 Hitter Projections

Hitter	Team	Age	G	AB	H	2B	3B	HR	R	RBI	RC	RC27	BB	SO	SB	CS	SB%	Avg	OBP	Slg	OPS
Graffanino,Tony	Mil	36	91	199	52	10	1	4	30	22	25	4.39	19	34	2	1	.67	.261	.335	.382	.717
Granderson,Curtis	Det	27	149	568	167	34	15	22	102	72	107	6.85	55	132	20	5	.80	.294	.359	.523	.882
Green,Shawn	NYM	35	112	403	112	24	1	14	57	54	62	5.48	42	66	6	3	.67	.278	.355	.447	.801
Greene,Khalil	SD	28	147	554	140	39	2	23	77	84	76	4.75	40	116	4	2	.67	.253	.310	.455	.765
Griffey Jr.,Ken	Cin	38	125	495	130	24	0	29	72	84	84	5.95	67	99	3	2	.60	.263	.353	.487	.840
Gross,Gabe	Mil	28	98	228	62	15	1	8	37	31	38	5.88	34	47	2	2	.67	.272	.369	.452	.821
Grudzielanek,Mark	KC	38	110	442	126	25	1	6	60	41	55	4.51	23	63	2	1	.67	.285	.329	.387	.716
Guerrero,Vladimir	LAA	32	155	596	193	38	2	33	99	115	131	8.37	68	67	8	4	.67	.324	.399	.560	.960
Guillen,Carlos	Det	32	149	562	167	34	5	17	91	85	95	6.14	61	95	11	7	.61	.297	.368	.466	.834
Guillen,Jose	Sea	32	148	565	155	29	2	23	77	88	82	5.17	36	112	4	2	.67	.274	.333	.455	.788
Gutierrez,Franklin	Cle	25	115	393	108	26	1	13	70	45	58	5.16	34	87	14	7	.67	.275	.334	.445	.779
Guzman,Cristian	Was	30	132	530	143	24	8	6	72	45	62	4.11	31	74	9	5	.64	.270	.313	.379	.692
Gwynn,Tony	Mil	25	72	158	43	6	2	1	22	13	19	4.15	15	26	4	4	.69	.272	.335	.354	.690
Hafner,Travis	Cle	31	150	549	159	38	1	33	96	115	118	7.85	99	125	1	1	.50	.290	.405	.543	.948
Hairston,Jerry	Tex	32	65	117	28	6	0	2	16	10	12	3.43	10	17	4	2	.67	.239	.331	.342	.673
Hairston,Scott	SD	28	119	277	76	16	2	14	42	39	47	6.05	27	55	2	1	.67	.274	.341	.498	.839
Hall,Bill	Mil	28	150	539	142	40	3	22	79	77	82	5.30	50	149	7	5	.58	.263	.328	.471	.800
Hall,Toby	CWS	32	46	138	35	7	0	3	11	16	15	3.79	6	13	0	0	.00	.254	.295	.370	.664
Hamilton,Josh	Cin	27	115	410	125	23	2	31	77	71	91	8.19	47	82	7	4	.64	.305	.382	.598	.979
Hannahan,Jack	Oak	28	71	231	64	15	0	6	33	36	37	5.69	40	59	3	2	.60	.277	.386	.420	.806
Hardy,J.J.	Mil	25	148	573	157	31	1	25	85	82	87	5.42	47	67	2	1	.67	.274	.330	.462	.793
Harris,Brendan	TB	27	127	467	129	30	2	11	63	60	65	4.97	40	84	4	2	.67	.276	.336	.420	.756
Harris,Willie	Atl	30	87	218	56	11	2	2	36	17	26	4.02	25	41	12	6	.67	.257	.339	.353	.692
Hart,Corey	Mil	26	140	489	145	33	7	23	85	79	91	6.70	40	94	24	9	.73	.297	.357	.534	.891
Hatteberg,Scott	Cin	38	55	180	49	10	0	4	22	22	25	4.96	24	19	0	0	.00	.272	.370	.394	.765
Hawpe,Brad	Col	29	150	522	154	32	4	27	77	105	107	7.54	83	123	1	1	.50	.295	.393	.527	.920
Headley,Chase	SD	24	126	467	145	37	4	18	85	81	99	7.97	77	130	1	1	.50	.310	.409	.522	.932
Helms,Wes	Phi	32	121	270	73	17	1	8	27	38	38	5.02	22	63	0	0	.00	.270	.334	.430	.764
Helton,Todd	Col	34	154	575	183	47	2	22	100	98	129	8.53	112	81	1	1	.50	.318	.433	.522	.954
Hermida,Jeremy	Fla	24	138	516	148	38	2	21	76	76	96	6.73	77	114	8	3	.73	.287	.384	.490	.874
Hernandez,Luis	Bal	24	51	125	31	4	1	0	12	10	10	2.71	6	16	2	2	.50	.248	.282	.296	.578
Hernandez,Ramon	Bal	32	120	440	116	23	0	15	52	70	59	4.72	38	68	1	1	.50	.264	.332	.418	.750
Hill,Aaron	Tor	26	154	571	167	41	2	13	82	68	86	5.51	43	78	4	2	.67	.292	.346	.440	.786
Hillenbrand,Shea	LAD	32	60	210	58	11	1	6	26	27	27	4.62	8	28	0	0	.00	.276	.327	.424	.751
Hinske,Eric	Bos	30	103	269	66	18	1	9	40	35	37	4.69	33	71	4	2	.67	.245	.334	.420	.755
Holliday,Matt	Col	28	156	612	199	47	5	33	111	121	135	8.40	56	117	10	5	.67	.325	.391	.580	.971
Hopper,Norris	Cin	29	90	220	70	8	1	0	31	15	29	4.90	14	19	11	4	.73	.318	.362	.364	.725
House,J.R.	Bal	28	45	110	33	8	0	4	14	18	19	6.42	9	15	0	0	.00	.300	.358	.482	.840
Howard,Ryan	Phi	28	149	554	168	31	1	53	101	144	149	10.04	105	177	1	0	1.00	.303	.419	.650	1.068
Hu,Chin-Lung	LAD	24	58	169	47	10	1	3	25	16	22	4.61	12	19	5	2	.71	.278	.326	.402	.728
Hudson,Orlando	Ari	30	151	563	159	33	6	12	77	68	85	5.42	62	90	8	4	.67	.282	.357	.426	.783
Huff,Aubrey	Bal	31	138	472	130	27	2	18	59	67	72	5.46	43	72	2	1	.67	.275	.341	.456	.797
Hunter,Torii	Min	32	152	581	159	36	2	27	88	98	90	5.44	43	108	15	8	.65	.274	.329	.482	.811
Iannetta,Chris	Col	25	67	237	65	13	2	7	33	32	37	5.59	33	50	0	0	.00	.274	.370	.435	.805
Ibanez,Raul	Sea	36	158	611	171	34	3	22	86	100	95	5.60	58	108	2	1	.67	.280	.344	.453	.798
Iguchi,Tadahito	Phi	33	146	558	160	32	2	18	90	76	90	5.79	63	99	16	6	.73	.287	.365	.444	.810
Infante,Omar	Det	26	56	145	39	8	1	3	18	15	18	4.37	10	23	3	1	.75	.269	.321	.400	.721
Inge,Brandon	Det	31	146	495	119	25	3	15	60	64	59	4.04	44	132	7	4	.64	.240	.311	.394	.705
Iwamura,Akinori	TB	29	144	521	153	23	8	8	89	37	80	5.53	65	110	12	8	.60	.294	.373	.415	.788
Izturis,Cesar	Pit	28	106	344	90	16	2	1	36	25	34	3.44	21	28	5	3	.62	.262	.306	.328	.634
Izturis,Maicer	LAA	27	121	400	114	23	3	6	60	50	57	5.09	43	42	10	5	.67	.285	.356	.403	.758
Jackson,Conor	Ari	26	136	468	138	35	1	16	71	76	84	6.60	62	54	2	1	.67	.295	.383	.476	.860
Jacobs,Mike	Fla	27	134	513	143	39	1	24	66	82	66	5.96	42	109	2	1	.67	.279	.336	.499	.835
Jenkins,Geoff	Mil	33	120	405	106	25	1	18	54	62	61	5.29	38	113	2	1	.67	.262	.341	.462	.803
Jeter,Derek	NYY	34	158	641	200	35	2	15	110	76	107	6.22	64	109	17	6	.74	.312	.385	.443	.828
Jimenez,DAngelo'	Was	30	74	165	44	9	1	4	23	19	24	5.07	26	26	3	2	.60	.267	.370	.406	.776
Johjima,Kenji	Sea	32	127	471	142	27	1	21	64	76	79	6.21	28	38	2	2	.50	.301	.357	.497	.854
Johnson,Dan	Oak	28	116	372	96	22	1	16	51	60	61	5.75	61	57	0	0	.00	.258	.366	.452	.817
Johnson,Kelly	Atl	26	147	539	152	30	8	19	98	76	96	6.43	87	109	10	5	.67	.282	.384	.473	.857
Johnson,Reed	Tor	31	100	279	77	15	1	5	40	29	35	4.46	17	54	4	2	.67	.276	.350	.391	.741
Jones,Adam	Sea	22	98	270	73	14	2	11	43	38	39	5.04	20	69	7	4	.64	.270	.323	.459	.782
Jones,Andruw	Atl	31	154	558	141	29	1	34	90	103	91	5.63	68	129	5	3	.62	.253	.343	.491	.834
Jones,Brandon	Atl	24	90	250	71	15	2	9	35	44	41	5.83	26	57	8	4	.67	.284	.354	.468	.822
Jones,Chipper	Atl	36	128	480	147	31	2	26	87	90	105	8.15	80	79	4	2	.67	.306	.406	.542	.948
Jones,Garrett	Min	27	78	175	44	11	1	7	24	29	24	4.73	14	39	1	1	.50	.251	.307	.446	.753
Jones,Jacque	ChC	33	120	443	123	25	1	14	56	61	62	4.99	32	87	6	3	.67	.278	.332	.433	.765
Kearns,Austin	Was	28	154	567	154	37	1	22	88	88	93	5.83	77	122	3	2	.60	.272	.368	.457	.824
Kemp,Matt	LAD	23	136	490	158	31	6	16	87	73	92	7.06	33	98	24	7	.77	.322	.365	.508	.873
Kendall,Jason	ChC	34	73	236	65	11	0	1	29	20	26	3.91	21	21	3	2	.60	.275	.369	.335	.704
Kendrick,Howie	LAA	24	128	496	158	39	3	12	74	71	81	6.14	15	79	11	5	.69	.319	.342	.482	.824
Kennedy,Adam	StL	32	110	323	87	16	2	4	39	32	38	4.10	25	48	9	5	.64	.269	.333	.368	.702
Kent,Jeff	LAD	40	144	535	155	35	2	22	82	90	93	6.33	60	82	2	2	.50	.290	.368	.486	.854
Keppinger,Jeff	Cin	28	80	255	82	14	1	3	35	26	40	5.98	23	14	2	1	.67	.322	.382	.420	.802
Kinsler,Ian	Tex	26	130	480	130	26	1	20	87	66	77	5.64	53	73	21	5	.81	.271	.351	.454	.805
Klesko,Ryan	SF	37	102	307	79	19	1	9	42	44	45	5.09	47	59	4	2	.67	.257	.358	.414	.771
Konerko,Paul	CWS	32	156	585	161	30	0	34	87	105	104	6.38	72	106	0	0	.00	.275	.360	.501	.861
Koshansky,Joe	Col	26	87	177	49	10	0	8	23	30	28	5.64	18	43	1	1	.50	.277	.344	.469	.813
Kotchman,Casey	LAA	25	137	447	122	32	2	12	60	66	67	5.33	51	44	2	2	.50	.273	.350	.434	.784
Kotsay,Mark	Oak	32	97	331	91	20	1	6	41	36	44	4.73	31	36	4	2	.67	.275	.339	.396	.735
Kouzmanoff,Kevin	SD	26	147	498	151	35	2	23	71	90	92	6.87	39	84	2	1	.67	.303	.362	.520	.882
Kubel,Jason	Min	26	128	428	118	28	2	15	55	68	66	5.50	40	75	5	2	.71	.276	.339	.456	.795

2008 Hitter Projections

PLAYER			BATTING												BASERUNNING			AVERAGES			
Hitter	Team	Age	G	AB	H	2B	3B	HR	R	RBI	RC	RC27	BB	SO	SB	CS	SB%	Avg	OBP	Slg	OPS
Laird,Gerald	Tex	28	101	315	80	16	2	9	45	37	39	4.28	23	70	5	2	.71	.254	.309	.403	.712
Lamb,Mike	Hou	32	121	308	86	15	1	10	46	41	46	5.39	30	49	0	0	.00	.279	.347	.432	.779
Lane,Jason	SD	31	80	196	48	11	0	10	27	33	28	4.89	21	36	2	1	.67	.245	.327	.454	.781
Langerhans,Ryan	Was	28	101	197	47	12	1	6	32	23	26	4.48	28	57	2	1	.67	.239	.339	.401	.740
LaRoche,Adam	Pit	28	152	528	145	41	0	25	74	89	91	6.18	58	124	1	0	1.00	.275	.350	.494	.844
LaRoche,Andy	LAD	24	138	465	128	28	0	19	77	73	78	5.95	66	84	7	4	.64	.275	.367	.458	.825
LaRue,Jason	KC	34	72	172	36	10	0	6	18	21	18	3.44	17	57	1	0	1.00	.209	.317	.372	.689
Lee,Carlos	Hou	32	155	601	175	38	1	31	93	108	107	6.45	54	71	11	5	.69	.291	.354	.512	.866
Lee,Derrek	ChC	32	136	515	153	35	1	25	82	80	100	7.10	69	111	7	4	.64	.297	.386	.515	.901
Lewis,Fred	SF	27	109	326	88	16	4	7	53	37	47	5.01	38	70	15	6	.71	.270	.350	.408	.758
Lind,Adam	Tor	24	95	310	92	19	1	14	40	55	54	6.41	24	68	1	1	.50	.297	.349	.500	.849
Linden,Todd	Fla	28	80	135	35	7	1	4	19	15	19	4.89	15	37	2	1	.67	.259	.342	.415	.757
Lo Duca,Paul	NYM	36	132	501	142	27	1	9	59	59	64	4.62	30	40	2	1	.67	.283	.331	.395	.727
Lofton,Kenny	Cle	41	113	415	114	17	4	5	65	34	54	4.57	44	45	16	6	.73	.275	.347	.371	.718
Logan,Nook	Was	28	92	226	59	10	2	0	30	14	24	3.63	17	51	15	5	.75	.261	.313	.323	.636
Loney,James	LAD	24	138	510	154	33	4	14	66	78	84	6.10	44	76	3	2	.60	.302	.359	.465	.823
Longoria,Evan	TB	22	147	500	142	29	0	27	92	93	92	6.64	44	111	5	2	.71	.284	.365	.504	.869
Lopez,Felipe	Was	28	156	610	161	30	4	14	86	64	81	4.59	64	121	24	10	.71	.264	.336	.395	.731
Lopez,Jose	Sea	24	134	466	126	25	3	10	59	62	56	4.26	19	54	3	2	.60	.270	.306	.401	.707
Loretta,Mark	Hou	36	122	445	127	23	1	5	53	42	58	4.73	41	44	2	1	.67	.285	.354	.375	.729
Lowell,Mike	Bos	34	140	490	138	34	1	17	64	81	77	5.67	47	62	2	1	.67	.282	.349	.459	.809
Ludwick,Ryan	StL	29	89	235	62	15	0	11	35	40	35	5.20	20	58	2	2	.50	.264	.329	.468	.798
Lugo,Julio	Bos	32	145	537	143	30	2	9	76	57	68	4.39	49	86	26	9	.74	.266	.331	.380	.711
Mackowiak,Rob	SD	32	108	272	71	13	1	7	35	33	35	4.48	27	67	4	2	.67	.261	.339	.393	.732
Markakis,Nick	Bal	24	161	606	186	43	3	23	97	106	113	6.90	61	94	14	6	.70	.307	.374	.502	.876
Martin,Russell	LAD	25	151	555	162	34	3	17	89	95	95	6.13	73	82	20	10	.67	.292	.379	.456	.835
Martinez,Ramon	LAD	35	76	150	39	7	0	1	16	19	16	3.75	13	19	1	0	1.00	.260	.323	.327	.650
Martinez,Victor	Cle	29	147	562	170	38	0	21	78	102	102	6.77	65	77	0	0	.00	.302	.381	.482	.863
Mathis,Jeff	LAA	25	61	147	35	9	1	3	20	16	16	3.68	10	30	1	1	.50	.238	.291	.374	.665
Matsui,Hideki	NYY	34	134	515	151	30	1	25	90	94	99	7.03	75	76	3	2	.60	.293	.386	.501	.887
Matsui,Kaz	Col	33	133	483	142	29	3	11	79	54	74	5.51	40	77	25	8	.76	.294	.350	.435	.785
Matthews Jr.,Gary	LAA	33	149	579	153	33	3	18	88	70	82	4.92	62	113	14	7	.67	.264	.337	.425	.762
Mauer,Joe	Min	25	132	500	160	34	3	12	79	76	97	7.35	73	55	9	3	.75	.320	.409	.472	.881
McCann,Brian	Atl	24	132	474	141	36	0	21	59	92	85	6.62	42	61	1	1	.50	.297	.360	.506	.866
McDonald,John	Tor	33	112	289	68	13	1	2	31	23	24	2.79	13	45	5	3	.62	.235	.273	.308	.581
McLouth,Nate	Pit	26	122	329	84	20	2	11	60	32	47	4.91	31	64	19	4	.83	.255	.332	.429	.761
McPherson,Dallas	LAA	27	129	409	101	21	3	25	58	66	59	4.93	27	146	6	3	.67	.247	.294	.496	.790
Mench,Kevin	Mil	30	110	350	98	24	2	13	45	51	53	5.28	26	40	2	1	.67	.274	.328	.461	.789
Metcalf,Travis	Tex	25	65	180	42	11	1	5	24	21	21	3.93	17	43	2	1	.67	.233	.290	.389	.688
Michaels,Jason	Cle	32	98	241	67	13	1	6	39	30	34	5.02	25	48	3	2	.60	.278	.353	.415	.768
Mientkiewicz,Doug	NYY	34	70	153	41	10	0	4	20	20	22	5.11	19	23	0	0	.00	.268	.364	.412	.775
Miles,Aaron	StL	31	134	421	117	16	2	2	52	33	46	3.91	26	43	3	2	.60	.278	.323	.340	.663
Millar,Kevin	Bal	36	140	463	121	28	1	15	60	63	68	5.15	60	90	1	1	.50	.261	.357	.423	.780
Milledge,Lastings	NYM	23	139	538	154	33	4	18	85	78	85	5.61	48	117	21	10	.68	.286	.350	.463	.813
Miller,Damian	Mil	38	61	157	39	9	0	3	16	18	18	3.97	15	39	0	0	.00	.248	.326	.363	.689
Mirabelli,Doug	Bos	37	50	120	25	6	0	5	11	16	13	3.56	12	41	0	0	.00	.208	.291	.383	.674
Molina,Bengie	SF	33	134	497	135	21	0	17	45	75	62	4.45	21	54	0	0	.00	.272	.305	.416	.722
Molina,Jose	NYY	33	84	219	54	12	0	3	20	23	21	3.29	9	45	2	1	.67	.247	.279	.342	.622
Molina,Yadier	StL	25	118	369	93	18	0	7	32	45	41	3.85	31	37	1	1	.50	.252	.317	.358	.675
Monroe,Craig	ChC	31	95	209	52	12	0	8	28	33	26	4.28	14	50	1	1	.50	.249	.302	.421	.723
Montero,Miguel	Ari	24	70	220	57	10	0	10	26	38	32	5.10	23	34	0	0	.00	.259	.335	.441	.776
Mora,Melvin	Bal	36	130	505	139	26	1	16	74	67	73	5.13	50	94	8	4	.67	.275	.351	.426	.777
Morales,Kendry	LAA	25	97	264	76	16	1	8	33	36	38	5.26	14	36	0	0	.00	.288	.326	.447	.773
Morgan,Nyjer	Pit	27	62	193	58	5	3	1	31	10	26	4.69	16	29	22	9	.71	.301	.357	.373	.730
Morneau,Justin	Min	27	152	548	155	31	2	32	83	112	100	6.60	57	88	1	1	.50	.283	.355	.522	.877
Munson,Eric	Hou	30	77	188	45	9	0	8	21	26	24	4.36	19	34	1	0	1.00	.239	.313	.415	.727
Murphy,David	Tex	26	75	208	57	15	2	5	27	27	30	5.10	20	35	3	2	.60	.274	.338	.438	.775
Murphy,Donnie	Oak	25	42	139	34	11	0	4	19	17	16	3.92	9	30	2	1	.67	.245	.295	.410	.705
Murton,Matt	ChC	26	90	220	67	13	1	7	33	28	38	6.42	23	30	3	1	.75	.305	.373	.468	.841
Nady,Xavier	Pit	29	140	479	130	27	1	20	60	71	68	5.04	30	103	3	2	.60	.271	.326	.457	.783
Napoli,Mike	LAA	26	100	336	80	17	1	19	61	58	54	5.42	55	98	7	3	.70	.238	.352	.464	.816
Navarro,Dioner	TB	24	119	432	104	20	1	10	50	46	49	3.86	44	66	4	2	.67	.241	.312	.361	.673
Nixon,Trot	Cle	34	106	268	71	16	1	7	38	38	39	5.15	38	49	1	0	1.00	.265	.362	.410	.773
Norton,Greg	TB	35	83	213	52	10	0	7	26	28	28	4.49	29	56	1	1	.50	.244	.337	.390	.727
Nunez,Abraham	Phi	32	98	204	49	7	1	1	24	17	19	3.17	22	37	1	1	.50	.240	.317	.299	.616
Ojeda,Augie	Ari	33	55	120	29	5	0	1	15	11	12	3.39	14	13	1	1	.50	.242	.321	.308	.629
Olivo,Miguel	Fla	29	119	386	92	19	2	13	43	51	41	3.60	14	103	4	2	.67	.238	.270	.399	.669
Ordonez,Magglio	Det	34	151	580	182	41	1	25	92	111	114	7.41	62	80	3	2	.60	.314	.383	.517	.900
Ortiz,David	Bos	32	156	588	175	45	1	41	109	130	140	8.79	106	120	2	1	.67	.298	.407	.587	.994
Ortmeier,Dan	SF	27	115	375	95	20	3	10	46	46	46	4.18	27	77	15	6	.71	.253	.305	.403	.708
Overbay,Lyle	Tor	31	130	425	120	31	1	13	56	58	70	5.95	54	79	2	1	.67	.282	.361	.456	.817
Owens,Jerry	CWS	27	120	430	118	15	2	3	65	34	52	4.16	41	65	38	13	.75	.274	.340	.340	.680
Pagan,Angel	ChC	26	65	120	30	5	1	3	16	11	14	3.96	9	23	5	2	.71	.250	.302	.383	.686
Patterson,Corey	Bal	28	132	439	118	22	3	13	63	47	58	4.58	23	83	29	8	.78	.269	.311	.421	.733
Paul,Josh	TB	33	57	117	28	5	0	1	13	12	11	3.18	11	28	1	1	.50	.239	.305	.308	.612
Paulino,Ronny	Pit	27	124	449	129	25	0	11	52	57	63	5.10	35	73	2	1	.67	.287	.342	.416	.758
Payton,Jay	Bal	35	110	340	93	17	2	8	43	41	42	4.39	19	37	3	2	.60	.274	.318	.403	.721
Pearce,Steve	Pit	25	109	353	111	32	2	12	61	65	68	7.22	29	49	11	3	.79	.314	.366	.518	.885
Pedroia,Dustin	Bos	24	139	523	157	40	2	9	77	57	83	5.85	53	38	6	3	.67	.300	.369	.436	.805
Pena,Carlos	TB	30	140	469	123	25	2	31	78	87	90	6.74	78	134	2	1	.67	.262	.373	.522	.896
Pena,Tony F	KC	27	140	485	130	24	5	3	57	43	49	3.54	14	79	8	5	.62	.268	.291	.357	.648

2008 Hitter Projections

Hitter	Team	Age	G	AB	H	2B	3B	HR	R	RBI	RC	RC27	BB	SO	SB	CS	SB%	Avg	OBP	Slg	OPS
Pena,Wily Mo	Was	26	132	412	114	19	1	23	61	69	67	5.81	32	124	3	2	.60	.277	.335	.495	.830
Pence,Hunter	Hou	25	146	602	184	41	9	27	90	100	115	7.05	47	114	15	6	.71	.306	.357	.538	.895
Peralta,Jhonny	Cle	26	154	584	161	35	2	20	93	79	90	5.51	62	148	3	2	.60	.276	.348	.445	.793
Phelps,Josh	Pit	30	91	141	40	7	1	7	19	25	24	6.18	12	36	0	0	.00	.284	.361	.496	.857
Phillips,Andy	NYY	31	87	209	58	9	1	7	30	28	30	5.13	18	35	1	1	.50	.278	.338	.431	.768
Phillips,Brandon	Cin	27	155	630	170	32	3	23	92	81	87	4.83	38	99	24	8	.75	.270	.318	.440	.757
Phillips,Jason	Tor	31	66	164	40	9	0	3	16	20	17	3.56	12	21	0	0	.00	.244	.307	.354	.661
Piazza,Mike	Oak	39	85	256	68	13	0	11	27	38	38	5.26	25	48	0	0	.00	.266	.336	.445	.781
Pie,Felix	ChC	23	147	533	151	30	7	16	82	62	80	5.29	40	111	23	11	.68	.283	.333	.456	.789
Pierre,Juan	LAD	30	162	685	204	26	7	1	97	45	86	4.45	40	40	57	21	.73	.298	.343	.361	.703
Pierzynski,A.J.	CWS	31	140	513	142	30	1	15	62	66	68	4.75	25	70	1	1	.50	.277	.323	.427	.750
Podsednik,Scott	CWS	32	91	282	74	15	2	3	43	20	33	3.95	26	50	20	9	.69	.262	.331	.362	.693
Polanco,Placido	Det	32	142	574	179	30	2	10	89	62	85	5.55	34	34	5	3	.62	.312	.360	.423	.783
Posada,Jorge	NYY	36	144	508	142	32	0	21	75	88	90	6.39	79	111	2	1	.67	.281	.386	.469	.854
Pujols,Albert	StL	28	157	586	194	45	1	42	122	126	156	10.27	98	61	4	3	.57	.331	.433	.626	1.059
Punto,Nick	Min	30	149	480	116	20	3	2	62	34	47	3.28	53	89	16	8	.67	.242	.317	.308	.625
Quentin,Carlos	Ari	25	110	380	100	23	2	13	60	59	57	5.26	37	65	4	2	.67	.263	.341	.455	.796
Quinlan,Robb	LAA	31	79	173	51	11	0	5	22	21	26	5.50	10	23	2	1	.67	.295	.337	.445	.782
Rabelo,Mike	Det	28	66	208	54	13	1	3	23	23	24	4.05	13	41	1	0	1.00	.260	.313	.375	.688
Raburn,Ryan	Det	27	75	242	66	15	2	10	39	42	40	5.81	27	56	7	3	.70	.273	.346	.475	.821
Ramirez,Aramis	ChC	30	148	568	168	37	2	31	81	108	105	6.83	46	74	1	0	1.00	.296	.355	.532	.887
Ramirez,Hanley	Fla	24	143	574	180	42	7	22	111	68	112	7.12	50	85	44	15	.75	.314	.374	.526	.900
Ramirez,Manny	Bos	36	146	538	162	34	1	33	93	113	119	8.23	88	116	0	0	.00	.301	.405	.552	.957
Rasmus,Colby	StL	21	141	490	127	38	2	24	85	66	85	6.01	64	102	20	5	.80	.259	.345	.492	.837
Redman,Tike	Bal	31	35	115	32	5	1	1	15	9	14	4.23	8	10	6	3	.67	.278	.331	.365	.696
Redmond,Mike	Min	37	75	248	71	13	0	1	22	29	28	4.11	14	24	0	0	.00	.286	.337	.351	.688
Renteria,Edgar	Atl	32	147	589	173	37	1	12	91	74	88	5.43	56	89	12	5	.71	.294	.357	.421	.778
Repko,Jason	LAD	27	93	228	56	11	2	6	35	26	27	3.99	18	49	9	4	.69	.246	.306	.390	.697
Reyes,Jose	NYM	25	160	668	193	34	13	14	120	67	106	5.57	59	75	69	20	.78	.289	.348	.442	.789
Reynolds,Mark	Ari	24	135	490	144	31	5	26	92	86	96	7.17	55	145	3	2	.60	.294	.369	.537	.905
Richar,Danny	CWS	25	120	415	115	23	5	13	64	44	63	5.37	38	69	8	5	.62	.277	.338	.451	.788
Rios,Alex	Tor	27	150	537	158	36	6	18	90	75	90	6.08	44	93	14	6	.70	.294	.353	.484	.837
Rivera,Juan	LAA	29	109	419	124	28	0	17	53	72	69	6.06	29	46	1	1	.50	.296	.343	.484	.827
Roberts,Brian	Bal	30	154	611	174	42	3	11	97	59	96	5.57	75	91	37	11	.77	.285	.364	.417	.781
Roberts,Dave	SF	36	101	321	84	12	5	2	48	23	39	4.16	35	50	23	7	.77	.262	.338	.349	.687
Rodriguez,Alex	NYY	32	159	601	180	29	1	47	125	133	139	8.46	93	134	19	6	.76	.300	.406	.586	.992
Rodriguez,Ivan	Det	36	125	489	139	29	2	13	60	62	66	4.88	21	92	4	2	.67	.284	.316	.431	.748
Rodriguez,Luis	Min	28	71	139	36	7	1	2	16	12	17	4.29	15	14	1	0	1.00	.259	.335	.367	.702
Rolen,Scott	StL	33	127	444	125	31	2	17	72	79	75	6.06	53	70	5	3	.62	.282	.367	.475	.842
Rollins,Jimmy	Phi	29	161	684	194	41	10	21	120	76	108	5.62	53	84	35	10	.78	.284	.339	.465	.804
Ross,Cody	Fla	27	100	287	75	18	1	15	45	48	46	5.62	29	64	2	1	.67	.261	.333	.488	.821
Ross,Dave	Cin	31	110	330	76	15	1	20	38	49	47	4.81	36	88	0	0	.00	.230	.310	.464	.773
Rowand,Aaron	Phi	30	151	571	164	39	2	21	91	77	89	5.63	37	111	8	4	.67	.287	.347	.473	.820
Ruiz,Carlos	Phi	29	130	457	129	33	3	12	58	69	72	5.66	49	58	6	3	.67	.282	.356	.446	.802
Ryan,Brendan	StL	26	67	221	59	8	2	2	34	12	25	3.94	16	24	10	3	.77	.267	.319	.348	.668
Saenz,Olmedo	LAD	37	90	170	42	10	0	8	21	29	24	4.88	17	40	0	0	.00	.247	.330	.447	.777
Salazar,Jeff	Ari	27	75	145	39	9	2	3	21	16	21	5.06	17	24	6	2	.75	.269	.346	.421	.766
Saltalamacchia,Jarrod	Tex	23	121	459	121	25	1	19	60	58	69	5.29	52	101	2	1	.67	.264	.340	.447	.786
Sanchez,Freddy	Pit	30	154	584	183	43	2	9	77	73	90	5.82	33	60	1	1	.50	.313	.355	.440	.795
Schierholtz,Nate	SF	24	117	344	103	22	5	10	44	45	54	5.73	15	50	8	4	.67	.299	.331	.480	.810
Schneider,Brian	Was	31	126	401	100	22	1	7	34	51	47	4.06	45	61	0	0	.00	.249	.328	.362	.690
Schumaker,Skip	StL	28	70	130	37	7	1	2	16	11	17	4.70	9	16	2	1	.67	.285	.331	.400	.731
Scott,Luke	Hou	30	120	390	108	26	4	21	56	66	74	6.77	52	87	4	2	.67	.277	.365	.526	.891
Scutaro,Marco	Oak	32	105	234	60	13	1	4	30	25	28	4.16	24	33	1	1	.50	.256	.328	.372	.700
Sexson,Richie	Sea	33	124	403	99	22	0	24	58	73	64	5.46	52	106	1	1	.50	.246	.339	.479	.818
Shealy,Ryan	KC	28	79	275	74	16	0	11	35	45	40	5.17	23	61	1	0	1.00	.269	.330	.447	.777
Sheffield,Gary	Det	39	128	490	137	22	1	26	89	87	90	6.54	76	69	13	5	.72	.280	.384	.488	.872
Shoppach,Kelly	Cle	28	63	176	45	12	0	8	23	30	25	4.96	15	57	0	0	.00	.256	.318	.460	.778
Sizemore,Grady	Cle	25	154	613	175	40	8	26	122	80	116	6.73	85	143	27	10	.73	.285	.384	.504	.888
Sledge,Terrmel	SD	31	82	174	44	8	1	7	22	25	25	4.96	22	40	2	1	.67	.253	.340	.431	.771
Smith,Jason	KC	30	66	132	31	5	2	5	16	16	14	3.57	6	40	1	1	.50	.235	.273	.417	.690
Smith,Seth	Col	25	71	148	43	11	1	4	18	19	23	5.64	11	21	2	1	.67	.291	.340	.459	.799
Snelling,Chris	Oak	26	87	328	83	17	2	7	48	43	43	4.53	47	79	3	2	.60	.253	.350	.381	.731
Snyder,Chris	Ari	27	120	380	96	22	0	15	41	56	55	5.04	49	75	0	0	.00	.253	.344	.429	.773
Soriano,Alfonso	ChC	32	153	625	174	40	2	35	100	86	103	5.82	39	142	23	9	.72	.278	.328	.517	.845
Sosa,Sammy	Tex	39	105	365	92	17	0	22	53	65	58	5.52	43	102	0	0	.00	.252	.336	.479	.815
Soto,Geovany	ChC	25	110	423	123	30	1	17	55	71	75	6.50	47	103	0	0	.00	.291	.362	.487	.849
Spiezio,Scott	StL	35	105	276	68	15	1	8	35	38	35	4.35	30	53	1	1	.50	.246	.329	.395	.724
Spilborghs,Ryan	Col	28	85	224	70	15	2	7	35	33	42	7.00	23	37	5	2	.71	.313	.379	.491	.870
Stairs,Matt	Tor	40	110	312	81	18	0	14	42	49	48	5.38	40	66	1	1	.50	.260	.351	.452	.803
Stewart,Ian	Col	23	132	494	134	34	3	13	66	65	70	4.99	43	106	10	5	.67	.271	.331	.431	.762
Stewart,Shannon	Oak	34	144	554	160	29	2	11	77	54	78	5.10	47	64	9	4	.69	.289	.349	.408	.757
Sullivan,Cory	Col	28	78	208	58	10	2	2	28	17	26	4.45	16	42	4	2	.67	.279	.336	.375	.711
Suzuki,Ichiro	Sea	34	160	659	213	23	5	8	101	57	102	5.83	46	73	30	9	.77	.323	.371	.410	.781
Suzuki,Kurt	Oak	24	123	432	112	26	0	10	60	63	56	4.54	49	70	1	1	.50	.259	.337	.389	.726
Sweeney,Mark	LAD	38	98	130	33	8	0	3	16	18	17	4.51	17	32	1	1	.50	.254	.349	.385	.734
Sweeney,Mike	KC	34	88	278	78	11	0	11	35	47	44	5.69	27	38	1	1	.50	.281	.355	.460	.815
Swisher,Nick	Oak	27	154	565	148	37	1	28	96	92	101	6.27	100	129	2	2	.50	.262	.380	.480	.860
Taguchi,So	StL	38	124	317	87	16	1	4	42	35	38	4.24	23	42	6	3	.67	.274	.329	.369	.699
Taveras,Willy	Col	26	132	472	143	15	3	2	75	28	60	4.57	27	68	34	12	.74	.303	.350	.360	.710
Teahen,Mark	KC	26	138	487	141	31	7	11	75	67	79	5.87	54	101	10	4	.71	.290	.363	.450	.812

446

2008 Hitter Projections

Hitter	Team	Age	G	AB	H	2B	3B	HR	R	RBI	RC	RC27	BB	SO	SB	CS	SB%	Avg	OBP	Slg	OPS
Teixeira,Mark	Atl	28	153	596	172	41	2	36	99	120	121	7.40	82	128	1	1	.50	.289	.382	.545	.927
Tejada,Miguel	Bal	32	153	608	183	34	1	24	90	105	102	6.21	46	72	4	2	.67	.301	.359	.479	.838
Terrero,Luis	CWS	28	56	140	38	7	1	6	20	17	20	4.95	10	32	5	3	.62	.271	.346	.464	.810
Thames,Marcus	Det	31	110	345	92	19	1	25	55	66	61	6.24	30	83	2	1	.67	.267	.329	.545	.874
Theriot,Ryan	ChC	28	140	512	145	30	3	3	76	47	68	4.73	50	47	26	7	.79	.283	.348	.371	.719
Thigpen,Curtis	Tor	25	66	196	52	13	1	3	25	23	26	4.66	21	30	2	1	.67	.265	.336	.388	.724
Thomas,Frank	Tor	40	137	462	121	23	0	28	65	87	84	6.40	78	90	0	0	.00	.262	.374	.494	.868
Thome,Jim	CWS	37	130	428	111	20	0	32	76	87	89	7.30	92	137	0	0	.00	.259	.395	.530	.925
Thorman,Scott	Atl	26	78	159	42	10	1	7	20	24	23	5.07	10	32	1	1	.50	.264	.316	.472	.787
Torrealba,Yorvit	Col	29	108	358	90	21	2	8	42	46	43	4.16	29	64	2	1	.67	.251	.315	.388	.703
Towles,J.R.	Hou	24	103	368	108	20	3	12	69	73	58	5.59	34	52	14	10	.58	.293	.355	.462	.817
Tracy,Chad	Ari	28	133	487	139	36	2	18	67	68	81	6.03	48	90	2	1	.67	.285	.353	.478	.832
Treanor,Matt	Fla	32	83	227	56	10	1	4	20	22	26	3.95	26	39	0	0	.00	.247	.335	.352	.687
Tulowitzki,Troy	Col	23	155	581	168	36	4	22	100	88	97	6.03	57	109	7	5	.58	.289	.360	.478	.838
Tyner,Jason	Min	31	89	233	68	9	1	0	33	17	27	4.18	15	22	6	3	.67	.292	.340	.339	.679
Uggla,Dan	Fla	28	143	568	152	39	3	28	100	85	93	5.77	57	126	4	3	.57	.268	.344	.495	.839
Upton,B.J.	TB	23	144	557	154	29	3	21	96	72	92	5.78	73	148	32	11	.74	.276	.362	.452	.815
Upton,Justin	Ari	20	130	490	136	32	9	19	76	74	84	6.02	56	100	16	9	.64	.278	.353	.496	.849
Uribe,Juan	CWS	29	151	536	132	27	4	21	66	74	66	4.23	32	107	2	2	.50	.246	.294	.429	.723
Utley,Chase	Phi	29	151	596	183	45	4	26	107	109	116	7.23	59	109	10	4	.71	.307	.384	.527	.910
Valentin,Javier	Cin	32	104	290	77	17	0	8	30	43	38	4.64	25	39	0	0	.00	.266	.326	.407	.733
Valentin,Jose	NYM	38	102	296	71	15	1	12	41	40	39	4.47	31	64	4	2	.67	.240	.316	.419	.735
Varitek,Jason	Bos	36	131	474	120	25	1	17	60	70	68	4.98	64	129	2	1	.67	.253	.349	.418	.767
Vazquez,Ramon	Tex	31	70	145	35	7	1	3	21	13	17	3.98	17	30	1	1	.50	.241	.325	.366	.691
Velez,Eugenio	SF	26	76	196	58	8	4	1	31	13	28	5.09	14	33	19	5	.79	.296	.343	.393	.736
Victorino,Shane	Phi	27	137	448	124	20	5	12	74	49	64	5.03	33	59	25	7	.78	.277	.336	.424	.760
Vidro,Jose	Sea	33	129	438	130	27	1	8	58	52	67	5.66	47	47	1	0	1.00	.297	.368	.418	.785
Vizquel,Omar	SF	41	128	443	113	18	2	3	52	39	46	3.56	43	45	11	6	.65	.255	.325	.325	.650
Votto,Joey	Cin	24	135	460	141	30	1	23	71	81	93	7.39	61	96	16	8	.67	.307	.388	.526	.914
Walker,Neil	LAA	22	130	442	116	30	2	11	69	54	60	4.71	43	73	9	5	.64	.262	.328	.414	.742
Ward,Daryle	ChC	33	80	125	33	8	0	4	14	20	18	5.09	13	24	0	0	.00	.264	.338	.424	.762
Weeks,Rickie	Mil	25	129	483	128	28	6	17	97	54	81	5.83	72	121	24	6	.80	.265	.374	.453	.827
Wells,Vernon	Tor	29	151	573	158	37	3	23	82	87	89	5.52	46	85	9	4	.69	.276	.333	.471	.804
Werth,Jayson	Phi	29	79	210	59	10	2	7	35	36	36	6.12	33	58	5	2	.71	.281	.386	.448	.834
Wigginton,Ty	Hou	30	139	509	137	32	1	20	65	72	74	5.13	42	106	4	3	.57	.269	.332	.454	.786
Wilkerson,Brad	Tex	31	111	337	81	22	2	15	55	45	51	5.12	51	105	4	3	.57	.240	.345	.451	.796
Willingham,Josh	Fla	29	138	501	139	30	3	24	72	84	89	6.36	65	107	6	2	.75	.277	.372	.493	.865
Willits,Reggie	LAA	27	141	472	137	22	2	1	81	38	67	5.02	73	79	31	12	.72	.290	.388	.352	.739
Wilson,Jack	Pit	30	150	563	156	30	3	10	71	54	71	4.50	36	62	3	3	.50	.277	.326	.394	.720
Wilson,Josh	TB	27	86	239	60	13	2	4	29	25	27	3.86	17	43	7	3	.70	.251	.309	.372	.681
Wilson,Preston	StL	33	97	265	67	15	1	11	34	42	36	4.66	22	71	6	3	.67	.253	.320	.442	.761
Winn,Randy	SF	34	134	521	147	33	3	12	69	57	74	5.06	42	77	12	6	.67	.282	.343	.426	.769
Wood,Brandon	LAA	23	122	392	98	26	1	17	53	58	55	4.81	33	115	11	3	.79	.250	.308	.452	.760
Wright,David	NYM	25	160	603	192	45	2	31	111	115	137	8.52	84	113	27	7	.79	.318	.407	.554	.961
Youkilis,Kevin	Bos	29	142	518	160	38	1	15	89	78	91	6.39	84	96	4	2	.67	.290	.399	.454	.852
Young,Chris	Ari	24	148	557	141	37	3	33	93	79	91	5.58	52	122	28	8	.78	.253	.320	.508	.828
Young,Delmon	TB	22	147	585	176	34	3	15	72	89	86	5.40	24	106	15	5	.75	.301	.331	.446	.777
Young,Dmitri	Was	34	131	485	139	30	2	17	60	70	77	5.79	40	92	1	0	1.00	.287	.346	.462	.808
Young,Michael	Tex	31	160	660	201	38	3	14	92	88	101	5.67	48	105	10	4	.71	.305	.354	.435	.789
Zaun,Gregg	Tor	37	124	417	102	24	0	11	52	55	54	4.46	61	71	1	0	1.00	.245	.344	.381	.725
Zimmerman,Ryan	Was	23	157	631	182	49	4	24	98	102	109	6.27	61	110	5	3	.62	.288	.353	.493	.846
Zobrist,Ben	TB	27	79	194	51	11	2	4	28	19	27	4.81	26	31	6	3	.67	.263	.353	.402	.755

447

Projected Career Totals for Active Players

Closed for Renovations

We've been publishing projected career totals for the past few years now. Each year we've included a very prominent note that says "These projections assume that the player will be healthy." The reason for this is that the multi-year version of our projection system does not have a random injury component. We've had plans to modify the system to incorporate injuries for quite a while now but just haven't found the time to get it done. Therefore we decided to forego publishing the totals since the assumption that every player will stay healthy over a long period of time is unrealistic.

We have one suggestion and one request:

1) For those of you interested in player career totals, we suggest you take a look at the Career Targets section of this book on page 463. This section will show you all the players who have a chance of hitting various milestones such as 500 homers, 3000 hits, 1000 stolen bases, etc.

2) We'd like your input. Please send us any thoughts or suggestions about this topic that you might have. Our e-mail address is info@baseballinfosolutions.com.

Projected Pitching Records

Bill James

John Dewan has always taken the lead in terms of publishing projections. Back in the 1980s, just after we all got personal computers with spreadsheets, I developed a spreadsheet that would "finish out" a player's career if you typed in the first part of his career. About 1990, John Dewan asked me if we could print those projections for next year in *The Bill James Handbook*.

"John," I said, "we can't print those. There's no scientific validity to them. That's just something I do to entertain myself, messing around with the numbers."

"OK," said John. "We won't tell people there is any validity to them. We'll tell them we're just messing around with the numbers." I'm simplifying a two-year argument into about four sentences, but we did eventually print the projections anyway, and this proved to be a popular feature of this book, which a lot of people use to help draft their fantasy teams. After a few years of publishing the projections and a certain amount of refining the system, we got a pretty good read on the accuracy of the method, and it eventually emerged as a serious tool for analyzing baseball, in certain contexts. There are several competitive projection systems around now, and even actual major league teams look at the projections, just to kind of line out what they have and what they still need for next year.

So about five years ago John Dewan says to me, "Why don't we run projections for pitchers?"

"No way," I said.

"Why?"

"It can't be done. Pitchers bounce up and down too much. There are too many injuries. Nobody can project what a pitcher will do next year with any accuracy."

"Well, I want to try anyway," John said.

"OK," I said. "But leave me out of it. I don't think it can be done."

So John and Pat Quinn went to work trying to project pitchers, and we've been publishing those projections for several years. And. . .guess what? The system actually works pretty well. The projections for pitchers are about as accurate, on average, as the projections for hitters.

Which is to say, sometimes they're just *completely* wrong. A year ago, we projected that Chris Carpenter would win 16 games in 2007, which turned out to be off by 16:

Chris Carpenter

	G	GS	IP	W	L	Pct.	SO	BB	ERA	Sv
Actual	1	1	6	0	1	.000	3	1	7.50	0
Projected	31	31	236	16	10	.615	187	63	3.55	0

We projected a better record for Clay Hensley than for Josh Beckett, which didn't turn out to be exactly correct:

Clay Hensley

	G	GS	IP	W	L	Pct.	SO	BB	ERA	Sv
Actual	13	9	50	2	3	.400	30	32	6.84	0
Projected	30	30	192	13	8	.619	129	71	3.28	0

Josh Beckett

	G	GS	IP	W	L	Pct.	SO	BB	ERA	Sv
Actual	30	30	201	20	7	.741	194	40	3.27	0
Projected	32	32	208	13	10	.565	191	75	3.68	0

But the projection for Beckett has its good points, and I'm sure the readers will forgive us for not foreseeing the injuries to Carpenter and Hensley. And Jason Schmidt. And B. J. Ryan. And Josh Johnson. And Anibal Sanchez.

OK, we didn't foresee *any* of the injuries, alright? We're not psychics; we're accountants. We didn't foresee that Brett Myers would be moved to the bullpen, or that Jonathan Papelbon wouldn't be moved to the starting rotation like the Red Sox promised us he would:

Brett Myers

	G	GS	IP	W	L	Pct.	SO	BB	ERA	Sv
Actual	51	3	69	5	7	.417	83	27	4.33	21
Projected	32	32	214	12	11	.522	179	73	4.29	0

Jonathan Papelbon

	G	GS	IP	W	L	Pct.	SO	BB	ERA	Sv
Actual	59	0	58	1	3	.250	84	15	1.85	37
Projected	27	27	184	14	6	.700	181	48	2.98	0

By the way, John Dewan and I are now having a dispute over the organization of the pitcher's record. The form that I am using here is the form that was used on Topps baseball cards when I was a kid. John doesn't like it; he thinks that Strikeouts should be to the right of Walks, not to the left. Maybe we'll poll the readers on this when the Bill James Online opens next spring.

Anyway, I was saying. . .we're not clairvoyant, we're just numbers guys. Given that premise, John and Pat's projection system actually does very well. Last year they projected that Jeff Suppan would have 114 strikeouts and 68 walks, and, son of a gun, he did:

Jeff Suppan

	G	GS	IP	W	L	Pct.	SO	BB	ERA	Sv
Actual	34	34	207	12	12	.500	114	68	4.62	0
Projected	33	33	206	11	12	.478	114	68	4.46	0

Of course, that's pretty much what Jeff Suppan does *every* year, but still. . .you can't say that about Josh Fogg, or Mike Wood, or Randy Messenger:

Josh Fogg

	G	GS	IP	W	L	Pct.	SO	BB	ERA	Sv
Actual	30	29	166	10	9	.526	94	59	4.94	0
Projected	31	31	170	8	10	.444	88	57	4.92	0

Mike Wood

	G	GS	IP	W	L	Pct.	SO	BB	ERA	Sv
Actual	21	4	51	3	2	.600	25	15	5.33	0
Projected	20	3	52	2	4	.333	28	18	5.37	0

Randy Messenger

	G	GS	IP	W	L	Pct.	SO	BB	ERA	Sv
Actual	60	0	64	2	4	.333	34	21	4.20	1
Projected	57	0	63	3	4	.429	47	32	4.86	0

We actually had good projections for a lot of pitchers. We had good projections for Chad Cordero, Tim Hudson, Roy Halladay, Billy Wagner and Trevor Hoffman. We had an excellent projection for Miguel Batista as a starter, except that his offensive support was much better than we had supposed:

Chad Cordero

	G	GS	IP	W	L	Pct.	SO	BB	ERA	Sv
Actual	76	0	75	3	3	.500	62	29	3.36	37
Projected	68	0	73	5	3	.625	68	25	3.33	32

Tim Hudson

	G	GS	IP	W	L	Pct.	SO	BB	ERA	Sv
Actual	34	34	224	16	10	.615	132	53	3.33	0
Projected	34	34	223	15	10	.600	147	71	3.75	0

Roy Halladay

	G	GS	IP	W	L	Pct.	SO	BB	ERA	Sv
Actual	31	31	225	16	7	.696	139	48	3.71	0
Projected	30	30	205	14	8	.636	142	47	3.38	0

Billy Wagner

	G	GS	IP	W	L	Pct.	SO	BB	ERA	Sv
Actual	66	0	68	2	2	.500	80	22	2.63	34
Projected	69	0	71	5	3	.625	87	20	2.66	38

Trevor Hoffman

	G	GS	IP	W	L	Pct.	SO	BB	ERA	Sv
Actual	61	0	57	4	5	.444	44	15	2.98	42
Projected	65	0	65	4	3	.571	63	15	2.77	45

Miguel Batista

	G	GS	IP	W	L	Pct.	SO	BB	ERA	Sv
Actual	33	32	193	16	11	.593	133	85	4.29	0
Projected	34	32	206	11	12	.478	124	84	4.37	0

We had very decent projections for Derek Lowe and Javier Vazquez:

Derek Lowe

	G	GS	IP	W	L	Pct.	SO	BB	ERA	Sv
Actual	33	32	199	12	14	.462	147	59	3.88	0
Projected	34	32	222	14	11	.560	135	62	3.81	0

Javier Vazquez

	G	GS	IP	W	L	Pct.	SO	BB	ERA	Sv
Actual	32	32	217	15	8	.652	213	50	3.74	0
Projected	33	33	217	13	11	.542	190	55	3.86	0

And we had equally good projections for Jarrod Washburn and Roy Oswalt, Andy Pettitte and Greg Maddux, Jered Weaver and Jason Marquis, Jeff Francis and A. J. Burnett and Cla Meredith and Scott Linebrink and Jay Witasick and Tyler Yates and Doug Davis and many others, but we can't print them all.

So Bill James has egg on his face once again, and probably on his shirt as well, but at the moment we're speaking figuratively, about the fact that he was wrong about this. You can, in fact, project pitcher's records with essentially the same accuracy that you can project hitter's records, at least in the modern world; we don't know about the days of Cy Young, when James was young and impressionable.

But this statement comes with one caveat. One reason the projections are as accurate as they are is that we don't make projections for very young and inexperienced pitchers. We had no projection here last year for Cole Hamels, for example, and we have no projection this year for Clay Buchholz. We have to see a baseline before we can make a projection.

Thanks.

Bill James

2008 Pitcher Projections

PLAYER			HOW MUCH			WHAT HE WILL GIVE UP					THE RESULTS					
Pitcher	Team	Age	G	GS	IP	H	HR	BB	SO	HB	W	L	Pct	Sv	BR/9	ERA
Accardo,Jeremy	Tor	26	61	0	68	62	4	21	57	1	5	3	.625	10	11.1	3.31
Acosta,Manny	Atl	27	41	0	47	41	3	36	45	2	3	3	.500	0	15.1	4.40
Affeldt,Jeremy	Col	29	72	0	55	56	5	26	38	2	3	3	.500	0	13.7	4.42
Albers,Matt	Hou	25	34	23	141	147	15	63	105	10	7	9	.438	0	14.0	4.72
Alfonseca,Antonio	Phi	36	58	0	42	48	3	18	26	1	2	3	.400	0	14.4	4.71
Armas Jr.,Tony	Pit	30	31	19	120	123	17	55	86	8	5	8	.385	0	14.0	4.95
Arroyo,Bronson	Cin	31	34	34	212	217	25	63	145	12	13	11	.542	0	12.4	4.08
Atchison,Scott	SF	32	38	0	55	52	4	16	51	1	4	3	.571	0	11.3	3.27
Ayala,Luis	Was	30	62	0	61	62	6	13	39	4	4	3	.571	4	11.7	3.69
Backe,Brandon	Hou	30	20	20	120	127	16	55	80	5	5	8	.385	0	14.0	4.88
Bacsik,Mike	Was	30	37	20	124	144	22	32	69	6	5	9	.357	0	13.2	5.15
Baek,Cha Seung	Sea	28	20	18	105	117	14	32	71	4	5	7	.417	0	13.1	4.63
Baker,Scott	Min	26	28	26	168	183	20	37	129	6	9	10	.474	0	12.1	4.13
Balfour,Grant	TB	30	40	0	40	36	4	22	52	1	2	2	.500	0	13.3	4.05
Bannister,Brian	KC	27	29	29	180	182	18	52	114	7	10	10	.500	0	12.0	3.85
Batista,Miguel	Sea	37	32	31	194	207	18	81	120	7	9	12	.429	0	13.7	4.50
Bazardo,Yorman	Det	23	15	4	41	47	4	16	25	3	2	3	.400	0	14.5	5.05
Beckett,Josh	Bos	28	29	29	203	184	22	64	187	7	14	8	.636	0	11.3	3.50
Bedard,Erik	Bal	29	32	32	210	196	19	78	207	7	13	11	.542	0	12.0	3.69
Beimel,Joe	LAD	31	82	0	66	69	5	27	37	1	4	4	.500	0	13.2	4.09
Belisle,Matt	Cin	28	28	28	169	195	22	46	119	8	9	10	.474	0	13.3	4.79
Bell,Heath	SD	30	83	0	90	78	6	26	97	1	7	3	.700	1	10.5	3.10
Bell,Rob	Bal	31	39	0	76	89	13	29	47	2	3	6	.333	0	14.2	5.57
Benitez,Armando	Fla	35	44	0	41	34	5	20	42	0	3	2	.600	0	11.9	3.73
Benoit,Joaquin	Tex	30	70	0	82	75	9	36	76	3	5	5	.500	1	12.5	3.95
Benson,Kris	Bal	33	20	20	130	137	18	43	77	4	6	8	.429	0	12.7	4.43
Bergmann,Jason	Was	26	25	25	158	146	20	60	139	7	9	9	.500	0	12.1	3.87
Betancourt,Rafael	Cle	33	69	0	86	72	7	18	86	0	7	2	.778	3	9.4	2.83
Billingsley,Chad	LAD	23	30	30	185	165	18	85	178	5	11	9	.550	0	12.4	3.79
Birkins,Kurt	Bal	27	31	4	55	63	6	25	47	4	2	4	.333	0	15.1	5.24
Blanton,Joe	Oak	27	32	32	220	233	19	54	128	5	13	12	.520	0	11.9	3.80
Bonderman,Jeremy	Det	25	28	28	175	182	20	55	147	4	10	9	.526	0	12.4	4.11
Bonser,Boof	Min	26	30	30	180	189	27	66	161	4	8	12	.400	0	13.0	4.60
Bootcheck,Chris	LAA	29	57	0	81	96	11	34	57	4	3	6	.333	0	14.9	5.56
Borkowski,Dave	Hou	31	67	0	74	86	9	26	51	4	3	5	.375	0	14.1	5.11
Borowski,Joe	Cle	37	65	0	60	57	8	20	52	1	4	3	.571	31	11.7	3.90
Bowie,Micah	Was	33	17	4	32	29	2	15	27	1	2	2	.500	0	12.7	3.66
Bradford,Chad	Bal	33	74	0	65	68	3	17	41	4	4	3	.571	0	12.3	3.60
Braun,Ryan	KC	27	33	0	55	55	3	28	50	1	3	3	.500	0	13.7	4.09
Bray,Bill	Cin	25	45	0	40	41	5	14	43	1	2	2	.500	0	12.6	4.05
Brocail,Doug	SD	41	74	0	84	84	5	29	59	3	5	4	.556	0	12.4	3.75
Brown,Andrew	Oak	27	52	0	68	58	5	32	68	4	4	3	.571	0	12.4	3.71
Broxton,Jonathan	LAD	24	84	0	83	68	5	31	103	1	6	3	.667	2	10.8	3.04
Bruney,Brian	NYY	26	60	0	55	51	6	41	56	4	3	3	.500	0	15.7	5.24
Buchholz,Taylor	Col	26	44	4	87	92	13	26	58	3	5	5	.500	0	12.5	4.34
Buehrle,Mark	CWS	29	30	30	200	213	24	45	114	5	11	11	.500	0	11.8	3.96
Bukvich,Ryan	CWS	30	52	0	43	46	8	28	35	1	1	3	.250	0	15.7	6.07
Burgos,Ambiorix	NYM	24	35	0	45	42	7	22	46	3	2	3	.400	0	13.4	4.60
Burnett,A.J.	Tor	31	27	27	190	164	18	76	179	10	12	9	.571	0	11.8	3.55
Burres,Brian	Bal	27	43	15	124	139	16	64	96	7	5	9	.357	0	15.2	5.52
Burton,Jared	Cin	27	60	0	60	60	4	28	50	3	4	3	.571	0	13.6	4.20
Bush,David	Mil	28	32	31	184	198	25	40	129	14	11	10	.524	0	12.3	4.26
Byrd,Paul	Cle	37	28	28	180	209	25	33	92	6	9	11	.450	0	12.4	4.45
Byrdak,Tim	Det	34	46	0	55	50	6	31	59	2	3	3	.500	0	13.6	4.25
Cabrera,Daniel	Bal	27	32	32	210	201	20	120	182	11	10	13	.435	0	14.2	4.54
Cabrera,Fernando	Bal	26	35	0	45	39	6	22	52	0	2	3	.400	0	12.2	4.00
Cain,Matt	SF	23	31	31	205	169	20	89	188	6	13	10	.565	0	11.6	3.42
Calero,Kiko	Oak	33	32	0	32	28	3	13	32	1	2	1	.667	0	11.8	3.66
Cali,Carmen	Min	29	35	0	32	38	3	17	23	1	1	2	.333	0	15.8	5.63
Cameron,Kevin	SD	28	52	0	60	58	4	30	51	1	3	3	.500	0	13.4	3.90
Camp,Shawn	TB	32	35	0	31	39	4	9	22	2	1	2	.333	0	14.5	5.52
Capellan,Jose	Det	27	25	0	35	35	4	16	28	1	2	2	.500	0	13.4	4.37
Capps,Matt	Pit	24	73	0	78	76	8	13	62	3	4	4	.500	35	10.6	3.35
Capuano,Chris	Mil	29	29	21	145	151	20	48	118	8	8	8	.500	0	12.8	4.41
Carlyle,Buddy	Atl	30	25	23	116	115	18	34	101	5	7	6	.538	0	11.9	4.11
Carmona,Fausto	Cle	24	31	31	224	229	20	65	151	14	13	12	.520	0	12.4	3.90
Carpenter,Chris	StL	33	24	24	172	160	17	46	137	6	11	8	.579	0	11.1	3.51
Casilla,Santiago	Oak	27	54	0	57	46	6	28	64	1	4	3	.571	0	11.8	3.63
Cassel,Jack	SD	27	12	8	45	53	4	15	33	2	2	3	.400	0	14.0	4.80
Chacin,Gustavo	Tor	27	15	15	85	92	12	30	48	4	4	6	.400	0	13.3	4.66
Chacon,Shawn	Pit	30	64	2	78	79	11	40	52	6	3	5	.375	0	14.4	5.08
Cherry,Rocky	Bal	28	27	0	44	44	4	19	42	2	2	3	.400	0	13.3	4.30
Chico,Matt	Was	25	28	28	157	172	23	62	97	4	6	11	.353	0	13.6	4.93
Chulk,Vinnie	SF	29	53	0	58	56	7	22	46	2	3	3	.500	0	12.4	3.88
Clement,Matt	Bos	33	15	15	95	89	10	43	82	7	6	5	.545	0	13.2	4.17
Coffey,Todd	Cin	27	55	0	50	58	6	15	36	3	3	3	.500	0	13.7	4.86
Colome,Jesus	Was	30	60	0	64	63	8	32	47	2	3	4	.429	0	13.6	4.50
Colon,Bartolo	LAA	35	14	12	70	73	10	22	51	2	4	4	.500	0	12.5	4.24
Condrey,Clay	Phi	32	48	0	64	76	6	20	35	3	3	4	.429	0	13.9	4.92
Contreras,Jose	CWS	36	31	31	196	200	23	70	141	11	10	12	.455	0	12.9	4.27

456

2008 Pitcher Projections

Pitcher	Team	Age	G	GS	IP	H	HR	BB	SO	HB	W	L	Pct	Sv	BR/9	ERA
Cook,Aaron	Col	29	25	25	160	185	14	49	61	6	9	9	.500	0	13.5	4.56
Cordero,Chad	Was	26	71	0	72	62	9	26	65	1	4	4	.500	36	11.1	3.50
Cordero,Francisco	Mil	33	61	0	61	54	4	25	68	2	4	2	.667	44	12.0	3.54
Cormier,Lance	Atl	27	20	16	105	128	16	48	66	3	4	7	.364	0	15.3	6.00
Corpas,Manny	Col	25	74	0	79	70	5	18	62	4	5	3	.625	34	10.5	3.08
Correia,Kevin	SF	27	50	15	131	129	15	55	101	5	6	8	.429	0	13.0	4.26
Cotts,Neal	ChC	28	30	0	30	27	4	16	27	2	2	2	.500	0	13.5	4.20
Coutlangus,Jon	Cin	27	44	0	30	28	2	19	28	3	2	2	.500	0	15.0	4.80
Crain,Jesse	Min	26	35	0	35	34	3	11	20	2	2	2	.500	0	12.1	3.86
Cruz,Juan	Ari	29	52	0	60	51	6	29	63	5	4	3	.571	0	12.8	3.75
Danks,John	CWS	23	23	23	116	133	23	48	103	4	4	9	.308	0	14.4	5.74
Davies,Kyle	KC	24	27	27	160	178	22	83	122	4	6	12	.333	0	14.9	5.46
Davis,Doug	Ari	32	32	32	188	192	19	85	143	5	10	11	.476	0	13.5	4.36
de la Rosa,Jorge	KC	27	25	8	72	83	10	37	52	2	2	6	.250	0	15.2	5.63
Delcarmen,Manny	Bos	26	57	0	58	53	3	27	58	2	4	2	.667	0	12.7	3.57
Dempster,Ryan	ChC	31	65	0	70	69	7	34	58	3	4	4	.500	32	13.6	4.37
DePaula,Julio	Min	25	27	0	37	39	4	16	25	2	2	2	.500	0	13.9	4.62
Dessens,Elmer	Col	37	20	3	30	33	4	9	18	0	2	2	.500	0	12.6	4.20
DiNardo,Lenny	Oak	28	34	23	141	159	15	55	83	6	6	10	.375	0	14.0	4.91
Dohmann,Scott	TB	30	50	0	54	55	7	25	53	2	2	4	.333	0	13.7	4.67
Donnelly,Brendan	Bos	36	30	0	30	26	3	10	28	2	2	1	.667	0	11.4	3.30
Dotel,Octavio	Atl	34	50	0	55	45	7	23	68	3	4	2	.667	26	11.6	3.44
Downs,Scott	Tor	32	77	0	54	54	6	20	43	2	3	3	.500	0	12.7	4.17
Duchscherer,Justin	Oak	30	55	0	60	55	6	16	50	2	4	3	.571	1	11.0	3.45
Duckworth,Brandon	KC	32	24	3	43	50	5	18	31	2	2	3	.400	0	14.7	5.23
Duke,Zach	Pit	25	25	18	128	155	11	35	68	4	6	8	.429	0	13.6	4.71
Durbin,Chad	Det	30	35	10	90	97	14	34	60	6	4	6	.400	0	13.7	5.00
Eaton,Adam	Phi	30	26	26	160	173	23	59	115	9	8	10	.444	0	13.6	4.89
Embree,Alan	Oak	38	63	0	68	67	8	20	59	1	4	4	.500	0	11.6	3.71
Escobar,Kelvim	LAA	32	30	30	200	191	16	75	173	6	12	10	.545	0	12.2	3.74
Eyre,Scott	ChC	36	61	0	55	52	5	28	50	1	3	3	.500	0	13.3	4.09
Eyre,Willie	Tex	29	23	2	48	53	5	19	32	2	2	3	.400	0	13.9	4.69
Farnsworth,Kyle	NYY	32	58	0	56	49	7	26	61	1	4	2	.667	0	12.2	3.86
Feldman,Scott	Tex	25	28	0	36	36	3	17	24	2	2	2	.500	0	13.8	4.25
Feliciano,Pedro	NYM	31	78	0	68	60	5	29	61	4	4	3	.571	0	12.3	3.57
Flores,Randy	StL	32	67	0	54	59	5	19	46	3	3	3	.500	0	13.5	4.50
Floyd,Gavin	CWS	25	25	16	118	138	19	51	87	11	4	9	.308	0	15.3	5.87
Fogg,Josh	Col	31	32	31	181	207	25	61	96	9	9	11	.450	0	13.8	5.02
Fossum,Casey	TB	30	22	5	42	49	6	17	32	4	2	3	.400	0	15.0	5.57
Francis,Jeff	Col	27	34	34	218	233	26	72	152	10	13	12	.520	0	13.0	4.42
Francisco,Frank	Tex	28	57	0	56	48	4	31	58	2	3	3	.500	0	13.0	3.70
Franklin,Ryan	StL	35	68	0	78	82	11	22	40	3	4	5	.444	6	12.3	4.27
Frasor,Jason	Tor	30	56	0	64	58	6	28	62	2	4	3	.571	0	12.4	3.80
Fuentes,Brian	Col	32	66	0	66	54	7	28	71	7	5	3	.625	4	12.1	3.55
Fultz,Aaron	Cle	34	48	0	42	40	4	17	34	2	3	2	.600	0	12.6	3.86
Gabbard,Kason	Tex	26	19	19	101	100	11	50	77	5	5	6	.455	0	13.8	4.54
Gagne,Eric	Bos	32	55	0	54	41	4	18	65	2	4	2	.667	32	10.2	3.00
Gallardo,Yovani	Mil	22	26	24	151	126	9	59	169	3	12	5	.706	0	11.2	3.16
Garcia,Freddy	Phi	32	10	10	62	63	8	19	44	2	4	3	.571	0	12.2	4.06
Gardner,Lee	Fla	33	60	0	75	78	6	21	51	3	5	4	.556	5	12.2	3.84
Garland,Jon	CWS	28	31	31	207	218	25	65	107	5	10	13	.435	0	12.5	4.22
Garza,Matt	Min	24	28	26	160	166	13	59	152	8	8	10	.444	0	13.1	4.11
Gaudin,Chad	Oak	25	32	32	202	206	20	90	149	8	10	12	.455	0	13.5	4.41
Geary,Geoff	Phi	31	55	0	74	80	6	21	49	5	4	4	.500	0	12.9	4.14
Germano,Justin	SD	25	29	23	137	152	17	34	92	9	7	8	.467	0	12.8	4.40
Glavine,Tom	NYM	42	32	32	194	202	19	64	102	4	11	10	.524	0	12.5	3.99
Glover,Gary	TB	31	69	0	74	82	10	26	50	2	3	5	.375	0	13.4	4.86
Gobble,Jimmy	KC	26	69	0	53	60	8	19	36	1	2	4	.333	0	13.6	5.09
Gonzalez,Edgar	Ari	25	31	12	102	115	15	26	69	6	5	7	.417	0	13.0	4.76
Gonzalez,Mike	Atl	30	40	0	35	27	1	17	39	1	3	1	.750	24	11.6	3.09
Gordon,Tom	Phi	40	66	0	60	49	6	21	62	1	5	2	.714	0	10.6	3.30
Gorzelanny,Tom	Pit	25	31	31	202	199	14	73	153	9	12	11	.522	0	12.5	3.79
Gosling,Mike	Cin	27	27	0	39	46	6	19	30	1	2	3	.400	0	15.2	5.77
Grabow,John	Pit	29	67	0	57	59	7	24	52	2	3	4	.429	0	13.4	4.42
Green,Sean	Sea	29	73	0	75	76	2	38	53	4	4	4	.500	0	14.2	4.08
Gregg,Kevin	Fla	30	69	0	81	79	8	31	75	4	5	4	.556	32	12.7	4.00
Greinke,Zack	KC	24	30	25	170	182	21	46	129	9	8	11	.421	0	12.5	4.29
Grilli,Jason	Det	31	55	0	82	88	10	33	52	5	4	5	.444	0	13.8	4.83
Guerrier,Matt	Min	29	73	0	86	85	9	24	58	3	5	5	.500	0	11.7	3.77
Guthrie,Jeremy	Bal	29	32	32	210	217	23	77	147	12	10	13	.435	0	13.1	4.33
Halladay,Roy	Tor	31	31	31	226	218	18	47	153	6	16	9	.640	0	10.8	3.31
Hamels,Cole	Phi	24	30	30	200	173	26	56	210	4	15	7	.682	0	10.5	3.33
Hammel,Jason	TB	25	29	24	130	145	14	53	113	5	6	9	.400	0	14.1	4.85
Hampson,Justin	SD	28	49	0	60	66	6	24	39	4	3	4	.429	0	14.1	4.80
Hampton,Mike	Atl	35	15	8	65	71	6	27	34	1	4	4	.500	0	13.7	4.57
Harang,Aaron	Cin	30	32	32	235	239	28	62	199	8	15	11	.577	0	11.8	3.91
Harden,Rich	Oak	26	20	18	125	102	10	53	119	2	9	5	.643	0	11.3	3.24
Haren,Dan	Oak	27	32	32	213	211	26	52	168	6	13	11	.542	0	11.4	3.72
Hawkins,LaTroy	Col	35	60	0	55	54	5	17	38	0	4	2	.667	0	11.6	3.60
Heilman,Aaron	NYM	29	81	0	87	77	7	30	72	4	6	4	.600	0	11.5	3.41
Hendrickson,Mark	LAD	34	39	12	110	128	13	31	62	2	5	7	.417	0	13.2	4.66

457

2008 Pitcher Projections

Pitcher	Team	Age	G	GS	IP	H	HR	BB	SO	HB	W	L	Pct	Sv	BR/9	ERA
Henn,Sean	NYY	27	27	2	37	39	3	18	29	2	2	2	.500	0	14.4	4.62
Hennessey,Brad	SF	28	72	0	71	74	8	27	39	4	3	5	.375	0	13.3	4.44
Hensley,Clay	SD	28	12	9	48	48	4	21	32	1	3	3	.500	0	13.1	4.13
Herges,Matt	Col	38	45	0	65	69	6	24	44	2	4	3	.571	0	13.2	4.29
Hernandez,Felix	Sea	22	32	32	216	209	20	71	205	5	13	11	.542	0	11.9	3.71
Hernandez,Livan	Ari	33	28	28	180	196	22	61	109	6	9	11	.450	0	13.2	4.55
Hernandez,Orlando	NYM	38	28	22	139	127	20	51	118	8	8	7	.533	0	12.0	3.95
Hill,Rich	ChC	28	33	33	206	173	28	69	223	10	14	9	.609	0	11.0	3.50
Hirsh,Jason	Col	26	28	28	169	155	20	64	133	9	11	8	.579	0	12.1	3.83
Hoey,Jim	Bal	25	43	0	48	43	3	23	53	3	3	2	.600	0	12.9	3.75
Hoffman,Trevor	SD	40	63	0	61	51	4	14	56	1	4	3	.571	39	9.7	2.80
Houlton,D.J.	LAD	28	22	0	34	36	5	13	26	2	2	2	.500	0	13.5	4.76
Howell,J.P.	TB	25	8	8	42	47	5	16	40	2	2	3	.400	0	13.9	4.93
Howry,Bob	ChC	34	80	0	85	76	8	24	69	3	6	3	.667	7	10.9	3.28
Hudson,Tim	Atl	32	32	32	221	219	17	64	140	9	15	9	.625	0	11.9	3.67
Isringhausen,Jason	StL	35	61	0	64	49	5	27	58	2	4	3	.571	28	11.0	3.09
Jackson,Edwin	TB	24	31	31	178	206	23	96	134	6	6	13	.316	0	15.6	5.76
James,Chuck	Atl	26	28	28	175	161	27	60	143	4	12	8	.600	0	11.6	3.86
Janssen,Casey	Tor	26	66	0	66	72	6	15	41	4	4	4	.500	0	12.4	4.09
Jenks,Bobby	CWS	27	59	0	62	54	3	22	66	2	4	2	.667	33	11.3	3.19
Jennings,Jason	Hou	29	25	23	150	164	17	66	99	4	7	10	.412	0	14.0	4.86
Jimenez,Kelvin	StL	27	32	0	42	47	3	19	32	2	2	3	.400	0	14.6	4.93
Johnson,Tyler	StL	27	53	0	38	35	4	20	37	3	2	2	.500	0	13.7	4.26
Jones,Todd	Det	40	60	0	60	62	4	20	42	2	4	3	.571	25	12.6	3.90
Julio,Jorge	Col	29	65	0	60	57	9	30	58	2	3	3	.500	0	13.4	4.50
Kazmir,Scott	TB	24	32	32	206	193	18	93	227	7	12	11	.522	0	12.8	3.89
Kennedy,Joe	Tor	29	45	8	96	106	10	37	58	6	4	6	.400	0	14.0	4.78
Kim,Byung-Hyun	Fla	29	31	18	110	114	13	49	98	10	5	7	.417	0	14.2	4.83
King,Ray	Mil	34	71	0	40	40	4	17	26	2	2	2	.500	0	13.3	4.28
Kinney,Josh	StL	29	30	0	35	31	3	16	34	2	2	2	.500	0	12.6	3.60
Kline,Steve	SF	35	71	0	42	42	3	17	25	1	2	3	.400	0	12.9	4.07
Lackey,John	LAA	29	32	32	228	230	19	68	184	11	13	12	.520	0	12.2	3.79
Lawrence,Brian	NYM	32	8	8	45	50	5	12	27	2	2	3	.400	0	12.8	4.20
League,Brandon	Tor	25	36	0	37	41	3	15	25	3	2	2	.500	0	14.4	4.86
Ledezma,Wil	SD	27	34	2	51	55	6	24	36	1	2	3	.400	0	14.1	4.94
Lee,Cliff	Cle	29	30	12	90	93	12	33	68	3	5	5	.500	0	12.9	4.40
Leicester,Jon	Bal	29	18	10	62	69	9	28	45	3	2	5	.286	0	14.5	5.37
Lester,Jon	Bos	24	25	25	175	173	18	89	149	6	10	10	.500	0	13.8	4.42
Lidge,Brad	Hou	31	65	0	68	54	7	29	94	4	5	3	.625	24	11.5	3.44
Lieber,Jon	Phi	38	27	27	167	185	22	29	107	4	10	8	.556	0	11.7	4.04
Lilly,Ted	ChC	32	34	34	208	196	31	77	174	6	12	11	.522	0	12.1	3.98
Lindstrom,Matt	Fla	28	72	0	72	81	6	35	67	5	3	5	.375	5	15.1	5.13
Linebrink,Scott	Mil	31	71	0	70	64	8	25	59	2	5	3	.625	1	11.7	3.60
Liriano,Francisco	Min	24	26	26	152	121	12	45	189	1	12	5	.706	0	9.9	2.84
Litsch,Jesse	Tor	23	26	26	148	160	18	41	92	10	7	9	.438	0	12.8	4.38
Littleton,Wes	Tex	25	52	0	67	68	9	21	45	3	3	4	.429	0	12.4	4.16
Livingston,Bobby	Cin	25	11	11	63	78	7	16	38	1	3	4	.429	0	13.6	5.00
Loaiza,Esteban	LAD	36	20	20	120	133	14	34	82	4	6	7	.462	0	12.8	4.35
Loe,Kameron	Tex	26	30	23	146	172	16	60	80	3	6	10	.375	0	14.5	5.18
Logan,Boone	CWS	23	71	0	56	58	6	25	53	5	2	4	.333	0	14.1	4.82
Lohse,Kyle	Phi	29	35	31	188	210	24	58	116	9	10	11	.476	0	13.3	4.69
Looper,Braden	StL	33	32	30	183	190	17	59	103	6	10	10	.500	0	12.5	3.98
Lopez,Javier	Bos	30	57	0	36	37	2	16	24	3	2	2	.500	0	14.0	4.25
Lowe,Derek	LAD	35	32	32	212	216	19	61	134	6	13	11	.542	0	12.0	3.78
Lowry,Noah	SF	27	30	30	194	192	20	82	129	6	9	12	.429	0	13.0	4.13
Lugo,Ruddy	Oak	28	53	0	76	67	3	46	55	3	4	4	.500	0	13.7	3.79
Lyon,Brandon	Ari	28	70	0	72	78	7	21	44	1	4	4	.500	0	12.5	4.13
MacDougal,Mike	CWS	31	59	0	52	51	3	26	47	3	3	3	.500	0	13.8	4.15
Maddux,Greg	SD	42	34	34	200	208	21	31	121	5	13	9	.591	0	11.0	3.60
Madson,Ryan	Phi	27	40	0	60	64	7	20	47	4	3	3	.500	0	13.2	4.50
Mahay,Ron	Atl	37	71	0	76	73	9	38	67	1	5	4	.556	0	13.3	4.26
Maholm,Paul	Pit	27	27	27	175	193	17	62	115	8	8	11	.421	0	13.5	4.58
Maine,John	NYM	27	31	31	200	190	26	81	169	5	12	11	.522	0	12.4	4.05
Majewski,Gary	Cin	28	50	0	55	63	3	21	33	3	3	3	.500	0	14.2	4.75
Marcum,Shaun	Tor	26	29	29	183	186	32	55	152	6	9	11	.450	0	12.1	4.38
Marmol,Carlos	ChC	25	66	0	81	68	9	44	85	6	5	4	.556	2	13.1	4.00
Maroth,Mike	StL	30	25	6	67	80	11	20	32	2	3	5	.375	0	13.7	5.37
Marquis,Jason	ChC	29	34	32	191	198	27	74	109	10	9	12	.429	0	13.3	4.66
Marshall,Sean	ChC	25	23	19	102	100	13	41	68	3	6	6	.500	0	12.7	4.15
Marte,Damaso	Pit	33	63	0	42	35	4	19	45	2	3	2	.600	0	12.0	3.64
Martinez,Pedro	NYM	36	22	22	125	99	11	29	135	7	10	4	.714	0	9.7	2.88
Mastny,Tom	Cle	27	42	0	53	49	2	26	52	3	3	3	.500	0	13.2	3.74
Matsuzaka,Daisuke	Bos	27	30	30	193	173	20	64	188	7	14	8	.636	0	11.4	3.54
McBride,Macay	Det	25	35	0	40	42	4	23	37	1	2	3	.400	0	14.8	5.18
McCarthy,Brandon	Tex	24	28	28	176	173	28	65	142	3	9	11	.450	0	12.3	4.30
McClung,Seth	Mil	27	45	0	50	50	6	31	44	3	2	3	.400	0	15.1	5.22
McGowan,Dustin	Tor	26	29	29	194	185	20	84	174	7	11	11	.500	0	12.8	4.04
McLemore,Mark	Hou	27	44	0	56	52	5	35	51	3	3	3	.500	0	14.5	4.50
Meche,Gil	KC	29	32	32	210	215	26	79	151	5	10	13	.435	0	12.8	4.33
Meredith,Cla	SD	25	82	0	82	82	7	18	63	3	5	4	.556	0	11.3	3.51
Mesa,Jose	Phi	42	55	0	51	53	6	23	34	2	3	3	.500	0	13.8	4.76

458

2008 Pitcher Projections

Pitcher	Team	Age	G	GS	IP	H	HR	BB	SO	HB	W	L	Pct	Sv	BR/9	ERA
Messenger,Randy	SF	26	64	0	73	81	7	31	49	1	3	5	.375	0	13.9	4.81
Miller,Justin	Fla	30	69	0	70	73	9	35	64	3	3	4	.429	0	14.3	5.01
Miller,Trever	Hou	35	70	0	49	47	6	22	46	5	3	3	.500	0	13.6	4.41
Millwood,Kevin	Tex	33	32	32	193	201	20	60	145	6	10	11	.476	0	12.5	4.01
Miner,Zach	Det	26	43	0	73	80	7	35	49	1	4	5	.444	0	14.3	4.81
Misch,Pat	SF	26	26	8	70	79	8	20	54	3	3	5	.375	0	13.1	4.50
Mitre,Sergio	Fla	27	28	28	165	193	17	55	103	11	8	10	.444	0	14.1	4.96
Moehler,Brian	Hou	36	46	0	66	83	9	18	36	2	3	5	.375	0	14.0	5.32
Morris,Matt	Pit	33	31	31	192	207	21	53	120	9	10	11	.476	0	12.6	4.17
Moseley,Dustin	LAA	26	40	11	100	117	12	34	61	5	4	7	.364	0	14.0	5.04
Mota,Guillermo	NYM	34	63	0	70	66	8	26	59	1	4	3	.571	0	12.0	3.73
Moyer,Jamie	Phi	45	31	31	190	201	27	53	111	7	11	10	.524	0	12.4	4.31
Moylan,Peter	Atl	29	80	0	85	80	6	39	68	8	5	4	.556	0	13.4	4.02
Mulder,Mark	StL	30	23	23	143	152	17	47	88	6	7	9	.438	0	12.9	4.34
Munter,Scott	SF	28	31	0	33	40	1	15	11	1	1	2	.333	0	15.3	5.18
Mussina,Mike	NYY	39	28	26	154	159	17	33	124	4	11	7	.611	0	11.5	3.74
Myers,Brett	Phi	27	65	5	95	94	14	33	83	3	6	5	.545	29	12.3	4.17
Myers,Mike	CWS	39	55	0	45	45	4	21	29	3	2	3	.400	0	13.8	4.40
Nathan,Joe	Min	33	63	0	70	50	4	25	81	1	5	3	.625	40	9.8	2.70
Neshek,Pat	Min	27	68	0	65	51	9	20	80	1	5	3	.625	0	10.0	3.05
Nippert,Dustin	Ari	27	39	0	46	47	4	21	41	1	2	3	.400	0	13.5	4.30
Nunez,Leo	KC	24	22	9	72	73	11	23	55	2	3	5	.375	0	12.2	4.25
OFlaherty,Eric'	Sea	23	59	0	51	54	1	22	42	5	3	3	.500	0	14.3	4.24
Ohman,Will	ChC	30	48	0	30	26	3	15	32	2	2	2	.500	0	12.9	3.90
Oliver,Darren	LAA	37	63	0	75	85	10	26	47	3	3	5	.375	0	13.7	4.92
Olsen,Scott	Fla	24	30	30	165	177	23	74	149	4	8	11	.421	0	13.9	4.96
Ortiz,Ramon	Col	35	40	5	82	93	14	26	48	5	4	5	.444	0	13.6	5.16
Osoria,Franquelis	Pit	26	48	0	57	70	5	20	33	7	2	4	.333	0	15.3	5.37
Oswalt,Roy	Hou	30	31	31	210	209	16	49	167	7	14	9	.609	0	11.4	3.51
Otsuka,Akinori	Tex	36	43	0	48	42	2	16	43	0	4	2	.667	8	10.9	3.00
Owings,Micah	Ari	25	29	28	166	173	17	57	124	13	9	10	.474	0	13.2	4.28
Padilla,Vicente	Tex	30	23	23	120	126	14	44	82	9	6	8	.429	0	13.4	4.50
Papelbon,Jonathan	Bos	27	60	0	60	43	5	16	66	3	4	2	.667	39	9.3	2.70
Paronto,Chad	Atl	32	35	0	35	38	2	14	23	2	2	2	.500	0	13.9	4.37
Parrish,John	Sea	30	43	0	46	49	3	34	41	2	2	3	.400	0	16.6	5.28
Patterson,John	Was	30	18	18	113	107	14	46	101	4	6	7	.462	0	12.5	4.06
Peavy,Jake	SD	27	31	31	212	180	20	67	217	7	15	8	.652	0	10.8	3.23
Pena,Tony	Ari	26	72	0	79	71	8	24	57	4	5	3	.625	7	11.3	3.53
Penny,Brad	LAD	30	32	32	195	198	16	62	139	5	12	10	.616	0	12.2	3.83
Peralta,Joel	KC	32	60	0	76	76	9	19	60	3	4	4	.500	0	11.6	3.79
Percival,Troy	StL	38	50	2	58	43	7	24	55	2	4	2	.667	0	10.7	3.26
Perez,Odalis	KC	31	18	18	96	106	12	26	61	2	5	6	.455	0	12.6	4.31
Perez,Oliver	NYM	26	30	30	190	176	31	100	196	9	9	12	.429	0	13.5	4.69
Perez,Rafael	Cle	26	56	0	73	67	5	22	62	2	5	3	.625	5	11.2	3.33
Petit,Yusmeiro	Ari	23	18	11	83	64	10	19	49	1	3	4	.429	0	12.0	4.14
Pettitte,Andy	NYY	36	32	32	205	212	18	58	156	2	14	9	.609	0	11.9	3.78
Pineiro,Joel	StL	29	30	27	173	189	22	56	109	6	8	11	.421	0	13.1	4.53
Pinto,Renyel	Fla	25	60	0	65	60	6	40	66	6	3	4	.429	0	14.7	4.57
Prior,Mark	ChC	27	20	20	75	66	10	26	85	4	5	4	.556	0	11.5	3.60
Proctor,Scott	LAD	31	75	0	80	77	13	33	68	4	4	5	.444	0	12.8	4.50
Putz,J.J.	Sea	31	63	0	68	56	6	17	71	2	4	3	.571	33	9.9	2.91
Qualls,Chad	Hou	29	76	0	80	78	9	24	62	5	5	4	.556	2	12.0	3.83
Ramirez,Elizardo	Cin	25	8	6	33	40	5	9	21	2	2	2	.500	0	13.9	5.18
Ramirez,Horacio	Sea	28	15	15	95	108	12	37	44	2	4	7	.364	0	13.9	5.02
Rauch,Jon	Was	29	89	0	89	79	10	28	75	1	6	4	.600	4	10.9	3.44
Redding,Tim	Was	30	25	25	155	175	22	60	108	5	6	11	.353	0	13.9	5.11
Redman,Mark	Col	34	13	8	50	57	6	17	29	2	3	3	.500	0	13.7	4.86
Reyes,Al	TB	38	61	0	63	52	8	23	66	3	4	3	.571	30	11.1	3.43
Reyes,Anthony	StL	26	24	20	109	102	16	35	93	6	6	6	.500	0	11.8	3.88
Reyes,Dennys	Min	31	45	0	30	31	2	16	25	1	1	2	.333	0	14.4	4.50
Rheinecker,John	Tex	29	40	11	84	99	8	29	49	3	4	6	.400	0	14.0	4.82
Rincon,Juan	Min	29	62	0	64	60	4	26	60	3	4	3	.571	0	12.5	3.66
Ring,Royce	Atl	27	40	0	30	26	2	15	29	1	2	1	.667	0	12.6	3.60
Riske,David	KC	31	59	0	66	57	9	27	57	3	4	4	.500	0	11.9	3.82
Rivera,Mariano	NYY	38	70	0	76	64	3	15	69	5	6	3	.667	35	9.9	2.72
Rivera,Saul	Was	30	85	0	90	87	3	38	67	4	5	5	.500	0	12.9	3.70
Robertson,Nate	Det	30	30	30	180	189	25	62	121	5	10	10	.500	0	12.8	4.40
Rodney,Fernando	Det	31	60	0	70	62	6	32	67	5	4	3	.571	1	12.7	3.86
Rodriguez,Francisco	LAA	26	64	0	69	48	5	30	92	1	5	3	.625	34	10.3	2.87
Rodriguez,Wandy	Hou	29	31	31	185	197	24	73	141	9	9	12	.429	0	13.6	4.72
Rogers,Kenny	Det	43	23	23	145	154	15	46	76	6	8	8	.500	0	12.8	4.22
Romero,J.C.	Phi	31	75	0	55	51	4	31	43	3	3	3	.500	0	13.9	4.25
Rowland-Smith,Ryan	Sea	25	39	0	57	58	4	28	58	3	3	4	.429	0	14.1	4.42
Ryan,B.J.	Tor	32	51	0	53	40	3	24	65	1	4	2	.667	32	11.0	3.06
Saarloos,Kirk	Cin	29	24	3	41	48	5	15	20	2	2	3	.400	0	14.3	5.27
Sabathia,C.C.	Cle	27	32	32	230	219	21	69	189	8	15	10	.600	0	11.6	3.56
Saito,Takashi	LAD	38	64	0	68	59	7	18	68	3	5	3	.625	38	10.6	3.31
Salas,Juan	TB	29	38	0	47	44	5	23	47	3	3	3	.500	0	13.4	4.21
Sampson,Chris	Hou	30	17	9	67	73	9	12	33	2	4	4	.500	0	11.7	4.03
Sanchez,Duaner	NYM	28	56	0	61	58	6	25	45	4	4	3	.571	4	12.8	3.98
Sanchez,Jonathan	SF	25	26	8	58	49	4	29	66	4	3	3	.500	0	12.7	3.57

459

2008 Pitcher Projections

Pitcher	Team	Age	G	GS	IP	H	HR	BB	SO	HB	W	L	Pct	Sv	BR/9	ERA
Santana,Ervin	LAA	25	28	25	160	164	20	57	124	9	8	10	.444	0	12.9	4.39
Santana,Johan	Min	29	32	32	216	174	24	57	228	4	16	8	.667	0	9.8	3.00
Santos,Victor	Bal	31	29	6	65	73	9	29	44	2	2	5	.286	0	14.4	5.40
Saunders,Joe	LAA	27	25	25	151	160	15	48	108	3	8	9	.471	0	12.6	4.05
Schilling,Curt	Bos	41	25	25	160	161	20	25	150	2	11	7	.611	0	10.6	3.54
Schmidt,Jason	LAD	35	22	22	145	125	13	56	139	4	10	6	.625	0	11.5	3.41
Schoeneweis,Scott	NYM	34	70	0	60	63	6	25	36	3	3	4	.429	0	13.6	4.50
Schroder,Chris	Was	29	51	0	60	49	6	28	70	5	4	3	.571	0	12.3	3.60
Seanez,Rudy	LAD	39	70	0	78	74	9	36	84	2	4	4	.500	0	12.9	4.15
Seay,Bobby	Det	30	58	0	50	50	4	19	39	3	3	3	.500	0	13.0	3.96
Seddon,Chris	Fla	24	14	8	35	41	5	14	26	4	1	2	.333	0	14.7	5.40
Sele,Aaron	NYM	38	34	0	51	61	6	17	26	2	2	3	.400	0	14.1	5.12
Shearn,Tom	Cin	30	14	12	65	71	9	30	51	1	3	4	.429	0	14.1	5.12
Sheets,Ben	Mil	29	27	27	185	181	21	40	161	3	13	8	.619	0	10.9	3.55
Sherrill,George	Sea	31	71	0	44	35	3	19	51	1	3	2	.600	0	11.2	3.07
Shields,James	TB	26	30	30	204	212	23	44	183	9	12	11	.522	0	11.7	3.84
Shields,Scot	LAA	32	68	0	72	61	5	26	67	2	5	3	.625	1	11.1	3.25
Shouse,Brian	Mil	39	74	0	49	51	3	18	32	3	3	3	.500	0	13.2	4.04
Silva,Carlos	Min	29	32	32	199	239	26	35	82	6	9	13	.409	0	12.7	4.61
Simontacchi,Jason	Was	34	6	6	35	42	6	12	19	2	1	3	.250	0	14.4	5.66
Slaten,Doug	Ari	28	57	0	31	29	2	13	32	1	2	1	.667	0	12.5	3.48
Smoltz,John	Atl	41	33	33	221	204	19	49	199	4	17	7	.708	0	10.5	3.22
Snell,Ian	Pit	26	31	31	210	211	27	73	182	5	11	12	.478	0	12.4	4.11
Snyder,Kyle	Bos	30	41	0	51	58	6	17	34	2	3	3	.500	0	13.6	4.76
Sonnanstine,Andy	TB	25	27	27	154	167	22	33	125	5	8	9	.471	0	12.0	4.15
Soriano,Rafael	Atl	28	68	0	74	56	9	20	77	3	6	2	.750	21	9.6	2.92
Sosa,Jorge	NYM	31	45	15	115	116	16	48	75	1	6	7	.462	0	12.9	4.38
Sowers,Jeremy	Cle	25	15	15	110	120	9	30	60	4	6	6	.500	0	12.6	4.01
Speier,Justin	LAA	34	65	0	64	55	8	20	56	4	4	3	.571	0	11.1	3.52
Speier,Ryan	Col	28	45	0	50	55	2	22	35	5	3	3	.500	0	14.8	4.68
Springer,Russ	StL	39	76	0	73	60	10	25	64	4	5	3	.625	0	11.0	3.45
Spurling,Chris	Mil	31	48	0	47	52	5	12	23	1	3	3	.500	0	12.4	4.21
Stanton,Mike	Cin	41	45	0	40	43	3	15	29	2	2	2	.500	0	13.5	4.05
Stokes,Brian	TB	28	42	0	51	60	6	20	35	2	2	4	.333	0	14.5	5.29
Street,Huston	Oak	24	61	0	68	54	4	17	71	1	5	3	.625	35	9.5	2.65
Stults,Eric	LAD	28	16	8	53	62	6	21	43	1	2	4	.333	0	14.3	5.26
Suppan,Jeff	Mil	33	32	32	204	225	23	68	113	9	11	12	.478	0	13.3	4.59
Switzer,Jon	TB	28	36	0	36	42	3	15	25	3	1	3	.250	0	15.0	5.25
Tallet,Brian	Tor	30	50	0	67	64	8	28	49	4	4	4	.500	0	12.9	4.16
Tankersley,Taylor	Fla	25	71	0	52	44	4	32	59	2	3	3	.500	5	13.5	3.81
Taschner,Jack	SF	30	59	0	48	43	4	24	52	2	3	3	.500	0	12.9	3.94
Tavarez,Julian	Bos	35	35	18	118	127	10	47	68	9	6	7	.462	0	14.0	4.58
Tejeda,Robinson	Tex	26	9	9	48	49	6	29	38	3	2	3	.400	0	15.2	5.25
Thompson,Brad	StL	26	50	10	109	118	14	32	55	9	5	7	.417	0	13.1	4.62
Thornton,Matt	CWS	31	68	0	63	60	8	34	60	1	3	4	.429	1	13.6	4.43
Timlin,Mike	Bos	42	57	0	62	62	6	15	39	3	4	3	.571	0	11.6	3.63
Tomko,Brett	SD	35	35	21	137	150	18	44	87	3	7	8	.467	0	12.9	4.53
Torres,Salomon	Pit	36	53	0	51	51	5	18	36	3	3	3	.500	0	12.7	4.06
Towers,Josh	Tor	31	21	10	81	100	13	14	47	4	3	6	.333	0	13.1	5.11
Traber,Billy	Was	28	34	1	39	45	4	11	28	3	2	3	.400	0	13.6	4.62
Trachsel,Steve	ChC	37	29	29	162	169	21	64	86	3	8	10	.444	0	13.1	4.50
Turnbow,Derrick	Mil	30	72	0	66	54	6	41	72	2	4	3	.571	0	13.2	3.82
Valverde,Jose	Ari	28	63	0	67	52	7	29	83	2	5	3	.625	40	11.1	3.36
Vargas,Claudio	Mil	30	27	18	115	125	20	44	85	5	5	7	.417	0	13.6	5.09
Vazquez,Javier	CWS	31	31	31	218	214	29	53	196	8	13	12	.520	0	11.4	3.80
Verlander,Justin	Det	25	31	31	202	188	20	66	163	13	13	9	.591	0	11.9	3.70
Villanueva,Carlos	Mil	24	49	10	122	110	17	47	106	4	8	6	.571	0	11.9	3.84
Villarreal,Oscar	Atl	26	43	0	65	64	7	25	45	3	4	3	.571	0	12.7	4.02
Villone,Ron	NYY	38	38	0	46	43	5	23	37	3	3	2	.600	0	13.5	4.30
Vizcaino,Luis	NYY	33	71	0	69	62	9	30	60	2	4	3	.571	0	12.3	3.91
Wagner,Billy	NYM	36	65	0	69	50	6	20	82	3	5	3	.625	35	9.5	2.74
Wainwright,Adam	StL	26	31	31	213	225	18	69	160	9	11	12	.478	0	12.8	4.06
Wakefield,Tim	Bos	41	29	29	181	174	24	63	123	10	11	9	.550	0	12.3	4.03
Walker,Jamie	Bal	36	77	0	61	60	8	14	44	2	4	3	.571	0	11.2	3.69
Walker,Tyler	SF	32	32	0	35	36	4	14	28	1	2	2	.500	2	13.1	4.37
Wang,Chien-Ming	NYY	28	30	30	204	215	12	55	89	6	14	9	.609	0	12.2	3.75
Washburn,Jarrod	Sea	33	31	31	193	199	24	58	111	7	10	11	.476	0	12.3	4.15
Wassermann,Ehren	CWS	27	55	0	38	40	1	17	28	4	2	2	.500	0	14.4	4.26
Weathers,David	Cin	38	70	0	75	70	7	31	54	3	5	4	.556	31	12.5	3.84
Weaver,Jeff	Sea	31	29	29	185	208	26	48	118	12	8	12	.400	0	13.0	4.72
Weaver,Jered	LAA	25	29	29	189	182	21	50	163	3	12	9	.571	0	11.2	3.57
Webb,Brandon	Ari	29	32	32	236	218	16	77	187	7	16	10	.615	0	11.5	3.39
Wellemeyer,Todd	StL	29	27	10	71	68	8	42	59	2	3	5	.375	0	14.2	4.56
Wells,David	LAD	45	20	20	135	158	17	23	74	4	7	8	.467	0	12.3	4.33
Wells,Kip	StL	31	32	23	155	165	18	71	111	8	7	10	.412	0	14.2	4.88
Westbrook,Jake	Cle	30	29	29	196	213	16	63	107	7	11	11	.500	0	13.0	4.18
Wheeler,Dan	TB	30	69	0	73	70	8	23	68	2	4	4	.500	0	11.7	3.82
Wickman,Bob	Ari	39	35	0	35	35	3	12	27	1	2	2	.500	0	12.3	3.86
Williams,Woody	Hou	41	26	23	140	149	20	39	87	6	7	8	.467	0	12.5	4.37
Willis,Dontrelle	Fla	26	34	34	209	219	20	73	153	12	12	11	.522	0	13.1	4.22
Wilson,Brian	SF	26	63	0	66	54	2	37	62	4	4	3	.571	26	13.0	3.55

2008 Pitcher Projections

Pitcher	Team	Age	G	GS	IP	H	HR	BB	SO	HB	W	L	Pct	Sv	BR/9	ERA
Wilson,C.J.	Tex	27	62	0	65	61	6	29	59	5	3	4	.429	4	13.2	4.02
Wise,Matt	Mil	32	46	0	40	38	4	13	31	1	3	2	.600	1	11.7	3.83
Wolf,Randy	LAD	31	18	18	100	101	13	36	81	5	5	6	.455	0	12.8	4.32
Wolfe,Brian	Tor	27	52	0	65	69	6	20	45	2	4	4	.500	0	12.6	4.02
Wood,Kerry	ChC	31	50	0	60	48	7	29	65	4	4	3	.571	0	12.2	3.75
Wood,Mike	Tex	28	33	2	69	80	10	22	39	5	3	5	.375	0	14.0	5.09
Wright,Jamey	Tex	33	27	6	92	99	10	45	52	7	4	6	.400	0	14.8	5.09
Wuertz,Mike	ChC	29	69	0	72	59	7	32	83	1	5	3	.625	0	11.5	3.50
Yates,Tyler	Atl	30	71	0	64	61	7	34	61	2	4	3	.571	0	13.6	4.36
Youman,Shane	Pit	28	24	8	71	79	5	29	43	1	3	4	.429	0	13.8	4.44
Young,Chris	SD	29	30	30	186	152	21	68	166	7	13	8	.619	0	11.0	3.34
Zambrano,Carlos	ChC	27	32	32	215	177	19	99	189	12	14	10	.583	0	12.1	3.52
Zito,Barry	SF	30	35	33	212	190	24	85	153	9	12	12	.500	0	12.1	3.74
Zumaya,Joel	Det	23	60	0	70	52	5	37	81	3	5	3	.625	4	11.8	3.34

Career Targets

by Bill James

Ichiro Suzuki, having been in the US for seven seasons, has had seven consecutive 200-hit seasons. The record is eight, and that streak, by Willie Keeler, ended in 1901. Wade Boggs also had seven.

Young Michael Young of Texas now has five consecutive 200-hit seasons, which, while not quite Ichiroic, is still an extremely impressive accomplishment—as in, neither Pete Rose nor Ty Cobb ever did that, nor Musial nor Aaron nor Tony Gwynn. The only guys ever to do that before Young are Willie Keeler, Boggs, Ichiro, Al Simmons, Charlie Gehringer and Chuck Klein—all Hall of Famers.

So then, are Young and Suzuki on target for 3,000 career hits? Probably not. Young at age 25, before his first 200-hit season, was almost 500 hits behind Pete Rose, and more than a thousand behind Cobb. What he has done is extremely impressive, and it makes him a 3,000 hit *candidate*, but he still has his work cut out for him. Ichiro, winning batting titles in Japan until age 26, started out about 450 hits behind Young.

The chart at right summarizes the 3,000-hit candidates in the major leagues today. The next page looks at the top candidates to break records or to achieve other milestone markers. Derek Jeter, with three consecutive 200-hit seasons and six in his career, almost certainly will get 3,000 hits, and is now on the cusp of emerging as a serious candidate for 4,000.

3,000 Hits	
% chance to reach milestone	
Biggio,Craig	done
Bonds,Barry	98%
Jeter,Derek	91%
Rodriguez,Alex	81%
Guerrero,Vladimir	50%
Renteria,Edgar	37%
Rollins,Jimmy	34%
Pujols,Albert	33%
Pierre,Juan	32%
Damon,Johnny	31%
Cabrera,Miguel	30%
Tejada,Miguel	29%
Crawford,Carl	28%
Griffey Jr.,Ken	26%
Reyes,Jose	26%
Young,Michael	24%
Suzuki,Ichiro	23%
Beltre,Adrian	23%
Rodriguez,Ivan	22%
Wright,David	21%
Helton,Todd	19%
Lee,Carlos	18%
Sizemore,Grady	17%
Furcal,Rafael	15%
Ramirez,Manny	15%
Castillo,Luis	14%
Holliday,Matt	14%
Cano,Robinson	13%
Jones,Andruw	13%
Anderson,Garret	12%
Abreu,Bobby	11%
Ramirez,Hanley	11%
Ordonez,Magglio	11%
Francoeur,Jeff	10%
Ramirez,Aramis	9%
Jones,Chipper	9%
Wells,Vernon	9%
Teixeira,Mark	7%
Beltran,Carlos	7%
Zimmerman,Ryan	7%
Green,Shawn	7%
Cabrera,Orlando	7%
Polanco,Placido	7%
Atkins,Garrett	6%
Soriano,Alfonso	5%
Konerko,Paul	5%
Vizquel,Omar	4%
Utley,Chase	4%
Roberts,Brian	4%
Ortiz,David	4%

Career Targets

762 Home Runs			**2,298 RBI**			**2,296 Runs Scored**			**4,257 Hits**	
% chance to break record			% chance to break record			% chance to break record			% chance to break record	
Bonds,Barry	done		Rodriguez,Alex	47%		Bonds,Barry	88%		Cabrera,Miguel	< 1%
Rodriguez,Alex	55%		Pujols,Albert	11%		Rodriguez,Alex	40%			
Pujols,Albert	11%		Cabrera,Miguel	9%		Rollins,Jimmy	10%			
Dunn,Adam	7%		Guerrero,Vladimir	8%		Sizemore,Grady	7%			
Howard,Ryan	5%		Jones,Andruw	7%		Pujols,Albert	7%			
Jones,Andruw	4%		Ramirez,Manny	1%		Reyes,Jose	6%			
Fielder,Prince	2%		Wright,David	< 1%		Jeter,Derek	4%			

900 Home Runs			**2,000 RBI**			**6,857 Total Bases**			**4,000 Hits**	
% chance to reach milestone			% chance to reach milestone			% chance to break record			% chance to reach milestone	
Rodriguez,Alex	17%		Bonds,Barry	99%		Rodriguez,Alex	24%		Jeter,Derek	7%
			Rodriguez,Alex	90%		Pujols,Albert	9%		Rodriguez,Alex	6%
			Ramirez,Manny	40%		Cabrera,Miguel	5%		Cabrera,Miguel	5%
			Guerrero,Vladimir	30%		Guerrero,Vladimir	2%		Rollins,Jimmy	3%
			Pujols,Albert	27%		Rollins,Jimmy	1%		Reyes,Jose	3%
			Jones,Andruw	26%					Crawford,Carl	2%
			Griffey Jr.,Ken	22%					Pujols,Albert	2%
			Cabrera,Miguel	21%					Guerrero,Vladimir	< 1%
			Ortiz,David	13%					Wright,David	< 1%
			Wright,David	10%						

800 Home Runs			**600 Home Runs**			**793 Doubles**			**Most Likely No-Hitter**	
% chance to reach milestone			% chance to reach milestone			% chance to break record			% chance to reach milestone	
Bonds,Barry	43%		Bonds,Barry	done		Cabrera,Miguel	13%		Kazmir,Scott	24%
Rodriguez,Alex	41%		Sosa,Sammy	done		Wright,David	7%		Bedard,Erik	23%
Pujols,Albert	7%		Griffey Jr.,Ken	99%		Zimmerman,Ryan	6%		Peavy,Jake	20%
Dunn,Adam	3%		Rodriguez,Alex	95%		Helton,Todd	6%		Santana,Johan	17%
Howard,Ryan	2%		Thome,Jim	55%		Sizemore,Grady	5%		Matsuzaka,Daisuke	13%
			Ramirez,Manny	43%		Beltre,Adrian	5%		Burnett,A.J.	12%
			Pujols,Albert	42%		Pujols,Albert	5%		Young,Chris	12%
			Jones,Andruw	41%		Rollins,Jimmy	4%		Lincecum,Tim	12%
			Dunn,Adam	33%		Ramirez,Hanley	3%		Vazquez,Javier	11%
			Howard,Ryan	24%		Cano,Robinson	3%		Perez,Oliver	11%

700 Home Runs			**500 Home Runs**			**1,000 Stolen Bases**	
% chance to reach milestone			% chance to reach milestone			% chance to reach milestone	
Bonds,Barry	done		Bonds,Barry	done		Reyes,Jose	33%
Rodriguez,Alex	89%		Sosa,Sammy	done		Pierre,Juan	15%
Pujols,Albert	20%		Griffey Jr.,Ken	done		Crawford,Carl	11%
Griffey Jr.,Ken	20%		Rodriguez,Alex	done			
Dunn,Adam	15%		Thomas,Frank	done			
Jones,Andruw	14%		Thome,Jim	done			
Howard,Ryan	11%		Ramirez,Manny	99%			
Fielder,Prince	7%		Sheffield,Gary	97%			
Ortiz,David	5%		Delgado,Carlos	93%			
Thome,Jim	< 1%		Jones,Andruw	89%			

300-Win Candidates

Bill James

When Tom Glavine rolled past 300 wins last summer there was the usual flurry of articles saying that he would be the last pitcher ever to do this—or, if not him, then Randy Johnson would. The end is near, anyway.

We do not believe that the end of 300-game winners is upon us. There is a sort of rule of thumb in history that the best careers represent about 18 years worth of league-leading performance—thus, as long as pitchers win 17 or more games in a season, there will probably be pitchers who win 300 in a career. But we'll let history decide that, and in any case, it does appear that it might be several years now before there is another 300-game winner.

Or not; Randy Johnson could come back, and Mike Mussina is now just three years away if he pitches well.

Name	2007 Age	R/L	W	L	EWL	Momentum	Chance
Randy Johnson	43	L	284	150	7.0	.790	.58
Johan Santana	28	L	93	44	15.7	.911	.29
John Smoltz	40	R	207	145	13.1	.815	.23
Jamie Moyer	44	L	230	178	11.4	.721	.13
Roy Oswalt	29	R	112	54	13.2	.865	.13
Brandon Webb	28	R	65	55	15.1	.875	.13
Mike Mussina	38	R	250	144	9.9	.631	.10
Andy Pettitte	35	L	201	113	12.5	.730	.08
John Lackey	28	R	79	58	15.2	.843	.08
C.C. Sabathia	26	L	100	63	15.6	.821	.08
Javier Vazquez	30	R	115	113	13.7	.798	.05
Tim Hudson	31	R	135	70	12.8	.789	.05
Curt Schilling	40	R	216	146	9.4	.696	.04
Tim Wakefield	40	R	168	146	12.1	.718	.03
Livan Hernandez	32	R	134	128	9.7	.804	.02
Barry Zito	29	L	113	76	10.9	.799	.02
David Wells	44	L	239	157	7.3	.616	.02
Derek Lowe	34	R	112	96	11.7	.770	.01
Roy Halladay	30	R	111	55	13.1	.732	.01
Mark Buehrle	28	L	107	75	9.9	.791	.01
Jon Garland	27	R	92	81	10.3	.782	.01
(Less than 1%: Matt Morris, Jeff Suppan, Woody Williams, Kevin Millwood.)							

Note: EWL = Established Win Level

Baseball Glossary

% Inherited Scored
The percentage of inherited baserunners a relief pitcher allows to score.

% Pitches Taken
The percentage of pitches that a batter does not swing at out of the total number of pitches thrown to him.

1st Batter Average
The Batting Average that a relief pitcher allows to the first batter he faces when he enters a game.

1st Batter OBP
The On-Base Percentage that a relief pitcher allows to the first batter he faces when he enters a game.

1st to 3rd (Baserunning)
Moved is the number of times a runner goes from 1st base to 3rd base on a SINGLE. Chances are the number of times a runner is on 1st base and a batter is credited with a SINGLE.

1st to Home (Baserunning)
Moved is the number of times a runner goes from 1st base to home on a DOUBLE. Chances are the number of times a runner is on 1st base and a batter is credited with a DOUBLE.

2nd to Home (Baserunning)
Moved is the number of times a runner goes from 2nd base to home on a SINGLE. Chances are the number of times a runner is on 2nd base and a batter is credited with a SINGLE.

Active Career Batting Leaders
A list of batting leaders among active (appearing in the most recent season) players. An active player is eligible when he meets the minimum requirements for the following categories:

> 1,000 At Bats—Batting Average, On-Base Percentage, Slugging Average, At Bats Per HR, At Bats Per GDP, At Bats Per RBI, Strikeout to Walk Ratio
> 100 Stolen Base Attempts—Stolen Base Success Percentage

Active Career Pitching Leaders
A list of pitching leaders among active (appearing in the most recent season) players. An active player is eligible when he meets the minimum requirements for the following categories:

750 Innings Pitched—Earned Run Average, Opponent Batting Average, all "Per 9 Innings" categories, Strikeout to Walk Ratio
250 Games Started—Complete Game Frequency
100 Decisions—Win-Loss Percentage

AVG Allowed ScPos
The Batting Average allowed by a pitcher while pitching with runners in scoring position.

AVG Bases Loaded
The Batting Average of a hitter while batting with the bases loaded.

Base Taken
A player is credited with a Base Taken whenever he moves up a base on a Wild Pitch, Passed Ball, Balk, Sacrifice Fly (other than the runner who scores), or Defensive Indifference.

Batting Average
Hits divided by at bats.

Blown Save
When a relief pitcher enters a game in a Save Situation (see definition for Save Situation) and allows the other team to score the tying or go-ahead run.

Bomb (Intentional Walk)
An Intentional Walk blows up (Bombs) when the next batter after the intentional walk does not ground into a double play and subsequently more than one run scores in the inning.

BR Gain (Baserunning)
BR Gain (or Loss if a negative number) is the total of all the types of extra baserunning advances minus the (triple) penalty for all the BR Outs compared with what would be expected based on the MLB averages.

BR Outs (Baserunning)
BR Outs include the sum of Outs Advancing, Doubled Offs, and when a runner is tagged out on the bases when another runner moves up on a Wild Pitch, Passed Ball, or scores on a Sacrifice Fly.

Career Targets
This method, once called the Favorite Toy, is a way to estimate the probability that a player will achieve a specific career goal. In this example, 3,000 hits will be used. The four components of the formula are Needed Hits, Years Remaining, Established Hit Level and Projected Remaining Hits.

Needed Hits. This is the number of Hits (or any statistic) that a player needs to reach a desired goal.

Years Remaining. This is the estimated number of years remaining in the player's career. It is determined using the player's age (on June 30th of the previous year; use 2003 when making the calculation after the 2003 season is complete). The formula is (42 - age) divided by two. This means a player who is 20 years old will have 11 remaining seasons, a player who is 25 years old will have 8.5 remaining seasons and a player who is 35 years old will have 3.5 remaining seasons. If the player is a catcher, then multiply his remaining seasons by .7. If a player is older than 39 (the Years Remaining calculation yields less than 1.5), consult the player's statistics for the most recent year. If the player either had 100 Hits or an Offensive Winning Percentage of .500 or greater, then the player will have 1.0 remaining seasons. If the player has both, he has 1.5 remaining seasons. If he has neither, he has .5 remaining seasons.

Established Hit Level. The Established Hit Level is a weighted average of the player's hits over the past three seasons. To calculate the Established Hit Level after the 2003 season is complete, add 2001 Hits, (2002 Hits multiplied by two) and (2003 Hits multiplied by three), then divide by six. If the Established Hit Level is less than 75% of the most recent performance (2003 Hits in this case), then the Established Hit Level is equal to .75 times the most recent performance.

Projected Remaining Hits. This is calculated by multiplying Years Remaining by the Established Hit Level.

The probability of achieving the specified goal is found by dividing Projected Remaining Hits by Need Hits, then subtracting .5. The maximum that any player has of achieving a goal is .97 raised to the power of (Need Hits / Established Hit Level). This prevents the possibility of a player reaching a goal from being higher than 100 percent, which is impossible.

Catcher's ERA
The ERA for a catcher is equal to the ERA of pitchers pitching while the catcher is playing behind the plate. It is calculated exactly like ERA for pitchers. Take the number of earned runs allowed while the catcher is playing, multiply it by 9 and then divide it by the total number of defensive innings that the catcher was behind the plate.

Cheap Win
A starting pitcher who wins the game with a game score under 50 gets credit for a cheap win. See Game Score.

Cleanup Slugging Average
The Slugging Average of a batter when he bats in the cleanup spot, or fourth, in the batting order.

Component ERA (ERC)
A statistic that estimates what a pitcher's ERA should have been, based on his pitching performance. The ERC formula is calculated as follows:

1. Subtract the pitcher's Home Runs Allowed from his Hits Allowed.
2. Multiply Step 1 by 1.255.

3. Multiply his Home Runs Allowed by four.
4. Add Steps 2 and 3 together.
5. Multiply Step 4 by .89.
6. Add his Walks and Hit Batsmen.
7. Multiply Step 6 by .475.
8. Add Steps 5 and 7 together.

This yields the pitcher's total base estimate (PTB), which is:

$$PTB = 0.89 \times (1.255 \times (H - HR) + 4 \times HR) + 0.475 \times (BB + HB)$$

For those pitchers for whom there is intentional walk data, use this formula instead:

$$PTB = 0.89 \times (1.255 \times (H - HR) + 4 \times HR) + 0.56 \times (BB + HB - IBB)$$

9. Add Hits and Walks and Hit Batsmen.
10. Multiply Step 9 by PTB.
11. Divide Step 10 by Batters Facing Pitcher. If BFP data is unavailable, approximate it by multiplying Innings Pitched by 2.9, then adding Step 9.
12. Multiply Step 11 by 9.
13. Divide Step 12 by Innings Pitched.
14. Subtract .56 from Step 13.

This is the pitcher's ERC, which is:

$$\frac{(H + BB + HB) \times PTB}{BFP \times IP} \times 9 - 0.56$$

If the result after Step 13 is less than 2.24, adjust the formula as follows:

$$\frac{(H + BB + HB) \times PTB}{BFP \times IP} \times 9 \times 0.75$$

Double Play %
Successful Double Plays divided by the number of Double Play opportunities. This statistic includes both the fielder who started the play and the pivot man.

Double Play Opportunity
A fielder is considered to have a double play opportunity when a ground ball is hit with a runner on first base and less than 2 outs and that fielder is involved in the play. This is used to calculate Double Play % and Pivot %.

Doubled Off
A runner is Doubled Off when he is out for failing to get back to his base before he, or the base, is tagged after a ball hit in the air is caught.

470

Earned Run Average

The number of earned runs that a pitcher surrenders per nine innings that he pitches. It is calculated by multiplying the total earned runs allowed by nine and dividing by the total number of innings pitched.

Easy Save

This label is used to separate Saves by difficulty level (Easy or Tough). A Save is considered Easy if the relief pitcher enters the game, pitches one inning or less, and the first batter he faces does not at least represent the tying run.

Fielding Percentage

The percentage of plays a player makes in the field without making an error out of the total number of opportunities. It is calculated by adding (Putouts plus Assists) and dividing by (Putouts plus Assists plus Errors).

Games Finished

The relief pitcher who is in the game for each team when the game ends is credited with a Game Finished.

Game Score

To determine the starting pitcher's Game Score:
Start with 50.
Add 1 point for each out recorded by the starting pitcher.
Add 2 points for each inning the pitcher completes after the fourth inning.
Add 1 point for each strikeout.
Subtract 2 points for each hit allowed.
Subtract 4 points for each earned run allowed.
Subtract 2 points for an unearned run.
Subtract 1 point for each walk.

GDP

Grounded into Double Play

GDP Opportunity

This is a situation where the batter has a chance to ground into a double play. It occurs with at least a runner on first base and less than two outs.

Ground / Fly Ratio (Grd/Fly, GB/FB)

Calculated for both batters and pitchers. For batters, it is the number of groundballs hit divided by the number of flyballs hit. For pitchers, it is exactly the same but uses the number of groundballs and flyballs allowed. Every fair batted ball is included except for bunts and line drives.

Hold

A relief pitcher is given a Hold anytime he enters a game in a Save Situation (see definition for Save Situation), records one out or more, and exits the game without giving up the lead. If the pitcher finishes the game, then he will only earn credit for a Save. He cannot receive credit for both a Hold and a Save.

Holds Adjusted Saves Percentage
Holds plus Saves divided by Holds plus Saves Opportunities.

Inherited Runner
When a relief pitcher enters the game, any runner who is on base at the time is considered an Inherited Runner.

Isolated Power
Slugging Average minus Batting Average.

K/BB Ratio
Strikeouts divided by Walks.

Late & Close
A situation in a game that is very similar to a Save Situation. The following requirements are necessary for a Late & Close game:
1. The game is in the seventh inning or later AND
2. The batting team is either leading by one run or tied OR
3. The tying run is on base, at bat, or on deck.

Leadoff On-Base Percentage
The On-Base Percentage of a batter when he bats leadoff, or first, in the batting order.

Long Outing
A Long Outing is one in which the starting pitcher throws more than 110 pitches. Prior to 2002, we use 120 pitches as the cutoff in the Manager's Record section.

Long Save
A Long Save is when the pitcher credited with a save pitches more than one inning.

Manufactured Runs
Manufactured Runs are of two types: Type 1 - Strict Manufactured Runs (MR-1) which involve at least one base resulting from one of four deliberate acts intended to manufacture a run; i.e. a sacrifice bunt, a stolen base, a hit and run play, or a bunt hit. Type 2 - Other Manufactured Runs (MR-2) are ones in which two of the four bases advanced do NOT result from the runner being forced along by a walk, a hit batsman, or a safe hit to the outfield; e.g. double, ground out, ground out, runner scores would be a MR-2. For a complete description with more examples, see the section on Manufactured Runs.

Not Good Outcome (Intentional Walk)
A Not Good Outcome (NG) for an Intentional Walk occurs when one run scored in the inning after the intentional walk (and the next batter after the intentional walk did not ground into a double play).

Offensive Winning Percentage (OWP)
A player's Offensive Winning Percentage is the winning percentage of a hypothetical team which has an offense consisting of nine of that player, and pitching and defense which is average for the player's league. It is calculated by taking the square of RC/27 (see the

definition for Runs Created per 27 Outs), dividing it by the sum of RC/27 and the square of the average runs scored per game in the league.

On Base (Baserunning)
Number of times a batter gets on base NOT including his home runs.

On-Base Percentage
(Hits plus Walks plus Hit by Pitcher) divided by (At Bats plus Walks plus Hit by Pitcher plus Sacrifice Flies).

$$\frac{H + BB + HBP}{AB + BB + HBP + SF}$$

Opponent Batting Average
Hits Allowed divided by (Batters Faced minus Walks minus Hit Batsmen minus Sacrifice Hits minus Sacrifice Flies minus Catcher's Interference).

$$\frac{H}{BFP - BB - HBP - SH - SF - CI}$$

Out Advancing
A runner is out advancing when he is tagged out attempting to score from 2nd base on a single or from 1st base on a double, or attempting to go from 1st base to 3rd base on a single.

PA*
Used in the denominator for the calculation of On-Base Percentage. It is calculated by subtracting (Sacrifice Hits plus Times Reached Base on Defensive Interference) from Plate Appearances (see definition for Plate Appearances).

Park Index
The Park Index of a given ballpark is the amount that the ballpark influences a given statistic. The following is a calculation of a park index using runs as the statistic:
1. Add Runs and Opponent Runs in home games.
2. Add At Bats and Opponent At Bats in home games. (If At Bats are unavailable, use home games.)
3. Divide Step 1 by Step 2.
4. Add Runs and Opponent Runs in road games.
5. Add At Bats and Opponent At Bats in road games. (If At Bats are unavailable, use road games.)
6. Divide Step 4 by Step 5.
7. Divide Step 3 by Step 6.
8. Multiply Step 7 by 100.

An index of 100 means the park is completely neutral and does not influence the particular statistic at all. A park index of 112 for runs indicates that teams score 12 percent more runs in this ballpark than a neutral park. A park index of 92 for runs means that teams tend to score 8 percent fewer runs in this ballpark than a neutral park.

PCS (Pitchers' Caught Stealing)

The number of runners officially scored as Caught Stealing where the pitcher initiated the play. The normal Caught Stealing is when a runner is out attempting to steal a base but the play was initiated by the catcher. PCS plays are often referred to as pickoffs, but differ when the runner breaks towards the next base as opposed to returning to the base he was currently on. Pickoffs occur when the pitcher throws to a base that a runner is leading from, and the runner is out attempting to return to that base. Pickoffs are not an official statistic.

Pitches per PA

The total number of pitches a hitter sees divided by his total Plate Appearances.

Pivot %

Successful Double Plays turned by pivot man divided by the number of Double Play opportunities with that pivot man involved.

Plate Appearances

At Bats plus Total Walks plus Hit By Pitcher plus Sacrifice Hits plus Sacrifice Flies plus Times Reached on Defensive Interference.

Platoon Advantage %

Platoon Advantage % is the percentage of players in the starting lineup who have the platoon advantage (i.e. bats right against a left-handed pitcher or bats left against a right-hander) against the starting pitcher; e.g. if the opposing starting pitcher is right handed and the batting team has six left-handed batters in its lineup, the platoon advantage for that game would be 67%.

Plus/Minus System

The Plus/Minus System is a method for evaluating defensive play on batted balls. It is made possible by a game scoring system in which each batted ball is rated for type (line drive, grounder, etc.), velocity within its type (hard, medium or soft), and location on the field. A player gets credit (a "plus" number) if he makes a play that at least one other player at his position missed during the season and he loses credit (a "minus" number") if he misses a play that at least one player made. The size of the credits are proportional to the percentage of times all players make the play, All plays for each player at his position are summed to get his total plus/minus for the season. A total of zero would be average and any other number would approximate how many plays more or less the player made than the average player at the position for the number of chances the player had to field batted balls.

Power/Speed Number

A single number that reflects a combination of power and speed. To achieve a high Power/Speed Number, a player must score high in both power and speed. To calculate the Power/Speed Number, multiply Home Runs by Stolen Bases by two, and divide by the sum of Home Runs and Stolen Bases.

$$\frac{2 \times HR \times SB}{HR + SB}$$

PPO (Pitcher Pickoff)
The number of baserunners thrown out when a pitcher throws to a base with a leading baserunner, and the runner is tagged out attempting to return to the base. PPO is not an official statistic and does not count toward Caught Stealing totals.

Quality Start
A game where the starting pitcher pitches for at least six innings and allows no more than three earned runs.

Quality Start Percentage
Quality Starts divided by Games Started (see the definition for Quality Start).

Quick Hooks
Used in the Manager's Record. For Quick Hooks and Slow Hooks a score is calculated for each game that is the sum of the number of Pitches plus 10 times the number of Runs Allowed. The bottom 25% of scores in the league are considered to be Quick Hooks.

Range Factor
The number of Successful Chances (Putouts plus Assists) times nine divided by the number of Defensive Innings Played. The average for a Regular Player at each position in 2007:

> Second Base: 4.91
> Third Base: 2.65
> Shortstop: 4.45
> Left Field: 2.05
> Center Field: 2.71
> Right Field: 2.13

Run Support Per 9 IP
The total number of runs scored by a pitcher's team while he is in the game multiplied by nine and divided by total Innings Pitched.

Runs Created
"Runs Created" is an estimate of the number of a team's runs which are created by each individual hitter. The Cincinnati Reds scored 820 runs last year, let us say. How many of those were created by Adam Dunn? How many by Ken Griffey Jr.? How many by Jason LaRue?

There are many different formulas for estimating runs created. . .did you want the one that involves swinging a dead cat in the cemetery under a full moon? Yeah, I don't blame you. . .worm-eaten persimmons are so hard to find in the modern world.

This is the one we use now; it is complicated enough. First, there is an "A" Factor in the formula, a "B" Factor, and a "C" factor. The "A" Factor, which represents the number of times the hitter is on base, is Hits, Plus Walks, Plus Hit Batsmen, Minus Caught Stealing, Minus Grounded Into Double Play. The "B" Factor, which represents the hitter's ability to advance other runners, is 1.125 times the player's Singles, plus 1.69 times his Doubles, plus 3.02 times his Triples, plus 3.73 times his Home Runs, plus .29 times his Walks and Hit Batsmen, not counting intentional walks, plus .492 times Sacrifice Hits, Sacrifice Flies and Stolen Bases, minus .04 times Strikeouts. The "C" Factor, which represents opportunities, is At Bats, Plus Walks, Plus Hit By Pitch, Plus Sacrifice Hits, Plus Sacrifice Flies.

Having made these initial calculations of the A, B and C factors, we then change the "A" factor to "A plus 2.4 times C".

We change the "B" factor to "B plus 3 times C".

We change the "C" factor to "9 times C".

Multiply A times B, divide by then new C ("9 times C"), and subtract .90 times by the original C.

This is our first, temporary estimate of the player's runs created. We what we have done here is to ask these questions:
1. How many runs would a team probably score that consisted of eight "ordinary" type of hitters, plus this particular hitter?
2. How many of those runs would be created by the eight ordinary type of hitters?
3. What is the difference-and thus, how many runs did our player create?

To estimate this, we have placed our player in the context of eight hitters with a .300 on base percentage (2.4 divided by 8) and a .375 advancement percentage (3 divided by 8). For each trip through the batting order, the eight ordinary-type hitters would produce 9/10 of a run (2.4 times 3, divided by 8). The "9" in the denominator is eight ordinary hitters plus our man. The "-.9" being subtracted at the end is the runs created by the "ordinary" hitters. In essence, we have placed the hitter in a neutral solution, measured the neutral solution without our hitter, measured it with our hitter, and then estimated the contribution of this hitter as being the difference between the two.

We're not quite done. After that, we adjust the player's runs created estimate for his performance in two "run-sensitive" situations. Suppose that a player whose overall batting average is .250 has batted 100 times with runners in scoring position, and has gone 30-for-100. That's five hits better than expected, 30 hits where we would have expected 25. His team will score an extra five runs because he has done that, and so we increase the player's runs created estimate by five runs. If the player has hit poorly with runners in scoring position, we decrease it by the shortfall in the same way.

Suppose that a player has batted 250 times with runners on base, 250 times with the bases empty, and that he has hit 20 home runs overall. We would expect him to have hit 10 with men on base, 10 with the bases empty, right?

Suppose that he didn't. Suppose that he hit 12 with the bases empty, 8 with men on base. His team would score two runs less than expected because he did this, and we would thus penalize him two runs for the shortfall.

This is our second runs created estimate-the player's runs created, adjusted for his batting performance in run-sensitive situations.

Suppose, however, that we figure the runs created for all of the individuals on a team, and we add them up, and it doesn't match the runs actually scored by the team? What if the formulas say that the team should have scored 800 runs, but they actually scored 820?

Then obviously, the formulas missed.   We're trying to measure the runs ACTUALLY created by each hitter as best we can, in the real world, not the theoretical impact of some combination of singles, doubles, triples and walks.   If the actual number is different than the estimates, we have to adjust the estimates to fit the facts. In this case-820 runs scored with only 800 runs created-we would multiply each runs created estimate by 820/800, or 1.025.   Then we round it off to an integer, and that's the player's estimated runs created.

Let go of that cat, Arthur.   Heck, the moon isn't full for three weeks, anyway.

Runs Created per 27 Outs (RC/27)

This statistic estimates the number of runs per game that a team made up of nine of the same player would score. To calculate RC/27, multiply Runs Created by league outs per team game, divide the result by outs made by the player (the sum of at bats plus sacrifice hits plus sacrifice flies plus caught stealing plus grounded into double plays, minus hits) The formula written out is:

$$\frac{\frac{RC \times 3 \times LgIP}{2 \times LgG}}{AB - H + SH + SF + CS + GDP}$$

SB Gain (Baserunning)

Stolen Base attempts must be successful greater than about two thirds of the time to have a positive result on the number of runs scored. SB gain is therefore the number of bases stolen minus two times the number of caught stealing (SB Gain = SB - 2CS.) For example, a runner steals 30 bases and is caught stealing 7 times. His SB Gain would be 30 - 2*7 = +16. Another runner steals 10 bases and is caught stealing 6 times. His SB Gain (actually a loss) would be 10 - 2*6 = -2.

Save Percentage

A pitcher's Saves divided by the total number of Save Situations he faces (see definition for Save Situation).

Save Situation

A relief pitcher is in a Save Situation when he enters the game with his team in the lead, has the opportunity to finish the game, is not the winning pitcher of record at the time, and meets any one of the three following conditions:

1.The pitcher's team is leading by no more than three runs and the pitcher has the chance to pitch for at least one inning,
OR
2.The pitcher enters the game with the potential tying run on base, at bat, or on deck,
OR
3.The pitcher pitches three or more effective innings regardless of the lead. The determination of a save in this situation is made by the official scorer.
It is not possible to have more than one save credited to a single team in a game.

SB Success Percentage
Stolen Bases divided by the number of Stolen Base attempts (Stolen Bases plus Caught Stealing).

$$\frac{SB}{SB + CS}$$

Scored (Baserunning)
The percentage of times a runner on base (not counting his own home runs) eventually scores a run.

Secondary Average
A number meant to reflect everything else except for batting average. A player will have a high Secondary Average if he hits for power, takes walks and steals bases. It is calculated with the following formula:

$$\frac{TB - H + BB + SB}{AB}$$

Similarity Score
A number which reflects the similarity between two different statistical lines, either for a player or for a team. A score of 1,000 means that the statistical lines are identical.

Slow Hooks
Used in the Manager's Record. For Quick Hooks and Slow Hooks a score is calculated for each game that is the sum of the number of Pitches plus 10 times the number of Runs Allowed. The top 25% of scores in the league are considered to be Slow Hooks.

Slugging Average
Total Bases divided by At Bats.

$$\frac{TB}{AB}$$

Speed Score
Speed Score is a number which evaluates how fast a player is. To calculate the Speed Score, start with the player's statistics over the last two seasons combined. A value will be

found for each of the following six categories and will be combined for a final score at the end:

1. Stolen Base Percentage. The value of this category is:

$$\left(\frac{SB + 3}{SB + CS + 7} - 0.4\right) \times 20$$

2. Frequency of Stolen Base Attempts. The value of this category is:

$$\frac{\sqrt{\dfrac{SB + CS}{Singles + BB + HBP}}}{0.07}$$

3. Percentage of Triples. This is calculated by taking the percentage of triples out of the number of balls put in play. To get the percentage, use this formula:

$$\frac{3B}{AB - HR - SO}$$

From this assign an integer from 0 to 10, based on the following chart:

Less than .001   0
.001   - .0023   1
.0023 - .0039   2
.0039 - .0058   3
.0058 - .0080   4
.0080 - .0105   5
.0105 - .013   6
.013   - .0158   7
.0158 - .0189   8
.0189 - .0223   9
.0223 or more   10

4. Runs Scored Percentage. This is calculated by taking the percentage of times the player scores a run out of the number of times the player is on base. To get the percentage, use this formula:

$$\frac{\left(\dfrac{R - HR}{H + HBP + BB - HR} - 0.1\right)}{0.04}$$

5. Grounded Into Double Play Frequency. To get the frequency, use this formula:

$$\frac{0.055 - \left(\dfrac{GIDP}{AB - HR - SO}\right)}{0.005}$$

6. Range Factor. The value of this category depends on the players position:

Catcher—1
First Baseman—2
Designated Hitter—1.5
Second Baseman—1.25 x Range Factor
Third Baseman—1.51 x Range Factor
Shortstop—1.52 x Range Factor
Outfield—3 x Range Factor

For an explanation on Range Factor, consult the definition in this glossary. Remember to figure range factors over a two-year period.

If any category value is greater than 10, then reduce it to 10. If any value is less than zero, then increase the value to zero. All category values must fall within the zero to 10 range. The Speed Score is then calculated by discarding the lowest of the six values, and taking the average of the remaining five.

Total Bases
Hits plus Doubles plus (2 times Triples) plus (3 times Home Runs).

$$H + 2B + (2 \times 3B) + (3 \times HR)$$

Tough Loss
A starting pitcher who loses the game with a game score over 50 gets credit for a tough loss. See Game Score.

Tough Save
This label is used to separate Saves by difficulty level (Easy or Tough). A Save is considered Tough if the relief pitcher enters the game with the tying run on base.

Winning Percentage
Wins divided by (Wins plus Losses).

480

Baseball Info Solutions

Baseball Info Solutions has been supplying top notch, unique, innovative baseball data to its customers since 2002. BIS provides comprehensive services to nearly half of the 30 Major League Baseball teams, as well as many sports agents, media, fantasy services, game companies, and private individuals.

BIS collects a statistical snapshot of every important moment of every Major League Baseball game with the most advanced technology, resulting in a database that includes traditional data, pitch-by-pitch data, and defensive positioning data. The company also has the highest quality pitch charting data available anywhere, including pitch type, location, and velocity.

John Dewan, the principal owner of BIS, has been on the cutting edge of baseball analysis for over 20 years. *The Fielding Bible*, John's award-winning book from 2006, is a fine example of the unique skill set John brings to BIS.

President Steve Moyer brings over 15 years of baseball industry experience to BIS. His hands-on, can-do business demeanor helps set BIS apart from its competition.

BIS continues to grow within the industry while emphasizing personal attention to its customers. This focus on personal attention is evidenced by the fact that if you contact the office with an inquiry you are very likely to be able to speak to the company president directly.

BIS also offers several baseball internships which run from mid-March through the end of the regular season. Past BIS interns are now working for MLB teams, sport agencies and ESPN. If interested, mail your qualifications after the New Year to:

Baseball Info Solutions
528 North New Street
Bethlehem, PA 18018-5752
610-814-0107
www.baseballinfosolutions.com

Notes

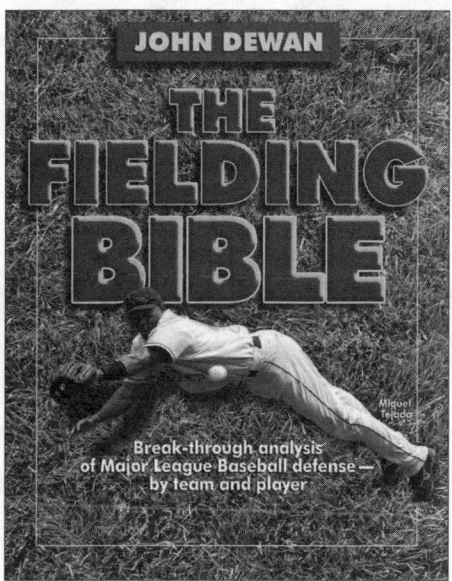

Career Registers for Your Favorite Team

We already know you love the comprehensive collection of stats in *The Bill James Handbook*, otherwise you wouldn't have bought it. But wouldn't it be nice to have the largest feature of the Handbook organized by team? For the first time ever, we are offering the Team Register, which compiles all the career statistics of each player on your favorite major league ball club, and it's FREE!

Just send an e-mail to info@actasports.com with "Handbook Free Gift" in the subject line, and include the following information:

Your First and Last Name
Mailing Address
E-Mail Address
Your Favorite MLB Team

As soon as we receive your e-mail, we will e-mail you a PDF version of a Team Register with all the players on your favorite team at the end of last season. So next year, you won't have to wonder how many wild pitches your Opening Day starter threw in 2007—you can check your personalized Team Register.

Limit one Team Register per customer.